Constitutional Law
Principles and Policies

ASPEN STUDENT TREATISE SERIES

CONSTITUTIONAL LAW
Principles and Policies

Fifth Edition

ERWIN CHEMERINSKY
Dean and Distinguished Professor of Law
Raymond Pryke Professor of First Amendment Law
University of California, Irvine School of Law

Wolters Kluwer

Published by Wolters Kluwer in New York.

Wolters Kluwer serves customers worldwide with CCH, Aspen Publishers, and Kluwer Law International products. (www.wolterskluwerlb.com)

To contact Customer Service, e-mail customer.service@wolterskluwer.com, call 1-800-234-1660, fax 1-800-901-9075, or mail correspondence to:

Wolters Kluwer
Attn: Order Department
PO Box 990
Frederick, MD 21705

Printed in the United States of America.

4 5 6 7 8 9 0

ISBN 978-1-4548-4947-6

Library of Congress Cataloging-in-Publication Data

Chemerinsky, Erwin, author.
   Constitutional law: principles and policies / Erwin Chemerinsky, Dean and Distinguished Professor of Law Raymond Pryke Professor of First Amendment Law University of California, Irvine School of Law.—Fifth Edition.
      pages cm.—(Aspen Student treatise series)
      ISBN 978-1-4548-4947-6
1. Constitutional law—United States. I. Title.
   KF4550.C429 2015
   342.73—dc23
                              2015008314

About Wolters Kluwer Law & Business

Wolters Kluwer Law & Business is a leading global provider of intelligent information and digital solutions for legal and business professionals in key specialty areas, and respected educational resources for professors and law students. Wolters Kluwer Law & Business connects legal and business professionals as well as those in the education market with timely, specialized authoritative content and information-enabled solutions to support success through productivity, accuracy and mobility.

Serving customers worldwide, Wolters Kluwer Law & Business products include those under the Aspen Publishers, CCH, Kluwer Law International, Loislaw, ftwilliam.com and MediRegs family of products.

CCH products have been a trusted resource since 1913, and are highly regarded resources for legal, securities, antitrust and trade regulation, government contracting, banking, pension, payroll, employment and labor, and healthcare reimbursement and compliance professionals.

Aspen Publishers products provide essential information to attorneys, business professionals and law students. Written by preeminent authorities, the product line offers analytical and practical information in a range of specialty practice areas from securities law and intellectual property to mergers and acquisitions and pension/benefits. Aspen's trusted legal education resources provide professors and students with high-quality, up-to-date and effective resources for successful instruction and study in all areas of the law.

Kluwer Law International products provide the global business community with reliable international legal information in English. Legal practitioners, corporate counsel and business executives around the world rely on Kluwer Law journals, looseleafs, books, and electronic products for comprehensive information in many areas of international legal practice.

Loislaw is a comprehensive online legal research product providing legal content to law firm practitioners of various specializations. Loislaw provides attorneys with the ability to quickly and efficiently find the necessary legal information they need, when and where they need it, by facilitating access to primary law as well as state-specific law, records, forms and treatises.

ftwilliam.com offers employee benefits professionals the highest quality plan documents (retirement, welfare and non-qualified) and government forms (5500/PBGC, 1099 and IRS) software at highly competitive prices.

MediRegs products provide integrated health care compliance content and software solutions for professionals in healthcare, higher education and life sciences, including professionals in accounting, law and consulting.

Wolters Kluwer Law & Business, a division of Wolters Kluwer, is headquartered in New York. Wolters Kluwer is a market-leading global information services company focused on professionals.

For my grandson —
Andrew Charles Chemerinsky

Summary of Contents

Contents

CHAPTER 1

Historical Background and Contemporary Themes
1

CHAPTER 2

The Federal Judicial Power
31

Contents

CHAPTER 3

The Federal Legislative Power   239

CHAPTER 4

The Federal Executive Power 351

CHAPTER 5

Limits on State Regulatory and Taxing Power 409

Contents

CHAPTER 6

The Structure of the Constitution's Protection of Civil Rights and Civil Liberties

501

CHAPTER 7

Procedural Due Process   569

CHAPTER 8

Economic Liberties   633

Contents

CHAPTER 9

Equal Protection   695

CHAPTER 10

Fundamental Rights   825

CHAPTER 11

First Amendment: Expression   965

CHAPTER 12

First Amendment: Religion   1247

Preface

The American Constitution is in many ways an amazing document. Written over 200 years ago for a vastly different world, it remains the vehicle for debating and resolving society's most profound political and moral issues. Although it can be discussed in terms of elegant abstract theories, it also has enormous practical effects on the most intimate and important aspects of people's lives.

Constitutional principles can and must be evaluated from a myriad of perspectives: issues of interpretation and how meaning should be given to the document; questions of institutional competence, especially as to the role of the judiciary in a democratic society; normative visions about theories of government and individual freedoms; and perhaps most important of all, in terms of how constitutional doctrines affect people's lives. Ultimately, constitutional law is about the meaning of a just society and how best to achieve it.

My goal is to write the most thorough and lucid discussion of American constitutional law that I can in approximately 1,400 pages. I want both to state clearly constitutional doctrines and to identify the competing policy considerations in each area.

Constitutional law is a vast field, and space limitation affected every aspect of the book. First, many aspects of constitutional law that are covered in parts of the law school curriculum other than constitutional law courses are omitted. Most notably, constitutional provisions concerning criminal procedure—such as the Fourth Amendment, the Fifth Amendment's double jeopardy and grand jury clauses, and the Sixth Amendment—are not included. Nor does the book cover aspects of federal court jurisdiction that are traditionally the focus of federal jurisdiction courses, such as the Eleventh Amendment and abstention doctrines.[1]

---

[1] These are covered in detail in Erwin Chemerinsky, Federal Jurisdiction (6th ed. 2012).

Second, the focus is primarily on the Supreme Court, and there is relatively little discussion of lower court decisions. There are many areas where lower court decisions are mentioned or cited, but there simply was not space for lengthy discussion of lower court approaches on various issues.

Finally, citations to secondary source materials are kept to a minimum. Although the literature on constitutional law is very rich, only a relatively small amount is cited in each area.

The material is divided into 12 chapters. Chapter 1 is an introduction and briefly describes the functions of the Constitution, the history of its drafting and ratification, and competing theories of constitutional interpretation.

Chapter 2 focuses on the federal judicial power and examines the authority for judicial review, justiciability doctrines, congressional control of federal court jurisdiction, and sovereign immunity of state governments.

Chapter 3 considers the federal legislative power, including various congressional powers, federalism as a limit on Congress's authority, and the problems of the administrative state.

Chapter 4 examines the federal executive power. A new section of this chapter focuses on presidential power in connection with the war on terrorism. Areas of overlap are acknowledged and dealt with by cross-references.

Chapter 5 discusses limits on state government power necessitated by the existence of a national government and of other states. Specifically, preemption, the dormant commerce clause, state taxation of interstate commerce, and the privileges and immunities clause are considered.

Chapter 6 examines the structure of the Constitution's protection of individual liberties. It discusses provisions in the Constitution's text, apart from the Bill of Rights, that concern individual rights. It also examines basic principles that apply to all the constitutional provisions dealing with individual liberties and civil rights, including the application of the Bill of Rights to the states, the requirement for government action, and the levels of scrutiny.

Chapter 7 focuses on procedural due process. The distinction between procedural and substantive due process is discussed at the outset. The chapter then examines what constitutes a deprivation of life, liberty, or property and what procedures must be followed when such a deprivation occurs.

Chapter 8 considers economic liberties under the Constitution. The chapter explores the use of substantive due process to protect economic rights, the contracts clause of Article I, §10, and the takings clause found in the Fifth Amendment.

Equal protection is examined in Chapter 9. This chapter begins by describing the analytical approach used in equal protection cases and focuses on the ways various types of discrimination have been treated by the Supreme Court.

Chapter 10 discusses fundamental rights. Because the Court often is unclear about whether a particular right, such as the right to marry, is found under due process or equal protection or both, it is clearest to place in one chapter all the Supreme Court decisions under these provisions that have concerned individual rights. The source of the various rights, of course, is discussed throughout the chapter.

Chapter 11 looks at the First Amendment's protection of expression, including the rights of speech, press, assembly, and association. Chapter 12 examines the First Amendment's protection of religion under both the free exercise clause and the establishment clause.

Since the publication of the fourth edition, the Supreme Court has handed down major rulings concerning standing, the Affordable Care Act and the scope of Congress's powers, Arizona's restrictive immigration law and preemption, marriage equality, many aspects of freedom of speech, separation of church and state, and religious rights of secular corporations. All of these and many other developments are discussed throughout the book.

The book is complete through the end of the Supreme Court's October 2013 term, which ended on June 30, 2014. It is current through December 31, 2014. In light of the often rapid pace of change in constitutional law, I expect to continue to write new editions at regular intervals. I welcome comments and suggestions from readers.

Erwin Chemerinsky

April 2015

Acknowledgments

Writing a one-volume constitutional law treatise often seemed overwhelming. I was enormously helped by many people.

First and foremost, I thank my family—Catherine, Jeffrey, Adam, Alex, Mara, and Kim—for their encouragement, their patience, and their support. This book is dedicated to my grandson, Andrew, who was born on November 12, 2014, as I was completing this manuscript.

I express my deep appreciation to my friend Stephen Siegel for reading a draft of each chapter and offering insightful comments. His criticisms improved the book greatly, and his praise was invaluable inspiration to keep going.

I also am very grateful to many others who read parts of the book and provided extremely useful suggestions: Scott Altman, Catherine Fisk, Candice Hoke, Bill Marshall, Ed Rubin, Sharon Rush, Larry Simon, Matt Spitzer, and Marcy Strauss. I also thank the many readers of earlier editions who offered comments and suggestions that are reflected throughout this book. Nadine Strossen and her students offered countless helpful suggestions.

I completed the first two editions of this book while on the faculty of the University of Southern California Law School. Dean Scott Bice and Dean Matt Spitzer provided constant support and encouragement. My work on the first two editions was enormously aided by my assistant, Margaret Miller. The third edition was completed at Duke Law School, and Dean Kate Bartlett provided great support.

This edition and the prior one were undertaken and completed at the University of California, Irvine. I am very grateful to my Chancellors and Provosts, Michael Drake, Michael Gottfredson, and Howard Gillman, who have been tremendously supportive of my work and the law school in every way. My assistant, Brandy Stewart, provides invaluable assistance on literally a daily basis.

The book simply could not have been completed without the help of Bob Nissenbaum at the Loyola Law School Library, which kindly "stored" a set of the Supreme Court Reporter at my house.

Also, as always, everyone at Wolters Kluwer has been terrific to work with. I am especially grateful to Carol McGeehan.

Last, but definitely not least, I was tremendously helped by a very talented group of research assistants. I express my deep thanks to Brian Mulhairn, Rod Castro, Chris Griggs, Amy Johnson, Melanie Petross, Melissa Pifko, Richard Rey, Karina Sterman, John Vetterly, and Cheryl Watkins for their work on the first edition; to Diara Fleming, Eric Godoy, Jorge Luna, Lori Minassian, Lisa Reush, Aneiko Webb, and especially Amy Kreutner for their work on the second edition; to Natasha Bell, Virginia Duke, Kim Kisabeth, Molly Penn, Michelle Riskind, and Garrick Sevilla for their work on the third edition; to Lori Speak and Tracey Steele for their work on the fourth edition; and to Fawn Bekam, Gillian Kuhlmann, and Jim Miller for their work on this edition.

Constitutional Law
Principles and Policies

CHAPTER 1

Historical Background and Contemporary Themes

§1.1   The Constitution's Functions
§1.2   Why a Constitution?
§1.3   A Brief History of the Creation and Ratification of the Constitution and Its Amendments
§1.4   How Should the Constitution Be Interpreted?
§1.5   Who Should Be the Authoritative Interpreter of the Constitution?

§1.1   THE CONSTITUTION'S FUNCTIONS

Creates National Government and Separates Power

The Constitution creates a national government and divides power among the three branches. Article I creates the legislative power and vests it in Congress. Article II places the executive power in the president of the United States. Article III provides that the judicial power of the United States shall be in the Supreme Court and such inferior courts as Congress creates.

The division of powers among the branches was designed to create a system of checks and balances and lessen the possibility of tyrannical rule. In general, in order for the government to act, at least two branches must agree. Adopting a law requires passage by Congress and the signature of the president (unless it is adopted over his or her veto). Enforcing a law generally requires that the executive initiate a prosecution and that the judiciary convict. Chapters 2, 3, and 4 examine the powers of the judiciary, the legislature, and the executive, respectively. The conflicts and tensions among the branches is a constant theme throughout these chapters.

The Constitution specifies the term of each office among the three branches, the qualifications necessary to hold office, and the manner by which the office is to be filled. Article I, for example, provides for popular election of members of the House of Representatives to two-year terms and for selection of senators by state legislators for six-year terms. The Seventeenth Amendment changed this and provided for popular election of senators. Article I also provides that each member of the House shall be at least 25 years old, a citizen of the United States for at least seven years, and an inhabitant of the state from which he or she is elected. A senator must be 30 years old, a citizen for at least nine years, and an inhabitant of the state from which he or she is elected.[1]

Article II outlines the method of choosing the president and vice president to a four-year term through the electoral college, a process that was modified by the Twelfth Amendment. The Twelfth Amendment eliminated the practice of making the runner-up in the presidential election the vice president, and established the procedure for the House of Representatives to choose the president when no candidate receives a majority in the electoral college.[2] Also, the Twenty-second Amendment provides that no person can be elected president more than twice. Article II also specifies that the president be at least 35 years old, a natural-born citizen, and a resident of the United States for at least 14 years.

Article III provides that federal judges shall have life tenure, and Article II specifies that they will be selected by the president with the "advice and consent of the Senate." Interestingly, the Constitution specifies no other qualifications for being a federal judge.[3]

The length of office terms and the manner of selecting officeholders are crucial in defining the character of American government. The framers intentionally chose a scheme whereby one body of Congress, the House of Representatives, was popularly elected and all citizens were represented equally; the other body, the Senate, was selected by state legislatures, and every state had two senators. The Seventeenth Amendment, adopted in 1913, provided that senators would be

§1.1 [1] The Supreme Court held that states may not set additional qualifications for membership in Congress. Specifically, in *United States Term Limits v. Thornton*, 514 U.S. 779 (1995), the Court declared unconstitutional a state law that prevented individuals from being listed on the ballot after serving three terms in the House or two in the Senate. The Court ruled that states may not set term limits for members of Congress because the Constitution specifies the only qualifications for election to the House or Senate. In *Cook v. Gralike*, 531 U.S. 510 (2001), the Court reaffirmed this and declared unconstitutional a Missouri law that required that candidates' support or opposition to term limits be indicated on the ballot.

[2] If no candidate receives a majority in the electoral college, the Twelfth Amendment provides that the House of Representatives shall choose the president, with each state casting one vote. The Amendment does not specify how the state is to decide how to vote.

[3] Over the last half century, there have been many congressional battles over the confirmation of Supreme Court Justices. In 1969, the Senate rejected President Nixon's nominations of Harold Carswell and Clement Haynsworth, and in 1987 it rejected the nomination of Robert Bork. In 1991, there was a highly publicized battle over the confirmation of Clarence Thomas, who was confirmed by a vote of 52 to 48, the smallest margin in history for any Justice confirmed by the Senate. In 2006, Samuel Alito was confirmed by a vote of 58 to 42.

directly elected by the voters. The president is chosen by the electoral college, not by majority vote, and the result has been that four times in history a president has been selected who received fewer popular votes than an opponent, most recently in November 2000.[4] Federal judges have life tenure so as to enhance the likelihood that their decisions will be based on the merits of the case and not on political pressure.

Divides Power Between the Federal and State Governments

The Constitution divides power vertically between the federal and state governments. "Federalism" is the term often used to refer to this vertical division of authority. The federalist structure of the government is much less apparent from the text of the Constitution than is the separation of powers. Article I begins by saying that "[a]ll legislative Powers herein granted shall be vested in a Congress." The implication is that Congress can act only if there is clear authority, with all other governance left to the states. But this is not made explicit in the text of the seven articles of the Constitution. Indeed, it was probably this lack of clarity that inspired the Tenth Amendment, which states: "The powers not delegated to the United States by the Constitution, nor prohibited by it to the States, are reserved to the States respectively, or to the people."

As discussed in detail in Chapter 3, there has been great debate throughout American history as to whether the Tenth Amendment reserves a zone of authority exclusively to the states and whether the judiciary should invalidate laws that infringe that zone.[5] Early in the last century, the Court aggressively used the Tenth Amendment as a limit on Congress's power. After 1937, the Court rejected this view and did not see the Tenth Amendment as a basis for declaring federal laws unconstitutional. Since the 1990s, however, the Tenth Amendment has been used by the Supreme Court to invalidate federal statutes that are deemed to "commandeer" or coerce the states into enacting laws or adopting regulations.[6]

---

[4] In the election of 1824, Andrew Jackson received the most popular votes with 152,933. John Quincy Adams received 115,696 votes. However, Jackson did not have a majority of the votes cast because William H. Crawford and Henry Clay each drew over 45,000 votes. Similarly, although Jackson received the most votes in the electoral college (99 compared to Adams's 84), Jackson did not receive a majority of the votes in the electoral college because Crawford and Clay received a total of 78 votes. In the subsequent election in the House of Representatives, Adams was elected president with 13 votes from the 24 states. Neal R. Peirce & Lawrence D. Longley, The People's President: The Electoral College in American History and the Direct Vote Alternative 50-51 (1981).

In the election of 1876, the Democrat Samuel J. Tilden received more popular votes than the Republican Rutherford B. Hayes. However, Hayes won 185 electoral college votes to Tilden's 184 and thereby gained the presidency. *Id.* at 53. In the election of 1888, Grover Cleveland received 95,096 more votes than Benjamin Harrison, but Harrison won the presidency with 233 votes in the electoral college compared to Cleveland's 168. *Id.* at 57-58. In the election of 2000, the Democrat Al Gore received more popular votes (50,992,335 votes) than the Republican George W. Bush (50,455,156 votes). Nevertheless, George W. Bush won the presidency by receiving 271 electoral college votes to Gore's 266.

[5] *See* §3.10.

[6] These cases are discussed in detail in §3.10.

One other provision that expressly relates to federalism is the supremacy clause found in Article VI of the Constitution. It declares that the "Constitution, and the Laws of the United States which shall be made in Pursuance thereof, and all Treaties made, or which shall be made, under the Authority of the United States, shall be the supreme Law of the Land." This provision sets up a clearly hierarchical relationship between the federal government and the states. Practically, the effect of the supremacy clause is that state and local laws are deemed preempted if they conflict with federal law. The issue of preemption is discussed in Chapter 5.

Finally, federalism limits the ability of states to impose burdens on each other. For example, since the country's earliest days, the Supreme Court has held that the grant of power to Congress to regulate commerce among the states limits the ability of states to regulate or tax commerce in a manner that places an undue burden on interstate commerce. This topic, sometimes called the dormant commerce clause, and the related issue of state taxation of interstate commerce, are discussed in Chapter 5.

Protects Individual Liberties

A third major function of the Constitution is to protect individual liberties. Although this is popularly regarded as the Constitution's most significant goal, there are few parts of the Constitution, apart from the Bill of Rights, that pertain to individual rights. Article I, §§9 and 10, respectively, say that neither the federal nor state governments can enact an ex post facto law or a bill of attainder.[7] An ex post facto law is one that criminally punishes conduct that was lawful when it was done or that increases the punishment for a crime after it was committed. A bill of attainder is a law that orders the punishment of a person without a trial. Article I, §10, also provides that no state shall impair the obligations of contracts.[8]

Article III, §2, ensures trial by jury of all crimes, except in cases of impeachment, in the state where the crime occurred. Article III, §3, limits the scope of treason to "levying War against [the United States], or in adhering to their Enemies, giving them Aid and Comfort." It also requires that a conviction be based on the testimony of two witnesses to an overt act or on a confession in open court. The punishment for treason is limited in that it cannot "work Corruption of Blood, or Forfeiture except during the Life of the Person attainted."

Article IV provides that the "Citizens of each State shall be entitled to all Privileges and Immunities of Citizens in the several States." This provision, which is discussed in detail in Chapter 5, limits the ability of a state to discriminate against out-of-state residents with regard to what are called "privileges and immunities." As described in Chapter 5, the Court has interpreted this phrase as referring to constitutional rights and the right of individuals to earn their livelihood.

---

[7] These clauses are discussed in Chapter 6, §§6.2.2 and 6.2.3, respectively.
[8] This provision is discussed in §8.2.

§1.1   The Constitution's Functions

The only other provisions of the Constitution, apart from the Bill of Rights, that deal with individual liberties focus on protecting the rights of slave owners. Article I, §9, prohibited Congress from banning the importation of slaves until 1808, and Article V, which concerns constitutional amendments, provides that this provision cannot be amended. Article IV, §2, contains the fugitive slave clause, which required that a slave escaping from one state, even to a non–slave state, be returned to his or her owner. Slavery was very much a part of the fabric of the Constitution and it was not abolished until the Thirteenth Amendment was adopted in 1865 after the conclusion of the Civil War.

There are many explanations for the absence of a more elaborate statement of individual rights in the Constitution. Some believe that the framers thought it unnecessary because rights were adequately protected by the limitations on power of the national government. Also, the framers might have been fearful that enumerating some rights could be taken as implicitly denying the existence of other liberties. Thus, the Ninth Amendment to the Constitution declares: "The enumeration in the Constitution, of certain rights, shall not be construed to deny or disparage others retained by the people."

As described below, several states ratified the Constitution, but with the insistence that a Bill of Rights be added.[9] Almost immediately after Congress began its first session, James Madison started drafting amendments to the Constitution. Seventeen amendments passed the House of Representatives and were sent to the Senate. The Senate approved 12 of them. Interestingly, one that the Senate did not approve would have prohibited state infringement of freedom of conscience, speech, press, and jury trial; Madison referred to this as "the most valuable amendment in the whole lot."[10]

Of the 12 amendments that passed the House and the Senate, the states ratified ten. One that was not ratified would have provided a formula for the apportionment of the House of Representatives. The other amendment that was not ratified by the states provided: "No law, varying the compensation for the services of the Senators and Representatives shall take effect, until an election of Representatives shall have intervened." Only five states ratified this amendment between 1789 and 1791, when the first ten amendments were approved by the states. Between 1973 and 1992, 33 more states ratified it and it became a part of the Constitution in 1992, even though the ratification process extended over a 200-year period.[11]

Two characteristics about the protection of individual rights in the Constitution should be noted. First, the Constitution's protections of individual liberties apply only to the government; private conduct generally does not have to comply with the Constitution. Only the Thirteenth Amendment, which prohibits slavery and involuntary servitude, directly protects individuals from private conduct. The

---

[9] *See* John P. Kaminski, Restoring the Grand Security: The Debate over a Federal Bill of Rights, 1787-1792, 33 Santa Clara L. Rev. 887 (1993).

[10] Quoted in *id.* at 919. For an excellent history of the drafting and ratification of the Bill of Rights, *see* Burt Neuborne, Madison's Music 195-221 (2015).

[11] The Twenty-seventh Amendment is discussed in more detail below in §1.3.

principle that the Constitution restricts only the government is sometimes called the "state action doctrine"; it is discussed in Chapter 6.

Second, the Bill of Rights provisions protecting individual liberties initially were deemed to apply only to the federal government and not to state or local governments.[12] Not until the twentieth century did the Supreme Court decide that most of the Bill of Rights apply to state and local governments through the due process clause of the Fourteenth Amendment.[13] This topic also is discussed in Chapter 6.

§1.2 WHY A CONSTITUTION?

As described above, the Constitution both empowers and limits government; it creates a framework for American government, but also limits the exercise of governing authority by protecting individual rights. The underlying question is why accomplish this through a Constitution?[1] Great Britain, for example, has no written constitution.

If no constitution existed in the United States, there likely would have been some initial informal agreement creating the institutions of government, and those institutions would have determined both the procedures of government and its substantive enactments. For example, the framers at the Constitutional Convention in Philadelphia in 1787 could have served as the initial legislature and, in that capacity, devised a structure of government embodied in a statute that could have been altered by subsequent legislatures.

A Constitution Is Unique Because It Is Difficult to Change

The key difference between this approach and the Constitution is that the latter is far more difficult to change. Whereas legislative enactments can be modified by another statute, the Constitution can be amended only by a much more elaborate and difficult procedure. Article V of the Constitution prescribes two alternative ways of amending the Constitution. One is for both houses of Congress, by two-thirds vote, to propose an amendment that becomes effective when ratified by

---

[12] *See* Barron v. Mayor & City Council of Baltimore, 32 U.S. (7 Pet.) 243 (1833).

[13] As discussed in §6.3.3, the Court has followed the approach of "selective incorporation," concluding that the Fourteenth Amendment does not incorporate all of the Bill of Rights, but only those parts that are deemed fundamental. All of the Bill of Rights, however, have been incorporated except the Third Amendment's right to not have soldiers quartered in a person's home, the Fifth Amendment's right to grand jury indictment in criminal cases, the Seventh Amendment's right to jury trial in civil cases, and the Eighth Amendment's right against excessive fines.

§1.2 [1] A systematic examination of this question is undertaken in Michael J. Klarman, What's So Great About Constitutionalism?, 93 Nw. U. L. Rev. 145 (1998).

three-fourths of the states. All 27 amendments to the Constitution were adopted through this procedure. The other mechanism outlined in Article V, though never used, is for two-thirds of the states to call for Congress to convene a constitutional convention that would propose amendments for the states to consider. These amendments, too, would require approval of three-fourths of the states in order to be ratified.[2]

Therefore, a defining characteristic of the American Constitution is that it is very difficult to alter. In focusing on the question, why have a Constitution, then, the real issue is: Why should a society generally committed to majority rule choose to be governed by a document that is very difficult to change? Professor Laurence Tribe puts the question succinctly: "[W]hy would a nation that rests legality on the consent of the governed choose to constitute its political life in terms of commitments to an original agreement—made by the people, binding on their children, and deliberately structured so as to be difficult to change?"[3]

It is hardly original or profound to answer this question by observing that the framers chose to create their government in a Constitution deliberately made difficult to change as a way of preventing tyranny of the majority, of protecting the rights of the minority from oppression by social majorities. If the structure of government was placed in a statute, there might be an overwhelming tendency to create dictatorial powers in times of crisis. If protections of individual liberties were placed in statutes only, a tyrannical government could overrule them. If terms of office were specified in a statute rather than in the Constitution, those in power could alter the rules to remain in power.

Thus, a constitution represents an attempt by society to limit itself to protect the values it most cherishes. A powerful analogy can be drawn to the famous story from mythology of Ulysses and the Sirens.[4] Ulysses, fearing the Sirens' song, which seduced sailors to their death, had himself bound to the ship's mast to protect himself from temptation. Ulysses's sailors plugged their ears with wax to be immune from the Sirens' call, whereas Ulysses, tied to the mast, heard the Sirens' song but was not harmed by it. Despite Ulysses's pleas for release, his sailors followed his earlier instructions and kept him bound and unable to heed the Sirens' song. His life was saved because he recognized his weakness and protected himself from it.

A constitution is society's attempt to tie its own hands, to limit its ability to fall prey to weaknesses that might harm or undermine cherished values. History teaches that the passions of the moment can cause people to sacrifice even the most basic principles of liberty and justice. The Constitution is society's attempt

---

[2] Thirty-two states have passed resolutions calling for a constitutional convention to draft a balanced budget amendment. *See* Stewart Dalzell & Eric J. Beste, Is the Twenty-Seventh Amendment 200 Years Too Late?, 62 Geo. Wash. L. Rev. 501, 506 (1994).

[3] Laurence Tribe, American Constitutional Law 10 (3d ed. 2000).

[4] The analogy to Ulysses is developed in Jon Elster, Ulysses and the Sirens: Studies in Rationality and Irrationality (1979). The story of Ulysses is from Homer's Odyssey, Book XII (Harper Colophon ed. 1985).

to protect itself from itself. The Constitution enumerates basic values—regular elections, separation of powers, individual rights, equality—and makes change or departure very difficult.

Although the analogy between the Constitution and Ulysses is appealing, there is a problem: Ulysses tied his own hands; a Constitution binds future generations. The survival of the Constitution likely is a reflection of the widespread belief, throughout American history, that it is desirable to be governed under it. Indeed, one enormous benefit of the Constitution is that it is written in terms sufficiently general and abstract that almost everyone in society can agree to them. For example, although people disagree about what speech should be protected and under what circumstances, there is almost universal agreement that there should be freedom of speech.[5] The Constitution thus serves as a unifying device, increasing the legitimacy of government and government actions. Professor Thomas Grey observed that the Constitution "has been, virtually from the moment of its ratification, a sacred symbol, the potent emblem . . . of the nation itself."[6]

Implications

Viewing the Constitution in this manner has important implications that underlie the discussion throughout this book. First, the Constitution needs to be understood as an intentionally anti-majoritarian document. Simple claims that American democracy is based on majority rule—such as in criticizing the judiciary for being anti-majoritarian—should be viewed suspiciously.[7]

Second, the Constitution should be appraised from the perspective of whether it has succeeded in restraining the majority, especially in times of crisis, and successfully protecting minorities' rights.[8] Obviously, while there have been successes, there also have been significant failures, such as in the internment of Japanese Americans during World War II,[9] the long history of discrimination against racial minorities and women, and the persecution of alleged communists during the McCarthy era.[10]

Third, viewing the Constitution as a way of protecting long-term values from short-term passions poses a basic problem in constitutional interpretation. Interpretation is crucial to allow a document written for an eighteenth-century agrarian

---

[5] *See* Herbert McClosky & Alida Brill, Dimensions of Tolerance: What Americans Believe About Civil Liberties 39 (1983) (in opinion polls 97 percent of Americans say that they believe in freedom of speech, but only 18 percent would permit the Nazi party to use a public building for a meeting and only 23 percent would allow a group denouncing the government to use a public facility).

[6] Thomas Grey, The Constitution as Scripture 1, 3 (1984); *see also* Sanford Levinson, Constitutional Faith (1988); Max Lerner, Constitution and Court as Symbols, 46 Yale L.J. 1290, 1296 (1937).

[7] For an excellent development of this point, *see* Edward L. Rubin, Getting Past Democracy, 149 U. Pa. L. Rev. 711 (2001).

[8] I address the question of whether the Supreme Court has succeeded or failed in Erwin Chemerinsky, The Case Against the Supreme Court (2014).

[9] *See* Korematsu v. United States, 323 U.S. 214 (1944), discussed in §9.3.2.

[10] *See, e.g.*, Dennis v. United States, 341 U.S. 494 (1951), discussed in §11.3.2.4.

slave society to govern in the technological world of the twenty-first century. Yet if each generation has broad license to interpret the Constitution, can it still serve as a constraint? The debate over how the Constitution should be interpreted is discussed specifically in §1.4 and, of course, throughout this book.

§1.3   A BRIEF HISTORY OF THE CREATION AND RATIFICATION OF THE CONSTITUTION AND ITS AMENDMENTS

The Constitution of the United States must be understood as a reaction to the events that preceded it. Many of its provisions—such as the Third Amendment, which prohibits quartering of soldiers in people's homes—only make sense in the context of history. Much of what is in the Constitution is the product of compromises made at the Constitutional Convention.

The Declaration of Independence, authored by Thomas Jefferson, was signed in 1776.[1] Although it has no binding legal authority, its ringing rhetoric often is invoked by courts and its complaints about British rule foreshadowed the protections that were placed in the Constitution and its Bill of Rights. After the Revolutionary War ended in 1781 (although the formal peace treaty was not signed until 1783), the 13 colonies ratified the Articles of Confederation.

Articles of Confederation

The Articles of Confederation were the first constitution of the United States. The Articles of Confederation created a very weak national government and embodied a strong commitment that state governments retained sovereignty. Indeed, the Articles of Confederation declared that "each state retains its sovereignty, freedom, and independence, and every Power, Jurisdiction, and right, which is not by this confederation expressly delegated to the United States, in Congress assembled." Under the Articles of Confederation there was no federal judiciary and no executive. There was a Confederation Congress, but its powers were greatly circumscribed. For example, under the Articles of Confederation, Congress had the authority to wage war, coin money, establish post offices, and deal with Indian tribes. However, the Congress had no power to tax and no authority to regulate commerce among the states. As Robert Clinton remarked, "Basically, the powers granted to Congress under the Articles represented the noncontroversial

---

§1.3 [1] For a fascinating account of the events leading up to the Declaration of Independence and how Thomas Jefferson came to write it, *see* David McCullough, John Adams (2001).

powers theretofore exercised by the Parliament and the Crown under the colonial system."[2]

Not surprisingly, serious problems developed under the Articles of Confederation. Most notably, states adopted laws that discriminated against goods and services from other states. For instance, New York, as a state with a port, imposed duties on goods destined for other states. To retaliate, these states then enacted taxes on commerce with New York. Many states tried to erect trade barriers to help their own economic interests. Congress, under the Articles of Confederation, was powerless to stop this.

Also, problems developed because of the lack of national executive or judicial authority. For instance, there was no way to ensure that states would comply with laws adopted by Congress.

Constitutional Convention

The Constitutional Convention met in Philadelphia from May 25 until September 17, 1787.[3] An interesting question is whether the Convention acted unlawfully in proposing a new constitution, rather than in amending the Articles of Confederation.[4] The Constitutional Convention's mandate was to propose changes to the Articles of Confederation. Moreover, the Articles of Confederation required unanimous consent for revisions, but Article VII of the Constitution specified that "[t]he Ratification of the Conventions of nine States shall be sufficient for the Establishment of this Constitution between the States."

The first vote at the Convention, on May 30, was the adoption of a resolution "that a national government ought to be established consisting of a supreme legislative, judiciary and executive."[5] Thus, the Convention immediately agreed on abandoning, rather than amending, the Articles of Confederation, and on creating a new constitution.

Two competing plans were introduced for the new government. One, termed the "Virginia plan," emphasized creating a national government with relatively strong powers and the ability to regulate the conduct of individuals. The other, called the "New Jersey plan," would have created a unicameral legislature in which all states had equal representation and would have established the Supreme Court as the only federal court. Compromises were reached. One compromise was to create two houses in Congress: one with proportional representation based on population and one in which each state would have equal representation. Another

---

[2] Robert N. Clinton, A Brief History of the Adoption of the United States Constitution, 75 Iowa L. Rev. 891, 893 (1990).

[3] The authoritative record of the Convention is Max Farrand, ed., The Records of the Federal Convention of 1787 (1966); see Leonard W. Levy, Making the Constitution, in Judgments: Essays on American Constitutional History 5 (L. Levy ed. 1972).

[4] See Bruce Ackerman & Neal Katyal, Our Unconventional Founding, 62 U. Chi. L. Rev. 475, 481-482 (1995).

[5] The Records of the Federal Convention of 1787 30 (Max Farrand ed. 1966).

compromise was to create a Supreme Court and to leave it up to Congress to decide whether to create lower federal courts.

After passing resolutions concerning the major aspects of the new government, the Convention formed a Committee on Detail to place the resolutions into a coherent document. The Committee on Detail, for example, drafted the list of the specific powers of Congress that are found in Article I of the Constitution. Then a Committee on Style was formed to reorder and renumber the provisions and revise the language where appropriate. After the Committee on Style presented its revised draft, there was a week of relatively hurried debate.[6] On September 17, 1787, the members of the Convention approved the document, signed it, and returned home to fight for its ratification.

The Ratification Process

There were heated debates in many states over whether to ratify the Constitution. Antifederalists, who opposed the ratification, emphasized the powers of the new national government and its ability to relegate state governments to a secondary and relatively unimportant role.[7] The antifederalists also stressed the absence of an enumeration of individual rights in the Constitution.

The opposition was strong in several states. For example, North Carolina refused to ratify the Constitution in 1788 and did not change its position until 1789.[8] Rhode Island did not ratify until 1790 after it was threatened with exclusion from the new nation. It is estimated that a majority of the delegates initially opposed ratification in Massachusetts, New Hampshire, New York, and Virginia.[9]

As part of the ratification debates, the Constitution was thoroughly analyzed and discussed. The most detailed and famous defense of the Constitution was a series of 85 essays written by Alexander Hamilton, James Madison, and John Jay to help persuade the New York Convention to ratify the Constitution. These are known as the Federalist Papers and are regularly cited by the Supreme Court as evidencing the framers' intent.

Pennsylvania was the first state to hold a ratifying convention, which initially met on November 20, 1787, and on December 12 voted to ratify the Constitution by a vote of 46 to 23.[10] Meanwhile, Delaware unanimously ratified the Constitution on December 7 after only three hours of debate. New Jersey and Georgia also ratified quickly, on December 18 and January 2, respectively.[11]

---

[6] *See, e.g.*, Clinton, *supra* note 2, at 910 (describing this as a "week of hurried and obviously impatient debate"). A key issue debated was whether there should be a right to a jury trial in civil cases, a proposal that was rejected. *Id.*

[7] *See* Wilson Carey McWilliams, The Anti-Federalists, Representations and Party, 84 Nw. U. L. Rev. 12 (1989); *see generally* The Complete Anti-Federalist (H. Storing ed. 1981).

[8] Forrest McDonald, A Constitutional History of the United States 31 (1982).

[9] *Id.*

[10] John P. Kaminski, Restoring the Grand Security: The Debate over a Federal Bill of Rights, 1787-1792, 33 Santa Clara L. Rev. 887, 897-899 (1993).

[11] *Id.* at 900.

The decision of Massachusetts, the second largest state, was pivotal. Initially, it was clear that a majority of the delegates were antifederalists and that the Constitution was likely to be defeated. Therefore the Federalists made a deal with antifederalist Governor John Hancock, who was also the president of the Massachusetts convention. The Federalists agreed not to oppose Hancock in the upcoming gubernatorial race and to propose him for vice president.[12] With Hancock's support, Massachusetts ratified the Constitution by the slim margin of 187 to 168.[13]

Maryland was the seventh state to ratify in April 1788, and South Carolina was the eighth state in May.[14] In Virginia, the antifederalists, led by Patrick Henry, mounted a strong opposition, but ultimately Virginia approved the Constitution by a margin of 89 to 79.[15] Likewise, there were heated battles in New York and New Hampshire. These states also eventually approved the Constitution; by June 1788, ten states had ratified the Constitution, one more than the nine that Article VII requires.

The Addition of the Bill of Rights

As described above, the antifederalists opposed the Constitution, in part, because it failed to enumerate individual rights. In fact, several states approved the Constitution, but with a request that the new government immediately create a bill of rights. The New York and Virginia legislatures passed resolutions calling for a constitutional convention to create a bill of rights.[16]

To prevent another constitutional convention from occurring, James Madison, then in the House of Representatives, undertook to coalesce the various amendment proposals. In proposing a Bill of Rights, Madison declared: "If [guarantees of individual rights] are incorporated in the Constitution, independent tribunals of justice will consider themselves in a peculiar manner the guardians of these rights; they will be an impenetrable bulwark against every assumption of power in the Legislature or Executive; they will be naturally led to resist every encroachment upon rights expressly stipulated for in the Constitution by the declaration of rights."[17] As mentioned above, 17 were passed by the House, 12 by the Senate, and 10 by the states.[18] These came to be known as the Bill of Rights.

New Jersey was the first state to approve the Bill of Rights on November 20, 1789, and Virginia was the last state on December 15, 1791.

---

[12] *Id.*

[13] *Id.* at 901.

[14] *Id.* at 902.

[15] *Id.* at 908.

[16] *Id.* at 908, 912.

[17] James Madison's Speech to the House of Representatives Presenting the Proposed Bill of Rights, June 8, 1789, reprinted in Daniel Farber & Suzanna Sherry, A History of the American Constitution (1990). For a discussion of Madison's role in drafting these amendments, *see* Burt Neuborne, Madison's Music 195-221 (2015).

[18] The Senate approved an eleventh of these initial 12 amendments in 1992 when Congress passed the Twenty-seventh Amendment.

Amendments

Since 1791, 17 more amendments have been added to the Constitution.[19] They fit into three major categories. One type of amendment overrules specific Supreme Court decisions. Four amendments have been adopted to overrule the Court's interpretation of the Constitution. The Eleventh Amendment overturned *Chisholm v. Georgia*[20] and provided that states could not be sued in federal court by citizens of other states or citizens of foreign countries. Section 1 of the Fourteenth Amendment overturned the Court's decision in *Dred Scott v. Sandford*[21] and made it clear that slaves are persons and that all persons born or naturalized in the United States are citizens. The Sixteenth Amendment overturned the holding in *Pollock v. Farmers' Loan & Trust Co.*[22] and permitted Congress to enact a personal income tax. Most recently, the Twenty-sixth Amendment overturned *Oregon v. Mitchell*[23] and provided anyone aged 18 or over the right to vote.

Second, some amendments were adopted to correct problems in the original Constitution. For example, the Twelfth Amendment, ratified in 1804, changed the procedure whereby the runner-up in a presidential election would become vice president. For obvious reasons, it was realized that it would be preferable that the vice president be of the same party as the president, rather than the president's opponent. The Twelfth Amendment also delineates the procedure that the House of Representatives shall use to choose a president if no candidate receives a majority of the votes in the electoral college.

Also, the Twenty-fifth Amendment, adopted in 1967, creates a procedure to choose a new vice president when there is a vacancy in that office. The procedure was used in 1973, when Gerald Ford was made vice president after Spiro Agnew resigned from the vice presidency. Less than a year later, the procedure was used for a second time when Richard Nixon resigned as president, Ford ascended to that office, and Nelson Rockefeller was made vice president. The Twenty-fifth Amendment also deals with the problem of a disabled president, a topic not addressed in the Constitution. The Twentieth Amendment, ratified in 1933, deals with the potential problem of the death of a president-elect, and specifies that terms of members of Congress begin on January 3 and the president and vice president are inaugurated on January 20. Previously, presidents had been inaugurated on March 4 and the goal was to shorten the interval between the election and the inauguration of a new president.

Third, and most commonly, amendments have been added to the Constitution to reflect changes in social attitudes. The Thirteenth Amendment, adopted in 1865 after the Civil War, prohibits slavery and involuntary servitude. The

---

[19] For an excellent history of the use of the amendment process, *see* David E. Kyvig, Explicit and Authentic Acts: Amending the U.S. Constitution, 1776-1995 (1996).

[20] 2 U.S. (2 Dall.) 419 (1793) (holding that states could be sued in federal court by citizens of other states).

[21] 60 U.S. (19 How.) 393 (1857).

[22] 157 U.S. 429 (1895).

[23] 400 U.S. 112 (1970).

Fourteenth Amendment was enacted in 1868 largely to protect the rights of the newly freed slaves and in its most important provisions says that no state can deny any person equal protection of the laws or deprive any person of life, liberty, or property without due process of law. The Fifteenth Amendment, ratified in 1870, provides that the right to vote shall not be denied on account of race or previous condition of servitude.

Several other amendments also seek to change and expand the electoral process. The Seventeenth Amendment, adopted in 1913, provides for popular election of senators.[24] The Nineteenth Amendment, approved in 1920, provides that "[t]he right of citizens of the United States to vote shall not be denied or abridged by the United States or by any State on account of sex." The Twenty-third Amendment, adopted in 1961, allows the District of Columbia to cast votes in the electoral college as if it were a state, but never more than the least populous state in the country. The Twenty-fourth Amendment, ratified in 1964, states that the right to vote in federal elections cannot be "denied or abridged by the United States or any State by reason of failure to pay any poll tax or other tax."

The Twenty-second Amendment, adopted in 1951, specifies that no person shall be elected more than twice to the office of president and "no person who has held the office of President, or acted as president, for more than two years of a term to which some other person was elected President shall be elected to the office of the President more than once." The amendment obviously was a reaction to President Franklin Roosevelt's being elected four times to the presidency; he was the only person in history to be elected more than twice.

The Eighteenth Amendment imposed prohibition and outlawed the "manufacture, sale, or transportation of intoxicating liquors." It was repealed in 1933, 14 years after it had been enacted, by the Twenty-first Amendment.

There is a story behind each amendment and each of the countless failed amendments.[25] Perhaps the most remarkable stories surround the adoption of the Fourteenth Amendment and the most recent amendment, the Twenty-seventh Amendment.

Of all the amendments since the Bill of Rights, the Fourteenth Amendment is the most important. It bestowed citizenship on the former slaves; prohibited states from denying any person equal protection; ensured that no person could be deprived of life, liberty, or property without due process of law; and empowered Congress to adopt legislation to implement it. It is through the Fourteenth Amendment that the Bill of Rights has been applied to the states.[26] Yet of all the amendments, the Fourteenth Amendment is the most questionable in terms of the procedures followed in its ratification.

---

[24] *See* Vikram Amar, Indirect Effects of a Direct Election: A Structural Examination of the Seventeenth Amendment, 49 Vand. L. Rev. 1347 (1996).

[25] *See* David E. Kyvig, Explicit and Authentic Acts: Amending the U.S. Constitution, 1776-1995 (1996).

[26] *See* §6.3.3.

Soon after the Fourteenth Amendment was proposed, the legislatures of Georgia, North Carolina, and South Carolina rejected it.[27] Congress was furious and saw this as an attempt by Southern states to undermine the North's victory in the Civil War. Therefore, in §5 of the Reconstruction Act, Congress specified that no rebel state would be readmitted to the Union and entitled to representation in Congress until it ratified the Fourteenth Amendment.[28]

New governments were created in these states, and the three states that had rejected it, along with most of the other Southern states, then ratified the Fourteenth Amendment. However, Ohio and New Jersey, which had ratified the amendment, subsequently passed resolutions withdrawing their ratification.

Nonetheless, on July 20, 1868, the secretary of state issued a proclamation that the required three-fourths of the states (28 of the then-existing 37 states) had ratified the amendment. His list included the Southern states that had initially rejected the amendment but had later approved it because of coercion from Congress, *and* Ohio and New Jersey, which had rescinded their ratification. The following day, Congress passed a concurrent resolution declaring that the Fourteenth Amendment was a part of the Constitution because it had been ratified by three-fourths of the states. The list of ratifying states included Ohio and New Jersey. Many years later, the Supreme Court recited this history and said that the "decision by the political departments of the Government as to the validity of the Fourteenth Amendment has been accepted."[29]

The Twenty-seventh Amendment also has an unusual, albeit less controversial, history. The Twenty-seventh Amendment states: "No law varying the compensation for the services of the Senators and Representatives shall take effect, until an election of Representatives shall have intervened."

The Twenty-seventh Amendment was drafted by James Madison when he was a member of the House of Representatives in 1789 and was one of 12 amendments passed by the Senate and sent to the states for ratification. Ten of the amendments were ratified and became the Bill of Rights, but only five states ratified this amendment. The amendment, however, contains no "expiration clause," that is, no requirement that it be ratified by a specified date in order to be effective. Therefore, in 1873, one additional state ratified the amendment.

The amendment never was the focus of much attention, but from time to time legislators in various states were successful in having it approved. From 1873 until 1992, 32 additional states approved the amendment. In 1992, Michigan was the thirty-eighth state to ratify it, providing the requisite approval of three-fourths

---

[27] *See* Coleman v. Miller, 307 U.S. 433, 448 (1939) (describing the history of the ratification of the Fourteenth Amendment).

[28] 14 Stat. 429 (1867) ("[W]hen said State, by a vote of its legislature elected under said constitution, shall have adopted the amendment to the Constitution of the United States, proposed by the Thirty-ninth Congress, and known as article fourteen, and when said article shall have become a part of the Constitution of the United States, said State shall be declared entitled to representation in Congress.").

[29] Coleman v. Miller, 307 U.S. at 450.

of the states. The amendment is now a part of the Constitution, even though it took over 200 years for it to be ratified.[30]

§1.4   HOW SHOULD THE CONSTITUTION BE INTERPRETED?

The Inevitable Need for Interpretation

A constant theme throughout this book and throughout all of constitutional law concerns how the document should be interpreted. In applying any law—be it a statute, regulation, or Constitution—judges must decide what it means. Three factors make constitutional interpretation uniquely complicated and produce a great many of the interpretive questions before the Supreme Court.

First, countless problems arise that the Constitution does not expressly consider. When may the president remove executive officers? When, if at all, do federal laws impermissibly infringe upon state sovereignty? May states adopt laws that place a substantial burden on interstate commerce? These problems are less a matter of deciding the meaning of a particular phrase in the Constitution and more a reflection of the reality that countless issues of governance are not dealt with in any of the language of the Constitution. Long ago, Chief Justice John Marshall expressed this when he explained that the Constitution was not meant to have the "prolixity of a legal code," but instead, "[i]ts nature . . . requires, that only its great outlines should be marked, its important objects designated. . . . [W]e must never forget that it is a constitution we are expounding. . . . [A]constitution, intended to endure for ages to come, and consequently, to be adapted to the various crises of human affairs."[1] Because the Constitution is just an outline, a blueprint for government, it does not address myriad questions that courts must face.

Second, even where there are constitutional provisions, much of the Constitution is written in open-textured language using phrases such as "commerce among the states," "necessary and proper," "freedom of speech," "due process of law," "liberty," "taking," "equal protection," and "cruel and unusual punishment." How should the Court decide the content and meaning of these and other similar clauses that are found throughout the Constitution?

There is no doubt that this open-textured language is what has allowed the Constitution to survive for over 200 years and to govern a world radically different

---

[30] *See* Sanford Levinson, Authorizing Constitutional Text: On the Purported Twenty-Seventh Amendment, 11 Const. Comment. 101, 102-107 (1994); William Van Alstyne, What Do You Think About the Twenty-Seventh Amendment, 10 Const. Comment. 9 (1993); Michael Stokes Paulsen, A General Theory of Article V: The Constitutional Lessons of the Twenty-Seventh Amendment, 103 Yale L.J. 677 (1993).

§1.4 [1] McCulloch v. Maryland, 17 U.S. (4 Wheat.) 316, 407, 415 (1819). *McCulloch* is discussed in detail in §3.2.

from the one that existed when it was drafted. But it is this very nature of the Constitution that requires that courts interpret it and decide its meaning.

Third, inevitably in constitutional law, courts must face the question of what, if any, government justifications are sufficient to permit the government to interfere with a fundamental right or to discriminate. Even though the First Amendment says that Congress shall make "no law" abridging freedom of speech, that provision never has been regarded as an absolute. Once it is recognized that there can be laws preventing perjury or, to use a classic example, forbidding falsely shouting "fire" in a crowded theater, the issue becomes how to draw a line as to when the government can regulate speech.[2]

Although the Fourteenth Amendment says that states shall not deny any person equal protection of the laws, inevitably states must draw distinctions among people. For instance, every state requires that people be 16 in order to get a driver's license, and that they have a low income in order to receive welfare benefits. These, and an infinite variety of other laws, can be challenged as treating people unequally, and courts must decide when differences in treatment are justified and when they deny equal protection. The point is that in interpreting and applying the Constitution, courts must decide what, if any, justifications permit deviating from the text, or interfering with a right, or discriminating.

Although these issues of interpretation arise in every area of constitutional law, there has been an especially heated scholarly and public debate over the question of whether it is appropriate for the Court to interpret the Constitution to protect rights that are not expressly stated in the text.[3] The paradigm issue concerning this debate has been whether the Court should have recognized a constitutional right of women to terminate their pregnancies in the absence of an explicit textual provision or framers' intent supporting such a right.[4]

The Debate Between Originalism and Nonoriginalism

Over the last few decades, the debate frequently has been characterized as one between originalism, sometimes synonymously called interpretivism, and nonoriginalism, sometimes termed noninterpretivism. Originalism is the view that "judges deciding constitutional issues should confine themselves to enforcing norms that are stated or clearly implicit in the written Constitution."[5] In contrast, nonoriginalism is the "contrary view that courts should go beyond that set of references and enforce norms that cannot be discovered within the four corners of the document."[6]

---

[2] The example of falsely shouting "fire" in a crowded theater comes from Justice Oliver Wendell Holmes's opinion in Schenck v. United States, 249 U.S. 47, 52 (1919), discussed in §11.3.2.2.

[3] See, e.g., Robert W. Bennett & Lawrence B. Solum, Constitutional Originalism: A Debate (2011); Robert H. Bork, The Tempting of America (1990); Mark Tushnet, Red, White, and Blue: A Critical Analysis of Constitutional Law (1988); John Hart Ely, Democracy and Distrust (1980).

[4] See Roe v. Wade, 410 U.S. 113 (1973).

[5] Ely, supra note 3, at 1. See Steven G. Calabresi, ed., Originalism: A Quarter Century of Debate (2007) (a collection of essays advocating originalism and discussing arguments for and against it).

[6] Id.

Originalists believe that the Court should find a right to exist in the Constitution only if it is expressly stated in the text or was clearly intended by its framers. If the Constitution is silent, originalists say it is for the legislature, unconstrained by the courts, to decide the law. Nonoriginalists think that it is permissible for the Court to interpret the Constitution to protect rights that are not expressly stated or clearly intended. Originalists believe that the meaning of a constitutional provision was set when it was adopted and that it can be changed solely by amendment; nonoriginalists believe that the Constitution's meaning can evolve by amendment and by interpretation. For example, originalists argue that it was wrong for the Court to strike down state laws prohibiting the use of contraceptives and forbidding abortion.[7] Because the Constitution is silent about reproductive freedom and there is no evidence that the framers intended to protect such a right, originalists argue that the matter is left entirely to the legislatures to govern as they deem appropriate. Nonoriginalists, by contrast, believe that it was appropriate for the Court to decide that the word "liberty" includes a right of privacy and that reproductive freedom is an essential aspect of privacy.

The disagreement between originalists and nonoriginalists is not only about whether the Court should recognize unenumerated rights. Originalists and nonoriginalists also disagree over how the Court should decide the meaning of particular constitutional provisions. For example, an issue arose before the Supreme Court as to whether the Fourth Amendment requires that police officers "knock and announce" before searching a residence.[8] Justice Thomas, following his originalist philosophy, decided the issue by considering the law as of 1791 when the Fourth Amendment was adopted and concluded that knock and announce is generally required because it was part of the law at that time. For a nonoriginalist, such historical practice might be of interest, but is not necessarily decisive because the meaning of the Constitution is not limited to what the framers experienced or intended. More recently, the Supreme Court, in an opinion by Justice Scalia, found that it violated the Fourth Amendment for the police to put a GPS device on a car without a valid warrant and track its movements for 28 days because that would have been regarded as a trespass under an English law case from 1765.[9]

Simply stated, the disagreement between originalists and nonoriginalists is basically over how the Constitution should evolve. Originalists explicitly state that amendment is the only legitimate means for constitutional evolution.[10] If there is to be a right to use contraceptives or a right to abortion, originalists would say that the Constitution must be amended.

---

[7] *See* Griswold v. Connecticut, 381 U.S. 479 (1965) (declaring unconstitutional Connecticut law prohibiting the use of contraceptives); Roe v. Wade, 410 U.S. 113 (1973) (declaring unconstitutional Texas law prohibiting abortion).

[8] Wilson v. Arkansas, 514 U.S. 927 (1995).

[9] United States v. Jones, 132 S. Ct. 945 (2012).

[10] *See, e.g.*, Raoul Berger, G. Edward White's Apology for Judicial Activism, 63 Tex. L. Rev. 367, 372 (1984); William Van Alstyne, Interpreting this Constitution: The Unhelpful Contributions of Special Theories of Judicial Review, 35 U. Fla. L. Rev. 209, 234-235 n.66 (1983).

In contrast, nonoriginalists believe that the Constitution's meaning is not limited to what the framers intended; rather, the meaning and application of constitutional provisions should evolve by interpretation.[11] The fact that the framers of the Fourteenth Amendment did not intend to prohibit gender discrimination or to apply the Bill of Rights to the states is not decisive for the nonoriginalist in deciding what the Constitution means. This discussion has been expressed as a debate over whether the document is a "living Constitution."

It is important to recognize that the Supreme Court, at various times, has professed adherence to each of these competing philosophies. In *South Carolina v. United States*, in 1905, the Court stated: "The Constitution is a written instrument. As such its meaning does not alter. That which it meant when adopted, it means now."[12] But there are equally strong statements from the Court rejecting an originalist approach. In *Home Building and Loan Assn. v. Blaisdell*, in 1934, the Court declared:

> It is no answer to say that this public need was not apprehended a century ago, or to insist that what the provision of the Constitution meant to the vision of that day it must mean to the vision of our time. If by the statement that what the Constitution meant at the time of its adoption it means today, it is intended to say that the great clauses of the Constitution must be confined to the interpretation which the framers, with the conditions and outlook of their time, would have placed upon them, the statement carries its own refutation. It was to guard against such a narrow conception that Chief Justice John Marshall uttered the memorable warning—"We must never forget that it is a constitution we are expounding."[13]

Countless other quotations from the Court can be found endorsing and rejecting both originalism and nonoriginalism.

The Range of Alternatives Within Originalism and Nonoriginalism

There are not only two approaches to interpreting the Constitution, but a wide range of alternative views exist within both originalism and nonoriginalism. Originalism and nonoriginalism are general categories more than unitary philosophies. Within originalism, there are those who might be termed strict originalists, who believe that the Court must follow the literal text and the specific intent of its drafters.[14] A strict originalist, for example, is likely to believe that the Court was wrong in ordering desegregation of public schools because the Congress that ratified the Fourteenth Amendment also approved the segregation of the District of

---

[11] *See, e.g.*, Gregg v. Georgia, 428 U.S. 153, 227 (1975) (Brennan, J., dissenting) (arguing that the cruel and unusual punishment clause should be interpreted according to contemporary norms); *see also* Peter Irons, Brennan v. Rehnquist: The Battle for the Constitution (1994); Bernard Schwartz, Brennan v. Rehnquist—Mirror Images in Constitutional Construction, 19 Okla. City U. L. Rev. 213 (1994).

[12] 199 U.S. 437, 448 (1905).

[13] 290 U.S. 398, 442-443 (1934).

[14] *See, e.g.*, Raoul Berger, Government by Judiciary (1977).

Columbia public schools. But there also are more moderate originalists who are "more concerned with the adopters' general purposes than with their intentions in a very precise sense."[15] A moderate originalist likely would argue that the Court was correct in ordering school desegregation because it advances the general purpose of the equal protection clause even if it does not follow the framers' specific views.

Because the framers' intent can be stated at many different levels of abstraction, the distinction between strict and moderate originalism is not always clear. Yet there is a difference between believing that the specific conceptions of the framers are binding and believing that the framers' general concepts are controlling, but that their particular conceptions need not be followed.[16]

In recent years, Justice Antonin Scalia has propounded a different version of originalism, one that focuses on finding the "original meaning" of constitutional provisions.[17] Justice Scalia says that original meaning is to be found in the historical practices and understandings of the time, not the views of the document's drafters.[18] As with other forms of originalism, Justice Scalia believes that the Constitution's meaning is fixed and unchanging until it is amended.

There are a great many varieties of nonoriginalism. This is inevitable because nonoriginalism describes what *doesn't* control interpretation; it does not specify what should be looked to in deciding the meaning of the Constitution. Some, including often the Supreme Court, say that tradition should be a, or even *the*, guide in interpreting the Constitution.[19] The tension between specific and abstract originalism replicates itself in the use of tradition as a method of interpretation. Justice Scalia, for example, has said that when the Court looks to tradition in deciding the meaning of due process, it should consider only traditions stated at the most specific level of abstraction.[20] Justice Brennan rejected this view and would allow the Court to follow traditions stated more generally.[21]

Another strand of nonoriginalism emphasizes the Court's role in implementing the processes of government. Some believe that the Court may decide cases based on contemporary values, but only when it is dealing with issues concerning

---

[15] Paul Brest, The Misconceived Quest for the Original Understanding. 60 B.U. L. Rev. 204, 205 (1980).

[16] The distinction between concepts and conceptions is from Ronald Dworkin, Taking Rights Seriously 134-136 (1978).

[17] *See, e.g.,* Antonin Scalia, A Matter of Interpretation: Federal Courts and the Law (1997).

[18] I have described and analyzed this approach to constitutional interpretation in more detail in Erwin Chemerinsky, The Jurisprudence of Justice Scalia: A Critical Appraisal, 22 U. Haw. L. Rev. 385 (2000).

[19] *See, e.g.,* Poe v. Ullman, 367 U.S. 497, 522-555 (1961) (Harlan, J., dissenting); Adamson v. California, 332 U.S. 46, 59-68 (1947) (Frankfurter J., concurring) (describing tradition as the basis for interpreting due process). Another view of tradition is advanced in Barry Friedman & Scott B. Smith, The Sedimentary Constitution, 147 U. Pa. L. Rev. 1 (1998) (constitutional interpretation should account for all that has occurred with regard to a constitutional provision throughout American history).

[20] *See, e.g.,* Michael H. v. Gerald D., 491 U.S. 110, 127 n.6 (1989) (plurality opinion).

[21] *Id.* at 137-141 (Brennan, J., dissenting). *See also* Laurence Tribe & Michael Dorf, On Reading the Constitution (1991) (discussing the debate over the use of tradition and its level of abstraction).

the process of government, such as in ensuring fair representation and adjudication.[22] Professor John Hart Ely, for example, argued that the Court is justified in being nonoriginalist when it follows a "participation-oriented, representation reinforcing approach."[23] Ely argues that nonoriginalism is appropriate when the Court is providing "procedural fairness in the resolution of individual disputes" or by "ensuring broad participation in the processes and distributions of government."[24] Ely maintains that the Court has special expertise in the area of procedure and also that judicial review in this realm is consistent with majority rule because it is perfecting democracy, whereas other judicial review must be limited because it is inconsistent with democratic principles.

Other nonoriginalists believe that the Court should discern and implement the "natural law" in interpreting the Constitution.[25] Still others say that the Court should identify and follow the deeply embedded moral consensus that exists in society.[26] Often nonoriginalists reject limiting the Constitution to the enumerations in the text or the framers' intent but don't articulate a specific philosophy for how meaning should be given to the Constitution.

The Basic Arguments for Originalism

The issue of how the Constitution should be interpreted confronts all branches and levels of government; all officeholders take an oath to uphold the Constitution and are therefore required to interpret the document. Yet the debate between originalism and nonoriginalism has focused on which approach the judiciary should follow in interpreting the Constitution.

Originalists make two primary arguments for their approach. First, some originalists argue that the very nature of interpreting a document requires that its meaning be limited to its specific text and its framers' intentions. Professor Walter Benn Michaels, for example, stated that "any interpretation of the Constitution that really is an interpretation . . . of the Constitution . . . is always and only an interpretation of what the Constitution originally meant."[27] Professor Edward Melvin wrote that "when a judge takes his oath to uphold the Constitution he promises to carry out the intention of its framers."[28]

---

[22] *See* Ely, *supra* note 3, at 73-75.

[23] *Id.* at 87.

[24] *Id.*

[25] *See, e.g.*, Harry V. Jaffa, Original Intent and the Framers of the Constitution: A Disputed Question (1994).

[26] *See, e.g.*, Larry G. Simon, The Authority of the Framers of the Constitution: Can Originalist Interpretation Be Justified?, 73 Cal. L. Rev. 1482, 1505-1510 (1985) (describing constitutional interpretation based on "deeply layered consensus"); Harry H. Wellington, Common Law Rules and Constitutional Double Standards: Some Notes on Adjudication, 83 Yale L.J. 221, 284 (1973).

[27] Walter Benn Michaels, Response to Perry and Simon, 58 S. Cal. L. Rev. 673, 673 (1985).

[28] Edward J. Melvin, Judicial Activism: The Violation of the Oath, 27 Cath. Law. 283, 284 (1982).

Second, and more commonly, originalists argue that their approach is desirable to constrain the power of unelected judges in a democratic society.[29] The argument is that the basic premise of American democracy is majority rule; "the political principle that governmental policymaking—. . . decisions as to which values among competing values shall prevail, and as to how those values shall be implemented—ought to be subject to control by persons accountable to the electorate."[30] The claim is that judicial review is a "deviant institution in American democracy" because it permits unelected judges to overturn the decisions of popularly accountable officials.[31] Alexander Bickel termed this the "counter-majoritarian difficulty," and it has been at the core of the debate over the proper method of judicial review.[32]

Originalists argue, therefore, that the Court is justified in invalidating government decisions only when it is following values clearly stated in the text or intended by the framers. Raoul Berger, for example, contends that "activist judicial review is inconsistent with democratic theory because it substitutes the policy choices of unelected, unaccountable judges for those of the people's representatives."[33] Robert Bork similarly remarked that a "Court that makes rather than implements value choices cannot be squared with the presuppositions of a democratic society."[34]

As to the former argument, that interpretation requires originalism, the nonoriginalist reply is that it is a tautology; it defines interpretation as requiring originalism and then concludes that only originalism is a legitimate method of interpretation. Nonoriginalists argue that both theories claim to be interpreting the Constitution and that neither is inherently the proper approach.

The second argument, based on democracy, has produced a variety of answers. Some nonoriginalists dispute the definition of democracy as majority rule that originalists rely on. They argue that neither descriptively nor normatively should American democracy be defined as majority rule.[35] The framers openly and explicitly distrusted majority rule, and therefore virtually every government institution that they created had strong anti-majoritarian features. As described above in §1.2, the Constitution exists primarily to shield some matters from easy change by

---

[29] *See, e.g.,* Robert Bork, Neutral Principles and Some First Amendment Problems, 47 Ind. L.J. 1 (1971).

[30] Perry, *supra* note 3, at 9; *see also* Ely, *supra* note 3, at 5, 7.

[31] Alexander Bickel, The Least Dangerous Branch 18 (1962).

[32] *Id.* at 16-17. Professor Barry Friedman has written an excellent series of articles tracing the history of the counter-majoritarian difficulty. *See, e.g.,* Barry Friedman, The History of the Counter-Majoritarian Difficulty, Part Four: Law's Politics, 148 U. Pa. L. Rev. 971 (2000); Barry Friedman, The History of the Counter-Majoritarian Difficulty, Part One: The Road to Judicial Supremacy, 73 N.Y.U. L. Rev. 333 (1998).

[33] Raoul Berger, Ely's Theory of Judicial Review, 42 Ohio St. L.J. 87, 87 (1981).

[34] Bork, *supra* note 29, at 6.

[35] *See, e.g.,* Erwin Chemerinsky, Foreword: The Vanishing Constitution, 103 Harv. L. Rev. 43, 74-76 (1989).

political majorities.[36] Judicial review implementing a counter-majoritarian document is inherently anti-majoritarian. Some critics of originalism argue that a preferable definition of American democracy includes both substantive values and procedural norms such as majority rule.[37] Nonoriginalist judicial review advancing these substantive values is therefore consistent with this broader definition of democracy.

However, some critics of originalism accept the originalists' definition of democracy as majority rule, but purport to offer a theory that reconciles judicial review with majority rule. John Ely, for example, argues that his process-based theory is consistent with democracy because judicial review reinforces majority rule when it ensures fair representation and procedures.[38] Michael Perry contends that judicial review is consistent with majority rule so long as Congress retains the power to restrict the jurisdiction of the Supreme Court.[39]

Also, some critics of originalism argue that originalist judicial review is itself inconsistent with majority rule and therefore cannot claim any advantage over nonoriginalism.[40] The claim is that all judicial review, including originalist review, involves unelected judges overturning policies enacted by electorally accountable officials.

Originalists often answer this by claiming that originalist judicial review is democratic because the people consented to the adoption of the Constitution.[41] But nonoriginalists reply that it is wrong to say that the people consented to the Constitution because less than 5 percent of the population participated in the ratification process.[42] More important, it is erroneous to say that originalist review is democratic because the people ratified the Constitution because not a person alive today — and not even most of our ancestors — voted in its favor.[43] Democracy is defined by originalists to require decisions by current majorities; majority rule does not exist if society is governed by decisions of past majorities that cannot be overruled by a majority of the current population.

---

[36] Justice Jackson eloquently expressed this view of the Bill of Rights:

> The very purpose of a Bill of Rights was to withdraw certain subjects from the vicissitudes of political controversy, to place them beyond the reach of majorities and officials and to establish them as legal principles to be applied by the courts. One's right to life, liberty, and property, to free speech, a free press, freedom of worship and assembly, and other fundamental rights may not be submitted to vote: they depend on the outcome of no elections.

West Va. State Bd. of Educ. v. Barnette, 319 U.S. 624, 638 (1943).

[37] *See, e.g.,* Mark Tushnet, Red, White and Blue: A Critical Analysis of Constitutional Law 71 (1988).

[38] Ely, *supra* note 3, at 101-104.

[39] Perry, *supra* note 3, at 126; the authority of Congress to restrict federal court jurisdiction is discussed at §2.9.

[40] *See, e.g.,* Erwin Chemerinsky, Interpreting the Constitution 17-20 (1987).

[41] Bork, *supra* note 29, at 3.

[42] Max Lerner, Constitution and Court as Symbols, 46 Yale L.J. 1290, 1296 (1937).

[43] Brest, *supra* note 15, at 225.

The Basic Arguments for Nonoriginalism

Three major arguments are often advanced to support nonoriginalism. First, nonoriginalists maintain that it is desirable to have the Constitution evolve by interpretation and not only by amendment. The cumbersome amendment process, requiring approval by two-thirds of both Houses of Congress and three-fourths of the states, makes it likely that few amendments will be added to the Constitution. Only 17 amendments have been added in more than two centuries. The claim is that nonoriginalist review is necessary if the Constitution is to meet the needs of a changing society.

Nonoriginalists argue, for example, that equal protection in the last half of the twentieth century must mean that government-mandated racial segregation is unacceptable, yet there is strong evidence that the framers of the Fourteenth Amendment approved this practice.[44] The drafters of the equal protection clause did not intend to protect women from discrimination,[45] but it is widely accepted that the clause should apply to gender discrimination. Indeed, the argument is made that under originalism it would be unconstitutional to elect a woman as president or vice president because the Constitution refers to these officeholders with the word "he," and the framers clearly intended that they be male.[46]

Moderate originalists respond to this by contending that all of these problems could be avoided under their approach because eliminating segregation, stopping gender discrimination, and allowing women to be elected president or vice president are consistent with the framers' general intentions. But nonoriginalists counter that moderate originalism fails in its goal of constraining judges and is actually indistinguishable from nonoriginalism. The intent behind a constitutional provision can be stated at many different levels of abstraction. Is the intent behind the equal protection clause protecting former slaves, protecting blacks, protecting racial minorities, protecting all "discrete and insular" minorities, or protecting everyone in society from unjust discrimination? Deciding the level of abstraction necessarily requires a value choice by the Justices.[47] Moreover, at the highest level of abstraction, the framers desired liberty and equality; almost any imaginable court decision can be justified as consistent with these values.

---

[44] The same Congress that ratified the Fourteenth Amendment also approved the segregation of the District of Columbia public schools. *See* Ronald Dworkin, Law's Empire 360 (1986). This legislation was later declared unconstitutional in *Bolling v. Sharpe*, 347 U.S. 497 (1954), discussed in §9.3.3.1. *But see* Michael McConnell, Originalism and the Desegregation Decisions, 81 Va. L. Rev. 947 (1995) (arguing that the framers of the Fourteenth Amendment did intend to desegregate public schools).

[45] *See, e.g.,* The Slaughter-House Cases, 83 U.S. (16 Wall.) 36, 81 (1872) (stating that the equal protection clause was meant only to protect racial minorities and never would be extended beyond this).

[46] Richard B. Saphire, Judicial Review in the Name of the Constitution, 8 U. Dayton L. Rev. 745, 796-797 (1983).

[47] Paul Brest, The Fundamental Rights Controversy: The Essential Contradictions of Normative Constitutional Scholarship, 90 Yale L.J. 1063, 1091-1092 (1981) ("The fact is that all adjudication requires making choices among the levels of generality on which to articulate principles, and all such choices are inherently non-neutral.").

§1.4 How Should the Constitution Be Interpreted?

A second major argument for nonoriginalism is that there is not an unambiguous, knowable framers' intent that can be found to resolve constitutional questions. Instead, the process of determining the framers' intent invariably is a process of interpretation that is affected by contemporary values; in other words, it is indistinguishable from nonoriginalism. In part, the argument is that there is not a single framer or group of framers. The framers include the drafters of a provision, the members of the House and Senate that voted for it, and the members of the state conventions and legislatures that ratified it.[48] Moreover, even if a particular group is chosen as authoritative for purposes of constitutional decision making, there is not a single intent but, rather, many and perhaps conflicting reasons for adopting a particular constitutional provision.[49] Ronald Dworkin remarked that "there are no, or very few, relevant collective intentions, or perhaps only collective intentions that are indeterminate rather than decisive one way or another."[50]

Nonoriginalists argue further that even if the group is determined and even if somehow a way of arriving at collective intent could be found, the historical materials are too incomplete to support authoritative conclusions. Jeffrey Shaman explains that the "Journal of the Constitutional Convention, which is the primary record of the Framers' intent, is neither complete nor necessarily accurate."[51] As Justice Jackson eloquently remarked: "Just what our forefathers did envision, or would have envisioned had they foreseen modern conditions, must be divined from materials almost as enigmatic as the dreams Joseph was called upon to interpret for Pharaoh."[52]

Third, some nonoriginalists argue that nonoriginalism is the preferable method of interpretation because it is the approach intended by the framers. In other words, the claim is that following originalism requires that originalism be abandoned because the framers did not intend this method of interpretation. Professor Jeff Powell stated: "It is commonly assumed that the 'interpretive intention' of the Constitution's framers was that the Constitution would be construed in accordance with what future interpreters could gather of the framers' own purposes, expectations, and intentions. Inquiry shows that assumption to be incorrect. Of the numerous hermeneutical options that were available in the framers' day . . . none corresponds to the modern notion of intentionalism."[53] In other words, the framers probably did not intend that their intent would govern later interpretations of the Constitution.

Originalists disagree with each of these arguments. As to the first, that nonoriginalism leads to better results, originalists argue that the appropriate method

---

[48] *See* John G. Wofford, The Blinding Light: The Use of History in Constitutional Interpretation, 31 U. Chi. L. Rev. 502, 508-509 (1964).

[49] Ely, *supra* note 3, at 18.

[50] Ronald Dworkin, The Forum of Principle, 56 N.Y.U. L. Rev. 469, 477 (1981).

[51] Jeffrey Shaman, The Constitution, the Supreme Court, and Creativity, 9 Hastings Const. L.Q. 257, 267 (1982).

[52] Youngstown Sheet & Tube Co. v. Sawyer, 343 U.S. 579, 592 (1952) (Jackson, J., concurring).

[53] H. Jefferson Powell, The Original Understanding of Original Intent, 98 Harv. L. Rev. 885, 948 (1985).

of changing the Constitution is through amendment, not interpretation. Original-ists argue that nonoriginalism improperly empowers unelected judges to displace the decisions of popularly elected officials and that, historically, nonoriginalism has produced undesirable decisions, such as those invalidating economic regula-tions in the first third of the last century.[54]

As to the second argument, on the difficulty of determining the framers' intent, originalists maintain that if the intent on a particular issue cannot be deter-mined, then it is a matter that should be left to the political process. Robert Bork wrote: "It follows that the choice of 'fundamental values' by the Court cannot be justified. Where constitutional materials do not clearly specify the value to be preferred, there is no principled way to prefer any claimed human value to any other."[55]

Finally, originalists argue that the framers did intend that their approach be followed in constitutional interpretation. Robert Bork declared that "not even a scintilla of evidence supports the argument that the framers and the ratifiers of the various amendments intended the judiciary to develop new individual rights, which correspondingly create new disabilities for democratic government. . . . If the framers really intended to delegate to judges the function of creating new rights by the method of moral philosophy, one would expect they would say so."[56]

Conclusion

This discussion of constitutional interpretation, of course, is not a compre-hensive presentation of the arguments on either side of the debate but rather a summary of some of the most frequently advanced points. The debate over how the Constitution should be interpreted will continue as long as there is a Consti-tution. Yet the issue of how the Constitution should be interpreted is crucial and manifests itself expressly or implicitly in all areas of constitutional law and all of the topics discussed in this book.

§1.5   WHO SHOULD BE THE AUTHORITATIVE INTERPRETER OF THE CONSTITUTION?

The Issue

Regardless of the method of interpretation, who should interpret the Con-stitution? The correct answer is that all government officials and institutions are required to engage in constitutional interpretation. All elected officeholders take

---

[54] *See* Bork, *supra* note 3, at 4449.

[55] Bork, *supra* note 29, at 8.

[56] Robert H. Bork, The Impossibility of Finding Welfare Rights in the Constitution, 1979 Wash. U. L.Q. 695, 697.

an oath to uphold the Constitution. Therefore, legislators—federal, state, and local—are obliged to consider the constitutionality of bills before ratifying them. The executive must consider constitutionality in deciding what laws to propose, which bills passed by the legislature to veto, and what executive policies to implement. Ever since *Marbury v. Madison*, the judiciary has had the authority to review the constitutionality of laws and of executive acts.[1] So the real question is not who should interpret the Constitution but, more specifically, who should be the authoritative interpreter of the Constitution? When there is a disagreement over how the Constitution should be interpreted, who resolves the conflict? This is an issue that arises in many ways throughout the book.

Approach 1: No Authoritative Interpreter

There are three possible answers to the question of who should be the authoritative interpreter of the Constitution. One approach is for no branch to be regarded as authoritative in constitutional interpretation. Each branch of the government would have equal authority to determine the meaning of constitutional provisions, and conflicts would be resolved through political power and compromise. If Congress and the president believe that a law is constitutional, they could disregard a judicial ruling of unconstitutionality. If the president believes a law to be unconstitutional, he or she could refuse to enforce it, notwithstanding declarations of its constitutionality from the legislature and judiciary.

This approach to constitutional interpretation finds support early in United States history from presidents such as Thomas Jefferson and Andrew Jackson. Jefferson wrote:

> [N]othing in the Constitution has given . . . [the judges] a right to decide for the Executive, more than the Executive to decide for them. Both magistrates are equally independent in the sphere of action assigned to them. The judges, believing the law constitutional, had a right to pass a sentence of fine and imprisonment; because that power was placed in their hands by the Constitution. But the Executive, believing the law to be unconstitutional, was bound to remit the execution of it, because that power has been confided to him by the constitution. That instrument meant that its coordinate branches should be checks on each other. But the opinion which gives to the judges the right to decide what laws are constitutional, and what not, not only for themselves in their own sphere of action, but for the legislature and executive also in their spheres, would make the judiciary a despotic branch.[2]

Similarly, in vetoing a bill to recharter the Bank of the United States, President Andrew Jackson declared:

---

§1.5 [1] 5 U.S. (1 Cranch) 137 (1803). *Marbury* is discussed in detail in §2.2.1.
[2] Thomas Jefferson, letter to Abigail Adams, September 11, 1804, 8 The Writings of Thomas Jefferson 310 (Ford ed. 1897).

The Congress, the Executive, and the Court must each for itself be guided by its own opinion of the Constitution. Each public officer who takes an oath to support the Constitution swears that he will support it as he understands it, and not as it is understood by others. It is as much the duty of the House of Representatives, of the Senate, and of the President to decide upon the constitutionality of any bill or resolution which may be presented to them for passage or approval as it is of the supreme judges when it may be brought before them for judicial decision. The opinion of the judges has no more authority over Congress than the opinion of Congress has over the judges, and on that point, the President is independent of both.[3]

In the 1980s, Attorney General Edwin Meese took exactly this position. Meese challenged the view that the judiciary is the ultimate arbiter of constitutional questions and argued that each branch has equal authority to decide for itself the meaning of constitutional provisions.[4] Meese remarked: "The Supreme Court, then, is not the only interpreter of the Constitution. Each of the three coordinate branches of government created and empowered by the Constitution—the executive and legislative no less than the judicial—has a duty to interpret the Constitution in the performance of its official functions."[5] More recently, advocates of "popular constitutionalism" have criticized what they regard as "judicial supremacy."[6] Although these terms are not defined with precision, a core aspect is to challenge the Court as ultimate arbiter of the meaning of the Constitution.[7]

Approach 2: Each Branch Is Authoritative in Certain Areas

A second approach to the question of who is the authoritative interpreter of the Constitution is that for each part of the Constitution one branch of government is assigned the role of being the final arbiter of disputes, but it is not the same branch for all parts of the Constitution. Thus, each branch would be the authoritative interpreter for some constitutional provisions. Because the Constitution does not specify who should interpret the document, some institution would need to allocate interpretive authority among the branches of government.

Arguably, the second approach is the one that best describes the current system of constitutional interpretation. The judiciary has declared that certain parts of the Constitution pose political questions and are matters to be decided by branches of

---

[3] Andrew Jackson, Veto Message, 2 Messages and Papers of the President 576, 581-583 (Richardson ed. 1896).

[4] Edwin Meese III, The Law of the Constitution, 61 Tul. L. Rev. 979 (1987). *See also* Edwin Meese III, Putting the Federal Judiciary Back on the Constitutional Track, 14 Ga. St. U. L. Rev. 781 (1998).

[5] *Id.* at 985-986. *See also* Edward J. Hartnett, A Matter of Judgment, Not a Matter of Opinion, 74 N.Y.U. L. Rev. 123 (1999).

[6] *See, e.g.,* Larry D. Kramer, The People Themselves: Popular Constitutionalism and Judicial Review (2004). For a critique of popular constitutionalism, *see* Erwin Chemerinsky, In Defense of Judicial Review: The Perils of Popular Constitutionalism, 2004 U. Ill. L. Rev. 673.

[7] In Packing the Court: The Rise of Judicial Power and the Coming Crisis of the Supreme Court 253 (2009), James MacGregor Burns writes that "the Constitution never granted the judiciary a supremacy over the government, nor had the Framers ever conceived it."

government other than the courts.[8] For example, the courts frequently have held that challenges to the president's conduct of foreign policy—such as whether the Vietnam War was constitutional—pose a political question not to be resolved by the judiciary.[9] By declaring a matter to be a political question, the Court states that it is for the other branches of government to interpret the constitutional provisions in question and determine whether the Constitution is violated. The effect of the political question doctrine is that for each part of the Constitution there is a final arbiter, but it is not the same branch for all constitutional provisions.

Approach 3: The Judiciary Is the Authoritative Interpreter

A third and final approach is to assign to one branch of government final authority for all constitutional interpretation. Although every governmental institution interprets the Constitution, one branch is assigned the role of umpire; its views resolve disputes and are final until reversed by constitutional amendment.[10] Arguably, *Marbury v. Madison* endorses this approach in Chief Justice John Marshall's famous declaration: "It is emphatically the province and duty of the judicial department to say what the law is."[11] Similarly, in *United States v. Nixon*, the Supreme Court held that it was the judiciary's duty to determine the meaning of the Constitution.[12] In rejecting the president's claim that it was for the executive to determine the scope of executive privilege, Chief Justice Warren Burger, writing for the Court, stated: "The President's counsel . . . reads the Constitution as providing an absolute privilege of confidentiality for all Presidential communications. Many decisions of this Court, however, have unequivocally reaffirmed the holding of *Marbury v. Madison* that '[i]t is emphatically the province and duty of the judicial department to say what the law is.' "[13]

But *Marbury* and *Nixon* also can be read as ambiguous and as not resolving the question of which of these three approaches is preferable. *Marbury* could be read narrowly as holding only that the Court is the final arbiter of the meaning of Article III of the Constitution, which defines the judicial power. The specific issue in *Marbury*, which is discussed in §2.2, is whether a section of the Judiciary Act of 1789 is consistent with Article III of the Constitution. Accordingly, *Marbury* could be interpreted, consistent with the second approach described above, as assigning to the judiciary only the responsibility for interpreting Article III.

In fact, *Marbury* even could be seen as consistent with the first approach, that there is no final arbiter of the meaning of the Constitution. By this view, *Marbury* simply holds that the judiciary may interpret the Constitution in deciding cases—it is one voice—and that it is not required to defer to legislative or executive interpretations. *Marbury*, according to this argument, says nothing about whether other

---

[8] The political question doctrine is discussed in detail in §2.8.

[9] *See* §2.8.4.

[10] For an excellent scholarly exposition and development of this view, *see* Larry Alexander & Frederick Schauer, On Extrajudicial Constitutional Interpretation, 110 Harv. L. Rev. 1359 (1997).

[11] 5 U.S. at 177, *Marbury* is discussed in §2.2.1.

[12] 418 U.S. 683 (1974), discussed in §4.3.

[13] *Id.* at 703.

branches of government are bound to follow the Court's interpretation. Chief Justice Marshall's declaration could be understood as emphatically declaring that courts do have a voice.

Likewise, *United States v. Nixon* could be viewed as a limited ruling that the judiciary has the final word in cases raising the question of access to evidence necessary for criminal trials. The Court in *Nixon* emphasized the judiciary's special role in ensuring fair trials.[14] Thus, the case could be seen as holding only that the Court is the final arbiter in matters relating to the judiciary's powers under Article III.

Like the debate over the method of constitutional interpretation, there is no definitive answer to the question of who should be the authoritative interpreter of the Constitution. There is an obvious benefit to having a single institution—the judiciary—resolve disputes. The federal judiciary, with its greater insulation from majoritarian politics, is arguably best suited to interpret and enforce the anti-majoritarian American Constitution. But there is also value in allowing each institution to decide for itself the meaning of the Constitution, or in allowing each branch a realm where it is the final arbiter of the Constitution's meaning. The anti-majoritarian nature of the federal judiciary is seen by some as a reason to restrict its role.

Although this issue does not often arise explicitly, it underlies many constitutional issues. For example, should there be a political question doctrine where the interpretation of particular constitutional provisions is left to the political branches of government, or should the judiciary decide these questions?[15] Can Congress use its power to create "exceptions and regulations" to the Supreme Court's appellate jurisdiction to attempt to change the law, such as by keeping the Court from hearing challenges to state abortion laws?[16] Can Congress use its powers under §5 of the Fourteenth Amendment to enact laws that interpret the amendment differently from the Supreme Court and thus effectively overrule Supreme Court decisions?[17] All of these issues require consideration of who is the authoritative interpreter of the Constitution.

[14] *Id.* at 709.
[15] *See* §2.8.
[16] This topic is discussed in §2.9.
[17] Discussed in §3.7.2.

CHAPTER 2

The Federal Judicial Power*

* Portions of this chapter are drawn from Erwin Chemerinsky, Federal Jurisdiction (6th ed. 2011).

§2.1 INTRODUCTION

Article III

Article III of the Constitution, a substantial departure from the Articles of Confederation, created the federal judiciary and defines its powers. The Confederation Congress had very limited authority to create courts, and the only national court established under the Articles was the Court of Appeals in Cases of Capture. This court existed for admiralty cases, specifically for instances in which American ships seized vessels, termed "prizes," belonging to enemy countries.[1] The

---

§2.1 [1] John P. Frank, Historical Bases of the Federal Judicial System, 13 Law & Contemp. Probs. 3, 8 (1948).

Confederation Congress also had the authority to establish courts to punish piracies, but this power was immediately delegated to the states and never exercised at the national level.[2]

The Constitutional Convention recognized the need for a federal judiciary and unanimously approved Edmund Randolph's resolution "that a National Judiciary be established."[3] Article III covers seven important topics concerning the federal judiciary.

First, the initial words of Article III — "the judicial Power of the United States shall be vested" — created a federal judicial system. Although there was substantial disagreement about the appropriate structure and authority of the federal courts, there was consensus that a national judiciary was necessary.

Second, Article III vests the judicial power "in one supreme Court and in such inferior courts as Congress may from time to time ordain and establish." A major dispute at the Constitutional Convention was whether lower federal courts should exist. The Committee of the Whole, echoing resolutions offered by Randolph, proposed that there should be both a Supreme Court and inferior courts.[4] This proposal drew strong opposition from those who thought that it was unnecessary and undesirable to create lower federal courts. Opponents of lower federal courts argued that state courts, subject to review by the Supreme Court, were sufficient to protect the interests of the national government. Furthermore, lower federal courts were perceived as an unnecessary expense and a likely intrusion on the sovereignty of state governments.

But others expressed distrust in the ability and willingness of state courts to uphold federal law. James Madison stated: "Confidence cannot be put in the State Tribunals as guardians of the National authority and interests."[5] Madison argued that state judges were likely to be biased against federal law and could not be trusted, especially in instances where there were conflicting state and federal interests. Appeal to the Supreme Court was claimed to be inadequate to protect federal interests because the number of such appeals would exceed the Court's limited capacity to hear and decide cases.

Thus, the question of whether state courts are equal to federal courts in their willingness and ability to uphold federal law — an issue that continues to be debated and that influences a great many aspects of the law of federal jurisdiction[6] — has its origins in the earliest discussions of the federal judicial power. The proposal to create lower federal courts was initially defeated, 5 votes to 4, with two states divided.[7]

---

[2] There also were ad hoc tribunals to resolve border disputes among the states. *See* Henry Melvin Hart, David L. Shapiro & Daniel J. Meltzer, Hart & Wechsler's The Federal Courts and the Federal System 4 n.17 (5th ed. 2003).

[3] 1 Max Farrand, The Records of the Federal Convention of 1787, at 21 (1913).

[4] *Id.* at 104-105.

[5] *Id.* at 27.

[6] *See, e.g.,* Burt Neuborne, The Myth of Parity, 90 Harv. L. Rev. 1105 (1977); *see also* Larry Yackle, Reclaiming the Federal Courts (1994).

[7] Farrand, *supra* note 3, at 125.

Madison and James Wilson then proposed a compromise. They suggested that the Constitution mandate the existence of the Supreme Court, but leave it up to Congress to decide whether to create inferior courts. Their proposal was adopted by a vote of eight states to two, with one state divided.[8] Congress, in its first judiciary act in 1789, established lower federal courts, and they have existed ever since.

Third, Article III ensures the independence of the federal judiciary by according all federal judges life tenure, "during good Behaviour," and salaries that cannot be decreased during their time in office.[9] A crucial lasting difference between federal and state court judges is the electoral accountability of the latter. In 42 states, state court judges are subject to some form of electoral review.[10] Some contend that this makes federal courts uniquely suited for the protection of constitutional rights.[11]

Fourth, Article III, §2, defines the federal judicial power in terms of nine categories of "cases" and "controversies." These nine categories fall into two major types of provisions. One set of clauses authorizes the federal courts to vindicate and enforce the powers of the federal government. For example, federal courts have authority to decide all cases arising under the Constitution, treaties, and laws of the United States. Additionally, the federal courts have authority to hear all cases in which the United States is a party. The federal government's powers in the area of foreign policy are protected by according the federal courts authority to hear all cases affecting ambassadors and other public ministers and consuls; to hear all cases of admiralty and maritime jurisdiction; and to hear cases between a state, or its citizens, and a foreign country, or its citizens.

A second set of provisions authorizes the federal courts to serve an interstate umpiring function, resolving disputes between states and their citizens. Thus, Article III gives the federal courts the authority to decide controversies between two or more states, between a state and citizens of another state,[12] between citizens of different states, and between citizens of the same state claiming land in other states.

---

[8] *Id.*

[9] Congress has created judges without life tenure and salary protection, such as bankruptcy judges, magistrate judges, judges on specialized tribunals such as the Tax Court, and administrative law judges. These judges are called "Article I judges," and their tribunals are sometimes called "legislative courts." The constitutional limits on Congress's ability to create such judges and courts are discussed in Erwin Chemerinsky, Federal Jurisdiction ch. 4 (6th ed. 2011). As an example of these constitutional limits, the Court recently ruled that bankruptcy courts, whose judges sit for 14-year terms, cannot issue final judgments over state law claims unless they stem from the bankruptcy itself. Stern v. Marshall, 131 S. Ct. 2594 (2011).

[10] *See* Larry Berkson, Scott Beller & Michele Grimaldi, Judicial Selection in the United States: A Compendium of Provisions (1981).

[11] *See, e.g.*, Neuborne, *supra* note 6, at 1127-1128; *but see* Michael E. Solimine & James L. Walker, Constitutional Litigation in Federal and State Courts: An Empirical Analysis of Judicial Parity, 10 Hastings Const. L.Q. 213, 230-231 (1983) ("It does not follow . . . that elections of state judges . . . will influence the subsequent decisions of elected judges.").

[12] This provision was essentially overturned by the adoption of the Eleventh Amendment, which provides that the judicial power of the United States does not extend to cases between a state and citizens of a different state or citizens of foreign nations. The Eleventh Amendment is discussed in detail below in §2.10.

The fifth major topic covered in Article III is the allocation of judicial power between the Supreme Court and the lower federal courts. Article III states that the Supreme Court has original jurisdiction over cases affecting ambassadors, other public ministers and consuls, and those in which a state shall be a party. In all other cases, the Supreme Court is granted appellate jurisdiction, both as to law and fact, subject to "such Exceptions and under such regulations as Congress shall make."

The Supreme Court has held that Congress can give the lower federal courts concurrent jurisdiction, even over those matters where the Constitution specifies that the Supreme Court has original jurisdiction.[13] Under contemporary practice, the Supreme Court's original jurisdiction is limited to disputes between two or more states.[14]

Sixth, Article III prescribes that the trial of all crimes, except in cases of impeachment, shall be by jury. Furthermore, it requires that the trial shall occur in the state where the crime was committed.

Finally, Article III provides that treason shall consist only in "levying war" against the United States or giving aid or comfort to the enemy and that no person shall be convicted of treason except on testimony of two witnesses or confession in open court. Article III concludes by stating that Congress has the power to prescribe the punishments for treason, but that "no Attainder of Treason shall work corruption of blood, or Forfeiture during the Life of the Person attained." In other words, the traitor's heirs and descendants may be punished only for their own wrongdoing.

Authority for Judicial Review

Interestingly, Article III never expressly grants the federal courts the power to review the constitutionality of federal or state laws or executive actions. Perhaps the silence reflects the shared understanding that courts possess the authority for constitutional review and it was thought unnecessary to enumerate this. Perhaps the silence reflects a failure to consider the issue in drafting the Constitution or even the assumption that courts would not have this authority. Courts would exist, as is the case in Great Britain, to hear civil and criminal cases, but not to declare unconstitutional government actions.

There were proposals at the Constitutional Convention to create a Council of Revision, composed of the president and members of the national judiciary. The Council of Revision would have reviewed "every act of the National Legislature before [it went into effect]."[15] The proposal was defeated every time it was raised. Opponents successfully argued that it was undesirable to involve the judiciary directly in the lawmaking process.

There have been 200 years of debate as to whether the rejection of the Council of Revision also was an implicit rejection of the power of the federal courts to declare

---

[13] *See, e.g.*, Ames v. Kansas ex rel. Johnson, 111 U.S. 449, 464 (1884) (allowing concurrent jurisdiction over suits by ambassadors).

[14] For a discussion of Supreme Court jurisdiction, *see* Chemerinsky, *supra* note 9, at 21-24.

[15] Farrand, *supra* note 3, at 21.

statutes unconstitutional.[16] Professor Henry Monaghan cogently remarked that it is "increasingly doubtful that any conclusive case can be made one way or the other."[17]

However, from the earliest days of the country, the Supreme Court has claimed the power to review the constitutionality of federal and state laws and executive actions. Section 2.2 reviews the seminal cases. Section 2.2.1 focuses on *Marbury v. Madison*.[18] Section 2.2.2 examines the initial cases establishing the authority for the Supreme Court to review state court judgments and proceedings: *Martin v. Hunter's Lessee*[19] and *Cohens v. Virginia*.[20] Because of these decisions, the power of judicial review is firmly established and is an integral part of American government, even though it is not expressly authorized in the text of the Constitution.[21]

Limits on the Federal Judicial Power

It is frequently stated and widely accepted that federal courts are courts of limited jurisdiction. There are two primary restrictions on federal judicial power. First, Article III of the Constitution defines the scope of federal court authority. For example, Article III circumscribes the maximum extent of federal court subject matter jurisdiction. Additionally, judicial interpretation of Article III has created crucial doctrines that restrict access to the federal courts. For example, the principles of standing, ripeness, mootness, and the political question doctrine were created through judicial interpretation of Article III. These principles—often termed justiciability doctrines—are discussed in §§2.3 through 2.8. Section 2.3 begins with an introduction to the justiciability doctrines, and the subsequent sections examine, in turn, the prohibition of advisory opinions, standing, ripeness, mootness, and the political question doctrine.

Second, Congress plays an important role in limiting federal court jurisdiction. The Supreme Court has held that a federal court may hear a matter only when there is both constitutional and statutory authorization. Thus, statutes limit the jurisdiction of the federal courts and the reach of the judiciary's power. Additionally, under Article III, §2, Congress has the power to create "exceptions and regulations" to the Supreme Court's appellate jurisdiction. However, what Congress may do in exercising this power is very much disputed. Congress's ability to restrict the jurisdiction of the Supreme Court and the lower federal courts is discussed in §2.9.

[16] *See, e.g.*, 2 William Crosskey, Politics and the Constitution 1008-1046 (1953) (arguing that judicial review was not intended); Raoul Berger, Congress v. The Supreme Court (1969) (arguing that judicial review was intended).

[17] Henry Paul Monaghan, The Constitution Goes to Harvard, 13 Harv. C.R.-C.L. 117, 125 (1978).

[18] 5 U.S. (1 Cranch) 137 (1803).

[19] 14 U.S. (1 Wheat.) 304 (1816).

[20] 19 U.S. (6 Wheat.) 264 (1821).

[21] This is not to suggest that the debate over the desirability of judicial review is over. *See, e.g.*, James MacGregor Burns, Packing the Court: The Rise of Judicial Power and the Coming Crisis of the Supreme Court 252-253 (2009) (arguing that judicial review is illegitimate and should not be accepted); Mark Tushnet, Taking the Constitution Away from the Courts (2000) (arguing for the elimination of constitutional judicial review).

Central Themes

Examination of constitutional and statutory limits on the federal judicial power—the focus of this chapter—inevitably entails consideration of separation of powers and federalism concerns. From a separation of powers perspective, a decision about the appropriate content of the constitutional and statutory limits on federal judicial power is a question about the proper role for the federal judiciary in the tripartite scheme of American government. Determining the courts' constitutional authority or deciding Congress's ability to control federal court jurisdiction inescapably involves separation of powers analysis.

Also, because state courts are the primary alternative to federal courts, the scope of federal judicial power is crucial in determining the authority of the state courts. Expansion of federal judicial authority may be defended on federalism grounds as necessary to protect the interests of the federal government from state intrusion. But, at the same time, increased federal court review can be opposed on federalism grounds as usurping power properly reserved to the states.

§2.2   THE AUTHORITY FOR JUDICIAL REVIEW

§2.2.1   Marbury v. Madison: *The Authority for Judicial Review of Congressional and Presidential Actions*

Marbury v. Madison is the single most important decision in American constitutional law.[1] It established the authority for the judiciary to review the constitutionality of executive and legislative acts. Although the Constitution is silent as to whether federal courts have this authority, the power has existed ever since *Marbury*.

Facts

The election of 1800 was fiercely contested, with the three most important candidates being the incumbent John Adams, Thomas Jefferson, and Aaron Burr.[2]

---

§2.2 [1] 5 U.S. (1 Cranch) 137 (1803).

[2] For an excellent review of the factual background and of the Supreme Court's decision, *see* Burt Neuborne, Madison's Music 146-194 (2015); William Van Alstyne, A Critical Guide to *Marbury v. Madison*, 1969 Duke L.J. 1. For a description of the events during the election of 1800, *see* David McCulloch, John Adams (2001). The 200th anniversary of *Marbury*, in 2003, produced a number of important, excellent articles reexamining the case and its impact. *See, e.g.*, Davison M. Douglas, The Rhetorical Uses of *Marbury v. Madison*: The Emergence of a "Great Case," 38 Wake Forest L. Rev. 375 (2003); Richard H. Fallon, Jr., *Marbury* and the Constitutional Mind: A Bicentennial Essay on the Wages of Doctrinal Tension, 91 Cal. L. Rev. 1 (2003); Louise Weinberg, Our *Marbury*, 89 Va. L. Rev. 1235 (2003).

Jefferson received a majority of the popular vote but tied in the electoral college vote with Burr. The clear loser among the three was President Adams.

In January 1801, Adams's Secretary of State, John Marshall, was named to serve as the third Chief Justice of the United States Supreme Court. Throughout the remainder of Adams's presidency, Marshall served as both Secretary of State and Chief Justice. Adams was a Federalist, and the Federalists were determined to exercise their influence before the Republican, Jefferson, took office. On February 13, 1801, Congress enacted the Circuit Court Act, which reduced the number of Supreme Court Justices from six to five, decreasing the opportunity for Republican control of the Court. The Act also eliminated the Supreme Court Justices' duty to serve as circuit judges and created 16 new judgeships on the circuit courts. However, this change was short-lived; in 1802, Congress repealed this statute, restoring the practice of circuit riding by Supreme Court Justices and eliminating the newly created circuit court judgeships. The constitutionality of congressional abolition of judgeships was not tested in the courts.

On February 27, 1801, less than a week before the end of Adams's term, Congress adopted the Organic Act of the District of Columbia, which authorized the president to appoint 42 justices of the peace. Adams announced his nominations on March 2, and on March 3, the day before Jefferson's inauguration, the Senate confirmed the nominees. Immediately, Secretary of State (and Chief Justice) John Marshall signed the commissions for these individuals and dispatched his brother, James Marshall, to deliver them. A few commissions, including one for William Marbury, were not delivered before Jefferson's inauguration. President Jefferson instructed his Secretary of State, James Madison, to withhold the undelivered commissions.

Marbury filed suit in the United States Supreme Court seeking a writ of mandamus to compel Madison, as Secretary of State, to deliver the commission. Marbury claimed that the Judiciary Act of 1789 authorized the Supreme Court to grant mandamus in a proceeding filed initially in the Supreme Court. Although Marbury's petition was filed in December 1801, the Supreme Court did not hear the case until 1803 because Congress, by statute, abolished the June and December 1802 Terms of the Supreme Court.[3]

Holding

The Supreme Court ruled against Marbury and held that it could not constitutionally hear the case as a matter of original jurisdiction. The Court held that although the Judiciary Act of 1789 authorized such jurisdiction, this provision of the statute was unconstitutional because Congress cannot allow original jurisdiction beyond the situations enumerated in the Constitution.

Before examining the Court's reasoning, it should be questioned whether the Court acted improperly in considering any of the issues presented besides the jurisdictional question. It is, of course, a long-standing principle that "the first

---

[3] The constitutionality of Congress abolishing Terms of the Supreme Court has never been tested, but it is hard to imagine that it would be deemed constitutional.

question necessarily is that of jurisdiction."[4] Because the Court held that it lacked jurisdiction, all of the other parts of the opinion—such as considering whether the commission had vested and the ability of the judiciary to review the executive's action—were arguably improper.

Perhaps these parts of the opinion were meant to show that the Court saw no way to decide the case without considering the constitutionality of the statute. Or perhaps these parts of the opinion were simply Chief Justice Marshall's way of chastising the Jefferson administration for its refusal to deliver the commissions. Politically, Marshall knew that a ruling in favor of Marbury would be futile; the Jefferson administration would ignore it, and that would undermine the Court's authority at the beginning of its history. Therefore, Marshall may have included the initial parts of the opinion to show that the Jefferson administration improperly denied Marbury his commission, knowing that it was the most Marshall could do for Marbury.

Indeed, it can be questioned whether John Marshall should have participated in deciding the case at all because of his conflict of interest. He was the Secretary of State who signed Marbury's commission and who was responsible for its delivery. In light of his participation in the events that gave rise to the litigation, there were strong grounds for Marshall to have recused himself.

Marshall likely perceived that the case presented a unique opportunity: the chance to claim the power of judicial review, but in a context least likely to draw opposition. The statutory provision being declared unconstitutional was one that enlarged the judiciary's power, and the Jefferson administration obviously welcomed the result. As Robert McCloskey wrote: "[The] decision was a masterwork of indirection, a brilliant example of Marshall's capacity to sidestep danger while seeming to court it, to advance in one direction while his opponents are looking in another."[5]

Issue 1: Does Marbury Have a Right to the Commission?

Chief Justice Marshall structured the opinion around three questions.[6] First, does Marbury have a right to the commission? Second, if so, "do the laws of his country afford him a remedy?"[7] Third, if so, can the Supreme Court issue this remedy? Chief Justice Marshall then answers each question in turn.[8]

As to the first question, the Court concluded that Marbury had a right to the commission because all appropriate procedures were followed. Chief Justice Marshall concluded: "It is . . . decidedly the opinion of the court, that when a commission has been signed by the President, the appointment is made; and that the

---

[4] Ex parte McCardle, 74 U.S. (7 Wall.) 506, 512 (1869).

[5] Robert McCloskey, The American Supreme Court 40 (1960).

[6] 5 U.S. at 154.

[7] Id.

[8] Professor Van Alstyne has done a superb job of showing that for each question an alternative answer would have been equally, or even more, plausible. See Van Alstyne, supra note 2.

commission is complete, when the seal of the United States has been affixed to it by the Secretary of State."[9]

The Court might have decided this issue differently. President Jefferson took the position that "if there is any principle of law never yet contradicted, it is that delivery is one of the essentials to the validity of the deed."[10] But the Court rejected this view and ruled that delivery was merely a custom and that therefore withholding Marbury's commission was "violative of a vested legal right."[11]

Issue 2: Do the Laws Afford Marbury a Remedy?

Chief Justice Marshall's initial answer to this question was that "[t]he very essence of civil liberty certainly consists in the right of every individual to claim the protection of the laws, whenever he receives an injury."[12] The specific issue was whether the Court could give Marbury a remedy against the executive branch of government. The Court answered this by declaring that "[t]he government of the United States has been emphatically termed a government of laws, and not of men."[13] In other words, no person — not even the president — is above the law.

The Court then drew a distinction as to when the judiciary could afford relief: The judiciary could provide remedies against the executive when there is a specific duty to a particular person, but not when it is a political matter left to executive discretion. Chief Justice Marshall wrote:

> [W]here the heads of departments are the political or confidential agents of the executive, merely to execute the will of the President, or rather to act in cases in which the executive possesses a constitutional or legal discretion, nothing can be more perfectly clear than that their acts are only politically examinable. But where a specific duty is assigned by law, and individual rights depend upon the performance of that duty, it seems equally clear that the individual who considers himself injured, has a right to resort to the laws of his country for a remedy.[14]

The Court returned to this distinction in considering the next issue: whether mandamus was an appropriate remedy.

Issue 3: Can the Supreme Court Issue This Remedy? Is Mandamus an Appropriate Remedy?

In considering the former question, the Court again used the distinction between ministerial acts, where the executive had a duty to perform, and political acts, within the discretion of the executive. Judicial review, including mandamus, was deemed appropriate only in the former realm. Chief Justice Marshall said:

---

[9] 5 U.S. at 162.
[10] Quoted in Van Alstyne, *supra* note 2, at 9.
[11] Quoted in Van Alstyne, *supra* note 2, at 9.
[12] 5 U.S. at 163.
[13] *Id.*
[14] *Id.*

"Questions, in their nature political, or which are, by the constitution and laws, submitted to the executive, can never be made in this court. . . . [But where the head of department] is directed by law to do a certain act affecting the absolute rights of individuals, . . . it is not perceived on what ground the courts of the country are further excused from the duty of giving judgment that right be done to an injured individual."[15]

Marbury thus establishes the power of the judiciary to review the constitutionality of executive actions. Some matters—such as whether to veto a bill or whom to appoint for an office—are entirely within the president's discretion and cannot be judicially reviewed. But where the executive has a legal duty to act or refrain from acting, the federal judiciary can provide a remedy, including a writ of mandamus.

The Court's claimed authority to review executive actions drew the most contemporary criticism.[16] But because the Court announced this power in a case in which it ruled in favor of the president, there was neither a confrontation nor disregard of a judicial order. The power of the federal courts to review presidential actions is the basis for many important Supreme Court decisions throughout American history. Perhaps most notably, in *United States v. Nixon*, the Court's holding—that the president had to comply with a subpoena to provide tapes of conversations for use in a criminal trial—led to the resignation of President Richard Nixon.[17]

Does the Law Authorize Mandamus on Original Jurisdiction?

Having concluded that Marbury had a right to the commission and that the Court had the authority to issue mandamus as a remedy, the Court then turned its attention to the issue of jurisdiction. As mentioned above, there is a strong argument that the Court should have begun with the jurisdictional question and discussed nothing else once it concluded that jurisdiction was absent.

Marbury argued that the Supreme Court had original jurisdiction to hear his suit for mandamus pursuant to §13 of the Judiciary Act of 1789. The Court agreed.[18] Yet a close reading of §13 of the Judiciary Act raises doubts as to the Court's conclusion. Section 13 stated, in part:

> The Supreme Court shall also have appellate jurisdiction from the circuit courts and courts of the several states, in the cases herein after specially provided for; . . . and shall have power to issue writs of prohibition . . . to the district courts, when proceeding as courts of admiralty and maritime jurisdiction, and writs of mandamus, in cases warranted by the principles and usages of law, to any court appointed, or persons holding office, under the authority of the United States.[19]

---

[15] *Id.* at 170-171.
[16] *See, e.g.*, 1 Charles Warren, The Supreme Court in United States History 232 (rev. ed. 1926).
[17] 418 U.S. 683 (1974), discussed in §4.3.
[18] 5 U.S. at 174.
[19] The Judiciary Act of 1789, 1 Stat. 73, 81 §13.

Although the Court read this statute as granting it original jurisdiction over requests for mandamus, alternative readings seem even more plausible.[20] For example, the statute might be read as pertaining only to the Court's appellate jurisdiction because that is the only type of jurisdiction mentioned. Alternatively, the statute might be understood as according the Court the authority to issue mandamus where appropriate, in cases properly within its jurisdiction. By this reading, the statute does not create original jurisdiction, but simply grants the Court the remedial powers when it has jurisdiction. Under either of these approaches, Marbury still would have lost, but the Court would have avoided the question as to whether the statute was constitutional and thus would have lost the opportunity to announce its power to declare statutes unconstitutional.

Does Mandamus on Original Jurisdiction Violate Article III?

Once it concluded that §13 of the Judiciary Act of 1789 authorized mandamus on original jurisdiction, the Court then considered whether this violated Article III. The Court concluded that Article III enumerated its original jurisdiction and that Congress could not enlarge it. Article III authorizes original jurisdiction for suits "affecting Ambassadors, other public Ministers and Consuls, and those in which a State shall be Party." The Court said that Congress could not add to this list cases seeking a writ of mandamus.

Chief Justice Marshall stated: "If it had been intended to leave it in the discretion of the legislature to apportion the judicial power between the supreme and inferior courts according to the will of that body, it would certainly have been useless to have proceeded further than to have denned the judicial power, and the tribunals in which it should be vested."[21] In other words, Marshall said that Article III's enumeration of original jurisdiction would be "mere surplusage, . . . entirely without meaning," if Congress could add more areas of original jurisdiction.[22]

Justice Marshall's analysis again is open to question. Article III's enumeration of the Court's original jurisdiction still has meaning even if Congress can increase it. Article III might be viewed as the floor, the minimum grant of jurisdiction that cannot be reduced by Congress.[23]

Irrespective of possible alternative interpretations, the Court's holding that Congress cannot increase the Supreme Court's original jurisdiction remains the law to this day. However, the Court's statement that the categories of original and appellate jurisdiction are mutually exclusive has not been followed. The Supreme Court subsequently held that Congress could grant the district courts concurrent jurisdiction over matters within the Court's original jurisdiction.[24] More generally, by viewing Article III as the ceiling of federal jurisdiction, *Marbury* helped establish

[20] *See* Van Alstyne, *supra* note 2, at 14-16.

[21] 5 U.S. at 174.

[22] *Id.*

[23] For a discussion of the scope of the Court's power on original jurisdiction and a critique of the reasoning in *Marbury, see* James F. Pfander, *Marbury,* Original Jurisdiction, and the Court's Supervisory Powers, 101 Colum. L. Rev. 1515 (2001).

[24] *See, e.g.,* Ames v. Kansas ex rel. Johnson, 111 U.S. 449 (1884).

the principle that federal courts are courts of limited jurisdiction, and that Congress may not expand the jurisdiction granted in Article III of the Constitution.

Can the Supreme Court Declare Laws Unconstitutional?

Having decided that the provision of the Judiciary Act of 1789 was unconstitutional, the Court then considered the final question: Did it nonetheless have to follow that provision or could the Court declare it unconstitutional? The Court began by stating: "The question, whether an act, repugnant to the Constitution, can become the law of the land, is a question deeply interesting to the United States; but, happily, not of an intricacy proportioned to its interest."[25] Marshall then offered several reasons why the Court could declare federal laws unconstitutional. Interestingly, although they are persuasive arguments, for each there is a reasonable answer.

Marshall argued, for example, that the Constitution imposes limits on government powers and that these limits are meaningless unless subject to judicial enforcement. Borrowing from Alexander Hamilton's Federalist No. 78, the Court stated: "The powers of the legislature are defined and limited; and that those limits may not be mistaken or forgotten, the constitution is written."[26] This is a powerful argument for judicial review, but it must be remembered that many other nations with written constitutions exist without according the judiciary the power to invalidate conflicting statutes.[27]

Marshall also argued that it is inherent to the judicial role to decide the constitutionality of the laws that it applies. In perhaps the most frequently quoted words of the opinion, Marshall wrote: "It is emphatically the province and duty of the judicial department to say what the law is."[28] However, the Court could interpret and apply a law without deciding its constitutionality. As mentioned above, there are other countries with judiciaries and constitutions, but without the power of the courts to declare laws unconstitutional.

Marshall then argued that the Court's authority to decide "cases" arising under the Constitution implied the power to declare unconstitutional laws conflicting with the basic legal charter. But as Professor David Currie explains, "jurisdiction over 'cases arising under this Constitution' need not mean that the Constitution is supreme over federal laws as well as over executive or state action."[29] In other words, the Court's power to decide cases under the Constitution still could have significant content even if the judiciary lacked the power to invalidate federal statutes. The Court would apply federal statutes to decide cases and could evaluate the constitutionality of state enactments.

---

[25] 5 U.S. at 176.

[26] 5 U.S. at 176. *See* The Federalist No. 78, at 446-469 (A. Hamilton) (Clinton Rossiter ed. 1961).

[27] *See, e.g.,* Mark Tushnet, Weak Courts, Strong Rights: Judicial Review and Social Welfare in Comparative Constitutional Law (2008) (arguing that judicial review is not necessary for the protection of individual rights).

[28] 5 U.S. at 177.

[29] David Currie, Federal Courts: Cases and Materials 27 (4th ed. 1990).

Chief Justice Marshall also defended judicial review on the ground that judges take an oath of office and that they would violate this oath if they enforced unconstitutional laws. But this argument is question-begging: Judges would not violate their oath by enforcing unconstitutional laws if they did not have the power to strike down such statutes.[30] In a famous state court dissenting opinion that argued against judicial review, Justice Gibson stated: "[The] oath to support the constitution is not peculiar to the judges, but is taken indiscriminately by every officer of the government, and is designed rather as a test of the political principles of the man, than to bind the officer in the discharge of his duty."[31]

Finally, Chief Justice Marshall argued that judicial review is appropriate because Article VI makes the Constitution "the *supreme law* of the land"; "the *constitution* itself is first mentioned; and not the laws of the United States generally, but those only which shall be made in *pursuance* of the constitution, have that rank."[32] Again, though, to say that the Constitution should control over all other laws does not necessarily mean that the judiciary has the power to invalidate laws. The supremacy clause in Article VI could be viewed as a declaration that Congress only should enact laws if they are authorized by the Constitution.

Brilliance of John Marshall's Opinion

The point of this discussion is not, of course, to argue that Chief Justice John Marshall was wrong or that judicial review is illegitimate. History has proved the opposite. Rather, the point is that constitutional judicial review was not axiomatic or unassailable; it had to be established by the Supreme Court, and John Marshall found the ideal occasion. He established judicial review while declaring unconstitutional a statute that he read as expanding the Court's powers. The particular statutory provision invalidated was minor, and Marshall's holding was a victory for his opponents.

The brilliance of Marshall's opinion cannot be overstated. Politically, he had no choice but to deny Marbury relief; the Jefferson administration surely would have refused to comply with a court order to deliver the commission. In addition, there was a real possibility that Jefferson might have sought the impeachment of the Federalist Justices in an attempt to gain Republican control of the judiciary. One judge, albeit a clearly incompetent jurist, already had been impeached, and not long after his removal the House of Representatives impeached Justice Samuel Chase on the grounds that he had made electioneering statements from the bench and had criticized the repeal of the 1801 Circuit Court Act.[33] Yet John Marshall did more than simply rule in favor of the Jefferson administration; he used

---

[30] *Id.*

[31] Eakin v. Raub, 12 Serg & Rawls 330 (Pa. 1825) (Gibson, J. dissenting); reprinted in Gerald Gunther, Constitutional Law 17 (13th ed. 1997).

[32] 5 U.S. at 180.

[33] *See* William Rehnquist, Grand Inquest: The Historic Impeachments of Justice Samuel Chase and President Andrew Johnson (1999).

the occasion of deciding *Marbury v. Madison* to establish the power of the judiciary and to articulate a role for the federal courts that survives to this day.

The Supreme Court did not declare another federal statute unconstitutional until 1857 in the infamous case of *Dred Scott v. Sandford*, which invalidated the Missouri Compromise and helped to precipitate the Civil War.[34] By then, the power of the Court to consider the constitutionality of federal laws was an accepted part of American government.

§2.2.2   The Authority for Judicial Review of State and Local Actions

Marbury established the power of the Supreme Court to review the constitutionality of federal executive actions and of federal statutes. Two other cases — *Martin v. Hunter's Lessee*[35] and *Cohens v. Virginia*[36] — were key in establishing the Court's authority to review state court decisions.[37] Although the Constitution does not explicitly say that the Supreme Court may review state court decisions, the Judiciary Act of 1789 provided for Supreme Court review of state court judgments. Section 25 of the Act allowed the Supreme Court to review state court decisions by a writ of error to the state's highest court in many situations.[38]

Martin v. Hunter's Lessee

The constitutional basis for such Supreme Court review was firmly established by the Court in *Martin v. Hunter's Lessee*.[39] In *Martin*, there were two conflicting claims to certain land within the State of Virginia. Martin claimed title to the land based on inheritance from Lord Fairfax, a British citizen who owned the property. The United States and England had entered into two treaties protecting the rights of British citizens to own land in the United States. However, Hunter claimed that Virginia had taken the land before the treaties came into effect and, hence, Martin did not have a valid claim to the property.

The Virginia Court of Appeals ruled in favor of Hunter and, in essence, in favor of the state's authority to have taken and disposed of the land. The United States Supreme Court issued a writ of error and reversed the Virginia decision. The Supreme Court held that the federal treaty was controlling and that it established Lord Fairfax's ownership and thus the validity of inheritance pursuant to his will. The Virginia Court of Appeals, however, declared that the Supreme Court lacked the authority to review state court decisions. The Virginia court stated that the "Courts of the United States, therefore, belonging to one sovereignty, cannot be appellate Courts in relation to the State Courts, which belong to

---

[34] 60 U.S. (19 How.) 393 (1857), discussed in §9.3.1.

[35] 14 U.S. (1 Wheat.) 304 (1816).

[36] 19 U.S. (6 Wheat.) 264 (1821).

[37] For a detailed discussion of these two cases, *see* David Currie, The Constitution in the Supreme Court: The Powers of the Federal Courts, 1801-1835, 49 U. Chi. L. Rev. 646 (1982).

[38] Act of September 24, 1789, ch. 20, 1 Stat. 73, 85-87.

[39] 14 U.S. (1 Wheat.) 304 (1816).

a different sovereignty—and, of course, their commands or instructions impose no obligation."[40]

The United States Supreme Court again granted review and, in a famous opinion by Justice Joseph Story, articulated the Court's authority to review state court judgments. Chief Justice John Marshall did not participate because he and his brother had contracted to purchase a large part of the Fairfax estate that was at issue in the litigation.[41] Justice Story persuasively argued that the Constitution presumed that the Supreme Court could review state court decisions. Story argued that the Constitution creates a Supreme Court and gives Congress discretion whether to create lower federal courts. But if Congress chose not to establish such tribunals, then the Supreme Court would be powerless to hear any cases, except for the few fitting within its original jurisdiction, unless it could review state court rulings.[42]

Additionally, Justice Story explained the importance of Supreme Court review of state courts. Justice Story said that although he assumed that "judges of the state courts are, and always will be, of as much learning, integrity, and wisdom as those of courts of the United States," the Constitution is based on a recognition that "state attachments, state prejudices, state jealousies, and state interests might sometimes obstruct, or control, or be supposed to obstruct or control, the regular administration of justice."[43] Furthermore, Justice Story observed that Supreme Court review is essential to ensure uniformity in the interpretation of federal law. Justice Story concluded that the very nature of the Constitution, the contemporaneous understanding of it, and many years of experience all established the Supreme Court's authority to review state court decisions.

Cohens v. Virginia

The Supreme Court has never questioned its constitutional authority to take appeals from state courts or to command state judiciaries to follow federal law. An important elaboration of the Court's power to take cases from state courts was *Cohens v. Virginia.*[44] Two brothers were convicted in Virginia state court of selling District of Columbia lottery tickets in violation of Virginia law. The defendants sought review in the United States Supreme Court because they claimed the Constitution prevented them from being prosecuted for selling tickets authorized by Congress. Virginia argued that the Supreme Court had no authority to review state court decisions in general, and, in particular, review was not allowed in criminal cases and in cases where a state government was a party.

The Supreme Court, in an opinion by Chief Justice John Marshall, reaffirmed the constitutionality of §25 of the Judiciary Act and the authority of the Supreme Court to review state court judgments. The Court emphasized that state courts often

---

[40] Quoted in Gunther, *supra* note 31, at 32.

[41] *Id.* at 30.

[42] 14 U.S. at 329.

[43] *Id.* at 346-347.

[44] 19 U.S. 264, 386-387 (1821).

could not be trusted to adequately protect federal rights because "[i]n many States the judges are dependent for office and for salary on the will of the legislature."[45] The Court thus declared that criminal defendants could seek Supreme Court review when they claimed that their conviction violated the Constitution.[46]

Cooper v. Aaron

The Supreme Court, of course, is not limited to reviewing state court decisions; federal courts also have the authority to review the constitutionality of state laws and the actions of state officials. This was resoundingly reaffirmed in *Cooper v. Aaron* in 1958.[47] A federal district court ordered the desegregation of the Little Rock, Arkansas, public schools. The state disobeyed this order, in part, based on a professed concern that compliance would lead to violence, and, in part, based on a claim that it was not bound to comply with judicial desegregation decrees.

In an unusual opinion, signed individually by each Justice, the Court rejected this position and emphatically declared: "Article VI of the Constitution makes the Constitution 'the supreme Law of the Land.' . . . *Marbury v. Madison* . . . declared the basic principle that the federal judiciary is supreme in the exposition of the law of the Constitution, and that principle has ever since been respected by this Court and the Country as a permanent and indispensable feature of our constitutional system. . . . Every state legislator and executive and judicial officer is solemnly committed by oath . . . 'to support this Constitution.' "[48]

§2.3 INTRODUCTION TO THE JUSTICIABILITY DOCTRINES

Perhaps the most important limit on the federal judicial power is imposed by a series of principles termed "justiciability" doctrines. The justiciability doctrines determine which matters federal courts can hear and decide and which must be dismissed. Specifically, justiciability includes the prohibition against advisory opinions, standing, ripeness, mootness, and the political question doctrine. Each of these justiciability doctrines was created and articulated by the United States Supreme Court. Neither the text of the Constitution, nor the framers in drafting the document, expressly mentioned any of these limitations on the judicial power.

---

[45] *Id.* at 386-387.

[46] Additionally, the Supreme Court held that the Eleventh Amendment did not bar Supreme Court appellate review of cases involving the state as a party because such review did not constitute a "suit" against the state. For a discussion of the Eleventh Amendment, *see* Erwin Chemerinsky, Federal Jurisdiction ch. 7 (6th ed. 2011). *See also* §2.10 *infra*, discussing the Eleventh Amendment.

[47] 358 U.S. 1 (1958).

[48] *Id.* at 18 (citations omitted).

Constitutional Versus Prudential Requirements

Although all of these requirements for federal court adjudication were judicially created, the Supreme Court has distinguished two different sources for these rules. First, the Court has declared that some of the justiciability doctrines are a result of its interpretation of Article III of the United States Constitution. Article III, §2, defines the federal judicial power in terms of nine categories of "cases" and "controversies." The Supreme Court repeatedly has said that the requirement for "cases" and "controversies" imposes substantial constitutional limits on federal judicial power.

Second, the Court has said that other justiciability doctrines are derived not from the Constitution but from prudent judicial administration. In other words, although the Constitution permits federal court adjudication, the Court has decided that in certain instances, wise policy militates against judicial review. These justiciability doctrines are termed "prudential."

The distinction between constitutional and prudential limits on federal judicial power is important because Congress, by statute, may override prudential, but not constitutional, restrictions. Because Congress may not expand federal judicial power beyond what is authorized in Article III of the Constitution, a constitutional limit on federal judicial review may not be changed by federal law. But since prudential constraints are not derived from the Constitution, Congress may instruct the federal courts to disregard such a restriction.[1]

It must be emphasized that both constitutional and prudential limits on justiciability are the product of Supreme Court decisions. The Court determines whether a particular restriction is constitutional or prudential in its explanation of whether the rule derives from Article III or from its views of prudent judicial administration. Some justiciability doctrines, such as standing, have both constitutional and prudential components. In other instances—for example, the political question doctrine—the Court has not announced whether it views the limitation as constitutional or prudential.

Policies Underlying Justiciability Requirements

A clear separation of the constitutional and prudential aspects of the justiciability doctrines is often difficult because both reflect the same basic policy considerations. In fact, all of the justiciability doctrines are premised on several important concerns. First, the justiciability doctrines are closely tied to separation of powers. Chief Justice Warren explained that the "words [cases and controversies] define the role assigned to the judiciary in a tripartite allocation of power to assure

---

§2.3 [1] *See, e.g.*, Warth v. Seldin, 422 U.S. 490, 501 (1975) ("Congress may grant an express right of action to persons who otherwise would be barred by prudential standing rules."). *Id.* at 500-501 (the requirements for injury and causation are constitutionally required; the ban on third-party standing and the prohibition against federal courts deciding generalized grievances are prudential); *but see* Lujan v. Defenders of Wildlife, 504 U.S. 555 (1992) (declaring that the ban on generalized grievances is constitutional, not prudential).

that the federal courts will not intrude into areas committed to the other branches of government."[2] The justiciability doctrines define the judicial role; they determine when it is appropriate for the federal courts to review a matter and when it is necessary to defer to the other branches of government.

Second, the justiciability doctrines conserve judicial resources, allowing the federal courts to focus their attention on the matters most deserving of review. For example, the justiciability doctrine termed "mootness" conserves judicial resources by allowing the federal courts to dismiss cases where there no longer is a live controversy. Many influential commentators have argued not only that the federal courts have finite resources in terms of time and money, but also that the federal judiciary has limited political capital.[3] That is, these commentators contend that federal courts generally depend on the other branches to voluntarily comply with judicial orders and that such acquiescence depends on the judiciary's credibility. Justiciability doctrines permit the judiciary to expend its political capital only when necessary and not to squander it on matters inappropriate for judicial review.[4]

Third, the justiciability doctrines are intended to improve judicial decision making by providing the federal courts with concrete controversies best suited for judicial resolution. The Supreme Court explained that the requirement for cases and controversies "limit[s] the business of federal courts to questions presented in an adversary context and in a form historically viewed as capable of resolution through the judicial process."[5] Because federal courts have limited ability to conduct independent investigations, they must depend on the parties to fully present all relevant information to them. It is thought that adverse parties, with a stake in the outcome of the litigation, will perform this task best. Many of the justiciability doctrines exist to ensure concrete controversies and adverse litigants.[6]

Finally, the justiciability doctrines also promote fairness, especially to individuals who are not litigants before the court. The justiciability doctrines generally prevent the federal courts from adjudicating the rights of those who are not parties to a lawsuit. It would be unfair to allow someone to raise a complaint on behalf of a person who is satisfied with a situation. Also, because judicial decisions almost inevitably affect many people other than the parties to the suit, it is thought fairest to reserve court review for situations where it is truly necessary.[7]

---

[2] Flast v. Cohen, 392 U.S. 83, 95 (1968).

[3] Jesse Choper, Judicial Review and the National Political Process: A Functional Reconsideration of the Role of the Supreme Court 55-59 (1980); Alexander Bickel, The Least Dangerous Branch 201-268 (1962); *but see* Erwin Chemerinsky, Interpreting the Constitution 134-138 (1987) (arguing that the Court's legitimacy is not fragile and conserving judicial credibility should not be a primary objective in constitutional interpretation).

[4] Bickel, *id.* at 116 (arguing that justiciability requirements create "a time lag between legislation and adjudication [and] strengthens the Court's hand in gaining acceptance for its principles").

[5] Flast v. Cohen, 392 U.S. at 95.

[6] *See, e.g.*, Baker v. Carr, 369 U.S. 186, 204 (1962) (standing ensures "concrete adverseness").

[7] Lea Brilmeyer, The Jurisprudence of Article III: Perspectives on the "Case or Controversy" Requirement, 93 Harv. L. Rev. 297, 306-310 (1979) (describing fairness as a basis for justiciability doctrines).

These policy considerations repeatedly recur in Supreme Court opinions concerning particular justiciability doctrines. Yet these justifications for limits on the judicial role must be balanced against the need for judicial review. Federal courts exist, in large part, to prevent and remedy violations of federal laws. Federal judicial review is particularly important in enjoining and redressing constitutional violations inflicted by all levels of government and government officers.[8] Thus, while justiciability doctrines serve the important goals described above, it is at least equally important that the doctrines not prevent the federal courts from performing their essential function in upholding the Constitution of the United States and preventing and redressing violations of federal laws.

The recurring issue is what should be the content of the justiciability doctrines to achieve this balance between restraint and review. Inevitably, the debate turns on a normative question concerning the proper role of the federal courts. Critics argue that the Court has gone too far in limiting justiciability and preventing federal courts from protecting and vindicating important constitutional rights. But the Court's defenders contend that the decisions have defined the properly limited role of the federal judiciary in a democratic society. This normative question about the appropriate role of the federal judiciary thus is common to discussions of each of the justiciability doctrines.

The debate over justiciability also centers on an issue of methodology: Should the rules of justiciability be as clear and predictable as possible, or should the doctrines be very flexible, permitting the federal courts discretion in choosing which cases to hear and which to decline? Some argue that the justiciability doctrines should be malleable, according judges great discretion in deciding which cases warrant federal judicial review. For example, the late Professor Alexander Bickel spoke of the "passive virtues"—the desirability of the Supreme Court using discretionary doctrines such as justiciability to decline review where prudence counsels judicial avoidance.[9]

But others contend that the rules defining jurisdiction should be as firm and predictable as is possible.[10] They argue that it is undesirable for federal courts to be able to manipulate justiciability doctrines to avoid cases or to make decisions about the merits of disputes under the guise of rulings about justiciability. Thus, another recurring theme is whether the Supreme Court has been sufficiently specific and consistent in defining justiciability requirements—a question that, of course, depends on the normative question about the proper approach to justiciability.

---

[8] For an excellent discussion of the importance of shaping justiciability doctrines to achieve this goal, *see* Susan Bandes, The Idea of a Case, 42 Stan. L. Rev. 227 (1990).

[9] Alexander Bickel, The Supreme Court 1960 Term: Foreword: The Passive Virtues, 75 Harv. L. Rev. 40 (1961).

[10] Gene Nichol, Rethinking Standing, 72 Cal. L. Rev. 68 (1984); Gerald Gunther, The Subtle Vices of the "Passive Virtues"—A Comment on Principle and Expediency in Judicial Review, 64 Colum. L. Rev. 1 (1964).

Other Limits on the Judicial Power

Additionally, there are other constitutional limits on federal judicial power, such as the Eleventh Amendment, which prevents federal court relief against state governments.[11] The Supreme Court also has identified a number of circumstances in which federal courts should abstain and refrain from deciding a matter even though it is justiciable and all jurisdictional requirements are met.[12]

Moreover, the Court has formulated other rules to guide its exercise of discretion. For example, the Court has stated that it will avoid deciding constitutional issues where there are nonconstitutional grounds for a decision, where the record is inadequate to permit effective judicial review, or where the federal issue is not properly presented.[13]

But the justiciability doctrines are, without a doubt, among the most significant principles defining access to the federal courts. The doctrines are enormously important, especially in constitutional litigation, in determining whether a case can be heard and decided by a federal judge. As such, the doctrines are crucial in defining the role of the federal courts in American society.

§2.4   THE PROHIBITION AGAINST ADVISORY OPINIONS

The core of Article III's limitation on federal judicial power is that federal courts cannot issue advisory opinions. In many states, state courts are authorized to provide opinions about the constitutionality of pending legislation or on constitutional questions referred to them by other branches of government.[1] Such advisory opinions are in many ways beneficial. By providing guidance to the legislature, these rulings can prevent the enactment of unconstitutional laws. Also, an advisory opinion can spare a legislature the effort of adopting statutes soon to be invalidated by the courts and can save time by allowing the legislature to correct constitutional infirmities at the earliest possible time.

---

[11] The Eleventh Amendment is discussed below in §2.10.

[12] For a discussion of the abstention doctrines, *see* Erwin Chemerinsky, Federal Jurisdiction chs. 12-14 (6th ed. 2011).

[13] *See, e.g.*, Ashwander v. TVA, 297 U.S. 288, 346 (1936) (Brandeis, J., concurring) (articulating principles governing Supreme Court review, including avoiding constitutional decisions where possible). For an excellent criticism of the use of these avoidance doctrines, *see* Lisa Kloppenberg, Playing It Safe: How the Supreme Court Sidesteps Hard Cases and Stunts the Development of Law (2001).

§2.4 [1] States permitting advisory opinions include Colorado, Florida, Maine, Massachusetts, New Hampshire, Rhode Island, and South Dakota. Laurence Tribe, American Constitutional Law 73 n.4 (3d ed. 1999); *see also* Henry Melvin Hart, David L. Shapiro & Daniel J. Meltzer, Hart & Wechsler's The Federal Courts and the Federal System 70 (5th ed. 2003).

Justifications for Prohibiting Advisory Opinions

Despite these benefits, it is firmly established that federal courts cannot issue advisory opinions. Many of the policies described in §2.3 are served by the prohibition of advisory opinions. First, separation of powers is maintained by keeping the courts out of the legislative process. The judicial role is limited to deciding actual disputes; it does not include giving advice to Congress or the president.

Second, judicial resources are conserved because advisory opinions might be requested in many instances in which the law ultimately would not pass the legislature. The federal courts can decide the matter if it turns into an actual dispute; otherwise, judicial review is unnecessary, a waste of political and financial capital.

Third, the prohibition against advisory opinions helps ensure that cases will be presented to the Court in terms of specific disputes, not as hypothetical legal questions. As the Court explained in *Flast v. Cohen*: "[T]he implicit policies embodied in Article III, and not history alone, impose the rule against advisory opinions. [The rule] implements the separation of powers [and] also recognizes that such suits often are not pressed before the Court with that clear concreteness provided when a question emerges precisely framed and necessary for decision from a clash of adversary argument exploring every aspect of a multifaceted situation embracing conflicting and demanding interests."[2]

Criteria to Avoid Being an Advisory Opinion

For a case to be justiciable and not an advisory opinion, two criteria must be met. First, there must be an actual dispute between adverse litigants. This requirement dates back to the earliest days of the nation. During the administration of President George Washington, Secretary of State Thomas Jefferson asked the Supreme Court for its answers to a long list of questions concerning American neutrality in the war between France and England.[3] In his letter to the Justices, Jefferson explained that the war between these countries had raised a number of important legal questions concerning the meaning of United States' treaties and laws. Jefferson's letter said that "[t]he President therefore would be much relieved if he found himself free to refer questions of this description to the opinions of the judges of the [Court], whose knowledge of the subject would secure us against errors dangerous to the peace of the United States."[4] For example, Jefferson asked the Justices, "May we, within our own ports, sell ships to both parties, prepared merely for merchandise? May they be pierced for guns?"[5]

The Justices wrote back to President Washington and declined to answer the questions asked. They explained that separation of powers would be violated if they were to give such advice to another branch of government. The Justices, in

---

[2] Flast v. Cohen, 392 U.S. 83, 96-97 (1968) (citations omitted).

[3] *See* Hart et al., *supra* note 1, at 65-67 (reprinting the correspondence between Jefferson and the Supreme Court).

[4] *Id.* at 65.

[5] *Id.* at 66.

their letter, stated: "[The] three departments of the government . . . being in certain respects checks upon each other, and our being judges of a court in the last resort, are considerations which afford strong arguments against the propriety of our extra-judicially deciding the questions alluded to."[6] The Justices concluded their letter in a gracious tone: "We exceedingly regret every event that may cause embarrassment to your administration, but we derive consolation from the reflection that your judgment will discern what is right, and that your usual prudence, decision, and firmness will surmount every obstacle to the preservation of the rights, peace, and dignity of the United States."[7]

For almost 200 years, then, it has been established that federal courts may not decide a case unless there is an actual dispute between adverse litigants. For example, federal courts must dismiss suits where the parties collude to bring the matter to federal court in the absence of a real controversy between them. In *United States v. Johnson*, the Supreme Court held that a suit brought by the plaintiff at the request of the defendant, who also financed and directed the litigation, had to be dismissed.[8] The Court explained that "the absence of a genuine adversary issue between the parties" meant that the case was not justiciable.[9]

Another example of the Court's insistence on an actual dispute between adverse litigants is *Muskrat v. United States*.[10] Congress adopted a statute expanding the participants in an allotment of land that was made to certain Native American tribes. In order to facilitate resolution of constitutional questions about the law, Congress subsequently adopted a statute permitting the filing of two lawsuits in the Court of Claims to determine the validity of the earlier law. Pursuant to this statutory authorization, a suit was initiated, but the Supreme Court ruled that it was not justiciable. The interests of the Native Americans and the government were not at all adverse. In the Court's view, Congress simply had adopted a statute authorizing the federal courts to issue an advisory opinion on the constitutionality of a statute.

Many of the other justiciability doctrines seek to ensure the existence of an actual dispute between adverse litigants. For instance, the standing requirement that a plaintiff demonstrate that he or she has suffered or imminently will suffer an injury is crucial in determining whether there is an actual dispute that the federal courts can adjudicate. Likewise, the ripeness doctrine determines whether a dispute has occurred yet or whether the case is still premature for review. Also, the mootness requirement states that federal courts should dismiss cases in which there no longer is an actual dispute between the parties, even though such a controversy might have existed at one time.

Second, in order for a case to be justiciable and not an advisory opinion, there must be a substantial likelihood that a federal court decision in favor of a claimant will bring about some change or have some effect. This requirement also

---

[6] *Id.*
[7] *Id.* at 67.
[8] 319 U.S. 302 (1943).
[9] *Id.* at 304.
[10] 219 U.S. 346 (1911).

dates back to the Supreme Court's earliest days. In *Hayburn's Case*, in 1792, the Court considered whether federal courts could express nonbinding opinions on the amount of benefits owed to Revolutionary War veterans.[11] Congress adopted a law permitting these veterans to file pension claims in the United States Circuit Courts. The judges of these courts were to inform the secretary of war of the nature of the claimant's disability and the amount of benefits to be paid. The secretary could refuse to follow the court's recommendation.

Although the Supreme Court never explicitly ruled the statute unconstitutional, five of the six Supreme Court Justices, while serving as Circuit Court judges, found the assignment of these tasks to be unconstitutional. The Justices explained that the duty of making recommendations regarding pensions was "not of a judicial nature."[12] They said that it would violate separation of powers because the judicial actions might be "revised and controuled [sic] by the legislature, and by an officer in the executive department. Such revision and controul we deemed radically inconsistent with the independence of that judicial power which is vested in the courts."[13]

In other cases as well, the Supreme Court has said that a case is a nonjusticiable request for an advisory opinion if there is not a substantial likelihood that the federal court decision will have some effect. For example, in *C. & S. Air Lines v. Waterman Corp.*, the Supreme Court said federal courts could not review Civil Aeronautics Board decisions awarding international air routes because the president could disregard or modify the judicial ruling.[14] The Court declared: "Judgments within the powers vested in courts by [Article III] may not lawfully be revised, overturned or refused faith and credit by another Department of Government. To revise or review an administrative decision which has only the force of a recommendation to the President would be to render an advisory opinion in its most obnoxious form."[15]

Subsequently, in *Plaut v. Spendthrift Farm, Inc.*, the Court applied the principle of *Hayburn's Case* to find unconstitutional a federal statute that overturned a Supreme Court decision dismissing certain cases.[16] In 1991, the Court ruled that actions brought under the securities laws, specifically §10(b) and Rule 10(b)(5), had to be brought within one year of discovering the facts giving rise to the violation and three years of the violation.[17] Congress then amended the law to allow cases to go forward that were filed before this decision if they could have been brought under the prior law.

In *Plaut*, the Supreme Court declared the new statute unconstitutional as violating separation of powers. Although the Court acknowledged that *Hayburn's Case*

---

[11] 2 U.S. (2 Call.) 409 (1792).

[12] *Id.* at 411.

[13] *Id.*

[14] 333 U.S. 103 (1948); *see also* United States v. Ferreira, 54 U.S. (13 How.) 40 (1852) (denying jurisdiction because the secretary of treasury could refuse to pay claims under a treaty if they were deemed to not be just and equitable).

[15] 333 U.S. at 113.

[16] 514 U.S. 211 (1995).

[17] *See* Lampf, Pleva, Lipkind, Prupis & Petigrow v. Gilbertson, 501 U.S. 350 (1991).

was distinguishable, the Court found *Hayburn's Case*'s underlying principle of finality applicable. Justice Scalia, writing for the Court, said that the Constitution "gives the Federal Judiciary the power, not merely to rule on cases, but to decide them."[18] He said that because the "judicial power is one to render dispositive judgments," the federal law "effects a clear violation of separation-of-powers."[19] The statute was unconstitutional because it overturned a Supreme Court decision and gave relief to a party that the Court had said was entitled to none.

The difficulty with Justice Scalia's analysis is that Congress always has the ability to overturn Supreme Court statutory interpretation by amending the law. The Court's concern was that Congress was reinstating cases that had been dismissed by the judiciary. But it is not clear why Congress cannot give individuals a cause of action, even if the courts previously ruled that none existed. For example, if the Court ruled that a group of plaintiffs could not obtain relief under a particular civil rights law, Congress surely could amend the law to overturn the decision and also could provide retroactive effect for the new statute. Critics of *Plaut* argue that it is exactly what Congress did with regard to the securities law after the Supreme Court's earlier ruling.

The Court refused to apply *Plaut* in a subsequent case concerning the Prison Litigation Reform Act (PLRA).[20] A provision of the PLRA provides that an injunction concerning prison conditions must be lifted by a federal court on a motion by the government after it has been in place for two years, unless the court finds that continuation of the order is needed to remedy ongoing constitutional violations.[21] This section of the Act also says that if the government moves to end the injunction, the federal court must act within 30 days; if it does not do so, then it must stay the injunction during the pendency of the proceedings.

The effect is that Congress, by statute, is ordering the suspension of a court injunction, essentially overturning a final judgment. But in *Miller v. French*,[22] the Court, in a 5-to-4 decision, distinguished *Plaut* and upheld this provision of the Act. Justice O'Connor, writing for the majority, stressed that "[p]rospective relief under a continuing, executory decree remains subject to alteration due to changes in the underlying law."[23] Thus, unlike *Plaut*, it is not the "last word of the judicial department."[24] Therefore, even though the PLRA provision had the effect of retroactively overturning a court's order, it was permissible because Congress can require federal courts to revise their injunctions to be in compliance with changes in the law.

An interesting and unusual issue based on *Plaut* arose after the Florida courts ordered the removal of the feeding tube from Theresa Marie Schiavo. She had been in a persistent vegetative state for more than ten years when the court held that she would have wanted food and water withdrawn under these circumstances. Congress adopted a statute, Act for Relief of the Parents of Theresa Marie Schiavo, vesting the federal courts with jurisdiction to adjudicate any claim on behalf of

---

[18] 514 U.S. at 218.
[19] *Id.* at 211, 224.
[20] 18 U.S.C. §3626.
[21] 18 U.S.C. §3626(b).
[22] 530 U.S. 327 (2000).
[23] *Id.*
[24] *Id.* at 347.

Ms. Schiavo under the Constitution or laws of the United States "relating to the withdrawal of foods, fluids, or medical treatment necessary to sustain her life." The statute provided that the district court should determine all claims de novo "notwithstanding any prior state court determination."

The Act raised issues under *Plaut* because it was Congress, by statute, attempting to overrule the prior judgment of the courts, albeit the Florida state courts. The Act was unambiguous that this was its goal and was explicit that it did not apply to anyone else in similar circumstances. The federal district court twice denied relief to Schiavo's parents, the Eleventh Circuit affirmed, and the Supreme Court denied review. Eleventh Circuit Judge Stanley Birch wrote a concurring opinion in which he cited *United States v. Klein* and argued that the federal law was unconstitutional because it "constitute[s] legislative dictation of how a federal court should exercise its judicial functions. . . . It invades the province of the judiciary and violates the separation of powers principle."[25]

More generally, a federal court decision is purely advisory if it has no effect. In fact, several of the other justiciability doctrines prevent review where there is not a sufficient likelihood that the federal court decision will make some difference. One of the requirements for standing is termed redressability: There must be a substantial likelihood that a favorable federal court decision will remedy the claimed injury. Also, if a case is moot, then the federal court decision will not have any effect because the controversy already has been resolved.

The difficulty, however, is predicting in advance whether there is a substantial enough chance that a federal court decision will have an effect so as to avoid being an advisory opinion. As Professor Bickel expressed, "the finality or lack of it in judicial judgments is rather a matter of degree."[26]

Therefore, for a case to be justiciable, and for it not to be a request for an advisory opinion, there must be an actual dispute between adverse litigants, and there must be a substantial likelihood that a favorable federal court decision will have some effect. These requirements must be met regardless of whether the plaintiff seeks monetary, injunctive, or declaratory relief.

Are Declaratory Judgments Impermissible Advisory Opinions?

For a time early in the last century, the Supreme Court expressed doubts about whether suits for declaratory judgments could be justiciable.[27] In fact, at one point, Justice Brandeis said, "What the plaintiff seeks is simply a declaratory judgment. To grant that relief is beyond the power conferred upon the federal judiciary."[28]

---

[25] Schiavo ex rel. Schindler v. Schiavo, 404 F.3d 1270, 1273-1274 (11th Cir. 2005) (Birch, J., concurring); *see also* Evan Caminker, *Schiavo* and *Klein*, 22 Const. Comment. 553 (2005).

[26] Alexander Bickel, The Least Dangerous Branch 117 (1962). Professor Currie points out that the federal government can always refuse to pay money judgments against it, yet this does not make such awards advisory opinions. *See* David Currie, Federal Courts 9 n.1 (4th ed. 1990).

[27] *See* Piedmont & Northern Ry. v. United States, 280 U.S. 469 (1930); Willing v. Chicago Auditorium Assn., 277 U.S. 274 (1928).

[28] *Id.* at 289.

But soon after this statement was uttered, the Supreme Court said that suits for declaratory judgments are justiciable so long as they meet the requirements for judicial review. In *Nashville, Chattanooga & St. Louis Railway v. Wallace*, the Court upheld the power of federal courts to issue declaratory judgments. A company sought a declaratory judgment that a tax was an unconstitutional burden on interstate commerce.[29] The Supreme Court explained that because the matter would have been justiciable as a request for an injunction, so was the suit for a declaratory judgment capable of federal court adjudication. Justice Stone, writing for the majority, explained, "The Constitution does not require that the case or controversy should be presented by traditional forms of procedure, invoking only traditional remedies. [Article III] did not crystallize into changeless form the procedure of 1789 as the only possible means for presenting a case or controversy."[30] The Court emphasized that the focus was on "substance" and "not with form" and that the case was justiciable "so long as the case retains the essentials of an adversary proceeding, involving a real, not a hypothetical, controversy."[31]

Wallace involved a request for relief pursuant to a state declaratory judgment statute. However, soon after *Wallace*, Congress adopted the Declaratory Judgment Act of 1934, authorizing a federal court to issue a declaratory judgment in a "case or actual controversy within its jurisdiction."[32] In *Aetna Life Insurance Co. v. Haworth*, the Supreme Court upheld the constitutionality of the Act.[33] The Court concluded that "[w]here there is such a concrete case admitting of an immediate and definitive determination of the legal rights of the parties in an adversary proceeding upon the facts alleged, the judicial function may be appropriately exercised although the adjudication of the rights of the litigants may not require the award of process or the payment of damages."[34] In other words, federal courts can issue declaratory judgments if there is an actual dispute between adverse litigants and if there is a substantial likelihood that the favorable federal court decision will bring about some change.

An interesting case that found a request for a declaratory judgment to be nonjusticiable was *Calderon v. Ashmus*.[35] The Antiterrorism and Effective Death Penalty Act of 1996 provides that there is a one-year statute of limitation for habeas corpus petitions, except in capital cases where the limitations period is reduced to six months if a state provides adequate counsel for collateral proceedings.[36] Death row inmates in California sought a declaratory judgment that California had not complied with the requirements for providing counsel and thus the six-month statute of limitations for habeas corpus petitions did not apply.

---

[29] 288 U.S. 249 (1933).

[30] *Id.* at 264.

[31] *Id.*

[32] 28 U.S.C. §2201. *See also* 28 U.S.C. §2202 (authorizing federal courts to enforce declaratory judgments by appropriate further relief).

[33] 300 U.S. 227 (1937).

[34] *Id.* at 221.

[35] 523 U.S. 740 (1998).

[36] 110 Stat. 1214, Pub. L. No. 104-132, April 24, 1996.

The United States Supreme Court unanimously held that the request for a declaratory judgment was not justiciable. The Court explained that the determination of whether the statute of limitations was six months or a year would not resolve the key controversy between the inmate and the prison: whether the prisoner was entitled to collateral relief. The Court stated that the "disruptive effects of an action such as this are particularly great when the underlying claim must be addressed in a federal habeas proceeding."[37] The effect of *Calderon* is that prisoners may individually receive a determination of the statute of limitations in their case in the context of a ruling on their habeas corpus petition, but no declaratory relief would be available.

Although the Supreme Court was unanimous, this is a puzzling ruling. As explained above, declaratory judgments exist so that people can know their rights in advance. Prisoners obviously have a need to know whether they have six months or a year to file their habeas petitions. *Calderon* means that prisoners will need to guess, and if a prisoner guesses wrong, assuming a year, when it is really six months, the court will deny the petition as time barred. In capital cases, that mistake can literally mean the difference between life and death. Although the determination of the statute of limitations would not resolve whether any particular prisoner was entitled to habeas corpus, it would have settled an important issue between the litigants and thus not have been an advisory opinion.

Importance of Prohibition of Advisory Opinions

Although the Supreme Court expressly refers to the ban on advisory opinions less frequently than the other justiciability doctrines, this should not be taken as an indication that it is less important. Quite the contrary, the other justiciability doctrines exist largely to ensure that federal courts will not issue advisory opinions, because the prohibition of advisory opinions is at the core of Article III. That is, it is because standing, ripeness, and mootness implement the policies and requirements contained in the advisory opinion doctrine that it is usually unnecessary for the Court to separately address the ban on advisory opinions.

§2.5   STANDING

§2.5.1   Introduction

Standing is the determination of whether a specific person is the proper party to bring a matter to the court for adjudication. The Supreme Court has declared that

---

[37] *Id.* at 1699.

"[i]n essence the question of standing is whether the litigant is entitled to have the court decide the merits of the dispute or of particular issues."[1]

Standing frequently has been identified by both Justices and commentators as one of the most confused areas of the law. Professor Vining wrote that it is impossible to read the standing decisions "without coming away with a sense of intellectual crisis. Judicial behavior is erratic, even bizarre. The opinions and justifications do not illuminate."[2] Thus, it is hardly surprising that standing has been the topic of extensive academic scholarship and that the doctrines are frequently attacked. Many factors account for the seeming incoherence of the law of standing. The requirements for standing have changed greatly in the past 40 years as the Court has formulated new standing requirements and reformulated old ones. The Court has not consistently articulated a test for standing; different opinions have announced varying formulations for the requirements for standing in federal court.[3] Moreover, many commentators believe that the Court has manipulated standing rules based on its views of the merits of particular cases.[4]

Most of all, though, the extensive attention to the standing doctrine reflects its importance in defining the role of the federal courts in American society. Basic policy considerations, about which there are strong arguments on both sides, are at the core of the law of standing. The Court has identified several values that are served by limiting who can sue in federal court.

Values Served by Limiting Standing

First, the standing doctrine promotes separation of powers by restricting the availability of judicial review.[5] The Supreme Court explained that standing "is founded in concern about the proper—and properly limited role—of the courts in a democratic society."[6] In *Allen v. Wright*, the Supreme Court declared that standing is "built on a single basic idea—the idea of separation of powers."[7] More recently, the Court explained: "The law of Article III standing, which is built on separation-of-powers principles, serves to prevent the judicial process from

---

§2.5 [1] Warth v. Seldin, 422 U.S. 490, 498 (1975).

[2] Joseph Vining, Legal Identity 1 (1978).

[3] The Court itself observed: "We need not mince words when we say that the concept of Art. III standing has not been defined with complete consistency in all of the various cases decided by this Court." Valley Forge Christian College v. Americans United for Separation of Church and State, 454 U.S. 464, 475 (1982).

[4] *See, e.g.*, Gene Nichol, Jr., Abusing Standing: A Comment on *Allen v. Wright*, 133 U. Pa. L. Rev. 635, 650 (1985); Mark Tushnet, The New Law of Standing: A Plea for Abandonment, 62 Cornell L. Rev. 663 (1977).

[5] *See* Antonin Scalia, The Doctrine of Standing as an Essential Element of the Separation of Powers, 17 Suffolk L. Rev. 881 (1983) (describing standing as a function of separation of powers). For a criticism of this view, *see* Nichol, Abusing Standing, *supra* note 4.

[6] Warth v. Seldin, 422 U.S. at 498.

[7] 468 U.S. 737, 752 (1984); *see also* Lewis v. Casey, 518 U.S. 343, 353 n.3 (1996) (Standing "has a separation of powers component, which keeps courts within certain traditional bounds vis-à-vis the other branches, concrete adverseness or not. That is where the 'actual injury' requirement comes from.").

being used to usurp the powers of the political branches."[8] The notion is that by restricting who may sue in federal court, standing limits what matters the judiciary will address and minimizes judicial review of the actions of the other branches of government. Indeed, the Court had said that the "standing inquiry is especially rigorous [because of separation of powers concerns] when reaching the merits of a dispute would force [it] to decide whether an action taken by one of the other two branches of the federal government was unconstitutional."[9]

However, concern for separation of powers also must include preserving the federal judiciary's role in the system of government.[10] Separation of powers can be undermined either by overexpansion of the role of the federal courts or by undue restriction. Standing thus focuses attention directly on the question of what is the proper place of the judiciary in the American system of government.

Second, standing is said to serve judicial efficiency by preventing a flood of lawsuits by those who have only an ideological stake in the outcome.[11] But in light of the high costs of litigation, one must wonder how large the burden really would be without the current standing restrictions. Standing also is justified in terms of conserving the Court's political capital. The Court once stated: "Should the courts seek to expand their power so as to bring under their jurisdiction ill-defined controversies over constitutional issues, they would become the organs of political theories. Such abuse of judicial power would properly meet rebuke and restriction from other branches."[12] But the question, of course, is what constitutes judicial abuse and what is appropriate court behavior.

Third, standing is said to improve judicial decision making by ensuring that there is a specific controversy before the court and that there is an advocate with a sufficient personal concern to effectively litigate the matter. The Supreme Court has frequently quoted its words from *Baker v. Carr*, that standing requires that a plaintiff allege "such a personal stake in the outcome of the controversy as to assure that concrete adverseness which sharpens the presentation of issues upon which the court so largely depends for illumination of difficult constitutional questions."[13]

Yet the need for specificity is likely to vary; some cases present pure questions of law in which the factual context is largely irrelevant. For example, if a city government tomorrow banned all abortions within its borders, the surrounding facts in the legal challenge almost surely would be immaterial. Also, the insistence on a personal stake in the outcome of the litigation is a very uncertain guarantee of high quality advocacy. The best litigator in the country who cared deeply about an issue could not raise it without a plaintiff with standing; but a pro se litigant, with no legal training, could pursue the matter on his or her own behalf.

Fourth, standing requirements are said to serve the value of fairness by ensuring that people will raise only their own rights and concerns and that people cannot

---

[8] Clapper v. Amnesty International, 133 S. Ct. 1138 (2013).

[9] Raines v. Byrd, 521 U.S. 811, 819 (1997).

[10] *See* Susan Bandes, The Idea of a Case, 42 Stan. L. Rev. 227 (1990).

[11] *See, e.g.*, United States v. Richardson, 418 U.S. 166, 192 (1974) (Powell, J., concurring).

[12] United Pub. Workers v. Mitchell, 330 U.S. 75, 90-91 (1947).

[13] 369 U.S. 186, 204 (1962).

be intermeddlers trying to protect others who do not want the protection offered. The Court explained: "[T]he courts should not adjudicate such rights unnecessarily, and it may be that in fact the holders of those rights either do not wish to assert them, or will be able to enjoy them regardless of whether the in-court litigant is successful or not."[14] But standing requirements might be quite unfair if they prevent people with serious injuries from securing judicial redress.[15]

Thus, although important values are served by the doctrine of standing, these same values also can often be furthered by expanding who has standing. Ultimately, the law of standing turns on basic normative questions about which there is no consensus.[16]

Requirements for Standing

The Supreme Court has announced several requirements for standing, all of which must be met in order for a federal court to adjudicate a case. The Court has said that some of these requirements are constitutional; that is, they are derived from the Court's interpretation of Article III and as constitutional restrictions they cannot be overridden by statute. Specifically, the Supreme Court has identified three constitutional standing requirements.[17] First, the plaintiff must allege that he or she has suffered or imminently will suffer an injury. Second, the plaintiff must allege that the injury is fairly traceable to the defendant's conduct. Third, the plaintiff must allege that a favorable federal court decision is likely to redress the injury. The requirement for injury is discussed in §2.5.2. The latter two requirements — termed causation and redressability — often have been treated by the Court as if they were a single test: Did the defendant cause the harm such that it can be concluded that limiting the defendant will remedy the injury?[18] Accordingly, these two requirements are considered together in §2.5.3.

In addition to these constitutional requirements, the Court also has identified three prudential standing principles. The Court has said that these are based not on the Constitution, but instead on prudent judicial administration. Unlike constitutional barriers, Congress may override prudential limits by statute. First, a

---

[14] Singleton v. Wulff, 428 U.S. 106, 113-114 (1976). For an excellent explanation of this fairness argument, *see* Lea Brilmayer, The Jurisprudence of Article III: Perspectives on the "Case or Controversy" Requirement, 93 Harv. L. Rev. 297, 306-310 (1979).

[15] *See* Richard Fallon, Of Justiciability, Remedies, and Public Law Litigation: Notes on the Jurisprudence of *Lyons*, 59 N.Y.U. L. Rev. 1 (1984).

[16] Indeed, some prominent commentators argue that the standing doctrine is unnecessary and that standing should simply be a question on the merits of the plaintiff's claim. *See* William Fletcher, The Structure of Standing, 98 Yale L.J. 221, 229 (1988) ("The essence of a true standing question is . . . [does] the plaintiff have a legal right to judicial enforcement of an asserted legal duty? This question should be seen as a question of substantive law, answerable by reference to the statutory or constitutional provision whose protection is invoked.").

[17] "To establish Article III standing, an injury must be 'concrete, particularized, and actual or imminent; fairly traceable to the challenged action; and redressable by a favorable ruling.'" Clapper v. Amnesty International, 133 S. Ct. at 1147.

[18] It should be noted that the Supreme Court indicated that causation and redressability are separate and independent standing barriers. Allen v. Wright, 468 U.S. at 758-759.

party generally may assert only his or her own rights and cannot raise the claims of third parties not before the court. Second, a plaintiff may not sue as a tax-payer who shares a grievance in common with all other taxpayers. However, the Supreme Court also has indicated that the bar on citizen suits, obviously quite similar to the limit on taxpayer suits, is constitutional and not prudential.[19] Third, a party must raise a claim within the zone of interests protected by the statute in question. These three standing requirements are discussed in §§2.5.4, 2.5.5, and 2.5.6, respectively.[20]

Although the requirements for standing must be met in every lawsuit filed in federal court, the issue frequently arises in cases presenting important constitutional and public law statutory questions. As such, standing is crucial in defining the scope of judicial protection of constitutional rights. Because standing is jurisdictional, federal courts can raise it on their own and it may be challenged at any point in the federal court proceedings.

§2.5.2 Injury

The Supreme Court has said that the core of Article III's requirement for cases and controversies is found in the rule that standing is limited to those who allege that they personally have suffered or imminently will suffer an injury. The Court explained: "The plaintiff must show that he has sustained or is immediately in danger of sustaining some direct injury as the result of the challenged official conduct and the injury or threat of injury must be both real and immediate, not conjectural or hypothetical."[21]

The injury requirement is viewed as advancing the values underlying the standing and justiciability doctrines. Requiring an injury is a key to ensuring that there is an actual dispute between adverse litigants and that the court is not being asked for an advisory opinion. The judicial role in the system of separation of powers is to prevent or redress particular injuries. Judicial resources are thought to be best saved for halting or remedying concrete injuries. An injury is said to give the plaintiff an incentive to vigorously litigate and present the matter to the court in the manner best suited for judicial resolution. An injury ensures that the plaintiff is not an intermeddler, but rather someone who truly has a personal stake in the outcome of the controversy.

---

[19] Lujan v. Defenders of Wildlife, 504 U.S. 555 (1992), discussed below.

[20] Specialized standing problems, such as standing for legislators and standing for government entities, are not covered. For a discussion of these topics, *see* Erwin Chemerinsky, Federal Jurisdiction (6th ed. 2011).

[21] *See, e.g.*, City of Los Angeles v. Lyons, 461 U.S. 95, 101-102 (1983) (citations omitted); *see also* Lujan v. Defenders of Wildlife, 504 U.S. 555, 560 (1992) ("[By injury in fact we mean] an invasion of a legally protected interest which is (a) concrete and particularized, . . . and (b) actual or imminent, not 'conjectural' or 'hypothetical.'").

Requirement for a Personally Suffered Injury

Two questions arise in implementing the injury requirement: What does it mean to say that a plaintiff must personally suffer an injury; and what types of injuries are sufficient for standing? Each issue warrants separate consideration.

The Supreme Court has declared that the "irreducible minimum" of Article III's limit on judicial power is a requirement that a party "show he personally has suffered some actual or threatened injury."[22] The Court has said that "we have repeatedly reiterated that 'threatened injury must be *certainly impending* to constitute injury in fact,' and that '[a]llegations of *possible* future injury' are not sufficient."[23]

Two environmental cases from the early 1970s illustrate this requirement. In *Sierra Club v. Morton*, the Sierra Club sought to prevent the construction of a ski resort in Mineral King Valley in California.[24] The issue was whether the plaintiff was "adversely affected or aggrieved" so as to be entitled to seek judicial review under the Administrative Procedures Act of the Interior Department's decision. The Sierra Club, a national membership organization dedicated to protecting the environment, asserted "a special interest in the conservation and the sound maintenance of the national parks, game refuges, and forests of the country."

The Supreme Court found this insufficient for standing purposes because there was no allegation that any of the Sierra Club's members ever had used Mineral King Valley. The Court stated: "The Sierra Club failed to allege that it or its members would be affected in any of their activities or pastimes by the . . . development. Nowhere in the pleadings or affidavits did the Club state that its members use Mineral King for any purpose, much less that they use it in any way that would be significantly affected by the proposed actions of respondents."[25] The Court concluded that "a mere interest in a problem, no matter how long standing the interest and no matter how qualified the organization is in evaluating the problem, is not sufficient."[26] Justice White is quoted in *The Brethren* as saying, "Why didn't the Sierra Club have one goddamn member walk through the park and then there would have been standing to sue?"[27] In fact, on remand, the Sierra Club amended its complaint to allege that its members had used the park for activities that would be disrupted by the ski resort, and it was then accorded standing.

Sierra Club can be contrasted with another decision handed down a year later involving a group seeking to protect the environment. In *United States v. Students Challenging Regulatory Agency Procedures (SCRAP)*, the Supreme Court upheld the standing of a group of students to seek review under the Administrative Procedures Act of an Interstate Commerce Commission decision to increase freight rates.[28] A

---

[22] Valley Forge Christian College v. Americans United for Separation of Church and State, 454 U.S. 464, 472 (1982).

[23] Clapper v. Amnesty International, 133 S. Ct. at 1147.

[24] 405 U.S. 727 (1972).

[25] *Id.* at 735.

[26] *Id.* at 739.

[27] Bob Woodward & Scott Armstrong, The Brethren 164 n.* (1979).

[28] 412 U.S. 669 (1973).

group of law students at George Washington University Law Center contended that the hike in railroad freight rates would discourage the use of recycled goods because of the extra cost of shipping them. The lawsuit claimed that a decrease in recycling would lead to more use of natural resources and thus more mining and pollution. The students maintained that their enjoyment of the forests, streams, and mountains in the Washington, D.C., area would be lessened as a result. The Supreme Court upheld the group's standing, concluding that aesthetic and environmental injuries are sufficient for standing so long as the plaintiff claims to suffer the harm personally.

A comparison of *Sierra Club* and *SCRAP* is revealing. The plaintiff's complaint must specifically allege that he or she has personally suffered an injury. Although what constitutes a sufficient injury is discussed in detail below, it is worth noting that these cases establish that an ideological interest in a matter is not enough for standing. Yet these cases also raise important policy questions. Why assume in *Sierra Club* that the only ones injured by the destruction of the park are those who already have used it? As Professor David Currie explained, why cannot a person upset by the destruction of the last grizzly bear be allowed to sue, even if he or she never has seen a grizzly?[29]

The Supreme Court has continued to apply *Sierra Club*.[30] In *Lujan v. National Wildlife Federation*, the plaintiffs challenged the federal government policy lessening the environmental protection of certain federal lands.[31] Two members of the National Wildlife Federation submitted affidavits that they used land "in the vicinity" of that which was reclassified and that the increased mining activity would destroy the area's natural beauty. The Supreme Court, however, said that this allegation was too general to establish a particular injury, and thus the defendant was entitled to prevail on summary judgment because of the plaintiffs' lack of standing. The Court quoted the district court's finding that thousands of acres were opened to development and "[a]t a minimum, [the] . . . affidavit is ambiguous regarding whether the adversely affected lands are the ones she uses."[32] In other words, the plaintiffs were not entitled to standing unless they could demonstrate that they used specific federal land that was being mined under the new federal regulations.

The Supreme Court subsequently applied this principle in *United States v. Hays* to hold that only a person residing within an election district may argue that the lines for the district were unconstitutionally drawn in violation of equal protection.[33] The Supreme Court has held that the government may use race in

---

[29] David Currie, Federal Courts: Cases and Materials 42 (4th ed. 1990).

[30] *See also* Director, Office of Workers' Compensation Programs, Department of Labor v. Newport News Shipbuilding and Dry Dock Co., 514 U.S. 122 (1995) (holding that the Director of the Office of Workers' Compensation Programs is not an aggrieved person under the Longshore and Harbor Workers' Compensation Act and thus did not have standing to seek review of decisions by the Benefits Review Board that deny individuals benefits).

[31] 497 U.S. 871, 883 (1990).

[32] *Id.* at 888 (citation omitted).

[33] 515 U.S. 737 (1995). The Court reaffirmed and applied this limitation on standing to challenge election districts in Shaw v. Hunt, 517 U.S. 899, 904-905 (1996), and Bush v. Vera, 517 U.S. 952 (1996) (plurality opinion).

drawing election district lines only if it meets strict scrutiny, even if the purpose is to increase the likelihood of electing minority-race representatives.[34] In *Hays*, the Court held that only individuals residing within a district suffer an injury from how the lines for that district are drawn. The Court said that a "plaintiff [who] resides in a racially gerrymandered district . . . has standing to challenge the legislature's action," but a plaintiff who resides outside the district fails to suffer "the injury our standing doctrine requires."[35]

It is understandable that the Court would want to limit who has standing to challenge election district lines, but it seems hard to justify restricting standing to those who actually reside within the districts. Why shouldn't a voter residing in a contiguous district, who claims to have been excluded because of the race-based districting, also have standing?[36] Drawing lines for one election district inevitably affects the lines for neighboring districts. It therefore seems arbitrary to say that those within the district suffer an injury under the equal protection clause and all others do not.

The need for a personal stake in order to have standing is also reflected in two recent, high profile cases concerning challenges to laws prohibiting marriage equality. In *Hollingsworth v. Perry*, the Court held, 5-4, that the supporters of an initiative lack standing to appeal a federal district court decision invalidating the initiative when state officials refuse to appeal.[37] After the California Supreme Court found a right to marriage equality for gays and lesbians under the California Constitution, California voters in November 2008 passed Proposition 8. It amended the California Constitution to provide that marriage had to be between a man and a woman.

Two same-sex couples who wanted marriage licenses brought a challenge to the initiative. A federal district court ruled in their favor and held that Proposition 8 denied equal protection and violated the fundamental right to marry.[38] The Court enjoined the defendant state officials from enforcing Proposition 8. The defendants choose not to appeal, but the supporters of the initiative sought to appeal. After briefing and oral argument, the United States Court of Appeals for the Ninth Circuit certified the question to the California Supreme Court as to whether under California law the supporters of an initiative could defend it when public officials refuse to do so. The California Supreme Court found that "the official proponents of the initiative are authorized under California law to appear

---

[34] *See e.g.*, Miller v. Johnson, 515 U.S. 900 (1995); Shaw v. Reno, 509 U.S. 630 (1993), discussed in §9.3.5.3 and §10.8.5.

[35] 515 U.S. at 745. Although the Court expressly said that the injury requirement was not met, the Court also said that the case presented a "generalized grievance." *Id.* at 745. This raises the question of whether the Court continues to believe that the generalized grievance requirement is a separate standing rule or simply another way of saying that there is not an injury sufficient for standing purposes.

[36] *But see* Pamela S. Karlan, All Over the Map: The Supreme Court's Voting Rights Trilogy, 1993 Sup. Ct. Rev. 245 (arguing that even voters who live in majority-minority districts should not have standing).

[37] 133 S. Ct. 2652 (2013).

[38] *Perry v. Schwarzenegger*, 704 F. Supp. 2d 921 (N.D. Cal. 2010). For a detailed description of this litigation, *see* Jo Becker, Forcing the Spring: Inside the Fight for Marriage Equality (2014).

and assert the state's interest in the initiative's validity and to appeal a judgment invalidating the measure when the public officials who ordinarily defend the measure or appeal such a judgment decline to do so."[39]

Nonetheless, the Court ruled, 5-4, that the supporters of the initiative lacked standing to appeal under Article III. The Court, in an opinion by Chief Justice Roberts, stressed that "to have standing, a litigant must seek relief for an injury that affects him in a 'personal and individual way.' "[40] The Court explained that the supporters of Proposition 8 only have an ideological interest in having it enforced and that an ideological injury is insufficient for standing. Chief Justice Roberts explained: "Article III standing 'is not to be placed in the hands of concerned bystanders, who will use it simply as a vehicle for the vindication of value interests.' No matter how deeply committed petitioners may be to upholding Proposition 8 or how 'zealous [their] advocacy,' that is not a 'particularized' interest sufficient to create a case or controversy under Article III."[41]

By contrast, in a case decided the same day, *United States v. Windsor,* the Court allowed the Bipartisan Legal Advisory Group (BLAG) of the House of Representatives to defend the constitutionality of §3 of the Defense of Marriage Act (DOMA) when the president and the attorney general refused to do so.[42] When Thea Spyer died, her spouse, Edith Windsor, was required by federal law to pay $363,000 in estate taxes. If the federal government had recognized their marriage, as their home state of New York did, Windsor would owe no taxes. But §3 of DOMA requires that for federal law and federal benefits, marriages had to be between a man and a woman. Windsor paid these taxes and then brought a challenge to §3 of DOMA.

The Obama administration's position was to enforce §3 of DOMA, as it did against Windsor, but not to defend it in court. The Bipartisan Legal Advisory Group of the House of Representatives voted 3-2 along party lines to intervene to defend §3 of DOMA.

In contrast to *Hollingsworth v. Perry,* the Court found that there was standing. The Court stressed that Windsor had suffered an economic injury — $363,000 — and the outcome of the lawsuit would determine whether she would get the money back. The Court explained: "Windsor suffered a redressable injury when she was required to pay estate taxes from which, in her view, she was exempt but for the alleged invalidity of §3 of DOMA."[43] The Court said that the question of whether BLAG could defend the statute was prudential and not jurisdictional. The Court found that "BLAG's sharp adversarial presentation of the issues satisfies the

---

[39] *Perry v. Brown,* 52 Cal. 4th 1116, 1127, 265 P.3d 1002, 1007 (2011), 134 Cal. Rptr. 3d 499.

[40] 133 S. Ct. at 2662 (citations omitted).

[41] *Id.* at 2663 (citations omitted). Justice Kennedy wrote the dissent, joined by Justices Thomas, Alito, and Sotomayor, and would have granted standing based on California law, as interpreted by the California Supreme Court, which would allow the supporters of an initiative to defend it in court.

[42] 133 S. Ct. 2675 (2013). The Court's analysis finding §3 of DOMA to violate equal protection is discussed in §9.7.4.

[43] *Id.* at 2685.

prudential concerns that otherwise might counsel against hearing an appeal from a decision with which the principal parties agree."[44]

What explains why the Court did not find standing in *Hollingsworth*, but did in *Windsor*?[45] The Court saw *Hollingsworth* as involving solely an ideological interest on the part of the supporters of Proposition 8 who wanted to appeal to defend it. By contrast, in *Windsor*, the Court saw a concrete injury: a woman who had to pay $363,000 in estate taxes because of §3 of DOMA.

The requirement for a personally suffered injury is also illustrated by the Supreme Court's recent decision in *Clapper v. Amnesty International*.[46] Section 702 of the Foreign Intelligence Surveillance Act of 1978 (FISA), added by the FISA Amendments Act of 2008, permits the attorney general and the Director of National Intelligence to acquire foreign intelligence information by intercepting communications between those in the United States and those in foreign countries.[47] A lawsuit was brought by attorneys, journalists, and business people who said that their communications were chilled by the possibility that their communications with individuals in foreign countries might be intercepted.

The Supreme Court, in a 5-4 decision, ordered that the case be dismissed for lack of standing. The Court, in an opinion by Justice Alito, stressed that none of the plaintiffs could show that their communications had been intercepted or were likely to be intercepted. Thus, they lacked the requisite injury required for standing. The Court explained: "First, it is speculative whether the Government will imminently target communications to which respondents are parties. . . . Second, even if respondents could demonstrate that the targeting of their foreign contacts is imminent, respondents can only speculate as to whether the Government will seek to use §1881a-authorized surveillance (rather than other methods) to do so. . . . Third, even if respondents could show that the Government will seek the Foreign Intelligence Surveillance Court's authorization to acquire the communications of respondents' foreign contacts under §1881a, respondents can only speculate as to whether that court will authorize such surveillance. . . . Fourth, even if the Government were to obtain the Foreign Intelligence Surveillance Court's approval to target respondents' foreign contacts under §1881a, it is unclear whether the Government would succeed in acquiring the communications of respondents' foreign contacts. And fifth, even if the Government were to conduct surveillance of respondents' foreign contacts, respondents can only speculate as to whether *their own communications* with their foreign contacts would be incidentally acquired."[48]

---

[44] *Id.* at 2688, 2701. Justice Scalia's dissent strongly disagreed that there was standing. *Id.* at 2698 (Scalia, J., dissenting) ("The majority's discussion of the requirements of Article III bears no resemblance to our jurisprudence.").

[45] Of course, one explanation is that the majority of the Justices wanted to reach the merits in *Windsor* and strike down §3 of DOMA, while a majority of the Justices were not ready to declare unconstitutional all state laws prohibiting same-sex marriage.

[46] 133 S. Ct. 1138 (2013).

[47] 50 U.S.C. §1881a.

[48] 133 S. Ct. at 1159-1160. The argument that the plaintiffs had an injury based on a claim that their speech was chilled is discussed below at text accompanying notes 76-77.

Justice Breyer, writing for the four dissenters, sharply disagreed and said that there was a sufficient likelihood that the plaintiffs' communications would be intercepted to meet the requirement for standing. He wrote: "The upshot is that (1) similarity of content, (2) strong motives, (3) prior behavior, and (4) capacity all point to a very strong likelihood that the Government will intercept at least some of the plaintiffs' communications. . . . Consequently, we need only assume that the Government is doing its job (to find out about, and combat, terrorism) in order to conclude that there is a high probability that the Government will intercept at least some electronic communication to which at least some of the plaintiffs are parties. The majority is wrong when it describes the harm threatened plaintiffs as 'speculative.' "[49]

A key difference between the majority and the dissent was how the test for future likelihood should be articulated. Justice Alito, writing for the Court, said that the injury has to be "certainly impending,"[50] while for the dissent what is required is a "reasonable probability" or "high probability."[51]

Application of Requirement for Personally Suffered Injury:

City of Los Angeles v. Lyons

Perhaps the most important application of the requirement for a personally suffered injury is the requirement that a plaintiff seeking injunctive or declaratory relief must show a likelihood of future harm. This was the holding in *City of Los Angeles v. Lyons*.[52] *Lyons* involved a suit to enjoin as unconstitutional the use of chokeholds by the Los Angeles Police Department in instances where the police were not threatened with death or serious bodily injury. Adolph Lyons, a 24-year-old black man, was stopped by the police for having a burnt-out taillight on his car. Justice Marshall describes the uncontested facts:

After one of the officers completed a patdown search, Lyons dropped his hands, but was ordered to place them back above his head, and one of the officers grabbed Lyons' hands and slammed them into his head. Lyons complained about the pain caused by the ring of keys he was holding in his hand. Within 5 to 10 seconds, the officer began to choke Lyons by applying a forearm against his throat. As Lyons struggled for air, the officer handcuffed him, but continued to apply the chokehold until he blacked out. When Lyons regained consciousness, he was lying facedown on the ground, choking, gasping for air, and spitting up blood and dirt. He had urinated and defecated. He was issued a traffic citation and released.[53]

---

[49] 133 S. Ct. at 1160 (Breyer, J., dissenting).
[50] 133 S. Ct. at 1150.
[51] 133 S. Ct. at 1165 (Breyer, J., dissenting).
[52] 461 U.S. 95 (1983).
[53] *Id.* at 115 (Marshall, J., dissenting).

At the time of the suit, 16 people in Los Angeles had died from the choke-hold—12 of them black men.[54] Lyons's complaint alleged that it was the official policy of the Los Angeles Police Department to use the chokeholds in situations where officers were not faced with a threat of bodily injury or death.

The Supreme Court, in a 5-to-4 decision, ruled that Lyons did not have standing to seek injunctive relief. Although Lyons could bring a suit seeking damages for his injuries, he did not have standing to enjoin the police because he could not demonstrate a substantial likelihood that he, personally, would be choked again in the future. Justice White, writing for the Court, explained: "Lyons' standing to seek the injunction requested depended on whether he was likely to suffer future injury from the use of the chokeholds by police officers."[55] The Court concluded that "absent a sufficient likelihood that he will again be wronged in a similar way, Lyons is no more entitled to an injunction than any other citizen of Los Angeles; and a federal court may not entertain a claim by any or all citizens who no more than assert that certain practices of law enforcement officers are unconstitutional."[56] *Lyons* thus establishes that in order for a person to have standing to seek an injunction, the individual must allege a substantial likelihood that he or she will be subjected in the future to the allegedly illegal policy.

Not surprisingly, the *Lyons* decision has been strongly criticized. First, some commentators have argued that the Court incorrectly assumed that Lyons would suffer an injury in the future only if he would be choked again. The Court's critics argue that Lyons would continue to suffer a psychological injury—fear of being subjected to a similar chokehold—so long as the police policy remained unchanged.[57]

Second, *Lyons* is criticized as representing a substantial departure from prior practice both with regard to standing and in terms of civil procedure. Never before had the Court determined standing on the basis of the remedy sought. In fact, under the Federal Rules of Civil Procedure a plaintiff is not even required to request injunctive relief in the complaint in order to receive it as a remedy.[58]

Third, critics argue that the *Lyons* rationale, if strictly followed, would have a devastating effect on a substantial amount of public law litigation. Under the *Lyons* holding, plaintiffs would have standing to seek injunctions only of ongoing practices that were likely to directly harm them in the future. For example, a student would have standing to challenge an ongoing public school practice of holding prayer sessions every morning. But in many instances, plaintiffs seek injunctions—as Adolph Lyons did—of policies sure to affect someone in the future, but where a particular victim cannot be identified in advance.

Indeed, many lower courts have applied *Lyons* to prevent judicial review of allegedly unconstitutional government policies. For example, lower federal courts have dismissed the following for lack of standing: requests for injunctions to

---

[54] *Id.* at 115-116 (Marshall, J., dissenting).
[55] *Id.* at 105.
[56] *Id.* at 111.
[57] Gene Nichol, Jr., Rethinking Standing, 72 Cal. L. Rev. 68, 100-101 (1982).
[58] For an excellent development of this and other criticisms, *see* Fallon, *supra* note 15.

regulate the use of the chemical mace by police; challenges to a state practice of paying police officers a bonus if their arrest led to a conviction; and attempts to halt strip searches conducted at county jails of those arrested for minor crimes.[59] Additionally, lower courts consistently have applied *Lyons* to prevent standing in suits seeking declaratory judgments where standing for injunctive relief would be unavailable.[60]

Yet defenders of the *Lyons* decision argue that Lyons was not completely denied the ability to secure review of the police department's use of chokeholds. The Court did not deny his standing to pursue a damages claim, and the constitutionality of the chokehold could be adjudicated there. The Court's rationale is that a person does not have standing to seek an injunction unless there is a reason to believe that he or she would directly benefit from the equitable relief. But critics of *Lyons* respond that unconstitutional government policies will remain in effect, especially in instances where damage suits cannot be brought or the government is willing to pay the damages in order to maintain its policy.

Since *Lyons*, the Supreme Court has reaffirmed that a plaintiff seeking injunctive or declaratory relief must show a likelihood of future injury. For example, in *County of Riverside v. McLaughlin*, the Court allowed plaintiffs standing to challenge a county arraignment policy that allowed long delays before arraignments over weekends and holidays.[61] The Court rejected a motion to dismiss based on *Lyons* and emphasized that plaintiffs were under arrest and in custody at the time that they filed their lawsuits. The plaintiffs' complaint alleged that they were suffering a current injury and that they "would continue to suffer that injury until they received the probable cause determination to which they were entitled."[62]

In contrast, in *Lujan v. Defenders of Wildlife*, the Supreme Court considered a challenge to a revision of a federal regulation that provided that the Endangered Species Act does not apply to United States government activities outside the United States or on the high seas.[63] The plaintiffs claimed that the failure to comply with the Act "with respect to certain funded activities abroad increases the rate of extinction of endangered and threatened species."[64]

---

[59]   Curtis v. City of New Haven, 726 F.2d 65 (2d Cir. 1984) (no standing to challenge police use of mace); Brown v. Edwards, 721 F.2d 1442 (5th Cir. 1984) (no standing to challenge state policy awarding money to constables for each arrest they made that led to a conviction); Jones v. Bowman, 664 F. Supp. 433 (N.D. Ind. 1987) (no standing to challenge strip searches of women performed by county jail); John Does 1-100 v. Boyd, 613 F. Supp. 1514 (D. Minn. 1985) (no standing to challenge strip searches of people brought to the city jail for minor offenses).

[60]   *See, e.g.*, Fair Employment Council of Greater Washington, Inc. v. BMC Marketing Corp., 23 F.3d 1268 (D.C. Cir. 1994) (suit for injunctive and declaratory relief to halt discriminatory placement practices dismissed based on *Lyons*); Knox v. McGinnis, 998 F.2d 1405 (7th Cir. 1993) (prisoner's suit to stop prison officials from using "black box" restraining device dismissed based on *Lyons*); Alabama Free Thought Association v. Moore, 893 F. Supp. 1522 (N.D. Ala. 1995) (dismissed based on *Lyons* request for injunctive and declaratory relief to halt judge from causing prayers to be uttered in the jury room and the placement of the Ten Commandments in the courtroom).

[61]   500 U.S. 44 (1991).

[62]   *Id.* at 51.

[63]   504 U.S. 555 (1992).

[64]   *Id.* at 562 (citations omitted).

The Court expressly applied *Lyons* and held that the plaintiffs lacked standing because they could not show a sufficient likelihood that they would be injured in the future by a destruction of the endangered species abroad. Two of the plaintiffs had submitted detailed affidavits describing their trips abroad and their viewing of endangered animals such as the Nile crocodile, the elephant, and the leopard. The Court said that the fact that the women had visited the areas in the past "proves nothing," and their desire to return in the future—"some day"—is insufficient for standing "without any description of concrete plans or indeed any specification of when the some day will be."[65]

Justice Blackmun wrote a vehement dissent and lamented that the requirement that a plaintiff have specific plans to return to a foreign country created only a silly formality that a plaintiff must purchase a plane ticket in order to sue.[66] Moreover, the dissent challenged the majority's assumption that a person is harmed by the destruction of the environment only if the individual has concrete plans to visit the harmed place. Justice Blackmun stated: "It cannot be seriously contended that a litigant's failure to use the precise or exact site where animals are slaughtered or where toxic waste is dumped into a river means that he or she cannot show injury."[67]

What Injuries Are Sufficient?

The second major question concerning injury as a standing requirement is what injuries are sufficient for standing? No formula exists for determining what types of injuries are adequate to allow a plaintiff standing to sue in federal court. The law is clear that injuries to common law, constitutional, and statutory rights are sufficient for standing. More than 40 years ago, Justice Frankfurter wrote that "[a] litigant ordinarily has standing to challenge governmental action of a sort that, if taken by a private person, would create a right of action cognizable by the courts. Or standing may be based on an interest created by the Constitution or a statute."[68] Past these categories, however, it is difficult to do more than identify the types of interests that the Court has regarded as adequate bases for standing and those that have been deemed insufficient.

---

[65] *Id.* at 564. *See also* Steel Co. v. Citizens for a Better Environment, 523 U.S. 83 (1998) (relying on *Lujan* to deny standing to plaintiffs who sought relief for past violations of a federal law, but did not seek compensation for themselves, and did not allege that the company was likely to violate the statute in the future).

[66] *Id.* at 592 (Blackmun, J., dissenting). For a thorough criticism of *Lujan*, *see* Cass Sunstein, What's Standing After *Lujan*: Of Citizen Suits, "Injuries," and Article III, 91 Mich. L. Rev. 163 (1992).

[67] *Id.* at 594 (Blackmun, J., dissenting).

[68] Joint Anti-Fascist Refugee Comm. v. McGrath, 341 U.S. 123, 152-153 (1951). Justice Frankfurter also expressed the view that only these categories could be a basis for standing; this certainly no longer is true, as discussed below.

Injuries to Common Law Rights

Injury to rights recognized at common law—property, contracts, and torts—are sufficient for standing purposes. In fact, for a time, the Court appeared to suggest that only such injuries would be enough for standing; that standing would be granted only if there would be a cause of action at common law for similar harms caused by a private actor. In *Tennessee Electric Power Co. v. Tennessee Valley Authority*, power companies attempted to enjoin the Tennessee Valley Authority from producing and selling electricity.[69] In denying the power companies standing to restrain their potential competitor, the Court explained that standing is unavailable "unless the right invaded is a legal right—one of property, one arising out of a contract, one protected against tortious invasion, or one founded on a statute which confers a privilege."[70] Although such injuries are obviously no longer exhaustive of those required for standing, violations of common law rights remain sufficient for standing purposes.[71]

Injuries to Constitutional Rights

Injuries to constitutional rights are also adequate to accord standing. Two qualifications are important. First, it is necessary to decide which constitutional provisions bestow rights. The Supreme Court has held that suits to halt the violation of certain constitutional provisions are nonjusticiable for lack of standing because they present "generalized grievances." For example, the Court refused to find standing for plaintiffs seeking to enjoin violations of constitutional clauses requiring a statement and account of all government expenditures and preventing members of Congress from serving in the executive branch.[72] These cases and the generalized grievance standing bar are discussed in detail in §2.5.5. In general, a person who claims discrimination or a violation of an individual liberty, such as freedom of speech or due process of law, will be accorded standing. But someone who seeks to prevent a violation of a constitutional provision dealing with the structure of government is unlikely to be accorded standing unless the person has suffered a particular harm distinct from the rest of the population.

Second, while an injury to a constitutional right is clearly a basis for standing, there remains the question of what facts are sufficient to establish such an injury. The Supreme Court's decision in *Laird v. Tatum* is illustrative.[73] In *Laird*,

---

[69] 306 U.S. 118 (1939).

[70] *Id.* at 137-138.

[71] The Supreme Court has ruled that "an assignee of a legal claim for money owed has standing, even when the assignee has promised to remit the proceeds of the litigation to the assignor." Sprint Communications Co. v. APCC Services, Inc., 554 U.S. 269 (2008). All of the Justices assumed that the claim for money was sufficient for standing, though split 5-4 as to whether the requirement for redressability is met when the plaintiff would not actually receive the funds. This is discussed below in the consideration of redressability.

[72] *See* Schlesinger v. Reservists Comm. to Stop the War, 418 U.S. 208 (1974); United States v. Richardson, 418 U.S. 166 (1974), discussed in §2.5.5, below.

[73] 408 U.S. 1 (1972).

the plaintiffs contended that their First Amendment rights were violated because their expression was chilled by the army's surveillance of domestic groups. The Court said that "negations of a subjective 'chill' are not an adequate substitute for a claim of specific present objective harm or a threat of specific future harm."[74] However, it should be noted that in other instances the Court has found a chilling effect on speech to be a sufficient basis for standing. For example, in 1987, the Supreme Court accorded an exhibitor of foreign films standing to challenge the Department of Justice's labeling the films as "political propaganda" under the Foreign Agents Registration Act.[75] The Court accepted as a sufficient injury the allegation that the showing of films was chilled. The underlying point is that deciding whether there is an injury to a constitutional right often requires an inquiry into the merits of the case to determine whether a constitutional right was violated.

The Court recently reaffirmed *Laird v. Tatum* in *Clapper v. Amnesty International*.[76] As explained above, *Clapper* involved a challenge to a law enacted in 2008 to amend the Foreign Intelligence Surveillance Act to allow the gathering of foreign intelligence information by intercepting communications between persons in the United States and those in foreign countries. A lawsuit was brought by lawyers, journalists, and business people who said that their speech was chilled by the fear that their communications might be intercepted. The Court rejected this injury as being sufficient for standing and stated: "Because '[a]llegations of a subjective "chill" are not an adequate substitute for a claim of specific present objective harm or a threat of specific future harm,' the plaintiffs in *Laird*—and respondents here—lack standing."[77]

Injuries to Statutory Rights

Violations of rights created by statute also are sufficient for standing purposes. The Supreme Court has explained that "Congress may create a statutory right or entitlement, the alleged deprivation of which can confer standing to sue even where the plaintiff would have suffered no judicially cognizable injury in the absence of statute."[78] *Trafficante v. Metropolitan Life Insurance Co.* illustrates this type of injury.[79] In *Trafficante*, two white residents of an apartment complex were accorded standing to challenge the owner's discrimination against black applicants in violation of the Civil Rights Act of 1968.[80] The Supreme Court concluded that the statute created a right to be free from the adverse consequences of racial discrimination and accepted the plaintiffs' claim that they were injured in being deprived of the right to live in an integrated community.[81]

---

[74] *Id.* at 13-14.

[75] Meese v. Keene, 481 U.S. 465 (1987), discussed in greater detail in §11.2.4.5.

[76] 133 S. Ct. 1138 (2013).

[77] *Id.* at 1152.

[78] Warth v. Seldin, 422 U.S. 490, 514 (1975).

[79] 409 U.S. 205 (1972).

[80] 42 U.S.C. §3604.

[81] *See, e.g.*, Havens Realty Corp. v. Coleman, 455 U.S. 363 (1982); Gladstone, Realtors v. Village of Bellwood, 441 U.S. 91 (1979).

The interesting question concerning injuries to statutory rights is how far Congress can expand standing pursuant to this authority. For instance, the Clean Air Act empowers "any person" to bring suit to enforce certain pollution control regulations.[82] In light of *Trafficante*, can Congress, by statute, create a right to clean air, the violation of which is a sufficient injury for standing purposes? The Court's decision in *Lujan v. Defenders of Wildlife* indicates that such broad authorizations for standing are not sufficient by themselves for standing.[83]

In *Lujan*, the Court considered a challenge brought under the Endangered Species Act, which provides, in part, that "any person may commence a civil suit" to enjoin a violation of the Act.[84] The Court held that Congress could not create standing in this manner. Justice Scalia, writing for the Court, stated: "To permit Congress to convert the undifferentiated public interest in executive officers' compliance with the law into an 'individual' right vindicable in the courts is to permit Congress to transfer from the president to the courts the Chief Executive's most important constitutional duty, to take Care that the laws be faithfully executed."[85]

The relationship between *Lujan* and *Trafficante* is unclear. Perhaps the Court will draw a distinction between statutes that create a specific statutory right, such as a right to interracial housing, and those that are essentially procedural in creating a right for any person to sue. This distinction is troubling, however, because if Congress can create a right for all citizens, such as a right to have endangered animals protected, then Congress should be able to authorize enforcement of the right.

Alternatively, the Court may interpret statutes authorizing any citizen to sue to expand standing to the maximum allowed by Article III. In other words, Congress in expressly permitting such citizen suits is seen as abrogating prudential requirements and allowing standing so long as it is constitutionally permissible. Support for this view is found in the Court's decision in *Bennett v. Spear*.[86] Ranch operators and irrigation districts filed an action under the citizen suit provision of the Endangered Species Act. The plaintiffs contended that the Act was violated in the proposed use of reservoir water to protect certain species of fish. The Supreme Court upheld the plaintiffs' standing and cited *Trafficante* as an instance where "standing was expanded to the full extent permitted under Article III."[87] Although the Court did not discuss *Lujan*, its reasoning implies that in *Trafficante*, and in *Bennett* itself, the citizen suit provision was a basis for standing because Article III's requirements also were met; in *Lujan*, the Article III standing requirements were not satisfied.

A subsequent standing case seems to confirm that Congress retains broad authority to create injuries that are the basis for standing. In *Federal Election Commission v. Akins*, the Court held that Congress, by statute, could create a right

---

[82] 42 U.S.C. §7604(a).

[83] 504 U.S. 555 (1992).

[84] 16 U.S.C. §1540(g).

[85] 504 U.S. 555, 562-563 (1992).

[86] 520 U.S. 154 (1997). *Bennett*'s discussion of the zone of interests test is explained below in §2.5.6.

[87] *Id.* at 165.

to information and that the denial of such information was an injury sufficient to satisfy Article III.[88] A group of voters brought suit challenging a decision by the Federal Election Commission that the American Israel Public Affairs Committee (AIPAC) was not a "political committee" subject to regulation and reporting requirements under the Federal Election Campaign Act of 1971. A federal statute authorizes suit by any person "aggrieved" by a Federal Election Commission decision.

The Court granted standing and concluded that Congress had created a right to information about political committees and that the plaintiffs were denied the information by virtue of the Federal Election Commission's decision. Justice Breyer, writing for the Court, explained: "The 'injury in fact' that respondents have suffered consists of their inability to obtain information—lists of AIPAC donors . . . and campaign-related contributions and expenditures—that on respondents' view of the law, the statute requires that AIPAC make public."[89] In other words, the statute created a right to information, albeit a right that would not exist without the statute, and the alleged infringement of that statutory right was deemed sufficient to meet Article III and to allow standing under the broad citizen suit provision for any aggrieved person.

Together *Bennett v. Spear* and *Federal Election Commission v. Akins* indicate that *Lujan* should not be read as a broad limit on Congress's ability to authorize suits. So long as the plaintiff meets Article III's injury requirement, and infringement of a statutory right is sufficient in this regard, standing is permitted under a federal statute permitting citizen suits.

Other Injuries Sufficient for Standing

Injuries to common law, constitutional, and statutory rights are sufficient for standing. But these are not the only types of injuries that permit federal court review. The Supreme Court has considered many other interests, finding some to be a sufficient basis for a claim of injury, but concluding that others were inadequate. No ascertainable principle exists to rationalize these rulings. For example, the Court has ruled that a claim of an aesthetic or environmental harm is sufficient to constitute an injury.[90] In *Lujan*, for example, the Court conceded that the "desire to use or observe an animal species, even for purely aesthetic purposes, is undeniably a cognizable interest for purposes of standing."[91] Also, the Court held that possible diminution of water allocations as a result of application of the Endangered Species Act was a sufficient injury for standing.[92] Most recently, in *Massachusetts v. E.P.A.*, the Court ruled that the harms from global warming are

---

[88] 524 U.S. 11 (1998).

[89] *Id.* at 21.

[90] *See* United States v. Students Challenging Regulatory Agency Procedures, 412 U.S. 669, 686 (1973). For a creative approach to the problem of standing in environmental cases, *see* Christopher Stone, Should Trees Have Standing?—Toward Legal Rights for Natural Objects, 45 S. Cal. L. Rev. 450 (1972).

[91] 504 U.S. at 562-563.

[92] Bennett v. Spear, 520 U.S. 154, 168 (1997).

sufficient to permit a state to sue the federal Environmental Protection Agency for failure to promulgate regulations to deal with greenhouse gas emissions.[93]

Additionally, the Court has allowed standing for those suffering economic harms[94] or facing possible criminal prosecutions for their actions.[95] The Court has stated that "a person indicted for violating a federal statute has standing to challenge its validity on grounds that, by enacting it, Congress exceeded its powers under the Constitution, thus intruding upon the sovereignty and authority of the States."[96] As Justice Ginsburg explained, a "defendant has a personal right not to be convicted under a constitutionally invalid law."[97] The Court has held that the loss of the right to sue in the forum of one's choice is an injury sufficient to convey standing.[98]

In *Clinton v. City of New York*, an important decision that declared the line-item veto unconstitutional, the Court found that a change in market conditions was a sufficient injury to meet the standing requirement.[99] President Clinton used the line-item veto to cancel a tax provision that would have benefited sellers in a transaction, but not a cooperative that was purchasing their company. Nonetheless, the Court concluded that the cooperative had suffered an injury because of the change in market conditions.

But other types of interests have been deemed insufficient for standing. For instance, in *Allen v. Wright*, the Supreme Court refused to allow standing to challenge the Internal Revenue Service's policy of providing tax exemptions to private schools that discriminated on the basis of race.[100] The Court said that the plaintiffs' claim that they were stigmatized by the government's policy was insufficient to constitute an injury for standing purposes. The Court explained: "[Stigmatic injury] accords a basis for standing only to those persons who are personally denied equal treatment. . . . If the abstract stigmatic injury were cognizable, standing would extend nationwide to all members of the particular racial groups against which the Government was alleged to be discriminating by its grant of a tax exemption to a racially discriminatory school."[101]

---

[93] 549 U.S. 497 (2007).

[94] Barlow v. Collins, 397 U.S. 159 (1970); Hardin v. Kentucky Utils. Co., 390 U.S. 1 (1968); FCC v. Sanders Bros. Radio Station, 309 U.S. 470 (1940).

[95] *See* Laurence Tribe, American Constitutional Law 115 (3d ed. 2000) ("A person subject to criminal prosecution, or faced with its imminent prospect, has clearly established the requisite 'injury in fact' to oppose such prosecution by asserting any relevant constitutional or federal rights.").

[96] Bond v. United States, 131 S. Ct. 2355, 2359 (2011).

[97] *Id.* at 2367 (Ginsburg, J., concurring).

[98] *See* International Primate Protection League v. Administrators of Tulane Educ. Fund, 500 U.S. 72 (1991) (allowing plaintiffs standing to challenge removal of a case from state to federal court, even though plaintiffs lacked standing to challenge the government's action, which was the basis for the lawsuit). *See also* Asarco Inc. v. Kadish, 490 U.S. 605 (1989) (a state court decision can create an injury, and therefore be the basis for standing, even if plaintiffs initially would have lacked standing to sue in federal court).

[99] 524 U.S. 417 (1998).

[100] 468 U.S. 737 (1984).

[101] *Id.* at 755-756. *Allen* also denied standing based on failure to meet the causation requirement; this is discussed below in §2.5.3.

Another example where the Court deemed a harm as insufficient to meet the injury requirement was in one of the companion cases to *Roe v. Wade*.[102] Although the Court found the claim of another plaintiff to be justiciable, the Court refused to hear the challenge brought by a married couple to a law prohibiting abortion. The couple claimed that their "marital happiness" was adversely affected because they were "forced to the choice of refraining from normal sexual relations or of endangering Mary Doe's health through a possible pregnancy."[103] The Court deemed this injury insufficient to confer standing.

It is difficult to identify a principle that explains why aesthetic or economic injuries are sufficient for standing, but stigma or marital happiness are not. The only conclusion is that in addition to injuries to common law, constitutional, and statutory rights, a plaintiff has standing if he or she asserts an injury that the Court deems sufficient for standing purposes.

§2.5.3 Causation and Redressability

Injury is necessary for standing, but not sufficient. A plaintiff also must allege and prove that the personal injury is "fairly traceable to the defendant's allegedly unlawful conduct and likely to be redressed by the requested relief."[104] These requirements have been labeled *causation*—the plaintiff must allege that the defendant's conduct caused the harm—and *redressability*—the plaintiff must allege that a favorable court decision is likely to remedy the injury. The Supreme Court has declared that both causation and redressability are constitutional requirements for standing.[105]

Initially, the Supreme Court treated causation and redressability as if they were a single test designed to determine whether a federal court decision would have some effect. Causation was deemed relevant because if the defendant is the cause of the plaintiff's injury, then it is likely that halting the defendant's behavior will stop the injury. Redressability focuses directly on the same inquiry: Will the federal court decision make a difference? Thus, in *Warth v. Seldin*, the Court said that in order to have standing a plaintiff must allege that "the asserted injury was the consequence of the defendants' actions, or that the prospective relief will remove the harm."[106]

But in *Allen v. Wright*, the Court indicated that these are separate requirements for standing.[107] In its most recent articulation of the standing doctrine, the Court has stated causation and redressability as distinct standing hurdles, both of which must be met for a federal court to hear a case.[108]

---

[102] 410 U.S. 113 (1973).

[103] *Id.* at 128 (citations omitted).

[104] Allen v. Wright, 468 U.S. 737, 751 (1984).

[105] *See, e.g.*, United States v. Hays, 515 U.S. 737, 743 (1995).

[106] 422 U.S. 490, 505 (1975).

[107] 468 U.S. 737, 753 n.19 (1984).

[108] *See, e.g.*, United States v. Hays, 515 U.S. at 743; Northeastern Florida Chapter of Associated Gen. Contractors of Am. v. Jacksonville, Florida, 508 U.S. 656, 663 (1993); Lujan v. Defenders of Wildlife, 504 U.S. 555, 560-561 (1992).

Key Cases Concerning Causation and Redressability

The causation and redressability tests are best understood in the context of the cases that first articulated the requirements: *Linda R.S. v. Richard D.*,[109] *Warth v. Seldin*,[110] *Simon v. Eastern Kentucky Welfare Rights Organization*,[111] *Duke Power Co. v. Carolina Environmental Study Group, Inc.*,[112] and *Allen v. Wright*.[113]

In *Linda R.S. v. Richard D.*, an unwed mother sought to have the father of her child prosecuted for failure to pay child support. The State of Texas had a policy of prosecuting fathers of legitimate children for not paying required child support, but did not prosecute fathers of illegitimate children. The plaintiff argued that this was unconstitutional discrimination on the basis of the child's legitimacy. The Supreme Court, however, dismissed the case for lack of standing. The Court reasoned that even an injunction commanding state prosecutions would not ensure that the mother would receive any additional child support money. The Court explained that "if appellant were granted the requested relief, it would result only in the jailing of the child's father. The prospect that prosecution, at least in the future, will result in payment of support can, at best, be termed only speculative."[114]

The importance of the causation and redressability doctrines as restrictions on federal jurisdiction was made clear in *Warth v. Seldin*. In *Warth*, several plaintiffs challenged the unconstitutionality of exclusionary zoning practices in Penfield, New York, a suburb of Rochester. The plaintiffs included Rochester residents who wanted to live in Penfield, but claimed that they could not because of the zoning practices that prevented construction of multifamily dwellings and low-income housing. Also, an association of home builders that wanted to construct such housing joined as plaintiffs in the suit.[115]

The Supreme Court held that these plaintiffs lacked standing—even though they alleged violations of their constitutional rights—because they could not demonstrate that appropriate housing would be constructed without the exclusionary zoning ordinances. The Court felt that the low-income residents seeking to live in Penfield might not be able to afford to live there even if the town's zoning ordinances were invalidated. Also, the builders might not choose to construct new housing in Penfield, regardless of the outcome of the lawsuit. Justice Powell, writing for the Court, stated: "But the record is devoid of any indication that these projects, or other like projects, would have satisfied petitioners' needs at prices

---

[109]   410 U.S. 614 (1973).
[110]   422 U.S. 490 (1975).
[111]   426 U.S. 26 (1976).
[112]   438 U.S. 59 (1984).
[113]   468 U.S. 737 (1984).
[114]   410 U.S. at 618.
[115]   Other plaintiffs included Rochester residents claiming injuries as taxpayers and an organization suing on behalf of its members who desired interracial association. Taxpayer standing is discussed in §2.5.5; standing for associations is discussed in §2.5.6.

they could afford, or that, were the court to remove the obstructions attributable to respondents, such relief would benefit petitioners."[116]

Similarly, in *Simon v. Eastern Kentucky Welfare Rights Organization*, the Court denied standing to plaintiffs who were clearly injured because the Court concluded that the plaintiffs failed to meet the requirements for causation and redressability.[117] The plaintiffs challenged an Internal Revenue Service revision of a Revenue Ruling limiting the amount of free medical care that hospitals receiving tax-exempt status were required to provide. Whereas previously tax-exempt charitable hospitals had to provide free care for indigents, under the new provisions only emergency medical treatment of indigents was required. The plaintiffs were individuals who claimed that they were denied needed medical care, and hence injured, by hospitals receiving tax-exempt status.

Again, the Supreme Court denied standing, concluding that causation and redressability were lacking. The Court said that it was "purely speculative" whether the new Revenue Ruling was responsible for the denial of medical services to the plaintiffs and that "the complaint suggests no substantial likelihood that victory in this suit would result in respondents receiving the hospital treatment they desire."[118]

In contrast, in *Duke Power Co. v. Carolina Environmental Study Group, Inc.*, the Supreme Court found the causation and redressability requirements to be satisfied. In *Duke Power*, 40 individuals and two organizations challenged the constitutionality of the Price-Anderson Act, which limited the liability of utility companies in the event of a nuclear reactor accident.[119] The plaintiffs argued that the Price-Anderson Act violated the due process clause because it allowed injuries to occur without compensation. The Supreme Court found standing to exist because the construction of a nuclear reactor in the plaintiffs' area subjected them to many injuries, including exposure to radiation, thermal pollution, and fear of a major nuclear accident. Furthermore, the Court accepted the lower court's conclusion that the causation and redressability tests were met because *but for* the Price-Anderson Act the reactor would not be built and the plaintiffs would not suffer these harms. After finding standing, the Court held that the Price-Anderson Act was constitutional.

In *Allen v. Wright*, parents of black public school children brought a class action suit challenging the failure of the Internal Revenue Service (IRS) to carry out its statutory obligation to deny tax-exempt status to racially discriminatory private schools. The plaintiffs claimed two injuries. One was that they and their children were stigmatized by government financial aid to schools that discriminate. As described above, the Court held that this injury was too abstract to confer standing. The plaintiffs also claimed that their children's chances to receive an integrated education were diminished by the continued tax breaks to discriminatory

---

[116] 422 U.S. at 505-506.

[117] 426 U.S. 26 (1976).

[118] *Id.* at 45-46.

[119] 42 U.S.C. §2210(e) (at the time *Duke Power* was decided, liability was limited to $560 million for a single nuclear accident).

schools. The parents argued that if the IRS enforced the law, the schools either would stop discriminating or have to charge more money because of the loss of the tax breaks. Either way, more white students likely would attend the public schools.

The Supreme Court acknowledged that this claim stated an injury, but denied standing based on an absence of "causation." The Court stated that "respondents' second claim of injury cannot support standing because the injury alleged is not fairly traceable to the Government conduct respondents challenge as unlawful. . . . From the perspective of the IRS, the injury to respondents is highly indirect and results from the independent action of some third party not before the court."[120] In an important footnote, the Court stated that even though a change in IRS policy might redress the injury that is insufficient for standing because the IRS did not cause the segregation. Justice O'Connor, writing for the Court, stated:

> The fairly traceable and redressability components of the constitutional standing inquiry were initially articulated by this Court as two facets of a single causation requirement. . . . Cases such as this, in which the relief requested goes well beyond the violation of law alleged, illustrate why it is important to keep the inquiries separate if the redressability component is to focus on the requested relief. Even if the relief respondents request might have a substantial effect on the desegregation of public schools, whatever deficiencies exist in the opportunities for desegregated education for respondents' children might not be traceable to IRS violations of the law.[121]

These cases illustrate that the causation/redressability standing requirements are a powerful barrier to federal court review. Although in cases such as *Linda v. Richard*, *Warth*, *Simon*, and *Allen* there were serious allegations of constitutional violations, access to the federal courts was denied.

The Court's most recent decisions concerning causation and redressability reveal that ideology continues to play a key role in how the Justices view these requirements. Both of the recent cases were split 5-4, with the Court divided along ideological lines. In *Massachusetts v. E.P.A.*, the Court held that Massachusetts could sue to challenge the Environmental Protection Agency's failure to promulgate rules to deal with greenhouse gas emissions even though it was uncertain how much such regulations would decrease the problem of global warming.[122] Justice Stevens, writing for a five-Justice majority, explained: "While it may be true that regulating motor-vehicle emissions will not by itself *reverse* global warming, it by no means follows that we lack jurisdiction to decide whether EPA has a duty to take steps to *slow* or *reduce* it. Because of the enormity of the potential consequences associated with manmade climate change, the fact that the effectiveness of a remedy might be delayed during the (relatively short) time it takes for a new motor-vehicle fleet to replace an older one is essentially irrelevant. Nor is it dispositive that developing countries such as China and India are poised to increase greenhouse gas emissions substantially over the next century: A reduction in domestic

---

[120] 468 U.S. at 757 (citations omitted).
[121] *Id.* at 753 n.19.
[122] 549 U.S. 497 (2007).

emissions would slow the pace of global emissions increases, no matter what happens elsewhere."[123]

Chief Justice Roberts's dissent, which was joined by Justices Scalia, Thomas, and Alito, argued that global warming is too general a problem affecting the entire world to meet the requirement for a particularized injury. The dissent, though, focused especially on the redressability requirement and argued that it was not met. Chief Justice Roberts declared: "The Court's sleight of hand is in failing to link up the different elements of the three-part standing test. What must be *likely* to be redressed is the particular injury in fact. The injury the Court looks to is the asserted loss of land. The Court contends that regulating domestic motor vehicle emissions will reduce carbon dioxide in the atmosphere, *and therefore* redress Massachusetts's injury. . . . The realities make it pure conjecture to suppose that EPA regulation of new automobile emissions will *likely* prevent the loss of Massachusetts coastal land."[124]

Similarly, in *Sprint Communications Co. v. APCC Services, Inc.*, the Court split 5-4 and ruled that the assignee of a claim for money owed has standing to sue in federal court even when the assignee has promised to remit the proceeds of the litigation to the assignor.[125] Justice Breyer, writing for the Court, said that "history and precedent are clear on the question before us: Assignees of a claim, including assignees for collection, have to be deemed redressed even if the money went to someone other than the plaintiff." The Court explained that redressability focuses "on whether the *injury* that a plaintiff alleges is likely to be redressed through the litigation—not on what the plaintiff ultimately intends to do with the money he recovers."[126]

Chief Justice Roberts once more wrote the dissent, which was joined by Justices Scalia, Thomas, and Alito. The dissent strongly disagreed that the redressability requirement was met when the money would not be received by the plaintiff, but rather by someone assigned the recovery. Chief Justice Roberts wrote: "The Court goes awry when it asserts that the standing inquiry focuses on whether the injury is likely to be redressed, not whether the *complaining party's* injury is likely to be redressed. That could not be more wrong. We have never approved federal-court jurisdiction over a claim where the entire requested relief will run to a party not before the Court."[127]

Criticism and Defenses of the Requirement

The causation/redressability standing requirement has been quite controversial. Its defenders argue that it simply implements the prohibition against advisory opinions; if a federal court decision will have little effect, if it will not redress the

---

[123] *Id.* at 525-526.

[124] *Id.* at 546 (Roberts, C.J., dissenting).

[125] 554 U.S. 269 (2008).

[126] *Id.* at 287.

[127] *Id.* at 303 (Roberts, C.J., dissenting).

injuries, then it is an advisory opinion. But its critics contend that it imposes an unjustified and unprincipled limit on the availability of the federal forum.

One criticism of the redressability requirement is that it is undesirable because it is an improper determination to make on the basis of the pleadings. All decisions about standing initially are made on the basis of the pleadings, assuming all allegations within them to be true. The criticism is that redressability is inherently a factual question—how likely is it that a favorable court decision will have a particular effect—that should not be made at the outset of a lawsuit. Traditionally, courts consider whether equitable relief will have the desired effect at the remedy stage, after there has been an opportunity for discovery and a hearing on the merits.

For example, in *Simon*, a plaintiff wanting to prove that the change in the Revenue Rulings was responsible for the lack of free care for indigents would seek to demonstrate that the hospitals economically would have little alternative but to provide free care rather than lose their tax-exempt status. But this would require discovery of the hospitals' financial records, something unavailable at the time standing is determined.

Similarly, in *Warth*, the Court implied that a plaintiff could have standing to challenge the exclusionary zoning only by producing specific plans for housing that the plaintiffs definitely could afford. But the more successful the exclusionary zoning, the less likely the plaintiffs could find a building company willing to go to the trouble and expense of drafting plans certain to be denied.

A second criticism of the causation/redressability requirement is that it is inherently unprincipled because it depends entirely upon how a court chooses to characterize the plaintiff's injury. If a court characterizes an injury one way, it is redressable; but if the court chooses a different characterization, redressability will be absent. For example, in *Linda R.S. v. Richard D.*, the Court characterized the plaintiff's injury as a lack of child support and concluded that there was not redressability because the plaintiff still might not receive payments even if her child's father was prosecuted. But if the Court characterized the plaintiff's injury as a denial of equal protection because of discrimination against mothers of illegitimate children, this injury would be remedied by a favorable court decision regardless of whether more money would be forthcoming as a result of the lawsuit.[128]

The Court's ability to manipulate the injury requirement is illustrated by comparing *Linda R.S. v. Richard D.* with *Orr v. Orr*.[129] In *Orr*, a man challenged an Alabama law that permitted courts to award alimony to women but not to men. Under the reasoning of *Linda v. Richard*, the case should have been dismissed for lack of standing: Even if the Court declared the Alabama law unconstitutional, that would not ensure that Mr. Orr would receive more money. But the Court in *Orr* refused to dismiss the case on standing grounds, finding the injury to be a denial of equal protection that would be remedied by a favorable court decision.

[128] Gene Nichol, Jr., Causation as a Standing Requirement: The Unprincipled Use of Judicial Restraint, 69 Ky. L.J. 185, 198 (1981).
[129] 440 U.S. 268 (1979), discussed in more detail in §9.4.3.

The importance of how the injury is characterized is illustrated by *Northeastern Florida Chapter of the Associated General Contractors of America v. Jacksonville, Florida.*[130] A Jacksonville, Florida ordinance created a preference for minority businesses in receiving city contracts. The city moved to dismiss for lack of standing on the grounds that the plaintiffs could not demonstrate that they would have bid successfully on the contracts. The Supreme Court ruled that the plaintiffs had standing because their injury is the denial of the ability to compete equally for all contracts and a favorable court ruling will redress that injury. Justice Thomas, writing for the Court, explained: "When the government erects a barrier that makes it more difficult for members of one group to obtain a benefit than it is for members of another group, a member of the former group seeking to challenge the barrier need not allege that he would have obtained the benefit but for the barrier in order to establish standing."[131] The Court emphasized that the injury "is the denial of equal treatment resulting from the imposition of the barrier not the ultimate inability to obtain the benefit."[132]

The Court relied on its earlier decision in *Regents of the University of California v. Bakke.*[133] Alan Bakke, a white male, was denied admission to the University of California at Davis Medical School and filed suit challenging the school's practice of setting aside 16 spots for minority students out of an entering class of 100. The state argued that Bakke lacked standing based on the redressability requirement. Even if the affirmative action program were declared unconstitutional, Bakke still might not be admitted to the medical school. In other words, if the Court characterized Bakke's injury as a denial of admission, there was no assurance that a favorable court decision would redress the injury. But the Court chose a different characterization of the harm. The Court stated that Bakke's injury was an inability to compete for all 100 slots, and therefore, a judicial decision declaring the setaside of 16 spots unconstitutional would remedy the injury and give him a chance to compete for all the slots.[134]

The Court's reasoning in *Northeastern Florida,* and before that in *Bakke* and *Orr,* seems clearly correct. When a plaintiff alleges a denial of equal protection, the injury is the denial of the ability to evenly compete. Even if ultimately the plaintiff would not receive the benefit, a favorable court decision redresses the harm by providing equal opportunity. Yet *Linda v. Richard* seems inconsistent with this because there the claimed denial of equal protection was not deemed sufficient for standing.

A third major criticism of the causation/redressability requirement is that it is inherently unprincipled in terms of what constitutes a sufficient likelihood of solution to justify standing. Causation and redressability are assessments of probability; how likely is it that the defendant is the cause of the plaintiff's injury and how likely is it that a favorable court decision will remedy the harm? But it is unclear

---

[130] 508 U.S. 656 (1993).
[131] *Id.* at 666.
[132] *Id.*
[133] 438 U.S. 265 (1978).
[134] *Id.* at 319-320.

where on the probability continuum it is sufficiently certain that a court should grant standing.

For example, in *Village of Arlington Heights v. Metropolitan Housing Development Corp.*, the Court allowed the plaintiffs standing to challenge a suburb's exclusionary zoning.[135] *Arlington Heights* was distinguished from *Warth* because in Arlington Heights, Illinois, builders had developed specific plans for low-income housing that had been rejected, whereas no such plans existed in Penfield, New York. The Court stated that there was a "sufficient probability" that this housing project would be built, affording the plaintiff a chance to live in Arlington Heights.[136] But even if the Court declared the exclusionary zoning unconstitutional, the housing still might not have been built. The developers did not have financing and required substantial government subsidies that had not yet been appropriated. The Court's critics argue that a comparison of *Warth* and *Arlington Heights* reveals that courts make an arbitrary choice about what is a sufficient likelihood that a favorable court decision will remedy the harm.

Another illustration of this subjectivity is *Larson v. Valente*.[137] Minnesota law required charitable organizations to register with the state and to comply with detailed reporting requirements. An exemption was created for religious organizations that received at least 50 percent of their contributions from members. A group called the Holy Spirit Association for the Unification of World Christianity filed suit challenging the constitutionality of the 50-percent requirement.

The state argued to the Supreme Court that the group lacked standing because it was not a religious organization; thus, regardless of the outcome of the lawsuit, it would have to register. The Supreme Court acknowledged that the church's status was uncertain and it would need to be determined on remand whether the group was a religious organization. Thus, it was quite uncertain whether a favorable court decision would have any effect for the plaintiff. But the Court nonetheless found standing because it concluded that it is "substantial and meaningful relief" to make it clear that if the church is a religious organization, it cannot be compelled to register. The Court said that "a plaintiff satisfies the redressability requirement when he shows that a favorable decision will relieve a discrete injury to himself. He need not show that a favorable decision will relieve his every injury."[138] The Court easily could have concluded either way in deciding whether there was a sufficient likelihood that the Court's decision would have an effect.

Subsequently, in *Lujan v. Defenders of Wildlife*, plaintiffs challenged a change in a federal regulation that provided that the Endangered Species Act would not be applied to federal government activity outside the United States.[139] The Court ruled that the plaintiffs lacked standing, in part because invalidating the new regulation might not change government behavior. Justice Scalia, writing for a plurality of four Justices, said that agencies might not comply with a revised regulation

---

[135] 429 U.S. 252 (1977).
[136] *Id.* at 264.
[137] 456 U.S. 228 (1982).
[138] *Id.* at 244 n.15.
[139] 504 U.S. 555 (1992).

in the future, thus preventing a federal court action from redressing the alleged harm. But if the possibility of noncompliance by government officials is sufficient to undermine redressability, countless cases would have to be dismissed because noncompliance with a judicial order is always a possibility.

Critics argue that the Court manipulates causation and redressability based on its views of the merits.[140] For example, in *Duke Power*, it is argued that the Court wanted to uphold the Price-Anderson Act and thus it found standing. But in *Simon*, where the Court did not want to address the issue, it denied standing. Again, the Court's defenders might argue that this judicial discretion is desirable and question whether the causation/redressability requirement is more unprincipled than other legal rules that are inherently discretionary.

Initially, the Court treated causation and redressability as if they imposed a single requirement for standing. In *Duke Power*, the Court said that "[t]he more difficult step in the standing inquiry is establishing that these injuries 'fairly can be traced to the challenged action of the defendant,' . . . or put otherwise, that the exercise of the Court's remedial powers would redress the claimed injuries."[141] In *Arlington Heights*, the Court said that the standing requirement demanded no more than a showing that there was a substantial likelihood that a favorable federal court decision will redress the injury.[142] But in *Allen v. Wright*, the Court stated that causation and redressability are independent requirements that must both be met in order for a plaintiff to have standing.[143] In its most recent decisions, the Court has continued to articulate these as separate requirements.[144]

This separation of causation and redressability has been criticized by commentators.[145] For example, commentators argue that in *Allen*, the IRS could be said to be the cause of segregation through its tax policy to exactly the same degree that eliminating the exemptions would reduce segregation. More generally, commentators question why standing should be denied if the defendant acted illegally and restraining the defendant's wrongful behavior will cure the plaintiff's injury.

Even after *Allen*, in most cases, it would seem that causation and redressability will involve an identical inquiry. If it can be demonstrated that the defendant is the cause of the injury, then halting the defendant's conduct usually will remedy the harm.

§2.5.4 The Limitation on Third-Party Standing

While the requirements for injury, causation, and redressability are deemed to be constitutional limits on standing, the Court also has articulated prudential standing barriers. One such nonconstitutional prudential limitation is the prohibition

---

[140] *See, e.g.*, Laurence Tribe, Constitutional Choices 344-346 (1985).

[141] 438 U.S. at 74 (citations omitted).

[142] 429 U.S. at 261-262.

[143] 468 U.S. 737 (1984).

[144] United States v. Hays, 515 U.S. at 743; Northeastern Florida Contractors v. Jacksonville, 508 U.S. at 663; Lujan v. Defenders of Wildlife, 504 U.S. at 562.

[145] *See, e.g.*, Gene Nichol, Abusing Standing: A Comment on *Allen v. Wright*, 133 U. Pa. L. Rev. 635 (1985).

against third-party standing. The Court has explained that "even when the plaintiff has alleged injury sufficient to meet the 'case or controversy' requirement, the Court has held that the plaintiff generally must assert his own legal rights and interests, and cannot rest his claim to relief on the legal rights or interests of third parties."[146] In other words, a plaintiff can assert only injuries that he or she has suffered; a plaintiff cannot present the claims of third parties who are not part of the lawsuit.

The prohibition against third-party standing—sometimes termed the rule against *jus tertii* standing—serves many of the underlying objectives of the standing doctrine.[147] The Court has emphasized that the people actually affected may be satisfied and thus the ban on third-party standing avoids "the adjudication of rights which those before the Court may not wish to assert."[148] Also, the Court has stated that requiring people to assert only their own injuries improves the quality of litigation and judicial decision making. In part, this is because the Court believes that the "third parties themselves usually will be the best proponents of their own rights."[149] Furthermore, it is thought that decisions might be improved in a concrete factual situation involving an injury to a party to the lawsuit.

But the Supreme Court has recognized four major exceptions to the prohibition against third-party standing. In these situations, the Court has ruled that a person who has suffered an injury has standing to raise the interests of third parties not before the court. It must be stressed that the person seeking to advocate the rights of third parties must meet the constitutional standing requirements of injury, causation, and redressability in addition to fitting within one of the four exceptions described below.

Exception: Where the Third Party Is Unlikely to Be Able to Sue

First, a person may assert the rights of a third party not before the court if there are substantial obstacles to the third party asserting his or her own rights and if there is reason to believe that the advocate will effectively represent the interests of the third party.[150] For example, in *Barrows v. Jackson*, the Court allowed third-party standing and permitted an individual sued for breaching a racially restrictive covenant to assert the rights of blacks in the community.[151] Barrows, a white person who had signed a racially restrictive covenant, was sued for breach of contract for allowing nonwhites to occupy the property. The defense was based on the rights of blacks, who were not parties to the lawsuit for breach of contract. The Court allowed third-party standing, permitting the white defendant to raise the interests

---

[146] Warth v. Seldin, 422 U.S. at 499. *See also* United Food and Commercial Workers v. Brown Group, 517 U.S. 544, 557 (1996) (discussing the bar against third-party standing as prudential).

[147] *See* Henry Monaghan, Third Party Standing, 84 Colum. L. Rev. 277, 278 n.6 (1984) (defining *jus tertii* standing).

[148] *See* Duke Power Co. v. Carolina Envtl. Study Group, Inc., 438 U.S. 59, 80 (1978); *see also* Singleton v. Wulff, 428 U.S. 106, 113-114 (1976).

[149] Singleton v. Wulff, 428 U.S. at 114.

[150] Secretary of State v. J.H. Munson Co., 467 U.S. 947, 956 (1984).

[151] 346 U.S. 249 (1953).

of blacks to rent and own property in the community. The Court stated that "it would be difficult if not impossible for the persons whose rights are asserted to present their grievance before any court."[152] Because blacks were not parties to the covenant, they had no legal basis for participating in the breach of contract suit.

Another example of this exception permitting third-party standing where the third party is unlikely to assert his or her own rights is *Eisenstadt v. Baird*.[153] A Massachusetts law made it a felony to distribute contraceptives, except by physicians or pharmacists, and then only to married individuals. Baird was prosecuted for distributing contraceptive foam to unmarried individuals in violation of this statute. His defense centered on the rights of individuals to have access to and use contraceptives. In other words, he attempted to raise the rights of third parties not before the Court. The Supreme Court allowed Baird standing to present this argument, concluding that "unmarried persons denied access to contraceptives in Massachusetts . . . are not themselves subject to prosecution and, to that extent, are denied a forum in which to assert their own rights."[154]

The Supreme Court also has held that parties in a litigation may raise the claims of prospective jurors to be free from discrimination in the use of peremptory challenges. In *Powers v. Ohio*, the Supreme Court held that in addition to the constitutional interests of the parties in having a jury selected without discrimination, prospective jurors are denied equal protection if they are excluded because of their race.[155] In *Powers*, the Court ruled that a criminal defendant could represent the interests of the prospective jurors, and in subsequent cases the Court extended this to civil litigants[156] and even to prosecutors. The Court applied *Powers* to find that a white defendant has standing to challenge the exclusion of African Americans from the grand jury that indicted him.[157]

This use of third-party standing fits within the well-recognized exception where individuals can represent the interests of parties who are unlikely to be able to represent their own interests. Prospective jurors who are struck on the basis of race will not know of the discriminatory pattern; nor are they likely to have an incentive to bring a challenge on their own.[158]

---

[152] *Id.* at 257.

[153] 405 U.S. 438 (1972).

[154] *Id.* at 446.

[155] 499 U.S. 400 (1991). The issue of discriminatory use of peremptory challenges is discussed more fully in §9.3.3.2.

[156] Edmonson v. Leesville Concrete Co., 500 U.S. 614 (1991).

[157] Campbell v. Louisiana, 523 U.S. 392 (1998).

[158] The Court in *Powers* also said that allowing third-party standing to represent the interests of prospective jurors is justified under the second exception, discussed below: where there is a close relationship between the litigant and the injured third party. 499 U.S. at 413 (citations omitted). This rationale seems more questionable because unlike other cases where this exception has been applied, there is no personal relationship between a litigant and prospective jurors.

Exception: Close Relationship Between Plaintiff and Third Party

A second exception to the ban against third-party standing permits an individual to assert the rights of third parties where there is a close relationship between the advocate and the third party. Usually, third-party standing is permitted in such circumstances where the individual seeking standing is part of the third party's constitutionally protected activity. For example, in *Pierce v. Society of Sisters*, a parochial school was accorded standing to challenge an Oregon law requiring all children to attend public school.[159] The parochial school argued that the law requiring public school attendance violated the rights of parents to control the upbringing of their children. The parochial school was allowed third-party standing because of the close relationship between the school and the parents and because the school was part of the regulated activity of providing parochial education.

Third-party standing based on this exception has been frequently allowed. For example, doctors often have been accorded standing to raise the rights of their patients in challenging laws limiting the patients' access to contraceptives and abortions.[160] In *Singleton v. Wulff*, two physicians were accorded standing to challenge a state statute that prohibited the use of state Medicaid benefits to pay for nontherapeutic abortions (abortions that were not necessary to protect the health or life of the mother).[161] The Court observed that the doctors were injured by the statute because it denied them payments for particular medical services. Moreover, the Court emphasized the closeness of the doctors' relationship to the patient and that "the constitutionally protected abortion decision is one in which the physician is intimately involved."[162] The Court concluded that "it generally is appropriate to allow a physician to assert the rights of women patients as against governmental interference with the abortion decision."[163]

The Court also has allowed vendors to assert the rights of their customers based on this exception to the rule against third-party standing. The most famous example of this is *Craig v. Boren*.[164] Oklahoma adopted a law permitting women to buy 3.2 percent beer at age 18, but denying men that privilege until age 21.[165] A bartender sought to challenge the law on behalf of male customers between the ages of 18 and 21. The bartender suffered economic loss from the law, thus fulfilling the injury requirement. Furthermore, the Court observed that generally "vendors and those in like positions have been uniformly permitted to resist efforts at

---

[159] 268 U.S. 510 (1925).

[160] *But see* Tileston v. Ullman, 318 U.S. 44 (1943) (denying standing to doctor to raise challenges to law prohibiting use of contraceptives on behalf of patients).

[161] 428 U.S. 106 (1976).

[162] *Id.* at 117.

[163] *Id.* at 118.

[164] 429 U.S. 190 (1976).

[165] The equal protection aspect of the case is discussed in §9.4.2.

restricting their operations by acting as advocates for the rights of third parties who seek access to their market or function."[166]

A much publicized case in which the Court refused to allow third-party standing based on this exception was *Gilmore v. Utah*.[167] Gary Gilmore was sentenced to death in the State of Utah, but chose not to pursue collateral challenges in federal court. His mother sought a stay of execution on his behalf. In a 5-to-4 decision, the Court refused to hear his mother's claim. The Court's per curiam opinion said that the defendant had waived his rights by not pursuing them. Four Justices, in a concurring opinion, said that the mother should be denied standing because there was no reason why her son could not protect and assert his own rights. The *Gilmore* case might be read as supporting the proposition that a close relationship is not enough for third-party standing; the advocate also must be part of the third party's exercise of the protected right. On the other hand, *Gilmore* might be thought of as a narrow decision in a unique factual context.

Gilmore was followed in *Whitmore v. Arkansas*, where the Supreme Court held that a death row inmate did not have standing to challenge the validity of a death sentence imposed on another inmate who elected to forgo his right of appeal to the state supreme court.[168] After Ronald Simmons chose not to appeal his death sentence, another inmate, James Whitmore, sought to intervene and appeal on Simmons's behalf. Additionally, Whitmore argued that under the Arkansas system of comparative review of death sentences, he could personally benefit from a change in Simmons's punishment. The Court rejected the assertion of third-party standing and held that "Whitmore provides no factual basis for us to conclude that the sentence imposed on a mass murderer like Simmons would even be relevant to a future comparative review of Whitmore's sentence."[169]

Another example where the Court refused to allow third-party standing was for a father who was suing on behalf of his daughter to challenge the use of the words "under God" in the Pledge of Allegiance in public schools.[170] In *Elk Grove Unified School District v. Newdow*, in a 5-to-3 decision (Justice Scalia recused himself in response to a motion made by Newdow based on Justice Scalia having given a speech in which he expressed his views on the case), the Court dismissed the case for lack of standing. The Court ruled that Michael Newdow lacked third-party standing to sue on behalf of his daughter. The Court stressed that the girl's mother, and not Newdow, had legal custody and the Court also emphasized a traditional unwillingness of federal courts to get involved in domestic relations matters. Justice Stevens's majority opinion declared: "In our view, it is improper for the federal courts to entertain a claim by a plaintiff whose standing to sue is founded on family law rights that are in dispute when prosecution of the lawsuit may have an adverse effect on the person who is the source of the claimed stand-

---

[166] *Id.* at 195. *See also* Carey v. Population Servs. Intl., 431 U.S. 678 (1977) (permitting vendor of contraceptives to challenge law on behalf of its customers).

[167] 429 U.S. 1012 (1976).

[168] 495 U.S. 149 (1990). For a discussion of *Gilmore* and *Whitmore, see* Ann Althouse, Standing, in Fluffy Slippers, 77 Va. L. Rev. 1177 (1991).

[169] 495 U.S. at 157.

[170] 542 U.S. 1 (2004).

ing. When hard questions of domestic relations are sure to affect the outcome, the prudent course is for the federal court to stay its hand rather than reach out to resolve a weighty question of federal constitutional law."[171]

It is difficult to fit the Court's decision in *Newdow* in the framework of traditional standing analysis. For example, apart from third-party standing, Michael Newdow had standing based on his own interests as a parent in the religious upbringing and education of his daughter. Also, it is long-standing practice that the Supreme Court defers to appellate courts' interpretations of state law and the Ninth Circuit carefully considered California family law in concluding that the award of legal custody did not preclude a noncustodial parent from suing on behalf of a child. Perhaps the Court dismissed *Newdow* on standing grounds to avoid a highly controversial political issue. But the question then becomes whether that is an appropriate use of the justiciability doctrines.

Exception: The Overbreadth Doctrine

The third exception to the prohibition against third-party standing is termed the "overbreadth doctrine." A person generally can argue that a statute is unconstitutional only as it is applied to him or her; the individual cannot argue that a statute is unconstitutional as it is applied to third parties not before the court. For example, a defendant in a criminal trial can challenge the constitutionality of the law that is the basis for the prosecution solely on the claim that the statute unconstitutionally abridges his or her constitutional rights. The overbreadth doctrine is an exception to the prohibition against third-party standing. It permits a person to challenge a statute on the ground that it violates the First Amendment rights of third parties not before the court, even though the law is constitutional as applied to that defendant.[172] In other words, the overbreadth doctrine provides that "[g]iven a case or controversy, a litigant whose own activities are unprotected may nevertheless challenge a statute by showing that it substantially abridges the First Amendment rights of other parties not before the court."[173]

The Court's decision in *Secretary of State of Maryland v. J.H. Munson Co.* illustrates the overbreadth doctrine.[174] A Maryland law prohibited charitable organizations from soliciting funds unless at least 75 percent of their revenues were used for "charitable purposes." The law was challenged by a professional fund-raiser who raised the First Amendment rights of his clients, charities who were not parties to the lawsuit. The Supreme Court permitted the fund-raiser standing to argue the constitutional claims of the charitable organizations. The state argued that third-party standing was inappropriate because the charities were fully able to litigate and protect their own rights. The Court rejected this contention, explaining that

---

[171] *Id.* at 17.

[172] The overbreadth doctrine is discussed in more detail in Chapter 11, on the First Amendment, in §11.2.2.

[173] Village of Schaumburg v. Citizens for a Better Envt., 444 U.S. 620, 634 (1980). For an excellent discussion of the overbreadth doctrine, *see* Richard Fallon, Making Sense of Overbreadth, 100 Yale L.J. 853 (1991).

[174] 467 U.S. 947 (1984).

"where the claim is that a statute is overly broad in violation of the First Amendment, the Court has allowed a party to assert the rights of another without regard to the ability of the other to assert his own claims and with no requirement that the person making the attack demonstrate that his own conduct could not be regulated by a statute drawn with the requisite narrow specificity."[175]

The overbreadth doctrine appears limited to First Amendment cases. This exception to the rule against third-party standing reflects a fear that an overbroad law will chill protected speech and that safeguarding expression justifies allowing third-party standing. The Court explained that "[l]itigants, therefore, are permitted to challenge a statute not because their own rights of free expression are violated, but because of a judicial prediction or assumption that the statute's very existence may cause others not before the court to refrain from constitutionally protected speech or expression."[176]

The Supreme Court has announced several limits on the overbreadth doctrine. For example, the Court has said that in order for a statute to be declared unconstitutional on overbreadth grounds there must be "substantial over-breadth"; that is, the law's excessive regulation must "not only be real, but substantial as well, judged in relation to the statute's plainly legitimate sweep."[177] Also, the Court has held that when confronted with an overbreadth challenge a court should attempt to construe the statute so as to avoid constitutional problems and, failing that, should, if possible, attempt to sever the unconstitutional part of the law from the remainder of the statute.[178] Additionally, the Supreme Court has declared that overbreadth cannot be used in challenging regulations of commercial speech.[179] The Court apparently believes that the incentive to engage in advertising is sufficiently strong to lessen any worries that such speech will be chilled.

Exception: Standing for Associations

An association or organization can sue based on injuries to itself or based on injuries to its members.[180] An organization's mere concern about a problem, of course, is not enough to meet the requirement for injury; the organization has standing only if it or its members would be affected in a tangible way by the challenged action. For example, in *Sierra Club v. Morton*, discussed earlier in this

---

[175] *Id.* at 957 (citation omitted). *Accord* Village of Schaumburg v. Citizens for a Better Envt., 444 U.S. 620, 634 (1980) (also invalidating a statute regulating charitable solicitation on overbreadth grounds).

[176] Broadrick v. Oklahoma, 413 U.S. 601, 612 (1973); Dombrowski v. Pfister, 380 U.S. 479, 486 (1965).

[177] Broadrick v. Oklahoma, 413 U.S. at 615 (also suggesting that overbreadth is limited to "pure speech" and not conduct that is expressive); *see also* New York v. Ferber, 458 U.S. 747, 770-771 (1982) (rejecting overbreadth challenge to law prohibiting distribution of child pornography because of the absence of substantial overbreadth).

[178] New York v. Ferber, 458 U.S. at 769 n.24.

[179] Village of Hoffman Estates v. Flipside, 455 U.S. 489, 497 (1982) ("the overbreadth doctrine does not apply to commercial speech").

[180] In *United Food and Commercial Workers v. Brown Group*, 517 U.S. 544, 556 (1996), the Court expressly discussed associational standing as an exception to the prohibition of third-party standing.

chapter, a national environmental protection organization was denied standing to sue to halt the construction of a ski resort in a national park because it failed to allege harm to itself or that any of its members ever had used the park.[181]

An organization has standing to sue on its own behalf if it has been injured as an entity. For example, an organization has standing to challenge conduct that impedes its ability to attract members, to raise revenues, or to fulfill its purposes.[182]

The Supreme Court's decision in *Havens Realty Corp. v. Coleman* is illustrative.[183] In *Havens*, several plaintiffs challenged a realty company's racial discrimination in providing information about housing. One of the plaintiffs was an organization dedicated to securing open housing. The organization claimed that the defendant's discriminatory practices undermined its ability to achieve its goals. The Court unanimously upheld standing for the organization, and for the other plaintiffs as well. The Court reasoned that the organization had standing because the defendant's practices injured the organization's ability to accomplish its purpose and required it to spend a great deal of its resources investigating and handling complaints of housing discrimination. The Court concluded that these injuries to the organization were sufficient for standing; that the organization successfully alleged "far more than simply a setback to the organization's abstract social interests."[184]

Alternatively, an organization might try to sue on behalf of its members. For example, in *NAACP v. Alabama ex rel. Patterson*, the NAACP was allowed standing, in a representational capacity for its members, to challenge a state law requiring it to disclose its membership lists.[185] In addition to asserting its own interests as an organization, the NAACP also raised the associational and speech rights of its members. The Court noted that the members who wish to remain anonymous might never come forward, and thus it was desirable to allow the NAACP to assert its members' challenges to the constitutionality of the disclosure law.

In *Hunt v. Washington State Apple Advertising Commission*, the Supreme Court articulated a three-part test for determining when an organization may sue on behalf of its members.[186] In *Hunt*, an organization funded by apple growers in the State of Washington contended that a North Carolina law concerning the marketing of apples violated the dormant commerce clause, which limits state interference with interstate commerce.[187] The Supreme Court said that "[a]n association has standing to bring suit on behalf of its members when: (1) its members would otherwise have standing to sue in their own right; (2) the interests it seeks to protect are germane to the organization's purpose; and (3) neither the claim asserted nor the relief requested requires the participation in the lawsuit of the individual members."[188]

---

[181] 405 U.S. 727, 735 (1972).

[182] Havens Realty Corp. v. Coleman, 455 U.S. 363, 379 (1982).

[183] *Id.*

[184] *Id.* at 379.

[185] 357 U.S. 449 (1958).

[186] 432 U.S. 333 (1977).

[187] The dormant commerce clause is discussed in §5.3.

[188] 432 U.S. at 343.

In *International Union, United Automobile Workers v. Brock*, the Court reaffirmed the *Hunt* three-part test for determining whether an organization may sue on behalf of its members.[189] The union, representing its members, sought to challenge the Trade Act of 1974, which limited the trade readjustment allowances that some individuals could receive in addition to unemployment compensation. Under the *Hunt* three-part test, the organization was entitled to standing to represent its members. The members could have sued on their own behalf because they were injured by the denial of readjustment allowances. Also, the lawsuit was related to the organization's purpose because the union exists to protect the interests of its members with regard to their jobs and compensation. There is no reason why the individual members needed to be parties to the lawsuit; their interests were fully represented by the union.

The defendant argued that the Court should overrule the three-part *Hunt* test, prevent the organization from suing, and instead require the members to bring a class action suit. The Supreme Court expressly rejected this position, stating that it would not "abandon settled principles of associational standing."[190] The Court explained that there are many benefits to allowing an existing organization to sue that would be lost if class action suits were required instead. For example, the Court observed that "[w]hile a class action creates an ad hoc union of injured plaintiffs who may be linked only by their common claims, an association suing to vindicate the interests of its members can draw upon a pre-existing reservoir of expertise and capital."[191] People join associations to advance their interests; associations should be able to pursue their objectives through litigation on behalf of the members.

In *United Food and Commercial Workers v. Brown Group*, the Court again reaffirmed the *Hunt* test and clarified that its third prong—that neither the claim nor the relief requires the participation of the individual members—is prudential and not constitutional.[192] A federal law, the Worker Adjustment and Retraining Notification Act (WARN), grants unions the authority to sue for damages on behalf of their members. The Court upheld the constitutionality of the law and explained that the first part of the *Hunt* test—the requirement that the members of the association would otherwise have standing to sue in their own right—implemented the constitutional requirement for an injury. The Court concluded that the third part of the test is prudential and that therefore Congress could override it in allowing the association to sue for damages on behalf of its members.

§2.5.5   *The Prohibition Against Generalized Grievances*

The Supreme Court has stated that there is a "prudential principle" preventing standing "when the asserted harm is a generalized grievance shared in a

---

[189] 477 U.S. 274 (1986); *see also* New York State Club Assoc. v. City of New York, 487 U.S. 1 (1988) (reaffirming the *Hunt* test).

[190] 477 U.S. at 290.

[191] *Id.* at 289.

[192] 517 U.S. 544 (1996).

substantially equal measure by all or a large class of citizens."[193] The prohibition against generalized grievances prevents individuals from suing if their only injury is as a citizen or a taxpayer concerned with having the government follow the law.

The term "generalized grievance" is confusing because it implies that no one would have standing to challenge a blatantly unconstitutional law applicable to everyone in the country. For example, would it be a generalized grievance, and everyone denied the ability to sue, if Congress were to adopt a law prohibiting all religious worship? The answer is clearly that standing would exist in such an instance to challenge the denial of free exercise of religion even though it would be an injury shared in substantially equal measure by all or a large class of citizens. In fact, the Court has explained, "[n]or . . . could the fact that many persons shared the same injury be sufficient reason to disqualify from seeking review . . . any person who had in fact suffered injury. . . . To deny standing to persons who are in fact injured simply because many others are also injured, would mean that the most injurious and widespread Government actions could be questioned by nobody."[194] The Court later explained that "where a harm is concrete, though widely shared, the Court has found injury in fact."[195]

Thus, the existence of a generalized grievance is not determined simply by the number of people affected. Rather, a generalized grievance is where the plaintiffs sue solely as citizens concerned with having the government follow the law or as taxpayers interested in restraining allegedly illegal government expenditures.

In other words, the bar against generalized grievance standing is inapplicable if a person claims that he or she has been denied freedom of speech or due process of law, even if everyone else in society has suffered the same harm. However, if the plaintiff alleges a violation of no specific constitutional right, but instead claims an interest only as a taxpayer or a citizen in having the government follow the law, standing is not allowed.

Sequence of Decisions: Three Sets of Cases

The prohibition against generalized grievances, and the current state of the law, can be best understood by examining three sets of cases: the initial decisions from about 90 years ago preventing taxpayer and citizen standing; the Warren Court's expansion of taxpayer standing; and the Burger Court's and Rehnquist Court's rulings virtually eliminating taxpayer and citizen suits in federal court.

The Supreme Court first articulated the barrier to taxpayer and citizen standing during the 1920s and 1930s. In *Frothingham v. Mellon*, the plaintiff, suing as a taxpayer, sought to restrain expenditures under the Federal Maternity Act of 1921, which provided financial grants to the states to reduce maternal and infant

---

[193] Warth v. Seldin, 422 U.S. 490, 499 (1975) (emphasis added) (citations omitted); Gladstone, Realtors v. Village of Bellwood, 441 U.S. 91, 99-100 (1979). However, in a subsequent decision the Supreme Court indicated that the ban on citizen standing is constitutional not prudential. Lujan v. Defenders of Wildlife, 504 U.S. 555 (1992). *Lujan* is discussed below.

[194] United States v. Students Challenging Regulatory Agency Procedures, 412 U.S. 669, 686-688 (1973).

[195] Federal Election Commission v. Akins, 524 U.S. 11, 24 (1998).

mortality.[196] The plaintiff asserted that the expenditures violated the Tenth Amendment's reservation of powers to the state governments. The Supreme Court ruled that the plaintiff lacked standing because her "interest in the moneys of the treasury . . . is comparatively minute and indeterminable."[197] The Court held that federal court review must be based on a plaintiff's alleging a direct injury and "not merely that he suffers in some indefinite way in common with people generally."[198]

Similarly, a few years later in *Ex parte Levitt*, the Supreme Court ruled that a person could not gain standing as a citizen claiming a right to have the government follow the law.[199] *Levitt* involved a citizen's suit to have Justice Hugo Black's appointment to the United States Supreme Court declared unconstitutional. The plaintiff contended that Justice Black could not be appointed to the Court because Black had voted, while a senator, to increase Supreme Court Justices' retirement benefits. This was alleged to violate Article I, §6, of the Constitution, which states that "No Senator shall during the time for which he was elected, be appointed to any civil office the emoluments whereof shall have increased during such time." The Court, however, held that the plaintiff lacked standing because "it is not sufficient [for standing] that he has merely a general interest common to all members of the public."[200]

Frothingham and *Levitt* establish the bar to taxpayer and citizen standing. The primary case deviating from this rule was the Warren Court's decision in *Flast v. Cohen*.[201] In *Flast*, the Court upheld a taxpayer's standing to challenge federal subsidies to parochial schools as violating the First Amendment's prohibition against government establishment of religion. Under the Elementary and Secondary Education Act of 1965, the federal government provided funds for instruction in secular subjects in parochial schools. The lower court dismissed the plaintiff's challenge to the Act based on *Frothingham*, concluding that the plaintiff's only claim was as a taxpayer and that such standing was not permitted.

The Supreme Court reversed, allowing standing. Both the majority and the dissent in *Flast* agreed that the rule preventing plaintiffs from asserting generalized grievances was prudential rather than constitutional in origin.[202] Chief Justice Warren, writing for the Court, said that the ability of the plaintiff to sue as a taxpayer depends on "whether there is a logical nexus between the status asserted and the claim sought to be adjudicated."[203]

Specifically, the Court said that in order to sue as a taxpayer the plaintiff needed to establish two factors. First, "the taxpayer must establish a logical link

---

[196] 262 U.S. 447 (1923). In a companion case, *Massachusetts v. Mellon*, 262 U.S. 447 (1923), the Supreme Court denied the State of Massachusetts standing to attack the constitutionality of the Maternity Act.

[197] 262 U.S. at 487.

[198] *Id.* at 488.

[199] 302 U.S. 633 (1937).

[200] *Id.* at 634.

[201] 392 U.S. 83 (1968).

[202] *Id.* at 101; at 119-120 (Harlan, J., dissenting).

[203] *Id.* at 102.

between that status and the type of legislative enactment attacked."[204] The Court said that this meant that a taxpayer could challenge only the expenditure of funds under the taxing and spending clause of the Constitution and not "an incidental expenditure of tax funds in the administration of an essentially regulatory statute."[205] Second, the "taxpayer must establish a nexus between that status and the precise nature of the constitutional infringement alleged."[206] In other words, the taxpayer must argue that Congress is violating a particular constitutional provision with the expenditure and not just that Congress is exceeding the scope of its powers under the Constitution.

The Court distinguished *Flast* from *Frothingham* because although both involved challenges to government spending programs, the First Amendment is a limit on Congress's taxing and spending authority, whereas the Tenth Amendment, at issue in *Frothingham*, is not.[207] *Flast* raised speculation that the Court had substantially expanded the availability of taxpayer standing.[208]

However, the Burger Court consistently rejected attempts at taxpayer and citizen standing and essentially narrowed *Flast* to the facts of that case. In *United States v. Richardson*, the plaintiff claimed that the statutes providing for the secrecy of the Central Intelligence Agency budget violated the Constitution's requirement for a regular statement and accounting of all expenditures.[209] The Court ruled that the plaintiff lacked standing because his case presented a generalized grievance; the plaintiff did not allege a violation of a personal constitutional right, but instead claimed injury only as a citizen and taxpayer. The Court held that the plaintiff lacked standing because he was "seeking to employ a federal court as a forum in which to air his generalized grievances about the conduct of government."[210]

The Court deemed irrelevant the plaintiff's claim that if he could not sue, no one could. The Court stated: "It can be argued that if respondent is not permitted to litigate this issue, no one can do so. In a very real sense, the absence of any particular individual or class to litigate these claims gives support to the argument that the subject matter is committed to the surveillance of Congress, and ultimately to the political process."[211]

Similarly, in a decision handed down the same day as *Richardson*, in *Schlesinger v. Reservists Committee to Stop the War*, the Court denied citizen and taxpayer standing.[212] In *Schlesinger*, the plaintiffs sued to enjoin members of Congress from serving in the military reserves. Article I, §6, of the Constitution prevents a senator or representative from holding civil office. Again, the Court refused to rule on the plaintiffs' claim of unconstitutionality, holding that the matter posed a generalized grievance.

---

[204] *Id.*

[205] *Id.*

[206] *Id.*

[207] *Id.* at 105.

[208] *See* Kenneth Davis, The Liberalized Law of Standing, 37 U. Chi. L. Rev. 450 (1970). Kenneth Davis, Standing: Taxpayers and Others, 35 U. Chi. L. Rev. 601 (1968).

[209] 418 U.S. 166 (1974).

[210] *Id.* at 175 (citations omitted).

[211] *Id.* at 179.

[212] 418 U.S. 208 (1974).

Standing was denied because the plaintiffs alleged injury only as a citizen or taxpayer with an interest in having the government follow the law and not a violation of a specific constitutional right. The Court stated: "Respondents seek to have the Judicial Branch compel the Executive Branch to act in conformity with the Incompatibility Clause, an interest shared by all citizens. . . . Our system of government leaves many crucial decisions to the political processes. The assumption that if respondents have no standing to sue no one would have standing, is not a reason to find standing."[213]

After *Richardson* and *Schlesinger*, it appeared that taxpayer standing was restricted to the one area where it had been approved in *Flast*: for alleged violations of the establishment clause of the First Amendment. But a few years later, in *Valley Forge Christian College v. Americans United for Separation of Church and State*, the Court denied taxpayer standing to challenge a federal government grant of surplus property as violating the establishment clause of the First Amendment.[214] The United States Department of Health, Education and Welfare gave a 77-acre tract of land, worth over $500 million, to Valley Forge Christian College. Americans United for Separation of Church and State sued to enjoin the transfer of the property on the ground that it was government aid to religion in violation of the establishment clause. The Supreme Court held that the plaintiffs lacked standing because they sued solely as taxpayers interested in having the government follow the law.[215]

Flast was distinguished from *Valley Forge* on two grounds. First, the plaintiffs in *Valley Forge* were challenging a decision by the Department of Health, Education and Welfare to transfer property, not a congressional statute.[216] One might wonder why this distinction matters. Both Congress and the executive branch are bound to obey the First Amendment. In fact, in *Flast* the named defendant was Wilbur Cohen, Secretary of the Department of Health, Education and Welfare. Second, the *Valley Forge* Court said that, unlike *Flast*, the objection was to a government action pursuant to Congress's power over government property, Article IV, §3, and not to a spending program under Article I, §8.[217] Again, one must question why this distinction makes any difference. All congressional actions, whether pursuant to Article I or other provisions, must comply with the First Amendment and the entire Bill of Rights. If *Flast* establishes that taxpayers have standing to halt violations of the establishment clause, it is hard to see why it matters whether the objectionable action was taken under Article I or Article IV authority.[218]

The Court further restricted taxpayer standing in the establishment clause context in *Hein v. Freedom from Religion Foundation*.[219] Upon taking office, President

---

[213] *Id.* at 227.

[214] 454 U.S. 464 (1982).

[215] *Id.* at 485-486.

[216] *Id.* at 479.

[217] *Id.* at 480.

[218] Subsequent to *Valley Forge*, the Court reaffirmed *Flast v. Cohen* in *Bowen v. Kendrick*, 487 U.S. 589 (1988). The Court allowed taxpayer standing to challenge the constitutionality of the Adolescent Family Life Act, which provided grants that required specific types of counseling to prevent teenage pregnancy. The Court explained that it had continually adhered to *Flast* and the narrow exception it had created for taxpayer standing to challenge government expenditures that violate the establishment clause.

[219] 551 U.S. 587 (2007).

George W. Bush created a White House office and several centers in executive branch offices to provide government funds to "faith-based institutions." This was designed to facilitate churches, synagogues, and mosques directly receiving federal money to provide social services. The White House Office of Faith-Based and Community Initiatives was funded entirely through general executive revenue. Taxpayers brought a suit challenging this as violating the establishment clause.

The Court ruled, without a majority opinion, that the taxpayers lacked standing. Justice Alito announced the judgment for the Court and distinguished *Flast v. Cohen* as involving expenditures under a specific federal statute, whereas the money for the White House Office of Faith-Based and Community Initiatives came from general executive revenue. Justice Alito, in an opinion joined by Chief Justice Roberts and Justice Kennedy, explained: "The link between congressional action and constitutional violation that supported taxpayer standing in *Flast* is missing here. Respondents do not challenge any specific congressional action or appropriation; nor do they ask the Court to invalidate any congressional enactment or legislatively created program as unconstitutional. That is because the expenditures at issue here were not made pursuant to any Act of Congress. . . . Those expenditures resulted from executive discretion, not congressional action."[220] In other words, the plurality opinion in *Hein v. Freedom from Religion Foundation* concludes that taxpayers lack standing to challenge expenditures of funds from general executive revenue as violating the establishment clause.

The other six Justices sharply criticized the plurality's distinction of *Flast*. The executive branch, no less than Congress, must comply with the First Amendment. Besides, all federal spending is pursuant to a federal statute; all executive branch revenues are authorized by Congress. Justices Scalia and Thomas concurred in the judgment and called for the overruling of *Flast v. Cohen*. Justice Scalia lamented the "meaningless distinctions" and wrote: "If this Court is to decide cases by rule of law rather than show of hands, we must surrender to logic and choose sides: Either *Flast v. Cohen* should be applied to (at a minimum) *all* challenges to the governmental expenditure of general tax revenues in a manner alleged to violate a constitutional provision specifically limiting the taxing and spending power, or *Flast* should be repudiated. For me, the choice is easy. *Flast* is wholly irreconcilable with the Article III restrictions on federal-court jurisdiction that this Court has repeatedly confirmed are embodied in the doctrine of standing."[221] By contrast, Justice Souter, in a dissent joined by Justices Stevens, Ginsburg, and Breyer, agreed that there was no meaningful distinction between money from general executive revenue and spending under a specific federal statute, but they would have followed *Flast* and allowed taxpayer standing.[222]

Most recently, in *Arizona School Tuition Organization v. Winn*, the Supreme Court again rejected a claim of taxpayer standing to present an alleged establishment

---

[220] *Id.* at 605.

[221] *Id.* at 618 (Scalia, J., dissenting).

[222] The Court also rejected taxpayer standing in *DaimlerChrysler Corp. v. Cuno*, 547 U.S. 332 (2006), where it rejected the argument that *Flast* should be extended to allow taxpayer standing to challenge government actions that allegedly violate the dormant commerce clause. The Court dismissed a challenge to a state program to give tax benefits to businesses relocating from out of state.

clause violation.[223] Arizona law allowed taxpayers who voluntarily contributed money to a "student tuition organization" (STO) to receive a dollar-for-dollar tax credit up to $500 of their annual tax liability. The challengers argued that this provides $50 million a year for private schools, primarily religious schools.

The Court, in a 5-4 decision, ordered the case dismissed for lack of standing and distinguished *Flast v. Cohen.* Justice Kennedy, writing for the Court, distinguished government expenditures from tax credits and stated: "The distinction between governmental expenditures and tax credits refutes respondents' assertion of standing. When Arizona taxpayers choose to contribute to STOs, they spend their own money, not money the State has collected from respondents or from other taxpayers."[224]

Justice Scalia, joined by Justice Thomas, concurred and again urged the overruling of *Flast v. Cohen*: "*Flast* is an anomaly in our jurisprudence, irreconcilable with the Article III restrictions on federal judicial power that our opinions have established. I would repudiate that misguided decision and enforce the Constitution."[225]

Justice Kagan wrote a vigorous dissent, joined by Justices Ginsburg, Breyer, and Sotomayor. She stated: "This novel distinction in standing law between appropriations and tax expenditures has as little basis in principle as it has in our precedent. Cash grants and targeted tax breaks are means of accomplishing the same government objective—to provide financial support to select individuals or organizations. Taxpayers who oppose state aid of religion have equal reason to protest whether that aid flows from the one form of subsidy or the other. Either way, the government has financed the religious activity. And so either way, taxpayers should be able to challenge the subsidy. Still worse, the Court's arbitrary distinction threatens to eliminate *all* occasions for a taxpayer to contest the government's monetary support of religion. Precisely because appropriations and tax breaks can achieve identical objectives, the government can easily substitute one for the other."[226]

After *Richardson, Schlesinger, Valley Forge, Hein,* and *Winn,* the only situation in which taxpayer standing appears permissible is if the plaintiff challenges a government expenditure pursuant to a specific statute as violating the establishment clause. After *Valley Forge,* for example, a local school system moved to dismiss a challenge to its aid to parochial schools on the ground that the plaintiffs lacked standing because they were suing as taxpayers. The Court summarily rejected this contention. The Court said: "Petitioners allege that respondents lacked taxpayer standing. The District Court and the Court of Appeals rejected the standing challenge. We affirm this finding, relying on the numerous cases in which we have adjudicated Establishment Clause challenges by state taxpayers to programs for aiding nonpublic schools."[227] But it also is clear from recent cases such as *Hein* and

---

[223] 131 S. Ct. 1436 (2011).
[224] *Id.* at 1147.
[225] *Id.* at 1450 (Scalia, J., concurring).
[226] *Id.* at 1450 (Kagan, J., dissenting).
[227] Grand Rapids School Dist. v. Ball, 473 U.S. 373 (1985).

Winn that the Court narrowly construes *Flast v. Cohen* and will not extend it beyond challenges to laws that directly provide money to religious institutions.

Generalized Grievance as a Constitutional Bar

In *Warth v. Seldin*, the Supreme Court declared that the bar on citizen and tax-payer suits was "prudential," not constitutional.[228] The Court apparently believed that citizens and taxpayers are hurt when the government violates the law, but that it was prudent for the federal courts to refuse to hear such cases. However, in *Lujan v. Defenders of Wildlife*, the Court treated the bar on citizen standing as constitutional.[229] The Endangered Species Act provided that "any person may commence a civil suit on his own behalf (A) to enjoin any person, including the United States and any other governmental instrumentality or agency . . . who is alleged to be in violation of any provision of this chapter."[230] The plaintiffs invoked this authority as the basis for a suit challenging a federal regulation providing that the United States would not comply with the Act outside the country except on the high seas.

The Court, in an opinion by Justice Scalia, held that the plaintiffs were assert-ing a generalized grievance and that Congress by statute cannot authorize stand-ing in such an instance. The prohibition against citizen standing was character-ized as being derived from Article III and therefore not susceptible to a statutory override. *Lujan* has potentially dramatic implications for the many federal statutes that authorize "citizen suits" as an enforcement mechanism.[231] Such provisions are especially common in environmental statutes and are included in laws such as the Clean Water Act,[232] the Surface Mining Control and Reclamation Act of 1977,[233] the Safe Drinking Water Act of 1974,[234] the Comprehensive Environmen-tal Response, Compensation and Liability Act,[235] the Clean Air Act,[236] the Noise Control Act,[237] and the Energy Conservation Act.[238] *Lujan* appears to mean that these provisions are unconstitutional except in instances where the plaintiff can otherwise demonstrate an injury sufficient for standing.

More generally, *Lujan* likely means that the bar against generalized griev-ances will be treated as constitutional and not prudential in the future. It is possi-ble, though, that the Court might distinguish taxpayer suits from citizen suits and argue that the former involves a clearer injury because of the dollars and cents

---

[228] 422 U.S. at 490.
[229] 504 U.S. 555 (1992).
[230] 16 U.S.C. §1540(g).
[231] For a discussion of these implications, *see* Cass Sunstein, What's Standing After *Lujan?* Of Cit-izen Suits, "Injuries," and Article III, 91 Mich. L. Rev. 163 (1992).
[232] 33 U.S.C. §1365(e).
[233] 30 U.S.C. §1270.
[234] 42 U.S.C. §300j-8.
[235] 42 U.S.C. §6972.
[236] 42 U.S.C. §7604.
[237] 42 U.S.C. §4911.
[238] 42 U.S.C. §6305.

loss (although extremely small), thus justifying taxpayer standing continuing to be regarded as prudential.

However, it should be noted that in a subsequent case addressing the generalized grievance doctrine, the Court reaffirmed that plaintiffs have standing so long as they can show a personal, concrete injury. In *Federal Election Commission v. Akins*, the Court held that plaintiffs had standing to challenge a decision of the Federal Election Commission that the American Israel Political Affairs Committee is not a "political committee" subject to the regulation and reporting requirements under the Federal Election Campaign Act of 1971.[239] The federal statute permitted standing to any "aggrieved party." The dissent argued that plaintiffs presented a generalized grievance; their desire for enforcement of the federal law was the same as everyone else's in the world.[240]

Justice Breyer, writing for the majority, expressly rejected this argument and emphasized that the federal statute created a right to information and the denial of this right was a concrete injury sufficient for standing. The Court explained that unlike *Richardson*, "there is a statute which . . . does seek to protect individuals such as respondents from the kind of harm that they say that they have suffered, i.e., failing to receive particular information about campaign-related activities."[241] *Federal Election Commission v. Akins* is an important post-*Lujan* clarification of the generalized grievance requirement because it clearly holds that Congress by statute can create rights that would not otherwise exist and the alleged violation of those rights is sufficient for standing, even under a broad citizen suit provision and even where the injury is widely shared in society.

Should There Be a Bar Against Generalized Grievances?

The generalized grievance standing doctrine can be defended on separation of powers grounds. This standing barrier reflects a belief that the judicial role is solely to prevent and remedy specific injuries suffered by individuals. The Court has no authority to halt government violations of the Constitution except when plaintiffs claim that their personal rights—be they rights created by common law, the Constitution, or statutes—are infringed. In *Richardson*, *Schlesinger*, *Valley Forge*, *Lujan*, and *Hein*, the Court expressly noted that the generalized grievance standing barrier reserves matters to the political branches of government, thereby promoting the separation of powers. Moreover, the generalized grievance standing barrier reflects a desire to exclude plaintiffs who sue entirely out of ideological interests and not on the basis of specific, concrete injuries.[242]

---

[239] 524 U.S. 11 (1998).

[240] *Id.* at 30.

[241] *Id.* at 22.

[242] Ideological plaintiffs are sometimes referred to as non-Hohfeldian plaintiffs. *See, e.g.*, Richard Fallon, Of Justiciability, Remedies and Public Law Litigation: Notes on the Jurisprudence of *Lyons*, 59 N.Y.U. L. Rev. 1, 3 n.12 (1984). The term originates from the scholar Wesley Newcomb Hohfeld, who devised a taxonomy of legal rights. *See* Wesley Hohfeld, Some Fundamental Legal Conceptions as

On the other hand, the generalized grievance standing doctrine can be criticized as the Court's abdicating the judicial role in upholding the Constitution. The argument is that the Court inappropriately deemed some parts of the Constitution to be enforceable only through the political process. No one is likely to have standing to challenge the practices objected to in *Richardson, Schlesinger, Valley Forge,* and *Hein.* The constitutional provisions involved there—the statements and accounts clause, the incompatibility clause, and the establishment clause—could be blatantly disregarded and yet the courts would be powerless to halt the violations. This is deeply troubling because the purpose of the Constitution and judicial review is to safeguard matters from majority rule—a value that is lost when provisions are enforceable only through the political process. The effect of the generalized grievance doctrine is to read these clauses out of the Constitution except to the extent the political branches want to voluntarily comply with them.

Also, critics argue that the Court's distinction between parts of the Constitution is unjustified. The Court draws a distinction between constitutional provisions creating individual rights—such as the equal protection clause—the violation of which creates standing, and provisions pertaining to the structure of government—such as the statements and accounts clause—the violation of which is a generalized grievance. But the desirability of drawing this distinction is open to question. Structural parts of the Constitution are integral to protecting individual rights. For example, if Congress were to adopt a law authorizing the current president to serve a ten-year term, in violation of Article II, would anyone have standing to sue? Perhaps this might be challenged as infringing the right to vote. But under a strict reading of the generalized grievance cases, citizens would lack standing because any plaintiff would be presenting a claim common to all in society.

Ultimately, two competing visions of the role of the federal judiciary are at stake. Under one, the role of federal courts is limited to remedying specific injuries suffered by individuals. This position sees a need for great deference to the political branches of government and fears the powers of the federal courts as an anti-majoritarian institution. An alternative view sees the federal judiciary as existing to ensure government compliance with the Constitution. Under this position, judicial deference does not include tolerating constitutional violations. The majority opinions in *Richardson, Schlesinger,* and *Valley Forge* and the plurality opinion in *Hein* endorsed the former view; the dissents expressed the latter position. The dispute is a fundamental disagreement over the role of the federal courts in American society.

Applied in Judicial Reasoning, 23 Yale L.J. 16 (1913). Because the claims of ideological plaintiffs do not fit into any of Hohfeld's categories of legal rights, such plaintiffs are termed "non-Hohfeldian."

§2.5.6   *The Requirement That the Plaintiff Be Within the Zone of Interests Protected by the Statute*

The Requirement Defined

A third prudential standing requirement, in addition to the ban on third-party standing and the prohibition against generalized grievances, is the rule that the plaintiff seeking standing must be within the zone of interests protected by the statute in question. This requirement applies when a person is challenging an administrative agency regulation that does not directly control the person's actions. Assuming that the constitutional standing requirements are met, the plaintiff may sue if it can show that it is within the group intended to benefit from the statute. For example, if there is a statute preventing widget companies from selling law books, a law book company might sue to challenge an administrative regulation permitting the widget company to sell law texts. Although the law book company is not directly controlled by the regulation, it may sue if it shows that it fulfills the constitutional standing requirements and that the statute limiting the widget company sales was intended to protect its interests.

The Supreme Court has stated that the plaintiff must allege that "the interest sought to be protected by the complainant is arguably within the zone of interests to be protected or regulated by the statute or constitutional guarantee in question."[243] In other words, if a plaintiff is suing pursuant to a statutory provision, in order to have standing the plaintiff must be part of the group intended to benefit from the law. Although the Court's statement of the test includes its application to constitutional provisions, for reasons discussed below, the zone of interests requirement is used only in statutory cases, usually involving administrative law issues.

The zone of interests test is particularly confusing, in part, because the Court has been inconsistent about whether it is a standing requirement. In some cases, in summarizing the law of standing, the Court has omitted the zone of interests test.[244] But in other decisions, the test has been included in a listing of the prudential standing requirements.[245] In fact, the Supreme Court's failure to mention the zone of interests test for several years convinced some commentators and lower courts that the Court had abandoned it as a separate standing requirement.[246] But in a decision in 1987, the Court again reaffirmed the zone of interests test as a separate standing requirement, albeit one that the Court said is "not meant to

---

[243] Association of Data Processing Serv. Orgs., Inc. v. Camp, 397 U.S. 150, 153 (1970).

[244] *See, e.g.*, Duke Power Co. v. Carolina Envtl. Study Group, 438 U.S. 59 (1978); Warth v. Seldin, 422 U.S. 490 (1975) (summarizing the law of standing, but omitting the zone of interests test).

[245] *See, e.g.*, Valley Forge Christian College v. Americans United for Separation of Church and State, 454 U.S. 464 (1982); Gladstone, Realtors v. Village of Bellwood, 441 U.S. 91, 99-100 (1979).

[246] *See, e.g.*, Robert Sedler, Standing, Justiciability, and All That: A Behavioral Analysis, 25 Vand. L. Rev. 479, 486-487 (1972); Department of Energy v. Louisiana, 690 F.2d 180, 187 (Emer. Ct. App. 1982).

be especially demanding."[247] More recently, in 2014, the Court again applied the zone of interests test and said that in the context of the Administrative Procedures Act "we have often 'conspicuously included the word "arguably" in the test to indicate that the benefit of any doubt goes to the plaintiff,' and have said that the test forecloses suit only when a plaintiff's 'interests are so marginally related to or inconsistent with the purposes implicit in the statute that it cannot reasonably be assumed that' Congress authorized that plaintiff to sue."[248] But despite this declaration that it is a relaxed standard, the Court has used this standing requirement to bar litigation.[249]

Creation of the Requirement

The zone of interests test was first articulated by the Supreme Court in *Association of Data Processing Service Organizations, Inc. v. Camp.*[250] The plaintiff challenged a ruling by the comptroller of the currency to allow banks to make data processing services available to other banks and bank customers. Although the data processors clearly were injured by the comptroller's decision, there was a question about whether they had standing to sue. Under the Administrative Procedures Act, a person may seek judicial review of an agency decision if he or she is "aggrieved by agency action within the meaning of a relevant statute."[251] The Court said that a person has standing under this provision if he or she has suffered an injury and if "the interest sought to be protected by the complainant is arguably within the zone of interests to be protected or regulated by the statute or constitutional guarantee in question."[252] The Court concluded that the data processors were arguably within the zone of interests protected by the Bank Service Corporation Act of 1962, which prohibited bank service corporations to "engage in any activity other than the performance of bank services for banks."[253]

The zone of interests test was applied by the Court in *Barlow v. Collins,*[254] decided the same day as *Camp. Barlow* also involved an attempt to secure judicial review of an agency decision under the Administrative Procedures Act. The secretary of agriculture issued a regulation permitting tenant farmers to assign payments under the Upland Cotton Program as security for land they were renting. The farmers sought review, objecting that the new regulation caused landlords to coerce them into making exorbitant payments for rent and supplies. The Court again found the zone of interests test to be met, concluding that the pertinent statutory provision was adopted to protect the tenant farmers.

---

[247] Clarke v. Securities Indus. Assn., 479 U.S. 388 (1987). *See also* Block v. Community Nutrition Inst., 467 U.S. 340 (1984).

[248] Lexmark Intl., Inc. v. Static Control Components, 134 S. Ct. 1377, 1389 (2014).

[249] *See* Air Courier Conference v. American Postal Workers Union, AFL-CIO, 498 U.S. 517 (1991), discussed below.

[250] 397 U.S. 150 (1970).

[251] 5 U.S.C. §702.

[252] 397 U.S. at 153.

[253] 12 U.S.C. §1864.

[254] 397 U.S. 159 (1970).

Is the Zone of Interests Test Desirable?

The zone of interests test has been defended on grounds similar to the prohibition against third-party standing. The idea is that those who invoke a statute's protections as a basis for standing should be the ones that the legislature intended to protect. Also, it is argued that the "zone of interests requirement . . . might improve the quality of adversary presentation, in part by providing a detailed fact setting that corresponds to the problems most likely to be encountered in the area of dispute, and in part by yielding parties sensitive to the perhaps conflicting interests of those most directly involved."[255]

But others have sharply criticized the zone of interests test.[256] Critics argue that the zone of interests test is unnecessary; if a person is asserting a judicially cognizable injury, and fulfills all of the other standing requirements, there is no reason for the federal court to deny review. Moreover, critics argue that the Court never has articulated how a judge is to decide the zone of interests protected by a particular statute.

Inconsistent Application of the Test

Subsequent cases are inconsistent in applying the requirement. In *Clarke v. Securities Industries Association,* the Supreme Court applied the zone of interests test, but explained that it is a requirement that generally should not preclude standing.[257] In *Clarke,* a trade association of securities brokers challenged a decision by the comptroller of the currency to allow a bank to offer discount brokerage services at locations around the country. The association claimed that this violated a federal law preventing banks from creating branch banks in other states.

The Supreme Court said that the plaintiff had standing because it was injured and because it was within the zone of interests intended to be protected by the statute. The Court explained: "In cases where the plaintiff is not itself the subject of the contested regulatory action, the test denies a right of review if the plaintiff's interests are so marginally related to or inconsistent with the purposes implicit in the statute that it cannot reasonably be assumed that Congress intended to permit the suit."[258] The Court explained that the zone of interests test was "not meant to be especially demanding; in particular, there need be no indication of congressional purpose to benefit the would-be plaintiff."[259] On the merits, the Court ruled in favor of the plaintiffs that the regulation was inconsistent with federal law.

The Court's most recent applications of the zone of interests test, like *Clarke,* involved situations in which the Court found that its requirements were met. In *Bennett v. Spear,* the Court found that the authorization for citizen suits within the

---

[255] Charles Wright, Arthur Miller & Edward Cooper, 13 Federal Practice and Procedure 511-512 (1984).

[256] *See, e.g.,* Richard Stewart, The Reformation of American Administrative Law, 88 Harv. L. Rev. 1669, 1731-1734 (1975).

[257] 479 U.S. 388 (1987).

[258] *Id.* at 399.

[259] *Id.* at 399-400.

Endangered Species Act eliminated the requirement that the plaintiffs be within the zone of interests created by the statute.[260] In *Bennett*, ranch operators and irrigation districts sued under the citizen suit provision of the Endangered Species Act to challenge the restriction of the use of reservoir water to protect two species of fish. Specifically, the Bureau of Reclamation determined that the operation of the Klamath Irrigation Project might affect two endangered species of fish and required the maintenance of water levels in the reservoir.

The ranch operators and irrigation districts sued and alleged an economic injury from the proposed federal action. The district court and court of appeals found that this was not within the zone of interests of the Endangered Species Act, which was intended to protect environmental interests. The United States Supreme Court reversed. Justice Scalia, writing for the Court, concluded that the authorization for citizen suits within the Act was meant to expand federal court standing to the maximum permitted under Article III. Therefore, the statute overrides prudential standing requirements, such as the zone of interests test. The Court concluded: "It is true that the plaintiffs here are seeking to prevent application of environmental restrictions rather than to implement them. But the 'any person' formulation applies to all of the causes of action authorized by [the law]—not only to private violators of environmental restrictions, and not only to actions against the secretary asserting underenforcement . . . , but also to actions against the secretary asserting overenforcement."[261]

In *National Credit Union Administration v. First National Bank & Trust Co.*, the Court found that banks had standing to challenge a change in federal regulations that would allow credit unions to compete more directly with the banks.[262] Although there was no indication that the federal law restricting credit union membership was intended to protect the economic interests of banks, the Court concluded that plaintiffs are not required to show that Congress intended to benefit them. Rather, plaintiffs need only demonstrate that the statute "arguably" protects their interests. Based on this relaxed standard, the Court concluded that the federal law restricting the operation of credit unions arguably protects the interests of their competitors.

Most recently, in *Lexmark International, Inc. v. Static Control Components, Inc.*,[263] the Court found that the zone of interests test was met in a claim under the Lanham Act for false and deceptive advertising.[264] Lexmark makes toner cartridges and Static Control makes components for them. Static Control alleged that Lexmark engaged in false advertising and sued under the Lanham Act. The Court said: "We thus hold that to come within the zone of interests in a suit for false advertising under [the Lanham Act], a plaintiff must allege an injury to a commercial interest in reputation or sales. A consumer who is hoodwinked into purchasing a disappointing product may well have an injury-in-fact cognizable under

---

[260] 520 U.S. 154 (1997).
[261] 520 U.S. at 166.
[262] 522 U.S. 479 (1998).
[263] 134 S. Ct. 1377 (2014).
[264] 15 U.S.C. §1125(a)

Article III, but he cannot invoke the protection of the Lanham Act."[265] The Court thus found that Static Control's claim was within the zone of interests protected by the Lanham Act: "Static Control's alleged injuries—lost sales and damage to its business reputation—are injuries to precisely the sorts of commercial interests the Act protects. Static Control is suing not as a deceived consumer, but as a 'perso[n] engaged in' 'commerce within the control of Congress' whose position in the marketplace has been damaged by Lexmark's false advertising."[266]

In contrast, in *Air Courier Conference v. American Postal Workers Union*, the postal workers' union challenged the United States Postal Service's suspension of its monopoly over "extremely urgent" letters under the Postal Express Statutes.[267] After the Postal Service suspended the application of its monopoly over certain routes, postal unions challenged the decision. The Supreme Court ruled that the unions lacked standing because they were not within the zone of interests protected by the Postal Express statutes. In an opinion by Chief Justice Rehnquist, the Court began by noting that "[t]he particular language of the statutes provides no support for respondents' assertion that Congress intended to protect jobs with the Postal Service."[268] Additionally, the Court noted that the legislative history did not indicate an intent to benefit postal workers. The Court distinguished other cases where the zone of interests test had been met by pointing to statutory language or legislative history creating interests in those instances.

Air Courier is important in showing that the zone of interests test is not toothless. The Court concluded that a person or group can claim to be within the zone of interests protected by law only if the statute's text or history justifies such a conclusion.

§2.6   RIPENESS

§2.6.1   *Introduction*

Ripeness Defined

Ripeness, like mootness (discussed in the next section), is a justiciability doctrine determining when review is appropriate. While standing is concerned with who is a proper party to litigate a particular matter, ripeness and mootness determine when that litigation may occur. Specifically, the ripeness doctrine seeks to separate matters that are premature for review, because the injury is speculative

---

[265] 134 S. Ct. at 1390.
[266] *Id.* at 1393.
[267] 498 U.S. 517 (1991).
[268] *Id.* at 524-525.

and never may occur, from those cases that are appropriate for federal court action.[1]

Although the phrasing makes the questions of who may sue and when they may sue seem distinct, in practice there is an obvious overlap between the doctrines of standing and ripeness. If no injury has occurred, the plaintiff might be denied standing or the case might be dismissed as not ripe. For example, in *O'Shea v. Littleton*, the Supreme Court declared nonjusticiable a suit contending that the defendants, a magistrate and a judge, discriminated against blacks in setting bail and imposing sentences.[2] The Court observed that none of the plaintiffs currently faced proceedings in the defendants' courtrooms and hence "the threat of injury from the alleged course of conduct they attack is too remote to satisfy the case-or-controversy requirement."[3] This decision could be placed under the label of either standing—no injury was alleged; or ripeness—the type of injury was adequate but had not yet occurred.

Similarly and more recently, in *Susan B. Anthony List v. Driehaus*, the Court considered a challenge to an Ohio statute that criminalized making false statements about candidates during political campaigns.[4] The Susan B. Anthony List, a political group that previously had been threatened with prosecution under the law, brought a suit for a declaratory judgment to have the law declared unconstitutional. The Court found that the plaintiffs met the requirements of Article III because they alleged a credible threat of enforcement. The Court referred to this as being about standing and ripeness, but made no attempt to distinguish between these doctrines. In fact, the Court said: "As the parties acknowledge, the Article III standing and ripeness issues in this case 'boil down to the same question.'"[5]

Perhaps the distinction between standing and ripeness is that standing focuses on whether the type of injury alleged is qualitatively sufficient to fulfill the requirements of Article III and whether the plaintiff has personally suffered that harm, whereas ripeness centers on whether that injury has occurred yet. Again, while the distinction will work in some instances, in others it is problematic because the question of whether the plaintiff has suffered a harm is integral to both standing and ripeness concerns. For example, in *Sierra Club v. Morton*, the Supreme Court dismissed, on standing grounds, a challenge by an environmental group to the construction of a ski resort in a national park.[6] The Court emphasized the failure of the plaintiff to allege that it or its members ever had used the park. This standing decision could be viewed as a ripeness ruling as well, if ripeness is understood as focusing on whether an injury that is sufficient to meet Article III has been suffered yet.

To the extent that the substantive requirements overlap and the result will be the same regardless of whether the issue is characterized as ripeness or standing, little turns on the choice of the label. However, for the sake of clarity, especially in

§2.6 [1] Abbott Labs. v. Gardner, 387 U.S. 136, 148 (1967).
[2] 414 U.S. 488 (1974).
[3] *Id.* at 489.
[4] 134 S. Ct. 2334 (2014).
[5] *Id.* at 2341 n.5.
[6] 405 U.S. 727 (1972), discussed in more detail in §2.5.2.

those cases where the law of standing and ripeness is not identical, ripeness can be given a narrower definition that distinguishes it from standing and explains the existing case law. Ripeness properly should be understood as involving the question of *when may a party seek preenforcement review of a statute or regulation*. Customarily, a person can challenge the legality of a statute or regulation only when he or she is prosecuted for violating it. At that time, a defense can be that the law is invalid, for example, as being unconstitutional.

There is an unfairness, however, to requiring a person to violate a law in order to challenge it. A person might unnecessarily obey an unconstitutional law, refraining from the prohibited conduct, rather than risk criminal punishments. Alternatively, a person might violate a statute or regulation, confident that it will be invalidated, only to be punished when the law is upheld. A primary purpose of the Declaratory Judgment Act was to permit people to avoid this choice and obtain preenforcement review of statutes and regulations.

The Declaratory Judgment Act does not allow preenforcement review in all instances. Rather, it permits federal court decisions only "[i]n a case of actual controversy."[7] In upholding the constitutionality of the Declaratory Judgment Act, the Supreme Court emphasized that the statute did not permit advisory opinions because it limited federal court action to justiciable cases.[8] Ripeness, then, is best understood as the determination of whether a federal court can grant preenforcement review; for example, when may a court hear a request for a declaratory judgment, or when must it decline review?

The Supreme Court has stated that in deciding whether a case is ripe it looks primarily to two considerations: "the hardship to the parties of withholding court consideration" and "the fitness of the issues for judicial decision."[9] Ripeness is said to reflect both constitutional and prudential considerations. The focus on whether there is a sufficient injury without preenforcement review seems inextricably linked with the constitutional requirement for cases and controversies, whereas the focus on the quality of the record seems prudential.[10]

The ripeness doctrine, limiting preenforcement review, serves many of the purposes underlying the other justiciability doctrines. Ripeness advances separation of powers by avoiding judicial review in situations where it is unnecessary for the federal courts to become involved because there is not a substantial hardship to postponing review. In the leading case of *Abbott Laboratories v. Gardner*, the Court explained that the "basic rationale" of the ripeness requirement is "to prevent the

---

[7] 28 U.S.C. §2201.

[8] Aetna Life Ins. Co. v. Haworth, 300 U.S. 227, 241 (1937); for a discussion of the constitutionality of the Declaratory Judgment Act and why it is not an authorization for unconstitutional advisory opinions, *see* §2.4.

[9] Abbott Labs. v. Gardner, 387 U.S. at 149.

[10] At times, the Court describes ripeness as constitutional; *see, e.g.*, Public Serv. Commn. of Utah v. Wycoff Co., 344 U.S. 237, 242-245 (1952); but at other times, the Court describes the ripeness test as prudential; *see, e.g.*, Buckley v. Valeo, 424 U.S. 1, 114-118 (1976). In large part, this difference might reflect the aspects of ripeness at issue in particular cases.

courts, through avoidance of premature adjudication, from entangling themselves in abstract disagreements."[11]

Additionally, the ripeness requirement, like all justiciability doctrines, enhances judicial economy by limiting the occasion for federal court jurisdiction and the expenditure of judicial time and revenues. Perhaps most of all, ripeness is said to enhance the quality of judicial decision making by ensuring that there is an adequate record to permit effective review.[12]

As is reflected in the cases described below, the federal courts have a great deal of discretion in determining whether a case is ripe. The questions of whether there is sufficient hardship to permit preenforcement review and whether the record is adequately focused cannot be reduced to a formula. The result is that it is often difficult to distinguish why in some instances ripeness was found, but in other seemingly similar circumstances it was denied.

§2.6.2   *Criteria for Determining Ripeness: The Hardship to Denying Review*

The first part of the ripeness inquiry is determining how significant is the harm to denying judicial review. The more a plaintiff can demonstrate substantial hardship to a denial of preenforcement review, the more likely a federal court is to find ripeness. Conversely, the more speculative and uncertain the harm, the less likely it is that review will be granted.[13]

Hardship from Choice Between Possibly Unnecessary Compliance and Possible Conviction

An examination of Supreme Court ripeness decisions reveals three situations in which the Court has found there to be enough hardship to justify preenforcement review. First, when an individual is faced with a choice between forgoing allegedly lawful behavior and risking likely prosecution with substantial consequences, the federal courts will deem the case ripe rather than insist that an individual violate the law and risk the consequences. *Abbott Laboratories v. Gardner* is illustrative.[14] The Food and Drug Administration (FDA) promulgated a regulation requiring the inclusion of generic names for prescription drugs on all labels and other printed materials. Violations of the regulation were punishable by civil and criminal sanctions. Thirty-seven drug companies, accounting for 90 percent

---

[11] 387 U.S. at 148.

[12] *Id.*

[13] For example, in *Texas v. United States*, 523 U.S. 296 (1998), the Supreme Court refused to rule as to whether the preclearance provision of the Voting Rights Act of 1965 applied to the possible appointment of a magistrate to oversee school districts that failed to meet performance standards. The Court noted that no magistrate had yet been appointed and that the appointment of a magistrate was a last resort to be used only if all other means failed. The Court concluded that the case was not ripe because it was too speculative whether a magistrate ever would be appointed.

[14] 387 U.S. 136 (1967).

of the supply of prescription drugs in the country, challenged the regulation as exceeding the scope of the FDA's authority under the pertinent statutes. The government argued that the case was not ripe until a drug company was prosecuted for violating the regulation.

The Supreme Court disagreed and permitted preenforcement review. The Court emphasized the substantial hardship to denying preenforcement review. The Court stated: "If petitioners wish to comply they must change all their labels, advertisements and promotional materials; they must destroy stocks of printed matter; and they must invest heavily in new printing type and new supplies. The alternative to compliance . . . would risk serious criminal and civil penalties for the unlawful distribution of 'misbranded' drugs."[15]

The ripeness requirement can be understood by contrasting *Abbott Laboratories* with another case decided the same day, *Toilet Goods Association v. Gardner*.[16] An FDA regulation permitted the FDA free access to all manufacturing processes involved in the production of color additives and authorized the suspension of certifications for sales if access is denied. A cosmetic manufacturing company sought a declaratory judgment invalidating the regulation. But unlike *Abbott Laboratories*, the Court said that the matter was not ripe because there was minimal hardship to denying review. The Court explained that "a refusal to admit an inspector here would at most lead only to a suspension of certification services to the particular party, a determination that can then be promptly challenged through an administrative procedure, which in turn is reviewable by a court."[17]

In numerous other cases as well, the Supreme Court found substantial hardship in denying judicial review because of the choice that a person faced between refraining from allegedly protected conduct or risking sanctions. For instance, in *Steffel v. Thompson*, the plaintiff sought a declaratory judgment upholding his right to distribute handbills in a shopping center.[18] On two occasions, the plaintiff attempted to distribute anti–Vietnam War literature at a shopping center; both times the owners of the property called the police. Although the plaintiff left to avoid arrest, his companions stayed and were arrested. The Supreme Court found the matter ripe because denying review would impose substantial hardship, forcing the plaintiff to choose between unnecessarily giving up possibly protected speech or risking arrest and criminal punishment. Justice Brennan, writing for the Court, spoke of the injury inflicted in placing "the hapless plaintiff between the Scylla of intentionally flouting state law and the Charybdis of forgoing what he believes to be constitutionally protected activity in order to avoid becoming enmeshed in a criminal proceeding."[19]

Similarly, in the earlier case of *Adler v. Board of Education of the City of New York*, the Court implicitly found ripe a challenge to a state law designed to eliminate "subversive persons" from the public school system.[20] The state statute contained

---

[15] *Id.* at 152-153.
[16] 387 U.S. 158 (1967).
[17] *Id.* at 165.
[18] 415 U.S. 452 (1974).
[19] *Id.* at 462.
[20] 342 U.S. 485, 488 n.4 (1952).

a list of subversive organizations, and membership in any of these groups was deemed a basis for disqualification from being employed in any school. Although Justice Frankfurter dissented, arguing that the case was not ripe, the Supreme Court upheld the statute on the merits. The Court's choice to decide the case apparently reflected a conclusion that there was substantial hardship to denying review in that teachers had to either refrain from joining these organizations or risk loss of their jobs.

Most recently, in *Susan B. Anthony List v. Driehaus*, the Court considered whether a group had standing to challenge an Ohio statute that prohibits "false statements" during the course of a political campaign.[21] The Court explained that the "question in this case is whether their preenforcement challenge to that law is justiciable—and in particular, whether they have alleged a sufficiently imminent injury for the purposes of Article III."[22]

A member of Congress initiated proceedings against the Susan B. Anthony List in the Ohio Elections Commission, which found probable cause to proceed, but the matter was dismissed after the congressman lost his reelection bid. The Susan B. Anthony Fund had brought a challenge to the Ohio law in federal court and the issue before the Supreme Court was whether its challenge to the Ohio law could continue after the Ohio Elections Commission proceedings were dismissed.

The Supreme Court unanimously ruled in favor of the Susan B. Anthony Fund and held that the matter was justiciable. Justice Thomas, writing for a unanimous Court, noted that "[w]hen an individual is subject to such a threat, an actual arrest, prosecution, or other enforcement action is not a prerequisite to challenging the law."[23] The Court found that the matter was ripe for review because the plaintiffs "have alleged a credible threat of enforcement."[24] The Court stressed that "the threat of future enforcement of the false statement statute is substantial."[25]

Thus, it is well established that a case is ripe because of the substantial hardship to denying preenforcement review when a person is forced to choose between forgoing possibly lawful activity and risking substantial sanctions. People should not be forced to exercise their rights at peril of criminal sanctions or loss of employment.

However, some Supreme Court cases deviate from this principle. For example, in *International Longshoremen's and Warehousemen's Union Local 37 v. Boyd*, the Court dismissed as not ripe a case in which resident aliens were forced to choose between giving up a job or risking permanent exclusion from the country.[26] For many years, some resident aliens in the United States went to work in Alaska during the summer. Because the case arose before Alaska became a state, the aliens sued to enjoin immigration officers from preventing their return to the United States. The Supreme Court, in an opinion by Justice Frankfurter, held that their suit was not ripe. The Court found that the situation was "hypothetical" and concluded that

---

[21] 134 S. Ct. 2334 (2014).
[22] *Id.* at 2338.
[23] *Id.* at 2342.
[24] *Id.* at 2343.
[25] *Id.* at 2345.
[26] 347 U.S. 222 (1954).

"[d]etermination of the scope and constitutionality of legislation in advance of its immediate adverse effect in the context of a concrete case involves too remote and abstract an inquiry for the proper exercise of the judicial function."[27] But this ignores the enormous hardship in forcing a person to choose between unnecessarily giving up a job or risking permanent exclusion from the country.

Like *Boyd*, the Supreme Court's decision in *United Public Workers v. Mitchell* is difficult to reconcile with the many cases holding that a case is ripe when a person is forced to choose between forgoing possibly constitutionally protected conduct or facing significant sanctions.[28] The issue in *Mitchell* was the ripeness of a challenge to the constitutionality of the Hatch Act of 1940, which prevented federal employees from taking "any active part in political management or political campaigns." The plaintiffs sought a declaratory judgment that the law violated their First Amendment rights and provided detailed affidavits listing the activities they wished to engage in. The Court found their claims to be not ripe. The Court said that the plaintiffs "seem clearly to seek advisory opinions upon broad claims. . . . A hypothetical threat is not enough. We can only speculate as to the kinds of political activity the appellants desire to engage in or as to the contents of their proposed public statements or the circumstances of their publication."[29] The Court found ripe the claims of one of the plaintiffs who was being fired for violating the Act and upheld the statute as applied to him.

The *Mitchell* Court's holding that employees had to violate the Hatch Act in order to challenge its constitutionality is unjust and inconsistent with the decisions described above. The plaintiffs in *Mitchell* suffered substantial hardship because of the Court's denial of review: They had to choose between refraining from political speech or risking loss of their jobs. In fact, 26 years later, the Court was presented with another constitutional challenge to the Hatch Act and found ripeness based on almost the same facts that were insufficient in *Mitchell*. In *United States Civil Service Commission v. National Association of Letter Carriers, AFL-CIO*, the Court found the case ripe because the plaintiffs alleged that they desired to engage in specific political activity.[30]

With reasoning quite similar to that in *Mitchell*, in *Renne v. Geary*, the Court dismissed on ripeness grounds a challenge to a provision in the California constitution that prohibits political parties and political party central committees from endorsing, supporting, or opposing candidates for nonpartisan offices.[31] The Court concluded that there was insufficient evidence that the plaintiffs were prevented from engaging in specific constitutionally protected conduct because of the law. The Court noted that "[t]he affidavit provides no indication whom the Democratic committee wished to endorse, for which office, or in what election. Absent a contention that [the provision] prevented a particular endorsement, and

---

[27] *Id.* at 224.

[28] 330 U.S. 75 (1947).

[29] *Id.* at 89-90.

[30] 413 U.S. 548 (1973). The First Amendment aspects of such restrictions on government employees are discussed in §11.3.8.2.

[31] 501 U.S. 312 (1991).

that the controversy had not become moot prior to the litigation, this allegation will not support an action in federal court."[32]

But the question arises as to why the identity of particular candidates matters for a facial challenge to the law. The record documented past enforcement of the statute, and the law undoubtedly would prevent endorsements in the future. As Justice Marshall argued in dissent: "Nothing in our analysis turn[s] on the identity of the candidates to be endorsed, the nature or precise language of the endorsements, or the mode of publicizing endorsements."[33]

Hardship Where Enforcement Is Certain

Thus, generally although not always, the Court has found substantial hardship on the basis of forcing a person to choose between refraining from possibly protected conduct and risking significant sanctions. A second situation in which the Court has found substantial hardship is where the enforcement of a statute or regulation is certain and the only impediment to ripeness is simply a delay before the proceedings commence. Where the application of a law is inevitable and consequences attach to it, the Court will find the matter ripe before the actual proceedings occur.

For example, in the *Regional Rail Reorganization Act Cases*, the Court deemed ripe a lawsuit brought by eight major railroads challenging the conveyance of their property to Conrail.[34] The district court found the case not justiciable on ripeness grounds because the reorganization plan had not yet been formulated and a special court had not yet ordered the reconveyances. But the Supreme Court held that the case was ripe, concluding: "Where the inevitability of the operation of a statute against certain individuals is patent, it is irrelevant to the existence of a justiciable controversy that there will be a time delay before the disputed provisions will come into effect."[35]

Similarly, in *Lake Carriers Association v. MacMullan*, the Court found ripe a challenge to a statute forbidding discharge of sewage from boats, even though prosecutions were definitely not imminent.[36] State officials had announced that they would not enforce the law until land-based pumpout facilities would be available, a construction process that would take a substantial amount of time. Reversing a district court decision dismissing the case as not ripe, the Supreme Court unanimously concluded that the matter was justiciable. The Court reasoned that it was inevitable that the law would be enforced and that as a result the boat owners had to begin installing new facilities on their boats in anticipation of the time when the law was implemented. This was sufficient to make the case ripe.

In *Buckley v. Valeo*, the plaintiffs were allowed to challenge the method of appointing members to the Federal Election Commission in anticipation of

[32] *Id.* at 320.
[33] *Id.* at 342 (Marshall, J., dissenting).
[34] 419 U.S. 102 (1974).
[35] *Id.* at 143.
[36] 406 U.S. 498, 507-508 (1972).

"impending future rulings and determinations by the Commission."[37] There was no doubt that the rulings would be forthcoming; thus, the Court concluded that the plaintiffs' "claims as they bear upon the method of appointment of the Commission's members may be presently adjudicated."[38]

Hardship Because of Collateral Injuries

A third way in which the Court has found substantial hardship is based on collateral injuries that are not the primary focus of the lawsuit. *Duke Power Co. v. Carolina Environmental Study Group, Inc.* is illustrative.[39] The plaintiffs challenged the constitutionality of the Price-Anderson Act, which limited the liability of private nuclear power plants to $560 million in the event of a nuclear accident.[40] The plaintiffs contended that the statute violated the due process clause because it allowed injuries to occur without ensuring adequate compensation to the victims. There were obvious ripeness problems with this claim because it was uncertain whether an accident ever would occur, if it occurred whether the losses would exceed the limit on liability, and if it occurred and did exceed the limit whether Congress would pay the difference. Nonetheless, the Court found the matter ripe on the basis of other injuries imposed by the Price-Anderson Act. The Court explained that *but for* the Price-Anderson Act, nuclear power plants for electricity generation would not be constructed. Thus, because of the Price-Anderson Act, a reactor was about to be constructed in the plaintiffs' area and would subject them to harms such as the exposure to radiation, thermal pollution, and fear of a nuclear accident. In other words, while the primary injury that was the focus of the lawsuit was not ripe — uncompensated losses from a nuclear accident — other injuries existed to make the case justiciable.[41]

Hardship Is a Prerequisite for Ripeness

If hardship is demonstrated in any of these three ways, the case is likely to be found ripe. However, if there appears minimal harm to denying review, the case will be dismissed as not ripe. *Poe v. Ullman* is a classic example of a case dismissed for lack of ripeness.[42] Married women for whom pregnancy was medically unadvisable and their doctors filed a lawsuit challenging a Connecticut law preventing the distribution or use of contraceptives. The Court deemed the case nonjusticiable because there had been only one prosecution under the law in more than 80 years. The Court noted that "contraceptives are commonly and notoriously

---

[37] 424 U.S. 1, 117 (1976).

[38] 424 U.S. 1, 117 (1976). Similarly, in *Palazzolo v. Rhode Island*, 533 U.S. 606 (2001), the Court found a takings claim to be ripe for review even though a plan had not been submitted to state court because similar requests for development had been denied.

[39] 438 U.S. 59 (1978). For an excellent analysis and criticism of this decision, *see* Jonathan Varat, Variable Justiciability and the Duke Power Case, 58 Tex. L. Rev. 273 (1980).

[40] 42 U.S.C. §2210.

[41] For a discussion of the standing aspects of *Duke Power, see* §2.5.3.

[42] 367 U.S. 497 (1961).

sold in Connecticut drug stores. . . . The undeviating policy of nullification by Connecticut of its anti-contraceptive laws throughout all the long years that they have been on the statute books bespeaks more than prosecutorial paralysis. . . . The fact that Connecticut has not chosen to press the enforcement of this statute deprives these controversies of the immediacy which is an indispensable condition of constitutional adjudication."[43] The Connecticut law was subsequently declared unconstitutional in *Griswold v. Connecticut* after the state prosecuted a family planning clinic.[44]

Yet the Court's decision in *Poe* was subjected to substantial criticism. The effect of the Connecticut law was to limit the availability of contraceptives, especially by preventing the opening of family planning clinics. Moreover, Justice Douglas, in dissent, argued that there was sufficient hardship to justify judicial review of the Connecticut statute: "What are these people—doctors and patients—to do? Flout the law and go to prison? Violate the law surreptitiously and hope they will not get caught? By today's decision we leave them no other alternatives. It is not the choice that they need have under the regime of the declaratory judgment and our constitutional system."[45]

Similarly, in *Reno v. Catholic Social Services*, the Supreme Court held that a challenge to Immigration and Naturalization Service (INS) regulations had to be dismissed on ripeness grounds because it was too speculative that anyone would be injured by the rules.[46] The Immigration Reform and Control Act of 1986 provided that before illegal aliens residing in the United States could apply for legalization, they had to apply for temporary resident status. Temporary resident status required a showing that a person continually resided in the United States since January 1, 1982, and maintained a continuous physical presence since November 6, 1986. The INS adopted many regulations to implement this law.

A class of plaintiffs, Catholic Social Services, challenged some of the INS regulations. The Supreme Court, in an opinion by Justice Souter, applied *Abbott Laboratories v. Gardner* and held that the case was not ripe for review. The Court said that it was entirely speculative whether any members of the class would be denied legalization because of the regulations. The Court said that the case might be ripe for review if the immigrants took the additional step of applying for legalization.

In other words, *Poe v. Ullman* and *Reno v. Catholic Social Services, Inc.* emphasize that a case will be dismissed on ripeness grounds if a federal court perceives the likelihood of harm as too speculative. Obviously, courts have a great deal of discretion in deciding what is a sufficient likelihood of hardship to meet the ripeness requirement.

---

[43] *Id.* at 502, 508.
[44] 381 U.S. 479 (1965), discussed in §10.3.2.
[45] 367 U.S. at 513 (Douglas, J., dissenting).
[46] 509 U.S. 43 (1993).

§2.6.3 Criteria for Determining Ripeness: The Fitness of the Issues and Record for Judicial Review

Is There Significant Gain to Waiting for an Actual Prosecution?

The existence of substantial hardship without judicial review is one of the two criteria articulated by the Court for determining ripeness. The other issue concerns the fitness of the issues for judicial review. The more a question is purely a legal issue the analysis of which does not depend on a particular factual context, the more likely it is that the Court will find ripeness. But the more judicial consideration of an issue would be enhanced by a specific set of facts, the greater the probability that a case seeking preenforcement review will be dismissed on ripeness grounds.

For example, in *Socialist Labor Party v. Gilligan*, the Supreme Court dismissed on ripeness grounds a challenge to a state law that allegedly limited the ability of the plaintiff to place candidates on the ballot for elections.[47] The law required candidates to sign an affidavit that they would not attempt to overthrow the government by force or violence. The Court concluded that "the record . . . now before this Court, is extraordinarily skimpy in the sort of proved or admitted facts that would enable us to adjudicate this claim."[48] The Court said that although the plaintiff might have standing to challenge the law, "their case has not given any particularity to the effect on them of Ohio's affidavit requirement."[49]

Another case in which the Court found an insufficient factual record to justify a conclusion of ripeness was *California Bankers Association v. Schultz*.[50] A bank, its customers, and bankers' organizations and associations sued to enjoin enforcement of a federal law that created record-keeping and reporting requirements for banks and other financial institutions. The claim, in part, was that the reporting requirements violated the First Amendment rights of bank customers. The Court said that the claim was not ripe, emphasizing the need for a concrete factual situation to facilitate judicial review. The Court concluded: "This Court, in the absence of a concrete fact situation in which competing associational and governmental interests can be weighed, is simply not in a position to determine whether an effort to compel disclosure of such records would or would not be barred."[51]

Relationship Between the Two Ripeness Criteria

The interaction of these two requirements for determining ripeness is not clear. Some commentators have suggested that ripeness can be found if either is met. Professor Tribe, for example, states that "[c]ases in which early legal challenges are held to be ripe normally present either or both of two features:

---

[47] 406 U.S. 583 (1972).
[48] *Id.* at 587.
[49] *Id.* at 588.
[50] 416 U.S. 21 (1974).
[51] *Id.* at 56.

significant present injuries . . . or legal questions that do not depend for their resolution on an extensive factual background."[52]

But the Court's decisions seem to indicate that both requirements must be met. For example, in *Poe v. Ullman*, the case was deemed not ripe even though it was a purely legal question that did not depend on an extensive factual background. In his dissenting opinion in *Poe*, Justice Harlan said: "I cannot see what further elaboration is required to enable us to decide the appellants' claims, and indeed neither the plurality nor the concurring opinion . . . suggests what more grist is needed before the judicial mill could turn."[53] Conversely, in *Socialist Workers Party v. Gilligan*, the Court admitted the existence of standing (and thus of an injury), but deemed the matter to be unripe because of the absence of an adequate record.[54]

Thus, while it appears that preenforcement review is possible only if there is both hardship to its denial and an adequate factual record, it is unclear whether a greater hardship might compensate for less in the way of a factual record or vice versa. Because the hardship requirement is constitutionally based, in all likelihood it is less flexible, whereas the prudential concern about the record is to be given less weight when there is a compelling need for immediate judicial review.

Finally, the relationship of ripeness to other doctrines should be noted. Ripeness is obviously closely related to requirements for exhaustion of administrative remedies before seeking federal court review; a case is not ripe until such exhaustion has occurred.[55] In fact, in cases claiming a government taking of property without just compensation, the Court has held that the matter is not ripe until compensation has been sought and denied through the available administrative procedures.[56]

§2.7 MOOTNESS

§2.7.1 Description of the Mootness Doctrine

An actual controversy must exist at all stages of federal court proceedings, at both the trial and appellate levels. If events subsequent to the filing of the case resolve the dispute, the case should be dismissed as moot. The Supreme Court, quoting Professor Henry Monaghan, explained that "mootness [is] the doctrine of standing in a time frame. The requisite personal interest that must exist at the

---

[52] Laurence Tribe, American Constitutional Law 80 (3d ed. 2000).

[53] 367 U.S. at 528 (Harlan, J., dissenting).

[54] 406 U.S. at 588.

[55] Myers v. Bethlehem Shipbuilding Corp., 303 U.S. 41 (1938).

[56] *See* San Remo Hotel v. City and County of San Francisco, 545 U.S. 323 (2005); Williamson County Regional Planning Commn. v. Hamilton Bank, 473 U.S. 172 (1984).

commencement of the litigation (standing) must continue throughout its existence (mootness)."[1]

Circumstances That Might Cause a Case to Be Moot

Many different types of events might render a case moot. For example, a case is moot if a criminal defendant dies during the appeals process or if a civil plaintiff dies where the cause of action does not survive death.[2] Also, if the parties settle the matter, a live controversy obviously no longer exists.[3] If a challenged law is repealed or expires, the case is moot.[4] Essentially, any change in the facts that ends the controversy renders the case moot. Thus, a defendant's challenge to a state law denying him pretrial bail was deemed moot after his conviction,[5] and a suit by students to enjoin a school's censorship of a student newspaper was dismissed as moot after the students graduated.[6]

Why Have a Mootness Doctrine?

The Supreme Court frequently has explained that the mootness doctrine is derived from Article III's prohibition against federal courts issuing advisory opinions.[7] By definition, if a case is moot, there no longer is an actual controversy between adverse litigants. Also, if events subsequent to the initiation of the lawsuit have resolved the matter, then a federal court decision is not likely to have any effect. Hence, neither of the prerequisites for federal court adjudication is fulfilled.[8]

---

§2.7 [1] United States Parole Commn. v. Geraghty, 445 U.S. 388, 397 (1980), quoting Henry Monaghan, Constitutional Adjudication: The Who and When, 82 Yale L.J. 1363, 1384 (1973).

[2] Dove v. United States, 423 U.S. 325 (1976).

[3] See, e.g., United Airlines, Inc. v. McDonald, 432 U.S. 385, 400 (1977) (Powell, J., dissenting) ("The settlement of an individual claim typically moots any issues associated with it."); Stewart v. Southern Ry., 315 U.S. 283 (1942). Settlement must be distinguished from a situation in which the defendant voluntarily agrees to refrain from a practice, but is free to resume it at any time. As discussed below, the latter does not moot the case.

[4] See, e.g., Burke v. Barnes, 479 U.S. 361, 365 (1987) (bill expired during pendency of appeal, rendering moot the question of whether the president's pocket veto prevented bill from becoming law); United States Dept. of Treasury v. Galioto, 477 U.S. 556 (1986) (amendment to federal statute rendered the case moot); Kremens v. Bartley, 431 U.S. 119, 128 (1977) (statutes providing for commitment of minors to institutions were repealed, rendering the case moot); but see City of Mesquite v. Aladdin's Castle, Inc., 455 U.S. 283 (1982) (repeal of a city ordinance was not moot where the city was likely to reenact it after completion of legal proceedings), discussed below.

[5] See, e.g., Murphy v. Hunt, 455 U.S. 478, 481-482 (1982) (challenge to a state law denying bail to those accused of violent sex crimes dismissed as moot after the defendant's conviction).

[6] Board of School Commrs. v. Jacobs, 420 U.S. 128, 130 (1975).

[7] See, e.g., Genesis Healthcare Corp. v. Symczyk, 133 S. Ct. 1523 (2013); SEC v. Medical Comm. for Human Rights, 404 U.S. 403, 406 (1972); Hall v. Beals, 396 U.S. 45, 48 (1969). But see Honig v. Doe, 484 U.S. 305, 330 (1988) (Rehnquist, C.J., concurring) (arguing that mootness doctrine is primarily prudential and not constitutionally based).

[8] See Church of Scientology of California v. United States, 506 U.S. 9, 11 (1992).

Additionally, many of the values underlying the justiciability doctrines also explain the mootness rules. Mootness avoids unnecessary federal court decisions, limiting the role of the judiciary and saving the courts' institutional capital for cases truly requiring decisions.[9] On the other hand, mootness might not save judicial resources; nor is it necessary to ensure a concrete factual setting in which to decide an issue. When a case is dismissed on appeal, there is a fully developed record and an opportunity for a definitive resolution of an issue. Dismissing such a case as moot might cause the same question to be litigated in many other courts until it is finally resolved by the Supreme Court.[10]

Perhaps it is because of these competing policy considerations that the Supreme Court has spoken of "the flexible character of the Article III mootness doctrine."[11] This flexibility is manifested in four exceptions to the mootness doctrine. Cases are not dismissed as moot if there are secondary or "collateral" injuries; if the issue is deemed a wrong capable of repetition yet evading review; if the defendant voluntarily ceases an allegedly illegal practice but is free to resume it at any time; and if it is a properly certified class action suit. These exceptions are discussed below.

Procedural Issues

Procedurally, mootness can be raised by a federal court on its own at any stage of the proceedings.[12] If a case is deemed moot by the United States Supreme Court, the Court will vacate the lower court's decision and remand the case for dismissal.[13] By vacating the lower court's decision, the Supreme Court leaves the legal issue unresolved for future cases to decide.

In *U.S. Bancorp Mortgage Co. v. Banner Mall Partnership*, the Court held that vacatur of a lower court opinion is not appropriate when a voluntary settlement of an underlying dispute makes a case moot.[14] The Court recognized that allowing such vacating of lower court opinions might facilitate settlements as losing parties may choose to settle in order to vacate an unfavorable opinion that could harm their position in future litigation. Also, vacating the lower court opinion could

---

[9] *See, e.g.*, Firefighter's Local 1784 v. Stotts, 467 U.S. 561, 596 (1984) (Blackmun, J., dissenting) (a central purpose of mootness doctrine is to avoid an unnecessary ruling on the merits).

[10] Chief Justice Rehnquist urged a new exception to the mootness doctrine for cases that become moot while pending before the Supreme Court. *See* Honig v. Doe, 484 U.S. 305, 330 (1988).

[11] United States Parole Commn. v. Geraghty, 445 U.S. at 400. For an excellent argument that mootness should be regarded as prudential and not constitutional, *see* Evan Lee, Deconstitutionalizing Justiciability: The Example of Mootness, 105 Harv. L. Rev. 605 (1992). Others argue that it is partially a prudential doctrine. *See, e.g.*, Matthew I. Hall, The Partially Prudential Doctrine of Mootness, 77 Geo. Wash. L. Rev. 562 (2009).

[12] *See, e.g.*, North Carolina v. Rice, 404 U.S. 244, 246 (1971).

[13] United States v. Munsingwear, Inc., 340 U.S. 36, 39 (1950) ("The established practice of the Court in dealing with a civil case from a court in the federal system which has become moot while on its way here or pending our decision on the merits is to reverse or vacate the judgment below and remand with a direction to dismiss.").

[14] 513 U.S. 18 (1994).

prevent an erroneous decision from remaining on the books. Nonetheless, the Court unanimously held that voluntary settlement does not justify vacatur of a lower court opinion. Nothing about the settlement undermines the reasoning of the lower court and warrants the vacating of its decision.[15]

Overview of the Exceptions to the Mootness Doctrine

Most of the cases dealing with the mootness issue have focused on the exceptions to the mootness doctrine. These are situations where a federal court should not dismiss a case as moot even though the plaintiff's injuries have been resolved. The common issue concerning each of these exceptions is whether the policy considerations served by them justify allowing review in a case where there is not an actual dispute between adverse litigants and where a favorable court decision will not effect a change. On the one hand, critics of these exceptions might argue that expediency does not justify a departure from Article III and that the Court wrongly has been much more flexible in carving exceptions to mootness than it has been in dealing with parallel doctrines such as standing. But others might argue that important policy objectives are served by the exceptions and that the exceptions effectuate the underlying purpose of Article III in ensuring judicial review of allegedly illegal practices.

§2.7.2   Exceptions to the Mootness Doctrine: Collateral Consequences

The first exception occurs when a secondary or "collateral" injury survives after the plaintiff's primary injury has been resolved. Although this is referred to as an exception to the mootness doctrine,[16] actually the case is not moot because some injury remains that could be redressed by a favorable federal court decision.

Criminal Cases

For example, a challenge to a criminal conviction is not moot, even after the defendant has completed the sentence and is released from custody, when the defendant continues to face adverse consequences of the criminal conviction. Criminal convictions, especially for felonies, cause the permanent loss of voting privileges in many states, prevent individuals from obtaining certain occupational licenses, and increase the severity of sentences if there is a future offense. Thus, the Court has concluded that even if the primary injury, incarceration, no longer exists, the secondary or collateral harms are sufficient to prevent the case from being dismissed on mootness grounds.

---

[15] *See* Jill E. Fisch, Rewriting History: The Propriety of Eradicating Prior Decisional Law Through Settlement and Vacatur, 76 Cornell L. Rev. 589 (1991).

[16] Sibron v. New York, 392 U.S. 40, 53 (1968) (describing collateral consequences as an exception to the mootness doctrine).

In *Sibron v. New York*, two defendants challenged the legality of evidence seized from them during a stop-and-frisk.[17] Although the defendants had completed their six-month sentences, the Court held that their challenge to the constitutionality of their convictions was not moot. The Court explained that "the obvious fact of life [is] that most criminal convictions do in fact entail adverse collateral legal consequences. The mere possibility that this will be the case is enough to preserve a criminal case from ending ignominiously in the limbo of mootness."[18]

Similarly, in *Carafas v. LaVallee*, a defendant convicted of burglary in state court was allowed to present a petition for habeas corpus in federal court challenging the constitutionality of his conviction despite the fact that he had been unconditionally released from custody.[19] The Court stated that "[i]n consequence of his conviction, he cannot engage in certain businesses; he cannot serve as an official of a labor union for a specified time; he cannot vote in any election held in New York State; he cannot serve as a juror. On account of these 'collateral consequences,' the case is not moot."[20]

The Court has explained that a challenge to a criminal conviction should be dismissed as moot "only if it is shown that there is no possibility that any collateral legal consequences will be imposed on the basis of the challenged conviction."[21] Therefore, a defendant convicted of two crimes, but sentenced to concurrent sentences, may challenge one of the convictions even though its reversal would not hasten his or her release from custody.[22] The Court has reasoned that the additional conviction might have future collateral consequences, such as by increasing the severity of a subsequent sentence if there is a new offense.

In fact, because the government has an interest in ensuring the conviction of criminals, the Supreme Court allows the state to continue to appeal matters even if the defendant has completed his or her sentence. In *Pennsylvania v. Mimms*, the Supreme Court granted the state's certiorari petition despite the fact that the defendant had completed the maximum three-year sentence.[23] The Court said that preventing the state from imposing the collateral consequences of a criminal conviction is of sufficient interest to the state to keep the case from being dismissed as moot.

Generally a challenge to a particular sentence, as opposed to a challenge to the conviction, is moot after the sentence has been served because there are no collateral consequences to the sentence itself. For example, in *North Carolina v. Rice*, a defendant contended that the state courts acted unconstitutionally in increasing his sentence on appeal.[24] The Supreme Court dismissed the case as moot because the additional sentence had been served by the time the case came before the Court.

---

[17] 392 U.S. 40 (1968).
[18] *Id.* at 55 (citations omitted).
[19] 391 U.S. 234 (1968).
[20] *Id.* at 237-238.
[21] Sibron v. New York, 392 U.S. at 57.
[22] *See, e.g.*, Benton v. Maryland, 395 U.S. 784, 791 (1969).
[23] 434 U.S. 106, 108 (1977); *see also* United States v. Villamonte-Marquez, 462 U.S. 579, 581 (1983).
[24] 404 U.S. 244, 246 (1977).

Civil Cases

In civil litigation, a case is not moot, even if the plaintiff's primary injury is resolved, so long as the plaintiff continues to suffer some harm that a favorable court decision would remedy. For instance, a plaintiff seeking both reinstatement and back pay for alleged discrimination can continue to pursue the case even if reinstatement is granted or no longer sought.[25] The claim for back pay is adequate to keep the case from being moot. In fact, even if the amount of money damages sought is quite small, it is still sufficient to present a live controversy to the federal court. The Supreme Court explained: "Undoubtedly, not much money and seniority are involved, but the amount of money and seniority at stake does not determine mootness. As long as the parties have a concrete interest in the outcome of the litigation, the case is not moot."[26]

Likewise, a plaintiff seeking both injunctive relief and money damages can continue to pursue the case, even after the request for an equitable remedy is rendered moot.[27] For example, the Supreme Court ruled that the release of plaintiffs on parole did not moot their suit, when in addition to a release from custody, they also sought money damages for the alleged violation of their constitutional rights.[28]

More generally, so long as the federal court's decision is likely to have some effect in the future, the case should not be dismissed even though the plaintiff's primary injury has passed. The Supreme Court's decision in *Super Tire Engineering Co. v. McCorkle* is particularly instructive.[29] During a labor strike, the employers whose plants were struck filed a lawsuit challenging a state law that permitted strikers to receive public assistance through state welfare programs. Although the strike ended before the completion of the federal court litigation, the Court held that the case was not moot because a federal court decision could substantially affect future labor-management negotiations.[30] Thus, while a plaintiff's emotional concern about the outcome of the case is not enough to keep it from being moot, any continuing injury means that there is a live controversy.

---

[25] *See, e.g.,* Firefighter's Local 1784 v. Stotts, 467 U.S. 561, 568 (1984).

[26] *Id.* at 571.

[27] Havens Realty Corp. v. Coleman, 455 U.S. 363, 370-371 (1982) (case not moot because plaintiffs would be entitled to $400 liquidated damages if defendants found liable); University of Texas v. Camenisch, 451 U.S. 390, 393 (1981) (case not moot when dispute for overpayment of money remained).

[28] Board of Pardons v. Allen, 482 U.S. 369, 371 n.1 (1987).

[29] 416 U.S. 115 (1974).

[30] The Court also reasoned that the case presented a wrong capable of repetition yet evading review, which is discussed below.

§2.7.3 Exceptions to the Mootness Doctrine: Wrongs Capable of Repetition Yet Evading Review

Definition

Perhaps the most important exception to the mootness doctrine is for "wrongs capable of repetition yet evading review." As the title of this exception implies, some injuries occur and are over so quickly that they always will be moot before the federal court litigation process is completed. When such injuries are likely to recur, the federal court may continue to exercise jurisdiction over the plaintiff's claim notwithstanding the fact that it has become moot.[31]

Roe v. Wade presented a paradigm example of a wrong capable of repetition yet evading review.[32] The plaintiff was pregnant when she filed her complaint challenging the constitutionality of a state law prohibiting abortion. However, obviously, by the time the case reached the Supreme Court, her pregnancy was completed and she no longer sought an abortion. Hence, her case was moot; intervening circumstances meant that there no longer was a live controversy between the plaintiff and the state. But the Supreme Court refused a request to dismiss the case on mootness grounds. The Court explained that the duration of pregnancy was inherently likely to be shorter than the time required for federal court litigation. The Court concluded that the challenge to the state laws prohibiting abortions "truly could be 'capable of repetition yet evading review.' "[33]

Requirements for the Exception

Two criteria must be met in order for a matter to fit within the wrong capable of repetition yet evading review exception to the mootness doctrine. In a recent case, the Supreme Court explained: That "exception applies where '(1) the challenged action is in its duration too short to be fully litigated prior to cessation or expiration; and (2) there is a reasonable expectation that the same complaining party will be subject to the same action again.' "[34]

First, the injury must be of a type likely to happen to the plaintiff again. In other words, an injury is not deemed capable of repetition merely because someone, at some time, might suffer the same harm; there must be a reasonable chance that it will happen again to the plaintiff. The Court explained that there must be a "reasonable expectation that the same complaining party would be subjected to the same action again."[35] For instance, in *Murphy v. Hunt*, a defendant's challenge

---

[31] A seminal case articulating this exception to the mootness doctrine was Southern Pac. Terminal Co. v. ICC, 219 U.S. 498, 514-515 (1911) (allowing a challenge to an Interstate Commerce Commission order that had expired because the Court concluded that consideration of such orders should not be defeated, "as they might be, . . . by short term orders, capable of repetition, yet evading review").

[32] 410 U.S. 113 (1973).

[33] *Id.* at 125 (citations omitted).

[34] Davis v. Federal Election Commn., 554 U.S. 724 (2008).

[35] Weinstein v. Bradford, 423 U.S. 147, 149 (1975).

to a state law denying pretrial bail to those accused of violent sex crimes was dismissed as moot after the defendant's conviction.[36] The Court said that the case did not fit into the exception for wrongs capable of repetition yet evading review because there was no likelihood that the defendant would be arrested for a similar offense and denied bail in the future. The Court noted that "there must be a reasonable expectation or a demonstrated probability that the same controversy will recur involving the same complaining party. We detect no such level of probability in this case."[37] But it must be noted that in other cases — such as in *Roe* and in the election cases described below — the Court did not specifically inquire whether the plaintiff in particular was likely to suffer the same harm in the future.

Second, it must be a type of injury of inherently limited duration so that it is likely to always become moot before federal court litigation is completed. For example, a ten-day restraining order on a protest demonstration was deemed to be capable of repetition but always likely to evade review because litigation never would be completed before the ten days expired.[38]

One area where the Court consistently has found cases to fit within the exception for wrongs capable of repetition yet evading review concerns court orders imposing prior restraints on speech. For example, in *Nebraska Press Association v. Stuart*, a trial judge imposed a limit on newspaper and broadcast reports concerning a pending murder trial.[39] Although the judge's order expired when the jury was empaneled, the Supreme Court held that it was a wrong capable of repetition yet evading review because similar orders might be imposed on the media again in the future, and they would escape judicial scrutiny because the restraints would be lifted long before the appellate process was completed.[40] Likewise, challenges to a court's order excluding the press from a pretrial hearing and to a court's order excluding the press from trial in a case involving a victim under age 18 were deemed to fit within this exception to the mootness doctrine.[41] In each instance, the Court reasoned that the media might be subjected to similar orders in the future and that the orders transpired so quickly as to prevent judicial review before they expired.

Another area where the Court often has applied this exception to the mootness doctrine is for challenges to election laws. Frequently, the election is over before the litigation is completed. For example, in *Moore v. Ogilvie*, a suit was brought challenging a state law requiring the obtaining of a certain number of signatures in order for an independent candidate to get on the ballot to run for president or vice president.[42] Although the election was held before the case was heard by the

---

[36] 455 U.S. 478 (1982).

[37] *Id.* at 482 (citations omitted).

[38] Carroll v. President & Commrs. of Princess Anne Cnty., 393 U.S. 175 (1968), discussed in §11.2.3.3.

[39] 427 U.S. 539 (1976), discussed in §11.2.3.3.

[40] *Id.* at 546.

[41] Globe Newspaper Co. v. Superior Court, 457 U.S. 596, 602 (1982) (exclusion from trial of victim of sex crime who was under age 18); Gannett Co. v. DePasquale, 443 U.S. 368, 377 (1979) (exclusion from pretrial hearing).

[42] 394 U.S. 814 (1969).

Supreme Court, the Court held that the case was not moot because it presented a "wrong capable of repetition, yet evading review."[43] The Court explained that the plaintiffs might again seek access to the ballot for independent candidates and that the matter would always escape review because litigation could never be completed before the election.

Similarly, in *First National Bank of Boston v. Bellotti*, the plaintiffs were allowed to pursue their challenge to a law prohibiting corporations from spending money to influence voters with regard to pending ballot initiatives.[44] The Court reasoned that the issue would likely arise in the future and there would never be enough time for the matter to be fully litigated, appealed, and decided before the completion of the election.

In *Dunn v. Blumstein*, a voter was allowed to continue to challenge a state law imposing a one-year residency requirement in the state in order to vote in state elections.[45] Although the plaintiff could vote by the time the case got to the Supreme Court, the Court held that the matter was a wrong capable of repetition yet evading review and thus should not be dismissed on mootness grounds.

In *Norman v. Reed*, the Court applied this exception to the mootness doctrine to allow a challenge to a law that created obstacles for new parties getting on the ballot.[46] Although the challenge concerned the ability to get on the ballot for an election held in 1990, the Court concluded that "[t]here would be every reason to expect the same parties to generate a similar, future controversy subject to identical time constraints if we should fail to resolve the constitutional issues that arose in 1990."[47] Thus, it was justiciable as a wrong capable of repetition yet evading review.

Likewise, in *Davis v. Federal Election Commission*, the Court allowed a challenge to a provision of the Federal Election Act to continue after the election was over.[48] Jack Davis twice ran for Congress, in 2004 and 2006, and spent enough of his own money for his campaign as to trigger the so-called millionaire's provision of the McCain-Feingold Bipartisan Campaign Finance Reform Act of 2001. Under this provision, the opponent of a candidate who spends more than $350,000 of his or her own money receives the benefit of higher contribution and expenditure limits. Davis filed his lawsuit challenging this provision while running for office, but the Supreme Court did not hear the case until after the election was over. Nonetheless, the Court unanimously rejected the government's argument that the case was moot (though it divided 5-4 in striking down the provision as violating the First Amendment). The Court found that this case was like others in which it held that challenges to laws regulating elections could continue after the elections were over.

But not all election cases fit within this exception to the mootness doctrine. For example, in *Illinois State Board of Elections v. Socialist Workers Party*, the plaintiffs

---

[43] *Id.* at 816 (citation omitted).
[44] 435 U.S. 765, 774 (1978).
[45] 405 U.S. 330 (1972).
[46] 502 U.S. 279 (1992).
[47] *Id.* at 288.
[48] 554 U.S. 724 (2008).

challenged actions by the State Board of Elections that interfered with their getting on the ballot.[49] The Court held that the case was moot after the election was completed because there was "no evidence creating a reasonable expectation that the . . . Board will repeat its purportedly unauthorized actions in subsequent elections."[50]

Golden v. Zwickler is even more difficult to reconcile with the other election cases.[51] In *Golden*, the plaintiff filed a lawsuit in 1966 challenging a New York statute prohibiting the distribution of handbills that did not state the identity of the author. The plaintiff wanted to distribute such anonymous leaflets in connection with the 1966 congressional election. The election was completed before the matter was fully resolved in the courts, but the plaintiff maintained that there was still a live controversy because he wanted to distribute anonymous handbills again in 1968. The Supreme Court deemed the case moot. The Court said that it was speculative whether the congressman whom the plaintiff sought to campaign for would run again.[52]

The question is whether it was more speculative that the plaintiff in *Golden* would want to distribute anonymous leaflets in the future than it was in *Moore v. Ogilvie* that the plaintiffs there would want to qualify as independent candidates for the ballot in the future. Was it more speculative in *Socialist Workers Party* that the plaintiffs would be frustrated in gaining access to the ballot than it was in *Bellotti* that the corporation would want to spend money in the future to oppose ballot initiatives?

In other words, the election cases reflect that the "wrong capable of repetition yet evading review exception" requires a court to determine that there is a sufficient likelihood that the harm will recur. But the courts have a great deal of discretion in deciding what is sufficient.

Perhaps the case best illustrating this discretion is *DeFunis v. Odegaard*.[53] The plaintiff, a white male, applied for admission to the University of Washington Law School and was denied acceptance. He sued the school, contending that he was discriminated against because of the school's preferential treatment of minority candidates. The trial court issued a preliminary injunction admitting the plaintiff to law school while the case was pending. By the time the case reached the United States Supreme Court, the plaintiff was in his final year of school and the school stipulated that the plaintiff would be allowed to complete his studies regardless of the outcome of the litigation. The Supreme Court held that the case was moot because "the controversy between the parties has thus clearly ceased to be definite and concrete and no longer touches the legal relations of parties having adverse legal interests."[54]

Some criticize the Court for not finding the case to constitute a wrong capable of repetition yet evading review. Professor David Currie quotes one critic as

[49] 440 U.S. 173 (1979).
[50] *Id.* at 187.
[51] 394 U.S. 103 (1969).
[52] *Id.* at 109-110.
[53] 416 U.S. 312 (1974).
[54] *Id.* at 316-317.

remarking that *DeFunis* "announced a new principle: 'Difficult cases are moot.' "[55] On the other hand, the Court explained that there was no chance that DeFunis again would be subjected to the law school admissions process. Moreover, there was no reason to believe that the issue would evade review because not every challenger would obtain a preliminary injunction securing law school attendance while the case was pending.[56]

In sum, a case is not dismissed, although the plaintiff's claim is moot, if the injury is one likely to recur and if the injury is of an inherently short duration that would make complete federal court review impossible. Courts have substantial discretion in deciding what is a sufficient likelihood of future injury or a sufficiently short time span for the injury to justify invoking this exception.

§2.7.4 Exceptions to the Mootness Doctrine: Voluntary Cessation

Exception Defined

A case is not to be dismissed as moot if the defendant voluntarily ceases the allegedly improper behavior but is free to return to it at any time. Only if there is no reasonable chance that the defendant could resume the offending behavior is a case deemed moot on the basis of voluntary cessation.[57]

The Court explained these principles in *United States v. W.T. Grant Co.*[58] The United States sued to enjoin a practice of several corporations having similar boards of directors; the government claimed that the interlocking directorates violated federal antitrust laws. In response to the suit, the defendants said that they had eliminated the interlocking directorships and would not resume the practice. The Supreme Court said that this was not sufficient to justify dismissal of the case because the "defendant is free to return to his old ways."[59] The Court stated that "voluntary cessation of allegedly illegal conduct does not deprive the tribunal of power to hear and determine the case, i.e., does not make the case moot."[60] The Court said that "[t]he case may nevertheless be moot if the defendant can demonstrate that there is no reasonable expectation that the wrong will be repeated. The burden is a heavy one."[61] The Court said the defendants'

---

[55] David Currie, Federal Courts: Cases and Materials 77 n.3 (4th ed. 1990).

[56] 416 U.S. at 316.

[57] *See* Friends of the Earth v. Laidlaw, 528 U.S. 167, 174 (2000).

[58] 345 U.S. 629 (1953). *See also* United States v. Concentrated Phosphate Export Assn., 393 U.S. 199, 203 (1968) (citations omitted) (case not moot where defendant is "free to return to his old ways").

[59] *Id.* at 632.

[60] *Id.*

[61] *Id.* at 633 (citations omitted). See Iron Arrow Honor Socy. v. Heckler, 464 U.S. 67 (1983) (an exclusively male honorary society on campus sought to enjoin the Department of Health and Human Services from requiring the university to exclude it; while the case was pending the university announced its decision to ban the club, regardless of the government's decision, rendering the case moot); Preiser v. Newkirk, 422 U.S. 395, 401-402 (1975) (case challenging transfer of prisoner to a medium or maximum security prison dismissed as moot because he had been moved back to a minimum security unit and there was no likelihood that the wrong would be repeated).

promise to not resume the offending practice is not enough to meet this burden and render the case moot.

The Court reaffirmed the narrowness of this exception in *Friends of the Earth, Inc. v. Laidlaw*.[62] Environmental groups brought a lawsuit pursuant to a citizen suit provision of the Clean Water Act (CWA) against the holder of a National Pollutant Discharge Elimination System (NPDES) permit, alleging that it was violating mercury discharge limits. The plaintiffs sought declaratory and injunctive relief, civil penalties, costs, and attorneys' fees. The defendant sought to have the case dismissed as moot on the ground that it had changed its conduct and complied with the permit requirements and had closed one of the facilities.

The Court reiterated that voluntary changes in behavior by a defendant are not sufficient to make a case moot because the defendant would be free to resume the behavior once the case was dismissed. Justice Ginsburg, writing for the Court, stated: "[T]he standard we have announced for determining whether a case has been mooted by the defendant's voluntary conduct is stringent: 'A case might become moot if subsequent events made it absolutely clear that the allegedly wrongful behavior could not reasonably be expected to recur.' The 'heavy burden of persua[ding]' the court that the challenged conduct cannot reasonably be expected to start up again lies with the party asserting mootness."[63] Indeed, Justice Ginsburg's statement of the test makes it clear that this is a very heavy burden: "[A] defendant claiming that its voluntary compliance moots a case bears the formidable burden of showing that it is absolutely clear the allegedly wrongful behavior could not reasonably be expected to recur."[64] This is quite different from standing where the burden is on the plaintiff to show that the constitutional and prudential requirements are met.[65] The Court, in *Laidlaw*, found that the defendant failed to meet its heavy burden and refused to dismiss the case based on its voluntary changes in behavior.

An interesting application of this exception involved a party that had prevailed in the lower court making the case moot while it was pending in the Supreme Court. In *City of Erie v. Pap's A.M.*,[66] the defendant, the owner of a nude dancing establishment, successfully challenged a city ordinance prohibiting public nudity that was adopted to close that business. While the case was pending in the Supreme Court, the business closed and the defendant moved for the Court to dismiss the matter on mootness grounds. The Court refused and said that the case was not moot because the company still had the license for the business and could reopen it at any time and also because the city continued to be injured by the injunction of the ordinance entered by the state court.[67] The defendant also said that he was 72 years old and retired. The Court said that this was not sufficient: "Several members of this Court can attest, however, that the 'advanced age' of Pap's owner, 72, does

---

[62] 528 U.S. 167 (2000).
[63] *Id.* at 189 (citation omitted).
[64] *Id.* at 190.
[65] *Id.*
[66] 529 U.S. 277 (2000).
[67] *Id.* at 287.

not make it 'absolutely clear' that a life of quiet retirement is his only reasonable expectation."[68]

Statutory Change

Usually, a statutory change is enough to render a case moot, even though the legislature possesses the power to reinstate the allegedly invalid law after the lawsuit is dismissed. For example, in *Kremens v. Bartley*, the state repealed statutes challenged as unconstitutional in that they permitted involuntary commitment of juveniles.[69] The Supreme Court said that the legislative action made the case moot. Likewise, in *Massachusetts v. Oakes*, the Court dismissed an overbreadth challenge to a Massachusetts law prohibiting nude photography of minors.[70] The law was amended while the case was pending, and the Court ruled that "overbreadth analysis is inappropriate if the statute being challenged has been amended or repealed."[71]

However, the Court also has held that a repeal of a challenged law does not render a case moot if there is a reasonable possibility that the government would reenact the law if the proceedings were dismissed. In *City of Mesquite v. Aladdin's Castle, Inc.*, a city law limited licensing of video arcades and amusement centers.[72] The plaintiff challenged the ordinance as being unconstitutionally vague in prohibiting licensing of operations that have "connections with criminal elements." The city repealed this language from the ordinance while the case was pending. Nonetheless, the Court held that the case was not moot. Justice Stevens, writing for the majority, explained: "It is well settled that a defendant's voluntary cessation of a challenged practice does not deprive a federal court of its power to determine the legality of the practice. . . . In this case the City's repeal of the objectionable language would not preclude it from reenacting precisely the same provision if the District Court's judgment were vacated."[73]

Similarly, in *Northeastern Florida Contractors v. Jacksonville*, the Court refused to dismiss as moot a challenge to a city ordinance that provided preference in contracting for minority-owned businesses.[74] The Court explained that "[t]here is no mere risk that Jacksonville will repeat its allegedly wrongful conduct; it already has done so. Nor does it matter that the new ordinance differs in certain respects from the old one. . . . [I]f that were the rule, a defendant could moot a case by repealing the challenged statute and replacing it with one that differs only in some insignificant respect."[75] The Court said that the new statute posed the same basic constitutional question, and thus the repeal of the earlier law did not moot the case.

---

[68] *Id.* at 288.

[69] 431 U.S. 119, 132 (1977).

[70] 491 U.S. 576 (1989).

[71] *Id.* at 582. *See also* Lewis v. Continental Bank Corp., 494 U.S. 472 (1990) (change in the law rendered the case moot).

[72] 455 U.S. 283 (1982).

[73] *Id.* at 289.

[74] 508 U.S. 656 (1993). The standing aspects of the case are discussed in §2.5.3.

[75] *Id.* at 662.

The difficulty is determining why in some situations a legislative repeal is deemed to make a case moot, yet in other cases it does not. In all instances, the legislature is free to reenact the law. In *Aladdin's Castle*, the Court said that "[t]he test for mootness in cases such as this is a stringent one. Mere voluntary cessation of allegedly illegal conduct does not moot a case. . . . A case might become moot if subsequent events made it absolutely clear that the allegedly wrongful behavior could not reasonably be expected to recur."[76] Yet in other cases described above, the Court concluded that legislative repeal was enough to make a case moot, although the law could have been readopted after the conclusion of the legal proceedings. The key appears to be that cases will not be dismissed as moot if the Court believes that there is a likelihood of reenactment of a substantially similar law if the lawsuit is dismissed.

Compliance with a Court Order

Compliance with a court order renders a case moot only if there is no possibility that the allegedly offending behavior will resume once the order expires or is lifted. For example, a case was not moot when a court order caused a union to end its boycott because the union could resume the boycott as soon as the order was removed.[77] Similarly, the voluntary cessation exception was applied to prevent dismissal of a case when a union stopped its picketing in response to a court injunction, but contested the constitutionality of that injunction and wished to challenge allegedly illegal harassment of its members.[78]

Vitek v. Jones illustrates the inability of court orders to render a case moot where the offending practices can resume if the orders are lifted.[79] In *Vitek*, the plaintiffs challenged the ability of state prisons to transfer prisoners to mental hospitals without providing adequate notice and an opportunity for a hearing. A court permanently enjoined these transfers imposed without due process protections. Although the transfers halted, the Court held that the case was not moot because "it is not absolutely clear absent the injunction that the allegedly wrongful behavior could not reasonably be expected to recur."[80]

But a case can be dismissed as moot if a court order produces a change in behavior and it is deemed unlikely that the offending conduct will resume. *County of Los Angeles v. Davis* is instructive.[81] The plaintiffs, representing present and future black and Mexican-American applicants to the Los Angeles County Fire Department, brought a class action suit challenging alleged discriminatory hiring practices. The district court found a violation of federal civil rights statutes and permanently enjoined the discriminatory practices. The fire department complied with

---

[76] 455 U.S. at 283, 289.

[77] Bakery Drivers v. Wagshal, 333 U.S. 437 (1948).

[78] Alice v. Medrano, 416 U.S. 802, 810 (1974).

[79] 445 U.S. 480 (1980). The procedural due process issues raised in *Vitek* are discussed in §7.4.2.

[80] *Id.* at 487 (citations omitted).

[81] 440 U.S. 625 (1979).

the injunction, discarding its preemployment screening test and hiring many new minority applicants.

The Supreme Court held that the case was moot. The Court explained that a case may become moot if "it can be said with assurance that there is no reasonable expectation that the alleged violation will recur, [and] interim relief or events have completely and irrevocably eradicated the effects of the alleged violation."[82] The Court said that the defendant had eliminated the use of the invalidated civil service examination and showed no propensity for reinstituting it and that the defendant had changed its hiring so that more than 50 percent of new recruits were racial minorities. As such, the Court deemed the case moot.

In short, under the voluntary cessation exception to the mootness doctrine the central question is whether the defendant has the ability to resort to the allegedly improper behavior that was voluntarily stopped. Only if the defendant can show that there is no reasonable chance that the conduct can resume should a federal court dismiss a case as moot when a defendant voluntarily halts a challenged practice.

§2.7.5   Exceptions to the Mootness Doctrine: Class Actions

The Supreme Court has taken a particularly flexible approach to the mootness doctrine in class action suits. In a series of cases, the Supreme Court has held that a properly certified class action suit may continue even if the named plaintiff's claims are rendered moot. The Court has reasoned that the "class of unnamed persons described in the certification acquired a legal status separate from the interest asserted by the [plaintiff]," and thus so long as the members of the class have a live controversy, the case can continue.[83] Furthermore, the Court has concluded that a plaintiff may continue to appeal the denial of class certification even after his or her particular claim is mooted.

Properly Certified Class Action Not Moot

Sosna v. Iowa was the first major departure from traditional mootness rules for class action suits.[84] The plaintiff, Mrs. Sosna, initiated a class action suit challenging an Iowa law requiring residence in the state for one year in order to obtain a divorce from an Iowa court. The class action was properly certified, and the district court ruled against the plaintiffs on the merits. While the appeals were pending, Mrs. Sosna satisfied the durational residency requirement, thus resolving her claim. The Supreme Court, in an opinion by then-Justice Rehnquist, held that the suit was not moot. The Court emphasized that the controversy "remains very much alive for the class of persons she has been certified to represent."[85] The Court

---

[82] *Id.* at 631.

[83] Sosna v. Iowa, 419 U.S. 393, 399 (1975).

[84] *Id.*

[85] *Id.* at 401. The Court also explained that the case could fit into the exception for wrongs capable of repetition yet evading review because of the fact that the residency requirement was shorter than the usual course of litigation. *Id.* at 401 n.9.

explained that a class action suit should not be dismissed on mootness grounds so long as the named plaintiff had a live controversy when the suit was filed, there was a properly certified class action, and there are members of the class whose claims are not moot.

The Supreme Court applied *Sosna* in other cases involving class action suits. For example, in *Gerstein v. Pugh*, a properly certified class action suit challenged the constitutionality of a Florida practice of holding individuals without a judicial hearing determining probable cause.[86] Although the named plaintiff's claim was resolved because the pretrial detention ended, the case was not moot because there was a properly certified class action and the members of the class continued to present a live controversy.

In several cases, decided the same year as *Sosna*, the Supreme Court concluded that the mootness doctrine required the dismissal of class action suits that were not properly certified when the named plaintiff's claim became moot.[87] The underlying rationale seems to be that when there is a properly certified class action, the entire class is the actual plaintiff, and as long as a live controversy exists for some of the plaintiffs, the case should not be deemed moot.

The Court expanded the exception for class action suits in *Franks v. Bowman Transportation Co.*[88] In *Franks*, the plaintiff brought a class action suit challenging alleged employment discrimination. By the time the case came to the Supreme Court, it was clear that the named plaintiff did not have a possible claim of discrimination even though other class members did. The Court said that even if the named plaintiff never had a legitimate claim for relief, a class action is not moot when it was properly certified and when some members continue to have live claims.

Appeals of Denial of Class Certification Not Moot

Sosna, Gerstein, and *Franks* all involved properly certified class actions. The Court first considered noncertified class actions in *United Airlines, Inc. v. McDonald*.[89] There the Court held that a member of the proposed class may intervene to challenge and appeal the denial of class certification after the named plaintiff's claims are mooted.

Subsequently, the Court held that a person seeking to initiate a class action suit may continue to appeal the denial of certification even after his or her own claims are rendered moot. In *United States Parole Commission v. Geraghty*, a prisoner who was denied parole on the basis of the Parole Commission's guidelines sought to bring a class action suit challenging the guidelines.[90] The district court refused

---

[86] 420 U.S. 103 (1975).

[87] *See, e.g.*, Indianapolis School Commrs. v. Jacobs, 420 U.S. 128 (1975); Weinstein v. Bradford, 423 U.S. 147 (1975); *see also* Pasadena City Bd. of Educ. v. Spangler, 427 U.S. 424 (1976); Franks v. Bowman Transportation Co., 424 U.S. 747 (1976).

[88] 424 U.S. 747 (1976).

[89] 432 U.S. 385, 393 (1977).

[90] 445 U.S. 388 (1980).

to certify a class action, and the plaintiff appealed. While the appeal was pending, the plaintiff was released from prison.

Even though a class action never was certified, the Court held that the case was not moot. The Court explained that the members of the proposed class still had a live controversy, justifying continued federal judicial consideration of whether the class should be certified. The Court stated "that an action brought on behalf of a class does not become moot upon expiration of the named plaintiff's substantive claim, even though class certification has been denied. The proposed representative retains a 'personal stake' in obtaining class certification sufficient to assure that Art. III values are not undermined. If the appeal results in a reversal of the class certification denial, and a class subsequently is properly certified, the merits of the class claim then may be adjudicated pursuant to the holding in *Sosna*."[91] Similarly, in *Deposit Guaranty National Bank v. Roper*, decided the same day as *Geraghty*, the Court held that the named plaintiffs in a proposed class action suit could continue to appeal the denial of class certification even after the plaintiffs settled their personal claims.[92] In *Roper*, the plaintiffs sought to bring a class action suit to challenge the interest charged by Bank Americard. The plaintiffs agreed to a settlement that paid them the full sum they claimed as damages. The Court said that the plaintiffs could continue to appeal the denial of class certification. The Court explained that the plaintiffs maintained a "personal stake in the appeal" because they had "a continuing individual interest in the resolution of the class certification question in their desire to shift part of the costs of litigation to those who will share in its benefits if the class is certified and ultimately prevails."[93] The Court explained that other class members had a live controversy, and allowing the settlement to end the litigation would give defendants an incentive to "buy off" named plaintiffs in class action litigation.[94]

The exception for class action suits makes sense in that it focuses on the interests of the class, rather than simply looking to the named plaintiff's claims. As long as the class presents a live controversy, the status of any particular member's claim is irrelevant. Thus, the Court has properly concluded that a properly certified class action is not moot simply because the named plaintiff's controversy is resolved. Nor should the mootness of the plaintiff's claim prevent an appeal of the denial of class certification. This mootness exception furthers the underlying purposes of the federal rules concerning class actions and is consistent with Article III, because there is an actual dispute between adverse litigants and a favorable federal court decision will make a difference for the class members.

---

[91]   *Id.* at 404.

[92]   445 U.S. 326 (1980).

[93]   *Id.* at 336.

[94]   *Id.* at 339. However, in Genesis Healthcare Corp. v. Symczyk, 133 S. Ct. 1523 (2013), the Court distinguished the class action contest and held that an employee action on behalf of himself "and others similarly situated" is moot when the lone plaintiff's individual claim becomes moot.

§2.8   THE POLITICAL QUESTION DOCTRINE

§2.8.1   *What Is the Political Question Doctrine?*

Definition

The Supreme Court has held that certain allegations of unconstitutional government conduct should not be ruled on by the federal courts even though all of the jurisdictional and other justiciability requirements are met. The Court has said that constitutional interpretation in these areas should be left to the politically accountable branches of government, the president and Congress. In other words, the "political question doctrine" refers to subject matter that the Court deems to be inappropriate for judicial review. Although there is an allegation that the Constitution has been violated, the federal courts refuse to rule and instead dismiss the case, leaving the constitutional question to be resolved in the political process.

Why Is the Political Question Doctrine Confusing?

In many ways, the political question doctrine is the most confusing of the justiciability doctrines. As Professor Martin Redish noted, "[t]he doctrine has always proven to be an enigma to commentators. Not only have they disagreed about its wisdom and validity . . . , but they also have differed significantly over the doctrine's scope and rationale."[1] First, the confusion stems from the fact that the "political question doctrine" is a misnomer; the federal courts deal with political issues all of the time. For example, in *United States v. Nixon*, the Court decided that President Nixon had to comply with a subpoena to produce tapes of presidential conversations that were needed as evidence in a criminal trial—a decision with the ultimate political effect of causing a president to resign.[2] The Supreme Court's direct involvement in the political process long has included ending racial discrimination in political primaries and elections.[3]

Second, the political question doctrine is particularly confusing because the Court has defined it very differently over the course of American history. The Court first spoke of political questions in *Marbury v. Madison*.[4] Chief Justice John Marshall wrote: "By the Constitution of the United States, the President is invested with certain important political powers, in the exercise of which he is to use his own discretion, and is accountable only to his country in his political character

---

§2.8 [1] Martin Redish, Judicial Review and the Political Question, 79 Nw. U. L. Rev. 1031 (1985).

[2] 418 U.S. 683 (1974), discussed in §4.3.

[3] *See, e.g.*, Nixon v. Herndon, 273 U.S. 536 (1927) (declaring unconstitutional racial discrimination in the Democratic political primary in Texas). The Court said that a claim that the matter was a political question because it involved the political process was "little more than a play upon words." *Id.* at 540.

[4] 5 U.S. (1 Cranch) 137 (1803), discussed above in §2.2.

and to his own conscience. The subjects are political. [B]eing entrusted to the executive, the decision of the executive is conclusive. Questions, in their nature political, or which are by the constitution and laws, submitted to the executive can never be made in this court."[5] Chief Justice Marshall contrasted political questions with instances where individual rights were at stake; the latter, according to the Court, never could be political questions.[6]

The Court's definition of political questions in *Marbury v. Madison* was quite narrow. Included only were matters where the president had unlimited discretion, and there was thus no allegation of a constitutional violation. For example, presidents have the choice about whether to sign or veto a bill or who to appoint for a vacancy on the federal judiciary. Because the Constitution vests the president with plenary authority in these areas, there is no basis for a claim of a constitutional violation regardless of how the president acts. But if there is a claim of an infringement of an individual right, in other words, if the plaintiff has standing, there is not a political question under the formulation presented in *Marbury v. Madison*.[7]

In sharp contrast, the political question doctrine now includes instances where individuals allege that specific constitutional provisions have been violated and that they have suffered a concrete injury.[8] The political question doctrine definitely is not limited to instances in which the president is exercising discretion and there is no claim of unconstitutional conduct. But the Court never has explained the differing content given to the term political question; in fact, the Court even invokes *Marbury* in its modern, very different cases.

The *Baker* Criteria and Their Limited Usefulness

Finally, and perhaps most important, the political question doctrine is confusing because of the Court's failure to articulate useful criteria for deciding what subject matter presents a nonjusticiable political question. The classic, oft-quoted statement of the political question doctrine was provided in *Baker v. Carr*.[9] The Court stated:

> Prominent on the surface of any case held to involve a political question is found a textually demonstrable commitment of the issue to a coordinate political department; or a lack of judicially discoverable and manageable standards for resolving it; or the impossibility of deciding without an initial policy determination of a kind clearly for nonjudicial discretion; or the impossibility of a court's undertaking independent resolution without expressing lack of the respect due coordinate

---

[5] *Id.* at 165-170.

[6] *Id.* at 170.

[7] Howard Fink & Mark Tushnet, Federal Jurisdiction: Policy and Practice 231 (2d ed. 1987) ("But notice the effect of *Marbury*'s classification: Standing is just the obverse of political questions. If a litigant claims that an individual right has been invaded, the lawsuit by definition does not involve a political question.").

[8] *See, e.g.*, Luther v. Borden, 48 U.S. (7 How.) 1 (1949) (declaring nonjusticiable a suit brought under the republican form of government clause even though the effect was to leave people in jail who contested the constitutionality of their conviction), discussed below in §2.8.3.

[9] 369 U.S. 186 (1962).

branches of government; or an unusual need for unquestioning adherence to a political decision already made; or the potentiality of embarrassment from multifarious pronouncements by various departments on one question.[10]

Virtually every case considering the political question doctrine quotes this language. But these criteria seem useless in identifying what constitutes a political question. For example, there is no place in the Constitution where the text states that the legislature or executive should decide whether a particular action constitutes a constitutional violation. The Constitution does not mention judicial review, much less limit it by creating "textually demonstrable commitments" to other branches of government. Similarly, most important constitutional provisions are written in broad, open-textured language and certainly do not include "judicially discoverable and manageable standards." The Court also speaks of determinations of a kind "clearly for a nonjudicial determination," but that hardly is a criterion that can be used to separate political questions from justiciable cases.

In other words, it is impossible for a court or a commentator to apply the *Baker v. Carr* criteria to identify what cases are political questions. As such, it hardly is surprising that the doctrine is described as confusing and unsatisfactory.

The political question doctrine can be understood only by examining the specific areas where the Supreme Court has invoked it. Specifically, the Court has considered the political question doctrine in the following areas: the republican form of government clause and the electoral process, foreign affairs, Congress's ability to regulate its internal processes, the process for ratifying constitutional amendments, instances where the federal court cannot shape effective equitable relief, and the impeachment process. Section 2.8.2 considers the basic normative question of whether there should be a political question doctrine. Sections 2.8.3 to 2.8.8 consider, in turn, each of the areas mentioned above.

§2.8.2   *Should There Be a Political Question Doctrine?*

Justifications for the Political Question Doctrine

The underlying normative issue is whether the political question doctrine should exist at all. Defenders of the doctrine make several arguments. First, and most commonly, it is argued that the political question doctrine accords the federal judiciary the ability to avoid controversial constitutional questions and limits the courts' role in a democratic society. Professor Alexander Bickel was the foremost advocate of this position.[11] Professor Bickel wrote:

Such is the foundation, in both intellect and instinct, of the political question doctrine: the Court's sense of lack of capacity, compounded in unequal part of

---

[10] *Id.* at 217.
[11] *See, e.g.,* Alexander Bickel, The Supreme Court, 1960 Term: Foreword: The Passive Virtues, 75 Harv. L. Rev. 40, 46 (1961); Alexander Bickel, The Least Dangerous Branch 184 (1962).

(a)   the strangeness of the issue and its intractability to principled resolution;

(b)   the sheer momentousness of it, which tends to unbalance judicial judgment;

(c)   the anxiety, not so much that the judicial judgment will be ignored, as that perhaps it should but will not be;

(d)   finally ("in a mature democracy"), the inner vulnerability, the self-doubt of an institution which is electorally irresponsible and has no earth to draw strength from.[12]

Professor Bickel contended that it was simply better for the federal courts to avoid deciding certain cases, especially so as to preserve what he perceived as the judiciary's fragile political legitimacy.[13] Justice Felix Frankfurter argued, on this basis, that the Court should not have decided whether malapportionment violates the Constitution,[14] and many commentators have suggested that the federal courts should not review impeachment proceedings conducted by Congress because any ruling would jeopardize the Court's credibility and prestige.[15]

A second argument for the political question doctrine is that it allocates decisions to the branches of government that have superior expertise in particular areas. For example, some argue that the Court rightly has treated many constitutional issues concerning foreign policy to be political questions because of the greater information and expertise of the other branches of government.[16]

Third, the political question doctrine is defended on the ground that the federal courts' self-interest disqualifies them from ruling on certain matters. Specifically, it is argued that the courts should not become involved in reviewing the process for ratifying constitutional amendments because amendments are the only way to overturn the Supreme Court's constitutional interpretations.[17] Justice Powell, for example, spoke of the dangers of having the Court "oversee the very constitutional process used to reverse [its] decisions."[18]

Finally, the political question doctrine is justified on separation of powers grounds as minimizing judicial intrusion into the operations of the other branches of government. The argument is that in certain cases an effective remedy would require judicial oversight of day-to-day executive or legislative conduct. For example, a lawsuit contending that there were constitutional deficiencies in training

---

[12] Bickel, *id.*, The Least Dangerous Branch at 184.

[13] *See also* Jesse Choper, Judicial Review and the National Political Process (1980) (arguing that separation of powers and federalism should be deemed political questions and left to the political process so that the federal courts can reserve their institutional legitimacy for individual rights cases).

[14] Baker v. Carr, 369 U.S. at 267 (Frankfurter, J., dissenting), discussed below.

[15] *See, e.g.*, Charles Black, Impeachment: A Handbook (1974) (discussing impeachment as a political question).

[16] *See, e.g.*, Fritz Scharpf, Judicial Review and the Political Question: A Functional Analysis, 75 Yale L.J. 517, 567 (1966).

[17] *See, e.g.*, Laurence Tribe, Constitutional Choices 22-23 (1985) (arguing that challenges to the constitutional amendment process should be treated as a political question).

[18] Quoted in Tribe, *id.* at 23.

the Ohio National Guard was deemed to be a political question because a remedy would involve judicial control and supervision over the Guard's activities.[19]

Criticisms of the Political Question Doctrine

On the other hand, critics, such as Professor Martin Redish, argue that "the political question doctrine should play no role whatsoever in the exercise of the judicial review power."[20] Such critics contend, first, that the judicial role is to enforce the Constitution—that it is inappropriate to leave constitutional questions to the political branches of government.[21] The argument is that matters are placed in a Constitution to insulate them from majoritarian control; judicial review serves to effectuate and uphold the Constitution. Thus, it is inappropriate to relegate constitutional issues to the political branches of government. Politically accountable bodies should not be entrusted to enforce any part of a document that is meant to restrain them.

Second, critics of the political question doctrine question the premise of scholars such as Professor Bickel and Justices such as Felix Frankfurter, who speak of the judiciary's fragile legitimacy. To the contrary, critics contend that the federal courts' credibility is quite robust, that there is no evidence that particular rulings have any effect on the judiciary's legitimacy, and that in any event, the courts' mission should be to uphold the Constitution and not worry about political capital.[22] The argument is that a judiciary that ducks controversial issues to preserve its credibility is likely to avoid judicial review where it is needed most, to restrain highly popular, unconstitutional government actions.

Third, critics of the political question doctrine argue that it confuses deference with abdication. The claim is that in areas where the federal courts lack expertise, they should be more deferential to the other branches of government. Likewise, the courts should be particularly deferential in reviewing the process of ratifying constitutional amendments that seek to overturn the Supreme Court's judgments. But deference need not mean abdication. Many foreign policy questions do not involve matters of expertise, but instead pose interpretive questions like those constantly resolved by the courts.[23] Also, a blatant disregard of the Constitution's requirements—for example, an amendment deemed by Congress to have been ratified even though not approved by the requisite number of states—should not be tolerated by the federal courts.[24] In other words, critics of the political question

[19] Gilligan v. Morgan, 413 U.S. 1 (1973), discussed below.

[20] Redish, *supra* note 1, at 1033; Erwin Chemerinsky, Interpreting the Constitution 99-105 (1987).

[21] Redish, *supra* note 1, at 1045-1046; Chemerinsky, *supra* note 20, at 99-100.

[22] Chemerinsky, *supra* note 20, at 133-138; *see also* Laurence Tribe, American Constitutional Law viii (3d ed. 2000) ("The highest mission of the Supreme Court . . . is not to conserve judicial credibility, but in the Constitution's own phrase, 'to form a more perfect Union.'").

[23] *See* Louis Henkin, Is There a Political Question Doctrine?, 85 Yale L.J. 597 (1976) (arguing against courts finding issues concerning foreign policy to be a political question).

[24] *See* Walter Dellinger, The Legitimacy of Constitutional Change: Rethinking the Amendment Process, 97 Harv. L. Rev. 386 (1983).

doctrine argue that the doctrine's defenders demonstrate only that on the merits, the Court should hesitate in some areas before ruling against the other branches of government; it is wrong to deem those areas to be nonjusticiable.

Is It Constitutional or Prudential?

Perhaps as a reflection of this debate, important questions remain unsettled concerning the political question doctrine. For example, it is uncertain whether the political question doctrine is constitutional, prudential, or both. Could Congress direct the federal courts to adjudicate a matter that the Supreme Court deemed to be a political question? Unlike the other justiciability doctrines, the political question doctrine is not derived from Article III's limitation of judicial power to "cases" and "controversies."

The political question doctrine might be treated as constitutional if it is thought to be based on separation of powers or textual commitments to other branches of government. On the other hand, the doctrine is prudential if it reflects the Court's concerns about preserving judicial credibility and limiting the role of an unelected judiciary in a democratic society.

§2.8.3   The "Republican Form of Government" Clause and Judicial Review of the Electoral Process

Article IV, §4, of the Constitution states that "The United States shall guarantee to every State in this Union a Republican form of government." The Supreme Court consistently has held that cases alleging a violation of this clause present nonjusticiable political questions. Several scholars have urged the Court to reconsider this rule and to find cases under the republican form of government clause to be justiciable.[25] Thus far, the Court has not done so, although Justice O'Connor remarked that "the Court has suggested that perhaps not all claims under the Guarantee Clause present nonjusticiable political questions" and acknowledged that "[c]ontemporary commentators have . . . suggested that courts should address the merits of such claims, at least in some circumstances."[26]

---

[25] *See, e.g.,* Erwin Chemerinsky, Cases Under the Guarantee Clause Should Be Justiciable, 65 U. Colo. L. Rev. 849 (1994); Deborah Merritt, The Guarantee Clause and State Autonomy: Federalism for a Third Century, 88 Colum. L. Rev. 1 (1988) (arguing that the guarantee clause should be seen as a basis for protecting federalism and states' rights from congressional interference); *but see* Ann Althouse, Time for Federal Courts to Enforce the Guarantee Clause?—A Response to Professor Chemerinsky, 65 U. Colo. L. Rev. 881 (1994); Louise Weinberg, Political Questions and the Guarantee Clause, 65 U. Colo. L. Rev. 887 (1994).

[26] New York v. United States, 505 U.S. 144 (1992).

Luther v. Borden

Luther v. Borden is the seminal case.[27] In the 1840s, Rhode Island was the only state without a state constitution. The state governed pursuant to a state charter that had been granted to it by King Charles II in 1663. As a result, in 1840, the Rhode Island legislature was badly malapportioned and controlled by a rural minority. Jamestown, for example, had one representative in the state legislature for every 180 citizens, but Providence had one representative for every 6,000 citizens.

In 1841, a convention met to draft a state constitution. A constitution was proposed and ratified. The existing government, which was sure to lose power under the new document, enacted a law prohibiting the constitution from going into effect. Nonetheless, elections were held—even though the existing government had declared voting in them to be a crime. Relatively few people participated, but a new government was chosen, headed by Thomas Dorr, who was elected governor. Dorr's government met for two days in an abandoned foundry and then disbanded.

In April 1842, a sheriff, Luther Borden, broke into the house of one of the election commissioners, Martin Luther, to search for evidence of illegal participation in the prohibited election. Luther sued Borden for trespassing. Borden claimed that the search was a lawful exercise of government power. Luther, however, contended that Borden acted pursuant to an unconstitutional government's orders; he maintained that the Rhode Island government violated the republican form of government clause.

The Supreme Court held that the case posed a political question that could not be decided by a federal court. The Court stated: "Under this article of the constitution it rests with Congress to decide what government is the established one in a State. For as the United States guarantee to each state a republican government, Congress must necessarily decide what government is established in the State before it can determine whether it is republican or not."[28] The Court also explained that the case posed a political question because if the state's government was declared unconstitutional, then all of its actions would be invalidated, creating chaos in Rhode Island.[29] Additionally, the Court, in siding with Rhode Island, spoke of a lack of criteria for deciding what constitutes a republican form of government.

Luther v. Borden has been followed consistently. There is not a single instance in which the Supreme Court has deemed a state government or state action to violate the republican form of government clause.[30] In *Taylor & Marshall v. Beckham,*

---

[27] 48 U.S. (7 How.) 1 (1849).

[28] 48 U.S. at 10.

[29] *Id.* at 13-14.

[30] There are instances in which the Supreme Court decided cases on the merits under the republican form of government clause, upholding the challenged government action. *See, e.g.,* Forsyth v. Hammond, 166 U.S. 506 (1897); Foster v. Kansas ex rel. Johnson, 112 U.S. 201 (1884); Kennard v. Louisiana ex rel. Morgan, 92 U.S. 480 (1875).

the Court refused to decide a claim that a state's resolution of a disputed gubernatorial race violated the republican form of government clause.[31]

Similarly, in *Pacific States Telephone & Telegraph Co. v. Oregon*, the Court again held that cases under this clause are not justiciable.[32] *Pacific States* involved a challenge to a state law, passed through a voter initiative, that taxed certain corporations. The defendant was a corporation sued by the State of Oregon for failure to pay taxes due under this law. The corporation argued that the statute was unconstitutional because the initiative process violated the republican form of government clause. The claim was that a republican form of government is one in which people elect representatives who then govern; direct democracy was said to be antithetical to a republican government. The Supreme Court held that the matter was not justiciable. The Court said that the issue was "political and governmental, and embraced within the scope of powers conferred upon Congress, and not therefore within the reach of judicial power."[33]

Reapportionment

Following these precedents, the Court declared nonjusticiable the first challenges to malapportioned state legislatures. By the middle of the last century, many state legislatures were badly malapportioned. Legislatures had not been reapportioned after substantial growth in urban areas, with the effect that rural residents were overrepresented and urban dwellers were substantially underrepresented in state legislatures. Legislators who benefited from this system were not about to voluntarily redraw districts at the expense of their seats. Also, the rurally dominated state legislatures drew district lines for electing members of the United States House of Representatives that obviously favored their areas.

In *Colegrove v. Green*, in 1946, the Supreme Court declared nonjusticiable a challenge to the congressional districting in Illinois.[34] In an opinion by Justice Frankfurter, the Court stated: "[T]he appellants ask of this Court what is beyond its competence to grant. [E]ffective working of our government revealed this issue to be of a peculiarly political nature and therefore not fit for judicial determination. Authority for dealing with such problems resides elsewhere."[35] The Court concluded that "[c]ourts ought not to enter this political thicket."[36] Similarly, in *South v. Peters*, in 1950, the Court held that "[f]ederal courts consistently refuse to exercise their equity powers in cases posing political issues arising from a state's geographical distribution of electoral strength among its political subdivisions."[37]

---

[31]   178 U.S. 548 (1900).
[32]   223 U.S. 118 (1912).
[33]   *Id.* at 151.
[34]   328 U.S. 549 (1946).
[35]   *Id.* at 552-554.
[36]   *Id.* at 556.
[37]   339 U.S. 276, 277 (1950).

Only in cases alleging racial discrimination in the drawing of election districts or in holding elections did the Supreme Court approve federal court involvement.[38]

But in 1962, in the landmark decision of *Baker v. Carr*, the Supreme Court deemed justiciable claims that malapportionment violates the equal protection clause.[39] Interestingly, the Court did not overrule *Luther v. Borden*, but instead distinguished cases brought under the equal protection clause from those pursued under the republican form of government clause. Justice Brennan explained that whereas "the Guaranty Clause is not a repository of judicially manageable standards . . . [j]udicial standards under the Equal Protection Clause are well-developed and familiar."[40] This seems to be a fatuous distinction because both clauses are equally vague and the principle of one-person one-vote could have been articulated and enforced under either constitutional provision.[41] Nonetheless, the Court's holding that challenges to malapportionment are justiciable was one of the most important rulings in American history.[42] The political process was not likely to correct the constitutional violation, and judicial review provided democratic rule.[43]

The Supreme Court and lower courts frequently have reaffirmed that challenges to election districts are justiciable. For example, in *United States Department of Commerce v. Montana*, the Court found justiciable a challenge by Montana voters to the method of apportioning members to the United States House of Representatives.[44] The Court unanimously found the challenge to be justiciable, though it concluded that there was no constitutional violation. The Court explained that objections to apportionment by Congress should be treated no differently than challenges to state government districting decisions.

Likewise, the Supreme Court has not hesitated to decide the constitutionality of using race in drawing election districts to increase the likelihood of electing African-American and Latino representatives.[45] Although the Supreme Court acknowledged that "[f]ederal court review of districting legislation represents a serious intrusion on the most vital of local functions," the Court has made it clear that strict scrutiny must be met in order for race to be used as a predominant factor in districting.[46]

---

[38] *See, e.g.*, Gomillion v. Lightfoot, 364 U.S. 339 (1960) (redrawing of Tuskegee, Alabama, districts to disenfranchise blacks); Terry v. Adams, 345 U.S. 461 (1953); Smith v. Allwright, 321 U.S. 649 (1944) (discrimination against blacks in political parties).

[39] 369 U.S. 186 (1962).

[40] *Id.* at 223-226.

[41] *See* Reynolds v. Sims, 377 U.S. 533 (1964) (articulating the one-person one-vote standard), discussed in §10.8.3.

[42] Chief Justice Earl Warren remarked that the most important decisions during his tenure on the Court were those ordering reapportionment. The Warren Court: An Editorial Preface, 67 Mich. L. Rev. 219, 220 (1968).

[43] *See, e.g.*, Louis Pollak, Judicial Power and the Politics of the People, 72 Yale L.J. 81, 88 (1962).

[44] 503 U.S. 442 (1992).

[45] *See, e.g.*, Shaw v. Hunt, 517 U.S. 899 (1996); Bush v. Vera, 517 U.S. 952 (1996); Miller v. Johnson, 515 U.S. 900 (1995); Shaw v. Reno, 509 U.S. 630 (1993), discussed in §9.3.5.3 and §10.8.4.

[46] Miller v. Johnson, 515 U.S. at 915.

Gerrymandering

In *Vieth v. Jubelirer*,[47] the Court dismissed a challenge to partisan gerrymandering and a plurality said that such suits are inherently nonjusticiable political questions. The issue was whether partisan gerrymandering violates equal protection. Republicans controlled the Pennsylvania legislature and they drew election districts to maximize Republican seats. This, of course, is not unique to Republicans or to Pennsylvania. Except in the places where there are independent district commissions, election districts for all levels of government are drawn to maximize seats for the political party drawing the districts.

Earlier, in *Davis v. Bandemer*, the Court held that challenges to gerrymandering are justiciable.[48] But in *Vieth*, the plurality concluded that *Davis* had proved impossible to implement and the plurality opinion, written by Justice Scalia, argued that challenges to partisan gerrymandering are nonjusticiable political questions. Justice Scalia, joined by Chief Justice Rehnquist and Justices O'Connor and Thomas, said that there are no judicially discoverable or manageable standards and no basis for courts to decide when partisan gerrymandering offends the Constitution.

Justice Kennedy, concurring in the judgment, provided the fifth vote for the majority. He agreed to dismiss the case because of the lack of judicially discoverable or manageable standards, but he said that he did not believe that such standards could not be developed in the future. Thus, he disagreed with the majority opinion that challenges to partisan gerrymandering are always political questions; he said that when standards are developed, such cases can be heard. Justices Stevens, Souter, and Breyer wrote dissenting opinions, which Justice Ginsburg joined, arguing that there are standards that courts can implement.

The puzzle is how lower courts should handle challenges to partisan gerrymandering after *Vieth*. The temptation may be to always dismiss such cases as nonjusticiable political questions. But five Justices expressly rejected that position. A majority of the Justices said that such challenges can be heard if there is a manageable legal standard. But who is to decide this? Is it for each district judge to evaluate in every case whether the parties have offered such a standard? Or must they wait until the Supreme Court pronounces a standard to exist? The Court just didn't say.

The Court offered no more clarity in a subsequent decision, *League of United Latin American Citizens v. Perry*,[49] where it again dismissed a challenge to partisan gerrymandering. After Republicans gained control of the Texas legislature in 2002, they redrew districts for Congress so as to maximize likely seats for Republicans. This replaced a plan that had been drawn up by a federal district court in 2001. The redistricting was very successful. The Texas congressional delegation went from 17 Democrats and 15 Republicans in the 2002 election to 11 Democrats and 21 Republicans in the 2004 election.

---

[47] 541 U.S. 267 (2004).
[48] 478 U.S. 109 (1986).
[49] 548 U.S. 399 (2006).

Many lawsuits were brought, and again the Court considered whether partisan gerrymandering is a nonjusticiable political question and, if it is justiciable, whether it violates equal protection. Once more, there was no majority opinion for the Court. Justice Kennedy announced the judgment of the Court and stated: "We do not revisit the justiciability holding but do proceed to examine whether appellants' claims offer the Court a manageable, reliable measure of fairness for determining whether a partisan gerrymander violates the Constitution."[50] He then went on to reject the challengers' argument that mid-decade redistricting for openly partisan reasons provided a "reliable standard" for the Court to use to invalidate the Texas plan.

Justices Scalia and Thomas reiterated their view, expressed in *Vieth*, that challenges to partisan gerrymandering are always nonjusticiable political questions. Chief Justice Roberts and Justice Alito agreed with the dismissal of the suit, but without saying whether they were finding it nonjusticiable or that partisan gerrymandering did not violate equal protection. Chief Justice Roberts wrote:

I agree with the determination that appellants have not provided "a reliable standard for identifying unconstitutional political gerrymanders." The question whether any such standard exists—that is, whether a challenge to a political gerrymander presents a justiciable case or controversy—has not been argued in these cases. I therefore take no position on that question, which has divided the Court, and I join the Court's disposition in Part II without specifying whether appellants have failed to state a claim on which relief can be granted, or have failed to present a justiciable controversy.[51]

Justices Stevens, Souter, Ginsburg, and Breyer again dissented from the aspect of the decision dismissing the challenge to partisan gerrymandering as being nonjusticiable. They would have reached the merits of the equal protection claim.

Although there still has not been a majority opinion holding that challenges to partisan gerrymandering are always political questions, after *Vieth* and *Perry* it is hard to imagine such a case succeeding. Five Justices—Chief Justice Roberts and Justices Scalia, Kennedy, Thomas, and Alito—likely would rule against any such challenge. The underlying normative issue is whether the federal judiciary should stay out of partisan gerrymandering because of the inherent lack of standards for determining when there is a constitutional violation, or whether the federal judiciary should review such claims to correct a serious problem in the political process that otherwise will go unremedied.

Review of Political Parties

A final area where the Court has considered the application of the political question doctrine to the electoral process involves judicial review of the activities of political parties. The Court repeatedly has held that the federal judiciary will

---

[50] *Id.* at 414.
[51] *Id.* at 493 (Roberts, C.J., concurring in part, concurring in the judgment in part, and dissenting in part).

prevent racial discrimination by political parties.[52] But other challenges to political parties, especially suits concerning the seating of delegates at national conventions, have been dismissed by the courts. In *O'Brien v. Brown*, the federal courts were asked to decide what group of delegates should be seated at the 1972 Democratic National Convention.[53] The case reached the Supreme Court three days before the convention began. Illinois delegates, led by Mayor Richard Daley, were excluded on the ground that they were not sufficiently representative of racial minorities. The Daley delegates argued that they were discriminated against and denied equal protection. Also, a group of California delegates pledged to Hubert Humphrey argued that the state's winner-take-all primary was unconstitutional. The court of appeals ruled that the case was not a political question and on the merits held for the California plaintiffs and against the Illinois plaintiffs.

The Supreme Court stayed the court of appeals decision. The Court cited *Luther v. Borden* and stated: "In light of the availability of the convention as a forum to review the recommendations of the Credentials Committee, in which process the complaining parties might obtain the relief they have sought from the federal courts, the lack of precedent to support the extraordinary relief granted by the Court of Appeals, and the large public interest in allowing the political process to function free from judicial supervision, we conclude the judgment of the Court of Appeals must be stayed."[54]

Subsequently, in *Cousins v. Wigoda*, the Court held that a state court should not interfere with the selection of delegates to a national political convention.[55] The Court did not expressly base its decision on the political question doctrine, but instead on the right of political association infringed by state oversight of the delegate selection process.

Summary

In sum, alleged violations of the republican form of government clause pose political questions, but claims that districting violates the equal protection clause are justiciable. The key normative question is whether it is desirable for the republican form of government clause to be immune from judicial application. By deeming cases under this provision always to be a political question, the Court in essence has read it out of the Constitution. Yet it seems no more lacking in content than any other open-textured constitutional provision.

---

[52] *See, e.g.*, Terry v. Adams, 345 U.S. 461 (1953); Smith v. Allwright, 321 U.S. 649 (1944) (discrimination against blacks in political parties), discussed in §6.4.4.2.

[53] 409 U.S. 1 (1972).

[54] *Id.* at 5.

[55] 419 U.S. 477 (1975).

§2.8.4   Foreign Policy

The Supreme Court frequently has held that cases presenting issues related to the conduct of foreign affairs pose political questions.[56] In *Oetjen v. Central Leather Co.*, in 1918, the Court declared: "The conduct of the foreign relations of our Government is committed by the Constitution to the Executive and Legislature 'the political' Departments of the Government, and the propriety of what may be done in the exercise of this political power is not subject to judicial inquiry or decision."[57]

Yet the Court also has emphasized that "it is error to suppose that every case or controversy which touches foreign relations lies beyond judicial cognizance."[58] For example, the Court has upheld, on the merits, the constitutionality of the president's use of executive agreements instead of treaties to implement major foreign policy agreements.[59] Also, the Court has ruled in favor of the constitutionality of the use of the treaty power for specific subject matters.[60]

Most recently, in *Zivotofsky v. Clinton*, the Court ruled that it was not a political question and the judiciary could rule on the constitutionality of a federal law that allows American parents who have a child born in Jerusalem to have the passport indicate Israel as the country of birth.[61] Since the establishment of Israel in 1948, American Presidents have taken a position of neutrality over which sovereign controls Jerusalem.

In 2002, Congress passed a bill with a section titled, "United States Policy with Respect to Jerusalem as the Capital of Israel." Among other things, the section directed the State Department to record "Israel" as the place of birth on a passport of a citizen born in Jerusalem, if the parents or guardians of a U.S. citizen born in Jerusalem so requested. President Bush signed the bill into law, but issued a signing statement expressing the view that this was an unconstitutional encroachment on presidential power. The Obama administration has taken the same position.

Menachem Zivotofsky was born in 2002 in Jerusalem to parents who are United States citizens. Zivotofsky's mother applied for a United States passport, listing his place of birth as "Jerusalem, Israel." A lawsuit was brought on Zivotofsky's behalf, but the lower courts ordered it dismissed as a political question. The Supreme Court reversed. In an opinion by Chief Justice Roberts, the Court said that the matter was justiciable, even though it involved foreign policy. The Court explained: "Resolution of Zivotofsky's claim demands careful examination of the textual, structural, and historical evidence put forward by the parties regarding

---

[56] For a defense of this use of the political question doctrine, *see* Theodore Blumoff, Judicial Review, Foreign Affairs, and Legislative Standing, 25 Ga. L. Rev. 227 (1991).

[57] 246 U.S. 297, 302 (1918). *See also* Chicago & S. Air Lines v. Waterman S.S. Corp., 333 U.S. 103, 111 (1948).

[58] Baker v. Carr, 369 U.S. at 211.

[59] *See, e.g.*, Dames & Moore v. Regan, 453 U.S. 654 (1981); United States v. Pink, 315 U.S. 203, 229 (1942); United States v. Belmont, 301 U.S. 324, 330 (1937); these cases are discussed in §4.6.2.

[60] *See, e.g.*, Missouri v. Holland, 252 U.S. 416, 433 (1920) (approving the constitutionality of a treaty with Great Britain concerning migratory birds).

[61] 132 S. Ct. 1421 (2012).

the nature of the statute and of the passport and recognition powers. This is what courts do. The political question doctrine poses no bar to judicial review of this case."[62]

Thus, it is difficult to identify any principle that determines which foreign policy issues are justiciable and which present political questions. The most that can be done is to describe the areas where the political question doctrine has been applied in the realm of foreign affairs.

Areas of Foreign Policy That Pose a Political Question

First, the Supreme Court has held that the determination of when war begins or when a war ends is left to the political branches of government. In *Commercial Trust Co. v. Miller*, the question presented was whether a congressional declaration that World War I had ended prevented application of the Trading with the Enemy Act.[63] In 1921, Congress, with the approval of the president, passed a joint resolution ending the war with Germany and proclaiming peace. The issue arose over whether the congressional proclamation suspended the application of the Act. The Court stated that the power to decide when a war ends is vested exclusively in Congress.[64] Quite similarly, the Court has held that the political branches decide when hostilities begin, and hence when it is appropriate to call up the militia.[65]

Second, the Supreme Court has held that the recognition of foreign governments is a political question,[66] as are related questions concerning disputes about the diplomatic status of individuals claiming immunity.[67] In other words, issues concerning who represents a foreign state, and in what capacity, are not justiciable.

Third, the Supreme Court has held that many issues concerning the ratification and interpretation of treaties pose political questions. For example, in *Terlinden v. Ames*, the Court held that it is a political question whether a treaty survives when one country becomes part of another.[68] Subsequently, a plurality of the Court held that a challenge to President Carter's rescission of the United States treaty with Taiwan posed a nonjusticiable political question. In *Goldwater v. Carter*, Senator Barry Goldwater argued that rescission of a treaty required approval of two-thirds of the Senate.[69] Senator Goldwater contended that just as the president cannot unilaterally repeal a law, neither is it constitutional for the president to rescind a treaty without the Senate's consent. Justice Rehnquist, writing for a plurality of

---

[62] Id. at 1430.

[63] 262 U.S. 51 (1923).

[64] *Id.* at 57.

[65] *See, e.g.*, Martin v. Mott, 25 U.S. (12 Wheat.) 19, 30 (1827).

[66] *See, e.g.*, United States v. Belmont, 301 U.S. 324, 330 (1937) (Court confirmed president's power to recognize and assume diplomatic relations with the Soviet Union); Oetjen v. Central Leather Co., 246 U.S. 297 (1918). The Court also has held that the recognition of Indian tribes is left to the political process. *See, e.g.*, United States v. Sandoval, 231 U.S. 28, 45-46 (1913).

[67] *See, e.g.*, In re Baiz, 135 U.S. 403 (1890).

[68] 184 U.S. 270 (1902).

[69] 444 U.S. 996 (1979).

four Justices, said that the case posed a political question. The plurality said that there were no standards in the Constitution governing rescission of treaties and that the matter was a "dispute between coequal branches of our Government, each of which has resources available to protect and assert its interests."[70]

Fourth, federal courts frequently have declared challenges to the president's use of the war powers to constitute a political question. During the Vietnam War, several dozen cases were filed in the federal courts arguing that the war was unconstitutional because there was no congressional declaration of war. Although the Supreme Court did not rule in any of these cases, either as to justiciability or on the merits, most of the lower courts deemed the challenges to the war to constitute a political question.[71] In the same way, challenges to the constitutionality of the president's military activities in El Salvador were dismissed by the lower federal courts as posing a political question.[72] Similarly, lower courts dismissed challenges to the constitutionality of the war in Iraq as posing a nonjusticiable political question.[73]

Should Foreign Policy Issues Be a Political Question?

The application of the political question doctrine to foreign policy is extremely controversial.[74] Some contend that it is appropriate for the judiciary to stay out of foreign policy because of the greater knowledge and expertise of the president and Congress in this area. The Supreme Court once stated: "[T]he very nature of executive decisions as to foreign policy is political, not judicial. Such decisions . . . are delicate, complex, and involve large elements of prophecy. . . . They are decisions of a kind for which the Judiciary has neither aptitude, facilities nor responsibility."[75] Furthermore, it is argued that the federal courts are particularly poorly suited to evaluating the constitutionality of a war and enforcing an order halting hostilities.

---

[70] *Id.* at 1004. Justice Powell concurred in the result, arguing that the matter was not yet ripe because Congress had not taken a position on the issue. *Id.* at 997 (Powell, J., concurring in the judgment).

[71] *See, e.g.*, Holtzman v. Schlesinger, 484 F.2d 1307, 1309 (3d Cir.), *cert. denied*, 416 U.S. 936 (1973); DaCosta v. Laird, 471 F.2d 1146, 1147 (2d Cir. 1973); Sarnoff v. Connally, 457 F.2d 809, 810 (9th Cir.), *cert. denied*, 409 U.S. 929 (1972); Orlando v. Laird, 443 F.2d 1039, 1043 (2d Cir.), *cert. denied*, 404 U.S. 869 (1971); Simmons v. United States, 406 F.2d 456, 460 (5th Cir.), *cert. denied*, 395 U.S. 982 (1969); *see also* Anthony D'Amato & Robert O'Neil, The Judiciary and Vietnam 51-58 (1972) (description of cases concerning the Vietnam War as a political question); Louis Henkin, Vietnam in the Courts of the United States: Political Questions, 63 Am. J. Intl. L. 284 (1969).

[72] *See, e.g.*, Crockett v. Reagan, 720 F.2d 1355 (D.C. Cir. 1983), *cert. denied*, 467 U.S. 1251 (1984); Sanchez-Espinoza v. Reagan, 770 F.2d 202 (D.C. Cir. 1985); Lowry v. Reagan, 676 F. Supp. 333 (D.D.C. 1987); *but cf.* Ramirez de Arellano v. Weinberger, 745 F.2d 1500 (D.C. Cir. 1984) (holding justiciable a claim by a United States citizen that the federal government had taken his property in Honduras for the purpose of using it as a military training site; no challenge to the legality of the military activities was present).

[73] *See* Doe v. Bush, 322 F.3d 109 (1st Cir. 2003).

[74] *See, e.g.*, Anne-Marie Slaughter Burley, Are Foreign Affairs Different?, 106 Harv. L. Rev. 1980 (1993).

[75] Chicago & S. Air Lines v. Waterman S.S. Corp., 333 U.S. 103, 111 (1948).

Yet critics of the political question doctrine argue that constitutional questions concerning foreign affairs should be adjudicated.[76] They contend that in many cases the constitutional questions do not depend on expert information. For example, deciding what constitutes a declaration of war is an interpretive question similar to others confronted by the Supreme Court. In instances that involve expertise, the Court can hear the case and defer to the other branches of government on the merits; there is no need to deem such matters to be nonjusticiable.

Critics of the political question doctrine argue that the constitutional provisions governing foreign policy are rendered essentially meaningless without judicial enforcement. Although in some instances the other branches of government might try to uphold the Constitution even in the absence of judicial review, at times this is likely impossible. For example, in *Goldwater v. Carter*, the plaintiffs contended that rescission of a treaty required approval of two-thirds of the Senate; that is, one-third of the senators should be able to block rescission.[77] Yet there is no way that one-third of the senators can have a voice or can enforce their position—even if it is impeccably correct constitutional law—without judicial review.

Because precedents concerning judicial review of constitutional issues pertaining to foreign affairs are conflicting and very controversial, it is inevitable that in the future the Court will need to decide again whether and when challenges to the conduct of foreign policy pose a political question.

§2.8.5   *Congressional Self-Governance*

On several occasions, the Court has considered whether the political question doctrine prevents federal court review of congressional decisions concerning its processes and members. Often, though certainly not always, the Court has held that congressional judgments pertaining to its internal governance should not be reviewed by the federal judiciary.

For example, in *Field v. Clark*, the Court dismissed a claim that a section of a bill passed by Congress was omitted from the final version of the law authenticated by the Speaker of the House and the vice president and signed by the president.[78] The Court emphasized that judicial review was unnecessary because Congress could protect its own interests by adopting additional legislation.

A key case rejecting the application of the political question doctrine to judicial review of internal congressional decisions is *Powell v. McCormack*.[79] In 1967, the House of Representatives refused to seat Representative Adam Clayton Powell, Jr., even though he had been elected by his constituents. A House subcommittee found that Powell deceived Congress by presenting false travel vouchers for reimbursements and had made illegal payments to his wife with government funds. Powell and 13 of his constituents sued, arguing that the refusal to seat him was

---

[76] *See, e.g.,* Redish, *supra* note 1, at 1052; Michael Tigar, Judicial Power, the Political Question Doctrine, and Foreign Relations, 17 UCLA L. Rev. 1135, 1141-1151 (1970).

[77] 444 U.S. 996 (1979).

[78] 143 U.S. 649 (1892).

[79] 395 U.S. 486 (1969).

unconstitutional because he was properly elected and met all of the requirements stated in the Constitution for service as a representative. Although he was not seated at all during that term of Congress, he was reelected in 1968 and he was seated in 1969. Nonetheless, the Supreme Court held that his suit was not moot because his claim for back pay for the time in which he was not seated remained a live controversy.

The Constitution specifically provides, in Article I, §5, that each house of Congress may, by a vote of two-thirds of its members, expel a member. However, the Court noted that the issue in *Powell v. McCormack* was not expulsion; he was excluded, not expelled.[80]

The defendants argued that the case posed a political question because the text of the Constitution in Article I, §5, provides that each house of Congress shall "be the Judge of the Qualifications of its Members." But the Court held that the House of Representatives had discretion only to determine if a member met the qualifications stated in Article I, §2 — requirements of age, citizenship, and residence.[81] In declaring that the case was justiciable and did not pose a political question, the Court stressed the importance of allowing people to select their legislators. The Court "concluded that Art. I. §5, is at most a 'textually demonstrable commitment' to Congress to judge only the qualifications expressly set forth in the Constitution."[82]

The defendants urged the Court to dismiss the case rather than interfere with or risk conflict with another branch of government. The Court rejected that such considerations should influence its ruling. The Court stated: "Our system of government requires that federal courts on occasion interpret the Constitution in a manner at variance with the construction given the document by another branch. The alleged conflict that such an adjudication may cause cannot justify the courts' avoiding their constitutional responsibility."[83]

In *Roudebush v. Hartke*, the Court held that Article I's provision making the Senate the "judge of the elections . . . of its members" did not preclude the state from ordering a recount in a senatorial election.[84] But the Court did state that the determination of which "candidate is entitled to be seated in the Senate [poses] a non-justiciable political question."[85]

In *United States v. Munoz-Flores*, the Court refused to apply the political question doctrine to bar a challenge to a federal assessment as violating the origination clause of the Constitution, which provides that "[a]ll bills for raising revenue

---

[80] *Id.* at 506-512.

[81] The Court relied on *Powell* to declare unconstitutional a state law that limited access to the ballot for candidates for the United States House of Representatives or the United States Senate after they had served a specified number of terms. United States Term Limits v. Thornton, 514 U.S. 779 (1995). The Court again emphasized that Article I sets the only permissible qualifications for a member of Congress.

[82] 395 U.S. at 548.

[83] *Id.* at 549.

[84] 405 U.S. 15, 19 n.6 (1972) (citations omitted).

[85] *Id.* at 19.

shall originate in the House of Representatives."[86] A federal statute required that courts collect a monetary assessment on any person convicted of a federal misdemeanor. The challenger argued that this was unconstitutional because the bill for the assessments arose in the Senate and not the House. The Court brushed aside concerns about the need for deference to Congress and the ability of the House of Representatives to protect its own interests. Justice Thurgood Marshall, writing for the Court, explained: "To be sure, the courts must develop standards for making the revenue and origination determinations, but the Government suggests no reason that developing such standards will be more difficult in this context than any other."[87]

The underlying normative question again is whether these decisions invoking the political question doctrine are proper deference to a coordinate branch of government or whether they are unjustified judicial abdication. From one view, the federal courts appropriately have refused to become involved in internal legislative matters. But from a different perspective, the courts have unjustifiably failed to enforce constitutional provisions and have eliminated an important check on Congress.

§2.8.6   The Process for Ratifying Constitutional Amendments

Article V of the Constitution prescribes the manner for amending the United States Constitution. When, if at all, should federal courts hear suits contending that the process was improperly followed? Some scholars, such as Professor Laurence Tribe, argue that the courts generally should not become involved in the only mechanism that exists to directly overturn the judiciary's interpretation of the United States Constitution.[88] But others, such as Professor Walter Dellinger, contend that the federal courts must ensure that the proper procedures are followed in amending the Constitution.[89] The argument is that the very safeguards that protect the Constitution from easy alteration are rendered impotent if the political process is allowed to disregard Article V.

Nor is it fanciful to imagine that Congress might violate the procedures for ratifying amendments, as the history of the adoption of the Fourteenth Amendment demonstrates.[90] After the Civil War, Congress adopted the Fourteenth Amendment, but it was quickly rejected by enough Southern and border states to prevent its passage. Congress, furious at what it perceived as an attempt to undo the outcome of the Civil War, enacted the Reconstruction Act, which provided, in part, for military rule of the rebel states and denied those states readmission into the Union until they had ratified the Fourteenth Amendment. After the Southern states ratified the amendment, two other states that had previously approved it

---

[86] 495 U.S. 385 (1990).

[87] *Id.* at 395-396.

[88] *See, e.g.,* Tribe, *supra* note 17, at 22-23.

[89] Walter Dellinger, The Legitimacy of Constitutional Change: Rethinking the Amendment Process, 97 Harv. L. Rev. 386 (1983).

[90] The history of the ratification of the Fourteenth Amendment is described in *Coleman v. Miller,* 307 U.S. 433 (1939), and reviewed in §1.3.

rescinded their ratification. Nonetheless, the Fourteenth Amendment was deemed adopted by counting all of the Southern states that were coerced into ratifying it and including the two states that rescinded their earlier approval.

Inconsistency Among the Cases

The Supreme Court has not been consistent in deciding whether the process of ratifying amendments is a nonjusticiable political question. In some instances, the Court has allowed judicial review. In 1798, in *Hollingsworth v. Virginia*, the Court held that the president may not veto amendments passed by Congress.[91] The Court concluded that the veto power contained in Article I, §7, was confined to statutes and did not include amendments. In a case involving the ratification of the Nineteenth Amendment, *Leser v. Garnett*, the Court held that a state's certification that it had ratified an amendment was sufficient to allow it to be counted as having approved the proposed constitutional change.[92] In *Dillon v. Gloss*, the Court upheld the constitutionality of Congress's creating time limits for the ratification of amendments.[93]

Yet on other occasions, the Court has indicated that the process of ratifying amendments poses a nonjusticiable political question. In *Coleman v. Miller*, a plurality of the Court declared that Congress has "sole and complete control over the amending process, subject to no judicial review."[94] The issue in *Coleman* was whether the time period for ratifying an amendment had expired. In 1924, Congress passed a proposed amendment to prohibit the use of child labor. In 1925, the Kansas legislature rejected the proposal, but in 1937, it was approved by that state's legislature. Kansas legislators who opposed the amendment sued, arguing that the time period for ratification had lapsed and that the earlier rejection was controlling.

The Supreme Court denied review. A plurality opinion written by Justice Black stated that the process of amending the Constitution is a "political question . . . . Article V . . . grants power over the amending of the Constitution to Congress alone. . . . The process itself is political in its entirety, from submission until an amendment becomes part of the Constitution, and is not subject to judicial guidance, control or interference at any point."[95]

An issue similar to that raised in *Coleman* was presented to the federal courts in *State of Idaho v. Freeman*.[96] Idaho ratified the proposed Equal Rights Amendment, but then rescinded its ratification. The plaintiffs filed suit arguing that the rescission was effective. Also, the plaintiffs contended that Congress had unconstitutionally extended the time period for ratification. The amendment, as proposed, contained a seven-year time limit for ratification. At the expiration of this

---

[91]   3 U.S. (3 Dal.) 378, 382 (1798).
[92]   258 U.S. 130 (1922).
[93]   256 U.S. 368 (1921).
[94]   307 U.S. 433, 459 (Black, J., concurring).
[95]   *Id.* at 457-459.
[96]   529 F. Supp. 1107 (D. Idaho 1981), *vacated*, 459 U.S. 809 (1982).

time period, Congress extended the limit by three years. The plaintiffs in *Idaho v. Freeman* argued that it was impermissible for Congress to approve the extension by majority vote; they argued that the Constitution requires a two-thirds vote of both houses of Congress to propose amendments.

The federal district court found that the case was justiciable and did not pose a political question. The court said that "the courts, as a neutral third party, and having the responsibility of guardian of the Constitution" should decide the issues presented.[97] On the merits the court ruled that the extension of time for the ratification of the amendment was unconstitutional. Before appellate review of the district court's decision was completed, the three-year extension for the ratification of the Equal Rights Amendment expired without ratification by three-fourths of the states. Accordingly, the Supreme Court vacated the district court's decision and ordered the case dismissed on mootness grounds.[98]

§2.8.7 *Excessive Interference with Coordinate Branches of Government*

Limiting Judicial Oversight and Intrusion

In many areas, the political question doctrine is intended to limit judicial oversight and control of the other branches of the federal government. For example, the Supreme Court's treatment of many aspects of foreign policy as political questions reflects a desire to avoid judicial intrusion into the domain of the other branches.

In *Gilligan v. Morgan*, the Supreme Court deemed not justiciable a lawsuit claiming that the government was negligent in failing to adequately train the Ohio National Guard.[99] The suit was initiated by students at Kent State University after the shooting of four students during an anti–Vietnam War protest on May 4, 1970. The plaintiffs contended that grossly inadequate training of the Guard was responsible for the unjustified use of lethal force and sought injunctive and declaratory relief.

The Supreme Court, in an opinion by Chief Justice Burger, dismissed the case as posing a political question. The Court said that allowing review "would plainly and explicitly require a judicial evaluation of a wide range of possibly dissimilar procedures and policies approved by different law enforcement agencies or other authorities. It would be inappropriate for a district judge to undertake this responsibility, in the unlikely event that he possessed the requisite technical competence to do so."[100] The Court emphasized that relief would require ongoing supervision and control of the activities of the Ohio National Guard.

Lower courts have continued to find that there is a political question when there is a challenge to the exercise of executive discretion. For instance, in *United States v. Mandel*, the Ninth Circuit concluded that the decision of the secretary of

[97] 529 F. Supp. at 1135 (citations omitted).
[98] 459 U.S. 809 (1982).
[99] 413 U.S. 1 (1973).
[100] *Id.* at 8.

interior to place an item on the commodity control list is not judicially review-able.[101] The court of appeals explained that "[t]hese are quintessentially matters of policy entrusted by the Constitution to the Congress and the President, for which there are not meaningful standards of judicial review."[102] But there also are a number of lower court cases that have refused to apply the political question doctrine on this basis. For example, in *Nation Magazine v. United States Department of Defense,* a federal district court found that the political question doctrine did not bar review of the method for issuing credentials to the press during the Persian Gulf War.[103]

The Supreme Court's use of the political question doctrine to deny review has been criticized.[104] For example, it is unclear why reviewing training of the Guard and requiring standards for improved training would be more intrusive than has been judicial review of school board or prison actions. Also, it is argued that the use of the political question doctrine was unnecessary; that courts always have the power to deny equitable relief when supervision and enforcement of the equitable decree would be too difficult.[105]

§2.8.8　*Impeachment and Removal from Office:* Nixon v. United States

In 1993, the Court extended the use of the political question doctrine and resolved a previously undecided issue by holding that challenges to the impeachment process are nonjusticiable. *Nixon v. United States* involved federal district court judge Walter Nixon, who had been convicted of making false statements to a grand jury.[106] Judge Nixon refused to resign from the bench and continued to collect his judicial salary while in prison. The House of Representatives adopted Articles of Impeachment. The Senate, in accord with its rules, created a committee to hold a hearing and make a recommendation to the full Senate. The committee recommended removal from office, and the entire Senate voted accordingly.

Nixon argued, however, that the Senate's procedure violated Article I, §3, of the Constitution, which provides that the "Senate shall have the sole Power to try all Impeachments." Nixon maintained that this meant that the entire Senate had to sit and hear the evidence; he contended that the use of a committee to hear testimony and make a recommendation was unconstitutional.

Chief Justice Rehnquist, writing for the Court, held that the language and structure of Article I, §3, demonstrate a textual commitment of impeachment to the Senate. The Court explained that the framers intended that there would be two proceedings against officeholders charged with wrongdoing: a judicial trial and legislative impeachment proceedings. Chief Justice Rehnquist noted that "[t]he Framers deliberately separated the two forums to avoid raising the specter

---

[101]　914 F.2d 1215 (9th Cir. 1990).
[102]　*Id.* at 1223.
[103]　762 F. Supp. 1558 (S.D.N.Y. 1991).
[104]　Redish, *supra* note 1, at 1055.
[105]　*Id.* at 1055-1056.
[106]　506 U.S. 224 (1993).

of bias and to ensure independent judgments. . . . Certainly, judicial review of the Senate's trial would introduce the same risk of bias as would participation in the trial itself."[107]

Moreover, the Court stated that judicial review of impeachment would be inconsistent with the framers' views of impeachment in the scheme of checks and balances. The framers saw impeachment as the only legislative check on the judiciary; judicial involvement would undercut this independent check on judges.[108]

Nixon holds that the judiciary will not review the Senate's use of a committee to hold a hearing and make a recommendation on an impeachment. *Nixon* leaves open the question of whether all challenges to impeachment are nonjusticiable political questions. For example, what if the president were impeached and convicted for an act that was completely lawful and within his constitutional powers? Or what if the Senate declared the president to be convicted on the basis of a committee's determination or a vote of less than two-thirds of the senators? Although these events are certainly improbable, it also is unlikely that the Court would declare an impeachment unconstitutional in the absence of compelling circumstances.

Justice Souter, in an opinion concurring in the judgment, recognized the potential need for judicial review. He wrote: "If the Senate were to act in a manner seriously threatening the integrity of its results, convicting, say, upon a coin-toss, or upon a summary determination that an officer of the United States was simply a bad guy, judicial interference might well be appropriate."[109]

§2.9   CONGRESSIONAL CONTROL OF FEDERAL COURT JURISDICTION

§2.9.1   Introduction

The previous section focused on judicially created limits on the federal judicial power, specifically the justiciability doctrines. Another possible check on federal court power is the ability of Congress to limit federal court jurisdiction. Unlike justiciability, where there is a large body of case law, there is relatively little law concerning the extent, if at all, that Congress can subtract from the federal courts' jurisdiction that is prescribed in Article III of the United States Constitution.

Proposals to Restrict Jurisdiction

The question of congressional power to restrict federal court jurisdiction might arise in the particularly compelling and controversial circumstance of whether Congress may deny the federal courts the power to hear specific types of

---

[107] *Id.* at 234.
[108] *Id.* at 233-237.
[109] *Id.* at 253 (Souter, J., concurring).

cases. For example, during the 1980s, there were proposals in Congress to prevent federal courts from hearing cases involving challenges to state laws permitting school prayers or state laws restricting access to abortions.[1]

Such proposals to restrict federal court jurisdiction over particular types of cases have been made at other times in American history. For example, during the 1950s, the Supreme Court invalidated some loyalty oaths for government workers and attorneys.[2] In response, the Jennings-Butler Bill was introduced in the United States Senate to prevent review of State Board of Bar Examiners' decisions concerning who could practice law in a state.[3] During the 1960s, jurisdictional stripping proposals were advanced in response to the Supreme Court's decision in *Miranda v. Arizona*, which held that confessions from criminal defendants would be admissible as evidence only if certain warnings were administered prior to interrogation.[4] A Senate proposal would have denied the Supreme Court or any lower federal court the authority "to review or to reverse, vacate, modify, or disturb in anyway, a rule of any trial court of any State in any criminal prosecution admitting in evidence as voluntarily made an admission or confession of any accused."[5] Altogether, between 1953 and 1968, over 60 bills were introduced into Congress to restrict federal court jurisdiction over particular topics.[6]

In the 1990s, Congress enacted significant restrictions on federal court jurisdiction. For example, the Antiterrorism and Effective Death Penalty Act of 1996 limits the availability of federal habeas corpus relief, especially by precluding successive habeas corpus petitions without the express permission of the court of appeals.[7] As discussed below, in *Felker v. Turpin*, the Court upheld this provision's restriction on Supreme Court review of court of appeals decisions by concluding that there remained some opportunity for Supreme Court review: writs for habeas corpus filed directly in the Court.[8]

Additionally, both the Antiterrorism and Effective Death Penalty Act and the Illegal Immigration Reform[9] and Immigrant Responsibility Act of 1996[10] significantly restrict federal court jurisdiction over certain immigration matters.[11] The

---

[1] §2.9 *See, e.g.*, S. 158, 97th Cong., 1st Sess. (1981) (bills restricting federal court jurisdiction in abortion cases); S. 481, 97th Cong., 1st Sess. (1981); H.R. 4756, 97th Cong., 1st Sess. (1981) (bills restricting federal court jurisdiction over cases that involve voluntary school prayers).

[2] *See, e.g.*, Schware v. Board of Bar Examiners, 353 U.S. 232 (1957); Konigsberg v. State Bar, 353 U.S. 252 (1957).

[3] S. 3386, 85th Cong., 2d Sess. (1958).

[4] 384 U.S. 436 (1966).

[5] Quoted in Gerald Gunther, Constitutional Law 47 (15th ed. 2004).

[6] Henry Melvin Hart, David L. Shapiro & Daniel J. Meltzer, Hart & Wechsler's The Federal Courts and the Federal System 377 (5th ed. 2003).

[7] Pub. L. No. 104-132, 110 Stat. 1214 (Apr. 24, 1996) (amended 1996, 1997).

[8] 518 U.S. 651 (1996), discussed below in text accompanying notes 58-64.

[9] Pub. L. No. 104-132, 110 Stat. 1214.

[10] Pub. L. No. 104-208, 110 Stat. 3009, amended Pub. L. No. 104-302, 110 Stat. 3656 (Oct. 11, 1996).

[11] For a discussion of these provisions and their constitutionality, *see* Lenni B. Benson, Back to the Future: Congress Attacks the Right to Judicial Review of Immigration Proceedings, 29 Conn. L. Rev. 1411 (1997); Note, The Constitutional Requirement of Judicial Review for Administrative Deportation Decisions, 110 Harv. L. Rev. 1850 (1997).

Antiterrorism and Effective Death Penalty Act greatly restricts the ability of federal courts to review deportation orders. The Act provides: "Any final order of deportation against an alien who is deportable by means of having committed a criminal offense [within the listed category] shall not be subject to review by any court."[12] Additionally, the Act expressly deletes the prior provision in federal law that permitted habeas corpus review of claims by aliens who were held in custody pursuant to deportation orders.[13] The law thus appears to foreclose all judicial review of deportation orders.[14]

Congress further restricted judicial review in the Illegal Immigration Reform and Immigrant Responsibility Act of 1996. This law repealed a long-standing provision that authorized judicial review in the circuit courts of appeals and guaranteed habeas corpus upon detention. Additionally, the Act limits review of removal orders directed at aliens by declaring that "all questions of law and fact . . . arising from any action taken or proceeding brought to remove an alien from the United States under this title . . . shall be available only in judicial review of a final order."[15] The Act also limits court review of discretionary decisions by the attorney general, stating that no court has jurisdiction to review such rulings by the attorney general as cancellation of removal,[16] voluntary departure,[17] or adjustment of status.[18]

Most dramatically, Congress enacted laws that restrict the ability of the federal courts to hear challenges brought by those detained as enemy combatants. The Detainee Treatment Act of 2005 precluded federal courts from hearing writs of habeas corpus brought by those detained by the Department of Defense at Guantánamo Bay, Cuba. The only access to federal courts available to such individuals would be in review by the District of Columbia Circuit of decisions by Combatant Status Review Tribunals or military commissions.

In June 2006, in *Hamdan v. Rumsfeld*,[19] the Supreme Court held that the restrictions on habeas corpus applied only prospectively and did not preclude judicial decisions concerning habeas petitions that were pending at the time the Detainee Treatment Act was adopted. In response to *Hamdan*, Congress passed and President Bush signed the Military Commissions Act of 2006.[20] The Act makes clear that the restrictions on habeas corpus apply retroactively. The Act states: "No court, justice or judge shall have jurisdiction to hear or consider an application for a writ of habeas corpus filed by or on behalf of an alien detained by the United States who has been determined by the United States to have been properly detained

---

[12] Antiterrorism and Effective Death Penalty Act, §440(a).

[13] *Id.* §401(e). The Act also provides that an alien convicted of an aggravated felony is to be "conclusively presumed" to be deportable. A petition for review or for habeas corpus on behalf of such an alien may only challenge whether the alien is in fact an alien. §242A(c).

[14] Lower courts generally have upheld the constitutionality of the restrictions found in the Antiterrorism and Effective Death Penalty Act. *See, e.g.*, Mansour v. INS, 123 F.3d 423 (6th Cir. 1997); Chow v. INS, 113 F.3d 659 (7th Cir. 1997); Yang v. INS, 109 F.3d 1185 (7th Cir. 1997).

[15] §242.

[16] §240(a).

[17] §240(b).

[18] §245.

[19] 548 U.S. 557 (2006).

[20] Pub. L. No. 109-366, 120 Stat. 2600 (2006).

as an enemy combatant or is awaiting such determination."[21] Moreover, the Act provides that this amendment "shall apply to all cases, without exception, pending on or after the date of the enactment of this Act which relate to any aspect of the detention, transfer, treatment, trial or conditions of an alien detained by the United States since September 11, 2001."[22]

This restriction of jurisdiction raises profound constitutional questions, especially as to whether this is an impermissible suspension of the writ of habeas corpus in violation of Article I, §9, of the Constitution. In June 2008, in *Boumediene v. Bush,* the Supreme Court ruled, 5-4, that this was unconstitutional.[23] Justice Kennedy wrote the opinion for the Court and explained that Article I, §9, of the Constitution allows Congress to suspend the writ of habeas corpus only in instances of rebellion or invasion and there was no claim that such a situation existed. The preclusion of federal courts hearing habeas petitions from detainees was deemed to be an impermissible suspension of the writ of habeas corpus. Justice Kennedy, writing for the Court, declared: "We hold that petitioners may invoke the fundamental procedural protections of habeas corpus. The laws and Constitution are designed to survive, and remain in force, in extraordinary times. Liberty and security can be reconciled; and in our system they are reconciled within the framework of the law. The Framers decided that habeas corpus, a right of first importance, must be a part of that framework, a part of that law."[24] Justice Scalia wrote a vehement dissent and lamented that the majority's decision "will almost certainly cause more Americans to be killed" as dangerous individuals would be released and commit terrorist acts.[25]

There have been other proposals for restricting federal court jurisdiction that have not been adopted. For example, in 2004, the House of Representatives passed bills to prevent federal courts, including the Supreme Court, from hearing constitutional challenges to the Pledge of Allegiance or to the federal Defense of Marriage Act. The bills would have precluded federal district courts from exercising original jurisdiction or the Supreme Court from exercising appellate jurisdiction. Neither bill passed the Senate, though both have been reintroduced into Congress.

Purpose of Jurisdiction Stripping

The obvious purpose of most jurisdiction stripping bills is to achieve a change in the substantive law by a procedural device. Opponents of the Supreme Court's decisions in controversial areas such as abortion, school prayer, loyalty oaths, and criminal procedure would prefer to overturn the rulings by enacting constitutional amendments. Although amendments have been proposed, especially to ban abortions and permit school prayers, they have not attracted sufficient strength in

---

[21] Section 7 of the Military Commission Act of 2006.
[22] Section 7(b) of the Military Commission Act of 2006.
[23] 553 U.S. 723 (2008).
[24] *Id.* at 798.
[25] *Id.* at 828 (Scalia, J., dissenting).

Congress to be forwarded to the states for possible ratification. Unable to directly overrule the Supreme Court, opponents of these decisions believe that they might achieve a substantive change in the law by limiting federal court jurisdiction. Without lower federal courts or the Supreme Court to protect particular rights, the litigation would be entirely in state courts with no review in the federal judicial system.

Proponents of jurisdictional restrictions are hopeful that state courts, especially without the prospect of federal judicial oversight, will be more sympathetic to their causes and thus be more likely than federal courts to sustain state laws regulating abortion or permitting school prayers. Thus, the goal of jurisdictional restrictions is the "de facto reversal, by means far less burdensome than those required of a constitutional amendment, of several highly controversial Supreme Court decisions dealing with matters such as abortion, school prayer, and busing."[26]

Constitutionality Uncertain

Although such proposals to limit federal court jurisdiction over particular topics have been advanced for decades, their constitutionality is uncertain. The scholarly literature is rich with articles arguing both sides of whether, and when, Congress may restrict federal court jurisdiction.[27] Distinct, though certainly interrelated, issues arise in analyzing Congress's power over the Supreme Court's jurisdiction and that of the lower federal courts.

Congress's authority to prevent Supreme Court review of cases involving topics such as abortion is based on the language of Article III, which provides that the "Supreme Court shall have appellate jurisdiction, both as to Law and Fact, with such Exceptions, and under such Regulations as the Congress shall make." Proponents of limits on Supreme Court jurisdiction contend that this provision authorizes congressional restriction and that such restrictions are an important check on the federal judicial power.[28] Critics argue that Congress cannot exercise

---

[26] Laurence Tribe, Jurisdictional Gerrymandering: Zoning Disfavored Rights out of the Federal Courts, 16 Harv. C.R.-C.L. L. Rev. 129, 129-130 (1981); *see also* Lawrence Sager, Foreword: Constitutional Limitations on Congress' Authority to Regulate the Jurisdiction of the Federal Courts, 95 Harv. L. Rev. 17, 69 (1981).

[27] Important scholarship on the issue includes Louise Weinberg, The Article III Box: The Power of Congress to Attack the Jurisdiction of Federal Courts, 78 Tex. L. Rev. 1405 (2000); Akhil Amar, The Two-Tiered Structure of the Judiciary Act of 1789, 138 U. Pa. L. Rev. 1499 (1990); Daniel J. Meltzer, The History and Structure III, 138 U. Pa. L. Rev. 1569 (1990); Martin H. Redish, Text, Structure, and Common Sense in Interpretation of Article III, 138 U. Pa. L. Rev. 1633 (1990); Barry Friedman, A Different Dialogue: The Supreme Court Congress and Federal Jurisdiction, 85 Nw. U. L. Rev. 1 (1990); Akhil Amar, Taking Article III Seriously: A Reply to Professor Friedman, 85 Nw. U. L. Rev. 442 (1990); Mark Tushnet, The Law, Politics, and Theory of Federal Courts: A Comment, 85 Nw. U. L. Rev. 454 (1990); Michael Wells, Congress' Paramount Role in Setting the Scope of Federal Jurisdiction, 85 Nw. U. L. Rev. 465 (1990).

[28] *See, e.g.*, Michael Perry, The Constitution, the Courts, and Human Rights 134 (1982); Charles Black, Decision According to Law, 17-19, 37-39 (1981); Gerald Gunther, Congressional Power to Curtail Federal Court Jurisdiction: An Opinionated Guide to the Ongoing Debate, 36 Stan. L. Rev. 895, 917-922 (1984).

its power to limit jurisdiction, any more than it can exercise any authority, in a manner that violates the Constitution. Opponents of jurisdiction stripping maintain that limiting review in particular controversial areas would unconstitutionally infringe constitutional rights and that, in effect, it would allow Congress to disregard the Constitution and permit state courts to ignore federal law.[29] Section 2.9.2 considers the constitutionality of such restrictions of Supreme Court jurisdiction.

Congress's authority to limit the jurisdiction of lower federal courts raises somewhat different questions. Under Article III of the Constitution, Congress has discretion as to whether to create any lower federal courts. Congress never has vested the full jurisdiction of Article III in the lower federal courts. In fact, on several occasions the Court has upheld statutory limits on lower federal court jurisdiction, concluding that because Congress has discretion whether to create lower federal courts; Congress also has discretion to define their jurisdiction.[30]

But opponents of jurisdictional restrictions argue that these instances are not precedent for congressional limits on the ability of federal courts to decide cases in specific controversial areas.[31] Also, a compelling problem arises when the restriction on federal court jurisdiction would mean the unavailability of any court, state or federal, to hear a case. Under such circumstances, there is an often-made argument that due process considerations require the existence of a federal court. The ability of Congress to restrict the jurisdiction of the lower federal courts is discussed in §2.9.3.

Although few jurisdictional restrictions have been adopted thus far in American history, the topic of congressional control of federal court jurisdiction is extremely important.[32] Doubts about the constitutionality of jurisdictional limitations partially account for Congress's failure to adopt such statutes.[33] The issue of jurisdiction restrictions also raises important questions concerning the role of the federal courts relative to Congress and the states. The scope of Congress's power to define federal court jurisdiction focuses attention on separation of powers and

[29] *See, e.g.,* Tribe, *supra* note 26; Sager, *supra* note 26; Henry Hart, The Power of Congress to Limit the Jurisdiction of Federal Courts: An Exercise in Dialectic, 66 Harv. L. Rev. 1362 (1953).

[30] *See, e.g.,* Yakus v. United States, 321 U.S. 414 (1944); Lockerty v. Phillips, 319 U.S. 182 (1943); Sheldon v. Sill, 49 U.S. (8 How.) 441 (1850); discussed at the text accompanying notes 93-158.

[31] *See generally* Tara Leigh Grove, The Exceptions Clause as a Structural Safeguard, 113 Colum. L. Rev. 929 (2013); Akhil Amar, A Neo-Federalist View of Article III: Separating the Two Tiers of Federal Jurisdiction, 65 B.U. L. Rev. 205 (1985); Robert Clinton, A Mandatory View of Federal Court Jurisdiction: A Guided Quest for the Original Understanding of Article III, 132 U. Pa. L. Rev. 741 (1984); Theodore Eisenberg, Congressional Authority to Restrict Lower Federal Court Jurisdiction, 83 Yale L.J. 498 (1974).

[32] Title I of the 1996 Antiterrorism and Effective Death Penalty Act precludes Supreme Court review, by appeal or certiorari, of any decision by circuit courts of appeals granting or denying authorization for a state prisoner to file a second or successive application for habeas corpus relief. In Felker v. Turpin, 518 U.S. 651 (1996), the Supreme Court unanimously upheld the constitutionality of this provision on the grounds that it did not foreclose all Supreme Court review; for example, the Court still could hear successive habeas petitions as part of its original jurisdiction. *Felker* is discussed in more detail below.

[33] Mark Tushnet, Legal Realism, Structural Review, and Prophecy, 8 U. Dayton L. Rev. 809, 813 (1983) (a "scholarly consensus that such restrictions are unconstitutional has been a political force [keeping] . . . Congress from enacting such legislation").

the allocation of power among the branches of the federal government. Proposals to restrict federal court jurisdiction additionally require analysis of the importance of ensuring the availability of a federal court to decide constitutional cases. Is it appropriate to trust state courts to have the final word in major constitutional litigation?

Court Has Jurisdiction to Decide Constitutionality

At the outset in discussing congressional control of federal court jurisdiction, it is necessary to note that the federal courts undoubtedly would have jurisdiction to decide the constitutionality of statutes denying federal courts the authority to hear particular types of cases. *Marbury v. Madison* long ago established the power of the federal judiciary to rule on the constitutionality of federal statutes.[34] This would include the authority to determine the constitutionality of statutes restricting jurisdiction. More subtly, courts always have been accorded jurisdiction to determine whether they have jurisdiction. *Marbury* establishes that federal courts may not apply an unconstitutional law to decide a case. Hence, the federal courts must decide whether a statute restricting jurisdiction is constitutional before it can be applied to deny review in a particular case.

§2.9.2   *Congressional Control of Supreme Court Jurisdiction*

The Issue

Can Congress prevent the Supreme Court from hearing cases on particular topics? For example, would it be constitutional for Congress to prevent the Supreme Court from hearing, by appeal, certiorari, or any other mechanism, cases involving challenges to state laws regulating abortions or permitting school prayers? Despite decades of heated debate in the scholarly literature, there is no consensus on the constitutionality of such restrictions on jurisdiction. Because Congress rarely has attempted such jurisdiction stripping—and never in a manner that has been interpreted as precluding *all* Supreme Court review—the question of constitutionality is uncertain. Each side in the debate claims support for its position from the text of the Constitution, from precedents, and from policy arguments about the most desirable interpretation of the Constitution. Each type of argument—from the text, from precedents, and from policy considerations—warrants examination.

Throughout this discussion, it is assumed that even if Supreme Court jurisdiction is limited, some court would remain available to hear the claim. The absence of any court, state or federal, undoubtedly would raise a serious due process issue.[35] Additionally, in certain circumstances it can be argued that there must be

---

[34] 5 U.S. (1 Cranch) 137, 178 (1803), discussed in §2.2.1.

[35] *See, e.g.,* Oestereich v. Selective Serv. Sys. Local Bd. No. 11, 393 U.S. 233, 243 n.6 (1968) (Harlan, J., concurring).

some federal court available to hear the case.[36] Constitutional issues arising from the absence of any court and from the preclusion of all federal judicial review are discussed in §2.9.3. For the sake of clarity, this section focuses solely on the question of congressional power to restrict Supreme Court jurisdiction and assumes that other judicial forums would remain open to hear the case even if the nation's highest court could not.

Dispute over Meaning of Constitutional Text

As is true of many constitutional arguments, the debate over congressional restrictions of Supreme Court jurisdiction begins with a dispute over the meaning of the text of the Constitution. Those who believe that Congress can limit Supreme Court jurisdiction to hear particular matters point to the language of Article III, §2: "[T]he supreme Court shall have appellate Jurisdiction, both as to Law and Fact, with such Exceptions, and under such Regulations as the Congress shall make." The claim is that the unambiguous language of Article III authorizes Congress to create exceptions to the Supreme Court's jurisdiction and that such exceptions include the ability to preclude review of particular topics, such as abortion or school prayer cases.[37]

Supporters of jurisdiction stripping proposals bolster their textual argument by claiming that the framers of the Constitution intended such congressional control as a check on the judiciary's power.[38] Evidence of this intent, it is argued, is found in the fact that the first Congress did not vest the Supreme Court with appellate jurisdiction over all of the types of cases and controversies enumerated in Article III. For example, under the Judiciary Act of 1789, the Supreme Court had authority only to review decisions of a state's highest court that ruled against a federal constitutional claim.[39] It was not until the twentieth century that the Supreme Court was accorded power to review decisions of a state court that ruled in favor of a constitutional right.[40]

Opponents of jurisdiction stripping proposals take a very different view of the language of Article III. Some argue that the term "Exceptions" in Article III was intended to modify the word "Fact."[41] The contention is that the framers were concerned about the Supreme Court's ability to overturn fact-finding by lower courts, especially when done by juries. Hence, Congress was given the authority to control the manner in which the Supreme Court reviews questions of fact. Under this view, Congress could create an exception to the Supreme Court's jurisdiction

---

[36] See generally Amar, supra note 31; Theodore Eisenberg, Congressional Authority to Restrict Lower Federal Court Jurisdiction, 83 Yale L.J. 498 (1974); discussed below in §2.9.3.

[37] See, e.g., Gunther, supra note 28, at 895; Paul M. Bator, Congressional Power over the Jurisdiction of the Federal Courts, 27 Vill. L. Rev. 1030 (1982).

[38] See, e.g., Herbert Wechsler, The Courts and the Constitution, 65 Colum. L. Rev. 1001, 1005-1006 (1965).

[39] Act of Sept. 24, 1789, 1 Stat 73; see Peter W. Low & John Calvin Jeffries, Federal Courts and the Law of Federal-State Relations 173 (5th ed. 2004).

[40] Act of Dec. 23, 1914, 38 Stat. 790.

[41] See Raoul Berger, Congress v. The Supreme Court 285-296 (1969).

for review of matters of fact, but Congress could not eliminate the Court's appellate jurisdiction for issues of law.[42]

Alternatively, it is argued that even though Congress is given authority to limit Supreme Court jurisdiction under the text of Article III, this power—like all congressional powers—cannot be used in a manner that violates the Constitution. Opponents of jurisdiction restriction contend that congressional preclusion of Supreme Court review of particular topics would violate other parts of the Constitution.[43] This issue, whether and to what extent there are constraints on jurisdiction restrictions imposed by other constitutional provisions, is discussed below.

Precedents for Both Arguments

Ex parte McCardle

In addition to textual arguments, each side invokes a Supreme Court precedent in support of its position. Advocates of proposals to limit Supreme Court jurisdiction point to *Ex parte McCardle*.[44] McCardle was a newspaper editor in Vicksburg, Mississippi, who was arrested by federal officials for writing a series of newspaper articles that were highly critical of Reconstruction and especially of the military rule of the South following the Civil War.[45] McCardle filed a petition for a writ of habeas corpus pursuant to a statute adopted in 1867 that permitted federal courts to grant habeas corpus relief to anyone held in custody in violation of the Constitution or laws of the United States by either a state government or the federal government. Under the 1867 law, the Supreme Court was empowered to hear appeals from lower federal courts in habeas corpus cases. Before 1867, under the Judiciary Act of 1789, which was supplemented but not replaced by the 1867 law, federal courts could hear habeas petitions only of those who were held in federal custody.

McCardle contended that the Military Reconstruction Act was unconstitutional in that it provided for military trials for civilians. He also claimed that his prosecution violated specific Bill of Rights provisions, including the First, Fifth, and Sixth Amendments. The United States government argued that the federal courts lacked jurisdiction to grant habeas corpus to McCardle under the 1867 Act. The federal government read the 1867 statute, despite its language to the contrary, as providing federal court relief only for state prisoners. The Supreme Court rejected this contention and set the case for argument on the merits of

---

[42] *But see* Gunther, *supra* note 28, at 901 (rejecting view that exceptions and regulations refers to matters of fact).

[43] *See, e.g.*, Leonard Ratner, Congressional Power over the Appellate Jurisdiction of the Supreme Court, 109 U. Pa. L. Rev. 157 (1960); Sager, *supra* note 26, at 17; Tribe, *supra* note 26, at 16.

[44] 74 U.S. (7 Wall.) 506 (1869). For an excellent discussion of this case, *see* William Van Alstyne, A Critical Guide to *Ex parte McCardle*, 15 Ariz. L. Rev. 229 (1973).

[45] Among other things, McCardle urged whites to boycott elections of officials for state constitutional conventions. He offered $1 for the name of each white person who voted, with the names to be published in his newspaper. *See* Van Alstyne, *id.* at 236 n.42.

McCardle's claim that the Military Reconstruction Act and his prosecution were unconstitutional.[46]

On March 9, 1868, the Supreme Court held oral arguments on McCardle's constitutional claims. Three days later, on March 12, 1868, Congress adopted a rider to an inconsequential tax bill that repealed that part of the 1867 statute that authorized Supreme Court appellate review of writs of habeas corpus. Members of Congress stated that their purpose was to remove the McCardle case from the Supreme Court's docket and thus prevent the Court from potentially invalidating Reconstruction. Representative Wilson declared that the "amendment [repealing Supreme Court authority under the 1867 Act is] aimed at striking at a branch of the jurisdiction of the Supreme Court . . . thereby sweeping the [McCardle] case from the docket by taking away the jurisdiction of the Court."[47]

On March 25, 1868, President Andrew Johnson vetoed the attempted repeal of Supreme Court jurisdiction. It should be noted that this was five days before the Senate was scheduled to begin its impeachment trial of President Johnson and that the grounds for impeachment focused solely on his alleged obstruction of Reconstruction. President Johnson declared: "I cannot give my assent to a measure which proposes to deprive any person restrained of his or her liberty in violation of the Constitution . . . , from the right of appeal to the highest judicial authority known to our government."[48] The Congress immediately overrode President Johnson's veto on March 27, 1868.

The Supreme Court then considered whether it had jurisdiction to hear McCardle's constitutional claims in light of the recently adopted statute denying it authority to hear appeals under the 1867 Act that was the basis for jurisdiction in McCardle's petition. The Court held that it could not decide McCardle's case because of Congress's authority to create exceptions and regulations to the Court's appellate jurisdiction.

Chief Justice Chase, writing for the Court, began by noting that the "first question necessarily is that of jurisdiction," and that the case had to be dismissed for want of jurisdiction if the 1868 Act repealed the Court's authority under the 1867 statute.[49] Chief Justice Chase then observed that although the Court's authority stems from the Constitution, it "is conferred 'with such exceptions and under such regulations as Congress shall make.' "[50] The Court concluded that the 1868 Act was an unmistakable exception to the Court's appellate jurisdiction, thus mandating the dismissal of McCardle's appeal. The Court stated: "The provision of the Act of 1867, affirming the appellate jurisdiction of this court in cases of habeas corpus

---

[46] Ex parte McCardle, 73 U.S. (6 Wall.) 318 (1868).
[47] Quoted in Van Alstyne, *supra* note 44, at 239.
[48] Quoted *id.* at 239-240.
[49] 74 U.S. at 512.
[50] *Id.* at 513. Although Supreme Court jurisdiction is self-executing, the Court always has acted as if Congress confers jurisdiction on it. In *Durousseau v. United States*, 10 U.S. (6 Cranch) 307, 314 (1810), the Court stated: "The appellate powers of this court are not given by the judicial act. They are given by the Constitution. But they are limited and regulated by the judicial act, and by such other acts as have been passed on the subject."

is expressly repealed. It is hardly possible to imagine a plainer instance of positive exception."[51] Accordingly, the Court dismissed the case for lack of jurisdiction.

Thus, supporters of contemporary proposals to restrict Supreme Court jurisdiction cite *McCardle* as precedent. They contend that *McCardle* establishes that Congress may prevent Supreme Court review of constitutional issues. The fact that Congress intends to change the substantive law by limiting jurisdiction is deemed irrelevant, for they quote the *McCardle* Court's statement that "[w]e are not at liberty to inquire into the motives of the legislature. We can only examine into its power under the Constitution; and the power to make exceptions to the appellate jurisdiction of this court is given by express words."[52]

But opponents of jurisdiction stripping proposals contend that *McCardle* is easily distinguished from contemporary attempts to prevent Supreme Court review of topics such as abortion and school prayer. In *McCardle*, even after the repeal of the 1867 Act, the Supreme Court still had authority to hear McCardle's claims under the 1789 Judiciary Act, which allowed federal courts to grant writs of habeas corpus to federal prisoners. In other words, in *McCardle*, the Supreme Court was considering the constitutionality of a statute that did not completely preclude Supreme Court review, but rather only eliminated one of two bases for its authority. The *McCardle* Court expressly indicated that it still had jurisdiction in habeas corpus cases notwithstanding the repeal of the 1867 Act. The Court, at the conclusion of its opinion, declared: "Counsel seem to have supposed, if effect be given to the repealing act in question, that the whole appellate power of the court, in cases of habeas corpus, is denied. But this is an error. The act of 1868 does not except from that jurisdiction any cases but appeals from Circuit Courts under the act of 1867. It does not affect the jurisdiction which was previously exercised."[53]

Ex parte Yerger

In fact, a year after its decision in *McCardle*, the Supreme Court in *Ex parte Yerger* held that it had authority to review habeas corpus decisions of lower federal courts under the Judiciary Act of 1789.[54] Like *McCardle*, *Yerger* involved a newspaper editor's challenge to the constitutionality of the Military Reconstruction Act. After the Supreme Court upheld its jurisdiction to decide Yerger's constitutional claims, the federal military authorities dismissed all charges against him, thereby again preventing Supreme Court review of the constitutionality of Reconstruction.[55]

In light of *Yerger*, opponents of jurisdiction restrictions claim that *McCardle* only establishes the limited proposition that if there are two statutory grounds for Supreme Court jurisdiction, Congress may repeal one of them. The Court in *McCardle* did not review McCardle's habeas petition under the authority of the

---

[51] 74 U.S. at 514.

[52] *Id.*

[53] *Id.* at 515.

[54] 75 U.S. (8 Wall.) 85 (1869).

[55] It should be noted that Chief Justice Chase indicated privately that had the Court reached the merits of McCardle's constitutional claims "the Court would doubtless have held that this imprisonment for trial before a military commission was illegal." Van Alstyne, *supra* note 44, at 238 n.46.

1789 Act because he had not pled that Act as the basis for federal court jurisdiction and because the Court was anxious to avoid ruling on the constitutionality of Reconstruction.[56] Moreover, McCardle was not in danger since he had been released from prison and even had resumed writing articles criticizing Reconstruction. Simply put, the opponents of jurisdiction stripping contend that *McCardle* is not a precedent for proposals that would eliminate all Supreme Court review of cases involving topics such as abortion or school prayer.[57]

Felker v. Turpin

In fact, the Supreme Court relied on this rationale in upholding a federal law that precluded Supreme Court review of some habeas corpus petitions.[58] Title I of the 1996 Antiterrorism and Effective Death Penalty Act prohibits state prisoners from bringing successive habeas corpus petitions unless approval is received from the United States court of appeals.[59] The law precluded United States Supreme Court review, by appeal or certiorari, of any decision by a court of appeals granting or denying authorization for a state prisoner to file a successive habeas corpus petition.[60]

In *Felker v. Turpin*, the Supreme Court unanimously upheld the constitutionality of this jurisdictional restriction.[61] Chief Justice Rehnquist, writing for the Court, emphasized that the law did not preclude *all* Supreme Court review of petitions from individuals denied the ability to file successive ones; the law did not repeal the Court's authority to entertain original habeas petitions.[62] The Court explained: "But since it does not repeal our authority to entertain a petition for habeas corpus, there can be no plausible argument that the Act has deprived this Court of appellate jurisdiction in violation of Article III, §2."[63]

The Supreme Court, however, has not granted an original habeas petition since 1925. *Felker* seems to stand for the proposition that any continuing basis for Supreme Court review, no matter how unlikely, is sufficient to make a restriction on jurisdiction constitutional.[64]

---

[56] *Id.* at 245-246.

[57] Some members of the Supreme Court have indicated that "there is a serious question whether the *McCardle* case could command a majority view today." Glidden Co. v. Zdanok, 370 U.S. 530, 605 n.11 (1962) (Douglas, J., and Black, J., dissenting).

[58] Felker v. Turpin, 518 U.S. 651 (1996).

[59] Pub. L. No. 104-132, 110 Stat. 1217, §106(b).

[60] §106(b)(3)(E).

[61] 518 U.S. 651 (1996).

[62] *Id.* at 661.

[63] *Id.*

[64] In a concurring opinion, Justice Stevens suggested that there might be other ways for the Supreme Court to review court of appeals decisions, such as through writs other than certiorari pursuant to the All Writs Act, §28 U.S.C. §1651. *Id.* at 666 (Stevens, J., concurring). Justice Stevens, however, gave no examples as to what these writs might be.

United States v. Klein

On the other hand, opponents of jurisdiction stripping contend that *United States v. Klein* supports their position that Congress cannot restrict Supreme Court appellate review in an effort to direct particular substantive results."[65] *Klein*, like *McCardle*, arose during Reconstruction. In 1863, Congress adopted a statute providing that individuals whose property was seized during the Civil War could recover the property, or compensation for it, upon proof that they had not offered aid or comfort to the enemy during the war. The Supreme Court subsequently held that a presidential pardon fulfilled the statutory requirement of demonstrating that an individual was not a supporter of the rebellion.[66]

In response to this decision and frequent pardons issued by the president, Congress quickly adopted a statute providing that a pardon was inadmissible as evidence in a claim for return of seized property. Moreover, the statute provided that a pardon, without an express disclaimer of guilt, was proof that the person aided the rebellion and would deny the federal courts jurisdiction over the claims. The statute declared that upon "proof of such pardon . . . the jurisdiction of the court in the case shall cease, and the court shall forthwith dismiss the suit of such claimant."[67]

The Supreme Court held that the statute was unconstitutional. While acknowledging Congress's power to create exceptions and regulations to the Court's appellate jurisdiction, the Supreme Court said that Congress cannot direct the results in particular cases. The Court stated:

> It seems to us that this is not an exercise of the acknowledged power of Congress to make exceptions and prescribe regulations to the appellate power. . . . What is this but to prescribe a rule for the decision of a cause in a particular way? . . . Can we do so without allowing one party to the controversy to decide it in its own favor? Can we do so without allowing that the legislature may prescribe rules of decision to the judicial department in the cases pending before it? . . . We think not. . . . We must think that Congress has inadvertently passed the limit which separates the legislative power from the judicial power.[68]

Thus, opponents of proposals to restrict Supreme Court jurisdiction argue that *Klein* establishes that Congress may not restrict Supreme Court jurisdiction in an attempt to dictate substantive outcomes. By analogy, it would be unconstitutional for Congress to restrict Supreme Court jurisdiction in an attempt to undermine the Court's protections in abortion and school prayer cases.

But supporters of jurisdiction restriction argue that *Klein* establishes only that Congress may not restrict Supreme Court jurisdiction in a manner that violates

---

[65] 80 U.S. (13 Wall.) 128 (1872). For an excellent discussion of this case, *see* Gordon G. Young, Congressional Regulations of Federal Courts' Jurisdiction and Processes: *United States v. Klein* Revisited, 1981 Wis. L. Rev. 1189.

[66] United States v. Padelford, 76 U.S. (9 Wall.) 531 (1869).

[67] 92 Stat. 2076.

[68] 80 U.S. at 146-147.

other constitutional provisions. Prior to *Klein*, the federal courts had the power to return seized property or award compensation pursuant to a federal statute. Why, then, could not Congress amend the statute to provide that a certain class of citizens, those pardoned, were not entitled to recover under the law? The answer cannot be a simple statement that Congress cannot direct substantive outcomes because Congress always is entitled to amend statutes and thereby determine subsequent results. For example, after the Supreme Court held that federal employment discrimination statutes did not require an employer to provide disability coverage for pregnancy, Congress amended the law to state that employers could not treat pregnancy different from other conditions.[69] The effect of the amendment was to change substantive outcomes, as all such amendments of statutes have that effect.

What is the difference between the statute in *Klein* and the statute reversing the Supreme Court's interpretation of Title VII? Both statutes, after all, reversed a Supreme Court holding and thereby determined the results in future litigation. Two features distinguish *Klein*. First, in the statute at issue in *Klein*, Congress was redefining the president's pardon power. The statute was arguably unconstitutional as an infringement of the executive's power under Article II of the Constitution.[70] Second, it can be argued that the statute in *Klein* unconstitutionally deprived property without just compensation or due process. Under the previous law, those pardoned had a vested right to the return of their property that had been seized. But the denial of jurisdiction prevented the federal courts from vindicating their protected property interest. Hence, the statute was unconstitutional. Thus, supporters of jurisdiction stripping argue that despite the Court's broad language in *Klein*, that decision does not support the general proposition that Congress may not restrict jurisdiction in order to direct substantive outcomes. Rather, it stands for the much more limited principle that Congress cannot limit the Supreme Court's jurisdiction in a manner that violates other constitutional provisions.

Robertson v. Seattle Audubon Society

In 1992, in *Robertson v. Seattle Audubon Society*, the Supreme Court unanimously rejected a claim that a federal law—the Department of Interior and Related Agencies Appropriations Act of 1990—was unconstitutional under *Klein*.[71] The Act both required the Bureau of Land Management to offer specified land for sale and also imposed restrictions on harvesting from other land. Additionally, the Act expressly noted two pending cases and said that "Congress hereby determines and directs that management of areas according to subsections (b)(3) and (b)(5) of this section on [the specified lands] is adequate consideration for the purpose of meeting the statutory requirements that are the basis for [the two lawsuits]."[72]

---

[69] General Elec. Co. v. Gilbert, 429 U.S. 125 (1976); Pregnancy Discrimination Act, 42 U.S.C. §2000e(k) (1978).

[70] 80 U.S. at 147.

[71] 503 U.S. 429 (1992).

[72] 103 Stat. §318(b)(6)(a), quoted in 503 U.S. at 434.

The Ninth Circuit held that this provision was unconstitutional under *Klein* because Congress was directing the outcome of the pending litigation. The Supreme Court disagreed, concluding that Congress had changed the law itself and did not direct findings or results under the old law.[73] The Court read *Klein* as applying in a situation where Congress directs the judiciary as to decision making under an existing law and not applying when Congress adopts a new law. By placing the Act into the latter category, the Court found *Klein* distinguishable and rejected the constitutional challenge.

Plaut v. Spendthrift Farm, Inc.

In *Plaut v. Spendthrift Farm, Inc.*, the Court declared unconstitutional a federal statute that overturned a Supreme Court decision dismissing certain cases.[74] In 1991, the Court ruled that actions brought under the securities laws, specifically §10(b) and Rule 10(b)(5), had to be initiated within one year of discovering the facts giving rise to the violation and within three years of the violation.[75] Congress then amended the law to allow cases to go forward that were filed before this decision if they could have been brought under the prior law.

In *Plaut*, the Supreme Court declared the new statute unconstitutional as violating separation of powers. Justice Scalia, writing for the Court, said that the Constitution "gives the Federal Judiciary the power, not merely to rule on cases, but to decide them."[76] He said that because the "judicial power is one to render dispositive judgments," the federal law "effects a clear violation of separation-of-powers."[77] The statute was unconstitutional because it overturned a Supreme Court decision and gave relief to a party that the Court had said was entitled to none.

Although *Plaut* was decided based on the principle of finality and the need to ensure that federal court rulings are not advisory opinions,[78] it can be analogized to *Klein*. In both cases, the federal statute commanded a result in federal court: In *Plaut*, it was hearing a case that the Court ordered dismissed; in *Klein*, it was dismissing cases that the Court had allowed to be heard.[79] In each case, the Court

---

[73] 503 U.S. at 437.
[74] 514 U.S. 211 (1995). *Plaut* is also discussed in §2.4, which considers the Court's conclusion that the federal statute overturning the earlier Supreme Court ruling is unconstitutional because it renders it an advisory opinion.
[75] *See* Lampf, Pleva, Lipkind, Prupis & Petigrow v. Gilbertson, 501 U.S. 350 (1991).
[76] 514 U.S. at 218.
[77] *Id.* at 219, 225.
[78] This aspect of *Plaut* is discussed in §2.4.
[79] In Miller v. French, 530 U.S. 327 (2000), the Court distinguished both *Plaut* and *Klein* and upheld a provision of the Prison Litigation Reform Act, 18 U.S.C. §3626, that required federal courts to stay injunctions that they had entered concerning prison conditions if they did not act within 30 days in response to a government's motion to end the injunction. The Court said that an injunction is not "the last word of the judicial department" because it is always open to modification. *Id.* at 347. Moreover, the Court said that Congress can change the substantive law and require that injunctions be modified to be in accord with the new law. The Court said that the change in the substantive law distinguished this Act from the law in *Klein*. *Id.* at 347. *Miller v. French* is discussed in more detail in §2.3, *supra*.

found a violation of separation of powers. Yet there also is a significant difference between the cases. *Plaut* did not involve any attempt by Congress to strip the federal courts of jurisdiction. Thus, its application to this area is only by analogy and in establishing separation of powers as a limit on Congress's ability to control results in federal court litigation.

Policy Arguments and Responses

Because neither the text nor precedents conclusively resolve the debate over congressional authority to restrict jurisdiction, the issue turns on competing policy considerations and ultimately the question of when jurisdictional restrictions violate other constitutional provisions. Supporters of proposals to limit Supreme Court jurisdiction under the "exceptions and regulations" clause argue that such congressional power is an essential democratic check on the power of an unelected judiciary. Professor Michael Perry, for example, argues that "the legislative power of Congress . . . to define, and therefore to limit, the appellate jurisdiction of the Supreme Court and the original and appellate jurisdiction of lower federal courts" is essential to reconcile judicial review with principles of democracy.[80] Professor Perry, and other commentators as well, argue that in a democracy all value choices should be subject to control by electorally accountable officials and congressional restrictions on jurisdiction are an essential majoritarian check on the judiciary.[81]

But opponents of restrictions on the Supreme Court's jurisdiction contend that this argument is based on a misdefinition of democracy and is inconsistent with the purposes of the Constitution. Professor Perry's argument is premised on a definition of democracy in purely procedural terms as majority rule. But others argue that the correct definition of American democracy must include substantive values, such as those contained in the Constitution.[82] The claim is that the purpose of the Constitution is to protect crucial values from majority rule and that it is undesirable to accord Congress the power to undermine Supreme Court decisions.

More specifically, opponents of Professor Perry's position argue that he is in a dilemma. On the one hand, jurisdiction restrictions may not achieve the desired effect of a majoritarian check on the federal judiciary. Limiting the federal courts' jurisdiction does not overrule prior judicial decisions.[83] For example, an act of

---

[80] Michael Perry, The Constitution, the Courts and Human Rights 138 (1982). In his initial exposition, Professor Perry said that he would accord Congress the power to restrict jurisdiction only in areas of nonoriginalist Supreme Court review—that is, review where the Court was protecting rights not expressly stated in the Constitution or intended by the framers. Subsequently, Professor Perry wrote that under his theory, the power would extend to both originalist and nonoriginalist decisions. Michael Perry, The Authority of Text, Tradition, and Reason: A Theory of Constitutional Interpretation, 58 S. Cal. L. Rev. 551, 580 n.89 (1985).

[81] *See, e.g.,* Charles Black, Decision According to Law 17-19, 37-39 (1981) (Congressional power to restrict jurisdiction is a necessary democratic check.).

[82] *See, e.g.,* Erwin Chemerinsky, Interpreting the Constitution 6-21 (1987).

[83] *See* Richard Kay, Limiting Federal Court Jurisdiction: The Unforeseen Impact on Courts and Congress, 65 Judicature 185, 187 (1981).

Congress restricting Supreme Court jurisdiction to hear challenges to state laws regulating abortion would not overturn the precedents protecting women's right to choose whether to have an abortion. The Supreme Court's prior decisions would remain the law, and both Congress and the states would be obligated to uphold them. In fact, because the Court could not hear additional cases on the subject, the effect of the jurisdiction restriction would be to freeze the existing law. Assuming state judges remain true to their oath of office and follow the Court's precedents, restrictions on jurisdiction will not achieve the hoped-for democratic check on the judiciary.

Alternatively, the restrictions on jurisdiction might bring about a substantive change in the law. The limit on federal court power might be perceived by some state legislatures as an open invitation to adopt laws disregarding Supreme Court precedents, and some state courts, without the prospect of Supreme Court review, might sustain such statutes. Although the defenders of jurisdiction restriction proposals might applaud this as desirable in a democracy, opponents of such bills contend that such disregard of the Constitution is repugnant. They maintain that the Constitution's ultimate purpose and the Court's primary function is to protect minorities and individual rights from majoritarian interference, and that this is lost if the majority can overrule Supreme Court precedents through the technique of jurisdiction restrictions.[84]

Thus, in terms of policy considerations, supporters of jurisdiction restrictions see the tool as a desirable democratic check on the judiciary. But opponents argue that the Constitution and the Court are intentionally anti-majoritarian and it is undesirable to create a majoritarian check on the process of constitutional interpretation.

Finally, critics of proposals to limit Supreme Court review argue that Congress cannot use its power to control jurisdiction in a way that violates other constitutional provisions. The claim is that congressional authority to create exceptions and regulations is limited, as is all congressional power, by the other parts of the Constitution. There are two primary ways in which it is argued that jurisdictional restrictions would violate the Constitution: They would undermine the Court's essential function in the system of government, and they would infringe specific constitutional rights.

In a famous article written as a dialogue, the late Professor Henry Hart said that "the exceptions must not be such as will destroy the essential role of the Supreme Court in the constitutional system."[85] Other commentators as well have argued that there is a limit on Congress's power to create exceptions: Congress cannot use its power to interfere with the Court's essential functions under the Constitution.[86]

---

[84] *See, e.g.*, Leonard Ratner, Majoritarian Constraints on Judicial Review: Congressional Control of Supreme Court Jurisdiction, 27 Vill. L. Rev. 929 (1982); Leonard Ratner, Congressional Power over the Appellate Jurisdiction of the Supreme Court, 109 U. Pa. L. Rev. 157 (1960); Sager, *supra* note 26, at 37-42.

[85] Henry Hart, The Power of Congress to Limit Jurisdiction of Federal Courts: An Exercise in Dialectic, 66 Harv. L. Rev. 1362, 1402 (1953).

[86] *See, e.g.*, Leonard Ratner, Majoritarian Constraints on Judicial Review: Congressional Control of Supreme Court Jurisdiction, 27 Vill. L. Rev. 929 (1982); Leonard Ratner, Congressional Power over

For example, it is argued that restrictions on jurisdiction would undermine the Court's essential function of ensuring the supremacy of federal law. If Congress were to restrict the Supreme Court's jurisdiction, states could ignore Supreme Court precedents with impunity, even though they remained the law of the land, and thus make state law supreme over federal. The notion of a national Constitution with uniform meaning throughout the country would be lost.[87]

Additionally, the Court's essential function in checking the legislature would be lost if Congress could enact an unconstitutional statute and immunize the law from judicial review. The power of the federal courts to review the constitutionality of federal statutes, established in *Marbury v. Madison*, would be largely meaningless if Congress could enact unconstitutional laws and also restrict jurisdiction to prevent federal court review.

But other prominent commentators who support the constitutionality of jurisdiction restrictions challenge the essential functions thesis. Professor Gerald Gunther calls it "question-begging" that confuses the familiar with the necessary.[88] Likewise, Professor Martin Redish terms it constitutional wishful thinking.[89] Their contention is that Article III gives Congress plenary power to create exceptions and make regulations, and that this is as much a part of the Constitution as separation of powers and federalism.

Opponents of jurisdiction restriction also argue that Congress cannot limit Supreme Court review in a manner that violates specific constitutional rights. The paradigm example is that it obviously would be unconstitutional if Congress were to create an exception to Supreme Court jurisdiction for appeals brought by blacks. Such a jurisdictional restriction would violate the guarantee of equal protection that is applied to the federal government through the Fifth Amendment. Similarly, it is argued that a restriction on jurisdiction that is designed to limit abortion or permit school prayers would violate these constitutional rights. The argument is that when Congress acts with the purpose and effect of limiting a constitutionally protected right, at a minimum its enactment should be subjected to strict scrutiny. A law that is intended to undermine a constitutional right and that has the potential impact of lessening that right should be sustained only if it is necessary to achieve a compelling government purpose. Because the restrictions on jurisdiction are motivated only by a desire to undermine the protection of the right, they would fail strict scrutiny.

But those who defend the constitutionality of jurisdictional restrictions contend that Congress may exempt particular areas from Supreme Court review. Professor Paul Bator, for example, argued that although Congress could not restrict jurisdiction in a racially discriminatory manner, "[i]t is, however, a fundamental

---

the Appellate Jurisdiction of the Supreme Court, 109 U. Pa. L. Rev. 157 (1960); Sager, *supra* note 26, at 37-42.

[87] On several occasions, the Supreme Court has stated that the central purpose of judicial review is to ensure the uniform application and enforcement of the Constitution. *See, e.g.,* Dodge v. Woolsey, 59 U.S. (18 How.) 331, 335 (1855); Cohens v. Virginia, 19 U.S. (6 Wheat.) 264, 386-387 (1821).

[88] Gunther, *supra* note 28, at 920.

[89] Martin H. Redish, Constitutional Limitations on Congressional Power to Control Federal Jurisdiction: A Reaction to Professor Sager, 77 Nw. L. Rev. 143, 145 (1982).

and egregious mistake to broaden this argument into an assertion that Congress is not free to differentiate among different subject matters, and to specify categories of cases arising under federal law which [cannot be reviewed in federal courts]."[90] The argument is that racial discrimination in itself violates the Constitution, but nothing in the Constitution requires the availability of Supreme Court review for particular types of claims. In fact, it is argued that the "exceptions and regulations" clause of Article III expressly authorizes Congress to remove particular matters from federal court jurisdiction.[91]

Thus, the debate over the constitutionality of congressional control of Supreme Court jurisdiction will rage on unsettled until Congress uses its authority and sets the stage for a definitive Supreme Court ruling. Even then, the context of the law likely will make a great deal of difference. For example, it is difficult to imagine the Court upholding a congressional enactment that blatantly violated the Constitution and simultaneously precluded Supreme Court review. Permitting such legislative disregard of the Constitution would mean that judicial review exists at the pleasure of Congress, and it would cast grave doubt on the holding in *Marbury v. Madison* that "[i]t is emphatically the province and duty of the judicial department to say what the law is."[92]

Similarly, a congressional restriction on jurisdiction that resulted in state court disregard of Supreme Court precedents would be unlikely to be upheld by the Court. Precluding review in such cases would mean upholding, in effect, state law that conflicted with federal law. State law then would be supreme; this would be a blatant violation of the supremacy clause in Article VI of the Constitution.

Yet these predictions, like all of the above analysis, must wait for their validation or refutation until the day comes when the Court considers the constitutionality of congressional limits on Supreme Court jurisdiction. Depending on one's views, it might be much better if that day never arrives.

§2.9.3 Congressional Control of Lower Federal Court Jurisdiction

Would a statute precluding lower federal courts from hearing challenges to state laws regulating abortion or permitting voluntary school prayer be constitutional? Again, the debate in the scholarly literature has been heated and lengthy, but here too, no consensus has emerged.[93] In fact, four different positions might be identified as to the constitutionality of congressional restrictions of lower federal court jurisdiction.

---

[90] Bator, *supra* note 37, at 1034.

[91] *See* Gunther, *supra* note 28, at 916-921.

[92] 5 U.S. (1 Cranch) 137, 177 (1803).

[93] *See, e.g.,* Amar, *supra* note 31; Robert Clinton, A Mandatory View of Federal Court Jurisdiction: A Guided Quest for the Original Understanding of Article III, 132 U. Pa. L. Rev. 741 (1984); Theodore Eisenberg, Congressional Authority to Restrict Lower Federal Court Jurisdiction, 83 Yale L.J. 498 (1974).

Approach 1: Federal Courts Must Have the Full Judicial Power

The first approach, and the only one that seems clearly untenable, is that lower federal courts created by Congress must have the full judicial power described in Article III. The text of Article III seems to support this view. Article III, §1, says that the judicial power of the United States shall be vested in one Supreme Court and such inferior courts as Congress shall establish. Article III, §2, states that the judicial power "shall extend to" nine categories of cases and controversies. Hence, the conclusion is that although Congress has a choice regarding whether to establish lower federal courts, once they are created, they must have the judicial power to decide all matters described in Article III. By this view, all attempts to restrict jurisdiction would be unconstitutional.[94]

The problem with this theory is that it has not been followed at any point in American history. The first Judiciary Act did not vest in federal courts the power to hear all matters outlined in Article III. For example, federal courts did not have the authority to hear all cases arising under the Constitution, treaties, and laws of the United States until 1875. In fact, under the first theory, amount in controversy requirements would be unconstitutional because they are a restriction on federal court jurisdiction not provided for in Article III. Yet such requirements have existed since the Judiciary Act of 1789. Thus, after more than 200 years of contrary practice, it no longer is possible to argue persuasively that the lower federal courts' jurisdiction cannot be limited in any way.

Approach 2: Congressional Discretion to Decide Jurisdiction

A second approach is that Congress has authority to determine the jurisdiction of the federal courts because Congress has discretion as to whether to establish such tribunals.[95] Article III, §1, provides that the judicial power of the United States shall be vested in one Supreme Court and in such "inferior courts as the Congress may from time to time ordain and establish." Therefore, in light of this literal language, Congress need not create lower federal courts at all. Some conclude from this that because Congress need not even establish such courts, Congress can create them with whatever jurisdiction it desires. In short, the second approach accords Congress virtually plenary authority to define the jurisdiction of the lower federal courts.[96]

---

[94] *See* Gordon G. Young, A Critical Reassessment of the Case Law Bearing on Congress's Power to Restrict the Jurisdiction of the Lower Federal Courts, 54 Md. L. Rev. 132 (1995) (arguing that Supreme Court precedents limit Congress's ability to restrict lower federal court jurisdiction).

[95] *See, e.g.*, Charles E. Rice, Congress and the Supreme Court's Jurisdiction, 27 Vill. L. Rev. 959, 960-962 (1982).

[96] Even under this approach, there is a strong argument that Congress could not use its power to determine jurisdiction in a manner that restricts other constitutional provisions. For example, it certainly would be unconstitutional if Congress were to adopt a law saying that no African Americans could file suit in a federal court. The nature of constitutional limits on the power to restrict federal jurisdiction is discussed below.

This second position finds strong support in Supreme Court precedents. *Sheldon v. Sill*, decided in 1850, is a seminal case concerning congressional power to determine the jurisdiction of the lower federal courts.[97] The Judiciary Act of 1789 prohibited diversity jurisdiction from being created by the assignment of a debt.[98] Under this principle, when there has been an assignment, a federal court may take the case under its diversity jurisdiction only if the case properly could have been brought to federal court prior to the assignment. Article III, which authorizes diversity jurisdiction, creates no such limitation precluding jurisdiction based on assignment.

The issue in *Sheldon v. Sill* was whether Congress could restrict diversity jurisdiction in this manner. Sheldon, a Michigan resident, owed money to Hastings, also a Michigan resident, on a bond and a mortgage. Hastings assigned the debt owed to him to Sill, a New York resident. Pursuant to this assignment, Sill sued Sheldon in federal court to recover the sum due. Sheldon moved to dismiss because under the Judiciary Act of 1789 federal courts could not hear cases where diversity was created by an assignment. But Sill contended that because Article III authorizes diversity jurisdiction and does not contain a limitation for diversity gained by assignment, this section of the Judiciary Act was unconstitutional.

The Supreme Court upheld the Judiciary Act's restriction on diversity jurisdiction. The Court declared: "Congress may withhold from any court of its creation jurisdiction of any of the enumerated controversies. Courts created by statute can have no jurisdiction but such as the statute confers."[99] The Court continued in even broader language: "The political truth is, that the disposal of the judicial power (except in a few specified instances) belongs to Congress; and Congress is not bound to enlarge the jurisdiction of the Federal courts to every subject, in every form which the Constitution might warrant."[100] *Sheldon v. Sill* thus stands as a strong precedent for the proposition that because Congress has discretion to create lower federal courts, Congress also possesses authority to determine their jurisdiction.

The Supreme Court has adopted this position in a number of other decisions. In *Kline v. Burke Construction Co.*, the Supreme Court held that the Anti-Injunction Act precluded a federal court from enjoining a simultaneous state court proceeding for breach of contract.[101] In upholding this limit on federal court power, the Court stated: "Only the jurisdiction of the Supreme Court is derived directly from the Constitution. Every other court created by the general government derives its jurisdiction wholly from the authority of Congress. That body may give, withhold or restrict such jurisdiction at its discretion, provided it be not extended beyond the boundaries fixed by the Constitution."[102] In *Lauf v. E.G. Shinner & Co.*, the Court considered the constitutionality of the Norris-LaGuardia Act, which limited the ability of the federal courts to issue injunctions in labor disputes and prevented federal courts from enforcing contracts whereby employees agreed to

---

[97] 49 U.S. (8 How.) 441 (1850).

[98] 1 Stat. 73, at §11.

[99] *Sheldon*, 49 U.S. (8 How.) at 449.

[100] *Id.* (citations omitted).

[101] 260 U.S. 226 (1922). The Anti-Injunction Act is discussed in Erwin Chemerinsky, Federal Jurisdiction §11.2 (6th ed. 2011).

[102] *Id.* at 234.

not join a union.[103] During the first decades of the twentieth century, the federal courts were hostile to the labor movement and often enjoined labor protests. Moreover, the Supreme Court held that states could not prohibit employers from requiring employees to agree to refrain from joining a union as a condition for employment.[104] The Norris-LaGuardia Act sought to protect labor by limiting the power of the federal courts.

In *Lauf*, an employer sought an injunction to prevent an unincorporated labor union from picketing an employer who refused to require employees to join the union. The federal district court ruled in favor of the employer and issued the injunction. The Supreme Court reversed. The Court held that the Norris-LaGuardia Act restricted the district court's authority to hear the matter or issue the remedy. The Court found the constitutional issue untroubling. Justice Roberts, writing for the Court, declared: "There can be no question of the power of Congress thus to define and limit the jurisdiction of the inferior courts of the United States."[105]

Additional litigation concerning congressional power to control lower federal court jurisdiction emerged as a result of the Emergency Price Control Act, which was adopted during World War II.[106] Under the Act, price controls adopted by the government could be challenged by filing a protest with the price control administrator.[107] Appeals from the administrator's decisions could be taken, within 30 days, to an emergency court of appeals, comprising three federal judges. No other federal court, except for the United States Supreme Court, had authority to determine the validity of a regulation or provide injunctive relief.

In *Lockerty v. Phillips*, the Court held that a federal district court lacked jurisdiction to hear challenges to price controls promulgated under the Emergency Price Control Act.[108] Without filing an administrative protest or seeking review in the emergency court of appeals, a group of wholesale meat dealers initiated suit in federal court to enjoin the enforcement of price controls. The plaintiffs contended that the Act was an unconstitutional delegation of legislative power to an administrative agency and that the price regulations denied them due process of law. The Supreme Court held that the federal court lacked jurisdiction to hear the suit. The Court stated that "[t]here is nothing in the Constitution which requires Congress to confer equity jurisdiction on any particular inferior federal court."[109] Furthermore, the Court spoke broadly of Congress's authority to prescribe the jurisdiction of the lower federal courts: "The Congressional power to ordain and establish inferior federal courts includes the power of investing them with jurisdiction either limited, concurrent, or exclusive, and of withholding jurisdiction from them in the exact degrees and character which to Congress may seem proper for the public good."[110]

---

[103] 303 U.S. 323 (1938).

[104] *See, e.g.*, Coppage v. Kansas, 236 U.S. 1 (1915).

[105] *Lauf*, 303 U.S. at 330.

[106] 56 Stat. 23 (1942).

[107] *Id.* §203(a), described in Lockerty v. Phillips, 319 U.S. 182, 186 (1943).

[108] 319 U.S. 182 (1943).

[109] *Id.* at 187.

[110] *Id.*

An even more serious challenge to the constitutionality of the Emergency Price Control Act arose in *Yakus v. United States*.[111] In *Yakus*, the government initiated a criminal prosecution in federal district court for the sale of beef for an amount in excess of that specified in the price controls. The defendant in the criminal proceeding argued that the price controls were unconstitutional. The government contended that the federal district court had no jurisdiction to hear this defense because the defendant had not raised the constitutional issue in a protest to the administrator or in the emergency court of appeals.

The Supreme Court agreed with the government and precluded the defendant from challenging the constitutionality of the price controls as a defense in the criminal action. The Court said that the defendant "forfeited" the opportunity to bring such a constitutional challenge by failing to use the prescribed administrative and judicial procedures.[112] The Court said that *Lockerty* had established the power of Congress to restrict the jurisdiction of the federal courts and to specify the emergency court of appeals as the only forum to hear challenges to price controls.

Justices Rutledge and Murphy filed a vehement dissent in *Yakus*. They argued that under *Marbury v. Madison*, a federal court had the inherent power to determine the constitutionality of a statute that it was asked to apply. The dissenters stated: "It is one thing for Congress to withhold jurisdiction. It is entirely another to confer it and direct that it be exercised in a manner inconsistent with constitutional requirements or, what in some instances may be the same thing, without regard to them."[113] They explained, "Once it is held that Congress can require the courts criminally to enforce unconstitutional laws or statutes, including regulations, or to do so without regard to their validity the way will have been found to circumvent the supreme law, and what is more, to make the courts party to doing so. This Congress cannot do."[114]

Supporters of the constitutionality of jurisdiction restrictions maintain that these decisions establish Congress's power to determine the scope of federal court authority. But opponents of jurisdiction stripping proposals contend that none of these cases are precedents for Congress to identify particular rights, such as abortion, and deny federal court jurisdiction over claims of government infringement. *Sheldon* and *Kline* did not involve constitutional claims. In *Lockerty* and *Yakus*, Congress specified one federal court to hear a particular issue; it did not preclude all federal court jurisdiction. Law is the hardest case to distinguish, but it is possible to argue that in the Norris-LaGuardia Act, Congress only limited the federal courts' ability to award a particular *remedy*—injunctions.[115] Congress did not foreclose all lower federal court review as is done in the contemporary proposals to strip

---

[111] 321 U.S. 414 (1944).

[112] *Id.* at 444.

[113] *Id.* at 468 (Rutledge, J., dissenting).

[114] *Id.*

[115] A distinction might be drawn between Congress's ability to restrict jurisdiction and Congress's ability to foreclose certain remedies from being used by federal courts. This issue emerged especially with regard to proposals for Congress to prevent lower federal courts from using busing as a remedy in school desegregation cases. The constitutionality of restriction of remedies is discussed at the end of this section.

jurisdiction in areas such as abortion or school prayer. Opponents of attempts to restrict lower federal court jurisdiction over matters such as abortion and school prayer argue that such congressional legislation is unprecedented and unconstitutional for the reasons described below.

Approach 3: Constitutional Requirement for Some Federal Courts

A third major approach urged by some commentators is that the existence of lower federal courts is constitutionally required, at least for some types of claims. While the first two approaches begin with the assumption that Congress has complete discretion as to whether to create lower federal courts, this position is premised on the contrary claim that, at least for some issues, lower federal courts must exist. The most famous version of this theory was advanced by Justice Joseph Story in dictum in *Martin v. Hunter's Lessee.*[116]

Justice Story stated that the full judicial power must be vested in some federal court. Justice Story argued that "[t]he language of the article throughout is manifestly designed to be mandatory upon the legislature. The judicial power of the United States *shall be vested* (not may be vested). If then, it is the duty of congress to vest the judicial power of the United States, it is a duty to vest the *whole judicial power.*"[117] Justice Story explained that if Congress could refuse to create lower federal courts, there would be at least some categories of cases that never could be heard in federal court. For instance, there are some matters that cannot be heard by state courts and that cannot be heard by the Supreme Court in its original jurisdiction. In such instances, lower federal courts must exist or no federal judicial tribunal would be available. Justice Story stated: "It would seem, therefore, to follow, that congress [is] bound to create some inferior courts, in which to vest all that jurisdiction which, under the constitution, is *exclusively* vested in the United States and of which the supreme court cannot take original cognizance."[118]

For example, under Supreme Court precedents, state courts may not grant habeas corpus to federal prisoners or issue writs of mandamus compelling performance by federal officers.[119] If there were no lower federal courts, there could be no federal court review of claims arising under the Constitution pursuant to a writ of habeas corpus or a writ of mandamus. The Supreme Court could not hear such matters as part of its original jurisdiction under Article III, and *Marbury v. Madison* conclusively establishes that Congress may not increase the Court's original jurisdiction.[120] Because state courts could not hear the claims, the Supreme Court

---

[116] 14 U.S. (1 Wheat.) 304, 328-331 (1816). *See* Michael G. Collins, Article III Cases, State Court Duties, and the Madisonian Compromise, 1995 Wis. L. Rev. 39 (arguing that history supports Justice Story's theory; that the framers thought that state courts would not adjudicate federal issues and that Congress was required to create lower federal courts to hear these claims).

[117] *Id.* at 328-329 (emphasis in original).

[118] *Id.* at 331 (emphasis in original).

[119] Tarble's Case, 80 U.S. (13 Wall.) 397 (1871) (state courts cannot grant habeas corpus to federal prisoners); M'Clung v. Sillman, 19 U.S. (6 Wheat.) 598 (1821).

[120] 5 U.S. (1 Cranch) 137 (1803). In fact, in *Marbury*, the Court ruled that it could not grant mandamus as part of its original jurisdiction.

could not gain appellate jurisdiction by reviewing state court decisions. In other words, without lower federal courts no federal judicial tribunal would be able to hear the matter. This clearly conflicts with Justice Story's conclusion: "[Congress] might establish one or more inferior courts; they might parcel out the jurisdiction among such courts, from time to time, at their own pleasure. But the whole judicial power of the United States should be, at all times, vested either in an original or appellate form, in some courts created under its authority."[121]

There is one instance in which a lower federal court followed this theory. In *Eisentrager v. Forrestal*, the United States Court of Appeals for the District of Columbia Circuit considered a habeas corpus petition from an individual who was imprisoned by United States military authorities in Germany.[122] The federal habeas corpus statute as then interpreted provided that a federal court could grant habeas relief only to prisoners held within the jurisdiction of the court.[123] Therefore, no federal court had jurisdiction to hear Eisentrager's claim that he was held in custody in violation of the United States Constitution. No state court could hear his habeas petition because of the Supreme Court's decision in *Tarble's Case* preventing state courts from granting habeas to federal prisoners.[124] The Supreme Court lacked original jurisdiction and could not hear the matter on appeal because there was no lower court from which an appeal could be taken.

The District of Columbia Circuit found the complete preclusion of jurisdiction to be unconstitutional and heard the case. The court said that because a state court cannot inquire into the validity of federal custody, federal jurisdiction must exist or else the government's action would be completely unreviewable. The court said that this is impermissible both under Justice Story's theory and because it would allow the government to suspend the writ of habeas corpus in violation of the Constitution.

Justice Story's argument and the holding adopted in *Eisentrager* would require the existence of lower federal courts in two situations. In instances where the Supreme Court cannot exercise original jurisdiction and where state courts cannot hear the matter, lower federal courts must exist to ensure jurisdiction in some federal court. Additionally, if Congress simultaneously restricts Supreme Court and lower federal court jurisdiction, the law would be unconstitutional because under Justice Story's theory some federal court must exist to hear cases and controversies specified in Article III. The proposals to prevent federal court jurisdiction in abortion or school prayer cases would be unconstitutional under this approach because they would preclude both the Supreme Court and the lower federal courts from hearing such matters.

Several alternative versions of Justice Story's approach have been advanced by contemporary commentators. Professor Akhil Amar argued that it is necessary

---

[121] 14 U.S. at 331. In addition to Justice Story's argument, it is possible to argue that restrictions on jurisdiction in such circumstances would deny due process of law; *see* the discussion in §2.10.2, text accompanying notes 135-157, *infra*.

[122] 174 F.2d 961 (D.C. Cir. 1949).

[123] *See* Ahrens v. Clark, 335 U.S. 188 (1948); *but see* Braden v. 30th Judicial Circuit Court of Kentucky, 410 U.S. 484 (1973).

[124] 80 U.S. (13 Wall.) 397 (1871).

to focus carefully on the text of Article III, §2.[125] This section says that the federal judicial power extends to "all" cases arising under the Constitution and laws of the United States, to "all" cases affecting ambassadors and public ministers, and to "all" cases of admiralty or maritime jurisdiction. But the other categories of cases and controversies are not preceded by the word "all." Professor Amar concluded that Justice Story's theory is accurate as to those categories where the Constitution is explicit that the federal judicial power exists to *all* such matters. In such instances, most notably for cases arising under federal law, jurisdiction must exist in some federal court.[126]

An even more expansive argument that lower federal courts are constitutionally required was advanced by Professor Theodore Eisenberg.[127] Professor Eisenberg argued that the framers of the Constitution intended that a federal court would be available, either via original jurisdiction or on appeal, to hear virtually every constitutional claim. The framers assumed that even if lower federal courts did not exist, the Supreme Court could perform the important task of ensuring compliance with the Constitution. But Professor Eisenberg contended that now, given the growth in the size of the country and rise in the volume of litigation, the Supreme Court cannot perform this function by itself. He maintained that Congress must create lower federal courts to ensure the existence of a federal forum for constitutional claims. He stated: "It is thus no longer reasonable to assert that Congress may simply abolish the lower federal courts. When Supreme Court review of all cases within Article III jurisdiction was possible, lower federal courts were perhaps unnecessary. As federal caseloads grew, however, lower federal courts became necessary components of the national judiciary."[128] He concluded that "[i]t can now be asserted that their existence in some form is constitutionally required."[129]

Professor Lawrence Sager developed yet another version of the argument that lower federal courts must exist where otherwise Supreme Court review would be impossible.[130] Professor Sager argued that the essential function of the federal judiciary is the "supervision of state conduct to ensure general compliance with the Constitution."[131] He contended that state courts cannot be fully trusted to perform this function because they lack the assurance of life tenure and salary protections accorded the federal judiciary. His conclusion is that a federal court must exist to hear constitutional challenges to state government actions.

---

[125] Amar, *supra* note 31; *but see* John Harrison, The Power of Congress to Limit the Jurisdiction of Federal Courts and the Text of Article III, 64 U. Chi. L. Rev. 203 (1997) (responding to and critiquing Amar's theory).

[126] *Id.* at 271-272.

[127] Eisenberg, *supra* note 93.

[128] *Id.* at 513.

[129] *Id.*

[130] Lawrence Gene Sager, Foreword: Constitutional Limitations on Congress' Authority to Regulate the Jurisdiction of the Federal Courts, 95 Harv. L. Rev. 17 (1981).

[131] *Id.* at 45. Also, other commentators base an argument for a constitutional requirement that federal courts exist on the intent of the Constitution's framers, *see, e.g.*, Clinton, *supra* note 93; Julius Goebel, History of the Supreme Court of the United States: Antecedents and Beginnings to 1801, at 246 (1971).

But other commentators strongly disagree with the positions advanced by Justice Story and contemporary scholars such as Professors Amar, Eisenberg, and Sager. Supporters of the constitutionality of jurisdiction restrictions contend that the language of Article III is unequivocal: Congress has complete discretion as to whether lower federal courts should exist.[132] Article III represented a compromise. Whereas one group at the Constitutional Convention wanted to ensure the existence of lower federal courts, another faction wanted the Supreme Court to be the exclusive federal judicial tribunal.[133] The compromise was to create a Supreme Court and to leave it to Congress to decide whether and under what circumstances lower federal courts should exist. Any argument that lower federal courts are required to exist disregards this history.

If anything, there might be a due process argument that state courts must be able to hear matters where the effect of jurisdiction stripping would mean that no court would be available. For example, there might be an argument that *Tarble's Case* cannot be applied to prevent a person held in prison in violation of the Constitution from securing some judicial remedy. This due process argument is discussed below, but it should be remembered that due process in this context would require only that some court exist, not that it necessarily would require a federal forum.

Approach 4: Specific Constitutional Limits

There is a fourth and final approach to the issue of congressional restriction of lower federal court jurisdiction. Congress has discretion both to create lower federal courts and to determine their jurisdiction, but Congress may not restrict the jurisdiction in a manner that violates other constitutional provisions. As in the previous section's discussion concerning congressional limitations on Supreme Court jurisdiction, the argument is that Congress's power to restrict jurisdiction—like all congressional powers—cannot be exercised in a manner that violates constitutional rights.

For example, Congress cannot restrict jurisdiction in a manner that would deny due process of law. There is a strong argument that due process would be violated if the effect of the jurisdictional restriction is that no court, state or federal, could hear a constitutional claim. In fact, on several occasions the Supreme Court went out of its way to narrowly construe federal statutes that appeared to preclude all judicial review.[134]

In *Johnson v. Robison*, the Court refused to interpret a statute limiting review of Veterans Administration decisions in a manner that would have foreclosed all

---

[132] *See, e.g.*, Gunther, *supra* note 28, at 895, 916.

[133] This history is described in §1.2.

[134] A distinction might be drawn between statutes that preclude review of statutory claims and those that preclude review of constitutional claims. In *Dalton v. Specter*, 511 U.S. 462 (1994), the Court upheld a federal law that precluded review of the president's closure of military bases under the Defense Base Closure and Realignment Act of 1990. The Court found that Congress could preclude all review of statutory claims, but suggested that Congress may not prevent all federal court review of constitutional claims.

judicial review.[135] Robison, a conscientious objector who had performed alternative service, challenged a federal statute that provided educational benefits to veterans but excluded conscientious objectors. A federal law appeared to preclude federal court review of Robison's claim. The statute provided: "[T]he decisions of the Administrator on any question of law or fact under any law administered by the Veterans Administration providing benefits for veterans . . . shall be final and conclusive and no official or any court of the United States shall have power or jurisdiction to review any such decision."[136]

The Court observed that there would be "serious question" about the constitutionality of this provision if it precluded all review. The Court, however, narrowly interpreted the statute and said that it did not apply in this case because this was not an objection to a decision made by the Veterans Administration, but instead a challenge to a statute adopted by Congress. The Court said that the purposes for the limit on judicial review—deference to the agency in awarding benefits—would not be undermined by allowing jurisdiction to hear challenges to the statute.

Similarly, in *Oestereich v. Selective Service System Local Board No. 11*, the Court narrowly interpreted a provision limiting review of Selective Service decisions.[137] During the 1960s, the Selective Service Commission retaliated against students involved in anti–Vietnam War protests by revoking their student deferments and classifying them as ready for induction. After the federal courts held that this was impermissible and enjoined the Selective Service Commission, Congress responded by adopting a statute limiting judicial review. The Act provided that "no judicial review shall be made of the classification or processing of any registrant . . . except as a defense to a criminal prosecution . . . after the registrant has responded affirmatively or negatively to an order to report for induction."[138] The statute appeared to limit challenges to its validity to two contexts: defenses to a criminal prosecution and habeas corpus.

Oestereich was a full-time student at a theological school preparing for the ministry and was therefore entitled to a draft exemption under federal statutes. But after he participated in an antiwar protest, he was reclassified, I-A, ready for induction. Despite the federal statute appearing to preclude jurisdiction, the Court held that Oestereich could bring a suit challenging the legality of his reclassification. The Court held that the law limiting judicial review was not meant to apply to a clearly lawless action by a draft board. Justice Harlan, in a concurring opinion, stated that it "is doubtful whether a person may be deprived of his personal liberty without the prior opportunity to be heard by some tribunal competent fully to adjudicate his claims."[139]

---

[135] 415 U.S. 361 (1974). *See also* Webster v. Doe, 486 U.S. 592 (1988) (refusing to find statute to preclude review of a claim by an employee of the CIA who alleged that he was fired because he was a homosexual).

[136] 38 U.S.C. §211(a) (1982).

[137] 393 U.S. 233 (1968).

[138] Military Selective Service Act of 1967, 50 U.S.C. §10(b)(3) (1982).

[139] 393 U.S. at 243-244 n.6.

In *United States v. Mendoza-Lopez*, the Court held that an alien who is prosecuted for illegal entry following deportation may assert in the constitutional proceeding the invalidity of the underlying administrative deportation order.[140] In narrowly construing statutes that appeared to preclude judicial review, the Court declared: "[W]here the defects in an administrative proceeding foreclose judicial review of that proceeding, an alternative means of obtaining judicial review must be made available before the administrative order may be used to conclusively establish an element of a criminal offense."[141]

In *McNary v. Haitian Refugee Center, Inc.*, the Supreme Court interpreted a federal statute to avoid finding that it precluded judicial review.[142] The Immigration Reform and Control Act of 1986 created a special amnesty program for specified alien farmworkers and barred judicial review of "a determination respecting an application," except in the federal court of appeals as part of judicial review of a deportation order.

The Supreme Court declared that there is a "well-settled presumption favoring interpretations of statutes that allow judicial review of administrative action."[143] The Court noted that it assumed that Congress was aware of this presumption and therefore "it is most unlikely that Congress intended to foreclose all forms of meaningful judicial review."[144] Hence, the Court concluded that the statute should be interpreted as not precluding judicial review.

Likewise, in *Reno v. Catholic Social Services*, the Court refused to find a preclusion of jurisdiction in INS regulations implementing the legalization program for illegal immigrants under the Immigration Reform and Control Act.[145] The Court explained that to find preclusion of review it "would have to impute to Congress an intent to preclude judicial review of the legality of the INS action entirely under those circumstances."[146] The Court noted that there is a "well-settled presumption" in favor of interpreting statutes to allow judicial review and that it "accordingly will find an intent to preclude such review only if presented with clear and convincing evidence."[147]

In *INS v. St. Cyr*, the Court interpreted jurisdictional preclusion in a federal immigration law as still permitting challenges in federal court via habeas corpus petitions.[148] In the Illegal Immigration Reform and Immigrant Responsibility Act of 1996 (IIRIRA), Congress limited both the attorney general's authority to waive deportation in certain cases and federal court jurisdiction over challenges to deportation. St. Cyr sought to argue that the limitation of waivers by the attorney general did not apply to him, but the statute precluded his seeking judicial review of the deportation order.

[140]   481 U.S. 828 (1987).
[141]   *Id.* at 838-839.
[142]   498 U.S. 479 (1991).
[143]   *Id.* at 480.
[144]   *Id.*
[145]   509 U.S. 43 (1993).
[146]   *Id.* at 63.
[147]   *Id.*
[148]   533 U.S. 289 (2001).

§2.9 Congressional Control of Federal Court Jurisdiction

The Supreme Court, in a 5-to-4 decision, held that the express statutory preclusion of judicial review of deportation proceedings did not bar a challenge from being brought through a writ of habeas corpus. Justice Stevens, writing for the Court, emphasized "the strong presumption in favor of judicial review of administrative action."[149] The Court recognized the statutory preclusion of direct judicial review of INS deportation orders, but said that this did not bar habeas corpus proceedings. Justice Stevens said that Congress "must articulate specific and unambiguous statutory directives" to repeal the availability of habeas jurisdiction.[150]

These cases establish that the Court will go out of its way to read statutes so that they do not foreclose all judicial review. In one instance, a lower federal court declared unconstitutional a federal statute that prevented any court from hearing a matter. In *Battaglia v. General Motors Corp.*, the United States Court of Appeals for the Second Circuit considered a federal statute that precluded all judicial review.[151] Previously, the Supreme Court held that employees were allowed to consider as part of their workweek time spent walking to their work stations, washing after work, and changing clothes.[152] Congress responded by adopting a statute, the Portal-to-Portal Act, specifying that time spent on such activities did not count as part of the workweek.[153] Moreover, the Act provided that "[n]o court of the United States, of any State, Territory or possession of the United States, or of the District of Columbia shall have jurisdiction . . . to enforce liability or impose punishments" for failure of the employer to pay for work time spent on such activities.[154]

The Second Circuit indicated that Congress could not restrict jurisdiction in a manner that prevented all courts from hearing claims. The court explained that "while Congress has the undoubted power to give, withhold, and restrict the jurisdiction of courts other than the Supreme Court, it must not so exercise that power as to deprive any person of life, liberty, or property without due process of law or to take private property without just compensation."[155]

This due process argument states only that *some* court, state or federal, must be available to hear claims. Proposals to restrict federal court jurisdiction to hear abortion and school prayer cases would not violate this requirement because state courts would remain open to decide constitutional challenges to state laws. Due process claims, however, might arise from jurisdiction restrictions in two circumstances.

One is if the state courts would refuse to hear federal constitutional claims in an instance where federal court jurisdiction was precluded. However, in numerous cases the Supreme Court has held that state courts cannot discriminate against federal claims and refuse to hear cases arising under federal law.

Alternatively, due process problems might arise in the face of federal jurisdictional restrictions in circumstances where state courts are precluded from hearing

---

[149] *Id.* at 298.
[150] *Id.* at 298-99.
[151] 169 F.2d 254 (2d Cir. 1948).
[152] Tennessee Coal, Iron & R.R. v. Muscoda Local 123, 321 U.S. 590 (1944).
[153] 61 Stat. 84 (1947), 29 U.S.C. §251.
[154] *Id.* §2(d).
[155] 169 F.2d at 257.

certain matters altogether by federal law. For example, as mentioned earlier, state courts cannot grant habeas corpus petitions of federal prisoners or issue mandamus to federal officers.[156] Under such circumstances, a restriction on federal court jurisdiction would foreclose all court review and pose due process problems.[157] Some commentators have argued that limits on federal court jurisdiction are thus unconstitutional when they have the effect of precluding *all* judicial review, state and federal. This, however, would not be the case with proposals to limit federal court jurisdiction over, for example, abortion or school prayer cases because state courts would remain available. Also, it might be argued that due process requires the state courts to hear the case, not that the restriction on federal jurisdiction is unconstitutional.

In addition to due process as a limit on Congress's power to restrict federal court jurisdiction, it is argued that other constitutional rights as well cannot be violated by jurisdictional restrictions. As was discussed in the previous section with regard to limits on Supreme Court jurisdiction, the paradigm example of an unconstitutional jurisdictional limitation would be a law that prevents blacks from suing in federal court. Some argue similarly that Congress cannot restrict jurisdiction with the purpose and effect of lessening the protection of constitutional rights, such as abortion or school prayer.[158]

But other commentators, who believe that jurisdictional restrictions are constitutional, challenge the analogy between racist restrictions on jurisdiction and those that prevent lower federal courts from hearing specific types of issues. They argue that while the Constitution forbids Congress from discriminating, it does not forbid Congress from singling out particular topics and assigning them to state court rather than federal court.[159] To the contrary, they maintain that the Constitution expressly authorizes Congress to determine the jurisdiction of the federal courts.

Congressional Restriction of Remedies

A related question is whether Congress can limit the remedies federal courts may employ even though it is not completely precluding jurisdiction. For example, can Congress prevent federal courts from using busing as a remedy in school desegregation cases? Some argue that this is unconstitutional because limiting remedies can have the effect of undermining the protection of a constitutional

---

[156] *See, e.g.*, Tarble's Case, 80 U.S. (13 Wall.) 397 (1871) (state courts cannot grant habeas corpus to federal prisoners); M'Clung v. Sillman, 19 U.S. (6 Wheat.) 598 (1821) (state courts cannot issue mandamus to federal officers).

[157] Earlier it was argued that restrictions on all federal court jurisdiction in such circumstances would violate Article III. This is a distinct argument that such jurisdictional limitations would violate due process.

[158] Laurence Tribe, Jurisdictional Gerrymandering: Zoning Disfavored Rights out of the Federal Courts, 16 Harv. C.R.-C.L. L. Rev. 129 (1981) (arguing strict scrutiny is used for laws that burden fundamental rights).

[159] *See, e.g.*, Gunther, *supra* note 28, at 918-919; Bator, *supra* note 37, at 1030, 1034.

right unless other equally effective remedies are available.[160] But others argue that Congress has even greater power to limit remedies than to restrict jurisdiction. They claim that "Congress has plenary authority to structure remedies,"[161] as well as the authority to confer federal jurisdiction on the condition that certain remedies not be used.

In *United States v. Dickerson,*[162] the Supreme Court declared unconstitutional a federal law that sought to overrule *Miranda v. Arizona.*[163] Congress, in a 1968 law, provided that confessions should be admissible in a federal court so long as they were voluntarily obtained, even if *Miranda* warnings were not properly administered. The challenge to the law was based, in part, on the argument that Congress could alter the remedies that federal courts could use for Fifth Amendment violations. The Supreme Court, in a 7-to-2 decision, declared the law unconstitutional. Chief Justice Rehnquist, writing for the Court, said that *Miranda* is a "constitutional rule" and that Congress by statute cannot overturn constitutional rules.

Dickerson does not resolve the question that long has been unresolved as to Congress's ability to limit remedies. But it does make clear that remedies that are deemed themselves to be constitutional rules cannot be modified by Congress.

§2.10   SOVEREIGN IMMUNITY AS A LIMIT ON THE FEDERAL JUDICIAL POWER

Importance of Sovereign Immunity

A major limit on the federal judicial power—and now on the authority of state courts as well—is the doctrine of sovereign immunity. Sovereign immunity in the federal courts is based on the Supreme Court's interpretation of the Eleventh Amendment. The Eleventh Amendment states: "The Judicial power of the United States shall not be construed to extend to any suit in law or equity, commenced or prosecuted against one of the United States by Citizens of another State, or by Citizens or Subjects of any foreign state." As interpreted, the Eleventh Amendment prohibits suits in federal courts against state governments in law, equity, or admiralty, by a state's own citizens, by citizens of another state, or by citizens of foreign countries. Additionally, in 1999 the Supreme Court held that

---

[160]   *See* Ronald D. Rotunda, Congressional Power to Restrict the Jurisdiction of the Lower Federal Courts and the Problem of School Busing, 64 Geo. L.J. 839 (1976); Sharon Susser Harzenski, Jurisdictional Limitations and Suspicious Motives: Why Congress Cannot Forbid Court-Ordered Busing, 50 Temp. L.Q. 14 (1976).

[161]   Mark V. Tushnet & Jennifer Jaff, Why the Debate over Congress' Power to Restrict the Jurisdiction of the Federal Courts Is Unending, 72 Geo. L.J. 1311, 1322 (1984).

[162]   530 U.S. 428 (2000).

[163]   18 U.S.C. §3501.

sovereign immunity bars suits against state governments in state court without their consent.[1] The Court thus has ruled that there is a broad principle of sovereign immunity that applies in both federal and state courts; the Eleventh Amendment is a reflection and embodiment of part of that principle. As Justice Kennedy, writing for the Court in *Alden v. Maine*, declared: "[S]overeign immunity derives not from the Eleventh Amendment but from the structure of the original Constitution itself."[2]

The Eleventh Amendment and sovereign immunity are particularly important in defining the relationship between the federal and state governments and in determining the scope of constitutional protections. An expansive reading of the Eleventh Amendment effectively immunizes the actions of state governments from federal court review, even when a state violates the most fundamental constitutional rights. Hence, the Eleventh Amendment protects state autonomy by immunizing states from suits in federal court, but it provides this independence by risking the ability to enforce basic federal rights. As Professors Low and Jeffries observed: "The stakes involved in interpreting the Eleventh Amendment are potentially very high. Virtually the entire class of modern civil rights litigation plausibly might be barred by an expansive reading of the immunity of the states from suit in federal court."[3]

Unwilling, however, to trust state courts completely to uphold and enforce the Constitution and federal laws, the Supreme Court has devised a number of ways to circumvent the broad prohibition of the Eleventh Amendment and to ensure federal court review of allegedly illegal state actions. The case law concerning the Eleventh Amendment often has been conflicting and inconsistent as the Court has struggled to articulate a standard that protects state autonomy while still ensuring state compliance with federal law. Commentators have labeled these decisions as a "tortuous line of Supreme Court cases"[4] and as "little more than a hodgepodge of confusing and intellectually indefensible judge-made law."[5]

In examining the Eleventh Amendment, §2.10.1 begins by describing the history of its ratification—a history that continues to be examined and relied upon in modern interpretations.[6] Although the Eleventh Amendment has been part of the Constitution since 1795, there still is no agreement as to its proper scope. In fact, several very different theories have been offered as to the appropriate meaning of the amendment. The choice of theory is likely to be determinative of most

---

§2.10 [1] Alden v. Maine, 527 U.S. 706 (1999).

[2] *Id.* at 728.

[3] Peter W. Low & John C. Jeffries, Jr., Federal Courts and the Law of Federal-State Relations 814 (5th ed. 2004).

[4] John R. Pagan, Eleventh Amendment Analysis, 39 Ark. L. Rev. 447, 449 (1986).

[5] John J. Gibbons, The Eleventh Amendment and State Sovereign Immunity: A Reinterpretation, 83 Colum. L. Rev. 1889, 1891 (1983).

[6] *See, e.g.*, Atascadero State Hosp. v. Scanlon, 473 U.S. 234, 247-302 (1985) (Brennan, J., dissenting); William A. Fletcher, A Historical Interpretation of the Eleventh Amendment: A Narrow Construction of an Affirmative Grant of Jurisdiction Rather Than a Prohibition Against Jurisdiction, 35 Stan. L. Rev. 1033 (1983) (detailing the history of the ratification of the Eleventh Amendment as a basis for an argument about its proper scope).

questions that arise concerning the effect of the Eleventh Amendment. These competing theories are described in §2.10.2.

Many particular issues concerning the application of the Eleventh Amendment have been addressed by the Supreme Court. Section 2.10.3 details this law and discusses which suits are prohibited by the amendment, as well as what type of litigation is allowed.

The Supreme Court has devised three primary mechanisms for circumventing the Eleventh Amendment and allowing federal courts to ensure state compliance with federal law. Specifically, the Court has allowed suits against state officers, permitted states to waive their Eleventh Amendment immunity and consent to suit, and sanctioned litigation against the states pursuant to statutes adopted under the Fourteenth Amendment. These techniques are described in §§2.10.4 to 2.10.6.

Underlying Policy Issues

Sovereign immunity is a topic of great significance in current law. From a practical perspective, there is great uncertainty in the current law concerning when state governments may be sued and which actions are barred. From a policy perspective, it raises profound questions about the appropriate role of the judiciary. On the one hand, supporters of sovereign immunity argue that it was a principle that predates the Constitution and is part of the very structure of that document. They maintain that safeguarding state governments, and particularly their treasuries, is deeply embedded in the Constitution. Supporters maintain that there are adequate other ways of holding state governments accountable, such as suits against state officers and suits by the federal government.

Critics of sovereign immunity argue that it is a principle not found in the text of the Constitution or intended by its framers.[7] Opponents of sovereign immunity argue that it wrongly favors government immunity over accountability and is inconsistent with the very notion of a government under law. People can be deprived of their life, liberty, or property, but be left with no remedy and thus no due process. State governments can violate the Constitution and nowhere be held accountable.

In *Alden v. Maine*, Justice Kennedy expressly addressed concerns about accountability and declared:

> The constitutional privilege of a State to assert its sovereign immunity in its own courts does not confer upon the State a concomitant right to disregard the Constitution or valid federal law. The States and their officers are bound by obligations imposed by the Constitution and by federal statutes that comport with the constitutional design. We are unwilling to assume the States will refuse to honor the Constitution or obey the binding laws of the United States. The good faith of the States thus provides an important assurance that "[t]his Constitution, and the

---

[7] I develop these criticisms of sovereign immunity in Erwin Chemerinsky, Against Sovereign Immunity, 53 Stan. L. Rev. 1201 (2001).

Laws of the United States which shall be made in Pursuance thereof . . . shall be the supreme Law of the Land." U.S. Const., Art. VI.[8]

Defenders of sovereign immunity say that the doctrine properly puts trust in governments. Critics argue that such trust has no role in constitutional jurisprudence; government at times will violate the law and must be held accountable.

§2.10.1   History of the Ratification of the Eleventh Amendment

Justices and commentators continue to base their arguments about the proper interpretation of the Eleventh Amendment on claims about the history of its ratification.[9] Therefore, a brief description of this history is appropriate.[10]

Did Article III Override Sovereign Immunity?
The Early Debate

As described earlier, Article III of the Constitution defined the federal judicial power in terms of nine categories of cases and controversies. Two of the clauses of Article III, §2, specifically deal with suits against state governments. These provisions permit suits "between a State and Citizens of another state" and "between a State . . . and foreign . . . Citizens." These are the clauses that the Eleventh Amendment modified, and these are the provisions that are frequently discussed in interpretations of the Eleventh Amendment.

A key matter in dispute is whether the above-quoted language of Article III was meant to override the sovereign immunity that kept states from being sued in state courts. As Justice Souter observed, "The 1787 draft in fact said nothing on the subject and it was this very silence that occasioned some, though apparently not widespread dispute among the framers and others over whether ratification of the Constitution would preclude a state sued in federal court from asserting sovereign immunity as it could have done on any nonfederal matter litigated in its own courts."[11] There is no record of any debate about this issue or these clauses at the Constitutional Convention.

---

[8] 527 U.S. at 754-755.

[9] For example, in *Seminole Tribe of Florida v. Florida*, 517 U.S. 44 (1996), both the majority and the dissent argue over the historical understanding of sovereign immunity and the meaning of the Eleventh Amendment. Justice Souter's dissent, in particular, focuses at length on the history surrounding the adopting of Article III and the ratification of the Eleventh Amendment. *See id.* at 100 (Souter, J., dissenting). Commentators, too, argue at length over the proper historical understanding of the Eleventh Amendment. *See, e.g.,* Carlos Manuel Vazquez, What Is Eleventh Amendment Immunity, 106 Yale L.J. 1683 (1997); Vicki C. Jackson, The Supreme Court, the Eleventh Amendment, and State Sovereign Immunity, 98 Yale L.J. 1 (1988); Fletcher, *supra* note 6, at 1033.

[10] For more detailed histories of the ratification of the Eleventh Amendment, *see* Clyde E. Jacobs, The Eleventh Amendment and Sovereign Immunity (1972); James E. Pfander, History and State Suability: An Explanatory Account of the Eleventh Amendment, 83 Cornell L. Rev. 1269 (1998); Fletcher, *supra* note 6.

[11] Seminole Tribe of Florida v. Florida, 517 U.S. at 100 (Souter, J., dissenting).

However, at the state ratification conventions the question of suits against state governments in federal court was raised and received a great deal of attention. States had incurred substantial debts, especially during the Revolutionary War, and there was a great fear of suits being brought against the states in federal court to collect on these debts. More generally, the concern was expressed that although sovereign immunity was a defense to state law claims in state court, it would be unavailable if the same matter were raised against a state in a diversity suit in federal court.

Thus, at the state ratification conventions there was a debate over whether states could be sued in federal court without their consent.[12] One group argued that the text of Article III clearly made states subject to suit in federal court. In Virginia, George Mason opposed ratification of the Constitution and particularly disliked the provisions that made the states liable in federal court:

> Claims respecting those lands, every liquidated account, or other claim against this state, will be tried before the federal court. Is not this disgraceful? Is this state to be brought to the bar of justice like a delinquent individual? Is the sovereignty of the state to be arraigned like a culprit, or private offender?[13]

Mason believed that Article III's explicit provision for suits against the states would have the effect of abrogating the states' sovereign immunity defense.[14]

Likewise, Patrick Henry opposed the Constitution at the Virginia convention, in part based on his belief that Article III unmistakably permitted litigation against states in federal court. He labeled as "incomprehensible" the claim that Article III allowed states to be plaintiffs, but not defendants.[15] Henry said "[t]here is nothing to warrant such an assertion. . . . What says the paper? That it shall have cognizance of controversies between a state and citizens of another state, without discriminating between plaintiff and defendant."[16]

Nor was this view that Article III overrides state sovereignty and permits suits against unconsenting states in federal court held only in Virginia or only by opponents of ratification. In Pennsylvania, North Carolina, and New York there were major objections to this part of the Constitution.[17] Many of the Constitution's supporters also agreed that Article III permitted states to be sued in federal court. In fact, they argued that this lack of immunity was desirable to ensure that states could not escape their liabilities or avoid litigation that was necessary to hold states properly accountable. Edmund Randolph, a member of the Committee of Detail at the Constitutional Convention, argued: "I ask the Convention of the free people of Virginia if there can be honesty in rejecting the government because justice is to be done by it? . . . Are we to say that we shall discard this government because it would make us all honest?"[18]

---

[12] *See, e.g.,* Jacobs, *supra* note 10, at 27-40; John J. Gibbons, *supra* note 5, at 1889, 1902-1914.

[13] The Debates in the Several States Conventions on the Adoption of the Federal Constitution 526-527 (Jonathan Elliot ed. 1937).

[14] 473 U.S. at 265 (Brennan, J., dissenting) (describing Mason's opposition to Article III).

[15] Elliot, *supra* note 13, at 543.

[16] *Id.*

[17] Gibbons, *supra* note 5, at 1902-1914.

[18] Elliot, *supra* note 13, at 575.

In Pennsylvania, Thomas Pickering argued that it was important for federal courts to be able to give relief against states to citizens of other states or nations who had been wronged and might be unable to receive fair treatment in a state's own courts.[19]

In sharp contrast, many other supporters of the Constitution argued that Article III did not override state sovereignty and that, notwithstanding its provisions, states could be sued in federal court only if they consented to be a party to the litigation. Alexander Hamilton wrote in the Federalist Papers:

> It is inherent in the nature of sovereignty not to be amenable to the suit of an individual *without its consent.* This is the general sense and the general practice of mankind; and the exemption, as one of the attributes of sovereignty, is now enjoyed by the government of every State in the Union. Unless, therefore, there is a surrender of this immunity . . . it will remain with the States.[20]

Similarly, Madison argued that states have sovereign immunity and Article III serves only to allow states to come to federal court as plaintiffs, not that it allows them to be sued as defendants without their consent.[21] Madison said that "jurisdiction in controversies between a state and citizens of another state is much objected to, and perhaps without reason. It is not in the power of individuals to call any state into court."[22]

This recounting of the ratification debates reveals that there was no consensus, even among the Constitution's supporters, about whether state sovereign immunity survived Article III.[23] Yet, as discussed more fully below, the Supreme Court has barred states from being sued by their own citizens, in large part based on its belief, supported by quotations from Madison and Hamilton, that Article III was not intended to authorize states to be sued without their consent.[24] In reviewing the Eleventh Amendment's history, the Supreme Court observed that "[a]t most, then, the historical materials show that . . . the intentions of the framers and Ratifiers were ambiguous."[25]

Chisholm v. Georgia

The dispute over whether sovereign immunity survived Article III was presented to the United States Supreme Court soon after ratification of the

---

[19] 14 John P. Kaminsky & Gaspare J. Saladino, The Documentary History of the Ratification of the Constitution 204 (1983).

[20] The Federalist Papers No. 81, at 487-488 (A. Hamilton) (C. Rossiter ed. 1961) (emphasis in original).

[21] Elliot, *supra* note 13, at 533.

[22] *Id.*

[23] Justice Souter, after a detailed recounting of this history, observed: "[T]he framers and their contemporaries did not agree about the place of common-law state sovereign immunity even as to federal jurisdiction resting on the citizen-state diversity clause." Seminole Tribe of Florida v. Florida, 517 U.S. at 142-143 (Souter, J., dissenting).

[24] *See* Hans v. Louisiana, 134 U.S. 1 (1890); *see also* Seminole Tribe of Florida v. Florida, 517 U.S. at 69-70 (reaffirming *Hans*, in part by defending the views of Marshall, Madison, and Hamilton).

[25] Welch v. Texas Dept. of Highways & Pub. Transp., 483 U.S. 468 (1987).

Constitution. The Judiciary Act of 1789 gave the Supreme Court original jurisdiction in cases between states and citizens of another state or citizens of foreign
states.[26] In fact, the first case filed in the United States Supreme Court involved
a suit by Dutch creditors trying to collect on Revolutionary War debts owed to
them by Maryland.[27] The Supreme Court, however, did not address the question of
Article III and its relation to sovereign immunity until 1794 in *Chisholm v. Georgia*.[28]
This decision is particularly important because the Eleventh Amendment was ratified specifically to overrule the Court's holding in *Chisholm*.

Chisholm involved an attempt by a South Carolina citizen to recover money
owed to him by the State of Georgia. Robert Farquhar, a South Carolina citizen,
had supplied materials to Georgia during the Revolutionary War. Although the
Georgia legislature appropriated the funds for this debt, the Georgia commissar-
ies refused to pay for the purchases. Farquhar died, and Alexander Chisholm,
the executor of his estate, sued Georgia to recover the money owed. Chisholm,
also a South Carolinian, sued in the Supreme Court based on the provision in the
Judiciary Act of 1789 that created original jurisdiction for suits against a state by
citizens of other states.

Chisholm was represented before the Supreme Court by Edmund Randolph,
who was also serving at the time as attorney general of the United States. Randolph,
who had been a delegate at the Constitutional Convention, argued that Article III
of the Constitution clearly permitted suits against states by citizens of other states.
The State of Georgia chose not to appear, believing that federal courts had no
jurisdiction over it unless it consented to be sued.

The Supreme Court, in a 4-to-1 decision, ruled in Chisholm's favor. Announc-
ing their decisions *seriatim*, four Justices seemed to have easily concluded that the
unmistakable language of Article III authorized suits against a state by citizens of
another state. Although later decisions criticized this view of Article III and the
decision in *Chisholm*,[29] it must be remembered that the four Justices in the majority
in *Chisholm* had impeccable credentials, especially in discussing the intent behind
constitutional provisions. Justices John Blair and James Wilson had been delegates
to the Constitutional Convention. Justice William Gushing presided over the state
ratification convention in Massachusetts. Chief Justice John Jay was a delegate to
the New York ratification convention and one of the authors of the Federalist
Papers.[30]

Only Justice Iredell dissented in *Chisholm*. He argued that the Judiciary Act did
not specifically authorize suits in assumpsit against states and such suits were not
permitted against the government in English common law. Thus, he concluded
that the general language of Article III was insufficient to authorize such a suit
against the State of Georgia without its consent.

---

[26] The Judiciary Act of 1789, ch. 20, 1 Stat. 73, 80, at §13.

[27] Vanstophorst v. Maryland, 2 U.S. (2 Dall.) 401 (1791).

[28] 2 U.S. (2 Dall.) 419 (1793).

[29] *See, e.g.*, Hans v. Louisiana, 134 U.S. 1 (1890) (criticizing the decision in *Chisholm v. Georgia*).

[30] John V. Orth, The Judicial Power of the United States: The Eleventh Amendment in American
History 22-23 (1987).

State legislators and governors were outraged by the Supreme Court's decision in *Chisholm v. Georgia.* Georgia adopted a statute declaring that anyone attempting to enforce the Supreme Court's decision is "hereby declared to be guilty of a felony, and shall suffer death, without the benefit of clergy by being hanged."[31] The intense reaction to *Chisholm* is reflected in the speed with which a constitutional amendment to overturn the decision was adopted. The Supreme Court decided *Chisholm* on February 14, 1794. By March 4, 1794, less than three weeks later, both houses of Congress had approved the Eleventh Amendment. Within a year, the requisite number of states ratified it, although it was three more years until the president issued a proclamation declaring the Eleventh Amendment to have been properly ratified.[32]

The consensus among historians is that states were particularly concerned about the *Chisholm* decision because they feared suits against them to collect unpaid Revolutionary War debts.[33] Also, there was fear that British creditors and American Tories whose property was seized during the war would sue the states to recover their assets.[34] The fact that such suits already had been filed in South Carolina, Georgia, Virginia, and Massachusetts indicated that it was not an idle fear.[35] Thus, within a few years after *Chisholm*, the Eleventh Amendment was adopted to prohibit federal courts from hearing suits against a state by citizens of another state or of a foreign country.

§2.10.2   *What Does the Eleventh Amendment Mean?*

Competing Theories of the Eleventh Amendment

Although the Eleventh Amendment is over 200 years old, there still is no agreement as to what it means or what it prohibits. In fact, several different theories have been developed to interpret it. The theory chosen determines the scope of the Eleventh Amendment and the circumstances under which states may be sued in federal courts.

The Rehnquist Court was split between two different theories. One theory—supported by a majority comprising Chief Justice Rehnquist and Justices O'Connor, Scalia, Kennedy, and Thomas—saw the Eleventh Amendment as a restriction on the subject matter jurisdiction of the federal courts that bars all suits against state governments. The competing theory—supported by Justices Stevens, Souter, Ginsburg, and Breyer—viewed the Eleventh Amendment as restricting the federal courts' subject matter jurisdiction only in precluding cases being brought against

---

[31] Low & Jeffries, *supra* note 3, at 810.

[32] For a description of this history, and a discussion of why there was such a delay in the issuance of the presidential proclamation, *see* Orth, *supra* note 30, at 20-21.

[33] 1 Charles Warren, The Supreme Court in United States History 99 (1922); Orth, *supra* note 30, at 7-8. *But see* Jacobs, *supra* note 10, at 70 ("[T]here is practically no evidence that Congress proposed and the legislatures ratified the Eleventh Amendment to permit the states to escape payment of existing obligations.").

[34] Orth, *supra* note 30, at 7.

[35] Warren, *supra* note 33, at 99.

states that are founded solely on diversity jurisdiction.[36] Four of these Justices have left the bench and have been replaced by Chief Justice Roberts and Justices Alito, Sotomayor, and Kagan. It appears the current Court also will split 5-4, with Roberts and Alito joining with Scalia, Kennedy, and Thomas, while Sotomayor and Kagan join with Ginsburg and Breyer.[37]

Hans v. Louisiana

In order to understand the alternative theories, it is important to note that the Supreme Court has interpreted the Eleventh Amendment as prohibiting suits against a state by its own citizens, as well as by citizens of other states and foreign countries.[38] Although the terms of the amendment only prohibit suits against a state by citizens of other states and foreign countries, the Supreme Court, in 1890, in *Hans v. Louisiana*, held that it would be "anomalous" to allow states to be sued by their own citizens.[39] Thus, since *Hans*, states have been immune to suits both by their own citizens and by citizens of other states.[40]

---

[36] Another theory of the Eleventh Amendment is that it reinstates the common law immunity from suit enjoyed by states prior to the adoption of Article III and, perhaps, prior to the Supreme Court's decision in *Chisholm v. Georgia*. For a thorough defense of this theory, *see* Vicki C. Jackson, The Supreme Court, the Eleventh Amendment, and State Sovereign Immunity, 98 Yale L.J. 1 (1988). In *Chisholm*, the Court held that Article III of the Constitution permits states to be sued by citizens of other states. Thus, some believe that the Eleventh Amendment in reversing *Chisholm* reinstated the common law immunity that states previously possessed. The claim is that originally states had common law immunity as to all suits against them. Article III and *Chisholm* denied immunity to the states from suits brought by citizens of other states. Thus, the Eleventh Amendment reinstituted the previously existing sovereign immunity. Under this theory, the Eleventh Amendment does not create a constitutional bar to suits against a state by its own citizens. The Eleventh Amendment by its terms and history has nothing to do with such suits. States had sovereign immunity to suits by their own citizens prior to the adoption of the Constitution, and Article III did not change this by authorizing suits against a state by citizens of other states and foreign countries. *Chisholm* and the Eleventh Amendment leave untouched a state's common law immunity to suits by citizens against their own states. Therefore, according to this view, the Court in *Hans* was not using the Eleventh Amendment as a constitutional bar, but was stating only the unchanged principle of common law immunity. In earlier cases, Justice Brennan advocated this theory. Employees of the Dept. of Pub. Health & Welfare v. Department of Pub. Health & Welfare, 411 U.S. 279, 309-322 (1973) (Brennan, J., dissenting). However, in his later opinions, Justice Brennan shifted to the approach discussed below that the Eleventh Amendment is a restriction only on diversity jurisdiction. *See, e.g.*, Pennsylvania v. Union Gas Co., 491 U.S. 1, 5 (1989); Atascadero State Hosp. v. Scanlon, 473 U.S. 234, 258-259 (1985) (Brennan, J., dissenting).

[37] For example, in Coleman v. Court of Appeals of Maryland, 132 S. Ct. 1327 (2012), the Roberts Court ruled 5-4 that state governments could not be sued under the self-care provision of the Family and Medical Leave Act. Justice Kennedy wrote the majority opinion joined by Chief Justice Roberts and Justices Scalia, Thomas, and Alito. Justice Ginsburg wrote the dissent, joined by Justices Breyer, Sotomayor, and Kagan. *Coleman* is discussed in §3.8.

[38] *See* discussion in §2.10.3 *infra*.

[39] 134 U.S. 1, 18 (1890).

[40] *See, e.g.*, Employees of the Dept. of Pub. Health & Welfare v. Department of Pub. Health & Welfare, 411 U.S. 279, 280 (1973) ("[A]n unconsenting State is immune from suits brought in federal courts by her own citizens as well as by citizens of another State."); In re New York, 256 U.S. 490, 497 (1921) (federal courts may not hear suits "brought by citizens of another state, or by citizens or

The underlying basis for the decision in *Hans*, and of the entire Eleventh Amendment, remains very much in dispute. In fact, Justices have very much disagreed over whether *Hans* was correct or whether it should be overruled. For example, in *Seminole Tribe of Florida v. Florida*, the Court's majority reaffirmed *Hans* and declared that the "decision found its roots not solely in the common law of England, but in the much more fundamental 'jurisprudence of all civilized nations.'"[41] In contrast, the dissent identified three critical errors in *Hans*: "[T]he *Hans* Court misread the Eleventh Amendment; [i]t also misunderstood the conditions under which common law doctrines were received or rejected at the time of the founding, and it fundamentally mistook the very nature of sovereignty in the young republic that was supposed to entail a state's immunity to federal question jurisdiction in federal court."[42] The majority views *Hans* as reflecting a constitutional principle, embodied in the Eleventh Amendment: that states have sovereign immunity when sued in federal court. The dissent sees *Hans* as wrongly decided and at most only recognizing common law immunity for state governments.

First Theory: Constitutional Limit on Subject Matter Jurisdiction for All Suits Against State Governments

One theory is that sovereign immunity creates a constitutional restriction on federal court subject matter jurisdiction for all suits against state governments. By this view, the Eleventh Amendment is part of a broader constitutional limitation on federal court jurisdiction created by sovereign immunity. Proponents of this view point to the initial language of the amendment, which appears to express a constitutional limitation on federal subject matter jurisdiction: "The Judicial power of the United States shall not be construed to extend to. . . ." In articulating this view, the Supreme Court declared that the Eleventh Amendment "affirm[s] that the fundamental principle of sovereign immunity limits the grant of judicial authority in Art. III."[43]

Although it is possible to argue that the constitutional bar applies only to suits brought by citizens of other states, those who advocate this first theory believe that *Hans* establishes sovereign immunity limits on federal court jurisdiction barring suits against a state by its own citizens. In cases involving suits against a state by its own citizens, the Supreme Court has declared that "the principle of sovereign immunity is a constitutional limitation on the federal judicial power established in Art. III"[44] and that "[t]he Eleventh Amendment is an explicit limitation of the judicial power of the United States."[45] In *Edelman v. Jordan*, for instance, the Supreme Court held that defendants could raise the Eleventh Amendment in the court of

---

subjects of a foreign state, because of the Eleventh Amendment; and not even one brought by its own citizens, because of the fundamental rule of which the Amendment is but an exemplification").

[41] 517 U.S. at 69.

[42] *Id.* at 130 (Souter, J., dissenting).

[43] Pennhurst State School & Hosp. v. Halderman, 465 U.S. 89, 98 (1984).

[44] *Id.*

[45] Missouri v. Fiske, 290 U.S. 18, 25 (1933).

appeals, although it had not been argued in the trial court.[46] Generally, except for jurisdictional arguments, matters may not be raised on appeal if they were not presented in the lower court. The Court concluded that the Eleventh Amendment partakes sufficiently of the characteristics of a jurisdictional bar that it may be raised for the first time on appeal.

In other words, the first approach to the Eleventh Amendment is that federal court subject matter jurisdiction is limited by the states' sovereign immunity. Justices holding this view have declared that the Eleventh Amendment reflects a "broad constitutional principle of sovereign immunity."[47] The principle of sovereign immunity is explicitly articulated in the text of the Eleventh Amendment for suits against a state by citizens of other states and was recognized by the Supreme Court in *Hans v. Louisiana* for suits against a state by its own citizens.

The Supreme Court, however, has not been completely consistent in treating the Eleventh Amendment as a restriction on subject matter jurisdiction. For example, it is firmly established that subject matter jurisdiction may not be gained in federal court by consent or waiver.[48] Agreement of the parties is never sufficient to create federal court jurisdiction when it otherwise would not be allowed. Yet the Supreme Court repeatedly and consistently has held that a state may waive its Eleventh Amendment immunity.[49] In *Hans*, for instance, the Court observed that a state is immune "unless the State consents to be sued."[50] But waiver should not be possible if the Eleventh Amendment is a restriction on subject matter jurisdiction.

Also, federal courts are required to raise objections to subject matter jurisdiction on their own when defects in jurisdiction become apparent. Subject matter jurisdiction is different from almost all other areas where courts must wait for the parties to raise objections. Yet the Supreme Court concluded that "we have never held that [the Eleventh Amendment] is jurisdictional in the sense that it must be raised and decided by this Court on its own motion."[51]

More fundamentally, it is difficult to justify the view that the Eleventh Amendment constitutionally prohibits federal courts from hearing suits against a state by its own citizens, and that sovereign immunity bars suits against state governments in state courts. The terms of the amendment speak only to suits against a state by citizens of other states and foreign countries.[52] The amendment was

---

[46] 415 U.S. 651, 677-678 (1974) (*Edelman* involved a suit against the Illinois Commissioner of the Department of Public Welfare brought by Illinois citizens).

[47] Pennsylvania v. Union Gas Co., 491 U.S. 1, 39 (1989) (Scalia, J., concurring in part and dissenting in part) (citations omitted).

[48] *See, e.g.*, Sosna v. Iowa, 419 U.S. 393, 398 (1975); Mitchell v. Maurer, 293 U.S. 237 (1934); Mansfield, C. & L.M. Ry. v. Swan, 111 U.S. 379, 382 (1884).

[49] Port Authority Trans-Hudson Corp. v. Feeney, 495 U.S. 299, 305-306 (1990). *Pennhurst*, 465 U.S. at 99; Ashton v. Cameron County Water Improvement Dist., 298 U.S. 513, 531 (1936). *See* discussion in §2.10.5, *infra*.

[50] 134 U.S. at 20.

[51] Patsy v. Board of Regents of Fla., 457 U.S. 496, 516 n.19 (1982).

[52] The Supreme Court acknowledged this, but declared: "Although the text of the amendment would appear to restrict only the Article III diversity jurisdiction of the federal courts, we have understood the 11th Amendment to stand not so much for what it says, but for the presupposition which it confirms." Seminole Tribe of Florida v. Florida, 517 U.S. 44, 54 (1996).

added to the Constitution to overrule the Supreme Court's decision in *Chisholm v. Georgia*,[53] which had upheld the right of a South Carolina resident to sue the State of Georgia. The focus was on protecting a state from suits by citizens of other states. Thus, neither the language nor the history of the Eleventh Amendment justifies reading it as creating a constitutional bar to suits against states by their own citizens.[54] Moreover, if sovereign immunity is a limit on federal judicial power even when not expressed in the text of the Constitution, then it is a principle of even greater significance than the document itself. This theory seems inconsistent with the supremacy clause, which declares that the Constitution is the supreme law of the land.

On the other hand, the advantage of this first approach is that it provides a clear rule: Federal courts may not hear suits against state governments regardless of the citizenship of the plaintiffs. Additionally, it is a view based on a need for federal court deference to state governments and for the use of federalism to protect states from federal encroachments. In fact, the Supreme Court has spoken of "the vital role of the doctrine of sovereign immunity in our federal system."[55]

Second Theory: Limit Only Diversity Suits

A second view of the Eleventh Amendment treats it as restricting only the diversity jurisdiction of federal courts.[56] Article III of the Constitution permits subject matter jurisdiction either based on the content of the litigation—for example, federal question jurisdiction—or based on the identity of the parties—for example, diversity jurisdiction. Article III, §2, identifies nine categories of cases and controversies that might be heard in federal court. One of these is "Cases, in Law and Equity, arising under this Constitution, the Laws of the United States, and Treaties made, or which shall be made, under their Authority." This is the provision that authorizes federal question jurisdiction. A different, later passage of Article III, §2, allows for "Controversies . . . between a State and Citizens of another state." This is an authorization for suits against a state based on diversity of citizenship.

The language of the Eleventh Amendment clearly is directed at modifying this latter provision. In fact, the amendment simply states: "The Judicial Power of the United States shall not be construed to extend to any suit . . . against one of the United States by Citizens of another state." Because *Chisholm* only involved this latter part of Article III, it makes sense to view the Eleventh Amendment as restricting only diversity suits against state governments. Therefore, according to this view, the Eleventh Amendment does not bar suits against states based on other parts of Article III. Most notably, the amendment does not preclude suits based

---

[53] 2 U.S. (2 Dall.) 419 (1793). *See* discussion in §2.10.1, *supra*.

[54] *See* Lawrence Marshall, Fighting the Words of the Eleventh Amendment, 102 Harv. L. Rev. 1342 (1989) (arguing from the text of the Eleventh Amendment that it is a prohibition against states being sued by citizens of other states).

[55] *Pennhurst*, 465 U.S. at 99.

[56] *See* Gibbons, *supra* note 5, at 1889; Fletcher, *supra* note 6, at 1033.

on federal question jurisdiction. Thus, all claims of state violations of the United States Constitution or federal laws could be heard in federal courts.[57]

Those who take this view also reject the Court's conclusion in *Alden v. Maine* that state governments cannot be sued in state court without their consent.

However, it should be noted that this view is inconsistent with the Supreme Court's decision in *Hans v. Louisiana*.[58] In *Hans*, a federal question was presented in a suit by a Louisiana resident against Louisiana; the issue was whether Louisiana had unconstitutionally impaired the obligation of contracts by refusing to pay interest owed on bonds it had issued. If the Eleventh Amendment only restricts diversity suits and does not affect federal question jurisdiction, then *Hans* was wrongly decided and the suit should not have been dismissed.[59] Several prominent scholars, such as Judge William Fletcher and Professor David Shapiro, and four Supreme Court Justices in dissenting opinions have taken exactly this position and contended that the decision in *Hans* was an error.[60]

Supreme Court's Current View

As explained previously, in recent years the Court has been split 5 to 4 between these two theories. In *Pennsylvania v. Union Gas Co.*, in 1989, only four Justices—Chief Justice Rehnquist and Justices O'Connor, Scalia, and Kennedy—took the position that the Eleventh Amendment reflects a "broad constitutional principle of sovereign immunity" that protects states from virtually all suits in federal court.[61] These four Justices were joined by Justice Thomas to create a clear majority approach.[62]

For the last quarter of a century, there have been four Justices adopting the latter view, that the Eleventh Amendment bars only suits founded solely on diversity jurisdiction. During the late 1980s, Justices Brennan, Marshall, Blackmun, and Stevens repeatedly expressed the view that "if federal jurisdiction is based on the existence of a federal question or some other clause of Article III, however, the

---

[57] There are alternative versions of the diversity theory. Professor William Fletcher argues that the amendment prohibits only suits founded solely on diversity jurisdiction; federal question suits against states are allowed. William A. Fletcher, The Diversity Explanation of the Eleventh Amendment: A Reply to Critics, 56 U. Chi. L. Rev. 1261 (1989). In contrast, Professor Larry Marshall contends that states may not be sued by citizens of other states in federal court under either diversity or federal question jurisdiction. Marshall, *supra* note 54.

[58] 134 U.S. 1 (1890).

[59] Professor William Marshall argues that neither the text of the Eleventh Amendment nor its history supports the claims for the diversity theory and that those who advocate this approach have failed to meet their burden of overcoming the 100 years of precedent since *Hans*. William P. Marshall, The Diversity Theory of the Eleventh Amendment: A Critical Evaluation, 102 Harv. L. Rev. 1372 (1989).

[60] Fletcher, *supra* note 6, at 1087-1091; David L. Shapiro, Wrong Turns: The Eleventh Amendment and the *Pennhurst* Case, 98 Harv. L. Rev. 61, 70 (1984); Seminole Tribe of Florida v. Florida, 517 U.S. at 100 (Stevens, J., dissenting), at 76 (Souter, Ginsburg, and Breyer, JJ., dissenting). *See also* Atascadero State Hosp. v. Scanlon, 473 U.S. at 301-302 (Brennan, Marshall, Blackmun, and Stevens, JJ., dissenting).

[61] 491 U.S. at 39 (Scalia, J., concurring in part and dissenting in part).

[62] *See* Seminole Tribe of Florida v. Florida, 517 U.S. at 46.

Eleventh Amendment has no relevance."[63] More recently, Justices Stevens, Souter, Ginsburg, and Breyer took this position.[64]

Of course, two Justices from each side of this divide have been replaced—Rehnquist and O'Connor by Roberts and Alito, Souter and Stevens by Sotomayor and Kagan. The expectation and indication so far is that the Court will continue to split 5-4, with the conservative position in the majority, on the issue of sovereign immunity.[65]

Underlying Value Question

Ultimately, the choice among the two theories is, in large part, a value question: How should state sovereignty be weighed against federal supremacy? For instance, the first theory accords great importance to sovereign immunity and federalism, but less weight to ensuring state compliance with the Constitution. In contrast, the second theory makes the opposite choice: subjecting states to liability whenever they violate federal law, but according relatively little weight to state sovereign immunity. Eleventh Amendment doctrines—and sovereign immunity more generally—thus reflect baseline assumptions about both the need for court review to ensure state compliance with federal law and the importance of immunizing state governments from federal jurisdiction.

§2.10.3 The Application of the Eleventh Amendment: What's Barred and What's Allowed

There have been literally dozens of Supreme Court decisions defining the scope of the Eleventh Amendment and delineating what suits are prohibited in federal court and what suits are permissible. This section describes this law. Postponed for consideration until the subsequent sections is discussion of three major ways around the Eleventh Amendment: suits against state officers for injunctive relief or money damages;[66] suits based on state consent to federal court jurisdiction; and suits pursuant to congressional statutes, especially those pursuant to civil rights laws.

---

[63] *See, e.g.*, Atascadero State Hosp. v. Scanlon, 473 U.S. at 234, 301 (Brennan, J., dissenting); *see also* Welch v. Texas Dept. of Highways & Pub. Transp., 483 U.S. 468, 496 (1987).

[64] Seminole Tribe of Florida v. Florida, 517 U.S. at 76, 96 (Stevens, J., dissenting; Souter, J., dissenting).

[65] *See* Coleman v. Court of Appeals of Maryland, 132 S. Ct. 1327 (2012) (holding, 5-4, that states cannot be sued under the self-care provision of the Family and Medical Leave Act, reflecting the continuing 5-4 divide between these theories of the Eleventh Amendment). *Coleman* is discussed below in §3.8.

[66] The distinction between "official capacity" and "individual capacity" suits is discussed in §2.10.2 at notes 45-52, *supra*.

Suits Barred

Most consistently, the Supreme Court has held that the Eleventh Amendment precludes suits against a state government by citizens of another state or citizens of a foreign country.[67] The very terms of the amendment clearly prohibit federal court jurisdiction over such litigation. Based on this provision, the Court has held that the Eleventh Amendment bars Indian tribes from suing state governments in federal court without their consent.[68]

Additionally, the Supreme Court repeatedly has held that the Eleventh Amendment bars suits against a state by its own citizens.[69] As described above, in *Hans v. Louisiana*, the Supreme Court applied the Eleventh Amendment to preclude a suit by a Louisiana resident against Louisiana to compel officials to pay money owed under state-issued bonds and coupons.[70] The Court held that a suit against an unconsenting state, even when brought by a citizen of that state, was "unknown to the law . . . [and] not contemplated by the Constitution when establishing the judicial power of the United States."[71] The Court concluded that it would be "anomalous" to allow a state to be sued by its own citizens in federal court when it cannot be sued by citizens of other states or nations. Although many commentators urged the overruling of *Hans*,[72] the Court repeatedly has reaffirmed it over the past decade.

Although the terms of the Eleventh Amendment speak only about federal jurisdiction over "suits in law or equity," the Supreme Court also has found admiralty suits against the states to be barred.[73] Likewise, despite the language of the amendment discussing suits by "Citizens of another State, or by Citizens or Subjects of any Foreign State," the Court has held that the Eleventh Amendment prohibits suits against a state by foreign nations[74] or Native American tribes.[75]

Additionally, although the Eleventh Amendment speaks only of restrictions on the federal judicial power, in *Alden v. Maine* the Court held that state governments

---

[67] *See, e.g.*, In re New York, 256 U.S. 490 (1921); Smith v. Reeves, 178 U.S. 436 (1900); Fitts v. McGhee, 172 U.S. 516 (1899). The protection of states against suits in federal court also applies to territories of the United States. *See, e.g.*, Fred v. Rogue, 916 F.2d 37, 38 (1st Cir. 1990); Rodriguez-Garcia v. Davila, 904 F.2d 90, 98 (1st Cir. 1990).

[68] Seminole Tribe of Florida v. Florida, 517 U.S 44 (1996); Blatchford v. Native Village of Noatak, 501 U.S. 775 (1991).

[69] Edelman v. Jordan, 415 U.S. 651 (1974); Missouri v. Fiske, 290 U.S. 18, 28 (1933); Hans v. Louisiana, 134 U.S. 1, 15 (1890).

[70] 134 U.S. 1 (1890). For an excellent discussion of the background of this case and the development of the Eleventh Amendment doctrines, *see* Orth, *supra* note 30.

[71] 134 U.S. at 15.

[72] *Id.* at 18. For detailed criticism of the *Hans* decision, *see* Fletcher, supra note 6, at 1033, 1087-1091; Shapiro, *supra* note 60; Seminole Tribe of Florida v. Florida, 517 U.S. at 100 (Souter, J., dissenting); Atascadero State Hosp. v. Scanlon, 473 U.S. 234, 259-260, 299-302 (1985) (Brennan, Marshall, Blackmun, and Stevens, JJ., dissenting).

[73] *See, e.g.*, Florida Dept. of State v. Treasure Salvors, Inc., 458 U.S. 670 (1982); In re New York, 256 U.S. 490 (1921).

[74] *See, e.g.*, Monaco v. Mississippi, 292 U.S. 313 (1934).

[75] *See, e.g.*, Seminole Tribe of Florida v. Florida, 517 U.S. 44 (1996).

cannot be sued in state court without their consent.[76] Probation officers in Maine sued, claiming that they were owed overtime pay under the federal Fair Labor Standards Act. The suit was initially filed in federal court, but was dismissed based on the Eleventh Amendment. The probation officers then sued in Maine state court. The Supreme Court, in a 5-to-4 decision, ruled that the state had sovereign immunity and could not be sued in state court, even on a federal claim, without its consent. Justice Kennedy wrote for the Court and acknowledged that the Constitution and its framers were silent about the ability to sue state governments in state courts. Justice Kennedy said, though, that it was unthinkable that the states would have ratified the Constitution had they thought that it made them subject to suit without their consent. The Court declared: "We hold that the powers delegated to Congress under Article I of the United States Constitution do not include the power to subject nonconsenting States to private suits for damages in state courts."[77]

In *Federal Maritime Commission v. South Carolina Ports Authority*,[78] the Supreme Court held that states cannot be named as defendants in federal administrative agency proceedings. A cruise ship company brought a claim against a state agency in the Federal Maritime Commission, claiming that it had been discriminated against in violation of federal maritime law. The Supreme Court, in a 5-to-4 decision, held that such actions are barred by sovereign immunity. The Court relied on *Alden v. Maine*'s conclusion that sovereign immunity is broader than the protections of the Eleventh Amendment. The Court said that the "preeminent purpose" of sovereign immunity is to protect the "dignity" of state governments and that such dignity would be impermissibly offended by allowing states to be named as defendants in agency proceedings without their consent.

Suits Allowed

In contrast, the Supreme Court has refused to apply the Eleventh Amendment in many instances. For example, the Eleventh Amendment does not bar federal court suits by the United States government against a state.[79]

Also, the Eleventh Amendment does not bar suits against a state by another state.[80] However, for such suits to be allowed the state must be suing to protect its own interests. If the state is suing to collect debts owed to individual citizens, then the litigation is barred from the federal courts by the Eleventh Amendment.[81] The apparent rationale is that it is important for there to be a neutral forum to resolve disagreements between the states, but the Court will not allow circumvention of the Eleventh Amendment by allowing states to litigate their citizens' claims.

---

[76] 527 U.S. 706.
[77] *Id.* at 711.
[78] 535 U.S. 743 (2002).
[79] *See, e.g.*, United States v. Mississippi, 380 U.S. 128, 140-141 (1965).
[80] *See, e.g.*, Colorado v. New Mexico, 459 U.S. 176, 182 n.9 (1982).
[81] *See, e.g.*, Maryland v. Louisiana, 451 U.S. 725, 745 n.21 (1981).

The Supreme Court also has carved an exception for suits in admiralty. In *Florida Department of State v. Treasure Salvors, Inc.*, the Supreme Court held that the Eleventh Amendment did not bar a federal court from issuing a warrant in an in rem action for a wreckage in an admiralty suit.[82] In *California v. Deep Sea Research*, the Court ruled that the Eleventh Amendment does not bar jurisdiction over an in rem admiralty suit where the state is not in possession of the property.[83]

The Court applied this exception in *Tennessee Student Assistance Corp. v. Hood*, to hold that states can be sued in bankruptcy proceedings to discharge debts since they are in rem in nature.[84] Two years later, in *Central Virginia Community College v. Katz*, the Supreme Court went even further and held that the Eleventh Amendment and sovereign immunity do not apply in bankruptcy proceedings at all.[85] Justice Stevens wrote for the Court in a 5-4 decision. He concluded that the clause in Article I, §8, of the Constitution, empowering Congress to create uniform rules for bankruptcy, was meant to override considerations of sovereign immunity. The Court declared that the clause, its history, and the initial bankruptcy legislation enacted by Congress all "demonstrate that [the bankruptcy clause] was intended not just as a grant of legislative authority to Congress, but also to authorize limited subordination of state sovereign immunity in the bankruptcy arena."[86]

In other words, the Court did not hold that the Bankruptcy Act's authorization of suits against states was sufficient to override sovereign immunity. Rather, more broadly, the Court concluded that sovereign immunity does not apply at all in proceedings properly arising under the bankruptcy powers of Congress.

The interesting question is why sovereign immunity is not implicated as to this power of Congress, but is present when Congress acts under other powers found in Article I, §8, such as pursuant to its authority to create patents and copyrights.[87] Is there something in the nature or history of the bankruptcy power that makes it different from other powers? Interestingly, eight of the Justices likely see no distinction. It was only Justice O'Connor who was in the majority in both cases and she did not write a separate opinion explaining why. *Katz* was a 5-4 decision, which came down just before Justice O'Connor left the Court; it is quite possible it would have come out differently with Justice Alito on the bench instead of Justice O'Connor.

The Eleventh Amendment only applies in federal court; it does not prevent a state from being sued in its own courts or in another state's courts.[88] Significantly, the Eleventh Amendment does not prevent the United States Supreme

---

[82] 458 U.S. 670 (1982). Four Justices indicated that the Eleventh Amendment might bar determination of the state's ownership of the wreckage.

[83] 523 U.S. 491 (1998).

[84] 541 U.S. 440 (2004).

[85] 546 U.S. 346 (2006).

[86] *Id.* at 362-363.

[87] *See* Florida Prepaid Postsecondary Ed. Expense Bd. v. College Savings Bank, 527 U.S. 627 (1989) (holding that Congress cannot authorize suits against states for patent infringement).

[88] Nevada v. Hall, 440 U.S. 410 (1979).

Court from hearing claims against the state as part of its appellate jurisdiction.[89] The Court has concluded that the Eleventh Amendment bars suits "commenced or prosecuted" in federal court, thus barring original jurisdiction before the Supreme Court or other federal courts, but not appellate jurisdiction in the form of Supreme Court review of state court decisions where the state is a party.[90] Thus, the Court declared: "We recognize what has long been implied in our consistent practice and uniformly endorsed in our cases: the Eleventh Amendment does not constrain the appellate jurisdiction of the Supreme Court over cases arising from state courts."[91]

Suits Against Cities

Perhaps most importantly, the Court long has held that the Eleventh Amendment does not bar suits against municipalities or political subdivisions of a state.[92] The ability to sue local governments in federal court is significant because it is this level of government that provides most social services in this country, such as police and fire protection, education, and sanitation. Therefore, if the Eleventh Amendment barred suits against municipalities, federal courts could not ensure compliance with the Constitution by those who are most likely to violate it.

The Supreme Court, however, has said that the state's Eleventh Amendment immunity does extend to local governments when there is so much state involvement in the municipalities' actions that the relief, in essence, runs against the state. In *Pennhurst State School & Hospital v. Halderman*, the Court held that relief against the county as well as against state officers was barred by the Eleventh Amendment.[93] The Court concluded that the county could not be sued in federal court because "funding for the county mental retardation programs comes almost entirely from the State . . . and the costs of the Masters have been borne by the State. . . . Finally, the MH/MR Act contemplates that the state and county officials will cooperate in operating the mental retardation programs."[94] Thus, the state's funding of a county program and cooperation were deemed sufficient to create an Eleventh Amendment barrier to suits against the county.

---

[89] *See, e.g.*, McKesson Corp. v. Division of Alcohol Beverages & Tobacco, Dept. of Bus. Reg. of Fla., 496 U.S. 18, 26 (1990); Maine v. Thiboutot, 448 U.S. 1, 9 n.7 (1980); Nevada v. Hall, 440 U.S. 410, 418-421 (1979).

[90] Monaco v. Mississippi, 292 U.S. 313 (1934) (Supreme Court cannot hear on its original jurisdiction claims against state governments).

[91] McKesson Corp. v. Div. of Alcohol Beverages & Tobacco, Dept. of Bus. Reg. of Fla., 496 U.S. at 26.

[92] *See, e.g.*, Mt. Healthy City School Dist. Bd. of Educ. v. Doyle, 429 U.S. 274 (1977); Lincoln County v. Luning, 133 U.S. 529 (1890). Some criticize these decisions on the ground that states should be able to transfer their immunity to local governments, which are created by the state and through which the states govern. *See, e.g.*, Margreth Barrett, Comment, The Denial of Eleventh Amendment Immunity to Political Subdivisions of the States: An Unjustified Strain on Federalism, 1979 Duke L.J. 1042.

[93] 465 U.S. 89, 123-124 (1979).

[94] *Id.* at 124.

This holding is a potentially marked expansion of local government immunity. Interestingly, the Court supported its conclusion by citation to only one Supreme Court precedent, *Lake County Estates, Inc. v. Tahoe Regional Planning Agency*.[95] In that case, however, the Supreme Court reached exactly the opposite result, holding that state funding of an interstate agency did not confer the protection of the Eleventh Amendment upon the agency.[96] The Court stated that it "has consistently refused to construe the amendment to afford protection to political subdivisions such as counties and municipalities, even though such entities exercise a 'slice of state power.' "[97] The Eleventh Amendment prevents suits against local governments only if a money judgment has to be paid directly by the state treasury. In *Pennhurst*, the state was not obligated to pay any money judgment issued against the county. Nor is it clear why state cooperation is sufficient to immunize municipalities, because in the *Lake County Estates* case the Supreme Court explicitly held that state cooperation in regional compacts did not bestow immunity on those entities.[98]

Immunity of State Agencies

Finally, the law concerning the immunity of state agencies, boards, and other entities from suit in federal courts is quite inconsistent. It is clear, however, that an agency of state government, such as the department of health or treasury, is a part of the state for purposes of the Eleventh Amendment.[99] The Court most directly confronted the question of when a suit is against a state in *Regents of University of California v. Doe*.[100] An individual worked for the Lawrence Livermore National Laboratory of the University of California pursuant to a contract with the United States Department of Energy. Under the terms of the contract, the federal government was responsible for any liabilities incurred by the State of California. The Ninth Circuit held that the plaintiff's suit against the state university was not barred by the Eleventh Amendment because there was no possibility of state financial liability.

The United States Supreme Court unanimously reversed. The Court stated that "it is the entity's potential legal liability, rather than its ability or inability to require a third party to reimburse it, or to discharge the liability in the first instance that is relevant."[101] The Court thus concluded that "[t]he Eleventh Amendment protects the State from the risk of adverse judgments even though the State may be indemnified by a third party."[102] In other words, if it is a suit against the state—and the University of California is clearly a part of the state—then the

---

[95] 440 U.S. 391 (1979).

[96] *Id.* at 400-402.

[97] *Id.* at 401.

[98] *Id.* at 400-402.

[99] *See, e.g.*, Florida Dept. of Health & Rehabilitative Servs. v. Florida Nursing Home Assn., 450 U.S. 147 (1981); Ford Motor Co. v. Department of Treasury, 323 U.S. 459 (1945).

[100] 519 U.S. 425 (1997).

[101] *Id.* at 430.

[102] *Id.* at 431.

Eleventh Amendment bars the suit even if there is no risk of actual state financial responsibility.

But nor did the Court completely reject possible state monetary liability as a factor to consider in evaluating whether a particular agency should be regarded as state rather than local. In fact, in *Regents of the University of California v. Doe*, the Court declared: "Of course, the question whether a money judgment against a state instrumentality or official would be enforceable against the State is of considerable importance to any evaluation of the relationship between the State and the entity or individual being sued."[103] Shortly after its decision in *Doe*, the Court concluded that the St. Louis Board of Police Commissioners is not the state for purposes of the Eleventh Amendment, even though the governor appoints a majority of its members.[104] In a footnote, the Court noted that financial responsibility rests with the local government, and thus it should be regarded as part of local rather than state government.

For state boards, corporations, and other entities, where the law is uncertain, the courts look to several factors. Professor John Pagan suggests that four criteria are used:

(1)   Will a judgment against the entity be satisfied with funds in the state treasury?[105]

(2)   Does the state government exert significant control over the entity's decisions and actions?

(3)   Does the state executive branch or legislature appoint the entity's policymakers?

(4)   Does the state law characterize the entity as a state agency rather than as a subdivision?[106]

Affirmative answers to these questions, especially the first, indicate that the entity will be protected by the Eleventh Amendment; negative answers suggest that the governing body will be deemed sufficiently independent of the state so that the Eleventh Amendment does not apply.

Suits Against Local Officials Deemed State Officers

The issue of when is it a suit against the state is likely to come up more frequently in light of the Supreme Court's decision in *McMillan v. Monroe County, Alabama*.[107] In *McMillan*, the Court held that a county sheriff in Alabama is a state official, not a local official, even though sheriffs are elected locally and paid by the county. Although the Court's holding was narrow and emphasized the Alabama

---

[103] *Id.* at 430.

[104] Auer v. Robbins, 519 U.S. 905, 908 n.1 (1997).

[105] As noted above, *Regents of the Univ. of Cal. v. Doe* is clear that a suit against a state is barred even if the state will be reimbursed from other funds.

[106] Pagan, *supra* note 4, at 447, 461.

[107] 520 U.S. 781 (1997).

Constitution's definition of sheriffs' responsibility, the reasoning in *McMillan* has potentially much broader applications. A key factor for the majority in *McMillan* was that the county sheriff in Alabama enforces state law. This is true in most states and is so for other county officials, such as coroners.

Although *McMillan* arose in the context of whether a sheriff's decisions establish local policy for purposes of §1983 and the Court did not discuss the Eleventh Amendment, the obvious implication is that the Eleventh Amendment applies once the sheriff is deemed a state officer. In fact, even before *McMillan*, the Fourth Circuit ruled that South Carolina sheriffs are state officials for Eleventh Amendment purposes.[108] It is likely after *McMillan* that many county officials will attempt to claim that they should be treated as state officers and that the Eleventh Amendment applies in the litigation.

Denial of Eleventh Amendment Immunity
Immediately Appealable

The Supreme Court has ruled that a denial of Eleventh Amendment immunity is immediately appealable. In *Puerto Rico Aqueduct and Sewer Authority v. Metcalf & Eddy*, the Court held that the Eleventh Amendment creates a constitutional immunity from suit and not simply an affirmative defense.[109] Accordingly, a denial of Eleventh Amendment immunity is immediately appealable in the same way that the denial of immunity to an individual officer can be immediately appealed.[110]

The three most significant limitations on the scope of the Eleventh Amendment are its inapplicability to suits against state officers, to situations where states waive their immunity, and to suits brought under some federal civil rights laws. These three exceptions are considered, respectively, in the next three sections.

§2.10.4   *Ways Around the Eleventh Amendment: Suits Against State Officers*

Origins of Permitting Suits Against Officers

In *Osborn v. Bank of the United States*, the Supreme Court concluded that the Eleventh Amendment precludes suits against a state only when the state is actually named as the defendant in the litigation.[111] Chief Justice John Marshall concluded that "in all cases where jurisdiction depends on the party, it is the party named in the record" that matters.[112] Thus, the Eleventh Amendment could be circumvented by naming a state officer as defendant instead of the state government itself. This principle actually was derived from English common law where the

---

[108] Cromer v. Brown, 88 F.3d 1315 (4th Cir. 1996).
[109] 506 U.S. 139 (1993).
[110] Mitchell v. Forsyth, 472 U.S. 511 (1985).
[111] 22 U.S. (9 Wheat.) 738 (1824).
[112] *Id.* at 857.

King had sovereign immunity, but other officials could be sued to remedy wrongs done by the government.[113]

Although the general rule is that suits against state officers are not barred by the Eleventh Amendment, the law is much more complicated, and the ability to sue the state officer in a particular case depends, to a large extent, on the nature of the relief sought and the claim presented. For example, suits for money damages to be paid from the state treasury are barred, even if the officer is named as the defendant.[114] Also, the Eleventh Amendment prohibits federal court pendent jurisdiction over state law claims against state officers.[115]

Overview of §2.10.4

These principles are examined in detail in this section, which considers the ability to sue state officers in federal court. Subsection 2.10.4.1 discusses suits against state officers for injunctive relief in federal court. Monetary relief in suits against state officers is examined in §2.10.4.2. Finally, exceptions to the ability to sue officers are discussed in §2.10.4.3. These exceptions include the prohibition against pendent state law claims against state officers, the preclusion of suits against officers to enforce federal laws that have a comprehensive enforcement mechanism, and a narrow exception for suits against state officers to quiet title to submerged land. Because state governments always act through their officers, suits against officers are clearly the most important way around the Eleventh Amendment.

§2.10.4.1　Suits Against State Officers for Injunctive Relief

Ex parte Young

The Eleventh Amendment does not preclude suits against state officers for injunctive relief, even when the remedy will enjoin the implementation of an official state policy. *Ex parte Young* is widely credited with establishing this principle,[116] and it has been heralded as "one of the three most important decisions the Supreme Court of the United States has ever handed down."[117]

Like many states around the turn of the last century, Minnesota adopted a law limiting railroad rates. The railroads and their shareholders believed that such regulations were unconstitutional and sought to enjoin their enforcement. The

---

[113] Orth, *supra* note 30, at 41.

[114] *See, e.g.*, Ford Motor Co. v. Department of Treasury, 323 U.S. 459, 464 (1945) (court looks to "essential nature and effect of the proceeding").

[115] Pennhurst State School & Hosp. v. Halderman, 465 U.S. 89 (1984).

[116] 209 U.S. 123 (1908). Actually, several earlier cases had held similarly that the Eleventh Amendment did not preclude suits against state officers. *See, e.g.*, Tindal v. Wesley, 167 U.S. 204 (1897); Osborn v. Bank of the United States, 22 U.S. (9 Wheat.) 738 (1824).

[117] Allied Artists Pictures Corp. v. Rhodes, 473 F. Supp. 560, 564 (E.D. Ohio 1979) (citations omitted).

railroads and shareholders could have violated the law and raised their constitutional challenge as a defense to prosecution. The statute, however, had severe penalties—a $2,500 fine for each violation and imprisonment of the railroad's agents for as long as five years.[118] Thus, shareholders in the Northern Pacific Railway instead instituted an action in federal court against the company and state officials responsible for enforcing the law to prevent compliance with the limits on railroad rates. Specifically, the plaintiffs sought an injunction against the attorney general of Minnesota, Edward T. Young, to prevent him from beginning any proceedings to enforce the challenged legislation.

While the lawsuit was pending, the federal district court issued a preliminary order enjoining Young from enforcing the law. Young, however, ignored the court's order and immediately filed a mandamus action against the railroad in state court to compel its compliance with the state law. Young then was cited by the federal court for contempt for disregarding its order. He was informed that he would be held in federal custody until such time as he dismissed the state action he had initiated against the railroads. Young petitioned for habeas corpus to the United States Supreme Court, claiming that the injunction violated the Eleventh Amendment.

The Supreme Court ruled against Young, holding that the Eleventh Amendment does not bar suits against state officers to enjoin violations of federal law.[119] In reaching this holding, the Court concluded that state officers have no authority to violate the Constitution and laws of the United States. Hence, their illegal acts are stripped of state authority, and such suits are not precluded by the Eleventh Amendment. The Court wrote:

> The act to be enforced is alleged to be unconstitutional, and if it be so, the use of the name of the State to enforce an unconstitutional act to the injury of complainants is a proceeding without the authority of and one which does not affect the State in its sovereign or governmental capacity. It is simply an illegal act upon the part of a state official in attempting to use the name of the State to enforce a legislative enactment which is void because unconstitutional. If the act which the state Attorney General seeks to enforce be a violation of the Federal Constitution, the officer in proceeding under such enactment comes into conflict with the superior authority of that Constitution, and he is in that case stripped of his official or representative character and is subjected in his person to the consequences of his individual conduct. The State has no power to impart to him any immunity from responsibility to the supreme authority of the United States.[120]

Criticism and Defense of *Ex parte Young*

Thus, if a state government is acting in violation of federal law, pursuant to an unconstitutional statute or otherwise, suit to enjoin the impermissible behavior

---

[118]   Clyde E. Jacobs, The Eleventh Amendment and Sovereign Immunity 139 (1972).

[119]   Ex parte Young, 209 U.S. at 159-160.

[120]   *Id.*

may be brought in federal court by naming the state officer as the defendant. The decision in *Ex parte Young* long has been recognized as a primary method of limiting the effect of the Eleventh Amendment and of ensuring state compliance with federal law. As Professor Charles Alan Wright noted, "the doctrine of *Ex parte Young* seems indispensable to the establishment of constitutional government and the rule of law."[121] Similarly, Professor Kenneth Culp Davis remarked, "From that day to this . . . *Young* has been the mainstay in challenging [state] governmental action[s]."[122] Because state governments always act through officers, state conduct in violation of the Constitution or federal laws can be halted by enjoining the state officers responsible for executing the state policy.

Many have criticized the *Young* decision as creating a fictional distinction between the state and its officers.[123] Indeed, a majority of the Court called *Young* "an obvious fiction."[124] The argument is that when a state officer is sued to enjoin the enforcement of an official state policy, the state is the real party in interest. The result—an injunction against enforcement of a state law—is the same as if the state had been sued directly. The infringement on state sovereignty is the same as if the state had been sued directly. Especially when the officer is acting in the scope of his or her duties, pursuant to an official state policy, it seems fictitious to say that the officer is "stripped" of state authority and the Eleventh Amendment's protection of the state is inapplicable.

Although the result in *Young* certainly has a fictional quality, this criticism is somewhat overstated. First, the state officer is the proper defendant in a lawsuit to prevent the officer's unconstitutional conduct. As Professor John Orth explains, "*Ex parte Young* was nonfictional in that Young was really and truly about to damage the interests of plaintiffs."[125] Second, *Young* distinguishes between the state and its officers in much the same way as the common law always has distinguished between a principal and its agent.[126] For example, a corporate officer who is performing acts that the corporation cannot legally authorize is said to be acting "ultra vires" or beyond the powers conferred by the corporation.[127] Such an officer cannot claim the authority of the corporation. Similarly, in *Young* the Court concluded that an officer acting illegally is stripped of state authority, and therefore the Eleventh Amendment does not bar suits against officers.

The caution against dismissing *Young* as a fiction is because of the importance of that decision in ensuring state compliance with the United States Constitution. As Professors Wright, Miller, and Cooper remarked: "To be sure the doctrine of *Ex*

---

[121] Charles Alan Wright, Law of Federal Courts 292 (6th ed. 2002).

[122] Kenneth Culp Davis, Suing the Government by Falsely Pretending to Sue an Officer, 29 U. Chi. L. Rev. 435, 437 (1962).

[123] *Id.* at 437.

[124] Idaho v. Coeur d'Alene Tribe, 521 U.S. 261, 270 (1997).

[125] Orth, *supra* note 30, at 133.

[126] *See, e.g.*, Restatement (Second) of Agency Authority §7, at 228, 383 (1958); Harold G. Reuschlein & William A. Gregory, Handbook on the Law of Agency and Partnership §13 (1979); Van Arsdale v. Metropolitan Title Guar. Co., 103 Misc. 2d 104, 425 N.Y.S. 2d 482 (1980); Webb v. Webb, 602 S.W.2d 127 (Tex. Civ. App. 1980) (distinguishing between authority of agent and principal).

[127] Orth, *supra* note 30, at 133.

parte Young has a fictive quality to it; nonetheless, it serves as an effective mechanism for providing relief against unconstitutional conduct by state officers and for testing, in the federal courts, the constitutionality of the state statutes under which they act."[128] Without *Young*, federal courts often would be powerless to prevent state violations of the Constitution and federal laws.

Is There State Action If an Officer Is Stripped of State Authority?

Allowing plaintiffs to circumvent the Eleventh Amendment by suing state officers creates two problems. First, if officers are stripped of the state's authority, then is there state action for purposes of the Fourteenth Amendment? It is clearly established that the Fourteenth Amendment only applies to state action; private conduct is not prohibited by the Constitution.[129] *Young* holds that officers acting in violation of the Constitution cannot claim to be the state for purposes of the Eleventh Amendment and, in fact, are stripped of all state authority. Therefore, a dilemma seems to arise: Either the officers are part of the state, in which case the Eleventh Amendment should apply, or the officers are not part of the state, in which case there is no state action and therefore no constitutional violation.

The Supreme Court addressed this problem a few years after *Young* in *Home Telephone & Telegraph v. Los Angeles*.[130] There the Court held that individual conduct not entitled to Eleventh Amendment immunity is nonetheless state action for purposes of the Fourteenth Amendment. In other words, under *Ex parte Young*, the officer is stripped of state authority solely for purposes of Eleventh Amendment analysis, a result that does not affect the determination of state action under the Fourteenth Amendment. Undoubtedly, this too seems fictional, manipulating the definition of state action to achieve the essential result of remedying unconstitutional conduct.

A second problem concerns injunctive relief that has the effect of awarding money damages against the state treasury. For example, equitable relief in the form of orders for restitution or injunctions that require substantial expenditures pose special Eleventh Amendment problems because of the underlying purpose of the amendment to protect state treasuries from federal courts. This issue is discussed in the next subsection, which focuses on monetary relief issues against state officers.

§2.10.4.2 Suits Against State Officers for Monetary Relief

What Monetary Consequences Against a State Are Permitted?

The Supreme Court is very concerned about federal court relief against state officers that has the effect of forcing state governments to pay money damages.

---

[128] Charles Alan Wright, Arthur R. Miller & Edward Cooper, 13 Federal Practice and Procedure §3524, at 154 (1984).

[129] *See, e.g.*, The Civil Rights Cases, 109 U.S. 3 (1883).

[130] 227 U.S. 278 (1913).

Thus, the Court has held that the Eleventh Amendment prevents an award of monetary relief from the state treasury even when the individual officer is the named defendant in the lawsuit. In *Ford Motor Co. v. Department of the Treasury,* the Court said: "[W]hen the action is in essence one for the recovery of money from the state, the state is the real, substantial party in interest and is entitled to invoke its sovereign immunity from suit even though individual officials are nominal defendants."[131]

A complex set of doctrines has developed for determining what monetary relief is allowed and what is prohibited. The current law in this regard can be summarized in three parts. First, the Eleventh Amendment does not prevent suits against state officers for money damages to be paid out of the officers' own pockets, even when the damages are retrospective compensation for past harms.[132] The Eleventh Amendment is concerned with protecting state treasuries, not individual officers. Hence, there is no reason to apply the amendment if the relief is to be paid by an officer to the injured victim of the officer's actions. Often this is described as a suit against the officer in his or her "individual capacity."

State indemnification policies are irrelevant for Eleventh Amendment analysis and do not prevent federal court relief against individual officers. That is, an officer of the state cannot claim Eleventh Amendment immunity on the grounds that state law requires that the officer be indemnified with funds from the state treasury.[133] In part, this is because the state has voluntarily chosen *to indemnify* the officer and should not be able to invoke the Eleventh Amendment because of its choice to provide compensation out of state resources. Also, in part, there is real concern that states could eliminate all relief against state and local government officers and even against local governments simply by enacting laws requiring indemnification from state funds. If the Eleventh Amendment prohibited awards against state officers where indemnification policies exist, states would lose nothing by adopting such policies because they never could be required to pay a penny. At the same time, injured victims would be wholly without federal remedies because they would be prohibited from suing both the state officers and the state government in federal court.

It should be noted that in order to successfully sue an officer for money damages it is necessary to overcome common law immunities that all individual officers possess, which protect them from money damage awards except under limited circumstances. These immunities are not based on the Eleventh Amendment.[134]

---

[131] 323 U.S. 459, 464 (1945).

[132] *See, e.g.,* Kentucky v. Graham, 473 U.S. 159 (1985) (discussing distinction between suits against an officer in an individual as opposed to an official capacity); Foulks v. Ohio Dept. of Rehabilitation & Corrections, 713 F.2d 1229 (6th Cir. 1983).

[133] *See, e.g.,* Leeds v. Sexson, 1 F.3d 1246 (9th Cir. 1993); Blaylock v. Schwinden, 862 F.2d 1352, 1354 (9th Cir. 1988); Wilson v. Beebe, 770 F.2d 578 (6th Cir. 1985) (en banc); Duckworth v. Franzen, 780 F.2d 645, 650 (7th Cir. 1985); Demery v. Kupperman, 735 F.2d 1139, 1147 (9th Cir. 1984).

[134] These immunities are discussed in detail in Erwin Chemerinsky, Federal Jurisdiction ch. 8 (6th ed. 2011).

Prospective Versus Retroactive Relief

Second, the Eleventh Amendment does not prohibit a federal court from giving injunctive relief against a state officer even though compliance with the injunction will cost the state a great deal of money in the future.[135] This is termed "prospective relief" or sometimes "ancillary relief." For example, in *Graham v. Richardson*, the Supreme Court held that Arizona and Pennsylvania officials were prohibited from denying welfare benefits to otherwise qualified recipients who were aliens.[136] The injunction compelling state officers to allow aliens access to welfare benefits cost the state treasuries large sums of money. The funds obviously would be paid from state resources and not out of the officers' own pockets. Nonetheless, the relief was permitted because it is firmly established that the Eleventh Amendment does not forbid a federal court from issuing an injunction, even when compliance will cause the state to expend substantial amounts of money.

Third, the Eleventh Amendment prevents a federal court from awarding retroactive relief—damages to compensate past injuries—when those damages will be paid by the state treasury.[137] Under such circumstances, it is irrelevant that the individual officer is the named defendant rather than the state itself.

The seminal case articulating the distinction between retroactive and prospective relief is *Edelman v. Jordan*.[138] In that case the plaintiffs sued Edelman, the Illinois commissioner of the Department of Public Welfare, objecting to the state's failure to comply with federal standards for processing welfare applications. The plaintiffs sought two types of relief: an injunction requiring the state to comply with federal guidelines in the future and an injunction requiring the state to give back payments of all of the funds that were previously improperly withheld.

The Supreme Court held that the Eleventh Amendment does not bar the order compelling state compliance in the future. The Court said that *Ex parte Young* establishes that federal courts may give injunctive relief against state officers, even when compliance will cost the state money.

The Court, however, refused to allow the injunction ordering payment of the previously owed sums. The Court said that the Eleventh Amendment bars such relief even though the officer and not the state is named as the defendant because the money obviously would be paid from the state treasury and not from the officer's own pocket. Furthermore, the fact that the relief is characterized as equitable does not matter; the Eleventh Amendment prohibits all awards of retroactive damages to be paid from the state treasury.

Thus, *Edelman* draws the extremely important distinction between prospective and retroactive relief. A federal court may order future compliance by state

---

[135] *See, e.g.,* Quern v. Jordan, 440 U.S. 332 (1979); Milliken v. Bradley, 433 U.S. 267 (1977); Edelman v. Jordan, 415 U.S. 651 (1974).

[136] 403 U.S. 365 (1971).

[137] *See, e.g.,* Edelman v. Jordan, 415 U.S. 651 (1974); Ford Motor Co. v. Department of the Treasury, 323 U.S. 459 (1945).

[138] 415 U.S. 651 (1974).

officials, but it may not compel payment of damages to compensate for past violations.[139]

Criticism and Defense of the Prospective/Retroactive Distinction

Does the distinction between prospective and retroactive relief make sense in determining the application of the Eleventh Amendment? Both prospective and retroactive relief can involve the expenditure of funds from the state treasury. In fact, in some cases, prospective compliance might cost much more than back payments.[140] Justice Rehnquist recognized this in *Edelman* when he stated that "the difference between the type of relief barred by the Eleventh Amendment and that permitted under *Ex parte Young* will not in many instances be that between day and night."[141] Nonetheless, Justice Rehnquist said that there was a difference when the expenditure of funds was "ancillary" to compliance with an injunction.

Furthermore, there are conceptual problems in trying to distinguish between retroactive and prospective relief. If an injury occurred in the past, is preventing it from continuing prospective or retroactive? For example, in *Edelman*, is the payment of the previously wrongfully withheld funds prospective in the sense that it is preventing individuals from being harmed in the future by the continued denial of funds that are owed to them, or is it retroactive in that it is compensation for a previous wrongful act?

Perhaps the difference between prospective and retroactive relief is primarily one of appearance. When a federal court issues retroactive relief that will be paid by the state, it appears that the court is taking a sum directly out of the state treasury. This is what the Eleventh Amendment seemed concerned with preventing. In contrast, prospective relief appears to be simply an order to comply with the law; the costs are incidental to the state's obligation to act in accordance with federal law.

Application of the Distinction

Not surprisingly, since *Edelman* the Supreme Court has struggled with determining whether relief is prospective and permitted or whether orders constitute retroactive awards and are therefore prohibited. For example, in *Milliken v. Bradley* the Court upheld a school desegregation order requiring the expenditure of state funds for educational aspects of a desegregation plan, including several remedial and compensatory education programs.[142] The Court found the remedy prospective and not barred by the Eleventh Amendment, concluding:

[139] *See, e.g.*, Cory v. White, 457 U.S. 85 (1982).
[140] *See, e.g.*, Milliken v. Bradley, 433 U.S. 267 (1977) (relief that required substantial state expenditures on education deemed to be prospective and not barred by the Eleventh Amendment).
[141] 415 U.S. at 667.
[142] 433 U.S. 267 (1977).

214

The decree to share the future costs of educational components in this case fits squarely within the prospective-compliance exception reaffirmed by *Edelman*. . . . The educational components, which the District Court ordered into effect *prospectively,* are plainly designed to wipe out continuing conditions of inequality produced by the inherently unequal dual school system long maintained by Detroit. . . . That the programs are also "compensatory" in nature does not change the fact that they are part of a plan that operates *prospectively* to bring about the delayed benefits of a unitary school system. We therefore hold that such prospective relief is not barred by the Eleventh Amendment.[143]

Milliken powerfully illustrates the difficulty in distinguishing prospective from retroactive relief. The orders were designed to remedy past injustices and hence could have been labeled retroactive. Yet they will go into effect in the future and could be termed prospective. As Professor David Currie explains: "*Milliken* was no more 'prospective' than that condemned in *Edelman* itself. In both cases the money was to be paid in the future in order to right a past wrong. If that is enough to make the order 'prospective,' there is no such thing as a retrospective order; nobody is ever ordered to have paid yesterday."[144]

Ancillary Relief

In applying the prospective-retroactive distinction, the Court has placed a great deal of emphasis on the language in *Edelman* that "ancillary" relief against state treasuries is not barred by the Eleventh Amendment. In *Hutto v. Finney*, the Supreme Court held that federal courts may award attorneys' fees to be paid from state treasuries to successful plaintiffs in civil rights actions pursuant to 42 U.S.C. §1988.[145] In *Hutto*, plaintiffs successfully challenged the conditions of confinement in the Arkansas prisons as violating the Eighth Amendment's prohibition against cruel and unusual punishment. The district court awarded attorneys' fees to the plaintiffs to be paid by the state. The Supreme Court held that the fee award did not violate the Eleventh Amendment. In part, the Court justified this conclusion by holding that the fee award was ancillary to the injunctive relief ordered in favor of the plaintiffs.[146] *Hutto* thus expanded the notion of permissible ancillary relief because in *Edelman* the Court spoke "not of ancillary orders to pay money but of orders having ancillary effects on the treasury."[147]

The concept of ancillary relief also was crucial in two other Supreme Court decisions, *Quern v. Jordan*[148] and *Green v. Mansour*.[149] After the Supreme Court decided *Edelman v. Jordan*, the federal district court ordered the State of Illinois to

---

[143]   433 U.S. at 289-290 (emphasis in original).

[144]   David P. Currie, Sovereign Immunity and Suits Against Government Officers, 1984 Sup. Ct. Rev. 149, 162.

[145]   437 U.S. 678 (1978).

[146]   The Court also based its decision on the ability of Congress to override the Eleventh Amendment pursuant to statutes adopted under §5 of the Fourteenth Amendment. *See* §2.10.6, *infra*.

[147]   Currie, *supra* note 144, at 162.

[148]   440 U.S. 332 (1979).

[149]   474 U.S. 64 (1985).

send to every member of the plaintiff's class a notice that they were denied money owed to them and informing them of the administrative procedures available for collecting the funds. In *Quern v. Jordan*, the Supreme Court held that the order to send such notices did not violate the Eleventh Amendment. The Court concluded that the notice was "properly viewed as ancillary to the prospective relief already ordered by the court."[150] It did not matter that the notices would have the effect of encouraging claims for retroactive benefits because the availability of such payments would rest "entirely with the state, its agencies, courts, and legislature, not with the federal court."[151] In sharp contrast, the Supreme Court, in *Green v. Mansour*, held that the Eleventh Amendment barred a federal court from compelling the state to send notices informing welfare recipients that they might wrongfully have been denied benefits. In response to a class action challenging Michigan's calculation of welfare benefits, the state voluntarily changed its practices to conform with federal requirements. The Supreme Court, in a 5-to-4 decision, said that under such circumstances notice relief was barred because it was not ancillary to other prospective relief. Unlike the situation in *Quern*, in *Green* there was "no claimed continuing violation of federal law, and therefore no occasion to issue an injunction."[152]

The dissent, however, was unpersuaded by this distinction and argued that the notice relief requested by the plaintiffs in *Green* was permissible because it was prospective and needed to remedy past illegal state practices.[153] Thus, the Court continues to struggle with determining what is prospective or retroactive and what is ancillary. This difficulty inevitably will continue; most remedies can be characterized either way. Nonetheless, a great deal depends on how such relief is labeled because the Eleventh Amendment bars retroactive expenditures to be paid by the state treasury, but not injunctions that result in prospective or ancillary costs to the state.

Official Versus Individual Capacity Suits

If the recovery is from the individual officer's pocket, the suit can be said to be against the officer in an "individual capacity." But if the recovery will be from the state treasury, the suit is against the officer in an "official capacity." As described above, official capacity suits are barred unless the plaintiff is seeking prospective relief. In *Will v. Michigan Department of State Police*, the Supreme Court held that suits against state governments, even in state courts, are not permitted under §1983 and that suits against state officers in their official capacity are barred under this rule.[154] However, in a footnote, the Court made it clear that this holding did not disturb the well-established rule of *Ex parte Young*: State officers

---

[150] 440 U.S. at 349.

[151] *Id.* at 348.

[152] 474 U.S. at 73.

[153] *Id.* at 76-77. *See also* Papasan v. Allain, 478 U.S. 265 (1986) (state possesses Eleventh Amendment immunity in suit against it for failure to apply the profits acquired from land granted by the federal government to education as it was required to do under the terms of the federal land grant).

[154] 491 U.S. 58 (1989).

may be sued, even in an official capacity for injunctive relief.[155] The key question, which frequently has perplexed lower courts, is: When should a suit be regarded as an official capacity suit and when is it an individual capacity suit? The Court provided much-needed clarification in *Hafer v. Melo*.[156] After being elected to the position of auditor general in Pennsylvania, Barbara Hafer fired 18 individuals. These individuals sued Hafer, contending that they were fired because of their Democratic political affiliation. Hafer, in defense, argued that the claims against her were barred by *Will* because in dismissing the employees she acted in an official capacity.

The Supreme Court unanimously held that the suit against Hafer was not barred by the Eleventh Amendment. The Court reaffirmed the distinction between official capacity and individual capacity suits. Official capacity suits are an attempt to sue the government entity by naming the officer as a defendant, whereas personal capacity suits "seek to impose individual liability upon a government officer for actions taken under color of state law."[157] The Court explained that a suit is not to be regarded as an official capacity suit simply because the government officer was acting in an official capacity. The Court stated that "the phrase 'acting in their official capacities' is best understood as a reference to the capacity in which the state officer is sued, not the capacity in which the officer inflicts the alleged injury."[158] In other words, if the suit against a state officer is for injunctive relief, under *Ex parte Young* as reaffirmed in *Will*, there is no Eleventh Amendment bar to federal court jurisdiction. Likewise, if the suit is against an officer for money damages where the relief would come from the officer's own pocket, there is no Eleventh Amendment bar even though the conduct was part of the officer's official duties. In such a suit, the officer could claim absolute or qualified immunity as a defense. The state's choice to indemnify the officer would not convert the suit from individual to official capacity.[159] However, there is an Eleventh Amendment bar if the suit against the officer would lead to monetary relief against the state treasury other than through indemnification.

The practical difficulty for judges is deciding whether a suit is official or individual capacity at the outset of the litigation. Some courts look to how the complaint is drafted[160] and some look to the defenses raised in determining the capacity in which the person is sued.[161] *Hafer* has not ended the confusion over the distinction between official capacity and individual capacity, but it has helped

---

[155] 491 U.S. at 71 n.10.

[156] 502 U.S. 21 (1991).

[157] 502 U.S. at 25.

[158] *Id.* at 26.

[159] *See, e.g.,* Darul-Islam v. Dubois, 997 F. Supp. 176 (D. Mass. 1998); Blaylock v. Schwinden, 862 F.2d 1352, 1354 (9th Cir. 1988); Wilson v. Beebe, 770 F.2d 578 (6th Cir. 1985) (en banc); Duckworth v. Franzen, 780 F.2d 645, 650 (7th Cir. 1985).

[160] *See, e.g.,* Arab African Intl. Bank v. Epstein, 958 F.2d 532 (3d Cir. 1992); Gregory v. Chehi, 843 F.2d 111 (3d Cir. 1988); Shabazz v. Coughlin, 852 F.2d 697 (2d Cir. 1988).

[161] *See, e.g.,* Pinaud v. County of Suffolk, 52 F.3d 1139 (2d Cir. 1995); Shabazz v. Coughlin, 852 F.2d at 697; Shockley v. James, 823 F.2d 1068 (7th Cir. 1987).

by making it clear that the fact that a government officer is acting in the scope of official duties is not enough to bar a suit as being in "official capacity."

§2.10.4.3   Exceptions to *Ex Parte Young*

There are now three major exceptions to *Ex parte Young*. First, state officers may not be sued on pendent state law claims. Second, state officers may not be sued to enforce federal statutes that contain comprehensive enforcement mechanisms. Finally, state officers cannot be sued to quiet title to submerged lands. Each of these exceptions is discussed in turn. Finally, the section concludes by considering the opinion by Justice Anthony Kennedy, joined only by Chief Justice Rehnquist, to limit dramatically the ability to sue state officers in federal court.

Bar on Suits Against State Officers Based on Pendent State Claims

Pendent jurisdiction—now called supplemental jurisdiction—provides that a federal court may hear state law claims that would otherwise not be within the federal judiciary's subject matter jurisdiction if those claims arise from a "common nucleus of operative fact" with a claim properly within the court's jurisdiction.[162] Therefore, under the traditional rule for pendent jurisdiction a federal court could hear and decide state law claims against state officers that arose from the same matter as federal law claims. The Supreme Court, however, in *Pennhurst State School and Hospital v. Halderman*, held that federal courts are barred by the Eleventh Amendment from enjoining state officers from violating state law.[163] The Court ruled that although federal courts may hear federal claims against state officers, they may not hear pendent state law claims. Justice Powell, writing for the majority, stated: "[A] claim that state officials violated state law in carrying out their official responsibilities is a claim against the State that is protected by the Eleventh Amendment. . . . We now hold that this principle applies as well to state law claims brought into federal court under pendent jurisdiction."[164]

The *Pennhurst* litigation began in 1974 when a resident of the Pennhurst State School and Hospital filed a lawsuit challenging conditions in this institution for the care of the mentally retarded operated by the State of Pennsylvania.[165] The class action suit claimed that inhumane and inadequate conditions

---

[162] 28 U.S.C. §1367; United Mine Workers v. Gibbs, 383 U.S. 715, 725 (1966) (articulating the test for pendent jurisdiction). *See* discussion in §5.4.

[163] 465 U.S. 89 (1984). For excellent criticisms of the Court's decision in *Pennhurst, see* David L. Shapiro, Wrong Turns: The Eleventh Amendment and the *Pennhurst* Case, 98 Harv. L. Rev. 61 (1984); George D. Brown, Beyond *Pennhurst*: Protective Jurisdiction, the Eleventh Amendment, and the Power of Congress to Enlarge Federal Jurisdiction in Response to the Burger Court, 71 Va. L. Rev. 343 (1985). For a defense of *Pennhurst, see* Ann Althouse, How to Build a Separate Sphere: Federal Courts and State Power, 100 Harv. L. Rev. 1485 (1987).

[164] 465 U.S. at 121.

[165] The Supreme Court provides a detailed description of the factual history of the *Pennhurst* litigation at *id.* at 92-97.

violated the class members' rights under the Eighth and Fourteenth Amendments to the United States Constitution, as well as federal statutes[166] and state laws.[167] Defendants included the hospital and various hospital officials, the Pennsylvania Department of Welfare and several of its officials, and various county commissioners and county mental retardation officials.

In 1977, after a lengthy trial, the district court rendered its decision in favor of the plaintiffs.[168] The United States Court of Appeals for the Third Circuit concluded that "[c]onditions at Pennhurst are not only dangerous, with the residents often physically abused or drugged by staff members, but also inadequate for the 'habilitation' of the retarded."[169] The court concluded that conditions violated the United States Constitution, federal law, and state law. The United States Court of Appeals for the Third Circuit affirmed, basing its decision entirely on the conclusion that the state was violating a federal statute—the "bill of rights" included in the Developmentally Disabled Assistance and Bill of Rights Act.[170] The appeals court found it unnecessary to determine whether there were also violations of the United States Constitution or other federal or state laws.

The United States Supreme Court reversed the decision of the Third Circuit.[171] The Court held that states were not required to comply with the "bill of rights" in the Developmentally Disabled Assistance and Bill of Rights Act. The Court said that Congress may require state compliance with conditions in federal grants only if the conditions are clear and unequivocal; this degree of clarity was absent in this Act.[172] On remand, the Third Circuit again affirmed the district court's decision, concluding that the plaintiffs were entitled to relief because of violations of Pennsylvania law.[173] The case again went to the United States Supreme Court, and again the Court reversed the Third Circuit's decision. The Court held that the Eleventh Amendment bars relief against state officers on the basis of state law.[174] The Court concluded that federal courts can give relief against state officers on federal law grounds because of the importance of securing compliance with federal law. Because the federal system has no such need to ensure enforcement of state law, there is no reason to create an exception to the Eleventh Amendment and allow suits against state officers on pendent state law claims in federal court.

Many commentators have criticized the Court's reasoning in the *Pennhurst* decision. First, the holding in *Ex parte Young*—that officers who act illegally are stripped of state authority and may be sued in federal court—should apply no less forcefully when the violation is of state as opposed to federal law. *Young*

---

[166] Rehabilitation Act of 1973, 29 U.S.C. §794 (1983), Assistance and Bill of Rights Act, Pub. L. No. 94-103, 89 Stat. 496 (1975), 42 U.S.C. §§6000-6083 (Supp. 1985).

[167] Pennsylvania Mental Health and Mental Retardation Act of 1966, 50 Pa. Const. Stat. Ann., §§4101-4704 (Purdon 1985).

[168] Halderman v. Pennhurst State School & Hosp., 446 F. Supp. 1295 (E.D. Pa. 1977).

[169] 612 F.2d 84, 107 (3d Cir. 1979) (en banc). The Third Circuit reversed and remanded, however, on the issue of appropriate relief.

[170] *Id.*

[171] 451 U.S. 1 (1981).

[172] *Id.* at 17.

[173] 673 F.2d 647 (3d Cir. 1982) (en banc).

[174] 465 U.S. 89, 120-121 (1984).

distinguishes between the state and its officers, much as the common law distinguishes between a principal and an agent. The decision states that the agent, the officer who acts illegally, is powerless to try to protect such actions by invoking the immunity of the principal, the state.

Because state authority protects only lawful actions of state officers, it follows directly that a state officer who violates state law also is stripped of state authority for purposes of the Eleventh Amendment. This is exactly what the Third Circuit held on remand in *Pennhurst,* concluding that it could give relief against state officers based on their violation of state statutes.[175] In fact, the basis for federal relief is even stronger in *Pennhurst* than in *Ex parte Young.* In *Young,* the state officer, the attorney general, was enforcing a statute adopted by the Minnesota legislature; while in *Pennhurst,* the officers were violating a statute adopted by the legislature. In *Ex parte Young,* the state authorized the officer's conduct, while in *Pennhurst,* it proscribed it. Thus, if there was no finding of state authority in *Young,* then none existed in *Pennhurst.*

Second, the Court's decision in *Pennhurst* substantially undermines the attractiveness of the federal forum for litigants and might have the effect of forcing many cases out of federal court. After *Pennhurst,* how should a litigant with both federal and state claims against a state officer proceed? There are three possible choices. One approach is to bring both the federal claims and the state claims in state court, in which case the federal forum would be lost. Alternatively, a litigant could bring the federal claims in federal court and the state claims in state court. This approach, however, risks having the federal claims completely barred by res judicata should the state court decide its case first.[176] If a state court decides in favor of the defendant on the state law claims, the defendant could then go to federal court and assert res judicata or collateral estoppel as a bar to a federal court decision on the federal claims. Because the claims arise from the same subject matter, and since all of the federal claims could have been raised in state court, all litigants who split their claims after *Pennhurst* risk the res judicata bar if the state court decides first.

The final possibility is for plaintiffs to file their claims sequentially—first going to federal court and, if unsuccessful, then going to state court with the state law claim. This approach, like splitting the claims, is wasteful of court and litigant resources. Moreover, the federal court's fact-finding would have collateral estoppel effect in the state court proceeding.

Litigants seeking to raise both federal and state claims against state officers in federal court possibly still have a few avenues open to them after *Pennhurst.* One way is to argue that *Pennhurst* does not preclude state claims based on a contention that the state officer acted in excess of his or her authority. The Court in *Pennhurst* said that sovereign immunity precludes injunctive relief "against state officials for failing to carry out their duties under state statutes" or "on violations

---

[175] 673 F.2d 647 (3d Cir. 1982) (en banc).

[176] *See, e.g.,* Migra v. Warren City School Dist., 465 U.S. 75 (1984); Kremer v. Chemical Constr. Corp., 456 U.S. 461 (1982); Allen v. McCurry, 449 U.S. 90 (1980) (state court decisions are accorded collateral estoppel and res judicata effects in federal court).

of state statutes that command purely discretionary duties."[177] The Court stated: "Since it cannot be doubted that the statutes at issue here gave petitioners broad discretion in operating Pennhurst, the conduct alleged in this case would not be ultra vires even under the standards of the dissent's cases."[178] Therefore, the Court in *Pennhurst* does not address the situation in which the state officer violates a state law that creates a nondiscretionary duty or acts in excess of lawful authority. Accordingly, *Pennhurst* might be construed as not precluding pendent state law claims against state officers in those circumstances.

An alternative way for litigants to bring state law claims into federal court after *Pennhurst* is to argue that the state law in question gives rise to a liberty or property interest protected by the due process clause of the Fourteenth Amendment. Under procedural due process doctrines, state law can create both liberty and property rights, either explicitly or by creating an expectation that gives rise to a vested right.[179] For example, in *Pennhurst*, the court of appeals found that state law required the state "to adopt the least restrictive environment approach for the care of the mentally retarded."[180] That is, under the Court's approach to procedural due process, the state law has created a liberty interest, and thus the state's violation of its own law constitutes a denial of liberty without due process.[181] In this manner, it appears that some state law claims can be construed as federal claims and therefore can be brought into federal court, avoiding the need for litigants to split their claims.

Suits Enforcing Federal Laws with Comprehensive Enforcement

In *Seminole Tribe v. Florida*,[182] the Court recognized an additional exception to *Ex parte Young*: State officers cannot be sued to enforce federal statutes that contain comprehensive enforcement mechanisms. The Indian Gaming Regulatory Act provides that an Indian tribe may conduct gambling activities only in accord with a valid compact between the tribe and the state where the tribe is located.[183] The law, enacted by Congress pursuant to its authority to regulate commerce with Indian tribes, requires that states negotiate in good faith with tribes for the formation of such compacts. The statute specifically authorizes suits against states to enforce its provisions.[184] The Seminole Tribe of Indians sued the State of Florida and its governor, Lawton Chiles, for failing to negotiate to create a compact

---

[177] 465 U.S. at 109-110.

[178] *Id.* at 110-111.

[179] *See, e.g.*, Paul v. Davis, 424 U.S. 693 (1976); Board of Regents v. Roth, 408 U.S. 564 (1972) (state law defines the existence of property and liberty for the purposes of procedural due process).

[180] 463 U.S. at 1251; *see also* John P. Dwyer, Pendent Jurisdiction and the Eleventh Amendment, 75 Cal. L. Rev. 129 (1987) (*Pennhurst* should be understood as preventing only suits for structural relief requiring ongoing federal court supervision of state officers).

[181] *See, e.g.*, Mitchell v. Plummer, 1998 WL 381992 (N.D. Cal. June 30, 1998); Jackson v. Ylst, 921 F.2d 882, 886 (9th Cir. 1990); Toussaint v. McCarthy, 801 F.2d 1080 (9th Cir. 1986); Spruyette v. Walters, 753 F.2d 498 (6th Cir. 1985).

[182] 517 U.S. 44 (1996).

[183] 25 U.S.C. §2710(d)(1)(C).

[184] 25 U.S.C. §2710(d)(7).

allowing gambling. The Tribe offered two theories as to why the suit was not barred by the Eleventh Amendment. First, a federal statute expressly abrogated the Eleventh Amendment and authorized a suit against the state government. The Court's rejection of this argument, and its narrowing of the ability of Congress to override the Eleventh Amendment, is discussed below in §2.10.6.

Second, the Tribe argued that *Ex parte Young* permitted the suit against the governor to enforce the federal statute. The Supreme Court carved a new exception to *Ex parte Young* and held that a state officer cannot be sued to enforce a federal law that contains a comprehensive enforcement mechanism. Chief Justice Rehnquist, writing for the Court, stated: "[W]here Congress has prescribed a detailed remedial scheme for the enforcement against a state of a statutorily created right, a court should hesitate before casting aside those limitations and permitting an action against a state officer based on *Ex parte Young*."[185] The Court found that the Indian Gaming Regulatory Act contained a detailed remedial scheme in that it provided for court-ordered negotiation and the submission of claims to a mediator.

This aspect of the *Seminole Tribe* decision raises two questions: one descriptive and the other normative. Descriptively, what is sufficient to justify a finding that a statute has a detailed remedial scheme sufficient to preclude suits against individual officers under *Ex parte Young*? Chief Justice Rehnquist's opinion offers no criteria and little discussion to guide lower courts. It should be noted that the primary enforcement mechanism in the Indian Gaming Regulatory Act was the ability to sue states in federal court—a provision declared unconstitutional in *Seminole Tribe*. Perhaps courts will analogize to a line of cases that hold that §1983 cannot be used as a cause of action to enforce federal statutes that contain comprehensive enforcement mechanisms.[186] As discussed in §8.8, the Supreme Court has interpreted this to be a narrow exception that applies when federal statutes intend an alternative to court enforcement to ensure compliance.

Normatively, the question is whether this exception to *Ex parte Young* is justified. *Young* is based on the premise that state officers are stripped of authority if they violate federal law. It is clearly established that suits against officers are permitted for violations of both federal statutes and the United States Constitution.[187] Therefore, under the reasoning of *Young*, a state officer is stripped of state authority, and amenable to suit, for violating any federal law, regardless of whether it has a detailed remedial scheme.

Moreover, the exception created by the Supreme Court assumes that Congress can choose to eliminate suits against officers to enforce federal laws. Even accepting this as true, the inquiry for each statute must be whether Congress intended to allow or preclude federal court review; does the remedial scheme for the law indicate that Congress wanted it to supplant suits in federal court for enforcement? Congress clearly chose to permit federal court enforcement of the

---

[185]   517 U.S. at 74.

[186]   *See* Middlesex County Sewage Auth. v. National Sea Clammers Assn., 453 U.S. 1 (1981).

[187]   *See, e.g.*, Green v. Mansour, 474 U.S. at 68 (injunctive relief is available to enforce federal laws).

Indian Gaming Regulatory Act as evidenced by its explicit authorization for suits against state governments. Therefore, it is puzzling that the Court would find that the remedial scheme in the statute evidences an intent by Congress to preclude suits under *Ex parte Young* to enforce the statute in federal court.

Exception for Suits to Quiet Title to Submerged Lands

In *Idaho v. Coeur d'Alene Tribe*, the Court carved a new, quite narrow exception to *Ex parte Young*: State officers cannot be sued to quiet title to submerged lands.[188] The case involved a dispute over whether the Tribe's ownership of lands extends to the banks and submerged lands of Lake Coeur d'Alene or is vested in the State of Idaho. The Supreme Court found that the suit against the state was barred by the Eleventh Amendment and that the suit against the state officials was precluded because "if the tribe were to prevail, Idaho's sovereign interest in its lands and waters would be affected to a degree fully as intrusive as almost any conceivable retroactive levy upon funds in its treasury."[189] Justice Kennedy, writing this part of the opinion on behalf of the Court's majority, explained that "[t]he requested injunctive relief would bar the state's principal officers from exercising their governmental powers and authority over the disputed lands and waters. The suit would diminish, even extinguish, the state's control over a vast reach of lands and waters long deemed by the state to be an integral part of its territory."[190] On the one hand, *Idaho v. Coeur d'Alene Tribe* can be viewed as a narrow case, involving an interest of particular importance to the State of Idaho. Indeed, Justice Kennedy's opinion concluded by speaking of the case's "particular and special circumstances."[191] On the other hand, the Court's decision precludes the Tribe from any federal court remedy for its claims; it can sue neither the state nor its officers. Preclusion of federal court jurisdiction is especially troubling in this context because of the special federal role in mediating disputes between Native American tribes and state governments. Moreover, the case opens the door to the Court finding other exceptions to *Ex parte Young* where the relief would have significant impact on a state government.

A Broader Exception to *Ex Parte Young*?

Justice Kennedy, in a part of the opinion in *Idaho v. Coeur d'Alene Tribe* joined only by Chief Justice Rehnquist, urged a much broader new exception to *Ex parte Young*. Declaring *Young* "an obvious fiction,"[192] Justice Kennedy argued that state officers should be subject to suit in federal court only in two narrow circumstances. First, state officers could be sued if "there is no state forum available to

---

[188] 521 U.S. 261 (1997).
[189] *Id.* at 287.
[190] *Id.* at 282.
[191] *Id.* at 287.
[192] *Id.* at 270.

vindicate federal interests."[193] Second, state officers could be sued in federal court when there is a showing of a particular need for federal court interpretation and enforcement of federal law. Justice Kennedy observed that this concern could lead "to expansive application of the *Young* exception" and that there was no indication that "states consented to these types of suits in the plan of the convention."[194] Justice Kennedy stated that such claims against state officers generally could be brought in state court and noted that "[n]either in theory nor in practice has it been shown problematic to have federal claims resolved in state courts."[195] Thus, Justice Kennedy advocated a case-by-case balancing approach, with federal courts exercising jurisdiction in a suit against a state officer only if there was a showing in that instance that one of the above two circumstances was present.

Justice Kennedy's approach, had it attracted support from a majority of the Court, would have radically altered constitutional litigation in the United States. Virtually all constitutional challenges to state laws and state government actions, now brought to federal court pursuant to *Ex parte Young*, would have been shifted to state courts. Rarely is a state forum unavailable and seldom under Justice Kennedy's approach could it be shown that there was a special need for federal court review. Justice Kennedy's approach would do no less than largely overrule *Ex parte Young*. Although this would have the virtue of furthering federalism by expanding state immunity from federal court review, it would undermine state accountability by eliminating the primary mechanism that is used to ensure state compliance with federal law.

Seven Justices rejected Justice Kennedy's attempt to reformulate *Ex parte Young*. In an opinion concurring in the judgment, Justice O'Connor, joined by Justices Scalia and Thomas, rejected replacing *Young*'s bright-line rule with a case-by-case balancing approach.[196] Additionally, the four dissenting Justices—Justices Stevens, Souter, Ginsburg, and Breyer—also rejected Justice Kennedy's attempt to carve a new, dramatic exception to *Ex parte Young*.[197]

§2.10.5   *Ways Around the Eleventh Amendment: Waiver*

Is Waiver Consistent with a Limit on Subject Matter Jurisdiction?

A second major way around the Eleventh Amendment is the state waiving its immunity and consenting to be sued in federal court. Although allowing such waivers seems inconsistent with viewing the Eleventh Amendment as a restriction on the federal courts' subject matter jurisdiction, it is firmly established that "if a State waives its immunity and consents to suit in federal court, the Eleventh Amendment does not bar the action."[198] Permitting states to waive their Eleventh

---

[193] *Id.*

[194] *Id.* at 274.

[195] *Id.* at 274-275.

[196] *Id.* at 288 (O'Connor, J., concurring and concurring in the judgment).

[197] *Id.* at 297 (Souter, J., dissenting).

[198] Atascadero State Hosp. v. Scanlon, 473 U.S. 234, 238 (1985).

Amendment immunity reflects the close relationship between the amendment and sovereign immunity.[199] Traditionally, sovereign immunity could be waived, and that principle has carried over to Eleventh Amendment jurisprudence. Professor Pagan suggests that "[w]hen a state consents to federal adjudication, it waives not the lack of subject matter jurisdiction, which a litigant never can waive, but rather the privilege of enforcing a limitation on the exercise of jurisdiction otherwise possessed by the court."[200]

Although this distinction seems ephemeral and is not followed in other areas of subject matter jurisdiction, nevertheless, the Supreme Court consistently has held that consenting states may be sued in federal court.[201] If a state waives its Eleventh Amendment immunity, then it may be sued directly in federal court, even for retroactive relief to be paid out of the state treasury.

However, the Court has stated clearly that the "test for determining whether a state has waived its [Eleventh Amendment] immunity from federal-court jurisdiction is a stringent one."[202] In *Edelman v. Jordan*, the Court declared that a state will be deemed to have waived its immunity "only where stated 'by the most express language or by such overwhelming implications from the text as [will] leave no room for any other reasonable construction.'"[203]

Explicit and Constructive Waivers

Two types of waivers exist: explicit waivers and constructive waivers. To be effective, an explicit waiver requires the state expressly to agree to be sued in federal court. A state's consent to be sued in its state courts is not sufficient to constitute a waiver of its Eleventh Amendment immunity.[204] Nor is a state's general waiver of its sovereign immunity enough. For example, a state statute authorizing the state to be sued "in any court of competent jurisdiction" is not an adequate waiver of Eleventh Amendment immunity.[205] The Court declared that "[a]lthough a State's general waiver of sovereign immunity may subject it to suit in state court, it is not enough to waive the immunity guaranteed by the Eleventh Amendment."[206] Rather, for a state statute or constitutional provision to constitute a waiver of Eleventh Amendment immunity, "it must specify the State's intention to subject itself to suit in *federal court*."[207] Thus, the Supreme Court's test is so stringent that it is

---

[199] Orth, *supra* note 30, at 123.

[200] Pagan, *supra* note 4, at 447, 488-489.

[201] *See, e.g.*, Florida Dept. of Health & Rehabilitative Servs. v. Florida Nursing Home Assn., 450 U.S. 147, 149-150 (1981); Edelman v. Jordan, 415 U.S. 651 (1974); Clark v. Barnard, 108 U.S. 436 (1883).

[202] Atascadero State Hosp. v. Scanlon, 473 U.S. at 241.

[203] 415 U.S. at 673 (citation omitted). *See also* Port Auth. Trans-Hudson Corp. v. Feeney, 495 U.S. 299, 305-306 (1990).

[204] *See, e.g.*, Florida Dept. of Health & Rehabilitative Servs. v. Florida Nursing Home Assn., 450 U.S. at 147, 149-150.

[205] Kennecott Copper Corp. v. State Tax Commn., 327 U.S. 573, 578-580 (1946).

[206] Atascadero State Hosp. v. Scanlon, 473 U.S. at 241.

[207] *Id.* at 241 (emphasis in original).

quite unlikely that very many explicit state waivers of Eleventh Amendment immunity will be found.

In *Port Authority Trans-Hudson Corp. v. Feeney*, the Court found an express waiver by a state of its Eleventh Amendment immunity.[208] The issue in *Feeney* was whether the Eleventh Amendment barred a suit against the Port Authority Trans-Hudson Corporation (PATH), an entity created by New York and New Jersey to operate transportation facilities. The Supreme Court assumed that PATH is a state agency entitled to Eleventh Amendment immunity.

The Court concluded that the states had waived their Eleventh Amendment immunity. Each state had adopted a law stating that it "consent[s] to suits, actions, or proceedings of any form or nature at law, in equity, or otherwise . . . against the Port Authority of New York."[209] Although this provision alone was insufficient to constitute a waiver because it did not consent to suit in *federal* court, there was another provision that was specific. The venue provision stated that "the foregoing consent is granted on the condition that venue . . . shall be within a county or judicial district, established by one of said States or by the United States, and situated wholly or partially within the Port of New York District."[210] Because the venue provision was part of the same law that consented to suit and because it clearly indicated that the states envisioned federal court litigation, the Court found that it was sufficient to waive the states' Eleventh Amendment immunity.

Constructive Waivers Not Allowed

Alternatively, there is the possibility of directly suing a state in federal court based on the state's constructive waiver of its Eleventh Amendment immunity. After some uncertainty in the law, it now appears that constructive waivers are disfavored and rarely will be found by the Court. As then-Justice Rehnquist declared, writing for the majority in *Edelman v. Jordan*, "[c]onstructive consent is not a doctrine commonly associated with the surrender of constitutional rights and we see no place for it here."[211]

The height of the doctrine of constructive consent was in *Parden v. Terminal Railway of Alabama State Docks Department*.[212] The issue in *Parden* was whether the state could be sued for violating provisions of the Federal Employers' Liability Act (FELA) in the operation of a state railroad. The Court held that the state's choice to operate a railroad in light of the federal statute reflected constructive consent by the state to be sued in federal court. Although the state had said explicitly it did

---

[208]   495 U.S. 299 (1990).

[209]   *Id.* at 306, quoting N.J. Stat Ann. §32:1-157 (1963); N.Y. Unconsol. Laws §7101 (McKinney 1979).

[210]   495 U.S. at 307, quoting N.J. Stat. Ann. §32:1-162; N.Y. Unconsol. Laws §7106 (McKinney 1979).

[211]   Edelman v. Jordan, 415 U.S. 651, 653 (1974). It is interesting that Justice Rehnquist analogizes a state's Eleventh Amendment immunity to an individual's constitutional rights.

[212]   377 U.S. 184 (1964). The Supreme Court overruled *Parden* in Welch v. Texas Dept. of Highways & Pub. Transp., 483 U.S. 468 (1987). *Welch* is discussed, in detail, at text accompanying notes 221-224, *infra*.

not consent to be sued, waiver was nonetheless found. Justice Brennan, writing for the majority, stated:

> Our conclusion is simply that Alabama, when it began operation of an interstate railroad approximately 20 years after enactment of the FELA, necessarily consented to such suit as was authorized by that Act. By adopting and ratifying the Commerce Clause, the States empowered Congress to create such a right of action against interstate railroads; by enacting the FELA in the exercise of this power, Congress conditioned the right to operate a railroad in interstate commerce upon amenability to suit in federal court as provided by the Act; by thereafter operating a railroad in interstate commerce, Alabama must be taken to have accepted that condition and thus to have consented to suit.[213]

Four Justices dissented, arguing that constructive waiver should be found only if there is an explicit statement from Congress that they intended to make states liable if they engaged in particular activities.

Subsequently, in *Employees of the Department of Public Health & Welfare v. Department of Public Health & Welfare*, the dissenting position in *Parden* was adopted by a majority of the Court.[214] The *Employees* case involved a suit against the State of Missouri to enforce the state's compliance with the Fair Labor Standards Act, which had been amended to apply to state and local governments. The majority distinguished *Parden* on the grounds that whereas states have a choice whether or not to operate railroads, they have little discretion in deciding whether to provide basic public services like public hospitals and police protection. Especially absent a clear declaration from Congress that it intended to make states liable for violations of the Act, there is no basis for finding a constructive waiver.[215]

The Court's refusal to find constructive waivers became even clearer a year after the *Employees* decision in *Edelman v. Jordan*.[216] In addition to trying to avoid the Eleventh Amendment by suing the state officers,[217] the plaintiffs also claimed that Illinois had waived its immunity to suits over its welfare program by voluntarily choosing to receive federal funds. Under the Social Security Act, states are not obligated to participate in the program of Aid to the Aged, Blind and Disabled. If, however, a state decides to participate, it receives federal funds but must comply with federal standards. The Court said that there was not a sufficient declaration of Congress's desire to permit suits against states in federal courts when states choose to receive federal welfare monies. The Court concluded that the "mere fact that a State participates in a program through which the Federal Government provides

---

[213] 377 U.S. at 192.

[214] 411 U.S. 279 (1973).

[215] *Id.* at 285. Justices Brennan and Marshall wrote dissenting opinions, in which they set out their views of the Eleventh Amendment, including the view that the Eleventh Amendment does not prevent a citizen's suit against his or her own state and that the Eleventh Amendment is a reinstatement of common law immunity.

[216] 415 U.S. 651 (1974).

[217] This aspect of Edelman v. Jordan is discussed in §2.10.4.2, *supra*.

assistance for the operation by the State of a system of public aid is not sufficient to establish consent on the part of the State to be sued in the federal courts."[218]

The holding in *Edelman* has been reaffirmed and applied by the Court in rulings that a state does not waive its Eleventh Amendment immunity by receiving federal funds under the Rehabilitation Act of 1973[219] or by agreeing to be bound by the requirements of the federal Medicaid Act.[220]

In 1987, the Supreme Court explicitly overruled its earlier decision in *Parden.* In *Welch v. Texas Department of Highways & Public Transportation,* the Court considered whether the Jones Act can be the basis for state liability in federal court.[221] The Jones Act is a federal statute creating remedies for injured seamen like those for injured railroad employees involved in the *Parden* case. Welch was injured while working for the State of Texas on the docks and sued to recover for his injuries.

The Supreme Court held that the Eleventh Amendment barred Welch's suit against Texas. The Court stated that "Congress has not expressed in unmistakable statutory language its intention to allow States to be sued in federal court under the Jones Act."[222] The Court emphasized that waiver will be found only if Congress clearly and unequivocally expresses its intent to make states liable. The Court declared that *Parden* was overruled to the extent that it was inconsistent with its holding in *Welch.*[223]

However, subsequent to *Welch,* the Supreme Court held that *Parden* was overruled only insofar as its holding that FELA constituted a waiver of the Eleventh Amendment. The Court ruled that suits still may be brought against states in state courts under FELA.[224]

In *College Savings Bank v. Florida Prepaid Postsecondary Expense Board,* the Supreme Court, in a 5-to-4 decision, again ruled that there is no constructive waiver of the Eleventh Amendment.[225] College Savings Bank is a company that devised a system for students to use to save money for their college education. Florida Prepaid, a Florida state agency, copied this system. College Savings Bank sued for patent infringement and for deceptive business practices in violation of the Lanham Act.[226] In *College Savings Bank v. Florida Prepaid,* the Court dealt with the latter claim and rejected the argument that the state had waived its sovereign immunity by engaging in the impermissible conduct. Justice Scalia, writing for the Court, stressed that there is no such thing as constructive waiver of the Eleventh Amendment.

---

[218] 415 U.S. at 673.

[219] Atascadero State Hosp. v. Scanlon, 473 U.S. 234 (1985).

[220] Florida Dept. of Health & Rehabilitative Servs. v. Florida Nursing Home Assn., 450 U.S. 147 (1981).

[221] Welch v. Texas Dept. of Highways & Pub. Transp., 483 U.S. 468 (1987).

[222] *Id.* at 475.

[223] *Id.* at 476.

[224] Hilton v. South Carolina Public Rys. Commn., 502 U.S. 197, 202 (1991).

[225] 527 U.S. 666 (1999).

[226] In a separate decision, *Florida Prepaid Postsecondary Education Expense Board v. College Savings Bank,* 527 U.S. 627 (1999), the Court held that the state could not be sued for patent infringement because Congress lacked the authority to permit such suits. This decision is discussed below.

Most recently, in *Sossaman v. Texas*,[227] the Court held that a state did not waive its sovereign immunity to suits for money damages under the Religious Land Use and Institutionalized Persons Act of 2000 (RLUIPA) by accepting federal funds.[228] The statute, in part, provides that states that receive federal funds for institutionalized persons, such as prisoners, cannot substantially burden their religious free exercise unless the action is necessary to achieve a compelling government purpose. The statute provides: "A person may assert a violation of [RLUIPA] as a claim or defense in a judicial proceeding and obtain appropriate relief against a government."[229]

The Court, though, found that the consent to suits for "appropriate relief" was not sufficiently specific to authorize money damages. Justice Thomas, writing for the Court, stated: "For these reasons, a waiver of sovereign immunity 'will be strictly construed, in terms of its scope, in favor of the sovereign.' RLUIPA's authorization of 'appropriate relief against a government,' is not the unequivocal expression of state consent that our precedents require. 'Appropriate relief' does not so clearly and unambiguously waive sovereign immunity to private suits for damages that we can 'be certain that the State in fact consents' to such a suit."[230]

In short, constructive waiver of Eleventh Amendment immunity is virtually nonexistent. If it ever will exist, it will be in situations where Congress indicates a clear intent to make states liable in federal court if they engage in a particular activity, and then a state voluntarily chooses to engage in that conduct.[231] The congressional desire to make states liable must be in "unmistakable language in the statute itself"[232] and it must be an area where the state realistically could choose not to engage in the activity.[233]

Nonetheless, there are important, unresolved questions concerning waivers. For example, is the removal of a case from state to federal court a waiver? The Supreme Court addressed but did not fully resolve the issue in *Lapides v. Board of Regents of University System of Georgia*.[234] The Court began by stating that the issue before it was "whether the State's act of removing a lawsuit from state court to federal court waives immunity."[235] The Court declared, "We hold that it does," but actually only decided a much narrower question: that a state's choice to remove a case from state to federal court is a waiver where there are state law claims and the state has waived its immunity as to these claims in state court. However, the reasoning in Justice Breyer's majority opinion has broader implications. He explained that "[i]t would seem anomalous or inconsistent for a State both (1) to invoke federal jurisdiction, thereby contending that the 'Judicial power of the United

---

[227] 131 S. Ct. 1651 (2011).

[228] 42 U.S.C. §2000cc *et seq.*

[229] §2000cc-2(a).

[230] 131 S. Ct. at 1658-1659.

[231] Pagan, *supra* note 4, at 491-492. *See also* Kit Kinports, Implied Waiver After *Seminole Tribe*, 82 Minn. L. Rev. 793 (1998).

[232] 473 U.S. at 243.

[233] Pagan, *supra* note 4, at 494-495.

[234] 535 U.S. 467 (2002).

[235] *Id.* at 617.

States' extends to the case at hand, and (2) to claim Eleventh Amendment immunity, thereby denying that the 'Judicial power of the United States' extends to the case at hand."[236] This would suggest that a state's invoking federal jurisdiction by removing a case from state to federal court is a waiver of sovereign immunity, but the issue has not yet been resolved by the Supreme Court.

A similar unresolved question concerns whether a state's participation in pretrial proceedings is a waiver.[237] Underlying these questions are issues concerning who within the state may waive its sovereign immunity; can the state attorney general do this, such as by removal, or can waiver be done only by a state legislature?

§2.10.6   Ways Around the Eleventh Amendment: Suits Pursuant to Federal Laws

Should Congress Be Able to Abrogate the Eleventh Amendment?

Many scholars have argued that Congress should be able to override the Eleventh Amendment and authorize suits against states in federal court. For example, Professors John Nowak and Laurence Tribe wrote articles contending that the Eleventh Amendment is a limit on the federal judiciary's powers, not on Congress's authority.[238] Both argue that questions of federalism are best resolved through the political process; therefore, Congress should have authority to balance federal and state interests and, where necessary, create state liability in federal court.[239]

Additionally, if the Eleventh Amendment is viewed as reinstating common law immunity,[240] then federal laws can authorize suits against the states because statutes can override the common law and federal statutes are supreme over the states.[241] Similarly, if the Eleventh Amendment is solely a prohibition of diversity suits against states in federal court, then states may be sued pursuant to any congressional statute.[242] But if the Eleventh Amendment is viewed as a limit on federal court subject matter jurisdiction, then, under traditional constitutional principles, statutes should not be able to authorize suits against the states. It has been established since *Marbury v. Madison* that Congress may not expand federal jurisdiction beyond the outer boundary created by the Constitution.[243]

---

[236] *Id.* at 618.

[237] Hill v. Blind Indus. and Servs. of Maryland, 179 F.3d 754 (9th Cir. 1999). Participation in pretrial proceedings in federal court is a waiver of sovereign immunity.

[238] *See* John E. Nowak, The Scope of Congressional Power to Create Causes of Action Against State Governments and the History of the Eleventh and Fourteenth Amendments, 75 Colum. L. Rev. 1413 (1975); Laurence H. Tribe, Intergovernmental Immunities in Litigation, Taxation, and Regulation: Separation of Powers Issues in Controversies About Federalism, 89 Harv. L. Rev. 682 (1976).

[239] For a criticism of the Nowak and Tribe positions, *see* Martha A. Field, The Eleventh Amendment and Other Sovereign Immunity Doctrines: Congressional Imposition of Suits upon the States, 126 U. Pa. L. Rev. 1203, 1258-1261 (1978).

[240] *See* discussion in §2.10.1, *supra*.

[241] For a development of this position, *see* Field, *supra* note 239, at 1253-1257.

[242] *See, e.g.,* Fletcher, *supra* note 6, at 1033.

[243] 5 U.S. (1 Cranch) 137 (1803).

The current law is that Congress may authorize suits against state governments only when it is acting pursuant to §5 of the Fourteenth Amendment. Congress may not override the Eleventh Amendment when acting under any other constitutional authority.

Statutes Adopted Under §5 of the Fourteenth Amendment

The seminal case holding that Congress can make states liable to suit in federal court pursuant to its powers under the post–Civil War amendments was *Fitzpatrick v. Bitzer*.[244] *Fitzpatrick* involved a suit brought directly against a state government pursuant to Title VII of the Civil Rights Act of 1964, which prohibits employment discrimination. Congress applied Title VII to the states pursuant to its powers under §5 of the Fourteenth Amendment. The Court reasoned that the Fourteenth Amendment specifically was intended to limit state sovereignty, and therefore congressional legislation under the Fourteenth Amendment can authorize suits directly against the states in federal court. Justice Rehnquist, writing for the majority, stated:

> When Congress acts pursuant to §5, not only is it exercising legislative authority that is plenary within the terms of the constitutional grant, it is exercising that authority under one section of a constitutional Amendment whose other sections by their own terms embody limitations on state authority. We think that Congress may, in determining what is "appropriate legislation" for the purpose of enforcing the provisions of the Fourteenth Amendment, provide for private suits against States or state officials which are constitutionally impermissible in other contexts.[245]

Soon after *Fitzpatrick*, the Supreme Court held, in *Hutto v. Finney*, that states may be sued for attorneys' fees pursuant to 42 U.S.C. §1988, a statute allowing successful plaintiffs in civil rights cases to recover attorneys' fees.[246] Despite the absence of an explicit authorization of suits against states in that statute, the Court said attorneys' fees against states are appropriate because of the clear congressional intent to include states and the statutory language that seemingly allows attorneys' fees to be awarded against all defendants.[247]

In subsequent cases, the Supreme Court has required Congress's intent to be very explicit in order to override state sovereignty pursuant to the Fourteenth Amendment. In *Quern v. Jordan*, the Court discussed whether 42 U.S.C. §1983 overrides the Eleventh Amendment.[248] Section 1983 is the basic civil rights law, creating an action in federal court against those acting under color of state law

---

[244] 427 U.S. 445 (1976).

[245] *Id.* at 456.

[246] 437 U.S. 678 (1978). In *Hutto*, the Court also said that attorneys' fees are permissible as a form of ancillary relief. *See* discussion in §2.10.4.2, *supra*.

[247] 437 U.S. at 693-698. *Hutto* was reaffirmed in Missouri v. Jenkins, 491 U.S. 274, 284 (1989) ("We reaffirm our holding in Hutto v. Finney that the Eleventh Amendment has no application to an award of attorneys' fees, ancillary to a grant of prospective relief, against a state.").

[248] 440 U.S. 332 (1979).

who violate the Constitution or federal laws.[249] If §1983 suits are not barred by the Eleventh Amendment, then any allegation of a state violation of federal law, statutory or constitutional, could be brought into federal court.

In *Quern v. Jordan*, Justice Rehnquist concluded that although §1983 was adopted pursuant to §5 of the Fourteenth Amendment, there was insufficient indication of an express congressional desire to make state governments liable under that statute. Justice Rehnquist wrote:

> [Section] 1983 does not explicitly and by clear language indicate on its face an intent to sweep away the immunity of the States; nor does it have a history which focuses directly on the question of state liability and which shows that Congress considered and firmly decided to abrogate the Eleventh Amendment immunity of the States.[250]

Justices Brennan and Marshall vehemently disagreed with this part of Justice Rehnquist's opinion, although they concurred in the result that it was permissible to compel Illinois to send notification to those who had been wrongfully denied welfare benefits. First, they argued that it was unnecessary to reach the question in *Quern* of whether §1983 overrides the Eleventh Amendment because the Court already had ruled that the notice ordered by the district court did not violate the Eleventh Amendment.[251] Thus, the majority's discussion of the relationship of §1983 to the Eleventh Amendment is completely unnecessary to the result and is therefore dicta. Second, the dissent objected to Justice Rehnquist's reliance on *Alabama v. Pugh*[252] as authority that §1983 does not override the Eleventh Amendment because that question had not been briefed or argued in *Pugh*.[253] Third, and perhaps most important, the dissenters argued that §1983 was meant to override state sovereignty and that the states are persons for purposes of liability under §1983.[254] Nonetheless, the Supreme Court subsequently stated that the "holding" in *Quern* was that §1983 does not abrogate the Eleventh Amendment.[255] In fact, the Supreme Court held that Eleventh Amendment principles mean that states may not even be sued in state court under §1983.[256]

Thus, although Congress may override the Eleventh Amendment pursuant to statutes adopted under §5 of the Fourteenth Amendment, there must be a clearer expression of congressional intent than existed for §1983. However, as *Hutto* indicates, the expression of congressional intent does not have to be in the text of the statute. Section 1988, in its text, does not expressly authorize attorneys' fees

---

[249] Section 1983 is discussed in detail in Erwin Chemerinsky, Federal Jurisdiction ch. 8 (6th ed. 2011).

[250] 440 U.S. at 345.

[251] 440 U.S. at 350 (Brennan, J., dissenting).

[252] 438 U.S. 781 (1978).

[253] 440 U.S. at 354 (Brennan, J., dissenting).

[254] *Id.* at 354-366. For criticisms of *Quern v. Jordan, see* Bruce McBirney, Note, *Quern v. Jordan*: A Misdirected Bar to Section 1983 Suits Against States, 67 Cal. L. Rev. 407, 420-427 (1979).

[255] Pennhurst State School & Hosp. v. Halderman, 465 U.S. 89, 99 (1984).

[256] Will v. Michigan Dept. of State Police, 491 U.S. 58 (1989).

against states, but the Court found that the legislative history was sufficiently clear to permit this.

Statutes Adopted Under Other Congressional Powers

In 1996, in *Seminole Tribe of Florida v. Florida*, the Supreme Court held that Congress may abrogate the Eleventh Amendment only when acting under its §5 powers and not under any other constitutional authority.[257] This overruled a series of cases decided in the late 1980s in which the Supreme Court held that Congress may authorize suits when acting pursuant to other constitutional powers so long as the federal law, in its text, clearly and expressly permits federal court jurisdiction over state governments.

This principle, overruled in *Seminole Tribe*, was first expressed in *Atascadero State Hospital v. Scanlon*, where the Supreme Court refused to allow suits against a state pursuant to the Rehabilitation Act of 1973.[258] The Act prohibits employment discrimination against an "otherwise qualified individual with handicaps" by any recipient of federal assistance.[259] There was strong evidence from the legislative history that Congress intended for states to be liable under the Act. Nonetheless, the Court, in a 5-to-4 decision, refused to allow a suit against the State of California on the grounds that Congress was not sufficiently explicit concerning its desire to make states liable in federal courts. The Court stated:

> We . . . affirm that Congress may abrogate the States' constitutionally secured immunity from suit in federal court only by making its intention unmistakably clear in the language of the statute. . . . A general authorization for suit in federal court is not the kind of unequivocal statutory language sufficient to abrogate the Eleventh Amendment. When Congress chooses to subject the States to federal jurisdiction, it must do so specifically.[260]

In *Pennsylvania v. Union Gas Co.*,[261] the Supreme Court held that Congress may authorize suits against states, so long as the law does so expressly in its text. In *Pennsylvania v. Union Gas Co.*, the Supreme Court confronted two questions: (1) Does the Comprehensive Environmental Response, Compensation, and Liability Act of 1980 (CERCLA),[262] as amended by the Superfund Amendments and

---

[257] 517 U.S. 44 (1996).

[258] 473 U.S. 234 (1985). In *Atascadero*, the Court also discussed the requirements for a state's waiver of its Eleventh Amendment immunity, an aspect of the case discussed in §2.10.5, *supra*.

[259] 29 U.S.C. §794 (1985). Rehabilitation Act Amendments of 1986, Pub. L. No. 99-506, 100 Stat. 1810, 29 U.S.C. §794 (1985) (The amendments replaced each occurrence of the words "handicapped individual" with the words "individuals with handicaps."). *See also* 1986 U.S. Code Cong. & Admin. News 3471, 3487.

[260] 473 U.S. at 245. The dissenting Justices argued that the Eleventh Amendment should be regarded only as limiting diversity suits against state governments; thus, all actions pursuant to federal statutes present federal questions and would be allowed to proceed in federal court. 473 U.S. at 247-248 (Brennan, J., dissenting). This aspect of the *Atascadero* dissent is discussed in §2.10.5, *supra*.

[261] 491 U.S. 1 (1989).

[262] 642 U.S.C. §9601.

Reauthorization Act of 1986 (SARA), authorize suits against state governments in federal court?[263] (2) If so, does Congress, when legislating pursuant to the commerce clause, have the authority to create such state government liability?

The Court answered both questions affirmatively. However, the Court did so without a majority opinion and was very splintered. Four Justices—Justices Brennan, Marshall, Blackmun, and Stevens—concluded that the statute permits suits against states[264] and that Congress may authorize such litigation under its commerce power.[265] These Justices ruled that CERCLA expressly defines "persons" to include states and other parts of the statute explicitly exclude states where Congress wanted to protect them from liability.

Three Justices—Chief Justice Rehnquist and Justices O'Connor and Kennedy—concluded that CERCLA did not expressly authorize suits against state governments.[266] Moreover, these Justices stated that even if CERCLA authorized such suits, the federal courts lacked jurisdiction because Congress could not override the Eleventh Amendment pursuant to its commerce power.[267]

Justice White agreed with the dissenters that the statute was not sufficiently specific to permit state governments to be sued in federal court. He reasoned that federal courts lacked jurisdiction because CERCLA "did not include an *unmistakable declaration* of abrogation of state immunity."[268] However, Justice White agreed with Justices Brennan, Marshall, Blackmun, and Stevens that Congress has the constitutional power to abrogate the states' immunity pursuant to its commerce power. In a short paragraph, Justice White stated that he concurred in the conclusion, although he said "I do not agree with much of [Justice Brennan's] reasoning."[269]

Justice Scalia's position was exactly the opposite of Justice White's. Justice Scalia stated that he believed that CERCLA clearly expressed a desire to impose liability on state governments in federal court. However, he forcefully argued that Congress should not be able to authorize suits against states under the commerce clause.[270]

Thus, there were five votes that CERCLA permits states to be sued for monetary liability in federal court: Justices Brennan, Marshall, Blackmun, Stevens, and Scalia. There also were five votes that Congress, acting pursuant to its commerce

---

[263] 100 Stat. 1613 (to be codified as 42 U.S.C. §9601).

[264] *Union Gas*, 491 U.S. at 13 (Congress intended to permit suits brought by private citizens against the state under CERCLA).

[265] *Id.* at 19 (Congress may abrogate states' immunity from suit when legislating pursuant to the plenary powers granted it by the Constitution).

[266] These three Justices concurred in Justice White's opinion stating that CERCLA did not clearly authorize suits against state governments in federal court. *Id.* at 50 (White, J., concurring).

[267] These three Justices concurred in Justice Scalia's opinion that Congress may not, pursuant to its commerce power, abrogate a state's Eleventh Amendment immunity. *Id.* at 42 (Scalia, J., concurring in part and dissenting in part).

[268] *Id.* at 46-47 (White, J., concurring) (emphasis in original).

[269] *Id.* at 57 (White, J., concurring).

[270] *Id.* at 42 (Scalia, J., concurring in part and dissenting in part).

clause authority, can create such federal court jurisdiction: Justices Brennan, Marshall, Blackmun, Stevens, and White.[271]

Thus, *Pennsylvania v. Union Gas* clearly held that Congress could override the Eleventh Amendment pursuant to any of its constitutional powers, so long as the law was explicit in its text in authorizing suits against state governments. This was overruled in *Seminole Tribe*. As described earlier, *Seminole Tribe* involved a suit under the Indian Gaming Regulatory Act, which required that states negotiate with Indian Tribes to form compacts to allow gambling on Native American land. The Act specifically authorized suits against states in federal court as an enforcement mechanism.[272]

The Supreme Court held that the federal statute authorizing suits against states in federal court was unconstitutional. Congress may authorize suits against states only when acting pursuant to §5 of the Fourteenth Amendment and not pursuant to other federal powers, such as the Indian commerce clause. Chief Justice Rehnquist, writing for the majority in the 5-to-4 decision, emphasized that *Pennsylvania v. Union Gas* was a plurality opinion. Chief Justice Rehnquist declared that "[t]he plurality's rationale . . . deviated sharply from our established federalism jurisprudence and essentially eviscerated our decision in *Hans*."[273] The Court concluded: "Reconsidering the decision in *Union Gas*, we conclude that none of the policies underlying stare decisis require our continuing adherence of its holding."[274]

Seminole Tribe produced a heated debate among scholars.[275] Many questions can be raised about the decision. First, was the Court justified in overruling the earlier, recent decisions that Congress could authorize suits against states under any constitutional power? What, after all, had changed in the seven years since the earlier rulings? The obvious answer is that in the intervening several years, Justice Thomas joined the Court, and he joined with the four dissenters in *Pennsylvania v. Union Gas*—Chief Justice Rehnquist and Justices O'Connor, Kennedy, and Scalia—to create the majority to overrule it. The issue in evaluating *Seminole Tribe*, in part, is about the proper role of stare decisis.

---

[271] In two cases decided the same Term, the Court applied *Pennsylvania v. Union Gas*, but found that Congress had not authorized suits against the states. In *Dellmuth v. Muth*, 491 U.S. 223 (1989), the Court ruled that states cannot be sued in federal court pursuant to the Education for All Handicapped Children Act, a federal law that ensures that disabled children may receive a free public education appropriate for their needs. The Supreme Court, in a 5-to-4 decision, ruled that the Act does not authorize suits against state governments in federal court.

In *Hoffman v. Connecticut Department of Income Maintenance*, 492 U.S. 96 (1989), by the same 5-to-4 margin, the Court held that states could not be sued in federal court pursuant to the then-existing provisions of the Bankruptcy Code.

[272] 25 U.S.C. §2710(d)(7).

[273] 517 U.S. at 45.

[274] *Id.* at 66.

[275] *See, e.g.*, Vicki Jackson, *Seminole Tribe*, the Eleventh Amendment, and the Potential Evisceration of *Ex parte Young*, 72 N.Y.U. L. Rev. 495 (1997); Carlos Manual Vasquez, What Is Eleventh Amendment Immunity?, 106 Yale L.J. 1683 (1997); Herbert Hovenkamp, Judicial Restraint and Constitutional Federalism: The Supreme Court's *Lopez* and *Seminole Tribe* Decisions, 96 Colum. L. Rev. 2213 (1996); Daniel J. Meltzer, The *Seminole* Decision and State Sovereign Immunity, 1996 Sup. Ct. Rev. 1; Henry Paul Monaghan, The Sovereign Immunity "Exception," 110 Harv. L. Rev. 102 (1996).

Second, is there a meaningful distinction between Congress's authority under §5 and other constitutional powers? The majority claims that §5 is different because it was meant as a limit on states and that the Fourteenth Amendment modifies the previously enacted Eleventh Amendment. The dissent argues that there is nothing in the history of the Eleventh Amendment that suggests that it was meant to preclude suits against states pursuant to federal statutes.[276] The dissent maintains that states consented to the exercise of congressional power in ratifying the Constitution.

Third, and most fundamentally, *Seminole Tribe* raises basic questions about federalism. Should the protection of state governments be left to Congress and should the need to ensure state compliance with federal law justify allowing Congress to authorize suits against states in federal court? This was the view underlying cases such as *Pennsylvania v. Union Gas*. Or is it the role of the Supreme Court to protect state sovereignty, especially from congressional encroachment? This is the assumption of *Seminole Tribe*. Ultimately, it is a choice about the meaning of federalism and the respective roles of Congress and the Supreme Court in defining and protecting it.

Which Statutes Were Enacted Under §5 of the Fourteenth Amendment?

The key question after *Seminole Tribe* is whether a statute was enacted under §5 or under another congressional power. A state can be sued in federal court only if the Court concludes that the law was enacted under §5. Often statutes, in their text and legislative history, are unclear about the constitutional basis for Congress's action.

The scope of Congress's power under §5 of the Fourteenth Amendment is discussed in detail in §3.7.2, and its power to authorize suits against state governments is considered in §3.8. By way of brief summary, because this is discussed in detail in Chapter 3, in *City of Boerne v. Flores*, the Court sharply limited the scope of Congress's power under §5 of the Fourteenth Amendment.[277] The Court ruled that pursuant to §5, Congress only may provide remedies for rights recognized by the courts and that Congress may not create new rights or expand the scope of rights. Any law must be narrowly tailored to solving constitutional violations; it must be "proportionate" and "congruent" to preventing and remedying constitutional violations. The Court declared the Religious Freedom Restoration Act unconstitutional as exceeding the scope of Congress's power under §5 of the Fourteenth Amendment. *City of Boerne v. Flores* makes many laws enacted under §5 potentially vulnerable to constitutional challenge. Therefore, if a Court concludes that a federal law was adopted under §5, a state may be sued for violating it, but there is a significant chance that the constitutionality of the law might be challenged under *City of Boerne v. Flores*.

---

[276] 517 U.S. at 111 (Souter, J., dissenting).
[277] 521 U.S. 507 (1997).

The Court has so far applied this limit on Congress's §5 powers in five cases concerning statutes authorizing suits against state governments. These cases are discussed in detail in §3.7, which discusses the scope of Congress's power under §5. In four of the cases—*Florida Prepaid Postsecondary Education Expense Board v. College Savings Bank*,[278] *Kimel v. Florida Board of Regents*,[279] *University of Alabama v. Garrett*,[280] and *Coleman v. Court of Appeals of Maryland*[281]—the Court in 5-to-4 decisions found that a law adopted by Congress exceeded the scope of Congress's §5 power and thus could not be used to sue state governments. In two cases—*Nevada Department of Human Resources v. Hibbs*[282] and *Tennessee v. Lane*[283]—the Court found that laws were within Congress's §5 powers because they involved claims that would receive heightened judicial scrutiny under equal protection and due process. Additionally, in *United States v. Georgia*,[284] the Court held that Congress may authorize suits against states for conduct that actually violates the Fourteenth Amendment.

In *Florida Prepaid*, the Court held that a federal law authorizing suits against states for patent infringement exceeded the scope of Congress's §5 authority. The Court said that the law was not "proportionate" or "congruent" because of the absence of proof of a pattern of such violations by state governments. In *Kimel*, the Court ruled that state governments could not be sued for violating the Age Discrimination in Employment Act. The Court held that the law prohibits much more than the Constitution, since age discrimination receives only rational basis review, and that the legislative record did not document a pattern of unconstitutional age discrimination by state governments. In *Garrett*, the Court held that state governments cannot be sued for violating Title I of the Americans with Disabilities Act, which prohibits employment discrimination based on disability and requires that employers make reasonable accommodations for disabilities. As in *Kimel*, the Court found that the law prohibits much that would not violate the Constitution, because disability discrimination receives only rational basis review under equal protection. The Court said that the legislative record did not sufficiently document unconstitutional discrimination by state governments against the disabled in employment to make the law "proportionate" or "congruent" to the problem.

In sharp contrast, in *Hibbs*, the Supreme Court held that state governments could be sued under the family leave provisions of the Family and Medical Leave Act. In a 6-to-3 decision, with the majority opinion written by Chief Justice William Rehnquist, the Court said that the law was intended to prevent gender discrimination because Congress was concerned that due to social roles women would suffer more than men in the workplace from a lack of family leave. Since gender discrimination, unlike age or disability discrimination, receives heightened scrutiny

---

[278] 527 U.S. 627 (1999).
[279] 528 U.S. 62 (2000).
[280] 531 U.S. 356 (2001).
[281] 132 S. Ct. 1327 (2012).
[282] 538 U.S. 721 (2003).
[283] 541 U.S. 509 (2004).
[284] 546 U.S. 151 (2006).

under equal protection, the Court said that Congress had greater authority to legislate under §5 and the law thus could be used to sue the state government.[285]

Similarly, in *Tennessee v. Lane*, the Court held that state governments may be sued for discriminating against people with disabilities, pursuant to Title II of the Americans with Disabilities Act, with regard to the fundamental right of access to the courts. Justice Stevens, writing for the Court, emphasized that there is a well-established fundamental right of access to the courts and that Congress may enforce it by authorizing suits against state governments. The Court left open the issue of whether states may be sued for other violations of Title II, which prohibits state and local governments from discriminating against people with disabilities in government programs, services, and activities.

In *United States v. Georgia*,[286] the Court held that a prisoner could sue a state under Title II of the Americans with Disabilities Act for alleged unconstitutional actions. Title II prohibits state and local governments from discriminating against persons with disabilities in government "programs, services, and activities." Justice Scalia, writing for a unanimous Court, declared: "Thus, insofar as Title II creates a private cause of action for damages against the States for conduct that *actually* violates the Fourteenth Amendment, Title II validly abrogates state sovereign immunity."[287]

Together *Lane* and *Hibbs* establish that Congress has more authority to act under §5 of the Fourteenth Amendment, and thus to authorize suits against state governments, when it is dealing with claims of discrimination or violations of rights that receive heightened scrutiny. The key normative question, discussed more fully in §3.8, is whether it makes sense for Congress's power under §5 to depend on the level of judicial scrutiny the Court has attached to the claim. Also, it must be remembered that *Hibbs* was a 6-to-3 decision with both Rehnquist and O'Connor in the majority, while *Lane* was 5-to-4 with O'Connor in the majority. Thus, this principle could change in the future.

After these cases, courts will need to consider many other federal laws and whether they fit within the scope of Congress's §5 powers and can be used to sue state governments. It should be remembered, however, that even if state governments cannot be sued for violating these statutes, enforcement still is possible via suits against individual state officers and in actions by the federal government. The underlying question is whether this is sufficient or whether suits against state governments are necessary for adequate enforcement. Ultimately, as with everything discussed in this section, the issue is over the appropriate balance between the desire for state immunity and the need for state accountability.

---

[285] But in *Coleman v. Court of Appeals of Maryland*, 132 S. Ct. 1327 (2012), the Court held that states could not be sued to enforce the self-care provisions of the Family and Medical Leave Act because they were not focused on remedying a history of gender discrimination.

[286] 546 U.S. 151 (2006).

[287] *Id.* at 159.

CHAPTER 3

The Federal Legislative Power

§3.1   THE DOCTRINE OF LIMITED FEDERAL LEGISLATIVE AUTHORITY

Congress Must Have Express or Implied Powers

A basic principle of American government is that Congress may act only if there is express or implied authority to act in the Constitution; states, however, may act unless the Constitution prohibits the action. Article I of the Constitution, which creates the federal legislative power, begins by stating: "All legislative powers herein granted shall be vested in a Congress of the United States which shall consist of a Senate and House of Representatives." Additionally, the Tenth Amendment declares: "The powers not delegated to the United States by the Constitution, nor prohibited by it to the States, are reserved to the States respectively, or to the people."

Therefore, in evaluating the constitutionality of any act of Congress, there are always two questions. First, does Congress have the authority under the Constitution to legislate? Second, if so, does the law violate another constitutional provision or doctrine, such as by infringing separation of powers or interfering with individual liberties? In contrast, when evaluating the constitutionality of a state law, there is a single question: Does the legislation violate the Constitution?

Put another way, a key difference between federal and state governments is that only the latter possess the police power. The police power allows state and local governments to adopt any law that is not prohibited by the Constitution.

There are a few areas where Congress does have the police power. Most notably, when Congress legislates for the District of Columbia or the territories, it possesses the same police power that state governments exercise.

The Reality of Broad Federal Powers

Yet this classic formulation of governmental powers does not fully reflect the reality of the federal government's authority. As described below, after 1937, the Supreme Court accorded Congress broad authority to regulate under constitutional provisions such as the commerce clause, the spending power, and the Reconstruction Amendments (the Thirteenth, Fourteenth, and Fifteenth Amendments). For example, as considered in detail below, from 1937 until 1995, not a single federal law was declared unconstitutional as exceeding the scope of Congress's commerce power.[1] Undoubtedly, the Supreme Court's expansive interpretation of congressional authority was, in part, based on a perceived need for a strong national government to deal with the problems of the twentieth century and, in part, a reaction to the intense criticism of the earlier decisions that had sharply limited the scope of federal powers.

---

§3.1 [1] In United States v. Lopez, 514 U.S. 549 (1995), the Court invalidated a federal law as exceeding the scope of the commerce power. The case, and its significance, is discussed in §3.4.5.

But in the last 20 years, the Supreme Court has changed course and in several important rulings has limited the scope of Congress's power under the commerce clause[2] and under §5 of the Fourteenth Amendment.[3] Also, the Court has revived the Tenth Amendment as a limit on federal power.[4]

Organization of the Chapter

In considering the federal legislative power, this chapter focuses on four major questions. First, what is the scope of congressional authority? Section 3.2 considers *McCulloch v. Maryland*,[5] which is crucial in defining the scope of congressional powers and the relationship of the federal and state governments.

Second, what is Congress's authority under specific constitutional provisions? Section 3.3 looks at the necessary and proper clause in Article I, §8 of the Constitution, §3.4 focuses on the commerce clause, §3.5 considers the taxing and spending power, §3.6 examines other powers granted in Articles I and IV of the Constitution, and §3.7 looks at the authority under the Reconstruction Amendments. Section 3.8 looks at Congress's power to authorize suits against state governments, and §3.9 considers Congress's authority to conduct investigations.

Third, does state sovereignty limit congressional power? Over the course of American history, the Supreme Court has shifted in its interpretation of the Tenth Amendment. Section 3.10 considers this issue.

Finally, what limits, if any, exist on Congress's ability to delegate legislative power? A classic statement about the federal government is that Congress may not delegate legislative power. Yet the rise of administrative agencies belies any realistic limit on such delegations. Administrative agencies possess legislative, executive, and judicial powers and thus pose a basic conflict with the traditional principle of separation of powers. The issues posed by these agencies are discussed in §3.11.

Although this chapter focuses on the legislative power, considerations of separation of powers and federalism underlie all of this material. The legislative power can be understood only relative to the other branches of the federal government. For example, although Congress's authority in the area of foreign policy is discussed in §3.6.1, it must be considered relative to the president's powers in this area, which are discussed in the next chapter in §4.6.

Moreover, federalism is a key recurring issue in defining the scope of Congress's powers. The allocation of power between the federal and state governments often is an express consideration for the Supreme Court as it decides whether to narrowly construe congressional authority or whether to find federal laws unconstitutional as infringing state sovereignty.

---

[2] *See* United States v. Morrison, 529 U.S. 598 (2000); United States v. Lopez, 514 U.S. 549 (1995), discussed below in §3.4.5.

[3] *See* Shelby County, Alabama v. Holder, 133 S. Ct. 2612 (2013); City of Boerne v. Flores, 521 U.S. 507 (1997), discussed below in §3.7.2.

[4] *See* National Federation of Independent Business v. Sebelius, 132 S. Ct. 2566 (2012); Printz v. United States, 521 U.S. 898 (1997); New York v. United States, 505 U.S. 144 (1992).

[5] 17 U.S. (4 Wheat.) 316 (1819).

§3.2   *McCULLOCH v. MARYLAND* AND THE SCOPE OF CONGRESSIONAL POWERS

Factual Background of *McCulloch*

McCulloch v. Maryland is the seminal case defining the scope of the federal legislative power and its relationship to state government authority.[1] The specific issue posed in *McCulloch* is whether the State of Maryland could collect a tax from the Bank of the United States. Chief Justice John Marshall used the case as an occasion to broadly construe Congress's powers and narrowly limit the authority of state governments to impede the federal government.

The controversy over the Bank of the United States began almost 30 years before *McCulloch*, in 1790, when there was a major dispute in both Congress and the executive branch as to whether Congress had the authority to create such a bank.[2] Secretary of the Treasury Alexander Hamilton strongly favored creating a Bank of the United States, but he was opposed by Secretary of State Thomas Jefferson and Attorney General Edmund Randolph. Both Jefferson and Randolph argued that Congress lacked the authority under the Constitution to create such a bank and that doing so would usurp state government prerogatives. Ultimately, Hamilton persuaded President George Washington to support creating the bank, but the debate continued in Congress. James Madison, then in the House of Representatives, echoed the views of Jefferson and Randolph, and opposed the bank. Despite this august opposition, the Federalists, who then solidly controlled Congress, successfully enacted legislation to create the Bank of the United States.

The bank existed for 21 years until its charter expired in 1811. However, after the War of 1812, the country experienced serious economic problems and the Bank of the United States was re-created in 1816. In fact, although he had opposed such a bank a quarter of a century earlier, as president, James Madison endorsed its re-creation. The United States government actually owned only 20 percent of the new bank.

The Bank of the United States did not solve the country's economic problems and, indeed, many blamed the bank's monetary policies for aggravating a serious depression. State governments were particularly angry at the bank, especially because the bank called in loans owed by the states. Thus, many states adopted laws designed to limit the operation of the bank. Some states adopted laws prohibiting its operation within their borders. Others, such as Maryland, taxed it. The Maryland law required that any bank not chartered by the state pay either an annual tax of $15,000 or a tax of 2 percent on all of its notes, which needed to be on special stamped paper.

The bank refused to pay the Maryland tax, and John James sued for himself and the State of Maryland in the County Court of Baltimore to recover the money owed under the tax. The defendant, McCulloch, was the cashier of that branch of the Bank of the United States. The trial court rendered judgment in favor of the plaintiff, and the Maryland Court of Appeals affirmed.

---

§3.2 [1] 17 U.S. (4 Wheat.) 316 (1819).

[2] A thorough discussion of the history of the Bank of the United States can be found in 1 Charles Warren, The Supreme Court in United States History, 499-540 (1st ed. 1922).

The Supreme Court, in a famous opinion by Chief Justice John Marshall, reversed. Marshall's opinion considered two major questions: First, does Congress have the authority to create the Bank of the United States; and second, is the state tax on the bank constitutional? It is notable that Marshall posed the first question because technically the sole issue before the Court was whether Maryland constitutionally could collect its tax. There are probably several reasons why Marshall began by considering Congress's power. Once it is established that Congress has the power to create the bank, it then is easier to explain why the states cannot tax or regulate it. Also, undoubtedly, John Marshall recognized this case as an ideal opportunity to articulate a broad vision of federal power, much as he used *Marbury v. Madison* to establish the power of judicial review.

Congress's Authority to Create the Bank of the United States

As to the first question, whether Congress has the authority to create the Bank of the United States, Marshall made four arguments. First, historical practice established the power of Congress to create the bank. Marshall began his opinion by declaring: "It has been truly said, that this can scarcely be considered as an open question, entirely unprejudiced by the former proceedings of the nation respecting it. The principle now contested was introduced at a very early period of our history, has been recognized by many successive legislatures, and has been acted upon by the judicial department, in cases of peculiar delicacy, as a law of undoubted obligation."[3]

In other words, Marshall invoked the history of the first Bank of the United States as authority for the constitutionality of the second bank. Marshall expressly noted that the first Congress enacted the bank after great debate and that it was approved by an executive "with as much persevering talent as any measure has ever experienced, and being supported by arguments which convinced minds as pure and as intelligent as this country can boast. . . ."[4] Although Marshall did not mention James Madison by name, Marshall remarked on how even those who opposed the first bank endorsed creating the second bank. Marshall concluded that "[i]t would require no ordinary share of intrepidity, to assert that a measure adopted under these circumstances, was a bold and plain usurpation, to which the constitution gave no countenance."[5]

Marshall's contention, that historical experience justifies the constitutionality of a practice, is a type of argument that often appears in Supreme Court opinions. For example, in *United States v. Midwest Oil Co.*, the Court declared that a "long-continued practice, known to and acquiesced in by Congress, would raise a presumption that the [action] had been [taken] in pursuance of its consent. . . ."[6] In *Youngstown Sheet & Tube Co. v. Sawyer*, Justice Felix Frankfurter expressed the view

---

[3]   *McCulloch*, 17 U.S. at 401.
[4]   *Id.* at 402.
[5]   *Id.*
[6]   236 U.S. 459, 474 (1915).

that a "systematic, unbroken executive practice, long pursued to the knowledge of Congress and never before questioned . . . may be treated as a gloss on 'executive power' vested in the President."[7] In *Dames & Moore v. Regan*, the Court approvingly invoked Justice Frankfurter's words in upholding an executive agreement to lift a freeze on Iranian assets in the United States as a part of a deal to have American hostages there released.[8]

The underlying question, however, is whether a description of a historical practice should have normative significance in resolving questions about its constitutionality. No court ever had ruled on the constitutionality of the Bank of the United States, and it is questionable why an unreviewed practice should create a presumption of constitutionality. Moreover, as Justice Holmes declared in oft-quoted language, that laws may be "natural and familiar . . . ought not to conclude our judgment upon the question whether [the] statutes . . . conflict with the Constitution of the United States."[9]

In considering the constitutionality of the Bank of the United States, Marshall's second major point was to refute the argument that states retain ultimate sovereignty because they ratified the Constitution. This view, sometimes called "compact federalism," sees the states as sovereign because they created the United States by ceding some of their power and by ratifying the Constitution. Chief Justice Marshall described this view when he stated: "The powers of the general government, it has been said, are delegated by the states, who alone are truly sovereign; and must be exercised in subordination to the states, who alone possess supreme dominion."[10] The implication is that if the states are sovereign, then they would have the authority to veto a federal action, such as the creation of the Bank of the United States.

Marshall emphatically rejected this view and contended that it was the people who ratified the Constitution, and thus the people are sovereign, not the states. Marshall wrote: "The government proceeds directly from the people; is 'ordained and established' in the name of the people. . . . The assent of the States, in their sovereign capacity, is implied, in calling a convention, and thus submitting that instrument to the people. But the people were at perfect liberty to accept or reject it; and their act was final. It required not the affirmance, and could not be negatived, by the state governments."[11]

Marshall's argument is rhetorically powerful; it concludes that "[t]he government of the Union . . . is, emphatically, and truly, a government of the people."[12] The Court thus rejected the view that the Constitution should be regarded as a compact of the states and that the states retain ultimate sovereignty under the Constitution.

---

[7] 343 U.S. 579, 610-611 (1952) (Frankfurter, J., concurring).

[8] 453 U.S. 654, 686 (1981).

[9] Lochner v. New York, 198 U.S. 45, 76 (1905) (Holmes, J., dissenting); Bowers v. Hardwick, 478 U.S. 186, 199 (1986) (Blackmun, J., dissenting).

[10] *McCulloch*, 17 U.S. at 402.

[11] *Id.* at 403-404.

[12] *Id.* at 404.

Yet Marshall's reasoning can be questioned. Article VII of the Constitution states: "The Ratification of the Conventions of nine States shall be sufficient for the Establishment of this Constitution between the States so ratifying the Same." The Constitution was not approved by a national plebiscite; it was ratified by the states. Marshall explains that it was natural that people would act within states, but this does not address the language of Article VII, which clearly indicates that the states themselves had to ratify the Constitution, not the people.

Nonetheless, Marshall's view has controlled throughout American history. There, however, have been challenges and reassertions of the theory of compact federalism. During the early part of the nineteenth century, John Calhoun defended slavery by claiming that states could interpose their sovereignty between Congress and the people and nullify federal actions.[13] During the 1950s and 1960s, opponents of federal civil rights initiatives again raised claims of state sovereignty.[14] More recently, in 1995, in *United States Term Limits v. Thornton,* Justice Thomas, in dissent, expressed the view that states retain ultimate sovereignty except in those areas where the Constitution expressly delegates power to the federal government.[15] Although it was surprising to see such a strong reassertion of this view in 1995, it was not at all surprising to see the Justices in the majority respond by quoting John Marshall's opinion in *McCulloch v. Maryland.*[16]

In discussing the constitutionality of the creation of the bank, the Court's third major point was to address the scope of congressional powers under Article I. It is important to note that the Court broadly described Congress's authority even before addressing the necessary and proper clause. Chief Justice Marshall admitted that the Constitution does not enumerate a power to create a Bank of the United States, but said that this is not dispositive as to Congress's power to establish such an institution. Marshall explained that "[a] constitution, to contain an accurate detail of all the subdivisions of which its great powers will admit, and of all the means by which they may be carried into execution, would partake of the prolixity of a legal code, and could scarcely be embraced by the human mind."[17] Marshall then uttered some of the most famous words in all of the United States Reports: "In considering this question, then, we must never forget that it is a *constitution* we are expounding."[18]

Felix Frankfurter described this sentence as "the single most important utterance in the literature of constitutional law—most important because [it was] most comprehensive and most comprehending."[19] Although Marshall's language seems tautological, his point is that the Constitution is different from a statute

---

[13] *See, e.g.,* Samuel H. Beer, To Make a Nation: The Rediscovery of American Federalism 224 (1993).

[14] *Id.* at 19-20.

[15] 514 U.S. 779, 845 (1995) (Thomas, J., dissenting).

[16] *Id.* at 839 (Kennedy, J., concurring).

[17] *McCulloch,* 17 U.S. at 407.

[18] *Id.* at 407 (emphasis added).

[19] Felix Frankfurter, John Marshall and the Judicial Function, 69 Harv. L. Rev. 217, 219 (1955).

and therefore should be interpreted differently.[20] Marshall's ultimate conclusion is that Congress is not limited only to those acts specified in the Constitution; Congress may choose any means, not prohibited by the Constitution, to carry out its lawful authority. Even though the Constitution does not mention a power to create a Bank of the United States, Congress can create one as a means to carrying out many of its other powers.

This is a dramatic expansion in the scope of congressional authority. If Congress were limited to the powers specifically enumerated in Article I, the range of laws would be finite. But if Congress can choose any means not prohibited by the Constitution to carry out its powers, it truly has an almost infinite range of options that can be enacted into law. Indeed, in opposing the initial creation of the Bank of the United States, Thomas Jefferson saw how broad Congress's power would be if it could choose any means to implement its authority: "Congress [is] authorized to defend the nation. Ships are necessary for defence; copper is necessary for ships; mines, necessary for copper; a company necessary to work the mines; and who can doubt this reasoning who has ever played at 'This Is the House that Jack Built.'"[21]

Yet if Congress's powers had been narrowly restricted to those enumerated in the Constitution, it is doubtful that the Constitution could have survived, at least without extensive amendments. The problems of the twentieth and twenty-first centuries, and the range of laws needed to deal with them, can be dealt with under an eighteenth-century Constitution only because of the broad construction of congressional powers found in *McCulloch*. What is notable, and often overlooked, is that the Court adopted this expansive view even before it considered the "necessary and proper clause."

The fourth and final point that Marshall made in explaining the constitutionality of the creation of the Bank of the United States concerns the meaning of the necessary and proper clause. Article I, §8, concludes by granting Congress the power "[t]o make all Laws which shall be necessary and proper for carrying into Execution the foregoing Powers, and all other Powers vested by this Constitution in the Government of the United States, or in any Department or Officer thereof."[22]

Chief Justice Marshall said that this provision makes it clear that Congress may choose any means not prohibited by the Constitution to carry out its express authority. In some of the most important words of the opinion, Marshall writes: "Let the end be legitimate, let it be within the scope of the constitution, and all means which are appropriate, which are plainly adapted to that end, which are not prohibited, but consist with the letter and spirit of the constitution, are constitutional."[23]

---

[20] For an excellent analysis of how Marshall implicitly adopts a structural view of interpreting the Constitution, *see* Charles Black, Structure and Relationship in Constitutional Law 22-33 (1969).

[21] Quoted in Charles Warren, *supra* note 2, at 501.

[22] The Necessary and Proper Clause is discussed below in §3.3.

[23] *McCulloch*, 17 U.S. at 421.

The contrary view is that the necessary and proper clause is a limit on Congress's powers, allowing Congress to adopt only those laws that are truly necessary. In fact, in other areas of constitutional law, the word "necessary" means indispensable. For example, when there is discrimination based on race or interference with a fundamental right, the government will prevail only if its action is necessary to achieve a compelling interest; *necessary* in this context means essential to achieve the goal.[24]

Yet John Marshall rejects that restrictive interpretation of the necessary and proper clause. *Necessary* here means useful or desirable, not indispensable or essential. In part, Marshall again explains that this is because of the nature of a Constitution. Marshall observed that the "provision is made in a constitution, intended to endure for ages to come, and consequently, to be adapted to the various crises of human affairs."[25]

Furthermore, Marshall noted that the necessary and proper clause is placed in Article I, §8, which expands Congress's powers, and not in Article I, §9, which limits them. Furthermore, its "terms purport to enlarge, not to diminish the powers vested in the government."[26]

The Court, however, rejected any contention that this gives Congress limitless authority. Marshall stated that "[s]hould congress, in the execution of its powers, adopt measures which are prohibited by the constitution; or should congress, under the pretext of executing its powers, pass laws for the accomplishment of objects not intrusted to the government; it would become the painful duty of this tribunal . . . to say, that such an act was not the law of the land."[27] Marshall thus reaffirmed *Marbury v. Madison* and the power of the judiciary to review the constitutionality of federal laws.

The Constitutionality of Maryland's Tax

Having concluded that Congress had the authority to create the Bank of the United States, Marshall then addressed the second major issue posed by the case: Did Maryland have the authority to tax the bank? This question required a much less detailed answer. Marshall explained that the power to create the bank includes a power to preserve its existence. However, he pointed out that "the power to tax involves the power to destroy; [and] that the power to destroy may defeat and render useless the power to create. . . ."[28]

Thus, the Court concluded that the state may not tax the Bank of the United States because such exactions could greatly impede its operation and potentially even tax it out of existence. An alternative approach would have been for the Court to allow state taxation up to the point of its interfering with or endangering the bank. But the Court rejected this argument, in part, because it did not want to

---

[24] *See, e.g.,* §9.3.2 (discussing the use of strict scrutiny for racial discrimination).
[25] *McCulloch*, 17 U.S. at 415.
[26] *Id.* at 420.
[27] *Id.* at 423.
[28] *McCulloch*, 17 U.S. at 431.

embark on assessing the impact of each and every tax. Also, the Court noted that a state tax on the Bank of the United States essentially was a state tax on those in other states. Those who were being taxed therefore were not represented in the state imposing the tax, and the tax was thus illegitimate. As described below, this is an essential aspect of limits on the ability of states to put a burden on commerce from other states: It is unfair to allow a state to regulate those who have no representation in the state.[29]

McCulloch v. Maryland thus establishes several crucial aspects of constitutional law. First, by rejecting "compact federalism," *McCulloch* emphatically declares that the federal government is supreme over the states and that the states have no authority to negate federal actions. Second, the Court expansively defines the scope of Congress's powers. Finally, the Court limits the ability of states to interfere with federal activities, such as by imposing taxes or regulations on the federal government. This framework for government articulated in *McCulloch* continues to this day.

§3.3   THE NECESSARY AND PROPER CLAUSE

Chief Justice Marshall's broad view of the meaning of the necessary and proper clause continues to this day. *United States v. Comstock*,[1] decided in June 2010, is one of the most important Supreme Court cases focusing on the meaning of the necessary and proper clause and it strongly reaffirms the approach taken in *McCulloch v. Maryland*. A federal statute, the Adam Walsh Child Protection Act of 2006, authorized federal courts to order the indefinite confinement of individuals in the custody of the federal Bureau of Prisons who are deemed to be "sexually dangerous." Earlier, in *Kansas v. Hendricks*, the Court ruled that it does not violate due process for a state to indefinitely imprison such individuals even after they have completed their prison sentences.[2] The issue in *Comstock* is whether Congress had the constitutional authority to provide for such indefinite detentions.

The Supreme Court, in an opinion by Justice Breyer, upheld the federal law and stressed that this was permissible as an exercise of Congress's power under the necessary and proper clause. Justice Breyer quoted at length from *McCulloch* and said: "We have since made clear that, in determining whether the Necessary and Proper Clause grants Congress the legislative authority to enact a particular federal statute, we look to see whether the statute constitutes a means that is rationally related to the implementation of a constitutionally enumerated power."[3] The Court explained that "the relevant inquiry is simply 'whether the means chosen are "reasonably adapted" to the attainment of a legitimate end under the commerce

[29] The dormant commerce clause is discussed in §5.3.

§3.3 [1] 130 S. Ct. 1949 (2010). For an excellent recent discussion of the necessary and proper clause, *see* John Manning, The Means of Constitutional Power, 128 Harv. L. Rev. 1 (2014).

[2] 521 U.S. 346 (1997).

[3] *Comstock*, 130 S. Ct. at 1956.

power' or under other powers that the Constitution grants Congress the authority to implement."[4] Using this approach, the Court decided that the indefinite commitment of sexually dangerous individuals fits within the scope of the necessary and proper clause. The Court stressed that Congress has the power, under the necessary and proper clause, to prescribe the sanctions for crimes that it creates. Continued commitment of the sexually dangerous fits within the scope of the necessary and proper clause as defined by Chief Justice Marshall in *McCulloch*.

However, it should be noted that in *National Federation of Independent Business v. Sebelius*, the Court emphasized that the necessary and proper clause must be used in conjunction with a valid exercise of another power of Congress.[5] The case involved the constitutionality of the Patient Protection and Affordable Care Act and specifically the "individual mandate," which requires that almost all Americans either purchase health insurance or pay a tax penalty.[6] There are exemptions for those with religious objections to medical care and those below a certain income level.

One of the arguments for the constitutionality of the individual mandate was based on the necessary and proper clause. Under the Affordable Care Act, insurance companies are required to provide coverage to all and no longer can deny policies based on preexisting conditions, or charge higher premiums based on health conditions, or impose yearly or lifetime caps on payments. No one disputes that Congress can impose these requirements on insurance companies under its power to regulate commerce among the states. But just imposing these requirements would almost surely fail: Many people would wait until they were ill to get insurance knowing that they could do so then and at no additional cost. Reducing the number of healthy people with insurance would dramatically increase its costs and ultimately the reforms of health insurance would prove impossible. The argument then was that Congress could impose the individual mandate under the necessary and proper clause as a way of carrying out its regulations of the health insurance industry.

Chief Justice Roberts expressed the views of five Justices in rejecting this argument.[7] Chief Justice Roberts explained that the necessary and proper clause must be used in conjunction with a valid exercise of another congressional power. He explained: "[T]he individual mandate cannot be sustained under the Necessary and Proper Clause as an essential component of the insurance reforms. Each of our prior cases upholding laws under that Clause involved exercises of authority

---

[4] *Id.* at 1957.

[5] 132 S. Ct. 2566 (2012).

[6] There also was an issue of whether the requirement that states expand their Medicaid coverage violates the Tenth Amendment. This is discussed below in §3.5.2.

[7] Chief Justice Roberts, joined by Justices Ginsburg, Breyer, Sotomayor, and Kagan, upheld the individual mandate as a valid exercise of Congress's taxing power. This is discussed below in §3.5.2. Chief Justice Roberts, writing for just himself, found that the individual mandate would not fit within the necessary and proper clause or the commerce clause. Justices Scalia, Kennedy, Thomas, and Alito wrote a joint opinion that would have declared the entire Act unconstitutional; they agreed with Chief Justice Roberts that the individual mandate would not fit within the necessary and proper clause or the commerce clause, but they also would have found that it was not constitutional as an exercise of Congress's taxing power.

derivative of, and in service to, a granted power. . . . The individual mandate, by contrast, vests Congress with the extraordinary ability to create the necessary predicate to the exercise of an enumerated power."[8] In other words, these five Justices said that since the individual mandate was not a valid exercise of Congress's commerce power,[9] the necessary and proper clause could not be used as the basis for enacting it.

Justice Ginsburg, joined by Justices Breyer, Sotomayor, and Kagan, disagreed and said that the individual mandate should be regarded as constitutional under the necessary and proper clause as a means for effectuating Congress's power of regulating the health insurance industry under its commerce power. She wrote: "Congress knew, however, that simply barring insurance companies from relying on an applicant's medical history would not work in practice. Without the individual mandate, . . . [i]nsurance premiums would skyrocket, the number of uninsured would increase, and insurance companies would exit the market. The minimum coverage provision is thus an 'essential par[t] of a larger regulation of economic activity'; without the provision, 'the regulatory scheme [w]ould be undercut.' Put differently, the minimum coverage provision, together with the guaranteed-issue and community-rating requirements, is 'reasonably adapted' to the attainment of a legitimate end under the commerce power: the elimination of pricing and sales practices that take an applicant's medical history into account."[10]

As explained below, Chief Justice Roberts joined with these four Justices in upholding the individual mandate as an exercise of Congress's taxing power.

§3.4   THE COMMERCE POWER

§3.4.1   Introduction to the Commerce Power

Article I, §8, of the Constitution contains 18 clauses enumerating specific powers of Congress.[1] Additionally, parts of Article IV authorize congressional action, as do clauses found in the Reconstruction Amendments (the Thirteenth, Fourteenth, and Fifteenth Amendments). Yet, of all these provisions bestowing power on Congress, none is more important than that in Article I, §8, which states: "The Congress shall have the power . . . [t]o regulate Commerce with foreign Nations, and among the several States, and with the Indian Tribes. . . ."

Practically speaking, this provision has been the authority for a broad array of federal legislation, ranging from criminal statutes to securities laws to civil rights

---

[8] *Id.* at 2592.

[9] This aspect of the decision is discussed below in §3.4.5.

[10] *Id.* at 2625-2626 (Ginsburg, J., dissenting) (citations omitted).

§3.4 [1] These clauses are reviewed in §3.6.

laws to environmental laws. From the perspective of constitutional law, the commerce clause has been the focus of most of the Supreme Court decisions that have considered the scope of congressional power and federalism.

Over the course of American history, the Supreme Court has adopted varying views as to the meaning of the commerce clause and the extent to which congressional powers under it are limited by the Tenth Amendment. Initially, in *Gibbons v. Ogden*, the Supreme Court adopted an expansive view of the scope of the commerce clause.[2] *Gibbons* is discussed in detail in the following subsection, §3.4.2. From the late nineteenth century until 1937, the Court adopted a much narrower construction of the commerce power and invalidated many federal laws as exceeding the scope of this authority. This era is discussed in §3.4.3.

From 1937 until 1995, not one federal law was declared unconstitutional as exceeding the scope of Congress's commerce power. The Court's expansive, and indeed almost unlimited, view of the commerce clause during this time period is discussed in §3.4.4. However, in 1995, in *United States v. Lopez*, the Supreme Court declared unconstitutional a federal law prohibiting a person from having a firearm within 1,000 feet of a school on the ground that it exceeded the limits of the commerce power.[3] Five years later, in *United States v. Morrison*, the Court declared unconstitutional as exceeding the scope of the commerce power a provision of the Violence Against Women Act that authorized victims of gender-motivated violence to sue their assailants.[4] *Lopez* and *Morrison*, and what they mean for the future of the commerce clause, are discussed in §3.4.5.

Throughout these eras, there are three questions the Court is considering. First, what is *commerce*; is it one stage of business or does it include all aspects of business and even life in the United States? Second, what does *among the several states* mean; is it limited to instances where there is a direct effect on interstate commerce or is any effect on interstate activities sufficient? Third, does the Tenth Amendment limit Congress; if Congress is acting within the scope of the commerce power, can a law be declared unconstitutional as violating the Tenth Amendment?

The following subsections about the commerce clause address how the first two of these questions have been dealt with over the course of American history. The Tenth Amendment, even though it is inextricably linked to these cases, is considered later, in more detail, in §3.10. Because the Tenth Amendment arguably is a limit on all congressional powers, and not just the commerce clause, it needs to be considered after the review of all congressional authority. However, it should be remembered that most of the Tenth Amendment cases have involved challenges to laws adopted under the commerce clause and thus are closely related to the materials covered in this section on the commerce clause.

---

[2] 22 U.S. (9 Wheat.) 1 (1824).
[3] 514 U.S. 549 (1995).
[4] 529 U.S. 598 (2000).

§3.4.2   Gibbons v. Ogden *and the Definition of the Commerce Power*

To this day, Supreme Court cases concerning the commerce clause begin their analysis by considering *Gibbons v. Ogden*.[5] The New York legislature granted a monopoly to Robert Fulton and Robert Livingston for operating steamboats in New York waters. Fulton and Livingston licensed Aaron Ogden to operate a ferry boat between New York City and Elizabethtown Port in New Jersey. Thomas Gibbons operated a competing ferry service and thus violated the exclusive rights given to Fulton and Livingston, and their licensee Ogden, under the monopoly. Gibbons maintained that he had the right to operate his ferry because it was licensed under a federal law as "vessels in the coasting trade." Nonetheless, Ogden successfully sued for an injunction in the New York state courts.

The United States Supreme Court reversed the New York courts, concluding that the 1793 federal law authorized Gibbons to operate a ferry in New York waters; thus, the New York–granted monopoly was preempted by federal law. The Court also found that the New York monopoly was an impermissible restriction of interstate commerce. This aspect of the commerce clause, as a restriction on state government actions apart from federal legislation, is discussed in Chapter 5.

What Is "Commerce"?

Chief Justice John Marshall, writing for the Court, considered the scope of Congress's commerce power in evaluating the constitutionality of the federal law that authorized the license issued to Gibbons. First, the Court considered what "commerce" means. Ogden's attorney argued that it should be limited "to traffic, to buying and selling or the interchange of commodities."[6] The Court disagreed: "Commerce undoubtedly is traffic, but it is something more: it is intercourse. It describes the commercial intercourse between nations, and parts of nations, in all its branches, and is regulated by prescribing rules for carrying on that intercourse."[7] In other words, according to *Gibbons*, commerce includes all phases of business, including navigation, which was the issue in that case.

What Is "Among the States"?

Second, the Court considered the meaning of "among the states." Is Congress limited to regulating commerce only when it is interstate; is intrastate commerce wholly outside Congress's power because it is not among the states? The Court answered by stating: "The word 'among' means intermingled with. A thing which is among others, is intermingled with them. Commerce among the States, cannot stop at the external boundary line of each State, but may be introduced into the interior."[8]

---

[5] 22 U.S. (9 Wheat.) 1 (1824).
[6] *Id.* at 189.
[7] *Id.* at 193.
[8] *Id.*

Yet the Court did not choose the broadest possible definition of *among*. *Among* is frequently defined in dictionaries as "in the midst of."[9] Had the Court adopted this definition, all commerce within the United States could be regulated by commerce, even that which is entirely intrastate, because everything is in the midst of the United States. But the Court said that as "[c]omprehensive as the word 'among' is, it may very properly be restricted to that commerce which concerns more States than one. . . . The completely internal commerce of a State, then, may be considered as reserved for the State itself."[10]

The Court made it clear, however, that Congress could regulate intrastate commerce if it had an impact on interstate activities. Chief Justice Marshall wrote: "But, in regulating commerce with foreign nations, the power of Congress does not stop at the jurisdictional lines of the several States. . . . The power of Congress, then, whatever it may be, must be exercised within the territorial jurisdiction of the several states."[11]

The Court had three possible definitions of *among* to choose from. One approach would have been to limit Congress to regulating interstate activities; intrastate commerce would have been beyond the scope of congressional power. A second approach would have been to define *among* as concerning more than one state. By this view, Congress may regulate when the commerce has interstate effects, even if the commerce occurs within a state. A third approach would have been to define *among* as "in the midst of." By this view, all commerce in the country could be regulated because all occurs "in the midst" of the several states.

In *Gibbons*, the Court chose the middle definition. The first and the last would have provided much clearer standards; the first would have excluded all intrastate commerce, while the last would have included all intrastate commerce in Congress's authority. The middle, in contrast, required line-drawing and case-by-case inquiry as to whether a particular activity has interstate effects. It necessitates that the Court decide how direct or substantial the effects must be. Are any interstate effects sufficient or must the impact be direct and substantial? As discussed below, this is a question that the Court has answered differently over time and continues to struggle with today.

Does State Sovereignty Limit Congressional Power?

The third and final issue in *Gibbons* was whether state sovereignty and the Tenth Amendment limit Congress's powers. If Congress is regulating commerce among the states, is there any limit on Congress because of state sovereignty? The Court emphatically rejected any such constraint: "This power, like all others vested in Congress, is complete in itself, may be exercised to its utmost extent, and acknowledges no limitations, other than are prescribed in the constitution. If, as has always been understood, the sovereignty of Congress, though limited to specified objects, is plenary as to those objects, the power over commerce with foreign

---

[9] *See, e.g.*, Webster Handy College Dictionary 28 (1981).
[10] *Gibbons*, 22 U.S. at 195-196.
[11] *Id.* at 196.

nations, and among the several States, is vested in Congress as absolutely as it would be in a single government."[12]

In other words, Congress has complete authority to regulate all commerce among the states. When acting under its commerce clause authority, Congress can regulate in the same way as it could if no state governments existed. The Court said that the sole check on Congress is the political process, not judicially enforced limits to protect the states.

Since *Gibbons*, the Court has not consistently followed this approach. As discussed in §3.10, from the late nineteenth century until 1937, the Court rejected *Gibbons*'s reasoning and found that the Tenth Amendment does reserve a zone of activities for the states. From 1937 until the 1990s, with the exception of one case in 1976,[13] the Court returned to the *Gibbons* view. However, in the 1990s, the Court has resumed using the Tenth Amendment as a limit on Congress's powers.[14] All of this is considered, in detail, in §3.10.

§3.4.3   The Commerce Clause Before 1937

In the years after *Gibbons* and before the Civil War, the Supreme Court rarely dealt with challenges to federal legislation adopted under Congress's commerce clause authority. There were a number of cases concerning challenges to state laws as unduly interfering with interstate commerce, and these are considered in §5.3.

Cases Before 1887

After the Civil War, there were a few cases concerning the scope of the commerce power. Interestingly, the cases were not consistent in their definition of this constitutional provision. Some of the cases continued *Gibbons*'s expansive definition of commerce. For example, in *The Daniel Ball*, the Court accorded Congress broad authority to license ships, even those operating entirely intrastate, so long as the boats were carrying goods that had come from another state or that ultimately would go to another state.[15] The Court explained that unsafe ships in intrastate commerce could affect and harm ships in interstate commerce.

Yet there also were a few cases that departed from *Gibbons* and invalidated federal legislation as exceeding the scope of the commerce power. The first case to overturn a federal law in this way was *United States v. Dewitt* in 1870.[16] A federal law outlawed the sale of naphtha and other illuminating oils that could ignite at less than 110 degrees Fahrenheit. The Court held that the law was "a police regulation, relating exclusively to the internal trade of the States."[17] The opinion seemed to

---

[12] *Id.* at 196-197.

[13] National League of Cities v. Usery, 426 U.S. 833 (1976), overruled in Garcia v. San Antonio Metro. Transit Auth., 469 U.S. 528 (1985). These cases are discussed in §3.10.

[14] *See* Printz v. United States, 521 U.S. 898 (1997); New York v. United States, 505 U.S. 144 (1992); both cases are discussed in §3.10 below.

[15] 77 U.S. (10 Wall.) 557 (1871).

[16] 76 U.S. (9 Wall.) 41 (1870).

[17] *Id.* at 45.

limit the scope of the commerce clause dramatically by declaring that this provision was "a virtual denial of any power to interfere with the internal trade and business of the separate States."[18]

In *The Trademark Cases,* in 1878, the Court invalidated the federal law that established a federal system for registering trademarks.[19] The Court concluded that the law was unconstitutional because it applied to wholly intrastate businesses and business transactions and therefore "is obviously the exercise of a power not confided to Congress."[20]

Apart from these few cases, the Supreme Court had little occasion to consider the scope of the commerce power before the late nineteenth century when Congress began using the commerce clause as the basis for enacting important economic regulations. The Interstate Commerce Act in 1887 and the Sherman Antitrust Act in 1890 ushered in a new era of federal economic and regulatory legislation. They also began a new era of much more activist judicial review.

Cases Between 1887 and 1937

Between the late nineteenth century and 1937, the Court was controlled by conservative Justices deeply committed to laissez-faire economics and strongly opposed to government economic regulations. Many federal laws were invalidated as exceeding the scope of Congress's commerce power or as violating the Tenth Amendment and the zone of activities reserved to the states. Many state laws were invalidated as interfering with freedom of contract, which the Court found to be protected as a fundamental right under the liberty of the due process clause.[21] So, for example, a federal law requiring a minimum wage during this period would be invalidated as exceeding the scope of Congress's power and as usurping states' prerogatives;[22] a state law requiring a minimum wage would be invalidated as impermissibly interfering with freedom of contract.[23]

This era of constitutional law is extremely important. It was the first time that the Supreme Court aggressively used its power of judicial review to invalidate federal and state laws. Constitutional law since 1937 has very much been a reaction to this earlier era. The Court did not invalidate another law as exceeding the scope of the commerce clause until 1995[24] and has generally very much deferred to federal and state economic regulations.

Although appreciating and understanding constitutional law in this era requires looking at all of these cases together, this chapter focuses solely on the

---

[18]   *Id.* at 44.

[19]   100 U.S. (10 Otto.) 82 (1878).

[20]   *Id.* at 96-97.

[21]   These cases are discussed in §8.1.

[22]   *See, e.g.,* Carter v. Carter Coal Co., 298 U.S. 238 (1936) (invalidating the wage and hour provisions of the Bituminous Coal Conservation Act of 1935).

[23]   *See, e.g.,* Morehead v. New York ex rel. Tipaldo, 298 U.S. 587 (1936) (invalidating a state minimum wage law for women).

[24]   United States v. Lopez, 514 U.S. 549 (1995), discussed in §3.4.5.

decisions concerning the scope of Congress's power. The Court's use of freedom of contract during this time period as a limit on state power is discussed in §8.1.

Between the late nineteenth century and 1937, the Court espoused a philosophy often termed "dual federalism." Dual federalism was the view that the federal and state governments were separate sovereigns, that each had separate zones of authority, and that it was the judicial role to protect the states by interpreting and enforcing the Constitution to protect the zone of activities reserved to the states.

Dual federalism was embodied in three important doctrines that the Court developed and followed during this time period. First, the Court narrowly defined the meaning of *commerce* so as to leave a zone of power to the states. Specifically, as described below, the Court held that commerce was one stage of business, distinct from earlier phases such as mining, manufacturing, or production. Under this view, only commerce itself could be regulated by Congress; the others were left for state regulation.

Second, the Court restrictively defined *among the states* as allowing Congress to regulate only when there was a substantial effect on interstate commerce. In all other areas, regulation again was left to the states.

Finally, the Court held that the Tenth Amendment reserved a zone of activities to the states and that even federal laws within the scope of the commerce clause were unconstitutional if they invaded that zone. For example, the Court held that regulation of production was left to the states and therefore a federal law that prohibited shipment in interstate commerce of goods made by child labor was unconstitutional, even though it was limited to interstate commerce, because it violated the Tenth Amendment.[25]

Each of these three doctrines requires further elaboration. However, it should be noted at the outset that the Court was not completely consistent in applying these principles. The Court was most likely to follow them when considering federal economic regulations; the Court was least likely to adhere to them, and most willing to uphold federal laws, when they concerned federal morals regulation. Thus, as described below, the Court invalidated federal antitrust laws[26] and employment regulation statutes,[27] but upheld federal laws prohibiting lotteries[28] and regulating sexual behavior.[29] Perhaps a principled distinction between these cases can be articulated, or more likely, the decisions were simply a product of the Court's particular brand of conservatism: economically conservative and thus aggressive in striking down economic regulations; morally conservative and thus deferential to laws directed at what was perceived as sin.

---

[25] Hammer v. Dagenhart (The Child Labor Case), 247 U.S. 251 (1918), discussed below.

[26] United States v. E.C. Knight Co., 156 U.S. 1 (1895), discussed below.

[27] *See, e.g.,* Carter v. Carter Coal Co., 298 U.S. 238 (1936).

[28] Champion v. Ames, 188 U.S. 321 (1903).

[29] *See, e.g.,* Hoke v. United States, 227 U.S. 308 (1913); Caminetti v. United States, 242 U.S. 470 (1917) (upholding the Mann Act, which made it a crime to take a woman across state lines for immoral purposes). Perhaps it can be said that these cases took Chief Justice John Marshall's definition of commerce as intercourse a bit too literally.

What Is "Commerce"?

The three doctrines described above created a powerful limit on the scope of Congress's power. First, the Court held that *commerce* was to be narrowly defined as one stage of business, separate and distinct from earlier phases such as mining, manufacturing, and production. In *United States v. E.C. Knight*, toward the beginning of this era, the Court held that the Sherman Antitrust Act could not be used to stop a monopoly in the sugar refining industry because the Constitution did not allow Congress to regulate manufacturing.[30] The United States government attempted to use the Sherman Antitrust Act to block the American Sugar Refining Company from acquiring four competing refineries. The acquisition would have given the company control of over 98 percent of the sugar refining industry.

Nonetheless, the Court held that federal law could not be applied because the monopoly was in the production of sugar, not in its commerce. The Court flatly declared: "Commerce succeeds to manufacture, and is not a part of it."[31] The Court was clear that this rigid distinction was based on a need for preserving a zone of activities to the states. The Court explained that although the commerce power was one of the "strongest bond[s] of the union, . . . the preservation of the autonomy of the States [w]as required by our dual form of government."[32]

This distinction between manufacturing and commerce seems arbitrary; a company would desire a monopoly in production because it would benefit from monopoly profits in commerce. The Court acknowledged this, but said that the relationship was too indirect to allow federal regulation under the commerce power. The Court said that it would be "far-reaching" to allow Congress to act "whenever interstate or international commerce may be ultimately affected."[33] The Court explained that the effect on commerce was only "indirect" and thus outside the scope of federal power.

This very limited definition of commerce continued throughout this era until 1937. For example, in *Carter v. Carter Coal Co.*, the Court declared unconstitutional the Bituminous Coal Conservation Act of 1935.[34] The law contained detailed findings as to the relationship between coal and the national economy and declared that the production of coal directly affected interstate commerce. The law provided for local coal boards to be established to determine prices for coal and to determine, after collective bargaining by unions and employers, wages and hours for employees. A shareholder in the Carter Coal Company sued it to stop it from complying with the law.

The Supreme Court, in an opinion by Justice Sutherland, declared the law unconstitutional. The Court focused on the unconstitutionality of federal regulation of wages and hours. The Court stated:

---

[30] 156 U.S. 1 (1895).
[31] *Id.* at 12.
[32] *Id.* at 13.
[33] *Id.*
[34] 298 U.S. 238 (1936).

[C]ommerce is the equivalent of the phrase "intercourse for the purposes of trade." Plainly, the incidents leading up to and culminating in the mining of coal do not constitute such intercourse. The employment of men, the fixing of their wages, hours of labor and working conditions, the bargaining in respect of these things—whether carried on separately or collectively—each and all constitute intercourse for the purposes of production, not of trade. . . . Mining brings the subject matter of commerce into existence. Commerce disposes of it.[35]

The Court again emphasized that this narrow definition of commerce was essential to protect the states. The Court lamented: "Every journey to a forbidden end begins with the first step; and the danger of such a step by the federal government in the direction of taking over the powers of the states is that the end of the journey may find the states so despoiled of their powers, or—what may amount to the same thing—so relieved of responsibilities . . . as to reduce them to little more than geographic subdivisions of the national domain."[36]

Decisions such as *E.C. Knight* and *Carter* rest on many assumptions: that it makes sense to distinguish commerce from other stages of business; that the Constitution requires that a rigid zone of activities be left to the states; and that it is the judicial role to protect this zone. From the late nineteenth century until 1937, these premises were fervently accepted by the Supreme Court.

What Does "Among the States" Mean?

The second major aspect of the Court's approach to the commerce clause during this era was the requirement that there be a direct effect on interstate commerce. For example, in the *Shreveport Rate Cases*, the Court upheld the ability of the Interstate Commerce Commission to set intrastate railroad rates because of their direct impact on interstate commerce.[37] Specifically, a railroad was ordered to charge the same rates for shipments to Marshall, Texas, whether from Shreveport, Louisiana, or from Dallas, Texas. The Court upheld the federal regulation and held that "Congress in the exercise of its paramount power may prevent the common instrumentalities of interstate and intrastate commercial intercourse from being used in their intrastate operations to the injury of interstate commerce."[38] The Court said that Congress "does possess the power to foster and protect interstate commerce, and to take all measures necessary or appropriate to that end, although intrastate transactions of interstate carriers may thereby be controlled."[39]

The distinction between direct and indirect effects is inherently elusive and difficult to draw. In contrast to the *Shreveport Rate Cases, A.L.A. Schechter Poultry Corp. v. United States*, often referred to as the "sick chickens" case, declared a federal law unconstitutional based on an insufficient effect on interstate commerce.[40]

---

[35]   *Id.* at 303-304.
[36]   *Id.* at 295-296.
[37]   Houston, East and West Texas Ry. Co. v. United States, 234 U.S. 342 (1914).
[38]   *Id.* at 353.
[39]   *Id.*
[40]   295 U.S. 495 (1935).

The National Industrial Recovery Act, a key piece of New Deal legislation, authorized the president to approve "codes of fair competition" developed by boards of various industries. Pursuant to this law, the president approved a Live Poultry Code for New York City. In part, the Code required sellers to sell only entire coops of chickens or half coops of chickens and made it illegal for buyers to reject individual chickens. The Code also regulated employment by requiring collective bargaining, prohibiting child labor, and establishing a 40-hour workweek and a minimum wage.

The Supreme Court declared the Code unconstitutional because there was not a sufficiently "direct" relationship to interstate commerce.[41] Although the Court acknowledged that virtually all of the poultry in New York was shipped from other states, the Court said that the Code was not regulating the interstate transactions; rather, the Code concerned the operation of businesses within New York. The Court emphasized that Congress could regulate only when there was a direct effect on interstate commerce. The Court explained: "In determining how far the federal government may go in controlling intrastate transactions upon the ground that they 'affect' interstate commerce, there is a necessary and well-established distinction between direct and indirect effects."[42] The federal government has the authority to regulate when there are direct effects on commerce, "[b]ut where the effect of intrastate transactions upon interstate commerce is merely indirect, such transactions remain within the domain of state power."[43]

The Court once again explained that this distinction was essential in order to protect state governments and ultimately the American system of government. The Court stated: "If the commerce clause were construed to reach all enterprises and transactions which could be said to have an indirect effect upon interstate commerce, the federal authority would embrace practically all the activities of the people and the authority of the State over its domestic concerns would exist only by sufferance of the federal government."[44] The Court thus declared that enforcing the distinction between direct and indirect effects on commerce "must be recognized as . . . essential to the maintenance of our constitutional system."[45]

The difficulty, of course, is in drawing a meaningful and useful distinction between direct and indirect effects. The Court struggled with this throughout the era. One approach that the Court often used was to allow Congress to regulate to protect the stream of commerce. The Court initially articulated this approach in *Swift & Co. v. United States*, which upheld the application of the Sherman Antitrust Act to an agreement among meat dealers to fix the price at which they would purchase meat from stockyards.[46] Although the stockyard was intrastate, the Court stressed how it was only a temporary stop for the cattle. Justice Holmes, writing for the Court, explained that the stockyards were in "a current of commerce

---

[41] The Court also declared the Code unconstitutional as an excessive delegation of legislative power. This aspect of the opinion is discussed in §3.10.

[42] *Schechter Poultry*, 295 U.S. at 546.

[43] *Id.* at 546.

[44] *Id.*

[45] *Id.* at 548.

[46] 196 U.S. 375 (1905).

among the States, and the purchase of the cattle is a part and incident of such commerce."[47]

Likewise, in *Stafford v. Wallace*, for example, the Court upheld the Packers and Stockyards Act of 1921, which authorized the secretary of commerce to regulate rates and prescribe standards for the operation of stockyards where livestock was kept.[48] The law was designed to protect consumers by lessening collusion between stockyard managers and packers and also by decreasing the ability of packers to set prices for livestock. The Supreme Court upheld the federal law emphasizing that the stockyards are in the stream of commerce. Chief Justice Taft, writing for the Court, explained that the "stockyards are but a throat through which the current flows, and the transactions which occur therein are only incident to this current from the West to the East, and from one State to another. Such transactions can not be separated from the movement to which they contribute and necessarily take on its character."[49]

The Court relied on this stream of commerce approach to allow Congress to prohibit the sale of impure or adulterated food or drugs,[50] to require retail labeling for items traveling in interstate commerce,[51] and to restrict the sale of intoxicating beverages to Indians.[52]

The Court, however, did not consistently apply its stream of commerce approach. For example, in *Railroad Retirement Board v. Alton R.R. Co.*, the Court declared unconstitutional the Railroad Retirement Act of 1934, which provided a pension system for railroad workers.[53] Railroads obviously were part of the stream of interstate commerce, and the Court had upheld other federal regulations of railroads. In *Southern Railway v. United States*, the Court upheld the Federal Safety Appliance Acts, which regulated couplers on railroad cars.[54] In *Baltimore & Ohio Railroad Co. v. Interstate Commerce Commission*, the Court upheld a federal law that set maximum hours for railroad workers.[55]

Yet in the *Alton R.R. Co.* case the Court struck down the requirement for a pension for railroad workers and distinguished the other cases as concerning the safety or efficiency of the railroads. The Court said that Congress could not use its commerce power to require a pension program for railroad employees because the law was only to help "the social welfare of the worker, and therefore [was] remote from any regulation of commerce."[56]

The key point is that the Court interpreted "among the states" as requiring a direct effect on interstate commerce. Yet the Court never formulated a clear or consistent way to distinguish direct from indirect effects. Why did intrastate rail-

---

[47] *Id.* at 388-389.
[48] 258 U.S. 495 (1922).
[49] *Id.* at 516.
[50] Hipolite Egg Co. v. United States, 220 U.S. 45 (1911).
[51] McDermott v. Wisconsin, 228 U.S. 115 (1913).
[52] United States v. Nice, 241 U.S. 591 (1916).
[53] 295 U.S. 330 (1935).
[54] 222 U.S. 20 (1911).
[55] 221 U.S. 612 (1911).
[56] 295 U.S. at 368.

road rates have a direct effect on interstate commerce, while regulations designed to limit the shipment of sick chickens in interstate commerce have only an indirect effect? The stream of commerce approach was sometimes used during this era to evaluate whether an activity was among the states. Yet the Court was no more consistent in applying this test. Why are prices at stockyards in the stream of commerce, but practices at poultry farms not part of that stream?

Does State Sovereignty Limit Congressional Power?

Finally, the Court held that even if an activity was commerce and was among the states, Congress still could not regulate if it was intruding into the zone of activities reserved to the states. The Court concluded that the Tenth Amendment reserved control of activities such as mining, manufacturing, and production to the states. Even federal laws regulating commerce among the states were unconstitutional if they sought to control mining, manufacturing, and production.

The Child Labor Case (Hammer v. Dagenhart) was the most significant decision to use the Tenth Amendment in this way.[57] A federal law prohibited the shipment in interstate commerce of goods produced in factories that employed children under age 14 or employed children between the ages of 14 and 16 for more than eight hours per day or six days a week. Although the law only regulated goods in interstate commerce, the Court declared it unconstitutional because it controlled production. The Court declared that "[t]he grant of power to Congress over the subject of interstate commerce was to enable it to regulate such commerce, and not to give it authority to control the States in their exercise of the police power over local trade and manufacture."[58] The Court said that regulating the hours of labor of children was entrusted "purely [to] state authority."[59] The Court expressly rejected the argument that federal legislation was necessary to prevent unfair competition; states that wanted to outlaw child labor would find it difficult to do so as long as other states allowed child labor.

Indeed, the Court spoke in apocalyptic terms as to the consequences if Congress was accorded such regulatory power: "The far reaching result of upholding the act cannot be more plainly indicated than by pointing out that if Congress can thus regulate matters entrusted to local authority by prohibition of the movement of commodities in interstate commerce, all freedom of commerce will be at an end, and the power of the States over local matters may be eliminated, and thus our system of government be practically destroyed."[60]

The Child Labor Case can be contrasted to another decision from that era, The Lottery Case (Champion v. Ames), where the Court upheld a federal law prohibiting the interstate shipment of lottery tickets.[61] In both The Child Labor Case and The Lottery Case, the federal law prohibited the shipment of a specified item — goods

[57] 247 U.S. 251 (1918).
[58] Id. at 273-274.
[59] Id. at 276.
[60] Id.
[61] 188 U.S. 321 (1903).

made by child labor or lottery tickets—in interstate commerce. In both, Congress obviously was seeking to stop intrastate activities: the use of child labor and gambling in lotteries. Yet in the former the Court declared the federal law unconstitutional, whereas in the latter the Court upheld the federal law.

In *The Lottery Case*, the Court made it clear that the power to regulate interstate commerce includes the ability to prohibit items from being in interstate commerce. The Court concluded that it was within Congress's commerce clause power to stop lottery tickets from being a part of interstate commerce. The Court declared: "If a State, when considering legislation for the suppression of lotteries within its own limits, may properly take into view the evils that inhere in the raising of money, in that mode, why may not Congress, invested with power to regulate commerce among the several States, provide that such commerce shall not be polluted by the carrying of lottery tickets from one State to another?"[62]

The Court explicitly rejected the argument that the federal law violated the Tenth Amendment and intruded on state government prerogatives. Also, the Court rejected the argument that according Congress such power would give Congress seemingly limitless authority and would endanger the constitutional structure. The Court simply said: "[T]he possible abuse of a power is not an argument against its existence."[63]

Thus, the Court did not consistently define the zone of activities reserved to the states. Yet the Court during this era clearly believed in dual sovereignty and used it to limit federal power.

Perhaps there are principled distinctions between these cases, or perhaps they simply reflect a conservative Court much more willing to defer to morals laws than to economic regulations. Whatever the cause, these three doctrines—the narrow definition of commerce, the restrictive interpretation of among the states, and the use of state sovereignty as a constraint on congressional power—all advanced dual federalism and all limited the scope of Congress's authority under the commerce clause.

§3.4.4   *The Commerce Clause from 1937 to 1995*

Causes for the Change in Doctrine

By 1937, there were enormous pressures for change in the direction of constitutional law. The decisions in *A.L.A. Schechter Poultry Corp. v. United States*[64] and *Carter v. Carter Coal Co.*,[65] discussed above, invalidated two important pieces of New Deal legislation, the National Industrial Recovery Act and the Bituminous Coal Conservation Act of 1935. Simultaneously, the Court's conservative philosophy and its commitment to restrict federal powers manifested itself in similar limits on the taxing and spending power, which is discussed in §3.5. For example, in *United*

---

[62] *Id.* at 356.
[63] *Id.* at 363.
[64] 295 U.S. 495 (1935).
[65] 298 U.S. 238 (1936).

States v. Butler, the Court declared unconstitutional the Agricultural Adjustment Act, which provided price supports for farmers on the ground that it attempted to control production.[66] At the same time, indeed throughout the era from the late nineteenth century until 1937, the Court frequently invalidated state economic regulations as impermissible interferences with freedom of contract.[67]

Although these cases concerning the *commerce* clause, the taxing and spending power, and state economic regulation are discussed in separate chapters, they all were a result of the Court's overall philosophy. The Court was deeply committed to laissez-faire economics, strongly opposed to economic regulations protecting employees, and very willing to use the power of judicial review to declare unconstitutional federal and state laws.

Many different types of pressures mounted for a dramatic change in constitutional law. The decisions were intellectually vulnerable because they seemed based on arbitrary distinctions and were frequently inconsistent. The distinction between commerce and other phases of business made little sense in that mining, manufacturing, and production all had obvious effects on commerce. The distinction between direct and indirect effects on commerce was inherently arbitrary. The decisions of the era—finding livestock to be in the stream of interstate commerce, but not chickens; allowing Congress to prohibit lottery tickets from being shipped in interstate commerce, but not goods made by child labor—were impossible to reconcile.

The economic crisis of the Depression made laissez-faire economics seem untenable. Unemployment was widespread and the wages of those with jobs were significantly reduced. Business failure was endemic and production was substantially lessened. Foreclosures of home and farm mortgages were common. The Court's opposition to national economic regulation seemed anachronistic and pernicious in the face of the Depression.

Not surprisingly, political pressure developed for change. President Franklin Roosevelt won a landslide reelection victory in 1936 and saw this as a strong endorsement for the New Deal programs that the Court was invalidating. In March 1937, Roosevelt proposed that Congress adopt legislation to increase the size of the Supreme Court.[68] Under the proposal, one Justice would be added to the Court for each Justice over age 70, up to a maximum of 15 Justices. In light of the ages of the Justices then on the Court, Roosevelt would have been able to add six new Justices and thus secure a majority on the Court to uphold the New Deal programs.

Roosevelt's Court-packing plan drew intense opposition, even from some supporters of New Deal programs, on the ground that it was a threat to the independence of the federal judiciary. It is worth noting, however, that nothing in the Constitution mandated or even suggested a number of Justices for the Court. The first Judiciary Act prescribed a Court of six. This was temporarily reduced to five

---

[66] 297 U.S. 1 (1936), discussed in §3.5.3.

[67] These cases are discussed in §8.1.

[68] For an excellent discussion of the development of the Court-packing plan and the controversy surrounding it, *see* Jeff Shesol, Supreme Power: Franklin Roosevelt vs. the Supreme Court (2010).

in 1801 and increased back to six in 1802. The number of Justices was increased to seven in 1807, to nine in 1837, and to ten in 1864. Generally, the increase in the size of the Court was a result of the addition of a new federal circuit court of appeals. Supreme Court Justices were responsible for "riding circuit" and sitting as federal appeals court judges; an additional Justice was created each time the country expanded and a new circuit was added.

In 1866, with unpopular President Andrew Johnson in the White House, Congress reduced the size of the Supreme Court to seven. This kept Johnson from filling an existing vacancy on the Court and meant that the next two vacancies also would go unfilled in order to bring the Court's size down from ten to seven. In 1869, after Ulysses Grant became president, the number on the Court was increased to nine, where it has been ever since.

In 1937, Justice Owen Roberts changed his position and was the fifth to uphold two laws of the type that previously had been invalidated: a state minimum wage law for women and a federal law regulating labor relations.[69] There is a debate over whether Roberts was influenced by the political pressure of the Court-packing plan or whether he planned to change his vote prior to Roosevelt's proposal. Whatever the cause, Robert's change in sentiment will forever be known as "the switch in time that saved nine."

Key Decisions Changing the Commerce Clause Doctrine

Three decisions — *NLRB v. Jones & Laughlin Steel Corp.* in 1937, *United States v. Darby* in 1941, and *Wickard v. Filburn* in 1942 — overruled the earlier decisions and expansively defined the scope of Congress's commerce power. Indeed, because of these three decisions, from 1937 until 1995 not one federal law was declared unconstitutional as exceeding the scope of Congress's commerce power.

NLRB v. Jones & Laughlin Steel Corp. involved a constitutional challenge to the National Labor Relations Act, which created a right of employees to bargain collectively, prohibited unfair labor practices such as discrimination against union members, and established the National Labor Relations Board to enforce the law.[70] The law contained detailed findings on the relationship between labor activity and commerce. The Act applied when there was an effect on commerce and, in fact, it expressly defined "affecting commerce" as meaning "in commerce, or burdening or obstructing commerce or the free flow of commerce, or having led or tending to lead to a labor dispute burdening or obstructing commerce or the free flow of commerce."[71]

The Court initially explained how the Jones & Laughlin Steel Corporation was clearly a part of interstate commerce. It was the fourth largest producer of steel with factories in Pennsylvania; mines in Pennsylvania, Minnesota, Michigan, and West

---

[69] West Coast Hotel Co. v. Parrish, 300 U.S. 379 (1937) (upholding a state minimum wage law for women), discussed in §8.2.3. NLRB v. Jones & Laughlin Steel Corp., 301 U.S. 1 (1937) (upholding federal regulation of the steel industry), discussed below.

[70] 301 U.S. 1 (1937).

[71] *Id.* at 31, quoting §2(7) of the Act.

Virginia; steel fabricating plants in Louisiana and New York; warehouses in Illinois, Michigan, Tennessee, and Ohio; and steamships operating on the Great Lakes.[72] The Court explained that overall the steel industry employed 33,000 individuals mining ore, 44,000 mining coal, 4,000 quarrying limestone, 16,000 manufacturing coke, 343,000 manufacturing steel, and 83,000 transporting its product.

In light of these findings, *NLRB v. Jones & Laughlin Steel Corp.* does not at first seem to be a radical departure from the earlier decisions. The Court explained how the steel business was part of the stream of commerce and how labor relations within it had a direct effect on commerce. However, the Court's opinion left no doubt that the decision marked a major shift in the law. The Court flatly declared that "the fact that the employees . . . were engaged in production is not determinative."[73] The Court spoke broadly of Congress's commerce power: "The fundamental principle is that the power to regulate commerce is the power to enact 'all appropriate legislation' for 'its protection and advancement,' 'to adopt measures' to 'promote its growth and insure its safety,' 'to foster, protect, control, and restrain.' That power is plenary and may be exerted to protect interstate commerce no matter what the source of the dangers which threaten it."[74]

Although the Court's holding in *Jones & Laughlin* might be squared with the decisions of the earlier era, the Court clearly signaled a major change in direction.[75] In fact, in a companion case, which has received much less attention, the Court upheld the application of the National Labor Relations Act to a relatively small clothes manufacturer.[76]

The radical nature of the Court's shift was apparent in the 1941 decision, *United States v. Darby*.[77] *Darby* involved a challenge to the constitutionality of the Fair Labor Standards Act of 1938. This Act prohibited the shipment in interstate commerce of goods made by employees who were paid less than the prescribed minimum wage (25 cents per hour at that time). In upholding the Act, the Court departed from all aspects of the pre-1937 commerce clause doctrines.

The Court rejected the view that production was left entirely to state regulation. The Court explained that Congress may control production by regulating shipments in interstate commerce. The Court wrote: "While manufacture is not of itself interstate commerce, the shipment of manufactured goods interstate is such commerce and the prohibition of such shipment by Congress is indubitably a regulation of commerce."[78] The Court spoke repeatedly of "the plenary power conferred on Congress by the commerce clause."[79] Perhaps most importantly, the

---

[72] *Id.* at 26.

[73] *Id.* at 40.

[74] *Id.* at 37 (citations omitted).

[75] Almost simultaneously, the Supreme Court abandoned its substantive due process doctrines that limited the ability of state and local governments to regulate the economy. *See* discussion in §8.2.3.

[76] NLRB v. Friedman-Harry Marks Clothing Co., 301 U.S. 58 (1937). *See also* United States v. Fainblatt, 306 U.S. 601 (1939) (upholding application of the Act to a small New Jersey company that employed only 60 people).

[77] 312 U.S. 100 (1941).

[78] *Id.* at 113.

[79] *Id.* at 115.

Court expressly overruled *Hammer v. Dagenhart* and emphatically rejected the view that the Tenth Amendment limits Congress's powers. In its most famous words, discussed more fully below in §3.10, the Court declared that "[t]he amendment states but a truism that all is retained which has not been surrendered."[80] In other words, a law is constitutional so long as it is within the scope of Congress's power; the Tenth Amendment would not be used by the judiciary as a basis for invalidating federal laws.

The third major decision, *Wickard v. Filburn*, left no doubts that the pre-1937 commerce clause doctrines had been completely abandoned.[81] Under the Agricultural Adjustment Act, the secretary of agriculture set a quota for wheat production and each farmer was given an allotment. Farmer Filburn owned a small dairy farm in Ohio and grew wheat primarily for home consumption and to feed his livestock. His allotment for 1941 was 222 bushels of wheat, but he grew 461 bushels and was fined $117. He claimed that the federal law could not constitutionally be applied to him because the wheat that he grew for home consumption was not a part of interstate commerce.

The Court, in an opinion written by Justice Robert Jackson, upheld the application of the federal law and ruled against farmer Filburn. The Court flatly rejected the limits on the commerce power that were enforced in the earlier era. The Court stated: "[Q]uestions of the power of Congress are not to be decided by reference to any formula which would give controlling force to nomenclature such as 'production' and 'indirect' and foreclose consideration of the actual effects of the activity in question upon interstate commerce."[82] In other words, the distinctions, which were crucial in the earlier era, between commerce and production, and between direct and indirect effects on commerce, no longer were followed. The Court declared: "Once an economic measure of the reach of the power granted to Congress in the Commerce Clause is accepted, questions of federal power cannot be decided simply by finding the activity in question to be 'production,' nor can consideration of its economic effects be foreclosed by calling them 'indirect.'"[83]

The Court upheld the application of the Agricultural Adjustment Act to homegrown wheat because of the cumulative effect of that wheat on the national market. The Court explained that homegrown wheat was the single most variable factor in the wheat market and that it could account for more than 20 percent of production.[84] Therefore, even though Filburn's wheat only had a negligible impact on interstate commerce, Congress could regulate his production because cumulatively homegrown wheat had a substantial effect on interstate commerce. The Court noted that even though Filburn's "own contribution to the demand for wheat may be trivial by itself, [it] is not enough to remove him from the scope of federal regulation where, as here, his contribution, taken together with that of many others similarly situated, is far from trivial."[85]

---

[80] *Id.* at 124.
[81] 317 U.S. 111 (1942).
[82] *Id.* at 120.
[83] *Id.* at 124.
[84] *Id.* at 127.
[85] *Id.* at 127-128.

The Test for the Commerce Clause After 1937

Taken together, *NLRB v. Jones & Laughlin Steel Corp.*, *United States v. Darby*, and *Wickard v. Filburn* expansively defined the scope of Congress's commerce clause power.[86] No longer did the Court distinguish between commerce and other stages of business such as mining, manufacturing, and production; instead, Congress could exercise control over all phases of business. No longer did the Court distinguish between direct and indirect effects on interstate commerce; rather, Congress could regulate any activity that taken cumulatively had an effect on interstate commerce. No longer was the Tenth Amendment a limit on congressional power; instead, a federal law would be upheld so long as it was within the scope of Congress's power, and the commerce clause was interpreted so broadly that seemingly any law would meet this requirement.

Thus, after 1937 until 1995, not one federal law was declared unconstitutional as exceeding the scope of Congress's commerce power. The law of the commerce clause during this era could be simply stated: Congress could regulate any activity if there was a substantial effect on interstate commerce. Of course, after *Wickard v. Filburn*, it was not necessary that the particular person or entity being regulated have a substantial effect on commerce; the requirement was only that the activity, looked at cumulatively across the country, have a substantial effect on commerce.

In fact, in some cases, the Court even deleted the word "substantial" and declared that Congress could regulate anything under the commerce clause so long as there was a rational basis for believing that there was an effect on commerce. In *Hodel v. Indiana*, in 1981, the Court stated: "A court may invalidate legislation enacted under the Commerce Clause only if it is clear that there is no rational basis for a congressional finding that the regulated activity affects interstate commerce, or that there is no reasonable connection between the regulatory means selected and the asserted ends."[87]

Under this test, it is difficult to imagine anything that Congress could not regulate under the commerce clause so long as it was not violating another consti-

---

[86] These were not the only decisions in this period that broadly defined the scope of Congress's commerce power. *See also* Kentucky Whip & Collar Co. v. Illinois Central R.R., 299 U.S. 334 (1937) (upholding a ban on shipments in interstate commerce of convict-made goods into states forbidding their use); United States v. Rock Royal Co-operative, 307 U.S. 533 (1939) (upholding a federal regulation of the handling of milk in the New York metropolitan area); United States v. Wrightwood Dairy Co., 315 U.S. 110 (1942) (upholding the power of Congress to regulate milk that was produced and sold intrastate, but was in competition with interstate dairy products).

[87] 452 U.S. 314, 323-324 (1981). It is worth noting that not all of the Justices agreed with this broad definition of the commerce power, though Justice Rehnquist wrote separately to stress that there must be a "substantial effect" in order for Congress to act: "It would be a mistake to conclude that Congress' power to regulate . . . is unlimited. Some activities may be so private or local in nature that they may not be in commerce. . . . [The] Court asserts that regulation will be upheld if Congress had a rational basis for finding that the regulated activity affects interstate commerce. . . . [But] it has long been established that . . . [t]here must instead be a showing that the regulated activity has a *substantial effect* on that commerce." Hodel v. Virginia Surface Mining & Reclamation Assn., Inc., 452 U.S. 264, 310-312 (1981) (Rehnquist, J., concurring in the judgment). As discussed below, in *United States v. Lopez*, 514 U.S. 549 (1995), the Court, in an opinion by Chief Justice Rehnquist, held that the test is that there must be a "substantial effect" on interstate commerce.

tutional provision. As such, since 1937, a wide array of federal legislation has been adopted under the aegis of the commerce clause. To illustrate the breadth of the Supreme Court's interpretation of the commerce clause, consider three types of federal laws adopted under it: regulatory laws, civil rights laws, and criminal laws.

Regulatory Laws

A key aspect of American government since 1937 has been the dramatic increase in the number of federal administrative and regulatory agencies and in the scope of authority they possess.[88] The Court's broad definition of the commerce clause power facilitated this expansion. The Court held that Congress can set the terms for items shipped in interstate commerce. This includes virtually anything that potentially can travel across state lines. For instance, the Court has held that Congress can regulate intangible items such as insurance policies or stock under its commerce power.[89]

Congress can regulate purely intrastate activities, including all aspects of business, if there is a rational basis for believing that there is an interstate effect. For example, the Court held that Congress could regulate strip mining on land even though the land was not a part of interstate commerce and even though regulating land use has been a traditional state government function.[90] The Court deferred to congressional findings that "many surface mining operations result in disturbances of surface areas that burden and adversely affect commerce and the public welfare by destroying or diminishing the utility of land . . . by causing erosion and landslides, by contributing to floods, by polluting the water, by destroying fish and wildlife habitat, by impairing natural beauty, by damaging the property of citizens, by creating hazards dangerous to life and property . . . , and by counteracting government programs and efforts to conserve soil, water, and other natural resources."[91]

Also, Congress can regulate intrastate activities if necessary to protect its regulation of interstate activities. In fact, the Court has held that Congress's regulatory power extends even after an item has been shipped in interstate commerce. For example, the Court upheld the authority of the Food and Drug Administration to impose labeling requirements for items that have been a part of interstate commerce.[92]

---

[88] The constitutional problems posed by these agencies are discussed in more detail in §3.11.

[89] *See* United States v. South-Eastern Underwriters Assn., 322 U.S. 533 (1944) (Congress's authority to regulate interstate insurance transactions); American Power & Light Co. v. SEC, 329 U.S. 90 (1946) (Congress's authority to regulate stock in public utilities).

[90] *See* Hodel v. Virginia Surface Mining & Reclamation Assn., Inc., 452 U.S. 264 (1981); Hodel v. Indiana, 452 U.S. 314 (1981).

[91] *Id.* at 277. In *Hodel v. Virginia Surface Mining and Reclamation Association*, the Court upheld the general constitutionality of the Surface Mining Control and Reclamation Act of 1977. In the companion case of *Hodel v. Indiana*, the Court upheld the prime farmland provisions of the Act that required a demonstration of the ability to restore cropland before it was subjected to strip mining operations.

[92] United States v. Sullivan, 332 U.S. 689 (1948) (affirming the conviction of a retail druggist for "misbranding" two pill boxes).

Civil Rights Laws

Among the most important laws ever adopted in American history is the 1964 Civil Rights Act, which, in part, prohibits private employment discrimination based on race, gender, or religion, and which forbids discrimination by places of public accommodation such as hotels and restaurants. Congress enacted this legislation under its commerce clause power, and the Supreme Court upheld it on that basis.

Logically, it might seem that the civil rights law would be most easily justified under Congress's authority pursuant to §5 of the Fourteenth Amendment. However, the Supreme Court, in 1883, had held that Congress only could regulate government conduct and could not regulate private behavior under the Fourteenth Amendments.[93] Therefore, in 1964, it was uncertain whether Congress could use its Fourteenth Amendment power to outlaw private discrimination in employment and public accommodations. Congress thus chose the commerce clause as the authority for this landmark legislation.[94]

In *Heart of Atlanta Motel Inc. v. United States*, the Court upheld the constitutionality of Title II of the Civil Rights Act, which prohibited discrimination by places of public accommodation.[95] The Heart of Atlanta Motel was located in downtown Atlanta and had 216 rooms and about 75 percent of its registered guests were from out of state.[96] The Court upheld the application of the Act to the motel, which had a policy of refusing to provide accommodations to blacks.

The Court said that in evaluating the law and its application "[t]he only questions are: (1) whether Congress had a rational basis for finding that racial discrimination by motels affected commerce, and (2) if it had such a basis, whether the means it selected to eliminate that evil are reasonable and appropriate."[97] The Court concluded that the "voluminous testimony [before Congress] presents overwhelming evidence that discrimination by hotels and motels impedes interstate travel."[98] The Court noted that it did not matter that Congress's motive, in part, was moral; many federal laws, stretching back to the *Lottery Case*, had been adopted under the commerce power to remedy moral wrongs. Also, the Court said that it did not matter if the motel was "of a purely local character"; the Court said "[i]f it is interstate commerce that feels the pinch, it does not matter how local the operation which applies the squeeze."[99]

In a companion case, *Katzenbach v. McClung*, the Court upheld the application of the Act to a small business: Ollie's Barbecue, a family-owned restaurant in

---

[93] The Civil Rights Cases, 109 U.S. 3 (1883). This decision is discussed in detail in §3.7.1 and §6.4.

[94] Earlier cases had upheld the ability of Congress to prohibit discrimination in the channels of interstate commerce. *See, e.g.*, Morgan v. Virginia, 328 U.S. 373 (1946); Boynton v. Virginia, 364 U.S. 454 (1960).

[95] 379 U.S. 241 (1964).

[96] *Id.* at 243.

[97] *Id.* at 258-259.

[98] *Id.* at 253.

[99] *Id.* at 258 (citation omitted).

Birmingham, Alabama.[100] The Court's recitation of the facts emphasized the interstate connections of the restaurant. For example, 46 percent of the meat that it purchased annually came from out of state.[101] The Court's decision, however, was not based on the interstate impact of this particular restaurant. Rather, the Court found that Congress rationally had concluded that discrimination by restaurants cumulatively had an impact on interstate commerce. The Court found that the testimony before Congress "afforded ample basis for the conclusion that established restaurants in such areas sold less interstate goods because of the discrimination, that interstate travel was obstructed directly by it, that business in general suffered and that many new businesses refrained from establishing there as a result of it."[102] The Court upheld the Civil Rights Act and its application to Ollie's Barbecue because "[t]he power of Congress [under the commerce clause] is broad and sweeping."[103]

Although both *Heart of Atlanta Motel* and *Katzenbach v. McClung* were unanimous decisions, Justices Douglas and Goldberg concurred in each and said that they would have preferred to have the law upheld as constitutional under §5 of the Fourteenth Amendment.[104] The scope of Congress's power under this constitutional provision is discussed in §3.7 below.

These decisions reflect the breadth of Congress's commerce power, but they are not surprising under the doctrines developed since 1937. Under *Wickard*, racial discrimination by hotels and restaurants, looked at cumulatively across the country, surely has an effect on interstate commerce. Nor is there any reason why it should matter that Congress's primary purpose was based more on a moral judgment to eliminate discrimination than on concern for enhancing the economy. The Court has been consistently unwilling to limit Congress to acting under the commerce clause only to advance economic efficiency.

Criminal Laws

Not surprisingly, Congress has used its broad commerce clause power to enact many federal criminal laws. Some of these laws were adopted before 1937, such as the Mann Act, which makes it a crime to take a woman across state lines for immoral purposes,[105] and the Lindbergh Act, which prohibits kidnapping.[106]

Perez v. United States illustrates the Court's willingness to uphold federal criminal laws adopted under the commerce power.[107] Title II of the Consumer Credit

[100] 379 U.S. 294 (1964).
[101] *Id.* at 297.
[102] *Id.* at 300.
[103] *Id.* at 305.
[104] 379 U.S. at 280 (Douglas, J., concurring) ("I would prefer to rest the assertion of legislative power [on] §5 of the Fourteenth Amendment"); *id.* at 293 (Goldberg, J., concurring) (Congress had the authority under both the commerce clause and under §5 of the Fourteenth Amendment).
[105] *See* Hoke v. United States, 227 U.S. 308 (1913); Caminetti v. United States, 242 U.S. 470 (1917).
[106] Gooch v. United States, 297 U.S. 124 (1936).
[107] 402 U.S. 146 (1971).

Protection Act prohibited loan sharking activities such as charges of excess interest, violence, and threats of violence to collect debts. The defendant had been convicted of violating the law, but argued to the Supreme Court that the law could not be constitutionally applied to him because his business wholly operated in New York and there was no proof that he had engaged in organized crime.

The Court rejected these arguments and upheld the federal law. The Court concluded that it was rational for Congress to believe that even intrastate loan sharking activities had a sufficient effect on interstate commerce. The Court said that particularized findings were not required in order for a law to be upheld; it was sufficient that Congress had a rational belief that even "purely intrastate [loan sharking] . . . nevertheless directly affect[s] interstate and foreign commerce."[108]

After *Perez*, Congress used this authority to adopt one of the broadest and most important contemporary statutes: the federal RICO law. Title IX of the Organized Crime Control Act of 1970 contains the Racketeer Influenced and Corrupt Organizations (RICO) Act, which makes it a federal crime for "any person employed by or associated with any enterprise engaged, or the activities of which affect, interstate or foreign commerce, to conduct or participate, directly or indirectly, in a pattern of racketeering activity."[109] Racketeering is broadly defined to include everything from prostitution, obscenity, and gambling to arson, extortion, and bribery.[110]

Is the Broad Definition of the Commerce Power Desirable?

These decisions illustrate the breadth of the commerce power between 1937 and 1995. The key question is whether this is a desirable recognition of the need for federal legislation or whether it is an undesirable abandonment of basic constitutional principles. On the one hand, the complex problems facing American society in the twentieth century necessitate that Congress have authority to act beyond the narrow confines created by the Court in the pre-1937 area.

On the other hand, a core principle of American constitutional law is that the federal government has limited powers with most governance left to the states. The Court's expansive approach to the commerce clause puts virtually nothing beyond the reach of Congress, so long as it does not violate another constitutional provision.

Closely related to this issue is the question whether the judiciary should protect the states or whether the only check on Congress is through the political process. This is discussed more fully in §3.8, below. These basic normative questions are key in evaluating the desirability of the shift in the law since 1995 as the Court has narrowed the scope of the commerce power.

---

[108] *Id.* at 155-156.
[109] 18 U.S.C. §1962(c).
[110] 19 U.S.C. §1961(1).

§3.4.5   The Commerce Clause After United States v. Lopez

Between 1936 and April 26, 1995, the Supreme Court did not find one federal law unconstitutional as exceeding the scope of Congress's commerce power. Then in *United States v. Lopez*,[111] by a 5-to-4 margin, the Supreme Court declared unconstitutional the Gun-Free School Zones Act of 1990, which made it a federal crime to have a gun within 1,000 feet of a school.[112] Splitting along ideological lines, the Court ruled that the relationship to interstate commerce was too tangential and uncertain to uphold the law as a valid exercise of Congress's commerce power. Chief Justice Rehnquist wrote the opinion of the Court and was joined by Justices O'Connor, Kennedy, Scalia, and Thomas. Justices Stevens, Souter, Ginsburg, and Breyer dissented.

The Court followed its decision in *Lopez* with *United States v. Morrison*,[113] in 2000, in which it declared unconstitutional the civil damages provision of the Violence Against Women Act, which created a federal cause of action for victims of gender-motivated violence.[114] *Morrison* had the identical split among the Justices as *Lopez*. As discussed below, *Morrison* goes significantly further than *Lopez* in limiting the scope of Congress's commerce power by holding that Congress cannot regulate a noneconomic activity by finding that, looked at cumulatively, it has a substantial effect on interstate commerce.

Additionally, in two subsequent cases, *United States v. Jones*[115] and *Solid Waste Agency of Northern Cook County v. United States Army Corps of Engineers*,[116] the Court interpreted federal laws narrowly to avoid "constitutional doubts" that would be raised by a broader interpretation. In each instance, the Court said that applying the federal law would raise serious questions as to whether Congress had exceeded its commerce power. To avoid these constitutional doubts the Court narrowly interpreted the federal laws.

However, in two subsequent cases concerning the scope of Congress's commerce power — *Pierce County, Washington v. Guillen*[117] and *Gonzales v. Raich*[118] — the Court rejected challenges and upheld federal statutes. Most recently, though, in *National Federation of Independent Business v. Sebelius*, five Justices indicated an additional limit on the commerce power: Congress can regulate economic activity, but not *inactivity*.[119]

These cases are discussed in turn below. There is no doubt that these cases, especially when considered together with the Court's narrowing in the scope of Congress's powers under §5 of the Fourteenth Amendment and its revival

---

[111] 514 U.S. 549 (1995).
[112] 18 U.S.C. §922(q)(2)(a); §921(a)(25).
[113] 529 U.S. 598 (2000).
[114] 42 U.S.C. §13981.
[115] 529 U.S. 848 (2000).
[116] 531 U.S. 159 (2001).
[117] 537 U.S. 129 (2003).
[118] 545 U.S. 1 (2005).
[119] 132 S. Ct. 2566 (2012).

of the Tenth Amendment,[120] are one of the most important developments in constitutional law in the last two decades.

United States v. Lopez

Alfonso Lopez was a twelfth-grade student at Edison High School in San Antonio, Texas, in 1992 when he was arrested for carrying a concealed .38-caliber handgun and five bullets. He was charged with violating the Gun-Free School Zones Act of 1990, which made it a federal offense "for any individual knowingly to possess a firearm at a place that the individual knows, or has reasonable cause to believe, is a school zone."[121] The law defines a school zone as "in, or on the grounds of, a public, parochial, or private school"[122] or "within a distance of 1,000 feet from the grounds of a public, parochial, or private school."[123] Lopez was convicted of violating this law and sentenced to six months of imprisonment and two years of supervised release.

Lopez appealed on the ground that the Gun-Free School Zones Act of 1990 was an unconstitutional exercise of Congress's commerce power. The United States Court of Appeals for the Fifth Circuit found that the law was unconstitutional because there were inadequate findings by Congress as to a sufficient relationship to interstate commerce.

The United States Supreme Court affirmed, but on different grounds. The Court's decision was not based on the absence of adequate findings by Congress; rather, the Court concluded that the law was unconstitutional because it was not substantially related to interstate commerce.

Chief Justice Rehnquist's opinion for the Court began by emphasizing that the Constitution creates a national government of enumerated powers.[124] In other words, the Court returned to the notion that Article I limits Congress's legislative powers to those that are express or implied in the Constitution.

After reviewing the history of decisions under the commerce clause, the Court identified three types of activities that Congress can regulate under this power. First, Congress can "regulate the use of the channels of interstate commerce."[125] The Court cited *Heart of Atlanta Motel, Inc. v. United States*, which upheld the federal law prohibiting discrimination by hotels and restaurants as an example of protecting the channels of interstate commerce.[126]

Second, the Court said that Congress may legislate "to regulate and protect the instrumentalities of interstate commerce."[127] The Court said that this includes

---

[120] The narrowing of Congress's power under §5 of the Fourteenth Amendment is discussed below in §3.7.1, and the revival of the Tenth Amendment as a limit on federal power is considered in §3.10.

[121] 18 U.S.C. §922(q)(2)(A).

[122] 18 U.S.C. §921(a)(25)(A).

[123] 18 U.S.C. §921(a)(25)(B).

[124] 514 U.S. 549, 552.

[125] *Id.* at 558.

[126] 379 U.S. 241 (1964), discussed above in §3.4.4.

[127] *Id.* at 558-559, citing NLRB v. Jones & Laughlin Steel Corp., 301 U.S. at 37.

the power to regulate persons and things in interstate commerce. The Court here cited several cases that upheld congressional power to regulate the railroads under its commerce power.[128]

Finally, the Court said that Congress may "regulate those activities having a substantial relation to interstate commerce."[129] Chief Justice Rehnquist said that the prior case law was uncertain as to whether an activity must "affect" or "substantially affect" interstate commerce to be regulated under this approach. Chief Justice Rehnquist concluded that the more restrictive interpretation of congressional power is preferable and that "the proper test requires an analysis of whether the regulated activity 'substantially affects' interstate commerce."[130]

The Court concluded that the presence of a gun near a school did not substantially affect interstate commerce and that therefore the federal law was unconstitutional. Chief Justice Rehnquist noted that nothing in the Act limited its application to instances where there was proof that the gun had been part of interstate commerce. The Court specifically rejected the federal government's claim that regulation was justified under the commerce clause because possession of a gun near a school may result in violent crime that can adversely affect the economy.

Concurring opinions were written by Justice Thomas and also by Justice Kennedy, whose opinion was joined by Justice O'Connor. Justice Thomas's opinion was notable because it urged a much narrower view of congressional power than adopted by the majority. Thomas's approach would have returned the Court to the limits on the commerce authority that the Court followed between 1887 and 1937. Justices Kennedy and O'Connor stressed federalism and the relationship between limiting Congress's authority and protecting state prerogatives. They also emphasized the lack of necessity for the federal law because the vast majority of states already had laws prohibiting guns near schools.

Justices Stevens, Souter, and Breyer wrote dissenting opinions. Justice Breyer's dissent was the most thorough and was joined by the other dissenting Justices: Stevens, Souter, and Ginsburg. The dissent criticized the majority for engaging in undue judicial activism; for abandoning almost 60 years of precedent; and for invalidating an important federal statute. Justice Breyer argued that the judiciary should uphold a federal law as a valid exercise of the commerce power so long as there is a "rational basis" that an activity affects interstate commerce.[131] Justice Breyer then explained why guns inherently are a part of interstate commerce and why guns near schools have an economic impact that justifies federal regulation under the commerce power.

---

[128] *See, e.g.*, Shreveport Rate Cases, 234 U.S. 342 (1914), discussed above in §3.4.3.
[129] 514 U.S. at 558.
[130] *Id.* at 559.
[131] *Id.* at 618 (Breyer, J., dissenting).

United States v. Morrison

United States v. Morrison presented the question as to whether the civil damages provision of the federal Violence Against Women Act is constitutional.[132] The provision authorizes victims of gender-motivated violence to sue for money damages. Congress enacted the Violence Against Women Act based on detailed findings of the inadequacy of state laws in protecting women who are victims of domestic violence and sexual assaults. For example, Congress found that gender-motivated violence costs the American economy billions of dollars a year and is a substantial constraint on freedom of travel by women throughout the country.

The case was brought by Christy Brzonkala, who allegedly was raped by football players while a freshman at Virginia Polytechnic Institute. The players were not criminally prosecuted and ultimately avoided even sanctions by the university. Brzonkala filed suit against her assailants and the university under the civil damages provision of the Violence Against Women Act.

The issue before the Supreme Court was whether the civil damages provision of the Act could be upheld, either as an exercise of Congress's commerce clause authority or as permissible under Congress's power pursuant to §5 of the Fourteenth Amendment. In a 5-to-4 decision, the Court held that Congress lacked the authority to adopt the provision under either of these powers.[133] The split was the same as in all of the recent federalism rulings: Chief Justice Rehnquist wrote the opinion for the Court, joined by Justices O'Connor, Scalia, Kennedy, and Thomas. Justices Stevens, Souter, Ginsburg, and Breyer dissented.

In *Morrison*, the Court reaffirmed the three-part test for Congress's commerce clause authority that was articulated in *United States v. Lopez*. Congress may regulate (a) the channels of interstate commerce, (b) the instrumentalities of interstate commerce and persons or things in interstate commerce, and (c) activities that have a substantial effect on interstate commerce. The United States government and the plaintiff, Christy Brzonkala, defended the law based on the third part of the test, on the ground that violence against women has a substantial effect on the national economy. There was a lengthy legislative history of the Violence Against Women Act in which Congress found that assaults against women, when looked at cumulatively across the country, have a substantial effect on interstate commerce. The Supreme Court expressly rejected this argument as insufficient to sustain the law. Chief Justice Rehnquist emphasized that Congress was regulating noneconomic activity that has traditionally been dealt with by state laws. He wrote: "Gender-motivated crimes of violence are not, in any sense of the phrase, economic activity. While we need not adopt a categorical rule against aggregating the effects of any noneconomic activity in order to decide these cases, thus far in our Nation's history our cases have upheld Commerce Clause regulation of intrastate activity only where that activity is economic in nature."[134] The Supreme

---

[132]   42 U.S.C. §13981.

[133]   The Court's discussion of Congress's power to enact the law pursuant to §5 of the Fourteenth Amendment is considered below in §3.7.1.

[134]   529 U.S. 598, 613 (2000).

Court found Congress's findings of impact on the economy to be inadequate to sustain the law under the commerce clause. Chief Justice Rehnquist declared: "But the existence of congressional findings is not sufficient, by itself, to sustain the constitutionality of Commerce Clause legislation. As we stated in *Lopez*, '[S]imply because Congress may conclude that a particular activity substantially affects interstate commerce does not necessarily make it so.'"[135] The Court said that Congress was relying on a "but-for" causal chain "from the initial occurrence of violent crime . . . to every attenuated effect upon interstate commerce."[136] The Court said that "[i]f accepted, petitioners' reasoning would allow Congress to regulate any crime as long as the nationwide, aggregated impact of that crime has substantial effects on employment, production, transit or consumption."[137] By this reasoning, the Court explained, Congress could regulate all violent crimes in the United States. The Court thus concluded: "We accordingly reject the argument that Congress may regulate noneconomic, violent criminal conduct based solely on that conduct's aggregated effect on interstate commerce. The Constitution requires a distinction between what is truly national and what is truly local."[138]

Justice Clarence Thomas wrote a concurring opinion in which he again objected, as in *Lopez*, to the "substantial effects" test as a way of justifying congressional action under the commerce power. He wrote: "[T]he very notion of a 'substantial effects' test under the Commerce Clause is inconsistent with the original understanding of Congress' powers and with this Court's early Commerce Clause cases. By continuing to apply this rootless and malleable standard, however circumscribed, the Court has encouraged the Federal Government to persist in its view that the Commerce Clause has virtually no limits. Until this Court replaces its existing Commerce Clause jurisprudence with a standard more consistent with the original understanding, we will continue to see Congress appropriating state police powers under the guise of regulating commerce."[139] In other words, Justice Thomas would go significantly further than the majority in limiting the scope of Congress's commerce power; the majority in *Morrison* would allow Congress to regulate economic activities based on their cumulative impact on the economy, but not Justice Thomas.

Justice Souter wrote a dissenting opinion, joined by Justices Stevens, Ginsburg, and Souter. Justice Souter stressed the need for judicial deference to congressional fact-finding: "Congress has the power to legislate with regard to activity that, in the aggregate, has a substantial effect on interstate commerce. The fact of such a substantial effect is not an issue for the courts in the first instance, but for the Congress, whose institutional capacity for gathering evidence and taking testimony far exceeds ours. By passing legislation, Congress indicates its conclusion, whether explicitly or not, that facts support its exercise of the commerce power. The business of the courts is to review the congressional assessment, not for

---

[135] *Id.* at 614 (citation omitted).
[136] *Id.* at 615.
[137] *Id.*
[138] *Id.* at 617-618.
[139] *Id.* at 627 (Thomas, J., concurring).

soundness but simply for the rationality of concluding that a jurisdictional basis exists in fact."[140]

Justice Souter stressed that Congress had conducted voluminous hearings and found that violence against women has an enormous effect on the American economy. He wrote: "But the sufficiency of the evidence before Congress to provide a rational basis for the finding cannot seriously be questioned. Indeed, the legislative record here is far more voluminous than the record compiled by Congress and found sufficient in two prior cases upholding Title II of the Civil Rights Act of 1964 against Commerce Clause challenges."[141]

Thus, *Morrison* goes further than *Lopez* in limiting the scope of Congress's commerce power by narrowing the ability of Congress to regulate based on findings of "substantial effect" on interstate commerce. At least in areas that the Court regards as traditionally regulated by the states, Congress cannot regulate noneconomic activity based on a cumulative substantial effect on interstate commerce.

Narrowly Interpreting Laws to Avoid "Constitutional Doubts"

In two subsequent cases, *United States v. Jones*[142] and *Solid Waste Agency of Northern Cook County v. United States Army Corps of Engineers*,[143] the Supreme Court has narrowly interpreted federal laws to avoid "constitutional doubts" as to whether Congress exceeded its commerce power. In each instance, the Court did not declare the federal statute unconstitutional, but instead used the recent restrictive interpretations of the commerce power as a reason for limiting the scope of the federal laws.

In *Jones*, the Court considered whether arson of a dwelling violates the federal law that makes arson of property in interstate commerce a federal crime.[144] The United States government argued that the residence was part of interstate commerce in that it had insurance policies and it received utility service. But the Supreme Court, in a unanimous decision, interpreted the arson act to not apply to arson of a dwelling. Justice Ginsburg wrote the opinion for the Court and said that allowing the law to be applied to arson of a residence would raise "constitutional doubts" as to whether Congress had exceeded the scope of its commerce clause power.[145] To avoid the constitutional issue, the Court interpreted the federal statute narrowly to not include arson of dwellings.

In *Solid Waste Agency of Northern Cook County v. United States Army Corps of Engineers*,[146] the Supreme Court held that the Army Corps of Engineers could not apply the federal Water Pollution Control Act to intrastate waters based on the presence of migratory birds. A consortium of suburbs of Chicago sought to buy an abandoned gravel pit to dispose of nonhazardous solid wastes. Water within the

---

[140]   *Id.* at 628 (Souter, J., dissenting).
[141]   *Id.* at 634.
[142]   529 U.S. 848 (2000).
[143]   531 U.S. 159 (2001).
[144]   18 U.S.C. §844.
[145]   529 U.S. at 858.
[146]   531 U.S. 159 (2001).

gravel pit was used by migratory birds. The Army Corps of Engineers had promulgated rules concerning when the Water Pollution Control Act applied, and one of these, the "migratory bird rule," was used to require compliance in the use of the abandoned gravel pit.

The Supreme Court, in a 5-to-4 decision, interpreted the federal Act narrowly to avoid "constitutional doubts" and thus held that the presence of migratory birds is not sufficient to bring intrastate waters within the scope of the Water Pollution Control Act. The government argued that the migratory bird rule was constitutional because "protection of migratory birds is a 'national interest of very nearly the first magnitude,' . . . and that, as the Court of Appeals found, millions of people spend over a billion dollars annually on recreational pursuits relating to migratory birds."[147] Chief Justice Rehnquist, writing for the Court, said that whether these justifications are sufficient under the commerce clause, especially in light of *Lopez* and *Morrison*, is a "significant constitutional question."[148]

To avoid the constitutional issue, the Court said that it would interpret the statute to not apply. Chief Justice Rehnquist explained: "These are significant constitutional questions raised by respondents' application of their regulations, and yet we find nothing approaching a clear statement from Congress that it intended §404(a) to reach an abandoned sand and gravel pit such as we have here. Permitting respondents to claim federal jurisdiction over ponds and mudflats falling within the 'Migratory Bird Rule' would result in a significant impingement of the States' traditional and primary power over land and water use. We thus read the statute as written to avoid the significant constitutional and federalism questions raised by respondents' interpretation, and therefore reject the request for administrative deference."[149]

Although interpreting laws narrowly to avoid constitutional doubts is not new, its application to the commerce clause gives a powerful tool to lawyers challenging the application of federal civil and criminal laws. They need not persuade the Court that a federal statute is unconstitutional on its face or as applied. Instead, they only need to show that the application of the law would raise "constitutional doubts." The Supreme Court never has explained how serious the constitutional doubts must be; nor has it indicated how plausible the narrowing construction has to be. Together, *Jones* and *Solid Waste Agency* indicate another way in which the Rehnquist Court's recent narrow interpretation of the commerce power is manifesting itself.

Upholding Federal Laws and Rejecting Commerce Clause Challenges

Two Supreme Court decisions since *Lopez* refused to extend limits on Congress's powers and upheld the federal statutes. In *Pierce County, Washington v.*

---

[147] *Id.* at 173.
[148] *Id.*
[149] *Id.* at 174.

Guillen,[150] the Court unanimously reaffirmed broad authority for Congress to legislate concerning road safety as part of its power to regulate the channels of interstate commerce. A federal statute provides that if a local government does a traffic study as part of applying for federal funds, that study is not discoverable. Congress's concern was that local governments would refrain from conducting such investigations if they could be used as evidence against them in suits arising from automobile accidents.

Guillen involved two separate accidents at intersections in the State of Washington and the local governments had recently conducted studies of traffic conditions at both locations. The plaintiffs sued the local governments and sought access to the traffic studies. The Washington Supreme Court declared unconstitutional the federal law that exempted these studies from discovery. The United States Supreme Court, in an opinion by Justice Clarence Thomas, unanimously reversed and upheld the federal law. Justice Thomas explained that "[i]t is well established that the Commerce Clause gives Congress authority to regulate the use of the channels of interstate commerce. . . . [The statutes] can be viewed as legislation aimed at improving safety in the channels of interstate commerce and increasing protection for the instrumentalities of interstate commerce. As such, they fall within Congress' Commerce Clause power."[151]

More dramatically, in *Gonzales v. Raich,*[152] the Court held that Congress constitutionally may use its power to regulate commerce among the states to prohibit the cultivation and possession of small amounts of marijuana for medicinal purposes. Although California has created an exemption to its state marijuana laws for medical uses, no such exemption exists to the federal law. In a 6-to-3 decision, with the majority opinion written by Justice Stevens, the Court upheld the federal law. Justices Kennedy, Souter, Ginsburg, and Breyer joined the majority opinion, and Justice Scalia concurred in the judgment. Justice Stevens explained that for almost 70 years Congress has had the authority to regulate activities that have a substantial effect on interstate commerce. The Court concluded that marijuana, looked at cumulatively, including that grown for medical purposes, has a substantial effect on interstate commerce. Justice Stevens's opinion relied on a precedent from over 60 years ago: *Wickard v. Filburn,* discussed above, which held that Congress may regulate the amount of wheat that farmers grow for their own home consumption.

How does *Gonzales v. Raich* fit into the Court's recent commerce clause jurisprudence? The Court did not change the test for the commerce clause that it has followed since *Lopez* in 1995: Congress, under the commerce clause, may regulate the channels of interstate commerce, the instrumentalities of interstate commerce and persons or things in interstate commerce, and activities that have a substantial effect on interstate commerce. Nor did the Court revisit its holding in *Morrison* that in regulating noneconomic activities, substantial effect cannot be based on cumulative impact. Instead, *Gonzales v. Raich* stands for the proposition that intrastate

---

[150] 537 U.S. 129 (2003).
[151] *Id.* at 146-147.
[152] 545 U.S. 1 (2005).

production of a commodity sold in interstate commerce is economic activity and thus substantial effect can be based on cumulative impact. Justice Scalia concurred in the judgment, and emphasized that Congress, pursuant to the necessary and proper clause, has the authority to control intrastate production of goods that are of a type that end up in interstate commerce.

Congress's Power to Regulate Activity, but Not Inactivity

In *National Federation of Independent Business v. Sebelius*, five Justices indicated an additional limit on Congress's commerce power: It may not regulate economic inactivity.[153] The Patient Protection and Affordable Care Act sought to remedy the problem of 50 million Americans being without health insurance. A crucial mechanism is that it requires that almost all individuals have health insurance and those that don't must pay a penalty to the Internal Revenue Service. Insurance companies are required to provide coverage to all and no longer can deny policies based on preexisting conditions, or charge higher premiums based on health conditions, or impose yearly or lifetime caps on payments.

As explained below, Chief Justice Roberts, joined by Justices Ginsburg, Breyer, Sotomayor, and Kagan, said that the individual mandate is a tax and within the scope of Congress's taxing power.[154] But five Justices—Chief Justice Roberts and the four dissenters who would have struck down the entire Act (Justices Scalia, Kennedy, Thomas, and Alito)—said that the individual mandate was not a constitutional exercise of Congress's commerce clause power. They said that Congress under the commerce clause may regulate economic *activity* that taken cumulatively has a substantial effect on interstate commerce. They saw the individual mandate as regulating *inactivity*, regulating those not engaged in commerce, and thus exceeding the scope of Congress's power. Chief Justice Roberts wrote: "As expansive as our cases construing the scope of the commerce power have been, they all have one thing in common: They uniformly describe the power as reaching 'activity.' . . . The individual mandate, however, does not regulate existing commercial activity. It instead compels individuals to *become* active in commerce by purchasing a product, on the ground that their failure to do so affects interstate commerce. Construing the Commerce Clause to permit Congress to regulate individuals precisely *because* they are doing nothing would open a new and potentially vast domain to congressional authority."[155]

Justice Ginsburg, joined by Justices Breyer, Sotomayor, and Kagan, strongly disagreed that the individual mandate was regulating "inactivity." They argued that everyone receives medical care and thus everyone is engaged in "activity"; over 99 percent of people will receive medical care in their lifetimes and 60 percent of the uninsured do so each year.[156] People either purchase insurance or they self-insure. Congress was regulating those who were engaged in the economic activity

---

[153]   132 S. Ct. 2566 (2012).
[154]   *See* §3.5.2.
[155]   132 S. Ct. at 2589.
[156]   *Id.* at 2618 (Ginsburg, J., concurring in part and dissenting in part).

of self-insuring because of the way in which it increased health insurance costs for everyone else in society: "Congress estimated that the cost of uncompensated care raises family health insurance premiums, on average, by over $1,000 per year."[157] Justice Ginsburg explained: "An individual's decision to self-insure . . . is an economic act with the requisite connection to interstate commerce."[158]

It is unclear how much this distinction between "activity" and "inactivity" will matter in the future. In fact, arguably the discussion of the commerce clause in *National Federation of Independent Business v. Sebelius* is just dicta because it was not necessary for the holding of the case, which upheld the individual mandate as an exercise of Congress's taxing power. On the one hand, it can be argued that this distinction is not likely to matter much in the future as Congress is unlikely to adopt other laws requiring that individuals purchase goods or services. On the other hand, the distinction between "activity" and "inactivity" seems inherently elusive; if a person is prosecuted for not stopping at a stop sign, is that punishing activity or inactivity? If a hotel refuses to serve African-American customers, is it being held liable for its activity or its inactivity?

Implications

Lopez was dramatic simply because it was the first time in almost 60 years that a federal law has been declared unconstitutional as exceeding the scope of Congress's commerce power. *Morrison, Jones, Solid Waste Agency,* and *National Federation of Independent Business* show that *Lopez* is not an aberration, but an important change in the Court's approach to the commerce clause. Interestingly, except for *Jones,* the limits on the commerce power were all in 5-to-4 decisions, with the five most conservative Justices in the majority. Although these Justices are most commonly associated with advocating judicial restraint, in these cases they abandoned almost 60 years of deference to the legislature under the commerce clause. On the other hand, it is not surprising that it would be conservative Justices who are most concerned with limiting the scope of congressional powers and protecting the prerogatives of state governments.

The test for the commerce power under *Lopez* is that Congress may act under the commerce clause in three areas. First, it may regulate the channels of interstate commerce. Second, it may regulate persons or things in interstate commerce. Third, it may regulate activities that have a substantial effect on interstate commerce; substantial activity may be found based on cumulative impact so long as Congress is regulating economic activity. There is still great uncertainty as to the meaning of each part of this test and as to how far the Supreme Court will limit Congress's power under the commerce clause.

---

[157] *Id.* at 2585 (Ginsburg, J., concurring in part and dissenting in part).
[158] *Id.* at 2624 (Ginsburg, J., concurring in part and dissenting in part).

§3.5 THE TAXING AND SPENDING POWER

§3.5.1 The Scope of the Taxing and Spending Power

Article I, §8, of the Constitution states that "Congress shall have Power To lay and collect Taxes, Duties, Imposts and Excises, to pay the Debts and provide for the common Defence and general Welfare of the United States; but all Duties, Imposts and Excises shall be uniform throughout the United States." Under the Articles of Confederation, the limited federal government had no taxing power and therefore no revenue to spend. Obviously, today the power to tax and spend is one of the most important of all congressional powers.

For What Purposes May Congress Tax and Spend?

Is Congress limited to taxing and spending only to carry out other powers specifically enumerated in Article I, or does Congress have broad authority to tax and spend for the general welfare? The Court adopted the latter, much more expansive, view in *United States v. Butler*.[1] *Butler* concerned the constitutionality of the Agricultural Adjustment Act of 1933, which sought to stabilize production in agriculture by offering subsidies to farmers to limit their crops. By restricting the supply of agricultural products, Congress sought to ensure a fair price and thus to encourage agricultural production.

Butler declared the Agricultural Adjustment Act unconstitutional on the ground that it violated the Tenth Amendment because it regulated production; the regulation of production, according to the Court, was left to the states.[2] This aspect of *Butler* has never been followed and is discussed in more detail in §3.10, which considers the Tenth Amendment. However, the *Butler* Court's holding concerning the scope of the taxing and spending powers remains good law.

The Court began by noting that the debate over the scope of the taxing and spending power goes back to a dispute between James Madison and Alexander Hamilton. Madison took the view that Congress was limited to taxing and spending to carry out the other powers specifically granted in Article I of the Constitution. The Court explained that "Madison asserted it amounted to no more than a reference to the other powers enumerated in the subsequent clauses of the same section; that, as the United States is a government of limited and enumerated powers, the grant of power to tax and spend for the general national welfare must be confined to the enumerated legislative fields committed to the Congress."[3]

In contrast, Hamilton took the position that Congress could tax and spend for any purpose that it believed served the general welfare, so long as Congress did not violate another constitutional provision. The Court noted that "Hamilton

---

§3.5 [1] 297 U.S. 1 (1936).

[2] The Court adopted a similar limit on Congress's commerce power between 1887 and 1937, holding that regulating production was left to the states. *See* §3.4.3.

[3] 297 U.S. at 65.

. . . maintained that the clause confers a power separate and distinct from those later enumerated, is not restricted in meaning by the grant of them, and Congress consequently has a substantive power to tax and to appropriate, limited only by the requirement that it shall be exercised to provide for the general welfare of the United States."[4]

The Court expressly endorsed Hamilton's position as "the correct one."[5] Thus, Congress has broad power to tax and spend for the general welfare so long as it does not violate other constitutional provisions. For example, a tax that was calculated or administered in a racially discriminatory fashion would be unconstitutional, not as exceeding the scope of Congress's Article I powers, but as violating the equal protection guarantee of the Fifth Amendment.[6]

Subsequent cases affirmed Congress's expansive authority under the taxing and spending clauses. In *Steward Machine Co. v. Davis*, the Court upheld the constitutionality of the federal unemployment compensation system created by the Social Security Act.[7] In *Helvering v. Davis*, the Court upheld the constitutionality of the Social Security Act's old age pension program, which was supported exclusively by federal taxes.[8] Justice Benjamin Cardozo, writing for the Court, stated: "The discretion [to decide whether taxing and spending advances the general welfare] belongs to Congress, unless the choice is clearly wrong, a display of arbitrary power, not an exercise of judgment. . . . Nor is the concept of the general welfare static. Needs that were narrow or parochial a century ago may be interwoven in our day with the well-being of the Nation."[9]

In light of the narrowing of Congress's commerce power, some have urged similar restrictions on Congress's spending power and even an overruling of *United States v. Butler*'s expansive interpretation of this authority.[10] Thus far, though, the Court has not indicated any such change in the law.

§3.5.2   The Taxing Power

Historically, the Court drew distinctions between direct and indirect taxes, and between revenue raising and regulatory taxes, in considering the constitutionality of taxes. Neither of these distinctions has any significance today.[11]

---

[4] *Id.* at 65.

[5] *Id.* at 66.

[6] As discussed in §9.1.1, equal protection applies to state and local governments through the Fourteenth Amendment and to the federal government through the Fifth Amendment.

[7] 301 U.S. 548 (1937).

[8] 301 U.S. 619 (1937).

[9] *Id.* at 640-641.

[10] John C. Eastman, Restoring the "General" to the General Welfare Clause, 4 Chapman L. Rev. 63 (2001).

[11] Another limit on Congress's taxing power that remains important is the export clause found in Article I, §9: "No Tax or Duty shall be laid on Articles exported from any State." The Supreme Court held that this provision prohibits Congress from assessing nondiscriminatory federal taxes on goods in export transit. United States v. International Business Machines Corporation, 517 U.S. 843 (1996). The Court also ruled that a tax on policies insuring exports is functionally the same as a tax on exports.

Direct and Indirect Taxes

Article I, §2, of the Constitution states that "direct Taxes shall be apportioned among the several States which may be included within this Union, according to their respective Numbers." Article I, §9, provides that "[n]o Capitation, or other direct, Tax shall be laid, unless in Proportion to the Census." In its initial cases considering these provisions, the Court narrowly defined a *direct* tax and thus accorded Congress broad authority to impose various kinds of taxes. Under the earlier cases, direct taxes seemed limited to taxes on real property; therefore, all other taxes could be imposed by Congress without concern about apportionment among the states. For example, in *Hylton v. United States*, in 1796, the Court held that a federal tax on carriages was indirect and therefore did not need to be apportioned among the states.[12]

In *Veazie Bank v. Fenno*, in 1869, the Court upheld the constitutionality of a federal tax on state bank notes.[13] The Court concluded that this was an indirect tax and declared that "direct taxes have been limited to taxes on land and appurtenances, and taxes on polls, or capitation taxes."[14] The Court repeated this view in *Springer v. United States*, where the Court upheld the constitutionality of the Civil War Income Tax.[15]

However, in *Pollock v. Farmer's Loan & Trust Co.*, the Court, by a 5-to-4 margin, declared unconstitutional the federal income tax.[16] The Court explained that because the income tax collected revenue gained from property, among other sources, it was a direct tax and had to be apportioned among the states. In 1913, 18 years after *Pollock*, the Sixteenth Amendment was ratified to overturn that decision and to allow a federal income tax. The Sixteenth Amendment provides: "The Congress shall have power to lay and collect taxes on incomes, from whatever source derived, without apportionment among the several States, and without regard to any census or enumeration."

The Court eventually abandoned the distinction between direct and indirect taxes.[17] In *Flint v. Stone Tracy Co.*, the Court upheld the Corporation Excise Tax of 1909, which imposed a tax on corporations doing business in states or territories.[18] Similarly, the Court upheld taxes such as those on estates[19] and gifts.[20] The constitutional provisions quoted above, requiring apportionment of direct taxes, seem limited, at most, to taxes on real property. In other words, unless Congress were to create a national property tax, all other taxes are very likely to be deemed indirect and therefore are constitutional even without apportionment among the states.

---

[12] 3 U.S. (3 Dall.) 171 (1796).

[13] 75 U.S. (8 Wall.) 533 (1869).

[14] *Id.* at 544.

[15] 102 U.S. (12 Otto.) 586, 602 (1880).

[16] 157 U.S. 429 (1895).

[17] *But see* Eisner v. Macomber, 252 U.S. 189 (1920) (stock dividends are not income prior to their sale or conversion and therefore are not taxable without apportionment).

[18] 220 U.S. 107 (1911).

[19] Bank & Trust Co. of New York v. Eisner, 256 U.S. 345 (1921).

[20] Bromley v. McCaughn, 280 U.S. 124 (1929).

Regulatory and Revenue Raising Taxes

Unlike the distinction between direct and indirect taxes, which is drawn in the text of the Constitution, the distinction between *regulatory* and *revenue raising taxes* was judicially created. However, like the distinction between direct and indirect taxes, the distinction between regulatory and revenue raising taxes no longer has any practical significance.

In the *Child Labor Tax Case, Bailey v. Drexel Furniture Co.*, the Court declared unconstitutional a federal tax on companies that shipped in interstate commerce goods made by child labor.[21] As discussed above, the Supreme Court earlier had declared unconstitutional a federal law that prohibited the shipment in interstate commerce of goods made by child labor.[22] The Court found that the law violated the Tenth Amendment and usurped prerogatives reserved to the states. Not surprisingly, the Court declared unconstitutional the federal tax that attempted to accomplish the same thing as the earlier federal law that had been invalidated.

The Court based its decision on a distinction between a true tax and a penalty for a violation of a commercial regulation. The Court explained that although taxes could have an "incidental" regulatory effect, a tax is unconstitutional when "in the extension of the penalizing features of the so-called tax . . . it loses its character as such and becomes a mere penalty with the characteristics of regulation and punishment."[23]

At the same time, in *Hill v. Wallace*, the Court declared unconstitutional a federal tax on grain future contracts.[24] The law imposed a tax on grain contracts unless the contracts had been approved by a board of trade that was sanctioned by the United States Department of Agriculture. As in the *Child Labor Tax Case*, the Court found that the regulation was unconstitutional because it was a penalty and not a true tax.

In *United States v. Constantine*, in 1935, the Court declared unconstitutional a federal tax on liquor dealers who had violated state liquor laws.[25] The Court again based its decision on a distinction between regulatory taxes and taxes that are designed to raise revenue. The Court stated: "[The tax] exhibits . . . an intent to prohibit and to punish violations of state law [and therefore] remove all semblance of a revenue act, and stamp the sum it exacts as a penalty."[26]

The problem with these cases is that they draw a false distinction between taxes that generate revenue and taxes that are penalties. Obviously, a tax can be both at the same time. Congress can use a tax law simultaneously to regulate and to generate funds. Therefore, deciding whether a tax should be characterized as regulatory or revenue generating is inherently arbitrary. Additionally, it is questionable why Congress cannot use taxes for a regulatory purpose; it is unclear what constitutional principle allows taxes for one purpose and not the other.

---

[21] 259 U.S. 20 (1922).
[22] Hammer v. Dagenhart, 247 U.S. 251 (1918), discussed in §3.4.3.
[23] 259 U.S. at 38.
[24] 259 U.S. 44 (1922).
[25] 296 U.S. 287 (1935).
[26] *Id.* at 295.

In fact, prior to the *Child Labor Tax Case* and *Hill v. Wallace*, the Court repeatedly had rejected such a distinction between regulatory taxes and revenue raising taxes. In *Veazie Bank v. Fenno*, the Court upheld a federal tax on state bank notes, even though the primary purpose of the tax was to eliminate such state notes.[27] In *United States v. Doremus*, the Court upheld the Narcotics Drug Act of 1914, which both taxed narcotics and imposed extensive regulations on their sale.[28] The Court rejected any distinction between regulatory taxes and those designed to raise revenues. The Court stated: "If the legislation enacted has some reasonable relation to the exercise of the taxing authority conferred by the Constitution, it cannot be invalidated because of the supposed [regulatory] motives which induced it."[29]

Similarly, in *McCrary v. United States*, the Court upheld a federal tax on colored oleomargarine.[30] The Court expressly rejected the argument that the tax was unconstitutional because it was a penalty and intended primarily for regulatory purposes. The Court declared: "Since . . . the taxing power conferred by the Constitution knows no limits except those expressly stated in that instrument, it must follow, if a tax be within the lawful power, the exertion of that power may not be judicially restrained because of the results to arise from its exercise."[31]

Therefore, it is not surprising that the distinction between regulatory taxes and revenue raising taxes was relatively short-lived. In 1937, the Court upheld a federal tax on firearm dealers.[32] The Court explained that "[e]very tax is in some measure regulatory. . . . But [it] is not any less a tax because it has a regulatory effect. . . . Inquiry into the hidden motives which may move Congress to exercise a power constitutionally conferred upon it is beyond the competency of the courts."[33] Subsequently, the Court upheld a federal tax on bookmakers and said that regulatory taxes are constitutional because "[u]nless there are provisions extraneous to any tax need, courts are without authority to limit the exercise of the taxing power."[34]

The Individual Mandate as an Exercise of Congress's Taxing Power

In *National Federation of Independent Business v. Sebelius*, the Court upheld the individual mandate in the Patient Protection and Affordable Care Act as a valid exercise of Congress's taxing power.[35] As explained above, the Affordable Care Act requires that almost all Americans purchase health insurance or pay a tax penalty; there are exemptions for those who oppose insurance on religious grounds or

---

[27] 75 U.S. (8 Wall.) 27 (1869).
[28] 249 U.S. 86 (1919).
[29] *Id.* at 93.
[30] 195 U.S. 27 (1904).
[31] *Id.* at 59.
[32] Sonzinsky v. United States, 300 U.S. 506 (1937).
[33] *Id.* at 513 (citations omitted).
[34] United States v. Kahriger, 345 U.S. 22, 31 (1953).
[35] 132 S. Ct. 2566 (2012).

who are of low income. The Court, in a 5-4 decision, said that the individual mandate is a tax and within the scope of Congress's taxing power.[36]

Chief Justice Roberts, joined by Justices Ginsburg, Breyer, Sotomayor, and Kagan explained that the mandate is calculated like a tax; for example, in 2014, it is 1 percent of income or $95 for those who do not purchase insurance. It is collected by the Internal Revenue Service and the funds go to the federal treasury; it will generate about $4 billion by 2017. The Court said that it was irrelevant that the Obama administration never called it a tax; the labels used by the government are not determinative. The Court concluded: "Our precedent demonstrates that Congress had the power to impose the exaction in §5000A under the taxing power, and that §5000A need not be read to do more than impose a tax. That is sufficient to sustain it." The "question of the constitutionality of action taken by Congress does not depend on recitals of the power which it undertakes to exercise."[37]

Justices Scalia, Kennedy, Thomas, and Alito wrote a joint dissent and strongly disagreed that the individual mandate fit within the scope of the taxing power. They stressed that the president and Congress refused to "frame" it as such.[38] Moreover, they said that "[o]ur cases establish a clear line between a tax and a penalty" and that the individual mandate is the latter.[39] The dissent objected that "to say that the Individual Mandate merely imposes a tax is not to interpret the statute but to rewrite it."[40]

Those defending the Court's conclusion argue that it rests on the well-established principle that Congress has broad power to tax for the general welfare and that it may tax behavior that it wants to discourage, such as going without health insurance. Those criticizing the Court's decision emphasize that the individual mandate was not adopted under the taxing power and should not be upheld on that basis.[41]

§3.5.3 The Spending Power

Broad Scope of the Spending Power

As described above, the Court has held that Congress has broad power to spend funds to advance the "general welfare."[42] In *United States v. Butler*, the Court held that Congress is not limited to spending only to achieve the specific powers

---

[36] As explained above, five Justices said that the individual mandate would not fit within the scope of the necessary and proper clause (*see* §3.3 above) or the commerce clause (*see* §3.4.5 above).

[37] 132 S. Ct. at 2598.

[38] *Id.* at 2651 (Scalia, Kennedy, Thomas, and Alito, JJ., dissenting).

[39] *Id.*

[40] *Id.* at 2656.

[41] *Id.* at 2651 ("The issue is not whether Congress had the *power* to frame the minimum-coverage provision as a tax, but whether it *did* so."). The dissent also objected that it made no sense that the majority treated the individual mandate as a tax for purposes of its constitutionality, but not as a tax for purposes of a federal statute, the Anti-Injunction Act, which prohibits federal courts from enjoining the collection of taxes.

[42] *See* §3.5.1.

granted in Article I of the Constitution.[43] Rather, Congress may spend in any way it believes would serve the general welfare, so long as it does not violate another constitutional provision. Thus, in *Steward Machine Co. v. Davis*,[44] the Court upheld provisions of the Social Security Act that provided unemployment compensation, and in *Helvering v. Davis*,[45] the Court upheld the provisions of the Social Security Act that provided for an old age pension program. In both cases, the Court emphasized the broad scope of Congress's spending power.

The Court has reaffirmed the broad scope of Congress's spending power. In *Sabri v. United States*,[46] the Court unanimously upheld the constitutionality of a federal law that prohibits bribery of state, local, and tribal officials of entities that receive at least $10,000 in federal funds.[47] An individual convicted under this law argued that his activities had nothing to do with the area of local government that received federal funds and that Congress exceeded the scope of its spending power. The claim was that Congress only could prohibit bribery as to those state, local, and tribal activities that actually got federal money.

The Supreme Court expressly rejected this argument. In an opinion by Justice David Souter, the Court explained: "Money is fungible, bribed officials are untrustworthy stewards of federal funds, and corrupt contractors do not deliver dollar-for-dollar value."[48] The Court expressly rejected the federalism challenge to the law and concluded that the criminal law was constitutional because Congress has the "power to bring federal power to bear directly on individuals who convert public spending into unearned private gain, not a means for bringing federal economic might to bear on a State's own choices of public policy."[49]

Conditions on Grants to State Governments

One important issue involving the spending power concerns the ability of Congress to place conditions on grants to state and local governments. The Court has held that Congress may place conditions on such grants, so long as the conditions are expressly stated, have some relationship to the purpose of the spending program, and are not unduly coercive.

In *Oklahoma v. Civil Service Commission*, the Court upheld a provision of the federal Hatch Act that granted federal funds to state governments on the condition that the states adopt civil service systems and limit the political activities of many categories of government workers.[50] The Court explained that Congress has broad power to set conditions for the receipt of federal funds even as to areas that Congress might otherwise not be able to regulate. The Court stated: "While the United States is not concerned with, and has no power to regulate, local political

---

[43] 297 U.S. 1 (1936), discussed above in §3.5.1.
[44] 301 U.S. 548 (1937).
[45] 301 U.S. 619 (1937).
[46] 541 U.S. 600 (2004).
[47] 18 U.S.C. §666(a)(2).
[48] 541 U.S. at 606.
[49] *Id.* at 608.
[50] 330 U.S. 127 (1947).

activities as such of state officials, it does have power to fix the terms upon which its money allotments to states shall be disbursed."[51]

The Court affirmed this decision in *South Dakota v. Dole*.[52] A federal law sought to create a 21-year-old drinking age by withholding a portion of federal highway funds from any state government that failed to impose such a drinking age. Specifically, 5 percent of federal highway funds would be denied to any state that did not create a 21-year-old drinking age.

The Court, in an opinion by Chief Justice Rehnquist, approved this condition on federal money. The Court emphasized that the condition imposed by Congress was directly related to one of the main purposes behind federal highway money: creating safe interstate travel. The Court recognized that at some point "the financial inducement offered by Congress might be so coercive as to pass the point at which pressure turns into compulsion."[53] But the Court said that in this case, the condition of federal highway money was a "relatively mild encouragement" and was constitutional "[e]ven if Congress might lack the power to impose a national minimum drinking age directly, we conclude that encouragement to state action . . . is a valid use of the spending power."[54]

In *Pennhurst State School and Hospital v. Halderman*, the Supreme Court held that Congress may place strings on grants to state and local governments so long as the conditions are expressly stated.[55] The Developmentally Disabled Assistance and Bill of Rights Act of 1975 created a federal grant program for state governments to provide for better care for the developmentally disabled. The Act included a "bill of rights" for the developmentally disabled. The Pennhurst State School and Hospital, a facility run by the State of Pennsylvania, was sued for violating the bill of rights contained in the Act.

The Court ruled in favor of the state, holding that "if Congress intends to impose a condition on the grant of federal moneys it must do so unambiguously."[56] The Court explained that conditions must be clearly stated so that states will know the consequences of their choosing to take federal funds. The Court concluded that the Act failed to require that states meet the bill of rights as a condition for accepting federal money.

However, the Court has recently enforced an important limit on Congress's ability to put conditions on grants to state and local governments: They cannot be unduly coercive. In *National Federation of Independent Business v. Sebelius*, the Court declared unconstitutional provisions of the Patient Protection and Affordable Care Act that required that states receiving federal Medicaid funds cover within their Medicaid programs those within 133 percent of the federal poverty level.[57]

---

[51] *Id.* at 143.

[52] 483 U.S. 203 (1987).

[53] *Id.* at 211 (citation omitted).

[54] *Id.* at 212.

[55] 451 U.S. 1, 17 (1981).

[56] *Id.* at 20.

[57] 132 S. Ct. 2566 (2012). Other aspects of the Court's decision are discussed above, including its consideration of the necessary and proper clause (§3.3), the commerce clause (§3.4.5), and the taxing power (§3.5.2).

The federal government pays 100 percent of these costs until 2019 and 90 percent thereafter. Any state that failed to comply would lose all of its Medicaid funds.

Chief Justice Roberts, writing for the Court in a 7-2 decision, said that "[i]n this case, the financial 'inducement' Congress has chosen is much more than 'relatively mild encouragement'—it is a gun to the head."[58] The Court explained that "Medicaid spending accounts for over 20 percent of the average State's total budget, with federal funds covering 50 to 83 percent of those costs. . . . The threatened loss of over 10 percent of a State's overall budget, in contrast, is economic dragooning that leaves the States with no real option but to acquiesce in the Medicaid expansion."[59]

Justice Ginsburg, joined by Justice Sotomayor, dissented, and argued that Congress should be able to condition Medicaid funds on states providing the required coverage. She argued that the majority did not dispute that Congress could tie Medicaid funds to conditions, but objected to tying all Medicaid funds to the new conditions of coverage. She said that this wrongly treats Medicaid as two programs, an old one and a new one, rather than as one program with expanded coverage. She wrote: "The ACA, in contrast, relates solely to the federally funded Medicaid program; if States choose not to comply, Congress has not threatened to withhold funds earmarked for any other program. Nor does the ACA use Medicaid funding to induce States to take action Congress itself could not undertake."[60] Justice Ginsburg expressed concern over how the line is to be drawn in the future as to what is impermissible compulsion: "When future Spending Clause challenges arrive, as they likely will in the wake of today's decision, how will litigants and judges assess whether a State has a legitimate choice whether to accept the federal conditions in exchange for federal funds? Are courts to measure the number of dollars the Federal Government might withhold for noncompliance? The portion of the State's budget at stake? And which State's—or States'—budget is determinative: the lead plaintiff, all challenging States (26 in this case, many with quite different fiscal situations), or some national median?"[61]

In sum, Congress possesses expansive power to spend for the general welfare so long as it does not violate another constitutional provision. Congress may impose conditions on grants to state and local governments so long as the conditions relate to the purpose of the spending, are clearly stated, and are not unduly coercive.

---

[58] *Id.* at 2604.
[59] *Id.* at 2604-2605.
[60] *Id.* at 2634 (Ginsburg, J., dissenting).
[61] *Id.* at 2640.

§3.6   OTHER CONGRESSIONAL POWERS UNDER ARTICLE I AND ARTICLE IV

Although the vast majority of Supreme Court cases concerning the scope of Congress's powers have involved laws adopted under the commerce clause and the taxing and spending powers, these are just a few of the many powers granted to Congress under the Constitution. Other powers are reviewed below in §3.6.1 and §3.6.2, which focus, respectively, on foreign policy and domestic affairs.

§3.6.1   Foreign Policy

Under Article I of the Constitution, Congress has several important powers with regard to foreign policy: to ratify treaties; to regulate foreign commerce; to define and punish "Piracies and Felonies committed on the high Seas and Offences against the law of Nations"; to declare war; to grant letters of marque and reprisal; to raise, support, and regulate an army and a navy; and to regulate immigration.

The crucial and difficult questions arise when there is a conflict between the president and Congress over control of foreign policy. Although the Court at times has spoken of the president's inherent power over foreign affairs,[1] the Court also has recognized broad congressional authority in this realm. The Court has declared that "[a]lthough there is in the Constitution no specific grant to Congress of power to enact legislation for the effective regulation of foreign affairs, there can be no doubt of the existence of this power in the law-making organ of the nation."[2]

Three areas are worth examining in some detail: the treaty power, the power to regulate immigration, and the war-making power. The corresponding powers of the president, especially with regard to treaties and war powers, are discussed in §4.6.

Treaties

The Constitution gives the president the authority, "by and with the Advice and Consent of the Senate, to make treaties provided two thirds of the Senators present concur." These treaties are the law of the land and prevail over all conflicting state laws. If there is a conflict between a treaty and a federal statute, the one adopted last in time controls. The Court has explained that when a statute and a treaty "relate to the same subject, the courts will always endeavor to construe them so as to give effect to both, if that can be done without violating the language of either; but if the two are inconsistent, the one last in date will control the other."[3]

---

§3.6 [1] United States v. Curtiss-Wright Export Corp., 299 U.S. 304 (1936), discussed in §4.6.1.

[2] Perez v. Brownell, 356 U.S. 44, 62 (1958).

[3] Whitney v. Robertson, 124 U.S. 190, 194 (1888); *see also* Chae Chan Ping v. United States (Chinese Exclusion Case), 130 U.S. 581 (1889) (a treaty is modified by a subsequent law only if Congress has clearly expressed such a purpose).

Treaties, of course, cannot violate the supreme law, which is the Constitution. In *Reid v. Covert*, the Court reversed the conviction of a United States military dependent who was convicted in Great Britain, without a jury trial, pursuant to jurisdiction under a treaty between the United States and Great Britain.[4] Justice Black, writing for the plurality, stated that "[n]o agreement with a foreign nation can confer power on the Congress, or on any other branch of Government, which is free from the restraints in the Constitution."[5]

The Court, however, has rejected the claim that state sovereignty and the Tenth Amendment limit the scope of the treaty power. In *Missouri v. Holland*, the Supreme Court upheld the constitutionality of a treaty between the United States and Great Britain protecting migratory birds.[6] The State of Missouri argued that the treaty violated the Tenth Amendment. The Court explained that the Constitution expressly grants the federal government the power to make treaties, and thus states could not claim that the treaty, or the statute adopted pursuant to it, violates the Tenth Amendment. The Court said: "The treaty in question does not contravene any prohibitory words to be found in the Constitution. The only question is whether it is forbidden by some invisible radiation from the general terms of the Tenth Amendment. . . . [Here] a national interest of very nearly the first magnitude is involved. It can be protected only by national action in concert with that of another power. The subject matter is only transitorily within the State and has no permanent habitat therein."[7]

The scope of Congress's power to adopt laws to implement treaties remains uncertain. Can Congress enact laws to do this that otherwise would not be within its powers? The Court might have addressed this, but didn't, in *Bond v. United States*.[8] Carol Ann Bond was prosecuted under a federal statute that had been enacted to implement the Chemical Weapons treaty after she tried to poison her former best friend. When Bond learned that her friend and her husband had an affair that resulted in her friend becoming pregnant, Bond put poison that could be absorbed through the skin on the car door, door knobs, and mail box of her former best friend in an attempt to injure her.

The Court was asked to decide the issue of Congress's ability to enact laws to implement treaties. But the Court declined to do so and instead ruled narrowly that there was no indication that Congress meant the prohibition of chemical weapons to apply to such a domestic dispute that is traditionally handled under state criminal law. Chief Justice Roberts wrote: "[T]he background principle that Congress does not normally intrude upon the police power of the States is critically important. In light of that principle, we are reluctant to conclude that Congress meant to punish Bond's crime with a federal prosecution for a chemical weapons attack."[9]

---

[4] 354 U.S. 1 (1957) (plurality opinion).
[5] *Id.* at 16.
[6] 252 U.S. 416 (1920).
[7] *Id.* at 433-435.
[8] 134 S. Ct. 2077 (2014). This case is also discussed in §4.6.2.
[9] *Id.* at 2092.

Justices Scalia and Thomas each wrote opinions concurring in the judgment, each of which was joined by the other and by Justice Alito. These Justices would have reached the issue not decided by the majority and would have made clear that Congress's power to enact statutes to implement treaties is limited.[10] They would have held that Congress cannot adopt laws to implement treaties unless the statutes otherwise would have fit within the scope of other congressional powers.

Although Congress must ratify treaties, congressional approval is not required for executive agreements. Executive agreements are agreements between the United States and a foreign country that are effective when signed by the president and the head of the foreign nation. The Supreme Court has accorded the president broad power to negotiate executive agreements, even when they entail major foreign policy commitments.[11] Executive agreements are discussed in detail in §4.6.1.

Also, it is important to note that the Supreme Court has not held that the Senate must approve rescission of a treaty. In *Goldwater v. Carter*, Senator Barry Goldwater challenged the constitutionality of President Jimmy Carter's rescission of the United States's treaty with Taiwan.[12] Goldwater argued that the president no more can unilaterally rescind a treaty than he can unilaterally rescind a statute. Adoption of both a statute and a treaty requires congressional action, and Goldwater therefore contended that rescission of either requires some congressional action. Specifically, Goldwater maintained that because the Constitution mandates that two-thirds of the Senate approve a treaty, the Constitution should be interpreted to require that two-thirds of the Senate approve rescission of a treaty.

The Court dismissed Senator Goldwater's challenge on justiciability grounds. The plurality opinion, by Justice Rehnquist, deemed that it was a nonjusticiable political question.[13] Justice Powell, in an opinion concurring in the judgment, contended that the case was not justiciable because it was not yet ripe for review since Congress had not acted.

Although the Court did not uphold the constitutionality of the president's rescinding treaties without Senate consent, in practical terms that was the effect of the Court's decision. The president can rescind treaties without worrying about judicial invalidation because the Court held that challenges are not justiciable. The Court's approach is troubling because it assumes that Congress has some way in which it can act to protect its constitutional powers. Yet the whole point of Senator Goldwater's suit is that one-third of the Senate should be able to block rescission of a treaty, and this is obviously impossible unless the judiciary imposes and enforces such a rule.

---

[10] *Id.* at 2103 (Thomas, J., concurring in the judgment).

[11] *See* Dames & Moore v. Regan, 453 U.S. 654 (1981); United States v. Pink, 315 U.S. 203 (1942).

[12] 444 U.S. 996 (1979) (plurality opinion).

[13] The political question doctrine and this aspect of the *Goldwater* decision are discussed in §2.8.4.

The Power to Regulate Immigration and Citizenship

Article I, §8, of the Constitution empowers Congress "to establish an uniform Rule of Naturalization." Congress has been accorded broad power to regulate immigration and citizenship. Indeed, the Court has held that "over no conceivable subject is the legislative power of Congress more complete than it is over the admission of aliens."[14] Congress thus has been recognized as having plenary power to set the conditions for entry into the country, the circumstances under which a person can remain, and the rules for becoming a citizen.[15]

Likewise, Congress has authority to set conditions for citizenship and retaining citizenship. Yet the Court has been less consistent in according Congress broad power to regulate citizenship than it has been in granting Congress power to regulate immigration. For example, in *Rogers v. Bellei*, the Court upheld a federal law that accorded citizenship to individuals born in foreign countries if the person has met certain residence requirements, such as having lived in the United States for at least five continuous years between the ages of 14 and 28 and if at least one parent is an American citizen.[16] Although *Rogers* grants Congress power to set such prospective conditions for citizenship, the Court has imposed limits on the ability of Congress to withdraw citizenship from naturalized citizens. In *Schneider v. Rusk*, the Court declared unconstitutional a federal law that withdrew citizenship from naturalized citizens who maintained continuous residence for three years in a country to which they formerly owed allegiance.[17]

The Court also has shifted its position as to whether Congress can withdraw citizenship to those who vote in foreign elections. For example, in *Perez v. Brownell*, the Court upheld a federal statute mandating loss of United States citizenship for those who voted in a political election in a foreign country.[18] The Court spoke broadly of Congress's power to legislate in the area of foreign policy and in setting the rules concerning citizenship. Yet in *Afroyim v. Rusk*, the Court held unconstitutional a federal law withdrawing citizenship from those who voted in foreign elections.[19] The Court declared: "[W]e reject the idea expressed in *Perez* that, aside from the Fourteenth Amendment, Congress has any general power, express or implied, to take away an American citizen's citizenship without his assent."[20] The Court concluded that "[t]he entire legislative history of the 1868 Act makes it abundantly clear that there was a strong feeling in the Congress that the only way the citizenship it conferred could be lost was by the voluntary renunciation or abandonment by the citizen himself."[21]

---

[14] Fiallo v. Bell, 430 U.S. 787, 792 (1977) (citations omitted). The issue of federal preemption of state regulation in this area is discussed in §5.2.3.

[15] *See id.* at 792-795; United States ex rel. Knauff v. Shaughnessy, 338 U.S. 537, 543 (1950).

[16] 401 U.S. 815 (1971).

[17] 377 U.S. 163 (1964).

[18] 356 U.S. 44 (1958); *see also* Mackenzie v. Hare, 239 U.S. 299 (1915) (upholding the loss of citizenship for a woman born in California when she married a man from England).

[19] 387 U.S. 253 (1967).

[20] *Id.* at 258.

[21] *Id.* at 266.

War Powers

In many ways, the Constitution is an invitation to a struggle over control of the power to declare and to conduct wars. Article I of the Constitution grants Congress the power to declare war and the authority to raise and support the army and the navy. Article II makes the president the commander-in-chief. Historically, presidents have used this power to send troops to foreign countries, even in wars, without express congressional approval.

The Supreme Court has rarely discussed the constitutionality of the president waging war without a formal congressional declaration of war. In part, this is because of the political question doctrine discussed in Chapter 2;[22] many challenges to the constitutionality of the Vietnam War were dismissed as nonjusticiable political questions.

One of the few cases to consider the president's power to act in the absence of congressional authorization arose in the unique context of the Civil War. In *Brig Amy Warwick*, the Court ruled that the president had the power to impose a blockade on Southern states without a congressional declaration of war.[23] The Court spoke broadly of the president's power to respond to invasions or rebellions: "If a war be made by invasion of a foreign nation, the president is not only authorized but bound to resist force by force. He does not initiate the war, but is bound to accept the challenge without waiting for any special legislative authority. And whether the hostile party be a foreign invader, or States organized in rebellion, it is nonetheless a war, although the declaration of it be unilateral."[24]

In discussing congressional authority in the area of the war powers, there are two distinct questions. First, what constitutes a declaration of war? Must it be a formal declaration of war, such as was adopted by Congress after the bombing of Pearl Harbor to authorize America's entry into World War II? Or may it be less explicit? For example, was the Gulf of Tonkin Resolution, which authorized the use of military force in Southeast Asia, sufficient to constitute a declaration of war for the Vietnam War? Might even continuous congressional approval of funding for a war be regarded as approval of the war?

Second, when may the president use American troops in hostilities without congressional approval? To what extent does the president's power as commander-in-chief authorize the use of troops in foreign countries without a formal declaration of war?

Neither of these questions ever has been clearly answered by the Supreme Court. In fact, given the Court's view that such foreign policy disputes constitute a political question, answers are unlikely to come from the judiciary. In 1973, Con-

---

[22] *See* §2.8.4. Also, there are likely to be problems in terms of who would have standing to sue. During the military conflict in Yugoslavia, Congressman Tom Campbell sued President Bill Clinton for not complying with the Constitution and with the War Powers Resolution. The federal district court dismissed on standing grounds, and the United States Court of Appeals affirmed. Campbell v. Clinton, 203 F.3d 19 (D.C. Cir. 2000).

[23] 67 U.S. (2 Black) 635 (1863).

[24] *Id.* at 668.

gress adopted the War Powers Resolution to address these two questions.[25] The War Powers Resolution was a response to the Vietnam War, in which two presidents, Lyndon Johnson and Richard Nixon, fought a highly unpopular war with great cost in lives and dollars without a formal declaration of war from Congress.

The War Powers Resolution states that the president as commander-in-chief may introduce the United States Armed Forces into hostilities or situations where hostilities appear imminent "only pursuant to (1) declaration of war, (2) specific statutory authorization, or (3) a national emergency created by attack upon United States, its territories or possessions, or its armed forces."[26] It requires that the president consult with Congress, where possible, before introducing troops into hostilities and that the president report to Congress within 48 hours after troops are introduced into hostilities or in situations that risk imminent involvement in hostilities.

Most importantly, the War Powers Resolution provides that the president shall withdraw troops after 60 days unless Congress has declared war or authorized a 60-day extension or is physically unable to meet as a result of an armed attack upon the United States.[27] The president can extend this by 30 days if he certifies to Congress in writing that "unavoidable military necessity respecting the safety of United States Armed Forces requires the continued use of such armed forces in the course of bringing about a prompt removal of such forces."[28]

Presidents repeatedly have expressed the view that the War Powers Resolution is unconstitutional and regularly have failed to comply with it.[29] On the one hand, the War Powers Resolution can be viewed as an impermissible limit on the president's powers as commander-in-chief.[30] On the other hand, the War Powers Resolution can be viewed as a constitutional and desirable assurance of checks and balances in the crucial area of waging war. Because the judiciary is likely to deem challenges to the War Powers Resolution to be a nonjusticiable political question, a Supreme Court decision on its constitutionality is unlikely. Therefore, its significance will depend on the willingness of Congress to enforce it, such as by cutting off funds for military efforts that it has not authorized.

§3.6.2 Domestic Affairs

Article I, §8, of the Constitution contains many provisions granting Congress power in the realm of domestic affairs. In addition to the powers described above, to

---

[25] 50 U.S.C. §1541. Although it is called "The War Powers Resolution," it is a properly adopted federal statute.

[26] 50 U.S.C. §1541(c).

[27] 50 U.S.C. §1544(b).

[28] *Id.*

[29] *See* Harold Koh, The National Security Constitution 39-40 (1990).

[30] *See, e.g.*, Louis Fisher, Congress: Does It Abdicate Its Power?: War and Spending Prerogatives: Stages of Congressional Abdication, 19 St. Louis U. Pub. L. Rev. 7 (2000). The War Powers Resolution might also be challenged as an impermissible legislative veto because it requires the president to withdraw troops without any congressional action if 60 days elapse. The legislative veto is discussed in detail in §3.11.2.

regulate commerce and to tax and spend, Congress is accorded seven other major powers over domestic affairs.

First, Congress can establish "uniform Laws on the subject of Bankruptcies throughout the United States." The Supreme Court has accorded Congress broad powers to set the rules for bankruptcies.[31] The Court has explained that the requirement for "uniform rules" of bankruptcies requires only that the law not be designed to help one debtor in a manner different from how other debtors are treated. For example, in the *Regional Railroad Reorganization Act Cases*, the Court upheld a bankruptcy law that treated railroads in one part of the country differently than those in other areas.[32] The Court explained that the law was "uniform" because all of the railroads covered by the law, and all of the creditors of these railroads, were treated the same under the Act.

Second, Congress has the power to "coin Money, regulate the Value thereof, and of foreign Coin, and fix the Standard of Weights and Measures" and "To provide for the punishment of counterfeiting the Securities and current Coin of the United States." In the *Legal Tender Cases*, the Court upheld Congress's power to provide that United States Treasury notes are legal tender and satisfy all obligations incurred before or after the legislation.[33] Likewise, during the 1930s, the Court upheld a federal law that abolished the gold standard for currency as part of its power to regulate the "Coin" and its value.[34]

Third, Congress has the authority "[t]o Establish Post Offices and Post Roads." The Court long has said that the "power possessed by Congress embraces the regulation of the entire postal system of the country" and to take "all measures necessary to secure its safe and speedy transit, and the prompt delivery of its contents."[35]

Fourth, Congress has the power "[t]o promote the Progress of Science and useful Arts, by securing for limited Times to Authors and Inventors the exclusive Right to their respective Writings and Discoveries." This, of course, grants Congress the power to provide for copyrights and patents, and it has done so since the earliest days of the country.

Fifth, the Constitution gives Congress the authority "[t]o constitute Tribunals inferior to the Supreme Court." This provision is in accord with Article III, §1, which provides: "The judicial Power of the United States, shall be vested in one supreme Court, and in such inferior Courts as the Congress may from time to time ordain and establish." As a compromise at the Constitutional Convention, it was decided to create the Supreme Court, but to leave it up to Congress as to whether there would be lower federal courts. The Judiciary Act of 1789 created such lower courts, and they have existed ever since.[36]

---

[31] *See* In re Klein, 42 U.S. (1 How.) 277 (1843).

[32] 419 U.S. 102 (1974).

[33] 79 U.S. (12 Wall.) 457 (1870).

[34] Norman v. Baltimore & Ohio R.R. Co., 294 U.S. 240 (1935).

[35] Ex parte Jackson, 96 U.S. (6 Otto.) 727, 732 (1878).

[36] The issue of Congress's power to restrict the jurisdiction of these courts is considered in §2.9.3.

Sixth, Congress has the power to create a "District [to be] the Seat of Government of the United States," to govern that area, and "to exercise like Authority over all Places purchased by the Consent of the Legislature of the State in which the Same shall be, for the Erection of Forts, Magazines, Arsenals, dock-yards, and other needful Buildings." In other words, Congress was granted power to create the District of Columbia and to govern it. Likewise, Congress is accorded power to regulate military buildings and federal buildings. Article IV, §3, provides that "Congress shall have Power to dispose of and make all needful Rules and Regulations respecting the Territory or other Property belonging to the United States." These provisions provide Congress with expansive power to regulate federal land and property. Indeed, the Court has spoken of "the complete power that Congress has over public lands."[37]

Seventh, Congress has the authority to approve interstate compacts. Article I, §10, says: "No State shall, without the consent of Congress, . . . enter into any Agreement or Compact with another State or with a Foreign Power." The Supreme Court has recognized that the clear implication of this provision is that Congress has the authority to approve compacts among states and that such a compact is the law of the United States.[38]

§3.7   CONGRESS'S POWERS UNDER THE RECONSTRUCTION-ERA AMENDMENTS

After the Civil War, three vitally important amendments were added to the Constitution. The Thirteenth Amendment, adopted in 1865, prohibits slavery and involuntary servitude, except as a punishment for a crime. It also provides, in §2, "Congress shall have power to enforce this article by appropriate legislation."

The Fourteenth Amendment, adopted in 1868, provides that all persons born or naturalized in the United States are citizens and that no state can abridge the privileges or immunities of such citizens; nor may states deprive any person of life, liberty, or property without due process of law or deny any person of equal protection of the laws. Section 5 of the Fourteenth Amendment states: "the Congress shall have power to enforce, by appropriate legislation, the provisions of this article."

The Fifteenth Amendment declares that "[t]he right of citizens of the United States to vote shall not be denied or abridged by the United States or by any State

---

[37] Kleppe v. New Mexico, 426 U.S. 529, 540-541 (1976) (citations omitted) (upholding a federal law that protected wild burros on federal land).

[38] *See* West Virginia ex rel. Dyer v. Sims, 341 U.S. 22 (1951) (approved compacts are the law of the United States); *see also* Virginia v. United States, 78 U.S. (11 Wall.) 39 (1870) (compact approved by Congress is the law of the United States).

on account of race, color, or previous condition of servitude." Section 2 again provides that Congress has the power to enforce it by appropriate legislation.

The three Reconstruction Amendments thus contain provisions that empower Congress to enact civil rights legislation. Two major questions arise concerning the scope of this power. First, may Congress regulate private conduct under this authority, or is Congress limited to regulating only government actions? Second, what is the scope of Congress's power under these amendments? For example, may Congress use this power to interpret the Constitution and even to overrule Supreme Court decisions?

§3.7.1   May Congress Regulate Private Conduct?

The *Civil Rights Cases*

In the *Civil Rights Cases*, in 1883, the Supreme Court greatly limited Congress's ability to use its power under the Reconstruction Amendments to regulate private conduct.[1] The Civil Rights Act of 1875 provided that all persons were "entitled to the full and equal enjoyment of the accommodations, advantages, facilities and privileges of inns, public conveyances, on land or water, theatres, and other places of public amusement; subject only to the conditions and limitations established by law, and applicable to citizens of every race and color, regardless of any previous condition of servitude." In other words, the law broadly prohibited private racial discrimination by hotels, restaurants, transportation, and other public accommodations.

By an 8-to-1 decision, the Court held that the Act was unconstitutional and adopted a restrictive view as to the power of Congress to use these provisions to regulate private behavior. As to the Thirteenth Amendment, the Court recognized that it applies to private conduct; it prohibits people from being or owning slaves. The Court, however, said that Congress's power was limited to ensuring an end to slavery; Congress could not use this power to eliminate discrimination. The Court explained that "it would be running the slavery argument into the ground to make it apply to every act of discrimination which a person may see fit to make as to the guests he will entertain, or as to the people he will take into his coach or cab or car, or admit to his concert or theatre, or deal with in other matters of intercourse or business."[2] Indeed, the Court stated that Congress could abolish "all badges and incidents of slavery," but it could not use its power under the Thirteenth Amendment to "adjust what may be called the social rights of men and races in the community."[3]

Astoundingly for a decision in 1883, less than two decades after the end of the Civil War, the Court suggested that slavery was a thing of the past and that there was little need for civil rights legislation to protect blacks. Justice Bradley, writing for the Court, stated: "When a man has emerged from slavery, and by the aid of

---

§3.7 [1] 109 U.S. 3 (1883).
   [2] *Id.* at 24-25.
   [3] *Id.* at 22.

beneficent legislation has shaken off the inseparable concomitants of that state, there must be some stage in the progress of his elevation when he takes the rank of a mere citizen and ceases to be the special favorite of the laws, and when his rights as a citizen, or a man, are to be protected in the ordinary modes by which other men's rights are protected."[4]

The Court also held that Congress lacked authority to enact the law under the Fourteenth Amendment. In fact, the Court broadly declared that the Fourteenth Amendment only applies to government action and that therefore it cannot be used by Congress to regulate private behavior. The Court stated that "the fourteenth amendment is prohibitory . . . upon the states. [Individual] invasion of individual rights is not the subject matter of the amendment."[5] The Court made it clear that Congress's authority was only over state and local governments and their officials, not over private conduct: "It does not authorize Congress to create a code of municipal law for the regulation of private rights; but to provide modes of redress against the operation of State laws, and the actions of State officers."[6]

The *Civil Rights Cases* remain good law in implicitly establishing that the provisions of §1 of the Fourteenth Amendment apply only to government action, not to private conduct.[7] However, as discussed below, the Court has held that Congress may prohibit private racial discrimination under the Thirteenth Amendment. Although some decisions suggested that Congress may prohibit private discrimination under the Fourteenth Amendment, in *United States v. Morrison*, in 2000, the Court reaffirmed the *Civil Rights Cases'* holding that Congress may not regulate private conduct under its §5 powers.

The Thirteenth Amendment

For almost 80 years, the Court continued to adhere to the holding of the *Civil Rights Cases* that Congress, pursuant to the Thirteenth Amendment, could not regulate private conduct. For example, in *Hodges v. United States*, in 1906, the Court declared unconstitutional a federal law that made it a crime for private individuals to intimidate blacks to keep them from performing their contracts of employment.[8] The Court explained that the Thirteenth Amendment was intended only to prohibit slavery, and the Court again stated its view that blacks should not be protected by special legislation. The Court said that the Reconstruction Amendments "declined to constitute them wards of the Nation . . . doubtless believing that thereby in the long run their best interests would be subserved, they taking their chances with other citizens in the states where they should make their homes."[9]

---

[4] *Id.* at 25.
[5] *Id.* at 10-11.
[6] *Id.* at 11.
[7] This is discussed in detail in §6.4, which considers the state action doctrine and exceptions to it.
[8] 203 U.S. 1 (1906).
[9] *Id.* at 20.

§3.7 Congress's Powers Under the Reconstruction-Era Amendments

Similarly, in *Corrigan v. Buckley*,[10] in 1926, and *Hurd v. Hodge*,[11] in 1948, the Court held that federal laws could not prohibit racially restrictive covenants, contracts among residents of a neighborhood that they would not sell their property to blacks or Jews.[12] However, in the last five decades, the Court has overruled these earlier decisions and has accorded Congress broad power under the Thirteenth Amendment to prohibit private racial discrimination. The seminal case is *Jones v. Alfred H. Mayer Co.*, which held that Congress could prohibit private discrimination in selling and leasing property.[13] The case involved a private real estate developer who refused to sell housing or land to African Americans. An African-American couple sued under 42 U.S.C. §1982, which provides that all citizens have "the same right, in every State and Territory, as is enjoyed by white citizens thereof to inherit, purchase, lease, sell, hold and convey real and personal property."

The Court held that §1982 applies to prohibit private discrimination and that Congress had the authority under the Thirteenth Amendment to adopt the law.[14] Indeed, the Court said that Congress has broad legislative power under the Thirteenth Amendment: "Congress has the power under the Thirteenth Amendment rationally to determine what are the badges and incidents of slavery, and the authority to translate that determination into effective legislation."[15]

Subsequently, the Court has upheld the constitutionality of other federal statutes regulating private behavior that were adopted under §2 of the Thirteenth Amendment.[16] In *Runyon v. McCrary*, the Court held that 42 U.S.C. §1981 applies to prohibit discrimination in private contracting and that this is within the scope of Congress's power under §2 of the Thirteenth Amendment.[17] Section 1981 provides that "[a]ll persons within the jurisdiction of the United States shall have the same right in every State and Territory to make and enforce contracts, to sue, be parties, give evidence, and to the full and equal benefit of all laws and proceedings for the security of persons and property as is enjoyed by white citizens." *Runyon* raised the question of whether §1981 prohibits private schools from excluding qualified African-American children solely because of their race.

The Supreme Court saw no basis for distinguishing *Jones v. Alfred H. Mayer Co.* and concluded "that §1981, like §1982, reaches private conduct."[18] The Court unanimously reaffirmed this conclusion in 1989, in *Patterson v. McLean Credit Union.*[19]

---

[10] 271 U.S. 323 (1926).

[11] 334 U.S. 24 (1948).

[12] In Shelley v. Kraemer, 334 U.S. 1 (1948), the Court held that court enforcement of racially restrictive covenants would violate the Fourteenth Amendment. *Shelley* is discussed in §6.4.4.3.

[13] 392 U.S. 409 (1968).

[14] The dissent especially focused on whether §1982 was meant to apply to private conduct. 392 U.S. at 454 (Harlan, J., dissenting).

[15] 392 U.S. at 440.

[16] The Court also has broadened the interpretation of §1982 as applying to personal as well as real property. *See* Sullivan v. Little Hunting Park, Inc., 396 U.S. 229 (1969) (discrimination in rental of property violates §1982).

[17] 427 U.S. 160 (1976).

[18] *Id.* at 173 (citation omitted).

[19] 491 U.S. 164 (1989).

The Court also has held that Congress had authority under the Thirteenth Amendment to enact 42 U.S.C. §1985(3), which creates a civil cause of action for conspiracies to violate civil rights.[20] In *Griffin v. Breckenridge*, the Court allowed a private suit by black victims of a racially motivated assault.[21] The incident occurred in 1966, when two white residents of Mississippi stopped a car with five black occupants and severely beat them. The Court found that there was a cause of action under §1985(3) because there was "nothing inherent in [the provision] that requires the action working the deprivation to come from the State."[22]

In *Jones, Runyon, Patterson,* and *Griffin,* the Court seemed to give Congress broad power under §2 of the Thirteenth Amendment to prohibit private racial discrimination. Yet it should be noted that in other cases, the Court has spoken in a more qualified manner about this power. In *Norwood v. Harrison,* the Court found that a Mississippi program to give free textbooks to private schools violated the Constitution.[23] In discussing Congress's power under §2 of the Thirteenth Amendment, the Court said that "some private discrimination is subject to special remedial legislation in certain circumstances."[24] Despite these qualifiers, *Jones, Runyon,* and *Patterson* give Congress authority to prohibit private racial discrimination as part of its authority to eliminate the badges and incidents of slavery.

The Fourteenth Amendment

Unlike the Thirteenth Amendment, which Congress can use to prevent private discrimination, it is now clear that §5 of the Fourteenth Amendment cannot be used to regulate private activity. Earlier, in *United States v. Guest,* five Justices, although not in a single opinion, concluded that Congress may outlaw private discrimination pursuant to §5 of the Fourteenth Amendment.[25] *Guest* involved the federal law that makes it a crime for two or more persons to go "in disguise on the highway, or on the premises of another, with intent to prevent or hinder his free exercise or enjoyment of any right or privilege."[26] The Court held that interference with the use of facilities in interstate commerce violated the law, whether or not motivated by a racial animus.

The majority opinion did not reach the question of whether Congress could regulate private conduct under §5 of the Fourteenth Amendment. However, six of the Justices—three in a concurring opinion and three in a dissenting opinion—expressed the view that Congress could prohibit private discrimination under its §5 powers. Justice Tom Clark, in a concurring opinion joined by Justices Hugo Black and Abe Fortas, said that "the specific language of §5 empowers the

---

[20] Section 1985(3) provides for liability "if two or more persons . . . conspire, or go in disguise on the highway . . . for the purpose of depriving, either directly or indirectly, any person or class of persons of the equal protection of the laws, or of equal privileges and immunities under the laws."

[21] 403 U.S. 88 (1971).

[22] *Id.* at 97.

[23] 413 U.S. 455 (1973).

[24] *Id.* at 470.

[25] 383 U.S. 745 (1966).

[26] 18 U.S.C. §241.

Congress to enact laws punishing all conspiracies with or without state action that interfere with Fourteenth Amendment rights."[27] Likewise, Justice William Brennan in an opinion that concurred in part and dissented in part, and that was joined by Chief Justice Earl Warren and Justice William Douglas, concluded that Congress may prohibit private discrimination pursuant to §5.[28]

But in *United States v. Morrison*,[29] the Supreme Court expressly reaffirmed the *Civil Rights Cases* and disavowed the opinions to the contrary in *United States v. Guest*. As described above in the discussion of Congress's commerce power, *Morrison* involved a constitutional challenge to the civil damages provision of the Violence Against Women Act, which authorized victims of gender-motivated violence to sue under federal law. The case involved a suit brought by a woman who allegedly was raped by football players at Virginia Tech University; the defendants were not criminally prosecuted and ultimately avoided even university discipline. The victim sued under the Violence Against Women Act, a law adopted by Congress after extensive hearings concerning the magnitude of gender-motivated violence, the great costs in economic losses and personal suffering, and the inadequacy of state laws and state courts.

The United States government intervened to defend the law, and it and the plaintiff argued that the civil damages provision was constitutional as an exercise of both Congress's commerce clause power and its authority under §5 of the Fourteenth Amendment. As explained above, the Court in a 5-to-4 decision held that the law exceeded the scope of the commerce power because Congress cannot regulate noneconomic activity based on a cumulative impact on interstate commerce.[30]

By the same 5-to-4 margin, the Court held that the law is not constitutional as an exercise of Congress's §5 power. Chief Justice Rehnquist, writing for the Court, said that Congress under this authority may regulate only state and local governments, not private conduct. Chief Justice Rehnquist relied on "the time-honored principle that the Fourteenth Amendment, by its very terms, prohibits only state action."[31] He said that the opinions in *United States v. Guest*, indicating congressional power to regulate private conduct, were only dicta.[32] Thus, the civil damages provision of the Violence Against Women Act was deemed to exceed the scope of Congress's §5 powers because it "is not aimed at proscribing discrimination by officials which the Fourteenth Amendment might not itself proscribe; it is directed not at any State or state actor, but at individuals who have committed criminal acts motivated by gender bias."[33]

Morrison is thus an important limit on Congress's powers under §5 of the Fourteenth Amendment. The Court's holding can be defended as being consistent with the long-standing principle that the amendment applies only to government

[27] 383 U.S. at 762 (Clark, J., concurring).
[28] *Id.* at 777 (Brennan, J., concurring in part and dissenting in part).
[29] 529 U.S. 598 (2000).
[30] *See* §3.4.5 above.
[31] 529 U.S. at 621.
[32] *Id.* at 623.
[33] *Id.* at 626.

conduct. But the decision can be criticized as an unduly narrow interpretation of a constitutional provision that was intended to have broad scope. The Violence Against Women Act was adopted because of perceived inadequacies in state courts and state laws. Critics of *Morrison* argue that §5 should be read as authorizing congressional action under such circumstances.

§3.7.2   *What Is the Scope of Congress's Power?*

A second major issue concerning Congress's power under the Reconstruction Amendments concerns the scope of authority under these provisions. Is Congress limited to providing remedies for violations of constitutional rights recognized by the Supreme Court; or may Congress use its power under these amendments to adopt an independent interpretation of the Constitution, even overruling Supreme Court decisions?

Alternative Views

There are two possible answers to these questions concerning the scope of Congress's powers under §5 of the Fourteenth Amendment. One view, which might be labeled the "nationalist" perspective, is that Congress may use its §5 authority to expand the scope of rights. *Katzenbach v. Morgan*, discussed below, appeared to adopt this approach. An alternative view, which might be called a "federalist perspective," is that Congress under §5 of the Fourteenth Amendment cannot create new rights or expand the scope of rights; Congress can act only to prevent or remedy violations of rights, and such laws must be narrowly tailored. In *City of Boerne v. Flores*, in 1997, discussed below, the Court unequivocally adopted this second perspective and the Court has reaffirmed this in several subsequent decisions.

The Nationalist Perspective of §5: *Katzenbach v. Morgan*

Katzenbach v. Morgan indicated that Congress, under §5 of the Fourteenth Amendment, may independently interpret the Constitution and even overturn the Supreme Court.[34] *Katzenbach* concerned the constitutionality of §4(e) of the Voting Rights Act of 1965, which provides that no person who has completed sixth grade in a Puerto Rican school, where instruction was in Spanish, shall be denied the right to vote because of failing an English literacy requirement. Earlier, in *Lassiter v. Northampton County Board of Elections*, the Supreme Court had upheld the constitutionality of an English language literacy requirement for voting.[35]

Congress, in the Voting Rights Act, sought to partially overturn *Lassiter* by providing that failing a literacy test could not bar a person from voting if the person was educated through the sixth grade in Puerto Rico. The Supreme Court

---

[34] 384 U.S. 641 (1966).
[35] 360 U.S. 45 (1959).

in *Katzenbach v. Morgan* upheld this provision as "a proper exercise of the powers granted to Congress by §5 of the Fourteenth Amendment."[36]

The Court offered two reasons to support this conclusion. One was that Congress could have concluded that granting Puerto Ricans the right to vote would empower them and help them to eliminate discrimination against them.[37] In essence, this is an argument that the law was constitutional because it was a remedy for discrimination.

Second, the Court held that Congress could find that the literacy test denied equal protection, even though this was contrary to the Court's earlier holding in *Lassiter.* This aspect of the ruling is much more significant because it accords Congress the authority to define the meaning of the Fourteenth Amendment.

A specific issue before the Supreme Court was whether Congress was limited to remedying what the Court had found to violate the Constitution or whether Congress could independently interpret the Constitution. The State of New York argued the former position that Congress could not use its §5 power to independently determine the meaning of the Fourteenth Amendment, but rather could only provide remedies for practices that the Court had deemed unconstitutional.[38]

The Court rejected this approach and spoke broadly of Congress's powers under §5 and expressly rejected the view that the legislative power is confined "to the insignificant role of abrogating only those state laws that the judicial branch was prepared to adjudge unconstitutional."[39] The Court explained that "[b]y including §5 the draftsmen sought to grant to Congress, by a specific provision applicable to the Fourteenth Amendment, the same broad powers expressed in the Necessary and Proper Clause."[40]

A concern raised by the dissent was that if Congress can use its power under §5 to interpret the Constitution, it conceivably could use this authority to dilute or even negate constitutional rights.[41] In a footnote, Justice Brennan, the author of the majority opinion, responded to this concern: "Contrary to the suggestion of the dissent, §5 does not grant Congress power to exercise discretion in the other direction and to enact 'statutes so as in effect to dilute equal protection and due

---

[36] 384 U.S. at 646-647.

[37] *Id.* at 652-653.

[38] This also was the position taken by Justice Harlan in a dissenting opinion joined by Justice Stewart. Justice Harlan wrote: "When recognized state violations of federal constitutional standards have occurred, Congress is of course empowered by §5 to take appropriate remedial measures to redress and prevent the wrongs. But it is a judicial question whether the condition with which Congress has thus sought to deal is in truth an infringement of the Constitution, something that is the necessary prerequisite to bringing the §5 power into play at all." 384 U.S. at 666 (Harlan, J., dissenting).

[39] *Id.* at 649.

[40] *Id.* at 650.

[41] In *Equal Employment Opportunity Commission v. Wyoming,* 460 U.S. 226, 260 (1983) (Burger, C.J., dissenting), four Justices in dissent argued that Congress could not use its power under §5 to interpret the Constitution. The issue in the case was whether the application of the Age Discrimination in Employment Act to state and local governments violated the Tenth Amendment. The majority rejected this argument, and the dissent both disagreed as to that and also contended that Congress lacked the power under §5 to legislate against age discrimination because the Supreme Court had not found such discrimination to violate the Fourteenth Amendment.

process decisions of this Court.' We emphasize that Congress's power under §5 is limited to adopting measures to enforce the guarantees of the Amendment; §5 grants Congress no power to restrict, abrogate, or dilute these guarantees."[42]

The Federalist Perspective of §5: *City of Boerne v. Flores*

Justice Brennan's majority opinion in *Katzenbach v. Morgan* thus appears to adopt a nationalist perspective according Congress the power to use its §5 authority to expand the scope of rights.[43] But in 1997, in *City of Boerne v. Flores*, the Court expressly rejected this view and shifted to the federalist perspective that Congress may not use its §5 powers to expand the scope of rights or to create new rights.

In *City of Boerne v. Flores*, the Supreme Court, in a 6-to-3 decision, declared the Religious Freedom Restoration Act (RFRA) unconstitutional as exceeding the scope of Congress's §5 powers.[44] The Act was adopted in 1993 to overturn a recent Supreme Court decision that had narrowly interpreted the free exercise clause of the First Amendment. In *Employment Div., Dept. of Human Resources of Oregon v. Smith*, in 1990, the Supreme Court significantly lessened the protections of the free exercise clause.[45] Oregon law prohibited the consumption of peyote, a hallucinogenic substance. Native Americans challenged this law, claiming that it infringed free exercise of religion because their religious rituals required the use of peyote. Under prior Supreme Court precedents, government actions burdening religion would be upheld only if they are necessary to achieve a compelling government purpose.[46] The Supreme Court, in *Smith*, changed the law and held that the free exercise clause cannot be used to challenge neutral laws of general applicability. The Oregon law prohibiting consumption of peyote was deemed neutral because it was not motivated by a desire to interfere with religion and it was a law of general applicability because it applied to everyone.

In response to this decision, in 1993, Congress overwhelmingly adopted the Religious Freedom Restoration Act, which was signed into law by President Clinton. The Religious Freedom Restoration Act was express in stating that its goal was to overturn *Smith* and restore the test that was followed before that decision.

---

[42] 384 U.S. at 651 n.10. Certainly, if this approach were followed, there could be questions as to what is an expansion of rights as opposed to a dilution. Often laws help some and hurt others and thus can be characterized as either an expansion or a contraction of rights depending on the perspective. For example, conservatives proposed that Congress use its power under §5 to declare that the word "person" in the Fourteenth Amendment means fetuses from the moment of conception. Under Justice Brennan's theory, would this be unconstitutional as a dilution of the right of women to obtain an abortion or would it be constitutional as an enlargement of the rights of fetuses? Another illustration would be affirmative action; is it constitutional as enlarging the rights and opportunities of minorities or is it unconstitutional as diluting the rights and opportunities of whites?

[43] For an excellent discussion of this decision, *see* William Cohen, Congressional Power to Interpret Due Process and Equal Protection, 27 Stan. L. Rev. 603, 606 (1975); Stephen Carter, The Morgan Power and the Forced Reconsideration of Constitutional Decisions, 53 U. Chi. L. Rev. 819, 824 (1986).

[44] 42 U.S.C. §2000bb.

[45] 494 U.S. 872 (1990). Employment Division v. Smith is discussed in detail in §12.3.2.

[46] *See, e.g.*, Sherbert v. Verner, 374 U.S. 398 (1963).

The Act requires courts considering free exercise challenges, including to neutral laws of general applicability, to uphold the government's actions only if they are necessary to achieve a compelling purpose. Specifically, RFRA prohibited "[g]overnment" from "substantially burden[ing]" a person's exercise of religion even if the burden results from a rule of general applicability unless the government can demonstrate the burden "(1) is in furtherance of a compelling governmental interest; and (2) is the least restrictive means of furthering that compelling governmental interest."[47]

City of Boerne v. Flores involved a church in Texas that was prevented from constructing a new facility because its building was classified a historic landmark. The church sued under the Religious Freedom Restoration Act, and the city challenged the constitutionality of the law. Justice Kennedy, writing for the Court, held that the Act is unconstitutional. The Court held that Congress under §5 of the Fourteenth Amendment may not create new rights or expand the scope of rights; rather Congress is limited to laws that prevent or remedy violations of rights recognized by the Supreme Court, and these must be narrowly tailored—"proportionate" and "congruent"—to the constitutional violation.[48]

Justice Kennedy explained that §5 gives Congress the power to enact laws "to enforce" the provisions of the Fourteenth Amendment. He stated: "Legislation which alters the meaning of the Free Exercise Clause cannot be said to be enforcing the Clause. Congress does not enforce a constitutional right by changing what the right is. It has been given the power 'to enforce,' not the power to determine what constitutes a constitutional violation. Were it not so, what Congress would be enforcing would no longer be, in any meaningful sense, the 'provisions of [the Fourteenth Amendment].' "[49]

Congress thus is limited to enacting laws that prevent or remedy violations of rights already recognized by the Supreme Court. Moreover, the Court said that "[t]here must be a congruence and proportionality between the injury to be prevented or remedied and the means adopted to that end."[50]

Justice Kennedy defended this conclusion by invoking the need to preserve the Court as the authoritative interpreter of the Constitution. Justice Kennedy quoted *Marbury v. Madison* and wrote: "If Congress could define its own powers by altering the Fourteenth Amendment's meaning, no longer would the Constitution be 'superior paramount law unchangeable by ordinary means.' It would be 'on a level with ordinary legislative acts, and like other acts, . . . alterable when the legislature shall please to alter it.' "[51] Justice Kennedy concluded this part of the majority opinion by declaring: "Shifting legislative majorities could change the Constitution and effectively circumvent the difficult and detailed amendment process contained in Article V."[52]

---

[47] 42 U.S.C. §2000bb-l.
[48] 521 U.S. at 519-520.
[49] *Id.* at 519.
[50] *Id.* at 520.
[51] *Id.* at 529, quoting Marbury v. Madison, 5 U.S. (1 Cranch) 137, 177 (1803).
[52] *Id.* at 529.

Justice Kennedy's majority opinion then declared RFRA unconstitutional on the grounds that it impermissibly expanded the scope of rights and that it was not proportionate or congruent as a preventive or remedial measure. He wrote: "RFRA is not so confined. Sweeping coverage ensures its intrusion at every level of government, displacing laws and prohibiting official actions of almost every description and regardless of subject matter. . . . Any law is subject to challenge at any time by any individual who alleges a substantial burden on his or her free exercise of religion. The reach and scope of RFRA distinguish it from other measures passed under Congress' enforcement power, even in the area of voting rights. The stringent test RFRA demands of state laws reflects a lack of proportionality or congruence between the means adopted and the legitimate end to be achieved."[53] RFRA prohibits much that would not violate the Constitution and thus was deemed to exceed the scope of Congress's §5 powers.

Although three Justices—O'Connor, Souter, and Breyer—dissented, none challenged Justice Kennedy's narrow view of Congress's powers under §5 of the Fourteenth Amendment. Rather, all three focused on the need for the Court to reconsider *Employment Division v. Smith*, which had narrowly interpreted the free exercise clause and prompted RFRA. Justice O'Connor, joined by Justice Breyer, declared: "I remain of the view that *Smith* was wrongly decided, and I would use this case to reexamine the Court's holding there."[54] Justice Souter, in a dissenting opinion, likewise urged the reconsideration of *Smith*.

Is *City of Boerne v. Flores* a desirable interpretation of Congress's §5 powers? On the one hand, it has the virtue of protecting the Supreme Court's role as the authoritative interpreter of the Constitution. The Court alone determines the meaning of substantive constitutional provisions; Congress is limited to enacting laws to enforce these rights. This avoids the risk expressed by Justice Harlan in his dissent in *Katzenbach v. Morgan* that Congress might try to use §5 to dilute or negate constitutional rights. Moreover, the narrow definition of Congress's §5 powers, like the recent restrictive interpretation of the commerce power, is consistent with the basic constitutional premise of a federal government with limited legislative authority and most governance left to the states.

On the other hand, *City of Boerne*'s restrictive interpretation can be criticized for denying Congress the power to expand the scope of rights. The Constitution's protection of rights long has been understood as the floor, the minimum liberties possessed by all individuals. The Ninth Amendment provides clear textual support for this view in its declaration: "The enumeration in the Constitution, of certain rights, shall not be construed to deny or disparage others retained by the people." The Ninth Amendment is a clear and open invitation for government to provide more rights than the Constitution accords. If the Court reads the Constitution to not include a right, Congress or the states may act to create and protect that right. In other words, the Court's interpretive judgment that a particular right is not *constitutionally* protected is in no way incompatible with a legislature's *statutory* recognition and safeguarding of the liberty.

---

[53] *Id.* at 532.
[54] *Id.* at 544-545 (O'Connor, J., dissenting).

Critics of *Boerne* also argue that Justice Kennedy begs the key question of what "enforce" means in §5 of the Fourteenth Amendment. One dictionary defines "enforce" as: "Urge, press home (argument, demand); impose (action, conduct upon person); compel observance of."[55] Another dictionary defines "enforce" as: "1. to give force to: strengthen; 2. to urge with energy; 3. constrain, compel; 4. to effect or gain by force; 5. to execute vigorously."[56] From the perspective of these definitions, Congress very much is "enforcing" the Fourteenth Amendment when it expands the scope of liberty under the due process clause or increases the protections of equal protection. In this sense, congressional expansion of rights is enforcing by strengthening the Fourteenth Amendment.

Justice Kennedy's use of *Marbury v. Madison* also can be questioned. He equates a Supreme Court decision failing to find a right in the Constitution with the conclusion that no right can be created by Congress. The former, however, in no way entails or implies the latter. The Court's conclusion that a particular right does not exist in the Constitution does not mean that the right cannot exist through other legal sources, such as federal or state legislation. Critics of *Boerne* contend that this is what RFRA did: The Court in *Smith* had decided that there was no constitutional right of individuals to have an exemption from neutral laws of general applicability that burden religion. Congress in RFRA created a statutory right that protects individuals from such laws, except in cases in which the government can meet strict scrutiny.

Thus, the debate over the proper interpretation of §5 involves arguments over the meaning of the Constitution's text, the intent of the Fourteenth Amendment's drafters, and basic policy questions concerning separation of powers, federalism, and individual rights.[57] The Warren Court of the 1960s, which was concerned with upholding federal civil rights laws and generally expanding the scope of individual rights, broadly defined Congress's §5 powers. The Rehnquist Court, which was concerned with limiting federal powers, narrowly interpreted this authority. So far, the Roberts Court, too, has narrowly interpreted Congress's powers under the post–Civil War amendments. Perhaps in the future the Court will shift back to the former view as it has shifted between broad and narrow definitions of Congress's commerce power over the course of American history.

Since *City of Boerne v. Flores*, there have been many Supreme Court decisions concerning the scope of Congress's powers under §5 of the Fourteenth Amendment. Almost all have been in the context of deciding whether a law fits under this authority so that it can be used to sue state governments. As discussed in detail in Chapter 2 (§2.10), the Supreme Court has held that Congress may authorize suits against state governments in laws enacted under §5, but not in statutes adopted

---

[55] The Concise Oxford Dictionary of Current English 375 (1929).

[56] Webster's Seventh New Collegiate Dictionary 275 (1965).

[57] Many excellent articles have been written discussing the scope of Congress's §5 powers in light of these decisions. *See, e.g.,* Evan H. Caminker, "Appropriate" Means-Ends Constraints on Section 5 Powers, 53 Stan. L. Rev. 1127 (2001); Robert C. Post & Reva B. Siegel, Protecting the Constitution from the People: Juricentric Restrictions on Section 5 Power, 78 Ind. L.J. 1 (2003); Ernest A. Young, Is the Sky Falling on the Federal Government? State Sovereign Immunity, the Section Five Power, and the Federal Balance, 81 Tex. L. Rev. 1551 (2003).

under other congressional powers.[58] Thus, to date, the application of *City of Boerne* and the elaboration of Congress's powers under §5 has come when the Court has considered whether a particular law can be used to sue state governments.

In the first three cases after *City of Boerne v. Flores*—*Florida Prepaid Postsecondary Education Expense Board v. College Savings Bank*,[59] *Kimel v. Florida Board of Regents*,[60] and *University of Alabama v. Garrett*,[61] the Supreme Court reaffirmed that Congress under §5 cannot expand the scope of rights and that any federal law must be a "proportionate" and "congruent" measure to prevent and remedy constitutional violations. All three cases involved the issue of whether a federal law was a valid exercise of Congress's §5 powers and thus a permissible basis for suing state governments in light of the Court's holding that Congress may authorize suits against states when acting under §5 of the Fourteenth Amendment. In all three cases, the Court found that the federal laws at issue did not fit within the scope of §5 under *City of Boerne v. Flores*. In *Nevada Department of Human Resources v. Hibbs*[62] and *Tennessee v. Lane*,[63] the Court held that the statutes were within the scope of Congress's §5 powers because they concerned claims that would receive heightened judicial scrutiny. In *United States v. Georgia*,[64] the Court held that Congress may authorize suits against states for their unconstitutional acts and thus may be sued under Title II of the Americans with Disabilities Act (ADA) for conduct that also violates the Constitution.

The principle that has emerged is that Congress can authorize suits against states for unconstitutional actions and also has much broader authority to legislate if it is a type of discrimination or a right that receives heightened scrutiny. But if it is a type of discrimination or a claim that receives only rational basis review, Congress's ability to legislate under §5 is very narrow.

These six cases are presented in detail in the next section, which discusses Congress's power to authorize suits against state governments.

The Fifteenth Amendment

The same basic issue arises with regard to the Fifteenth Amendment: May Congress act only to remedy constitutional violations, or may Congress use this authority to interpret the Fifteenth Amendment and even adopt interpretations contrary to that of the Supreme Court? In *South Carolina v. Katzenbach*, the Supreme Court upheld the constitutionality of the Voting Rights Act of 1965.[65] The Voting Rights Act empowered the attorney general to suspend literacy tests and other restrictions on voting in those states where less than 50 percent of the citizens had voted or were registered to vote. In addition, once these findings were made, the

---

[58] Seminole Tribe v. Florida, 517 U.S. 44 (1996), discussed in §2.10.
[59] 527 U.S. 627 (1999).
[60] 528 U.S. 62 (2000).
[61] 531 U.S. 356 (2001).
[62] 538 U.S. 721 (2003).
[63] 541 U.S. 509 (2004).
[64] 546 U.S. 151 (2006).
[65] 383 U.S. 301 (1966).

state could not adopt any new standards with regard to voting without obtaining preclearance from the attorney general.

The Court upheld the constitutionality of the Voting Rights Act of 1965 as an exercise of Congress's power under §2 of the Fifteenth Amendment. Although the Court spoke broadly of Congress's authority, it emphasized that the provisions of the Voting Rights Act were a remedy for proven violations of the Fifteenth Amendment.

In *City of Rome v. United States*, the Court went even further and suggested that Congress has the authority under §2 to interpret the meaning of the Fifteenth Amendment.[66] *Rome* involved a challenge to changes that a city adopted after the Voting Rights Act was enacted in 1965. Specifically, the city had annexed a substantial number of outlying areas and thus altered the racial composition of its electorate and also had adopted an at-large system for selecting city commissioners. The federal district court found no evidence that these changes were motivated by a discriminatory purpose. Also, on the same day *Rome* was decided, the Court held in *City of Mobile v. Bolden* that at-large election systems are constitutional unless there is proof of a discriminatory purpose.[67] Therefore, the City of Rome's actions did not appear to be in violation of the Fourteenth or Fifteenth Amendments.

Nonetheless, the Supreme Court ruled against the city based on the Voting Rights Act. Although *City of Mobile v. Bolden* held that proof of a discriminatory intent was a prerequisite to finding a constitutional violation, the Court in *City of Rome* concluded that Congress could "prohibit changes that have a discriminatory impact."[68] *City of Rome* can be read narrowly or broadly. The narrow reading sees it as simply approving a remedy for violations of voting rights; allowing proof of discriminatory impact to show a violation of the Act was meant as a remedy for a proven history of the denial of voting rights. The broad reading sees it as authorizing Congress independently to interpret the meaning of the Fifteenth Amendment and even to adopt a view contrary to that of the Supreme Court. The Court had said that discriminatory impact was insufficient to show a violation of the Fourteenth Amendment, but the Court upheld a statute allowing discriminatory impact to suffice to establish liability.

Shelby County, Alabama v. Holder

In *Shelby County v. Holder*, the Court again considered the constitutionality of key provisions of the Voting Rights Act, but unlike in the prior decisions, this time the Court declared aspects of the law unconstitutional.[69] Section 2 of the Voting

---

[66] 446 U.S. 156 (1980).

[67] 446 U.S. 55 (1980). *Mobile* is discussed in detail in §9.3.3.2.

[68] 446 U.S. at 177.

[69] 133 S. Ct. 2612 (2013). Earlier, in *Northwest Austin Municipal Utility District v. Holder*, the Court had before it a constitutional challenge to these provisions of the Voting Rights Act and said that the "Act's preclearance requirements and its coverage formula raise serious constitutional questions." 557 U.S. 193, 203 (2009). But the Court avoided the question of whether Congress had the constitutional power to extend §5 of the Voting Rights Act by interpreting the law to allow local governments to "bail out" of the Act's requirements by showing that they had not engaged in recent race discrimination.

Rights Act prohibits state and local governments from having election practices or systems that have a discriminatory effect against minority voters. Lawsuits can be brought to enforce it. But Congress believed that this was not sufficient to stop discrimination in voting. Congress knew that litigation is expensive and time consuming. Congress also knew that Southern states especially had the practice of continually changing their voting systems to disenfranchise minority voters.

Section 5 of the Voting Rights Act provides that jurisdictions with a history of race discrimination in voting may change their election systems only if they get "preclearance" from the attorney general or a three-judge federal district court. Section 4(B) of the Act defines those jurisdictions that must get preclearance, nine states and many local governments with a history of race discrimination in voting.

Each time the law was about to expire, Congress extended it. In 1982, Congress held extensive hearings, modified the formula under §4(B) of the Act, and extended the provisions for another 25 years. As the law was set to expire in 2007, Congress held 21 hearings and produced a record that is over 15,000 pages. The Senate voted 98-0 to extend the law for another 25 years and there were only 33 no votes in the House of Representatives. President George W. Bush signed the extension into law.

In *Shelby County, Alabama v. Holder*, the Court, 5 to 4, held §4(B) unconstitutional and thereby also effectively nullified §5 because it applies only to jurisdictions covered under §4(B).[70] It is the first time since the nineteenth century that the Court declared unconstitutional a federal civil rights statute. Chief Justice Roberts wrote for the Court and stressed that the formula in §4(B), last modified in 1982, rests on data from the 1960s and the 1970s and that race discrimination in voting has changed since then. The Court declared: "Nearly 50 years later, things have changed dramatically. Shelby County contends that the preclearance requirement, even without regard to its disparate coverage, is now unconstitutional. Its arguments have a good deal of force. In the covered jurisdictions, '[v]oter turnout and registration rates now approach parity. Blatantly discriminatory evasions of federal decrees are rare. And minority candidates hold office at unprecedented levels.' The tests and devices that blocked access to the ballot have been forbidden nationwide for over 40 years."[71] Thus, "[c]overage today is based on decades-old data and eradicated practices."[72]

The Court stressed the intrusion on the covered states as they could not exercise the power to choose how to hold elections, but instead the "States must beseech the Federal Government for permission to implement laws that they would otherwise have the right to enact and execute on their own, subject of course to

---

The Court thus did not rule on the constitutionality of §5 or construe the scope Congress's power to enact laws under §2 of the Fifteenth Amendment.

[70] There is the possibility that a federal court under §3 of the Voting Rights Act could impose a preclearance requirement on a jurisdiction by finding that it has intentionally discriminated against minority voters. This has not happened yet.

[71] 133 S. Ct. at 2625 (citations omitted).

[72] *Id.* at 2627.

any injunction in a §2 action."[73] The Court also emphasized that §§4(B) and 5, by requiring only some states to get preclearance, violated the principle of equal state sovereignty. The Court stated: "Not only do States retain sovereignty under the Constitution, there is also a 'fundamental principle of *equal* sovereignty' among the States. . . . [D]espite the tradition of equal sovereignty, the Act applies to only nine States (and several additional counties)."[74]

Justice Ginsburg wrote a dissent joined by Justices Breyer, Sotomayor, and Kagan. The dissent stressed that race discrimination in voting remains and was documented by Congress. The dissent argued that the Court should be deferential to this judgment and the exercise of power by Congress. Justice Ginsburg stated: "In the Court's view, the very success of §5 of the Voting Rights Act demands its dormancy. Congress was of another mind. Recognizing that large progress has been made, Congress determined, based on a voluminous record, that the scourge of discrimination was not yet extirpated. The question this case presents is who decides whether, as currently operative, §5 remains justifiable, this Court, or a Congress charged with the obligation to enforce the post-Civil War Amendments 'by appropriate legislation.' With overwhelming support in both Houses, Congress concluded that, for two prime reasons, §5 should continue in force, unabated. First, continuance would facilitate completion of the impressive gains thus far made; and second, continuance would guard against backsliding. Those assessments were well within Congress' province to make and should elicit this Court's unstinting approbation."[75]

The majority and the dissent in *Shelby County* disagree over basic issues: how significant is the problem of race discrimination in voting today; how much of an intrusion is preclearance on the states and how much should that matter; how much deference is due Congress when it legislates under §5 of the Fourteenth Amendment and §2 of the Fifteenth Amendment? In assessing Chief Justice Roberts's opinion, it is important to note that he does not invoke the test from *City of Boerne v. Flores*, in terms of the scope of Congress's power. Rather, the Court finds that §4(B) of the Voting Rights Act is unconstitutional because it fails to treat all the states the same—what the Court terms the principle of "equal sovereignty." But the text of the Constitution obviously mentions no such principle and the Congress that ratified the Fourteenth and Fifteenth Amendments did not believe in this as it imposed Reconstruction on the South. Countless federal laws treat some states differently from others.[76]

In theory, Congress can enact a new version of §4(B) based on contemporary data. In reality, it is hard to imagine Congress being able to ever agree on a new formula to require that some of their jurisdictions get preclearance. Moreover, it would seem that any formula that treats some states differently from others would violate the Court's principle of equal state sovereignty.

---

[73] *Id.* at 2624.

[74] *Id.* at 2623-2624.

[75] *Id.* at 2632-2633 (Ginsburg, J., dissenting).

[76] *Id.* at 2649 (Ginsburg, J., dissenting). Justice Ginsburg gave several examples of federal laws that treat some states differently from others.

§3.8 CONGRESS'S POWER TO AUTHORIZE SUITS AGAINST STATE GOVERNMENTS

The Eleventh Amendment and Congress's Power to Override It

The Eleventh Amendment states: "The Judicial power of the United States shall not be construed to extend to any suit in law or equity, commenced or prosecuted against one of the United States by Citizens of another State, or by Citizens or Subjects of any foreign state." The Supreme Court long has interpreted this provision as barring suits against state governments without their consent both by their own citizens and by citizens of other states.[1]

In *Fitzpatrick v. Bitzer*, the Court ruled that Congress could authorize suits against state governments if it acts pursuant to §5 of the Fourteenth Amendment.[2] In *Fitzpatrick*, the Court held that state governments may be sued for violating Title VII of the 1964 Civil Rights Act, which prevents employment discrimination based on race, gender, and religion.[3] The Court, in an opinion by then-Justice Rehnquist, explained that the Fourteenth Amendment followed the Eleventh Amendment and thus can modify it. More importantly, the Court said that the Fourteenth Amendment was intended as a limit on state power. Justice Rehnquist explained: "When Congress acts pursuant to §5, not only is it exercising legislative authority that is plenary within the terms of the constitutional grant, it is exercising that authority under one section of a constitutional Amendment whose other sections by their own terms embody limitations on state authority. We think that Congress may, in determining what is 'appropriate legislation' for the purpose of enforcing the provisions of the Fourteenth Amendment, provide for private suits against States or state officials which are constitutionally impermissible in other contexts."[4]

In *Pennsylvania v. Union Gas Co.*, in 1989, the Supreme Court held, 5 to 4, that Congress may override the Eleventh Amendment and authorize suits against state governments pursuant to any of its constitutional powers, so long as the law in its text expressly authorizes such suits.[5] In this case, the Court ruled that state governments could be sued pursuant to a federal environmental law, CERCLA, because Congress was clear in acting under the commerce clause in authorizing suits against state governments.

Seven years later, in *Seminole Tribe v. Florida*,[6] the Supreme Court expressly overturned *Pennsylvania v. Union Gas*. The simple reality is that between 1989, when *Union Gas* was decided, and 1996, when *Seminole Tribe* was decided, there was a significant change in the composition of the Supreme Court. Four of the Justices

---

§3.8 [1] Hans v. Louisiana, 134 U.S. 1 (1890). The Eleventh Amendment and sovereign immunity are discussed in detail in §2.10.

[2] 427 U.S. 445 (1976).

[3] 42 U.S.C. §2000e.

[4] 427 U.S. at 456.

[5] 491 U.S. 1 (1989).

[6] 517 U.S. 44 (1996).

in majority in *Pennsylvania v. Union Gas* had left the Court: Justices Brennan, Marshall, Blackmun, and White. All four of the dissenters in *Pennsylvania v. Union Gas* remained on the Court. They were joined by Justice Clarence Thomas and overruled *Pennsylvania v. Union Gas* by a 5-to-4 margin.

Chief Justice Rehnquist wrote for the Court and stressed that *Pennsylvania v. Union Gas* is an unprecedented expansion in Congress's power to authorize suits against state governments. He explained:

> Even when the Constitution vests in Congress complete law-making authority over a particular area, the Eleventh Amendment prevents congressional authorization of suits by private parties against unconsenting States. The Eleventh Amendment restricts the judicial power under Article III, and Article I cannot be used to circumvent the constitutional limitations placed upon federal jurisdiction.[7]

The Court held that Congress only can authorize suits against state governments, and override the Eleventh Amendment, when it acts pursuant to §5 of the Fourteenth Amendment.[8]

A year after *Seminole Tribe*, the Court decided *City of Boerne v. Flores* and narrowed the scope of Congress's §5 powers. There is an obvious and crucial interrelationship of these two cases: In deciding whether a state can be sued under a federal statute, the court must decide whether the law is a valid exercise of Congress's §5 powers. If the Court upholds the law as permissible under §5, the state may be sued; otherwise the litigation cannot go forward against the state government. Five times so far the Court has considered whether a law is a valid exercise of power under Congress's §5 authority and whether the law can be used to sue a state government. In the first three cases — *Florida Prepaid Postsecondary Education Expense Board v. College Savings Bank*,[9] *Kimel v. Florida Board of Regents*,[10] and *University of Alabama v. Garrett*,[11] the Court applied *City of Boerne v. Flores* and found the law invalid as an exercise of Congress's §5 powers and precluded the suit against the state government. But in the two most recent cases — *Nevada Department of Human Resources v. Hibbs*[12] and *Tennessee v. Lane*[13] — the Court found statutes to fit within Congress's §5 authority and allowed suits against the states. In *United States v. Georgia*, the Court held that Congress may authorize suits to remedy constitutional violations.[14] These cases are described below and followed by a consideration of the principle that emerges from them.[15]

---

[7] *Id.* at 72-73.

[8] For an excellent criticism of *Seminole Tribe, see* Laura S. Fitzgerald, Beyond *Marbury*: Jurisdictional Self-Dealing in *Seminole Tribe*, 52 Vand. L. Rev. 407 (1999); Vicki C. Jackson, *Seminole Tribe*, the Eleventh Amendment, and the Potential Evisceration of *Ex parte Young*, 72 N.Y.U. L. Rev. 495 (1997).

[9] 527 U.S. 627 (1999).

[10] 528 U.S. 62 (2000).

[11] 531 U.S. 356 (2001).

[12] 538 U.S. 721 (2003).

[13] 541 U.S. 509 (2004).

[14] 546 U.S. 151 (2006).

[15] Also, in Sossamon v. Texas, 131 S. Ct. 1651 (2011), the Court held that a state could not be sued for money damages under the Religious Land Use and Institutionalized Persons Act, which

Florida Prepaid Postsecondary Expense Education
Board v. College Savings Bank

College Savings Bank, a New Jersey company, devised a system, which it patented, for students to use to save money to later pay for their college education. Florida Prepaid, an agency of the Florida government, copied this system for use by Florida residents to save money to attend Florida schools. College Savings Bank sued Florida Prepaid for, among other things,[16] patent infringement.

In 1992, Congress expressly amended the patent laws to authorize suits against state governments for patent infringement.[17] The Supreme Court, however, held that the law was not a valid exercise of power under §5 of the Fourteenth Amendment and thus could not be used to sue the state government. Although patents unquestionably are property and the Fourteenth Amendment protects property from being deprived by state governments without due process, the Court found that the authorization of suits was impermissible because it was not "proportionate" or "congruent" to remedy constitutional violations.

Chief Justice Rehnquist, writing for the Court, stated: "In enacting the Patent Remedy Act, however, Congress identified no pattern of patent infringement by the States, let alone a pattern of constitutional violations. Unlike the undisputed record of racial discrimination confronting Congress in the voting rights cases, Congress came up with little evidence of infringing conduct on the part of the States."[18] The Court held that the law was not valid under §5 because "[t]he legislative record thus suggests that the Patent Remedy Act does not respond to a history of 'widespread and persisting deprivation of constitutional rights' of the sort Congress has faced in enacting proper prophylactic §5 legislation."[19]

Florida Prepaid follows from *Seminole Tribe* and *City of Boerne*. The Court reaffirmed that Congress can authorize suits against states only pursuant to §5, and it concluded, based on *City of Boerne*, that the law authorizing suits for patent infringement did not fit within this power. However, what is striking about *Florida Prepaid* is that it involved patent law, an area in which federal courts have exclusive jurisdiction. Barring patent infringement suits against state governments in federal court means that a state government can infringe patents without ever facing a lawsuit.[20]

---

allows "appropriate relief against a government." The Court said that this was not sufficiently specific in authorizing money damages to overcome sovereign immunity. This part of the Act was adopted under Congress's spending power, not under its power under §5 of the Fourteenth Amendment.

[16] College Savings Bank also sued for a violation of the Lanham Act, but the Supreme Court, in a separate opinion, also found that this was barred by sovereign immunity. College Sav. Bank v. Florida Prepaid Postsecondary Expense Educ. Bd., 527 U.S. 666 (1999).

[17] 35 U.S.C. §271.

[18] 527 U.S. at 640.

[19] *Id.*

[20] Although the state government cannot be sued, the state official may be sued. Ex parte Young, 209 U.S. 123 (1908). Thus, the state official may be sued for an injunction to stop future infringements, but the state government may not be sued for damages.

Kimel v. Florida Board of Regents

Several cases were consolidated in *Kimel v. Florida Board of Regents*.[21] The named case involved a suit by current and former faculty and librarians at Florida State University, including Daniel Kimel, Jr. They alleged that the university's failure to provide promised pay adjustments discriminated against older workers and thus violated the ADEA. A companion case was brought by Wellington Dickson, an employee of the Florida Department of Corrections, who claimed that he was denied promotions because of his age. Another of the consolidated cases involved faculty members at a state university in Alabama who claimed age discrimination.

The Supreme Court held that all of these claims against state agencies are barred by the Eleventh Amendment. By a 7-to-2 margin, with only Kennedy and Thomas dissenting, the Court concluded that the ADEA is an express authorization of suit against the states. The Court then ruled 5 to 4 that the ADEA is not a valid exercise of Congress's power under §5 and that therefore it cannot be used to sue state governments.

Justice O'Connor wrote the majority opinion and was joined by Chief Justice Rehnquist and Justices Scalia, Kennedy, and Thomas. The Court concluded that the burdens the ADEA imposes on state and local governments are disproportionate to any unconstitutional behavior that might exist. The Court emphasized that under prior decisions, only rational basis review is used for age discrimination.[22] The Court explained that there is not a "history of purposeful discrimination" based on age and that "age also does not define a discrete and insular minority because all persons, if they live out their normal life spans," will experience it.[23] Indeed, the Court said that states "may discriminate based on age without offending the Fourteenth Amendment if the age classification is rationally related to a legitimate state interest."[24] The Court said that age often is a relevant criteria for employers.

Therefore, the Court concluded that the broad prohibition of age discrimination in the ADEA was deemed to exceed the scope of Congress's power. The Court declared: "Judged against the backdrop of our equal protection jurisprudence, it is clear that the ADEA is so out of proportion to a supposed remedial core preventive object that it cannot be understood as responsive to, or designed to prevent, unconstitutional behavior."[25]

The Court stressed that the ADEA prohibits a great deal of conduct that is otherwise constitutional. The Court also emphasized that there were not "findings" by Congress of substantial age discrimination by state governments. Therefore, the Court stated that because of "the lack of evidence of widespread and unconstitutional age discrimination by the States, we hold that the ADEA is not a valid exercise of power under section 5 of the Fourteenth Amendment."

---

[21] 528 U.S. 62 (2000).

[22] *See, e.g.*, Vance v. Bradley, 440 U.S. 93 (1979); Massachusetts Bd. of Retirement v. Murgia, 427 U.S. 307 (1976).

[23] 528 U.S. at 83.

[24] *Id.*

[25] *Id.* at 86.

Where does this leave state employees who are victims of age discrimination? Justice O'Connor concludes the majority opinion by saying that their recourse is under state law in state courts. She states: "Our decision does not signal the end of the line for employees who find themselves subject to age discrimination at the hands of state employers. . . . State employees are protected by state age discrimination statutes, and may recover money damages from their state employers, in almost every State of the Union. Those avenues of relief remain available today, just as they were before the decision."[26] State courts and state law are the only recourse for an attorney seeking redress for a state employee who has suffered age discrimination.

University of Alabama v. Garrett

In *University of Alabama v. Garrett,*[27] the Court considered whether state governments may be sued for violating Title I of the Americans with Disabilities Act, which prohibits employment discrimination against the disabled and requires reasonable accommodation for disabilities by employers. The plaintiffs' key argument to the Court was that the elaborate legislative history documenting government discrimination against the disabled made the Americans with Disabilities Act different from other laws the Court had considered in the last few years. The Supreme Court, in a 5-to-4 decision, rejected this argument and held that state governments may not be sued for violating Title I of the ADA.

Patricia Garrett was the director of nursing at the University of Alabama, Birmingham hospital. She was diagnosed with breast cancer and took time off work to have surgery, chemotherapy, and radiation. When she returned to work, she was informed that her position as director of nursing was no longer available. She sued under Title I of the ADA.

Chief Justice Rehnquist's majority opinion began by stating that the ADA was a substantial expansion of rights compared to the Constitution. He explained that under equal protection, discrimination based on disability only need meet a rational basis test, being rationally related to a legitimate government purpose.[28] The ADA prohibits much more than would fail a rational basis test, and its requirement for reasonable accommodation of disabilities is significantly greater than the Constitution requires.

The Court then concluded that Title I of the ADA is not "proportionate" or "congruent" to preventing and remedying constitutional violations. Chief Justice Rehnquist declared: "The legislative record of the ADA, however, simply fails to show that Congress did in fact identify a pattern of irrational state discrimination in employment against the disabled."[29] Justice Breyer attached a 39-page appendix to his dissenting opinion in which he listed the numerous references in the leg-

[26] *Id.* at 17.
[27] 531 U.S. 356 (2001).
[28] 531 U.S. at 366, citing City of Cleburne v. Cleburne Living Center, 473 U.S. 432 (1985).
[29] *Id.* at 965.

islative history to government discrimination against the disabled.[30] Chief Justice Rehnquist's majority opinion found these insufficient. He said that some were just anecdotes.[31] He said that most involved local governments, not state governments, and local governments are not protected by state sovereign immunity.[32] He said that some of the evidence concerns government discrimination against the disabled in providing services, and that is Title II, not Title I, of the ADA. He observed that "[i]n 1990, the States alone employed more than 4.5 million people. It is telling, we think, that given these large numbers, Congress assembled only such minimal evidence of unconstitutional state discrimination in employment against the disabled."[33]

Chief Justice Rehnquist contrasted the legislative record for the Voting Rights Act of 1965, which he said was in "stark" contrast to the ADA. He noted the statistical findings by Congress in enacting the Voting Rights Act, such as "an otherwise inexplicable 50-percentage-point gap in the registration of white and African-American voters in some States."[34] He concluded that the congressional findings for the ADA were insufficient in comparison. He wrote: "[I]n order to authorize private individuals to recover money damages against the States, there must be a pattern of discrimination by the States which violates the Fourteenth Amendment, and the remedy imposed by Congress must be congruent and proportional to the targeted violation. Those requirements are not met here, and to uphold the Act's application to the States would allow Congress to rewrite the Fourteenth Amendment law laid down by this Court in *Cleburne*. Section 5 does not so broadly enlarge congressional authority."[35]

Chief Justice Rehnquist, however, added a footnote to make clear that the Court was not declaring the ADA unconstitutional as applied to state governments, but rather only holding that state governments could not be sued by individuals for violations.[36] He explained that the federal government still could sue the states to enforce the law and that suits against individual government officers for injunctive relief were also permissible.[37] But damages actions against state governments are barred.

Nevada Department of Human Resources v. Hibbs

In contrast, in *Nevada Department of Human Resources v. Hibbs*,[38] the Supreme Court held that the family leave provision of the Family and Medical Leave Act (FMLA) fits within the scope of Congress's §5 powers and can be used to sue state governments. The FMLA requires that employers, including government employ-

---

[30] *Id.* at 389-390 (Breyer, J., dissenting).
[31] *Id.* at 370-371.
[32] *Id.*
[33] *Id.* at 370.
[34] *Id.* at 373.
[35] *Id.* at 374.
[36] *Id.* at 374 n.9.
[37] *Id.*
[38] 538 U.S. 721 (2003).

ers, provide their employees with unpaid leave time for family and medical care. The Supreme Court in *Hibbs*, by a 6-to-3 margin, held that the family leave provision is a valid congressional abrogation of state sovereign immunity.[39] Chief Justice Rehnquist, writing for the Court, stressed that the "FMLA aims to protect the right to be free from gender-based discrimination in the workplace."[40] The Court said that Congress, recognizing social realities, found that the absence of family leave policies disadvantaged women in the workplace. Although the FMLA is gender neutral in that it requires leaves be granted to both men and women, and Hibbs was male, the Court said that Congress clearly intended the law to prevent gender discrimination in employment.

Chief Justice Rehnquist distinguished *Kimel* and *Garrett* on the grounds that they involved types of discrimination that receive only rational basis review, whereas gender discrimination triggers intermediate scrutiny under equal protection. The Court explained: "Here, however, Congress directed its attention to state gender discrimination, which triggers a heightened level of scrutiny. Because the standard for demonstrating the constitutionality of a gender-based classification is more difficult to meet than our rational basis test, . . . it was easier for Congress to show a pattern of constitutional violations."[41]

Tennessee v. Lane

The Court followed and extended *Hibbs* in *Tennessee v. Lane*.[42] The case involved a criminal defendant who literally climbed on his hands and knees to get to a second-floor courtroom because it was not accessible to those with disabilities. He sued the state government pursuant to Title II of the Americans with Disabilities Act,[43] which prohibits state and local governments from discriminating against people with disabilities in government programs, services, and activities.

The Court, in a 5-to-4 decision, held that Lane's suit against the state was not barred by sovereign immunity. The Court, in an opinion by Justice Stevens, emphasized that there is a well-established fundamental right of access to the courts. The Court recognized that Congress has greater latitude to legislate under §5 when dealing with a claim that receives heightened judicial scrutiny, whether because it is a fundamental right or a type of discrimination that receives heightened scrutiny. *Tennessee v. Lane* does not address whether states can be sued under Title II when there is not a fundamental right that is implicated.

---

[39] For an excellent discussion of the issue presented in *Hibbs, see* Robert C. Post & Reva B. Siegel, Legislative Constitutionalism and Section Five Power: Policentric Interpretation of the Family and Medical Leave Act, 112 Yale L.J. 1943 (2003).

[40] 538 U.S. at 728.

[41] *Id.* at 736.

[42] 541 U.S. 509 (2004).

[43] 42 U.S.C. §12131.

United States v. Georgia

United States v. Georgia also involved Title II of the Americans with Disabilities Act, specifically a suit by a paraplegic prisoner.[44] The Court, in a unanimous opinion written by Justice Scalia, held that sovereign immunity did not bar the suit because the prisoner alleged violations of his constitutional rights under the Eighth Amendment. The Court explained: "Thus, insofar as Title II creates a private cause of action for damages against the States for conduct that *actually* violates the Fourteenth Amendment, Title II validly abrogates state sovereign immunity."[45]

United States v. Georgia thus holds that Congress may authorize suits against states pursuant to §5 of the Fourteenth Amendment for actions that actually violate the Fourteenth Amendment. *Hibbs* and *Lane* hold that for rights or types of discrimination that receive heightened scrutiny, Congress has much greater authority to permit suits against state governments than for claims that receive only rational basis review.

Coleman v. Court of Appeals of Maryland

The most recent case, *Coleman v. Court of Appeals of Maryland*, makes no new law in this area, though it is important in making clear that the four newest Justices—Roberts, Alito, Sotomayor, and Kagan—will vote in the same way as the Justices they replaced, meaning that the Court remains split 5-4 in favor of limiting Congress's ability to authorize suits against state and local governments.[46] Like *Hibbs*, *Coleman* involved a provision of the Family and Medical Leave Act, but in *Coleman* the provision was one that requires employers, including state employers, to grant 12 weeks of unpaid leave for self-care for a serious medical condition.[47]

Justice Kennedy wrote the plurality opinion, joined by Chief Justice Roberts and Justices Thomas and Alito. Justice Kennedy reiterated that Congress may abrogate a state's sovereign immunity only through legislation adopted under §5 of the Fourteenth Amendment. Justice Kennedy explained that "[w]hether a congressional Act passed under §5 can impose monetary liability upon States requires an assessment of both the 'evil' or 'wrong' that Congress intended to remedy, and the means Congress adopted to address that evil."[48] He explained that whereas *Hibbs* found that the family leave provision was meant to remedy sex discrimination, and thus fit within Congress's §5 power, "[t]he same cannot be said for requiring the States to give all employees the opportunity to take self-care leave. . . . Without widespread evidence of sex discrimination or sex stereotyping

---

[44] 546 U.S. 151 (2006).
[45] *Id.* at 159.
[46] 132 S. Ct. 1327 (2012).
[47] The Family and Medical Leave Act of 1993, 107 Stat. 6, 29 U.S.C. §2601 *et seq.*
[48] 132 S. Ct. at 1333-1334.

in the administration of sick leave, it is apparent that the congressional purpose in enacting the self-care provision is unrelated to these supposed wrongs."[49]

Justice Scalia concurred in the judgment and again urged abandoning the test that has been followed since *City of Boerne v. Flores* for determining whether a law fits within Congress's §5 power. He wrote: "[O]utside of the context of racial discrimination (which is different for *stare decisis* reasons), I would limit Congress's §5 power to the regulation of conduct that *itself* violates the Fourteenth Amendment. Failing to grant state employees leave for the purpose of self-care—or any other purpose, for that matter—does not come close."[50]

Justice Ginsburg wrote for the four dissenters and saw this case as controlled by *Hibbs*. The dissent would have found that the self-care provision of the Family and Medical Leave Act "validly enforces the right to be free from gender discrimination in the workplace."[51] She explained: "The FMLA's purpose and legislative history reinforce the conclusion that the FMLA, in its entirety, is directed at sex discrimination. Indeed, the FMLA was originally envisioned as a way to guarantee—without singling out women or pregnancy—that pregnant women would not lose their jobs when they gave birth. The self-care provision achieves that aim."[52]

Future Implications

There are two key questions in appraising these recent decisions: Descriptively what are they likely to mean in terms of the ability to sue state governments to enforce other federal civil rights laws; and normatively are they desirable in their protection of state sovereign immunity and in the distinctions drawn as to when state governments may be sued?

Descriptively, the law seems to be that if it is a claim that receives heightened scrutiny, based on the type of discrimination or the presence of a fundamental right, Congress has broad authority to legislate. Indeed, based on *Hibbs*, there is no need for a congressional finding of pervasive constitutional violations when Congress is dealing with areas that receive heightened judicial scrutiny. In *Hibbs*, Congress never found any *unconstitutional* gender discrimination. On the other hand, if it is a claim that receives only rational basis review, then even an elaborate legislative record, as in *Garrett*, is unlikely to be enough to allow suits against state governments. Unless Congress finds pervasive unconstitutional state conduct, it cannot authorize suits against the states.

Normatively, there are questions as to whether the distinctions drawn in these cases are desirable and more generally whether Congress should be able to authorize suits against state governments. The Court offered little explanation as to why the level of scrutiny matters in determining the scope of Congress's powers under §5. Perhaps it is that in areas receiving heightened scrutiny there already are sufficient findings of historical violations such that there is no need for congressional

---

[49] *Id.* at 1334.
[50] *Id.* at 1338-1339 (Scalia, J., concurring in the judgment).
[51] *Id.* at 1339 (Ginsburg, J., dissenting).
[52] *Id.* at 1340.

documentation. But critics, including the dissenting Justices, argue that Congress's power under §5 is not altered by the level of scrutiny used by the courts.

Defenders of the Court's decisions in *Florida Prepaid, Kimel,* and *Garrett* contend that the rulings are an appropriate protection of state sovereign immunity and a proper limit on Congress's §5 powers.[53] They argue that sovereign immunity is an important aspect of the Constitution's protection of state governments and that Congress's power to authorize suits against state governments must be limited. As explained above in the discussion of *City of Boerne v. Flores,* its defenders argue that the decision properly interpreted §5 based on the text of the provision, its framers' intent, and the need to preserve the Supreme Court's role in determining the meaning of the Constitution.

But critics of these decisions disagree with their premise that sovereign immunity is an inherent part of the Constitution's design. Indeed, those objecting to the decisions contend that sovereign immunity is not authorized by the text of the Constitution,[54] and that such immunity undermines the basic constitutional principle of government accountability.[55] Critics also argue, as discussed above, that *City of Boerne* was wrongly decided and that Congress should have the authority under §5 to expand the scope of rights. The critics contend that all of these recent decisions are undue conservative judicial activism: The five most conservative Justices are striking down important federal laws based on principles nowhere found in the Constitution.

This debate is likely to continue for the foreseeable future as the federal courts continue to apply *City of Boerne* and *Seminole Tribe.* Ultimately, the disagreement is over basic constitutional principles concerning separation of powers, federalism, and the protection of individual rights under the Constitution. There also is the prospect of change in the near future because of the presence of two new Justices. *Hibbs* was a 6-to-3 decision, with Chief Justice Rehnquist and Justice O'Connor in the majority. *Lane* was a 5-to-4 ruling, with Justice O'Connor in the majority. The most recent case, *Coleman v. Court of Appeals of Maryland,* indicates that Chief Justice Roberts and Justice Alito will be with Justices Scalia, Kennedy, and Thomas in limiting Congress's ability to authorize suits against state governments, while Justices Sotomayor and Kagan will be with Justices Ginsburg and Breyer in wanting to allow suits against states under federal statutes.

---

[53] *See, e.g.,* James Eugene Fitzgerald, State Sovereign Immunity: Searching for Stability, 48 UCLA L. Rev. 1203 (2001); Alfred Hill, In Defense of Our Law of Sovereign Immunity, 42 B.C. L. Rev. 485 (2001); William J. Rich, Privileges or Immunities: The Missing Link in Establishing Congressional Power to Abrogate State Eleventh Amendment Immunity, 28 Hastings Const. L.Q. 235 (2001).

[54] The Eleventh Amendment's text only bars suits against state governments by citizens of other states or citizens of foreign countries. There is strong historical evidence that this was meant to preclude only suits based on diversity of citizenship against state governments. *See* William A. Fletcher, A Historical Interpretation of the Eleventh Amendment: A Narrow Construction of an Affirmative Grant of Jurisdiction Rather Than a Prohibition Against Jurisdiction, 35 Stan. L. Rev. 1033 (1983); John J. Gibbons, The Eleventh Amendment and State Sovereign Immunity: A Reinterpretation, 83 Colum. L. Rev. 1889 (1983).

[55] *See, e.g.,* Erwin Chemerinsky, Against Sovereign Immunity, 53 Stan. L. Rev. 1201 (2001).

§3.9 CONGRESS'S POWER TO INVESTIGATE

Broad Power to Investigate

The Supreme Court has recognized that Congress, as an inherent part of its legislative authority, has broad power to conduct investigations. In recent years, important and highly publicized congressional investigations have been conducted into the Watergate break-in and cover-up, the Iran-Contra affair, and, most recently, the Whitewater scandal.

The ability to gather information has been regarded as a predicate to effective legislation and as important to providing a legislative check on executive actions. The Supreme Court has explained that Congress thus may conduct "inquiries concerning the administration of existing laws as well as proposed or possibly needed statutes. It includes surveys of defects in our social, economic or political system for the purpose of enabling the Congress to remedy them."[1] The power to investigate also includes "probes into departments of the Federal Government to expose corruption, inefficiency, or waste."[2]

Contempt Power

The authority to investigate necessarily requires the power to compel testimony. Thus, the Supreme Court has recognized that Congress has the power to hold in contempt those who refuse to answer congressional inquiries. In *McGrain v. Daugherty*, the Court held that Congress could hold in contempt and order the arrest of a witness who refused to answer questions in connection with an investigation about the Justice Department.[3] Indeed, Congress's contempt power is codified in a federal statute that provides that "[e]very person who having been summoned as a witness by the authority of either House of Congress to give testimony or to produce papers upon any matter under inquiry before either House . . . or any committee of either House of Congress, willfully makes default, or who, having appeared, refuses to answer any question pertinent to the question under inquiry, shall be deemed guilty of a misdemeanor."[4]

The statute makes it clear that the power to investigate, and thus the contempt power, can be exercised by committees. This makes sense because realistically the entire House or Senate is too large to conduct investigations and virtually always must use a committee to do this. Although the Supreme Court generally has been very deferential to congressional investigations, it has held that a committee must be empowered by resolution and the investigation must be within the scope of its authorization. Thus, in *Gojack v. United States*, the Court overturned a contempt

---

§3.9 [1] Watkins v. United States, 354 U.S. 178, 187 (1957).
[2] *Id.*
[3] 273 U.S. 135 (1927).
[4] 2 U.S.C. §192.

citation issued by a congressional subcommittee because it had not been granted authority to conduct the investigation or to compel witnesses to appear.[5]

However, where there is authority for a committee to conduct an investigation, the Court is likely to construe it broadly to effectuate Congress's broad power to conduct inquiries. *Barenblatt v. United States* involved the authority of a congressional committee to force a college professor to answer questions about his membership in the Communist Party.[6] The Supreme Court affirmed the finding of contempt and held that delegations to committees to conduct investigations should be interpreted broadly. The Court explained that "the proper meaning of an authorization to a congressional committee is not to be derived alone from its abstract terms unrelated to the definite content furnished them by the course of congressional actions."[7]

Cases like *Barenblatt*, which involved the power of the House Un-American Activities Committee, reveal the possible abuses of the investigative power. During and after the McCarthy era, this committee conducted far-reaching investigations into the Communist threat and harassed countless individuals who were suspected of having ties or leanings to the Communist Party.[8]

First and Fifth Amendment Protections

Occasionally, the Court stepped in on behalf of witnesses during this time period. For example, in *Watkins v. United States*, a witness subpoenaed by the House Un-American Activities Committee refused to answer questions about the activities of others; he said that he would answer all questions about his own activities.[9] The Court overturned the contempt citation, in part, based on the vague delegation of power to the committee and, in part, based on concerns about the effect of the investigation on First Amendment rights of freedom of speech and association.[10]

A key protection for witnesses is their ability to invoke the privilege against self-incrimination. It is firmly established that a witness may invoke the Fifth Amendment before Congress or one of its committees, just as a witness may invoke the Fifth Amendment in a court.[11] However, Congress can overcome the Fifth Amendment privilege by granting the witness immunity, providing a legally binding promise that the testimony will not be used against the person.[12]

---

[5] 384 U.S. 702 (1966).

[6] 360 U.S. 109 (1959).

[7] *Id* at 117.

[8] For a moving account of the experience of one witness, *see* Lillian Hellman, Scoundrel Time (1976).

[9] 354 U.S. 178 (1957).

[10] *Id*. at 188.

[11] *See, e.g.*, Quinn v. United States, 349 U.S. 155, 161 (1955).

[12] *See* Kastigar v. United States, 406 U.S. 441 (1972). A famous example of this was when Oliver North was forced, by the grant of immunity, to answer questions about the Iran-Contra affair. Ultimately, his conviction was overturned because of a violation of this immunity. United States v. North, 920 F.2d 940 (D.C. Cir. 1990); 910 F.2d 843 (D.C. Cir. 1990).

At times, such as in the *Watkins* case, described above, the Court has recognized a First Amendment limit on congressional investigations. *Watkins* indicates that the First Amendment is implicated when a witness is forced to answer questions about his or her speech or associational activities. However, after *Watkins*, in *Barenblatt*, also discussed above, the Court rejected a First Amendment defense to a congressional investigation into the Communist Party. The Court said that in evaluating a Fifth Amendment claim it would engage in a "balancing . . . of the competing private and public interests at stake."[13] The Court held that the need to investigate the Communist Party, and its alleged infiltration into education, outweighed the infringement of First Amendment rights.

The experience of the last half century reveals that the congressional power to investigate is an important power that can discover and publicize wrongdoing, such as with Watergate and the Iran-Contra affair. At the same time, the McCarthy-era witch hunts show how the power can be abused. The Supreme Court's decisions indicate that the primary check on this power must come from the political process. Courts generally are reluctant to get involved, so long as there is properly delegated authority and so long as the Fifth Amendment privilege against self-incrimination is protected.

§3.10   THE TENTH AMENDMENT AND FEDERALISM AS A LIMIT ON CONGRESSIONAL AUTHORITY

Competing Approaches to the Tenth Amendment

The Tenth Amendment states: "The powers not delegated to the United States by the Constitution, nor prohibited by it to the States, are reserved to the States respectively, or to the people." The key question about the Tenth Amendment is whether it is a judicially enforceable limit on Congress's powers; can federal laws be declared unconstitutional as violating this constitutional provision? Over the course of American history, the Court has been inconsistent in answering this question and has shifted between two different approaches.

One approach is that the Tenth Amendment is not a separate constraint on Congress, but rather is simply a reminder that Congress only may legislate if it has authority under the Constitution. Under this approach, a federal law never would be found unconstitutional as violating the Tenth Amendment, but it could be invalidated as exceeding the scope of Congress's powers under Article I of the Constitution or for violating another constitutional provision.

The alternate approach is that the Tenth Amendment protects state sovereignty from federal intrusion. Under this approach, the Tenth Amendment is a key protection of states' rights and federalism. The Tenth Amendment reserves a

---

[13] 360 U.S. at 126.

zone of activity to the states for their exclusive control, and federal laws intruding into this zone should be declared unconstitutional by the courts.

As described below, in the nineteenth century, the Court took the former position and held that a federal law was constitutional so long as Congress was acting within the scope of its authority. In the first third of the twentieth century until 1937, the Court adopted the latter view and found that the Tenth Amendment reserved to the states control over production and federal laws attempting to regulate production were unconstitutional. From 1937 until the 1990s, the Court shifted back to the former approach. In fact, during this period, there was only one case where a federal law was found to violate the Tenth Amendment and this case was later expressly overruled.[1] In the 1990s, however, the Court resurrected the Tenth Amendment as a limit on congressional power.

The Issues Concerning the Tenth Amendment

The dispute over the meaning of the Tenth Amendment concerns two inter-related issues of constitutional policy.[2] First, how important is the protection of state sovereignty and federalism? Second, should it be the role of the judiciary to protect state prerogatives or should this be left to the political process?

As to the former question, many Supreme Court decisions protecting federalism say relatively little about the underlying values that are being served. When the Court does speak of the values of federalism, usually three benefits of protecting state governments are identified: decreasing the likelihood of federal tyranny, enhancing democratic rule by providing government that is closer to the people, and allowing states to be laboratories for new ideas.

The first justification for protecting states from federal intrusions is that the division of power vertically, between federal and state governments, lessens the chance of federal tyranny. Professor Andrew Rapczynski noted that "[p]erhaps the most frequently mentioned function of the federal system is the one it shares to a large extent with separation of powers, namely the protection of the citizen against governmental oppression—the 'tyranny' that the framers were so concerned about."[3]

How do state governments prevent federal tyranny? Perhaps most important, the framers thought that the possibility of federal abuses could be limited by restricting the authority of the federal government. The framers envisioned that the vast majority of governance would be at the state and local levels and that

---

§3.10 [1] National League of Cities v. Usery, 426 U.S. 833 (1976); overruled in Garcia v. San Antonio Metro. Transit Auth., 469 U.S. 528 (1985), discussed below.

[2] For excellent discussions of this issue, *see* David Shapiro, Federalism: A Dialogue (1995); Edward L. Rubin & Malcolm Feeley, Federalism: Some Notes on a National Neurosis, 41 UCLA L. Rev. 903 (1994). *See also* Erwin Chemerinsky, Empowering Government: Federalism for the 21st Century (2008).

[3] Andrew Rapczynski, From Sovereignty to Process: The Jurisprudence of Federalism After *Garcia*, 1985 Sup. Ct. Rev. 341, 380.

federal actions would be relatively rare and limited.[4] Moreover, the danger of tyranny at the federal level is much more ominous than autocratic rule at the state or local level. Professor Rapczynski continues: "Should the federal government ever be captured by an authoritarian movement or assert itself as a special cohesive interest, the resulting oppression would almost certainly be much more severe and durable than any state would be capable."[5]

Yet the notion of radically limited federal powers seems anachronistic in the face of a modern national market economy and decades of extensive federal regulations. Additionally, there has been a major shift over time as to how abusive government is best controlled. Now it is thought that if a federal action intrudes upon individual liberties, the federal judiciary will invalidate it as unconstitutional. Judicial review is seen as an important check against tyrannical government actions.

A second frequently invoked value of federalism is that states are closer to the people and thus more likely to be responsive to public needs and concerns.[6] Professor David Shapiro summarizes this argument when he writes: "[O]ne of the stronger arguments for a decentralized political structure is that, to the extent that the electorate is small, and elected representatives are thus more immediately accountable to individuals and their concerns, government is brought closer to the people and democratic ideals are more fully realized."[7] This argument has intuitive appeal. It suggests that the smaller the area governed, the more responsive the government will be to the interests of the voters.

However, it must be recognized that this value of federalism could be inconsistent with the first value discussed above. To the extent that voters at the state and local level prefer tyrannical rule or, more likely, rule that abuses a particular minority group, greater responsiveness increases the dangers of government tyranny. In other words, the substantive result of decreasing tyranny will not always be best achieved by the process approach of maximizing electoral responsiveness; indeed, the reverse might well be the result. In fact, there is a greater danger of special interests capturing government at smaller and more local levels. James Madison wrote of the danger of "factions" in Federalist No. 10, and modern political science literature offers support for his fears.[8]

Moreover, it is not clear what size of government unit is necessary for such responsiveness. For example, is a state the size of California, or for that matter a city the size of Los Angeles, sufficiently more homogeneous in its interests as to increase the likelihood of responsive government? Professor Shapiro writes: "[T]he goal of realizing democratic values to the maximum extent feasible may not be significantly enhanced by reducing the relevant polity from one of some 280,000,000 (the United States) to one of, say 30,000,000 (the State of California)."[9]

---

[4] Alexander Hamilton explained that "[the] necessity of local administration for local purposes would be a complete barrier against the oppressive use of such power."

[5] Rapczynski, *supra* note 3, at 388. *See also* John C. Yoo, The Judicial Safeguards of Federalism, 70 S. Cal. L. Rev. 1311 (1997).

[6] Rapczynski, *supra* note 3, at 391.

[7] Shapiro, *supra* note 2, at 92.

[8] James Madison, Federalist No. 10, The Federalist Papers (C. Rossiter ed. 1961).

[9] Shapiro, *supra* note 2, at 93.

§3.10 The Tenth Amendment and Federalism

A final argument that is frequently made for protecting federalism is that states can serve as laboratories for experimentation. Justice Brandeis apparently first articulated this idea when he declared: "To stay experimentation in things social and economic is a grave responsibility. Denial of the right to experiment might be fraught with serious consequences to the Nation. It is one of the happy incidents of the federal system that a single courageous State may, if its citizens choose, serve as a laboratory; and try novel social and economic experiments without risk to the rest of the country."[10]

The Justices, too, have invoked this notion. Justice Powell, dissenting in *Garcia*, lamented that "the Court does not explain how leaving the States virtually at the mercy of the Federal Government, without recourse to judicial review, will enhance their opportunities to experiment and serve as laboratories."[11] Likewise, Justice O'Connor, dissenting in *Federal Energy Regulatory Commission v. Mississippi*, stated that the "Court's decision undermines the most valuable aspects of our federalism. Courts and commentators frequently have recognized that the 50 states serve as laboratories for the development of new social, economic, and political ideas."[12]

However, any federal legislation preempting state or local laws limits experimentation. Indeed, the application of constitutional rights to the states limits their experimenting with providing fewer safeguards of individual liberties. The key question is when is it worth experimenting, and when is experimentation to be rejected because of a need to impose a national mandate? The value of states as laboratories provides no answer to this issue.

There also is a related process question: Who is in the best position to decide when further experimentation is warranted or when there is enough knowledge to justify federal actions? A strong argument can be made that the need for using states as laboratories is a policy argument to be made to Congress against federal legislation and not a judicial argument that should be used to invalidate particular federal laws on the grounds that they unduly limit experimentation. Additionally, Congress and even federal agencies can design experiments and try differing approaches in varying parts of the country.[13]

A second major question is whether it is the role of the judiciary to enforce the Tenth Amendment and protect state sovereignty or whether it is an issue left to the political process. One view is that judicial enforcement of federalism as a limit on Congress is unnecessary because the political process will adequately protect state government interests. Professor Herbert Wechsler, in a landmark article, provided the intellectual foundation for this approach.[14] Wechsler argued that the interests of the states are represented in the national political process and that the

---

[10] New State Ice Co. v. Liebmann, 285 U.S. 262, 311 (1932) (Brandeis, J., dissenting).

[11] 469 U.S. at 567-568 n.13 (Powell, J., dissenting).

[12] 456 U.S. 742, 787-788 (1982) (O'Connor, J., dissenting).

[13] Rubin & Feeley, *supra* note 2, at 925.

[14] The Political Safeguards of Federalism: The Role of the States in the Composition, and Selection of the National Government, 54 Colum. L. Rev. 543 (1954).

nature of that process provides sufficient protection of state sovereignty, thus making it unnecessary for the courts to enforce federalism as a limit on Congress.[15]

But the assumption that states' interests are adequately represented in the national political process is questionable.[16] At the time the Constitution was written, states chose senators and thus were directly represented in Congress. But now, with popular election of senators, why believe that the states' interests as states are adequately protected in Congress?[17] The assumption must be that the voters, in choosing representatives and senators, weigh heavily the extent to which the individual legislator votes in a manner that serves the interests of the state as an entity. Yet simple observation of congressional elections shows that the issues are usually basic ones about the economy, health care, and the personalities of the candidates. The interests of the voters are the focus of attention, not the institutional interests of state and local governments. Indeed, it may well be that the "primary constituencies of the national representatives may . . . be precisely those that advocate an extension of the federal power to the disadvantage of the states."[18]

Thus, the debate over the meaning of the Tenth Amendment that has lasted throughout American history is likely to continue. This debate turns on the two questions considered above: What policies are served by protection of state sovereignty, and should it be the judicial role to enforce the Tenth Amendment and protect the states?

The Tenth Amendment in the Nineteenth Century

The Court in the nineteenth century viewed the Tenth Amendment simply as a reminder that Congress must have authority under the Constitution in order to legislate, not as a judicially enforceable limit on the legislative power. In *Gibbons v. Ogden*, Chief Justice John Marshall adopted the former view.[19] The Court took the position that so long as Congress is acting within the scope of its commerce clause power, the law will not be declared unconstitutional as violating state sovereignty. Chief Justice Marshall declared: "This power, like all others vested in Congress, is complete in itself, may be exercised to the utmost extent, and acknowledges no limitations, other than are prescribed in the constitution. [If], as has always been understood, the sovereignty of Congress, though limited to specified objects, is plenary as to those objects, the power over commerce with foreign nations, and among the several states, is vested in Congress as absolutely as it would be in a single government."[20]

---

[15] Professor Jesse Choper has advanced a similar thesis. *See* Jesse Choper, Judicial Review and the National Political Process (1980).

[16] *See* Saikrishna B. Prakash & John C. Yoo, The Puzzling Persistence of Process-Based Federalism Theories, 79 Tex. L. Rev. 1459 (2001); Larry Kramer, Putting the Politics into the Political Safeguards of Federalism, 100 Colum. L. Rev. 215 (2000).

[17] *See* Rapczynski, *supra* note 3, at 341, 393.

[18] *Id.*

[19] 22 U.S. (9 Wheat.) 1 (1824). *Gibbons* is discussed more fully in §3.4.2.

[20] *Id.* at 196-197.

In other words, once Congress is within the scope of its power, it can legislate the same as if there were no states at all. By this view, the Tenth Amendment is simply a reminder that Congress must have authority under the Constitution to legislate, but the Tenth Amendment is not a basis for invalidating laws that are within the scope of Congress's legislative power. The sole check on Congress is the political process, not judicially enforced limits to protect the states.

The Tenth Amendment from the Late Nineteenth Century Until 1937

As described earlier in this chapter, from the late nineteenth century until 1937, the Court greatly circumscribed the scope of Congress's powers, especially its commerce power.[21] At the same time and as part of the same overall approach, the Court held that the Tenth Amendment reserves a zone of activities to the states for their exclusive control. Federal laws intruding into this zone were declared unconstitutional. Specifically, the Court held that control over production, such as manufacturing, was left to the states and that Congress could not intrude into this zone, even if exercising its authority under the commerce clause or the spending power.

The Child Labor Case (Hammer v. Dagenhart) was the most significant case to construe the Tenth Amendment in this way.[22] A federal law prohibited the shipment in interstate commerce of goods produced in factories employing children under age 14 or employing children between the ages of 14 and 16 for more than eight hours per day or six days a week. Although the law was limited to regulating goods in interstate commerce, the Court declared it unconstitutional because it controlled production. The Court declared that "[t]he grant of power to Congress over the subject of interstate commerce was to enable it to regulate such commerce, and not to give it authority to control the States in their exercise of the police power over local trade and manufacture."[23] The Court said that regulating the hours of labor of children was entrusted "purely [to] state authority."[24]

Defenders of the law argued that the protection of state autonomy was illusory because the national market restricted the ability of the states to choose whether to allow or prohibit child labor. If a few states allowed child labor, goods produced there would be less expensive than those made in states that prohibited child labor. The market would favor the goods that were cheaper by virtue of their production by inexpensive child labor. Over time, the pressure would be enormous for all states to allow child labor. The Court flatly rejected this as a sufficient basis for federal legislation. In fact, the Court said: "The far-reaching result of upholding the act cannot be more plainly indicated than by pointing out that if Congress can thus regulate matters entrusted to local authority by prohibition of the movement of commodities in interstate commerce, all freedom of commerce

---

[21] *See* §3.4.4.
[22] 247 U.S. 251 (1918).
[23] *Id.* at 273-274.
[24] *Id.* at 276.

will be at an end, and the power of the states over local matters may be eliminated, and thus our system of government practically destroyed."[25]

The Tenth Amendment was used in this era as a limit not only on the commerce power but also on other federal legislative authority. In *Bailey v. Drexel Furniture Co. (The Child Labor Tax Case)*, a federal tax on goods produced by child labor and shipped in interstate commerce was declared unconstitutional.[26] Again, the Court's concern was that Congress was attempting to control production and thereby intrude into a zone that the Court saw as reserved to the states. Similarly, in *United States v. Butler*, the Court declared unconstitutional the Agricultural Adjustment Act of 1933, which gave subsidies to farmers to stabilize agricultural production.[27] The law imposed a tax on agricultural producers and used the revenues to subsidize farmers to limit production. The reduction in production was sought to decrease the supply of certain agricultural products to ensure an adequate price for them and thus a sufficient incentive for continued production. The Court declared this unconstitutional as impermissibly controlling production, an area left to the states by the Tenth Amendment.

The Tenth Amendment
Between 1937 and the 1990s

Between 1937 and the 1990s, there was only one case where a federal law was declared unconstitutional as violating the Tenth Amendment and that decision was later expressly overruled. During this era, the Court expressly rejected the view that the Tenth Amendment is an independent limit on the legislative power and instead viewed it simply as a reminder that Congress may legislate only if there is authority in the Constitution.

The key case was *United States v. Darby* in 1941.[28] *Darby* involved a challenge to the constitutionality of the Fair Labor Standards Act of 1938, which prohibited the shipment in interstate commerce of goods made by employees who were paid less than the prescribed minimum wage (25 cents an hour at that time) or who worked more than the prescribed maximum number of hours. The Court upheld the Act as a lawful exercise of Congress's commerce clause authority. The Court flatly rejected the claim that the law violated the Tenth Amendment and declared: "The Amendment states but a truism that all is retained which has not been surrendered."[29] The Court expressly overruled *Hammer v. Dagenhart* and its view that control of production was left to the exclusive regulation of the states. The Court made it clear that a law is constitutional so long as it is within the scope of Congress's power; the Tenth Amendment would not be used as a basis for invalidating federal laws.

---

[25] *Id.*

[26] 259 U.S. 20 (1922), discussed in §3.5.2.

[27] 297 U.S. 1 (1936). *Butler*, and its discussion of the scope of the spending power, is considered in §3.5.3.

[28] 312 U.S. 100 (1941). *Darby* is discussed more fully in §3.4.4.

[29] *Id.* at 124.

The only case between 1937 and the 1990s to deviate from this view and find that a law violated the Tenth Amendment was *National League of Cities v. Usery* in 1976.[30] In *Usery*, the Court, by a 5-to-4 margin, declared unconstitutional the application of the Fair Labor Standards Act, which required the payment of the minimum wage to state and local employees. The Court began with the premise that "there are limits upon the power of Congress to override state sovereignty, even when exercising its otherwise plenary powers to tax or to regulate commerce."[31] The Court found that requiring states to pay their employees the minimum wage violated the Tenth Amendment because the law "operate[s] to directly displace the States' freedom to structure integral operations in areas of traditional governmental functions."[32]

The Court explained that forcing state and local governments to pay their employees the minimum wage would require that they either raise taxes or cut other services to pay these costs. The Court said that this would displace decisions traditionally left to the states and "may substantially restructure traditional ways in which the local governments have arranged their affairs."[33]

In other words, *National League of Cities v. Usery* held that Congress violates the Tenth Amendment when it interferes with traditional state and local government functions. The Court, however, did not attempt to define what is such a traditional function; the Court only held that forcing payment of the minimum wage was unconstitutional.

It should be noted that the key fifth vote for the majority was found in the concurring opinion of Justice Harry Blackmun. Blackmun said that he saw the majority as adopting "a balancing approach [that] . . . does not outlaw federal power in areas such as environmental protection, where the federal interest is demonstrably greater and where state facility compliance with imposed federal standards would be essential."[34]

Many predicted that *Usery* marked a rebirth of state sovereignty and the Tenth Amendment as a major limit on congressional power.[35] In the years after *Usery*, the Supreme Court had many opportunities to clarify its ruling. In each, the Court rejected a Tenth Amendment challenge to a federal law and distinguished *Usery*. In each, Justice Blackmun voted with the majority, often as the crucial fifth vote refusing to extend or apply *National League of Cities v. Usery*.

In *Hodel v. Virginia Surface Mining & Reclamation Association*, in 1980, the Court made it clear that *Usery* applied only when Congress was regulating state

---

[30] 426 U.S. 833 (1976).

[31] *Id.* at 842.

[32] *Id.* at 852.

[33] *Id.* at 849.

[34] *Id.* at 856 (Blackmun, J., concurring).

[35] *See, e.g.,* Laurence Tribe, Unraveling *National League of Cities*: The New Federalism and Affirmative Rights to Essential Government Services, 90 Harv. L. Rev. 1065 (1977); Frank Michelman, States' Rights and States' Roles: The Permutations of "Sovereignty" in *National League of Cities v. Usery*, 86 Yale L.J. 1165 (1977) (forecasting major implications from the decision, including it being used to create an affirmative right to government services).

governments, not when Congress was regulating private conduct.[36] In *Hodel*, the Court upheld a federal law that regulated strip mining and required reclamation of strip mined land. The Court clarified its test for the Tenth Amendment in light of *Usery*. The Court said that for a federal law to violate the Tenth Amendment, it needed to regulate "the States as States"; it must "address matters that are indisputably attribute[s] of state sovereignty"; it must directly impair the states' ability to "structure integral operations in areas of traditional governmental functions"; and it must not be such that "the nature of the federal interest . . . justifies state submission."[37] The Court in *Hodel* found that the law, the Surface Mining Control and Reclamation Act of 1977, was constitutional because it did not regulate the states as states.

The next case to consider the application of *National League of Cities v. Usery* was *United Transportation Union v. Long Island R.R. Co.*, in which the Supreme Court held that the application of the Railway Labor Act to a state-owned railroad did not violate the Tenth Amendment.[38] Although the Act was being applied to the state as a state, the Court said that there was no violation of the Tenth Amendment because there was no evidence that the application of the federal law "would be likely to hamper the state government's ability to fulfill its role in the Union and endanger its separate and independent existence."[39] Of course, if this was the test, relatively few federal laws would violate the Tenth Amendment because few would "endanger" a state's "separate and independent existence."

The Court next considered the application of *National League of Cities v. Usery* in *Federal Energy Regulatory Commission (FERC) v. Mississippi*.[40] As in *Hodel* and *Long Island R.R.*, the Court again distinguished *Usery* and upheld the federal law. However, unlike *Hodel* and *Long Island R.R.*, which were unanimous, *FERC v. Mississippi* was a 5-to-4 decision. In fact, the split was exactly the same as in *Usery*, except that Justice Blackmun switched sides and this time voted to uphold the federal law.[41]

FERC v. Mississippi involved a challenge to the Public Utilities Regulatory Policies Act of 1978, which required that state utility commissions consider FERC proposals. The Court emphasized that the federal regulation at issue only forced states to consider adopting the federal standards; it did not force them to do so. Thus, the majority found no violation of the Tenth Amendment. The dissent, in contrast, found that compelling states to consider adopting federal regulations was, in essence, to conscript the state regulatory process and thus to violate the Tenth Amendment.[42]

The final case to distinguish *National League of Cities v. Usery* was *Equal Employment Opportunity Commission v. Wyoming*, which considered whether forcing states

---

[36] 452 U.S. 264 (1981).

[37] *Id.* at 287-288.

[38] 455 U.S. 678 (1982).

[39] *Id.* at 687.

[40] 456 U.S. 742 (1982).

[41] The only other difference was that Justice O'Connor had replaced Justice Stewart in the time between the two decisions. Justice Stewart had been in the majority in *Usery*. Justice O'Connor joined the other Justices who had been in that majority, except for Justice Blackmun, in dissent in *FERC*.

[42] 456 U.S. at 786 (O'Connor, J., dissenting).

to comply with the Age Discrimination in Employment Act violated the Tenth Amendment.[43] Again, the decision was 5 to 4, with Justice Blackmun joining the four dissenters from *Usery* to create the majority. Justice Brennan, writing for the Court, held that the Tenth Amendment was not violated because the Act did not "directly impair the State's ability to structure integral operations in areas of traditional governmental functions."[44] Yet the distinction between *Usery* and *EEOC v. Wyoming* is a difficult one to explain. The federal law eliminating mandatory retirement ages means that state and local governments will have to retain employees with more seniority and thus higher wages. Imposing such a cost on the states, together with controlling who will perform the tasks, seems to be exactly what *Usery* disapproved.[45]

After *Hodel, Long Island R.R., FERC v. Mississippi*, and *EEOC v. Wyoming*, little remained of *National League of Cities v. Usery*. In 1985, in *Garcia v. San Antonio Metropolitan Transit Authority*, the Supreme Court expressly overruled *Usery*.[46] The decision was 5 to 4, with Justice Blackmun again joining the four dissenters from *Usery* to create the majority. *Garcia*, like *Usery*, focused on whether the application of the Fair Labor Standards Act to state and local governments violated the Tenth Amendment.

Justice Blackmun, writing for the Court, offered two reasons for overruling *Usery*. First, the *Usery* approach had proved unworkable. He wrote: "We therefore now reject, as unsound in principle and unworkable in practice, a rule of state immunity from federal regulation that turns on a judicial appraisal of whether a particular government function is 'traditional' or 'integral.'"[47] Justice Blackmun, writing for the more liberal wing of the Court, argued for judicial restraint in enforcing the Tenth Amendment in terms usually associated with the more conservative Justices: "Any rule of state immunity that looks to the 'traditional,' 'integral,' or 'necessary' nature of governmental functions inevitably invites an un-elected federal judiciary to make decisions about which state policies it favors and which ones it dislikes."[48]

Second, Justice Blackmun argued that the protection of state prerogatives should be through the political process and not from the judiciary. The Court stated: "Of course, we continue to recognize that the States occupy a special and specific position in our constitutional system and that the scope of Congress's authority under the Commerce Clause must reflect that position. But the principal and basic limit on the federal commerce power is that inherent in all congressional 'action—the built-in' restraints that our system provides through state

---

[43]   460 U.S. 226 (1983).

[44]   *Id.* at 239.

[45]   This was the position of the dissent. *See id.* at 259-265 (Burger, C.J., dissenting). Although this decision never has been overruled, and the Age Discrimination in Employment Act applies to the states, the Court has held that state governments may not be sued for violating it because of state sovereign immunity. Kimel v. Florida Bd. of Regents, 528 U.S. 62 (2000), which is discussed above in §3.8.

[46]   469 U.S. 528 (1985).

[47]   *Id.* at 545-547.

[48]   *Id.* at 556.

participation in federal governmental action. The political process ensures that the laws that unduly burden the States will not be promulgated."[49]

There were three dissenting opinions. Justice Powell's dissent focused on the majority's first major point as to whether it was possible to define "traditional" or "integral" government functions.[50] Powell argued that the Court could define the parameters of the Tenth Amendment just as the Court has defined numerous other ambiguous constitutional provisions. Justice O'Connor's dissent responded to the majority's second major point and challenged the view that the political process would adequately protect the interests of state governments.[51] Finally, Justice Rehnquist wrote a short dissent lamenting the majority's approach, but predicting that, in time, the conservative's position on the Tenth Amendment again would prevail.[52]

As discussed below, in the 1990s, the Court revived the Tenth Amendment as a limit on Congress's power. However, *Garcia* has not been overruled and *Usery* has not been reinstated. Therefore, the Fair Labor Standards Act does apply to state governments. However, in *Alden v. Maine*,[53] in 1999, the Supreme Court held that sovereign immunity precludes suits against state governments to enforce this law in either federal or state courts. *Alden* is discussed in detail in §2.10.

The Tenth Amendment in the 1990s and Beyond

Justice Rehnquist's prediction came true. So far, since 1991, there have been four Supreme Court cases relying on the Tenth Amendment. The first indication of this resurrection occurred in *Gregory v. Ashcroft* in 1991.[54] State court judges in Missouri challenged a provision of the Missouri constitution that set a mandatory retirement age as violating the federal Age Discrimination in Employment Act. The Supreme Court held that a federal law will be applied to important state government activities only if there is a clear statement from Congress that the law was meant to apply. The Court did not use the Tenth Amendment to invalidate the federal law on its face or as applied.[55] Instead, the Court used the Tenth Amendment and federalism considerations as a rule of construction. The Court ruled that a federal law that imposes a substantial burden on a state government will be applied only if Congress clearly indicated that it wanted the law to apply. The Age Discrimination in Employment Act lacks such a clear statement, and hence the Court refused to apply it to preempt the Missouri mandatory retirement age. Justice O'Connor, writing for the Court, discussed the importance of autonomous

---

[49] *Id.* at 551.

[50] *Id.* at 561 (Powell, J., dissenting).

[51] *Id.* at 587.

[52] *Id.* at 580.

[53] 527 U.S. 706 (1999).

[54] 501 U.S. 452 (1991).

[55] Subsequently, in Kimel v. Florida Board of Regents, 528 U.S. 62 (2000), the Court held that state governments cannot be sued for violating the Age Discrimination in Employment Act. *Kimel* is discussed above in §3.8.

state governments as a check on possible federal tyranny and stressed the significance of the Tenth Amendment as a constitutional protector of state sovereignty.

A year later, in *New York v. United States*, the Court—for only the second time in 55 years and the first since the overruled *National League of Cities* decision—invalidated a federal law as violating the Tenth Amendment.[56] A federal law, the 1985 Low-Level Radioactive Waste Policy Amendments Act, created a statutory duty for states to provide for the safe disposal of radioactive wastes generated within their borders. The Act provided monetary incentives for states to comply with the law and allowed states to impose a surcharge on radioactive wastes received from other states. Additionally, and most controversially, to ensure effective state government action, the law provided that states would "take title" to any wastes within their borders that were not properly disposed of by January 1, 1996, and then would "be liable for all damages directly or indirectly incurred."

The Supreme Court ruled that Congress, pursuant to its authority under the commerce clause, could regulate the disposal of radioactive wastes. However, by a 6-to-3 margin, the Court held that the "take title" provision of the law was unconstitutional because it gave state governments the choice between "either accepting ownership of waste or regulating according to the instructions of Congress."[57] Justice O'Connor, writing for the Court, said that it was impermissible for Congress to impose either option on the states. Forcing states to accept ownership of radioactive wastes would impermissibly "commandeer" state governments, and requiring state compliance with federal regulatory statutes would impermissibly impose on states a requirement to implement federal legislation. The Court concluded that it was "clear" that because of the Tenth Amendment and limits on the scope of Congress's powers under Article I, "[t]he Federal Government may not compel the States to enact or administer a federal regulatory program."[58] The Court explained that allowing Congress to commandeer state governments would undermine government accountability because Congress could make a decision, but the states would take the political heat and be held responsible for a decision that was not theirs.[59]

Although the Court said that it was not "revisit[ing]" the holdings of earlier cases, such as *Garcia*, the Court clearly rejected *Garcia*'s conclusion that the federal judiciary would not use the Tenth Amendment to invalidate federal laws. Indeed, it appears that if a federal law compels state legislative or regulatory activity, the statute is unconstitutional even if there is a compelling need for the federal action. Justice O'Connor's opinion for the Court expressly rejected the argument that a compelling government interest is sufficient to permit a law that otherwise would violate the Tenth Amendment.[60]

[56] 505 U.S. 144 (1992).

[57] *Id.* at 173.

[58] *Id.* at 188.

[59] For an excellent analysis of the commandeering principle and its implications, *see* Vicki C. Jackson, Federalism and the Uses and Limits of Law: *Printz* and Principle, 111 Harv. L. Rev. 2180 (1998); Evan H. Caminker, State Sovereignty and Subordinacy: May Congress Commandeer State Officers to Implement Federal Laws?, 95 Colum. L. Rev. 1001 (1995).

[60] 505 U.S. at 161.

The central holding of *New York v. United States* is that it is unconstitutional for Congress to compel state legislatures to adopt laws or state agencies to adopt regulations. The Court, however, indicated that Congress was not powerless. Congress may set standards that state and local governments must meet and thereby preempt state and local actions. Also, Congress may attach strings on grants to state and local governments and through these conditions induce state and local actions that it cannot directly compel.[61]

The third major case interpreting the Tenth Amendment is *Printz v. United States*.[62] The issue was whether the Brady Handgun Violence Prevention Act violated the Tenth Amendment in requiring that state and local law enforcement officers conduct background checks on prospective handgun purchasers. In a 5-to-4 decision, with Justice Scalia writing for the Court and with the same split among the Justices as in most of the other recent federalism cases, the Court found the provision unconstitutional.

Justice Scalia's majority opinion emphasized that Congress was impermissibly commandeering state executive officials to implement a federal mandate. He observed that historically, and particularly in the early years of the United States, Congress had not exercised such a power.[63] Reaffirming *New York v. United States*, the Court held that Congress violates the Tenth Amendment when it conscripts state governments. In addition to finding the Brady Law unconstitutional on this ground because it compels state officers to act, Justice Scalia said that the law also violates separation of powers. He explained that the Constitution vests all executive power in the president and that Congress impermissibly had given the executive authority to implement the law to state and local law enforcement personnel. Justice Scalia wrote: "The Brady Act effectively transfers this responsibility to thousands of [chief law enforcement officers] in the 50 States, who are left to implement the program without meaningful Presidential control (if indeed meaningful Presidential control is possible without the power to appoint and remove). The insistence of the Framers upon unity in the Federal Executive—to insure both vigor and accountability—is well known. That unity would be shattered, and the power of the President would be subject to reduction, if Congress could act as effectively without the President as with him, by simply requiring state officers to execute its laws."[64]

Justice Stevens—in a dissenting opinion joined by Justices Souter, Ginsburg, and Breyer—disagreed with the premise of *New York v. United States* and *Printz* and declared: "When Congress exercises the powers delegated to it by the Constitution, it may impose affirmative obligations on executive and judicial officers of state and local governments as well as ordinary citizens. This conclusion is firmly supported by the text of the Constitution, the early history of the Nation, decisions

---

[61] *Id.* at 166-167. The ability of Congress to place strings on grants to state and local governments is discussed in §3.5.3.

[62] 521 U.S. 898 (1997). For an excellent analysis of *Printz, see* Evan H. Caminker, *Printz*, State Sovereignty, and the Limits of Formalism, 1997 Sup. Ct. Rev. 199 (1997).

[63] *Id.* at 907.

[64] *Id.* at 922.

of this Court, and a correct understanding of the basic structure of the Federal Government."[65]

Justice Stevens also stressed the need for the Brady Act. He wrote: "The Act's legislative history notes that 15,377 Americans were murdered with firearms in 1992, and that 12,489 of these deaths were caused by handguns. . . . The partial solution contained in the Brady Act, a mandatory background check before a handgun may be purchased, has met with remarkable success. Between 1994 and 1996, approximately 6,600 firearm sales each month to potentially dangerous persons were prevented by Brady Act checks; over 70% of the rejected purchasers were convicted or indicted felons."[66]

The final Tenth Amendment decision thus far was *Reno v. Condon.*[67] Unlike the other recent cases, in *Reno v. Condon* the Supreme Court rejected a Tenth Amendment challenge and upheld the federal law. The case involved a challenge to the Driver's Privacy Protection Act, a federal law that prohibited states from disclosing personal information gained by departments of motor vehicles, such as home addresses and phone numbers, Social Security numbers, and medical information.[68] California Senator Barbara Boxer introduced the bill after an actress in Los Angeles, Rebecca Schaeffer, was stalked and murdered by a man who obtained her home address from the California Department of Motor Vehicles.

The United States Court of Appeals for the Fourth Circuit declared the law unconstitutional as violating the Tenth Amendment because it commanded the states to not disclose the information. The Supreme Court unanimously reversed in an opinion by Chief Justice Rehnquist. The Court explained that the law was constitutional as an exercise of Congress's commerce clause power because "Congress found that many States . . . sell this personal information to individuals and businesses [and] [t]hese sales generate significant revenues for the States."[69]

The Court also stressed that the law is not limited to state governments; it also regulates private entities that possess the drivers' license information. Chief Justice Rehnquist noted: "The DPPA's provisions do not apply solely to States. The Act also regulates the resale and redisclosure of drivers' personal information by private persons who have obtained that information from a state DMV."[70]

Perhaps most important, the Court said that the law did not violate the Tenth Amendment because it was a prohibition of conduct, not an affirmative mandate as in *New York v. United States* and *Printz v. United States.* Chief Justice Rehnquist stated: "It does not require the South Carolina Legislature to enact any laws or regulations, and it does not require state officials to assist in the enforcement of federal statutes regulating private individuals. We accordingly conclude that the DPPA is consistent with the constitutional principles enunciated in *New York* and *Printz.*"[71]

---

[65] *Id.* at 939 (Souter, J., dissenting).
[66] *Id.* at 940.
[67] 528 U.S. 141 (2000).
[68] 18 U.S.C. §2721.
[69] 528 U.S. at 143-144.
[70] *Id.* at 146.
[71] *Id.* at 151.

Reno v. Condon thus is important because the Court limited the scope of the Tenth Amendment's restrictions on Congress. Congress may prohibit state governments from engaging in harmful conduct, particularly if the law applies to private entities as well; but Congress may not impose affirmative duties on state governments. Certainly, it can be questioned whether this distinction between prohibition and obligation makes sense. Most duties can be characterized either way. The Driver's Privacy Protection Act could be characterized as imposing the affirmative duty on states to keep information secret. Conversely, the Brady Act, at issue in *Printz*, could be characterized as a prohibition on state and local governments from issuing gun permits without doing background checks. Also, it can be questioned whether an otherwise impermissible regulation of state governments should become acceptable because it includes private actors as well.

The Court returned to the Tenth Amendment and the anti-commandeering principle in striking down the Medicaid coverage requirements imposed on states in the Patient Protection and Affordable Care Act.[72] As discussed in §3.5.2, the Court found that the conditions on federal Medicaid funds to the state were unduly coercive and thus they constituted commandeering that violates the Tenth Amendment. No state is required to accept federal Medicaid money, but any state that chooses to do so—and every state does—must meet federally imposed conditions.

The Affordable Care Act required that states cover within their Medicaid programs those within 133 percent of the federal poverty level.[73] The federal government pays 100 percent of these costs until 2019 and 90 percent thereafter. Any state that failed to comply would lose all of its Medicaid funds.

Chief Justice Roberts, writing for the Court in a 7-2 decision, said that this is "a gun to the head of the states."[74] The Court said that the states' dependence on federal Medicaid dollars and the size of this amount within state budgets meant that the federal law "is economic dragooning that leaves the States with no real option but to acquiesce in the Medicaid expansion."[75]

This is significant because it is the first time that the Court has found impermissible commandeering based on conditions on federal funds. *New York* and *Printz* each involved more directly federal mandates imposed on the states. In *National Federation of Independent Business v. Sebelius*, the Court concluded that conditions on federal money to the states violate the Tenth Amendment if they are unduly coercive. The Court, though, did not define how is it to be determined if there is "undue coercion."

---

[72] National Federation of Independent Business v. Sebelius, 132 S. Ct. 2566 (2012).

[73] 132 S. Ct. 2566 (2012). Other aspects of the Court's decision are discussed above, including its consideration of the necessary and proper clause (§3.3 above), the commerce clause (§3.4.5 above), and the taxing power (§3.5.2 above).

[74] *Id.* at 2604.

[75] *Id.* at 2604-2605.

§3.11   DELEGATION OF LEGISLATIVE POWER AND THE PROBLEMS OF THE ADMINISTRATIVE STATE

§3.11.1   *The Nondelegation Doctrine and Its Demise*

The Rise of the Administrative State

Article I of the Constitution, of course, vests the legislative power in Congress. Although federal agencies and departments have existed in some form since the beginning of American history, it is only in the last century that Congress has routinely delegated its legislative power to executive agencies. The creation of the Interstate Commerce Commission in 1887 ushered in a new era for the federal government: the creation of federal administrative agencies with broad powers. Over the course of the next century, a vast array of federal agencies have been created, such as the Federal Communication Commission, the Securities and Exchange Commission, the Food and Drug Administration, the Environmental Protection Agency, the Nuclear Regulatory Commission, and many others.

The Constitution does not expressly mention such agencies and, in fact, in many ways they are in tension with basic constitutional principles. Virtually all of these agencies possess rule-making power, and these rules have the force of law. This seems in conflict with the notion that Congress alone possesses the federal legislative power. Yet for many reasons, Congress has delegated broad legislative power to administrative agencies. In many areas, the need for complex regulations seems better handled in a specialized agency than in Congress. Also, the sheer quantity of regulations exceeds the capacity of Congress. Additionally, there is a political dimension: Expansive delegation of legislative power to administrative agencies allows Congress to act, but avoid the political heat that specific regulations might engender.[1]

Administrative agencies, however, do not possess only the legislative power. They also have the executive power to enforce the regulations that they have promulgated and the judicial power to adjudicate violations of their rules. Many agencies employ administrative law judges who hear cases brought by agency officials against those accused of violating the agency's regulations.

In other words, federal agencies possess the legislative power to make rules, the executive power to enforce them, and the judicial power to adjudicate them. This combination of functions in a single agency seems in conflict with elemental concepts of separation of powers.

---

§3.11 [1] These and other justifications for broad delegations of power are discussed in Richard Stewart, The Reformation of American Administrative Law, 88 Harv. L. Rev. 1667 (1975).

The Nondelegation Doctrine

One solution to these constitutional problems posed by administrative agencies is the nondelegation doctrine: the principle that Congress may not delegate its legislative power to administrative agencies. The nondelegation doctrine forces a politically accountable Congress to make the policy choices, rather than leave this to unelected administrative officials.

The height of the Court's enforcement of the nondelegation doctrine was in the mid-1930s in two decisions that invalidated New Deal legislation. The National Industrial Recovery Act, a key piece of New Deal legislation, authorized the president to approve "codes of fair competition" developed by boards of various industries. In *Panama Refining Co. v. Ryan*, in 1935, the Court declared unconstitutional a provision of the National Industrial Recovery Act that authorized the president to prohibit the shipment in interstate commerce of oil produced in excess of state-imposed production quotas.[2] The Court concluded that the law was an impermissible delegation of legislative power to the president, and the Court emphasized the lack of any standards in the Act to limit the president's discretion.

In *Schechter Poultry Corp. v. United States*, also in 1935, the Court declared unconstitutional a regulation adopted under the National Industrial Recovery Act.[3] Pursuant to this law, the president approved a Live Poultry Code for New York City. In part, the Code required sellers to sell only entire coops of chickens or half coops of chickens, and it made it illegal for buyers to reject individual chickens. The Code also regulated employment by requiring collective bargaining, prohibiting child labor, and establishing a 40-hour workweek and a minimum wage.

As described above in §3.4.3, the Court declared the regulation unconstitutional as exceeding the scope of Congress's commerce power. The Court also found the regulation unconstitutional as an impermissible delegation of legislative power. The Court declared that "Congress is not permitted to abdicate or to transfer to others the essential legislative function with which it is thus vested."[4] The Court recognized the need for regulations to deal with the "host of details with which the national legislature cannot deal directly."[5] But the Court said that "the constant recognition of the necessity and validity of such provisions, and the wide range of administrative authority which has been developed by means of them cannot be allowed to obscure the limitations of the authority to delegate, if our constitutional system is to be maintained."[6]

The Demise of the Nondelegation Doctrine

In the 80 years since *Panama Oil* and *Schechter*, not a single federal law has been declared an impermissible delegation of legislative power. Although these

---

[2] 293 U.S. 388 (1935).
[3] 295 U.S. 495 (1935).
[4] *Id.* at 529.
[5] *Id.* at 530.
[6] *Id.*

decisions have not been expressly overruled, they never have been followed either. All delegations, no matter how broad, have been upheld. Although the Court says that when Congress delegates its legislative power it must provide criteria—"intelligible principles"—to guide the agency's exercise of discretion,[7] all delegations, even without any criteria, have been upheld. Undoubtedly, this reflects a judicial judgment that broad delegations are necessary in the complex modern world and that the judiciary is ill-equipped to draw meaningful lines.[8]

In recent years, the Supreme Court has continued to reject challenges to federal statutes on the ground that they impermissibly delegate legislative power. In *Mistretta v. United States*, the Court approved a broad delegation of power to the United States Sentencing Commission to promulgate sentencing guidelines to determine the punishments for those convicted of federal crimes.[9] The Sentencing Commission is composed of seven members appointed by the president, at least three of whom must be federal judges. Organizationally, the commission is a part of the judicial branch of government. By an 8-to-1 margin, with only Justice Scalia dissenting, the Court upheld the law and rejected the claim that it was an impermissible delegation of legislative power to the judicial branch of government. Justice Blackmun, writing for the Court, stated that "Congress may delegate to the Judicial Branch nonadjudicatory functions that do not trench upon the prerogatives of another Branch and that are appropriate to the central mission of the Judiciary."[10]

Justice Scalia, in dissent, argued that the commission was given broad discretion to make "value judgments and policy assessments" in creating the Sentencing Guidelines.[11] Although he recognized that judicial limits on the delegation of legislative power are problematic, he said that "the power to make law cannot be exercised by anyone other than Congress, except in conjunction with the lawful exercise of executive or judicial power."[12] Scalia contended that the commission's authority to promulgate sentencing guidelines was an unconstitutional delegation of legislative power to a judicial agency.

Scalia is not the only Justice to urge a resurrection of the nondelegation doctrine. In the early 1980s, then-Justice Rehnquist took a similar position. In *Industrial Union Dept. v. American Petroleum Institute*, the Court considered provisions of the Occupational Safety and Health Act that authorized the secretary of labor to adopt standards that are "reasonably necessary or appropriate to provide safe or healthful employment" and to "set the standard which most adequately assures, to the extent feasible, on the basis of the best available evidence, that no employee will suffer material impairment of health."[13] Justice Rehnquist, in a dissenting opinion, argued that these provisions should have been invalidated as an excessive

---

[7] *See, e.g.*, Whitman v. American Trucking Associations, Inc., 531 U.S. 457 (2001); National Cable Television Association v. United States, 415 U.S. 336 (1974).

[8] *See* Stewart, *supra* note 1, at 1695-1697.

[9] 488 U.S. 361 (1989).

[10] *Id.* at 388.

[11] *Id.* at 414 (Scalia, J., dissenting).

[12] *Id.* at 417.

[13] 448 U.S. 607 (1980).

delegation of legislative power. He wrote: "When fundamental policy decisions underlying important legislation about to be enacted are to be made, the buck stops with Congress and the President insofar as he exercises his constitutional role in the legislative process."[14]

These isolated dissents, however, detract little from the strong consensus over the last half century in favor of allowing broad delegations of legislative power to administrative and regulatory agencies of all types.[15] Indeed, two more recent cases have emphatically refused to revive the nondelegation doctrine. In *Loving v. United States*, the Supreme Court rejected a nondelegation doctrine challenge to the president's prescription of aggravating factors for the imposition of the death penalty in the military.[16] The Uniform Code of Military Justice permits the imposition of the death penalty for crimes such as premeditated murder. The Code, however, does not delineate "aggravating" and "mitigating" factors to be considered in imposing the death penalty, as is now required by the Supreme Court. The president, by executive order, specified these aggravating and mitigating factors. Loving, an Army private convicted of two murders and sentenced to death, argued that the president lacked the authority to promulgate the aggravating factors that enabled the military court to sentence him to death.

The Court rejected this contention and upheld the death sentence. The Court emphasized the long tradition, dating back to English history, of the chief executive making rules for the military.[17] The Court also stressed that it gives "Congress the highest deference in ordering military affairs."[18] Justice Kennedy, writing for the Court, thus concluded that "Congress [may] delegate authority to the president to define the aggravating factors that permit the imposition of a statutory death penalty."[19]

Most recently, in *Whitman v. American Trucking Associations, Inc.*, the Court unanimously rejected a challenge to the federal Clean Air Act as an impermissible delegation of legislative power.[20] The United States Court of Appeals for the District of Columbia Circuit declared unconstitutional the Environmental Protection Agency's air quality regulations, particularly as to ozone levels, on the ground that there was an impermissible delegation of power.[21] The court emphasized the lack of an "intelligible principle" to explain why the statute permits one level of pollution, but not another, when all amounts entail some risk to public health.[22]

To the surprise of many, the Court unanimously upheld the delegation and the constitutionality of the EPA's air quality regulations. Justice Scalia wrote for the

---

[14] *Id.* at 687 (Rehnquist, J., concurring); *see also* American Textile Manufacturers v. Donovan, 452 U.S. 490, 543 (1981) (Rehnquist, J., dissenting).

[15] *See also* Touby v. United States, 500 U.S. 160 (1991) (upholding and rejecting a nondelegation doctrine challenge to the federal Controlled Substances Act).

[16] 517 U.S. 748 (1996).

[17] *Id.* at 764.

[18] *Id.* at 768.

[19] *Id.*

[20] 531 U.S. 457 (2001).

[21] *See* American Trucking Assns. v. United States EPA, 195 F.3d 4 (D.C. Cir. 1999).

[22] Interestingly, the D.C. Circuit emphasized that the Environmental Protection Agency failed to interpret the statute to provide intelligible principles. 195 F.3d at 8.

Court. He began by declaring that the Constitution "permits no delegation of [legislative] powers."[23] But he noted that only twice in history, in two cases decided in 1935, had the Court invalidated delegations. Justice Scalia said that Congress must give "intelligible principles" to guide the agency in its exercise of discretion and concluded that "the scope of discretion [the statute] allows is in fact well within the outer limits on nondelegation precedents."[24] He emphasized that the law does not permit the EPA to consider implementation costs in promulgating clean air act rules, something that considerably narrows the discretion of the agency. Justice Scalia concluded his majority opinion by declaring that the requirement that the "EPA . . . set air quality standards at the level that is 'requisite'—that is, not lower or higher than is necessary—to protect the public health with an adequate margin of safety, fits comfortably within the scope of discretion permitted by our precedent."[25]

Descriptively, after these decisions a successful challenge to a federal law as an impermissible delegation of legislative power seems unlikely. No such challenge has succeeded in 80 years despite countless expansive delegations of legislative power. Still, there is the possibility that the Supreme Court might find a statute so devoid of "intelligible principles" as to be unconstitutional.[26]

Normatively, the Court's refusal to enforce a nondelegation doctrine can be criticized as undermining government accountability as political decisions are made by unelected administrative officials and as undermining the basic philosophy of separation of powers embodied in the Constitution. On the other hand, the broad delegations can be defended as essential in a complex world requiring technical and detailed regulations that probably exceed the scope and ability of Congress.

§3.11.2 *The Legislative Veto*

The Legislative Veto Defined

In light of the demise of the nondelegation doctrine, the issue arises as to how the power of administrative agencies will be checked and controlled. Congress, of course, could enact a law overturning an agency's rule, but requiring legislative action obviously limits the circumstances in which Congress can or will exercise its checking function.

Therefore, in the 1930s, not coincidentally corresponding to the time of great growth in federal administrative agencies, Congress created the "legislative veto" as a check on the actions of administrative agencies. Congress included in statutes provisions authorizing Congress or one of its houses or committees to overturn an

---

[23] 531 U.S. at 472.
[24] *Id.* at 474.
[25] *Id.* at 475-476.
[26] For contemporary analysis of the nondelegation doctrine, *see* Larry Alexander & Saikrishna Prakash, 70 U. Chi. L. Rev. 1297 (2003); Gary Lawson, Delegation and Original Meaning, 88 Va. L. Rev. 202 (2002).

agency's action by doing something less than adopting a new law. A typical form of a legislative veto provision authorized Congress to overturn an agency's decision by a resolution of one house of Congress. Legislative vetoes also took the form of overturning agency rules by resolution of both houses of Congress or even by action of a congressional committee. Over 200 federal laws contained legislative veto provisions.[27]

The Unconstitutionality of the Legislative Veto

In *Immigration and Naturalization Service (INS) v. Chadha*, the Supreme Court declared unconstitutional the legislative veto.[28] Chadha was an East Indian who had been born in Kenya and had a British passport. After his visa expired, Chadha was ordered to show cause as to why he should be allowed to remain in the United States. An immigration judge ruled in favor of Chadha and ordered that his deportation be stayed.

However, the House of Representatives adopted a resolution overturning this decision and thereby ordering Chadha's deportation. Federal law gave either house of Congress the authority to overturn an INS decision to suspend deportation.[29] Representative Eilberg, chair of the House Judiciary Subcommittee on Immigration, Citizenship, and International Law, introduced a resolution opposing the granting of citizenship to six individuals, including Chadha, on the ground that they "did not meet [the] statutory requirements, particularly as it relates to hardship."[30]

The Supreme Court, in an opinion by Chief Justice Burger, declared this legislative veto to be unconstitutional. Burger's opinion can be described as a syllogism. The major premise of the syllogism is that Congress may legislate only if there is *bicameralism*, passage by both the House and the Senate, and *presentment*, giving the bill to the president to sign or veto. Burger's opinion recited the constitutional provisions requiring bicameralism and presentment and quoted from the Federalist Papers as to the importance of these procedural requirements.[31]

The minor premise of the syllogism was that the legislative veto was legislation without bicameralism or presentment. Chief Justice Burger declared that the action "was essentially legislative in purpose and effect."[32] The effect of the legislative veto was to "alter the legal rights, duties, and relations of persons, including the Attorney General, Executive Branch officials and Chadha." Accordingly, the Court concluded that it was legislation and that it did not fit into any of the limited situations under the Constitution where one branch of Congress can act alone.[33]

Thus, the conclusion followed, as it always does with a syllogism: The legislative veto is unconstitutional. Chief Justice Burger expressly rejected the position

---

[27] INS v. Chadha, 462 U.S. 919, 967 (1983) (White, J., dissenting).
[28] 462 U.S. 919 (1983).
[29] 8 U.S.C. §1254(c)(2), quoted at 462 U.S. at 925.
[30] Quoted at 462 U.S. 926.
[31] *Id.* at 945-950.
[32] *Id.* at 952.
[33] *Id.*

that the legislative veto was necessary to ensure adequate checks and balances. Burger wrote: "The choices we discern as having been made in the Constitutional Convention impose burdens on governmental processes that often seem clumsy, inefficient, even unworkable, but those hard choices were consciously made by men who had lived under a form of government that permitted arbitrary governmental acts to go unchecked. There is no support in the Constitution or decisions of this Court for the proposition that the cumbersomeness and delays often encountered in complying with explicit Constitutional standards may be avoided, either by the Congress or the President."[34]

Justice White wrote a strong dissenting opinion that emphasized the need for the legislative veto as a check on the broad delegations of legislative power. He explained that although the legislative veto was not contemplated by the framers of the Constitution, nor were the expansive delegations found in countless statutes creating administrative agencies. He explained that "[w]ithout the legislative veto, Congress is faced with a Hobson's choice: either to refrain from delegating the necessary authority, leaving itself with a hopeless task of writing laws with the requisite specificity to cover endless special circumstances across the entire policy landscape, or in the alternative, to abdicate its lawmaking function to the Executive Branch and independent agencies."[35]

While Chief Justice Burger's majority opinion was highly formalistic, Justice White's dissent was functional.[36] Burger emphasized the formal structure prescribed in the Constitution for adopting laws and dismissed the functional concern that the legislative veto was essential to check administrative power. White, in contrast, stressed the fact that over 200 federal laws contained legislative vetoes reflecting Congress's judgment that this was an essential tool for checking the exercise of delegated powers. Indeed, White lamented that the majority in *Chadha* invalidated "in one fell swoop provisions in more laws enacted by Congress than the Court had cumulatively invalidated in its history."[37]

The dispute among the Justices in *Chadha* was over the proper form of analysis in separation of powers cases. Should the evaluation of the constitutionality of the legislative veto rest entirely on the text of the Constitution and the framers' intent, or should the Court consider the functional justification for legislative vetoes? Neither the majority nor the dissent addressed whether the legislative veto is actually an effective tool for checking administrative agencies.[38] *Chadha* involved a legislative veto of an adjudicatory proceeding; Congress, by resolution of the House of Representatives, overturned an immigration judge's decision to allow Chadha to remain in the country. Almost immediately after *Chadha*, the Court extended its

[34] *Id.* at 959.

[35] *Id.* at 968 (White, J., dissenting).

[36] *See* Peter Strauss, Formal and Functional Approaches to Separation-of-Powers Questions: A Foolish Inconsistency?, 72 Cornell L. Rev. 765, 782 (1987).

[37] 462 U.S. at 1002.

[38] *See, e.g.,* Harold Bruff & Ernest Gellhorn, Congressional Control of Administrative Regulation: A Study of Legislative Vetoes, 90 Harv. L. Rev. 1369 (1977) (reviewing the exercise of legislative vetoes and questioning whether they are actually an effective check on the exercise of delegated powers).

holding to preclude legislative vetoes of agency rules.[39] It is thus clearly established that if Congress wants to overturn an executive action, there must be bicameralism, passage by both houses of Congress, and presentment, giving the bill to the president for signature or veto. Anything less is a legislative veto, and legislative vetoes are unconstitutional.

Other Checks on Administrative Powers

Although *Chadha* invalidated an important means of congressional control of agency discretion, others certainly remain. For example, Congress can overturn agency decisions so long as there is bicameralism and presentment. Additionally, of course, Congress controls the purse strings of administrative agencies, and there undoubtedly are informal political checks, such as through oversight committees. Another political check on agency power comes from the power of the president to appoint agency members, often subject to Senate approval. The appointment and removal power is discussed more fully in §4.2.

The basic question, though, remains: In light of the demise of the nondelegation doctrine and the unconstitutionality of legislative vetoes, are there sufficient checks on administrative agencies?

§3.11.3   Delegation of Executive Power to Congress and Its Officials

Although Congress has broad authority to delegate legislative power to administrative agencies, the Court has made it clear that Congress cannot delegate executive power to itself or to its agents. For example, in *Buckley v. Valeo*, the Court declared unconstitutional a provision of a federal law that allowed the speaker of the House of Representatives and the president pro tempore of the Senate to appoint members of the Federal Election Commission.[40] The Federal Election Commission Act created an eight-person commission, with four members to be appointed by the president and two each by the Speaker of the House and the president pro tem of the Senate. The Supreme Court declared this unconstitutional as an impermissible delegation of appointment power to Congress. The Court explained that the Constitution specifies who may possess the appointment power and never contemplates giving this authority to Congress.

In *Bowsher v. Synar*, the Court declared unconstitutional a provision of the Gramm-Rudman-Hollings Deficit Reduction Act as an impermissible delegation of executive power to legislative officials.[41] In an attempt to eliminate the federal budget deficit, Congress adopted a law that set the maximum allowable deficit for each of the following five years. If spending exceeded the deficit ceiling, the comptroller general, the head of the General Accounting Office, was instructed to

---

[39] *See, e.g.*, Process Gas Consumers Group v. Consumers Energy Council of America, 463 U.S. 1216 (1983).

[40] 424 U.S. 1 (1976).

[41] 478 U.S. 714 (1986). The Act was the Balanced Budget and Emergency Deficit Control Act of 1985.

impose across-the-board spending cuts as prescribed and limited in the Act. The comptroller general is a legislative official, and the General Accounting Office is a legislative agency.

The Supreme Court declared this to be an unconstitutional delegation of the executive power to the legislature. The Court explained that the comptroller general was granted the executive power to administer the law and concluded that it was impermissible for Congress to delegate the executive power to itself or its officers. Chief Justice Burger, writing for the Court, stated: "[As] *Chadha* makes clear, once Congress makes its choice in enacting legislation, its participation ends. Congress can thereafter control the execution of its enactment only indirectly by passing new legislation. By placing the responsibility for the executive of the Balanced Budget and Emergency Deficit Control Act in the hands of an officer who is subject to removal only by itself, Congress in effect has retained control over the execution of the Act and has intruded into the executive function. The Constitution does not permit such intrusion."[42]

Similarly, in *Metropolitan Washington Airports Authority v. Citizens for the Abatement of Aircraft Noise*, the Supreme Court declared unconstitutional a federal law that gave authority to review decisions of an airport authority to a Board of Review that consisted of nine members of Congress.[43] Virginia and the District of Columbia created the Metropolitan Washington Airports Authority to operate Reagan and Dulles Airports in the Washington, D.C., metropolitan area. Congress created a Board of Review with the authority to overturn decisions of the authority. Eight of the nine members were to be members of Congress. Virginia and the District of Columbia then amended their statutes to create this Board of Review, composed of congressional members as prescribed by Congress.

The Supreme Court declared this unconstitutional as Congress impermissibly delegating an executive power to itself. Alternatively, the Court said that if the board was exercising executive power, the requirements of bicameralism and presentment prescribed in *Chadha* were not met.

The underlying question is whether it makes sense for the Court to allow Congress to delegate the legislative power to the executive, but to refuse to allow Congress to delegate the executive power to the legislature. Perhaps it is unjustified formalism and a refusal to allow the flexibility that is necessary to govern in the complex world of the twenty-first century. Or perhaps it is a reflection of a judicial judgment that there is less reason to be concerned when a branch of government is relinquishing its power than when it is assuming the authority assigned to another branch.

---

[42] *Id.* at 733-734.
[43] 501 U.S. 252 (1991).

CHAPTER 4

The Federal Executive Power

§4.1   EXPRESS AND INHERENT PRESIDENTIAL POWERS

Is There Inherent Presidential Power?

Article II of the Constitution begins, "The executive Power shall be vested in a President of the United States of America." Article II then enumerates specific powers of the president.

From the earliest days of the country, there has been a debate over whether this language was intended to grant the president inherent powers not expressly enumerated in Article II. Some commentators, beginning with Alexander Hamilton, have argued that the difference in the wording of Articles I and II reveals the framers' intention to create inherent presidential powers.[1] Article I initially states that "All legislative Powers herein granted shall be vested in a Congress of the United States." Since Article II does not limit the president to powers "herein granted," it is argued that the president has authority not specifically delineated in the Constitution.

Others, beginning with James Madison,[2] have disputed this interpretation of Article II, contending that the opening language of Article II was "simply to settle the question whether the executive branch should be plural or single and to give the executive a title."[3] According to this position, the president has no powers that are not enumerated in Article II and, indeed, such unenumerated authority would be inconsistent with a Constitution creating a government of limited authority.

The debate between Hamilton and Madison over inherent presidential power reflects the difficulty of resolving this issue by reference to the text of the Constitution or the framers' intent.[4] As Justice Robert Jackson eloquently wrote: "Just what our forefathers did envision, or would have envisioned had they foreseen modern conditions, must be divined from materials almost as enigmatic as the dreams Joseph was called upon to interpret for Pharaoh. A century and a half of partisan debate and scholarly speculation yields no net result but only supplies more or less apt quotations from respected sources on each side of any question. They largely cancel each other. And court decisions are indecisive because of the judicial practice of dealing with the largest questions in the most narrow way."[5]

Youngstown Sheet & Tube Co. v. Sawyer

The leading case addressing the scope of inherent presidential power—the ability of the president to act without express constitutional or statutory authority—is *Youngstown Sheet & Tube Co. v. Sawyer.*[6] In early 1952, the United Steelworkers Union announced a planned nationwide strike as a result of a labor-management dispute. A few hours before the strike was to begin, President Harry Truman issued Executive Order 10340, which directed the secretary of commerce to take possession of the steel mills and to keep them running. Truman believed that the steel strike could endanger the national defense and the war effort in Korea because steel was indispensable for all weapons. The secretary of commerce,

---

§4.1 [1] Alexander Hamilton, First Letter of Pacificus (June 29, 1793), reprinted in William H. Goldsmith, The Growth of Presidential Power: A Documented History 398, 401 (1974).

[2] James Madison, First Letter of Helvidius, reprinted in Goldsmith, *supra* note 1, at 405.

[3] Edward S. Corwin, The Steel Seizure Case: A Judicial Brick Without Straw, 53 Colum. L. Rev. 53, 53 (1953).

[4] The debate between Hamilton and Madison over the scope of inherent presidential power occurred when President George Washington issued a Neutrality Proclamation, declaring that the United States would remain impartial toward countries involved in a war in Europe. Hamilton argued that the president had the authority to issue the Proclamation even though Article II did not enumerate such a power; Madison argued against such presidential authority.

[5] Youngstown Sheet & Tube Co. v. Sawyer, 343 U.S. 579, 634 (1952) (Jackson, J., concurring) (footnote omitted).

[6] 343 U.S. 579 (1952).

Charles Sawyer, issued the order, and the president reported this action to Congress. Congress took no action in response to the seizure.

The Supreme Court, by a 6-to-3 margin, declared the seizure of the steel mills unconstitutional. Seven different opinions were written. Interestingly, although Justice Black's opinion was a majority opinion for the Court, the Justices in the majority gave several different answers to the question of when the president may act without express constitutional or statutory authority.

In fact, four different approaches can be identified in the opinions in *Youngstown*; these varying approaches also are reflected in numerous other cases. The four approaches, discussed below, are:

(1)   There is no inherent presidential power; the president may act only if there is express constitutional or statutory authority.

(2)   The president has inherent authority unless the president interferes with the functioning of another branch of government or usurps the powers of another branch.

(3)   The president may exercise powers not mentioned in the Constitution so long as the president does not violate a statute or the Constitution.

(4)   The president has inherent powers that may not be restricted by Congress and may act unless the Constitution is violated.

Approach 1: No Inherent Presidential Power

One approach, found in Justice Black's majority opinion, is to deny the existence of any inherent presidential power: The president may act only pursuant to express or clearly implied statutory or constitutional authority. Justice Black stated that "[t]he President's power, if any, to issue the order must stem either from an act of Congress or from the Constitution itself."[7]

Justice Black concluded that President Truman's order to seize control of the steel mills was unconstitutional because "[t]here is no statute that expressly authorizes the President to take possession of property as he did here" and "it is not claimed that express constitutional language grants this power to the President."[8]

This approach is premised on the belief that inherent authority is inconsistent with a written Constitution establishing a government of limited powers.[9] As William Howard Taft, former president and Supreme Court Chief Justice, declared: "The true view of the Executive functions is . . . that the President can exercise no power which cannot be fairly and reasonably traced to some specific grant of power . . . either in the Federal Constitution or in an act of Congress passed in pursuance

---

[7] *Id.* at 585.

[8] *Id.* at 585, 587.

[9] *See, e.g.,* Raoul Berger, The Presidential Monopoly of Foreign Relations, 71 Mich. L. Rev. 1, 27, 32-33 (1972) (allowing inherent presidential powers ignores the framers' clear intent to form a government of limited powers).

thereof. There is no undefined residuum of power which he can exercise because it seems to him to be in the public interest."[10]

Approach 2: Interstitial Executive Power

A second approach allows the president to act without express statutory or constitutional authority so long as the president is not usurping the powers of another branch of government or keeping another branch from performing its duties. Justice Douglas, in a concurring opinion in *Youngstown*, appeared to take this approach. Douglas argued that the seizure was unconstitutional because the president was forcing the expenditure of federal funds to compensate the steel mill owners for the taking of their property. Douglas contended that the president was therefore impermissibly usurping Congress's spending power. Douglas wrote: "The President might seize and the Congress by subsequent action might ratify the seizure. But until and unless Congress acted, no condemnation would be lawful. The branch of government that has the power to pay compensation for a seizure is the only one able to authorize a seizure or make lawful one that the President has effected. That seems to me to be the necessary result of the condemnation provision of the Fifth Amendment."[11]

Unlike the no-inherent-presidential-power approach, this view recognizes the ability of the president to act without express constitutional or statutory authority, so long as the president is not infringing or usurping the powers of Congress or the courts. This approach is premised on the belief that there is a need for the president to exercise powers not specifically enumerated in the Constitution or not expressly granted by Congress. For example, the Constitution makes no mention of a presidential power to recognize foreign governments or to remove presidential appointees from office, nor has Congress ever granted such powers in a statute. Yet it is conceded that the president has these powers.[12]

Approach 3: Legislative Accountability

A third approach is that the president may take any action not prohibited by the Constitution or a statute.[13] Several of the opinions in *Youngstown* took this approach. For example, Justice Frankfurter argued that Congress had explicitly

---

[10] William Howard Taft, Our Chief Magistrate and His Powers 139-140 (1916).

[11] 343 U.S. at 631-632 (Douglas, J., concurring).

[12] Another example of the Court following this approach would be *United States v. Nixon*, 418 U.S. 683 (1974), where the Court held that the president has executive privilege, the ability to keep memoranda to or conversations with the president secret. But the Court said that executive privilege must yield when it keeps the courts from having needed evidence in a criminal trial. Executive privilege is discussed in detail in §4.3.

[13] One of the earliest separation of powers cases, *Little v. Barreme*, 6 U.S. (2 Cranch) 170 (1804), took this approach. In *Little*, the Court upheld an award of damages against a ship captain who followed a specific order of the president to seize a ship coming to the United States from France. The Court stated that while the president might have the inherent authority to order the seizure of ships, Congress, by the Nonintercourse Act, had expressly limited the president's authority.

rejected giving the president the authority to seize industries and that this was a clear decision to preclude such an action. Justice Frankfurter declared: "[N]othing can be plainer than that Congress made a conscious choice of policy in a field full of perplexity and peculiarly within legislative responsibility for choice. In formulating legislation for dealing with industrial conflicts, Congress could not more clearly and emphatically have withheld authority than it did in 1947."[14]

Likewise, Justice Robert Jackson found the president's action unconstitutional because Congress had denied the president the authority to seize industries. Justice Jackson's concurring opinion is perhaps the most famous opinion dealing with presidential power because he delineated three zones of presidential authority. First, Jackson said that "[w]hen the President acts pursuant to an express or implied authorization of Congress, his authority is at its maximum, for it includes all that he possesses in his own right plus all that Congress can delegate."[15] Under such circumstances, the president's acts are presumptively valid.

Second, Jackson said that "[w]hen the President acts in absence of either a congressional grant or denial of authority, he can only rely upon his own independent powers, but there is a zone of twilight in which he and Congress may have concurrent authority, or in which its distribution is uncertain."[16] Under these circumstances, Jackson said that it is impossible to formulate general rules as to the constitutionality of actions in this area; rather, constitutionality is likely "to depend on the imperatives of events and contemporary imponderables rather than on abstract theories of law."[17]

Third, Jackson argued that "[w]hen the President takes measures incompatible with the expressed or implied will of Congress, his power is at its lowest ebb."[18] Because the president is disobeying a federal law, such presidential actions will be allowed only if the law enacted by Congress is unconstitutional.

Analysis of presidential power often starts with Justice Jackson's three-part test. Interestingly, his first and third zones involve situations in which Congress has acted, and thus the issue is the constitutionality of the federal law. The second approach concerns inherent powers—when the president is acting without constitutional or statutory authority. This is the situation in issues such as executive privilege, impoundment, rescission of treaties, executive agreements, removal of executive officials from office, and the like. Justice Jackson offered no criteria to guide the courts in dealing with these issues.

In *Youngstown*, Justice Jackson concluded that the president's seizure of the steel mills fit into the third category because "Congress has not left seizure of private property an open field but has covered it by three statutory policies inconsistent with this seizure."[19]

It should be noted that the dissenting Justices in *Youngstown* appeared to agree with this third approach to inherent powers, but disagreed as to whether

---

[14] 343 U.S. at 602 (Frankfurter, J., concurring).
[15] *Id.* at 635 (Jackson, J., concurring).
[16] *Id.* at 637.
[17] *Id.*
[18] *Id.*
[19] *Id.* at 639.

Congress had acted. Chief Justice Vinson's dissenting opinion argued, in part, that the president had notified Congress of the seizure and that Congress never acted to disapprove the action.[20] He concluded that "there is no evidence whatever of any Presidential purpose to defy Congress or act in any way inconsistent with the legislative will."[21] In other words, Vinson, like Jackson and Frankfurter, looked to whether Congress had disapproved the president's actions; unlike these other Justices, Vinson found no such disapproval.

Approach 4: Broad Inherent Authority

Finally, there is the view that the president has inherent authority, at least in some areas, and may act unless such conduct violates the Constitution. In other words, in this fourth area, federal laws restricting the president's power are unconstitutional. Chief Justice Vinson's dissenting opinion in *Youngstown* suggests such inherent authority when he approvingly invokes "President [Theodore] Roosevelt['s] . . . 'Stewardship Theory' of Presidential power, stating that the executive as subject only to the people, and, under the Constitution, bound to serve the people affirmatively in cases where the Constitution does not explicitly forbid him to render the service."[22]

The strongest expression of this approach was in *United States v. Curtiss-Wright Export Corp.*[23] The case involved a congressional authorization permitting the president to restrict arms sales to two warring Latin American nations. In upholding a broad delegation of power to the president, Justice Sutherland wrote: "The two classes of powers [domestic and foreign] are different, both in respect of their origin and their nature. The broad statement that the federal government can exercise no powers except those specifically enumerated in the Constitution . . . is categorically true only in respect of our internal affairs."[24] Justice Sutherland argued that power to conduct foreign policy does not stem from the Constitution, but instead is intrinsic to nationality.[25]

Over the last decade and a half, there have been claims of broad inherent presidential power to protect national security and fight terrorism.[26] In the years following the attack on September 11, 2001, the Bush administration asserted inherent power, including the power to engage in warrantless eavesdropping in

---

[20] *Id.* at 703 (Vinson, C.J., dissenting).

[21] *Id.* at 703.

[22] *Id.* at 688. However, as discussed above, it should be noted that Vinson also emphasized the absence of congressional action disapproving the seizure of the steel mills.

[23] 299 U.S. 304 (1936). *Curtiss-Wright* is discussed in more detail below in §4.6.1.

[24] *Id.* at 315-316.

[25] There are cases taking this approach in the domestic realm. In *In re Neagle*, 135 U.S. 1 (1890), the Court held that the president had inherent authority to assign a United States Marshal as a personal bodyguard for Supreme Court Justice Stephen Field. In *In re Debs*, 158 U.S. 564 (1895), the Court upheld President Cleveland's authority to use troops and to seek an injunction without statutory authority to end the Pullman strike.

[26] For an excellent discussion of *Youngstown* and its application to the war on terrorism, *see* Christopher Bryant & Carl Tobias, *Youngstown* Revisited, 29 Hastings Const. L.Q. 373 (2002).

violation of the requirements of the Foreign Intelligence Security Act.[27] Unlike the third approach, which would allow federal statutes to control executive power, the fourth approach would make such laws unconstitutional as impermissibly restricting inherent presidential powers.

The Importance of the Approach

All four of these approaches have some support in *Youngstown* and some support in other cases. No Supreme Court case definitively makes one of these approaches correct and the others wrong. Ultimately, the choice of approach must be based on a decision about the appropriate scope of presidential power and how best to check the president. The first approach grants the president only the powers found in the Constitution or a statute; the fourth approach grants the president broad authority so long as the Constitution is not violated. The second approach allows the courts to invalidate presidential actions that interfere with the other branches of government; the third approach sees it as Congress's responsibility to act to stop presidential infringements.

As an example of the importance of the choice of the approach, consider the issue of impoundment. During the early 1970s, President Richard Nixon claimed that he had the power to impound funds appropriated by Congress and to refuse to spend them. Under the first approach, impoundment is unconstitutional because there is no constitutional or statutory authority to support the practice.[28] Under the second approach, impoundment also is likely unconstitutional because it usurps Congress's power of the purse. If Congress overrides the president's veto and decides to expend funds, the president could still preclude the spending by impounding the money; this would undermine the legislative power. Under approach three, impoundment likely was constitutional until Congress adopted the Impoundment Control Act of 1974,[29] which effectively forbids the practice. Finally, under approach four, if impoundment is regarded as an inherent power of the president, then it is constitutional and the Impoundment Control Act is an impermissible restriction.

In other words, the choice of the approach is crucial in determining the analysis used and the likely outcome. In most cases, however, the approach used is implicit rather than expressly defended.

---

[27] The President's powers in the war on terrorism are discussed below in §4.6.4. For a defense of broad inherent presidential powers, *see* John Yoo, The Power of War and Peace: The Constitution and Foreign Affairs After 9/11 (2005). For a critique of this view, *see* David Cole, What Bush Wants to Hear, New York Review of Books, Nov. 17, 2005.

[28] *See, e.g.,* State Highway Commission of Missouri v. Volpe, 347 F. Supp. 950 (W.D. Mo. 1972), *aff'd* 479 F.2d 1099 (8th Cir. 1973); Local 2677 v. Phillips, 358 F. Supp. 60 (D.D.C. 1973) (finding impoundment unconstitutional); *cf.* Train v. New York, 420 U.S. 35 (1975) (rejecting the argument that the Federal Water Pollution Control Act authorized impoundment of funds).

[29] 31 U.S.C. §1301.

Can Congress Expand Presidential Power?
The Line-Item Veto

This section thus far has considered the inherent powers of the president. A related issue is the extent to which Congress, by statute, may increase presidential powers beyond what are found in the Constitution. In *Clinton v. City of New York*,[30] the Supreme Court considered the constitutionality of a federal statute that created authority for a presidential line-item veto. The statute empowered the president to veto (or more precisely to "cancel") particular parts of appropriation bills while allowing the rest to go into effect.[31] Congress could overturn such a veto by a majority vote of both houses.

The Supreme Court, in an opinion by Justice Stevens, declared this statutory increase in presidential power unconstitutional. Justice Stevens explained that the president, by exercising the line-item veto, was changing a law adopted by Congress; the final version of the law is different after the veto than what Congress passed. The Court concluded that the Constitution does not allow such presidential authority. Justice Stevens wrote: "In both legal and practical effect, the President has amended two Acts of Congress by repealing a portion of each. '[R]epeal of statutes, no less than enactment, must conform with Art. I.' There is no provision in the Constitution that authorizes the President to enact, to amend, or to repeal statutes."[32] The Court emphasized that the procedures for enacting and vetoing laws contained in the Constitution must be strictly adhered to and that any changes must come from a constitutional amendment, not legislative action.[33]

Justice Breyer, joined by Justices O'Connor and Scalia, dissented, and stressed the practical need for a line-item veto. He explained that when the Constitution was written, the national budget was $4 million and each appropriation could be in a separate bill.[34] Today, though, with a federal budget of $1.5 trillion, "a typical budget appropriations bill may have a dozen titles, hundreds of sections, and spread across more than 500 pages of the Statutes at Large. Congress cannot divide such a bill into thousands, or tens of thousands, of separate appropriations bills, each one of which the President would have to sign, or to veto, separately."[35]

Justice Breyer disagreed with the majority's conclusion that the president was amending the law by exercising the line-item veto. Justice Breyer explained: "When the President 'canceled' the two appropriation measures now before us, he did not repeal any law nor did he amend any law. He simply followed the law, leaving the statutes, as they are literally written, intact."[36]

In large part, the difference between the majority in *Clinton v. City of New York* is the difference between a formalist and a functional approach to separation of powers that reappears throughout the material in this chapter. Justice Stevens's

---

[30] 524 U.S. 417 (1998).
[31] Line Item Veto Act (Act), 110 Stat. 1200, 2 U.S.C. §691.
[32] 524 U.S. at 438 (citation omitted).
[33] *Id.* at 439.
[34] *Id.* at 471 (Breyer, J., dissenting).
[35] *Id.* at 473.
[36] *Id.* at 474.

majority opinion was highly formalistic in stressing the procedures prescribed in the Constitution for enacting laws and eschewing any consideration of the practical benefits of a line-item veto. In contrast, Justice Breyer's dissenting opinion emphasized the need for a line-item veto in light of the myriad ways in which the budget process has changed with the growth of government over 200 years.

The Issues and the Organization of the Chapter

The remainder of the chapter considers specific areas of presidential power, examining both areas of express authority and claimed inherent powers. Section 4.2 considers the appointment and removal power. Section 4.3 examines executive privilege. Section 4.4 focuses on presidential immunity to civil and criminal suits. Section 4.5 discusses the pardon power. Section 4.6 examines the president's authority in foreign policy and includes specific discussion of presidential power in connection with the war on terrorism. Finally, §4.7 considers the ultimate check on presidential power: impeachment and removal from office, and especially the events surrounding the impeachment of President Bill Clinton.

The material discussed in this chapter, of course, concerns the basic theme of separation of powers. Therefore, these topics are closely related to many of the issues discussed in the prior chapter on the federal legislative power. Some of the same basic policy questions arise. To what extent should the Court take a formalist approach to executive power, following solely the text and the framers' intent, or to what extent should the Court take a functional approach and be guided by the underlying values of separation of powers? What is the proper balance between checking the president to ensure accountability and according the president the discretion necessary to govern? These questions recur in the areas discussed below.

§4.2   APPOINTMENT AND REMOVAL POWER

Article II, §2, provides that the president "shall nominate, and by and with the Advice and Consent of the Senate, shall appoint Ambassadors, other public Ministers and Consuls, Judges of the Supreme Court, and all other Officers of the United States, whose Appointments are not herein otherwise provided for, and which shall be established by Law: but the Congress may by Law vest the Appointment of such inferior Officers, as they think proper, in the President alone, to the Courts of Law, or in the Heads of Departments."[1] No constitutional provision addresses the removal power. Section 4.2.1 considers the appointment power, and §4.2.2 focuses on the law concerning the removal power.

---

§4.2 [1] For an excellent discussion of the appointments power, its historical use, and constitutional issues surrounding it, *see* Michael Gerhardt, The Federal Appointments Process: A Constitutional and Historical Analysis (2000).

§4.2.1   The Appointment Power

Relatively few Supreme Court cases have posed questions concerning the appointment power. Three major issues have arisen. Article II, in the language quoted above, says that the president alone appoints ambassadors, Supreme Court Justices, and officers of the United States; but Congress can vest the appointment of inferior officers in the president, or the federal courts, or the heads of departments. Thus, the question arises: Who is an "inferior officer" within the meaning of Article II? Second, may Congress assign the appointment power in other ways besides those enumerated in Article II? Specifically, when, if at all, may Congress give the appointment power to itself or its officers? Third, what is the President's power to make "recess appointments"?

Who Are "Inferior Officers"?

In several cases, the Court has held that Congress has the ability to determine who is an inferior officer of the United States. In *Ex parte Siebold*, in 1880, the Supreme Court ruled that Congress could authorize the federal circuit courts to appoint election supervisors.[2] The Court recognized that although generally appointments are made by the president, "there is no absolute requirement to this effect in the Constitution."[3] The Court said that "as the Constitution stands, the selection of the appointing power, as between the functionaries named, is matter resting in the discretion of Congress."[4] The Court explained that the judiciary could refuse to exercise the appointment power only if doing so would be an "incongruity" with the judicial power.[5] The Court offered no examples of the situations where court appointment would be incongruous with the judicial function, though it did conclude that there was no constitutional problem with court appointment of election supervisors.

In *United States v. Eaton*, in 1898, the Court upheld department of state regulations that allowed executive officials to appoint a "vice consul" during the temporary absence of the consul.[6] The Court concluded that a vice consul is a subordinate officer "[b]ecause the subordinate officer is charged with the performance of the duty of the superior for a limited time and under special and temporary conditions."[7]

Similarly, in *Rice v. Ames*, in 1901, the Court held that Congress could have federal court judges appoint extradition commissioners.[8] The Court regarded it as a simple issue, in light of the text of Article II, and dealt with it in less than a paragraph. The Court declared: "Congress having provided for commissioners, who are not judges in the constitutional sense, had a perfect right under Article II,

---

[2] 100 U.S. 371 (1880).
[3] *Id.* at 397-398.
[4] *Id.* at 398.
[5] *Id.* at 398.
[6] 169 U.S. 331 (1898).
[7] *Id.* at 343.
[8] 180 U.S. 371 (1901).

section 2, paragraph 2 of the Constitution, to invest the District or Circuit Courts with the power of appointment."[9]

The Supreme Court returned to this issue in *Morrison v. Olson* in 1988.[10] In light of the events of the Watergate cover-up and investigation, Congress adopted the Ethics in Government Act of 1978.[11] Title VI of the Act allowed for the appointment of an "independent counsel" to investigate and prosecute wrongdoing by high-level federal government officials. If the attorney general determined that further investigation or prosecution is warranted, a panel of federal court judges "shall appoint an independent counsel and shall define that independent counsel's prosecutorial jurisdiction."[12] The law provides that the panel shall consist of three federal court judges, one of whom must be a judge of the United States Court of Appeals for the District of Columbia Circuit, and no two of the judges can be from the same court.

The Court, by a 7-to-1 margin, with Justice Kennedy not participating and Justice Scalia dissenting, upheld the constitutionality of having federal judges appoint the independent counsel. Chief Justice Rehnquist, writing for the Court, emphasized that it was permissible for Congress to vest appointment in the federal courts because the independent counsel is an "inferior" rather than a "principal" officer.[13] First, the Court said that the independent counsel is an "inferior" officer because, under the statute, he or she can be removed by the attorney general for sufficient cause.[14] Second, the Court noted that the independent counsel possesses inferior power compared to the attorney general, who has broad authority and participates in formulating policy for the executive branch.[15] Similarly, the Court noted that the independent counsel is appointed for a limited tenure with its jurisdiction limited by the instructions from the appointing court.[16]

Moreover, the Court concluded that there was no incongruity in having judges appoint the independent counsel. Indeed, the Court said that in light of the desire for independence in investigating alleged wrongdoing within the executive branch, "the most logical place to put [the appointment power] was in the Judicial Branch."[17]

Nor did the Court find that it violated Article III to give federal judges the appointment power.[18] The Court emphasized that the Act does not give to the federal courts any authority "to supervise the independent counsel in the exercise of his or her investigative or prosecutorial authority."[19] The Court said that such supervision would be a violation of separation of powers, and thus the Court

---

[9] *Id.* at 378.

[10] 487 U.S. 654 (1988).

[11] 28 U.S.C. §§591-599. The Act expired in 1999 and was not renewed, 28 U.S.C. §599 (Pocket Parts, 2001).

[12] *Id.* §593(b).

[13] *Morrison*, 487 U.S. at 671.

[14] *Id.*

[15] *Id.*

[16] *Id.*

[17] *Id.* at 672.

[18] *Id.* at 677.

[19] *Id.* at 677-679.

disapproved of the federal courts exercising such tasks as issuing orders regulating conflicts of interest or requiring the delay of a federal prosecution until the completion of related state criminal proceedings.[20]

Justice Scalia wrote a lone dissent. Scalia emphasized that the power to prosecute is "a quintessentially executive activity" and that it usurps presidential power for Congress to vest this authority in the independent counsel.[21] Scalia said that it "effects a revolution in our constitutional jurisprudence" to allow the independent counsel once it has been determined that "(1) purely executive functions are at issue here, and (2) those functions have been given to á person whose actions are not fully within the supervision and control of the President."[22] Scalia said that the Constitution presumes that all executive powers are within control of the president, and thus it is unconstitutional for Congress to vest the prosecutorial power in the independent counsel.

Like so many separation of powers issues, *Morrison v. Olson* turns, at least in part, on the choice between a functional or a formalist approach to separation of powers.[23] From a functional perspective, there is an obvious benefit to having investigations of executive officials conducted outside the executive branch. The independent counsel is desirable because an independent individual, appointed by Article III judges, is conducting the investigation and prosecution, rather than this being done by Justice Department prosecutors who are ultimately answerable to the attorney general and the president. However, from a formalist perspective, Justice Scalia emphasizes that the executive power is vested solely in the president. For Scalia, any grant of prosecutorial authority to an independent counsel is unconstitutional.

It should be noted, however, that the majority in *Morrison v. Olson* largely avoided this functionalist/formalist dispute by relying heavily on the text of Article II, which expressly allows Congress to empower the federal courts to appoint inferior officers. Once the Court concluded that the independent counsel was an inferior officer, it saw no problem with the appointment being vested in the lower federal courts. After the experience with the Whitewater special prosecutor, the independent counsel law became even more controversial and was not renewed when it expired in 1999.[24]

Most recently, the Court addressed the issue of who may possess the appointment power in *Free Enterprise Fund v. Public Company Accounting Oversight Board.*[25] The Sarbanes-Oxley Act of 2002 created tighter regulation of the accounting industry, including a new Public Company Accounting Oversight Board. The Board is composed of five members, appointed to staggered five-year terms by the Securities

---

[20] *Id.* at 681.

[21] *Id.* at 684.

[22] *Id.* at 706 (Scalia, J., dissenting).

[23] *Id.* at 708.

[24] *See* Peter L. Strauss, Formal and Functional Approaches to Separation of Powers Questions—A Foolish Inconsistency?, 72 Cornell L. Rev. 488 (1987).

[25] 130 S. Ct. 3138 (2010).

and Exchange Commission.[26] One of the issues presented was whether vesting appointment in the Securities and Exchange Commission was constitutional.[27]

The Supreme Court unanimously upheld the constitutionality of such appointments. As discussed below, the Court invalidated the limit on removal of Board members and ruled the Securities and Exchange Commission could remove the members of the Public Accounting Oversight Board at will. This made members of the Board "inferior" officers and thus Congress could vest their appointment in the head of the department: the Securities and Exchange Commission. The Court rejected the argument that a multimember body could not be the head of a department and declared: As a constitutional matter, "we see no reason why a multimember body may not be the 'Hea[d]' of a 'Departmen[t]' that it governs."[28]

Who Else May Possess the Appointment Power?

The Court has made it clear that Congress cannot give the appointment power to itself or to its officers. Article II specifies several possibilities as to who may possess the appointment power; Congress is not among them. In *Buckley v. Valeo*, the Court held unconstitutional a federal law that empowered the Speaker of the House of Representatives and the president pro tempore of the Senate to appoint four of the six members of the Federal Election Commission.[29]

The Court emphasized the text of Article II, which specifies who may possess the appointment power. The Court said that under Article II, Congress could vest the appointment power for inferior offices in the president, the heads of departments, or the lower federal courts. The Speaker of the House and the president pro tem of the Senate are obviously none of these, and therefore, the Court found that they could not possess the appointment power. This is consistent with other Court decisions that have held that Congress cannot delegate power to itself or its officers.[30]

What Is the President's Authority to Make Recess Appointments?

Article II of the Constitution says that "The President shall have Power to fill up all Vacancies that may happen during the Recess of the Senate by granting Commissions which shall Expire at the End of their next Session." In *NLRB*

---

[26] 15 U.S.C. §7211.

[27] The other issue, discussed below, was whether the restriction on presidential removal of Board members violated the Constitution.

[28] 130 S. Ct. at 3163.

[29] 424 U.S. 1 (1976).

[30] *See, e.g.,* Bowsher v. Synar, 478 U.S. 714 (1986), discussed in §3.11.3. *See also* Metropolitan Washington Airports Authority v. Citizens for the Abatement of Aircraft Noise, 501 U.S. 252 (1991) (declaring unconstitutional a federal law that gave to members of Congress the power to appoint and serve on a board to review decisions of an authority to run airports in the District of Columbia metropolitan area). This case is discussed more fully in §3.11.3.

v. Noel Canning, the Supreme Court for the first time in history interpreted this provision.[31]

The National Labor Relations Board (NLRB) has five members and three members are required for a quorum.[32] In 2011, President Obama made three appointments to fill vacancies on the Board. Senate Republicans, however, filibustered these nominations. On December 17, 2011, the Senate, by unanimous consent, had adopted a resolution providing that it would take a series of brief recesses beginning the following day. Pursuant to that resolution, the Senate held *pro forma* sessions every Tuesday and Friday until it returned for ordinary business on January 23, 2012. On January 4, 2012—between the January 3 and January 6 *pro forma* sessions—President Obama used his recess appointment power to appoint these three individuals to the NLRB.

The NLRB, with these three individuals participating, ruled against Noel Canning, a bottling company, in a labor dispute. Noel Canning appealed to the United States Court of Appeals for the District of Columbia Circuit arguing that the decision was invalid because there was not a lawful quorum; it contended that the three recess appointments were unconstitutional. The D.C. Circuit concluded that the recess appointments were invalid because the President could make recess appointments only during recesses between sessions of Congress and only for vacancies occurring during those recesses.[33]

The Supreme Court unanimously found that President Obama's recess appointments to the National Labor Relations Board were invalid. The majority ruled narrowly on the ground that the Senate was not in recess in this instance, but four Justices strongly objected, wanting to impose much greater restrictions on the President's power to make recess appointments.

Justice Breyer wrote the opinion for the majority, which was joined by Justices Kennedy, Ginsburg, Sotomayor, and Kagan. The Court began by stressing that "*in interpreting the Clause, we put significant weight upon historical practice.*"[34] *Based especially on this history, the Court concluded that* recesses, within meaning of the recess appointments clause, include intra-session recesses of substantial length and that the recess appointments clause extends to vacancies arising before recesses.

As to the former, the Court wrote: "In our view, the phrase 'the recess' includes an intra-session recess of substantial length. Its words taken literally can refer to both types of recess."[35] The Court explained that this serves the underlying goal of the recess appointments clause: "The Clause gives the President authority to make appointments during 'the recess of the Senate' so that the President can ensure the continued functioning of the Federal Government when the Senate is away. The Senate is equally away during both an inter-session and an intra-session recess,

---

[31]   134 S. Ct. 2550 (2014).

[32]   New Process Steel, L.P. v. NLRB, 560 U.S. 674 (2010) (in the absence of a lawfully appointed three-member quorum, the Board cannot exercise its powers).

[33]   Noel Canning v. NLRB, 705 F.3d 490 (D.C. Cir. 2013).

[34]   134 S. Ct. at 2559 (emphasis in original)

[35]   *Id.* at 2561.

and its capacity to participate in the appointments process has nothing to do with the words it uses to signal its departure."[36]

As to the latter, the Court concluded that the president may make recess appointments *both* for vacancies that occur during the recess and for those that preceded the recess. The Court said that "[t]he Clause's purpose strongly supports" this view because it "permit[s] the President to obtain the assistance of subordinate officers when the Senate, due to its recess, cannot confirm them."[37] The Court also stressed that historical practice supports this view. The Court said that this power extends to make recess appointments during "substantial recesses" and "that a recess lasting less than 10 days is presumptively too short."[38]

But the Court concluded that these recess appointments were invalid because the Senate was not in recess, and especially not in recess for a period of greater than ten days. The Court explained that "the *pro forma* sessions count as sessions, not as periods of recess. We hold that, for purposes of the Recess Appointments Clause, the Senate is in session when it says it is, provided that, under its own rules, it retains the capacity to transact Senate business. The Senate met that standard here."[39] The Court rejected the Obama administration's argument that these were "sham" sessions and did not keep the Senate from being in recess. The Court emphasized the deference that must be given to the Senate in deciding whether it was in recess. The Court concluded "that when the Senate declares that it is in session and possesses the capacity, under its own rules, to conduct business, it is in session for purposes of the Clause."[40] Because at most the Senate was in recess for the three days between its *pro forma* sessions, that was not long enough to trigger the President's ability to make recess appointments.

Justice Scalia wrote an opinion concurring in the judgment, joined by Chief Justice Roberts and Justices Thomas and Alito. In tone, it was much more like a dissent. Justice Scalia emphasized his reading of the text of Article II and rejected the majority's heavy reliance on historical practice. Justice Scalia said: "First, [the recess appointment power] may be exercised only in 'the Recess of the Senate,' that is, the intermission between two formal legislative sessions. Second, it may be used to fill only those vacancies that 'happen during the Recess,' that is, offices that become vacant during that intermission."[41]

All nine Justices found the recess appointments to the NLRB to be invalid. The majority did so on the relatively narrow grounds that the Senate was not in recess for a period of ten days or longer. The Justices concurring in the judgment would have imposed much greater limits on the recess appointment power, restricting it to recesses between sessions of Congress and to vacancies occurring during those recesses. To a large extent, the difference was about interpreting the Constitution, with the majority focusing a great deal on historical practice and the dissent focusing on the language of Article II.

[36] *Id.*
[37] *Id.* at 2568.
[38] *Id.* at 2567.
[39] *Id.* at 2574.
[40] *Id.* at 2575.
[41] *Id.* at 2592 (Scalia, J., concurring in the judgment).

§4.2.2   *The Removal Power*

As mentioned at the beginning of this section, there is no provision of the Constitution concerning the president's authority to remove executive branch officials. The principle that has emerged from the cases is that, in general, the president may remove executive officials unless removal is limited by statute. Congress, by statute, may limit removal both if it is an office where independence from the president is desirable, and if the law does not prohibit removal but, rather, limits removal to instances where good cause is shown.

No single case has clearly articulated this principle. Rather it comes from the experience of the impeachment of Andrew Johnson and from five Supreme Court decisions that have considered the removal power. Each of these is reviewed below, and then the section concludes by describing the law concerning the removal power that emerges from this authority.

The Impeachment of Andrew Johnson

Consideration of the removal power must begin with an incident that was never directly reviewed in the courts: the impeachment of President Andrew Johnson for firing the secretary of war in violation of a federal law that prohibited the removal.[42] After the assassination of President Abraham Lincoln, there was great consternation that a Southerner, Andrew Johnson from Tennessee, was the president at the end of the Civil War. The perception was that Johnson's sympathies were with the South and that he was obstructing Reconstruction and the North's claim of the benefits of its victory. Congress passed the Tenure in Office Act of 1867 to prevent him from removing key members of the cabinet.

Secretary of War Edwin Stanton openly challenged the president's authority, and Johnson fired Stanton, even though that violated the Tenure in Office Act. The House of Representatives voted Articles of Impeachment based almost entirely on this removal. The vote in the Senate, however, was one short of the two-thirds necessary for removal, and Johnson completed his term as president.

Myers v. United States

Although the courts did not get involved at the time of Johnson's impeachment, the Supreme Court discussed it at some length in the first major decision to consider the removal power: *Myers v. United States*, in 1926.[43] *Myers* involved the firing of the postmaster of Portland, Oregon, in violation of a federal law that provided that postmasters could be removed during their four-year terms only "with the advice and consent of the Senate."

Chief Justice William Howard Taft, a former president of the United States, wrote broadly of the president's ability to remove executive officials. He declared

---

[42] For a detailed description of the facts of this impeachment, *see* Raoul Berger, Impeachment: Constitutional Problems (1973).

[43] 272 U.S. 52 (1926).

that "[t]he power to remove . . . is an incident of the power to appoint."[44] He thus concluded that "the President has the exclusive power of removing executive officers of the United States whom he has appointed by and with the advice and consent of the Senate."[45] Taft explained that the ability of the president to control the personnel in administrative positions is central to the executive power. Taft reviewed the debates in the first session of Congress and concluded that it was the framers' intent to place the removal power in the president.[46]

Although the Tenure in Office Act that was the basis for Andrew Johnson's impeachment had been repealed in 1887, Taft's opinion expressly argued that the Act was an unconstitutional infringement of the power of the presidency. Thus, *Myers* stands for the broad proposition that any congressional limits on the removal power are unconstitutional.

Humphrey's Executor v. United States

Less than a decade after *Myers*, the Court took a much different position and recognized that Congress could, for some officers and under some circumstances, limit the removal power. In *Humphrey's Executor v. United States*, the Court unanimously upheld the ability of Congress to limit the removal of a commissioner of the Federal Trade Commission.[47]

Under the Federal Trade Commission Act, the president could fire a commissioner only for "inefficiency, neglect of duty, or malfeasance in office." The Court explained that Congress, pursuant to its powers under Article I, could create independent agencies and insulate their members from presidential removal unless good cause for firing existed. The Court declared: "The authority of Congress, in creating quasi-legislative or quasi-judicial agencies, to require them to act in discharge of their duties independently of executive control cannot well be doubted; and that authority includes, as an appropriate incident, power to fix the period during which they shall continue in office, and to forbid their removal except for cause in the meantime."[48]

The difficulty facing the Court was how to reconcile this ruling with *Myers*. The Court distinguished *Myers* saying that its holding applied only to "purely executive officers" and that beyond that the opinion was merely dicta and therefore "[did] not come within the rule of stare decisis."[49] The Court said that officers in "quasi-legislative" or "quasi-judicial" positions are different and that Congress may limit the removal of these individuals.

The practical effect is to draw a distinction between cabinet officials and those who are in independent regulatory agencies. For the former, such as the postmaster in *Myers* or the secretary of state or attorney general, Congress may not limit

---

[44] *Id.* at 161.
[45] *Id.* at 106.
[46] *Id.* at 106.
[47] 295 U.S. 602 (1935).
[48] *Id.* at 623.
[49] *Id.* at 629.

removal because the cabinet is there to carry out the president's policies. But for independent regulatory agencies—such as the Federal Trade Commission, the Securities and Exchange Commission, and the Federal Communications Commission—Congress may limit removal to situations where there is just cause for firing.

From a functional perspective, this distinction makes sense. Congress, in creating independent regulatory agencies, intended that they be relatively insulated from political control. But from a more formalistic perspective, the distinction is troubling. The Constitution creates a single executive and provides no authority for executive agencies that operate outside the president's control.[50]

Weiner v. United States

The Court has continued to adhere to this functional approach, and in *Weiner v. United States* the Court went further and held that even without a statutory limit on removal, the president could not remove executive officials where independence from the president is desirable.[51] *Weiner* involved the president's firing a member of the War Claims Commission. Unlike the Federal Trade Commission Act in *Humphrey's Executor*, the statute creating the War Claims Commission did not expressly limit the president's removal power.

However, the Court concluded that the functional need for independence of the War Claims Commission limited the president's removal power. The Court explained that Congress's intent was for the War Claims Commission to award claims based on merit rather than on political influence. The Court said that there was a "sharp differentiation" between "those who are part of the Executive establishment and those whose tasks require absolute freedom from Executive interference."[52]

Bowsher v. Synar

The "sharp differentiation" described in *Weiner* is not always so clear in practice. Nor have subsequent decisions offered much in the way of clarification. In *Bowsher v. Synar*, the Court articulated one clear and important limit on the removal power: Congress cannot give itself the power to remove executive officials.[53] The only exception, of course, is that Congress always can remove an executive official through the impeachment process.

---

[50] *See, e.g.*, Steven G. Calabresi & Saikrishna B. Prakash, The President's Power to Execute the Laws, 104 Yale L.J. 541 (1994); Steven G. Calabresi & Kevin H. Rhodes, The Structural Constitution: Unitary Executive, Plural Judiciary, 105 Harv. L. Rev. 1153 (1992). *But see* Lawrence Lessig & Cass R. Sunstein, The President and the Administration, 94 Colum. L. Rev. 1 (1994). In *Printz v. United States*, 521 U.S. 898 (1997), Justice Scalia's majority opinion expressly declared that the Constitution creates a unitary executive and invalidated the Brady Handgun Control Act, in part, because it assigned the executive task of enforcing federal law to state and local governments. *Printz* is discussed in detail in §3.10. Whether there is a "unitary executive" and, if so, what this means is very much disputed.

[51] 357 U.S. 349 (1958).

[52] *Id.* at 353.

[53] 478 U.S. 714 (1986). *Bowsher* is also discussed in §3.11.3.

In *Bowsher*, the Supreme Court declared unconstitutional the Balanced Budget and Emergency Deficit Control Act of 1985, also known as the Gramm-Rudman-Hollings Deficit Reduction Act. The Act prescribed a maximum allowable budget deficit for each of five years. If spending exceeded the deficit ceiling, the comptroller general of the United States, who is the head of a congressional agency—the General Accounting Office—was instructed to impose budget cuts. The Supreme Court declared this unconstitutional as an impermissible delegation to a legislative official of the executive power to implement the law.

The Court in *Bowsher* emphasized that the comptroller general could be removed only by Congress and concluded that it was impermissible for the executive power to be exercised by a person who was totally insulated from presidential removal. The Court held that "Congress cannot reserve for itself the power of removal of an officer charged with the execution of the laws except by impeachment."[54]

Morrison v. Olson

In *Morrison v. Olson*, the Court distinguished *Bowsher* and upheld the constitutionality of limits on the president's ability to remove the independent counsel.[55] The law creating the independent counsel provided that he or she could be removed by the attorney general only for cause. If an independent counsel were removed, the attorney general would have to file a report with the panel of judges who made the appointment and with the House and Senate Judiciary Committees.

The Supreme Court upheld the constitutionality of this limit on the removal power. The Court's discussion of the removal power began by distinguishing *Bowsher v. Synar*, where the Court had declared unconstitutional Congress's exercise of the removal power over an individual performing executive tasks.[56] In contrast, in *Morrison v. Olson*, the Court observed that Congress had no role in removing the independent counsel.

The Court noted that earlier cases, such as *Humphrey's Executor* and *Weiner*, had drawn a distinction between purely executive tasks and those that were quasi-legislative or quasi-judicial. The Court said that while it did "not mean to suggest that an analysis of the functions served by the officials at issue is irrelevant . . . the real question is whether the removal restrictions are of such a nature that they impede the president's ability to perform his constitutional duty."[57]

The Court stressed that the independent counsel, who exists to investigate and prosecute alleged wrongdoing in the executive branch of government, ideally should be independent of the president. The Court also emphasized that the statute does not prohibit all removal; rather, it allows the attorney general

---

[54] *Id.* at 726.

[55] 487 U.S. 654 (1988). The constitutionality of Congress vesting the appointment of the independent counsel in the federal courts is discussed above in §4.2.1.

[56] *Id.* at 685-686.

[57] *Id.* at 691.

to fire an independent counsel for "good cause."[58] Hence, the Court concluded that the limits on the removal of the independent counsel did not violate the Constitution.

Free Enterprise Fund v. Public Company Accounting Oversight Board

The Court's most recent examination of the removal power occurred in *Free Enterprise Fund v. Public Company Accounting Oversight Board*.[59] As explained above, the Sarbanes-Oxley Act created a Public Company Accounting Oversight Board (PCAOB) to oversee the accounting industry. The members of the Board are appointed by the Securities and Exchange Commission and are removable by the Commission only for "good cause." The issue was whether this is constitutional in light of the fact that the president cannot remove Board members and can remove members of the Securities and Exchange Commission also only for "good cause." Chief Justice Roberts, writing for the Court in a 5-4 decision, phrased the issue as: "May the President be restricted in his ability to remove a principal officer, who is in turn restricted in his ability to remove an inferior officer, even though that inferior officer determines the policy and enforces the laws of the United States?"[60]

The Court held this unconstitutional and declared: "We hold that such multilevel protection from removal is contrary to Article II's vesting of the executive power in the President. The President cannot 'take Care that the Laws be faithfully executed' if he cannot oversee the faithfulness of the officers who execute them. Here the President cannot remove an officer who enjoys more than one level of good-cause protection, even if the President determines that the officer is neglecting his duties or discharging them improperly. That judgment is instead committed to another officer, who may or may not agree with the President's determination, and whom the President cannot remove simply because that officer disagrees with him. This contravenes the President's 'constitutional obligation to ensure the faithful execution of the laws.'"[61]

The Court distinguished cases that had allowed limits on removal such as *Humphrey's Executor, Weiner, Bowsher, and Morrison* on the ground that they involved limits on only the president's ability to remove. Unlike the PCAOB, there were not two levels of protection from presidential removal: The president can remove the members of the Securities and Exchange Commission only for good cause and they, in turn, can remove members of the PCAOB only for good cause.

Justice Breyer wrote for the four dissenting Justices and lamented the formalistic approach of the majority.[62] He explained: "[I]n my view the statute does not significantly interfere with the President's 'executive Power.' It violates no separation-of-powers principle. And the Court's contrary holding threatens to disrupt

---

[58] *Id.* at 691.
[59] 130 S. Ct. 3138 (2010).
[60] *Id.* at 3147.
[61] *Id.*
[62] *Id.* at 3164 (Breyer, J., dissenting).

severely the fair and efficient administration of the laws. I consequently dissent."[63] He argued that it is desirable to have an independent Board and this requires protection from removal. Justice Breyer also argued that there are many other situations where there are double layers of protection from removal, such as in the military, and these are constitutionally suspect after the majority's holding.

The Principle That Emerges

The experience of President Andrew Johnson's impeachment and the Supreme Court's decisions in *Myers, Humphrey's Executor, Weiner, Bowsher, Morrison,* and *Free Enterprise Fund* hardly produce a consistent pattern or a clear rule. As the law now stands, in general, the president has the power to remove executive officials, but Congress may limit the removal power if it is an office where independence from the president would be desirable. Congress cannot, however, completely prohibit all removal, and it cannot give the removal power to itself (other than by exercising its impeachment power). Nor can Congress prescribe a double layer of protection from presidential removal whereby "inferior officers" may be removed only for just cause by "officers" who may be removed by the President only for just cause.

Therefore, in approaching an issue concerning the removal power, analysis can be divided into two questions. First, is the office one in which independence from the president is desirable? If so, Congress may limit the removal power, and *Weiner* indicates that the judiciary may limit removal even in the absence of a statutory restriction. There is no clear test for when independence from the president is desirable. The distinction drawn in *Humphrey's Executor* between purely "executive tasks" and those that are "quasi-legislative" or "quasi-judicial" seems difficult to apply in practice. Nor is *Morrison v. Olson's* test, as to whether "the removal restrictions are of such a nature that they impede the President's ability to perform his constitutional duty," clear or easy to apply. Ultimately, the analysis must be functional and contextual: Are there good reasons why the office should be independent of the president?[64]

Second, are Congress's limits on removal constitutional? Congress cannot completely prohibit presidential removal, but it can limit removal to where there is "good cause." Nor can Congress give itself the sole power to remove an executive official or structure removal so that there is a double layer of insulation from presidential removal.

---

[63] *Id.* at 3164-3165.
[64] 487 U.S. at 692.

§4.3   EXECUTIVE PRIVILEGE

The Need for Executive Privilege

Executive privilege refers to the ability of the president to keep secret conversations with or memoranda to or from advisors. The Constitution does not mention such authority, but presidents have claimed it throughout American history. In part, executive privilege is seen as necessary in order for presidents to receive candid advice. As the Supreme Court explained: "Human experience teaches that those who expect public dissemination of their remarks may well temper candor with a concern for appearances and for their own interests to the detriment of the decision making process."[1]

Also, executive privilege is sometimes defended as important to protect national security; diplomacy is regarded as requiring secrecy. In justifying a broad presidential power in the realm of foreign affairs, the Court noted that "[s]ecrecy in respect of information gathered . . . may be highly necessary, and the premature disclosure of it productive of harmful results."[2] The Supreme Court did not expressly consider the constitutionality and scope of executive privilege until 1974 in the landmark case of *United States v. Nixon.*[3] The only other major Supreme Court case to address executive privilege was *Cheney v. United States District Court for the District of Columbia.*[4]

United States v. Nixon

Facts

On June 17, 1972, a burglary occurred at the Democratic National Headquarters in the Watergate building in Washington, D.C. Over the course of the next year, it was discovered that the burglars were connected to the Campaign to Re-elect the President and that high-level White House officials were involved in a cover-up.[5] In the summer of 1973, Senator Sam Ervin from North Carolina chaired closely watched hearings of the Senate Select Committee on Watergate.

---

§4.3 [1] United States v. Nixon, 418 U.S. 683, 705 (1974).

[2] United States v. Curtiss-Wright Export Corp., 299 U.S. 304, 320 (1936). *Curtiss-Wright* is discussed in more detail below in §4.6.1.

[3] 418 U.S. 683 (1974). In 1807, Chief Justice John Marshall, sitting as a circuit judge, issued a subpoena to President Thomas Jefferson for a document requested by Aaron Burr in his defense to a treason charge. United States v. Burr, 25 F. Cas. 30, 34 (C.C.D. Va. 1807) (case No. 14,692D). President Jefferson supplied it, but said that he was doing so voluntarily and not in compliance with the court order. *See* Raoul Berger, Executive Privilege: Constitutional Myth (1974). For a discussion of *Nixon* in a historical context and its relationship to the legal proceedings surrounding Aaron Burr, *see* John C. Yoo, The First Claim: The Burr Trial, *United States v. Nixon,* and Presidential Power, 83 Minn. L. Rev. 1435 (1999).

[4] 542 U.S. 367 (2004).

[5] For a fascinating account of the discovery of this information, *see* Bob Woodward & Carl Bernstein, All the President's Men (1974).

One of the dramatic moments occurred when a presidential aide, Alexander Butterfield, revealed that there was a secret taping system in the Oval Office and that presidential conversations were routinely recorded.

Because top Justice Department officials, including the former attorney general, John Mitchell, were suspected of involvement in the cover-up, there was political pressure for an independent investigation. Attorney General Elliot Richardson appointed Harvard law professor Archibald Cox to serve as a special prosecutor.

Cox subpoenaed tapes of White House conversations, and the president challenged the subpoena in court. On October 12, 1973, the United States Court of Appeals for the District of Columbia sided with the special prosecutor and gave the president one week to file an appeal. On October 19, the president announced that he would turn over edited transcripts of the tapes and that he would ask Senator John Stennis (who was reported to be quite hard of hearing) to listen to the tapes and verify their accuracy. President Nixon also announced that he would comply with no additional subpoenas and turn over no additional tapes.

On Saturday, October 20, special prosecutor Archibald Cox declared Nixon's position unacceptable; there was a court order to turn over tapes, not transcripts. More important, he would seek whatever tapes he needed. President Nixon ordered Attorney General Richardson to fire Cox; Richardson refused and resigned. Nixon then asked the Justice Department's number two official to fire Cox; William Ruckelshaus also refused and resigned. The request was then made to the number three person in the Justice Department, Solicitor General Robert Bork. Bork then fired Cox in what came to be known as the Saturday Night Massacre.[6]

The first resolutions calling for Richard Nixon's impeachment were introduced into the House of Representatives, and intense political pressure caused the appointment of a new special prosecutor, Leon Jaworski. On March 1, 1974, a grand jury for the United States District Court for the District of Columbia indicted seven top officials of the Nixon administration and the Campaign to Re-elect the President for obstruction of justice and conspiracy to defraud. President Nixon was named an "unindicted co-conspirator."

On April 18, 1974, a subpoena *duces tecum* was issued, at the request of the special prosecutor, for the president to turn over tapes and other materials to use as possible evidence in the upcoming criminal trial. On April 30, President Nixon announced that he was disclosing edited transcripts of 43 conversations, including 20 that were the subject of the subpoena. On May 1, the president moved to quash the subpoena. On May 20, the United States District Court denied the motion to quash and directed the president to provide all of the items that had been subpoenaed. The Supreme Court granted review prior to consideration by the court of appeals.

Meanwhile, the House Judiciary Committee was considering Articles of Impeachment against President Nixon. Impeachment hearings were held in July 1974, while the *Nixon* case was pending before the Supreme Court. The Supreme

---

[6] For a detailed account of this incident and its aftermath, *see* Theodore H. White, Breach of Faith: The Fall of Richard Nixon (1975).

Court announced its decision in *Nixon* on July 25, 1974, and unanimously ruled that Nixon had to comply with the subpoena. The House Judiciary Committee voted its first article of impeachment on July 25 for obstruction of justice in connection with the Watergate break-in and cover-up. On July 29 and 30, the committee voted two additional articles of impeachment for abuse of power and for failure to comply with a Judiciary Committee subpoena.

On August 6, 1974, President Nixon complied with the subpoena and made the transcripts of the tapes available to the public. The tapes showed that President Nixon clearly had obstructed justice by ordering the Federal Bureau of Investigation not to investigate the Watergate matter. Three days later, on Thursday, August 9, 1974, President Nixon became the only president in history to resign.

The Holding

Chief Justice Burger wrote the opinion for a unanimous Court in *United States v. Nixon*.[7] The Court began by rejecting the president's contention that the case posed a nonjusticiable political question because it was an intra-branch dispute and that the president alone had authority to control prosecutions.[8] The Court said that the president had the authority to delegate this power and that he had done so, through the actions of the attorney general, in creating the office of the special prosecutor. Indeed, the Court noted that the regulations creating the office of the special prosecutor, adopted after the Saturday Night Massacre, "give the special prosecutor explicit power to contest the invocation of executive privilege in the process of seeking evidence deemed relevant to the performance of these specially delegated duties."[9] Moreover, the Court said that there was no doubt that the special prosecutor and the president were adversaries, even though both were executive officials.[10]

After explaining that the subpoena followed the procedures and requirements of Federal Rule of Civil Procedure 17(c), the Court turned its attention to the issue of executive privilege. The Court made three major points. First, the Court held that it is the role of the Court to decide whether the president has executive privilege and, if so, its scope. Nixon claimed that the Constitution gave the president executive privilege and that the president alone determined its reach. The Court flatly rejected this contention: "The President's counsel, as we have noted, reads the Constitution as providing an absolute privilege of confidentiality for all Presidential communications. Many decisions of this Court, however, have unequivocally reaffirmed the holding of *Marbury v. Madison*, that '[i]t is emphatically the province and duty of the judicial department to say what the law is.'"[11]

---

[7] Justice William Rehnquist did not participate, almost certainly because he had been a top-level Justice Department official in the Nixon administration before being appointed to the Supreme Court in 1971. For a fascinating account of how the *Nixon* opinion was written within the Court, *see* Bob Woodward & Scott Armstrong, The Brethren (1979).

[8] For a discussion of the political question doctrine, *see* §2.8.

[9] 418 U.S. at 694-695.

[10] *Id.* at 697.

[11] *Id.* at 703 (citation omitted).

One can question, though, whether *Marbury* really stands for this proposition. *Marbury* obviously establishes the power of judicial review of executive actions, but as Professor Gerald Gunther argued, "there is nothing in *Marbury v. Madison* that precludes a constitutional interpretation which gives final authority to another branch."[12]

Second, the Court recognized the existence of executive privilege. The Court recognized that the need for candor in communications with advisors justified executive privilege; indeed, the Court said that a need for confidentiality was "too plain to require further discussion."[13] Although Article II of the Constitution does not expressly grant this power to the president, the Court said that "the privilege can be said to derive from the supremacy of each branch within its own assigned area of constitutional duties. Certain powers and privileges flow from the nature of enumerated powers; the protection of the confidentiality of Presidential communications has similar constitutional underpinnings."[14]

United States v. Nixon thus recognizes executive privilege as an inherent presidential power. It is in contrast with decisions, such as Justice Hugo Black's majority opinion in *Youngstown Sheet & Tube Co. v. Sawyer*, that reject any inherent powers.[15] As discussed above in §4.1, Justice Black concluded that in the absence of statutory authorization, a presidential action must be based on "some provision of the Constitution."[16] Third, the Court held that executive privilege is not absolute, but rather must yield when there are important countervailing interests. The Court explained that "neither the doctrine of separation of powers, nor the need for confidentiality of high-level communications, without more, can sustain an absolute, unqualified presidential privilege of immunity from judicial process under all circumstances."[17]

More specifically, the Court said that an absolute privilege would interfere with the ability of the judiciary to perform its constitutional function. The Court explained: "The impediment that an absolute, unqualified privilege would place in the way of the primary constitutional duty of the Judicial Branch to do justice in criminal prosecutions would plainly conflict with the function of the courts under Article III."[18] The Court thus concluded that the need for evidence at a criminal trial outweighed executive privilege. The Court said that allowing "the privilege to withhold evidence that is demonstrably relevant in a criminal trial would cut deeply into the guarantee of due process of law and gravely impair the basic function of the courts."[19]

United States v. Nixon is the most important case concerning executive privilege; *Nixon* recognizes the existence of executive privilege, but refuses to make it

---

[12] Gerald Gunther, Judicial Hegemony and Legislative Autonomy: The *Nixon* Case and the Impeachment Process, 22 UCLA L. Rev. 30, 33-34 (1974).

[13] 418 U.S. at 705.

[14] *Id.* at 705-706 (footnote omitted).

[15] 343 U.S. 579 (1952), discussed in §4.1.

[16] *Id.* at 587.

[17] 418 U.S. at 706.

[18] *Id.* at 707.

[19] *Id.* at 712.

absolute. *Nixon* also is a powerful reaffirmation of the power of judicial review and of the essential principle that no person, not even the president, is above the law. But *Nixon*, too, had its critics. Professor Gerald Gunther, for example, argued that the Court erred in granting expedited review and that the better course would have been to allow the impeachment process to run its course.[20] The House Judiciary Committee already had voted Articles of Impeachment against Nixon, and some believe that the better course would have been for the judiciary to avoid deciding the issue of the tapes until the congressional proceedings were completed.[21]

Nixon v. Administrator of General Services

Another Supreme Court decision to consider executive privilege also involved Richard Nixon: *Nixon v. Administrator of General Services*.[22] After President Nixon resigned, Congress adopted the Presidential Recordings and Material Preservation Act, which directed the administrator of General Services to take custody of Nixon's tapes and papers. The administrator was to arrange for their screening, return those that were private, and ensure public access for the rest.

Former President Nixon complained that the statute unconstitutionally violated separation of powers and that it would impede the ability of future presidents to receive candid advice. The Court recognized that even a former president may claim executive privilege, but the Court said that the screening process created by the law was sufficient to safeguard this interest. Justice Brennan, writing for the Court, explained that there "is no reason to believe that the restriction on public access ultimately established by regulation will not be adequate to preserve executive confidentiality."[23]

Despite these decisions, only some of the questions about executive privilege have been resolved. *United States v. Nixon* emphatically declares that there is such a privilege under the Constitution, but that it is not absolute. It does not, for example, justify a president's refusal to comply with a subpoena for evidence needed at a criminal trial. However, the Court has not indicated what other circumstances, if any, might outweigh claims of executive privilege.

Cheney v. U.S. District Court for the District of Columbia

In *Cheney v. U.S. District Court for the District of Columbia*, the Supreme Court considered executive privilege in an unusual procedural context.[24] A lawsuit was filed claiming that an energy task force, chaired by Vice President Dick Cheney,

---

[20] Gunther, *supra* note 12, at 31.

[21] The obvious difficulty with the Court waiting for the impeachment process to finish was that a criminal trial was imminent and the subpoenaed tapes were relevant as evidence. Delaying the criminal trial risked denying defendant's right to a speedy trial. Having the trial go forward without the tapes as evidence effectively would have been ruling in Nixon's favor.

[22] 433 U.S. 425 (1977).

[23] *Id.* at 450. *See also* Nixon v. Warner Communications, Inc., 435 U.S. 589 (1978) (denying news organizations and media companies the right to copy the tapes that were played at trial).

[24] 542 U.S. 367 (2004).

violated the Federal Advisory Committee Act. The plaintiffs sought and received a discovery order. The defendants then sought a writ of mandamus from the Court of Appeals to stop enforcement of the discovery order. In the context of considering whether the Court of Appeals should have issued a writ of mandamus, the Supreme Court discussed executive privilege and when it is to be considered. The Court did not resolve whether executive privilege applied here, or even whether mandamus should be issued. The Court remanded the case for further consideration.

But the Court did discuss executive privilege and expressly distinguished *United States v. Nixon*. Justice Kennedy's majority opinion explained that "unlike this case, which concerns respondents' requests for information for use in a civil suit, *Nixon* involves the proper balance between the Executive's interest in the confidentiality of its communications and the 'constitutional need for production of relevant evidence in a criminal proceeding.' "[25] The Court said that the distinction between criminal and civil cases "is not just a matter of formalism"; the "need for information for use in civil cases, while far from negligible, does not share the urgency or significance of the criminal subpoena requests in *Nixon*."[26] The Court also explained that the subpoenas in *Nixon* were narrowly focused, while the discovery sought in *Cheney* was broad.

The Court concluded that the executive was not required to invoke executive privilege in order to seek to keep the information secret. Justice Kennedy's majority opinion explained that "contrary to the District Court's and the Court of Appeals' conclusions, *Nixon* does not leave them the sole option of inviting the Executive Branch to invoke executive privilege while remaining otherwise powerless to modify a party's overly broad discovery requests."[27] The Court was concerned that "once executive privilege is asserted, coequal branches of the Government are set on a collision course. The Judiciary is forced into the difficult task of balancing the need for information in a judicial proceeding and the Executive's Article II prerogatives. This inquiry places courts in the awkward position of evaluating the Executive's claims of confidentiality and autonomy, and pushes to the fore difficult questions of separation of powers and checks and balances."[28] Thus, the Court said that secrecy issues could be raised without formal invocation of executive privilege by the president. The Court remanded the case for further proceedings consistent with its opinion.

---

[25] *Id.* at 383.
[26] *Id.* at 384.
[27] *Id.* at 389.
[28] *Id.*

§4.4   PRESIDENTIAL IMMUNITY TO CRIMINAL AND CIVIL SUITS

It remains unsettled whether a president may be criminally prosecuted while in office or whether the sole remedy is impeachment and removal.[1] However, it is established that a president may not be sued for injunctions or for money damages for actions taken while in office. Also, it is clear that a president, while in office, may be sued for conduct that occurred before taking office.

Criminal Prosecutions

No case has addressed whether a sitting president can be criminally prosecuted. In March 1974, a federal grand jury considered indicting then-President Richard Nixon and decided instead to make him an unindicted co-conspirator because it was unsure whether it could indict a sitting president.

On the one hand, there is a strong argument that impeachment and removal should be the sole remedy against a president. The danger is that criminal prosecution inevitably would interfere with the president's ability to perform and that the impeachment process is the appropriate remedy for wrongdoing. On the other hand, no principle is more basic than that no person is above the law, and that justifies allowing the president, like all others, to be charged and tried for crimes.

Civil Cases

The Court has held that a president may be sued neither for injunctions nor for money damages for conduct while in office. Discussion of presidential immunity generally begins with *Mississippi v. Johnson*, in which the State of Mississippi sued President Andrew Johnson to enjoin the Reconstruction Acts.[2] The Court stated that there was a single issue presented: "Can the President be restrained by injunction from carrying into effect an act of Congress alleged to be unconstitutional?"[3] The Court held that it did not have "jurisdiction . . . to enjoin the President in the performance of his official duties."[4]

Mississippi v. Johnson does not decide whether a president can be criminally prosecuted or even whether a president can be sued for money damages. The case concerned only injunctive relief against a president. After *Mississippi v. Johnson*, the Court has broadly approved the ability to sue other government officers for injunctive relief as a means of securing compliance with the Constitution.[5] Although these cases have not directly addressed the ability to sue a sitting president for an

---

§4.4 [1] For a discussion of whether the president may be criminally prosecuted while in office, *see* Nexus: A Journal of Opinion, 2 NEXUS 7 (1997).

[2] 71 U.S. (4 Wall.) 475 (1866).

[3] *Id.* at 498.

[4] *Id.* at 501.

[5] Ex parte Young, 209 U.S. 123 (1908).

injunction, they indicate that the Court generally has been very willing to allow suits for injunctions to go forward.[6]

The Court has directly faced the issue of money damages and held that a president, or ex-president, may not be sued for money damages for conduct in office. In *Nixon v. Fitzgerald*, in a 5-to-4 decision, the Court held that the president's "unique status under the Constitution" and the "singular importance" of the duties of the office justify absolute immunity.[7] A. Ernest Fitzgerald, an analyst in the Air Force, alleged that his job was eliminated in unconstitutional retaliation for his exposing cost overruns in the Defense Department in testimony to Congress.

In ruling that the suit against the president for money damages was barred, the Court emphasized that it feared that frequent suits against the president would detract from his or her ability to perform effectively. The Court concluded not only that a sitting president was immune from suit, but also that "a former President . . . is entitled to absolute immunity from damages liability predicated on his official acts."[8]

The Court explained that there are other checks against the president, ranging from formal ones, such as impeachment, to more informal ones, such as political pressure. Yet the dissent responded that these checks do not provide compensation to an individual injured by unconstitutional presidential actions. The dissent lamented that the decision "places the President above the law."[9]

Although *Nixon v. Fitzgerald* held that a president or ex-president may not be sued for damages for conduct during the president's term in office, the case does not resolve whether a president may be sued for conduct prior to taking office. This issue was resolved by the Court in *Clinton v. Jones*.[10] Bill Clinton was sued for sexual harassment that allegedly occurred while he was governor of Arkansas. Clinton moved in federal district court to dismiss the suit, or at least to have it stayed until he was no longer the president. The federal district court ruled that a president does not have absolute immunity to suits for conduct prior to becoming president, but the court used its discretion to stay the trial until after the completion of Clinton's tenure in the White House.[11] The United States Court of Appeals for the Eighth Circuit affirmed and the Supreme Court granted certiorari.

In a unanimous decision, the Court ruled against Clinton and held that a suit against a president should be neither stayed nor dismissed if it is based on conduct that allegedly occurred prior to his taking office. Justice Stevens wrote the opinion for the Court. The Court explained that immunity exists to safeguard the exercise of discretion by an officeholder; thus, there is no basis for "immunity for unofficial conduct."[12] The Court expressly rejected President Clinton's claim that civil

---

[6] In *Young, id.*, the Court held that a state officer who violates the Constitution is stripped of authority and may be sued for an injunction. Arguably, then, a president who violates the Constitution also could be sued for injunctive relief.

[7] 457 U.S. 731, 750-751 (1982).

[8] *Id.* at 749.

[9] *Id.* at 767 (White, J., dissenting).

[10] 520 U.S. 681 (1997).

[11] Jones v. Clinton, 869 F. Supp. 690 (E.D. Ark. 1994).

[12] 520 U.S. 861 at 682.

suits would unduly interfere with the president's carrying out the important and unique constitutional functions of the office. Justice Stevens wrote: "[I]n the more than 200-year history of the Republic, only three sitting Presidents have been subjected to suits for their private actions. If the past is any indicator, it seems unlikely that a deluge of such litigation will ever engulf the Presidency. As for the case at hand, if properly managed by the District Court, it appears to us highly unlikely to occupy any substantial amount of petitioner's time."[13]

On the one hand, Justice Stevens was hardly prescient; the civil suit against Clinton took a huge amount of the president's time and ultimately led to impeachment. Some believe that it is for exactly this reason, the inevitable distraction and burden of civil suits, that litigation against the president should be stayed until he is out of office. On the other hand, *Clinton v. Jones* is a powerful statement that no one, not even the president, is above the law and delaying suits for as much as eight years often may preclude meritorious suits from going forward. The Supreme Court, though, unanimously and unequivocally held that presidents may be sued for acts that allegedly occurred prior to taking office.

Other Executive Officials

Although the president has absolute immunity to suits for damages, other executive officials generally have only qualified immunity.[14] In addition to the president, only a few executive officials are accorded absolute immunity. Prosecutors, both federal and state, have absolute immunity to suits for money damages for prosecutorial actions.[15] But the Supreme Court has declared that qualified immunity represents the "norm for executive officials."[16]

The current standard for qualified immunity—or, as it is sometimes called, "good faith immunity"—was articulated in *Harlow v. Fitzgerald*.[17] In a companion suit to *Nixon v. Fitzgerald*, discussed above, Fitzgerald sued other executive branch officials who were involved in his firing. The Court concluded that the other officials were protected by qualified, not absolute, immunity. The Court announced

---

[13] *Id.* at 702.

[14] It should be noted that members of Congress are granted absolute immunity to suits for damages and for injunctive relief because of the "speech and debate clause" of Article I, §6. *See* Eastland v. United States Servicemen's Fund, 421 U.S. 491 (1975). Also, judges have absolute immunity to suits for money damages for their judicial actions. *See* Stump v. Sparkman, 435 U.S. 349 (1978). Section 1983 was amended to preclude suits for injunctive relief against judges. Pub. L. No. 104-317, §309(c) (1996) as codified in 42 U.S.C. §1983. A full discussion of absolute and qualified immunity is beyond the scope of this book, but can be found in Erwin Chemerinsky, Federal Jurisdiction ch. 8 (6th ed. 2011).

[15] Suits against state and local prosecutors are brought pursuant to 42 U.S.C. §1983. Suits against federal prosecutors for violating constitutional rights are brought pursuant to *Bivens v. Six Unknown Named Agents of Federal Bureau of Narcotics*, 403 U.S. 388 (1971), which recognizes a cause of action, for money damages, directly under the Constitution. The Court has said that the issue of immunities is the same whether the suit is against federal, state, or local officials. Harlow v. Fitzgerald, 457 U.S. 800, 809 (1982).

[16] Buckley v. Fitzsimmons, 509 U.S. 259, 273 (1993).

[17] 457 U.S. 800 (1982).

the test for qualified immunity that still controls: "[G]overnment officials performing discretionary functions, generally are shielded from liability for civil damages insofar as their conduct does not violate clearly established statutory or constitutional rights of which a reasonable person would have known."[18]

In other words, the test for qualified immunity is entirely objective: Did the officer violate a clearly established right that a reasonable person would know? Earlier cases allowed proof of liability by showing that an officer acted subjectively in bad faith.[19] The *Harlow* Court rejected the subjective test as too disruptive of government operations. The Court felt that it was too easy for plaintiffs to allege malice with the hope of finding evidence during discovery. Such discovery was time-consuming, and additionally, it was difficult for trial courts to grant summary judgment on the malice question because subjective intent is a factual question that generally requires a trial.[20]

In its most recent formulation of the standard for qualified immunity, the Court said that a "Government official's conduct violates clearly established law when, at the time of the challenged conduct, '[t]he contours of [a] right [are] sufficiently clear' that every 'reasonable official would have understood that what he is doing violates that right.' We do not require a case directly on point, but existing precedent must have placed the statutory or constitutional question beyond debate."[21]

§4.5 PARDON POWER

Article II, §2, grants the president the "Power to grant Reprieves and Pardons for Offenses against the United States, except in Cases of Impeachment." This is a broad power, and it includes the ability to pardon or reduce the sentence for all accused or convicted of federal crimes. The only exception is that stated in the text: The president cannot issue a pardon to those who have been impeached. In 2001, following controversial pardons by President Bill Clinton in the final days of his presidency, proposals were suggested for restrictions on the pardon power, including allowing Congress to overturn a presidential pardon.[1] But such changes would require a constitutional amendment, which seems unlikely.

In discussing the pardon power, there are three major questions that must be addressed: For what offenses may a pardon be issued? What forms may a pardon take? What, if any, conditions can be imposed?

---

[18] *Id.* at 818.
[19] *See* Wood v. Strickland, 420 U.S. 308 (1975); Scheuer v. Rhodes, 416 U.S. 232 (1974).
[20] 457 U.S. at 816-817.
[21] Ashcroft v. Al-Kidd, 131 S. Ct. 2074, 2083 (2011).
§4.5 [1] *See* Cong. Rec., Statements on Introduced Bills and Joint Resolutions, 146 Cong. Rec. §538-05 (2000); Cong. Record, Expressing the Sense of the Congress That the President Should Not Have Granted Clemency to Terrorists, 146 Cong. Rec. H8012-03.

For What Offenses?

The president can issue a pardon for all crimes against the United States, whether or not there has been a conviction. The Supreme Court declared more than a century ago that the pardon power "extends to every offence known to the law, and may be exercised at any time after its commission, either before legal proceedings are taken, or during their pendency, or after conviction and judgment."[2]

Thus, President Gerald Ford issued a broad pardon to his predecessor, President Richard Nixon, for all crimes that Nixon might have committed as president. Nixon had not been impeached because he resigned, although Articles of Impeachment had been voted against him by the House Judiciary Committee. Nixon had not been indicted because the grand jury did not know if it could indict a sitting president. Ford's pardon was extremely broad, covered crimes that may never have been investigated, and included actions that almost certainly would have been the basis for an impeachment.[3] The scope of the pardon power always has been expansively defined; it has not been limited only to crimes that have been indicted; and Nixon did resign before his impeachment.[4]

The pardon power extends to all criminal offenses, but does not include the ability to relieve an individual of civil liability. For example, in *Ex parte Grossman*, the Court held that the president could issue a pardon as to criminal contempt of court, but not as to civil contempt.[5]

What Form?

The president has discretion to decide the form of the pardon. The classic form of the pardon is to excuse the individual for the criminal acts. It means that "in the eye of the law the offender is as innocent as if he had never committed the offense."[6]

Alternatively, the pardon can take the form of reducing the sentence, but not excusing the crime. In *Biddle v. Perovich*, the Supreme Court upheld the authority of the president to reduce a death sentence to life imprisonment.[7]

Pardons generally are issued on an individual basis, but the president also may give amnesty to an entire group. For example, in 1868, President Andrew Johnson issued a proclamation that granted a "universal amnesty and pardon for

---

[2] Ex parte Garland, 71 U.S. (4 Wall.) 333, 380 (1866).

[3] *See* Hugh C. Macgill, The Nixon Pardon: Limits on the Benign Prerogative, 7 Conn. L. Rev. 56 (1974).

[4] An interesting issue that arose during the Clinton presidency is whether a president can pardon himself. Obviously, there is no law on point. On the one hand, Article II contains no limit on this; on the other, there is a clear conflict of interest in such a pardon. *See* Note, Pardon Me?: The Constitutional Case Against Presidential Self Pardons, 106 Yale L.J. 779 (1996).

[5] 267 U.S. 87, 121-122 (1925).

[6] Ex parte Garland, 71 U.S. (4 Wall.) at 380; United States v. Padelford, 76 U.S. (9 Wall.) 531 (1869).

[7] 274 U.S. 480 (1927).

participation in [the Civil War], extended to all who have borne any part therein."[8] The pardon was granted "unconditionally and without reservation, to all and every person who directly or indirectly participated in the late insurrection or rebellion" and was "a full pardon and amnesty for the offence of treason against the United States, or of adhering to their enemies during the late civil war, with restoration of all rights, privileges, and immunities under the Constitution, and the laws which have been made in pursuance thereof."[9] The proclamation explained that its purpose was "to secure permanent peace, order, and prosperity throughout the land, and to renew and fully restore confidence and fraternal feeling among the whole people."[10]

Congress responded to this pardon by adopting a law that a pardon was inadmissible as evidence in a claim for return of seized property.[11] The statute also provided that a pardon, without an express disclaimer of guilt, was proof that the person aided the rebellion and would deny the federal courts jurisdiction over the claims. The statute declared that upon "proof of such pardon . . . the jurisdiction of the court in the case shall cease, and the court shall forthwith dismiss the suit of such claimant."[12]

The Supreme Court declared the law unconstitutional as a violation of separation of powers and an infringement of the judiciary's prerogatives. The Court concluded that Congress cannot direct how the court will rule in a particular case.[13] The Court did not find that the law undermined the president's pardon power, but rather focused on Congress's powers to create "exceptions and regulations" to the Supreme Court's appellate jurisdiction.[14] President Jimmy Carter also exercised the pardon power when he issued a proclamation of amnesty to those who had evaded service in the Vietnam War by violating the Military Selective Service Act.[15]

What Conditions?

The Supreme Court has made it clear that the president may grant a pardon subject to conditions.[16] In *Schick v. Reed*, the Court upheld the president's

---

[8] Quoted in Armstrong v. United States, 80 U.S. (13 Wall.) 154, 155 (1872), quoting Proclamation No. 15, 15 Stat. 711 (1868).

[9] *Id.*

[10] *Id.*

[11] 16 Stat. 235.

[12] *Id.*

[13] United States v. Klein, 80 U.S. (13 Wall.) 128 (1987).

[14] This issue is discussed more fully in §2.9.

[15] Proclamation No. 4483, 3 C.F.R. 4 (1977) pardoning all Vietnam-era violators of the Military Selective Service Act. This Proclamation granted a full and unconditional pardon to all persons who violated the Military Selective Service Act between August 4, 1964, and March 28, 1973, or were convicted of having violated the Military Selective Service Act during that time, regardless of the time of conviction.

[16] For an excellent discussion of conditions on presidential pardons, and the appropriate role for the courts, *see* Harold J. Krent, Conditioning the President's Conditional Pardon Power, 89 Cal. L. Rev. 1665 (2001).

commuting a death sentence on the condition that the person never would be eligible for parole.[17] Even though the new punishment, life imprisonment without the possibility of parole, was not authorized under the federal law, the Court approved it because it is a lesser punishment than that to which the individual was initially sentenced. The Court observed that the president, of course, may not increase the punishment, but any decrease is permissible as a condition of a pardon.[18]

The pardon power is only the authority to reduce a person's sentence. The president cannot award any other compensation to an individual as part of the conditions attached to a pardon. In *Knote v. United States*, the Court observed that "[h]owever large . . . may be the power of pardon possessed by the President, and however extended may be its application, there is this limit to it, as there is to all his powers—it cannot touch moneys in the treasury of the United States, except expressly authorized by act of Congress. The Constitution places this restriction upon the pardoning power."[19]

But this is one of the few limits on the pardon power. Ultimately, the key point about the pardon power is its breadth. The president has expansive authority to pardon virtually all who have been accused or convicted of a federal crime.

§4.6   FOREIGN POLICY

§4.6.1   *Are Foreign Policy and Domestic Affairs Different?*

United States v. Curtiss-Wright Export Corp.

A basic question, for which there is no definitive answer, is whether the president inherently has greater powers in the area of foreign policy compared with domestic affairs. The most explicit statement of such a distinction is found in *United States v. Curtiss-Wright Export Corp.*[1] Because of concern that United States munitions manufacturers were arming both sides of a war in South America, Congress adopted a law that empowered the president to issue a proclamation making illegal further sales of arms to the warring nations. The case arose at a time when the Court was invalidating laws pertaining to domestic affairs as impermissible delegations of legislative power to the executive.[2]

---

[17] 419 U.S. 256 (1974).

[18] *Id.* at 267.

[19] 95 U.S. (5 Otto) 149, 154 (1877).

§4.6 [1] 299 U.S. 304 (1936). For an excellent discussion of presidential power and foreign policy, *see* Saikrishna B. Prakash & Michael D. Ramsey, The Executive Power over Foreign Affairs, 111 Yale L.J. 231 (2001).

[2] *See, e.g.,* Schechter Poultry Corp. v. United States, 295 U.S. 495 (1935), discussed in §3.11.1.

The Court, however, upheld the delegation to the president to stop munitions shipments and spoke generally of a fundamental difference between domestic and foreign policy. Justice Sutherland, writing for the Court, declared that "[t]he two classes of power are different, both in respect of their origin and their nature. The broad statement that the federal government can exercise no powers except those specifically enumerated in the Constitution, and such implied powers as are necessary and proper to carry into effect the enumerated powers, is categorically true only in respect of our internal affairs."[3]

Justice Sutherland explained that authority over domestic affairs was possessed by the states before the ratification of the Constitution and that they, by approving the Constitution, bestowed power on the national government. As to foreign policy, however, the power is inherently in the national government by virtue of it being sovereign.

Moreover, Justice Sutherland maintained that the realities of conducting foreign policy require that the president possess much greater inherent powers than in the realm of domestic affairs. The Court explained: "In this vast external realm, with its important, complicated, delicate, and manifold problems, the President alone has the power to speak or listen as a representative of the nation."[4] For instance, the president has access to intelligence information that is generally unavailable to Congress.[5]

Although *Curtiss-Wright* is still cited by the Supreme Court as authority for broad inherent presidential power in the area of foreign policy,[6] Justice Sutherland's reasoning has been thoroughly criticized by many scholars. First, some contend that his view is inconsistent with a written Constitution that contains provisions concerning foreign policy. If Sutherland's view were correct, there would have been no reason for the Constitution to enumerate any powers in the area of foreign affairs; all powers would exist automatically as part of national sovereignty. The detailing of authority for conducting foreign policy rebuts the assumption that the president has complete control over foreign affairs simply by virtue of being chief executive.[7]

Second, many have criticized the historical account that is the foundation for Justice Sutherland's opinion. Professor Charles Lofgren notes that the "history on which [*Curtiss-Wright*] rest[s] is 'shockingly inaccurate'" and not based on either the text of the Constitution or the framers' intent.[8] In his view, the framers intended that the presidency, like all branches of the federal government, have limited powers, not the expansive inherent authority described in *Curtiss-Wright*.

---

[3] 299 U.S. at 315-316.

[4] *Id.* at 319.

[5] *Id.* at 320.

[6] *See, e.g.*, Dames & Moore v. Regan, 453 U.S. 654, 661 (1981); Goldwater v. Carter, 444 U.S. 996, 1003-1005 (1979) (Rehnquist, J., concurring).

[7] David M. Levitan, The Foreign Relations Power: An Analysis of Mr. Justice Sutherland's Theory, 55 Yale L.J. 467, 493-494 (1946).

[8] Charles Lofgren, *United States v. Curtiss-Wright Export Corporation*: A Historical Reassessment, 83 Yale L.J. 1, 32 (1973).

The debate over the differences between foreign policy and domestic affairs has occurred in two major areas: treaty-making and war powers. In addition to rulings on the merits, frequently challenges to the president's conduct of foreign policy are dismissed on justiciability grounds, especially as posing political questions.[9] The effect is that the president's power is upheld; if a case challenging the president is dismissed on justiciability grounds, the president's actions are uncontrolled.

§4.6.2 Treaties and Executive Agreements

Article II, §2, states that the president "shall have Power, by and with the Advice and Consent of the Senate, to make Treaties, provided two thirds of the Senators present concur." Two major issues arise: First, when may executive agreements be used instead of treaties? Second, what limits, if any, exist on the ability of the president to negotiate or rescind a treaty?

Executive Agreements

A treaty is an agreement between the United States and a foreign country that is negotiated by the president and is effective when ratified by the Senate.[10] An executive agreement, in contrast, is an agreement between the United States and a foreign country that is effective when signed by the president and the head of the other government. In other words, if the document is labeled "treaty," Senate approval is required. If the document is titled "executive agreement," no Senate ratification is necessary.

Although the Constitution does not mention executive agreements, it is well established that such agreements are constitutional. Indeed, executive agreements can be used for any purpose; that is, anything that can be done by treaty can be done by executive agreement. Never in American history has the Supreme Court declared an executive agreement unconstitutional as usurping the Senate's treaty-approving function. Even major foreign policy commitments have been implemented through executive agreements. For example, in 1940, the "Destroyer-Bases Agreement" substantially expanded American involvement in World War II when President Roosevelt agreed to loan Great Britain 50 naval destroyers in exchange for the United States receiving free 99-year leases to develop military bases on several sites in the Caribbean and Newfoundland.[11]

---

[9] See §2.8.4.

[10] For an argument that there is a new form of presidential-congressional international agreement, approved by both Houses of Congress, but not requiring approval of two-thirds of the Senate, see Brace Ackerman & David Golove, The Constitutionality of NAFTA, 198 Harv. L. Rev. 799 (1995); but see Laurence Tribe, Taking Text and Structure Seriously: Reflections on Free Form Method in Constitutional Interpretation, 108 Harv. L. Rev. 1221 (1995) (strongly objecting to such an approach).

[11] Richard W. Leopold, The Growth of American Foreign Policy 565-566 (1962).

The Court has sided with the president each time there has been a challenge to an executive agreement. In *United States v. Pink*[12] and *United States v. Belmont*,[13] the Supreme Court upheld an executive agreement, the Litvinov Agreement, whereby the United States recognized the Soviet Union in exchange for the Soviet Union assigning to the United States its interests in a Russian insurance company in New York. The Soviet Union had nationalized the interest in this insurance company in 1918 and 1919. The United States would use these assets to pay claims that it and others had against the Soviet Union.[14]

The Court upheld the executive agreement and explained that because it was not a treaty, Senate approval was not required. New York courts had refused to enforce the Litvinov Agreement, but the Court ruled that states must comply with executive agreements. Executive agreements, like treaties, prevail over state law and policy. Justice Douglas, writing for the Court in *Pink*, explained: "A treaty is a 'Law of the Land' under the supremacy clause [of Article VI] of the Constitution. Such international compacts and agreements as the Litvinov Assignment have a similar dignity."[15] Similarly, in *United States v. Belmont*, the Court stated that "in the case of all international compacts and agreements . . . complete power over international affairs is in the national government and is not and cannot be subject to any curtailment or interference on the part of the several states."[16]

A later example of the Supreme Court upholding an executive agreement was *Dames & Moore v. Regan* in 1981.[17] Shortly before leaving office in 1981, President Jimmy Carter negotiated an agreement with Iran whereby that country would free American hostages being held in Tehran in exchange for the United States lifting a freeze on Iranian assets in the United States. After Iran seized the American embassy in Iran and held its occupants hostage, President Carter froze all assets of the Iranian government in the United States. The executive agreement lifted this freeze and also provided for an end to all suits pending against Iran in United States courts. Such claims would be resolved instead in a new Iran–United States Claims Tribunal.

The executive agreement was challenged by Dames & Moore, which had filed a lawsuit in federal district court against Iran for breach of contract for almost $3.5 million. The Supreme Court, in an opinion by Justice Rehnquist, rejected the constitutional challenge to the executive agreement. The Court emphasized that a series of federal statutes authorized the president's actions. Justice Rehnquist stated: "Because the President's action in nullifying the attachments and ordering the transfer of the assets was taken pursuant to specific congressional authorization, it is 'supported by the strongest of presumptions and the widest latitude of

---

[12]   315 U.S. 203 (1942).

[13]   301 U.S. 324 (1937).

[14]   In *Pink*, the Court also rejected a claim that the agreement was an impermissible taking of property without just compensation in violation of the Fifth Amendment. The Court noted that the Litvinov Agreement did not bar compensation for claims, although it did give the United States priority as a creditor.

[15]   315 U.S. at 230.

[16]   301 U.S. at 331.

[17]   453 U.S. 654 (1981).

judicial interpretation, and the burden of persuasion would rest heavily upon any who might attack it.'"[18]

The Court explained that the executive agreement was constitutional because federal statutes authorized such presidential actions and because there was a history of such executive settlement of claims.[19] Justice Rehnquist quoted Justice Frankfurter's words from *Youngstown* that "a systematic, unbroken, executive practice, long pursued to the knowledge of the Congress and never before questioned . . . may be treated as a gloss on 'Executive Power' vested in the President by §1 of Article II."[20]

On the one hand, *Pink, Belmont,* and *Dames & Moore* can be read narrowly as establishing only that executive agreements prevail over conflicting state law and are permissible when authorized by federal statutes.[21] The opinions in all three cases were narrow, rather than broad, and leave open the possibility that some future executive agreement might be invalidated as usurping the Senate's treaty-approving power.

On the other hand, never has the Court invalidated an executive agreement for undermining the Senate's role in ratifying treaties. In fact, in 1951 and 1952, Senator Bricker proposed a constitutional amendment, known as the Bricker Amendment, which would have provided that "executive agreements shall not be made in lieu of treaties."[22] So long as the president is not violating another constitutional provision or a federal statute, there seems little basis for challenging the constitutionality of an executive agreement.

Treaties

Treaties, agreements between the United States and a foreign country that are negotiated by the president and ratified by the Senate, are permitted unless they violate the Constitution. It is firmly established that if there is a conflict between a treaty and a federal statute, the one adopted last in time controls.

Article VI of the Constitution states that the "Constitution, and the Laws of the United States which shall be made in Pursuance thereof; and all Treaties made, or which shall be made, under the Authority of the United States, shall be the supreme Law of the Land." The United States government has broad powers to enter into

---

[18] *Id.* at 674, quoting Youngstown Sheet & Tube Co. v. Sawyer, 343 U.S. 579, 637 (1952) (Jackson, J., concurring) (citations omitted).

[19] However, some scholars challenge the Court's claim that federal statutes authorized the president's actions. Professor Harold Koh, for example, says that the Court found "legislative 'approval'" when Congress had given none." Harold Koh, The National Security Constitution: Sharing Power After the Iran-Contra Affair 140 (1990). Professor Koh criticizes the Supreme Court for not demanding "more specific legislative approval for the president's far-reaching measures." *Id.* at 139-140.

[20] 453 U.S. at 686, quoting Youngstown Sheet & Tube Co. v. Sawyer, 343 U.S. 579, 610-611 (1952) (Frankfurter, J., concurring).

[21] Although there is no Supreme Court holding on point, it appears, then, that a federal statute would prevail if it were in conflict with an executive agreement. *See* United States v. Guy W. Capps, Inc., 204 F.2d 655 (4th Cir. 1953), *aff'd on other grounds*, 348 U.S. 296 (1955) (invalidating an executive agreement between the United States and Canada because of its conflict with a federal statute).

[22] Leopold, *supra* note 11, at 555, 716-717.

treaties with foreign countries. Indeed, the Supreme Court has explained that "the treaty power of the United States extends to all proper subjects of negotiation between our government and the governments of other nations . . . [and] it is not perceived that there is any limit to the questions which can be adjusted touching any matter which is properly the subject of negotiation with a foreign country."[23]

Treaties, however, cannot violate the Constitution. In *Reid v. Covert*, the Court held that American civilian dependents of military personnel in a foreign country must be accorded a trial that meets the dictates of the Constitution.[24] Justice Black explained that "no agreement with a foreign nation can confer power on the Congress, or on any other branch of Government, which is free from the restraints of the Constitution."[25]

However, treaties cannot be challenged as violating the Tenth Amendment and infringing state sovereignty. *Missouri v. Holland*[26] was decided in 1920, during an era when the Court aggressively used the Tenth Amendment to safeguard states from federal encroachment.[27] The United States and Great Britain entered into a treaty to protect migratory birds. Earlier, the lower federal courts had declared unconstitutional a federal statute that attempted to protect such birds.[28] Nonetheless, the Supreme Court upheld the constitutionality of the Migratory Bird Treaty.

Justice Holmes, writing for the Court, spoke broadly of the power to enter into treaties and rejected any Tenth Amendment limit on the treaty power. Holmes noted that Article II expressly authorizes treaties and that Article VI makes treaties the supreme law of the land. Indeed, Justice Holmes indicated that the treaty power is broader than the authority Congress possesses to enact statutes. He wrote: "Acts of Congress are the supreme law of the land only when made in pursuance of the Constitution, while treaties are declared to be so when made under the authority of the United States. . . . It is obvious that there may be matters of the sharpest exigency for the national well being that an act of Congress could not deal with but that a treaty followed by such an act could."[29]

As the Court revitalizes the Tenth Amendment,[30] perhaps the Court might reconsider *Missouri v. Holland* and the possibility of invalidating the provisions of a treaty as infringing state sovereignty. If a particular law violates the Tenth Amendment, for example, by placing an undue burden on state governments, then it is questionable why the same action would be constitutional if undertaken through a treaty. It is true that treaties are authorized in Article II and mentioned in the supremacy clause of Article VI, but laws are authorized in Article I and also

---

[23] Geofroy v. Riggs, 133 U.S. 258, 266-267 (1890).

[24] 354 U.S. 1 (1957).

[25] *Id.* at 16.

[26] 252 U.S. 416 (1920). For a contemporary analysis of Missouri v. Holland, *see* Mark Strasser, Domestic Relations, *Missouri v. Holland,* and the New Federalism, 12 Wm. & Mary Bill Rts. J. 179 (2003).

[27] *See* §3.10.

[28] *See, e.g.,* United States v. McCullagh, 221 Fed. 288 (D. Kan. 1915).

[29] 252 U.S. at 433.

[30] *See* Printz v. United States, 521 U.S. 898 (1997); New York v. United States, 505 U.S. 144 (1992). These cases are discussed in §3.10.

mentioned in the supremacy clause of Article VI. Since treaties cannot violate the Constitution, it is questionable why the Tenth Amendment issue should depend on whether the legal requirement is in a statute or treaty.[31]

The Court was asked to reconsider *Missouri v. Holland* and Congress's ability to use the treaty power to enact federal statutes in *Bond v. United States*,[32] but declined to do so. Carol Ann Bond was thrilled when she learned that her best friend was pregnant, but then horrified to discover that her husband was the father of the coming baby. She put poison that could be absorbed through the skin on the car door, door knobs, and mail box of her former best friend in an attempt to injure her. (Her friend received a minor chemical burn on a thumb, but otherwise was fine.)

Bond was prosecuted under a federal law that was enacted to implement the federal chemical weapon treaty and that prohibits knowingly using a chemical weapon. The Court was asked to decide the issue of Congress's ability to enact laws to implement treaties and perhaps the continued validity of *Missouri v. Holland*. But the Court declined to do so and instead ruled narrowly that there was no indication that Congress meant the prohibition of chemical weapons to apply to such a local dispute that is traditionally handled under state criminal law. Chief Justice Roberts wrote: "Of course Bond's conduct is serious and unacceptable—and against the laws of Pennsylvania. But the background principle that Congress does not normally intrude upon the police power of the States is critically important. In light of that principle, we are reluctant to conclude that Congress meant to punish Bond's crime with a federal prosecution for a chemical weapons attack."[33]

Justices Scalia and Thomas each wrote opinions concurring in the judgment, each of which was joined by the other and by Justice Alito. These Justices would have reached the issue not decided by the majority and would have made clear that Congress's power to enact statutes to implement treaties is limited. Justice Thomas, for example, wrote: "Yet to interpret the Treaty Power as extending to every conceivable domestic subject matter—even matters without any nexus to foreign relations—would destroy the basic constitutional distinction between domestic and foreign powers. It would also lodge in the Federal Government the potential for a police power over all aspects of American life. A treaty-based power of that magnitude—no less than a plenary power of legislation—would threaten the liberties that derive from the diffusion of sovereign power."[34]

If there is a conflict between a treaty and a federal statute, the one adopted last in time controls. The Court has said that if a treaty and statute "relate to the same subject, the courts will always endeavor to construe them so as to give effect to both, if that can be done without violating the language of either; but if the two

---

[31] For an excellent debate over whether federalism is a limit on the treaty power, *see* Curtis A. Bradley, The Treaty Power and American Federalism, 97 Mich. L. Rev. 390 (1998) (arguing for a national perspective in which federalism does not limit the treaty power); David M. Golove, Treaty-Making and the Nation: The Historical Foundations of the Nationalist Conception of the Treaty Power, 98 Mich. L. Rev. 1075 (2000) (arguing that federalism limits the treaty power).

[32] 134 S. Ct. 2077 (2014).

[33] *Id.* at 2092.

[34] *Id.* at 2103 (Thomas, J., concurring in the judgment).

are inconsistent, the one last in date will control the other."[35] This is the same rule that applies when two statutes conflict. Because treaties and statutes are co-equal as law, there is no reason to treat them differently in this respect or to give treaties preference over statutes.

The other major issue that has arisen before the Supreme Court concerning treaties is whether the president may unilaterally rescind them. This question was raised in *Goldwater v. Carter*, but the Court dismissed the case on justiciability grounds.[36] President Carter rescinded the United States's treaty with Taiwan as part of recognizing the People's Republic of China. Senator Barry Goldwater sued contending that the Senate must approve rescission of a treaty, just as it must approve the rescission of a statute.

The Court, without a majority opinion, dismissed the case. Justice Rehnquist, writing for the plurality, said that the case was a nonjusticiable political question. He wrote that "the basic question presented . . . in this case is 'political' and therefore nonjusticiable because it involves the authority of the President in the conduct of our country's foreign relations."[37] Justice Powell concurred in the judgment, agreeing that the case should be dismissed as nonjusticiable, but focusing on ripeness grounds. Powell argued that the case was not ripe until and unless Congress acted to disapprove the rescission of the treaty.

The effect of the dismissal in *Goldwater v. Carter* is to empower the president to rescind treaties. Although the Court did not reach the merits, dismissing the challenge means that the president can rescind treaties in the future without worrying about judicial invalidation. The problem with the Court's approach is that if the plaintiffs in *Goldwater* were correct that the Senate must approve rescission of the treaty, one-third of the senators should be able to block rescission. Yet there is no way that one-third of the senators can have a voice or can enforce their position without judicial review and participation.

§4.6.3   War Powers

As discussed in Chapter 3, the Constitution is an invitation for a struggle between the president and Congress over control of the war power. The Constitution, in Article I, grants Congress the power to declare war and the authority to raise and support the army and the navy. Article II makes the president the commander-in-chief. This issue, and especially the tensions between Congress and the president over the war powers, is discussed in detail in §3.6.1.

Absence of Case Law Concerning War Powers

Rather than repeat that analysis, several points can be highlighted here. First, the Supreme Court rarely has spoken as to the constitutionality of the president

---

[35] Whitney v. Robertson, 124 U.S. 190, 194 (1888); *see also* The Chinese Exclusion Case (Chae Chan Ping v. United States), 130 U.S. 581 (1889).
[36] 444 U.S. 996 (1979).
[37] *Id.* at 1002.

using troops in a war or war-like circumstances without congressional approval. In fact, the only Supreme Court case to address the issue was in the unique context of the Civil War and the actions of the president to deal with the rebellion. In the *Prize Cases*, the Court ruled that the president had the power to impose a blockade on Southern states without a congressional declaration of war.[38] No other Supreme Court case has addressed the constitutionality of presidential war making without a congressional declaration of war. Therefore, little exists in the way of law as to the circumstances in which the president may use troops without congressional approval or as to what Congress may do to suspend American involvement in a war.[39]

Challenges Likely to Be Dismissed as Political Questions

Second, challenges to the president's use of troops in a foreign country are likely to be dismissed on political question grounds. The Supreme Court often has generally remarked that challenges to the conduct of foreign policy present a non-justiciable political question. For example, the Court observed that "[t]he conduct of the foreign relations of our Government is committed by the Constitution to the Executive and Legislative—the political—Departments of the Government, and the propriety of what may be done in the exercise of this political power is not subject to judicial inquiry or decision."[40]

The challenges to foreign policy that are probably most likely to be deemed political questions are those directed to the constitutionality of the president's use of the war powers. During the Vietnam War, dozens of cases were filed in the federal courts arguing that the war was unconstitutional because there was no declaration of war. Although the Supreme Court did not rule in any of these cases, either as to justiciability or on the merits, most of the lower federal courts considered the cases to present nonjusticiable political questions.[41] In the same way, challenges to the constitutionality of President Reagan's military activities in El Salvador were dismissed by the lower federal courts as posing a political question.[42] Likewise, challenges to American involvement in the Persian Gulf War were dismissed on

---

[38] 67 U.S. (2 Black) 635 (1863).

[39] There is, however, a voluminous academic literature on the topic. Some thorough discussions include Mark E. Brandon, War and American Constitutional Order, 56 Vand. L. Rev 1815 (2003); Michael D. Ramsey, Textualism and War Powers, 69 U. Chi. L. Rev. 1543 (2002); John C. Yoo, The Continuation of Politics by Other Means: The Original Understanding of War Powers, 84 Cal. L. Rev. 167 (1996); Louis Fisher, Presidential War Power (1995); John Hart Ely, War and Responsibility: Constitutional Lessons of Vietnam and Its Aftermath (1993).

[40] Oetjen v. Central Leather Co., 246 U.S. 297, 302 (1918); *see also* Chicago & S. Air Lines, Inc. v. Waterman S.S. Corp., 333 U.S. 103, 111 (1948).

[41] *See, e.g.*, Holtzman v. Schlesinger, 484 F.2d 1307, 1309 (3d Cir.), *cert. denied*, 416 U.S. 936 (1973); DaCosta v. Laird, 471 F.2d 1146, 1147 (2d Cir. 1963); Orlando v. Laird, 443 F.2d 1039, 1043 (2d Cir.), *cert. denied*, 404 U.S. 869 (1971); *see also* Louis Henkin, Vietnam in the Courts of the United States: Political Questions, 63 Am. J. Intl. L. 284 (1969).

[42] *See, e.g.*, Crockett v. Reagan, 720 F.2d 1355 (D.C. Cir. 1983), *cert. denied*, 467 U.S. 1251 (1984); Sanchez-Espinoza v. Reagan, 770 F.2d 202 (D.C. Cir. 1985); Lowry v. Reagan, 676 F. Supp. 333 (D.D.C. 1987).

political question grounds.[43] Similarly, during the American bombing in Yugoslavia, a lawsuit challenging its constitutionality by a member of the House of Representatives was dismissed on standing grounds.[44] Hence, it is unlikely that courts will become involved in answering the key questions about the war powers.

Uncertainty as to What Constitutes a "Declaration of War"

Third, it is unresolved as to what constitutes a declaration of war sufficient to fulfill the requirements of Article I of the Constitution. Must it be a formal declaration of war, such as was adopted by Congress after the bombing of Pearl Harbor to authorize America's entry into World War II? Or may it be less explicit? For example, was the Gulf of Tonkin Resolution, which authorized the use of military force in Southeast Asia, sufficient to constitute a declaration of war for the Vietnam War? Might even repeated congressional approval of funding for a war be regarded as sufficient even without passage of a resolution explicitly approving the war?

Uncertainty as to How Congress May Limit the President

Fourth, it is unclear whether and how Congress can put other limits on the president's use of troops in foreign countries. This issue arises most notably as to whether the War Powers Resolution is constitutional. The War Powers Resolution states that the president as commander-in-chief may introduce the United States Armed Forces into hostilities or situations where hostilities appear imminent "only pursuant to (1) a declaration of war, (2) specific statutory authorization, or (3) a national emergency created by attack upon the United States, its territories or possessions, or its armed forces."[45] It requires that the president consult with Congress, where possible, before introducing troops into hostilities and that the president report to Congress within 48 hours after troops are introduced into hostilities or in situations that risk imminent involvement in hostilities.

Most important, the War Powers Resolution provides that the president shall withdraw troops after 60 days unless Congress has declared war or authorized a 60-day extension or is physically unable to meet as a result of an armed attack upon the United States.[46] The president can extend this by 30 days if he certifies to Congress in writing that "unavoidable military necessity respecting the safety of United States Armed Forces requires the continued use of such armed forces in the course of bringing about a prompt removal of such forces."[47] The constitutionality of the War Powers Resolution is discussed in §3.6.1.

The issue arose during the Reagan presidency as to whether the Boland Amendment was constitutional in limiting the president's ability to provide funds

---

[43] Ange v. Bush, 752 F. Supp. 509 (D.D.C. 1990).
[44] Campbell v. Clinton, 52 F. Supp. 2d 34 (D.D.C. 1999), *aff'd* 203 F.3d 19 (D.C. Cir. 1999).
[45] 50 U.S.C. §1541(c).
[46] 50 U.S.C. §1544(b).
[47] *Id.*

for the Contras in Nicaragua. Specifically, the amendments to the appropriation bills barred any "agency or entity of the United States involved in intelligence activities" from spending funds "to support military or paramilitary operations in Nicaragua."[48]

It is now known that some high-level members of the Reagan administration intentionally violated the Boland Amendment by raising funds from third parties to fund the Contras and by selling arms to Iran to fund the Contras.[49] Some have defended these actions on the ground that the Boland Amendment was an impermissible restriction on the president's power to conduct foreign policy. For example, a Republican minority report to a House Committee report declared: "[The] Constitution gives the President some power to act on his own in foreign affairs. . . . Congress may not use its control over appropriations, including salaries, to prevent the executive or judiciary from fulfilling Constitutionally mandated obligations."[50]

But Congress controls the power of the purse and therefore should be able to control government spending. The Boland Amendment was a restriction on expenditures. Moreover, Article I gives Congress the power to regulate foreign commerce. The Boland Amendment was constitutional under this authority as well, and the president has no authority to disobey a constitutional statute in the conduct of foreign or domestic affairs.

These questions—what constitutes a declaration of war and when may the president wage war without such a declaration—are among the most basic and most important of all constitutional questions. Yet in light of the Court's historical unwillingness to tackle these issues and its propensity for finding them to be political questions, answers from the judiciary are unlikely in the future.

§4.6.4   Presidential Power and the War on Terrorism

The tragic events of September 11, 2001, led to new controversies over the scope of presidential power. For example, President George W. Bush claimed broad authority to detain enemy combatants to protect national security. Those who defended the president's position argued that the Constitution envisioned expansive presidential power to deal with external threats and that this power especially is needed in dealing with the risk of terrorist attacks on the United States.[51] But critics argued that the Constitution rejects such unchecked executive power and that President Bush's actions were unprecedented and unconstitutional.[52] Two of the most important issues thus far have been the power of the president to detain individuals and the constitutionality of the use of military tribunals to try individuals suspected of terrorist activity.

---

[48] 101 Stat. 1011 (1987).

[49] *See* Lawrence E. Walsh, Final Report of the Independent Counsel for Iran/Contra Matters (1993); Michael E. Ledeen, Perilous Statecraft: An Insider's Account of the Iran-Contra Affair (1988).

[50] Report of the Congressional Committees Investigating the Iran-Contra Affair, S. Rep. No. 100-216, H. Rep. No. 100-433 (1987) at 473 (Minority report).

[51] *See* John Yoo, The Powers of War and Peace (2005).

[52] *See* Erwin Chemerinsky, The Conservative Assault on the Constitution ch. 2 (2010).

Detentions

In three cases decided on June 28, 2004, the Supreme Court considered the right of those being detained as part of the war on terrorism to have access to the courts. In *Hamdi v. Rumsfeld*,[53] the Court, by an 8-to-1 margin, held that an American citizen apprehended in a foreign country and held as an enemy combatant must be accorded due process and a meaningful factual hearing. In *Padilla v. Rumsfeld*, the Court dismissed on jurisdictional grounds a challenge by an American citizen apprehended in the United States and held as an enemy combatant.[54] The Court ruled that Jose Padilla needed to sue in federal court in South Carolina where he is being held, rather than in New York where the case was litigated. But at least five Justices clearly signaled that they would rule in favor of Padilla and hold that the government has no authority to detain an American citizen arrested in the United States as an enemy combatant. In *Rasul v. Bush*, the Court held that those being detained in Guantánamo Bay, Cuba have the right to have a habeas corpus petition heard in federal court.[55] Although only *Hamdi* was a constitutional ruling, all of the decisions are important, especially because they were the Supreme Court's first rulings about the government's actions in the war on terrorism since September 11. Four years later, in *Boumediene v. Bush*, the Supreme Court held unconstitutional the denial of habeas corpus to noncitizens held as enemy combatants.[56]

Hamdi v. Rumsfeld

Yaser Hamdi is an American citizen who was apprehended in Afghanistan and brought to Guantánamo Bay. There it was discovered that he is an American citizen and he was taken to a military prison in South Carolina. He has been held as an enemy combatant and never has been charged with any crime. His situation is identical to that of John Walker Lindh, except that Lindh was indicted and pled guilty to crimes.

The United States Court of Appeals for the Fourth Circuit agreed with the government that an American citizen apprehended in a foreign country and held as an enemy combatant is not entitled to any form of due process or judicial review.[57] The Supreme Court reversed, though without a majority opinion.

There were two issues before the Supreme Court. First, does the federal government have the authority to hold an American citizen apprehended in a foreign country as an enemy combatant? In a 5-to-4 ruling, the Court decided in favor of the government. Justice O'Connor wrote the plurality opinion, which was joined by Chief Justice Rehnquist and Justices Kennedy and Breyer. Hamdi contended that his detention violated the Non-Detention Act, which states that "[n]o citizen shall be imprisoned or otherwise detained by the United States except pursuant to an Act of Congress."[58]

---

[53] 542 U.S. 507 (2004).
[54] 542 U.S. 426 (2004).
[55] 542 U.S. 466 (2004).
[56] 553 U.S. 723 (2008).
[57] 316 F.3d 450 (4th Cir. 2003).
[58] 18 U.S.C. §4001(a).

But the plurality concluded that Hamdi's detention was authorized pursuant to an Act of Congress: the Authorization for Use of Military Force that was passed after September 11. Justice O'Connor stated that this constituted sufficient congressional authorization to meet the requirements of the Non-Detention Act and to permit detaining an American citizen apprehended in a foreign country as an enemy combatant. Justice O'Connor's plurality opinion was joined by Chief Justice Rehnquist and Justices Kennedy and Breyer. Justice Thomas was the fifth vote for the government on this issue and in a separate opinion he concluded that the president has inherent authority, pursuant to Article II of the Constitution, to hold Hamdi as an enemy combatant. Only Justice Thomas of the five Justices who composed the majority addressed the president's claim of inherent power as commander-in-chief to detain American citizens as enemy combatants.

The other four Justices vehemently disagreed. In a powerful dissenting opinion, Justice Scalia, joined by Justice Stevens, argued that there is no authority to hold an American citizen in the United States as an enemy combatant without charges or trial unless Congress expressly suspends the writ of habeas corpus. Justice Souter, in an opinion joined by Justice Ginsburg concurring in the judgment in part and dissenting in part, contended that it violates the Non-Detention Act to hold an American citizen as an enemy combatant. Justice Souter argued that Congress must expressly authorize such detentions and that it had not done so.

The second issue before the Court was what, if any, process must be accorded to Hamdi? The Court ruled, with only Justice Thomas dissenting, that Hamdi must be accorded due process. (Justice Scalia, joined by Justice Stevens, did not reach this issue because he believed that there was no authority to detain Hamdi.) Justice O'Connor explained that Hamdi is entitled to have his habeas corpus petition heard in federal court and that imprisoning a person is obviously the most basic form of deprivation of liberty. Thus, due process is required and the procedures required are to be determined by applying the three-part balancing test under *Mathews v. Eldridge*,[59] which instructs courts to weigh the importance of the interest to the individual, the ability of additional procedures to reduce the risk of an erroneous deprivation, and the government's interests.

Although the Court did not specify all of the procedures that must be followed in Hamdi's case, the Justices were explicit that Hamdi must be given a meaningful factual hearing. At a minimum, this includes notice of the charges, the right to respond, and the right to be represented by an attorney. The Court, however, suggested that hearsay evidence might be admissible and the burden of proof even could placed on Hamdi. The Court remanded the case for the determination of what procedural due process requires when an American citizen apprehended in a foreign country is detained as an enemy combatant. Only Justice Thomas rejected this conclusion and accepted the government's argument that the president could detain enemy combatants without any form of due process.

In the fall of 2004, following the Supreme Court's decision, the government and Hamdi reached an agreement. In exchange for Hamdi being released from

---

[59] 424 U.S. 319 (1976). *Mathews v. Eldridge* and the test for procedural due process are discussed in detail in §7.4.

custody, he agreed to leave the country, renounce his citizenship, and never to take up arms against the United States. Thus, Hamdi's case was not the occasion for the Court to spell out the procedures required.

Padilla v. Rumsfeld

Jose Padilla is an American citizen who was apprehended at Chicago's O'Hare Airport in May 2002. He allegedly was planning to build and detonate a "dirty bomb" in the United States. Although he has been imprisoned since May 2002, he has not been indicted or tried for any crime. Instead, the government is holding him as an enemy combatant. Padilla's situation is different from Hamdi's because Padilla was arrested in the United States for a crime allegedly planned to occur in this country.

After his arrest, Padilla was taken to New York. An attorney filed a petition in the Southern District of New York to meet with him. Shortly thereafter, Padilla was transferred to a military prison in South Carolina. But the litigation over his detention and rights remained in New York and ultimately in the Second Circuit. The Supreme Court, in a 5-to-4 decision, with the majority opinion written by Chief Justice Rehnquist, concluded that the New York court lacked jurisdiction to hear Padilla's habeas corpus petition. The Court said that a person must bring a habeas petition where he or she is being detained against the person immediately responsible for the detention. Padilla needed to file his habeas petition in South Carolina against the head of the military prison there.

Justice Stevens wrote for the four dissenters and lamented that Padilla, who already had been held for over two years, must begin all over again. But it appears clear that Padilla has five votes on the Supreme Court that it is illegal to hold him as an enemy combatant. In a footnote near the end of his dissenting opinion, Justice Stevens expressly stated that he agreed with the Second Circuit that there was no legal authority to detain Padilla as an enemy combatant.[60] Justice Scalia was emphatic in his dissent in *Hamdi* that an American citizen cannot be held without trial as an enemy combatant unless Congress suspends the writ of habeas corpus.[61]

Subsequently, the United States District Court ruled in Padilla's favor and held that the government either had to criminally charge Padilla or release him from custody.[62] However, the Fourth Circuit reversed and found presidential power to detain an American citizen as an enemy combatant.[63] In November 2005, the United States issued an indictment of Padilla so that he would no longer be held as an enemy combatant and the United States Supreme Court dismissed the matter as moot.[64] In 2007, Padilla was convicted of materially assisting a foreign terrorist organization and sentenced to 17 years, 4 months in prison.

---

[60] 542 U.S. at 463 n.8 (Stevens, J., dissenting).

[61] 542 U.S. at 554 (Scalia, J., dissenting).

[62] 389 F. Supp. 2d 678 (D.S.C. 2005).

[63] 423 F.3d 386 (4th Cir. 2005).

[64] Padilla v. Hanft, 547 U.S. 1062 (2006). Justices Stevens and Souter dissented from the denial of certiorari.

Rasul v. Bush

Beginning January 2002, the United States government has held over 600 individuals as prisoners at a military facility in Guantánamo, Cuba. The first cases before the Supreme Court involved two habeas corpus petitions that had been filed on behalf of the Guantánamo detainees. *Rasul v. Bush*, the title under which both cases were decided by the Supreme Court, was brought by the father of an Australian detainee, the father of a British detainee, and the mother of another British detainee. *Al Odah v. United States* was brought by fathers and brothers of 12 individuals being held at Camp X-Ray in Guantánamo.

In both cases, the government moved to dismiss contending that the federal courts lacked authority to hear habeas corpus petitions by those being held in Guantánamo. In March 2003, the United States Court of Appeals for the District of Columbia Circuit affirmed the dismissal of the case for lack of jurisdiction and ruled that no court in the country could hear the petitions brought by the Guantánamo detainees.[65] The Court of Appeals based this conclusion on the Supreme Court's decision in *Johnson v. Eisentrager*.[66] In *Johnson v. Eisentrager*, 21 German nationals sought habeas corpus after they were arrested in China for working in Japan on behalf of the German government before Germany surrendered. They were taken into custody by the United States Army and convicted by a United States Military Commission of violating laws of war by engaging in continued military activity in Japan after Germany's surrender, but before Japan had surrendered. The defendants were convicted and repatriated to Germany to serve their sentences in a prison whose custodian was an American army officer. The prisoners sought habeas corpus in federal court and the Supreme Court found that there was not jurisdiction in a federal district to hear the petition. The D.C. Circuit found that the Guantánamo detainees are like the petitioners in *Johnson* and thus held that the petition in this case be dismissed.

The Supreme Court, in a 6-to-3 decision, reversed the Court of Appeals, and held that a federal court may hear the habeas corpus petition of those being held in Guantánamo. Justice John Paul Stevens wrote the opinion for the Court. He emphasized that *Johnson v. Eisentrager* is distinguishable in many important respects. In *Johnson*, those detained were accorded a trial in a military tribunal; but those being held in Guantánamo have never had any form of trial or due process. Also, the Court stressed that unlike the situation in *Johnson*, Guantánamo is functionally under the control and sovereignty of the United States government.

The Court in *Rasul v. Bush* did not address what type of hearing ultimately must be accorded to those in Guantánamo. Rather, the case was limited to the issue of whether a federal court could hear their habeas corpus petition.

---

[65] 321 F.3d 1134 (D.C. Cir. 2003).
[66] 339 U.S. 763 (1950).

Boumediene v. Bush

On remand, the government argued that the Guantánamo detainees failed to state a claim upon which relief could be granted. Two judges in the United States District Court for the District of Columbia came to opposite conclusions.[67] One judge found that those in Guantánamo stated claims under the Constitution and under the Geneva accords; the other judge disagreed and found no cause of action for those being detained in Guantánamo. The cases were initially argued to the United States Court of Appeals for the District of Columbia Circuit in September 2005, but it was not until June 2008 in *Boumediene v. Bush* that the Court returned to the issue of the Guantánamo detainees and their access to habeas corpus.

After the Supreme Court rejected this argument in *Rasul v. Bush*,[68] Congress adopted the Detainee Treatment Act,[69] which provided that federal courts could not hear writs of habeas corpus by "enemy combatants." In *Hamdan v. Rumsfeld,* the Court ruled that the Detainee Treatment Act does not apply retroactively to those held prior to its enactment.[70]

Congress responded to *Hamdan* by enacting the Military Commission Act.[71] The Military Commission Act provides that noncitizens held as enemy combatants shall not have access to federal courts via a writ of habeas corpus or otherwise, except that if there is a military proceeding, the detainee may seek review of its decision in the United States Court of Appeals for the District of Columbia Circuit.

In a 5-4 decision, with Justice Kennedy writing an opinion joined by Justices Stevens, Souter, Ginsburg, and Breyer, the Court held that the preclusion of habeas corpus jurisdiction was unconstitutional. Justice Kennedy explained that Article I, §9, of the Constitution allows Congress to suspend habeas corpus in times of rebellion or invasion. The government did not claim that either of these situations were present.

The Court concluded that this provision applies to the detainees held in Guantánamo: "We hold that Art. I, §9, cl. 2, of the Constitution has full effect at Guantánamo Bay. If the privilege of habeas corpus is to be denied to the detainees now before us, Congress must act in accordance with the requirements of the Suspension Clause."[72] Moreover, the Court decided that the remedy provided, review in the D.C. Circuit, did not substitute for habeas corpus. The Court thus declared: "We hold that petitioners may invoke the fundamental procedural protections of habeas corpus. The laws and Constitution are designed to survive, and remain in force, in extraordinary times. Liberty and security can be reconciled; and in our system they are reconciled within the framework of the law. The Framers

---

[67] In re Guantánamo Detainee Cases, 355 F. Supp. 2d 443 (D.D.C. 2005) (holding cause of action exists for those being held in Guantánamo); Khalid v. Bush, 355 F. Supp. 2d 311 (D.D.C. 2005) (holding no cause of action exists for those being held in Guantánamo).

[68] 542 U.S. 466 (2004).

[69] Pub. L. No. 109-148, 119 Stat. 2739.

[70] 548 U.S. 557 (2006) (discussed below).

[71] 28 U.S.C. §2241(e).

[72] 548 U.S. at 771.

decided that habeas corpus, a right of first importance, must be a part of that framework, a part of that law."[73]

Chief Justice Roberts dissented, joined by Justices Scalia, Thomas, and Alito, and said that the Court should have deferred to the choices made by Congress and the president. He wrote: "Today the Court strikes down as inadequate the most generous set of procedural protections ever afforded aliens detained by this country as enemy combatants. The political branches crafted these procedures amidst an ongoing military conflict, after much careful investigation and thorough debate. The Court rejects them today out of hand, without bothering to say what due process rights the detainees possess, without explaining how the statute fails to vindicate those rights, and before a single petitioner has exhausted the procedures under the law. And to what effect? The majority merely replaces a review system designed by the people's representatives with a set of shapeless procedures to be defined by federal courts at some future date."[74] Chief Justice Roberts argued that the procedures provided in the Military Commission Act were sufficient to avoid there being a suspension of the writ of habeas corpus.

Justice Scalia wrote an even more vehement dissent, joined by the other dissenting Justices, in which he argued that the judiciary has no business being involved in the matter at all. He wrote: "What competence does the Court have to second-guess the judgment of Congress and the President on such a point? None whatever. But the Court blunders in nonetheless. Henceforth, as today's opinion makes unnervingly clear, how to handle enemy prisoners in this war will ultimately lie with the branch that knows least about the national security concerns that the subject entails."[75]

The majority and the dissent articulated vastly different views about the role of the federal courts during the war on terrorism. For the majority, the Constitution and access to the federal courts to enforce it are essential even in times of crisis. From this perspective, the decision was a profound reaffirmation of the rule of law. For the dissent, the decision was dangerous judicial meddling in a realm properly left to president and Congress. Justice Scalia said that he believed that people would needlessly die because of the majority's opinion. The issue is profoundly important in terms of the appropriate role of the Constitution, the judiciary, and the rule of law in the war on terrorism.

Military Tribunals

Another major issue concerning the war on terrorism concerns the legality of using military tribunals. On November 13, 2001, President Bush issued an Executive Order providing for military tribunals to try non-American citizens accused of participating in or assisting terrorism.[76] The Department of Defense has issued regulations for conducting such proceedings.

---

[73] *Id.* at 798.

[74] *Id.* at 801 (Roberts, C.J., dissenting).

[75] *Id.* at 831 (Scalia, J., dissenting).

[76] Detention, Treatment, and Trial of Certain Non-Citizens in the War Against Terrorism, 66 Fed. Reg. 57,833 (Nov. 13, 2001).

The use of military tribunals raises important and difficult constitutional questions. Does the president have the authority as commander-in-chief to create military tribunals, or is creating courts entirely a congressional power under the Constitution?[77] Does it violate the Fifth and Sixth Amendments to try individuals in military tribunals, where these protections are not fully provided?[78]

The Supreme Court in *Ex parte Quirin*, during World War II, upheld the use of military tribunals.[79] *Quirin* involved the military tribunal of eight Nazi saboteurs who landed on American soil during World War II; they were carrying explosives and wearing uniforms. President Franklin Roosevelt issued an executive order providing for their trial in a military tribunal. The detainees filed a habeas corpus petition in federal court. Although the president's executive order precluded judicial review, the Supreme Court agreed to hear the case and the proceedings in the military tribunal were suspended. Less than 24 hours after oral arguments concluded, the Court issued a short per curium order upholding the use of military tribunals. The order stated that the president had constitutional authority to try the individuals before a military commission.

The individuals were then tried and convicted. On August 1, 1942, the commission found the defendants guilty and recommended death sentences. On August 8, the president accepted the recommendations, but commuted the sentences for the two individuals who defected to the United States. The other six defendants were executed by electrocution on that day.

On October 29, 1942, the Court released its opinion in *Quirin*—three and a half months after it had announced its decision and over two and a half months after six defendants had been executed. The Court's opinion initially rejected the claim that the president's executive order barred it from having jurisdiction. The Court said that "there is certainly nothing in the Proclamation to preclude access to the courts for determining its applicability to the particular case."[80] In discussing the merits of the case, the Court said "[b]y universal agreement and practice, the law of war draws a distinction between . . . lawful and unlawful combatants."[81] The former are to be treated as prisoners of war, but the latter are "offenders against the law of war subject to trial and punishment by military tribunals."[82] The Court stressed that it had "no occasion now to define with meticulous care the ultimate boundaries of the jurisdiction of military tribunals to try persons according to the law of war."[83]

---

[77] *See* Neal Katyal & Laurence H. Tribe, 111 Yale L.J. 1259 (2002).

[78] *See, e.g.,* Laura A. Dickersson, Using Legal Process to Fight Terrorism: Detentions, Military Commissions, International Tribunals and the Rule of Law, 75 S. Cal. L. Rev. 1407 (2002); Carl Tobias, Detentions, Military Commissions, Terrorism, and Domestic Case Precedent, 76 S. Cal. L. Rev. 1371 (2003); Jonathan Turley, Tribunals and Tribulations: The Antithetical Elements of Military Governance in a Madisonian Democracy, 70 Geo. Wash. L. Rev. 649 (2002).

[79] 317 U.S. 1 (1942). For excellent descriptions of the background of this case, *see* Louis Fisher, Nazi Saboteurs on Trial (2003); Christopher Bryant & Carl Tobias, *Quirin* Revisited, 2003 Wis. L. Rev. 309.

[80] 317 U.S. at 25.

[81] *Id.* at 30-31.

[82] *Id.* at 31.

[83] *Id.* at 45-46.

There is great disagreement over whether *Quirin* is precedent for the current attempt to use military tribunals for suspected terrorists. Supporters, including the Bush administration, argue that *Quirin* is on point and specifically authorizes the use of military tribunals in this situation. Critics, though, argue that *Quirin* is a discredited decision that should not be followed.[84] Moreover, it is argued that *Quirin* is distinguishable because the Court there stressed that it was a declared war and there was a statute authorizing military tribunals.[85]

The legality of military tribunals created pursuant to President Bush's executive order was addressed by the Supreme Court in *Hamdan v. Rumsfeld*.[86] The Court, in a 5-3 opinion,[87] found that the military tribunals were not authorized by act of Congress and that they violated the Uniform Code of Military Justice and the Geneva Conventions. The Court especially emphasized the ability to exclude a defendant during the presentation of evidence, and even to prevent the defendant from being told of this evidence. Justice Stevens, writing for the Court, concluded: "Common Article 3 [of the Geneva Conventions] obviously tolerates a great degree of flexibility in trying individuals captured during armed conflict; its requirements are general ones, crafted to accommodate a wide variety of legal systems. But *requirements* they are nonetheless. The commission that the President has convened to try Hamdan does not meet those requirements."[88] The Court did not reach any of the constitutional issues presented.

The legality of military tribunals, like so many issues posed by the war on terrorism, raises profound questions about separation of powers, individual rights, and the applicability of the Constitution and of international law to American activities. Those who defended the Bush administration's actions argued forcefully for the need for broad executive powers to deal with the terrorist threat. Those who criticized the Bush administration's actions made powerful arguments that checks and balances are essential, and that basic rights need not and should not be compromised.

Detentions and military commissions, of course, are not the only constitutional issues that have arisen in the context of the war on terrorism. There are important questions concerning the constitutionality of warrantless electronic eavesdropping, the use of torture, the scope of the state secrets doctrine, and the application of the Constitution outside the United States.[89]

---

[84] *See, e.g.,* Katyal & Tribe, *supra* note 77, at 1290-1291.

[85] *Id.* at 1284-1292. Also, it is argued that the law of habeas corpus is very different now. Tobias, *supra* note 78, at 355-363.

[86] 548 U.S. 557 (2006).

[87] Chief Justice Roberts was recused because he had been a judge in the Court of Appeals decision that had upheld the military tribunals.

[88] 548 U.S. at 635.

[89] In *Munaf v. Geren*, 553 U.S. 674 (2008), the Court held that the habeas statute extends to American citizens held overseas by American forces operating subject to an American chain of command. However, the Court ruled that federal district courts may not exercise their habeas jurisdiction to enjoin the United States from transferring individuals alleged to have committed crimes and detained within the territory of a foreign sovereign to that sovereign for criminal prosecution.

§4.7   IMPEACHMENT AND REMOVAL FROM OFFICE

The ultimate check on presidential power is impeachment and removal. Article II, §4, of the Constitution provides: "The President, Vice President and all civil Officers of the United States, shall be removed from Office on Impeachment for, and Conviction of Treason, Bribery, or other high Crimes and Misdemeanors." Article I, §2, provides that the House of Representatives has the sole power to impeach. If there is an impeachment by the House, then a trial is held in the Senate. Article I, §3, gives the Senate the sole power to try impeachments and prescribes that "no Person shall be convicted without the Concurrence of two thirds of the Members present."[1]

Two major issues remain unresolved concerning these provisions. First, what are "high Crimes and Misdemeanors"? At one end of the spectrum is the view that these offenses are limited to acts that violate the criminal law and that can be deemed a serious threat to society.[2] At the opposite pole is the statement of Gerald Ford, when as a congressman from Michigan he proposed the impeachment of Supreme Court Justice William Douglas largely because of Douglas's liberal views: "[A]n impeachable offense is whatever a majority of the House of Representatives considers [it] to be."[3]

Second, what procedures must be followed when there is an impeachment and removal proceeding? For example, is it permissible for the Senate to have a committee hear the evidence and make a recommendation to the entire body, or must the Senate sit as a tribunal to hear the case? Are completely closed-door proceedings, as were used in the Senate during the Clinton impeachment, permissible?[4]

There is no definitive answer to either of these questions.[5] There is no Supreme Court case addressing either. In fact, none is likely in the future because the Supreme Court has held that challenges to the impeachment and removal process pose nonjusticiable political questions.[6] Ironically, the only Supreme Court case to deal with issues of impeachment was titled *Nixon v. United States.*[7] The case had nothing to do with Richard Nixon, but rather involved federal district court judge Walter Nixon, who had been convicted of making false statements to a grand jury. Judge Nixon refused to resign from the bench and continued to collect his judicial salary while in prison.

---

§4.7 [1] Article I, §3, also provides that if the president is being tried by the Senate, the Chief Justice of the United States shall preside.

[2] *See* Charles L. Black, Jr., Impeachment: A Handbook 39-40 (1974) (a violation of the criminal law is not essential, but a good indicator of a high crime or misdemeanor).

[3] 116 Cong. Rec. 11913 (1970).

[4] *See* Marjorie Cohn, Open and Shut: Senate Impeachment Deliberations Must Be Public, 51 Hastings L.J. 365 (2000).

[5] For an excellent scholarly treatment of these and other issues surrounding impeachment, *see* Michael J. Gerhardt, The Federal Impeachment Process: A Constitutional and Historical Analysis (2000).

[6] This issue is more fully discussed in §2.8.8.

[7] 506 U.S. 224 (1993).

After the House impeached Nixon, the Senate, in accord with its rules, created a committee to hold a hearing and make a recommendation to the full Senate. The committee, not surprisingly, recommended removal from office, and the entire Senate voted accordingly.

Nixon argued, however, that the Senate's procedure was unconstitutional and that the entire Senate had to sit and hear the evidence. The Supreme Court ruled that Nixon's challenge must be dismissed as a nonjusticiable political question. Chief Justice Rehnquist, writing for the Court, emphasized that the framers intended that there would be two proceedings against officeholders charged with wrongdoing: a judicial trial and legislative impeachment proceedings. He stated: "The Framers deliberately separated the two forums to avoid raising the specter of bias and to ensure independent judgments. . . . Certainly judicial review of the Senate's trial would introduce the same risk of bias as would participation in the trial itself."[8]

The Court's desire that the judiciary stay out of the impeachment process is certainly understandable. Impeachment is the ultimate political remedy. Federal judges are removable only by impeachment, and judicial involvement in the impeachment process could undercut the independence of this check.

But the provisions concerning impeachment are part of the Constitution, and if the judiciary cannot stop violations, the constitutional limits become unenforceable. Perhaps the political question doctrine would not be applied in a really egregious case of Congress disregarding constitutionally mandated procedures. In a concurring opinion, Justice Souter noted that "[i]f the Senate were to act in a manner seriously threatening the integrity of its results, convicting, say, upon a coin-toss, or upon a summary determination that an officer of the United States was simply a bad guy, judicial interference might well be appropriate."[9]

Because *Nixon* makes challenges to impeachments nonjusticiable, it will be for Congress to decide what are "high crimes and misdemeanors" and what procedures are appropriate concerning impeachment and removal. Although there are not judicial precedents to guide Congress, there is historical experience. Three times there have been serious efforts to impeach the president.

Impeachment of Andrew Johnson

Andrew Johnson was the first president to be impeached. He was impeached in 1867 for firing Secretary of War Edwin Stanton in violation of the Tenure in Office Act.[10] After the end of the Civil War, Congress became increasingly frustrated with Johnson, a Southerner from Tennessee, presiding over Reconstruction. Congress adopted the Tenure in Office Act of 1867 to keep Johnson from firing Lincoln's cabinet. The Act declared that such a firing would be deemed a

---

[8] *Id.* at 234.

[9] *Id.* at 254 (Souter, J., concurring in the judgment).

[10] *See, e.g.,* Michael Les Benedict, The Impeachment and Trial of Andrew Johnson (1973); Milton Lomask, Andrew Johnson: President on Trial (1973); Gene Smith, High Crimes and Misdemeanors: The Impeachment and Trial of Andrew Johnson (1977).

"high misdemeanor," indicating that Congress was considering the possibility of impeachment from the outset. The Supreme Court subsequently said that the Tenure in Office Act violated separation of powers.[11] Nonetheless, the House impeached and Johnson avoided removal by just one vote in the Senate.

Effort to Impeach Richard Nixon

The second serious attempt to impeach a president occurred in 1974 and was directed against Richard Nixon. The House Judiciary Committee voted three articles of impeachment. One was for obstruction of justice in connection with the Watergate cover-up; one was for using government agencies, such as the FBI and the IRS, for political advantages; and the final article was for failing to comply with subpoenas. Before the matter could be considered by the entire House, Nixon resigned.[12]

Impeachment of Bill Clinton

President Bill Clinton was impeached by the House of Representatives in 1998, but the Senate did not convict him. After the Supreme Court decided *Clinton v. Jones*, discussed above, and allowed Paula Jones's civil suit against Bill Clinton to proceed, the United States District Court permitted Jones's attorney to depose President Clinton and ask questions about Clinton's other sexual relationships.

Monica Lewinsky, a former White House aide, had described to her friend Linda Tripp a sexual relationship that Lewinsky had with the president that included many phone calls, private meetings, phone sex, and oral sex. Tripp informed Jones's lawyers of this, and on the eve of President Clinton's deposition in the Jones case, Ms. Tripp secretly met for hours with lawyers for Ms. Jones and briefed them about Ms. Lewinsky.

On January 17, 1998, Clinton's deposition was taken and he was asked about Ms. Lewinsky. Clinton denied having an "extramarital sexual affair" with Monica Lewinsky. In response to repeated questioning, Clinton said: "I have never had sexual relations with Monica Lewinsky. I've never had an affair with her."

The possibility that the president had committed perjury was brought to the attention of Attorney General Janet Reno. She authorized Independent Counsel Kenneth Starr, who was investigating the Whitewater land scandal for possible presidential involvement, to broaden his investigation to consider whether the president had committed perjury or obstructed justice. Starr conducted a lengthy investigation, including having the president testify before a grand jury.

On August 17, 1998, Clinton testified before the grand jury. His testimony later became the basis for a separate accusation of perjury. In his grand jury testimony, President Clinton refused to answer any specific questions of a sexual nature about his relationship with Monica Lewinsky; instead, he read and referred to the following prepared statement:

---

[11] Myers v. United States, 272 U.S. 52 (1926), discussed in §4.2.2.
[12] *See* §4.2.2.

When I was alone with Ms. Lewinsky on certain occasions in early 1996 and once in early 1997, I engaged in conduct that was wrong. These encounters did not consist of sexual intercourse; they did not constitute "sexual relations" as I understood that term to be defined at my January 17, 1998, deposition; but they did involve inappropriate intimate contact. These inappropriate encounters ended, at my insistence, in early 1997. . . .

While I will provide the grand jury whatever other information I can, because of privacy considerations affecting my family, myself, and others, and in an effort to preserve the dignity of the Office I hold, this is all I will say about the specifics of these particular matters.[13]

Mr. Clinton did engage in extended hypothetical and definitional discussions as to what would or would not constitute sexual relations or fall within his definition of the term "sexual relations." The following was the most important exchange, with Clinton answering the questions:

A. You are free to infer that my testimony is that I did not have sexual relations, as I understood this term to be defined.

Q. Including touching her breast, kissing her breast, or touching her genitalia?

A. That's correct.

In the fall of 1998, Independent Counsel Kenneth Starr released a very detailed report documenting the relationship between Monica Lewinsky and Bill Clinton.[14] The report detailed the progress of their relationship, many phone calls over a long period of time, sexual touchings, and oral sex. The House Judiciary Committee then conducted impeachment hearings and voted four Articles of Impeachment against the president. The vote in the House Judiciary Committee was entirely along partisan lines, with all of the Republican members voting for impeachment and almost all of the Democrats voting against.

The first Article of Impeachment alleged that Clinton "willfully corrupted and manipulated the judicial process of the United States for his personal gain and exoneration, impeding the administration of justice [through his perjury before the grand jury concerning this prior relationship with an intern and his prior sworn testimony]."[15]

Article Two stated that Clinton violated his duty to faithfully execute the laws of the United States in that he "willfully corrupted and manipulated the judicial process of the United States for his personal gain and exoneration, impeding the administration of justice [through acts of deception and perjury]."[16]

---

[13] President Clinton's Videotaped Grand Jury Testimony, Segment 5, Aug. 17, 1998, 1998 WL 644128.

[14] *See* Starr Report, 1998 WL 801023 (F.D.C.H.).

[15] H.R. Res. 611, 105th Cong. (1998) (enacted), reprinted in 144 Cong. Rec. H11, 774 (daily ed. Dec. 18, 1998).

[16] *Id.*, reprinted in 144 Cong. Rec. H11, 774 (daily ed. Dec. 18, 1998).

Article Three stated that Clinton "prevented, obstructed, and impeded the administration of justice, and has to that end engaged personally, and through his subordinates and agents, in a course of conduct or scheme designed to delay, impede, cover up, and conceal the existence of evidence and testimony related to a Federal civil rights action brought against him in a duly instituted judicial proceeding."[17]

Finally, the fourth Article of Impeachment stated that Clinton "engaged in conduct that resulted in misuse and abuse of his high office, impaired the due and proper administration of justice and the conduct of lawful inquiries, and contravened the authority of the legislative branch and the truth seeking purpose of a coordinate investigative proceeding, in that, as President, William Jefferson Clinton refused and failed to respond to certain written requests for admission and willfully made perjurious, false and misleading sworn statements in response to certain written requests for admission propounded to him as part of the impeachment inquiry."[18]

On December 19, 1998, the House of Representatives passed two Articles of Impeachment. The first article passed by a vote of 228 to 206, with five Democrats defecting to vote for impeachment and five Republicans defecting to vote against impeachment. Article Three passed by a vote of 221 to 212, with five Democrats defecting to vote for impeachment and 12 Republicans defecting to vote against impeachment. On Article Two, alleging perjury in the civil deposition, 28 Republicans crossed party lines to vote against the article, defeating the article 205 to 229. On Article Four, alleging perjury in the president's answer to Congress, 81 Republicans crossed party lines in favor of the president, while one Democrat crossed party lines in favor of Article Four, for a final vote of 285 to 148.

The United States Senate then held a trial of President Clinton on the two Articles of Impeachment. The Chief Justice of the United States, as prescribed by the Constitution, presided. In accord with Senate rules, the senators' deliberations were entirely in closed session.[19] Neither Article of Impeachment received the two-thirds vote needed to remove the president.[20]

It is unclear what lesson is to be learned from any of these experiences concerning what constitutes "high crimes and misdemeanors." The Johnson and the Clinton impeachments were highly partisan, and all of the prior efforts at presidential impeachment raise the fundamental question of what should be regarded as an impeachable offense. Perhaps most of all, these incidents show that there is no legal definition of what constitutes a high crime or misdemeanor, and the answer in Congress always is likely to be political.

---

[17] *Id.*, reprinted in 144 Cong. Rec. H11, 774 (daily ed. Dec. 18, 1998).

[18] *Id.*, reprinted in 144 Cong. Rec. H11, 774-775 (daily ed. Dec. 18, 1998).

[19] For an excellent criticism of secret Senate deliberations, *see* Marjorie Cohn, Open and Shut: Senate Impeachment Deliberations Must Be Public, 51 Hastings L.J. 365 (2000).

[20] For a discussion of some of the longer-term implications of the Clinton impeachment, *see* Michael J. Klarman, Constitutional Fetishism and the Clinton Impeachment Debate, 85 Va. L. Rev. 631 (1999); Randall K. Miller, Presidential Sanctuaries After the Clinton Sex Scandal, 22 Harv. J.L. & Pub. Pol. 647 (1999).

CHAPTER 5

Limits on State Regulatory and Taxing Power

§5.1   INTRODUCTION

Chapters 2, 3, and 4 focused on the scope of federal powers. This chapter examines limits on state authority. State and local governments possess the police power, which means that they can take any action unless there is a constitutional prohibition. State authority, of course, is different from that of the federal government, which can act only if there is constitutional authority.[1]

State and local governments are limited by the Constitution's protections of individual rights, which are discussed in the remaining chapters. Also, the Constitution explicitly identifies a few instances where states may not act. Article I, §10, states: "No State shall enter into any Treaty, Alliance, or Confederation; grant Letters of Marque and Reprisal; coin Money; emit Bills of Credit; make any Thing but gold and silver Coin a Tender in Payment of Debts; . . . or grant any Title of Nobility."[2]

Preemption

This chapter focuses on limits on state power that derive from the existence of a national government and of other states.[3] There are two possibilities when considering whether a state or local law is invalidated because of these restrictions. One situation is where Congress has acted. If Congress has passed a law and it is a lawful exercise of congressional power, the question is whether the federal law preempts state or local law. Article VI of the Constitution provides that the "Constitution and the Laws of the United States which shall be made in Pursuance thereof; and all Treaties made, or which shall be made under the Authority of the United States, shall be the Supreme Law of the Land." Because of the supremacy clause, if there is a conflict between federal law and state or local law, the latter is deemed preempted.[4] Preemption is discussed in §5.2.

---

§5.1 [1] Federal authority is discussed in §2.2.

[2] The provision also prohibits bills of attainder and ex post facto laws, which are discussed in §6.2, and laws that impair the obligations of contracts, which are discussed in §8.3.

[3] The material covered in this chapter applies to regulation by both state and local governments. Because local governments are created by state governments and exercise powers granted by the states, they must follow the principles that are applied to the states. Therefore, although for ease of expression this chapter often refers only to "states," it is important to note that local governments are included as well.

[4] *See* Gade v. National Solid Wastes Management Assn., 505 U.S. 88, 108 (1992) (preemption is derived from the supremacy clause). For a critique of this view linking preemption to the supremacy clause, *see* Stephen A. Gardbaum, The Nature of Preemption, 79 Cornell L. Rev. 767 (1994).

Dormant Commerce Clause

The other situation is where Congress has not acted—or at least the judiciary decides that federal law does not preempt state or local law. Nonetheless, even though there is not preemption, state and local laws can be challenged under two principles: the dormant commerce clause and the privileges and immunities clause. The dormant commerce clause—or, as it is sometimes called, "the negative commerce clause"—is the principle that state and local laws are unconstitutional if they place an undue burden on interstate commerce. The Supreme Court has inferred this limit on state regulatory power from the grant of power to Congress to regulate commerce among the states. Even if Congress has not acted, even if its commerce power lies dormant, state and local governments cannot place an undue burden on interstate commerce. Section 5.3 considers the dormant commerce clause. Section 5.4 considers the application of this principle in a specific and important context: state and local taxation.

Privileges and Immunities Clause

Another basis for attacking state and local laws in the absence of preemption is the privileges and immunities clause of Article IV, §2. This provision states: "The Citizens of each State shall be entitled to all Privileges and Immunities of Citizens in the several States." As described in §5.5, the Supreme Court has interpreted the privileges and immunities clause as limiting the ability of states to discriminate against out-of-staters with regard to constitutional rights or important economic activities. This clause primarily has been applied by the Supreme Court when there have been challenges to state and local laws that discriminate against out-of-staters with regard to their ability to earn a livelihood.

Underlying Policy Themes

A central issue throughout this chapter is the appropriate degree of judicial oversight or of judicial deference to state and local governments. At one extreme, it is possible to argue that state and local governments should be unfettered by the federal government as much as possible. From this view, preemption should be restricted to those situations where Congress has expressly preempted state and local laws. Also from this view, there should not be a dormant commerce clause or only a very narrow one. State and local regulation generally should be limited only if Congress clearly precludes state and local actions.

At the other extreme, some argue that it is essential for the judiciary to preserve the federal nature of American government. From this perspective, preemption is not something to avoid, but rather preemption should be found whenever doing so will better effectuate the interests of federal law and of the federal government. Likewise, the dormant commerce clause is an essential restriction on abuses by state governments so as to preserve a free flow of goods and services throughout the economy.

Thus, the material in this chapter is very much about federalism. What is the appropriate and desirable allocation of power between the federal government and the states and also among the state governments? What is the proper role of the judiciary in reviewing state and local regulations?

§5.2   PREEMPTION OF STATE AND LOCAL LAWS

§5.2.1   Introduction

As described above, Article VI of the Constitution contains the supremacy clause, which provides that the Constitution, and laws and treaties made pursuant to it, are the supreme law of the land. If there is a conflict between federal and state law, the federal law controls and the state law is invalidated because federal law is supreme.[1] As the Supreme Court declared: "[U]nder the Supremacy Clause, from which our pre-emption doctrine is derived, 'any state law, however clearly within a State's acknowledged power, which interferes with or is contrary to federal law, must yield.' "[2]

The difficulty, of course, is in deciding whether a particular state or local law is preempted by a specific federal statute or regulation.[3] As in so many other areas of constitutional law, there is no clear rule for deciding whether a state or local law should be invalidated on preemption grounds. The Supreme Court once remarked that there is not "an infallible constitutional test or an exclusive constitutional yardstick. In the final analysis, there can be no one crystal clear distinctly marked formula."[4]

Ways of Finding Preemption

Traditionally, the Supreme Court has identified two major situations where preemption occurs. One is where a federal law expressly preempts state or local law. The other situation is where preemption is implied by a clear congressional intent to preempt state or local law.

§5.2 [1] *See* Gade v. National Solid Wastes Management Assn., 505 U.S. 88, 108 (1992) (deriving preemption from the supremacy clause); *but see* Stephen A. Gardbaum, The Nature of Preemption, 79 Cornell L. Rev. 767 (1994); S. Candice Hoke, Transcending Conventional Supremacy: A Reconstruction of the Supremacy Clause, 24 Conn. L. Rev. 829 (1992) (arguing that only some preemption should be based on the supremacy clause).

[2] Gade v. National Solid Wastes Management Assn., 505 U.S. at 108 (citations omitted). In Gibbons v. Ogden, 22 U.S. (9 Wheat.) 1 (1824), Chief Justice John Marshall said: "[A]cts of the State Legislatures . . . [that] interfere with, or are contrary to the laws of Congress [are to be invalidated because] [i]n every such case, the act of congress . . . is supreme; and the law of State though enacted in the exercise of powers not controverted, must yield to it."

[3] The preemption can be by a federal law or by a federal regulation adopted pursuant to a federal statute. The Supreme Court has said that "state laws can be pre-empted by federal regulations as well as by federal statutes." Hillsborough County, Fla. v. Automated Med. Lab., Inc., 471 U.S. 707, 713 (1985).

[4] Hines v. Davidowitz, 312 U.S. 52, 67 (1941).

§5.2 Preemption of State and Local Laws

In *Gade v. National Solid Wastes Management Association*, the Court summarized the tests for preemption:

> Preemption may be either express or implied, and is compelled whether Congress' command is explicitly stated in the statute's language or implicitly contained in its structure and purpose. Absent explicit preemptive language, we have recognized at least two types of implied preemption: field preemption, where the scheme of federal regulation is so pervasive as to make reasonable the inference that Congress left no room for the States to supplement it, and conflict preemption, where compliance with both federal and state regulations is a physical impossibility, or where state law stands as an obstacle to the accomplishment and execution of the full purposes and objectives of Congress.[5]

Problems with Applying the Test for Preemption

Although these categories, or minor variations, are frequently used, they are not distinct. For example, even if there is statutory language expressly preempting state law, Congress rarely is clear about the scope of what is preempted or how particular situations should be handled. Courts must decide what is preempted, and this inevitably is an inquiry into congressional intent.[6] Conversely, implied preemption is often a function of both perceived congressional intent and the language used in the statute or regulation.

The Supreme Court has recognized that in both express and implied preemption, the key is discerning congressional intent. The Court has said that "[t]he question of whether a certain state action is preempted by federal law is one of congressional intent."[7] It has remarked that "'[t]he purpose of Congress is the ultimate touchstone' in every preemption case."[8] The problem, of course, is that Congress's intent, especially as to the scope of preemption, is rarely expressed or clear. Therefore, although the Court purports to be finding congressional intent, it often is left to make guesses about purpose based on fragments of statutory language, random statements in the legislative history, and the degree of detail of the federal regulation.

The Court frequently has said that congressional intent must be clear to find preemption because of a desire, stemming from federalism concerns, to minimize invalidation of state and local laws. Thus, the Court has observed: "Congress . . .

---

[5] 505 U.S. at 98 (citations omitted). In an earlier case, *Pennsylvania v. Nelson*, 350 U.S. 497, 502-505 (1956), the Supreme Court identified three situations where preemption could be found: "First, the scheme of federal regulation is so pervasive as to make reasonable the inference that Congress left no room for the states to supplement it. . . . Second the federal statutes touch a field in which the federal interest is so dominant that the federal system must be assumed to preclude enforcement of state laws on the same subject. . . . Third, [where] enforcement of state . . . acts presents a serious danger of conflict with the administration of the federal program."

[6] Lorillard Tobacco Co. v. Reilly, 533 U.S. 525, 540-541 (2001) ("Congressional purpose is the 'ultimate touchstone' of our inquiry.") *See* Catherine Fisk, The Last Article About the Language of ERISA Preemption?: A Case Study of the Failure of Textualism, 33 Harv. J. Legis. 37 (1996) (arguing that the distinction between express and implied preemption is one without much difference).

[7] Gade v. National Solid Wastes Management, 505 U.S. at 96 (citations omitted).

[8] *See* Medtronic Inc. v. Lohr, 518 U.S. 470, 485 (1996), quoting Retail Clerks v. Schermerhorn, 375 U.S. 96, 103 (1963).

should manifest its intention [to preempt state and local laws] clearly. . . . The exercise of federal supremacy is not lightly to be presumed."[9] Similarly, the Court declared: "[B]ecause the States are independent sovereigns in our federal system, we have long presumed that Congress does not cavalierly preempt state-law causes of action. In all preemption cases, and particularly in those in which Congress has legislated in a field which the States have traditionally occupied, we 'start with the assumption that the historic police powers of the States were not to be superseded by the Federal Act unless that was the clear and manifest purpose of Congress.'"[10]

Three Situations Where Preemption Claims Arise

For the sake of clarity, this section is organized parallel to the test for preemption articulated by the Supreme Court in *Gade v. National Solid Wastes Management Association* that is quoted above and that has been frequently repeated by the Court.[11] There are three major situations where preemption is found. First, express preemption occurs where there is explicit preemptive language. This type of preemption is discussed in §5.2.2.

Second, there is implied preemption. The Court has identified three types of implied preemption. One is termed "field preemption"—where the scheme of federal law and regulation is "so pervasive as to make reasonable the inference that Congress left no room for the States to supplement it."[12] Field preemption is discussed in §5.2.3.

Another type of implied preemption occurs when there is a conflict between federal and state law. Even if federal law does not expressly preempt state law, preemption will be found where "compliance with both federal and state regulations is a physical impossibility."[13] Preemption based on such conflicts is discussed in §5.2.4.

Implied preemption also will be found if state law impedes the achievement of a federal objective. Even if federal and state laws are not mutually exclusive and even if there is no congressional expression of a desire to preempt state law, preemption will be found if state law "stands as an obstacle to the accomplishment and execution of the full purposes and objectives of Congress."[14] Preemption based on state law interfering with the achievement of a federal objective is discussed in §5.2.5.[15]

Although these types of preemption are presented as distinct categories, in practice they often overlap and they certainly are not mutually exclusive. As is discussed below, all of these categories frequently turn on a determination of

---

[9] New York State Dept. of Soc. Servs. v. Dublino, 413 U.S. 405, 413 (1973) (citation omitted).

[10] Medtronic, Inc. v. Lohr, 518 U.S. at 485, quoting Hillsborough County v. Automated Med. Labs., Inc., 471 U.S. 707, 715 (1985).

[11] 505 U.S. at 96. *See, e.g.,* Freightliner Corp. v. Myrick, 514 U.S. 280, 287 (1995); Wisconsin Public Intervenor v. Mortier, 501 U.S. 597, 604-605 (1991).

[12] Rice v. Santa Fe Elevator Corp., 331 U.S. 218, 230 (1947).

[13] Florida Lime & Avocado Growers, Inc. v. Paul, 373 U.S. 132, 142-143 (1963).

[14] Hines v. Davidowitz, 312 U.S. 52, 67 (1941).

[15] The Court has regarded both preemption based on mutual exclusivity and preemption based on interference with a federal objective as forms of "conflict preemption." For the sake of clarity, they are discussed separately here.

congressional intent. The common problem is that Congress's intent concerning preemption frequently is unclear.[16] Congress often is silent on the preemption question. Even when Congress expresses a desire for preemption, it rarely indicates the scope of preemption or provides guidance for the myriad of situations that will arise.

Perhaps it is for this reason that there has been a dramatic increase in preemption decisions by the United States Supreme Court.[17] Preemption issues arise in literally every area of federal law and federal regulation.

Finally, there is a third major situation where preemption might be found: States generally cannot tax or regulate federal government activities. Although this can be viewed as a form of preemption because state laws are invalidated based on the supremacy clause, this type of preemption is different from the others because it does not depend on congressional intent. This type of preemption is discussed in §5.2.6.

The Underlying Policy Issues

Ultimately, preemption doctrines are about allocating governing authority between the federal and state governments. A broad view of preemption leaves less room for governance by state and local governments. It is for this reason that, at times, the Court has declared that the preemption analysis "start[s] with the assumption that the historic powers of the States [are] not to be superseded by . . . Federal Act unless that [is] the clear and manifest purpose of Congress."[18] But a very narrow preemption doctrine minimizes the reach of federal law and risks undermining the federal objectives. Therefore, it is somewhat surprising that the Rehnquist and the Roberts Courts, with their commitment to federalism and protecting states' rights, have been quite willing to find federal preemption.[19] One

---

[16] The Court has declared that "any understanding of the scope of a preemption statute must rest primarily on a 'fair understanding of *congressional purpose.*'" Medtronic, Inc. v. Lohr, 518 U.S. at 485 (emphasis in original). The Court explained that "Congress's intent, of course, primarily is discerned from the language of the pre-emption statute and the statutory framework surrounding it. Also relevant, however, is the structure and purpose of the statute as a whole, as revealed not only in the text, but through the reviewing court's reasoned understanding of the way in which Congress intended the statute and its surrounding regulatory scheme to affect business, consumers, and the law." *Id.*

[17] *See* Hoke, *supra* note 1, at 830 n.5.

[18] Rice v. Santa Fe Elevator Corp., 331 U.S. 218, 230 (1947). Justice Thomas has argued against implied preemption on federalism grounds. He wrote: "I have become increasingly skeptical of this Court's 'purposes and objectives' pre-emption jurisprudence. Under this approach, the Court routinely invalidates state laws based on perceived conflicts with broad federal policy objectives, legislative history, or generalized notions of congressional purposes that are not embodied within the text of federal law. . . . [I]mplied pre-emption doctrines that wander far from the statutory text are inconsistent with the Constitution." Wyeth v. Levine, 555 U.S. 555, 583 (2009) (Thomas, J., concurring in the judgment).

[19] *See, e.g.*, Lorillard Tobacco Co. v. Reilly, 533 U.S. 525 (2001); Buckman Co. v. Plaintiffs' Legal Comm., 531 U.S. 341 (2001); Crosby v. National Foreign Trade Council, 530 U.S. 363 (2000); Geier v. American Honda Motor Co., Inc., 529 U.S. 861 (2000) (all finding federal law to preempt state law).

way to empower states is to narrow the reach of federal preemption, but this has not occurred.

The basic question is how willing courts should be to find preemption. Should there be a strong presumption against a court concluding that there is preemption? If so, what should be sufficient to overcome this preemption? Or should courts be willing to find preemption whenever doing so would effectuate the purposes of federal law?

§5.2.2   *Express Preemption of State Laws*

Federal Laws Can Explicitly Preclude State Regulations

Whenever Congress has the authority to legislate, Congress can make federal law exclusive in a field. The clearest way for Congress to do this is to expressly preclude state or local regulation in an area. Thus, some federal laws contain clauses that expressly preempt state and local laws. For example, the federal Employee Retirement Income Security Act of 1974 (ERISA) states that it "supersede[s] any and all State laws insofar as they may now or hereafter relate to any employee benefit plan."[20]

Jones v. Rath Packing Co. is a case involving this type of preemption.[21] The Federal Meat Inspection Act stated: "Marking, labeling, packaging, or ingredient requirements in addition to, or different than, those made under this Act may not be imposed by any State."[22] The federal law and a state law both required that every package of bacon contain an amount at least equal to that stated on the package. They differed, however, in that the federal law permitted deviations because of moisture loss, while the state law did not permit variations from the stated amount on that basis. The Court found that the express language of the statute dictated the preemption of the state law.

Another example of a statute containing express preemptive language is the Airline Deregulation Act of 1978, which provides: "[N]o State . . . shall enact or enforce any law, rule, regulation, standard, or other provision having the force and effect of law relating to rates, routes, or services of any air carrier."[23] In *Morales v. Trans-World Airlines, Inc.*, the Court applied this provision to find that price advertising guidelines promulgated by the National Association of Attorneys General could not be applied to airlines because they related to "rates."[24] The Court broadly interpreted the language of the Act as expressly preempting all state laws "having a connection with or reference to airline 'rates, routes, or services.'"[25]

---

[20]   29 U.S.C. §1144(a).
[21]   430 U.S. 519 (1977).
[22]   *Id.* at 530-531.
[23]   49 U.S.C. §1305(a)(1). Repealed by Pub. L. No. 103-272, §7(b), July 5, 1994, 108 Stat. 1379.
[24]   504 U.S. 374, 384 (1992).
[25]   *Id.*

The Court said that Congress's purpose was "[t]o ensure that the States would not undo federal deregulation with regulation of their own."[26]

Similarly, in *American Airlines, Inc. v. Wolens*, the Court held that the Airline Deregulation Act preempted an action under a state consumer fraud law against an airline for deceptive practices concerning its frequent flyer program.[27] The Court explained that the matter concerned the "services" of an air carrier, and thus the application of the state law was preempted by federal law. However, the Court found that the Act did not preempt a state law claim for breach of contract because the action was based on the airline's own promises and not duties imposed by the state government.

The Scope of Preemption Is Rarely Clear

The problem is that even when an express preemption clause exists, it rarely provides guidance as to the scope of preemption. The Supreme Court's decision in *Riegel v. Medtronic, Inc.* is illustrative.[28] The federal Medical Devices Act preempts states from imposing "requirements" greater than federal law for medical devices approved by the federal government.[29] The case involved a man who was seriously injured when a balloon catheter exploded during angioplasty surgery. He sued the manufacturer and the issue was whether the preemption of greater state "requirements" precluded state tort liability.

In an 8-1 decision, the Court found preemption. Justice Scalia, writing for the Court, explained that liability under state common law, like state regulation, could impose additional duties on manufacturers of medical devices. He declared that "[a]bsent other indication, reference to a State's 'requirements' includes its common-law duties."[30] Justice Ginsburg, in a dissenting opinion, said that if Congress wanted to preclude state tort liability it could have done so and that "requirements" should not be interpreted as preempting common law claims. She lamented that there was no indication from the legislative history of a desire to preempt tort claims and that it is "difficult to believe that Congress would, without comment, remove all means of judicial recourse" for consumers injured by FDA-approved devices.[31] Thus, even though there was an express preemption provision,

---

[26] *Id.* at 378.

[27] 513 U.S. 219 (1995).

[28] 552 U.S. 312 (2008).

[29] Specifically, it states: "Except as provided in subsection (b) of this section, no State or political subdivision of a State may establish or continue in effect with respect to a device intended for human use any requirement (1) which is different from, or in addition to, any requirement applicable under this chapter to the device, and (2) which relates to the safety or effectiveness of the device or to any other matter included in a requirement applicable to the device under this chapter." 21 U.S.C. §360(k)(a).

[30] *Id.* at 324.

[31] *Id.* at 337 (Ginsburg, J., dissenting). Earlier in *Medtronic, Inc. v. Lohr*, 518 U.S. 470 (1996), the Court held that the preemption provision in the Medical Device Amendments (MDA) of 1976 did not preclude an individual from bringing common law claims for negligent design, negligent manufacturing, and failure to warn to recover for injuries suffered when her pacemaker failed. The Court stated: "Moreover, because there is no explicit private cause of action against manufacturers contained in the

there still was the need to interpret it and decide what constitutes forbidden state "requirements."

Two cases concerning the ability of states to regulate cigarettes also show the need for judicial interpretation of express preemption provisions. *Cipollone v. Liggett Group, Inc.*, which involved the ability of states to allow liability against tobacco companies, illustrates the inability to decide preemption issues solely based on a textual provision.[32] A lawsuit was brought against cigarette manufacturers by a victim of lung cancer and her husband. The suit alleged that the companies had breached express warranties contained in their advertising, because they had failed to warn consumers about the hazards of smoking, because they had fraudulently misrepresented those hazards to consumers, and because they had conspired to deprive the public of medical information about smoking.

The Federal Cigarette Labeling and Advertising Act required that there be a warning of smoking's health hazards on all packages of cigarettes sold. A section of a law adopted in 1965, captioned "Preemption," provided: "No statement relating to smoking and health, other than [the federally prescribed warning] . . . shall be required on any cigarette package [and no such] statement . . . shall be required in the advertising of any cigarettes." A 1969 law provided: "No requirement or prohibition based on smoking and health shall be imposed under State law with respect to the advertising or promotion of any cigarettes the packages of which are labeled."[33]

The issue in *Cipollone* was whether these provisions preempted a state from awarding damages on claims for torts such as failure to warn and fraudulent misrepresentation. The Court held that the 1965 provision did not preempt state damage actions but, rather, only state laws and regulations mandating specific warnings on cigarette labels or in cigarette advertising. The Court emphasized that "there is no general, inherent conflict between federal preemption of state warning requirements and the continued vitality of state common law damages actions."[34]

The Court, however, ruled that the broader language in the 1969 Act did preempt state damage actions for failure to warn and fraudulent misrepresentation.[35] The plurality opinion said that it had long recognized "the phrase 'state law' to include common law as well as statutes and regulations."[36] Specifically, the

---

MDA, and no suggestion that the Act created an implied private right of action, Congress would have barred most, if not all, relief for persons injured by defective medical devices. Medtronic's construction of [the statute] would therefore have the perverse effect of granting complete immunity from design defect liability to an entire industry that, in the judgment of Congress, needed more stringent regulation in order to provide for the safety and effectiveness of medical devices intended for human use." *Id.* at 487. However, in *Riegel*, the Court distinguished *Medtronic* on the ground that it did not involve the premarket approval that was present in *Riegel*.

[32] 505 U.S. 504 (1992).

[33] 15 U.S.C. §334(b).

[34] *Cipollone*, 505 U.S. at 518.

[35] As to this part of the decision, there was a plurality opinion by Justice Stevens—joined by Rehnquist, White, and O'Connor—and an opinion concurring in the judgment by Justices Scalia and Thomas.

[36] *Cipollone*, 505 U.S. at 522.

Court concluded that failure to warn suits were preempted insofar as they claimed that advertisements "should have included additional, or more clearly stated, warnings."[37]

But the Court ruled that the claim for breach of express warranties was not preempted. The plurality opinion said that the warranties were created by the cigarette companies and not the federal or state law. Therefore, even if the warranties were stated in the federally required warnings, this did not prevent suits against the companies for breaching those warranties.

As to the fraudulent misrepresentation claims, the Court ruled that federal law preempted the state from allowing liability for advertising that allegedly undermined the effect of the federally mandated warning labels. However, the Court said that federal law did not preempt fraudulent misrepresentation claims based on intentional concealment of information through channels other than advertising. Also, claims of conspiracy to misrepresent or to conceal material facts were deemed to be not preempted.

Cipollone powerfully illustrates that express preemption provisions require judicial interpretation as to what specific types of state law are preempted. This issue also is present in a second, subsequent case concerning state regulation of tobacco advertising. In *Lorillard Tobacco Co. v. Reilly*,[38] the Court invalidated a Massachusetts law that prohibited outdoor advertising for cigarettes, such as billboards, within 1,000 feet of a playground or school.[39] The Supreme Court relied on the language of a federal law adopted in 1969 that proscribes any "requirement or prohibition based on smoking and health . . . imposed under State law with respect to the advertising or promotion" of cigarettes.[40] The Court reviewed the history of federal regulation of cigarette advertising and concluded: "In the 1969 amendments, Congress not only enhanced its scheme to warn the public about the hazards of cigarette smoking, but also sought to protect the public, including youth, from being inundated with images of cigarette smoking in advertising. In pursuit of the latter goal, Congress banned electronic media advertising of cigarettes. And to the extent that Congress contemplated additional targeted regulation of cigarette advertising, it vested that authority in the FTC."[41]

Justice Stevens, in a dissenting opinion, argued that the state law was not preempted because it regulated the location and not the content of cigarette advertisements.[42] The majority, however, rejected this distinction and declared: "But the content/location distinction cannot be squared with the language of the preemption provision, which reaches all 'requirements' and 'prohibitions' 'imposed under State law.' A distinction between the content of advertising and the loca-

---

[37] *Id.* at 524.

[38] 533 U.S. 525 (2001).

[39] The Court found that the Massachusetts law was preempted in its regulation of advertising of cigarettes. As for the regulation of advertising of cigars and smokeless tobacco, which are not the subject of federal regulation, the Court found that the law violated the First Amendment. The latter aspect of the case is discussed in §11.3.7.7, in the consideration of commercial speech.

[40] 15 U.S.C. §1334.

[41] *Lorillard Tobacco*, 533 U.S. at 548.

[42] *Id.* at 590.

tion of advertising in the FCLAA also cannot be reconciled with Congress' own location-based restriction, which bans advertising in electronic media, but not elsewhere."[43] The majority said that general zoning regulations limiting outdoor advertisements could be applied to cigarettes, but not laws targeting just tobacco products.

The Court also faced this issue concerning the scope of an express preemption provision in *Bates v. Dow Agrosciences LLC*.[44] Peanut farmers sued a pesticide manufacturer claiming that the use of a particular pesticide caused severe crop damage. The manufacturer argued that there was preemption based on the Federal Insecticide, Fungicide, and Rodenticide Act (FIFRA).[45] The specific provision that allegedly preempted state law provided: "Such State shall not impose or continue in effect any requirements for labeling or packaging in addition to or different from those required under this subchapter."[46] The Court expressly distinguished *Cipollone* and said that unlike the statute there, FIFRA "prohibits only state-law labeling and packaging requirements that are 'in addition to or different from' the labeling and packaging requirements under FIFRA."[47] A state law would not be preempted if it was consistent with the requirements of FIFRA.

The Court thus narrowly construed the express preemption clause as not precluding the suit by the Texas peanut farmers. The Court stressed that this was an area of traditional state control and thus the preemption clause was to be read narrowly. The Court stated: "The long history of tort litigation against manufacturers of poisonous substances adds force to the basic presumption against preemption. If Congress had intended to deprive injured parties of a long available form of compensation, it surely would have expressed that intent more clearly."[48]

Another example of the difficulty of construing the scope of express preemption provisions is *Chamber of Commerce v. Whiting*.[49] Federal immigration law expressly preempts "any State or local law imposing civil or criminal sanctions (other than through licensing and similar laws) upon those who employ . . . unauthorized aliens."[50] An Arizona statute—the Legal Arizona Workers Act—provided that the licenses of state employers that knowingly or intentionally employ unauthorized aliens may be, and in certain circumstances must be, suspended or revoked.[51] The Supreme Court focused on the language in the federal law that has an exemption for "licensing and similar laws." The Court found that Arizona's law, which would revoke business "licenses" for those who employ undocumented immigrants, falls within this exception. The Court declared: "We hold that Arizona's licensing law

---

[43] *Id.* at 548.
[44] 544 U.S. 431 (2005).
[45] 7 U.S.C. §136.
[46] §136v(b).
[47] 544 U.S. at 447.
[48] *Id.* at 448.
[49] 131 S. Ct. 1968 (2011).
[50] 8 U.S.C. §1324a(h)(2).
[51] The Arizona law also required that all Arizona employers use a federal electronic verification system to confirm that the workers they employ are legally authorized workers.

falls well within the confines of the authority Congress chose to leave to the States and therefore is not expressly preempted."[52]

But the dissenting Justices disagreed over the meaning of the word "licensing." Justice Breyer, joined by Justice Ginsburg, wrote: "Arizona calls its state statute a 'licensing law,' and the statute uses the word 'licensing.' But the statute strays beyond the bounds of the federal licensing exception, for it defines 'license' to include articles of incorporation and partnership certificates, indeed *virtually every* state-law authorization for *any* firm, corporation, or partnership to do business in the State. Congress did not intend its 'licensing' language to create so broad an exemption, for doing so would permit States to eviscerate the federal Act's preemption provision, indeed to subvert the Act itself, by undermining Congress' efforts (1) to protect lawful workers from national-origin-based discrimination and (2) to protect lawful employers against erroneous prosecution or punishment."[53]

The key point is that provisions in federal statutes expressly preempting state and local laws inevitably require interpretation as to their scope and effect, as illustrated by the disagreement among the Justices in *Chamber of Commerce v. Whiting* as to the meaning of the word "licensing." The explosion of litigation concerning the preemption provision in the Employee Retirement Income Security Act of 1974 (ERISA) also demonstrates this. ERISA broadly preempts state laws that "relate to" employee benefit plans.[54] A key problem, though, is the inherent ambiguity in the phrase "relates to." As Professor Fisk observed: "[R]elates to is a term that requires a modifier in order to have a concrete meaning and the spectrum of possible modifiers—directly, slightly, remotely—suggests a wide spectrum of possible meanings."[55] Employers and others have argued that many state laws—from family leave to workers' compensation to health care finance and malpractice claims—are preempted by ERISA because they "relate to" employee benefit plans.[56]

In the decades since ERISA was enacted, the Court has rendered decisions with written opinions in dozens of ERISA preemption cases and also decided many others without a written opinion.[57] In 1992, Justice Stevens said that overall in the

---

[52] 131 S. Ct. at 1981. The Court also rejected an implied preemption challenge to the Arizona law. Implied preemption is discussed below.

[53] *Id.* at 1987 (Breyer, J., dissenting). Justice Sotomayor also dissented, though on different grounds. She argued that "the saving clause can only be understood to preserve States' authority to impose licensing sanctions after a final federal determination that a person has violated IRCA by knowingly employing an unauthorized alien." *Id.* at 1998 (Sotomayor, J., dissenting).

[54] 29 U.S.C. §1144(a).

[55] Fisk, *supra* note 6, at 47. The Supreme Court acknowledged the lack of clarity even in express preemption provisions in *New York State Conference of Blue Cross & Blue Shield Plans v. Travelers Ins. Co.*, 514 U.S. 645, 655 (1995).

[56] *See* Fisk, *supra* note 6, at 47-52 (summarizing ERISA challenges).

[57] Fisk, *supra* note 6, at 58 n.104; *see* Egelhoff v. Egelhoff ex rel. Breiner, 532 U.S. 141 (2001); Pegram v. Herdrich, 530 U.S. 211 (2000); UNUM Life Ins. Co. of Am. v. Ward, 526 U.S. 358 (1999); Boggs v. Boggs, 520 U.S. 833 (1997); New York State Conference of Blue Cross & Blue Shield Plans v. Travelers Ins. Co., 514 U.S. 645 (1995); John Hancock Mut. Life Ins. Co. v. Harris Trust & Sav. Bank, 510 U.S. 86 (1993): District of Columbia v. Greater Washington Bd. of Trade, 506 U.S. 125 (1992); Ingersoll-Rand Co. v. McClendon, 498 U.S. 133 (1990); FMC Corp. v. Holliday, 498 U.S. 52 (1990); Massachusetts v. Morash, 490 U.S. 107 (1989); Mackey v. Lanier Collection Agency & Serv. Inc., 486

country there had been 2,800 judicial opinions on ERISA preemption,[58] and a 1995 study found 3,153 cases. Twenty years later, the number undoubtedly is vastly larger. The sheer quantity of ERISA litigation shows that an express preemption provision leaves open countless questions about the scope of that preemption.[59]

All of these cases indicate that even when there is an express preemption provision, a court inevitably must decide "the domain expressly preempted by that language." This leaves the court tremendous discretion and often leads to seemingly arbitrary and inconsistent answers.

§5.2.3   "Field Preemption"

Field Preemption Defined

Even if there is not express preemption, the Supreme Court has ruled that it will find implied preemption if there is a clear congressional intent that federal law should exclusively occupy a field. The Court has said that such preemption exists if "either . . . the nature of the regulated subject matter permits no other conclusion, or that the Congress has unmistakably so ordained."[60] In other words, the Court will find field preemption either if Congress expresses a clear intent that federal law will be exclusive in an area or if comprehensive federal regulation evidences a congressional desire that federal law should completely occupy the field. The Court has said that "[a]bsent explicit preemptive language, Congress's intent to supersede state law altogether may be found from a scheme of federal regulation so pervasive as to make reasonable the inference that Congress left no room for the States to supplement it."[61]

The difficulty is in deciding when congressional intent is sufficiently specific or federal regulation sufficiently detailed so as to preclude all state regulation in a field. Again, as expressed above, there are no clear criteria for courts to decide this, and inevitably courts must make a judgment call based on whether the interests behind the federal law will be best served by the law being exclusive in a field.

The Court's decision in *Chamber of Commerce v. Brown* is illustrative of this problem.[62] California law prohibits employers that receive state grants or more than $10,000 in state program funds per year from using the funds "to assist, promote, or deter union organizing."[63] Although the Court acknowledged that the National Labor Relations Act contains no express preemption provision, the Court said that it reflects a policy choice that both employers and employees be allowed to

---

U.S. 825 (1988); Fort Halifax Packing Co. v. Coyne, 482 U.S. 1 (1987); Pilot Life Ins. Co. v. Dedeaux, 481 U.S. 41 (1987); Metropolitan Life Ins. Co. v. Massachusetts, 471 U.S. 724 (1985); Shaw v. Delta Air Lines, Inc., 463 U.S. 85 (1983); Alessi v. Raybestos-Manhattan, Inc., 451 U.S. 504 (1981).

[58] District of Columbia v. Greater Washington Bd. of Trade, 506 U.S. at 135 n.3.

[59] Fisk, *supra* note 6, at 59 n.106.

[60] Florida Lime & Avocado Growers, Inc. v. Paul, 373 U.S. 132, 142 (1963).

[61] Rice v. Santa Fe Elevator Corp., 331 U.S. 218, 230 (1947); *see also* Pacific Gas & Elec. Co. v. State Energy Resources Conservation & Dev. Commn., 461 U.S. 190, 203-204 (1983).

[62] 554 U.S. 60 (2008).

[63] Cal. Govt. Code Ann. §§16645.2(a), 16645.7(a).

speak with regard to the issue of union organizing and that this be left largely to "market forces." The Court concluded that the California law interfered with this by imposing a restriction on employer speech. But, as Justice Breyer argued in dissent, all California did was to prevent employers from using *state* funds to discourage union organizing.[64] He explained: "[T]he law normally gives legislatures broad authority to decide how to spend the people's money. A legislature, after all, generally has the right *not* to fund activities that it would prefer not to fund—even where the activities are otherwise protected."[65] Thus, the disagreement between the majority and the dissent was over the scope of field preemption under a federal statute that is silent about preemption.

Foreign Policy and Immigration as an Example

One place where the Court often has found field preemption is in the area of foreign policy and immigration.[66] The federal government has exclusive authority in dealing with foreign nations, and therefore state regulations in this area are preempted. The problem, though, is deciding how far this preemption extends in invalidating state and local laws that have an indirect effect on foreign policy or immigration.

Hines v. Davidowitz is a classic example of preemption of state regulation in the field of immigration.[67] A Pennsylvania law required aliens to register with the state, carry a state-issued registration card, and pay a small registration fee. The Supreme Court deemed this law preempted by emphasizing that alien registration "is in a field which affects international relations, the one aspect of our government that from the first has been most generally conceded imperatively to demand broad national authority."[68]

The Court stressed the extensive federal regulation in the area, including a "broad and comprehensive plan describing the terms and conditions upon which aliens may enter this country, how they may acquire citizenship, and the manner in which they may be deported."[69] Indeed, a federal law specifically required alien registration with the federal government.

Two aspects of *Hines* are particularly noteworthy. First, the Court found preemption of a state law that complemented the federal law; the state law in no way interfered with the federal law or its implementation.[70] Field preemption means that federal law is exclusive in the area and preempts state laws even if they serve the same purposes as the federal law and do not impede the implementation of federal law.

---

[64] 554 U.S. at 76-77 (Breyer, J., dissenting).

[65] *Id.* at 79.

[66] For an excellent discussion of this issue, *see* Karl Manheim, State Immigration Laws and Federal Supremacy, 22 Hastings Const. L.Q. 939 (1995).

[67] 312 U.S. 52 (1941).

[68] *Id.* at 68.

[69] *Id.* at 69.

[70] Kenneth Starr et al., The Law of Preemption: A Report of the Appellate Judges Conference 23 (1991).

Second, the Court found field preemption in *Hines* even in the absence of express preemptive language in the federal statute. Congress certainly could have explicitly preempted state alien registration in the federal law that required aliens to register. But Congress did not do this. The dissent in *Hines* emphasized this point:

> At a time when the exercise of the federal power is being rapidly expanded through Congressional action, it is difficult to overstate the importance of safeguarding against such diminution of state power by vague inferences as to what Congress might have intended if it had considered the matter or by reference to our own conceptions of a policy which Congress has not expressed and which is not plainly to be inferred from the legislation which it has enacted. The Judiciary of the United States should not assume to strike down a state law which is immediately concerned with the social order and safety of its people unless the statute plainly and palpably violates some right granted or secured to the national government by the Constitution or similarly encroaches upon the exercise of some authority delegated to the United States for the attainment of objects of national concern.[71]

The dispute between the majority and the dissent in *Hines*—over whether preemption should be found in the absence of an explicit congressional declaration—continues to this day. As described above, ultimately it is a tension between the desire to effectuate the interests of the federal government and the desire to limit the instances where state power is limited.

Later cases have followed *Hines* and have found that state laws concerning immigration are preempted. In *Takahashi v. Fish and Game Commission*, the Court declared preempted a state law that precluded aliens who were not eligible for citizenship under federal law from obtaining commercial fishing licenses.[72] The Court used expansive language to find the state law preempted: "The Federal Government has broad constitutional powers in determining what aliens shall be admitted to the United States, the period they may remain, regulation of their conduct before naturalization, and the terms and conditions of their naturalization. Under the Constitution the states are granted no such powers. . . . State laws which impose discriminatory burdens upon the entrance or residence of aliens lawfully within the United States conflict with this constitutionally derived federal power to regulate immigration."[73]

Similarly, in *Toll v. Moreno*, the Court found a state law preempted that denied in-state tuition to "non-immigrant aliens" that it accorded to citizens and to "immigrant aliens."[74] A nonimmigrant alien, for example, was a child of officers or employees of international organizations who were in the United States because of their work. The Court found preemption based on "the broad principle that 'state regulation not congressionally sanctioned that discriminates against aliens

---

[71] *Hines*, 312 U.S. at 75 (Stone, J., dissenting) (citations omitted).
[72] 334 U.S. 410 (1948).
[73] *Id.* at 419.
[74] 458 U.S. 1 (1982).

lawfully admitted to the country is impermissible if it imposes additional burdens not contemplated by Congress.' "[75]

In contrast, in *De Canas v. Bica,* the Court found that there was not preemption of a state law that precluded employment of undocumented aliens if that employment would adversely affect resident workers.[76] The Court noted that the "[p]ower to regulate immigration is unquestionably exclusively a federal power."[77] Nonetheless, the Court concluded that there was not preemption because Congress intended that the states be allowed, "to the extent consistent with federal law, [to] regulate the employment of illegal aliens."[78]

The most recent, and likely the most important, Supreme Court decision concerning preemption in the area of immigration law is *Arizona v. United States.*[79] In 2010, Arizona adopted a law, S.B. 1070, which among other things requires officers to check a person's immigration status if there is reasonable suspicion that the person is in the United States illegally (§2) and authorizes officers to make a warrantless arrest of a person where there is probable cause to believe that the person committed a public offense that makes the person removable from the United States (§6). S.B. 1070 also requires that noncitizens carry registration papers showing they are lawfully in the United States (§3), and makes it a crime for those who are not lawfully present to apply for or be hired for work (§5).[80] Arizona's S.B. 1070 declares its purpose to be decreasing the presence in the state of undocumented immigrants through aggressive law enforcement and attrition.

The Supreme Court, in a 5-3 ruling, affirmed the district court's preliminary injunction as to three of these provisions. Justice Kennedy wrote for the majority and was joined by Chief Justice Roberts and Justices Ginsburg, Breyer, and Sotomayor. Justice Kagan was recused, while Justice Scalia dissented, joined by Justices Thomas and Alito.

Justice Kennedy began by accepting the argument of the United States that immigration is solely in the control of the federal government. Anything done with regard to immigration has foreign policy implications and states cannot have their own foreign policy. The Court quoted its 1942 ruling in *Hines v. Davidowitz* that states cannot "contradict or complement" federal immigration efforts and "[o]ne of the most important and delicate of all international relationships . . . has

---

[75] *Id.* at 12-13, quoting De Canas v. Bica, 424 U.S. 351, 358 n.6 (1976). *See also* Graham v. Richardson, 403 U.S. 365 (1971) (declaring unconstitutional a state law that denied welfare benefits to aliens as violating equal protection and interfering with the exclusive federal authority to regulate immigration).

[76] 424 U.S. 351 (1976).

[77] *Id.* at 354. However, the Court also did say that it "has never held that every state enactment which in any way deals with aliens is a regulation of immigration and *per se* preempted by this constitutional power, whether latent or exercised." *Id.* at 355.

[78] *Id.* at 361.

[79] 132 S. Ct. 2492 (2012). This law is separate from the Arizona statute revoking business licenses for employers who employ undocumented immigrants. That law was upheld by the Supreme Court in *Chamber of Commerce v. Whiting,* 131 S. Ct. 1968 (2011), which is discussed above.

[80] Support Our Law Enforcement and Safe Neighborhoods Act, 2010 Ariz. Sess. Laws, Ch. 113.

to do with the protection of the just rights of a country's own nationals when those nationals are in another country."[81]

In fact, the Court found that the Arizona requirement (§3) that noncitizens carry papers at all times showing that they are lawfully in the country was pre-empted based on *Hines*, which had held that alien registration was exclusively in the province of the federal government. The Court found the criminal prohibition against those unlawfully in the country from seeking or receiving employment in Arizona (§5C) was preempted based on Congress's explicit choice to impose sanctions on employers and not employees. Justice Kennedy explained: "The legislative background of [the federal law] underscores the fact that Congress made a deliberate choice not to impose criminal penalties on aliens who seek, or engage in, unauthorized employment."[82]

The Court found that §6, which allows police to arrest and detain without warrants where there is probable cause that a person is unlawfully in the United States, is preempted because it was solely in the discretion of the federal government to decide whether to detain a person for possible deportation. The Court declared: "By authorizing state officers to decide whether an alien should be detained for being removable, §6 violates the principle that the removal process is entrusted to the discretion of the Federal Government. A decision on removability requires a determination whether it is appropriate to allow a foreign national to continue living in the United States. Decisions of this nature touch on foreign relations and must be made with one voice."[83]

Finally, the Court reversed the preliminary injunction as to the provision that allows police to question individuals about their immigration status if they are stopped for other reasons and if there is reasonable suspicion that they are not lawfully in the United States. The Court stressed that it was too uncertain as to how this would be implemented to allow it to decide constitutionality at this stage. The Court explained: "The nature and timing of this case counsel caution in evaluating the validity of §2(B). The Federal Government has brought suit against a sovereign State to challenge the provision even before the law has gone into effect. There is a basic uncertainty about what the law means and how it will be enforced. At this stage, without the benefit of a definitive interpretation from the state courts, it would be inappropriate to assume §2(B) will be construed in a way that creates a conflict with federal law."[84] But this provision was substantially narrowed as the Court said that police cannot extend the duration of a stop to check immigration status and also that state and local police cannot arrest individuals whom they determine to be illegally in the country. Moreover, the Court left open the possibility of an "as applied" challenge to this provision of S.B. 1070 if it could be shown that it was being applied in a racially discriminatory fashion.

Justice Scalia wrote a vehement dissent as to those parts of the law that the majority had deemed preempted. His central thesis was that Arizona, as a sovereign

---

[81] 132 S. Ct. at 2498-2499.
[82] *Id.* at 2504.
[83] *Id.* at 2506-2507.
[84] *Id.* at 2510.

state, had the authority to decide who could be within its borders. He wrote: "As a sovereign, Arizona has the inherent power to exclude persons from its territory, subject only to those limitations expressed in the Constitution or constitutionally imposed by Congress."[85] The dissent accepted Arizona's central argument that S.B. 1070 supplemented federal immigration laws and did not conflict with them.

Arizona v. United States is an important and powerful affirmation that states are significantly limited in their ability to regulate immigration.

The question also arises as to how far the federal preemption of state laws affecting foreign policy extends. The issue arose in the 1950s in the context of whether states could prohibit advocacy of overthrow of the government. Initially, in *Pennsylvania v. Nelson*, in 1956, the Court found that a Pennsylvania sedition statute was preempted by the federal Smith Act, which prohibited the knowing advocacy of the overthrow of the United States government by force or violence.[86] The federal law contained no preemptive language, Congress did not express an intent to preempt state law, and there was no conflict between the Pennsylvania law and the Smith Act. Nonetheless, the Court concluded that there was preemption. The Court said that the "scheme of federal regulation is so pervasive as to make reasonable the inference that Congress left no room for the States to supplement it."[87] The Court emphasized that the law touched foreign policy and thus concerned a "field in which the federal interest is so dominant that the federal system must be assumed to preclude the enforcement of state laws on the same subject."[88]

But three years later, in *Uphaus v. Wyman*, the Court held that Congress had not preempted all state sedition laws.[89] An individual was held in contempt for failing to comply with a subpoena that was issued by the New Hampshire attorney general as part of an investigation into possible subversive activity in the state. The Court found that states were allowed to prohibit subversive activity, and it narrowly construed *Nelson* as only "proscrib[ing] . . . a race between federal and state prosecutors to the courthouse door."[90]

The comparison between *Nelson* and *Uphaus* is revealing in terms of the problems with field preemption. The decision as to whether the Smith Act preempts similar and related state laws turns entirely on a judgment by the Court as to whether it is a field that should be left entirely to the federal government. Although the Court is influenced by statutory language and legislative intent, inevitably these are sufficiently ambiguous as to require a choice by the Court.

Two later cases illustrate preemption in the area of foreign policy. In *Crosby v. National Foreign Trade Council*,[91] the Court considered a Massachusetts law that prohibited the state and its agencies from purchasing goods or services from companies that do business with Burma (Myanmar). The state adopted this law because

---

[85] *Id.* at 2511 (Scalia, J., concurring in part and dissenting in part). Justices Thomas and Alito also each wrote separate opinions concurring in part and dissenting in part.

[86] 350 U.S. 497 (1956).

[87] *Id.* at 502 (citations omitted).

[88] *Id.* at 504 (citations omitted).

[89] 360 U.S. 72 (1959).

[90] *Id.* at 76.

[91] 530 U.S. 363 (2000).

of human rights violations in that nation. The Supreme Court unanimously found that the state law was preempted by federal law. Justice Souter, writing for the Court, explained that Congress had enacted a sanctions law against Burma. He found that this preempted states from imposing their own sanctions.

The decision, though unanimous, can be questioned because Congress had not expressed or implied any intent to preempt states from imposing sanctions and the state law was not inconsistent with the federal law. The state was simply choosing how it would spend its taxpayers' money and who it would do business with. Many state and local governments adopted similar laws refusing to contract with companies doing business in South Africa at the time of apartheid. On the other hand, the Court's unanimous ruling can be seen as following the tradition of having federal laws occupy the field with regard to foreign policy.

The Court also found preemption because of potential foreign policy issues in *American Insurance Assn. v. Garamendi*.[92] California's Holocaust Victim Insurance Relief Act required any insurer that did business in California and that sold insurance policies in Europe that were in effect during Holocaust era to disclose certain information about those policies to the California Insurance Commissioner or risk losing its license. The state was concerned that insurance companies were "stonewalling" and refusing to disclose information about their Holocaust-era policies. The law applied only to insurance companies doing business in California and only required disclosure of information.

Nonetheless, in a 5-to-4 decision with an unusual split among the Justices, the Court found the California law preempted based on the "implied dormant foreign affairs power of the President." Justice Souter wrote the opinion for the Court and the four dissenters were Justices Stevens, Scalia, Thomas, and Ginsburg. The majority acknowledged that neither the statute nor executive agreements contained a preemption clause and that there was no conflict between the California law and any federal law. Nonetheless, the Court concluded that the California law limited the ability of the president to negotiate executive agreements in this area and thus was preempted.[93] Justice Souter's majority opinion stressed that "resolving Holocaust-era insurance claims that may be held by residents of this country is a matter well within the Executive's responsibility for foreign affairs."[94] The Court concluded that the choice of the president to not aggressively pursue policies in the area precluded California from making a contrary choice.

On the one hand, *Garamendi*, like *Crosby*, reflects the Court according broad authority to the federal government in matters touching foreign policy and thus expansively defining field preemption. But the decision also is troubling in that it finds preemption where there is no express clause in any federal law or executive agreement precluding state regulation and where there is no conflict between the state law and anything the federal government had done. From a federalism

---

[92] 539 U.S. 396 (2003).

[93] The Court relied on its earlier decision in *Zschernig v. Miller*, 389 U.S. 429 (1968), where the Court had invalidated an Oregon probate statute prohibiting inheritance by a nonresident alien, absent showings that the foreign heir would take the property "without confiscation" by his home country and that American citizens would enjoy reciprocal rights of inheritance there.

[94] *Garamendi*, 539 U.S. at 423.

perspective, such a broad view of field preemption dramatically limits the choices state governments may make.

Federal Regulations as Field Preemption

The same issue arises in other areas, besides foreign policy and immigration, where there is extensive federal regulation and a claim that the field excludes state and local actions. Perhaps the most frequently cited case concerning field preemption is *Rice v. Santa Fe Elevator Corporation.*[95] The issue in *Rice* was whether states could regulate grain elevators licensed by the federal government. The Court concluded that such regulation was preempted even though Congress did not expressly preclude state regulation. The Court saw the purpose of the federal law as eliminating dual state and federal regulation of grain warehouses and found preemption based on Congress's desire to make preemption exclusive in the field. But the dissent argued, as the dissent has contended in many cases finding preemption, that Congress had the power to preempt state laws, if it wanted to do so, and that preemption should not be found absent such statutory provisions.[96]

Another prominent example of the Supreme Court finding field preemption based on extensive federal regulation is *City of Burbank v. Lockheed Air Terminal, Inc.*[97] The issue was whether a city ordinance prohibiting jet flights at a local airport between 11:00 P.M. and 7:00 A.M. was preempted by the Federal Aviation Act and the Noise Control Act amendments to it.[98] Although there was no provision in either law expressly preempting state regulation, the Court declared: "It is the pervasive nature of the scheme of federal regulation of aircraft noise that leads us to conclude that there is preemption."[99] The Court exhaustively reviewed the legislative history of the federal laws and expressed concern that allowing such local regulations would impede the ability of federal regulators to control air traffic flow.[100] The Court concluded: "Control of noise is of course deep-seated in the police power of the States. Yet the pervasive control vested in EPA and in FAA under the 1972 Act seems to us to leave no room for local curfews or other local controls."[101]

Yet the Court has refused to find preemption in other areas where there is extensive federal regulation. For instance, in *Hillsborough County, Fla. v. Automated Medical Laboratories, Inc.*, the Court concluded that federal regulations governing the collection of blood plasma from paid donors did not preempt local

---

[95] 331 U.S. 218 (1947).

[96] *Id.* at 239 (Frankfurter, J., dissenting).

[97] 411 U.S. 624 (1973).

[98] Federal Aviation Act of 1958, Pub. L. No. 85-726, Aug. 23, 1958, 72 Stat. 731 (repeated by Pub. L. No. 103-272, §7(b), July 5, 1994, 108 Stat. 1379), amended by the Noise Control Act of 1972, Pub. L. No. 92-574, §7(b), Oct. 27, 1972, 86 Stat. 1239 (repealed by Pub. L. No. 103-272, §7(b), July 5, 1994, 108 Stat. 1379).

[99] *City of Burbank*, 411 U.S. at 633.

[100] *Id.* at 639.

[101] *Id.* at 638.

ordinances.[102] A city adopted rules requiring that all paid blood donors be tested for hepatitis and be given a blood alcohol test. The Food and Drug Administration, pursuant to federal law, had adopted many regulations of such paid donations. The blood bank argued that the comprehensive federal regulation preempted the local ordinance.

The Supreme Court disagreed and emphasized the absence of any intent by Congress to preempt the entire field. The Court stressed that "the regulation of health and safety matters is primarily, and historically, a matter of local concern."[103] The Court also said that the judiciary should be more reluctant to find preemption of a field based on regulations as opposed to statutes. The Court said: "We are even more reluctant to infer preemption from the comprehensiveness of regulations than from the comprehensiveness of statutes. As a result of their specialized functions, agencies normally deal with problems in far more detail than does Congress. To infer preemption whenever an agency deals with a problem comprehensively is virtually tantamount to saying that whenever a federal agency decides to step into a field, its regulations will be exclusive. Such a rule, of course, would be inconsistent with the federal-state balance embodied in our supremacy clause jurisprudence."[104]

In other areas, too, the Court has refused to find field preemption even though there is extensive federal regulation. For instance, in *Goldstein v. California*, the Court refused to find that a state law prohibiting record piracy was preempted by federal copyright laws.[105] Even though copyright traditionally has been regulated exclusively by the federal government, the Court refused to find preemption because of the absence of any expression by Congress of a desire to prevent such state regulation. Similarly, in *New York State Department of Social Services v. Dublino*, the Court found that federal law did not preempt a state law that required that welfare recipients participate in an employment program.[106] The Court acknowledged the extensive federal regulations, but found no indication that Congress meant to preclude state regulation in the area.

Making Sense of Field Preemption

As the above cases indicate, there is no clear rule as to when courts will find field preemption. However, several criteria can be identified that are crucial in determining whether there is field preemption. First, is it an area where the federal government traditionally has played a unique role? For example, the Supreme Court has found field preemption with regard to foreign policy and immigration based on the federal government's preeminent and exclusive role in these areas.

Second, has Congress expressed an intent in the text of the law or in the legislative history to have federal law be exclusive in the area? For instance, in *Rice*,

---

[102] 471 U.S. 707 (1985).
[103] *Id.* at 719.
[104] *Id.* at 717.
[105] 412 U.S. 546 (1973).
[106] 413 U.S. 405 (1973).

described above, the Court found that the purpose behind the federal law was to eliminate dual federal and state regulations of grain elevators.

Third, would allowing state and local regulations in the area risk interfering with comprehensive federal regulatory efforts? Field preemption can be found in the absence of such interference, but the potential for impeding the federal scheme can be crucial in a court finding preemption. In the *Burbank* case described above, a key factor in the Court finding preemption was its fear that a multiplicity of city curfew ordinances for airports would undermine the ability of the Federal Aviation Administration to regulate airspace in a safe and efficient manner.

Fourth, is there an important traditional state or local interest served by the law? Although the Court often has found preemption even when the state or local law serves an important and traditional purpose, such as noise control in *Burbank*, in other cases the Court has emphasized the significance of the state interest in avoiding preemption. For instance, in *Maurer v. Hamilton*, the Court upheld a state law preventing the carrying of cars over the cabs of auto transport trucks, even though there was extensive regulation by the Interstate Commerce Commission, because of the traditional and important state interest in regulating highway safety.[107] At the very least, the Court is more likely to avoid finding field preemption if it regards the state interest as particularly important and in an area that has been traditionally regulated by state and local governments.

These factors, of course, are not mutually exclusive, and the presence of more than one favoring exclusive federal control greatly enhances the likelihood that preemption will be found. But it must be recognized that the Court usually has great discretion in deciding whether a particular area has been left exclusively to federal law and, if so, how far the preemption extends. Although the Court often says that it looks to congressional intent to decide if there is field preemption,[108] rarely is the intent clear; the Court is thus left to decide whether a field is preempted and, if so, the scope of that preemption.

§5.2.4   Conflicts Between State and Federal Laws

Preemption If Impossible to Comply with Federal and State Law

If federal law and state law are mutually exclusive, so that a person could not simultaneously comply with both, the state law is deemed preempted. The Supreme Court has explained that such preemption exists when "compliance with both federal and state regulation is a physical impossibility."[109]

McDermott v. Wisconsin is illustrative.[110] Federal law required labeling of maple syrup in a manner that Wisconsin law prohibited. A company could not

---

[107] 309 U.S. 598 (1940).

[108] *See, e.g.*, Hillsborough County v. Automated Med. Labs, Inc., 471 U.S. at 714 ("The question whether the regulation of an entire field has been reserved by the Federal Government is, essentially, a question of ascertaining the intent underlying the federal scheme.").

[109] Florida Lime & Avocado Growers, Inc. v. Paul, 373 U.S. 132, 142-143 (1963).

[110] 228 U.S. 115 (1913).

simultaneously comply with both federal and state law, so the state law was deemed preempted. Similarly, in *Hisquierdo v. Hisquierdo*, the Court found that a federal law prohibiting attachment of railroad retirement income preempted a state community property law that would have expressly divided railroad retirement income in the case of divorce.[111]

Problems in Deciding If There Is a Conflict

The difficulty with regard to this type of preemption is in deciding whether there is a conflict between federal and state law. The fact that federal law and state law are different does not necessarily mean that there is an impermissible conflict. Rather, it could be that the federal government has set a minimum standard and permits states to set stricter standards. However, it also may be that the federal regulation was meant to be *the* standard, and the differing state standard is thus preempted.

An example of this difficulty is *Florida Lime & Avocado Growers, Inc. v. Paul.*[112] The Department of Agriculture adopted regulations for measuring the maturity of avocados. California adopted a stricter rule, which prohibited the transportation or sale of avocados that had less than 8 percent oil. The result was that some Florida avocados, which were permissible under the federal regulation, were prohibited under the California law. The issue before the Supreme Court was whether there was mutual exclusivity between the federal and state regulations.

The federal and state laws are mutually exclusive if the federal regulation is seen as setting the exclusive standard for avocados. However, the federal and state law are not mutually exclusive if the federal regulation is viewed as setting only the minimum standard for saleable avocados, with states allowed to set stricter standards. Nothing in the federal law or regulation answered this question.

The Court concluded the latter—that the federal regulation was the floor, but not the ceiling; it was the minimum standard, but states were allowed to set stricter regulations if they wished. In part, the Court emphasized the traditional role of states in regulating the marketing of food products.[113] The Court also relied in part on the history of the adoption of the federal regulation. The Court observed that the federal regulation was motivated less by a desire to ensure palatable avocados than by successful lobbying efforts of Florida avocado growers. The Court remarked that "the pattern which emerges is one of maturity regulations drafted and administered locally by the growers' own representatives, and designed to do no more than promote orderly competition among the South Florida growers."[114]

---

[111] 439 U.S. 572 (1979); *see also* McCarty v. McCarty, 453 U.S. 210 (1981) (finding that federal law concerning military retirement pay prevented it from being divided under state community property law). The Court found preemption in these cases even though it acknowledged the unique state interest in matters of family law, and it said that state law would be deemed preempted only if it did "major damage to clear and substantial federal interests." 439 U.S. at 581.

[112] 373 U.S. 132 (1963).

[113] *Id.* at 146.

[114] *Id.* at 151.

Numerous other cases reflect the same problem: When states set stricter standards in an area than does federal law, it is necessary to decide whether the federal government meant its law to be exclusive or only intended to set a minimum standard that states may exceed. Unfortunately, almost never does the statute or regulation answer this question and rarely is there any legislative history on point. Thus, mutual exclusivity preemption, like the other areas of preemption, involves the Court making a judgment about what Congress or a federal agency intended when they said nothing about their intent.

This issue often arises in the context of state environmental laws. For instance, in *Midatlantic National Bank v. New Jersey Department of Environmental Protection*, there was a seemingly direct conflict between a state's environmental law and a federal bankruptcy statute.[115] New Jersey law prohibited the abandonment of property of the estate on which toxic wastes had been dumped unless the site had been completely decontaminated. The federal bankruptcy law expressly allowed the trustee in bankruptcy to "abandon any property that is burdensome to the estate or that is of inconsequential value to the estate."[116] These provisions appear to be mutually exclusive: Federal law allowed abandonment of the property, while state law prohibited it.

The Court, however, found that there was not preemption of the state law. The Court reviewed the Bankruptcy Code's legislative history and concluded that "Congress did not intend for the Bankruptcy Code to preempt all state laws that otherwise constrain the exercise of a trustee's power."[117] Also, the Court looked to federal environmental laws and said that they evidence a congressional "goal of protecting the environment against toxic pollution."[118] In other words, even in the face of a clear conflict between federal and state law and apparent manifest mutual exclusivity, the Court used its view of Congress's overall intent to reject a preemption claim.

Another illustration in the environmental area is *Wisconsin Public Intervenor v. Mortier*.[119] The issue was whether the Federal Insecticide, Fungicide, and Rodenticide Act preempted local governmental regulation of pesticide use. The Court found that the stricter local rules were permissible because the federal law set the minimum standard and did not preempt the entire field.

Subsequently, the Court considered conflict preemption in the product liability area, in *Geier v. American Honda Motor Co., Inc.*[120] Alexis Geier bought a 1987 model Honda Accord. She was seriously injured when the car crashed into a tree. She sued saying that the absence of airbags was a design defect that was responsible for her injuries. The Department of Transportation had promulgated rules pursuant to the National Traffic and Motor Vehicle Safety Act for 1987 automobiles. The regulations required that cars have passive restraint systems and gave manufactur-

---

[115]   474 U.S. 494 (1986).
[116]   11 U.S.C. §554(a), quoted in Midatlantic Natl. Bank v. New Jersey Dept. of Envtl. Protection, 474 U.S. at 509.
[117]   *Id.* at 505.
[118]   *Id.* at 505 (citations omitted).
[119]   501 U.S. 597 (1991).
[120]   529 U.S. 861 (2000).

ers three choices: One was airbags; another was lap and shoulder belts, which were in Geier's car. The defendant argued that Geier's suit was preempted by federal law because it built the car in compliance with the federal safety requirements.

The problem with this is that the National Traffic and Motor Vehicle Safety Act, which was the basis for the Department of Transportation regulations, had a savings clause that nothing within the law was meant to preempt any other cause of action that might exist.[121] Geier argued that this provision prevented a finding of federal preemption.

The Supreme Court rejected Geier's argument and found federal preemption notwithstanding the savings clause. Justice Breyer, writing for the majority, said that this was not a situation of express preemption, but instead conflicts preemption.[122] Allowing state liability for cars made in compliance with the federal safety standard was deemed to conflict with the federal law. Justice Breyer said that the savings clause did not foreclose preemption because there is no indication that Congress wanted to permit lawsuits when cars were made in compliance with the Department of Transportation's safety regulations.[123]

Geier is important because it provides a basis for defendants to claim preemption to tort liability when products are made in compliance with a federal safety standard. The case also is significant in showing the need for judicial interpretation of savings clauses[124] and, more generally, judicial determination of whether there really is a conflict between federal and state law.

Making Sense of Conflict Preemption

As in all areas of preemption law, there are potentially cases where it is easy to identify conflict preemption. For instance, if the federal government requires conduct that the state prohibits, conflict preemption will be found. As indicated above, however, there also are many harder cases that depend on determining federal intent in order to decide whether the federal law and the state law are mutually exclusive. As is the case throughout preemption law, this intent is rarely expressed or clear and courts thus must make a judgment about how best to effectuate the policy behind a particular federal law.

---

[121] The savings clause stated: "Compliance with any Federal motor vehicle safety standard issued under this subchapter does not exempt any person from any liability under common law." 15 U.S.C. §1397(k) (1988 ed.). This provision is now codified at 49 U.S.C. §30103(e).

[122] *Geier*, 529 U.S. at 866-867, 877.

[123] *Id.* at 869-870.

[124] This issue, judicial construction of a savings clause in determining whether there is federal preemption, also was the issue in *United States v. Locke*, 529 U.S. 89 (2000) (savings clause of the Oil Pollution Control Act allowing states to impose additional liabilities and requirements with regard to the discharge of oil are limited to regulations governing liability and compensation for oil pollution, and do not extend to rules regulating vessel operation, design, or manning).

§5.2.5   State Laws That Impede Achievement of Federal Objectives

Even if Congress has not expressly preempted state law, and even if federal law does not occupy the field and there is no conflict between the federal and state laws, preemption still can be found if a court concludes that the state law interferes with a federal goal. The Court has explained that state law will be deemed preempted if it "stands as an obstacle to the accomplishment and execution of the full purposes or objectives of Congress."[125] For example, in *Nash v. Florida Industrial Commission,* the Court found preemption of a state law that denied unemployment benefits to those who filed an unfair labor practice charge with the National Labor Relations Board.[126] The Court saw encouraging the filing of such charges to be a key purpose of the National Labor Relations Act, and therefore a state law that imposed a punishment for doing so was deemed preempted.

Similarly, in *Perez v. Campbell,* the Court concluded that federal bankruptcy law preempted a state law that suspended the driver's licenses of those who did not pay judgments arising from automobile accidents, even if the debt had been discharged in bankruptcy.[127] The Court said that the purpose of the federal bankruptcy law was to provide uniform standards for determining when a debt was discharged and that to allow states to regulate would undermine this purpose.

In some very important recent cases, the Supreme Court has considered preemption in the context of liability of prescription drugs. The Court has held that makers of brand name drugs may be sued for failure to adequately warn consumers, even when the warning labels had been approved by the Food and Drug Administration. But it also has held that suits against makers of generic drugs are preempted, both for failure to warn claims and design defect claims.

In *Wyeth v. Levine,* the Court considered whether the Food and Drug Administration's approval of warning labels on a prescription drug preempted state tort liability on a failure to warn theory.[128] The Court ruled against preemption, finding that allowing tort liability would further the federal regulatory goal: informing doctors and patients of the dangers of prescription drugs. The drug company argued both that there was conflicts preemption and that allowing tort liability would undermine the federal objective of having an expert agency decide the content of warnings.

The Court rejected both of these arguments, concluding that nothing in federal law precludes drug companies from providing more information and that allowing tort liability would further the federal objectives. Justice Stevens concluded the majority opinion by declaring: "In short, Wyeth has not persuaded us that failure-to-warn claims like Levine's obstruct the federal regulation of drug labeling. Congress has repeatedly declined to pre-empt state law, and the FDA's recently adopted position that state tort suits interfere with its statutory mandate is

---

[125] Hines v. Davidowitz, 312 U.S. at 67.
[126] 389 U.S. 235 (1967).
[127] 402 U.S. 637 (1971).
[128] 555 U.S. 555 (2009).

entitled to no weight. Although we recognize that some state-law claims might well frustrate the achievement of congressional objectives, this is not such a case."[129]

But two years later, in *Pliva v. Mensing*, the Court ruled that makers of generic drugs cannot be sued on a failure to warn theory.[130] The case involved a drug sometimes prescribed for those with diabetes to speed digestion. It is now known that in about 30 percent of cases prolonged users will suffer horrible irreversible neurological side effects. But the Court, in a 5-4 decision with Justice Thomas writing for the majority, concluded that suits against generic drug companies on a failure to warn theory are preempted by federal law.

Justice Thomas, joined by Chief Justice Roberts and Justices Scalia, Kennedy, and Alito, reasoned that the Food and Drug Act allows a generic drug to be sold so long as it is chemically the same as the brand name drug and so long as it has the warning label approved for the brand name drug. The Court said that because the generic drug had to have the warning label approved for the brand name drug and could not change it, a suit on a failure to warn theory was preempted by federal law.[131]

Justice Thomas acknowledged the incongruity that after *Wyeth* the makers of brand name drugs can be sued for a failure to warn, but not the makers of generic drugs. This was the key point of the dissenting opinion written by Justice Sotomayor, and joined by Justices Ginsburg, Breyer, and Kagan: It made no sense to allow a suit against the maker of a brand name drug and bar a suit against the maker of a generic drug that is the identical chemical compound. But Justice Thomas, writing for the Court, acknowledged this and said it was because of how Congress wrote the statutes: "Had Mensing and Demahy taken Reglan, the brand-name drug prescribed by their doctors, *Wyeth* would control and their lawsuits would not be pre-empted. But because pharmacists, acting in full accord with state law, substituted generic metoclopramide instead, federal law pre-empts these lawsuits. We acknowledge the unfortunate hand that federal drug regulation has dealt Mensing, Demahy, and others similarly situated. But 'it is not this Court's task to decide whether the statutory scheme established by Congress is unusual or even bizarre.' "[132]

The Court followed this decision in *Mutual Pharmaceuticals v. Bartlett*, which extended *Pliva v. Mensing* and found that design defect suits against generic drug makers are also preempted by federal law.[133] Karen Bartlett took a generic form of the prescription pain reliever, Sulindac. She then experienced a horrific side effect, called toxic epidermal necrolysis. Sixty to sixty-five percent of the surface of her skin deteriorated, was burned off, or turned into an open wound. She spent months in a medically induced coma, underwent 12 eye surgeries, and was

[129] *Id.* at 581.

[130] 131 S. Ct. 2567 (2011).

[131] The Court framed this in terms of "conflicts preemption," pointing to the impossibility of a drug company complying with the federal requirement and changing the content of its warning labels. *Id.* at 2577 ("We find impossibility here.").

[132] *Id.* at 2580-2581.

[133] 133 S. Ct. 2466 (2013).

tube-fed for a year. She is now severely disfigured, has a number of physical disabilities, and is nearly blind.

The Supreme Court held that her claim for a design defect was preempted by federal law. Justice Alito wrote for the Court in a 5-4 decision. The Court concluded: "In the instant case, it was impossible for Mutual to comply with both its state-law duty to strengthen the warnings on sulindac's label and its federal-law duty not to alter sulindac's label. Accordingly, the state law is pre-empted."[134]

The Court explained that New Hampshire law requires that manufacturers not sell drugs, or other products, that are "unreasonably dangerous." The Court said that in the context of prescription drugs it would be necessary to redesign a drug to increase its usefulness or reduce its risk of danger. But the maker of a generic drug cannot redesign it; federal law requires that for it to be sold it must be identical to the brand name version. Therefore, Justice Alito reasoned that the only way for a generic drug company to reduce the risk would be to strengthen the warning for consumer. *Pliva v. Mensing*, though, held that generic drug companies cannot change the warning label, but instead must include exactly the same warning label approved for the brand name drug.

The result is that makers of generic drugs cannot be sued on a design defect theory or a failure to warn theory. Justices Breyer and Sotomayor each wrote dissenting opinions and disputed the majority's contention that it is impossible to comply with both federal and state law. They said said that there was a way for the drug company to do this: Cease selling the product in the state or decide to pay the penalty for doing so.

Problem with Deciding If State Law Impedes a Federal Objective

The difficulty in applying this type of preemption is often in determining the federal objective and whether a particular type of state law is inconsistent with it. A comparison of two cases — *Pacific Gas & Electric v. State Energy Resources Conservation & Development Commission*[135] and *Gade v. National Solid Wastes Management Association*[136] — powerfully illustrates this problem. *Pacific Gas & Electric* involved a California law that imposed a moratorium on the construction of nuclear power plants until the State Energy Commission determined that there was a safe means of disposing of high-level nuclear wastes that had been approved by a federal agency.

The utility argued that this law was preempted by the federal government both because Congress intended to preempt the field of nuclear regulation and because the state law interfered with the federal objective of encouraging the development of nuclear power. Although these are two distinct types of implied preemption, both turn on congressional intent. The Supreme Court rejected both preemption arguments and upheld the state law by concluding that Congress's intent was to ensure safety, while the state's goal was economic.

---

[134] *Id.* at 2473.
[135] 461 U.S. 190 (1983).
[136] 505 U.S. 88 (1992).

As to the field preemption argument, the Court said Congress intended that the federal government have exclusive authority to regulate safety, "but that the States retain their traditional responsibility in the field of regulating electrical utilities for determining questions of need, reliability, cost, and other related state concerns."[137] The Court concluded that the California law was not preempted because its main purpose was economics and not safety. The Court noted that "California has maintained, and the Court of Appeals agreed, that [the law] was aimed at economic problems, not radiation hazards. . . . Without a permanent means of disposal, the nuclear waste problem could become critical, leading to unpredictably high costs to contain the problem or, worse, shutdowns in reactors."[138] The Court said that because it "accept[s] California's avowed economic purpose . . . the statute lies outside the occupied field of nuclear safety regulation."[139]

The utility also argued that the state law was preempted because it impeded the federal goal of encouraging the development of nuclear reactors as a source of electrical power. The Court acknowledged that "[t]here is little doubt that a primary purpose of the Atomic Energy Act was, and continues to be, the promotion of nuclear power."[140] Yet the Court rejected the preemption argument by characterizing Congress's purpose as encouraging nuclear power only to the extent that it was economically feasible. Justice White, writing for the Court, said that "Congress has left sufficient authority in the States to allow the development of nuclear power to be slowed or even stopped for economic reasons."[141]

Thus, in determining whether the California law interfered with achieving the federal objective, the Court had to make two major choices: One was in characterizing the federal objective; the other was in characterizing the state law and its purpose. If the Court saw a broad purpose for the Atomic Energy Act in encouraging the development of nuclear power, then the state law, which obviously limited it, would be preempted. The Court avoided preemption by more narrowly characterizing the federal goal as promoting nuclear reactors only when they were economically feasible.

Additionally, if the Court characterized California's purpose as ensuring safety before construction of nuclear power, then the law would have been preempted. The Court avoided preemption by accepting California's claim that its goal was economics, even though the law was written in terms of preventing construction of nuclear plants unless the *safety* of disposal was ensured.

The *Pacific Gas & Electric* case thus illustrates how preemption determinations are very much based on the record and context of the particular case. It also shows how much the outcome turns on the manner in which the Court chooses to characterize the purposes of the federal and state laws.

---

[137] *Pacific Gas & Electric*, 461 U.S. at 205.
[138] *Id.* at 213-214.
[139] *Id.* at 216.
[140] *Id.* at 221.
[141] *Id.* at 223.

The Court applied *Pacific Gas & Electric* to hold that federal law did not preempt state tort actions against state utilities. In *Silkwood v. Kerr-McGee Corp.*, the Court held that a state could award punitive damages for the escape of plutonium from a nuclear power plant.[142] The Court decided that federal law preempted states from setting their own safety standards, but did not preclude states from awarding a tort remedy for harms suffered because of the operation of the plant, even though the plant was in compliance with federal law. In a dissenting opinion, Justice Blackmun explained that "[w]hatever compensation standard a State imposes . . . a licensee remains free to continue operating under federal standards and to pay for the injury that results."[143]

Similarly, in *English v. General Electric Co.*, the Court found that federal law did not preclude a state action for intentional infliction of emotional distress by an employee who claimed retaliation for reporting nuclear safety violations.[144]

On the one hand, these cases seem inconsistent with *Pacific Gas & Electric*: In these cases, the states were not regulating only for economics but for safety. Tort damages, especially punitive damages, are a means for controlling behavior. On the other hand, as in *Pacific Gas & Electric*, the Court avoided preemption by narrowly construing the federal purpose; had the Court broadly characterized the federal goal, preemption would have been clear.

The problems with this type of preemption are evident if these cases are compared with *Gade v. National Solid Wastes Management Association*.[145] The issue in *Gade* was whether the federal Occupational Safety and Health Act of 1970, and federal regulations promulgated pursuant to it, preempted an Illinois law that protected the health and safety of workers who handled hazardous wastes. Both the federal and the state regulations required training of hazardous waste operators, a written examination, refresher courses, and fines for violations.

Justice O'Connor, writing for the plurality, stated: "Looking to the 'provisions of the whole law, and to its object and policy,' we hold that nonapproved state regulation of occupational safety and health issues for which a federal standard is in effect is impliedly preempted as in conflict with the full purposes and objectives of the OSH Act."[146] Justice O'Connor explained that Congress created a system where states could have their regulations approved by the federal Occupational Safety and Health Administration and then their regulations would replace federal law. She concluded that this evidenced a desire by Congress that there be only one set, either federal or state, of occupational safety and health standards. Thus,

---

[142]   464 U.S. 238 (1984).

[143]   *Id.* at 264 (Blackmun, J., dissenting).

[144]   496 U.S. 72 (1990).

[145]   505 U.S. 88 (1992).

[146]   *Id.* at 98-99 (citations omitted). Justice Kennedy, concurring in part and concurring in the judgment, would have found express preemption of the state law because the federal law allowed state regulations to displace federal ones if approved by the federal government. *Id.* at 112-113. Interestingly, Justices O'Connor and Kennedy relied on the same provision as the basis for preemption, but Justice O'Connor would have termed it implied preemption, while Justice Kennedy viewed it as express preemption. It again illustrates the difficulty in drawing a clear distinction between these two types of preemption.

the plurality felt that "the OSH Act precludes any state regulation of an occupational safety or health issue with respect to which a federal standard has been established, unless a state plan has been submitted and approved."[147]

The state argued that its regulation should be allowed because it also had the purpose of protecting public safety and not only the health of its workers. The Court recognized that the state law had this effect, but rejected it as insufficient to prevent preemption. Justice O'Connor, writing here for the majority, said that "in the absence of the approval of the Secretary, the OSH Act preempts all state law that constitutes, in a direct, clear and substantial way, regulation of worker health and safety."[148]

In many ways, *Gade* seems inconsistent with *Pacific Gas & Electric*. In *Pacific Gas & Electric*, the Court accepted the state's claim that it had two reasons for stopping the construction of new nuclear power plants: safety and economics. Although safety regulation would not be allowed, the economic motivation was sufficient to save the law.[149] In *Gade*, too, the state presented two justifications for its law: protecting worker health and promoting public safety. Although a traditional state function is protecting public safety, the Court found that states could not regulate worker health without federal approval. Nonetheless, the Court found preemption in *Gade*.

Indeed, the state law in *Pacific Gas & Electric* seemed inconsistent with the federal objective of encouraging the development of nuclear power, while the state law in *Gade* was consistent with the federal goal of protecting worker health. Yet the Court avoided preemption in *Pacific Gas & Electric* by narrowly construing the federal goal as encouraging nuclear power only where it was economically efficient, and found preemption in *Gade* by broadly viewing the federal goal as preempting all state regulation of worker safety unless approved by the federal government.

The point is that preemption based on state laws interfering with a federal goal turns on how the court characterizes the federal purpose. If a court wants to avoid preemption, it can narrowly construe the federal objective and interpret the state goal as different from or consistent with the federal purpose. But if a court wants to find preemption, it can broadly view the federal purpose and preempt a vast array of state laws as it did in *Gade*.

---

[147] *Id.* at 102.

[148] *Id.* at 107 (citations omitted).

[149] Another example of this was in *Ray v. Atlantic Richfield Co.*, 435 U.S. 151 (1978). A Washington law required all tankers in Puget Sound to either have safety features in addition to those required by federal law or have a tug escort. The Court said that if the law required only safety features, it would have been preempted. But the Court said that the law was not preempted because the state could have required tug escorts for all tankers; therefore, allowing a choice between tug escorts or greater safety standards was permissible.

§5.2.6   Preemption of State Taxation or Regulation of the Federal Government

Supremacy Clause Prevents Such State Taxation or Regulation

All of the types of preemption discussed above are based on a court finding that a particular federal law or specific federal regulations preempt state regulation in that area. A distinct type of preemption arises when a state attempts to tax or regulate the federal government. The general rule is that a state cannot tax or regulate the federal government because of the supremacy clause of Article VI. In other words, the state law is preempted, not because of its conflict with a federal statute or rule, but because it is inconsistent with the supremacy of the federal government.

This principle was first expressed in *McCulloch v. Maryland* where the Supreme Court declared unconstitutional a state tax on the Bank of the United States.[150] Chief Justice John Marshall, writing for the Court, explained that "the power to tax [is the] power to destroy" and concluded that it therefore was unconstitutional for states to tax the federal government or its instrumentality.

When Are State Taxes of Federal Activities Allowed?

In applying this type of preemption the issue is how far it extends to preempt general state taxes or regulations, especially ones that only incidentally affect the federal government. In the area of taxes, the Court long has held that state and local property taxes cannot be applied to federal property unless there is express authorization from Congress.[151]

The Court has been more inconsistent in dealing with whether states could apply their income taxes to federal employees. Initially, the Court held that it was unconstitutional for states to tax the income of federal workers.[152] In fact, the Court also ruled that the federal government could not tax the income of state employees.[153] But the Court ultimately reversed these cases and held that states may tax federal employees—and the federal government may tax state workers—so long as the tax is applied to the individual and not to the government entity.[154]

For example, in *James v. Dravo Contracting Co.*, the Supreme Court held that a state gross receipts tax could be applied to a federal contractor.[155] The Court acknowledged that the gross receipts tax "may . . . increase the cost to the Government," but held that so long as the tax was on the private entity and not

---

[150] 17 U.S. (4 Wheat.) 316 (1819), discussed in greater detail in §3.2.
[151] *See* Van Brocklin v. Anderson, 117 U.S. 151 (1886).
[152] *See* Dobbins v. Commissioners of Erie County, 41 U.S. (16 Pet.) 435 (1842).
[153] Collector v. Day, 78 U.S. (11 Wall.) 113 (1870).
[154] *See, e.g.*, Alabama v. King & Boozer, 314 U.S. 1 (1941); Graves v. New York ex rel. O'Keefe, 306 U.S. 466 (1939); Helvering v. Mountain Producers Corp., 303 U.S. 376 (1938); Helvering v. Gerhardt, 304 U.S. 405 (1938); James v. Dravo Contracting Co., 302 U.S. 134 (1937).
[155] 302 U.S. 134 (1937).

the government, a nondiscriminatory state tax could be applied to businesses contracting with the federal government.[156]

Similarly, in *Alabama v. King & Boozer*, the Court allowed a state to collect a sales tax from a business that sold materials to the federal government.[157] The Court emphasized that the "legal incidence" of the tax was borne by the contractor and not by the federal government.[158]

The Court has extended this principle to allow states to tax users of federal property so long as there is no liability of the United States government for the taxes, even if there is nonpayment by the person or entity owing the taxes. For example, in *United States v. County of Fresno*, the Court allowed a local tax on employee housing for those working for the United States Forest Service in national forests.[159]

The difficulty often is in deciding whether a particular entity should be regarded as independent of the federal government or sufficiently a part of it so as to be protected from state and local taxation. In *United States v. New Mexico*, the Court allowed a state tax on federal contractors even though they had the authority to draw funds directly from the federal government.[160] The Court emphasized that the legal incidence of the tax fell on an entity that otherwise was private, and therefore the tax was allowed.[161]

Similarly, in *Washington v. United States*, the Court upheld a state tax on construction materials that was ultimately borne by the federal government when it purchased construction work from a contractor.[162] The Court expressed a desire "to be sympathetic with States in their urgent quest for new taxes" and concluded that "[i]f the immunity of federal contractors is to be expanded beyond its narrow constitutional limits, it is Congress that must take responsibility for the decision."[163]

The general principle is a "legal incidence" test: If the tax will be directly borne by the federal government, it is unconstitutional as violating the supremacy clause of Article VI unless Congress expressly allows the tax.[164] But the tax is permissible if it will be borne by a private actor, even if the ultimate effect will be to increase costs for the federal government.

---

[156] *Id.* at 160.

[157] 314 U.S. 1 (1941).

[158] *Id.* at 12.

[159] 429 U.S. 452 (1977). *See also* City of Detroit v. Murray Corp. of Am., 355 U.S. 489 (1958) (upholding the application of a state personal property tax on a federal contractor because there was no potential liability of the federal government).

[160] 455 U.S. 720 (1982).

[161] The Court thus implicitly overruled its earlier decision in Kern-Limerick, Inc. v. Scurlock, 347 U.S. 110 (1954), which had invalidated a state tax on a private contractor that was identified as a federal purchasing agent.

[162] 460 U.S. 536 (1983).

[163] *Id.* at 546, quoting United States v. Mexico, 455 U.S. 720, 737-738 (1982).

[164] *See, e.g.,* United States v. State Tax Commn. of Miss., 421 U.S. 599, 608 (1975) (articulating the legal incidence test).

When Is State Regulation of Federal Activities Allowed?

In general, state laws apply to federal activities unless the application of the state law would conflict with or interfere with a federal law or policy. For example, state traffic laws apply to federal workers while on the job; but states cannot apply their environmental laws to federal activities if they would interfere with the federal government.

So long as the state law is neutral and applied to the federal government in the same manner as to all others, the question in each instance is whether the application of the state law would interfere with the operation of the federal government. For instance, states cannot apply their licensing and restrictions of professionals to limit the ability of the federal government to use its employees as it chooses. In *Johnson v. Maryland*, the Court held that federal postal employees could not be arrested by a state for lacking a valid state driver's license.[165] Likewise, in *Sperry v. Florida*, the Court held that a state could not use its unauthorized practice of law statute to prevent patent agents licensed by the United States Patent Office from giving advice.[166]

A classic example of the Court finding a state law preempted because it interfered with federal activities was *Mayo v. United States*.[167] A federal law allowed the Department of Agriculture to purchase and distribute fertilizer, while a Florida law required that every bag of fertilizer be stamped to show payment of an inspection fee. The Court found that the state law was invalid and broadly declared that "the activities of the Federal Government are free from regulation by any state."[168] The more precise statement of the law would be that the activities of the federal government are free from any state regulation that hinders or impedes the federal activities.

§5.3   THE DORMANT COMMERCE CLAUSE

§5.3.1   What Is the Dormant Commerce Clause?

Definition

The *dormant commerce clause* is the principle that state and local laws are unconstitutional if they place an undue burden on interstate commerce. There is no constitutional provision that expressly declares that states may not burden interstate

---

[165]   254 U.S. 51 (1920).
[166]   373 U.S. 379 (1963).
[167]   319 U.S. 441 (1943).
[168]   *Id.* at 445.

commerce. Rather, the Supreme Court has inferred this from the grant of power to Congress in Article I, §8, to regulate commerce among the states.

If Congress has legislated, the question is whether the federal law preempts the state or local law—the issue discussed above. Even if Congress has not acted or no preemption is found, the state or local law can be challenged on the ground that it excessively burdens commerce among the states. In other words, even if Congress has not acted—even if its commerce power lies dormant—state and local laws still can be challenged as unduly impeding interstate commerce. As Felix Frankfurter explained: "[T]he doctrine [is] that the commerce clause, by its own force and without national legislation, puts it into the power of the Court to place limits on state authority."[1]

The commerce clause thus has two distinct functions. One is an authorization for congressional actions. The scope of Congress's power to legislate under the commerce clause is discussed in §3.4. The other function of the commerce clause is in limiting state and local regulation. This is the dormant, or "negative," commerce clause.[2]

Organization of the Section

Section 5.3.2 considers whether there should be a dormant commerce clause, reviewing both the justifications for the dormant commerce clause and the arguments against it. Section 5.3.3 provides an overview of the dormant commerce clause analysis. Initially, in §5.3.3.1, the Court's nineteenth-century dormant commerce clause cases are reviewed. Then, in §5.3.3.2, the modern approach to the dormant commerce clause is summarized.

As discussed below, the key question in dormant commerce clause analysis is whether the state or local law discriminates against out-of-staters or whether it treats in-staters and out-of-staters alike. Section 5.3.4 describes the importance of this inquiry and how it is decided whether state and local laws discriminate against out-of-staters.

Section 5.3.5 considers the analysis when the state or local law does not discriminate against out-of-staters, but rather treats in-staters and out-of-staters alike. In general, the Court uses a balancing test in such cases and invalidates a state or local law under the dormant commerce clause if its burden on interstate commerce exceeds its benefits.[3]

Section 5.3.6 discusses the analysis when the state or local law is deemed to discriminate against out-of-staters. In general, the Court is extremely suspicious of such laws, and they usually are declared unconstitutional. Specifically, the Court

---

§5.3 [1] Felix Frankfurter, The Commerce Clause Under Marshall, Taney & Waite 18 (1937).

[2] There is a vast literature on the dormant commerce clause. Some of the most important and best articles include Donald Regan, The Supreme Court and State Protectionism: Making Sense of the Dormant Commerce Clause, 84 Mich. L. Rev. 1091 (1986); Julian N. Eule, Laying the Dormant Commerce Clause to Rest, 91 Yale L.J. 425 (1982); Noel T. Dowling, Interstate Commerce and State Power—Revised Version, 47 Colum. L. Rev. 547 (1947); Noel T. Dowling, Interstate Commerce and State Power, 27 Va. L. Rev. 1 (1940).

[3] See, e.g., Pike v. Bruce Church, Inc., 397 U.S. 137, 142 (1970).

has indicated that such laws will be allowed only if they are necessary—the least restrictive way—to achieve an important government purpose.[4]

There are, however, exceptions to the dormant commerce clause, that is, situations where laws that otherwise would violate the dormant commerce clause will be allowed. One exception is if Congress approves the state or local action. Congress has plenary power to regulate commerce among the states and may authorize laws that otherwise would violate the dormant commerce clause.[5] This exception is discussed in §5.3.7.1.

The other major exception is termed "the market participant exception." Under the market participant exception, a state or local government may favor its own citizens in receiving benefits from state or local governments or in dealing with government-owned businesses.[6] The market participant exception is considered in §5.3.7.2.

One important application of the dormant commerce clause concerns the constitutionality of state and local taxes that burden interstate commerce. Although occasionally cases concerning taxes are mentioned in this section, the next section, §5.4, considers in detail the constitutionality of state and local taxes under the dormant commerce clause.

Relationship to Other Constitutional Provisions

The dormant commerce clause is not the only way of challenging state laws that burden interstate commerce, especially if the state or local law discriminates against out-of-staters. For example, if the state or local government discriminates against out-of-staters with regard to a fundamental right or important economic activities, a challenge can be brought under the privileges and immunities clause of Article IV, §2. The privileges and immunities clause is discussed in §5.5.

Also, laws that discriminate against out-of-staters can be challenged under the equal protection clause of the Fourteenth Amendment.[7] Equal protection is discussed in Chapter 9.

§5.3.2   Should There Be a Dormant Commerce Clause?

Congress always has the authority under its commerce power to preempt state or local regulation of commerce. Therefore, Congress could invalidate any state or local law that it deems to place an undue burden on interstate commerce. The crucial issue with regard to the dormant commerce clause is whether the judiciary,

---

[4] *See, e.g.,* Fort Gratiot Sanitary Landfill, Inc. v. Michigan Dept. of Natural Resources, 504 U.S. 353, 359 (1992); Maine v. Taylor, 477 U.S. 131, 138 (1986).

[5] *See, e.g.,* Northeast Bancorp, Inc. v. Board of Governors, 472 U.S. 159 (1985); Prudential Ins. Co. v. Benjamin, 328 U.S. 408 (1946).

[6] *See, e.g.,* White v. Massachusetts Council of Constr. Employers, Inc., 460 U.S. 204 (1983); Hughes v. Alexandria Scrap Corp., 426 U.S. 794 (1976).

[7] *See, e.g.,* Metropolitan Life Ins. Co. v. Ward, 470 U.S. 869 (1985) (equal protection violated by a state tax on insurance companies that was higher on out-of-state insurance companies than was paid by in-state companies).

in the absence of congressional action, should invalidate state and local laws because they place an undue burden on interstate commerce.

Justifications for the Dormant Commerce Clause

As discussed below, the dormant commerce clause has existed since early in American history. There are several justifications for it. First, there is a historical argument for the dormant commerce clause: The framers intended to prevent state laws that interfered with interstate commerce. A key impetus for the Constitutional Convention in 1787 was the absence of any federal commerce power under the Articles of Confederation.[8] Commerce among the states was obstructed as states charged other states for use of port facilities or for shipping goods through the state. It is inferred from this history that the framers meant to prevent such protectionist state legislation. Justice Robert Jackson expressed this view when he stated:

> Our system, fostered by the Commerce Clause, is that every farmer and every craftsman shall be encouraged to produce by the certainty that he will have free access to every market in the Nation, that no home embargoes will withhold his exports, and no foreign state will by customs duties or regulations exclude them. Likewise, every consumer may look to the free competition from every producing area in the Nation to protect him from exploitation by any. Such was the vision of the Founders; such has been the doctrine of this Court which has given it reality.[9]

Second, there is an economic justification for the dormant commerce clause: The economy is better off if state and local laws impeding interstate commerce are invalidated. Certainly, this is reflected in the views of Justice Jackson quoted above. If a state acts to help itself at the expense of other states, the other states are sure to retaliate with protectionist legislation of their own. The resulting impediments of commerce are likely to stifle production and harm the overall economy. As Professor Regan notes, "protectionism is inefficient because it diverts business away from presumptively low-cost producers without any colorable justification in terms of a benefit that deserves approval from the point of view of the nation as a whole."[10]

Third, there is a political justification for the dormant commerce clause: States and their citizens should not be harmed by laws in other states where they lack political representation. In *McCulloch v. Maryland*, the Supreme Court invalidated Maryland's tax on the Bank of the United States, in part, because it was a tax that ultimately would be borne by those in other states who obviously did not have representation in the Maryland political process.[11] Similarly, the political process cannot be trusted when a state is advantaging itself at the expense of out-of-staters who have no representation. Justice Stone explained: "Underlying the stated rule

---

[8] *See* §1.3.
[9] H.P. Hood & Sons, Inc. v. DuMond, 336 U.S. 525, 539 (1949).
[10] Regan, *supra* note 2, at 1118.
[11] 17 U.S. (4 Wheat.) 316, 428-431 (1819), discussed in more detail in §3.2.

has been the thought, often expressed in judicial opinion, that when the regulation is of such a character that its burden falls principally upon those without the state, legislative action is not likely to be subjected to those political restraints which are normally exerted on legislation where it affects adversely some interests within the state."[12]

These justifications, of course, are not mutually exclusive, but quite consistent. All emphasize reasons why states should not be able to obstruct interstate commerce and especially why states should not be able to discriminate against those from other states.

Arguments Against the Dormant Commerce Clause

The argument against the dormant commerce clause is, in part, textual. The drafters of the Constitution could have included a provision prohibiting states from interfering with interstate commerce. For instance, the framers included the privileges and immunities clause of Article IV, §2, which limits the ability of states to discriminate against out-of-staters with regard to the privileges and immunities of citizenship. Article I, §10, contains many restrictions on state power; a limit on the ability to burden interstate commerce is not among them. Justice Clarence Thomas made this argument in urging the abandonment of the dormant commerce clause as an "exercise of judicial power in an area for which there is no textual basis."[13] Justice Antonin Scalia similarly has lamented that the "'negative commerce clause' . . . is 'negative' not only because it negates state regulation of commerce, but also because it does not appear in the Constitution."[14]

Also, opponents of the dormant commerce clause argue that the Constitution gives Congress the power to regulate commerce and Congress can invalidate state laws that unduly burden interstate commerce. The contention is that this should not be a task for an unelected federal judiciary.[15] Thus, the argument against the dormant commerce clause is based partially on separation of powers—the task of reviewing state laws should be done by Congress and not by the courts—and partially on federalism—minimizing the instances where state and local laws are invalidated. Justice Thomas made this argument as well when he wrote: "In my view, none of this policy-laden decision making is proper. Rather, the Court should confine itself to interpreting the text of the Constitution, which itself seems to prohibit in plain terms certain of the more egregious state taxes on interstate

[12] South Carolina Highway Dept. v. Barnwell Bros., Inc., 303 U.S. 177, 185 n.2 (1938).

[13] Camps Newfound/Owatonna, Inc. v. Town of Harrison, Me., 520 U.S. 564, 612 (1997) (Thomas, J., dissenting). *See also* American Trucking Assns., Inc. v. Michigan Pub. Serv. Commn., 545 U.S. 429, 439 (2005) (Thomas, J., concurring in the judgment) ("'[t]he negative Commerce Clause has no basis in the text of the Constitution, makes little sense, and has proved virtually unworkable in application,' and, consequently, cannot serve as a basis for striking down a state statute").

[14] Oklahoma Tax Commn. v. Jefferson Lines, Inc., 514 U.S. 175, 200 (1995) (Scalia, J., dissenting).

[15] *See* Eule, *supra* note 2; Martin H. Redish & Shane V. Nugent, The Dormant Commerce Clause and the Constitutional Balance of Federalism, 1987 Duke L.J. 569, 573 (1987) (the dormant commerce clause "lacks any basis in constitutional democratic theory").

commerce . . . and leaves to Congress the policy choices necessary for any further regulation of interstate commerce."[16]

Defenders of the dormant commerce clause respond that it is unrealistic to expect Congress to review the vast array of state and local laws that might be challenged as burdening interstate commerce. As Justice Jackson expressed: "[T]hese restraints are individually too petty, too diversified and too local to get the attention of a Congress hard pressed with more urgent matters."[17] The claim is that achieving the benefits of the dormant commerce clause necessitates judicial action. Furthermore, it is argued that judicial deference to the political process is unwarranted because those adversely affected by a state's law are not represented in the state. But critics of the dormant commerce clause reject these concerns as sufficient to justify the dormant commerce clause. Justice Thomas declared: "The negative Commerce Clause has no basis in the text of the Constitution, makes little sense, and has proved virtually unworkable in application."[18]

Basic Policy Questions

The dormant commerce clause, of course, is firmly established and has been a part of constitutional law for almost two centuries. These policy arguments are important, however, in evaluating the appropriate scope of the dormant commerce clause. Should the courts be aggressive in striking down state and local laws that burden the national economy, or should the courts adopt a general posture of deference and invalidate laws only in the exceptional and extreme circumstances? In part, the answer to this question turns on a view about the importance of the dormant commerce clause; how important is it that state and local laws that interfere with interstate commerce be invalidated? In part, too, the answer depends on a view of the appropriate allocation of power between Congress, the states, and the judiciary.

§5.3.3   An Overview of the Dormant Commerce Clause

§5.3.3.1   The Dormant Commerce Clause Before 1938

Gibbons v. Ogden

The dormant commerce clause can be traced back to *Gibbons v. Ogden*.[19] The issue in *Gibbons* was whether the State of New York could grant an exclusive monopoly for operating steamboats in New York waters and thereby prevent a person

---

[16] Camps Newfound/Owatonna, Inc. v. Town of Harrison, Me., 520 U.S. at 620 (Thomas, J., dissenting).

[17] *See, e.g.*, Duckworth v. Arkansas, 314 U.S. 390, 400 (1941) (Jackson, J., concurring).

[18] Camps Newfound/Owatonna, Inc. v. Town of Harrison, Me., 520 U.S. at 611 (Thomas, J., dissenting).

[19] 22 U.S. (9 Wheat.) 1 (1824). *Gibbons* also is discussed in §3.4.2 concerning the scope of Congress's power under the commerce clause.

with a federal license from operating in New York. Chief Justice John Marshall, writing for the Court, used *Gibbons* as the occasion for broadly defining the scope of Congress's power under the commerce clause. Marshall said that "commerce" refers to all stages of business and that "among the states" includes matters that affect more than one state and are not purely internal.[20]

Chief Justice John Marshall also used *Gibbons* for considering the commerce clause as an independent limit on state power, even where Congress has not acted. Marshall explained that "when a State proceeds to regulate commerce with foreign nations, or among the several States, it is exercising the very power that is granted to Congress, and is doing the very thing which Congress is authorized to do."[21]

This argument would seem to imply that Congress's commerce power is exclusive, that any state regulation of commerce is inconsistent with federal power. The idea appears to be that the power to regulate commerce is the authority to decide that commerce should not be regulated and that states therefore should not be able to act with regard to commerce unless specifically authorized by Congress.[22] Chief Justice Marshall, however, did not go nearly this far in limiting state authority. Rather, Marshall drew a distinction between a state's exercise of its police power and a state exercising the federal power over commerce.

Marshall said, for example, that state inspection laws are constitutional even though they may have a "considerable influence on commerce" because they are a "portion of that immense mass of legislation, which embraces everything within the territory of a State not surrendered to the general government: all [of] which can be most advantageously exercised by the States themselves. Inspection laws, quarantine laws, health laws of every description, as well as laws for regulating the internal commerce of a State, and those which respect turnpike roads, ferries, etc., are component parts of this mass."[23]

In several cases following *Gibbons*, the Court applied this approach in evaluating state laws under the commerce clause. For example, in *Wilson v. Black-Bird Creek Marsh Co.*, the Court considered whether a state could construct a dam that obstructed an interstate waterway.[24] The Court rejected a challenge by the owner of a federally licensed ship because construction of the dam was a permissible exercise of the state's police power. Similarly, in *Mayor, Aldermen and Commonality of New York v. Miln*, the Court upheld a state law that required passenger identification lists for all ships arriving from other states or countries.[25] The Court said that law was "not a regulation of commerce but of police" apparently because it was based on a desire to protect public safety by guarding against the arrival of undesirables.

The problem with Marshall's approach is that it assumes two distinct categories — state laws adopted under the police power and state laws that regulate

---

[20] These aspects of *Gibbons* are reviewed in §3.4.2.
[21] *Gibbons*, 22 U.S. at 199-200.
[22] Justice Johnson expressed this view in a concurring opinion in *Gibbons, id.* at 227.
[23] *Id.* at 203.
[24] 27 U.S. (2 Pet.) 245 (1829).
[25] 36 U.S. (11 Pet.) 102 (1837).

commerce among the states—that are not at all separate. Obviously, state laws adopted under the police power can place an enormous burden on interstate commerce, such as when a state offers a health or safety justification for discriminating against out-of-staters. Therefore, the issue, unresolved in *Gibbons*, is when state laws, including those adopted under the police power, violate the dormant commerce clause because they unduly burden interstate commerce.

Cooley v. Board of Wardens: National Versus Local Subject Matter

The Court has struggled ever since *Gibbons* with attempting to articulate criteria for when state laws burdening commerce are to be upheld as valid exercises of the police power and when they should be invalidated as violating the dormant commerce clause.[26] *Cooley v. Board of Wardens* is a particularly important case in which the Court drew a distinction between subject matter that is national, in which event state laws are invalidated under the dormant commerce clause, and subject matter that is local, in which event state laws are allowed.[27] *Cooley* involved a Pennsylvania law that required all ships entering or leaving the Port of Philadelphia to use a local pilot or to pay a fine, which went to support retired pilots.

The Court upheld the Pennsylvania law and said that the crucial question was whether the subject is of a nature that requires uniform national regulation or diverse local regulation. Justice Benjamin Curtis, writing for the Court, said: "Now the power to regulate commerce, embraces a vast field, containing not only many, but exceedingly various subjects, quite unlike in their nature; some imperatively demanding a single uniform rule, operating equally on the commerce of the United States in every port; and some, like the subject now in question, as imperatively demanding that diversity, which alone can meet the local necessities of navigation."[28] The Court found that regulating pilots was a local matter both because of differences among ports and also because a federal law adopted in 1789 expressly allowed states to regulate piloting.

There are, however, several problems with the *Cooley* test. First, it allows state regulations, no matter how protectionist or how much they interfere with interstate commerce, so long as the subject matter is deemed local. In *Cooley*, the state's obvious goal was to help local pilots at the expense of out-of-state pilots. If the goal was to protect safety, this could have been accomplished by requiring a license, based on experience or a test, in order to pilot a ship into the Port of Philadelphia. Moreover, the concern for safety is belied by the law's allowing nonlocal pilots to be used if a fee was paid to a fund that benefited local pilots.

---

[26] *See, e.g.*, The Passenger Cases, 48 U.S. (7 How.) 283 (1849) (where the Court split 5 to 4, with every Justice writing a separate opinion, and invalidated a state law on every incoming passenger to pay for the costs of health inspections and treatment); *see also* The License Cases, 46 U.S. (5 How.) 504 (1847).

[27] 53 U.S. (12 How.) 299 (1851).

[28] *Id.* at 319.

Second, there is not a clear distinction between what is national, demanding local regulation, and what is local, requiring diverse regulation. *Cooley* articulates no criteria for making this determination, and it seems inherently arbitrary; in almost any area there likely are some benefits from national uniformity and some gains from local diversity.

Nonetheless, the *Cooley* test was applied throughout the nineteenth century and into the twentieth century. In *Welton v. Missouri*, the Court used the *Cooley* approach to invalidate a law that required peddlers of out-of-state merchandise to pay a tax and obtain a license, whereas no similar requirements existed for in-state merchants.[29] The Court said that "transportation and exchange of commodities is of national importance, and admits and requires uniformity of regulation."[30] Similarly, in *Wabash, St. Louis & Pacific Railway Co. v. Illinois*, the Court used the *Cooley* approach to invalidate a state law that regulated railway rates for goods brought to or from other states.[31] The Court emphasized that there would be enormous burdens on interstate commerce if all states adopted such laws and thus concluded that it was an area that required national uniformity and not local regulation.

But during this same time the Court upheld other state laws on the ground that they were in areas where diverse regulation was desirable. For instance, in *Smith v. Alabama*, the Court upheld a state law requiring that all locomotive engineers operating in the state be licensed by a state board of examiners.[32] Likewise, in *Erb v. Morasch*, the Court upheld a city's ordinance that restricted train speed within the city.[33] In *Atchison Topeka & Santa Fe Railway Co. v. Railroad Commission*, the Court upheld a state law that required electric headlights of prescribed brightness on all trains operating within the state.[34]

DiSanto v. Pennsylvania: Direct Versus Indirect Effects on Commerce

Another effort to define a test for the dormant commerce clause was in *DiSanto v. Pennsylvania*, in 1927, where the Court drew a distinction between state laws that directly interfered with interstate commerce, and thus were invalid, as opposed to those that only had an indirect effect and were permissible.[35] *DiSanto* involved a state law that required a state-issued license in order to sell tickets for foreign travel. The state claimed that the law was necessary to prevent fraud, which had occurred in the ticket industry. The Court rejected this justification and concluded that the law was unconstitutional because it had a direct effect on interstate commerce. The Court explained that a "statute which by its necessary operation

---

[29] 91 U.S. 275 (1876).
[30] *Id.* at 281.
[31] 118 U.S. 557 (1886).
[32] 124 U.S. 465 (1888).
[33] 177 U.S. 584 (1900).
[34] 283 U.S. 380 (1931).
[35] 273 U.S. 34 (1927).

directly interferes with or burdens foreign commerce is a prohibited regulation and invalid, regardless of the purpose with which it was passed."[36]

The problem, of course, with a "direct/indirect" test is that it falsely assumes that there is a clear, in kind, difference between laws that directly burden commerce and those with only an indirect effect. The reality is that burdens are a matter of degree, and the determination of whether something is direct or indirect is a choice about where to draw the line. Justice Stone, dissenting in *DiSanto*, recognized this and criticized the direct/indirect test as "too mechanical, too uncertain in its application, and too remote from actualities to be of value."[37]

§5.3.3.2   An Overview of the Modern Approach to the Dormant Commerce Clause

Shift to a Balancing Approach

All of the approaches summarized above — the police power/commerce power test of *Gibbons*, the local/national subject matter test of *Cooley*, and the direct/indirect test of *DiSanto*—attempted to draw rigid categories of areas where federal law was exclusive and those where states could regulate. The modern approach is based not on rigid categories but, rather, on courts balancing the benefits of a law against the burdens that it imposes on interstate commerce. It should be noted, however, that the Court never has expressly overruled any of the earlier tests and sometimes invokes them in explaining a particular result.[38]

The Court's shift to a balancing approach in dormant commerce clause analysis is evident from comparing two cases, *South Carolina State Highway Dept. v. Barnwell Bros.*[39] and *Southern Pacific Co. v. Arizona.*[40] In *Barnwell*, the Court upheld a state law that imposed length and width requirements for trucks operating in the state. The Court emphasized the state's important interest in protecting highway safety and in preserving its roadways. In contrast, in *Southern Pacific*, the Court declared unconstitutional a state law that limited the length of railroad trains operating in the state. The Court in *Southern Pacific* expressly articulated a balancing test when it said: "Hence the matters for ultimate determination here are the nature and extent of the burden which the state regulation of interstate trains, adopted as a safety measure, imposes on interstate commerce, and whether the relative

---

[36] *Id.* at 37.

[37] *Id.* at 44 (Stone, J., dissenting).

[38] *See, e.g.,* Brown-Forman Distillers Corp. v. New York State Liquor Auth., 476 U.S. 573 (1986) (using the direct/indirect test to invalidate a state law that regulated the price of alcoholic beverages and operated to the disadvantage of out-of-staters); California v. Zook, 336 U.S. 725, 728 (1949) (using the local/national subject matter test and saying that "[a]bsent congressional action, the familiar test is that of uniformity versus locality").

[39] 303 U.S. 177 (1938).

[40] 325 U.S. 761 (1945). The shift to the balancing test is generally credited to the scholarship of Noel Dowling, *supra* note 2, which was cited in *Southern Pacific Co. v. Arizona* and countless times since.

weights of the state and national interests involved are such [as to make the law permissible]."[41] The difference is that in *Barnwell*, the Court believed that the burdens on interstate commerce were outweighed by the benefits in terms of road safety; whereas in *Southern Pacific*, the Court decided that the burdens on interstate transportation were greater than the safety benefit to the state from its law.

In other words, the central issue in dormant commerce clause cases is whether the benefits of the state law outweigh its burdens on interstate commerce. By definition, such a balancing test gives courts enormous discretion because it is attempting to weigh and compare two completely different things: burdens on interstate commerce and the benefits to a state or local government.

Balancing Test Used Depends on Whether There Is Discrimination

The way in which the Court balances is not the same in all dormant commerce clause cases, but instead varies depending on whether the state or local law discriminates against out-of-staters or treats in-staters and out-of-staters alike. As discussed below, if the Court concludes that a state is discriminating against out-of-staters, then there is a strong presumption against the law and it will be upheld only if it is necessary to achieve an important purpose. In contrast, if the Court concludes that the law is nondiscriminatory, then the presumption is in favor of upholding the law and it will be invalidated only if it is shown that the law's burdens on interstate commerce outweigh its benefits.

Criticism of the Balancing Approach

Some Justices—most notably Rehnquist, Scalia, and Thomas—have objected to this balancing test and have argued in favor of upholding all state laws that are deemed nondiscriminatory.[42] Scalia contended: "This process is ordinarily called 'balancing,' but the scale analogy is not really appropriate, since the interests on both sides are incommensurate. It is more like judging whether a particular line is longer than a particular rock is heavy. . . . Weighing the governmental interests of a State against the needs of interstate commerce is, by contrast, a task squarely within the responsibility of Congress, and ill-suited to the judicial function."[43]

The question, of course, is what should replace the balancing test. The categorical approaches that proceeded it were not terribly useful in deciding whether a particular law violated the dormant commerce clause. Justice Scalia's answer is

---

[41] *Id.* at 770.

[42] Many scholars also have taken this position. *See, e.g.,* Regan, *supra* note 2; Robert Sedler, Negative Commerce Clause as a Restriction on State Regulation and Taxation: An Analysis in Terms of Constitutional Structure, 31 Wayne L. Rev. 885 (1985); Mark Tushnet, Rethinking the Dormant Commerce Clause, 1979 Wis. L. Rev. 125.

[43] Bendix Autolite Corp. v. Midwesco Enters., Inc., 486 U.S. 888, 897 (1988) (Scalia, J., dissenting); *see also* CIS Corp. v. Dynamics Corp., 481 U.S. 69 (1987) (Scalia, J., concurring in the judgment).

to eliminate dormant commerce clause review where the state is not discriminating against out-of-staters. Scalia wrote: "I would therefore abandon the balancing approach to these negative Commerce Clause cases . . . and leave essentially legislative judgments to the Congress. . . . In my view, a state statute is invalid under the Commerce Clause if, and only if, it accords discriminatory treatment to interstate commerce in a respect not required to achieve a lawful state purpose."[44]

The question that Justice Scalia raises is whether there should be any dormant commerce clause review when a state law is deemed nondiscriminatory. Even nondiscriminatory laws can put a significant burden on interstate commerce, and ensuring a free flow of commerce among the states is best achieved by eliminating these hindrances. On the other hand, there is less reason to distrust the political process when it is treating in-staters and out-of-staters alike. Limiting the scope of the dormant commerce clause minimizes the judicial role and maximizes the deference paid to state and local governments.

Summary of Current Approach

The overall approach to the dormant commerce clause thus can be simply summarized.[45] The crucial initial question, discussed in the next section, is whether a state law discriminates against out-of-staters or whether it treats all alike regardless of residence. As discussed in §5.3.5, laws that do not discriminate are generally upheld and will be struck down only if found to place a burden on interstate commerce that outweighs the benefits from the law. However, as discussed in §5.3.6, laws that discriminate against out-of-staters are usually invalidated and will be upheld only if deemed to be necessary to achieve an important government purpose. Indeed, the Supreme Court has reaffirmed that "[s]tate laws that discriminate against interstate commerce face a virtually per se rule of invalidity."[46] It should be kept in mind that there are two exceptions where laws that otherwise would violate the dormant commerce clause will be allowed: congressional approval and the market participant exception, both discussed in §5.3.7.

---

[44] *Bendix*, 486 U.S. at 897-898. Justice Thomas offers another alternative: invalidating discriminatory state taxes under the import-export clause of the Constitution, and not having any dormant commerce clause at all. Camps Newfound/Owatonna v. Harrison, Me., 520 U.S. 564, 620, 636-637 (1997) (Thomas, J., dissenting). For a critique of this alternative, *see* Brannon P. Denning, Justice Thomas, the Import-Export Clause, and *Camps Newfound/Owatonna v. Harrison*, 70 U. Colo. L. Rev. 155 (1998).

[45] The approach described here is very similar to that described in Professor Julian Eule's excellent article, Laying the Dormant Commerce Clause to Rest, *supra* note 2.

[46] Granholm v. Heald, 544 U.S. 460, 476 (2005).

§5.3.4   *The Central Question: Is the State Discriminating Against Out-of-Staters?*

Importance of Determining Whether a Law Is Discriminatory

The obvious threshold issue under the dormant commerce clause is whether the state or local law affects interstate commerce. Ever since *Gibbons v. Ogden*, the Court has broadly defined the scope of commerce among the states for purposes of dormant commerce clause analysis.[47] For example, in *Philadelphia v. New Jersey*, the Court expansively declared that "all objects of interstate trade merit Commerce Clause protection."[48]

If the state or local law affects interstate commerce, then the dormant commerce clause may be applied. The key initial question is whether the state law discriminates against out-of-staters or whether it treats in-staters and out-of-staters alike. As described above and as detailed below, the answer to this inquiry is likely to be decisive in dormant commerce clause analysis; state laws that discriminate rarely are upheld, while nondiscriminatory laws are infrequently invalidated.

This makes sense in light of the purposes of the dormant commerce clause. The framers were most concerned about stopping protectionist state legislation where a state would discriminate against out-of-staters to benefit its citizens at the expense of out-of-staters. Also, it is thought that protectionist laws are most likely to interfere with the economy. Besides, if a law applies to in-staters and out-of-staters equally, then at least some of those affected are represented in the political process that produced and can review the law.

Determining If a State Law Is Discriminatory: Facially Discriminatory Laws

Sometimes it is obvious that a state or local law is discriminatory because the statute expressly draws a distinction between in-staters and out-of-staters. Many of the Supreme Court cases concerning the dormant commerce clause have involved such facially discriminatory laws. These facially discriminatory laws can take many forms. For example, sometimes states expressly place out-of-state businesses at a disadvantage compared to in-state businesses or act to help in-state businesses at the expense of out-of-state businesses. In *Lewis v. BT Investment Managers*, the Court considered the constitutionality of a state law that prevented out-of-state banks from owning investment advisory businesses within the state.[49] In *Baldwin v. G.A.F. Seelig, Inc.*, the Court reviewed a state law that restricted prices of milk

---

[47] In fact, some cases that adopted a narrower view of the scope of the commerce clause have been overruled. *See, e.g.*, Hudson County Water Co. v. McCarter, 209 U.S. 349 (1908) (holding that water is not an article of commerce), overruled in Sporhase v. Nebraska, 458 U.S. 941 (1982); Geer v. Connecticut, 161 U.S. 519 (1896) (birds are not an article of commerce), overruled in Hughes v. Oklahoma, 441 U.S. 322 (1979).

[48] 437 U.S. 617, 622 (1978).

[49] 447 U.S. 27 (1980).

produced out of the state and prevented it from being sold at a price lower than in-state milk.[50] In *Reynoldsville Casket Co. v. Hyde*, the Court declared unconstitutional a state law that allowed a longer tolling period for the statute of limitations for suits against out-of-staters than for suits against in-staters.[51] In *Camps Newfound/ Owatonna, Inc. v. Town of Harrison, Maine*, the Court found a Maine law that gave tax exemptions for charitable property to be discriminatory and to violate the dormant commerce clause because it singled out institutions that served mostly state residents for beneficial tax treatment; institutions that principally did interstate business were penalized.[52] In one of its most recent dormant commerce clause decisions, the Court held that a Michigan law that allowed in-state wineries, but not out-of-state wineries, to send wine to consumers through the mail was facially discriminatory and violated the dormant commerce clause.[53]

Sometimes states attempt to keep their natural resources and thus limit their accessibility to out-of-staters. In *Philadelphia v. New Jersey*, the Court reviewed a New Jersey law that effectively kept landfills in the state exclusively for New Jersey's use by preventing the importation of any wastes from out of state.[54] In *Hughes v. Oklahoma*, the Court considered an Oklahoma law that prevented the transport of minnows obtained in Oklahoma for sale outside the state.[55] In *New England Power Co. v. New Hampshire*, the Court reviewed a state law that prohibited a utility in the state from conveying electricity out of the state except with the permission of the state's public utility commission.[56]

The Court has held that reciprocity requirements—where a state allows out-of-staters to have access to markets or resources only if they are from states that grant similar benefits to their citizens—are facially discriminatory. For instance, in *Great Atl. & Pac. Tea Co. v. Cottrell*, the Court unanimously invalidated a Mississippi law that provided that milk could be shipped into Mississippi from another state only if it had a public health certificate and only if the other state would accept milk from Mississippi on a reciprocal basis.[57] Likewise, in *Sporhase v. Nebraska*, the Court found that a state law was discriminatory when it denied a permit to draw

---

[50]   294 U.S. 511 (1935).

[51]   514 U.S. 749 (1995).

[52]   519 U.S. 316 (1997).

[53]   Granholm v. Heald, 544 U.S. 460 (2005). The issue that divided the majority and the dissent was whether a state's power to regulate alcoholic beverages under the Twenty-first Amendment (which repealed prohibition) allowed such a law. The Court held, 5-4, that a state cannot exercise its power under the Twenty-first Amendment in a manner that violates other constitutional principles, including the dormant commerce clause.

[54]   437 U.S. 617 (1978); *see also* Chemical Waste Management, Inc. v. Hunt, 504 U.S. 334 (1992) (declaring unconstitutional a state law that required that out-of-state companies pay a hazardous waste disposal fee, but in-state companies did not); Oregon Waste Sys., Inc. v. Department of Envtl. Quality of the State of Or., 511 U.S. 93 (1994) (declaring unconstitutional a state law that charged more for disposal of out-of-state waste than for disposal of in-state generated waste).

[55]   441 U.S. 322 (1979).

[56]   455 U.S. 331 (1982).

[57]   424 U.S. 366 (1976).

water for use in another state unless that state granted reciprocal rights to draw water for use in Nebraska.[58]

The Court also has made it clear that local regulations that treat out-of-staters in a disparate manner will be treated as discriminatory even though they also discriminate against those in other parts of that state. In *Dean's Milk Co. v. Madison,* the Court considered a city's ordinance that required that all milk sold in the city had to be pasteurized within five miles of the city.[59] The law prevented milk that was pasteurized in other states from being sold in the city, but it also precluded milk that was pasteurized in other parts of that state from being sold in the city. Nonetheless, the Court concluded that the law was discriminatory against out-of-staters. The Court said: "In thus erecting an economic barrier protecting a major local industry against competition from without the State, Madison plainly discriminates against interstate commerce."[60] In a footnote, the Court said that it was irrelevant that the law also discriminated against in-staters: "It is immaterial that Wisconsin milk from outside the Madison area is subjected to the same proscription as that moving in interstate commerce."[61]

Similarly, in *Fort Gratiot Sanitary Landfill, Inc. v. Michigan Department of Natural Resources,* the Court found that a state law was discriminatory when it limited the ability of a county to accept waste for disposal from other counties, states, or countries.[62] The Court said that it was immaterial that the county was also discriminating against other counties in that state. The Court said: "[A] State (or one of its political subdivisions) may not avoid the strictures of the Commerce Clause by curtailing the movement of articles of commerce through subdivisions of the State, rather than through the State itself."[63]

These are not the only ways in which a state or local law can facially discriminate against out-of-staters but, rather, are illustrative of the many forms that such laws can take. The crucial point is that a law will be regarded as facially discriminatory if its terms draw a distinction between in-staters and out-of-staters.

Determining If State Laws Are Discriminatory: Facially Neutral Laws

What, though, if a state law is facially neutral in that its terms treat in-staters and out-of-staters alike, but the purpose and/or effect of the law is to discriminate? The Court has on many occasions found facially neutral state and local laws to be discriminatory based on their purpose and/or effect.[64] Unfortunately, the Court never has articulated clear criteria for deciding when proof of a discriminatory

---

[58] 458 U.S. 941 (1982).
[59] 340 U.S. 349 (1951).
[60] *Id.* at 354.
[61] *Id.* at 354 n.4.
[62] 504 U.S. 353 (1992).
[63] *Id.* at 361.
[64] *See, e.g.,* C & A Carbone, Inc. v. Town of Clarkstown, 511 U.S. 383 (1994); Hunt v. Washington State Apple Advertising Commission, 432 U.S. 333 (1977).

purpose and/or effect is sufficient for a state or local law to be deemed discriminatory. Indeed, the cases in this area seem quite inconsistent.

At times, the Court has found that proof of a discriminatory impact against out-of-staters is sufficient for a law to be regarded as discriminatory.[65] In *Hunt v. Washington State Apple Advertising Commission,* the Court found discrimination based on the disparate impact of a law against out-of-staters.[66] A North Carolina law required that all closed containers of apples sold or shipped into the state bear "no grade other than the applicable U.S. grade or standard."[67] The law was facially neutral in that all apples sold in the state—whether produced in state or out of state—had to comply with this rule.

Nonetheless, the Court found that the law should be treated as discriminatory because of its effect on the sale of Washington apples. Washington had a system for grading apples that was different from and more stringent than the federal standard. The Court explained:

> The challenged statute has the practical effect of not only burdening interstate sales of Washington apples, but also discriminating against them. This discrimination takes various forms. The first, and most obvious, is the state's consequence of raising the costs of doing business in the North Carolina market for Washington apple growers and dealers, while leaving those of North Carolina counterparts unaffected. . . . Second, the statute has the effect of stripping away from the Washington apple industry the competitive and economic advantages it has earned for itself through its expensive inspection and grading system. . . . Third, by prohibiting Washington growers and dealers from marketing apples under their State's grades, the statute has a leveling effect which insidiously operates to the advantage of local apple producers.[68]

The Court also found discrimination based on the disparate impact of a facially neutral law in *C & A Carbone, Inc. v. Town of Clarkstown.*[69] A city adopted an ordinance that required all nonhazardous solid waste in the town to be deposited at a transfer station. The law allowed recyclers to continue to receive solid waste, but they had to bring their nonrecyclables to the transfer station. In other words, the companies could not ship nonrecyclable waste themselves and they had to pay a fee at the transfer station even if they had already sorted the waste.

The ordinance was facially neutral and applied to both in-state and out-of-state companies. Nonetheless, the Court deemed the law discriminatory because of its effect on out-of-staters: "While the immediate effect of the ordinance is to direct local transport of solid waste to a designated site within the local jurisdiction,

---

[65] This is very different from the equal protection context where the Court has held that proof of discriminatory impact is not sufficient, but, rather, when a law is facially neutral, proving race or gender discrimination requires demonstrating a discriminatory purpose for the law. *See* Washington v. Davis, 426 U.S. 229 (1976); *see also* McCleskey v. Kemp, 481 U.S. 279 (1987); Personnel Administrator v. Feeney, 442 U.S. 256 (1979). These cases are discussed in §9.3.3.2.

[66] 432 U.S. 333 (1977).

[67] *Id.* at 339 (citing N.C. Gen. Stat. §106-189.1 (1973)).

[68] *Id.* at 350-351.

[69] 511 U.S. 383 (1994).

its economic effects are interstate in reach. . . . [T]he flow control ordinance discriminates, for it allows only the favored operator to process waste that is within the limits of the town. The ordinance is no less discriminatory because in-state or in-town processors are also covered by the prohibition."[70]

Hunt and *C & A Carbone* clearly establish that a facially neutral law can be found discriminatory if there is proof of a discriminatory impact. Yet in other cases, the Court has found that proof of discriminatory impact is not sufficient, even where there was strong evidence of a discriminatory purpose. Most notably, in *United Haulers Assn. v. Oneida-Herkimer Solid Waste Management Authority*,[71] the Court found constitutional an ordinance very similar to that which it struck down in *C & A Carbone*. In *C & A Carbone*, the city had a "flow control ordinance" for trash that required that haulers bring it to a private facility, whereas in *United Haulers*, the ordinance required that the trash be brought to a state-created public benefit corporation.

The Court found that this distinction was crucial. Chief Justice Roberts, writing for the Court, explained: "We find this difference constitutionally significant. Disposing of trash has been a traditional government activity for years, and laws that favor the government in such areas—but treat every private business, whether in-state or out-of-state, exactly the same—do not discriminate against interstate commerce for purposes of the Commerce Clause. Applying the Commerce Clause test reserved for regulations that do not discriminate against interstate commerce, we uphold these ordinances because any incidental burden they may have on interstate commerce does not outweigh the benefits they confer on the citizens of Oneida and Herkimer Counties."[72]

But the dissent by Justice Alito, joined by Justices Stevens and Kennedy, saw this as a distinction without a difference. It was still the government discriminating in favor of in-state businesses at the expense of out-of-state businesses by requiring that trash be brought to the in-state facility. For this dissent, this discrimination was enough to trigger strict scrutiny and invalidate the ordinance.

For example, in *Exxon Corp. v. Governor of Maryland*, the Court found that a state law was not discriminatory even though it greatly harmed out-of-state oil companies and favored local businesses.[73] A Maryland law prohibited a producer or refiner of petroleum products from operating a retail service station within the state. Because virtually all petroleum products sold in Maryland were produced and refined out of state, the law meant that these out-of-state oil companies could not own service stations in Maryland. The obvious beneficiary was local businesses.

Justice Blackmun explained the discriminatory impact of the Maryland law: "[G]iven the structure of the retail gasoline market in Maryland, the effect . . . is to exclude a class of predominately out-of-state gasoline retailers while providing protection from competition to a class of nonintegrated retailers that is

---

[70] *Id.*
[71] 550 U.S. 330 (2007).
[72] *Id.* at 334.
[73] 437 U.S. 117 (1978).

overwhelmingly comprised of local businessmen."[74] The statistical disparity was enormous: "Of the class of stations statutorily insulated from the competition of the out-of-state integrated firms . . . more than 99 percent were operated by local business interests. Of the class of enterprises excluded entirely from participation in the retail gasoline market, 95 percent were out-of-state firms, operating 98 percent of the stations in the class."[75]

Nonetheless, the majority found that the law was not discriminatory. The majority declared: "[T]he Act creates no barriers whatsoever against interstate independent dealers; it does not prohibit the flow of interstate goods, place added costs upon them, or distinguish between in-state and out-of-state companies in the retail market. The absence of any of these factors fully distinguishes this case from those in which a State has been found to have discriminated against interstate commerce."[76]

Another example where proof of discriminatory impact was insufficient, even though there also was proof of discriminatory purpose, was *Minnesota v. Clover Leaf Creamery Co.*[77] A Minnesota law prohibited the sale of milk in plastic disposable containers, but allowed its sale in paper disposable containers. The law had a substantial discriminatory effect in favor of in-state businesses and against out-of-state businesses because Minnesota had a substantial paper industry but no plastics industry. The law thus created a demand for paper products traditionally produced in state and prevented the out-of-state plastics industry from having access to this Minnesota market. Moreover, the state trial court found that the "actual basis" of the statute "was to promote the economic interests of certain segments of the local dairy and pulpwood industries at the expense of the economic interests of other segments of the dairy industry and the plastics industry."[78]

Yet the Court found that the law was nondiscriminatory. The Court said: "Minnesota's statute does not effect 'simple protectionism,' but 'regulates evenhandedly' by prohibiting all milk retailers from selling their products in plastic, nonreturnable milk containers, without regard to whether the milk, the containers, or the sellers are from outside the State. This statute is therefore unlike statutes discriminating against interstate commerce, which we have consistently struck down."[79]

Thus, in *Hunt* and *C & A Carbone*, disparate impact against out-of-staters was sufficient for finding a law discriminatory, but in *United Haulers*, *Exxon*, and *Clover Leaf Creamery Co.*, proof of discriminatory impact, even with evidence of a protectionist purpose, was insufficient for the Court to deem the law discriminatory. In making sense of these cases, it is important to note that they do not disagree as to the legal standard: All of the cases indicate that proof of discriminatory impact is sufficient for a facially neutral law to be deemed discriminatory. The cases turned

---

[74] *Id.* at 137.
[75] *Id.* at 138.
[76] *Id.* at 126.
[77] 449 U.S. 456 (1981).
[78] *Id.* at 460.
[79] *Id.* at 471-472.

not on differences about the rule, but on the Court's appraisal of the particular facts and its assessment of whether there was discrimination.

In other words, proof of either a protectionist purpose for the law or a substantial discriminatory impact is sufficient to establish that a law is discriminatory. A court will assess each situation and decide whether there is sufficient evidence of discriminatory purpose and/or effect. Although there are no clear criteria for this inquiry, several factors seem particularly important. First, a law is likely to be found discriminatory if its effect is to exclude virtually all out-of-staters from a particular state market, but not if it only excludes one group of out-of-staters. In *Exxon*, only out-of-state petroleum producers and refiners were kept from operating in the state; other out-of-staters could own service stations in the state. In *Clover Leaf Creamery Co.*, the out-of-state plastics industry was disadvantaged, but out-of-state paper companies could sell milk containers in the state.

Second, a law is likely to be found discriminatory if it imposes costs on out-of-staters that in-staters would not have to bear. In *Hunt*, the Court emphasized the costs imposed on Washington apple producers compared to the North Carolina apple industry.

Third, the Court is more likely to find discrimination if it believes that a law is motivated by a protectionist purpose, helping in-staters at the expense of out-of-staters. The Court often has said that the central purpose of the dormant commerce clause is to prevent such protectionist legislation.[80]

In sum, a law will be found discriminatory either if it facially discriminates against out-of-staters or if it is facially neutral and is deemed to have a discriminatory purpose and/or impact. The following section discusses the analysis if a law is found to be nondiscriminatory, and then §5.3.6 considers the analysis if a law is deemed discriminatory. As discussed below, the conclusion as to whether the law is discriminatory or evenhanded is likely to be decisive in determining whether the law will be invalidated or upheld.

§5.3.5   *The Analysis When a State Is Not Discriminating*

Balancing Test

If the court decides that a particular law is not discriminatory against out-of-staters, then a simple balancing test is used: The court balances the law's burdens on interstate commerce against its benefits. The law will be found unconstitutional if the court decides that the burdens from the law exceed its benefits. The Court articulated this in *Pike v. Bruce Church, Inc.*: "Where the statute regulates evenhandedly to effectuate a legitimate local public interest, and its effects on interstate commerce are only incidental, it will be upheld unless the burden imposed on such commerce is clearly excessive in relation to the putative local benefits."[81]

---

[80] *See, e.g.*, H.P. Hood & Sons v. DuMond, 336 U.S. 525, 533, 538 (1949).

[81] 397 U.S. 137, 142 (1970). For a discussion of the origins of this balancing test, *see* David S. Day, Revisiting *Pike*: The Origins of the Nondiscrimination Tier of the Dormant Commerce Clause, 27 Hamline L. Rev. 46 (2004).

The balancing test obviously gives courts enormous discretion because there is no formula or standard for how to compare the burdens on interstate commerce with the benefits to the state or local government; indeed, the court is comparing two very different things.[82] Generally, although certainly not always, a court upholds the law once it decides that it is not discriminatory. For example, in *Exxon Corp. v. Governor of Maryland*, discussed above, the Court upheld a state law that prevented out-of-state petroleum producers or refiners from operating service stations in the state.[83] The Court concluded that the law had a minimal burden on interstate commerce: "Some refiners may choose to withdraw entirely from the Maryland market, but there is no reason to assume that their share of the entire supply will not be replaced promptly by other interstate refiners. The source of the consumers' supply may switch from company-operated stations to independent dealers, but interstate commerce is not subjected to an impermissible burden simply because an otherwise valid regulation causes some business to shift from one interstate supplier to another."[84]

Similarly, in *Minnesota v. Clover Leaf Creamery Co.*, the Court upheld a state law prohibiting the use of nonrecyclable plastic containers for milk after finding that it was not discriminatory.[85] The Court said that the law did not greatly burden interstate commerce because it helped out-of-state paper companies. Moreover, the Court said that the environmental benefits of the law outweighed any harms to interstate commerce. The Court said: "Even granting that the out-of-state plastics industry is burdened relatively more heavily than the Minnesota pulpwood industry, we find that this burden is not clearly excessive in light of the substantial state interest in promoting conservation of energy and other natural resources and easing solid waste disposal problems."[86]

An earlier case using the balancing test to uphold a state law that burdened interstate commerce, but that did not discriminate against out-of-staters, was *Parker v. Brown*.[87] California attempted to fix the prices for California raisins by requiring that two-thirds of all crops be given to a state agency that then set their price.[88] The Court ruled that the California law was constitutional because it protected the economic viability of an important crop at a time of economic vulnerability. The Court accepted the state's argument that without the assurance of an adequate price, raisin production could be dramatically decreased.[89]

---

[82] Justice Scalia has pointed to this as a reason why the balancing test should be eliminated. *See* Bendix Autolite Corp. v. Midwesco Enter., Inc., 486 U.S. 888, 897 (1988) (Scalia, J., dissenting).

[83] 437 U.S. 117 (1978).

[84] *Id.* at 127.

[85] 449 U.S. 456 (1981).

[86] *Id.* at 473.

[87] 317 U.S. 341 (1943).

[88] The Court rejected an antitrust challenge by holding that the Sherman Act did not apply to a state.

[89] *See also* Cities Serv. Gas Co. v. Peerless Oil & Gas Co., 340 U.S. 179 (1950) (upholding a state law fixing the price of natural gas to help conserve that resource); Milk Control Bd. v. Eisenberg Farm Prod., 306 U.S. 346 (1939) (upholding a Pennsylvania law that set the prices for milk that ultimately would be shipped out of state; the Court emphasized the need for the price controls to ensure dairy production).

Another example of the Court upholding a law that was deemed nondiscriminatory is *CTS Corp. v. Dynamics Corp. of America*.[90] An Indiana law limited corporate takeovers by requiring that a purchaser who acquired "control shares" in an Indiana corporation would acquire voting rights only if the transaction was approved by a majority vote of the preexisting disinterested shareholders. At the outset of its analysis, the Court concluded that the law was not discriminatory against out-of-staters. Justice Powell, writing for the Court, explained: "[The] principal objects of dormant Commerce Clause scrutiny are statutes that discriminate against interstate commerce. The Indiana Act is not such a statute. It has the same effects on tender offers whether or not the offerer is a domiciliary or resident of Indiana. Thus, it visits its effects equally upon both interstate and local business."[91]

The Court upheld the law because it concluded that its benefits outweighed its burdens on interstate commerce. The Court said that a "State has an interest in promoting stable relationships among parties involved in the corporations it charters, as well as in ensuring that investors in such corporations have an effective voice in corporate affairs. There can be no doubt that the Act reflects these concerns."[92] At the same time, the Court found that the burden on interstate commerce was not great. The Court noted that the "Act does not prohibit any entity—resident or nonresident—from offering to purchase, or from purchasing, shares in Indiana corporations or from attempting thereby to gain control. It only provides regulatory procedures designed for the better protection of the corporations' shareholders."[93]

Another example where the Court upheld a nondiscriminatory law is *American Trucking Associations, Inc. v. Michigan Public Service Commission*.[94] The issue was whether a flat $100 fee that Michigan charges trucks engaging in intrastate commerce violates the dormant commerce clause. The Court, in an opinion by Justice Breyer, stressed that the law "does not facially discriminate against interstate or out-of-state activities or enterprises. The statute applies evenhandedly to all carriers that make domestic journeys. It does not reflect an effort to tax activity that takes place, in whole or in part, outside the State. Nothing in our case law suggests that such a neutral, locally focused fee or tax is inconsistent with the dormant Commerce Clause."[95]

But a finding that a law does not discriminate is not an assurance that the law will be upheld; there have been some cases where nondiscriminatory laws have been invalidated. In *Bibb v. Navajo Freight Lines*, the Court declared unconstitutional a state law that required that all trucks in the state use curved mudguards to prevent spatter and enhance road safety.[96] The Court found that the law put a substantial burden on interstate commerce because straight mudguards were legal in 45 other states and curved mudguards were illegal in one other state.

---

[90] 481 U.S. 69 (1987).
[91] *Id.* at 87.
[92] *Id.* at 91.
[93] *Id.* at 93.
[94] 545 U.S. 429 (2005).
[95] *Id.* at 434.
[96] 359 U.S. 520 (1959).

Trucks would have to either avoid Illinois or stop at the border to change their mudguards. Moreover, the trial court found that curved mudflaps have "no" safety benefits over straight ones and actually create "hazards previously unknown" by increasing the heat around the truck's tires.[97] The Court thus declared the law unconstitutional and said that it was "one of those cases—few in number—where local safety measures that are nondiscriminatory place an unconstitutional burden on interstate commerce."[98]

Must the State Use the Least Restrictive Alternative?

In weighing the burdens on interstate commerce against the benefits of the law, will a court consider whether the state could achieve the benefits in a manner that places less of a burden on interstate commerce? In stating the test to be used in evaluating nondiscriminatory laws, the Court generally includes a "least restrictive alternative" component. In *Pike v. Bruce Church, Inc.*, the Court, after stating the balancing test quoted above, said: "And the extent of the burden that will be tolerated will of course depend on the nature of the local interest involved, and on whether it could be promoted as well with a lesser impact on interstate activities."[99] Similarly, in *Minnesota v. Clover Leaf Creamery Co.*, after finding that the Minnesota law preventing nonrecyclable plastic milk containers was not discriminatory and that it served important environmental interests, the Court said that the law was constitutional because "no approach with 'a lesser impact on interstate activities' is available."[100]

Yet the Court never has invalidated a nondiscriminatory state law on the ground that the goal could be achieved through a means that is less burdensome on interstate commerce. The cases where laws have been declared unconstitutional under the dormant commerce clause based on the existence of a less restrictive alternative all involved discrimination.[101] Moreover, the "least restrictive alternative" generally is used in constitutional law only where heightened scrutiny is applied;[102] the balancing test applied when laws are not discriminatory is not that type of rigorous judicial review. Thus, although the Court articulates a least restrictive alternative component of its balancing test, it is questionable whether it is likely to be used in evaluating nondiscriminatory state and local laws.

State Laws Regulating the Size of Trucks and Trains

The largest group of cases decided by the Supreme Court concerning nondiscriminatory state laws involved regulations of the size of trucks. The outcome of the cases has varied depending on the facts of the case—the specific content

---

[97] *Id.* at 525.

[98] *Id.* at 529.

[99] 397 U.S. at 142.

[100] 449 U.S. at 473 (citation omitted).

[101] *See, e.g.,* Dean Milk Co. v. Madison, 340 U.S. 349 (1951), discussed below in §5.3.6.

[102] *See* §6.5 (reviewing the levels of scrutiny).

of the state law and the particular evidence concerning its burden on commerce and its safety benefits. For example, in *South Carolina State Highway Department v. Barnwell*, the Court upheld a South Carolina law that prohibited the use on state highways of motor trucks and semitrailer motor trucks whose width exceeds 90 inches and whose weight, including load, exceeds 20,000 pounds.[103] The effect of the South Carolina law was to exclude 85 to 90 percent of the motor trucks used in interstate transport.[104]

Yet the Court upheld the law emphasizing the need for judicial deference to state highway regulations.[105] The Court described how the weight limits might protect South Carolina's roads and how the width restrictions could enhance safety because "as the width of trucks is increased it obstructs the view of the highway, causing much inconvenience and increased hazard in its use."[106]

But in other cases, the Court has invalidated state laws restricting truck size. In *Raymond Motor Transportation, Inc. v. Rice*, the Court unanimously declared unconstitutional a Wisconsin law that generally prevented the operation on state highways of trucks longer than 55 feet and of double-trailer trucks.[107] The law prohibited 65-foot double-trailer trucks, while allowing 55-foot single trucks.

The Court concluded that the "regulations violate the Commerce Clause because they place a substantial burden on interstate commerce and they cannot be said to make more than the most speculative contribution to highway safety."[108] The Court explained that the law put a "substantial burden on the interstate movement of goods" by limiting the ability of trucks to enter Wisconsin.[109] Additionally, the Court said that the State "failed to make even a colorable showing that its regulations contribute to highway safety."[110]

Similarly, in *Kassel v. Consolidated Freightways Corp.*, the Court declared unconstitutional an Iowa law banning 65-foot double trailers.[111] The Court again weighed the "asserted safety purpose against the degree of interference with interstate commerce."[112] The Court said that the "State failed to present any persuasive evidence that 65-foot doubles are less safe than 55-foot singles. . . . Statistical studies supported the view that 65-foot doubles are at least as safe overall as 55-foot singles and 60-foot doubles."[113] Moreover, the Court found that the Iowa law "substantially

---

[103] 303 U.S. 177 (1938).

[104] *Id.* at 182.

[105] *Id.* at 189. In fact, the Court said that its task was "to ascertain upon the whole record whether it is possible to say that the legislative choice is without rational basis." *Id.* at 191-192. The rational basis test is the type of judicial review that is most deferential to the legislature. *See* §6.5 (discussing the standards of review). Subsequently, the Court made it clear that the later cases articulating a balancing test replaced the approach followed in *Barnwell. See* Raymond Motor Transp., Inc. v. Rice, 434 U.S. 429, 443 (1978).

[106] *Barnwell*, 303 U.S. at 196.

[107] 434 U.S. 429 (1978).

[108] *Id.* at 447.

[109] *Id.* at 445.

[110] *Id.* at 448.

[111] 450 U.S. 662 (1981).

[112] *Id.* at 670.

[113] *Id.* at 671, 673.

burdens interstate commerce" by forcing these trucks to avoid Iowa or to detach the trailers and ship them separately.[114]

These cases indicate that the Court will evaluate state laws restricting truck size on a case-by-case basis considering the specific evidence as to the safety benefits of the laws compared to their burden on interstate commerce. The same is true when the Court evaluates state laws limiting train size, although there is probably less of a presumption of deference when a state is regulating railroads as compared to highways. In *Southern Pacific Co. v. Arizona*, the Supreme Court declared unconstitutional a state law that limited train lengths to 14 passenger or 70 freight cars.[115] The Court said that "[e]nforcement of the law in Arizona [must] inevitably result in an impairment of . . . efficient railroad operation because the railroads are subjected to regulation which is not uniform in its application. . . . [The] carrier [must] conform to the lowest train limit restriction of any of the states through which its trains pass, whose laws thus control the carriers' operations both within and without the regulating state."[116] The Court deemed the law unconstitutional because it said that "viewed as a safety measure, [it] affords at most slight and dubious advantage, if any, over unregulated train lengths."[117]

The Court distinguished the earlier ruling in *Barnwell* by noting the differences between railroads and highways.[118] This distinction seems questionable because there is a national interest in the free flow of both trucks and trains. The *Southern Pacific* case is best understood as reflecting the Court's conclusion that the Arizona law put a substantial burden on commerce, but did little to enhance safety.

Laws Where States Attempt to Regulate Out-of-State Businesses

The Court has consistently declared unconstitutional state laws that regulate the out-of-state conduct of businesses. In *Edgar v. MITE Corp.*, the Court declared unconstitutional an Illinois law that required the secretary of state to adjudicate the fairness of tender offers for the purchase of corporate stock and to reject the transaction if the offer was inequitable or would work a fraud on the sellers.[119] The Court said that the law was a "direct restraint on interstate commerce" because the state was controlling "conduct beyond the boundary of the state."[120] The state law regulated sales of stock that occurred outside Illinois. The Court applied the balancing test and found that the law was unconstitutional because it substantially burdened interstate commerce by "hindering the reallocation of economic

---

[114] *Id.* at 674.
[115] 325 U.S. 761 (1945).
[116] *Id.* at 773.
[117] *Id.* at 779
[118] *Id.* at 783.
[119] 457 U.S. 624 (1982).
[120] *Id.* at 642.

resources to their highest-valued use," but there was "nothing to be weighed in the balance to sustain the law."[121]

Brown-Forman Distillers Corp. v. New York State Liquor Authority involved a New York law that required liquor distillers selling wholesale in the state to file a monthly price schedule, to sell at those prices in New York, and to sell at the lowest prices the distiller charged wholesale in any other state for the same month.[122] The Court found the latter provision to violate the dormant commerce clause because it had the "practical effect of . . . control[ling] liquor prices in other states."[123] The Court explained: "While New York may regulate the sale of liquor within its borders, and may seek low prices for its residents, it may not project its legislation into other States by regulating the price to be paid for liquor in those states."[124]

Similarly, in *Healy v. The Beer Institute*, the Court declared unconstitutional a Connecticut law that required beer companies to post their prices each month and to attest that the prices were not higher than their prices in the four states bordering Connecticut.[125] The Court noted that "the Commerce Clause . . . precludes the application of a state statute to commerce that takes place wholly outside the State's borders, whether or not the commerce has effects within the State."[126] The Court said therefore that "[t]he critical inquiry is whether the practical effect of the regulation is to control conduct beyond the boundaries of the State."[127] The Connecticut law was declared unconstitutional because it affected the prices charged out of the state.

Conclusion

If a law does not discriminate against out-of-staters, the Court balances its burdens on interstate commerce against its benefits. The inquiry is very much fact dependent, and the outcome obviously turns on how the Court appraises the burdens and the benefits and how the Court weighs them.[128] As described earlier, the

---

[121] *Id.* at 643.

[122] 476 U.S. 573 (1986).

[123] *Id.* at 643.

[124] *Id.* at 582-583 (citations omitted). The Court also expressly rejected the state's argument that the Twenty-first Amendment provided constitutional authority for the law. The Twenty-first Amendment repealed prohibition and gave states the authority to regulate the "transportation or importation into any State . . . for delivery or use therein" of alcoholic beverages. The Court said that "[t]he Commerce Clause operates with full force whenever one State attempts to regulate the transportation and sale of alcoholic beverages destined for distribution and consumption in a foreign country or another State." *Id.* at 585. The Court came to the same conclusion in *Granholm v. Heald*, 544 U.S. 460 (2005), where it held that the Twenty-first Amendment does not allow states to regulate alcoholic beverages in a manner that violates the dormant commerce clause and thus a state law that allowed in-state wineries, but not out-of-state wineries, to ship wine to consumers through the mail violates the dormant commerce clause.

[125] 491 U.S. 324 (1989).

[126] *Id.* at 336 (citations omitted).

[127] *Id.*

[128] The one exception to this, as described above, is that the Court consistently has declared unconstitutional state laws that have the effect of regulating conduct in other states.

test has been criticized for being unpredictable and arbitrary.[129] Indeed, Justices Scalia and Thomas have urged the abandonment of the balancing test. Justice Scalia contends that the balancing test "is ill suited to the judicial function and should be undertaken rarely if at all."[130] However, the majority of the Court has shown no indication of taking this position and abandoning dormant commerce clause analysis of nondiscriminatory laws. The balancing test, however subjective and unpredictable, is firmly established and frequently applied.

§5.3.6   The Analysis When a State Is Discriminating

Presumption Against Constitutionality

There is a strong presumption against discriminatory laws that burden interstate commerce. A state or local law that discriminates against out-of-staters will be upheld only if it is proved that the law is necessary to achieve an important government purpose. The Court has declared that a discriminatory law "invokes the strictest scrutiny of any purported legitimate local purpose and of the absence of nondiscriminatory alternatives."[131] The Court has observed that "State laws that discriminate against interstate commerce face 'a virtually *per se* rule of invalidity.' "[132]

Thus, judicial review of discriminatory laws involves scrutiny of both the ends served by the law and the means used. As to the ends, in many cases, the Court has said that a law that discriminates will be upheld if it is necessary to achieve a "legitimate local purpose."[133] Yet this is puzzling phrasing. Requiring only a "legitimate" purpose is characteristic of highly deferential rational basis review and not the "strictest scrutiny," which the Court says is appropriate when a law discriminates against out-of-staters.[134] Moreover, the cases described below indicate that the Court requires more than just a legitimate purpose; a discriminatory state or local law must serve an important purpose in order to be upheld.

At the very least, a state law that discriminates against interstate commerce must be justified by a purpose that is "unrelated to economic protectionism."[135] The Court has explained that "[s]hielding in-state industries from out-of-state competition is almost never a legitimate local purpose, and state laws that amount

---

[129] *See* text accompanying notes 42-44, *supra.*

[130] CTS Corp. v. Dynamics Corp., 481 U.S. at 95 (1987) (Scalia, J., dissenting).

[131] Hughes v. Oklahoma, 441 U.S. 322, 337 (1979).

[132] Granholm v. Heald, 544 U.S. 460, 476 (2005).

[133] *See, e.g.,* Granholm v. Heald, 544 U.S. at 489; Maine v. Taylor, 477 U.S. 131, 138 (1986); Sporhase v. Nebraska, 458 U.S. 941, 954 (1982); Hunt v. Washington State Apple Advertising Comm., 432 U.S. 333 (1977).

[134] Maine v. Taylor, 477 U.S. 131, 144 (1986), quoting Hughes v. Oklahoma, 441 U.S. at 337 ("the proffered justification for any local discrimination against interstate commerce must be subjected to 'the strictest scrutiny' ").

[135] Fort Gratiot Sanitary Landfill, Inc. v. Michigan Dept. of Natural Resources, 504 U.S. 353, 359 (1992); New Energy Co. of Indiana v. Limbach, 486 U.S. 269, 274 (1988).

to simple economic protectionism consequently have been subject to a virtually per se rule of invalidity."[136]

As to the review of the means used, it is clearly established that a discriminatory law will be upheld only if the "purpose could not be served as well by available nondiscriminatory means."[137] For example, in *Dean Milk Co. v. City of Madison,* the Court declared unconstitutional Madison, Wisconsin's requirement that milk sold there had to be pasteurized within five miles of the city.[138] The Court found that the law discriminated against milk from other states, notably Illinois, and explained that Madison could achieve its goal of ensuring safe milk by less discriminatory alternatives such as by sending its inspectors to importing producers or by relying on inspections by federal authorities.[139]

Similarly, in *Hughes v. Oklahoma,* the Court declared unconstitutional a state law that prevented the shipment of minnows out of the state.[140] After concluding that the law was facially discriminatory against out-of-staters by attempting to restrict use of the resource to in-staters, the Court stated: "Far from choosing the least discriminatory alternative, Oklahoma has chosen to 'conserve' its minnows in the way that most overtly discriminates against interstate commerce. The State places no limits on the numbers of minnows that can be taken by licensed minnow dealers; nor does it limit in any way how these minnows may be disposed of within the State."[141]

The strong presumption against state laws that discriminate against out-of-staters means that usually such laws are declared unconstitutional under the dormant commerce clause. But the test is not always fatal; occasionally, the Supreme Court finds that a discriminatory law is necessary to serve an important purpose. For example, in *Maine v. Taylor,* the Supreme Court upheld a Maine law that prohibited the importing of live baitfish into the state.[142] The Court found that the discriminatory law protected Maine's "unique and fragile fisheries" from "significant threats" from parasites that were prevalent in out-of-state baitfish, but not common in Maine.[143] Also, the Court observed that nonnative species of fish that were inadvertently included with baitfish could pose a threat by "preying on native species, or by disrupting the environment in more subtle ways."[144]

The Court upheld the Maine law because it concluded that there was no less discriminatory way to prevent these threats. The Court noted that there was "no satisfactory way to inspect shipments of live baitfish for parasites or commingled species."[145] The Court concluded that "Maine's ban on the importation of live

---

[136] Maine v. Taylor, 477 U.S. at 148 (citations omitted); *see also* Granholm v. Heald, 544 U.S. at 576.
[137] *Id.*
[138] 340 U.S. 349 (1951).
[139] *Id.* at 354-355.
[140] 441 U.S. 322 (1979).
[141] *Id.* at 337-338.
[142] 477 U.S. 131 (1986).
[143] *Id.* at 141.
[144] *Id.*
[145] *Id.*

baitfish serves legitimate local purposes that could not adequately be served by available nondiscriminatory alternatives."[146]

In considering how the Court has applied this test to various types of laws that discriminate against out-of-staters, several categories of laws can be identified: laws that limit the access by out-of-staters to in-state resources; laws that limit access to local markets by out-of-state businesses; and laws that require use of local businesses. Each of these types of discriminatory laws is reviewed in turn. These categories are not exhaustive, but rather are a way of grouping some of the more common situations that arise where states discriminate against out-of-staters.

Laws That Limit Access to In-State Resources

Many cases have involved attempts by states to reserve state resources for in-staters. Such laws will be invalidated unless the state identifies a valid purpose that cannot be achieved in a less discriminatory way. The reality is that it is extremely difficult to identify any legitimate reason why in-staters should have access to a state's resources that is denied to out-of-staters. For example, in *City of Philadelphia v. New Jersey*, described above, the state attempted to reserve its scarce landfill space for in-state refuse.[147] The Court found this to be an impermissible protectionist action and declared the law unconstitutional. Likewise, in *Fort Gratiot Sanitary Landfill, Inc. v. Michigan Department of Natural Resources*, the Court declared unconstitutional a law that prevented a landfill operator from accepting out-of-county waste.[148] Similarly, in *Hughes v. Oklahoma*, also described above, the Court declared unconstitutional a state law that essentially reserved profiting from minnow fishing exclusively for in-state residents.[149]

Although *Philadelphia*, *Fort Gratiot*, and *Hughes* involved natural resources, the same principle applies to all types of resources in a state. For instance, in *H.P. Hood & Sons v. Du Mond*, the Court declared unconstitutional a New York law that prevented a company from constructing an additional depot for receiving milk.[150] The effect of the New York law was to keep more milk for in-staters at the expense of those in Massachusetts. The Court declared the law unconstitutional as violating the dormant commerce clause because there was not a permissible nonprotectionist purpose for it. In *New England Power Co. v. New Hampshire*, the Court declared unconstitutional a state law that prevented electricity produced in the state from being conveyed outside the state.[151]

The law need not prohibit use of in-state resources to violate the dormant commerce clause; a discriminatory fee for use of a state's resources also will be declared unconstitutional. In *Chemical Waste Management, Inc. v. Hunt*, the Court invalidated a state law that imposed a fee on out-of-staters that disposed hazardous

---

[146] *Id.* at 151.
[147] 437 U.S. 617 (1978).
[148] 504 U.S. 353 (1992).
[149] 441 U.S. 322 (1979).
[150] 336 U.S. 525 (1949).
[151] 455 U.S. 331 (1982).

wastes in the state, but collected no such fee from in-staters.[152] The law limited the ability of out-of-staters to use the state's land by charging a fee that was not imposed on hazardous waste generated within the state. Similarly, in *Oregon Waste Systems, Inc. v. Department of Environmental Quality of the State of Oregon*, the Court declared unconstitutional an Oregon law that charged a greater fee for disposal of wastes generated out of state than for wastes generated in state.[153] The law imposed a $2.25 per ton surcharge on disposal of out-of-state waste, but only a $0.85 per ton surcharge on waste generated in state. The Court declared this unconstitutional because there was no evidence that it was based on actual costs imposed on the state in disposing of waste from other states.

In all of these cases, states were attempting to preserve a resource—land, minnows, milk, electricity—for in-staters by limiting shipments out of state. All were invalidated as violating the dormant commerce clause.

Laws That Limit Access to Local Markets by Out-of-Staters

Another common type of dormant commerce clause case before the Supreme Court involves a state's attempt to gain an economic advantage for its citizens by limiting the ability of out-of-staters to compete in the state market. Such laws can take many forms. The most blatant type of law is a state law that expressly excludes out-of-staters from doing business in the state. For instance, in *Lewis v. BT Investment Managers*, the Court declared unconstitutional a Florida law that barred out-of-state banks from owning Florida investment advisory businesses.[154] The law explicitly precluded competition from out-of-state banks.

Sometimes states impose regulations that have the effect of limiting the ability of out-of-staters to do business in a state by imposing additional costs on them. For example, in *Hunt v. Washington State Apple Advertising Commission*, the Court declared unconstitutional a North Carolina law that prevented the marketing of apples with gradings in addition to those prescribed by the federal government.[155] As described above, the Court saw the law as increasing the costs for Washington apple producers and thus helping in-state growers gain an advantage.

More recently, in *Granholm v. Heald*, the Supreme Court invalidated state laws that allowed in-state wineries to ship wine directly to consumers through the mail, but prevented out-of-state wineries from doing so.[156] Justice Kennedy, writing for the Court, described this as the type of protectionist legislation that clearly violates the dormant commerce clause.

Four Justices dissented and would have allowed the law based on the Twenty-first Amendment, which repealed prohibition and allows states to regulate the sale of alcoholic beverages. The majority, however, rejected this argument and

---

[152] 504 U.S. 334 (1992).
[153] 511 U.S. 93 (1994).
[154] 447 U.S. 27 (1980).
[155] 432 U.S. 333 (1977).
[156] 544 U.S. 460 (2005).

concluded that a state must exercise its power under the Twenty-first Amendment in a manner consistent with other constitutional requirements. Justice Kennedy's majority opinion concluded by declaring: "States have broad power to regulate liquor under §2 of the Twenty-first Amendment. This power, however, does not allow States to ban, or severely limit, the direct shipment of out-of-state wine while simultaneously authorizing direct shipment by in-state producers. If a State chooses to allow direct shipment of wine, it must do so on evenhanded terms. Without demonstrating the need for discrimination, New York and Michigan have enacted regulations that disadvantage out-of-state wine producers. Under our Commerce Clause jurisprudence, these regulations cannot stand."[157]

Maine v. Taylor—one of the rare cases where discrimination against out-of-staters was allowed—also was a case where out-of-staters were denied access to a state's market.[158] As described above, the Court allowed this restriction because admitting out-of-state baitfish into Maine risked introducing parasites and predators into its waters. In other words, the Court perceived the Maine objective not as economically helping the Maine baitfish industry at the expense of out-of-staters, but as protecting Maine's fragile marine ecology.

Laws That Require Use of Local Businesses

Sometimes state and local governments attempt to help their citizens at the expense of out-of-staters by requiring that tasks be performed locally. *Cooley v. Board of Wardens*, discussed above, was an example of this in that Pennsylvania required either the use of a local pilot or the payment of a fee for bringing a ship into the Port of Philadelphia.[159]

Another example, also discussed above, was *Dean Milk Co. v. City of Madison*, where the Court declared unconstitutional a law requiring that all milk sold in the city be pasteurized within five miles of it.[160] The law obviously advantaged businesses in or near the city, at the expense of those farther away. Subsequently, in *C & A Carbone, Inc. v. Town of Clarkstown*, the Court declared unconstitutional a local ordinance that required that all nonrecyclable waste be taken to a local waste transfer station.[161] The Court noted that the requirement "ensures that the town-sponsored facility will be profitable" and diverted business away from other counties and states.[162]

Another example of a law requiring use of local businesses was *Pike v. Bruce Church, Inc.*, where the Court invalidated an Arizona regulation that required cantaloupes grown there to be packed in the state rather than in another state.[163] The Court said that it "has viewed with particular suspicion state statutes requiring

---

[157] *Id.* at 493.
[158] 477 U.S. 131 (1986).
[159] 53 U.S. (12 How.) 299 (1851).
[160] 340 U.S. 349 (1951).
[161] 511 U.S. 383 (1994).
[162] *Id.* at 393.
[163] 397 U.S. 137 (1970).

business operations to be performed in the home State that could more efficiently be performed elsewhere."[164]

Likewise, in *Wyoming v. Oklahoma*, the Court declared unconstitutional an Oklahoma law that required that coal-burning power plants use at least 10 percent Oklahoma coal.[165] The Court found that the requirement for use of locally produced coal was "protectionist and discriminatory."[166]

Although *Cooley* upheld a state law that required use of local pilots, more recent cases have consistently found such laws unconstitutional. Attempting to help in-state businesses at the expense of out-of-staters is exactly the type of protectionism forbidden by the dormant commerce clause.

Conclusion

State laws that discriminate against out-of-staters are almost always declared unconstitutional. Such a law will be allowed only if it is proved that the law is necessary—the least restrictive means—to achieve a nonprotectionist purpose. Although the Court repeatedly has said that it must be a "legitimate" purpose, it also has said that the "strictest scrutiny" is to be applied, which implies that there must be an important or even a compelling reason for the law.

§5.3.7   Exceptions

There are two exceptions where laws that otherwise would violate the dormant commerce clause will be allowed. One exception is if Congress approves the state law. Even a clearly unconstitutional, discriminatory state law will be allowed if approved by Congress because Congress has plenary power to regulate commerce among the states. The second exception is termed the "market participant exception": A state may favor its own citizens in receiving benefits from government programs or in dealing with government-owned businesses. Each exception is discussed in turn.

§5.3.7.1   Congressional Approval

State Laws Are Allowed If Approved by Congress

The Supreme Court consistently has held that the Constitution empowers Congress to regulate commerce among the states and that therefore state laws burdening commerce are permissible, even when they otherwise would violate the dormant commerce clause, if they have been approved by Congress. The Court thus declared: "If Congress ordains that the States may freely regulate an aspect of

---

[164] *Id.* at 145.
[165] 502 U.S. 437 (1992).
[166] *Id.* at 145.

interstate commerce, any action taken by a State within the scope of the congressional authorization is rendered invulnerable to Commerce Clause challenge."[167] This means that Congress may "confer . . . upon the States an ability to restrict the flow of interstate commerce that they would not otherwise enjoy."[168]

Of course, if Congress has acted, the commerce power no longer is dormant. The issue would be whether the federal law is a constitutional exercise of the commerce power; if so, the law must be followed even if it means upholding laws that otherwise would violate the Constitution. It is interesting that this is one of the few areas where Congress has the clear authority to overrule a Supreme Court decision interpreting the Constitution. If the Court deems a matter to violate the dormant commerce clause, Congress can respond by enacting a law approving the action, thereby effectively overruling the Supreme Court.[169] However, although the law will not violate the dormant commerce clause, it still can be challenged under other constitutional provisions. Congressional approval does not excuse a violation of equal protection, or the privileges and immunities clause, or other constitutional provisions besides the dormant commerce clause. For instance, in *Metropolitan Life Insurance Co. v. Ward*, the Court found that a state tax that discriminated against out-of-state insurance companies violated the equal protection clause, even though a federal law permitted such discriminatory taxes, and thus there was not a violation of the dormant commerce clause.[170]

Examples

This principle has been long followed. In *In re Rahrer*, the Court upheld a state law restricting the importation and sale of alcoholic beverages.[171] Earlier, the Court had declared unconstitutional an almost identical law from another state,[172] but Congress then adopted a law expressly permitting such state regulation of alcoholic beverages. In light of the new federal statute, the Court shifted positions and allowed the state law. The Court said that "[t]he power to regulate is solely in the general government, and it is an essential part of that regulation to prescribe the regular means for accomplishing the introduction and incorporation of articles into and with the mass of property in the country or State."[173]

In *Prudential Insurance Co. v. Benjamin*, the Court said that Congress could approve state taxes that discriminate against interstate commerce and that otherwise would be unconstitutional.[174] A state imposed a tax on insurance companies,

---

[167] Western & Southern Life Ins. Co. v. State Bd. of Equalization of Cal., 451 U.S. 648, 652-653 (1981).

[168] Lewis v. BT Investment Managers, Inc., 447 U.S. 27, 44 (1980).

[169] This also potentially occurs when Congress legislates under §5 of the Fourteenth Amendment. *See* §3.7.2.

[170] 470 U.S. 869 (1985).

[171] 140 U.S. 545 (1891).

[172] Leisy v. Hardin, 135 U.S. 100 (1890).

[173] *Rahrer*, 140 U.S. at 562.

[174] 328 U.S. 408 (1946); the subject of state taxation of interstate commerce is discussed below in §5.4.

but exempted in-state companies. The Court said that the federal McCarran Act "was a determination by Congress that state taxes, which in its silence might be held invalid as discriminatory, do not place on interstate insurance business a burden which it is unable generally to bear or should not bear in the competition with local business."[175] The Court declared that Congress's "broad authority" over commerce means that if Congress acts, "limitations imposed for the preservation of their powers become inoperative."[176]

Similarly, in *Western and Southern Life Insurance Co. v. State Board of Equalization of California*, the Court said that a state law imposing a discriminatory and retaliatory tax on out-of-state insurance companies was permissible because the McCarran-Ferguson Act removes entirely any commerce clause restriction on a state's power to tax the insurance business.[177] The Court said that this Act "removed all Commerce Clause limitations on the authority of the States to regulate and tax the business of insurance."[178] Therefore, the tax was permitted even though it otherwise would have violated the dormant commerce clause.

In *Northeast Bancorp. v. Board of Governors*, the Court applied this principle and upheld Connecticut and Massachusetts laws that allowed out-of-state holding companies to acquire in-state banks if they were from another state in the region that accorded reciprocal privileges to Connecticut and Massachusetts companies.[179] The Court said that a federal law, the Bank Holding Company Act of 1956, expressly authorized such state regulation. The Court recognized that absent congressional approval, the Connecticut and Massachusetts laws would violate the dormant commerce clause.[180] But the Court said: "Here the commerce power of Congress is not dormant, but has been exercised. . . . When Congress so chooses, state actions which it plainly authorizes are invulnerable to constitutional attack under the Commerce Clause."[181]

§5.3.7.2   The Market Participant Exception

Defined

The market participant exception provides that a state may favor its own citizens in dealing with government-owned business and in receiving benefits from government programs. In other words, if the state is literally a participant in the market, such as with a state-owned business, and not a regulator, the dormant commerce clause does not apply. Discrimination against out-of-staters is allowed that otherwise would be impermissible. However, it must be emphasized that even

---

[175] *Id.* at 431.
[176] *Id.* at 434.
[177] 451 U.S. 648 (1981).
[178] *Id.* at 653.
[179] 472 U.S. 159 (1985).
[180] *Id.* at 174.
[181] *Id.*

though the laws will be permissible under the dormant commerce clause, the laws might be vulnerable to other constitutional challenges such as those based on the privileges and immunities clause of Article IV or equal protection.[182]

The Court initially articulated the market participant exception in *Hughes v. Alexandria Scrap Corp.*[183] In *Hughes*, the Court upheld a Maryland law designed to rid the state of abandoned automobiles by having the state pay for inoperable cars. The state required minimal documentation of ownership from in-staters, but required more elaborate proof from out-of-staters through either a certificate of title, a police certificate vesting title, or a bill of sale from a police auction. The Court said that the state was a market participant by purchasing the cars and that therefore its discriminatory actions against out-of-staters did not violate the dormant commerce clause. The Court declared: "Nothing in the purposes animating the Commerce Clause forbids a State, in the absence of congressional action, from participating in the market and exercising the right to favor its own citizens over others."[184]

The Court applied *Hughes* in *Reeves, Inc. v. Stake*, where the Court upheld a cement company owned by South Dakota charging less to in-state purchasers and more to out-of-state purchasers.[185] The Court said the "basic distinction . . . between States as market participants and States as market regulators makes good sense and sound law."[186] The Court said that there "is no indication of a constitutional plan to limit the ability of the States themselves to operate freely in the free market."[187] The Court said that South Dakota, as the seller of cement, was clearly a market participant and thus was able to favor in-state purchasers over those from out of the state.

The market participant exception is not limited to state-owned businesses; states also may favor their citizens in receiving benefits from government programs. For example, in *White v. Massachusetts Council of Construction Employers*, the Court upheld a city's ordinance that required that all construction projects financed by the city must use a workforce composed of at least 50 percent residents of the city.[188] The Court began by noting that "*Alexandria Scrap* and *Reeves* . . . stand for the proposition that when a state or local government enters the market as a participant it is not subject to the restraints of the Commerce Clause."[189] The Court said that the city could favor its residents over out-of-staters in employment for government-funded construction projects because "it was a market participant."[190]

---

[182] The privileges and immunities clause is discussed in §5.5; equal protection is considered in Chapter 9.

[183] 426 U.S. 794 (1976).

[184] *Id.* at 810.

[185] 447 U.S. 429 (1980).

[186] *Id.* at 436.

[187] *Id.* at 437.

[188] 460 U.S. 204 (1983).

[189] *Id.* at 208.

[190] *Id.* at 215. Although the law did not violate the dormant commerce clause, it still could be challenged under other constitutional provisions such as the privileges and immunities clause of Article IV. In *United Building & Construction Trades Council v. Mayor & Council of Camden*, 465 U.S. 208 (1984), the Court declared unconstitutional a city's ordinance that required that 40 percent of the

Limitation on the Market Participant Exception

The Court has imposed one important limit on the scope of the market participant exception: State businesses may favor in-state purchasers, but they may not attach conditions to a sale that discriminate against interstate commerce. In *South-Central Timber Development, Inc. v. Wunnicke*, the Court declared unconstitutional an Alaska law that required that purchasers of state-owned timber have the timber processed in Alaska before it is shipped out of state.[191] The Court said that "[t]he limit of the market-participant doctrine must be that it allows a State to impose burdens on commerce within the market in which it is a participant, but allows it to go no further. The State may not impose conditions, whether by statute, regulation, or contract, that have a substantial regulatory effect outside of that particular market."[192] The Court explained that "[u]nless the market is relatively narrowly defined, the doctrine has the potential of swallowing up the rule that States may not impose substantial burdens on interstate commerce even if they act with the permissible state purpose of fostering local industry."[193]

Thus, the Court drew a distinction between the ability of a state to prefer its own citizens in the "initial disposition of goods when it is a market participant" and a "State's attachment of restrictions on dispositions subsequent to the goods coming to rest in private hands."[194]

Should There Be a Market Participant Exception?

The market participant exception can be criticized on several grounds.[195] First, the dormant commerce clause is meant to stop protectionist actions by state governments; protectionism should not be allowed regardless of whether the state is acting in a proprietary or a regulatory capacity. Second, there is not a clear distinction between situations where the government is acting as a regulator and when it is a market participant.

For example, in *New England Power Co. v. New Hampshire*, the Court declared unconstitutional a law that limited the ability of electricity to be shipped out of the state without the permission of the state's public utility commission.[196] The state was trying to retain for its citizens the benefits of the electricity created by the state-owned water, which created the hydroelectric power. The Court said

---

employees on city-funded construction projects be residents of the city. The Court found that the law violated the privileges and immunities clause and expressly distinguished *White* as holding only that the law did not violate the dormant commerce clause; the issue of the privileges and immunities clause is distinct, and there is not a market participant exception to this constitutional provision. *Id.* at 213. The privileges and immunities clause is discussed below in §5.5.

[191] 467 U.S. 82 (1984) (plurality opinion).
[192] *Id.* at 97.
[193] *Id.* at 97-98 (citations omitted).
[194] *Id.* at 98.
[195] For a criticism of the market participant exception, *see* Karl Manheim, New-Age Federalism and the Market Participant Doctrine, 22 Ariz. St. L.J. 559 (1990).
[196] 455 U.S. 331 (1982).

that the state "has done more than regulate the use of a resource that it assertedly owns; it has restricted the sale of electric energy, a product entirely distinct from the river waters used to produce it."[197] But if a state can prefer its own citizens with regard to state-owned resources, it is not clear why this distinction should matter.

On the other hand, the market participant exception can be defended as allowing citizens in a state to recoup the benefits of the taxes that they pay. Professor Laurence Tribe says that the exception is justified by "the sense of fairness in allowing a community to retain the public benefits created by its own public investment."[198] The market participant exception also is defended on the ground that "state spending programs are less coercive than regulatory programs or taxes with similar purposes" and they "seem less hostile to other states and less consistent with the conception of union than discriminatory regulation or taxation."[199]

These benefits, however, can be challenged. Under other constitutional provisions, such as the privileges and immunities clause and equal protection, states are prohibited from favoring in-staters over out-of-staters in receiving benefits from the government.[200] Moreover, there is no inherent reason why there is less coercion or less hostility when the state is discriminating against out-of-staters as a market participant than when it is acting in other capacities.

§5.4   STATE TAXATION OF INTERSTATE COMMERCE

§5.4.1   The Test Used to Evaluate State Taxes of Interstate Commerce

One way in which states can burden interstate commerce is by taxing it. In general, the same basic principles apply to state taxation of interstate commerce as to state regulation of commerce: Discriminatory taxes are virtually never allowed, while nondiscriminatory taxes are much more likely to be permitted. Yet the topic of state taxation of interstate commerce requires separate consideration because the

---

[197] *Id.* at 338.

[198] Laurence Tribe, Constitutional Choices 145 (1985).

[199] Regan, *supra* note 2, at 1194.

[200] *See, e.g.,* United Building & Construction Trades Council v. Mayor & Council of Camden, 465 U.S. 208 (1984) (declaring unconstitutional under the privileges and immunities clause a city law that favored hiring of city residents for city-funded construction projects); Shapiro v. Thompson, 394 U.S. 618 (1969) (declaring unconstitutional, as violating equal protection, a state law that created a one-year residency requirement for receipt of welfare benefits).

Court, both historically and currently, has formulated distinct tests for evaluating state taxes that burden interstate commerce.[1]

Historical Approach

From 1873 until 1977, the Court applied the rule that a state may not directly tax interstate commerce.[2] The Court applied this rule to invalidate a wide variety of state taxes, including a gross receipts tax on interstate sales,[3] a sales tax on interstate sales,[4] and a license tax on solicitors of orders for interstate sales.[5] The Court, however, allowed taxes that were deemed to have only an indirect burden on interstate commerce.[6]

The historical approach can be criticized for many reasons. The direct/indirect distinction is inherently arbitrary and unpredictable. The effect of a tax on interstate commerce is a matter of degree, and where the line is drawn between what is direct as opposed to indirect is inherently arbitrary.

Moreover, this approach to taxation of interstate commerce was completely different from how the Court evaluated state regulations of interstate commerce. A state law that was deemed to tax interstate commerce directly would be automatically declared unconstitutional. But a state law that regulated interstate commerce, even in a discriminatory manner, would be subjected to the analysis under the dormant commerce clause. As Professor Hartman asked: "What is there in the commerce clause that justifies the Court's conclusion that the states have concurrent power to regulate interstate commerce but do not have the power to tax any facet of interstate commerce?"[7]

Current Approach

In *Complete Auto Transit, Inc. v. Brady*, the Court abandoned this historical approach and adopted a test that treats state taxation of interstate commerce similarly to state regulation of interstate commerce.[8] *Complete Auto Transit* addressed the constitutionality of a Mississippi tax on gross revenues for the privilege of doing business in the state. Complete Auto took cars shipped from out of state by General Motors and hauled them to car dealers. The issue was whether the

---

§5.4 [1] For a detailed review of state taxation of interstate commerce, *see* Jerome R. Hellerstein & Walter Hellerstein, State Taxation (2d ed. 1993).

[2] *See, e.g.*, Spector Motor Serv. v. O'Connor, 340 U.S. 602 (1951). For a discussion of this rule and how it has been changed, *see* William B. Lockhart, A Revolution in State Taxation of Commerce?, 65 Minn. L. Rev. 1025 (1981).

[3] Freeman v. Hewit, 329 U.S. 249 (1946).

[4] McLeod v. J.E. Dilworth Co., 322 U.S. 327 (1944).

[5] Mills v. Portland, 268 U.S. 325 (1925).

[6] *See, e.g.*, United States Glue Co. v. Oak Creek, 247 U.S. 321 (1918) (upholding net income tax on interstate businesses); McGoldrick v. Berwind-White Coal Mining Co., 309 U.S. 33 (1940) (upholding sales tax on interstate transactions).

[7] Paul J. Hartman, State Taxation of Interstate Commerce: A Survey and an Appraisal, 46 Va. L. Rev. 1051, 1071-1072 (1960).

[8] 430 U.S. 274 (1977).

Mississippi tax was unconstitutional because it was applied to an activity that was a part of interstate commerce.

The Supreme Court unanimously upheld the Mississippi law and emphasized that the challenger did "not allege that its activity which Mississippi taxes does not have a sufficient nexus with the State; or that the tax discriminates against interstate commerce; or that the tax is unfairly apportioned; or that it is unrelated to services provided by the State."[9] The Court made it clear that this functional approach to evaluating state taxes of interstate commerce was meant to replace the earlier rule that it saw "as a triumph of formalism over substance, providing little guidance even as to formal requirements."[10]

Since 1977, the Court has consistently followed the four-part test articulated in *Complete Auto Transit, Inc. v. Brady*. A state tax does not violate the commerce clause if

(1)   it is applied to an activity with a substantial nexus to the taxing state;

(2)   it is fairly apportioned so as to tax only the activities connected to the taxing state;

(3)   it does not discriminate against out-of-staters; and

(4)   it is fairly related to services provided by the state.

Each of these four requirements is discussed in turn below.[11]

Remedies

Generally, relief for unconstitutional state taxes must be sought in state court pursuant to state law causes of action, but Supreme Court review is available to ensure adequate remedies for constitutional violations. The Eleventh Amendment to the United States Constitution precludes suits against state governments in federal court.[12] Additionally, the Tax Injunction Act prevents federal courts from enjoining the collection of any state tax "where a plain, speedy, and efficient remedy may be had in the courts of such State."[13] The Court has interpreted the Tax Injunction Act as also precluding federal court declaratory relief against state taxes.[14] Moreover, the Supreme Court has said that principles of comity and federal-

---

[9] *Id.* at 277-278.

[10] *Id.* at 281.

[11] For an analysis and critique of this test, *see* Jesse H. Choper & Tung Yin, State Taxation and the Dormant Commerce Clause: The Object-Measure Approach, 1998 Sup. Ct. Rev. 193 ("Our thesis is that the *Complete Auto* test embodies the basic values underlying the Dormant Commerce Clause, but that it is more complicated than it needs to be, primarily because several of its parts are functionally redundant.").

[12] *See* Erwin Chemerinsky, Federal Jurisdiction ch. 7 (6th ed. 2011) (describing the law concerning the Eleventh Amendment).

[13] 28 U.S.C. §1341; *see* Chemerinsky, *supra* note 12, at ch. 11 (discussing the Tax Injunction Act).

[14] California v. Grace Brethren Church, 457 U.S. 393 (1982).

ism keep federal courts from entertaining damage actions against state taxes when state law furnishes an adequate legal remedy.[15]

The Court extended this to say that state courts also could not award declaratory or injunctive relief under 42 U.S.C. §1983 against state taxes.[16] In *National Private Truck Council, Inc. v. Oklahoma Tax Commission*, the Court held that §1983 was not available in state courts to provide relief from state taxes that violate the dormant commerce clause when there is an adequate state remedy in the form of refunds of collected taxes.[17]

The result is that federal courts and even federal law are generally not available for relief against states for taxes that violate the dormant commerce clause. Such suits to remedy unconstitutional taxes generally must be brought in state court. Nonetheless, the Supreme Court has made it clear that it will review state court decisions to ensure that state courts carry out their duty to compensate victims of unconstitutional taxes that violate the commerce clause.[18]

§5.4.2   The Requirement for a Substantial Nexus to the Taxing State

A state tax will be allowed under the commerce clause only if there is a substantial nexus — a significant connection — between the taxing state and the activity or the property being taxed. If an activity or an entity has little connection to a state, it is unfair for the state to impose a tax.

Early Cases

An earlier case applying this requirement was *Braniff Airways, Inc. v. Nebraska State Board of Equalization and Assessment*, which allowed Nebraska to tax Braniff Airways' flight equipment in that state, even though it had no real property there.[19] The Court found that the airline's 18 scheduled flights a day to and from Nebraska were a sufficient nexus to permit the tax.

Another important earlier case concerning the requirement for a nexus was *Northwestern States Portland Cement Co. v. Minnesota*, where the Court held that it was constitutional for a state to collect a net income tax from an out-of-state corporation whose only local activity was the solicitation of sales through the use of sales

---

[15] Fair Assessment in Real Estate Assn. v. McNary, 454 U.S. 100 (1981).

[16] Earlier the Supreme Court had ruled that violations of the dormant commerce clause are a constitutional violation for purposes of §1983. Dennis v. Higgins, 498 U.S. 439 (1991). The Court has not in any way overruled this holding, but has limited its impact by holding that suits against the state cannot be brought in federal or state court pursuant to §1983.

[17] 515 U.S. 582 (1995).

[18] *See, e.g.,* Harper v. Virginia Dept. of Taxation, 509 U.S. 86 (1993); McKesson Corp. v. Division of Alcoholic Beverages and Tobacco, 496 U.S. 18 (1990).

[19] 347 U.S. 590 (1954).

personnel.[20] The Court found that the solicitation of business within the state was a sufficient nexus to permit the tax.[21]

Relationship to Due Process

There are actually two distinct constitutional sources for the nexus requirement: the commerce clause and due process. The Court has indicated that due process requires that a company have "minimum contacts" with a state in order to be subjected to its taxes.[22] For example, in *Asarco Inc. v. Idaho State Tax Commission*[23] and *F.W. Woolworth Co. v. Taxation and Revenue Department of New Mexico*,[24] the Supreme Court declared that state taxes on dividend income derived by resident corporations that had no other contact with the taxing state violated due process.

The Supreme Court, however, has indicated that the requirement for minimum contacts and the substantial nexus requirement might be different in particular cases; proving minimum contacts does not necessarily demonstrate the significant connection required by the commerce clause. In *Quill Corporation v. North Dakota*, the Court held that there is not a substantial nexus when an interstate seller solicits sales in a state only by mail with orders then shipped into the state by mail or common carrier.[25] The Court expressly found that because the company "has purposefully directed its activities at North Dakota residents, the magnitude of those contacts are more than sufficient for due process purposes, and the tax is related to the benefits Quill receives from access to the State."[26]

However, the Court found that even though due process was met, the nexus test under the commerce clause was not satisfied. The Court said that "a mail order house may have the minimum contacts with a taxing State as required by the Due Process Clause, and yet lack the substantial nexus with the State required by the Commerce Clause. These requirements are not identical and are animated by different constitutional concerns and policies."[27] The Court explained that due process is ultimately about the fairness of the government's activity, whereas the

---

[20] 358 U.S. 450 (1959).

[21] Congress soon adopted a law, overruling this decision, that provided that "mere solicitation" in a state is not a sufficient connection to permit a state net income tax on the business. 15 U.S.C. §381 *et seq.*

[22] *See, e.g.,* Wisconsin v. J.C. Penney, 311 U.S. 435 (1940) (taxing property outside a state that does not have minimum contacts to the taxing state violates due process); *see also* Moorman Mfg. v. Bair, 437 U.S. 267 (1978) (rejecting a due process challenge to a state tax on an out-of-state company that earned 20 percent of its income in the taxing state).

[23] 458 U.S. 307 (1982).

[24] 458 U.S. 354 (1982).

[25] 458 U.S. 298 (1992).

[26] *Id.* at 308. Earlier in *National Bellas Hess, Inc. v. Department of Revenue*, 386 U.S. 753 (1967), the Supreme Court held that it was unconstitutional for a state to collect use taxes from out-of-state mail order sellers who had neither outlets nor sales representatives in the state. The Court found that the tax violated both due process, because of the lack of contacts with the state, and the commerce clause, because of its burden on interstate commerce. In *Quill Corp.*, the Court overruled the due process aspect of *National Bellas Hess*, but affirmed its commerce clause holding, expressly ruling that a law could be consistent with due process but still violate the commerce clause.

[27] 458 U.S. at 299.

dormant commerce clause is about the effects of state actions on the national economy.

The Court concluded that there is not a sufficient nexus to the taxing state when an interstate seller solicits by mail and ships orders by mail or common carrier. The Court said that a company must have a physical presence in the state in order to have a substantial nexus and be subjected to its use tax.

§5.4.3 The Requirement for Fair Apportionment

Reason for the Requirement

A state tax may be applied only to the portion of a company's business that is in some way connected to the taxing state. This condition is termed the requirement for "fair apportionment." Fair apportionment is closely related to the first requirement for a nexus: A state may tax a business only if it has a substantial connection to the state, and it may tax only that which is rationally connected to the state.

The requirement for apportionment is based on the desire to protect interstate businesses from cumulative taxation. If every state could tax the entirety of a company's business, the company would face enormous liabilities. Therefore, the apportionment requirement ensures that each state taxes only that which has some connection to it.

Apportionment Permissible as Long as It Is Reasonable

In *Container Corp. v. Franchise Tax Board*, the Court upheld a California tax that was based on the business's total payroll, its property, and sales that are located in the taxing state.[28] The Court explained that "[h]aving determined that a set of activities constitute a unitary business, a State must then apply a formula apportioning the income of that business within and without the State. Such an apportionment formula must, under both the Due Process Clause and the Commerce Clause, be fair."[29]

The Court then articulated a test for apportionment that is quite deferential to the government: "[W]e will strike down the application of an apportionment formula if the taxpayer can prove by clear and cogent evidence that the income attributed to the State is in fact out of all appropriate proportion to the business transacted in that State, or has led to a grossly distorted result."[30] The Court said that the challenger has the burden of proving that the apportionment is not fair and to succeed "must demonstrate that there is no rational relationship between the income attributed to the State and the intrastate value of the enterprise."[31]

[28] 463 U.S. 159 (1983).
[29] *Id.* at 169 (citations omitted).
[30] *Id.* at 170 (citations omitted).
[31] *Id.* at 180 (citations omitted).

Similarly, in *Moorman Manufacturing Co. v. Bair*, the Court upheld an Iowa tax that looked at one factor—income in the state—rather than the three factors that were used in the California tax considered in *Container Corp.*[32] Iowa required a company to pay a 20 percent tax on its profits because 20 percent of its sales occurred in Iowa, even though the company's products were made entirely in Illinois. The Court upheld the Iowa tax because it was a rational apportionment, even though it meant that the company was subjected to some degree of duplicative taxation.[33]

Likewise, with regard to property taxes, the Court has held that there must be fair apportionment.[34] In *Norfolk and Western Railway Co. v. State Tax Commission*, the Court said that the formula for a property tax on a railroad's stock must "bear a rational relationship . . . to property values connected with the taxing State."[35]

Oklahoma Tax Commission v. Jefferson

The Supreme Court considered the apportionment requirement in *Oklahoma Tax Commission v. Jefferson Lines, Inc.*[36] The issue was whether Oklahoma violated the commerce clause by collecting a sales tax from Oklahoma to another state. The Court said that "[t]he difficult question in this case is whether the tax is properly apportioned within the meaning of the second prong of *Complete Auto*'s test."[37]

The Court said that in evaluating apportionment it considered "internal consistency" and "external consistency." Internal consistency exists "when the imposition of a tax identical to the one in question by every other State would add no burden to interstate commerce that intrastate commerce would not also bear."[38] External consistency, in contrast, "looks not to the logical consequences of cloning, but to the economic justification for the State's claim upon the value taxed, to discover whether a State's tax reaches beyond that portion of value that is fairly attributable to economic activity within the taxing State."[39]

The Court found that there was no problem with internal consistency because if every state were to impose a tax identical to Oklahoma's, no sale would be subject to more than one tax. The Court found that the requirement for external consistency was met because "[a] sale of services can ordinarily be treated as a local state event just as readily as a sale of tangible goods can be located solely within the State of delivery."[40] Because the Court found that the other prongs of the *Complete Auto* test also were met, the Court upheld the Oklahoma tax as constitutional.

[32]   437 U.S. 267 (1978).

[33]   *See also* Tyler Pipe Indus., Inc. v. Washington State Dept. of Revenue, 483 U.S. 232 (1987).

[34]   The same is also true of value added taxes that tax the value added at each stage of production or distribution. *See* Trinova Corp. v. Michigan Dept. of Treasury, 498 U.S. 358 (1991) (approving a value added tax that used a reasonable apportionment formula).

[35]   390 U.S. 317, 322 (1968).

[36]   514 U.S. 175 (1995).

[37]   *Id.* at 184.

[38]   *Id.* at 185.

[39]   *Id.*

[40]   *Id.* at 188.

In sum, the requirement for apportionment ultimately is about fairness: It is unfair to have multiple states imposing significant taxes on the same things.[41] Although some overlap is permissible and sometimes inevitable, the Court seeks to have a state tax only that which is connected to it. States have great discretion in deciding how to measure this, so long as the approach is reasonable.

§5.4.4   The Prohibition of Discrimination Against Out-of-Staters

Prohibition of Discriminatory Taxes

Under dormant commerce clause analysis, discussed above, there is a strong presumption against state discrimination against out-of-staters. The same is true with regard to state taxation of interstate commerce. In fact, discriminatory taxes of this sort are always declared unconstitutional. The Supreme Court has declared: "No State, consistent with the Commerce Clause, may impose a tax which discriminates against interstate commerce . . . by providing a direct commercial advantage to local business."[42] The Court has said that "[s]tate laws discriminating against interstate commerce are 'virtually *per se* invalid.' "[43]

The Supreme Court has made it clear that states cannot use their tax systems to help in-state businesses at the expense of out-of-state businesses.[44] For instance, in *New Energy Co. of Indiana v. Limbach*, the Court declared unconstitutional an Ohio law that provided a tax credit for ethanol motor fuel that was produced in state, but no credit for ethanol produced out of state.[45] The law obviously created an incentive to purchase from in-staters and not out-of-staters and thus was deemed to violate the commerce clause.

Nor can states attempt to profit by taxing out-of-staters in a manner that it does not tax in-staters. In *Associated Industries of Missouri v. Lohman*, the Court declared unconstitutional a state's use tax "on the privilege of storing, using, or consuming within the State any article of personal property purchased outside the State."[46] The use tax was meant to compensate for the failure to pay a sales tax that

---

[41] *See* Western Live Stock v. Bureau of Revenue, 303 U.S. 250, 256 (1938) (expressing the concern that without protection under the dormant commerce clause, "it would bear cumulative burdens not imposed on local commerce. The multiplication of state taxes measured by the gross receipts from interstate transactions would spell the destruction of interstate commerce and renew the barriers to interstate trade which it was the object of the commerce clause to remove."); *see also* J.D. Adams Mfg. Co. v. Storen, 304 U.S. 307 (1938): Gwin, White & Prince, Inc. v. Henneford, 305 U.S. 434 (1939) (expressing need to avoid cumulative taxation).

[42] Boston Stock Exchange v. State Tax Commn., 429 U.S. 318, 329 (1977) (citations omitted).

[43] Fulton Corp. v. Faulkner, 516 U.S. 325, 331 (1996), quoting Oregon Waste Sys., Inc. v. Department of Envtl. Quality of Or., 511 U.S. 93, 99 (1994).

[44] *See, e.g.*, Hale v. Bimco Trading, Inc., 306 U.S. 375, 380-381 (1939) (declaring unconstitutional a state law that imposed an inspection fee on out-of-staters that was 60 times greater than that imposed on in-staters); Robbins v. Taxing Dist. of Shelby County, 466 U.S. 388 (1884) (invalidating tax on out-of-state solicitors); Welton v. Missouri, 91 U.S. 275 (1876) (imposing a tax on out-of-state merchants but not on in-state merchants).

[45] 486 U.S. 269 (1988).

[46] 511 U.S. 641, 644 (1994).

was collected for goods purchased in the state. The Court found that the tax was unconstitutional because it violated the "cardinal rule of nondiscrimination, for it exempts from its scope all sales of goods occurring within the State."[47] The Court stressed that the burdens imposed on interstate and intrastate commerce were not equal, and therefore the tax was unconstitutional.[48]

Similarly, in *Oregon Waste Systems, Inc. v. Department of Environmental Quality of the State of Oregon,* the Court declared unconstitutional an Oregon law that charged a $2.25 per ton surcharge on disposal of out-of-state waste, but only a $0.85 per ton surcharge on waste generated in state.[49] The Court declared this unconstitutional because there was no evidence that it was based on actual costs borne by the state in disposing of waste from other states.

The Court applied *Oregon Waste Systems* in *Fulton Corp. v. Faulkner.*[50] North Carolina imposed an "intangibles tax" on a fraction of the value of corporate stock owned by state residents; the amount of the tax was inversely proportionate to a company's liability to the corporation's exposure to North Carolina's income tax. In other words, the lower the level of income taxes paid by the company, the greater the intangibles tax. The Court explained that "[t]here is no doubt that the intangibles tax facially discriminates against interstate commerce."[51] The more a company did business out of state, the higher the level of the intangibles tax.

The Court declared this tax unconstitutional and rejected the state's claim that the tax was designed to compensate for the burden of the general corporate income tax paid by corporations doing business in North Carolina.[52] The Court said that for a tax to be compensatory, three requirements must be met: The tax must serve some purpose for which the state may otherwise impose a burden on interstate commerce; the tax on interstate commerce must approximate, but not exceed, the tax on intrastate commerce; and the different taxes on in-staters and out-of-staters must fall on substantially equivalent events. The Court concluded that the North Carolina tax failed all of these requirements.

Determining If a Tax Is Discriminatory

Sometimes, such as in the cases mentioned above, state tax laws are facially discriminatory; that is, the terms of the law treat in-staters and out-of-staters differently. The harder cases are instances where the tax law is facially neutral, but has a disparate impact on out-of-staters.

For example, in *Commonwealth Edison v. Montana,* the Court considered the constitutionality of Montana's severance tax on coal.[53] The amount of the tax varied depending on the energy content of the coal, its method of extraction, and its market value. The tax produced almost 20 percent of Montana's revenues, with 50

47. *Id.* at 647.
48. *Id.* at 648.
49. 511 U.S. 93 (1994).
50. 516 U.S. 325 (1996).
51. *Id.* at 333.
52. *Id.* at 334-336.
53. 453 U.S. 609 (1981).

percent of the severance tax revenue going to a permanent trust fund to alleviate the environmental problems caused by coal mining. The tax appeared to have a discriminatory impact on out-of-staters because 90 percent of Montana's coal was shipped to other states; the tax burden thus was primarily borne by utilities and citizens in other states.

The Court, however, rejected this argument and found that the law was not discriminatory. The Court explained that the "Montana tax is computed at the same rate regardless of the final destination of the coal, and there is no suggestion here that the tax is administered in a manner that departs from this even-handed formula."[54]

An example in which a court deemed discriminatory a facially neutral tax law is *West Lynn Creamery, Inc. v. Healy*.[55] Massachusetts imposed a tax on all milk dealers, but the funds from the tax went into a fund to pay subsidies to in-state dairy farmers. The Court found that the law was unconstitutional because its impact was the same as a discriminatory tax law. In essence, the state was taxing both in-staters and out-of-staters, but in effect refunding the taxes paid by in-staters through the subsidy system. The net effect was that the tax was borne disproportionately by out-of-staters and thus was unconstitutional.

Another illustration of a facially neutral tax being found discriminatory based on its effects was *American Trucking Associations, Inc. v. Scheiner*.[56] A state imposed a flat tax on trucks to use roads in the state; the amount of the tax was not related to the amount of time that the vehicle was in the state or the number of miles traveled there. The Court said that such a tax violates the commerce clause when it has the effect of imposing a higher tax burden on a multistate carrier than would be borne by a solely in-state carrier.[57]

Congressional Approval

As described above in the discussion of the dormant commerce clause, state discrimination against interstate commerce that would otherwise be unconstitutional is permissible if approved by Congress. The same is true with regard to discriminatory taxes; if Congress has approved them, they do not violate the commerce clause. Congress's plenary power to regulate commerce among the states means that it can approve regulations or taxes that would be invalidated in the absence of congressional action. Simply put, if Congress has acted, its commerce power is no longer dormant and thus there is not a basis for a dormant commerce clause challenge.

In fact, the cases described above in §5.3.7.1 concerning congressional approval almost all involved instances where discriminatory taxes were allowed because they were approved in federal legislation. For example, in *Prudential*

---

[54]   *Id.* at 618.

[55]   512 U.S. 186 (1994).

[56]   483 U.S. 266 (1987).

[57]   In *American Trucking Assns., Inc. v. Smith*, 496 U.S. 167 (1990), the Court held that this rule did not apply retroactively to taxes on highway use that were applied prior to the date of the decision.

Insurance Co. v. Benjamin,[58] and in *Western & Southern Life Insurance Co. v. State Board of Equalization of California,*[59] the Court approved taxes that discriminated against out-of-state insurance companies because a federal law—the McCarran-Ferguson Act—expressly authorized states to adopt such discriminatory laws. The Court allowed taxes that otherwise would have been unconstitutional because the Act "removed all limitations on the authority of the States to regulate and tax the business of insurance."[60]

Other Constitutional Provisions

In addition to challenges based on the dormant commerce clause, discriminatory taxes also can be challenged under other constitutional provisions such as the equal protection clause and the privileges and immunities clause. For example, in *Metropolitan Life Insurance Co. v. Ward,* the Court declared unconstitutional a state law that imposed a higher tax on out-of-state insurance companies than on in-state companies.[61] As explained above, a federal law allowed such discriminatory taxes on out-of-state insurance companies so that the state law did not violate the dormant commerce clause. However, the Court explained that congressional approval is irrelevant with regard to equal protection analysis, and the Court found that the discriminatory tax violated the equal protection clause of the Fourteenth Amendment. The Court concluded that the state lacked a legitimate purpose to justify the discriminatory tax because it was designed to protect local insurance companies from out-of-state competition.[62]

Also, discriminatory taxes can be challenged under the privileges and immunities clause of Article IV, §2. For example, in *Toomer v. Witsell,* the Court declared unconstitutional a South Carolina law that charged its citizens $25 for a fishing permit, but charged out-of-state citizens $2,500 for the same permit.[63] Discriminating against out-of-staters with regard to their ability to earn their livelihood was deemed to violate the privileges and immunities clause. The privileges and immunities clause is discussed in more detail below in §5.5.

---

[58] 328 U.S. 408 (1946), the subject of state taxation of interstate commerce is discussed below in §5.4.

[59] 451 U.S. 648 (1981).

[60] *Id.* at 653.

[61] 470 U.S. 869 (1985).

[62] *See also* Williams v. Vermont, 472 U.S. 14 (1985) (finding a violation of equal protection when a state gave a tax credit for cars purchased out of state while a person lived in the state, but not for cars purchased out of state before a person moved to the state).

[63] 334 U.S. 385 (1948).

§5.4.5   The Requirement for Fair Relationship to Services Provided by the State

Does the State Provide Some Benefit to the Taxpayer?

The final requirement under *Complete Auto Transit, Inc. v. Brady* is that the tax must have a fair relationship to services provided by the state. A state can tax out-of-staters only if it is providing them some benefit so that it is fair to collect the tax. The Court said that "[t]he simple but controlling question is whether the state has given anything for which it can ask return."[64]

Essentially, this requires that the tax be based on the extent of the taxpayer's activities in the state. The Supreme Court has explained: "When a tax is assessed in proportion to a taxpayer's activities or presence in a State, the taxpayer is shouldering its fair share of supporting the State's provision of police and fire protection, the benefit of a trained work force, and the advantages of a civilized society."[65]

This requirement is thus closely related to the first and second prongs of the test: If a taxpayer has a substantial nexus to the state and the tax is fairly apportioned, generally it should meet the fourth requirement as well. Yet there is a difference between the requirement for fair apportionment and the requirement for a fair relationship to services provided by the state. Although both are ultimately about fairness, the former—fair apportionment—is primarily about preventing duplicative taxes on the same activity in multiple states; the latter—fair relationship to services provided—is primarily about ensuring that the taxpayer has received some benefit to justify bearing the tax.

Examples

In *General Motors Corp. v. Washington*, the Court upheld a Washington tax on engaging in business in the state that was measured by a company's gross wholesale sales in the state.[66] The Court allowed the tax because it deemed the tax to be "fairly related" to the "[taxpayer's] activities within the state."[67]

Similarly, in *Commonwealth Edison v. Montana*, the Court upheld a Montana tax on coal extracted in the state. The Court explained: "We have little difficulty concluding that the Montana tax satisfies the fourth prong of the *Complete Auto Transit* test. Because the tax is measured as a percentage of the value of the coal taken, the Montana tax is in proper proportion to appellant's activity within the State and, therefore, to their 'consequent enjoyment of the opportunities and protections which the State has afforded in connection with those activities.'"[68]

---

[64] Wisconsin v. J.C. Penney Co., 311 U.S. 435, 444 (1940).

[65] Commonwealth Edison v. Montana, 453 U.S. 609, 627 (1981) (citations omitted).

[66] 377 U.S. 436 (1964).

[67] *Id.* at 441; *see also* Standard Pressed Steel Co. v. Department of Revenue of Washington, 419 U.S. 560 (1975) (upholding the same tax as applied to sales of aerospace parts from a Pennsylvania company to a Washington company).

[68] *Id.* at 441.

Conclusion

Both state regulations and state taxes that burden interstate commerce can be challenged under the dormant commerce clause. In many ways, the analysis is the same regardless of whether it is a regulation or a tax. For example, discrimination against out-of-staters in either context is very likely to be declared unconstitutional.[69] Also, congressional approval precludes dormant commerce clause challenges to state laws even if they otherwise would be unconstitutional.

But there also is a difference in the way the Court treats state taxes as opposed to state regulations. For almost two decades, since *Complete Auto Transit, Inc. v. Brady*, the Supreme Court has applied a four-part test in evaluating state taxes that burden interstate commerce. The Supreme Court has held that a state tax does not violate the commerce clause if

(1)   it is applied to an activity with a substantial nexus to the taxing state;

(2)   it is fairly apportioned so as to tax only the activities connected to the taxing state;

(3)   it does not discriminate against out-of-staters; and

(4)   it is fairly related to services provided by the state.

§5.5   THE PRIVILEGES AND IMMUNITIES CLAUSE OF ARTICLE IV, §2

§5.5.1 Introduction

Article IV, §2, states: "The Citizens of each State shall be entitled to all Privileges and Immunities of Citizens in the several States." The Supreme Court has interpreted this provision as limiting the ability of a state to discriminate against out-of-staters with regard to fundamental rights or important economic activities. The Court has said that "[t]he section, in effect, prevents a State from discriminating against citizens of other States in favor of its own."[1] As discussed below, most cases under the privileges and immunities clause involve challenges to state and local

---

[69] In a 1998 article, Jesse H. Choper & Tung Yin, s*upra* note 11, at 193, have proposed a simplified test for evaluating state taxes under the dormant commerce clause. They suggest that "a nondiscriminatory tax on an activity that can be reached only by one state should generally be upheld without the need for apportionment; but a nondiscriminatory tax on an activity that can be reached by more than one state must be apportioned to be valid."

§5.5 [1] Hague v. Committee for Industrial Organization, 307 U.S. 496, 511 (1939).

laws that discriminate against out-of-staters with regard to their ability to earn a livelihood.[2] Such discrimination will be allowed only if it is substantially related to achieving a substantial state interest.[3]

Discrimination against citizens of other states is a prerequisite for application of the privileges and immunities clause.[4] The Supreme Court long has held that the term "citizen" in the privileges and immunities clause is limited to individuals who are United States citizens.[5] Thus, corporations cannot sue under the privileges and immunities clause because, by definition, they are not citizens.[6] Nor can aliens sue under the privileges and immunities clause.

Relationship to the Dormant Commerce Clause

The dormant commerce clause and the privileges and immunities clause overlap: Both can be used to challenge state and local laws that discriminate against out-of-staters. In fact, the Supreme Court has spoken of the "mutually reinforcing relationship" between the dormant commerce clause and the privileges and immunities clause.[7]

There are, however, some key differences.[8] First, the privileges and immunities clause can be used only if there is discrimination against out-of-staters. The dormant commerce clause, as explained above, can be used to challenge state and local laws that burden interstate commerce regardless of whether they discriminate against out-of-staters. However, under the dormant commerce clause, laws that discriminate are much more likely to be invalidated.

Second, corporations and aliens can sue under the dormant commerce clause, but not the privileges and immunities clause. The privileges and immunities clause is expressly limited to "citizens," whereas no such limitation exists with regard to the dormant commerce clause.

Third, there are two exceptions to the dormant commerce clause that do not apply to the privileges and immunities clause. If Congress approves state laws, then

---

[2] For an excellent discussion of the clause and its purposes, *see* Jonathan Varat, State "Citizenship" and Interstate Equality, 48 U. Chi. L. Rev. 487 (1981).

[3] *See* United Bldg. & Constr. Trades Council v. Mayor and Council of Camden, 465 U.S. 208 (1984).

[4] *See* Zobel v. Williams, 457 U.S. 55, 59 n.5 (1982) (finding that an Alaskan law that gave refunds based on duration of state residence did not violate the privileges and immunities clause. The Court said that the law did not discriminate between citizens and noncitizens, but among citizens based on duration of residence. The Court did find that the law violated equal protection.).

[5] The Court has held that in determining whether a person is a citizen of a state, residency in the state is synonymous with state citizenship. *See* United Bldg. & Constr. Trades Council v. Mayor and Council of Camden, 465 U.S. 208, 216 (1984) ("[I]t is now established that the terms 'citizen' and 'resident' are essentially interchangeable for purposes of analysis of most cases under the Privileges and Immunities Clause.") (citations omitted).

[6] Blake v. McClung, 172 U.S. 239 (1898); Paul v. Virginia, 75 U.S. (8 Wall.) 168 (1868); *see also* Hemphill v. Orloff, 277 U.S. 537 (1928) (trust cannot sue under the privileges and immunities clause because of its corporate form).

[7] Hicklin v. Orbeck, 437 U.S. 518, 531 (1978).

[8] *See* Brannon P. Denning, Why the Privileges and Immunities Clause of Article IV Cannot Replace the Dormant Commerce Clause Doctrine, 88 Minn. L. Rev. 384 (2003).

they do not violate the dormant commerce clause; if Congress has acted, its commerce power no longer is dormant.[9] But congressional approval does not excuse a law that violates the privileges and immunities clause.

Also, as described in §5.4, there is a market participant exception to the dormant commerce clause that allows states to favor their own citizens in receiving benefits from government programs and in dealing with government-owned businesses. No such exception exists for the privileges and immunities clause. Thus, in *White v. Massachusetts Council of Construction Employers, Inc.*, the Court found that a city law requiring that 50 percent of those hired to work on city construction projects be residents of the city did not violate the dormant commerce clause because of the market participant exception.[10] But a year later in *United Building & Construction Trades Council v. Mayor and Council of Camden*, the Court declared unconstitutional a city's ordinance requiring that at least 40 percent of the employees on city projects be city residents.[11] The Court found that the law violated the privileges and immunities clause and explained that the market participant exception only applies with regard to dormant commerce clause challenges.

Relationship to Other Constitutional Provisions

The privileges and immunities clause of Article IV should be distinguished from another constitutional provision that uses similar language: the privileges or immunities clause of the Fourteenth Amendment. The Fourteenth Amendment declares that "No State shall make or enforce any law which shall abridge the privileges or immunities of citizens of the United States." As described in §6.3.2, the Supreme Court has given this clause an extremely narrow construction.[12] Although the privileges or immunities clause of the Fourteenth Amendment has rarely been used, the privileges and immunities clause of Article IV remains an important tool for challenging discriminatory state and local legislation.

Also, it should be remembered that discriminatory laws can be challenged under the dormant commerce clause and the equal protection clause as well as via the privileges and immunities clause.

---

[9] *See* text accompanying notes 167-181, §5.3.7.1, *supra.*

[10] 460 U.S. 204 (1983).

[11] 465 U.S. 208 (1984).

[12] The Court, however, did rely on the privileges or immunities clause of the Fourteenth Amendment in *Saenz v. Roe*, 526 U.S. 489 (1999), in declaring unconstitutional a California law that limited a new resident of California, for the first year in the state, to receiving welfare benefits at the level of the previous state of residence. The privileges and immunities clause of Article IV did not apply because the state was not distinguishing between in-staters and out-of-staters, but instead was drawing a distinction among its own residents (new versus longer-term residents).

Analysis Under the Privileges and Immunities Clause

When a challenge is brought under the privileges and immunities clause, there are two basic questions.[13] First, has the state discriminated against out-of-staters with regard to privileges and immunities that it accords its own citizens? Section 5.5.2 considers the meaning of "privileges and immunities." Second, if there is such discrimination, is there a sufficient justification for the discrimination? The privileges and immunities clause is not absolute; but it does create a strong presumption against state and local laws that discriminate against out-of-staters with regard to fundamental rights or important economic activities. Section 5.5.3 examines what is a sufficient justification for discrimination against out-of-staters with regard to privileges and immunities of citizenship.

§5.5.2   What Are the "Privileges and Immunities" of Citizenship?

Definitions

The classic statement of the meaning of the phrase "privileges and immunities" of citizenship was provided by Justice Bushrod Washington in *Corfield v. Coryell* when he said that the clause protects interests "which are fundamental; which belong, of right, to the citizens of all free governments. [They] may be comprehended under the following general heads: Protection by the government, the enjoyment of life and liberty, with the right to acquire and possess property of every kind, and to pursue and obtain happiness and safety; subject nevertheless to such restraints as the government may prescribe for the general good of the whole."[14]

In *Paul v. Virginia*, the Court said that "[i]t was undoubtedly the object of the clause . . . to place the citizens of each State upon the same footing with citizens of other States. . . . It relieves them from the disabilities of alienage in other States; it inhibits discriminating legislation against them by other States; it gives them the right of free ingress into other States, and egress from them; it insures to them in other States the same freedom possessed by the citizens of those States in the acquisition and enjoyment of property and in the pursuit of happiness."[15]

Subsequently, in 1984 the Court said that the clause applies "[o]nly with respect to those privileges and immunities bearing upon the vitality of the Nation as a single entity." The Court also has said that the issue is whether the interest is "sufficiently fundamental to the promotion of interstate harmony."[16]

---

[13] The Supreme Court has expressly referred to this as "a two-step inquiry." United Bldg. & Constr. Trades Council v. Mayor and Council of Camden, 465 U.S. 208, 218 (1984).

[14] 6 F. Cas. 546, 551, 4 Wash. C.C. 371, No. 3230 (Cir. Ct. E.D. Pa. 1823). In *Corfield*, the court of appeals upheld a New Jersey law that prevented nonresidents from gathering clams from state waters. The court said that clams were the property of the state. Subsequently, the Supreme Court has rejected that view that natural resources, such as animals, are property and not items of commerce. *See, e.g.*, Hughes v. Oklahoma, 441 U.S. 222 (1979).

[15] 75 U.S. (8 Wall.) 168, 180 (1868).

[16] United Bldg. & Constr. Trades Council v. Mayor and Council of Camden, 465 U.S. at 218.

Yet these and similar statements are quite abstract and provide relatively little guidance in identifying what are the "privileges and immunities of citizenship" under Article IV. It is well settled that the privileges and immunities clause is meant to limit the ability of states to discriminate against citizens from other states, but it is not at all clear as to what constitutes the area — privileges and immunities — where discrimination is forbidden. Indeed, the Supreme Court has acknowledged that "the contours of [the clause] are not well developed."[17]

Examining the cases concerning the privileges and immunities clause reveals that the Court primarily has applied it in two contexts: when a state is discriminating against out-of-staters with regard to fundamental rights and when a state is discriminating against out-of-staters with regard to important economic activities. The latter almost always arises in the context of a state discriminating against out-of-staters with regard to their ability to earn a livelihood. The Court has refused to apply the privileges and immunities clause in situations where the discrimination against out-of-staters has involved neither fundamental rights nor important economic activities.

Constitutional Rights

The rights enumerated in the Bill of Rights seem the most obvious and the most basic "privileges and immunities of citizenship."[18] However, generally, there is no need to use the privileges and immunities clause to protect constitutionally guaranteed rights. If a state were to prevent out-of-staters from engaging in religious worship, a challenge certainly could be brought under the privileges and immunities clause. But, in reality, the suit would be brought under the First Amendment as applied to the states through the Fourteenth Amendment.[19]

Although such cases arise only relatively rarely, the privileges and immunities clause can be used to challenge state and local laws that discriminate against out-of-staters with regard to the exercise of constitutional rights. For example, in *Canadian Northern Railway Co. v. Eggen*, the Court held that a state cannot deny out-of-staters meaningful access to its courts.[20] Also, in *Blake v. McClung*, the Court

---

[17] Baldwin v. Montana Fish and Game Commn., 436 U.S. 371, 380 (1978).

[18] *See* Duncan v. Louisiana, 391 U.S. 145, 166 (1968) (Black, J., concurring) ("What more precious 'privilege' of American citizenship could there be than that privilege to claim the protection of our great Bill of Rights?").

[19] The application of the Bill of Rights to the states through the process of incorporation is discussed in §6.3.3.

[20] 252 U.S. 553 (1920). Actually, in *Eggen*, the Supreme Court held that a state does not violate the privileges and immunities clause when it imposes a longer statute of limitations for suits that arose out of state where that state's statute of limitations has expired. The Court said that "[t]he constitutional requirement is satisfied if the nonresident is given access to the courts of the State upon terms which in themselves are reasonable and adequate for the enforcing of any rights he may have, even though they may not be technically and precisely the same in extent as those accorded to resident citizens." 252 U.S. at 562. Nonetheless, the Supreme Court cites *Eggen* as establishing that "access to the courts of the State" is a right protected under the privileges and immunities clause. *See* Baldwin v. Fish and Game Commn. of Montana, 436 U.S. at 383. It is very questionable whether the discrimination approved in *Eggen* would be allowed today. In *Reynoldsville Casket Co. v. Hyde*, 514 U.S. 749 (1995),

ruled that the right to own and dispose of property is protected under the privileges and immunities clause.[21] In *Blake*, the Supreme Court held that a state may not favor in-state creditors over out-of-state creditors in the disposition of property of an insolvent corporation.

In *Doe v. Bolton*, the Supreme Court concluded that a state could not limit the ability of out-of-staters to obtain abortions in the state.[22] *Doe* was a companion case to *Roe v. Wade*[23] and involved a Georgia law that allowed residents to obtain an abortion if a physician determined that continuing the pregnancy would endanger a woman's life or health, or the fetus would be born with a serious defect, or the pregnancy resulted from rape. The Court declared the law unconstitutional and invalidated the residency requirement based on the privileges and immunities clause. The Court said: "Just as the Privileges and Immunities Clause . . . protects persons who enter other States to ply their trade, so must it protect persons who enter Georgia seeking the medical services that are available there. A contrary holding would mean that a State could limit to its own residents the general medical care available within its borders. This we could not approve."[24]

Doe establishes that a state cannot discriminate against out-of-staters with regard to access to the constitutionally protected right to abortion. But it also goes further than just preventing discrimination concerning constitutional rights; it expressly says that a state cannot discriminate against out-of-staters with regard to access to medical care, even though there is no constitutional right to medical care.

But most recently, in *McBurney v. Young*, the Court held "that the Privileges and Immunities Clause protects only those privileges and immunities that are 'fundamental.'"[25] *McBurney* involved a challenge to Virginia's Freedom of Information Act (FOIA), which provides that "all public records shall be open to inspection and copying by any citizens of the Commonwealth." But the Virginia law grants no such right to information to those who are not citizens of Virginia. Several other states have similar laws, limiting access to information under public records laws to in-state residents.

The Supreme Court upheld the Virginia law concluding that it violated neither the privileges and immunities clause of Article IV nor the dormant commerce clause. Justice Alito wrote the opinion for a unanimous Court and held that the Virginia law does not violate the privileges and immunities clause because it does not keep anyone from earning a living in Virginia and it does not discriminate with regard to a fundamental right. The Court noted that the Constitution does not require that a government open its papers to the press and the public or mandate that a state have a public records law.[26] The Court said that such laws are of recent vintage and had no analogue at common law or through the nineteenth

---

the Court declared unconstitutional a state law that allowed a longer tolling period for the statute of limitations for suits against out-of-staters than for suits against in-staters.

[21]   172 U.S. 239 (1898).
[22]   410 U.S. 179 (1973).
[23]   410 U.S. 113 (1973).
[24]   *Doe*, 410 U.S. 179, 200 (1973).
[25]   133 S. Ct. 1709, 1714 (2013).
[26]   *Id.* at 1719.

century and thus there was not a fundamental right for purposes of the privileges and immunities clause.[27]

Important Economic Activities

The vast majority of cases under the privileges and immunities clause involve states discriminating against out-of-staters with regard to their ability to earn their livelihood. As described below, the Court has found a violation of the privileges and immunities clause if a state excludes out-of-staters from practicing a trade or profession, or charges a discriminatory licensing fee, or mandates that a preference be given to in-staters for employment.

The most extreme form of discrimination is where the state completely bars out-of-staters from engaging in a particular trade or profession in the state. In *Supreme Court of New Hampshire v. Piper*, the Court invalidated a New Hampshire law that required residence in the state in order to be admitted to the bar.[28] The Court explained that the practice of law is a "privilege and immunity" protected under the clause: "[A]ctivities of lawyers play an important part in commercial intercourse. The lawyer's role in the national economy is not the only reason that the opportunity to practice law should be considered a fundamental right. We believe that the legal profession has a noncommercial role and duty that reinforce the view that the practice of law falls within the ambit of the Privileges and Immunities Clause."[29]

Even if a state is not excluding out-of-staters, it is denying a privilege and immunity of citizenship if it charges out-of-staters more for a licensing fee than it charges in-staters. An early case demonstrating this was *Ward v. Maryland*, which invalidated a Maryland law that required nonresidents to pay $300 per year for a license to trade in goods not manufactured in Maryland, while resident traders had to pay a smaller fee ranging from $12 to $150.[30]

Similarly and more subsequently, in *Toomer v. Witsell*, the Court declared unconstitutional a South Carolina law that required nonresidents to pay a license fee of $2,500 for each commercial shrimp boat, but residents only had to pay a fee of $25.27. The Court said that "commercial shrimping . . . , like other common callings, is within the purview of the privileges and immunities clause."[31] The Court said that "one of the privileges which the clause guarantees to citizens of

---

[27] Additionally, the Court rejected the claim that the Virginia law violated the dormant commerce clause. The dormant commerce clause is the principle that a state law is unconstitutional if it places an undue burden on interstate commerce. Justice Alito wrote that "Virginia's FOIA law neither 'regulates' nor 'burdens' interstate commerce; rather, it merely provides a service to local citizens that would not otherwise be available at all." *Id.* at 1720.

[28] 470 U.S. 274 (1985).

[29] *Id.* at 281 (citations omitted); *see also* Supreme Court of Virginia v. Friedman, 487 U.S. 59 (1988) (declaring unconstitutional a state's residency requirement for admission to the state bar by motion).

[30] 79 U.S. (12 Wall.) 418 (1870).

[31] 334 U.S. 385 (1948).

State A is that of doing business in State B on terms of substantial equality with citizens of that State."[32]

In *Mullaney v. Anderson*, the Court declared unconstitutional an Alaska law that required Alaska residents to pay $5 for a license fee, but nonresidents to pay $50.[33] The Court followed the same reasoning as in *Toomer* and invalidated the law.

Another type of impermissible discrimination is where a state requires that its residents be given a preference in employment. In *Hicklin v. Orbeck*, the Supreme Court unanimously declared unconstitutional an Alaska law that required that Alaska residents be given priority in hiring for jobs on oil and gas projects.[34] Under the "Local Hire Under State Leases" law, Alaska required that preference be given to Alaska residents over nonresidents in employment on all oil and gas leases. The Court found that this "discrimination against nonresidents cannot withstand scrutiny under the Privileges and Immunities Clause."[35]

Likewise, in *United Building & Construction Trades Council of Camden v. Mayor and Council of Camden*, the Court applied the privileges and immunities clause to a city's ordinance requiring that at least 40 percent of the employees of contractors and subcontractors working on city construction projects be residents of the city.[36] The Court explained that "the pursuit of a common calling is one of the most fundamental of those privileges protected by the Clause. Many, if not most, of our cases expounding the Privileges and Immunities Clause have dealt with this basic and essential activity."[37]

All of these cases make it clear that the privileges and immunities clause limits the ability of a state or local government to discriminate against out-of-staters with regard to their ability to earn a livelihood. However, if there is neither such economic discrimination nor discrimination with regard to constitutional rights, then there is not a violation of the privileges and immunities clause.

Baldwin v. Fish and Game Commission of Montana is illustrative.[38] Montana charged out-of-staters much more for elk hunting licenses than it charged in-staters. The Court rejected a challenge based on the privileges and immunities clause because it felt that elk hunting was neither a constitutional right nor an important economic activity. The Court explained that "[e]lk hunting by nonresidents in Montana is a recreation and a sport. . . . It is not a means to the nonresident's livelihood. . . . Equality in access to Montana elk is not basic to the mainte-

---

[32] *Id.* at 403.

[33] 342 U.S. 415 (1952).

[34] 437 U.S. 518 (1978).

[35] *Id.* at 526.

[36] 465 U.S. 208 (1984). The Court did not invalidate the statute as violating the privileges and immunities clause, but instead found that the record was inadequate to evaluate whether the test was met and remanded the case for further proceedings. *Id.* at 223.

[37] *Id.* at 219. Earlier, the Supreme Court had ruled that such city preferences for hiring city residents did not violate the dormant commerce clause because of the market participant exception. *See* White v. Massachusetts Council of Constr. Employers, Inc., 460 U.S. 204 (1983), discussed in §5.3.7.2. The Court in *United Building* expressly ruled that there was no such exception to the privileges and immunities clause. 465 U.S. at 220.

[38] 436 U.S. 371 (1978).

nance or well-being of the union."[39] The Court thus concluded that "[w]hatever rights or activities may be 'fundamental' under the Privileges and Immunities Clause, . . . elk hunting by nonresidents in Montana is not one of them."[40]

Conclusion

There is not a clear or comprehensive definition of "privileges and immunities." The clause is used to prevent states from discriminating against out-of-staters with regard to activities that are deemed "fundamental." These activities include, but are not necessarily limited to, constitutional rights and the ability to earn a livelihood. But recreational activities, like elk hunting, do not fit within this clause.

§5.5.3   What Is Sufficient Justification for Discrimination?

The Test

The Supreme Court has declared that "the privileges and immunities clause is not an absolute."[41] The Court has said that a state may discriminate against out-of-staters, even with regard to constitutional rights or the ability to earn a livelihood, only if there is a "substantial reason" for the difference in treatment compared with in-staters, and only if the law is closely related to the justification.[42] More specifically, the Court has explained: "The Clause does not preclude discrimination against nonresidents where: (i) there is a substantial reason for the difference in treatment; and (ii) the discrimination against nonresidents bears a substantial relationship to the State's objective. In deciding whether the discrimination bears a close or substantial relationship to the State's objective, the Court has considered the availability of less restrictive means."[43]

The Test Applied

The Court applied this test in several cases and rejected claims that discrimination against out-of-staters was justified. In *Supreme Court of New Hampshire v. Piper*, the state offered many justifications for limiting admission to the bar to citizens. For example, the state argued that nonresidents were less likely to know local rules and procedures; to act in an ethical manner; to be available for court proceedings; and to do pro bono work in the state.[44] For each justification, the Court found that it did not meet "the test of substantiality, and that the means chosen do not bear the necessary relationship to the State's objectives."[45] The Court said

---

[39] *Id.* at 388.
[40] *Id.*
[41] *Toomer*, 334 U.S. at 396.
[42] *Id.*
[43] Supreme Court of New Hampshire v. Piper, 470 U.S. at 284.
[44] *Id.* at 285.
[45] *Id.* at 285 (citations omitted).

that there was no reason to believe that in-state residents were more likely to know the law or act ethically. The Court found that problems with unavailability of non-resident lawyers could be solved by requiring the designation of local counsel. Additionally, the Court thought that any absence of pro bono work could be dealt with by requiring such efforts.

In *Hicklin v. Orbeck*, the Court invalidated the Alaska law giving preference for employment on oil and gas contracts to Alaska residents.[46] The Court found that reducing unemployment in the state was not a sufficient justification for the law. Although lessening unemployment is certainly an important interest for the state, the Court concluded that a state violates the privileges and immunities clause when it "attempt[s] to ease its unemployment problem by forcing employers within the State to discriminate against nonresidents."[47]

Conclusion

A state may discriminate against out-of-staters with regard to "privileges and immunities" only if the discrimination is "substantially related" to a "substantial state interest." Because the Court uses least restrictive alternative analysis under the privileges and immunities clause, it appears that the discrimination must be proved necessary to achieve a substantial government interest. Thus far, the Court has not found that any law meets this rigorous test.

[46] 437 U.S. 518 (1978).
[47] 437 U.S. at 528.

CHAPTER 6

The Structure of the Constitution's Protection of Civil Rights and Civil Liberties

§6.1   INTRODUCTION

The prior chapters focused primarily on the structure of American government and the allocation of power among the branches of the federal government, between the federal government and the states, and among the states. The remainder of the book considers individual liberties and civil rights.

It is traditional to draw a distinction between constitutional issues concerning the structure of government and those that concern civil liberties and civil rights. Yet in many ways such a distinction is more misleading than illuminating. There is no doubt that the framers thought that a careful structure of government with divided and separated powers was the best way to safeguard individual rights.

Also, it is important to note that the issues of separation of powers and federalism, which underlie all of the materials in the earlier chapters, are crucial in the discussion of individual rights. A key issue throughout the remainder of the book is the extent to which the judiciary should protect civil liberties and civil rights when doing so means striking down the actions of popularly elected officials. This, of course, is an issue of separation of powers. Likewise, there is the important question of the extent to which individual rights should be applied to state governments and how aggressively they should be enforced; this is very much about federalism.

The text of the Constitution contains few provisions concerning individual liberties. In part, this was because the framers thought that an enumeration of rights was unnecessary in that they had created a government with limited powers and thus without the authority to violate basic liberties. In part, too, the framers were concerned that the enumeration of some rights in the text of the Constitution inevitably would be incomplete and thus would deny protection to those not listed. The Ninth Amendment was added to address this latter concern and provides: "The enumeration in the Constitution, of certain rights, shall not be construed to deny or disparage others retained by the people."[1]

Several states, however, were concerned about the absence of an enumeration of rights and ratified the Constitution with a request that it would be amended to add a Bill of Rights. In the first Congress, James Madison drafted 16 amendments, 12 of which were ratified by Congress and 10 by the states.[2] These amendments became known as the Bill of Rights.

Section 6.2 examines the few provisions in the text of the Constitution, apart from the Bill of Rights, that protect individual freedom. Section 6.3 considers the application of the Bill of Rights to states. As discussed below, the Supreme Court initially concluded that the Bill of Rights applied only to the federal government.[3] The Fourteenth Amendment's clause, that "No State shall make or enforce any law which shall abridge the privileges or immunities of citizens of the United States," might have been a basis for applying the Bill of Rights to the states. However, in the *Slaughter-House Cases*, in 1872, the Supreme Court interpreted the clause in an extremely narrow manner and thus precluded its use as a vehicle for applying the Bill of Rights to the states. In the twentieth century, the Supreme Court applied

---

§6.1 [1] The Ninth Amendment as a basis for protecting individual rights is discussed in §1.1 and §10.3.2.

[2] *See* §1.3. For an excellent history of Madison's work in drafting the amendments and the process by which they were revised and ratified, *see* Burt Neuborne, Madison's Music 195-221 (2015).

[3] Barron v. Mayor and City Council of Baltimore, 32 U.S. (7 Pet.) 243 (1833), discussed below in §6.3.1.

most of the Bill of Rights to the states by finding that the provisions were incorporated into the due process clause of the Fourteenth Amendment.[4]

Section 6.4 examines the application of constitutional rights to private entities and individuals. The basic rule, often termed "the state action doctrine," is that such rights apply only to the government; private entities and individuals are not required to comply with the Constitution. The rationale for this doctrine and its exceptions are considered in §6.4.

Finally, §6.5 reviews the levels of scrutiny. In most areas concerning constitutional civil liberties and civil rights—from privacy to freedom of speech to equal protection—the outcome is very likely to depend on the level of scrutiny the court applies. The level of scrutiny is the test used by the judiciary in evaluating the constitutionality of a law; it determines how deferential a court will be to the government or how exacting it will be in its review.

This chapter, then, examines the way in which civil rights and civil liberties are protected by the Constitution. It covers some basic principles—incorporation, state action, and the levels of scrutiny—that apply to almost all of the constitutional provisions concerning individual rights and equal protection.

§6.2   TEXTUAL PROVISIONS, APART FROM THE BILL OF RIGHTS, PROTECTING INDIVIDUAL RIGHTS

The seven Articles of the United States Constitution contain relatively few provisions concerning individual rights. As mentioned above, this probably was both because a detailing of liberties was thought unnecessary in light of the federal government's limited powers and because a delineation of rights was thought dangerous because the list inevitably would be incomplete.

§6.2.1   A Review of the Textual Provisions Protecting Rights

Article I, §9, which places limits on Congress's powers, declares that "[t]he privilege of the Writ of Habeas Corpus shall not be suspended, unless when in Cases

---

[4] Discussed below in §6.3.3. Most recently, the Court found that the Second Amendment applies to state and local governments. McDonald v. City of Chicago, 561 U.S. 742 (2010). The plurality found that the Second Amendment was incorporated through the due process clause of the Fourteenth Amendment. Justice Thomas, the fifth vote for the majority, found that the Second Amendment was applied to the states through the privileges or immunities clause of the Fourteenth Amendment. *McDonald* is discussed below in §6.3.3.

of Rebellion or Invasion, the public Safety may require it."[1] It should be noted that although the Constitution prevents Congress from suspending the writ of habeas corpus, the availability and scope of habeas corpus is a matter of federal statutes. Thus, it is federal laws, specifically 28 U.S.C. §§2254 and 2255, that determine the power of federal courts to issue writs of habeas corpus. If Congress greatly narrowed the availability of habeas corpus, the action might be challenged as suspending the writ of habeas corpus. However, the Supreme Court is likely to give Congress great latitude in regulating habeas corpus because historically habeas relief was quite limited.[2] Until 1867, only federal prisoners could seek habeas corpus relief from federal courts, and until 1915, habeas corpus could be used only to challenge a court's jurisdiction. But the Court's deference to Congress in regulating habeas corpus is not limitless. For example, in *I.N.S. v. St. Cyr,* the Court held that aliens may use a writ of habeas corpus to challenge their deportation, even though Congress had expressly precluded appellate judicial review of deportation orders.[3] The Court explained that interpreting the law to also preclude habeas corpus review would raise serious constitutional questions because of the Constitution's limit on Congress's power to suspend the writ of habeas corpus. More dramatically, in *Boumediene v. Bush,* the Supreme Court declared unconstitutional a federal law that prohibited noncitizens held as enemy combatants from bringing habeas corpus petitions in federal courts.[4] The Court ruled that this was an impermissible suspension of the writ of habeas corpus.

Article I, §9, also states: "No Bill of Attainder or ex post facto Law shall be passed." Article I, §10, which contains limits on state government powers, similarly provides: "No State shall . . . pass any Bill of Attainder, ex post facto Law, or law impairing the Obligation of Contracts." The prohibition of bills of attainder and ex post facto laws is discussed below. The contracts clause of Article I, §10, is discussed in §8.3.

Article III, §2, states that "[t]he trial of all Crimes, except in Cases of Impeachment, shall be by jury; and such Trial shall be held in the State where the said Crimes shall have been committed." Article III, §3, also provides: "Treason against the United States, shall consist only in levying War against them or, in adhering to their Enemies, giving them Aid and Comfort. No person shall be convicted of Treason unless on the Testimony of two Witnesses to the same overt Act, or on Confession in open Court." Section 3 concludes by declaring that although Congress may prescribe the punishment for treason, there shall be no "Corruption

---

§6.2 [1] For a discussion of this clause, its meaning, and current law concerning habeas corpus, *see* Erwin Chemerinsky, Federal Jurisdiction ch. 15 (6th ed. 2011).

[2] In 1996, the Supreme Court upheld a federal law limiting successive habeas corpus petitions and rejected the argument that this constituted a suspension of the writ of habeas corpus. Under the Antiterrorism and Effective Death Penalty Act of 1996, an individual can bring a successive habeas petition only with the permission of the United States Court of Appeals. Pub. L. No. 104-132, 110 Stat. 1217. The Supreme Court is precluded from reviewing the Court of Appeals decision as to whether to allow the successive petition. The Supreme Court unanimously upheld these provisions and held "that they do not amount to a 'suspension' of the writ contrary to Article I, §9." Felker v. Turpin, 518 U.S. 651, 654 (1996). *Felker* is discussed in more detail in §2.9.2.

[3] 533 U.S. 289 (2001).

[4] 553 U.S. 723 (2008), discussed in §4.6.4.

of Blood, or Forfeiture except during the Life of the Person attained." In other words, only the traitor can be punished; family members and future generations cannot be sanctioned because of someone else's wrongdoing.

Article IV, §2, contains the "privileges and immunities clause," which states: "The Citizens of each State shall be entitled to all Privileges and Immunities of Citizens in the several States." This provision, which has been interpreted to limit the ability of states to discriminate against out-of-state citizens, is discussed in §5.4.4.

Finally, Article VI concludes that "no religious Test shall ever be required as a Qualification to any Office of public Trust under the United States." In *Torcaso v. Watkins*, the Supreme Court used the free exercise clause of the First Amendment to impose a similar requirement on state governments.[5] In *Torcaso*, the Supreme Court declared unconstitutional a state constitutional provision that required a declaration of a belief in God as a prerequisite to taking public office. Although these provisions are not trivial, they are minor compared with the protection of liberties found in the Bill of Rights. The seven Articles of the Constitution are primarily about the structure of government and not individual rights.

§6.2.2   The Prohibition of Bills of Attainder

What Is a Bill of Attainder?

Article I, §§9 and 10, respectively, prohibit the federal and state governments from adopting bills of attainder. Simply stated, a bill of attainder is a law that directs the punishment of a particular person. A classic bill of attainder would be a law that prescribes that "Erwin Chemerinsky shall be put to death." Such a law negates all due process and procedural protections. In essence, it is trial by legislature, undermining the basic rights to a fair trial and usurping the role of the judiciary. The Supreme Court has explained that "the Bill of Attainder Clause was intended not as a narrow, technical . . . prohibition, but rather as an implementation of the separation of powers, a general safeguard against legislative exercise of the judicial function, or more simply—trial by legislature."[6]

In evaluating whether a law is a bill of attainder, there are two issues. First, does the law impose a punishment? Second, does the law designate particular individuals for the punishment or does the law describe conduct that will be punished? The former is a bill of attainder; the latter is not. For a law to be a bill of attainder the law must be a punishment imposed by the legislature on a specific person or a particular group of people.

---

[5] 367 U.S. 488 (1961).
[6] United States v. Brown, 381 U.S. 437, 442 (1965).

Does the Law Impose a Punishment?

The Supreme Court repeatedly has held that a law must impose a punishment in order to be considered a bill of attainder.[7] The Court has broadly defined what constitutes a punishment sufficient to constitute a bill of attainder and has rejected the much more limited approach that was used in England before the Constitution was adopted. In England, a distinction was drawn between "bills of attainder" and "bills of pains and penalties."[8] The former referred to laws that required that a specific individual or group be put to death. The latter referred to laws that required the imprisonment or confiscation of property from a specific individual or group.

However, from the earliest days of the United States, the Supreme Court has rejected any such distinction and has held that the prohibition of bills of attainder applies to all "legislative acts, no matter what their form, that apply either to named individuals or to easily ascertainable members of a group in such a way as to inflict punishment on them without a judicial trial."[9] Indeed, in *Fletcher v. Peck*, Chief Justice John Marshall explained that "[a] bill of attainder may affect the life of an individual, or may confiscate property, or may do both."[10]

The Court has broadly defined what constitutes a punishment under the bill of attainder clauses. In one of its most recent cases to consider the bill of attainder clause, the Supreme Court articulated criteria to be considered in evaluating whether a law imposes punishment. In *Selective Service System v. Minnesota Public Interest Research Group*, the Court rejected a bill of attainder challenge to a state law that denied college financial assistance to men who did not register for the draft.[11] Chief Justice Burger, writing for the Court, stated:

> In deciding whether a statute inflicts forbidden punishment, we have recognized three necessary inquiries: (1) whether the challenged statute falls within the historical meaning of legislative punishment; (2) whether the statute, "viewed in terms of the type and severity of burdens imposed, reasonably can be said to further nonpunitive legislative purposes"; and (3) whether the legislative record "evinces a congressional intent to punish."[12]

Obviously, punishment includes traditional sanctions such as death, imprisonment, and fines. It also is broader than that and includes exclusion from employment and other benefits. Thus, the Supreme Court has explained that punishments include "imprisonment, banishment, and the punitive confiscation of property by the sovereign . . . [and] a legislative enactment barring designated

---

[7] *See, e.g.*, Selective Servs. Sys. v. Minnesota Pub. Interest Research Group, 468 U.S. 841 (1984); Nixon v. Administrator of General Serv., 433 U.S. 425 (1977); United States v. Brown, 381 U.S. 437 (1965).

[8] This history is reviewed in United States v. Brown, 381 U.S. 437, 441-442 (1965); and in Nixon v. Administrator of General Servs., 433 U.S. 425, 473-474 (1977).

[9] United States v. Lovett, 328 U.S. 303, 315 (1946).

[10] 10 U.S. (6 Cranch) 87, 138 (1810).

[11] 468 U.S. 841 (1984).

[12] *Id.* at 852 (citations omitted).

individuals or groups from participation in specified employments or vocations, a mode of punishment commonly employed against those legislatively banded as disloyal."[13] Not surprisingly then, the outcome of cases concerning bill of attainder claims often turns on whether the court regards the law as imposing a punishment. After the Civil War, the Supreme Court invalidated as bills of attainder laws that required individuals, as a condition for practicing a profession, to take an oath that they had not helped the Confederacy.[14] The Court held that excluding a person from working as a member of the clergy or as an attorney was a punishment sufficient to constitute a bill of attainder. The Court explained that "[t]he deprivation of any rights, civil or political, previously enjoyed, may be punishment . . . [and] [d]isqualification from the pursuits of a lawful avocation, or from positions of trust, . . . may also, and often has been, imposed as a punishment."[15]

In *United States v. Lovett*, the Court concluded that there was a bill of attainder when the House of Representatives decided not to pay the salary of three employees who it deemed to be subversives.[16] Another illustration is *United States v. Brown*, where the Court invalidated as a bill of attainder a federal law that made it a crime for a member of the Communist Party to serve as an officer or an employee of a labor union.[17]

Yet in other cases, the Supreme Court rejected claims under the bill of attainder clauses by finding that there was not a punishment. Most notably, in *Nixon v. Administrator of General Services*, the Court upheld the constitutionality of the Presidential Recordings and Materials Preservations Act that provided for government custody and review of Richard Nixon's presidential papers.[18] The Court thoroughly reviewed the claim that the law was a bill of attainder because it applied solely to Richard Nixon and, in fact, mentioned him by name. The Court, however, concluded that it was not a bill of attainder, but instead "an act of non-punitive legislative policymaking."[19] The Court explained that this was not a traditional form of punishment and that it was not Congress's intent to punish. Rather, Congress acted to ensure the integrity and public availability of the presidential papers, while still safeguarding secrecy, where necessary, for them.

In light of the very broad definition of punishment, the Court's holding in *Nixon v. General Services Administration* can be questioned. The law confiscated Nixon's papers, at least long enough to permit screening by an archivist and to ensure public access. Taking someone's property, even if only temporarily, seems

---

[13] Nixon v. Administrator of General Servs., 433 U.S. at 474.

[14] Cummings v. Missouri, 71 U.S. (4 Wall.) 277 (1866) (invalidating the requirement for members of the clergy); Ex parte Garland, 71 U.S. (4 Wall.) 333 (1866) (invalidating the requirement for attorneys).

[15] Cummings v. Missouri, 71 U.S. at 320.

[16] 328 U.S. 303 (1946).

[17] 381 U.S. 437 (1965), invalidating §504 of the Labor-Management Reporting and Disclosure Act of 1959.

[18] 433 U.S. 425 (1977). The issues concerning executive privilege for presidential papers are discussed in §4.3.

[19] *Id.* at 477.

a punishment. Since the law applied only to Nixon, in many ways it resembles a classic bill of attainder.

In other cases, too, the Court rejected bill of attainder challenges by concluding that there was not a punishment. In *Fleming v. Nestor*, the Court upheld a federal law that denied Social Security benefits to aliens who had been deported; it was immaterial how long the individual had been in the United States or had contributed to Social Security.[20] The Court said that there must be "unmistakable evidence of punitive intent" for a law to be declared unconstitutional as a bill of attainder and that "only the clearest proof could suffice to establish the unconstitutionality of a statute on such a ground."[21]

No easy litmus test can be identified for determining what is a punishment. If a sanction resembles a traditional punishment, ranging from the death penalty to imprisonment to fines to precluding practicing a trade or profession, then it likely will be found a punishment for the purpose of the bill of attainder clauses. Also, if the Court believes that the legislature's purpose was to punish, it likely will be regarded as a punishment under the bill of attainder clauses.

Does the Law Designate Particular Individuals for Punishment?

It is necessary, but not sufficient, that a law impose a punishment in order to be considered a bill of attainder. The law also must designate particular individuals for punishment, rather than impose punishments on those who commit specific acts. At the extremes, it is relatively easy to tell the difference. A law requiring that Erwin Chemerinsky be put to death is obviously a bill of attainder; the legislature has imposed punishment on a specific person and thus undermined the protections of a trial within the judiciary. At the opposite extreme, a law that says that any person who intentionally kills shall be punished is a traditional criminal law and not a bill of attainder.

The hard cases are those where punishment is imposed on individuals who commit a particular act, but only a small defined class of individuals are likely to be punished. Is the legislature impermissibly designating who shall be punished, or is the legislature acting appropriately in defining criminal behavior? For example, in *United States v. Lovett*, the House of Representatives decided that three federal employees had engaged in subversive activity, and a law was passed denying these individuals any payments unless the president appointed them to a position and they were confirmed by the Senate.[22] This is a clear example of a bill of attainder because Congress identified specific individuals and directed that they be punished; they were denied paid employment with the federal government. There were no judicial proceedings to determine guilt or impose a sentence.

Harder cases were those where Congress provided that membership in a group, such as the Communist Party, was the basis for punishment. In addition

---

[20] 363 U.S. 603 (1960).
[21] *Id.* at 617, 619.
[22] 328 U.S. 303 (1946).

to concerns based on freedom of association,[23] there is the issue of whether such laws constitute bills of attainder. The Supreme Court has not been consistent. On the one hand, in *American Communications Association v. Douds*, the Court upheld a provision of the Labor Management Relations Act that required that union officers file affidavits with the National Labor Relations Board stating that they are not a member of the Communist Party and that they do not favor the overthrow of the United States government by force or violence.[24] Unions that failed this requirement could not receive assistance from or use the services of the National Labor Relations Board. The Supreme Court upheld this law and concluded that "Congress could rationally find that the Communist Party is not like other parties in its utilization of positions of union leadership as means by which to bring about strikes and other obstructions of commerce for purposes of political advantage."[25]

In contrast, in *United States v. Brown*, the Supreme Court declared unconstitutional a federal law that made it a crime for a member of the Communist Party to serve as an officer or manager of a labor union.[26] The Court concluded that the law was an impermissible bill of attainder because it identified specific individuals—members of the Communist Party—and imposed on them a punishment, exclusion from union positions. The Court said that it was a bill of attainder because Congress had adopted "a general rule to the effect that persons possessing characteristics . . . should not hold office, and simply inserted in place of a list of those characteristics as an alternative, shorthand criterion— membership in the Communist Party."[27]

Is it possible to distinguish *Douds* from *Brown*? In both, punishment was imposed on members of the Communist Party. In fact, in both, the likely consequence was to keep members of the Communist Party from being officers of labor unions. Perhaps the difference is that *Brown* involved criminal penalties of individuals, whereas *Douds* concerned denial of services from the National Labor Relations Board to the union. Perhaps the difference is timing, with *Douds* decided in 1950, during the anti-Communist hysteria, and *Brown* decided 15 years later. But the difficult question remains: Why is one a bill of attainder and the other permissible sanctions imposed for specified criminal behavior? A later case concerning this question is *Selective Service System v. Minnesota Public Interest Research Group*.[28] The Court upheld a federal law that denied student assistance to those men who had not registered for the draft. The challengers argued that the law was a bill of attainder because it denied benefits to a designated group of individuals. The Court rejected this argument, in part, because the law punished those who failed to comply with the law and, in part, because the individuals could avoid the punishment by registering for the draft at any time. In other words, the Court said that it was not a bill of attainder because it did not designate a particular group for punishment, but instead denied aid for a continuing failure to register for the

---

[23] *See* §11.5, discussing freedom of association.
[24] 339 U.S. 382 (1950).
[25] *Id.* at 391.
[26] 381 U.S. 437 (1965).
[27] *Id.* at 455.
[28] 468 U.S. 841 (1984).

draft. The Court observed that a statute that "leaves open perpetually the possibility of qualifying for aid does not fall within the historical meaning of forbidden legislative punishment."[29]

Ultimately, again, there is not a litmus test for determining whether the punishment is impermissibly directed at a person or a group or appropriately imposed on those who violate the law. In deciding this issue, courts will consider whether the punishment is imposed on either a specific person or a fixed group and whether the law itself prescribes the punishment or whether judicial proceedings remain necessary. The clearer it is that the punishment is imposed on a person or a group without any judicial proceedings, the more likely it is that the law will be found to constitute a bill of attainder.

§6.2.3   The Prohibition Against Ex Post Facto Laws

Article I, §§8 and 9, prohibit the federal and state governments, respectively, from enacting ex post facto laws. Simply stated, an ex post facto law is one that criminally punishes conduct that was lawful when it was done. It is an ex post facto law if after a person acts legally, the legislature adopts a criminal law and attempts to punish the person retroactively. The Supreme Court has held that it also is an ex post facto law if the government retroactively increases the punishment under a law.

This section focuses on two questions. First, what are the requirements for a law to be deemed "ex post facto"? An ex post facto law must involve a retroactive criminal punishment; a law with purely civil effects cannot be challenged under the ex post facto clauses. Also, it must be a law; a judicial decision, even with retroactive effects, does not violate the ex post facto clauses. Second, what changes in the criminal law are ex post facto laws?

What Are the Requirements for an Ex Post Facto Law?

From the earliest days of the country, the Supreme Court has held that ex post facto laws must involve criminal consequences. Retroactive civil consequences cannot be challenged as an ex post facto law, although they can be challenged under the due process clause.[30]

The Supreme Court initially considered the ex post facto clauses in *Calder v. Bull* in 1798.[31] The issue in *Calder* was whether there was an ex post facto law when a Connecticut statute overturned the decision of a probate court and ordered a new hearing on the validity of a will. The Court rejected the claim that this was

---

[29] *Id.* at 853.

[30] *See* Usery v. Turner Elkhorn Mining Co., 428 U.S. 1 (1976) (articulating a rational basis test for the evaluation of retroactive civil laws).

[31] 3 U.S. (3 Dall.) 386 (1798). Justice Clarence Thomas has urged the Court to reconsider *Calder*'s holding that the ex post facto clause applies only in criminal cases. Eastern Enters. v. Apfel, 524 U.S. 498, 502 (1998) (Thomas, J., concurring).

an ex post facto law. Justice Chase articulated a test for ex post facto laws that still applies two centuries later:

> 1st. Every law that makes an action done before the passing of the law, and which was innocent when done, criminal; and punishes such action. 2d. Every law that aggravates a crime, or makes it greater than it was, when committed. 3d. Every law that changes the punishment, and inflicts a greater punishment, than the law annexed to the crime, when committed. 4th. Every law that alters the legal rules of evidence, and receives less, or different, testimony, than the law required at the time of the commission of the offence, in order to convict the offender.[32]

Several of the Justices, in their separate opinions, emphasized that the ex post facto clauses apply only in the criminal context. Justice Iredell, for example, explained that the Connecticut statute was not an ex post facto law because "the true construction of the prohibition extends to criminal, not to civil, cases."[33] Similarly, Justice Patterson said that the clause referred "to crimes, pains and penalties, and no further."[34]

Similarly, in *Fletcher v. Peck*, Chief Justice John Marshall explained that "[a]n ex post facto law is one which renders an act punishable in a manner in which it was not punishable when it was committed."[35] In many other cases as well, the Supreme Court ruled that the ex post facto clauses do not invalidate civil legislation.[36] Thus, the Court has said that it is "settled that this prohibition is confined to laws respecting criminal punishments, and has no relation to retrospective legislation of any other description."[37]

An important implication of the ex post facto clause applying only in criminal cases is that it does not apply in deportation proceedings. The Supreme Court has characterized these actions as civil and thus held that "whatever might have been said at an earlier date for applying the ex post facto clause, it has been the unbroken rule of this Court that it has no application to deportation."[38] It can be questioned whether the characterization of a proceeding as civil or criminal, espe-

---

[32] 3 U.S. (3 Dall.) at 390. This test from *Calder* continues to be relied upon by the Supreme Court in its analysis of current issues under the ex post facto clause. *See, e.g.*, Rogers v. Tennessee, 532 U.S. 451, 456 (2001); Carmell v. Texas, 529 U.S. 513, 521-522 (2000); Lynce v. Mathis, 519 U.S. 433, 441 (1997).

[33] 3 U.S. at 399 (Iredell, J., concurring).

[34] *Id.* at 397 (Patterson, J., concurring).

[35] 10 U.S. at 138. *Fletcher* might be read as including as ex post facto laws civil statutes that take property and benefit the government. This view of the ex post facto clause has not been followed.

[36] Harisades v. Shaughnessy, 342 U.S. 580 (1952); Mahler v. Eby, 264 U.S. 32 (1924); Cummings v. Missouri, 71 U.S. (4 Wall.) 277 (1866); Ex parte Garland, 71 U.S. (4 Wall.) 333 (1866); Locke v. New Orleans, 71 U.S. (4 Wall.) 172 (1866); Watson v. Mercer, 33 U.S. (6 Pet.) 88 (1834).

[37] Johannessen v. United States, 225 U.S. 227, 242 (1912). The only case that suggests that civil matters might fall within the ex post facto clause is *Burgess v. Salmon*, 97 U.S. 381 (1878), which held that a tax on tobacco could not be applied retroactively. Subsequent cases reinterpreted *Burgess* as involving an essentially criminal matter being disguised in a civil statute. *See* Weaver v. Graham, 450 U.S. 24, 29 n.10 (1981).

[38] Galvan v. Press, 347 U.S. 522, 531 (1954); *see also* Immigration and Naturalization Serv. v. Lopez-Mendoza, 468 U.S. 1032, 1039 (1984); Harisades v. Shaughnessy, 342 U.S. 580, 594 (1952).

cially when there are such harsh consequences, should matter so much. Yet the Supreme Court has clearly and consistently rejected the application of the ex post facto clause to deportation actions.

Although retroactive civil legislation cannot be challenged as an ex post facto law, it can be objected to as violating due process. In *Usery v. Turner Elkhorn Mining Company*, the Court said that retroactive civil laws violate due process if they are not rationally related to a legitimate government purpose.[39] In *Usery*, the Court upheld a federal law that provided benefits to victims of black lung disease and that imposed some of these costs on mine owners. Even though the law created retroactive financial liability, it was upheld as constitutional.

Also, retroactive civil laws can be challenged under the contracts clause of Article I, §10, if they impair the obligations of contracts. The contracts clause is discussed in §8.3.

The other major limit on the ex post facto clause is that it applies only to criminal *statutes*; it does not apply to judicial decisions that have retroactive effect.[40] The Court has explained that title text of the ex post facto clauses refers to "laws" and that the traditional understanding is that only statutes and ordinances are included within that term. However, Supreme Court has held that retroactive changes in judicially created rules can be challenged under the due process clause.[41]

The Supreme Court subsequently announced a limit on the ability to use the due process clause to challenge retroactive changes in judicially created rules. In *Rogers v. Tennessee*, the Court held that a new judicial decision with retroactive application does not violate due process if it was not "unexpected or indefensible."[42] Tennessee traditionally had followed a common law rule that a person could not be convicted of murder if the defendant died more than year and a day after the action. Rogers was convicted of second degree murder even though his victim died more than a year and a day after his crime. The Tennessee Supreme Court used his case as the occasion for eliminating the "year and a day rule." Rogers objected that this was a violation of due process of law.

The Court repeated the basic rule that changes in judicially created rules are to be analyzed under due process, not the ex post facto clause, and it noted that "limitations on ex post facto judicial decision making are inherent in the notion of due process."[43] But in a 5-to-4 decision the Court found no violation of due process. Justice O'Connor, writing for the majority, said that the elimination of the year and a day rule "was not unexpected or indefensible. The year and a day rule is widely viewed as an outdated relic of the common law."[44] She noted that the vast majority of jurisdictions had abolished it and that at the time of Rogers's crime it had "only the most tenuous foothold as part of the criminal law of the State of Tennessee."[45] Because the change in the law was not "unexpected or indefen-

---

[39] 428 U.S. 1 (1976).
[40] Frank v. Magnum, 237 U.S. 309 (1915); Ross v. Oregon, 227 U.S. 150 (1913).
[41] Rogers v. Tennessee, 532 U.S. 451, 456 (2001).
[42] 532 U.S. 451 (2001).
[43] *Id.* at 1697.
[44] *Id.* at 1701.
[45] *Id.* at 1701.

sible," the Court concluded that there is "nothing to indicate that the Tennessee court's abolition of the rule in petitioner's case represented an exercise of the sort of unfair and arbitrary judicial action against which the Due Process Clause aims to protect."[46]

What Changes in the Law with Criminal Consequences Are Ex Post Facto Laws?

The paradigm ex post facto law is one that criminally punishes conduct that was lawful when it was done. Additionally, a retroactive increase in punishment also is an impermissible ex post facto law.[47] For example, in *Miller v. Florida*, the Supreme Court held that the ex post facto clause precludes sentencing a defendant under sentencing guidelines promulgated after the crime was committed.[48] Under the prior sentencing standards, the sentence for the crime would have been between three and four years; under the new guidelines, the sentence would have been between five and a half and seven years. Similarly, earlier in *Lindsey v. Washington*, the Court declared unconstitutional a state law that created a mandatory sentence, even though the same sentence previously was possible, although not mandatory.[49] Also, in *Weaver v. Graham*, the Supreme Court held that the retroactive reduction in the availability of "good time credits" for prisoners was an ex post facto law because it had the effect of increasing punishment.[50] In *Lynce v. Mathis*, the Court applied this and held that a statute that retroactively canceled early release credits after they were awarded violates the ex post facto clause of the Constitution.[51]

However, the Court subsequently distinguished these cases and held that a retroactive decrease in the availability of parole suitability hearings does not violate the ex post facto clause. In *California Department of Corrections v. Morales*, the Court explained that decreasing the frequency of parole hearings does not change the definition of the crime or the sentence imposed.[52] In an opinion by Justice Thomas, the Court said that the ex post facto clause does not bar any legislative change that has any conceivable risk of affecting a prisoner's punishment. Thomas said that under such an approach "the judiciary would be charged with the micromanagement of an endless array of legislative adjustments of parole and sentencing procedures."[53] The Court concluded that decreasing the frequency of

---

[46] *Id.* at 1703.

[47] The key, though, for the ex post facto clause is that the change must be imposed retroactively. *See, e.g.*, Johnson v. United States, 529 U.S. 694, 699 (2000) (change in law was not applied retroactively, so it does not violate the ex post facto clause).

[48] 482 U.S. 423 (1987). In contrast, the Court has held that nonretroactive application of new sentencing guidelines does not violate the ex post facto clause. *See* Johnson v. United States, 529 U.S. 694 (2000).

[49] 301 U.S. 397 (1937).

[50] 450 U.S. 24 (1981).

[51] 519 U.S. 433 (1997).

[52] 514 U.S 499, 504-505 (1995).

[53] *Id.* at 507.

parole suitability hearings "creates only the most speculative and attenuated possibility of producing the prohibited effect of increasing the measure of punishment for covered crimes, and such conjectural effects are insufficient under any threshold we might establish under the Ex Post Facto Clause."[54]

In *Garner v. Jones*, the Supreme Court reaffirmed *Morales* and held that a change in Georgia law that increased the intervals between consideration for parole did not violate the ex post facto clause.[55] The parole board in Georgia adopted a rule that extended the reconsideration for parole from three years to at least eight years. The Supreme Court concluded that this did not violate the ex post facto clause. The Court said that a change in the law was not an ex post facto law because it did not create a sufficient risk of decreasing the likelihood for parole.[56] The Court emphasized that the parole board had substantial discretion, and the lengthening of the time for reconsideration was just part of the uncertainty inherent to a discretionary process.[57]

In evaluating laws, the key question is whether the change can be regarded as a "punishment." For example, the Supreme Court held that a state's decision to change the method of execution from hanging to the electric chair was not an ex post facto law because it was not perceived as a greater punishment.[58] At the time, electrocution was perceived as a more humane form of execution than hanging.

Also, the Court has ruled that a law that retroactively provided for the civil commitment of sex offenders after they served their sentence was not an ex post facto law because it was not punitive. In *Kansas v. Hendricks*, the Court considered a challenge to a state's Sexually Violent Predator Act, which provided for the civil commitment of sex offenders who were deemed to be a continuing danger.[59] The defendant objected to the law, which was enacted after his conviction, being applied to him once he had completed his sentence. But the Court, in a 5-to-4 ruling, held that this was not an ex post facto law. Justice Thomas, writing for the majority, said that Hendricks failed to meet the burden of showing that the law was punitive.[60] The Court stressed that the new statute provided for civil commitment and was not intended to impose an additional punishment for the crime.[61] Justice Breyer, writing for the dissent, sharply disagreed and said that the law was not about treatment, but incarceration, and that is inherently punitive.

The Court followed similar reasoning in *Smith v. Doe*,[62] where the Court held that the Alaska Sex Offender Registry statute was not punitive and thus that its application to those who were convicted before its enactment did not violate the

---

[54] *Id.* at 507.

[55] 529 U.S. 244 (2000).

[56] *Id.* at 257.

[57] *Id.* at 259.

[58] Malloy v. South Carolina, 237 U.S. 180 (1915).

[59] 521 U.S. 346 (1997). In *United States v. Comstock*, 130 S. Ct. 1949 (2010), the Supreme Court upheld a similar federal statute as being within the scope of Congress's power under the "necessary and proper" clause. However, no issue was presented as to whether this was an impermissible ex post facto law. *Comstock* is discussed in §3.3.

[60] *Id.* at 361.

[61] *Id.* at 371.

[62] 538 U.S. 84 (2003).

ex post facto clause. The Court concluded that Alaska sought to create a civil, nonpunitive regulatory scheme. Although there obviously are very serious consequences in requiring that an individual register as a sex offender, the Court said that law was a reasonable way to achieve the state's nonpunitive objectives.

Finally, a procedural change in the law is unlikely to be found an ex post facto law unless it deprives the defendant of a defense or increases the punishment imposed. Earlier cases suggested that an ex post facto law exists if the government changes procedural rules in a manner that increases the likelihood that a person will be convicted. This makes sense because such retroactive procedural changes increase the chance of criminal punishments being imposed. For instance, in *Thompson v. Utah*, the Supreme Court found that it was an impermissible ex post facto law for a state to retroactively decrease the size of juries from 12 to 8.[63] From a practical perspective, the smaller the jury the fewer the number of people who can prevent a conviction by voting to acquit.

Yet in subsequent cases the Court rejected the view that changes in procedure constitute an ex post facto law.[64] The Supreme Court has expressly declared that "[e]ven though it may work to the disadvantage of a defendant, a procedural change is not ex post facto."[65] Indeed, repeatedly, the Court has rejected ex post facto challenges to retroactive procedural changes.

In *Collins v. Youngblood*, the Court held that it was not an ex post facto law for a state to retroactively allow courts of appeals to correct errors in punishment.[66] The state had retroactively authorized a fine as well as imprisonment for those convicted of aggravated sexual abuse. The court of appeals, pursuant to a law adopted after the defendant's crime, revised the punishment because it concluded that the retroactive fine was an ex post facto law. The defendant argued that the change in appellate procedure that allowed the court of appeals to revise sentences was itself an ex post facto law. The Supreme Court, in an opinion by Chief Justice Rehnquist, disagreed and said that decreasing the likelihood that a conviction will be overturned on appeal is not sufficient to make it an ex post facto law. The Court indicated that an ex post facto law must retroactively increase punishment or deny a defense to a defendant that would have been available at the time the crime was committed.

Similarly, in *Dobbert v. Florida*, the Supreme Court upheld the imposition of the death sentence under a capital punishment statute that was revised subsequent to the defendant's conviction and sentence.[67] At the time the defendant murdered his

---

[63] 170 U.S. 343 (1898).

[64] Actually, earlier cases were very inconsistent as to whether procedural changes constituted ex post facto laws. For example, in *Thompson v. Missouri*, 171 U.S. 380 (1898), the Court rejected an ex post facto challenge to a change in evidence law that allowed more circumstantial evidence to be introduced against a criminal defendant. In *Hopt v. Utah*, 110 U.S. 574 (1884), the Court rejected an ex post facto challenge to a law that allowed a convicted felon to be called as a witness to the detriment of the defendant. In *Beazell v. Ohio*, 269 U.S. 167 (1925), the Court found that it was not an ex post facto law when the state retroactively limited the right of jointly indicted defendants to receive separate trials.

[65] Dobbert v. Florida, 432 U.S. 282, 293 (1977).

[66] 497 U.S. 37 (1990).

[67] 432 U.S. 282 (1977).

two children, Florida law provided for the imposition of the death penalty on those convicted of a capital felony unless the majority of the jury recommended mercy. Subsequent to the murders, the Florida Supreme Court declared this law unconstitutional. Florida then adopted a new law that substantially changed the procedures in capital cases. The revision provided for a separate proceeding where the jury considered whether to recommend the death penalty and where the defendant could present mitigating evidence. Additionally, the new law required that in order to impose the death penalty the judge had to make a written finding that there were insufficient mitigating circumstances to outweigh the aggravating circumstances. The law also provided for automatic appellate review of all death sentences.

The defendant argued that this retroactive change in the law created an impermissible ex post facto law. The Court said that it was not an ex post facto law because "the change in the statute was clearly procedural."[68] Moreover, the Court said that the change in the law was not a punishment, but was "ameliorative," because it actually helped the defendant and decreased the likelihood of punishment.[69]

It thus now is clearly established that a retroactive procedural change is not an ex post facto law simply because it works to the detriment of a criminal defendant. In order to be an ex post facto law, the procedural reform must deny a defense or increase the punishment for a crime.

However, a change in the rules of evidence that changes the likelihood of conviction is an ex post facto law. In *Calder v. Bull*, quoted above, the Court listed four types of laws that are impermissible under the ex post facto clause; the fourth was "[e]very law that alters the legal rules of evidence, and receives less, or different, testimony, than the law required at the time of the commission of the offence, in order to convict the offender."[70] The Supreme Court applied this in *Carmell v. Texas* to find that a state law retroactively changing the rules of evidence constituted an ex post facto law.[71] Texas law allowed a defendant to be convicted of sex offenses solely based on the testimony of the victim so long as the victim informed someone of the crime within six months of its commission. The law, though, had an exception if the victim was younger than 14 years old. In 1993, Texas changed the law to extend the exception to victims under 18 years old.

The defendant was convicted of sex offenses against his step-daughter that occurred prior to this change in the law. The Supreme Court held that to apply the new law to him was an impermissible ex post facto law. The Court explained that by allowing only the victim's testimony to convict, rather than the victim and corroboration, the state had lessened the amount of evidence required.[72] The Court said that there is no difference between a law that lessens the burden of proof and one that reduces the amount of evidence necessary to convict; both are impermissible ex post facto laws.

---

[68] *Id.* at 293.
[69] *Id.* at 294.
[70] 3 U.S. (3 Dall.) at 390.
[71] 529 U.S. 513 (2000).
[72] *Id.* at 530.

§6.3   THE APPLICATION OF THE BILL OF RIGHTS TO THE STATES

§6.3.1   The Rejection of Application Before the Civil War

The Bill of Rights, of course, is the first ten amendments to the Constitution. The first eight amendments detail protection of individual rights. Some, such as the First Amendment's protection of freedom of speech and religion and the criminal procedure protections of the Fourth, Fifth, and Sixth Amendments, are the subject of frequent litigation. Others, such as the Third Amendment's right against having soldiers quartered in a person's home, have almost no contemporary significance. The Ninth Amendment provides: "The enumeration in the Constitution, of certain rights, shall not be construed to deny or disparage others retained by the people."[1] The Tenth Amendment states: "The powers not delegated to the United States by the Constitution, nor prohibited by it to the States, are reserved to the States respectively, or to the people."[2]

Barron v. Mayor & City Council of Baltimore

Early in American history, the Supreme Court ruled that the protection of individual liberties in the Bill of Rights applied only to the federal government, not to state or local governments. In *Barron v. Mayor & City Council of Baltimore*, the Supreme Court expressly held that the Bill of Rights was a restriction of federal actions, not state and local conduct.[3] Barron sued the city for taking his property without just compensation in violation of the Fifth Amendment. He contended that the city ruined his wharf by diverting streams and thereby made the water too shallow for boats.

The issue was whether the takings clause of the Fifth Amendment applied to the city.[4] Chief Justice John Marshall, writing for the Court, began by declaring: "The question . . . is . . . of great importance, but not of much difficulty."[5] He explained that the Bill of Rights was clearly intended to apply only to the federal government. He wrote: "The constitution was ordained and established by the people of the United States for themselves, for their own government, and not for the government of the individual states."[6] He said that if the framers had intended the Bill of Rights to apply to the states, "they would have declared this purpose in plain and intelligible language."[7]

---

§6.3 [1] The Ninth Amendment is discussed in more detail in §§10.1.1 and 10.3.2.

[2] The Tenth Amendment is discussed in detail in §3.10.

[3] 32 U.S. (7 Pet.) 243 (1833).

[4] The takings clause is discussed in §8.4. As discussed there, it is unlikely that this action would be considered a taking under current law because it does not confiscate the property and it still leaves some reasonable economically viable use of the property.

[5] *Id.* at 247.

[6] *Id.*

[7] *Id.* at 250.

The counterargument is that at least some provisions of the Bill of Rights, such as the takings clause, do not limit themselves only to the federal government. The Fifth Amendment begins, "No person shall," and concludes "nor shall private property be taken for public use, without just compensation." It does not say that the federal government cannot commit such a taking. The First Amendment, in contrast, begins, "Congress shall make no law." Chief Justice John Marshall expressly rejected this textual argument and said that "the limitations on power, if expressed in general terms, are naturally, and we think, necessarily applicable to the government created by the instrument."[8]

If the Bill of Rights applies only to the federal government, the obvious concern is that state and local governments then are free to infringe even the most precious liberties. Chief Justice Marshall observed that "[e]ach state established a constitution for itself, and in that constitution, provided such limitations and restrictions on the power of its particular government, as its judgment dictated."[9]

Thus, the Court concluded that the Fifth Amendment was "intended solely as a limitation on the exercise of power by the government of the United States, and is not applicable to the legislation of the States."[10] *Barron* meant that the Bill of Rights applied only to the federal government.

From a modern perspective, it is troubling that state and local governments were free to violate basic constitutional rights. Yet at the time of its decision, *Barron* made sense because of faith in state constitutions and because of the shared understanding that the Bill of Rights was meant to apply only to the federal government. As Professor John Hart Ely noted: "In terms of the original understanding, *Barron* was almost certainly decided correctly."[11]

§6.3.2   A False Start: The Privileges or Immunities Clause and the Slaughter-House Cases

The Fourteenth Amendment, adopted after the Civil War, declares: "No State shall make or enforce any law which shall abridge the privileges or immunities of citizens of the United States."[12] It might be argued that this provision was meant to apply the Bill of Rights to the states. After all, aren't the Bill of Rights the most basic "privileges or immunities" of citizenship? Indeed, Justice Hugo Black declared that "the words 'No State shall make or enforce any law which shall abridge the privileges or immunities of citizens of the United States' seem to me an eminently reasonable way of expressing the idea that henceforth the Bill of Rights shall apply to the States."[13]

---

[8] *Id.* at 247.

[9] *Id.*

[10] *Id.* at 250-251.

[11] John Ely, Democracy and Distrust 196 n.58 (1980).

[12] The history of the adoption of the Fourteenth Amendment is described in §1.3.

[13] Duncan v. Louisiana, 391 U.S. 145, 166 (1968) (Black, J., dissenting).

The Debate over the Framers' Intent

The historical accuracy of Justice Black's claim concerning the privileges or immunities clause is uncertain. On the one hand, the choice of the words "privileges" and "immunities" suggests that the framers intended to protect fundamental rights from state and local interference. The words "privileges" and "immunities" were already a part of the Constitution in Article IV, §2, which prevents a state from denying citizens of other states the privileges and immunities it accords its own citizens.[14] More than 40 years before the adoption of the Fourteenth Amendment, Justice Washington stated that the privileges and immunities clause in Article IV protected rights "which are, in their nature, fundamental; which belong, of right, to the citizens of all free governments."[15]

During the congressional debate over the Fourteenth Amendment, representatives and senators said that the Fourteenth Amendment privileges or immunities clause was meant to protect basic rights from state interference. Senator Howard, for example, quoted Justice Washington's earlier statement as to the meaning of privileges and immunities and declared: "Such is the character of the privileges and immunities spoken of in the second section of the fourth article of the Constitution. To these privileges and immunities . . . should be added the personal rights guarantied and secured by the first eight amendments of the Constitution."[16] Likewise, Representative Bingham, who is credited with drafting the provision, stated that "the privileges and immunities of citizens of the United States [are] chiefly defined in the first eight amendments to the Constitution."[17]

Yet the historical claim that the privileges or immunities clause was meant to apply the Bill of Rights to the states is very much disputed. Charles Fairman, in an exhaustive study of the framers' intent on this issue, concluded: "[The theory that the] privileges or immunities clause incorporated Amendments I to VIII found no recognition in the practice of Congress, or the action of state legislatures, constitutional conventions, or courts. . . . Congress would not have attempted such a thing, the country would not have stood for it, the legislatures would not have ratified."[18]

As is so often the case in discussing the framers' intent, there probably was not a single view within the Congress that passed the Fourteenth Amendment, or the states that ratified it, as to whether the privileges or immunities clause was meant to apply the Bill of Rights to the states.[19] Some of the members of Congress and the state legislatures probably believed that the privileges or immunities clause

---

[14] The privileges and immunities clause is discussed in §5.5.

[15] Corfield v. Coryell, 6 F. Cas. 546, 551 (C.C.E.D. Pa. 1823) (No. 3,230). In a recent opinion, Justice Thomas exhaustively reviews the history of the privileges or immunities clause in arguing that it is the appropriate vehicle for applying the Bill of Rights to the states. McDonald v. City of Chicago, 561 U.S. 742, 805-806 (2010) (Thomas, J., concurring in the judgment).

[16] Cong. Globe, 39th Cong., 1st Sess. 2765 (1866).

[17] Cong. Globe, 42d Cong., 1st Sess. App. 84 (1871).

[18] Charles Fairman, Does the Fourteenth Amendment Incorporate the Bill of Rights?, 2 Stan. L. Rev. 132, 137 (1949).

[19] See Timothy S. Bishop, Comment, The Privileges or Immunities Clause of the Fourteenth Amendment: The Original Intent, 79 Nw. U. L. Rev. 142, 174 (1984) (supporting the view that there was a range of intentions in Congress concerning the meaning of the privileges or immunities clause).

included the Bill of Rights; some probably didn't think so; and many probably didn't consider the question.

The *Slaughter-House Cases*

Apart from claims based on the framers' intent, a strong argument can be made that the privileges or immunities clause should be interpreted as applying the Bill of Rights to the states. The claim would be that the provisions of the Bill of Rights are the basic "privileges" and "immunities" possessed by all citizens. That argument, however, was foreclosed in the first Supreme Court case to interpret the Fourteenth Amendment: the *Slaughter-House Cases*.[20]

Seeing a huge surplus of cattle in Texas, the Louisiana legislature gave a monopoly in the livestock landing and the slaughterhouse business for the City of New Orleans to the Crescent City Livestock Landing and Slaughter-House Company. The law required that the company allow any person to slaughter animals in the slaughterhouse for a fixed fee.

Several butchers brought suit challenging the grant of the monopoly. They argued that the state law impermissibly violated their right to practice their trade. The butchers invoked many of the provisions of the recently adopted constitutional amendments. They argued that the restriction created involuntary servitude, deprived them of their property without due process of law, denied them equal protection of the laws, and abridged their privileges or immunities as citizens.

The Supreme Court narrowly construed all of these provisions and rejected the plaintiffs' challenge to the legislature's grant of a monopoly. At the outset, the Court said that it recognized the importance of the case before it. Justice Miller, writing for the Court, said: "No questions so far reaching and pervading in their consequences, so profoundly interesting to the people of this country, and so important in their bearing upon the relations of the United States, and of the several States . . . have been before this court during the official life of any of its present members."[21]

The Court then said that the purpose of the Thirteenth and Fourteenth Amendments was solely to protect former slaves. Justice Miller wrote that "[t]he most cursory glance at these articles discloses a unity of purpose, when taken in connection with the history of the times . . . [that there was] one pervading purpose found in them all . . . : the freedom of the slave race, the security and firm establishment of that freedom, and the protection of the newly-made freeman and citizen from the oppression of those who had formerly exercised unlimited dominion over him."[22]

The Court proceeded to interpret each provision very narrowly and solely to achieve this limited goal. Interestingly, except for the privileges or immunities

---

For an excellent criticism of both Justice Black and Professor Fairman's historical arguments, *see* Alfred H. Kelly, Clio and the Court: An Illicit Love Affair, 1965 Sup. Ct. Rev. 119, 132-134.

[20] 83 U.S. (16 Wall.) 36 (1872).

[21] *Id.* at 67.

[22] *Id.* at 67-71.

clause, all of the other restrictive interpretations of the Fourteenth Amendment in the *Slaughter-House Cases* were subsequently overruled. For example, the Court said that the equal protection clause only was meant to protect blacks and offered the prediction that "[w]e doubt very much whether any action of a State not directed by way of discrimination against the negroes as a class, or on account of their race, will ever be held to come within the purview of this provision."[23] This prediction obviously proved false, and the equal protection clause has been applied, since the 1960s, to prevent discrimination based on characteristics such as gender, alienage, and legitimacy.[24]

Likewise, the Court rejected the application of the due process clause to protect a right to practice one's trade. The Court declared, with no elaboration or explanation, that "it is sufficient to say that under no construction of that provision that we have ever seen, or any that we deem admissible, can the restraint imposed by the State of Louisiana upon the exercise of their trade by the butchers of New Orleans be held to be a deprivation of property within the meaning of the last provision."[25] Yet by the late nineteenth century and in the first third of this century, the Court found that the due process clause did protect a right to practice a person's trade or profession. Throughout the twentieth century the Court used the due process clause to safeguard privacy and autonomy rights such as the right to marry, the right to custody of one's children, the right to purchase and use contraceptives, and the right to abortion.[26]

However, the Supreme Court's extremely narrow interpretation of the privileges or immunities clause never has been expressly overruled and has precluded the use of that provision to apply the Bill of Rights.[27] Specifically, the Court held that the privileges or immunities clause was not meant to protect individuals from state government actions and was not meant to be a basis for federal courts to invalidate state laws. Justice Miller wrote: "[S]uch a construction . . . would constitute this court a perpetual censor upon all legislation of the States, on the civil rights of their own citizens, with authority to nullify such as it did not approve as consistent with those rights, as they existed at the time of the adoption of this amendment. . . . We are convinced that no such results were intended by the Congress which proposed these amendments, nor by the legislatures of the States which ratified them."[28]

Indeed, the Court was explicit that "privileges and immunities . . . are left to the State governments for security and protection, and not by this article placed

---

[23] *Id.* at 81.

[24] Equal protection is discussed in Chapter 9.

[25] *Slaughter-House Cases*, 83 U.S. at 80-81.

[26] *See* Chapter 10, discussing the protection of these rights.

[27] As discussed below, in *Saenz v. Roe*, 526 U.S. 489 (1999), the Court revived the privileges or immunities clause of the Fourteenth Amendment and used it to protect the right to travel. The Court has not used the privileges or immunities clause since *Saenz v. Roe*, though Justice Thomas would have used it to apply the Second Amendment to the states. McDonald v. City of Chicago, 561 U.S. 742, 805-806 (2010) (Thomas, J., concurring in the judgment).

[28] *Slaughter-House Cases*, 83 U.S. at 498.

under the special care of the federal government."[29] This means that the privileges or immunities clause is removed as a basis for applying the Bill of Rights to the states or for protecting any rights from state interference.

The Court then considered the meaning of privileges and immunities. Interestingly, the Court gave a list of rights that were protected under the Constitution even before the privileges or immunities clause was adopted. Justice Miller wrote that privileges and immunities included "the right of the citizen . . . to come to the seat of the government to assert any claim he may have upon that government, to transact any business he may have with it, to seek its protections, to share its offices, to engage in administering its functions. He has the right of free access to its seaports . . . and courts of justice in the several States . . . [and] to demand the care and protection of the Federal government . . . when on the high seas or within the jurisdiction of a foreign government."[30]

All of these rights existed before the privileges or immunities clause was adopted. Therefore, the *Slaughter-House Cases* interpreted the provision in a manner to rob it of all meaning. This was noted by the dissenting Justices. Justice Field, in dissent, lamented: "If [the privileges and immunities clause] only refers, as held by the majority of the court . . . to such privileges and immunities as were before its adoption specially designated in the Constitution or necessarily implied as belonging to citizens of the United States, it was a vain and idle enactment, which accomplished nothing, and most unnecessarily excited Congress and the people on its passage."[31]

In fact, such has been the case: The privileges or immunities clause was rendered a nullity by the *Slaughter-House Cases*, and it has been ever since. Professor Edward Corwin remarked that "[u]nique among constitutional provisions, the privileges and immunities clause of the Fourteenth Amendment enjoys the distinction of having been rendered a practical nullity by a single decision of the Supreme Court rendered within five years after its ratification."[32]

Interestingly, many scholars, including prominent conservatives such as Clarence Thomas (prior to being appointed to the Supreme Court), have urged a revival of the privileges or immunities clause.[33] The words of the clause suggest that it clearly protects rights—those that can be deemed privileges or immunities of citizenship—from state interference.

---

[29] *Id.*

[30] *Id.* at 499.

[31] *Id.* at 521 (Field, J., dissenting).

[32] Legislative Reference Service, Library of Congress, The Constitution of the United States of America 965 (Edward S. Corwin ed. 1953).

[33] Clarence Thomas, The Higher Law Background of the Privileges or Immunities Clause, 12 Harv. J.L. & Pub. Poly. 63, 68 (1989); Philip B. Kurland, The Privileges or Immunities Clause: "Its Hour Come Round at Last?," 1972 Wash. U. L.Q. 405, 418-420. Justice Thomas would have used the privileges or immunities clause to apply the Second Amendment to state and local governments. McDonald v. City of Chicago, 561 U.S. 742, 805-806 (2010) (Thomas, J., concurring in the judgment).

The Revival of the Privileges or Immunities Clause: *Saenz v. Roe*

In 1999, essentially for the first time in American history,[34] the Supreme Court used the privileges or immunities clause of the Fourteenth Amendment to invalidate a state law. *Saenz v. Roe* involved a California law that limited welfare benefits for new residents in the state to the level of the state that they moved from for their year of residence; Justice Stevens, writing for the Court, said that prior decisions clearly established that the right to travel is a fundamental right.[35] He explained that one aspect of this is the right of new residents to be treated the same as longer term residents of a state, and he said that this aspect of the right to travel is protected by the privileges or immunities clause of the Fourteenth Amendment. He wrote: "Despite fundamentally differing views concerning the coverage of the Privileges or Immunities Clause of the Fourteenth Amendment, most notably expressed in the majority and dissenting opinions in the *Slaughter-House Cases*, it has always been common ground that this Clause protects the . . . right to travel [and] the citizen's right to be treated equally in her new State of residence."[36]

The state argued to the Supreme Court that it was justified in restricting welfare benefits for new residents to avoid California's being a magnet for those moving to the state solely to collect its higher welfare benefits. Justice Stevens's majority opinion emphatically rejected this argument: "First, although it is reasonable to assume that some persons may be motivated to move for the purpose of obtaining higher benefits, the empirical evidence reviewed by the District Judge, which takes into account the high cost of living in California, indicates that the number of such persons is quite small—surely not large enough to justify a burden on those who had no such motive. Second, California has represented to the Court that the legislation was not enacted for any such reason. Third, even if it were, as we squarely held in *Shapiro v. Thompson* (1969), such a purpose would be unequivocally impermissible."[37]

Notably, *Saenz v. Roe* was a 7-to-2 decision with only Chief Justice Rehnquist and Justice Thomas dissenting. Each lamented the revival of the privileges or immunities clause as a basis for protecting rights. Chief Justice Rehnquist wrote: "The Court today breathes new life into the previously dormant Privileges or Immunities Clause of the Fourteenth Amendment—a Clause relied upon by this Court in only one other decision, *Colgate v. Harvey* (1935), overruled five years later by *Madden v. Kentucky* (1940). . . . Because I do not think any provision of the Constitution—and surely not a provision relied upon for only the second time since its enactment 130 years ago—requires this result, I dissent."[38]

---

[34] In *Edwards v. California*, 314 U.S. 160 (1941), four Justices relied on the privileges or immunities clause as creating a right to interstate travel and as a basis for invalidating a California law that made it a crime to bring an indigent person into the state. In *Colgate v. Harvey*, 296 U.S. 404 (1935), the Supreme Court invalidated a state tax that applied solely to income and dividends earned outside the state. In part, the Court said that this was unconstitutional because it infringed a "privilege . . . attributable to national citizenship." *Id.* at 430. However, four years later, the Court overruled *Colgate* in *Madden v. Kentucky*, 309 U.S. 83 (1940).

[35] 526 U.S. 489 (1999). The right to travel is discussed in detail in §10.7.

[36] *Id.* at 503.

[37] *Id.* at 506 (citations omitted).

[38] *Id.* at 511 (Rehnquist, C.J., dissenting).

Similarly, Justice Thomas objected that the Court's "majority attributes a meaning to the Privileges or Immunities Clause that likely was unintended when the Fourteenth Amendment was enacted and ratified."[39] Justice Thomas said that he would be "open to reevaluating its meaning in an appropriate case. Before invoking the Clause, however, we should endeavor to understand what the framers of the Fourteenth Amendment thought that it meant. We should also consider whether the Clause should displace, rather than augment, portions of our equal protection and substantive due process jurisprudence."[40] But he objected that "[t]he majority's failure to consider these important questions raises the specter that the Privileges or Immunities Clause will become yet another convenient tool for inventing new rights, limited solely by the 'predilections of those who happen at the time to be Members of this Court.' "[41]

It is interesting to note that Justice Scalia, one of the Court's foremost opponents of protecting nontextual constitutional rights, voted with the majority. He did not write a separate opinion, so it is not possible to discern whether this means he sees the privileges or immunities clause as a basis for protecting rights that he is unwilling to find under equal protection or due process.

In the decade and a half since *Saenz* was decided, the Court has not again based a decision on, or even discussed, the privileges or immunities clause of the Fourteenth Amendment. In *McDonald v. City of Chicago*, the plurality rejected the argument that it should use the privileges or immunities clause to apply the Second Amendment to the states and declared: "We see no need to reconsider that interpretation [of the *Slaughter-House Cases*] here. For many decades, the question of the rights protected by the Fourteenth Amendment against state infringement has been analyzed under the Due Process Clause of that Amendment and not under the Privileges or Immunities Clause. We therefore decline to disturb the *Slaughter-House* holding."[42] Perhaps this reflects, as explained below, the Court simply following prior decisions in using the due process clause to apply the Bill of Rights to state and local governments; or perhaps this reflects that, at least for the time being, *Saenz* is an anomaly in using the privileges or immunities clause.

§6.3.3   The Incorporation of the Bill of Rights into the Due Process Clause of the Fourteenth Amendment

Initial Incorporation Cases

Because of the *Slaughter-House Cases*, the application of the Bill of Rights to the states could not be through the privileges or immunities clause. In the early twentieth century, the Supreme Court suggested an alternative approach: finding

---

[39] *Id.* at 521 (Thomas, J., dissenting).
[40] *Id.* at 528.
[41] *Id.* at 528 (citations omitted).
[42] 561 U.S. 742, 758 (2010).

that at least some of the Bill of Rights provisions are part of the liberty protected from state interference by the due process clause of the Fourteenth Amendment.

In 1897, in *Chicago, Burlington & Quincy Railroad Co. v. City of Chicago*, the Supreme Court ruled that the due process clause of the Fourteenth Amendment prevents states from taking property without just compensation.[43] Although the Court did not speak explicitly of the Fourteenth Amendment incorporating the takings clause, that was the practical effect of the decision.

In 1908, in *Twining v. New Jersey*, the Court expressly recognized the possibility that the due process clause of the Fourteenth Amendment incorporates provisions of the Bill of Rights and thereby applies them to state and local governments.[44] The Court rejected criminal defendants' claim that a state court had violated their constitutional rights by instructing the jury that it could draw a negative inference from their failure to testify at trial. However, the Court said that it "is possible that some of the personal rights safeguarded by the first eight Amendments against National action may also be safeguarded against state action, because a denial of them would be a denial of due process of law. . . . If this is so, it is not because those rights are enumerated in the first eight Amendments, but because they are of such a nature that they are included in the conception of due process of law."[45]

For example, in *Gitlow v. New York*, in 1925, the Court for the first time said that the First Amendment's protection of freedom of speech applies to the states through its incorporation into the due process clause of the Fourteenth Amendment.[46] The Court declared: "For present purposes we may and do assume that freedom of speech and of the press—which are protected by the First Amendment from abridgment by Congress—are among the fundamental personal rights and liberties protected by the due process clause of the Fourteenth Amendment from impairment by the States."[47] In *Gitlow*, the Court actually rejected the constitutional challenge to a state law that made it a crime to advocate the violent overthrow of government by force or violence.[48] Two years later, in *Fiske v. Kansas*, the Court for the first time found that a state law regulating speech violated the due process clause of the Fourteenth Amendment.[49]

In 1933, in *Powell v. Alabama*, the Court found that a state's denial of counsel in a capital case denied due process, thereby in essence applying the Sixth Amendment to the states in capital cases.[50] The infamous Scottsboro trial involved two African-American men who were convicted of rape without the assistance of an attorney at trial and with a jury from which all blacks had been excluded. The Supreme Court concluded that the due process clause of the Fourteenth Amendment protects fundamental rights from state interference and that this can include Bill of Rights provisions. But the Court said that "[i]f this is so, it is not

[43]   166 U.S. 226 (1897).
[44]   211 U.S. 78 (1908).
[45]   *Id.* at 99.
[46]   268 U.S. 652 (1925).
[47]   *Id.* at 666.
[48]   The First Amendment issues in *Gitlow* are discussed in §11.3.2.3.
[49]   274 U.S. 380 (1927).
[50]   287 U.S. 45 (1932).

because those rights are enumerated in the first eight Amendments, but because they are of such a nature that they are included in the 'conception of due process of law.'[51] The Court held that in a capital case, "it [is] clear that the right to the aid of counsel is of this fundamental character."[52]

The Debate over Incorporation

Once the Court found that the due process clause of the Fourteenth Amendment protected fundamental rights from state infringement, there was a major debate over which liberties are safeguarded. For many years, this debate raged among Justices and commentators. On the one side, there were the total incorporationists who believed that all of the Bill of Rights should be deemed to be included in the due process clause of the Fourteenth Amendment. Justices Black and Douglas were the foremost advocates of this position.[53]

On the other side, there were the selective incorporationists who believed that only some of the Bill of Rights were sufficiently fundamental to apply to state and local governments. Justice Cardozo, for example, wrote that "[t]he process of absorption . . . [applied to rights where] neither liberty nor justice would exist if they were sacrificed."[54] Justice Cardozo said that the due process clause included "principles of justice so rooted in the tradition and conscience of our people as to be ranked as fundamental" and that were therefore "implicit in the concept of ordered liberty."[55] Justice Frankfurter said that due process precludes those practices that "offend those canons of decency and fairness which express the notions of justice of English-speaking peoples."[56]

The debate between total and selective incorporation was obviously extremely important because it determined the reach of the Bill of Rights and the extent to which individuals could turn to the federal courts for protection from state and local governments. The debate primarily was centered on three issues.[57]

First, the debate was over history and whether the framers of the Fourteenth Amendment intended for it to apply the Bill of Rights to the states. Both sides of the debate claimed that history supported their view. As described above, Justice Black believed that the privileges or immunities clause of the Fourteenth Amendment was meant to incorporate the Bill of Rights. For example, in *Adamson v. California,* Justice Black stated: "My study of the historical events that culminated in the Fourteenth Amendment . . . persuades me that one of the chief objects . . . [of] the first section . . . was to make the Bill of Rights applicable to the states."[58]

---

[51] *Id.* at 67-68 (citations omitted).

[52] *Id.* at 68.

[53] *See, e.g.,* Adamson v. California, 332 U.S. 46, 71-72 (1947) (Black, J., dissenting).

[54] Palko v. Connecticut, 302 U.S. 319, 326 (1937).

[55] *Id.* at 325.

[56] Adamson v. California, 332 U.S. 46, 67 (1947) (Frankfurter, J., concurring).

[57] For a detailed description of the debate and the issues, *see* Jerold Israel, Selective Incorporation Revisited, 71 Geo. L.J. 253, 336-338 (1982).

[58] 332 U.S. 46, 71-72 (1947) (Black, J., dissenting).

Those on the other side of the debate challenged this history and argued that the framers did not intend for the Fourteenth Amendment to apply the Bill of Rights to the states. Charles Fairman, for example, examined the history of the Fourteenth Amendment and argued that the original intent was not to apply the Bill of Rights to the states.[59] Indeed, Professor Fairman argues that Congress never would have approved such a result and certainly the states never would have ratified it.

The historical argument ultimately is unresolvable with advocates on both sides arguing that history definitively supports their position.[60] The arguments on both sides, of course, assume that the framers' intent should be given significant weight in determining whether the Bill of Rights applies to the states. Moreover, both sides can marshal quotes from framers to support their positions.[61] In all likelihood, there were members of the Congress that passed the Fourteenth Amendment and of the state legislatures that ratified it who believed that it applied the Bill of Rights to the states and others who rejected this view.[62] The historical argument can never be decisively resolved because there is not a single discernible intent on the issue of incorporation. Additionally, the historical argument begs the question as to how much weight should be given to the framers' intent even if it could be ascertained.

Second, the incorporation debate was over federalism. Applying the Bill of Rights to the states imposes a substantial set of restrictions on state and local governments. Not surprisingly, opponents of total incorporation argued based on federalism: the desirability of preserving state and local governing autonomy by freeing them from the application of the Bill of Rights. Defenders of total incorporation responded that federalism is not a sufficient reason for tolerating violations of fundamental liberties.

Supporters of selective incorporation reply that states on their own are capable of advancing individual rights. Justice Frankfurter, for instance, argued that "[a] construction which gives to due process no independent function but turns it into a summary of the specific provisions of the Bill of Rights would . . . deprive the States of opportunity for reforms in legal process designed for extending the area of freedom."[63] Those who favored total incorporation counter that history shows that there are instances where states and state courts will not adequately protect rights; safeguarding precious liberties should not rest on faith in the states.

---

[59] Fairman, *supra* note 18, at 5, 132.

[60] *See, e.g.*, Michael Curtis, No State Shall Abridge: The Fourteenth Amendment and the Bill of Rights (1986) (arguing that history supports the total incorporation position); Michael Curtis, The Bill of Rights as a Limitation on State Authority: A Reply to Professor Berger, 16 Wake Forest L. Rev. 45 (1980) (same); Raoul Berger, Incorporation of the Bill of Rights into the Fourteenth Amendment: A Nine Lived Cat, 42 Ohio St. L.J. 435 (1981) (arguing that historical analysis rejects the total incorporation position); Raoul Berger, Incorporation of the Bill of Rights: A Reply to Michael Curtis' Response, 44 Ohio St. L.J. 1 (1983) (same).

[61] For a criticism of the use of history in the incorporation, *see* Kelly, *supra* note 19, at 119, 132-134.

[62] Timothy S. Bishop, Comment, The Privileges or Immunities Clause of the Fourteenth Amendment, 79 Nw. U. L. Rev. 142 (1984) (reviewing the historical record and identifying the split of opinions).

[63] Adamson v. California, 332 U.S. at 68 (Frankfurter, J., concurring).

Third, the debate was over the appropriate judicial role. Defenders of total incorporation, such as Justice Black, argued that selective incorporation gives judges far too much discretion in deciding what rights are fundamental. He maintained that this allowed judges to "roam at will in the limitless area of their own beliefs as to reasonableness . . . which the Constitution entrusts to the representatives of the people."[64]

In contrast, advocates of selective incorporation denied that this allowed subjective choices by Justices. They maintained that total incorporation would mean more judicial oversight of state and local actions and thus less room for democracy to operate. Justice Frankfurter argued: "The judicial judgment in applying the Due Process Clause must move within the limits of accepted notions of justice and is not to be based upon the idiosyncrasies of a merely personal judgment. . . . An important safeguard against such merely individual judgment is an alert deference to the judgment of the State court under review."[65]

Although the debate over incorporation seems largely resolved, in recent years, Justice Clarence Thomas has repeatedly argued that the establishment clause of the First Amendment should not apply to state and local governments. He has explained that the "Establishment Clause of the First Amendment states that 'Congress shall make no law respecting an establishment of religion.' On its face, this provision places no limit on the States with regard to religion. The Establishment Clause originally protected States, and by extension their citizens, from the imposition of an established religion by the Federal Government."[66] Justice Thomas has said that the "Establishment Clause is a federalism provision, which, for this reason, resists incorporation."[67] By this view, the establishment clause was meant solely as a limit on the federal government to keep it from establishing a church that would rival state churches. To this point, no other Justice has joined Justice Thomas's call to reexamine the incorporation of the establishment clause. This likely reflects the judgment of the other Justices that the establishment clause does protect individual freedom and thus is safeguarded as part of the liberty protected by the due process clause of the Fourteenth Amendment.

The Current Law as to What's Incorporated

In one sense, the selective incorporationists prevailed in this debate; never has the Supreme Court endorsed the total incorporationist approach. However, from a practical perspective, the total incorporationists largely succeeded in their objective because, one by one, the Supreme Court found almost all of the provisions to be incorporated.

---

[64] *Id.* at 92 (Black, J., dissenting).
[65] *Id.* at 68 (Frankfurter, J., concurring).
[66] Zelman v. Simmons-Harris, 536 U.S. 639, 677 (2002) (Thomas, J., concurring).
[67] Elk Grove Unified School Dist. v. Newdow, 542 U.S. 1, 45 (2004); *see also* Town of Greece v. Galloway, 134 S. Ct. 1811, 1835-1837 (2014) (Thomas, J., concurring in part and concurring in the judgment).

§6.3 The Application of the Bill of Rights to the States

Over time, the Court has articulated varying tests for deciding whether a provision of the Bill of Rights is incorporated. In *Duncan v. Louisiana*, the Supreme Court summarized these formulations and said: "The question has been asked whether a right is among those 'fundamental principles of liberty and justice which lie at the base of all our civil and political institutions,' whether it is 'basic in our system of jurisprudence,' and whether it is a 'fundamental right, essential to a fair trial.' "[68]

To be specific, the Court has found the following provisions of the Bill of Rights to be incorporated:

- the First Amendment's establishment clause,[69] free exercise clause,[70] and protections of speech,[71] press,[72] assembly,[73] and petition;[74]
- the Second Amendment's right to bear arms;[75]
- the Fourth Amendment's protection against unreasonable search and seizures and the requirement for a warrant based on probable cause;[76] also, the exclusionary rule, which prevents the government from using evidence obtained in violation of the Fourth Amendment;[77]
- the Fifth Amendment's prohibition of double jeopardy,[78] protection against self-incrimination,[79] and requirement that the government pay just compensation when it takes private property for public use;[80]
- the Sixth Amendment's requirements for a speedy[81] and public trial,[82] by an impartial jury,[83] with notice of the charges,[84] the chance to confront adverse witnesses[85] and to have compulsory process to obtain favorable witnesses,[86] and to have assistance of counsel if the sentence involves possible imprisonment;[87]
- the Eighth Amendment's prohibition against excessive bail[88] and cruel and unusual punishment.[89]

---

[68] Duncan v. Louisiana, 391 U.S. 145, 148-149 (1968) (citations omitted).
[69] Everson v. Board of Educ., 330 U.S. 1 (1947); Wallace v. Jaffree, 472 U.S. 38 (1985).
[70] Cantwell v. Connecticut, 310 U.S. 296 (1940).
[71] Gitlow v. New York, 268 U.S. 652 (1925).
[72] Near v. Minnesota, 283 U.S. 697 (1931).
[73] DeJonge v. Oregon, 299 U.S. 353 (1937).
[74] Hague v. CIO, 307 U.S. 496 (1939).
[75] McDonald v. City of Chicago, 130 S. Ct. 3020 (2010).
[76] Wolf v. Colorado, 338 U.S. 25 (1949).
[77] Mapp v. Ohio, 367 U.S. 643 (1961).
[78] Benton v. Maryland, 395 U.S. 784 (1969).
[79] Malloy v. Hogan, 378 U.S. 1 (1964).
[80] Chicago, Burlington & Quincy R.R. Co. v. City of Chicago, 166 U.S. 226 (1897).
[81] Klopfer v. North Carolina, 386 U.S. 213 (1967).
[82] In re Oliver, 333 U.S. 257 (1948).
[83] Irvin v. Dowd, 366 U.S. 717 (1961).
[84] In re Oliver, 333 U.S. 257 (1948).
[85] Pointer v. Texas, 380 U.S. 400 (1965).
[86] Washington v. Texas, 388 U.S. 14 (1967).
[87] Gideon v. Wainwright, 372 U.S. 335 (1963).
[88] Schilb v. Kuebel, 404 U.S. 357 (1971).
[89] Robinson v. California, 370 U.S. 660 (1962); Harmelin v. Michigan, 501 U.S. 957 (1991).

In reviewing these decisions, what is particularly striking is the relative recency of incorporation of most of these provisions. It was not until 1963, in *Gideon v. Wainwright*,[90] that the right to counsel was required in all cases where there is a possible prison sentence. It was not until 1964, in *Malloy v. Hogan*,[91] that the privilege against self-incrimination was incorporated. Indeed, most of the Bill of Rights provisions concerning criminal procedure were not incorporated until the Warren Court decisions of the 1960s.

In 2010, in *McDonald v. City of Chicago*, the Court held that the Second Amendment is incorporated and applies to state and local governments.[92] From 1791 when the Second Amendment was adopted until 2008, the Court never found any law to violate this provision. The Court viewed the Second Amendment as protecting a right to have guns for the purpose of militia service.[93] But in 2008, in *District of Columbia v. Heller*,[94] the Court held that the Second Amendment is not limited to this and ruled that it protects a right to have guns for personal safety, especially in the home. The District of Columbia, of course, is a part of the federal government so the Court has no occasion to consider whether the Second Amendment applies to state and local governments. Two years later, in *McDonald v. City of Chicago*, the Court, by the same 5-4 margin as in *Heller*, held that the Second Amendment is incorporated into the Fourteenth Amendment. Justice Alito's plurality opinion, joined by Chief Justice Roberts and Justices Scalia and Kennedy, did so through the due process clause of the Fourteenth Amendment, while Justice Thomas, concurring in the judgment, used the privileges or immunities clause.

There are still four provisions of the Bill of Rights that never have been incorporated and do not apply to state and local governments.[95]

First, the Third Amendment right to not have soldiers quartered in a person's home never has been deemed incorporated. The reason almost certainly is that a Third Amendment case presenting the incorporation question never has reached the Supreme Court. If ever such a case would arise, the Supreme Court surely would find this provision applies to the states.[96]

Second, the Court has held that the Fifth Amendment's right to a grand jury indictment in criminal cases is not incorporated.[97] Thus, states need not use grand juries and can choose alternatives such as preliminary hearings and prosecutorial informations.

---

[90] 372 U.S. 335 (1963); for an excellent history of this litigation, *see* Anthony Lewis, Gideon's Trumpet (1965).

[91] 378 U.S. 1 (1964).

[92] 130 S. Ct. 3020 (2010).

[93] *See, e.g.*, United States v. Miller, 307 U.S. 74 (1939).

[94] 554 U.S. 570 (2008).

[95] Justice Alito's plurality opinion in *McDonald v. City of Chicago* reviewed the history of incorporation and stated: "[T]he only rights not fully incorporated are (1) the Third Amendment's protection against quartering of soldiers; (2) the Fifth Amendment's grand jury indictment requirement; (3) the Seventh Amendment right to a jury trial in civil cases; and (4) the Eighth Amendment's prohibition on excessive fines." 130 S. Ct. at 3035 n.13.

[96] *See* Engblom v. Carey, 677 F.2d 957 (2d Cir. 1982) (finding that the Third Amendment is incorporated).

[97] Hurtado v. California, 110 U.S. 516 (1884).

Third, the Court has ruled that the Seventh Amendment right to jury trial in civil cases is not incorporated.[98] States therefore can eliminate juries in some or even all civil suits without violating the United States Constitution.

Finally, the Court never has ruled as to whether the prohibition of excessive fines in the Eighth Amendment is incorporated.[99]

All of the rest of the Bill of Rights, as detailed above, has been deemed incorporated.[100] Technically, the Bill of Rights still applies directly only to the federal government; *Barron v. Mayor & City Council of Baltimore* never has been expressly overruled.[101] Therefore, whenever a case involves a state or local violation of a Bill of Rights provision, to be precise it involves that provision as applied to the states through the due process clause of the Fourteenth Amendment. For example, if a criminal defendant in a state court proceeding is challenging the legality of a search, the defendant is raising the Fourth Amendment as applied to the states through the due process clause of the Fourteenth Amendment.

The Content of Incorporated Rights

If a provision of the Bill of Rights applies to the states, is its content identical as to when it is applied to the federal government? Or as it is sometimes phrased, does the Bill of Rights provision apply "jot for jot"?[102]

The Supreme Court has not consistently answered these questions. In some cases, the Court has expressly stated that the Bill of Rights provision applied in exactly the same manner whether it is a federal or a state government action. For example, the Supreme Court has declared that it is "firmly embedded in our constitutional jurisprudence . . . that the several States have no greater power to restrain the individual freedoms protected by the First Amendment than does the Congress of the United States."[103] Similarly, the Court has said that "the guarantees of the First Amendment, the prohibition of unreasonable searches and seizures of the Fourth Amendment, and the right to counsel guaranteed by the Sixth Amendment, are all to be enforced against the States under the Fourteenth Amendment according to the same standards that protect those personal rights against federal encroachment."[104] The Court said that it "rejected the notion that

---

[98]   Minneapolis & St. Louis R.R. Co. v. Bombolis, 241 U.S. 211 (1916).

[99]   Browning-Ferris Indus. of Vt. Inc. v. Kelco Disposal, Inc., 492 U.S. 257, 262, 276 n.2 (1989).

[100]   For an excellent discussion of the Bill of Rights, including the significance of incorporation, *see* Akhil Reed Amar, The Bill of Rights Creation and Reconstruction (1998).

[101]   32 U.S. (7 Pet.) 243 (1833).

[102]   *See* Duncan v. Louisiana, 391 U.S. at 181 (Harlan, J., dissenting) (using the "jot-for-jot" language).

[103]   Wallace v. Jaffree, 472 U.S. 38, 48-49 (1985). *Wallace* involved a First Amendment establishment clause challenge to school prayers. *See* §12.2.5.1. Some Justices, at times, have suggested that they believed that the First Amendment's protection of freedom of speech applies differently to states than to the federal government. *See, e.g.,* Roth v. United States, 354 U.S. 476 (1957) (Harlan, J., concurring); Beauharnais v. Illinois, 343 U.S. 250 (1952) (Jackson, J., dissenting).

[104]   Malloy v. Hogan, 378 U.S. at 10.

the Fourteenth Amendment applies to the states only a 'watered-down, subjective version of the individual guarantees of the Bill of Rights.' "[105]

However, in other instances, the Court has ruled that some Bill of Rights provisions apply differently to the states than to the federal government. In *Williams v. Florida*, the Supreme Court held that states need not use 12-person juries in criminal cases, even though that is required by the Sixth Amendment for federal trials.[106] The Court upheld the constitutionality of 6-person juries in state criminal trials and explained that the jury of 12 was "a historical accident, unnecessary to effect the purposes of the jury system."[107]

In *Apodaca v. Oregon*[108] and *Johnson v. Louisiana*,[109] the Supreme Court held that states may allow nonunanimous jury verdicts in criminal cases. Although the Sixth Amendment has been interpreted to require unanimous juries in federal criminal trials, the Supreme Court ruled that states may allow convictions based on 11-to-1 or 10-to-2 jury votes. However, the Court has ruled that conviction by a nonunanimous 6-person jury violates due process.[110]

From a practical perspective, except for the requirements of a 12-person jury and a unanimous verdict, the Bill of Rights provisions that have been incorporated apply to the states exactly as they apply to the federal government. This might be criticized on federalism grounds as unduly limiting the states. But rights such as freedom of speech are fundamental liberties, and there is no reason why their content should vary depending on the level of government.

Although the debate over incorporation raged among Justices and scholars during the 1940s, 1950s, and 1960s, now the issue seems settled. Except for the few provisions mentioned above, the Bill of Rights do apply to state and local governments and, in almost all instances, with the same content regardless of whether it is a challenge to federal, state, or local actions.

§6.4   THE APPLICATION OF CIVIL RIGHTS AND CIVIL LIBERTIES TO PRIVATE CONDUCT: THE STATE ACTION DOCTRINE

§6.4.1   *The Requirement for State Action*

The Constitution's protections of individual liberties and its requirement for equal protection apply only to the government. Private conduct generally does not have

---

[105] *Id.* at 10-11 (citations omitted).
[106] 399 U.S. 78 (1970).
[107] *Id.* at 102.
[108] 406 U.S. 404 (1972).
[109] 406 U.S. 356 (1972).
[110] Burch v. Louisiana, 441 U.S. 130 (1979).

to comply with the Constitution. This is often referred to as the "state action" doctrine, although "state action" is something of a misnomer. The Constitution applies to government at all levels—federal, state, and local—and to the actions of government officers at all levels.[1] The Constitution, however, generally does not apply to private entities or actors.

The *Civil Rights Cases*

In 1879, not long after the ratification of the Fourteenth Amendment, the Supreme Court declared that "[t]he provisions of the Fourteenth Amendment . . . all have reference to State action exclusively, and not to any action of private individuals."[2] The *Civil Rights Cases*, in 1883, are generally credited with mandating the requirement for state action.[3] The Civil Rights Act of 1875 provided that all persons were "entitled to the full and equal enjoyment of the accommodations, advantages, facilities, and privileges of inns, public conveyances on land or water, theaters, and other places of public amusement."[4] The law specifically prohibited discrimination based on race and color or on the basis of any previous condition of servitude. In other words, the law prohibited private race discrimination and provided both criminal and civil penalties.

The Supreme Court, with only Justice John Harlan dissenting, declared the law unconstitutional.[5] The Court ruled that the Fourteenth Amendment applies just to state and local government actions, not to private conduct. Justice Bradley, writing for the Court, said that the "Fourteenth Amendment . . . is prohibitory upon the States. . . . Individual invasion of individual rights is not the subject-matter of the amendment."[6] The Court explained that private action was governed by state law and not by the United States Constitution: "The wrongful act of an individual, unsupported by any such authority is simply a private wrong, or a crime of that individual; an invasion of the rights of the injured party, it is true, whether they affect his person, his property, or his reputation; but if not sanctioned in some way by the State, or done under State authority, his rights remain in full force, and may presumably be vindicated by resort to the laws of the State for redress."[7]

---

§6.4 [1] The phrase "state action doctrine" reflects the fact that cases involving this issue usually involve the question of whether the Fourteenth Amendment—which governs state and local conduct—applies to private conduct. But all levels of government obviously must comply with the Constitution.

[2] Virginia v. Rives, 100 U.S. 313, 318 (1879); *see also* United States v. Cruikshank, 92 U.S. 542, 554-555 (1875).

[3] 109 U.S. 3 (1883).

[4] 8 Stat. 336 (1875).

[5] Civil Rights Cases, 109 U.S. 3 (1883). Many historians have argued that the *Civil Rights Cases* were a validation of the Compromise of 1877, which ended Reconstruction. *See* C. Vann Woodward, Reunion and Reaction: The Compromise of 1877 and the End of Reconstruction 245 (1966); Eugene Gressman, The Unhappy History of Civil Rights Legislation, 50 Mich. L. Rev. 1323, 1336-1340 (1952).

[6] *Id.* at 11.

[7] *Id.* at 17.

The Court therefore concluded that Congress under §5 of the Fourteenth Amendment could not regulate private conduct but, rather, only could legislate against wrongs by state governments. The Court also ruled that Congress could not adopt the law pursuant to its authority under §2 of the Thirteenth Amendment because the refusal to serve a person was no more than "an ordinary civil injury" and not a "badge of slavery."[8]

This restrictive interpretation of Congress's powers under the Thirteenth Amendment has been overruled in later cases, and it is now clearly established that Congress has broad power under this provision to prohibit private racial discrimination.[9] However, in *United States v. Morrison*,[10] the Supreme Court reaffirmed the holding in the *Civil Rights Cases* that Congress lacks the power under §5 of the Fourteenth Amendment to regulate private conduct.

The central holding of the *Civil Rights Cases*—that the Fourteenth Amendment applies only to the government, not to private conduct—remains the law and is a central principle of constitutional law. Indeed, the Supreme Court frequently has spoken of "the essential dichotomy . . . between deprivation by the State, subject to [constitutional] scrutiny under its provisions, and private conduct . . . against which the Fourteenth Amendment offers no shield."[11] In other words, the Constitution offers no protection against private wrongs no matter how discriminatory or how much they infringe fundamental rights.

When Does the Constitution Apply to Private Actions?

The blanket rule that the Constitution only applies to the government must be qualified in a few respects. First, the Thirteenth Amendment to the Constitution is the one provision that directly regulates private conduct. Section 1 of the Thirteenth Amendment states: "Neither slavery nor involuntary servitude, except as a punishment for crime whereof the party shall have been duly convicted, shall exist within the United States, or any place subject to their jurisdiction." In other words, the Thirteenth Amendment forbids people from being or owning slaves. For example, the Supreme Court has said that the Thirteenth Amendment forbids compelling a person to work for another individual to repay a debt.[12]

---

[8] *Id.* at 24.

[9] *See, e.g.*, Jones v. Alfred H. Mayer Co., 392 U.S. 409 (1968); Runyon v. McCrary, 427 U.S. 160 (1976). These cases and Congress's power under the Thirteenth Amendment are discussed in §3.7.

[10] 529 U.S. 598 (2000). This aspect of *Morrison* is discussed in detail in §3.7. Jackson v. Metropolitan Edison Co., 419 U.S. 345, 349 (1974).

[11] Jackson v. Metropolitan Edison Co., 419 U.S. 345, 349 (1974).

[12] United States v. Reynolds, 235 U.S. 133 (1914); *see also* Bailey v. Alabama, 219 U.S. 219 (1911) (it is unconstitutional to imprison a person for failure to pay a debt). However, the Supreme Court has held that injunctions to halt labor disputes do not violate the Thirteenth Amendment. *See* International Union v. Wisconsin Employment Relations Bd., 336 U.S. 245 (1949). The Court also has ruled that the military draft does not violate the Thirteenth Amendment, Arver v. United States, 245 U.S. 366, 390 (1918), and that it does not violate the Thirteenth Amendment for a state to require that all able-bodied men, between the ages of 21 and 45, work on road construction for a period of time. Butler v. Perry, 240 U.S. 328 (1916).

§6.4 The Application of Civil Rights and Civil Liberties to Private Conduct

Second, there are exceptions to the state action requirement—situations where private conduct has to comply with the Constitution. Cases concerning these exceptions have been called a "conceptual disaster area,"[13] and even the Supreme Court has admitted that the "cases deciding when private action might be deemed that of the state have not been a model of consistency."[14] These exceptions are reviewed below in §6.4.4. Section 6.4.4.1 introduces the exceptions and considers inconsistencies and overlap. Section 6.4.4.2 focuses on the public function exception—the principle that private conduct must comply with the Constitution if it involves a task that has been traditionally, exclusively done by the government. Section 6.4.4.3 considers the entanglement exception—the principle that the Constitution applies if the government affirmatively authorizes, encourages, or facilitates unconstitutional conduct.

Finally, it should be noted that statutes, both federal and state, can apply constitutional norms to private conduct. The state action doctrine provides that the Constitution only applies to the government. But government can enact laws that require that private conduct meet the same standards that the Constitution requires of the government. For example, the constitutional requirement for equal protection applies just to the government. Congress, however, has enacted laws, such as the Civil Rights Act of 1964, that prohibit private discrimination by private employers and by places of public accommodation.[15] Another illustration is a California law that requires that private schools and universities provide the same protection of speech that a person would receive at a public school or university.[16] Actions, of course, are brought directly under such statutes and are governed by the terms of the laws; the Constitution still does not apply.

The following section, §6.4.2, considers the rationales for the state action doctrine. Then §6.4.3 discusses the threshold question of whether an action is by the government. Finally, as mentioned above, §6.4.4 examines the exceptions to the state action requirement.

At the outset, it must be recognized that there are inconsistencies and tensions among the decisions in this area, especially the cases concerning the exceptions. Because the government is involved in so much private conduct, inevitably seemingly arbitrary lines have to be drawn as to what constitutes state action. Additionally, because the government always can regulate private behavior, it is difficult to articulate principles as to when the failure to do so is a constitutional

---

[13] Charles L. Black, Jr., Foreword: "State Action," Equal Protection, and California's Proposition 14, 81 Harv. L. Rev. 69, 95 (1967).

[14] Edmonson v. Leesville Concrete Co., 500 U.S. 614, 632 (1991).

[15] Congress's authority to adopt such laws is discussed in §3.7.

[16] Cal. Educ. Code, §48950(a) ("School districts operating one or more high schools and private secondary schools shall not make or enforce any rule subjecting any high school pupil to disciplinary sanctions solely on the basis of conduct that is speech or other communication that, when engaged in outside the campus, is protected by governmental restriction by the First Amendment to the United States Constitution or Section 2 of Article I of the California Constitution."). *See also* §94367(a) (identical provision applied to private postsecondary schools). For a discussion of the desirability of this law, *see* Julian N. Eule, Transporting First Amendment Norms to the Private Sector: With Every Wish There Comes a Curse, 45 UCLA L. Rev. 1537 (1998); Erwin Chemerinsky, More Speech Is Better, 45 UCLA L. Rev. 1635 (1998).

violation. The inconsistencies in the cases also reflect social realities. From the late 1940s through the 1960s, the Court often found state action in order to combat racial discrimination. Later cases, especially those concerning other constitutional rights, generally did not find state action, and the tensions among the decisions never have been resolved.

§6.4.2   Why Have a State Action Requirement?

Costs of a State Action Requirement

There are obvious costs to the state action requirement: Absent statutory restrictions, private conduct can infringe or trample even the most basic rights. Freedom of speech, privacy, and equality—this society's most cherished values—can be violated without any redress in the courts.[17] Private infringements of basic freedoms can be just as harmful as government violations. Speech can be lost or chilled just as much through private sanctions as through public ones. Private discrimination causes and perpetuates social inequalities at least as pernicious as those caused by government actions.

Why, then, is there a state action doctrine? There are three major answers—one based on the text of the Constitution, one based on history, and one based on the policy arguments that the state action doctrine enhances individual autonomy and safeguards federalism.

Textual Explanation for the State Action Requirement

The text of the Constitution seems to limit its application to just the government. The Fourteenth Amendment, for example, declares that "nor shall any State" deny equal protection or deprive a person of life, liberty, or property without due process of law. The First Amendment says that "Congress" shall make no law abridging freedom of speech or of the press. Except for the Thirteenth Amendment, none of the Constitution's provisions are directed to private actors.

The question arises, however, as to whether the government's failure to stop private infringements of rights is itself a constitutional violation. In other words, does the government deny equal protection if it permits private racial discrimination? Does the government allow a deprivation of liberty in violation of the Fourteenth Amendment if it permits private employers to fire their employees for speech and associational activities? In a sense, "the state can be said to authorize all conduct that it does not prohibit."[18]

---

[17] In a sense, to speak of private parties infringing constitutional rights begs the critical question of whether such rights exist against private infringements. The point here is that these are values widely accepted as important throughout society, and the state action doctrine means that the Constitution does not limit their private infringement.

[18] Harold Horowitz & Kenneth Karst, *Reitman v. Mulkey*: A Telophase of Substantive Equal Protection, 1967 Sup. Ct. Rev. 39, 55.

Because the state has the power to stop the private infringement of individual rights, its failure to do so constitutes a state decision to permit the violations. In fact, in the first case to interpret the Fourteenth Amendment, 13 years before the *Civil Rights Cases*, the Court declared: "Denying includes inaction as well as action, . . . the omission to protect, as well as the omission to pass laws for protection."[19]

Indeed, as discussed below, much of the confusion concerning the exceptions to the state action doctrine comes from the fact that it is analytically possible to conceptualize any private infringement of constitutional values as a result of government inaction. At times, especially in combating private racial discrimination, the Court has wanted to rely on this rationale to apply the Constitution; but usually the Court has rejected it and attempted to maintain a distinction between government and private conduct. Not surprisingly, the doctrine ends up confusing and the cases seem often inconsistent.

Historical Explanation for the State Action Doctrine

Historically, the state action doctrine made sense because it was thought that the common law protected individuals from private interference of their rights.[20] Blackstone's famous commentaries on the law repeatedly expressed the view that individuals possessed natural rights and that the common law protected these from infringement. Professor Robert Cover noted that Blackstone "almost uniformly[21] . . . [found] coincidence of common law and natural law."[22]

Therefore, at the time the Constitution was written, it was thought that the common law completely safeguarded personal liberties from private infringements. Individuals were protected from state government infringements by state constitutions. The Bill of Rights completed the safeguards by protecting rights from federal encroachment.

But some constitutional rights, such as freedom of speech, have little protection in the common law. Also, over time, the Court has recognized many rights that have not become a part of the common law. Therefore, the historical congruence between the common law and constitutional rights has enormously diminished over time, making the state action requirement more troubling.

Policy Justifications for the State Action Doctrine

The Supreme Court has articulated two major policy rationales for the state action doctrine. First, it preserves a zone of private autonomy. The Supreme Court has explained that the state action requirement "preserves an area of individual

---

[19] United States v. Hall, 26 F. Cas. 79, 81 (C.C.S.D. Ala. 1871) (No. 15,282).

[20] This historical analysis is more fully described in Erwin Chemerinsky, Rethinking State Action, 80 Nw. U. L. Rev. 503, 511-516 (1985).

[21] *See, e.g.,* William Blackstone, Commentaries on the Laws of England 41, 111, 116-117, 122, 219, 226 (1979 ed.).

[22] Robert Cover, Justice Accused 15 (1975); *see also* Duncan Kennedy, The Structure of Blackstone's Commentaries, 28 Buff. L. Rev. 205, 241 (1979).

freedom by limiting the reach of federal law and federal judicial power."[23] The state action doctrine means that private actors have the freedom to ignore the Constitution and the limits contained within it.[24] A vast array of private actions might be constrained and challenged in the courts if there were not a state action requirement for the application of the Constitution.

Yet it should be noted that the state action doctrine also sacrifices individual freedom because it permits the violation of rights. In each case when a question of state action arises, both the freedom of the alleged violator and the freedom of the alleged victim are at stake. Thus, some scholars have advocated that the Court should engage in an explicit balancing test rather than choose entirely based on the identity of the actors.[25] From this perspective, the court would balance the competing claims of freedom rather than always rule for the nongovernment defendant.[26] Indeed, some scholars maintain that the Supreme Court already balances, without expressly admitting it, in deciding whether to apply the exceptions to the state action doctrine.[27]

Second, the Supreme Court says that the state action doctrine enhances federalism by preserving a zone of state sovereignty.[28] The *Civil Rights Cases* held that federal constitutional rights do not govern individual behavior and, furthermore, that Congress lacks the authority to apply them to private conduct.[29] Structuring the legal relationships of private citizens was for the state, not for the national government.

However, in the almost a century and a half since the *Civil Rights Cases*, the federal government has come to regulate private legal relationships in a vast array of circumstances. More important, it should be questioned whether federalism justifies allowing infringements of basic rights. If states are not adequately protecting those rights from private interference, does concern for state sovereignty justify allowing the violation to go unremedied?

Although interesting questions can be raised about the rationales for the state action doctrine, there is no doubt that it is a firmly established part of constitutional law. Yet the questions remain important as courts continue to struggle with the scope of the exceptions to the doctrine. The confusion in the cases

---

[23] Lugar v. Edmondson Oil Co., 457 U.S. 922, 936 (1982).

[24] For an excellent defense of this position, *see* William P. Marshall, Diluting Constitutional Rights: Rethinking "Rethinking State Action," 80 Nw. U. L. Rev. 558 (1985).

[25] Horowitz & Karst, *supra* note 18, at 75-76; Black, *supra* note 13, at 108; Frank Goodman, Professor Brest on State Action and Liberal Theory and a Postscript to Professor Stone, 130 U. Pa. L. Rev. 1331, 1340 (1982).

[26] Defenders of the state action doctrine might respond to this by arguing that the requirement for state action avoids the need for difficult constitutional balancing. Without a state action doctrine, every aspect of private behavior could be challenged under the Constitution and would have to be balanced against the competing rights. This obviously would have a cost in terms of judicial resources. Also, some would argue that it is better for courts to avoid such constant weighing of competing social values.

[27] Robert J. Glennon & John E. Nowak, A Functional Analysis of the Fourteenth Amendment "State Action" Requirement, 1976 Sup. Ct. Rev. 221, 227, 232.

[28] Lugar v. Edmondson Oil Co., 457 U.S. at 936.

[29] 109 U.S. at 11.

concerning these exceptions is explained, in large part, by the strength of the competing considerations.

§6.4.3   Is It the Government?

A threshold question in any constitutional case is whether the defendant is the government. Obviously, if a law is being challenged, there is no question that the Constitution applies. Likewise, the Constitution applies to the conduct of government officers in all branches and at all levels. Therefore, in the vast majority of cases presenting constitutional issues, there is no dispute over whether there is state action. Occasionally, however, the issue arises as to whether a particular entity or individual is the government.[30]

When Is an Entity a Part of the Government?

Clearly, legislative bodies at all levels—Congress, state, and local—are the government, and their enactments are state action. Likewise, the rules and decisions of government agencies at all levels are state action. However, what about government-created corporations?

In *San Francisco Arts & Athletics, Inc. v. United States Olympic Committee*, the Court held that the United States Olympic Committee was not a part of the government and was not required to comply with the Constitution even though it was chartered by Congress, regulated by federal law, and partially federally funded.[31] The issue was whether the United States Olympic Committee (USOC) violated the First Amendment by denying a group the ability to call its activities "the gay Olympics." The Court said that the USOC was a private entity and "[t]he fact that Congress granted it a corporate charter does not render the USOC a Government agent."[32] The Court concluded that neither government regulation nor government funding was sufficient to make the USOC into a government actor for constitutional purposes.[33]

In contrast, in *Lebron v. National Railroad Passenger Corp.*, the Court found that the National Railroad Passenger Corporation, Amtrak, must comply with the Constitution.[34] Amtrak is a corporation created by federal law, with a board appointed by the president and substantial federal funding. However, the statute creating Amtrak declares that it "will not be an agency or establishment of the United States government."[35]

Michael Lebron signed a contract to display an advertisement on a huge billboard—approximately 103 feet long and 10 feet high—at Amtrak's Penn Station

---

[30] There also are related, but distinct, questions as to when private conduct might be treated as if it is the government. These are discussed below.

[31] 483 U.S. 522, 543 (1987).

[32] *Id.* at 543.

[33] The issue of whether government funding or government regulation is sufficient to create state action is discussed below in §6.4.4.3.

[34] 513 U.S. 374 (1995).

[35] 45 U.S.C. §541.

in New York City. Lebron's advertisement was a photomontage criticizing the Coors beer company's conservative political activities and especially its involvement in Central America. Amtrak refused to allow the advertisement to be displayed on the ground that political advertising was not permitted at Penn Station. Lebron filed suit, and the issue before the Supreme Court was whether Amtrak must comply with the Constitution.

The Supreme Court ruled that Amtrak is the government for state action purposes. Justice Scalia, writing for the majority, declared: "We hold that where, as here, the Government creates a corporation by special law, for the furtherance of governmental objectives, and retains for itself permanent authority to appoint a majority of the directors of that corporation, the corporation is part of the Government for purposes of the First Amendment."[36]

The Court emphasized that Amtrak was created by a federal statute to serve the national interest of providing railroad passenger service.[37] Eight of the nine members of Amtrak's board of directors are appointed by the president of the United States, and the ninth is named by a majority of the board.[38] Additionally, the United States holds all of the preferred stock in Amtrak and subsidizes Amtrak's perennial losses.[39] Therefore, even though the statute creating Amtrak declares it to be a private corporation and not a part of the federal government, the Court concluded that, in reality, Amtrak is a government entity and must comply with the Constitution.

Lebron makes it clear that government-created corporations such as the Overseas Private Investment Corporation, the Communications Satellite Corporation (COMSAT), the Corporation for Public Broadcasting, and the Legal Services Corporation should be considered part of the government.[40] Indeed, the Court said that "[g]overnment-created-and-controlled corporations are (for many purposes at least) part of the government itself."[41]

Additionally, there is growing consideration throughout the country of privatizing various government functions. Proposals have included privatizing airports, highways, and even prisons. If such privatization occurs, the inevitable question will be whether the private entity will be required to comply with the Constitution. *Lebron* provides a strong indication that the Constitution must be followed. The Court stated: "It surely cannot be that government, state or federal, is able to evade the most solemn obligations imposed in the Constitution by simply resorting to the corporate form."[42]

The difficulty is whether any meaningful distinction can be drawn between *Lebron* and the earlier decision in *San Francisco Arts & Athletics, Inc. v. United States Olympic Committee.* In *Lebron*, government creation of the corporation, together with a great deal of federal involvement, was sufficient for state action. But in *United States Olympic Committee*, government chartering of a corporation, together

---

[36] *Lebron*, 513 U.S. at 397-400.

[37] *Id.* at 384-385.

[38] *Id.* at 396.

[39] *Id.* at 385.

[40] The Supreme Court described these examples, and their statutory authority, at *id.* at 390.

[41] *Id.* at 396.

[42] *Id.*

with regulation and funding, was not enough for state action. The difference seems to be one of degree rather than kind. The government not only created Amtrak, but owned all of its stock, appointed its directors, and ultimately managed it—substantially greater involvement than with regard to the United States Olympic Committee.

When Do the Actions of Individuals Constitute State Action?

If a person is employed by the government and acting as a government officer, there is no doubt that there is state action and the Constitution applies.[43] Sometimes, though, issues arise as to whether a particular person should be regarded as a state agent.[44] The Court has made it clear that a government officer is acting under color of law, and is a state actor, if he or she is acting in an official capacity, even if the conduct is not authorized by state law.

For example, the Court has found that doctors and psychiatrists who provide medical care in prisons are government actors. In *O'Connor v. Donaldson*, a prisoner sued a psychiatrist, who also was the administrator of a state mental health facility.[45] In *Estelle v. Gamble*, a prisoner sued a doctor, who also was the chief medical officer at the prison hospital, for malpractice.[46] In *West v. Atkins*, a prisoner sued a private physician who provided medical care in the prison pursuant to a contract with the state.[47] In all of these instances, the Supreme Court found that the doctors were acting under color of state law.

Yet in *Polk County v. Dodson*, the Supreme Court ruled that a public defender, employed by the state to represent indigent criminal defendants, is not a state actor and therefore is not under color of state law.[48] The Court found that the public defender should not be thought of as a state actor because the public defender's loyalties are not to the government but rather to the client, even though a public defender is a government officer performing in an official capacity.

It is difficult to reconcile *Polk County* with *O'Connor, Estelle,* and *West.* A doctor employed by the government provides the same care as a private physician. Just as the attorney's primary loyalties are to the client, so are the psychiatrist's or physician's fundamental duties to the patient and not to the government employer. In *West*, the Court explained that a public defender is different from a doctor because a doctor's "professional and ethical obligation to make independent

---

[43] Almost all constitutional litigation challenging the constitutionality of state and local actions is brought pursuant to 42 U.S.C. §1983. Section 1983 requires that the action be "under color of law." The Supreme Court has said that this is the same inquiry as to whether there is state action. Lugar v. Edmondson Oil Co., 457 U.S. 922, 928-932 (1982); United States v. Price, 383 U.S. 787, 794 n.7 (1966).

[44] It should be noted that a government officer is acting under color of law, and as a state actor, if he or she is acting in an official capacity, even if the conduct is not authorized by state law. Home Telephone and Telegraph Co. v. Los Angeles, 227 U.S. 278 (1913).

[45] 422 U.S. 563 (1975).

[46] 429 U.S. 97 (1976).

[47] 487 U.S. 42 (1988).

[48] 454 U.S. 312 (1981).

medical judgments [does] not set him in conflict with the State and other prison authorities."[49] But it is unclear why a professional employed by the government does not act under color of law simply because the individual has other professional obligations or opposes the state.

Also, the issue of whether a private person must comply with the Constitution arises in instances where the individual acts in concert with government officials. For example, in *Soldal v. Cook County*, the Supreme Court found that the private owner of a mobile home park was acting under color of state law when he acted with sheriff's deputies to seize an individual's property.[50] An individual's mobile home was taken off its foundation and towed away by the park owner and sheriff's deputies to collect an unpaid debt. The Court found that this conduct constituted state action in violation of the Fourth Amendment because there was not a lawful eviction order or other judicial authorization.

§6.4.4 The Exceptions to the State Action Doctrine

§6.4.4.1 Introduction to the Exceptions

There are two exceptions to the state action doctrine. One is the "public function exception," which says that a private entity must comply with the Constitution if it is performing a task that has been traditionally, exclusively done by the government. The other is the "entanglement exception," which says that private conduct must comply with the Constitution if the government has authorized, encouraged, or facilitated the unconstitutional conduct.[51]

Inconsistencies Among the Cases

At the outset in examining the exceptions to the state action doctrine it must be recognized that the cases do not neatly fit together. Some of the decisions seem clearly inconsistent with one another, and the Court often has made little effort to reconcile them. There are several explanations for this. In part, it reflects inherent problems with state action; the government always has the power to regulate private behavior, and there never can be a clear line for when the failure to do so

---

[49] 487 U.S. at 51.

[50] 506 U.S. 56 (1992).

[51] In *Brentwood Academy v. Tennessee Secondary School Athletic Association*, 531 U.S. 288 (2001), discussed below, the Supreme Court found state action based on "entwinement." Notably, the Court did not use the term "entanglement." Nor did the Court invoke the public function exception. This indicates that perhaps there is a third exception distinct from the other two. As discussed below, "entanglement" has been held to require a finding of government encouragement, but the Court in *Brentwood Academy* found state action based on entwinement with the government without a finding of government encouragement. On the other hand, the Court did not hold or imply that it was creating a new exception to the state action doctrine, but instead purported to apply existing law for determining whether there is state action. *Brentwood Academy*, and its impact on the state action exceptions, is discussed below at text accompanying notes 90-94.

constitutes state action and a constitutional violation. Likewise, the government is involved, to some extent, in almost every activity. It is difficult, if not impossible, to draw a meaningful line as to the point where the involvement is great enough to require the private action to comply with the Constitution.

The inconsistencies also reflect the way in which some of the state action decisions were written and decided. As explained below, cases with regard to both of the exceptions articulated broad principles that could make a wide range of private conduct actionable under the Constitution. Because those cases have not been overruled, but also not always followed, there is tension among the decisions.

The inconsistencies also reflect social realities. From the late 1940s through the 1960s, the Court expansively defined what constitutes state action as part of trying to combat racial discrimination. These decisions understandably articulated broad principles that could make a great deal of private conduct reviewable under the Constitution. Since the 1960s, especially in cases involving other constitutional provisions, the Court has applied a much narrower definition of state action. There are inconsistencies among the cases that the Court never has acknowledged or resolved.

In fact, a review of the decisions indicates that the Court has been much more likely to apply the exceptions in cases involving race discrimination than in cases involving other constitutional claims. Indeed, the United States Court of Appeals for the Second Circuit expressly held that the scope of the exceptions to the state action doctrine turns on whether it is a claim of race discrimination or another constitutional right.[52] Yet this distinction seems difficult to defend. State action is about whether the Constitution should apply because of the government's involvement or because the act is one that is traditionally governmental in nature. It is unclear why this inquiry depends at all on the particulars of the constitutional claim.

The inconsistency among the cases also reflects the reduced need to rely on the Constitution to reach private racial discrimination. The adoption of the Civil Rights Act of 1964, which prohibited private discrimination by places of public accommodation and private employers, greatly lessened the need for constitutional litigation to end discrimination. For example, prior to the 1964 Civil Rights Act, the Court had to consider whether there was state action when the government leased premises to a restaurant that racially discriminated.[53] But after the 1964 Civil Rights Act, the state action inquiry would have been unnecessary because the law prohibited the restaurant from racially discriminating even if there was no government involvement.

Cases Often Involve Both Exceptions

The two exceptions—the public function exception and the entanglement exception—are discussed, in turn, below. It should be noted that many cases

---

[52] *See* Lebron v. National R.R. Passenger Corp., 12 F.3d 388, 392 (2d Cir. 1993), *rev'd on other grounds*, 513 U.S. 374 (1995).

[53] Burton v. Wilmington Parking Auth., 365 U.S. 715 (1961), discussed below.

involve discussion of both exceptions and therefore are considered below under each of the exceptions. Also, in some cases, the Court is not clear as to which exception it is discussing. This, too, contributes to the doctrinal confusion concerning the state action doctrine.[54]

§6.4.4.2   The Public Function Exception

The Public Function Exception Defined

The first exception to the state action doctrine is often termed the "public function exception." The current formulation of the public function exception was articulated in *Jackson v. Metropolitan Edison Co.*, where the Supreme Court held that there is state action "in the exercise by a private entity of powers traditionally exclusively reserved to the State."[55]

In *Jackson*, the Supreme Court held that a private utility company did not have to provide due process before it terminated a customer's service. The Court has ruled that a government-owned utility must provide notice and a hearing before cutting off service.[56] The argument was that a private utility, with a state-granted monopoly, performs a public function and should also have to provide due process. But the Court rejected this argument and explained that running a utility is "not traditionally the exclusive prerogative of the State" and therefore the Constitution was inapplicable.[57] In other words, since there long have been private utility companies, running a utility is not regarded as a public function to which the Constitution always applies.

Rationale for the Public Function Exception

The public function exception serves important purposes. The government should not be able to avoid the Constitution by delegating its tasks to a private actor. Also, there are some acts that seem inherently governmental in nature; a private entity performing them therefore also should be limited by the Constitution. A paradigm illustration of these purposes is the so-called White Primary Cases, described below, where the Supreme Court held that a private political party holding a primary election could not racially discriminate.[58] Conducting an election for government office is a classic government function, and the government should not be able to avoid the Constitution by delegating the task to a private entity.

---

[54] For example, in *Brentwood Academy v. Tennessee Secondary School Athletic Association*, 513 U.S. 288 (2001), discussed in detail below, the Court speaks of neither the public function nor the entanglement exception, but instead of the government's "entwinement" with the private entity.

[55] 419 U.S. 345, 352 (1974).

[56] Memphis Light, Gas and Water Division v. Craft, 436 U.S. 1 (1978).

[57] *Id.* at 353.

[58] *See* Terry v. Adams, 345 U.S. 461 (1953); Smith v. Allwright, 321 U.S. 649 (1944), discussed below.

The question, of course, becomes how to formulate the test for when a private entity should be regarded as performing a public function. Should intent matter; that is, should the Court consider whether the government delegated the task precisely to allow constitutional violations? Should the frequency with which the task is performed by nongovernment actors matter? *Jackson* says that it must be a task that has been traditionally, exclusively done by the government. But it is unclear why it shouldn't be sufficient if it is a task that has usually been done by the government, or even often done by the government, even if it has not been exclusively done by the government. Should the nature of the rights involved matter? For example, it seems highly questionable that the result in *Jackson* would have been the same if the utility engaged in racial discrimination. Yet nothing in the formulation of the public function exception makes its application turn on the underlying constitutional claim.

There are three major areas, in addition to *Jackson*, where the Court has considered the public function exception: the management of private property, the control of the electoral process, and the running or regulating of schools. These cases are examined in turn.

Management of Private Property

One of the first cases to apply the public function exception was *Marsh v. Alabama*.[59] *Marsh* involved an attempt by a Jehovah's Witness to distribute literature in a company town, Chickasaw, Alabama, which was owned by the Gulf Shipbuilding Corporation. The company ran all aspects of the town and refused to allow solicitation without prior written permission. The issue before the Supreme Court was whether the government could criminally punish a criminal defendant who distributed religious literature on the premises of the company-owned town contrary to the wishes of the town's management.

The Supreme Court ruled that running a city is a public function, and therefore it must be done in compliance with the Constitution, whether by the government or a private entity. The Court's explanation was broad. The Court said that "[t]he more an owner, for his advantage, opens up his property for use by the public in general, the more do his rights become circumscribed by the constitutional and statutory rights of those who use it."[60] This could justify applying the Constitution to all businesses and places of public accommodation that open their doors for use by the public in general.

The Court then went even further at the conclusion of the opinion. The Court said: "When we balance the Constitutional rights of owners of property against those of the people to enjoy freedom of press and religion, as we must here, we remain mindful of the fact that the latter occupy a preferred position."[61] The Court concluded that private property rights of the company did not "justify

[59] 326 U.S. 501 (1946).
[60] *Id.* at 506.
[61] *Id.* at 509.

the States permitting a corporation to govern a community of citizens so as to restrict their fundamental liberties."[62]

This suggests that the determination of state action is a balancing test where the court weighs the interests of the private property owner and the constitutional rights involved. From this perspective, any state failure to prohibit serious violations of constitutional rights by private entities is actionable under the Constitution.

The Court never has gone nearly this far in its application of the public function exception and, in fact, in *Jackson* cited *Marsh* for the limited proposition that a private entity performs a public function when it exercises power that has been traditionally exclusively reserved to the state.[63] Yet the language in *Marsh* is much broader than that and has never been expressly overruled.

Marsh was followed in *Evans v. Newton*.[64] In *Evans*, the Supreme Court held that a city could not avoid desegregating a park by turning its control over to a private entity. The park had been created in Macon, Georgia, by a testamentary trust in the will of Senator Augustus Bacon, which required that it be used only by white persons. The city was designated as the trustee and operator of the park. Rather than desegregate the park, the city resigned as trustee and sought to turn the park over to private control.

The Supreme Court held that running the park was a public function and that it had to comply with the Constitution even if managed by a private entity. Justice Douglas, writing for the Court, explained: "The service rendered even by a private park of this character is municipal in nature. It is open to every white person, there being no selective element other than race. . . . A park . . . is more like a fire department or police department that traditionally serves the community. Mass recreation through the use of parks is plainly in the public domain."[65]

Again, this is broad language that might make any place of recreation, such as an amusement park or even a golf course, a "public function." The Court never has gone that far. The Civil Rights Act of 1964 made this less necessary because it prohibited discrimination by places of public accommodation, such as hotels, restaurants, and amusement parks.

Following the Supreme Court's decision in *Evans v. Newton*, the state court concluded that under Georgia law the land should revert to the heirs, for uses other than as a park, because the terms of the trust could not be followed. In *Evans v. Abney*, the Supreme Court held that returning the land to the family did not violate the Constitution because no longer was the property being used for the public function of providing a park.[66]

The other area where the Court considered the application of *Marsh v. Alabama* concerned the ability of privately owned shopping centers to exclude speakers. The evolution of the law here reflects how the Supreme Court has greatly narrowed the public function exception. In *Amalgamated Food Employees*

---

[62] *Id.*
[63] *Jackson*, 419 U.S. at 352.
[64] 382 U.S. 296 (1966).
[65] *Id.* at 301-302.
[66] 396 U.S. 435 (1970).

§6.4 The Application of Civil Rights and Civil Liberties to Private Conduct

Union Local 590 v. Logan Valley Plaza, in 1968, the Supreme Court held that a privately owned shopping center could not exclude striking laborers from picketing a store within it.[67] The Court expressly analogized to *Marsh* and said that "[t]he similarities between the business block in *Marsh* and the shopping center . . . are striking. . . . The shopping center here is clearly the functional equivalent of the business district of Chickasaw involved in *Marsh.*"[68] The Court emphasized that the shopping center was open to the public and functionally was the same as the commercial center of a town.

Just four years later, in *Lloyd Corp. v. Tanner,* the Supreme Court held that a privately owned shopping center could exclude anti–Vietnam War protestors from distributing literature on its premises.[69] The Court distinguished *Logan Valley* on the ground that it involved a labor protest related to the functioning of a store in the shopping center, whereas the speech in *Lloyd* was an antiwar protest unrelated to the conduct of the business.

Although there is a common sense basis for this distinction, constitutionally it is difficult to defend. The Supreme Court long has held that the core of the First Amendment is that the government cannot regulate speech based on its content.[70] Yet *Lloyd* makes the content of the speech decisive in determining whether it will be allowed. Under *Lloyd,* speech in shopping centers is constitutionally protected and cannot be the basis for a trespassing conviction only if its content concerns the functioning of the shopping centers. Also, it is difficult to explain why the determination of whether a private shopping center is a state actor for First Amendment purposes should turn on the message being expressed.

In *Hudgens v. National Labor Relations Board,*[71] the Court recognized these problems and expressly overruled *Logan Valley.* The Court said that "the reasoning of the Court's opinion in *Lloyd* cannot be squared with the reasoning of the Court's opinion in *Logan Valley.*"[72] The Court explained that if the First Amendment applies to privately owned shopping centers, then the law cannot permit a distinction based on the content of the speech.[73] The Court concluded that the proper conclusion was that the First Amendment does not apply to privately owned shopping centers regardless of the content of the speech.

The shift from *Logan Valley* to *Lloyd* to *Hudgens,* in part, can be explained by the changing composition of the Supreme Court. Between 1968, when *Logan Valley* was decided, and 1972, when *Lloyd* was decided, President Richard Nixon had made four appointments to the Supreme Court: Chief Justice Warren Burger and Justices Harry Blackmun, William Rehnquist, and Lewis Powell. In *Hudgens,* all four of these Justices were in the majority voting to overrule *Logan Valley.*

On the one hand, shopping centers are the modern equivalent of a town square, and they do perform a public function in providing a gathering place for

---

[67] 391 U.S. 308 (1968).
[68] *Id.* at 317-318.
[69] 407 U.S. 551 (1972).
[70] *See* §11.2.1.
[71] 424 U.S. 507 (1976).
[72] *Id.* at 518.
[73] *Id.* at 520.

people and an obvious place to disseminate information. It is difficult to distinguish the company town in *Marsh*, especially in light of the Court's broad language in that decision, from shopping centers and its conclusion in *Hudgens*.

On the other hand, shopping centers do not meet the *Jackson* test for public functions; obviously, they are not a task that has been traditionally, exclusively done by the government. Also, private owners generally have the ability to control their business, except as regulated by statutes. Part of ownership is the ability to exclude messages that one disagrees with or that might interfere with business activities.

It should be noted, however, that after *Hudgens*, the Supreme Court rejected the argument that shopping center owners have a constitutional right to exclude speakers. In *PruneYard Shopping Center v. Robins*, the Supreme Court held that a state could create a state constitutional right of access to shopping centers for speech purposes.[74] The California Supreme Court found such a right under the California constitution. The shopping center contended that forcing it to allow speakers violated its First Amendment rights and constituted a taking of its property without just compensation.[75] The United States Supreme Court rejected both of these arguments and held that states could recognize a state constitutional right of access to shopping centers, even though no such right exists under the United States Constitution.

In sum, *Marsh* remains good law, but it is unclear how far it extends beyond the circumstance of the company town.[76] It is now clearly established that privately owned shopping centers need not comply with the First Amendment.

Election Cases

Another example of the public function exception is the *White Primary Cases*, where the Supreme Court ruled that holding an election for government office is a public function that must meet the constitutional requirement for equal protection. Early in the last century, Texas law excluded blacks from participating in political primary elections. The Texas statute provided that "in no event shall a negro be eligible to participate in a Democratic party primary election held in the State of Texas."[77] The Supreme Court declared this unconstitutional in *Nixon v. Herndon*.[78] Texas then revised its law to provide that the party's State Executive Committee could prescribe qualifications for voting in political primary elections.

---

[74] 447 U.S. 74 (1980).

[75] The takings aspect of this case is discussed in §8.4.2.1, and the free speech aspects are discussed in §11.4.3.

[76] *See* David R. Keyser, Note, First Amendment and the Problem of Access to Migrant Labor Camps, 67 Cornell L. Rev. 560 (1976); *see, e.g.*, Asociacion de Trabajadores Agricolas de Puerto Rico v. Green Giant Co., 518 F.2d 130 (3d Cir. 1975); Petersen v. Talisman Sugar Corp., 478 F.2d 73, 81 (5th Cir. 1973); Folgueras v. Hassle, 331 F. Supp. 615, 621 (W.D. Mich. 1971) (applying *Marsh* to migrant labor camps).

[77] Nixon v. Herndon, 273 U.S. 536, 540 (1927).

[78] *Id.*

When this was used to exclude blacks from voting in these elections, the Supreme Court again declared this unconstitutional in *Nixon v. Condon.*[79]

Texas then revised its law again, this time to allow the state party convention to make its own rules for participation in the party's primary elections. The Democratic Party of Texas, a private entity, then conducted primary elections, but refused to allow African Americans to participate. The party argued that it was a private entity and therefore did not need to comply with the equal protection clause of the Constitution. The Supreme Court disagreed,[80] holding that running an election for government office, even a primary election, is a public function and must be in accord with the Constitution. The Court declared: "When primaries become a part of the machinery for choosing officials, state and national, as they have here, the same tests to determine the character of discrimination or abridgement should be applied to the primary as are applied to the general election."[81]

The Court explained that the government could not avoid the Constitution by delegating its tasks to private entities. The Court said that the Constitution is "not to be nullified by a State through casting its electoral process in a form which permits a private organization to practice racial discrimination in the election. Constitutional rights would be of little value if they could be thus indirectly denied."[82]

Subsequently, there was a challenge to the exclusion of blacks from participating in preprimaries held by the Jaybird Democratic Association, a Texas political organization.[83] The Jaybirds contended that they were a private club and not a political party or an electoral body. The Supreme Court noted, however, that candidates nominated by the Jaybirds were enormously successful and that usually they ran unopposed. The Court thus found that there was state action. Justice Black wrote: "The only election that has counted in this Texas county for more than fifty years has been that held by the Jaybirds from which Negroes were excluded. . . . It is immaterial that the state does not control that part of this elective process which it leaves for the Jaybirds to manage. The Jaybird primary has become an integral part, indeed the only effective part, of the elective process that determines who shall rule and govern in the county. The effect of the whole procedure . . . is to do precisely what the Fifteenth Amendment forbids—strip Negroes of every vestige of influence in selecting the officials who control the local county matters that intimately touch the daily lives of citizens."[84]

In many ways, the *White Primary Cases* are the paradigm instance of the public function exception, but also an example from which it is difficult to generalize. Running an election is a task that has been traditionally, exclusively done by

---

[79] 286 U.S. 73 (1932).

[80] Actually, the Supreme Court initially upheld this on the ground that the party was a private entity and therefore did not need to comply with the Constitution. Grovey v. Townsend, 295 U.S. 45 (1935). The Court overruled this decision in *Smith v. Allwright,* 321 U.S. 649, 666 (1944).

[81] *Id.* at 664.

[82] *Id.*

[83] Terry v. Adams, 345 U.S. 461 (1953).

[84] *Id.* at 469-470.

the government. Texas decided to stop doing so precisely to facilitate discrimination. Perhaps the *White Primary Cases* are most useful as a precedent if the government ever would choose to stop performing a traditional task so as to avoid the Constitution. For example, if the government were to rely on contracts with private prisons in order to avoid constitutional constraints, the *White Primary Cases* indicate that delegations to avoid the Constitution will not succeed.

Running and Regulating Schools

A third example where the public function exception might be applied is when a private entity is managing or regulating schools. Education long has been a province of the government, and there is a strong argument that a private entity is performing a public function when it educates children. The problem, though, is that *Jackson* narrowly defines public function, and it seems impossible to say that running or regulating schools is a task that has traditionally been done exclusively by the government. Not surprisingly, the Court has refused to apply the public function exception in this area.

In *Rendell-Baker v. Kohn*, the Supreme Court held that there was no state action when a private school that received almost all of its funding from the government fired a teacher because of her speech.[85] The Court said that the question is not whether the school performs a "public function," but rather "the question is whether the function performed has been 'traditionally the *exclusive* prerogative of the State.'"[86] The Court recognized that providing special education was an important social function, but said that there was not state action because such private schools long have existed.

In *National Collegiate Athletic Association v. Tarkanian*, the Court concluded that the NCAA was a private entity and that it therefore did not have to provide due process before it suspended the basketball coach at a state university.[87] The Court said that although fostering and regulating collegiate athletics is a "critical" function, "by no means is it a traditional, let alone an exclusive, state function."[88]

The *Tarkanian* Court relied, in part, on the earlier decision in *San Francisco Arts & Athletics, Inc. v. United States Olympic Committee*, where the Court declared: "Neither the conduct nor the coordination of amateur sports has been a traditional government function."[89] In the *Olympic Committee* case, the Supreme Court found that the United States Olympic Committee did not perform a public function and therefore did not violate the Constitution when it prevented a group from calling its activities the "Gay Olympic Games."

---

[85] 457 U.S. 830 (1982). *Rendell-Baker* also involved the question of whether there was sufficient government entanglement for the Constitution to apply. This aspect of the decision is discussed below.

[86] *Id.* at 842 (emphasis in original) (citations omitted).

[87] 488 U.S. 179 (1988).

[88] *Id.* at 197 n.18.

[89] 483 U.S. 522, 545 (1987). The Court's discussion of whether the United States Olympic Committee is part of the government is considered in §6.4.3, text accompanying notes 31-33.

But in *Brentwood Academy v. Tennessee Secondary School Athletic Association*, the Court found that a private entity regulating high school athletics was a state actor based on the government's "entwinement" with its activities.[90] Justice Souter, writing for the Court, reiterated the basic test for the entanglement exception: "that state action may be found . . . only if, there is such a 'close nexus between the State and the challenged action' that seemingly private behavior 'may be fairly treated as that of the State itself.' "[91] Justice Souter said that there is no single test for determining state action, but said that the facts in this case justified concluding that there was sufficient government "entwinement" for the Constitution to apply.

Justice Souter emphasized that 84 percent of the members of the private entity were public schools, that the state traditionally had delegated regulating interscholastic athletics to the entity, that most of its funds came from public schools, and that most of its meetings were held on government property. Together, these factors justified applying the Constitution to the private entity's activities.

The Court expressly distinguished *NCAA v. Tarkanian*, which is obviously similar in that it involved an entity regulating interscholastic sports, albeit at the college level. Justice Souter said that the difference is that *Tarkanian* involved an entity, the National Collegiate Athletic Association, that operates in all states, whereas *Brentwood* was concerned with an entity operating only in one state.[92] Justice Souter said that "the NCAA's policies were shaped not by the University of Nevada alone, but by several hundred member institutions, most of them having no connection with Nevada, and exhibiting no color of Nevada law. Since it was difficult to see the NCAA, not as a collective membership, but as surrogate for the one State, we held the organization's connection with Nevada too insubstantial to ground a state action claim."[93] In contrast, the Tennessee Secondary School Athletic Association obviously was just in one state.

Certainly, it can be questioned whether this distinction should make a difference in deciding if the Constitution applies. The nature and extent of government involvement are very similar, with the only difference being that in *Tarkanian* it was government entities in many states and in *Brentwood Academy* it was within a single state. But should this matter in determining whether there is sufficient government involvement for the Constitution to apply? Perhaps the difference is symbolic; people are much more likely to attribute the Tennessee Secondary School Athletic Association's decisions to the government than they are to do this for the NCAA.

More important, the key question concerning the *Brentwood Academy* case is whether it creates a new, broader exception to the state action doctrine. Notably, Justice Souter does not use the word "entanglement" in his majority opinion, but instead the word "entwinement." Justice Clarence Thomas, in a dissenting opinion, objected that "[w]e have never found state action based upon mere

---

[90] 531 U.S. 288 (2001).
[91] *Id.* at 298 (citation omitted).
[92] 531 U.S. at 299.
[93] *Id.* at 301.

'entwinement.' "[94] "Entanglement," in cases like *Rendell-Baker*, had been found to require government encouragement of constitutional violations by private actors. But no encouragement was found in *Brentwood Academy*. Instead, the Court found that significant government involvement with the private entity was sufficient for a finding of state action. This is a much more expansive exception to the state action doctrine than found in prior cases. But the exception is not defined with any precision. Although the Court identifies the factors that cause it to find the Tennessee Secondary Schools Athletic Association to be a state actor, it offers no criteria for determining more generally when there is enough entwinement for state action.

§6.4.4.3   The Entanglement Exception

The other major exception to the state action doctrine is termed the "entanglement exception." Under this exception, the Constitution applies if the government affirmatively authorizes, encourages, or facilitates private conduct that violates the Constitution. Either the government must cease its involvement with the private actor or the private entity must comply with the Constitution.

The key question, then, is what degree of government involvement is sufficient to make the Constitution applicable? What types of government encouragement are sufficient for state action? Unfortunately, the entanglement exception cases are even more inconsistent than those concerning the public function exception.

The entanglement exception cases have arisen primarily in four areas: judicial and law enforcement actions, government licensing and regulation, government subsidies, and voter initiatives permitting discrimination. These categories are admittedly arbitrary in that many cases involve all or most of these government activities, just as cases often involve both the public functions and the entanglement exception. Nonetheless, the categories at least provide useful groupings for considering the cases.

Judicial and Law Enforcement Actions

The most famous illustration, and one of the most important state action cases, is *Shelley v. Kraemer*, where the Supreme Court held that courts cannot enforce racially restrictive covenants.[95] The issue in *Shelley* was whether courts could enforce contracts whereby members of a neighborhood agreed not to sell their property to blacks. The argument was that private contractual agreements need not comply with the Constitution and that court enforcement was simply implementing private choices. The Supreme Court, in an opinion by Chief Justice Fred Vinson, disagreed and held that courts may not enforce racially restrictive covenants.

The Court explained that court enforcement has the government, through its judicial branch, facilitating discrimination. The "participation of the State consists

---

[94] 531 U.S. at 305 (Thomas, J., dissenting).
[95] 334 U.S. 1 (1948).

in the enforcement of the restrictions."[96] The Court thus concluded that the "action of state courts and judicial officers in their official capacities is to be regarded as action of the State within the meaning of the Fourteenth Amendment."[97] It is government-employed judges enforcing the contract law of the state, which does not forbid racial discrimination, that implements discrimination by enforcing a racially restrictive covenant.

Although *Shelley* long has been controversial,[98] there seems little doubt that judges are government actors and that judicial remedies are state action. Nor was it controversial when the Supreme Court held in *New York Times Co. v. Sullivan*, 15 years after *Shelley*, that the common law of libel is state action that must comply with the First Amendment.[99] The Court said that although the defamation action was a "civil lawsuit between private parties, the Alabama courts have applied a state rule of law which [allegedly] . . . impose[s] invalid restrictions on their constitutional freedoms. . . . It matters not that the law has been applied in a civil action and that it is common law only. . . . The test is not the form in which state power has been applied but, whatever the form, whether such power has in fact been exercised."[100] From this perspective, *Shelley* seems unremarkable: A branch of the government, the judiciary, was enforcing the law of the state, albeit the common law, to enforce racial discrimination by enforcing the discriminatory covenants.

Yet *Shelley* remains controversial because ultimately everything can be made state action under it. If any decision by a state court represents state action, then ultimately all private actions must comply with the Constitution. Anyone who believes that his or her rights have been violated can sue in state court. If the court dismisses the case because the state law does not forbid the violation, there is state action sustaining the infringement of the right, just as there would have been state action had the court dismissed the case in *Shelley*. All private violations of rights exist because state law allows them. It is difficult to imagine anything that cannot potentially be transformed into state action under this reasoning.

The Court, of course, never has taken *Shelley* this far, but nor has it articulated any clear limiting principles. In fact, the Court only rarely has applied *Shelley* as a basis for finding state action.[101] In *Bell v. Maryland*, the Supreme Court avoided deciding whether there is inherently state action if the state prosecutes a person

---

[96] *Id.* at 13.

[97] *Id.* at 14.

[98] *See, e.g.,* Herbert Wechsler, Toward Neutral Principles of Constitutional Law, 73 Harv. L. Rev. 1, 29 (1959) (criticizing *Shelley*).

[99] 376 U.S. 254 (1964), discussed in detail in §11.3.5.2.

[100] *Id.* at 265.

[101] In *Pennsylvania v. Board of Girard College*, 353 U.S. 230 (1957), the Court, without expressly citing *Shelley*, found that there was state action when public officials ran a private trust, for a school for orphans, in a racially discriminatory manner. *See also* Evans v. Newton, 382 U.S. 296 (1966) (finding state action when the city delegated running a private park, segregated pursuant to the terms of a will, to a private entity that racially discriminated); Evans v. Abney, 396 U.S. 435 (1970) (finding no state action when the park was returned to private ownership and not used any longer as a park or place of public accommodation so as to fulfill the intent of the grantor), discussed above.

for trespass.[102] *Bell* involved nine African-American students who were convicted in Maryland state court of criminal trespass as a result of their participation in a sit-in at a restaurant that refused to serve blacks. The majority decision, written by Justice Brennan, remanded the case to the state court for consideration in light of recently adopted state and local public accommodation laws.[103] Nonetheless, some of the Justices addressed the question of whether state enforcement of trespass laws is inherently state action.

Justice Douglas argued that although "[p]rivate property is involved, . . . it is property that is serving the public."[104] Justice Douglas expressly relied on *Shelley v. Kraemer* and said that "[w]e should put these restaurant cases in line with *Shelley v. Kraemer*, holding that what the Fourteenth Amendment requires in restrictive covenant cases it also requires from restaurants."[105] Douglas's basic point was that Maryland enforced the policy of segregation with its police, prosecutors, and courts, and thus there was state action.

Justice Black dissented and explicitly disagreed with Justice Douglas. Black argued that there was no state action when the government enforced the desires of private property owners. Justice Black stated: "It seems pretty clear that the reason judicial enforcement of the restrictive covenants in *Shelley* was deemed state action was not merely the fact that a state court had acted, but rather that it had acted 'to deny petitioners, on the grounds of race or color, the enjoyment of property rights in premises which petitioners are willing and financially able to acquire and which the grantors are willing to sell.'"[106] In other words, Justice Black read *Shelley* narrowly as applying only in a situation where the buyer and seller both wanted the transaction. The sit-in was different because the owner of the restaurant did not want the protest activity. Justice Black thus concluded that "mere judicial enforcement of the trespass law is not sufficient" for state action.[107]

Logically, there is great merit in Justice Douglas's argument. The use of the police to arrest civil rights protestors, of prosecutors to prosecute them, and of courts to convict them is state action. Yet if this is state action, isn't it possible that state action always exists? For example, any time a private property owner chooses to exclude a speaker, such as in a private shopping center, there would be state action in using police, prosecutors, and courts for trespass actions. Those who favor a state action doctrine recoil from such a possibility and see the courts monitoring whom people invite to their houses for dinner. Those who oppose the state action doctrine believe that the court should simply balance the competing

---

[102] 378 U.S. 226 (1964). For an excellent analysis of these cases, *see* Christopher W. Schmidt, The Sit-ins and the State Action Doctrine, 18 Wm. & Mary Bill Rts. J. 767 (2010).

[103] *See also Lombard v. Louisiana*, 373 U.S. 267 (1963), where the Supreme Court overturned the trespass convictions of sit-in demonstrators on the ground that the city had condemned the sit-in and thus encouraged the violation of rights; *Peterson v. Greenville*, 373 U.S. 244 (1963), overturning the convictions of black youths who refused to leave a restaurant when denied service at a lunch counter.

[104] 378 U.S. at 252 (Douglas, J.).

[105] *Id.* at 259.

[106] *Id.* at 330 (Black, J., dissenting) (citations omitted).

[107] *Id.* at 332.

interests; the need to end discrimination outweighs the property rights of a business open to the public, but not the rights of a person holding a dinner party.[108]

There are two other areas where the Court has found the involvement of courts as a basis for state action: use of courts for prejudgment attachment and the use of peremptory challenges at trials. In *Lugar v. Edmonson Oil Co.*, the Supreme Court found that there was state action when a creditor obtained a writ of prejudgment attachment from a court.[109] The Court concluded that the involvement of the court in issuing the writ and of the sheriff in enforcing it was sufficient for state action.

The *Lugar* Court articulated a two-part test for state action analysis that other cases have invoked.[110] "First the deprivation must be caused by the exercise of some right or privilege created by the state, or a rule of conduct imposed by the state, or by a person for whom the state is responsible. . . ." Second, the party charged with the deprivation must be a person who may be fairly said to be a state actor "because he is a state official, because he has acted together with or has obtained significant aid from state officials, or because his conduct is otherwise chargeable to the state."[111] In *Lugar*, state law provided for prejudgment attachment, meeting the first prong; and the sheriff carried out the attachment, meeting the second requirement.

Lugar can be contrasted to the Supreme Court's earlier decision in *Flagg Brothers v. Brooks.*[112] In *Flagg Brothers*, the Supreme Court held that a private creditor's self-help repossession did not constitute state action, and thus due process was not required prior to the sale of her belongings. After an individual was evicted from her home, the sheriff arranged for storage of her possessions at a warehouse. The warehouse demanded that she pay the storage fees or it would sell her property. The customer claimed a right to due process before the sale, but the Supreme Court concluded that since the warehouse company was privately owned, the Constitution did not apply.

The customer's primary contention was that the State of New York "delegated" to the company "a power 'traditionally exclusively reserved to the State.' "[113] The customer argued that resolving disputes is a traditional function of government and that the government had delegated this task to the creditor by giving it the authority to sell the goods to pay the debt. The Supreme Court expressly rejected this argument and said that there were many ways in which the dispute could have been resolved: The debtor could have sought a waiver of the creditor's rights to sell her goods; the debtor could have sought to replevy her goods under state law; the debtor had a statutory damages action available for violations of the law. The Supreme Court said that in light of all these options, it could not be said that the government delegated to the creditor "an exclusive prerogative of the sovereign."[114]

---

[108] Justice Douglas expressly made this argument in *Bell v. Maryland, id.* at 252-253.

[109] 457 U.S. 922 (1982).

[110] *See, e.g.,* Georgia v. McCollum, 500 U.S. 42, 52 (1992); Edmonson v. Leesville Concrete Co., 500 U.S. 614, 620 (1991), discussed below.

[111] *Lugar,* 457 U.S. at 937.

[112] 436 U.S. 149 (1978).

[113] *Id.* at 157 (citations omitted).

[114] *Id.* at 160.

The key difference between *Lugar* and *Flagg Brothers* was the direct involvement of a state officer, the sheriff, in the former case, while the latter was entirely private self-help. Yet the difference in state involvement seems more a matter of degree than one of kind as the Supreme Court tried to make it seem. In both cases, state law provided the procedures for the debtors' action. In *Lugar*, state law provided the procedure for prejudgment attachment; in *Flagg Brothers*, state law provided for the self-help action. In fact, in *Flagg Brothers* involvement of the sheriff was unnecessary precisely because the state's law allowed the repossession action without assistance of the sheriff. Therefore, it can be questioned whether the distinction between *Lugar* and *Flagg Brothers* based on the involvement of the sheriff should make such a difference.

The other major area where the Court has considered court involvement to be state action concerns the exercise of peremptory challenges. Peremptory challenges are the ability of a litigant to excuse prospective jurors without showing cause. In *Batson v. Kentucky*, the Supreme Court held that equal protection prohibits prosecutors from using peremptory challenges in a discriminatory fashion in criminal cases.[115] The issue then arose as to whether *Batson* should be applied when private litigants—such as parties in private civil litigation or even criminal defendants—exercise peremptory challenges in a discriminatory fashion.

In *Edmonson v. Leesville Concrete Co.*, the Supreme Court held that *Batson* applies in private civil litigation.[116] The Court applied the *Lugar* two-part test, described above, and found that there is state action when private parties exercise peremptory challenges in a civil case in a racially discriminatory manner. As to the first prong of the test, the Court explained that it is state and federal laws that authorize peremptory challenges in state and federal courts. As to the second prong of the test, the Court emphasized the involvement of the government in jury selection from subpoenaing individuals for jury service to compelling completion of questionnaires to judicial supervision of the voir dire process. Moreover, juries function as a traditional and important government decision-making body. As a result, the Court found that discriminatory use of peremptory challenges denies equal protection, even if done by private litigants.

The Court took this a step further a year later in *Georgia v. McCollum*, where the Court considered "whether a criminal defendant's exercise of a peremptory challenge constitutes state action for purposes of the Equal Protection Clause."[117] If anyone is the antithesis of the government, it is a criminal defendant who is being prosecuted. Yet for purposes of jury selection, the Court found that a criminal defendant is a state actor in exercising peremptory challenges. The Court followed exactly the same reasoning as in *Edmonson*: Laws create peremptory challenges, and jury selection is a government function accomplished through the power of the state and overseen by a judge.

Putting aside the issue of whether these limits on peremptory challenges are desirable, which is discussed in §9.3.3.2, the key question is whether it makes sense

[115] 476 U.S. 79 (1986).
[116] 500 U.S. 614, 631 (1991).
[117] 505 U.S. 42, 50 (1992).

to treat private civil litigants and especially criminal defendants as state actors. The power to exercise peremptory challenges is created by law, exercised in a government proceeding, and supervised by a government employee. Yet private civil litigants and criminal defendants are not the government, and there are serious questions as to whether they should be treated as if they are the state.

Government Licensing and Regulation

The Court also has considered the entanglement exception in instances when the government licenses or regulates an activity. In general, government licensing or regulating is insufficient for a finding of state action, unless there is other government encouraging or facilitating of unconstitutional conduct. Yet here, too, the cases are not easily reconciled.

Burton v. Wilmington Parking Authority, decided in 1961, is the key case where government licensing and regulation was deemed sufficient for state action.[118] Wilmington, Delaware, operated a parking authority that leased space to a private restaurant, the Eagle Coffee Shoppe, that denied a person service solely because he was black. The Supreme Court found that the government was so entangled with the restaurant that there was a "symbiotic relationship" sufficient to create state action. For example, the government had responsibility for upkeep and maintenance of the building, and this was done with public funds. The parking facility was used by the restaurant's customers. At the same time, the government benefited from revenues from the restaurant and its customers. The Court thus concluded that the parking "Authority, and through it the State, has not only made itself a party to the refusal of service, but has elected to place its power, property, and prestige behind the admitted discrimination. The State has so far insinuated itself into a position of interdependence with Eagle that it must be recognized as a joint participant in the challenged activity."[119]

The Court also emphasized that the government could have prevented discrimination by placing a clause in the lease prohibiting it. The Court said: "But no state may effectively abdicate its responsibilities by either ignoring them or by merely failing to discharge them whatever the motive may be. It is of no consolation to an individual denied the equal protection of the laws that it was done in good faith."[120]

By this reasoning, however, virtually everything is state action. All corporations are chartered by a state government. The state always could insist, as a condition for incorporation, that the corporation comply with the Constitution. All who receive government money could be required, as a condition of receipt, to comply with the Constitution. All who are regulated by the government could have, as one condition of regulation, a mandate to comply with the Constitution.

The Supreme Court, however, has not followed this path and, in fact, virtually always has found that government licensing or regulation is not sufficient to create

[118] 365 U.S. 715 (1961).
[119] *Id.* at 725.
[120] *Id.*

state action. For example, in *Moose Lodge Number 107 v. Irvis*, the Supreme Court held that the state grant of a liquor license to a private club was not sufficient government entanglement for the Constitution to apply.[121] The Moose Lodge restricted membership to whites and refused to allow guests to bring blacks into the dining room and bar. The Court emphasized that the Pennsylvania Liquor Control Board played no role in establishing or enforcing the membership or guest policies of the lodge. The Court concluded that "there is nothing approaching the symbiotic relationship between lessor and lessee that was present in *Burton*."[122] Yet following the reasoning of *Burton*, the state certainly could have prevented discrimination by making that a condition of the liquor license, and the state was conferring a substantial benefit on the private club by granting it the license. The Court, however, felt that this was insufficient for state action.

A year later, in *Columbia Broadcasting System v. Democratic National Committee*, the Court, without a majority opinion, ruled that television stations, licensed by the government, could refuse to accept editorial advertisements from anti–Vietnam War groups.[123] Several of the Justices took the position that federal licensing of broadcast stations is not sufficient government involvement for state action.[124] Other Justices took the position that even if there was state action, it did not violate the First Amendment for the stations to refuse to accept the advertisements.

A few years later, in *Jackson v. Metropolitan Edison Co.*, the Court held that government regulation of a utility was not sufficient to create state action.[125] The issue in *Jackson* was whether a private utility, operating under a state-granted monopoly, had to provide due process before terminating a customer's service. The Court ruled that there was not state action and declared: "The mere fact that a business is subject to state regulation does not by itself convert its action into that of the State for purposes of the Fourteenth Amendment. Nor does the fact that the regulation is extensive and detailed, as in the case of most public utilities, do so."[126]

In *American Manufacturers Mutual Insurance Co. v. Sullivan*, the Court again emphasized the difficulty of finding state action based on government regulation.[127] Pennsylvania law provides that an employer or insurer may withhold

---

[121] 407 U.S. 163 (1972).

[122] *Id.* at 175.

[123] 412 U.S. 94 (1973).

[124] *See id.* at 114-121 (Burger, C.J., Stewart, J., and Rehnquist, J.). *But see id.* at 172-181 (Brennan, J., and Marshall, J., dissenting) (arguing that the refusal of stations to accept the advertisements violated the First Amendment).

[125] 419 U.S. 345 (1974). *Jackson* also involved the issue of whether running a utility is a public function, which is discussed above in §6.4.4.2.

[126] *Id.* at 350 (citations omitted). An earlier Supreme Court decision, *Public Utilities Commission v. Pollak*, 343 U.S. 451 (1952), considered a constitutional challenge to the broadcasting of radio programming over buses that were operated by a private company pursuant to a license from the city. The Supreme Court rejected the constitutional claim. In *Jackson*, the Supreme Court said that it "is not entirely clear whether the Court alternatively held that Capital Transit's action was action of the 'State' for First Amendment purposes, or whether it merely assumed, arguendo, that it was and went on to resolve the First Amendment question adversely to the bus riders." 419 U.S. at 356. Therefore, *Pollak* is, at best, a very questionable authority for finding that government regulation is a basis for state action.

[127] 526 U.S. 40 (1999).

workers' compensation payment for disputed medical treatment pending an independent review to determine whether the treatment is "reasonable and necessary." *Sullivan* involved a challenge by workers whose payment had been withheld claiming that the insurance companies and employers were state actors because they were acting pursuant to the state law and its extensive regulation. The Supreme Court, in an opinion by Chief Justice William Rehnquist, rejected this argument and found no state action.

The Court said that the issue was whether "a private insurer's decision to withhold payment for disputed medical treatment may be fairly attributable to the State so as to subject insurers to the constraints of the Fourteenth Amendment."[128] The Court said that this requires a "close nexus" between the state and the private conduct and that "[w]hether such a 'close nexus' exists . . . depends on whether the State has exercised coercive power or has provided such significant encouragement, either overt or covert, that the choice must in law be deemed to be that of the State. Action taken by private entities with the mere approval or acquiescence of the State is not state action."[129]

The plaintiffs argued that the state encouraged withholding of payments by enacting a law expressly authorizing this. But the Court said that this was insufficient to find that an employer withholding a payment was a state actor. Chief Justice Rehnquist explained: "We have never held that the mere availability of a remedy for wrongful conduct, even when the private use of that remedy serves important public interests, so significantly encourages the private activity as to make the State responsible for it."[130] Together *Moose Lodge, CBS v. DNC, Jackson,* and *Sullivan* make it very difficult to find state action based on government licensing or regulation. *Burton* never has been overruled. Yet practically speaking, it may be a relic of the era, before the Civil Rights Act of 1964, when the Supreme Court tried to find ways to apply the Constitution to forbid private discrimination. Indeed, in *Sullivan,* the Court described it as "one of our early cases dealing with 'state action' under the Fourteenth Amendment" and as applying a test "refined" in later cases.[131] At the most, *Burton* leaves open the possibility that the Court in the future might find a sufficient "symbiotic relationship" that in an extraordinary case could support a finding of state action based on government licensing or regulation. Courts are most likely to find state action on this basis if it can be shown that the government's actions are likely to be perceived as approving the private conduct or if there is some way in which the government has encouraged the wrongful behavior. Also, if the private behavior simply could not have occurred without the government's assistance, the entanglement exception is more likely to be applied.

---

[128] *Id.* at 51.

[129] *Id.* at 52 (citations omitted).

[130] *Id.* at 53. This statement could be quite significant as courts deal with the issue of when private dispute resolution constitutes state action. *See* Richard Reuben, Public Justice: Toward a State Action Theory of Alternative Dispute Resolution, 85 Cal. L. Rev. 577 (1997).

[131] 526 U.S. at 58.

Government Subsidies

A third type of government entanglement is government financial support. Here, too, there are some cases indicating that this can be used as a basis for finding state action. But later decisions make it highly doubtful that subsidies, no matter how large, by themselves could justify applying the Constitution.

In *Norwood v. Harrison*, the Supreme Court unanimously found that there was state action when the government gave free textbooks to private schools that engaged in racial discrimination.[132] A Mississippi program provided free textbooks to public and private schools, without reference to whether the schools engaged in racial discrimination. The Supreme Court noted the great growth in private school education in Mississippi in the years after desegregation was required.[133] The Court stated that a "State's constitutional obligation requires it to steer clear, not only of operating the old dual system of racially segregated schools, but also of giving significant aid to institutions that practice racial or other invidious discrimination."[134] The Court's holding meant that either the schools had to stop discriminating if they wanted the books or, if they kept their policy of discrimination, the state had to halt giving them the books.

Likewise, in *Gilmore v. City of Montgomery*, the Supreme Court held that a city could not give racially segregated private schools exclusive use of public recreational facilities.[135] Montgomery, Alabama, allowed segregated private schools to have exclusive possession of football stadiums, baseball diamonds, basketball courts, and tennis courts for athletic contests and other school-sponsored events. The Court found state action because the "city's actions significantly enhanced the attractiveness of segregated private schools, formed in reaction against the federal court school order, by enabling them to offer complete athletic programs."[136]

Norwood and *Gilmore* both involved challenges to state government assistance to segregated private schools in states—Mississippi and Alabama—with a long history of school segregation. Outside this contest, however, the Court has been unwilling to find government subsidy to be a basis for finding state action.

In *Rendell-Baker v. Kohn*, the Supreme Court held that there was not state action when a private school, receiving over 90 percent of its funds from the state, fired a teacher because of her speech activities.[137] The Court made it clear that government funding, by itself, is not a basis for finding state action. The Court said that "the school's receipt of public funds does not make the discharge decisions acts of the State."[138] The Court explained that the school was not different from other private businesses whose business depends on contracts with the government and that the "[a]cts of such private contractors do not become acts of the government by reason of their significant or even total engagement in performing

---

[132] 413 U.S. 455 (1973).
[133] *Id.* at 457.
[134] *Id.* at 467.
[135] 417 U.S. 556 (1974).
[136] *Id.* at 569.
[137] 457 U.S. 830 (1982).
[138] *Id.* at 840.

public contracts."[139] The Court said that because the school's actions were not "compelled or even influenced by any state regulation," the Constitution did not apply.[140]

In *Blum v. Yaretsky*, there was a strong argument that the government's funding of Medicaid patients caused their transfer to other less well-equipped facilities. State policy required that private facilities receiving Medicaid funding create "utilization review committees" to determine the level of care needed.[141] After a decision from a utilization review committee, the state would terminate its Medicaid payments for patients unless they were transferred from "skilled nursing facilities" to "health related facilities." Because the state paid over 90 percent of the medical expenses for the patients, its decision clearly was responsible for the transfer decisions. The patients argued that they should be given due process with regard to their transfer.

The Supreme Court, however, ruled that there was not state action because it was the decision of the private nursing home to transfer the patients. The Court found neither the extent of state regulation nor the size of state funding to be a basis for finding state action. Furthermore, the Court found that the state financial incentives for the transfers were insufficient to constitute state action. The Court said that "a State normally can be held responsible for a private decision only when it has exercised such significant encouragement, either overt or covert, that the choice must in law be deemed to be that of the State."[142]

There is an obvious tension between *Norwood* and *Gilmore*, on the one hand, and *Rendell-Baker* and *Blum*, on the other. In *Norwood* and *Gilmore*, partial aid—books and athletic facilities—was sufficient for state action. In *Rendell-Baker* and *Blum*, almost total subsidies were not enough. The cases, however, are most easily distinguished on the ground that in *Norwood* and *Gilmore* the government gave its aid with the intent of undermining school desegregation. In *Rendell-Baker* and *Blum*, the Court did not act with the purpose of encouraging constitutional violations.

In other words, the Court is most likely to find that government subsidies are state action when the government's purpose is to undermine the protection of constitutional rights. Absent such a government motivation, it is very difficult to find that government funding is sufficient for a finding of state action.

Initiatives Encouraging Violations of Rights

In *Reitman v. Mulkey*, the Supreme Court found unconstitutional a voter initiative that repealed open housing laws and prevented the enactment of such future antidiscrimination laws.[143] A ballot initiative adopted by the voters declared: "Neither the State nor any subdivision or agency thereof shall deny, limit or abridge, directly or indirectly, the right of any person, who is willing or desires to sell, lease

---

[139] *Id.* at 841.
[140] *Id.*
[141] 457 U.S. 991 (1982).
[142] *Id.* at 1004.
[143] 387 U.S. 369 (1967).

or rent any part or all of his real property, to decline to sell, lease or rent such property to such person or persons as he, in his absolute discretion, chooses."[144]

The Court concluded that the provision "would encourage and significantly involve the State in private racial discrimination contrary to the Fourteenth Amendment."[145] The Court observed that no longer was discrimination solely a matter of private choice. Rather, "[t]he right to discriminate, including the right to discriminate on racial grounds, was now embodied in the State's basic charter, immune from legislative, executive, or judicial regulation at any level of the state government."[146] Because the initiative was intended to authorize discrimination in housing, and because it does authorize such discrimination, the Court found that it was unconstitutional.

On the one hand, this makes sense because the initiative's purpose and effect were to encourage private discrimination. In that sense, this seems an almost paradigm example of the entanglement exception because it is government encouragement.[147] On the other hand, does this mean that any repeal of an antidiscrimination law is impermissible encouragement of discrimination? If so, then isn't the failure to adopt antidiscrimination laws also encouragement of discrimination? And then, isn't the same true about the failure to adopt laws that prohibit all violations of constitutional rights? Again, it would seem that *Reitman v. Mulkey*, like cases such as *Shelley* and *Burton*, could make anything state action.

The Court never has gone nearly this far, although it has invalidated other initiatives that overturned antidiscrimination laws.[148] In *Hunter v. Erickson*, the Supreme Court declared unconstitutional an initiative in Akron, Ohio, that repealed open housing laws and required voter approval of any such future law.[149] The Court found that the initiative was an "explicitly racial classification treating racial housing matters differently from other racial and housing matters."[150]

In *Washington v. Seattle School Dist. No. 1*, the Supreme Court declared unconstitutional a Washington initiative that provided that no school board could require any student to attend a school other than the school geographically nearest or next nearest the student's place of residence.[151] The initiative precluded pupils

---

[144] *Id.* at 371.

[145] *Id.* at 376.

[146] *Id.* at 377.

[147] For an excellent critique and alternative explanation of *Reitman, see* Charles L. Black, Jr., Foreword: State Action, Equal Protection, and California's Proposition 14, 81 Harv. L. Rev. 69 (1967). Professor Black argued that the initiative was unconstitutional because it created a legal obstacle to a racial minority's use of the political process; they only could enact protective legislation by amending the state constitution.

[148] *See also* Romer v. Evans, 517 U.S. 620 (1996) (declaring unconstitutional a Colorado initiative that repealed laws prohibiting discrimination against gays, lesbians, and bisexuals and preventing future laws to protect such individuals). *Romer v. Evans* is discussed in §9.7.4.

[149] 393 U.S. 385 (1969).

[150] *Id.* at 389. In contrast, in *James v. Valtierra*, 402 U.S. 137 (1971), that Court upheld a state constitutional provision that prevented the creation of low-rent housing except if it was approved by a majority vote in the locality where the housing was to be built. The Court emphasized that there was no proof that the requirement was intended to discriminate based on race.

[151] 458 U.S. 457 (1982).

from being assigned for purposes of desegregation, and this goal—frustrating desegregation—made the initiative unconstitutional.[152]

The Court distinguished the companion case of *Crawford v. Board of Education*, where the Court upheld a California initiative that provided that state courts could not order mandatory assignment or transportation of students unless a federal court would do so to remedy a violation of the Fourteenth Amendment.[153] The Court found that there was no racial classification in the law, and the repeal of remedies not required by the Constitution is permissible.

Distinguishing *Crawford* from the other cases is difficult. There was not a racial classification within the California initiative, and it only limited remedies not required by the Constitution. Yet the initiative in *Crawford* had as its objective limiting busing just as the initiatives in *Reitman* and *Hunter* sought to limit open housing laws and as the initiative in *Washington* also aimed to decrease busing. The point at which the state's encouragement of discrimination becomes unconstitutional is never clearly defined in these cases.

Most recently, in *Schuette v. Coalition to Defend Affirmative Action*, the Court distinguished *Hunter* and *Washington* and upheld a Michigan initiative that restricted affirmative action.[154] Michigan voters passed an initiative that prohibited the state or its political subdivisions from discriminating or giving preferences based on race or gender in education, contracting, or employment. Challenges were brought arguing that the restriction on affirmative action in education violated the Constitution. The United States Court of Appeals for the Sixth Circuit declared this unconstitutional based on *Hunter* and *Washington*.[155] The Court of Appeals explained that virtually any group could gain benefits in admission through the Board of Regents for the university or the state legislature, but not racial minorities. They would need to go through the much more arduous process of amending the state constitution.

The Supreme Court, in a 6-2 decision, without a majority opinion, upheld the Michigan initiative. Justice Kennedy wrote the plurality opinion, joined by Chief Justice Roberts and Justice Alito, and said that *Hunter* and *Washington* were limited to initiatives that were intentionally discriminatory against racial minorities, something the plurality found absent as to the Michigan initiative. Justice Scalia wrote an opinion concurring in the judgment, joined by Justice Thomas, in which he argued that *Hunter* and *Washington* should be overruled. Justice Breyer was the final vote for the majority and he expressed the need for deference to the political process and emphasized that the earlier cases involved a restructuring of the political process that changed the political level at which policies were enacted, while this case involves an amendment that took decision-making authority away from unelected actors and placed it in the hands of the voters. Justice Sotomayor wrote a powerful dissent in which she defended her views of race and society, including the importance of racially sensitive admissions policies.

---

[152] *Id.* at 468.

[153] 458 U.S. 527 (1982).

[154] 134 S. Ct. 1623 (2014).

[155] Coalition to Defend Affirmative Action v. Regents of the Univ. of Mich., 701 F.3d 466 (6th Cir. 2012) (en banc).

The bottom line from *Schuette* is that no state needs to have affirmative action programs for its colleges and universities and that a state may eliminate these, including by an initiative. As for *Hunter* and *Washington*, they have not been overruled, but they have been limited and it is uncertain what remains of the so-called political restructuring doctrine that they created.

Inevitably, the determination of state action is inextricably linked to the Court's view as to whether there is a violation of equal protection. In *Reitman, Hunter,* and *Washington*, the Court saw the initiatives as being motivated by impermissible discriminatory purposes and found denials of equal protection. In *Schuette*, the six Justices in the majority saw no violation of equal protection; in their view, a state did not need to have affirmative action programs and could repeal them, including by an initiative.

Conclusion to the Entanglement Exception

In sum, the cases under the entanglement exception are often inconsistent. In almost every area, there is a Warren Court decision expansively defining the exception to find that private race discrimination violates the Constitution. Later, in each area, there are Burger and Rehnquist Court decisions greatly narrowing the scope of the exception. Yet the earlier cases are never overruled, and the distinctions often seem arbitrary. In light of these seemingly inconsistent rulings, it is not surprising that Professor Charles Black called the state action doctrine "a conceptual disaster area."[156]

Yet, overall, it is possible to say that the Court is most likely to find state action based on entanglement if it can be shown that the government's purpose was to undermine protection of constitutional rights or if the government is facilitating private conduct that otherwise would not occur. To find state action based on entanglement, there must be some government action that can be identified as affirmatively authorizing, encouraging, or facilitating constitutional violations.

§6.5   THE LEVELS OF SCRUTINY

The Meaning of the Levels of Scrutiny

In constitutional litigation concerning individuals' rights and equal protection, the outcome often very much depends on the "level of scrutiny" used. The level of scrutiny is the test that is applied to determine if the law is constitutional. Throughout the remaining chapters, which consider particular rights and equal protection, there is frequent mention of the levels of scrutiny.

---

[156] Black, *supra* note 147, at 95.

In a sense, the level of scrutiny provides instructions for balancing. It informs courts as to how to arrange the weights on the constitutional scale in evaluating particular laws. If it is an area where there is reason for great suspicion of the government or a fundamental right is at stake, the government will be required, by the level of scrutiny, to meet a heavy burden. But if it is an area of general deference to the legislature, the government will have a minimal burden to carry.

The *Carolene Products* Footnote

In a very famous footnote in *United States v. Carolene Products Co.*, the Supreme Court articulated the idea that different constitutional claims would be subjected to varying levels of review.[1] The Supreme Court upheld a federal law prohibiting "filled milk," a substance made by mixing vegetable oil with skim milk. The Court emphasized the need for deference to Congress, and in footnote 4, the Court declared:

> There may be narrower scope for operation of the presumption of constitutionality when legislation appears on its face to be within a specific prohibition of the Constitution, such as those of the first ten amendments. . . . It is unnecessary to consider now whether legislation which restricts those political processes which can ordinarily be expected to bring about repeal of undesirable legislation, is to subjected to more exacting judicial scrutiny under the general prohibitions of the Fourteenth Amendment. . . . Nor need we enquire . . . whether prejudice against discrete and insular minorities may be a special condition, which tends seriously to curtail the operation of those political processes ordinarily to be relied upon to protect minorities, and which may call for a correspondingly more searching judicial inquiry.[2]

In other words, courts generally should presume that laws are constitutional. However, "more searching judicial inquiry" is appropriate when it is a law that interferes with individual rights, or a law that restricts the ability of the political process to repeal undesirable legislation, or a law that discriminates against a "discrete and insular minority." It is a framework of general judicial deference to the legislature, but with particular areas of more intensive judicial review.

The Levels of Scrutiny Defined

The minimal level of review is the "rational basis test." All laws challenged under the due process clause or equal protection must meet at least rational basis review. Under the rational basis test, a law will be upheld if it is *rationally related to a legitimate government purpose.*[3] In other words, the government's objective only need

---

§6.5 [1]   304 U.S. 144, 152 n.4 (1938). *See* J.M. Balkin, The Footnote, 83 Nw. U. L. Rev. 275 (1989); Bruce A. Ackerman, Beyond *Carolene Products*, 98 Harv. L. Rev. 713 (1985).

[2]   304 U.S. at 52-53 n.4.

[3]   *See, e.g.*, Pennell v. City of San Jose, 485 U.S. 1 (1988); U.S. R.R. Retirement Bd. v. Fritz, 449 U.S. 166 (1980); Allied Stores v. Bowers, 358 U.S. 522 (1959); Williamson v. Lee Optical, 348 U.S. 483 (1955); Day-Brite Lighting, Inc. v. Missouri, 342 U.S. 421 (1952).

be a goal that it is legitimate for government to pursue. In fact, the goal need not be the actual purpose of the litigation but, rather, any conceivable legitimate purpose is sufficient.[4] The means chosen need be only a reasonable way to accomplish the objective.

Under the rational basis test, the challenger of a law has the burden of proof. That is, the law will be upheld unless the challenger proves that the law does not serve any conceivable legitimate purpose or that it is not a reasonable way to attain the end. The rational basis test is enormously deferential to the government, and only rarely has the Supreme Court invalidated laws as failing rational basis review.[5]

The middle tier of review is termed "intermediate scrutiny." Under intermediate scrutiny, a law will be upheld if it is *substantially related to an important government purpose.*[6] In other words, the government's objective must be more than just a legitimate goal for government to pursue; the court must regard the purpose as "important." The means chosen must be more than a reasonable way of attaining the end; the court must believe that the law is substantially related to achieving the goal.

As discussed in succeeding chapters, intermediate scrutiny is used in evaluating laws involving gender discrimination,[7] discrimination against nonmarital children,[8] discrimination against undocumented alien children with regard to education,[9] and regulation of commercial speech[10] and of speech in public forums.[11] It appears clear that the government has the burden of proof under intermediate scrutiny. For instance, in the area of gender discrimination, the Court remarked that "[p]arties who seek to defend gender-based government action must demonstrate an 'exceedingly persuasive justification' for that action."[12] Likewise, in the area of commercial speech, where intermediate scrutiny also is applied, the Court has declared that "[t]he party seeking to uphold a restriction on commercial speech carries the burden of justifying it."[13]

---

[4] *See* United States R.R. Retirement Bd. v. Fritz, 449 U.S. 166 (1980); Schweiker v. Wilson, 450 U.S. 221 (1981).

[5] *See, e.g.*, Romer v. Evans, 517 U.S. 620 (1996); City of Cleburne v. Cleburne Living Ctr., Inc., 473 U.S. 432 (1985); Zobel v. Williams, 457 U.S. 55 (1982); United States Dept. of Agriculture v. Moreno, 413 U.S. 528 (1973) (all declaring laws unconstitutional as violating the rational basis test). These cases are discussed in §9.2.2.

[6] *See, e.g.*, Craig v. Boren, 429 U.S. 190, 197 (1976); Lehr v. Robertson, 463 U.S. 248, 266 (1983).

[7] *See, e.g.*, United States v. Virginia, 518 U.S. 515 (1996); Craig v. Boren, 429 U.S. 190 (1976).

[8] *See, e.g.*, Lehr v. Robertson, 463 U.S. 248 (1983).

[9] *See* Plyler v. Doe, 457 U.S. 202 (1982).

[10] *See* Central Hudson Gas & Electric Corp. v. Public Serv. Commn., 447 U.S. 557 (1980); Rubin v. Coors Brewing Co., 514 U.S. 476 (1995); Lorillard Tobacco Co. v. Reilly, 533 U.S. 525 (2001).

[11] *See, e.g.*, Ward v. Rock Against Racism, 491 U.S. 781 (1989).

[12] United States v. Virginia, 518 U.S. 515, 529 (1996). However, in a subsequent gender discrimination case, *Nguyen v. Immigration and Naturalization Service*, 533 U.S. 53 (2001), the Court's majority opinion did not use this language, although the dissent did. *See id.* at 2071.

[13] Edenfield v. Fane, 507 U.S. 761, 770 (1993).

An unresolved question concerning intermediate scrutiny is whether less restrictive alternative analysis ever should be used for intermediate scrutiny.[14] The cases are conflicting, although it is clear that, at the very least, the means must be narrowly tailored to achieve the goal when intermediate scrutiny is applied.

Finally, the most intensive type of judicial review is strict scrutiny. Under strict scrutiny, a law will be upheld *if it is necessary to achieve a compelling government purpose.*[15] In other words, the court must regard the government's purpose as vital, as "compelling." Also, the law must be shown to be "necessary" as a means to accomplishing the end.[16] This requires proof that the law is the least restrictive or least discriminatory alternative. If the law is not the least restrictive alternative, then it is not "necessary" to accomplish the end.[17] At times, the Court has said that strict scrutiny "means that such classifications are constitutional only if they are narrowly tailored to further compelling governmental interests."[18] The problem with this phrasing is that "narrowly tailored" is used under both intermediate and strict scrutiny. Also, "narrowly tailored" fails to communicate as clearly as "necessary" that least restrictive alternative analysis is applied under strict scrutiny.

Under strict scrutiny, the government has the burden of proof.[19] That is, the law will be struck down unless the government can show that the law is necessary to accomplish a compelling government purpose. Strict scrutiny, of course, is the most intensive type of judicial review, and laws generally are declared unconstitutional when it is applied. Professor Gerald Gunther said that it is "strict in theory and fatal in fact."[20]

Strict scrutiny is used when the Court evaluates discrimination based on race or national origin, generally for discrimination against aliens (although there are exceptions), and for interference with fundamental rights such as the right to vote, the right to travel, the right to privacy, and interference with freedom of speech. All of these areas, of course, are discussed in the following chapters.

---

[14] For example, in *Board of Trustees of the State University of New York v. Fox*, 492 U.S. 469 (1989), the Court rejected least restrictive alternative analysis for commercial speech, but in *Rubin v. Coors Brewery Co.*, 514 U.S. 300 (1995), the Supreme Court invalidated a regulation of commercial speech because the government could achieve its goal through means less intrusive of speech. These cases are discussed in §11.3.7.3. In its subsequent commercial speech cases, the Court has held that the government regulation does not have to be the least restrictive alternative, though it must be narrowly tailored and substantially related to the goals sought. *See* Lorillard Tobacco Co. v. Reilly, 533 U.S. 525 (2001); Greater New Orleans Broad. Assn. v. United States, 527 U.S. 173 (1999). *See also* Ward v. Rock Against Racism, 491 U.S. 781 (1989) (rejecting least restrictive alternative analysis in evaluating government regulation of public forums).

[15] *See, e.g.*, Adarand Constructors v. Pena, 515 U.S. 200 (1995); Sugarman v. Dougall, 413 U.S. 634 (1973); Sherbert v. Verner, 374 U.S. 398 (1963).

[16] *See, e.g.*, Wygant v. Jackson Bd. of Educ., 476 U.S. 267, 280 (1986) ("Under strict scrutiny the means chosen to accomplish the State's asserted purpose must be specifically and narrowly tailored to accomplish that purpose.").

[17] *See, e.g.*, Simon & Schuster v. Members of the N.Y. State Crime Victims Bd., 502 U.S. 105 (1991).

[18] Grutter v. Bollinger, 509 U.S. 306, 326 (2003).

[19] Miller v. Johnson, 515 U.S. 900, 919-921 (1995); Burson v. Freeman, 504 U.S. 191, 198 (1992); City of Richmond v. J.A. Croson Co., 488 U.S. 469 (1989).

[20] Gerald Gunther, Foreword: In Search of Evolving Doctrine on a Changing Court: A Model for a Newer Equal Protection, 86 Harv. L. Rev. 1, 8 (1972).

The levels of scrutiny are thus extremely important in almost all areas involving individual rights and equal protection. The level of scrutiny used is very likely to determine the outcome. If rational basis review is applied, the law is likely to be upheld. If strict scrutiny is used, the law is likely to be struck down.

Criticisms of the Levels of Scrutiny

Although the levels of scrutiny are firmly established in the law, there are many who criticize the rigid tiers of review. Critics argue both that the levels of scrutiny are not descriptively accurate because there are more than just three levels of review and that they are not normatively desirable.

On a descriptive level, the criticism is that there actually is a spectrum of standards of review and not just the three levels of scrutiny. The argument is that in some cases where the Court says that it is using rational basis review, it is actually employing a test with more "bite" and not the customary very deferential rational basis test.[21] Likewise, the claim is that in some cases intermediate scrutiny is applied in a very deferential manner, and in some cases it is applied in a much more rigorous way. Also, there are instances where the Court has formulated alternative tests, such as the "undue burden test" for evaluating government restrictions of abortion.[22] The overall claim is that although the Court articulates three rigid tiers of review, the reality is a range of standards.[23]

On a normative level, the criticism is that the levels of scrutiny are undesirable and that they should be replaced by a "sliding scale" approach. Justices Thurgood Marshall and John Paul Stevens, among others, have endorsed such a sliding scale.[24] The argument is that the Court should consider factors such as the constitutional and social importance of the interests adversely affected and the invidiousness of the basis on which the classification was drawn. The claim is that under the rigid tiers of review the choice of the level of scrutiny is usually decisive and unduly limits the scope of analysis. Those who advocate a sliding scale believe that it would lead to more candid discussion of the competing interests and overall better decision making.

However, a majority of the Supreme Court never has endorsed such a sliding scale, but instead continues to articulate and apply the levels of scrutiny. Indeed, they are referred to in and applied in each of the following chapters.

---

[21] *See, e.g.,* City of Cleburne v. Cleburne Living Ctr., Inc., 473 U.S. 432 (1985), discussed in §9.2.

[22] Casey v. Planned Parenthood, 505 U.S. 833 (1992).

[23] For an excellent defense of this position, *see* Jeffrey Shaman, Cracks in the Structure: The Coming Breakdown of the Levels of Scrutiny, 45 Ohio St. L.J. 161 (1984).

[24] *See, e.g.,* Plyler v. Doe, 457 U.S. 202, 231 (1982) (Marshall, J., concurring); Craig v. Boren, 429 U.S. 190, 212 (1976) (Stevens, J., concurring); San Antonio Indep. School Dist. v. Rodriguez, 411 U.S. 1, 109-110 (1973) (Marshall, J., dissenting).

CHAPTER 7

Procedural Due Process

§7.1   THE DISTINCTION BETWEEN PROCEDURAL AND SUBSTANTIVE DUE PROCESS

Definitions

The Fifth and Fourteenth Amendments, respectively, provide that neither the United States nor state governments shall deprive any person "of life, liberty, or property without due process of law." This clause has been interpreted as imposing two separate limits on government, usually called "procedural due process" and "substantive due process."

Procedural due process, as the phrase implies, refers to the procedures that the government must follow before it deprives a person of life, liberty, or property. Classic procedural due process issues concern what kind of notice and what form of hearing the government must provide when it takes a particular action.

Substantive due process, as that phrase connotes, asks whether the government has an adequate reason for taking away a person's life, liberty, or property. In other words, substantive due process looks to whether there is a sufficient justification for the government's action. Whether there is such a justification depends very much on the level of scrutiny used.[1] For example, if a law is in an area where only rational basis review is applied, substantive due process is met so long as the law is rationally related to a legitimate government purpose. But if it is in an area where strict scrutiny is used, such as for protecting fundamental rights, then the government will meet substantive due process only if it can prove that the law is necessary to achieve a compelling government purpose.

An illustration can be found in the constitutional right of parents to custody of their children. The Supreme Court has held that parents have a liberty interest in the custody of their children.[2] Therefore, procedural due process requires that the government provide notice and a hearing, and that there be clear and convincing evidence of a need to terminate custody, before parental rights are permanently ended.[3] Because the right to custody is deemed a fundamental right, substantive due process requires that the government prove that terminating custody is necessary to achieve a compelling purpose, such as the need to prevent abuse or neglect of the child.[4]

Another example of the distinction between procedural and substantive due process can be found in challenges to large punitive damage awards. Procedural due process requires that there be safeguards such as instructions to the jury to guide their discretion, and judicial review to ensure the reasonableness of the awards.[5] Substantive due process prevents excessive punitive damage awards, regardless of the procedures followed.[6]

Thus, it is possible to distinguish procedural and substantive due process based on the remedy sought. If the plaintiff is seeking to have a government action declared unconstitutional as violating a constitutional right, substantive due process is involved. But when a person or a group is seeking to have a government action declared unconstitutional because of the lack of adequate safeguards, such as notice and a hearing, procedural due process is the issue.

---

§7.1 [1] The levels of scrutiny are defined and discussed in §6.5. The Supreme Court has explained that the due process clause "cover[s] a substantive sphere as well, 'barring certain government actions regardless of the fairness of the procedures used to implement them.'" County of Sacramento v. Lewis, 523 U.S. 833, 840 (1998).

[2] *See, e.g.,* Santosky v. Kramer, 455 U.S. 745 (1982); Little v. Streater, 452 U.S. 1 (1981); Stanley v. Illinois, 405 U.S. 645 (1972), discussed in §7.3.3 (procedural due process) and §10.2.2 (substantive due process).

[3] *See* Santosky v. Kramer, 455 U.S. 745 (1982).

[4] *See, e.g.,* Stanley v. Illinois, 405 U.S. 645 (1972) (rights of unmarried fathers); *but see* Michael H. v. Gerald D., 491 U.S. 110 (1989) (denying rights to unmarried fathers where the mother was married to another man at the time of the birth of the child), discussed in §10.2.2.

[5] *See* Honda Motor Co., Ltd. v. Oberg, 512 U.S. 415 (1994); TXO Prod. Corp. v. Alliance Resources Corp., 509 U.S. 443 (1993); Pacific Mut. Life Ins. Co. v. Haslip, 499 U.S. 1 (1991).

[6] *See* Philip Morris USA v. Williams, 549 U.S. 346 (2007); State Farm Mut. Automobile Ins. v. Campbell, 548 U.S. 408 (2003); BMW of North Am., Inc. v. Gore, 517 U.S. 559 (1996) (finding a punitive damage award to be grossly excessive); discussed below in §7.4.3.

§7.1 The Distinction Between Procedural and Substantive Due Process

Procedural and substantive due process can involve some of the same questions. For example, for both, it often is necessary to define what is "liberty" or "property." If there is not a denial of life, liberty, or property, then the government does not have to provide procedural or substantive due process. Indeed, the same case can present issues of both procedural and substantive due process. In *District Attorney's Office for the Third Judicial District v. Osborne*,[7] the Court considered both procedural and substantive due process claims for a right to postconviction DNA testing. Osborne, who had been convicted of rape and other crimes, claimed that sophisticated DNA testing would exonerate him. The Court rejected the procedural due process claim by concluding that the procedures created by Alaska law were sufficient to meet due process.[8] Chief Justice Roberts, writing for the Court in a 5-4 decision, stated: "We see nothing inadequate about the procedures Alaska has provided to vindicate its state right to postconviction relief in general, and nothing inadequate about how those procedures apply to those who seek access to DNA evidence."[9] The Court also rejected a substantive due process right, concluding that the matter is best left to the legislatures. The Court explained: "Establishing a freestanding right to access DNA evidence for testing would force us to act as policymakers, and our substantive-due-process rulemaking authority would not only have to cover the right of access but a myriad of other issues."[10]

The Controversy over Substantive Due Process

The concept of procedural due process never has been controversial, although there certainly have been major disputes over what constitutes liberty and property interests and what procedures should be required. In contrast, the very idea of substantive due process has been contested. The argument is that due process denotes procedures and that it is incorrect to use the due process clause as the place for protecting substantive rights.[11]

The criticism of substantive due process has many facets. In part, critics argue that due process is the wrong provision to use to protect substantive rights. The argument is that within the Fourteenth Amendment, the privileges or immunities clause—the provision that states no state "shall abridge the privileges or immunities of citizens of the United States"—is the appropriate place for safeguarding substantive rights. However, as discussed in §6.3.2, in the *Slaughter-House Cases*,[12] in 1872, the Court gave the clause an extremely narrow interpretation that has

---

[7] 557 U.S. 52 (2009).

[8] Alaska is one of the few states that does not create a statutory right to such testing, but under judicial decisions allows it if the defendant shows (1) that the conviction rested primarily on eyewitness identification evidence, (2) that there was a demonstrable doubt concerning the defendant's identification as the perpetrator, and (3) that scientific testing would likely be conclusive on this issue. 557 U.S. at 65.

[9] *Id.* at 69.

[10] *Id.* at 73.

[11] John Hart Ely remarked that "[s]ubstantive due process is a contradiction in terms—sort of like 'green pastel redness.'" John H. Ely, Democracy and Distrust 18 (1980).

[12] 83 U.S. 36 (1872), discussed in §6.3.2.

prevented it from being used to safeguard individual liberties.[13] As a result, the Court turned to the due process clause to protect substantive rights. Critics argue that this is inappropriate.

Also, the objections to substantive due process inevitably are combined with arguments against the Supreme Court protecting rights that are not expressly enumerated in the Constitution. In other words, the objections generally are not only to the place in the Constitution where the rights are found, but also to the Court's finding and protecting the rights at all. Critics argue that the Court acts illegitimately when it protects rights that are not explicitly stated in the Constitution or intended by its framers.[14]

Finally, the criticism of substantive due process cannot be separated from attacks on how the Supreme Court has used the doctrine over the course of American history. There have been two major uses of substantive due process. Early in the twentieth century, before 1937, the Court used it to safeguard economic liberties and to protect freedom of contract as a fundamental right. The paradigm case of this era was *Lochner v. New York*, where the Court declared unconstitutional a law that imposed a limit on the number of hours bakers could work.[15] In the more contemporary era, substantive due process has been used to protect rights of privacy and personal autonomy. *Roe v. Wade*, which legalized abortion, is the most famous example of this modern substantive due process.[16] Needless to say, both sets of cases are controversial, and often the criticisms are presented as attacks on the idea of substantive due process.

In response to these criticisms, defenders argue that "due process" does denote substantive limits on government. Over a century ago, the Supreme Court declared that due process "is a restraint on the legislative as well as on the executive and judicial powers of the government, and cannot be so construed as to leave congress free to make any 'due process of law,' by its mere will."[17] The clause does not speak solely of due process but, rather, of "due process of law," and it is argued that an action is not in accord with the law of the land if it violates the substantive guarantees of the Constitution.[18]

Thus, the due process clause has been found to incorporate provisions of the Bill of Rights that are deemed fundamental and to protect these rights from state

---

[13] In 1999, for essentially the first time in American history (the other was a 1935 decision that was overruled in 1940), the Court used the privileges or immunities clause to invalidate a state law. Saenz v. Roe, 526 U.S. 489 (1999) (finding that the right to travel is protected under the privileges or immunities clause). *Saenz* is discussed in §6.3.2.

[14] *See, e.g.*, Raoul Berger, Government by Judiciary (1977); Robert H. Bork, Neutral Principles and Some First Amendment Problems, 47 Ind. L.J. 1 (1971). This debate over protecting unenumerated rights is discussed in §1.4.

[15] 198 U.S. 45 (1905), discussed in §§8.1 and 8.2.2.

[16] 410 U.S. 113 (1973), discussed in §10.3.3.1.

[17] Murray's Lessee v. Hoboken Land & Improv. Co., 59 U.S. (18 How.) 272, 276 (1856); *see also* Hurtado v. California, 110 U.S. 516, 531 (1884).

[18] *See* Laurence Tribe, The Puzzling Persistence of Process-Based Constitutional Theories, 89 Yale L.J. 1063, 1066 n.9 (1980); *see also* Edward S. Corwin, Liberty Against Government 89-115 (1948) (arguing that due process includes a notion of acting in accord with the law of the land).

and local interference.[19] This is substantive due process in that it uses the due process clause to protect rights and only allows interference if there is a sufficient justification.

Supporters of substantive due process also defend the legitimacy of the Court protecting rights that are not expressly stated or implied in the Constitution. This approach to judicial review, often called "nonoriginalism," posits that it is desirable for the Supreme Court to identify and safeguard unenumerated rights.[20] Of course, *Roe v. Wade* has its defenders, as well as its critics, and this is a part of the debate over substantive due process.

Organization of the Material on Due Process

This chapter focuses on procedural due process. Procedural due process can be broken down into three basic questions:

(1)   Has there been a deprivation
(2)   of life, liberty, or property
(3)   without due process of law?

Section 7.2 focuses on the first of these questions, what constitutes a "deprivation"? Section 7.3 examines the meaning of life, liberty, and property within the due process clause. Finally, §7.4 considers what procedures are required when there has been a deprivation of life, liberty, or property.

A central theme throughout this chapter, as throughout the book, concerns judicial methodology. How should the Court decide whether there is a liberty or property interest requiring due process? How should the Court decide the procedures that government must follow?

As mentioned earlier, over the course of American history, substantive due process has been used primarily in two contexts. One was the protection of economic liberties in the last century prior to 1937. This is discussed in Chapter 8 as part of the consideration of economic rights under the Constitution. The other use of substantive due process has been to safeguard rights of privacy and personhood. This is considered in Chapter 10. Of course, any law, even outside these areas, can be challenged under substantive due process. However, except in these areas, only a rational basis test has been used and the law is virtually sure to be upheld.

One major area of procedural due process is omitted: the procedures that must be followed in criminal cases. There are, of course, many specific constitutional provisions concerning this important issue. Although it is very much an issue of constitutional law and concerns procedures in perhaps their most significant application, criminal procedure is beyond the scope of this book.

---

[19] Incorporation is discussed in §6.3.3.
[20] Nonoriginalism, and the debate over judicial review, is discussed in §1.4.

§7.2 WHAT IS A "DEPRIVATION"?

The text of the due process clause prohibits the government from "depriving" a person of life, liberty, or property without due process of law. A crucial question, therefore, concerns the meaning of *deprive*. Three main issues have arisen in this regard. First, is government negligence sufficient to create a deprivation or must there be a reckless or intentional government action? Second, when is the government's failure to protect a person from privately inflicted harms a deprivation? Third, does the availability of state remedies prevent a finding that the state has deprived due process?

Is Negligence Sufficient to Constitute a Deprivation?

The Supreme Court has held that allegations and proof of negligence are insufficient to demonstrate a deprivation of due process; establishing a denial of due process requires demonstrating an intentional deprivation or at least a reckless government action. This was the holding in two companion cases decided in 1986, *Daniels v. William*[1] and *Davidson v. Cannon*.[2] In *Daniels*, a prisoner claimed that his freedom from bodily harm, a protected liberty interest, was denied without due process when he tripped on a pillow that was negligently left on a staircase by a prison guard. In *Davidson*, a prisoner claimed that prison authorities violated his due process rights by failing to protect him from attack by another prisoner. The prisoner had been threatened and had informed the prison authorities, but they had inadvertently forgotten about the message, and the prisoner was subsequently seriously injured by the attack. Under New Jersey law, the prisoner could not bring an action to recover for the injuries against the guards or prison officials in state court.[3]

The Supreme Court ruled that neither prisoner presented a constitutional claim under the due process clause. The Court concluded that "the Due Process Clause is simply not implicated by a *negligent* act of an official causing unintended loss of or injury to life, liberty, or property. . . . Not only does the word 'deprive' in the Due Process Clause connote more than a negligent act, but we should not open the federal courts to lawsuits where there has been no affirmative abuse of power."[4] The effect of *Daniels* and *Davidson* extends beyond prisoner suits, to all due process claims: A deprivation of due process exists only if there is an allegation of an intentional violation by government or government officers.

The Supreme Court has not yet expressly ruled on whether other states of mind—such as recklessness, deliberate indifference, or gross negligence—are sufficient to constitute a deprivation of due process. Although there is some

---

§7.2 [1] 474 U.S. 327 (1986).

[2] 474 U.S. 344 (1986).

[3] N.J. Stat. Ann. §59:5-2(b)(4) ("Neither a public entity nor a public employee is liable for . . . any injury caused by a prisoner to any other prisoner.").

[4] *Daniels*, 474 U.S. at 328, 330 (emphasis in original) (citations omitted).

division among lower courts, generally they have held that deliberate indifference or recklessness is sufficient to constitute a due process violation, but that gross negligence is not adequate.[5] In *County of Sacramento v. Lewis*, discussed below, the Court held that in emergency circumstances the government only may be held liable if its officers' conduct "shocks the conscience."[6] In doing so, the Court said that liability in emergency circumstances could not be found based on deliberate indifference because "the very term 'deliberate indifference' implies [that] the standard is sensibly employed only when actual deliberation is practical."[7] This implicitly suggests that deliberate indifference is permissible in nonemergency situations where deliberation is possible.

The Court's decisions in *Daniels* and *Davidson* can be questioned. First, especially in *Davidson*, why is the absence of a state remedy not a denial of due process? In *Davidson*, state law prohibited the plaintiff from suing the prison or its employees to recover for the injuries inflicted by another prisoner. There is a strong argument that the state deprived liberty without due process by failing to provide any remedy for prisoners injured in this manner.[8]

The Court said that the absence of proceedings is irrelevant because there was no denial of due process.[9] But this ignores the fact that the absence of proceedings itself is arguably a denial of due process.

Second, the distinction between negligent and intentional deprivations of life, liberty, and property should be questioned. The term "deprivation" signifies a loss; the Court thus cannot justify limiting the due process clause to intentional deprivations based on a textual analysis of the Constitution. Nor can the Court justify its conclusions based on an assumption that injuries inflicted by intentional conduct are inherently more serious than negligent actions. Negligent government conduct can be tremendously violative of rights. Consider, for example, governmental execution of an innocent person.

As mentioned above, in *County of Sacramento v. Lewis*,[10] the Court carved an exception to *Daniels* and *Davidson* and held that in emergency circumstances the government can be held liable only if its officers' conduct shocks the conscience. This requires showing that the officers acted with the intent of causing harm to the victim. The case involved a high-speed police chase that ended tragically. An officer mistakenly heard another officer and chased a boy on a motorcycle. The high-speed chase ended in a crash that killed a passenger, another teenage boy.

The Supreme Court, in an opinion by Justice Souter, reversed a Ninth Circuit opinion that had adopted "deliberate indifference" as the appropriate standard for evaluating the government's conduct. The Court said that in emergency

---

[5] *See* Slade v. Board of School Directors of City of Milwaukee, 702 F.3d 1027, 1032 (7th Cir. 2012) (gross negligence insufficient for a claim under due process); Wilson v. Lawrence County, 260 F.3d 946, 956 (8th Cir. 2001) (recklessness sufficient for a claim under due process).

[6] 523 U.S. 833 (1998).

[7] *Id.* at 851.

[8] *See* Christina B. Whitman, Government Responsibility for Constitutional Torts, 85 Mich. L. Rev. 225, 274 (1986).

[9] *Davidson*, 474 U.S. at 348.

[10] 523 U.S. 833 (1998).

situations, like a high-speed chase, the government can be held liable only if the officer's behavior "shocks the conscience."[11] The Court adopted a very restrictive definition of this requirement and concluded that this requires showing that the officers acted with the intent of harming the victim. Justice Souter stated: "[W]e hold that high-speed chases with no intent to harm suspects physically or to worsen their legal plight do not give rise to liability under the Fourteenth Amendment."[12] The Court found that the officer's behavior was not done with such an intent to harm and thus could not be the basis for liability.

County of Sacramento v. Lewis thus makes it extremely difficult to hold the government liable based on actions taken in emergency circumstances. The definition of emergency is based on whether there was the opportunity for deliberation before the officers acted.

When Is the Government's Failure to Protect a Person from Privately Inflicted Harms a Deprivation?

In *DeShaney v. Winnebago County Department of Social Services*, the Supreme Court broadly held that the government generally has no duty to protect individuals from privately inflicted harms.[13] The guardians of a four-year-old child sued the Department of Social Services for its failure to protect the child from beatings his father inflicted that ultimately resulted in irreversible brain damage. The plaintiffs maintained that the department was informed of the abuse over a 26-month period, but failed to act.

The Supreme Court held that there was no constitutional violation because the child was not in the custody of the government and because the abuse occurred in the hands of a private party. Chief Justice Rehnquist, writing for the Court, stated:

> [N]othing in the language of the Due Process Clause itself requires the State to protect the life, liberty, and property of its citizens against invasion by private actors. The Clause is phrased as a limitation on the State's power to act, not as a guarantee of certain minimal levels of safety and security.[14]

The Court expansively declared that "[a]s a general matter . . . a State's failure to protect an individual against private violence simply does not constitute a violation of the Due Process Clause."[15] The Supreme Court recognized two narrow situations where the government has a duty to provide protection from privately inflicted harms. One is where the government has limited the ability of a person to protect himself or herself, such as when there is incarceration or institutionaliza-

---

[11] *Id.* at 846.
[12] *Id.* at 854.
[13] 489 U.S. 189, 195-196 (1989).
[14] *Id.* at 195.
[15] *Id.* at 197.

tion.[16] The other is where there is a special relationship between the government and the injured individual, such as when the government took an affirmative step to place the person in danger.

DeShaney reflects a deeply entrenched belief that the Constitution is a charter of negative liberties—rights that restrain the government—and not a creator of affirmative rights to government services.[17] But *DeShaney* also can be criticized as resting on faulty distinctions and premises. In a strongly worded dissent, Justice Blackmun accused the majority of gross insensitivity and of resorting to "formalistic reasoning" in drawing an artificial distinction between action and inaction.[18] Characterizing the Department of Social Service's conduct as inaction seems arbitrary; the Court could have described the government's failure to protect Joshua DeShaney as the "active, if reckless, management of a case in which it was deeply involved."[19] Justice Blackmun argued that, at a minimum, once the government began to investigate the case, especially because the child had no other protections, it had the obligation to do so carefully and competently.

The Supreme Court followed and extended *DeShaney* in *Town of Castle Rock v. Gonzales*.[20] Like *DeShaney*, the case had tragic facts. Jessica Gonzales obtained a restraining order limiting contact between her estranged husband and their three daughters. Colorado has a law requiring enforcement of restraining orders and the order itself included language mandating enforcement by the police. One night, Gonzales discovered that her three daughters were missing. She immediately suspected her husband had taken them and called the police. The police refused to help her. Five times that evening she contacted the police, including once by going to the station house, and each time they were unhelpful. Later that night, her husband killed the three girls and he died in a shoot-out with the police.

Jessica Gonzales sued under the due process clause for the failure of the police to enforce the restraining order. The United States Court of Appeals for the Tenth Circuit, in an *en banc* decision, ruled in her favor and expressly distinguished *DeShaney*. The court explained that Gonzales's claim was for procedural due process; the state law and the restraining order being written in mandatory language created a property interest and Gonzales was deprived of this property without due process of law. *DeShaney*, in contrast, was a substantive due process case.

The Supreme Court, in a 7-to-2 decision, with Justice Scalia writing for the majority, reversed. The Court reaffirmed, as discussed below in §7.3.2, that there is a property interest only if there is an entitlement. The Court said that a "benefit

---

[16] *Id.* at 199-200. *See* Youngberg v. Romeo, 457 U.S. 307 (1982) (duty of state to provide for safety and medical needs of involuntarily committed mental patients); Estelle v. Gamble, 429 U.S. 97 (1976) (state has constitutional duty to provide medical care for incarcerated prisoners).

[17] For a thorough exploration and critique of this view, *see* Susan Bandes, The Negative Constitution: A Critique, 88 Mich. L. Rev. 2271 (1990). The issue of when the government's failure to act constitutes state action is discussed in §6.4.

[18] 489 U.S. at 212 (Blackmun, J., dissenting).

[19] The Supreme Court, 1988 Term: Leading Cases, 103 Harv. L. Rev. 137, 173 (1989).

[20] 545 U.S. 748 (2005).

is not a protected entitlement if government officials may grant or deny it in their discretion."[21] The Court explained that police always have discretion as to how to enforce a law and prosecutors always have discretion as to whether to initiate a criminal action. Thus, the Court concluded that there is not a property interest for purposes of due process. Moreover, the Court noted that "it is by no means clear that an individual entitlement to enforcement of a restraining order could constitute a 'property' interest for purposes of the Due Process Clause. Such a right would not, of course, resemble any traditional conception of property."[22]

The bottom line is that it does not matter whether the claim is called substantive or procedural due process, or whether the law is written in mandatory or discretionary terms. The government generally has no duty to provide protection from private inflicted harms. Only if the government literally creates the danger or a person is in government custody, is there any constitutional duty for the government to provide protection. State and local governments may create duties and remedies under their law, but they do not exist under the Constitution.

Does the Availability of State Remedies Prevent a Finding That the State Has Deprived Due Process?

The Supreme Court has held that there is not a deprivation of due process if the plaintiff seeks a postdeprivation remedy for the loss of liberty or property resulting from a random and unauthorized act of a government officer and the state provides an adequate postdeprivation remedy. This principle was initially articulated in *Parratt v. Taylor*.[23]

In *Parratt*, a prisoner ordered a $23.50 hobby kit, which was lost by prison guards. The prisoner filed suit contending that he was deprived of liberty without due process. The Court concluded that the plaintiff did not allege a violation of the due process clause because he was seeking only a postdeprivation remedy for the lost hobby kit and the state provided such a remedy through its tort law. The Court emphasized that this case did not involve an issue of inadequate predeprivation due process; there is nothing that the state could have done to prevent the hobby kit from being lost. Nor was it a claim that the state itself was responsible for the injury. Instead, the loss resulted from the random and unauthorized act of a government officer, and due process could mean only a chance for a remedy after the loss. Justice Rehnquist said that this was a request for procedural due process "simpliciter" and was fulfilled by the existence of adequate state law remedies.[24]

While *Parratt* involved a negligent deprivation of property, its holding was extended to intentional losses of property in *Hudson v. Palmer*.[25] In *Hudson*, prison guards searched a prisoner's cell and intentionally destroyed some of his noncontraband personal property. The Court ruled that there was not a deprivation

---

[21] *Id.* at 756.
[22] *Id.* at 766.
[23] 451 U.S. 527 (1981).
[24] *Id.* at 543-544.
[25] 468 U.S. 517 (1984).

under the due process clause. As in *Parratt*, the plaintiff was not challenging a government policy, nor was the plaintiff requesting a predeprivation hearing. Because the plaintiff was seeking only a postdeprivation remedy, and the state provided one, there was no denial of due process even though the intentional act caused the destruction of property.

Taken to an extreme, *Parratt* could defeat a wide variety of constitutional claims against state and local governments. The Court conceivably could extend *Parratt* to mean that the state cannot be said to deprive due process so long as the state provides adequate remedies for any violation. Because the Bill of Rights is applied to the states through the due process clause of the Fourteenth Amendment, arguably any state or local violation of rights is not a deprivation of due process so long as the state courts are available to provide a remedy.

The Supreme Court, however, has made it clear that *Parratt* is limited to situations when a random and unauthorized act of a government official causes a deprivation of liberty or property, and the plaintiff is seeking only a postdeprivation remedy, and the state provides an adequate postdeprivation remedy. In *Zinermon v. Burch*,[26] the Court clearly articulated these limits on *Parratt*. In *Zinermon*, the plaintiff voluntarily committed himself to a state mental hospital. After his release, he sued hospital officials, contending that they should have known that he was incompetent to give informed consent to his admission. The plaintiff argued that the failure of hospital administrators and doctors to initiate the state's involuntary commitment proceedings deprived him of liberty without due process. The question before the Supreme Court was whether, in light of *Parratt v. Taylor*, the existence of remedies in the state court system precluded constitutional claims under §1983.

Although the Court ruled that *Parratt* applies to claims of deprivation of liberty as well as for loss of property,[27] the Court concluded that *Parratt* was distinguishable. First, the Court made it clear that *Parratt* applies only when the plaintiff is objecting to a failure to provide adequate procedural due process. *Parratt* does not apply if the plaintiff claims a violation of a substantive constitutional right, whether it is a right secured by the Bill of Rights or protected under substantive due process.

This distinction makes sense. In the procedural due process cases, the issue is whether the government has provided adequate mechanisms such as notice and a hearing. But in substantive due process cases, the question is whether the government's action is justified by a sufficiently important purpose. In other words, if the constitutional violation is a lack of adequate procedures, state procedures can remedy the infringement. But if the constitutional violation is a lack of adequate justification for the government's action, then the existence of state procedures is not relevant.

The Supreme Court has applied *Parratt* to one substantive claim: complaints for alleged takings of private property for public use without just compensation. In *Williamson County Regional Planning Commission v. Hamilton Bank*, the Court

---

[26] 494 U.S. 113 (1990).
[27] *Id.* at 132.

dismissed as premature a claim that the planning commission's zoning ordinance constituted a taking without just compensation.[28] Expressly drawing on the principles of *Parratt*, the Court held that an individual cannot claim that the state has taken private property for public use until the property owner has "unsuccessfully attempted to obtain just compensation through the procedures provided by the State for obtaining such compensation."[29] Although *Williamson* represents an extension of *Parratt* to substantive claims, there is a close similarity between takings and due process claims. In both instances, plaintiffs are seeking a postdeprivation remedy for harms to property; in both the Court believes that a federal remedy is unnecessary if the state provides adequate procedures for redress.

Second, the *Zinermon* Court emphasized that *Parratt* applies only to the failure to provide procedural due process that results from the random and unauthorized acts of government officials.[30] In both *Parratt* and *Hudson*, the Court emphasized that the deprivations of property were the result of random and unauthorized acts, not official policy.[31]

In *Logan v. Zimmerman Brush Co.*, the Court also declared that *Parratt* was limited to instances of a "random and unauthorized act by a state employee."[32] In *Logan*, an employee claimed that he was terminated from his job because of a physical disability. He challenged his firing through the proper state administrative agency, but the agency negligently failed to hold a hearing within the statutorily prescribed time limit. The employer secured a dismissal of the plaintiff's claim with prejudice. The defendant argued that the case should be dismissed based on *Parratt*. The Supreme Court disagreed, stating that "[u]nlike the complainant in *Parratt*, Logan is challenging not the [agency's] error, but the 'established state procedure' that destroys his entitlement without according him proper procedural safeguards."[33]

In *Zinermon*, the Court held that the government's action was not random and unauthorized because officials with the authority to supply a hearing failed to provide one even though they should have foreseen the need for such procedural protections. The Court explained that the plaintiff "was deprived of a substantial liberty interest . . . by the very state officials charged with the power to deprive mental patients of their liberty and the duty to implement procedural safeguards. Such a deprivation is foreseeable, due to the nature of mental illness, and will occur, if at all, at a predictable point in the process."[34]

---

[28] 473 U.S. 172 (1985).

[29] *Id.* at 195. In *Palazzolo v. Rhode Island*, 533 U.S. 606 (2001), the Supreme Court reaffirmed *Williamson County*, but held that there was no need to present a specific plan to the state agency when it was clear from past refusals and from the regulation that it would be declined. In *San Remo Hotel v. City and County of San Francisco*, 545 U.S. 323 (2005), the Court reaffirmed *Williamson*, though four Justices called for its reconsideration.

[30] 494 U.S. at 128-129.

[31] *Parratt*, 451 U.S. at 541; *Hudson*, 468 U.S. at 533.

[32] 455 U.S. 422, 435-436 (1982).

[33] *Id.* at 436.

[34] *Zinermon*, 494 U.S. at 138-139.

After *Zinermon*, when does *Parratt v. Taylor* apply? That is, when does the existence of adequate state remedies preclude a due process claim? *Parratt* applies only when

(1)   the plaintiff seeks a postdeprivation remedy;
(2)   for a random and unauthorized act of a government official;
(3)   that resulted in a deprivation of liberty or property without adequate procedural due process;
(4)   where the officials responsible could not have provided a hearing to prevent foreseeable harms; and
(5)   adequate state remedies exist.

Or, phrased differently, *Parratt* does *not* apply if the plaintiff objects to the absence of a predeprivation remedy; or if the harms resulted from an official government policy; or if there is an alleged violation of a substantive right; or the officials responsible could have prevented foreseeable harm; or there are inadequate state remedies.

Some Justices have indicated a desire to expand *Parratt* beyond these narrow limits.[35] As described above, taken to an extreme, *Parratt* can be extended to say that there never is a state deprivation of due process so long as the state provides an adequate remedy. This approach would end almost all constitutional challenges to state and local actions because almost always there is some state procedure, such as state court remedies, available. The Supreme Court has shown no inclination to take *Parratt* in this direction.

§7.3   IS IT A DEPRIVATION OF "LIFE, LIBERTY, OR PROPERTY"?

§7.3.1   The "Rights-Privileges" Distinction and Its Demise

The "Rights-Privileges" Distinction Defined

The government has to provide due process only if there has been a deprivation of life, liberty, or property. Until 1970, the Supreme Court narrowly defined what constitutes a liberty or property interest. The Court repeatedly held that there was a liberty or a property interest only if there was a *right*. A government-bestowed *privilege* was not a basis for requiring due process.

A classic articulation of the rights-privileges distinction was in the ruling of then state court justice Oliver Wendell Holmes that the government did not have to provide due process before firing a police officer for his political activities: "The

---

[35] Albright v. Oliver, 510 U.S. 266, 283-286 (1994) (Kennedy, J., concurring).

petitioner may have a constitutional right to talk politics, but he has no constitutional right to be a policeman."[1] Under this view, the government was not required to provide due process if a person was fired from a government job,[2] or had government benefits terminated,[3] or had an occupational license revoked.[4] All of these were regarded as privileges, not rights, so that no due process was required if the government made the decision to remove them.

The Unconstitutional Conditions Doctrine

Although the rights-privileges distinction was firmly embedded in the law, it also was established that the government could not condition a privilege on the requirement that a person give up a constitutional right. This principle is termed the "unconstitutional conditions doctrine."[5] For example, the government cannot condition welfare benefits on the requirement that a person agree never to criticize the government. To do so would impermissibly condition a privilege, welfare, on the relinquishing of a constitutional right.

The Court has not been completely consistent in adhering to the unconstitutional conditions doctrine. For example, in *Speiser v. Randall*, the Court declared unconstitutional a statute that denied tax exemptions to those who could not prove that they did not advocate the violent overthrow of the government.[6] The Court explained that the government may not act indirectly to "produce a result which [it] could not command directly."[7]

Yet in *Rust v. Sullivan*, the Supreme Court held that the federal government could condition aid to family planning clinics on the requirement that they not provide abortion counseling or referrals.[8] The Court held that the government has the discretion to decide what activities to fund. It is difficult to explain why this is not an impermissible unconstitutional condition; the government is conditioning the receipt of government aid on the requirement that health professionals in the clinics relinquish their right to speak about abortion. In *Legal Services Corporation v. Velazquez*, the Supreme Court characterized *Rust* as involving the government as using private speakers to transmit its message.[9] In *Velazquez*, the Court declared unconstitutional a federal law that prevented recipients of federal Legal Services

---

§7.3 [1] McAuliffe v. New Bedford, 155 Mass. 216, 29 N.E. 517 (1892).

[2] *See, e.g.*, Bailey v. Richardson, 182 F.2d 46 (D.C. Cir. 1950), *aff'd by an equally divided Court*, 341 U.S. 918 (1951).

[3] Fleming v. Nestor, 363 U.S. 603 (1960).

[4] *See, e.g.*, Barsky v. Board of Regents, 347 U.S. 442, 451 (1954).

[5] There is a large body of excellent scholarship on the unconstitutional conditions doctrine. *See, e.g.*, Kathleen Sullivan, Unconstitutional Conditions, 102 Harv. L. Rev. 1413 (1989); Richard Epstein: Foreword: Unconstitutional Conditions, State Power, and the Limits of Consent, 102 Harv. L. Rev. 4 (1988).

[6] 357 U.S. 513 (1958).

[7] *Id.* at 526.

[8] 500 U.S. 173 (1991), discussed in §11.2.4.4.

[9] 531 U.S. 533, 541 (2001).

Corporation funds from challenging the validity of welfare laws and regulations.[10] These cases are discussed in detail in §11.2.4, which examines the unconstitutional condition doctrine in the area of freedom of speech.

Criticism of the Rights-Privileges Distinction

By the 1960s, there was substantial criticism of the rights-privileges distinction as a basis for determining whether there was an interest requiring due process. In a classic article, Professor Charles Reich argued that the rights-privileges distinction is an anachronism in an era where people depend on government for so much that is essential for survival. Government benefits such as education, welfare, Social Security, licenses, and jobs are relied upon by people in their lives and thus hold the same place in a person's life as property traditionally occupied.[11]

Thus, Reich argued there is the same need to prevent arbitrary government action. He wrote: "Society today is built around entitlements. . . . Many of the most important of these entitlements now flow from government. . . . Such sources of security, whether private or public, are no longer regarded as luxuries or gratuities; to the recipients they are essentials, fully deserved, and in no sense a form of charity."[12] Reich contended that the rights-privileges distinction should be discarded and that due process should be provided when the government terminates the "new property."

By the end of the 1960s, this view was accepted by a majority of the Supreme Court. In the landmark case of *Goldberg v. Kelly*, the Supreme Court held that individuals receiving welfare have a property interest in continued receipt of benefits and the government must provide due process before it terminates benefits.[13] Justice Brennan, writing for the Court, expressly quoted Charles Reich and declared: "It may be realistic today to regard welfare entitlements as more like 'property' than a 'gratuity.' Much of the existing wealth in this country takes the form of rights that do not fall within traditional common-law concepts of property."[14]

After the Court recognized that welfare benefits, once bestowed, become property requiring due process before termination, the rights-privileges distinction obviously had been discarded. A few years after *Goldberg*, in *Roth v. Board of Regents*, the Court said this explicitly: "[T]he Court has fully and finally rejected the wooden distinction between 'rights' and 'privileges' that once seemed to govern the applicability of procedural due process rights."[15]

---

[10] Most recently, in *United States Agency for International Development v. Alliance for Open Society International*, 133 S. Ct. 2321 (2013), the Court held that it violated the First Amendment to require that recipients of federal funds for combatting HIV/AIDS have an explicit policy condemning prostitution and sex trafficking. This case is discussed in §11.2.4.4.

[11] Charles A. Reich, The New Property, 73 Yale L.J. 733 (1964); *see also* Charles A. Reich, Individual Rights and Social Welfare: The Emerging Legal Issues, 74 Yale L.J. 1245 (1965).

[12] Reich, *id.*, Individual Rights and Social Welfare, 74 Yale L.J. at 1255.

[13] 397 U.S. 254 (1970).

[14] *Id.* at 262 n.8.

[15] 408 U.S. 564, 571 (1972).

The question then becomes, if the rights-privileges distinction is not to be used in defining "liberty" and "property," how is the Court to decide if such an interest is present? This is examined in the following sections. The constant question is whether the Court has resurrected the rights-privileges distinction, not expressly, but in the way in which it has defined property and liberty.

§7.3.2   Deprivations of "Property"

Property as an "Entitlement"

There never has been doubt that the government must provide due process before it deprives a person of real or personal property. After the demise of the rights-privileges distinction, the question becomes: When are government benefits, such as jobs or payments, to be considered property?

In *Roth*, the Court attempted to define property. The Court said that "[t]o have a property interest in a benefit, a person clearly must have more than an abstract need or desire for it. He must have more than a unilateral expectation of it. He must, instead, have a legitimate claim of entitlement to it. It is a purpose of the ancient institution of property to protect those claims upon which people rely in their daily lives, reliance that must not be arbitrarily undermined."[16] The Court explained that "[p]roperty interests, of course, are not created by the Constitution. Rather, they are created and their dimensions are defined by existing rules or understandings that stem from an independent source such as state law—rules or understandings that secure benefits and that support claims of entitlement to those benefits."[17]

In other words, *Roth* defines property, as Charles Reich did, as an "entitlement." The problem is that in defining entitlement, the above-quoted language from *Roth* offers two inconsistent approaches. One approach is that an entitlement is defined by the importance of the interest to the individual. If people rely on a government benefit in "their daily lives," then it should be regarded as a property interest that "must not be arbitrarily undermined."[18]

But the Court then goes on to say that the existence of an entitlement is determined by an "independent source such as state law" and the "rules or understandings" that it creates.[19] By this view, an entitlement exists if there is a reasonable expectation to continued receipt of a benefit.

In other words, the former approach to defining entitlement would find a property interest if there is an important benefit regardless of the content of the state law. The latter definition, however, would find a property interest only if the

---

[16]   408 U.S. at 577.

[17]   *Id.*

[18]   *Id.*

[19]   *Id.* In *Town of Castle Rock v. Gonzales*, 545 U.S. 748 (2005), the Court reaffirmed that a property interest exists only if there is an "entitlement" and an entitlement does not exist if the government has discretion as to whether to provide a benefit. *Gonzales* is discussed in detail, above, in §7.2.

state law creates a reasonable expectation to receipt of a benefit, regardless of the importance of the interest.

Each definition has problems. If the existence of property is determined solely by the importance of the benefit, there seems no principled way to decide which government benefits are sufficiently significant to constitute property. The government provides a vast array of services and programs that people rely upon. How is the Court to decide which are important enough to constitute property and require due process when they are ended?

Defining property based on whether the law creates a reasonable expectation to continued receipt of a benefit solves this problem because it provides a basis for deciding what constitutes property apart from the importance of the interest. But it creates a different major difficulty: Could the state simply deny the existence of property by expressly stating that individuals should have no expectation to continued receipt? In other words, if property is defined by expectations, the state can defeat property interests by making it clear that people should have no expectations. In essence, the rights-privileges distinction is re-created under a different label; the state could deny a property interest merely by making it clear that the benefit or program was something that the government could terminate at any point. Indeed, the more arbitrary the government is, the less there can be reasonable expectations to continued receipt of the benefit, and the less likely there will be a requirement for due process.

To this day, the Court has not resolved this tension. The Court generally has adopted the second approach to defining property—that is, as a reasonable expectation to continued receipt of a benefit. Yet the Court has been inconsistent in its willingness to embrace the consequence that the government then can deny a property interest merely by informing people that they should not expect the benefit to continue.

Government Employment as Property

The primary area where the Court has struggled with defining property is in the context of deciding when government employment constitutes an entitlement. *Roth* itself involved this issue. A teacher employed by Wisconsin State University was not rehired and contended that the failure to provide a hearing in connection with the nonrenewal denied due process. The Supreme Court found that there was not a property interest because under the contract the teacher could not have a reasonable expectation that he would be rehired. The Court explained that the "important fact in this case is that [the contract] specifically provided that the . . . employment was to terminate on June 30. They did not provide for contract renewal absent sufficient cause. Indeed, they made no provision for renewal whatsoever."[20]

In other words, *Roth* defined property not based on the importance of the job to the individual, but rather based on the expectation of continued employment. Justice Marshall in dissent challenged this view and argued that "[e]mployment is

---

[20] *Id.* at 578.

one of the greatest, if not the greatest, benefits that governments offer in modern-day life. When something as valuable as the opportunity to work is at stake, the government may not reward some citizens and not others without demonstrating that its actions are fair and equitable."[21] The dispute between the majority and the dissent in *Roth* is over which of the two definitions of property described above should control.

In a companion case to *Roth*, *Perry v. Sindermann*, the Court made it clear that it was defining property based on a reasonable expectation to continued receipt of a benefit.[22] Sinderman was a professor at Odessa Junior College, and although the college did not have a tenure system, its faculty guide stated that it "wishes the faculty member to feel that he has permanent tenure as long as his teaching services are satisfactory and as long as he displays a cooperative attitude."[23] The Court said that the absence of a formal tenure system was not dispositive in deciding whether there was a property interest. The Court explained that the teacher had raised "a genuine issue as to his interest in continued employment, [which,] though not secured by a formal contractual tenure provision, was secured by a no less binding understanding fostered by the college administration."[24]

But, as described above, does this approach mean that the government can prevent there from being a property interest in a government job simply by making it clear to the employees that they should have no expectation of the job continuing? Justice Rehnquist suggested this in *Arnett v. Kennedy*.[25] The issue in *Arnett* was whether the government could fire a nonprobationary employee without a pretermination hearing. There was no majority opinion by the Court, but six of the Justices recognized that there was a property interest in the job. The ruling was that there was not a denial of due process because the government provided a pretermination review and a posttermination hearing.[26]

However, Justice Rehnquist, joined by Chief Justice Burger and Justice Stewart, would not have found a property interest requiring due process. Rehnquist emphasized that the property interest in the job is only that which the statute provides. He also wrote that "where the grant of a substantive right is inextricably intertwined with the limitations on the procedures which are to be employed in determining that right, a litigant in the position of appellee must take the bitter with the sweet."[27] The other six Justices appeared to reject this and objected that the Rehnquist "[v]iew misconceives the origin of the right to procedural due process. That right is conferred, not by legislative grace, but by constitutional guarantee."[28]

This view, however, appeared to attract support from a majority of the Supreme Court in *Bishop v. Wood*.[29] The plaintiff, a city police officer, was considered a

---

[21] *Id.* at 589 (Marshall, J., dissenting).
[22] 408 U.S. 593 (1972).
[23] *Id.* at 600.
[24] *Id.* at 599.
[25] 416 U.S. 134 (1974).
[26] See *id.* at 163-164 (Rehnquist, J., plurality opinion).
[27] *Id.* at 153-154.
[28] *Id.* at 167 (Powell, J., concurring).
[29] 426 U.S. 341 (1976).

"permanent employee" under state law. Nonetheless, the federal district court found that as a matter of state law, the police officer "held his position at the will and pleasure of the city."[30] Therefore, the Court concluded that he did not have a property interest in his job and that he was not entitled to due process with regard to his termination. This means that the government can prevent there from being a property interest simply by making it clear that it retains the right to fire the individual at will. As such, it seems little different from the rights-privileges distinction that the Court so expressly repudiated in cases like *Goldberg* and *Roth*.

Subsequent to *Bishop*, the Court has clarified that if there is a property right, the issue of what procedures are required is a matter of federal constitutional law to be decided by the courts. In *Cleveland Board of Education v. Loudermill*, the Supreme Court considered a state civil service law that provided that employees were entitled only to posttermination administrative review.[31] There was no dispute that the law created a property interest in that it required that employees only be terminated if there was "cause." The Court then said that due process required a predischarge opportunity to be heard and that state law could not alter this requirement. The Court said that it was "settled that the bitter with the sweet approach misconceives the constitutional guarantee" and that when there is a property interest, the Constitution—and not the state law—determines the procedures to be followed.[32]

Loudermill, however, only addresses the question of what procedures are required when there has been a deprivation of life, liberty, or property, which is addressed in §7.4. *Loudermill* does not overrule or change *Bishop*'s holding: In deciding if there is a property interest in a government job, the relevant inquiry is the expectations created by the law and customs surrounding the position.

Government Benefits

The same equivocation between the two definitions of entitlement described above is also present in cases concerning when government benefits are property. *Goldberg*, for example, found that welfare benefits were property because of the importance of these benefits in the lives of the recipients.[33] Likewise, in *Bell v. Burson*, the Supreme Court held that the government had to provide a hearing before suspending a person's driver's license based on the person's alleged responsibility for an accident.[34] The Court explained that "[o]nce licenses are issued . . . continued possession may become essential in the pursuit of a livelihood. Suspension of issued licenses thus involves state action that adjudicates important interests of the licensees."[35]

---

[30] *Id.* at 345 (citation omitted).
[31] 470 U.S. 532 (1985).
[32] *Id.* at 54.
[33] 397 U.S. at 262-263.
[34] 402 U.S. 535 (1971).
[35] *Id.* at 539.

Similarly, in *Goss v. Lopez*, the Supreme Court found that there was a property interest in continued receipt of an education when the government creates a public school system and requires children to attend.[36] The Court explained that "on the basis of state law, appellees plainly had legitimate claims of entitlement to a public education."[37] Even though the government had no constitutional duty to provide a public education, the Court found that there was a property interest in continued schooling created by state laws and a liberty interest in not being stigmatized by suspension. The Court emphasized the importance of education, terming it "perhaps the most important function of state and local governments," and concluding that "the total exclusion from the educational process for more than a trivial period" is a deprivation of property and liberty requiring due process.[38]

Yet in later cases, the Court has defined property less on the basis of the importance of the interest and more based on the content of the expectations created by the laws. For instance, in *Memphis Light, Gas & Water Division v. Craft*, the Supreme Court held that a public utility company could not terminate a customer's service unless it provided due process because state law provided that service could be cut off only for "cause."[39] Also, in *O'Bannon v. Town Court Nursing Center*, the Supreme Court held that residents in a nursing home had no property interest and thus no right to due process before a government agency revoked their home's certification to receive payments from the government.[40] Although the ability to remain in the home of their choice was obviously quite important to the patients, the Court found that the patient did not have a property interest in remaining in a particular home. The Court said that the patients have no "interest in receiving benefits for care in a particular facility that entitles them . . . to a hearing before the Government can decertify the facility."[41]

In a subsequent case defining whether there is a property interest in benefits, *American Manufacturers Mutual Insurance Company v. Sullivan*,[42] the Court also looked to whether state law creates an entitlement. *Sullivan* involved whether a Pennsylvania law that allowed insurance companies to withhold payment for medical treatment pending utilization review violated due process. The Court found that there was not state action in the decisions of the insurance companies.[43] Additionally, the Court went on and said that there was not a property interest. Chief Justice Rehnquist, writing for the Court, said that "for an employee's property interest in the payment of medical benefits to attach under state law, the employee must clear two hurdles. First, he must prove that an employer is liable for a work-related injury, and second, he must establish that the particular medical treatment

---

[36] 419 U.S. 565, 574 (1975).

[37] *Id.* at 573.

[38] *Id.* at 576 (citation omitted).

[39] 436 U.S. 1 (1978). Earlier, the Supreme Court had held that a private utility company does not have to provide due process before terminating a customer's service because there is no state action. *See* Jackson v. Metropolitan Edison Co., 419 U.S. 345 (1974), discussed in §6.4.4.2.

[40] 447 U.S. 773 (1980).

[41] *Id.* at 784.

[42] 526 U.S. 40 (1999).

[43] This aspect of the case is discussed in §6.4.4.3.

at issue is reasonable and necessary. Only then does the employee's interest parallel that of the beneficiary of welfare assistance in *Goldberg* and the recipient of disability benefits in *Mathews*."[44] Chief Justice Rehnquist said that the beneficiaries did not have a property interest because they "have yet to make good on their claim that the particular medical treatment was reasonable and necessary."[45]

Although this would seem to be just dicta given the Court's conclusion earlier in the opinion that there was no state action, Chief Justice Rehnquist's analysis is revealing of the Court's approach to defining whether there is a property interest. The plaintiffs in the case claimed that they should have a hearing before the insurance company could withhold payments on the ground that they were not reasonable and necessary. Chief Justice Rehnquist, however, said that there is no property interest until the plaintiffs proved that the payments were reasonable and necessary. In other words, the plaintiffs somehow would have to prove the very matter in dispute before getting a hearing in order to claim a property interest. The Court bases this conclusion on its reading of the state statutes, thus clearly indicating that it is defining what constitutes property based on the entitlement approach and not on the importance of the interest to the individual.

Summary

In sum, there is a property interest requiring due process if there is an entitlement. There are two possible alternative ways of defining when there is an entitlement; each has some support in the case law, though the latter has been favored by the Supreme Court. One approach is to define entitlement based on the importance of the interest to the individual. Some cases found a property interest because of the crucial significance of the interest in a person's life. The alternative approach is to define entitlement as a reasonable expectation to continued receipt of a benefit. Under this definition, the existence of an entitlement depends on whether the law creates a justifiable expectation that the benefit will be received in the future.

The Supreme Court, especially in cases concerning when government employment becomes a property interest, has defined property based on the expectations created by the relevant law. The problem, however, with this definition is that it allows the government to undermine the existence of property simply by instructing people not to expect continued receipt of the benefit. In this way, the definition of property is functionally little different from the discredited rights-privileges distinction.

§7.3.3 Deprivations of "Liberty"

In *Roth v. Board of Regents*, the Court also attempted to clarify the meaning of "liberty." The Court said:

---

[44] *Id.* at 60-61.
[45] *Id.* at 61.

While this Court has not attempted to define with exactness the liberty . . . guaranteed [by the Fifth and Fourteenth Amendments], the term denotes not merely freedom from bodily restraint but also the right of the individual to contract, to engage in any of the common occupations of life, to acquire useful knowledge, to marry, establish a home and bring up children, to worship God according to the dictates of his own conscience, and generally to enjoy those privileges long recognized . . . as essential to the orderly pursuit of happiness by free men. In a Constitution for a free people, there can be no doubt that the meaning of "liberty" must be broad indeed.[46]

Roth thus includes in its definition of liberty those rights that are expressly stated in the text, such as free exercise of religion, and rights that are not enumerated, such as the right to marry.

There, of course, is no doubt that constitutional rights are a liberty interest. The difficult question arises as to what other interests fit under the rubric of "liberty" and require due process. Again, there are two different ways for the Court to approach this and define liberty. One would be for the Court to determine what is "liberty" based on the importance of the interest at stake. The other way would be for the Court to determine whether there is a liberty interest based on the expectations engendered by state law. Again, both are present in the case law. Specifically, considered below are cases involving freedom from physical restraint, parental rights, deportation proceedings, prisoners' rights, and reputation as a liberty interest. Although this is by no means an exhaustive list of what is considered to be a liberty interest, it does encompass the vast majority of Supreme Court cases pertaining to the meaning of liberty in the context of procedural due process.

Freedom from Physical Restraint

The most obvious and most basic aspect of liberty is freedom from physical restraint.[47] Institutionalizing a person, by definition, takes away that individual's liberty. Indeed, attempts to define liberty throughout the past century usually begin by saying that liberty is more than "merely freedom from bodily restraint."[48] The Court has declared that "the freedom 'from bodily restraint,' lies 'at the core of the liberty protected by the Due Process Clause.'"[49] In *Hamdi v. Rumsfeld,* in holding that an American citizen detained as an enemy combatant was entitled to due process, Justice O'Connor's plurality opinion noted that Hamdi presented "the most

---

[46] 408 U.S. at 572 (citations omitted).

[47] For a discussion of this aspect of liberty and the implications it has, especially for substantive due process, *see* Sherry Colb, Freedom from Incarceration: Why Is This Right Different from All Other Rights?, 69 N.Y.U. L. Rev. 781 (1994). A Supreme Court decision that was based on this right is *Zadvydas v. Davis,* 533 U.S. 678 (2001), which held that the indefinite detention of nondeportable aliens violates federal law. Discussed below in text accompanying notes 78-80.

[48] *See, e.g.,* Meyer v. Nebraska, 262 U.S. 390, 399 (1923); Roth v. Board of Regents, 408 U.S. at 572.

[49] Turner v. Rogers, 131 S. Ct. 2507, 2518 (2011).

elemental of liberty interests—the interest in being free from physical detention by one's own government."[50]

Obviously, many provisions of the Bill of Rights concern the procedures that the government must follow before it deprives a person of liberty in criminal proceedings. These provisions include the prohibition of excessive bail found in the Eighth Amendment[51] and the many procedural safeguards at trial including the Sixth Amendment's rights to a speedy and public trial before an impartial jury, with the assistance of counsel and the right to confront adverse witnesses. The Court also has found that due process requires basic protections such as the presumption of innocence[52] and the requirement for proof beyond a reasonable doubt.[53] Criminal procedure protections, both found in the text of the Constitution and based on the due process clause, are beyond the scope of this book.

A person's freedom from bodily restraint also can be taken away by civil proceedings, most notably through civil commitment. The Supreme Court "repeatedly has recognized that civil commitment for any purpose constitutes a significant deprivation of liberty that requires due process protection."[54] Thus, in *O'Connor v. Donaldson*, the Supreme Court ruled that "a State cannot constitutionally confine without more a nondangerous individual who is capable of surviving safely in freedom by himself or with the help of willing and responsible family members of friends."[55]

The Court, however, rejected the argument that there must be proof beyond a reasonable doubt—the standard in criminal cases—in civil commitment proceedings. The Court declared: "We have concluded that the reasonable doubt standard is inappropriate in civil commitment proceedings because, given the uncertainties of psychiatric diagnosis, it may impose a burden that the state cannot meet and thereby erect an unreasonable barrier to needed medical treatment."[56] Thus, the Court concluded that a state may institutionalize a person through civil commitment only if there is "clear and convincing evidence" of the need for commitment.

The procedural protections accorded to adults in civil commitment proceedings are not required for children who are being institutionalized by their parents.[57] In *Parham v. J.R.*, the Supreme Court held that it generally assumes that

---

[50] 542 U.S. 507 (2004), discussed below in §7.4.3.

[51] *But see* United States v. Salerno, 481 U.S. 739 (1987) (upholding the constitutionality of the Federal Bail Reform Act that allows pretrial detention of an individual without bail if there is a showing, with clear and convincing evidence, that a person is a threat to the community).

[52] *See, e.g.,* Taylor v. Kentucky, 436 U.S. 478 (1978).

[53] *See, e.g.,* In re Winship, 397 U.S. 358 (1970).

[54] Addington v. Texas, 441 U.S. 418, 425 (1979); *see also* Jones v. United States, 463 U.S. 354, 361 (1983).

[55] 422 U.S. 563, 576 (1975); *see also* Specht v. Patterson, 386 U.S. 605 (1967) (due process denied to an indefinite commitment to a mental institution for a person convicted of a sex crime for which there was a mandatory ten-year punishment).

[56] Addington v. Texas, 441 U.S. 418, 432 (1979).

[57] Children are entitled to basic procedural protections in criminal proceedings, such as proof beyond a reasonable doubt (In re Winship, 397 U.S. 358 (1970)) and the assistance of an attorney (In re Gault, 387 U.S. 1 (1967)).

parents act in the best interests of their children so that all a child is entitled to before commitment is a screening proceeding by a doctor or other neutral fact-finder.[58] In other words, a child institutionalized by a parent need not be accorded an adversarial hearing, but only review by a neutral individual who approves the commitment.[59]

Parham is based on a long line of cases that hold that parents generally have the right to make decisions concerning the upbringing of their children.[60] The Court followed this authority and ruled that the deference to parents extends even to situations where children are being civilly committed. But it can be questioned whether this deference is appropriate when there is such a dramatic restriction of a child's freedom, with such long-term consequences, as occurs with civil commitment. Although it may be the exception, rather than the rule, there is the danger that a parent, together with a cooperative doctor, could institutionalize a child under inappropriate circumstances.

Parental Rights

The Supreme Court has recognized that parents have a fundamental right to the custody of their children.[61] The Court has spoken of the "fundamental liberty interest of natural parents in the care, custody, and management of their child."[62] Indeed, the Court recognized that a parent's "desire for and right to the companionship, care, custody, and management of his or her children is . . . far more precious than any property right."[63] Thus, the Court has held that when the government seeks to terminate parental rights, "it must provide the parents with fundamentally fair procedures."[64]

For example, in *Santosky v. Kramer*, the Supreme Court held that the state must prove, by "clear and convincing evidence," the need to terminate parental rights.[65] The Court has extended this to recognize a liberty interest of unmarried

---

[58] 442 U.S. 584 (1979).

[59] The child, of course, has a liberty interest in not being institutionalized, even by a parent. Therefore, *Parham* really is about the procedures required, the subject of §7.4, rather than the issue of whether there is a liberty interest. However, because civil commitment is discussed here, *Parham* is important to note.

[60] *See, e.g.*, Pierce v. Society of Sisters, 268 U.S. 510 (1925) (state law prohibiting parochial school education unconstitutionally interferes with the right of parents to control the upbringing of their children); Meyer v. Nebraska, 262 U.S. 390 (1923) (state law prohibiting education in the German language unconstitutionally interferes with the right of parents to control the upbringing of their children); discussed in §§10.2 and 10.2.4.

[61] *See, e.g.*, Santosky v. Kramer, 455 U.S. 745 (1982); Stanley v. Illinois, 405 U.S. 645 (1972). In 1996, the Supreme Court held that it violates due process to condition an appeal from the termination of parental rights on payment of filing fees for the appeal. M.L.B. v. S.L.J., 519 U.S. 102 (1996).

[62] Santosky v. Kramer, 455 U.S. at 753.

[63] *Id.* at 758-759 (citations omitted).

[64] *Id.* at 754. The specific procedures that must be provided are discussed in more detail in §7.4. For example, discussed there is *Lassiter v. Department of Social Services*, 452 U.S. 18 (1981), where the Court held that indigent parents are not automatically entitled to government-appointed counsel at parental termination proceedings.

[65] *Id.* at 769.

fathers to custody of their children and thus a need for due process before their parental rights are permanently terminated.[66] In *Stanley v. Illinois*, the Supreme Court held that a state may not deny an unmarried father of custody absent a hearing and a finding that the father was an unfit parent.[67]

However, the Court refused to recognize any rights for an unmarried father where the mother was married to another man. In *Michael H. v. Gerald D.*, the Supreme Court held that a state could create an irrebuttable presumption that a married woman's husband is the father of her child.[68] In *Michael H.*, the Court refused to recognize any parental rights for a biological father even though he had lived with the mother and the child for almost a year and a half. The Court said that the biological father had no right to a hearing to determine paternity and could be denied all parental rights, including visitation.

Michael H. raises basic questions about how the Court should determine what constitutes a liberty interest. Justice Scalia, in an opinion joined only by Chief Justice Rehnquist, said that the Court should recognize a liberty interest only if there is a tradition of providing protection, when the tradition is stated at the most specific level of abstraction.[69] Scalia said that such specificity was necessary "[b]ecause . . . general traditions provide such imprecise guidance, they permit judges to dictate rather than discern society's views."[70] In contrast, Justice Brennan vehemently objected to such a narrow definition of liberty. Brennan argued that it was well established that fathers have a fundamental interest in their children and that this is sufficient for a liberty interest, regardless of whether the mother is married to someone else. In other words, the basic dispute between Brennan and Scalia in *Michael H.* was over how the Court should go about interpreting the meaning of "liberty."

It also should be noted that the Court has not recognized a liberty interest for foster families. In *Smith v. Organization of Foster Families for Equality & Reform*, the Court explained why foster parents inherently have a different interest than natural parents, but the Court avoided deciding whether the interest is protected as a "liberty" under the due process clause.[71] The Court unanimously upheld a state law that provided for the removal of children from foster care with ten days' notice. A hearing was to be provided to such parents only if they requested one. The Court said that even assuming that there was such a liberty interest, the state did not deny due process in failing to provide an automatic hearing for individuals who had been foster parents for a child for less than 18 months.

---

[66] *See* Stanley v. Illinois, 405 U.S. 645 (1972).

[67] *Id.* at 651-652. However, in *Quilloin v. Walcott*, 434 U.S. 246 (1978), the Court distinguished *Stanley* and held that a state may deny an unmarried father rights if he never sought custody of his child and never assumed any significant responsibility with regard to the child. In *Quilloin*, the Court allowed a husband to adopt his wife's illegitimate child, who had been continually in her custody for 11 years, despite the biological father's objections.

[68] 491 U.S. 110 (1989), discussed in more detail in §10.2.2.

[69] *Id.* at 127 n.6.

[70] *Id.* at 128 n.6.

[71] 431 U.S. 816 (1977).

Deportation and Exclusion Proceedings

The Supreme Court has recognized that deportation involves a loss of liberty and that therefore due process must be provided before an alien is deported.[72] For example, notice must be given before a deportation proceeding.[73] Individuals facing possible deportation have a right to a hearing and have a right to representation by an attorney at the hearing.[74] The Supreme Court has held that there must be "clear, unequivocal, and convincing" proof before a person can be deported.[75]

On the other hand, the Court has refused to recognize a liberty interest in entering the country and has allowed exclusion without any due process.[76] In *Shaughnessy v. United States ex rel. Mezei*, the Supreme Court held that "[w]hatever the procedure authorized by Congress is, it is due process as far as an alien denied entry is concerned."[77]

However, the Supreme Court subsequently distinguished *Shaughnessy* and held that the indefinite detention of those who are legally present in the country violates federal law. In *Zadvydas v. Davis*,[78] the Court considered the permissibility of the government's policy of indefinitely detaining nondeportable aliens. Zadvydas, for example, was an alien lawfully in the United States who committed a crime and served a prison sentence. Under federal law, the Immigration and Naturalization Service sought to deport him after the completion of his sentence. Because he was born in a displaced person's camp in Lithuania after World War II, no country would recognize him as a citizen or accept him. The United States simply kept him—and thousands others in a similar situation—locked up indefinitely.

The Supreme Court, in a 5-to-4 decision, held that the indefinite detention of nondeportable aliens is not authorized by federal law. Justice Breyer, writing for the Court, emphasized that all who enter the United States lawfully are protected under the due process clause and that freedom from incarceration is obviously one of the most basic aspects of liberty. Justice Breyer explained that if federal law were interpreted to allow indefinite detention, there would be serious constitutional doubts about the statute. To avoid the constitutional doubts, the Court construed the law to not authorize indefinite detention.

Justice Scalia dissented and disagreed with the majority's premise that nondeportable aliens have a liberty interest in being free from incarceration.[79] He argued that under federal law, aliens who commit crimes have no right to remain in the country at all, and they should not gain that right because another nation will not accept them in a deportation proceeding. Justice Kennedy dissented and

---

[72] *See* Chew v. Colding, 344 U.S. 590 (1953); Sung v. McGrath, 339 U.S. 33 (1950).

[73] *See, e.g.*, Hirsh v. INS, 308 F.2d 562 (9th Cir. 1962).

[74] *See, e.g.*, Snajder v. INS, 29 F.3d 1203 (7th Cir. 1994).

[75] Woodby v. INS, 385 U.S. 276, 285 (1966).

[76] *See* Shaughnessy v. United States ex rel. Mezei, 345 U.S. 206 (1953); United States ex rel. Knauff v. Shaughnessy, 338 U.S. 537 (1950); *see* Charles D. Weisselberg, The Exclusion and Detention of Aliens: Lessons from the Lives of Ellen Knauff and Ignatz Mezei, 143 U. Pa. L. Rev. 933 (1995).

[77] 345 U.S. 206, 212 (1953).

[78] 533 U.S. 678 (2001).

[79] *Id.* at 703 (Scalia, J. dissenting).

maintained that due process required only that nondeportable aliens be given procedural due process, notice and a hearing, before being held, and that this was provided.[80]

Liberty Interests for Prisoners

In defining "liberty," the Court has struggled most with cases involving prisoners. Interestingly, the Court has shifted its approach several times. Initially, the Court indicated that prisoners have a liberty interest when an important matter is at stake. The Court, however, later moved away from this approach and repeatedly held that liberty interests for prisoners are a function of statutes and regulations; prisoners have liberty interests when the relevant statutes and regulations create them. However, in *Sandin v. Conner*, the Supreme Court backed away from this approach and held that regardless of the content of statutes and regulations, there is a liberty interest only if there is a significant deprivation of freedom, which is atypical to the usual conditions of confinement.[81]

In *Morrissey v. Brewer*, the Supreme Court held that revocation of parole is a deprivation of liberty that requires the provision of due process.[82] The Court emphasized the importance of the interest to the individual. When out on parole an individual can be "gainfully employed and is free to be with family and friends and to form the other enduring attachments of normal life."[83] This, of course, is taken away if parole is revoked, and the Supreme Court found that there was a liberty interest in remaining on parole because ending parole "inflicts a grievous loss on the parolee and often on others."[84] In other words, *Morrissey* found a liberty interest based on the significance of the interest to the parolee, rather than focusing on the specifics of the state law involved.

Likewise, a year later, in *Gagnon v. Scarpelli*, the Supreme Court ruled that the revocation of probation is a deprivation of liberty requiring due process.[85] The Court explained that "revocation of probation . . . is constitutionally indistinguishable from the revocation of parole."[86]

Soon after these cases, however, the Court shifted its approach and based its determination of whether there is a liberty interest on the content of the statutes or rules, rather than on the importance of the interest to the individual. For example, in *Wolff v. McDonnell*, the Supreme Court held that prisoners have a liberty interest in "good time credits" awarded under state law.[87] The Court explained that although a state need not give prisoners good time credits, "the State having created the right to good time . . . , the prisoner's interest has real substance and is sufficiently embraced within Fourteenth Amendment liberty to entitle him to

---

[80] *Id.* at 718-724 (Kennedy, J. dissenting).
[81] 515 U.S. 472 (1995).
[82] 408 U.S. 471 (1972).
[83] *Id.* at 482.
[84] *Id.*
[85] 411 U.S. 778 (1973).
[86] *Id.* at 782 n.3.
[87] 418 U.S. 539 (1974).

those minimum procedures . . . required by the Due Process Clause to insure that the state-created right is not arbitrarily abrogated."[88] The Court said that a "person's liberty is equally protected, even when the liberty itself is a statutory creation of the state."[89] In other words, *Wolff* found a liberty interest based on the expectations created by state law, rather than based on the significance of the credits for the individual prisoner.

The Court applied *Wolff* in *Meachum v. Fano*, where the Supreme Court held that prisoners do not have a liberty interest in remaining in a minimum, as opposed to a maximum, security facility, unless the state or federal law clearly creates such an expectation.[90] A prisoner argued that a transfer from a minimum to a maximum security facility obviously meant that he had less liberty. The Court disagreed and declared: "We reject at the outset the notion *that any* grievous loss visited upon a person by the State is sufficient to invoke the procedural protections of the Due Process Clause. . . . That life in one prison is much more disagreeable than in another does not in itself signify that a Fourteenth Amendment liberty interest is implicated."[91]

In dissent, Justice Stevens, joined by Justices Brennan and Marshall, disagreed and argued that "neither the Bill of Rights nor the laws of sovereign States create the liberty which the Due Process Clause protects. . . . It is . . . basic freedom which the Due Process Clause protects, rather than the particular rights or privileges conferred by specific laws or regulations."[92] The conflict between the dissent and the majority was over how to determine when a prisoner has a liberty interest. For the dissent, a deprivation of liberty occurs when a prisoner is denied important freedoms regardless of the content of statutes or regulations. For the majority, a deprivation of liberty occurs if there is the removal of a freedom created by a statute or regulation.[93]

After *Wolff* and *Meachum*, the question became what statutes and rules create liberty interests? The Supreme Court focused on whether a law or rule was sufficiently mandatory so as to create a reasonable expectation on the part of the prisoner. For example, in *Greenholtz v. Inmates of Nebraska Penal and Correctional Complex*, the Supreme Court held that the existence of a parole system is not enough to create a liberty interest in parole; rather, there must be specific requirements in the law that transform parole from a mere hope to an entitlement under particular circumstances.[94] The Court found that Nebraska created a liberty interest in parole because state law allowed the denial of parole only under specific statutorily defined reasons and because the law allowed denial only if there were specific findings to support the decision. The Court emphasized that the word "shall" in

---

[88] *Id.* at 557.

[89] *Id.* at 558.

[90] 427 U.S. 215 (1976).

[91] *Id.* at 224-225.

[92] *Id.* at 230 (Stevens, J., dissenting).

[93] *See also* Montanye v. Haymes, 427 U.S. 236 (1976) (no loss of liberty when a prisoner is transferred from one prison to another).

[94] 442 U.S. 1 (1979).

the state law created a legitimate expectation to release on parole unless one of the statute's exceptions was met.[95]

The contrast in approach between *Morrissey v. Brewer* and *Greenholtz* is striking. *Morrissey* found a liberty interest in parole because it determines a person's freedom. *Greenholtz* held that there is a liberty interest in parole only if the state law makes it one by its mandatory language.

The *Greenholtz* approach was followed in a series of cases spanning over two decades. For example, the Supreme Court has held that a prisoner has a liberty interest in not being placed in disciplinary segregation or being transferred to another, more restrictive facility, only if state law creates such an expectation. In *Hewitt v. Helms*, the Supreme Court found that a prison had to provide due process before placing a prisoner in administrative segregation because state law had created such a liberty interest.[96] The Court explained that generally prisoners have no liberty interest in being confined in one place as opposed to another. But the Court said that the state had done more than issue procedural guidelines; it had used "language of an unmistakably mandatory character" and made it clear that a prisoner would not be placed in administrative segregation "absent specific substantive predicates."[97]

In contrast, in *Olim v. Wakinekona*, the Court refused to find a liberty interest for a prisoner in not being transferred from a prison in Hawaii to a maximum security prison in California.[98] The Court focused on the discretionary nature of the transfer decision and the absence of any mandatory language in the regulation in concluding that there was not a deprivation of liberty. The Court explained that "a State creates a protected liberty interest by placing substantive limitations on official discretion."[99]

Similarly, in *Connecticut Board of Pardons v. Dumschat*, the Supreme Court found that a prisoner did not have a liberty interest in having a review of a request for commutation of a life sentence.[100] The Court explained that state law did not create an expectation that sentences would be commuted, even though in practice the review board commuted most of the life sentences in the cases it considered. The Court said that the Connecticut law governing commutation of sentences did not provide "particularized standards or criteria [to] guide the State's decisionmakers."[101]

In other words, in deciding whether a prisoner has a liberty interest, the Court would examine the statutes and regulations governing the prison. If they

---

[95] *Id.* at 12. *See also* Board of Pardons v. Allen, 482 U.S. 369 (1987); the Court found a liberty interest in parole because the mandatory language in the parole statute created an expectation of release. The Court explained that "the presence of general or broad release criteria—delegating significant discretion to the decisionmaker" did not prevent a liberty interest because the statute allowed denial of parole only if one of several specific justifications was met. *Id.* at 375-376.

[96] 459 U.S. 460 (1983).

[97] *Id.* at 471-472.

[98] 461 U.S. 238 (1983).

[99] *Id.* at 249.

[100] 452 U.S. 458 (1981).

[101] *Id.* at 467 (Brennan, J., concurring).

were written in mandatory language and created a legitimate expectation of a benefit, then the Court would find a liberty interest. The Court expressly stated this in *Kentucky Department of Corrections v. Thompson*, where it declared: "We have . . . articulated a requirement . . . that the regulations contain explicitly mandatory language, i.e., specific directives to the decisionmaker that if the regulations' substantive predicates are present, a particular outcome must follow in order to create a liberty interest."[102] In *Thompson*, the Supreme Court held that prisoners in Kentucky did not have a liberty interest in visitation, even visitation from family members, because the regulations "lack the requisite relevant mandatory language."[103]

Although in all of these cases the Court emphasized the content of the laws and regulations, there were some cases that did not fit this pattern and where the Court found a liberty interest primarily based on the importance of the interest to the prisoner. For example, in *Vitek v. Jones*, the Court held that a prisoner is deprived of liberty when transferred from a prison to a mental hospital.[104] The Court, in part, focused on the content of the state's prison regulations and concluded that they created an expectation that the inmate would be kept in prison facilities and not moved to a mental hospital without a proven need for treatment. But the Court also emphasized that there was a loss of liberty because confinement to a mental hospital likely would mean the imposition of mandatory treatment and also a realistic possibility of stigma. The clear implication of *Vitek* is that prisoners have a liberty interest in not being transferred to a mental hospital regardless of the content of the specific laws or regulations for that prison.

Also, in *Washington v. Harper*, the Supreme Court recognized that prisoners have a liberty interest in avoiding the involuntary administration of antipsychotic medications.[105] The Court made it clear that independent of any state law or regulation, prisoners have a liberty interest in being free from the involuntary administration of psychotropic drugs.[106] The Court found that the state's law met the requirements for procedural and substantive due process before the administration of these drugs. Prison regulations required that the prisoner be given at least 24 hours' notice before the administration of this medication, and it provided the opportunity for a hearing before health professionals and prison officials. The Court found that this was procedurally adequate to meet the requirements of due process.[107]

Thus, up until June 1995, a liberty interest for prisoners could be found either if the prison statutes and regulations were written in mandatory language and created such an interest, or if the interest was so important that the Court would deem it to be a part of liberty regardless of the content of the statutes or regulations. In *Sandin v. Conner*, however, the Court called into question the approach of finding liberty interests based on the content of statutes and regulations.

---

[102] 490 U.S. 454, 463 (1989).
[103] *Id.* at 464.
[104] 445 U.S. 480 (1980).
[105] 494 U.S. 210 (1990).
[106] *Id.* at 221-222.
[107] Sandin v. Conner, 515 U.S. 472 (1995).

§7.3 Is It a Deprivation of "Life, Liberty, or Property"?

Sandin involved a Hawaii prisoner who was placed in disciplinary segregation for vocally objecting to a body cavity search. The United States Court of Appeals for the Ninth Circuit had found that there was a liberty interest based on Hawaii prison regulations that provided that an individual only would be placed in disciplinary segregation if there was "substantial evidence" of misconduct.[108] The Supreme Court reversed and strongly criticized the approach of finding liberty interests based on the language of statutes and regulations.

The Court said that this approach had produced two undesirable consequences. First, "it creates disincentives for States to codify prison management procedures in the interest of uniform treatment."[109] The Court explained that rather than create a judicially enforceable liberty interest requiring due process, a state might choose not to place matters in regulations. This, the Court said, is undesirable because it does not provide standards to guide prison employees in how to exercise their discretion.

Second, the Court said that the "approach has led to the involvement of federal courts in the day-to-day management of prisons, often squandering judicial resources with little offsetting benefit to anyone."[110] Chief Justice Rehnquist, writing for the Court, listed a series of cases where prisoners sued objecting to such matters as being given a sack lunch rather than a tray lunch or receiving a paperback dictionary.[111] Rehnquist said that the federal courts' actions have run counter to the Court's view "that federal courts ought to afford appropriate deference and flexibility to state officials trying to manage a volatile environment."[112] The Court thus concluded "that the search for a negative implication from mandatory language in prisoner regulations has strayed from the real concerns undergirding the liberty protected by the Due Process Clause."[113] The Court then sought to clarify when a prisoner has a liberty interest. The Court said:

> Following *Wolff*, we recognize that States may under certain circumstances create liberty interests which are protected by the Due Process Clause. But these interests will be generally limited to freedom from restraint which, while not exceeding the sentence in such an unexpected manner as to give rise to the Due Process Clause of its own force, nonetheless imposes atypical and significant hardship on the inmate in relation to the ordinary incidents of prison life.[114]

As examples, the Court cited *Vitek v. Jones* and *Washington v. Harper*.

In other words, after *Sandin v. Conner*, a statute or regulation creates a liberty interest for prisoners only if it "imposes atypical and significant hardship . . . in relation to the ordinary incidents of prison life." *Sandin* raises many questions. First, what is such a hardship? There is every reason to believe that the Court will

---

[108] Conner v. Dakai, 15 F.3d 1463 (9th Cir. 1993).
[109] *Sandin*, 515 U.S. at 481.
[110] *Id.* at 483.
[111] *Id.*
[112] *Id.* at 482.
[113] *Id.* at 483.
[114] *Id.* at 483-484.

be narrow in defining this. Certainly, any decision that affects the length of confinement—such as revoking parole or good time credits when created by mandatory language in state law—should be regarded as a deprivation of liberty. But *Sandin* holds that being placed in disciplinary segregation is not such an interest. This seems to mean that absent a claim that a sanction is cruel and unusual punishment, prisoners will not succeed in seeking judicial review of prison discipline.

In other words, if the prisoner is claiming that the government's action is causing or increasing incarceration, then courts are likely to recognize a deprivation of liberty; but if the prisoner is challenging conditions of confinement, then a due process challenge is much less likely to succeed. For example, in *Young v. Harper*, the Supreme Court unanimously found that the revocation of preparole release was a deprivation of liberty.[115] Oklahoma, because of prison overcrowding, released a prisoner before he was eligible for parole. When space became available in the prison, it demanded the reincarceration of the individual, claiming that he always had been in government custody, even while on preparole release. The Supreme Court, however, disagreed and found that the release from custody gave the individual obvious freedom, which was a liberty interest requiring due process before reincarceration. On the other hand, many lower courts have refused to find a liberty interest, based on *Sandin*, when the prisoner is challenging discipline imposed within the prison.[116]

Subsequently, in *Wilkinson v. Austin*, the Court applied *Sandin* to find that placing a prisoner in a "super-max" facility is a deprivation of liberty requiring due process.[117] The Court, in an opinion by Justice Kennedy, explained that prisoners in such facilities spend 23 hours a day in their cell without contact with other human beings. All meals are taken alone in the inmate's cell. A light is on 24 hours a day. Justice Kennedy noted that inmates suffer "severe limitations on all human contact" for a prolonged period of time; placement is indefinite, with only an annual review.[118] Thus, the Court found that under *Sandin*, super-max facilities "impose an atypical and significant hardship within the correctional context."[119]

Second, from a normative perspective, it must be questioned whether *Sandin* provides sufficient protection for prisoners from arbitrary treatment. Prisons obviously have enormous power over every aspect of a prisoner's life. *Sandin* holds that this authority does not have to be accompanied by due process unless there is both mandatory language in the relevant law and it is a significant, atypical deprivation of freedom. The Court defends this based on a need to encourage prisons to write

---

[115] 520 U.S. 143 (1997).

[116] *See, e.g.*, Stone-Bey v. Barnes, 913 F. Supp. 1226 (N.D. Ind. 1996) (one-year disciplinary segregation was not a deprivation of liberty); Frazier v. Coughlin, 81 F.3d 313 (2d Cir. 1996) (confinement in special housing unit for 12 days while awaiting disciplinary proceedings and then in close supervision unit for 11 months was not deprivation of liberty); Dominique v. Weld, 73 F.3d 1156 (1st Cir. 1996) (loss of work release privileges and transfer to a higher security prison were not deprivations of liberty).

[117] 545 U.S. 209 (2005).

[118] *Id.* at 211.

[119] *Id.* at 225. The Court, however, found that the procedures provided, including the ability to contest placement in a super-max facility and several levels of administrative review, was sufficient to meet due process.

regulations and based on a desire to minimize federal court oversight of prisons. Yet the issue is whether this leaves prisoners, who have no way to protect themselves, sufficient safeguards against arbitrary and capricious treatment.

The transformation of the law with regard to defining liberty interests for prisoners is revealing. Initially, the Court found a liberty interest when prisoners suffered a "grievous loss." In an effort to narrow the scope of liberty interests, the Court ruled that liberty interests exist when there is a statute or regulation that in mandatory language limits the government's discretion over the prisoner. The more liberal Justices on the Court repeatedly objected to this approach and argued that a liberty interest should be found when there is a significant deprivation of freedom, regardless of the content of the statutes or regulations.

Now, however, it is the conservatives on the Court—the majority in *Sandin* was Rehnquist, O'Connor, Scalia, Kennedy, and Thomas—who have abandoned finding liberty interests based on mandatory language. They seek to narrow greatly the circumstances where liberty interests will be found. It will require future cases to determine when, if at all, the Court will find such interests under the *Sandin* test and how it is to be reconciled with all of the earlier cases, none of which were expressly overruled in *Sandin*.

Reputation as a Liberty Interest

The Court has been inconsistent as to whether harm to reputation is a deprivation of liberty requiring due process. In *Goss v. Lopez*, the Supreme Court held that students have a liberty interest in not being disciplined by a public school, in part, because suspension from school would damage the student's reputation.[120] The Court explained that the disciplinary charges "could seriously damage the students' standing with their fellow pupils and their teachers as well as interfere with later opportunities for higher education and employment."[121]

Similarly, in *Wisconsin v. Constantineau*, the Court found that an individual's liberty was denied when the chief of police posted a notice in all local retail liquor stores forbidding sales of liquor to the person.[122] The individual objected that the posting was done without any notice or a hearing. The Court agreed and stated: "Where a person's good name, reputation, honor, or integrity is at stake because of what the government is doing to him, notice and an opportunity to be heard are essential."[123]

However, just a few years later, in *Paul v. Davis*, the Court held that harm to reputation, by itself, is not a deprivation of liberty.[124] In *Paul*, the Louisville, Kentucky, chief of police circulated a flyer of those "known" to have committed shoplifting. The individual whose picture and name was included objected saying that his reputation, a liberty interest, was denied without any due process. The

---

[120] 419 U.S. 565 (1975).
[121] *Id.* at 575.
[122] 400 U.S. 433 (1971).
[123] *Id.* at 437.
[124] 424 U.S. 693 (1976).

Supreme Court, however, disagreed and held that an "interest in reputation alone . . . is neither liberty nor property guaranteed against state deprivation without due process of law."[125]

The Court emphasized that liberty interests are created either by the Bill of Rights or by state law. The Court explained that in addition to the provisions of the Bill of Rights that are incorporated into the due process clause of the Fourteenth Amendment, liberty and property "interests attain this constitutional status by virtue of the fact that they have been initially recognized and protected by state law."[126] In other words, in deciding if there is a liberty interest, the Court is to look at the positive law and not base its decision on a conclusion about the importance of the interest to the individual.

The Court reaffirmed *Paul v. Davis* in *Siegert v. Gilley*.[127] In *Siegert*, an unfavorable recommendation letter was the basis for a civil rights suit. The Supreme Court held that there was not a claim for a denial of liberty because harm to reputation, by itself, is not a loss of liberty.

The issue of whether a person has a liberty interest in his or her reputation is important. On the one hand, recognizing a liberty interest makes sense in light of the obvious importance of a person's reputation within a community and the fact that this is recognized in state laws, such as those creating liability for defamation. On the other hand, the Court in *Paul* clearly was struggling to limit the meaning of liberty and sought to do this by recognizing only liberty interests that are expressly mentioned in the Constitution or created by statute. The Court found that reputation met neither of these requirements.

The Court has indicated, however, that due process is required when there is harm to reputation if it is accompanied by a tangible detriment, such as loss of employment. In *Owen v. City of Independence*, the Supreme Court explained that "[d]ue process requires a hearing on the discharge of a government employee 'if the employer creates and disseminates a false and defamatory impression about the employee in connection with his termination.'"[128] The question, of course, is why reputation matters only if it is accompanied by a loss of a job. Harm to reputation might prevent a person from getting a job in the future, and it might be difficult, if not impossible, for a person to prove that effect.

§7.3.4 Deprivations of "Life"

Unlike the terms "property" and "liberty," which have produced a great deal of litigation over their meaning, the term "life" in the due process clause is rarely the subject of controversy. In part, this is because there are fewer instances in which it is alleged that the state impermissibly took a person's life without due process than

---

[125] *Id.* at 712.
[126] *Id.* at 710.
[127] 500 U.S. 226 (1991).
[128] 445 U.S. 622, 661 (1980), quoting Codd v. Velger, 429 U.S. 624 (1977).

there are claims of state wrongful deprivations of liberty or property. In part, too, it is because when such cases arise, they are not over the meaning of "life."

In the substantive due process context, issues over life have arisen in two areas. One is the controversy over abortion rights. Even here, however, the debate is rarely couched in terms of the meaning of the word "life" in the due process clause but, instead, is usually about whether women have a right to terminate their pregnancies and whether fetuses should be considered persons under the Constitution.[129] The other area of controversy is over whether there is a right of individuals to refuse life-saving medical treatment. This, too, is not about the meaning of the word "life" in the due process clause, but rather about whether individuals have a liberty interest in refusing treatment and the circumstances under which the state can interfere with such choices.[130]

Otherwise, claims concerning state deprivations of life are litigated under constitutional provisions other than due process. For example, challenges to the constitutionality of the death penalty usually involve the Eighth Amendment, and if they do involve due process, they concern the requirements of due process in capital cases rather than the definition of life.

Also, the Supreme Court has ruled that claims against the police for excessive force or impermissible use of deadly force cannot be brought under the due process clause. The Court has said that they are properly brought under the Fourth Amendment as impermissible seizures or perhaps under the Eighth Amendment as cruel and unusual punishment, but not under due process.[131]

§7.4 WHAT PROCEDURES ARE REQUIRED?

§7.4.1 When Is Procedural Due Process Required?

As described in §7.1, procedural due process refers to the procedures that the government must follow when it takes away a person's life, liberty, or property. Yet not every deprivation of life, liberty, or property presents a procedural due process question. For example, if the government adopts a law prohibiting abortion, it is unquestionably a deprivation of liberty under current law, and yet there would not be a procedural due process issue. The plaintiffs challenging the anti-abortion law would not be objecting to the procedures followed by the government, but rather would be challenging the substantive constitutionality of the law.

---

[129] *See, e.g.,* Roe v. Wade, 410 U.S. 113 (1973), discussed in §10.3.3.

[130] *See, e.g.,* Washington v. Glucksberg, 521 U.S. 702 (1997) (no liberty interest in a right to physician-assisted suicide); Cruzan v. Director, Mo. Dept. of Health, 497 U.S. 261 (1990) (a liberty interest exists in refusing unwanted medical treatment), discussed in §10.5.

[131] *See* Graham v. Connor, 490 U.S. 386 (1989); Tennessee v. Garner, 471 U.S. 1 (1985).

In other words, procedural due process issues arise when an individual or group is claiming a right to a fair *process* in connection with their suffering a deprivation of life, liberty, or property. The classic cases illustrating this are *Bi-Metallic Investment Co. v. State Board of Equalization*[1] and *Londoner v. Denver*.[2] In *Bi-Metallic*, Colorado's State Board of Equalization sought to impose an order increasing the valuation of all taxable property in Denver by 40 percent. Challengers objected, arguing that the government violated the Fourteenth Amendment because it failed to provide them an opportunity to be heard and thus denied them of property without due process of law.

The Supreme Court said that even assuming that none of the taxpayers were given an opportunity to be heard, there still was no violation of due process. The Court explained: "General statutes within the state power are passed that affect the person or property of individuals, sometimes to the point of ruin, without giving them a chance to be heard. Their rights are protected in the only way that they can be in a complex society, by their power, immediate or remote, over those who make the rule."[3]

In contrast, in *Londoner*, the issue was whether individual property owners had to be accorded a hearing before the city assessed them for the costs of local improvements. The Supreme Court said that "due process of law requires that at some stage of the proceedings, before the tax becomes irrevocably fixed, the taxpayer shall have an opportunity to be heard, of which he must have notice, either personal, by publication, or by a law fixing the time and place of the hearing."[4]

Perhaps most simply stated, procedural protections are required under the due process clause when there is a possible issue about how the law applies to a specific person. For example, imagine that the legislature adopts a law cutting welfare benefits for all recipients by 50 percent. No procedural due process question seems to be present there; it is a situation indistinguishable from *Bi-Metallic*. In contrast, imagine that the legislature says that welfare benefits will be cut by 50 percent for all individuals who already have received benefits for 12 months. In the latter situation, there is a need in each case for a determination as to whether the government should reduce that person's benefits. Procedural due process requires that there be a fair process for this determination just as was the case in *Londoner*.

In other words, procedural due process must be provided when (a) there is a deprivation of life, liberty, or property; and (b) potential factual issues exist concerning a particular individual or group. Procedural due process issues generally are not present when there is a challenge to the constitutionality of a statute or regulation and the issue is not the fairness of the process being followed. These challenges are commonly brought under substantive due process or under the specific constitutional right at issue.

---

§7.4 [1] 239 U.S. 441 (1915).
[2] 210 U.S. 373 (1908).
[3] *Bi-Metallic*, 239 U.S. at 445.
[4] 210 U.S. at 385-386.

§7.4.2   What Is the Test for Determining What Process Is Due?

When the government must provide due process, it must always supply certain basic safeguards such as notice of the charges or issue,[5] the opportunity for a meaningful hearing,[6] and an impartial decision maker.[7] These long have been regarded as the core elements of due process. In *Mullane v. Central Hanover Bank & Trust Co.*, the Court declared the much quoted words: "Many controversies have raged about the cryptic and abstract words of the Due Process Clause but there can be no doubt that at a minimum they require that deprivation of life, liberty, or property by adjudication be proceeded by notice and opportunity for hearing appropriate to the nature of the case."[8]

Yet even when notice and a hearing are required, there are a multitude of ways of providing them. For example, what type of notice is required; must it be notice that is personally served or is notice by posting or even by publication sufficient? What type of hearing must be supplied; is a full-trial type, adversarial hearing required or is a much more informal proceeding sufficient? What procedural safeguards must be accorded at the hearing? Must the government provide the right to be represented by an attorney at the hearing and, if so, is the government required to provide indigents with a free lawyer if they cannot afford one? When must the hearing occur; must it be before the deprivation can occur or is a postdeprivation hearing sufficient? What *is* the standard of proof and who has the burden of proof? Who is a permissible decision maker; must it be a judge or can others suffice? And these are just some of the choices that must be made in deciding what due process requires.

Obviously, the answers to these questions are not the same in all situations where there has been a deprivation of life, liberty, or property. One possible answer would be for the Court to allow the government to decide the answer to these questions as part of the definition of the property or liberty interest. In *Arnett v. Kennedy*, then-Justice Rehnquist, joined by Chief Justice Burger and Justice Stewart, took this position.[9] Rehnquist argued that the "grant of a substantive right is inextricably intertwined with the limitations on the procedures which are to be employed . . . [and that] a litigant . . . must take the bitter with the sweet."[10]

However, a majority of the Court later expressly rejected this position. In *Cleveland Board of Education v. Loudermill*, the Supreme Court held that the nature

---

   [5] *See, e.g.*, Mullane v. Central Hanover Bank & Trust Co., 339 U.S. 306 (1950) (discussing notice as a requirement of due process).

   [6] *See, e.g.*, Goldberg v. Kelly, 397 U.S. 254 (1970) (hearing required before termination of welfare benefits).

   [7] *See, e.g.*, Caperton v. A.T. Massey Coal Co., Inc., 556 U.S. 868 (2009) (due process violated by having a judge participate where parties had made substantial expenditures for the judge's election campaign) (discussed below); Gibson v. Berryhill, 411 U.S. 564 (1973) (unconstitutional to have decision makers who potentially would personally gain from their decisions).

   [8] 339 U.S. 306, 313 (1950). *See, e.g.*, Richards v. Jefferson County, Alabama, 517 U.S. 793 (1996) (the opportunity to be heard is essential to due process, and prior litigation to challenge the constitutionality of a tax did not prevent different taxpayers from bringing a constitutional challenge).

   [9] 416 U.S. 134 (1974).

   [10] *Id.* at 153-154.

of the procedures required by due process is a constitutional question to be answered by the judiciary, not a statutory question for the legislature.[11] The Court explained that the "'minimum [procedural] requirements [are] a matter of federal law, they are not diminished by the fact that the State may have specified its own procedures that it may deem adequate for determining the preconditions to adverse official action.'"[12] The Court said that the "bitter with the sweet" approach "misconceives the constitutional guarantee."[13] If there is a deprivation of life, liberty, or property, constitutionally adequate procedures are required.

If the statutes and regulations are irrelevant in deciding what is required under due process, there is a need for the Court to decide how to answer the many questions that arise concerning the nature of the procedures that are required. The Court has refused to provide uniform answers to these questions, but instead has said that "due process . . . is not a technical conception with a fixed content unrelated to time, place and circumstances, . . . [but rather] is flexible and calls for such procedural protections as the particular situation demands."[14]

In *Mathews v. Eldridge*, the Court articulated a balancing test for deciding what procedures are required when there has been a deprivation of life, liberty, or property and due process is required.[15] As discussed below, the Supreme Court repeatedly has applied it in deciding what process is due. The Court in *Mathews* articulated three factors that should be balanced:

> First, the private interest that will be affected by the official action; second, the risk of an erroneous deprivation of such interest through the procedures used, and the probable value, if any, of additional or substitute procedural safeguards; and finally, the Government's interest, including the function involved and the fiscal and administrative burdens that the additional or substitute procedural requirement would entail.[16]

In other words, in answering the myriad of questions about what procedures must be provided, the Supreme Court instructs that three factors be balanced. The first factor is the importance of the interest to the individual. The more important the interest, the more in the way of procedural safeguards the Court will require. The second consideration is the ability of additional procedures to increase the accuracy of the fact-finding. The more the Court believes that the additional procedures will lead to better, more accurate, less erroneous decisions, the more likely it is that the Court will require them. Finally, the Court looks at the burdens imposed on the government by requiring the procedures. The more expensive the procedures will be, the less likely it is that the Court will require them.

The *Mathews* test can be praised because it focuses a court's attention on what seem to be the right questions in deciding the nature of the procedural protections.

---

[11] 470 U.S. 532 (1985).
[12] *Id.* at 541, quoting Vitek v. Jones, 445 U.S. 480, 491 (1980).
[13] *Id.*
[14] Mathews v. Eldridge, 424 U.S. 319, 334 (1976) (citations omitted).
[15] 424 U.S. 319 (1976).
[16] *Id.* at 335.

It seems clearly correct that the nature of the proceeding should be a function of the interest involved, the degree to which the procedure will make a difference, and the cost to the government. An expensive trial-type hearing would be out of place for a minor interest in a situation where there is little likelihood of a factual dispute.[17] But an adversarial hearing is essential, despite its expense, if there is a fundamental right at stake, such as the right of parents to the custody of their children.

Yet *Mathews* also can be criticized for failing to provide any real guidance as to how courts should balance the competing interests. The reality is that courts have enormous discretion in evaluating each of the three factors and especially how to balance them. Such multipart balancing inherently provides little constraint on judicial decisions. Indeed, Justice Rehnquist once remarked that under *Mathews*, "[t]he balance is simply an ad hoc weighing which depends to a great extent upon how the Court subjectively views the underlying interests at stake."[18]

Moreover, the *Mathews* test has been criticized for giving insufficient weight to the intrinsic benefits of procedural protections and for giving disproportionate weight to quantifiable variables such as cost.[19] Due process, it is argued, is important not only to enhance the accuracy of decision makers; it also is about treating individuals fairly and with dignity when important decisions are made about their lives. *Mathews* can be criticized for failing to recognize these values.

Nonetheless, it is firmly established that in deciding what procedures are required, the Court employs the *Mathews*-three-part balancing test. Considered below is how the Court has applied this test in many different contexts, including government benefit programs, government employment, family rights, educational institutions, children's rights, prisoners' rights, punitive damages, creditors' claims, and forfeiture proceedings. These, of course, are not exhaustive of the situations where procedural due process is required, but these are areas where the Court has attempted to balance the interests and determine the appropriate procedures to be followed.

§7.4.3 *The* Mathews v. Eldridge *Test Applied*

In applying the *Mathews v. Eldridge* test in a variety of contexts, the Supreme Court has had to consider five basic questions. Not all have been addressed in all of the contexts discussed below. First, what type of notice is required?[20] Second, when

---

[17] *See, e.g.*, Henry J. Friendly, Some Kind of Hearing, 123 U. Pa. L. Rev. 1267, 1276 (1975) ("It should be realized that procedural requirements entail the expenditure of limited resources, that at some point the benefit to individuals from an additional safeguard is substantially outweighed by the cost of providing such protection, and that the expense of protecting those likely to be found undeserving will probably come out of the pockets of the deserving.").

[18] Cleveland Bd. of Educ. v. Loudermill, 470 U.S. 532, 562 (1985) (Rehnquist, J., dissenting).

[19] *See, e.g.*, Jerry Mashaw, The Supreme Court's Due Process Calculus for Administrative Adjudication in *Mathews v. Eldridge*: Three Factors in Search of a Theory of Value, 44 U. Chi. L. Rev. 28 (1976).

[20] For example, in *City of West Covina v. Perkins*, 525 U.S. 234 (1999), the Supreme Court unanimously ruled that the government does not need to give a person notice of how to get his or her

must the hearing be provided; must it be before the deprivation or can it be after the deprivation? Third, what type of hearing is required? For example, must it be an adversarial hearing and must the government provide an attorney? Fourth, who has the burden of proof and what is the standard of proof (i.e., preponderance of the evidence, clear and convincing evidence, or proof beyond a reasonable doubt) to be applied? Fifth, who should be the decision maker?

For example, in *Hamdi v. Rumsfeld*, the Supreme Court held that an American citizen apprehended in a foreign country and held as an enemy combatant is entitled to due process.[21] The Court remanded the case for the application of the *Mathews v. Eldridge* test to determine what procedures are required. However, Justice O'Connor's plurality opinion held that at a minimum, due process would necessitate notice of the charges, a meaningful factual hearing, and representation by counsel.[22] But Justice O'Connor also suggested that allowing hearsay and placing the burden of proof on the defendant may be permissible.[23] The precise procedures required never were resolved on remand because Hamdi and the government reached an agreement where Hamdi was released from custody in exchange for renouncing his citizenship, leaving the country, and promising never to take up arms against the United States.

Another recent case involved the due process requirement for an impartial decision maker. In *Caperton v. A.T. Massey Coal Co., Inc.*,[24] a jury in West Virginia state court had awarded a $50 million judgment against the defendant, A.T. Massey Coal Co., Inc. Officials of Massey Coal spent $3 million in independent expenditures to get their candidate of choice, Brent Benjamin, elected to the West Virginia Supreme Court. This was a substantial percentage of all the money spent for Benjamin and the effort was successful; Benjamin defeated the incumbent justice by 50,000 votes. Benjamin denied a motion for his recusal and was in the majority in the 3-2 decision to overturn the jury verdict.

The Supreme Court, in a 5-4 decision, ruled that Benjamin's participation violated due process. Justice Kennedy wrote for the Court and began his opinion by noting: "It is axiomatic that '[a] fair trial in a fair tribunal is a basic requirement of due process.' "[25] The Court said that the test under due process is whether "under a realistic appraisal of psychological tendencies and human weakness, the interest poses such a risk of actual bias or prejudgment that the practice must be forbidden if the guarantee of due process is to be adequately implemented."[26] The Court noted that the expenditures by Massey Coal officials had a "significant

---

property back after it has been taken pursuant to a valid search warrant. The Court said that individualized notice was not required by due process because there was adequate public information about the available mechanisms for obtaining the property back. On the other hand, in *Jones v. Flower*, 547 U.S. 220 (2006), the Court held that before a state may take property and sell it for unpaid property taxes, the government must take additional steps to provide notice when notice of a tax sale is mailed to the owner and returned undelivered.

[21] 542 U.S. 507 (2004). *Hamdi* is discussed in detail in §4.6.4.

[22] *Id.* at 533.

[23] *Id.* at 533-534.

[24] 556 U.S. 868 (2009).

[25] *Id.* at 876 (citation omitted).

[26] *Id.* at 883.

and disproportionate effect" in electing Justice Benjamin. The Court stated: "We conclude that there is a serious risk of actual bias — based on objective and reasonable perceptions — when a person with a personal stake in a particular case had a significant and disproportionate influence in placing the judge on the case by raising funds or directing the judge's election campaign when the case was pending or imminent. The inquiry centers on the contribution's relative size in comparison to the total amount of money contributed to the campaign, the total amount spent in the election, and the apparent effect such contribution had on the outcome of the election."[27] An impartial decision maker is essential to due process and this is denied if a party to the litigation played a substantial part in getting the judge elected by spending significant money for his or her election to the bench.

Government Benefits and Services

In *Goldberg v. Kelly*, the case that in many ways began the procedural due process revolution, the Court held that the government must provide notice and a hearing before terminating a person's welfare benefits.[28] The Court emphasized the importance of welfare for basic subsistence and the need to protect welfare recipients from arbitrary termination of benefits. The Court said that a "quasi-judicial trial" was not required,[29] but it did mandate that there be an adversarial hearing, with the right to present evidence and witnesses, in front of a neutral decision maker.

In contrast, in *Mathews v. Eldridge*, the Supreme Court held that when the government terminates Social Security disability benefits, it need provide only a post-termination hearing.[30] In applying the first part of the balancing test, concerning the importance of the interest to the individual, the Court distinguished *Goldberg v. Kelly* and welfare benefits from Social Security payments. The Court explained that welfare benefits were based on financial need, but "[e]ligibility for disability benefits, in contrast, is not based upon financial need."[31] Also, the Court believed that individuals who lose Social Security disability benefits still can obtain other sources of income, such as welfare.

The Court then turned its attention to the second part of the balancing test concerning the ability of additional procedures to reduce the likelihood of an erroneous deprivation. The Court said that decisions about "whether to discontinue

---

[27] *Id.* at 884. Justice Kennedy concluded his majority opinion by describing this as an "extraordinary situation" and thus saw this as rarely recurring. *Id.* at 887. Chief Justice Roberts, writing for the four dissenters, saw this as opening the door to far more frequent requests for recusal and listed 40 unanswered questions in the majority's opinion. *Id.* at 893 (Roberts, C.J., dissenting). In light of the Supreme Court's subsequent decision in *Citizens United v. Federal Election Commission*, 130 S. Ct. 876 (2010), holding that corporations (and by implication, unions) can engage in unlimited independent expenditures, there is the prospect for the issue to arise much more frequently as to when expenditures for a judicial candidate create a sufficient risk of "actual bias" as to require recusal.

[28] 397 U.S. 254 (1970).

[29] *Id.* at 266.

[30] 424 U.S. 319 (1976).

[31] *Id.* at 340.

disability benefits will turn, in most cases, upon routine, standard, and unbiased medical reports by physician specialists."[32] Thus, the Court said that the "potential value of an evidentiary hearing, or even oral presentation to the decision maker, is substantially less in this context than in *Goldberg*."[33]

Finally, the Court considered the last part of the balancing test: the costs to the government of requiring pretermination hearings. The Court believed that there would be substantial expense as individuals receiving benefits would likely exhaust all appeals if they could keep receiving funds until the procedures were completed.[34] The Court said that there would thus be both financial and administrative burdens on the government if it was required to provide due process before terminating Social Security disability benefits.

Based on this three-part balancing test, the Court "conclude[d] that an evidentiary hearing is not required prior to the termination of disability benefits."[35] Justice Brennan, joined by Justice Marshall, wrote a short dissent. Brennan objected that it was purely "speculative" as to whether those losing Social Security disability benefits would suffer only limited harms because of the existence of other sources of income, such as welfare payments. Brennan pointed out that "in the present case, it is indicated that because disability benefits were terminated there was a foreclosure upon the Eldridge home and the family's furniture was repossessed, forcing Eldridge, his wife, and their children to sleep in one bed."[36]

After *Mathews*, the Court generally has been more likely to be satisfied with posttermination hearings than it was earlier. For example, prior to *Mathews*, in *Bell v. Burson*, the Supreme Court held that there had to be a hearing before suspending a person's driver's license if the individual was involved in an automobile accident and could not show proof of financial responsibility.[37] But after *Mathews*, in *Mackey v. Montrym*, the Court held that a hearing after suspension of a driver's license was sufficient when an individual's license was suspended for refusal to take a breathalyzer test.[38] The Court emphasized that the need to protect public safety from drunk drivers justified allowing suspension of licenses prior to the hearing.

Yet there are some circumstances, even after *Mathews*, where the Court has required some form of pretermination hearing. For example, in *Memphis Light, Gas and Water Division v. Craft*, the Court held that a government-owned utility must provide due process before terminating a customer's service.[39] The Court required that notice be given to the customer of the pending termination and that there be an informal procedure where the customer could be heard. The Court emphasized that there was no requirement for an adversarial hearing before an

---

[32] *Id.* at 344 (citation omitted).
[33] *Id.* at 344-345.
[34] *Id.* at 347.
[35] *Id.* at 349.
[36] *Id.* at 350 (Brennan, J., dissenting).
[37] 402 U.S. 535 (1971).
[38] 443 U.S. 1 (1979).
[39] 436 U.S. 1 (1978).

impartial decision maker; an informal pretermination hearing before an employee who could correct errors in billing would be sufficient.

Another area where the Court has applied the *Mathews* test in connection with government benefits concerns the ability of the government to limit attorneys' fees for challenges to its decisions. In *Walters v. National Association of Radiation Survivors*, the Court considered the constitutionality of a federal statute that limits to $10 the fee that may be paid to an attorney who represents a veteran challenging a termination of benefits for service-connected death or disability.[40] The law was adopted in 1862 during the Civil War.[41] The Court expressly applied the *Mathews* test and upheld the constitutionality of this provision. The Court emphasized "the deference owed to Congress" and concluded that Congress had the important goals of providing more informal procedures and of protecting claimants' benefits from being diverted to lawyers.[42]

The Court also found that the law did not interfere with accurate determinations because complex cases "are undoubtedly a tiny fraction of the total cases pending."[43] The Court looked at statistics concerning the outcome of proceedings before the Board of Veterans' Appeals and found that those represented by attorneys have only a "slightly better success rate" than those represented by service representatives or those who are unrepresented.[44]

Finally, the Court said that the benefits were more like those in *Mathews* than those in *Goldberg v. Kelly* in that veterans' benefits were not based on need. Thus, the Court upheld the federal law because it perceived that the benefits were not likely to be crucial for subsistence, that the presence of an attorney would not significantly increase the accuracy of the decision making, and that there were important government interests in preventing attorneys from collecting more than $10.

The Court's deference to Congress in *Walters* can be questioned in light of its decision in *Loudermill* that the requirements of due process are to be decided by the judiciary as a constitutional issue and not by the legislature. Justice Stevens, in a dissenting opinion joined by Justices Brennan and Marshall, argued that the law is unconstitutional because it interferes with "the right of an individual to consult an attorney of his choice in connection with a controversy with the Government."[45]

Nonetheless, the Court reaffirmed *Walters* in *United States Department of Labor v. Triplett.*[46] In *Triplett*, the Court upheld the constitutionality of the Black Lung Benefits Act of 1972 that prohibited attorneys' fees for representing claimants except where the fees are approved by the Department of Labor or a court. The

---

[40] 473 U.S. 305 (1985), considering the constitutionality of 38 U.S.C. §3404(c). The statutory provision involved in *Walters* has been amended and recodified as 38 U.S.C. §5904. It says "the total fee payable to the attorney may not exceed 20 percent of the total amount of any past-due benefits awarded on the basis of the claim." 38 U.S.C. §5904(d)(1).

[41] The initial fee was $5 per claim, and this was increased to $10 in 1864. *Id.* at 359-360 (Stevens, J., dissenting).

[42] *Id.* at 321.

[43] *Id.* at 330.

[44] *Id.* at 331.

[45] *Id.* at 368 (Stevens, J., dissenting).

[46] 494 U.S. 715 (1990).

Court approvingly cited *Walters*,[47] but concluded that it did not need to reach the due process question because there was no showing that the Act prevented individuals from securing legal representation in Black Lung Benefits Act proceedings.

The Court subsequently considered what process is due in the area of government contracts. In *Lujan v. G&G Fire Sprinklers*, the Court found that due process was met in the government's withholding payments on contracts because of the availability of a judicial remedy.[48] The California Labor Code authorizes the state to withhold payments to a contractor based on a subcontractor's failure to comply with prevailing wage requirements in the public works contract. The contractor, in turn, could withhold payments from the subcontractor under such circumstances. The Court found that the availability of legal actions in court was sufficient to meet the requirements of due process. Chief Justice Rehnquist, writing for a unanimous Court, explained that if the state "makes ordinary judicial process available . . . for resolving its contractual dispute, that process is due process."[49]

Government Employment

In *Arnett v. Kennedy*, the Supreme Court, without a majority opinion, ruled that the government could fire a public employee for misconduct without a full hearing prior to termination.[50] The Court said that it was sufficient that there was the opportunity for a pretermination review within the department followed by a posttermination hearing.

The Court reaffirmed this in *Cleveland Board of Education v. Loudermill*, where it expressly applied the *Mathews* balancing test.[51] In *Loudermill*, the Court concluded that due process was satisfied if the government provided a fired employee both an informal pretermination proceeding where it was possible to respond to charges and then a later posttermination hearing.

As to the first aspect of the *Mathews* balancing test, the Court found that continued employment by the government is a "significant" interest for the individual.[52] As to the second part of the balancing test, the Court concluded that an informal pretermination proceeding was essential to avoid erroneous terminations. As to the third prong of the test, the Court recognized that any pretermination proceeding would entail costs to the government. But the Court said that the importance of the interest to the individual and the need to avoid errors justified requiring an informal pretermination proceeding despite these costs. The Court emphasized that "the pretermination hearing, though necessary, need not be elaborate."[53]

Arnett, and especially *Loudermill*, seem to provide exactly the type of compromise that *Mathews* envisioned. The Court recognizes the importance of providing a pretermination hearing to employees, but also acknowledges the costs to the

[47] 473 U.S. at 721.
[48] 532 U.S. 189 (2001).
[49] *Id.* at 197.
[50] 416 U.S. 134 (1974).
[51] 470 U.S. 532 (1985).
[52] *Id.* at 543.
[53] *Id.* at 545.

government of doing this. So the Court strikes a compromise: an informal pre-termination proceeding to be followed, if necessary, by a formal posttermination hearing.

In *Gilbert v. Homar*,[54] the Supreme Court held that the government did not have to provide a police officer suspended after being arrested on drug charges notice and a hearing *before* his suspension. The Court expressly applied the balancing test from *Mathews v. Eldridge* in concluding that a postdeprivation hearing was sufficient to meet the requirements of the due process clause.[55] The Court explained that the loss to the individual was relatively minimal and could be restored through a postdeprivation hearing. But the Court said that the government had a significant interest in immediately suspending employees charged with felonies, especially if they occupy positions of public trust such as police officers.

Family Rights

The Supreme Court has been inconsistent in the degree of due process it has required in cases concerning parental rights. On the one hand, there have been cases where the Court has stressed the importance of the interest and required substantial procedural protections. For example, the Supreme Court has held that a state must prove, by "clear and convincing evidence," the need to terminate parental rights at a hearing before such rights are terminated.[56]

The Court also has recognized the right of an individual to deny paternity. In *Little v. Streater*, the Court held that the government must pay for blood tests for indigent defendants in paternity cases.[57] The Court explained that a defendant unable to afford the cost of the blood tests would lack a "meaningful opportunity to be heard" because there was no other way to refute the allegation of paternity.[58] The Court explained that "a cost requirement, valid on its face, may offend due process because it operates to foreclose a particular party's opportunity to be heard."[59]

But on the other hand, the Court has held that the government need not automatically provide an attorney to indigent parents at parental termination proceedings. In *Lassiter v. Department of Social Services*, the Court explicitly applied the *Mathews* test and concluded that the obligation to provide counsel depends on the circumstances of the particular case and is not required in all instances where the government seeks to end parental rights.[60] The Court said that it had recognized an automatic right to government-appointed counsel for indigents "only where the litigant may lose his physical liberty if he loses the litigation."[61]

---

[54] 520 U.S. 924 (1997).

[55] *Id.* at 931-32.

[56] Santosky v. Kramer, 455 U.S. 745, 769 (1982).

[57] 452 U.S. 1 (1981).

[58] *Id.* at 16, quoting Boddie v. Connecticut, 401 U.S. 371, 377 (1970).

[59] *Id.*

[60] 452 U.S. 18 (1981).

[61] *Id.* at 25.

The Court recognized that a "parent's desire for and right to the companionship, care, custody, and management of his or her children is an undeniably important interest that undeniably warrants deference."[62] The Court said that "the State has an urgent interest in the welfare of the child" that also is served by "ensuring accurate and just results at parental termination hearings."[63]

Nonetheless, the Court did not find that due process always requires the provision of counsel for indigent parents at such proceedings. The Court said that sometimes the presence of an attorney would matter little in the outcome of the proceedings. The Court declared that "the presence of counsel for Ms. Lassiter could not have made a determinative difference."[64] The Court said that "Ms. Lassiter had expressly declined to appear at the 1975 child custody hearing, . . . had not even bothered to speak to her retained lawyer after being notified of the termination hearing, . . . [and failed] to make an effort to contest the termination proceeding."[65]

The Court said that "wise public policy" might cause states to provide an attorney for all indigent parents at termination proceedings and those concerning neglect or dependency.[66] The Court also recognized that in some instances the government would be required to appoint counsel where "the parent's interests were at their strongest, the State's interests were at their weakest, and the risks of errors were at their peak."[67] But the Court concluded that the Constitution does not "require the appointment of counsel in every parental termination proceeding."[68]

The likelihood of error without the appointment of counsel was the decisive factor for the majority in *Lassiter*. The dissent, written by Justice Blackmun and joined by Justices Brennan and Marshall, argued that attorneys always should be provided to prevent errors. Often parents will not know enough about their rights and the procedures to make a showing as to how an attorney would make a difference. In some cases, it would take an attorney to make the argument as to why an attorney is necessary; but no lawyer is provided until after such a showing. Justice Blackmun thus lamented that "[b]y intimidation, inarticulateness, or confusion, a parent can lose forever all contact and involvement with his or her offspring."[69]

In a separate dissenting opinion, Justice Stevens questioned the application of the *Mathews* balancing test to a fundamental liberty interest outside the property context.[70] He argued that the utilitarian calculus employed under *Mathews* is ill-suited for cases involving basic freedoms. He said that even if the costs to the state were great, procedural protections such as the right to counsel in termination

---

[62] *Id.* at 27 (citation omitted).

[63] *Id.*

[64] *Id.* at 33.

[65] *Id.*

[66] *Id.* at 33-34.

[67] *Id.* at 31.

[68] *Id.*

[69] *Id.* at 47 (Blackmun, J., dissenting).

[70] *Id.* at 59-60 (Stevens, J., dissenting).

proceedings are essential because "protecting our liberty from deprivation by the State without due process of law is priceless."[71]

In its most recent case applying *Mathews* in the family law context, in *Turner v. Rogers*, the Court considered whether a man was entitled to counsel before he was sentenced to 12 months in jail for his failure to pay child support.[72] The Court stressed that it was considering this in the context of a privately initiated proceeding, rather than one begun by the government. The Court said that although the interest in being free from incarceration was a strong one, counsel was not required in every such case so long as adequate alternative procedures were provided. The Court declared: "[T]he Due Process Clause does not always require the provision of counsel in civil proceedings where incarceration is threatened."[73]

The Court elaborated the type of alternative procedures that could reduce the risks of erroneous deprivations: "(1) notice to the defendant that his 'ability to pay' is a critical issue in the contempt proceeding; (2) the use of a form (or the equivalent) to elicit relevant financial information; (3) an opportunity at the hearing for the defendant to respond to statements and questions about his financial status, (*e.g.*, those triggered by his responses on the form); and (4) an express finding by the court that the defendant has the ability to pay."[74] In this instance, the Court found that there was a violation of due process because there was neither an attorney provided nor these alternative procedural safeguards before a person was incarcerated.

Educational Institutions

As described above, in *Goss v. Lopez*, the Supreme Court concluded that suspension of a student from school is a deprivation of liberty and property requiring due process.[75] The Court thus held that "[a]t the very minimum, . . . students facing suspension and the consequent interference with a protected property interest must be given *some* kind of notice and afforded *some* kind of hearing."[76] The Court said that for a suspension of ten days or less, the student must be provided oral or written notice of the charges and "an explanation of the evidence the authorities have and an opportunity to present his side of the story."[77]

The Court said that at least in cases involving short suspensions, notice of the charges and an opportunity to explain was sufficient to meet due process; the Constitution did not require a trial-type hearing with the right to counsel and the ability to call witnesses. The Court indicated, however, that more formal proceedings might be required in cases involving longer suspensions or expulsions.

Goss can be criticized both by those who believe that it does not provide any meaningful protection for students and by those who believe that it ensures too

---

[71] *Id.* at 60 (Stevens, J., dissenting).
[72] 131 S. Ct. 2507 (2011).
[73] *Id.* at 2518.
[74] *Id.* at 2519.
[75] 419 U.S. 565 (1975).
[76] *Id.* at 579 (emphasis in original).
[77] *Id.* at 581.

much protection. From the former perspective, notice of the charges and an opportunity to explain to a school administrator is unlikely to provide much protection for the student. From the latter perspective, *Goss* is undue judicial interference with school discipline that will disrupt school administration.[78]

In subsequent cases, the Court seemed to sympathize with the latter perspective and minimized the procedural protections required. For instance, in *Ingraham v. Wright*, the Court held that the imposition of corporal punishment involves a deprivation of liberty, but did not require that the school provide any type of due process prior to its imposition.[79] The Court recognized that liberty includes "freedom from bodily restraint and punishment" and that therefore where school authorities "deliberately decide to punish a child for misconduct by restraining the child and inflicting appreciable physical pain, . . . Fourteenth Amendment liberty interests are implicated."[80]

Yet the Court refused to require that the school provide any procedures with regard to the imposition of corporal punishment. The Court said that it was sufficient for due process that the state provided tort law remedies against abuses. The Court emphasized that "[h]earings—even informal hearings—require time, personnel, and a diversion of attention from normal school pursuits. School authorities may well choose to abandon corporal punishment rather than incur the burdens of complying with the procedural requirements."[81] The Court thus felt that tort suits against abuses were adequate to meet the Constitution's requirement for due process.

It can be questioned whether the decision in *Ingraham* gives sufficient weight to the importance of due process prior to the imposition of corporal punishment. A hearing prior to paddling might prevent the erroneous imposition of pain. A tort suit afterward cannot eliminate the pain already suffered.[82]

The Court's deference to educational institutions also was evident in its decision in *Board of Curators v. Horowitz*.[83] *Horowitz* involved a medical student who was dismissed because of perceived poor clinical performance and who argued that due process was required with regard to the dismissal. The student had been placed on probation and was evaluated by a panel of seven doctors who found her performance inadequate. The decision to expel the student from the medical school program was then approved by the dean and a university administrator.

The Supreme Court found that this was adequate to meet due process even though no hearing was provided to the student. The Court perceived the matter as involving academic judgment and therefore was distinguishable from a disciplinary proceeding such as that involved in *Goss*. The Court declined to "formalize the academic dismissal process by requiring a hearing . . . [and] to further enlarge the

---

[78]   *See id.* at 591-596 (Powell, J., dissenting).

[79]   430 U.S. 651 (1977). The Court also held that the imposition of corporal punishment was not cruel and unusual punishment in violation of the Eighth Amendment.

[80]   *Id.* at 674.

[81]   *Id.* at 680.

[82]   *See id.* at 695 (White, J., dissenting).

[83]   435 U.S. 78 (1978).

judicial presence in the academic community and thereby risk deterioration of many beneficial aspects of faculty-student relationship."[84]

The deference evident in cases such as *Ingraham* and *Horowitz* mirrors a shift to great deference to school authorities in other constitutional areas as well. For example, the Supreme Court has evidenced great deference to schools in punishing students for their speech[85] and in allowing random drug testing of students.[86] The underlying question is whether this is necessary deference to the expertise of school officials or whether it needlessly compromises the rights of students and fails to provide adequate protection against arbitrary actions.

Children's Rights

Even outside the school context, the Court generally has required less in the way of procedural due process when children are deprived of liberty than when adults suffer the same deprivation. For example, although the Supreme Court has held that civil commitment of an adult requires notice and a hearing except in exigent circumstances,[87] the Court has ruled that a state may permit parents to commit their children without such protections.[88] The Court said that it assumes that parents act in the best interests of their children, even if the parent is institutionalizing the child. A child is entitled only to a screening by a health professional or other neutral fact-finder before commitment. No adversarial hearing is required even though the consequence of commitment is that the child will be involuntary institutionalized.

In *Schall v. Martin*, the Supreme Court upheld a state law that provided for pretrial detention of juveniles accused of serious crimes.[89] The Court emphasized that the detention was not punitive, did not involve sending the child to prison, and was accompanied by a prompt hearing. The Court expressly applied the *Mathews* test and acknowledged that confinement was a significant deprivation of liberty. The Court, however, felt that the procedures in the statute protected against erroneous deprivation of liberty because there was notice, a right to an expedited hearing with the ability to be represented by an attorney, and the right to counsel. Finally, the Court emphasized the importance of the government's interest in "protecting both the community and the juvenile himself from the consequences of future criminal conduct."[90]

---

[84]   *Id.* at 90. *See also Regents of University of Michigan v. Ewing,* 474 U.S. 214 (1985), where the Court held that in dismissing a medical school student, the university was not obligated to allow the student a second chance to take a standardized test. *Ewing* did not involve a procedural due process question, but rather seemed to be about the substantive due process issue of whether the school's action was so arbitrary as to be unconstitutional.

[85]   *See, e.g.,* Morse v. Frederick, 551 U.S. 393 (2007); Bethel School Dist. No. 403 v. Fraser, 478 U.S. 675 (1986), discussed in §11.4.4.

[86]   *See, e.g.,* Board of Educ. of Indep. School Dist. No. 92 of Pottowatomie County v. Earls, 536 U.S. 822 (2002); Vernonia School Dist. 47J v. Acton, 515 U.S. 646 (1995).

[87]   Addington v. Texas, 441 U.S. 418 (1979).

[88]   Parham v. J.R., 442 U.S. 584 (1979).

[89]   467 U.S. 253 (1984).

[90]   *Id.* at 264.

The underlying question in evaluating these cases is whether it is justifiable to treat children differently from adults in these circumstances. Is it appropriate to assume that parents will act in their children's best interests when institutionalizing them; or is there too great a danger that a parent and a cooperative doctor might institutionalize a child without sufficient reasons? Is it appropriate to allow a child to be subjected to pretrial detention prior to conviction in circumstances where it would not be allowed for an adult so as to protect the child and the community; or is this an impermissible deprivation of liberty without due process? In many contexts, the Supreme Court has recognized lesser rights for children.[91] The question here is whether this is appropriate when the deprivation is as fundamental as confinement.

Prisoners' Rights

As described earlier, the Supreme Court has found that those on probation and parole have liberty interests in avoiding revocation of these privileges. The Court also has found that prisoners have liberty interests under certain circumstances, although this has been narrowed by the Supreme Court's decision in *Sandin v. Conner.*[92] In instances where the Court has found a deprivation of liberty, the Court's conclusion as to the degree of due process required has varied enormously depending on the setting. In transfers of a prisoner from a prison to a mental facility, the Court has required extensive procedural protections. In contrast, in imposition of prison discipline, the Court has found relatively informal procedures to be sufficient. The Court has considered the degree of procedures required in parole and probation revocation hearings, parole determinations, prison discipline, and the administration of psychiatric confinement and treatment for prisoners. Each is examined in turn.

In *Morrissey v. Brewer*, the Supreme Court held that in a preliminary hearing for revocation of probation or parole, a probationer or parolee is entitled to notice of the alleged violation of probation or parole, an opportunity to appear and to present evidence in his own behalf, a conditional right to confront adverse witnesses, an independent decision maker, and a written report of the hearing.[93] The Court found that a final hearing on parole or probation revocation must provide even more elaborate procedural protections. The Court said that at the time of the final determination there must be

> (a) written notice of the claimed violations . . . ;
> (b) disclosure to the [probationer or] parolee of the evidence against him;

---

[91] *See, e.g.,* Morse v. Frederick, 551 U.S. 393 (2007); Vernonia School Dist. 47J v. Acton, 515 U.S. 646 (1995); Bethel School Dist. v. Fraser, 478 U.S. 675 (1986).

[92] 515 U.S. 472 (1995), discussed above in §7.3.3.

[93] 408 U.S. 471, 486-487 (1972).

(c) [the] opportunity to be heard in person and to present witnesses and documentary evidence;

(d) the right to confront and cross-examine adverse witnesses (unless the hearing officer specifically finds good cause for not allowing confrontation);

(e) a neutral and detached hearing body such as a traditional parole board, members of which need not be judicial officers or lawyers; and

(f) a written statement by the factfinders as to the evidence relied on and reasons for revoking [probation or] parole.[94]

In *Gagnon v. Scarpelli*, however, the Court held that there was no automatic right to an attorney at probation revocation hearings.[95] The Court said that the decision "as to the need for counsel must be made on a case-by-case basis in the exercise of a sound discretion by the state authority charged with responsibility for administering the probation and parole system."[96] This is similar to the Court's approach to the provision of counsel to indigent parents at parental termination proceedings in the *Lassiter* case described above: There is no automatic right to an attorney, but the court should provide one to indigents where it appears important to do so.

The Supreme Court has found that relatively informal proceedings suffice when a prisoner has a liberty interest in a determination of eligibility for parole. In *Greenholtz v. Inmates of Nebraska Penal and Correctional Complex*, the Court found that the state law had created a liberty interest in parole determinations, but said that the existing system of notice and hearing was sufficient for due process.[97] The inmates objected that they were given notice only of the month of their hearing and did not know the exact date until the day of the proceedings. The Supreme Court said that this was permissible notice because "[t]here is no claim that either the timing of the notice or its substance seriously prejudices the inmate's ability to prepare adequately for the hearing."[98]

Moreover, the Court in *Greenholtz* approved the decision-making process even though it did not involve a formal hearing. The parole board conducted an initial screening for all inmates eligible for parole, but did not hear evidence at that stage. If the board determined that the inmate was a reasonable candidate for parole, the board would then hold a nonadversarial hearing. The inmate could make a presentation and could be represented by a lawyer, but the inmate did not have the opportunity to hear or respond to the opposing evidence. The parole board issued a written statement of reasons if it denied parole. The Court found that this procedure was sufficient even though a trial-type hearing never was provided. The Court made it clear that a fair procedure must exist, but gave to parole boards great discretion in designing that process and in making the ultimate parole decisions.

---

[94] *Id.* at 489. In *Gagnon v. Scarpelli*, 411 U.S. 778, 786 (1973), the Court approvingly quoted this language and added the word "probationer" every time "parolee" appears.

[95] 411 U.S. 778 (1973).

[96] *Id.* at 790.

[97] 442 U.S. 1 (1979).

[98] *Id.* at 14 n.6.

In *Wolff v. McDonnell*, the Supreme Court refused to recognize a right to counsel at proceedings to revoke a prisoner's good time credits.[99] In *Wolff*, the Court did require that the revocation of good time credits generally must be accompanied by written notice of the charges, an opportunity to call witnesses and present other evidence, and a written statement explaining the ultimate decision.[100] The Court stated that an "inmate facing disciplinary proceedings should be allowed to call witnesses and present documentary evidence in his defense when permitting him to do so will not be unduly hazardous to institutional safety or correctional goals."[101]

However, the Court soon backed away from this and said that it usually would defer to prison officials who determined that allowing the inmate to call witnesses would be disruptive.[102] The Court explained that precluding the calling of witnesses was permissible so long as there was not evidence that prison officials were abusing their discretion.

The Court has required notice and a hearing before a prisoner is transferred from a prison to a mental hospital or before antipsychotic medications are involuntarily administered. In *Vitek v. Jones*, the Supreme Court held that the transfer of a prisoner from a prison to a mental hospital was a deprivation of liberty.[103] The Court affirmed the order of the district court that held that before such a transfer could occur there had to be

(a) written notice to the prisoner that the transfer was being considered;

(b) a hearing at which the evidence justifying the transfer is presented and where there is the opportunity for the prisoner to cross-examine and to present witnesses;

(c) an attorney to represent the prisoner, including one supplied by the government if the inmate was indigent;

(d) an impartial decision maker; and

(e) a written decision with a statement of the evidence relied upon and the reasons for approving the transfer.[104]

Vitek is striking in how much more it required in procedural protections than any of the other cases concerning prisoners' rights. Indeed, few cases involving procedural due process in any context have required this much. Most notably, this is one of the few instances, outside criminal trials, where the Court has required the government to provide indigent individuals with an attorney. This reflects the Court's judgment as to the severity of the deprivation of liberty if a prisoner is transferred to a mental hospital and also its concern that the mentally ill inmate may be unable to represent himself or herself.[105]

---

[99] 418 U.S. 539, 569-570 (1974).

[100] *Id.* at 539.

[101] *Id.* at 566.

[102] Baxter v. Palmigiano, 425 U.S. 308 (1976).

[103] 445 U.S. 480 (1980).

[104] *Id.* at 494-495.

[105] *Id.* at 496-497. The Court said: "A prisoner thought to be suffering from a mental disease or defect requiring involuntary treatment probably has an even greater need for legal assistance,

§7.4 What Procedures Are Required?

In *Washington v. Harper*, the Court found that prisoners have a liberty interest in avoiding the involuntary administration of antipsychotic medications.[106] The Court concluded that due process was satisfied because the prison provided the inmate notice of the intent to administer the drugs, a hearing at which there was the opportunity to present evidence and cross-examine witnesses, independent decision makers in doctors and prison officials who were not otherwise involved in the treatment decision, and judicial review of the panel's decision. The Court expressly applied the *Mathews* test and analogized to *Vitek v. Jones* in concluding that these procedures were constitutionally adequate.

Finally, in *Wilkinson v. Austin*,[107] the Supreme Court held that placing a prisoner in a super-max facility is a deprivation of liberty.[108] But the Court applied the *Mathews* test to conclude that due process was met by the Ohio system because there were criteria specifying when an individual could be placed in such a facility, there was a requirement of notifying the inmate of the reasons for the confinement, there was the opportunity for a hearing to contest the placement, and there were three levels of administrative review.

The range of procedures required for prisoners can be understood as reflecting the Court's sense about the severity of the deprivation. In instances where the Court perceives a more serious deprivation, such as revocation of probation or parole or the transfer of a prisoner to a mental hospital or administration of antipsychotic medications, the Court requires more procedural protections. In instances where the Court regards the deprivation as more minor, such as the administration of discipline within a prison, the Court requires less procedural protections. Yet the Court can be criticized for not recognizing the need for more protection when parole decisions are made or good time credits are revoked because these choices can make the difference for an inmate between remaining incarcerated or going free.

Punitive Damages

In the 1990s, there were a number of Supreme Court cases involving due process challenges to punitive damage awards.[109] The Supreme Court has held that punitive damage awards require procedural safeguards such as instructions to the jury to guide the exercise of their discretion, judicial review of the award to ensure its reasonableness, and appellate review. Also, the Court has ruled that grossly excessive punitive damage awards deny due process.

---

for such a prisoner is more likely to be unable to understand or exercise his rights. In these circumstances, it is appropriate that counsel be provided to indigent prisoners whom the State seeks to treat as mentally ill."

[106] 494 U.S. 210 (1990).

[107] 545 U.S. 209 (2005).

[108] This aspect of the decision is discussed above in §7.3.3.

[109] In *Browning Ferris Indus., Inc. v. Kelco Disposal, Inc.*, 492 U.S. 257 (1989), the Court held that large punitive damage awards cannot be challenged as violating the excessive fines clause of the Eighth Amendment, but the Court left open the question of whether they could be challenged under due process.

In *Pacific Mutual Life Insurance Co. v. Haslip*, the Supreme Court upheld a punitive damage award 200 times the size of the actual loss.[110] A woman purchased health insurance, but the agent pocketed the premiums rather than providing the policy. When the woman was hospitalized, she discovered that she did not have insurance and sued the agent and also sued the company on a respondeat superior basis. The jury awarded punitive damages against the company 200 times the size of her loss. The Supreme Court upheld the award. The Court emphasized that there was a long history of punitive damages in our legal system and that there were adequate procedural safeguards to protect against unreasonable awards. The Court emphasized the judge's instructions to the jury and the availability of judicial review of damage awards at both the trial and the appellate levels.

Similarly, in *TXO Production Corp. v. Alliance Resources Corp.*, the Court upheld a very large punitive damage award: one that was 500 times the size of the compensatory damages.[111] A Texas company filed a quit claim on a piece of property in West Virginia. The West Virginia company defended its ownership and also filed a counterclaim for malicious prosecution. The company sought punitive damages on the counterclaim, which the jury granted. The jury awarded $19,000 in compensatory damages and $10 million in punitive damages. There was no majority opinion for the Court, but Justice Stevens's plurality emphasized that punitive damage awards are not to be deemed unconstitutional simply based on their size compared to the compensatory damages. Justice Stevens emphasized that punitive damages were to be upheld so long as there were procedural safeguards such as instructions to the jury and judicial review to ensure reasonableness.

In *Honda Motor Corp. v. Oberg*, the Court declared unconstitutional an Oregon law that precluded appellate review of punitive damage awards.[112] A provision of the Oregon constitution essentially prohibited the appellate court from overturning a jury's damage awards. The Supreme Court declared this unconstitutional and again emphasized that punitive damage awards are limited by due process and that the constraint is procedural. Appellate review, the Court said, is an essential constitutional prerequisite.

Thus, up until 1996, the Court dealt with the issue of punitive damages entirely from a procedural perspective. But in *BMW of North America, Inc. v. Gore*, the Court found that a punitive damage award of $2 million against BMW for repainting automobiles without disclosing that to customers was "grossly excessive."[113] A doctor paid $40,000 for a new BMW only to discover later that part of the car had been repainted because of acid rain damage and that he had not been informed of this when purchasing the car. He sued BMW, and the jury awarded him $4,000 in compensatory damages and $4 million in punitive damages, which the Alabama Supreme Court reduced to $2 million.

---

[110] 499 U.S. 1 (1991).
[111] 509 U.S. 443 (1993).
[112] 512 U.S. 415 (1994).
[113] 517 U.S. 559 (1996).

§7.4 What Procedures Are Required?

The Court, in an opinion by Justice Stevens, concluded that grossly excessive punitive damages deny due process.[114] The Court, in a 5-to-4 decision, ruled that it is impermissible for a jury in one state to award punitive damages for conduct in other states that is lawful in those places. Justice Stevens explained that "it follows from . . . principles of state sovereignty and comity that a State may not impose economic sanctions on violators of its laws with the intent of changing the tortfeasors' lawful conduct in other States."[115]

Moreover, the Court articulated three criteria to be used in evaluating whether a punitive damages award is grossly excessive. First, what is the degree of "reprehensibility" of the defendant's conduct?[116] Obviously, the more reprehensible—the more fraudulent or malicious—the behavior, the greater the sum of punitive damages that are justified. Second, what is the ratio of punitive damages to the actual harm suffered by the plaintiff?[117] Although earlier cases, such as *Haslip* and *TXO*, establish that the ratio is not decisive by itself, the Court indicated that the ratio is an important factor to be considered. Finally, what are the sanctions for comparable misconduct on other state laws?[118] The larger the disparity between the punitive damages and other possible sanctions for the behavior, the more likely it is that a punitive damages award will be found excessive.[119]

BMW of North America, Inc. v. Gore is thus important in that it is the first time that a punitive damages award has been found excessive by the Supreme Court. It also is significant in that the Court articulated criteria for determining when punitive damage awards are grossly excessive and limited the ability of a jury to award punitive damages for a defendant's conduct in other states.[120]

In *State Farm Mutual Automobile Insurance Co. v. Campbell*, the Supreme Court reaffirmed *Gore*'s holding that grossly excessive punitive damage awards violate due process and clarified the three-part test articulated in *Gore*.[121] *Campbell* involved a claim against a national automobile insurance company for bad faith and fraud in refusing to settle a claim. The jury awarded $1 million in compensatory damages and $145 million in punitive damages. The Supreme Court, however, found that the award of punitive damages was grossly excessive.

Justice Kennedy wrote the majority opinion in the 6-to-3 decision. Justice Kennedy applied the three-part test articulated in *BMW v. Gore*. First, the Court

---

[114] *Id.* at 568.

[115] *Id.* at 572.

[116] *Id.* at 575.

[117] *Id.* at 580.

[118] *Id.* at 583.

[119] In *United States v. Bajakajian*, 524 U.S. 321 (1998), the Supreme Court invalidated a government forfeiture as unconstitutional under the excessive fines clause of the Eighth Amendment. Although the Court used this provision, rather than due process, its analysis was very similar to that in *BMW v. Gore* in that the Court said that the test was "gross disproportionality" and considered factors such as the seriousness of the offense and other punishments that could be imposed for the conduct.

[120] After *BMW v. Gore*, the Court held that the determination of whether a punitive damages award is "grossly excessive" is a question of law and therefore is to be reviewed *de novo* by a federal court of appeals. Cooper v. Leatherman Tool Co., 532 U.S. 424 (2001).

[121] 538 U.S. 408 (2003).

again said that reprehensibility is the most important consideration. The Court found that State Farm's fraud was relatively low on the reprehensibility scale. More important, the Court stressed that the jury was wrong in punishing State Farm for its conduct outside Utah, where the claim arose. The Court explained: "A State cannot punish a defendant for conduct that may have been lawful where it occurred. Nor, as a general rule, does a State have a legitimate concern in imposing punitive damages to punish a defendant for unlawful acts committed outside the State's jurisdiction."[122] In other words, punitive damages are now limited to punishing a defendant for that type of conduct in that state.

Second, the Court again said that it is appropriate in determining the reasonableness of a punitive damage award to consider the "ratio between harm, or potential harm, to the plaintiff and the punitive damage award."[123] The Court stressed that it "decline[s] again to impose a bright-line ratio which a punitive damage award cannot exceed."[124] But then, in language that has caused great confusion in the lower courts, Justice Kennedy stated: "Our jurisprudence and the principles it has now established demonstrate, however, that, in practice, few awards exceeding a single-digit ratio between punitive and compensatory damages, to a significant degree, will satisfy due process."[125] Of course, the crucial question after *Campbell*, and one where there has been no further clarification from the Court, is when a larger ratio is permissible. The Court emphatically did not prohibit all ratios greater than single digits, but it said that only rarely would ratios significantly greater than that be upheld. The Court indicated that ratios greater than single digits would be allowed "where a particularly egregious act has resulted in only a small amount of economic damages."[126] But what circumstances would justify which ratios is left for further cases to clarify.

Finally, the Court briefly discussed the third prong of the *BMW v. Gore* test: other punishments in the jurisdiction for the conduct. The Court said that the fact that State Farm's conduct would be criminal fraud was relevant in assessing the seriousness with which the state regards the defendant's conduct. However, the Court said that "[g]reat care" must be taken "to avoid use of the civil process to assess criminal penalties that can be imposed only after the heightened protections of a criminal trial have been observed."[127] The Court said that "[p]unitive damages are not a substitute for the criminal process, and the remote possibility of criminal sanction does not automatically sustain a punitive damage award."[128]

State Farm v. Campbell clarifies the law, but also creates great uncertainty: What conduct of a defendant in the state can be considered in imposing punitive damages? When are ratios greater than single digits allowed? What relevance do criminal penalties have in assessing the constitutionality of a punitive damage award? There are already dozens of lower court decisions on these questions, often with

---

[122] *Id.* at 421.
[123] *Id.* at 424.
[124] *Id.* at 425.
[125] *Id.*
[126] *Id.*
[127] *Id.* at 428.
[128] *Id.*

conflicting answers, and there obviously will be the need for future clarification by the Supreme Court.

The Court returned to the issue of punitive damages in *Philip Morris USA v. Williams*.[129] A jury awarded the widow of a smoker a damage award against a tobacco company of $800,000 in compensatory damages and $79.5 million in punitive damages. The Supreme Court held that this award violated due process because it punished the defendant for harms suffered by individuals other than the plaintiff. Justice Breyer, writing for the Court in a 5-4 decision, stated: "In our view, the Constitution's Due Process Clause forbids a State to use a punitive damages award to punish a defendant for injury that it inflicts upon nonparties or those whom they directly represent, *i.e.*, injury that it inflicts upon those who are, essentially, strangers to the litigation."[130] This is a major new substantive limit on punitive damages: They may be imposed only to punish a defendant for the harms suffered by that plaintiff and not for harms incurred by others who are not part of the litigation.

However, the Court said that a jury in considering the reprehensibility of a defendant's conduct may consider the extent of harm to third parties. The Court explained: "Respondent argues that she is free to show harm to other victims because it is relevant to a different part of the punitive damages constitutional equation, namely, reprehensibility. That is to say, harm to others shows more reprehensible conduct. Philip Morris, in turn, does not deny that a plaintiff may show harm to others in order to demonstrate reprehensibility. Nor do we. Evidence of actual harm to nonparties can help to show that the conduct that harmed the plaintiff also posed a substantial risk of harm to the general public, and so was particularly reprehensible—although counsel may argue in a particular case that conduct resulting in no harm to others nonetheless posed a grave risk to the public, or the converse. Yet for the reasons given above, a jury may not go further than this and use a punitive damages verdict to punish a defendant directly on account of harms it is alleged to have visited on nonparties."[131]

Although conceptually such a distinction can be drawn, it is likely to cause serious confusion for juries. A jury cannot base its punitive damages on harm to third parties, but it may consider harm to third parties in assessing the reprehensibility of a defendant's conduct.

The Court remanded the case to the Oregon courts for reconsideration in light of its decision. The Oregon courts reaffirmed the entire punitive damage award, concluding that the defendant had not properly objected under state law requirements. The Supreme Court once more granted review, but then after oral argument dismissed the case as certiorari having been improvidently granted.[132]

The final case thus far to consider punitive damages did so in the context not of due process, but of maritime law. In *Exxon Shipping Co. v. Baker*, the Court held that in admiralty law there cannot be more than a 1:1 ratio between compensatory

---

[129] 549 U.S. 306 (2007).
[130] *Id.* at 353.
[131] *Id.* at 355.
[132] 556 U.S. 178 (2009).

and punitive damages.[133] The case arose from the Exxon Valdez oil spill. A jury awarded $507 million in compensatory damages and $5 billion in punitive damages, which was ultimately reduced by the federal Court of Appeals to $2.5 billion. The Supreme Court reversed this and held that under maritime law punitive damages cannot be greater than the compensatory damages.

Although the Court focused exclusively on maritime law and did not invoke the Constitution, its reasoning was not based on admiralty or maritime principles. Rather, Justice Souter, writing for the Court, expressed concern about the great discretion that juries have in deciding the amount of punitive damages. He said that there is not evidence of significant "runaway" punitive damage awards, but stated that "[t]he real problem, it seems, is the stark unpredictability of punitive awards."[134] The solution, the Court decided, is to limit punitive damages to no more than the amount of compensatory damages in maritime cases. The Court stated: "A punitive-to-compensatory ratio of 1:1 thus yields maximum punitive damages in that amount."[135]

Undoubtedly, the Court will return to the issue of punitive damages in the years ahead and the presence of new Justices could cause a reexamination of the law in this area. For example, *Williams* was a 5-4 decision, with Justice Souter in the majority. This is an area where ideology does not predict votes; Justices Souter and Breyer were in the majority in the opinions limiting punitive damages, with Justices Scalia and Thomas in dissent. The two newest Justices—Sotomayor and Kagan—have not yet participated in a punitive damages case and their positions can change the direction of the law in this area.

Creditors' Claims

In a series of cases, the Supreme Court has considered what procedures must be followed when creditors assert remedies against debtors such as garnishment of wages, replevin of goods, and prejudgment attachment. In all instances, the Supreme Court held that due process is required, although the procedures vary depending on the nature of the remedy sought.

In *Sniadach v. Family Finance Corp. of Bay View*, the Supreme Court declared unconstitutional a Wisconsin statute that permitted a creditor to garnish a person's wages without a judgment and without any notice or hearing.[136] The Court emphasized that garnishment is a remedy "which may impose tremendous hardship on wage earners with families to support."[137] The Court also expressed concern over the "grave injustices" that can result when there is no hearing until after the garnishment occurs.[138] Therefore, the Court held that absent notice and a prior hearing, prejudgment garnishment violates due process.

---

[133] 554 U.S. 471 (2008).
[134] *Id.* at 499.
[135] *Id.* at 515.
[136] 395 U.S. 337 (1969).
[137] *Id.* at 340.
[138] *Id.*

§7.4 What Procedures Are Required?

The cases have been inconsistent in dealing with attempts by creditors to take personal property without due process. In *Fuentes v. Shevin*, the Supreme Court applied *Sniadach* to creditor's replevin of goods and held that this procedure also required due process before it occurs.[139] State replevin laws in Florida and Pennsylvania permitted businesses to have goods seized through an ex parte application and the posting of a bond. The Court concluded that the "prejudgment replevin provisions work a deprivation of property without due process of law insofar as they deny the right to a prior opportunity to be heard before chattels are taken from their possessor."[140] Although the Court said that the hearing must provide a "real test," it also said that the "nature and form of such prior hearings . . . are legitimately open to many potential variations."[141] The Court also recognized that there are "extraordinary situations that justify postponing notice and opportunity for a hearing," but the Court said that these must be "truly unusual."[142]

However, in *Mitchell v. W.T. Grant Co.*, the Court approved a Louisiana law that allowed a creditor to have goods sequestered based on an ex parte procedure.[143] The law allowed creditors to seize and sequester goods if the following procedures were present: a detailed affidavit, a requirement that a judge rather than a clerk make the determination that issuance of the writ was appropriate, and an immediate postdeprivation hearing including the possibility of damages for wrongful sequestration.[144] The Court distinguished *Fuentes* based on these detailed procedures that were present in the Louisiana law, but not in the Florida and Pennsylvania statutes considered in *Fuentes*. The Court said that *Fuentes* was decided against "a factual and legal background sufficiently different . . . that it does not require the invalidation of the Louisiana sequestration statute."[145]

Yet there obviously is tension between *Fuentes* and *Mitchell*: The former says that prejudgment replevin requires a predeprivation hearing; the latter says that it does not, so long as there are adequate safeguards. The Court acknowledged this tension and attempted to reconcile the cases in *North Georgia Finishing, Inc. v. Di-Chem, Inc.*[146] Relying on *Fuentes*, the Court declared unconstitutional a Georgia law that allowed a creditor to garnish the property of a debtor without notice or a prior hearing, without a detailed affidavit, without a decision by a judge, and without a requirement for a prompt postdeprivation hearing.[147]

It appears that after *North Georgia Finishing* a state law is required to provide for notice and a hearing before it allows a remedy such as a prejudgment replevin, sequestration, or garnishment of property, unless there is a very detailed postdeprivation remedy such as in *Mitchell*. For the postdeprivation remedy to be adequate, it must require that before any replevin, sequestration, or garnishment of

---

[139] 407 U.S. 67 (1972).
[140] *Id.* at 96.
[141] *Id.*
[142] *Id.* at 90.
[143] 416 U.S. 600 (1974).
[144] *Id.* at 615-619.
[145] *Id.* at 615.
[146] 419 U.S. 601 (1975).
[147] *Id.* at 606-608.

property there must be a detailed affidavit, a decision by a judge to issue the writ, the posting of a bond, and a prompt postdeprivation hearing.

Subsequently, in *Connecticut v. Doehr*, the Supreme Court held unconstitutional a state law allowing prejudgment attachment of real property without prior notice or hearing and without a showing of exigent circumstances.[148] The Connecticut law permitted a judge to allow the prejudgment attachment of real estate without prior notice or hearing based on the plaintiff's affidavit that there is probable cause to sustain the validity of the claim. The Court applied the *Mathews* test and declared this unconstitutional. The Court said that under the first prong of the *Mathews* test, important interests of the individual are at stake in prejudgment attachment. The Court explained: "[T]he property interests that attachment affects are significant. For a property owner like Doehr, attachment ordinarily clouds title; impairs the ability to sell or otherwise alienate the property; taints any credit rating; reduces the chance of obtaining a home equity loan or additional mortgage; and can even place an existing mortgage in technical default."[149]

As to the second part of the *Mathews* test, the Court concluded that under the Connecticut law "the risk of erroneous deprivation . . . is substantial."[150] The Court distinguished *Mitchell* as involving quite different circumstances. The Court said that in *Mitchell*, "the plaintiff had a vendor's lien to protect, the risk of error was minimal because the likelihood of recovery involved uncomplicated matters that lent themselves to documentary proof, and the plaintiff was required to put up a bond."[151]

Finally, as to the last part of the *Mathews* test, the Court found that there was no government interest in allowing prejudgment attachment without due process. The Court emphasized that there were no additional financial or administrative burdens for the state because it already was providing immediate postdeprivation hearings.

The Court indicated that prejudgment attachment without notice and hearing would be allowed only if there were exigent circumstances that provided a reason to believe there are extraordinary and compelling circumstances. For example, prejudgment attachment without prior notice and a hearing would be allowed if there were specific reasons to believe that the debtor would dissipate the assets if given notice and a hearing before attachment.[152]

All of these cases, from *Sniadach* to *Doehr*, reflect the Court's recognition of the enormous harms that can result to an individual from prejudgment garnishment, replevin, or attachment. The Court also clearly realizes that there is a great risk of erroneous deprivation if these remedies can be imposed ex parte without prior notice and a hearing. Thus, unless there are exigent circumstances, the Court almost always has required notice and a hearing prior to the remedy being imposed.

---

[148] 501 U.S. 1 (1991).
[149] *Id.* at 11.
[150] *Id.* at 12.
[151] *Id.* at 15 (citation omitted).
[152] Although the majority of the Court did not reach the issue, four of the Justices—White, Marshall, Stevens, and O'Connor—went on to say that due process requires the posting of a bond or other security in addition to requiring a hearing or a showing of exigent circumstances. *Id.* at 18-19.

Forfeiture Proceedings

One of the major changes in American law in recent decades has been the tremendous growth in the number of laws that allow government forfeiture proceedings.[153] In *United States v. James Daniel Good Real Property*, the Supreme Court held that absent exigent circumstances, due process requires the government to provide notice and a hearing before seizing real property pursuant to civil forfeiture.[154] An individual in Hawaii was convicted in state court of violating the Hawaii marijuana and hashish law and sentenced to a year in jail, five years' probation, and fined $1,000. Four and a half years later, the United States brought an in rem action in federal court seeking to forfeit the person's house and the property on which it was located because it had been used to commit or facilitate a drug offense. An ex parte proceeding was held, and a federal magistrate authorized the seizure.

The Supreme Court applied the *Mathews* test and held that except in exigent circumstances, there must be notice and a meaningful opportunity to be heard before there is government seizure of real property.[155] As to the first part of the test, the Court noted that a person's right "to maintain control over his home, and to be free from governmental interference, is a private interest of historic and continuing importance."[156] Under the second part of the *Mathews* test, the Court said that "[t]he practice of ex parte seizure . . . creates an unacceptable risk of error."[157] The Court explained that an ex parte proceeding provides little or no protection for the innocent owner or for instances where the government makes a mistake.

Finally, as to the last prong of the *Mathews* test, the Court found that requiring notice and a hearing before seizure would impose little burden on the government. The Court said: "Requiring the Government to postpone seizure until after an adversary hearing creates no significant administrative burden. A claimant is already entitled to an adversary hearing before a final judgment of forfeiture. No extra hearing would be required in the typical case, since the Government can wait until after the forfeiture judgment to seize the property."[158]

The Court said that the government can seize real property without notice and a hearing only if there are extraordinary exigent circumstances. The Court said, however, that "[t]o establish exigent circumstances, the Government must show that less restrictive measures—i.e., a lis pendens, restraining order, or bond—would not suffice to protect the Government's interests in preventing the sale, destruction, or continued unlawful use of the real property."[159]

---

[153] The Court has held that the size of such forfeitures is limited by the excessive fines clause of the Eighth Amendment. Austin v. United States, 509 U.S. 602 (1993); *see also* United States v. Bajakajian, 524 U.S. 321 (1998).

[154] 510 U.S. 43 (1993).

[155] *Id.*

[156] *Id.* at 53-54.

[157] *Id.* at 55.

[158] *Id.* at 54.

[159] *Id.* at 55.

However, the Court has concluded that due process does not require that there be an innocent owner defense in government forfeiture proceedings.[160] John Bennis was arrested for having sex with a prostitute in his automobile. Bennis was convicted of gross indecency. Additionally, a Michigan court ordered the car forfeited as a public nuisance because it had been used in committing the crime. The automobile, however, was jointly owned with Bennis's wife, Tina Bennis. She argued that due process was violated by the state's failure to accord her an innocent owner defense to the seizure.

In a 5-to-4 decision, with Chief Justice Rehnquist writing the majority opinion, the Court ruled in favor of the state and rejected this due process claim. Rehnquist wrote that "a long and unbroken line of cases holds that an owner's interest in property may be forfeited by reason of the use to which the property is put even though the owner did not know that it was to be put to such use."[161] The Court said that the forfeiture action was permissible because "[t]he State here sought to deter illegal activity that contributes to neighborhood deterioration and unsafe streets. The Bennis automobile, it is conceded, facilitated and was used in criminal activity."[162] In other words, property being used in a crime is subject to forfeiture even if the owner did not consent or know of that use.

Justice Stevens wrote a vehement dissent. He emphasized that the car was incidental to the crime and that "[t]he logic of the Court's analysis would permit the States to exercise virtually unbridled power to confiscate vast amounts of property where professional criminals have engaged in illegal acts."[163] Stevens argued that forfeitures are appropriately directed at contraband or at the proceeds of criminal activity or at the tools of a criminal's trade. The car used for the act of prostitution in *Bennis* fit into none of these categories. Moreover, Stevens said that the seizure was unconstitutional because Tina Bennis "is entirely without responsibility for that act. Fundamental fairness prohibits the punishment of innocent people."[164]

Subsequently, the Court in *United States v. Bajakajian*,[165] considered when forfeitures are so large as to be unconstitutional as an excessive fine in violation of the Eighth Amendment. Although the Court used the excessive fines clause and not due process, the analysis was very similar to that used to evaluate whether punitive damages are unconstitutional. *Bajakajian* involved an individual who violated the federal law that requires reporting if a person is leaving the country with more than $10,000 in cash. Bajakajian was caught exiting with $357,000, which he claimed to be his life savings. The government took the entire amount in a forfeiture action.

---

[160] Bennis v. Michigan, 516 U.S. 442 (1996). In 1996, the Court also ruled that government forfeiture proceedings do not have double jeopardy consequences and hence do not bar subsequent criminal actions for the same conduct; nor are forfeitures precluded by earlier criminal prosecutions. United States v. Ursery, 518 U.S. 267 (1996).

[161] *Bennis*, 516 U.S. at 446.

[162] *Id.* at 453.

[163] *Id.* at 458 (Stevens, J., dissenting).

[164] *Id.* at 466.

[165] 524 U.S. 321 (1998).

§7.4 What Procedures Are Required?

The Supreme Court, in a 5-to-4 decision, found that the forfeiture was unconstitutional because it was "grossly disproportionate" to the offense. Justice Thomas wrote the opinion for the Court, joined by Justices Stevens, Souter, Ginsburg, and Breyer. Justice Thomas's majority opinion stressed that even though the courts generally should defer to government forfeitures, there is a constitutional limit. Here the Court found the forfeiture to be "grossly disproportionate" in light of the minor nature of the offense, the small penalties provided for in the criminal statute, and the amount taken by the government.

Most recently, in *Kaley v. United States*, the Court considered whether individuals had a due process right to challenge the sufficiency of the basis for a grand jury indictment when it resulted in the seizure of property that would prevent them from being able to pay for an attorney.[166] The Court held that when challenging the legality of a pretrial asset seizure, a criminal defendant who has been indicted is not constitutionally entitled to contest a grand jury's determination of probable cause to believe the defendant committed the crimes charged. Justice Kagan, writing for the majority, explained: "A defendant has no right to judicial review of a grand jury's determination of probable cause to think a defendant committed a crime."[167]

The Court then considered the application of the *Mathews* balancing test and concluded that it did not require that there be the opportunity to challenge a grand jury's indictment that resulted in the seizure of property. The Court said "to begin the *Mathews* analysis, the Government has a substantial interest in freezing potentially forfeitable assets without an evidentiary hearing about the probable cause underlying criminal charges. At the least, such an adversarial proceeding—think of it as a pre-trial mini-trial (or maybe a pre-trial not-so-mini-trial)—could consume significant prosecutorial time and resources. The hearing presumably would rehearse the case's merits, including the Government's theory and supporting evidence."[168] The Court acknowledged that the individuals' interest in having the counsel of their choice is "a vital interest."[169]

The Court concluded, though, that under the balancing test due process did not require a hearing to challenge the grand jury indictment: "The *Mathews* test's remaining prong—critical when the governmental and private interests both have weight—thus boils down to the 'probable value, if any,' of a judicial hearing in uncovering mistaken grand jury findings of probable cause. . . . [I]n this context—when the legal standard is merely probable cause and the grand jury has already made that finding—both our precedents and other courts' experience indicate that a full-dress hearing will provide little benefit."[170]

Chief Justice Roberts dissented, joined by Justices Breyer and Sotomayor. They argued that depriving people of the assets to pay for their attorney of choice denied due process. Chief Justice Roberts explained: "Here . . . the Government

---

[166] 134 S. Ct. 1090 (2014).
[167] *Id.* at 1100.
[168] *Id.* at 1101.
[169] *Id.* at 1102.
[170] *Id.* at 1104.

seeks to use the grand jury's probable cause determination to strip the Kaleys of their counsel of choice. The Kaleys can take no comfort that they will be able to vindicate that right in a future adversarial proceeding. Once trial begins with someone other than chosen counsel, the right is lost, and it cannot be restored based on what happens at trial. . . . If the Kaleys are to have any opportunity to meaningfully challenge that deprivation, they must have it before the trial begins."[171]

Conclusion

A review of the cases concerning what procedures are required reveals that everything depends on context and the Court's perception of it. This seems inevitable under the *Mathews* three-part balancing test, which accords enormous discretion in weighing such diverse interests as the importance of the interest to the individual, the ability of additional procedures to increase the accuracy of the fact-finding, and the government's interest in administrative efficiency.

---

[171] *Id.* at 1114 (Roberts, C.J., dissenting).

CHAPTER 8

Economic Liberties

§8.1 INTRODUCTION

What Are Economic Liberties?

Some constitutional rights can be grouped together under the category of "economic liberties." Economic liberties generally refer to constitutional rights concerning the ability to enter into and enforce contracts; to pursue a trade or profession; and to acquire, possess, and convey property.

For example, the contracts clause found in Article I, §10, of the Constitution provides that "no state shall pass any law impairing the obligation of contracts." Also, several constitutional provisions protect property rights. The Fifth Amendment's takings clause states "nor shall private property be taken for public use, without just compensation." The Fifth and Fourteenth Amendments, respectively, provide that neither the federal nor state governments can take a person's property (or life or liberty) without due process of law. At times, the Court also has used the due process clause to protect other economic liberties such as freedom of contract, freedom to pursue a livelihood, and freedom to practice a trade or profession.

This chapter focuses on all of these economic liberties. Material covered in other chapters also is relevant to the topic. For example, Chapter 5 considers the dormant commerce clause and the privileges and immunities clause of Article IV, §2, which limit the ability of states to burden interstate commerce or to discriminate against out-of-staters. Chapter 7 focuses on procedural due process and therefore considers the procedural protections the government must follow before taking away property, life, or liberty. Chapter 9 examines equal protection, which also might be a basis for challenging many economic regulations.

Historical Overview

The framers obviously were concerned about protecting economic rights and thus included in the Constitution provisions such as the contracts clause and the takings clause. Indeed, Charles Beard, in a famous book published early last century, argued that the primary impetus for the Constitution was a desire to protect property and wealth.[1] Although later historians have challenged Beard's analysis and conclusions,[2] there is no doubt that the framers intended to protect economic rights.

The Supreme Court's protection of economic liberties has varied enormously over time. In the early nineteenth century, the Court invoked natural law principles to protect property rights.[3] Also, throughout the nineteenth century, the Court aggressively used the contracts clause to limit the ability of states to interfere with existing contractual obligations.[4]

Beginning in the late nineteenth century and continuing until 1937, the Court found that freedom of contract was a basic right under the liberty and property provisions of the due process clause. During this period of constitutional history, sometimes referred to as the *Lochner* era,[5] the Court aggressively protected economic rights under the due process clause. Many state laws, such as minimum wage and maximum hour statutes, were declared unconstitutional as violating the Fourteenth Amendment by impermissibly interfering with freedom of contract. The contracts clause was not used often during this era; the protection of freedom of contracts under the due process clause made the contracts clause superfluous.

---

§8.1 [1] Charles Beard, An Economic Interpretation of the Constitution (1913).

[2] *See, e.g.,* Forrest McDonald, We the People: The Economic Origins of the Constitution (1958).

[3] Fletcher v. Peck, 10 U.S. (6 Cranch) 87 (1810); Calder v. Bull, 3 U.S. (3 Dall.) 386 (1798), discussed in §8.2.1.

[4] *See* §8.3.

[5] The label comes from the decision in Lochner v. New York, 198 U.S. 45 (1905) (invalidating a maximum hours law for bakers), which is regarded as a paradigm case in the era. *Lochner* is discussed below in §8.2.2.

Freedom of contracts under the due process clause limited the government's ability both to impair existing contracts and to regulate the content of future contracts; the contracts clause always has been confined to the former.

It is extremely important to note that during this same era the Court used federalism to limit the ability of Congress to regulate the economy. From the late nineteenth century until 1937, the Court narrowly defined the scope of Congress's powers under the commerce clause, and it also found that the Tenth Amendment reserved a zone of authority exclusively to the states.[6] In other words, if a state adopted a minimum wage or a maximum hour law, it likely would have been invalidated for violating the due process clause of the Fourteenth Amendment. But if the federal government adopted the same law, it would have been declared unconstitutional as exceeding the scope of Congress's powers or as violating states' rights and the Tenth Amendment. The decisions during this era concerning the scope of Congress's powers are discussed in §3.4.3 and §3.10. Although the doctrines used were different, they were inspired by the same philosophy: a strong commitment to a laissez-faire economy and to protecting business from government regulations.

After 1937, the law changed dramatically, and the Court adopted a policy of great deference to government economic regulations. No longer did the Court protect freedom of contract under the liberty of the due process clause. Nor did the Court impose limits on Congress's ability to regulate the economy based on federalism or on narrow definitions of federal powers.

This reluctance to protect economic liberties also has manifested itself in cases under the contracts clause. Only twice since 1937 has the Court found that any law violates the contracts clause in Article I, §10.[7] However, the Court has used the takings clause to protect property rights.[8]

Organization of the Chapter

Section 8.2 examines economic substantive due process. As described in §7.1, under substantive due process the issue is whether a government action is justified by a sufficient purpose. This is in contrast to procedural due process, discussed in Chapter 7, which focuses on whether the government has provided adequate procedural safeguards in taking away a person's life, liberty, or property.[9] The discussion of substantive due process is placed first simply because it has dominated the Court's approach to economic liberties in the twenty-first century. In the first third of the twentieth century, the Court's use of substantive due process to protect economic rights made most of the other constitutional provisions in the area unnecessary. Since 1937, the Court's tremendous reluctance to use economic

---

[6] Discussed in §3.4.3 and §3.10.

[7] Allied Structural Steel v. Spannaus, 438 U.S. 234 (1978); United States Trust Co. v. New Jersey, 431 U.S. 1 (1977). *See* discussion in §8.3.

[8] Discussed below in §8.4.

[9] For a more detailed discussion of the difference between procedural and substantive due process, *see* §7.1.

substantive due process has been paralleled by a general unwillingness to safe-guard economic liberties.

Section 8.3 focuses on the contracts clause. It briefly describes the Court's active use of this provision in the nineteenth century and then examines contemporary decisions limiting the scope of this clause.

Finally, §8.4 discusses the takings clause. Four major questions are considered: What is a "taking"; what is "property"; when is a taking for "public use"; and what is the requirement for "just compensation"?

Normative Questions

Throughout this chapter the key normative issue concerns the appropriate degree of judicial protection of economic liberties. How important are rights of property and contracting? What was the framers' intent concerning these rights? Does the legislature have a special expertise concerning these rights that justifies a greater degree of judicial deference compared to when the Court deals with political and civil liberties, such as freedom of speech and the right to vote? What, if anything, was wrong with the *Lochner*-era decisions? Since 1937, has the Court unduly or appropriately deferred to government economic regulations?

§8.2   ECONOMIC SUBSTANTIVE DUE PROCESS

§8.2.1   *Economic Substantive Due Process During the Nineteenth Century*

The Early Antecedents: Using Natural Law to Protect Property

In several cases very early in American history, the Supreme Court suggested that the Constitution protected natural rights that a person possesses to own and keep property. In *Calder v. Bull*, the Court considered a Connecticut law that set aside the decision of a probate court that had denied inheritance to those designated as beneficiaries under a will.[1] After the new law was adopted, the probate court changed its ruling and allowed inheritance. The Supreme Court upheld the constitutionality of the law.[2] Although Justice Chase was part of the majority, he expressed the view that the government could neither violate the provisions of the Constitution nor infringe rights that are part of the natural law. Justice Chase wrote: "I cannot subscribe to the omnipotence of a state legislature, or that it is

---

§8.2 [1] 3 U.S. (3 Dall.) 386 (1798).

[2] The Court expressly rejected the argument that the law was an ex post facto law in violation of Article I, §10. The Court said that the ex post facto clause only applies to criminal laws. *See id.* at 391. The ex post facto clause is discussed in §6.2.3.

absolute and without control. . . . There are certain vital principles in our free Republic governments, which will determine and overrule an apparent and flagrant abuse of legislative power; as to authorize manifest injustice by positive law; or to take away that security for personal liberty, or private property, for the protection whereof the government was established. An ACT of the legislature (for I cannot call it a law) contrary to the great first principles of the social compact, cannot be considered a rightful exercise of legislative authority."[3]

Justice Iredell, in a separate opinion, agreed with the result, but expressly disagreed with Justice Chase's claim that courts can rely on natural law principles to declare laws unconstitutional. Justice Iredell wrote: "If . . . the Legislature of the Union, or the Legislature of any member of the Union, shall pass a law, within the general scope of their constitutional power, the Court cannot pronounce it to be void, merely because it is, in their judgment, contrary to the principles of natural justice. The ideas of natural justice are regulated by no fixed standard; the ablest and purest men have differed on the subject; and all that the Court could properly say, in such an event, would be, that the Legislature (possessed of an equal right of opinion), had passed an act which, in the opinion of the judges, was inconsistent with abstract principles of natural justice."[4] The disagreement between Justices Chase and Iredell is thus the first debate over judicial activism and judicial restraint found in the United States Reports.

In *Fletcher v. Peck*, the Supreme Court relied, in part, on natural law principles in declaring a state law unconstitutional.[5] *Fletcher* involved a challenge to a Georgia statute that rescinded an earlier law that granted land to certain individuals. In 1795, members of the Georgia legislature had been bribed to convey about 35 million acres of land to private companies at a price of approximately 1½ cents per acre. In 1796, the Georgia legislature rescinded the grant of land, but, by then, much of the property already had been conveyed to innocent investors.

The Supreme Court, in an opinion by Chief Justice John Marshall, held that it was unconstitutional for Georgia to rescind its grant of land. The Court indicated that the legislative power is limited by both "the general principles of our political institutions" and "the words of the constitution."[6] Because title had been conveyed to innocent owners, the law rescinding the grant was deemed to unconstitutionally interfere with vested rights. The Court found that these rights were protected both by the text of the Constitution and by the natural law. In *Terrett v. Taylor*, the Supreme Court declared unconstitutional a Virginia law that would have taken title of certain property away from the Episcopalian Church.[7] Justice Joseph Story, writing for the Court, stated that such interference with vested property rights violated "principles of natural justice" and "fundamental laws of every free government."[8]

---

[3] *Id.* at 387-388 (emphasis by capitalization in original).
[4] *Id.* at 399 (Iredell, J.).
[5] 10 U.S. (6 Cranch) 87 (1810).
[6] *Id.* at 139.
[7] 13 U.S. (9 Cranch) 43 (1815).
[8] *Id.* at 52.

In *Calder, Fletcher,* and *Terrett,* the Court expressed the view that natural rights concerning property limited government actions. The decisions reflected the belief in natural law that existed in the early nineteenth century and that undoubtedly influenced the framers of the Constitution.[9]

The Initial Rejection of Economic Substantive Due Process

The Supreme Court rejected the first attempts to use the due process clause to protect economic rights from government interference. In *Murray's Lessee v. Hoboken Land & Improvement Co.,* the Court denied a due process challenge to an attempt by the government to collect delinquent taxes.[10] The Court emphasized that due process is met so long as the government's *procedures* are in accord with the law.[11]

In the *Slaughter-House Cases,* in 1873, the Court expressly rejected a substantive due process claim.[12] The *Slaughter-House Cases* involved a challenge to a Louisiana law that granted a private company a 25-year monopoly in the livestock landing and slaughterhouse business. The law also required that the company allow any person to use the facilities to slaughter animals for a fixed fee.

Several butchers brought a lawsuit challenging the constitutionality of the grant of a monopoly. In addition to arguing that the law was involuntary servitude in violation of the Thirteenth Amendment, that it violated the privileges or immunities clause, and that it violated the equal protection clauses of the Fourteenth Amendment,[13] the plaintiffs contended that it denied their right to practice their trade and thus violated the due process clause. The Supreme Court rejected all of these arguments. As to due process, the Court emphasized that this clause concerned the procedures that government must follow and thus could not be used to challenge the law for interfering with the right of butchers to practice their trade. Indeed, the Court said that "under no construction of that provision that we have ever seen, or any that we deem admissible, can the restraint imposed by the State of Louisiana upon the exercise of their trade by the butchers of New Orleans be held to be a deprivation of property within the meaning of that provision."[14] The Court flatly rejected the idea that the due process clause could be used to safeguard a right to practice a trade or profession from arbitrary government interference.

Justices Field and Bradley strongly dissented. In addition to disagreeing with the majority as to the meaning of the privileges or immunities clause, Field and

---

[9] *See* Edward S. Corwin, The "Higher Law" Background of American Constitutional Law, 42 Harv. L. Rev. 149, 365 (1928-1929); Gordon Wood, The Creation of the American Republic, 1776-1787 (1969); Bernard Bailyn, The Ideological Origins of the American Revolution (1967).

[10] 59 U.S. (18 How.) 272 (1856).

[11] At about the same time, a New York court used substantive due process under the state constitution to declare unconstitutional a New York law that prohibited the use or possession of liquor. Wynehamer v. People, 13 N.Y. 378 (1856). The Court emphasized that the law applied even to liquor owned prior to the enactment of the law. The Court said that when "a law annihilates the value of property, the owner is deprived of it within the spirit of a constitutional provision intended expressly to shield private rights from the exercise of arbitrary power." *Id.* at 398.

[12] 83 U.S. (16 Wall.) 36 (1872). The *Slaughter-House Cases* are discussed in §6.3.2.

[13] These aspects of the *Slaughter-House Cases* are discussed in §6.3.2.

[14] *Id.* at 81.

Bradley also differed as to the content of the due process clause. They saw the due process clause as limiting the ability of states to adopt arbitrary laws, especially ones that interfered with natural rights. Justice Bradley, for example, declared: "[T]he individual citizen, as a necessity, must be left free to adopt such calling, profession, or trade as may seem to him most conducive to that end. Without this right he cannot be a freeman. This right to choose one's calling is an essential part of that liberty which is the government's object to protect; and a calling when chosen, is a man's property and right. Liberty and property are not protected where these rights are arbitrarily assailed."[15] In other words, Justice Bradley interpreted the words "liberty" and "property" in the due process clause as protecting a right to practice a trade or profession and believed that arbitrary interference with these rights violated the Fourteenth Amendment. Although this position was rejected by a majority of the Court in the *Slaughter-House Cases*, it soon became the majority view of the Supreme Court.

The Court's Suggestion of Economic Substantive Due Process

Beginning in the 1870s, government regulation significantly increased as industrialization changed the nature of the economy. Simultaneously, business turned to the courts to have the new regulatory laws declared unconstitutional. Professor Arnold Paul explains that "the great pace of industrialization and, more particularly, . . . the swift concentration of economic power in the large corporation" created pressure for government to adopt regulatory laws.[16] Professor Paul notes: "Midwestern and Southern farmers . . . complained bitterly of monopolistic rates by railroads, grain elevators, and banks. Factory workers and miners . . . periodically rebelled at low wages, long hours and bad working conditions. . . . Under the pressure of social discontent, legislators had begun to act in the 1870s and 1880s in regard to railroad and grain elevator rates, labor relations, and other matters affecting large business concerns. In turn, corporations' lawyers had been pressing the courts to protect more vigilantly the rights of property against legislative regulation."[17]

At the same time, over these decades, scholars and judges increasingly espoused a belief in a laissez-faire, unregulated economy. In part, this was based on a philosophy of social Darwinism that society would thrive with the least government regulation so as not to interfere with allowing the "best" to advance and prosper.[18] In part, it was based on a belief that government regulations unduly interfered with the natural rights of people to own and use their property and with a basic liberty interest in freedom of contract.[19] And, in part, support for a laissez-faire philosophy simply reflected hostility by businesses to the increased

---

[15] *Id.* at 116 (Bradley, J., dissenting).

[16] Arnold Paul, Conservative Crisis and the Rule of Law 1-2 (1960).

[17] *Id.* at 5.

[18] A widely cited advocate of this view was Herbert Spencer in Social Statics (1851).

[19] Leading proponents of this view were Thomas M. Cooley in Constitutional Limitations (1868) and Christopher Tiedeman in A Treatise on the Limitations of the Police Power in the United States (1886).

government regulation designed to protect workers, unions, consumers, and competitors.

Loan Association v. Topeka, decided one year after the *Slaughter-House Cases*, is regarded as one of the first instances of the Court's using natural law principles to limit government regulatory power.[20] In *Loan Association v. Topeka*, the Court invalidated a city law that imposed a tax to fund bonds to attract private businesses to Topeka. Without expressly referring to the Constitution because the case arose as a diversity suit, the Court invalidated the law as "purely in aid of private or personal [objects] beyond the legislative power and an unauthorized invasion of private or personal objects beyond the legislative power and an unauthorized invasion of private right. . . . [There] are limitations on such power which grow out of the essential nature of all free governments."[21]

Over the next two decades, in a series of cases, the Supreme Court rejected due process challenges to government economic regulations. Yet in these cases, Supreme Court dicta indicated that it would invalidate laws as violating due process if they interfered with natural principles of justice. Although these cases articulated the principles of substantive economic due process, the Court did not use them to declare laws unconstitutional.

For example, in *Munn v. Illinois*, in 1877, the Court upheld a state law that set maximum rates for grain-storage warehouses.[22] The Court indicated, however, that "under some circumstances" regulation of business would be found to violate due process.[23] The Court said that the central question was whether the "private property is 'affected with a public interest,' . . . [because] when one devotes his property to a use in which the public has an interest, he, in effect, grants to the public an interest in that use, and must submit to be controlled by the public for the common good."[24] The Court expressly declared that it was for the judiciary to evaluate the reasonableness of state regulations. The Court stated: "Undoubtedly, in mere private contracts, relating to matters in which the public has no interest, what is reasonable must be ascertained judicially."[25]

In the *Railroad Commission Cases*, in 1886, the Court upheld a state law regulating railroad rates, but the Court indicated that due process could be used to challenge such rates in the future.[26] The Court stated that the "power to regulate is not a power to destroy. Under pretence of regulating fares and freights, the State cannot require a railroad corporation to carry persons or property without reward; neither can it do that which in law amounts to a taking of private property for public use without just compensation, or without due process of law."[27] Indeed,

---

[20] 87 U.S. (20 Wall.) 655 (1874).

[21] *Id.* at 662, 663.

[22] 94 U.S. 113 (1877).

[23] *Id.* at 125.

[24] *Id.* at 126.

[25] *Id.* at 134.

[26] 116 U.S. 307 (1886).

[27] *Id.* at 331. For a thorough discussion of the use of due process to challenge railroad rate regulations, *see* Stephen Siegel, Understanding the *Lochner* Era: Lessons from the Controversy over Railroad and Utility Rate Regulation, 70 Va. L. Rev. 187 (1984).

just a few years later, the Court found a state railroad regulation to violate the due process clause and held that "[t]he question of [the] reasonableness of a rate of charge for transportation by a railroad company is eminently a question for judicial investigation, requiring due process of law for its determination."[28]

In *Mugler v. Kansas*, in 1887, the Court upheld as constitutional a state law that prohibited the sale of alcoholic beverages.[29] But the Court strongly indicated that state laws would be invalidated as violating due process unless they truly were an exercise of the state's police power. The Court said that if "a statute purporting to have been enacted to protect the public health, public morals, or the public safety, has no real or substantial relation to those objects, or is a palpable invasion of rights secured by the fundamental law, it is the duty of the courts so to adjudge, and thereby give effect to the Constitution."[30]

Munn v. Illinois, the *Railroad Commission Cases*, and *Mugler v. Kansas* were important for articulating that due process was a limit on the government's regulatory power, even though in each of these cases the Court ruled in favor of the government. The Court expressed the philosophy that was to dominate constitutional law for the first third of the twentieth century. Moreover, at about the same time, in 1886, the Supreme Court held that corporations were "persons" under the due process and equal protection clauses.[31] This meant, of course, that corporations could use the Constitution and the philosophy expressed in cases such as *Munn*, the *Railroad Commission Cases*, and *Mugler* to challenge government regulations.

In *Allgeyer v. Louisiana*, the Supreme Court applied these principles and declared unconstitutional a state law that prohibited payments on marine insurance policies issued by out-of-state companies that were not licensed or approved to do business in the state.[32] The Court found that the Louisiana law interfered with freedom of contract and that it thus violated the due process clause of the Fourteenth Amendment. The Court, in language that was frequently quoted in the following decades, declared: "The liberty mentioned in that amendment . . . [is] deemed to embrace the right of citizen[s] to be free in the enjoyment of all his faculties, to be free to use them in all lawful ways; to live and work where he will; to earn his livelihood by any lawful calling; to pursue any livelihood or avocation, and for that purpose to enter into all contracts which may be proper, necessary, and essential to his carrying out to a successful completion the purposes above mentioned."[33]

Thus, in *Allgeyer*, the Court moved from speaking only in dicta of due process as a limit on economic regulations to invalidating a state law based on it.[34] *Allgeyer*

---

[28] Chicago, Milwaukee & St. Paul Ry. Co. v. Minnesota, 134 U.S. 418 (1890).

[29] 123 U.S. 623 (1887).

[30] *Id.* at 661.

[31] Santa Clara County v. Southern Pac. R.R. Co., 118 U.S. 394 (1886).

[32] 165 U.S. 578 (1897).

[33] *Id.* at 589.

[34] Actually, a year earlier, in *Missouri Pac. Ry. Co. v. Nebraska*, 164 U.S. 403 (1896), the Court, without explaining its reasons, declared unconstitutional a state requirement that a railroad permit construction on its property of a grain elevator. The Court found that this was the government using its power to help private owners and not to serve the public.

expressed the key themes of economic substantive due process that were to be followed for the next 40 years until 1937.

§8.2.2   *Economic Substantive Due Process During the* Lochner *Era*

Lochner v. New York

In 1905, in *Lochner v. New York*, the Supreme Court declared unconstitutional a New York law that set the maximum hours that bakers could work.[35] The New York law provided that no employee shall "work in a biscuit, bread or cake bakery or confectionery establishment more than sixty hours in any one week, or more than ten hours in any one day." The Supreme Court declared the law unconstitutional as violating the due process clause of the Fourteenth Amendment because it interfered with freedom of contract and because it did not serve a valid police purpose. The Court articulated three major principles that were followed until 1937. Indeed, because *Lochner* reflects the philosophy and doctrines of these times, this period is often called the "*Lochner* era."

First, the Court, in *Lochner* and throughout this era, stated that freedom of contract is a basic right protected as liberty and property rights under the due process clause of the Fourteenth Amendment. In *Allgeyer*, as discussed above, the Court had said that liberty includes the right "to enter into all contracts which may be proper, necessary, and essential" to carrying out a trade or profession.[36] Similarly, the Court in *Lochner* expressly declared: "The general right to make a contract in relation to his business is part of the liberty of the individual protected by the Fourteenth Amendment. . . . The right to purchase or sell labor is part of the liberty protected by this amendment."[37]

Second, the Court said that the government could interfere with freedom of contract only to serve a valid police purpose: to protect the public safety, public health, or public morals. The Court in *Lochner* explained that the government could regulate freedom of contract pursuant to its "police powers" and "[t]hose powers . . . relate to the safety, health, morals, and general welfare of the public. Both property and liberty are held on such reasonable conditions as may be imposed by the governing power of the State in the exercise of those powers."[38]

Third, the Court said that it was the judicial role to carefully scrutinize legislation interfering with freedom of contract to make sure that it served a police purpose. In *Lochner*, the Court said: "Is this a fair, reasonable and appropriate exercise of the State, or is it an unreasonable, unnecessary and arbitrary interference with the right of the individual to his personal liberty or to enter into those contracts in relation to labor which may seem to him appropriate or necessary for the support of himself and his family?"[39]

[35] 198 U.S. 45 (1905).
[36] 165 U.S. at 589.
[37] 198 U.S. at 53.
[38] *Id.*
[39] *Id.* at 56.

The Court intended that many laws that purport to be exercises of the police power in reality are to redistribute wealth or to help a particular group at the expense of others. The Court in *Lochner* said: "It is impossible for us to shut our eyes to the fact that many laws of this character, while passed under what is claimed to be the police power for the purpose of protecting the public health or welfare, are, in reality, passed for other motives."[40]

The *Lochner* Court applied these three principles to declare the New York law unconstitutional. The Court saw the maximum hours law as interfering with free-dom of contract because it prevented bakery owners and bakers from contracting for as many hours of work as they wished. The Court rejected the argument that the maximum hours law served a police purpose. The Court declared: "There is no contention that bakers as a class are not equal in intelligence and capacity to men in other trades or manual occupations, or that they are not able to assert their rights and care for themselves without the protecting arm of the State, interfering with their independence of judgment and of action. They are in no sense wards of the State. . . . [A] law like the one before us involves neither the safety, the mor-als nor the welfare of the public, and that the interest of the public is not in the slightest degree affected by such an act."[41] Protecting the health of bakers was not a sufficient justification to allow the state to interfere with freedom of contract. The Court said that if this was allowed, then "the hours of employers could be regulated, and doctors, lawyers, scientists, all professional men, as well as artisans and athletes, could be forbidden to fatigue their brains and bodies by prolonged hours of exercise."[42]

The Court emphasized that limiting hours of work for bakers had no rela-tionship to public health. The Court said: "Clean and wholesome bread does not depend upon whether the baker works but ten hours per day or only sixty hours a week. . . . [The law provides] for the inspection of premises where the bakery is being carried on, with regard to furnishing proper wash-rooms and water-closets, [with] regard to providing proper drainage, plumbing, and painting."[43]

Therefore, the Court concluded that "the limit of the police power has been reached and passed in this case. . . . The act is not, within any fair meaning of the term a health law, but is an illegal interference with the rights of individuals, both employers and employees, to make contracts regarding labor upon such terms as they may think best, or which they may agree upon with the other parties to such contracts."[44]

Lochner was a 5-to-4 decision, and strong dissents were written. Justice John Harlan emphasized the need for judicial deference to legislative choices.[45] He stressed that the legislation was a reasonable way to protect the health of bakers who suffered serious medical problems because of exposure to flour dust and intense heat. He quoted one study that found that the "average age of a baker

[40] *Id.* at 64.
[41] *Id.* at 57.
[42] *Id.* at 60.
[43] *Id.* at 57, 61.
[44] *Id.* at 58, 61.
[45] *Id.* at 69 (Harlan, J., dissenting).

is below that of other workmen; they seldom live over their fiftieth year, most of them dying between the ages of forty and fifty."[46]

Justice Oliver Wendell Holmes, in a short but famous dissent, expressly rejected the majority's premise that the Constitution should be used to limit government regulation and protect a laissez-faire economy. Justice Holmes wrote: "The Fourteenth Amendment does not enact Mr. Herbert Spencer's Social Statics. . . . [A] constitution is not intended to embody a particular economic theory, whether of paternalism and the organic relation of the citizen to the State or of laissez-faire."[47]

Cases Following *Lochner*

Lochner v. New York thus announced three themes that were followed until 1937: Freedom of contract was a right protected by the due process clauses of the Fifth and Fourteenth Amendments; the government could interfere with freedom of contract only to serve a valid police purpose of protecting public health, public safety, or public morals; and the judiciary would carefully scrutinize legislation to ensure that it truly served such a police purpose. This position is classic substantive due process: The due process clause was used not to ensure that the government followed proper procedures, but to ensure that laws served an adequate purpose. The Court scrutinized both the ends served by the legislation, to ensure that there really was a valid police purpose, and the means, to ensure that the law sufficiently achieved its purported goal.

Over the next three decades, the Court followed the principles articulated in *Lochner*, finding many laws unconstitutional as interfering with freedom of contract. It is estimated that almost 200 state laws were declared unconstitutional as violating the due process clause of the Fourteenth Amendment.[48] Yet during this time, the Court upheld many state and federal economic regulations as sufficiently related to a valid police purpose. It is difficult to reconcile some of the decisions from this era. The cases, reviewed below, concerned statutes protecting unions, setting maximum hours, requiring a minimum wage, regulating prices, safeguarding consumers, and regulating business entry into a field.

Laws Protecting Unionizing

With regard to laws protecting unions, in *Adair v. United States*[49] and *Coppage v. Kansas*,[50] the Court declared unconstitutional federal and state laws that prohibited

---

[46] *Id.* at 71.

[47] *Id.* at 75 (Holmes, J., dissenting).

[48] Benjamin Wright, The Growth of American Constitutional Law 154 (1942) (159 Supreme Court cases found state laws to violate due process and equal protection; 25 more were found to violate due process and another constitutional provision). It should be remembered that the Court's commitment to laissez-faire economics also caused it to invalidate federal economic regulations as exceeding the scope of the commerce clause or as violating the Tenth Amendment. *See* §§3.4.3; 3.10.

[49] 208 U.S. 161 (1908).

[50] 236 U.S. 1 (1915).

employers from requiring that employees not join a union. In the early part of the twentieth century, as workers attempted to unionize, many states and the federal government adopted laws to facilitate unionization by prohibiting employers from insisting, as a condition of employment, that employees agree not to join a union. The Supreme Court declared the laws unconstitutional as impermissibly infringing freedom of contract. In *Adair*, the Court said that "it is not within the functions of government, at least in the absence of contract between the parties, to compel any person in the course of his business and against his will to accept or retain the personal services of another."[51] In *Coppage*, the Court said that it was not a legitimate exercise of the police power for the government to attempt to equalize bargaining power between employer and employee. The Court said that an individual "has no inherent right to [join a union] . . . and still remain in the employ of one who is unwilling to employ a union man."[52]

In *Truax v. Corrigan*, the Court declared unconstitutional a state law restricting the use of injunctions in labor disputes.[53] Employers frequently used the courts to enjoin labor protests and union activities. Arizona adopted a law limiting the ability of courts to issue such injunctions. The Court declared this law unconstitutional as violating the due process and equal protection clauses of the Fourteenth Amendment.

Maximum Hours Laws

In *Lochner*, the Court declared unconstitutional a state law setting maximum hours for bakers. Yet in *Holden v. Hardy*, less than a decade before *Lochner*, the Court had upheld a maximum hours law for coal miners.[54] The legislature sought to protect the health of miners by limiting their exposure to coal dust. In *Lochner*, the Court distinguished *Holden* as a legitimate exercise of the police power of the state and concluded that there "is nothing in *Holden v. Hardy* which covers the case now before us."[55]

Three years after *Lochner*, in *Muller v. Oregon*, the Court upheld a maximum hours law for women.[56] *Muller* is especially famous because attorney, and later Supreme Court Justice, Louis Brandeis wrote a detailed 113-page brief purporting to document that women's reproductive health required limiting nondomestic work. After *Lochner* held that there had to be proof that a law was closely related to advancing public health, public safety, or public morals, attorneys began filing detailed briefs, filled with social science data, seeking to show the need for the law. Often termed "Brandeis briefs" because of what Louis Brandeis filed in *Muller*, these documents used social science data to demonstrate the need for a particular law.

---

[51]   208 U.S. at 174.
[52]   236 U.S. at 19.
[53]   257 U.S. 312 (1921).
[54]   169 U.S. 366 (1898).
[55]   198 U.S. at 55.
[56]   208 U.S. 412 (1908).

In *Muller*, the Court upheld the maximum hours law for women because there was "widespread belief that women's physical structure, and the functions she performs in consequence thereof, justify special legislation restricting or qualifying the conditions under which she should be permitted to toil."[57] The Court said that regulating the hours worked by women was justified because of "women's physical structure and the performance of maternal functions."[58]

In *Bunting v. Oregon*, the Court upheld a maximum hours law for manufacturing jobs.[59] The state established a ten-hour workday for those involved in manufacturing positions. The distinction between *Bunting* and *Lochner* is difficult to articulate or understand.

Minimum Wage Laws

Although the Court upheld several maximum hours laws, it declared unconstitutional many state minimum wage laws. In *Adkins v. Children's Hospital*, the Court declared unconstitutional a law that set a minimum wage for women.[60] As discussed above, the Court upheld a maximum hours law for women.[61] But the Court in *Adkins* said that a minimum wage law was different: It interfered with freedom of contract, but did not serve any valid police purpose. The Court rejected the argument that without a minimum wage women would be forced to earn money in an immoral manner. In fact, the Court stressed the growing equality of women, as reflected in the recent adoption of the Nineteenth Amendment that guaranteed women the right to vote. The Court said: "But the ancient inequality of the sexes, otherwise than physical, has continued with diminishing intensity. In view of the great changes which have taken place . . . in the contractual, political, and civil status of women, culminating in the Nineteenth Amendment, it is not unreasonable say that these differences have now come almost, if not quite, to the vanishing point."[62]

The Court reaffirmed *Adkins* in 1936, in *Morehead v. New York ex rel. Tipaldo*, which also declared unconstitutional a state minimum wage law for women.[63] In *Morehead*, like in *Adkins*, the Court found that the minimum wage law impermissibly interfered with freedom of contract because it did not serve a valid state police purpose.

Consumer Protection Legislation

Another type of legislation that was invalidated concerned price regulations. Laws setting the maximum prices for theater tickets,[64] employment agencies,[65] and

---

[57] *Id.* at 420.
[58] *Id.* at 421
[59] 243 U.S. 426 (1917).
[60] 261 U.S. 525 (1923).
[61] Muller v. Oregon, 208 U.S. 412 (1908).
[62] 261 U.S. at 553.
[63] 298 U.S. 587 (1936).
[64] Tyson & Brother v. Banton, 273 U.S. 418 (1927).
[65] Ribnik v. McBride, 277 U.S. 350 (1928).

gasoline[66] were declared unconstitutional as interfering with freedom of contract. The Court repeatedly distinguished *Munn v. Illinois*, which had upheld price controls for grain storage on the ground that it affected the public interest.[67] The Court stressed the importance of freedom of contract and narrowly defined the permissible scope of the government's police power.

Other types of consumer protection laws were invalidated as well. In *Weaver v. Palmer Bros.*, the Court declared unconstitutional a state law prohibiting the use of shoddy in making bedding.[68] "Shoddy" was rags and other debris that were stuffed in mattresses. The Court rejected the claim that the ban was needed to protect public health and found that the law interfered with freedom of contract for those who wished to buy and sell such products. The Court said that the public interest in health could be served by regulation, such as by mandating sterilization of the material. In *Jay Burns Baking Co. v. Bryan*, the Court declared unconstitutional a law that required standardized weights for bread loaves.[69]

Laws Regulating Business Entry

Similarly, the Court followed the principles articulated in *Lochner* to declare unconstitutional laws that made it more difficult for businesses to enter a particular field. For instance, in *New State Ice Co. v. Liebmann*, the Supreme Court declared unconstitutional a law that prohibited any person to manufacture ice unless they first obtained a permit from the government; a certificate would be denied if existing service was adequate.[70] The Court said that under the due process clause, "a regulation which has the effect of denying or unreasonably curtailing the common right to engage in a lawful business . . . cannot be upheld."[71] The Court noted that the law existed to create a monopoly and said that it is the same as the use of state authority "to prevent another shoemaker from making or selling shoes because shoemakers already in that occupation can make and sell all the shoes that are needed."[72]

In *Adams v. Tanner*, the Court declared unconstitutional a state law that prohibited private employment agencies that charged a fee to be paid by employees.[73]

The Court emphasized that the law interfered with freedom of contract between the agencies and employees without protecting public safety, public health, or public morals.

---

[66] Williams v. Standard Oil Co., 278 U.S. 235 (1929).

[67] 94 U.S. 113 (1877), discussed above in §8.2.1. In some cases, the Court did uphold price regulations. *See* Block v. Hirsh, 256 U.S. 135 (1921) (price controls for rental housing); German Alliance Ins. Co. v. Lewis, 233 U.S. 389 (1914) (price controls for fire insurance).

[68] 270 U.S. 402 (1926).

[69] 264 U.S. 504 (1924).

[70] 285 U.S. 262 (1932).

[71] *Id.* at 278.

[72] *Id.* at 279.

[73] 244 U.S. 590 (1917).

What, If Anything, Was Wrong with the *Lochner*-Era Decisions?

These cases show that a vast array of legislation to protect workers, consumers, and even businesses was invalidated by the Supreme Court in the first third of the twentieth century under the doctrine of substantive due process. For more than 70 years, commentators and Justices have repudiated the *Lochner*-era decisions. But what, if anything, was wrong with these rulings?

One criticism is that the doctrines formulated by the Court were undesirable; that the Court was wrong in protecting freedom of contract as a fundamental right and that it erred in concluding that the government only could interfere with this right to enhance public health, public safety, or public morals. Critics argue that the government should be able to regulate to achieve many other goals, including protecting workers, consumers, and the public generally. Freedom of contract should not be an obstacle to necessary regulations.

Critics say that it was absurd to talk of bakers having freedom to bargain to work fewer hours; unequal bargaining power made real freedom of contract illusory. Thus, critics argue that the Court should have allowed legislatures to set maximum hours for bakers, minimum wages, and prices. The Court's commitment to laissez-faire economics was misguided and ultimately favored some, such as employers and corporations, over others, such as workers and consumers.

A second criticism of the *Lochner*-era decisions focuses on their inconsistency. The Court allowed maximum hour laws for women, but not minimum wage laws. It permitted maximum hour laws for coal miners and manufacturing workers, but not for bakers. The Court allowed government price controls for grain elevators, but not for gasoline. This criticism focuses less on the Court's doctrines and more on their inconsistent application.

A third attack on the *Lochner*-era decisions stresses the degree of judicial activism. The criticism is that unelected judges were unduly substituting their values for those of popularly elected legislatures to protect rights that were not expressly stated in the Constitution. The focus of this criticism is less on the Court's value choices or on its inconsistency and more on the Court's invalidating laws adopted through the democratic process.

These three criticisms are not mutually exclusive, but they do point in different directions about the appropriate content of constitutional law. The first criticism suggests that the Court should defer to laws regulating the economy and especially those protecting workers and consumers. The second criticism indicates that the Court should articulate and more consistently follow constitutional principles. The last criticism suggests judicial deference, not just in the area of economic regulations, but across other areas of constitutional law as well, especially when there is not an express constitutional provision on point.

It should be noted that the *Lochner*-era decisions have their defenders as well.[74] These scholars argue that the Court was correct in protecting freedom of contract as a basic aspect of liberty and in carefully scrutinizing laws regulating the economy.

---

[74] *See, e.g.*, Richard Epstein, Takings: Private Property and the Power of Eminent Domain (1985); Bernard Siegan, Economic Liberties and the Constitution (1980).

§8.2.3 Economic Substantive Due Process Since 1937

Pressures for Change

By the mid-1930s, enormous pressures were mounting for the Court to abandon the laissez-faire philosophy of the *Lochner* era. The Depression created a widespread perception that government economic regulations were essential. With millions unemployed and with wages incredibly low for those with jobs, employees had no realistic chance of bargaining in the workplace. As Professor Laurence Tribe remarked: "In large measure . . . it was the economic realities of the Depression that graphically undermined *Lochner*'s premises. . . . The legal 'freedom' of contract and property came increasingly to be seen as an illusion, subject as it was to impersonal economic forces. Positive government intervention came to be more widely accepted as essential to economic survival, and legal doctrines would henceforth have to operate from that premise."[75]

The intellectual foundations of the *Lochner* era also were under attack. *Lochner* rested on the assumption that freedom of contract and related property rights were part of the natural liberties possessed by individuals. Legal realists attacked this premise and persuasively argued that the law reflected political choices; using freedom of contract to invalidate state laws was a political choice that favored employers over employees and corporations over consumers.[76] As such, the Supreme Court's decision in *Lochner* and its progeny could not be regarded as "restoring the natural order which had been upset by the legislature . . . [because] there was no 'natural' economic order to upset or restore."[77] If it was all about making political choices, there was no reason for the Court to overturn the decisions made by the political process.

At the same time, there were strong political pressures for change. After Franklin Roosevelt was elected to a second term as president in 1936, he proposed a "Court-packing plan," where the president could appoint one additional Justice for every Justice on the Court who was over age 70, up to a maximum of 15 Justices.[78] Roosevelt was particularly upset that the Court had invalidated several key pieces of New Deal legislation as part of its commitment to a laissez-faire philosophy.[79]

---

[75] Laurence Tribe, American Constitutional Law 578 (2d ed. 1988).

[76] *See, e.g.,* Roscoe Pound, The Call for a Realist Jurisprudence, 44 Harv. L. Rev. 697 (1931); Ray A. Brown, Due Process, Police Power, and the Supreme Court, 40 Harv. L. Rev. 943 (1927); Thomas Reed Powell, The Judiciality of Minimum Wage Legislation, 37 Harv. L. Rev. 37 (1924). For a discussion of the importance of legal realist writings in undermining the intellectual foundations of Lochnerism, *see* Howard Gillman, The Constitution Besieged: The Rise and Demise of the *Lochner* Era (1993); Morton Horwitz, The Transformation of American Law, 1870-1960 (1992).

[77] Tribe, *supra* note 75, at 578-579.

[78] The Court-packing plan, and the reactions to it, are discussed in §3.4.4.

[79] These cases are discussed in §3.4.3.

Initial Suggestions of the Demise of Lochnerism

Even before Roosevelt proposed his Court-packing plan, there were initial indications that the Court was ready to allow more government economic regulations. In *Nebbia v. New York*, in 1934, the Supreme Court upheld a New York law that set prices for milk.[80] On the one hand, this can be viewed as a narrow decision based on strong evidence of the importance of milk and a legislative finding that "the evils [in the market] . . . could not be expected to right themselves through the ordinary play of the forces of supply and demand, owing to the peculiar and uncontrollable factors affecting the industry."[81] Although, as discussed above, the *Lochner* Court had invalidated some price controls, it had upheld others in businesses that it deemed to affect the public interest.[82] *Nebbia* might be seen as a limited ruling following those cases.

Yet the language of the Court's opinion in *Nebbia* was broader than that; the Court seemed to question the basic premises of the *Lochner* era. The Court said, for example, "But neither property rights nor contract rights are absolute; for government cannot exist if the citizen may at will use his property to the detriment of his fellows, or exercise his freedom of contract to work them harm. . . . [T]his court from the early days [has] affirmed that the power to promote the general welfare is inherent in government."[83] The Court went even further in declaring a need for judicial deference to legislative choices: "So far as the requirement of due process is concerned and in the absence of other constitutional restraints, a state is free to adopt whatever economic policy may reasonably be deemed to promote public welfare, and to enforce that policy by legislation adapted to its purpose. The courts are without authority either to declare such policy, or, when it is declared by the legislature, to override it."[84] In other words, in *Nebbia*, the Court appeared to question the premises of the *Lochner* era that the government only could regulate to achieve a police purpose and that the Court needed to review laws aggressively to ensure that they truly served a police purpose.

In the same year, 1934, in *Home Building & Loan Association v. Blaisdell*, the Supreme Court upheld the constitutionality of a Minnesota law that prevented the foreclosure of homeowners' mortgages for a two-year period.[85] Although mortgage holders had a right under the contracts to foreclose when homeowners failed to make timely payments, the state adopted an emergency measure in response to the Depression preventing foreclosures from 1933 until 1935. As discussed below in §8.3, the Court expressly rejected the argument that the law impaired the obligations of contracts in violation of Article I, §10. Even though the case focused

---

[80]   291 U.S. 502 (1934).

[81]   *Id*. at 518.

[82]   Munn v. Illinois, 94 U.S. 113 (1877) (price controls for grain elevators); Block v. Hirsh, 256 U.S. 135 (1921) (price controls for rental housing); German Alliance Ins. Co. v. Lewis, 233 U.S. 389 (1914) (price controls for fire insurance).

[83]   291 U.S. at 523-524.

[84]   *Id*. at 537.

[85]   290 U.S. 398 (1934).

on the contracts clause and not substantive due process, it indicates the Court's increasing willingness by 1934 to defer to government economic regulations.

Yet despite these 1934 decisions, the substantive economic due process of the *Lochner* era was not over. In 1936, in *Morehead v. Tipaldo*, the Supreme Court declared unconstitutional a New York law that set a minimum wage for women.[86] The Court, in a 5-to-4 decision, flatly declared: "[T]he State is without power by any form of legislation to prohibit, change, or nullify contracts between employers and adult women workers as to the amount of wages to be paid."[87] Also, during 1936, the Court continued to declare unconstitutional federal economic regulations as exceeding the scope of Congress's commerce power and for violating federalism.[88]

The End of Lochnerism

In 1937, in two cases—one involving substantive due process and one involving the scope of Congress's commerce power—Justice Owen Roberts switched sides and cast the fifth vote to uphold the laws. Perhaps this was a reaction to the Court-packing plan or perhaps he made up his mind in these cases before even learning about that threat. Regardless, in these two decisions, the Court signaled the end of the laissez-faire jurisprudence that had dominated constitutional law for several decades.

In *West Coast Hotel v. Parrish*,[89] the Supreme Court upheld a state law that required a minimum wage for women employees and expressly overruled *Adkins v. Children's Hospital* and *Morehead v. Tipaldo*. Chief Justice Hughes, writing for the Court, made it clear that the Court was abandoning the principles of *Lochner v. New York*. He noted that the minimum wage law was challenged as interfering with freedom of contract and he replied: "What is this freedom of contract? The Constitution does not speak of freedom of contract. It speaks of liberty and prohibits the deprivation of liberty without due process of law. . . . [R]egulation which is reasonable in relation to its subject and is adopted in the interests of the community is due process."[90]

Moreover, the Court was emphatic that the government was not limited to regulating only to advance the public safety, public health, or public morals. The Court said: "There is an additional and compelling consideration which recent economic experience has brought into a strong light. The exploitation of a class of workers who are in an unequal position with respect to bargaining power and are thus relatively defenseless against the denial of a living wage is not only detrimental to their health and well being but casts a direct burden for their support upon

---

[86] 298 U.S. 587 (1936).

[87] *Id.* at 611.

[88] *See, e.g.*, Carter v. Carter Coal Co., 298 U.S. 238 (1936), discussed in §3.4.3; A.L.A. Schechter Poultry Corp. v. United States, 295 U.S. 495 (1935), discussed in §3.4.3.

[89] 300 U.S. 379 (1937).

[90] *Id.* at 391.

the community."[91] For 40 years, the Court had refused to allow the government to regulate to equalize bargaining power; now it was permitted.

In these paragraphs, the Court unequivocally declared that it no longer would protect freedom of contract as a fundamental right, that government could regulate to serve any legitimate purpose, and that the judiciary would defer to the legislature's choices so long as they were reasonable.

One year after *West Coast Hotel v. Parrish*, the Supreme Court reaffirmed its holding and the new policy of judicial deference to government economic regulations. In *United States v. Carolene Products Co.*, the Court upheld the Filled Milk Act of 1923 that prohibited "filled milk," a substance obtained by mixing milk and vegetable oil.[92] The Court said that economic regulations should be upheld so long as they are supported by a conceivable rational basis, even if it cannot be proved that it was the legislature's actual intent. Justice Stone, writing for the Court, said: "[T]he existence of facts supporting the legislative judgment is to be presumed, for regulatory legislation affecting ordinary commercial transactions is not to be pronounced unconstitutional unless in the light of the facts made known or generally assumed it is of such a character as to preclude the assumption that it rests upon some rational basis."[93]

In a famous footnote, the Court articulated a double standard of review. Generally, the Court would defer to the government and uphold laws so long as they were reasonable. But this deference would not extend to laws interfering with fundamental rights or discriminating against discrete and insular minorities. In footnote 4, the Court said:

> There may be narrower scope for operation of the presumption of constitutionality when legislation appears on its face to be within a specific prohibition of the Constitution, such as those of the first ten amendments. . . . It is unnecessary to consider now whether legislation which restricts those political processes which can ordinarily be expected to bring about repeal of undesirable legislation, is to be subjected to more exacting judicial scrutiny under the general prohibitions of the Fourteenth Amendment. . . . Nor need we enquire . . . whether prejudice against discrete and insular minorities may be a special condition, which tends seriously to curtail the operation of those political processes ordinarily to be relied upon to protect minorities, and which may call for a correspondingly more searching judicial inquiry.[94]

In other words, courts generally would presume that laws are constitutional. However, this deference would be replaced by a "more searching judicial inquiry" when it is a law that interferes with individual rights, or a law that restricts the ability of the political process to repeal undesirable legislation, or a law that discriminates against a "discrete and insular minority."[95]

---

[91] *Id.* at 399.
[92] 304 U.S. 144 (1938). *See* Geoffrey Miller, The True Story of *Carolene Products*, 1987 Sup. Ct. Rev. 397.
[93] 304 U.S. at 152.
[94] *Id.* at 152-153 n.4.
[95] The levels of scrutiny that this ultimately created are discussed in §6.5.

At the same time that the Court abandoned the substantive due process principles of *Lochner*, the Court also overruled the limits that it had placed on Congress's power during that era. In *NLRB v. Jones & Laughlin Steel Corp.*, in 1937, the Court upheld the National Labor Relations Act and its application to the steel industry.[96] In *United States v. Darby*, the Court upheld the Fair Labor Standards Act and its minimum wage and maximum hours provisions.[97] In *Darby*, the Court expressly rejected challenges based on both substantive economic due process and federalism. *Darby* powerfully illustrated that both the state and federal governments would be accorded very broad powers to regulate the economy.

Between 1937 and 1941, the composition of the Court changed dramatically. The conservative Justices — Van Devanter, McReynolds, Butler, and Sutherland — left the Court and were replaced by Roosevelt appointees. In fact, between 1937 and 1941, Roosevelt made eight appointments to the Supreme Court, and this created a solid majority committed to repudiating *Lochner*-era jurisprudence and to deferring to government economic regulations.

Economic Substantive Due Process Since 1937

Since 1937, not one state or federal economic regulation has been found unconstitutional as infringing liberty of contract as protected by the due process clauses of the Fifth and Fourteenth Amendments.[98] The Court has made it clear that economic regulations — laws regulating business and employment practices — will be upheld when challenged under the due process clause so long as they are rationally related to serve a legitimate government purpose.

The government's purpose can be any goal not prohibited by the Constitution. In fact, it does not need to be proved that the asserted purpose was the legislature's actual objective. Any conceivable purpose is sufficient. The law only need seem a reasonable way of attaining the end; it does not need to be narrowly tailored to achieving the goal.

The reality is that virtually any law can meet this very deferential requirement. Several cases reveal how unlikely it is that any economic regulation will be found to violate due process. In *Lincoln Federal Labor Union v. Northwestern Iron & Metal Co.*, the Court unanimously upheld a state "right-to-work" law — a law that mandated that no person could be denied a job for failure to join a union.[99] The Court stressed that it had long repudiated the "*Allgeyer-Lochner-Adair-Coppage* constitutional doctrine."[100] The Court said that states could legislate against "injurious practices in their internal commercial and business affairs, so long as their laws do not run afoul of some specific federal constitutional provision, or some valid federal law."[101]

---

[96]   307 U.S. 1 (1937), which is discussed in §3.4.4.

[97]   312 U.S. 100 (1941).

[98]   *See* Geoffrey Stone et al., Constitutional Law 832 (5th ed. 2005) ("Indeed, the Court has not invalidated an economic regulation on substantive due process grounds since 1937").

[99]   335 U.S. 525 (1949).

[100]   *Id.* at 535-536.

[101]   *Id.* at 536.

In *Williamson v. Lee Optical*, the Supreme Court upheld an Oklahoma statute that prohibited an optician to fit or duplicate lenses without a prescription from an optometrist or an ophthalmologist.[102] The federal district court had declared the law unconstitutional as failing the rational basis test because a prescription was unnecessary if a person broke a pair of glasses; an optician could measure the power of the lenses and duplicate them without a new prescription.

The Supreme Court, in an opinion by Justice William Douglas, reversed and stressed the need for judicial deference to legislative choices. He wrote: "The Oklahoma law may exact a needless, wasteful requirement in many cases. But it is for the legislature, not the courts, to balance the advantages and disadvantages of the new requirement."[103] The Court then hypothesized possible legitimate purposes for the law: "[The] legislature might have concluded that the frequency of occasions where a prescription is necessary was sufficient to justify this regulation of the fitting of eyeglasses. [Or] the legislature might have concluded that eye examinations were so critical, not only for correction of vision but also for the detection of latent ailments or diseases, that every change in frames and every duplication of a lens should be accompanied by a prescription from a medical expert."[104] The Court concluded by recognizing that the law might be illogical in some of its applications, but noted that the "day is gone when the Court uses the Due Process Clause to strike down state laws regulatory of business and industrial conditions, because they may be unwise, improvident, or out of harmony with a particular school of thought."[105]

In all likelihood, the Oklahoma law was adopted to protect business for optometrists and ophthalmologists and was not motivated by a desire to improve health. But *Williamson* shows that so long as the Court can conceive of some legitimate purpose and so long as the law is reasonable, a law will be upheld.

Similarly, in *Ferguson v. Skrupa*, the Court upheld a Kansas law that made it unlawful for a person to engage in the business of debt adjusting, except incident to the practice of law.[106] A debt adjuster would make a deal with a debtor to pay money to the adjuster on a regular basis and the adjuster would then distribute it to the debtor's creditors based on an agreed upon plan. The effect of the Kansas law was to put out of business individuals, who were not lawyers, who had been debt adjusters.

Justice Black, writing for the Court, said: "Under the system of government created by our Constitution, it is up to legislatures, not courts, to decide on the wisdom and utility of legislation. There was a time when the Due Process Clause was used by this Court to strike down laws which were thought unreasonable, that is, unwise or incompatible with some particular economic or social philosophy. . . . [That doctrine] has long since been discarded. It is now settled that States have power to legislate against what are found to be injurious commercial and business

---

[102] 348 U.S. 483 (1955).
[103] *Id.* at 487.
[104] *Id.*
[105] *Id.* at 488.
[106] 372 U.S. 726 (1963).

affairs, so long as their laws do not run afoul of some specific federal constitutional prohibition, or some valid federal law."[107]

Ferguson shows that no longer did the Court interpret the due process clause to protect a right to practice a trade or profession or even freedom of contract. The Kansas law undoubtedly was an anticompetitive measure to give lawyers a monopoly in debt adjustments. Nonetheless, the Court proclaimed deference to the legislature and upheld the law.

The extent of this deference is reflected in the Supreme Court's ruling that even retroactive laws, so long as they do not impose criminal punishments, will be upheld so long as they meet the rational basis test. Laws that retroactively make an action illegal or increase the punishment for a crime violate the ex post facto clauses contained in Article I, §§9 and 10.[108] But the Supreme Court long has held that the ex post facto clauses apply only in the criminal context; laws without criminal consequences cannot be challenged under these provisions, but instead must be challenged as denying due process.[109]

In *Turner v. Elkhorn Mining Co.*, the Court held that retroactive legislation without criminal effects would be upheld so long as it was rationally related to a legitimate government purpose.[110] *Turner* involved a challenge to the Federal Coal Mine Health and Safety Act, which, in part, provided compensation to former coal miners who suffered from pneumoconiosis, "black lung disease."

Coal operators challenged the aspect of the law that required them to compensate former employees who terminated their work in the industry before the Act was passed.

Justice Thurgood Marshall, writing for the Court, stressed the need for deference to legislative choices: "It is by now well established that legislative Acts adjusting the burdens and benefits of economic life come to the Court with a presumption of constitutionality, and that the burden is on one complaining of a due process violation to establish that the legislature acted in an arbitrary and irrational way."[111] The Court thus concluded that the retroactive civil liability did not violate due process.[112] There is an obvious unfairness to imposing retroactive

---

[107] *Id.* at 729.

[108] The ex post facto clauses are discussed in §6.2.3.

[109] *See, e.g.*, Calder v. Bull, 3 U.S. (3 Dall.) 386, 390 (1798); discussed in §6.2.3.

[110] 428 U.S. 1 (1976). *See also* United States v. Carlton, 512 U.S. 26 (1994) (a retroactive tax law will be upheld so long as the law is rationally related to a legitimate government purpose).

[111] *Id.* at 15.

[112] The Court distinguished the earlier case, *R.R. Retirement Bd. v. Alton R. Co.*, 295 U.S. 330 (1935), that had declared unconstitutional a federal law that required that railroads provide pensions for former employees. The Court in *Turner* said that assuming that *Alton* "retains vitality," it is distinguishable because compensating coal miners "is to satisfy a specific need created by the dangerous conditions under which the former employee labored." 428 U.S. at 19. It is very questionable whether *Alton* retains vitality because it was a 1935 decision reflecting *Lochner*-era jurisprudence and because *Turner* articulates a rational basis test for evaluating retroactive laws that do not have criminal consequences.

civil liability.[113] Yet the Court concluded in *Turner* that only a rational basis test will be used in evaluating such laws.

In one case since *Turner*, the Court invalidated a retroactive law, but there was no majority opinion for the Court. In *Eastern Enterprises v. Apfel*,[114] the Court invalidated a federal law that made coal companies responsible for paying the medical benefits of former coal miners.[115] Four Justices—Justice O'Connor joined by Chief Justice Rehnquist and Justices Scalia and Thomas—found this to be an impermissible taking of property without just compensation.[116] But five Justices rejected this conclusion and expressly said that there was not a taking.

Justice Kennedy cast the key fifth vote for invalidating the law, concluding that the retroactive liability violated due process. Although he said that the majority's takings analysis was "incorrect,"[117] he said that the Act imposes a "staggering financial burden" on coal companies.[118] He further stated that the case "represents one of the rare instances where the Legislature has exceeded the limits imposed by due process [because] . . . the remedy created by the Coal Act bears no legitimate relation to the interest which the Government asserts in support of the statute."[119] Justice Kennedy emphasized the unfairness of imposing liability on companies that had done nothing to create an expectation of health benefits being paid to former workers. However, no other Justice joined Justice Kennedy's opinion invalidating the law on substantive due process grounds.

Is It Too Much Deference?

As mentioned above, since 1937, not one law has been declared unconstitutional by the Supreme Court as violating economic substantive due process.[120] Ultimately, the question is whether this is appropriate judicial deference to legislative choices in regulating the economy or whether it is judicial abdication of an important role in protecting economic liberties. Are the decisions since 1937 an

---

[113] For an excellent discussion of the issue of retroactivity, *see* Julian Eule, Temporal Limits on the Legislative Mandate: Entrenchment and Retroactivity, 1987 Am. B. Found. Res. J. 379, 427-459.

[114] 524 U.S. 498 (1998).

[115] Coal Act, 26 U.S.C. §9701 *et seq.*

[116] The takings clause is discussed below in §8.4.

[117] 524 U.S. at 540 (Kennedy, J., concurring in the judgment and dissenting in part).

[118] *Id.* at 539.

[119] *Id.* at 548.

[120] The Court, however, has declared unconstitutional punitive damages awards as being "grossly excessive" and thus a violation of due process. *See* Philip Morris USA v. Williams, 549 U.S. 346 (2007) (due process requires that punitive damages may punish a defendant only for harms suffered by the plaintiff and not by others who are not part of the litigation); State Farm Mut. Ins. v. Campbell, 538 U.S. 4008 (2003) (finding grossly excessive a punitive damage award of $145 million with compensatory damages of $1 million for insurance company's bad faith refusal to settle a claim); BMW of North Am., Inc. v. Gore, 517 U.S. 559 (1996) (finding grossly excessive a punitive damages award of $2 million for the undisclosed repainting of automobiles where the punitive damages award included conduct in states where the defendant's conduct was lawful and where the compensatory damages award was $4,000). These cases are discussed in detail in §7.4.3.

overreaction to the *Lochner*-era decisions?[121] Or do the decisions reflect a properly limited judicial role in scrutinizing economic regulations? Answering these normative questions requires consideration of whether there should be constitutional protection of economic rights, such as freedom of contract and a right to practice a trade or profession.[122] Also, there must be consideration of the proper judicial role and whether there are reasons why the judiciary should be especially deferential to legislatures in this area.[123]

The bottom line is that since 1937 economic substantive due process has been unavailable to challenge government economic and social welfare laws and regulations.[124] Protection of economic rights, since 1937, such that it has been, has come under two specific constitutional provisions: the contracts clause of Article I, §10, and the takings clause of the Fifth Amendment.

§8.3   THE CONTRACTS CLAUSE

§8.3.1   Introduction

Article I, §10, provides that "No State shall . . . pass any . . . law impairing the Obligation of Contracts." It is firmly established that the provision applies only if a state or local law interferes with existing contracts. In other words, the contracts clause does not apply to the federal government; challenges to federal interference with contracts must be brought under the due process clause where they will receive the deferential rational basis review described above. Also, the contracts clause does not limit the ability of the government to regulate the terms of future contracts; it applies only if the state or local government is interfering with performance of already existing contracts.[1]

Historical Overview

The contracts clause seems to have been motivated by a desire to prevent states from adopting laws to help debtors at the expense of creditors.[2] The framers were concerned that in times of recession or depression, state legislatures might

---

[121] *See* Robert McCloskey, Economic Due Process and the Supreme Court: An Exhumation and Reburial, 1962 Sup. Ct. Rev. 34, 43 (the "extreme of the past had generated the extreme of the present").

[122] *See* Siegan, *supra* note 74, at 302-303 (arguing for greater protection of economic liberties).

[123] *See* Cass Sunstein, Naked Preferences and the Constitution, 84 Colum. L. Rev. 1689 (1984).

[124] Likewise, equal protection challenges to economic regulations are subjected to a rational basis test and are unlikely to succeed. This is discussed in §9.2.

§8.3 [1] *See* Ogden v. Saunders, 25 U.S. (12 Wheat.) 213 (1827).

[2] Benjamin Wright, The Growth of American Constitutional Law 41 (1967).

adopt laws to protect debtors who were unable to pay what was owed. The contracts clause was meant to stop such debtor relief legislation that had the effect of interfering with contractual rights. The goal was not only to protect creditors but also to encourage credit by assuring lenders that they would be repaid.

In the first half of the nineteenth century, the Court aggressively used the contracts clause to invalidate state and local laws that interfered with rights under existing contracts. Although the contracts clause continued to be used by the Court in the latter half of the nineteenth century, by the twentieth century the contracts clause rarely was mentioned in Supreme Court decisions. During the *Lochner* era, from about 1897 until 1937, the contracts clause was made superfluous by the Court's protection of freedom of contract under the due process clauses of the Fifth and Fourteenth Amendments.[3] The freedom of contract protected under these provisions limited both government regulation of future contracts and government interference with existing contracts. Because the contracts clause only applies to the latter, preventing impairment of existing contracts, the Court's use of due process to protect freedom of contracts subsumed the content of the contracts clause.

The modern era of contracts clause law began in 1934, even before the end of economic substantive due process. In *Home Building & Loan Association v. Blaisdell,* the Supreme Court upheld a Minnesota law, enacted in response to the Depression, that prevented mortgage holders from foreclosing on mortgages for a two-year period.[4] Even though this was exactly the kind of debtor relief legislation that the contracts clause was meant to forbid, the Court upheld it and emphasized the emergency nature of the legislation.[5]

Since 1937, the Court's deference to government economic regulation has resulted in the contracts clause rarely being used to invalidate state and local laws. In fact, only twice since 1937 has the Supreme Court found laws to violate the contracts clause.[6] Under current law, a government interference with private contracts will be struck down only if there is a "substantial impairment" of the contract and only if the law fails to reasonably serve a "significant and legitimate public purpose."[7] However, a government interference with government contracts will receive greater scrutiny than its interference with private contracts because of distrust of the government when it is acting in its own "self-interest."[8]

The normative questions concerning the appropriate content of the contracts clause are very similar to those raised above concerning substantive due process. How aggressively should the Court protect contract rights?[9] How much should the Court defer to the legislature, even when contractual rights are impaired?

---

[3] The *Lochner*-era decisions are described above in §8.2.2.

[4] 290 U.S. 398 (1934).

[5] This case is discussed in more detail below in §8.3.3.

[6] *See* Allied Structural Steel Co. v. Spannaus, 438 U.S. 234 (1978); United States Trust Co. v. New Jersey, 431 U.S. 1 (1977), discussed below in §8.3.3.

[7] Energy Reserves Group v. Kansas Power & Light, 459 U.S. 400, 411-412 (1983).

[8] United States Trust Co. v. New Jersey, 431 U.S. at 26.

[9] For an argument for a more aggressive use of the contracts clause, *see* Richard Epstein, Toward a Revitalization of the Contracts Clause, 51 U. Chi. L. Rev. 703 (1984).

§8.3.2   The Contracts Clause Before 1934

The Contracts Clause and the Marshall Court

In the early part of the nineteenth century, the Supreme Court actively used the contracts clause to limit the ability of state and local governments to interfere with existing contracts.[10] The initial cases involved state laws that impaired contracts with the government. In *Fletcher v. Peck*, the Supreme Court declared unconstitutional a Georgia statute that rescinded an earlier law that granted land to certain individuals.[11] In 1795, members of the Georgia legislature had been bribed to convey about 35 million acres of land to private companies at a price of approximately 1½ cents per acre. In 1796, the Georgia legislature rescinded the grant of land, but by then much of the property had been conveyed to innocent investors.

The Supreme Court, in an opinion by Chief Justice John Marshall, held that it was unconstitutional for Georgia to rescind its grant of land. The Court said that the law violated the contracts clause and also that it infringed on natural law principles.[12]

In *New Jersey v. Wilson*, the Supreme Court declared unconstitutional a state law that repealed a tax exemption that the colonial legislature had granted to land 50 years earlier.[13] The Court concluded that repealing the law violated the contracts clause of Article I, §10.

In *Dartmouth College v. Woodward*, perhaps the most famous contracts clause decision of this era, the Court declared unconstitutional a New Hampshire law that changed the charter that had been issued to Dartmouth College.[14] The charter made Dartmouth College a private institution, and New Hampshire attempted to change this to place the school under public control. The Supreme Court declared this unconstitutional as a violation of the contracts clause, even though Chief Justice Marshall's opinion admitted that "[i]t is more than possible that the preservation of rights of this description was not particularly in the view of the framers of the Constitution."[15] In a concurring opinion, Justice Joseph Story indicated that the state, in granting the charter, could have reserved the power to amend the charter.[16]

Although these cases all involved the government modifying its own promises and obligations, the Marshall Court then applied the contracts clause to keep the government from interfering with private contracts. In *Sturges v. Crowninshield*, the

---

[10] For an excellent discussion of the contracts clause during this period, *see* Stephen Siegel, Understanding the Nineteenth Century Contract Clause: The Role of the Property-Privilege Distinction and "Takings" Clause Jurisprudence, 60 S. Cal. L. Rev. 1 (1986).

[11] 10 U.S. (6 Cranch) 87 (1810).

[12] *Id.* at 136-139.

[13] 11 U.S. (7 Cranch) 164 (1812).

[14] 17 U.S. (4 Wheat.) 518 (1819).

[15] *Id.* at 644.

[16] *Id.* at 680 (Story, J., concurring).

Supreme Court held that a state's bankruptcy law could not be applied retroactively to discharge a debt incurred before the law was adopted.[17]

But in *Ogden v. Saunders*, the Supreme Court limited *Sturges* and the scope of the contracts clause to interference with already existing contracts; the contracts clause does not apply to limit the ability of the government to regulate the terms of future contracts.[18] The Court reasoned that a contract implicitly includes the law as of the time of the agreement, and therefore the law cannot be viewed as an impairment of a contract. Chief Justice John Marshall dissented. This was the only dissent he ever wrote in a constitutional case. Marshall argued, based on natural law principles, that the government should not be able to dictate the terms of future contracts so as to protect debtors in case they became insolvent. Marshall's position, however, never attracted majority support from the Supreme Court, and it always has been the law that the contracts clause does not apply to statutes that regulate the terms of future contracts.

The Contracts Clause in the Nineteenth Century After the Marshall Court

Throughout the remainder of the nineteenth century, the Supreme Court continued to enforce the contracts clause and to follow the basic principles set forth during the Marshall Court era. For example, the Supreme Court found violations of the contracts clause when a state attempted to repeal a tax exemption[19] and when a state attempted to restore property that had been foreclosed.[20]

Yet the Court during the nineteenth century also articulated some limits on the scope of the contracts clause. First, the Court indicated that it would narrowly construe charters from state governments and thereby limit the circumstances in which they could be regarded as contracts limiting state regulation. In *Charles River Bridge v. Warren Bridge*, the state gave a company a charter to construct and operate a toll bridge.[21] Subsequently, the state gave a second company a charter to build a toll-free bridge. The first company argued that the second charter decreased the value of its contract and thus violated the contracts clause. The Supreme Court found no constitutional violation. It concluded that the first contract created only authority to build a bridge; it did not give an exclusive right to do so. Accordingly, the second contract did not impair the obligations of the first.

Second, the Supreme Court said that while the government could not impair contractual duties, it could modify the remedies available under a contract. In *Bronson v. Kinzie*, the Supreme Court held that a state may shorten the statute of limitations period or specify what items may be used to satisfy a judgment.[22] The Court said that if "the laws of the State passed afterwards had done nothing more

---

[17] 17 U.S. (4 Wheat.) 122 (1819).

[18] 25 U.S. (12 Wheat.) 213 (1827).

[19] Piqua Branch of the State Bank of Ohio v. Knoop, 57 U.S. (16 How.) 369 (1853).

[20] Bronson v. Kinzie, 42 U.S. (1 How.) 311 (1843).

[21] 36 U.S. (11 Pet.) 420 (1837).

[22] 42 U.S. (1 How.) 311 (1843).

than change the remedy upon contracts . . . they would be liable to no contractual objection."[23] The Court explained that "[w]hatever belongs merely to the remedy may be altered according to the will of the State, provided the alteration does not impair the obligation of the contract."[24] For example, in *Curtis v. Whitney*, the Court applied this principle to uphold a state law that provided that a deed to property may not be issued unless the prior owner was given at least three months' notice.[25]

The difficulty, of course, with this distinction is deciding when interference with a remedy is impairment of the contract. The Supreme Court later admitted that the line was an "obscure" one, but it was used to allow more latitude for state regulation.[26]

Third, and most important, the Supreme Court indicated that the contracts clause was not absolute; that the government could interfere even with existing contracts to achieve a valid police purpose. In *Stone v. Mississippi*, the issue was whether the state impaired the obligations of contracts by prohibiting lotteries after it earlier had chartered a lottery company.[27] The Court upheld the new law and emphasized that "[a]ll agree that the legislature cannot bargain away the police power of a state. . . . [N]o legislature can curtail the power of its successors to make such laws as they deem proper in matters of police."[28] The Court said that the power to stop lotteries "is governmental, to be exercised at all times by those in power, at their discretion."[29]

Similarly, in *Manigault v. Springs*, the Court upheld a state law authorizing the building of a dam on a creek, even though it violated a contract among landowners that no such dam would be constructed.[30] The Court upheld the law, even though it disrupted a carefully bargained agreement, because the state was exercising its police power. The Court explained that the police power "is an exercise of the sovereign right of the government to protect the lives, health, morals, comfort, and general welfare of the people, and is paramount to any rights under contracts between individuals."[31] The Court declared that "parties entering into contracts may not estop the legislature from enacting laws intended for the public good."[32]

By holding that the government may interfere with contracts to achieve a valid police purpose, the Court opened the door to allowing a vast array of government regulations even when they have the effect of interfering with contract rights. Indeed, this "'exception' might swallow the contract clause. If any effort that might be described as an attempt to protect the 'general welfare' can justify a

---

[23] *Id.* at 315.
[24] *Id.* at 316.
[25] 80 U.S. (13 Wall.) 68 (1871).
[26] *See* W.B. Worthen Co. v. Kavanaugh, 295 U.S. 56, 60 (1935).
[27] *See* Stone v. Mississippi, 101 U.S. (11 Otto) 814 (1880).
[28] *Id.* at 817-818.
[29] *Id.* at 821.
[30] 199 U.S. 473 (1905).
[31] *Id.* at 480.
[32] *Id.*

retroactive interference with rights acquired by contract, the clause furnishes little or no barrier to contractual impairments."[33]

The Contracts Clause in the First Third of the Twentieth Century

The Supreme Court's aggressive protection of freedom of contract under the due process clauses made the contracts clause superfluous during the first third of the twentieth century. Indeed, the freedom of contract protected under due process was even broader than that safeguarded by the contracts clause; due process limited government regulation of existing or future contracts, whereas the contracts clause applied only to interference with already existing contracts. Moreover, government regulation would be allowed under both due process and the contracts clause if it was deemed to serve a valid police purpose. Although the Court occasionally used the contracts clause,[34] it was applied relatively infrequently during this period because the Court relied on substantive economic due process to protect the same rights.

§8.3.3   The Contracts Clause Since 1934

Home Building & Loan Association v. Blaisdell

The key case defining the scope of the contracts clause since 1934 is *Home Building & Loan Association v. Blaisdell*.[35] *Blaisdell* involved a Minnesota law that created a moratorium on foreclosure of mortgages from 1933 until no later than May 1, 1935. Because of the Depression, the state was concerned about people losing their homes due to mortgage foreclosures and the state acted to prevent foreclosures, even though the mortgage contracts accorded the lenders this remedy. The Minnesota law was thus exactly the kind of debtor relief legislation that the contracts clause was meant to forbid.

The Supreme Court upheld the Minnesota law and dismissed the framers' intent for the contracts clause as being irrelevant. Chief Justice Hughes wrote:

> It is no answer to say that this public need was not apprehended a century ago, or to insist that what the provision of the Constitution meant to the vision of that day it must mean to the vision of our time. If by the statement that what the Constitution meant at the time of its adoption it means today, it is intended to say that the great clauses of the Constitution must be confined to the interpretation which the framers, with the conditions and outlook of their time, would have placed upon them, the statement carries its own refutation. It was to guard against such a narrow conception that Chief Justice Marshall uttered the memorable warning—We must never forget that it is a constitution we are expounding—a

---

[33]   Geoffrey Stone et al., Constitutional Law 1558 (5th ed. 2005).
[34]   *See, e.g.*, W.B. Worthen Co. v. Kavanaugh, 295 U.S. 56 (1935) (eliminating a foreclosure remedy violates the contracts clause); W.B. Worthen Co. v. Thomas, 292 U.S. 426 (1934) (law exempting insurance payments from creditors' claims violates the contracts clause).
[35]   290 U.S. 398 (1934).

constitution intended to endure for ages to come, and consequently, to be adapted to the various crises of human affairs.[36]

This is as strong a statement as can be found anywhere in the United States Reports that the framers' intent is not controlling in contemporary constitutional adjudication.[37]

The Court upheld the Minnesota law because it was an emergency measure of limited duration "to protect the vital interests of the community."[38] The Court stressed that the law "was not for the mere advantage of particular individuals but for the protection of a basic interest of society."[39]

Blaisdell is extremely important in limiting the scope of the contracts clause. It reaffirms that the government can interfere with existing contracts if it has a valid police purpose, and it describes the police power broadly enough to include debtor relief, protecting people from foreclosure of their mortgages, as a valid governmental objective. Indeed, since *Blaisdell*, there only have been two cases, both described below, where a state law has been found to violate the contracts clause.[40]

Government Interference with Private Contracts

The current law under the contracts clause distinguishes government interference with private contracts from government interference with its own contractual obligations. As to government interference with private contracts, the current test was articulated in *Energy Reserves Group v. Kansas Power & Light.*[41] A contract for natural gas provided that the price to be paid would be increased if government regulators fixed a higher price than that specified in the contract. Subsequently, Kansas adopted a law that provided that the price to be paid for natural gas under a contract could not be increased because of prices set by federal authorities. The state law prevented the natural gas producer from charging the higher prices that it was entitled to under the contract.

The Supreme Court upheld the Kansas law and explained the analysis to be used in contracts clause cases:

> The threshold inquiry is whether the state law has, in fact, operated as a substantial impairment of a contractual relationship. . . . If the state regulation constitutes a substantial impairment, the State, in justification, must have a significant and legitimate purpose behind the regulation, such as the remedying of a broad and general social or economic problem. . . . Once a legitimate public purpose has

---

[36] *Id.* at 442-443 (citations omitted) (emphasis omitted).

[37] For a discussion of the debate over whether the framers' intent should be authoritative, *see* §1.4.

[38] 290 U.S. at 439.

[39] *Id.* at 445.

[40] Allied Structural Steel Co. v. Spannaus, 438 U.S. 234 (1978); United States Trust Co. v. New Jersey, 431 U.S. 1 (1977).

[41] 459 U.S. 400 (1983).

been identified, the next inquiry is whether [the law] is reasonable and is of a character appropriate to the public purpose justifying the legislation's adoption. Unless the State itself is a contracting party, as is customary in reviewing economic and social regulation, courts properly defer to legislative judgments as to the necessity and reasonableness of a particular measure.[42]

In other words, when a state or local government interferes with existing private contracts, a three-part test is used: (1) is there a substantial impairment of a contractual relationship; (2) if so, does it serve a significant and legitimate public purpose; and (3) is it reasonably related to achieving the goal? The test is very similar to traditional rational basis review.

As to the first part of the test, whether there is a substantial impairment of the contract, in *General Motors v. Romein*, the Court rejected a challenge to a state law that changed the workers' compensation program on the ground that it did not interfere with existing contracts.[43] In 1981, the Michigan Supreme Court interpreted a recently adopted Michigan statute to allow employers to reduce workers' compensation payments to disabled employees who could receive compensation from other employer-funded sources. In 1987, the Michigan legislature overturned this ruling by statute and required that employers make retroactive payments.

Employers sued and said that the change in the law constituted an impairment of the obligation of contracts. The Supreme Court rejected this challenge because it concluded that there was "no contractual agreement regarding the specific workers' compensation terms allegedly at issue."[44] The Court explained: "The 1987 statute did not change the legal enforceability of the employment contract here. . . . Moreover, petitioners suggestion that we should read every workplace regulation into the private arrangements of employers and employees would expand the definition of contract so far that the constitutional provision would lose its anchoring purpose . . . [and] [i]nstead, the Clause would protect against all changes in legislation."[45]

As to the second and third prongs of the test, state and local laws are upheld, even if they interfere with contractual rights, so long as they meet a rational basis test. Not surprisingly, virtually all laws have been found to meet this deferential scrutiny. For example, in *El Paso v. Simmons*, the Supreme Court upheld a state law that clearly changed the terms of a contract.[46] Under a 1910 contract, Texas sold public lands. The contract provided that if interest was not paid in a timely fashion, the state could terminate the contract and reclaim the land. However, the contract said that an owner could reinstate a claim to the land by paying the delinquent interest owed. In 1941, Texas adopted a law saying that reinstatement had to occur within five years after there was a forfeiture for nonpayment.

The Supreme Court upheld the Texas law, even though it obviously limited the rights of landowners to reclaim land that had been forfeited. The Court said

---

[42] *Id.* at 411-413 (citations omitted).
[43] 503 U.S. 181 (1992).
[44] *Id.* at 186-187.
[45] *Id.* at 190.
[46] 379 U.S. 497 (1965).

that the law had a legitimate purpose in that it was intended "to restore confidence in the stability and integrity of land tides" and to end the "imbroglio over land titles in Texas."[47] The Court found that the law was reasonably designed to achieve these goals and thus did not violate the contracts clause.

Similarly, in *Exxon Corp. v. Eagerton*, the Supreme Court upheld a state law that prevented oil and gas producers from passing on the costs of a severance tax, even though their contracts permitted them to do so.[48] The Court emphasized that the law was constitutional, notwithstanding its impairment of contract rights, because it is a "generally applicable rule of conduct designed to advance a broad societal interest."[49]

In *Keystone Bituminous Coal Association v. DeBenedictis*, the Court found that a state law limiting coal mining impaired existing contracts, but nonetheless upheld the law because it served a significant government interest.[50] A state law prohibited coal mining that would cause subsidence damage to property. The coal mine companies frequently had entered into agreements with those owning the surface rights whereby the companies were allowed to mine, even if it caused subsidence of the land. In other words, the law prevented exactly what the coal miners had bargained to be able to do. Although the Court recognized that the law interfered with contractual rights, it upheld the law because it was a reasonable way to prevent or repair environmental damage caused by coal mining.

There is only one case since 1934 where the Supreme Court has declared unconstitutional a state law that interfered with private contracts: *Allied Structural Steel Co. v. Spannaus*.[51] An Illinois company operated an office in Minnesota and provided a pension plan for its employees. The terms of the plan provided that the company could, at any time, amend the plan or terminate the plan and distribute the assets to the employees. Employees were entitled to collect under the plan if they worked for the company until they reached age 65 and if the plan was in effect at that time. Minnesota adopted a Private Pension Benefits Protection Act that required employers to pay a "pension funding charge" if they terminated a pension plan or closed a Minnesota office. The charge was to ensure that pensions would be available for individuals when they reached retirement age. Allied Structural Steel closed its Minnesota facility and was assessed a $185,000 fee.

The Court found that the Minnesota law violated the contracts clause. Justice Potter Stewart, writing for the Court, began by declaring that the "Contract Clause remains part of the Constitution. It is not a dead letter."[52] The Court found that the Minnesota statute was a substantial impairment of the obligation of contracts. The Court reasoned that the employer had a contract with its employees that permitted the termination of the contract at any point. The state, by forcing the company to make pension payments, was essentially abrogating this provision.

---

[47] *Id.* at 513.
[48] 462 U.S. 176 (1983).
[49] *Id.* at 191.
[50] 480 U.S. 470 (1987).
[51] 438 U.S. 234 (1978).
[52] *Id.* at 240.

The Court said that the law was unconstitutional because it was not narrowly tailored emergency legislation like that in *Blaisdell.* Justice Stewart stated: "[T]his law can hardly be characterized, like the law at issue in the *Blaisdell* case, as one enacted to protect a broad society interest rather than a narrow class. This legislation, imposing a sudden, totally unanticipated, and substantial retroactive obligation upon the company to its employees, was not enacted to deal with a situation remotely approaching the broad and desperate economic conditions of the early 1930s. . . . [If] the Contract Clause means anything at all, it means that Minnesota could not constitutionally do what it tried to do to the company in this case."[53]

The Court's decision in *Allied Structural Steel* can be questioned on many levels. First, was there a substantial impairment of a contract? Justice Brennan, in dissent, argued that the "Act does not relieve either the employer or his employees of any existing contract obligation. Rather, the Act creates an additional, supplemental duty of the employer, no different in kind from myriad duties created by a wide variety of legislative measures, which defeat settled expectations but have nonetheless been sustained by this Court."[54]

Second, was the Court using more than the rational basis test? Protecting pensions and ensuring income for people at retirement is surely a legitimate government purpose, and the law seems a reasonable way to achieve this goal. Therefore, it seems that the Court was applying heightened scrutiny that is not usually used in evaluating government regulation of private contracts.

Because *Allied Structural Steel* has not been followed by the Supreme Court in the last two decades, it is difficult to know whether it is an anomaly or whether it is a precedent that might someday be used to revitalize the contracts clause. Thus far, the contracts clause cases since *Allied Structural Steel*—such as *Energy Resources Group, Exxon,* and *Keystone Bituminous Coal*—have distinguished *Allied Structural Steel* and have refused to find a violation of the contracts clause.[55]

Government Interference with Government Contracts

In *United States Trust Co. v. New Jersey,* the Supreme Court indicated that government interference with government contracts will be subjected to heightened scrutiny.[56] In 1962, New Jersey and New York adopted laws prohibiting the use of toll revenues from the Port Authority of New Jersey and New York to subsidize railroad passenger service. The laws were meant to assure those holding Port Authority bonds that the toll funds would remain available to pay that debt. A decade later, during the energy crisis of the 1970s, the states adopted laws to repeal the earlier prohibition and to permit the use of toll funds to improve rail transit.

The Supreme Court declared that the states had violated the contracts clause. The Court emphasized its distrust of the government when it is abrogating its own

---

[53] *Id.* at 248-249.

[54] *Id.* at 255 (Brennan, J., dissenting).

[55] *Compare* Pension Benefit Guaranty Corp. v. R.A. Gray Co., 467 U.S. 717 (1984) (upholding the retroactive application of liability for pensions pursuant to federal law).

[56] 431 U.S. 1 (1977).

contracts. Justice Blackmun, writing for the Court, stated: "[C]omplete deference to a legislative assessment of reasonableness and necessity is not appropriate when the State's self-interest is at stake. A governmental entity can always find a use for extra money, especially when taxes do not have to be raised. If a State could reduce its financial obligation whenever it wanted to spend the money for what it regarded as an important public purpose, the Contract Clause would provide no protection at all."[57]

The Court recognized that conserving energy and protecting the environment are important public purposes, but the Court said that infringing the contract rights was "neither necessary to achievement of the plan nor reasonable in light of the circumstances."[58] The Court emphasized that the government could have achieved its goals through other means and also that the government knew of the need for railroad service to protect the environment and conserve energy when it adopted the initial law in 1962.

Thus, although the Court did not articulate a level of scrutiny, its use of least restrictive alternative analysis and the word "necessary" seems indicative of strict scrutiny. Because there has not been another Supreme Court case since *United States Trust Co. v. New Jersey* concerning government interference with government contracts, the precise test remains uncertain. Nonetheless, it is clear that laws impairing the government's obligations under its own contracts will be subjected to much more careful review than will laws interfering with private contracts.

§8.4   THE TAKINGS CLAUSE

§8.4.1   Introduction

Both the federal government and the states have the power of eminent domain—the authority to take private property when necessary for government activities. However, the Constitution contains an important limit on this power: The Fifth Amendment states "nor shall private property be taken for public use without just compensation." This was the first provision of the Bill of Rights to be applied to the states.[1]

---

[57] *Id.* at 25.
[58] *Id.* at 29.
§8.4 [1] *See* Chicago, Burlington & Quincy R.R. v. Chicago, 166 U.S. 226 (1897), discussed in §6.3.3.

Overview of the Issues

Analysis under the takings clause can be divided into four questions. First, is there a "taking"? As described below, there are two basic ways of finding a taking. A possessory taking occurs when the government confiscates or physically occupies property. Alternately, a regulatory taking is when government regulation leaves no reasonable economically viable use of property.

Second, is it "property"? Obviously, only if the object of the taking is "property" does the Fifth Amendment provision apply. Generally, the Court has relied on other sources of law, usually state law, in deciding whether there is a property interest.

Third, if there is a taking of property, the next question becomes: Is the taking for "public use"? If the taking is not for public use, the government must give the property back. However, as also is discussed below, the Court has very broadly defined public use so that almost any taking will meet the requirement. The Court has said that a taking is for public use so long as it is "rationally related to a conceivable public purpose"[2]; in other words, so long as it meets the rational basis test.

Fourth, assuming that it is a taking for public use, the final question becomes: Is "just compensation" paid? The key is that just compensation is measured in terms of the loss to the owner; the gain to the taker is irrelevant.

Purposes of the Takings Clause

The takings clause is the most important protection of property rights in the Constitution. In part, the takings clause is about ensuring that the government does not confiscate the property of some to give it to others.[3] Long ago, in *Calder v. Bull*, the Court condemned such a practice as violating the natural law principles on which the Constitution was founded.[4]

In part, too, it is about loss spreading. If the government takes away a person's property to benefit society, then society should pay. The Supreme Court has explained that a principal purpose of the takings clause is "to bar the Government from forcing some people alone to bear public burdens which, in all fairness and justice, should be borne by the public as a whole."[5]

Yet, as described below, very difficult questions arise in determining when the government incurs this obligation to pay just compensation. Almost any government regulation decreases the value of someone's property. The Court thus has long noted that "[g]overnment hardly could go on if to some extent values incident to property could not be diminished without paying for every change in the

---

[2] Kelo v. City of New London, Conn., 545 U.S. 469 (2005); Hawaii Hous. Auth. v. Midkiff, 465 U.S. 1097 (1984).

[3] For a discussion of the importance of property rights, *see* Margaret Jane Radin, Property and Personhood, 34 Stan. L. Rev. 957 (1982); Frank Michelman, Property as a Constitutional Right, 38 Wash. & Lee L. Rev. 1097 (1981).

[4] 3 U.S. (3 Ball.) 386 (1798), discussed above in §8.2.1.

[5] Armstrong v. United States, 364 U.S. 40, 49 (1960).

general law."[6] No bright-line test ever has been, or likely ever will be, formulated to determine when government actions that decrease the value of property become a taking. Indeed, the Court has admitted that it "has been unable to develop any 'set formula' for determining when 'justice and fairness' require that economic injuries caused by public action be compensated by the government."[7] Rather, the Court has engaged in "ad hoc, factual inquiries" that turn "upon the particular circumstances in that case."[8] The result is a very large body of cases concerning the takings clause, but little in the way of coherent principles to make sense of them.

§8.4.2   What Is a "Taking"?

The vast majority of litigation concerning the takings clause of the Fifth Amendment has focused on the question: What is a "taking"? It is the obvious threshold issue for takings clause analysis because the constitutional provision applies only if a court finds that a taking has occurred.

For the sake of clarity, two different types of takings can be identified, although the Supreme Court has not always used these categories and has not always consistently defined them. A "possessory" taking occurs when the government confiscates or physically occupies property. A "regulatory" taking occurs when the government's regulation leaves no reasonable economically viable use of the property.

§8.4.2.1   Possessory Takings

Government Confiscation or Physical Occupation Is a Taking

The Supreme Court generally has found a taking when the government confiscates or physically occupies property. The Supreme Court declared: "When faced with a constitutional challenge to a permanent physical occupation of real property, this Court has invariably found a taking."[9] Indeed, as Professor Frank Michelman notes, "[a]t one time it was commonly held that in the absence of explicit expropriation, a compensable 'taking' could occur *only* through physical encroachment and occupation."[10] Michelman points out that the "one incontestable case for compensation (short of physical expropriation) seems to occur when the government brings it about that its agents, or the public at large, 'regularly' use or 'permanently' occupy, space or a thing which theretofore was understood to be under private ownership."[11]

---

[6] Pennsylvania Coal v. Mahon, 260 U.S. 393, 413 (1922).

[7] Penn Cent. Transp. Co. v. New York City, 438 U.S. 104, 124 (1978).

[8] *Id.* at 124 (citations omitted).

[9] Loretto v. Teleprompter Manhattan CATV Corp., 458 U.S. 419, 427 (1982).

[10] Frank Michelman, Property, Utility, and Fairness: Comments on the Ethical Foundations of "Just Compensation" Law, 80 Harv. L. Rev. 1165, 1884 (1967).

[11] *Id.*

Thus, government confiscation of property pursuant to its eminent domain power always has been considered a classic taking. In *Webb's Fabulous Pharmacies, Inc. v. Beckwith*, the Supreme Court applied this to find a taking when the government took the interest accruing on an interpleader account.[12] A Florida statute provided that when there was an interpleader account—a sum of money deposited with the court to which there are competing claims—the interest on the account would be the property of the government. The Supreme Court said that this was a classic taking because it was the government's expropriation of private property.[13]

Also, there is a taking when the government physically occupies property. Physical occupation can occur in a variety of forms. For example, in *Pumpelly v. Green Bay Co.*, the Supreme Court found a taking when the government's construction of a dam permanently flooded a person's property.[14] The Supreme Court said that "where real estate is actually invaded by superinduced additions of water, earth, sand, or other material, or by having any artificial structure placed on it, so as to effectually destroy or impair its usefulness, it is a taking, within the meaning of the Constitution."[15] The Court has characterized *Pumpelly* as involving "a physical occupation of the real estate of the private owner, and a practical ouster of his possession."[16]

In *United States v. Causby*, the Supreme Court found a taking when the government's regular use of airspace for military flights destroyed use of land as a chicken farm.[17] The Court explained that the government's action was "as complete as if the United States had entered upon the surface of the land and taken exclusive possession of it."[18] The Court said that the harm to the owner was a "product of a direct invasion of [his] domain."[19]

In *Stop the Beach Renourishment, Inc. v. Florida Department of Environmental Protection*, the Court concluded that there was not a taking when the state denied ownership of newly created beachfront property to property owners who had previously owned the land up to the shoreline.[20] After damage from hurricanes, additional landfill was added to combat the effects of erosion. The Florida Supreme Court ruled against the property owners who previously had owned the land up to the water. They argued that this decision was an impermissible taking.

---

[12] 449 U.S. 155 (1980).

[13] *Id.* at 163-164. *See also Connolly v. Pension Benefit Guar. Corp.*, 475 U.S. 211 (1986), concluding that there was not a taking when a statute required that an employer withdrawing from a multiemployer pension plan pay its proportionate share of the plan's unfunded benefits. The Court said that it was not a taking because under the Act "the government does not physically invade or permanently appropriate any of the employer's assets for its own use." *Id.* at 225.

[14] 80 U.S. (13 Wall.) 166 (1872).

[15] *Id.* at 181.

[16] Northern Transp. Co. v. Chicago, 99 U.S. 635, 642 (1878).

[17] 328 U.S. 256 (1946).

[18] *Id.* at 261.

[19] *Id.* at 265-266. *See also* Griggs v. County of Allegheny, 369 U.S. 84 (1962) (overflights held a taking); Portsmouth Harbor Land & Hotel Co. v. United States, 260 U.S. 327 (1922) (military's repeated firing of guns over property was a taking).

[20] 130 S. Ct. 2592 (2010).

An underlying issue presented to the Supreme Court was whether a judicial decision can constitute a taking. The Court split 4-4 on this issue, with Justice Stevens not participating. Justice Scalia, joined by Chief Justice Roberts and Justices Thomas and Alito, concluded that judicial actions can constitute a taking and declared: "In sum, the Takings Clause bars *the State* from taking private property without paying for it, no matter which branch is the instrument of the taking."[21] But the other four Justices—Kennedy, Ginsburg, Breyer, and Sotomayor—concluded that this issue did not need to be addressed. All eight of the Justices agreed that in this case there was no taking because under Florida law the beachfront property owners had no property right to the newly created land.

The Court has made it clear that government confiscation or occupation of property constitutes a taking no matter how small the amount of property. In *Loretto v. Teleprompter Manhattan CATV Corp.*, the Supreme Court found a taking in a city ordinance requiring apartment building owners to make space available for cable television facilities.[22] Although the amount of space involved was only about one cubic foot, the Court applied "the traditional rule that a permanent physical occupation of property is a taking."[23]

The Court in *Loretto* reviewed many earlier cases and concluded that they "clearly establish that permanent physical occupations [of] land by such installations as telegraph and telephone lines, rails, and underground pipes or wires are takings even if they occupy only relatively insubstantial amounts of space and do not interfere with the landowner's use of the rest of his land."[24] The Court thus concluded that a requirement that owners make available space for cable television was a permanent physical occupation and thus a taking.[25]

When Is There a Physical Occupation?

These cases establish that there is a taking if the government confiscates land or physically occupies it. A difficult issue concerns whether there is a government physical occupation of property when the government requires public access to property. The cases are not consistent in answering this question.

In *Kaiser Aetna v. United States*, the Supreme Court found that there was a taking when the government required that a private waterway be opened for public use.[26] The owners of a pond in Hawaii spent a substantial amount of money to dig a channel connecting it to the Pacific Ocean. The United States Corps of Engineers deemed this to be a "navigable water" and thus open to use by the United States

---

[21] *Id.* at 2602.

[22] 458 U.S. 419 (1982).

[23] *Id.* at 441.

[24] *Id.* at 430.

[25] *Compare FCC v. Florida Power Corp.*, 480 U.S. 245 (1987), where the Court distinguished *Loretto* and found that there was not a taking when the Federal Communication Commission regulated the rates that utility companies charged cable television companies for use of utility poles. The Court said that in *Loretto* the government required landlords to give space to cable companies, but the FCC regulation does not give any right to space and instead sets the price when space is given.

[26] Kaiser Aetna v. United States, 444 U.S. 164 (1979).

and the general public. The Court said that this was a taking because the government was transforming private property into public property and in essence allowing the public to occupy the property.[27]

In contrast, in *PruneYard Shopping Center v. Robins*, the Court rejected the claim that there was a taking when the California Supreme Court interpreted the California constitution as requiring that shopping centers be open to speech activities.[28] After an earlier ruling to the contrary, the Supreme Court in *Hudgens v. NLRB* held that there was not a First Amendment right of access to privately owned shopping centers for speech purposes.[29] However, in *PruneYard*, the California Supreme Court found that there was a *state* constitutional right to use shopping centers for speech activities.[30] The owners appealed this ruling to the Supreme Court and argued that mandating access to the shopping center was a taking because it meant that there would be a physical invasion of the property.

The Supreme Court, in an opinion by Justice Rehnquist, concluded that there was not a taking. The Court said that "[t]here is nothing to suggest that preventing appellants from prohibiting this sort of activity will unreasonably impair the value or use of their property as a shopping center. . . . In these circumstances, the fact that they may have 'physically invaded' appellants' property cannot be viewed as determinative."[31]

Justice Rehnquist, who also wrote the majority opinion in *Kaiser Aetna*, distinguished the two cases. He said that in *Kaiser Aetna* there was a substantial interference with "reasonable investment backed expectations," but in *PruneYard* the plaintiffs failed to show that excluding speakers was "essential to the use or economic value of their property."[32]

At the very least, these cases illustrate that the distinction between a possessory taking and a regulatory interference is often unclear. Is requiring that shopping centers allow speech activity a possessory taking because it involves a physical invasion of the property; or is it to be considered under the looser standard of regulatory takings because it is a regulation that decreases value? Indeed, in many of the cases, the characterization of whether it is to be considered a possessory taking or a regulatory taking seems arbitrary. In *Causby*, are the flights that destroyed the chicken farm a government occupation or rather a government action that decreases the value of property? Although the Court invokes the categories of possessory and regulatory takings as if they are clear and distinct, such is often not the case.[33]

---

[27] *Compare* United States v. Riverside Bayview Homes, 474 U.S. 121 (1985) (finding no taking when a government regulation required a permit before the discharge of landfill materials into navigable waters).

[28] 447 U.S. 74 (1980), also discussed in §§6.4.4.2 and 11.4.3.

[29] 424 U.S. 507 (1976); discussed in §6.4.4.2 (no state action in private shopping center's exclusion of speech); §11.4.3 (no First Amendment right of access to private property for speech purposes).

[30] 23 Cal. 3d 899, 595 P.2d 341 (1979).

[31] 447 U.S. at 83-84.

[32] *Id.* at 84.

[33] *See, e.g.,* Yee v. Escondido, 503 U.S. 519 (1992) (distinguishing possessory and regulatory takings).

Also, *Kaiser Aetna* and *PruneYard* indicate that there is not a clear rule as to when the government's requiring physical access to property constitutes a taking. In *PruneYard*, the Supreme Court said that it would weigh "such factors as the character of the government action, its economic impact, and its interference with reasonable investment-backed expectations."[34] These criteria, however, are so general as to allow courts great latitude in deciding when there is a taking because the government requires physical access to property.

Is There an Emergency Exception?

Some cases suggest that in an emergency situation there is not a taking, even though the government confiscates or physically occupies property. Again, the cases are not consistent.

In *United States v. Caltex, Inc.*, the Supreme Court found that there was not a taking when the government destroyed a company's oil facilities in the Philippines to keep them from being taken over by the Japanese during the early days of World War II.[35] The Court acknowledged that the government had destroyed the property intentionally to keep it from being used by the enemy. But the Court refused to find that this was a taking requiring compensation. The Court said: "The terse language of the Fifth Amendment is no comprehensive promise that the United States will make whole all who suffer from every ravage and burden of war. This Court has long recognized that in wartime many losses must be attributed solely to the fortunes of war, and not to the sovereign. No rigid rules can be laid down to distinguish compensable losses from noncompensable losses. Each case must be judged on its own facts."[36]

Yet not all of the cases have found such an exception to the takings clause, even in wartime. In *United States v. Pewee Coal Co.*, the Supreme Court found that the government's seizure of a coal mine during a national labor strike constituted a taking even though it was done during wartime.[37] The plurality opinion concluded that there was a taking requiring compensation because there had been an "actual taking of possession and control."[38]

In fact, in a subsequent case, the Supreme Court rejected the notion of any exception to the requirement for compensation for possessory takings. In *Lucas v. South Carolina Coastal Council*, Justice Scalia, writing for the Court, said: "In general (at least with regard to permanent invasions), no matter how minute

---

[34] 447 U.S. at 83.

[35] 344 U.S. 149 (1952).

[36] *Id.* at 155-156. Consider also *United States v. Central Eureka Mining Co.*, 357 U.S. 155 (1958), where the Court found that there was not a taking when the government ordered that nonessential gold mines stop production during World War II. The Court emphasized that the government "did not occupy, use, or in any manner take physical possession of the gold mines or the equipment connected with them." *Id.* at 165-166.

[37] 341 U.S. 114 (1951).

[38] *Id.* at 116.

the intrusion, and no matter how weighty the public purpose behind it, we have required compensation."[39]

§8.4.2.2 Regulatory Takings

Pennsylvania Coal v. Mahon

Traditionally, courts limited "takings" to situations where the government expropriated property or physically occupied it.[40] In the landmark case of *Pennsylvania Coal v. Mahon*, the Court said that a taking also could be found if government regulation of the use of property went "too far."[41] *Pennsylvania Coal v. Mahon* involved a Pennsylvania statute that prohibited the mining of coal in any manner that would cause the subsidence of property. The effect of the law was to prevent companies from exercising certain mining rights; they were required to leave columns of coal underground to support the surface. Unlike the cases described above, the government did not confiscate, occupy, destroy, or invade the property; the government regulated its use. Thus, the issue before the Supreme Court was whether this government regulation constituted a taking.

Justice Oliver Wendell Holmes wrote for the Court and found that there was a taking. He said that "when [regulation] reaches a certain magnitude, in most if not in all cases there must be an exercise of eminent domain and compensation to support the act."[42] Justice Holmes recognized that the government could not function if it had to compensate every person whose property values decreased because of a government action,[43] but he said that "while property may be regulated to a certain extent, if regulation goes too far it will be recognized as a taking."[44] Justice Holmes concluded that the Pennsylvania law limiting mining was a taking because "mak[ing] it commercially impracticable to mine certain coal has nearly the same effect for constitutional purposes as appropriating or destroying it."[45]

---

[39] 505 U.S. 1003 (1992).

[40] Michelman, *supra* note 10, at 1184. *See, e.g.,* Mugler v. Kansas, 123 U.S. 623, 668-669 (1887) (concluding that a state's prohibition of alcoholic beverages was not a taking and declaring that "a prohibition . . . upon the use of property for purposes that are declared, by valid legislation, to be injurious to the health, morals, or safety of the community, cannot in any sense, be deemed a taking or an appropriation of property for the public benefit").

[41] 260 U.S. 393, 415 (1922).

[42] *Id.* at 413.

[43] *Id.*

[44] *Id.* at 415.

[45] *Id.* at 414. *But see* Keystone Bituminous Coal Assoc. v. DeBenedictis, 480 U.S. 470 (1987) (upholding a Pennsylvania law that limited the amount of coal that could be removed so as to prevent subsidence of land).

When Does a Regulation Become a Taking?

The problem that has confounded courts and commentators ever since *Mahon* is what is "too far"; when does regulation become a taking?[46] The Supreme Court has repeatedly acknowledged that no formula or rule can be devised to answer this question. In fact, in *Mahon*, Justice Holmes recognized that it was "a question of degree and therefore cannot be disposed of by general propositions."[47] On many other occasions as well, the Court has said that the issue of when regulation constitutes a taking cannot be reduced to a formula or a rule, but inevitably is a matter of considering the facts in each case.[48]

The Court has articulated general criteria that should be considered in evaluating whether a regulation is a taking. The Court said:

> [W]e have eschewed the development of any set formula for identifying a "taking" forbidden by the Fifth Amendment, and have relied instead on ad hoc, factual inquiries into the circumstances of each particular case. To aid in this determination, however, we have identified three factors which have "particular significance": (1) the economic impact of the regulation on the claimant; (2) the extent to which the regulation has interfered with investment-backed expectations; and (3) the character of the governmental action.[49]

These criteria obviously accord courts a tremendous amount of discretion, and it is not surprising that cases concerning regulatory takings are often inconsistent and difficult to reconcile. As the criteria indicate, the Court especially focuses on the economic effect of the government regulations and the extent to which they interfere with reasonable expectations of the property owner.

One important principle that emerges from the cases and that is crucial in judicial consideration of regulatory takings is that government regulation is a taking if it leaves no reasonable economically viable use of property; government regulation is not a taking simply because it decreases the value of a person's property, so long as it leaves reasonable economically viable uses.

Comparison of two Supreme Court cases illustrates this principle. In *Penn Central Transportation Co. v. New York City*, the Supreme Court held that there was not a taking when the government designated a building as a historical landmark and prevented the owner from constructing a substantial expansion on top of the building.[50] The Court emphasized that the regulation did not deny the owners all profitable use of the building and, in fact, had not even precluded all development

---

[46] For an excellent discussion of the issue, tracing it back to *Mahon, see* Carol Rose, *Mahon* Reconstructed: Why the Takings Issue Is Still a Muddle, 57 S. Cal. L. Rev. 561 (1984).

[47] *Id.* at 416.

[48] *See, e.g.*, Penn Cent. Transp. Co. v. New York City, 438 U.S. 104, 124 (1978); Goldblatt v. Town of Hempstead, 369 U.S. 590, 594 (1962); United States v. Central Eureka Mining Co., 357 U.S. 155, 168 (1958).

[49] Connolly v. Pension Benefit Guar. Corp., 475 U.S. 211, 225 (1986); *see also* Penn Cent. Transp. Co. v. New York City, 438 U.S. at 124; PruneYard Shopping Ctr. v. Robins, 447 U.S. at 82-83.

[50] 438 U.S. 104 (1978).

of the air rights above the building.[51] Because designating the building a historic landmark had the effect only of decreasing the value of the property, and because it served an important purpose, the Court concluded that there was not a taking requiring just compensation.

Penn Central can be compared to the Supreme Court's subsequent decision in *Lucas v. South Carolina Coastal Council*.[52] After a person purchased beachfront property for almost $1 million, the state adopted a coastal protection plan that prevented the construction of any permanent habitable structures on the property. The state trial court concluded that this prohibition rendered the property "valueless."[53] Justice Scalia, writing for the Court, said that it was established that there is a taking "where regulation denies all economically beneficial or productive use of the land."[54] Scalia observed: "[T]here are good reasons for our frequently expressed belief that when the owner of real property has been called upon to sacrifice all economically beneficial uses in the name of the common good, that is, to leave his property economically idle, he has suffered a taking."[55] The Court concluded that the coastal protection law was a taking of Lucas's property unless there had been a similar restriction on development at the time he acquired the land.[56]

It thus is clear that, at the very least, there is not a regulatory taking when the government's action leaves reasonable economically viable use of the property. Also, crucial in evaluating whether there is a regulatory taking is the relationship of the government's actions to the property owner's expectations. For example, people who purchase property knowing of common law legal regulations cannot subsequently claim that those regulations are a taking. In *Lucas*, for example, the Supreme Court said that the State of South Carolina only could avoid its regulation being deemed a taking if it could "identify background principles of nuisance and property law that prohibit the uses [Lucas] now intends in the circumstances in which the property is presently found."[57]

However, it appears that the Court is drawing a distinction between common law rules that existed prior to purchase and other regulations. The Court ruled

---

[51] *Id.* at 137.

[52] 505 U.S. 1003 (1992).

[53] Quoted in *Lucas, id.*

[54] *Id.* at 1016.

[55] *Id.* at 1019.

[56] In a footnote, Justice Scalia indicated that less than complete elimination of economic value could be the basis for a taking. Scalia wrote:

> Regrettably, the rhetorical force of our "deprivation of all economically feasible use" rule is greater than its precision, since the rule does not make clear the "property interest" against which the loss is to be measured. When, for example, a regulation requires a developer to leave 90% of a rural tract in its natural state, it is unclear whether we would analyze the situation in which the owner has been deprived of all economically beneficial use of the burdened portion of the tract, or as one in which the owner has suffered a mere diminution in the value of the tract as a whole. Unsurprisingly, this uncertainty regarding the composition of the denominator in our "deprivation" fraction has produced inconsistent pronouncements by the Court.

Id. at 1016 n.7.

[57] *Id.* at 1004.

that the latter may be challenged even if they were already in place at the time of purchase. In *Palazzolo v. Rhode Island*, the Court held that a property owner could bring a takings claim as to regulations and laws that were in place at the time the property was acquired.[58]

Palazzolo formed a company to purchase and develop coastal property in Rhode Island. After several proposals for development were rejected by the state, the corporation stopped functioning and ultimately was dissolved under the state's law. Palazzolo was deemed the owner under the terms of this law. Subsequently, he presented additional proposals for development, which were denied by the Coastal Commission. He sued claiming a taking because the government was preventing all development of his property. The Rhode Island Supreme Court rejected this argument, in part, because the rules were already in place at the time Palazzolo acquired the property.[59]

The Supreme Court rejected this argument and reversed. The Court said that if it accepted such an argument, then "the postenactment transfer of title would absolve the State of its obligation to defend any action restricting land use, no matter how extreme or unreasonable. A State would be allowed, in effect, to put an expiration date on the Takings Clause. This ought not to be the rule. Future generations, too, have a right to challenge unreasonable limitations on the use and value of land."[60] Thus, the Court unambiguously held that takings claims may be brought by owners to challenge regulations that were in place at the time that the property was acquired.[61]

---

[58]   533 U.S. 606 (2001).

[59]   The Rhode Island Supreme Court had also ruled that the claim was not ripe for review because the basis for the takings suit was a proposed development that had never been presented to the state agency. The Supreme Court reversed and held that the takings claim was ripe for review because it was clear that the proposal for development would be rejected. In *Williamson County Regl. Planning Commn. v. Hamilton Bank of Johnson City*, 473 U.S. 173, 186 (1985), the Court ruled that a takings claim challenging the application of land-use regulations is not ripe unless "the government entity charged with implementing the regulations has reached a final decision regarding the application of the regulations to the property at issue." The Supreme Court, though, reversed because it found no doubt as to the likely outcome for such a request by Palazzolo. Justice Kennedy explained that any claim of uncertainty in the administrative process was "belied by the unequivocal nature of the wetland regulations at issue and by the Council's application of the regulations to the subject property. . . . There is no indication the Council would have accepted the application had petitioner's proposed beach club occupied a smaller surface area. To the contrary, it ruled that the proposed activity was not a 'compelling public purpose.' " *Palazzolo*, 533 U.S. at 618.

[60]   533 U.S. at 627.

[61]   The Court, however, rejected that there was a showing of a regulatory taking in these facts. The Court explained that the record was undisputed that Palazzolo could build a residence on an 18-acre parcel, a $200,000 development value. Thus, it could not be said that all economically viable use was forbidden as a basis for a regulatory takings claim. The Court said that Palazzolo might have other arguments for a regulatory taking, such as that this upland section of the property is distinct from the wetlands section and should not affect a takings claim for the latter. But the Court said that such an argument was not presented to the lower court and thus was not properly before it. In light of this holding, it can be questioned whether the Court's discussion of the ability to bring a takings challenge to preexisting regulations is just dicta, unnecessary to its holding that there is not a taking on these facts.

How can this language be reconciled with the statement in *Lucas* that takings challenges are limited by the preexisting law? It is possible that *Palazzolo* is implicitly overruling this statement from *Lucas*. More likely, the Court is drawing a distinction between challenges to common law rules, which cannot be brought if they were in place when the property was acquired, and takings claims as to regulations and statutes, which can be made even if they were there when the owner obtained the property. Drawing a distinction among types of law, deferring more to court-created common law than to legislatively enacted statutes, seems questionable.

Yet it is well established that the common law does limit a person's use of his or her property. A prominent example of this is that a person has no right to use his or her property to create a nuisance to others. For example, in *Hadachek v. Sebastian*, the Supreme Court held that a brickyard could be ordered to cease its operations, without just compensation being paid, because of its adverse effects on the surrounding area.[62] Similarly, in *Northwestern Fertilizing Co. v. Hyde Park*, the Court ruled that the government could close a fertilizer plant without it being a taking, when it constituted a nuisance.[63] In both of these cases, the activities originally were built away from the population in the city, but growth and expansion then brought people in proximity to the activities.

In *Miller v. Schoene*, the State of Virginia ordered the destruction of a large number of ornamental red cedar trees to prevent the spread of cedar rust, a highly infectious plant disease.[64] The state acted to protect many apple orchards in the vicinity. The Court sided with the state and did not require that it provide compensation to the owners of the ornamental red cedar trees. The Court said that when the government is forced to make a choice between the preservation of two types of property—either the cedar trees or the apple orchards—"the state does not exceed its constitutional powers by deciding upon the destruction of one class of property in order to save another which, in the judgment of the legislature, is of greater value to the public."[65]

It is very difficult to generalize about regulatory takings beyond the statement that a taking exists if the government denies all economically viable use of property in a manner that interferes with reasonable expectations for use. Five major areas where the Court has considered regulatory takings involve zoning ordinances, conditions on development of property, limits on conveyance of property, rent and rate controls, and imposition of government liability.

Zoning Ordinances

Zoning ordinances limit the way in which a person may use his or her property and, therefore, frequently have the effect of diminishing the property's economic value. Generally, though, the Court has refused to find a taking, concluding

---

[62] 239 U.S. 394, 410 (1915).
[63] 97 U.S. 659, 669 (1878).
[64] 276 U.S. 272 (1928).
[65] *Id.* at 279.

that the regulation does not eliminate all reasonable economically viable uses of the property.

Village of Euclid v. Ambler Realty Co. was one of the first Supreme Court cases to consider a challenge to a zoning ordinance.[66] A tract of vacant land was zoned for industrial uses and had a market value of about $10,000 per acre. The land was rezoned so that it could be used only for residential purposes, and its value was reduced to about $2,500 an acre. Nonetheless, the Supreme Court rejected a due process challenge to the revised zoning ordinance. The Court emphasized the government's strong police purpose in the zoning regulation. The Court said: "[T]he segregation of residential, business, and industrial buildings will make it easier to provide fire apparatus available for the character and intensity of the development in each section; that it will increase the safety and security of home life; greatly tend to prevent street accidents, especially to children, by reducing the traffic and resulting confusion in residential sections; decrease noise and other conditions which produce or intensify nervous disorders; preserve a more favorable environment in which to raise children."[67]

Subsequent cases generally have followed this reasoning and have rejected takings challenges to zoning ordinances.[68] For example, in *Goldblatt v. Town of Hempstead,* a city's zoning ordinance prevented further excavation of a stone and gravel quarry that had been in operation for over 30 years.[69] The Court rejected the takings claim and noted that "[i]t is an oft-repeated truism that every regulation necessarily speaks as a prohibition. If this ordinance is otherwise a valid exercise of the town's police powers, the fact that it deprives the property of its most beneficial use does not render it unconstitutional."[70] The Court said that the zoning ordinance was not a taking because "there is no evidence . . . which even remotely suggests that prohibition of further development will reduce the value of the lot in question."[71]

Similarly, in *Agins v. Tiburon,* the Supreme Court rejected a takings clause challenge to a zoning ordinance that required that property be used for single family homes rather than multiple family dwellings.[72] Whereas previously the owners might have constructed apartment or condominium buildings, the City of Tiburon adopted a zoning ordinance limiting construction to single family homes. The effect of the ordinance was to substantially reduce the value of the property. But the Supreme Court concluded that there was not a taking also because the owner still had reasonable economically viable use of the property and because

---

[66] 272 U.S. 365 (1926).

[67] *Id.* at 394.

[68] There are instances of the Supreme Court invalidating zoning ordinances based on other constitutional challenges. *See, e.g.,* Washington ex rel. Seattle Title & Trust Co. v. Roberge, 278 U.S. 116 (1928) (finding a violation of due process when a zoning ordinance required approval of two-thirds of the residents in order to develop property); City of Cleburne v. Cleburne Living Ctr., 473 U.S. 432 (1985) (finding that a zoning ordinance violated equal protection in preventing a home for the mentally disabled), discussed in §9.2.

[69] 369 U.S. 590 (1962).

[70] *Id.* at 592.

[71] *Id.* at 594.

[72] 447 U.S. 255 (1980).

the government had an important interest in "assuring careful and orderly development of residential property."[73]

The Court has followed this reasoning in other cases where the government's regulation limits development or use of property. In *Keystone Bituminous Coal Association v. DeBenedictis*, the Court refused to find a taking when a Pennsylvania law prevented mining that could cause subsidence of buildings and a Pennsylvania agency required that 50 percent of the coal be kept in the land underneath structures.[74] The law and the agency's interpretation of it had the effect of preventing some mining, even in instances where the coal company had purchased surface rights.[75] Nonetheless, the Supreme Court found that there was not a taking. The Court quoted *Agins* as establishing that "land use regulation can effect a taking if it does not substantially affect legitimate state interests . . . or denies an owner economically viable use of land."[76]

The *Keystone* Court concluded that there was not a taking because the law served legitimate state interests and because it allowed economically viable development of the property. The Court explained that the legislature's goal was to protect public safety by preventing subsidence of land. The Court also observed that there was not a taking because the law did not eliminate all economically viable use of the property. The Court said: "When the coal that must remain beneath the ground is viewed in the context of any reasonable unit of petitioner's coal mining operations and financial-backed expectations, it is plain that petitioners have not come close to satisfying their burden of proving that they have been denied the economically viable use of that property."[77]

Likewise, as discussed above, in *Palazzolo v. Rhode Island*, the Court found that there was not a taking when environmental protection laws prevented development of property because some economically viable use remained.[78] Although coastal protection laws prevented most development of the property, the owner was still allowed to build a residence on an 18-acre parcel worth about $200,000. This was enough, based on the facts before the Court, to preclude a finding of a regulatory taking even though far more valuable developments were prevented.

All of these cases indicate that it is very difficult to persuade the Supreme Court that restrictions on use of property, through zoning or other laws, constitute a taking. The Court only is willing to find a taking if the law prevents virtually all economically viable uses of the property, as was the situation in *Lucas*.

---

[73] *Id.* at 262. In *Agins*, the Court said that it was not a taking because the government action was "substantially related" to a legitimate government purpose. But in *Lingle v. Chevron U.S.A., Inc.*, 544 U.S. 528 (2005), the Supreme Court held that *Agins*'s phrasing was in error and that, to avoid being a taking, the government action only need be rationally related to a legitimate government purpose. In *Lingle*, the Court upheld a Hawaii law that limited the rent that national oil companies could charge to local service stations.

[74] 480 U.S. 470 (1987).

[75] The contracts clause aspect of the case is discussed above in §8.3.3.

[76] *Keystone*, 480 U.S. at 485, quoting *Agins*, 447 U.S. at 260.

[77] *Id.* at 499. The Court distinguished *Pennsylvania Coal v. Mahon*, in part, on the ground that in the earlier case there was evidence of substantial interference with the investment-backed expectations, but that was not proved in *Keystone*. *Id.*

[78] 533 U.S. 606 (2001).

Government Conditions on Development

The above cases concerned government prohibitions or restrictions on the use of property: restricting use of property to residential purposes; preventing mining of a quarry; requiring property be used for single family homes; and limiting the mining of underground coal to 50 percent of that present. What, however, if the government allows the development of property, but subject to specific conditions that the developer must meet? When are government conditions on development to be considered a taking?

In two decisions, the Supreme Court has announced that a condition on development of property is a taking if the burden imposed by the condition is not roughly proportionate to the government's justification for regulating. In *Nollan v. California Coastal Commission*, the government conditioned a permit for development of beachfront property on the owner's granting the public an easement to cross the property for beach access.[79] The Court, in an opinion by Justice Scalia, said that there would be a taking if the government were to require the property owners to grant an easement. He wrote: "Had California simply required the [appellants] to make an easement across their beachfront property available to the public on a permanent basis . . . we have no doubt that there would have been a taking. We think a 'permanent physical occupation' has occurred . . . where individuals are given a permanent and continuous right to pass to and from, so that real property may continuously be traversed, even though no particular individual is permitted to station himself permanently upon the premises."[80]

The Court said that police power allows the government to place a condition on development if it is rationally related to preventing harms caused by the new construction. For example, the government could put conditions on development of beachfront property to protect use of the beach from the effects of the new building. But the Court said that there is a taking if "the condition . . . utterly fails to further the end advanced as the justification. . . . In short, unless the permit condition serves the same governmental purposes as the development ban, the building restriction is not a valid regulation of land use but an out-and-out plan of extortion."[81]

The Court clarified *Nollan* in a more subsequent case, *Dolan v. City of Tigard*.[82] The government gave the owner of a store a permit to expand the building on the condition that land be set aside for a public greenway along a creek to minimize flooding and a bicycle path to relieve traffic congestion. The issue was whether these conditions on development constituted a taking.

The Supreme Court said that a two-part test was to be applied. First, is there a "nexus . . . between the legitimate state interest and the permit condition created by the city"?[83] This is the requirement created by *Nollan*. The Court found that

---

[79] 483 U.S. 825 (1987).
[80] *Id.* at 831-832.
[81] *Id.* at 837.
[82] 512 U.S. 374 (1994).
[83] *Id.* at 374, quoting *Nollan*, 483 U.S. at 837.

this requirement was met in *Dolan*. The Court said that there was an "obvious" relationship between the conditions on development and the goals in regulating.[84] For example, development within the area of the flood plan would increase runoff into the creek, and requiring an area for flood control as a condition on development was a way to solve that problem. Likewise, the pedestrian and bicycle path was to deal with the increased traffic congestion caused by the additional development.

Second, the Court said that it would evaluate whether the exactions on development were roughly proportionate to the government's justifications for regulating.[85] The Court said that this is a reasonableness test, but to avoid it being confused with the rational basis test, it would be called a "rough proportionality" standard.[86] The Court said that "[n]o precise mathematical calculation is required, but the city must make some sort of individualized determination that the required dedication is related both in nature and extent to the impact of the proposed development."[87]

Therefore, if the government imposes a condition on the development of property, two requirements must be met. First, it must be shown that the condition is rationally related to the government's purpose for regulating. Second, it must be shown that the burden created by the condition is roughly proportionate to the government's justification for regulating. Phrased slightly differently, it is a taking if either the government regulation is not rationally connected to the government's reason for regulating or the burden imposed by the condition is not roughly proportionate to the benefits gained because of the condition. The regulation thus must both be rationally related to the goal and impose burdens that are proportionate to the reasons for regulating.

The Court's most recent case considering when conditions on development constitute a taking involved a situation where, unlike in *Nollan* and *Dolan*, the permit for development was denied. In other words, in *Nollan* and *Dolan*, the property owner went ahead with the development and then argued that the conditions were a taking, while in *Koontz v. St. Johns River Water Management District*, the property owner choose to not get a permit for development but nonetheless to challenge the conditions as a taking.[88]

Coy Koontz wanted to develop some of his property on wetlands in Florida. He was told that he could do this only if he (1) reduced the size of his development and deeded to the District a conservation easement on the resulting larger remainder of his property or (2) hired contractors to make improvements to District-owned wetlands several miles away. Rather than do this, he brought a lawsuit arguing that these conditions constituted a taking.

The Court, in a 5-4 decision with Justice Alito writing for the majority, ruled in favor of Koontz. There were two parts to the Court's holding. First, the Court

---

[84] *Id.* at 388.
[85] *Id.*
[86] *Id.*
[87] *Id.* at 391.
[88] 133 S. Ct. 2586 (2013).

held that "[t]he principles that undergird our decisions in *Nollan* and *Dolan* do not change depending on whether the government *approves* a permit on the condition that the applicant turn over property or *denies* a permit because the applicant refuses to do so."[89]

Second, the Court said that it was a taking even though the government gave Koontz the option of spending money rather than providing an easement on his property. The Court said that "[s]uch so-called 'in lieu of' fees are utterly commonplace and they are functionally equivalent to other types of land use exactions. For that reason and those that follow, we reject respondent's argument and hold that so-called 'monetary exactions' must satisfy the nexus and rough proportionality requirements of *Nollan* and *Dolan*."[90]

Justice Kagan wrote for the four dissenters and focused on the latter, expressing concern that there will not be a way of distinguishing between impermissible land use exactions and property taxes. She expressed concern that the Court's holding "threatens to subject a vast array of land-use regulations, applied daily in States and localities throughout the country, to heightened constitutional scrutiny."[91] She explained: "By applying *Nollan* and *Dolan* to permit conditions requiring monetary payments—with no express limitation except as to taxes—the majority extends the Takings Clause, with its notoriously 'difficult' and 'perplexing' standards, into the very heart of local land-use regulation and service delivery. Cities and towns across the nation impose many kinds of permitting fees every day. Some enable a government to mitigate a new development's impact on the community, like increased traffic or pollution—or destruction of wetlands. Others cover the direct costs of providing services like sewage or water to the development. Still others are meant to limit the number of landowners who engage in a certain activity, as fees for liquor licenses do. All now must meet *Nollan* and *Dolan's* nexus and proportionality tests. . . . And the flexibility of state and local governments to take the most routine actions to enhance their communities will diminish accordingly."[92]

Temporarily Denying an Owner Development of Property

In *Tahoe-Sierra Preservation Council, Inc. v. Tahoe Regional Planning Agency*, the Court held that temporarily denying an owner the ability to develop property is not a taking so long as the government's action is reasonable.[93] Lake Tahoe is a beautiful area, with pristine waters. The local government became concerned that developments were causing significant changes and imposed a moratorium on further development pending studies being conducted. Owners, who could not develop their property, argued that the moratorium was a taking and that they should be compensated.

---

[89] *Id.* at 2595.
[90] *Id.* at 2599.
[91] *Id.* at 2604 (Kagan, dissenting).
[92] *Id.* at 2607.
[93] 535 U.S. 302 (2002).

The issue before the Court was whether a 32-month moratorium on development was a taking requiring the government to pay just compensation. In a 6-to-3 decision, with Justice Stevens writing for the majority, the Court concluded that there was not a taking. The Court rejected a categorical rule concerning delays in development, instead holding that it depended on the context and circumstances. The Court said that judges should apply the balancing test that it earlier articulated in *Penn Central*.[94] Under this approach, a moratorium on development is not a taking so long as the government's action is reasonable. The Court concluded that the 32-month delay for purposes of an environmental study was reasonable given the strong government interest in preserving the beauty of the Lake Tahoe area.

Limits on Conveyance of Property

Is there a taking if the government limits conveyance or transfer of the property? The cases are inconsistent. In *Andrus v. Allard*, the Supreme Court considered whether the Eagle Protection Act constituted a taking in its prohibition of the sale of bald or golden eagle parts, including those obtained before the statute's adoption.[95] The Court explained that it was not a taking because it did not eliminate all use of the property; possession or transportation still was allowed. The Court notes that the "regulations here do not compel the surrender of the artifacts, and there is no physical invasion or restraint upon them. Rather, a significant restriction has been imposed on one means of disposing of artifacts. But the denial of one traditional property right does not always amount to a taking. . . . It is, to be sure, undeniable that the regulations here prevent the most profitable use of appellees' property. Again, however, that is not dispositive. When we review regulations, a reduction in the value of the property is not necessarily equated with a taking."[96]

But in *Hodel v. Irving*, the Court found that there was a taking when the government prevented inheritance of certain property.[97] In the nineteenth century, a federal law divided some land on a Sioux Nation reservation into individual allotments. A Department of Interior regulation adopted in 1910 allowed inheritance of this property, and over time the property was divided into increasingly smaller sections. Indeed, the parcels were so small and divided as to prevent meaningful use of the property. Congress then passed a law preventing inheritance of small parcels that occupied less than 2 percent of the total land and that had earned its owner less than $100 in its prior year. Such land would revert to ownership by the tribe.

The Supreme Court found this regulation to be a taking. Justice O'Connor, writing for the Court, said: "[The] regulation here amounts to virtually the abrogation of the right to pass on a certain type of property . . . to one's heirs. In one form

---

[94] 438 U.S. at 124, quoted above at text accompanying notes 50 and 51.
[95] 444 U.S. 51 (1979).
[96] *Id.* at 65-66.
[97] 481 U.S. 704 (1987).

or another, the right to pass on property to one's family in particular has been part of the Anglo-American legal system since feudal times."[98]

There is an obvious tension between *Andrus v. Allard* and *Hodel v. Irving.* In the latter, the limit on conveyance by inheritance was deemed a taking; in the former, the limit on conveyance by sale was found not to be a taking. Indeed, three Justices in *Hodel* saw it as implicitly overruling *Andrus.* In *Hodel,* Justice Scalia, in an opinion joined by Rehnquist and Powell, said that "the present statute [is] indistinguishable from the statute that was at issue in *Allard.* . . . [In] finding a taking today our decision effectively limits *Allard* to its facts."[99] But in another concurring opinion, three other Justices disagreed that *Hodel* had overruled *Andrus v. Allard.* Justice Blackmun, joined by Brennan and Marshall, said that "nothing in today's opinion . . . limit[s] *Allard.* Indeed, I am of the view that the unique negotiations giving rise to the property rights and expectations at issue here make this case the unusual one."[100]

At the very least, it is unclear when restrictions on conveyance constitute a taking. Perhaps the difference between *Andrus* and *Hodel* is based on an unarticulated perception of the difference of the government's interest in regulating: The Court gave more weight to protecting an endangered species than to reuniting small parcels of land. Or perhaps the cases cannot be reconciled, and it will require a future Supreme Court decision to clarify when restrictions on conveyance are a taking.

Rent and Rate Controls

Government limits on the rents or rates that can be charged by property owners obviously limit the profits that can be received from the property. Not surprisingly, there have been many takings clause challenges. Virtually always, the Supreme Court has rejected these objections and found that there is not a taking because the controls leave economically viable use of the property.

The Supreme Court initially considered rent control laws in the context of wartime where sudden increases in demand for housing in particular areas caused windfall profits for owners of rental property. The Court upheld rent controls as constitutional and as not being a taking.[101] The Court has extended this to rent control in nonwartime situations as well.

In *Pennell v. City of San Jose,* the Court upheld a rent control ordinance that allowed landlords to raise rents up to 8 percent and provided due process for tenants to object to rent increases of greater than that amount.[102] The Court rejected the argument that the rent control was necessarily a taking. The Court emphasized that the statute required hearings to determine whether any particular rent was unreasonable. The Court said that it therefore could not, without a specific example before it, conclude that the law effected a taking. The Court stated that the

---

[98] *Id.* at 716.
[99] *Id.* at 719 (Scalia, J., concurring).
[100] *Id.* at 718 (Blackmun, J., concurring).
[101] *See* Bowles v. Wilmington, 321 U.S. 503 (1944).
[102] 485 U.S. 1 (1988).

ordinance "represents a rational attempt to accommodate the conflicting interests of protecting tenants from burdensome rent increases while at the same time
ensuring that landlords are guaranteed a fair return on their investment."[103]

Similarly, in *Federal Communication Commission v. Florida Power Corporation*, the
Court ruled that there was not a taking when the government set rates for cable
companies using utility poles.[104] The Supreme Court again emphasized that the
rate regulation did not confiscate property from owners and it did not deny them
use of their property; rather, it just set rates to serve the public's interest in facilitating the development of cable systems.

The Court also considered government rate-setting in the context of regulations of utility rates. Because utility companies often are granted monopolies by
the government, it is common for states to set utility rates. The Supreme Court has
accorded the government broad discretion in rate-setting and has concluded that
rates only will be found to be a taking if they are so unreasonable as to be considered confiscatory.[105]

Imposition of Government Liability

In *Eastern Enterprises v. Apfel*, four Justices concluded that the imposition of ret-
roactive civil liability was a taking; five Justices, though, rejected this argument.[106]
The Coal Act made coal companies responsible for paying the medical benefits
of former coal miners.[107] Justice O'Connor, joined by Chief Justice Rehnquist and
Justices Scalia and Thomas, said that this was an impermissible regulatory taking.
Justice O'Connor expressly relied on the balancing test from *Kaiser Aetna v. United
States* that a taking be determined by weighing "the economic impact of the regu-
lation, its interference with reasonable investment backed expectations, and the
character of the government action."[108]

Five Justices, however, rejected this conclusion and said that there was not a
taking. Justice Kennedy, concurring in the judgment and dissenting in part, found
that the law violated due process by imposing unreasonable retroactive civil liability. But he expressly said that the plurality's takings analysis was "incorrect."[109]
Justice Kennedy said that the takings clause allows the government to act so long
as it meets the condition of paying just compensation. He said that in this instance
the law should be invalidated under due process. He wrote: "Given that the constitutionality of the Coal Act appears to turn on the legitimacy of Congress's

---

[103] *Id.* at 13. *See also* Yee v. Escondido, 503 U.S. 519 (1992) (no taking from a rent control ordinance that set rents for a mobile home park and set factors for any increase in rent; the effect was that
the tenant could sell the spot to the next tenant and accrue the value); Lingle v. Chevron, USA, Inc.,
544 U.S. 528 (2005) (no taking when the government limited the rents that national oil companies
could charge local service stations).

[104] 480 U.S. 245 (1987).

[105] *See* Duquesne Light Co. v. Barasch, 488 U.S. 299 (1989).

[106] 524 U.S. 498 (1998).

[107] 26 U.S.C. §9701 *et seq.*

[108] 444 U.S. 164, 175 (1979).

[109] 524 U.S. at 539 (Kennedy, J., concurring in the judgment and dissenting in part).

judgment rather than on the availability of compensation, the more appropriate constitutional analysis arises under general due process principles rather than under the Takings Clause."[110]

Justice Stevens wrote a dissenting opinion joined by the other three Justices in which he argued that government-imposed liability is not a taking. He explained: "The dearth of Takings Clause authority is not surprising, for the application of the Takings Clause bristles with conceptual difficulties. If the Clause applies when the government orders A to pay B, why does it not apply when the government simply orders A to pay the government when it assesses a tax?"[111]

Thus, while five Justices are unwilling to see such government regulation as a taking, four Justices in the plurality opinion came to an opposite conclusion. It is possible that with future changes in the composition of the Court there could be a shift and challenges would be possible under the takings clause to many other government laws.

Conclusion on Regulatory Takings

A review of the cases reveals that the Court generally has been reluctant to find government regulations to be a taking. The Court frequently and expressly has recognized that government would be unduly shackled if it had to compensate every time it frustrated someone's expectations or decreased the value of somebody's property. There is no formula; the cases concerning regulatory takings reflect ad hoc balancing and the inevitable discretion in deciding what is "too much" regulation. Overall, though, the Court has not found a taking so long as the government regulation met a rational basis test and so long as the regulation did not prevent almost all economically viable use of the property.

§8.4.3   What Is "Property"?

Broad Definition of Property

By its very terms, the takings clause applies only if a court concludes that "property" has been taken by the government. At times, the Court has expressed a broad view of what constitutes property for purposes of the takings clause. In *United States v. General Motors Corp.*, the Supreme Court said that "property" as used in the takings clause refers to the entire "group of rights inhering in the citizen's [ownership]."[112] The Court explained that it is not limited to the "vulgar and untechnical sense of the physical thing with respect to which the citizen exercises rights recognized by law. [Instead it] . . . denote[s] the group of rights inhering in the citizen's relation to the physical thing, as the right to possess, use and dispose

---

[110] *Id.* at 545.
[111] *Id.* at 553 (Stevens, J., dissenting).
[112] 323 U.S. 373 (1945).

of it. . . . The constitutional provision is addressed to every sort of interest the citizen may possess."[113]

Positivist Approach to Defining Property

The Court, however, frequently has taken a very positivist approach, looking to the state law defining the property interest, in deciding whether there is property under the Constitution. For example, in *Webb's Fabulous Pharmacies, Inc. v. Beckwith*, the Supreme Court found that the interest on an interpleader account—a sum of money deposited with a court because of conflicting claims to it—is property because of a state law that provided that the interest goes with the principal.[114]

The Court relied on *Webb's Fabulous Pharmacies* in *Phillips v. Washington Legal Foundation* to hold that the interest paid on lawyers' trust accounts is property within the meaning of the takings clause.[115] *Phillips* involved Interest on Lawyer Trust Account (IOLTA) programs that exist in every state. Lawyers are required to keep client funds in trust accounts. Sometimes the money is too small or in the account for too short a time to pay measurable interest. States adopted laws saying that such funds should be pooled and the resulting interest should be used for legal services.

Many unsuccessful constitutional challenges had been brought to these programs.[116] In *Phillips*, the Supreme Court concluded that the interest was property, though it did not decide whether the IOLTA laws were a taking or what just compensation would require. Chief Justice Rehnquist, writing for the Court in a 5-to-4 decision, said that the "rule that 'interest follows principal' has been established under English common law since at least the mid-1700s."[117] Relying on this history and on *Webb's Fabulous Pharmacy*, the Court held that "the interest income generated by funds held in IOLTA accounts is the 'private property' of the owner."[118] However, as discussed below, in *Brown v. Legal Foundation of Washington*, the Supreme Court held that IOLTA programs are constitutional and no just compensation is required because owners do not lose anything of value from their operation.[119]

In contrast to these decisions, in *Dames & Moore v. Regan*, the Supreme Court refused to find a loss of property rights when the president lifted a freeze on Iranian assets in the United States as part of an agreement for the release of American hostages in Iran.[120] Iranian assets in the United States had been attached. The attachment was removed pursuant to an executive agreement between the United States

---

[113] *Id.* at 378.

[114] 449 U.S. 155 (1980), discussed above in §8.4.2.1.

[115] 524 U.S. 156 (1998).

[116] *See* Phillips v. Washington Legal Found., 524 U.S. 156 (1998); Schneider v. California Dept. of Corr., 151 F.3d 1194 (9th Cir. 1998); Garneau v. City of Seattle, 147 F.3d 802 (9th Cir. 1998).

[117] 524 U.S. at 165.

[118] *Id.* at 171.

[119] 538 U.S. 216 (2003).

[120] 453 U.S. 654 (1981), also discussed in §4.6.2 (considering the constitutionality of the executive agreement).

and Iran, and the agreement also put a limit on Iran's liability to its creditors in the United States. The creditors argued that lifting the attachment was a taking of their property. The Supreme Court rejected this argument and said that the "attachments . . . [were] 'revocable,' 'contingent,' and in every sense subordinate to the President's power. . . . We conclude that because of the President's authority to prevent or condition attachments, and because of the orders he issued to this effect, petitioner did not acquire any 'property' interest in its attachments of the sort that would support a constitutional claim."[121] Because the law made the attachments "revocable," the creditors could not claim a property right in them.[122]

In *Lucas v. South Carolina Coastal Council,* the Court said that whether there was a taking when a coastal preservation law prevented development of property depended on whether the restrictions existed at the time the property was purchased.[123] In other words, again, property is defined based on the rights and expectations created by the positive law.

Less Traditional Forms of Property

The Court has followed this approach in dealing with less traditional property as well. The Court has been inconsistent as to when other, less traditional types of property—such as intangibles or government benefits—are protected by the takings clause.

The Court has clearly indicated that some forms of property, besides real and personal property, are protected under the clause. For example, in *Ruckelshaus v. Monsanto Co.,* the Supreme Court held that trade secrets are property.[124] The Federal Insecticide, Fungicide, and Rodenticide Act (FIFRA) required an applicant for registration of a product to submit detailed data and authorized the Environmental Protection Agency to publicly disclose some of the information. The Supreme Court held that trade secrets were property within the meaning of the takings clause. The Court explained that "[t]rade secrets have many of the characteristics of more tangible forms of property. A trade secret is assignable. A trade secret can form the res of a trust, and it passes to a trustee in bankruptcy. . . . This general perception of trade secrets as property is consonant with a notion of 'property' that extends beyond land and tangible goods and includes the products of an individual's labour and invention."[125] The Court thus concluded that the "health, safety, and environmental data cognizable [under state law] as a trade secret property right is protected by the Taking Clause of the Fifth Amendment."[126]

---

[121] *Id.* at 674 n.6.

[122] The Court recognized that there would be a taking if some claims were not satisfied because of the limit on Iran's liability. However, the Court said that this issue was not yet ripe for review because no one had been denied compensation and that there was an adequate remedy in the Court of Claims if a taking did occur. *Id.* at 689.

[123] 505 U.S. at 1026, also discussed above in §8.4.2.2.

[124] 467 U.S. 986 (1984).

[125] *Id.* at 1002-1003 (citations omitted).

[126] *Id.* at 1004.

It is notable that in defining property, the Court in *Ruckelshaus* both analogized to the traditional features of property protected under the Fifth Amendment and relied on state law in determining whether there is a property interest in trade secrets. Some would contend that this is too narrow and that the Court should focus not only on whether the government has created a property right, but also on natural law principles or on conceptions of personhood in defining what is property for purposes of the Fifth Amendment.[127]

The Court's failure to use this latter approach is revealed in several cases where it refused to find a property interest. For example, in *Bowen v. Gilliard*, the Supreme Court rejected the argument that government-granted welfare benefits were property under the takings clause.[128] A federal law provided that recipients of benefits under the Aid to Families with Dependent Children program must assign to the government child support payments received from a noncustodial parent. The argument was that this constituted a taking of property from the child because the support payments were for the child, whereas the welfare benefits were for the entire household. In other words, the claim was that property, the child support payments, was taken and that it was an inadequate substitution to provide welfare benefits to the whole family.

The Supreme Court rejected this contention. The Court said: "Congress is not, by virtue of having instituted a social welfare program, bound to continue it at all, much less at the same benefit level. Thus, notwithstanding the technical legal arguments that have been advanced, it is imperative to recognize that the amendments at issue merely incorporate a definitional element into an entitlement program. It would be quite strange indeed if, by virtue of an offer to provide benefits to needy families through the entirely voluntary AFDC program, Congress or the States were deemed to have taken some of those very family members' property."[129]

Bowen v. Gilliard can be questioned in a number of respects. First, the Court has recognized that welfare benefits are property for purposes of the due process clause. In *Goldberg v. Kelly*, the Supreme Court expressly held that welfare is property and that the government must therefore provide due process—notice and a hearing—before terminating benefits.[130] The Court relied heavily on the writings of Professor Charles Reich that government-created benefits, such as welfare, play the same role in a person's life as traditional property.[131] To the extent that *Bowen* seems to endorse a different view, it is difficult to understand why welfare would be considered property under the due process clause of the Fifth Amendment, but not under the takings clause of the Fifth Amendment.

Second, it can be argued that the Court in *Bowen* did not properly follow its usual analysis of property, which focuses on the positive law in defining whether there is a property interest. Under the state law, the child support payments were to be used solely for the child; they were the child's property. The government

[127] *See* Richard Epstein, Takings (1985); Margaret Jane Radin, Property and Personhood, 34 Stan. L. Rev. 957 (1982).
[128] 483 U.S. 587 (1987).
[129] *Id.* at 604-605.
[130] 397 U.S. 254 (1970), discussed in §§7.3.1 and 7.4.3.
[131] *See, e.g.,* Charles Reich, The New Property, 73 Yale L.J. 733 (1964).

took these away by its law requiring that they be turned over to the government. Perhaps the grant of benefits to the family could be conceived of as just compensation sufficient to meet the Fifth Amendment's requirements, but there is a strong argument that there was a taking of property from the child.

§8.4.4   What Is a Taking for "Public Use"?

Taking Must Be for Public Use

The Fifth Amendment authorizes the government only to take private property for "public use." If the taking were deemed to be for private use, the taking would be invalidated and the government would have to return the property to the owner. The Supreme Court often has declared that "one person's property may not be taken for the benefit of another person without a justifying public purpose, even though compensation be paid."[132] The framers' obvious concern was that the government might use its eminent domain power to play Robin Hood and take from some private owners and give to others.

Very Broad Definition of Public Use

However, the Supreme Court has expansively defined "public use" so that virtually any taking will meet the requirement. The Supreme Court has indicated that a taking is for public use as long as it is an exercise of the state's police power.[133] In other words, a taking is for public use if a rational basis test is met; it is for public use so long as the government acts out of a reasonable belief that the taking will benefit the public.

The Court expressed this view in *Berman v. Parker*.[134] In *Berman*, the District of Columbia used its eminent domain power to acquire slum properties and planned to sell or lease them to private interests for development. The owners argued that this was the government taking from one private owner to give it to another and thus not a taking for "public use." The Supreme Court, in an opinion by Justice William Douglas, disagreed and expansively defined the meaning of *public use*. He wrote: "We deal, in other words, with what traditionally has been known as the police power. . . . Subject to specific constitutional limitations, when the legislature has spoken, the public interest has been declared in terms well-nigh conclusive. In such cases, the legislature, not the judiciary is the main guardian of the public needs to be served by social legislation. . . . *Once the object is within the authority of Congress, the right to realize it through the exercise of eminent domain is clear.*"[135]

---

[132] Thompson v. Consolidated Gas Corp., 300 U.S. 55, 80 (1937); *see also* Cincinnati v. Vester, 281 U.S. 439, 447 (1930); Missouri Pac. Ry. Co. v. Nebraska, 164 U.S. 403, 416 (1896).

[133] For an excellent discussion of the relationship of the police power to the takings clause, *see* Joseph Sax, Takings and the Police Power, 74 Yale L.J. 36 (1964).

[134] 348 U.S. 26 (1954).

[135] *Id.* at 32-33 (emphasis added).

Thus, a taking is for public use so long as the government is taking property to achieve a legitimate government purpose and so long as the taking is a reasonable way to achieve the goal. The Court reaffirmed this in *Hawaii Housing Authority v. Midkiff*.[136] The State of Hawaii was concerned that so much land was owned by a relatively few people, a result of Hawaii's precolonial property system, which restricted ownership to the islands' chiefs and nobility. The state therefore used its eminent domain power to take the property, with just compensation, and with the plan of selling ownership to a much larger number of people. The owners were furious and argued that the government was impermissibly taking from some private owners to give to others.

The Supreme Court unanimously found that this was a taking for public use. The Court reviewed *Berman v. Parker* and said that it establishes the proposition that "[t]he public use requirement is thus coterminous with the scope of a sovereign's police powers."[137] The Court emphasized the need for great deference to the legislature in deciding whether a taking is for public use. Justice O'Connor, writing for the Court, said: "[T]he Court has made it clear that it will not substitute its judgment for a legislature's judgment as to what constitutes a public use unless the use be palpably without reasonable foundation."[138]

The Court was explicit that a taking is for public use so long as the government meets the rational basis test. The Court declared: "[W]here the exercise of the eminent domain power is rationally related to a conceivable public purpose, the Court has never held a compensated taking to be proscribed by the Public Use Clause."[139] The Court concluded that Hawaii's action was for public use because it acted out of a reasonable belief that distributing ownership among a larger number of people would benefit the public.

In a particularly controversial case, *Kelo v. City of New London, Connecticut,* the Court reaffirmed that a taking is for "public use" so long as the government acts out of a reasonable belief that the taking will benefit the public.[140] An economically depressed city sought, through a private economic development corporation, to take private property for purposes of a new economic development project. The owners, who did not want to sell their property, objected that it was not for "public use."

The Supreme Court, in a 5-to-4 decision, ruled in favor of the city. Justice Stevens wrote for the Court, joined by Justices Kennedy, Souter, Ginsburg, and Breyer. The Court relied on *Berman* and *Midkiff* to hold that a taking is for public use so long as the government acts out of a reasonable belief that the taking will benefit the public. The Court said that the city's action was for public use because it reasonably believed that its action would create over 1,000 new jobs and increase economic growth.

---

[136] 467 U.S. 229 (1984).
[137] *Id.* at 240.
[138] *Id.* at 241 (citations omitted).
[139] *Id.*
[140] 545 U.S. 469 (2005).

The decision generated enormous controversy and the media presented it as a dramatic change in the law, while in reality the Court applied exactly the principle that was articulated decades ago: A taking is for public use so long as the government acts out of a reasonable belief that the taking will benefit the public. Certainly, there can be disagreement over whether the government should take private property for purposes of economic development, and some states already have laws that restrict this, but it is important to recognize that the case in no way changed the constitutional law in this area.[141] However, after *Kelo* many states adopted laws preventing the government from using its eminent domain power in that manner.[142]

§8.4.5   What Is the Requirement for "Just Compensation"?

The Constitution clearly envisions that the government will take private property for public use, but it requires that the government pay for it. The standard of payment is "just compensation."

The Supreme Court has consistently ruled that just compensation is measured in terms of the loss to the owner; the gain to the taker is irrelevant. Long ago, Justice Oliver Wendell Holmes declared that the measure is "what has the owner lost, not what has the taker gained."[143] The Supreme Court has said that the loss should be valued in terms of the market value to the owner,[144] as of the time of the taking.[145] However, the government does not need to pay for any increases in the market value that occurred solely because of its plan to take the property.[146]

The Court applied this principle, that just compensation is measured in terms of the loss to the owner not the gain to the taker, in *Brown v. Legal Foundation of Washington*.[147] In *Brown*, the Court upheld Interest on Lawyer Trust Account (IOLTA) programs that provide almost $200 million for legal services for the poor. Every state has an IOLTA program, which applies to client trust accounts that are too small or too temporary to generate measurable interest greater than the cost

---

[141] Justice Kennedy wrote a concurring opinion stressing that there are limits and that it would not be public use if the government took from one private owner solely to enrich another. 545 U.S. at 493 (Kennedy, J., concurring). Justice O'Connor, in dissent, lamented that the majority's approach would allow the government to take private property simply to put it to more economically advantageous use. 545 U.S. at 494-505 (O'Connor, J., concurring). Justice Thomas, in dissent, urged a major change in the law, contending that public use should require that the government be the actual user of the private property. 545 U.S. at 505 (Thomas, J., dissenting).

[142] *See* D. Zachary Hudson, Note, Eminent Domain Due Process, 119 Yale L.J. 1280, 1282 (2010) ("many states altered their eminent domain statutes or amended their constitutions to ensure that economic development could not serve as a legitimate basis for exercising the state's eminent domain power"); Amanda W. Goodin, Rejecting the Return to Blight in Post-*Kelo* State Legislation, 82 N.Y.U. L. Rev. 177, 195 (2007).

[143] Boston Chamber of Commerce v. Boston, 217 U.S. 189, 195 (1910).

[144] *See, e.g.,* United States v. 564.54 Acres of Land, 441 U.S. 506 (1979).

[145] *See, e.g.,* Kirby Forest Indus., Inc. v. United States, 467 U.S. 1 (1984).

[146] *See, e.g.,* United States v. Fuller, 409 U.S. 488 (1973).

[147] 538 U.S. 216 (2003).

of administering the account. Earlier, the Court ruled that the interest was private property within the meaning of the takings clause.[148]

But in *Brown*, the Supreme Court, in a 5-to-4 decision with Justice Stevens writing for the majority, joined by Justices O'Connor, Souter, Ginsburg, and Breyer, affirmed the Ninth Circuit's conclusion that such programs are constitutional and not an impermissible taking of private property without just compensation. The Court explained that under the takings clause, just compensation is measured in terms of the loss to the owner, determined by the reasonable market value of the property. IOLTA programs, by definition, apply only as to client accounts that would not otherwise generate interest and thus impose no loss to the owner requiring just compensation.

If there is a taking, the property owner can bring a legal action against the government to receive just compensation. One form of action is an "inverse condemnation suit," where an individual claims that a government action constitutes a taking. In *First English Evangelical Lutheran Church of Glendale v. County of Los Angeles*, the Supreme Court held that even if the government ceases its regulation in response to an inverse condemnation suit, the government nonetheless must pay damages for the time, however temporary, that it had taken the private property.[149] In other words, the Court held that the government is required to pay just compensation for the entire time of its action, including the period before the judicial adjudication that it was a taking. The Court said that "[i]nvalidation of the ordinance . . . is not a sufficient remedy to meet the demands of the Just Compensation Clause."[150] Rather, the government must pay just compensation when there is a taking, even if it is a temporary taking.[151] However, as discussed above, the Supreme Court has held that temporarily denying an owner the ability to develop property is not a taking so long as the government's action is reasonable.[152]

---

[148] Phillips v. Washington Legal Found., 524 U.S. 156 (1998), discussed above in §8.4.3.

[149] 482 U.S. 304 (1987).

[150] *Id.* at 316.

[151] In *City of Monterey v. Del Monte Dunes*, 526 U.S. 687 (1999), the Court concluded that the determination of the reasonableness of the rejection of development of property was a question for the jury.

[152] Tahoe-Sierra Pres. Council, Inc. v. Tahoe Regl. Planning Agency, 535 U.S. 302 (2002).

CHAPTER 9

Equal Protection

§9.1   INTRODUCTION

§9.1.1   *Constitutional Provisions Concerning Equal Protection*

Equal Protection Clause

The Constitution as originally drafted and ratified had no provisions ensuring equal protection of the laws. This, of course, is not surprising for a document written for a society where blacks were enslaved and where women were denied political and civil rights. After the Civil War, widespread discrimination against former slaves led to the passage of the Fourteenth Amendment,[1] which provides in part: "No state shall . . . deny to any person within its jurisdiction the equal protection of the laws."

The promise of this provision went unrealized for almost a century as the Supreme Court rarely found any state or local action to violate the equal protection clause until the mid-1950s. Indeed, Justice Oliver Wendell Holmes derisively referred to the provision as "the last resort of constitutional arguments."[2] Holmes probably was referring to the possibility of challenging almost any law as discriminating against someone and to the Court's consistent reluctance to use the equal protection clause to invalidate state or local laws.

Brown v. Board of Education, in 1954, ushered in the modern era of equal protection jurisprudence.[3] Since *Brown*, the Supreme Court has relied on the equal protection clause as a key provision for combating invidious discrimination and for safeguarding fundamental rights.

Application to the Federal Government

There is no provision in the Constitution that says that the federal government cannot deny equal protection of the laws. However, in *Bolling v. Sharpe*,[4] a companion case to *Brown v. Board of Education* that concerned the segregation of the District of Columbia public schools, the Court held that equal protection applies to the federal government through the due process clause of the Fifth Amendment.

Obviously, it would be unacceptable to allow the federal government to discriminate based on race or gender in a manner prohibited the states by the

---

§9.1 [1] The history of the ratification of the Fourteenth Amendment is described in §1.3.

[2] Buck v. Bell, 274 U.S. 200, 208 (1927).

[3] 347 U.S. 483 (1954).

[4] 347 U.S. 497 (1954).

Fourteenth Amendment. To avoid this embarrassment, the Court interpreted the Fifth Amendment as including an implicit requirement for equal protection.[5] The Court simply declared that "discrimination may be so unjustifiable as to be violative of due process."[6]

It is now well settled that the requirements of equal protection are the same whether the challenge is to the federal government under the Fifth Amendment or to state and local actions under the Fourteenth Amendment. The Supreme Court has expressly declared that "[e]qual protection analysis in the Fifth Amendment area is the same as that under the Fourteenth Amendment."[7] But technically, equal protection applies to the federal government through judicial interpretation of the due process clause of the Fifth Amendment and to state and local governments through the Fourteenth Amendment.

§9.1.2 A Framework for Equal Protection Analysis

The Basic Question

All equal protection cases pose the same basic question: Is the government's classification justified by a sufficient purpose? Many government laws draw a distinction among people and thus are potentially susceptible to an equal protection challenge. For example, those under age 16 might claim to be discriminated against by the age requirement for obtaining a driver's license, and those denied government benefits might argue that they are discriminated against by eligibility guidelines. If these laws, or any government actions, are challenged based on equal protection, the issue is whether the government can identify a sufficiently important objective for its discrimination.[8]

What is a sufficient justification depends entirely on the type of discrimination. For instance, the Supreme Court has declared that it is extremely suspicious

[5] For a discussion of this, *see* Kenneth Karst, The Fifth Amendment's Guarantee of Equal Protection, 55 N.C. L. Rev. 540 (1977).

[6] *Bolling*, 347 U.S. at 499.

[7] Buckley v. Valeo, 424 U.S. 1, 93 (1976).

[8] Understandably, the Supreme Court never has attempted to define "equality" for purposes of the equal protection clause, and commentators have offered many different models. Often commentators will contrast two conceptions of equal protection: one that focuses on equal treatment and the other that looks at equal results. *See, e.g.,* Sheila Foster, Difference and Equality: A Critical Assessment of the Concept of "Diversity," 1993 Wis. L. Rev. 105, 148-150; Michel Rosenfeld, Decoding *Richmond*: Affirmative Action and the Elusive Meaning of Constitutional Equality, 87 Mich. L. Rev. 1729, 1735-1737 (1989). The equal treatment approach focuses on whether the government is treating people equally without discrimination. If so, equal protection is met, even if the results are unequal. The equal results approach emphasizes the outcomes of the government's actions. For example, as discussed later in this chapter, a major issue of equal protection law is whether proving discriminatory impact of a law is sufficient to establish an equal protection violation. Those who take the equal treatment approach would say that there is no violation of equal protection unless there is proof that the law had a discriminatory purpose. In contrast, those who take the equal results approach would say that there is an equal protection approach if a facially neutral law has a discriminatory impact.

of race discrimination and therefore the government may use racial classifications only if it proves that they are necessary to achieve a compelling government purpose. This is known as "strict scrutiny." In contrast, a 14-year-old who claimed that the denial of a driver's license violated equal protection would prevail only by proving that the law was not rationally related to a legitimate government purpose. This is known as "rational basis" review.

Question 1: What Is the Classification?

To be more specific, all equal protection issues can be broken down into three questions: What is the classification? What level of scrutiny should be applied? Does the particular government action meet the level of scrutiny?

The first question is: What is the government's classification? How is the government drawing a distinction among people? Equal protection analysis always must begin by identifying how the government is distinguishing among people. Sometimes this is clear; sometimes it is the focus of the litigation.

As described below, there are two basic ways of establishing a classification. In one, the classification exists on the face of the law—that is, the law in its very terms draws a distinction among people based on a particular characteristic. For example, a law that prohibits blacks from serving on juries is an obvious facial racial classification.[9] A law that says that only those aged 16 and older can have drivers' licenses is obviously an age classification.

Alternatively, sometimes laws are facially neutral, but there is a discriminatory impact to the law or discriminatory effects from its administration. For instance, a law that requires that all police officers be at least 5′10″ tall and 150 pounds is, on its face, only a height and weight classification. Statistics, however, show that over 40 percent of men, but only 2 percent of women, will meet this requirement. The result is that the law has a discriminatory impact against women in hiring for the police force.

As described below, the Supreme Court has made it clear that discriminatory impact is insufficient to prove a racial or gender classification. If a law is facially neutral, demonstrating a race or gender classification requires proof that there is a discriminatory purpose behind the law.[10] Thus, women challenging the height and weight requirements for the police force must show that the government's purpose was to discriminate based on gender.

In other words, there are two alternative ways of proving the existence of a classification: showing that it exists on the face of the law or demonstrating that a facially neutral law has a discriminatory impact and a discriminatory purpose.

---

[9] See Strauder v. West Virginia, 100 U.S. 303 (1879) (invalidating state law limiting jury service to "white male persons").

[10] See, e.g., Personnel Administrator of Mass. v. Feeney, 442 U.S. 256 (1979) (discriminatory impact is insufficient to prove a gender classification; there must be proof of discriminatory purpose); Washington v. Davis, 426 U.S. 229 (1976) (discriminatory impact is insufficient to prove a racial classification; there must be proof of discriminatory purpose), discussed below in §9.3.3.2.

Question 2: What Is the Appropriate Level of Scrutiny?

Once the classification is identified, the next step in analysis is to identify the level of scrutiny to be applied.[11] The Supreme Court has made it clear that differing levels of scrutiny will be applied depending on the type of discrimination.

Discrimination based on race or national origin is subjected to strict scrutiny.[12] Also, generally, discrimination against aliens is subjected to strict scrutiny, although there are several exceptions where less than strict scrutiny is used.[13] Under strict scrutiny, a law is upheld if it is proved necessary to achieve a compelling government purpose.[14] The government must have a truly significant reason for discriminating, and it must show that it cannot achieve its objective through any less discriminatory alternative. The government has the burden of proof under strict scrutiny, and the law will be upheld only if the government persuades the court that it is necessary to achieve a compelling purpose. Strict scrutiny is virtually always fatal to the challenged law.[15]

Intermediate scrutiny is used for discrimination based on gender[16] and for discrimination against nonmarital children.[17] Under intermediate scrutiny a law is upheld if it is substantially related to an important government purpose.[18] In other words, the Court need not find the government's purpose "compelling," but it must characterize the objective as "important." The means used need not be necessary, but must have a "substantial relationship" to the end being sought. Under intermediate scrutiny, the government has the burden of proof. The Supreme Court explained that the "burden of justification is demanding and that it rests entirely on the state."[19]

Finally, there is the rational basis test. Rational basis review is the minimum level of scrutiny that all laws challenged under equal protection must meet. All laws not subjected to strict or intermediate scrutiny are evaluated under the rational basis test. Under rational basis review, a law will be upheld if it is rationally related to a legitimate government purpose.[20] The government's objective need not be compelling or important, but just something that the government legitimately may do. The means chosen only need be a rational way to accomplish the end.

---

[11] The levels of scrutiny are reviewed in detail in §6.5.

[12] *See* §9.3.

[13] *See* §9.5.

[14] *See, e.g.,* Palmore v. Sidoti, 466 U.S. 429, 432 (1984).

[15] Professor Gerald Gunther, in a classic article, described it as "strict in theory and fatal in fact." Foreword: In Search of Evolving Doctrine on a Changing Court: A Model for a Newer Equal Protection, 86 Harv. L. Rev. 1, 8 (1972).

[16] *See* §9.4.

[17] *See* §9.6.

[18] *See, e.g.,* Craig v. Boren, 429 U.S. 190, 197 (1976); Lehr v. Robertson, 463 U.S. 248, 266 (1983).

[19] *See* United States v. Virginia, 518 U.S. 515, 533 (1996), discussed more fully below in §9.4.

[20] *See, e.g.,* Pennell v. City of San Jose, 485 U.S. 1, 14 (1988); U.S. Retirement Bd. v. Fritz, 449 U.S. 166, 175, 177 (1980); Allied Stores v. Bowers, 358 U.S. 522, 527 (1959).

The challenger has the burden of proof under rational basis review. The rational basis test is enormously deferential to the government, and only rarely have laws been declared unconstitutional for failing to meet this level of review.[21]

How has the Court decided which level of scrutiny to use for particular classifications? Although the Court has shown little willingness in the past three decades to subject additional classifications to strict or intermediate scrutiny, how will it evaluate such requests? This has renewed importance in the context of the debate over whether sexual orientation discrimination should receive heightened scrutiny.[22] Several criteria are applied in determining the level of scrutiny.

For example, the Court has emphasized that immutable characteristics such as race, national origin, gender, and the marital status of one's parents warrant heightened scrutiny.[23] The notion is that it is unfair to penalize a person for characteristics that the person did not choose and that the individual cannot change.

The Court also considers the ability of the group to protect itself through the political process. Women, for example, make up more than half the population, but traditionally they have been severely underrepresented in political offices. Aliens do not have the ability to vote, and thus the political process cannot be trusted to represent their interests.[24]

The history of discrimination against the group also is relevant to the Court in determining the level of scrutiny. A related issue is the Court's judgment concerning the likelihood that the classification reflects prejudice as opposed to a permissible government purpose.[25] For example, the Court's choice of strict scrutiny for racial classifications reflects its judgment that race is virtually never an acceptable justification for government action. In contrast, the Court's use of intermediate scrutiny for gender classifications reflects its view that the biological differences between men and women mean that there are more likely to be instances where sex is a justifiable basis for discrimination.

Although the levels of scrutiny are firmly established in constitutional law and especially in equal protection analysis, many criticize the rigid tiers of review. For example, Justices Thurgood Marshall and John Paul Stevens, among others, have

---

[21] *See, e.g.,* Romer v. Evans, 517 U.S. 620 (1996); City of Cleburne v. Cleburne Living Ctr. Inc., 473 U.S. 432 (1985); Zobel v. Williams, 457 U.S. 55 (1982); United States v. Moreno, 413 U.S. 528 (1973) (all discussed below).

[22] In United States v. Windsor, 133 S. Ct. 2675 (2013), the Court declared unconstitutional §3 of the Defense of Marriage Act as violating equal protection without indicating the level of scrutiny used. *Windsor* is discussed below in §9.7.4. Some Circuits have adopted "heightened" scrutiny for sexual orientation discrimination, *see, e.g.,* SmithKline Beecham Corp. v. Abbott Laboratories, 740 F.3d 471 (9th Cir. 2014), while others continue to use rational basis review, *see, e.g.,* DeBoer v. Snyder, 772 F.3d 388 (6th Cir. 2014).

[23] *See, e.g.,* Fullilove v. Klutznick, 448 U.S. 448, 496 (1980); Kahn v. Shevin, 416 U.S. 351, 356 (1974).

[24] *See, e.g.,* Graham v. Richardson, 403 U.S. 365, 367 (1971).

[25] *See* City of Cleburne v. Cleburne Living Ctr., 473 U.S. 432, 440 (1985) ("[W]hen a statute classifies by race, alienage, or national origin, [t]hese factors are so seldom relevant to the achievement of any legitimate state interest that laws grounded in which considerations are deemed to reflect prejudice and antipathy. . . . For these reasons and because such discrimination is unlikely to be soon rectified by legislative means, these laws are subjected to strict scrutiny and will be sustained only if they are suitably tailored to serve a compelling state interest.").

argued that there should be a sliding scale of review rather than the three levels of scrutiny.[26] They maintain that the Court should consider such factors as the constitutional and social importance of the interests adversely affected and the invidiousness of the basis on which the classification was drawn. They contend that under the rigid tiers of review the choice of the level of scrutiny is usually decisive and unduly limits the scope of judicial analysis. Those who favor a sliding scale believe that it would lead to more candid discussion of the competing interests and therefore provide overall better decision making.

Some critics suggest that although the Court speaks in terms of three tiers of review, in reality there is a spectrum of standards of review.[27] The claim is that in some cases where the Court says that it is using rational basis review, it is actually employing a test with more "bite" than the customarily very deferential rational basis review. Similarly, it is argued that in some cases intermediate scrutiny is applied in a very deferential manner that is essentially rational basis review, while in other cases intermediate scrutiny seems indistinguishable from strict scrutiny. Even strict scrutiny, some argue, is used in different ways in varying cases.[28] The argument is that although the Court articulates three tiers of review, the reality is a range of standards.

Question 3: Does the Government Action Meet the Level of Scrutiny?

The level of scrutiny is the rule of law that is applied to the particular government action being challenged as denying equal protection. In evaluating the constitutionality of a law, the Court evaluates both the law's ends and its means. For strict scrutiny the end must be deemed compelling for the law to be upheld; for intermediate scrutiny the end has to be regarded as important; and for the rational basis test there just has to be a legitimate purpose.

In evaluating the relationship of the means of the particular law to the end, the Supreme Court often focuses on the degree to which a law is underinclusive and/or overinclusive.[29] A law is underinclusive if it does not apply to individuals who are similar to those to whom the law applies. For example, a law that excludes those under age 16 from having drivers' licenses is somewhat underinclusive because some younger drivers undoubtedly have the physical ability and the emotional maturity to be effective drivers.

---

[26] *See, e.g.*, Plyler v. Doe, 457 U.S. 202, 211 (1982) (Marshall, J., concurring); Craig v. Boren, 429 U.S. 190, 212 (1976) (Stevens, J., concurring); San Antonio Indep. School Dist. v. Rodriguez, 411 U.S. 1, 109-110 (1973) (Marshall, J., dissenting).

[27] *See* Jeffrey M. Shaman, Cracks in the Structure: The Coming Breakdown of the Levels of Scrutiny, 45 Ohio St. L.J. 161 (1984); *see also* Suzanne B. Goldberg, Equality without Tiers, 77 S. Cal. L. Rev. 481 (2004).

[28] For example, some argue that the Supreme Court's decision in *Grutter v. Bollinger*, 539 U.S. 306 (2003), which upheld affirmative action by colleges and universities and which used strict scrutiny, was more deferential than traditional strict scrutiny. Lackland H. Bloom, *Grutter* and *Gratz*: A Critical Analysis, 41 Hous. L. Rev. 459 (2004). *Grutter v. Bollinger* is discussed below in §9.3.5.

[29] These concepts were articulated and explained in Joseph Tussman & Jacobus tenBroek, The Equal Protection of the Laws, 37 Cal. L. Rev. 341, 348-353 (1949).

A law is overinclusive if it applies to those who need not be included in order for the government to achieve its purpose. In other words, the law unnecessarily applies to a group of people. For example, the government's decision to evacuate and intern all Japanese Americans on the West Coast during World War II was radically overinclusive.[30] Although the government's purported interest was in preventing espionage, individuals were evacuated and interned without any determination of their threat. Obviously, the law was enormously overinclusive because it harmed a large number of people unnecessarily.

A law can be both underinclusive and overinclusive. The decision to evacuate Japanese Americans during World War II was certainly both. If the goal was to isolate those who were a threat to security, interning only Japanese Americans was underinclusive in that it did not identify those of other races who posed a danger. At the same time, as explained above, the federal government's action was extremely overinclusive because few, if any, Japanese Americans posed any threat. In fact, not a single Japanese American during World War II was ever charged with espionage.[31]

The fact that a law is underinclusive and/or overinclusive does not mean that it is sure to be invalidated. Quite the contrary, virtually all laws are underinclusive, overinclusive, or both. The Court has recognized that laws often are underinclusive because the government may choose to proceed "one step at a time."[32] But underinclusiveness and overinclusiveness are used by courts in evaluating the fit between the government's means and its ends. If strict scrutiny is used, a relatively close fit is required; in fact, the government will have to show that the means is necessary—the least restrictive alternative—to achieve the goal. Under intermediate scrutiny a closer fit, less underinclusiveness or overinclusiveness, will be required than under the rational basis test.

Thus, equal protection analysis involves three questions: What is the classification? What level of scrutiny should be applied? Does the particular government action meet the level of scrutiny? Cases posing an equal protection issue always involve a dispute over one or more of these questions.[33]

---

[30] *See* Korematsu v. United States, 323 U.S. 214 (1944), discussed below in §9.3.3.1.

[31] *See* Nanette Dembitz, Racial Discrimination and the Military Judgment: The Supreme Court's *Korematsu* and *Endo* Decisions, 45 Colum. L. Rev. 175 (1945).

[32] Williamson v. Lee Optical, 348 U.S. 483, 489 (1955).

[33] In a provocative article, Professor Peter Westen argued that equality "is an idea that should be banished from moral and legal discourse as an explanatory norm." Peter Westen, The Empty Idea of Equality, 95 Harv. L. Rev. 537, 542 (1982). Professor Westen argues that equality is unnecessary as a concept because it always is necessary to develop standards to decide which inequalities are acceptable and which intolerable. Westen says that once these standards exist, they can be the basis for decisions, making the concept of equality superfluous. Moreover, he claims that equality is an undesirable concept that distorts legal analysis. Many commentators wrote replies to Professor Westen. *See, e.g.,* Steven Burton, Comment on "Empty Ideas": Logical Positivist Analysis of Equality and Rules, 91 Yale L.J. 1136 (1982); Erwin Chemerinsky, In Defense of Equality: A Reply to Professor Westen, 81 Mich. L. Rev. 575 (1983). Critics of Professor Westen argue, in part, that he demonstrates only that equality is insufficient because other concepts are needed; he does not prove that equality is unnecessary. Moreover, critics argue that equality serves many important purposes, such as to remind us to care about how people are treated relative to one another and to create a presumption in favor of treating people alike and placing a burden on those who would discriminate.

The Protection of Fundamental Rights Under Equal Protection

Usually, equal protection is used to analyze government actions that draw a distinction among people based on specific characteristics, such as race, gender, age, disability, or other traits. Sometimes, though, equal protection is used if the government discriminates among people as to the exercise of a fundamental right.

An early case using equal protection in this way was *Skinner v. Oklahoma*.[34] The Oklahoma Habitual Criminal Sterilization Act required surgical sterilization for individuals who have been convicted three or more times for crimes involving "moral turpitude." The Supreme Court declared the law unconstitutional as violating equal protection because it discriminated among people in their ability to exercise a fundamental liberty: the right to procreate. Justice William Douglas, writing for the Court, said: "We are dealing here with legislation which involves one of the basic civil rights of man. Marriage and procreation are fundamental to the very existence and survival of the race. The power to sterilize, if exercised, may have subtle, far-reaching and devastating effects."[35] In other words, the Court found that the right to procreate was a fundamental right and essentially used strict scrutiny under the equal protection clause to analyze the government's discrimination as to its exercise.

The Court has used the equal protection clause to protect other fundamental rights such as voting,[36] access to the judicial process,[37] and interstate travel.[38] The use of equal protection to safeguard these fundamental rights was, in part, based on the Supreme Court's desire to avoid substantive due process, which had all of the negative connotations of the *Lochner* era. However, the effect is the same whether a right is deemed fundamental under the equal protection clause or under the due process clause: Government infringements are subjected to strict scrutiny. Correspondingly, if a right is not fundamental, then only rational basis review is used for claims concerning it under both equal protection and due process. For example, in *Washington v. Glucksberg*, the Supreme Court held that the right to privacy under the due process clause does not create a fundamental right to physician-assisted suicide.[39] In the companion case, *Vacco v. Quill*, the Court held that rational basis review should also be used for an equal protection challenge to laws prohibiting physician-assisted suicide.[40]

---

[34] 316 U.S. 535 (1942).

[35] *Id.* at 541.

[36] *See, e.g.*, Bush v. Gore, 531 U.S. 98 (2000); Harper v. Virginia Bd. of Elections, 383 U.S. 663 (1966); Reynolds v. Sims, 377 U.S. 533 (1964).

[37] *See, e.g.*, Boddie v. Connecticut, 401 U.S. 371 (1971) (right to fee waiver for indigents in filing for divorce); Douglas v. California, 372 U.S. 353 (1963) (right to counsel on appeal for indigents); Griffin v. Douglas, 351 U.S. 12 (1956) (right to free transcripts on appeal for indigents).

[38] *See, e.g.*, Shapiro v. Thompson, 394 U.S. 618 (1969) (declaring unconstitutional as violating the right to travel a state law creating a one-year residency requirement for receiving welfare). The Court also has protected the right to travel under the privileges or immunities clause of the Fourteenth Amendment. *See* Saenz v. Roe, 526 U.S. 489 (1999).

[39] 521 U.S. 702 (1997). The topic of physician-assisted death is discussed in §10.5.

[40] 521 U.S. 793 (1997).

Chapter 10 discusses fundamental rights, including both those that the Court has protected under the equal protection clause and those safeguarded under due process. This chapter focuses on the use of equal protection to analyze discrimination among people based on traits such as race, gender, alienage, legitimacy, age, disability, wealth, and sexual orientation.

Discrimination Against an Individual Is Sufficient for a Claim

The Supreme Court has been clear that equal protection does not require allegations that the government has discriminated against a group or on the basis of group characteristics; there is a claim under the equal protection clause even for discrimination against a "class of one." In *Village of Willowbrook v. Olech*, the Court held that there is a claim under equal protection when a person alleges to have suffered arbitrary and discriminatory treatment by the government.[41] A homeowner in Willowbrook was told by the city that the grant of a 33-foot easement on the property was a requirement for connection to the city's water supply. The homeowner objected that others had gotten such service by granting just a 15-foot easement. The homeowner sued and claimed a denial of equal protection.

In a brief per curiam opinion, the Court held that the plaintiff stated a claim upon which relief could be granted. The Court emphasized that equal protection safeguards individuals and not groups. The Court said: "Our cases have recognized successful equal protection claims brought by a 'class of one,' where the plaintiff alleges that she has been intentionally treated differently from others similarly situated and that there is no rational basis for the difference in treatment."[42] The Court noted that there were allegations of improper motive, but it did not need to consider them because the allegations of arbitrary government action "are sufficient to state a claim for relief under traditional equal protection analysis."[43] *Olech* is an important case in allowing equal protection claims by any person who claims to have been subjected to arbitrary government treatment.[44] For example, in land use litigation, a person who claims to have been denied a zoning variance or a conditional use permit that others received can sue under equal protection. Unless a suspect class is involved, government actions only have to meet rational basis review. But *Olech* means that such claims cannot be dismissed for failure to state a claim. There is a claim under equal protection when it is alleged that the government is arbitrarily treating some differently from others.

However, in *Engquist v. Oregon Department of Agriculture*, the Court held that government employees cannot bring class-of-one equal protection claims.[45] Anup

[41] 528 U.S. 562 (2000).

[42] *Id.* at 564.

[43] *Id.* at 565.

[44] Justice Breyer, in a concurring opinion, recognized this possibility, but said that in this case there was a claim of improper subjective motivation and that this is enough "to minimize any concern about transforming run-of-the-mill zoning cases into cases of constitutional right." *Id.* at 566 (Breyer, J., dissenting).

[45] 553 U.S. 591 (2008).

§9.1 Introduction

Engquist was fired from her position in the Oregon Department of Agriculture and sued, alleging among other things that "she was fired not because she was a member of an identified class (unlike her race, sex, and national origin claims), but simply for 'arbitrary, vindictive, and malicious reasons.' "[46] The Court rejected this claim and declared: "Our traditional view of the core concern of the Equal Protection Clause as a shield against arbitrary classifications, combined with unique considerations applicable when the government acts as employer as opposed to sovereign, lead us to conclude that the class-of-one theory of equal protection does not apply in the public employment context."[47]

Chief Justice Roberts, writing for the Court, stressed the distinction between the government acting as regulator and the government acting as proprietor or employer. The Court also said that there are situations where discretion makes differences in treatment inevitable and thus should not lead to possible liability under an equal protection class-of-one theory. The Court explained: "There are some forms of state action, however, which by their nature involve discretionary decisionmaking based on a vast array of subjective, individualized assessments. In such cases the rule that people should be 'treated alike, under like circumstances and conditions' is not violated when one person is treated differently from others, because treating like individuals differently is an accepted consequence of the discretion granted. In such situations, allowing a challenge based on the arbitrary singling out of a particular person would undermine the very discretion that such state officials are entrusted to exercise."[48] This certainly raises the possibility of other situations where the Court will not allow class-of-one equal protection claims.

The Court's focus, though, was solely on the government employment context and it expressed great concern that allowing class-of-one equal protection claims would "constitutionalize" too many grievances by government employees.[49] In this way, *Engquist* is similar to the Roberts Court's earlier decision in *Garcetti v. Ceballos*, which held that the First Amendment does not protect the speech of government employees on the job within the scope of their duties.[50] Both cases express great reluctance to have courts overseeing the relationship between government employers and government employees by allowing constitutional claims.

---

[46] *Id.* at 595.

[47] *Id.* at 598.

[48] *Id.* at 603.

[49] *Id.* at 609 ("In short, ratifying a class-of-one theory of equal protection in the context of public employment would impermissibly 'constitutionalize the employee grievance.'").

[50] 547 U.S. 410 (2006), discussed in §11.3.8.

§9.2   THE RATIONAL BASIS TEST

§9.2.1   *Introduction*

Formulations of the Rational Basis Test

The rational basis test is the minimal level of scrutiny that all government actions challenged under equal protection must meet. In other words, unless the government action is a type of discrimination that warrants the application of intermediate or strict scrutiny, rational basis review is used.

The rational basis test has been phrased in varying ways by the Supreme Court. For example, in *Lindsley v. Natural Carbonic Gas Co.*, the Court declared: "When the classification in such a law is called in question, if any state of facts reasonably can be conceived that would sustain it, the existence of that state of facts at the time the law was enacted must be assumed. . . . One who assails the classification in such a law must carry the burden of showing that it does not rest upon any reasonable basis, but is essentially arbitrary."[1] A similarly deferential definition of the rational basis test was articulated by the Court in *McGowan v. Maryland*: "[T]he Court has held that the 14th Amendment permits the State a wide scope of discretion in enacting laws which affect some groups of citizens differently from others. The constitutional safeguard is offended only if a classification rests on grounds wholly irrelevant to the achievement of the State's objective. State legislatures are presumed to have acted within their constitutional power despite the fact that, in practice, their laws result in some inequality. Statutory discrimination will not be set aside if any state of facts reasonably may be conceived to justify it."[2]

At other times, the Court has phrased the rational basis test in more rigorous terms. For example, in *Royster Guano Co. v. Virginia*, the Court said: "[T]he classification must be reasonable, not arbitrary and must rest upon some ground of difference having a fair and substantial relation to the object of the legislation, so that all persons similarly situated shall be treated alike."[3]

Although the Court has phrased the test in different ways, the basic requirement is that a law meets rational basis review if it is rationally related to a legitimate government purpose. For instance, in *New Orleans v. Dukes*, and in many other cases, the Court said that the equal protection clause is satisfied so long as the classification is "rationally related to a legitimate state interest."[4] Also, the Court has been consistent that the challenger has the burden of proof when rational

---

§9.2 [1] 220 U.S. 61, 78-79 (1911).
[2] 366 U.S. 420, 425-426 (1961).
[3] 253 U.S. 412, 415 (1920).
[4] 427 U.S. 297, 303 (1976).

basis review is applied. There is a strong presumption in favor of laws that are challenged under the rational basis test.[5]

As the Court declared in *Hodel v. Indiana*: "Social and economic legislation . . . that does not employ suspect classifications or impinge on fundamental rights must be upheld against equal protection attack when the legislative means are rationally related to a legitimate government purpose. Moreover, such legislation carries with it a presumption of rationality that can only be overcome by a clear showing of arbitrariness and irrationality."[6] In other words, the law will be upheld unless the challenger can prove that the government has no legitimate purpose or that the means used are not a reasonable way to accomplish the goal.

Underlying Issues

The Supreme Court generally has been extremely deferential to the government when applying the rational basis test. As the above-quoted tests indicate, and as discussed below, the Court often has said that a law should be upheld if it is possible to conceive any legitimate purpose for the law, even if it was not the government's actual purpose. The result is that it is very rare for the Supreme Court to find that a law fails the rational basis test.

This approach raises important questions.[7] First, is this appropriate deference to the legislative process or undue judicial abdication? Since 1937, the Court has made it clear that it will defer to government economic and social regulations unless they infringe on a fundamental right or discriminate against a group that warrants special judicial protection.[8] This position can be defended as proper judicial restraint, as the Court allows the more democratic branches of government to make decisions except in areas where there is reason for heightened judicial scrutiny.[9] Legislation often involves arbitrary choices favoring some over others, and judicial deference leaves these decisions to the political process.[10]

But it also can be argued that the Court has gone too far in its deference under the rational basis test. Unfair laws are allowed to stand because a conceivable

[5] *See* McGowan v. Maryland, 366 U.S. 420, 425-426 (1961) ("State legislatures are presumed to have acted within their constitutional power despite the fact that, in practice, their laws result in some inequality.").

[6] 452 U.S. 314, 331-332 (1981).

[7] For an excellent collection of articles on the rational basis test, *see* Symposium, Equal Protection After the Rational Basis Era: Is It Time to Reassess the Current Standards of Review?, 4 U. Pa. J. Const. L. 235-449 (2002).

[8] This, of course, was the philosophy articulated in the famous *Carolene Products*, footnote 4. *See* United States v. Carolene Prods. Co., 304 U.S. 144, 152-153 n.4 (1938), discussed in §6.5.

[9] "Unless a statute employs a classification that is inherently invidious or that impinges on fundamental rights, areas in which the judiciary has a duty to intervene in the democratic process, this Court properly exercises only a limited review power over Congress, the appropriate representative body through which the public makes democratic choices among alternative solutions to social and economic problems." Schweiker v. Wilson, 450 U.S. 221, 230 (1981).

[10] *See* Scott Bice, Rationality Analysis in Constitutional Law, 65 Minn. L. Rev. 1, 19 (1980) (Often "the legislature is simply a 'market-like arena' in which individuals and special interest groups trade with each other through representatives to further their own private ends.").

legitimate purpose can be identified for virtually any law. Frequently, these are laws enacted to help a particular group with political clout at the expense of others who are less politically powerful. For example, in *Kotch v. Board of River Port Pilot Commissioners*, the Court upheld a Louisiana law that conditioned receiving a harbor pilot's license on completion of an apprenticeship term, even though "with occasional exception, only relatives and friends" of pilots were selected as apprentices.[11] The Court said that it was sufficient that "the benefits to morale and esprit de corps . . . might have prompted the legislature to permit Louisiana pilot officers to select those whom they serve."[12] Critics of the rational basis test argue that in *Kotch*, and many other similar cases, the Court is upholding unfair, discriminatory laws because of its almost complete deference to the legislative process.

Another underlying issue in considering the rational basis test is whether the Court has been consistent in applying it. Although in general the Court has been enormously deferential, there have been several cases where laws have been declared unconstitutional under rational basis review. For example, in *City of Cleburne v. Cleburne Living Center*, the Court used rational basis review to invalidate a zoning ordinance that prevented the operation of a home for the mentally disabled.[13] In *Metropolitan Life Insurance Company v. Ward*, the Court declared unconstitutional a state law that attempted to encourage growth of an in-state insurance industry by taxing in-state companies at much lower rates than out-of-state companies doing business in the state.[14] In *United States Department of Agriculture v. Moreno*, the Court invalidated, as violating the rational basis test, a federal law that prevented a household from receiving food stamps if it included individuals who were not related to one another.[15] Subsequently, in *Romer v. Evans*, the Court found that a voter initiative in Colorado that repealed laws prohibiting discrimination based on sexual orientation and that precluded the adoption of new protections failed rational basis review.[16]

Many argue that the Court in these cases applied a different, more rigorous version of the rational basis test, one with "bite."[17] The claim is that there is not a singular rational basis test, but one that varies between complete deference and substantial rigor. On the other hand, it might be argued that the test is consistent and that the Court is simply deciding that certain laws lack a legitimate purpose or are so arbitrary as to be unreasonable.

---

[11] 330 U.S. 552, 555 (1947).

[12] *Id.* at 563.

[13] 473 U.S. 432 (1985). In University of Ala. v. Garrett, 531 U.S. 356 (2001), the Supreme Court expressly declared that rational basis review is used for disability discrimination.

[14] 470 U.S. 869 (1985).

[15] 413 U.S. 528 (1973).

[16] 517 U.S. 620 (1996). *Romer* is discussed in detail below in §9.7.4.

[17] *See* Jeffrey Shaman, Cracks in the Structure: The Coming Breakdown of the Levels of Scrutiny, 45 Ohio St. L.J. 161 (1984); Gerald Gunther, Foreword: In Search of Evolving Doctrine on a Changing Court: A Model for a Newer Equal Protection, 86 Harv. L. Rev. 1, 18-24 (1972).

§9.2.2   The Requirement for a "Legitimate Purpose"

In assessing whether there is a legitimate purpose for a law, there are two interrelated questions. What constitutes a "legitimate" purpose? How is it to be decided whether there is such a purpose present; must it be the actual purpose behind the law or is it enough that such a purpose is conceivable?

What Is a "Legitimate" Purpose?

At the least, the government has a legitimate purpose if it advances a traditional "police" purpose: protecting safety, public health, or public morals. *Railway Express Agency v. New York* is an example of a case where a law was found constitutional as promoting public safety.[18] The Supreme Court upheld a law that prohibited the operation of an "advertising vehicle," but created an exception for "business notices upon business delivery vehicles, so long as such vehicles are engaged in the usual business or regular work of the owner and not used mainly for advertising."[19] The Court concluded that the law had the legitimate purpose of enhancing traffic safety because the city might perceive that the prohibited advertisements could be more distracting.

In *Williamson v. Lee Optical*, the Court emphasized public health as a basis for finding a law constitutional.[20] An Oklahoma law made it illegal for any person other than an optometrist or ophthalmologist to fit eyeglass lenses or to duplicate or replace lenses except with a written prescription from an optometrist or an ophthalmologist. The law thus precluded opticians from fitting new lenses into old frames or supplying duplicate lenses without a prescription. The law seemed to have a clearly protectionist purpose: helping optometrists and ophthalmologists at the expense of opticians. But the Court upheld the law as potentially advancing public health. Justice William Douglas, writing for the Court, explained: "[T]he legislature may have concluded that eye examinations were so critical, not only for correctness of vision but also for detection of latent ailments or diseases, that every change in frames and every duplication of a lens should be accompanied by a prescription from a medical expert."[21]

McGowan v. Maryland illustrates the Court's use of public morals as a sufficient basis for upholding a law under the rational basis test.[22] *McGowan* involved a challenge to a state law that required businesses to be closed on Sundays, but contained many exceptions, including sales of automobiles, boating accessories, flowers, food, and souvenirs. The Court upheld the law, accepting the state's justification that there is a benefit to having a uniform day of rest, "a day which all

---

[18]   336 U.S. 106 (1949).

[19]   *Id.* at 107-108.

[20]   348 U.S. 483 (1955). *Williamson* also involved a due process challenge that is discussed in §8.2.3.

[21]   *Id.* at 487.

[22]   366 U.S. 420 (1961). *McGowan* also is discussed in connection with the establishment clause in §12.2.3.

members of the family and community have the opportunity to spend and enjoy together."[23]

Yet the Court also has indicated that there are situations where moral justifications for laws do not satisfy the requirement for a legitimate purpose. In *Romer v. Evans*, the Supreme Court declared unconstitutional Colorado Amendment 2, a voter-approved initiative that repealed all laws protecting gays, lesbians, and bisexuals from discrimination and that prohibited all future government action to protect these individuals from discrimination.[24] Justice Kennedy, writing for the Court, explained that there was no legitimate purpose in singling out a particular group and precluding it from using the political process. The majority opinion said "that laws of the kind now before us raise the inevitable inference that the disadvantage imposed is born of animosity toward the class of persons affected."[25]

Justice Scalia, in a dissenting opinion joined by Chief Justice Rehnquist and Justice Thomas, argued that Amendment 2 was a permissible moral judgment by the voters of Colorado "to preserve traditional sexual mores against efforts of a politically powerful minority to revise those mores through use of the laws."[26] The majority, however, rejected this view and declared: "We must conclude that Amendment 2 classifies homosexuals not to further a proper legislative end but to make them unequal to everyone else. This Colorado cannot do."[27] The majority found Amendment 2 unconstitutional because it failed to serve any legitimate purpose.

Public safety, public health, and public morals are legitimate government purposes, but they are not the only ones. Virtually any goal that is not forbidden by the Constitution will be deemed sufficient to meet the rational basis test. As the Supreme Court declared in *Berman v. Parker*: "Public safety, public health, morality, peace and quiet, law and order, these are some of the more conspicuous examples of the traditional application of the police power to municipal affairs. Yet they merely illustrate the scope of the power and do not delimit it."[28]

For example, in *New Orleans v. Dukes*, the Supreme Court upheld an ordinance that banned all pushcart food vendors in the French Quarter, except those who had continuously operated there for eight or more years.[29] The Court accepted the city's claim that "street peddlers and hawkers tend to interfere with the charm and beauty of a historic area and disturb tourists and disrupt their enjoyment of that charm and beauty, and that such vendors . . . might thus have a deleterious effect on the economy of the city."[30] The Court said that the distinction among vendors based on their length of work in the French Quarter was legitimate because "[t]he

---

[23] *Id.* at 450.
[24] 517 U.S. 620 (1996).
[25] *Id.* at 634.
[26] *Id.* at 636 (Scalia, J., dissenting).
[27] *Id.* at 635.
[28] 348 U.S. 26, 32 (1954).
[29] 427 U.S. 297 (1976).
[30] *Id.* at 304-305.

city could reasonably decide that newer businesses were less likely to have built up substantial reliance interests in continued operation."[31]

Obviously, a desire to infringe freedom of religion or deny freedom of speech, in a manner that would violate the First Amendment, would not be deemed a legitimate purpose. Also, the Court has explained that "if the constitutional conception of equal protection of laws means anything, it must at the very least mean a bare congressional desire to harm a politically unpopular group cannot constitute a *legitimate* governmental purpose."[32] Thus, in *U.S. Department of Agriculture v. Moreno,* the Court declared unconstitutional a federal law that excluded from participation in the food stamp program any household containing an individual who is unrelated to any other member of the household. The Court explained that the express congressional purpose of discriminating against "hippies" could not constitute a legitimate purpose.[33]

Similarly, favoring in-state businesses over out-of-state businesses does not constitute a legitimate purpose, especially in light of the policies underlying the "dormant commerce clause" and the privileges and immunities clause of Article IV, which seek to prevent such favoritism.[34] For example, in *Metropolitan Life Insurance Co. v. Ward,* the Court declared unconstitutional a state law that imposed a higher tax on out-of-state insurance companies than on in-state companies.[35] The Court said that the state's only avowed purpose was to improve the local economy, but that doing so at the expense of out-of-staters was not a legitimate purpose.[36]

Likewise, in *Williams v. Vermont,* the Court declared unconstitutional a Vermont automobile tax that exempted cars purchased by Vermont residents in other states, but did not exempt cars bought outside Vermont before a person moved into the state.[37] The Court invalidated the law because it could identify no purpose other than favoring residents over nonresidents. The Court noted that "we can see no relevant difference between motor vehicle registrants who purchase their cars out-of-state while they were Vermont residents and those who came to Vermont only after buying a car elsewhere."[38]

In other cases, as well, the Court invalidated laws that served no purpose other than favoring long-term state residents over new arrivals. In *Hooper v. Bernalillo County Assessor,* the Court declared unconstitutional a state property tax exemption that was available only to persons who were residents of the state before a specific date.[39] Similarly, in *Zobel v. Williams,* the Court invalidated an Alaska law that distributed state money to Alaska residents based on their length of residency in

---

[31] *Id.* at 305.

[32] U.S. Dept. of Agric. v. Moreno, 413 U.S. 528, 534 (1973); *see also* Romer v. Evans, 517 U.S. 620 (1996).

[33] *Id.*

[34] The dormant commerce clause and the privileges and immunities clause are discussed in detail in Chapter 5.

[35] 470 U.S. 869 (1985).

[36] *Id.* at 877 n.5.

[37] 472 U.S. 14 (1985).

[38] *Id.* at 27.

[39] 472 U.S. 612 (1985).

Alaska.[40] In both of these cases the Court emphasized that there was no legitimate interest in rewarding people solely for their length of residence in a state.

However, these cases are the exceptional ones where laws failed the rational basis test. Since 1937, the Court has sided with the government in the vast majority of instances in which rational basis review has been used.

Must It Be the Actual Purpose, or Is a Conceivable Purpose Enough?

The Court's enormous judicial deference under the rational basis test is, in part, due to its willingness to accept any conceivable legitimate purpose as sufficient, even if it is not the government's actual purpose. In other words, a law will be upheld so long as the government's lawyer can identify some conceivable legitimate purpose, regardless of whether that purpose was the government's actual motivation. The Court has declared that under rational basis review, the actual purpose behind a law is irrelevant and the law must be upheld "if any state of facts reasonably may be conceived to justify" its discrimination.[41]

In *U.S. Railroad Retirement Board v. Fritz*, the Supreme Court upheld a federal law designed to prevent retired railroad workers from receiving benefits under both the Social Security system and the railroad retirement system.[42] The law allowed those who were already retired and receiving dual benefits to continue to get them, but those who were still employed could not get dual benefits unless they had worked for the railroads for 25 years. The result was that a person who had worked 10 years for the railroads and was already retired could get dual benefits, but a person who had worked for 24 years and was still employed could not collect dual benefits.

In upholding the law, the Court said: "Where, as here, there are plausible reasons for Congress's action, our inquiry is at an end. It is, of course, constitutionally irrelevant whether this reasoning in fact underlies the legislative decision because this Court never has insisted that a legislative body articulate its reasons for enacting a statute. This is particularly true where the legislature must necessarily engage in a process of line drawing."[43] The Court accepted the government's claim that the Congress could have believed that those who had acquired a statutory entitlement to dual benefits while still employed in the railroad industry "had a greater equitable claim to those benefits than [those] who were no longer in railroad employment when they became eligible for dual benefits."[44]

The dissent, however, objected and said that "[a] challenged classification may be sustained only if it is rationally related to the achievement of an actual legitimate governmental purpose."[45] The dissent contended that the law should

---

[40] 457 U.S. 55 (1982).
[41] McGowan v. Maryland, 366 U.S. 420, 426 (1961).
[42] 449 U.S. 166 (1980).
[43] *Id.* at 179 (citations omitted).
[44] *Id.* at 178.
[45] *Id.* at 186 (Brennan, J., dissenting).

be invalidated because it failed to serve any purpose that Congress actually intended.

Repeatedly, the Court has taken the position that a conceivable legitimate purpose is sufficient. In *Schweiker v. Wilson*, the Court upheld a federal law that denied certain Supplemental Security Income benefits to recipients, aged 21 to 65, who were in public mental institutions that did not receive Medicaid funds for their care.[46] The Supreme Court accepted the government's argument that the law was reasonable in calculating benefits, but the dissent objected and urged much less deference for laws when there is no articulated legislative purpose. Justice Louis Powell, joined by three other Justices, remarked in dissent: "[T]he Court should receive with some skepticism post hoc hypotheses about legislative purpose, unsupported by the legislative history. When no indication of legislative purpose appears other than the current position of the [government], the Court should require that the classification have a fair and substantial relation to the asserted purpose."[47] The dissent thus contended that a tougher version of the rational basis test should be used when the government asserts a conceivable purpose rather than the actual purpose for a law.

Subsequently, in *Federal Communications Commission v. Beach Communications, Inc.*, the Court reaffirmed that any conceivable legislative purpose is sufficient and even went so far as to say that "those attacking the rationality of the legislative classification have the burden to [negate] every conceivable basis which might support it."[48] The case involved a challenge to a provision of the Federal Cable Communications Policy Act that created an exemption to certain regulations for cable television facilities that serve one or more buildings under common ownership or operation. Justice Clarence Thomas, writing for the Court, said: "[B]ecause we never require a legislature to articulate its reasons for enacting a statute, it is entirely irrelevant for constitutional purposes whether the conceived reason for the challenged distinction actually motivated the legislature. . . . [A] legislative choice is not subject to courtroom fact finding and may be based on rational speculation unsupported by evidence or empirical data."[49] Justice Stevens, in a concurring opinion, lamented that "judicial review under the 'conceivable set of facts' test is tantamount to no review at all."[50]

This issue—whether any conceivable legitimate purpose is sufficient or whether it must be the actual purpose—is crucial in determining the impact of rational basis review. If any conceivable purpose is sufficient, very few laws will fail the rational basis test. Government lawyers can invent some legitimate conceivable purpose for virtually every law. The critics argue that rational basis review is meaningful only if the Court limits itself to looking at the actual purpose for a law.

On the other hand, those who defend the Supreme Court point out that rarely is there a single, identifiable purpose for a law. Legislators might have radically

---

[46] 450 U.S. 221 (1981).
[47] *Id.* at 244-245 (Powell, J., dissenting).
[48] 508 U.S. 307, 315 (1993).
[49] *Id.* at 315.
[50] *Id.* at 323 n.3 (Stevens, J., concurring).

different reasons for supporting a specific legislative act. Justice Rehnquist once remarked that actual purpose review "assumes that individual legislators are motivated by one discernible actual purpose, and ignores the fact that different legislators may vote for a single piece of legislation for widely different reasons."[51] Moreover, once a law is struck down for lack of an adequate actual purpose, Congress simply could reenact the law and assert a permissible goal.

Ultimately, the issue is over how much "bite" there should be in the rational basis test. Allowing any conceivable legitimate purpose to suffice makes the rational basis test a rule of almost complete deference to the government. Limiting the judiciary to considering only the actual purpose behind a law would dramatically increase the chance that laws would be struck down under rational basis review.

§9.2.3 The Requirement for a "Reasonable Relationship"

Deference in Determining If There Is a "Reasonable Relationship"

Under rational basis review, the Court also must decide "whether the classifications drawn in a statute are reasonable in light of its purpose."[52] However, the Court repeatedly has expressed that this is "the most relaxed and tolerant form of judicial scrutiny."[53] Thus, the Court has said that under the rational basis test, laws will be upheld unless the government's action is "clearly wrong, a display of arbitrary power, not an exercise of judgment."[54]

Tolerance for Underinclusiveness

As a result, under the rational basis test the Court will allow laws that are both significantly underinclusive and overinclusive. As described above, laws are underinclusive when they do not regulate all who are similarly situated. Underinclusive laws raise the concern that the government has enacted a law that targets a particular politically powerless group or that exempts those with more political clout. But the Supreme Court has said that when rational basis review is used, even substantial underinclusiveness is allowed because the government "may take one step at a time, addressing itself to the phase of the problem which seems most acute to the legislative mind."[55]

For example, in *Railway Express Agency, Inc. v. New York*, the Court upheld an ordinance that banned all advertising on the sides of trucks unless the ad was for the business of the truck's owner.[56] It was argued that this distinction was irrational

---

[51] Kassel v. Consol. Freightways Corp., 450 U.S. 662, 702-703 (1981) (Rehnquist, J., dissenting).
[52] McLaughlin v. Florida, 379 U.S. 184, 191 (1964).
[53] City of Dallas v. Stanglin, 490 U.S. 19, 26 (1989).
[54] Mathews v. De Castro, 429 U.S. 181, 185 (1976), quoting Helvering v. Davis, 301 U.S. 619, 640 (1937).
[55] Williamson v. Lee Optical, 348 U.S. 483, 489 (1955).
[56] 336 U.S. 106 (1949).

as a way to achieve the government's purpose of decreasing distractions for drivers and promoting traffic safety.[57] The Court concluded that the government might have perceived some difference among the ads and that it was immaterial whether the government failed to deal with even greater distractions to motorists. The Court declared: "It is no requirement of equal protection that all evils of the same genus be eradicated or none at all."[58]

Tolerance for Overinclusiveness

Likewise, even substantial overinclusiveness is tolerated under rational basis review. A law is overinclusive if it regulates individuals who are not similarly situated—that is, if it covers more people than it needs to in order to accomplish its purpose. Overinclusive laws are unfair to those who are unnecessarily regulated, and they risk "burden[ing] a politically powerless group which would have been spared if it had enough clout to compel normal attention to the relevant costs and benefits."[59]

Nonetheless, the Supreme Court has indicated that even significant overinclusiveness is allowed under rational basis review. For example, in *New York Transit Authority v. Beazer,* the Supreme Court upheld a city's regulation that prevented those in methadone maintenance programs from holding positions with the Transit Authority.[60] The Court noted that "[t]he evidence indicates that methadone is an effective cure for the physical aspects of heroin addiction" and that " 'the strong majority' of patients who have been on methadone maintenance for at least a year are free from illicit drug use."[61] Thus, the exclusion of all methadone addicts was substantially overinclusive relative to the goal of safety. The vast majority of those in methadone programs posed no safety risk.

But the Supreme Court upheld the law under the rational basis test. The Court said that any alternative rule is likely to be less precise "and will ensuredly be more costly" than the total ban on those using drugs.[62]

Tolerance of Laws That Are Both Underinclusive and Overinclusive

Many laws are both underinclusive and overinclusive. Yet these laws, too, are usually tolerated under the rational basis test. The Supreme Court has declared: "Even if the classification involved here is to some extent both underinclusive and overinclusive, and hence the law drawn by Congress imperfect, it is nevertheless

---

[57] *Id.* at 109-110.
[58] *Id.* at 110.
[59] Laurence H. Tribe, American Constitutional Law 1449 (2d ed. 1988).
[60] 440 U.S. 568 (1979).
[61] *Id.* at 575.
[62] *Id.* at 590.

the rule that . . . perfection is by no means required."[63] For example, in *Beazer*, the law prohibiting methadone addicts from working for the Transit Authority was upheld even though it was both overinclusive and underinclusive. The law was overinclusive in excluding from employment the vast majority of methadone users who posed no safety risk, and it was underinclusive in that it allowed employment of others who would be a safety threat.

In *Vance v. Bradley*, the Supreme Court upheld a mandatory retirement age of 60 for those in the Foreign Service.[64] The Court recognized that the law was overinclusive in that it applied to many who were capable of continuing to work effectively, and it was underinclusive in that it did not apply to many who were under that age and were no longer capable of performing adequately. Nonetheless, the Supreme Court held that age discrimination receives rational basis review only under the equal protection clause and upheld the law even though the "classification involved here is to some extent both underinclusive and overinclusive."[65]

Cases Where Laws Are Deemed Arbitrary and Unreasonable

These decisions indicate that the Supreme Court is extremely deferential under the rational basis test and usually will find that laws are reasonable. There are, however, a few cases where the Court has found that laws are so arbitrary as to fail rational basis review.

For example, in *City of Cleburne, Texas v. Cleburne Living Center, Inc.*, the Supreme Court declared unconstitutional a city ordinance that required a special permit for the operation of a group home for the mentally disabled.[66] The Court expressly held that rational basis review was the appropriate standard for evaluating government actions discriminating against the mentally disabled.[67] The Court nevertheless declared the ordinance unconstitutional.

The city offered a number of justifications for the law; the Court concluded either that they were not legitimate purposes or that the ordinance was not a reasonable way of accomplishing the goals. For example, the city argued that property owners in the area opposed having a facility for the mentally disabled, and the city expressed concern that students from a junior high school across the street might harass occupants of a group home.[68] The Court held that these justifications

---

[63] Vance v. Bradley, 440 U.S. 93, 108 (1979), quoting Phillips Chem. Co. v. Dumas School Dist., 361 U.S. 376, 385 (1960).

[64] 440 U.S. 93 (1979).

[65] *Id.* at 108.

[66] 473 U.S. 432 (1985).

[67] *Id.* at 446 ("To withstand equal protection review, legislation that distinguishes between the mentally retarded and others must be rationally related to a legitimate governmental purpose."). The choice of rational basis review for discrimination based on mental disability is discussed more fully below in §9.7.2.

[68] *Id.* at 448-449.

were based on prejudices against the mentally disabled and that indulging such private biases is not a legitimate government purpose.[69]

The city also contended that the home was located on a "five hundred year flood plain."[70] The Court dismissed this concern because in the same area the city allowed facilities such as nursing homes, homes for convalescents and the aged, hospitals, and sanitariums.[71] Likewise, the Court rejected the city's concern over the number who would live in the home because no similar restrictions on size existed for nursing homes, boarding houses, fraternities, or others.

Although the Court expressly declared that it was applying rational basis review, it appears that there was more "bite" to the Court's approach than usual for this level of scrutiny. The Court often has declared that the rational basis test allows the government to proceed one step at a time; substantial underinclusiveness is tolerated.[72] Therefore, under usual rational basis review, the government would be able to regulate homes for the mentally disabled, but not apply the standards to hospitals or nursing homes. But the Supreme Court's decision also can be seen as a straightforward application of rational basis review: Drawing a distinction between a home for the mentally disabled and all other facilities is based on nothing other than irrational prejudices and thus fails even deferential scrutiny. In a subsequent decision, *University of Alabama v. Garrett*,[73] the Court declared that *Cleburne* held that only rational basis review is to be used for disability discrimination.

Another instance where the Court declared unconstitutional a government action because of its irrationality is *Allegheny Pittsburgh Coal Co. v. County Commission*.[74] The Court unanimously invalidated a county tax assessor's practice of valuing real property at 50 percent of its most recent sale price. Property would not be reassessed until it was again sold. The result was that properties with identical values would have widely divergent assessments depending on the timing of the sales. The plaintiff's property was assessed at a value of 8 to 35 times more than similar property in the county, even though the West Virginia constitution ensured that taxes would be "equal and uniform."

The Court said that although the judiciary should generally defer to distinctions drawn in tax laws, the county assessor's practices were arbitrary and unsupported by state law.[75] The Court concluded that "[t]he relative undervaluation of comparable property in Webster County over time therefore denies petitioners the equal protection of the law."[76]

---

[69] *Id.*

[70] *Id.* at 449.

[71] *Id.*

[72] *See* text accompanying notes 55-58, above.

[73] 531 U.S. 356 (2001). In *Garrett*, the Court held that Congress lacked the authority to authorize suits against the states for employment discrimination based on disability under Title I of the Americans with Disabilities Act. This is discussed in detail in §3.7.2.

[74] 488 U.S. 336 (1989).

[75] *Id.* at 345.

[76] *Id.* at 346.

However, just a few years later, in *Nordlinger v. Hahn*,[77] the Supreme Court upheld a California law that was very similar in its effects to what was declared unconstitutional in *Allegheny Pittsburgh Coal.* Proposition 13, adopted by California voters as an initiative in 1976, limits real property taxes to 1 percent of assessed valuation of the property as of 1975-1976 and permits reassessment only when sold. The result is enormous disparities in the property taxes for otherwise identical property. A person who purchased property in the 1970s, when property values were low, would pay little in property taxes; but a person who bought the identical house next door in the 1980s, when property values were high, would pay far more in property taxes.

Nonetheless, the Court upheld Proposition 13 as being rationally related to a legitimate government purpose.[78] The Court said that there were many conceivable purposes for the law including encouraging stable neighborhoods by offering an economic disincentive for people to move, avoiding taxes on appreciation that was the result of inflation, and allowing people to know their tax burden at the time of purchase.

What is the difference between *Allegheny Pittsburgh Coal* and *Nordlinger?* In *Allegheny Pittsburgh Coal,* the challenge was not to the state's tax law, but instead to the administrative practices of the county tax assessor. In *Nordlinger,* the objection was to the tax law itself. *Nordlinger* reflects the Court's general unwillingness to review tax laws that inherently must draw distinctions. *Allegheny Pittsburgh Coal* thus seems limited to challenges of arbitrary and unjustifiable administrative decisions. Yet this distinction can be questioned because the practices challenged in *Allegheny Pittsburgh Coal* and *Nordlinger* had the identical effect: Property with the same value would be taxed at widely different amounts depending on the time of sale.

The Court returned to the issue of equal protection challenges to tax laws in *Armour v. City of Indianapolis.*[79] A city adopted a new system for funding sewer improvement projects. Under the prior law, residents could pay the cost of connecting to the sewer system in a lump sum or over time. The effect of the new law was to reduce the cost to those who were paying over time, but provide no refund to those who had already paid in full. The latter challenged this as denying them equal protection.

The Supreme Court held that city had a rational basis for its distinction between residents who had already paid their share of project costs and those who had not and, thus, did not violate the equal protection clause. The Court explained that "we have repeatedly pointed out that '[l]egislatures have especially broad latitude in creating classifications and distinctions in tax statutes'" and that "administrative considerations can justify a tax-related distinction."[80] Justice Breyer, writing for the majority in a 6-3 decision, distinguished *Allegheny Pittsburgh Coal* as involving "a clear state law requirement clearly and dramatically violated"

---

[77] 505 U.S. 1 (1992).
[78] *Id.* at 11-13.
[79] 132 S. Ct. 2073 (2012).
[80] *Id.* at 2079, 2080.

and said that *Allegheny* is "the 'rare case where the facts precluded' any alternative reading of state law and thus any alternative rational basis."[81]

By contrast, Chief Justice Roberts, joined by Justices Scalia and Alito, dissented and found *Allegheny Pittsburgh Coal* indistinguishable. He wrote: "The Court reminds us that *Allegheny Pittsburgh* is a 'rare case.' It is and should be; we give great leeway to taxing authorities in this area, for good and sufficient reasons. But every generation or so a case comes along when this Court needs to say enough is enough, if the Equal Protection Clause is to retain any force in this context. *Allegheny Pittsburgh* was such a case; so is this one."[82]

Cases such as *Cleburne* and *Allegheny Pittsburgh Coal* indicate that rational basis review is not completely toothless. Yet it also must be remembered that these are the rare and exceptional cases where laws failed the rational basis test.

§9.3   CLASSIFICATIONS BASED ON RACE AND NATIONAL ORIGIN

Of all the infinite array of distinctions drawn by American governments in almost 240 years, none has been more important than race discrimination. Some injustices are so enormous as to defy comprehension. Slavery, the apartheid that followed it in much of the country, and the systematic race discrimination that has existed throughout the nation are a profound embarrassment and a human tragedy of incalculable dimensions.

Organization of This Section

In discussing discrimination based on race and national origin, we begin in §9.3.1 by looking at race discrimination and slavery before the Civil War. Section 9.3.2 explains that strict scrutiny is used for evaluating race and national origin classifications. Section 9.3.3 then focuses on the question of how the existence of a race or national origin classification can be proved. There are two ways of proving such discrimination. First, the classification may exist on the face of the law; that is, the law in its very terms draws a distinction among people based on race or national origin. The types of racial classifications that might exist on the face of the law are discussed in §9.3.3.1. Alternatively, if a law is facially neutral, a racial classification can be proved by demonstrating that the law has a discriminatory purpose and a discriminatory impact. This way of proving discrimination is discussed in §9.3.3.2.

---

[81] *Id.* at 2084.
[82] *Id.* at 2087 (Roberts, C.J., dissenting).

No area of race discrimination has produced more litigation or has been more difficult for the courts than the problem of school segregation. Section 9.3.4 examines the issues surrounding remedies for school segregation.

Finally, §9.3.5 discusses racial classifications that benefit minorities. This, of course, is the controversial issue of affirmative action that has produced a number of major Supreme Court decisions in recent years.

§9.3.1   *Race Discrimination and Slavery Before the Thirteenth and Fourteenth Amendments*

Constitutional Provisions Protecting Slavery

Prior to the adoption of the Thirteenth Amendment in 1865, slavery was constitutional. Prior to the adoption of the Fourteenth Amendment in 1868, there was no constitutional assurance of equal protection and thus no limit on race discrimination. Despite the majestic words of the Declaration of Independence that "all men are created equal," blacks were anything but equal under the Constitution.

Several constitutional provisions expressly protected aspects of the institution of slavery. Article I, §2, requires apportionment of the House of Representatives based on the "whole number of free Persons" and "three fifths of all other Persons." Article I, §9, prevented Congress from banning the importation of slaves until 1808, and Article V of the Constitution prohibited this provision from being altered by constitutional amendment. Article IV, §2, contains the fugitive slave clause, which provided: "No Person held to Service or Labour in one State, under the Laws thereof, escaping into another, shall, in Consequence of any Law or Regulation therein, be discharged from such Service or Labour, but shall be delivered up on Claim of the Party to whom such Service or Labour may be due."

Southern states simply would not have accepted a Constitution that abolished slavery. Additionally, many of the most influential drafters at the Constitutional Convention were slave owners. For example, such prominent framers as George Washington, James Madison, and John Rutledge all owned slaves.[1] The result was a Constitution that protected the institution of slavery. As Professor Donald Robinson explains: "There is no evidence that any framer thought that the Constitution contained power to abolish slavery. They all knew how the Deep Southerners felt, and however much some of them may have regretted the hold that slavery had on the South, they were all fully sympathetic with the determination of the Deep Southerners to resist abolition in the present circumstances. . . . [The] framers, as of 1787, agreed unanimously to place the institution of slavery, as it existed within the South, not 'in the course of ultimate extinction,' as Lincoln argued, but beyond national regulation."[2]

---

§9.3 [1] *See* Donald L. Robinson, Slavery in the Structure of American Politics 1765-1820, 209-210 (1971).

[2] *Id.* at 245-246.

Court Decisions Protecting the Institution of Slavery

The judiciary consistently enforced the institution of slavery by ruling in favor of slave owners and against slaves.[3] For example, the Court enforced the fugitive slave clause and prevented Northern states from protecting escaped slaves. In *Prigg v. Pennsylvania*, the Supreme Court declared unconstitutional a state law that prevented the use of force or violence to remove any person from the state to return the individual to slavery.[4] The Fugitive Slave Act of 1793, adopted by the second Congress, required that judges return escaped slaves. In *Prigg*, the Supreme Court relied on this Act and the fugitive slave clause to invalidate the Pennsylvania law. Justice Joseph Story, writing for the Court, began by noting that "[f]ew questions which have ever come before this court involve more delicate and important considerations; and few upon which the public at large may be presumed to feel a more profound and pervading interest."[5]

The Court then held that the Constitution prohibited states from interfering with the return of fugitive slaves. The Court explained that the "object of this clause was to secure to the citizens of the slaveholding states the complete right and title of ownership in their slaves, as property, in every state in the Union into which they might escape from the state where they were held in servitude."[6] Indeed, the Court said that the fugitive slave clause "was so vital . . . that it cannot be doubted that it constituted a fundamental article, without the adoption of which the Union could not have been formed."[7] Thus, the Court concluded that "we have not the slightest hesitation in holding that under and in virtue of the Constitution, the owner of a slave is clothed with entire authority, in every state in the Union, to seize and recapture his slave."[8] Likewise, the Court also held that states could punish those who harbored fugitive slaves.[9]

At no point prior to the Civil War did the Supreme Court significantly limit slavery or even raise serious questions about its constitutionality.[10] Nor were state courts, even in the North, a significant force in ending slavery. For example, in *State v. Post*, the Supreme Court of New Jersey rejected a claim that the state constitution abolished slavery.[11] The Court said that "it has been often adjudged, both by the State and Federal courts, that slavery still exists; that the master's right of property in the slave has not been affected either by the declaration of independence, or the constitution of the United States."[12]

---

[3] For an excellent description of these cases and this history, *see* Robert M. Cover, Justice Accused: Antislavery and the Judicial Process (1975).

[4] 41 U.S. (16 Pet.) 539 (1842).

[5] *Id.* at 610.

[6] *Id.* at 611.

[7] *Id.*

[8] *Id.* at 613.

[9] Moore v. Illinois, 55 U.S. (14 How.) 13, 18 (1852).

[10] In *The Antelope*, 23 U.S. (10 Wheat.) 66 (1825), the Supreme Court suggested that slavery was inconsistent with national law and therefore had to be authorized by statute.

[11] 20 N.J.L. 368 (1845).

[12] *Id.* at 376.

The importance of slavery as a social and political issue during this period cannot be overstated. Every discussion of the relationship between the federal and state governments was directly or indirectly about the slavery question. It was the central dispute of the time and affected almost all other issues.

Dred Scott v. Sandford

In 1819, a major national controversy surrounded the admission of Missouri as a state and whether it, and other areas covered by the Louisiana Purchase, would be free or slave states. In a compromise that was intended to resolve the issue, known as the Missouri Compromise, Congress admitted Missouri as a slave state, but prohibited slavery in the territories north of the latitude of 36′30′. Territories below this line could decide whether to allow slavery and could make that choice when admitted as states.

In *Dred Scott v. Sandford*, the Supreme Court declared the Missouri Compromise unconstitutional and broadly held that slaves were property, not citizens.[13] Dred Scott, a slave owned in Missouri by John Emerson, was taken into Illinois, a free state. After Emerson died, his estate was administered by John Sanford, a resident of New York.[14] Scott sued Sanford in federal court, basing jurisdiction on diversity of citizenship, and claimed that his residence in Illinois made him a free person.

The United States Supreme Court ruled against Scott in a decision that fills over 200 pages in the United States Reports. Chief Justice Roger Taney, writing for the Court, began by stating the issue: "The question is simply this: Can a negro, whose ancestors were imported into this country, and sold as slaves, become a member of the political community formed and brought into existence by the Constitution of the United States, and as such become entitled to all of the rights, and privileges, and immunities, guarantied by that instrument to the citizen?"[15]

The Supreme Court held that slaves were not citizens and thus could not invoke federal court diversity of citizenship jurisdiction. The Court explained that when the Constitution was ratified, slaves were considered "as a subordinate and inferior class of beings, who had been subjugated to the dominant race, and whether emancipated or not, yet remained subject to their authority, and had no rights or privileges but such as those who held the power and the Government might choose to grant them."[16] The Court reviewed the laws that existed in 1787 and concluded that a "perpetual and impassable barrier was intended to be erected between the white race and the one which they had reduced to slavery."[17] The Court said that slaves were not citizens and could not sue as citizens in the federal courts.

Even though the Court concluded that it lacked jurisdiction to hear Scott's suit, it went further and declared the Missouri Compromise unconstitutional. The

---

[13] 60 U.S. (19 How.) 393 (1857).
[14] Sanford's name is misspelled in the United States Reports as "Sandford."
[15] *Id.* at 403.
[16] *Id.* at 404-405.
[17] *Id.* at 409.

Supreme Court ruled that Congress could not grant citizenship to slaves or their descendants; this would be a taking of property from slave owners without due process or just compensation. The Court concluded: "[T]he right of property in a slave is distinctly and expressly affirmed in the Constitution. . . . [I]t is the opinion of the court that the act of Congress which prohibited a citizen from holding and owning property of this kind in the territory of the United States north of the line therein mentioned, is not warranted by the Constitution, and is therefore void."[18] The Court said that Scott therefore was not made free by being taken into Illinois and that his status on return to Missouri was to be determined by Missouri law.

Although the Supreme Court undoubtedly thought that it was resolving the controversy over slavery in *Dred Scott v. Sandford*, the decision had exactly the opposite effect. The ruling became the focal point in the debate over slavery and, by striking down the Missouri Compromise, the decision helped to precipitate the Civil War.[19]

Discrimination in Northern States

Although Northern states generally did not allow slavery and often adopted laws to undermine that reprehensible institution,[20] these states certainly did not provide equality for blacks before the Civil War. Laws in Northern states did not guarantee equal protection but, rather, institutionalized discrimination in diverse ways such as by prohibiting interracial marriage and requiring separation of the races in schools.[21]

The Post–Civil War Amendments

After the completion of the Civil War, in 1865, Congress enacted and the states ratified the Thirteenth Amendment, which prohibits slavery and involuntary servitude. Yet it was obvious that the Thirteenth Amendment would not by itself secure the rights of former slaves; Southern states systematically discriminated against blacks in every imaginable way. Congress therefore approved and the states ratified the Fourteenth Amendment in 1868.[22] Section 1 of the Fourteenth Amendment overrules the *Dred Scott* decision by declaring that all persons "born or naturalized in the United States . . . are citizens of the United States and of the

---

[18] *Id.* at 451-452.

[19] For example, the famous Lincoln-Douglas debates involved extended arguments about the *Dred Scott* decision and its meaning. For an excellent discussion of this, *see* David Zarefsky, Lincoln, Douglas and Slavery: In the Crucible of Public Debate 51-53 (1990).

[20] *See* Derrick A. Bell, Jr., Race, Racism and American Law 34-36 (1973).

[21] *See* Roberts v. City of Boston, 59 Mass. (5 Cush.) 198 (1850) (upholding segregation in public education); Bell, *supra* note 20, at 195-196 (describing Northern laws imposing segregation).

[22] Initially, Southern states rejected the Fourteenth Amendment. These states approved the amendment only after Congress, in the Reconstruction Act, made ratification a condition for admission to the Union. By then, two Northern states rescinded their ratification. The Fourteenth Amendment was deemed ratified when three-fourths of the states—counting the Southern states that ratified under protest and the two states that had rescinded their ratification—had approved it. The history of the ratification of the Fourteenth Amendment is described in §1.3.

State wherein they reside." Section 1 also guarantees that no state shall deprive any citizen of the privileges or immunities of citizenship,[23] or deprive any person of life, liberty, or property without due process of law, or deny any person "equal protection of the laws."

§9.3.2 Strict Scrutiny for Discrimination Based on Race and National Origin

Recognition of Strict Scrutiny

It now is clearly established that racial classifications will be allowed only if the government can meet the heavy burden of demonstrating that the discrimination is necessary to achieve a compelling government purpose.[24] In other words, the government must show an extremely important reason for its action *and* it must demonstrate that the goal cannot be achieved through any less discriminatory alternative.[25] The Court has expressly declared that all racial classifications—whether disadvantaging or helping minorities—must meet strict scrutiny.[26]

Ironically, the Supreme Court first articulated the requirement for strict scrutiny for discrimination based on race and national origin in *Korematsu v. United States*, which upheld the constitutionality of the relocation of Japanese Americans during World War II.[27] The Court declared: "[A]ll legal restrictions which curtail the civil rights of a single racial group are immediately suspect. That is not to say that all such restrictions are unconstitutional. It is to say that courts must subject them to the most rigid scrutiny. Pressing public necessity may sometimes justify the existence of such restrictions; racial antagonism never can."[28]

Justifications for Strict Scrutiny

The Supreme Court has identified many reasons why strict scrutiny is appropriate for race and national origin classifications. These justifications are important both in understanding the Court's approach to racial discrimination and also in evaluating whether other types of discrimination warrant heightened scrutiny.

The Court long has recognized that the primary purpose of the Fourteenth Amendment was to protect African Americans; in fact, the initial Supreme Court decisions construing the equal protection clause suggested that it could be used

---

[23] The privileges or immunities clause is discussed in §6.3.2.

[24] *See, e.g.*, Wygant v. Jackson Bd. of Educ., 476 U.S. 267, 274 (1986); Palmore v. Sidoti, 466 U.S. 429, 432 (1984).

[25] Wygant v. Jackson Bd. of Educ., 476 U.S. at 267, 280 n.6.

[26] *See, e.g.*, Adarand Constructors, Inc. v. Pena, 515 U.S. 200 (1995) (federal affirmative action programs must meet strict scrutiny); Richmond v. J.A. Croson Co., 488 U.S. 469 (1989) (state and local affirmative action programs must meet strict scrutiny). The topic of affirmative action is discussed in detail in §9.3.5.

[27] 323 U.S. 214 (1944), discussed in more detail below at §9.3.3.1.

[28] *Id.* at 216.

only to protect blacks.[29] The Court has emphasized that the long history of racial discrimination makes it very likely that racial classifications will be based on stereotypes and prejudices. Chief Justice Warren Burger wrote: "A core purpose of the Fourteenth Amendment was to do away with all governmentally imposed discrimination based on race. Classifying persons according to their race is more likely to reflect racial prejudice than legitimate public concerns."[30]

Additionally, heightened scrutiny for government actions discriminating against racial and national origin minorities is justified because of the relative political powerlessness of these groups. In the famous *Carolene Products* footnote, the Supreme Court indicated that "prejudice against discrete and insular minorities may be a special condition, which tends seriously to curtail the operation of those political processes ordinarily to be relied upon to protect minorities" and thus "may call for a correspondingly more searching judicial inquiry."[31] Prejudice and the history of discrimination make it less likely that racial and national origin minorities can protect themselves through the political process.

Also, the Court has emphasized that race is an immutable trait.[32] It is unfair to discriminate against people for a characteristic that is acquired at birth and cannot be changed.

For all of these reasons, it is firmly established that race and national origin classifications must meet the most exacting standard of judicial review. Such discrimination will be tolerated only if the government can prove that it is necessary to achieve a compelling government purpose.

§9.3.3 *Proving the Existence of a Race or National Origin Classification*

There are two alternative ways of demonstrating the existence of a race or national origin classification. In one way, the classification exists on the face of the law; that is, the text of the law draws a distinction among people based on race or national origin. Alternatively, if a law is facially neutral, a race or national origin classification might be proved by demonstrating discriminatory administration or discriminatory impact; however, the Supreme Court has held that this requires proof of a discriminatory purpose. Section 9.3.3.1 looks at racial classifications on the face of the law, and §9.3.3.2 considers facially neutral laws with a discriminatory impact or with discriminatory administration.

---

[29] The Slaughter-House Cases, 83 U.S. 36, 81 (1872).

[30] Palmore v. Sidoti, 466 U.S. at 429, 432.

[31] United States v. Carolene Prods. Co., 304 U.S. 144, 153 n.4 (1938), discussed in §6.5.

[32] *See, e.g.,* Frontiero v. Richardson, 411 U.S. 677, 686 (1973); Lockhart v. McCree, 476 U.S. 162, 175 (1986); Regents of the Univ. of Cal. v. Bakke, 438 U.S. 265, 360-361 (1978) (Blackmun, J., concurring and dissenting).

§9.3.3.1   Race and National Origin Classifications on the Face of the Law

Facial race and national origin classifications exist when a law, in its very terms, draws a distinction among people based on those characteristics. There are three major types of such laws.

Race-Specific Classifications That Disadvantage Racial Minorities

First, there are laws that expressly impose a burden or disadvantage on people because of their race or national origin. For example, in *Strauder v. West Virginia*, the Supreme Court declared unconstitutional a West Virginia law that limited jury service to "white male persons who are twenty-one years of age and who are citizens of this State."[33] The Court explained that the Fourteenth Amendment was "designed to ensure to the colored race the enjoyment of all the civil rights that under the law are enjoyed by white persons, and to give to that race the protection of the general government, in that enjoyment, whenever it should be denied by the States."[34] The Court declared the law unconstitutional because it expressly singled out and disadvantaged blacks.

Similarly, in *Buchanan v. Warley*, the Supreme Court declared unconstitutional a state law that prevented blacks from buying homes in white neighborhoods.[35] The Court declared this unconstitutional as impermissible race discrimination.

Any government action that uses race as a basis for a burden or disadvantage is a classification of this type. For example, in *Palmore v. Sidoti*, the Supreme Court deemed unconstitutional a state court's denying a mother custody of a child because she had married a person of a different race.[36] The state court had concluded that the child's best interests would be served by awarding custody to the father because the child might be taunted and stigmatized for living in a biracial household. The Supreme Court unanimously declared this unconstitutional and concluded: "The Constitution cannot control such prejudices but neither can it tolerate them. Private biases may be outside the reach of the law, but the law cannot, directly or indirectly, give them effect. . . . The effects of racial prejudice, however real, cannot justify a racial classification removing an infant child from the custody of its natural mother found to be an appropriate person to have such custody."[37]

There is only one situation in which the Court expressly upheld racial classifications burdening minorities: the rulings affirming the constitutionality of the evacuation of Japanese Americans during World War II.[38] During World War II,

---

[33] 100 U.S. (10 Otto) 303 (1879).
[34] *Id.* at 306.
[35] 245 U.S. 60 (1917).
[36] 466 U.S. at 429.
[37] *Id.* at 433-434.
[38] Korematsu v. United States, 323 U.S. 214 (1944).

110,000 Japanese Americans—adults and children, aliens and citizens—were forcibly uprooted from their homes and placed in concentration camps. In some camps, they were housed in horse stalls and kept prisoners behind barbed wire.[39] The government's purported justification was national security; a fear that Japanese Americans on the West Coast might aid an invading Japanese army or be a threat to commit acts of espionage and sabotage. No evidence of a specific threat was required to evacuate and intern a person. Race alone was used to determine who would be uprooted and incarcerated and who would remain free.

The Court considered the constitutionality of the government's actions in three decisions. In *Hirabayashi v. United States*, the Supreme Court upheld the constitutionality of a curfew applicable only to Japanese Americans.[40] Regulations required that all persons of Japanese ancestry residing in designated areas must be in their residences between 8:00 P.M. and 6:00 A.M. Although the regulations were explicitly discriminatory, the Supreme Court upheld them and concluded that "[t]he challenged orders were defense measures for the avowed purpose of safeguarding the military area in question, at a time of threatened air raids and invasion by the Japanese forces."[41]

In *Korematsu v. United States*, the Supreme Court went even further and upheld the constitutionality of the evacuation of Japanese Americans.[42] The Court accepted the government's claim that there was a serious risk to national security from Japanese Americans who were disloyal to the United States and that there was no way of screening to identify such individuals. Justice Black, writing for the Court, said: "Like curfew, exclusion of those of Japanese origin was deemed necessary because of the presence of an unascertained number of disloyal members of the group, most of whom we have no doubt were loyal to this country. It was because we could not reject the finding of the military authorities that it was impossible to bring about an immediate segregation of the disloyal from the loyal that we sustained the validity of the curfew order as applying to the whole group. In the instant case, temporary exclusion of the entire group was rested by the military on the same ground."[43] The Court emphasized that it was upholding the order because it was wartime and "hardships are part of war."[44]

Korematsu is objectionable because the government used race alone as the basis for predicting who was a threat to national security and who would remain free.[45] The racial classification was enormously overinclusive: All Japanese Americans were evacuated and interned because a few might be disloyal. In fact, there was no evidence of a threat from any Japanese Americans, and subsequent research by Professor Peter Irons has shown that government attorneys intentionally

---

[39] William R. Manchester, The Glory and the Dream 300-301 (1974) (describing the conditions in internment camps).

[40] 320 U.S. 81 (1943).

[41] *Id.* at 94-95.

[42] 323 U.S. 214 (1944).

[43] *Id.* at 218-219.

[44] *Id.* at 219.

[45] *See, e.g.*, Eugene Rostow, The Japanese American Cases—A Disaster, 54 Yale L.J. 489 (1945).

exaggerated the risk to persuade the Court to accept the evacuation order.[46] The racial classification also was enormously underinclusive: Those of other races who posed a threat of disloyalty were not interned and evacuated. Even though winning the war undoubtedly was a compelling purpose, the means was not necessary to attaining that end. As Justice Murphy lamented in dissent, the evacuation of Japanese Americans was "one of the most sweeping and complete deprivations of constitutional rights in the history of this nation."[47]

In *Ex parte Endo*, decided the same day as *Korematsu*, the Supreme Court held that the continued detention of Japanese Americans was unwarranted.[48] The Court's holding was narrow, simply concluding that the executive orders that provided the authority for the evacuation of Japanese Americans did not expressly authorize the continued detention of loyal Japanese Americans. The Court did observe that "[a] citizen who is concededly loyal presents no problem of espionage or sabotage. Loyalty is a matter of the heart and mind, not of race, creed, or color."[49] Yet the Court never declared the evacuation and internment of Japanese Americans unconstitutional.

Perhaps these cases are best understood as examples of the Court's tremendous deference to the military, especially in time of war. Yet it can be argued that the Constitution and the Court's role are most important precisely in such times when pressure and even hysteria to violate rights and discriminate will be most likely to occur.

Racial Classifications Burdening Both Whites and Minorities

A second type of racial classification that can exist on the face of the law is government actions that burden both whites and minorities. For example, antimiscegenation laws—statutes that prohibit interracial cohabitation and marriage—apply to both whites and blacks. In fact, the Supreme Court initially upheld such laws on the ground that they did not discriminate; the Court saw them as treating blacks and whites equally. In *Pace v. Alabama*, the Court upheld an Alabama law that provided for harsher penalties for adultery and fornication if the couple were composed of a white and a black than if the couple were both of the same race.[50]

Subsequently, however, the Court recognized that such racial classifications are impermissible under the equal protection clause because they are based on assumptions of the inferiority of blacks to whites. In *McLaughlin v. Florida*, the Supreme Court declared unconstitutional a Florida law that prohibited the

---

[46] *See* Peter Irons, Justice at War (1983).

[47] Korematsu v. United States, 323 U.S. at 235 (Murphy, J., dissenting). In fact, in the Civil Liberties Act of 1988, 50 U.S.C. §1989 (1988), Congress issued a public apology to Japanese Americans and promised to make restitution to those who were interned.

[48] 323 U.S. 283 (1944). For an excellent discussion of this case, *see* Patrick O. Gutridge, Remember *Endo?*, 116 Harv. L. Rev. 1933 (2003).

[49] *Id.* at 302.

[50] 106 U.S. (16 Otto) 583 (1883).

habitual occupation of a room at night by unmarried interracial couples.[51] The Court indicated that *Pace* "represents a limited view of the Equal Protection Clause that has not withstood analysis in the subsequent decisions of this Court."[52] The Court emphasized that the state offered no acceptable justification for why a race neutral law could not adequately serve its purposes of punishing premarital sexual relations.

In *Loving v. Virginia*, the Supreme Court declared unconstitutional a state's miscegenation statute that made it a crime for a white person to marry outside the Caucasian race.[53] The Court expressly repudiated the state's argument that the law was permissible because it burdened both whites and minorities. The Court said that "we reject the notion that the mere equal application of a statute concerning racial classifications is enough to remove the classifications from the Fourteenth Amendment's proscription of all invidious racial discriminations."[54] The Court explained: "There can be no question but that Virginia's miscegenation statutes rest solely upon distinctions drawn according to race. The statutes proscribe generally accepted conduct if engaged in by members of different races. . . . There can be no doubt that restricting the freedom to marry solely because of racial classifications violates the central meaning of the Equal Protection Clause."[55]

Another example of a law that violates equal protection even though it applied to whites and blacks is the statute invalidated in *Anderson v. Martin*, which required that the race of candidates for office be listed on the ballot.[56] The Court explained that "[t]he vice lies not in the resulting injury but in the placing of the power of the State behind a racial classification that induces racial prejudice at the polls."[57]

Similarly, in *Hunter v. Erickson*, the Supreme Court declared unconstitutional an ordinance, adopted by referendum, that required that laws regulating real estate transactions "on the basis of race, color, religion, national origin or ancestry must first be approved by a majority of the electors voting on the question at a regular or general election before said ordinance shall be effective."[58] The Court explained that the law in question was an "explicitly racial classification treating racial housing matters differently from other racial and housing matters."[59] Blacks, much more than whites, were obviously harmed by creating obstacles to enactment of open housing laws, and thus the Court found the ordinance to violate equal protection.[60]

---

[51] 379 U.S. 184, 196 (1964).

[52] *Id.* at 188.

[53] 388 U.S. 1 (1967).

[54] *Id.* at 8 (citations omitted).

[55] *Id.* at 11-12.

[56] 375 U.S. 399 (1964).

[57] *Id.* at 402.

[58] 393 U.S. 385 (1969).

[59] *Id.*

[60] *Id.* at 141. In contrast, in *James v. Valtierra*, 402 U.S. 137 (1971), the Court upheld an amendment to the California constitution, that had been adopted by initiative, that prohibited the government from constructing low-rent housing projects unless approved by a majority of those voting in a community election. The Court held that the law was not a racial classification because it "required

In the same vein, in *Washington v. Seattle School District No. 1*, the Court declared unconstitutional a law adopted by initiative that prevented school boards from requiring students to attend schools not nearest or next nearest to the student's place of residence.[61] The Supreme Court ruled the law unconstitutional because "it uses the racial nature of an issue to define the governmental decisionmaking structure and thus imposes substantial and unique burdens on racial minorities."[62] Although the law nowhere mentioned race and applied in the same way to all races, the Court found that it was a racial classification because, like in *Hunter*, the law "removes the authority to address a racial problem—and only a racial problem—from the existing decisionmaking body, in such a way as to burden minority interests."[63]

However, in *Schuette v. Coalition to Defend Affirmative Action*, the Court distinguished *Hunter* and *Washington* and upheld a Michigan initiative that restricted affirmative action.[64] Michigan's Proposal 2 was an initiative passed by voters that prohibited the state or its political subdivisions from discriminating or giving preferences based on race or gender in education, contracting, or employment. The United States Court of Appeals for the Sixth Circuit declared this unconstitutional in the area of education based on *Hunter* and *Washington*.[65] The Court of Appeals explained that virtually any group could gain benefits in admission through the political process; the Board of Regents for the university or the state legislation could give preference in admission to those who lived in the state or those from a specific area of the state or those whose parents went to a state school. But racial minorities could not use this political process for benefits in admission; to gain racially sensitive admissions policies, they would need to go through the much more arduous process of amending the state constitution.

The Supreme Court, in a 6-2 decision, without a majority opinion, upheld the Michigan initiative. Justice Kennedy wrote the plurality opinion, joined by Chief Justice Roberts and Justice Alito, and said that *Hunter* and *Washington* were limited to initiatives that were intentionally discriminatory against racial minorities, something the plurality found absent as to the Michigan initiative. Justice Kennedy

---

referendum approval for any low-rent public housing project, not only for projects which will be occupied by a racial minority."

[61] 458 U.S. 457 (1982). The law included a number of exceptions that permitted such assignments for nonracial reasons, such as to alleviate overcrowding, or for racial reasons if court-ordered as a remedy.

[62] *Id.* at 470.

[63] *Id.* at 474. In contrast, in *Crawford v. Bd. of Educ.*, 458 U.S. 527 (1982), the Supreme Court upheld an initiative that prohibited state courts from ordering mandatory pupil assignment or transportation unless a federal court would do so to remedy a violation of the federal equal protection clause. The Court said that the law was not a racial classification and that states could say that they would do no more than the Fourteenth Amendment requires. Perhaps *Crawford* is distinguishable from *Washington* on the ground that the latter altered the political process in a manner different from the former; *Washington* limited the powers of the school board in all instances from using race unless court ordered, while *Crawford* only limited the school board when the actions were greater than those required to comply with the Fourteenth Amendment. On the other hand, both involved initiatives limiting desegregation, making the Court's distinction questionable.

[64] 134 S. Ct. 1623 (2014).

[65] Coalition to Defend Affirmative Action v. Regents of the Univ. of Mich., 701 F.3d 466 (6th Cir. 2012) (en banc).

explained that "[t]hose cases were ones in which the political restriction in question was designed to be used, or was likely to be used, to encourage infliction of injury by reason of race."[66]

Justice Scalia wrote an opinion concurring in the judgment, joined by Justice Thomas, in which he argued that *Hunter* and *Washington* should be overruled. Justice Scalia declared: "Patently atextual, unadministrable, and contrary to our traditional equal-protection jurisprudence, *Hunter* and *Seattle* should be overruled."[67]

Justice Breyer was the final vote for the majority and he expressed the need for deference to the political process. He emphasized that the earlier cases involved a restructuring of the political process that changed the political level at which policies were enacted, while this case involves an amendment that took decision-making authority away from unelected actors and placed it in the hands of the voters.

Justice Sotomayor wrote a powerful dissent in which she defended her views of race and society, including the importance of racially sensitive admissions policies. She concluded her opinion by declaring: "Race matters. Race matters in part because of the long history of racial minorities' being denied access to the political process. . . . Race also matters because of persistent racial inequality in society—inequality that cannot be ignored and that has produced stark socioeconomic disparities. . . . Race matters because of the slights, the snickers, the silent judgments that reinforce that most crippling of thoughts: 'I do not belong here.' . . . This refusal to accept the stark reality that race matters is regrettable. The way to stop discrimination on the basis of race is to speak openly and candidly on the subject of race, and to apply the Constitution with eyes open to the unfortunate effects of centuries of racial discrimination."[68]

The bottom line from *Schuette* is that no state needs to have affirmative action programs for its colleges and universities and that a state may eliminate these, including by an initiative. As for *Hunter* and *Washington*, they have not been overruled, but they have been limited and it is uncertain what remains of the so-called political restructuring doctrine that they created.

Laws Requiring Separation of the Races

Statutes requiring separation of the races are a third type of racial classification that can exist on the face of the law. During the Reconstruction era that followed the Civil War, the South was under military rule and Congress enacted many laws to protect civil rights.[69] Substantial progress was made in protecting the rights of the former slaves.

---

[66] 134 S. Ct. at 1638.

[67] *Id.* at 1643 (Scalia, J., concurring in the judgment).

[68] *Id.* at 1676 (Sotomayor, J., dissenting).

[69] For example, the Civil Rights Act of 1866 provided that blacks and whites should have the same right to make and enforce contracts, sue, give evidence, and acquire property. These provisions now are codified at 42 U.S.C. §§1981 and 1982 and are discussed in §3.7. In 1871, Congress adopted the Ku Klux Klan Act, which provided criminal penalties and civil liability for any person acting under

By the 1880s, Reconstruction was over. In part, it ended through a compromise in 1877 to resolve a disputed presidential election. Although it appeared that Democrat Samuel Tilden won a majority of the popular vote, Democrats in Congress agreed to the election of Republican Rutherford Hayes in exchange for an end of military rule in the South. Also, in 1883, in the *Civil Rights Cases*, the Supreme Court declared unconstitutional the Civil Rights Act of 1875 that prohibited discrimination by places of public accommodations such as inns, theaters, and places of public amusement.[70] The Supreme Court broadly held that the Fourteenth Amendment only applies to government action, not to private conduct, and that therefore Congress acting under §5 of the Fourteenth Amendment can regulate only government actions.[71]

As Reconstruction ended, many states, especially in the South, adopted laws that discriminated against blacks. Private violence against blacks increased dramatically; more than 3,000 lynchings were reported in the last two decades of the nineteenth century.[72] Every Southern state enacted statutes that required separation of the races in virtually every aspect of life. Called "Jim Crow laws," these statutes created a system of apartheid in which the government mandated segregation in public accommodations, transportation, schools, and almost everything else.[73]

Plessy v. Ferguson

In *Plessy v. Ferguson*, in 1896, the Supreme Court upheld laws that mandated that blacks and whites use "separate, but equal facilities."[74] A Louisiana law adopted in 1890 required railroad companies to provide separate but equal accommodations for whites and blacks; the law required there to be separate coaches, divided by a partition, for each race.[75] In 1892, Louisiana prosecuted Homer Adolph Plessy, a man who was seven-eighths Caucasian, for refusing to leave the railroad car assigned to whites.

---

color of state law who violates the Constitution or laws of the United States or who engages in a conspiracy to violate civil rights. These provisions are now codified at 18 U.S.C. §§241 and 242 (criminal provisions), 42 U.S.C. §1983 (civil liability), and 42 U.S.C. §1985 (civil liability for conspiracies). In 1875, Congress passed the Civil Rights Act prohibiting discrimination by places of public accommodations such as inns, theaters, and places of public amusement. This law was declared unconstitutional in the *Civil Rights Cases*, 109 U.S. 3 (1883). This case is discussed in detail in §6.4.1.

[70] 109 U.S. 3 (1883), discussed in §6.4.1.

[71] The former aspect of the holding, that the Fourteenth Amendment applies only to government action, remains good law and is called the "state action doctrine"; it is discussed in detail in §6.4. The latter aspect of the holding, that Congress only can regulate government conduct under §5 of the Fourteenth Amendment, is probably no longer good law as five Justices in *United States v. Guest*, 383 U.S. 745 (1966), expressed the view that Congress could use this provision to regulate private conduct. This is discussed in §3.7.1.

[72] Daniel Farber, William N. Eskridge, Jr. & Philip P. Frickey, Constitutional Law: Themes for the Constitution's Third Century 37 (1993).

[73] *See* C. Vann Woodward, The Strange Career of Jim Crow (1957). For an excellent history of the Supreme Court's treatment of racial classifications, *see* Michael J. Klarman, From Jim Crow to Civil Rights: The Supreme Court and the Struggle for Racial Equality (2004).

[74] 163 U.S. 537 (1896).

[75] *Id.* at 540.

The Supreme Court concluded that laws requiring "separate, but equal" facilities are constitutional and declared: "[W]e cannot say that a law which authorizes or even requires the separation of the two races in public conveyances is unreasonable, or more obnoxious to the Fourteenth Amendment than the acts of Congress requiring separate schools for colored children in the District of Columbia, the constitutionality of which does not seem to have been questioned, or the corresponding acts of state legislatures."[76]

The Court explicitly addressed the claim that such laws are based on an assumption of the inferiority of blacks and thus they stigmatize them with a second-class status. The Court replied: "We consider the underlying fallacy of the plaintiff's argument to consist in the assumption that the enforced separation of the two races stamps the colored race with a badge of inferiority. If this be so, it is not by reason of anything found in the act, but solely because the colored race chooses to put that construction upon it."[77]

Justice Harlan was the sole dissenter and wrote that "[e]very one knows that the statute in question had its origin in the purpose, not so much to exclude white persons from railroad cars occupied by blacks, as to exclude colored people from coaches occupied by or assigned to white persons."[78] Justice Harlan concluded eloquently:

> [I]n view of the Constitution, in the eye of the law, there is in this country no superior, dominant, ruling class of citizens. There is no caste here. Our Constitution is color-blind, and neither knows nor tolerates classes among citizens. In respect of civil rights, all citizens are equal before the law. The humblest is the peer of the most powerful. . . . In my opinion, the judgment this day rendered will, in time, prove to be quite as pernicious as the decision made by this tribunal in the *Dred Scott* case. . . . The destinies of the two races, in this country, are indissolubly linked together, and the interests of both require that the common government of all shall not permit the seeds of race hate to be planted under the sanction of law.[79]

"Separate but equal" thus became the law of the land even though separate was anything but equal. In several subsequent cases, the Court reaffirmed *Plessy v. Ferguson*. For example, in *McCabe v. Atchison, Topeka & Santa Fe Railway Co.*, the Supreme Court upheld an Oklahoma law that required separation of the races on railroads, but ruled that if there was a dining car for whites, one also had to be available for blacks.[80]

"Separate but equal" was expressly approved in the realm of education. In *Cumming v. Board of Education*, in 1899, the Court upheld the government's operation of a high school open only for white students while none was available for blacks. The Court emphasized that local authorities were to be allowed great discretion in allocating funds between blacks and whites and that "any interference

---

[76] *Id.* at 550-551.
[77] *Id.* at 551.
[78] *Id.* at 557.
[79] *Id.* at 559-560 (Harlan, J., dissenting).
[80] 235 U.S. 151 (1914).

on the part of Federal authority with the management of such schools cannot be justified except in the case of a clear and unmistakable disregard of rights secured by the supreme law of the land."[81]

In *Berea College v. Kentucky*, in 1908, the Supreme Court affirmed the conviction of a private college that had violated a Kentucky law that required the separation of the races in education.[82] Similarly, in *Gong Lum v. Rice*, the Supreme Court concluded that Mississippi could exclude a child of Chinese ancestry from attending schools reserved for whites.[83] The Court said that the law was settled that racial segregation was permissible and that it did not "think that the question is any different, or that any different result can be reached . . . where the issue is as between white pupils and the pupils of the yellow races."[84]

The Initial Attack on "Separate but Equal"

In several cases between 1938 and 1954, the Supreme Court found that states denied equal protection by failing to provide educational opportunities for blacks that were available to whites.[85] Interestingly, most of these decisions involved the failure of states to provide the equal opportunity for legal education for blacks. The Court did not question the doctrine of separate but equal; instead it concluded that the lack of opportunities for blacks was unconstitutional.

In *Missouri ex rel. Gaines v. Canada*, the Supreme Court held that it was unconstitutional for Missouri to refuse to admit blacks to its law school, but instead to pay for blacks to attend out-of-state law schools.[86] The Court explained that the "basic consideration is not as to what sort of opportunities other States provide, . . . but as to what opportunities Missouri itself furnishes to white students and denies to negroes solely upon the ground of color."[87] In response, Missouri did not admit blacks to its law school, but instead created a new law school for blacks.[88]

In *Sweatt v. Painter*, in 1950, the Supreme Court for the first time ordered that a white university admit a black student.[89] The University of Texas Law School had denied Heman Sweatt admission on the ground that he could attend the recently created Prairie View Law School. Although the Court was urged to reconsider *Plessy v. Ferguson*, it refused and instead found that the schools obviously were not equal. The University of Texas Law School had 16 full-time faculty members and substantial facilities. Prairie View Law School opened in 1947 with no full-time

---

[81] 175 U.S. 528 (1899).

[82] 211 U.S. 45 (1908).

[83] 275 U.S. 78 (1927).

[84] *Id.* at 87.

[85] In one earlier case, *Buchanan v. Warley*, 245 U.S. 60 (1917), the Supreme Court declared unconstitutional a Kentucky law that required racial separation in housing.

[86] 305 U.S. 337 (1938).

[87] *Id.* at 349.

[88] *See also* Sipuel v. Board of Regents, 332 U.S. 631 (1948) (declaring unconstitutional Oklahoma's refusal to provide legal education for blacks while maintaining a law school available only to whites). The state again responded by creating a law school only for blacks, and the Supreme Court denied further relief. Fisher v. Hurst, 333 U.S. 147 (1948).

[89] 339 U.S. 629 (1950).

faculty and no library, though by the time the Court decided the case there were five full-time professors and a small library.[90] The Court concluded: "[W]e cannot find substantial equality in the educational opportunities offered white and Negro law students by the State. . . . It is difficult to believe that one who had a free choice between these law schools would consider the question close."[91]

In *McLaurin v. Oklahoma State Regents*, the Supreme Court held that once blacks were admitted to a previously all-white school, the university could not force them to sit in segregated areas of classrooms, libraries, and cafeterias.[92] The Court ruled that such segregation hindered the student's "ability to study, to engage in discussions, and exchange views with other students, and, in general, to learn his profession."[93]

The reality, of course, was that the laws required racial separation, but not equality. Only one of 41 law schools in the South was for blacks; only one of 30 medical schools admitted blacks; and none of 36 engineering schools admitted blacks.[94] Those facilities that existed for blacks were inferior by every measure.

Brown v. Board of Education

In the 1952-1953 Term, the Supreme Court granted review in five cases that challenged the doctrine of separate but equal in the context of elementary and high school education.[95] At the time, 17 states and the District of Columbia practiced segregation in the public schools.[96] The school systems challenged in the five cases before the Supreme Court involved schools that were totally unequal. For example, one of the cases was a challenge to South Carolina's educational system.[97] The white schools had one teacher for every 28 pupils; the black schools had one teacher for every 47 students. The white schools were brick and stucco; the black schools were made of rotting wood. The white schools had indoor plumbing; the black schools had outhouses.[98]

The five cases were argued together during the 1952-1953 Term. The Justices could not agree as to a decision, and the cases were set for reargument for the following year. According to Justice William Douglas's autobiography, had the Supreme Court ruled then, the decision would have been 5 to 4 to affirm *Plessy v. Ferguson* and the separate but equal doctrine:

> When the cases had been argued in December of 1952, only four of us—Minton, Burton, Black, and myself—felt that segregation was unconstitutional. . . . It was

---

[90] *Id.* at 633.

[91] *Id.* at 633-634.

[92] 339 U.S. 637 (1950).

[93] *Id.* at 641.

[94] Richard Kluger, Simple Justice: The History of *Brown v. Board of Education* and Black America's Struggle for Equality 257 (1977).

[95] For a superb discussion of this litigation and its history, *see* Kluger, *id.*

[96] Kluger, *id.* at 327.

[97] Briggs v. Elliott, 342 U.S. 350 (1952), decided with Brown v. Board of Educ., 349 U.S. 294 (1954).

[98] Kluger, *supra* note 94, at 332.

clear that if a decision had been reached in the 1952 Term, we would have had five saying that separate but equal schools were constitutional, that separate but unequal schools were not constitutional, and that the remedy was to give the states time to make the two systems of schools equal.[99]

The Supreme Court asked the parties to brief several questions that primarily focused on the intent of the framers of the Fourteenth Amendment. In the summer between the two Supreme Court Terms, Chief Justice Fred Vinson died of a heart attack and President Dwight Eisenhower appointed California governor Earl Warren to be the new Chief Justice. The cases were argued on October 13, 1953, and through intense effort Chief Justice Warren persuaded all of the Justices to join a unanimous decision holding that separate but equal was impermissible in the realm of public education.[100]

On May 17, 1954, the Supreme Court released its decision in *Brown v. Board of Education*.[101] *Brown*, one of the five cases decided together, involved a challenge to the segregation of the Topeka, Kansas, public schools. The opinion, authored by Chief Justice Warren, began by explaining that the constitutionality of segregation in education could not be resolved based on the framers' intent. The Court said that the historical sources of the Fourteenth Amendment "[a]t best . . . are inconclusive" and that the enormous changes in the nature of education made history of little use in resolving the issue.[102] The Court thus concluded that "[i]n approaching this problem, we cannot turn the clock back to 1868 when the Amendment was adopted, or even to 1896 when *Plessy v. Ferguson* was written. We must consider public education in the light of its full development and its present place in American life throughout the Nation."[103]

The Court did not focus on the obvious inequalities between the black and white schools in many of the cases before it. Rather, the Court said that "there are findings below that the Negro and white schools involved have been equalized, or are being equalized, with respect to buildings, curricula, qualifications and salaries of teachers, and other 'tangible factors.' Our decision, therefore, cannot turn on merely a comparison of those tangible factors in the Negro and white schools involved in each of the cases. We must look instead to the effect of segregation itself on public education."[104]

The Court probably characterized the issue this way, in part, because there had been factual findings by some of the district courts of equalization between the black and white schools[105] and, in part, to reach the basic question: Is separate but equal constitutional in public education? Indeed, the Court stated the issue

---

[99] William O. Douglas, The Court Years: 1939-1975 113 (1980).

[100] *See* Kluger, *supra* note 94, at 694-699.

[101] 347 U.S. 483 (1954).

[102] *Id.* at 489-490. *But see* Michael McConnell, Originalism and the Desegregation Decisions, 81 Va. L. Rev. 947 (1995) (arguing that the framers of the Fourteenth Amendment meant to prohibit "separate but equal" laws).

[103] *Id.* at 492-493.

[104] *Id.* at 492.

[105] *See id.* at 492 n.9.

presented as: "Does segregation of children in public schools solely on the basis of race, even though the physical facilities and other 'tangible' factors may be equal, deprive the children of the minority group of equal educational opportunities?"[106]

The Court answered this question by declaring that state-mandated segregation inherently stamps black children as inferior and impairs their educational opportunities. Chief Justice Warren wrote: "To separate them from others of similar age and qualifications solely because of their race generates a feeling of inferiority as to their status in the community that may affect their hearts and minds in a way unlikely ever to be undone."[107] The Court supported this conclusion with a citation to psychology literature that purported to show that segregation causes black children to feel inferior and interferes with their learning.[108]

The Court ended its relatively short opinion by declaring: "We conclude that in the field of public education the doctrine of 'separate but equal' has no place. Separate educational facilities are inherently unequal."[109] The Court did not prescribe a remedy, but asked for reargument in the next Term on that issue. A year later, in *Brown II*, the Supreme Court remanded the cases to the lower courts to use traditional equity principles to fashion remedies "to admit to public schools on a racially nondiscriminatory basis with all deliberate speed the parties to these cases."[110] The issue of the remedies in school desegregation cases is discussed in detail in §9.3.4 below.

Brown's significance cannot be overstated. Richard Kluger eloquently wrote:

> Every colored American knew that *Brown* did not mean that he would be invited to lunch with the Rotary the following week. It meant something more basic and more important. It meant that black rights had suddenly been redefined; black bodies had suddenly been reborn under a new law. Blacks' value as human beings had been changed overnight by the declaration of the nation's highest court. At a stroke, the Justices had severed the remaining cords of *de facto* slavery. The Negro could no longer be fastened with the status of official pariah. No longer could the white man look right through him as if he were, in the title words of Ralph Ellison's stunning 1952 novel, Invisible Man. No more would he be a grinning supplicant for the benefactions and discards of the master class; no more would he be a party to his own degradation. He was both thrilled that the signal for the demise of his caste status had come from on high and angry that it had taken so long and first exacted so steep a price in suffering.[111]

Not surprisingly, *Brown* was harshly criticized by supporters of segregation. For example, 96 Southern congressmen, virtually all representatives from Southern states, published a "Declaration of Constitutional Principles," which scathingly attacked *Brown*:

---

[106] *Id.* at 493.
[107] *Id.* at 494.
[108] *Id.* at 494 n.11.
[109] *Id.* at 495.
[110] 349 U.S. 294, 301 (1955).
[111] Kluger, *supra* note 94, at 749.

We regard the decision of the Supreme Court in the school cases as clear abuse of the judicial power. It climaxes a trend in the Federal judiciary undertaking to legislate in derogation of the authority of Congress, and to encroach upon the reserved rights of the states and the people. The original Constitution does not mention education. Neither does the Fourteenth Amendment nor any other amendment. . . . Though there has been no constitutional amendment or act of Congress changing this established legal principle almost a century old, the Supreme Court of the United States, with no legal basis for such action, undertook to exercise their naked judicial power and substituted their personal political and social ideas for the established law of the land. . . . We decry the Supreme Court's encroachment on rights reserved to the states and to the people, contrary to established law and to the Constitution. We commend the motives of those states which have declared the intention to resist forced integration by any lawful means.[112]

Even among its supporters, *Brown* drew criticism. Some argued that the Court erred by relying on social science studies to support its conclusion, rather than expressing a moral judgment that segregation was wrong.[113] Indeed, Professor (and former University of California President) Mark Yudof argued that "[v]irtually everyone who has examined the question now agrees that the Court erred" in relying upon the social science data.[114] The concern is that the studies were "methodologically unsound"[115] and that reliance on them made the decision vulnerable if future research came to differing conclusions.

The Invalidation of Segregation in Other Contexts

Others criticized *Brown* for focusing exclusively on education and thus failing to provide a basis for declaring segregation unconstitutional in other contexts.[116] Following *Brown*, in a series of per curiam opinions, the Supreme Court affirmed lower court decisions declaring unconstitutional state laws requiring segregation in all of the remaining areas of Southern life. For example, in *Mayor and City Council of Baltimore City v. Dawson*, the Supreme Court, in a memorandum disposition without an opinion, affirmed a lower court decision declaring unconstitutional a law requiring segregation in the use of public beaches and bathhouses.[117] The Court did the exact same thing in *Holmes v. City of Atlanta*[118] in declaring

---

[112] Text of 96 Congressmen's Declaration on Integration, N.Y. Times, Mar. 12, 1956, at 19, col. 2-3.

[113] *See, e.g.*, Edmond Cahn, Jurisprudence, 30 N.Y.U. L. Rev. 150 (1955).

[114] Mark Yudof, School Desegregation: Legal Realism, Reasoned Elaboration, and Social Science Research in the Supreme Court, 42 Law & Contemp. Probs. 57, 70 (1978).

[115] *Id.*

[116] Herbert Wechsler criticized *Brown* for lacking a sufficient "neutral principle" to justify its conclusion. *See* Herbert Wechsler, Toward Neutral Principles of Constitutional Law, 73 Harv. L. Rev. 1 (1959). For excellent responses to Wechsler, *see* Louis Pollak, Racial Discrimination and Judicial Integrity: A Reply to Professor Wechsler, 108 U. Pa. L. Rev. 1 (1959); Charles L. Black, Jr., The Lawfulness of the Segregation Decision, 69 Yale L.J. 421 (1960).

[117] 350 U.S. 877 (1955).

[118] 350 U.S. 879 (1955).

unconstitutional segregation of municipal golf courses; in *Gayle v. Browder*[119] in declaring unconstitutional the segregation of a municipal bus system; in *Johnson v. Virginia*[120] in declaring unconstitutional segregation of courtroom seating; and in *Turner v. City of Memphis*[121] in declaring unconstitutional segregation of public restaurants.

Although these decisions, of course, reached the necessary result, the Court can be criticized for deciding without any opinion. The decision in *Brown* was based on the importance of education and the harms of segregation in that area. The unconstitutionality of segregation in beaches, golf courses, or buses required a separate explanation, one that the Court never offered.[122]

Nonetheless, it is clearly established that laws requiring separation of the races are racial classifications that will be allowed only if strict scrutiny is met. For example, in *Johnson v. California*, the Supreme Court held that strict scrutiny must be used in evaluating the routine racial segregation of prisoners.[123] In California, when a male prisoner enters a new institution—whether at the start of a sentence or as a result of a transfer to a different prison—the inmate is placed in a reception center for up to 60 days. During this time, the prisoner is evaluated for purposes of determining the inmate's placement within the institution. Most prisoners are "double celled" during this time, with two inmates being housed together in a cell. Although several factors are considered in assigning prisoners during this period, race is very much taken into account. In fact, prison officials conceded that there is virtually a "zero percent" chance that inmates of different races will be housed together.[124]

Prison officials argued that such racial segregation was necessary to prevent violence. Prison gangs are endemic in California prisons and they are organized along racial lines. Prison officials expressed their belief that violence and conflict would result if prisoners were not segregated.

The Supreme Court, in a 5-to-3 decision, stressed that all racial classifications must meet strict scrutiny; that is, they will be upheld only if the government can prove that its action is necessary to achieve a compelling purpose.[125] The government claimed that segregation of prisoners did not constitute discrimination because all prisoners were treated the same: Every prisoner, regardless of race, was placed in a cell with an inmate of the same race. Black prisoners were treated no differently than white or Latino or Asian inmates. But the Court noted that *Brown v. Board of Education* rejected that argument 50 years ago and clearly held that segregation based on race constitutes a racial classification and must meet strict scrutiny under equal protection.

The Court expressly rejected applying the rational basis test that is usually used for constitutional claims by prisoners. The Court was clear and emphatic that

---

[119] 352 U.S. 903 (1956).
[120] 373 U.S. 61 (1963).
[121] 369 U.S. 350 (1962).
[122] *See* Wechsler, *supra* note 116, at 22-23.
[123] 543 U.S. 499 (2005).
[124] *Id.* at 502.
[125] *Id.* at 821.

strict scrutiny must be used in evaluating claims of racial discrimination by prisoners. Justice O'Connor, writing for the Court, stated: "Because the CDC's policy is an express racial classification, it is 'immediately suspect.' We therefore hold that the Court of Appeals erred when it failed to apply strict scrutiny to the CDC's policy and to require the CDC to demonstrate that its policy is narrowly tailored to serve a compelling state interest."[126] The Court then remanded the case for the application of strict scrutiny.

§9.3.3.2 Facially Neutral Laws with a Discriminatory Impact or with Discriminatory Administration

The Requirement for Proof of a Discriminatory Purpose

Some laws that are facially race neutral are administered in a manner that discriminates against minorities or has a disproportionate impact against them. The Supreme Court has held that there must be proof of a discriminatory purpose in order for such laws to be treated as racial or national origin classifications.

Washington v. Davis was a key case articulating this requirement.[127] Applicants for the police force in Washington, D.C., were required to take a test, and statistics revealed that blacks failed the examination much more often than whites. The Supreme Court, however, held that proof of a discriminatory impact is insufficient, by itself, to show the existence of a racial classification. Justice White, writing for the majority, said that the Court never had held that "a law or other official act, without regard to whether it reflects a racially discriminatory purpose, is unconstitutional *solely* because it has a racially disproportionate impact."[128] The Court explained that discriminatory impact, "[s]tanding alone, . . . does not trigger the rule that racial classifications are to be subjected to the strictest scrutiny and are justifiable only by the weightiest of considerations."[129]

In other words, laws that are facially neutral as to race and national origin will receive more than rational basis review only if there is proof of a discriminatory purpose. The Court justified this conclusion, in part, based on its view that the purpose of the equal protection clause "is the prevention of official conduct discriminating on the basis of race."[130] The Court also emphasized that allowing discriminatory impact to suffice in proving a racial classification "would raise serious

---

[126] *Id.* at 508.

[127] 426 U.S. 229 (1976). Prior to *Washington v. Davis*, in *Mayor of Phil. v. Education Equality League*, 415 U.S. 605 (1974), the Supreme Court rejected an equal protection challenge to the mayor's appointment of members of the school board. Statistics showed a significant underrepresentation of African Americans, but the Court held that such statistical proof was insufficient to prove discrimination.

[128] 426 U.S. at 239 (emphasis in original).

[129] *Id.* at 242 (citation omitted).

[130] *Id.* at 239.

questions about, and perhaps invalidate, a whole range of tax, welfare, public service, regulatory, and licensing statutes that may be more burdensome to the poor and to the average black than to the more affluent white."[131]

Many times the Court has reaffirmed this principle that discriminatory impact is not sufficient to prove a racial classification. For example, in *Mobile v. Bolden*, the Supreme Court held that an election system that had the impact of disadvantaging minorities was not to be subjected to strict scrutiny unless there was proof of a discriminatory purpose.[132] *Mobile v. Bolden* involved a challenge to Mobile, Alabama's use of an at-large election for its city council. The city was predominately white, with a sizeable African-American population. The long history of racially polarized voting meant that only whites were elected in the at-large system. Nonetheless, the Supreme Court found no equal protection violation because there was not sufficient evidence of a discriminatory purpose. The Court declared: "[O]nly if there is purposeful discrimination can there be a violation of the Equal Protection Clause. . . . [T]his principle applies to claims of racial discrimination affecting voting just as it does to other claims of racial discrimination."[133]

Similarly, in *McCleskey v. Kemp*, the Supreme Court held that proof of discrimination impact in the administration of the death penalty was insufficient to show an equal protection violation.[134] Statistics powerfully demonstrated racial inequality in the imposition of capital punishment. A study conducted by Professor David Baldus found that the death penalty was imposed in 22 percent of the cases involving black defendants and white victims; in 8 percent of the cases involving white defendants and white victims; in 1 percent of the cases involving black defendants and black victims; and in 3 percent of the cases involving white defendants and black victims.[135] Baldus found that "prosecutors sought the death penalty in 70 percent of the cases involving black defendants and white victims; 15 percent of the cases involving black defendants and black victims; and 19 percent of the cases involving white defendants and black victims."[136] After adjusting for many other variables, Baldus concluded that "defendants charged with killing white victims were 4.3 times as likely to receive a death sentence as defendants charged with killing blacks."[137]

The Supreme Court, however, said that for the defendant to demonstrate an equal protection violation, he "must prove that the decisionmakers in *his* case acted with discriminatory purpose."[138] Because the defendant could not prove that the prosecutor or jury in his case was biased, no equal protection violation existed.

---

[131] *Id.* at 248.

[132] 446 U.S. 55 (1980).

[133] *Id.* at 67. *See also* Rogers v. Lodge, 458 U.S. 613 (1982) (declaring unconstitutional an at-large voting system by finding intentional discrimination based on evidence of past discrimination in voting and schooling, limited black participation in the political process, and the failure of any black to be elected to the city council).

[134] 481 U.S. 279 (1987).

[135] *Id.* at 286.

[136] *Id.* at 287.

[137] *Id.*

[138] *Id.* at 292 (emphasis in original).

Moreover, the Court said that to challenge the law authorizing capital punishment, the defendant "would have to prove that the Georgia Legislature enacted or maintained the death penalty statute *because of an* anticipated racially discriminatory effect."[139]

Cases such as *Washington v. Davis, Mobile v. Bolden,* and *McCleskey v. Kemp* clearly establish that proof of a discriminatory impact is not sufficient by itself to prove an equal protection violation; there also must be proof of a discriminatory purpose.[140] It should be noted that civil rights statutes can, and often do, allow violations to be proved based on discriminatory impact without evidence of a discriminatory purpose. For example, Title VII of the 1964 Civil Rights Act allows employment discrimination to be established by proof of discriminatory impact,[141] and the 1982 Amendments to the Voting Rights Act of 1965 permit proof of discriminatory impact to establish a violation of that law.[142] But the Court has said that under the Constitution, proof of discriminatory impact is, by itself, insufficient to establish a denial of equal protection.

Should Discriminatory Purpose Be Required?

Whether discrimination can be proved by showing a discriminatory impact is crucial in determining the reach of the equal protection clause. Undoubtedly, there are many areas where a significant discriminatory impact can be proved, but there is not sufficient evidence of a discriminatory purpose. Current law means that the government need not offer a racially neutral explanation for these effects and, indeed, need do no more than meet a rational basis test.

On the one hand, this can be justified by the view that the equal protection clause is concerned with stopping discriminatory acts by the government, not in bringing about equal results. Moreover, there is concern that countless laws might have some discriminatory impact given the enormous inequalities between whites and racial minorities that continue to exist. Also, it is argued that there will be laws that have the impact of benefiting minorities and that these can counterbalance those that have a detrimental effect. Professor Robert Bennett suggested: "If members of racial minorities stochastically obtain benefits and suffer detriments as one or another piece of legislation is passed without attention to its racial impact, they are obtaining, not being deprived of equal protection of the laws. To forbid all

---

[139] *Id.* at 298.

[140] The Court also has held that proving a violation of 42 U.S.C. §1982 and the Thirteenth Amendment requires proof of a discriminatory purpose. In *Memphis v. Greene*, 451 U.S. 100 (1981), the Court found no constitutional violation when a city closed down a street that was used mainly by blacks. The Court said that "the record discloses no racially discriminatory motive on the part of the City Council [and] a review of the justification for the official action challenged in this case demonstrates that its disparate impact on black citizens could not [be] fairly characterized as a badge or incident of slavery." *Id.* at 126.

[141] *See* Griggs v. Duke Power Co., 401 U.S. 424 (1971).

[142] *See, e.g.,* Johnson v. DeGrandy, 512 U.S. 997 (1994); Thornburg v. Gingles, 478 U.S. 30 (1986); *see also* City of Rome v. United States, 446 U.S. 156 (1980) (Congress has the power to allow proof of discriminatory impact to establish a violation of voting rights).

legislation that disadvantages them would give them the gains from political bargaining without the losses."[143]

On the other hand, as discussed below, proving discriminatory purpose is very difficult; rarely will such a motivation be expressed, and benign purposes can be articulated for most laws.[144] Therefore, many laws with both a discriminatory purpose and effect might be upheld simply because of evidentiary problems inherent in requiring proof of such a purpose. Scholars such as Professor Charles Lawrence argue that this is especially true because racism is often unconscious and such "unconscious racism . . . underlies much of the disproportionate impact of governmental policy."[145] In a society with a long history of discrimination, there can be a presumption that many laws with a discriminatory impact likely were motivated by a discriminatory purpose.[146]

Furthermore, it is argued that equal protection should be concerned with the results of government actions and not just their underlying motivations. Professor Laurence Tribe explained: "The goal of the equal protection clause is not to stamp out impure thoughts, but to guarantee a full measure of human dignity for all. . . . [M]inorities can also be injured when the government is 'only' indifferent to their suffering or 'merely' blind to how prior official discrimination contributed to it and how current official acts will perpetuate it."[147]

Ultimately, the issue of whether discriminatory purpose should be required, or whether discriminatory impact should be sufficient to prove an equal protection violation, turns on a determination of the fundamental mission of the equal protection clause. Is the clause only about equal treatment by the government or should it also be concerned with equal results?

Is Proof of a Discriminatory Effect Also Required?

The cases discussed thus far involve situations where there is proof of a racially discriminatory impact of a facially neutral law. A distinct question that arises much less often is whether proof of discriminatory purpose is sufficient, by itself, to establish an equal protection violation or whether there must be both discriminatory impact and discriminatory purpose. Although the Supreme Court has never expressly addressed the question, it appears that both are required.

In *Palmer v. Thompson*, the Supreme Court found that equal protection was not violated when a city closed down its previously segregated swimming pool rather than allow it to be integrated.[148] The Court said that "no case in this Court has held that a legislative act may violate equal protection solely because of the

---

[143] Robert Bennett, "Mere" Rationality in Constitutional Law: Judicial Review and Democratic Theory, 67 Cal. L. Rev. 1049, 1076 (1979).

[144] *See* Daniel R. Ortiz, The Myth of Intent in Equal Protection, 41 Stan. L. Rev. 1105 (1989).

[145] Charles Lawrence, The Id, the Ego, and Equal Protection: Reckoning with Unconscious Racism, 39 Stan. L. Rev. 317, 355 (1987).

[146] *See* David Strauss, Discriminatory Intent and the Taming of *Brown*, 56 U. Chi. L. Rev. 935 (1989).

[147] Laurence H. Tribe, American Constitutional Law 1516-1519 (2d ed. 1988).

[148] 403 U.S. 217 (1971).

motivations of the men who voted for it."[149] The Court said that "there is an element of futility in a judicial attempt to invalidate a law because of the bad motives of its supporters. If the law is struck down for this reason, rather than because of its facial content or effect, it would presumably be valid as soon as the legislature or relevant governing body repassed it for different reasons."[150]

Palmer thus suggests that discriminatory purpose, alone, is insufficient to prove that a facially neutral law constitutes a race or national origin classification. Together with *Washington v. Davis* and its progeny, it appears that a facially neutral law will be regarded as creating a race or national origin classification only if there is proof of *both* a discriminatory impact to the law and a discriminatory purpose behind it.

In *United States v. Armstrong*, the Court said that to prove impermissible discriminatory prosecution based on race, a defendant seeking to establish an equal protection violation must show discriminatory purpose and effect.[151] In *Armstrong*, the Court rejected two black defendants' requests for discovery on a selective prosecution claim because the defendants failed to show governmental refusal to prosecute similarly situated whites. The Court, in an 8-to-1 decision, said that in order to get such discovery regarding discriminatory prosecution, "the defendant [must] produce some evidence that similarly situated defendants of other races could have been prosecuted, but were not."[152] *Armstrong* is particularly important because of its express declaration that an equal protection challenge to a facially race neutral law requires showing both discriminatory purpose and discriminatory effect.

How Is a Discriminatory Purpose Proved?

The crucial question then becomes: How can it be proved that a facially neutral law is motivated by a discriminatory purpose? The Supreme Court has made it clear that showing such a purpose requires proof that the government desired to discriminate; it is not enough to prove that the government took an action with knowledge that it would have discriminatory consequences. In *Personnel Administrator of Massachusetts v. Feeney*, the Court declared: "'Discriminatory purpose,' however, implies more than intent as volition or intent as awareness of consequences. It implies that the decisionmaker . . . selected or reaffirmed a particular course of action at least in part 'because of,' not merely 'in spite of,' its adverse effects upon an identifiable group."[153]

Feeney involved a challenge to a Massachusetts law that gave preference in hiring for state jobs to veterans. At the time of the litigation, over 98 percent of the veterans in the state were male; only 1.8 percent were female.[154] The result

[149] *Id.* at 224.
[150] *Id.* at 225.
[151] 517 U.S. 456, 465 (1996).
[152] *Id.* at 469.
[153] 442 U.S. 256, 279 (1979) (citations omitted).
[154] *Id.* at 270.

was a substantial discriminatory effect against women in hiring for state jobs. Nonetheless, the Supreme Court held that there was not a gender classification because the law creating a preference for veterans was facially gender neutral and there was not proof that the state's purpose in adopting the law was to disadvantage women.[155]

The Court's adoption of this narrow definition of intent can be questioned. The Court essentially rejected the tort definition of intent as acting with knowledge of foreseeable consequences and instead adopted a criminal law definition of intent meaning the desire to cause those results. Professor Larry Simon argues that "a showing of significant disproportionate disadvantage to a racial minority group, *without more*, gives rise to an inference that the action may have been taken or at least maintained or continued with knowledge that such groups would be relatively disadvantaged. . . . [I]t raises a possibility sufficient to oblige the government to come forward with a credible explanation showing that the action was (or would have been) taken apart from prejudice."[156] But the Supreme Court has not taken this approach and instead has required proof that the government desired the discriminatory consequences.

In *Village of Arlington Heights v. Metropolitan Housing Development Corp.*, the Supreme Court explained the different ways in which discriminatory purpose can be proved.[157] *Arlington Heights* involved a challenge to a city's refusal to rezone a parcel of land to allow construction of low and moderate income housing. The plaintiffs alleged that this had a discriminatory effect in excluding blacks from the city. The Supreme Court identified several ways in which a discriminatory purpose can be demonstrated.

First, the impact of a law may be so clearly discriminatory as to allow no other explanation than that it was adopted for impermissible purposes. The Court said: "The impact of the official action—whether it 'bears more heavily on one race than another'—may provide an important starting point. Sometimes a clear pattern, unexplainable on grounds other than race, emerges from the effect of the state action even when the governing legislation appears neutral on its face."[158] The Court cited to several examples of this, including *Yick Wo v. Hopkins*[159] and *Gomillion v. Lightfoot*.[160]

In *Yick Wo*, a city's ordinance required that laundries be located in brick or stone buildings unless a waiver was obtained from the board of supervisors. The plaintiff alleged that over 200 petitions by those of Chinese ancestry had been denied, but all but one of the petitions filed by non-Chinese individuals were granted. The Supreme Court unanimously reversed Yick Wo's conviction for violating the ordinance and explained: "[T]he facts shown establish an administra-

---

[155] Gender discrimination is discussed in detail in §9.4. *Feeney* makes it clear that proving a gender classification is identical to proving a racial classification.

[156] Larry G. Simon, Racially Prejudiced Government Actions: A Motivation Theory of the Constitutional Ban Against Racial Discrimination, 15 San Diego L. Rev. 1041, 1111 (1978).

[157] 429 U.S. 252 (1977).

[158] *Id.* at 266 (citations omitted).

[159] 118 U.S. 356 (1886).

[160] 364 U.S. 339 (1960).

tion directed so exclusively against a particular class of persons as to warrant and require the conclusion, that, whatever may have been the intent of the ordinances as adopted, they are applied by the public authorities charged with the administration, and thus representing the State itself, with a mind so unequal and oppressive as to amount to a practical denial by the State of equal protection of the laws."[161]

Gomillion v. Lightfoot involved a challenge to the government's redrawing of the city's boundaries to exclude blacks from participating in city elections.[162] Tuskegee, Alabama, was transformed from a square shape into a 28-sided figure. All but 4 or 5 of the 400 blacks in the city were placed outside its boundaries, but no whites were excluded. The Court said that the "conclusion would be irresistible, tantamount for all practical purposes to a mathematical demonstration, that the legislature is solely concerned with segregating white and colored voters by fencing Negro citizens out of town so as to deprive them of their pre-existing municipal vote."[163]

Thus, one way of proving discriminatory purpose is to show a statistical pattern that can be explained only by a discriminatory purpose.[164] However, the Court in *Arlington Heights* cautioned: "[S]uch cases are rare. Absent a pattern as stark as that in *Gomillion* or *Yick Wo*, impact alone is not determinative, and the Court must look to other evidence."[165]

A second way of proving discriminatory purpose is through the history surrounding the government's action. In *Arlington Heights*, the Court said: "The historical background of the decision is one evidentiary source, particularly if it reveals a series of official actions taken for invidious purposes. . . . The specific sequence of events leading up to the challenged decision also may shed some light on the decisionmaker's purposes."[166]

Again, the Court in *Arlington Heights* cited several examples of this. *Guinn v. United States* declared unconstitutional an Oklahoma law that required a literacy test for voting, but in effect excluded white citizens from this requirement through a "grandfather" clause.[167] Although the law expressly prohibited discrimination based on race in voting, it also created a literacy test that had an exemption for all who were eligible to vote in 1866 and their descendants. The obvious purpose and clear effect was to disenfranchise blacks.

Lane v. Wilson[168] invalidated an Oklahoma law adopted in response to the Court's decision in *Guinn*. The state said that those who voted in the general election in 1914 were automatically eligible to vote, but those who were potentially eli-

---

[161] 118 U.S. at 373.

[162] 364 U.S. 339 (1960).

[163] *Id.* at 341.

[164] *See, e.g.,* Castaneda v. Partida, 430 U.S. 482 (1977) (proof that 79 percent of the county's population was Spanish-surnamed, but only 39 percent of grand jurors were Spanish-surnamed from 1962-1972 was sufficient to establish a prima facie case of discrimination and shift the burden to the government to offer a race neutral explanation for these statistics).

[165] 429 U.S. at 266 (footnotes omitted).

[166] *Id.* at 267 (citations omitted).

[167] 238 U.S. 347 (1915).

[168] 307 U.S. 268 (1939).

gible and not registered could register only in a 12-day period from April 30, 1916, to May 11, 1916. Although the law was facially race neutral, the circumstances of its adoption left no doubt as to its discriminatory purpose.

Another example mentioned in *Arlington Heights* is *Griffin v. School Board of Prince Edward County,* which declared unconstitutional a county's decision, in response to desegregation orders, to close its public schools and to pay for children to attend segregated private schools.[169] Again, the history surrounding this action made its discriminatory purpose clear.

A third way of proving discriminatory purpose is through the legislative or administrative history of a law. The Court in *Arlington Heights* explained: "The legislative or administrative history may be highly relevant, especially where there are contemporary statements by members of the decisionmaking body, minutes of its meetings, or reports."[170] The Court said that in "extraordinary instances" the legislators might be called to testify, but the Court recognized that privileges accorded to legislators, such as by the speech and debate clause, might preclude questioning.[171]

Evidence of a Discriminatory Purpose Shifts the Burden

If the plaintiff produces evidence of a discriminatory purpose, the burden shifts to the government to prove that it would have taken the same action without the discriminatory motivation. The Supreme Court in *Arlington Heights* recognized that "[r]arely can it be said that a legislature or administrative body operating under a broad mandate made a decision motivated solely by a single concern, or even that a particular purpose was the 'dominant' or 'primary' one."[172] The Court said that "[w]hen there is a proof that a discriminatory purpose has been a motivating factor in the decision, this judicial deference is no longer justified."[173]

In a footnote, the Court said that if there is proof that a decision is "motivated in part by a racially discriminatory purpose," the burden would shift to the government to prove that "the same decision would have resulted even had the impermissible purpose not been considered."[174] The Court cited to a First Amendment case, *Mt. Healthy School District v. Doyle,* which held that if a government employee proves that his or her speech caused a firing or demotion, the burden shifts to the government to prove that it would have taken the same action even if the speech never had occurred.[175] The Court, however, did not describe how the government might prove that it would have taken the same action anyway or how a court can decide what might have happened under different circumstances.

The Court applied this approach in *Hunter v. Underwood,* which considered an Alabama law that permanently denied the right to vote to anyone convicted of a

---

[169] 377 U.S. 218 (1964), discussed in more detail below in §9.3.4.
[170] 429 U.S. at 268.
[171] *Id.*
[172] *Id.* at 265.
[173] *Id.* at 265-266.
[174] *Id.* at 270-271 n.21.
[175] 429 U.S. 274 (1977).

crime involving "moral turpitude."[176] The Supreme Court held that it was unconstitutional race discrimination for the state to disenfranchise those convicted of misdemeanors.[177] The Court reiterated the approach that it articulated in *Arlington Heights*: "Once racial discrimination is shown to have been a 'substantial' or 'motivating' factor behind enactment of the law, the burden shifts to the law's defenders to demonstrate that the law would have been enacted without this factor."[178] The evidence in the case indicated both that excluding a misdemeanant from voting had a substantial discriminatory impact against blacks and that racial discrimination was a key purpose of the legislature when the law was adopted in 1901. The Court found no persuasive evidence that the law would have been adopted without this motivation and thus concluded that it was unconstitutional because "its original enactment was motivated by a desire to discriminate against blacks on account of race and the section continues to this day to have that effect."[179]

In other words, if a law is racially neutral, a challenger must show a discriminatory purpose and a discriminatory effect. If such proof is provided, the government has the opportunity to demonstrate that it would have taken the same action regardless of race or national origin. If the Court accepts the government's justification and rejects the claim of a discriminatory purpose, only rational basis review is used. If the Court is convinced that there is a discriminatory purpose, the law is treated as a race or national origin classification and the law will be invalidated. The formal application of strict scrutiny is unnecessary because persuading the Court that the purpose behind the law is discriminatory forecloses the government's ability to show a compelling purpose for it.

Application: Discriminatory Use of Peremptory Challenges

One of the most important areas where the Supreme Court has followed and applied this analysis is in holding unconstitutional the discriminatory use of peremptory challenges. Laws providing for peremptory challenges—the ability of attorneys to exclude prospective jurors without having to prove cause for excusing them—are facially race neutral. But peremptory challenges based on race or gender are motivated by a discriminatory intent and have a discriminatory impact. Thus, the Court has held that race- or gender-based peremptory challenges deny equal protection whether exercised by a prosecutor,[180] a criminal defendant,[181] or a civil litigant.[182]

Initially, in *Swain v. Alabama*, the Supreme Court held that racial discrimination by a prosecutor could be proved only by showing a pattern of discrim-

---

[176] 471 U.S. 222 (1985).

[177] Earlier, in a case unrelated to race discrimination, the Court held that states could permanently disenfranchise those convicted of felonies. Richardson v. Ramirez, 418 U.S. 24 (1974).

[178] 471 U.S. at 228.

[179] *Id.* at 233.

[180] Batson v. Kentucky, 476 U.S. 79 (1986).

[181] Georgia v. McCollum, 505 U.S. 42 (1992).

[182] Edmonson v. Leesville Concrete Co., Inc., 500 U.S. 614 (1991).

inatory peremptory challenges over a series of cases.[183] A defendant could not allege a denial of equal protection by the prosecution based on how peremptory challenges were exercised in that case; systematic discrimination had to be proved.[184] In *Batson v. Kentucky*, the Supreme Court overruled *Swain v. Alabama* and explained that "[a] single invidiously discriminatory governmental act is not immunized by the absence of such discrimination in the making of other comparable decisions."[185]

Batson thus holds that the discriminatory use of peremptory challenges by a prosecutor denies equal protection. *Batson* set forth a three-step process for determining whether there is impermissible discrimination in jury selection. First, the criminal defendant must set forth a prima facie case of discrimination by the prosecutor.[186] The Supreme Court has not articulated precise standards for determining what is a prima facie case. In *Batson*, the Court said that "the defendant first must show that he is a member of a cognizable racial group, and that the prosecutor has exercised peremptory challenges to remove from the venire members of the defendant's race."[187] But in practice what is enough for a prima facie case is unclear. The Court simply expressed "confidence that trial judges, experienced in supervising voir dire" would be able to "consider all relevant circumstances" and decide if there is a prima facie case of discrimination.[188]

The Court clarified this first prong of the test in *Johnson v. California*.[189] The California Supreme Court concluded that showing a prima facie case required strong evidence that it was more likely than not that race was used as the basis for peremptory challenges. In an 8-to-1 decision, the Supreme Court reversed and said that a defendant need only produce evidence sufficient to permit the trial judge to draw an inference that discrimination has occurred. The Court left unclear what is sufficient to meet this requirement, but there is no doubt that the Court was setting a low threshold and made it easier for parties to object that their opponent has impermissibly used race or gender in the exercise of peremptory challenges.

Second, once the defendant has presented a prima facie case of discrimination, the burden shifts to the prosecutor to offer a race neutral explanation for the peremptory challenges. The Court said that the proponent of a strike "must give a 'clear and reasonably specific' explanation of his 'legitimate reasons' for exercising the challenges."[190] Subsequently, in *Purkett v. Elem*, the Supreme Court said that "[t]he second step of this process does not demand an explanation that is

---

[183] 380 U.S. 202 (1965).

[184] The Court had found that statistical proof of discrimination in grand jury composition was sufficient to shift the burden of proof to the government to offer a nonracial explanation. In *Castaneda v. Partida*, 430 U.S. 482 (1977), statistics showed that 79 percent of the county's population had Spanish surnames, but only 39 percent of the grand jurors had Spanish surnames between 1962 and 1972. The Supreme Court held that this was sufficient to shift the burden to the state to offer a race neutral explanation.

[185] 476 U.S. at 95 (citations omitted).

[186] *Id.* at 96 (citations omitted).

[187] *Id.* (citations omitted).

[188] *Id.* at 97.

[189] 543 U.S. 499 (2005).

[190] 476 U.S. at 98 n.20 (citations omitted).

persuasive, or even plausible. . . . It is not until the *third* step that the persuasiveness of the justification becomes relevant."[191] In other words, the second step is simply the prosecutor offering the explanation; the third step is where the justification is evaluated.

In the third step, the trial court must decide whether the race neutral explanation is persuasive or whether the "defendant has established purposeful discrimination."[192] In two cases since *Batson,* the Supreme Court has elaborated this step and made it easier for courts to find a neutral explanation for the strikes of prospective jurors. In *Hernandez v. New York,* the Court found that there was a sufficient race neutral explanation when a prosecutor said that he had struck two prospective Latino jurors because they spoke Spanish and therefore might not accept the translator's version of the testimony from witnesses who were going to testify in Spanish.[193]

In *Purkett v. Elem,* the Supreme Court said that "a 'legitimate reason' is not a reason that makes sense, but a reason that does not deny equal protection."[194] *Purkett* did not elaborate; it is a short per curiam opinion, and there had been neither briefing nor oral arguments in the case.[195] The Court upheld a trial court's conclusion that there was not discriminatory purpose when a prosecutor struck a prospective juror because of "long, unkempt hair, a mustache, and a beard."[196] If any "legitimate reason," even one that does not make sense, is sufficient, *Batson* will be substantially weakened. It almost always will be possible for a prosecutor to articulate some race neutral reason for a strike, such as the physical appearance of the prospective juror. However, in its last case in this line of decisions, the Court stressed the need for trial and appellate courts to examine the record carefully in determining whether race or gender was impermissibly used in the exercise of peremptory challenges. In *Miller-El v. Dretke,*[197] the Court found that the defendant proved the prosecutor violated equal protection by showing that the prosecutor's office had a policy of striking black prospective jurors when there was a black defendant; that blacks were struck when whites with similar circumstances were not; that blacks were asked different questions than whites; and that the prosecutor "shuffled" the jury when prospective black jurors were coming up. Justice Souter's opinion for the Court in a 6-to-3 decision should send a clear message to trial and appellate courts dealing with this issue: They are required to examine the record closely, as the Supreme Court did, to see if race or gender has been impermissibly used in the exercise of peremptory challenges.

Although *Batson* involved only the issue of discriminatory peremptory strikes by prosecutors, the Court subsequently expanded it to apply to civil litigants and criminal defendants. In *Edmonson v. Leesville Concrete Co., Inc.,* the Supreme Court

---

[191] 514 U.S. 765, 767-768 (1995).
[192] *Batson,* 476 U.S. at 98.
[193] 500 U.S. 352 (1991).
[194] 514 U.S. at 769.
[195] *See id.* at 770 (Stevens, J., dissenting).
[196] *Id.* at 769.
[197] 545 U.S. 231 (2005).

ruled that *Batson* applies in private civil litigation.[198] The Court explained that there is state action because peremptory challenges are authorized by state law and supervised by courts.[199] In *Georgia v. McCollum*, the Supreme Court held that criminal defendants may not exercise peremptory challenges in a discriminatory manner.[200] Although criminal defendants are the antithesis of the government, the Court followed its earlier rulings that prospective jurors have a right to be free from discrimination in jury selection[201] and that there is state action when a private party exercises peremptory challenges.

In *J.E.B. v. Alabama ex rel. T.B.*, the Supreme Court extended *Batson* to apply to gender-based discrimination in the use of peremptory challenges.[202] The Court, in an opinion by Justice Blackmun, stressed the long history of discrimination against women in the legal system and concluded that gender, like race, was an impermissible basis for peremptory challenges. The Court indicated, however, that *Batson* only would apply to types of discrimination that would receive heightened scrutiny under equal protection analysis.[203] In addition to race and gender, this would include discrimination against nonmarital children and aliens; neither, however, is likely to be a basis for peremptory challenges, especially since aliens are usually not allowed to serve on juries. An unresolved issue is whether *Batson* will apply to peremptory challenges based on religion.[204]

§9.3.4   Remedies: The Problem of School Segregation

Introduction: The Problem of Remedies

If a court finds that there is an equal protection violation, it then must fashion a remedy. In some cases, the remedy is simply invalidating the discriminatory law. For example, in *Strauder v. West Virginia*, the remedy was declaring unconstitutional the law prohibiting blacks from serving on juries;[205] in *Loving v. Virginia*, the remedy was invalidating the law prohibiting interracial marriage;[206] in *Hunter*

---

[198] 500 U.S. 614 (1991).

[199] *Edmonson*, and especially its conclusions with regard to state action, is discussed in more detail in §6.4.4.3.

[200] 505 U.S. 42 (1992).

[201] Powers v. Ohio, 499 U.S. 400 (1991). In Campbell v. Louisiana, 523 U.S. 392 (1998), the Court extended this to grand jurors.

[202] 511 U.S. 127 (1994). For an excellent analysis of this decision, *see* Nancy S. Marder, Beyond Gender: Peremptory Challenges and the Roles of the Jury, 73 Tex. L. Rev. 1041 (1995).

[203] *Id.* at 129-145.

[204] *See* United States v. Clemmons, 892 F.2d 1153 (3d Cir. 1989), *cert. denied*, 496 U.S. 927 (1990); State v. Davis, 504 N.W.2d 767 (Minn.), *cert. denied*, 511 U.S. 1115 (1993); Dunham v. Frank's Nursery & Crafts, Inc., 919 F.2d 1281 (7th Cir. 1990); *see also* Benjamin H. Barton, Religion-Based Peremptory Challenges After *Batson v. Ky.* and *J.E.B. v. Ala.*: An Equal Protection and First Amendment Analysis, 94 Mich. L. Rev. 191 (1995).

[205] 100 U.S. 303 (1879), *supra* notes 33-34.

[206] 388 U.S. 1 (1967), *supra* notes 53-55.

v. Underwood, the remedy was voiding the law that permanently denied the vote to those convicted of misdemeanors.[207]

In some cases, the Court must go further and fashion an injunction. For example, in desegregation cases, the Court generally will issue an order prohibiting the offending conduct. If a state had a law requiring segregation of a park or a beach, the Court would declare the law unconstitutional and also issue an injunction preventing continued segregation of the facility.

Fashioning a remedy was most difficult, by far, in the area of school desegregation. Initially, there was massive resistance by Southern states to compliance with *Brown*'s mandate. Additionally, in the area of schools, it was not sufficient simply to order removal of the "whites only" sign. Pupils and teachers had to be reassigned. Because schools tend to serve neighborhoods and residential segregation was prevalent, desegregating schools proved extremely difficult. Moreover, aggressive desegregation efforts, especially those including busing, often provoked "white flight" from the school district to neighboring suburbs and private schools. Desegregation was thus made even more difficult, if not impossible, because of the absence of a substantial number of white students in city school systems.

In examining the problem of fashioning remedies in school desegregation cases, five topics are examined.[208] First, the history of massive resistance is reviewed. Second, the problem of proving discrimination in the schools' context is considered. Third, the fashioning of remedies, what courts can and cannot do and under what circumstances, is discussed. Fourth, the section examines Supreme Court decisions concerning when federal desegregation remedies should be ended. Finally, the section concludes by considering the most recent Supreme Court decision on school desegregation, which limited the ability of school boards to use race as a factor in assigning students to schools to achieve desegregation.

Massive Resistance

Southern states openly and aggressively resisted compliance with *Brown v. Board of Education* and the ordered end to school segregation. State legislatures adopted resolutions of "nullification" and "interposition" that declared that the Supreme Court's decisions were without effect.[209] State officials attempted to obstruct desegregation in every imaginable way.

---

[207] 471 U.S. 222 (1985).

[208] Although the vast majority of cases have involved elementary and high schools, the same basic principles apply with regard to segregation in colleges and universities. In *United States v. Fordice*, 505 U.S. 717 (1992), the Supreme Court ordered Mississippi to end its dual system of college education. Mississippi operated three white universities, one predominately black university, and two primarily black and two primarily white regional colleges. Ninety-nine percent of the white students were enrolled in the white schools; 71 percent of the black students attended the black schools. The Supreme Court held that the state had a duty to remedy the segregation that resulted from its actions. The Court said that the state's constitutional duty to end segregation continues until "it eradicates policies and practices traceable to its prior de jure dual system that continues to foster segregation." *Id.* at 728.

[209] For a review of these laws, *see* Robert B. McKay, "With All Deliberate Speed" —A Study of School Desegregation, 31 N.Y.U. L. Rev. 991, 1039-1049 (1956). For an excellent description of the

§9.3 Classifications Based on Race and National Origin

The Supreme Court first responded to this in *Cooper v. Aaron* in 1958.[210] The Little Rock school system was ordered desegregated during the 1957-1958 school year, but the governor called out the Arkansas National Guard to keep blacks out. Black students began attending the previously all-white high school only after President Dwight Eisenhower used federal troops to protect them. The Little Rock school system then asked for a stay of the integration plan. The United States Supreme Court responded with an unusual opinion that was signed by each of the nine Justices. The Court began its opinion by declaring: "As this case reaches us it raises questions of the highest importance to the maintenance of our federal system of government. It necessarily involves a claim by the Governor and Legislature of a State that there is no duty on state officials to obey federal court orders resting on this Court's considered interpretation of the United States Constitution."[211]

The Court declared that "[t]he constitutional rights of respondents are not to be sacrificed or yielded to the violence and disorder which have followed upon the actions of the Governor and Legislature."[212] The Court invoked *Marbury v. Madison*[213] to respond to the state's claim that it did not have to comply with the Supreme Court's decision. The Court said: "[*Marbury*] declared the basic principle that the federal judiciary is supreme in the exposition of the law of the Constitution, and that principle has ever since been respected by this Court and the Country as a permanent and indispensable feature of our constitutional system. It follows that the interpretation of the Fourteenth Amendment enunciated by this Court in the *Brown* case is the supreme law of the land. . . . No state legislator or executive or judicial officer can war against the Constitution without violating his undertaking to support it."[214] The Court strongly reaffirmed *Brown* and said that it could not be nullified either "openly and directly by state legislators or state executive or judicial officers" or "indirectly by them through evasive schemes for segregation whether attempted 'ingeniously or ingenuously.'"[215]

Cooper v. Aaron, however, did not end efforts by Southern states to circumvent *Brown* and prevent desegregation. Some areas attempted to close their public schools rather than desegregate.[216] Others sought to comply with *Brown* by creating voluntary transfer plans that allowed students to attend the school of their choice; segregation continued unabated under these plans.[217] Some school systems adopted "one grade a year" desegregation plans that would mean almost 20 years before a school system was fully desegregated.[218]

---

events following *Brown, see* Charles J. Ogletree, Jr., All Deliberate Speed (2004); Peter Irons, Jim Crow's Children: The Broken Promise of the *Brown* Decision (2002).

[210] 358 U.S. 1 (1958). For a description of how the opinion in *Cooper v. Aaron* came to be written, *see* Seth Stern & Stephen Wermeil, Justice Brennan: Liberal Champion 142-152 (2010).

[211] *Id.* at 4.

[212] *Id.* at 16.

[213] 5 U.S. (1 Cranch) 137 (1803), discussed in §2.2.1.

[214] 358 U.S. at 18.

[215] *Id.* at 17.

[216] *See* Griffin v. School Bd. of Prince Edward Cnty., 377 U.S. 218 (1964), *infra* notes 225-227.

[217] *See* Goss v. Board of Educ., 373 U.S. 683 (1963).

[218] *See* Rogers v. Paul, 382 U.S. 198 (1965).

These and other state efforts succeeded in frustrating desegregation. In 1964, a decade after *Brown*, in the South, just 1.2 percent of black school children were attending school with whites.[219] In South Carolina, Alabama, and Mississippi not one black child attended a public school with a white child in the 1962-1963 school year.[220] In North Carolina, only one-fifth of 1 percent—or 0.026 percent—of the black students attended desegregated schools in 1961, and the figure did not rise above 1 percent until 1965.[221] Similarly, in Virginia, in 1964, only 1.63 percent of blacks were attending desegregated schools.[222]

Except for *Cooper v. Aaron*, the Supreme Court did not hear a school desegregation case for almost a decade after *Brown*. In a series of cases in the mid- and late 1960s, the Court declared unconstitutional various obstructionist techniques used throughout the South. In 1963, in *Goss v. Board of Education*, the Supreme Court invalidated Knoxville, Tennessee's law that allowed students who were assigned to new schools as part of desegregation to transfer from schools where they were a racial minority to ones where they would be in the racial majority.[223] In other words, a white student who was placed in a predominately black school could transfer back to a white school and a black student who was placed in a predominately white school could do the same. The Supreme Court declared this unconstitutional because "[i]t is readily apparent that the transfer system . . . lends itself to perpetuation of segregation."[224]

In *Griffin v. School Bd. of Prince Edward Cnty.*, in 1964, the Supreme Court declared it unconstitutional for school systems to close rather than desegregate.[225] In 1959, Prince Edward County, Virginia, closed its school system rather than comply with a desegregation order. The Court ordered the schools reopened and explained that "[w]hatever nonracial grounds might support a State's allowing a county to abandon public schools, the object must be a constitutional one, and grounds of race and opposition to desegregation do not qualify as constitutional."[226] The Court also expressed its frustration with the resistance to desegregation and declared that "[t]here has been entirely too much deliberation and not enough speed."[227]

In 1969, in *Green v. County School Board*, the Supreme Court declared unconstitutional a "freedom of choice plan" that was a common approach used to frustrate desegregation.[228] A school system in rural Virginia adopted a desegregation plan whereby students could choose which school to attend. Three years after it was enacted, no white student was attending a black school and only 15 percent of the black students were attending white schools. The Court said that "[i]t is incumbent

[219] Michael J. Klarman, *Brown*, Racial Change, and the Civil Rights Movement, 80 Va. L. Rev. 7, 9 (1994).
[220] *Id.* at 9.
[221] *Id.*
[222] *Id.*
[223] 373 U.S. 683 (1963).
[224] *Id.* at 686.
[225] 377 U.S. 218 (1964).
[226] *Id.* at 231.
[227] *Id.* at 229.
[228] 391 U.S. 430 (1968).

upon the school board to establish that its proposed plan promises meaningful and immediate progress toward disestablishing state-imposed segregation. . . . Of course, the availability to the board of other more promising courses of action may indicate a lack of good faith; and at the least it places a heavy burden upon the board to explain its preference for an apparently less effective method."[229] The Court emphatically declared that school boards have "the affirmative duty to take whatever steps might be necessary to convert to a unitary system in which racial discrimination would be eliminated root and branch."[230]

These Supreme Court decisions ending obstruction to desegregation were accompanied by an important federal law: the Civil Rights Act of 1964. Title VI prohibited discrimination by schools receiving federal funds. This became especially significant when Congress enacted the Elementary and Secondary Education Act of 1965, which appropriated $2.5 billion for schools. Additionally, the 1964 Civil Rights Act authorized the United States attorney general to intervene in desegregation suits.

The combination of federal court action and the federal law had an effect in bringing about desegregation.[231] One by one the obstructionist techniques were defeated. Finally, by the mid-1960s, desegregation began to proceed. By 1968, the integration rate in the South rose to 32 percent, and by 1972-1973, 91.3 percent of Southern schools were desegregated. To point to one example of success, the federal court's desegregation order in Oklahoma City effectively eliminated one-race schools and meant that few blacks or whites were attending schools that were more than 90 percent of one race. Indeed, it was demonstrated that ending the court's desegregation order would cause the resegregation of the Oklahoma City schools.[232]

Yet there is no doubt that despite over 60 years of judicial action, school segregation continues.[233] Indeed, racial segregation in American schools has been increasing. A study by Professor Gary Orfield found that "[f]rom 1988 to 1998, most of the progress of the previous two decades in increasing integration in the region was lost. The South is still more integrated than it was before the civil rights revolution, but it is moving backward at an accelerating rate."[234]

For example, the percentage of African-American students attending majority white schools has steadily decreased since 1986. In 1954, at the time of *Brown v. Board of Education*, only 0.001 percent of African-American students in the South attended majority white schools. In 1964, a decade after *Brown*, it was just 2.3

---

[229] *Id.* at 439.

[230] *Id.* at 437-438.

[231] An empirical study shows that *Brown v. Board of Education* had a substantial effect in changing decisions by federal district courts. *See* Francine Sanders, *Brown v. Bd. of Educ.*: An Empirical Reexamination of the Effects on Federal District Courts, 29 Law & Socy. Rev. 703 (1995).

[232] *See* Board of Educ. of Oklahoma City v. Dowell, 498 U.S. 237 (1991) (the Court held that once unitary status has been achieved in a school system, the desegregation order should be lifted, even if it will result in the resegregation of the public schools).

[233] *See* Gary Orfield & Susan E. Eaton, Dismantling Desegregation: The Quiet Reversal of *Brown v. Board of Education* 53, 66-69 (1996).

[234] Gary Orfield, Schools More Separate: Consequences of a Decade of Resegregation 2 (2001).

percent. From 1964 to 1986, there was significant progress: from 13.9 percent in 1967, to 23.4 percent in 1968, to 37.6 percent in 1976, to 42.9 percent in 1986, to 43.5 percent in 1988. But since then the percentage of African-American students attending minority white schools has gone in the opposite direction. By 1991, the percentage of black students attending majority white schools in the South had decreased to 39.2 percent and over the course of the 1990s it went to 36.6 percent in 1994, to 34.7 percent in 1996, to 32.7 percent in 1998. These statistics show that nationally the percentage of African-American students attending majority black schools and schools where over 90 percent of the students are black also has increased. In 1986, 62.9 percent of black students attended schools that were 50 to 100 percent composed of minority students; by 1998-1999, this percentage had increased to 70.2 percent.[235]

Orfield's research shows that during the last decade the problem of racially segregated schools continued to get worse.[236] By 2006-2007, 73 percent of African-American students attended schools that were between 50 and 100 percent minority students; 38.5 percent attended schools that were between 90 and 100 percent minority students. Orfield's research also shows that the nation's teaching force, too, is largely segregated; students rarely encounter teachers of races different from their own.

Quite significantly, Professor Orfield shows that the same is true for Latino students. The historic focus for desegregation efforts has been to integrate African-American and white students. The burgeoning Latino population requires that desegregation focus on this racial minority as well. The percentage of Latino students attending schools where the majority of students are of minority races, or almost exclusively of minority races, increased steadily over the 1990s and the last decade. In the 2006-2007 school year, 78 percent of Latino students attended schools that were between 50 and 100 percent minority students, and 40 percent attended schools that were between 90 and 100 percent minority students. Professor Orfield notes that "[Latinos] have been more segregated than blacks for a number of years, not only by race and ethnicity but also by poverty."[237]

The reality is that most children in the United States are educated only with children of their own race.[238] In 2012-2013, in the Boston public schools, only 12 percent of the students were white.[239] In Chicago, just 8.8 percent of children in the schools were white. In Dallas, only 4.8 percent of children in the public schools were white and in Los Angeles, 9.2 percent of the students were white. In Washington, D.C., 85 percent of children were black or Hispanic and 11 percent

---

[235] Id. at 29.

[236] Gary Orfield, Reviving the Goal of Integrated Society: A 21st Century Challenge (Los Angeles, California: The Civil Rights Project of UCLA, 2009).

[237] Orfield, supra note 234, at 2.

[238] For excellent discussion of the resegregation in education, see John Charles Boger & Gary Orfield, eds., School Resegregation (2005); Charles T. Clotfelter, After Brown: The Rise and Retreat of School Desegregation (2004); see also Erwin Chemerinsky, The Conservative Assault on the Constitution (2010) (ch. 1, Separate and Unequal Schools).

[239] National Center for Education Statistics, Characteristics of the 100 Largest Public Elementary and Secondary Schools in the United States, 2012-2013, nces.ed.gov, last visited Dec. 27, 2013.

were white. In part, this is because of the obstacles the Supreme Court created since the 1970s, discussed below, to proving discrimination, to federal courts fashioning remedies, and to continuation of desegregation efforts.

Proving Discrimination in the School Context

There obviously was no difficulty in proving discrimination in states that by law had required separation of the races in education. But in Northern school systems, where segregated schools were not the product of state laws, the issue arose as to what had to be proved in order to demonstrate an equal protection violation and justify a federal court remedy.

The Supreme Court addressed this issue in *Keyes v. School District No. 1, Denver, Colorado*.[240] The Supreme Court recognized that it was not a case where schools were segregated by statute, but the Court said, "[n]evertheless, where plaintiffs prove that the school authorities have carried out a systematic program of segregation affecting a substantial portion of the students, schools, teachers, and facilities within the school system, it is only common sense to conclude that there exists a predicate for a finding of the existence of a dual school system."[241] Once it is proved that there were segregative actions affecting a significant number of students, an equal protection violation is demonstrated that justifies a system-wide federal court remedy because "common sense dictates the conclusion that racially inspired school board actions have an impact beyond the particular schools that are the subjects of those actions."[242]

Keyes thus held that absent laws requiring school segregation, plaintiffs must prove intentional segregative acts affecting a substantial part of the school system. The Court said that "a finding of intentionally segregative school board actions in a meaningful portion of a school system . . . creates a presumption that other segregated schooling within the system is not adventitious."[243] Such proof shifts "the burden of proving that other segregated schools within the system are not also the result of intentionally segregative actions."[244]

The Court therefore drew a distinction between *de jure* segregation, which existed throughout the South, and *de facto* segregation, which existed in the North. The latter constitutes a constitutional violation only if there is proof of discriminatory purpose. This approach is consistent with the Supreme Court cases, reviewed above, holding that when laws are facially neutral, proof of a discriminatory impact alone is not sufficient to show an equal protection violation; there also must be proof of a discriminatory purpose.[245] But requiring proof of discriminatory purpose also created a substantial obstacle to desegregation in Northern school systems where residential segregation—which was a product of a myriad

---

[240] 413 U.S. 189 (1973).
[241] *Id.* at 201.
[242] *Id.* at 203.
[243] *Id.* at 208.
[244] *Id.*
[245] *See* §9.3.3.2.

of discriminatory policies—caused school segregation. Justice Powell wrote a lengthy concurring opinion in *Keyes* urging that the Court abandon the distinction between *de jure* and *de facto* segregation and require that all schools act to end school segregation.[246]

The Court applied these principles to find intentional discrimination in two cases involving Ohio school systems. In *Columbus Board of Education v. Penick*, the Court considered the Columbus, Ohio, school system, which was substantially race segregated: In 1976, half of the schools were 90 percent black or 90 percent white; 70 percent of the students attended schools that were at least 80 percent black or 80 percent white.[247] The district court had found that as of 1954, Columbus had maintained "an enclave of separate, black schools on the near east side of Columbus."[248] The Court said that this was sufficient to establish an equal protection violation because "[p]roof of purposeful and effective maintenance of a body of separate black schools in a substantial part of the system itself is prima facie proof of a dual school system and supports a finding to this effect absent sufficient contrary proof by the Board."[249]

Similarly, in *Dayton Board of Education v. Brinkman*, the Supreme Court considered a school system in Ohio where 43 percent of the students were black, but 51 of the 69 schools in the system were virtually all-black or all-white.[250] Again, there was a lower court finding that at the time of *Brown* the city was intentionally operating a dual school system. The Supreme Court said that this triggered a duty to desegregate. The Court explained that "the Board had to do more than abandon its prior discriminatory purpose. The Board has had an affirmative responsibility to see that pupil assignment policies and school construction and abandonment practices are not used and do not serve to perpetuate or re-establish the dual school system."[251]

Thus, proof of racial separation in schools is not sufficient to establish an equal protection violation or provide a basis for federal court remedies. As is true in other areas of equal protection law, there must be either proof of laws that mandated segregation or evidence of intentional acts to segregate the schools.[252] Proof of intentional discrimination as to a substantial part of the school system will justify a system-wide remedy, unless the school system can demonstrate that the segregation in those areas was not a consequence of its segregative acts.

[246] 413 U.S. at 223-236 (Powell, J., dissenting).

[247] 443 U.S. 449, 452 (1979).

[248] *Id.* at 436.

[249] *Id.* at 458.

[250] 443 U.S. 526, 529 (1979).

[251] *Id.* at 538.

[252] For a defense of the Court's distinction between *de facto* and *de jure* segregation, *see* Frank Goodman, De Facto School Segregation: A Constitutional and Empirical Analysis, 60 Cal. L. Rev. 275, 319 (1972). For a criticism of the distinction, *see* David Strauss, Discriminatory Intent and the Taming of *Brown*, 56 U. Chi. L. Rev. 935, 962 (1989); Owen Fiss, Racial Imbalance in the Public Schools: The Constitutional Concepts, 78 Harv. L. Rev. 564 (1965).

Judicial Power to Impose Remedies
in School Desegregation Cases

In *Swann v. Charlotte-Mecklenburg Board of Education*, the Supreme Court addressed the issue of the federal courts' power to issue remedies in school deseg-regation cases.[253] The Supreme Court said that district courts have broad authority in formulating remedies in desegregation cases. The Court stated that mathemat-ical ratios—such as comparisons of the race in particular schools with the overall race of the district—are a "useful starting point in shaping a remedy to correct past constitutional violations."[254] This does not mean that "every school in every community must always reflect the racial composition of the school system as a whole" and, in fact, "some small number of one-race, or virtually one-race, schools within a district" may be unavoidable.[255] However, such a result always should receive close judicial review in a school system that was once segregated by law.

The Court upheld broad power of the district court to take "affirmative action in the form of remedial altering of attendance zones . . . to achieve truly nondis-criminatory assignments."[256] The Court also said that courts could use busing as a remedy where needed. The Court said that bus transportation is an important "tool of school desegregation" and is a constitutionally acceptable remedy unless "the time or distance of travel is so great as to either risk the health of the children or significantly impinge on the educational process."[257]

In *Milliken v. Bradley*, in 1974, the Supreme Court imposed a substantial limit on the courts' remedial powers in desegregation cases.[258] A federal district court had imposed a multidistrict remedy for *de jure* segregation in one of the districts. The Supreme Court ruled this impermissible and held that "[b]efore the bound-aries of separate and autonomous school districts may be set aside by consolidat-ing the separate units for remedial purposes or by imposing a cross-district rem-edy, it must first be shown that there has been a constitutional violation within one district that produces a significant segregative effect in another district."[259] Thus, the Court concluded that "without an interdistrict violation and interdistrict effect there is no constitutional wrong calling for an interdistrict remedy."[260]

Milliken has a devastating effect on the ability to achieve desegregation in many areas. In a number of major cities, inner-city school systems are substantially black and are surrounded by almost all-white suburbs. Desegregation obviously requires the ability to transfer students between the city and suburban schools. There simply are not enough white students in the city, or enough black students in the suburbs, to achieve desegregation without an interdistrict remedy. Yet *Milliken* precludes an interdistrict remedy unless there is proof of an interdistrict violation.

---

[253]   402 U.S. 1 (1971).
[254]   *Id.* at 25.
[255]   *Id.* at 24, 26.
[256]   *Id.* at 28.
[257]   *Id.* at 30-31.
[258]   418 U.S. 717 (1974).
[259]   *Id.* at 744-745.
[260]   *Id.* at 745.

In other words, a multidistrict remedy can be formulated for those districts whose own policies fostered discrimination or if a state law caused the interdistrict segregation. Otherwise, the remedy can include only those districts found to violate the Constitution. Such proof is often not available, although there have been some cases where the requirements of *Milliken* have been met.[261]

Milliken can be defended based on the traditional principle that a court has authority to impose a remedy only after it is proved that the person or entity violated the law. Moreover, the *Milliken* Court emphasized that "[n]o single tradition in public education is more deeply rooted than local control over the operation of schools; local autonomy has long been thought essential both to the maintenance of community concern and support for public schools and to quality of the educational process."[262]

But critics of *Milliken* argue that the segregated pattern in major metropolitan areas—blacks in the city and whites in the suburbs—did not occur by accident, but rather was the product of a myriad government policies. Additionally, the reality is that in many areas *Milliken* means no desegregation. Critics argue that together with *San Antonio Independent School District v. Rodriguez*[263]—which held that disparities in school funding do not violate equal protection—the result is separate and unequal schools: wealthy white suburban schools spending a great deal on education surrounding much poorer black city schools that spend much less on education.

When Should Federal Desegregation Remedies End?

In several cases, the Supreme Court has considered when a federal court desegregation order should be ended. The Court first addressed this issue in *Pasadena City Board of Education v. Spangler*.[264] *Pasadena* involved a school system that had been segregated by law. A federal court order succeeded in desegregation: In 1970, no schools within the district were racially imbalanced. By 1974, 5 of the 32 schools in the district were over half black. The district court ordered that attendance lines be redrawn on an annual basis so that blacks would not be a majority in any school in the district. The Supreme Court deemed this improper. The Court noted that residential shifts were inevitable in cities and that they might alter the racial composition of the schools. The Court said that "having once implemented a racially neutral attendance pattern in order to remedy the perceived constitutional violations on the part of the defendants, the District Court had fully performed its function of providing the appropriate remedy for previous racially discriminatory attendance patterns."[265]

---

[261] *See, e.g.*, United States v. Board of School Commrs., 456 F. Supp. 183 (S.D. Ind. 1978); Evans v. Buchanan, 416 F. Supp. 328 (D. Del. 1976), *aff'd in part and vacated in part*, 637 F.2d 1101 (7th Cir.), *cert. denied*, 449 U.S. 838 (1980) (approving interdistrict remedies); *see also* Hills v. Gatreaux, 425 U.S. 284 (1976) (approving an interdistrict remedy for housing discrimination).

[262] 418 U.S. at 741-742.

[263] 411 U.S. 1 (1973), discussed in §§9.7.3 and 10.10.

[264] 427 U.S. 424 (1976).

[265] *Id.* at 436-437.

In three cases in the 1990s, the Supreme Court hastened the end of federal court desegregation orders. In *Board of Education of Oklahoma City v. Dowell,* the issue was whether a desegregation order should continue when its end would mean a resegregation of the public schools.[266] Oklahoma schools had been segregated by a state law mandating separation of the races. A federal court order was successful in desegregating the Oklahoma City public schools. Evidence proved that ending the desegregation order would result in resegregation. Nonetheless, the Supreme Court held that once a "unitary" school system had been achieved, a federal court's desegregation order should end, even if it will mean resegregation of the schools.

The Court did not define "unitary system" with any specificity. The Court simply said that the desegregation decree should be ended if the board "has complied in good faith" and "the vestiges of past discrimination have been eliminated to the extent practicable."[267] The Court said that in evaluating this "the District Court should look not only at student assignments, but to every facet of school operations—faculty, staff, transportation, extra-curricular activities and facilities."[268]

In *Freeman v. Pitts,* the Supreme Court held that a federal court desegregation order should end when it is complied with, even if other desegregation orders for the same school system remain in place.[269] A federal district court ordered desegregation of various aspects of a school system in Georgia that previously had been segregated by law. Part of the desegregation plan had been met; the school system had achieved desegregation in pupil assignment and in facilities. Another aspect of the desegregation order, concerning assignment of teachers, had not yet been fulfilled. The school system planned to construct a facility that likely would benefit whites more than blacks. Nonetheless, the Supreme Court held that the federal court could not review the discriminatory effects of the new construction because the part of the desegregation order concerning facilities had already been met. The Court said that once a portion of a desegregation order is met, the federal court should cease its efforts as to that part and remain involved only in those aspects of the plan that have not been achieved.

Finally, in *Missouri v. Jenkins,* the Court ordered an end to a school desegregation order for the Kansas City schools.[270] Missouri law once required the racial segregation of all public schools. It was not until 1977 that a federal district court ordered the desegregation of the Kansas City, Missouri, public schools. The federal court's desegregation effort made a difference. In 1983, 24 schools in the district had an African-American enrollment of 90 percent or more. By 1993, no elementary-level student attended a school with an enrollment that was 90 percent or more African American. At the middle school and high school levels, the

---

[266] 498 U.S. 237 (1991).

[267] *Id.* at 249-250.

[268] *Id.* at 250 (citations omitted).

[269] 503 U.S. 467 (1992).

[270] 515 U.S. 70 (1995). Earlier in *Missouri v. Jenkins,* 495 U.S. 33 (1990), the Supreme Court ruled that a federal district court could order that a local taxing body increase taxes to pay for compliance with a desegregation order, although the federal court should not itself order an increase in the taxes.

percentage of students attending schools with an African-American enrollment of 90 percent or more declined from about 45 percent to 22 percent.

The Court, in an opinion by Chief Justice Rehnquist, ruled in favor of the state on every issue. There were three parts to the Court's holding. First, the Court ruled that the district court's order that attempted to attract nonminority students from outside the district was impermissible because there was no proof of an inter-district violation. The social reality is that many city school systems are now primarily composed of minority students, while surrounding suburban school districts are almost all white. Effective desegregation requires an interdistrict remedy. Chief Justice Rehnquist, however, applied *Milliken v. Bradley* to conclude that the interdistrict remedy—incentives to attract students from outside the district into the Kansas City schools—was impermissible because there was proof only of an intradistrict violation.

Second, the Court ruled that the district court lacked authority to order an increase in teacher salaries. Although the district court believed that an across-the-board salary increase to attract teachers was essential for desegregation, the Supreme Court concluded that it was not necessary as a remedy.

Finally, the Court ruled that the continued disparity in student test scores did not justify continuance of the federal court's desegregation order. The Court concluded that the Constitution requires equal opportunity and not any result, and therefore disparities between African-American and white students on standardized tests were not a sufficient basis for concluding that desegregation had not been achieved. The Supreme Court held that once a desegregation order is complied with, the federal court effort should be ended. Disparity in test scores is not a basis for continued federal court involvement.

During the Vietnam War, Senator George Aiken said that the United States should declare victory and withdraw from Vietnam.[271] It appears that in *Board of Education of Oklahoma City v. Dowell*, *Freeman v. Pitts*, and *Missouri v. Jenkins*, the Supreme Court is declaring victory over school segregation and urging the federal courts to withdraw.[272]

Limits on Voluntary Desegregation Efforts

The cases described above have the effect of limiting the ability of federal courts to remedy desegregation. The Court's most recent decision about school segregation, *Parents Involved in Community Schools v. Seattle School Dist. No. 1*, limits the ability of school boards to remedy racial separation.[273] The case involved

---

[271] Albin Krebs, George Aiken, Longtime Senator and G.O.P. Maverick, Dies at 92, N.Y. Times, Nov. 20, 1984, at B-10.

[272] Lower courts have followed these decisions and ordered the end to desegregation efforts. For example, the United States Court of Appeals for the Fourth Circuit upheld a determination that the Charlotte-Mecklenburg school district had achieved unitary status and thus the desegregation order was to end. Belk v. Charlotte-Mecklenburg Bd. of Educ., 269 F.3d 305 (4th Cir. 2001).

[273] 551 U.S. 701 (2007). For an excellent analysis of this issue, *see* Neil S. Siegel, Race-Conscious Student Assignment Plans: Balkanization, Integration, and Individualized Consideration, 56 Duke L.J. 781, 835-838 (2006).

public school systems in Louisville, Kentucky and Seattle, Washington that had adopted plans that used race as one factor in assigning students to schools to achieve greater racial diversity. Louisville, which had a program that included all students from kindergarten through twelfth grade, had previously been a system segregated by law and had been subject to a judicial desegregation order, which had been lifted not long before it adopted its own desegregation plan. Seattle never had been segregated by law and had a plan that used race as a factor in assigning students to high schools to achieve greater racial diversity.

The Court, in a 5-4 decision, found both plans to be unconstitutional. Chief Justice Roberts's opinion was joined in its entirety only by Justices Scalia, Thomas, and Alito. Justice Kennedy concurred in part, but also concurred only in the judgment in part, and his separate opinion is thus crucial to determining the scope and impact of the decision.

All five Justices in the majority agreed that the government must meet strict scrutiny—its actions must be necessary to achieve a compelling purpose—even if it is using race to achieve school desegregation. Chief Justice Roberts, writing for the majority, declared: "It is well established that when the government distributes burdens or benefits on the basis of individual racial classifications, that action is reviewed under strict scrutiny."[274]

Chief Justice Roberts, writing for a plurality of four, found that Seattle and Louisville lacked a compelling interest for their desegregation efforts. Chief Justice Roberts stressed that the school systems were not seeking to remedy constitutional violations and he rejected the argument that diversity in classrooms was an interest sufficient to meet strict scrutiny. Chief Justice Roberts, writing for the plurality stated: "However closely related race-based assignments may be to achieving racial balance, that itself cannot be the goal, whether labeled 'racial diversity' or anything else. To the extent the objective is sufficient diversity so that students see fellow students as individuals rather than solely as members of a racial group, using means that treat students solely as members of a racial group is fundamentally at cross-purposes with that end."[275] By contrast, Justice Kennedy and the four dissenters said that desegregating schools is a compelling government interest. Justice Kennedy stated: "In the administration of public schools by the state and local authorities it is permissible to consider the racial makeup of schools and to adopt general policies to encourage a diverse student body, one aspect of which is its racial composition."[276]

But all five Justices in the majority agreed that the school districts failed to show that race neutral means cannot achieve desegregation. Justice Kennedy, like the four Justices in the plurality, said that race can be used in assigning students only if there is no other way of achieving desegregation. Justice Kennedy identified several alternatives that school systems can use to achieve greater racial diversity in their schools: "School boards may pursue the goal of bringing together students of diverse backgrounds and races through other means, including strategic site

---

[274] 551 U.S. at 720.

[275] *Id.* at 733.

[276] *Id.* at 788 (Kennedy, J., concurring in part and concurring in the judgment in part).

selection of new schools; drawing attendance zones with general recognition of the demographics of neighborhoods; allocating resources for special programs; recruiting students and faculty in a targeted fashion; and tracking enrollments, performance, and other statistics by race. These mechanisms are race conscious but do not lead to different treatment based on a classification that tells each student he or she is to be defined by race, so it is unlikely any of them would demand strict scrutiny to be found permissible."[277]

Justice Breyer wrote a lengthy dissent joined by Justices Stevens, Souter, and Ginsburg.[278] He described how American public schools are increasingly racially segregated and lamented that the Court's decision will have the effect of placing many effective desegregation plans in jeopardy. Justice Breyer attached an appendix to his dissent that listed the many voluntary desegregation plans that will be in jeopardy in light of the invalidation of the Louisville and Seattle programs. The dissent questioned whether meaningful desegregation can be achieved without such efforts.

The majority and the dissent have dramatically different views about the importance of diversity in public schools and the meaning of *Brown v. Board of Education*. Chief Justice Roberts sees in the Constitution a command for colorblindness and concluded his opinion by declaring: "Before *Brown*, schoolchildren were told where they could and could not go to school based on the color of their skin. The school districts in these cases have not carried the heavy burden of demonstrating that we should allow this once again—even for very different reasons. For schools that never segregated on the basis of race, such as Seattle, or that have removed the vestiges of past segregation, such as Jefferson County, the way to achieve a system of determining admission to the public schools on a nonracial basis, is to stop assigning students on a racial basis. The way to stop discrimination on the basis of race is to stop discriminating on the basis of race."[279]

By contrast, Justice Breyer and the dissent express the need for deference to school boards in desegregating schools and see the majority as abandoning the promise of *Brown v. Board of Education*. Justice Breyer concludes his dissent by stating: "The last half century has witnessed great strides toward racial equality, but we have not yet realized the promise of *Brown*. To invalidate the plans under review is to threaten the promise of *Brown*. The plurality's position, I fear, would break that promise. This is a decision that the Court and the Nation will come to regret."[280]

§9.3.5 Racial Classifications Benefiting Minorities

No topic in constitutional law is more controversial than affirmative action. Three issues are discussed. First, what level of scrutiny should be used for racial classifications benefiting minorities? Second, what purposes for affirmative action

[277] *Id.* at 789.
[278] *Id.* at 803 (Breyer, J., dissenting).
[279] *Id.* at 747-748 (Roberts, C.J.).
[280] *Id.* at 868 (Breyer, J., dissenting).

programs are sufficient to meet the level of scrutiny? Third, what techniques of affirmative action are sufficient to meet the level of scrutiny?

§9.3.5.1   What Level of Scrutiny for Racial Classifications Benefiting Minorities?

Strict Scrutiny Used

It now is clearly established that strict scrutiny is used to evaluate all government affirmative action plans. In *Adarand Constructors, Inc. v. Pena*, the Supreme Court said: "[A]ll racial classifications, imposed by whatever federal, state, or local governmental actor, must be analyzed by a reviewing court under strict scrutiny."[281] The Court reaffirmed that strict scrutiny is the test for affirmative action programs in its most recent case, *Fisher v. University of Texas, Austin*, where it declared: "Strict scrutiny requires the university to demonstrate with clarity that its purpose or interest is both constitutionally permissible and substantial, and that its use of the classification is necessary . . . to the accomplishment of its purpose."[282]

Initial Cases Considering the Level of Scrutiny

The Supreme Court, however, arrived at this conclusion only after struggling with the issue of the level of scrutiny for over a decade. The Court first considered the issue of affirmative action in *Regents of the University of California v. Bakke*.[283] *Bakke* involved a challenge to the University of California at Davis Medical School's set-aside of 16 slots in the entering class of 100 for minority students. There was no majority opinion for the Supreme Court. Four Justices—Brennan, White, Marshall, and Blackmun—said that intermediate scrutiny was the appropriate test for racial classifications benefiting minorities. They said that "a number of considerations . . . lead us to conclude that racial classifications designed to further remedial purposes must serve important governmental objectives and must be substantially related to achievement of those objectives."[284] These four Justices voted to uphold the University of California at Davis Medical School's affirmative action program.

Four Justices—Stevens, Burger, Stewart, and Rehnquist—concluded that the affirmative action program violated Title VI of the 1964 Civil Rights Act, which prohibited discrimination by institutions receiving federal funds.[285] They did not reach the constitutional issue or discuss the level of scrutiny. However, five

---

[281] 515 U.S. 200, 227 (1995).
[282] 133 S. Ct. 2411, 2418 (2013). Also, as described above, in *Parents Involved in Community Schools v. Seattle School Dist. No. 1*, 551 U.S. 701, 720 (2007), the Court reaffirmed that strict scrutiny is the appropriate test when the government uses race as a factor in assigning students to schools.
[283] 438 U.S. 265 (1978).
[284] *Id.* at 359 (citations omitted).
[285] *Id.* at 418 (Stevens, J., concurring in the judgment in part and dissenting in part).

Justices—Brennan, White, Marshall, Blackmun, and Powell—rejected this view and concluded that the analysis under Title VI and the Constitution is identical.

Finally, Justice Powell, writing just for himself, said that strict scrutiny should be used for affirmative action. He said that "[r]acial and ethnic distinctions of any sort are inherently suspect and thus call for the most exacting judicial examination."[286] Powell concluded that the set-aside was unconstitutional, but that it was permissible for race to be used as one factor in admissions decisions to enhance diversity. Thus, the vote was 5 to 4 invalidating the set-aside—Powell, Stevens, Burger, Rehnquist, and Stewart voting for this conclusion—but 5 to 4 that it is permissible for universities to use race as a factor in admissions to increase diversity—Powell, Brennan, Marshall, White, and Blackmun coming to this conclusion. Whether diversity is a permissible goal for affirmative action and when set-asides are permissible are discussed below in §§9.3.5.2 and 9.3.5.3, respectively.

Two years later, in *Fullilove v. Klutznick*, the Supreme Court again considered an affirmative action program, but did not produce a majority opinion concerning the appropriate level of scrutiny.[287] The Court upheld a federal law that required that 10 percent of federal public works monies given to local governments be set aside for minority-owned businesses. Chief Justice Burger, in an opinion joined by Justices White and Powell, concluded that the affirmative action program was justified to remedy past discrimination, but said that the "opinion does not adopt, either expressly or implicitly, the formulas of analysis articulated in cases such as *Regents of the University of California v. Bakke*."[288]

Three Justices—Marshall, Brennan, and Blackmun—concurred in the judgment to uphold the affirmative action program, but argued again that intermediate scrutiny should be used for racial classifications serving a remedial purpose.[289] Finally, three Justices—Stewart, Rehnquist, and Stevens—dissented and said that strict scrutiny was the appropriate test.[290] Justice Stewart, joined by Justice Rehnquist, wrote: "Under our Constitution, the government may never act to the detriment of a person solely because of that person's race. . . . The rule cannot be any different when the persons injured by a racially biased law are not members of a racial minority."[291]

The Emergence of Strict Scrutiny as the Test

It was not until 1989, in *Richmond v. J.A. Croson Co.*, that the Supreme Court expressly held that strict scrutiny should be used in evaluating state and local affirmative action programs.[292] The Court invalidated a Richmond, Virginia, plan to

---

[286] *Id.* at 291.

[287] 448 U.S. 448 (1980).

[288] *Id.* at 492.

[289] *Id.* at 519 (Marshall, J., concurring in the judgment).

[290] *Id.* at 523 (Stewart, J., dissenting with whom Rehnquist, J., joined); at 532 (Stevens, J., dissenting).

[291] *Id.* at 525-526 (Stewart, J., dissenting).

[292] 488 U.S. 469 (1989).

set aside 30 percent of public works monies for minority-owned businesses.[293] Five Justices—O'Connor, Rehnquist, White, Kennedy, and Scalia—wrote or joined in opinions declaring that strict scrutiny was the appropriate test in evaluating such affirmative action plans.[294] As Justice Marshall lamented in his dissenting opinion: "Today, for the first time, a majority of the Court has adopted strict scrutiny as its standard of Equal Protection Clause review of race-conscious remedial measures."[295]

But a year later, in *Metro Broadcasting, Inc. v. Federal Communications Commission*, the Supreme Court held that congressionally approved affirmative action programs need only to meet intermediate scrutiny.[296] The Supreme Court, in a 5-to-4 decision, upheld FCC policies that gave a preference to minority-owned businesses in broadcast licensing. The majority expressly said: "We hold that benign race-conscious measures mandated by Congress, even if those measures are not 'remedial' in the sense of being designed to compensate victims of past governmental or society discrimination, are constitutionally permissible to the extent that they serve important governmental objectives within the power of Congress and are substantially related to the achievement of those objectives."[297]

The majority opinion in *Metro Broadcasting* was written by Justice Brennan and joined by Justices White, Marshall, Blackmun, and Stevens. The dissent was composed of Justices O'Connor, Kennedy, Scalia, and Rehnquist. Between *Metro Broadcasting*, in 1990, and *Adarand Constructors, Inc. v. Pena*,[298] in 1995, four of the Justices in the majority, but none of the Justices in the dissent, resigned.[299] In *Adarand*, the four dissenters from *Metro Broadcasting* were joined by Justice Thomas to create a majority to overrule *Metro Broadcasting*.[300] The Court thus concluded that "[f]ederal racial classifications, like those of a State, must serve a compelling governmental interest, and must be narrowly tailored to further that interest."[301]

Justice O'Connor, writing for the plurality in *Adarand*, said that although the Court was adopting strict scrutiny as the appropriate test for all affirmative action, it wanted to "dispel the notion that strict scrutiny is strict in theory, but fatal in fact."[302] O'Connor said that "[w]hen race-based action is necessary to further a

---

[293] The permissibility of set-asides as an affirmative action technique is discussed below in §9.3.5.

[294] In addition to Justice O'Connor's opinion, which was joined by Chief Justice Rehnquist and Justice White, using strict scrutiny, Justice Scalia, *id.* at 520, and Justice Kennedy, *id.* at 518, wrote concurring opinions using strict scrutiny.

[295] 488 U.S. at 551 (Marshall, J., dissenting).

[296] 497 U.S. 547 (1990).

[297] *Id.* at 564-565.

[298] 515 U.S. 200 (1995).

[299] Between *Metro Broadcasting* and *Adarand*, the Supreme Court also decided *Shaw v. Reno*, 509 U.S. 630 (1993), which held that strict scrutiny should be applied when race is used in drawing election districts to increase the likelihood that minorities would be elected. This was later reaffirmed in *Miller v. Johnson*, 515 U.S. 900 (1995), *Shaw v. Hunt*, 517 U.S. 899 (1996), and *Bush v. Vera*, 517 U.S. 952 (1996). These cases are discussed in more detail below in §9.3.5.3.

[300] 515 U.S. at 227.

[301] *Id.* at 235.

[302] *Id.* at 237 (citations omitted).

compelling interest, such action is within constitutional constraints if it satisfies the 'narrow tailoring' test this Court has set out in previous cases."[303] In contrast, Justice Scalia wrote separately to argue that the government never could have a compelling interest in using racial classifications to remedy prior discrimination.[304]

In its subsequent affirmative actions cases, *Grutter v. Bollinger*[305] and *Gratz v. Bollinger*,[306] the Court reaffirmed that "all racial classifications imposed by government must be analyzed by a reviewing court under strict scrutiny."[307] The Court explained: "We apply strict scrutiny to all racial classifications to 'smoke out' illegitimate uses of race by assuring that [government] is pursuing a goal important enough to warrant use of a highly suspect tool."[308] In its most recent affirmative action decision, *Fisher v. University of Texas, Austin*, the Court said: "Judicial review must begin from the position that any official action that treats a person differently on account of his race or ethnic origin is inherently suspect. Strict scrutiny is a searching examination, and it is the government that bears the burden to prove that the reasons for any [racial] classification [are] clearly identified and unquestionably legitimate."[309]

The Arguments for and Against Strict Scrutiny

Those who favor strict scrutiny for affirmative action programs argue that all racial classifications—whether invidious or benign—should be subjected to strict scrutiny. Justice Thomas, in *Adarand*, espoused this view: "In my mind, government-sponsored racial discrimination based on benign prejudice is just as noxious as discrimination inspired by malicious prejudice. In each instance, it is racial discrimination, plain and simple."[310] The view is that the Constitution requires that the government treat each person as an individual without regard to his or her race; strict scrutiny is used to ensure that this occurs.

Moreover, supporters of strict scrutiny for affirmative action argue that all racial classifications stigmatize and breed racial hostility, and therefore all should be subjected to strict scrutiny. Justice O'Connor, in *Croson*, stated: "Classifications based in race carry a danger of stigmatic harm. Unless they are strictly reserved for remedial settings, they may in fact promote notions of racial inferiority and lead to politics of racial hostility."[311] Professor Michael Perry made a similar point that affirmative action "inevitably foments racial resentment and thereby strains the effort to gain wider acceptance for the principle of moral equality of the races."[312]

---

[303] *Id.*

[304] *Id.* at 239 (Scalia, J., concurring in part and concurring in the judgment).

[305] 539 U.S. 306 (2003).

[306] 539 U.S. 244 (2003).

[307] *Grutter*, 539 U.S. at 326.

[308] *Id.*

[309] 133 S. Ct. at 2419.

[310] 515 U.S. at 241 (Thomas, J., concurring in part and concurring in the judgment).

[311] 488 U.S. at 493.

[312] Michael J. Perry, Modern Equal Protection: A Conceptualization and Appraisal, 79 Colum. L. Rev. 1023, 1048 (1979). An additional argument against affirmative action is based on a claim that

On the other side of the debate, supporters of affirmative action argue that there is a significant difference between the government using racial classifications to benefit minorities and the government using racial classifications to disadvantage minorities. There is a long history of racism and discrimination against minorities, but no similar history of persecution of whites. Professor Richard Lempert forcefully explains the significance of this difference:

> Why does racial discrimination excite us when so many other kinds of discrimination do not? It is because of the way we interpret history, associating racial discrimination with practices that now appear self-evidently evil: forcing blacks from their homeland, enslaving blacks, lynching blacks for actions that among whites would not be criminal, intimidating blacks who sought to exercise their rights, in sum, systematically disadvantaging a people in almost every way that mattered because of the color of their skin. A claim made by a white person as a member of the dominant majority draws its moral force from our collective horror at centuries of oppressing black people. It would be ironic indeed if evils visited on blacks had lent enough force to the moral claims of whites to prevent what appears to many at this point to be the most effective means eliminating the legacy of those evils.[313]

Those who argue for a lower level of scrutiny for judicial review of affirmative action programs also emphasize the last point made by Professor Lempert: Achieving social equality requires affirmative action at this point in American history. The tremendous continuing disparities between blacks and whites in areas such as education, employment, and public contracting necessitate remedial action. Applying strict scrutiny would greatly impede such remedial efforts because relatively little ever has survived this rigorous review.

Also it is argued that there is a major difference between a majority discriminating against a minority and the majority discriminating against itself. Professor John Hart Ely explained: "When the group that controls the decision making process classifies so as to advantage a minority and disadvantage itself, the reasons for being unusually suspicious, and consequently, employing a stringent brand of review are lacking. A White majority is unlikely to disadvantage itself for reasons of racial prejudice; nor is it likely to be tempted either to underestimate the needs and deserts of Whites relative to those of others, or to overestimate the cost of devising an alternative classification that would extend to certain Whites the disadvantages generally extended to Blacks."[314]

---

it causes a "mismatch" between minority students and the institutions where they are most likely to succeed. *See* Richard Sander & Stuart Taylor, Jr., Mismatch: How Affirmative Action Hurts Students It's Intended to Help, and Why Universities Won't Admit It (2012). *But see* William C. Kidder & Angela Onwuachi-Willig, Still Hazy After All these Years: The Data and Theory Behind "Mismatch," 92 Tex. L. Rev. 895 (2014).

[313] Richard Lempert, The Force of Irony: On the Morality of Affirmative Action and *United Steelworkers v. Weber*, 95 Ethics 86, 88-89 (1984).

[314] John Hart Ely, The Constitutionality of Reverse Racial Discrimination, 41 U. Chi. L. Rev. 723, 735 (1974).

§9.3.5.2   What Purposes for Affirmative Action Programs Are Sufficient to Meet the Level of Scrutiny?

Affirmative action is used to achieve many different goals and takes various forms. Each goal and each type of government action needs to be analyzed separately for the chosen level of scrutiny. Four major objectives for affirmative action are identified: remedying past discrimination, enhancing diversity, providing role models for those in minority communities, and increasing services for minority communities. Each is analyzed in turn, and then §9.3.5.3 considers the forms that affirmative action might take.

Remedying Past Discrimination

The most frequently identified objective for affirmative action is to remedy past discrimination. Those who advocate affirmative action say that it is not enough to stop current discrimination. Efforts must be made to erase the effects of past discrimination, and this necessarily involves affirmative action. Those who oppose affirmative action say that it is sufficient to prohibit race discrimination and to allow all to be considered based on their merits.

The problem is that remedying past discrimination can mean many different things and cannot be treated as a single concept. For example, in its most limited sense, remedying past discrimination can mean that a person or entity who is proved to have violated the law can be required to provide a benefit to an individual who personally suffered past discrimination. For example, if a person can prove that he or she was denied a job on account of race, a court order that the discriminating employer hire that person is a form of affirmative action; the person is now being hired to remedy past discrimination. Even the most vehement opponents of affirmative action on the Supreme Court, such as Justices Scalia and Thomas, are willing to accept this.[315]

Remedying past discrimination also can have a broader meaning: It can be used to require that a proven violator of the law provide a remedy to a class of persons who were the subject of discrimination, even though the benefits are not limited to the individuals who were the proven victims of discrimination. For example, in *United States v. Paradise*, the Supreme Court upheld a federal court order, to remedy proven intentional discrimination by the Alabama Department of Public Safety, that a qualified black had to be hired or promoted every time a white was hired or promoted.[316] Justice Brennan, writing for the plurality, found that the "relief ordered survives even strict scrutiny analysis"[317] and "the race-conscious relief at issue here is justified by a compelling interest in remedying discrimination."[318]

---

[315] *See, e.g.*, Richmond v. J.A. Croson Co., 488 U.S. at 520 (Scalia, J., concurring in judgment).
[316] 480 U.S. 149 (1987).
[317] *Id.* at 167.
[318] *Id.* at 170.

A third possible meaning to remedying past discrimination could be requiring that those in a field or industry where there is proved discrimination provide a remedy, even if it is not demonstrated that the particular entity violated the law, and even though the recipient need not be shown to have personally suffered discrimination. In *Fullilove v. Klutznick*, the Supreme Court upheld a federal law that set aside public works monies for minority-owned businesses.[319] The Court emphasized that Congress found a long history of discrimination in the construction industry and that the affirmative action program was justified as a remedy. Affirmative action was used to help a group that had suffered past discrimination, though the beneficiaries of the remedy were not limited to those who could prove that they had specifically suffered discrimination.

Although *Fullilove* has not been expressly overruled, it is doubtful whether it survives later rulings. In *Croson*,[320] Justice O'Connor said: "Like the claim that discrimination in primary and secondary schooling justifies a rigid racial preference in medical school admissions, an amorphous claim that there has been past discrimination in a particular industry cannot justify use of an unyielding racial quota."[321] In *Adarand*,[322] the Court held that federal affirmative action efforts are to be treated the same as those by state and local governments. Thus, although *Fullilove* has not been expressly overruled, the Court would be unlikely to accept such affirmative action efforts in the future where there is neither proof of discrimination by the entity nor proof that the particular recipients' rights were violated.

Finally, and most broadly, affirmative action might be used to remedy general societal discrimination. These efforts are based on the legacy of racism that has pervaded all aspects of society and attempt to place minorities in the same position that they would be in if the centuries of discrimination had not occurred. This type of affirmative action also can be defended as a form of reparations to a class of persons who have suffered from discrimination over a long period of time.

However, the Supreme Court has not accepted this as a sufficient justification for affirmative action. In *Wygant v. Jackson Board of Education*, Justice Powell, writing for the plurality, stated: "This Court never has held that societal discrimination alone is sufficient to justify a racial classification. Rather, the Court has insisted upon some showing of prior discrimination by the governmental unit involved before allowing limited use of racial classifications in order to remedy such discrimination."[323]

Thus, under current law, it is clear that affirmative action will be allowed if it is directed at entities that are proved to have engaged in illegal discrimination and if it is limited to providing a remedy to those who are proven victims of that discrimination. It also is clear that affirmative action will not be allowed if it is based on a desire to remedy the long history of racism throughout society. The more uncertain area is when the Court will allow affirmative action efforts directed

---

[319] 448 U.S. 448 (1980).
[320] 488 U.S. 469 (1989).
[321] *Id.* at 499.
[322] 515 U.S. 200 (1995).
[323] 476 U.S. 267, 274 (1986).

at particular entities or sectors of the economy where discrimination has been proved to occur, but where the beneficiaries are not themselves the proved victims of this discrimination.

Enhancing Diversity

Another important objective of affirmative action is enhancing diversity. Entirely apart from remedying past discrimination, race might be used in decision making to provide more diversity than would exist through a completely color-blind system.

This justification for affirmative action is most frequently invoked with regard to decisions by colleges and universities, both in admitting students and in hiring faculty members. The argument is that race is a powerful factor influencing a person's experiences and perceptions. Education of all is enhanced when there is a diverse student body and faculty.

In *Regents of the University of California v. Bakke*, Justice Powell argued that "the interest of diversity is compelling in the context of a university's admissions program."[324] Ideally, such diversity would occur through race-blind admissions and hiring policies. But where that would not be the case, and because of the legacy of discrimination it often won't occur, affirmative action is used to enhance diversity.

While Justice Powell was just writing for himself in *Bakke*, in *Grutter v. Bollinger*, in a 5-to-4 decision, with Justice O'Connor writing for the majority, the Court ruled that colleges and universities have a compelling interest in creating a diverse student body and that they may use race as one factor, among many, to benefit minorities and enhance diversity. The Court said that the "benefits [of diversity] are substantial" and diversity "promotes cross-racial understanding, helps to break down racial stereotypes, and enables students to better understand persons of different races."[325] The Court accepted the university's argument that the education of all students is enhanced with a diverse student body. The dissent, though, strongly challenged the basis for this conclusion, contending that the Court's deference to the university was not appropriate under strict scrutiny and that diversity was not a sufficient interest to justify the use of racial classifications.[326]

Although increasing diversity is most frequently used to justify affirmative action in the educational context, there are other situations where this goal has been accepted. In *Metro Broadcasting, Inc. v. Federal Communications Commission*, the Supreme Court upheld a federal system to give preference to minority-owned businesses in licensing broadcast stations.[327] The Court emphasized the value of diversity of views and programming over the broadcast media and accepted the government's argument that racial diversity in licensing would enhance this goal.

---

[324] 438 U.S. at 314.
[325] 539 U.S. at 330.
[326] *Id.* at 380.
[327] 497 U.S. 547 (1990).

The dissent in *Metro Broadcasting* expressly rejected this as a sufficient justification for affirmative action. Justice O'Connor said that "[m]odern equal protection doctrine has recognized only one such interest: remedying the effects of racial discrimination. The interest in increasing diversity of broadcast viewpoints is clearly not a compelling interest."[328] As explained above, *Metro Broadcasting* has been overruled, at least in its holding that intermediate scrutiny should be used in evaluating federal affirmative action efforts. The Court, however, did not discuss whether the diversity rationale accepted in *Metro Broadcasting* remains an acceptable justification for affirmative action outside the education context. But it seems unlikely that the current Court would accept this. Indeed, although *Grutter* clearly accepts that diversity is a compelling interest in higher education, this conclusion may be reconsidered in future years in light of the change in the composition of the Supreme Court. In its most recent affirmative action decision, *Fisher v. University of Texas, Austin*, the Court did not reconsider that question, but instead simply said, "[b]ut the parties here do not ask the Court to revisit that aspect of *Grutter*'s holding."[329]

As described above, in *Parents Involved in Community Schools v. Seattle School Dist. No. 1*, Chief Justice Roberts, writing for a plurality of four, rejected diversity as a compelling government interest in the context of elementary and high schools and strongly proclaimed the view that the Constitution requires that the government be color-blind.[330] Justice Kennedy and the four dissenters accepted that diversity is a compelling government interest,[331] but it must be remembered that Justice Kennedy dissented in *Grutter* and has never voted to uphold any affirmative action program.

Providing Role Models

Affirmative action also can be justified as a way to provide role models in society. For example, affirmative action in hiring faculty members can be justified as a means to providing positive role models for minority students. At the same time, white students undoubtedly benefit from seeing minorities in positions of authority. More generally, affirmative action in college and university admissions might be justified because of the likelihood that this will supply positive role models in the long term. For instance, increasing the number of black doctors and black lawyers will have this benefit over time.

The Supreme Court, however, has rejected this as a justification for affirmative action. In *Wygant v. Jackson Board of Education*, the Court declared unconstitutional a school system's plan to lay off white teachers with more seniority instead of minority teachers with less seniority.[332] Justice Powell, writing for the plurality, stated: "The role model theory allows the Board to engage in discriminatory hiring and layoff practices long past the point required by legitimate remedial

---

[328] *Id.* at 612 (O'Connor, J., dissenting).
[329] 133 S. Ct. at 2419.
[330] 551 U.S. at 733.
[331] *Id.* at 788 (Kennedy, J., concurring in part and concurring in the judgment).
[332] 476 U.S. 267 (1986).

purposes. . . . Moreover, because the role model theory does not necessarily bear a relationship to the harm caused by the past discriminatory hiring practices, it actually could be used to escape the obligation to remedy such practices by justifying the small percentage of black teachers by reference to the small number of black students."[333]

Enhancing Services Provided to Minority Communities

The legacy of discrimination is that minority communities generally have less access to professional services than predominately white areas. Affirmative action can be justified as a way to deal with this problem. For example, affirmative action in medical school admissions might be used to improve the delivery of health care services to communities that currently are underserved.[334] The hope is that training more African-American doctors will increase the number of doctors desiring to practice in the African-American community.

However, again, it appears that this justification for affirmative action is not accepted as sufficient by the Supreme Court. In *Bakke*, Justice Powell rejected this argument and said that there was no proof that training more black doctors would mean that there would be more doctors actually practicing in minority communities.[335] Also, there might be other ways of achieving this goal more directly, such as by providing incentives for doctors to work in areas that are underserved.

§9.3.5.3   What Techniques of Affirmative Action Are Sufficient to Meet the Level of Scrutiny?

Although the goals of affirmative action are varied, the means of affirmative action are even more numerous. There are a vast array of techniques for affirmative action depending on whether it is affirmative action in employment, in education, in contracting or licensing, or in political representation. For example, affirmative action in employment can range from aggressive recruitment of minorities to goals and timetables to set-asides to rigid quotas. And these are only a few of the possible forms of affirmative action.

Thus far, the Supreme Court has considered several techniques of affirmative action: numerical set-asides, using race as one factor in decision making to help minorities, deviations from seniority systems, and drawing election districts to enhance the likelihood that minority representatives will be selected. Each is discussed in turn.[336]

---

[333] *Id.* at 275-276.

[334] The University of California at Davis used this argument in attempting to justify its affirmative action program. *See Bakke*, 438 U.S. at 310 (opinion of Powell, J.).

[335] *Id.* at 310-311.

[336] The focus is exclusively on the constitutionality of affirmative action programs. There also is a distinct question of whether a particular program violates federal civil rights statutes. *See, e.g.,* Johnson

Numerical Set-Asides

The Supreme Court has made it clear that numerical set-asides will be allowed, if at all, only if needed to remedy clearly proven past discrimination. In *Regents of the University of California v. Bakke*, five Justices—Justice Powell on equal protection grounds and four Justices on statutory grounds—found impermissible the University of California at Davis Medical School's set-aside of 16 slots in the entering class of 100 for minority students.[337]

In *Fullilove v. Klutznick*, the Supreme Court upheld a federal law that required that 10 percent of federal public works monies to local governments be set aside for minority-owned businesses.[338] Six of the Justices concluded that Congress had adopted the affirmative action program to remedy a long history of discrimination in the construction industry.

Although *Fullilove* has not been expressly overruled, it is questionable whether it survives later decisions. In *Richmond v. J.A. Croson Co.*, the Supreme Court invalidated an affirmative action program in Richmond, Virginia, that set aside 30 percent of public works monies for minority-owned businesses.[339] The Court emphasized that the set-aside was not narrowly tailored because it also benefited "Spanish-speaking, Oriental, Indian, Eskimo or Aleut persons . . . that may never have suffered from discrimination in the construction industry in Richmond."[340] The Court also said that "there does not appear to have been any consideration of the use of race-neutral means to increase minority business participation in city contracting."[341]

In *Adarand Constructors, Inc. v. Pena*, the Supreme Court held that set-asides created by federal law also must meet strict scrutiny.[342] *Adarand* involved a challenge to the federal government's practice of giving general contractors on government projects a financial incentive to hire minority businesses as subcontractors. The Supreme Court did not rule on the constitutionality of the program, but rather remanded the case for it to be evaluated under strict scrutiny.

Fullilove is thus of questionable precedential value because the Court in *Croson* said that set-asides would not be allowed to remedy general discrimination in an industry or field and because *Adarand* said that the same principles apply to federal affirmative action as to state and local programs. A set-aside, such as in *Fullilove*, would be allowed only if strict scrutiny was met.

---

v. Transportation Agency, 480 U.S. 616 (1987) (upholding a voluntary affirmative action program as not violating Title VII that was designed to increase the number of women in traditionally male positions); Local 93, Intl. Assn. of Firefighters v. Cleveland, 478 U.S. 501 (1986) (upholding as not violating Title VII a voluntary affirmative action program to benefit those who were not the actual victims of discrimination); Sheet Metal Workers v. EEOC, 478 U.S. 421 (1986) (upholding an affirmative action plan imposed on a union that was found to have discriminated); United Steel Workers v. Weber, 443 U.S. 193 (1979) (upholding a private employer's affirmative action plan under Title VII).

[337] 438 U.S. 265 (1978).
[338] 448 U.S. 448 (1980).
[339] 488 U.S. 469 (1989).
[340] *Id.* at 506.
[341] *Id.* at 507.
[342] 515 U.S. 200 (1995).

The other Supreme Court case upholding set-asides was *United States v. Paradise.*[343] A federal district court found that the Alabama Department of Public Safety had intentionally discriminated against blacks in hiring and promotions. The court ordered as a remedy that, for a period of time, whenever a white was hired or promoted, a qualified black had to be hired or promoted. The Supreme Court upheld this as constitutional, and the plurality opinion declared that this met strict scrutiny because it was designed to remedy past discrimination.[344]

Using Race as One Factor in Decisions to Help Minorities

On three occasions the Supreme Court has indicated that the government may use race as one factor among several in decision making to help minorities and to enhance diversity, but in the most recent case the Court rejected this in the context of desegregating elementary and high schools. In *Bakke,* Justice Powell said that the University of California at Davis Medical School could use race as one criterion in admissions decisions.[345] He wrote that "[i]n such an admissions program, race or ethnic background may be deemed a 'plus' in a particular applicant's file, yet it does not insulate the individual from comparison with all other candidates for the available seats. . . . [A]n admissions program operated in this way is flexible enough to consider all pertinent elements of diversity in light of the particular qualifications of each applicant, and to place them on the same footing for consideration, although not necessarily according them the same weight."[346] Although Justice Powell was writing only for himself, four other Justices—Brennan, White, Marshall, and Blackmun—also clearly indicated that they believed that this technique of affirmative action is constitutional.

In *Metro Broadcasting,* the Supreme Court held that the Federal Communications Commission could use race as one factor in licensing decisions to increase the number of minority-owned stations.[347] Although *Adarand* overruled *Metro Broadcasting*'s holding that intermediate scrutiny is used in evaluating congressionally approved affirmative action efforts, it did not discuss whether this also overruled the conclusion that race could be used as one factor in decisions to increase diversity.

In *Grutter v. Bollinger,* in a 5-to-4 decision, with Justice O'Connor writing for the majority, the Court upheld the University of Michigan Law School's affirmative action program.[348] The Court ruled that colleges and universities have a compelling interest in creating a diverse student body and that they may use race as one factor, among many, to benefit minorities and enhance diversity. However, in a companion case, *Gratz v. Bollinger,*[349] the Court, 6 to 3, invalidated an affirmative

---

[343] 480 U.S. 149 (1987).
[344] *Id.* at 167-171.
[345] 438 U.S. at 316-318.
[346] *Id.* at 313.
[347] 497 U.S. 547 (1990).
[348] 539 U.S. 306 (2003).
[349] 539 U.S. 244 (2003).

action program for undergraduate admissions that added 20 points to the applications for minority students. The University of Michigan undergraduate admissions office assigned points to various features in an applicant's profile; additional points were added to those who were from minority races. In an opinion by Chief Justice Rehnquist, the Court ruled that the undergraduate program was not sufficiently "narrowly tailored" to meet the strict scrutiny used for government racial classifications.

The bottom line is that the Court in *Grutter* and *Gratz* adhered to the position articulated by Justice Powell in *Regents of the University of California v. Bakke* almost 40 years ago: Diversity is a compelling interest in education and universities may use race as a factor to ensure diversity, but quotas or numerical quantification of benefits is impermissible.

- The underlying question is whether this is a distinction that makes a difference. Practically speaking, can colleges and universities effectively add points so long as it is not done explicitly and officially? Is there really a difference between a college having a set-aside and a college using race as a factor in admissions decisions and keeping track of the number of minority students to ensure "critical mass"? Interestingly, seven of the nine Justices on the Court at the time of *Grutter* and *Gratz* saw no difference. Four Justices—Rehnquist, Scalia, Kennedy, and Thomas—would have struck both programs down; three Justices—Stevens, Souter, and Ginsburg—would have upheld both. Only Justices O'Connor and Breyer saw a meaningful difference.

In *Parents Involved in Community Schools v. Seattle School Dist. No. 1*,[350] Chief Justice Roberts writing for a plurality of four rejected achieving racial diversity as a compelling interest in the context of elementary and high schools. Justice Kennedy and the four dissenters accepted this as a compelling interest, but Justice Kennedy joined with the plurality to strike down programs in Seattle and Louisville that used race as a factor in assigning students to schools because of the existence of race neutral alternatives to achieve this objective.

Finally, in *Fisher v. University of Texas, Austin*, the Court held that for an affirmative action program to be upheld, the college or university must prove that no less discriminatory alternative can achieve diversity.[351] In 2004, the Regents of the University of Texas realized that they had a less diverse student body than existed in 1996. A new admissions plan was adopted.

Under it, about 75 percent of the entering class was taken from the top 10 percent of high schools across the state. Texas is sufficiently racially segregated that this will produce some racial diversity. The other 25 percent of the class was taken by calculating an admissions score for each student. The score was the sum of two numbers: an academic achievement index, which was the applicant's grades

---

[350] 551 U.S. 701 (2007) (described above).

[351] 133 S. Ct. at 2420. For a fascinating discussion of the Court's internal deliberations in *Fisher*, *see* Joan Biskupic, Breaking In: The Rise of Sonia Sotomayor and the Politics of Justice 190-210 (2014) (indicating that the Court's initial vote was to overrule *Grutter*, but that a vehement dissent from Justice Sotomayor caused the Court to adopt a compromise approach).

and test scores, and a personal achievement index, which was arrived at by grading two essays and looking at six factors, one of which was diversity.

Abigail Fisher applied to the University of Texas in 2008 and was rejected and brought a lawsuit against the University of Texas challenging its use of race as denying equal protection.[352] The federal district court and the Fifth Circuit ruled in favor of the University of Texas saying that it had followed *Grutter* and had permissibly used race as one factor among many in its admissions decisions.

Justice Kennedy, writing for the majority in a 7-1 decision, reversed and remanded on the ground that Texas had failed to prove that there was no other way to achieve diversity. The Court stated: "The University must prove that the means chosen by the University to attain diversity are narrowly tailored to that goal. On this point, the University receives no deference."[353]

The Court elaborated as to what is required: "Narrow tailoring also requires that the reviewing court verify that it is 'necessary' for a university to use race to achieve the educational benefits of diversity. This involves a careful judicial inquiry into whether a university could achieve sufficient diversity without using racial classifications. Although '[n]arrow tailoring does not require exhaustion of every *conceivable* race-neutral alternative,' strict scrutiny does require a court to examine with care, and not defer to, a university's 'serious, good faith consideration of workable race-neutral alternatives.' . . . The reviewing court must ultimately be satisfied that no workable race-neutral alternatives would produce the educational benefits of diversity."[354]

After *Fisher*, it remains uncertain as to what will be sufficient to demonstrate that no race neutral alternative can achieve diversity. On remand, in 2014, the United States Court of Appeals for the Fifth Circuit again upheld the University of Texas affirmative action plan, concluding that no less restrictive alternative would achieve diversity.[355] This case could return to the Supreme Court and provide it another opportunity to address the issue of affirmative action in higher education.

Deviations from Seniority Systems

In *Wygant v. Jackson Board of Education*, the Supreme Court declared unconstitutional a city's attempt to achieve faculty diversity in its schools by laying off white teachers with more seniority than black teachers who were retained.[356] The Jackson, Michigan school system, as part of a settlement to a discrimination suit, hired a number of African-American teachers. When layoffs were required, the Board of Education decided that teachers with the most seniority would be retained, except that at no time would the percentage of minorities to be laid off exceed the percentage of minorities employed at the time of the layoffs. The result

---

[352] She enrolled at Louisiana State University, from which she graduated in 2012.
[353] 133 S. Ct. at 2420.
[354] *Id.*
[355] 758 F.3d 633 (5th Cir. 2014).
[356] 476 U.S. 267 (1986).

was that some white teachers were laid off even though they had more seniority than some of the black teachers who kept their jobs.

The Court rejected this as an acceptable means of affirmative action. The Court said that even if prior discrimination was proved, the layoff provision was not a constitutionally acceptable means of achieving even the compelling purpose of remedying prior discrimination. Justice Powell, writing for the plurality, said that "as a means of accomplishing purposes that otherwise may be legitimate, the Board's layoff plan is not sufficiently narrowly tailored. Other, less intrusive means of accomplishing similar purposes, such as the adoption of hiring goals, are available."[357]

Drawing Election Districts to Increase Minority Representation

Sometimes government will draw election districts so as to increase the likelihood that minority groups will be able to choose a representative.[358] This might be done by grouping African Americans or Latinos together in a single district where they are the majority. Between 1993 and 1996, the Supreme Court decided four cases on the constitutionality of using race in districting to help racial minorities:[359] *Shaw v. Reno*,[360] *Miller v. Johnson*,[361] *Shaw v. Hunt*,[362] and *Bush v. Vera*.[363] In these cases, the Court addressed three major issues.

First, in each case, the Supreme Court ruled that the use of race in drawing election districts must meet strict scrutiny. *Shaw v. Reno* held, and each subsequent case reaffirmed, that the use of race in drawing election districts is permissible only if the government can show that it is necessary to achieve a compelling purpose. Although this is consistent with recent Supreme Court cases mandating strict scrutiny for government affirmative action efforts, the dissent made a strong argument that affirmative action in voting is different from affirmative action in areas such as employment or education. In the latter areas, racial classifications benefiting minorities arguably disadvantage a white individual who is not hired or admitted

---

[357] *Id.* at 283-284.

[358] Another form of affirmative action in the voting context is limiting who can participate in particular elections. In *Rice v. Cayetano*, 528 U.S. 495 (2000), the Court considered the constitutionality of a Hawaii statute that limited voters selecting the Office of Hawaiian Affairs to those who were persons of Hawaiian or native Hawaiian descent. The Supreme Court invalidated this as violating the Fifteenth Amendment concluding that it was impermissible denial or abridgement of voting rights based on race.

[359] Also, in *United States v. Hays*, 515 U.S. 737 (1995), the Supreme Court held that only an individual who lives in the district where race allegedly was used in drawing election districts has standing to bring a challenge. This was reaffirmed in *Shaw v. Hunt*, 517 U.S. 899, 904 (1996). This is discussed more fully in §2.5.3.

[360] 509 U.S. 630 (1993).

[361] 515 U.S. 900 (1995).

[362] 517 U.S. 899 (1996).

[363] 517 U.S. 952 (1996).

because of the affirmative action program. But in voting, every person still gets to vote and every vote is counted equally.[364]

Moreover, there is a long history of government drawing district lines to keep racial and ethnic groups together. Justice Ginsburg, dissenting in *Miller v. Johnson*, observed: "To accommodate the reality of ethnic bonds, legislatures have long drawn voting districts along ethnic lines. Our Nation's cities are full of districts identified by their ethnic character—Chinese, Irish, Italian, Jewish, Polish, Russian, for example."[365]

Second, the Court indicated two ways in which it can be demonstrated that race was used in drawing election districts and thus strict scrutiny is to be applied. One is if a district has a "bizarre" shape that, in itself, makes clear that race was the basis for drawing the lines. *Shaw v. Reno* and *Shaw v. Hunt* involved an election district in North Carolina that had a quite unusual shape—it was very long and very narrow—and that had an African-American majority. The Supreme Court said that it was apparent from the shape of the district that race had been used in drawing the district lines to create a majority black district.[366]

Alternatively, if the use of race in districting cannot be inferred from the shape of the district, strict scrutiny is justified if it is proved that race was a "predominant" factor in drawing the lines. In *Miller v. Johnson*, the Court considered an election district in Georgia that also had been created to provide a majority black district. Justice Kennedy, writing for the Court, said that if it is not obvious from the shape of the district that race was used in drawing its lines, the judiciary should use strict scrutiny if it is demonstrated that race was a "predominant" factor in districting.[367]

Bush v. Vera, which involved congressional districts in Texas, reaffirmed this.[368] Justice O'Connor, writing for a plurality, stated: "Strict scrutiny does not apply merely because redistricting is performed with consciousness of race. Nor does it apply to all cases of intentional creation of majority-minority districts. . . . For strict scrutiny to apply, the plaintiffs must prove that other legitimate districting principles were 'subordinated' to race."[369] The plurality concluded that strict scrutiny was appropriate in evaluating the Texas districts because the evidence demonstrated that racial motivations had a qualitatively greater influence on the drawing of district lines than political motivations.[370]

---

[364] This is the point that Justice Souter emphasized in dissent in *Shaw v. Reno*, 509 U.S. at 681-682 (Souter, J., dissenting).

[365] 515 U.S. at 944-945 (Ginsburg, J., dissenting).

[366] 509 U.S. at 658. The Court reiterated this in *Shaw v. Hunt*, 517 U.S. at 906.

[367] 515 U.S. at 920.

[368] 517 U.S. 952 (1996).

[369] *Id.* at 958-959.

[370] In an opinion concurring in the judgment, Justice Thomas, joined by Justice Scalia, argued that strict scrutiny is appropriate whenever race is intentionally used in districting, even if it is not the predominant purpose. *Id.* at 999-1003 (Thomas, J., concurring in the judgment). Thus, although Justice O'Connor's plurality opinion was joined only by Chief Justice Rehnquist and Justice Kennedy, there is no doubt that the four dissenting Justices strongly preferred the plurality's approach over that of Justice Thomas.

Third, the Court considered what justifications are sufficient to meet strict scrutiny. For example, the Court held that §5 of the Voting Rights Act, which requires that the Justice Department approve changes in election systems in states where there has been a history of race discrimination with regard to voting, does not justify the use of race in districting.[371] The views of the Justice Department about the desirability of maximizing minority districts do not constitute a compelling interest sufficient to meet strict scrutiny.

The more difficult question is whether compliance with the 1982 Amendments to §2 of the Voting Rights Act is sufficient to meet strict scrutiny. Section 2 prohibits election systems, such as in districting, that have discriminatory effects against racial minorities. In *Shaw v. Hunt* and *Bush v. Vera*, the Court avoided the question of whether complying with this statutory provision is a compelling interest by finding that §2 would not have been violated by the failure to use race in districting in these cases.[372]

However, in *Bush*, Justice O'Connor wrote a separate opinion concurring in the judgment where she expressed the view that "compliance with the results test of §2 of the Voting Rights Act is a compelling state interest."[373] It is unclear whether on the current Court there is a majority who believe that race may be used in districting when it is necessary to achieve compliance with §2 of the Voting Rights Act.

Since these decisions, there has been one important clarification by the Court that allows greater use of race in the districting process. In *Easley v. Cromartie*, the Supreme Court considered the constitutionality of districts for congressional seats in North Carolina. A three-judge federal district court held that North Carolina's legislature had impermissibly used race as the "predominant factor" in drawing the 12th Congressional District's boundaries. The Supreme Court, in a 5-to-4 decision, reversed the district court and found that its fact-finding was "clearly erroneous."[374] Rarely does the Court reverse a trial court on that basis.

Justice Breyer, writing for the majority, drew a distinction between the use of race for political reasons as opposed to for the purpose of affirmative action. At the outset of the opinion, Justice Breyer explained: "The issue in this case is evidentiary. We must determine whether there is adequate support for the District Court's key findings, particularly the ultimate finding that the legislature's motive was predominantly racial, not political."[375] Justice Breyer emphasized that in this inquiry the burden of proof is on the plaintiff asserting the impermissible use of race and that courts must show deference to legislative choices in districting.

The Court was clear that the government may use race as a factor in districting if the goal is political, such as protecting a safe seat for an incumbent or creating a

---

[371] *See* Shaw v. Hunt, 517 U.S. at 912. In *Shelby County, Alabama v. Holder*, 133 S. Ct. 2612 (2013), the Court effectively invalidated §5 of the Voting Rights Act of 1965 by declaring unconstitutional §4(B) of the Act, which is the formula that determines the jurisdictions that need to get preclearance. *Shelby County* is discussed in Chapter 3.

[372] Shaw v. Hunt, 517 U.S. at 915; Bush v. Vera, 517 U.S. at 979.

[373] 517 U.S. 990 (O'Connor, J., concurring). This opinion is particularly unusual because Justice O'Connor also wrote the plurality opinion; in other words, she wrote both the plurality opinion and a separate concurring opinion.

[374] 532 U.S. 234, 237 (2001).

[375] *Id.* at 258.

district that has a majority of one political party.[376] Justice Breyer carefully reviewed the evidence relied on by the district court and found that it was consistent with the legislature using race to create a majority Democratic district. African Americans in North Carolina vote Democratic about 95 percent of the time, and thus creating a majority black district could be seen as serving the legislature's political goal of having a safely Democratic seat. Justice Breyer said that the facts support a political rationale equally as much as an affirmative action explanation for the districting.

After discussing the evidence, Justice Breyer concluded: "The basic question is whether the legislature drew District 12's boundaries because of race rather than because of political behavior (coupled with traditional, nonracial districting considerations). . . . And given the fact that the party attacking the legislature's decision bears the burden of proving that racial considerations are 'dominant and controlling,' given the 'demanding' nature of that burden of proof, and given the sensitivity, the 'extraordinary caution,' that district courts must show to avoid treading upon legislative prerogatives, the attacking party has not successfully shown that race, rather than politics, predominantly accounts for the result."[377]

The problem for litigation is that rarely will a case involve only racial or political considerations; these are not mutually exclusive goals. In all likelihood, a legislature choosing to create a majority African-American or Latino district did so both for political reasons and to increase the likelihood of electing minority representatives.

Justice Breyer, writing for the Court, offered guidance to lower courts hearing such cases. He said: "In a case such as this one where majority-minority districts (or the approximate equivalent) are at issue and where racial identification correlates highly with political affiliation, the party attacking the legislatively drawn boundaries must show at the least that the legislature could have achieved its legitimate political objectives in alternative ways that are comparably consistent with traditional districting principles. That party must also show that those districting alternatives would have brought about significantly greater racial balance."[378]

In other words, the Court clearly said that there is a strong presumption that districting is permissible, even if it is clear that race was a major factor. The challenger must demonstrate that race and not politics was the predominant consideration. This requires showing that the legislature's political goals could have been achieved without consideration of race. This will be a difficult burden to meet and one that thus allows much greater use of race in districting than before.

---

[376] Earlier, the Supreme Court ruled that political considerations may be the basis for districting, often called "gerrymandering," so long as there is not unconstitutional vote dilution. Davis v. Bandemer, 478 U.S. 109 (1986). In subsequent cases, *League of United Latino American Citizens v. Perry*, 548 U.S. 399 (2006), and *Vieth v. Jubelirer*, 541 U.S. 267 (2004), the Court, without a majority opinion, ruled that challenges to partisan gerrymandering were nonjusticiable political questions.

[377] 532 U.S. at 257.

[378] *Id.* at 258.

§9.4   GENDER CLASSIFICATIONS

There is a long history of discrimination against women in almost every aspect of society. Women were not accorded the right to vote until the Nineteenth Amendment was ratified in 1920. No woman ever has been elected president or vice president, and there have been only four women on the Supreme Court, all appointed since 1980. As of 2014, there are only 26 women who are CEOs of Fortune 500 companies, or 5.2 percent of all CEOS of these corporations.[1]

In examining gender discrimination under the Constitution, three issues are addressed. First, §9.4.1 examines the level of scrutiny used for gender discrimination. Second, §9.4.2 considers how gender discrimination can be proved. Finally, §9.4.3 focuses on gender classifications benefiting women.

§9.4.1   The Level of Scrutiny

It was not until 1971 that the Supreme Court first invalidated a gender classification.[2] This section begins by briefly reviewing the early cases approving gender discrimination and then considers the more recent cases holding that intermediate scrutiny is the appropriate test for evaluating gender classifications challenged under the equal protection clause. Finally, the section concludes by examining the arguments concerning whether strict scrutiny should be the standard for sex-based discrimination.

Early Cases Approving Gender Discrimination

The Supreme Court first addressed a gender discrimination issue in 1871 in *Bradwell v. Illinois*, which upheld an Illinois law that prohibited women from being licensed to practice law.[3] A very short majority opinion ruled against Myra Bradwell without considering gender discrimination. Justice Miller, writing for the Court, rejected the argument that practicing law was a "privilege" of citizenship protected under the privileges or immunities clause of the Fourteenth Amendment.[4]

However, Justice Bradley, in a concurring opinion, directly addressed the claim of sex discrimination and opined that the state was justified in excluding women from the practice of law: "The paramount destiny and mission of women are to fulfill the noble and benign offices of wife and mother. This is the law of the creator. And the rules of civil society must be adapted in the general constitutional

---

§9.4 [1] *See* http://www.catalyst.org/knowledge/women-ceos-fortune-1000 (last visited on Dec. 24, 2014); *see also* Eva Patterson, et al., The Id, the Ego, and Equal Protection in the Twenty-First Century, 40 Conn. L. Rev. 1175, 1189 (2008).

[2] Reed v. Reed, 404 U.S. 71 (1971) (giving preference to men over women in administering estates), discussed below.

[3] 83 U.S. (16 Wall.) 130 (1872).

[4] *Id.* at 134-137.

of things, and cannot be based on exceptional cases."[5] He concluded that "in view of the peculiar characteristics, destiny, and mission of woman, it is within the province of the Legislature to ordain what offices, positions and callings shall be filled and discharged by men."[6]

The Court reaffirmed *Bradwell* in 1894, in *In re Lockwood.*[7] The Supreme Court ruled that Virginia could exclude a woman from practicing law even though she had been admitted to the bars of the Supreme Court and the District of Columbia.

In between *Bradwell* and *Lockwood,* the Supreme Court in *Minor v. Happersett,* in 1874, upheld the constitutionality of excluding women from voting.[8] Although recognizing that women are citizens under the Constitution, the Court said that denying women the right to vote is permissible because voting is not a "privilege or immunity" of United States citizenship. The Nineteenth Amendment overruled this decision and declared that "[t]he right of citizens of the United States to vote shall not be denied or abridged by the United States or by any State on account of sex."[9]

In several cases during the first third of the twentieth century, the Supreme Court upheld laws that expressly discriminated based on gender. During this period of constitutional history, often referred to as the *Lochner* era, the Supreme Court aggressively protected freedom of contract and invalidated many regulatory laws for violating that right.[10] However, the Court was much more willing to uphold such laws if women were being regulated. For example, although *Lochner v. New York* declared unconstitutional a maximum hours law for bakers,[11] three years later, in *Mutter v. Oregon,* the Supreme Court upheld a maximum hours law for women employed in factories.[12] The Court in *Mutter* said: "That women's physical structure and the performance of maternal functions place her at a disadvantage in the struggle for subsistence is obvious. . . . Differentiated by these matters from the other sex, she is properly placed in a class by herself, and legislation designed for her protection may be sustained, even when like legislation is not necessary for men and could not be sustained."[13]

Following this rationale, the Court upheld a state law that prohibited women from being employed in restaurants between 10:00 P.M. and 6:00 A.M.[14] However, the Court initially rejected a state law that created a minimum wage for women. The Court said that "while the physical differences must be recognized in appropriate cases . . . women of mature age . . . may [not] be subjected to restrictions upon their liberty of contract which could not lawfully be imposed in the case

---

[5] *Id.* at 141 (Bradley, J., concurring).

[6] *Id.* at 142.

[7] 154 U.S. 116 (1894).

[8] 88 U.S. (21 Wall.) 162 (1874).

[9] For an excellent discussion of the importance of the Nineteenth Amendment for gender equality, *see* Riva B. Siegel, She the People: The Nineteenth Amendment, Sex Equality, Federalism, and the Family, 115 Harv. L. Rev. 947 (2002).

[10] These cases are discussed in §8.3.2.

[11] 198 U.S. 45 (1905), discussed in §8.3.2.

[12] 208 U.S. 412 (1908).

[13] *Id.* at 421-422.

[14] Radice v. New York, 264 U.S. 292 (1924).

of men under similar circumstances."[15] The Court later overruled this holding and in *West Coast Hotel v. Parrish*—a key case signaling the end of the *Lochner* era—upheld a minimum wage law for women, declaring: "What can be closer to the public interest than the health of women and their protection from unscrupulous and overreaching employers? And if the protection of women is a legitimate end of the exercise of state power, how can it be said that the requirement of the payment of a minimum wage fairly fixed to meet the very necessities of existence is not an admissible means to that end?"[16]

Even after World War II and the entrance of many women into the labor market, the Supreme Court continued to allow gender discrimination based on stereotypes. In *Goesaert v. Cleary*, the Supreme Court upheld a Michigan law that prevented the licensing of women as bartenders unless the woman was the wife or daughter of a male who owned the bar where she would work.[17] Justice Frankfurter declared that "Michigan could, beyond question, forbid all women from working behind a bar."[18] He said that "the vast changes in the social and legal position of women . . . [do] not preclude States from drawing a sharp line between the sexes, certainly in matters such as the regulation of the liquor traffic."[19] The Court said that the law's discrimination among women was permissible because "the line they have drawn is not without a basis in reason";[20] "the oversight assured through ownership of bar by a barmaid's husband or father minimizes hazards that may confront a barmaid without such protecting oversight."[21]

In 1961, in *Hoyt v. Florida*, the Court upheld a state law that made men eligible for jury service unless they requested and were granted an exception, whereas women were automatically exempted unless they waived it and expressed a desire to be included on the jury rolls.[22] The Court applied the rational basis test and upheld the law. The Court said that "[d]espite the enlightened emancipation of women from the restrictions and protections of bygone years, and their entry into many parts of community life formerly considered to be reserved to men, woman is still regarded as the center of the home and family life."[23] Thus, a state could exempt women "from the civic duty of jury service unless she herself determines that such service is consistent with her own special responsibilities."[24]

---

[15] Adkins v. Children's Hosp., 261 U.S. 525, 553 (1923).

[16] 300 U.S. 379, 398 (1937).

[17] 335 U.S. 464 (1948).

[18] *Id.* at 465.

[19] *Id.* at 465-466.

[20] *Id.* at 467.

[21] *Id.* at 466.

[22] 368 U.S. 57 (1961).

[23] *Id.* at 61-62.

[24] *Id.* at 62. *Hoyt* was later overruled in *Taylor v. Louisiana*, 419 U.S. 522 (1975). *See also* J.E.B. v. Alabama ex rel. T.B., 511 U.S. 127 (1994) (gender-based use of peremptory challenges denies equal protection).

The Emergence of Intermediate Scrutiny

In 1971, in *Reed v. Reed*, the Supreme Court for the first time invalidated a gender classification, but the Court professed to apply only rational basis review.[25] An Idaho law specified the hierarchy of persons to be appointed as administrators of an estate when a person died intestate. Specifically, the law created 11 categories in rank order—parents were first, children second, and so on—and said that if there were two competing applicants in the same category, the male was to be preferred over the female.

The Court articulated the standard of review in traditional rational basis terms. It said: "A classification must be reasonable, not arbitrary and must rest upon some ground of difference having a fair and substantial relation to that object of the legislation, so that all persons similarly circumstanced shall be treated alike."[26] The Supreme Court said that the issue was whether gender had a rational relationship to the ability to administer the estate. Obviously, gender is irrelevant, and the Court held the law unconstitutional, concluding: "To give a mandatory preference to members of either sex over members of the other, merely to accomplish the elimination of hearings on the merits, is to make the very kind of arbitrary legislative choice forbidden by the Equal Protection Clause of the Fourteenth Amendment; and whatever may be said as to the positive values of avoiding intra-family controversy, the choice in this context may not lawfully be mandated solely on the basis of sex."[27]

Although the Court purported to be using just the rational basis test and did not express the view that gender was a suspect classification, its reasoning was not characteristic of rational basis review. If the law had said, "when there are two people in a category who are equally qualified, one will be chosen by random selection," that surely would have been permissible under rational basis review. Therefore, the use of gender had to have been regarded by the Court as worse than random selection and an inappropriate ground to use to simplify administration. In other words, the Court implicitly had to regard gender as an impermissible basis for government decisions.

In *Frontiero v. Richardson*, four Justices took the position that gender classifications should be subjected to strict scrutiny.[28] A federal law allowed a man to automatically claim his wife as a dependent and thereby receive a greater allowance for quarters and for medical benefits. A woman, however, only could gain these benefits if she could prove that her spouse was dependent on her for over half of his support.

Justice Brennan—writing for a plurality that included Justices Douglas, White, and Marshall—said that "classifications based on sex, like classifications based upon race, alienage or national origin, are inherently suspect, and must therefore

---

[25] 404 U.S. 71 (1971) (citations omitted).
[26] *Id.* at 76.
[27] *Id.* at 76-77.
[28] 411 U.S. 677 (1973).

be subjected to strict judicial scrutiny."[29] Justice Brennan explained: "There can be no doubt that our Nation has had a long and unfortunate history of sex discrimination. Traditionally such discrimination was rationalized by an attitude of 'romantic paternalism' which, in practical effect, put women, not on a pedestal, but in a cage."[30] Justice Brennan argued that the characteristics that justify strict scrutiny of racial classifications also are present as to gender discrimination: "[W]omen still face pervasive, although at times more subtle, discrimination in our educational institutions, in the job market, and perhaps most conspicuously, in the political arena. Moreover, since sex, like race and national origin, is an immutable characteristic determined solely by birth, the imposition of special disabilities upon members of a particular sex would seem to violate the basic concept of our system that legal burdens should bear some relationship to individual responsibility."[31]

Justice Stewart concurred in the judgment and said that he would find the law unconstitutional based on the reasoning used in *Reed v. Reed*. According to journalists Bob Woodward and Scott Armstrong, Stewart believed that gender classifications should be subjected to strict scrutiny, but he was sure that the Equal Rights Amendment would be ratified and thought that the Court should wait until then to apply strict scrutiny to gender discrimination.[32] Justices Powell, Burger, and Blackmun concurred in the judgment and wrote separately to disagree with the application of strict scrutiny to gender. They explicitly noted that the Court should wait and see whether the Equal Rights Amendment was ratified. Justice Rehnquist was the sole dissenter. The Equal Rights Amendment, which in all likelihood would have meant strict scrutiny for gender classifications,[33] fell 3 states short of the 38 needed for ratification.

Because there was not a majority supporting strict scrutiny in *Frontiero*, the level of scrutiny for gender classifications remained uncertain. In the two years after *Frontiero*, the Court decided several gender cases without articulating a level of scrutiny; some of the cases sustained gender classifications while other decisions invalidated them. For example, in *Kahn v. Shevin*, a year after *Frontiero*, the Supreme Court upheld a state law that provided a property tax exemption for widows but not for widowers.[34] The Court did not articulate a level of scrutiny, but ruled that the law was constitutional because "[w]hether from overt discrimination or from the socialization process of a male-dominated culture, the job market is inhospitable to the woman seeking any but the lowest paid job."[35]

---

[29] *Id.* at 688 (plurality opinion).

[30] *Id.* at 684 (citations omitted).

[31] *Id.* at 686.

[32] Bob Woodward & Scott Armstrong, The Brethren 302 (1979).

[33] Barbara A. Brown et al., The Equal Rights Amendment: A Constitutional Basis for Equal Rights for Women, 80 Yale L.J. 871 (1971).

[34] 416 U.S. 351 (1974).

[35] *Id.* at 353 (1974). Other cases upholding gender classifications included *Geduldig v. Aiello*, 417 U.S. 484 (1974), discussed below in §9.4.2, which held that it was not gender discrimination for a state to refuse to pay for pregnancy-related disabilities; and *Schlesinger v. Ballard*, 419 U.S. 498 (1975), discussed below in §9.4.3, which held that it was permissible for the navy to require a man to leave the service if he had not been promoted within 9 years, but a woman could go 13 years without a promotion before she had to leave the navy.

In contrast, in *Taylor v. Louisiana*,[36] the Court effectively overruled *Hoyt v. Florida* and held that excluding women from jury service violated the defendant's right to a fair trial with an impartial jury drawn from a cross section of the community. The Court emphasized the Sixth Amendment and said that the "right to a proper jury cannot be overcome on merely rational grounds."[37]

In *Stanton v. Stanton*, the Court declared unconstitutional a Utah law that required that parents support their female children until age 18, but that male children be supported until age 21.[38] The Court said that the statute was based on "old notions" about social roles; "[no] longer is the female destined solely for the home and the rearing of the family, and only the male for the market place and the world of ideas. Women's activities and responsibilities are increasing and expanding."[39] Again, the Court decided without a holding as to the level of scrutiny. In fact, the Court said that the law was unconstitutional "under any test, compelling state interest, or rational basis, or something in between."[40]

Finally, in 1976, in *Craig v. Boren*, the Supreme Court agreed upon intermediate scrutiny as the appropriate level of review for gender classifications and declared: "To withstand constitutional challenge, previous cases establish that classifications by gender must serve important governmental objectives and must be substantially related to those objectives."[41] The Court declared unconstitutional an Oklahoma law that allowed women to buy low alcohol, 3.2 percent beer, at age 18, but men could not buy such beer until age 21. Although traffic safety is undoubtedly an "important" government interest, the Court concluded that gender discrimination was not substantially related to that objective. The Court observed that "the statistics broadly establish that .18 percent of females and 2 percent of males [between ages 18 and 21] were arrested [for drunk driving]. While such a disparity is not trivial in a statistical sense, it hardly can form the basis for employment of a gender line as a classifying device. . . . [A] correlation of 2 percent must be considered an unduly tenuous 'fit.' Indeed, prior cases have consistently rejected the use of sex as a decisionmaking factor even though the statutes in question certainly rested on far more predictive empirical relationships than this."[42]

Since *Craig v. Boren*, the Supreme Court, on many occasions, has reaffirmed and applied intermediate scrutiny for gender classifications.[43] As described below,

---

[36]   419 U.S. 522 (1975).

[37]   *Id.* at 534. In *J.E.B. v. Ala. ex rel. T.B.*, 511 U.S. 127, 135 n.5 (1994), the Supreme Court held that gender discrimination in the exercise of peremptory challenges denies equal protection and observed that *Taylor v. Louisiana* had overruled *Hoyt v. Florida*.

[38]   421 U.S. 7 (1975).

[39]   *Id.* at 14-15. *See also Weinberger v. Wiesenfeld*, 420 U.S. 636 (1975), discussed below in §9.5.3, declaring unconstitutional a provision of the Social Security Act that allowed a woman whose husband dies to receive benefits based on his earnings, but did not allow a man whose wife dies to receive benefits based on her earnings.

[40]   *Id.* at 17.

[41]   429 U.S. 190, 197 (1976).

[42]   *Id.* at 201-202.

[43]   *See, e.g.*, United States v. Virginia, 518 U.S. 515 (1996); Califano v. Westcott, 443 U.S. 76, 89 (1980); Caban v. Mohammed, 441 U.S. 380, 388 (1979); Orr v. Orr, 440 U.S. 268, 279 (1979); Califano v. Webster, 430 U.S. 313, 316-317 (1977).

in §9.5.3, the Court has held that intermediate scrutiny is to be used for both gender classifications discriminating against women and those discriminating against men. For example, in *Kirchberg v. Feenstra*, the Court expressly used intermediate scrutiny to invalidate a Louisiana law that gave a husband, as "head and master" of property jointly owned with his wife, the unilateral right to dispose of such property without his spouse's consent.[44] In *Mississippi University for Women v. Hogan*, the Court applied intermediate scrutiny to declare unconstitutional a state policy of operating a nursing school that was available only to women.[45]

In *United States v. Virginia*, the Supreme Court declared unconstitutional the exclusion of women by the Virginia Military Institute (VMI).[46] Virginia, in response to an order from the United States Court of Appeals for the Fourth Circuit, had created the Virginia Women's Institute for Leadership at Mary Baldwin College. The Court found this insufficient to excuse VMI's gender discrimination; women still were denied an opportunity available only for men.

Justice Ginsburg applied intermediate scrutiny and said that "[p]arties who seek to defend gender-based government action must demonstrate an exceedingly persuasive justification for that action. . . . The burden of justification is demanding and it rests entirely on the State." Justice Ginsburg said that the justification "must not rely on overbroad generalizations about the different talents, capacities, or preferences of males and females."[47] VMI's exclusion of women was found unconstitutional because it was based entirely on gender stereotypes. Indeed, the Court emphasized that successful gender integration of the federal military academies belied any claims of a need to exclude women from VMI.

Although it is clearly established that intermediate scrutiny is the test for gender classifications, there have been occasional cases since *Craig v. Boren* where gender classifications have been upheld without the Court expressly using intermediate scrutiny or mentioning a level of scrutiny. *Rostker v. Goldberg*[48] and *Michael M. v. Superior Court*[49] —both discussed below in §9.5.3—are examples of this. In *Rostker*, the Supreme Court upheld a federal law requiring men, but not women, to register for the draft. In *Michael M.*, the Court upheld a state's statutory rape law that punished men for having sexual intercourse with a woman under age 18, but did not punish a woman for having sex with a man under age 18. In neither case did the Court articulate a level of scrutiny, and in both the Court showed great deference to the government.

---

[44] 450 U.S. 455, 459 (1981).
[45] 458 U.S. 718, 724 (1982).
[46] 518 U.S. 515 (1996).
[47] *Id.*
[48] 453 U.S. 57 (1981).
[49] 450 U.S. 464 (1981).

What Should Be the Level of Scrutiny?

Many of the factors that explain the use of strict scrutiny for racial classifi-cations also apply to gender discrimination.[50] For example, there is a long his-tory of discrimination against women in virtually every aspect of society. Ruth Bader Ginsburg, writing as a law professor, observed: "When the post–Civil War amendments were added to the Constitution, women were not accorded the vote. [Married] women in many states could not contract, hold property, litigate on their own behalf, or even control their own earnings. The fourteenth amendment left all that untouched."[51] As a result, gender classifications, like race and national origin classifications, are usually based on stereotypes rather than important gov-ernment interests.[52] Many purported biological differences that are invoked to justify legal distinctions are in reality just stereotypes, such as in the cases reviewed above where women were kept from being licensed as bartenders or from being automatically considered for jury service.

Also, as Justice Brennan observed in arguing for strict scrutiny in *Frontiero*, sex, like race and national origin, is an immutable characteristic.[53] Strict scrutiny is warranted because of the need for a strong presumption against laws that dis-criminate against people based on traits that were not chosen and that cannot be changed. Gender, like race, is an immediately visible characteristic. Moreover, women, like racial minorities, tend to be significantly underrepresented in the political process.

Those who argue for intermediate rather than strict scrutiny for gender classi-fications make several arguments. In part, the argument is historical: The framers of the Fourteenth Amendment meant only to outlaw race discrimination.[54] Also, it is argued that biological differences between men and women make it more likely that gender classifications will be justified, and thus less than strict scrutiny is appropriate to increase the chances that desirable laws will be upheld.

Also, it is claimed that women are a political majority who are not isolated from men and thus cannot be considered a discrete and insular minority. Professor Ely remarked: "I may be wrong in supposing that because women now are in a posi-tion to protect themselves they will, that we are thus unlikely to see in the future the sort of official discrimination that has marked our past. But if women don't protect themselves from sex discrimination in the future, it will be because for one

---

[50] *See* Richard A. Wasserstrom, Racism, Sexism, and Preferential Treatment: An Approach to the Topics, 24 UCLA L. Rev. 581 (1977).

[51] Ruth Bader Ginsburg, Sexual Equality Under the Fourteenth and Equal Rights Amendments, 1979 Wash. U. L.Q. 161, 162-163.

[52] *See* Kenneth Karst, Foreword: Equal Citizenship Under the Fourteenth Amendment, 91 Harv. L. Rev. 1, 23 (1977).

[53] 411 U.S. at 686.

[54] *See, e.g.*, Strauder v. West Virginia, 100 U.S. 303, 310 (1879); Slaughter-House Cases, 83 U.S. (16 Wall.) 36, 81 (1872) (declaring that the purpose of the equal protection clause was only to limit racial discrimination).

reason or another, substantive disagreement or more likely the assignment of a low priority to the issue, they don't choose to."[55]

In more recent years, the debate over whether strict or intermediate scrutiny should be used for gender classifications has been complicated by the affirmative action debate. Many of those who previously favored strict scrutiny for gender classifications now are concerned that such review would make it much more difficult for the government to engage in affirmative action to benefit women.[56] Because intermediate scrutiny is generally successful in challenging invidious discrimination against women, there is concern that the primary effect of strict scrutiny might be to limit programs that help women. There, of course, are still many advocates of strict scrutiny for gender and many who continue to believe that intermediate scrutiny is the best approach.

§9.4.2   Proving the Existence of a Gender Classification

Two Basic Ways of Proving a Gender Classification

There are two major ways of proving a gender classification; they are identical to the two methods of demonstrating a racial classification discussed in §9.3.4. First, the gender classification can exist on the face of the law; that is, the law in its very terms draws a distinction among people based on gender. All of the cases discussed thus far concerning gender discrimination are of this type. For example, facial gender classifications mentioned above include the Oklahoma law that women could buy low-alcohol beer at age 18, but men not until 21;[57] the Louisiana law that men, not women, could dispose of property without consent of their spouse;[58] and the Virginia policy that excluded women from attending the Virginia Military Institute.[59]

Second, if a law is facially gender neutral, proving a gender classification requires demonstrating that there is both a discriminatory impact to the law and a discriminatory purpose behind it. In *Personnel Administrator of Massachusetts v. Feeney*, the Supreme Court upheld a state law that gave a preference in hiring to veterans even though it had a substantial discriminatory impact against women.[60] Helen Feeney repeatedly took civil service examinations for particular positions and received among the highest scores in the state but was placed below lists of veterans with lower scores. At the time the litigation was commenced, "over 98 percent of the veterans in Massachusetts were male; only 1.8 percent were female. And over one-quarter of the Massachusetts population were veterans."[61]

---

[55] John Hart Ely, Democracy and Distrust 169 (1980).

[56] *See, e.g.*, Associated Gen. Contractors of Cal. v. San Francisco, 813 F.2d 922 (9th Cir. 1986) (upholding affirmative action program for women as meeting intermediate scrutiny, but declaring unconstitutional affirmative action program based on race as failing strict scrutiny).

[57] Craig v. Boren, 429 U.S. 190 (1976).

[58] Kirchberg v. Feenstra, 450 U.S. 455 (1981).

[59] United States v. Virginia, 518 U.S. 515 (1996).

[60] 442 U.S. 256 (1979).

[61] *Id.* at 270.

Nonetheless, the Supreme Court rejected the claim of gender discrimination. The Court said that the law providing a preference for veterans was gender neutral and that discriminatory impact is not sufficient to prove the existence of sex-based classification; there also must be proof of a discriminatory purpose. The Court concluded that "nothing in the record demonstrates that this preference for veterans was originally devised or subsequently re-enacted because it would accomplish the collateral goal of keeping women in a stereotypic and predefined place in the Massachusetts civil service."[62] The ways of proving a discriminatory purpose based on gender are identical to the ways of proving a discriminatory racial purpose, described above in §9.3.4.

When Is It "Discrimination"?

In *Geduldig v. Aiello*,[63] the Supreme Court held that it was not a denial of equal protection for a state's disability insurance system to exclude pregnancy-related disabilities, but include disabilities affecting only men.[64] California's disability law provided payments for disabilities lasting more than 8 days and less than 26 weeks, but denied any coverage for disabilities caused by pregnancy. The Supreme Court held that this was not a gender classification warranting more than rational basis review. The Court explained: "There is no risk from which men are protected and women are not. Likewise, there is no risk from which women are protected and men are not."[65]

In a footnote, the Court elaborated: "The lack of identity between the excluded disability and gender as such under this insurance program becomes clear upon the most cursory analysis. The program divides potential recipients into two groups: pregnant women and nonpregnant persons. While the first

---

[62] *Id.* at 279. The Court said that it was not sufficient for the plaintiffs to prove that Massachusetts adopted the preference knowing that it would have a discriminatory impact. The Court said: "'Discriminatory purpose,' however, implies more than intent as volition or intent as awareness of consequences. It implies that the decisionmaker, in this case a state legislature, selected or reaffirmed a particular course of action at least in part 'because of,' not merely 'in spite of,' its adverse effects upon an identifiable group." *Id.* at 279.

[63] 417 U.S. 484 (1974).

[64] In the same year as *Geduldig*, the Supreme Court declared unconstitutional a school board regulation that required that pregnant women take maternity leave at a fixed point in their pregnancies. Cleveland Bd. of Educ. v. LaFleur, 414 U.S. 632 (1974). The Court declared this unconstitutional as creating an impermissible "irrebuttable presumption" that women could not perform adequately after that point of their pregnancy. Except for a few cases from this time period, the Court has not applied the irrebuttable presumptions doctrine. *See also* Stanley v. Illinois, 405 U.S. 645 (1972) (using the irrebuttable presumptions doctrine to invalidate a state law that automatically placed a child for adoption if an unwed mother did not want custody). The problem with the irrebuttable presumption doctrine is that laws constantly create conclusive presumptions. A law that requires that a person be age 16 to get a driver's license creates an irrebuttable presumption as does the statute requiring a license in order to practice law. The existence of an irrebuttable presumption is thus not enough to find a law unconstitutional; there also must be reasons to distrust the law because it discriminates based on a suspect classification or impinges a fundamental right.

[65] *Id.* at 496-497.

group is exclusively female, the second includes members of both sexes."[66] The Court said that the exclusion of pregnancy met rational basis review because the state has a legitimate interest in maintaining the fiscal integrity of its program and making choices in allocating its funds.[67]

The Court's reasoning can be criticized because it appears that it is saying that pregnancy is not a sex-based characteristic.[68] The entire burden from the exclusion of pregnancy is borne by women, making the discriminatory nature of the exclusion obvious. California's exclusion of pregnancy from coverage would impact not only currently pregnant persons, but also all capable of becoming pregnant; women might choose to delay or forgo a pregnancy because of the inability to receive payments under the disability program. Thus, the law distinguished between persons capable of becoming pregnant and those not capable of becoming pregnant. It is hard to imagine a clearer sex-based distinction.

Congress, by statute, effectively overruled *Geduldig* when it enacted the Pregnancy Discrimination Act, which defined sex discrimination to include pregnancy discrimination and prohibits discrimination on that basis.[69] Although *Geduldig*'s impact has been negated in the area of pregnancy by the Pregnancy Discrimination Act, its reasoning is still applied by the Court in other contexts. In *Bray v. Alexandria Women's Health Clinic,* the Supreme Court considered whether those blocking access to abortion clinics were engaged in a form of gender discrimination in violation of federal civil rights statutes.[70] The Supreme Court, in an opinion by Justice Scalia, expressly invoked *Geduldig* in rejecting the claim that there was a gender-based animus behind the protests.[71] Scalia said that there were two categories of individuals: persons protesting and persons receiving abortions. The Court said that there was not gender discrimination because women were both in the former category, protestors, and in the latter category, those seeking abortion.

§9.4.3 Gender Classifications Benefiting Women

Interestingly, the majority of Supreme Court cases concerning gender discrimination have involved laws that benefit women and disadvantage men.[72] Three prin-

---

[66] *Id.* at 497 n.20.

[67] In a companion case, General Electric Co. v. Gilbert, 429 U.S. 125 (1976), the Supreme Court held that Title VII is not violated when a company excludes pregnancy from its disability plans.

[68] There is an excellent literature on the meaning of equality in the context of pregnancy and whether equality requires that women be treated the same as men or whether equality requires that the law account for the differences between men and women. *See, e.g.*, Christine Littleton, Reconstructing Sexual Equality, 75 Cal. L. Rev. 1279 (1987); Wendy Williams, Equalities Riddle: Pregnancy and the Equal Treatment/Special Treatment Debate, 13 N.Y.U. Rev. L. & Soc. Change 325 (1985); Sylvia Law, Rethinking Sex and the Constitution, 132 U. Pa. L. Rev. 955 (1984).

[69] 42 U.S.C. §2000e(k).

[70] 506 U.S. 263 (1993).

[71] *Id.* at 269-270.

[72] There obviously also have been cases where women are discriminated against. *See, e.g.*, United States v. Virginia, 518 U.S. 515 (1996) (holding unconstitutional the exclusion of women from the

ciples emerge from these decisions. First, gender classifications benefiting women based on role stereotypes generally will not be allowed. Second, gender classifications benefiting women designed to remedy past discrimination and differences in opportunity generally are permitted. Third, gender classifications benefiting women can be based on biological differences between men and women.

Gender Classifications Based on Role Stereotypes

The Supreme Court frequently has invalidated laws that benefit women and disadvantage men when the Court perceives the law as being based on stereotypical assumptions about gender roles. Many of these laws were based on the stereotype of women being economically dependent on their husbands, but men being economically independent of their wives. For example, in *Orr v. Orr*, the Court invalidated an Alabama law that allowed women, but not men, to receive alimony in case of divorce.[73] The Court explained that "[u]nder the statute, individualized hearings at which the parties' relative financial circumstances are considered *already* occur. . . . Needy males could be helped along with needy females with little if any additional burden."[74]

Similarly, the Supreme Court declared unconstitutional many laws that automatically allowed women economic benefits, such as when their husbands died, but permitted men the same benefits only if they proved dependence on their wives' income. In *Weinberger v. Wiesenfeld*, the Supreme Court deemed unconstitutional a provision of the Social Security Act that allowed a widowed mother, but not a widowed father, to receive benefits based on the earnings of the deceased spouse.[75] The Court said that the law was based on the stereotype "that male workers' earnings are vital to the support of their families, while the earnings of female wage earners do not significantly contribute to their families' support."[76]

The Court applied *Weinberger* in *Califano v. Goldfarb* to hold unconstitutional a provision in the Federal Old-Age, Survivors and Disability Insurance Benefits program whereby a woman automatically would receive benefits based on the earnings of her husband, but a man would receive such benefits only if he could prove that he received at least half of his support from his wife.[77] The Court declared the law unconstitutional because it was based, at least in part, on a "presumption that wives are usually dependent."[78] The Court said that "such assumptions do not

---

Virginia Military Institute); Kirchberg v. Feenstra, 450 U.S. 455 (1981) (declaring unconstitutional a law that allows men, but not women, to dispose of property without their spouse's consent); Dothard v. Rawlinson, 433 U.S. 321 (1977) (upholding law excluding women from "contact positions" in all-male prisons).

[73] 440 U.S. 268 (1979).
[74] *Id.* at 281.
[75] 420 U.S. 636 (1975).
[76] *Id.* at 643.
[77] 430 U.S. 199 (1977).
[78] *Id.* at 217.

suffice to justify a gender-based discrimination in the distribution of employment-related benefits."[79]

In *Wengler v. Druggists Mutual Insurance Company*, the Court applied the same principle to rule unconstitutional a state law that automatically allowed widows benefits, but only allowed widowers benefits if they proved that they were dependent on their wives' income or were physically incapacitated.[80] In all of these cases — *Orr, Weinberger, Goldfarb*, and *Wengler* — the Court rejected laws that benefited women because they were based on the stereotype of economically dependent women and economically independent men.

Other stereotypes also have been rejected as a sufficient basis for gender classifications benefiting women. Some laws are based on stereotypes about women's role in the family and raising children as compared with men. For example, in *Caban v. Mohammed*, the Supreme Court invalidated a state statute that required the consent of the mother, but not the consent of the father, before a child born out of wedlock was placed for adoption.[81] The Court expressly rejected the claim that the statute was warranted by "a fundamental difference between maternal and paternal relations. [Such relations are not] invariably different in importance. . . . The present case demonstrates that an unwed father may have a relationship with his children fully comparable to that of a mother."[82]

But in other cases, the Court has recognized a difference between mothers and fathers of nonmarital children. In *Parham v. Hughes*, the Court upheld a state law that permitted the mother, but not the father, to sue for the wrongful death of a nonmarital child.[83] The Court explained that the distinction was not between men and women because men also could sue for wrongful death by establishing paternity under the state's procedures. The Court said that the law drew a distinction among men between those who had established paternity, and could sue, and those who had not.

Similarly, in *Lehr v. Robertson*, the Supreme Court upheld a state law that allowed a child to be adopted without notice to the father if the father had not lived with the mother and child or registered his intent to claim paternity with a "putative father's registry" maintained by the state.[84] Again, in *Lehr*, as in *Parham*, the Court saw the distinction as being among fathers: those who had taken legal steps to establish paternity as opposed to those who had not. This is distinguishable from *Caban* where the only distinction was between men and women.

Sometimes the stereotype is about what occupations are primarily for women and which are for men. In *Mississippi University for Women v. Hogan*, the Court declared unconstitutional a state policy of operating a nursing school that excluded men.[85] Justice O'Connor, writing for the Court, said that the gender

---

[79] *Id.*
[80] 446 U.S. 142 (1980).
[81] 441 U.S. 380 (1979).
[82] *Id.* at 388-389.
[83] 441 U.S. 347 (1979).
[84] 463 U.S. 248 (1983).
[85] 458 U.S. 718 (1982).

classification was not designed to remedy past discrimination, but based on an occupational stereotype: "Rather than compensate for discriminatory barriers faced by women, MUW's policy tends to perpetuate the stereotyped view of nursing as an exclusively woman's job. By assuring that Mississippi allots more openings to its state-supported nursing schools to women than it does to men, MUW's admissions policy lends credibility to the old view that women, not men, should be nurses, and makes the assumption that nursing is a field for women a self-fulfilling prophecy."[86]

Thus, in all of these cases the Supreme Court invalidated laws benefiting women because they were based on stereotypes about women and their roles in the family and the economy. Yet in some cases the Court has upheld laws benefiting women even though they seem to be based on stereotypes. In *Michael M. v. Superior Court*, the Supreme Court upheld California's statutory rape law that defined statutory rape as "an act of sexual intercourse accomplished with a female not the wife of the perpetrator, where the female is under the age of 18 years."[87] The case involved a 17-year-old boy who was convicted under the law for having sex with a 16-year-old girl. The girl was not prosecuted because the statute "makes men alone criminally liable for the act of sexual intercourse."[88]

The gender-based law was adopted because of sexual stereotypes. Justice Brennan, in a dissenting opinion, reviewed the historical background of the law and said that it "was initially enacted on the premise that young women, in contrast to young men, were to be deemed legally incapable of consenting to an act of sexual intercourse. Because their chastity was considered particularly precious, those young women were felt to be uniquely in need of the State's protections."[89]

The Court, however, upheld the gender-based statutory rape law. Justice Rehnquist, writing for the plurality, said that the state could attack the problem of teenage pregnancy and sexual activity by regulating and punishing men, but not women. Justice Rehnquist explained: "Because virtually all of the significant harmful and inescapably identifiable consequences of teenage pregnancy fall on the young female, a legislature acts well within its authority when it elects to punish only the participant who, by nature, suffers few of the consequences of his conduct. It is hardly unreasonable for a legislature acting to protect minor females to exclude them from punishment. Moreover, the risk of pregnancy itself constitutes a substantial deterrence to young females. No similar natural sanctions deter males."[90] The Court concluded that a gender neutral law was less likely to be effective because girls would be less likely to file complaints or be witnesses if they, too, faced potential criminal liability.[91]

In analyzing *Michael M.*, there is no doubt that preventing teenage pregnancy is an important government interest; the issue is whether a gender-based law is

[86] *Id.* at 729-730.
[87] 450 U.S. 464, 466 (1981).
[88] *Id.* at 466.
[89] *Id.* at 494-495 (Brennan, J., dissenting).
[90] *Id.* at 473.
[91] *Id.* at 473-474.

substantially related to that goal.[92] Justice Stevens, in dissent, argued that "the fact that a female confronts greater risk of harm than a male is a reason for applying the prohibition to her, not a reason for granting her a license to use her own judgment on whether or not to assume the risk. . . . Would a rational parent making rules for the conduct of twin children simultaneously forbid the son and authorize the daughter to engage in conduct that is especially harmful to the daughter?"[93]

Another case, decided the same year, where the Court accepted stereotypes as the basis for a gender classification benefiting women was *Rostker v. Goldberg*, which upheld male-only draft registration.[94] The Military Selective Service Act requires every male between the ages of 18 and 26 to register for possible conscription. The Court expressed the need for "healthy deference to legislative and executive judgments in the area of military affairs."[95]

The Court premised its holding on the fact that women, unlike men, are not eligible for combat and that Congress and the president had evidenced an intent to retain that policy in the future.[96] The Court said that the exclusion of women from combat justifies Congress's decision to have only men register for possible conscription.[97] Justice Rehnquist, writing for the Court, recognized that women could serve in noncombat roles, but said that "Congress simply did not consider it worth the added burdens of including women in draft and registration plans. . . . Most significantly, Congress determined that staffing noncombat positions with women would be positively detrimental to the important goal of military flexibility."[98]

The dissent argued that the law was founded on sex-based stereotypes and that male-only registration is unconstitutional even assuming that it is constitutional to exclude women from serving in combat. Justice Marshall began his dissenting opinion: "The Court today places its imprimatur on one of the most potent remaining public expressions of 'ancient canards' about the proper role of women."[99] The dissent argued that registering women could be useful in the event that it became desirable to draft women for noncombat positions in the armed forces.[100]

---

[92] For criticisms of gender-based statutory rape laws, *see, e.g.,* Kristin Bumiller, Rape as a Legal Symbol: An Essay on Sexual Violence and Racism, 42 U. Miami L. Rev. 75 (1987) (arguing that many violent rapes are prosecuted as statutory rapes); Wendy Williams, The Equality Crisis: Reflection on Culture, Courts, and Feminism, 7 Women's Rts. L. Rep. 175 (1982) (criticizing the *Michael M.* decision).

[93] *Id.* at 499 (Stevens, J., dissenting).

[94] 453 U.S. 57 (1981).

[95] *Id.* at 66.

[96] *Id.* at 76-77.

[97] *Id.* at 77.

[98] *Id.* at 81-82.

[99] *Id.* at 86 (Marshall, J., dissenting).

[100] Of course, the assumption that women cannot serve in combat is itself open to serious question and could be challenged as being based on stereotypes. *See, e.g.,* Kenneth Karst, The Pursuit of Manhood and the Desegregation of the Armed Forces, 38 UCLA L. Rev. 499 (1991); Lori Kornblum, Women Warriors in a Men's World: The Combat Exclusion, 2 Law & Ineq. 351 (1984) (arguing that women should not be excluded from combat). In fact, the Combat Exclusion Policy was lifted as of January 24, 2013, following a unanimous recommendation by the Joint Chiefs of Staff. Both men and women are now eligible to serve in front line combat and complete combat operations.

Ultimately, cases like *Michael M.* and *Goldberg* force consideration of when biological differences between men and women justify gender discrimination.[101] To ignore physical differences between men and women leads to absurd results such as in *Geduldig* where the Court essentially said that pregnancy is not a sex-based classification. Yet allowing laws to be based on perceived physical differences between men and women risks upholding laws that are really based on stereotypes.

Gender Classifications Benefiting Women as a Remedy

The Court has indicated that gender classifications benefiting women will be allowed when they are designed to remedy past discrimination or differences in opportunity. For example, in *Califano v. Webster*, the Supreme Court upheld a provision in the Social Security Act that calculated benefits for women in a more advantageous way than was used for men.[102] The Court said that the difference in the formula was not based on stereotypes, but rather the permissible goal "of redressing our society's longstanding disparate treatment of women."[103] The Court concluded that using a formula that helped women was constitutional because it "operated directly to compensate women for past economic discrimination."[104]

In *Schlesinger v. Ballard*, the Court upheld a navy regulation that required the discharge of male officers who had gone 9 years without a promotion, but allowed women to remain 13 years without a promotion.[105] The Court decided that this was constitutional because men had more opportunities for promotion than women. Justice Stewart, writing for the Court, explained: "Congress may quite rationally have believed that women line officers had less opportunity for promotion than did their male counterparts, and that a longer period of tenure for women officers would, therefore, be consistent with the goal to provide women officers with fair and equitable career advancement programs."[106]

Thus far, the Court has not considered a constitutional challenge to an affirmative action program designed to benefit women. Although intermediate scrutiny is the test for all gender-based classifications, many of the same issues will arise as in the context of race-based affirmative action, including what interests justify affirmative action and what techniques are permissible.[107]

---

[101] *See also* Dothard v. Rawlinson, 433 U.S. 321 (1977) (upholding the exclusion of women from "contact positions" in all-male prisons).

[102] 430 U.S. 313 (1977).

[103] *Id.* at 317.

[104] *Id.* at 318.

[105] 419 U.S. 498 (1975).

[106] *Id.* at 508.

[107] In Johnson v. Transportation Agency, 480 U.S. 616 (1987) (holding that a voluntary affirmative action program based on gender did not violate Title VII).

Gender Classifications Benefiting Women Because of Biological Differences Between Men and Women

In *Nguyen v. Immigration and Naturalization Service*,[108] the Court allowed a third type of gender classification: gender classifications benefiting women because of biological differences between men and women. The Court allowed a difference in INS rules favoring mothers over fathers because of the greater certainty as to the identity of the mother as compared to the father and the greater opportunity that mothers have in establishing a relationship with their children.

The case involved how children can become citizens when they are born outside the United States to unmarried parents and one of their parents is a United States citizen and one is not. The relevant federal statute imposed different and greater requirements for the child's acquisition of citizenship if the citizen parent is the father as opposed to the mother.[109] Specifically, the statute required one of three affirmative steps to be taken if the citizen parent is the father, but not if the citizen parent is the mother: legitimation, a declaration of paternity under oath by the father, or a court order of paternity.

The Court upheld this and said that "Congress' decision to impose requirements on unmarried fathers that differ from those on unmarried mothers is based on the significant difference between their respective relationships to the potential citizen at the time of birth."[110] First, the Court said that the difference in the rule serves the government's interest in being sure that there is a biological relationship between the parent and the child. The Court explained that there, of course, is no doubt as to the relationship between the mother and the child, but paternity is not so certain. The dissent, though, argued that with DNA testing paternity can be established to a virtual certainty.[111]

Second, the Court said that another governmental interest furthered in a substantial manner by the law "is the determination to ensure that the child and the citizen parent have some demonstrated opportunity or potential to develop not just a relationship that is recognized, as a formal matter, by the law, but one that consists of the real, everyday ties that provide a connection between child and

---

[108] 533 U.S. 53 (2001). Earlier, in *Miller v. Albright*, 523 U.S. 420 (1998), the Supreme Court upheld a distinction drawn by §309 of the Immigration and Nationality Act, 8 U.S.C. §1409, between the child of an alien father and a citizen mother, on the one hand, and the child of an alien mother and a citizen father, on the other. The citizenship of the former (the alien father and citizen mother) is established at birth; but the citizenship of the latter is not established unless and until either the father or his child takes certain affirmative steps to create or confirm their relationship. The Court, without a majority opinion, upheld the federal law. Six Justices voted to uphold the law, but there were three opinions, each getting two votes. Justice Stevens, joined by Chief Justice Rehnquist, found that the law was justified by a sufficient interest. Justice O'Connor, joined by Justice Kennedy, concurred in the judgment, but would have rejected the claim based on a lack of standing. Justice Scalia, joined by Justice Thomas, concurred in the judgment and said that Congress alone decides the basis for granting citizenship. Justice Ginsburg, joined by Justices Souter and Breyer, dissented and argued that the law was impermissible gender discrimination.

[109] U.S.C. §1409.

[110] 533 U.S. at 62.

[111] *Id.* at 80.

citizen parent and, in turn, the United States."[112] The Court said that "[i]n the case of a citizen mother and a child born overseas, the opportunity for a meaningful relationship between citizen parent and child inheres in the very event of birth."[113] The Court explained that "[t]he same opportunity does not result from the event of birth, as a matter of biological inevitability, in the case of the unwed father. Given the 9-month interval between conception and birth, it is not always certain that a father will know that a child was conceived, nor is it always clear that even the mother will be sure of the father's identity."[114]

Justice Breyer, in a dissenting opinion, questioned whether this counts as an important government interest. Moreover, he disagreed that mothers should be presumed inherently to have more of a relationship with a child than the father; a mother could have no contact after birth, while the father could raise the child. He wrote: "[T]he idea that a mother's presence at birth supplies adequate assurance of an opportunity to develop a relationship while a father's presence at birth does not would appear to rest only on an overbroad sex-based generalization."[115]

Nguyen's significance is in allowing a gender classification benefiting women based on biological differences between men and women. The issues, however, whenever the Court purports to rely on biological differences as a justification for differences in treatment, are whether these differences are real or social constructs and whether they should matter. The majority and dissent in *Nguyen* disagree over exactly these questions.

§9.5   ALIENAGE CLASSIFICATIONS

§9.5.1   *Introduction*

Definition

Alienage classifications refer to discrimination against noncitizens. This type of discrimination should be distinguished from national origin classifications, which discriminate against individuals because of the country that a person, or his or her ancestors, came from. Obviously, the two types of classifications can overlap. A government, for example, might choose to discriminate against aliens—noncitizens—from a particular country. Alternatively, the two categories can be distinct; the government might discriminate against all aliens regardless of their initial country.

---

[112] *Id.* at 64.
[113] *Id.*
[114] *Id.* at 65.
[115] *Id.* at 86.

§9.5 Alienage Classifications

Although America is very much a nation of immigrants, discrimination against aliens long has been widespread. Whether it is founded on economic protectionism, xenophobia, or other motivations, aliens frequently have been denied benefits and privileges accorded to citizens. The issue arises when such discrimination is a denial of equal protection of the laws.

Protection Under the Equal Protection Clause

Aliens are protected from discrimination because the equal protection clause explicitly says that no "person" shall be denied equal protection of the laws. The clause does not mention the word "citizen," although it is used in the privileges or immunities clause, which also is found in §1 of the Fourteenth Amendment. Long ago, in *Yick Wo v. Hopkins*, in 1886, the United States Supreme Court declared: "The Fourteenth Amendment to the Constitution is not confined to the protection of citizens. . . . [Its] provisions are universal in their application, to all persons within the territorial jurisdiction without regard to any differences of race, of color, or of nationality; and the equal protection of the laws is a pledge of the protection of equal laws."[1]

As explained above,[2] equal protection is applied to the federal government through the due process clause of the Fifth Amendment. This provision, too, speaks of persons, and the Supreme Court has held that it protects aliens from unjustified discrimination.[3]

Relationship to Preemption Analysis

Often state and local laws that discriminate against aliens can be challenged on preemption grounds as well as for violating equal protection. The Supreme Court has held that federal immigration laws wholly occupy the field and preempt state efforts to regulate immigration.[4] For example, in *Toll v. Moreno*, the Supreme Court used preemption analysis to invalidate a state law denying resident aliens in-state tuition at the University of Maryland.[5]

Sometimes state and local laws can be challenged based both on equal protection and on preemption analysis. In *Graham v. Richardson*, the Supreme Court declared unconstitutional a state law denying welfare benefits to aliens.[6] The Court found both that it violated equal protection and that it was preempted by federal control over the field of immigration law.

---

§9.5 [1] 118 U.S. 356, 369 (1886); *see also* Shaughnessy v. United States ex rel. Mezei, 345 U.S. 206, 212 (1953); Wong Wing v. United States, 163 U.S. 228, 238 (1896).

[2] *See* §9.1.1.

[3] *See* Mathews v. Diaz, 426 U.S. 67, 77-78 (1976).

[4] *See, e.g.,* De Canas v. Bica, 424 U.S. 351 (1976); Nyquist v. Mauclet, 432 U.S. 1 (1977); *DeCanas* is discussed in §5.2.3.

[5] 458 U.S. 1 (1982).

[6] 403 U.S. 365 (1971).

Overview of Organization

As described below in §9.5.2, the general rule is that strict scrutiny is used to evaluate discrimination against noncitizens. There are, however, several exceptions where less than strict scrutiny is used. Section 9.5.3 describes the case law establishing that alienage classifications related to self-government and the democratic process only need meet rational basis review.

The Supreme Court has recognized that Congress has plenary power to regulate immigration and thus has been very deferential to federal statutes and presidential orders that discriminate against aliens. Again, only a rational basis test is applied rather than the usual strict scrutiny for alienage classifications. This is discussed in §9.5.4.

Finally, the Supreme Court has indicated that undocumented aliens are protected by equal protection, and it appears that intermediate scrutiny will be used at least in evaluating government actions discriminating against undocumented immigrants with regard to education.[7] This is examined in §9.5.5.

§9.5.2 Strict Scrutiny as the General Rule

Initial Cases Generally Allowing Discrimination

In 1971, in *Graham v. Richardson*, discussed below, the Supreme Court held that strict scrutiny was to be applied to discrimination against aliens.[8] Prior to this decision, the Court had been extremely deferential to discrimination against aliens so long as it related to a "special public interest." Three cases decided in 1915 applied and defined this concept. In *Truax v. Reich*, the Supreme Court declared unconstitutional an Arizona law that required that employers with more than five employees hire at least 80 percent qualified voters or native-born citizens.[9] In part, the Court relied on preemption analysis, declaring: "The authority to control immigration, to admit or exclude aliens, is vested solely in the Federal Government. The assertion of an authority to deny to aliens the opportunity of earning a livelihood when lawfully admitted to the state would be tantamount to the assertion of the right to deny them entrance and abode, for in ordinary cases they cannot live where they cannot work."[10] The Court said that the Arizona law was arbitrary and that "[n]o special public interest with respect to any particular business is shown that could possibly be deemed to support the enactment."[11]

However, in two other cases that year, the Supreme Court allowed exclusions of aliens from government jobs; the Court found the "special public interest" that

---

[7] *See* Plyler v. Doe, 457 U.S. 202 (1982).
[8] 403 U.S. 365 (1971) (holding unconstitutional state law denying welfare benefits to aliens).
[9] 239 U.S. 33 (1915).
[10] *Id.* at 42.
[11] *Id.* at 43.

had been lacking in *Truax*.[12] In *Heim v. McCall*, the Supreme Court upheld a New York law that prohibited the employment of aliens on public works contracts for the construction of the New York City subways.[13] The Court said that there is a "special power of the state" over government employment and that the discrimination against aliens in this realm was permissible.[14] Similarly, in *Crane v. New York*, the Court upheld a New York law that made it a crime to employ aliens on public works contracts.[15]

The Court subsequently held, in *Terrace v. Thompson*, that states have a "special public interest" in excluding aliens from owning land.[16] The Court said that each state has "wide discretion" to make its own policies concerning ownership of land and that "each State, in the absence of any treaty provision to the contrary, has power to deny to aliens the right to own land within its borders."[17] The Court further declared that "[t]he quality and allegiance of those who own, occupy and use the farm lands within its borders are matters of highest importance, and affect the safety and power of the state itself."[18]

The Court also extended the "special public interest" doctrine to exclude aliens from receiving occupational licenses. In *Clarke v. Deckebach*, the Supreme Court ruled that states could prevent aliens from being licensed to operate pool halls.[19]

This approach to alienage classifications, which effectively gave states broad latitude to discriminate against noncitizens in a wide array of areas, continued until *Takahashi v. Fish and Game Commission* in 1948.[20] In *Takahashi*, the Supreme Court declared unconstitutional a California law that denied aliens the privilege of receiving licenses for commercial fishing in coastal waters. The Court, in part, relied upon principles of preemption and said: "State laws which impose discriminatory burden upon the entrance or residence of aliens lawfully within the United States conflict with the constitutionally derived power to regulate immigration."[21] Additionally, the Court found the California law to deny aliens equal protection, and the Court rejected the argument that California had a "special public interest" in conserving its natural resources for use only by citizens.[22]

---

[12] An earlier case, *Patsone v. Pennsylvania*, 232 U.S. 138 (1914), found that a state had a special public interest in excluding aliens from hunting wild game.

[13] 239 U.S. 175 (1915).

[14] *Id.* at 194.

[15] 239 U.S. 195 (1915).

[16] 263 U.S. 197 (1923).

[17] *Id.* at 217.

[18] *Id.* at 221.

[19] 274 U.S. 392 (1927).

[20] 334 U.S. 410 (1948).

[21] *Id.* at 419.

[22] *See also* Oyama v. California, 332 U.S. 633 (1948) (declaring unconstitutional a state law that land paid for by an alien, ineligible to own land, but conveyed to a citizen, was held for the benefit of the alien).

Emergence of Strict Scrutiny

In 1971, in *Graham v. Richardson*, the Supreme Court used strict scrutiny in declaring unconstitutional a Pennsylvania law that made noncitizens ineligible to receive public assistance and an Arizona law that limited receipt of benefits to those who are citizens or had resided in the state for at least 15 years.[23] The Court said that "classifications based on alienage, like those based on nationality or race, are inherently suspect and subject to close judicial scrutiny. Aliens as a class are a prime example of a 'discrete and insular minority for whom heightened judicial solicitude is appropriate.'"[24] The Court said that *Takahashi* "cast doubt on the continuing validity of the special public interest doctrine in all contexts" and that "a State's desire to preserve limited welfare benefits for its own citizens is inadequate to justify" the discrimination against aliens.[25] The Court also emphasized that state laws that restrict the eligibility of aliens for welfare benefits conflict with federal immigration policy; once the federal government has decided to admit aliens, states cannot discriminate against those present.[26]

The Court applied *Graham* in two cases decided in 1973: *Sugarman v. Dougall*[27] and *In re Griffiths*.[28] In *Sugarman*, the Supreme Court declared unconstitutional a New York law that prevented aliens from holding civil service jobs. The Court said that excluding aliens denied equal protection and that a "flat ban on the employment of aliens in positions that have little, if any, relation to a State's legitimate interest, cannot withstand scrutiny under the Fourteenth Amendment.[29]

In re Griffiths invalidated, as violating equal protection, a state law that excluded aliens from being licensed as attorneys. The Court reaffirmed that strict scrutiny was the appropriate test for discrimination against aliens and held that it was impermissible for states to require citizenship as a condition for practicing law.

The Court applied these decisions in later cases. In *Examining Board v. Flores de Otero*, the Supreme Court declared unconstitutional a Puerto Rico statute that permitted only United States citizens to engage in the private practice of engineering.[30] The Court said that the earlier decisions "establish that state classification based on alienage are subject to strict judicial scrutiny."[31] The Court said that excluding aliens from private practice as engineers has no "rational relationship to skill, competence, or professional responsibility."[32]

Likewise, in *Nyquist v. Mauclet*, the Supreme Court used strict scrutiny to invalidate a New York law that limited financial aid for higher education to citizens, those who had applied for citizenship, and those who declared an intent to apply

---

[23] 403 U.S. 365, 367 (1971).
[24] *Id.* at 372, citing United States v. Carolene Products Co., 304 U.S. 144, 152-153 n.4 (1938).
[25] *Id.* at 374.
[26] *Id.* at 378.
[27] 413 U.S. 634 (1973).
[28] 413 U.S. 717 (1973).
[29] *Sugarman*, 413 U.S. at 647.
[30] 426 U.S. 572 (1976).
[31] *Id.* at 602.
[32] *Id.* at 606.

as soon as they were eligible.[33] The Court emphasized the discriminatory nature of the statute, observing that the law "is directed at aliens and . . . only aliens are harmed by it."[34]

What Level of Scrutiny Is Appropriate?

Thus, it is clearly established that strict scrutiny is the appropriate test for discrimination against aliens, subject to the exceptions described below. The Court justified strict scrutiny by characterizing aliens as a "discrete and insular minority." Aliens cannot vote and thus cannot protect themselves through the political process.[35] Additionally, there is a long history of discrimination against aliens, often based on prejudice or economic protectionism.

Critics of using strict scrutiny for alienage classifications emphasize how they are different from discrimination based on race or gender. Alienage is not immutable; aliens are capable of being citizens after a relatively short time period.[36] Moreover, some believe that it is appropriate to allow the government more latitude than strict scrutiny permits in reserving benefits for citizens.

In balancing these factors, the Supreme Court gave most weight to the inability of aliens to protect themselves at the ballot box and in the political arena. The usual rule of judicial deference to the legislative process is least appropriate when a group is disenfranchised and thus does not have any opportunity to influence that process. The group has no political clout and thus is highly vulnerable. Exacting judicial review is thus used to ensure that discrimination is necessary and not simply a reflection of prejudice or the political power of others.

§9.5.3   Alienage Classifications Related to Self-Government and the Democratic Process

The Exception Explained and Applied

Although strict scrutiny is the general rule when the government discriminates against aliens, the Supreme Court has carved an important exception: Only rational basis review is used for alienage classifications related to self-government and the democratic process. The Supreme Court has said that "a democratic

---

[33] 432 U.S. 1 (1977).

[34] *Id.* at 9.

[35] *See* Gerald M. Rosberg, The Protection of Aliens from Discriminatory Treatment by the National Government, 1977 Sup. Ct. Rev. 275, 308-309 (arguing for strict scrutiny based on the political powerlessness of aliens).

[36] Justice Rehnquist made this argument in opposing heightened scrutiny for alienage classifications. *See* Nyquist v. Mauclet, 432 U.S. at 20 (Rehnquist, J., dissenting). However, it should be noted that alienage is immutable until the requisite waiting period has passed.

society can be ruled by its people."[37] Hence, the Court has declared that a state may deny aliens the right to vote or hold political office[38] or serve on juries.[39]

Rather than use strict scrutiny and find these interests to be compelling, the Court has altered the level of scrutiny when the alienage classification relates to self-government and the democratic process. In *Foley v. Connelie*, the Supreme Court said that when the discrimination is against aliens in these areas, "[t]he State need only justify its classification by a showing of some rational relationship between the interest sought to be protected and the limiting classification."[40]

In *Foley*, the Supreme Court used the rational basis test to uphold a state law that required citizenship in order for a person to be a police officer. The Court emphasized that police officers are integral to self-government; they enforce the laws that are the product of the democratic process. The Court concluded: "[I]t would be . . . anomalous to conclude that citizens may be subjected to the broad discretionary powers of noncitizen police officers. . . . It is not surprising, therefore, that most States expressly confine the employment of police officers to citizens, whom the State may reasonably presume to be more familiar with and sympathetic to American traditions."[41] The Court said that a state may "confine the performance of this important public responsibility to citizens of the United States."[42]

The Court followed this reasoning in *Ambach v. Norwich*, upholding a state law that required citizenship for a person to be an elementary or secondary school teacher.[43] The Court said that teachers are integral to self-government because they are responsible for inculcating democratic values in youth. The Court explained that a "teacher has an opportunity to influence the attitudes of students toward government, the political process, and a citizen's social responsibilities. This influence is crucial to the continued good health of a democracy."[44] Therefore, the Court applied *Foley* and said that only rational basis review was appropriate in scrutinizing the state law. The Court found that a state had a legitimate interest in excluding aliens from elementary and secondary school classrooms.

In *Cabell v. Chavez-Salido*, the Supreme Court followed *Foley* and *Ambach* and held that a state may require citizenship in order for a person to be a probation officer.[45] The Court said that probation officers serve both as law enforcement officers and also as teachers in the sense that they perform an educational function for those they supervise. The Court therefore used only the rational basis test and upheld the law.

But in *Bernal v. Fainter*, the Supreme Court refused to apply this exception to a state law that created a citizenship requirement in order for a person to be a notary

---

[37] Foley v. Connelie, 435 U.S. 291, 296 (1978).

[38] *Sugarman*, 413 U.S. at 634, 647.

[39] Perkins v. Smith, 426 U.S. 913 (1976).

[40] 435 U.S. at 296.

[41] *Id.* at 299-300.

[42] *Id.* at 300.

[43] 441 U.S. 68 (1979).

[44] *Id.* at 79.

[45] 454 U.S. 432 (1982).

public.[46] The Court reaffirmed that "[a]s a general matter, a state law that discriminates on the basis of alienage can be sustained only if it can withstand strict judicial scrutiny."[47] The Court emphasized that this is a "narrow" exception that applies only if it is specifically tailored to those who "participate directly in the formulation, execution, or review of broad public policy, and hence perform functions that go to the heart of representative government."[48]

The Court said that notary publics do not perform responsibilities that go to the heart of representative government.[49] Therefore, strict scrutiny was applied and the state law was deemed to violate equal protection.

Is the Exception Justified?

In evaluating this exception, there are two interrelated questions: Should a state be able to reserve prerogatives and privileges for citizens; and, if so, what level of scrutiny should be used? For example, it can be questioned whether it is appropriate to exclude aliens from voting.[50] Aliens pay taxes, and denying them the vote creates "taxation without representation." Moreover, even if a state can reserve matters going to the "heart of representative government" for citizens, it is hard to see why a math teacher or an art teacher is performing such a function.

Additionally, the Court's decisions can be criticized for so openly manipulating the level of scrutiny. The Court could have used strict scrutiny and found the interest in preserving self-government and the democratic process to be compelling. The issue in each case then would be whether discrimination in that area was necessary for self-government. Instead, the Court chose rational basis review and thus virtually ensured that such discrimination would be allowed.

§9.5.4   Congressionally Approved Discrimination

Another exception to the usual rule of strict scrutiny for alienage classifications is where the discrimination is a result of a federal law. The Supreme Court has ruled that the federal government's plenary power to control immigration requires judicial deference and that therefore only rational basis review is used if Congress has created the alienage classification or if it is the result of a presidential order.

Deference to Federal Laws Discriminating Against Aliens

In *Mathews v. Diaz*, the Supreme Court unanimously upheld a federal statute that denied Medicaid benefits to aliens unless they had been admitted for

---

[46] 467 U.S. 216 (1984).

[47] *Id.* at 219.

[48] *Id.* at 222 (citation omitted).

[49] *Id.* at 225.

[50] *See* Gerald M. Rosberg, Aliens and Equal Protection: Why Not the Right to Vote?, 75 Mich. L. Rev. 1092 (1977).

permanent residence and resided for at least five years in the United States.[51] The Court said that "the relationship between the United States and our alien visitors has been committed to the political branches of the federal government. Since decisions in these matters may implicate our relations with foreign powers, and since a wide variety of classifications must be defined in light of the changing political and economic circumstances, such decisions are frequently of a character more appropriate to either the Legislature or the Executive than to the Judiciary."[52]

The Court thus drew a distinction between alienage classifications imposed by the federal government and those created by state and local governments.[53] Strict scrutiny is used for the latter, but the Court said that the federal law was upheld because it was not "wholly irrational" and served the "legitimate" interests of the federal government in preserving the fiscal integrity of the program.[54]

However, in *Hampton v. Wong*,[55] the Supreme Court clarified this and articulated a distinction between decisions by Congress or the president and those by federal administrative agencies; rational basis review is used only for the former. The Court invalidated a federal civil service regulation that denied employment to aliens. The Court said that "if the rule were expressly mandated by the Congress or the President, we might presume that any interest which might rationally be served by the rule did in fact give rise to its adoption."[56] The Court therefore explained that if the civil service regulation had been adopted via a federal law or a presidential order, "it would be justified by the national interest in providing an incentive for aliens to become naturalized, or possibly even as providing the President with an expendable token for treaty negotiating purposes."[57]

But the Civil Service Commission that adopted the regulation had no involvement in making decisions concerning immigration or foreign policy. Nor was there anything to "indicate that the Commission actually made any considered evaluation of the relative desirability of a simple exclusionary rule on the one hand, or of the value . . . of enlarging the pool of qualified employees on the other."[58] The Civil Service regulation was invalidated even though it would have been constitutional if adopted by other federal government institutions.

Is This Exception Justified?

The Court defended the exception to the usual rule of strict scrutiny based on its need to defer to decisions by Congress and the president as to matters of

---

[51] 426 U.S. 67 (1976).
[52] *Id.* at 81.
[53] The Court distinguished *Graham v. Richardson*, 403 U.S. 365 (1971), because it involved a state denying welfare benefits, and thus "concerns the relationship between aliens and the States rather than between aliens and the Federal government." 426 U.S. at 84-85.
[54] *Id.* at 83, 85.
[55] 426 U.S. 88 (1976).
[56] *Id.* at 103.
[57] *Id.* at 105.
[58] *Id.* at 115.

immigration and foreign policy. This is consistent with the Court's general practice of deference in these areas.[59]

But it can be questioned whether the federal government's power to limit who enters the country should give it a right to discriminate once people are here.[60] Professor Gerald Rosberg argues: "[T]he reasons for treating alienage as a suspect classification apply as forcefully to the federal government as to the states. . . . The Court's repeated insistence that Congress has plenary power to act against aliens in any way it wants must be seen as an invitation to Congress to act capriciously and without significant concern for the legitimate interest of resident aliens."[61]

§9.5.5 Undocumented Aliens and Equal Protection

Plyler v. Doe

In *Plyler v. Doe*, the Supreme Court declared unconstitutional a Texas law that provided a free public education for children of citizens and of documented aliens, but required that undocumented aliens pay for their schooling.[62] Justice Brennan, writing for the Court, initially emphasized that "[a]liens, even aliens whose presence in this country is unlawful, have long been recognized as 'persons' guaranteed due process of law by the Fifth and Fourteenth Amendments."[63]

The Court did not expressly articulate a level of scrutiny, but it did say that "[u]ndocumented aliens cannot be treated as a suspect class because their presence in this country in violation of federal law is not a constitutional irrelevancy. Nor is education a fundamental right."[64] But the Court also made it clear that it was using more than rational basis review. The state's claim of a desire to reserve benefits for its own citizens likely would meet a rational basis test. Thus, it appears that the Court was using intermediate scrutiny in evaluating the discrimination against undocumented alien children with regard to education.[65]

The Court stressed the blamelessness of the children: They were being punished by being denied an education because of their parents' choice to bring them into the country. Moreover, the Court also emphasized the importance of education and the unfairness of leaving children without this crucial service. Justice Brennan concluded the majority opinion by explaining that "it hardly can be

---

[59] *See* §2.8.4 (discussing application of the political question doctrine in these areas).

[60] For an excellent argument that the denial of benefits to legal immigrants under the 1996 Welfare Reform Act is unconstitutional, *see* Michael J. Wishnie, Laboratories of Bigotry?: Devolution of the Immigration Power, Equal Protection, and Federalism, 76 N.Y.U. L. Rev. 493 (2001).

[61] Gerald M. Rosberg, The Protection of Aliens from Discriminatory Treatment by the National Government, 1977 Sup. Ct. Rev. 275, 336-338.

[62] 457 U.S. 202 (1982).

[63] *Id.* at 210.

[64] *Id.* at 223.

[65] Justice Powell, in a concurring opinion, explicitly said that "[o]ur review in a case such as this is properly heightened" and he cited to *Craig v. Boren*, 429 U.S. 190 (1976), which articulated the standard of intermediate scrutiny for gender classifications. 457 U.S. at 238 (Powell, J., concurring).

argued rationally that anyone benefits from the creation within our borders of a sub-class of illiterate persons many of whom will remain in the State, adding to the problems and costs of both State and National Governments attendant upon unemployment, welfare, and crime."[66]

The dissent argued that rational basis review was appropriate and that the judiciary should defer to the legislature on matters of how to allocate resources for education.[67] Chief Justice Burger said that heightened scrutiny was inappropriate because there was no suspect classification and there was no fundamental right. The dissent maintained that "[t]he solution to this seemingly intractable problem is to defer to the political processes, unpalatable as that may be to some."[68]

The Supreme Court has not overruled *Plyler* or even called it into question, though there have been other laws discriminating against undocumented immigrants.[69] In November 1994, California voters approved Proposition 187, which denies all government services—such as education, welfare, and medical care—to undocumented aliens. Under *Plyler*, this is clearly unconstitutional, at least as to education and likely as to the other services as well. The federal district court declared most provisions of the law unconstitutional on federal preemption grounds and the case settled while on appeal before the Ninth Circuit as the state, with a newly elected Democratic governor, decided not to pursue the appeal.[70] But if other states adopt similar laws, the Court may have occasion to revisit *Plyler*.

§9.6   DISCRIMINATION AGAINST NONMARITAL CHILDREN

Intermediate Scrutiny Is Used

It is now clearly established that intermediate scrutiny is applied in evaluating laws that discriminate against nonmarital children—that is, children whose parents were not married. In *Clark v. Jeter*, the Supreme Court declared unconstitutional a state law that required a nonmarital child to establish paternity within six

---

[66] *Id.* at 241.

[67] *Id.* at 252-253 (Burger, C.J., dissenting).

[68] *Id.* at 254.

[69] There have been two decisions concerning undocumented aliens since *Plyler*. In *Martinez v. Bynum*, 461 U.S. 321 (1983), the Supreme Court upheld a state law that allowed school districts to charge students for their education if they lived apart from their parents for the sole purpose of attending school in the district. The Court emphasized that this was "[a] bona fide residence requirement, appropriately defined and uniformly applied"; it was not directed at aliens and was designed to ensure that cities could provide education for their residents. *Id.* at 328. In *Reno v. Flores*, 507 U.S. 292 (1993), the Court held that it was constitutional for the Immigration and Naturalization Service to retain custody of alien children who were being held pending deportation proceedings when there were no relatives or guardians in the United States to whom the children could be released.

[70] League of United Latin Am. Citizens v. Wilson, 890 F. Supp. 755 (C.D. Cal. 1995).

years of birth in order to seek support from his or her father.[1] The Court expressly stated that intermediate scrutiny is used for discriminatory classifications based on illegitimacy.[2] The Court felt that the six-year limitations period was impermissible because financial needs may not emerge until later and because it did not offer the child a sufficient opportunity to present his or her own claims.

Intermediate scrutiny is justified because of the unfairness of penalizing children because their parents were not married. The Supreme Court observed: "The status of illegitimacy has expressed through the ages society's condemnation of irresponsible liaisons beyond the bonds of marriage. But visiting this condemnation on the head of an infant is illogical and unjust. Moreover, imposing disabilities on the illegitimate child is contrary to the basic concept of our system that legal burdens should bear some relationship to individual responsibility or wrongdoing. Obviously, no child is responsible for his birth and penalizing the illegitimate child is ineffectual, as well as an unjust, way of deterring the parent."[3]

As with other classifications that receive heightened scrutiny, there is a long history of discrimination, and it is immutable in the sense that there is nothing the individual can do to change his or her status.[4] As the Supreme Court noted: "[T]he legal status of illegitimacy, however defined, is, like race or national origin, a characteristic determined by causes not within the control of the illegitimate individual, and it bears no relation to the individual's ability to participate in and contribute to society."[5]

But the Court also has distinguished discrimination against nonmarital children from the types of classifications that receive strict scrutiny. Illegitimacy is different from race, which receives strict scrutiny, or gender, which receives intermediate scrutiny, in that "illegitimacy does not carry an obvious badge."[6] Additionally, "the discrimination against illegitimates has never approached the severity or pervasiveness of the historic legal and political discrimination against women and Negroes."[7]

In applying intermediate scrutiny in this area, three principles emerge from the Court's decisions. First, laws that provide a benefit to all marital children, but no nonmarital children, always are declared unconstitutional. Second, laws that provide a benefit to some nonmarital children, while denying the benefit to other nonmarital children, are evaluated on a case-by-case basis under intermediate scrutiny. Third, laws that create statutes of limitations for the time period for evaluating paternity must provide enough time for those with an interest in the child to

---

§9.6 [1] 486 U.S. 456 (1988).

[2] *Id.* at 461.

[3] Weber v. Aetna Cas. & Surety Co., 406 U.S. 164, 175 (1972).

[4] *See* Henry O. Krause, Equal Protection for the Illegitimate, 65 Mich. L. Rev. 477, 488-489 (1966).

[5] Mathews v. Lucas, 427 U.S. 495, 505 (1976).

[6] *Id.* at 506.

[7] *Id.*

present his or her rights and must be substantially related to the state's interest in preventing false claims.[8]

Laws Denying Benefits to All Nonmarital Children

The Supreme Court consistently has invalidated laws that deny a benefit to all nonmarital children that is accorded to all marital children. In *Levy v. Louisiana*, the Supreme Court declared unconstitutional a state law that prevented nonmarital children from suing under a wrongful death statute for losses because of a mother's death.[9] All marital children could sue, but no nonmarital children. The Court found this unreasonable: "Legitimacy or illegitimacy of birth has no relation to the nature of the wrong allegedly inflicted on the mother. . . . [I]t is invidious to discriminate against [the children] when no action, conduct or demeanor of theirs is possibly relevant to the harm that was done the mother."[10]

In a companion case, *Gloria v. American Guarantee & Liability Insurance Co.*, the Supreme Court declared unconstitutional a state law that prevented parents from suing for the wrongful death of their nonmarital children.[11] The Court concluded that "[w]here the claimant is plainly the mother, the State denies equal protection of the laws to withhold relief merely because the child, wrongfully killed, was born to her out of wedlock."[12]

Similarly, in *New Jersey Welfare Rights Organization v. Cahill*, the Supreme Court ruled unconstitutional a state law that discriminated against nonmarital children in receiving public assistance.[13] A New Jersey law limited receipt of benefits under the "Assistance to Families of the Working Poor" program to families where there were two married adults and a child. The Supreme Court said that allowing all marital children to receive these benefits, but no nonmarital children, violated equal protection.

In the same year that *Cahill* was decided, the Supreme Court also declared unconstitutional a Texas law that created a legal obligation for fathers to support

---

[8] An additional issue that arises concerning nonmarital children is the rights of fathers to prevent adoption and to assert custody. Although these cases involve the rights of nonmarital fathers, they have been litigated as gender discrimination issues and as questions concerning the right to custody. Thus, the cases are discussed in more detail in §9.4.3 and §10.2.2. In *Stanley v. Illinois*, 405 U.S. 645 (1972), the Supreme Court declared unconstitutional a state law that denied the father of any hearing or due process before a nonmarital child was placed for adoption. Similarly, in *Caban v. Mohammed*, 441 U.S. 380 (1979), the Supreme Court invalidated a state law that required consent of the mother, but not the father, before a child was placed for adoption. But in *Lehr v. Robertson*, 463 U.S. 248 (1983), the Court upheld a state law that allowed nonmarital children to be placed for adoption without notice to their fathers if there was an available procedure for the fathers to assert paternity and the procedure was not used. Also, in *Michael H. v. Gerald D.*, 491 U.S. 110 (1989), the Supreme Court held that a state could deny all rights to an unmarried father when the mother was married to someone else; the Court upheld a California law that created an irrebuttable presumption that a married woman's husband is the father of her child.

[9] 391 U.S. 68 (1968).

[10] *Id.* at 72.

[11] 391 U.S. 73 (1968).

[12] *Id.* at 76.

[13] 411 U.S. 619 (1973).

their marital children, but no similar duty with regard to nonmarital children. In *Gomez v. Perez*, in concluding that the law violated equal protection, the Court stated: "[A] state may not invidiously discriminate against illegitimate children by denying them substantial benefits accorded children generally. We therefore hold that once a State posits a judicially enforceable right of behalf of children to needed support from their natural fathers there is no constitutionally sufficient justification for denying such an essential right to a natural child simply because its natural father has not married its mother."[14]

In *Trimble v. Gordon*, the Supreme Court deemed unconstitutional a law that prevented nonmarital children from inheriting from fathers who died intestate (without a will).[15] An Illinois law allowed marital children to inherit from either parent, but a nonmarital child only could inherit from his or her mother. Although the Court recognized the need to establish paternity for unwed fathers, it concluded that this did not justify the complete denial of benefits to all nonmarital children whose fathers died intestate.

In all of these cases, the laws in question allowed all marital children to receive a benefit that was denied to all nonmarital children. In each instance, the Supreme Court found that the discrimination violated equal protection.

Laws That Provide a Benefit to Some Nonmarital Children

No similar bright-line rule exists when the law provides a benefit to some nonmarital children that it denies to other nonmarital children. In other words, rather than discriminating between marital and nonmarital children, these laws distinguish among nonmarital children. Such statutes are subjected to intermediate scrutiny and evaluated on a case-by-case basis with the courts determining whether there is an important interest served and whether the law is substantially related to that goal.

In *Lalli v. Lalli*, the Supreme Court upheld a state law that provided that a nonmarital child could inherit from his or her father only if paternity was established during the father's lifetime.[16] In other words, some nonmarital children could inherit—those whose paternity was established during the father's life—while other nonmarital children could not inherit—those whose paternity was not so established. The Court said that the state had an important interest in preventing fraud and that requiring paternity to be established during the father's lifetime was substantially related to that objective.

In *Labine v. Vincent*, the Supreme Court upheld a state law that denied inheritance from a nonmarital father unless the child had been formally acknowledged by the father during the father's life.[17] Although the Court does not expressly say so, it appears that in *Labine*, as in *Lalli*, the Court accepted the state's argument

---

[14] 409 U.S. 535, 538 (1973).
[15] 430 U.S. 762 (1977).
[16] 439 U.S. 259 (1978).
[17] 401 U.S. 532 (1971).

that requiring paternity to be established in this way is substantially related to the government's interest in preventing fraud.[18]

Another case upholding a distinction among nonmarital children was *Mathews v. Lucas*.[19] The Supreme Court sustained a provision of the Social Security Act that allowed children to receive survivors' benefits only if they could establish both paternity and that the father was providing financial support. The law created a presumption of dependency for all marital children and all nonmarital children who were entitled to inherit under state law. The law allowed other nonmarital children to inherit only if they could prove financial dependency on their fathers. The Court found that the distinction among nonmarital children was constitutional because it did not preclude any child from receiving benefits and because it allowed the government to reduce its administrative burdens. Requiring every child to prove dependency would have been a substantial additional burden on the government; allowing all children to inherit without having to prove dependency would have been a greater cost on the government, which it was not constitutionally required to absorb.

However, not all laws discriminating among nonmarital children have been upheld. In *Jimenez v. Weinberger*, the Supreme Court invalidated a provision of the Social Security Act that allowed intestate inheritance of disability benefits by all marital children and by nonmarital children who had been "legitimated."[20] Other nonmarital children could inherit benefits only if they proved that they were living with or being supported by the father at the time the disability began. In other words, nonmarital children who were neither living with the father nor being supported by him when the disability arose could not get benefits.

The Supreme Court said that this was unconstitutional and explained: "Assuming that the appellants are in fact dependent on the claimant, it would not serve the purposes of the Act to conclusively deny them an opportunity to establish their dependency and their right to insurance benefits, and it would discriminate between the two subclasses of afterborn illegitimates without any basis for the distinction since the potential for spurious claims is exactly the same as to both subclasses."[21]

In other words, if the law's distinction is between marital and nonmarital children, the law is likely to be invalidated. But if the distinction is among nonmarital children, the Court will apply intermediate scrutiny in evaluating the law.

Statutes of Limitations for Establishing Paternity

In response to Supreme Court decisions invalidating laws denying benefits to all nonmarital children, some states adopted relatively short statutes of limitations

---

[18] In *Labine*, the Court expressed the view that laws regulating inheritance should not be scrutinized under equal protection. This view obviously has not survived later cases, and it now is clearly established that such cases will be reviewed under equal protection.

[19] 427 U.S. 495 (1976).

[20] 417 U.S. 628 (1974).

[21] *Id.* at 636.

for establishing paternity. The Supreme Court has been consistently hostile to these limitation periods.

In *Mills v. Habluetzel*, the Supreme Court ruled unconstitutional a state law that required that paternity for an unmarried father had to be established within a year of the child's birth.[22] The Supreme Court said that in evaluating such limitations periods a two-step analysis would be used: "First, the period for obtaining support granted by Texas to illegitimate children must be sufficiently long in duration to present a reasonable opportunity for those with an interest in such children to assert claims on their behalf. Second, any time limitation placed on that opportunity must be substantially related to the State's interest in avoiding the litigation of stale or fraudulent claims."[23] The Supreme Court found that one year was too short to give adequate opportunity to protect the child and is shorter than needed to achieve the state's interest of preventing fraud.

In *Pickett v. Brown*, the Supreme Court applied *Mills* to declare unconstitutional a state law that created a two-year statute of limitations for paternity and child support actions for nonmarital children.[24] Again, the Court said that the time period was unduly restrictive and compromised the child's interests without significantly discouraging or detecting fraud.

Most recently, in *Clark v. Jeter*, the Supreme Court found that a state law creating a six-year statute of limitations was unconstitutional.[25] The Court said that "[e]ven six years does not necessarily provide a reasonable opportunity to assert a claim on behalf of an illegitimate child."[26] The Court also concluded that the six-year "statute of limitations is not substantially related to Pennsylvania's interest in avoiding the litigation of stale or fraudulent claims."[27]

Thus far, the Court has not upheld any restrictive statutes of limitations for establishing paternity. Nor is it possible to imagine why the state would need such a restriction. So long as the father and child remain alive, paternity can be established at any point in time.

§9.7   OTHER TYPES OF DISCRIMINATION: RATIONAL BASIS REVIEW

There is an infinite variety of ways that governments draw distinctions among people. For instance, laws that determine who can practice law, who can have a driver's license, who can receive welfare, who can be a police officer, and who can

---

[22] 456 U.S. 91 (1982).
[23] *Id.* at 99-100.
[24] 462 U.S. 1 (1983).
[25] 486 U.S. at 463.
[26] *Id.*
[27] *Id.* at 464.

have a broadcast license all involve classifications. Any of these laws can be challenged as denying equal protection. Each, of course, would be subjected only to rational basis review, unless the discrimination was with regard to race, national origin, gender, alienage, or legitimacy. Thus far, these are the only types of discrimination for which the Supreme Court has approved either intermediate or strict scrutiny.[1]

The Supreme Court has expressly rejected heightened scrutiny for some other types of discrimination. Specifically, the Court has ruled that only rational basis review should be used for discrimination based on age, disability, and wealth even though these classifications share much in common with the types of discrimination for which heightened scrutiny is used. Also, while the Supreme Court has not yet ruled, almost all of the federal courts to consider the issue have held that rational basis review should be used for discrimination based on sexual orientation. These four types of discrimination—age, disability, wealth, and sexual orientation—are discussed in turn.

§9.7.1   Age Classifications

Many of the factors that justify heightened scrutiny for race, national origin, gender, alienage, and legitimacy classifications also exist with regard to age discrimination. There is a history of discrimination against the elderly with judgments often based on stereotypes. A person's age is immutable in the sense that a person cannot voluntarily change it and it is a characteristic that is visible.

Yet the Supreme Court has expressly declared that only rational basis review should be used under equal protection analysis for age discrimination. In *Massachusetts Board of Retirement v. Murgia*, the Supreme Court upheld a state law that required police officers to retire at age 50.[2] The Court gave several reasons for choosing rational basis review for age classifications. The Court said: "While the treatment of the aged in this Nation has not been wholly free of discrimination, such persons, unlike, say, those who have been discriminated against on the basis of race or national origin, have not experienced a history of purposeful unequal treatment or been subjected to unique disabilities on the basis of stereotyped characteristics not truly indicative of their abilities."[3] Moreover, the Court said that "even old age does not define a 'discrete and insular' group in need of extraordinary protection from the political process. Instead, it marks a stage that each of us will reach if we live our normal span."[4]

The Court examined the state law under the rational basis standard and upheld it. The Court said that "[s]ince physical ability generally declines with age,

***

§9.7 [1] It also is likely that heightened scrutiny will be used for discrimination based on religion. *See, e.g.,* Griffin v. Illinois, 351 U.S. 12 (1956) (mentioning religion along with race and national origin as impermissible grounds for discrimination). However, such cases are likely to arise under the free exercise or establishment clauses of the First Amendment rather than under equal protection.

[2] 427 U.S. 307 (1976).

[3] *Id.* at 313.

[4] *Id.* at 313-314.

mandatory retirement at age 50 serves to remove from police service those whose fitness for uniformed work presumptively has diminished with age. This clearly is rationally related to the State's objective."[5]

Similarly, in *Vance v. Bradley*, the Supreme Court upheld a federal law that mandated retirement at age 60 for participants in the Foreign Service Retirement System.[6] The statutory scheme drew a distinction between those covered by the Social Security system, where there was not a mandatory retirement age, and the Foreign Service Retirement System, which did require retirement at age 60. The Court used the rational basis test and said that it upheld the law because the challengers failed "to demonstrate that Congress has no reasonable basis for believing that conditions overseas generally are more demanding than conditions in the United States and that at age 60 or before many persons begin something of a decline in mental and physical reliability."[7] The Court said that the federal government had a legitimate interest in having a vigorous foreign service and that a mandatory retirement age was rationally related to that end.[8]

The age classifications upheld in *Murgia* and *Vance* were significantly overinclusive and underinclusive. Each law required retirement for many individuals who were still capable of performing competently or even superbly. Moreover, the laws had no effect on those younger who already had "declined in mental and physical reliability." The Supreme Court, however, said that when the rational basis test is used, "perfection is by no means required . . . ; [a] provision does not offend the Constitution simply because the classification is not made with mathematical nicety."[9]

Although the rational basis test makes it very difficult to challenge age classifications under the Constitution, the federal Age Discrimination in Employment Act prohibits age discrimination in employment and specifically outlaws mandatory retirement ages.[10]

§9.7.2 Discrimination Based on Disability

The Supreme Court also has ruled that only rational basis review should be used for discrimination based on disability. However, in *City of Cleburne, Texas v. Cleburne Living Center, Inc.*, the Supreme Court used the rational basis test to declare unconstitutional a city ordinance that required a special permit for the operation of a group home for the mentally disabled.[11] The Court declared that "[t]o withstand equal protection review, legislation that distinguishes between the mentally retarded and others must be rationally related to a legitimate governmental purpose."[12]

---

[5] *Id.* at 315.

[6] 440 U.S. 93 (1979).

[7] *Id.* at 111.

[8] *Id.* at 106.

[9] *Id.* at 108 (citations omitted).

[10] *See* Barbara Lindemann & Paul Grossman, Employment Discrimination Law 545-648 (3d ed. 1996) (describing provisions of the Age Discrimination in Employment Act).

[11] 473 U.S. 432 (1985).

[12] *Id.* at 446.

The Court rejected the city's justifications for discriminating against the mentally disabled, finding either that each was not a "legitimate purpose" or that the law was not "rational" as a way to achieve the goal. For example, the city argued that students from a junior high school across the street might harass occupants of a group home.[13] The Court said that this argument was based on prejudices against the mentally disabled and that indulging such private biases is not a legitimate government purpose.[14]

The city also contended that the home was located on a "five hundred year flood plain."[15] But the Court said that the city's professed concern was belied by its allowing in the area facilities such as nursing homes, homes for convalescents and the aged, hospitals, and sanitariums.[16] Also, the Court rejected the city's concern over the number who would live in the home because no similar restrictions on size existed for nursing homes, boarding houses, fraternities, or others.

It can be argued that the Court's review was more rigorous than usual for rational basis analysis. Under traditional rational basis review, significant under-inclusiveness is tolerated and the government may proceed one step at a time.[17] Thus, under usual rational basis review, the government would be able to regulate homes for the mentally disabled, but not apply the standards to hospitals or nursing homes.

The Supreme Court, however, later reaffirmed that *Cleburne* stands for the proposition that only rational basis review is to be used for discrimination based on disability.[18] In *Heller v. Doe*, the Supreme Court upheld a state law that allowed mentally retarded individuals to be civilly committed if there was clear and convincing evidence justifying institutionalization, but required that there be proof beyond a reasonable doubt before an individual could be committed because of mental illness.[19] In a 5-to-4 decision, the Supreme Court applied rational basis review and concluded that there were reasonable distinctions between the mentally retarded and the mentally ill.[20]

The Court said that the state's law was constitutional because mental retardation is subject to more objective measures than mental illness. Also, the Court said that the "prevailing methods of treatment for mentally retarded, as a general rule, are much less invasive than are those given the mentally ill."[21]

---

[13] *Id.* at 449.

[14] *Id.* at 450.

[15] *Id.*

[16] *Id.*

[17] *See* §9.2.3, text accompanying notes 55-58, *infra.*

[18] For example, in *University of Ala. v. Garrett*, 531 U.S. 356 (2001), the Court held that only rational basis review is used for disability discrimination, and as a result, Congress cannot use its power under §5 of the Fourteenth Amendment to authorize suits against states for employment discrimination based on disability. *Garrett* is discussed in detail in §3.7.2.

[19] 509 U.S. 312 (1993).

[20] The Court said that it was applying only rational basis review because arguments for heightened scrutiny had not been made in the lower courts. *Id.* at 319.

[21] *Id.* at 324.

Justice Blackmun dissented and argued for heightened scrutiny for laws that "discriminate against individuals with mental retardation."[22] Justice Souter—joined by Justices O'Connor, Blackmun, and Stevens—contended that the law failed rational basis review. Souter said that proving mental retardation is not always easier than proving mental illness and that institutionalization and treatment of the mentally retarded also involves a substantial loss of freedom.

Although disability classifications receive only rational basis review under the equal protection clause,[23] a federal statute broadly prohibits such discrimination: the Americans with Disabilities Act.[24]

§9.7.3   Wealth Discrimination

For a time it appeared that the Court would use heightened scrutiny for laws discriminating against the poor. In *Griffin v. Illinois*, in 1956, the Supreme Court held that it violated equal protection to deny free trial transcripts to indigent criminal defendants who were appealing their conviction.[25] The Court said that "[i]n criminal trials a State can no more discriminate on account of poverty than on account of religion, race, or color."[26] Likewise, in *Harper v. Virginia Board of Elections*, the Supreme Court declared unconstitutional a poll tax for state and local elections and said that "[l]ines drawn on the basis of wealth and property, like those of race, are traditionally disfavored."[27]

Subsequently, however, the Supreme Court clearly held that only rational basis review should be used for wealth classifications. In *Dandridge v. Williams*, the Supreme Court upheld a state law that put a cap on welfare benefits to families regardless of their size.[28] Children in larger families therefore received less per person than those in smaller families. The Supreme Court said that rational basis review was appropriate because the law related to "economics and social welfare."[29] The Court thus accepted the state's interest in allocating scarce public benefits as sufficient to justify the law. The Court said that "the Constitution does not empower this Court to second-guess state officials charged with the difficult responsibility of allocating limited public welfare funds among the myriad of potential recipients."[30]

---

[22] *Id.* at 335 (Blackmun, J., dissenting).

[23] *See also* New York City Transit Auth. v. Beazer, 440 U.S. 568 (1979) (using rational basis review for discrimination against methadone addicts), discussed in §9.2.3.

[24] 42 U.S.C. §12101 *et seq.*

[25] 351 U.S. 12 (1956).

[26] *Id.* at 17. *See also* Douglas v. California, 372 U.S. 353 (1963) (equal protection violated by a state's failure to provide counsel for criminal defendants on their first appeal of a conviction).

[27] 383 U.S. 663, 668 (1966). *See also* Hill v. Stone, 421 U.S. 289 (1975) (declaring unconstitutional property ownership requirement for voting).

[28] 397 U.S. 471 (1970).

[29] *Id.* at 485.

[30] *Id.* at 487. *See also Lindsey v. Normet*, 405 U.S. 56 (1972), where the Court rejected a challenge to a state's summary eviction procedure. The Court said that the "Constitution does not provide judicial remedies for every social and economic ill. We are unable to perceive in that document any constitutional guarantee of access to dwellings of a particular quality." *Id.* at 74.

In *San Antonio School District v. Rodriguez*, the Supreme Court expressly held that poverty is not a suspect classification and that discrimination against the poor should only receive rational basis review.[31] *Rodriguez* involved a challenge to Texas's system of relying heavily on local property taxes to pay for public education. The result was that poor areas were taxed at high rates, but still had little to spend on education. Wealthy areas could tax at low rates and had a great deal to spend on schooling.[32] The plaintiffs argued, in part, that the disparity in funding discriminated against the poor in violation of the equal protection clause.[33]

The Supreme Court, in a 5-to-4 decision, held that discrimination against the poor does not warrant heightened scrutiny.[34] The Court also rejected the claim that the law should be regarded as discriminating against the poor as a group. Justice Powell, writing for the Court, stated: "[A] cursory examination, however, demonstrates that neither of the two distinguishing characteristics of wealth classifications can be found here. First, in support of their charge that the system discriminates against the 'poor,' appellees have made no effort to demonstrate that it operates to the peculiar disadvantage of any class fairly definable as indigent. . . . [T]here is no basis on the record in this case for assuming that the poorest people, defined by reference to any level of absolute impecunity, are concentrated in the poorest districts. Second, . . . lack of personal resources has not occasioned an absolute deprivation of the desired benefit."[35]

A few years later, in *Maher v. Roe*, the Supreme Court rejected an argument that the government violated equal protection when it refused to fund abortions, even though it was paying for childbirth and other medical care costs.[36] The Court said that it "has never held that financial need alone identifies a suspect class for purposes of equal protection analysis."[37]

On the one hand, the Court's refusal to find that poverty is a suspect classification can be justified by distinguishing that characteristic from those where heightened scrutiny is used. Poverty is not immutable; most discrimination against the poor is a result of the effects of the law, rather than a product of intentional discrimination. Additionally, the Court clearly wanted to avoid creating a constitutional right to government benefits such as welfare, food, shelter, or medical care.

But the poor as a group do share many characteristics with groups that are protected by intermediate and strict scrutiny. The poor lack political power, especially in a political system where money is so crucial for influence. Additionally, there is a long history of discrimination against the poor in a wide array of areas

[31] 411 U.S. 1 (1973).

[32] *See* John E. Coons et al., Private Wealth and Public Education 212-217 (1970). Nor are such disparities a thing of the past.

[33] The plaintiffs also argued that education should be regarded as a fundamental right. The Court rejected this claim as well. This aspect of *Rodriguez* is discussed in §10.11.

[34] 411 U.S. at 17-29.

[35] *Id.* at 22-23. *See also* Kadrmas v. Dickinson Pub. Schs., 487 U.S. 450 (1988) (reaffirming that discrimination against the poor in education warrants only rational basis review; upholding the constitutionality of a school district charging a fee for bus service).

[36] 432 U.S. 464 (1977), discussed in §10.3.3.3.

[37] *Id.* at 471.

throughout society. Moreover, some prominent scholars have argued that there should be a right to minimum entitlements under the Constitution; that every person should be assured of food, shelter, and medical care to survive.[38]

§9.7.4 Discrimination Based on Sexual Orientation

The Supreme Court has not yet ruled as to whether discrimination based on sexual orientation warrants the application of intermediate or strict scrutiny. Discrimination based on sexual orientation has many characteristics that are present in other areas where heightened scrutiny is used. There is a long history of discrimination against gays, lesbians, and bisexuals. Laws discriminating on this basis generally reflect prejudices and stereotypes, rather than any actual differences. Also, research supports the view that sexual orientation is immutable and not a matter of individual choice.[39]

The federal courts of appeals are split over the question of whether heightened scrutiny should be used for sexual orientation discrimination.[40] There have been two Supreme Court cases invalidating laws discriminating against gays and lesbians; one used rational basis review and the other did not indicate the level of scrutiny being applied.

In 1996, the Supreme Court used the rational basis test to invalidate a Colorado initiative that encouraged discrimination based on sexual orientation.[41] Colorado Amendment 2 repealed all state and local laws that prohibited discrimination against gays, lesbians, and bisexuals. The popularly approved initiative also prevented future laws to protect these individuals. In *Romer v. Evans,* the Supreme Court found that Amendment 2 impermissibly discriminated based on sexual orientation. Justice Kennedy, writing for the Court, said: "Homosexuals, by state decree, are put in a solitary class with respect to transactions and relations in both the private and the governmental sphere. The amendment withdraws from homosexuals, but no others, specific legal protection from the injuries caused by discrimination, and it forbids reinstatement of these laws and policies."[42]

The Court said that the initiative failed even rational basis review. Justice Kennedy explained that "the amendment has the peculiar property of imposing a broad and undifferentiated disability on a single named group, an exceptional

---

[38] *See, e.g.,* Charles L. Black, Jr., Further Reflections on the Constitutional Justice of Livelihood, 86 Colum. L. Rev. 1103 (1986); Peter B. Edelman, The Next Century of Our Constitution: Rethinking Our Duty to the Poor, 39 Hastings L.J. 1 (1987); Frank I. Michelman, Foreword: On Protecting the Poor Through the Fourteenth Amendment, 83 Harv. L. Rev. 7 (1969).

[39] *See* Janet E. Halley, The Politics of the Closet: Towards Equal Protection for Gay, Lesbian and Bisexual Identity, 36 UCLA L. Rev. 915, 937 (1989).

[40] *Compare* SmithKline Beecham Corp. v. Abbott Laboratories, 740 F.3d 471 (9th Cir. 2014) (using heighted scrutiny for sexual orientation discrimination), *with* DeBoer v. Snyder, 772 F.3d 388 (6th Cir. 2014) (using rational basis review).

[41] Romer v. Evans, 517 U.S. 620 (1996).

[42] *Id.* at 627.

and . . . invalid form of legislation."[43] The Court concluded that there was no legitimate purpose for denying gays, lesbians, and bisexuals the same use of the political process available to everyone else. Justice Kennedy observed that the only apparent purpose behind the law was "animosity toward the class of persons affected," and this fails even the rational basis test.[44]

Romer v. Evans is significant because it was the first time the Court has invalidated discrimination based on sexual orientation. Although the Court used just rational basis review, the decision indicated judicial willingness to protect gays, lesbians, and bisexuals from discrimination. *Romer* establishes that animus against gays and lesbians, even when presented as a purported "moral" basis for a law, is not sufficient to meet the rational basis test.

After *Romer*, in *Lawrence v. Texas*, the Supreme Court held that a state cannot prohibit private, consensual homosexual activity.[45] Overruling its earlier decision in *Bowers v. Hardwick*,[46] the Court held that the right to privacy protects the right of consenting adults to engage in same-sex sexual activity in their bedrooms. However, as discussed in the Chapter 10, which considers *Lawrence* in more detail, Justice Kennedy's majority opinion focused on privacy and due process, not equal protection.[47] Moreover, Justice Kennedy's opinion did not state the level of scrutiny being used and thus it is unclear, even under the right to privacy, whether rational basis review or heightened scrutiny is to be applied to laws that prevent private, consensual same-sex sexual activity.

United States v. Windsor, decided in 2013, is the other Supreme Court decision finding a law discriminating on the basis of sexual orientation to deny equal protection.[48] Section 3 of the federal Defense of Marriage Act (DOMA) defines the term "marriage" for all purposes under federal law, including the provision of federal benefits, as "only a legal union between one man and one woman as husband and wife."[49] In *Windsor*, in a 5-4 decision, the Court declared §3 of DOMA unconstitutional as denying equal protection to gays and lesbians.

New York law would recognize the marriage of Edith Windsor and Thea Spyer, a couple that lived together for 42 years in Manhattan and got married in Canada in 2007. But federal law would not recognize their marriage because of §3 of the federal Defense of Marriage Act. If the federal government recognized their marriage, Spyer's estate would not have owed any estate taxes. But because of §3 of DOMA, Spyer's estate owed $363,053 in federal estate taxes, which Windsor paid.

The Court began by noting that marriage has traditionally been defined by the states. The Court observed that "[b]y history and tradition the definition and regulation of marriage . . . has been treated as being within the authority and

---

[43] *Id.* at 632.

[44] *Id.* at 634.

[45] 539 U.S. 558 (2003).

[46] 478 U.S. 186 (1986).

[47] An opinion concurring in the judgment by Justice O'Connor invalidated the law based on equal protection. However, Justice O'Connor gave no indication that she was using heightened scrutiny. 539 U.S. at 579 (O'Connor, J., concurring in the judgment).

[48] 133 S. Ct. 2675 (2013).

[49] Pub. L. No. 104-199, 110 Stat. 2419; 1 U.S.C. §7.

realm of the separate States."[50] The Court said that "DOMA seeks to injure the very class New York seeks to protect. By doing so it violates basic due process and equal protection principles applicable to the Federal Government."[51]

The Court explained that DOMA is unconstitutional because it was based on an impermissible desire to disadvantage gays and lesbians. The Court quoted the House Report on DOMA, which said the Act was based on "both moral disapproval of homosexuality, and a moral conviction that heterosexuality better comports with traditional (especially Judeo-Christian) morality."[52] This is consistent with the Court's holding in *Romer v. Evans*, described above, which held that the government cannot base a law on disapproval of homosexuality.

The Court concluded that §3 of DOMA was unconstitutional because it failed to serve a legitimate government purpose. The Court declared: "The federal statute is invalid, for no legitimate purpose overcomes the purpose and effect to disparage and to injure those whom the State, by its marriage laws, sought to protect in personhood and dignity. By seeking to displace this protection and treating those persons as living in marriages less respected than others, the federal statute is in violation of the Fifth Amendment."[53]

Chief Justice Roberts and Justices Scalia and Alito each wrote dissenting opinions. Chief Justice Roberts emphasized that the Court held only that this provision of DOMA was unconstitutional and expressed no views on state laws prohibiting same-sex marriages. Justice Scalia's dissent argued that the Court effectively had created a right to same-sex marriage and that there was no meaningful distinction between the federal law and state laws denying marriage equality. Justice Alito argued that marriage had throughout history been limited to opposite-sex couples and that Congress, too, could define marriage in this way.

Windsor left open many questions. What level of scrutiny should be used for sexual orientation discrimination? Justice Kennedy's majority opinion says that §3 of DOMA fails to serve a "legitimate" purpose, which means that the Court held that it failed rational basis review. But the Court did not expressly state what level of scrutiny should be used.

Most importantly, are state laws that prohibit marriage equality constitutional? The Court could have resolved this question in *Hollingsworth v. Perry*,[54] decided on the same day as *Windsor*, but instead dismissed that case on standing grounds. After *Windsor*, the United States Courts of Appeals for the Fourth, Seventh, Ninth, and Tenth Circuits found state laws prohibiting marriage equality to be unconstitutional.[55] But the United States Court of Appeals for the Sixth Circuit concluded that such laws are constitutional.[56]

---

[50] 133 S. Ct. at 2690.

[51] *Id.* at 2693.

[52] *Id.*

[53] *Id.* at 2696.

[54] 133 S. Ct. 2652 (2013), discussed in Chapter 2.

[55] *See, e.g.,* Bostic v. Schaefer, 760 F.3d 352 (4th Cir. 2014), *cert. denied,* 135 S. Ct. 308 (2014) (declaring Virginia law unconstitutional); Kitchen v. Herbert, 755 F.3d 1193 (10th Cir.), *cert. denied,* 135 S. Ct. 308 (2014) (declaring Utah law unconstitutional).

[56] DeBoer v. Snyder, 772 F.3d 388 (6th Cir. 2014).

CHAPTER 10

Fundamental Rights

§10.1 INTRODUCTION

§10.1.1 Constitutional Bases for Fundamental Rights

The Idea of a Fundamental Right

The Supreme Court has held that some liberties are so important that they are deemed to be "fundamental rights" and that generally the government cannot infringe upon them unless strict scrutiny is met. This chapter examines many of these liberties, including rights protecting family autonomy, procreation, sexual activity and sexual orientation, medical care decision making, travel, voting, access to the courts, and the right to bear arms. Freedom of speech and religious freedom also are deemed fundamental rights and are considered in Chapters 11 and 12, respectively. Economic rights are discussed in Chapter 8. Criminal procedure protections—such as the Fourth Amendment's safeguard from unreasonable searches and seizure, the Fifth Amendment's protection from self-incrimination and double jeopardy, the Sixth Amendment's assurance of a speedy trial before an impartial jury, and the Eighth Amendment's right to bail and prohibition of cruel and unusual punishment—are beyond the scope of this book.

The rights considered in this chapter share much in common. Almost all of these rights are not mentioned in the text of the Constitution.[1] Thus, as discussed below, all raise the important issue of how the Court should decide whether a liberty should be regarded as a fundamental right. Also, for almost all of these rights, the Supreme Court has indicated that strict scrutiny should be used, which means that the government must justify its interference by proving that its action is necessary to achieve a compelling government purpose.[2]

Due Process and Equal Protection as a Source for Rights

Almost all of these rights have been protected by the Court under the due process clauses of the Fifth and Fourteenth Amendments and/or the equal protection clause of the Fourteenth Amendment. Some of the rights have been protected solely under the due process clause. For example, thus far, the Supreme

---

§10.1 [1] The only exceptions are the Second Amendment right to bear arms and the right to vote, which is protected by the Fifteenth Amendment. Additionally, however, the Supreme Court has said that the right to vote is a fundamental right protected under the equal protection clause of the Fourteenth Amendment. *See, e.g.*, Harper v. Virginia State Bd. of Elections, 383 U.S. 663 (1966), discussed in §10.8 below.

[2] The levels of scrutiny are reviewed and discussed in §6.5. One notable exception to the use of strict scrutiny for fundamental rights is the right to abortion. In *Planned Parenthood v. Casey*, 505 U.S. 833 (1992), the Supreme Court said that government regulations of abortions before viability would be allowed unless they placed an "undue burden" on access to abortions. The right to abortion, and the undue burden test, is discussed in §10.3.3. For some of the rights discussed in this chapter—specifically, the right to engage in private consensual homosexual activity, the right to refuse medical care, and the right to bear arms—the Court has not yet specified the level of scrutiny.

Court has considered a constitutional right to refuse medical care as an aspect of the "liberty" protected in the due process clause.[3] Other rights have so far been protected under the equal protection clause. For example, the right to travel has been safeguarded under equal protection and also the privileges or immunities clause of the Fourteenth Amendment.[4] Also, the right to vote has been protected under both this clause and the Fifteenth Amendment, which prohibits government racial discrimination concerning voting.[5]

Most of these rights, though, have been protected by the Court under both due process and equal protection. For example, the Court has invalidated state laws restricting access to contraceptives both as violating equal protection and as infringing on the right to privacy.[6] In some cases, the Justices disagree among themselves as to whether the right is protected under due process or equal protection. In *Zablocki v. Redhail*, the majority opinion found the right to marry to be a fundamental right protected under the liberty of the due process clause,[7] but the concurring opinion by Justice Powell used an equal protection approach.[8]

Relatively little depends on whether the Court uses due process or equal protection as the basis for protecting a fundamental right. Under either provision, the Court must decide whether a claimed liberty is sufficiently important to be regarded as fundamental, even though it is not mentioned in the text of the Constitution. Also, once a right is deemed fundamental, under due process or equal protection, strict scrutiny is generally used.

The major difference between due process and equal protection as the basis for protecting fundamental rights is in how the constitutional arguments are phrased. If a right is safeguarded under due process, the constitutional issue is whether the government's interference is justified by a sufficient purpose. But if the right is protected under equal protection, the issue is whether the government's discrimination as to who can exercise the right is justified by a sufficient purpose. Although the difference is generally just semantics and phrasing, there can be a real distinction: If a law denies the right to everyone, then due process

---

[3] *See* Cruzan v. Director, Missouri Dept. of Health, 497 U.S. 261 (1990) (competent adults have the right, as part of liberty protected under the due process clause, to refuse medical treatment). Discussed below in §10.5.

[4] *See, e.g.,* Shapiro v. Thompson, 394 U.S. 618 (1969) (residency requirements for receipt of welfare benefits violate the right to travel protected under the equal protection clause), discussed below in §10.7.2; Saenz v. Roe, 526 U.S. 489 (1999) (using the privileges or immunities clause to protect the right to travel), discussed below in §10.7.1 and in Chapter 6 at §6.3.2.

[5] *See, e.g.,* Harper v. Virginia State Bd. of Elections, 383 U.S. 663 (1966) (poll taxes in state and local elections violate the equal protection clause of the Fourteenth Amendment). The Twenty-fourth Amendment outlaws poll taxes in federal elections.

[6] Eisenstadt v. Baird, 405 U.S. 438 (1972) (finding that a law prohibiting distribution of contraceptives to unmarried individuals violated equal protection); Carey v. Population Servs. Intl., 431 U.S. 678 (1977) (declaring unconstitutional a law that provided that only a licensed pharmacist could provide contraceptives to persons over age 16 and that no one could provide them to those under age 16).

[7] 434 U.S. 374 (1978) (declaring unconstitutional a state law preventing a person from obtaining a marriage license if he or she had minor children not in his or her custody and if their support payments were not up to date).

[8] *Id.* at 400 (Powell, J., concurring).

would be the best grounds for analysis; but if a law denies a right to some, while allowing it to others, the discrimination can be challenged as offending equal protection or the violation of the right can be objected to under due process.[9]

The Ninth Amendment

The Ninth Amendment is often mentioned in discussions of fundamental rights, especially rights not expressly mentioned in the text of the Constitution. The Ninth Amendment states: "The enumeration in the Constitution of certain rights, shall not be construed to disparage others retained by the people." The Supreme Court rarely has invoked the Ninth Amendment. A notable exception is *Griswold v. Connecticut*, where Justice Goldberg, in a concurring opinion, reviewed the history of the Ninth Amendment and relied upon it to justify invalidating a law prohibiting use of contraceptives.[10]

The Ninth Amendment generally is not seen as the source of rights in that rights are not protected under it; there are no Ninth Amendment rights. Rather, the Ninth Amendment is used to provide a textual justification for the Court to protect nontextual rights, such as the right to privacy. From this perspective, the Ninth Amendment is not a repository of rights or even a provision that is itself interpreted, but instead is a justification for the Court safeguarding unenumerated liberties.[11]

§10.1.2   *Framework for Analyzing Fundamental Rights*

Litigation and judicial decision making in cases about individual rights can be understood as addressing one or more of four questions. First, is there a fundamental right? Second, is the right infringed? Third, is the government's action justified by a sufficient purpose? And fourth, are the means sufficiently related to the goal sought?

First Issue: Is There a Fundamental Right?

If a right is deemed fundamental, the government usually will be able to prevail only if it meets strict scrutiny; but if the right is not fundamental, generally only the rational basis test is applied.[12] This is the framework for judicial review articulated in the famous *Carolene Products* footnote 4 more than a half century ago:

---

[9] For an excellent discussion of the relationship between the parts of the Fourteenth Amendment, *see* Ira Lupu, Untangling the Strands of the Fourteenth Amendment, 77 Mich. L. Rev. 981 (1979).

[10] 381 U.S. 479, 486 (1965) (Goldberg, J., concurring).

[11] For an excellent collection of essays on the Ninth Amendment, *see* Randy Barnett, ed., The Rights Retained by the People, vols. 1 & 2 (1993).

[12] Strict scrutiny also would be required if there is discrimination based on race, national origin, or alienage. *See* §§9.3, 9.5.

§10.1 Introduction

The judiciary will defer to the legislature unless there is discrimination against a "discrete and insular" minority or infringement of a fundamental right.[13]

The constitutional interpretation debate, discussed in more detail in §1.4, has been primarily about how the Court should decide what rights are fundamental and particularly whether it should find fundamental rights that are not supported by the text or the clear intent of the framers. Many different theories have been advanced to explain when the Court should or shouldn't deem rights to be fundamental.

For example, originalists take the position that fundamental rights are limited to those liberties explicitly stated in the text or clearly intended by the framers. An originalist would say that the Court acts impermissibly and usurps the democratic process if it finds other rights to be fundamental.[14] Nonoriginalism, in contrast, is the view that it is permissible for the Court to protect fundamental rights that are not enumerated in the Constitution or intended by its drafters.

Although as described in §1.4 the debate often has been characterized as a dispute between originalists and nonoriginalists, many other theories also have been advanced for identifying fundamental rights. For example, in addition to strict originalism that limits the Court to rights stated in the text or intended by the framers, there also is moderate originalism, which is the view that the judiciary should implement the framers' general intent, but not necessarily their specific views.[15]

Alternatively, at times, the Court often has looked to history and tradition in deciding what rights not mentioned in the text are fundamental. For instance, the Supreme Court has said that fundamental rights include those liberties that are "deeply rooted in this Nation's history and tradition."[16] In addition to the difficulty of deciding what counts as a sufficient tradition for recognizing a right as fundamental, there also is the question of the abstraction at which the right is stated. At a sufficiently general level of abstraction, any liberty can be justified as consistent with the nation's traditions. At a very specific level of abstraction, few nontextual rights would be justified.[17]

There are many other theories as well for deciding what is a fundamental right. Some argue that the Court's preeminent role is perfecting the processes of government and that the Court only should recognize nontextual rights that concern ensuring adequate representation and the effective operation of the political process.[18] Others would argue that the Court should use natural law principles in

---

[13] United States v. Carolene Prods. Co., 304 U.S. 144, 152 n.4 (1938), discussed in detail in §6.5.

[14] *See* §1.4, text accompanying notes 1-7.

[15] *See, e.g.*, Paul Brest, The Misconceived Quest for the Original Understanding, 60 B.U. L. Rev. 204, 205 (1980), discussed in §1.4, at text accompanying notes 14-17.

[16] Moore v. City of East Cleveland, 431 U.S. 494, 503 (1977).

[17] Justice Scalia, for example, has argued that nontextual rights should be protected under the due process clause only if there is a tradition, stated at the most specific level of abstraction, for protecting the rights. *See* Michael H. v. Gerald D., 491 U.S. 110, 127 n.6 (1989). For a powerful criticism of this view, *see* Laurence Tribe & Michael Dorf, On Reading the Constitution (1991).

[18] *See, e.g.*, John Hart Ely, Democracy and Distrust (1980), discussed in §1.4, text accompanying notes 22-24.

deciding what rights to protect as fundamental.[19] Still other scholars maintain that the Court should recognize nontextual fundamental rights that are supported by a deeply embedded moral consensus that exists in society.[20]

These theories, and the arguments for and against them, are reviewed in §1.4. Throughout this chapter, an underlying question is whether a particular liberty should be deemed a fundamental right, and that inevitably raises the methodological question of how the Court should decide this issue. Inevitably, it provokes debate about the proper role of an unelected judiciary in a democratic society and also about what activities are so important that the courts should find a fundamental right to exist.

Second Issue: Is the Constitutional Right Infringed?

If there is a fundamental right, the next question must be: Has the government infringed upon the right? There, of course, is no doubt that a constitutional right is infringed upon and the government's action must be justified when the exercise of the right is prohibited. For example, if there is a fundamental right to purchase and use contraceptives, a law that outlaws all distribution and use of birth control obviously is an infringement.[21] But when is burdening the exercise of a fundamental right also to be considered an infringement requiring the application of strict scrutiny?[22]

The Supreme Court has said that in evaluating whether there is a violation of a right it considers "[t]he directness and substantiality of the interference."[23] But there has been surprisingly little discussion of what constitutes a direct and substantial interference with a right. The Court has held, for example, that it is impermissible for the government to condition a benefit on a person agreeing to give up a constitutional right. Sometimes referred to as the "unconstitutional conditions doctrine," this is the principle that the government infringes upon a right if it demands that a person forgo a constitutional right in order to receive a government benefit. In its simplest form, there is an unconstitutional condition if the government were to require welfare recipients to refrain from criticizing the government in order to receive welfare benefits.[24]

Many cases, such as in the abortion context, have forced the Court to consider what constitutes an infringement of a right. Is denying of public funding for

---

[19] *See, e.g.*, Harry V. Jaffa, Original Intent and the Framers of the Constitution (1994).

[20] *See, e.g.*, Harry H. Wellington, Common Law Rules and Constitutional Double Standards: Some Notes on Adjudication, 83 Yale L.J. 221, 284 (1973).

[21] *See* §10.3.2.

[22] For an excellent discussion of this issue, *see* Michael C. Dorf, Incidental Burdens on Fundamental Rights, 109 Harv. L. Rev. 1175 (1996).

[23] Zablocki v. Redhail, 434 U.S. 374, 387 n.12 (1978), discussed at §10.2.1; Lyng v. Castillo, 477 U.S. 635, 638 (1986).

[24] There is a rich literature on the unconstitutional conditions doctrine. *See, e.g.*, Kathleen Sullivan, Unconstitutional Conditions, 102 Harv. L. Rev. 1413 (1989). The unconstitutional condition and its application to freedom of speech are discussed in §11.2.4.4.

abortions an infringement?[25] Is a waiting period for abortions or a requirement for spousal notification an infringement?[26] For any right the same basic issue can emerge: Under what circumstances is the government's action an infringement?

Third Issue: Is There a Sufficient Justification for the Government's Infringement of a Right?

If a right is deemed fundamental, the government must present a compelling interest to justify an infringement. Alternatively, if a right is not fundamental, only a legitimate purpose is required for the law to be sustained.[27]

The Supreme Court never has articulated criteria for determining whether a claimed purpose is to be deemed "compelling." The most that can be said is that the government has the burden of persuading the Court that a truly vital interest is served by the law in question. For example, the Court has recognized as "compelling" interests the winning of a war[28] and ensuring that children receive adequate care.[29]

Fourth Issue: Is the Means Sufficiently Related to the Purpose?

Under strict scrutiny it is not enough for the government to prove a compelling purpose behind a law; the government also must show that the law is *necessary* to achieve the objective. This requires that the government prove that it could not attain the goal through any means less restrictive of the right. In comparison, under rational basis review, the means only has to be a *reasonable* way to achieve the goal and the government is not required to use the least restrictive alternative.

There is no formula for deciding whether a means is necessary or whether a less restrictive means can suffice. The government's burden when there is an infringement of a fundamental right is to prove that no other alternative, less intrusive of the right, can work.

In some cases, all four of these issues are in controversy. In other cases, the focus might be on just one or two of the questions. Inevitably, all four require that the judiciary make value choices: What is important enough to be a fundamental right; what is intrusive enough to be deemed an invasion; what is significant enough to be regarded as a compelling interest; and what is narrowly tailored enough to be regarded as a necessary means? These four questions recur throughout the cases discussed in this chapter.

---

[25] *See, e.g.,* Harris v. McRae, 448 U.S. 297 (1980); Maher v. Roe, 432 U.S. 464 (1977), discussed below in §10.3.3.

[26] *See* Planned Parenthood v. Casey, 505 U.S. 833 (1992) (24-hour waiting period is constitutional; spousal notification requirements are unconstitutional), discussed below in §10.3.3.

[27] The question of what constitutes a legitimate purpose is discussed in §9.2.2.

[28] *See* Korematsu v. United States, 323 U.S. 214 (1944) (justifying evacuation of Japanese Americans based on wartime necessity), discussed in §9.3.3.1.

[29] *See, e.g.,* Zablocki v. Redhail, 434 U.S. 374 (1978) (accepting the need to protect children as a compelling interest), discussed in §10.2.1.

§10.2   CONSTITUTIONAL PROTECTION FOR FAMILY AUTONOMY

Origins of Protection

In *Meyer v. Nebraska*, in 1923, the Supreme Court declared unconstitutional a state law that prohibited the teaching in school of any language except English.[1] The Court broadly defined the term "liberty" in the due process clause to protect basic aspects of family autonomy. The Court said: "Without doubt, [liberty] denotes not merely freedom from bodily restraint, but also the right of the individual to contract, to engage in any of the common occupations of life, to acquire useful knowledge, to marry, establish a home and bring up children, to worship God according to the dictates of his own conscience, and generally to enjoy those privileges long recognized at common law as essential to the orderly pursuit of happiness by free men."[2]

Since *Meyer*, the Court has expressly held that certain aspects of family autonomy are fundamental rights and that government interference will be allowed only if strict scrutiny is met. These liberties include the right to marry, the right to custody of one's children, the right to keep the family together, and the right to control the upbringing of one's children. None of these rights, of course, is absolute. But the government must meet the heavy burden of strict scrutiny in order to justify an infringement of any of these rights. Each is discussed in turn. The closely related rights concerning procreation and reproductive autonomy are discussed in the next section, §10.3.

§10.2.1   The Right to Marry

Cases Recognizing the Right to Marry as Fundamental

The Supreme Court first recognized the right to marry as a fundamental right protected under the liberty of the due process clause in *Loving v. Virginia*.[3] In *Loving*, the Court declared unconstitutional Virginia's antimiscegenation statute that prohibited a white person from marrying anyone other than another white person. The first part of the Court's opinion explained why the law violated equal protection.[4] The Court concluded by saying that the law also deprived the Lovings, an interracial couple prosecuted in Virginia for violating the antimiscegenation law, of constitutionally protected liberty without due process of law. The Court declared: "The freedom to marry has long been recognized as one of the vital

---

§10.2 [1] 262 U.S. 390 (1923), discussed in §10.2.4.

[2] *Id.* at 399. For a critique of the Supreme Court's decisions protecting family autonomy, *see* David D. Meyer, The Paradox of Family Privacy, 53 Vand. L. Rev. 527 (2000).

[3] 388 U.S. 1 (1967).

[4] *Id.* This aspect of *Loving* is discussed in §9.3.3.1.

personal rights essential to the orderly pursuit of happiness by free men. Marriage is one of the 'basic civil rights of man,' fundamental to our very existence and survival."[5] The Court thus concluded that the law "surely . . . deprive[s] all the State's citizens of liberty without due process of law."[6]

In *Boddie v. Connecticut*, the Court ruled that a state law requiring the payment of filing fees and court costs in order to receive a divorce violated indigent individuals' due process rights.[7] At the outset of its analysis, the Supreme Court observed: "As this Court on more than one occasion has recognized, marriage involves interests of basic importance in our society."[8] Obviously, preventing individuals from obtaining a divorce precludes them from exercising their right to marry someone else. In subsequent cases, the Supreme Court upheld the constitutionality of filing fees in other contexts, such as for filing bankruptcy petitions[9] and appeals of welfare denials.[10] The Court distinguished these situations from divorce filing fees on the ground that *Boddie*, unlike the others, implicated a fundamental liberty: the right to marry.[11] The Court's most extended discussion of the right to marry was in *Zablocki v. Redhail*.[12] A Wisconsin law prevented an individual from obtaining a marriage license without court approval if the person had a minor child not in his or her custody for whom there was a court order to pay support. The court could grant permission to marry only if there was proof that all child support payments were up to date.

The Supreme Court began by reviewing the cases where it had spoken of the right to marry as a fundamental right and said that "[i]t is not surprising that the decision to marry has been placed on the same level of importance as decisions relating to procreation, childbirth, child rearing, and family relationships."[13] The Court explained that "it would make little sense to recognize a right of privacy with respect to other matters of family life and not with respect to the decision to enter the relationship that is the foundation of the family in our society."[14]

Moreover, the Court said that if the "right to procreate means anything at all, it must imply some right to enter the only relationship in which the State of Wisconsin allows sexual relations legally to take place."[15]

The Court accepted the state's claim that it had a substantial state interest in ensuring that child support was paid for minor children.[16] But the Court found that the law was not sufficiently related to that end and thus concluded that it violated equal protection. The Court explained that the law prevented individuals

---

[5] *Id.* at 12 (citation omitted).

[6] *Id.*

[7] 401 U.S. 371 (1971).

[8] *Id.* at 376.

[9] United States v. Kras, 409 U.S. 434 (1973).

[10] Ortwein v. Schwab, 410 U.S. 656 (1973).

[11] These cases are discussed in more detail in §10.9.

[12] 434 U.S. 374 (1978).

[13] *Id.* at 386.

[14] *Id.*

[15] *Id.*

[16] The Court also recognized a substantial interest in providing counseling to individuals as to the importance of their fulfilling prior support obligations. *Id.* at 388.

who were unable to pay the owed child support from getting married, but "without delivering any money at all into the hands of the applicant's prior children."[17] Also, the Court noted that the state had many alternative ways of ensuring that child support was paid that were less restrictive of the right to marry, such as through wage garnishment, civil contempt, and criminal prosecutions.[18]

Justices Stewart and Powell wrote separate concurring opinions in *Zablocki* and argued that the case should have been decided under due process rather than equal protection analysis.[19] Although they would have used a different constitutional basis for finding the right to marry, their conclusion was the same: The law impermissibly interfered with the right to marry.[20]

The importance of the right to marry is reflected in the Court's willingness to protect it even for prison inmates. In *Turner v. Safley*, the Supreme Court declared unconstitutional a state law that prevented prisoners from getting married unless the superintendent gave permission.[21] The superintendent, by law, only could grant such permission if there were "compelling reasons" for allowing the marriage. Generally only a pregnancy or the birth of a child was considered "compelling."

The Court said that prisoners retained the right to marry because of the importance of expressing "emotional support and public commitment"; because marriage "may be an exercise of religious faith"; because most inmates will be released at some point so that there is "the expectation that [the marriages] ultimately will be fully consummated"; and because "marital status often is a precondition to the receipt of government benefits."[22] Unlike the usual strict scrutiny for fundamental rights, the government may interfere with prisoners' rights if the action is reasonably related to a legitimate penological interest.[23] But the Court concluded that "the almost complete ban on the decision to marry is not reasonably related to legitimate penological objectives."[24] The prison could regulate the time and circumstances of the marriage ceremony and could prevent the married couple from cohabiting, but the state could not forbid all marriages.

The most important contemporary issue with regard to the scope of this right is whether it includes a right to marry for gay and lesbian couples. In 2003, the Massachusetts Supreme Judicial Court became the first state to find a constitutional right to marry under its state constitution.[25] Over the following decade,

---

[17] *Id.* at 389.

[18] *Id.* at 389-390.

[19] *Id.* at 391 (Stewart, J., concurring in the judgment); *id.* at 396 (Powell, J., concurring in the judgment).

[20] Justice Stewart disagreed as to whether the right to marry is a fundamental right. He wrote: "I do not agree with the Court that there is a 'right to marry' in the constitutional sense. That right, or more accurately that privilege, is under our federal system peculiarly one to be defined and limited by state law." *Id.* at 392 (Stewart, J., concurring). However, Stewart also said that the right to marry is protected under the due process clause. *Id.*

[21] 482 U.S. 78 (1987).

[22] *Id.* at 96.

[23] *Id.* at 78.

[24] *Id.* at 99.

[25] Goodrich v. Department of Pub. Health, 440 Mass. 309, 790 N.E.2d 941 (2003).

litigation ensued in both state courts and federal courts as to whether laws denying marriage equality violated the right to marry or deprived equal protection to gays and lesbians. Additionally, some state legislatures passed laws allowing marriage equality and in November 2012, voters in Maine, Maryland, and Washington passed initiatives to permit gays and lesbians to marry in those states.

In June 2013, in *United States v. Windsor*, the Supreme Court declared unconstitutional §3 of the federal Defense of Marriage Act, which defined the term "marriage" under federal law, including the provision of federal benefits, as "only a legal union between one man and one woman as husband and wife."[26] In *Windsor*, in a 5-4 decision, the Court declared §3 of DOMA unconstitutional as denying equal protection to gays and lesbians. *Windsor* is discussed in detail in §9.7.4. The Court emphasized that marriage has traditionally been regulated by the states and that there was "no legitimate purpose" served by the federal government refusing to recognize marriages that a state allowed and recognized.[27] The Court did not address whether the law violated the fundamental right to marry.

After *Windsor*, the United States Courts of Appeals for the Fourth, Seventh, Ninth, and Tenth Circuits found state laws prohibiting marriage equality to be unconstitutional.[28] The Tenth Circuit emphasized the right to marry, while the others focused on equal protection. By contrast, the United States Court of Appeals for the Sixth Circuit concluded that such laws are constitutional and neither deny equal protection nor violate the right to marry.[29] Because of these decisions, as of December 2014, same-sex couples can marry in 35 states and it is likely that the Supreme Court will soon decide whether state laws prohibiting marriage equality violate the United States Constitution.

Cases Finding No Violation of the Right to Marry

Not every law that impacts on the right to marry has been declared unconstitutional. As explained above, the Supreme Court has said that there must be a direct and substantial interference with the right in order to trigger heightened scrutiny.[30] In *Califano v. Jobst*, the Court upheld the constitutionality of a provision of the Social Security Act that terminated benefits for disabled children, who were covered as dependents of wage earners, at the time they got married.[31] The law had an exception if a child married a person who also was entitled to benefits under the Act.

The Court acknowledged that the termination of benefits might have an impact on a person's desire to marry,[32] but the Court said that a "general rule

---

[26] Pub. L. No. 104-199, 110 Stat. 2419; 1 U.S.C. §7.

[27] 133 S. Ct. 2675, 2696 (2013).

[28] *See, e.g.*, Bostic v. Schaefer, 760 F.3d 352 (4th Cir. 2014), *cert. denied*, 135 S .Ct. 308 (2014) (declaring Virginia law unconstitutional); Kitchen v. Herbert, 755 F.3d 1193 (10th Cir.), *cert. denied*, 135 S. Ct. 308 (2014) (declaring Utah law unconstitutional).

[29] DeBoer v. Snyder, 772 F.3d 388 (6th Cir. 2014).

[30] Zablocki v. Redhail, 434 U.S. at 387.

[31] 434 U.S. 47 (1977).

[32] *Id.* at 58.

is not rendered invalid simply because some persons who might otherwise have married were deterred by the rule or because some who did marry were burdened thereby."[33] The Court unanimously concluded that it was permissible for Congress to assume that "a married person is less likely to be dependent on his parents for support than one who is unmarried."[34]

Similarly, in *Bowen v. Owens*, the Court rejected a challenge to another provision of the Social Security Act. The Act provided survivor benefits from a wage earner's account to a widowed spouse who remarried after age 60, but denied such benefits to a similarly situated divorced widowed spouse.[35] The law in essence created a divorce penalty allowing nondivorced widowed spouses to continue to receive benefits, but denying continuing benefits to divorced spouses who remarried.

The Court said that "it was rational for Congress to assume that divorced widowed spouses are generally less dependent upon the resources of their former spouses than are widows and widowers."[36] Thus, "[p]resumably Congress concluded that remarriage sufficiently reduced that lesser dependency to the point where it could conclude that benefits no longer were appropriate."[37]

Cases such as *Califano v. Jobst* and *Bowen v. Owens*, in part, undoubtedly are about judicial deference to legislative decisions about how to allocate scarce funds in a program like Social Security. Lines inevitably must be drawn, and the Court is understandably reluctant to second-guess the legislature unless there is discrimination against a suspect class or a clear infringement of a fundamental right. *Califano v. Jobst* and *Bowen v. Owens* also reflect the Court's unwillingness to find that a right is violated unless there has been a direct and substantial interference. These cases, however, in no way deny that the right to marry is regarded as a fundamental right and that generally the government must meet strict scrutiny before interfering with this basic liberty.

§10.2.2   *The Right to Custody of One's Children*

Custody as a Fundamental Right

The Supreme Court also has recognized that parents have a fundamental right to custody of their children. The Court has remarked that a "natural parent's desire for and right to the companionship, care, custody, and management of his or her children is an interest far more precious than any property right."[38] Thus, the government can permanently terminate custody only if it meets the

---

[33] *Id.* at 54.

[34] *Id.* at 53.

[35] 476 U.S. 340 (1986).

[36] *Id.* at 348-349.

[37] *Id.* at 350. Justices Marshall, Brennan, and Blackmun dissented on the grounds that there was no rational basis for treating widowed spouses and surviving divorced spouses differently upon divorce. *Id.* at 350 (Marshall, J., dissenting); *id.* at 354 (Blackmun, J., dissenting).

[38] Santosky v. Kramer, 455 U.S. 745, 758-759 (1982) (citations omitted).

requirements of both procedural and substantive due process: Parents must be given notice and a hearing, and the government must prove that terminating custody is necessary to achieve a compelling goal.[39]

In *Santosky v. Kramer*, the Supreme Court said that the government must provide "clear and convincing evidence" before permanently terminating a parent's rights.[40] The Court noted that a long line of cases had recognized that "freedom of personal choice in matters of family life is a fundamental liberty interest protected by the Fourteenth Amendment."[41] The Court spoke specifically of "[t]he fundamental liberty interest of natural parents in the care, custody, and management of their child."[42] The Court thus concluded that "[b]efore a State may sever completely and irrevocably the rights of parents in their natural child, due process requires that the State support its allegations by at least clear and convincing evidence."[43]

The Court has made it clear that there must be a very substantial reason before parental custody can be terminated. The Court observed: "We have little doubt that the Due Process Clause would be offended 'if a State were to attempt to force the breakup of a natural family, over the objection of the parents and their children, without some showing of unfitness and for the sole reason that to do so was thought to be in the children's best interest.'"[44]

Rights of Unmarried Fathers

Many of the cases concerning parents' right to custody have involved claims by unmarried fathers. The cases in this area are often difficult to reconcile. In *Stanley v. Illinois*, the Supreme Court declared unconstitutional a state law that automatically made children of an unmarried mother wards of the state at the time of her death.[45] Joan and Peter Stanley had lived together for 18 years and had three children together at the time of her death. Nonetheless, the children were taken from the father and placed into the state's guardianship without any showing that he was an unfit parent simply because the Stanleys had never been married.

The Supreme Court's analysis began by quoting from earlier decisions that had recognized "[t]he rights to conceive and raise one's children have been deemed 'essential,' 'basic civil rights of man,' and 'rights far more precious than property rights.'"[46] The Court concluded that both due process and equal

---

[39] Procedural due process in the context of terminating parental rights is discussed in §7.3.3. In 1996, the Supreme Court held that due process is violated by a requirement that parents pay a filing fee to appeal the permanent termination of custody. M.L.B. v. S.L.J., 519 U.S. 102 (1996).

[40] 455 U.S. 746 (1982).

[41] *Id.* at 753.

[42] *Id.*

[43] *Id.* at 747-748.

[44] Quilloin v. Walcott, 434 U.S. 246, 255 (1978) (quoting Smith v. Organization of Foster Families for Equality & Reform, 431 U.S. 816, 862-863 (1977) (Stewart, J., concurring in the judgment).

[45] 405 U.S. 645 (1972).

[46] *Id.* at 651 (citations omitted).

protection were violated by the state's terminating a father's rights without any showing that he was unfit as a parent.[47]

In other cases, however, the Supreme Court has ruled that the government can terminate the rights of unmarried fathers without being required to provide due process.[48] *Lehr v. Robertson* involved a nonmarital father who had not supported his two-year-old child and had not registered his interest in paternity in a putative father's registry maintained by the state.[49] The Supreme Court held that the state could terminate the father's parental rights without providing notice or a hearing.

The Court distinguished *Stanley* because in that case the father had been actively involved in his children's lives. The Court observed: "When an unwed father demonstrates a full commitment to the responsibilities of parenthood by coming forward to participate in the rearing of his child, his interest in personal contact with his child acquires substantial protection under the due process clause. But the mere existence of a biological link does not merit equivalent constitutional protection."[50]

In *Michael H. v. Gerald D.*, the Supreme Court went even further in limiting the rights of nonmarried fathers. The Supreme Court held that even an unmarried father who participated actively in the child's life is not entitled to due process if the mother was married to someone else.[51] Specifically, the Supreme Court ruled that a state may create an irrebuttable presumption that a married woman's husband is the father of her child even though it negates all of the biological father's rights.

Michael H. involved a married woman who conceived a child as a result of an affair. The biological father was regularly involved in the child's life and sought a court order granting visitation rights. California law, however, created a presumption that a married woman's husband is the father of her child if they were cohabitating and if the husband is not impotent or sterile. The California law allowed this presumption to be rebutted only within two years after the child's birth and only if the husband or wife filed a motion in court. The California court relied on this statute to deny the biological father all parental rights, including visitation.

The Supreme Court, in a 5-to-4 decision, held that this was constitutional. The Court said that the biological father did not have a liberty interest in a relationship with his child because there was no tradition of protecting the father's

---

[47] Similarly, in *Caban v. Mohammed*, 441 U.S. 380 (1979), the Supreme Court declared unconstitutional a state law that required the mother's consent, but not the father's, before a nonmarital child was placed for adoption. The Court, however, invalidated the law as impermissible gender discrimination and did not discuss the issue in terms of the nonmarried father's right to custody of his child. The gender discrimination aspect of this case is discussed in §9.4.3.

[48] The Court also has said that a state may terminate a nonmarital father's rights if it provides due process and determines that it would be in the child's best interests. In *Quilloin v. Walcott*, 434 U.S. 246 (1978), the Court allowed a child to be placed for adoption over the father's objections because he had been accorded procedural due process and the hearing had determined that the adoption would be in the child's best interests.

[49] 463 U.S. 248 (1983).

[50] *Id.* at 261.

[51] 491 U.S. 110 (1989).

rights when the mother is married to someone else. Justice Scalia, writing for the plurality, remarked: "What counts is whether the States in fact award substantive parental rights to the natural father of a child conceived within, and born into, an extant marital union that wishes to embrace the child. We are not aware of a single case, old or new, that has done so. This is not the stuff of which fundamental rights qualifying as liberty interests are made."[52]

Justice Scalia, writing at this point just for himself and Chief Justice Rehnquist, said that the Supreme Court should protect rights under the due process clause only if there is a tradition, stated at the most specific level of abstraction, for safeguarding the liberty.[53] Scalia's point was that the general tradition of protecting an unmarried father's rights was irrelevant because there was not a specific tradition of protecting unmarried fathers when the child was conceived as a result of an adulterous relationship. Scalia wrote: "The need, if arbitrary decisionmaking is to be avoided, [is] to adopt the most specific tradition as the point of reference. . . . Although assuredly having the virtue (if it be that) of leaving judges free to decide as they think best when the unanticipated occurs, a rule of law that binds neither by text nor by any particular, identifiable tradition is no rule of law at all."[54]

Justice Stevens, the fifth vote for the majority's result, wrote separately to say that he would not foreclose "the possibility that a natural father might ever have a constitutionally protected interest in his relationship with a child whose mother was married to, and cohabitating with, another man at the time of the child's conception and birth."[55] Justice Stevens upheld the California law and the denial of custody in *Michael H.* because the state offered a procedure whereby the biological father could have established paternity and preserved his rights.

Justice Brennan wrote a vehement dissent disagreeing with both the majority's conclusions and its reasoning. Justice Brennan emphasized the Constitution's protections for parents' rights to custody of the children, including rights of unmarried fathers. Brennan explained that in a diverse society parental rights might arise in a wide variety of different types of family arrangements: "In construing the Fourteenth Amendment to offer shelter only to those interests specifically

---

[52] *Id.* at 127.

[53] *Id.* at 127 n.6.

[54] *Id.* Justice Scalia also followed this approach in *Reno v. Flores*, 507 U.S. 292 (1993), which upheld the Immigration and Naturalization Service's regulations concerning detention of children. A child who did not have a parent, close relative, or guardian in the United States would remain in federal custody. The Court rejected the argument that the government had to provide care in a manner that was narrowly tailored to promote the child's best interests. The Court said that "[t]he best interests of the child is . . . not an absolute and exclusive constitutional criterion for the government's exercise of the custodial responsibility that it undertakes, which must be reconciled with many other responsibilities. Thus, child-care institutions operated by the state in exercise of its *parens patriae* authority . . . are not constitutionally required to be funded at a level to provide the *best* schooling or the *best* health care available." *Id.* at 304 (emphasis in original). Justice Scalia rejected the claim that children have a right to a private custodian rather than the government and stated: "The mere novelty of such a claim is reason enough to doubt that substantive due process sustains it; the alleged right cannot be considered 'so rooted in the traditions and conscience of our people' as to be ranked as fundamental." *Id.*

[55] 491 U.S. at 133 (Stevens, J., concurring in the judgment).

protected by historical practice . . . the plurality ignores the kind of society in which our Constitution exists. We are not an assimilative, homogenous society, but a facilitative, pluralistic one, in which we must be willing to abide someone else's unfamiliar or even repellant practice because the same tolerant impulse protects our own idiosyncrasies."[56] Brennan's point was that family rights should not be narrowly defined as existing only within certain types of families and that the Court should not restrictively define traditions in determining the scope of constitutional rights.

Michael H. v. Gerald D. is an important case for many reasons. The opinions directly focused on the basic question of how the Court should decide the content of fundamental rights: Is tradition determinative and, if so, must it be a tradition stated at the most specific level of abstraction?[57]

Also, the case is important in addressing the issue of who should be deemed to have a constitutionally protected interest in a relationship with a child. The Court, especially the plurality, believed that society's interest in protecting the family requires that only the two individuals deemed by law to be parents should have constitutionally safeguarded rights concerning the children. But in contemporary society, many individuals might have a relationship with a child: biological parents, stepparents, grandparents, foster parents, and so on. The issue is whether the Court should recognize and protect these interests under the Constitution.[58]

§10.2.3 The Right to Keep the Family Together

Protection for the Extended Family

The Supreme Court has recognized a fundamental right to keep the family together that includes an extended family. The key case was *Moore v. City of East Cleveland*.[59] A city's zoning ordinance limited the number of unrelated people who could live together in one household and defined "unrelated" to keep a grandmother from living with her two grandsons who were first cousins. Justice Powell, writing for the plurality, concluded that "liberty" in the due process clause includes protection for family rights. Justice Powell acknowledged that "[s]ubstantive due process has at times been a treacherous field for this Court. There *are* risks when the judicial branch gives enhanced protection to certain substantive liberties without the guidance of more specific provisions of the Bill of Rights."[60] But Powell said that "history counsels caution and restraint. But it does not counsel

---

[56] *Id.* at 141 (Brennan, J., dissenting).

[57] For a powerful criticism of Justice Scalia's approach of defining tradition at the most specific level of abstraction, *see* Laurence Tribe & Michael Dorf, On Reading the Constitution (1991).

[58] In Smith v. Organization of Foster Families for Equality & Reform, 431 U.S. 816 (1977), the Court distinguished between natural families and foster families and rejected a due process challenge to a state law that allowed removal of a child from a foster family without notice or a hearing if the child had been there less than 18 months.

[59] 431 U.S. 494 (1977).

[60] *Id.* at 502.

abandonment, nor does it require what the city urges here: cutting off any protection of family rights at the first convenient, if arbitrary boundary—the boundary of the nuclear family."[61]

The plurality opinion concluded that the Constitution protects family rights, not just for parents and children but for the extended family as well. Justice Powell observed that child-rearing decisions "long have been shared with grandparents or other relatives who occupy the same household."[62] Thus, the East Cleveland zoning ordinance was declared unconstitutional for infringing on the rights of the extended family.

Families Must Be Relatives

The Court has limited the reach of *Moore v. City of East Cleveland* two major ways. First, individuals must be related to one another to be considered a family. For example, in *Moore*, the Court distinguished the earlier decision in *Village of Belle Terre v. Boraas*, where the Court had upheld a similar zoning ordinance that limited the number of unrelated people who could live together in one household.[63] In *Belle Terre*, a group of college students who wanted to share a house brought a constitutional challenge to the ordinance. The Court in *Moore* emphasized that *Belle Terre* had involved only "*unrelated* individuals" and, in fact, the zoning ordinance there had an exception for "all who were related by 'blood, adoption, or marriage.' "[64]

The Court invoked the same distinction between relatives and nonrelatives in *Smith v. Organization of Foster Families for Equality and Reform*, which concerned the rights of foster parents.[65] The Supreme Court held that the state did not violate due process in providing preremoval hearings only to foster parents who had been with a child for 18 months or more. The Court observed that although its prior decisions had involved a biological relationship, "[n]o one would seriously dispute that a deeply loving and interdependent relationship between an adult and a child in his or her care may exist even in the absence of a blood relationship."[66]

However, the Court also saw key differences between biological parents and foster parents. The Court said that "whatever emotional ties may develop between foster parent and foster child have their origins in an arrangement in which the State has been a partner from the outset."[67] Also, the Court stressed that protecting a liberty interest for foster parents often would be at the expense of the liberty of natural parents.

The Court concluded that it did not need to resolve the nature of the liberty interest of foster parents because the state law provided adequate protections

---

[61] *Id.*

[62] *Id.* at 505.

[63] 416 U.S. 1 (1974).

[64] 431 U.S. at 498.

[65] 431 U.S. 816 (1977).

[66] *Id.* at 844.

[67] *Id.* at 845.

even assuming rights of foster parents.[68] The Court said that due process did not require that there be a hearing every time a child was removed from a foster home and that it was sufficient for the government to provide preremoval due process for those foster parents who had been with a child for more than 18 months.

Infringement Must Be Direct and Substantial

The other important limit on *Moore* has been the Court's refusal to find an infringement of the right to keep the family together unless there is a direct and substantial interference. In *Lyng v. Castillo*, the Supreme Court upheld a federal law that provided food stamps to households rather than to individuals.[69] The law treated relatives—parents, children, and siblings—who live together as a family, even if in reality they do not customarily purchase food and prepare meals together. More distant relatives and unrelated individuals are not grouped together. The result was that families were treated worse than unrelated individuals; a family was considered as a single unit in receiving benefits, but others could individually receive benefits.

Nonetheless, the Supreme Court held that the federal law was constitutional because the statute does not "'directly and substantially' interfere with family living arrangements and thereby burden a fundamental right."[70] The Court emphasized that the law "does not order or prevent any group of persons from dining together."[71] The Court saw no indication that the statute would have a substantial effect on a family's choices about whether to live together. The Court observed: "Indeed, in the overwhelming majority of cases it probably has no effect at all. It is exceedingly unlikely that close relatives would choose to live apart simply to increase their allotment of food stamps, for the cost of separate housing would almost certainly exceed the incremental value of the additional stamps."[72]

Similarly, in *Bowen v. Gilliard*, the Court upheld a federal law that used the income of all parents and siblings living in the home in determining eligibility under the Aid to Families with Dependent Children program.[73] The Court emphasized the need for "deferential" review in making decisions concerning benefits.[74] The Court quoted earlier authority as establishing that "discretion belongs to Congress unless the choice is clearly wrong, a display of arbitrary power, not an exercise of judgment."[75] The Court said that in determining eligibility and in allocating benefits, Congress has "plenary power to define the scope and the duration of the entitlement to benefits and to increase, to decrease, or to terminate

[68] *Id.* at 847.
[69] 477 U.S. 635 (1986).
[70] *Id.* at 638.
[71] *Id.*
[72] *Id.*
[73] 483 U.S. 587 (1987).
[74] *Id.* at 598.
[75] *Id.* (quoting Mathews v. De Castro, 429 U.S. 181, 185 (1976)).

those benefits based on the relative importance of the recipients' needs and the resources available to fund the program."[76]

Lyng v. Castillo and *Bowen v. Gilliard* are, in large part, about the Court's unwillingness to review aggressively countless choices that the legislature must make in allocating very scarce benefits dollars. They also illustrate that a federal law that incidentally burdens a right—such as by discouraging family members from living together—is not an infringement sufficient to trigger strict scrutiny.

§10.2.4   *The Right to Control Upbringing of Children*

Initial Recognition of the Right

The first Supreme Court cases recognizing family autonomy involved the right of parents to control the upbringing of their children. In *Meyer v. Nebraska,* in 1923, the Supreme Court declared unconstitutional a state law that prohibited teaching in any language other than English in the public schools.[77] The Court invalidated the law, not on First Amendment grounds, but by using substantive due process and finding that the statute violated the right of parents to make decisions for their children.[78]

Similarly, two years later, in *Pierce v. Society of Sisters,* the Supreme Court held unconstitutional a state law that required children to attend public schools.[79] The Court explained that "[t]he fundamental theory of liberty upon which all governments in this Union repose excludes any general power of the state to standardize its children by forcing them to accept instruction from public teachers only. The child is not the mere creature of the state; those who nurture him and direct his destiny have the right, coupled with the high duty, to recognize and prepare him for his additional obligations."[80]

But the Court also has recognized that the right to make parenting decisions is not absolute and can be interfered with by the state if necessary to protect a child. For example, in *Prince v. Massachusetts,* the Court upheld the application of child labor laws to a nine-year-old girl who was soliciting for the Jehovah's Witnesses religion at the direction of her parents.[81] The Court acknowledged that there is a "private realm of family life which the state cannot enter."[82] But the Court said that "the family itself is not beyond regulation in the public interest. . . . Acting to guard the general interest in youth's well being, the state as parens patriae may

---

[76] *Id.* (quoting Atkins v. Parker, 472 U.S. 115, 129 (1985)).

[77] 262 U.S. 390 (1923).

[78] In part, this is because the First Amendment had not yet been incorporated into the Fourteenth Amendment and applied to the states. *See* Gitlow v. New York, 268 U.S. 652 (1925) (finding that the First Amendment applies to the states through its incorporation into the due process clause of the Fourteenth Amendment).

[79] 268 U.S. 510 (1925).

[80] *Id.* at 535.

[81] 321 U.S. 158 (1944).

[82] *Id.* at 166.

restrict the parent's control by requiring school attendance, regulating or prohibiting the child's labor and in many other ways."[83] The Court said that the need to protect children from being exploited and harmed justified upholding laws prohibiting child labor, even if the work was at the direction of the parents and even if it was undertaken for religious purposes.[84]

Deference to Parents

In weighing the competing claims of parents and of the state on behalf of children, the Supreme Court has given great deference—some say too much deference—to parents.[85] In *Wisconsin v. Yoder*, the Supreme Court held that Amish parents had a constitutional right, based on their right to control the upbringing of their children and based on free exercise of religion, to exempt their 14- and 15-year-old children from a compulsory school attendance law.[86] The Court said that "a State's interest in universal education, however highly we rank it, is not totally free from a balancing process when it impinges on fundamental rights and interests, such as those specifically protected by the Free Exercise Clause of the First Amendment, and the traditional interest of parents with respect to the religious upbringing of their children."[87]

The Court gave great weight to the parents' claim that additional education would threaten their children's religious beliefs and to the uniquely insulated nature of the Amish culture. The Court accepted the argument that applying the mandatory schooling law to 14- and 15-year-old Amish children would interfere with free exercise of religion and with the ability of parents to make decisions concerning their children. The Court noted that there was no evidence of "any harm to the physical or mental health of the child or to the public safety, peace, order, or welfare."[88] The Court thus concluded that "[u]nder the doctrine of *Meyer v. Nebraska* we think it entirely plain that the Act . . . interferes with the liberty of parents and guardians to direct the upbringing and education of children under their control."[89]

The key question, of course, is whether making sure that children have basic schooling to at least age 16 is a compelling interest that justifies interfering with parents' choice to terminate formal schooling at an earlier age. The Court based its decision on the nature of the Amish community where additional formal schooling was unnecessary. But the concern is that without more formal schooling Amish children could not choose for themselves what life path to take as adults.

The Court's substantial deference to parents also is reflected in *Parham v. J.R.*[90] *Parham* presented the question of what type of procedural due process must

---

[83] *Id.*

[84] The free exercise aspect of this case is discussed in §12.3.2.2.

[85] *See* James G. Dwyer, Parents' Religion and Children's Welfare: Debunking the Doctrine of Parents' Rights, 82 Cal. L. Rev. 1371 (1994).

[86] 406 U.S. 205 (1972).

[87] *Id.* at 214.

[88] *Id.* at 230.

[89] *Id.* at 232-233.

[90] 442 U.S. 584 (1979).

be accorded to children when their parents commit them to an institution.[91] The Supreme Court had earlier ruled that except in an emergency, before an adult can be committed to an institution there must be notice and a hearing.[92] But the Court said that the assumption must be that a parent is acting in the best interests of a child when making a commitment decision.

The Court recognized that some parents might abuse the power to institutionalize a child, but said that this was not a sufficient basis for treating commitment of children like commitment of adults. Chief Justice Burger, writing for the Court, stated: "That some parents may at times be acting against the interests of their children . . . creates a basis for caution, but is hardly a reason to discard wholesale those pages of human experience that teach that parents generally do act in the child's best interests. The statist notion that governmental power should supersede parental authority in *all* cases because *some* parents abuse and neglect children is repugnant to American tradition."[93]

Thus, the Court concluded that before a child can be institutionalized by a parent there only need be a screening by a doctor or other neutral fact-finder. A child, unlike an adult, did not have to be given notice and an evidentiary hearing. The dissenting opinion by Justice Brennan, joined by Justices Marshall and Stevens, emphasized the "massive curtailment of liberty" inherent to institutionalization and the need to protect children from the possibility of erroneous commitment.[94] The dissent said that "[c]hildren incarcerated in public mental institutions are constitutionally entitled to a fair opportunity to contest the legitimacy of their confinement. They are entitled to some champion who can speak on their behalf and who stands ready to oppose a wrongful commitment. . . . And fairness demands that children abandoned by their supposed protectors to the rigors of institutional confinement be given the help of some separate voice."[95]

Parham and *Yoder* reveal the extent of the Court's willingness to defer to parenting decisions. Yet in both cases there is a strong argument that the Court undervalued the importance of protecting children by preventing unneeded institutionalization and ensuring their education.

Grandparents' Rights Statutes

The Supreme Court most recently considered the right of parents to control the upbringing of their children in the context of a state law protecting grandparents' rights. All 50 states have laws that accord rights to grandparents. The underlying constitutional issue is whether such statutes impermissibly interfere with the right of parents to control the upbringing of their children. In *Troxel v. Granville*,[96]

---

[91] *Parham* also is discussed in §7.3.3, which focuses on procedural due process.
[92] Addington v. Texas, 441 U.S. 418 (1979).
[93] 442 U.S. at 602-603 (emphasis in original) (citation omitted).
[94] *Id.* at 626 (Brennan, J., concurring in part and dissenting in part).
[95] *Id.* at 638-639 (Brennan, J., dissenting).
[96] 530 U.S. 57, 58 (2000).

the Supreme Court declared unconstitutional Washington's law, but the absence of a majority opinion and the focus on the specifics of the statute in question left in doubt the permissibility of other versions of grandparents' rights laws.

The case had tragic facts. A father of two young daughters committed suicide. For the first year after his death, the girls continued to regularly visit with their paternal grandparents. Then their mother largely ended this visitation, restricting it to a few times a year. The grandparents sued in Washington State trial court under the state law that protects grandparents' rights. Section 26.10.160(3) of the Revised Code of Washington permits "[a]ny person" to petition a superior court for visitation rights "at any time" and authorizes that court to grant such visitation rights whenever "visitation may serve the best interest of the child." The Washington trial court ruled in favor of the grandparents and ordered extensive visitation, but the Washington Supreme Court declared this unconstitutional as violating the mother's right to control the upbringing of her children.

There was no majority opinion for the Court; Justice O'Connor wrote for a plurality of four and was joined by Chief Justice Rehnquist and Justices Ginsburg and Breyer. Justice O'Connor began by noting the fundamental nature of the right involved: "The liberty interest at issue in this case—the interest of parents in the care, custody, and control of their children—is perhaps the oldest of the fundamental liberty interests recognized by this Court."[97] The plurality found that the Washington law, as applied in this case, was unconstitutional as infringing on this fundamental right.

Justice O'Connor observed that the "Washington nonparental visitation statute is breathtakingly broad. According to the statute's text, '[a]ny person may petition the court for visitation rights at any time,' and the court may grant such visitation rights whenever 'visitation may serve the best interest of the child.'"[98] Justice O'Connor said that this gives the judge undue ability to overturn the decisions of a fit parent: "Thus, in practical effect, in the State of Washington a court can disregard and overturn any decision by a fit custodial parent concerning visitation whenever a third party affected by the decision files a visitation petition, based solely on the judge's determination of the child's best interests."[99]

Justice O'Connor stressed that in this case there were no allegations that the mother was unfit. Nor, she stressed, had all visitation been ended; the mother had restricted visitation to one visit per month and special holidays. Thus, Justice O'Connor concluded: "Considered together with the Superior Court's reasons for awarding visitation to the Troxels, the combination of these factors demonstrates that the visitation order in this case was an unconstitutional infringement on Granville's fundamental right to make decisions concerning the care, custody, and control of her two daughters."[100] Justice O'Connor noted that the Court was

---

[97] *Id.* at 65.
[98] *Id.* at 60.
[99] *Id.* at 67.
[100] *Id.* at 72.

not considering the unconstitutionality of other grandparents' rights statute, but rather only the Washington law as applied.

Justice Souter concurred in the judgment and said that he would affirm the Washington Supreme Court's decision declaring the law facially unconstitutional as infringing the right of parents to control the upbringing of their children.[101] Justice Thomas also concurred in the judgment, but his opinion was more cryptic. He began by stating: "I write separately to note that neither party has argued that our substantive due process cases were wrongly decided and that the original understanding of the Due Process Clause precludes judicial enforcement of non-enumerated rights under that constitutional provision."[102] He then said that because no one had raised this issue, strict scrutiny was the appropriate test and that the Washington law failed. The clear implication is that Justice Thomas would have agreed with Justice Scalia's dissent, which rejected a right of parents to control the upbringing of their children, if only that issue had been raised.

In addition to Justice Scalia's dissent, which disputed the existence of fundamental rights under the due process clause,[103] Justice Stevens dissented and said that he would have denied certiorari and let the Washington legislature draft a better law in response to the Washington Supreme Court's decision.[104] Justice Kennedy also dissented and expressed the view that the Washington Supreme Court was wrong in concluding that the "best interests" standard in the grandparents' rights statute was unconstitutional.[105]

Troxel did more to confuse than clarify the law in the area of grandparents' rights laws. On the one hand, the case can be read broadly as reaffirming that parents have a fundamental right to control the upbringing of their children and as providing a basis for invalidating orders for grandparent visitation over the objection of fit parents. On the other hand, *Troxel* can be read as a very narrow decision that involved a particularly broad law applied in a situation where the parent was fit and regular grandparent visitation still occurred. The absence of a majority opinion makes it even more difficult to assess the impact of the decision other than the certainty that it will lead to challenges to grandparents' rights laws throughout the country.

---

[101] *Id.* at 76.
[102] *Id.*
[103] *Id.* at 91.
[104] *Id.* at 93.
[105] *Id.* at 94.

§10.3   CONSTITUTIONAL PROTECTION FOR REPRODUCTIVE AUTONOMY

§10.3.1   *The Right to Procreate*

Buck v. Bell

The Supreme Court has held that the right to procreate is a fundamental right, and therefore government-imposed involuntary sterilization must meet strict scrutiny. Initially, the Court rejected this position and in *Buck v. Bell* upheld the ability of the government to involuntarily sterilize the mentally retarded.[1] In *Buck*, the Supreme Court stated that it was constitutional for the State of Virginia to sterilize Carrie Buck, an 18-year-old woman, pursuant to a law that provided for the involuntary sterilization of the mentally retarded who were in state institutions. Justice Oliver Wendell Holmes, in some of the most offensive language found anywhere in the United States Reports, declared: "It is better for all the world, if instead of waiting to execute degenerate offspring for crime, or to let them starve for their imbecility, society can prevent those who are manifestly unfit from continuing their kind. . . . Three generations of imbeciles are enough."[2]

The Court described Carrie Buck as a "feeble minded white woman."[3] In fact, in 1980, Carrie Buck was found to be alive and living with her sister, who also had been sterilized by the state. Carrie Buck was discovered to be a woman of normal intelligence.[4] She was one of almost 60,000 "forced eugenic sterilizations" that had been performed in the United States by 1935.[5]

Skinner v. Oklahoma

In *Skinner v. Oklahoma*, in 1942, the Court rejected this approach and declared unconstitutional the Oklahoma Habitual Criminal Sterilization Act that allowed courts to order the sterilization of those convicted two or more times for crimes involving "moral turpitude."[6] Justice Douglas, writing for the Court, began by stating: "This case touches a sensitive and important area of human rights. Oklahoma deprives certain individuals of a right which is basic to perpetuation of a race — the right to have offspring."[7]

---

§10.3 [1] 274 U.S. 200 (1927). For an excellent history of this case, *see* Paul A. Lombardo, Three Generations, No Imbeciles: Eugenics, the Supreme Court, and *Buck v. Bell* (2008).

[2] *Id.* at 207.

[3] *Id.* at 205.

[4] *See* Stephen Jay Gould, Carrie Buck's Daughter, 2 Const. Comment. 331, 336 (1985).

[5] *See* Erwin Chemerinsky, The Case Against the Supreme Court 4 (2014).

[6] 316 U.S. 535, 536 (1942).

[7] *Id.*

The Court found that the Oklahoma law violated equal protection and spoke broadly of the right to procreate as a fundamental right: "We are dealing here with legislation which involves one of the basic civil rights of man. Marriage and procreation are fundamental to the very existence and survival of the race. The power to sterilize, if exercised, may have subtle, far-reaching and devastating effects. In evil or reckless hands it can cause races or types which are inimical to the dominant group to whither and disappear. There is no redemption for the individual whom the law touches. . . . He is forever deprived of a basic liberty."[8]

The Court did not expressly overrule *Buck v. Bell*,[9] but it is hard to see how it survives the forceful language in Justice Douglas's majority opinion. Perhaps *Skinner* reflects the waning of the eugenics movement that had inspired the laws challenged in both cases. Also, it is possible that fighting the Nazis in World War II, and their attempt to create a master race, made these laws unpalatable. What is clear is that the right to procreate is deemed a fundamental right, and any attempt by the government to impose involuntary sterilization has to meet strict scrutiny.

§10.3.2   *The Right to Purchase and Use Contraceptives*

Griswold v. Connecticut

In *Griswold v. Connecticut*, the Supreme Court declared unconstitutional a state law that prohibited the use and distribution of contraceptives.[10] A Connecticut law said: "Any person who uses any drug, medicinal article, or instrument for the purpose of preventing conception shall be fined not less than fifty dollars or imprisoned not less than sixty days nor more than one year or be both fined and imprisoned."[11] The law also made it a crime to assist, abet, or counsel a violation of the law.

The case involved a criminal prosecution of Estelle Griswold, the executive director of the Planned Parenthood League of Connecticut, and a physician, who openly ran a family planning clinic from November 1 to November 10, 1961. They were prosecuted for providing contraceptives to a married woman.

The Supreme Court, in an opinion by Justice Douglas, found that the right to privacy was a fundamental right. Douglas, however, expressly rejected the argument that the right was protected under the liberty of the due process clause. Douglas stated: "[W]e are met with a wide range of questions that implicate the Due Process Clause of the Fourteenth Amendment. Overtones of some suggest that Lochner v. New York should be our guide. But we decline that invitation as we did [in many other cases.]"[12]

---

[8] *Id.* at 541.

[9] Indeed, Justice Douglas attempted to distinguish *Buck v. Bell* on the ground that it treated all similarly situated people the same and thus did not violate equal protection, while the Oklahoma law drew an arbitrary distinction among criminals in determining who would be sterilized. *Id.* at 540.

[10] 381 U.S. 479 (1965).

[11] *Id.* at 480.

[12] *Id.* at 481-482 (citations omitted).

Instead, Douglas found that privacy was implicit in many of the specific provisions of the Bill of Rights, such as the First, Third, Fourth, and Fifth Amendments. Douglas declared: "The foregoing cases suggest that specific guarantees in the Bill of Rights have penumbras, formed by emanations from those guarantees that help give them life and substance. Various guarantees create zones of privacy. . . . We have had many controversies over these penumbral rights of privacy and repose. These cases bear witness that the right of privacy which presses for recognition here is a legitimate one."[13]

Douglas then concluded that the Connecticut law violated the right to privacy in prohibiting married couples from using contraceptives. Douglas said: "Would we allow the police to search the sacred precincts of the marital bedrooms for telltale signs of the use of contraceptives? The very idea is repulsive to the notions of privacy surrounding the marriage relationship."[14]

It is notable both as to where Douglas found the right to privacy in the Constitution and as to what Douglas deemed offensive to that right. In an attempt to avoid substantive due process, Douglas, who had lived through the *Lochner* era, found privacy in the "penumbra" of the Bill of Rights. This approach has been much criticized[15] and has not been followed by subsequent cases. It also does not seem to achieve Douglas's goal of avoiding substantive due process because the Bill of Rights is applied to the states through the due process clause of the Fourteenth Amendment; the penumbral approach is thus ultimately a due process analysis.

Also, it is important to note that Douglas did not focus on a right to avoid procreation or to make reproductive choices. Rather, Douglas focused on the need to protect the privacy of the bedroom from intrusion by the police and the ability to control information about contraceptive use. It was not until later cases, discussed below, that the Court expressly protected access to contraceptives as part of reproductive autonomy.

There were several other opinions in *Griswold*. Justice Goldberg, joined by Chief Justice Warren and Justice Brennan, wrote a concurring opinion emphasizing the Ninth Amendment as authority for the Court to protect nontextual rights such as privacy.[16] Justice Harlan concurred in the judgment and argued that the right to privacy should be protected under the liberty of the due process clause. He said that "the proper constitutional inquiry . . . is whether this Connecticut statute infringes the Due Process Clause of the Fourteenth Amendment because the enactment violates basic values 'implicit in the concept of ordered liberty.'"[17]

---

[13] *Id.* at 484-485 (citations omitted).

[14] *Id.* at 485-486.

[15] *See* Robert G. Dixon, The "New" Substantive Due Process and the Democratic Ethic: A Prolegomenon, 1976 BYU L. Rev. 43, 84 (In *Griswold*, Douglas "skipped through the Bill of Rights like a cheerleader — 'Give me a P . . . give me an R . . . give me an I . . . ,' and so on, and found P-R-I-V-A-C-Y as a derivative or penumbral right.").

[16] 381 U.S. at 486.

[17] *Id.* at 500. Harlan referred to his earlier opinion in *Poe v. Ullman*, 367 U.S. 497, 522 (1961) (Harlan, J., dissenting), where he had dissented from the dismissal of a challenge to the Connecticut law on ripeness grounds. There he had argued that the law violates the right to privacy, which is protected under the liberty of the due process clause.

Justice White also concurred in the judgment and argued that the law did not even meet a rational basis test.[18] White said that he "wholly fail[ed] to see how the ban on the use of contraceptives by married couples in any way reinforces the State's ban on illicit sexual relationships."[19]

Justices Black and Stewart wrote dissenting opinions. They contended that the law was constitutional because there is no right to privacy mentioned in the Constitution. Justice Black wrote: "The Court talks about a constitutional 'right of privacy' as though there is some constitutional provision or provisions forbidding any law ever to be passed which might abridge the 'privacy' of individuals. But there is not."[20] Black thus concluded: "I get nowhere in this case by talk about a constitutional 'right of privacy' as an emanation from one or more constitutional provisions. I like my privacy as well as the next one, but I am nevertheless compelled to admit that government has a right to invade it unless prohibited by some specific constitutional provision."[21]

A Fundamental Right to Control Reproduction

Subsequent to *Griswold*, the Supreme Court recognized a right to purchase and use contraceptives based on a right of individuals to make decisions concerning procreation. In *Eisenstadt v. Baird*, the Supreme Court declared unconstitutional a Massachusetts law that prohibited distributing contraceptives to unmarried individuals and that only allowed physicians to distribute them to married persons.[22] An individual was convicted for giving a woman a package of contraceptive foam at the completion of a lecture on birth control at Boston University. The Court found that the Massachusetts law denied equal protection because it discriminated against nonmarried individuals.

Justice Brennan, writing for the Court, stated: "If the right of privacy means anything, it is the right of the *individual*, married or single, to be free from unwarranted governmental intrusion into matters so fundamentally affecting a person as the decision whether to bear or beget a child."[23] Moreover, the Court said that prohibiting the distribution of contraceptives served no legitimate government purpose. Justice Brennan remarked that "[i]t would be plainly unreasonable to assume that Massachusetts has prescribed pregnancy and the birth of an unwanted child as punishment for fornication."[24] Nor could prohibiting distribution of contraceptives be defended as a health measure.[25]

---

[18] *Id.* at 505 (White, J., concurring in the judgment) (arguing that the rational basis test is the appropriate level of scrutiny).

[19] *Id.*

[20] *Id.* at 508 (Black, J., dissenting).

[21] *Id.* at 509-510.

[22] 405 U.S. 438 (1972).

[23] *Id.* at 453.

[24] *Id.* at 448.

[25] There were several other opinions in *Eisenstadt*. Justice Douglas said that the law should have been invalidated as violating the First Amendment. *Id.* at 455 (Douglas, J., concurring). Justices White and Blackmun concurred in the result on the ground that there was no evidence that contraceptives

Eisenstadt expands on *Griswold* in recognizing a right to control reproduction as a fundamental right. *Eisenstadt* also is significant in recognizing a right for unmarrieds, as well as marrieds, and in protecting a right to distribute contraceptives as well as to use them.

The Court followed this reasoning in *Carey v. Population Services International*.[26] In *Carey*, the Court declared unconstitutional a New York law that made it a crime to sell or distribute contraceptives to minors under age 16; for anyone other than a licensed pharmacist to distribute contraceptives to persons over age 15; and for anyone to advertise or display contraceptives. The Court reviewed the cases concerning family and procreational autonomy and said that "[t]he decision whether or not to beget or bear a child is at the very heart of this cluster of constitutionally protected choices."[27] The Court thus said that strict scrutiny must be met for the government to justify a law restricting access to contraceptives. Justice Brennan, writing for the Court, said: "'Compelling' is of course the key word; where a decision as fundamental as that whether to bear or beget a child is involved, regulations imposing a burden on it may be justified only by compelling state interests, and must be narrowly drawn to express only those interests."[28]

Thus, the Court found that limiting distribution of contraceptives to licensed pharmacists unduly restricted access to birth control and infringed on the right to control procreation.[29] Additionally, the Court found that the law violated the rights of those under age 16 to have access to contraceptives.[30] The Court explained: "Since the State may not impose a blanket prohibition, or even a blanket requirement of parental consent, on the choice of a minor to terminate her pregnancy, the constitutionality of a blanket prohibition of the distribution of contraceptives to a minor is a fortiori foreclosed."[31] The Court doubted that prohibiting distribution of contraceptives would deter teenage sexual activity and, in any event, thought it irrational that the state would want an unwanted pregnancy to be the punishment for fornication.[32]

---

had been distributed to an unmarried person. *Id.* at 464-465 (White, J., concurring in the result). Chief Justice Burger was the sole dissenter and argued that requiring that contraceptives be distributed by a licensed pharmacist was a valid health measure. *Id.* at 465 (Burger, C.J., dissenting).

[26] 431 U.S. 678 (1977).

[27] *Id.* at 685.

[28] *Id.* at 686.

[29] *Id.* at 689 ("Limiting the distribution of nonprescription contraceptives to licensed pharmacists clearly imposes a significant burden on the right of individuals to use contraceptives if they choose to do so. The burden, of course, is not as great as that under a total ban on distribution. Nevertheless, the restriction of distribution channels to a small fraction of the total number of possible retail outlets renders contraceptive devices considerably less accessible to the public, reduces the opportunity for privacy of selection and purchase, and lessens the possibility of price competition.").

[30] The Court also invalidated the restriction on advertising and displaying contraceptives as violating the First Amendment. *Id.* at 700.

[31] *Id.* at 694.

[32] There were several other opinions in *Carey*. Justice White, concurring in part and concurring in the result, emphasized that the state retained power to prohibit extramarital sexual relations and disagreed that minors have a constitutional right to use contraceptives over the objections of their parents and the state. *Id.* at 702 (White, J., concurring in part and concurring in the result). Justice Powell, concurring in part and concurring in the judgment, argued that strict scrutiny and the com-

Ultimately, cases such as *Eisenstadt* and *Carey*, and *Griswold* before them, force attention to the basic question of how the Court should interpret the Constitution. These decisions reflect the Court's judgment that a basic right, such as the ability to control procreation, is constitutionally protected even though it is nowhere mentioned in the text of the Constitution and was not considered by its framers. Little is more basic to autonomy than the decision of whether to become a parent. The Court's critics maintain that the absence of such a right in the text or the framers' intent means that the entire matter should be left to the legislature.

§10.3.3   The Right to Abortion

§10.3.3.1   The Right to Abortion from *Roe* to *Casey*

Overview

In 1973, in *Roe v. Wade*, the Supreme Court held that the Constitution protects a right for a woman to choose to terminate her pregnancy prior to viability—the time at which the fetus can survive on its own outside the womb.[33] Specifically, the Court ruled that the government may not prohibit abortions prior to viability and that government regulation of abortions had to meet strict scrutiny.

By the 1990s, there was a great deal of uncertainty as to whether *Roe* would be overruled and states would be allowed to prohibit abortion. In 1992, in *Planned Parenthood v. Casey*, the Supreme Court reaffirmed *Roe v. Wade* and again held that the government may not ban abortions prior to viability.[34] However, the Court ruled that the government may regulate abortions before viability so long as it does not place an "undue burden" on access to abortions.

In examining the right to abortion, analysis is divided into five parts. First, this subsection reviews the Supreme Court's conclusion that the Constitution protects the right of women to choose to terminate their pregnancies prior to viability. *Roe v. Wade* and *Planned Parenthood v. Casey* are examined in detail. Second, §10.3.3.2 considers what types of state regulations of abortion are permissible and which are unconstitutional, including the most recent abortion decisions concerning laws prohibiting so-called partial birth abortions. Next, §10.3.3.3 looks at the decisions

---

pelling interest test should not be applied in evaluating state laws regulating adult sexual relations. *Id.* at 703 (Powell, J., concurring in part and concurring in the judgment). Justice Stevens, concurring in part and concurring in the judgment, emphasized that prohibiting distribution of contraceptives to minors violated due process because it denied them of a choice that could prevent disease and unwanted pregnancy. *Id.* at 712-713 (Stevens, J., concurring in part and concurring in the judgment). Chief Justice Burger and Justice Rehnquist dissented emphasizing the ability of the government to act to discourage teenage sexual activity and the absence of any such rights in the Constitution. *Id.* at 717 (Rehnquist, J., dissenting).

[33] 410 U.S. 113 (1973). For a detailed description of the abortion debate before *Roe, see* Linda Greenhouse & Reva B. Siegel, Before *Roe v. Wade*: Voices that Shaped the Abortion Debate Before the Supreme Court's Ruling (2010).

[34] 505 U.S. 833 (1992).

concerning laws that prohibit the use of government funds or facilities for performing abortions. There have been many cases, and all have concluded that the government is not constitutionally obligated to pay for abortions or use government facilities for them.

Section 10.3.3.4 examines a particular type of government regulation that has been declared unconstitutional: spousal consent and spousal notification requirements for married women's abortions. Finally, §10.3.3.5 reviews the law concerning the ability of a state to require parental notice and/or consent for an unmarried minor's abortion. The Court has ruled that a state may require parental notice and/or consent for an unmarried minor's abortion so long as it creates an alternative procedure whereby a minor can obtain an abortion by going before a judge. The judge can approve the abortion by finding that it would be in the minor's best interests or by concluding that she is mature enough to decide for herself.

Few decisions in Supreme Court history have provoked the intense controversy that has surrounded the abortion rulings. The debate, in part, is over constitutional methodology. Should the Court protect such a right that is not mentioned in the text and was not clearly intended by the framers?[35] This, of course, is the same methodological question that can be asked about all of the unenumerated rights concerning family and reproductive autonomy protected by the Court. Also, the heated battle over abortion reflects the strong sentiments on both sides. There simply is no middle ground between those who believe that abortion is murder and those who reject that view and believe that a woman should not be forced by the state to be an incubator.

Roe v. Wade

Roe v. Wade, of course, is the key case recognizing a constitutional right to abortion.[36] *Roe* involved a challenge to a Texas law that prohibited all abortions except those necessary to save the life of the mother. A companion case, *Doe v. Bolton*, presented a challenge to a Georgia law that outlawed abortions except if a doctor determined that continuing the pregnancy would endanger a woman's life or health, if the fetus likely would be born with a serious defect, or if the pregnancy resulted from rape.[37]

In *Roe*, Justice Blackmun, writing for the Court, exhaustively reviewed the history of abortion from ancient attitudes through English law through American history and to the present. Blackmun also described the development of medical technology to provide safe abortions. With this as background, Blackmun focused on the right to privacy. After reviewing earlier cases dealing with family and reproductive autonomy, Blackmun concluded: "This right of privacy, whether it be founded in the Fourteenth Amendment's conception of personal liberty and

---

[35] For a criticism of *Roe* on this basis, *see* John Hart Ely, The Wages of Crying Wolf: A Comment on *Roe v. Wade*, 82 Yale L.J. 920, 947-949 (1973); for a defense of *Roe* on this basis, *see* Philip Heymann, The Forest and the Trees: *Roe v. Wade* and Its Critics, 53 B.U. L. Rev. 765, 772-774 (1973).

[36] 410 U.S. 113 (1973).

[37] 410 U.S. 179 (1973).

restrictions upon state action, as we feel it is, or, . . . in the Ninth Amendment's reservation of rights to the people, is broad enough to encompass a woman's decision whether or not to terminate her pregnancy."[38] It is notable that the Court did not find privacy, as Douglas did in *Griswold,* in the penumbra of the Bill of Rights, but instead as part of the liberty protected under the due process clause.

The Court then explained why prohibiting abortion infringes on a woman's right to privacy. Justice Blackmun observed that "[m]aternity, or additional offspring, may force upon the woman a distressful life and future. Psychological harm may be imminent. Mental and physical health may be taxed by child care. There is also the distress, for all concerned, associated with the unwanted child."[39] Forcing a woman to continue a pregnancy against her will obviously imposes enormous physical and psychological burdens.

The Court observed, however, that the right to abortion is not absolute and that it must be balanced against other considerations, such as the state's interest in protecting "prenatal life."[40] The Court said that strict scrutiny was to be used in striking the balance because the right to abortion was a fundamental right. The Court reiterated that where "fundamental rights are involved, . . . regulation limiting these rights may be justified only by a compelling state interest and . . . legislative enactments must be narrowly drawn to express only legitimate state interests at stake."[41]

The Court rejected the state's claim that fetuses are persons and that there was a compelling interest in protecting potential life. The Court observed that there was no indication that the term "person" in the Constitution ever was meant to include fetuses.[42] Moreover, the Court noted that there was no consensus as to when human personhood begins, but rather enormous disagreement among various religions and philosophies. The Court said: "We need not resolve the difficult question of when life begins. When those trained in the respective disciplines of medicine, philosophy and theology are unable to arrive at any consensus, the judiciary, at this point in the development of man's knowledge, is not in a position to speculate as to the answer."[43]

The Court said that in balancing the competing interests, the state had a "compelling interest" in protecting maternal health after the first trimester because it was then that abortions became more dangerous than childbirth.[44] The Court further concluded that "[w]ith respect to the State's important and legitimate interest in potential life, the 'compelling' point is at viability. This is so because the fetus then presumably has the capability of meaningful life outside the mother's womb."[45]

Thus, the Court divided pregnancy into three trimesters. During the first trimester, the government could not prohibit abortions and could regulate abortions only as it regulated other medical procedures, such as by requiring that they be

---

[38] 410 U.S. at 153.
[39] *Id.* at 153.
[40] *Id.* at 155.
[41] *Id.* at 155 (citations omitted).
[42] *Id.* at 157-158.
[43] *Id.* at 159.
[44] *Id.* at 163.
[45] *Id.* at 163.

performed by a licensed physician. During the second trimester, the government also could not outlaw abortions, but the government "may, if it chooses, regulate the abortion procedure in ways that are reasonably related to maternal health."[46] Finally, for the stage subsequent to viability, the government may prohibit abortions except if necessary to preserve the life or health of the mother.

Roe was a 7-to-2 decision with only Justices Rehnquist and White dissenting.[47] Both of the dissenting Justices emphasized that the question of abortion was one that should have been left to the legislative process. Justice White, for example, objected: "As an exercise of raw judicial power, the Court perhaps has the authority to do what it does today; but in my view its judgment is an improvident and extravagant exercise of the power of judicial review."[48] White said that the issue "should be left with the people and to the political processes the people have devised to govern their affairs."[49]

The Court relied on its decision in *Roe* to invalidate Georgia's abortion law in *Doe v. Bolton*. Once the Court recognized that women have a constitutional right to abortions prior to viability, it follows that a state law is unconstitutional if it prohibits abortion except when pregnancy endangers the mother's health, the fetus is seriously deformed, or the woman has been raped.

The Debate over *Roe v. Wade*

Dozens and dozens of scholarly articles have been written about *Roe*. Three major criticisms of *Roe* can be identified. One, already mentioned, is that the Court was wrong to protect a right to abortion because the right is neither mentioned in the text nor intended by the framers. John Ely, for example, argued: "What is frightening about *Roe* is that this superprotected right is not inferable from the language of the Constitution, the framers' thinking respecting the specific problem in issue, any general value derivable from the provisions they included, or the nation's governmental structure. . . . The problem with *Roe* is not so much that it bungles the question it sets itself, but rather that it sets itself a question the Constitution has not made the Court's business. . . . [*Roe* is] a very bad decision. . . . It is bad because it is bad constitutional law, or rather because it is *not* constitutional law and gives almost no sense of an obligation to try to be."[50]

But defenders of *Roe* answer this criticism by pointing to the other rights that the Court has protected concerning family and reproductive autonomy. The Court has safeguarded the right to marry, the right to custody, the right to keep

---

[46] *Id.* at 164.

[47] Several Justices—Chief Justice Burger, Justice Douglas, and Justice Stewart—wrote separate concurring opinions. Chief Justice Burger said that he would allow a state to require that two physicians certify an abortion before one could be performed. *Id.* at 208 (Burger, C.J., concurring). Justice Douglas argued that prohibiting abortions threatens women's lives and thus is unconstitutional. *Id.* at 217 (Douglas, J., concurring). Justice Stewart wrote separately to emphasize that the right to abortion was properly protected under the liberty of the due process clause. *Id.* at 167 (Stewart, J., concurring).

[48] *Id.* at 222 (White, J., dissenting).

[49] *Id.* at 222.

[50] Ely, *supra* note 35, at 935-936, 943, 947.

the family together, the right to control the upbringing of children, the right to procreate, the right to purchase and use contraceptives, the right to refuse medical treatment, and the right to engage in private, adult homosexual activity even though these liberties are not mentioned in the Constitution and were not intended by the framers. Professor Laurence Tribe, for example, notes that "nearly everyone supposes that at least some of these dimensions of personal autonomy and independence are aspects of the 'liberty' which the Fourteenth Amendment says no state may deny to any person 'without due process of law.'"[51] Thus, *Roe* cannot be criticized simply because the Constitution and its framers were silent about abortion.

Ultimately, this first objection to *Roe* turns on a much wider ongoing debate over how the Court should interpret the Constitution and when, if at all, it is permissible for the judiciary to protect unenumerated rights. This debate is reviewed in detail in §1.4 and recurs throughout this chapter.

A second major criticism of *Roe* is that the Court gave insufficient weight to the state's interest in protecting fetal life. Some who criticize *Roe* focus less on the issue of judicial methodology and more on the Court's substantive judgment that protecting the fetus was not a sufficiently compelling interest to justify the prohibition of abortion. Professor (now Judge) John Noonan said that "[t]o judge from the weight the Court gave the being in the womb—found to be protectable in any degree only in the last two months of pregnancy—the Court itself must have viewed the unborn as pure potentiality or a mere theory before viability. The Court's opinion appeared to rest on the assumption that the biological reality could be subordinated or ignored by the sovereign speaking through the Court."[52]

Those who defend *Roe* respond in two ways. One is that the Court was correct in not deciding the question of when personhood begins. There are many possibilities for defining the point at which the fetus is a human person entitled to constitutional protection: conception, implantation into the uterine wall, individuation (when the fetus takes on individual characteristics), quickening (when the mother feels the first movement of the fetus), viability, birth. Professor Frances Olsen explains that "any determination of the beginning of human life can be criticized as arbitrary. . . . The value of life is not a simple attribute of any particular life form, something that can be discovered. Culturally created, the value of life rests on social meanings, and importantly on sexual politics."[53] Thus, the claim is that the Court acted properly in leaving each woman to decide for herself when human personhood begins.

An alternative response to the argument that the Court gave too little weight to protecting the fetus is that even if the fetus is regarded as a person, the law should not force the woman to be an incubator against her will. Professor Judith Jarvis Thomson argued that even granting that the fetus is a person from the moment of conception, the law should not force one person to use their body to sustain the life

---

[51] Laurence Tribe, Abortion: The Clash of Absolutes 99 (1990).
[52] John Noonan, Jr., The Root and Branch of *Roe v. Wade*, 63 Neb. L. Rev. 668, 673 (1984).
[53] Frances Olsen, Unraveling Compromise, 103 Harv. L. Rev. 105, 127-128 (1989).

of another.[54] She says, for example, that the law would not require a person to be physically connected with another even if it was the only way to save a life. Parents are not required to donate organs or blood to save their children.[55] By this view, nor should women be forced to donate their wombs and their bodies to sustain fetal life.[56]

A third criticism of *Roe* is that the Court erred in using due process rather than equal protection as the basis for its decision. The argument is that laws prohibiting abortion apply exclusively to women, and thus they should be declared unconstitutional as gender discrimination.[57] Professor Catharine MacKinnon wrote: "Under this sex equality analysis, criminal abortion statutes of the sort invalidated in *Roe v. Wade* violate equal protection of the laws. They make women criminals for a medical procedure only women need, or make others criminals for performing a procedure on women that only women need, when much of the need for this procedure as well as barriers to access to it have been created by social conditions of sex inequality. Forced motherhood is sex inequality."[58]

The response to this argument is that an equality analysis, like a privacy approach, still comes down to the same basic question: Does the government's interest in protecting fetal life justify prohibiting abortion? Under equal protection law, gender discrimination is permissible if intermediate scrutiny is met; that is, if the government's action is substantially related to an important government interest.[59] If protecting fetal life is regarded as an important government interest, then laws prohibiting abortion are justified even though they are a form of gender discrimination.[60] The argument is that nothing is gained by shifting to an equal protection analysis; either the state's interest in protecting fetal life is not a sufficient interest, in which case abortion laws are unconstitutional under both privacy and equal protection, or the state has an interest sufficient to justify prohibiting abortion under either approach.

[54] Judith Jarvis Thomson, A Defense of Abortion, 1 Phil. & Pub. Aff. 47, 48-49 (1971).

[55] *See also* Donald Regan, Rewriting *Roe v. Wade*, 77 Mich. L. Rev. 1569 (1979).

[56] For responses to this position, *see* Philip Bobbitt, Constitutional Fate 163 (1982) ("This argument seems to treat the embryonic child as a stranger who merely happens to be inconveniently placed proximate to the mother. There is much law, however, for the proposition that one owes a duty to care to one's child. This puts us back in the position of deciding when a child's life begins, a position the *Roe* Court was doctrinally forced to take in its argument despite its disclaimers and one which sound constitutional decision ought to avoid completely."); *see also* Michael Tooley, Abortion and Infanticide 43-49 (1983).

[57] *See, e.g.*, Ruth Bader Ginsburg, Some Thoughts on Autonomy and Equality in Relation to *Roe v. Wade*, 63 N.C. L. Rev. 375, 383 (1985); Sylvia Law, Rethinking Sex and the Constitution, 132 U. Pa. L. Rev. 955, 987 (1984).

[58] Catharine MacKinnon, Reflections on Sex Equality Under Law, 100 Yale L.J. 1281, 1319 (1991).

[59] *See, e.g.*, Craig v. Boren, 429 U.S. 190 (1976); §9.4.1.

[60] Also, it should be noted that the Court used strict scrutiny in *Roe* based on privacy being a fundamental right. A gender discrimination analysis only would use intermediate scrutiny under the approach used to evaluate sex discrimination since 1976.

Webster v. Reproductive Health Services

By the 1990s, the change in the composition of the Supreme Court raised questions as to whether *Roe v. Wade* would be overruled. In 1989, in *Webster v. Reproductive Health Services,* four Justices seemed poised to overrule *Roe.*[61] A Missouri law declared the state's view that life begins at conception, prohibited the use of government funds or facilities from performing or "encouraging or counseling" a woman to have an abortion, and allowed abortions after 20 weeks of pregnancy only if a test was done to ensure that the fetus was not viable. The Supreme Court upheld the Missouri law, but without a majority opinion.[62]

Chief Justice Rehnquist, in a plurality opinion joined by Justices White and Kennedy, strongly criticized *Roe.* Rehnquist attacked the trimester distinctions that were used by *Roe* to balance the rights of the mother and the state's interest in protecting the fetus. Rehnquist wrote: "[T]he rigid *Roe* framework is hardly consistent with the notion of a Constitution cast in general terms. . . . The key elements of the Roe framework—trimesters and viability—are not found in the text of the Constitution or in any place else one would expect to find a constitutional principle."[63]

Even more important, Rehnquist said: "[W]e do not see why the State's interest in protecting potential human life should come into existence only at the point of viability, and that there should therefore be a rigid line allowing state regulation after viability, but prohibiting it before viability. . . . The State's interest, if compelling after viability, is equally compelling before viability."[64] Although Rehnquist's opinion did not expressly urge the overruling of *Roe v. Wade,* that was the unmistakable implication of declaring that the state has a compelling interest in protecting fetal life from the moment of conception. Rehnquist and White were the two dissenters in *Roe,* and they had consistently argued for overruling it.[65]

Justice Scalia wrote a separate opinion concurring in part and concurring in the judgment. He said that the plurality opinion "effectively would overrule *Roe v. Wade.*"[66] He said: "I think that should be done, but would do it more explicitly."[67] He argued that the failure to overrule *Roe* "needlessly . . . prolong[s] this Court's self-awarded sovereignty over a field where it has little proper business since the answers to most of the cruel questions posed are political and not juridical."[68]

Justice O'Connor provided the fifth vote for the result in *Webster,* but she ruled only on the specifics of the Missouri law and did not opine on the question

---

[61] 492 U.S. 490 (1989).

[62] The constitutionality of restrictions on government funding of abortion is discussed in §10.3.3.3; the constitutionality of state regulations of abortion is discussed in §10.3.3.2.

[63] *Id.* at 518.

[64] *Id.* at 519.

[65] *See, e.g.,* Thornburgh v. American College of Obstetricians and Gynecologists, 476 U.S. 747, 797 (1986) (White, J., dissenting).

[66] 492 U.S. at 532 (Scalia, J., concurring in part and concurring in the judgment).

[67] *Id.*

[68] *Id.*

of whether *Roe* should be overruled.[69] O'Connor noted that the Missouri law did not prohibit abortions, and thus "there is no necessity to accept the state's invitation to reexamine the constitutional validity of *Roe*."[70] She said that "[w]hen the constitutional invalidity of a State's abortion statute actually turns on the constitutional validity of *Roe v. Wade*, there will be time enough to reexamine *Roe*. And to do so carefully."[71]

The dissent in *Webster* saw a Court on the verge of overruling *Roe*. Justice Blackmun, joined by Justices Brennan and Marshall, lamented: "Today, *Roe v. Wade* and the fundamental constitutional right of women to decide whether to terminate a pregnancy, survive but are not secure. . . . [T]he plurality discards a landmark case of the last generation and casts into darkness the hopes and visions of every woman in this country who had come to believe that the Constitution guaranteed her right to exercise some control over her unique ability to bear children. . . . For today, at least, the law of abortion stands undisturbed. For today, the women of this Nation still retain the liberty to control their destinies. But the signs are evident and very ominous, and a chill wind blows."[72]

Planned Parenthood v. Casey

Between 1989, when *Webster* was decided, and 1992, when *Planned Parenthood v. Casey*[73] was before the Court, Justices Brennan and Marshall had resigned and were replaced, respectively, by Justices Souter and Thomas. It was thought that either of them, and particularly Justice Clarence Thomas, might cast the fifth vote to overrule *Roe v. Wade*. Indeed, the United States, through the Solicitor General, urged the Court in *Casey* to use it as the occasion for overruling *Roe*.

The Court, however, did not do so. By a 5-to-4 margin, the Supreme Court reaffirmed that states cannot prohibit abortion prior to viability. However, the plurality opinion by Justices O'Connor, Kennedy, and Souter overruled the trimester distinctions used in *Roe* and also the use of strict scrutiny for evaluating government regulation of abortions. Instead, the plurality said that government regulation of abortions prior to viability should be allowed unless there is an "undue burden" on access to abortion. Justices Blackmun and Stevens concurred in the judgment and would have reaffirmed the trimester distinctions and the use of strict scrutiny.

Specifically, Justices O'Connor, Kennedy, and Souter wrote an unusual joint opinion. Their opinion began: "Liberty finds no refuge in a jurisprudence of doubt."[74] Obviously, this is meant to explain the shift in Justice O'Connor's position from *Webster*, where she said that the Supreme Court should not reevaluate *Roe* until the Court reviewed a law prohibiting abortion. In *Casey*, Justice O'Connor — and

---

[69] *Id.* at 522 (O'Connor, J., concurring in part and concurring in the judgment).

[70] *Id.* at 525.

[71] *Id.* at 526.

[72] *Id.* at 537, 557, 560 (Blackmun, J., dissenting).

[73] 505 U.S. 833 (1992).

[74] 505 U.S. at 844.

all of the Justices—reconsidered *Roe* even though the Pennsylvania law before the Court did not prohibit abortions. Rather, the Pennsylvania law regulated them by creating a 24-hour waiting period for abortions, requiring physicians to inform women of the availability of information about the fetus, requiring parental consent for unmarried minors' abortions, creating requirements for reporting and record keeping, and requiring spousal notification before abortions.

The joint opinion, with Justices Blackmun and Stevens joining, declared at the outset: "[T]he essential holding of *Roe v. Wade* should be retained and once again reaffirmed."[75] The joint opinion reviewed the cases protecting family and reproductive autonomy and concluded that these fundamental rights are protected even though they are not mentioned in the text of the Constitution, were not intended by the framers, and are not part of tradition stated at the most specific level of abstraction. The joint opinion said that the right to abortion is constitutionally protected because of the importance of the choice and the intrusion in forcing a woman to remain pregnant against her will. The joint opinion stated: "[T]he liberty of the woman is at stake in a sense unique to the human condition and so unique to the law. The mother who carries a child to full term is subject to anxieties, to physical constraints, to pain that only she must bear. . . . Her suffering is too intimate and personal for the state to insist, without more, upon its own vision of the woman's role. . . . The destiny of the woman must be shaped to a large extent on her own conception of her spiritual imperatives and her place in society."[76]

The joint opinion then engaged in a lengthy discussion about the importance of stare decisis and the circumstances that justify overruling an earlier precedent. The joint opinion explained that the Court is warranted in overruling precedents if the earlier decisions had proved unworkable, if there was an evolution of legal principles that undermined the doctrinal foundation of the precedents, or if there was a change in the factual predicate for the decisions.[77] The opinion concluded "that the basic decision in *Roe* was based on a constitutional analysis which we cannot now repudiate."[78]

The joint opinion reaffirmed viability as the key dividing line during pregnancy: Before viability, the government may not prohibit abortion, but after viability, abortions may be prohibited except where necessary to protect the woman's life or health. The joint opinion, however, overruled the trimester framework articulated in *Roe*. It declared: "We reject the trimester framework, which we do not consider to be part of the essential holding of *Roe*. . . . The trimester framework suffers from these basic flaws in its formulation: it misconceives the nature of the pregnant woman's interest; and in practice it undervalues the State's interest in potential life, as recognized in *Roe*."[79]

---

[75] *Id.* at 846.
[76] *Id.* at 852.
[77] *Id.* at 854-860.
[78] *Id.* at 869.
[79] *Id.* at 873.

More generally, the joint opinion said that the test for evaluating the constitutionality of a state regulation of abortion is whether it places an "undue burden" on access to abortion. The joint opinion explained: "[T]he undue burden standard is the appropriate means of reconciling the State's interest with the woman's constitutionally protected liberty. . . . A finding of an undue burden is a short-hand for the conclusion that a state regulation has the purpose or effect of placing a substantial obstacle in the path of a woman seeking an abortion of a nonviable fetus."[80] The joint opinion said, however, that "[t]o promote the State's profound interest in potential life, throughout pregnancy the State may take measures to ensure that the woman's choice is informed, and measures designed to advance this interest will not be invalidated as long as their purpose is to persuade the woman to choose childbirth over abortion. These measures must not be an undue burden on the right."[81]

The joint opinion then applied these principles to the specific aspects of the Pennsylvania law. The joint opinion upheld the 24-hour waiting period, the requirement that the woman be told of the availability of detailed information about the fetus, and the reporting and recording requirements.[82] As to these provisions that were upheld, the majority comprised the three Justices in the joint opinion and the four Justices who would have overruled *Roe v. Wade* and allowed the entire law. Finally, the joint opinion said that the spousal notification requirement is unconstitutional. This is discussed below in §10.3.3.4.

Justices Stevens and Blackmun wrote opinions concurring in part,[83] concurring in the judgment in part, and dissenting in part. These Justices would have used strict scrutiny and continued the basic framework outlines in *Roe*. Justice Blackmun, for example, said: "Application of this analytical framework is no less warranted than when it was approved by seven Members of this Court in *Roe*. Strict scrutiny of state limitations on reproductive choice still offers the most secure protection of the woman's right to make her own reproductive decisions, free from state coercion. . . . The factual premises of the trimester framework have not been undermined."[84] Thus, Justice Blackmun would have invalidated all of the challenged provisions in the Pennsylvania law.[85]

Nonetheless, Blackmun expressed great pleasure that *Roe*'s basic holding was reaffirmed. He said: "But now, just when so many expected the darkness to fall, the flame has grown bright. . . . Make no mistake, the joint opinion of Justices

---

[80] *Id.* at 876-877.

[81] *Id.* at 878.

[82] *Id.* at 879-901. The constitutionality of these regulations is discussed in §10.3.3.3 below. The joint opinion also upheld the parental consent requirement, which is discussed in §10.3.3.5.

[83] Justice Stevens's opinion is concurring in part and dissenting in part, *id.* at 911; Justice Blackmun's opinion is concurring in part, concurring in the judgment in part, and dissenting in part, *id.* at 922.

[84] *Id.* at 930 (Blackmun, J., concurring in part, concurring in the judgment in part, and dissenting in part).

[85] *Id.* at 934.

O'Connor, Kennedy, and Souter is an act of personal courage and constitutional principle."[86]

Chief Justice Rehnquist and Justice Scalia each wrote opinions concurring in the judgment in part and dissenting in part. They joined each other's opinions, and Justices White and Thomas joined each. These four Justices expressly said that they believed that *Roe v. Wade* should be overruled. Chief Justice Rehnquist wrote: "We believe that *Roe* was wrongly decided, and that it can and should be overruled consistently with our traditional approach to *stare decisis* in constitutional cases."[87] Justice Scalia similarly said that he reached the conclusion that states can prohibit abortion "for the same reason that I reach the conclusion that bigamy is not constitutionally protected—because of two simple facts: (1) the Constitution says absolutely nothing about it, and (2) the longstanding traditions of American society have permitted it to be legally proscribed."[88] Justice Scalia responded, point by point, to most of the key aspects in the joint opinion.

The four dissenting Justices would have upheld all of the aspects of the Pennsylvania law. They also unequivocally expressed that they would allow states to prohibit abortions or to regulate them however they choose.

What Is an Undue Burden on the Right to Abortion?

In *Stenberg v. Carhart*, the majority opinion expressly adopted and applied the undue burden test that three Justices had urged in *Casey*.[89] In *Stenberg*, the Court declared unconstitutional a state law that prohibited the procedure called "partial birth abortion." This aspect of the decision is discussed below, but its greatest significance is that it is the first time that a majority of the Court said that the undue burden test is to be used in evaluating laws regulating abortion. Subsequently, in *Gonzales v. Carhart*, the Court again used the undue burden test, though this time to uphold a federal law prohibiting "partial birth" abortion.[90]

The key question after *Casey*, *Stenberg*, and *Gonzales v. Carhart* is what constitutes an undue burden on the right to abortion. Specific types of regulations are discussed below. However, in general, there are some important problems with applying the undue burden test.

First, the undue burden test combines three distinct questions into one inquiry. As explained above in §10.1.2, when the Supreme Court considers cases involving individual liberties, there are four issues: Is there a fundamental right; is the right infringed; is the infringement justified by a sufficient purpose; are the means sufficiently related to the end sought? The undue burden test combines the latter three questions. Obviously, "undue burden" pertains to whether there is an infringement of the right, but the joint opinion in *Casey* also uses it to analyze whether the law is justified. No level of scrutiny is articulated by the joint opinion;

---

[86] *Id.* at 922-923.
[87] *Id.* at 944 (Rehnquist, C.J., dissenting).
[88] *Id.* at 980 (Scalia, J., dissenting).
[89] 530 U.S. 914, 921 (2000).
[90] 550 U.S. 124 (2007).

there is no statement that the goal of the law must be compelling or important or that the means have to be necessary or substantially related to the end. Undue burden is thus confusing to apply because it melds together three distinct issues.

Second, the joint opinion's statement of the undue burden test has an internal tension. The joint opinion says that a law is an undue burden "if its purpose or effect is to place a substantial obstacle in the path of a woman seeking an abortion before the fetus attains viability."[91] But the joint opinion then says "[t]o promote the State's profound interest in potential life, throughout pregnancy the State may take measures to ensure that the woman's choice is informed, and measures designed to advance this interest will not be invalidated as long as their purpose is to persuade the woman to choose childbirth over abortion. These measures must not be an undue burden on the right."[92]

The problem is that the joint opinion says both that the state cannot act with the purpose of creating obstacles to abortion and that it can act with the purpose of discouraging abortion and encouraging childbirth. Every law adopted to limit abortion is for the purpose of discouraging abortions and encouraging childbirth. How is it to be decided which of these laws is invalid as an undue burden and which is permissible? The joint opinion simply says that the regulation "must not be an undue burden on the right." But this, of course, is circular; it offers no guidance as to which laws are an undue burden and which are not.

The Court implied that an undue burden exists only if a court concludes that a regulation will prevent women from receiving an abortion. In *Casey*, the joint opinion said that spousal notification requirement was an undue burden because it is "likely to prevent a significant number of women from obtaining an abortion."[93] The joint opinion, however, said that there was inadequate evidence that a 24-hour waiting period would prevent women from obtaining abortions and thus found that it was constitutional. The Court thus seems to be saying that an undue burden exists only if there is proof that the regulation will keep someone from getting an abortion. However, it must be questioned why burdens, no matter how substantial, are allowed unless they are actually proven to prevent abortions. Also, it is unclear how challengers will be able to prove that particular regulations create insurmountable obstacles to obtaining abortions.

Third, there is the issue of how many women must be adversely affected by a regulation of abortions in order for it to be considered an undue burden. In *Casey*, the plurality found that the requirement for spousal notification before a married woman could receive an abortion was an undue burden because *some* women might be adversely affected. Although the plurality found that spousal notification boule keep a "significant number of women from obtaining an abortion," it also unequivocally stated: "The analysis does not end with the one percent of women upon whom the statute operates; it begins there. Legislation is measured for consistency with the Constitution by its impact on those whose conduct it affects. For example, we would not say that a law which requires a newspaper

---

[91] 505 U.S. at 878 (joint opinion of O'Connor, Kennedy, and Souter, JJ.).
[92] *Id.*
[93] *Id.* at 893.

to print a candidate's reply to an unfavorable editorial is valid on its face because most newspapers would adopt the policy even absent the law. The proper focus of constitutional inquiry is the group for whom the law is a restriction, not the group for whom the law is irrelevant."[94]

By contrast, in *Gonzales v. Carhart*, the Court said that for a law to be unconstitutional there must be a showing that it would be an undue burden for a "large fraction of women."[95] In other words, under the plurality's approach in *Casey* the focus is on whether a law is an undue burden likely to keep some women from having access to abortion. But under the more recent decision in *Gonzales v. Carhart*, a law regulating abortion is unconstitutional only if it would be an undue burden for a large fraction of women. This is a significant change in the law and one that will make it more likely that courts will uphold regulations of abortion.

Despite these ambiguities in the undue burden test, *Casey* is clear and emphatic in reaffirming that states may not prohibit abortions prior to viability and that states may prohibit abortions after viability except where necessary to protect the woman's life or health. Likewise, in its subsequent decision in *Stenberg*, the Court began its opinion by declaring: "[B]efore viability the woman has a right to choose to terminate her pregnancy."[96]

§10.3.3.2   Government Regulation of Abortions

There are many different ways in which government can regulate the performance of abortions. After *Planned Parenthood v. Casey*, the government can regulate abortions performed prior to viability so long as there is not an undue burden on access to abortions.[97] The Supreme Court has considered the constitutionality of a number of types of restrictions including waiting periods, informed consent requirements, fetal viability tests, reporting and recording requirements, and the conduct of medical care personnel.[98] Each is discussed in turn below. Additionally, the Supreme Court has ruled on the constitutionality of other restrictions such as denial of government funding for abortions, spousal consent and notification requirements, and parental notice and consent requirements. These are discussed in §10.3.3.3, §10.3.3.4, and §10.3.3.5, respectively.

In addition to these requirements, that have been considered by the Supreme Court and that are discussed below, many state governments are adopting new limits on abortions, such as requirements that doctors performing abortions have

---

[94]   *Id.* at 894.

[95]   550 U.S. at 168.

[96]   530 U.S. at 921 (citing *Casey*, 505 U.S. 833).

[97]   505 U.S. at 878.

[98]   Additionally, the Supreme Court has ruled that the government may deny funding to family planning clinics that perform abortion counseling or make abortion referrals. Rust v. Sullivan, 500 U.S. 173 (1991). The Court held that such restrictions are not a violation of the First Amendment. *Rust* is discussed in §11.2.4.4.

admitting privileges at nearby hospitals,[99] that doctors performing abortions must first to perform an ultrasound and display that sonogram and describe the fetus to women seeking abortions,[100] limits on medically induced abortions,[101] and prohibitions of pregnancy at earlier stages of pregnancy.[102] It is likely that challenges to these restrictions will soon come before the Court for it to decide whether they constitute an undue burden.

Waiting Periods

Prior to *Casey*, the Supreme Court had invalidated waiting periods for adult women's abortions. In *City of Akron v. Akron Center for Reproductive Health, Inc.*, the Court declared unconstitutional a part of a city ordinance that prohibited a physician from performing an abortion until 24 hours after the pregnant woman signed a consent form.[103] The district court had found that such waiting periods increase the costs of obtaining an abortion by requiring women to make two trips to the facility and could increase the risk of complications because of delays in performing abortions.[104] The Supreme Court agreed and found that waiting periods failed to serve any valid state purpose. Justice Powell, writing for the Court, explained that the city had "failed to demonstrate that any legitimate state interest is furthered by an arbitrary and inflexible waiting period. There is no evidence suggesting that the abortion procedure will be performed more safely. Nor are we convinced that the State's legitimate concern that the woman's decision be informed is reasonably served by requiring a 24-hour delay as a matter of course."[105]

However, in *Planned Parenthood v. Casey*, the Supreme Court used the undue burden test, rather than strict scrutiny as in *Akron*, and upheld the constitutionality of a waiting period.[106] In fact, the joint opinion in *Casey* reviewed the invalidation of the waiting period in *Akron* and declared: "We consider that conclusion to be wrong. The idea that important decisions will be more informed and deliberate if they follow some period of reflection does not strike us as unreasonable, particularly where the statute directs that important information become part of the background of the decision."[107]

The joint opinion in *Casey* argued that a waiting period is not an undue burden on access to abortion. The joint opinion acknowledged that the district court

---

[99] *See, e.g.*, Planned Parenthood of Greater Texas Surgical Services v. Abbott, 748 F.3d 583 (5th Cir. 2014) (upholding admitting privileges requirement); Jackson Women's Health Organization v. Currier, 760 F.3d 448 (5th Cir. 2014) (declaring unconstitutional admitting privileges requirement).

[100] *See, e.g.*, Stuart v. Camnitz, 774 F.3d 238 (4th Cir. Dec. 22, 2014) (declaring requirement unconstitutional as violating First Amendment rights of doctors).

[101] *See, e.g.*, Cline v. Oklahoma Coalition for Reproductive Justice, 313 P.3d 215 (Okla. 2013) (declaring unconstitutional restrictions on medically induced abortions).

[102] *See, e.g.*, Isaacson v. Horne, 716 F.3d 1213 (9th Cir. 2013) (declaring unconstitutional state law prohibiting abortions after the twentieth week of pregnancy).

[103] 462 U.S. 416, 449 (1983).

[104] *Id.* at 450.

[105] *Id.*

[106] 505 U.S. at 885-886.

[107] *Id.* at 885.

had found that because of travel and scheduling problems there often would be more than a day's delay before an abortion could be received and thus that waiting periods would increase the cost and risks of abortions.[108] But the joint opinion concluded that 24-hour waiting periods are constitutional. It declared: "Yet, as we have stated, under the undue burden standard a State is permitted to enact persuasive measures which favor childbirth over abortion, even if those measures do not further a health interest. And while the waiting period does limit a physician's discretion, that is not, standing alone, a reason to invalidate it."[109] The four Justices who favored overruling *Roe*—Rehnquist, White, Scalia, and Thomas—provided the other votes necessary to uphold the waiting period requirement.

What is troubling about the Court's reasoning in *Casey* concerning waiting periods is the absence of a clear explanation for why the Court concluded that waiting periods were not an undue burden, especially in light of the district court's findings of fact. In fact, there seems a tension between the reasons the *Casey* joint opinion gave for finding spousal notification to be an undue burden and its analysis of waiting periods. In invalidating a requirement for spousal notification for a married woman's abortion (discussed in detail below), the joint opinion said: "The analysis does not end with the one percent of women upon whom the statute operates; it begins there. Legislation is measured for consistency with the Constitution by its impact on those whose conduct it affects. . . . The proper focus of constitutional inquiry is the group for whom the law is a restriction, not the group for whom the law is irrelevant."[110] The district court found that waiting periods would be particularly burdensome for poorer women. It is unclear why the Court felt that this was not enough to meet the undue burden test.

"Informed Consent" Requirements

The Supreme Court has had several occasions to consider "informed consent" requirements: laws that require that women be advised about the fetus and its characteristics at that stage of pregnancy. Again, prior to *Casey*, the Supreme Court had consistently invalidated these requirements, but after *Casey* they are much more likely to be upheld.

In *Planned Parenthood of Central Missouri v. Danforth*, the Supreme Court held that the government may require written informed consent to abortions, just as it requires for other surgical procedures.[111] The issue is whether the government may require more than that with regard to abortions and mandate that doctors give women information intended to discourage abortions. In *City of Akron v. Akron Center for Reproductive Health*, the Supreme Court declared unconstitutional a part of a city ordinance that required that physicians inform women seeking abortions

---

[108] *Id.* at 886.

[109] *Id.*

[110] *Id.* at 894.

[111] 428 U.S. 52, 67 (1976); *see also* City of Akron v. Akron Center for Reproductive Health, Inc., 462 U.S. at 446 (upholding informed consent requirements that are the same as for other surgical procedures).

about the development of her fetus, that the "unborn child is a human life from the moment of conception,"[112] the date of possible viability, and the physical and emotional consequences that may result from an abortion.[113] The Court said that "much of the information required is designed not to inform the woman's consent but rather to persuade her to withhold it altogether. . . . By insisting upon recitation of a lengthy and inflexible list of information, Akron unreasonably has placed obstacles in the path of the doctor upon whom the woman is entitled to rely for advice in connection with her decision."[114]

Similarly, in *Thornburgh v. American College of Obstetricians and Gynecologists*, the Court invalidated a Pennsylvania law that required, in part, that women be given seven different kinds of information at least 24 hours before they give consent for abortions.[115] This information included telling the woman that there may be unforeseeable detrimental physical and psychological effects to having an abortion, the possible availability of prenatal and childbirth medical care, and the father's liability to pay child support.[116] Also, the physician had to inform the woman of the availability of printed materials that describe the anatomical and physiological characteristics of the "unborn child" at two-week gestational increments.[117] The Court said that, as in *Akron*, the Pennsylvania law was unconstitutional because it was motivated by a desire to discourage women from having abortions and because it imposed a rigid requirement that a specific body of information be communicated regardless of the needs of the patient or the judgment of the physician.

In *Casey*, however, the Court upheld a provision virtually identical to that invalidated in *Thornburgh* and the joint opinion said: "To the extent *Akron I* and *Thornburgh* find a constitutional violation where the government requires . . . the giving of truthful, nonmisleading information about the nature of the abortion procedure, the attendant health risks and those of childbirth, and the 'probable gestational age' of the fetus, those cases are inconsistent with *Roe*'s acknowledgment of an important interest in potential life, and are overruled."[118] Specifically, the Court upheld a section of the statute that required that women be told information and that they be informed of the availability of other materials that describe the fetus, provide information about medical care for childbirth, and list adoption providers.

The shift from *Akron* and *Thornburgh* to *Casey* reflects the Court's abandoning the position that the state may not regulate abortions in a way to encourage childbirth. The issue that *Casey* leaves unresolved is how far the government can go in this direction in the form of informed consent laws. For example, do *Akron* and *Thornburgh* remain good law that the government could not require that women be given detailed descriptions of the fetus, or shown photographs, or told that human life begins at conception? There is a strong argument that all of these go

---

[112] 462 U.S. at 444.
[113] *Id.* at 442.
[114] *Id.* at 444-445 (citations omitted).
[115] 476 U.S. 747, 760 (1986).
[116] *Id.* at 760-761.
[117] *Id.* at 761.
[118] *Id.* at 838 (citations omitted).

much further than the Pennsylvania law in *Casey* and thus that the Court might find them to be an undue burden on access to abortion.

Fetal Viability Tests

In *Colautti v. Franklin*, the Court ruled unconstitutional a state law that required that before performing an abortion, a doctor make a determination, "based on his experience, judgment, or professional competence that the fetus is not viable."[119] If the physician concluded that the fetus might be viable, the statute imposed a series of requirements designed to ensure the survival of the fetus. The Court found that the law was unduly vague, especially in speaking of fetuses that "may be viable" and in not specifying the physician's duty of care to the mother relative to the fetus.[120] The Court said that "the determination of whether a particular fetus is viable is, and must be, a matter for the judgment of the responsible attending physician."[121]

In *Webster v. Reproductive Health Services*, however, the Supreme Court upheld a state law that required testing and evaluation of fetal viability for all abortions performed after the twentieth week of pregnancy.[122] The plurality opinion recognized that such tests will increase the costs of abortions and limit the discretion of the physician.[123] Nonetheless, the plurality said it was "satisfied that the requirement of these tests permissibly furthers the State's interest in protecting potential human life."[124]

Justice O'Connor, in an opinion concurring in part and concurring in the judgment, said that this provision should be upheld because it is not an undue burden on access to abortions: "It is clear to me that requiring the performance of examinations and tests useful to determining whether a fetus is viable, when viability is possible, and when it would not be medically imprudent to do so, does not impose an undue burden on a woman's abortion decision."[125]

Reporting and Recording Requirements

The Court generally has upheld laws that require the recording and reporting of information concerning abortions so long as the information is protected as confidential. In *Planned Parenthood of Central Missouri v. Danforth*, the Court upheld a statutory provision that required that physicians performing abortions complete forms, maintain records for seven years, and allow inspection of them by health officials.[126] The Court said that "[r]ecordkeeping and reporting requirements that

---

[119]   439 U.S. 379, 391 (1979).
[120]   *Id.* at 393.
[121]   *Id.* at 396, quoting Planned Parenthood of Central Mo. v. Danforth, 428 U.S. at 64.
[122]   492 U.S. at 517.
[123]   *Id.* at 519.
[124]   *Id.* at 519-520.
[125]   *Id.* at 530.
[126]   428 U.S. at 79-80.

are reasonably directed to the preservation of maternal health and that properly respect a patient's confidentiality and privacy are permissible."[127]

In *Thornburgh v. American College of Obstetricians and Gynecologists*, the Court declared unconstitutional a reporting and recording requirement because the law mandated the reporting of more information than in *Danforth* and especially because there were not sufficient assurances of confidentiality.[128] The Court observed that the Pennsylvania law in *Thornburgh* required, as the law in *Danforth* did not, "information as to method of payment, as to the woman's personal history, and as to the bases for medical judgment."[129] The Court said that the records "while claimed not to be 'public,' are available nonetheless to the public for copying."[130] The Court concluded that "[a]lthough the statute does not specifically require the reporting of the woman's name, the amount of information about her and the circumstances under which she had an abortion are so detailed that identification is likely. Identification is the obvious purpose of these extreme reporting requirements."[131]

In *Casey*, the Court again upheld a record-keeping and reporting requirement. The law required a report to be filed for each abortion performed that included the name of the physician, the woman's age, the number of prior pregnancies and abortions the woman had experienced, medical complications from the abortion, the weight of the fetus, and whether the woman was married.[132] In the case of state-funded institutions, the information is publicly available.

The Court found that the regulations served an important purpose without being an undue burden on access to abortions. The Court explained: "Although they do not relate to the State's interest in informing the woman's choice, they do relate to health. The collection of information with respect to actual patients is a vital element of medical research, and so it cannot be said that the requirements serve no purpose other than to make abortion more difficult."[133] Moreover, the Court said that there was no indication that the reporting requirement was so onerous as to substantially increase the costs of abortion and therefore be an undue burden on access to abortion.

These cases indicate that the government may require record keeping and reporting, but it must ensure that the patient's identity remains confidential and that it cannot be easily ascertained from other information in the report. *Thornburgh* is distinguishable from *Danforth* and *Casey* because of the perceived lack of protection for confidentiality under the Pennsylvania law reviewed in *Thornburgh*.

---

[127] *Id.* at 80.
[128] 476 U.S. at 766.
[129] *Id.*
[130] *Id.*
[131] *Id.* at 766-767.
[132] 505 U.S. at 900.
[133] *Id.* at 900-901.

Medical Procedures

Many state laws have regulated how doctors actually perform abortions. Almost all of these have been declared unconstitutional. However, these decisions were prior to *Casey*, and it is possible that under the undue burden test, the Court will be more inclined to allow such laws.

For example, in *Planned Parenthood of Central Missouri v. Danforth*, the Supreme Court invalidated a law that prohibited saline amniocentesis as a method of abortion after the first trimester.[134] The Court said that "the record conclusively demonstrates . . . [that] saline amniocentesis [is] an accepted medical procedure in this country."[135] In fact, the Court said that prohibiting this technique "as a practical matter, . . . forces a woman and her physician to terminate her pregnancy by methods more dangerous to her health than the method outlawed."[136]

In *Akron v. Akron Center for Reproductive Health*, the Supreme Court invalidated a part of a city's ordinance that required that all abortions after the first trimester be performed in hospitals.[137] The Court said that there was "impressive evidence that—at least during the early weeks of the second trimester— . . . abortions may be performed as safely in an outpatient clinic as in a full-service hospital. We conclude, therefore, that present medical knowledge convincingly undercuts Akron's justification for requiring that *all* second-trimester abortions be performed in a hospital."[138]

Several cases have involved laws regulating the performance of abortions on potentially viable fetuses. For instance, in *Planned Parenthood of Kansas City, Mo. v. Ashcroft*, the Court upheld a state law that required the presence of a second physician during an abortion performed after viability.[139] Although the law did not expressly contain an exception for emergency abortions, the Court construed the statute to include such a requirement so as to meet constitutional muster.[140]

However, in *Thornburgh v. American College of Obstetricians and Gynecologists*, the Court invalidated a similar requirement that there be two physicians when abortions are performed on potentially viable fetuses.[141] The Court said that the statute in *Thornburgh*, unlike that in *Ashcroft*, is not "worded sufficiently to imply an emergency exception. Pennsylvania's statute contains no such comforting or helpful language and evinces no intent to protect a woman whose life may be at risk."[142] The Court said that the "Pennsylvania Legislature knows how to provide

---

[134] 428 U.S. at 75.

[135] *Id.* at 77.

[136] *Id.* at 79.

[137] 462 U.S. at 436, 437. *See also* Planned Parenthood v. Ashcroft, 462 U.S. 476 (1983) (invalidating a requirement that second trimester abortions be performed in hospitals).

[138] 462 U.S. at 437 (citations omitted).

[139] 462 U.S. at 486. *See also Colautti v. Franklin*, 439 U.S. 379 (1979), discussed above, that required that fetuses that may be viable be aborted in the manner most likely to ensure that it would be born alive. The Court declared the provisions void on vagueness grounds.

[140] *Id.* at 485.

[141] 476 U.S. at 771.

[142] *Id.* at 770-771.

a medical-emergency exception when it chooses to do so [and] . . . that the legislature's failure to provide a medical-emergency exception was . . . intentional."[143]

Laws Prohibiting "Partial Birth" Abortions

The Supreme Court twice has considered the constitutionality of laws that prohibit so-called partial birth abortions. In *Stenberg v. Carhart*, the Court considered the constitutionality of a Nebraska law that prohibited a procedure commonly referred to as "partial birth" abortions.[144] Nebraska's statute was typical of laws enacted in 30 other states in prohibiting the removal of a living fetus or a substantial part of a living fetus with the intent of ending the fetus's life. Specifically, the Nebraska law defined "partial birth abortions" as "an abortion procedure in which the person performing the abortion partially delivers vaginally a living unborn child before killing the unborn child and completing the delivery."[145] The statute further clarified this by prohibiting "deliberately and intentionally delivering into the vagina a living unborn child, or a substantial portion thereof, for the purpose of performing a procedure the person performing such procedure knows will kill the unborn child and does kill the unborn child."[146]

Justice Breyer—in a majority opinion joined by Justices Stevens, O'Connor, Souter, and Ginsburg—held this unconstitutional as an impermissible undue burden on a woman's right to abortion. Justice Breyer said that the law was unconstitutional for two separate reasons. First, "the law lacks any exception for the preservation of the life of the mother."[147] The Court noted that the law applied to both previability and postviability abortions. The Court emphasized that the district court had found, as a matter of fact, that the procedures prohibited were safer for the woman than the alternatives. Thus, the law was an impermissible undue burden on a woman's right to choose because it contained no exception permitting the prohibited procedures to protect the woman's health.

Second, the Court concluded that the law "imposes an undue burden on a woman's ability to choose a [dilation and evacuation] abortion, thereby unduly burdening the right to choose abortion itself."[148] Justice Breyer explained that the Nebraska law was intended to prohibit "dilation and extraction," which involves removal of a fetus, or a substantial part of the fetus, before ending the fetus's life. But the statute has the unintended effect of also prohibiting "dilation and evacua-

---

[143] *Id.* at 771. The Court has invalidated other types of regulations of how abortions are performed. For example, in *Planned Parenthood Association of Kansas City v. Ashcroft*, 462 U.S. 476 (1983), the Court upheld a statutory requirement that a tissue sample be taken from each abortion for a pathologist's report. In *City of Akron v. Akron Center for Reproductive Health*, 462 U.S. 416 (1983), the Court declared unconstitutional a provision of a city law that required that physicians performing abortions "insure that the remains of the unborn child are disposed of in a humane and sanitary manner." *Id.* at 451. The Court found that this provision was impermissibly vague and thus a violation of due process.

[144] 530 U.S. 914 (2000).

[145] Neb. Rev. Stat. §28-326(9).

[146] *Id.*

[147] *Stenberg*, 530 U.S. 914, 929 (2000).

[148] *Id.*

tion," a procedure where the cervix is dilated and the contents removed. Because a physician cannot know if the fetus is still alive when the removal is done, the law would prohibit this common abortion procedure.

Justice O'Connor wrote a concurring opinion in which she emphasized that the Nebraska law was unconstitutional because it lacked an exception for the health of the woman and that it had the unintended effect of prohibiting a common form of previability abortions. She said: "If Nebraska's statute limited its application to the [dilation and extraction] procedure and included an exception for the life and health of the mother, the question presented would be quite different than the one we face today."[149] Justice O'Connor clearly signaled that she would be much more likely to uphold a narrower partial birth abortion ban and thus sent a message to legislatures as to how to draft such laws in a manner likely to be upheld by the Supreme Court.

Other Justices wrote opinions sharply disagreeing about the nature of the states' interest in the case. Justice Ginsburg emphasized that the law does not "save any fetus from destruction," and that it was adopted "because the State legislators wish to chip away at the private choice shielded in *Roe v. Wade*."[150] In sharp contrast, Justice Thomas lamented that the "Court inexplicably holds that the States cannot constitutionally prohibit a method of abortion that millions find hard to distinguish from infanticide."[151] Underlying the majority and the dissenting opinions obviously were contrasting views as to whether abortion rights should be constitutionally protected at all; Justice Breyer began by reaffirming *Roe* and *Casey*; Chief Justice Rehnquist and Justices Scalia and Thomas in their dissents called for these cases to be overruled.[152]

Seven years later, in *Gonzales v. Carhart*, the Court upheld the federal Partial Birth Abortion Ban Act.[153] The federal Partial Birth Abortion Act has no health exception and though narrower than the Nebraska law, it is more broadly written than the Court said it would allow in *Stenberg*. Nonetheless, the Court upheld the federal act. Justice Kennedy wrote the opinion for the Court and was joined by Chief Justice Roberts and Justices Scalia, Thomas, and Alito. The key to the case was not in the difference in wording between the federal law and the Nebraska act; it was Justice Alito having replaced Justice O'Connor and thus shifting the Court from 5-4 to invalidate partial birth abortion laws to 5-4 to uphold them.

The Court concluded that the government's interest in preventing partial birth abortion was sufficient to uphold the law. The Court explained: "The Act's ban on abortions that involve partial delivery of a living fetus furthers the Government's objectives. No one would dispute that, for many, [partial birth abortion] is a procedure itself laden with the power to devalue human life. Congress could nonetheless conclude that the type of abortion proscribed by the Act requires specific regulation because it implicates additional ethical and moral concerns that justify

---

[149] *Id.* at 953 (Ginsburg, J., concurring).

[150] *Id.* at 953 (Ginsburg, J., concurring).

[151] *Id.* at 980 (Thomas, J., dissenting).

[152] Justice Kennedy also dissented and in a strongly worded opinion disagreed with the majority's use of the undue burden test. *Id.* at 956 (Kennedy, J., dissenting).

[153] 550 U.S. 124 (2007).

a special prohibition." Congress determined that the abortion methods it proscribed had a "disturbing similarity to the killing of a newborn infant," and thus it was concerned with "draw[ing] a bright line that clearly distinguishes abortion and infanticide."[154]

The Court found that the federal law is constitutional even though it has no exception for allowing the procedure where necessary to protect the health of the mother. The dissent argued that the banned procedure is in many cases the safest for the woman.[155] Alternative procedures last longer and involve increased risks of perforation of the uterus, blood loss, and infection. Moreover, the most frequently used alternative is to dismember the fetus in the uterus and remove it piece by piece. This is no less "barbaric" and is more dangerous because it requires repeated surgical intrusions into the uterus. The majority rejected this argument and said that there was medical uncertainty over what was safest and stated that "[m]edical uncertainty does not foreclose the exercise of legislative power in the abortion context any more than it does in other contexts. The medical uncertainty over whether the Act's prohibition creates significant health risks provides a sufficient basis to conclude in this facial attack that the Act does not impose an undue burden."[156]

The Court also noted the alternatives to partial birth abortion. And as explained above, Justice Kennedy said that the law is facially constitutional because it is not an undue burden for a "large fraction of women."[157]

It also is important to note that the Court changed the rhetoric of abortion rights and expressed much more support for government regulation of abortion. Justice Kennedy's majority opinion repeatedly referred to the fetus as the "unborn child."[158] He wrote: "[r]espect for human life finds an ultimate expression in the bond of love the mother has for her child. . . . While we find no reliable data to measure the phenomenon, it seems unexceptionable to conclude some women come to regret their choice to abort the infant life they once created and sustained. Severe depression and loss of esteem can follow."[159]

Justice Ginsburg, writing for the four dissenters, strongly objected that this statement is at odds with prior Supreme Court decisions protecting the right to reproductive freedom, and is demeaning to women. She wrote: "This way of thinking reflects ancient notions about women's place in the family and under the Constitution—ideas that have long since been discredited. Though today's majority may regard women's feelings on the matter as 'self-evident,' this Court has repeatedly confirmed that '[t]he destiny of the woman must be shaped . . . on her own conception of her spiritual imperatives and her place in society.' "[160]

---

[154] *Id.* at 138.
[155] *Id.* at 170 (Ginsburg, J., dissenting).
[156] *Id.* at 164.
[157] *Id.* at 167-168.
[158] *Id.* at 134, 160.
[159] *Id.* at 159.
[160] *Id.* at 185 (Ginsburg, J., dissenting).

As for the future, the Court left open the possibility of an "as applied" challenge to the law, where a woman and her doctor could argue that in her case the law was an undue burden by prohibiting the safest form of abortion.

§10.3.3.3 Government Restrictions on Funds and Facilities for Abortions

Decisions Holding No Requirement for Government Funding

The Supreme Court repeatedly has held that the government is not constitutionally required to subsidize abortions even if it is paying for childbirth. In three cases in 1977, the Court upheld the ability of the government to deny funding for "nontherapeutic abortions" — that is, abortions that were not performed to protect the life or health of the mother. In *Beal v. Doe*, the Supreme Court held that the federal Medicaid Act did not require that states fund nontherapeutic first trimester abortions as part of participating in the joint federal-state program.[161] In *Maher v. Roe*, the Supreme Court upheld the constitutionality of a state law that denied the use of Medicaid funds for nontherapeutic first trimester abortions, although the law provided funding for medically necessary first trimester abortions.[162] And in *Poelker v. Doe*, the Court found that it was constitutional for a city to refuse to pay for nontherapeutic first trimester abortions in its public hospital.[163]

In two cases in 1980, the Supreme Court went further and upheld the constitutionality of laws that denied public funding for medically necessary abortions except where necessary to save the life of the mother. In *Harris v. McRae*, the Court upheld a federal law, the Hyde Amendment, that prohibited the use of federal funds for performing abortions "except where the life of the mother would be endangered if the fetus were carried to term" or except for cases of rape or incest "when such rape or incest has been reported promptly to a law enforcement agency or public health service."[164] Similarly, in *Williams v. Zbarez*, the Supreme Court found constitutional a state law that prohibited the use of state funds for performing abortions except where the mother's life was in danger.[165]

In *Webster v. Reproductive Health Services*, in 1989, the Court upheld a state law that prohibited the use of public employees and facilities to perform or assist the performance of abortions except where necessary to save the mother's life.[166] The Court said that this law was indistinguishable from the earlier cases that allowed the government to deny funding of abortions.[167]

---

[161] 432 U.S. 438 (1977).

[162] 432 U.S. 464 (1977).

[163] 432 U.S. 519 (1977).

[164] 448 U.S. 297, 302 (1980).

[165] 448 U.S. 358 (1980).

[166] 492 U.S. 490, 509-511 (1989).

[167] In *Rust v. Sullivan*, 500 U.S. 173 (1991), the Court held that the government does not violate the First Amendment if it denies funding to family planning clinics that perform abortion counseling or make abortion referrals. *Rust* is discussed in §11.2.4.4.

The Court's Reasoning in Allowing the Denial
of Public Funding

In all of these cases, the Court gave the same basic reasons as to why it is constitutional for the government to deny funding or facilities for abortions, even though it pays for childbirth. First, the Court often said that the existence of a constitutional right does not create a duty for the government to subsidize the exercise of the right. For example, in *Harris v. McRae*, the Court said: "It cannot be that because government may not prohibit the use of contraceptives, or prevent parents from sending their children to a private school, government, therefore, has an affirmative constitutional obligation to ensure that all persons have the financial resources to obtain contraceptives or send their children to private schools."[168]

This is in accord with a more general principle that the government rarely has an affirmative constitutional duty to provide benefits or to facilitate the exercise of rights. The Court has explained: "[O]ur cases have recognized that the Due Process Clauses generally confer no affirmative right to governmental aid, even where such aid may be necessary to secure life, liberty, or property interests of which the government itself may not deprive the individual."[169]

Second, the Court said that denial of public funding places a woman in no different position than she would have been if there was no Medicaid program or no public hospital. In *Maher v. Roe*, the Court said that the state law denying use of Medicaid funds "places no obstacles—absolute or otherwise—in the pregnant woman's path to an abortion. An indigent woman who desires an abortion suffers no disadvantage as a consequence of Connecticut's decision to fund childbirth. . . . The indigency that may make it difficult—and in some cases perhaps, impossible—for some women to have abortions is neither created nor in any way affected by the Connecticut regulation."[170] Similarly, in *Harris v. McRae*, the Court said that the prohibition of the use of federal funds for abortions "leaves an indigent woman with at least the same range of choices in deciding whether to obtain a medically necessary abortion as she would have had if Congress chose to subsidize no health care costs at all."[171]

Third, the Court emphasized that the government constitutionally could make the choice to encourage childbirth over abortion. In *Maher*, the Court wrote that *Roe* "implies no limitation on the authority of a State to make a value judgment favoring childbirth over abortion, and to implement that judgment by the allocation of public funds."[172]

[168] 448 U.S. at 318.
[169] Webster v. Reproductive Health Serv., 492 U.S. at 507, quoting DeShaney v. Winnebago County Dept. of Social Servs., 489 U.S. 189, 196 (1989).
[170] 432 U.S. at 474.
[171] 448 U.S. at 317.
[172] 432 U.S. at 474.

Criticism of the Abortion Funding Decisions

The primary criticism of these decisions is that the denial of public funding has both the purpose and effect of preventing abortions and thus should be regarded as a violation of the right. Critics argue that the government should not be able to use its resources to encourage childbirth over abortion. In dissent in *Harris,* Justice Brennan argued: "[T]he state must refrain from wielding its enormous power and influence in a manner that might burden the pregnant woman's freedom to choose whether to have an abortion."[173]

There are only two outcomes to a pregnancy (unless there is a miscarriage): childbirth or abortion. Those who disagree with the Court's abortion funding decisions maintain that it should be left to each woman, on her own, to decide between childbirth and abortion. It violates the right for the government to offer incentives or pressures for one option over the other. In essence, denying funding for abortions is a penalty for the exercise of a constitutional right.[174]

Abortion is less costly to the government than childbirth.[175] Therefore, the only possible justification for the government's paying for childbirth but not abortion is a judgment that abortion is wrong. Critics of the Court's decisions argue that the government should not be able to act with the purpose and effect of preventing the exercise of a constitutional right.[176]

§10.3.3.4 Spousal Notice and Consent Requirements

The Supreme Court has held that the government cannot require either spousal consent or spousal notification as a prerequisite for a married woman's obtaining an abortion.

Unconstitutionality of Spousal Consent Requirements

In *Planned Parenthood of Central Missouri v. Danforth,* the Supreme Court declared unconstitutional a state law that required a husband's written consent before a married woman could receive an abortion unless a physician certified that the abortion was necessary to protect the woman's life.[177] The Court recognized that the husband has a "deep and proper concern and interest . . . in his wife's pregnancy and in the growth and development of the fetus she is carrying."[178] The Court, however, said that "the obvious fact is that when the wife and the husband disagree on this decision, the view of only one of the two marriage partners can

---

[173] 448 U.S. at 330 (Brennan, J., dissenting).

[174] *See* Kathleen Sullivan, Unconstitutional Conditions, 102 Harv. L. Rev. 1413, 1498-1499 (1989).

[175] Beal v. Doe, 432 U.S. at 463 (Blackmun, J., dissenting).

[176] *See* Michael Perry, Why the Supreme Court Was Plainly Wrong in the Hyde Amendment Case: A Brief Comment on *Harris v. McRae,* 32 Stan. L. Rev. 1113, 1115-1116 (1980).

[177] 428 U.S. at 67-68.

[178] *Id.* at 69.

prevail. Inasmuch as it is the woman who physically bears the child and who is the more directly and immediately affected by the pregnancy, as between the two, the balance weighs in her favor."[179]

Unconstitutionality of Spousal Notification Requirements

In *Planned Parenthood v. Casey*, the Supreme Court invalidated a state law that required spousal notification before a married woman could receive an abortion.[180] The joint opinion of Justices O'Connor, Kennedy, and Souter noted the tragic prevalence of men abusing their wives and said that a spousal notification requirement could trigger such abuse. The joint opinion observed: "In well-functioning marriages, spouses discuss intimate decisions such as whether to bear a child. But there are millions of women in this country who are the victims of regular physical and psychological abuse at the hands of their husbands. Should these women become pregnant, they may have very good reasons for not wishing to inform their husbands of their decision to obtain an abortion. . . . The spousal notification requirement is thus likely to prevent a significant number of women from obtaining an abortion."[181]

The joint opinion again recognized that a husband has an interest in whether his wife has an abortion, but the Justices said: "Before birth, however, the issue takes on a very different cast. It is inescapable biological fact that state regulation with respect to the child a woman is carrying will have a far greater impact on the mother's liberty than on the father's."[182] The Court said that the choice whether to have an abortion must be left to the woman, without any requirement for spousal notification.

§10.3.3.5   Parental Notice and Consent Requirements

The Supreme Court has held that a state may require parental notice and/or consent for an unmarried minor's abortion, but only if it creates an alternative procedure where a minor can obtain an abortion by going before a judge who can approve the abortion by finding that it would be in the minor's best interest or by concluding that the minor is mature enough to decide for herself.

Parental Consent

In *Planned Parenthood of Central Missouri v. Danforth*, the Supreme Court invalidated a state law that prevented an unmarried woman under age 18 from receiving an abortion unless her parents consented or a physician certified that the

---

[179] *Id.* at 71.
[180] 505 U.S. at 887-898.
[181] *Id.* at 892-895.
[182] *Id.* at 896.

abortion was necessary to protect the woman's life.[183] Subsequently, in *Bellotti v. Baird*, the Court declared unconstitutional a similar law from another state that prevented an unmarried woman under age 18 from receiving an abortion unless both of her parents granted consent or unless a court authorized the abortion for good cause.[184] The Court recognized that parents have a constitutional right to control the upbringing of their children, but also acknowledged that females of all ages have a right to abortion. The Court thus attempted to strike a compromise: A state could require parental consent for unmarried minors' abortions, but only if it created a bypass procedure where a minor could obtain an abortion by persuading a judge that it would be in her best interests or that she is mature enough to decide for herself.

Justice Powell, writing for the plurality, stated: "[I]f the State decides to require a pregnant minor to obtain one or both parents' consent to an abortion, it also must provide an alternative procedure whereby authorization for the abortion can be obtained. A pregnant minor is entitled to such a proceeding to show either: (1) that she is mature enough and well enough informed to make her abortion decision, in consultation with her physician, independently of her parents' wishes; or (2) that even if she is not able to make this decision independently, the desired abortion would be in her best interests."[185]

Parental Notification

In *H.L. v. Matheson*, the Supreme Court upheld a Utah law that required that a physician "[n]otify, if possible, the parents or guardian of the woman upon whom the abortion is to be performed, if she is a minor."[186] The Court said that although "a state may not constitutionally legislate a blanket, unreviewable veto power of parents to veto their daughter's abortion, a statute setting out a 'mere requirement of parental notice' does not violate the constitutional rights of an immature, dependent minor."[187] The Court emphasized that parents have a constitutional right to raise their children and that therefore the state has an important interest in making sure that parents are notified prior to an abortion on a teenage girl. The Court also stressed that the "Utah statute gives neither parents nor the judges a veto power over the minor's abortion decision."[188] The Court said that the fact that the notice requirement might "inhibit some minors from seeking abortions is not a valid basis to void the statute."[189]

---

[183] 428 U.S. at 72.

[184] 443 U.S. 622 (1979).

[185] *Id.* at 643-644. *See also* Planned Parenthood Assn. of Kansas City v. Ashcroft, 462 U.S. 476 (1983) (upholding a parental consent procedure that provided for judicial bypass as outlined in *Bellotti*).

[186] 450 U.S. 398, 400 (1981). The law also required spousal notification for married women, a requirement declared unconstitutional in *Casey* and described above in §10.3.3.4.

[187] *Id.* at 409.

[188] *Id.* at 411.

[189] *Id.* at 413.

Subsequently, the Supreme Court upheld parental notification requirements so long as they have the judicial bypass procedures outlined in *Bellotti*. In *Ohio v. Akron Center for Reproductive Health*, the Court upheld a law that required that notice be given to at least one parent of an unmarried minor before an abortion could be performed.[190] The law allowed an abortion without such notification if a judge approved it either by finding it would be in the minor's best interests or by concluding that she is mature enough to decide for herself.

In *Hodgson v. Minnesota*, the Supreme Court upheld the constitutionality of an even more burdensome law that required that notice be given to both of a minor's parents before an abortion could be performed.[191] The Court specifically ruled that a two-parent notification requirement without a judicial bypass procedure was unconstitutional, but that such a requirement is permissible so long as there is a mechanism for judicial bypass.[192]

Is the Court's Approach a Desirable Compromise?

On the one hand, these cases concerning parental notice and consent reflect a compromise between giving parents total control over their daughters' access to abortion and permitting females of all ages to decide for themselves whether to have an abortion. Generally, parental consent is required for all surgical procedures for unemancipated children, and the Court's decisions can be defended on the ground that parents presumptively should participate in these decisions. The Court's approach preserves parental involvement, while not giving parents veto power.

But on the other hand, it can be argued that judicial bypass is an unrealistic approach. Teenagers are likely to lack resources and knowledge to petition courts.[193] Moreover, the standard gives the judge little guidance in making the decision. How is a judge to decide whether an abortion is in the minor's best interests? Some judges probably believe an abortion is always in a teenager's best interests, while others might think that abortion is wrong and never in a person's best interests. Also, how is the judge to decide if a minor is mature enough to decide for herself, and does it make sense that if a minor is not mature enough to decide to have an abortion, she then will have a baby to care for?

---

[190] 497 U.S. 502 (1990).

[191] 497 U.S. 417 (1990).

[192] In *Ayotte v. Planned Parenthood*, 546 U.S. 320 (2006), the Court considered a New Hampshire law that did not require parental notification if the life of the minor was in jeopardy, but would require parental notification if the health of the minor would be in jeopardy by waiting. The Court said that it would be unconstitutional to deny an abortion in such circumstances, but concluded that this would not require invalidating the entire statute. The Court remanded the case to fashion a narrower declaratory and injunctive remedy. The Court stated: "Only a few applications of New Hampshire's parental notification statute would present a constitutional problem. So long as they are faithful to legislative intent, then, in this case the lower courts can issue a declaratory judgment and an injunction prohibiting the statute's unconstitutional application." *Id.* at 969.

[193] For a critique of the Court's approach, *see* Jennifer C. Friedman, Parental Notice in State Abortion Statutes: Filling the Gap in Constitutional Jurisprudence, 29 Colum. Hum. Rts. L. Rev. 437 (1998); Katheryn D. Katz, The Pregnant Child's Right to Self-Determination, 62 Alb. L. Rev. 1119 (1999).

§10.4 CONSTITUTIONAL PROTECTION FOR SEXUAL ACTIVITY AND SEXUAL ORIENTATION

In *Lawrence v. Texas*, the Court held that states may not prohibit private consensual sexual activity between consenting adults of the same sex.[1] *Lawrence* is thus an extremely important decision reaffirming constitutional protection for privacy and applying it to private, consensual homosexual activity.

Seventeen years earlier, in *Bowers v. Hardwick*, the Court ruled that the right to privacy does not protect a right to engage in private consensual homosexual activity.[2] Michael Hardwick was arrested for engaging in homosexual activity in his bedroom. A police officer came to his apartment on a totally unrelated matter. A roommate answered the door and directed the officer to Hardwick's room. The officer said that he witnessed the homosexual behavior and arrested Hardwick for violating the Georgia sodomy law that provided: "A person commits the offense of sodomy when he performs or submits to any sexual act involving the sex organs of one person and the mouth or anus of another. . . . A person convicted of the offense of sodomy shall be punished by imprisonment for not less than one nor more than 20 years."[3] After a preliminary hearing, the district attorney decided not to present the case to the grand jury or pursue criminal charges. Hardwick, however, filed a suit in federal court challenging the constitutionality of the Georgia law.

The Supreme Court, in a 5-to-4 decision, upheld the Georgia statute. Justice White wrote the opinion for the Court, joined by Chief Justice Burger and Justices Rehnquist, Powell, and O'Connor. Justice White began by contending that the earlier decisions protecting privacy pertained to matters of family and reproduction; homosexual activity, he argued, did not fit within these rights. White wrote: "[W]e think . . . that none of the rights announced in those cases bears any resemblance to the claimed constitutional right of homosexuals to engage in acts of sodomy that is asserted in this case. No connection between family, marriage, or procreation on the one hand and homosexual activity on the other has been demonstrated."[4]

White said that the Court should protect rights as fundamental only if they are supported by the Constitution's text, the framers' intent, or a tradition of being safeguarded. He said: "The Court is most vulnerable and comes nearest to illegitimacy when it deals with judge-made constitutional law having little or no cognizable roots in the language or design of the Constitution."[5] White said that neither the text nor tradition justified finding a fundamental right to engage in homosexual activity.

In *Lawrence*, the Court expressly overruled *Bowers v. Hardwick*. *Lawrence* arose when police in Texas received an anonymous tip of a disturbance in an apartment. They went to investigate and entered the apartment; they found two men engaged

---

§10.4 [1] 539 U.S. 558 (2003).
[2] 478 U.S. 186 (1986).
[3] *Id.* at 188 n.1.
[4] *Id.* at 190-191.
[5] *Id.* at 194.

in sexual activity. The men were convicted and fined $200 under a Texas law prohibiting "deviate sexual intercourse," defined as sexual activity between same-sex couples. In a forceful opinion in *Lawrence*, Justice Kennedy, writing for the Court, expressly overruled *Bowers* and spoke of constitutional protection for all individuals in the most intimate and private aspects of their lives.[6] Justice Kennedy stated:

> To say that the issue in *Bowers* was simply the right to engage in certain sexual conduct demeans the claim the individual put forward, just as it would demean a married couple were it to be said marriage is simply about the right to have sexual intercourse. The laws involved in *Bowers* and here are, to be sure, statutes that purport to do no more than prohibit a particular sexual act. Their penalties and purposes, though, have more far-reaching consequences, touching upon the most private human conduct, sexual behavior, and in the most private of places, the home. The statutes do seek to control a personal relationship that, whether or not entitled to formal recognition in the law, is within the liberty of persons to choose without being punished as criminals. . . . It suffices for us to acknowledge that adults may choose to enter upon this relationship in the confines of their homes and their own private lives and still retain their dignity as free persons. When sexuality finds overt expression in intimate conduct with another person, the conduct can be but one element in a personal bond that is more enduring. The liberty protected by the Constitution allows homosexual persons the right to make this choice.[7]

Lawrence is important in many respects. First, *Lawrence* means that laws in 13 states prohibiting private consensual homosexual activity are unconstitutional. As Justice Kennedy pointed out, these statutes often are the basis for discrimination against gays and lesbians. Second, *Lawrence* is a powerful affirmation of a right to privacy under the Constitution. Justice Kennedy's majority opinion emphasized that the Court has safeguarded privacy, even though it is not enumerated in the Constitution, for almost a century in decisions involving family autonomy, contraception, and abortion. Third, *Lawrence*, more than any other case in American history, recognizes that sexual activity is a fundamental aspect of personhood and that it is entitled to constitutional protection. In a dissent, Justice Scalia objected that the Court's decision would put in jeopardy laws prohibiting, among other activities, "adultery" and "masturbation."[8] Finally, and perhaps most important, *Lawrence* is the most important decision to date recognizing the rights of gays and lesbians to equal dignity and equal treatment under the Constitution.[9]

However, the Court in *Lawrence* did not articulate the level of scrutiny to be used. Nowhere did the Court speak of a fundamental right or mention strict scrutiny. On the other hand, the Court did rely on privacy cases where strict scrutiny

---

[6] Justice O'Connor concurred in the judgment and would have invalidated the Texas law based on equal protection, holding the law unconstitutional because it prohibited sex acts between same-sex couples that were allowed between opposite-sex couples. She would not have overruled *Bowers*.

[7] 539 U.S. at 567.

[8] *Id.* at 590 (Scalia, J., dissenting).

[9] For excellent history of the litigation in *Lawrence, see* Dale Carpenter, Flagrant Conduct: The Story of *Lawrence v. Texas* (2012).

had been used. Also, Texas justified the law as advancing its moral judgment and traditionally this is enough to meet rational basis review. The Court's rejection of this can be seen as implying heightened scrutiny. But the silence of the decision about the level of scrutiny leaves this issue open until the Supreme Court returns to it and offers needed clarification.[10]

§10.5   CONSTITUTIONAL PROTECTION FOR MEDICAL CARE DECISIONS

The Supreme Court has considered constitutional protection for medical care decisions in three contexts. One involves circumstances where there is a constitutional right to have the government provide care. A second concerns whether there is a right to refuse medical care. Finally, the Court has considered whether there is a constitutional right to physician-assisted suicide.

A Right to Medical Care

Generally, the Constitution creates no affirmative right to government services and thus does not generally obligate the government to provide medical care to those who need it.[1] In *DeShaney v. Winnebago County Department of Social Services*, the Court said that "our cases have recognized that the Due Process Clauses generally confer no affirmative right to governmental aid, even where such aid may be necessary to secure life, liberty, or property interests of which the government itself may not deprive the individual."[2] In line with this philosophy, the Supreme Court ruled that the government constitutionally may refuse to subsidize abortions, even if the government pays for childbirth.[3]

---

[10] The Eleventh Circuit, for example, has read *Lawrence* as using only rational basis review and thus applied this deferential test in upholding a state law that prohibited sale, distribution, or possession of "sex toys." Williams v. Attorney General of Alabama, 378 F.3d 1232 (11th Cir. 2004).

§10.5 [1] For an argument that the Constitution should be interpreted to create a right to such minimum entitlements, *see* Peter B. Edelman, The Next Century of Our Constitution: Rethinking Our Duty to the Poor, 39 Hastings L.J. 1 (1987); Charles L. Black, Jr., Further Reflections on the Constitutional Justice of Livelihood, 86 Colum. L. Rev. 1103 (1986); Frank I. Michelman, Foreword: On Protecting the Poor Through the Fourteenth Amendment, 83 Harv. L. Rev. 7 (1969); *but see* Robert Bork, The Impossibility of Finding Welfare Rights in the Constitution, 1979 Wash. U. L.Q. 695.

[2] 489 U.S. 189, 196 (1989).

[3] These cases are reviewed in §10.3.3.3.

DeShaney recognized that the government has a duty to provide services in extraordinary circumstances, such as when a person is in government custody or the government itself created the danger.[4] Thus, prisoners or others that the government has institutionalized have the strongest claim of a right to government-provided medical care. The Supreme Court expressed this distinction in *Youngberg v. Romeo*: "As a general matter, a State is under no constitutional duty to provide substantive services for those within its border. When a person is institutionalized—and wholly dependent on the State—it is conceded . . . that a duty to provide certain services and care does exist, although even then a State necessarily has considerable discretion in determining the nature and scope of its responsibilities."[5]

In *Estelle v. Gamble*, the Court found that it was cruel and unusual punishment for a prison to refuse to provide medical treatment after an inmate had injured his back.[6] The Court said that the government has an "obligation to provide medical care for those whom it is punishing by incarceration."[7] A prisoner has no choice but to rely on the government to provide needed medical care. If the government fails to do so, the inmate's medical needs will not be met; in "the worst cases, such a failure may actually produce physical 'torture or a lingering death.'"[8] The Court in *Estelle* said that "deliberate indifference to serious medical needs of prisoners constitutes the 'unnecessary and wanton infliction of pain.'"[9]

In *Youngberg v. Romeo*, the Court considered the rights of a mentally disabled person who was confined in a state institution. The Court said that the government had a "duty to provide adequate food, shelter, clothing, and medical care. These are the essentials of care that the State must provide. . . . [The patients] enjoy constitutionally protected interests in conditions of reasonable care and safety, reasonably nonrestrictive confinement conditions, and such training as may be required by these interests."[10]

Under current law, it is very unlikely that the Court will find that the government has a duty to provide medical care except when people are incarcerated or institutionalized by the government. Although the Court has not defined the right to care for these individuals with any precision, it is clear that in this limited context there is a constitutional right to medical care.

The Right to Refuse Treatment

Generally, there is a constitutional right of individuals to refuse medical treatment, but it certainly is not absolute and can be regulated by the state. For example, in *Jacobson v. Massachusetts*, the Supreme Court upheld a Massachusetts

---

[4] *DeShaney* is discussed in detail in §7.2.
[5] 457 U.S. 307, 317 (1982).
[6] 429 U.S. 97 (1976).
[7] *Id.* at 103.
[8] *Id.* at 103 (citations omitted).
[9] *Id.* at 104 (citations omitted).
[10] 457 U.S. at 324.

law that required vaccinations.[11] The Court allowed the law because of the government's compelling interest in stopping the spread of communicable diseases.

In *Washington v. Harper*, the Court said that prisoners had the right to be free from the involuntary administration of antipsychotic drugs.[12] The Court observed that prisoners possess "a significant liberty interest in avoiding the unwanted administration of antipsychotic drugs under the Due Process Clause of the Fourteenth Amendment."[13] The Court therefore said that "[t]he forcible injection of medication into a nonconsenting person's body represents a substantial interference with that person's liberty."[14] However, the Court said that this interest was adequately protected by providing an inmate with notice and a hearing before a tribunal of medical and prison personnel at which the inmate could challenge the decision to administer the drugs.

The most important case, thus far, concerning a right to refuse medical care is *Cruzan v. Director, Missouri Department of Health*.[15] Nancy Cruzan suffered severe head injuries in an automobile accident and was in a persistent vegetative state. There was virtually no chance of her regaining consciousness. Her parents wished to terminate food and hydration and thus to end her life. The state intervened to prevent this.

There were three parts to the Court's holding in *Cruzan*. First, the Court said that competent adults have a constitutional right to refuse medical care. Eight of the nine Justices, all but Justice Scalia, recognized such a right. Chief Justice Rehnquist, writing the opinion of the Court, said: "The principle that a competent person has a constitutionally protected liberty interest in refusing unwanted medical treatment may be inferred from our prior decisions."[16]

The majority opinion then said: "[F]or purposes of this case, we assume that the United States Constitution would grant a competent person a constitutionally protected right to refuse lifesaving hydration and nutrition."[17] Although Chief Justice Rehnquist's majority opinion only "assumed" that there was a right to refuse food and water to bring about death, five Justices in *Cruzan*—Justice O'Connor concurring and the four dissenting Justices—said that such a right exists. Justice O'Connor began her concurring opinion by saying: "I agree that a protected liberty interest in refusing unwanted medical treatment may be inferred from our prior decisions and that the refusal of artificially delivered food and water is encompassed within that liberty interest."[18] Justice Brennan—in a dissenting opinion joined by Marshall, Blackmun, and Stevens—said that there is a "fundamental right to be free of unwanted artificial nutrition and hydration."[19]

---

[11] 197 U.S. 11 (1905).

[12] 494 U.S. 210 (1990). The procedural due process aspects of *Washington v. Harper* are discussed in §7.3.3.

[13] *Id.* at 221-222.

[14] *Id.* at 229.

[15] 497 U.S. 261 (1990).

[16] *Id.* at 278.

[17] *Id.* at 279.

[18] *Id.* at 287 (O'Connor, J., concurring).

[19] *Id.* at 302 (Brennan, J., dissenting).

Thus, eight Justices said that there is a right to refuse treatment under the liberty of the due process clause, and five expressly said that this includes a right to refuse food and water to bring about death. Only Justice Scalia expressly rejected such a right. Scalia said: "I would have preferred that we announce, clearly and promptly, that the federal courts have no business in this field; that American law has always accorded the State the power to prevent, by force if necessary, suicide — including suicide by refusing to take appropriate measures necessary to preserve one's life."[20]

The second major aspect of the Court's holding in *Cruzan* was that a state may require clear and convincing evidence that a person wanted treatment terminated before it is cut off. Chief Justice Rehnquist's majority opinion acknowledged the state's important interest in protecting life and in ensuring that a person desired the end of treatment before it is suspended. He said that "[t]he choice between life and death is a deeply personal decision of obvious and overwhelming finality. We believe Missouri may legitimately seek to safeguard the personal element of this choice through the imposition of heightened evidentiary requirements."[21]

Finally, the *Cruzan* Court said that a state may prevent family members from terminating treatment for another. The right to end treatment belongs to each individual, and a state may prevent someone else from making the decision. Chief Justice Rehnquist said: "[W]e do not think that the Due Process Clause requires the State to repose judgment on these matters with anyone but the patient herself. . . . [T]here is no automatic ensurance that the view of close family members will necessarily be the same as the patient's would have been had she been confronted with the prospect of her situation while competent."[22]

Family members may be in a conflict of interest situation; they may choose to terminate care to minimize their own emotional or financial burdens. Hence the Court said that "the State may choose to defer only to [the] wishes [of the patient], rather than confide the decision to close family members."[23]

Cruzan left many questions unresolved. First, *Cruzan* did not articulate a level of scrutiny to be used in evaluating government regulation of personal decisions concerning refusal of medical treatment. Although the majority opinion recognized such a right to exist, it did not use the label "fundamental" or imply that strict scrutiny was appropriate. But nor did it suggest that a lower level of scrutiny was to be used; the Court just did not say.

Second, *Cruzan* did not resolve what is sufficient to constitute clear and convincing proof of a person's desire to terminate treatment. The Court noted that most states limit the use of "oral testimony entirely in determining the wishes of parties in transactions which, while important, simply do not have the consequences that a decision to terminate a person's life does."[24] This implies that a

---

[20] *Id.* at 293 (Scalia, J., concurring).
[21] *Id.* at 281.
[22] *Id.* at 286.
[23] *Id.* at 286-287.
[24] *Id.* at 284.

written "living will" would be sufficient to meet the clear and convincing test, but that a state can entirely prevent oral testimony.

Third, *Cruzan* does not address the situation where a competent person designates a surrogate or guardian to make the decision concerning terminating life-saving treatment. In fact, in a footnote at the end of the opinion, Rehnquist said: "We are not faced in this case with the question whether a State might be required to defer to the decision of a surrogate if competent and probative evidence established that the patient herself had expressed a desire that the decision to terminate life-sustaining treatment be made for her by that individual."[25]

Physician-Assisted Death

In *Washington v. Glucksberg*[26] and *Vacco v. Quill*,[27] the Supreme Court rejected facial challenges to state laws prohibiting aiding a suicide and the claim that there is a constitutional right to physician-assisted death. These decisions have the effect of upholding laws that exist in the vast majority of states prohibiting aiding another in committing suicide. However, although the decisions were rendered without a single dissent, they left open the possibility of legal protection for such a right both at the state level and in future Supreme Court rulings.

The Court had before it two decisions of United States Courts of Appeals that found a constitutional right to physician-assisted death. The United States Court of Appeals for the Ninth Circuit, in an *en banc* decision, found that terminally ill individuals have a fundamental liberty interest, protected under the due process clause of the Fourteenth Amendment, to physician-assisted death.[28] The Ninth Circuit declared unconstitutional a Washington law that "[a] person is guilty of promoting a suicide attempt when he knowingly causes or aids another person to commit suicide."[29] The court concluded that "the Constitution encompasses a due process liberty interest in controlling the time and manner of one's death—that there is, in short, a constitutionally recognized 'right to die.' "[30]

Just a few weeks after the Ninth Circuit's ruling, the United States Court of Appeals for the Second Circuit declared unconstitutional a New York law that prohibits aiding another in committing suicide.[31] Several physicians and gravely ill patients challenged the New York statute that "[a] person is guilty of manslaughter in the second degree when . . . [h]e intentionally causes or aids another person

---

[25] *Id.* at 287 n.12.

[26] 521 U.S. 702 (1997).

[27] 521 U.S. 793 (1997). For an excellent summary of the arguments against a right to physician-assisted death, *see* Yale Kamisar, Against Suicide: Even a Very Limited Form, 72 U. Det. Mercy L. Rev. 735 (1995). For an excellent defense of such a right, *see* Robert A. Sedler, Are Absolute Bans on Assisted Suicide Constitutional? I Say No, 72 U. Det. Mercy L. Rev. 725 (1995); Robert A. Sedler, Constitutional Challenges to Bans on "Assisted Suicide": The View from Without and Within, 21 Hastings Const. L.Q. 777 (1994).

[28] Compassion in Dying v. Washington, 79 F.3d 790 (9th Cir. 1996) (*en banc*).

[29] Wash. Rev. Code §9A.36.060(1) (2d Cir. 1994).

[30] 79 F.3d at 816.

[31] Quill v. Vacco, 80 F.3d 716 (2d Cir. 1996).

to commit suicide."[32] The Second Circuit found that the New York law violated the equal protection clause of the Fourteenth Amendment. The court explained that patients on artificial life support already have the right to physician-assisted suicide based on *Cruzan v. Director, Missouri Department of Health,* discussed above. The Second Circuit said that in light of this decision, those not receiving artificial life support are discriminated against because they do not have a right to physician-assisted suicide. The court concluded that this latter group is denied equal protection.

The United States Supreme Court reversed both of these court of appeals decisions. Chief Justice Rehnquist wrote for the majority in each case. In *Washington v. Glucksberg,* the Court rejected the claim that the Washington law prohibiting assisted suicide violated a fundamental right protected under the due process clause. Rehnquist's opinion began by observing that a right is protected as fundamental under the due process clause only when supported by history or tradition. Rehnquist then stated that "for over 700 years, the Anglo-American common-law tradition has punished or otherwise disapproved of both suicide and attempting suicide."[33]

Rehnquist noted that "[i]n almost every State—indeed, in almost every western democracy—it is a crime to assist suicide."[34] After reviewing the history of laws prohibiting suicide and assistance of suicide, Rehnquist stated: "Despite changes in medical technology and notwithstanding an increased emphasis on the importance of end-of-life decision-making, we have not retreated from this prohibition [of assisting suicide]."[35] The Court thus concluded that "[t]o hold for respondents, we would have to reverse centuries of legal doctrine and practice, and strike down the considered policy choice of almost every state."[36]

Because the Court determined that "the asserted 'right' to assistance in committing suicide is not a fundamental liberty interest protected by the due process clause,"[37] the Washington law was to be upheld so long as it met a rational basis test. The Court found that the law reasonably served many legitimate interests. The Court found, for example, that the state has important interests in the preservation of life,[38] in protecting the integrity and ethics of the medical profession,[39] in protecting vulnerable groups,[40] and in stopping the path to voluntary and even involuntary euthanasia.[41] Chief Justice Rehnquist said that the experience in the Netherlands indicated that "regulation of the practice may not have prevented

---

[32] N.Y. Penal L. §125.15 (McKinney 1987). Also, New York has a separate statute that makes it a felony when a person "intentionally causes or aids another person to commit suicide." N.Y. Penal L. §120.30.

[33] 521 U.S. at 702.

[34] *Id.*

[35] *Id.* at 703.

[36] *Id.* at 702.

[37] *Id.* at 703-704.

[38] *Id.*

[39] *Id.*

[40] *Id.*

[41] *Id.* at 734.

abuses in cases involving vulnerable persons, including severely disabled neonates and elderly persons suffering from dementia."[42]

Similarly, in *Vacco v. Quill*, the Supreme Court held that laws prohibiting physician-assisted suicide do not violate the equal protection clause. Chief Justice Rehnquist, again writing for the majority, initially noted that the prohibition of assisted suicide neither discriminated against a suspect class, such as against a racial minority, nor violated a fundamental right, since *Washington v. Glucksberg* had expressly repudiated that contention.[43] Under equal protection analysis this means that the law was to be upheld so long as it met a rational basis test.

Moreover, the Court rejected the claim that New York's law discriminated against anyone. The Court noted that New York's law treated everyone equally: All have the right to refuse medical care, and all are prohibited from assisting another in committing a suicide.[44] The Court disagreed with the Second Circuit's conclusion that those not on artificial life support are discriminated against as compared with those who can receive physician-assisted suicide by demanding the termination of a respirator or artificial nutrition or hydration. The Court said that this "distinction comports with fundamental legal principles of causation and intent."[45] The Court explained that "when a patient refuses life-sustaining medical treatment, he dies from an underlying fatal disease or pathology; but if a patient ingests lethal medication prescribed by a physician he is killed by that medication."[46]

The Court also emphasized the importance of intent in laws prohibiting assisted suicide. The Court noted that "in some cases, painkilling drugs may hasten a patient's death, but the physician's purpose and intent is, or may be, only to ease his patient's pain. A doctor who assists a suicide, however, 'must necessarily and indubitably, intend that the patient be made dead.'"[47] The Court said that the law traditionally has recognized this distinction in distinguishing between allowing refusal of treatment and prohibiting suicide.

Washington v. Glucksberg and *Vacco v. Quill* thus seem to emphatically reject a constitutional right to physician-assisted death. Not a single Justice in either case voted to declare unconstitutional either state law. Yet the cases also left open some doors to future legal protection of a right to physician-assisted death.

First, states may enact statutes protecting such a right. The Court's decision emphasized the absence of constitutional limits on state laws. In other words, the issue of a right to die is left to the political process; states may prohibit or allow physician-assisted suicide largely unconstrained by the Constitution. For example, in 1994, Oregon enacted, through a ballot initiative, a "Death with Dignity Act," which legalized physician-assisted suicide for competent, terminally ill adults.[48]

---

[42] *Id.*

[43] Vacco v. Quill, 521 U.S. at 793.

[44] *Id.* at 794.

[45] *Id.*

[46] *Id.*

[47] *Id.* at 802.

[48] Or. Rev. Stat. §127.800 (1996). A federal district court declared the law unconstitutional on the ground that it does not provide sufficient safeguards for terminally ill patients, Lee v. Oregon,

Second, five Justices, in concurring opinions and opinions concurring in the judgment, left open the possibility that laws prohibiting physician-assisted death might be declared unconstitutional as applied in specific cases. Justice O'Connor submitted the identical short concurring opinion in both decisions. Justice O'Connor said that while there "is no generalized right to 'commit suicide,'" the Court need not address the "narrower question whether a mentally competent person who is experiencing great suffering has a constitutionally cognizable interest in controlling the circumstances of his or her death."[49] Justice O'Connor concluded her concurring opinion by reiterating that "there is no need to address the question whether suffering patients have a constitutionally cognizable interest in obtaining relief from the suffering that they may experience in the last days of their lives."[50] Justices Ginsburg and Breyer concurred in this opinion.

Additionally, Justice Stevens wrote an opinion concurring in the judgment in both cases that was joined by Justices Souter, Ginsburg, and Breyer.[51] Justice Stevens said that he wrote "separately to make it clear that there is also room for further debate about the limits that the Constitution places on the power of the States to punish the practice."[52] Justice Stevens said that although the Court rejected the facial challenges to the New York and Washington laws, that "does not foreclose the possibility that some applications of the statute[s] might well be invalid."[53] Justice Stevens explained that in particular cases an individual's claim of such a right might be strong and the state's interests much less.

Likewise, Justice Breyer wrote an opinion concurring in the judgment, and he was clearer than the other Justices in explaining when a constitutional right to physician-assisted suicide might be recognized in particular instances. Justice Breyer observed that the core of a person's claim would be "avoidance of severe physical pain (connected with death)."[54] Justice Breyer said that the New York and Washington laws were constitutional because they "do not prohibit doctors from providing patients with drugs sufficient to control pain despite the risk that those drugs themselves will kill."[55] Justice Breyer concluded that "[w]ere the legal circumstances different—for example, were state law to prevent the provision of palliative care, including the administration of drugs as needed to avoid pain at the end of life—then the law's impact upon serious and otherwise unavoidable physical pain (accompanying death) would be more at issue."[56]

---

891 F. Supp. 1429 (D. Or. 1995), but this decision was vacated by the Ninth Circuit, Lee v. Oregon, 107 F.3d 1382 (9th Cir. 1997). Additionally, the Supreme Court held that the United States Attorney General may not use authority under the federal Controlled Substances Act to deny the authority to write prescriptions to doctors who participate under the Oregon law. Gonzales v. Oregon, 546 U.S. 243 (2006). Voters in Washington and Vermont have passed "death with dignity" initiatives and the Montana Supreme Court has interpreted the state's constitution as protecting such a right.

[49] 521 U.S. at 737.
[50] *Id.* at 738.
[51] *Id.*
[52] *Id.* at 739.
[53] *Id.* at 791.
[54] *Id.*
[55] *Id.* at 792.
[56] *Id.*

In other words, five Justices left open the possibility of challenging the application of laws prohibiting physician-assisted death in particular cases. The strongest challenge might be brought if a state law prevented the provision of pain-relieving medication that likely would hasten a terminally ill patient's death. Similarly, a challenge might succeed if brought by a person whose pain was so severe that it could not be relieved by medication.

Ultimately, the question of whether there should be a right to physician-assisted death, like all difficult constitutional questions, turns on one's view of constitutional interpretation and the role of the judiciary. Should this be regarded as one of the most important aspects of personhood and autonomy, as the Ninth Circuit concluded? Or is this a matter appropriately left to the political process, as the Supreme Court ruled?

§10.6   CONSTITUTIONAL PROTECTION FOR CONTROL OVER INFORMATION

A basic aspect of privacy is the ability of people to control information about themselves.[1] In an era of computer data banks, the existence and scope of this right are of obvious importance. Surprisingly, though, thus far the Court has rarely addressed this issue directly.[2]

Whalen v. Roe

Whalen v. Roe[3] is the primary Supreme Court case concerning constitutional protection for control over information. *Whalen* involved a New York law that required that physicians provide reports identifying patients receiving prescription drugs that have a potential for abuse. The state maintained a centralized computer file that listed the names and addresses of the patients, as well as the identity of the prescribing doctors. Challengers argued that this database infringed the right to privacy because individuals have a right to avoid disclosure of personal matters.[4]

---

§10.6 [1] *See generally* Alan Westin, The Right to Privacy (1964). *See also* Paul M. Schwartz, Property, Privacy, and Personal Data, 117 Harv. L. Rev. 2055 (2004).

[2] Although the Supreme Court has not yet used the right to privacy under the due process clause to provide a right to control information, other constitutional provisions are relevant. For example, the Fourth Amendment limits the ability of the government to gather information about individuals, generally requiring a warrant based on probable cause before a person can be searched.

[3] 429 U.S. 589 (1977).

[4] *Id.* at 598-599. The challengers also argued that the law infringed on the right to make decisions concerning medical care. *Id.* at 599-600.

The Court, however, rejected this privacy argument. The Court noted that the law created liability for Health Department employees who failed, either deliberately or negligently, to maintain proper security.[5] The Court said that the state has an important interest in monitoring the use of prescription drugs that might be abused. The Court stated: "[D]isclosures of private medical information to doctors, to hospital personnel, to insurance companies, and to public health agencies are often an essential part of modern medical practice even when the disclosure may reflect unfavorably on the character of the patient. Requiring such disclosures to representatives of the State having responsibility for the health of the community does not automatically amount to an impermissible invasion of privacy."[6]

The Court did not reject the possibility that the right to privacy might be recognized in the future to include a right to control information. Justice Stevens concluded the majority opinion by declaring: "We are not unaware of the threat to privacy implicit in the accumulation of vast amounts of personal information in computerized data banks or other massive government files. The collection of taxes, the distribution of welfare and social security benefits, the supervision of public health, the direction of our Armed Forces, and the enforcement of the criminal laws all require the orderly preservation of great quantities of information, much of which is personal in character and potentially embarrassing or harmful if disclosed."[7] Justice Stevens said, however, that *Whalen* did not pose such an issue: "We therefore need not, and do not, decide any question which might be presented by the unwarranted disclosure of accumulated private data—whether intentional or unintentional—or by a system that did not contain comparable security provisions. We simply hold that this record does not establish an invasion of any right or liberty protected by the Fourteenth Amendment."[8]

NASA v. Nelson

The Court returned to the question of whether informational privacy is protected under due process in *National Aeronautics and Space Administration v. Nelson*.[9] After September 11, 2001, new requirements imposed uniform identification standards for both federal civil servants and contractor employees. Government employees and employees of government contractors were required to disclose whether they had "used, possessed, supplied, or manufactured illegal drugs" in the last year. If so, the employee was required to provide details, including information about "treatment or counseling received." The employee must also sign a release authorizing the government to obtain personal information from schools, employers, and others during its investigation. Individuals who worked at the Jet Propulsion Laboratory, pursuant to a contract with NASA, brought a challenge on the ground that the required disclosure violated the right to privacy.

---

[5] *Id.* at 600.
[6] *Id.* at 602.
[7] *Id.* at 605.
[8] *Id.* at 605-606.
[9] 131 S. Ct. 746 (2011).

The Supreme Court unanimously rejected the challenge. Justice Alito wrote the opinion for the majority and began by saying, "We assume, without deciding, that the Constitution protects a privacy right of the sort mentioned in *Whalen*."[10] *But the Court held that the background checks were constitutional and declared:* "The Government's interests as employer and proprietor in managing its internal operations, combined with the protections against public dissemination provided by the Privacy Act of 1974, satisfy any 'interest in avoiding disclosure' that may 'arguably ha[ve] its roots in the Constitution.' "[11]

Justice Scalia, joined by Justice Thomas, concurred in the judgment and expressly rejected any constitutional right to information privacy. Justice Scalia stated: "A federal constitutional right to 'informational privacy' does not exist."[12]

Other Reporting Requirements

The Court also has upheld reporting requirements in other areas even though they pose some risk to privacy. For example, the Court has upheld several laws that required keeping of records and reporting of information concerning the performance of abortions. These cases are discussed above in §10.3.3.2.

Also, in *California Bankers Association v. Schultz*, the Court upheld the constitutionality of the Bank Secrecy Act of 1970, which required banks to maintain records of financial transactions and to report certain domestic and foreign transactions.[13] The Court rejected claims based on the Fourth and Fifth Amendments and concluded that the law was constitutional because of the government's need to monitor financial transactions and to prevent fraudulent conduct.

Thus, although there is a strong argument that the Constitution should be interpreted to protect a right to control information, there is thus far little support for such a right from the Supreme Court.

§10.7   CONSTITUTIONAL PROTECTION FOR TRAVEL

The Supreme Court has held that there is a fundamental right to travel and to interstate migration within the United States. Therefore, laws that prohibit or burden travel within the United States must meet strict scrutiny. A key example is that strict scrutiny is used in evaluating durational residency requirements; these are laws requiring that a person reside within a jurisdiction for a specified amount of time in order to receive a benefit. However, the Court has said that there is not a right to international travel, and thus restrictions on foreign travel only have to meet a rational basis test.

---

[10] *Id.* at 751.
[11] *Id.*
[12] *Id.* at 764 (Scalia, J., concurring in the judgment).
[13] 416 U.S. 21 (1974).

In discussing the right to travel, §10.7.1 describes the cases recognizing the right to travel as a fundamental right. Next, §10.7.2 considers what constitutes an infringement of the right to travel and especially examines the cases concerning when durational residency requirements are an infringement of this right. Finally, §10.7.3 reviews the decisions concerning foreign travel.

§10.7.1 The Recognition of the Right to Travel as a Fundamental Right

The Initial Cases

Although the text of the Constitution does not mention a right to travel, it long has been recognized by the Supreme Court. For example, in *The Passenger Cases*, in 1849, the Supreme Court declared unconstitutional a state law imposing a tax on aliens arriving from foreign ports.[1] Even the dissenting Justices in the case acknowledged a basic right to interstate travel. Chief Justice Taney, in dissent, remarked: "We are all citizens of the United States; and, as members of the same community, must have the right to pass and repass through every part of it without interruption, as freely as in our own States. And a tax imposed by a State for entering its territories or harbours, is inconsistent with the rights which belong to the citizens of other States as members of the Union, and with the objects which that Union was intended to attain."[2]

The Court followed this principle in *Crandall v. Nevada*, in 1867, which declared unconstitutional a state law that imposed a tax on a railroad or stage coach for every passenger that it transported out of state.[3] The impact of the law was to tax individuals leaving the state because the levy was passed on to customers. The Court noted that the law "imposes a tax upon the passenger for the privilege of leaving the State, or passing through it by the ordinary mode of passenger travel."[4]

The Court ruled that the law was unconstitutional and spoke forcefully about the importance of the right to travel: "The people of these United States constitute one nation. They have a government in which all of them are deeply interested. This government has necessarily had a capital established by law, where its principal operations are conducted. . . . That government has a right to call to this point any or all of its citizens to aid in its service . . . and this right cannot be made to depend upon the pleasure of a State over whose territory they must pass to reach the point where these services must be rendered. . . . [T]he citizen . . . has a right of free access . . . and this right is in its nature independent of the will of any State whose soil he must pass in the exercise of it."[5]

---

§10.7 [1] 48 U.S. (7 How.) 283 (1849).
[2] *Id.* at 492 (Taney, C.J., dissenting).
[3] 73 U.S. (6 Wall.) 35 (1867).
[4] *Id.* at 42.
[5] *Id.* at 43-44.

Edwards v. California

Interestingly, the Supreme Court's next major case addressing the right to travel was not for almost three-quarters of a century until *Edwards v. California* in 1941.[6] *Edwards* invalidated a California law that made it a crime to bring a nonresident into the state knowing the individual to be "an indigent person." The majority opinion, written by Justice Byrne, declared the law unconstitutional as violating the commerce clause and did not address the right to travel.[7] However, four Justices in concurring opinions—Justices Douglas, Black, Murphy, and Jackson—argued that the right to travel is a fundamental right protected under the privileges or immunities clause of the Fourteenth Amendment.[8] This is one of the few times that any members of the Court have invoked the privileges or immunities clause since it was essentially read out of the Constitution in the *Slaughter-House Cases* in 1873.[9]

Justice Douglas declared: "[T]he right of persons to move freely from State to State . . . is so fundamental. . . . The right to move freely from State to State is an incident of national citizenship protected by the privileges and immunities clause of the Fourteenth Amendment against state interference."[10] Justice Jackson acknowledged that the Court had rejected every claim under the privileges or immunities clause, but he said: "This Court should, however, hold squarely that it is a privilege of citizenship of the United States, protected from state abridgment, to enter any state of the Union, either for temporary sojourn or for the establishment of permanent residence therein and for gaining resultant citizenship thereof. If national citizenship means less than this, it means nothing."[11]

United States v. Guest

In *United States v. Guest*, the Supreme Court expressly declared that there is a fundamental right to interstate travel.[12] Individuals were prosecuted for a conspiracy to interfere with civil rights because of their actions against African Americans. The indictment charged that the defendants had conspired to deprive blacks of their "full and equal enjoyment of the goods, services, facilities . . . and other places of public accommodations; . . . [t]he right to full and equal utilization

---

[6] 314 U.S. 160 (1941). In *LaTourette v. McMaster*, 248 U.S. 465 (1919), the Court upheld the constitutionality of a two-year residency requirement in order for an individual to be licensed as a stockbroker by the state. Residency requirements are discussed below at text accompanying notes 26-66.

[7] *Id.* at 173-174.

[8] *Id.* at 178 (Douglas, J., concurring); *id.* at 183 (Jackson, J., concurring).

[9] 83 U.S. (16 Wall.) 36 (1872). In the *Slaughter-House Cases*, the Supreme Court ruled that the privileges or immunities clause was not meant to give federal courts the power to invalidate state laws, and the Court defined the provision narrowly so as to include only rights that were protected before it was enacted. The *Slaughter-House Cases* are discussed in detail in §6.3.2.

[10] *Edwards*, 314 U.S. at 177-178.

[11] *Id.* at 183 (Jackson, J., concurring).

[12] 383 U.S. 745 (1966). *Guest* is perhaps most important because five Justices, in separate opinions, expressed the position that Congress under §5 of the Fourteenth Amendment could regulate private conduct. This was subsequently disavowed and rejected by the Supreme Court in *United States v. Morrison*, 529 U.S. 598 (2000). The issue of regulating private conduct is discussed in §3.7.1.

on the same terms as white citizens of the public streets and highways . . . ; the right to travel freely to and from the State of Georgia and to use highway facilities and other instrumentalities of interstate commerce."[13] The indictment said that the defendants accomplished this "[b]y shooting Negroes; [b]y beating Negroes; [b]y killing Negroes; [b]y damaging and destroying property of Negroes; [b]y pursuing Negroes in automobiles and threatening them with guns."[14]

The Court reversed a decision by the district court dismissing the indictment, and it declared: "The constitutional right to travel from one State to another, and necessarily to use the highways and other instrumentalities of interstate commerce in doing so, occupies a position fundamental to the concept of our Federal Union. It is a right that has been firmly established and repeatedly recognized."[15]

The Court explained that the right to travel was absent from the text of the Constitution because as a right so basic, it was simply assumed to exist. Justice Stewart, writing for the Court, explained: "Although the Articles of Confederation provided that 'the people of each State shall have free ingress and regress to and from any other State,' that right finds no mention in the Constitution. The reason, it has been suggested, is that a right so elementary was conceived from the beginning to be a necessary concomitant of the stronger Union that the Constitution created. In any event, freedom to travel throughout the United States has long been recognized as a basic right under the Constitution."[16]

Saenz v. Roe

In *Saenz v. Roe*, the Supreme Court used the privileges or immunities clause of the Fourteenth Amendment as the basis for protecting the right to travel.[17] The Court declared unconstitutional a California law that restricted a new resident's welfare benefits to the level of the state where the person moved from for the first year of residence. Justice Stevens, writing for the Court in a 7-to-2 decision, reviewed the history of the Court's protection of the right to travel. He noted that the right to travel "protects the right of a citizen of one State to enter and to leave another State, the right to be treated as a welcome visitor rather than an unfriendly alien when temporarily present in the second State, and, for those travelers who elect to become permanent residents, the right to be treated like other citizens of that State."[18] He said that the third aspect of travel, the right of new residents to be treated the same as longer residents of the state, is protected by the privileges or immunities clause of the Fourteenth Amendment.[19]

Justice Stevens was explicit that this aspect of the right to travel is protected as a fundamental right. He wrote: "That newly arrived citizens 'have two political capacities, one state and one federal,' adds special force to their claim that they

[13] *Id.* at 747-748 n.1.
[14] *Id.* at 748.
[15] *Id.* at 757.
[16] *Id.* at 758.
[17] 526 U.S. 489 (1999). The privileges or immunities clause is discussed in §6.3.2.
[18] *Id.* at 500.
[19] *Id.* at 502.

have the same rights as others who share their citizenship. Neither mere rationality nor some intermediate standard of review should be used to judge the constitutionality of a state rule that discriminates against some of its citizens because they have domiciled in the State for less than a year. The appropriate standard may be more categorical than that articulated in *Shapiro*, but it is surely no less strict."[20]

Why Is the Right to Travel a Fundamental Right?

These cases clearly establish that the right to travel within the United States is a fundamental right. There are many reasons why it is regarded as a basic liberty. In part, the justification is historical: Ever since the Articles of Confederation, the right to free movement among the states has been acknowledged as a basic liberty.

The right to travel is closely related to the policies underlying the commerce clause and particularly the dormant commerce clause, which prevents states from burdening interstate commerce, and the privileges and immunities clause of Article IV, which prevents states from discriminating against out-of-staters with regard to basic liberties. All of these constitutional protections concern ensuring the free flow of goods and services throughout the United States and the full access of every person to the markets of every state. Justice Harlan, writing separately in *Guest*, explained: "[T]he right to unimpeded travel, regarded as a privilege and immunity of national citizenship, was historically seen as a method of breaking down state provincialism, and facilitating the creation of a true federal union."[21]

There is a political significance to the right to travel as well; it is the right to relocate to a place with a different political climate and environment. Professor John Ely explained: "The right at issue in the modern cases . . . [is] not simply a right to travel to or through a state but rather a right to move there—the right . . . to relocate. . . . To a large extent, America was founded by persons escaping from environments they found oppressive. . . . [A] dissenting member [of a community] . . . should have the option of exiling and relocating in a community whose values he or she finds more compatible."[22]

§10.7.2 What Constitutes an Infringement of the Right to Travel?

Jones v. Helms

Not every law that burdens travel will be deemed an infringement of the right. For example, in *Jones v. Helms*, the Supreme Court upheld a Georgia law that provided that a parent who willfully and voluntarily abandoned his or her minor child is guilty of a misdemeanor, but a parent who does so and then leaves the state is guilty of a felony.[23] The defendant argued that the enhanced penalties for those

---

[20] *Id.*

[21] *Id.* at 767 (Harlan, J., concurring in part and dissenting in part).

[22] John Ely, Democracy and Distrust 178-179 (1980).

[23] 452 U.S. 412 (1981).

who leave the state impermissibly burden the right to travel. The Supreme Court disagreed and upheld the law.

At the outset, the Court reaffirmed the "fundamental nature" of the right to travel.[24] The right, however, is not absolute, and the Court said that the state had a right to prevent the exit of a person who committed a crime within the state. The Court explained: "Despite the fundamental nature of this right, there nonetheless are situations in which a State may prevent a citizen from leaving. . . . Manifestly, a person who has committed an offense against the laws of Georgia may be stopped at its borders and temporarily deprived of his freedom to travel elsewhere within or without the State."[25]

The Court applied this and held that the Georgia law was constitutional because it applied to individuals who committed a crime in Georgia and then fled the state. In other words, *Jones v. Helms* holds that a state may enhance the penalties for those who move from the state after committing a crime. Although the Court concluded that there was no infringement of the right to travel, essentially what the Court said was that states have a compelling interest in discouraging those who commit crimes from fleeing.

Durational Residency Requirements

The Supreme Court has articulated and applied the right to travel primarily in evaluating laws that impose durational residency requirements. A durational residency requirement stipulates that a person must live in the jurisdiction for a specified amount of time in order to receive a benefit. Prominent examples, discussed below, involve waiting periods required for receipt of welfare benefits, voting, and divorces. The Supreme Court has recognized that durational residency requirements discourage interstate travel, and especially migration. The Court, therefore, has said that strict scrutiny should be applied in this area.

The seminal decision was *Shapiro v. Thompson*, which declared unconstitutional laws that imposed a one-year residency requirement in the state as a prerequisite for eligibility for welfare.[26] The Supreme Court said that the law discriminates as to who can receive welfare benefits based on duration in the state; as such, the Court said that the law imposes a burden on those who have recently traveled and migrated to the state. The Court said that "[s]ince the classification here touches on the fundamental right of interstate movement, its constitutionality must be judged by the stricter standard of whether it promotes a compelling state interest. Under this standard, the waiting-period requirement clearly violates the Equal Protection Clause."[27] Simply put, the state laws discourage people from moving to the state because they would not be able to receive welfare benefits for a year, and this situation infringes on the right to travel.

---

[24] *Id.* at 418.
[25] *Id.* at 419.
[26] 394 U.S. 618 (1969).
[27] *Id.* at 638.

§10.7 Constitutional Protection for Travel

The Court reviewed the justifications proffered by the states for the waiting period for travelers and found that none was sufficient to meet strict scrutiny. For example, the states argued that the durational residency requirement was designed to preserve the fiscal integrity of the public assistance programs.[28] The Court, however, rejected this as a permissible purpose and, in fact, said "the purpose of inhibiting migration by needy persons into the State is constitutionally impermissible."[29] The Court declared that "a State may no more try to fence out those indigents who seek higher welfare benefits than it may try to fence out indigents generally."[30] The laws declared unconstitutional in *Shapiro* violated the right to travel because their purpose was to discourage migration of indigent persons into the state and because the likely impact of the laws would be to prevent such travel.

In subsequent cases, the Court applied *Shapiro* to invalidate other durational residency requirements. For instance, in *Memorial Hospital v. Maricopa County*, the Court declared unconstitutional a government rule that required a year's residency in the county as condition to receiving nonemergency hospitalization or medical care at the county's expense.[31] The Court reviewed the prior decisions in this area and said that they "stand for the proposition that a classification which operates to penalize those persons . . . who have exercised their constitutional right of interstate migration must be justified by a compelling state interest."[32]

The Court found the residency requirement for medical care at issue in *Memorial Hospital* indistinguishable from the residency requirement for welfare benefits that was declared unconstitutional in *Shapiro*. The Court forcefully reaffirmed the fundamental nature of the right to travel: "Not unlike the admonition of the Bible that, 'Ye shall have one manner of law, as well for the stranger, as for one of your own country,' . . . the right of interstate travel must be seen as insuring new residents the same right to vital government benefits and privileges in the States to which they migrate as are enjoyed by other residents. The State of Arizona's durational residence requirement for free medical care penalizes indigents for exercising their right to migrate to and settle in that state."[33]

The Supreme Court followed this reasoning in invalidating and limiting the length of durational residency requirements for voting. In *Dunn v. Blumstein*, the Court declared unconstitutional a state law that created a one-year residency requirement for voting eligibility.[34] Vanderbilt law professor James Blumstein challenged Tennessee's waiting period in order to register to vote. The Court noted that the state law drew a distinction among residents solely on the basis of their recent migration and travel.

The Court said that it was thus clear that "the durational residence requirement directly impinges on the exercise of a . . . fundamental personal right, the

---

[28] *Id.* at 627.
[29] *Id.* at 629.
[30] *Id.* at 631.
[31] 415 U.S. 250 (1974).
[32] *Id.* at 258.
[33] *Id.* at 261-262 (citation omitted).
[34] 405 U.S. 330 (1972).

right to travel."[35] The Court explained that "it is clear that the freedom to travel includes the 'freedom to enter and abide in any State in the Union.' Obviously durational residence laws single out the class of bona fide state and county residents who have recently exercised this constitutionally protected right, and penalize such travelers directly."[36]

The Court rejected each of the state's justifications and invalidated the law. For example, the state said that the durational residency requirement was justified by its desire to have knowledgeable voters. The Court ruled that a state cannot exclude residents from voting based on an assessment of their knowledge, sophistication with local issues, or how they might vote.[37]

Subsequently, the Supreme Court has qualified *Dunn v. Blumstein* and has allowed some residency requirements for voting. The Court has permitted durational residency requirements of up to 50 days for voting to give the government time to check election rolls, prevent fraud, and administer the electoral system.[38]

Also, in *Rosario v. Rockefeller*, the Court upheld a state law that allowed a voter to participate in a primary election only if he or she registered for the political party 30 days before the prior general election.[39] Because general elections are usually a year or more before the next primary, a person had to be in the state a year or so in advance of the primary election in order to vote in it. The result was a de facto residency requirement. Yet the Supreme Court upheld it concluding that each party had an interest in ensuring that only its previously registered members could vote in its primary.[40]

One area where the Court has upheld durational residency requirements is for divorces within a state. In *Sosna v. Iowa*, the Court upheld the constitutionality of a state law that required one year of residency in the state before a person could obtain a divorce.[41] The Court distinguished earlier cases invalidating durational residency requirements for receipt of government benefits, such as *Shapiro* and *Maricopa County*. The Court said: "But none of those cases intimated that the States might never impose durational residency requirements, and such a proposition was in fact expressly disclaimed. What those cases had in common was that the durational residency requirements they struck down were justified on the basis of budgetary or recordkeeping considerations which were held insufficient to outweigh the constitutional claims of the individuals."[42]

The Court felt that the state's durational residency requirement was "of a different stripe."[43] The Court said that the difference was that a person moving into

---

[35] *Id.* at 338.

[36] *Id.*

[37] *Id.* at 339.

[38] Marston v. Lewis, 410 U.S. 679 (1973).

[39] 410 U.S. 752 (1973).

[40] *But see* Kusper v. Pontikes, 414 U.S. 51 (1973) (declaring unconstitutional a law that prevented a person from voting in a party's primary election if the person had voted in the opposing party's primary in the prior 23 months).

[41] 419 U.S. 393 (1975).

[42] *Id.* at 406.

[43] *Id.*

the state "would eventually qualify" for eligibility for divorce and "could ultimately have obtained the same opportunity for adjudication which she asserts ought to have been hers at an earlier point in time."[44]

Yet this distinction seems questionable because all people precluded by a durational residency requirement will "eventually qualify." Those denied welfare benefits in *Shapiro* or medical care in *Maricopa County* ultimately could obtain the same benefits after waiting for a year. It is not clear why the ability to wait for divorce makes that durational residency requirement permissible, but waiting for welfare or medical care is an impermissible durational residency requirement.

The Court accepted other justifications for the residency requirement including the state's belief that such requirements for divorce make it less likely that the decree will be collaterally attacked in other courts. The Court concluded: "We therefore hold that the state interest in requiring that those who seek a divorce from its courts be genuinely attached to the State, as well as a desire to insulate divorce decrees from the likelihood of collateral attack, requires a different resolution of the constitutional issues presented than was the case in *Shapiro, Dunn,* and *Maricopa County*."[45] But the concern over collateral attacks could be dealt with by enforcing the constitutional requirement for full faith and credit; it is unclear why this requires a durational residency requirement.

All of these cases — *Shapiro, Maricopa County, Dunn,* and *Sosna* — involved laws that denied benefits to new arrivals in the state. The Supreme Court also has ruled that laws that do not totally deny benefits, but provide less to new arrivals, are unconstitutional.[46] In *Zobel v. Williams,* the Court declared unconstitutional an Alaska law that distributed oil revenues to those in the state according to a formula that was calculated based on the duration of a person's residence in the state.[47] The Court found that the law failed the rational basis test and invalidated it as denying equal protection. For instance, the law did not further the state's goal of encouraging people to develop ties with the state because it applied retroactively to those who had been residents but not prospectively to those making choices in the future. Also, the Court rejected the state's goal of rewarding people for past contributions to the state; the Court said that mere duration in the state was not a reliable proxy to use in measuring what a person had given or contributed to the state.

Similarly, in *Hooper v. Bernalillo County Assessor,* the Court declared unconstitutional a state law that provided a property tax exemption to Vietnam War veterans who had become residents of the state prior to a specified date.[48] Again, as in *Zobel,* the Court used the rational basis test and found the law unconstitutional. Duration of residency in the state, especially as measured by an arbitrary date, was deemed an impermissible basis for determining who should receive a property tax exemption. The Court explained: "The State may not favor established residents over

---

[44] *Id.*
[45] *Id.* at 409.
[46] Saenz v. Roe, 526 U.S. 489 (1999), discussed below.
[47] 457 U.S. 55 (1982).
[48] 472 U.S. 612 (1985).

new residents based on the view that the State may take care 'of its own,' if such is denned by prior residence. Newcomers, by establishing bona fide residence in the State, become the State's 'own' and may not be discriminated against solely on the basis of their arrival in the State after [the specified date.]"[49]

Likewise, in *Attorney General of New York v. Soto-Lopez*, the Court invalidated a state law that provided a preference in hiring to veterans who were residents of the state when they entered the armed services, but no preference for veterans who were residents of other states when they joined the armed forces.[50] The plurality opinion, written by Justice Brennan, said that prior cases established that "even temporary deprivations of very important benefits and rights can operate to penalize migration."[51]

The plurality concluded that the state law failed strict scrutiny and that the state could not draw a distinction between its residents based on when they began to live in the state. Justice Brennan stated: "Once veterans establish bona fide residence in a State, they become the State's own and may not be discriminated against solely on the basis of the date of their arrival in the State. . . . For as long as New York chooses to offer its resident veterans a civil service employment preference, the Constitution requires that it do so without regard to residence at the time of entry into the services."[52]

Finally, in *Saenz v. Roe*, the Court declared unconstitutional a California law that limited welfare benefits for new residents in a state to the level of the state that they moved from for their first year of residence.[53] As explained above, the Court said that the privileges or immunities clause protects the right of a new resident in the state to be treated the same as longer term residents. Justice Stevens, writing for the Court, explained: "Because this case involves discrimination against citizens who have completed their interstate travel, the State's argument that its welfare scheme affects the right to travel only 'incidentally' is beside the point. Were we concerned solely with actual deterrence to migration, we might be persuaded that a partial withholding of benefits constitutes a lesser incursion on the right to travel than an outright denial of all benefits. But since the right to travel embraces the citizen's right to be treated equally in her new State of residence, the discriminatory classification is itself a penalty."[54] The Court found it irrelevant that a federal law expressly allowed states to draw a distinction in benefit levels between new residents and longer term residents; Congress has no power to authorize states to violate the Fourteenth Amendment.[55]

These cases establish that durational residency requirements or laws that provide benefits based on length of residency will have to meet strict scrutiny. Such state laws are very likely to be declared unconstitutional.

---

[49] *Id.* at 623.
[50] 476 U.S. 898 (1986).
[51] *Id.* at 907.
[52] *Id.* at 911-912.
[53] 526 U.S. 489 (1999).
[54] *Id.* at 491.
[55] *Id.* at 503.

Residency Requirements Are Different

The Supreme Court repeatedly has distinguished residency requirements from durational residency requirements. Residency requirements provide a benefit to current residents that is not available to nonresidents. The key is that all current residents benefit; no distinction is drawn based on length of time in the state. In contrast, durational residency requirements draw a distinction among current residents based on their length of time in the state. Because durational residency requirements are seen as potentially inhibiting interstate travel, they must meet strict scrutiny.

Phrased slightly differently, if the law distinguishes only between residents and nonresidents, it is treated as a residency requirement and not viewed as infringing on the right to travel. The law might be challenged under the privileges and immunities clause for discriminating against out-of-state citizens[56] or even under equal protection for this discrimination, but it cannot be objected to as infringing on the right to travel. But when the law distinguishes among current residents based on their length of time in the state, that is a durational residency requirement and must meet strict scrutiny because of the potential impact on the right to travel.

In *Soto-Lopez*, Justice Brennan expressed this distinction saying that the Court has "always carefully distinguished between bona fide residence requirements, which seek to differentiate between residents and nonresidents, [and residence requirements] such as durational, fixed date, and fixed point residence requirements, which treat established residents differently based on the time they migrated into the State."[57]

In several cases, the Court has allowed residency requirements. In *Holt Civic Club v. City of Tuscaloosa*, the Court upheld denying the right to vote in city elections to persons outside the city limit, although they were within the city's policing and licensing jurisdiction.[58]

Also, the Court has upheld residency requirements for public employment. In *McCarthy v. Philadelphia Civil Service Commission*, the Court, in a short per curiam opinion, upheld a fire department regulation that required residence in the city as a condition for employment.[59] An employee who moved from Philadelphia to New Jersey lost his job and argued that the firing violated his right to travel. The Court disagreed and distinguished the earlier cases. The Court said that none of the prior decisions "questioned the validity of a condition placed upon municipal employment that a person be a resident *at the time* of his application. In this case appellant claims a constitutional right to be employed by the city of Philadelphia *while* he is living elsewhere. There is no support in our cases for such a claim."[60]

---

[56] *See* §5.5.
[57] 476 U.S. at 903 n.3.
[58] 439 U.S. 60 (1978).
[59] 424 U.S. 645 (1976).
[60] *Id.* at 646-647.

In *Martinez v. Bynum*, the Court again drew a distinction between residency requirements and durational residency laws. In *Martinez*, the Court found constitutional a law that denied free public education to children who lived apart from their parents and were in the school district for the primary purpose of attending school there.[61] The Court said that "[t]he Constitution permits a State to restrict eligibility for tuition-free education to its bona fide residents."[62] The Court explained that "[a] bona fide residence requirement, appropriately defined and uniformly applied, furthers the substantial state interest in assuring that services provided for its residents are enjoyed only by residents. Such a requirement with respect to attendance in public free schools does not violate the Equal Protection Clause of the Fourteenth Amendment. It does not burden or penalize the constitutional right of interstate travel, for any person is free to move to a State and to establish residence there."[63]

Yet depending on how it is phrased, what appears to be a residency requirement actually might be a durational residency requirement. In *Vlandis v. Kline*, the Supreme Court declared unconstitutional a state law requiring that nonresident tuition be paid by those students who were nonresidents when they applied for admission.[64] Residents of the state who moved there after applying never could receive in-state tuition benefits, whereas residents who had been in the state since the time of their application would get the benefit. The Court acknowledged that a residency requirement would be permissible because "a State has a legitimate interest in protecting and preserving . . . the right of its own bona fide residents to attend [its colleges and universities] on a preferential tuition basis."[65] But the Court found that the permanent preclusion of in-state tuition for residents who moved to the state after applying was unconstitutional.[66] After *Saenz v. Roe*, discussed above, courts will have to decide whether in-state tuition preferences impermissibly prefer longer term residents over newer ones, or whether such laws are permissible efforts by states to define when a person becomes a resident.

§10.7.3 Restrictions on Foreign Travel

The Supreme Court has held that there is not a fundamental right to international travel and that therefore only a rational basis test will be used in evaluating restrictions on foreign travel. The Supreme Court's initial decisions in this area had

---

[61] 461 U.S. 321 (1983).

[62] *Id.* at 333.

[63] *Id.* at 328.

[64] 412 U.S. 441 (1973).

[65] *Id.* at 452-453.

[66] The Court used the "irrebuttable presumptions" doctrine; the Court emphasized that the law irrebuttably presumed that a person moving to the state after applying to school there was not a resident of the state. The problem with the irrebuttable presumption doctrine is that many laws create irrebuttable presumptions. For example, the laws requiring a license to practice law or that someone be age 16 for a driver's license create irrebuttable presumptions. The question is when such presumptions should be allowed and when not. The irrebuttable presumptions doctrine was used in a few cases in the 1970s, but not since. The doctrine also is discussed in §9.4.2 n.64.

broad dicta that suggested such a right, but subsequent cases have clearly held that the Court does not recognize a fundamental right to foreign travel.

Initial Cases

In *Kent v. Dulles*, the issue was whether Congress had delegated to the secretary of state the authority to deny passports to Communists and to persons who were going abroad to further Communist causes.[67] Also, the secretary promulgated regulations requiring people to complete an affidavit denying affiliation with the Communist Party. The Court did not rule on whether such regulations were constitutional, but instead focused on the narrower question of whether Congress had delegated this authority to the secretary of state. The Court concluded that if Congress had delegated such authority, there would be important constitutional questions. The Court said that absent a clear statement from Congress that it meant to allow such restrictions, the Court would conclude that no such delegation existed.

However, in explaining why it would interpret the statute to avoid the constitutional question, the Court spoke expansively about a right to foreign travel. Justice Douglas, writing for the Court, stated: "The right to travel is a part of the 'liberty' of which the citizen cannot be deprived without the due process of law under the Fifth Amendment. . . . Freedom of movement across frontiers in either direction, and inside frontiers as well, was a part of our heritage. Travel abroad, like travel within the country, may be necessary for a livelihood. It may be as close to the heart of the individual as the choice of what he eats, or wears, or reads. Freedom of movement is basic in our scheme of values."[68]

In *Aptheker v. Secretary of State*, the Court declared unconstitutional a provision of the Subversive Activities Control Act of 1950, which prohibited the issuance of a passport to a member of the Communist Party.[69] The Court emphasized the impact of the law on foreign travel and thus also on association. Justice Goldberg, writing for the Court, said: "The denial of a passport, given existing domestic and foreign laws, is a severe restriction upon, and in effect a prohibition against, worldwide foreign travel. . . . Since freedom of association is itself guaranteed in the First Amendment, restrictions imposed upon the right to travel cannot be dismissed by asserting that the right to travel could be fully exercised if the individual would first yield up his membership in a given association."[70]

The Court invalidated the law, explaining that it "sweeps too widely and too indiscriminately across the liberty guaranteed in the Fifth Amendment."[71] For example, the Court noted that the law creates "an irrebuttable presumption that individuals who are members of specified organizations will, if given passports,

[67] 357 U.S. 116 (1958).

[68] *Id.* at 125-126.

[69] 378 U.S. 500 (1964).

[70] *Id.* at 507.

[71] *Id.* at 514.

engage in activities inimical to the security of the United States."[72] The law contained no criteria as to what activities would justify denial of a passport; membership alone was sufficient. The Court concluded that "[t]he broad and enveloping prohibition indiscriminately excludes plainly relevant considerations such as the individual's knowledge, activity, commitment, and purposes in and places for travel."[73]

However, a year after *Aptheker*, in *Zemel v. Rusk*, the Supreme Court upheld the constitutionality of the secretary of state's refusal to issue passports for travel to Cuba.[74] Unlike *Kent* and *Aptheker*, where the issue was the constitutionality of denying passports to particular individuals, in *Zemel* the issue was the permissibility of refusing passports to all people wanting to travel to a particular place. The Court emphasized that this was a foreign policy decision to which the Court should defer. Chief Justice Warren, writing for the Court, said: "It must be remembered . . . that the issue involved in *Kent* was whether a citizen could be denied a passport because of his political beliefs or associations. . . . In this case, however, the Secretary has refused to validate appellant's passport not because of any characteristic peculiar to appellant, but rather because of foreign policy considerations affecting all citizens."[75]

In rejecting claims based on both the right to travel and the First Amendment right to gather information by traveling to foreign countries, the Court stressed the foreign policy justifications for the restrictions. Chief Justice Warren said: "That the restriction which is challenged in this case is supported by the weightiest considerations of national security is perhaps best pointed up by recalling that the Cuban missile crisis of October 1962 preceded the filing of appellant's complaint by less than two months."[76]

Later Cases Using Rational Basis Review

Later cases have made it clear that only rational basis review is used for restrictions on foreign travel. The Court has repudiated the broad language in cases like *Kent* and *Aptheker* and narrowly construed the holdings in those decisions.

For example, in *Califano v. Aznavorian*, the Court upheld a provision of the Social Security Act that caused a person to lose Supplemental Security Income benefits for any month during all of which the individual was out of the United States and until the person had been back in the country for 30 consecutive days.[77] The Court expressly distinguished the right to interstate travel from the right to foreign travel; only the former is deemed fundamental. The Court stated: "The constitutional right of interstate travel is virtually unqualified. By contrast, the 'right' of international travel has been considered to be no more than an aspect

---

[72] *Id.* at 511.
[73] *Id.* at 514.
[74] 381 U.S. 1 (1965).
[75] *Id.* at 13.
[76] *Id.* at 16.
[77] 439 U.S. 170 (1978).

of the 'liberty' protected by the Due Process Clause of the Fifth Amendment. . . . Thus, legislation which is said to infringe the freedom to travel abroad is not to be judged by the same standard applied to laws that penalize the right of interstate travel, such as durational residency requirements imposed by the States."[78]

The Court also emphasized that the law did not prohibit anyone from traveling and thus was distinguishable from the earlier cases that involved the denial of passports. The Court said that the "justifications for the legislation in question are not, perhaps compelling. But its constitutionality does not depend on compelling justifications. It is enough if the provision is rationally based."[79]

This express use of the rational basis test for restrictions on foreign travel was reaffirmed in later cases. In *Haig v. Agee*, the Court upheld the authority of the secretary of state to revoke the passport of a former CIA agent who had threatened to identify CIA officers and agents and to take measures to drive them out of countries where they were operating.[80] The Court emphasized the ability of the government to regulate international travel to further its foreign policy objectives. Chief Justice Burger, writing for the Court, said: "Revocation of a passport undeniably curtails travel, but the freedom to travel abroad . . . is subordinate to national security and foreign policy considerations; as such, it is subject to reasonable governmental regulation. The Court has made it plain that the freedom to travel outside the United States must be distinguished from the right to travel within the United States."[81]

Similarly, in *Regan v. Wald*, the Court used the rational basis test to uphold a federal regulation that prevented travel to Cuba.[82] The Court found that the case was indistinguishable from *Zemel* and again stressed that the restrictions were a foreign policy decision. Justice Rehnquist, writing for the Court, said: "Matters relating 'to the conduct of foreign relations . . . are so exclusively entrusted to the political branches of government as to be largely immune from judicial inquiry or interference.' Our holding in *Zemel* was merely an example of this classical deference to the political branches in matters of foreign policy."[83]

Is There Sufficient Protection of a Right to Foreign Travel?

Thus, the Court repeatedly has distinguished interstate travel from foreign travel, finding only the former to be a fundamental right and using just rational basis review in evaluating limits on international travel. The primary justification for this distinction is the foreign policy aspects of international travel. Cases such as *Zemel*, *Agee*, and *Wald* indicate that the Court is very likely to uphold restrictions if the government asserts a foreign policy justification. In fact, the earlier cases,

---

[78] *Id.* at 176-177.
[79] *Id.* at 178.
[80] 453 U.S. 280 (1981).
[81] *Id.* at 306.
[82] 468 U.S. 222 (1984).
[83] *Id.* at 242-243 (citation omitted).

Kent and *Aptheker*, can be reconciled because the government did not rely primarily on a foreign policy objective for denying passports to Communists.

Yet it can be questioned as to whether the more recent cases give sufficient weight to the importance of protecting a right to foreign travel. Freedom of international travel provides many of the same benefits—informational, educational, economic, and political—as domestic travel. The rational basis test means that restrictions are unlikely to be invalidated and that there is relatively little constitutional protection for a right to international travel.

§10.8   CONSTITUTIONAL PROTECTION FOR VOTING

§10.8.1   The Right to Vote as a Fundamental Right

Constitutional Provisions Protecting the Right to Vote

Many of the amendments to the Constitution concern the right to vote. The Fifteenth Amendment says: "The right of citizens of the United States to vote shall not be denied or abridged by the United States or by any State on account of race, color, or previous condition of servitude." The Nineteenth Amendment, adopted in 1920, extended the right to vote to women and says that the "right of citizens of the United States to vote shall not be denied or abridged by the United States or by any State on account of sex."

The Twenty-fourth Amendment, ratified in 1964, prohibits poll taxes in elections for federal office. Specifically, it provides: "The right of citizens of the United States to vote in any primary or other election for President or Vice President, for electors for President or Vice President, or for Senator or Representative in Congress, shall not be denied or abridged by the United States or any State by reason of failure to pay any poll tax or other tax."

The Twenty-sixth Amendment, adopted in 1971, extends the right to vote to all citizens who are 18 years of age or older. It says: "The right of citizens of the United States, who are eighteen years of age or older, to vote shall not be denied or abridged by the United States or by any State on account of age."

Fundamental Right Under Equal Protection

In addition to these textual provisions, the Supreme Court repeatedly has declared that the right to vote is a fundamental right protected under equal protection.[1] The right to vote is regarded as fundamental because it is essential in a

---

§10.8 [1] *See, e.g.,* Kramer v. Union Free School Dist., 395 U.S. 621, 626 (1969); Harper v. Virginia St. Bd. of Elections, 383 U.S. 663, 666 (1966); Reynolds v. Sims, 377 U.S. 533, 555 (1964).

democratic society; it is obviously through voting that the people choose their government and hold it accountable. The Court has explained that "[t]he right to vote freely for the candidate of one's choice is of the essence of a democratic society, and any restrictions on that right strike at the heart of representative government."[2] Hence, "any unjustified discrimination in determining who may participate in political affairs or in the selection of public officials undermines the legitimacy of representative government."[3]

Indeed, the Court long has said that the right to vote is a "fundamental political right" because it is "preservative of all rights."[4] Voting is itself a form of expression, but it also is the way in which people choose a government that will safeguard all of their liberties and interests. As the Court observed: "No right is more precious in a free country than that of having a voice in the election of those who make the laws under which, as good citizens, we must live. Other rights, even the most basic, are illusory if the right to vote is undermined."[5]

Thus, it is clearly established that laws infringing on the right to vote must meet strict scrutiny. The Court has explained that "[e]specially since the right to exercise the franchise in a free and unimpaired manner is preservative of other basic civil and political rights, any alleged infringement of the right of citizens to vote must be carefully and meticulously scrutinized."[6]

In reviewing the many cases concerning voting rights, three types of government restrictions can be identified. First, §10.8.2 examines laws that deny some citizens the right to vote. Second, §10.8.3 considers dilutions of voting power. The Court has said that "the right of suffrage can be denied by a debasement or dilution of the weight of a citizen's vote just as effectively as by wholly prohibiting the free exercise of the franchise."[7] Section 10.8.4 examines inequalities in counting votes as a denial of equal protection and focuses on the Supreme Court's landmark decision in *Bush v. Gore*.[8] Section 10.8.5 reviews racial discrimination with regard to voting. Many of the restrictions on voting have been intended to limit voting by African Americans. Finally, §10.8.6 focuses on laws that limit the ability of candidates and parties to have access to the ballot.

§10.8.2 Restrictions on the Ability to Vote

Are Elections Constitutionally Required?

The Constitution expressly provides for elections for members of Congress and for the president. Arguably, Article IV, §4, of the Constitution requires

---

[2] Reynolds v. Sims, 377 U.S. at 555.
[3] Kramer v. Union Free School Dist., 395 U.S. at 626.
[4] Yick Wo v. Hopkins, 118 U.S. 356, 370 (1886).
[5] Wesberry v. Sanders, 376 U.S. 1, 17 (1964).
[6] Harper v. Virginia St. Bd. of Elections, 383 U.S. at 667.
[7] Reynolds v. Sims, 377 U.S. at 555.
[8] 531 U.S. 98 (2000).

elections for state and local offices in its declaration that "[t]he United States shall guarantee to every State in this Union a Republican Form of Government." However, the Supreme Court consistently has held that cases brought under this clause pose a nonjusticiable political question.[9]

An interesting and unresolved question is when, if at all, the Constitution would be violated if state and local governments chose to eliminate elections for particular offices. For example, would it be unconstitutional for a state to abolish the election for governor and have its chief executive chosen by the state legislature?[10] Generally, the Court has allowed state and local governments to select their office-holders through means other than elections. The Court expressly upheld the ability of a state to have its legislature choose its governor when no candidate received a majority of the popular votes.[11] There are cities where the elected city council chooses a city manager, rather than holding elections for the executive official, such as the mayor.[12] The Supreme Court ruled that where a county school board is an administrative and not a legislative body, its members need not be elected.[13]

While the extent of the ability of state and local governments to completely abolish elections for particular offices is an unresolved issue, it is clearly settled that once there is an election, any laws that deny or limit the ability of citizens to vote must meet strict scrutiny. For example, as described below, the Supreme Court has used strict scrutiny in evaluating poll taxes, property ownership requirements for voting, and durational residency requirements.

However, there are some areas where the Court did not use strict scrutiny and upheld restrictions on voting: literacy tests and laws preventing those convicted of felonies from voting. Finally, the Court has allowed laws that create closed political primaries—ones where voting is limited to members of that party—so long as the restrictions are reasonable. Each of these types of restrictions is discussed in turn.

Poll Taxes

The Twenty-fourth Amendment prohibits poll taxes in elections for federal offices. Additionally, the Supreme Court in *Harper v. Virginia State Board of Elections* held that poll taxes are unconstitutional as a denial of equal protection for all other elections.[14] At the outset in *Harper*, the Court said that "once the franchise is granted to the electorate, lines may not be drawn which are inconsistent with the Equal Protection Clause."[15] The Court concluded that limiting voting to those who paid a poll tax was impermissible discrimination. Justice Douglas, writing for

[9] *See* §2.8.3.
[10] *See* Rodriguez v. Popular Democratic Party, 457 U.S. 1 (1982) (upholding a Puerto Rican law that provided that vacancies in the legislature would be filled by the political party with which the officeholder had been affiliated).
[11] Fortson v. Morris, 385 U.S. 231 (1966).
[12] *See* Kramer v. Union Free School Dist., 395 U.S. at 629 (indicating that it is constitutional to have an elected city council choose the mayor, who has broad administrative powers).
[13] Sailors v. Board of Educ. of the County of Kent, 387 U.S. 105 (1967).
[14] 383 U.S. 663 (1966).
[15] *Id.* at 665.

the Court, explained: "[A] State violates the Equal Protection Clause . . . whenever it makes the affluence of the voter or payment of any fee an electoral standard. Voter qualifications have no relation to wealth nor to paying or not paying this or any other tax."[16]

The Court rejected the state's argument that the poll tax of $1.50 was minimal and thus not a significant burden on the right to vote. The Court said: "To introduce wealth or payment of a fee as a measure of a voter's qualifications is to introduce a capricious or irrelevant factor. The degree of the discrimination is irrelevant. . . . [A]s a condition of obtaining a ballot, the requirement of fee paying causes an invidious discrimination that runs afoul of the Equal Protection Clause."[17]

Property Ownership Requirements

Laws requiring property ownership as a requirement for voting seem to run afoul of *Harper*'s forceful declaration that wealth cannot be a basis for denying individuals the ability to vote. Yet the Court's record in dealing with such property ownership requirements is mixed.

In *Kramer v. Union Free School District*, the Supreme Court declared unconstitutional a state law that restricted voting in school district elections to those who owned taxable real property in the district or who had custody of children enrolled in the local public schools.[18] The Court said that strict scrutiny was appropriate because the law kept some citizens from voting in school elections. The state's primary justification for the restrictions was to limit participation to those who were "primarily interested in school affairs."[19] The Court found that it was not permissible for the government to measure interest by property ownership or the presence of children in the school system. Thus, the Court said that the "requirements . . . are not sufficiently tailored to limiting the franchise to those 'primarily interested' in school affairs to justify the denial of the franchise."[20]

Kramer was followed in other cases that invalidated laws limiting voting to property owners. In *Cipriano v. City of Houma*, the Court declared unconstitutional a statute that provided that only property owners could vote on whether a municipal utility could issue municipal bonds.[21] *City of Phoenix v. Kolodziejski* extended this to prevent states from limiting the vote to real property owners in elections to approve the issuance of general obligation bonds.[22] In both *Cipriano* and *Kolodziejski*, the Court emphasized that all citizens in the cities had an interest in the availability of municipal services, and thus all should be able to participate in the elections. In *Kolodziejski*, the Court said: "Presumptively, when all citizens are affected in important ways by a governmental decision subject to a referendum,

---

[16] *Id.* at 666.
[17] *Id.* at 668.
[18] 395 U.S. 621 (1969).
[19] *Id.* at 632.
[20] *Id.* at 633 (citations omitted).
[21] 395 U.S. 701 (1969).
[22] 399 U.S. 204 (1970).

the Constitution does not permit weighted voting or the exclusion of otherwise qualified citizens from the franchise."[23]

However, *Kramer* does not mean that all property ownership requirements for voting are invalid. In *Salyer Land Co. v. Tulare Lake Basin Water Storage District*, the Supreme Court upheld state laws that limited voting in water storage district elections to property owners and that apportioned votes according to assessed valuation of land within the districts.[24] The Court emphasized that landowners had a far greater interest in the outcome of the election than other citizens. The Court explained: "Landowners as a class were to bear the entire burden of the district's costs, and the State could rationally conclude that they, to the exclusion of residents, should be charged with responsibility for its operation."[25] The Court also noted that although the water district has some governmental authority, it does not provide general public services ordinarily attributed to a governing body. Thus, it concluded "that nothing in the Equal Protection Clause precluded California from limiting the voting for directors of appellee district by totally excluding those who merely reside within the district."[26]

The Court followed and applied *Salyer* in *Ball v. James*.[27] *Ball*, like *Salyer*, involved a water district election. In *Ball*, votes were allocated based on property ownership: The basic rule was one acre, one vote. Unlike *Salyer*, decisions by the governing body in *Ball* had a wide impact. The district was a major supplier of hydroelectric power, and about 40 percent of its water went to urban areas for nonagricultural uses.

Nonetheless, the Court found that the property ownership requirement for voting was justified. The Court explained that only the landowners were subject to the acreage-based taxing power of the water district. The Court did not deny that others had an interest in and were affected by the decisions of the district. But the Court said that "[t]he Salyer opinion did not say that the selected class of voters for a special public entity must be the only parties at all affected by the operation of the entity, or that their entire economic well-being must depend on that entity. Rather, the question was whether the effect of the entity's operations on them was disproportionately greater than the effect on those seeking the vote."[28]

The question is whether *Salyer* and *Ball* can be reconciled with cases like *Kramer*, *Cipriano*, and *Kolodziejski*. The latter cases seem to establish the impermissibility of using property ownership as a condition to voting; the assumption of each is that all citizens, regardless of whether they own property, have an interest in the conduct of their government. But *Salyer* and *Ball* seem to establish that property ownership can be required as a condition for voting if some are more directly affected and if the governing body has limited authority. But in *Kramer*, there was an argument that property owners and parents are more directly affected by school

---

[23] *Id.* at 209.
[24] 410 U.S. 719 (1973).
[25] *Id.* at 731.
[26] *Id.*
[27] 451 U.S. 355 (1981).
[28] *Id.* at 371.

district decisions. Also, in *Kramer*, the school board has limited governing authority as compared to a city council. Distinguishing these cases is thus extremely difficult.

Durational Residency Requirements

The Supreme Court has held that a city may limit voting in city elections to its residents. In *Holt Civic Club v. City of Tuscaloosa*, the Court ruled that a city could exclude nonresidents from voting in its elections, even though the city had some governing authority over unincorporated communities.[29]

In *Carrington v. Rash*, the Supreme Court invalidated a state law that denied voting to members of the armed forces who moved into the state in connection with service, regardless of how long they had lived in the area or how much property they owned.[30] The difference between *Holt* and *Carrington* is that the former limited voting to residents of the city, while the latter denied the right to vote to some residents based on how they came to live in the city.

Waiting periods for voting for new residents have been sharply limited by the Supreme Court. In *Dunn v. Blumstein*, the Court declared unconstitutional a one-year durational residency requirement for voting eligibility.[31] The Court emphasized that the durational residency requirement would discourage interstate travel and migration and thus violated the fundamental right to travel.[32] Durational residency requirements penalize those who have recently exercised their right to interstate travel and migration. The Court explained: "Obviously durational residence laws single out the class of bona fide state and county residents who have recently exercised this constitutionally protected right, and penalize such travelers directly."[33]

This is not to say that all durational residency requirements for voting are impermissible. In *Marston v. Lewis*, the Court allowed a 50-day residency requirement for voting to provide election officials sufficient time to check election rolls, prevent fraud, and administer the election.[34]

Literacy Tests

Surprisingly, the Supreme Court has concluded that literacy tests are permissible as a qualification for voting, although they have been outlawed by federal statutes. The Court first confronted literacy tests in 1915 in *Guinn v. United States*, and the Court upheld the ability of states to require passing a literacy test as a condition for voting.[35] However, in *Guinn*, the Court invalidated a "grandfather clause" that exempted from the literacy test anyone, or the lineal descendants

---

[29] 439 U.S. 60 (1978).
[30] 380 U.S. 89 (1965).
[31] 405 U.S. 330 (1972).
[32] Discussed above in §10.7.2.
[33] *Id.* at 338.
[34] 410 U.S. 679 (1973).
[35] 238 U.S. 347 (1915).

of anyone, who could have voted on January 1, 1866. Obviously, the effect was to deny the vote to blacks who were ineligible to vote at the end of the Civil War. But apart from the grandfather clause, the Court was explicit that literacy tests are permissible: "No time need be spent on the question of the validity of the literacy test, considered alone, since, as we have seen, its establishment was but the exercise by the state of a lawful power vested in it, not subject to our supervision, and, indeed, its validity is admitted."[36]

Subsequently, in 1959, in *Lassiter v. Northampton County Board of Elections*, the Court upheld a North Carolina statute that conditioned voting eligibility on a person's ability to read and write any section of the Constitution in the English language.[37] Justice Douglas, writing for the Court, emphasized that "[t]he States have long been held to have broad powers to determine the conditions under which the right of suffrage may be exercised, absent of course discrimination which the Constitution condemns."[38]

Thus, the Court concluded that literacy tests may be used because the ability to read and write is relevant to the ability to exercise the franchise intelligently. Justice Douglas wrote: "The ability to read and write likewise has some relation to standards designed to promote intelligent use of the ballot. Literacy and illiteracy are neutral on race, creed, color, and sex, as reports around the world show. Literacy and intelligence are obviously not synonymous. Illiterate people may be intelligent voters. Yet in our society where newspapers, periodicals, books, and other printed matter canvass and debate campaign issues, a State may conclude that only those who are literate should exercise the franchise."[39]

The Court's decision rests on two assumptions: that literacy tests are race neutral in their purpose and effect, and that literacy tests meet strict scrutiny. As to the former, the history of literacy tests indicates that they generally were motivated by a desire to exclude blacks from voting and that was definitely their impact. As to the latter, the issue is whether literacy tests were necessary to achieve a compelling interest. In an era of radio and television news, even illiterate voters could be well informed. Nor is literacy a prerequisite for handling a ballot because alternatives, such as orally presented ballots or other forms of assistance, could allow illiterate voters to participate in elections.

However, although literacy tests are constitutional, they have been outlawed by federal statute. Congress initially limited literacy tests[40] and then amended the Voting Rights Act to completely prohibit them.[41] The Supreme Court upheld these laws as a valid exercise of Congress's powers under §5 of the Fourteenth

---

[36] *Id.* at 366.

[37] 360 U.S. 45 (1959).

[38] *Id.* at 50 (citation omitted).

[39] *Id.* at 51-52.

[40] *See, e.g.,* Katzenbach v. Morgan, 384 U.S. 641 (1966) (upholding Congress's power under §5 of the Fourteenth Amendment to prohibit denying the right to vote to anyone educated through the sixth grade in a Puerto Rican school on account of literacy); Louisiana v. United States, 380 U.S. 145 (1965) (upholding a provision of the Voting Rights Act that allowed the attorney general to prohibit literacy tests in any state where less than half of the eligible voters were registered to vote).

[41] Oregon v. Mitchell, 400 U.S. 112 (1970).

Amendment even though they had the effect of overturning an earlier Court decision.[42]

Prisoners' and Convicted Criminals' Rights to Vote

Many cases have concerned the ability of the state to restrict voting by those being held in prison or those convicted of crimes. To summarize the cases described below, states cannot deny the right to vote to those being held waiting for trial and, in fact, must provide them absentee ballots if they have no other way of voting. However, once a person has been convicted of a felony, a state may permanently disenfranchise the individual. But, at least where there was evidence of a racially discriminatory purpose behind the law, a state was prevented from permanently denying the right to vote to those convicted of crimes involving moral turpitude.

In a series of cases, the Court considered the duty of the government to provide absentee ballots to those being held in jail while waiting for trial. In *McDonald v. Board of Election Commissioners*, the Court rejected a constitutional challenge to a state law that allowed absentee ballots only for those who had a disability that made it impossible for them to get to the polls or those who would be outside the county on the day of the election.[43] The effect was to deny absentee ballots to those who were in jail while waiting for trial.

The Court, in an opinion by Chief Justice Warren, emphasized that there was no evidence that the inmates actually were deprived of the ability to vote. Even without absentee ballots, there were many ways that the government could facilitate the right to vote for those in jail: polling places at the jail, guarded transportation to outside polling places, or even temporary reductions in bail to allow inmates the chance to vote.[44] Because the record did not demonstrate that inmates were actually kept from voting, the Court concluded: "It is thus not the right to vote that is at stake here but a claimed right to receive absentee ballots."[45]

However, in *O'Brien v. Skinner*, the Court held that the government must provide absentee ballots to jail inmates where it is proved that they have no other way of voting.[46] In *O'Brien*, the record demonstrated that the state refused to provide jail inmates absentee ballots and did not create polling places at jails or transport inmates outside to vote. Actually, the state law was even more irrational: Inmates being held outside their county of residence could receive an absentee ballot, but those in jail within their home county could not obtain an absentee ballot.

Together *McDonald* and *O'Brien* establish that the government cannot completely deny the right to vote to jail inmates who are being held waiting for trial. The state does not have to provide an absentee ballot so long as it creates alternative mechanisms to ensure access to voting. However, if no alternatives exist, then there will be a duty for the government to provide inmates an absentee ballot.

---

[42] *See, e.g.*, Katzenbach v. Morgan, 384 U.S. 641 (1966), discussed in detail in §3.7.2.

[43] 394 U.S. 802 (1969).

[44] *Id.* at 808 n.6.

[45] *Id.* at 807.

[46] 414 U.S. 524 (1974).

Once, however, a person has been convicted of a felony, a state may permanently deny the individual of the right to vote. In *Richardson v. Ramirez*, the Court relied on the language of §2 of the Fourteenth Amendment to uphold the ability of states to disenfranchise felons and ex-felons.[47] Section 2, in part, says that "Representatives shall be apportioned among the several states according to their respective numbers, counting the whole number of persons in each State, excluding Indians not taxed." However, the provision says that representation shall be decreased if a state denies the right to vote to any male citizens, 21 years of age or older, "except for participation in rebellion, or other crimes." In other words, the provision says that there would be no penalty in terms of representation in the House of Representatives if a state denied the right to vote to those who participated in rebellion or other crimes.

The Court, in an opinion by Justice Rehnquist, reviewed the legislative history of this provision and also noted that at the time the Fourteenth Amendment was ratified, "29 States had provisions in their constitutions which prohibited, or authorized the legislature to prohibit, exercise of the franchise by persons convicted of felonies or infamous crimes."[48] The Court also relied on earlier decisions, from the late nineteenth century, that denied bigamists and polygamists the right to vote in territorial Utah and Idaho.[49] The Court concluded that a state may deny the right to vote to those convicted of felonies, even if they had completed their sentences and paroles.

Richardson raises the question of whether it is even rational to permanently deny the right to vote to a person who has completed his or her sentence. The permanent and irrevocable denial of the right to vote seems unjustified by any legitimate purpose, let alone a compelling one. After a person has completed his or her sentence, it is unclear why the state should be able to continue to punish a person by denying the right to vote. There is no reason to believe that a person convicted of a felony is less able to vote intelligently or more likely to corrupt the election process. Justice Rehnquist's opinion stresses the text of §2 of the Fourteenth Amendment, but that only addresses whether a state will be punished by a decrease in representation if it denies ex-felons the right to vote.

However, in *Hunter v. Underwood*, the Court invalidated an Alabama law that denied the right to vote to those who had been convicted of crimes involving moral turpitude.[50] A federal district court found that the provision had been adopted with the purpose of disenfranchising blacks and that it had that effect.[51] The Supreme Court accepted these findings and said: "Without deciding whether [the law] would be valid if enacted today without any impermissible motivation, we simply observe that its original enactment was motivated by a desire to discriminate against blacks on account of race and the section continues to this day to have that effect."[52]

---

[47] 418 U.S. 24 (1974).
[48] *Id.* at 48.
[49] *See* Murphy v. Ramsey, 114 U.S. 15 (1885); Davis v. Season, 133 U.S. 333 (1890).
[50] 471 U.S. 222 (1985).
[51] *Id.* at 227-228.
[52] *Id.* at 233.

Limiting Voting in Primaries Based on Party Affiliation

Another type of restriction on voting occurs when a state requires party affiliation as a condition for voting in primary elections. On the one hand, there is the desire to restrict participation in primaries to those who are members of the party. If nothing else, there is fear that members of the opposing party might sabotage a party's primary by participating and deliberately voting for the weakest candidate. But on the other hand, limiting voting to those who are registered members of the political party denies individuals, especially independents, of their right to vote and participate in primary elections.

The Court has attempted to strike a compromise: allowing a state to limit voting in a primary to those in the party so long as this is measured in a reasonable way. In *Rosario v. Rockefeller*, the Court upheld a New York law that required voters to select a political party 30 days before a general election in order to vote in the next political primary.[53] The Court explained that the law was designed to prevent raiding, a practice "whereby voters in sympathy with one party designate themselves as voters of another party so as to influence or determine the results of the other party's primary."[54]

However, the Court subsequently made it clear that there are limits as to how far the state may go in pursuing this objective. In *Kusper v. Pontikes*, the Court declared unconstitutional a state law that prohibited a person from voting in a political primary election if he or she had voted in another party's primary in the prior 23 months.[55] The difference between *Rosario* and *Kusper* is in the length of the restriction. In *Rosario*, the disqualification from participating in a different party's primary was for about a year and a half, from the October before the general election until the next primary election, usually about 18 months later. In *Kusper*, the disqualification was 23 months. The question, though, is whether this difference in time really should be decisive.

In *Tashjian v. Republican Party of Connecticut*, the Court declared unconstitutional a state law that limited voting in a political party's primary election to those who were members of that party.[56] The Connecticut Republican Party adopted a rule that permitted independent voters—those not registered with any political party—to vote in Republican primaries for federal and state offices. Connecticut law, unlike the party rule, limited voting in a primary to those registered in that political party. The Court emphasized that the rationale underlying *Rosario*—preventing voters from one party from participating in the primary of the other and sabotaging its choices—was inapplicable with regard to independent voters. Also, the Court emphasized that the party itself wished to open its election.[57]

In a subsequent decision, *California Democratic Party v. Jones*, the Court declared unconstitutional a "blanket primary" and placed in doubt the constitutionality of

---

[53]   410 U.S. 752 (1973).
[54]   *Id.* at 760.
[55]   414 U.S. 51 (1973).
[56]   479 U.S. 208 (1986).
[57]   *Id.* at 224.

other forms of open primaries.[58] California voters adopted an initiative that allowed a voter to cast a ballot in either party's political primary. Justice Scalia, writing for the Court in a 7-to-2 decision, concluded that this impermissibly violated the First Amendment's protection of political association. Justice Scalia explained that "[i]n no area is the political association's right to exclude more important than in the process of selecting its nominee."[59]

Forcing a political party to allow nonparty members to participate in the selection of its nominee was thus deemed to violate the First Amendment. Justice Scalia concluded: "California's blanket primary . . . forces political parties to associate with—to have their nominees, and hence their positions, determined by—those who, at best, have refused to affiliate with the party, and, at worst, have expressly affiliated with a rival."[60] Justice Scalia said that evidence supports the fear that nonadherents can play a decisive role in choosing a nominee. He rejected the various justifications offered by the state for the blanket primary, such as increasing participation in the political process.

The key question after *Jones* is whether other forms of open primaries will be allowed. The Court only invalidated blanket primaries, but the decision certainly casts doubt on all state laws that force parties to include nonmembers to participate in choosing their candidates. In some states, voters must request a ballot of a particular party at the time of voting during the primary. This is different from California's blanket primary that allowed a person to vote for any candidate for each office. Is the requirement for requesting a ballot for a specific party, and whatever affiliation that conveys, enough to distinguish *Jones*?

Subsequently, in *Washington State Grange v. Washington State Republican Party*, the Court upheld a different form of a blanket primary.[61] Voters in Washington State passed an initiative providing that candidates must be identified on the primary ballot by their self-designated party preference; that voters may vote for any candidate; and that the two top vote-getters for each office, regardless of party preference, advance to the general election. The political parties claimed that the new law, on its face, violates a party's associational rights by usurping its right to nominate its own candidates and by forcing it to associate with candidates it does not endorse.

The Supreme Court upheld this form of a primary and distinguished *Jones*. Justice Thomas, writing for the Court, explained how the Washington system is different from that struck down in *Jones*: "[U]nlike the California primary, the [Washington] primary does not, by its terms, choose parties' nominees. The essence of nomination—the choice of a party representative—does not occur under [Washington law]. The law never refers to the candidates as nominees of any party, nor does it treat them as such. To the contrary, the election regulations specifically provide that the primary 'does not serve to determine the nominees of a political party but serves to winnow the number of candidates to a final list of

[58] 530 U.S. 567 (2000).
[59] *Id.* at 574.
[60] *Id.* at 576.
[61] 552 U.S. 442 (2008).

two for the general election.' The top two candidates from the primary election proceed to the general election regardless of their party preferences."[62]

In other words, even though voters could vote in the primary outside their political party and even though candidates could identify themselves by political party without the endorsement of the party, the system was deemed facially constitutional. Thus, the form of the blanket primary is likely to be crucial in determining its constitutionality.

Requirement for Photo Identification for Voting

The final type of government regulation of voting is the most recent to be considered by the Court: a state law that required photo identification in order to vote. In *Crawford v. Marion County*,[63] the Court, without a majority opinion, upheld the facial constitutionality of an Indiana law requiring voter identification. Justice Stevens announced the judgment of the Court and his opinion was joined by Chief Justice Roberts and Justice Kennedy. Justice Stevens, quoting *Anderson v. Celebrezze*,[64] said that the general rule is that "evenhanded restrictions that protect the integrity and reliability of the electoral process itself are not invidious. Rather than applying any 'litmus test' that would neatly separate valid from invalid restrictions, we concluded that a court must identify and evaluate the interests put forward by the State as justifications for the burden imposed by its rule, and then make the 'hard judgment' that our adversary system demands."[65]

Justice Stevens then proceeded to balance the burden on the right to vote against the state's interest in preventing fraud. As for the former, Justice Stevens found a minimal burden especially because most people have some form of picture identification and those that don't can cast a provisional ballot and later verify their identity. As for the latter, Justice Stevens said that there was an important state interest in preventing voter fraud and preserving confidence in the election system. He wrote: "There is no question about the legitimacy or importance of the State's interest in counting only the votes of eligible voters. Moreover, the interest in orderly administration and accurate recordkeeping provides a sufficient justification for carefully identifying all voters participating in the election process. While the most effective method of preventing election fraud may well be debatable, the propriety of doing so is perfectly clear."[66] Justice Stevens was clear that the Court was rejecting a facial challenge to the law, but there is still the possibility of an "as applied" challenge if it can be shown that in operation the law unduly burdens the right to vote.

Justice Scalia concurred in the judgment in an opinion joined by Justices Thomas and Alito. Justice Scalia said that strict scrutiny is appropriate when it

---

[62] *Id.* at 453.
[63] 553 U.S. 181 (2008).
[64] 460 U.S. 780 (1983).
[65] 553 U.S. at 190.
[66] *Id.* at 196.

comes to regulation of voting only if the burden is "severe."[67] Justice Scalia argued that the Indiana law should be allowed because it is reasonable: "The universally applicable requirements of Indiana's voter-identification law are eminently reasonable. The burden of acquiring, possessing, and showing a free photo identification is simply not severe, because it does not 'even represent a significant increase over the usual burdens of voting.' And the State's interests are sufficient to sustain that minimal burden. That should end the matter."[68] It should be noted that six Justices rejected Justice Scalia's approach that only "severe" burdens on the right to vote trigger strict scrutiny.

Finally, Justices Souter, Ginsburg, and Breyer dissented. Justice Souter explained: "Indiana's 'Voter ID Law' threatens to impose nontrivial burdens on the voting right of tens of thousands of the State's citizens, and a significant percentage of those individuals are likely to be deterred from voting. The statute is unconstitutional under the balancing standard; . . . a State may not burden the right to vote merely by invoking abstract interests, be they legitimate, or even compelling, but must make a particular, factual showing that threats to its interests outweigh the particular impediments it has imposed. The State has made no such justification here, and as to some aspects of its law, it has hardly even tried."[69] Justice Souter argued that there is no evidence of voter fraud that would be cured by photo identification and that it would cause many individuals to be unable to vote.

The case is important in prescribing a balancing test rather than strict scrutiny for such laws regulating the right to vote. Also, like in other recent cases, including *Washington State Grange*, the Court expresses a strong aversion to facial challenges but leaves open the possibility of an applied challenge. Many additional states have adopted laws requiring photo identification for voting and challenges to these statutes likely soon will make it to the Supreme Court, presenting both challenges under equal protection and under §2 of the Voting Rights Act of 1965.

§10.8.3   Dilution of the Right to Vote

The Rule of One-Person, One-Vote

One district for the legislature often would be far more populous than another district for the same body. Likewise, districts within a state for electing members of the House of Representatives often were significantly malapportioned. Malapportionment in many areas was a result of population shifts to urban areas. Districts often were not redrawn after urban migration, causing cities to be underrepresented compared with more rural areas. Legislators who benefited from the malapportionment were unlikely to change the districting.

---

[67] *Id.* at 205 (Scalia, J., concurring in the judgment).
[68] *Id.* at 209.
[69] *Id.* at 209 (Souter, J., dissenting).

§10.8 Constitutional Protection for Voting

Initially, the Supreme Court ruled that challenges to malapportionment posed a nonjusticiable political question.[70] However, in *Baker v. Carr*, the Court concluded that equal protection challenges to malapportionment were justiciable.[71] Soon after, the Court articulated the rule of one-person, one-vote; that is, for any legislative body all districts must be about the same in population size.

The first case to announce this principle was *Gray v. Sanders*, in 1963.[72] *Gray* involved a challenge to the Georgia system of selecting representatives for the Georgia House of the General Assembly on a county basis. An inequality resulted because counties varied widely in population size. Justice Douglas, writing for the Court, explained why this is unconstitutional: "How then can one person be given twice or 10 times the voting power of another person in a statewide election merely because he lives in a rural area or because he lives in the smallest rural county? Once the geographical unit for which a representative is to be chosen is designated, all who participate in the election are to have an equal vote—whatever their race, whatever their sex, wherever their occupation, whatever their income, and whatever their home may be in that geographic unit. This is required by the Equal Protection Clause of the Fourteenth Amendment."[73]

Thus, the Court said that equal protection requires that all districts be about the same in population size; anything else impermissibly dilutes the voting power of those in the more populous districts. In its conclusion, the Court declared: "The conception of political equality from the Declaration of Independence, to Lincoln's Gettysburg Address, to the Fifteenth, Seventeenth, and Nineteenth Amendments can mean only one thing—one person, one vote."[74]

The Court followed this rationale in *Wesberry v. Sanders* and declared unconstitutional districts for the House of Representatives where some districts had twice as many people as others.[75] Specifically, one district had 823,680 people, compared with another district that had 394,312. The Court, in an opinion by Justice Black, discussed, at length, the framers' theory of representative democracy and again concluded that the rule is "one person, one vote."[76] The Court concluded: "While it may not be possible to draw congressional districts with mathematical precision, that is no excuse for ignoring our Constitution's plain objective of making equal representation for equal numbers of people the fundamental goal of the House of Representatives. That is the high standard of justice and common sense which the Founders set for us."[77]

In *Reynolds v. Sims*, the Court applied these principles to declare the malapportionment of a state legislature unconstitutional and to order its reapportionment.[78] Under then-existing law, the Alabama legislature had a 35-member state

---

[70] Colegrove v. Green, 328 U.S. 549 (1946), discussed in §2.8.3.
[71] 369 U.S. 186 (1962), discussed in §2.8.1.
[72] 372 U.S. 368 (1963).
[73] *Id.* at 379.
[74] *Id.* at 381.
[75] 376 U.S. 1 (1964).
[76] *Id.* at 18.
[77] *Id.*
[78] 377 U.S. 533 (1964).

senate elected from 35 districts that varied in population from 15,417 to 634,864.[79] There also was a 100-member state house of representatives with population varying from 31,175 to 634,864.[80]

Chief Justice Warren, writing for the Court, explained that geographical area made no sense in drawing districts; only population was a permissible basis. He said: "Legislators represent people, not trees or acres. Legislators are elected by voters, not farms or cities or economic interests. As long as ours is a representative form of government, and our legislatures are those instruments of government elected directly by and directly representative of the people, the right to elect representatives in a free and unimpaired fashion is a bedrock of our political system."[81]

Malapportionment inevitably means vote dilution; those voters in the more populous district have proportionately less influence in the political process than those in the small districts. The Court explained: "[I]f a State should provide that the votes of citizens in one part of the State should be given two times, or five times, or 10 times the weight of votes of citizens in another part of the State, it could hardly be contended that the right to vote of those residing in disfavored areas had not been effectively diluted."[82]

The Court thus concluded that both houses of a state legislature must be apportioned by population. A state is not allowed to mirror Congress where the House is apportioned by population and Senate seats are allocated two to each state regardless of population. The Court declared: "We hold that, as a basic constitutional standard, the Equal Protection Clause requires that the seats in both houses of a bicameral state legislature must be apportioned on a population basis. Simply stated, an individual's right to vote for state legislators is unconstitutionally impaired when its weight is in a substantial fashion diluted when compared with votes of citizens living in other parts of the State."[83]

In a companion case to *Reynolds*, *Lucas v. Forty-Fourth General Assembly*, the Court said that it was irrelevant that voters, by initiative, had approved the malapportionment.[84] The Court explained that one-person, one-vote is a constitutional mandate and that voter approval does not justify a violation, any more than voter approval would permit the violation of any other constitutional right. The Court observed that "[a]n individual's constitutionally protected right to cast an equally weighted vote cannot be denied even by a vote of a majority of a State's electorate."[85]

The principle of one-person, one-vote has been extended to all forms of local governments. In *Avery v. Midland County*, the Court said that one-person, one-vote applied to county commissioners who had "general government powers over the

[79]   *Id.* at 545-546.
[80]   *Id.*
[81]   *Id.* at 562.
[82]   *Id.*
[83]   *Id.* at 568.
[84]   377 U.S. 713 (1964).
[85]   *Id.* at 736.

entire geographic area served by the body."[86] In *Hadley v. Junior College District*, the principle was applied to an elected body with limited governing authority: a junior college district.[87] The elected body had the authority to tax, to employ teachers, and to manage the educational program. The Court rejected earlier attempts to distinguish legislative officials from administrative ones. The Court said that all elected officials must be selected in a manner that avoids vote dilution.[88] The Court stated: "[A]s a general rule, whenever a state or local government decides to select persons by popular election to perform governmental functions, [equal protection] requires that each qualified voter must be given an equal opportunity to participate in that election, and when members of an elected body are chosen from separate districts, each district must be established on a basis that will insure, as far as practicable, that equal numbers of voters can vote for proportionately equal numbers of officials."[89]

Only in limited and unique circumstances has the Court ever permitted deviation from one-person, one-vote. For example, in a case involving a water storage district, described above, the Court permitted a one-acre, one-vote rule.[90] The Court emphasized the limited governing authority of the water district and how its decisions uniquely affected landowners.[91] But in almost all other instances, the Court has said that one-person, one-vote must be met.[92]

The rule of one-person, one-vote does not require mathematical exactness in the size of districts, but only relatively small deviations are tolerated. More latitude is given to deviations in districting for state and local offices than for districts for the United States House of Representatives. In *Kirkpatrick v. Preisler*, the Court invalidated districting for the House of Representatives where the "most populous district was 3.13 percent above the mathematical ideal, and the least populous was 2.84 percent below."[93] The Court emphasized that the government must "make a good-faith effort to achieve precise mathematical equality."[94] In *White v. Weiser*, the Court declared unconstitutional even smaller deviations in districts for the House of Representatives.[95] The Court repeatedly has emphasized that, especially with regard to elections for federal offices, any deviation must be justified. For

[86]   390 U.S. 474, 485 (1968).

[87]   397 U.S. 50 (1970).

[88]   The Court thus implicitly rejected the view that it had earlier articulated that it was permissible to depart from one-person, one-vote in elections for bodies exercising only administrative tasks. *See* Sailors v. Board of Educ., 387 U.S. 105 (1967) (allowing departure from one-person, one-vote in school board election).

[89]   397 U.S. at 56.

[90]   Ball v. James, 451 U.S. 355 (1981).

[91]   *See also* Town of Lockport v. Citizens for Community Action at the Local Level, Inc., 430 U.S. 259 (1977) (allowing a law that requires changes in the county charter to be approved by a majority of the voters in the county who live in cities and the majority who live in unincorporated areas of the county).

[92]   *See also* Board of Estimates v. Morris, 489 U.S. 688 (1989) (requiring that one-person, one-vote be met for New York City's Board of Estimates, which consisted of the five borough presidents, and the city's mayor, comptroller, and city council president).

[93]   394 U.S. 526, 528-529 (1969).

[94]   *Id.* at 530-531.

[95]   412 U.S. 783 (1973).

example, in *Karcher v. Daggett*, the Court declared unconstitutional districting for the House of Representatives where the deviation between them was 0.7 percent.[96] This deviation was impermissible because the state could offer no justification as to why it was needed.

The Court, though, has allowed more deviation in districts for electing state and local officials. In *Mahan v. Howell*, the Court expressly said that "broader latitude has been afforded the States under the Equal Protection Clause in state legislative redistricting."[97] For example, in *Mahan*, the Court allowed deviations where the overrepresented districts exceeded the ideal by 6.8 percent and the underrepresented districts were 9.6 percent away from the target. Similarly, in *Gaffney v. Cummings*, the Court upheld a legislative apportionment where the maximum deviation was 7.83 percent and concluded that the differences were insignificant.[98] In *White v. Regester*, the Court allowed an apportionment scheme where the total variation between the largest and the smallest district was 9.9 percent, though the Court indicated that this was near the maximum allowable deviation.[99]

In assessing whether districts are drawn appropriately, an inevitable question arises: Who counts? Is it all persons legally within the area, or all citizens in the area, or all potential voters in the area, or all registered voters, or all who voted in the last election? The choice can make an enormous difference as to whether particular districting is constitutional or a violation of equal protection. The Supreme Court has not ruled that one of these approaches must be used, though in *Bums v. Richardson* it held that it is permissible for the government to use the number of registered voters as its basis for drawing districts.[100] Yet this could lead to enormous inequity in the size of the districts if one district had many more people than another, but no more registered voters because it had more children, more noncitizens, or more people who don't vote.

There is no doubt that the reapportionment decisions have had an enormous effect on American government. Although they were extremely controversial in the 1960s, by the 1990s, they were seen as a paradigm instance of the judiciary acting to perfect the political process and reinforce democracy.[101] Reapportionment was very unlikely to occur without judicial action because officeholders were not likely to give up their seats voluntarily. The decisions dramatically changed the composition of state legislatures and thus undoubtedly affected the laws adopted.

Yet some still criticize the cases as being excessive judicial activism because there was not authority in the text or the framers' intent for the rule of one-person,

---

[96] 462 U.S. 725 (1983).

[97] 410 U.S. 315, 322 (1973).

[98] 412 U.S. 735 (1973).

[99] 412 U.S. 755 (1973). *See also* Brown v. Thomson, 462 U.S. 835 (1983) (allowing a maximum deviation of 89 percent in drawing congressional districts).

[100] 384 U.S. 73 (1966).

[101] *See* John Ely, Democracy and Distrust 101-102 (1980). For an excellent discussion of the nature of the right to an undiluted vote, *see* Heather K. Gerken, Understanding the Right to an Undiluted Vote, 114 Harv. L. Rev. 1663 (2001).

one-vote.[102] The critics see the decisions as improper judicial interference, unsupported by the text of the Constitution or the framers' intent, with the political process.

Do Deviations from Majority Rule Violate Equal Protection?

Sometimes laws provide for voting principles other than simple majority rules. For example, a law might require that a super-majority must approve a candidate or an initiative. Are such laws unconstitutional because they effectively expand the strength of the votes of those in the minority and, therefore, proportionately lessen the value of the votes of those in the majority?[103]

The Supreme Court consistently has allowed state and local governments to depart from simple majority rule. In *Gordon v. Lance*, for example, the Supreme Court upheld the constitutionality of a state law that prevented the city from incurring bonded indebtedness or increasing taxes except by approval of 60 percent of the voters in a referendum election.[104] The Court expressly rejected the argument that the super-majority requirement was a denial of one-person, one-vote because it gave disproportionate power to the majority. The Court explained: "Certainly, any departure from strict majority rule gives disproportionate power to the minority. But there is nothing in the language of the Constitution, our history, or our cases that requires that a majority always prevail on every issue."[105]

Also, in *Town of Lockport v. Citizens for Community Action at the Local Level, Inc.*, the Court upheld a state law that provided that a new county charter could go into effect only if it was approved in a referendum election by the majority of the voters who live in cities within the county *and* the majority of voters who live in the city.[106] In essence, this, too, was a super-majority voting requirement. A simple majority of the total number of votes was not sufficient; a majority of two distinct groups—city and noncity dwellers—was required. The Court upheld this as constitutional.

Thus, although one-person, one-vote must be maintained, it is not violated by a super-majority voting rule. Yet it is difficult to see the difference between a super-majority voting rule and malapportionment. In each instance, those with less voting strength are helped by the government. Yet deviations from one-person, one-vote are almost always intolerable, although super-majority voting requirements are allowed.

---

[102] Robert Bork, The Tempting of America 87 (1990) (criticizing the decisions on the ground that the "Warren majority's new constitutional doctrine was supported by nothing").

[103] *See, e.g.*, J. Harvie Wilkinson, III, The Supreme Court, the Equal Protection Clause, and the Three Faces of Constitutional Equality, 61 Va. L. Rev. 945 (1975) (arguing that super-majority voting rules dilute the votes of those who are in the majority, but not the super-majority).

[104] 403 U.S. 1 (1971).

[105] *Id.* at 6.

[106] 430 U.S. 259 (1977).

Gerrymandering

Gerrymandering is the practice by a political party of drawing election districts to benefit itself and harm its opponent; political gerrymandering occurs when the party controlling the legislature draws districts to maximize safe seats for that party. Typically, a state legislature draws election districts for seats in the United States House of Representatives and for the state legislature.

There are many ways in which a political party can adhere to one-person, one-vote, but still engage in gerrymandering. For example, in a large geographic area where Democrats are 60 percent of the voters and Republicans are 40 percent, ten seats in the legislature could be reflected in six majority Democratic districts and four majority Republican districts. But if the Democrats controlled the legislature, they could try to create ten districts, each comprising 60 percent Democratic and 40 percent Republican voters. Or they could try to create one or two districts that were 100 percent Republican voters and create eight districts that were solidly Democratic. Depending on how lines were drawn to group or spread people, districting could make an enormous difference in the political composition of the legislature. Sophisticated computer programs have made partisan gerrymandering more accurate and more successful.

In *Gaffney v. Cummings*, the Court indicated that it would be very reluctant to invalidate districts based on gerrymandering.[107] In *Gaffney*, districts were drawn to create a legislature reflecting the approximate political strength of the Democratic and Republican parties within the state. The Court found no equal protection violation and declared: "It would be idle, we think, to contend that any political consideration taken into account in fashioning a reapportionment plan is sufficient to invalidate it. . . . Politics and political considerations are inseparable from districting and apportionment. . . . The reality is that districting inevitably has and is intended to have substantial political consequences."[108] The Court expressed acceptance of politics in districting so long as one-person, one-vote is maintained and there is no discrimination against any racial or other group.

In *Davis v. Bandemer*, the Supreme Court considered a more difficult form of gerrymandering: Where the incumbent party controlling the legislature draws districts to help it remain in control.[109] Republicans had a majority in the Indiana legislature and created a committee composed exclusively of Republicans to draw the new election districts. Under the plan, Democratic House candidates won 51.9 percent of the statewide vote, but only 43 of the 100 seats. Democratic Senate candidates won 53.1 percent of the statewide vote and 13 of 25 seats up for election.

The Court initially said that challenges to such gerrymandering are justiciable. Although the Court recognized that the issue was different from that in the malapportionment cases, it said that "[n]evertheless, the issue is one of representation, and we decline to hold that such claims are never justiciable."[110]

---

[107] 412 U.S. 735 1973).
[108] *Id.* at 752-753.
[109] 478 U.S. 109 (1986).
[110] *Id.* at 124.

The plurality opinion by Justice White said that in order for a group to prove a violation of equal protection it must prove "both intentional discrimination against an identifiable political group and an actual discriminatory effect on that group."[111] The plurality stated, however, that the Constitution does not require that there be proportional representation in the legislature based on political party strength in the state or that seats be allocated to the contending parties in proportion to their likely strength in statewide elections. The plurality said that "the mere lack of proportional representation will not be sufficient to prove unconstitutional discrimination."[112]

The plurality concluded that "unconstitutional discrimination occurs only when the electoral system is arranged in a manner that will consistently degrade a voter's or a group of voters' influence on the political process as a whole."[113] In other words, gerrymandering is unconstitutional "only where the electoral system substantially disadvantages certain voters in their opportunity to influence the political process effectively. . . . [S]uch a finding of unconstitutionality must be supported by evidence of continued frustration of the will of a majority of the voters or effective denial to a minority of voters of a fair chance to influence the political process."[114] Thus, the results of a single election are not sufficient to prove impermissible gerrymandering.

Justice White, and the three other Justices in the plurality, found no constitutional violation with regard to the districting of the Indiana legislature. Justices O'Connor, Rehnquist, and Burger would have dismissed the case on justiciability grounds and thus concurred in the judgment.[115] Justices Powell and Stevens agreed with the plurality that the case was justiciable, but would have found that the districting in Indiana denied equal protection.[116]

The result was a very fragmented opinion. Six Justices found that challenges to gerrymandering are justiciable. Seven Justices voted to uphold the districts used in Indiana, four by finding no constitutional violation and three by concluding that the case was not justiciable. *Davis* does not answer the question of what will be sufficient to prove that gerrymandering constitutes an effective denial to a minority of voters of a fair chance to influence the political process. *Davis* was clear that a single election is not sufficient and that substantial disadvantaging in the political process must be shown. But it is unclear as to what proof will be enough.

In *Vieth v. Jubelirer*, the Court dismissed a challenge as being a nonjusticiable political question.[117] The plurality opinion by Justice Scalia would have overruled *Davis*, but there was no majority opinion. The case involved the Republican-controlled Pennsylvania legislature drawing election districts to maximize seats for Republicans. The plurality opinion, written by Justice Scalia, concluded that

---

[111]   *Id.* at 127.
[112]   *Id.* at 132.
[113]   *Id.*
[114]   *Id.* at 133.
[115]   *Id.* at 144 (O'Connor, J., concurring in the judgment).
[116]   *Id.* at 161 (Powell, J., concurring in part and dissenting in part).
[117]   541 U.S. 267 (2004). The case, and its relationship to the political question doctrine, is discussed in §2.8.3.

challenges to partisan gerrymandering are nonjusticiable political questions. Justice Scalia, joined by Chief Justice Rehnquist and Justices O'Connor and Thomas, said that there are no judicially discoverable or manageable standards and no basis for courts to decide when partisan gerrymandering offends the Constitution.

Justice Kennedy, concurring in the judgment, provided the fifth vote for the majority. He agreed to dismiss the case because of the lack of judicially discoverable or manageable standards, but he said that he did not believe that such standards could not be developed in the future.[118] Thus, he disagreed with the majority opinion that challenges to partisan gerrymandering are always political questions; he said that when standards are developed, such cases can be heard.

The difficulty for lower courts will be in deciding what the case means. Five Justices voted to dismiss the case as a political question. But five Justices—Justice Kennedy and the four dissenters—rejected the proposition that challenges to partisan gerrymandering are always political questions. Whether gerrymandering ever violates the Constitution, and if so when, is left open to future cases to resolve.

Two years after *Vieth*, in *League of United Latin American Citizens v. Perry*, the Court again without a majority opinion refused to address the constitutionality of partisan gerrymandering, this time in the State of Texas.[119] Justice Kennedy announced the judgment for the Court and found that there was not sufficient evidence to show vote dilution. Justices Scalia and Thomas would have dismissed on justiciability grounds, concluding that challenges to partisan gerrymandering inherently present a political question. Chief Justice Roberts and Justice Alito said that the plaintiffs did not present a standard for determining when gerrymandering violates equal protection. They said that they took no position as to whether a standard might be developed, but they agreed that the case should be dismissed as nonjusticiable for failure to state a claim.

The bottom line after *Vieth* and *Perry* is that it is highly unlikely that the current Court will find gerrymandering to be unconstitutional. Justice Kennedy has left open the possibility of developing a standard in the future, but it is unclear what this would be or whether it ever will be found.

§10.8.4 Inequalities in Counting Votes Within a State

On December 12, 2000, the United States Supreme Court for the first time in American history effectively decided a presidential election with its ruling in *Bush v. Gore*.[120] In explaining this landmark case, first the events leading up to it are described and then the opinions are summarized. Finally, questions are raised concerning the controversial decision and its likely future impact.[121]

---

[118] *Id.* at 306 (Kennedy, J., concurring in the judgment).

[119] 548 U.S. 399 (2006).

[120] 531 U.S. 98 (2000).

[121] There are a number of books analyzing the decision. *See* Alan Dershowitz, Supreme Injustice: How the Supreme Court Hijacked Election 2000 (2002); Richard A. Posner, Breaking the Deadlock (2001); Jeffrey Toobin, Too Close to Call: The Thirty-Six Day Battle to Decide the 2000 Election (2002).

The Events Leading Up to *Bush v. Gore*

The presidential election of Tuesday, November 7, 2000, was one of the closest in American history. By early Wednesday morning it was clear that the Democratic candidate, Vice President Al Gore, won the national popular vote but that the outcome of the electoral vote was uncertain. The presidency turned on Florida and its 25 electoral votes. Early on election night, the television networks called Gore the winner in Florida, only to retract their prediction later in the evening. In the early hours of Wednesday, November 8, the networks declared Bush the winner of Florida and the presidency, only to recant that a short time later and to conclude that the outcome in Florida, and thus of the national election, was too close to call.

On November 8, the Florida Division of Elections reported that Bush had received 2,909,135 votes and Gore had received 2,907,351 votes. Florida law provides for a recount of votes if the election is decided by less than one-half of a percent of the votes cast.[122] Because the difference in votes between the two candidates was less than one-half of a percent, Gore immediately asked for a machine recount of the tally of votes in four counties: Volusia, Palm Beach, Broward, and Miami-Dade. On November 9, Florida's Secretary of State Katherine Harris declined to extend the statutory deadline for county vote totals beyond November 14. By this point the machine recount had narrowed Bush's lead to a mere 327 votes.

Upon learning of the close margin between him and Bush, Gore petitioned and received permission to have a hand recount in the four counties in question. On Saturday, November 9, Bush sued in federal district court to block the manual recount, but his request was denied.

However, Secretary of State Harris declared that she would enforce the November 14 deadline and that she would not accept late recounts from counties in Florida. She said that the Florida election statute required counties to report their votes within one week of the election, unless one of the statutory exceptions was met. These exceptions included "proof of fraud that affects the outcome of the election," "substantial noncompliance with statutory election procedures, and a reasonable doubt exists as to whether the certified results expressed the will of the voters," or where compliance with the deadline is "prevented as a result of an act of God, or extenuating circumstances beyond their control." The four counties submitted their response and requested acceptance of late completion of totals; each one was denied by Harris. A suit was brought against Harris in Florida district court to compel her to accept the time for the reporting of the results. On Friday, November 17, the Florida state trial court ruled in favor of Harris. On Monday, November 20, the Florida Supreme Court held a nationally televised hearing. On Tuesday night, November 21, the Florida Supreme Court unanimously reversed the trial court and ordered that the secretary of state accept hand recounts from the four counties if

---

[122] The Florida Statute, §102.141(4), provides: "(4) If the returns for any office reflect that a candidate was defeated or eliminated by one-half of a percent or less of the votes cast for such office . . . the board responsible for certifying the results of the vote on such race or measure shall order a recount of the votes cast with respect to such office or measure."

they were completed by Sunday, November 26, at 5:00 P.M., or Monday morning, if the secretary of state was not open for business on Sunday afternoon.

The Florida Supreme Court ruled that Florida's secretary of state abused her discretion in refusing to extend the deadline for certifying elections so as to provide the needed time for the recounts. The court said that it was confronted with a conflict between two statutes. One statute, Fla. Stat. §102.111, provides that local election canvassing boards must submit their results "by 5:00 of the seventh day following an election." This law was amended in 1989, by §102.112, which provides that election results may be ignored and board members shall be fined if these deadlines are not met.

However, another statute, Fla. Stat. §102.166(4)(a), specifically allows any candidate to request a manual recount. This provision states: "[A]ny candidate whose name appeared on the ballot . . . or any political party whose candidates' name appeared on the ballot may file a written request with the county canvassing board for a manual recount." The law provides that the written request may be made prior to the time the board certifies the returns or within 72 hours after the election, whichever occurs later.

The Florida Supreme Court expressly noted that these statutes "conflict." The court relied on "traditional rules of statutory construction" —such as that specific laws prevail over general ones and the more recently enacted law takes precedence over the older one—and concluded that Harris erred in denying the extension of time for the counting.

The Florida Supreme Court also said that "a statutory provision will not be construed in such a way that renders meaningless or absurd any other statutory provision." In order to effectuate the law allowing recounts, the court concluded that there must be time for doing so. The court said that the secretary of state's refusal to accept hand recounts was wrong because it completely negated the statute that expressly provided for this.

On Friday, November 24, the day after Thanksgiving, the United States Supreme Court granted certiorari in this case and scheduled oral argument for the following Friday, December 1. In an unprecedented order, the Court permitted the broadcasting of the oral argument immediately after it was finished. A few days later, in *Bush v. Palm Beach County Canvassing Board*,[123] the United States Supreme Court remanded the case back to the Florida Supreme Court for clarification of its earlier decision. The United States Supreme Court, in a per curiam opinion, said that it was unclear whether the Florida court's decision was based on its interpretation of the Florida constitution or Florida statutes. The former apparently would be an impermissible basis for decision, while the latter would be acceptable, based on the United States Supreme Court's interpretation of federal election laws. On Monday, December 11—the same day the Florida Supreme Court held oral argument in *Bush v. Gore*—the court issued a statement saying that its decision was based on interpreting Florida's statutes, not its constitution.

Meanwhile, on Sunday, November 26, some counties asked for additional time to complete their counting. For example, Palm Beach County asked for two

[123] 531 U.S. 70 (2000).

additional hours beyond the Sunday 5:00 P.M. deadline set by the Florida Supreme Court, particularly because the state supreme court expressly had allowed the secretary of state to wait until Monday morning before receiving the recount totals. The secretary of state refused all requests for extensions. On Sunday night, November 26, the Florida Elections Canvassing Commission certified the election results: Bush was determined to be the winner of Florida by 537 votes and thus the winner of Florida's 25 electoral votes.

On Monday, November 27, Gore filed suit in Florida under the Florida law providing for "contests" of election results.[124] This provision, §102.168(3)(c), provides that "[r]eceipt of a number of illegal votes or rejection of a number of legal votes sufficient to change or place in doubt the result of the election" shall be grounds for a contest. The statute authorizes a court, if it finds that there are successful grounds for a contest, to "provide any relief appropriate under such circumstances."[125]

On Saturday and Sunday, December 2 and 3, a Florida state trial court held a hearing as to whether Gore had met the statutory requirements for a successful contest. On Monday, December 4, the Florida trial court ruled against Gore on the grounds that Gore failed to prove a "reasonable probability" that the election would have turned out differently if not for problems in counting ballots.

The Florida Supreme Court granted review and scheduled oral arguments for Thursday, December 6. On Friday afternoon, December 7, the Florida Supreme Court, by a 4-to-3 decision, reversed the trial court. The Florida Supreme Court ruled that the trial court had used the wrong standard in insisting that Gore demonstrate a "reasonable probability" that the election would have been decided differently. The Florida Supreme Court said that the statute requires only a showing of "[r]eceipt of a number of illegal votes or rejection of a number of legal votes sufficient to change or place in doubt the result of the election."[126]

The Florida Supreme Court ordered "the Supervisor of Elections and the Canvassing Boards, as well as the necessary public officials, in all counties that have not conducted a manual recount or tabulation of the undervotes . . . to do so forthwith, said tabulation to take place in the individual counties where the ballots are located."[127] The Florida Supreme Court also determined that Palm Beach County and Miami-Dade County, in their earlier manual recounts, had identified a net gain of 215 and 168 legal votes for Vice President Gore, and that these should

---

[124] It should be noted that other lawsuits, unrelated to the specific issues in *Bush v. Gore*, were going on simultaneously. For example, voters in Palm Beach County brought a lawsuit seeking a new election there based on the so-called butterfly ballot, which they claimed violated Florida law and caused several thousand votes intended for Gore to be mistakenly cast for Pat Buchanan. A Florida trial court then concluded that it lacked the constitutional authority to order a new election and the Florida Supreme Court denied review. Also, there were lawsuits in two counties claiming that election officials had illegally filled in missing information on requests for absentee ballots. Both Florida trial court judges held that this was not a basis for refusing to count absentee ballots because the actions of the election officials did not in any way taint the ballots themselves.

[125] Fla. Stat. §102.168(8).

[126] Gore v. Harris, 772 So. 2d 1243 (Fla. 2000).

[127] *Id.* at 1262.

be included in the vote total even though they were reported after the deadline of Sunday, November 26.

Just hours after the Florida Supreme Court's decision, on Friday night, December 8, a Florida trial court judge ordered that the counting of the uncounted votes commence the next morning and that it be completed by Sunday afternoon, December 9, at 2:00 P.M. The judge said that he would resolve any disputes.

On Saturday morning, counting commenced as ordered. At the same time, Bush asked the United States Supreme Court to stay the counting and grant certiorari in the case. In the early afternoon on Saturday, the United States Supreme Court, in a 5-to-4 ruling, stayed the counting of the votes in Florida.[128] Justice Stevens dissented on the grounds that there was not an irreparable injury, which is a requirement for such a stay.[129] Justice Scalia wrote a short opinion, not joined by any other Justice, in which he said that the requirements for a stay were met. He said that Bush had shown a likelihood of prevailing on the merits and also irreparable injury. Justice Scalia said that there were two such harms: First, there would be a cloud over the legitimacy of a Bush presidency if the counting showed Gore ahead, but the counting was disallowed by the Supreme Court; and second, handling of the ballots would lead to their degradation and prevent a more accurate counting later if that were ordered by the Court.[130]

On Monday, December 11, the United States Supreme Court held oral arguments. Again, they were broadcast immediately after their completion. On Tuesday night, December 12, at approximately 10:00 P.M., Eastern Standard Time, the Court released its opinion in *Bush v. Gore.*

The Decision in *Bush v. Gore*

In a per curiam opinion joined by five of the Justices, the Supreme Court ruled 5 to 4 that counting the uncounted ballots without standards denies equal protection and that counting could not continue because Florida wished to choose its electors by the December 12 "safe harbor" date set by federal law. The per curiam opinion was joined by Chief Justice Rehnquist and Justices O'Connor, Scalia, Kennedy, and Thomas. Additionally, Chief Justice Rehnquist wrote an opinion concurring in the judgment, which was joined by Justices Scalia and Thomas, arguing that the Florida Supreme Court had impermissibly changed Florida's election law in a manner that violates federal law. Each of the other four Justices wrote dissenting opinions.

The per curiam opinion began its analysis by reiterating that the right to vote is a fundamental right and that "[w]hen the state legislature vests the right to vote for President in its people, the right to vote as the legislature has prescribed is fundamental; and one source of its fundamental nature lies in the equal weight accorded to each vote and the equal dignity owed to each voter."[131]

---

[128]   Bush v. Gore, 531 U.S. 1046 (2000).
[129]   *Id.* at 1048.
[130]   *Id.* at 1047.
[131]   Bush v. Gore, 531 U.S. 98, 107 (2000).

The Court said that the central problem was that the Florida Supreme Court ordered the counting of the uncounted ballots, but failed to prescribe standards. The per curiam opinion stated: "The problem inheres in absence of specific standards to ensure its equal application. The formulation of uniform rules to determine intent based on these recurring circumstances is practicable and, we conclude, necessary."[132] The Court said that this results in similar ballots being treated differently. The Court also objected to the procedures being followed in the recount: "In addition to these difficulties the actual process by which the votes were to be counted under the Florida Supreme Court's decision raises further concerns. That order did not specify who would recount the ballots. The county canvassing boards were forced to pull together ad hoc teams comprised of judges from various Circuits who had no previous training in handling and interpreting ballots. Furthermore, while others were permitted to observe, they were prohibited from objecting during the recount."[133]

The Court thus concluded that counting the uncounted ballots pursuant to the order of the Florida Supreme Court would deny equal protection: "The recount process, in its features here described, is inconsistent with the minimum procedures necessary to protect the fundamental right of each voter in the special instance of a statewide recount under the authority of a single state judicial officer."[134] The Court was explicit that it was deciding just the matter before it and was not setting a general precedent. The per curiam opinion declared: "Our consideration is limited to the present circumstances, for the problem of equal protection in election processes generally presents many complexities."[135]

The Court then confronted the key question: Should the case be remanded to the Florida Supreme Court for it to set standards for the counting or should the Court order an end to the counting process? The Court, in its per curiam opinion, said that Florida indicated that it wished to observe the December 12 date set by federal law, which created a conclusive presumption that a state's electors chosen by that date would be recognized by Congress. The Court thus ordered an end to the counting, stating:

> The Supreme Court of Florida has said that the legislature intended the State's electors to "participat[e] fully in the federal electoral process," as provided in 3 U.S.C. §5. That statute, in turn, requires that any controversy or contest that is designed to lead to a conclusive selection of electors be completed by December 12. That date is upon us, and there is no recount procedure in place under the State Supreme Court's order that comports with minimal constitutional standards. Because it is evident that any recount seeking to meet the December 12 date will be unconstitutional for the reasons we have discussed, we reverse the judgment of the Supreme Court of Florida ordering a recount to proceed.
>
> Seven Justices of the Court agree that there are constitutional problems with the recount ordered by the Florida Supreme Court that demand a remedy. The

---

[132] *Id.*
[133] *Id.* at 110.
[134] *Id.* at 109.
[135] *Id.*

only disagreement is as to the remedy. Because the Florida Supreme Court has
said that the Florida Legislature intended to obtain the safe-harbor benefits of 3
U.S.C. §5, Justice Breyer's proposed remedy—remanding to the Florida Supreme
Court for its ordering of a constitutionally proper contest until December 18—
contemplates action in violation of the Florida election code, and hence could not
be part of an "appropriate" order authorized by Fla. Stat. §102.168(8) (2000).[136]

Thus, the per curiam ordered an end to the counting of votes in Florida based on
its interpretation of the Florida election law.

Chief Justice Rehnquist wrote a separate opinion concurring in the judgment, which was joined by Justices Scalia and Thomas. The Rehnquist opinion
focused on 3 U.S.C. §5, which provides that the state's selection of electors "shall
be conclusive, and shall govern in the counting of the electoral votes" if the electors are chosen under laws enacted prior to election day, and if the selection
process is completed six days prior to the meeting of the electoral college. Chief
Justice Rehnquist said that this prevents a state from changing its electoral process
after the election and that Florida's Supreme Court had done this by usurping the
authority Florida law had vested in the Florida secretary of state and the Florida
circuit courts. Chief Justice Rehnquist concluded that the Florida Supreme Court
"significantly departed from the statutory framework in place on November 7, and
authorized open-ended further proceedings which could not be completed by
December 12, thereby preventing a final determination by that date."[137]

Each of the other four Justices wrote dissenting opinions. Justice Stevens,
joined by Justices Ginsburg and Breyer, challenged the per curiam's premise that
there was a denial of equal protection. He argued that the procedure created by
the Florida Supreme Court, with a trial judge resolving disputes, could prevent
unequal treatment of like ballots. He explained: "Admittedly, the use of differing
substandards for determining voter intent in different counties employing similar
voting systems may raise serious concerns. Those concerns are alleviated—if not
eliminated—by the fact that a single impartial magistrate will ultimately adjudicate all objections arising from the recount process."[138]

Justice Stevens said that if the lack of standards for counting is the problem,
the solution is to send the case back to Florida for the creation of standards and
subsequent counting. He concluded his dissent with powerful language: "The
endorsement of that position by the majority of this court can only lend the cre-
dence to the most cynical appraisal of the work of judges throughout the land. It
is confidence in the men and women who administer the judicial system that is the
true backbone of the rule of law. Time will one day heal the wound to that confidence that will be inflicted by today's decision. One thing, however, is certain.
Although we may never know with complete certainty the identity of the winner of
this year's Presidential election, the identity of the loser is perfectly clear. It is the
Nation's confidence in the judge as an impartial guardian of the rule of law."[139]

[136] *Id.* at 111.
[137] *Id.* at 122 (Rehnquist, C.J., concurring in the judgment).
[138] *Id.* at 123 (Stevens, J., dissenting).
[139] *Id.* at 128.

Justice Souter's dissenting opinion, joined by the other three dissenting Justices, objected to the Court hearing the case at all. Justice Souter argued that there were no significant federal issues raised and that the case should have been left to the Florida courts to resolve.[140] Justice Ginsburg's dissent argued that there was no denial of equal protection and that in any event the appropriate solution was to have the case sent back to Florida for the counting to continue.[141]

Finally, Justice Breyer acknowledged that there were equal protection problems with counting votes without standards, but argued that the Court was wrong in ending the counting rather than remanding the case for counting with standards.[142] He stressed that there is nothing magical about the December 12 deadline; states could still choose their electors after that date and could be confident that Congress would recognize them. He ended his opinion forcefully: "I fear that in order to bring this agonizingly long election process to a definitive conclusion we have not adequately attended to that necessary 'check upon our own exercise of power,' 'our own sense of self-restraint.' Justice Brandeis once said of the Court, 'The most important thing we do is not doing.' What it does today, the Court should have left undone. I would repair the damage done as best we now can, by permitting the Florida recount to continue under uniform standards."[143]

Issues to Consider Concerning *Bush v. Gore*

There are many issues to consider regarding *Bush v. Gore*. First, was the case justiciable? Gore did not raise justiciability issues in his briefs or at oral argument. Yet justiciability is jurisdictional; the Court must raise it on its own. The question is whether Bush had standing to raise the equal protection claims of the Florida voters. Also, was the case ripe for review at the time it was decided by the United States Supreme Court? Should the Court have found that the matter was a political question and left it to Congress to ultimately resolve?[144]

Second, was the Court correct in finding a denial of equal protection? Seven of the Justices expressed concern over a denial of equal protection from counting votes without uniform standards. However, it is notable that Justices Souter and Breyer, who shared this concern with the majority, did not file opinions "concurring in part and dissenting in part," but rather just dissented. How, exactly, was equal protection denied? Also, there is the issue of whether the Court has created a new principle of equality in voting that will be the basis for future successful challenges to variations within a state in election practices.

Third, was the Court justified in ending the counting in Florida? The Court, in its per curiam opinion, said that the Florida Supreme Court had indicated that it wanted to follow the December 12 deadline set by the federal "safe harbor" statute. Since it was December 12, the Supreme Court ordered an end to the counting.

---

[140] *Id.* at 129 (Souter, J., dissenting).
[141] *Id.* at 136 (Ginsburg, J., dissenting).
[142] *Id.* at 146 (Breyer, J., dissenting).
[143] *Id.* at 158.
[144] *See* Erwin Chemerinsky, *Bush v. Gore* Was Not Justiciable, 76 Notre Dame L. Rev. 1093 (2001).

But because it was an issue of Florida state law, should the Supreme Court have remanded the case for the Florida Supreme Court to decide the content of Florida law under the unprecedented circumstances?

On December 13, 2000, the day after *Bush v. Gore* was decided, Al Gore conceded the election to George W. Bush. Rightly or wrongly, for the first time in history, the Supreme Court decided a presidential election.

§10.8.5   Racial Discrimination in Voting Rights

The Fifteenth Amendment precludes denial of the right to vote on account of race or previous condition of servitude. Race discrimination with regard to voting also receives strict scrutiny under the equal protection clause of the Fourteenth Amendment as a racial classification and as an infringement of the fundamental right to vote.

For example, any laws that would exclude a racial minority from voting are sure to be declared unconstitutional as denying equal protection. In *Nixon v. Herndon*, the Supreme Court invalidated a Texas law that excluded blacks from voting in political primary elections.[145] Subsequently, when the state attempted to stop holding political primary elections, the state delegated this task to private entities, the parties themselves. The Court concluded that this, too, was unconstitutional and ruled that because the parties were performing a public function, they had to meet the requirements of equal protection.[146]

Even laws that are facially neutral will be declared unconstitutional when they were motivated by a discriminatory purpose and have a discriminatory impact. For instance, in *Guinn v. United States*, the Supreme Court declared unconstitutional a literacy test for voting that contained a "grandfather clause" that exempted from the requirement all who could vote, and their descendants, in 1865.[147] The obvious motivation was to exclude blacks from voting, while providing an exception that benefited solely whites.

In *Gomillion v. Lightfoot*, the Court found a denial of equal protection when city borders were redrawn to exclude black voters.[148] Tuskegee, Alabama, redrew its boundaries in a manner that changed its shape from a square to a 28-sided figure. Virtually all of the African-American voters were placed outside the city. The racial discrimination was obvious and thus so was the unconstitutionality of the districting.[149]

---

[145] 273 U.S. 536 (1927).

[146] *See* Terry v. Adams, 345 U.S. 461 (1953); Smith v. Allwright, 321 U.S. 649 (1944); Nixon v. Condon, 286 U.S. 73 (1932), discussed in §6.4.4.2 (discussing holding elections for public office as a public function).

[147] 238 U.S. 347 (1915).

[148] 364 U.S. 339 (1960).

[149] *See also* Hunter v. Underwood, 471 U.S. 222 (1985) (declaring unconstitutional a state law denying the right to vote to those convicted of crimes involving moral turpitude because the law was motivated by a discriminatory purpose), discussed in §§9.3.3.2 and 10.8.2.

Two difficult questions concern whether at-large elections are unconstitutional where they have a discriminatory effect and whether the government may use race in drawing election districts to help racial minorities. The latter issue—the ability of the government to use race in districting to benefit minorities— is discussed in detail in §9.3.5.3.

At-Large Elections and Multimember Districts

At-large elections and multimember districts can have a substantial discriminatory effect. An at-large election is an election in which all of the voters cast votes for all of the officials. In other words, there are multiple representatives for a given area and each member of the electorate votes for all of them. For instance, if there is a three-person city council, the city could divide the area into three districts with each electing a representative. In contrast, in an at-large election, each voter in the city would cast three votes for members of the city council.

At-large elections can have a serious discriminatory impact. If a city using at-large elections has a white majority and has a history of racially polarized voting, the result generally will be that no black will be elected even if blacks are a substantial minority in the city. The Supreme Court has explained that "[a]t-large voting schemes and multi-member districts tend to minimize the voting strength of minority groups by permitting the political majority to elect *all* representatives of the district. A distinct minority, whether it be a racial, ethnic, economic, or political group, may be unable to elect any representatives in an at-large election; yet may be able to elect several representatives if the political unit is divided into single-member districts."[150]

However, the Supreme Court never has held that multimember legislative districts are unconstitutional per se. In *Whitcomb v. Chavis*, the Court upheld a multimember district and said that such districts are permissible unless the challenger proves that such a district "unconstitutionally operate[s] to dilute or cancel the voting strength of racial or political elements."[151]

However, in *White v. Regester*, the Court found that a multimember district violated equal protection because it discriminated against Mexican Americans.[152] The federal district court had found that "the multimember district, as designed and operated . . . invidiously excluded Mexican-Americans from effective participation in political life, specifically in the election of representatives to the Texas House of Representatives."[153] Without elaboration, the Court said that it was "not inclined to overturn these findings."[154]

---

[150] *Id.* at 616.

[151] 403 U.S. 124, 144 (1971). *See also* Wise v. Lipscomb, 437 U.S. 535 (1978) (refusing to hold that multimember districts are per se unconstitutional).

[152] 412 U.S. 755 (1973).

[153] *Id.* at 769.

[154] *Id.*

Whitcomb and *White* together established that at-large elections and multimember districts are not inherently unconstitutional, but proof of racial discrimination in the use of such an election arrangement makes it unconstitutional. These cases did not resolve what is sufficient to prove racial discrimination.

City of Mobile, Alabama v. Bolden is the key case, and it held that at-large elections and multimember districts are allowed, even if there is proof of a discriminatory impact, unless there is also proof of a discriminatory purpose.[155] Mobile, Alabama, is governed by a three-person commission, with each member chosen in an at-large election. Although blacks constituted more than 35 percent of the city, no black had been elected to the commission.[156] The long history of racially polarized voting and the at-large election system meant that the commission always was all-white.

Nonetheless, the Court found no equal protection violation. The plurality opinion reiterated the basic principle that proof of a discriminatory impact is insufficient to establish an equal protection violation;[157] there also must be proof of a discriminatory purpose. The Court said that Mobile's at-large system for electing city commissioners "violates the Fourteenth and Fifteenth Amendments only if it is motivated by a racially discriminatory purpose."[158] The plurality said that in order to demonstrate that an at-large election system denies equal protection, it must be proved that it was "conceived or operated as [a] purposeful devic[e] to further racial . . . discrimination."[159] The plurality distinguished *White v. Regester* by finding that in *White* there had been proof of invidious racial discrimination. In contrast, the plurality concluded in *Mobile* that equal protection and the Fifteenth Amendment were not violated because there was not proof of a discriminatory purpose.[160]

However, soon after *Mobile,* in *Rogers v. Lodge*, the Court found that an at-large election system was unconstitutional because there was sufficient proof of a discriminatory purpose behind the election system.[161] *Rogers* involved a challenge to an at-large election scheme for a large rural county in Georgia. The district court found that the "at-large system in Burke Country was being maintained for the invidious purpose of diluting the voting strength of the black population."[162]

The Court emphasized the fact that blacks were a substantial majority of the population in the county, yet a distinct minority of the registered voters.[163] The Court also noted that no black ever had been elected to the county commission. The Court pointed to a long history of purposeful discrimination against blacks in voting in the county including the use of poll taxes, literacy tests, and white

---

[155] 446 U.S. 55 (1980).
[156] *Id.* at 98-99 (White, J., dissenting).
[157] *See* §9.3.3.2.
[158] 446 U.S. at 62.
[159] *Id.* at 66 (citation omitted).
[160] The requirement for proof of discriminatory purpose in challenging facially neutral laws on equal protection grounds is discussed in §9.3.3.2.
[161] 458 U.S. 613 (1982).
[162] *Id.* at 622.
[163] *Id.* at 623.

primaries.[164] Furthermore, schools within the county were racially segregated until 1969 and still remained largely segregated. The Court additionally observed that blacks had been excluded from participating in the political process, in party affairs, and in primary elections. All of these factors justified the conclusion that there was a discriminatory purpose behind the at-large election system.

    Mobile v. Bolden and *Rogers v. Lodge* are consistent in that both clearly say that proof of a discriminatory purpose is required in order to challenge an at-large election scheme. But it is difficult to explain why there was not enough proof of discriminatory intent in the former, while the evidence in the latter was found to be sufficient. Both involve Southern cities with a long history of overt racial discrimination, including in voting. In neither had a black candidate been elected. But the Court saw a meaningful difference in the proof between the two cases and found only sufficient evidence of discriminatory purpose in the latter.

    The 1982 Amendments to the Voting Rights Act of 1965 largely obviated the need to distinguish the two cases and figure out what is sufficient to establish discriminatory purpose.[165] The amendment was in response to *Mobile v. Bolden* and prohibits election systems that dilute the voting power of a racial minority. In other words, the 1982 Amendments to the Voting Rights Act of 1965 eliminate the need for proof of discriminatory purpose in challenging an election system as being racially discriminatory.[166]

§10.8.6   Restrictions on Parties and Candidates

Strict Scrutiny Is Used

    A final aspect of the right to vote concerns the rights of candidates and parties to get a place on the ballot. The Supreme Court has held that strict scrutiny is appropriate for restrictions in this area. The Court observed that restrictions on access to the ballot "burden[] . . . two different, although overlapping, kinds of rights—the right of individuals to associate for the advancement of political beliefs, and the right of qualified voters, regardless of their political persuasion,

---

[164] *Id.* at 624.

[165] 42 U.S.C. §1973.

[166] *See* Johnson v. DeGrandy, 512 U.S. 997, 1000 (1994) (a court should find a violation only if the "totality of the circumstances" demonstrates that the challenged apportionment system was designed to suppress minority voting strength); Thornburg v. Gingles, 478 U.S. 30, 50-51 (1986) (articulating criteria that must be met in order to establish a prima facie case of vote dilution: (1) the minority must be sufficiently large and geographically compact as to be able to comprise a majority of a district; (2) the minority group must be shown to be "politically cohesive"; (3) racially polarized voting must be shown by demonstrating that it is likely that whites would vote as a block to defeat minority candidates). In *Bush v. Vera*, 517 U.S. 952 (1996), Justice O'Connor, in a concurring opinion, said that she believed that compliance with §2 of the Voting Rights Act was a compelling interest sufficient to permit the use of race in districting. *Id.* at 990 (O'Connor, J., concurring). This, and the use of race in districting to help minorities, is discussed in §9.3.5.3.

to cast their votes effectively. Both of these rights, of course, rank among our most precious freedoms."[167]

However, in later cases, the Court at times has refused to apply strict scrutiny. In *Clements v. Fashing*, the plurality said: "Far from recognizing candidacy as a 'fundamental right,' we have held that the existence of barriers to a candidate's access to the ballot 'does not of itself compel close scrutiny.' "[168]

Most likely, these conflicting statements can be reconciled by focusing on the degree of burden placed on ballot access. If the Court believes that a law creates a substantial barrier to ballot access, strict scrutiny will be used; but if the burden is not seen as significant, strict scrutiny is not used. In other words, substantial interference with access to the ballot warrants strict scrutiny, and the Court's declaration in *Clements* simply means that not every restriction on ballot access is deemed "substantial." In fact, in *Clements*, the Court said: "In approaching candidate restrictions, it is essential to examine in a realistic light the extent and nature of their impact on voters. In assessing challenges to state election laws that restrict access to the ballot, this Court has not formulated a 'litmus-paper test for separating those restrictions that are valid from those that are invidious under the Equal Protection Clause.' Decision in this area of constitutional adjudication is a matter of degree, and involves a consideration of the facts and circumstances behind the law, the interests the State seeks to protect by placing restrictions on candidacy, and the nature of the interests of those who may be burdened by the restrictions."[169]

Restrictions on Minor Parties and Their Candidates

Most of the cases in this area have involved restrictions on the ability of "third parties" and their candidates to gain a place on the ballot. *Williams v. Rhodes* was one of the first cases to use strict scrutiny to declare unconstitutional a state restriction.[170] An Ohio law required new political parties to meet rigorous requirements in order to qualify for the ballot for presidential elections. For example, the party had to hold a primary election that met detailed standards, obtain petitions by qualified voters that totaled 15 percent of the number of ballots cast in the last election, and file by February 7 of the election year. Established parties needed only to have received 10 percent of the vote in the last gubernatorial election.

The Court found that the restrictions failed to meet strict scrutiny and hence were unconstitutional. The state had claimed that the restrictions were necessary to preserve the two-party system. But the Court said: "The fact is, however, that the Ohio system does not merely favor a 'two-party system'; it favors two particular parties—the Republicans and Democrats—and in effect tends to give them a

---

[167] Williams v. Rhodes, 393 U.S. 23, 30 (1968).
[168] 457 U.S. 957, 963 (1982) (citations omitted).
[169] *Id.* at 963.
[170] 393 U.S. 23 (1968).

complete monopoly. There is, of course, no reason why two parties should retain a permanent monopoly on the right to have people vote for or against them."[171]

The state also claimed an interest in encouraging two parties so that the winner in an election would receive a majority of the votes and in minimizing confusion for the voters by limiting choices. The Court said that these, too, were not compelling interests. The Court concluded: "Considering these Ohio laws in their totality, this interest cannot justify the very severe restrictions on voting and associational rights which Ohio has imposed."[172]

Similarly, in *Anderson v. Celebrezze*, the Court declared unconstitutional an Ohio law that required independent candidates for president to file more than seven months before the election.[173] The Court relied primarily on the First Amendment and again said that restrictions on ballot access infringe on fundamental rights. The Court said that "[t]he right to vote is 'heavily burdened' if that vote may be cast only for major-party candidates at a time when other parties or candidates are clamoring for a place on the ballot. The exclusion of candidates also burdens voters' freedom of association, because an election campaign is an effective platform for the expression of views on the issues of the day, and a candidate serves as a rallying point for like-minded citizens."[174] The Court concluded that the early filing date substantially burdened the ability of independent candidates to qualify for the ballot and rejected the state's claim that the requirement was justified to educate voters, ensure equal treatment of all candidates, or promote political stability.

In *Illinois State Board of Elections v. Socialist Workers Party*, the Court followed these precedents and declared unconstitutional a state law that required new political parties or independent candidates to obtain the signatures of 5 percent of the number of voters who voted at the prior election in order to get on the ballot for elections for city offices.[175] The law required 25,000 signatures for such individuals or parties to have access to the ballot for statewide offices. Once more, the Court said that restrictions on access to the ballot infringe on fundamental rights and thus must be proved to be "necessary to serve a compelling interest."[176] The Court found that the law was unconstitutional because it "produced the incongruous result that a new party or an independent candidate needs substantially more signatures to gain access to the ballot than a similarly situated party or candidate for statewide office."[177]

Similar Illinois laws were declared unconstitutional in *Moore v. Ogilvie*[178] and *Norman v. Reed*.[179] *Moore* involved a state law that required independent candidates for president and vice president to obtain 25,000 signatures with at least

---

[171] *Id.* at 32.
[172] *Id.*
[173] 460 U.S. 780 (1983).
[174] *Id.* at 787-788 (citations omitted).
[175] 440 U.S. 173 (1979).
[176] *Id.* at 184.
[177] *Id.* at 176-177.
[178] 394 U.S. 814 (1969).
[179] 502 U.S. 279 (1992).

200 signatures being obtained from at least 50 of the state's 102 counties. *Norman* involved a law that required a new party to obtain at least 25,000 signatures to be on the ballot for a county election, but if there were districts within the county, 25,000 had to be obtained from each district. In both *Moore* and *Norman*, the Court used strict scrutiny and found that requiring a substantial number of signatures from differing areas was unconstitutional.

However, the Court has made it clear that not all restrictions on access to the ballot by parties and candidates are unconstitutional. In *Jenness v. Fortson*, the Court said that a state can require that a third party make a threshold showing of support in order to get on the ballot so long as the requirement is not unduly burdensome and is evenly applied.[180] The Court said that "[t]here is surely an important state interest in requiring some preliminary showing of a significant modicum of support before printing the name of a political organization's candidate on the ballot — the interest, if no other, in avoiding confusion, deception, and even frustration of the democratic process at the general election."[181] In *Jenness*, the Court upheld a requirement that a candidate for elective public office who does not win a primary election may appear on the ballot for the general election only by filing a nominating petition signed by at least 5 percent of the number of registered voters at the last general election.

In *Storer v. Brown*, the Court upheld a state law that denied ballot position in a general election to an independent candidate if he or she had registered affiliation with another political party in the year prior to the primary election and required that the candidate file petitions with signatures of at least 5 percent of the entire vote cast at the last general election.[182] The law required that signatures be obtained during a 24-day period after the primary election. The Court found the restrictions justified to achieve the compelling purpose of preserving political stability. The Court said: "A State need not take the course California has, but California apparently believes with the founding fathers that splintered parties and unrestrained factionalism may do significant damage to the fabric of government. It appears obvious to us that the one-year disaffiliation provision furthers the State's interest in the stability of its political system. We also consider that interest as not only permissible, but compelling and as outweighing the interest the candidate and his supporters may have in making a late rather than an early decision to seek independent ballot status."[183]

Likewise, in *American Party of Texas v. White*, the Court upheld a state law that allowed major parties to get on the ballot automatically if they received at least 200,000 votes in the last general election, but created detailed requirements for minor parties.[184] Parties that received less than 2 percent of the votes in the last election were required to hold precinct, county, and state nominating conventions and had to obtain signatures of at least 1 percent of the number of voters who

---

[180]   403 U.S. 431 (1971).
[181]   *Id.* at 442.
[182]   415 U.S. 724 (1974).
[183]   *Id.* at 736.
[184]   415 U.S. 767 (1974).

participated in the last gubernatorial election. The Court upheld these requirements and emphasized that they allowed minority parties a "real and essentially equal opportunity for ballot qualification."[185] Similarly, in *Monro v. Socialist Workers Party*, the Court upheld a requirement that minor party candidates receive at least 1 percent of the votes cast in order to have a place on the general election ballot.[186]

There is an obvious tension among these cases. The Court seems equivocal, if not inconsistent, as to whether limiting the number of parties or candidates on the ballot is a compelling interest. Is it a compelling interest to restrict the number of candidates so as to lessen voter confusion and to foster political stability? Cases such as *Williams* and *Anderson* seem to reject such restrictions as sufficient to meet strict scrutiny, but *Storer* and *White* appear to accept this justification. These conflicting precedents mean that courts have a great deal of discretion in evaluating restrictions on the ability of third parties to have access to the ballot. Ultimately, a court must decide if a law is a significant limit on ballot access, as in the *Williams* and *Anderson* cases, or whether it is an evenhanded requirement that does not unduly restrict access, as in the *Storer* and *White* cases.

Subsequently, the Supreme Court considered another restriction that had an adverse effect on minor party candidates: laws prohibiting candidates from running on more than one party's ticket. In *Timmons v. Twin Cities Area New Party*,[187] the Supreme Court upheld the constitutionality of a Minnesota law that prohibited such "fusion" candidates. Although the Court recognized that fusion candidates were common in early eras when there were more political parties, the Court found no constitutional problems with a state's forbidding a party listing on the ballot a candidate who was running for a different party as well.

Chief Justice Rehnquist, writing for the Court, explained that a party's right to select its own candidate does not necessarily entitle it to have its candidate listed on the ballot. The Court rejected the claim that preventing fusion candidates unduly limits the rights of minor parties. The Court said that the party still could endorse the candidate of its choice; it just could not also be separately listed on the ballot.

More important, Chief Justice Rehnquist said that even if there was an adverse effect on minor party candidates, the law still was constitutional because states have "a strong interest in the stability of their political systems. . . . The Constitution permits the Minnesota legislature to decide that political stability is best served through a healthy two-party system."[188] The Court said that while a state cannot exclude third parties, it "need not remove all of the many hurdles third parties face in the American political arena today."[189]

Justice Stevens wrote a dissenting opinion, joined by Justices Ginsburg and Souter. Justice Stevens particularly questioned the majority's conclusion that Minnesota had "weighty interests" in "ballot integrity" and "political stability."[190]

---

[185] *Id.* at 788.
[186] 479 U.S. 189 (1986).
[187] 520 U.S. 351 (1997).
[188] *Id.* at 366-367.
[189] *Id.* at 367.
[190] *Id.* at 369-370.

He said that the state's justifications were "far-fetched."[191] Justice Stevens questioned the assumption that the two-party system was vulnerable and said that "fusion candidacy is the best marriage of the virtues of the minor party challenge to entrenched viewpoints and the political stability of the two party system."[192]

Filing Fee Requirements

Another type of limit on the ability of candidates to have a place on the ballot is filing fee requirements. In *Bullock v. Carter*, the Court declared unconstitutional a state law that required payment of a substantial filing fee in order for candidates to qualify for the ballot.[193] In addition to a basic fee, there was an elaborate system of additional charges. For example, candidates for local office also had to pay a percentage of their aggregate salary. In counties with populations of 1 million or more, candidates for offices of two-year terms could be assessed up to 10 percent of their annual salary and candidates for offices of four-year terms could be assessed up to 15 percent of their aggregate annual salary. The Court noted that there were filing fees under this law as high as $8,900.[194]

The Court said that "[b]ecause the Texas filing-fee scheme has a real and appreciable impact on the exercise of the franchise, and because this impact is related to the resources of the voters supporting a particular candidate, we conclude . . . that the laws must be closely scrutinized."[195] The Court rejected the state's argument that candidates could be made to bear the costs of elections. The Court said that "[i]t seems appropriate that a primary system designed to give the voters some influence at the nominating stage should spread the cost among all of the voters in an attempt to distribute the influence without regard to wealth."[196]

The Court followed the same reasoning in *Lubin v. Panish* in declaring unconstitutional a filing fee requirement to be listed on the primary election ballot or to be a write-in candidate.[197] Specifically, a candidate for the county board of supervisors challenged a filing fee of $701.60 in order to be placed on the ballot in a primary election. The Court acknowledged the state's interest in limiting the number of candidates listed on the ballot, but it said that this could not be accomplished by filing fees. The Court stated: "Selection of candidates solely on the basis of ability to pay a fixed fee without providing any alternative means is not reasonably necessary to the accomplishment of the State's legitimate election interests. Accordingly, we hold that in the absence of reasonable alternative means of ballot access, a State may not, consistent with constitutional standards, require from an indigent candidate filing fees he cannot pay."[198]

---

[191] *Id.* at 376 (Stevens, J., dissenting).
[192] *Id.* at 380-381.
[193] 405 U.S. 134 (1972).
[194] *Id.* at 145.
[195] *Id.* at 144.
[196] *Id.* at 148.
[197] 415 U.S. 709 (1974).
[198] *Id.* at 718.

These cases indicate that only the most minimal filing fees will be allowed if there is a showing that they impede the ability of a candidate to be listed on the ballot. The underlying concern is the unfairness and inequity of denying access to the ballot to those who are too poor to pay the fee. Also, the Court believes that the state has other ways—such as those upheld in cases such as *Jenness, Storer,* and *White*—to limit the number of candidates on the ballot.

Other Restrictions on Candidacy

In *Clements v. Fashing,* the Court upheld a state law that prevented a person from running for the state legislature if he or she was currently holding office in the state as a judge, a clerk of a court, the secretary of state, or the attorney general.[199] The Court found that the waiting period imposed by not allowing current officeholders to run for other positions did not create a significant barrier to candidacy.[200] The Court said that the state had an especially important interest in keeping judges from running for other offices so as to minimize the likelihood that accusations could be made that a judicial officer made a politically motivated decision.

The Court consistently has rejected property ownership as a prerequisite for being a candidate. In *Turner v. Fouche,* the Court declared unconstitutional a state law that limited school board membership to those who owned real property.[201] The Court said that the requirement violated the "constitutional right to be considered for public service without the burden of invidiously discriminatory disqualifications."[202] Similarly, in *Quinn v. Millsap,* the Court held that the government cannot require property ownership as a prerequisite to running for and holding public office.[203] Requiring property ownership obviously is a form of wealth discrimination, and it also is a very imprecise way of measuring a person's interests or knowledge.

Finally, in *Burdick v. Takushi,* the Court upheld a state law that completely prohibited write-in votes in primary and general elections.[204] The Court stressed that the law made it possible for virtually any candidate to be listed on the ballot. For example, being listed on the primary ballot required only 15 to 25 signatures. *Burdick* cannot be read as general authorization for states to eliminate write-in votes. Such restrictions are likely to be allowed only if it is very easy for candidates to qualify for listing on the ballot.

---

[199] 457 U.S. 957 (1982).
[200] *Id.* at 967.
[201] 396 U.S. 346 (1970).
[202] *Id.* at 362.
[203] 491 U.S. 95 (1989).
[204] 504 U.S. 428 (1992).

§10.9   CONSTITUTIONAL PROTECTION FOR ACCESS TO COURTS

Protection Under Due Process and Equal Protection

The Supreme Court has spoken of "the fundamental constitutional right of access to the courts."[1] The Court long has said that the right to be heard in court is an essential aspect of due process. For example, in *Windsor v. McVeigh*, in 1876, the Court spoke of the right to be heard as a principle that "lies at the foundation of all well-ordered systems of jurisprudence" and is "founded in the first principles of natural justice."[2]

Additionally, the Court has held that discrimination among people as to access to the courts is subjected to strict scrutiny under equal protection. The Court has quoted the Magna Charta: "To no one will we sell, to no one will we refuse, or delay, right or justice. . . . No free man shall be taken or imprisoned, or . . . upon him nor send upon him, but by the lawful judgment of his peers or by the law of the land."[3] The Court has said that "[i]n this tradition, our own constitutional guaranties of due process and equal protection both call for procedures in criminal trials which allow no invidious discriminations between persons and different groups of persons."[4]

Access to the courts also is protected by specific guarantees in the Bill of Rights, most notably by the Sixth Amendment's guarantee of the right to counsel in criminal cases. In *Gideon v. Wainwright*, the Supreme Court held that this right applies to the states,[5] and subsequently the Court clarified that states are constitutionally required to provide indigent defendants an attorney in all criminal cases where there is a punishment of imprisonment.[6] In *Gideon*, the Court forcefully declared that "reason and reflection require us to recognize that in our adversary system of criminal justice, any person haled into court, who is too poor to hire a lawyer, cannot be assured a fair trial unless counsel is provided for him."[7]

Although at times the Court has spoken generally of a right of access to the courts, the decisions all have involved challenges to particular impediments. The Supreme Court has considered the scope of the right of access to the courts under due process and equal protection in three major areas: the right to appeal, challenges to filing fee requirements, and prisoners' access to the judiciary. Each is discussed in turn.

---

§10.9 [1] Bounds v. Smith, 430 U.S. 817, 828 (1977). However, as discussed below, in *Lewis v. Casey*, 518 U.S. 343 (1996), the Court substantially undercut *Bounds* by finding that there was no right to prison law libraries and that only rational basis review was to be used for restrictions on prisoners' access to the courts. *Lewis*, however, accepted *Bounds*'s statement that there is a "right of access to the courts." *Id.* at 349 (emphasis omitted).

[2] 93 U.S. 274, 277, 280 (1876). *See also* Hovey v. Elliot, 167 U.S. 409, 417 (1897).

[3] Griffin v. Illinois, 351 U.S. 12, 16-17 (1956).

[4] *Id.* at 17.

[5] 372 U.S. 335 (1963).

[6] Scott v. Illinois, 440 U.S. 367 (1979).

[7] 372 U.S. at 344.

The Right to Appeal

Neither the text of the Constitution nor the Bill of Rights mentions a right to appeal. Nor has the Supreme Court held that due process requires appellate review of criminal convictions or civil judgments.[8] But the Court has ruled that when appeals are made available, the government cannot discriminate or create barriers that limit the ability of indigents to exercise this right. Specifically, the Court has considered the government's duty to provide transcripts, to supply counsel, and to waive filing fees for indigents on appeal.

In *Griffin v. Illinois*, the Supreme Court concluded that the government must provide transcripts on appeal for indigent criminal defendants.[9] Illinois law created a right to appeal criminal convictions, but direct appellate review was available only if the defendant provided the appellate court with a bill of exceptions or a report of the trial proceedings certified by the trial judge. It sometimes was impossible to prepare such documents without a stenographic transcript of the trial proceedings. Under state law these were provided free of charge only to defendants who had been sentenced to death. *Griffin* involved a defendant who had been sentenced for armed robbery and was kept from appealing solely because he lacked the funds to pay for a transcript.

The Supreme Court did not hold that there is a constitutional right to appeal, but did say that if state law creates such a right, the state may not "den[y] the poor an adequate appellate review accorded to all who have enough money to pay the costs in advance."[10] The Court concluded that the state must purchase a stenographic transcript if the defendant could not afford one. Justice Frankfurter, in a concurring opinion, went further and declared: "The right to an appeal from a conviction for crimes today is so established that this leads to the easy assumption that it is fundamental to the protection of life and liberty and therefore a necessary ingredient of due process of law."[11]

The Court has followed *Griffin* and held that it is unconstitutional for the government to give the judge discretion as to whether indigent defendants will be given transcripts. In *Eskridge v. Washington*, the Court declared unconstitutional a Washington law that allowed trial judges to provide a free transcript if "justice will thereby be promoted."[12] The Court said that *Griffin* was controlling and that "destitute defendants must be afforded as adequate appellate review as defendants who have enough money to buy transcripts."[13] Indeed, the Court has extended the right to a free transcript for indigent defendants to petitions for a writ of habeas

---

[8] *See* McKane v. Durston, 153 U.S. 684 (1894) (state is not obligated to provide an appeal for all criminal defendants).

[9] 351 U.S. 12 (1956).

[10] *Id.* at 18.

[11] *Id.* at 20 (Frankfurter, J., concurring). In *M.L.B. v. S.L.J.*, 519 U.S. 102 (1996), the Supreme Court relied on *Griffin* to hold unconstitutional a Mississippi law that conditioned an indigent mother's right to appeal judgment terminating her parental rights on prepayment of costs. *M.L.B.* is discussed below.

[12] 357 U.S. 214, 215 (1958).

[13] *Id.* at 216 (citation omitted).

corpus[14] and to extraordinary writs in state court such as petitions for writs of error coram nobis to have convictions overturned.[15] The Court thus has concluded that indigent criminal defendants in all cases must be provided with free transcripts. The Court has explained that "*Griffin* does not represent a balance between the need of the accused and the interests of society; its principle is a flat prohibition against pricing indigent defendants out of as effective an appeal as would be available to others able to pay their own way."[16]

The Court also has found that the government must provide a free attorney to indigent defendants for their appeals, but the Court has limited this to first appeals where courts must review the case and has not extended the right to second, discretionary appeals or to collateral attacks on convictions. In *Douglas v. California*,[17] decided the same day as *Gideon v. Wainwright*,[18] the Court ruled that the government must provide indigent criminal defendants free counsel on appeal, at least for their initial appeal, which state law requires the courts of appeals to hear. The Court explained: "There is lacking that equality demanded by the Fourteenth Amendment where the rich man, who appeals as of right, enjoys the benefit of counsel's examination into the record, research of the law, and marshalling of arguments on his behalf, while the indigent, already burdened by a preliminary declaration that his case is without merit, is forced to shift for himself. The indigent, where the record is unclear or errors are hidden, has only the right to a meaningless ritual, while the rich man has a meaningful appeal."[19]

However, the Court subsequently limited this right to initial appeals that are created as a matter of right by state law, that is, appeals that state appellate courts are obligated to hear and decide. In *Ross v. Moffitt*, the Court held that the government is not required to appoint counsel for an indigent defendant's discretionary appeal to the highest state court or to the United States Supreme Court.[20] *Ross* involved a criminal defendant who was provided with an attorney for his initial appeal to the state court of appeals, but was denied an attorney to seek discretionary review in the North Carolina Supreme Court or to file a petition for writ of certiorari in the United States Supreme Court.

The Supreme Court acknowledged that the lack of an attorney is a significant disadvantage in seeking such review, but it nonetheless found no constitutional violation in the government's refusing to pay for a lawyer at these stages for indigent defendants. The Court explained: "The duty of the State under our cases is not to duplicate the legal arsenal that may be privately retained by a criminal defendant in a continuing effort to reverse his conviction, but only to assure the indigent defendant an adequate opportunity to present his claims fairly in the

---

[14] *See* Long v. District Court of Iowa, 385 U.S. 192 (1966) (holding that the government must provide a free transcript on habeas corpus to indigent criminal defendants).

[15] Lane v. Brown, 372 U.S. 477 (1963) (holding that the government must provide a free transcript to criminal defendants filing a writ of error coram nobis in state court).

[16] Mayor v. Chicago, 404 U.S. 189, 196-197 (1971).

[17] 372 U.S. 353 (1963).

[18] 372 U.S. 335 (1963).

[19] *Douglas*, 372 U.S. at 358-359.

[20] 417 U.S. 600 (1974).

context of State's appellate process. We think respondent was given that opportunity under the existing North Carolina system."[21]

Similarly, the Court has held that the government is not required to provide free counsel to indigent defendants to bring collateral attacks on their convictions, such as through writs of habeas corpus. In *Pennsylvania v. Finley*, the Court said: "We have never held that prisoners have a constitutional right to counsel when mounting collateral attacks upon their convictions and we decline to so hold today. Our cases establish that the right to appointed counsel extends to the first appeal as of right, and no further."[22] In *Murray v. Giarratano*, the Court went even further and held that the government is not required to provide indigent defendants sentenced to death with free counsel to pursue collateral attacks on their convictions and sentences.[23] The Court reiterated that the government has the constitutional duty to provide counsel to indigent defendants only for their first appeal as of right and not for discretionary appeals or for collateral attacks. The Court expressly rejected the argument that a defendant facing a death sentence is entitled to special protection on appeal.

On the one hand, the Court's distinction between initial appeals as of right and all other review of a conviction can be defended because it ensures every criminal defendant of counsel for at least one appeal. The right to meaningful appeal is thus preserved for all criminal defendants regardless of their wealth. On the other hand, in the right to counsel cases, the Court drew exactly the distinction among types of appeals that it rejected in the right to transcript cases. As reviewed above, the Court has required that the government provide free transcripts to indigent defendants for all of their appeals and collateral attacks. Moreover, if the concern is equal justice, as the Court eloquently declared in cases like *Griffin* and *Douglas*, this is not provided by denying poor defendants attorneys for discretionary appeals and collateral attacks.[24]

A final area where the Court has considered the right to appeal is in invalidating filing fees for appeals. In *Smith v. Bennett*, the Supreme Court ruled that it was unconstitutional for the government to deny a defendant the ability to file a petition for a writ of habeas corpus because he could not afford a $4 filing fee.[25] The Court broadly declared that "to interpose any financial consideration between an indigent prisoner of the State and his exercise of a state right to sue for his liberty is to deny that prisoner the equal protection of the laws."[26] The Court said that its earlier decisions, such as *Griffin*, established that "there can be no equal justice where the kind of trial a man gets depends on the amount of money he has."[27]

---

[21] *Id.* at 616.

[22] 481 U.S. 551, 555 (1987).

[23] 492 U.S. 1 (1989).

[24] For an excellent criticism of *Murray, see* Geraldine S. Moohr, *Murray v. Giarratano:* A Remedy Reduced to a Meaningless Ritual, 39 Am. U. L. Rev. 765 (1990).

[25] 365 U.S. 708 (1961).

[26] *Id.* at 709.

[27] *Id.* at 710 (citation omitted).

Filing Fees

Despite this strong statement of a right of equal access to the courts for rich and poor, the Court has been very inconsistent as to whether the government is constitutionally obligated to waive filing fees for indigent individuals in civil proceedings.[28] In fact, generally, the Court has refused to find that filing fees impermissibly violate equal protection or due process.

In *Boddie v. Connecticut*, the Supreme Court found that it was unconstitutional to deny indigent individuals access to the courts for filing a divorce petition because of their inability to pay a filing fee.[29] Connecticut law required the payment of a $60 fee in order to file a petition for divorce. The Boddies were welfare recipients who were denied the ability to file divorce papers because of their inability to afford the filing fee.

The Supreme Court held that this was unconstitutional and said that "a State may not, consistent with the obligations imposed on it by the Due Process Clause of the Fourteenth Amendment, preempt the right to dissolve this legal relationship without affording all citizens access to the means it has prescribed for doing so."[30] The Court emphasized that only the courts could grant divorce and that the defendants therefore were "faced with exclusion from the only forum effectively empowered to settle their disputes. Resort to the judicial process by these plaintiffs is no more voluntary in a realistic sense than that of the defendant called upon to defend his interests in court."[31]

The Court in *Boddie* spoke expansively of how " 'within the limits of practicability,' a State must afford to all individuals a meaningful opportunity to be heard if it is to fulfill the promise of Due Process Clause."[32] Thus, it held that the government was constitutionally obligated to waive filing fees for indigent individuals seeking a divorce.

However, in subsequent cases, the Court refused to extend *Boddie* to require a waiver of filing fees in other civil proceedings. In *United States v. Kras*, the Court held that the government was not required to waive filing fees for indigents seeking to file for bankruptcy.[33] Robert Kras was unemployed and lived in a two-room apartment with his wife, his two young children, his mother, and her child. His eight-month-old son had cystic fibrosis and had substantial medical bills. Kras's sole assets were $50 worth of clothing and essential household goods.[34] He and his family were receiving public assistance. He sought to file for bankruptcy for relief

---

[28] For an excellent review and discussion of these cases, *see* Frank Michelman, The Supreme Court and Litigation Access Fees: The Right to Protect One's Rights, Part I, 1973 Duke L.J. 1153; Part II, 1974 Duke L.J. 527; Gary Goodpaster, The Integration of Equal Protection, Due Process Standards, and the Indigent's Right of Free Access to the Courts, 56 Iowa L. Rev. 223 (1970).

[29] 401 U.S. 371 (1971).

[30] *Id.* at 383.

[31] *Id.* at 376-377.

[32] *Id.* at 379 (citation omitted).

[33] 409 U.S. 434 (1973).

[34] *See id.* at 452 (Stewart, J., dissenting).

from $6,000 in debts. He submitted an affidavit that he could not afford the $60 filing fee or promise that he could afford to pay it in installments.

The Supreme Court, however, concluded that the Constitution did not require that the government waive its filing fee for bankruptcy. The Court distinguished *Boddie* on two grounds. First, divorces relate to the constitutional right to marry; a person only could exercise that right if he or she received a divorce from an existing spouse. The Court said that "[t]he denial of access to the judicial forum in *Boddie* touched directly . . . on the marital relationship and on the associational interests that surround the establishment and dissolution of that relationship. . . . The *Boddie* appellants' inability to dissolve their marriages seriously impaired their freedom to pursue other protected associational activities. Kras's alleged interest in the elimination of his debt burden, and in obtaining his desired new start in life, although important and so recognized by enactment of the Bankruptcy Act, does not rise to the same constitutional level."[35]

Second, the Court emphasized that the state has a monopoly in granting divorces. A person wishing a divorce has no other way to get one than through the courts. But, the Court said, there are alternative ways for a person to solve the problem of debts. The Court remarked: "In contrast with divorce, bankruptcy is not the only method available to a debtor for the adjustment of his legal relationship with his creditors. . . . However unrealistic the remedy may be in a particular situation, a debtor, in theory, and often in actuality, may adjust his debts by negotiated agreement with his creditors. . . . Resort to the court, therefore, is not Kras' sole path to relief. *Boddie*'s emphasis on exclusivity finds no counterpart in the bankrupt's situation."[36]

Finally, the Court emphasized that the law allowed a person to pay the filing fee in installments of as little as $1.28 a week. The Court said that "[t]his is a sum less than the payments Kras makes on his couch of negligible value in storage, and less than the price of a movie and little more than the cost of a pack or two of cigarettes."[37]

This observation provoked an eloquent response from Justice Thurgood Marshall: "But no one who has had close contact with poor people can fail to understand how close to the margin of survival many of them are. A sudden illness, for example, may destroy whatever savings they have accumulated, and by eliminating a sense of security may destroy the incentive to save in the future. A pack or two of cigarettes may be, for them, not a routine purchase but a luxury indulged in only rarely. The desperately poor almost never go to see a movie, which the majority seems to believe is an almost weekly activity. They have more important things to do with what little money they have—like attempting to provide some comforts for a gravely ill child, as Kras must do."[38] Justice Marshall stated: "It is perfectly proper for judges to disagree about what the Constitution requires. But

---

[35]   *Id.* at 444-445 (citations omitted).
[36]   *Id.* at 445-446.
[37]   *Id.* at 449.
[38]   *Id.* at 460 (Marshall, J., dissenting).

it is disgraceful for an interpretation of the Constitution to be premised upon unfounded assumptions about how people live."[39]

In *Ortwein v. Schwab*, the Court followed the reasoning in *Kras* and held that the government was not obligated to waive filing fees for judicial review of adverse welfare decisions.[40] An individual sought judicial review of a reduction in his welfare benefits, but he could not afford the $25 filing fee. The Supreme Court found no violation of due process or equal protection in precluding judicial review because of the inability to pay the fee. The Court relied on *Kras* and again distinguished *Boddie* on the ground that a denial or reduction in welfare benefits did not implicate constitutional rights. Interestingly, in *Ortwein*, like in *Boddie*, the state had a monopoly for resolving disputes: Only judicial review could reverse the denial of welfare benefits. Nonetheless, the Court found no constitutional violation in denying judicial review because of an inability to pay the filing fee.

Although *Boddie* and *Ortwein* make it very difficult to challenge filing fee requirements, it is still possible in areas where fundamental rights are at issue and where the state has a monopoly in providing redress. In *M.L.B. v. S.L.J.*, the Supreme Court declared unconstitutional a state requirement that parents pay a fee for preparation of the trial record in order to appeal a termination of custody.[41] A Mississippi court entered an order permanently terminating a mother's custody of her child. The mother sought to appeal from the termination decree, but Mississippi required that she pay in advance record preparation fees estimated at $2,352.36. Because she lacked funds to pay the fees, her appeal was dismissed.

The Court, in an opinion by Justice Ginsburg, found this unconstitutional. Justice Ginsburg began by stressing the fundamental rights involved: "Choices about marriage, family life, and the upbringing of children are among associational rights this Court has ranked as 'of basic importance in our society,' rights sheltered by the Fourteenth Amendment against the State's unwarranted usurpation, disregard, or disrespect."[42]

The Court noted that access to the courts, as reflected in prior decisions, embodied "both equal protection and due process concerns."[43] The Court said that generally access fees only have to meet rational basis review, but that there is an exception in that "access to judicial processes in cases criminal or 'quasi criminal in nature,' [may not] turn on ability to pay."[44] The Court said that proceedings to permanently terminate parental custody fit into the latter category because "termination adjudications involve the awesome authority of the State 'to destroy permanently all legal recognition of the parental relationship.'"[45] Thus, the imposition of costs for the record preparation was declared unconstitutional.

---

[39] *Id.*
[40] 410 U.S. 656 (1973).
[41] 519 U.S. 102 (1996).
[42] 519 U.S. at 117.
[43] *Id.*
[44] *Id.*
[45] *Id.*

Even after *M.L.B.*, it is unlikely that the Court will find such a right in many other instances; if there is not a right to fee waivers for indigents seeking bankruptcy or appealing a denial of welfare benefits it is hard to imagine many situations where the Constitution requires a fee waiver. *Boddie* has been narrowly construed to create a right to fee waivers only in cases raising issues related to constitutional rights. *Kras* and *Ortwein* therefore are powerful precedents casting doubt on any general right of access to the courts.[46]

Prisoners' Right of Access to the Courts

One area, though, where, the Court previously had been protective of a right of access to the courts is for prisoners. In *Ex parte Hull*, the Court said that "the state and its officers may not abridge or impair petitioner's right to apply to a federal court for a writ of habeas corpus."[47] In *Hull*, the Court declared unconstitutional actions by prison officials in repeatedly seizing and destroying habeas corpus petitions prepared by a prison inmate.

In *Johnson v. Avery*, the Supreme Court declared unconstitutional a state prison regulation that provided that no inmate could advise or assist another inmate in preparing writs or giving legal assistance.[48] The Court said that unless the state provides reasonable alternatives in assisting inmates with postconviction proceedings, it may not enforce a regulation that bars inmates from assisting other prisoners. The Court said that "the basic purpose of the writ is to enable those unlawfully incarcerated to obtain their freedom[;] it is fundamental that access of prisoners to the courts for the purpose of presenting their complaints may not be denied or obstructed."[49]

The Court followed this reasoning in *Procunier v. Martinez* and declared unconstitutional a prison regulation that prevented law students and paralegals from conducting attorney-client interviews with clients.[50] The Court said that "[t]he Constitutional Protection for Access to Courts constitutional guarantee of due process of law has as a corollary the requirement that prisoners be afforded access to the courts in order to challenge unlawful convictions and to seek redress for violations of their opportunity to seek and receive the assistance of attorneys."[51] The Court concluded that the state had no interest in barring all law students and paralegals from the prison.

In *Bounds v. Smith*, the Court extended this reasoning and held that prisons were obligated to provide law library facilities and appropriate supplies to

[46] For criticism of these decisions, *see* Gay Gellhorn, Justice Thurgood Marshall's Jurisprudence of Equal Protection of the Laws and the Poor, 26 Ariz. St. L.J. 429 (1994); Karen Gross & Shari Rosenberg, In Forma Pauperis in Bankruptcy: Reflections on and Beyond *United States v. Kras*, 2 Am. Bankr. Inst. L. Rev. 57 (1994).

[47] 312 U.S. 546, 549 (1941).

[48] 393 U.S. 483 (1969).

[49] *Id.* at 485.

[50] 416 U.S. 396 (1974).

[51] *Id.* at 419.

inmates.[52] The Court said that the government has the affirmative obligation to provide prisoners with facilities that can facilitate access to the courts. The Court said: "[T]he fundamental constitutional right of access to the courts requires prison authorities to assist inmates in the preparation and filing of meaningful legal papers by providing prisoners with adequate assistance from persons trained in the law."[53] It is notable that the Court spoke explicitly of a "fundamental constitutional right of access to the courts."

Thus, the Court in *Bounds* said that prisons must provide inmates with adequate law libraries or adequate assistance from persons trained in the law.[54] The Court said that prior "decisions have consistently required States to shoulder affirmative obligations to assure all prisoners meaningful access to the courts. It is indisputable that indigent inmates must be provided at state expense with paper and pen to draft legal documents, with notarial services to authenticate them, and with stamps to mail them."[55] The Court rejected the argument that prisoners were incapable of effectively using law libraries. The Court concluded: "We hold, therefore, that the fundamental constitutional right of access to the courts requires prison authorities to assist inmates in the preparation and filing of meaningful legal papers by providing prisoners with adequate law libraries or adequate assistance from persons trained in the law."[56]

In *Lewis v. Casey*,[57] however, the Court narrowed, and even repudiated, parts of *Bounds v. Smith*. A federal district court in Arizona found systematic inadequacies in the law libraries and legal assistance available to prisoners including the failure to adequately update legal materials, the unavailability of photocopiers, the lack of access to law libraries for "lock-down prisoners," and the inadequacy of legal assistance for illiterate and non-English-speaking inmates.[58] An injunction was entered to remedy these inadequacies and was affirmed on appeal by the United States Court of Appeals for the Ninth Circuit.

The Supreme Court, in an opinion by Justice Scalia, reversed. First, the Court ruled that "in order to establish a violation of *Bounds*, an inmate must show that the alleged inadequacies of a prison's library facilities or legal assistance program caused him 'actual injury'—that is, 'actual prejudice with respect to contemplated or existing litigation, such as the inability to meet a filing deadline or to present a claim.'"[59] In other words, the Court specifically rejected the view that *Bounds* created a right of access to law libraries for prisoners.[60] Indeed, the Court said that the language in *Bounds* that spoke of a "right of access to the courts [has] no

---

[52] 430 U.S. 817 (1977).
[53] *Id.* at 828.
[54] *Id.*
[55] *Id.* at 824-825.
[56] *Id.* at 828.
[57] 518 U.S. 343 (1996).
[58] *Id.* at 344-345.
[59] *Id.* at 348 (citation omitted).
[60] *Id.* at 349.

antecedent in our pre-*Bounds* cases, and we now disclaim them."[61] The Court concluded that the inmates lacked standing because they failed to demonstrate the requisite injuries from the inadequacy of the prison's law library.[62]

Second, the Court said that the system-wide relief contained in the district court's injunction was unjustified. Justice Scalia concluded that the trial court "failed to accord adequate deference to the judgment of the prison authorities."[63] The Court emphasized that the right of access for prisoners, like all prisoners' rights, is evaluated under rational basis review; that is, "a prison regulation impinging on inmates' constitutional rights 'is valid if it is reasonably related to legitimate penological interests.' "[64] Justice Scalia said that it was reasonable for the prison to restrict access to legal materials for inmates in "lockdown" because of security concerns.[65] Also, Scalia objected to the breadth of the district court's injunction and said that the process used by the district court offended "comity" and "a model of what should not" be done.[66]

Lewis v. Casey dramatically undermines *Bounds v. Smith*. Whereas *Bounds* spoke of a fundamental right of access to the courts for prisoners, *Lewis* says that only rational basis review is to be used. While *Bounds* broadly declares a right of access to the courts for prisoners, *Lewis* disavows that language. *Bounds* creates a right of access to law libraries for prisoners, but *Lewis* expressly repudiates such a right and says that the prisoner must show an actual, specific injury to not having adequate access to the courts.

After *Lewis v. Casey*, prisoners still have the right to use the courts to remedy their grievances and challenge their convictions and sentences, but the right is only minimally protected. The inmate will need to demonstrate that the barrier to access directly prevented adequate relief. Even then, the prison can prevail by meeting the rational basis test.

Lewis v. Casey is thus consistent with the current Supreme Court's increased hostility to prisoners' claims.[67] But *Lewis* also is very troubling in that it likely will leave many prisoners without meaningful access to the courts. The Court's focus on standing means that in order for a prisoner to sue he or she likely will need to meet the almost impossible burden of showing that he or she would have won in court if only better law library facilities had been available.

[61] *Id.* at 354.
[62] Standing is discussed in detail in §2.5.
[63] 518 U.S. at 361.
[64] *Id.*, quoting Turner v. Safley, 482 U.S. 78, 89 (1987).
[65] *Id.*
[66] *Id.* at 362.
[67] *See* discussion in §7.3.3.

§10.10   THE SECOND AMENDMENT RIGHT TO BEAR ARMS

There long has been a debate about the meaning of the Second Amendment, which provides: "A well regulated Militia being necessary to the security of a free State, the right of the people to keep and bear Arms, shall not be infringed." One side of the debate sees the latter clause as being key and interprets the Second Amendment as creating an individual right to possess firearms. The other side of the debate emphasizes the first clause and says that it is a right only for purposes of service in the militia.

From 1791, when the Second Amendment was ratified, until 2008, the Supreme Court never had found any law regulating possession of firearms to be unconstitutional. In the handful of cases dealing with the Second Amendment, the Court held that it protected a right of individuals to have firearms for the purpose of militia service. For example, in *United States v. Miller*, the Supreme Court expressly declared that the Second Amendment was limited to safeguarding possessing of firearms for militia service.[1] The Court upheld a federal law prohibiting possessing sawed-off shotguns by explaining that they were not weapons used in militia service at the time the Bill of Rights was ratified. The Court was clear that it believed that the Second Amendment was about protecting a right to have firearms for militia service. The Court said: "With obvious purpose to assure the continuation and render possible the effectiveness of such forces the declaration and guarantee of the Second Amendment were made. It must be interpreted and applied with that end in view. . . . The signification attributed to the term Militia appears from the debates in the Convention, the history and legislation of Colonies and States, and the writings of approved commentators."[2]

However, in 2008, in *District of Columbia v. Heller*, the Court for the first time invalidated a law regulating guns and found that the Second Amendment is not limited to protecting a right to have firearms for militia service.[3] The case concerned the constitutionality of a 32-year-old District of Columbia ordinance that prohibited possession of handguns and imposed significant restrictions on long guns. The Supreme Court, in a 5-4 decision, invalidated the ordinance as violating the Second Amendment.

Not surprisingly, the Court split along ideological lines with Justice Scalia's opinion being joined by Chief Justice Roberts and Justices Kennedy, Thomas, and Alito. Justices Stevens and Breyer wrote dissenting opinions, which were joined by Justices Souter and Ginsburg.

Justice Scalia began with the text of the Second Amendment and said that it had a prefatory clause, concerning militias, and an operative clause, about the right to bear arms. He said that a prefatory clause cannot negate an operative clause. He wrote: "The Second Amendment is naturally divided into two parts: its prefatory clause and its operative clause. The former does not limit the latter

---

§10.10 [1] 307 U.S. 174 (1939).
[2] *Id.* at 178.
[3] 554 U.S. 570 (2008).

grammatically, but rather announces a purpose."[4] Justice Scalia carefully traced the history of gun rights in England and the states prior to the ratification of the Constitution. He said: "We therefore believe that the most likely reading of all four of these pre-Second Amendment state constitutional provisions is that they secured an individual right to bear arms for defensive purposes."[5] Justice Scalia then looked at the postratification commentary, the pre–Civil War cases, the post–Civil War legislation and cases, and said that all of these confirm that the Second Amendment was not meant to be limited to a right to have firearms for militia service.

The Court concluded by declaring: "We are aware of the problem of handgun violence in this country, and we take seriously the concerns raised by the many *amici* who believe that prohibition of handgun ownership is a solution. The Constitution leaves the District of Columbia a variety of tools for combating that problem, including some measures regulating handguns. But the enshrinement of constitutional rights necessarily takes certain policy choices off the table. These include the absolute prohibition of handguns held and used for self-defense in the home. Undoubtedly some think that the Second Amendment is outmoded in a society where our standing army is the pride of our Nation, where well-trained police forces provide personal security, and where gun violence is a serious problem. That is perhaps debatable, but what is not debatable is that it is not the role of this Court to pronounce the Second Amendment extinct."[6]

Justice Stevens wrote a dissent, joined by Justices Souter, Ginsburg, and Breyer, which just as carefully traced the history of the Second Amendment and came to an opposite conclusion: that it creates a right to have firearms for the purpose of militia service.[7] Justice Stevens, too, focused on the text and accused the majority of ignoring the first half of the Second Amendment and reading it as if it said, "The right of the people to keep and bear arms shall not be infringed." He said that James Madison drafted the Second Amendment, as with all of the Bill of Rights, and the initial draft including an exemption from militia service for conscientious objectors, confirming that it was about a right to have arms for militia service. Justice Stevens reviewed the same sources as Justice Scalia—English history, the experience in the states, the postratification commentary—and concluded that they lead to an opposite conclusion. Justice Stevens gave great weight to precedent and the fact that all prior decisions of the Court concerning the Second Amendment found that it protected only a right to have guns for the purpose of militia service.

Justice Stevens concluded his dissent by stating: "The Court properly disclaims any interest in evaluating the wisdom of the specific policy choice challenged in this case, but it fails to pay heed to a far more important policy choice—the choice made by the Framers themselves. The Court would have us believe that over 200 years ago, the Framers made a choice to limit the tools available to elected officials

----

[4] *Id.* at 577.
[5] *Id.* at 602.
[6] *Id.* at 636.
[7] *Id.* at 636 (Stevens, J., dissenting).

wishing to regulate civilian uses of weapons, and to authorize this Court to use the common-law process of case-by-case judicial lawmaking to define the contours of acceptable gun-control policy. Absent compelling evidence that is nowhere to be found in the Court's opinion, I could not possibly conclude that the Framers made such a choice."[8]

Justice Breyer wrote a separate dissent, joined by all of the dissenting Justices, in which he argued that a reasonableness test should be used for the Second Amendment and that the District of Columbia ordinance was reasonable in light of the problem of handgun violence in the United States. He wrote: "[The] District's decision represents the kind of empirically based judgment that legislatures, not courts, are best suited to make. In fact, deference to legislative judgment seems particularly appropriate here, where the judgment has been made by a local legislature, with particular knowledge of local problems and insight into appropriate local solutions."[9]

The key question after *Heller* is what level of scrutiny should be used for this right. The Court did not say. Justice Scalia, writing for the majority, stated: "Under any of the standards of scrutiny that we have applied to enumerated constitutional rights, banning from the home 'the most preferred firearm in the nation to "keep" and use for protection of one's home and family,' would fail constitutional muster."[10] In a footnote, he indicated that more than rational basis review would be appropriate but did not elaborate beyond that as to the appropriate level of scrutiny.[11]

The Court was clear that the Second Amendment is not absolute. Justice Scalia wrote: "Like most rights, the right secured by the Second Amendment is not unlimited. From Blackstone through the 19th-century cases, commentators and courts routinely explained that the right was not a right to keep and carry any weapon whatsoever in any manner whatsoever and for whatever purpose. . . . Although we do not undertake an exhaustive historical analysis today of the full scope of the Second Amendment, nothing in our opinion should be taken to cast doubt on longstanding prohibitions on the possession of firearms by felons and the mentally ill, or laws forbidding the carrying of firearms in sensitive places such as schools and government buildings, or laws imposing conditions and qualifications on the commercial sale of arms."[12]

Because the District of Columbia is a part of the federal government, the Court had no occasion to consider whether the Second Amendment applies to state and local governments. In the nineteenth century, the Court had ruled that the Second Amendment applies only to the federal government.[13] Immediately following *Heller*, the National Rifle Association and others filed lawsuits in federal

---

[8] *Id.* at 680.
[9] *Id.* at 705 (Breyer, J., dissenting).
[10] *Id.* at 628-629.
[11] *Id.* at 628 n.27.
[12] *Id.* at 626-627.
[13] *See, e.g.,* United States v. Cruikshank, 92 U.S. 542 (1876).

court challenging local gun control laws so as to present the issue to the Supreme Court of whether the Second Amendment applies to state and local governments.

In *McDonald v. City of Chicago*, the Supreme Court ruled that the Second Amendment applies to state and local governments.[14] Once more, the Court was split exactly along ideological lines. Justice Samuel Alito wrote for the Court and was joined by Chief Justice Roberts and Justices Scalia, Kennedy, and Thomas. Justices Stevens, Ginsburg, Breyer, and Sotomayor dissented.

The case involved ordinances adopted by Chicago and Oak Park, Illinois. Oak Park, Illinois, has an ordinance that makes it "unlawful for any person to possess . . . any firearm," a term that includes "pistols, revolvers, guns and small arms . . . commonly known as handguns."[15] A Chicago ordinance provides that "[n]o person shall . . . possess . . . any firearm unless such person is the holder of a valid registration certificate for such firearm."[16] Chicago law also prohibits registration of most handguns, thus effectively banning handgun possession by almost all private citizens who reside in the city. It is important, therefore, to note that in both *Heller* and *McDonald*, the Court focused only on laws that prohibit virtually all possession of handguns. The Court had no occasion to consider the constitutionality of more limited regulations.

The five Justices in the majority split 4-1 as to the constitutional approach that the Court should use in applying the Second Amendment to state and local governments. Justice Alito, joined by Chief Justice Roberts and Justices Scalia and Kennedy, found that the Second Amendment is incorporated into the due process clause of the Fourteenth Amendment. Justice Alito carefully reviewed the history of the application of the Bill of Rights to the states and how almost all of its provisions have been found to apply to state and local governments through the process of incorporation. The plurality concluded that the Second Amendment was likewise a right that should be found to apply to state and local governments through incorporation into the due process clause.

Justice Thomas concurred in the judgment as to this part of the decision and said that he would find that the Second Amendment applies to state and local governments through the privileges or immunities clause of the Fourteenth Amendment.[17] Justice Alito, writing for the plurality, rejected this and relied solely on due process.

The most important implication of the case is the obvious one: Now state and local gun control laws, including state and local tort liability for gun manufacturers and dealers, can be challenged on Second Amendment grounds. Until *McDonald*, such constitutional claims were not possible.

However, it is important to recognize that *McDonald*, like *Heller* two years earlier, did not recognize an absolute right, and left open the possibility of significant

---

[14] 130 S. Ct. 3020 (2010).

[15] Oak Park, Ill., Municipal Code §§27-2-1 (2007), 27-1-1 (2009).

[16] Chicago, Ill., Municipal Code §8-20-040(a) (2009).

[17] *McDonald*, 130 S. Ct. at 3058 (Thomas, J., concurring in part and concurring in the judgment in part).

regulation and liability. In both *McDonald* and *Heller*, the Court emphasized that it had found a right to have firearms in one's home for the purpose of personal safety. In *Heller*, the Court stressed "the need for defense of self, family, and property is most acute" in the home, and found a Second Amendment right to possess handguns because they are "the most preferred firearm in the nation to 'keep' and use for protection of one's home and family."[18] Justice Alito echoed this view in *McDonald*.

Moreover, in both cases, the Court stressed that the government can regulate firearms, including by keeping them from places such as airports and schools. The Court said that the government also can regulate who may possess firearms, such as in laws denying possession to those with a prior felony conviction or a history of serious mental illness.[19] Thus, the Court in *McDonald* stated: "We repeat those assurances here. Despite municipal respondents' doomsday proclamations, incorporation does not imperil every law regulating firearms."[20]

The key question left unanswered in both decisions concerns the level of scrutiny to be used for Second Amendment challenges. As of December 2014, the federal courts of appeals are split as to whether it should be strict scrutiny, intermediate scrutiny, or some form of "interest balancing" test.[21] Undoubtedly, the outcome of many Second Amendment challenges will depend on this unresolved question.

§10.11   CONSTITUTIONAL PROTECTION FOR A RIGHT TO EDUCATION

The Supreme Court has refused to recognize a fundamental right to education. In *San Antonio Independent School District v. Rodriguez*, the Supreme Court expressly rejected the claim that education is a fundamental right.[1] *Rodriguez* involved a challenge to the Texas system of funding public schools largely through

---

[18] 554 U.S. at 628.

[19] *Id.*

[20] 130 S. Ct. at 3048.

[21] *See, e.g.*, Tyler v. Hillsdale County Sheriff's Dept., 775 F.3d 308 (6th Cir. Dec. 18, 2014) (applying strict scrutiny); United States v. Booker, 644 F.3d 12, 25 (1st Cir. 2011) (applying intermediate scrutiny); United States v. Chester (*Chester II*), 628 F.3d 673, 683 (4th Cir. 2010) ("[W]e conclude that intermediate scrutiny is more appropriate than strict scrutiny for Chester and similarly situated persons."); NRA v. ATF (*NRA I*), 700 F.3d 185, 195 (5th Cir. 2012) ("[T]he appropriate level of scrutiny depends on the nature of the conduct being regulated and the degree to which the challenged law burdens the right.").

§10.11 [1] 411 U.S. 1 (1973).

local property taxes. Texas's financing system meant that poor areas had to tax at a high rate, but had little to spend on education; wealthier areas could tax at low rates, but still had much more to spend on education. For example, one poorer district spent $356 per pupil, while a wealthier district spent $594 per student.[2]

The plaintiffs challenged this system on two grounds: It violated equal protection as impermissible wealth discrimination, and it denied the fundamental right to education. The Court rejected the former argument by holding that poverty is not a suspect classification and that therefore discrimination against the poor only need meet rational basis review.[3]

Moreover, the Court rejected the claim that education is a fundamental right. The Court said: "It is not the province of this Court to create substantive constitutional rights in the name of guaranteeing equal protection of the laws. Thus, the key to discovering whether education is 'fundamental' is not to be found in comparisons of the relative social significance of education as opposed to subsistence or housing. Nor is it to be found by weighing whether education is as important as the right to travel. Rather, the answer lies in assessing whether there is a right to education explicitly or implicitly guaranteed by the Constitution."[4] Justice Powell, writing for the majority, then concluded: "Education, of course, is not among the rights afforded explicit protection under our Federal Constitution. Nor do we find any basis for saying it is implicitly so protected."[5]

Although education obviously is inextricably linked to the exercise of constitutional rights such as freedom of speech and voting, the Court nonetheless decided that education, itself, is not a fundamental right. The Court said: "[T]he logical limitations on appellees' nexus theory are difficult to perceive. How, for instance, is education to be distinguished from the significant personal interests in the basics of decent food and shelter? Empirical examination might well buttress an assumption that the ill-fed, ill-clothed, and ill-housed are among the most ineffective participants in the political process, and that they derive the least enjoyment from the benefits of the First Amendment."[6] The Court also noted that the government did not completely deny an education to students; the challenge was to inequities in funding.[7]

The Court concluded that strict scrutiny was inappropriate because there was neither discrimination based on a suspect classification nor infringement of a fundamental right. The Court found that the Texas system for funding schools met the rational basis test.

In *Kadrmas v. Dickinson Public Schools*, the Court reaffirmed that education is not a fundamental right under the equal protection clause.[8] *Kadrmas* involved a

---

[2] *Id.* at 12-13.
[3] *Id.* at 28-29. The equal protection aspect of *Rodriguez* is more fully discussed in §9.7.3.
[4] *Id.* at 33.
[5] *Id.* at 35.
[6] *Id.* at 37.
[7] *Id.* at 39.
[8] 487 U.S. 450 (1988).

challenge brought by a poor family to a state law authorizing local school systems to charge a fee for use of school buses. The Court again reiterated that poverty is not a suspect classification and that discrimination against the poor only has to meet rational basis review.[9] The Court said that education was not denied because the fee did not preclude the student from attending school. Hence, the Court said that rational basis review was appropriate and concluded that the plaintiffs "failed to carry the 'heavy burden' of demonstrating the challenged statute is both arbitrary and irrational."[10]

Although the Court never has held that there is a fundamental right to education, the Court has recognized education's importance. In *Plyler v. Doe*, the Supreme Court declared unconstitutional a Texas law that provided a free public education to citizens and to children of documented immigrants, but required undocumented immigrants to pay for their public education.[11] The Court ruled that the law denied equal protection and, in part, based this conclusion on the importance of education. Justice Brennan, writing for the Court, stated: "Public education is not a 'right' granted to individuals by the Constitution. But neither is it merely some governmental 'benefit' indistinguishable from other forms of social welfare legislation. Both the importance of education in maintaining our basic institutions, and the lasting impact of its deprivation on the life of the child, mark the distinction. . . . [E]ducation provides the basic tools by which individuals might lead economically productive lives to the benefit of us all. In sum, education has a fundamental role in maintaining the fabric of our society."[12]

The Court emphasized the great harms to children if they are denied an education. The Court also stressed the unfairness of penalizing children because of the choices made by their parents. Thus, without declaring education to be a fundamental right or using strict scrutiny, the Court invalidated the Texas law.

The Court's refusal to find a fundamental right to education is consistent with its general unwillingness to hold that there are constitutional rights to affirmative services provided by the government. But there is a strong argument that education is different; education is essential for the exercise of constitutional rights, for economic opportunity, and ultimately for achieving equality. Chief Justice Warren eloquently expressed this view in *Brown v. Board of Education*: "Today, education is perhaps the most important function of state and local governments. Compulsory school attendance laws and the great expenditures for education both demonstrate our recognition of the importance of education to our democratic society. It is required in the performance of our most basic public responsibilities, even service in the armed forces. It is the very foundation of good citizenship. Today it is a principal instrument in awakening the child to cultural values, in preparing him for later professional training, and in helping him to adjust normally to

---

[9] *Id.* at 458.
[10] *Id.* at 463 (citation omitted).
[11] 457 U.S. 202 (1982). *Plyler* is discussed in more detail in §9.5.5.
[12] *Id.* at 221 (citation omitted).

his environment. In these days, it is doubtful that any child may reasonably be expected to succeed in life if he is denied the opportunity of an education."[13]

In fact, several state courts have found a fundamental right to education under their state constitutions and have concluded that inequities in school funding are impermissible as a matter of state constitutional law.[14] Perhaps someday the Supreme Court will revisit *Rodriguez* and come to the same conclusion.

[13] 347 U.S. 483, 493 (1954).
[14] *See, e.g.*, Serrano v. Priest, 557 P.2d 929 (Cal. 1977); Abbott v. Burke, 575 A.2d 359 (N.J. 1990); Tennessee Small School Sys. v. McWherter, 851 S.W.2d 139 (Tenn. 1993); McDuffy v. Secretary of Educ., 615 N.E.2d 516 (Mass. 1993); Rose v. Council for Better Educ., 790 S.W.2d 186 (Ky. 1989); Edgewood Indep. School Dist. v. Kirby, 777 S.W.2d 391 (Tex. 1989).

CHAPTER 11

First Amendment: Expression

§11.1   INTRODUCTION

The First Amendment states: "Congress shall make no law respecting an establishment of religion, or prohibiting the free exercise thereof; or abridging the freedom of speech, or of the press; or the right of the people peaceably to assemble, and to petition the Government for a redress of grievances." The next chapter, Chapter 12, considers the religion clauses. This chapter focuses on the other provisions of the First Amendment, all of which concern aspects of freedom of expression.

§11.1.1   Historical Background

Reaction Against English Restrictions

The First Amendment undoubtedly was a reaction against the suppression of speech and of the press that existed in English society. Until 1694, there was an elaborate system of licensing in England, and no publication was allowed without a government-granted license. Blackstone, in his famous commentaries on the law, remarked that "[t]he liberty of the press consists in laying no *previous* restraints upon publications, and not in freedom from censure for criminal matter when published. . . . [To] subject the press to the restrictive power of a licenser . . . is to subject all freedom of sentiment to the prejudices of one man, and make him the arbitrary and infallible judge of all controverted points in learning, religion, and government."[1] It is widely accepted that the First Amendment was meant, at the very least, to abolish such prior restraints on publication.[2]

---

§11.1 [1] 4 William Blackstone, Commentaries on the Law of England, 151-152 (1769) (emphasis in original).

[2] Some have contended that this was all the First Amendment was meant to do. *See, e.g.*, Patterson v. Colorado, 205 U.S. 454, 462 (1907) ("the main purpose of such constitutional provisions is 'to prevent all such *previous restraints* upon publications as had been practiced by other governments,'

Speech in England also was restricted by the law of seditious libel that made criticizing the government a crime.[3] The English Court of the Star Chamber announced the principle that the King was above public criticism and that, therefore, statements critical of the government were forbidden. Chief Justice Holt, writing in 1704, explained the perceived need for the prohibition of seditious libel: "If people should not be called to account for possessing the people with an ill opinion of the government, no government can subsist. For it is very necessary for all governments that the people should have a good opinion of it."[4] Truth was not a defense to the crime because the goal was to prevent and punish all criticism of the government; if anything, true speech was perceived as worse because it might do more to damage the image and reputation of the government. Professor Zechariah Chaffee said that "the First Amendment was . . . intended to wipe out the common law of sedition, and make further prosecutions for criticism of the government, without any incitement to law-breaking, forever impossible in the United States of America."[5]

Colonial Experience

The record for protection of freedom of speech in the colonies was mixed. There were fewer prosecutions for seditious libel than in England during the time period, but there were other controls, formal and informal, over dissident speech. Professor Levy said that each community "tended to be a tight little island clutching its own respective orthodoxy and . . . eager to banish or extralegally punish unwelcome dissidents."[6]

Of the prosecutions that occurred for seditious libel, the most famous was the trial of John Peter Zenger in 1735 for publishing criticisms of the governor of New York. Zenger's lawyer argued that truth should be a defense to the crime of seditious libel. Although the court rejected this argument, Zenger's lawyer persuaded the jury to disregard the law and to acquit Zenger.[7]

Purposes of the First Amendment

There is thus little doubt that the First Amendment was meant to prohibit licensing of publication such as existed in England and to forbid punishment for seditious libel. Beyond this, though, there is little indication of what the framers

---

and they do not prevent the subsequent punishment of such as may be deemed contrary to the public welfare") (emphasis in original). Professor Leonard Levy initially argued that the purpose of the First Amendment was solely to prohibit prior restraints, Leonard W. Levy, Legacy of Suppression (1960), but later changed his mind and argued for a broader intent behind the First Amendment. See Leonard W. Levy, Emergence of a Free Press (1985).

[3] A classic history of the First Amendment, which reviews this background, is Zechariah Chaffee, Jr., Free Speech in the United States (1941).

[4] 14 Thomas Howell, A Collection of State Trials 1095, 1128 (1704).

[5] Chaffee, *supra* note 3, at 21.

[6] Leonard Levy, The Emergence of a Free Press 16 (1985).

[7] *See* Vincent Buranelli, The Trial of Peter Zenger (1957).

intended. Certainly, nothing in the historical record sheds light on most of the free speech issues that face society and the courts in the twenty-first century. Professor Rodney Smolla remarked that "[o]ne can keep going round and round on the original meaning of the First Amendment, but no clear, consistent vision of what the framers meant by freedom of speech will ever emerge."[8]

In fact, ascertaining the framers' intent is made more difficult by the fact that Congress in 1798—with many of the Constitution's drafters and ratifiers participating—adopted the Alien and Sedition Acts of 1798.[9] The law prohibited the publication of "false, scandalous, and malicious writing or writings against the government of the United States, or either house of the Congress of the United States, or the President of the United States, with intent to defame . . . ; or to bring them . . . into contempt or disrepute; or to excite against them . . . hatred of the good people of the United States, or to stir up sedition within the United States, or to excite any unlawful combinations therein, for opposing or resisting any law of the United States, or any act of the President of the United States."[10] The law did allow truth as a defense and required proof of malicious intent.

The Federalists under President John Adams aggressively used the law against their rivals, the Republicans. The Alien and Sedition Act was a major political issue in the election of 1800, and after he was elected president, Thomas Jefferson pardoned those who had been convicted under the law. The Alien and Sedition Act was repealed, and the Supreme Court never ruled on its constitutionality. However, in *New York Times v. Sullivan*, in 1964, the Court declared: "Although the Sedition Act was never tested in this Court, the attack upon its validity has carried the day in the court of history."[11]

Not surprisingly, then, Supreme Court cases dealing with freedom of expression focus less on the framers' intent than do cases involving many other constitutional provisions. There is relatively little that can be discerned as to the drafters' views other than their desire to prohibit prior restraints, such as the licensing scheme, and their rejection of the crime of seditious libel.

§11.1.2   Why Should Freedom of Speech Be a Fundamental Right?

The Complexity of the Inquiry

Inevitably, the courts must decide what speech is protected by the First Amendment and what can be regulated by the government. Although the First Amendment is written in absolute language that Congress shall make "no law," the Supreme Court never has accepted the view that the First Amendment prohibits all government regulation of expression. Justice Hugo Black took the absolutist view

---

[8] Rodney A. Smolla, Smolla and Nimmer on Freedom of Speech at 1-18 (1994).
[9] 1 Stat. 596, Act of July 14, 1798.
[10] *Id.*
[11] 376 U.S. 254, 276 (1964). *New York Times v. Sullivan* is discussed below in §11.3.5.2.

of the First Amendment,[12] but he is virtually alone among Supreme Court Justices.[13] Indeed, the Court expressly declared that it "reject[ed] the view that freedom of speech and association, . . . as protected by the First and Fourteenth Amendments, are absolutes."[14]

No matter how appealing the absolute position may be to the First Amendment's staunchest supporters, it is simply untenable. Even one example of an instance where government must be able to punish speech is sufficient to refute the desirability of an absolutist approach. For example, perjury laws or laws that prohibit quid pro quo sexual harassment ("sleep with me or you are fired") both punish speech, but no one would deny that such statutes are imperative.

Line-drawing is inevitable as to what speech will be protected under the First Amendment and what can be proscribed or limited. Moreover, lines must be drawn about where and when speech will be allowed. Even an absolutist view surely would not permit spectators to yell out while a court is in session and prevent the judge from hearing the proceeding. Lines also must be drawn in defining what is speech. Justice Black attempted to make his view plausible by distinguishing between speech and conduct, allowing the government to regulate the latter, but not the former. This distinction, too, requires line-drawing as to when nonverbal communication should be regarded as speech.[15]

Because even for originalists there is little guidance from history or the framers' intent as to the meaning of the First Amendment, the Supreme Court inevitably must make value choices as to what speech is protected, under what circumstances, and when and how the government may regulate. Such analysis is possible only with reference to the goals that freedom of speech is meant to achieve.

Why Is Speech Protected?

There thus is a voluminous literature debating why freedom of speech should be regarded as a fundamental right. The issue is important in general in understanding freedom of expression, but also is crucial in appraising specific First Amendment issues and how they have been handled by the Supreme Court.

There is not a single, universally accepted theory of the First Amendment, but rather several different views as to why freedom of speech should be regarded as a fundamental right. To a large extent, the theories are not mutually exclusive, although the choice of a theory can influence views on many specific issues. The four major theories, reviewed below, are that freedom of speech is protected to

---

[12] *See, e.g.*, Hugo Black, The Bill of Rights, 35 N.Y.U. L. Rev. 865, 874, 879 (1960) ("The phrase 'Congress shall make no law' is composed of plain words, easily understood. The language is absolute. . . . [T]he Framers themselves did this balancing when they wrote the [First Amendment]. . . . Courts have neither the right nor the power to make a different judgment.").

[13] Justice William O. Douglas also, at times, took this view. Konigsberg v. State Bar of Cal., 366 U.S. 36, 56 (1961) (Black, J., dissenting, joined by Douglas, J.).

[14] Konigsberg v. State Bar of Cal., 366 U.S. at 49.

[15] The issue of when conduct that communicates is protected by the First Amendment is discussed below in §11.3.6.

further self-governance, to aid the discovery of truth via the marketplace of ideas, to promote autonomy, and to foster tolerance. Justice Louis Brandeis offered an eloquent explanation for why freedom of speech is protected that includes all of these rationales. He wrote:

> Those who won our independence believed that the final end of the state was to make men free to develop their faculties, and that in its government the deliberative forces should prevail over the arbitrary. They valued liberty both as an end and as a means. They believed liberty to be the secret of happiness and courage to be the secret of liberty. They believed that freedom to think as you will and to speak as you think are means indispensable to the discovery and spread of political truth; that without free speech and assembly discussion would be futile; that with them, discussion affords ordinarily adequate protection against the dissemination of noxious doctrine; that the greatest menace to freedom is an inert people; that public discussion is a political duty; and that this should be a fundamental principle of American government. They recognized the risks to which all human institutions are subject. But they knew that order cannot be secured merely through fear of punishment for its infraction; that it is hazardous to discourage thought, hope, and imagination; that fear breeds repression; that repression breeds hate; that hate menaces stable government; that the path of safety lies in the opportunity to discuss freely supposed grievances and proposed remedies; and that the fitting remedy for evil counsels is good ones.[16]

Self-Governance

Freedom of speech is crucial in a democracy: Open discussion of candidates is essential for voters to make informed selections in elections; it is through speech that people can influence their government's choice of policies; public officials are held accountable through criticisms that can pave the way for their replacement. Alexander Meiklejohn wrote that freedom of speech "is a deduction from the basic American agreement that public issues shall be decided by universal suffrage."[17] He argued that "[s]elf-government can exist only insofar as the voters acquire the intelligence, integrity, sensitivity, and generous devotion to the general welfare that, in theory, casting a ballot is assumed to express."[18] Professor Vincent Blasi argued that freedom of speech serves an essential "checking value" on government.[19] He wrote that free speech checks the abuse of power by public officials and said that through speech voters retain "a veto power to be employed when the decisions of officials pass certain bounds."[20]

There is little disagreement that political speech is at the core of that protected by the First Amendment. The Supreme Court has spoken of the ability to criticize government and government officers as "the central meaning of the First

---

[16] Whitney v. California, 274 U.S. 357, 375 (1927) (Brandeis, J., concurring).
[17] Alexander Meiklejohn, Free Speech and Its Relation to Self-Government 27 (1948).
[18] Alexander Meiklejohn, The First Amendment Is an Absolute, 1961 Sup. Ct. Rev. 245, 255.
[19] Vincent Blasi, The Checking Value in First Amendment Theory, 1977 Am. B. Found. Res. J. 523.
[20] Id. at 542.

Amendment."[21] Some commentators have argued that political speech should be the *only* speech protected by the First Amendment. Robert Bork, perhaps the foremost advocate of this position, argued that the "notion that all valuable types of speech must be protected by the first amendment confuses the constitutionality of laws with their wisdom. Freedom of non-political speech rests, as does freedom for other valuable forms of behavior, upon the enlightenment of society and its elected representatives."[22]

The Supreme Court never has accepted this view that the First Amendment protects only political speech. Indeed, the Court has declared that the "guarantees for speech and press are not the preserve of political expression or comment upon public affairs, essential as those are to healthy government."[23] In part, this is probably because of the difficulty of defining what is political speech. Virtually everything from comic strips to commercial advertisements to even pornography can have a political dimension.[24] In part, too, the refusal to narrowly limit the First Amendment in this way reflects the importance of freedom of speech to other topics ranging from scientific debates to accurate commercial information in the marketplace.

Discovering Truth

Another classic argument for protecting freedom of speech as a fundamental right is that it is essential for the discovery of truth. Justice Oliver Wendell Holmes invoked the powerful metaphor of the "marketplace of ideas" and wrote that "the best test of truth is the power of the thought to get itself accepted in the competition of the market, and that truth is the only ground upon which their wishes safely can be carried out."[25] The argument is that truth is most likely to emerge from the clash of ideas.

John Stuart Mill expressed this view when he wrote that the "peculiar evil of silencing the expression of an opinion is that it is robbing the human race, posterity as well as the existing generation—those who dissent from the opinion, still more than those who hold it."[26] He said that an opinion may be true and may be wrongly suppressed by those in power, or a view may be false and people are informed by its refutation. Justice Brandeis embraced this view when he said that the "fitting remedy for evil counsels is good ones" and that "[i]f there be time to expose through discussion the falsehood and fallacies, to avert the evil by the

---

[21] New York Times v. Sullivan, 376 U.S. 254, 273 (1964).

[22] Robert Bork, Neutral Principles and Some First Amendment Problems, 47 Ind. L.J. 1, 28 (1971).

[23] Time, Inc. v. Hill, 385 U.S. 374, 388 (1967).

[24] As the Supreme Court recently observed, "The Free Speech Clause exists principally to protect discourse on public matters, but we have long recognized that it is difficult to distinguish politics from entertainment, and dangerous to try. 'Everyone is familiar with instances of propaganda through fiction. What is one man's amusement, teaches another's doctrine.'" Brown v. Entertainment Merchants Association, 131 S. Ct. 2729, 2733 (2011) (citation omitted).

[25] Abrams v. United States, 250 U.S. 616, 630 (1919) (Holmes, J., dissenting).

[26] John Stuart Mill, On Liberty 76 (1859).

processes of education, the remedy to be applied is more speech, not enforced silence."[27]

The marketplace of ideas rationale for freedom of speech has been sharply criticized by scholars.[28] Critics argue that it is wrong to assume that all ideas will enter the marketplace of ideas, and even if they do, some may drown out others because some have more resources to have their voices heard. Professor Laurence Tribe observed that "[e]specially when the wealthy have more access to the most potent media of communication than the poor, how sure can we be that 'free trade in ideas' is likely to generate truth?"[29] Professor Jerome Barron said that "if ever there were a self-operating marketplace of ideas, it has long ceased to exist."[30]

Moreover, critics of the marketplace metaphor argue that it is wrong to assume that truth necessarily will trump over falsehood; history shows that people may be swayed by emotion more than reason. Professor Edwin Baker argued that "the belief that the marketplace leads to truth, or even to the best or most desirable decision, is implausible."[31] He said that it assumes that people will use "their rational capabilities in order to eliminate distortion caused by the form and frequency of message presentation. . . . This [assumption] cannot be accepted. . . . People consistently respond to emotional or irrational appeals."[32]

Moreover, even if truth ultimately prevails, enormous harms can occur in the interim. Professor Harry Wellington powerfully made this point when he wrote: "In the long run, true ideas do tend to drive out false ones. The problem is that the short run may be very long, that one short run follows hard upon another, and that we may become overwhelmed by the inexhaustible supply of freshly minted, often very seductive, false ideas. . . . [M]ost of us do believe that the book is closed on some issues. Genocide is an example. . . . Truth may win, and in the long run it may almost always win, but millions of Jews were deliberately and systematically murdered in a very short period of time . . . . Before those murders occurred, many individuals must have come 'to have false beliefs.' "[33]

However, the response to these criticisms is to concede the problems with the marketplace of ideas, but to argue that the alternative—government determination of truth and censorship of falsehoods—is worse. The marketplace of ideas may be terribly flawed, but allowing the government to decide what is true and right and suppress all else is much worse. Inevitably, government will censor to serve its own ends, such as by silencing its critics, and even a benevolent government will make mistakes as to what is true and false. Professor Nimmer thus remarked that "[i]f acceptance of an idea in the competition of the market is not

---

[27] Whitney v. California, 274 U.S. at 375, 377 (Brandeis, J., concurring).

[28] *See, e.g.,* C. Edwin Baker, Human Liberty and Freedom of Speech (1989); Stanley Ingber, The Marketplace of Ideas: A Legitimizing Myth, 1984 Duke L.J. 1.

[29] Laurence H. Tribe, American Constitutional Law 786 (2d ed. 1988).

[30] Jerome Barron, Access to the Press—A New First Amendment Right, 80 Harv. L. Rev. 1641, 1641 (1967).

[31] Baker, *supra* note 28, at 12.

[32] *Id.*

[33] Harry Wellington, On Freedom of Expression, 88 Yale L.J. 1105, 1130, 1132 (1979).

the 'best test,' [what] is the alternative? It can only be acceptance of an idea by some individual or group narrower than that of the public at large."[34]

Advancing Autonomy

A third major rationale often expressed for protecting freedom of speech as a fundamental right is that it is an essential aspect of personhood and autonomy. Professor Baker said that "[t]o engage voluntarily in a speech act is to engage in self-definition or expression. A Vietnam war protestor may explain that when she chants 'Stop This War Now' at a demonstration, she does so without any expectation that her speech will affect continuance of the war . . . ; rather, she participates and chants in order to *define* herself publicly in opposition to the war. This war protestor provides a dramatic illustration of the importance of this self-expressive use of speech, independent of any effective communication to others, for self-fulfillment or self-realization."[35]

Protecting speech because it aids the political process or furthers the search for truth emphasizes the instrumental values of expression. Protecting speech because it is a crucial aspect of autonomy sees expression as intrinsically important.[36] Justice Thurgood Marshall observed that "[t]he First Amendment serves not only the needs of the polity but also those of the human spirit—a spirit that demands self-expression."[37]

This view, too, has been criticized. Robert Bork, for example, argued that there is no inherent reason to find speech to be a fundamental right compared with countless other activities that might be regarded as a part of autonomy or that could advance self-fulfillment. Bork said that the self-fulfillment/autonomy rationale does "not distinguish speech from any other human activity. An individual may develop his faculties or derive pleasure from trading on the stock market, working as a barmaid, engaging in sexual activity, or in any of thousands of other endeavors. Speech can be preferred to other activities only by ranking forms of personal gratification. One cannot, on neutral grounds, choose to protect speech on this basis more than one protects any other claimed freedom."[38]

Moreover, critics of this view maintain that it ignores the ways in which protecting freedom of speech for some can undermine the autonomy and self-fulfillment of others. For example, some have argued for restricting hate speech or pornography because of how such expression demeans and injures others.[39]

---

[34] Melville Nimmer, Nimmer on Freedom of Speech, 1-12 (1984).

[35] C. Edwin Baker, Scope of the First Amendment Freedom of Speech, 25 UCLA L. Rev. 964, 994 (1978).

[36] *See, e.g.*, Martin Redish, The Value of Free Speech, 130 U. Pa. L. Rev. 591 (1982) (arguing that self-realization should be regarded as the exclusive value of the First Amendment).

[37] Procunier v. Martinez, 416 U.S. 396, 427 (1974) (Marshall, J., concurring).

[38] Bork, *supra* note 22, at 25.

[39] *See, e.g.*, Mari Matsuda, Public Response to Racist Speech: Considering the Victim's Story, 87 Mich. L. Rev. 2320 (1989); Richard Delgado, Words That Wound: A Tort Action for Racial Insults, Epithets, and Name-Calling, 17 Harv. C.R.-C.L. L. Rev. 133 (1982) (arguing for restrictions of hate speech); Catharine MacKinnon, Feminism Unmodified 146-213 (1987) (arguing for restriction of

Promoting Tolerance

Another explanation for protecting freedom of speech as a fundamental right that has received substantial attention is that it is integral to tolerance, which should be a basic value in our society. Professor Lee Bollinger is a primary advocate of this view, and he argued: "[The free speech principle] involves a special act of carving out one area of social interaction for extraordinary self-restraint, the purpose of which is to develop and demonstrate a social capacity to control feelings evoked by a host of social encounters."[40] The free speech principle is thus concerned with nothing less than helping to shape "the intellectual character of the society."[41]

The claim is that tolerance is a desirable, if not essential, value, and that protecting unpopular or distasteful speech is itself an act of tolerance. Moreover, such tolerance serves as a model that encourages more tolerance throughout society. But critics question why tolerance should be regarded as a basic value.[42] For example, critics argue that society need not be tolerant of the intolerance of others, such as those who advocate great harm, even genocide. Preventing such harms is claimed to be much more important than being tolerant of those who argue for them.

Conclusion

These four theories are not mutually exclusive.[43] None is sufficient to explain all of the cases, and none is without problems.[44] Yet all are important in understanding why freedom of speech is protected, in considering what expression should be safeguarded and what can be regulated, and in appraising the Supreme Court's decisions in this area.

---

pornography because of its harmful effects on women). Hate speech is discussed in §11.3.3.4; pornography is discussed in §11.3.4.2.

[40] Lee Bollinger, The Tolerant Society: Freedom of Speech and Extremist Speech in America 9-10 (1986).

[41] *Id.* at 120.

[42] *See* David Strauss, Why Be Tolerant?, 53 U. Chi. L. Rev. 1485 (1986).

[43] *See* Rodney A. Smolla, Free Speech in an Open Society 14-17 (1992) (arguing for multiple justifications for freedom of speech); Steven Shiffrin, The First Amendment and Economic Regulation: Away from a General Theory of the First Amendment, 78 Nw. U. L. Rev. 1212 (1983) (many values underlie the First Amendment; no need to reduce the First Amendment to a single theory).

[44] *See* Ronald Cass, The Perils of Positive Thinking: Constitutional Interpretation and Negative First Amendment Theory, 34 UCLA L. Rev. 1405 (1987) (criticizing the foundational theories of the First Amendment).

§11.1.3   The Issues in Free Expression Analysis

Overview of Chapter Organization

In examining the First Amendment's protection of freedom of expression, analysis is divided into five sections. First, §11.2 examines ways of evaluating any government action restricting freedom of speech. For example, any law can be reviewed to determine whether it is content-based or content-neutral, a distinction that the Court has said is crucial in determining whether strict scrutiny or intermediate scrutiny should be used.[45] Also, any law regulating speech is unconstitutional if it is unduly vague or overbroad. The Court additionally has said that prior restraints of speech are strongly disfavored, and thus any government action restricting speech can be challenged if it constitutes a prior restraint. Finally, there is the basic question in evaluating any law as to whether it constitutes a restriction of speech; what government actions sufficiently burden expression as to trigger First Amendment analysis?

Second, §11.3 focuses on types of speech that are unprotected or less protected by the First Amendment. The Supreme Court has declared that some types of expression are unprotected and may be prohibited and punished. There are other categories of speech that are deemed less protected so that the government has more latitude in regulating them. These categories, reviewed in §11.3, include incitement of illegal activity, fighting words and provocation of hostile audiences, obscenity and sexually oriented speech, defamatory speech, conduct that communicates, commercial speech, speech by government employees and by attorneys, and labor protests.

Third, §11.4 considers the places that are available for speech. Many First Amendment cases involve a claim of a right of access to government-owned property for speech purposes or present a challenge to restrictions on the use of public property for expression. The Supreme Court has drawn distinctions among types of government properties and has articulated rules as to when the government may regulate speech in each.

Fourth, §11.5 examines freedom of association. Although association is not expressly mentioned in the First Amendment, the Supreme Court has held that it is a fundamental right because of its close relationship to speech and assembly.[46]

Finally, §11.6 focuses on freedom of the press. Many issues concerning press freedom are discussed throughout the chapter. For example, prior restraints of the press — a crucial aspect of the Constitution's protection of the media — are discussed in §11.2. Section 11.6 considers the extent to which the First Amendment is a shield that protects the press from government regulation, such as from being taxed or forced to disclose information or required to allow others to use it. The section also considers whether and when freedom of the press creates a right for the press to have access to government papers, activities, and facilities.

---

[45] Turner Broad. Sys. v. FCC, 512 U.S. 622 (1994).
[46] *See, e.g.*, NAACP v. Alabama ex rel. Patterson, 357 U.S. 449 (1958).

Part of what makes First Amendment analysis difficult is that many of these issues can be present in the same case, and there is no prescribed order for analysis. For instance, if the government were to prohibit sexually explicit displays in public parks, the law might be challenged as vague and overbroad, it might be analyzed as to whether the speech is obscenity unprotected by the First Amendment, and it might be considered as to whether it is a permissible restriction of speech in a public forum. All these, and others, are issues presented. There is no reason why one question should inherently precede the others. Simply put, it is not possible to comprehensively flowchart the First Amendment as a defined series of questions in a required sequential order. There are many ways of approaching and evaluating government actions restricting expression.

§11.2   FREE SPEECH METHODOLOGY

Overview

This section considers doctrines that can be used to evaluate government restrictions of speech. Section 11.2.1 describes the distinction between content-based and content-neutral laws regulating speech and the significance of this difference. Section 11.2.2 considers the vagueness and overbreadth doctrines; even in regulating unprotected speech, laws are unconstitutional if they are unduly vague or overbroad. Section 11.2.3 examines the strong presumption against prior restraints and especially focuses on classic forms of prior restraints such as court orders suppressing speech and licensing systems. Finally, §11.2.4 discusses the basic question of what constitutes an infringement of speech.

§11.2.1   The Distinction Between Content-Based and Content-Neutral Laws

Importance of the Distinction

The Supreme Court frequently has declared that the very core of the First Amendment is that the government cannot regulate speech based on its content. In *Police Department of Chicago v. Mosley*, for example, the Court said: "[A]bove all else, the First Amendment means that government has no power to restrict expression because of its message, its ideas, its subject matter or its content."[1] In countless First Amendment cases, involving many of the issues discussed throughout this chapter, the Court has invoked the content-based/content-neutral distinction as the basis for its decisions.

---

[1] §11.2 408 U.S. 92, 95-96 (1972).

§11.2 Free Speech Methodology

The Court has declared that "[c]ontent-based regulations are presumptively invalid."[2] In *Turner Broadcasting System v. Federal Communications Commission*, the Court said that the general rule is that content-based restrictions on speech must meet strict scrutiny, while content-neutral regulation only need meet intermediate scrutiny.[3] Justice Kennedy, writing for the Court, explained that "[g]overnment action that stifles speech on account of its message, or that requires the utterance of a particular message favored by the Government, contravenes this essential [First Amendment] right."[4] Justice Kennedy thus noted: "For these reasons, the First Amendment, subject only to narrow and well understood exceptions, does not countenance governmental control over the content of messages expressed by private individuals."[5] Hence, the Court endorsed a two-tier system of review. The Court uses "the most exacting scrutiny to regulations that suppress, disadvantage, or impose differential burdens upon speech because of its content."[6] But, "[i]n contrast, regulations that are unrelated to the content of speech are subject to an intermediate level of scrutiny."[7]

As discussed in §11.3, there are some categories of speech that are unprotected or less protected by the First Amendment, such as incitement or illegal activity, obscenity, and defamation. These categories, by definition, are content-based. But apart from these categories, content-based discrimination must meet strict scrutiny, and the Court indicated that content-based distinctions within these categories also must pass strict scrutiny.[8]

Why Does the Distinction Matter So Much?

Why is there so much concern about content neutrality?[9] Obviously, the fear is that the government will target particular messages and attempt to control thoughts on a topic by regulating speech.[10] As the Court noted, "Laws of this sort pose the inherent risk that the Government seeks not to advance a legitimate

---

[2] R.A.V. v. City of St. Paul, 505 U.S. 377, 382 (1992); United States v. Alvarez, 132 S. Ct. 2537, 2544 (2012) (plurality opinion).

[3] 512 U.S. 622 (1994).

[4] *Id.* at 640.

[5] *Id.*

[6] *Id.* at 641; *see also* United States v. Playboy Entertainment Group, Inc., 529 U.S. 803 (2000) (using strict scrutiny for a content-based restriction on speech), discussed below in text accompanying notes 21-24.

[7] *Id.*; *see also* Hill v. Colorado, 530 U.S. 703 (2000) (upholding a law, without using strict scrutiny, because the law was deemed content-neutral), discussed below in text accompanying notes 46-47.

[8] *See* R.A.V. v. City of St. Paul, 505 U.S. 377 (1992), discussed below in §11.3.3.2.

[9] For an excellent explanation of the basis for the content-based/content-neutral distinction, *see* Geoffrey Stone, Content-Neutral Restrictions, 54 U. Chi. L. Rev. 46 (1987); for an excellent argument that the Court has given undue weight to this distinction, *see* Martin Redish, The Content Distinction in First Amendment Analysis, 34 Stan. L. Rev. 113 (1981) (arguing, in part, that content-based restrictions limit less speech than content-neutral ones).

[10] As the Court noted, "[such restrictions] raise the specter that the government may effectively drive certain ideas or viewpoints from the marketplace." Simon & Schuster, Inc. v. Members of the N.Y. State Crime Victims Bd., 502 U.S. 105, 116 (1991).

regulatory goal, but to suppress unpopular ideas or information or to manipulate the public debate through coercion rather than persuasion."[11]

A viewpoint restriction does this directly. The government could try to control dissent and advance its own interests by stopping speech that expresses criticism of government policy, while allowing praise. A subject matter restriction on speech can accomplish the same goal. In the 1960s, a law prohibiting speech about the war—a subject matter restriction—obviously would have had a far greater impact on antiwar speech. The Court has explained that "[t]o allow a government the choice of permissible subjects for public debate would be to allow the government control over the search for political truth."[12]

Forty years ago, Professor Kenneth Karst persuasively argued that equality is at the core of the First Amendment.[13] All speech, regardless of its content, must be treated the same by the government. To allow the government to target particular views or subjects permits the government to greatly distort the marketplace of ideas.

How Is It Determined Whether a Law Is Content-Based?

The requirement that the government be content-neutral in its regulation of speech means that the government must be both viewpoint neutral and subject matter neutral.[14] Viewpoint neutral means that the government cannot regulate speech based on the ideology of the message.[15] For example, it would be clearly unconstitutional for the government to say that pro-choice demonstrations are allowed in the park but antiabortion demonstrations are not allowed. In *Boos v. Berry*, the Court declared unconstitutional a District of Columbia ordinance that prohibited the display of signs critical of a foreign government within 500 feet of that government's embassy.[16] The law, in its very terms, drew a distinction among speech based on the viewpoint expressed.[17]

Subject matter neutral means that the government cannot regulate speech based on the topic of the speech.[18] A case from 1980, *Carey v. Brown*, is illustrative.[19] Chicago adopted an ordinance prohibiting all picketing in residential neighborhoods unless it was labor picketing connected to a place of employment. The

---

[11] Turner Broad. Sys. v. Federal Communications Commn., 512 U.S. 622, 641 (1994).

[12] Consolidated Edison Co. of N.Y., Inc. v. Public Serv. Commn., 447 U.S. 530, 538 (1980).

[13] Kenneth Karst, Equality as a Central Principle in the First Amendment, 43 U. Chi. L. Rev. 20 (1975); *see also* Geoffrey Scone, Content Regulation and the First Amendment, 25 Wm. & Mary L. Rev. 189 (1983).

[14] *See, e.g.,* Perry Educ. Assn. v. Perry Local Educators' Assn., 460 U.S. 37, 45 (1983).

[15] *See* Amy Sabrin, Thinking About Content: Can It Play an Appropriate Role in Government Funding of the Arts?, 102 Yale L.J. 1209, 1220 (1993).

[16] 485 U.S. 312 (1988).

[17] The Court, however, said that this was a law that was viewpoint neutral, though content-based. It is difficult to see how a law that restricts speech that is likely to be embarrassing to a foreign government, but allows that which is supportive, is not viewpoint based.

[18] Sabrin, *supra* note 15, at 1217.

[19] 447 U.S. 455 (1980).

Supreme Court held this regulation unconstitutional. The Court explained that the law allowed speech if it was about the subject of labor, but not otherwise. The Court said that whenever the government attempts to regulate speech in public places, it must be subject matter neutral.[20]

Similarly, in *United States v. Playboy Entertainment Group, Inc.*, the Court found that a law that regulated only sexual speech was a subject matter restriction and had to meet strict scrutiny.[21] A provision of the federal Cable Act prohibited "signal bleed" of sexual images;[22] signal bleed occurs when people receive images from cable stations to which they do not subscribe. The law required that cable companies either completely eliminate signal bleed of sexual images or that sexual programming be shown exclusively during late-night hours. In finding the law unconstitutional, Justice Kennedy declared: "The speech in question is defined by its content; and the statute which seeks to restrict it is content based."[23] He explained that the law "applies only to channels primarily dedicated to 'sexually explicit adult programming or other programming that is indecent.' The statute is unconcerned with signal bleed from any other channels. . . . It focuses *only* on the content of the speech and the direct impact it has on its listeners. This is the essence of content-based regulation."[24] The Court found that the law failed strict scrutiny because it was not the least restrictive alternative for achieving the government's interest.

The Court followed the same reasoning in its subsequent decision in *Ashcroft v. American Civil Liberties Union.*[25] The case involved the constitutionality of the Child Online Protection Act, a federal law that regulated sexually oriented commercial websites. The statute applied only to commercial websites that included material that appealed to the prurient interest and would be offensive to contemporary community standards. The law required that such websites do age verification and provided several ways in which they could do so.

A federal district court issued a preliminary injunction and the United States Court of Appeals for the Third Circuit affirmed. The Supreme Court also upheld the preliminary injunction. The majority opinion was written by Justice Anthony Kennedy, and joined by Justices Stevens, Souter, Ginsburg, and Thomas. Justice Kennedy's opinion said that the law is a content-based restriction of speech, applying only to sexual speech, and that it therefore must meet strict scrutiny. The Court said that the preliminary injunction was upheld because there was a substantial likelihood that the plaintiffs would prevail in their argument that the law does not meet strict scrutiny. Justice Kennedy explained that filtering devices, which are installed on individual computers, likely are a less restrictive alternative for protecting children from exposure to sexually explicit material. The Court remanded

---

[20] The ability of government to regulate speech in public places is discussed in §11.4.
[21] 529 U.S. 803 (2000).
[22] Telecommunications Act of 1996, §505, 47 U.S.C. §561.
[23] 529 U.S. at 803.
[24] *Id.*
[25] 542 U.S. 656 (2004).

the case to the federal district court for a determination of whether such filtering devices are a less restrictive alternative.[26]

In *Republican Party of Minnesota v. White*, the Court again found a law unconstitutional as a subject matter restriction on speech.[27] A Minnesota law prohibited candidates for elected judicial office from making statements about disputed legal or political issues. The Supreme Court, in a 5-to-4 decision, with Justice Scalia writing for the Court (joined by Chief Justice Rehnquist and Justices O'Connor, Kennedy, and Thomas), struck down the law as a content-based restriction that failed to meet strict scrutiny. It was undisputed that the law was a subject matter restriction: It prohibited speech on some issues, but allowed it on others. The Court rejected the government's argument that statements about disputed legal or political issues would undermine judicial impartiality. The dissent, in contrast, would have accepted this as a sufficient interest to meet strict scrutiny.

A law regulating speech is content-neutral if it applies to all speech regardless of the message. For example, a law prohibiting the posting of all signs on public utility poles would be content-neutral because it would apply to every sign regardless of its subject matter or viewpoint.[28] In *Turner Broadcasting System v. Federal Communications Commission*, the Supreme Court found that a federal law requiring cable companies to carry local broadcast stations was content-neutral because they were required to include all stations, whatever their programming.[29] A law might also be content-neutral if it regulates conduct and it has an effect on speech without regard to its content. For example, a sales tax, applicable to all purchases including reading material, might have a significant incidental effect on speech, but it is content-neutral.[30]

How is it determined whether a law is viewpoint or subject matter based? Sometimes laws, on their very face, draw a distinction based on the content of the message. For instance, a law prohibiting antiwar demonstrations in the park or the ordinance prohibiting labor picketing in residential neighborhoods would be examples of content-based restrictions on the face of the law.

However, the Supreme Court has indicated that a facial content-based restriction will be deemed content-neutral if it is motivated by a permissible content-neutral purpose. The Court articulated this rule in *Renton v. Playtime Theatres, Inc.*[31]

---

[26] On remand, the federal district court, 478 F. Supp. 2d 775 (E.D. Pa. 2007), declared the law unconstitutional and issued a permanent injunction and the United States Court of Appeals for the Third Circuit affirmed, 534 F.3d 181 (3d Cir. 2008).

[27] 536 U.S. 765 (2002).

[28] *See* Members of the City Council of Los Angeles v. Taxpayers for Vincent, 466 U.S. 789 (1984), discussed at §11.4.2.5.

[29] 512 U.S. 622 (1994). In *Turner Broadcasting*, the Supreme Court remanded the case for the application of intermediate scrutiny. After a remand, the Supreme Court held that the regulation met intermediate scrutiny because of the government's important interest in protecting the over-the-air, free broadcast media. 520 U.S. 180 (1997).

[30] *See, e.g.*, Leathers v. Medlock, 499 U.S. 439 (1991) (upholding the application of a general sales tax to cable television that was not applicable to the print media because it did not suppress ideas and did not target a small group of speakers).

[31] 475 U.S. 41, 47-48 (1986).

In *Renton,* the Court rejected a First Amendment challenge to a zoning ordinance that prohibited adult motion picture theaters from locating within 1,000 feet of any residential zone, single or multifamily dwelling, church, park, or school. The ordinance was clearly content-based in its very terms: It applied only to theaters that showed films with sexually explicit content.

The Court, though, treated the law as content-neutral because it said that the law was motivated by a desire to control the secondary effects of adult movie theaters, such as crime, and not to restrict the speech.[32] The Court said that "the Renton ordinance is completely consistent with our definition of 'content-neutral' speech regulations as those that are *justified* without reference to the content of the regulated speech."[33] *Renton* thus makes the test of whether a law is content-based or content-neutral not its terms but, rather, its justification. A law that is justified in content-neutral terms is deemed content-neutral even if it is content-based on its face.

Renton has been strongly criticized by commentators.[34] Critics argue that *Renton* "permits an end run around the First Amendment: The government can always point to some neutral, non-speech justification for its actions."[35] Justice Brennan expressed his "continued disagreement with the proposition that an otherwise content-based restriction on speech can be recast as 'content-neutral' if the restriction 'aims' at 'secondary-effects' of the speech. . . . [S]uch secondary effects offer countless excuses for content-based suppression of political speech."[36]

The *Renton* approach seems to confuse whether a law is content-based or content-neutral with the question of whether a law is justified by a sufficient purpose. The law may have been properly upheld as needed to combat crime and the secondary effects of adult theaters, but it nonetheless was clearly content-based: It applied only to theaters showing films with sexually explicit content.[37]

In several subsequent cases, the Court distinguished *Renton*. For example, in *Boos v. Berry,* the government argued that the restriction of speech critical of foreign governments near their embassies was justified based on an international law obligation to shield diplomats from speech that offends their dignity.[38] Justice O'Connor, writing for the plurality in declaring this part of the law unconstitutional, distinguished *Renton* because the ordinance restricting speech near embassies was justified *only* by reference to the content of the speech. "Respondents and the United States do not point to the 'secondary effects' of picket signs in front of embassies. They do not point to congestion, to interference with ingress or egress, to visual clutter, or to the need to protect the security of embassies. Rather,

---

[32] *Id.* at 48.

[33] *Id.* at 48 (emphasis in original) (citations omitted).

[34] For an excellent summary of these criticisms, *see* Marcy Strauss, From Witness to Riches: The Constitutionality of Restricting Witness Speech, 38 Ariz. L. Rev. 291 (1996).

[35] *Id.* at 317.

[36] Boos v. Berry, 485 U.S. at 334-335 (Brennan, J., concurring in part and concurring in the judgment).

[37] *See* Kimberly Smith, Comment, Zoning Adult Entertainment: A Reassessment of *Renton,* 79 Cal. L. Rev. 119, 142 (1991).

[38] 485 U.S. at 322.

they rely on the need to protect the dignity of foreign diplomatic personnel by shielding them from speech that is critical of their governments. This justification focuses *only* on the content of the speech and the direct impact that speech has on its listeners."[39]

The Court also distinguished *Renton* in *City of Cincinnati v. Discovery Network, Inc.*, where the Court declared unconstitutional a prohibition on the use of news-racks on public property for the distribution of commercial handbills.[40] The city argued that the ordinance was justified by concern over the secondary effects of such newsracks with regard to safety and aesthetics. The Court rejected this argu-ment and characterized the ordinance as content-based. Justice Stevens, writing for the Court, said: "Under the city's newsrack policy, whether any particular news-rack falls within the ban is determined by the content of the publication resting inside that newsrack. Thus, by any commonsense understanding of the term, the ban is 'content-based.' "[41]

Justice Stevens expressly distinguished *Renton* and said that the city's "reli-ance on *Renton* is misplaced."[42] He said that "[i]n contrast to the speech at issue in *Renton*, there are no secondary effects attributable to . . . newsracks [containing commercial handbills] that distinguish them from the newsracks Cincinnati per-mits to remain on its sidewalks."[43]

But in other cases, the Court has applied *Renton*. In *City of Erie v. Pap's A.M.*,[44] the Court upheld a city ordinance that prohibited public nudity, even though it was motivated by a desire to close down a nude dancing club. Justice O'Connor, writing for the plurality, expressly invoked *Renton* and declared: "[T]he regulation . . . is . . . properly evaluated as a content-neutral regulation because the interest in combating the secondary effects associated with those clubs is unrelated to the suppression of the erotic message conveyed by nude dancing."[45]

In *Hill v. Colorado*,[46] the Court upheld a Colorado law that prohibits approach-ing without consent within 8 feet of a person, who is within 100 feet of a health care facility, for purposes of oral protest, education, or counseling. Justice Stevens, writing for the Court, emphasized the content neutrality of the law as the basis for upholding it. He quoted the determination by the Colorado Supreme Court that the "restrictions apply equally to all demonstrators, regardless of viewpoint, and the statutory language makes no reference to the content of the speech."[47] Justice Stevens explained that the "State's interest in protecting access and pri-vacy, and providing the police with clear guidelines, are unrelated to the content

---

[39] *Id.* at 321 (emphasis in original).

[40] 507 U.S. 410 (1993).

[41] *Id.* at 429.

[42] *Id.* at 430.

[43] *Id.*

[44] 529 U.S. 277 (2000).

[45] *Id.* at 294. *City of Erie* is discussed more fully below in §11.3.4.4 text accompanying notes 249-253.

[46] 530 U.S. 703 (2000).

[47] *Id.* at 720 (quoting Hill v. Thomas, 973 P.2d 1246, 1256 (Colo. 1999)).

of the demonstrators' speech." As in *Renton*, the Colorado law on its face seemed content-based—it stopped speech that was for "protest, education, or counseling"—but the Court found it to be content-neutral because it was motivated by a desire to stop adverse effects of speech.

Thus, at this point, it appears that a law that on its face regulates speech based on its viewpoint or message will be presumed to be content-based, but the government can refute this by persuading a court that the regulation is justified by a content-neutral desire to avoid undesirable secondary effects of the speech. The content-neutral justification must be unrelated to the desire to suppress speech, and it must be unique to the speech suppressed as compared to the speech allowed.

Renton, *Boos*, and *Discovery Network* all involved laws that on their face drew content-based distinctions. A more difficult issue is whether a facially neutral law may be argued to be content-based because of its purpose and/or effects. The Court has not expressly addressed when facially neutral laws will be found to be content-based because of their purpose or impact.

However, the Court has implicitly recognized the ability to prove content restrictions in these ways. For example, *Renton* emphasizes the justifications of a law in determining whether it is content-based or content-neutral; there is no reason why this should be relevant only when laws are facially discriminatory. Moreover, in the decisions concerning flag burning and the First Amendment, the Court relied on the content-based purpose and effect of the laws.[48] The Supreme Court held that government cannot prohibit flag burning because such laws in effect say that the flag can be used to express the view of patriotism, but not the view of dissent. Such viewpoint regulation is not allowed. Scholars have persuasively argued that laws should be treated as content-based if their purpose is to restrict particular messages[49] or if their effect is to discriminate against specific topics or views.[50]

However, in *Hill v. Colorado*,[51] the Court found a law to be content-neutral, even though its effect was unquestionably content-based. As described above, the Colorado law prohibited approaching a person, without consent, within 100 feet of a health care facility, for purposes of oral protest, education, or counseling. There was no doubt that the effect of this law was to stop antiabortion speech. Yet the Court said that the law was content-neutral because it was facially neutral, applying to all speech regardless of its message, and because it was motivated by the desire to protect those entering health care facilities.

Quite similarly, in *McCullen v. Coakley*, the Court found that a Massachusetts law that created a 35-foot buffer zone around reproductive health care facilities

---

[48] *See, e.g.*, Texas v. Johnson, 491 U.S. 397 (1989) (invalidating Texas law prohibiting flag desecration); discussed below in §11.3.6.2.

[49] *See* Laurence H. Tribe, American Constitutional Law 794 (2d ed. 1988) ("law should be deemed content-based if it is discriminatory on its face or if it was motivated by (i.e., would not have occurred but for) an intent to single out constitutionally protected speech for control or penalty") (emphasis omitted).

[50] *See* Stone, *supra* note 9, at 81-86; Susan Williams, Content Discrimination and the First Amendment, 139 U. Pa. L. Rev. 615 (1991).

[51] 530 U.S. 703 (2000).

was content-neutral, though it invalidated the law on the ground that it was not sufficiently narrowly tailored in restricting speech on public sidewalks.[52] The Court concluded that "the Act does not draw content-based distinctions on its face."[53] The Court acknowledged that by "limiting the buffer zones to abortion clinics, the Act has the 'inevitable effect' of restricting abortion-related speech more than speech on other subjects."[54] But it said that "a facially neutral law does not become content based simply because it may disproportionately affect speech on certain topics."[55]

Thus, although the law is not completely clear, it appears that a content-based restriction on the face of the law will be treated as content-neutral if it is motivated by a desire to prevent adverse secondary effects of the speech. A law that is facially content-neutral can be treated as content-based if its purpose and/or effects are content-based. The Court, however, has been much less clear or consistent about this.

Of course, even if a law is deemed to be content-based that does not make it automatically unconstitutional; strict scrutiny is then applied. For example, in *United States v. Alvarez*, the Court considered the constitutionality of a federal law that made it a crime for a person to falsely claim to have received military honors or decorations.[56] Justice Kennedy wrote for a plurality of four and concluded that the law imposed a content-based restriction on speech and thus had to meet the most "exacting scrutiny." He explained that the government failed this test because it did not prove any harm from false claims of military honors and because the government could achieve its goals through less restrictive alternatives.[57] Perhaps most importantly for the future, he rejected the government's argument that false speech is inherently outside the scope of the First Amendment.[58]

Another example of the Court applying strict scrutiny and then finding a law unconstitutional is *Brown v. Entertainment Merchants Association*, which considered the constitutionality of a California law that made it a crime to sell or rent violent video games to minors under 18 without parental consent.[59] The Court began by observing that video games are a form of speech and that the First Amendment protects minors as well as adults.[60] The Court found that the California law was

---

[52] 134 S. Ct. 2518, 2531 (2014), discussed below at §11.4.2.2.

[53] *Id.* at 2531.

[54] *Id.*

[55] *Id.*

[56] 132 S. Ct. 2537 (2012).

[57] *Id.* at 2549.

[58] Justice Breyer concurred in the judgment, joined by Justice Kagan. He said that he would use intermediate rather than strict scrutiny and that the law failed this test because it was not narrowly tailored. *Id.* at 2551 (Breyer, J., concurring in the judgment). It is not clear, though, as to why Justice Breyer thought that intermediate scrutiny was appropriate rather than the usual strict scrutiny for content-based restrictions on speech.

[59] 131 S. Ct. 2729 (2011).

[60] *Id.* at 2735-2736 ("[M]inors are entitled to a significant measure of First Amendment protection, and only in relatively narrow and well-defined circumstances may government bar public dissemination of protected materials to them." (citation omitted)).

content-based— its application depended entirely on the content of the video game— and said that therefore "it is invalid unless California can demonstrate that it passes strict scrutiny—that is, unless it is justified by a compelling government interest and is narrowly drawn to serve that interest."[61]

California argued that playing interactive video games has a deleterious effect on children and makes them more prone to commit acts of violence. The Court, though, rejected this argument. Justice Scalia, writing for the majority, concluded: "California cannot meet [strict scrutiny.] At the outset, it acknowledges that it cannot show a direct causal link between violent video games and harm to minors. . . . The State's evidence is not compelling. . . . They show at best some correlation between exposure to violent entertainment and minuscule real-world effects, such as children's feeling more aggressive or making louder noises in the few minutes after playing a violent game than after playing a nonviolent game."[62]

Although content-based laws usually fail strict scrutiny, that is not always so. For example, in *Burson v. Freeman*, the Court upheld a state law that prohibited either the soliciting of votes or the display or distribution of campaign materials within 100 feet of the entrance of a polling place.[63] The law was a content-based restriction on speech, but the Court concluded that this was the "rare case" in which strict scrutiny was satisfied. Justice Blackmun explained that "[a] long history, a substantial consensus, and simple common sense show that some restricted zone around polling places is necessary to protect [the] fundamental right [to vote]. Given the conflict between those two rights [speech and voting], we hold that requiring solicitors to stand 100 feet from the entrances to polling places does not constitute an unconstitutional compromise."[64]

When the Government Must Make Content-Based Choices

There are some situations in which the government inevitably must make choices based on the content of the speech. For example, when the government runs a theater or publishes a newspaper or runs a library or subsidizes speech, it is inevitable that the government will make choices based on the content of the message. Obviously, the government will not choose randomly among all possible plays or books.

---

[61] *Id.* at 2738.

[62] *Id.* at 2739.

[63] 504 U.S. 191 (1992).

[64] *Id.* at 211 (plurality opinion). Justice Alito, joined by Chief Justice Roberts, concurred in the judgment, and would have found the California law unconstitutionally vague, but said that the research indicates that playing video games may be different from other media in terms of their effects on children and the Court should not foreclose laws protecting children. Justice Thomas dissented and argued that there is no First Amendment protection for children based on the law that existed when the First Amendment was ratified. Justice Breyer dissented and would have upheld the law because it did not preclude children from having the video games, but only required parental consent, which the Court has allowed as a form of regulation of sexually explicit materials.

The Court has held that in such situations the government may make content-based choices, so long as the government is viewpoint neutral. In *National Endowment for the Arts v. Finley*, the Court upheld federal restrictions on the funding of artists.[65] The National Endowment for the Arts (NEA) provides grants to artists. Since 1965, when it was created, it has disbursed over $3 billion in funds to individuals and organizations. The federal statute creating the NEA gives it substantial discretion in awarding funds; it is empowered to give money based on "artistic and cultural significance, giving emphasis to American creativity and cultural diversity," "professional excellence," and encouragement of "public knowledge, education, understanding, and appreciation of the arts."[66] In 1990, the statute was amended to provide that the NEA also should "tak[e] into consideration general standards of decency and respect for the diverse beliefs and values of the American public."[67]

Justice O'Connor's opinion for the Court emphasized that the federal law did not require that the NEA consider decency and respect for values; rather, the statute permitted such consideration. The Court rejected the vagueness challenge and noted that "when the Government is acting as patron rather than as sovereign, the consequences of imprecision are not constitutionally severe."[68] In other words, when the government is giving subsidies, imprecise criteria are permitted, even if they would not be tolerated in a regulatory scheme.

Justice O'Connor also rejected the claim that the law was impermissible viewpoint discrimination. The Court stressed that the government must make choices among applicants, and it said that the statute's language does "not engender the kind of directed viewpoint discrimination that would prompt this Court to invalidate a statute on its face."[69] The Court said that there was no allegation of viewpoint discrimination in the application of the law and that facially the law was constitutional.[70]

Integral to the Court's decision was its conclusion that it was viewpoint neutral for the federal law to authorize the NEA to consider "decency and respect" for values. Yet these terms inherently focus attention on viewpoint. What is decent or indecent depends entirely on the evaluator's views. Likewise, determining whether art shows respect for values requires a viewpoint-based assessment. However, all of the Justices, except for the sole dissent of Justice Souter, saw the law as viewpoint neutral and as employing permissible criteria for the government to use in disbursing funds.

In *Board of Regents v. Southworth*,[71] the Court repeated that in situations in which the government must make content-based choices, viewpoint neutrality still must be maintained. In *Southworth*, the Court considered the constitutionality of mandatory student activity fees at a public university. The Court rejected a First Amendment

---

[65] 524 U.S. 569 (1998).
[66] 20 U.S.C. §954(c)(1)-(10).
[67] *Id.* §954(d)(1); *Finley*, 524 U.S. at 576.
[68] 524 U.S. at 589.
[69] *Id.* at 583.
[70] *Id.* at 586-587.
[71] 529 U.S. 217 (2000).

challenge by students who objected to being forced to subsidize causes that they opposed. The Court said that the fees helped to facilitate a diversity of ideas on campus and that they were permissible so long as they were administered in a viewpoint neutral manner. Justice Kennedy, writing for a unanimous Court, declared: "The proper measure, and the principal standard of protection for objecting students, we conclude, is the requirement of viewpoint neutrality in the allocation of funding support."[72] Because the student challengers stipulated in the district court that the program was viewpoint neutral, the Court upheld its constitutionality.

Together *Finley* and *Southworth* provide important guidance for situations when the government inevitably must make content-based choices. In such situations, the government may do so, but it must be viewpoint neutral.[73]

§11.2.2   Vagueness and Overbreadth

Vagueness

A law is unconstitutionally vague if a reasonable person cannot tell what speech is prohibited and what is permitted.[74] Unduly vague laws violate due process whether or not speech is regulated.[75] For example, in *Kolender v. Lawson*, the Court declared unconstitutional California's loitering law and declared that "the void-for-vagueness doctrine requires that a penal statute define the criminal offense with sufficient definiteness that ordinary people can understand what conduct is prohibited and in a manner that does not encourage arbitrary and discriminatory enforcement."[76]

Similarly, in *City of Chicago v. Morales*, the Supreme Court invalidated a law on due process vagueness grounds.[77] Chicago adopted an antigang ordinance that required gang members to disperse if ordered to do so by police officers; their failure to do so was itself a crime. Specifically, if the police reasonably believed that at least one person in a group of two or more was a gang member and they were loitering, their failure to follow a police order to leave the area was a misdemeanor offense punishable by imprisonment. Justice Stevens, writing in part for a majority and in part for a plurality, stressed the vagueness of the law. The definition of

---

[72] *Id.* at 232.

[73] In at least some cases, the problem of the government making content-based choices may be solved by a new development in free speech law: the Court's holding that the First Amendment does not apply when the government itself is the speaker. The Court expressly held this in *Pleasant Grove City, Utah v. Summum*, 555 U.S. 460 (2009). If it is a government museum or playhouse or park, the government can make content-based choices because it is the speaker and the First Amendment does not apply at all. *Pleasant Grove* and this exception to the First Amendment are discussed in detail below in §11.2.5.

[74] *See, e.g.,* Connally v. General Constr. Co., 269 U.S. 385, 391 (1926) (a law is unconstitutionally vague "when people of common intelligence must necessarily guess at its meaning").

[75] *See, e.g.,* Papachristou v. Jacksonville, 405 U.S. 156 (1972) (declaring vagrancy law unconstitutional).

[76] 461 U.S. 352, 357 (1983).

[77] 527 U.S. 41 (1999).

loitering—being in a place for no apparent purpose—was vague. The behavior needed to avoid arrest was uncertain; could the individuals move a block away or go around the block and come back? The Court said that the ambiguity in the law meant that it failed due process.

In part, the vagueness doctrine is about fairness; it is unjust to punish a person without providing clear notice as to what conduct was prohibited. Vague laws also risk selective prosecution; under vague statutes and ordinances the government can choose who to prosecute based on their views or politics. Justice O'Connor said that "[t]he more important aspect of the vagueness doctrine is not actual notice, but the other principle element of the doctrine—the requirement that a legislature establish minimal guidelines to govern law enforcement. Where the legislature fails to provide such minimal guidelines, a criminal statute may permit a standardless sweep that allows policemen, prosecutors and juries to pursue their personal predilections."[78] In a subsequent case, the Court explained that "[a] conviction fails to comport with due process if the statute under which it is obtained fails to provide a person of ordinary intelligence fair notice of what is prohibited, or is so standardless that it authorizes or encourages seriously discriminatory enforcement."[79]

But courts are particularly troubled about vague laws restricting speech out of concern that they will chill constitutionally protected speech. The Court has observed that freedom of speech is "delicate and vulnerable, as well as supremely precious in our society . . . [and] the threat of sanctions may deter their exercise almost as potently as the actual application of sanctions."[80] Further, in *NAACP v. Button*, the Court said that "standards of permissible statutory vagueness are strict in the area of free expression. . . . Because First Amendment freedoms need breathing space to survive, government may regulate in the area only with narrow specificity."[81] In *Button*, the Court declared unconstitutional a Virginia law that prohibited attorneys from soliciting prospective clients that had been used against the NAACP for informing individuals of their rights and referring them to lawyers.

Thus, the Supreme Court has declared laws regulating speech to be void on vagueness grounds when they are so ambiguous that the reasonable person cannot tell what expression is forbidden and what is allowed.[82] For instance, in *Smith v. Goguen*, the Court invalidated a state law that prohibited treating a flag "contemptuously."[83] The Court said that the law "fails to draw reasonably clear

---

[78] Kolender v. Lawson, 461 U.S. 352, 358 (1983) (citations omitted).

[79] United States v. Williams, 553 U.S. 285 (2008).

[80] NAACP v. Button, 371 U.S. 415, 433 (1963).

[81] *Id.* at 415, 432-433 (citations omitted).

[82] It should be noted that the Court has drawn a distinction with regard to vagueness between laws regulating speech and those subsidizing speech. In *National Endowment for the Arts v. Finley*, 524 U.S. 569, 589 (1998), the Court said that "when the Government is acting as patron rather than as sovereign, the consequences of imprecision are not constitutionally severe." *Finley* is discussed in detail above in text accompanying notes 65-70.

[83] 415 U.S. 566, 569 (1974).

lines between the kinds of nonceremonial treatment that are criminal and those that are not."[84]

Similarly, in *Baggett v. Bullitt*, the Court declared unconstitutional a state's loyalty oath that, among other things, prevented any "subversive person" from being employed in the state and required a person to swear that he or she was not such an individual or a part of any subversive organization.[85] The Court found "the oath requirements and the statutory provisions on which they are based . . . invalid on their face because their language is unduly vague, uncertain, and broad."[86] The Court stressed that the ambiguities inherent in the term "subversive" and in the language of the statute gave individuals little guidance as to what speech and associational activities were proscribed.

In *Houston v. Hill*, the Court declared unconstitutional a city's ordinance that made it unlawful to interrupt police officers in the performance of their duties.[87] The Court emphasized that the law was not "narrowly tailored to prohibit only disorderly conduct or fighting words" and objected that the law "effectively grants police the discretion to make arrests selectively on the basis of the content of the speech."[88]

There is not and never will be a litmus test for evaluating when a law is too vague and thus offends the Constitution. Ambiguity is inherent in language, and all laws will have some vagueness. But the Court has made it clear that greater precision is required when laws regulate speech, and statutes will be invalidated if a judge concludes that they provide inadequate notice as to what speech is prohibited and what is allowed. The void-for-vagueness doctrine is thus a powerful tool in First Amendment litigation because it allows facial challenges to laws even by those whose speech otherwise would be unprotected by the First Amendment.[89]

Overbreadth

A law is unconstitutionally overbroad if it regulates substantially more speech than the Constitution allows to be regulated, and a person to whom the law constitutionally can be applied can argue that it would be unconstitutional as applied to others. In other words, in an area where the government can regulate speech, such as obscenity, a law that regulates much more expression than the Constitution allows to be restricted will be declared unconstitutional on overbreadth grounds.

---

[84] *Id.* at 574.

[85] 377 U.S. 360, 362 (1964).

[86] *Id.* at 366.

[87] 482 U.S. 451 (1987).

[88] *Id.* at 465 n.15.

[89] However, the Supreme Court also has said that "[a] plaintiff who engages in some conduct that is clearly proscribed cannot complain of the vagueness of the law as applied to the conduct of others." Holder v. Humanitarian Law Project, 130 S. Ct. 2705, 2719 (2010) (citations omitted). In *Holder*, the Court rejected a vagueness challenge to a federal law that prohibits "material support" for foreign terrorist organizations, 18 U.S.C. §2339(B). The Court stressed that the law was not vague as to the plaintiff's proposed action. The Court stated: "[T]he statutory terms are clear in their application to plaintiffs' proposed conduct, which means that plaintiffs' vagueness challenge must fail." *Id.* at 2720. *Holder* is discussed in more detail below in §11.3.2.5.

An individual whose speech is unprotected by the First Amendment and who could constitutionally be punished under a more narrow statute may argue that the law is unconstitutional because of how it might be applied to third parties not before the Court.

Schad v. Borough of Mt. Ephraim is illustrative.[90] A city's ordinance prohibiting all live entertainment was challenged by an adult bookstore that had live nude dancers. The Court assumed (and in a later case held) that nude dancing is not protected by the First Amendment.[91] But the law prohibited much more speech than just nude dancing: It outlawed all live entertainment—all plays, all concerts, all athletic events. The nude dancing establishment was allowed to challenge the law, in part, because of how it regulated the speech of others not before the Court.

There are thus two major aspects to the overbreadth doctrine. First, a law must be substantially overbroad; that is, it must restrict significantly more speech than the Constitution allows to be controlled. In *Broadrick v. Oklahoma*, the Court said that "particularly where conduct and not merely speech is involved, we believe that the overbreadth of a statute must not only be real, but substantial as well, judged in relation to the statute's plainly legitimate sweep."[92] In *Broadrick*, the Court upheld the constitutionality of an Oklahoma law that prohibited political activities by government employees.[93] The challengers argued that the law was overbroad because it prohibited constitutionally protected activity such as the wearing of political buttons or the displaying of bumper stickers. The Supreme Court acknowledged some overbreadth, but upheld the law because it was "not substantially overbroad and that whatever overbreadth may exist should be cured through case-by-case analysis of the fact situations to which its sanctions, assertedly, may not be applied."[94] In other words, the Court said that the law should not be declared unconstitutional on its face because it was not substantially overbroad, but that particular applications of the law could be declared unconstitutional in future cases.

In subsequent cases, the Court made it clear that the requirement for substantial overbreadth applies in all cases, whether the law regulates conduct that communicates or "pure speech."[95] The Court has declared that "[a] statute may be invalidated on its face . . . only if the overbreadth is substantial."[96] In *City Council v. Taxpayers for Vincent*, the Court upheld a municipal ordinance that prohibited the

---

[90] 452 U.S. 61 (1981).

[91] *See* Barnes v. Glen Theatre, Inc., 501 U.S. 560 (1991) (holding that nude dancing is not protected speech under the First Amendment). *Barnes* is discussed below in §11.3.4.4.

[92] 413 U.S. 601, 615-616 (1973).

[93] The constitutionality of political activities by government employees is discussed in more detail in §11.3.8.2.

[94] *Id.* at 615-616.

[95] The distinction between conduct that communicates and pure speech is discussed in §11.3.6. Cases holding that substantial overbreadth is required in order for a law to be invalidated include *City Council of Los Angeles v. Taxpayers for Vincent*, 466 U.S. 789, 800 (1984), and *New York v. Ferber*, 458 U.S. 747, 772 (1982).

[96] Board of Airport Commrs. of Los Angeles v. Jews for Jesus, Inc., 482 U.S. 569, 574 (1987).

posting of signs on public property and emphasized that "substantial overbreadth" was required in order for a law to be invalidated.[97]

In *Vincent*, the Court also addressed the question of what is "substantial overbreadth." The Court said that "[t]he concept of substantial overbreadth is not readily reduced to an exact definition. It is clear, however, that the mere fact that one can conceive of some impermissible applications of a statute is not sufficient to render it susceptible to an overbreadth challenge. . . . In short, there must be a realistic danger that the statute itself will significantly compromise recognized First Amendment protections of parties not before the Court for it to be facially challenged on overbreadth grounds."[98]

It appears, then, that substantial overbreadth might be demonstrated by showing a significant number of situations where a law could be applied to prohibit constitutionally protected speech. For example, in *Houston v. Hill*, the Court declared unconstitutional an ordinance that made it unlawful to interrupt police officers in the performance of their duties.[99] An individual was convicted of violating the law for shouting at police officers to divert their attention from arresting his friend. The Court declared the law unconstitutional and said that the "ordinance criminalizes a substantial amount of constitutionally protected speech, and accords the police unconstitutional discretion in enforcement. The ordinance's plain language is admittedly violated scores of times daily . . . , yet only some individuals — those chosen by the police in their unguided discretion — are arrested. Far from providing the 'breathing space' that 'First Amendment freedoms need to survive,' the ordinance is susceptible of regular application to protected expression. We conclude that the statute is substantially overbroad."[100]

More recently, in *United States v. Stevens*, the Court declared unconstitutional a law that prohibited the creation, sale, or possession of depictions of animal cruelty.[101] The Court refused to recognize depictions of animal cruelty as a new category of unprotected speech, analogous to child pornography, in which the government could punish creation, distribution, or even possession of the expression. Additionally, the Court found that the law was unconstitutionally overbroad. Chief Justice Roberts, writing for the Court in an 8-1 decision, explained that the statute "create[s] a criminal prohibition of alarming breadth. To begin with, the text of the statute's ban on a 'depiction of animal cruelty' nowhere requires that the depicted conduct be cruel."[102] The Court explained that because the statute applies to any conduct that is illegal, hunting videos would fit within its prohibition

---

[97] 466 U.S. 789, 800 (1984).
[98] *Id.* at 800-801.
[99] 482 U.S. 451 (1987).
[100] *Id.* at 466-467.
[101] 130 S. Ct. 1577 (2010).
[102] *Id.* at 1587.

since hunting is illegal in some states. This made the statute impermissibly over-broad in its sweep.[103]

In contrast, if the Court believes that the law will apply to relatively few situations where speech is constitutionally protected, it will not be declared overbroad. For example, in *New York v. Ferber*, the Court upheld a state law prohibiting child pornography, although it acknowledged that the statute could be applied to material with serious literary, scientific, or educational value.[104] The Court said that the law was constitutional because these applications of the statute would not "amount to more than a tiny fraction of the materials within the statute's reach."[105] These applications thus could be dealt with on a case-by-case basis if prosecutions arose, rather than by declaring the entire law unconstitutional.

It also is possible that a law can be shown to be overbroad by demonstrating great harm to particularly important speech. Professor Richard Fallen has persuasively argued that substantial overbreadth should be determined by a balancing test, with a court weighing the state's substantive interest in being able to "employ a standard that is broader than the less restrictive substitutes" against "the First Amendment interest in . . . avoiding the chilling of constitutionally protected conduct."[106] In other words, Professor Fallen argued that the "farther that chilled conduct lies from the central concerns of the First Amendment, . . . the more a federal court should hesitate about declaring a [law] void for overbreadth."[107]

The second major aspect of the overbreadth doctrine is that a person to whom the law constitutionally may be applied can argue that it would be unconstitutional as applied to others. The usual rule of standing is "that a person to whom a statute may constitutionally be applied will not be heard to challenge that statute on the ground that it may conceivably be applied unconstitutionally to others, in other situations not before the Court."[108] But overbreadth is an exception to this general standing principle that requires people to assert only their own rights.[109]

---

[103] On December 10, 2010, President Obama signed H.R. 5566, the Animal Crush Video Prohibition Act of 2010, which was designed to overturn the Supreme Court's decision in *Stevens*. The law prohibits material that (1) depicts actual conduct in which one or more living nonhuman mammals, birds, reptiles, or amphibians is intentionally crushed, burned, drowned, suffocated, impaled, or otherwise subjected to serious bodily injury (as defined in §1365 and including conduct that, if committed against a person and in the special maritime and territorial jurisdiction of the United States, would violate §2241 or 2242); and (2) is obscene.

[104] 458 U.S. 747 (1982). Child pornography and the First Amendment is discussed in §11.3.4.3.

[105] *Id.* at 773.

[106] Richard Fallen, Jr., Making Sense of Overbreadth, 100 Yale L.J. 853, 894 (1991).

[107] *Id.*

[108] Broadrick v. Oklahoma, 413 U.S. at 610. The prohibition against such "third-party" standing is discussed in §2.5.4.

[109] *See, e.g.*, Virginia v. American Booksellers Assn., Inc., 484 U.S. 383, 392-393 (1988); Secretary of State v. J.H. Munson, 467 U.S. 947, 956 (1984). This is an exception to the usual standing rules because individuals are allowed to argue that a law is unconstitutional as applied to others, unlike the requirements of the usual standing rules. This is discussed in §2.5.4.

Secretary of State v. J.H. Munson Co. illustrates this aspect of the overbreadth doctrine.[110] A Maryland statute prohibited charitable organizations from soliciting funds unless at least 75 percent of their revenue was used for "charitable purposes." The law was challenged by a professional fund-raiser who raised the First Amendment rights of his clients, charities who were not parties to the lawsuit. The Supreme Court permitted the fund-raiser standing to argue the constitutional claims of charitable organizations. The Court said that "where the claim is that a statute is overly broad in violation of the First Amendment, the Court has allowed a party to assert the rights of another without regard to the ability of the other to assert his own claims and with no requirement that the person making the attack demonstrate that his own conduct could not be regulated by a statute drawn with the requisite narrow specificity."[111]

The overbreadth doctrine is thus regarded by the Supreme Court as "strong medicine"[112] because it involves the facial invalidation of a law and because it permits individuals standing to raise the claims of others not before the Court. Individuals who otherwise could be constitutionally punished are allowed to go free. The Court explained that "there are substantial costs created by the overbreadth doctrine when it blocks the application of a law to constitutionally unprotected speech, or especially to constitutionally unprotected conduct."[113] The Court has justified the overbreadth doctrine because the "First Amendment needs breathing space."[114] The concerns are that overbroad laws will chill significant constitutionally protected speech and that individuals to whom the law is unconstitutional may refrain from expression rather than bring a challenge to the statute. Justice Brennan explained that the overbreadth doctrine is "necessary because persons whose expression is constitutionally protected may well refrain from exercising their rights for fear of criminal sanctions provided by a statute susceptible of application to protected expression."[115]

This rationale for the overbreadth doctrine is illustrated by the Court's holding that it does not apply in challenges to laws regulating commercial speech.[116] The Court believes that the incentive to engage in advertising is sufficiently strong as to lessen any worries that such speech will be chilled.

---

[110] 467 U.S. 947 (1984).

[111] *Id.* at 957 (citations omitted); *see also* Village of Schaumburg v. Citizens for a Better Environment, 444 U.S. 620, 634 (1980) (also invalidating a statute regulating charitable solicitation on overbreadth grounds).

[112] Broadrick v. Oklahoma, 413 U.S. at 613.

[113] Virginia v. Hicks, 539 U.S. 113, 119 (2003) (rejecting an overbreadth challenge to a city ordinance restricting access to a housing development by those who had received notices barring them from being there).

[114] *Id.* at 611.

[115] Gooding v. Wilson, 405 U.S. 518, 521 (1972). The Court explained that it has provided "this expansive remedy [of the overbreadth doctrine] out of concern that the threat of enforcement of an overbroad law may deter or 'chill' constitutionally protected speech—especially where the overbroad statute imposes criminal sanctions." Virginia v. Hicks, 539 U.S. at 119.

[116] *See, e.g.,* Village of Hoffman Estates v. Flipside, Hoffman Estates, Inc., 455 U.S. 489, 497 (1982) ("the overbreadth doctrine does not apply to commercial speech").

Because the overbreadth doctrine is perceived as "strong medicine," the Court has said that it will avoid invalidating laws by allowing courts to construe statutes narrowly and thus avoid overbreadth. In *Osborne v. Ohio*, the Court used this approach to avoid declaring a child pornography law unconstitutional on overbreadth grounds.[117] The law prohibited private possession of child pornography and, by its terms, outlawed possession of nude photographs. The Supreme Court has long recognized that nudity, by itself, is not enough to place pictures outside the scope of the First Amendment.[118] The Ohio Supreme Court adopted a narrowing construction of the law so that it applied only to "the possession or viewing of material or performance of a minor who is in a state of nudity, where such nudity constitutes a lewd exhibition or involves a graphic focus on the genitals, and where the person depicted is neither the child nor the ward of the person charged."[119] The United States Supreme Court accepted this narrowing construction as avoiding "penalizing persons for viewing or possessing innocuous photographs of naked children."[120] The Court thus found that the law was not impermissibly overbroad.

In contrast, in *Gooding v. Wilson*, the absence of narrowing constructions by state courts led to a law prohibiting fighting words being invalidated on overbreadth grounds.[121] A Georgia law made it a crime for "[a]ny person who shall, without provocation, use to or of another, and in his presence opprobrious words or abusive language, tending to cause a breach of the peace."[122] The Court said that the law could be upheld under the First Amendment "only if, as authoritatively construed by the Georgia courts, it is not susceptible of application to speech, although vulgar or offensive, that is protected by the First and Fourteenth Amendments."[123] The Court reviewed Georgia court decisions and, finding no such limiting construction, declared the law unconstitutionally overbroad.

The Court also avoids the "strong medicine" of overbreadth by attempting to sever the unconstitutionally overbroad part of the law from the remainder of the statute. In *Brockett v. Spokane Arcades, Inc.*, the Court did exactly this, upholding an obscenity law, while striking down the part of the law that defined "lust" as unduly broad.[124]

Relationship Between Vagueness and Overbreadth

The concepts of vagueness and overbreadth are closely related; laws often are challenged under both of these doctrines simultaneously. Both vagueness and overbreadth involve facial challenges to laws. But these concepts are best

---

[117] 495 U.S. 103 (1990).
[118] *See, e.g.,* Erznoznik v. City of Jacksonville, 422 U.S. 205 (1975).
[119] 495 U.S. at 113.
[120] *Id.*
[121] 405 U.S. 518 (1972).
[122] *Id.* at 519.
[123] *Id.* at 520.
[124] 472 U.S. 491, 498 (1985). *Brockett* is discussed in §11.3.4.2.

understood as overlapping, not identical. Sometimes a law might be overbroad, but not vague. For example, in *Board of Airport Commissioners of Los Angeles v. Jews for Jesus, Inc.*, the Court declared unconstitutional an ordinance prohibiting any person "to engage in First Amendment activities within the Central Terminal Area at Los Angeles International Airport."[125] The Court found that the law was impermissibly overbroad because it prohibited "*all* protected expression. . . . [I]t prohibits even talking and reading, or the wearing of campaign buttons or symbolic clothing."[126] The Court did not find that the law was vague; quite the contrary, the Court thought that the law was clear in prohibiting all forms of First Amendment activity and thus concluded that it was clearly overbroad.

Sometimes a law can be vague, but not overbroad. For example, if the Los Angeles ordinance declared unconstitutional in *Board of Airport Commissioners* was rewritten to prohibit all speech not protected by the First Amendment, it would, by definition, not be overbroad. It would forbid only expression which by law could be regulated. But the law would be vague because a reasonable person could not know what was outlawed and what was permitted.

Often, though, laws that are vulnerable to vagueness challenges also can be objected to on overbreadth grounds. For instance, in *Coates v. Cincinnati*, the Court declared unconstitutional an ordinance that made it a criminal offense for "three or more persons to assemble . . . on any of the sidewalks . . . and there conduct themselves in a manner annoying to persons passing by."[127] The Court said that the law "is unconstitutionally vague because it subjects the exercise of the right of assembly to an unascertainable standard, and unconstitutionally broad because it authorizes the punishment of constitutionally protected conduct."[128] The law was vague because "[c]onduct that annoys some people does not annoy others"[129] and people would have to guess as to what behavior would be punished. The law was overbroad in that political demonstrations would be prohibited if spectators found them annoying.

§11.2.3   Prior Restraints

§11.2.3.1   What Is a Prior Restraint?

Definition

The Supreme Court has declared that "prior restraints on speech and publication are the most serious and least tolerable infringement on First Amendment

---

[125] 482 U.S. 569, 571 (1987).
[126] *Id.* at 574-575 (emphasis in original).
[127] 402 U.S. 611 (1971).
[128] *Id.* at 614.
[129] *Id.*

rights."[130] The Supreme Court frequently has said that "[a]ny system of prior restraints of expression comes to this Court bearing a heavy presumption against its constitutional validity."[131] As explained above, the First Amendment was, in part, a reaction against the licensing requirements for publication that had existed in England. It was this legacy that prompted Blackstone to declare that "the liberty of the press is, indeed, essential to the nature of a free state; but this consists in laying no previous restraints upon publication, and not in freedom from censure for criminal matter when published."[132] Although it is clear that "the prohibition of laws abridging the freedom of speech is not confined to previous restraints,"[133] there is no doubt that prior restraints are regarded as a particularly undesirable way of regulating speech.

Yet a clear definition of "prior restraint" is elusive. It is too broad to say that a prior restraint is a government action that prevents speech from occurring. All laws outlawing speech would constitute prior restraints by this definition. Nor is the traditional distinction between censorship before speech and after the fact punishments sufficient. All punishment for speech—whether under prior restraints or other laws—occurs after the expression takes place. All government actions regulating speech—whether prior restraints or not—exist before the speech occurs.

The clearest definition of prior restraint is as an administrative system or a judicial order that prevents speech from occurring. For example, in *Alexander v. United States*, the Court said that "[t]he term prior restraint is used 'to describe administrative and judicial orders forbidding certain communications when issued in advance of the time that such communication are to occur.'"[134] As Professor Smolla observed, "[i]n practice, most prior restraints involve either an administrative rule requiring some form of license or permit before one may engage in expression, or a judicial order directing an individual not to engage in expression, on pain of contempt."[135]

While court injunctions stopping speech and licensing systems are classic forms of prior restraints, they are not the only types of government actions that constitute prior restraints.[136] For example, a prior restraint clearly would exist if the government were to seize every copy of a particular newspaper.

---

[130] Nebraska Press Assn. v. Stuart, 427 U.S. 539, 559 (1976).

[131] New York Times v. United States, 403 U.S. 713, 714 (1971).

[132] 4 William Blackstone, Commentaries 151-152.

[133] Schenck v. United States, 249 U.S. 47, 51 (1919).

[134] 509 U.S. 544, 550 (1993), quoting M. Nimmer, Nimmer on Freedom of Speech §4.03 p. 4-14 (1984).

[135] Rodney Smolla, Smolla and Nimmer on Freedom of Speech, 8-4 (1994).

[136] *See, e.g.*, Bantam Books, Inc. v. Sullivan, 372 U.S. 58 (1963) (finding that there was a prior restraint when the Rhode Island Commission to Encourage Morality in Youth encouraged booksellers not to sell certain materials that it deemed objectionable). Although there was no court or administrative order preventing the sale of the books, the Court found sufficient coercive pressure so as to constitute a prior restraint. *Bantam Books* is discussed more fully below in §11.2.4.5.

Cases Refusing to Find a Prior Restraint

The Court has been reluctant to characterize government actions as prior restraints even when they seem to share many of the characteristics of what has traditionally fit under this rubric.[137] For example, in *Pittsburgh Press Co. v. Pittsburgh Commission on Human Relations*, the Court found that an agency's order to newspapers to stop publishing gender-based employment advertisements did not constitute a prior restraint.[138] The Pittsburgh Commission on Human Relations issued an order prohibiting newspapers from placing help-wanted advertisements in categories captioned "Jobs-Male Interest," "Jobs-Female Interest," and "Male-Female." As an order stopping speech, this seems to fit within the definition of a prior restraint, albeit one that could be justified by the desire to eliminate sex discrimination in the workplace.

But the Supreme Court held that it was not a prior restraint. The Court said: "The special vice of a prior restraint is that communication will be suppressed, either directly or by inducing excessive caution in the speaker, before an adequate determination that it is unprotected by the First Amendment. The present order does not endanger arguably protected speech. Because the order is based on a continuing course of repetitive conduct, this is not a case in which the Court is asked to speculate as to the effect of publication. . . . Moreover, the order is clear and sweeps no more broadly than necessary."[139]

It is puzzling why any of these factors mean that the order is not a prior restraint. A clear judicial order directed only at stopping unprotected speech is undoubtedly a prior restraint, as would be a court order directed at continuing conduct. The most significant distinction between the administrative order and court orders was alluded to in a footnote: The agency could not punish violators with contempt as can courts.[140]

Subsequently, in *Alexander v. United States*, the Court held that the seizure and destruction of books, magazines, and films from a person convicted of an obscenity law violation did not constitute a prior restraint.[141] Ferris Alexander, an owner of more than a dozen bookstores and theaters dealing in sexually explicit material, was convicted of selling seven items (four magazines and three videotapes) that were deemed to be obscene. He was sentenced to six years in prison and fined

---

[137] A counter example to this was in *Lowe v. SEC*, 472 U.S. 181 (1985), where the Court used the prior restraint doctrine as a basis for interpreting a statute. The Investment Advisors Act of 1940 provides for injunctions and criminal penalties against anyone using the mail in conjunction with an advisory business who is not registered with the SEC or exempt from regulation. The SEC sought an injunction against Lowe to keep him from publishing a newsletter because of a prior criminal conviction and because his registration had been revoked. The Court concluded that Lowe's publication of a financial newsletter did not make him an investment advisor under the Act. The Court emphasized that to enjoin him from publishing would be a prior restraint and so interpreted the statute to avoid its application.

[138] 413 U.S. 376 (1973).

[139] *Id.* at 390.

[140] *Id.* at 390 n.4.

[141] 509 U.S. 544 (1993).

$100,000. In addition, pursuant to the federal RICO statute, the court ordered that the contents of all of his stores be seized.[142] The books and magazines were literally burned by the government; the videotapes were crushed. Nine million dollars of merchandise was destroyed, even though only seven items had been found to be obscene.

The Court, in a 5-to-4 decision, upheld this action as constitutional and ruled that it did not constitute a prior restraint. Chief Justice Rehnquist, writing for the majority, said that there was not a prior restraint because "the RICO forfeiture order does not forbid petitioner from engaging in any expressive activities. It only deprives him of specific assets that were found to be related to his previous racketeering violations. . . . Unlike . . . injunctions, the forfeiture order in this case imposes no legal impediment to—no prior restraint on—petitioner's ability to engage in any expressive activity he chooses."[143] The majority's view was that the government may seize the assets of businesses convicted of violating RICO, and it is irrelevant if those assets are in the form of books and videos that are protected by the First Amendment.

The Court's decision, allowing $9 million worth of books, magazines, and films to be destroyed without any finding that they were obscene or unprotected by the First Amendment, is deeply troubling. It is difficult to understand why the destruction is not a prior restraint. Burning the printed materials and crushing the videotapes prevent them from being used just as a court order or a licensing system would. Although Alexander could set up a new business with new copies of the materials, the government's action seems a clear prior restraint as to everything that was destroyed. Justice Kennedy, in a dissenting opinion, explained: "The admitted design and the overt purpose of the forfeiture in this case are to destroy an entire speech business and all its protected titles, thus depriving the public of access to lawful expression. This is restraint in more than theory. It is censorship all too real."[144]

The definition of a prior restraint became even more puzzling after the Court's ruling in *Madsen v. Women's Health Center* that a court order restricting speech in a 36-foot buffer zone around an abortion clinic did not constitute a

---

[142]   RICO refers to the Racketeer Influenced and Corrupt Organization Act, 18 U.S.C. §1963.

[143]   509 U.S. at 550. Earlier, in *Arcara v. Cloud Books, Inc.*, 478 U.S. 697 (1986), the Court found that a court order closing down an adult bookstore as a nuisance did not constitute a prior restraint. The Court said:

> The closure order sought in this case differs from a prior restraint in two significant respects. First, the order would impose no restraint at all on the dissemination of particular materials, since respondents are free to carry on their bookselling business at another location, even if such locations are difficult to find. Second, the closure order would not be imposed on the basis of an advance determination that the distribution of particular materials is prohibited—indeed, the imposition of the closure order has nothing to do with any expressive conduct at all.

Id. at 705-706 n.2.

[144]   *Id.* at 565-66 (Kennedy, J., dissenting).

prior restraint.[145] A state court trial judge issued an order that, in part, created a buffer zone around the entrance to a clinic that provided abortions so as to protect the ability of people to enter and leave the facility.

The Court rejected the argument that the court order was a prior restraint. The Court said that the injunction did not prevent the demonstrators from expressing their message in other places, but they "are simply prohibited from expressing it within the 36-foot buffer zone."[146] The Court also said that the court order creating the buffer zone was based not on the demonstrators' expression, "but because of their prior unlawful conduct," which repeatedly had interfered with the free access of patients and staff.[147]

Madsen involved a court order limiting speech in the future, which is a classic form of prior restraint. It is unclear why a prior restraint requires that the court order stop all expression in all places. For example, does *Madsen* mean that it would not be a prior restraint for a court to issue an order banning a demonstration in a park because, in theory, the demonstration could occur someplace else? Moreover, the need to secure access to the abortion clinic in light of the past behavior obstructing the entrance is clearly sufficient to warrant such a court order; but it is confusing as to why the adequacy of the reason for the court order keeps it from being a prior restraint.

Thus, it is very difficult to formulate a clear and accurate definition of what constitutes a prior restraint. The definition articulated in *Alexander*—that the "term prior restraint is used 'to describe administrative and judicial orders forbidding certain communications when issued in advance of the time that such communication are to occur' "[148]—seems the best. Yet it is inconsistent with the Court's decisions in *Pittsburgh Press, Alexander,* and *Madsen.*

§11.2.3.2   Why Are Prior Restraints So Bad?

Are Prior Restraints Really So Bad?

There is little doubt that the Court went out of its way in these cases to avoid finding the orders to be prior restraints because of the strong presumption against constitutionality that would be triggered by such a conclusion. As expressed above, the Court has said that "[a]ny system of prior restraints of expression comes to this Court bearing a heavy presumption against its constitutional validity"[149] and the government "thus carries a heavy burden of showing justification for the imposition of such a restraint."[150]

---

[145] 512 U.S. 753 (1994).
[146] *Id.* at 764 n.2.
[147] *Id.*
[148] 509 U.S. at 550.
[149] Bantam Books, Inc. v. Sullivan, 372 U.S. 58, 70 (1963).
[150] Organization for a Better Austin v. Keefe, 402 U.S. 415, 419 (1971).

But why are prior restraints so bad? After the fact punishments, if large enough, can prevent speech just as much as any prior restraint.[151] Also, prior restraints have the virtue that they are usually specific in the form of a court order stopping particular speech or the denial of a license for certain expression.[152] There usually is some due process in the form of a judicial or administrative hearing before the prior restraint.[153]

The Evils of Prior Restraints

A classic argument as to why prior restraints are the worst form of speech regulations was advanced by noted First Amendment scholar Thomas Emerson: "A system of prior restraint is in many ways more inhibiting than a system of subsequent punishment: It is likely to bring under government scrutiny a far wider range of expression; it shuts off communication before it takes place; suppression by a stroke of the pen is more likely to be applied than suppression through a criminal process; the procedures do not require attention to the safeguards of the criminal process; the system allows less opportunity for public appraisal and criticism; the dynamics of the system drive toward excesses, as the history of all censorship shows."[154]

Prior restraints prevent speech from ever occurring. The Court explained that "[b]ehind the distinction is a theory deeply etched in our law: A free society prefers to punish the few who abuse rights of speech *after they* break the law than to throttle them and all others beforehand."[155] Inevitably, prior restraints could be imposed based on predictions of danger that would not actually materialize and thus would not be the basis for subsequent punishments.[156]

The Collateral Bar Rule

Perhaps the most persuasive argument as to why prior restraints are worse than other ways of regulating speech is the collateral bar rule: A person violating an unconstitutional law may not be punished, but a person violating an unconstitutional prior restraint generally may be punished. Specifically, the collateral

---

[151] *See, e.g.*, John C. Jeffries, Jr., Rethinking Prior Restraint, 92 Yale L.J. 409 (1983) (questioning the usefulness and desirability of the prior restraint doctrine).

[152] *See, e.g.*, William T. Mayton, Toward a Theory of First Amendment Process: Injunctions of Speech, Subsequent Punishment, and the Costs of the Prior Restraint Doctrine, 67 Cornell L. Rev. 245 (1982).

[153] Hans Linde, Courts and Censorship, 66 Minn. L. Rev. 171, 186 (1981); *see also* Martin Redish, The Proper Role of the Prior Restraint Doctrine in First Amendment Theory, 70 Va. L. Rev. 53, 58 (1984) (arguing that preliminary orders stopping speech are undesirable and that the prior restraint doctrine should invalidate injunctions only if they are imposed prior to a full and fair judicial hearing).

[154] Thomas Emerson, The System of Freedom of Expression 506 (1970).

[155] Southeastern Promotions, Ltd. v. Conrad, 420 U.S. 546, 559 (1975) (emphasis added).

[156] *See, e.g.*, Vincent Blasi, Toward a Theory of Prior Restraint: The Central Linkage, 66 Minn. L. Rev. 11, 49-54 (1981).

bar rule provides that "a court order must be obeyed until it is set aside, and that persons subject to the order who disobey it may not defend against the ensuing charge of criminal contempt on the ground that the order was erroneous or even unconstitutional."[157]

For example, in *Walker v. City of Birmingham*, the Court upheld the contempt convictions of defendants, civil rights protestors, who had violated a court order preventing them from engaging in demonstrations on city streets without a permit.[158] The Court ruled that the protestors—Dr. Martin Luther King, Jr. and seven other African-American ministers—were barred from challenging the constitutionality of the court order because they had violated it. The Court said: "This Court cannot hold that the petitioners were constitutionally free to ignore all the procedures of the law and carry their battle to the streets. . . . [R]espect for judicial process is a small price to pay for the civilizing hand of law, which alone can give abiding meaning to constitutional freedom."[159] The Court indicated that the collateral bar rule precluded challenges to punishment for violating a court order, unless the injunction was "transparently invalid or had only a frivolous pretense to validity."[160]

The Court has ruled that the collateral bar rule applies only to procedurally proper court orders. In *Carroll v. President and Commissioners of Princess Anne County*, the Court refused to apply the collateral bar rule when individuals violated a court order preventing demonstrations for ten days when the restraining order resulted from an ex parte proceeding, where no notice was given to those affected, and no attempt was made to communicate with them.[161] The Court said that "[t]he 10-day order here must be set aside because of a basic infirmity in the procedure by which it was obtained. It was issued ex parte, without notice to petitioners and without any effort, however informal, to invite or permit their participation in the proceedings."[162] The Court forcefully concluded: "[T]here is no place within the area of basic freedoms guaranteed by the First Amendment for such orders where no showing is made that it is impossible to serve or to notify the opposing parties and to give them an opportunity to participate."[163]

The collateral bar rule explains why prior restraints are worse than after the fact punishments. A law prohibiting expression and imposing punishments for violations always can be challenged as unconstitutional. But an unconstitutional court order cannot be challenged if it has been violated. The collateral bar rule is justified as necessary to protect respect for the judiciary and compliance with its orders. Yet it seems unjust to punish a person for constitutionally protected speech.

---

[157] Stephen Barnett, The Puzzle of Prior Restraint, 29 Stan. L. Rev. 539, 552 (1977).
[158] 388 U.S. 307 (1967).
[159] 388 U.S. at 321.
[160] *Id.* at 315.
[161] 393 U.S. 175 (1968).
[162] *Id.* at 180.
[163] *Id.*

The Court, at times, has applied the collateral bar rule to licensing schemes as well as to court orders. In *Poulos v. New Hampshire*, the Court affirmed an individual's conviction for conducting a religious service in a public park without the required license.[164] The Court said that the defendant could not challenge the denial of a license as arbitrary and unconstitutional when the licensing system is valid on its face and when he proceeded without a license rather than challenge its denial. The Court said: "The valid requirements of license are for the good of the applicants and the public. . . . Delay is unfortunate but the expense and annoyance of litigation is a price citizens must pay for life in an orderly society. . . . Nor can we say that a state's requirement that redress must be sought through appropriate judicial procedure violates due process."[165]

But in *Shuttlesworth v. City of Birmingham*, the Court overturned the convictions of civil rights protestors who violated a city's ordinance by having a demonstration without the required permit.[166] The Court found the permit law unconstitutional because it gave city officials unfettered discretion in granting and denying permits. The Court refused to apply the collateral bar rule and prevent a challenge. In fact, the Court said that "a person faced with such an unconstitutional licensing law may ignore it and engage with impunity in the exercise of the right of free expression for which the law purports to require a license."[167]

The difference between *Poulos* and *Shuttlesworth* is that the former involved a law that was valid on its face because it contained adequate standards and safeguards, whereas the latter case concerned a law that was facially invalid because of the absence of criteria to limit administrative discretion. *Shuttlesworth* establishes that courts will not preclude a person who failed to apply for a license from challenging a licensing law as facially unconstitutional, such as in giving too much discretion to government officials in awarding licenses. But *Poulos* likely remains good law in that a licensing law that is valid on its face must be complied with; a failure to follow the procedures or to challenge the denial of a permit through available administrative and judicial challenges will preclude later assertion that the speech was protected by the First Amendment. Yet even here, the justification for the collateral bar rule in preserving respect for courts and in ensuring compliance with judicial orders is absent in administrative licensing systems.

§11.2.3.3   Court Orders as a Prior Restraint

Near v. Minnesota

One classic form of prior restraint is a court order stopping speech from occurring. In *Near v. Minnesota*, the Court clearly held that judicial orders preventing

---

[164] 345 U.S. 395 (1953).
[165] *Id.* at 409.
[166] 394 U.S. 147 (1969).
[167] *Id.* at 151.

speech constitute a prior restraint.[168] A Minnesota law provided for the abatement, as a public nuisance, of a "malicious, scandalous, and defamatory newspaper, magazine or other periodical."[169] The statute was applied to the Saturday Press that published a series of articles that made defamatory and anti-Semitic accusations. A trial court issued an injunction that perpetually enjoined the Saturday Press from publishing or circulating "any publication . . . whatsoever containing a malicious, scandalous and defamatory matter."[170]

The Court declared the injunction unconstitutional and said that "it has been generally, if not universally, considered that it is the chief purpose of the guaranty to prevent previous restraints upon publication. . . . The fact that for approximately one hundred and fifty years there has been almost an entire absence of attempts to impose previous restraints upon publications . . . is significant of the deep-seated conviction that such restraints would violate constitutional right."[171] The Court emphasized that the appropriate way of dealing with unprotected speech was after the fact punishment, not a prior restraint. "[The] fact that liberty of the press may be abused by miscreant purveyors of scandal does not make any the less necessary the immunity of the press from previous restraint in dealing with official misconduct. Subsequent punishment for such abuses as may exist is the appropriate remedy."[172]

The Court in *Near* did not say that all court orders stopping speech are unconstitutional, but said that such injunctions would be allowed "only in exceptional cases."[173] The Court then outlined the situation where it envisioned allowing such prior restraints: "No one would question but that a government might prevent actual obstruction to its recruiting service or the publication of the sailing dates of transports or the number and location of troops. On similar grounds, the primary requirements of decency may be enforced against obscene publications. The security of the community life may be protected against incitements to acts of violence and the overthrow by force of orderly government."[174]

Requirement for Narrow Tailoring

The Court has been clear that any court order regulating speech must be narrowly tailored. The Court has stated that any injunction restricting speech must "'burden no more speech than necessary' to accomplish its objective."[175] An injunction "issued in the area of First Amendment rights must be couched in the narrowest terms that will accomplish the pin-pointed objective permitted by constitutional mandate and the essential needs of the public order."[176]

---

[168] 283 U.S. 697 (1931).
[169] *Id.* at 701-702.
[170] *Id.* at 705.
[171] *Id.* at 713, 718.
[172] *Id.* at 720.
[173] *Id.* at 716.
[174] *Id.*
[175] Madsen v. Women's Health Center, 512 U.S. 753, 765 (1994).
[176] Carroll v. President and Commrs. of Princess Anne County, 393 U.S. 175, 183 (1968).

The Court reaffirmed this in *Tory v. Cochran.*[177] A trial court found that Ulysses Tory had defamed renowned attorney Johnnie Cochran and issued an injunction preventing Tory and his wife from saying anything about Cochran or his law firm in any public forum. The Supreme Court, without reaching the question of whether injunctions are ever permissible in defamation cases, concluded that the injunction was unconstitutionally overbroad. The Court reaffirmed that any injunction of speech must be narrowly tailored to achieve its objectives.

National Security

Near spoke of national security—such as to prevent publication of the details of when and where a military action would occur—as justifying prior restraints. *New York Times v. United States*, the Pentagon Papers case, is the primary decision thus far considering national security as the basis for a court order stopping speech.[178] The New York Times, and then the Washington Post, published excerpts from a top secret, 47-volume Defense Department history of the Vietnam War. The United States government sought federal court injunctions precluding publication on national security grounds. The federal district courts refused to issue such orders. The District of Columbia Circuit affirmed, while the Second Circuit reversed and approved the injunction. The case proceeded quickly: Just 18 days elapsed from the first article in The New York Times until the decision in the Supreme Court.

The Supreme Court held, by a 6-to-3 margin, that a court order stopping publication violated the First Amendment. There were ten different opinions: a per curiam opinion and a separate opinion by each Justice. The per curiam opinion was brief and simply reiterated the heavy presumption against prior restraints, concluding that the government failed to meet this burden.[179]

Justices Black and Douglas each wrote separate opinions, which strongly condemned any prior restraint. Justice Black, for example, wrote that "every moment's continuance of the injunctions against these newspapers amounts to a flagrant, indefensible, and continuing violation of the First Amendment. . . . Now, for the first time in the 182 years since the founding of the Republic, the federal courts are asked to hold that the First Amendment does not mean what it says, but rather means that the Government can halt the publication of current news of vital importance to the people in this country."[180] Likewise, Justice Douglas said that "[t]he dominant purpose of the First Amendment was to prohibit . . . the widespread use of the common law of seditious libel to punish the dissemination of material that is embarrassing to the powers-that-be. The present cases will, I think, go down in history as the most dramatic illustration of that principle."[181]

[177] 554 U.S. 734 (2005).
[178] 403 U.S. 713 (1971).
[179] *Id.* at 714.
[180] *Id.* at 715 (Black, J., concurring).
[181] *Id.* at 723-724.

Although Justices Black and Douglas seemed to take an absolute position against prior restraints to protect national security, one wonders whether even they would allow such restrictions if there was compelling proof of a need to protect national security. For example, if a newspaper during World War II was going to report that America had broken the Nazi code, probably even Black and Douglas would have allowed an injunction to stop that information from being published and to preserve an enormous strategic advantage in the war.

Justice Brennan wrote a concurring opinion in which he argued for the use of strict scrutiny for prior restraints. He said that the "First Amendment stands as an absolute bar to the imposition of judicial restraints in circumstances of the kind presented by these cases."[182] He wrote that "the First Amendment tolerates absolutely no prior judicial restraints of the press predicated upon surmise or conjecture that untoward consequences may result. Our cases . . . have indicated that there is a single, extremely narrow class of cases in which the First Amendment's ban on prior judicial restraint may be overridden. Our cases thus far indicates that such cases may arise only when the Nation 'is at war.' "[183] He thus said that the attempt to enjoin publication of the Pentagon Papers fell far short of the high standard that needed to be met for a prior restraint.

Justices White and Marshall each wrote separate opinions and emphasized the absence of statutory authority for the courts to impose such an injunction. Justice White said that the government had failed to meet its burden "at least in the absence of express and appropriately limited congressional authorization for prior restraints in circumstances such as these."[184] Justice Marshall argued that Congress had failed to give the president the power to seek injunctions to stop publication of information. He wrote: "Either the Government has the power under statutory grant to use traditional criminal law to protect the country or, if there is no basis for arguing that Congress has made the activity a crime, it is plain that Congress has specifically refused to grant the authority the Government seeks from this Court. In either case this Court does not have the authority to grant the requested relief."[185]

Although Justices White and Marshall stressed the absence of statutory authority for the injunction, it can be questioned as to what difference it would have made if a statute had existed. The First Amendment obviously limits Congress as much as the president, and it is not apparent why an otherwise unconstitutional prior restraint is made more palatable because Congress has approved it.

Justice Stewart, the final Justice in the majority, contended that the president had the power to seek an injunction to protect national security, but he concluded that the executive had failed to justify the need for the prior restraint in this case. He stated: "I am convinced that the Executive is correct with respect to some of the documents involved. But I cannot say that disclosure of any of them will surely result in direct, immediate, and irreparable damage to our Nation or its people.

---

[182] *Id.* at 725 (Brennan, J., concurring).
[183] *Id.* at 726.
[184] *Id.* at 731 (White, J., concurring).
[185] *Id.* at 747.

That being so, there can under the First Amendment be but one judicial resolution of the issues before us."[186]

There were three dissenting opinions, by Chief Justice Burger, Justice Harlan, and Justice Blackmun. Each urged allowing an injunction of publication until there could be more thorough review of the material. Chief Justice Burger said that the haste of review meant that "we literally do not know what are we acting on. As I see it, we have been forced to deal with litigation concerning rights of great magnitude without an adequate record, and surely without time for adequate treatment."[187] Justice Harlan likewise lamented as to the "frenzied train of events"[188] and said that the doctrine prohibiting prior restraints does not reach "to the point of preventing courts from maintaining the status quo long enough to act responsibly in matters of such national importance as those involved here."[189]

Justice Blackmun wrote the strongest dissent and also objected to the precipitous handling of the case. He said: "I hope that damage has not already been done. If, however, damage has been done, and if, with the Court's action today, these newspapers proceed to publish the critical documents and there results therefrom 'the death of soldiers, the destruction of alliances, the greatly increased difficulty of negotiation with our enemies, the inability of our diplomats to negotiate,' to which list I might add the factors of prolongation of the war and of further delay in the freeing of United States prisoners, then the Nation's people will know where the responsibility for these sad consequences rests."[190]

New York Times v. United States is thus a strong pronouncement against prior restraints, even in the name of national security, unless there is proof of a compelling need for an injunction. The Court's decision ultimately rested on the failure of the government to point to materials in the historical study that needed to be kept secret in order to protect national security.

New York Times leaves two major questions open. First, what circumstances, if any, would justify a court order preventing publication so as to protect national security? Second, what difference, if any, would it make if there was a statute authorizing a prior restraint?

No Supreme Court case has dealt with these issues since the Pentagon Papers case. One case that might have presented these questions was resolved before it reached the Supreme Court. In *United States v. Progressive, Inc.*, a federal district court issued an injunction to keep a magazine from publishing an article on how to build a hydrogen bomb.[191] Unlike the Pentagon Papers case, there was a provision in the Atomic Energy Act that appeared to authorize the injunction, and the government claimed that preventing nuclear proliferation was a justification

---

[186] *Id.* at 730 (Stewart, J., concurring).
[187] *Id.* at 751 (Burger, C.J., dissenting).
[188] *Id.* at 753 (Harlan, J., dissenting).
[189] *Id.* at 759.
[190] *Id.* at 763 (Blackmun, J., dissenting).
[191] 467 F. Supp. 990 (W.D. Wis. 1979).

sufficient to warrant the prior restraint. The case, however, was dismissed while on appeal because others published the same information in other places.[192]

The only other Supreme Court case to consider prior restraints to protect national security was *Snepp v. United States*, where the Court held that the government could insist that a former CIA agent turn his book over for prepublication review.[193] Frank Snepp, a former CIA agent and the author of *Decent Interval*, a history of the fall of Vietnam, had signed a Security Agreement allowing such review. The Court held that the agreement was binding and furthermore said that "even in the absence of an express agreement—the CIA could have acted to protect substantial government interests by imposing reasonable restrictions on employee activities that in other contexts might be protected by the First Amendment."[194] Because the book already had been published, the Court approved the government seizing the assets from the book's sale because of the violation of the agreement.

On the one hand, *Snepp* is a case with unique facts: There had been a voluntary agreement authorizing the prior restraint, and there was a perception of a special need for government oversight of the writings of former CIA agents. Yet *Snepp* also is noteworthy as the broadest holding by the Supreme Court approving of a prior restraint for national security and absent of any evidence that the contents of Snepp's book were damaging to national security.

Court Orders to Protect Fair Trials

The other major area where the Court has considered court orders as prior restraints is in injunctions against pretrial coverage of legal proceedings so as to enhance a criminal defendant's ability to receive a fair trial. In *Nebraska Press Association v. Stuart*, the Supreme Court ruled that the strong presumption against prior restraints means that such gag orders on the press will be allowed only in the rarest of circumstances, if at all.[195] *Nebraska Press* involved a defendant who was tried for committing six murders in a small town in Nebraska. The trial court issued an injunction restraining the media from publishing or broadcasting accounts of confessions or admissions made by the accused or facts strongly implicating him.

Chief Justice Burger's opinion for the Court began by reviewing the historical conflict between a free press and ensuring a fair trial. The Court said that these rights cannot be ranked in relationship to one another. Both are fundamental and, the Court said, one cannot be achieved at the expense of the other. The Court concluded that there was a very strong presumption against court orders

---

[192] For a review of the history of the litigation and a discussion of the issues presented, *see* L.A. Powe, Jr., The H-Bomb Injunction, 61 U. Colo. L. Rev. 55 (1990).
[193] 444 U.S. 507 (1980).
[194] *Id.* at 510.
[195] 427 U.S. 539 (1976).

preventing pretrial publicity as a way to protect a fair trial because the "barriers to prior restraint [must] remain high."[196]

In reviewing the case before the Court, Chief Justice Burger indicated three requirements that had to be met to justify a gag order on the press to protect a defendant's right to a fair trial. First, there has to be a showing of extensive publicity without a prior restraint that will jeopardize the ability to select a fair and impartial jury. The Court found that this requirement was met in the case. Chief Justice Burger said that "the trial judge was justified in concluding that there would be intensive and pervasive pretrial publicity . . . [and] [h]e could also reasonably conclude, based on common human experience, that publicity might impair the defendant's right to a fair trial."[197]

Yet it can be questioned as to whether pretrial publicity, even when it is at its most extensive, affects the jury's verdict. In many high profile cases, from the *McMartin Preschool* case to the rape trial of William Kennedy Smith to the first trial of the police officers for beating Rodney King to the O.J. Simpson murder trial, there was extensive publicity, but also acquittals. In each case, there were concerns that the pretrial publicity made a conviction likely. Perhaps these cases indicate the ability of juries to decide based on the facts presented at trial and not on the basis of pretrial reports in the press.

Second, to justify a prior restraint it must be determined that "measures short of an order restraining all publication [would not] have insured the defendant a fair trial."[198] The Court provided a long list of alternatives to gag orders on the press, including changing venue, postponing the trial to allow public attention to subside, searching questioning of prospective jurors "to screen out those with fixed opinions as to guilt or innocence,"[199] clear instructions to the jury as to what may be considered in reaching a verdict, and sequestration of jurors. The Court found that in the *Nebraska Press* case there was not a finding that these alternatives would have been insufficient to protect the defendant's right to a fair trial.

Finally, even if the first two requirements are met, a prior restraint is permissible only if it is determined that one would be a workable and effective method of securing a fair trial.[200] For example, there is a significant likelihood that media outlets outside the scope of the court's order will cover the case and that this will reach prospective jurors.

The Court said that it was not creating an absolute ban on prior restraints to protect a defendant's right to a fair trial,[201] but from a practical perspective, the Court did just that.[202] It is hard to imagine a case where all three requirements can

---

[196]   *Id.* at 561.

[197]   *Id.* at 562-563.

[198]   *Id.* at 563.

[199]   *Id.* at 564.

[200]   *Id.* at 565.

[201]   *Id.* at 570.

[202]   It should be noted that three Justices—Brennan, Stewart, and Marshall—took the position that prior restraints never would be justified to protect a defendant's right to a fair trial, *id.* at 572 (Brennan, J., concurring), and a fourth, Justice White, expressed "grave doubt" that such a prior restraint ever would be justified. *Id.* at 570 (White, J., concurring).

be met. Even assuming that extensive pretrial publicity threatens a defendant's right to a fair trial, it is difficult to see how a court could conclude that all alternatives to a gag order would fail or that a prior restraint would be successful in keeping prospective jurors from receiving information. Indeed, as Professor Smolla observed, "[l]ower courts have treated *Nebraska Press* as tantamount to an absolute prohibition on such prior restraints, consistently refusing to permit orders limiting press coverage of judicial proceedings."[203]

Nor has the Supreme Court ever approved a prior restraint to protect a defendant's right to a fair trial since *Nebraska Press*. In *Oklahoma Publishing Co. v. District Court*, the Court declared unconstitutional a judge's order enjoining the news media from publishing, broadcasting, or disseminating the name or picture of an 11-year-old boy who was accused of murder.[204] In a brief per curiam opinion, the Court said that the media had lawfully obtained the information, and thus there could be no injunction to prevent its truthful reporting.[205]

The Supreme Court has never addressed the question of when it is permissible for courts to impose gag orders on attorneys and other trial participants. Such restrictions are increasingly common, and there are lower court cases both invalidating and upholding such orders. Professor Smolla notes that the law in this area is in "significant disarray" and that "[a]ppellate courts tend to reverse such gag orders when they do not pose serious and imminent threats to the fairness of the proceedings. When the order is narrowly tailored to eliminate serious and imminent threats, however, appellate courts are inclined to sustain such orders."[206]

On the one hand, attorneys are officers of the Court, and the Supreme Court has approved greater restrictions on attorney speech than for others in society.[207] Restricting the speech of trial participants seems less restrictive than an injunction on the press. But on the other hand, a gag order on lawyers is a prior restraint and should have to overcome the same strong presumption as other prior restraints. Moreover, limiting speech by trial participants effectively restricts the media's ability to cover proceedings with complete and accurate information.

---

[203] Smolla, *supra* note 135, at 8-41. *See id.* at 570 n.12 (collecting cases rejecting such prior restraints). One of the few cases where a lower court imposed a prior restraint was in United States v. Noriega, 752 F. Supp. 1032 (S.D. Fla.), *aff'd* In re Cable News Network, 917 F.2d 1543 (11th Cir.), *cert. denied*, Cable News Network, Inc. v. Noriega, 498 U.S. 976 (1990), where a federal district court enjoined CNN from broadcasting tapes of conversations between deposed Panamanian dictator Manuel Noriega and his attorneys. For a persuasive argument that the district court erred in granting this prior restraint because the *Nebraska Press* requirements were not met, *see* Smolla, *supra* note 135, at 8-53. *See also* Procter and Gamble Co. v. Bankers Trust Co., 78 F.3d 219 (6th Cir. 1996) (holding unconstitutional a prior restraint on Business Week to prevent publication of material that had been produced during discovery and was sealed pursuant to a court order).

[204] 430 U.S. 308 (1977).

[205] *Id.* at 310-311. The case is consistent with a body of decisions holding that the government may not create liability for the invasion of privacy for the truthful reporting of information lawfully obtained from government records. These cases are discussed in §11.3.5.5.

[206] Smolla, *supra* note 135, at 8-67.

[207] *See* Gentile v. State Bar of Nevada, 501 U.S. 1030 (1991), discussed in §11.3.9.

Obscenity[208]

In *Paris Adult Theatre I v. Slaton*, the Court held that it is permissible for courts to issue injunctions to prevent the exhibition of obscene materials.[209] The Court said that the state "imposed no restraint on the exhibition of the films . . . until after a full adversary proceeding and a final judicial determination by the Georgia Supreme Court that the materials were constitutionally unprotected."[210] Because only constitutionally unprotected material was enjoined and because there were procedural safeguards, the Court found no First Amendment violation to the prior restraint.

But the Court has made it clear that the government only can stop the showing of particular obscene material; it cannot attempt to close down an establishment because it has been "habitually used" for commercial exhibition of obscene material.[211] In *Vance v. Universal Amusement Co., Inc.*, the Court declared unconstitutional a Texas public nuisance statute authorizing injunctions against habitual use of premises for the commercial exhibition of obscene material.[212] In a per curiam opinion, the Court noted that the law "authorizes prior restraints of indefinite duration on the exhibition of motion pictures that have not been finally adjudicated to be obscene."[213] The Court objected that under the law a temporary restraining order could be issued to close down a theater based on an ex parte application.

But the Court has qualified this by holding the government may close down a business if it is used for prostitution, even if it also sells materials that are protected by the First Amendment. The Court ruled that the First Amendment has no "relevance to a statute directed at imposing sanctions on nonexpressive activity."[214] In *Arcara v. Cloud Books, Inc.*, the Court upheld a court order that closed down an adult bookstore that was used as a place of prostitution. The Court emphasized that the owners could "carry on their bookselling business at another location" and that "the imposition of the closure order has nothing to do with any expressive conduct at all."[215]

---

[208] Obscenity as a category of unprotected speech is discussed in §11.3.4.2.

[209] 413 U.S. 49 (1973).

[210] *Id.* at 55.

[211] However, as described above, in *Alexander v. United States*, 509 U.S. 544 (1993), the Court held that the government's use of the RICO law to seize the assets of a store selling adult books and movies after its conviction of obscenity violations did not constitute a prior restraint.

[212] 445 U.S. 308 (1980).

[213] *Id.* at 316.

[214] Arcara v. Cloud Books, Inc., 478 U.S. 697, 707 (1986).

[215] *Id.* at 705 n.2.

§11.2.3.4   Licensing as a Prior Restraint

Requirements for Licensing

Another form of prior restraint—in fact, the classic type of prior restraint—is where the government requires a license or permit in order for speech to occur. The Supreme Court has held that such laws are allowed only if the government has an important reason for licensing and only if there are clear criteria leaving almost no discretion to the licensing authority. In addition, there must be procedural safeguards, such as a requirement for prompt determinations as to license requests and judicial review of license denials.

For example, in *Lovell v. City of Griffin*, the Supreme Court declared unconstitutional an ordinance that prohibited the distribution of literature of any kind, in any way, without first obtaining written permission from the city manager.[216] The Court declared the law unconstitutional as an impermissible prior restraint. Chief Justice Hughes, writing for the Court, said: "[T]he ordinance is invalid on its face. Whatever the motive which induced its adoption, its character is such that it strikes at the very foundation of the freedom of the press by subjecting it to license and censorship. The struggle for freedom of the press was primarily directed against the power of the licensor."[217]

Important Reason for Licensing

Thus, three requirements must be met in order for a licensing scheme to be valid. First, there must be an important reason for licensing. For example, in *Cox v. New Hampshire*, the Court upheld an ordinance that required that those wishing to hold a parade or demonstration obtain a permit and that allowed a permit to be denied only if the area already was in use by another group.[218] The Court emphasized that the city had an important reason for licensing: to receive notice of demonstrations so as to be able to "afford opportunity for proper policing"[219] and to preserve order by ensuring only one parade at a particular place at a specific time. The Court stressed that the "licensing board was not vested with arbitrary power or an unfettered discretion."[220]

In *Watchtower Bible and Tract Society of New York, Inc. v. Village of Stratton*, the Court invalidated a city ordinance that prohibited door-to-door advocacy without first registering with the mayor and receiving a permit.[221] The Court, in an opinion by Justice Stevens, stressed that such door-to-door advocacy and solicitation is speech protected by the First Amendment. The Court explained that the

---

[216] 303 U.S. 444 (1938).
[217] *Id.* at 451.
[218] 312 U.S. 569 (1941).
[219] *Id.* at 576.
[220] *Id.*
[221] 536 U.S. 150 (2002).

licensing requirement would put a substantial burden on speech by preventing anonymous speech, by preventing spontaneous speech, and by discouraging speakers who do not wish to seek a license. The Court carefully examined the government's justifications and concluded that there was not an important reason for licensing. For example, the Court said that the privacy of residents could be protected by their posting, "No Solicitation" signs. Nor was the Court persuaded that the licensing requirement decreased the likelihood of crime. Justice Stevens explained that "it seems unlikely that the absence of a permit would preclude criminals from knocking on doors and engaging in conversations not covered by the ordinance."[222]

Clear Standards Leaving Almost No Discretion to the Government

Second, there must be clear standards leaving almost no discretion to the licensing authority. The Court is very concerned that discretion could be used for content-based censorship; the government could grant permits to speech that it liked, but deny licenses to disfavored expression.

For example, in *Saia v. New York*, the Supreme Court declared unconstitutional an ordinance that required a permit in order to use a sound amplification system on a motor vehicle.[223] Although the Court has upheld restrictions on such sound trucks,[224] an ordinance that gives unfettered discretion to government officials to decide who can use such vehicles violates the First Amendment. Similarly, in *Kunz v. New York*, the Court declared unconstitutional an ordinance that prohibited the holding of a religious meeting on a public street without a permit.[225] The Court said that the government "cannot vest restraining control over the right to speak . . . in an administrative official where there are no appropriate standards to guide his action."[226]

In many other cases as well,[227] the Court has declared unconstitutional permit laws because of the extent of discretion vested in government officials. For example, in *City of Lakewood v. Plain Dealer Publishing Co.*, the Supreme Court declared unconstitutional a city's ordinance that required a permit for placing a newspaper vending machine on public property and gave the mayor complete discretion to decide whether to issue a permit.[228] The Court noted that prior decisions clearly established that "a licensing statute placing unbridled discretion in the hands of a government official or agency constitutes a prior restraint and may result in

---

[222] *Id.* at 169.

[223] 334 U.S. 558 (1948).

[224] *See* Kovacs v. Cooper, 336 U.S. 77 (1949).

[225] 340 U.S. 290 (1951).

[226] *Id.* at 295.

[227] *See, e.g.*, Shuttlesworth v. City of Birmingham, 394 U.S. 147 (1969) (invalidating ordinance requiring a permit for parades); Staub v. City of Baxley, 355 U.S. 313 (1958) (invalidating permit requirement for solicitation of members of dues-paying organizations).

[228] 486 U.S. 750 (1988).

censorship."[229] Moreover, the Court said that without clearly delineated standards, it is too easy for licensing officials to invent some reason for denying a permit, and it is too difficult for courts to review the administrative discretion.

In *Forsyth County, Georgia v. Nationalist Movement,* the Court followed the same reason in declaring unconstitutional an ordinance that required a permit in order for a demonstration to occur and that vested discretion in the government to set the amount of the fee up to $1,000.[230] The Court found that the licensing law was impermissible because "[t]here are no articulated standards either in the ordinance or in the county's established practice. The administrator is not required to rely on any objective factors. He need not provide any explanation for his decision, and that decision is unreviewable."[231] The Court concluded that "[n]othing in the law or its application prevents the official from encouraging some views and discouraging others through the arbitrary application of the fees. The First Amendment prohibits the vesting of such unbridled discretion in a government official."[232]

Procedural Safeguards

Finally, in order for a licensing or permit system to be constitutional there must be procedural safeguards. Any system of prior restraints must have a prompt decision made by the government as to whether the speech will be allowed;[233] there must be a full and fair hearing before speech is prevented;[234] and there must be a prompt and final judicial determination of the validity of any preclusion of speech.[235]

In *Freedman v. Maryland,* the Court unanimously declared unconstitutional a Maryland law that made it unlawful to exhibit a motion picture without having first obtained a license.[236] The Court noted that such a licensing system presents grave dangers for freedom of speech. The Court said that such a system would be allowed "only if it takes place under procedural safeguards designed to obviate the dangers of . . . censorship."[237] The "burden of proving that the film is unprotected expression must rest on the censor."[238] There must be a requirement for a prompt

---

[229] *Id.* at 757.

[230] 505 U.S. 123 (1992).

[231] *Id.* at 133.

[232] *Id.*

[233] *See, e.g.,* Teitel Film Corp. v. Cusack, 390 U.S. 139 (1968) (a 50-day delay before seeking an injunction, during which time the speech could not be disseminated, violated the First Amendment).

[234] *See, e.g.,* Carroll v. President and Commrs. of Princess Anne County, 393 U.S. 175 (1968) (ex parte court orders are impermissible in restraining speech because of the lack of adversarial presentation).

[235] *See* National Socialist Party of Am. v. Village of Skokie, 432 U.S. 43 (1977) (improper to leave an injunction in place pending an appeal that could take up to a year; either the injunction had to be lifted or the appeal had to be expedited).

[236] 380 U.S. 51 (1965).

[237] *Id.* at 58.

[238] *Id.*

determination by the government whether to issue or deny the license request.[239] Also, prompt judicial review must be available for all permit denials. The Court said that "only a judicial determination in an adversary proceeding ensures the necessary sensitivity to freedom of expression."[240]

The Court repeatedly has held that such procedural safeguards are required for government actions that operate like licensing systems, such as postal stop orders for obscene materials[241] and customs seizures of obscene materials.[242] In *FW/PBS, Inc. v. City of Dallas*, the Court declared unconstitutional a city ordinance that required licensing of "sexually oriented businesses" because of the absence of the procedural safeguards prescribed in *Freedman*.[243] The Court noted that the law failed to require prompt determination of license requests or to provide for judicial review of license denials.[244]

In *Riley v. National Federation of the Blind*, the Court invalidated a state law that required a license for professional fund-raisers who were soliciting on behalf of charitable organizations.[245] The Court said that even assuming that such licensing was justified, "a regulation must provide that the licensor 'will, within a specified brief period, either issue a license or go to court.' That requirement is not met here."[246] The Court found the licensing law unconstitutional because of the lack of any requirement for a prompt determination of license requests.

However, in its subsequent cases, the Court has not adhered to *Freedman* and has relaxed the procedural safeguards that the government must meet in licensing. For example, in *Thomas and Windy City Hemp Development Board v. Chicago Park District*, the Court rejected the application of some of the procedural safeguards from *Freedman* to requirements for obtaining a license in order to use a park.[247] Specifically, the Court rejected the procedures under which the "Park District, like the Board of Censors in *Freedman*, must initiate litigation every time it denies a permit and that the ordinance must specify a deadline for judicial review of a challenge to a permit denial."[248] The Court explained that it never has "required that a content-neutral permit scheme regulating speech in a public forum must adhere to the procedural requirements set forth in *Freedman*."[249]

In *City of Littleton, Colorado v. Z.J. Gifts D-4, L.L.C.*, the Court also dealt with the application of the *Freedman* procedural requirements to a licensing system.[250] The Court reaffirmed that a city's licensing of adult businesses must comply with

---

[239] *Id.* at 59.

[240] *Id.* at 58.

[241] Blount v. Rizzi, 400 U.S. 410 (1971).

[242] United States v. Thirty-Seven Photographs, 402 U.S. 363 (1971).

[243] 493 U.S. 215 (1990).

[244] The plurality opinion by Justice O'Connor said that it was not necessary that the government have the burden of going to court if it wished to deny a license; she argued that it was permissible that those denied licenses would have to initiate the review in the courts. *Id.* at 230.

[245] 487 U.S. 781 (1988).

[246] *Id.* at 802 (citation omitted).

[247] 534 U.S. 316 (2002).

[248] *Id.* at 322.

[249] *Id.*

[250] 541 U.S. 774 (2004).

the First Amendment and that this must include judicial review of license denials. However, the Court said that the ordinance itself need not specify the availability of prompt judicial review so long as timely judicial review is available.

§11.2.4 What Is an Infringement of Freedom of Speech?

§11.2.4.1 Introduction: Besides Prohibitions and Prior Restraints, What Infringes Speech?

Prohibitions and Prior Restraints

A threshold question in many cases is whether the government has infringed freedom of speech and therefore whether First Amendment analysis is applicable.[251] Often it is clear that a law infringes freedom of speech and is susceptible to First Amendment challenge. For example, a statute that prohibits speech and authorizes criminal punishments obviously has to meet constitutional scrutiny. Section 11.3, below, reviews many of these laws, such as those prohibiting speech that incites illegal conduct, obscenity, and false advertising. Although these are categories of unprotected speech and regulation is allowed, there is no doubt that the laws interfere with expression and must meet First Amendment standards. Also, there is no doubt that prior restraints are infringements of expression and must meet First Amendment standards. Court orders preventing speech and licensing systems precluding speech without a permit thus always are subject to constitutional attack. Such prior restraints are discussed above in §11.2.3.

What Other Government Actions Are an Infringement?

But what types of government actions—apart from prohibitions via laws, court orders, or licensing systems—are infringements of speech triggering First Amendment analysis? A wide variety of government actions sufficiently burden speech so as to be considered an infringement and thus be subjected to First Amendment scrutiny.[252] A finding that a law substantially burdens or infringes speech does not, of course, mean that it is automatically unconstitutional; but it does mean that the law will have to meet heightened scrutiny unless it regulates a category of unprotected speech. As explained above, the general rule is that content-based regulations of speech must meet strict scrutiny, while content-neutral regulation must meet intermediate scrutiny.[253]

---

[251] A closely related question is what is "speech." This is discussed in §11.3.6.1.

[252] For an excellent discussion of when incidental burdens on fundamental rights, including freedom of speech, should trigger heightened scrutiny, *see* Michael C. Dorf, Incidental Burdens on Fundamental Rights, 109 Harv. L. Rev. 1175, 1200-1210 (1996).

[253] *See* Turner Broad. Sys., Inc. v. Federal Communications Commn., 512 U.S. 622 (1994), discussed above in §11.2.1.

Laws that significantly burden speech are ones that allow civil liability for expression; that prevent compensation for speech; that compel expression; that condition a benefit on a person forgoing speech; and that pressure individuals not to speak. These are discussed, in turn, in the following subsections. Additionally, laws that regulate conduct might have an incidental effect on speech because of the communicative content of behavior. First Amendment analysis of such conduct that communicates is discussed in §11.3.6.

§11.2.4.2 Civil Liability and Denial of Compensation for Speech [254]

Civil Liability

The Court repeatedly has held that civil liability for speech, even in the context of private civil litigation, is an interference with speech and therefore must meet First Amendment scrutiny. In *New York Times v. Sullivan*, the Court held that state defamation law was limited by the First Amendment.[255] *New York Times v. Sullivan*, discussed more fully below in §11.3.5.2, involved a defamation suit brought by the Montgomery, Alabama, police commissioner against The New York Times and four black clergymen for an advertisement criticizing the handling of demonstrations. A jury awarded the plaintiff $500,000 under Alabama's defamation law.

The Supreme Court expressly held that the First Amendment applied. Justice Brennan, writing in one of the most famous and important free speech cases in history, declared: "What a State may not constitutionally bring about by means of a criminal statute is likewise beyond the reach of its civil law of libel. The fear of damage awards under a rule such as that invoked by the Alabama courts here may be markedly more inhibiting than the fear of prosecution under a criminal statute."[256] The Court noted that the "judgment awarded in this case—without the need for any proof of actual pecuniary loss—was one thousand times greater than the maximum fine provided by the Alabama criminal [libel law], and one hundred times greater than that provided by the Sedition Act. . . . Whether or not a newspaper can survive a succession of such judgments, the pall of fear and timidity imposed upon those who would give voice to public criticism is an atmosphere in which the First Amendment freedoms cannot survive."[257]

---

[254] There are other ways that the government can impose economic costs for speech, such as firing government employees or terminating contracts with government contractors. The Supreme Court has held that these actions also are limited by the First Amendment. They are discussed in §11.3.8.

[255] 376 U.S. 254 (1964). For a recent discussion urging a reconsideration of civil liability and the First Amendment, *see* Daniel J. Solove & Neil M. Richards, Rethinking Free Speech and Civil Liability, 109 Colum. L. Rev. 1650 (2013).

[256] 376 U.S. at 277.

[257] *Id.* at 277-278.

The Supreme Court has followed this and held that liability for such torts as invasion of privacy,[258] false light,[259] and intentional infliction of emotional distress[260] must be consistent with the First Amendment.[261] These torts, and the applicable First Amendment limits, are discussed below in §11.3.5.

Although it is litigation between two private parties, there is clearly state action in such tort litigation. It is the state's law—whether statutory or common law—that is the basis for liability and recovery. Also, the courts, a branch of the government, oversee the judicial proceedings and ultimately impose any judgment. In *Shelley v. Kraemer*, the Supreme Court held that judges cannot enforce racially restrictive covenants because court action is a form of state action.[262] Similarly, court action in private civil litigation is state action, and thus any civil liability must comport with First Amendment standards.

Prohibitions on Compensation

The Supreme Court has clearly indicated that another way in which the government can infringe freedom of speech is by prohibiting individuals from being paid for their expression. In *Simon & Schuster v. Members of the New York State Crime Victims Board*, the Court declared unconstitutional a state law that prevented an accused or convicted criminal from profiting from selling the story of his or her crime to any media.[263] The so-called Son of Sam Law placed any funds received from works describing the crime into an escrow account that was used for restitution to victims of the crime and for paying the criminal's other creditors.

The New York law did not prohibit any speech; it only prevented individuals from keeping profits from selling the tales of their criminal activity. Nonetheless, the Supreme Court found the law to violate the First Amendment. The Court said that "[a] statute is presumptively inconsistent with the First Amendment if it imposes a financial burden on speakers because of the content of their speech."[264] The Supreme Court stressed that the state law was content-based: "It singles out income derived from expressive activity for a burden the State places on no other income, and it is directed only at works with a specified content."[265] The Court thus applied strict scrutiny and concluded that while compensating crime victims was a compelling interest, the state could achieve its goal through a means less restrictive of speech.

---

[258] Florida Star v. B.J.F., 491 U.S. 524 (1989).

[259] Time, Inc. v. Hill, 385 U.S. 374 (1967).

[260] Hustler Magazine v. Falwell, 485 U.S. 46 (1988).

[261] However, in *Cohen v. Cowles Media Co.*, 501 U.S. 663 (1991), the Supreme Court held that the First Amendment was not violated by a suit for breach of contract brought against a reporter and newspaper for breaking a confidentiality agreement and disclosing the identity of a source. The Court emphasized that contract law is neutral with regard to speech, and its application did not violate the First Amendment.

[262] 334 U.S. 1 (1948), discussed in §6.4.4.3.

[263] 502 U.S. 105 (1991).

[264] *Id.* at 115.

[265] *Id.* at 116.

In *United States v. National Treasury Employees Union*, the Court declared unconstitutional a federal law that prevented government employees from receiving monetary honoraria for their off-the-job speeches and writings, even if they were totally unrelated to their work.[266] The Court said that "[a]lthough [the law] neither prohibits any speech nor discriminates among speakers based on the content or viewpoint of their messages, its prohibition on compensation unquestionably imposes a significant burden on expressive activity."[267] The Court noted that preventing compensation for speech often has the practical effect of stopping the speech. Justice Stevens, writing for the Court, observed: "Publishers compensate authors because compensation provides a significant incentive toward more expression. By denying respondents that incentive, the honoraria ban induces them to curtail their expression if they wish to continue working for the Government."[268]

Simon & Schuster and *National Treasury Employees Union* thus establish that restrictions on payments for speech—whether content-based or content-neutral—are infringements on expression and must meet First Amendment scrutiny. Just as potential civil liability can deter speech, so can preventing monetary compensation decrease speech by eliminating an economic incentive for First Amendment activity.[269]

§11.2.4.3 Compelled Speech

The Right to Not Speak

The cases reviewed thus far concerning what constitutes an infringement of speech all have involved the government prohibiting or penalizing speech— criminally, civilly, or by withholding compensation. The government also can infringe the First Amendment by compelling speech. Just as there is a right to speak, so, it is clear, there is a right to be silent and refrain from speaking.

The classic case in this regard was *West Virginia State Board of Education v. Barnette*, which declared unconstitutional a state law that required that children salute the flag.[270] Justice Robert Jackson, writing for the Court, eloquently said: "[T]he compulsory flag salute and pledge requires affirmation of a belief and an attitude of mind. . . . If there is any fixed star in our constitutional constellation, it is that no official, high or petty, can prescribe what shall be orthodox in politics, nationalism, religion or other matters of opinion or force citizens to confess by word or act their faith therein."[271]

---

[266] 513 U.S. 454 (1995). The Court declared the law unconstitutional as applied to lower level government employees and left the issue unresolved as to whether the law would be constitutional as applied to top level executive officials.

[267] *Id.* at 468.

[268] *Id.*

[269] A related topic concerns when tax liability on the press violates the First Amendment. This is discussed below in §11.6.2.1.

[270] 319 U.S. 624 (1943).

[271] *Id.* at 633, 642.

The Court followed this principle in other cases, such as in *Wooley v. Maynard*, where it ruled that an individual could not be punished for blocking out the portion of his automobile license plate that contained the New Hampshire state motto, "Live Free or Die."[272] The Court said that "the right of freedom of thought protected by the First Amendment . . . includes both the right to speak freely and the right to refrain from speaking at all. . . . The right to speak and the right to refrain from speaking are complementary components of the broader concept of 'individual freedom of mind.' "[273]

By contrast, in *Rumsfeld v. Forum for Academic and Institutional Rights*, the Court rejected a claim that requiring universities to allow military recruiters equal access to campus interviewing as a condition for receipt of federal funds was impermissible compelled speech.[274] Most law schools refused to allow the United States military to use campus facilities for recruiting because of the military's policy of excluding gays and lesbians. The Solomon Amendment denied federal funding to universities that denied the military equal access to campus facilities.

The United States Court of Appeals for the Third Circuit found that the Solomon Amendment impermissibly forced colleges and universities to express support for a policy of which they disapproved. The Supreme Court unanimously rejected this argument and stated: "The Solomon Amendment neither limits what law schools may say nor requires them to say anything. Law schools remain free under the statute to express whatever views they may have on the military's congressionally mandated employment policy, all the while retaining eligibility for federal funds. As a general matter, the Solomon Amendment regulates conduct, not speech. It affects what law schools must *do*—afford equal access to military recruiters—not what they may or may not *say*."[275]

The Right to Speak Anonymously

The right to not speak includes a right to not disclose one's identity when speaking. In *Talley v. California*, the Supreme Court declared unconstitutional a ban on anonymous handbills.[276] The Court observed that the "obnoxious press licensing law of England, which was also enforced on the Colonies was due in part to the knowledge that exposure of the names of printers, writers and distributors would lessen the circulation of literature critical of the government."[277] Justice Black, writing for the Court, said that "[p]ersecuted groups and sects from time to time

---

[272] 430 U.S. 705 (1977).

[273] *Id.* at 714 (citations omitted).

[274] 547 U.S. 47 (2006).

[275] *Id.* at 60. The Court also rejected the claim that the Solomon Amendment was an unconstitutional condition on federal funds on the ground that the policy did not violate the First Amendment and therefore since the government could do this directly it could do so as a condition for receipt of federal funds. This is discussed below in §11.2.4.4.

[276] 362 U.S. 60 (1960).

[277] *Id.* at 64.

throughout history have been able to criticize oppressive practices and laws either anonymously or not at all."[278]

Subsequently, in *McIntyre v. Ohio Elections Commission*, the Court declared unconstitutional a law that prohibited the distribution of anonymous campaign literature.[279] The Court expressly quoted *Talley*'s statement that "[a]nonymous pamphlets, leaflets, brochures, and even books have played an important role in the progress of mankind."[280] The Court noted the long tradition of authors writing under pseudonyms, including Mark Twain, O. Henry, Benjamin Franklin, Voltaire, George Eliot, Charles Dickens, and perhaps Shakespeare.[281]

Justice Stevens, writing for the Court, stated: "The decision in favor of anonymity may be motivated by fear of economic or official retaliation, by concern about social ostracism, or merely by a desire to preserve as much of one's privacy as possible. . . . Accordingly, an author's decision to remain anonymous, like other decisions concerning omissions or additions to the content of a publication, is an aspect of the freedom of speech protected by the First Amendment."[282] Moreover, Justice Stevens said that anonymity also provides a way for a speaker "who may be personally unpopular to ensure that readers will not prejudge her message simply because they do not like its proponent."[283]

The Court followed and applied *McIntyre* in *Buckley v. American Constitutional Law Foundation*.[284] A Colorado law regulated the gathering of signatures on petitions for ballot initiatives. Specifically, the law required that initiative-petition circulators be registered voters, that they wear an identification badge bearing the circulator's name, and that proponents of an initiative report the names and addresses of all paid circulators and the amount paid to each circulator.

The Court found that the requirement that those circulating petitions be registered voters unduly restricted who was able to perform this task. Justice Ginsburg, writing for the Court, explained why the provision violates the First Amendment: "The provision 'limit[s] the number of voices who will convey the initiative proponents' message' and, consequently, cut[s] down 'the size of the audience proponents can reach' sufficient in number to qualify for the ballot, and thus limited proponents' ability to make the matter the focus of statewide discussion. [T]he requirement imposes a burden on political expression that the State has failed to justify."[285]

The Court also found the disclosure requirements in the law to be unconstitutional. The Court said that the requirement that solicitors wear an identification badge would chill political participation without any significant gain. Justice Ginsburg noted: "Colorado's current badge requirement discourages participation in the petition circulation process by forcing name identification without

[278] *Id.*
[279] 514 U.S. 334 (1995).
[280] *Id.* at 341, quoting Talley v. California, 362 U.S. at 64.
[281] *Id.* at 342 n.4.
[282] *Id.* at 341-342.
[283] *Id.* at 342.
[284] 525 U.S. 182 (1999).
[285] *Id.* at 195.

sufficient cause."[286] Likewise, the Court struck down the requirement that the identity of paid solicitors had to be disclosed. The Court stressed the Constitution's protection of anonymous speech and the lack of a sufficient interest to warrant disclosure. As in *McIntyre*, the Court was concerned with how disclosure could chill constitutionally protected speech and political activities.

The underlying issue in cases such as *McIntyre* and *Buckley* is how to balance the benefits of secrecy and disclosure.[287] Anonymity may encourage some to participate in the political process who otherwise would be unwilling to do so. But disclosure often provides key information for regulators and for voters in appraising candidates and organizations. In the years ahead, the Court will need to consider other requirements in state and federal law for disclosure in political campaigns.[288]

Compelled Use of Private Property for Speech Purposes

A related question is whether the government impermissibly compels expression when it forces people to use their property for speech by others. The cases in this area are difficult to reconcile. In some instances, the Court has held that the First Amendment is violated if the government forces owners to make their property available for expressive purposes.

For example, in *Miami Herald Publishing Co. v. Tornillo*, the Supreme Court unanimously invalidated a state law that required newspapers to provide space to political candidates who had been verbally attacked in print.[289] The Court emphasized that freedom of the press gave to the newspaper the right to decide what was included or excluded.[290]

Similarly, in *Pacific Gas & Electric Co. v. Public Utilities Commission of California*, the Court declared unconstitutional a utility commission regulation that required that a private utility company include in its billing envelopes materials prepared by a public interest group.[291] The utility commission sought to provide a more balanced presentation of views on energy issues; the public interest group's statements were to be a counterpoint to the statements by the utility companies. But the Court found that such compelled access violated the First Amendment. Justice Powell, writing for the Court, said that "[c]ompelled access like that ordered in this case both penalizes the expression of particular points of view and forces speakers to alter their speech to conform with an agenda they do not set."[292]

---

[286] *Id.* at 200.

[287] In *Doe v. Reed*, 130 S. Ct. 2811 (2010), the Court held that disclosing petitions for a ballot referendum does not inherently violate the First Amendment, though the Court left open the possibility of challenge if it could be shown that disclosure would lead to threats, intimidation, or reprisals. *Doe v. Reed* is discussed in detail in §11.5.3.

[288] Disclosure in the context of campaign finance laws is discussed in §11.5.3.

[289] 418 U.S. 241 (1974).

[290] *But see* Red Lion Broad. Co. v. Federal Communications Commn., 395 U.S. 367 (1969). *Tornillo* and *Red Lion* are discussed in more detail in §11.6.2.4.

[291] 475 U.S. 1 (1986).

[292] *Id.* at 9.

In contrast, in *PruneYard Shopping Center v. Robins*, shopping center owners argued that their First Amendment rights were violated by a California Supreme Court ruling that protestors had a right to use their property for speech under the state constitution.[293] The shopping center owners specifically invoked *Wooley v. Maynard* and said that forcing them to allow speech was impermissible coerced expression. The Supreme Court disagreed and found no violation of the First Amendment from a state constitutional rule that created a right of access to shopping centers for speech purposes.

The Court expressly distinguished *Wooley* and explained that the shopping center is "not limited to the personal use of appellants, . . . [but] is instead a business establishment that is open to the public to come and go as they please. The views expressed by members of the public in passing out pamphlets or seeking signatures for a petition thus will not likely be identified with those of the owner."[294] Moreover, the Court said that "no specific message is dictated by the State to be displayed on appellants' property . . . [and] appellants can expressly disavow any connection with the message by simply posting signs in the area where the speakers or handbillers stand."[295]

The distinction between *PruneYard* and *Tornillo* is that the latter concerned freedom of the press and the ability of editors to determine what to publish. It is more difficult, though, to reconcile *PruneYard* with *Pacific Gas & Electric*. The Court's distinction that the owners in *PruneYard* had not objected to the particular message being conveyed, as they had in *Pacific Gas & Electric*, seems very questionable. The shopping center owners very much wanted to exclude the speakers from using their property. If there is a right of private property owners to avoid compelled use of their property, their right to do this should not depend on the content of their views relative to the demonstrators.

Forced Association

Another context in which the right not to speak arises is when the government seems to be forcing associational activities.[296] For example, the Supreme Court has limited the ability of the government to require union members or lawyers to pay dues for ideological activities. In *Abood v. Detroit Board of Education*, the Court considered a state law that required that all local government employees pay a union service charge.[297] Union members paid this amount as their dues; nonmembers were required to pay a charge of the same amount. The Court said that the nonmembers could be forced to pay a charge to subsidize the collective bargaining activities of the union. The Court explained that nonmembers would

---

[293]   447 U.S. 74 (1980). The Supreme Court previously had held that there is not a First Amendment right of access to privately owned shopping centers for speech purposes. Hudgens v. NLRB, 424 U.S. 507 (1976). The issue of a constitutional right of access to shopping centers for speech is discussed in §6.4.4.2 and §11.4.3.

[294]   447 U.S. at 87.

[295]   *Id.*

[296]   Freedom of association is discussed below in §11.5.

[297]   431 U.S. 209 (1977).

benefit from the gains of collective bargaining and would be "free riders" if not required to pay for these activities. Although nonmembers may disagree with the union's labor-related activities, or even to the existence of the union, the Court found no violation of the First Amendment in forcing nonmembers to pay for the union's collective bargaining conduct.

But the Court said that it violated the First Amendment to force the nonmembers to pay for ideological causes with which they disagreed. The Court explained that it was unconstitutional to use the mandatory service charges "to contribute to political candidates and to express political views unrelated to its duties as exclusive bargaining representative."[298] The Court said that the "heart of the First Amendment is the notion that an individual should be free to believe as he will, and that in a free society one's beliefs should be shaped by his mind and his conscience rather than coerced by the State."[299]

The union was free to use its members' dues or collect voluntary contributions for its ideological activities. The Court said that "the Constitution requires only that expenditures be financed from charges . . . paid by employees who do not object to advancing those ideas and who are not coerced into doing so against their will by the threat of loss of governmental employment."[300]

The Court reaffirmed and applied *Abood* in *Keller v. State Bar of California*.[301] The Court said that compulsory bar dues could be used only if "reasonably incurred for the purpose of regulating the legal profession or improving the quality of the legal service available to the people of the State."[302] The Court explained that bar dues could be collected from all members to pay for bar-related activities. But the Court said that "[c]ompulsory dues may not be expended to endorse or advance a gun control or nuclear weapons freeze initiative; at the other end of the spectrum petitioners have no valid constitutional objection to their compulsory dues being spent for activities connected with disciplining members of the Bar or proposing ethical codes for the profession."[303]

Abood and *Keller* draw a commonsense distinction, albeit one difficult to apply in practice. Both cases recognize that there is a need for compulsory dues in contexts such as collective bargaining and bar membership. But the Court also acknowledged that it violates the First Amendment to force a person to contribute money for a cause with which he or she disagrees. Therefore, the Court attempted to distinguish between activities that relate directly to the purpose of the group, such as collective bargaining activities or bar regulation, and those activities that are ideological in nature. The problem is that in practice it can be problematic to apply this distinction. For example, is a union's lobbying activity for legislation

---

[298] *Id.* at 234.

[299] *Id.* at 234-235.

[300] *Id.* at 235-236. In *Davenport v. Washington Education Association*, 551 U.S. 177 (2007), the Court held that that it does not violate the First Amendment for a state to require that its public-sector labor unions receive affirmative authorization from a nonmember before spending that nonmember's agency-shop fees for election-related purposes.

[301] 496 U.S. 1 (1990).

[302] *Id.* at 14 (citation omitted).

[303] *Id.* at 16.

beneficial to its members something that nonmembers can be forced to subsidize since they too would benefit?

In recent years, the Court has sharply questioned *Abood* and has refused to extend it. In *Knox v. Service Employees Union Local 1000*, the Court held that non-union members must "opt in" to supporting the political activities of the union, that it is not sufficient that they can opt out.[304] Justice Alito, in an opinion joined by Chief Justice Roberts and Justices Scalia, Kennedy, and Thomas, instead questioned the Court's decisions of the last 35 years that have allowed unions to require that nonmembers opt out of providing funds for political activities. He wrote: "Similarly, requiring objecting nonmembers to opt out of paying the noncharge-able portion of union dues—as opposed to exempting them from making such payments unless they opt in—represents a remarkable boon for unions. Courts 'do not presume acquiescence in the loss of fundamental rights.' "[305]

In light of this objection to the traditional opt-out procedure, the Court held that for special assessments nonunion members can be charged for politi-cal activities only if they affirmatively choose to provide funds. The Court stated: "Therefore, when a public-sector union imposes a special assessment or dues increase, the union must provide a fresh *Hudson* notice *and may not exact any funds from nonmembers without their affirmative consent.*"[306] Although the case was about special assessments, its reasoning would seem to apply to all situations and require that nonunion members opt in to supporting the political activities of the union.[307]

Subsequently, in *Harris v. Quinn*,[308] the Court again questioned and limited *Abood*. Illinois law deemed personal assistants— home health care workers— as state employees and allowed them to unionize. They voted to unionize and chose to be part of the SEIU. Some nonunion members objected to paying to support the collective bargaining activities of the union. In other words, unlike *Knox*, which involved supporting the union's political activities, *Harris v. Quinn* concerned whether these individuals could be required to support the collective bargaining activities of the union.

Justice Alito, writing for the majority, began by declaring that "[t]he *Abood* Court's analysis is questionable on several grounds."[309] Among other criticisms, he said that "*Abood* failed to appreciate the conceptual difficulty of distinguishing in public-sector cases between union expenditures that are made for collective-bargaining purposes and those that are made to achieve political ends. In the pri-vate sector, the line is easier to see. . . . *Abood* likewise did not foresee the practical

---

[304] 132 S. Ct. 2277 (2012).

[305] *Id.* at 2290.

[306] *Id.* at 2296. For a criticism of the Court's reasoning and a discussion of its implications, *see* Catherine Fisk & Erwin Chemerinsky, Political Speech and Associational Rights After *Knox v. SEIU*, 98 Cornell L. Rev. 1023 (2013).

[307] Justice Breyer, in dissent, observed: "The decision is particularly unfortunate given the fact that each reason the Court offers in support of its 'opt-in' conclusion seems in logic to apply, not just to special assessments, but to ordinary yearly fee charges as well." 132 S. Ct. at 2306 (Breyer, J., dis-senting).

[308] 134 S. Ct. 2618 (2014).

[309] *Id.* at 2632.

problems that would face objecting nonmembers. Employees who suspect that a union has improperly put certain expenses in the 'germane' category must bear a heavy burden if they wish to challenge the union's actions."[310]

Despite these criticisms, the Court did not overrule *Abood*, but instead said that it would not extend it to home health care workers who it regarded as being different from "full-fledged government employees." The Court declared: "Because of *Abood*'s questionable foundations, and because the personal assistants are quite different from full-fledged public employees, we refuse to extend *Abood* to the new situation now before us. *Abood* itself has clear boundaries; it applies to public employees."[311]

Justice Kagan, writing for the four dissenters, strongly defended *Abood* and said that the Illinois law fit within it in requiring that state employees who were not union members pay their "fair share" of union dues to support the collective bargaining of the union that they benefit from. Justice Kagan stated: "*Abood* held that a government entity may, consistently with the First Amendment, require public employees to pay a fair share of the cost that a union incurs negotiating on their behalf for better terms of employment. That is exactly what Illinois did in entering into collective bargaining agreements with the Service Employees International Union Healthcare (SEIU) which included fair-share provisions. Contrary to the Court's decision, those agreements fall squarely within *Abood*'s holding. . . . *Abood* is not, as the majority at one point describes it, 'something of an anomaly,' allowing uncommon interference with individuals' expressive activities. Rather, the lines it draws and the balance it strikes reflect the way courts generally evaluate claims that a condition of public employment violates the First Amendment."[312]

It is uncertain whether *Knox* and *Harris* are steps to overruling *Abood* or a reflection of a desire to limit it. Interestingly, in other contexts, though, the Court has allowed the government to require individuals to make financial contributions that violate their beliefs. For example, the Court distinguished *Abood* and *Keller* and upheld mandatory student activity fees at public universities. In *University of Wisconsin v. Southworth*, the Court unanimously upheld the permissibility of requiring college students to pay money each semester for a fund that subsidizes student activities.[313] A challenge was brought by conservative University of Wisconsin law students to their having to contribute to groups with which they disagreed. They argued under *Abood* and *Keller* that this was forced association that violated their First Amendment rights.

The Supreme Court rejected the challenge. The Court emphasized the importance of student activity fees in colleges and universities in providing a diversity of speakers and events. Justice Kennedy, writing for the Court, said that such a fee is constitutional so long as the funds are distributed in a viewpoint neutral manner.[314] In this case, the students had stipulated as to the viewpoint neutral

---

[310] *Id.* at 2632-2633.
[311] *Id.* at 2638.
[312] *Id.* at 2645 (Kagan, J., dissenting).
[313] 529 U.S. 217 (2000).
[314] Viewpoint neutrality is discussed above in §11.2.1.

disbursement of the funds, so no First Amendment violation was found. Future cases are likely to focus on how to determine whether funds are spent in a viewpoint neutral manner given the inherent need to make choices among competing requests for money.

One other area where the Court has considered mandatory assessments is in the context of government requirements that agricultural producers contribute to funds for product advertising. In two decisions, *Glickman v. Wileman Brothers & Elliott*[315] and *United States v. United Foods, Inc.*,[316] the Court has come to opposite conclusions about the constitutionality of such programs. In *Glickman*, the Court upheld regulations issued pursuant to the Agricultural Marketing Agreement Act of 1937 that required fruit producers to financially contribute toward generic advertising for fruit in certain markets. Wileman Brothers & Elliott, California fruit producers, challenged the regulation as impermissible compelled speech and association.

The Supreme Court, in a 5-to-4 decision, rejected the challenge and upheld the federal law. Justice Stevens, writing for the majority, said that "requiring respondents to pay the assessments cannot be said to engender any crisis of conscience. None of the advertising in this record promotes any particular message other than encouraging producers to buy California tree fruit."[317] Justice Stevens said that neither the challengers' desire to differentiate their own product nor their belief that the money is not being well spent provides a basis for a First Amendment violation.[318]

But in *United States v. United Foods, Inc.*, the Court came to an opposite conclusion and invalidated the requirement for mandatory assessments for product advertising contained in the Mushroom Promotion, Research, and Consumer Information Act. The Act authorizes the secretary of agriculture to establish a Mushroom Council composed of mushroom producers and importers. The council can impose mandatory assessments on handlers of fresh mushrooms to be used for generic advertising to promote mushroom sales.

In a 6-to-3 decision, the Supreme Court declared the mandatory assessments on mushroom producers unconstitutional. Justice Kennedy, writing for the majority, began by emphasizing that the challengers were forced to express "the message . . . that mushrooms are worth consuming whether or not they are branded," instead of its preferred message that its brand was superior to the others.[319] Justice Kennedy said: "First Amendment values are at serious risk if the government can compel a particular citizen, or a discrete group of citizens, to pay special subsidies for speech on the side it favors," and therefore, "the compelled funding for the advertising must pass First Amendment scrutiny."[320]

The Court then proceeded to distinguish *Glickman*. For example, Justice Kennedy said that "in *Glickman*, the mandatory assessments for speech were

---

[315] 521 U.S. 457 (1997).
[316] 533 U.S. 405 (2001).
[317] 521 U.S. at 472.
[318] *Id.* at 472-473.
[319] 533 U.S. at 411.
[320] *Id.*

ancillary to a more comprehensive program restricting regulatory autonomy," whereas "[h]ere . . . the advertising itself . . . is the principal object of the marketing scheme."[321] Justice Kennedy also said that in *Glickman*, California tree fruit producers were constrained in other aspects of their marketing; but no similar restrictions applied to mushroom producers who are not bound by the statute to "associate as a group which makes cooperative decisions."[322] Justice Kennedy said that it does not matter that the "party who protests the assessment here is required simply to support speech by others, not to utter the speech itself."[323] The Court expressly cited to *Abood* and *Keller* to support its conclusion that "the mandated support is contrary to the First Amendment principles set forth in cases involving expression by groups which include persons who object to the speech, but who nevertheless, must remain members of the group by law."[324]

Subsequently, in *Johanns v. Livestock Marketing Association*, the Court upheld a requirement that cattle producers pay a fee into a fund for generic advertising to encourage consumption of beef.[325] Some beef producers objected and said that they wished to have their own advertisements to distinguish their products, such as for organic beef. The Supreme Court, in an opinion by Justice Scalia, rejected the First Amendment challenge and upheld the federal law. Justice Scalia stressed that this was government speech; the government, through its board, was running the speech rather than forcing the private companies to advertise. Justice Scalia said that the government may pay for such ads out of general revenue or out of a targeted assessment.

The key question is whether there is a meaningful distinction between *Glickman*, *United Foods*, and *Johanns*, other than that they involve different agricultural products. For the majority in *United Foods*, there was a persuasive distinction based on the presence of other regulations of tree fruit producers in *Glickman*; but Justice Breyer failed to see why this matters in assessing the permissibility of mandatory assessments.[326]

Johanns is based on the distinction between the government speaking and the government forcing others to speak. Ultimately, the underlying normative question is whether the government violates the First Amendment when it forces producers to contribute to a fund for generic advertising. On this, the cases seem inconsistent.

Hurley v. Irish-American Gay, Lesbian, and Bisexual Group of Boston[327] also involved an issue of forced association, although in a different context from *Abood*, *Keller*, *Southworth*, or the agricultural advertising cases. Every St. Patrick's Day, the Veterans Council, a private group, organizes a parade in Boston. The Veterans Council refused to allow the Irish-American Gay, Lesbian, and Bisexual Group of Boston to participate in its parade. The Irish-American Gay, Lesbian, and Bisexual Group

---

[321] *Id.* at 411-412.
[322] *Id.* at 412.
[323] *Id.* at 413.
[324] *Id.*
[325] 544 U.S. 550 (2005).
[326] 533 U.S. at 409-410 (Breyer, J., dissenting).
[327] 515 U.S. 557 (1995).

sued in Massachusetts state court based on the state's public accommodations law that prohibited discrimination by business establishments based on sexual orientation. The Massachusetts Supreme Judicial Court sided with the Irish-American Gay, Lesbian, and Bisexual Group.

The United States Supreme Court unanimously reversed. The Court, in an opinion by Justice Souter, said that organizing a parade is inherently expressive activity and that it violated the First Amendment to force the organizers to include messages that they find inimical. Justice Souter explained that compelling the Veterans Council to include the Irish-American Gay, Lesbian, and Bisexual Group "violates the fundamental rule . . . under the First Amendment, that a speaker has the autonomy to choose the content of his own message."[328]

The Court expressly invoked the principle discussed above that there is a First Amendment right not to speak. Justice Souter wrote that "the Council clearly decided to exclude a message it did not like from the communication it chose to make, and that is enough to invoke its right as a private speaker to shape its expression by speaking on one subject while remaining silent on another."[329]

Conclusion

Thus, all of these cases, although in very different contexts, established that compelled speech and association violates the First Amendment. The right not to speak is as much a constitutional freedom as is the right to speak.

§11.2.4.4 Unconstitutional Conditions

The Unconstitutional Conditions Doctrine Defined

The unconstitutional conditions doctrine is the principle that the government cannot condition a benefit on the requirement that a person forgo a constitutional right. The corollary is that the "government may not deny a benefit to a person because he exercises a constitutional right."[330]

Speiser v. Randall is a classic example of the application of the unconstitutional conditions doctrine.[331] A California law provided that in order for an individual to receive a veterans' property tax exemption he or she had to sign a declaration disavowing a belief in overthrowing the United States government by force or violence. The Court said that "[t]o deny an exemption to claimants who engage in certain forms of speech is in effect to penalize them for this speech."[332]

---

[328] *Id.* at 572.

[329] *Id.* at 575.

[330] Regan v. Taxation with Representation of Washington, 461 U.S. 540, 545 (1983), quoting Perry v. Sindermann, 408 U.S. 593, 597 (1972).

[331] 357 U.S. 513 (1958).

[332] *Id.* at 518.

Conditioning a benefit on a requirement that individuals give up their First Amendment rights obviously pressures individuals to forgo constitutionally protected speech. The *Speiser* Court explained that the condition "will have the effect of coercing the claimants to refrain from the proscribed speech."[333] Put another way, the unconstitutional conditions doctrine prevents the government from penalizing those who exercise their constitutional rights by withholding a benefit that otherwise would be available.[334] In *Perry v. Sindermann*, the Court, in explaining that the government could not deny employment to a person for exercising First Amendment rights, declared: "For if the government could deny a benefit to a person because of his constitutionally protected speech or associations, his exercise of those freedoms would in effect be penalized and inhibited. This would allow the government to 'produce a result which it could not command directly.'"[335]

Inconsistent Application

The Court, however, has not consistently applied the unconstitutional conditions doctrine. The cases in this area seem quite inconsistent. The doctrine was followed in *Federal Communications Commission v. League of Women Voters of California*.[336] The Supreme Court declared unconstitutional a federal statute that prohibited any noncommercial educational broadcasting station that received a grant from the Corporation for Public Broadcasting from engaging in editorializing. The Court said that the government could not condition funds on a requirement that the stations relinquish their right to editorialize.

In *Legal Services Corporation v. Velazquez*, the Court used the unconstitutional conditions doctrine to invalidate a restriction on the activities of lawyers receiving funds from the federal Legal Services Corporation.[337] Those receiving such monies are subject to many restrictions, such as a prohibition against bringing class action suits, challenging laws regulating abortions, and representing undocumented immigrants. *Velazquez* involved a challenge to the prohibition against challenges to welfare statutes and regulations by lawyers receiving legal services funding. Attorneys could represent claimants in seeking benefits, but the lawyers could not challenge the validity of the laws.

In a 5-to-4 decision, with Justice Kennedy writing the majority opinion, the Court declared this unconstitutional. As the Court noted, "[t]he prohibitions apply to all of the activities of an LSC grantee, including those paid for by non-LSC funds."[338] The Court said that the government essentially had created a "limited

---

[333] *Id.* at 519.

[334] There is a large and rich literature on the unconstitutional conditions doctrine. *See, e.g.*, Kathleen Sullivan, Unconstitutional Conditions, 102 Harv. L. Rev. 1413 (1989); Richard Epstein, Foreword: Unconstitutional Conditions, State Power, and the Limits of Consent, 102 Harv. L. Rev. 4 (1989); Seth Kreimer, Allocational Sanctions: The Problem of Negative Rights in a Positive State, 132 U. Pa. L. Rev. 1293 (1984).

[335] 408 U.S. 593, 597 (1972) (citation omitted).

[336] 468 U.S. 364 (1984).

[337] 531 U.S. 533 (2001).

[338] *Id.* at 538.

forum" and had impermissibly attempted to control the content of the speech within it. Lawyers were prevented from making certain types of arguments on behalf of their clients. Ultimately, the Court felt that this was the government trying to control both sides of a lawsuit. As Justice Kennedy explained: "Restricting LSC attorneys in advising their clients and in presenting arguments and analyses to the courts distorts the legal system by altering the traditional role of the attorneys."[339]

Although the Court did not expressly invoke the unconstitutional conditions doctrine, conceptually that is exactly what the Court did; Congress was deemed to have placed an impermissible restriction on what lawyers could argue. Justice Kennedy concluded his majority opinion by stating: "Congress was not required to fund an LSC attorney to represent indigent clients; and when it did so, it was not required to fund the whole range of legal representations or relationships. The LSC and the United States, however, in effect ask us to permit Congress to define the scope of the litigation it funds to exclude certain vital theories and ideas. The attempted restriction is designed to insulate the Government's interpretation of the Constitution from judicial challenge. The Constitution does not permit the Government to confine litigants and their attorneys in this manner. We must be vigilant when Congress imposes rules and conditions which in effect insulate its own laws from legitimate judicial challenge."[340]

Most recently, *Agency for International Development v. Alliance for Open Society International, Inc.* held that it violated the First Amendment for the government to require as a condition of federal funding that organizations adopt a policy expressing opposition to prostitution and human trafficking.[341] The United States Leadership Against HIV/AIDS, Tuberculosis, and Malaria Act of 2003 (Leadership Act) authorized the appropriation of billions of dollars to fund efforts by nongovernmental organizations to assist in the fight.[342] One of the conditions for receipt of federal money was that "no funds may be used by an organization 'that does not have a policy explicitly opposing prostitution and sex trafficking.' "[343] The Court found that this requirement that organizations adopt a policy as a condition for federal funds violated the First Amendment. The Court explained: "The Policy Requirement compels as a condition of federal funding the affirmation of a belief that by its nature cannot be confined within the scope of the Government program. In so doing, it violates the First Amendment and cannot be sustained."[344]

Yet other cases have allowed the government to condition a benefit on individuals forgoing their First Amendment rights. In *Regan v. Taxation with Representation of Washington*, the Court upheld a provision of the federal tax law that conditioned tax-exempt status on the requirement that the organization not participate in lobbying or partisan political activities.[345] The Court said that "Congress has not

---

[339] *Id.* at 534.
[340] *Id.* at 548.
[341] 133 S. Ct. 2321 (2013).
[342] 117 Stat. 711, as amended, 22 U.S.C. §7601 *et seq.*
[343] §7631(f).
[344] 133 S. Ct. at 2332.
[345] 461 U.S. 540 (1983).

infringed any First Amendment rights or regulated any First Amendment activity. Congress has simply chosen not to pay for TWR's lobbying."[346] The Court said that it found "no indication that the statute was intended to suppress any ideas or any demonstration that it has had that effect."[347]

On the one hand, *Regan* can be defended as reflecting the principle that the government is not required to subsidize the exercise of First Amendment rights. The *Regan* Court said exactly this: "We have held in several contexts that a legislature's decision not to subsidize the exercise of a fundamental right does not infringe the right, and thus is not subject to strict scrutiny."[348] On the other hand, the government was conditioning a very valuable tax benefit on the requirement that the recipient forgo engaging in First Amendment protected speech. In essence, the government was penalizing organizations that exercised their rights to petition Congress for redress of grievances and to participate in political campaigns.[349]

The Court also refused to apply the unconstitutional conditions doctrine in *Rust v. Sullivan*.[350] *Rust* involved a challenge to a federal regulation that prohibited recipients of federal funds for family-planning services from providing "counseling concerning the use of abortion as a method of family planning or provide referral for abortion as a method of family planning."[351] The regulations prohibited recipients of federal money from referring a pregnant woman to an abortion provider, even upon specific request. Also, the rules "broadly prohibit a [recipient of funds] . . . from engaging in activities that 'encourage, promote, or advocate abortion as a method of family planning.'"[352]

Chief Justice Rehnquist, writing for the Court, upheld the regulation on the ground that the government could decide what activity to subsidize. He wrote: "[The] Government can, without violating the Constitution, selectively fund a program to encourage certain activities it believes to be in the public interest, without at the same time funding an alternate program which seeks to deal with the problem in another way. In so doing, the Government has not discriminated on the basis of viewpoint; it has merely chosen to fund one activity to the exclusion of another. 'A legislature's decision not to subsidize the exercise of a fundamental right does not infringe the right.'"[353]

It is difficult to reconcile *Rust* with the unconstitutional conditions doctrine because the regulations expressly conditioned a benefit, federal funds, on the requirement that the recipients forgo constitutionally protected speech. The federal regulation was content-based in that it denied funds only if the content of the

---

[346] *Id.* at 546. The Court relied on *Cammarano v. United States,* 358 U.S. 498 (1959), which upheld a Treasury Regulation that denied business expense deductions for lobbying activities. *Cammarano* held that Congress is not required by the First Amendment to subsidize lobbying. *Id.* at 513.

[347] 461 U.S. at 548.

[348] *Id.* at 549.

[349] *See* Sullivan, *supra* note 334, at 1441.

[350] 500 U.S. 173 (1991).

[351] *Id.* at 179.

[352] *Id.* at 180.

[353] *Id.* at 193 (citations omitted).

speech was abortion counseling and referrals, and the rule was obviously motivated by an intent to prevent speech. Justice Blackmun, in dissent, said: "Until today, the Court never has upheld viewpoint-based suppression of speech simply because that suppression was a condition upon the acceptance of public funds. Whatever may be the Government's power to condition the receipt of its largess upon the relinquishment of constitutional rights, it surely does not extend to a condition that suppresses the recipient's cherished freedom of speech based solely upon the content or viewpoint of that speech."[354]

Moreover, it is difficult to reconcile *Rust* with the Court's subsequent decision in *Rosenberger v. Rector of the University of Virginia*, where it held that the state violated the First Amendment in refusing to provide funds to a Christian student group that published a religious magazine.[355] In *Rosenberger*, like in *Rust*, it was a choice by the government to fund some speech but not others. Yet in *Rosenberger*, this choice was deemed unconstitutional. Justice Kennedy, writing for the majority in *Rosenberger*, distinguished *Rust*: "[In *Rust*], the government did not create a program to encourage private speech but instead used private speakers to transmit specific information pertaining to its own program. We recognized that when the government appropriates public funds to promote a particular policy of its own it is entitled to say what it wishes. . . . It does not follow, however, . . . that viewpoint-based restrictions are proper when the University does not itself speak or subsidize transmittal of a message it favors but instead expends funds to encourage diversity of views from private speakers."[356]

Yet it can be asked why this is a distinction that makes a difference. Whether the government has created the program to encourage private speech or is relying on existing private speakers, the issue is the same: Can the government condition funds on the content of the speech? In *Rust*, the Court said yes if the speech is abortion counseling and referrals; in *Rosenberger*, the Court said no if the speech has religious content.

It also is quite difficult to reconcile *Legal Services Corporation v. Velazquez* with *Rust v. Sullivan*. In both cases, the government was denying funding to groups if they engaged in particular activities. But in the former the conditions on federal money were upheld, while in the latter they were struck down. Justice Kennedy's majority opinion in *Velazquez* expressly addressed this. He said that the Court has held that "viewpoint-based funding decisions can be sustained in instances in which the government is itself the speaker, or instances, like *Rust*, in which the government used private speakers to transmit information pertaining to its own program."[357] But as Justice Scalia argued in dissent, the question is why the government is limited to these circumstances when it chooses to put restrictions on how its funds are used.[358] Perhaps the difference is in the Court's willingness to see litigation as a "forum" and thus not accept viewpoint restrictions.

---

[354] *Id.* at 207 (Blackmun, J., dissenting).
[355] 515 U.S. 819 (1995). *Rosenberger* is discussed in detail in §12.2.4.
[356] *Id.* at 834.
[357] 531 U.S. at 541.
[358] *Id.* at 550 (Scalia, J., dissenting).

Overall, it is very difficult to reconcile the cases concerning the unconstitutional conditions doctrine. Perhaps they reflect an implicit balancing by the Court with the Justices weighing the burden on speech imposed by a condition against the government's justification for the requirement. Or perhaps the cases cannot be reconciled, and the decisions simply turn on the views of the Justices in particular cases. If the Court wishes to strike down a condition, it declares it to be an unconstitutional condition; if the Court wishes to uphold a condition, it declares that the government is making a permissible choice to subsidize some activities and not others.

§11.2.4.5   Government Pressures: Is It Government Speech or a Form of Government Censorship?

Is it an infringement of speech if the government places pressure on individuals or entities to refrain from First Amendment behavior without actually prohibiting or in any way penalizing speech? The cases are mixed in dealing with this issue. In *Bantam Books, Inc. v. Sullivan,* the Court held that it was unconstitutional for the Rhode Island Commission to Encourage Morality in Youth to identify "objectionable" books because they were unsuitable for children and to write to sellers urging them to stop selling those books.[359] The letter also informed the recipient that the commission recommended obscenity prosecutions to prosecutors and turned its list of distributors of objectionable books over to local police. In fact, a police officer often followed up and visited the recipient of a letter to see what actions had been taken. The Supreme Court found that such pressure constituted an unconstitutional prior restraint of speech, even though no books were actually banned and no prosecutions were undertaken.

Another type of impermissible pressure was identified in *Lamont v. Postmaster General,* where a federal statute instructed the postal service to identify "communist political propaganda" and deliver it only to those who requested, in writing, such materials.[360] The law did not ban any material or impose any punishments for receipt. Nonetheless, the Court found that the law created obvious pressure against receiving material labeled "communist political propaganda" and thus violated the First Amendment. Justice Douglas, writing for the Court, said that "[t]his requirement is almost certain to have a deterrent effect, especially as respects those who have sensitive positions. . . . Public officials like school teachers who have no tenure, might think they would invite disaster if they read what the Federal Government says contains the seeds of treason. Apart from them, any addressee is likely to feel some inhibition in sending for literature which federal officials have condemned as 'communist political propaganda.'"[361]

However, other cases point in the opposite direction. In *Meese v. Keene,* the Court held that the government could label a film without violating the First

---

[359]   372 U.S. 58 (1963).
[360]   381 U.S. 301 (1965).
[361]   *Id.* at 307.

Amendment.[362] Pursuant to the Foreign Agents Registration Act, the federal government identified some Canadian films as political propaganda. One, titled "If You Love This Planet," had won the Academy Award for Best Short Documentary in 1982 and depicted an antinuclear weapons speech given by the president of the American group Physicians for Social Responsibility. A second film, titled "Acid Rain: Requiem or Recovery?," also produced by the National Film Board of Canada, focused on the harms from acid rain.

By labeling the films as "propaganda" under the Foreign Agents Registration Act, the exhibitors of the movies were required to place the words "political propaganda" at the beginning of the films. Additionally, the producer of the films, the National Film Board of Canada, was required to provide the government with a list of all major distributors of the films and with a list of all of the groups that had requested the films for viewing.

The government's actions, like in *Bantam Books* and *Lamont*, did not prohibit any speech, but created obvious pressure against showing such movies. However, the Court found no violation of the First Amendment. The Court emphasized that "[t]he statute itself neither prohibits nor censors the dissemination of advocacy materials by agents of foreign principles. . . . The term 'political propaganda' does nothing to place regulated expressive material 'beyond the pale of legitimate discourse.' . . . To the contrary, Congress simply required the disseminators of such material to make additional disclosures that would better enable the public to evaluate the import of the propaganda."[363] The Court distinguished *Lamont* on the ground that there was actual physical detention of mail, but no restraint of films in *Meese v. Keene.*

The underlying issue in these cases concerns when the government's own speech should be regarded as impermissible pressure and thus an infringement of the First Amendment. Would a government-imposed rating system for records or television programs simply be, in the words of *Meese*, "additional disclosures that would better enable the public to evaluate" the speech? Or would it be a form of pressure to self-censorship as in *Bantam Books* and *Lamont*? Are letters from government agencies or commissions pressuring stores not to sell certain adult-oriented magazines simply the government expressing its views or is it an infringement of the First Amendment because of the government's prosecutorial powers?[364] Are speeches by high-level political officials condemning certain speech, such as rap lyrics, an exercise of the officials' expressive rights or are they impermissible pressure in light of *Bantam Books*? Cases such as *Bantam Books, Lamont,* and *Meese* point in opposite directions.

Ultimately, the task for courts is to evaluate the degree of pressure against speech. If the pressure is more than minimal, cases such as *Bantam Books* and *Lamont* suggest that First Amendment scrutiny is required. *Meese v. Keene* might be

---

[362] 481 U.S. 465 (1987).

[363] *Id.* at 478, 480-481.

[364] Penthouse Intl., Ltd. v. Meese, 939 F.2d 1011 (D.C. Cir. 1991) (finding that letters sent from a government commission to stores accusing them of selling obscene materials did not violate the First Amendment).

distinguished on the ground that the Court saw little adverse effect on speech by the government labeling material as "political propaganda."

§11.2.5   Government Speech

The Supreme Court has held that when the government is the speaker the First Amendment does not apply at all or provide a basis for challenging the government's action. The Court most clearly held this in *Pleasant Grove, Utah v. Summum*.[365]

Pioneer Park in Pleasant Grove, Utah, has 15 monuments, 11 of which were privately donated. One of these is a large Ten Commandments monument donated by the Fraternal Order of Eagles in 1971.

Summum is a religious organization founded in 1975 and headquartered in Salt Lake City, Utah. On two separate occasions in 2003, Summum's president wrote a letter to the Pleasant Grove's mayor requesting permission to erect a "stone monument," which would contain "the Seven Aphorisms of Summum" and be similar in size and nature to the Ten Commandments monument. The city refused the request and Summum sued. Summum claimed that for the city to allow a monument from some religion but not others violated the First Amendment.

The federal district court ruled against Summum, but the Tenth Circuit reversed and found that the government was engaged in impermissible content-based discrimination by denying access to the Summum monument, but permitting the Ten Commandments display.

The Supreme Court unanimously reversed and ruled in favor of the City of Pleasant Grove, with Justice Samuel Alito writing for the Court. The Court held that by allowing placement of donated permanent monuments in a public park, the city was exercising a form of government speech not subject to scrutiny under the free speech clause.

Justice Alito began by declaring that "[t]he Free Speech Clause restricts government regulation of private speech; it does not regulate government speech."[366] The Court quoted its prior decision in *Johanns v. Livestock Marketing Assn.*,[367] declaring that "[t]he Government's own speech . . . is exempt from First Amendment scrutiny." Justice Alito also explained that "[a] government entity may exercise this same freedom to express its views when it receives assistance from private sources for the purpose of delivering a government-controlled message."[368] In other words, the fact that the Ten Commandments monument had been donated by a private group did not prevent the government from adopting it and making it government speech. Justice Alito declared: "[I]t is clear that the monuments in Pleasant Grove's Pioneer Park represent government speech."[369]

---

[365] 555 U.S. 460 (2009).
[366] *Id.* at 467.
[367] 544 U.S. 550, 553 (2005), discussed above.
[368] 555 U.S. at 468.
[369] *Id.* at 470.

This is not the first case to invoke the notion that the First Amendment does not apply when the government is the speaker; *Rust v. Sullivan* and *Johanns v. Livestock Marketing Assn.*, discussed above, also use this rationale. But *Pleasant Grove* is the first time that the Court has said that the government can adopt private speech as its own and thereby avoid the First Amendment.

This has potentially broad implications. Could a city allow a pro-war demonstration in a city park while denying access to an antiwar demonstration by adopting the former as its government speech? Justice Alito recognized the danger that the "government speech doctrine not be used as a subterfuge for favoring certain private speakers over others based on viewpoint."[370] But it is unclear how this can be avoided under the principle that the government can adopt private speech as government speech and the First Amendment then does not apply. A distinction can be drawn between the permanent monument in *Pleasant Grove* and a transitory demonstration, but it is not clear why that should matter under the First Amendment. This problem led Justice Stevens in a concurring opinion to express concern about the "recently minted government speech doctrine."[371]

After *Pleasant Grove*, a key question will be whether the government is the speaker or whether the government is creating a forum for private speech. The First Amendment applies only in the latter instance.[372]

§11.3   TYPES OF UNPROTECTED AND LESS PROTECTED SPEECH

§11.3.1   *Introduction*

Categories of Unprotected and Less Protected Speech

The Supreme Court has identified some categories of unprotected speech that the government can prohibit and punish. Incitement of illegal activity, fighting words, and obscenity are examples of such categories of unprotected speech.[1]

---

[370] *Id.*

[371] *Id.* at 1139 (Stevens, J., concurring).

[372] Also, if the government is the speaker and the monument, as in *Pleasant Grove*, is a religious symbol, then this would seem to heighten the establishment clause issue. The Court in *Pleasant Grove* expressly said it was not addressing that question.

§11.3 [1] In a 2010 case, the Supreme Court declared: "From 1791 to the present, however, the First Amendment has permitted restrictions upon the content of speech in a few limited areas, and has never include[d] a freedom to disregard these traditional limitations. These historic and traditional categories long familiar to the bar, including obscenity, defamation, fraud, incitement, and speech integral to criminal conduct, are well-defined and narrowly limited classes of speech, the prevention and punishment of which have never been thought to raise any Constitutional problem." United States v. Stevens, 130 S. Ct. 1577, 1584 (2010).

Additionally, there are categories of less protected speech where the government has more latitude to regulate than usual under the First Amendment. For instance, government generally can regulate commercial speech if intermediate scrutiny is met. Also, the Court has indicated that some types of sexually oriented speech, although protected by the First Amendment, are deemed to be of "low value," and thus are more susceptible to government regulation.

These categories are defined based on the subject matter of the speech and thus represent an exception to the usual rule that content-based regulation must meet strict scrutiny. For a long time it was thought that the government had broad latitude to prohibit and regulate speech within the categories of unprotected expression. The conventional view was that laws in these areas would be upheld so long as they met the rational basis test that all government actions must satisfy. However, in *R.A.V. v. City of St. Paul*,[2] discussed below, the Court indicated that generally content-based distinctions within categories of unprotected speech must meet strict scrutiny. In *R.A.V.*, the Court declared unconstitutional a city's ordinance that prohibited hate speech based on race, color, religion, or gender that was likely to "anger, alarm, or cause resentment." The Court said that even though fighting words are a category of unprotected speech, the law impermissibly drew content-based distinctions among fighting words, such as by prohibiting expression of hate based on race, but not based on political affiliation.[3] It is unclear after *R.A.V.* how much its reasoning will limit the ability of government to regulate within the categories of unprotected speech.

The categories of unprotected and less protected speech reflect value judgments by the Supreme Court that the justifications for regulating such speech outweigh the value of the expression. For each of the categories discussed below, the Court's judgment can be questioned. For example, is the Court correct that obscenity is "utterly without redeeming social importance" and therefore is unprotected by the First Amendment?[4] Is the Court right that commercial speech is less important than other types of speech and therefore worthy only of intermediate scrutiny? Also, it is important to consider whether other categories of unprotected speech should be recognized because of the harms of such speech relative to its benefits. For example, in recent years the Court has consistently refused to find that violent speech is a category of unprotected or less protected speech.[5]

Moreover, the categorical approach requires careful attention to how the types of unprotected speech are defined. For instance, the definitions of "incitement" or "obscenity" are enormously important because they determine whether the government can punish the speech or whether the expression is safeguarded by the First Amendment. A recurring theme throughout this section is whether

---

[2] 505 U.S. 377 (1992).

[3] *Id.* at 387-388.

[4] Roth v. United States, 354 U.S. 476, 484 (1957).

[5] *See, e.g.*, Brown v. Entertainment Merchants Assn., 131 S. Ct. 2729, 2734 (2011) (declaring unconstitutional a state law prohibiting sale or rental of violent video games to minors under 18 without parental consent); United States v. Stevens, 130 S. Ct. 1577, 1585 (2010) (declaring unconstitutional federal law prohibiting depictions of violence or cruelty to animals).

the Court's definitions of the categories are sufficiently specific and a desirable way of separating protected from unprotected speech.

§11.3.2   Incitement of Illegal Activity

§11.3.2.1   Introduction

Importance of the Topic

The topic of incitement is important for many reasons. It was the first area that produced a large body of Supreme Court cases.[6] Thus, the doctrines articulated in this area—such as the clear and present danger test—have been carried over to many other areas of First Amendment law.

The issue of incitement also is important because it poses a basic value question: How should society balance its need for social order against its desire to protect freedom of speech? When, if at all, may speech that advocates criminal activity or the overthrow of the government be stopped to promote order and security?

Some commentators have argued that all such advocacy of illegal conduct should be deemed unprotected by the First Amendment. Robert Bork, for example, contended that "[a]dvocacy of law violation is a call to set aside the results that political speech has produced. The process of the 'discovery and spread of political truth' is damaged or destroyed if the outcome is defeated by a minority that makes law enforcement, and hence the putting of political truth into practice, impossible or less effective. There should, therefore, be no constitutional protection for any speech advocating violation of law."[7]

The Supreme Court never has taken this view. Justice Brandeis explained that "even advocacy of [law] violation, however reprehensible morally, is not a justification for denying free speech where the advocacy falls short of incitement and there is nothing to indicate that the advocacy would be immediately acted on."[8] The strong presumption in favor of protecting speech is viewed as justifying safeguarding even advocacy of illegality unless there is a substantial likelihood of imminent harm. Also, advocacy of law violations, or even civil disobedience, is seen as a powerful way of expressing a message. But the Court also never has taken the position that such speech is completely protected by the First Amendment, and the government is limited to punishing the criminal acts themselves.

---

[6] For an excellent discussion of the First Amendment prior to these cases, which occurred in the World War I and post–World War I era, *see* David Rabban, The First Amendment in Its Forgotten Years, 90 Yale L.J. 514 (1981).

[7] Robert Bork, Neutral Principles and Some First Amendment Problems, 47 Ind. L.J. 1, 31 (1971).

[8] Whitney v. California, 274 U.S. 357, 376 (1927) (Brandeis, J., concurring).

Overview of the Development
of the Law of Incitement

Thus, the Court has been confronted with the task of defining when advocacy of illegality constitutes unprotected incitement and when it is safeguarded by the First Amendment.[9] Over the course of the last century, the Supreme Court has used at least four major different approaches in this area. Interestingly, often the later tests have replaced earlier ones without overruling them or even acknowledging their differences.

During World War I and the years immediately following it, the Supreme Court articulated and applied the "clear and present danger test." During the 1920s and 1930s, the Court often did not use this formulation, but instead used a "reasonableness test" that allowed the government to punish advocacy of illegality so long as it was reasonable to do so. The reasonableness test is the one approach that has been expressly repudiated by later Court decisions. In the 1950s, during the *McCarthy* era, the Court reformulated the clear and present danger test as a risk formula; whether speech was protected depended on the gravity of the evil compared with its likelihood. But since the late 1960s, the Court has narrowly defined incitement to maximize protection of speech. Under this approach, advocacy can be punished only if there is a likelihood of imminent illegal conduct and the speech is directed to causing imminent illegality. These four approaches are discussed in the following subsections.

§11.3.2.2   The "Clear and Present Danger" Test

The Context

There was substantial criticism within the country of American involvement in World War I.[10] There was significant opposition to the draft, and it is estimated that there were over 350,000 draft evaders or delinquents during the war.[11] At about the same time, the success of the Bolshevik revolution in Russia led to fears of a leftist uprising in this country.[12]

In response to all of this, two months after America's entry into World War I, Congress enacted the Espionage Act of 1917. The law, in part, made it a crime when the nation was at war for any person willfully to "make or convey false reports or false statements with intent to interfere" with the military success or "to promote

---

[9] For an excellent in-depth discussion of the law in this area, *see* Kent Greenawalt, Speech, Crime, and the Uses of Language (1989).

[10] *See* Rabban, *supra* note 6, at 581-582; Zechariah Chaffee, Free Speech in the United States 108-111 (1941).

[11] Robert J. Goldstein, Political Repression in Modern America from 1870 to the Present 105 (1978).

[12] *See* Chaffee, *supra* note 10, at 110-111; Mitchell Tilner, Ideological Exclusion of Aliens: The Evolution of Policy, 2 Geo. Immigr. L.J. 46-48 (1987) (describing the Palmer raids, where Attorney General Mitchell Palmer deported aliens because of their speech and associational activities).

the success of its enemies."[13] The law also made it a crime to willfully "obstruct the recruiting or enlistment service of the United States."[14] Convictions could be punished by sentences of up to 20 years imprisonment and fines of up to $10,000. In 1918, Congress adopted a law even more restrictive of speech. The Sedition Act of 1918 prohibited individuals from saying anything with the intent to obstruct the sale of war bonds; to "utter, print, write, or publish any disloyal, profane, scurrilous, or abusive language" intended to cause contempt or scorn for the form of the government of the United States, the Constitution, or the flag; to urge the curtailment of production of war materials with the intent of hindering the war effort; or to utter any words supporting the cause of any country at war with the United States or opposing the cause of the United States.[15]

The Cases

In a series of cases, the Supreme Court upheld the constitutionality of both the laws and their application to speech that, in hindsight, was mild and ineffectual.[16] The Court articulated the clear and present danger test and found it was met in the cases before it.[17] In *Schenck v. United States*, individuals were convicted for circulating a leaflet arguing that the draft violated the Thirteenth Amendment as a form of involuntary servitude.[18] The leaflet said, "Do not submit to intimidation," and "Assert Your Rights," but did not expressly urge violation of any law; it advocated repealing the draft law.

There was not any evidence that the leaflet had any effect in causing a single person to resist the draft. But the Court, in an opinion by Justice Oliver Wendell Holmes, dismissed this as irrelevant. He said: "Of course the document would not have been sent unless it had been intended to have some effect, and we do not see what effect it could be expected to have upon persons subject to the draft except to influence them to obstruct the carrying of it out."[19]

The Court said that although in "many places and in ordinary times" the speech would have been protected by the First Amendment, the wartime circumstances

---

[13]   Act of June 15, 1917, ch. 30, tit. I, §3, 40 Stat. 219.

[14]   *Id.*

[15]   Act of May 16, 1918, 40 Stat. 553.

[16]   In addition to Supreme Court rulings, there were notable decisions by lower federal courts concerning the acts. For example, in *Masses Publishing Co. v. Patten*, 244 F. 535 (S.D.N.Y. 1917), *rev'd*, 246 F. 24 (2d Cir. 1917), Judge Learned Hand attempted to draw a clear distinction between incitement and discussion. He wrote that "one may not counsel or advise others to violate the law as it stands. Words are not only the keys of persuasion, but the triggers of action." *Id.* at 540. Criticism of the law is constitutionally protected, advocacy of its violation is not. In *Shaffer v. United States*, 255 F. 886 (9th Cir. 1919), the court upheld the application of the Espionage Act of 1917 against a book critical of American involvement in World War I. The court said that the test is "whether the natural and probable tendency and effect of [the publication] are such as are calculated to produce the result condemned by statute." *Id.* at 887.

[17]   For a thorough review of these cases, *see* Zechariah Chaffee, Jr., Free Speech in the United States (1941).

[18]   249 U.S. 47 (1919).

[19]   *Id.* at 51.

were crucial. In some of the most famous words in the United States Reports, Justice Holmes said: "But the character of every act depends upon the circumstances in which it is done. The most stringent protection of free speech would not protect a man in falsely shouting fire in a theatre, and causing a panic. . . . The question in every case is whether the words used are used in such circumstances and are of such a nature as to create a clear and present danger that they will bring about the substantive evils that Congress has a right to prevent."[20] With relatively little elaboration, the Court found that this test was met and upheld Schenck's conviction.

A week after *Schenck* was announced, the Court upheld convictions under the 1917 Act in *Frohwerk v. United States*[21] and *Debs v. United States*.[22] In *Frohwerk*, two individuals who published a German language newspaper were convicted and sentenced to ten years in prison because of their articles criticizing the war. Justice Holmes, again writing for the Court, acknowledged that there was no evidence that the articles had any adverse effect on the war effort. But he said that "on the record it is impossible to say that it might not have been found that the circulation of the paper was in quarters where a little breath would be enough to kindle a flame and that the fact was known and relied upon by those who sent the paper out."[23]

In *Debs v. United States*, the Court affirmed the conviction of Socialist Party leader Eugene Debs, who had been sentenced to jail for ten years for violating the 1917 Act. Debs's speech, which primarily was advocacy of socialism, included some mild criticism of the draft. At one point in a long speech, Debs remarked that he had to be "prudent" and not say all that he thought, but that "you need to know that you are fit for something better than slavery and cannon fodder."[24] The Court found it irrelevant that this was a small part of the speech. Justice Holmes said that the speech was not protected if "one purpose of the speech, whether incidental or not does not matter, was to oppose . . . this war, and if, in all the circumstances, that would be its probable effect."[25] The Court invoked *Schenck* as resolving the First Amendment issue raised by Debs.

What did the clear and present danger test mean? Its phrasing connotes three requirements: (1) likelihood of (2) imminent, (3) significant harm.[26] Yet in none of these three cases was harm to the war effort from the speech likely or imminent. The famous analogy to shouting fire in a crowded theater invokes a situation where speech obviously poses a great likelihood of imminent substantial harm.

[20] *Id.* at 52.
[21] 249 U.S. 204 (1919).
[22] 249 U.S. 211 (1919).
[23] 249 U.S. at 209.
[24] 249 U.S. at 214.
[25] *Id.* at 214-215.
[26] In *Abrams v. United States*, 250 U.S. 616 (1919), discussed below, Justice Holmes, in a dissenting opinion, phrased the clear and present danger test in a slightly different way. He said: "It is only the present danger of immediate evil or an intent to bring it about that warrants Congress in setting a limit to the expression of opinion." *Id.* at 628 (Holmes, J., dissenting). This implies that *either* the intent to cause a clear and present danger or the actual creation of such a risk can be punished. In other words, completely ineffectual speech can be punished if the speaker intended harms.

But the speech in *Schenck*, *Debs*, and *Frohwerk* seems far from that and in hindsight seems quite mild, especially when compared to criticisms of America's involvement in the Vietnam War.

Interestingly, later in the year in which these cases were decided, Justice Holmes dissented in a case in which the Supreme Court upheld convictions for violating the 1918 Act. In *Abrams v. United States*, the Supreme Court affirmed the convictions of a group of Russian immigrants who circulated leaflets, in English and in Yiddish, objecting to America sending troops to Eastern Europe after the Russian revolution.[27] Although the defendants' speech had nothing to do with World War I or the draft, they were convicted of encouraging resistance and conspiracy to urge curtailment of the production of war materials and sentenced to 20 years in prison. The Supreme Court, relying on *Schenck* and *Frohwerk*, upheld the convictions.

Justice Holmes wrote an eloquent dissent in which he articulated the marketplace of ideas metaphor for the First Amendment. Justice Holmes said that he never had seen any reason to doubt that *Schenck*, *Frohwerk*, and *Debs* were rightly decided: "I do not doubt for a moment that by the same reasoning that would justify punishing persuasion to murder, the United States constitutionally may punish speech that produces or is intended to produce a clear and imminent danger that it will bring about forthwith certain substantive evils that the United States constitutionally may seek to prevent. The power undoubtedly is greater in time of war than in time of peace because war opens dangers that do not exist at other times."[28]

Unlike in *Schenck*, *Frohwerk*, and *Debs*, Holmes thought that the clear and present danger test was not met in *Abrams*. He said: "Now nobody can suppose that the surreptitious publishing of a silly leaflet by an unknown man, without more, would present any immediate danger that its opinions would hinder the success of the government arms or have any appreciable tendency to do so."[29] It can be asked, however, whether the same description might not have been used in *Schenck*: a silly leaflet, circulated by an unknown man, without more.[30]

§11.3.2.3   The Reasonableness Approach

The Emphasis on Deference to Legislatures

During the 1920s and the 1930s, the Court decided a series of cases involving criminal syndicalism laws—statutes that made it a crime to advocate the overthrow of the United States government or industrial organization by force or violence. The Court decided these cases without invoking the clear and present danger

---

[27]   250 U.S. 616 (1919).

[28]   250 U.S. at 627-628 (Holmes, J., dissenting).

[29]   *Id.* at 628.

[30]   *See* Thomas Healy, The Great Dissent: How Oliver Wendell Holmes Changed His Mind and Changed the History of Free Speech in America (2013) (describing Holmes's shift in *Abrams*).

test. Rather, the Court appeared to use a reasonableness approach; it upheld the laws and their applications so long as the government's law and prosecution were reasonable.

Gitlow v. New York, the first case that indicated that the First Amendment applied to the states through its incorporation into the due process clause of the Fourteenth Amendment, upheld a conviction under the New York criminal anarchy statute.[31] Benjamin Gitlow was convicted for publishing the "Left Wing Manifesto" and thereby violating the statute prohibiting advocating "overthrowing and overturning organized government by force, violence, and unlawful means."

Although there was no evidence that the speech had any effects, the Court upheld the conviction. The Court said that a "State may punish utterances endangering the foundations of organized government and threatening its overthrow by unlawful means. These imperil its own existence as a constitutional State. Freedom of speech and press . . . does not deprive a State of the primary and essential right of self preservation."[32] The Court then proclaimed the need for deference to legislative judgments in this area: "By enacting the present statute the State has determined, through its legislative body, that utterances advocating the overthrow of organized government by force, violence and unlawful means, are so inimical to the general welfare and involve such danger of substantive evil that they may be penalized in the exercise of the police power. That determination must be given great weight. Every presumption is to be indulged in favor of the validity of the statute."[33]

Justice Holmes dissented and urged the application of the clear and present danger test.[34] He said that there was no "present danger" of an attempt to overthrow the government. He wrote: "It is said that this manifesto was more than a theory, that it was an incitement. Every idea is an incitement. . . . Eloquence may set fire to reason. But whatever may be thought of the redundant discourse before us it had no chance of starting a present conflagration."[35]

In *Whitney v. California*, the Court again upheld a conviction under a state criminal syndicalism law.[36] Anita Whitney was convicted of attending a meeting in Oakland, California, to organize a branch of the Communist Labor Party. She actually took a moderate position at the convention, although it adopted a more radical approach. The Court upheld the California law and Whitney's conviction under it. Again, the Court proclaimed the need for deference to the legislature. The Court said: "[A] State in the exercise of its police power may punish those who abuse [freedom of speech] by utterances inimical to the public welfare, tending to incite to crime, disturb the public peace, or endanger the foundations of organized government and threaten its overthrow by unlawful means. . . . By enacting the provisions of the Syndicalism Act the State has declared, through its legislative body, that [criminal syndicalism] . . . involves such danger to the public peace

---

[31] 268 U.S. 652 (1925).
[32] *Id.* at 668.
[33] *Id.*
[34] *Id.* at 672 (Holmes, J., dissenting).
[35] *Id.* at 673.
[36] 274 U.S. 357 (1927).

and the security of the State, that these acts should be penalized in the exercise of its police power. That determination must be given great weight."[37]

Justice Brandeis concurred in an opinion joined by Justice Holmes. In language quoted above in §11.1.2, Justice Brandeis eloquently and powerfully articulated the reasons why freedom of speech should be protected as a fundamental right. Brandeis also urged the use of the clear and present danger test. He said: "Fear of serious injury cannot alone justify suppression of free speech and assembly. Men feared witches and burnt women. It is the function of speech to free men from the bondage of irrational fears. To justify suppression of free speech there must be reasonable ground to fear that serious evil will result if free speech is practiced. There must be reasonable ground to believe that the danger apprehended is imminent. There must be reasonable ground to believe that the evil to be prevented is a serious one."[38] Interestingly, despite his ringing pronouncement, Justice Brandeis did not dissent in *Whitney*; instead, he concurred and upheld the California law and the jury's conviction under it.

Convictions Overturned Under the Reasonableness Approach

In several cases after *Gitlow* and *Whitney*, the Supreme Court overturned convictions under criminal syndicalism laws. In each, the Court still did not use the clear and present danger test but, rather, found the convictions unreasonable. In *Fiske v. Kansas*, the Supreme Court for the first time overturned a state court conviction as violating the First Amendment as applied to the states through the Fourteenth Amendment.[39] In *Fiske*, the Court concluded that there was no evidence of criminal syndicalism because there were no declarations by the defendant, or his organization, urging unlawful acts. The Court said that the conviction was "an arbitrary and unreasonable exercise of the police power of the State."[40]

Similarly, in *DeJonge v. Oregon*, the Court overturned a conviction for holding a meeting of the Communist Party.[41] Again, the Court emphasized that no one at the meeting advocated illegal acts or the overthrow of the government. The Court said that "peaceable assembly for lawful discussion cannot be made a crime. The holding of meetings for peaceable political action cannot be proscribed."[42]

The majority in all of these cases used an approach that now would be termed rational basis review. None applied the clear and present danger test or anything akin to heightened scrutiny.[43] Thus, the reasonableness approach is inconsistent

---

[37] *Id.* at 371.

[38] *Id.* at 376 (Brandeis, J., concurring).

[39] 274 U.S. 380 (1927).

[40] *Id.* at 387.

[41] 299 U.S. 353 (1937).

[42] *Id.* at 365. *See also* Herndon v. Lowry, 301 U.S. 242 (1937) (overturning a conviction of an individual who was a paid organizer of the Communist Party because there was no evidence that he had advocated illegal activity).

[43] Interestingly, in other areas, not involving advocacy of illegal activity, the Court during the 1930s and 1940s expressly used the clear and present danger test. *See, e.g.*, Bridges v. California, 314

with the now firmly established heightened scrutiny for fundamental rights. Indeed, the Supreme Court has declared that "*Whitney* has been thoroughly discredited by later decisions."[44]

§11.3.2.4   The Risk Formula Approach

Dennis v. United States

During the late 1940s and early 1950s, Senator Joseph McCarthy led a crusade to identify and exclude Communists in government. It was the age of suspicion—a time where merely being suspected of being a part of a Communist or radical group was enough to cause a person to lose a job or appear on a blacklist.[45]

Amidst this hysteria, in 1951, the Supreme Court decided *Dennis v. United States.*[46] Individuals were convicted and sentenced to long prison terms for teaching four books written by Stalin, Marx and Engels, and Lenin. Although there was no accusation that they had done anything other than teach these works, they were convicted of violating the Smith Act. Section 2 of the Smith Act made it unlawful for any person "to knowingly or willfully advocate, abet, advise, or teach the duty, necessity, desirability, or propriety of overthrowing or destroying any government in the United States by force or violence, or by the assassination of any officer of such government."[47] Section 3 made it "unlawful for any person to attempt to commit, or to conspire to commit, any of the acts"[48] prohibited in §2. The defendants were convicted of conspiring to organize the Communist Party of the United States, which was described as a group that taught and advocated the overthrow of the United States government. The Court, in a plurality opinion written by Chief Justice Vinson, said that the appropriate test was the clear and present danger approach articulated in *Schenck* and not the reasonableness test of *Gitlow* or *Whitney*. Chief Justice Vinson said that the measure of the clear and present danger test is the formula announced by Judge Learned Hand: "In each case [courts] must ask whether the gravity of the 'evil,' discounted by its improbability, justifies such invasion of free speech as is necessary to avoid the danger."[49]

The plurality concluded that the harms of an overthrow of the government are so enormous that the government need not show that the danger is imminent or probable in order to punish speech. Chief Justice Vinson said: "Obviously, the words cannot mean that before the Government may act, it must wait until the putsch is about to be executed, the plans have been laid and the signal is

---

U.S. 252 (1941) (speech critical of courts could be held in contempt only if there was a clear and present danger), discussed below in §11.3.9; Cantwell v. Connecticut, 310 U.S. 296 (1940) (speech that provokes a hostile audience can be punished only if there is a clear and present danger).

[44] Brandenburg v. Ohio, 395 U.S. 444, 447 (1969).
[45] *See* Victor Navasky, Naming Names (1980).
[46] 341 U.S. 494 (1951).
[47] Act of June 28, 1940, 54 Stat. 670, 671.
[48] 54 Stat. at 671.
[49] 341 U.S. at 570 (citation omitted).

awaited. . . . The damage which such attempts create both physically and politically to a nation makes it impossible to measure the validity in terms of, the probability of success, or the immediacy of a successful attempt."[50]

In other words, the approach taken by the plurality in *Dennis* makes probability and imminence—two seeming requirements of a clear and present danger test—irrelevant. If the harm is great enough, such as the overthrow of the government, then speech advocating it can be punished without any showing of likelihood or imminence. Indeed, the plurality acknowledged that its approach was different from that advocated by Justices Holmes and Brandeis in their opinions in *Gitlow* and *Whitney*. But Chief Justice Vinson said that Justices Holmes and Brandeis "were not confronted with any situation comparable to the instant one—the development of an apparatus designed and dedicated to the overthrow of the Government, in the context of world crisis after crisis."[51]

Justice Frankfurter wrote a concurring opinion in which he urged the application of the reasonableness test as in *Gitlow* and *Whitney*. He urged deference to the legislature: "Primary responsibility for adjusting the interests which compete in the situation before us of necessity belongs to the Congress."[52] He said that "[f]ree speech cases are not an exception to the principle that we are not legislators, that direct policy-making is not our province. . . . It is not for us to decide how we would adjust the clash of interests which this case presents were the primary responsibility for reconciling it ours. Congress has determined that the danger created by advocacy of overthrow justifies the ensuing restriction on freedom of speech."[53]

Justice Jackson, in his concurring opinion, argued against the application of the clear and present danger test on the ground that it was too protective of speech. He said that "[t]he authors of the clear and present danger test never applied it to a case like this, nor would I. If applied as it is proposed here, it means that the Communist plotting is protected during its period of incubation; its preliminary stages of organization and preparation are immune from the law; the Government can move only after imminent action is manifest, when it would, of course, be too late."[54]

Justices Black and Douglas each wrote impassioned dissenting opinions. Each emphasized that the convictions were solely for engaging in speech. Justice Black lamented that the defendants were "not charged with an attempt to overthrow the Government. They were not charged with overt acts of any kind designed to overthrow the Government. They were not even charged with saying anything or writing anything designed to overthrow the Government. The charge was that they agreed to assemble and to talk and publish certain ideas at a later date."[55] Justice Douglas said that to punish expression "[t]here must be some immediate injury to

---

[50] *Id.* at 509.

[51] *Id.*

[52] *Id.* at 525 (Frankfurter, J., concurring).

[53] *Id.* at 539, 550.

[54] *Id.* at 570.

[55] *Id.* at 579 (Black, J., dissenting).

society that is likely if speech is allowed."[56] He said: "How it can be said that there is a clear and present danger that this advocacy will succeed is . . . a mystery. . . . In America, [the Communists] are miserable merchants of unwanted ideas; their wares remain unsold."[57]

The Court's decision in *Dennis* can be assessed on many levels. From a doctrinal perspective, it can be asked whether the *Dennis* test is, as the plurality proclaimed, an application of the clear and present danger test. The *Dennis* risk formula means that if the harm is great enough, such as the overthrow of the government, the danger need be neither clear nor present. However, in cases such as *Schenck*, *Debs*, and *Frohwerk*, the Court affirmed convictions even though there was no proof of imminent, likely harms.

From a broader policy perspective, *Dennis* can be evaluated in terms of whether the government should be able to punish advocacy of its overthrow, no matter how remote or unlikely that it will occur. The Justices in the majority in *Dennis* believed that because the harm is so great, even the smallest increase in risk is unacceptable. But, especially from the perspective of hindsight, *Dennis* seems terribly misguided; individuals were punished for doing no more than reading and talking about four books that are now a regular part of many college courses.

Smith Act Cases After *Dennis*

In the years following *Dennis*, the Supreme Court decided several cases under the Smith Act. In *Yates v. United States*, the Court overturned the convictions of several individuals for conspiracy to violate the Smith Act.[58] The Court emphasized that there was a crucial "distinction between advocacy of abstract doctrine and advocacy directed at promoting unlawful action."[59] The Court did not overrule *Dennis*, but distinguished it. Justice Harlan, writing for the Court, said that *Dennis* held that "the indoctrination of a group in preparation for future violent action, as well as exhortation to immediate action . . . is not constitutionally protected when the group is of sufficient size and cohesiveness, is sufficiently oriented towards action, and other circumstances are such as reasonably to justify the apprehension that action will occur."[60] But the Court said that was not present in *Yates*. Justice Harlan explained that the essential distinction is that those to whom the advocacy is addressed must be urged to *do* something, now or in the future, rather than merely to *believe* in something.[61]

The problem, of course, is deciding whether speech is advocacy of doctrine or advocacy to action. In many instances, this is likely to be an ephemeral distinction based entirely on how a judge chooses to characterize the speech. As Justice Holmes said, "[e]very idea is an incitement."[62]

---

[56] *Id.* at 585 (Douglas, J., dissenting).
[57] *Id.* at 588-589.
[58] 354 U.S. 298 (1957).
[59] *Id.* at 318.
[60] *Id.* at 321.
[61] *Id.* at 324-325 (emphasis in original).
[62] Gitlow v. New York, 268 U.S. at 673.

Yates did not mark the end of the Court's willingness to uphold convictions under the Smith Act. For example, in *Scales v. United States*, the Court upheld a conviction for being a member of an organization that advocates the overthrow of the government.[63] The Court stressed that for the government to punish such association there must be proof that an individual actively affiliated with a group, knowing of its illegal objectives, and with the specific intent of furthering those goals.[64] The Court concluded that there was sufficient evidence in the record "to make a case for the jury on the issue of illegal Party advocacy."[65] In contrast, in *Noto v. United States*, the Court reversed a conviction under the Smith Act for conspiracy because of inadequate evidence to meet these requirements.

§11.3.2.5   The *Brandenburg* Test

The Court's Shift to a More Speech Protective Approach

By the mid-1960s, the Court appeared to be much more protective of speech. In *Bond v. Floyd*, the Court held that the Georgia legislature could not refuse to seat Julian Bond because of his support for a statement strongly critical of the Vietnam War and the draft.[66] The Court invoked *Yates v. United States* and concluded that Bond's statements were advocacy of ideas protected by the First Amendment.

Also, in *Watts v. United States*, the Court reversed the conviction of an individual for violating the law that made it a crime to "knowingly and willfully . . . [threaten] to take the life of or to inflict bodily harm upon the President."[67] An individual was convicted under this law for saying, "If they ever make me carry a rifle the first man I want to get in my sights is L.B.J. They are not going to make me kill my black brothers."[68] The Court said that Watts's statement was "political hyperbole," not a real threat, and thus was protected by the First Amendment.[69]

Brandenburg v. Ohio

The key case, though, defining when the government may punish advocacy of illegality is *Brandenburg v. Ohio*.[70] A leader of a Ku Klux Klan group was convicted under the Ohio criminal syndicalism law. Evidence of his incitement was a film of the events at a Klan rally, which included racist and anti-Semitic speech, and several items that appeared in the film, including a number of firearms. In a per

---

[63] 367 U.S. 203 (1961).

[64] These requirements for punishing association are discussed in more detail in §11.5.2, which discusses freedom of association.

[65] 367 U.S. at 251.

[66] 385 U.S. 116 (1966).

[67] 394 U.S. 705 (1969).

[68] *Id.*

[69] *Id.* The Court has reaffirmed that "true threats" are not protected by the First Amendment, *see, e.g.,* Virginia v. Black, 538 U.S. 343 (2003), though it never has clearly defined what is a true threat.

[70] 395 U.S. 444 (1969).

curiam opinion, the Court acknowledged that *Whitney* had upheld the California criminal syndicalism law, but the Court cited *Dennis* as discrediting *Whitney*'s reasoning. The Court said that these later decisions, referring to *Dennis*, "have fashioned the principle that the constitutional guarantees of free speech and free press do not permit a State to forbid or proscribe advocacy of the use of force or of law violation except where such advocacy is directed to inciting or producing imminent lawless action and is likely to incite or produce such action."[71]

Brandenburg clearly seems to be the Supreme Court's most speech protective formulation of an incitement test.[72] A conviction for incitement under *Brandenburg* only is constitutional if several requirements are met: imminent harm, a likelihood of producing illegal action, and an intent to cause imminent illegality. None of the earlier tests had contained an intent requirement. Also, none ever had so clearly stated a requirement for a likelihood of imminent harm.

Therefore, on a doctrinal level, it is puzzling that the Court presented the *Brandenburg* test as if it followed from the *Dennis* formulation, rather than that it was a substantial expansion in the protection of speech. In *Dennis*, the Court expressly denied that there was a requirement for proof of an imminent danger of likely harm.

Brandenburg does not answer, however, how imminence and likelihood are to be appraised. Are these requirements to be assessed relative to the harms to be prevented, so that the more serious the danger, the less in the way of imminence or likelihood that will be required? Or is some showing of imminence and likelihood necessary no matter how great the harm? If imminence and likelihood are judged relative to the nature of the danger, then *Brandenburg* in essence creates a risk formula like the *Dennis* test, even though one is not expressly stated in the *Brandenburg* formulation. Nor does the Court in *Brandenburg* define "intent" and what must be proved to establish it.[73]

Cases Applying the *Brandenburg* Test

There were very few Supreme Court cases in the decade after *Brandenburg* applying or explaining its standard. *Hess v. Indiana* involved an individual who was convicted of disorderly conduct for declaring, "We'll take the fucking street later," after the police had cleared a demonstration from the street.[74] The Court said that

---

[71] *Id.* at 447.

[72] Gerald Gunther, Learned Hand and the Origins of Modern First Amendment Doctrine: Some Fragments of History, 27 Stan. L. Rev. 719, 755 (1975) (describing the *Brandenburg* test as the "most speech-protective standard yet evolved by the Supreme Court").

[73] This issue has arisen in a series of suits against the media for criminal acts allegedly copying or inspired by media depictions. In each instance, the courts have ruled in favor of the media based on the lack of evidence that the speech was directed to causing imminent illegality. *See, e.g.*, NEC, Inc. v. Neimi, 434 U.S. 1354 (1978); Waller v. Osborne, 763 F. Supp. 1144 (N.D. Ga. 1991). In *Rice v. Paladin Enterprises*, 128 F.3d 233 (4th Cir. 1997), the Fourth Circuit ruled holding the publisher of a book on how to be a contract killer did not violate the First Amendment. For a discussion of the case from the perspective of one of the plaintiff's attorneys, *see* Rodney Smolla, Deliberate Intent (2001).

[74] 414 U.S. 105 (1973).

the speech was protected by the First Amendment. The Court explained that "at best . . . , the statement could be taken as counsel for present moderation; at worst, it amounted to nothing more than advocacy of illegal action at some indefinite future time."[75] The Court said that this was insufficient to meet the *Brandenburg* test because there was "no evidence . . . that his words were intended to produce, and likely to produce, *imminent* disorder."[76]

In *NAACP v. Claiborne Hardware Co.*, the Court overturned a judgment against the NAACP for a boycott of white-owned businesses that it alleged engaged in racial discrimination.[77] In part, the trial court had based the liability of the NAACP for damages from the boycott on a speech by an NAACP official that included the statement, "If we catch any of you going in any of them racist stores, we're gonna break your damn neck."[78] The Court held that this speech was protected by the First Amendment under the *Brandenburg* test and thus could not be the basis for liability. The Court explained:

> In the passionate atmosphere in which the speeches were delivered, they might have been understood as inviting an unlawful form of discipline or, at least, intending to create a fear of violence whether or not improper discipline was specifically intended. . . . This Court has made clear, however, that mere *advocacy* of the use of force or violence does not remove speech from the protection of the First Amendment. . . . The emotionally charged rhetoric of Charles Evers' speeches did not transcend the bounds of protected speech set forth in *Brandenburg*.[79]

Brandenburg, *Hess*, and *NAACP* indicate that the Court has redefined the test for incitement in much more speech protective terms. Under this law, an individual can be convicted for incitement only if it is proved that there was a likelihood of imminent illegal conduct and if the speech was directed at causing imminent illegal conduct. Yet perhaps the major difference between these cases and the earlier decisions such as *Schenck*, *Gitlow*, *Whitney*, and *Dennis* is the social climate. The prior cases all were issued in tense times where there were strong pressures to suppress speech. Only in the unfortunate event that such times occur again will it be possible to know if the *Brandenburg* test better succeeds in protecting dissent in times of crisis.

An important issue, related to *Brandenburg* but also distinct, is the constitutional protection for threatening speech. The Supreme Court has held that there is no First Amendment protection for a "true" threat.[80] There is a split among the Circuits, however, as to how to determine whether speech should be regarded as a "true threat." Some Circuits have said that this is determined from the perspective

---

[75] *Id.* at 108.
[76] *Id.* at 109 (emphasis in original).
[77] 458 U.S. 886 (1982).
[78] *Id.* at 902.
[79] *Id.* at 927-928.
[80] *See* United States v. Watts, 394 U.S. 705, 708 (1969); Madsen v. Women's Health Ctr., 512 U.S. 753, 773 (1994).

of the reasonable listener,[81] while other Circuits have said that this is assessed from the perspective of the reasonable speaker.[82] The issue is related to *Brandenburg* because it involves speech that threatens violence, yet it is a distinct issue because the focus is not on the likely consequences but on the need to protect people from the adverse effects of feeling threatened. In this way, the issue of threats shares much in common with the cases discussed in the next section.

Speech That Materially Assists a Foreign Terrorist Organization

In *Holder v. Humanitarian Law Project*,[83] the Court considered an issue that raises many of the same issues presented in the incitement cases, but the Court did not apply the *Brandenburg* test. Federal law prohibits providing "material assistance" to a "foreign terrorist organization."[84] Material assistance is defined to include such activities as "training," "personnel," and "expert advice or assistance." Two groups of Americans brought a lawsuit seeking to establish First Amendment protection for their assistance for groups that had been designated by the Department of State as foreign terrorist organizations. One group of Americans sought to help a Kurdish group, which sought to form a separate country, use international law and the United Nations to peacefully resolve disputes. The other group of Americans sought to help a group in Sri Lanka, which also sought to form a separate nation, apply for humanitarian assistance.

The Court, in a 6-3 decision, ruled that this speech could constitutionally be punished. Initially, the Court rejected the vagueness challenge to the law, con-cluding that most of the activities of the plaintiffs were clearly within the statute's prohibition of expert advice, assistance, and training.[85] The Court then concluded that the speech could be punished so long as it was done in coordination with a foreign terrorist organization. Chief Justice Roberts, writing for the Court, stressed that the plaintiffs could speak out on any topic they wished, but if the speech was done in concert with a foreign terrorist organization, it was not protected by the First Amendment. He wrote: "Under the material-support statute, plaintiffs may say anything they wish on any topic. They may speak and write freely about the PKK and LTTE, the governments of Turkey and Sri Lanka, human rights, and international law. They may advocate before the United Nations. . . . Congress has not, therefore, sought to suppress ideas or opinions in the form of 'pure political speech.' Rather, Congress has prohibited 'material support,' which most often does not take the form of speech at all. And when it does, the statute is care-fully drawn to cover only a narrow category of speech to, under the direction

---

[81] *See, e.g.*, Lovell v. Poway Unified School Dist., 90 F.3d 367 (9th Cir. 1996); United States v. Orozco-Santillian, 903 F.2d 1262 (9th Cir. 1990); United States v. Gilbert, 884 F.2d 454 (9th Cir. 1989).

[82] United States v. Kelner, 534 F.2d 1020 (2d Cir. 1976).

[83] 130 S. Ct. 2705 (2010).

[84] 18 U.S.C. §2339(B).

[85] *Holder*, 130 S. Ct. at 2719-2721.

of, or in coordination with foreign groups that the speaker knows to be terrorist organizations."[86]

Justice Breyer's dissenting opinion, joined by Justices Ginsburg and Sotomayor, criticized the majority for allowing the punishment of speech without any proof that it was likely to cause harms.[87] Justice Breyer reviewed the Supreme Court's decisions concerning incitement, especially *Brandenburg*, and said that they do not justify allowing punishment of the speech of the sort the plaintiffs sought to engage in. He explained that prior "cases [have] permit[ed] pure advocacy of even the most unlawful activity—as long as that advocacy is not directed to inciting or producing imminent lawless action and . . . likely to incite or produce such action."[88]

§11.3.3   Fighting Words, the Hostile Audience, and the Problem of Racist Speech

§11.3.3.1   Introduction

The prior section focused on when speech can be punished because it advocates illegal acts or the overthrow of the government. This section considers a related, though distinct, question: When may speech be punished because of the risk that it might provoke an audience into using illegal force against the speaker? In other words, the former cases involved concern that an audience might follow the speaker into lawlessness; these cases concern the danger that the audience might be lawless in its reaction against the speaker.

The Court has formulated two doctrines that deal with this issue. One is the Court's holding that "fighting words"—speech that is directed at another and likely to provoke a violent response—are unprotected by the First Amendment. The other is a series of cases concerning when a speaker may be punished because of the reaction of the audience. These doctrines are discussed in §11.3.3.2 and §11.3.3.3, respectively.

Closely related to these topics, but again distinct, is the question of whether and when the government may prohibit and punish expression of hate. This topic, which has attracted a great deal of attention in recent years because of the development of hate speech codes at campuses across the country, is discussed in §11.3.3.4.

---

[86] *Id.* at 2722-2723.
[87] *Id.* at 2727 (Breyer, J., dissenting).
[88] *Id.* at 2737.

§11.3.3.2 Fighting Words

Fighting Words as Unprotected Speech

In *Chaplinsky v. New Hampshire*, in 1942, the Supreme Court expressly held that "fighting words" are a category of speech unprotected by the First Amendment.[89] Chaplinsky, a Jehovah's Witness, was distributing literature for his religion on a street corner on a Saturday afternoon and gave a speech denouncing other religions as a "racket." In addition, he said at one point to a listener, "You are a God damned racketeer" and "a damned Fascist and the whole government of Rochester are Fascists or agents of Fascists."[90]

The Supreme Court upheld Chaplinsky's conviction for this speech. The Court said that "[a]llowing the broadest scope to the language and purpose of the Fourteenth Amendment, it is well understood that the right of free speech is not absolute at all times and under all circumstances. There are certain well-defined and narrowly limited classes of speech, the prevention and punishment of which have never been thought to raise any constitutional problem. These include the lewd and obscene, the profane, the libelous, and *the insulting or fighting words—those which by their very utterance inflict injury or tend to incite an immediate breach of the peace.*"[91] The Court said that "such utterances are no essential part of any exposition of ideas, and are of such slight social value as a step to truth that any benefit that may be derived from them is clearly outweighed by the social interest in order and morality. Resort to epithets or personal abuse is not in any proper sense communication of information or opinion safeguarded by the Constitution."[92]

Chaplinsky appears to recognize two situations where speech constitutes fighting words: where it is likely to cause a violent response against the speaker and where it is an insult likely to inflict immediate emotional harm. Each aspect raises questions about whether such speech should be outside the protection of the First Amendment. As to the former, the danger that the listener will be provoked to fight, the issue is whether the appropriate response is to punish the speaker or punish the person who actually resorts to violence. As to the latter, speech that inflicts an emotional injury, the question—which is key in the discussion of hate speech considered below—is whether speech should be punished because it is upsetting or deeply offensive to an audience.[93]

Refusal to Uphold Fighting Words Convictions

The Supreme Court never has overturned *Chaplinsky*; fighting words remain a category of speech unprotected by the First Amendment. But in the nearly

---

[89] 315 U.S. 568 (1942).

[90] *Id.* at 569.

[91] *Id.* at 571-572 (emphasis added).

[92] *Id.* at 571 (citation omitted).

[93] *See* Kent Greenawalt, Insults and Epithets: Are They Protected Speech?, 42 Rutgers L. Rev. 287 (1990).

three-quarters of a century since *Chaplinsky*, the Court has never again upheld a fighting words conviction. Every time the Court has reviewed a case involving fighting words, the Court has reversed the conviction, but without overruling *Chaplinsky*.

The Court has used three techniques in overturning these convictions. First, the Court has narrowed the scope of the fighting words doctrine by ruling that it applies only to speech directed at another person that is likely to produce a violent response. Second, the Court frequently has found laws prohibiting fighting words to be unconstitutionally vague or overbroad. Third, the Court has found laws that prohibit some fighting words—such as expression of hate based on race or gender—to be impermissible content-based restrictions of speech.

Each of these techniques is discussed, in turn, below. The cumulative impact of these decisions is to make it unlikely that a fighting words law could survive. If the law is narrow, then it likely would be deemed an impermissible content-based restriction because it outlaws some fighting words, but not others, based on the content of the speech. If the law is broad, then it probably would be invalidated on vagueness or overbreadth grounds.

Narrowing the Fighting Words Doctrine

In *Street v. New York*, the Supreme Court said that there is a "small class of 'fighting words' which are 'likely to provoke the average person to retaliation, and thereby cause a breach of the peace.'"[94] In *Street*, the Court reversed the conviction of an individual who had burned an American flag after learning that James Meredith had been shot.[95] He declared, "We don't need no damn flag. . . . If they let that happen to Meredith we don't need an American flag."[96] The Court said that while some might have found the speech inherently inflammatory, it was not fighting words unprotected by the First Amendment.

This was further clarified in *Cohen v. California*, where the Court held that unprotected fighting words occur only if the speech is directed to a specific person and likely to provoke violent response.[97] Cohen was convicted for disturbing the peace for having in a courthouse a jacket that had on its back the words, "Fuck the Draft." The state argued, in part, that the inscription on the jacket constituted fighting words because of the possible violent response from people who saw and were angered by the message.[98] The Court, in an opinion by Justice Harlan, rejected this and stated: "While the four-letter word displayed by Cohen in relation to the draft is not uncommonly employed in a personally provocative fashion, in this instance it was clearly not directed to the person of the hearer. No individual

---

[94] 394 U.S. 576, 592 (1969) (citation omitted).

[95] The decisions concerning First Amendment protection for flag burning are discussed in §11.3.6.2.

[96] 394 U.S. at 598-599 (Warren, C.J., dissenting).

[97] 403 U.S. 15 (1971).

[98] *Cohen* is discussed in more detail below in §11.3.4.6 as to the Constitution's protection of profane and indecent language.

actually or likely to be present could reasonably have regarded the words on appellant's jacket as a direct personal insult."[99]

The Court applied this requirement in *Texas v. Johnson* where it held that flag burning was a form of speech protected by the First Amendment.[100] As in *Street*, one argument made by the government was that the flag destruction was likely to provoke a violent response from the audience and thus was a form of fighting words. The Court rejected this contention for the reason given in *Cohen*: The speech was not directed at a particular person. Justice Brennan, writing for the Court, said: "[N]o reasonable onlooker would have regarded [the] generalized expression of dissatisfaction with the policies of the Federal Government as a direct personal insult or an invitation to exchange fisticuffs."[101]

Fighting Words Laws Invalidated as Vague and Overbroad

In most cases since *Chaplinsky* involving fighting words, the Court has reversed the convictions by declaring the laws to be unconstitutionally vague and overbroad. For example, in four cases decided in 1972, *Gooding v. Wilson*,[102] *Rosenfeld v. New Jersey*,[103] *Lewis v. City of New Orleans*,[104] and *Brown v. Oklahoma*,[105] the Court overturned fighting words laws by finding them to be impermissibly vague and overbroad.

Gooding, discussed earlier, involved an individual who was convicted for his behavior at an antiwar demonstration where he said to a police officer, "White son of a bitch, I'll kill you," and "You son of a bitch, I'll choke you to death."[106] He was convicted under a Georgia law that prohibited any person to "use to or of another, and in his presence opprobrious words or abusive language, tending to cause a breach of the peace."[107] The Court found that the statute was impermissibly overbroad and emphasized the failure of the state courts to narrowly construe the law to prohibit only unprotected fighting words.

Rosenfeld, *Lewis*, and *Brown* all involved the angry use of profanity in a manner likely to provoke an audience. In each case, the Court overturned a fighting words conviction and vacated in light of *Gooding v. Wilson*. In *Rosenfeld*, the defendant, speaking at a school board meeting, repeatedly used the word "mother-fucker" in describing teachers and school board members. In *Lewis*, a woman called the police, who were arresting her son, "god-damn-mother-fucker police." In *Brown*, an individual in a speech referred to police officers as "mother-fucking fascist pig cops" and spoke of one particular officer as a "black mother-fucking pig." In each

---

[99] 403 U.S. at 20.
[100] 491 U.S. 397 (1989), discussed more fully below in §11.3.6.2.
[101] *Id.* at 409.
[102] 405 U.S. 518 (1972).
[103] 408 U.S. 901 (1972).
[104] 408 U.S. 913 (1972).
[105] 408 U.S. 914 (1972).
[106] 405 U.S. at 518, 520 n.1.
[107] *Id.* at 529 (Burger, C.J. dissenting).

of the instances, the Court reversed the convictions, making it clear that speech is protected even if it is uttered in anger, filled with profanities, and likely to anger the audience.

In *City of Houston v. Hill*, also described above, the Court overturned a city ordinance that made it a crime for a person to oppose, molest, abuse, or interrupt any policeman in the execution of his duty.[108] The Court explained that "the ordinance's plain language is admittedly violated scores of times daily. . . . It is not limited to fighting words nor even to obscene or opprobrious language, but prohibits speech that in any manner . . . interrupt[s] an officer. The Constitution does not allow such speech to be made a crime."[109]

These cases indicate that a fighting words law will be upheld only if it is narrowly tailored to apply just to speech that is not protected by the First Amendment.[110] Otherwise, the statute or ordinance will be deemed void on vagueness grounds or invalidated as being impermissibly overbroad.

R.A.V. v. City of St. Paul

However, a very narrow fighting words law likely will be declared unconstitutional as impermissibly drawing content-based distinctions as to what speech is prohibited and what is allowed. This was the result in *R.A.V. v. City of St. Paul*.[111] A St. Paul ordinance prohibited placing "on public or private property symbols, objects, characterizations, or graffiti, including, but not limited to, a burning cross or Nazi swastika, which one knows or has reasonable grounds to know arouses anger, alarm or resentment in others on the basis of race, color, creed, religion or gender."[112] The Minnesota Supreme Court gave the ordinance a narrowing construction so that it applied only to fighting words or incitement not protected by the First Amendment.

All nine Justices on the United States Supreme Court voted to overturn the conviction of a man who burned a cross on a black family's lawn and hold the ordinance unconstitutional. Justice Scalia wrote the majority opinion, which was joined by Rehnquist, Kennedy, Souter, and Thomas. Justice Scalia began by explaining that even within categories of unprotected speech, the government is limited in its ability to draw content-based distinctions. He wrote:

> We have sometimes said that these categories of expression are not within the area of constitutionally protected speech, or that the protection of the First

[108] 482 U.S. 451, 461 (1987).

[109] *Id.* at 462, 466.

[110] Although the Court has not upheld a fighting words conviction in almost 75 years, it continues to state that fighting words are a category of speech unprotected by the First Amendment. For example, in *Virginia v. Black*, 538 U.S. 343, 359 (2003), the Court declared: "[A] state may punish those words 'which by their very utterance inflict injury or tend to incite an immediate breach of the peace.' We have consequently held that fighting words . . . are generally proscribable under the First Amendment."

[111] 505 U.S. 377 (1992).

[112] *Id.* at 380.

Amendment does not extend to them. Such statements must be taken in context. . . . What they mean is that these areas of speech can, consistently with the Constitution, be regulated *because of their constitutionally proscribable content* (obscenity, defamation, etc.) —not that they are categories of speech entirely invisible to the First Amendment so that they may be made the vehicles for content discrimination unrelated to their distinctively proscribable content. Thus, the government may proscribe libel; but it may not make the further content discrimination of proscribing *only* libel critical of the government.[113]

The Court then addressed fighting words as a category of unprotected speech. Justice Scalia wrote: "It is not true that 'fighting words' have at most a 'de minimis' expressive content . . . or that their content is *in all respects* 'worthless and undeserving of constitutional protection'; sometimes they are quite expressive indeed. We have not said that they constitute '*no* part of the expression of ideas,' but only that they constitute 'no essential part of any exposition of ideas.' "[114] The Court said that "the exclusion of fighting words from First Amendment protection means that they are regarded as essentially a 'nonspeech' element of communication. Fighting words are thus analogous to a noisy sound truck: Each is . . . a mode of speech; both can be used to convey an idea; but neither has, in and of itself, a claim upon the First Amendment. As with the sound truck, however, so also with fighting words: The government may not regulate use based on hostility—or favoritism—towards the underlying message expressed."[115]

Justice Scalia said that there was not an absolute prohibition of content-based discrimination within categories of unprotected speech. He wrote that "[w]hen the basis for the content discrimination consists entirely of the very reason the entire class of speech at issue is proscribable, no significant danger of idea or viewpoint discrimination exists."[116] As an example, Justice Scalia said that the government may choose to prohibit sexually oriented materials that are the most patently offensive or that most appeal to the prurient interest, but that it could not prohibit only sexually oriented materials that convey a political message.

Justice Scalia also indicated that apparent content-based distinctions would be permissible if they were designed to prevent secondary effects so that "the regulation is justified without reference to the content of the speech."[117] Justice Scalia here cited to *Renton v. Playtime Theatres*, discussed above, where the Court said that it is not content-based discrimination if the government's purpose is preventing secondary effects of speech. Scalia said that "a particular content-based subcategory of a proscribable class of speech can be swept up incidentally within the reach of a statute directed at conduct rather than, speech. Thus, for example, sexually derogatory 'fighting words,' among other words, may produce a violation

---

[113] *Id.* at 383-384 (citations omitted).
[114] *Id.* at 384-385 (emphasis in original).
[115] *Id.* at 386 (citations omitted).
[116] *Id.* at 388.
[117] *Id.* at 389 (citation and emphasis omitted).

of Title VII's general prohibition against sexual discrimination in employment practices."[118]

Thus, Justice Scalia's opinion indicates that content-based distinctions within a category of unprotected speech will have to meet strict scrutiny, subject to two exceptions. One is that a content-based distinction is permissible if it directly advances the reason why the category of speech is unprotected; for example, an obscenity law could prohibit the most sexually explicit material without having to ban everything that is obscene. Second, a law will not be deemed to be content-based if it is directed at remedying secondary effects of speech and is justified without respect to content.

Justice Scalia applied these principles to invalidate the St. Paul ordinance. The Court explained that the law drew a distinction among expressions of hate: It prohibited hate speech based on race, religion, or gender, but not based on political affiliation or sexual orientation. Justice Scalia said: "[T]he ordinance applies only to 'fighting words' that insult, or provoke violence, 'on the basis of race, color, creed, religion, or gender.' Displays containing abusive invective, no matter how vicious or severe, are permissible unless they are addressed to one of the specified disfavored topics. Those who wish to use 'fighting words' in connection with other ideas—to express hostility, for example, on the basis of political affiliation, union membership, or homosexuality—are not covered."[119]

Justice White wrote an opinion concurring in the judgment that was joined by Blackmun, O'Connor, and Stevens. Justice Blackmun also wrote a separate concurring opinion, as did Justice Stevens. These opinions argued that the St. Paul ordinance was unconstitutional on overbreadth grounds. Justice White's opinion objected to the majority's conclusion that content-based distinctions within categories of unprotected speech generally must meet strict scrutiny. He expressed concern that after *R.A.V.*, "[s]hould the government want to criminalize certain fighting words, the Court now requires it to criminalize all fighting words."[120]

Likewise, Justices Blackmun and Stevens in their concurring opinions argued that the government should have latitude to draw distinctions within categories of unprotected speech. Justice Blackmun expressed concern that the "Court has been distracted from its proper mission by the temptation to decide the issue over 'politically correct speech' and 'cultural diversity,' neither of which is presented here."[121] Justice Stevens argued that "[c]onduct that creates special risks or causes special harms may be prohibited by special rules."[122] He thus argued that content-based distinctions within categories of unprotected speech often were justified.

R.A.V. can be appraised on many levels.[123] First, it can be analyzed in terms of its significance for the fighting words doctrine. *R.A.V.* means that a fighting words

---

[118] *Id.* at 389.

[119] *Id.* at 391.

[120] *Id.* at 401 (White, J., concurring in the judgment).

[121] *Id.* at 415-416 (Blackmun, J., concurring in the judgment).

[122] *Id.* at 416 (Stevens, J., concurring in the judgment).

[123] *See, e.g.,* Steven Shiffrin, Racist Speech, Outsider Jurisprudence, and the Meaning of America, 80 Cornell L. Rev. 43, 65 (1994); Elena Kagan, Regulation of Hate Speech and Pornography After *R.A.V.,* 60 U. Chi. L. Rev. 873 (1993).

law will be upheld only if does not draw content-based distinctions among types of speech, such as by prohibiting fighting words based on race, but not based on political affiliation. The problem, though, is that it will be extremely difficult for legislation to meet this requirement without being so broad that the law will be invalidated on vagueness or overbreadth grounds.

Second, *R.A.V.* can be analyzed in terms of the Court's holding that there is a strong presumption against content-based discrimination within categories of unprotected speech. This was the issue that most divided the Justices in the majority from those concurring in the judgment. On the one hand, Justice Scalia makes a powerful argument that the government should not be able to prohibit only obscenity or fighting words that contain messages critical of the government. But on the other hand, the dissent makes a persuasive point that inevitably in regulating categories of unprotected speech, the government will not forbid all such speech, but draw lines. Such lines are vulnerable after *R.A.V.*

Finally, in examining *R.A.V.*, there is the question of whether the case should have been found to meet the exceptions that Justice Scalia recognized where content-based discrimination is allowed. Justice Scalia's majority opinion indicated two circumstances where content-based distinctions within categories of unprotected speech would be allowed. One instance where Scalia would allow content discrimination is where the distinction advances the reason why the category is unprotected. Yet there is a strong argument that this was true with regard to the St. Paul ordinance; the law seemingly was based on a judgment that fighting words based on race, religion, or gender are most likely to cause the harms that the fighting words doctrine means to prevent.

The other exception is where the restriction of speech is meant to prevent secondary effects. The St. Paul ordinance is written specifically in terms of secondary effects; it proscribes speech that would "anger, alarm, or cause resentment." The problem is in deciding whether these are "secondary effects" or are to be viewed as a content-based regulation of speech.

§11.3.3.3　The Hostile Audience Cases

Application of the Clear and Present Danger Test

In some cases, especially in the 1940s and the 1950s, the Supreme Court applied the clear and present danger test in dealing with the issue of when the government may punish individuals for speech that provokes a hostile audience reaction. For example, in *Terminiello v. Chicago*, the Court overturned a conviction for disturbing the peace because it was not shown that the speech posed a clear and present danger of lawlessness.[124] Terminiello was convicted for disturbing the peace because of a speech that he gave in which he attacked his opponents as "slimy scum," "snakes," and "bedbugs." Despite the presence of many police offi-

---

[124] 337 U.S. 1 (1949).

cers, disturbances broke out. The trial court's instructions to the jury said that the defendant could be convicted for speech that "stirs the public to anger, invites dispute, brings about a condition of unrest, or creates a disturbance."[125]

The Court overturned the conviction and found that the jury instruction was not sufficiently protective of speech. The Court declared: "A function of free speech under our system is to invite dispute. It may indeed best serve its high purpose when it induces a condition of unrest, creates dissatisfaction with conditions as they are, or even stirs people to anger. [That] is why freedom of speech, though not absolute, [is] nevertheless protected against censorship or punishment, *unless shown likely to produce a clear and present danger of a serious substantive evil that rises far above public inconvenience, annoyance or unrest.*"[126]

Similarly, in *Cantwell v. Connecticut,* the Supreme Court overturned a conviction for disturbing the peace because of the absence of proof of a clear and present danger.[127] Jesse Cantwell, a Jehovah's Witness, was prosecuted for playing a phonograph record on a street corner that attacked the Roman Catholic religion. The Court said that "[w]hen clear and present danger of riot, disorder, interference with traffic upon the public streets, or other immediate threat to public safety, peace, or order, appears, the power of the State to prevent or punish is obvious. Equally obvious is it that a State may not unduly suppress free communication of views, religious or otherwise, under the guise of conserving desirable conditions."[128] The Court overturned the conviction because the speech posed "no such clear and present menace to public peace and order."[129]

Although in *Terminiello* and *Cantwell* the Court applied the clear and present danger test to protect speech, in *Feiner v. New York* the test was used to uphold a conviction.[130] In *Feiner,* an individual was convicted for a speech that he gave that sharply criticized the president and local political officials for their inadequate record on civil rights. Some members of the crowd seemed angered by the speech, and the police asked the speaker to leave. After the speaker refused, the police arrested him. The Supreme Court upheld the conviction for disturbing the peace. The Court quoted *Cantwell,* that the government may prevent or punish speech that poses a clear and present danger. The Court concluded: "It is one thing to say that the police cannot be used as an instrument for the suppression of unpopular views, and another to say that, when as here the speaker passes the bounds of argument or persuasion and undertakes incitement to riot, they are powerless to prevent a breach of the peace."[131]

The problem with the clear and present danger test in this context is that it allows an audience reaction, if hostile enough, to be a basis for suppressing a speaker. A speaker who is acting completely lawfully can be silenced because of illegal behavior—the threats of violence and use of force—by members of

---

[125] *Id.* at 3.
[126] *Id.* at 4 (emphasis added).
[127] 310 U.S. 296 (1940).
[128] *Id.* at 308.
[129] *Id.* at 311.
[130] 340 U.S. 315 (1951).
[131] *Id.* at 321.

the audience. Indeed, Justice Black, dissenting in *Feiner*, said that the appropriate response of the police should have been to control the crowd, and only if that was impossible and a threat to breach of the peace was imminent could the police arrest the speaker. Justice Black argued: "I reject the implication of the Court's opinion that the police had no obligation to protect petitioner's constitutional right to talk. The police of course have power to prevent breaches of the peace. But if, in the name of preserving order, they ever can interfere with a lawful public speaker, they first must make all reasonable efforts to protect him. Here the policeman did not even pretend to try to protect petitioner."[132]

Audience Control Approach

In later cases, the Supreme Court appeared to follow the approach articulated in Justice Black's dissent in *Feiner*, although it never overruled the earlier cases using the clear and present danger test. For example, in *Edwards v. South Carolina*, the Court overturned a conviction for civil rights protestors who had staged a march to the South Carolina capitol.[133] A significant hostile crowd gathered, although there was no violence or threats of violence. The speakers were arrested after they ignored a police order to disperse. The Court emphasized that "police protection at the scene was at all times sufficient to meet any foreseeable possibility of disorder."[134] The Court distinguished *Feiner* based on the absence of any violence or threats of violence in the march to the state capitol.

In *Cox v. Louisiana*, an individual was convicted for giving a speech objecting to the racial segregation of lunch counters and urging a sit-in.[135] Some members of the audience found the speech inflammatory, and the speaker was arrested a day after the demonstration. The Court overturned the conviction and again emphasized the ability of the police to control the crowd. The Court stated: "It is virtually undisputed, however, that the students themselves were not violent and threatened no violence. The fear of violence seems to have been based upon the reaction of the groups of white citizens looking on from across the street. . . . There is no indication, however, that any member of the white group threatened violence. . . . [A police officer testified that] they could have handled the crowd."[136]

Similarly, in *Gregory v. City of Chicago*, the Court unanimously overturned convictions for disturbing the peace for a group of civil rights demonstrators who had been arrested when an angry group threatened the marchers.[137] The civil rights protestors were marching to the mayor's house when some members of an opposing group reacted angrily, made threats against the demonstrators, and threw rocks at them. The Court overturned the conviction because the law did not limit convictions to instances where there was a threat of imminent violence, the police

---

[132] *Id.* at 326 (Black, J., dissenting).
[133] 372 U.S. 229 (1963).
[134] *Id.* at 232-233.
[135] 379 U.S. 536 (1965).
[136] *Id.* at 550.
[137] 394 U.S. 111 (1969).

have made all reasonable efforts to protect the demonstrators, and the police have requested that the demonstration be stopped.[138]

Perhaps these cases can be read as applications of the clear and present danger test with the Court concluding that there was not sufficient evidence under the circumstances to justify a conclusion of an imminent threat to a breach of the peace. But an alternative, and seemingly better, way of reading the cases is as being more speech protective than the clear and present danger test; that is, as being much closer to Justice Black's approach in *Feiner* than to its majority opinion. From this perspective, the First Amendment requires that the police try to control the audience that is threatening violence and stop the speaker only if crowd control is impossible and a threat to breach of the peace imminent.[139]

§11.3.3.4   The Problem of Racist Speech

Can the Government Restrict Racist Speech?

Over the past few decades, there has been an important debate among scholars as to whether, and when, the government may punish racist speech.[140] Over 200 colleges and universities have adopted hate speech codes of various types. Additionally, many governments have adopted laws prohibiting racist speech.

Those who favor restrictions on hate speech emphasize how racist hate speech undermines the constitutional value of equality. For example, in the context of colleges and universities, hate speech makes traditionally excluded minorities feel unwelcome and perpetuates their exclusion. Moreover, it is argued that hate speech is a form of verbal assault that the law should punish.

But those who oppose such hate speech restrictions maintain that it is wrong to stop speech because it is distasteful and offensive. Additionally, opponents argue that it is impossible to formulate a definition of racist speech that is not unconstitutionally vague and overbroad. Furthermore, opponents of hate speech

---

[138] *Id.* at 113 (Black, J., concurring) (describing the factual background in detail).

[139] One of the more highly publicized instances concerning the ability of the government to prevent speech because of a possible violent audience reaction was in Skokie, Illinois, where the city attempted to stop the Nazi party from marching because of threats from the community. The United States Court of Appeals for the Seventh Circuit held that the Nazis had a right to speak and declared unconstitutional ways in which Skokie tried to stop them. Collin v. Smith, 578 F.2d 1197 (7th Cir. 1978). The Supreme Court refused to issue a stay of the Seventh Circuit's ruling. Smith v. Collin, 436 U.S. 953 (1978). The Skokie case is discussed in more detail below at text accompanying notes 148-150.

[140] *See, e.g.,* Charles R. Lawrence, III, If He Hollers Let Him Go: Regulating Racist Speech on Campus, 1990 Duke L.J. 431; Mari Matsuda, Public Response to Racist Speech: Considering the Victim's Story, 87 Mich. L. Rev. 2320 (1989); David Kretzmer, Freedom of Speech and Racism, 8 Cardozo L. Rev. 445 (1987); Richard Delgado, Words That Wound: A Tort Action for Racial Insults, Epithets, and Name-Calling, 17 Harv. C.R.-C.L. L. Rev. 133 (1982) (all favoring restrictions on hate speech); *see also* Lee Bollinger, The Tolerant Society (1986); Marjorie Heins, Banning Words: A Comment on Words That Wound, 18 Harv. C.R.-C.L. L. Rev. 585 (1983) (arguing for tolerance for expressions of hate).

codes argue that practical experience indicates that they are most likely to be used against minorities. The opponents maintain that unless the speech meets the traditional definition of an assault, racist speech, however vile, is protected by the First Amendment.

Group Libel

The Supreme Court has not directly addressed this debate, but several decisions are relevant to it. Over a half century ago, the Supreme Court held that group libel is not protected by the First Amendment. In *Beauharnais v. Illinois*, the Supreme Court upheld a state law that prohibited any publication that portrayed "depravity, criminality, unchastity, or lack of virtue of a class of citizens, of any race, color, creed, or religion [which exposes such citizens] to contempt, derision, or obloquy or which is productive of breach of the peace or riots."[141] The Court, in an opinion by Justice Frankfurter, affirmed the conviction of individuals who urged the mayor and city council of Chicago to protect white neighborhoods from "encroachment, harassment, and invasion . . . by the Negro" and called for "one million self respecting white people in Chicago to unite."[142]

The Court said that just as a state could punish defamation, so may a state "punish the same utterance directed at a defined group."[143] The Court stressed the strife caused by expressions of hate based on race and religion. Justice Frankfurter's opinion concluded that the government did not need to meet the clear and present danger test because "[l]ibelous utterances not being within the area of constitutionally protected speech, it is unnecessary, neither for us or for the State courts, to consider the issues behind the phrase 'clear and present danger.' "[144]

Beauharnais is the strongest authority for the government to regulate racist speech, and it never has been overruled. Yet for many reasons it is questionable whether *Beauharnais* is still good law.[145] *Beauharnais* is based on the assumption that defamation liability is unlimited by the First Amendment—a premise expressly rejected by the Supreme Court a decade later in *New York Times v. Sullivan*.[146] The speech that led to the conviction in *Beauharnais*, however vile, was political speech, and it is doubtful that the Court would allow punishment of individuals for expressing opinions about racial groups or calling for government actions. The Court's decision in *R.A.V. v. City of St. Paul*, described above, strongly indicates that expression of hate is not a category of speech entirely outside First Amendment

---

[141] 343 U.S. 250 (1952).

[142] *Id.* at 251.

[143] *Id.* at 258.

[144] *Id.* at 266.

[145] Indeed, the United States Court of Appeals for the Seventh Circuit has expressly said that it does not believe that *Beauharnais* survives and is any longer good law. American Booksellers Assn. v. Hudnut, 771 F.2d 323 (7th Cir. 1985); Collin v. Smith, 578 F.2d 1197, 1204-1205 (7th Cir. 1978).

[146] 376 U.S. 254 (1964), discussed below in §11.3.5.2.

protection.[147] Moreover, the Illinois statute upheld in *Beauharnais* almost certainly would be declared unconstitutional today based on vagueness and overbreadth grounds.

A reflection of the unwillingness of courts to follow *Beauharnais* is found in the protection of the ability of Nazis to stage a march in the predominantly Jewish suburb of Skokie, Illinois. In 1977, the leaders of the National Socialist Party of America announced that it planned to hold a peaceful demonstration in Skokie, a town where there were many survivors of Nazi concentration camps.

A trial court issued an injunction preventing the marchers from wearing Nazi uniforms, displaying swastikas, or expressing hatred against Jewish people. The court relied in part on testimony concerning a large counterdemonstration and the fear of a violent confrontation between the two groups. Although the state appellate courts upheld this injunction, the United States Supreme Court granted certiorari and summarily reversed the state courts.[148] The Court emphasized that appellate review of the trial court's injunction could take a year or more to complete and said that a stay was required unless there was immediate appellate review.

On remand, the Illinois Court of Appeals modified the injunction so that it only prohibited display of the swastika. The Illinois Supreme Court reversed and vacated the entire injunction as violating the First Amendment.[149]

Meanwhile, Skokie adopted several ordinances that were intended to prevent the Nazis from speaking there. For example, the laws required applicants for parade permits to purchase a substantial amount of insurance, prohibited dissemination of material that "promotes and incites hatred" based on race or religion, and outlawed wearing military-style uniforms in demonstrations. The United States Court of Appeals for the Seventh Circuit declared these ordinances unconstitutional and expressly said that it no longer regarded *Beauharnais* as good law.[150] After winning in the courts, the Nazi party canceled its rally in Skokie and held a small protest march in Chicago.

The Skokie controversy reflects many basic First Amendment principles. Expression of hate is protected speech, and the government may not outlaw symbols of hate such as swastikas. Moreover, the government cannot suppress a speaker because of the reaction of the audience. Skokie was not allowed to prevent the Nazis from marching because their demonstration would deeply offend and upset Holocaust survivors or even might provoke a violent response.

Hate Speech as Fighting Words

Another approach that government might take to regulating racist hate speech is by banning it as a form of fighting words. As described above, *Chaplinsky*

---

[147] *See also* Dawson v. Delaware, 503 U.S. 159 (1992) (holding that it was reversible error for a jury to be instructed that a defendant was a member of the Aryan Brotherhood, which was stipulated to be a "white racist gang," because it was irrelevant and violated the First Amendment).

[148] National Socialist Party of Am. v. Village of Skokie, 432 U.S. 43, 44 (1977).

[149] 69 Ill. 2d 605, 373 N.E.2d 21 (1978).

[150] Collin v. Smith, 578 F.2d 1197 (7th Cir. 1978). The Supreme Court denied a stay of this decision. Smith v. Collin, 436 U.S. 953 (1978).

v. New Hampshire held that fighting words are a category of speech unprotected by the First Amendment.[151] Many colleges and universities have based their hate speech codes around the fighting words exception to the First Amendment.

There are, however, many problems with such an approach to regulating hate speech. In the nearly 75 years since *Chaplinsky*, the Supreme Court never again has upheld a fighting words conviction. Most of the fighting words cases since *Chaplinsky* have found the laws unconstitutional on vagueness or overbreadth grounds. The laws and campus codes regulating hate speech have been frequently challenged on exactly these grounds: that they are impermissibly vague and overbroad. In fact, the federal courts that thus far have considered the constitutionality of university hate speech codes have invalidated them on vagueness and overbreadth grounds.[152]

Moreover, the Supreme Court's decision in *R.A.V. v. City of St. Paul* makes it difficult for hate speech codes to survive judicial analysis; if they prohibit only some forms of hate, they will be invalidated as impermissible content-based discrimination. But if the codes are more expansive and general, they likely will fail on vagueness and overbreadth grounds.

Although some scholars have made powerful arguments for hate speech codes and even for a new categorical exception to the First Amendment, *R.A.V.* indicates that the current Court is unwilling to move in that direction. Public colleges and universities are unlikely to be allowed to prohibit expressions of hate or racism on campus. However, they likely will be able to prohibit harassment directed at particular individuals, just as they may prohibit all forms of directed harassment.[153]

Cross Burning

In *Virginia v. Black*, the Court held that governments may prohibit cross burning done with the intent to intimidate, but that this intent must be proved in the particular case.[154] A Virginia law prohibited cross burning "with an intent to intimidate a person or group of persons." The law also provided that an act of cross burning was "prima facie evidence of an intent to intimidate a person or group of persons." Before the Court were two Virginia cases involving individuals convicted

---

[151] 315 U.S. 568 (1942), discussed above at §11.3.3.2.

[152] *See* UWM Post, Inc. v. Board of Regents of Univ. of Wisconsin, 774 F. Supp. 1163 (E.D. Wis. 1991); Iota XI Chapter of Sigma Chi Fraternity v. George Mason Univ., 773 F. Supp. 792 (E.D. Va. 1991), *aff'd*, 993 F.2d 386 (4th Cir. 1993); Doe v. University of Michigan, 721 F. Supp. 852 (E.D. Mich. 1989).

[153] An important and unresolved related question concerns the relationship between sexual harassment law in the workplace and the First Amendment. For example, is the First Amendment violated by a finding of sexual harassment because of a hostile environment based on the pervasive presence of pornographic material in a workplace? *See, e.g.*, Eugene Volokh, Freedom of Speech and Workplace Harassment, 39 UCLA L. Rev. 1791 (1992); Kingsley R. Browne, Title VII as Censorship: Hostile-Environment Harassment and the First Amendment, 52 Ohio St. L.J. 481 (1991); Marcy Strauss, Sexist Speech in the Workplace, 25 Harv. C.R.-C.L. L. Rev. 1 (1990). *See also* Robinson v. Jacksonville Shipyards, Inc., 760 F. Supp. 1486 (M.D. Fla. 1991) (finding liability for sexual harassment based largely on the pervasive presence of pornography creating a hostile and intimidating environment).

[154] 538 U.S. 343 (2003).

under the law. One involved Ku Klux Klan members who were convicted for burning a cross at a rally on a relatively isolated farm; the other involved two men who were convicted for burning a cross on the lawn of a home recently purchased by an African-American family.

There were three parts to the Court's holding. First, the Court ruled that the government cannot prohibit all cross burning. Justice O'Connor, writing for the Court, explained that burning a cross is symbolic expression and the government cannot ban symbols just because they are powerful and offensive. Only Justice Thomas dissented as to this aspect of the decision and argued that cross burning is conduct not speech and that its history makes clear that is inherently threatening and intimidating.[155] Second, the Court concluded that cross burning done with the intent to threaten or intimidate—that constitutes a "true threat"—is not protected by the First Amendment. Justice O'Connor wrote that "'[t]rue threats' encompass those statements when the speaker means to communicate a serious intent to commit an act of unlawful violence to a particular individual or group of individuals. The speaker need not actually intend to carry out the threat."[156] Third, the Court said that there must be proof in the individual case that the speech was a true threat.[157] The Virginia law was unconstitutional in providing that the act of cross burning was itself prima facie evidence of an intent to threaten or intimidate.

Thus, the Court concluded that the Klan members could not be punished for burning a cross on a relatively isolated farm. The absence of onlookers meant that the action could not reasonably be seen as a true threat. But the Court remanded the convictions of the men who had burned a cross on the lawn of a home owned by an African-American family. The Court clearly signaled that this was obviously a true threat.

The Court in *Virginia v. Black* struck a middle course: Cross burning is protected speech and cannot be completely outlawed, but the government may prohibit it when done in a manner that constitutes a true threat.

Penalty Enhancements for Hate-Motivated Crimes

The Supreme Court has held that the government may provide for penalty enhancements for hate-motivated crimes. In *Wisconsin v. Mitchell*, the Court upheld a state law that imposed greater punishments if it could be proved that a victim was chosen because of his or her race.[158] The Supreme Court emphasized that such penalty enhancements are directed at conduct, not at speech. The Court said that greater punishment for hate-motivated crimes was justified because of their harms to society. Chief Justice Rehnquist, writing for a unanimous Court, explained that "the law singles out for enhancement bias-inspired conduct because this conduct

---

[155] *Id.* at 360 n.2 (Thomas, J., dissenting).

[156] *Id.* at 359-360.

[157] The question of what is a "true threat" has not been answered by the Supreme Court and is pending before the Court in October Term 2014. Elonis v. United States, 730 F.3d 321 (3d Cir. 2013), *cert. granted*, 134 S. Ct. 2819 (2014).

[158] 508 U.S. 476 (1993).

is thought to inflict greater individual and societal harm. For example, . . . bias-motivated crimes are more likely to provoke retaliatory crimes, inflict distinct emotional harms on their victims, and incite community unrest. The State's desire to redress these perceived harms provides an adequate explanation for its penalty-enhancement provision over and above mere disagreement with offenders' beliefs or biases."[159]

Although the evidence of hate motivation might be speech, that is also true under other civil rights laws. For example, proof of discriminatory purpose in the employment discrimination context can be speech expressing racist views. The Supreme Court explained that where the law punishes conduct it may consider racist intentions as a basis for enhancing penalties.

In *Apprendi v. New Jersey*, the Court held that proof of an impermissible racial motivation in such a penalty enhancement statute must be proved beyond a reasonable doubt and is a question for the jury in a case tried to a jury.[160] An individual fired a gun into a home owned by an African-American family. He told the police that he did this because he did not want a black family living in his neighborhood. Although he later retracted this statement, the trial court found, by a preponderance of the evidence, that the crime was racially motivated and increased the sentence under New Jersey's hate crime statute. The Supreme Court, however, ruled that any factor that increases a sentence, other than a prior conviction, must be proved beyond a reasonable doubt.[161] Therefore, under hate crime laws, like Wisconsin's and New Jersey's, that provide for penalty enhancements for hate-motivated crimes, the hate motivation must be proved beyond a reasonable doubt to the jury.

§11.3.4   Sexually Oriented Speech

§11.3.4.1   Introduction

Overview of Organization

A major topic in First Amendment law is the ability of the government to regulate sexually oriented speech. First, the Supreme Court has held that obscenity is a category of speech unprotected by the First Amendment and has struggled to define what is "obscene." These cases are discussed in §11.3.4.2. This section also considers whether obscenity should be a category of unprotected speech and the proposals that some have advanced that pornography should be banned as a form of discrimination against women.

Second, the Court has indicated that child pornography is not protected by the First Amendment, even if it does not fit within the definition of obscenity. This is considered in §11.3.4.3.

---

[159] *Id.* at 487-488.
[160] 530 U.S. 466 (2000).
[161] *Id.*

Third, the Court has indicated the government has more latitude to regulate sexually oriented speech, even if it is not obscenity or child pornography that is unprotected by the First Amendment. For example, the Court has allowed the use of zoning ordinances to limit the locations of adult bookstores and movie theaters and permitted the government to ban nude dancing. These cases are discussed in §11.3.4.4.

Section 11.3.4.5 examines the techniques that the government may and may not use in regulating sexually oriented materials. Governments have tried many techniques ranging from licensing schemes to prohibition of private possession to seizing assets of businesses convicted of violating obscenity laws.

Finally, §11.3.4.6 considers the related question of the constitutional protection for profane and indecent language. The Supreme Court generally has held that profane and indecent language is protected by the First Amendment, although there are exceptions where limits are allowed, notably over the broadcast media and in schools.

§11.3.4.2   Obscenity

Obscenity as a Category of Unprotected Speech

In *Roth v. United States*, the Supreme Court held that obscenity is a category of speech unprotected by the First Amendment.[162] Justice Brennan, writing for the Court, described the issue as "whether obscenity is utterance within the area of protected speech and press."[163] The Court concluded that "implicit in the history of the First Amendment is the rejection of obscenity as utterly without redeeming social importance."[164] The Court thus declared: "We hold that obscenity is not within the area of constitutionally protected speech or press."[165]

The Court in *Roth* observed that "sex and obscenity are not synonymous. Obscene material is material which deals with sex in a manner appealing to the prurient interest."[166] In a footnote, the Court defined prurient as "material having a tendency to excite lustful thoughts."[167]

Since *Roth*, the Supreme Court has reaffirmed that obscenity is a category of speech unprotected by the First Amendment.[168] For example, in *Paris Adult Theater I v. Slaton*, the Court stated: "We categorically disapprove the theory . . . that obscene, pornographic films acquire constitutional immunity from state regulation simply because they are exhibited for consenting adults only. . . . [W]e

---

[162] 354 U.S. 476 (1957).

[163] *Id.* at 481.

[164] *Id.* at 484.

[165] *Id.* at 485.

[166] *Id.* at 487.

[167] *Id.* at n.20. For a description of Justice Brennan's choice to use this term, *see* Seth Stern & Stephen Wermiel, Justice Brennan: Liberal Champion 122-123 (2010).

[168] *See, e.g.,* Alexander v. United States, 509 U.S. 544 (1993); Paris Adult Theater I v. Slaton, 413 U.S. 49 (1973); Miller v. California, 413 U.S. 15 (1973).

hold that there are legitimate state interests at stake in stemming the tide of commercialized obscenity, even assuming it is feasible to enforce effective safeguards against exposure to juveniles and to the passersby."[169]

Should Obscenity Be a Category of Unprotected Speech?

Many disagree with the Court that obscenity should be deemed a category of unprotected speech.[170] They argue that the very definition of obscenity used in *Roth* focuses on controlling thoughts—something that should be beyond the reach of the government. David Richards explained that there "is no reason whatsoever to believe that the freedom to determine the sexual content of one's communications or to be an audience to such communications is not as fundamental to this self-mastery as the freedom to decide upon any other communicative contents."[171]

Those who favor allowing the government to prohibit obscenity make several arguments. One is that a community should be able to determine its moral environment. In *Paris Adult Theater I v. Slaton*, the Court accepted this justification for regulating obscenity and spoke of "the interest of the public in the quality of life and the total community environment [and] the tone of commerce in the great city centers."[172] Henry Clor argued that the "ethical convictions of social man do not simply rest upon his explicit opinions. They rest also upon a delicate network of moral and aesthetic feelings, sensibilities, tastes. These 'finer feelings' could be blunted and eroded by a steady stream of impressions which assault them. Men whose sensibilities are frequently assaulted by prurient and lurid impressions may become desensitized. . . . This is what is meant by 'an erosion of the moral fabric.' "[173]

However, those who oppose a First Amendment exception for obscenity argue that the government should not be able to decide what is moral and suppress speech that does not advance that conception. In fact, the Supreme Court has held in other contexts that the government may not prohibit speech simply because it advances ideas that the government deems immoral. For example, in *Kingsley International Pictures Corp. v. Regents*, the Court held that a state could not prohibit the film *Lady Chatterley's Lover* because it shows adultery and thus "portrays acts of sexual immorality [as] desirable, acceptable or proper patterns of behavior."[174] The Court said that what the state "has done, [is] to prevent the exhibition of a motion picture because that picture advocates an idea—that adultery under certain circumstances may be proper behavior. Yet the First Amendment's

---

[169]   413 U.S. at 57-58.
[170]   *See, e.g.,* David Cole, Playing by Pornography's Rules: The Regulation of Sexual Expression, 143 U. Pa. L. Rev. 111 (1994); David A.J. Richards, Free Speech and Obscenity Law: Toward a Moral Theory of the First Amendment, 123 U. Pa. L. Rev. 45 (1974).
[171]   Richards, *id.,* at 82.
[172]   413 U.S. at 49, 58.
[173]   Henry Clor, Obscenity and Public Morality 170-171 (1969).
[174]   360 U.S. 684, 699 (1959).

basic guarantee is of freedom to advocate ideas. The State, quite simply, has thus struck at the very heart of constitutionally protected liberty."[175] It is not for the government to stop speech to advance any particular idea of what is moral.

A second major argument for excluding obscenity from First Amendment protection is that it causes antisocial behavior, particularly violence against women. In *Paris Adult Theater I v. Slaton*, Chief Justice Burger, writing for the Court, said that obscenity "possibly [endangers] the public safety itself. The Hill-Link Minority Report of the Commission on Obscenity and Pornography indicates that there is at least an arguable correlation between obscene material and crime."[176] Professor Catharine MacKinnon, who advocates creating a new categorical exception for pornography as a form of discrimination against women, argued that "[r]ecent experimental research on pornography shows that . . . exposure to [it] increases normal men's immediately subsequent willingness to aggress against women under laboratory conditions. . . . It also significantly increases attitudinal measures known to correlate with rape."[177] The Meese Commission on Pornography believed that experimental studies found that exposure to violent pornography increased a willingness to be violent in laboratory experiments.[178]

But others challenge these studies and whether they establish that obscenity increases the likelihood of antisocial behavior.[179] The Report of the Commission on Obscenity and Pornography, a commission appointed by President Richard Nixon, reviewed the empirical literature and concluded that there was no evidence that "exposure to explicit sexual, materials plays a significant role in the causation of delinquent or criminal behavior."[180] Moreover, it is questioned whether the laboratory experiments that measure aggression in laboratory settings or conduct on mock juries indicate anything about whether obscenity causes antisocial behavior in society. Also, it is argued that these studies show, at most, that depictions of violence—whether erotic or not—correlate with more violence in laboratory experiments; they maintain that there is no evidence that nonviolent sexual depictions increase aggressive or violent behavior.[181]

A third argument often made for excluding obscenity from First Amendment protection is that it should be regarded as a sex aid, not as speech. Professor Fred Schauer argued that "hardcore pornography is designed to produce a purely physical effect. [It is] essentially a physical rather than a mental stimulus. . . . The pornographic item is in a real sense a sexual surrogate. . . . Consider further rubber, plastic, or leather sex aids. It is hard to find any free speech aspects in their sale or use. . . . The mere fact that in pornography the stimulating experience is initiated

---

[175] *Id.* at 688.
[176] *Id.*
[177] Catharine R. MacKinnon, Pornography, Civil Rights, and Speech, 20 Harv. C.R.-C.L. L. Rev. 1, 52, 54 (1985); *see also* Catharine R. MacKinnon, Only Words (1994).
[178] Report of the Attorney General's Commission on Pornography (1986).
[179] *See* Nadine Strossen, Defending Pornography (1995).
[180] Report of the Commission on Obscenity and Pornography 26-27 (1970).
[181] *See* Deana Pollard, Regulating Violent Pornography, 43 Vand. L. Rev. 125, 128-129 (1990) (reviewing social science studies on the effects of pornography).

by visual rather than tactile means is irrelevant. Neither means constitutes communication in the cognitive sense."[182]

Yet in response it is argued that other forms of speech produce physical reactions. A movie or book is not deprived of First Amendment protection because it provokes tears. A beautiful symphony is not unprotected because of the physical reactions it evokes. Moreover, it is argued that sexual material does have a cognitive dimension. Professor David Cole observed that the argument that sexual speech is "noncognitive" because it is designed to produce a physical effect is predicated on an impoverished view of sexuality. He wrote: "[Sexual] expression, like human sexuality itself, cannot be 'purely physical.' Rather, it is deeply and inextricably interwoven with our identities, our upbringing, our emotions, our relationships to other human beings, and the ever-changing narratives and images that our community finds stimulating."[183]

Defining Obscenity

So long as the Court continues to hold that obscenity is unprotected by the First Amendment, it is essential to define this category. In fact, some argue that obscenity should not be a category of unprotected expression because of the impossibility of formulating a definition that is not impermissibly vague or overbroad. Justice Brennan, who wrote the opinion in *Roth*, dissented in *Paris Adult Theater* and said: "I am convinced that the approach initiated 16 years ago in *Roth* . . . cannot bring stability to this area of the law without jeopardizing fundamental First Amendment values."[184]

In the years after *Roth*, the Court struggled to formulate a definition of obscenity.[185] The difficulty of these efforts was expressed by Justice Potter Stewart when he declared in *Jacobellis v. Ohio*: "I shall not today attempt further to define the kinds of material I understand to be embraced within that shorthand description; and perhaps I could never succeed in intelligibly doing so. But I know it when I see it, and the motion picture involved in this case is not that."[186] Beginning in 1967, in *Redrup v. New York*, the Court overturned an obscenity conviction in a per curiam decision without an opinion[187] — something that the Court did over 30 times in obscenity cases in the next six years.

In *Miller v. California*, in 1973, the Court reaffirmed that obscene material is not protected by the First Amendment and formulated the test for obscenity that continues to be used.[188] The Court said that "the basic guidelines for the trier of fact must be: (a) whether 'the average person, applying contemporary community

---

[182] Frederick Schauer, Speech and "Speech"—Obscenity and "Obscenity": An Exercise in the Interpretation of Constitutional Language, 67 Geo. L.J. 899, 922-923 (1979).

[183] Cole, *supra* note 170, at 127.

[184] 413 U.S. at 73 (Brennan, J., dissenting).

[185] *See, e.g.*, Mishkin v. New York, 383 U.S. 502 (1966); Ginzburg v. United States, 383 U.S. 463 (1966); Memoirs v. Massachusetts, 383 U.S. 413 (1966).

[186] 378 U.S. 184, 197 (1964) (Stewart J., concurring).

[187] 386 U.S. 767 (1967).

[188] 413 U.S. 15, 36 (1973).

standards' would find that the work, taken as a whole, appeals to the prurient interest; (b) whether the work depicts or describes, in a patently offensive way, sexual conduct specifically defined by the applicable state law; and (c) whether the work, taken as a whole, lacks serious literary, artistic, political or scientific value."[189]

In other words, under *Miller*, three requirements must be met in order for material to be deemed obscene. First, the material must appeal to the prurient interest for the average person, applying contemporary community standards. The problem here is with defining what is the "prurient interest." As indicated above, "prurient" means that which excites lustful or lascivious thoughts. The Court has done little to clarify what this means. In *Brockett v. Spokane Arcades, Inc.*, the Court declared unconstitutional a Washington obscenity law because it failed to distinguish between a "normal" interest in sex and "a shameful" or "morbid" interest.[190] The Court held that only the latter was the prurient interest, but it left everyone to guess as to how to draw this distinction.

Under *Miller*, "prurient interest" is determined by a community standard. This is puzzling because it is unlikely that the ability of material to cause sexual arousal will vary geographically. It also is troubling because it could have the effect of forcing national distributors to make sure that their products meet the most restrictive laws. Justice Brennan expressed this concern: "Under [this approach] distributors [will] be forced to cope with the community standards of every hamlet into which their goods may wander. Because these variegated standards are impossible to discern, national distributors . . . must inevitably be led to retreat to debilitating self-censorship."[191]

Nonetheless, the Court has adhered to the view that prurient interest is to be decided by a community standard. For example, the Court has ruled that juries applying federal obscenity laws define prurient interest from a community perspective. The Court said that "[t]he fact that distributors of allegedly obscene materials may be subjected to varying community standards in the various federal judicial districts does not render a federal statute unconstitutional because of the failure of application of uniform national standards of obscenity."[192]

Second, in order for material to be obscene it must be patently offensive under the law prohibiting obscenity. The Court in *Miller* gave an example of this and said that a law could define this as: "(a) Patently offensive representations or descriptions of ultimate sexual acts, normal or perverted, actual or simulated; (b) Patently offensive representations or descriptions of masturbation, excretory functions, and lewd exhibition of the genitals."[193]

In *Ward v. Illinois*, the Supreme Court held that the law did not need to provide an "exhaustive list of the sexual conduct" that would be patently offensive.[194] The Court said that it was sufficient that a law included the examples included in *Miller*.

---

[189] *Id.* at 24.
[190] 472 U.S. 491 (1985).
[191] Hamling v. United States, 418 U.S. 87, 144 (1974) (Brennan, J., dissenting).
[192] *Id.* at 106.
[193] 413 U.S. at 15, 25.
[194] 431 U.S. 767 (1977).

However, in *Jenkins v. Georgia,* the Court ruled that there are limits on what a state may deem to be patently offensive.[195] In *Jenkins,* the Court concluded that the film *Carnal Knowledge,* a mainstream movie with actors including Jack Nicholson and Ann Margaret, could not be found obscene because "[t]here is no exhibition whatever of the actors' genitals, lewd or otherwise. . . . There are occasional scenes of nudity, but nudity alone is not enough to make material legally obscene under the *Miller* standards."[196] The Court stated that "the film could not, as a matter of constitutional law, be found to depict sexual content in a patently offensive way, and is therefore not outside the protection of the First and Fourteenth Amendments because it is obscene."[197]

Finally, in order for material to be obscene, it must, taken as a whole, lack serious redeeming artistic, literary, political, or scientific value. In *Pope v. Illinois,* the Court held that social value is to be determined by a national standard—how the work would be appraised across the country—and not a community standard.[198] The Court said that "the value of [a] work [does not] vary from community to community. . . . The proper inquiry [is] whether a reasonable person would find such value in the material."[199]

Should There Be a New Exception for Pornography?

Some commentators, most notably Catharine MacKinnon and Andrea Dworkin, have argued that a new exception should be created to the First Amendment that excludes pornography as a form of sex discrimination against women. They argue that pornography is "the graphic sexually explicit subordination of women through pictures and/or words."[200] They propose an ordinance that would outlaw such depictions if, for example, "[w]omen are presented as sexual objects who enjoy pain or humiliation; or . . . [w]omen are presented as sexual objects who experience sexual pleasure in being raped; or . . . women are presented as sexual objects for domination, conquest, violation, exploitation, possession, or use, or through postures or positions of servility or submission or display."[201]

MacKinnon argues that pornography causes harmful attitudes and actions toward women in society.[202] She maintains that restrictions on pornography are justified to advance equality for women. She argues furthermore that women are coerced into the making of pornography and that the prohibition of pornography

---

[195]   418 U.S. 153 (1974).

[196]   *Id.* at 161.

[197]   *Id.*

[198]   481 U.S. 497 (1987).

[199]   *Id.* at 500-501.

[200]   *See* American Booksellers Assn., Inc. v. Hudnut, 771 F.2d 323 (7th Cir. 1985) (describing Indianapolis ordinance based on MacKinnon-Dworkin proposal).

[201]   *Id.* at 324.

[202]   *See, e.g.,* Catharine MacKinnon, Only Words (1994); Catharine MacKinnon, Feminism Unmodified (1987); Catharine MacKinnon, Pornography, Civil Rights and Speech, 20 Harv. C.R.-C.L. L. Rev. 1, 18-20 (1985).

is necessary to provide protection. She contends that obscenity is inadequate as an approach to sexually oriented material because it requires that the work be looked at as a whole and because of its focus on the prurient interest.[203]

Critics of the MacKinnon approach argue that it is vague and extremely broad in terms of what it would deem to be pornography unprotected by the First Amendment.[204] Professor Thomas Emerson argued that "[t]he sweep of the [MacKinnon] ordinance is breathtaking. It would subject to governmental ban virtually all depictions of rape, verbal or pictorial, and a substantial proportion of other sexual encounters. More specifically, it would outlaw such works of literature as the *Arabian Nights*, Henry Miller's Tropic of Cancer, John Cleland's Fanny Hill, William Faulkner's Sanctuary, and Norman Mailer's Ancient Evenings, to name a few."[205] Furthermore, if MacKinnon is correct that pornography expresses a political message about women, she then is proposing a viewpoint based restriction of speech of the sort that is virtually never allowed.

The United States Court of Appeals for the Seventh Circuit, in *American Booksellers Assn. v. Hudnut,* declared unconstitutional a version of the MacKinnon ordinance that had been enacted in Indianapolis.[206] The court found that the ordinance was impermissible viewpoint discrimination because it attempted to outlaw depictions of certain images of women. The court said: "The ordinance discriminates on the ground of the content of the speech. Speech treating women in the approved way . . . is lawful no matter how sexually explicit. Speech treating women in the disapproved way—as submissive in matters sexual or as enjoying humiliation—is unlawful no matter how significant the literary, artistic, or political qualities of the work taken as a whole. The state may not ordain preferred viewpoints in this way."[207]

The debate over pornography raises basic questions about the First Amendment. May the government restrict some speech in an attempt to advance equality by controlling how a group is treated or portrayed? How much proof of harm from speech, such as pornography, must there be in order to justify regulation?

§11.3.4.3   Child Pornography

New York v. Ferber

In *New York v. Ferber,* the Supreme Court held that the government may prohibit the exhibition, sale, or distribution of child pornography even if it does not meet the test for obscenity.[208] A New York law prohibited any person knowingly

---

[203] MacKinnon, Feminism Unmodified, at 152-158.

[204] For an excellent response to the MacKinnon position, *see* Nadine Strossen, Defending Pornography (1995).

[205] Thomas Emerson, Pornography and the First Amendment: A Reply to Professor MacKinnon, 3 Yale L. & Poly. Rev. 130, 131-132 (1985).

[206] 771 F.2d 323 (7th Cir. 1985).

[207] *Id.* at 325.

[208] 458 U.S. 747 (1982).

to produce, promote, direct, exhibit, or sell any material depicting a "sexual performance" by a child under age 16. The statute defined "sexual performance" as any performance that includes "actual or simulated sexual intercourse, deviate sexual intercourse, sexual bestiality, masturbation, sado-masochistic abuse, or lewd exhibition of the genitals."[209] An individual was convicted under the law for selling two films showing young boys masturbating, and the Supreme Court unanimously upheld the conviction.

The Court said that "[i]t is evident beyond the need for elaboration that a State's interest in 'safeguarding the physical and psychological well-being of a minor' is 'compelling.' . . . [T]he use of children as subjects of pornographic materials is harmful to the physiological, emotional, and mental health of the child."[210] The Court said that child pornography is closely related to child abuse because children are harmed by the permanent record of their involvement in pornography and children are exploited in the making of pornography.

The Court emphasized that child pornography did not have to fit under the *Miller* test for obscenity in order to be banned. Justice White, writing for the Court, said: "[The] test for child pornography is separate from the obscenity standard enunciated in *Miller*. . . . The *Miller* formulation is adjusted in the following respects: A trier of fact need not find that the material appeals to the prurient interest of the average person; it is not required that sexual conduct portrayed be done so in a patently offensive manner; and the material at issue need not be considered as a whole."[211]

New York v. Ferber did not attempt to define child pornography; it simply upheld the definition contained in the New York law. Also, the case did not resolve the question of whether child pornography can be banned if it has serious socially redeeming value. Justice O'Connor, in an opinion concurring in the judgment, argued that the government's compelling interest in protecting children justified its banning child pornography even if it has artistic, literary, political, or scientific value.[212] But Justice Brennan concurred in the judgment and argued that the First Amendment protected material that has serious socially redeeming value.[213] Nor have any cases since *Ferber* resolved these issues.[214]

Ashcroft v. Free Speech Coalition

But since *Ferber*, the Court has been clear that in order to be considered child pornography, the material must use children in its production. In *Ashcroft v. Free Speech Coalition*, the Court declared unconstitutional the Child Pornography Prevention Act of 1996, which prohibits child pornography whether it is based on

---

[209] *Id.* at 750-751.

[210] *Id.* at 757-758.

[211] *Id.* at 764.

[212] *Id.* at 774-775 (O'Connor, J., concurring).

[213] *Id.* at 776-777 (Brennan, J., concurring in the judgment).

[214] In Massachusetts v. Oakes, 491 U.S. 576 (1989), five Justices expressed concern about the overbreadth of a Massachusetts child pornography law, but did not resolve the issue because of a change in the statute while the litigation was under way.

actual pictures of children or computer-generated images.[215] The law prohibited "visual depiction" that "appeared to be" or "conveyed the impression" of a minor engaging in sexually explicit conduct. The Act thus banned material that included adults who are childlike in appearance, as well as computer-generated images.

The Court, in an opinion by Justice Kennedy, stressed that the material prohibited by the Act did "not involve, let alone harm, any children."[216] The Court explained that the government's interest in banning child pornography is in safeguarding children. The Court expressed concern that many works dealing with teenage sexuality might be found to violate the law. The Court found that there was insufficient evidence to support the government's contention that enforcement of child pornography laws would be impeded without a ban of the sort in the Act.

Thus, *Ashcroft v. Free Speech Coalition* is an important clarification of *Ferber*. The government cannot ban child pornography based on its condemnation of the material. Rather, the government's interest is limited to protecting children from being used in the making of the material.

Congress responded to *Ashcroft v. Free Speech Coalition* by enacting the Prosecutorial Remedies and Other Tools to End the Exploitation of Children Today Act of 2003.[217] The Act more narrowly defines child pornography and it prohibits offers to provide and requests to obtain child pornography. The law was challenged on overbreadth grounds in that it applies even if the material provided or requested is not actually child pornography, but instead is speech protected by the First Amendment.[218] In *United States v. Williams*, the Court upheld the Act and concluded that "offers to provide or requests to obtain child pornography are categorically excluded from the First Amendment," even if the material involved is not child pornography and is speech protected under the First Amendment.[219]

Justice Scalia's majority opinion emphasizes that the criminal law can punish attempts and thus argues that the government may punish the attempt to purchase or request child pornography even if it is not actually present. Justice Scalia illustrates this by noting that a drug dealer who sells baking powder believing it is cocaine can be punished for an attempted drug transaction. The analogy is powerful because selling baking powder is no more a crime than selling computer-generated images of children in sexual situations.

The problem with this argument, as Justice Souter explains in his dissent, is that there is no constitutional right to sell baking powder, but there is a First Amendment right to request or sell computer-generated images of children in sexual situations.[220] When the government punishes the sale of baking powder, it is not compromising any constitutional rights. But when the government punishes speech safeguarded by the First Amendment, a fundamental right is sacrificed.

---

[215] 535 U.S. 234 (2002).
[216] *Id.* at 241.
[217] 117 Stat. 650. 18 U.S.C. §2252A(a)(3)(B).
[218] Overbreadth is discussed above in §11.2.2.
[219] 553 U.S. 285, 299 (2008).
[220] *Id.* at 318-320 (Souter, J., dissenting).

There is a tension between *Williams* and *Free Speech Coalition. Free Speech Coalition* unequivocally held that people cannot be punished for possessing, selling, distributing, or requesting nonobscene sexually explicit material unless it actually used children in its production. But the effect of *Williams* is exactly that: The government can punish people for offering or requesting this material if they have the mistaken belief that it is child pornography. On the other hand, the cases can be distinguished in that *Williams* follows basic criminal law principles in holding that a person can be punished for attempting to engage in illegal activity even if the material involved turns out not to actually be contraband.

§11.3.4.4   Protected, but Low Value, Sexual Speech

Zoning Ordinances

The Supreme Court also has indicated that there is a category of sexual speech that does not meet the test for obscenity and thus is protected by the First Amendment, but is deemed to be low value speech, and thus the government has latitude to regulate such expression. The Court never has defined the contours of this category, but it clearly involves sexually explicit material. For example, the Court has upheld the ability of local governments to use zoning ordinances to regulate the location of adult bookstores and movie theaters. In *Young v. American Mini-Theaters, Inc.*, the Supreme Court upheld a city's ordinance that limited the number of adult theaters that could be on any block and that prevented such enterprises from being in residential areas.[221] A theater is deemed to be "adult" if it presented material that met the ordinance's definitions of "specified sexual activities" or "specified anatomical areas."

Justice Stevens, writing for the Court, began by noting that "[t]here is no claim that distributors or exhibitors of adult films are denied access to the market or, conversely, that the viewing public is unable to satisfy its appetite for sexually explicit fare. Viewed as an entity, the market for this commodity is essentially unrestrained."[222] Justice Stevens's opinion then argued that the sexually explicit material should be regarded as "low value" speech and thus is more susceptible to government regulation. He wrote: "But few of us would march our sons and daughters off to war to preserve the citizen's right to see 'Specified Sexual Activities' exhibited in the theaters of our choice. Even though the First Amendment protects communication in this area from total suppression, we hold that the State may legitimately use the content of these materials as the basis for placing them in a different classification from other motion pictures."[223]

Likewise, in *City of Renton v. Playtime Theatres, Inc.*, the Supreme Court relied on *Young* to uphold a zoning ordinance that excluded adult motion picture theaters

---

[221] 427 U.S. 50 (1976).
[222] *Id.* at 62.
[223] *Id.* at 70-71.

from being within 1,000 feet of any residential zone, church, park, or school.[224] The effect was to exclude such theaters from about 95 percent of the land in the city. Of the remaining land, a substantial part was occupied by a sewage disposal and treatment plant, a horse racing track, a warehouse and manufacturing facility, an oil tank farm, and a shopping center. Nonetheless, the Supreme Court upheld the ordinance saying that the result was "largely dictated by our decision in *Young.*"[225]

However, unlike *Young*, where the Court acknowledged the regulation as content-based, the Court in *Renton* described the ordinance as being content-neutral because the "City Council's '*predominate* concerns' were with the secondary effects of adult theaters, and not with the content of adult films themselves."[226] The Court said that the ordinance was designed to "prevent crime, protect the city's retail trade, maintain property values, and generally protect and preserve the quality of the city's neighborhoods, commercial districts, and the quality of urban life, not to suppress the expression of unpopular views."[227] In other words, the Court defined content neutrality not by the terms of the law but, rather, by the legislature's predominant purpose.

The Court said that the "appropriate inquiry . . . is whether the Renton ordinance is designed to serve a substantial governmental interest and allows for reasonable alternative avenues for communication."[228] The Court found that the city's goals were substantial interests and that there were alternative places for the movie theaters, albeit in very limited places.

Young and *Renton* thus establish broad power for cities to use zoning ordinances to regulate the location of adult entertainment establishments. Some, including the dissenting Justices in these cases, have objected to the Court's creating a hierarchy of speech and finding that sexually oriented speech is subject to more government regulation than other types of expression. For example, Justice Stewart, writing for the four dissenters in *Young*, argued: "What this case does involve is the constitutional permissibility of selective interference with protected speech whose content is thought to produce distasteful effects. It is elementary that a prime function of the First Amendment is to guard against just such interference."[229] In *Young*, Justice Stevens argued that the speech is less protected because people would not send their children to war to fight for it; yet if this is the standard, little, if any, speech, and certainly not unpopular expression, would be deemed protected by the First Amendment.

Young and particularly *Renton* also raise the question of how far a city can go in its zoning. In *Renton*, adult entertainment establishments were excluded from almost 95 percent of the city; what if it were 98 or 99 percent? The Court does not

---

[224] 475 U.S. 41 (1986). *Renton* is also discussed in §11.2.1.
[225] *Id*. at 46.
[226] *Id*. at 47 (emphasis in original).
[227] *Id*. at 48 (citation omitted).
[228] *Id*.
[229] 427 U.S. at 85 (Stewart, J., dissenting).

indicate the point at which such restrictions are effective preclusions of speech protected by the First Amendment.[230]

Nude Dancing

Another example of the Court's treatment of sexually oriented speech as being of "low value" is its willingness to allow the government to prohibit nude dancing.[231] Initially, in *Schad v. Borough of Mt. Ephraim*, the Supreme Court indicated that nude dancing was protected by the First Amendment.[232] In *Schad*, the Court declared unconstitutionally overbroad a city's ordinance that prohibited all live entertainment and was used to close down a nude dancing establishment. The Court said that "nude dancing is not without its First Amendment protections from official regulation."[233] But the Court concluded that even if nude dancing were unprotected speech, the ordinance was substantially overbroad in that it prohibited all concerts, all plays, all forms of live entertainment.

The Supreme Court initially upheld government regulation of nude dancing in a series of cases involving liquor licenses. For example, in *California v. LaRue*, the Court said that the government could regulate live performances in establishments it licenses to sell liquor.[234] The Court spoke of the "broad sweep of the Twenty-first Amendment [that] has been recognized as conferring something more than the normal state authority over public health, welfare, and morals."[235] The Court said that the government constitutionally could conclude "that certain sexual performances and the dispensation of liquor ought not to occur [together]."[236]

Similarly, in *City of Newport v. Iacobucci*, the Court upheld a city ordinance banning nude dancing in bars.[237] The Court accepted the city's rationale that "nude dancing in establishments serving liquor was 'injurious to the citizens' of the city"[238] and concluded that "the broad powers of the States to regulate the sale of liquor, conferred by the Twenty-first Amendment, outweighed any First

---

[230] In *City of Los Angeles v. Alameda Books*, 535 U.S. 425 (2002), the Court, without a majority opinion, upheld a city ordinance preventing two adult businesses from being located in the same building structure. The plurality opinion by Justice O'Connor expressed deference to the city's judgment that the ordinance serves the objective of preventing undesirable secondary effects. Justice Kennedy concurred in the judgment, and said that the case should be remanded to give the city the opportunity to prove the need for the ordinance at trial.

[231] *See also* City of Dallas v. Stanglin, 490 U.S. 19 (1989) (upholding an ordinance limiting use of certain dance halls to those between ages 14 and 18).

[232] 452 U.S. 61 (1981).

[233] *Id.* at 66.

[234] 409 U.S. 109 (1972).

[235] *Id.* at 114.

[236] *Id.* at 118.

[237] 479 U.S. 92 (1986). *See also* New York State Liquor Auth. v. Bellanca, 452 U.S. 714 (1981) (per curiam) (upholding a city's ordinance prohibiting nude dancing in establishments with liquor licenses).

[238] 479 U.S. at 96.

Amendment interest in nude dancing and that a State could therefore ban such dancing as a part of its liquor license program."[239]

In *Barnes v. Glen Theatre, Inc.*, the Supreme Court went even further and held that the government may completely ban nude dancing.[240] Specifically, the Court ruled that an Indiana statute prohibiting public nudity could be used to require that female dancers must, at a minimum, wear "pasties" and a "G-string" when they dance. There was no majority opinion for the Court in its 5-to-4 decision. Chief Justice Rehnquist wrote the plurality opinion joined by Justices O'Connor and Kennedy and initially noted that "nude dancing of the kind sought to be performed here is expressive conduct within the outer perimeters of the First Amendment, though we view it as only marginally so."[241]

The plurality saw nude dancing as a form of conduct that communicates and applied the test used for regulating symbolic speech: "[A] government regulation is sufficiently justified if it is within the constitutional power of the Government; if it furthers an important or substantial governmental interest; if the governmental interest is unrelated to the suppression of free expression; and if the incidental restriction on alleged First Amendment freedoms is no greater than is essential to the furtherance of that interest."[242]

The plurality upheld the prohibition of nude dancing because it served the goal of "protecting societal order and morality."[243] The Court said that this was the goal of laws outlawing public nudity and that the prohibition of nude dancing was not directed at the message conveyed. Chief Justice Rehnquist said that "the requirement that the dancers don pasties and G-strings does not deprive the dance of whatever erotic message it conveys; it simply makes the message slightly less graphic. The perceived evil that Indiana seeks to address is not erotic dancing, but public nudity."[244]

Justice Scalia, concurring in the judgment, took a different approach. He argued: "[T]he challenged regulation must be upheld, not because it survives some lower level of First Amendment scrutiny, but because as a general law regulating conduct and not specifically directed at expression, it is not subject to First Amendment scrutiny at all."[245] Scalia also expressly rejected the dissent's argument that public nudity laws exist only to protect unwilling viewers from offense. He wrote: "The purpose of Indiana's nudity law would be violated, I think, if 60,000 fully consenting adults crowded into the Hoosier Dome to display their genitals to one another, even if there were not an offended innocent in the crowd.

[239] *Id.* at 95 (citation omitted).

[240] 501 U.S. 560 (1991).

[241] *Id.* at 566.

[242] *Id.* at 567 (citation omitted). The topic of symbolic speech is discussed in detail below in §11.3.6.

[243] *Id.* at 568.

[244] *Id.* at 571.

[245] *Id.* at 572 (Scalia, J., concurring in the judgment). In other cases, as well, Justice Scalia has advanced the view that the First Amendment's protections of speech and religion are not violated by neutral laws of general applicability that burden these rights. *See, e.g.*, Cohen v. Cowles Media Co., 501 U.S. 663 (1991); Employment Division v. Smith, 494 U.S. 872 (1990). *Cohen* is discussed below in §11.6.2.2, and *Smith* is discussed in §12.3.2.3.

Our society prohibits, and all human societies have prohibited, certain activities not because they harm others, but because they are considered, in the traditional phrase, . . . immoral."[246]

Justice Souter also concurred in the judgment and focused on the secondary effects of nude dancing. He said "that legislation seeking to combat the secondary effects of adult entertainment need not await localized proof of those effects [and that] the State of Indiana could reasonably conclude that forbidding nude entertainment of the type offered at the Kitty Kat Lounge [furthers] its interest in preventing prostitution, sexual assault, and associated crimes."[247]

Justice White wrote a dissenting opinion joined by Justices Brennan, Marshall, and Blackmun and emphasized that stopping nude dancing was suppressing a message. Justice White said: "[T]he nudity of the dancer is an integral part of the emotions and thoughts that a nude dancing performance evokes. The sight of a fully clothed, or even a partially clothed, dancer generally will have a far different impact on a spectator than that of a nude dancer, even if the same dance is performed. The nudity itself is itself an expressive component of the dance, not merely incidental 'conduct.' "[248]

The Court reaffirmed *Barnes*, though under different reasoning, in *City of Erie v. Pap's A.M.*[249] The city adopted an ordinance prohibiting public nudity, with the clear objective of shutting down Kandyland, a nude dancing club. In a 6-to-3 decision, but like in *Barnes* without a majority opinion, the Court upheld the ordinance.

Justice O'Connor wrote for the plurality and emphasized that the city was justified in prohibiting nude dancing so as to stop the undesirable secondary effects, such as crime, associated with the activity. She declared: "We conclude that Erie's asserted interest in combating the negative secondary effects associated with adult entertainment establishments like Kandyland is unrelated to the suppression of the erotic message conveyed by nude dancing. The asserted interests of regulating conduct through a public nudity ban and of combating the harmful secondary effects associated with nude dancing are undeniably important."[250]

The dissenting opinions by Justices Stevens and Souter stressed the absence of any proof that nude dancing increases crime or causes undesirable secondary effects. Justice Souter said that "I do not believe, however, that the current record allows us to say that the city has made a sufficient evidentiary showing to sustain its regulation," and admitted that he had erred in *Barnes* in not demanding such proof.[251] Justice Stevens indicated the lack of an adequate evidentiary basis for the law in more pointed terms. He noted that the ordinance allowed dancers wearing pasties and a G-string. He said that there was no evidence that fully nude dancers cause any more crime than those minimally clothed.[252]

---

[246] 501 U.S. at 575.
[247] *Id.* at 585 (Souter, J., concurring in the judgment).
[248] *Id.* at 584 (White, J., dissenting).
[249] 529 U.S. 277 (2000).
[250] *Id.* at 296.
[251] *Id.* at 310 (Souter, J., dissenting).
[252] *Id.* at 317 (Stevens, J., dissenting).

Yet Justice O'Connor's plurality opinion said that such proof is unnecessary. She said that city council members could rely on the experience of other cities and their own observations to reasonably conclude that nude dancing increases crime. *City of Erie v. Pap's A.M.* thus may have its greatest significance in allowing local governments to regulate sexually oriented speech, like nude dancing, without needing evidence to prove its harms. But the decision also is most vulnerable to criticism for allowing the government to regulate speech that the plurality concedes to be constitutionally protected without requiring any proof of the harms that justified the law.[253]

Should There Be Such a Category of Low Value Sexual Speech?

Ultimately, cases like *Young, Renton, Barnes,* and *Erie* raise the question of whether there should be a category of minimally protected sexually oriented speech. Answering this inquiry turns on the general question of whether there should be a hierarchy of protected speech and the specific question of whether sexually oriented speech that is not obscene should be regarded of low value.

Also, there is the crucial issue of what justifications are sufficient to warrant regulation of this speech. *Young, Renton,* Justice Souter's opinion in *Barnes,* and Justice O'Connor's opinion in *Erie* all focus on the need to regulate speech to stop secondary effects. But almost all speech has some secondary effects; parades and demonstrations, for example, cause litter. What the opinions do not address is what secondary effects warrant restriction of speech and how much proof there must be of these consequences. Also, these cases raise the question of whether a state's interest in advancing a certain moral vision is sufficient to warrant restriction of the speech.

Finally, it must be noted that the Court has never defined the content of this category of low value sexually oriented speech. The Court has made it clear that nudity, alone, is not enough to place speech in this category. In *Erznoznik v. City of Jacksonville,* the Court declared unconstitutional an ordinance that declared it a public nuisance for any drive-in movie theater to exhibit any motion picture "in which the human male or female bare buttocks, human female bare breasts, or human bare pubic areas are shown, if such motion picture [is] visible from any public street or public place."[254] The Court noted that the law "sweepingly forbids display of all films containing *any* uncovered buttocks or breasts, irrespective of context or pervasiveness. . . . [A]ll nudity cannot be deemed obscene even as to minors."[255] Nudity alone, therefore, is not enough to make speech less protected,

---

[253] Justice Scalia, in a concurring opinion joined by Justice Thomas, disputed the plurality's view that the speech is constitutionally protected. Justice Scalia said that since the ordinance was a neutral law of general applicability, it could not be challenged on First Amendment grounds. This is the same approach that Scalia took in *Barnes* and that a majority of the Court adopted as to the free exercise clause. Employment Division v. Smith, 494 U.S. 872 (1990), discussed in detail in §12.3.2.3.

[254] 422 U.S. 205, 207 (1975).

[255] *Id.* at 213.

and the contours of the category of less protected sexual speech never have been defined.[256]

§11.3.4.5   Government Techniques for Controlling Obscenity and Child Pornography

What Can Be Prohibited?

The Supreme Court has made it clear that the government can prohibit the sale, distribution, and exhibition of obscene materials even to willing recipients. In *Paris Adult Theatre I v. Slaton*, the Court said that "[t]he States have the power to make a morally neutral judgment that public exhibition of obscene material, or commerce in such material, has a tendency to injure the community as a whole, to endanger the public safety, or to jeopardize . . . the States' 'right to maintain a decent society.' "[257]

However, the Court also has held that the government cannot prohibit or punish the private possession of obscene material, although it may outlaw the private possession of child pornography.[258] In *Stanley v. Georgia*, the Court held that "the mere private possession of obscene matter cannot constitutionally be made a crime."[259] The Court emphasized that a person in his or her home has the right to choose what to read or watch. Justice Thurgood Marshall, writing for the Court, said: "[I]f the First Amendment means anything, it means that a State has no business telling a man, sitting alone in his house, what books he may read or what films he may watch."[260]

Although *Stanley* never has been overruled, the Court also has been consistently unwilling to extend it. For example, in *United States v. Reidel*, the Court held that *Stanley* did not protect a right to receive obscene materials.[261] A federal law prohibits the shipment of obscene materials in the mails. The defendant argued that the right to possess such material as recognized in *Stanley* means that there must be a right to receive it. The Supreme Court disagreed and held that the government may prohibit shipment of such materials. The Court expressly distinguished *Stanley* and said that the defendant was "in a wholly different position . . . [because he] has no complaints about governmental violations of his private thoughts or fantasies, but stands squarely on a claimed First Amendment right to

---

[256] *See also* the discussion of profane and indecent language and the First Amendment below in §11.3.4.6.

[257] 413 U.S. at 69 (citation omitted).

[258] Regulation of sexually explicit material over the broadcast media is discussed below in §11.3.4.6.

[259] 394 U.S. 557, 559 (1969).

[260] *Id.* at 565.

[261] 402 U.S. 351 (1971).

do business in obscenity and use the mails in the process. . . . *Stanley* did not overrule *Roth* and we decline to do so now."[262]

Even more significantly, the Court in *Osborne v. Ohio* held that the government may prohibit and punish the private possession of child pornography.[263] The Court emphasized that the government has an important interest in attempting to dry up the market for child pornography so as to protect children and may therefore punish even private possession. Justice White explained that the government's interests in outlawing private possession of child pornography "far exceed" the justifications for prohibiting private possession that were raised in *Stanley*.[264] White said that the law was designed "to protect the victims of child pornography" by "hop[ing] to destroy a market for the exploitative use of children."[265]

There is an obvious tension among these cases. On the one hand, *Stanley* reflects the powerful intuition that it is unseemly for the government to be monitoring and punishing what people read and watch in their bedrooms. Yet *Osborne* allows the government to do exactly that. Moreover, if there is a right to read what a person wants or to view what a person chooses in his or her home, the right has little meaning if the government can criminally punish virtually every means of getting the material. Alternatively, if the government is justified in prohibiting the sale or distribution of obscene materials because of the harms that they cause, that would warrant prohibiting private use as well.

Are Prior Restraints Allowed?

As described above, the Court has held that prior restraints of obscene material are allowed.[266] Prior restraints of obscene materials can take many forms. Classic forms of prior restraints such as court orders stopping speech and licensing can be used to control obscenity. In *Paris Adult Theater I v. Slaton*, the Court held that it is permissible for courts to issue injunctions to prevent the exhibition of obscene materials.[267] Because only constitutionally unprotected material was enjoined and because there were procedural safeguards, the Court found no First Amendment violation to the prior restraint.[268]

The Court also has held that the government may require that movies obtain a license in order to be exhibited. In *Times Film Corp. v. Chicago*, the Court said that

---

[262] *Id.* at 356. *See also* United States v. Orito, 413 U.S. 139 (1973); United States v. 12 200-Foot Reels of Film, 413 U.S. 123 (1973); United States v. Thirty-seven Photographs, 402 U.S. 363 (1971).

[263] 495 U.S. 103 (1990).

[264] *Id.* at 108.

[265] *Id.* at 109.

[266] *See* §11.2.3.

[267] 413 U.S. 49 (1973).

[268] However, in *Vance v. Universal Amusement Co.*, 445 U.S. 308 (1980), the Court declared unconstitutional a law that allowed the closure of theaters that "habitually showed" obscene materials. The Court emphasized that the government could stop the showing of particular movies, but not close the establishments. But in *Alexander v. United States*, 509 U.S. 544 (1993), the Court held that the government could seize the assets of businesses convicted of obscenity law violations. *Alexander* is discussed in detail in §11.2.3.1.

the city could require the submission of all motion pictures for a determination that they were not obscene before they were shown.[269] Yet the specter of government licensing is very troubling; surely the government could not require that publishers obtain a license for books or magazines, to ensure that they are not obscene, before they are published.

Although licensing of motion pictures once was common, it now has largely disappeared. Thus, the Court has had little opportunity to consider whether such systems are still constitutional. The Court has held that if there is to be such a licensing system, there must be stringent procedural safeguards. In *Freedman v. Maryland*, the Court ruled unconstitutional a Maryland law that made it unlawful to exhibit a motion picture without having first obtained a license.[270] The Court said that such a system would be allowed "only if it takes place under procedural safeguards designed to obviate the dangers of . . . censorship."[271] The procedural safeguards must include the burden of proof being on the government, a requirement for a prompt determination of license requests, and prompt judicial review of license denials.

The Court also has ruled that such procedural safeguards are required for government actions that operate like licensing systems, such as postal stop orders for obscene materials[272] and customs seizures of obscene materials.[273] In *FW/PBS, Inc. v. Dallas*, the Court declared unconstitutional a city ordinance that required licensing of sexually oriented businesses because of the absence of the procedural safeguards prescribed in *Freedman*.[274] The Court noted that the law failed to require prompt determination of license requests or provide for judicial review of license denials.[275]

In addition to court orders and licensing, there are other forms that prior restraints can take. For instance, government seizure of materials is another type of prior restraint; if the government were to seize all copies of a publication or a film, that obviously would operate as an even more effective prior restraint than a court order or a licensing system. In *Marcus v. Search Warrant*, the Court said that the government cannot seize allegedly obscene materials unless there is a prior judicial determination in an adversary hearing that the material is not protected by the First Amendment.[276]

However, in subsequent cases, the Court has substantially weakened this protection. In *Heller v. New York*, the Court ruled that no such prior judicial

---

[269] 365 U.S. 43 (1961).

[270] 380 U.S. 51 (1965).

[271] *Id.* at 58.

[272] Blount v. Rizzi, 400 U.S. 410 (1971).

[273] United States v. Thirty-seven Photographs, 402 U.S. 363 (1971).

[274] 493 U.S. 215 (1990).

[275] The plurality opinion by Justice O'Connor said that it was not necessary that the government have the burden of going to court if it wished to deny a license; she argued that it was permissible that those denied licenses would have to initiate the review in the courts. *Id.* at 230. Similarly, in City of Littleton, Colorado v. Z.J. Gifts D-4, L.L.C., 541 U.S. 774 (2004), the Court concluded that a law requiring licensing of adult businesses need not expressly provide for prompt judicial review so long as it is available.

[276] 367 U.S. 717 (1961).

determination is required before a single copy of a film is seized so as to preserve it as evidence.[277] The Court in *Heller* stressed that the exhibitor retained other copies of the film and could continue to show it while the legal action was pending.[278]

Even more dramatically, in *Alexander v. United States*, the Supreme Court held that the government could seize and destroy the assets of businesses convicted of obscenity law violations.[279] Ferris Alexander, the owner of a chain of adult bookstores and movie theaters in Minnesota, was convicted of selling seven obscene items. He was sentenced to six years in prison and fined $100,000. Additionally, the government, pursuant to the federal RICO law, seized the contents of all of his stores. Nine million dollars worth of films, books, and magazines were seized; the books and magazines were burned by the government and the videotapes crushed. Because only seven of the items were deemed obscene, millions of dollars of First Amendment protected material was destroyed.

Yet the Supreme Court, in a 5-to-4 decision, upheld the government's action as constitutional. As described above, the Court rejected the argument that the seizure and destruction constituted an impermissible prior restraint of speech. The Court concluded that it was permissible for the government, pursuant to the RICO law, to seize the assets of businesses engaged in "racketeering activities." Obscenity is deemed such an activity under the federal RICO law, and the Court said that it was immaterial that the material seized was books, magazines, and films. Once seized, the Court said, the government had no obligation to keep the material, and thus the government was allowed to burn books and crush videotapes.

The decision is enormously troubling because the Court allowed the destruction of First Amendment material—books, magazines, and tapes—without any determination that they were obscene. Alexander already had been punished by a six-year prison sentence and a $100,000 fine; the destruction of books, magazines, and tapes was unnecessary as a punishment and inconsistent with the First Amendment's protection of this material.

§11.3.4.6   Profanity and Sexually Oriented Language

Constitutional Protection for Profane and Indecent Language

Although profanities and indecent language are not obscene, government often has tried to punish them. The Supreme Court has held that such language is generally protected by the First Amendment, but there are notable exceptions. The strongest declaration of First Amendment protection for such speech was in *Cohen v. California*.[280] Cohen was convicted of disturbing the peace for being in

---

[277]   413 U.S. 483 (1973).

[278]   *See also* New York v. P.J. Video, 475 U.S. 868 (1986) (there is not a requirement for heightened probable cause when a single copy of a film is seized in this manner).

[279]   509 U.S. 544 (1993), discussed above in §11.2.3.1.

[280]   403 U.S. 15 (1971).

a courtroom with a jacket that said "Fuck the Draft." The Supreme Court over-turned the conviction.

Justice Harlan, writing for the Court, said: "We cannot indulge the facile assumption that one can forbid particular words without also running a substantial risk of suppressing ideas in the process. Indeed, governments might soon seize upon the censorship of particular words as a convenient guise for banning the expression of unpopular views."[281] Justice Harlan explained that "the principle contended for by the State seems inherently boundless. How is one to distinguish this from any other offensive word? Surely the State has no right to cleanse public debate to the point where it is grammatically palatable to the most squeamish among us."[282]

Cohen reflects the basic First Amendment principle that the government may not prohibit or punish speech simply because others might find it offensive.[283] Cohen clearly was expressing a political message. Indeed, as Professor Frank Haiman observed, no other words would have so succinctly and forcefully captured the idea; surely "fornicate the draft" or "ban the draft" would not have been nearly as effective in conveying the message.[284]

The Court in *Cohen* rejected many arguments made by the state for punishing the speech. The Court, for example, said that the speech was not fighting words because it was not directed to a particular person. The Court also rejected the argument that the speech could be punished to protect a "captive audience." Justice Harlan wrote: "[T]he mere presumed presence of unwitting listeners or viewers does not serve automatically to justify curtailing all speech capable of giving offense. While this Court has recognized that government may properly act in many situations to prohibit intrusion into the privacy of the home of unwelcome views and ideas which cannot be banned from the public dialogue, we have at the same time consistently stressed that we are often 'captives' outside the sanctuary of the home and subject to objectionable speech. The ability of government, consonant with the Constitution, to shut off discourse solely to protect others from hearing it is, in other words, dependent upon a showing that substantial privacy interests are being invaded in an essentially intolerable manner."[285] Under *Cohen*, it would be extremely difficult for a person to complain of being a captive audience when outside the home.[286]

---

[281] *Id.* at 26.

[282] *Id.* at 25.

[283] *See, e.g.,* Texas v. Johnson, 491 U.S. 397 (1989) (flag burning is protected by the First Amendment), discussed at §11.3.6.2.

[284] Frank Haiman, Speech and Privacy: Is There a Right Not to Be Spoken To?, 67 Nw. U. L. Rev. 153, 189 (1972).

[285] 403 U.S. at 21.

[286] The "captive audience doctrine" is a concept that is raised in a number of cases, but its significance has never been defined by the Court. For example, in *Lehman v. Shaker Heights*, 418 U.S. 298 (1974), Justice Douglas, concurring in the judgment, argued that a city could prohibit political advertisements on buses so as to protect unwilling riders from exposure. *Id.* at 308 (Douglas, J., concurring in the judgment). *See also* Public Utilities Commn. v. Pollak, 343 U.S. 451 (1952) (holding that radio broadcasts on buses did not violate the First Amendment, but with Justices Douglas and Frankfurter writing opinions disagreeing and emphasizing the captive audience). For an excellent discussion of

Exception: In Schools

One situation where the Court has held that government may prohibit and punish profane and indecent language is in schools. In *Bethel School District No. 403 v. Fraser*, the Court held that the government constitutionally could punish a student for indecent speech.[287] Matthew Fraser gave a speech at a school assembly nominating another student for a position in student government. The short speech actually had no profanities, but it was filled with sexual innuendo. Fraser was punished for the speech by being suspended for a few days and being prevented from speaking at his graduation as scheduled.

The Court said that the government could punish Fraser because such speech is "wholly inconsistent with the 'fundamental value' of public school education."[288] The Court stressed that schools are responsible for inculcating civilized discourse in youth and therefore may punish profane and indecent language. The Court also emphasized the need for deference to school officials and said that "[t]he determination of what manner of speech in the classroom or in school assembly is inappropriate properly rests with the school board."[289] *Bethel v. Fraser* is thus consistent with the Court's willingness, discussed below, to defer to schools in regulating student expression.

Exception: The Broadcast Media

Another situation where the government can prohibit profane and indecent language is over the broadcast media. In *FCC v. Pacifica Foundation*, the Court upheld the ability of the Federal Communications Commission to prohibit and punish indecent language over television and radio.[290] A radio station in New York, as part of a program on language, played comedian George Carlin's monologue on the "seven dirty words." The monologue, titled "Filthy Words," repeatedly used these words and made fun of the way people are uncomfortable with certain language.

The Supreme Court recognized that the government could not prohibit all use of these words but said that it could ban them from being aired over the broadcast media. The Court, in an opinion by Chief Justice Burger, said that the broadcast media is uniquely pervasive and intrusive into the home. The Court said that "[p]atently offensive, indecent material presented over the airwaves confronts the citizen, not only in public, but also in the privacy of the home, where the individual's right to be left alone plainly outweighs the First Amendment rights of an intruder."[291] The Court said that warnings were insufficient because people might

---

the captive audience doctrine, *see* Marcy Strauss, Redefining the Captive Audience Doctrine, 19 Hastings Const. L.Q. 85 (1991).

[287] 478 U.S. 675 (1986). The issue of speech rights in public schools is discussed in more detail in §11.4.4.

[288] *Id.* at 685-686.

[289] *Id.* at 683.

[290] 438 U.S. 726 (1978).

[291] *Id.* at 748.

tune in during the middle of a broadcast. The Court also said that regulation is allowed because "broadcasting is uniquely accessible to children, even those too young to read. Although Cohen's written message might have been incomprehensible to a first grader, Pacifica's broadcast could have enlarged a child's vocabulary in an instant."[292]

Pacifica is troubling because it allows the government to deny material to willing listeners and viewers in order to prevent offense to others. Also, it says that the government can cleanse the broadcast media so that it is palatable for children. In reality, Chief Justice Burger undoubtedly underestimates the vocabulary of children and how young they are when they are exposed to such words. Additionally, the Court's rationale seems to mean that the government could ban such language in newspapers or magazines delivered to the home; they too pervade the home and are accessible to children.

The Court returned to the issue of profanities over the broadcast media, though without addressing constitutional questions, in *F.C.C. v. Fox Television Stations, Inc.*[293] After *Pacifica*, the Federal Communications Commission adopted a policy that it would not punish single uses of profanities, so-called fleeting expletives. But during the administration of President George W. Bush, the FCC adopted a new policy that any use of the "F" word was deemed sexual and fleeting expletives would be punished. The FCC indicated this in connection with the use of profanities by several performers—Bono, Cher, and Nicole Richie—at music awards shows.

Fox Television Stations, which faced sanctions for these profanities, brought a challenge to the new policy and the United States Court of Appeals for the Second Circuit found it to violate the Administrative Procedures Act for being "arbitrary and capricious" in that it was a change in long-standing policy without an adequate justification. The Supreme Court, in a 5-4 decision, reversed. Justice Scalia, writing for the Court, said that "the Commission's new enforcement policy and its order finding the broadcasts actionably indecent were neither arbitrary nor capricious."[294] The Court found that the FCC's change in policy was adequately justified and accepted its rationale of protecting children from profanities. Justice Scalia stated: "Programming replete with one-word indecent expletives will tend to produce children who use (at least) one-word indecent expletives. Congress has made the determination that indecent material is harmful to children, and has left enforcement of the ban to the Commission. If enforcement had to be supported by empirical data, the ban would effectively be a nullity."[295]

The Court did not address the First Amendment issue because that had not been ruled on by the court of appeals. The Court remanded the case on that question and in 2010, the United States Court of Appeals for the Second Circuit found that the policy violated the First Amendment.[296] The Supreme Court

---

[292] *Id.* at 749.
[293] 556 U.S. 502 (2009).
[294] *Id.* at 517.
[295] *Id.* at 518.
[296] Fox Television Stations, Inc. v. F.C.C., 613 F.3d 317 (2d Cir. 2010).

affirmed, but on narrow grounds. The Court said that the FCC's change in policy failed to give sufficient notice to the television networks that fleeting expletives or nudity were impermissible. Justice Kennedy, writing for the Court, explained: "The Commission failed to give Fox or ABC fair notice prior to the broadcasts in question that fleeting expletives and momentary nudity could be found actionably indecent. Therefore, the Commission's standards as applied to these broadcasts were vague, and the Commission's orders must be set aside."[297]

What About Other Media?

The Court has not been willing to extend *Pacifica* beyond the over-the-air—free—broadcast media. In cases involving telephones, cable television, and the Internet, the Court has largely rejected *Pacifica* and has struck down federal regulations of "indecent" speech.

Telephones

In *Sable Communications v. FCC*,[298] the Court declared unconstitutional a federal statute, designed to eliminate the "dial-a-porn" industry; the law prohibited obscene or indecent telephone conversations. The Supreme Court drew a distinction between the "obscene" and the "indecent." The Court said that while the law was constitutional in prohibiting obscene speech, it was unconstitutional in prohibiting indecent speech.

The Court emphasized that the government could not ban speech simply because it was "indecent." The Court noted that "there is no 'captive audience' problem here; callers will generally not be unwilling listeners."[299] Moreover, the Court said that Congress's goal of protecting children could be achieved through means less restrictive of speech. Justice White, writing for the Court, said that the "Congressional record contains no legislative findings that would justify us in concluding that there is no constitutionally acceptable less restrictive means, short of a total ban, to achieve the Government's interest in protecting minors."[300]

Cable Television

In two cases, the Court has considered the application of *Pacifica* to cable television. *Denver Area Educational Telecommunications Consortium, Inc. v. FCC*[301] involved First Amendment challenges to three provisions of the Cable Television Consumer Protection and Competition Act of 1992 that regulate the broadcasting of "patently offensive" sexually oriented material on cable television.[302] One

---

[297] FCC v. Fox Television Stations, Inc., 132 S. Ct. 2307, 2320 (2012).
[298] 492 U.S. 115 (1989).
[299] *Id.* at 128.
[300] *Id.* at 129.
[301] 518 U.S. 727 (1996).
[302] 47 U.S.C. §532(h), 532(j).

provision permits a cable system operator to prohibit the broadcasting of programming that depicts sexual or excretory activities or organs in a "patently offensive manner."[303] A second challenged section requires that cable systems allowing such material segregate it on a single channel and block the channel from viewer access unless the viewer, in writing, requests it.[304] The final provision allows cable systems to "prohibit sexually oriented material on public, educational, or governmental channels."[305]

Without a majority opinion, the Court upheld the first provision, but invalidated the latter two sections. As to the first clause, which allowed cable systems to refuse to carry sexually explicit broadcasting, Justice Breyer wrote a plurality opinion that was joined by Stevens, O'Connor, and Souter. Justice Breyer explicitly eschewed choosing or applying a level of scrutiny, saying it was "unwise and unnecessary" to do so.[306] Nonetheless, the plurality said that the first provision is constitutional because it serves "an extremely important justification, one that this Court has often found compelling — the need to protect children from exposure to patently offensive sex-related material."[307] The plurality opinion expressly analogized to *Pacifica* and said that the Cable Act was even less restrictive of speech than what the Court had upheld in the earlier case; the Cable Act permits, but does not require, cable systems to prohibit sexually explicit material. The plurality also rejected the argument that the law was impermissibly vague.

Justice Thomas, in an opinion joined by Chief Justice Rehnquist and Justice Scalia, concurred in the judgment and said that cable system operators have the First Amendment right to decide what programming to broadcast.[308] Accordingly, the First Amendment is not violated by allowing cable companies to refuse to carry sexually explicit material.

Justice Kennedy, joined by Justice Ginsburg, dissented as to this part of the opinion. Justice Kennedy criticized the plurality's refusal to adopt a level of scrutiny and argued that strict scrutiny was the appropriate test: "When the government identifies certain speech on the basis of its content as vulnerable to exclusion from a common carrier or public forum, strict scrutiny applies. These laws cannot survive that exacting review."[309]

As to the second part of the Act, Justice Breyer wrote a majority opinion — joined by Justices Stevens, O'Connor, Kennedy, Souter, and Ginsburg — declaring unconstitutional the requirement that sexual material be segregated and available only on request. Justice Breyer explained that this part of the Act was mandatory on cable companies carrying sexual material and imposed substantial restrictions on access. For example, there could be a 30-day delay before receiving such material and "the written notice requirement will further restrict viewing by subscribers

---

[303] §10(a).

[304] §10(b).

[305] §10(c).

[306] 518 U.S. 741.

[307] *Id.*

[308] *Id.* at 824 (Thomas, J., concurring in the judgment in part and dissenting in part).

[309] *Id.* at 781 (Kennedy, J., concurring in part, concurring in the judgment in part, and dissenting in part).

who fear for their reputations should the operator, advertently or inadvertently, disclose the list of those who wish to watch the 'patently offensive' channel."[310] Moreover, the Court said that less restrictive alternatives could protect children, such as a system where parents could request blocking by telephone or employ lockboxes.[311]

Justice Thomas, joined again by Rehnquist and Scalia, dissented on the ground that the provision was "narrowly tailored to achieve [a] well-established compelling interest. . . . [G]overnment may support parental authority to direct the moral upbringing of their children by imposing a blocking requirement as a default position."[312]

Finally, as to the third provision, Justice Breyer, wrote a plurality opinion, joined by Justices Stevens and Souter, finding unconstitutional the provision of the Cable Act that permitted cable systems to prohibit sexually explicit material over public access channels. The plurality distinguished leased channels, where the authority to prohibit such material was upheld, from public access channels, where it was declared unconstitutional. The plurality found that there was not proof of "a compelling need, nationally, to protect children from significantly harmful material" on these channels.[313] Justice Kennedy, again joined by Justice Ginsburg, concurred in the judgment and argued that the public access channels are public forums and that the content-based restriction on speech failed strict scrutiny.[314] Justice Thomas, once more joined by Chief Justice Rehnquist and Justice Scalia, dissented on the ground that cable system operators have a First Amendment right to decide what programming to include or exclude.

In light of the fragmented Court,[315] it is difficult to draw generalizations from the *Denver Area* decision. The plurality's express refusal to adopt a level of scrutiny makes it even harder to assess the impact of the case. It appears that any restrictions on sexual material over new media will be carefully examined by the Court, but it is extremely difficult to predict the likely outcome of such ad hoc review.

Even more dramatically, in *United States v. Playboy Entertainment Group, Inc.*, the Supreme Court used strict scrutiny to declare unconstitutional a provision of the Cable Act regulating sexual speech.[316] Section 505 of the Cable Act requires cable television operators who provide channels "primarily dedicated to sexually-oriented programming" to either "fully scramble or otherwise fully block" those channels or to limit their transmission to hours when children are unlikely to be viewing, set by administrative regulation as the time between 10 P.M. and 6 A.M. The section is thus intended to prevent "signal bleed" of sexual images—the situation where people receive images from cable channels to which they do not subscribe.

Justice Kennedy, writing for the Court in a 5-to-4 decision, emphasized that the law is a content-based restriction on speech. The law regulates signal bleed of

---

[310] *Id.* at 754.

[311] *Id.* at 758.

[312] *Id.* at 832.

[313] *Id.* at 767.

[314] Public forums are discussed in detail in §11.4.

[315] Justices Stevens, Souter, and O'Connor also wrote separate opinions.

[316] 529 U.S. 803 (2000).

sexual images, but not any other type. He declared: "Since §505 is a content-based speech restriction, it can stand only if it satisfies strict scrutiny. If a statute regulates speech based on its content, it must be narrowly tailored to promote a compelling Government interest. If a less restrictive alternative would serve the Government's purpose, the legislature must use that alternative."[317]

This is very important because it is the first time that the Court has applied strict scrutiny to government regulation of sexually explicit, nonobscene speech. In the prior sexual speech cases—ranging from *Young, Renton,* and *Erie* to *Pacifica* and *Denver Area*—the Court has emphasized the low value of such speech and eschewed articulating a level of scrutiny. In *Playboy Entertainment,* though, the Court expressly used strict scrutiny in striking down the restriction of sexual speech.

Justice Kennedy's majority opinion conceded that the government has a compelling interest in protecting children and unconsenting adults from exposure to sexual material. But Justice Kennedy concluded that the government had a less restrictive alternative to achieve these goals: Subscribers, on request, could fully block adult-oriented channels. He explained: "Simply put, targeted blocking is less restrictive than banning, and the Government cannot ban speech if targeted blocking is a feasible and effective means of furthering its compelling interests."[318] The opportunity for targeted blocking was the key way in which the Court distinguished *Pacifica* and the over-the-air broadcast media. Justice Kennedy explained: "There is a key difference between cable television and the broadcasting media, which is the point on which this case turns: Cable systems have the capacity to block unwanted channels on a household-by-household basis."[319]

Justice Breyer's dissenting opinion challenged whether this was a realistic less restrictive alternative in light of how few people actually use it.[320] The difference between the majority and the dissent raises an important question, rarely addressed by the Supreme Court: How should it be assessed whether there is a less restrictive alternative? What evidence is necessary for a court to conclude that an alternative is sufficiently effective as to be the basis for invalidating a law under strict scrutiny? This is what the majority and the dissent were disagreeing over in *Playboy Entertainment,* and it is a question that can arise in any area where strict scrutiny and least restrictive alternative analysis is used.

The Internet

A final medium for which the Supreme Court has considered government regulation of indecent speech is the Internet. Thus far, the Court has been very protective of the Internet as a medium of communication and has shown a great reluctance to uphold restrictions of the content of the Internet.

In *Reno v. American Civil Liberties Union,* the Supreme Court first considered the Internet and invalidated key provisions of the Communications Decency Act

---

[317] *Id.* at 804.
[318] *Id.*
[319] *Id.*
[320] *Id.* at 835 (Breyer, J., dissenting).

of 1996.[321] The law made it a federal crime to transmit obscene or indecent material over the Internet in a manner likely to be accessible to a minor. Specifically, §223(a) of the Act prohibited the knowing transmission of obscene or indecent messages to any recipient under 18 years of age. A second provision, §223(d), prohibited the knowing sending or displaying of patently offensive messages in a manner that is available to a person under 18 years of age. There were two important affirmative defenses provided for under the law. One covers those who take "good faith, reasonable, effective, and appropriate actions" to restrict access by minors to the prohibited communications. The other covers those who restrict access to covered material by requiring certain designated forms of age proof, such as a verified credit card or an adult identification number or code.

The Supreme Court, in a 7-to-2 decision, declared the prohibition of indecent material over the Internet unconstitutional. Justice Stevens wrote for the Court and expressly distinguished *Pacifica*. He noted that the Federal Communications Commission regulation of television and radio was applied to a time when children might be listening, whereas the Communications Decency Act applies to all hours. Also, *Pacifica* involved sanctions by a regulatory agency; the Communications Decency Act imposed criminal penalties on violators.

The Court stressed the vagueness of the statute. Justice Stevens observed: "Given the absence of a definition of either term, this difference in language will provoke uncertainty among speakers about how the two standards relate to each other and just what they mean. Could a speaker confidently assume that a serious discussion about birth control practices, homosexuality, or the consequences of prison rape would not violate the CDA? This uncertainty undermines the likelihood that the CDA has been carefully tailored to the congressional goal of protecting minors from potentially harmful materials."[322] The Court explained that the vagueness of the law was of great concern because it was a content-based restriction of speech and because it was a criminal statute.

The Court recognized that the government has a compelling interest in protecting children from exposure to sexual material, but it said that the government cannot restrict speech available to adults so as to safeguard children. Ultimately, the Court said that it was striking down the law because of its breadth. Justice Stevens explained: "The breadth of the CDA's coverage is wholly unprecedented. . . . [T]he scope of the CDA is not limited to commercial speech or commercial entities. Its open-ended prohibitions embrace all nonprofit entities and individuals posting indecent messages or displaying them on their own computers in the presence of minors. The general, undefined terms 'indecent' and 'patently offensive' cover large amounts of nonpornographic material with serious educational or other value."[323]

In *Ashcroft v. American Civil Liberties Union*,[324] the Court returned to the issue of government regulation of sexual speech over the Internet and considered the

---

[321]   521 U.S. 844 (1997).
[322]   *Id.* at 846.
[323]   *Id.* at 878.
[324]   542 U.S. 656 (2004).

constitutionality of the Child Online Protection Act, which seeks to protect children from exposure to sexual material on the Internet. After *Reno v. ACLU* invalidated key provisions of the Communications Decency Act, Congress passed the Child Online Protection Act, which requires that operators of commercial websites restrict access by children to material that the average person "applying contemporary community standards" would find is designed to pander to the minors' prurient interest.[325] This law is different from the Communications Decency Act in that it applies only to commercial websites and it defines the objectionable material in terms of what would be offensive under community standards. The law requires that such websites take actions to exclude children, such as by requiring credit cards or age verification services. Thus, perhaps most important, the Act is different from its predecessor because it does not prohibit material so long as the commercial website takes the necessary steps to exclude children.

Nonetheless, the federal district court issued a preliminary injunction and the United States Court of Appeals for the Third Circuit affirmed based on how the Act would limit speech on the Internet to that which would be palatable in the most restrictive state.[326] The court of appeals explained that the use of "contemporary community standards" greatly restricts speech when applied to a national medium like the Internet, which cannot be limited to users in particular geographic areas. The United States Supreme Court reversed, holding that the phase "contemporary community standards" is not unduly vague.[327] Several Justices discussed how contemporary community standards might be determined for a medium such as the Internet. The Court allowed the preliminary injunction to stand and remanded the case. The Third Circuit, on remand, reaffirmed the preliminary injunction.

The Supreme Court, in a 5-to-4 decision, affirmed and concluded that there was a substantial likelihood that the law would be declared unconstitutional. Justice Kennedy wrote for the Court, joined by Justices Stevens, Souter, Ginsburg, and Thomas. Justice Kennedy said that the law was a content-based restriction, since it applied only to sexual content over the Internet, and thus must meet strict scrutiny.[328]

Although the Court accepted the government's goal of protecting children from exposure to sexual material as a compelling interest, the Court found that the law was likely unconstitutional because it was not the least restrictive alternative. The Court said that filters, installed by parents, were more likely to be effective than the federal statute. The Court noted that 40 percent of sexual material on the Internet comes from overseas and thus would not be regulated by the Act, but could be blocked by filters.[329] Moreover, the Court noted that "filters also may be more effective because they can be applied to all forms of Internet communication, including e-mail, not just communications available via the World Wide Web."[330]

[325] 47 U.S.C. §609.
[326] *See* ACLU v. Reno, 217 F.3d 162 (3d Cir. 2000).
[327] 535 U.S. 564 (2002).
[328] 542 U.S. at 670.
[329] *Id.* at 667.
[330] *Id.*

On remand, the United States District Court found the law unconstitutional and issued a permanent injunction, and the United States Court of Appeals for the Third Circuit affirmed.[331]

The Court's preference for Internet filters, as opposed to laws prohibiting material on the Internet, also was evident in its decision in *United States v. American Library Association*.[332] The Court, without a majority opinion, upheld a federal law requiring libraries receiving federal funds to install filters to block sexually explicit material. Chief Justice Rehnquist's plurality opinion stressed that libraries need not buy all materials or allow access to all materials on the Internet. Thus, it is constitutional for Congress to condition federal funds on a requirement that local libraries place filters on their computers that are available to users. Justices Kennedy and Breyer emphasized that under the law patrons may request librarians to lift filters. They said that since none of the plaintiffs in the suit had been denied access to any materials it was premature to consider the constitutional issue.

Underlying Issues

The many decisions concerning government regulation of sexual speech over various media raise important underlying questions. First, should there be a category of "indecent" speech? All of these cases involve laws regulating sexually oriented nonobscene speech. Some cases, such as *Reno v. ACLU*, emphasize the inherent vagueness to the term "indecent." Other cases, such as *Pacifica*, seem untroubled by the ambiguity as to what is "indecent."

Second, if there is a category of "indecent" speech, what level of scrutiny should be used in evaluating government regulations? Most of the cases do not articulate a level of scrutiny—and *Denver Area* expressly refuses to choose one—but treat it as minimally protected speech. *Playboy Entertainment* and *Ashcroft v. ACLU*, however, use strict scrutiny on the grounds that a law regulating sexual speech is a content-based restriction.

Finally, does the Court's medium-by-medium approach make sense? The Court has dealt separately with over-the-air broadcast stations, telephones, cable, and the Internet. In *Denver Area*, the Court expressly acknowledged analyzing each medium separately. But technology seems to undermine such a distinction. People today often receive all of these media through a single source. The Court's very different treatment of the same speech over different forms of electronic communications thus is likely to be questioned and reconsidered in the years ahead. Justice Thomas made exactly this point and wrote: "The extant facts that drove this Court to subject broadcasters to unique disfavor under the First Amendment simply do not exist today. . . . These dramatic changes in factual circumstances might well support a departure from precedent under the prevailing approach to *stare decisis*."[333]

---

[331] 478 F. Supp. 2d 775 (E.D. Pa. 2007); 534 F.3d 181 (3d Cir. 2008).
[332] 539 U.S. 194 (2003).
[333] F.C.C. v. Fox Televisions Stations, Inc., 556 U.S. 502, 530-31 (2009) (Thomas, J., concurring).

§11.3.5   Reputation, Privacy, Publicity, and the First Amendment: Torts and the First Amendment

§11.3.5.1   Introduction

First Amendment Limits on Tort Liability

Many tort claims seek to impose liability for speech. For example, the tort of defamation—libel and slander—is liability for speech injurious to reputation. Similarly, the "false light" tort is liability for speech that creates a false impression about a person and his or her activities. Speech can be the basis for a claim for infliction of emotional distress. Also, speech that discloses private information or exploits the commercial likeness of another might be the basis for a tort for invasion of privacy or for violating the right of publicity. This section considers, in turn, each of these torts and First Amendment limits upon them.

In *New York Times v. Sullivan*, the Supreme Court expressly held that the First Amendment limits the ability of the government to impose tort liability.[334] Although tort litigation is generally between two private parties, there is state action in that it is the state's law, whether statutory or common law, that allows recovery. Besides, it is a branch of the government, the judiciary, that is imposing liability for the speech.[335] The Court in *New York Times v. Sullivan* declared that "[w]hat a State may not constitutionally bring about by means of a criminal statute is likewise beyond the reach of its civil law. . . . The fear of damage awards . . . may be markedly more inhibiting than the fear of prosecution under a criminal statute."[336] As the Court recently reaffirmed, "The Free Speech Clause of the First Amendment . . . can serve as a defense in state tort suits."[337]

§11.3.5.2   Defamation

Overview

In *New York Times v. Sullivan*, the Court held that recovery for defamation—libel and slander—is limited by the First Amendment.[338] The challenge for the Court in this area is to balance the need to protect reputation, the obvious central concern of defamation law, with the desire to safeguard expression, which can be chilled and limited by tort liability.

Since *New York Times*, the Supreme Court has attempted to strike this balance by developing a complex series of rules that depend on the identity of the plaintiff and the nature of the subject matter. As described below, there are four major

---

[334] 376 U.S. 254 (1964).
[335] *See* §6.4.4.3 discussing court action as state action.
[336] 376 U.S. at 277.
[337] Snyder v. Phelps, 131 S. Ct. 1207, 1215 (2011).
[338] 376 U.S. at 254.

categories of situations: where the plaintiff is a public official or running for public office, where the plaintiff is a public figure, where the plaintiff is a private figure and the matter is of public concern, and where the plaintiff is a private figure and the matter is not of public concern.

Public Officials as Defamation Plaintiffs

If the plaintiff is a public official or running for public office, the plaintiff can recover for defamation only by proving with clear and convincing evidence the falsity of the statements and actual malice. Actual malice means that the defendant knew that the statement was false or acted with reckless disregard of the truth.

New York Times v. Sullivan is the seminal case in this area. L.B. Sullivan, an elected commissioner of Montgomery, Alabama, sued The New York Times and four African-American clergymen for an advertisement that had been published in the newspaper on March 29, 1960. The ad criticized the way in which police in Montgomery had mistreated civil rights demonstrators. There is no dispute that the ad contained false statements: It said that the demonstrators sang "My Country 'Tis of Thee," but they actually sang the national anthem; it said that Dr. Martin Luther King, Jr., had been arrested seven times, but it really was only four; it said that nine students were expelled for the demonstration, but their suspension was for a different protest at lunch counters; and the ad mistakenly said that the dining hall had been padlocked. Pursuant to a judge's instructions that the statements were libelous per se and that general damages could be presumed, the jury awarded a $500,000 verdict for Sullivan.

The Supreme Court held that the tort liability violated the First Amendment. Justice Brennan, writing for the Court, began by stating that the case was considered "against the background of a profound national commitment to the principle that debate on public issues should be uninhibited, robust, and wide-open, and that it may well include vehement, caustic, and sometimes unpleasantly sharp attacks on government and public officials."[339] The Court explained that criticism of government and government officials was at the core of speech protected by the First Amendment. The fact that some of the statements were false was not sufficient to deny the speech of protection; the Court said that false "statement is inevitable in free debate and [it] must be protected if the freedoms of expression are to have the 'breathing space' that they 'need . . . to survive.' "[340]

Accordingly, the Court said that it was not enough that truth was a defense under Alabama's libel law — requiring that defendants prove the truth of their statements will chill speech. The Court thus concluded that the First Amendment prevents a "public official from recovering damages for a defamatory falsehood relating to his official conduct unless he proves that the statement was made with

---

[339] *Id.* at 270.
[340] *Id.* at 271-272. Justice Brennan noted that "[a]lthough the Sedition Act was never tested in this Court, the attack upon its validity has carried the day in the court of history." *Id.* at 276.

'actual malice' — that is, with knowledge that it was false or with reckless disregard of whether it was false or not."[341]

New York Times is one of the most important First Amendment decisions in history because of its application of the Constitution as a limit on tort liability and because of its strong protection for political speech.[342] Yet it also has its critics who maintain that the Court went too far in protecting false statements and in not providing adequate protection for political speech.[343]

Under *New York Times*, there are four requirements in this category: (1) the plaintiff must be a public official or running for public office; (2) the plaintiff must prove his or her case with clear and convincing evidence; (3) the plaintiff must prove falsity of the statement; and (4) the plaintiff must prove actual malice — that the defendant knew the statement was false or acted with reckless disregard of the truth. Each is discussed in turn.

First, the plaintiff must be a public official or running for public office for the case to fit within this category. Although *New York Times* involved a plaintiff who was a government official, the Court extended this to those running for public office.[344] For example, the Court has said that *New York Times* applies to "anything which might touch on an official's fitness for office."[345]

The Supreme Court never has held that all government employees are to be considered public officials under *New York Times*, but nor has the Court formulated a precise test for determining which public employees are public officials. In *New York Times*, in a footnote, the Court said that it had "no occasion here to determine how far down into the lower ranks of government employees the 'public official' designation would extend."[346]

The primary Supreme Court decision clarifying who is a "public official" was *Rosenblatt v. Baer*.[347] In *Rosenblatt*, the plaintiff was a fired supervisor of a county-owned ski resort. The Court said that "public officials" are "at the very least . . . those among the hierarchy of government employees who have, or appear to the public to have substantial responsibility for the control of governmental affairs."[348] The Court said that public officials are those who hold positions of such "apparent importance that the public has an independent interest in the qualifications and performance of the person who holds it."[349]

It is certainly possible to imagine government employees who do not fit within this definition. Yet for any government employee, even at the "lowest" rung of the

---

[341] *Id.* at 279-280.

[342] *See, e.g.*, Harry Kalven, The *New York Times* Case: A Note on the Central Meaning of the First Amendment, 1964 Sup. Ct. Rev. 191.

[343] *See, e.g.*, Richard Epstein, Was *New York Times v. Sullivan* Wrong?, 53 U. Chi. L. Rev. 782 (1986); Robert Nagel, How Useful Is Judicial Review in Free Speech Cases?, 69 Cornell L. Rev. 302 (1984).

[344] *See* Monitor Patriot Co. v. Roy, 401 U.S. 265 (1971) (defamation of a candidate for public office covered by the *New York Times* standard).

[345] Garrison v. Louisiana, 379 U.S. 64, 77 (1964).

[346] 376 U.S. at 283 n.23.

[347] 383 U.S. 75 (1966).

[348] *Id.* at 85.

[349] *Id.* at 86.

hierarchy, it is possible that issues could arise concerning their performance on the job and thus be of importance to the public. Thus, no clear definition exists as to who is a public official for purposes of the *New York Times* test.[350]

Second, the plaintiff in this category must prove his or her case with clear and convincing evidence; preponderance of the evidence, the usual standard in civil cases, is not enough. In *New York Times v. Sullivan*, the Court said that the plaintiff had the burden of proving falsity of the statement and actual malice with "convincing clarity."[351] The Court subsequently termed this standard as a requirement for "clear and convincing evidence."[352]

To ensure that this requirement is met, appellate courts are required to conduct an independent, de novo review to ensure that there is clear and convincing evidence that defendant uttered false statements with actual malice. In *Bose Corp. v. Consumers Union of United States, Inc.*, the Court said that under the "actual malice" standard of *New York Times*, "[a]ppellate judges in such a case must exercise independent judgment and determine whether the record established actual malice with convincing clarity."[353]

Third, the plaintiff must prove the falsity of the statements. At the very least, this means that the defendant in this category cannot be forced to prove truth of the statements. A difficult issue arises here in drawing a distinction between expression of opinion and false statements of fact. In *Gertz v. Welch*, the Court observed that "[u]nder the First Amendment there is no such thing as a false idea. However pernicious an opinion may seem, we depend for its correction not on the conscience of judges and juries but on the competition of other ideas. But there is no constitutional value in false statements of fact."[354]

But separating opinion from fact is inherently difficult. Is calling a public official "stupid" a statement of fact, because IQ can be measured, or of opinion? Is calling a person a "crook" fact or opinion? The Supreme Court addressed the fact/opinion distinction in *Milkovich v. Lorain Journal Co.*[355] Michael Milkovich was the wrestling coach at a public high school and prevailed in a lawsuit overturning sanctions that had been imposed on him because of an altercation that occurred at a match. A column in a local newspaper said that the school had prevailed with the "big lie," implying that Milkovich had lied under oath.[356]

The Court in *Milkovich* said that the language in *Gertz*, quoted above, was not "intended to create a wholesale defamation exemption for anything that might be labeled 'opinion.'"[357] However, the Court also made it clear that only

---

[350] Generally, lower courts have found government officials of all sorts to be public officials. *See, e.g.*, Crane v. Arizona Republic, 972 F.2d 1511 (9th Cir. 1992) (prosecutor is a public official); Stevens v. Tillman, 885 F.2d 394 (7th Cir. 1988) (elementary school principal is a public official); McKinley v. Baden, 777 F.2d 1017 (5th Cir. 1985) (police officer is a public official).

[351] 376 U.S. at 285-286.

[352] Gertz v. Welch, 418 U.S. 323, 331-332 (1974); Beckley Newspapers Corp. v. Hanks, 389 U.S. 81, 83 (1967).

[353] 466 U.S. 485, 514 (1984).

[354] 418 U.S. at 339-340.

[355] 497 U.S. 1 (1990).

[356] *Id.* at 4.

[357] *Id.* at 18.

false statements of fact could be the basis for defamation liability. Chief Justice Rehnquist, writing for the Court, said "a statement on matters of public concern must be provable as false before there can be liability under state defamation law, at least in situations, like the present, where a media defendant is involved. . . . [A] statement of opinion relating to matters of public concern which does not contain a provably false factual connotation will receive full constitutional protection."[358]

Therefore, the focus is not on whether a statement is opinion, but whether it contains, directly or by clear implication, factual statements. False statements of fact are a prerequisite for defamation liability. Yet this still leaves unresolved the key question: When are statements "rhetorical hyperbole" protected by the First Amendment[359] and when are they factual statements that can be the basis for defamation actions? All *Milkovich* holds is that labeling a statement as opinion is not sufficient, by itself, to preclude defamation liability.

Fourth and finally in this category, there must be proof of actual malice; that is, the defendant knew that the statement was false or acted with reckless disregard of the truth. The Court has explained that this requires proof that the statements were made with "a high degree of awareness of their probable falsity."[360] The Court has said that "actual malice is a term of art denoting deliberate or reckless falsification."[361]

In *St. Amant v. Thompson*, the Supreme Court said that actual malice requires that the defendant "in fact entertained serious doubts as to the truth of his publication."[362] In *St. Amant*, a candidate for public office made highly critical statements about the conduct of the sheriff. The Supreme Court overturned defamation liability and emphasized that actual malice could not be proved by showing that the defendant failed to verify the accuracy of facts or even investigate. Actual malice requires that the defendant have a subjective awareness of probable falsity; that there be proof that the defendant had serious doubts about the accuracy of the statements before making them.[363]

The Court has held that even the intentional fabrication of quotations is not enough, by itself, to prove actual malice if the statements were substantially accurate in reflecting what was said. *Masson v. New Yorker* concerned a defamation suit brought by Jeffrey Masson, a psychoanalyst, against Janet Malcolm, a writer for *New Yorker* magazine.[364] Although the case did not involve a public official, it did involve a plaintiff who was a public figure, and as described below, this meant that the *New York Times* test applied. The article was based on more than 40 hours of interviews

---

[358]   *Id.* at 19-20.

[359]   *Id.* at 17.

[360]   Garrison v. Louisiana, 379 U.S. 64, 74 (1964).

[361]   Masson v. New Yorker Magazine, Inc., 501 U.S. 496, 499 (1991).

[362]   390 U.S. 727, 731 (1968).

[363]   *Id.* at 731. In *Herbert v. Lando*, 441 U.S. 153 (1979), the Court held that a defamation plaintiff may have discovery as to the knowledge of a defendant and its decision-making processes concerning publication as part of proving actual malice. The Court explained that the subjective nature of the actual malice standard requires that such discovery be available. *Herbert* involved a defamation action against the television show "60 Minutes" for a story it did on the plaintiff's alleged participation in atrocities during the Vietnam War.

[364]   501 U.S. 496 (1991).

and contained many quotations; none of the quotes, however, were actual statements made during the interviews.

The Court, in an opinion by Justice Kennedy, said that quotation marks do not convey that what is within them is a word-for-word transcription of an actual statement. Rather, the Court said that a quotation implies a substantially accurate representation of a person's statement. The issue, therefore, is not whether the quotation published is a verbatim reflection of what was said, but whether it is substantially accurate. Falsely attributing a statement to a person can be the basis for defamation liability, but there has to be proof that the statements substantially change the meaning of what was said.

Thus, actual malice is a difficult standard to meet. It is a subjective standard that requires that the plaintiff prove that the defendant knew that the statement was false or acted with serious doubts about its truth.

Public Figures as Plaintiffs

The Supreme Court has held that the same rules apply in defamation suits brought by public figures. The Court initially applied the *New York Times* test to public figures in *Curtis Publishing Co. v. Butts*[365] and *Associated Press v. Walker.*[366] Both of these cases involved plaintiffs who did not hold public office, but were very prominent in their communities. *Butts* involved game-fixing allegations directed at a football coach at a state university who actually was employed by a private corporation that administered the school's athletic programs. *Walker* involved a former army general accused of leading an angry crowd that obstructed federal marshals who were facilitating the enrollment of James Meredith and the desegregation of the University of Mississippi.

There was not a majority opinion in either case. Justice Harlan, writing for the plurality, said that although the plaintiffs were not public officials, "the public interest in the circulation of the materials involved, and the publisher's interest in circulating them, is not less than that involved in *New York Times.*"[367] While the plurality would have allowed public figures to recover with less than proof of actual malice, a majority of the Justices rejected that view. Chief Justice Warren said that "differentiation between 'public figures' and 'public officials' and adoption of separate standards of proof for each have no basis in law, logic, or First Amendment policy."[368] Justices Brennan and White agreed that actual malice should be required when public figures are defamation plaintiffs, and Justices Black and Douglas took an absolutist position that would have barred any defamation liability. Thus, five Justices said that public figures cannot recover for defamation with less than proof of actual malice.

In *Rosenbloom v. Metromedia, Inc.*, a plurality of the Court went even further and held that the actual malice test should be used so long as the matter is of

---

[365] 388 U.S. 130 (1967).
[366] *Id.*
[367] 388 U.S. at 154.
[368] *Id.* at 163 (Warren, C.J., concurring in the result).

public concern, even if the plaintiff was neither a public official nor a public figure.[369] Justice Brennan, writing for the plurality, said that "[i]f a matter is a subject of public or general interest, it cannot suddenly become less so merely because a private individual is involved, or because in some sense the individual did not 'voluntarily' choose to become involved."[370]

However, a majority of the Court never accepted this view and, in fact, it was expressly rejected in *Gertz v. Welch*, where the Court expressly drew the distinction between public and private figures.[371] *Gertz* involved a defamation suit brought by a prominent Chicago attorney, Elmer Gertz, who was attacked in a John Birch society publication for his representation of the family of a young man killed by a police officer. The Court said that the issue was "whether a newspaper or broadcaster that publishes defamatory falsehoods about an individual who is neither a public official nor a public figure may claim a constitutional privilege against liability for the injury inflicted by those statements."[372]

The Court drew a distinction between defamation plaintiffs who are public figures and those who are private figures. Justice Powell, writing for the Court, said: "The *New York Times* standard defines the level of constitutional protection appropriate to the context of defamation of a public person. [But] the state interest in compensating injury to the reputation of private individuals requires that a different rule should obtain with respect to them."[373] The Court explained that "public figures, like public officials, usually enjoy significantly greater access to the channels of effective communication and hence have a more realistic opportunity to counteract false statements than private individuals usually enjoy."[374] Moreover, public figures generally have made the choice to thrust themselves into the limelight and thus have "voluntarily exposed themselves to increased risk of injury from defamatory falsehood."[375]

The difficulty is in defining who is a "public figure." The distinction has enormous practical importance: A public figure can recover for defamation only by meeting the *New York Times* standard; as discussed below, a private figure can recover compensatory damages for defamation by proving falsity of the statement and negligence. There is a huge difference between actual malice and negligence.

The Court in *Gertz* did relatively little to clarify who is a public figure. The Court said that "[f]or the most part those who attain this status have assumed roles of especial prominence in the affairs of society. Some occupy positions of such persuasive power and influence that they are deemed public figures for all purposes. More commonly, those classified as public figures have thrust themselves to the forefront of particular public controversies in order to influence the resolution of the issues involved."[376] The Court recognized that individuals might become

[369] 403 U.S. 29 (1971).
[370] *Id.* at 43.
[371] 418 U.S. 323 (1974).
[372] *Id.* at 332.
[373] *Id.* at 342-343.
[374] *Id.* at 344.
[375] *Id.* at 345.
[376] *Id.*

public figures through no purposeful action of their own, but the Court said that "instances of truly involuntary public figures must be exceedingly rare."[377] The Court concluded that Gertz was not a public figure because "[h]e plainly did not thrust himself into the vortex of this public issue, nor did he engage the public's attention in an attempt to influence its outcome."[378]

No subsequent Supreme Court case has formulated a precise definition of who is a public figure. The later cases all indicate, however, that in order to be a public figure a person must voluntarily, affirmatively thrust himself or herself into the limelight. For example, in *Time, Inc. v. Firestone*, the Court held that Mary Alice Firestone, the wife of a member of the very wealthy Firestone family, was a private figure.[379] Ms. Firestone was prominent in social circles and often in the newspapers; she even hired a clipping service to keep track of publicity about her. *Time* magazine wrongly reported that her divorce was granted on grounds of adultery and was sued for defamation. The Court held that Ms. Firestone was a private figure because she "did not assume any role of especial prominence in the affairs of society, other than perhaps Palm Beach society, and she did not thrust herself to the forefront of any particular public controversy in order to influence the resolution of the issues involved in it."[380]

Similarly, in *Wolston v. Reader's Digest Association*, the Court found that an individual was a private figure even though he had been convicted of contempt for his refusal to appear before a grand jury investigating espionage by the Soviet Union.[381] An article, published 16 years after the conviction, described Wolston as a Soviet agent. The Supreme Court said that Wolston was neither a general public figure nor even a limited public figure even though there had been extensive publicity about his refusal to testify before the grand jury. The Court said that the plaintiff had not "engaged the attention of the public in an attempt to influence the resolution of the issues involved."[382] As in *Time v. Firestone*, the Court stressed that the plaintiff did not "voluntarily thrust" or "inject . . . himself into the forefront."[383]

In *Hutchinson v. Proxmire*, the Court ruled that an individual who received a "Golden Fleece of the Month Award" from Senator William Proxmire was a private figure.[384] Ronald Hutchinson received substantial federal funding for research into aggressive monkey behavior. Senator Proxmire ridiculed the grant with his "Golden Fleece Award." The Court said that Hutchinson could sue Senator Proxmire for defamation because the statement was not protected by the Speech or Debate Clause.[385] The Court also ruled that Hutchinson was a private figure

[377] *Id.*
[378] *Id.* at 352.
[379] 424 U.S. 448 (1976).
[380] *Id.* at 453.
[381] 443 U.S. 157 (1979).
[382] *Id.* at 168.
[383] *Id.* at 166.
[384] 443 U.S. 11 (1979).
[385] *Id.* at 133.

because he "at no time . . . assumed any role of public prominence."[386] The Court said that "[n]either his applications for federal grants nor his publications in professional journals can be said to have invited that degree of public attention and comment on his receipt of federal grants essential to meet the public figure level."[387]

These cases do not offer a clear definition of who is a public figure. They do indicate a restrictive view of who is a public figure requiring that a person take voluntary, affirmative steps to thrust himself or herself into the limelight. At the very least, they make it very difficult for anyone to be found an involuntary public figure.

Private Figures, Matters of Public Concern

If the plaintiff is a private figure and the matter is of public concern, a state can allow a plaintiff to recover compensatory damages if there is proof that the statements were false and of negligence by the defendant. However, proof of presumed or punitive damages requires proof of actual malice. "Private figures" are obviously plaintiffs who are not public officials or public figures. "Matter of public concern" has never been defined, but generally it refers to issues in which the public has a legitimate interest.

In *Gertz v. Welch*, the Court said that "so long as they do not impose liability without fault, the States may define for themselves the appropriate standard of liability for a publisher or broadcaster of defamatory falsehood injurious to a private individual."[388] The Court said that this was based on the important state interest of compensating private individuals for injuries to their reputations. But the Court said that "this countervailing state interest extends no further than compensation for actual injury. . . . [T]he States may not permit recovery of presumed or punitive damages, at least when liability is not based on a showing of knowledge of falsity or reckless disregard for the truth."[389]

In *Dun & Bradstreet, Inc. v. Greenmoss Builders, Inc.*, the Supreme Court said that a distinction must be drawn in suits against private figures between speech that involves matters of public concern and that which does not.[390] *Dun & Bradstreet* involved a confidential report prepared by a credit reporting agency for subscribers that falsely said that a company had filed a petition for bankruptcy. In a plurality opinion by Justice Powell, the Court said that "not all speech is of equal First Amendment importance. It is speech on 'matters of public concern' that is 'at the heart of the First Amendment's protection.' . . . In contrast, speech on matters of purely private concern is of less First Amendment concern."[391] The plurality thus said that the *Gertz* requirement that presumed or punitive damages require proof

---

[386] *Id.* at 135.
[387] *Id.*
[388] 418 U.S. at 347.
[389] *Id.* at 349.
[390] 472 U.S. 749 (1985).
[391] *Id.* at 758-759 (citation omitted).

of actual malice only applies in suits involving private figures and matters of public concern.

Dun & Bradstreet thus brings back into defamation law the "matters of public concern" standard that *Rosenbloom* had introduced and that was seemingly rejected in *Gertz*. Defining matters of public concern is inherently difficult. If "public concern" is defined in terms of the public's actual interest, the media's judgment to publish is likely strong, if not conclusive, evidence of people's interest in the material. But if "public concern" is defined from a more objective viewpoint, then courts are in the position of deciding what people, in their enlightened best interest, should want to know about. Such judgments are obviously troubling under the First Amendment.

Thus, it is established that if the plaintiff is a private figure and the matter is of public concern, a state can allow recovery of compensatory damages if the plaintiff proves falsity of the statement and negligence by the speaker. But presumed or punitive damages require proof of actual malice. The Court has expressly ruled that the plaintiff must bear the burden of proof in this category, just as when the plaintiff is a public official or a public figure. In *Philadelphia Newspapers, Inc. v. Hepps*, the Court held that the First Amendment requires that the plaintiff prove falsity of the statement.[392] A newspaper ran a series of articles linking the owner of a chain of stores to organized crime. The state court had ruled that the defendant had the burden of proving truth of the statements because the plaintiff was neither a public official nor a public figure. The Court said that "[t]o ensure that true speech on matters of public concern is not deterred, we hold that the common-law presumption that defamatory speech is false cannot stand when a plaintiff seeks damages against a media defendant for speech of public concern."[393]

Philadelphia Newspapers, Inc. v. Hepps articulates a rule for when there is a media defendant. The Court has never invoked the distinction between media and nonmedia defendants. On the one hand, the media obviously plays a crucial role in informing the public and can claim special protection as the "press" under the First Amendment. On the other hand, defining the "media" is likely to be extremely difficult; nonmedia individuals and entities also can play an important role in informing the public. As discussed below, the Court generally has been reluctant to provide any special rights for the institutional press.[394] In *Dun & Bradstreet v. Greenmoss Builders*, five Justices — though in separate opinions — expressly rejected any distinction between media and nonmedia defendants for purposes of defamation liability. Justice White, in an opinion concurring in the judgment, said that he agreed with the four dissenters "that the First Amendment gives no more protection to the press in defamation suits than it does to others exercising their freedom of speech."[395]

---

[392] 475 U.S. 767 (1986).
[393] *Id.* at 776-777.
[394] *See* §§11.6.1 and 11.6.2.
[395] 472 U.S. at 773 (White, J., concurring in the judgment).

Private Figures, Matters Not of Public Concern

There only has been one case, *Dun & Bradstreet v. Greenmoss Builders*, that thus far has considered the category of private figures and speech that is not of public concern. In *Dun & Bradstreet*, the Court ruled that in this category presumed and punitive damages do not require proof of actual malice. Justice Powell, writing for the plurality, said that "in light of the reduced constitutional value of speech involving no matters of public concern, we hold that the state interest adequately supports awards of presumed and punitive damages—even absent a showing of actual malice."[396] The plurality said that the credit report did not involve a matter of public concern because it was circulated only to five subscribers, was required to be kept confidential, and was thus of interest only to its "specific business audience."[397]

Chief Justice Burger and Justice White wrote separate opinions concurring in the judgment. Each argued that *Gertz* should be overruled, but said that if it remained the law, it should not be extended to suits involving matters that are not of public concern.[398]

The Supreme Court never has considered what should be the standard of liability or even who must bear the burden of proof when it is a private figure as plaintiff and the matter is not of public concern. The Court only has ruled that in this category presumed or punitive damages do not require proof of actual malice.

Conclusion

This law of defamation has been criticized on many grounds. The categories at times seem arbitrary and ill-defined; a great deal depends on whether a plaintiff is classified as a public figure or whether a matter is deemed a matter of public concern. Some argue that the Court's approach has provided too much protection for speech and not enough for reputation.[399] Others argue that the approach does not provide enough protection for speech and that the current law chills speech and, indeed, "perpetuates a system of censorship by libel lawyers—a system in which the relevant question is not whether a story is libelous, but whether the subject is likely to sue, and if so, how much it will cost to defend."[400]

But the current approach also can be defended as drawing sensible compromises between the important values of speech and reputation. The categories obviously try to strike a balance: They give more weight to speech that is relevant to the political process and of public interest; they give more weight to reputation when a

---

[396] *Id.* at 761.

[397] *Id.* at 762.

[398] *Id.* at 764 (Burger, C.J., concurring in the judgment); *id.* at 774 (White, J., concurring in the judgment).

[399] *See id.* at 771 (White, J., concurring in the judgment); Epstein, *supra* note 343, at 801.

[400] David Anderson, Libel and Press Self-Censorship, 53 Tex. L. Rev. 422, 424-425 (1975); *see also* Rodney A. Smolla, Let the Author Beware: The Rejuvenation of the American Law of Libel, 132 U. Pa. L. Rev. 1 (1983).

person has not voluntarily entered the public domain and when the matter is not of public concern.[401]

§11.3.5.3   False Light

Application of the *New York Times* Standard

Another tort, closely related to defamation, is for "false light." In other words, a person is liable for placing another "before the public in a false light."[402] The distinction between the false light tort and defamation is difficult to draw; the former is viewed as an aspect of privacy, while the latter is about reputation. Yet both ultimately are about causing a person to be falsely perceived in the public's eye.

Not surprisingly, the Supreme Court has said that recovery for false light must meet the constitutional standards applied in defamation actions. In *Time, Inc. v. Hill,* the Court said that recovery for false light under a state's privacy statute was not permissible when there were "matters of public interest in the absence of proof that the defendant published the report with knowledge of its falsity or in reckless disregard of the truth."[403] *Time, Inc. v. Hill* involved a family that had been kidnapped and held hostage by three escaped convicts for 19 hours. Although they were treated civilly by the kidnappers, a play about the incident, which was reported in a magazine, portrayed the kidnappers as violent toward the hostages. The family sued under the false light tort. The Supreme Court overturned the jury's finding of liability for the magazine by ruling that the *New York Times* standard had not been met.

Time, Inc. v. Hill comes to the logical conclusion that the false light tort must meet the same standards as applied in defamation actions. Otherwise plaintiffs could circumvent *New York Times v. Sullivan* by suing for false light rather than defamation. However, *Time, Inc. v. Hill* applied the actual malice test that clearly no longer would apply under those facts; the plaintiffs were private figures, not public officials or public figures.

In *Cantrell v. Forest City Publishing Co.,*[404] the Court avoided the issue of whether *Gertz v. Welch* has undercut the holding of *Hill,* at least when the plaintiff in a false light suit is not a public figure. The Court found that the plaintiff proved actual malice because the defendant had made up facts concerning her reaction to her husband's death in a bridge collapse. Because the plaintiff established actual mal-

---

[401] A few years ago, the Court granted review on an issue concerning defamation law that is splitting the lower courts, whether injunctions are a permissible remedy in defamation cases. The Court, however, did not decide that question, instead finding the injunction in the particular case to be unconstitutionally overbroad. Tory v. Cochran, 544 U.S. 734 (2005). However, the Court was clear that any injunction must be narrowly tailored and it overturned as violating this requirement an injunction that prevented the defamation defendant (and his wife) from saying anything about the plaintiff, Johnnie Cochran, in any public forum.

[402] Restatement (Second) of Torts §652(E) (1977).

[403] 385 U.S. 374, 388 (1967).

[404] 419 U.S. 245 (1974).

ice, the Court said that "this case presents no occasion to consider whether a State may constitutionally apply a more relaxed standard of liability for a publisher or broadcaster of false statements injurious to a private individual under a false light theory of invasion of privacy, or whether the constitutional standard announced in *Time, Inc. v. Hill* applies to all false light cases."[405]

There is a strong argument that false light liability should be treated under exactly the same standards as defamation because they are closely related. But there also is a persuasive argument that all false light claims should have to meet the rigorous "actual malice" test because the state has less interest in protecting the privacy interest in false light claims than the reputational interest in defamation actions. The lower courts are split as to which approach should be used.[406]

§11.3.5.4   Intentional Infliction of Emotional Distress

Application of the *New York Times* Standard

In *Hustler Magazine v. Falwell,*[407] the Supreme Court held that recovery for the tort of intentional infliction of emotional distress had to meet the *New York Times* standards. Specifically, the Court ruled that public officials and public figures who are targets of parody cannot recover for intentional infliction of emotional distress unless there is proof of actual malice.

Hustler Magazine published a parody in which it depicted Jerry Falwell, a nationally famous minister and founder of the Moral Majority, as having his first sexual experience with his mother in an outhouse. At the bottom of the page, in small print, there was the disclaimer, "ad parody—not to be taken seriously."[408] The Supreme Court, in a unanimous opinion written by Chief Justice Rehnquist, emphasized the importance of First Amendment protection for parody and satire. The Court said that the motive behind the ad was irrelevant. It explained: "[W]hile such a bad motive may be deemed controlling for purposes of tort liability in other areas of the law, we think that the First Amendment prohibits such a result in the area of public debate about public figures. Were we to hold otherwise, there can be little doubt that political cartoonists and satirists would be subjected to damage awards without any showing that their work falsely defamed its subject."[409]

The Court thus held that the *New York Times* standard of actual malice had to be met in suits by public officials and public figures for intentional torts. Chief Justice Rehnquist wrote: "We conclude that public figures and public officials may

---

[405] *Id.* at 250-251.
[406] *See, e.g.,* Wood v. Hustler Magazine, Inc., 736 F.2d 1084 (5th Cir. 1984), *cert. denied,* 469 U.S. 1107 (1985) (defamation standards apply); Dodrill v. Arkansas Democrat Co., 265 Ark. 628, 590 S.W.2d 840 (1979), *cert. denied sub nom.* Little Rock Newspapers, Inc. v. Dodrill, 444 U.S. 1076 (1980) (actual malice applies in all false light cases). *See* Rodney A. Smolla, Smolla and Nimmer on Freedom of Speech, 11-48 n.22 (1994).
[407] 485 U.S. 46 (1988).
[408] *Id.* at 48.
[409] *Id.* at 53.

not recover for the tort of intentional infliction of emotional distress by reason of publications such as the one here at issue without showing in addition that the publication contains a false statement of fact which was made with 'actual malice,' i.e., with knowledge that the statement was false or with reckless disregard as to whether or not it was true."[410]

Any other result in *Hustler Magazine v. Falwell* would have meant that defamation plaintiffs could circumvent the rigorous *New York Times* standard simply by suing for infliction of emotional distress. Moreover, the decision reflects the strong First Amendment protection for speech about public officials and public figures, even when it is caustic and offensive.[411]

The Court returned to the issue of tort liability for intentional infliction of emotional distress, and strongly reaffirmed the First Amendment limits, in *Snyder v. Phelps*.[412] For the past 20 years, the members of the Westboro Baptist Church have picketed military funerals to communicate their belief that God hates the United States for its tolerance of homosexuality, particularly in America's military. Fred Phelps, who founded the church, and six Westboro Baptist parishioners (all relatives of Phelps) traveled to Maryland to picket the funeral of Marine Lance Corporal Matthew Snyder, who was killed in Iraq in the line of duty. The picketing took place on public land approximately 1,000 feet from the church where the funeral was held. The protestors followed the instructions from local law enforcement officers. The picketers peacefully displayed their signs, which conveyed very offensive messages.

Albert Snyder, Matthew Snyder's father, saw the tops of the picketers' signs when driving to the funeral, but did not learn what was written on the signs until watching a news broadcast later that night. Albert Snyder sued Phelps, his family members who were with him at the funeral, and the Westboro Baptist Church for the state tort claims of intentional infliction of emotional distress, intrusion upon seclusion, and civil conspiracy. A jury in federal court ruled in favor of Snyder and the district court judge allowed a $10 million judgment, including both compensatory and punitive damages, to stand.

The United States Court of Appeals for the Fourth Circuit reversed, concluding that such liability violates the First Amendment. The Supreme Court, with only Justice Alito dissenting, affirmed. Chief Justice Roberts wrote the opinion for the Court. He stressed that the speech, while offensive, involved a matter of public concern. He wrote: "[S]peech on 'matters of public concern' . . . is 'at the heart of the First Amendment's protection.' . . . Accordingly, 'speech on public issues occupies the highest rung of the hierarchy of First Amendment values, and is entitled to special protection.' "[413] Relying on prior cases, he said that "speech deals with matters of public concern when it can 'be fairly considered as relating to any matter of political, social, or other concern to the community,' or when it is a subject

---

[410] *Id.* at 56.

[411] For an excellent discussion of this case and its significance, *see* Rodney A. Smolla, *Jerry Falwell v. Larry Flynt: The First Amendment on Trial* (1988); Robert Post, The Constitutional Concept of Public Discourse, 103 Harv. L. Rev. 601 (1990).

[412] 131 S. Ct. 1207 (2011).

[413] *Id.* at 1215.

of legitimate news interest; that is, a subject of general interest and of value and concern to the public."[414] He concluded that "[t]he 'content' of Westboro's signs plainly relates to broad issues of interest to society at large, rather than matters of 'purely private concern.' "[415]

It was important to the Court that the protestors were lawfully present and not disruptive in any way. They followed the guidelines provided them by the police. Nor was the Court receptive to Snyder's claim of intrusion. Chief Justice Roberts stated: "Here, Westboro stayed well away from the memorial service. Snyder could see no more than the tops of the signs when driving to the funeral. And there is no indication that the picketing in any way interfered with the funeral service itself. We decline to expand the captive audience doctrine to the circumstances presented here."[416]

Ultimately, *Snyder v. Phelps* reaffirms that speech cannot be punished or be the basis for liability just because it is offensive, even deeply offensive. The case indicated that there cannot be liability for intentional infliction of emotional distress for speech that is otherwise protected by the First Amendment. But this does not mean that there never can be such liability; if it is for speech that is otherwise unprotected— such as for "true threats"— there could be tort liability. After *Snyder v. Phelps*, the federal government and many states have adopted laws creating buffer zones around military funerals as a way of trying to balance speech interests with those of privacy and sensibility of grieving family members.

§11.3.5.5 Public Disclosure of Private Facts

Information Obtained from Public Records and Truthfully Reported

The tort of public disclosure of private facts, a tort for invasion of privacy, exists if there is publication of nonpublic information that is not "of legitimate concern to the public" and that the reasonable person would find offensive to have published.[417] Unlike defamation where the information is false and a retraction conceivably could lessen the harm to reputation, the tort of public disclosure of private facts involves the publication of true information and the harm that is done once publication occurs.

The Supreme Court has held that the First Amendment prevents liability for public disclosure of private facts if the information was lawfully obtained from public records and is truthfully reported. In *Cox Broadcasting Corp. v. Cohn*, a broadcast reporter obtained and reported the name of a rape victim from court records that were available to the public.[418] A Georgia law prohibited the publication of a

---

[414] *Id.* at 1216.
[415] *Id.*
[416] *Id.* at 1220.
[417] Restatement (Second) of Torts §652(D) (1977).
[418] 420 U.S. 469 (1975).

rape victim's identity. The father of the girl who had been raped and murdered sued for invasion of privacy. The Supreme Court said that the First Amendment barred liability because the information had been lawfully obtained from court records and truthfully reported. The Court stressed that the First Amendment protects the publication of information "obtained from public records—more specifically, from judicial records which are maintained in connection with a public prosecution and which themselves are open to public inspection."[419]

The Court followed this same reasoning in *Smith v. Daily Mail Publishing Co.*, where the Court declared unconstitutional a state law that prohibited the publication of the name of a child who was a defendant in a criminal proceeding.[420] The Court relied on *Cox Broadcasting* and held that "if a newspaper lawfully obtains truthful information about a matter of public significance then state officials may not constitutionally punish publication of the information, absent a need to further a state interest of the highest order."[421] Likewise, in *Oklahoma Publishing Co. v. District Court*, the Court declared unconstitutional a court order that prevented the publication of a juvenile's name and photograph that had been lawfully obtained in a court proceeding.[422] The Court found that *Cox Broadcasting* was controlling and said that "the First and Fourteenth Amendments will not permit a state court to prohibit the publication of widely disseminated information obtained at court proceedings which were in fact open to the public."[423]

In *Florida Star v. B.J.F.*,[424] the Court applied *Cox Broadcasting* and *Smith* to hold that there cannot be liability for invasion of privacy when there is the truthful reporting of information lawfully obtained from public records, at least unless there is a state interest of the highest order justifying liability. A newspaper reporter obtained a rape victim's name from publicly released police records. The name was published in the newspaper, even though Florida law prohibited the publication of the name of a victim of a sexual offense. A jury awarded the victim $75,000 in compensatory damages and $25,000 in punitive damages.

The Supreme Court overturned this liability. The Court began by refusing to hold that "truthful publication may never be punished consistent with the First Amendment."[425] But the Court said that liability for the truthful reporting of information lawfully obtained from public records and concerning a matter of public significance would be allowed only if there was an interest of the highest order. The Court explained that the rape victim's name was lawfully obtained from police records and was truthfully communicated. The Court rejected the claim that protecting the privacy of rape victims was a sufficient interest to justify liability. The Court emphasized the failings of the Florida law that created liability

---

[419] *Id.* at 491.

[420] 443 U.S. 97 (1979).

[421] *Id.* at 103.

[422] 430 U.S. 308 (1977).

[423] *Id.* at 310. *See also* Globe Newspapers Co. v. Superior Court, 457 U.S. 596 (1982) (declaring unconstitutional a state law that completely prohibited the press from attending rape trials in which the victim is a minor).

[424] 491 U.S. 524 (1989).

[425] *Id.* at 532.

for publishing a rape victim's identity, including that it allowed liability where the information was released by the government, that it permitted liability without any scienter requirement, and that it applied only to actions of the mass media.

The Court stressed that its "holding . . . is limited."[426] The Court said: "We do not hold that truthful publication is automatically constitutionally protected, or that there is no zone of personal privacy within which the State may protect the individual from intrusion by the press, or even that a State may never punish publication of the name of a victim of a sexual offense. We hold only that where a newspaper publishes truthful information which it has lawfully obtained, punishment may lawfully be imposed, if at all, only when narrowly tailored to a state interest of the highest order."[427]

These cases can be criticized for giving too much weight to freedom of speech and not enough to protecting privacy. Some argue that there is little public benefit to knowing a rape victim's identity, but significant harm to the victim who does not want her name published.[428] Moreover, fear of such publicity may discourage other rape victims from reporting the crime. But the Court's rulings reflect the principle that the First Amendment must virtually always protect the publication of true information.[429] Moreover, there is an important First Amendment value in allowing the press to report what is contained in government records. *Cox Broadcasting, Smith,* and *Florida Star* all involved liability for information gained lawfully from government documents.

This principle, protecting publication of material gained from public records, has been followed in other cases as well. In *Landmark Communications, Inc. v. Virginia,* the Supreme Court held unconstitutional a state statute that created criminal liability for divulging or publishing truthful information regarding confidential proceedings of a judicial inquiry board.[430] A newspaper was convicted for violating this statute for accurately reporting that the Virginia Judicial Inquiry and Review Commission was initiating an investigation of a state court judge.

The Court said that "the publication Virginia seeks to punish under its statute lies near the core of the First Amendment, and the Commonwealth's interests advanced by the imposition of criminal sanctions are insufficient to justify the actual and potential encroachments on freedom of speech and of the press which follow therefrom."[431] The Court said that the "Commonwealth has offered little more than assertion and conjecture to support its claim that without criminal sanctions the objectives of the statutory scheme would be seriously undermined."[432]

---

[426] *Id.* at 541.

[427] *Id.*

[428] *See, e.g.,* Ruth Gavison, Too Early for a Requiem, 43 S. Cal. L. Rev. 437, 448 (1992).

[429] Marc A. Franklin, Constitutional Libel Law: The Role of Content, 34 UCLA L. Rev. 1657, 1674 n.79 (1987).

[430] 435 U.S. 829 (1978).

[431] *Id.* at 838.

[432] *Id.* at 841. In *Butterworth v. Smith,* 494 U.S. 624 (1990), the Court declared unconstitutional a state law that prohibited grand jury witnesses from ever publicly disclosing their own testimony. The Court again emphasized that the information was truthfully reported and that there was no justification for prohibiting witnesses from disclosing their own testimony.

Information from Nongovernment Sources

All of these cases involve the truthful publication of information gained from the government. In *Bartnicki v. Vopper*, the Court considered privacy claims when the information was illegally obtained from nongovernment sources.[433]

Gloria Bartnicki worked for the Pennsylvania Educators' Association and helped local teachers' unions as they negotiated new contracts with school boards. She was in Wyoming, Pennsylvania, and while on her cellular telephone had a conversation with the president of the local teachers' union. They clearly thought that they were having a private conversation, but unknown to them, it was illegally intercepted and recorded. A tape of the phone conversation was given to the president of a local taxpayers' union that was opposing a pay raise for the teachers. The tape was given to a local radio talk show host, Fred Vopper, who played it twice on his program. Bartnicki sued the radio station and Vopper on various state and federal claims.

The Supreme Court, in a 6-to-3 decision with Justice Stevens writing for the majority, concluded that allowing liability in these circumstances would violate the First Amendment. Justice Stevens repeatedly emphasized the narrowness of the Court's holding. He said that the press was protected here because it did not participate in the illegal interception and recording, and because the tape concerned a matter of public importance. Justice Stevens concluded: "In this case, privacy concerns give way when balanced against the interest in publishing matters of public importance. . . . One of the costs associated with participation in public affairs is an attendant loss of privacy. We think it clear that a stranger's illegal conduct does not suffice to remove the First Amendment shield from speech about a matter of public concern."[434]

Justice Breyer wrote a concurring opinion, joined by Justice O'Connor, to stress the narrowness of the Court's holding. He said: "I join the Court's opinion because I agree with its 'narrow' holding, limited to the special circumstances present here: (1) the radio broadcasters acted lawfully (up to the time of final public disclosure); and (2) the information publicized involved a matter of unusual public concern, namely a threat of potential physical harm to others."[435] The latter refers to a statement made during the conversation by the president of the local teachers' union that if the school board did not agree to their demands, they would have to go "blow away the porch" of the school board president's house. Although this clearly seems to be hyperbole in a private conversation, it was given great weight by Justice Breyer.

Chief Justice Rehnquist wrote a dissenting opinion, joined by Justices Scalia and Thomas, in which he stressed the chilling effect that the ruling would have on speech. He said that people would be less likely to use cell phones for communication once they learned that illegally intercepted calls could be broadcast so long as the media did not participate in the interception or recording.

---

[433] 532 U.S. 514 (2001).
[434] *Id.* at 536.
[435] *Id.* at 535-536 (Breyer, J., concurring).

Although both the majority and concurring opinions repeatedly emphasize the narrowness of the decision, it seems broader in its significance than they acknowledge. This is the first time that the Court has considered a privacy claim when the information comes from nongovernment sources. Also, it is the first time that the Court has dealt with information that was illegally obtained. Nonetheless, the Court found that freedom of speech and press outweigh the privacy interests involved.

Future Approaches

In the years ahead, the Court likely often will have to return to the tension between freedom of the press and the right of privacy. The proliferation of media, especially the Internet, and a constant obsession with celebrity make this inevitable. Perhaps the Court will use the categories developed in the defamation context and draw distinctions based on the identity of the plaintiff. Public officials and public figures obviously have less expectation of privacy than private figures.

The Court also is likely to struggle in defining what is a matter of "public concern." *Florida Star* mentions that even when information is obtained from government records, it must be of public concern in order for publication to be protected by the First Amendment. In *Bartnicki*, the Court said that there could not be liability, in part, because the conversation involved a matter of "public importance."

The problem, however, again will be in defining "public concern." If it is determined by the public's interest in the information, then virtually always the media will prevail. But if it is determined by a court based on how much the public really should be interested in the information, judges will be in the role of deciding what is in the enlightened best interest of the people.

§11.3.5.6 Right of Publicity

Protection of Commercial Value

The right of publicity protects the ability of a person to control the commercial value of his or her name, likeness, or performance. In *Zacchini v. Scripps-Howard Broadcasting Co.*, the Court held that a state may allow liability for invasion of this right when a television station broadcast a tape of an entire performance without the performer's authorization.[436] A television station broadcast a 15-second tape of a circus act where an individual was a "human cannonball" shot from a cannon into a net. The Supreme Court held that the broadcast station could be held liable because it broadcast the entire performance without authorization. The Court noted, however, that the plaintiff would have to prove damages and

---

[436] 433 U.S. 562 (1977).

noted that it was quite possible that "respondent's newsbroadcast increased the value of petitioner's performance by stimulating the public's interest in seeing the act live."[437]

The *Zacchini* Court emphasized that "the State's interest is closely analogous to the goals of patent and copyright law, focusing on the right of the individual to reap the reward of his endeavors."[438] The Court has held that the First Amendment does not protect the right to publish speech owned by another. In *Harper & Row v. Nation Enterprises*, the Court held that a magazine could be held liable for publishing copyrighted material.[439] An article in *Nation* magazine contained 300 words from a 200,000-word manuscript written by former President Gerald Ford that had been under contract for publication, in excerpt form, in *Time* magazine. *Time* canceled its contract after the *Nation* article appeared.

The Supreme Court held that the First Amendment did not protect *Nation* from liability for copyright infringement. Justice O'Connor, writing for the Court, said that "[i]n our haste to disseminate news, it should not be forgotten that the Framers intended copyright itself to be the engine of free expression. By establishing a marketable right to use of one's expression, copyright supplies the economic incentive to create and disseminate ideas."[440] The Court also rejected the argument that the publication should be considered to be "fair use" under the copyright law. Justice O'Connor said: "In view of the First Amendment protections already embodied in the Copyright Act's distinction between copyrightable expression and uncopyrightable facts and ideas, and the latitude for scholarship and comment traditionally afforded by fair use, we see no warrant for expanding the doctrine of fair use to create what amounts to a public figure exception to copyright."[441]

Zacchini and *Harper & Row* both reflect the Court's willingness to allow liability for publications that decrease the commercial value of the speech of others. Yet what is troubling about these cases is that in both instances liability was created for reporting in news stories. *Zacchini* involved a story on a news broadcast; *Harper & Row* involved an article that contained verbatim quotes in a larger story. Neither case involved the appropriation of the name or likeness or performance of another for commercial exploitation, though, of course, the magazine hoped to sell more copies because it had the article based on the Ford manuscript and the television station hoped to increase its viewers by broadcasting the act of the human cannonball.

[437] *Id.* at 575 n.12.
[438] *Id.* at 573.
[439] 471 U.S. 539 (1985).
[440] *Id.* at 558.
[441] *Id.* at 560.

§11.3.6   Symbolic Speech: Conduct That Communicates

§11.3.6.1   What Is Speech?

Conduct as Speech

People often communicate through symbols other than words. Marches, picketing, armbands, and peace signs are just a few examples of obviously expressive conduct. To deny First Amendment protection for such forms of communication would mean a loss of some of the most effective means of communicating messages. Also, words are obviously symbols, and there is no reason why the First Amendment should be limited to protecting just these symbols to the exclusion of all others.

Thus, the Supreme Court long has protected conduct that communicates under the First Amendment. For example, in *Stromberg v. California*, the Court declared unconstitutional a state law that prohibited the display of a "red flag."[442] In *West Virginia State Board of Education v. Barnette*, the Supreme Court invalidated a law that required that students salute the flag.[443] The Court found that the state statute impermissibly compelled expression and emphasized that saluting, or not saluting, a flag is a form of speech.[444] The Court explained that "[s]ymbolism is a primitive but effective way of communicating ideas. The use of an emblem or flag to symbolize some system, idea, institution, or personality is a short cut from mind to mind."[445]

Conduct of all sorts can convey a message. Yet if taken to the extreme, it would mean that virtually every criminal law would have to meet strict scrutiny because any criminal defendant could argue that his or her conduct was meant to communicate a message. Two interrelated questions thus emerge: When should conduct be analyzed under the First Amendment; and what should be the test for analyzing whether conduct that communicates is protected by the First Amendment?

When Is Conduct Communicative?

The Supreme Court observed that "[i]t is possible to find some kernel of expression in almost every activity a person undertakes—for example, walking down the street, or meeting one's friends at a shopping mall—but such a kernel is not sufficient to bring the activity within the protection of the First Amendment."[446] In *Spence v. Washington*, the Court considered the issue of when conduct should be regarded as communicative.[447] An individual who taped a peace sign on an

---

442   283 U.S. 359 (1931).
443   319 U.S. 624 (1943).
444   The compelled speech aspect of *Barnette* is discussed above in §11.2.4.3.
445   319 U.S. at 632.
446   City of Dallas v. Stanglin, 490 U.S. 19, 25 (1989).
447   418 U.S. 405 (1974).

American flag after the killing of students at Kent State was convicted of violating a state law prohibiting flag desecration.

The Supreme Court, in a per curiam opinion, reversed the conviction and found that the act was speech protected by the First Amendment. The Court said that "this was not an act of mindless nihilism. Rather, it was a pointed expression of anguish by appellant about the then-current domestic and foreign affairs of his government."[448] The Court emphasized two factors in concluding that the conduct was communicative: "An intent to convey a particularized message was present, and in the surrounding circumstances the likelihood was great that the message would be understood by those who viewed it."[449]

In other words, under this approach, conduct is analyzed as speech under the First Amendment if, first, there is the intent to convey a specific message and, second, there is a substantial likelihood that the message would be understood by those receiving it. Problems in applying this test are inevitable. How is it to be decided whether a person intended an act to communicate a message? Is it subjective, in which case a person always can claim such an intent in a hope to avoid punishment, or is it objective from the perspective of the reasonable listener, in which case it collapses the first part of the test into the second? How is it to be decided whether the message is sufficiently understood by the audience? Moreover, why should protection of speech depend on the sophistication and perceptiveness of the audience? There, for example, might be great works of art where people fail to comprehend the message intended by an artist.

Examples of Expressive Conduct

There are many examples of conduct that the Supreme Court has properly recognized as communicative.[450] For example, in *Tinker v. Des Moines Independent Community School District*, the Court held that wearing a black armband to protest the Vietnam War was speech protected by the First Amendment.[451] The Court explained that "the wearing of an armband for the purpose of expressing certain views is the type of symbolic act that is within the First Amendment; it is closely akin to 'pure speech.' "[452] In terms of the *Spence* test, there is little doubt that the armband was worn to communicate a message and that those seeing it, in the context of the times, would understand it as a symbol of protest against the Vietnam War.

---

[448] *Id.* at 410.

[449] *Id.* at 410-411.

[450] *See also Schacht v. United States*, 398 U.S. 58 (1970), declaring unconstitutional a federal law that allowed wearing a military uniform only "if the portrayal does not tend to discredit" the armed forces. This law obviously was content-based: The symbol of the uniform could be used to express a promilitary view, but not an antimilitary sentiment.

[451] 393 U.S. 503 (1969). *Tinker* also is discussed in §11.4.4 concerning the issue of when schools may regulate speech.

[452] *Id.* at 505.

§11.3.6.2 When May the Government Regulate Conduct That Communicates?

The *O'Brien* Test

Finding that conduct communicates does not mean that it is immune from government regulation. The question then arises as to whether the government has sufficient justification for regulating the conduct. In *United States v. O'Brien*, the Court formulated a test for evaluating the constitutional protection for conduct that communicates.[453] *O'Brien* involved individuals who burned their draft cards to protest the Vietnam War in violation of a federal law, amended in 1965 to make it a crime to knowingly "destroy" or "knowingly mutilate" draft registration certificates.

The Court said that "when 'speech' and 'nonspeech' elements are combined in the same course of conduct, a sufficiently important governmental interest in regulating the nonspeech element can justify incidental limits on First Amendment freedoms."[454] The Court then articulated a test for evaluating conduct that communicates under the First Amendment. Chief Justice Warren, writing for the Court, said: "[A] governmental regulation is sufficiently justified if it is within the constitutional power of the Government; if it furthers an important or substantial governmental interest; if the governmental interest is unrelated to the suppression of free expression; and if the incidental restriction on First Amendment freedoms is no greater than is essential to the furtherance of that interest."[455]

In other words, the government can regulate conduct that communicates if it has an important interest unrelated to suppression of the message and if the impact on communication is no more than necessary to achieve the government's purpose. The test is thus very similar, if not identical, to intermediate scrutiny.

The *O'Brien* Court found that this test was met in the government's prohibition of draft card burning. The Court identified several justifications, unrelated to suppression of speech, for the prohibition of draft card destruction or mutilation. The Court said, for example, that requiring the presence of draft cards facilitates emergency military mobilization, aids communication with a person's draft board because the address is listed on the card, and reminds individuals to notify their draft board of any change in address or changes related to draft status.

All of these justifications can be questioned. It seems highly unlikely that the military ever would induct people by pulling them over, inspecting draft cards, and conscripting those who were draft eligible. Moreover, people can communicate with their draft boards or remember to notify them of a change of address without carrying their draft card.

The clear purpose of the amendment to the Selective Service Act was to stop draft card burning as a form of political protest. Yet the Court said that this motive was irrelevant. The Court said that "[i]t is a familiar principle of constitutional law

[453] 391 U.S. 367 (1968).
[454] *Id.* at 376.
[455] *Id.* at 377.

that this Court will not strike down an otherwise constitutional statute on the basis of an alleged illicit legislative motive."[456] The Court explained that "[i]nquiries into congressional motives or purposes are a hazardous matter."[457]

The Court, however, frequently engages in exactly such inquiry into motives. In the area of equal protection law, for example, courts determine whether there is a discriminatory purpose behind a law.[458] In First Amendment analysis, whether a law is content-based or content-neutral often turns on whether the government's purpose is to suppress a particular message.[459] It is unclear why the Court categorically rejects motive analysis in this context. Moreover, the *O'Brien* test itself seems to require analysis of motive, at least in some areas. Under this approach, government can regulate conduct that communicates only if it has an important *purpose* unrelated to suppression of the message. Despite *O'Brien*'s statement that motive is irrelevant, it is quite important under the test it formulated.

Flag Desecration

A major area where the Supreme Court has applied the *O'Brien* test is with regard to flag burning and flag desecration laws. After initial cases that protected flag desecration on narrow grounds, but without resolving the issue, the Court in 1989 and again in 1990 made it clear that flag burning is a constitutionally protected form of speech.

In *Street v. New York*, the Court overturned a conviction of an individual who burned a flag in anger after learning that James Meredith had been shot.[460] The individual exclaimed, "We don't need no damn flag. [If] they let that happen to Meredith we don't need an American flag."[461] The Court said that the law was unconstitutional because it allowed the individual to be punished solely for speaking contemptuously about the flag; indeed, it was impossible to tell in *Street* whether the punishment was for the speech about the flag or for its destruction.

In *Smith v. Goguen*, the Court declared unconstitutional on vagueness grounds a state law that made it a crime for any individual to "publicly mutilate, trample upon, deface or treat contemptuously the flag of the United States."[462] An individual was convicted for sewing, to the seat of his pants, a small cloth replica of the flag. The Court found that the state law was void on vagueness grounds because of the inherent ambiguity in deciding what is contemptuous treatment of the flag.

In *Spence v. Washington*, described above, the Court found that the First Amendment protected the right of an individual to tape a peace symbol to a

---

[456] *Id.* at 383.
[457] *Id.*
[458] *See, e.g.,* Washington v. Davis, 426 U.S. 229 (1976), discussed in §9.3.3.2.
[459] *See* City of Renton v. Playtime Theatres, 475 U.S. at 47; this aspect of the case is discussed in §11.2.1.
[460] 394 U.S. 576 (1969).
[461] *Id.* at 579.
[462] 415 U.S. 566 (1974).

flag.[463] The Court emphasized that the protestor's "message was direct, likely to be understood, and within the contours of the First Amendment."[464]

The Court went even further in 1989 in *Texas v. Johnson*, where it declared unconstitutional a state law prohibiting any person to "deface, damage or otherwise physically mistreat" a flag in a way that the actor knows "will seriously offend one or more persons likely to observe or discover his action."[465] An individual was convicted of violating the law and sentenced to a year in prison for burning a flag as part of a protest at the Republican National Convention.

Justice Brennan, writing for the majority in the 5-to-4 decision, held that the Texas law was unconstitutional. Brennan emphasized that unlike *O'Brien*, the government's interest was not unrelated to suppression of the message; to the contrary, the law's purpose was to keep the flag from being used to communicate protest or dissent. Brennan also stressed that the Texas law did not prevent all flag destruction, but rather applied only when there would be offense to others. The Court said that "[i]f there is a bedrock principle underlying the First Amendment, it is that the Government may not prohibit the expression of an idea simply because it finds the idea itself offensive or disagreeable."[466]

Chief Justice Rehnquist wrote a dissenting opinion that was joined by Justices White and O'Connor. Rehnquist emphasized the importance of the flag as a national symbol and maintained that flag burning is "no essential part of any exposition of ideas" and whatever message was transmitted by the defendant's flag burning could have "been conveyed . . . in a dozen different ways."[467] Rehnquist said that "flag burning is the equivalent of an inarticulate grunt or roar that is most likely to be indulged in not to express any particular idea, but to antagonize others."[468]

Texas v. Johnson produced an enormous amount of controversy and proposals to amend the Constitution to prohibit flag burning. In an effort to avoid such an amendment, Congress adopted the Flag Protection Act of 1989, which made it a crime for any person to knowingly mutilate, deface, defile, burn, or trample upon the flag. Unlike the Texas law, punishment was not limited to situations where the conduct would offend another.

In *United States v. Eichman*, the Supreme Court declared this law unconstitutional.[469] The split was identical to that in *Texas v. Johnson*: Brennan, Marshall, Blackmun, Scalia, and Kennedy were in the majority; Rehnquist, White, Stevens, and O'Connor dissented. Justice Brennan again wrote the opinion for the Court and said that the statute had the "same fundamental flaw" as the Texas law that had been invalidated a year earlier.[470] The law's primary purpose was to keep the flag from being used to communicate protest or dissent. The Court said that this

---

[463] 418 U.S. 405 (1974).
[464] *Id.* at 415.
[465] 491 U.S. 397, 400 (1989).
[466] *Id.* at 414.
[467] *Id.* at 430-431 (Rehnquist, J., dissenting).
[468] *Id.* at 432.
[469] 486 U.S. 310 (1990).
[470] *Id.* at 317.

was a purpose directly focused on the message and that therefore strict scrutiny was the appropriate test.

From one perspective, these decisions can be criticized for failing to recognize that the flag is a unique symbol and deserving of protection. As Rehnquist expressed in an earlier case, the "true nature of the State's interest [is] preserving the flag as an important symbol of nationhood and unity."[471]

But on the other hand, it is precisely the strong emotional attachment to the flag that makes its desecration a uniquely powerful form of expression. Also, laws that prohibit flag burning or defacement are inherently content-based: The government is trying to preserve the flag as a symbol that communicates patriotism, but not of protest or dissent. Such a content-based restriction of speech only can be justified if strict scrutiny is met. The government's claim that flag destruction must be prohibited to preserve the flag as a symbol of national unity assumes that flag burning undermines the ability of the flag to serve as such a symbol. No such evidence exists. In fact, the more flag burning is met by intense reaction, the more the flag as a symbol is reinforced.

Nude Dancing

In the flag burning cases, *Texas v. Johnson* and *United States v. Eichman*, the Court did not apply the *O'Brien* test because it concluded that the restriction on speech was directly related to the message. However, in *Barnes v. Glen Theatre, Inc.*, the plurality applied the *O'Brien* test to conclude that nude dancing was not protected by the First Amendment.[472] *Barnes*, which is discussed above in §11.3.4.4, involved the constitutionality of the application of a state's law prohibiting public nudity to prevent nude dancing.

The plurality opinion by Chief Justice Rehnquist characterized nude dancing as conduct that communicates and expressly applied the *O'Brien* test. The Court found that it is within a state's police power to prohibit public nudity, that there is an important interest unrelated to suppression of the message because of the state's interest in morality, and that the impact on communication was no greater than necessary because the dancers could still express their message, albeit with clothes. Justice Scalia, in an opinion concurring in the judgment, said that there was no basis for a First Amendment challenge because the state law was applicable to everyone and was not motivated by a desire to interfere with speech.[473] Justice Souter also wrote an opinion concurring in the judgment and emphasized the secondary effects of nude dancing, such as on property values.

What is troubling about the majority's application of the *O'Brien* test is the absence of a purpose for prohibiting nude dancing that is unrelated to suppression of the message. The state's justification was a purely moral one—its view that the message and its means of expression are immoral. Moreover, the Court's judgment that the dancers could continue with scanty clothes misses the plaintiff's

---

[471] Spence v. Washington, 418 U.S. at 421 (citation omitted).
[472] 501 U.S. 560 (1991).
[473] *Id.* at 576.

argument that nude dancing uniquely communicates in a way different from even minimal clothing.

In *City of Erie v. Pap's A.M.*, the Supreme Court reaffirmed the power of local governments to ban nude dancing, though on different grounds.[474] Erie, Pennsylvania, adopted an ordinance that prohibited public nudity. The unquestioned objective of the law was to close down the Kandyland nude dancing establishment.

The Supreme Court, in a 6-to-3 decision, upheld the decision, but there was no majority opinion. Justice O'Connor wrote for the plurality and recognized that nude dancing is conduct that communicates. The plurality opinion said that the government could ban such conduct so as to prevent the undesirable secondary effects of nude dancing, such as crime in the area. She wrote: "We conclude that Erie's asserted interest in combating the negative secondary effects associated with adult entertainment establishments like Kandyland is unrelated to the suppression of the erotic message conveyed by nude dancing. The asserted interests of regulating conduct through a public nudity ban and of combating the harmful secondary effects associated with nude dancing are undeniably important."[475]

Justice O'Connor dismissed the dissent's objection that there was no sufficient evidence of the adverse effects of nude dancing. Justice Stevens, for example, said that there is no evidence that dancers with pasties and G-strings, allowed under the ordinance, would cause less crime than completely nude dancers.[476] But the plurality opinion said that the city could rely on the experience elsewhere and the observations of the city council members in concluding that nude dancing causes undesirable consequences.[477]

The decision is important in reaffirming the ability of local governments to regulate sexual speech such as nude dancing. But Justice O'Connor's approach is troubling in allowing the restriction of speech based on its harms without requiring any proof of the adverse effects.

§11.3.6.3   Spending Money as Political Speech

Political Speech as the Core of the First Amendment

Political speech—speech in connection with elections and the electoral process—is at the very core of the First Amendment. If there is a hierarchy of protected speech, political speech occupies the top rung. The Supreme Court has declared that "the First Amendment has its 'fullest and most urgent application' to speech

---

[474] 529 U.S. 277 (2000).

[475] *Id.* at 296.

[476] *Id.* at 323 (Stevens, J., dissenting).

[477] Justice Scalia, in a concurring opinion joined by Justice Thomas, argued that the law prohibiting public nudity could not be challenged on First Amendment grounds because it was a neutral law of general applicability. *Id.* at 307-309 (Scalia, J., concurring).

uttered during a campaign for political office."[478] The Court has explained that "[w]hatever differences may exist about interpretations of the First Amendment, there is practically universal agreement that a major purpose of that Amendment was to protect the free discussion of governmental affairs. This of course includes discussion of candidates, structures and forms of government, the manner in which government is operated or should be operated, and all such matters relating to political processes."[479]

Thus, restrictions on political speech are subjected to strict scrutiny. For example, in *Brown v. Hartlage*, the Court held that it violated the First Amendment when a court voided an election based on a state's corrupt practices law because a candidate had promised to work for a lower salary.[480] The Court said that "[w]hen a State seeks to restrict directly the offer of ideas by a candidate to the voters, the First Amendment surely requires that the restriction be demonstrably supported by not only a legitimate state interest, but a compelling one, and that the restriction operate without unnecessarily circumscribing protected expression."[481] The Court held that the candidate's promise to work at a lower salary was speech during a campaign and that the government's interest in preventing corruption did not justify invalidating the election.

Strict scrutiny does not mean that all restrictions on political speech will be invalidated. For instance, in *Burson v. Freeman*, the Court upheld a state law that prohibited either the soliciting of votes or the display or distribution of campaign materials within 100 feet of the entrance of a polling place.[482] The plurality opinion by Justice Blackmun said that strict scrutiny was appropriate because the law was a content-based restriction on speech and a restriction of political speech. But the plurality concluded that this was the "rare case" in which strict scrutiny was satisfied. Justice Blackmun explained that "[a] long history, a substantial consensus, and simple common sense show that some restricted zone around polling places is necessary to protect [the] fundamental right [to vote]. Given the conflict between those two rights [speech and voting], we hold that requiring solicitors to stand 100 feet from the entrances to polling places does not constitute an unconstitutional compromise."[483]

Spending Money in a Campaign as Speech

In light of the strong protection for political speech, the issue arose as to whether the spending of money in connection with political campaigns is a form of speech protected by the First Amendment and, if so, when the government

---

[478] Eu v. San Francisco County Democratic Central Committee, 489 U.S. 214, 223 (1989), quoting Monitor Patriot Co. v. Roy, 401 U.S. at 272.

[479] Mills v. Alabama, 384 U.S. 214, 218-219 (1966). In *Mills*, the Court declared unconstitutional the conviction of a newspaper for editorializing on election day under a law that made it a crime to solicit votes on election day.

[480] 456 U.S. 45 (1982).

[481] *Id.* at 53-54.

[482] 504 U.S. 191 (1992).

[483] *Id.* at 211.

may regulate such expression. The seminal case addressing this issue was *Buckley v. Valeo*, which held that spending money is a form of political speech and articulated the framework for campaign finance law and the First Amendment.[484] *Buckley* involved a challenge to the 1974 amendments to the Federal Election Campaign Act of 1971,[485] a law adopted after the abuses uncovered during the Watergate investigation.

The 1974 amendments were a sweeping reform of campaign financing. First, the law created a limit on campaign contributions. The law imposed a $1,000 ceiling on political contributions made by an individual or a group to candidates for federal office, and a $5,000 limit on contributions by a political committee to a candidate. The law also imposed an annual limit of $25,000 for each contributor. Second, the law created a limit on campaign expenditures. Individuals were limited to spending $1,000 "relative to a clearly identified candidate." The Act also sets limits on expenditures by a candidate from personal funds or the funds from his or her immediate family; the restriction was $50,000 for presidential or vice presidential candidates, $35,000 for Senate candidates, and $25,000 for House candidates. Third, the law created disclosure requirements for individuals and committees giving money to political campaigns. Finally, the law created public funding for presidential elections.

The Court began a lengthy per curiam opinion by noting that the "Act's contribution and expenditure limitations operate in an area of the most fundamental First Amendment activities. Discussion of public issues and debate on the qualifications of candidates are integral to the operation of the system of government established by our Constitution."[486] The Court expressly refused to apply the *O'Brien* test, described above, that is used for conduct that communicates. The Court said that "[t]he expenditure of money simply cannot be equated with such conduct as destruction of a draft card. Some forms of communication made possible by the giving and spending of money involve speech alone, some involve conduct primarily, and some involve a combination of the two."[487] The Court said that even if *O'Brien* was applied, the Act would be treated as a law designed to suppress speech and thus would have to meet strict scrutiny.

Thus, *Buckley* clearly treats spending money in a political campaign as a form of political speech. The Court said that "[a] restriction on the amount of money a person or group can spend on political communication during a campaign necessarily reduces the quantity of expression by restricting the number of issues discussed, the depth of their exploration, and the size of the audience reached. This is because virtually every means of communicating ideas in today's mass society requires the expenditure of money."[488]

---

[484] 424 U.S. 1 (1976). For an excellent description of the background of the case, *see* Richard Hasen, The Nine Lives of *Buckley v. Valeo*, in First Amendment Stories, Richard Garnett & Andrew Koppelman, eds., 2011).

[485] 2 U.S.C. §441 *et seq.*

[486] Buckley v. Valeo, 405 U.S. at 14.

[487] *Id.* at 16.

[488] *Id.* at 19.

The Court drew a distinction between the contribution limits and the expenditure limits, upholding the former and invalidating the latter. In part, the distinction was based on the way in which each affected speech; the Court saw expenditure limits as restricting the nature and quantity of speech that would occur, but saw little direct effect on speech through contribution limits. The Court explained that "[t]he expenditure limitations contained in the Act represent substantial rather than merely theoretical restraints on the quantity and diversity of political speech. . . . By contrast, . . . a limitation on the amount of money a person may give to a candidate or campaign organization [involves] little direct restraint on his political communication, for it permits the symbolic expression of support evidenced by a contribution but does not in any way infringe the contributor's freedom to discuss candidates and issues."[489]

In part, too, the Court's distinction was based on the stronger justifications for contribution as opposed to expenditure limits. The Court said that restrictions on the amount that a person or group could contribute to any particular candidate were justified to prevent "the actuality and appearance of corruption resulting from large individual financial contributions."[490] The Court explained that "[t]o the extent that large contributions are given to secure a political quid pro quo from current and potential office holders, the integrity of our system of representative democracy is undermined. . . . Of almost equal concern as the danger of actual quid pro quo arrangements is the impact of the appearance of corruption stemming from public awareness of the opportunities for abuse inherent in a regime of large individual financial contributions."[491]

In contrast, the Court said that independent expenditures to support a candidate do not have the same risk of corruption or the appearance of corruption. The Court expressly rejected the argument that the government could restrict expenditures so as to equalize political influence. The Court said that "the concept that government may restrict the speech of some elements of our society in order to enhance the relative voice of others is wholly foreign to the First Amendment, which was designed to secure the widest possible dissemination of information from diverse and antagonistic sources and to secure unfettered interchange of ideas for the bringing about of political and social changes desired by the people."[492]

The Court used this same reasoning to invalidate ceilings on overall campaign expenditures by candidates seeking office. The law said that presidential candidates could not spend more than $10 million in seeking nominations and $20 million in the general election campaign and that House candidates could not spend more than $70,000 in a campaign. Spending limits for Senate campaigns depended on the size of the state. The Court again rejected the argument that the government could seek to *equalize* spending in election campaigns. The Court said that reducing "skyrocketing costs of political campaigns" did not justify the

---

[489] *Id.* at 19-21.
[490] *Id.* at 26.
[491] *Id.* at 26-27.
[492] *Id.* at 48-49 (citations omitted).

restrictions on spending; the Court explained that "the First Amendment denies government the power to determine that spending to promote one's political views is wasteful, excessive, or unwise. In the free society ordained by our Constitution it is not the government but the people — individually as citizens and candidates and collectively as associations and political committees—who must retain control over the quantity and range of debate on public issues in political campaigns."[493]

The Court upheld the disclosure requirements imposed by the law because they provide important information to the electorate about candidates, they "deter actual corruption and avoid the appearance of corruption," and they provide crucial information for enforcing the contribution limits in the law.[494] The Court noted, however, that there might be instances involving minor or dissident parties "where the threat to the exercise of First Amendment rights is so serious and the state interest furthered by disclosure so insubstantial that the Act's requirements cannot be constitutionally supplied."[495] The Court said that there was no proof of such an impact in the case before it.

Finally, the Court upheld the provision of the law that provided for public funding of presidential elections. The Court said that such government financing does not restrict speech, but rather increases expression in connection with election campaigns. The Court said that the provision is a "congressional effort, not to abridge, restrict, or censor speech, but rather to use public money to facilitate and enlarge public discussion and participation in the electoral process, goals vital to a self-governing people."[496] The Court said that expenditure limits were permissible as a condition for receipt of such federal money because "acceptance of public financing entails voluntary acceptance of an expenditure ceiling."[497]

Criticisms of *Buckley*

Buckley v. Valeo had an enormous practical impact on the nature of political campaigns. The Court's invalidation of expenditure limits led to the proliferation of political action committees and the continued skyrocketing of the costs of election campaigns. There is widespread criticism that this leads to enormous inequalities in political influence and directly affects who can run for office and who can get elected.[498]

---

[493] *Id.* at 57.

[494] *Id.* at 67.

[495] *Id.* at 71. *See* Brown v. Socialist Workers '74 Campaign Committee, 459 U.S. 87 (1982) (invalidating disclosure requirements as applied to the Socialist Workers Party). The issue of disclosure is discussed in more detail in §11.5.3 concerning freedom of association.

[496] *Id.* at 92-93.

[497] *Id.* at 95. However, in *FEC v. National Conservative Political Action Comm.*, 470 U.S. 480 (1985), the Court declared unconstitutional a statutory provision prohibiting groups from spending more than $1,000 for candidates receiving federal funding.

[498] *See, e.g.*, Jamin B. Raskin & John Bonifaz, The Constitutional Imperative and Practical Superiority of Democratically Financed Elections, 94 Colum. L. Rev. 1160 (1994). For excellent recent discussions of campaign finance and proposals for reform, *see* Richard Hasen, Plutocrats United: Campaign Money, the Supreme Court, and the Distortion of American Elections (forthcoming 2015); Robert Post, Citizens Divided: Campaign Finance Reform and the Constitution (2014).

Buckley has been criticized on many levels. First, the Court's treatment of spending money as speech, rather than as conduct that communicates, has been questioned.[499] Spending money may facilitate speech, and it is a way of expressing support for a candidate, but it is arguably distinguishable from "pure" speech. The contention is that the *O'Brien* test should have been applied, which is less protective of speech, rather than the strict scrutiny test used by the Court.

Second, the Court's distinction between expenditure and contribution limits has been questioned.[500] Elected officials can be influenced by who spends money on their behalf, just as they can be influenced by who directly contributes money to them. The perception of corruption might be generated by large expenditures for a candidate, just as it can be caused by large contributions. Alternatively, some attack the distinction between contributions and expenditures, arguing that the restrictions on the former also should have been declared unconstitutional as violating the First Amendment.[501] Justice Clarence Thomas declared: "I would reject the framework established by *Buckley v. Valeo.* . . . Instead, I begin with the premise that there is no constitutionally significant difference between campaign contributions and expenditures: both forms of speech are central to the First Amendment."[502]

In *Nixon v. Shrink Missouri Government PAC*,[503] the Supreme Court reaffirmed *Buckley*'s distinction between contributions and expenditures, but four Justices sharply disagreed. Three Justices—Kennedy, Scalia, and Thomas—expressly declared their desire to overrule *Buckley*'s approval of contribution limits. One Justice, Stevens, indicated his disagreement with *Buckley*'s premise that spending money is speech and that government restrictions must meet strict scrutiny. Thus, he likely would be willing to overrule *Buckley*'s prohibition of expenditure limits.

Justice Kennedy wrote a strong dissent in which he lamented that "[t]he Court's decision has lasting consequences for political speech in the course of elections, the speech upon which democracy depends."[504] He accused the Court of being "almost indifferent" to freedom of speech and said that he would overrule *Buckley*.[505] Justice Thomas, joined by Justice Scalia, wrote a lengthier dissent, which began by declaring: "In the process of ratifying Missouri's sweeping repression of

---

[499]   *See, e.g.*, J. Skelly Wright, Politics and the Constitution: Is Money Speech?, 85 Yale L.J. 1001 (1976). Justice Stevens expressed this view that spending money in campaigns should be regarded as conduct and not speech. He stated: "Money is property; it is not speech. Speech has the power to inspire volunteers to perform a multitude of tasks on a campaign trail, on a battleground, or even on a football field. Money, meanwhile, has the power to pay hired laborers to perform the same tasks. It does not follow, however, that the First Amendment provides the same measure of protection to the use of money to accomplish such goals as it provides to the use of ideas to achieve the same result." Nixon v. Shrink Missouri Government PAC, 528 U.S. 377, 398 (2000) (Stevens, J., concurring).

[500]   *See, e.g.*, Lillian R. BeVier, Money and Politics: A Perspective on the First Amendment and Campaign Finance Reform, 73 Cal. L. Rev. 1045 (1985).

[501]   Colorado Republican Federal Campaign Committee v. Federal Election Commn., 518 U.S. 604, 640-641 (1996) (Thomas, J., concurring in the judgment and dissenting in part).

[502]   *Id.* at 631, 640.

[503]   528 U.S. 377 (2000), discussed below.

[504]   *Id.* at 405 (Kennedy, J., dissenting).

[505]   *Id.* at 405, 409.

political speech, the Court today adopts the analytical fallacies of our flawed decision in *Buckley v. Valeo*. . . . Under the guise of applying *Buckley*, the Court proceeds to weaken the already enfeebled constitutional protection that *Buckley* afforded campaign contributions. As I indicated [previously], our decision in *Buckley* was in error, and I would overrule it."[506]

While Justices Kennedy, Thomas, and Scalia would overrule *Buckley* and declare contribution limits unconstitutional, Justice Stevens questioned *Buckley*'s premise that spending money is speech and its rejection of expenditure limits. Justice Stevens, in a concurring opinion, said: "Money is property; it is not speech. . . . These property rights are not entitled to the same protection as the right to say what one pleases."[507]

With Chief Justice Roberts and Justice Alito having joined the Court—and in light of their votes with Justices Scalia, Kennedy, and Thomas in *Citizens United v. Federal Election Commission* to protect campaign spending by corporations and unions[508]—there now could be five votes on the Court to find that contribution limits are unconstitutional. As discussed below, in *McCutcheon v. Federal Election Commission*, the Court, in a 5-4 decision with these Justices comprising the majority, declared unconstitutional aggregate contribution limits, restrictions on the total amount that a person can contribute to candidates for federal office or political parties in a two-year period.[509]

Third, many have criticized the Court for giving inadequate weight to the value of equality of influence in political campaigns.[510] Allowing unlimited expenditures allows the wealthy to drown out the voices of those with less money. It thus permits those with money to have much more influence in election campaigns and ultimately with elected officials.[511] Critics argue that equality is a compelling interest that justified the limits on expenditures that the Court invalidated.

The Continuing Distinction Between Contributions and Expenditures

Since *Buckley*, the Court has adhered to the distinction between contributions and expenditures. For example, in *California Medical Association v. Federal Election Commission*, the Supreme Court upheld a provision of the Federal Election Campaign Act that limited the amount that individuals and associations could

---

[506] *Id.* at 410 (Thomas, J., dissenting). In Federal Election Commission v. Colorado Republican Federal Campaign Committee, 533 U.S. 431, 465 (2001) (Thomas, J., dissenting), Justice Thomas again declared: "I continue to believe that *Buckley v. Valeo* should be overruled."

[507] *Id.* at 398-399 (Stevens, J., concurring).

[508] 130 S. Ct. 876 (2010), discussed below.

[509] 134 S. Ct. 1434 (2014).

[510] *See, e.g.*, Marlene Arnold Nicholson, *Buckley v. Valeo*: The Constitutionality of the Federal Election Campaign Act Amendments of 1974, 1977 Wis. L. Rev. 323, 336.

[511] *See, e.g.*, Edward B. Foley, Equal-Dollars-Per-Voter: A Constitutional Principle of Campaign Finance, 94 Colum. L. Rev. 1204 (1994); Jamin Raskin & John Bonifaz, Equal Protection and the Wealth Primary, 11 Yale L. & Poly. Rev. 273 (1993).

contribute to a political action committee.[512] The Court followed the same reasoning as in *Buckley*, concluding that restricting the amount of contributions does not significantly limit speech. The Court said that the speech value of contributions to political action committees is even less than when the money is given to candidates; the money is used for political expression only when spent by the political action committee.

In contrast, in *FEC v. National Conservative PAC*, the Court declared unconstitutional expenditure limits imposed on political action committees by the Presidential Election Campaign Fund Act.[513] The law said that a political action committee could not spend more than $1,000 on behalf of a presidential candidate who accepted public financing. As in *Buckley*, the Court stressed that restrictions on expenditures limited speech; the ability of political action committees to speak in campaigns was restricted by the laws. The Court noted that political action committees allow people to pool their resources to express themselves. The Court concluded, as in *Buckley*, that the expenditure limits violated the First Amendment.

The distinction between contribution and expenditure limits is based on the Court's judgment that contributions to candidates create a greater danger of corruption and the appearance of corruption than expenditures and also that expenditures are much more directly related to speech than contributions. Applying this reasoning, the Court held that contribution limits during ballot referendum campaigns were unconstitutional because there was not the same danger of corruption as when money is given to candidates. In *Citizens Against Rent Control v. City of Berkeley*, the Court declared unconstitutional an ordinance that limited to $250 an individual's contribution to a committee supporting or opposing a ballot referendum.[514] The Court explained that contributions in connection with a ballot initiative do not have the same danger of buying influence with a candidate or of creating the perception of undue influence.

In *Colorado Republican Federal Campaign Committee v. Federal Election Commission*, the Court invoked the distinction between contributions and expenditures to declare unconstitutional a federal law that limited expenditures by a political party on behalf of a candidate.[515] The Federal Election Commission found that expenditures by the Colorado Republican Party attacking the Democratic Party's likely senatorial candidate, Tim Wirth, exceeded the dollar limits imposed upon a political party's expenditures in connection with a general election campaign for congressional office. The plurality's opinion concluded that "the First Amendment prohibits the application of this provision to the kind of expenditure at issue here—an expenditure that the political party had made independently, without coordination with any candidate."[516]

---

[512] 453 U.S. 182 (1981).
[513] 470 U.S. 480 (1985).
[514] 454 U.S. 290 (1981).
[515] 518 U.S. 604 (1996).
[516] *Id.* at 608 (plurality opinion).

Justice Breyer, writing for the plurality, said that the First Amendment protects the right of political parties to make unlimited independent expenditures. He declared: "We do not see how a Constitution that grants to individuals, candidates, and ordinary political committees the right to make unlimited independent expenditures could deny the same right to political parties."[517] The plurality did not rule on whether restrictions on "coordinated" expenditures violate the First Amendment, but instead remanded the case as to that issue.

Justice Kennedy, joined by Chief Justice Rehnquist and Justice Thomas, agreed that the First Amendment is violated by restrictions on expenditures by political parties, but would not have remanded the case for possible proceedings on the constitutionality of restrictions on coordinated expenditures.[518] From his perspective, all restrictions on expenditures by parties are unconstitutional, although some future case might pose the issue of whether restrictions on party contributions are constitutional. Likewise, Justice Thomas would have declared unconstitutional the restrictions on expenditures by parties, but would not have remanded the case.[519] In fact, Justice Thomas argued that the Court should overrule the distinction drawn in *Buckley* between contributions and expenditures and find restrictions on the former to violate the First Amendment.[520]

Justice Stevens, joined by Justice Ginsburg, dissented and argued that all expenditures by political parties should be treated as contributions.[521] He contended that restrictions on spending by political parties avoid "both the appearance and the reality of a corrupt political process."[522] He also maintained that the spending limits are constitutional because "the Government has an important interest in leveling the electoral playing field by constraining the cost of federal campaigns."[523]

After a remand, in *Federal Election Commission v. Colorado Republican Federal Campaign Committee*, the Court rejected a facial challenge to the ban on coordinated expenditures by political parties on behalf of specific candidates.[524] Justice Souter wrote for the majority in a 5-to-4 decision and held that coordinated expenditures are functionally the same as contributions and thus carry the same risk of corruption and the appearance of corruption. Justice Souter said that the case posed two issues: "does limiting coordinated spending impose a unique burden on parties, and is there reason to think that coordinated spending by a party would raise the risk of corruption posed when others spend in coordination with a candidate?"[525]

As to the former, the Court rejected the claim that the ban on coordinated expenditures disadvantages parties more than other groups that wish to donate money in that manner. As to the latter, the Court explained that allowing

[517] *Id.* at 618.
[518] *Id.* at 630-631 (Kennedy, J., concurring in the judgment and dissenting in part).
[519] *Id.* at 631 (Thomas, J., concurring in the judgment and dissenting in part).
[520] *Id.* at 635-636.
[521] *Id.* at 648 (Stevens, J., dissenting).
[522] *Id.*
[523] *Id.* at 649.
[524] 533 U.S. 431 (2001).
[525] *Id.* at 445.

coordinated expenditures would create a way to circumvent contributing limits. Justice Souter observed: "The idea was that coordinated expenditures are as useful to the candidate as cash, and that such 'disguised contributions' might be given 'as a quid pro quo for improper commitments from the candidate' (in contrast to independent expenditures, which are poor sources of leverage for a spender because they might be duplicative or counterproductive from a candidate's point of view)."[526]

The Court said that evidence supports the government's concern that coordinated expenditures can be used to circumvent expenditure limits. Justice Souter concluded: "We hold that a party's coordinated expenditures, unlike expenditures truly independent, may be restricted to minimize circumvention of contribution limits."[527]

The Supreme Court also reaffirmed *Buckley*'s distinction between contributions and expenditures in *Nixon v. Shrink Missouri Government PAC*.[528] *Nixon* involved a Missouri law that set contribution limits for candidates to state government office. The statute set limits ranging from $1,075 for candidates to statewide office, such as the governor or attorney general, to $275 for candidates for state representative or for any office for which there are fewer than 100,000 people represented.

The United States Court of Appeals for the Eighth Circuit declared Missouri's contribution limits unconstitutional.[529] The court of appeals stated that the Missouri law had to meet strict scrutiny in its restriction of contributions and held that the government failed to meet this burden by proving a corruption problem in the state that justified such limits. The court said that the First Amendment required "some demonstrable evidence that there were genuine problems that resulted from contributions in amounts greater than the limits in place."[530]

If the Supreme Court had affirmed the Eighth Circuit, then contribution limits that have been established in many states would be vulnerable.[531] The Court then would have needed to define what type of proof or what sort of corruption would be sufficient to justify specific contribution limits. This obviously would have opened the door to challenges to every contribution limit, and many likely would have been struck down.

Instead, the Supreme Court in *Nixon*, by a 6-to-3 margin, upheld the Missouri law. Justice Souter wrote the opinion for the Court and began by reciting at length the key aspects of *Buckley v. Valeo*: that spending money for a campaign is speech and restrictions must meet strict scrutiny and that contribution limits are constitutional, while expenditure limits are unconstitutional.[532] Justice Souter then said that the Missouri contribution limits were constitutional for the same reasons that

---

[526] *Id.* at 446.

[527] *Id.* at 465.

[528] 528 U.S. 377 (2000).

[529] Shrink Missouri Government PAC v. Nixon, 161 F.3d 519 (8th Cir. 1998).

[530] *Id.* at 521.

[531] For a description of the various state laws, *see* E. Feigenbaum & J. Palmer, Campaign Finance Law 98 (1998).

[532] 528 U.S. at 385-389.

the contribution limits were upheld in *Buckley*; large contributions risk corruption and the appearance of corruption. The Court acknowledged that there may be laws where the judiciary will need to examine whether there is sufficient evidence of a problem to justify the restrictions, but the Court said that "this case does not present a close call requiring further definition of whatever the State evidentiary obligation may be."[533]

Nor was the Court willing to consider whether inflation since *Buckley* makes contribution limits of the sort approved then too low now. Although the challengers pressed this argument, the Court understandably was reluctant to try and calibrate what specific contribution limits are appropriate for particular states or times.[534]

In short, the Court decided *Nixon* by reaffirming and applying *Buckley v. Valeo*. Indeed, Justice Souter concluded the majority opinion by stating: "There is no reason in logic or evidence to doubt the sufficiency of *Buckley* to govern this case in support of the Missouri statute."[535]

Most recently, in 2014, in *McCutcheon v. Federal Election Commission*, which is discussed below, the Court declined to reconsider the distinction between expenditures and contributions and declared: "The parties and *amici curiae* spend significant energy debating whether the line that *Buckley* drew between contributions and expenditures should remain the law. Notwithstanding the robust debate, we see no need in this case to revisit *Buckley*'s distinction between contributions and expenditures and the corollary distinction in the applicable standards of review."[536]

The Bipartisan Campaign Finance Reform Act

The Bipartisan Campaign Finance Reform Act of 2002 was the result of years of hearings and debate. Congress sought to close loopholes and solve problems that had developed under the *Buckley* framework. First, the law sought to restrict "soft money" in political campaigns. "Soft money" is money raised and spent by political parties that was not covered by limits on contributions to candidates or committees. Corporations and unions that could not legally contribute directly to candidates or their committees circumvented this by giving money to the political parties, which then spent the funds. Similarly, individuals who already had contributed the maximum amount owed by law got around the limit by giving to the political parties.

As the Supreme Court noted in *McConnell v. Federal Election Commission*,[537] the amount of soft money raised and spent by political parties has increased enormously, from $21.6 million in 1984 to $498 million in 2000.[538] The soft money contributions often were much larger than would be allowed by federal law. For exam-

---

[533] *Id.* at 393.

[534] However, in *Randall v. Sorrell*, 548 U.S. 230 (2006), discussed below, the Court found that contribution limits were so low as to violate the First Amendment.

[535] 528 U.S. at 397-398.

[536] 134 S. Ct. 1434, 1445 (2014).

[537] 540 U.S. 93 (2003).

[538] *Id.* at 124.

ple, in 1996, "the top five corporate soft-money donors gave, in total, more than $9 million in nonfederal funds to the two national political party candidates. In the most recent election cycle the political parties raised almost $600 million—60% of their total soft-money fundraising—from just 800 donors, each of which contributed a minimum of $120,000."[539]

The *McConnell* Court upheld these limits on soft money. The Supreme Court reaffirmed that contribution limits do not have to meet strict scrutiny and said that the restrictions on soft money serve "the Government's important interest in preventing corruption and the appearance of corruption."[540] The Court upheld the restrictions on soft money to prevent circumvention of contribution limits that the Court upheld in *Buckley* and subsequent cases. Thus, the Court deemed constitutional the specific provisions of the Act limiting soft money, including the prohibition on the national political parties raising or spending soft money; the regulation of state political parties from spending soft money on federal election activity; the ban on federal officeholders or candidates raising or spending soft money; and the ban on state candidates spending soft money on public communications that promote or attack federal candidates.

Second, the Act sought to restrict issue advertisements by corporations and unions that clearly were intended to support or oppose particular candidates. In *Buckley*, the Court said that the limits in federal election law, such as disclosure and reporting requirements, applied only to funds used for communications "that expressly advocate the election or defeat of a clearly identifiable candidate."[541] On the other hand, advertisements focusing on issues were not subject to these regulations. As a result, the limits created by *Buckley* could be circumvented just by omitting the magic words, "Elect Jane Doe," or "Vote for John Smith." As the Court noted, "[c]orporations and unions spent hundreds of millions of dollars of their general funds to pay for these ads, and those expenditures, like soft-money donations to the political parties, were unregulated."[542]

The Act applies campaign finance law to broadcast advertisements by corporations and unions that mention a federal candidate and are targeted to the relevant electorate within 30 days of a primary election or 60 days of a general election. Also, the Act requires that such "electioneering communication" by corporations and unions be paid for by "hard money" and that such expenditures be disclosed to the Federal Election Commission. The law additionally provides that coordinated electioneering communication be treated as contributions to candidates or parties.

The Supreme Court in *McConnell* upheld these provisions as constitutionally permissible ways of preventing circumvention of federal law by issue advertisements. However, seven years later, in *Citizens United v. Federal Election Commission*, the Supreme Court overruled this aspect of *McConnell* and held that the restrictions

---

[539] *Id.*
[540] *Id.* at 141.
[541] 424 U.S. at 80.
[542] *McConnell*, 540 U.S. at 128.

on independent expenditures violated the First Amendment.[543] In a 5-4 decision, with Justice Kennedy writing for the majority, the Court held that corporations and unions have free speech rights and the limits on independent expenditures are unconstitutional restrictions of core political speech. The Court declared: "[T]he Government may not suppress political speech on the basis of the speaker's corporate identity. No sufficient governmental interest justifies limits on the political speech of nonprofit or for-profit corporations."[544] This constitutional protection for corporate and union expenditures, and the Court's decision in *Citizens United*, are discussed more fully below.

Third, the Bipartisan Campaign Finance Reform Act also prohibited individuals 17 years old or younger from making contributions to candidates and political parties. The provision obviously was intended to prevent parents from circumventing contribution limits by donating money in the names of their children. The Supreme Court in *McConnell*, however, said that "the Government offers scant evidence of this form of evasion."[545] Moreover, the Court stressed that "[m]inors enjoy the protection of the First Amendment" and that the prohibition of all contributions by those under 17 was "overinclusive."[546] In essence, the Court said that the law should not stop a 16-year-old from contributing the money from his or her paper route to a political candidate.

Finally, in *McConnell*, the Court upheld the provision of the Act that requires that broadcasters keep publicly available records of politically related broadcasting. The Court stressed the authority of the government to regulate broadcasting and rejected the argument that the requirements would be unduly burdensome on broadcasters.[547]

Although a key aspect of the Court's decision in *McConnell* was subsequently overruled in *Citizens United*, *McConnell* remains an important decision especially in upholding the restrictions on "soft money." Of course, because the ruling on this issue, like that on corporate and union expenditures, was 5-4, there is the possibility for reconsideration in the near future.[548]

When Are Contribution Limits Unconstitutional?

As explained above, in *Nixon v. Shrink Missouri Government PAC*,[549] the Court rejected a challenge to contribution limits as being so low as to violate the First Amendment and expressed the need for deference to the government in draw-

---

[543] 130 S. Ct. 876 (2010).

[544] *Id.* at 913.

[545] 540 U.S. at 232.

[546] *Id.*

[547] *Id.* at 238-239.

[548] As discussed below, two other provisions of the Bipartisan Campaign Finance Reform Act also have been declared unconstitutional: the limit on aggregate contributions that a person can make to a candidate or a committee for a candidate, and the "millionaire's provision," which increases the amount that a person can receive in contributions when his or her opponent spends more than $350,000 of personal funds.

[549] 528 U.S. 377 (2000).

ing such lines. However, in *Randall v. Sorrell*, the Court found Vermont's limits on contributions to be so restrictive as to violate the First Amendment.[550] Vermont imposed both expenditure limits and contribution limits with regard to state elections. The Court, relying on *Buckley*, found the expenditure limits to be unconstitutional and stated: "Over the last 30 years, in considering the constitutionality of a host of different campaign finance statutes, this Court has repeatedly adhered to *Buckley*'s constraints, including those on expenditure limits."[551]

The Court, in a 6-3 decision, also found the contribution limits in the Vermont law to be unconstitutional. Vermont law limited contributions so that the amount that any single individual can contribute to the campaign of a candidate for state office during a "two-year general election cycle" is limited to $400 for governor, lieutenant governor, and other statewide offices; $300 for state senator; and $200 for state representative.[552] Justice Breyer, writing for the Court, explained: "[W]e must recognize the existence of some lower bound. At some point the constitutional risks to the democratic electoral process become too great."[553] The Court noted that the contribution limits in the Vermont law were lower than those upheld in *Buckley* or in any other Supreme Court decision, that they were the lowest in the country, and that they were not indexed to keep pace with inflation. The Court concluded: "[The] contribution limits are not narrowly tailored. Rather, the Act burdens First Amendment interests by threatening to inhibit effective advocacy by those who seek election, particularly challengers; its contribution limits mute the voice of political parties; they hamper participation in campaigns through volunteer activities; and they are not indexed for inflation."[554]

The Court looked at a number of factors in coming to this conclusion and did not prescribe a bright-line test for determining when contribution limits are too small. This opens the door to challenges to other contribution limits—in local, state, or federal laws—as being unduly restrictive.

More recently, in *McCutcheon v. Federal Election Commission*, the Court declared unconstitutional the aggregate contribution limits found in the Bipartisan Campaign Finance Reform Act.[555] Specifically, *McCutcheon* is a challenge to a part of the Act that provides that an individual contributor cannot give more than $46,200 to candidates or their authorized agents or more than $70,800 to anyone else in a two-year election cycle. Within the $70,800 limit, a person cannot contribute more than $30,800 per calendar year to a national party committee.

Chief Justice Roberts wrote a plurality opinion, joined by Justices Scalia, Kennedy, and Alito, finding that these provisions violate the First Amendment. Chief Justice Roberts explained that limits on contributions are allowed only to prevent corruption and the appearance of corruption, and that this is limited to stopping quid pro quo corruption. He declared: "Moreover, while preventing corruption or its appearance is a legitimate objective, Congress may target only a

[550] 548 U.S. 230 (2006).
[551] *Id.* at 242.
[552] *Id.* at 238.
[553] *Id.* at 248.
[554] *Id.* at 261.
[555] 134 S. Ct. 1434 (2014).

specific type of corruption — '*quid pro quo*' corruption."[556] He concluded that the aggregate contribution limits do not sufficiently further these goals and are thus unconstitutional. He wrote: "Spending large sums of money in connection with elections, but not in connection with an effort to control the exercise of an office-holder's official duties, does not give rise to such *quid pro quo* corruption. Nor does the possibility that an individual who spends large sums may garner influence over or access to elected officials or political parties. And because the Government's interest in preventing the appearance of corruption is equally confined to the appearance of *quid pro quo* corruption, the Government may not seek to limit the appearance of mere influence or access."

Justice Thomas concurred in the judgment and argued that all contribution limits should be deemed to violate the First Amendment, and urged the Court to overrule *Buckley v. Valeo*. He declared: "I adhere to the view that this Court's decision in *Buckley v. Valeo* denigrates core First Amendment speech and should be overruled."[557]

Justice Breyer wrote for the dissenters and lamented that the Court has "eviscerated" federal campaign finance law and has too narrowly defined the government's interests in regulating contributions. He wrote: "The Court's legal analysis is faulty: It misconstrues the nature of the competing constitutional interests at stake. It understates the importance of protecting the political integrity of our governmental institutions. It creates a loophole that will allow a single individual to contribute millions of dollars to a political party or to a candidate's campaign. Taken together with *Citizens United v. Federal Election Commission*, today's decision eviscerates our Nation's campaign finance laws, leaving a remnant incapable of dealing with the grave problems of democratic legitimacy that those laws were intended to resolve."[558]

McCutcheon will be important in challenges to local, state, and federal limits on contributions. It makes clear that restrictions are allowed only to prevent corruption or the appearance of corruption, that this is limited to quid pro quo corruption, and that any limits must be narrowly tailed to preventing this.

"Millionaire's Provisions" and Public Finance

As described above, in *Buckley v. Valeo*, the Court invalidated a provision of federal law that limited the amount that a person could spend on his or her own campaign. Congress, in the Bipartisan Campaign Finance Reform Act, attempted to deal with concern over the advantage of personal wealth in election campaigns by allowing increased contribution limits for opponents when a candidate spends more than $350,000 of his or her own money.[559] Known as the "millionaire's provision," this trebles the contribution limits — from $2,300 to $6,900 — for those

---

[556] *Id.* at 1450.

[557] *Id.* at 1462 (Thomas, J., concurring in the judgment).

[558] 134 S. Ct. at 1465 (Breyer, J., dissenting).

[559] 2 U.S.C. §441a-1(a).

giving to the campaigns of candidates opposing individuals who spend more than $350,000 of their own funds.

In *McConnell v. Federal Election Commission*, the Court held the challenge to this provision was not ripe for review. But in *Davis v. Federal Election Commission*, the Court, in a 5-4 decision, declared the "millionaire's provision" unconstitutional.[560] Justice Alito, writing for the Court, stressed that the provision increased contribution limits for only one side in the election: the opponents of a candidate who spent more than $350,000 of his or her personal funds. The Court said that it would have been constitutional if Congress had done this for both sides, but increasing the contribution limit for one side and not the other violated the First Amendment. Justice Alito, writing for the Court, explained: "[The law] does not raise the contribution limits across the board. Rather, it raises the limits only for the non-self-financing candidate and does so only when the self-financing candidate's expenditure of personal funds causes the OPFA threshold to be exceeded. We have never upheld the constitutionality of a law that imposes different contribution limits for candidates who are competing against each other, and we agree with Davis that this scheme impermissibly burdens his First Amendment right to spend his own money for campaign speech."[561]

On the one hand, *Davis* can be understood as following a basic principle of fairness; the government should not be allowed to increase contribution for one side and not the other. On the other hand, the Court can be criticized, as it is by the dissent, for being insensitive to the inequity that exists when a candidate has a huge personal fortune to spend in an election campaign. The "millionaire's provision" actually was allowing more speech and nonetheless was struck down.

The Court followed and extended *Davis* in *Arizona Free Enterprise Club's Freedom Club PAC v. Bennett*.[562] The case involved an Arizona voter-passed initiative law, adopted after a major political scandal, which provided for public funding of elections for state offices. Under the Arizona Citizens Clean Elections Act, no candidate was required to accept public funding for his or her election. A candidate wishing to receive such money could qualify for receiving public funds by obtaining a specified amount of donations. Candidates choosing to take public funds had to agree, among other things, to limit their expenditure of personal funds to $500, to participate in at least one public debate, to adhere to an overall expenditure cap, and to return all unspent public moneys to the state.

The concern, though, was if the amount of public funds was fixed, it could be exceeded by an opponent who did not take public funds. The Arizona law said that if an opponent not taking public funds spends more than a designated sum, a publicly financed candidate receives roughly one additional dollar for every dollar spent by the opposing privately financed candidate. The publicly financed candidate also receives roughly one dollar for every dollar spent by independent expenditure groups to support the privately financed candidate or to oppose the publicly financed candidate. But there was a cap on these additional funds; matching

---

[560] 554 U.S. 724 (2008).
[561] *Id.* at 738.
[562] 131 S. Ct. 2806 (2011).

funds top out at two times the initial authorized grant of public funding to the publicly financed candidate.

The Supreme Court, in a 5-4 decision, declared this law unconstitutional. Chief Justice Roberts wrote for the Court and was joined by Justices Scalia, Kennedy, Thomas, and Alito. The Court said that the Arizona law was unconstitutional because it penalized candidates who spent their own money in elections. The "penalty" was that their increased spending would be met with greater public funds for an opponent accepting such money. The Court said that the Arizona law violated the First Amendment because it would chill candidates, and their supporters, from spending money in elections. The Court said: "The logic of *Davis* largely controls our approach to this case. Much like the burden placed on speech in *Davis*, the matching funds provision 'imposes an unprecedented penalty on any candidate who robustly exercises [his] First Amendment right[s].' "[563]

The Court rejected the argument that the laws served a compelling interest in preventing corruption and the appearance of corruption or of equalizing influence in the electoral process. The Court said that ultimately the Arizona law was about attempting to "level the playing field for elections" and that "[w]e have repeatedly rejected the argument that the government has a compelling state interest in 'leveling the playing field' that can justify undue burdens on political speech."[564]

Justice Kagan wrote for the four dissenters. She stressed that the Arizona law in no way restricted or regulated any speech. The sole effect of the Arizona Citizens Clean Election Act was to increase money for candidates taking public funds. Justice Kagan said that the majority opinion repeatedly characterizes the Act as limiting speech, "[b]ut Arizona's matching funds provision does not restrict, but instead subsidizes, speech."[565] If one accepts that spending money in elections is a form of speech protected by the First Amendment, then the Arizona law actually *increases* speech.

It is important to note that the Court explicitly left open the possibility that other public funding systems might be allowed.[566] It would seem that these would need to provide a lump sum to all candidates receiving public funding; there could be no increase based on the amount spent by an opponent. The dissent argued that problem with this is that it makes it far harder to design a public funding system that will attract the participation of candidates. The amount needed for a successful campaign varies tremendously depending on the election, the opponents, the overall spending, and the like. It is much less likely that candidates will choose to participate in public funding where their money is not increased when candidates not taking such money can spend far more.

---

[563] *Id.* at 2818.

[564] *Id.* at 2825.

[565] *Id.* at 2829 (Kagan, J., dissenting).

[566] *Id.* at 2828 ("We have said that governments 'may engage in public financing of election campaigns' and that doing so can further 'significant governmental interest[s],' such as the state interest in preventing corruption. But the goal of creating a viable public financing scheme can only be pursued in a manner consistent with the First Amendment.").

Is Corporate Spending Protected Speech?

In *First National Bank of Boston v. Bellotti*, the Supreme Court declared unconstitutional a Massachusetts law that prohibited banks or businesses from making contributions or expenditures in connection with ballot initiatives and referenda.[567] The law had an exception if the initiative materially affected the property, business, or assets of the corporation. Justice Powell, writing for the Court, concluded that the value of speech is in informing the audience. Any restriction on speech, regardless of its source, therefore undermines the First Amendment. Powell explained: "The speech proposed by appellants is at the heart of the First Amendment's protection. . . . If the speakers here were not corporations, no one would suggest that the State could silence their proposed speech. It is the type of speech indispensable to decisionmaking in a democracy, and this is no less true because the speech comes from a corporation rather than an individual. The inherent worth of the speech in terms of its capacity for informing the public does not depend upon the identity of its source, whether corporation, association, union, or individual."[568]

The Court said that limiting corporations to speaking and spending only on topics related to their activities is an impermissible content-based restriction of speech. Moreover, the Court explained that corporate spending in connection with ballot initiatives has much less risk of corruption, or the appearance of corruption, than contributions to candidates. Justice Powell wrote that initiatives "are held on issues, not candidates for public office. The risk of corruption perceived in cases involving candidate elections . . . simply is not present in a popular vote on a public issue."[569] The Court also expressly rejected the argument that restrictions on corporate spending were justified to keep businesses from drowning out the voices of others in election campaigns.

Bellotti has been sharply criticized by many commentators. The primary objection is that the Court gave inadequate weight to the value of equality and how corporate speech can distort the marketplace of ideas because of corporate wealth and resources.[570] Professor Mark Tushnet, for example, declared: "The First Amendment has replaced the due process clause as the primary guarantor of the privileged. Indeed, it protects the privileges more perniciously than the due process clause ever did. . . . Today, in contrast, the First Amendment stands as a general obstruction to all progressive legislative efforts. . . . Under [*Buckley*] and [*Bellotti*], however, [corporate] investments in politics—or politicians—cannot be regulated significantly."[571]

In two subsequent cases, the Court allowed restrictions on corporate expenditures in election campaigns. In *Austin v. Michigan Chamber of Commerce*, the Court upheld a restriction on corporate contributions or expenditures, expressly relying

[567] 435 U.S. 765 (1978).
[568] *Id.* at 776-777.
[569] *Id.* at 790.
[570] *See* Daniel Lowenstein, Campaign Spending and Ballot Propositions: Recent Experience, Public Choice Theory and the First Amendment, 29 UCLA L. Rev. 505 (1982).
[571] Mark Tushnet, An Essay on Rights, 62 Tex. L. Rev. 1363, 1387 (1984).

on the ability of the state to limit corporate speech so as to limit the distortions caused by corporate wealth.[572] A Michigan law prohibited corporations from using their revenues to contribute to candidates or to make expenditures for or against candidates. The corporations, however, could create a separate fund to solicit contributions and could spend money from this segregated fund.[573]

Justice Marshall said that the Michigan law was directed at "the corrosive and distorting effects of immense aggregations of wealth that are accumulated with the help of the corporate form and that have little or no correlation to the public's support for the corporation's political ideals. The Act does not attempt 'to equalize the relative influence of speakers on elections'; rather, it ensures that expenditures reflect actual public support for the political ideas espoused by the corporations."[574]

The Court was explicit in accepting the argument that "[c]orporate wealth can unfairly influence elections."[575] Thus, the Court concluded that the government was justified in restricting both corporate expenditures and contributions. The Court emphasized that the corporation still could spend money; it just had to be raised separately from corporate funds.[576]

The Court followed this in *McConnell v. Federal Election Commission* in upholding a provision of the Bipartisan Campaign Finance Reform Act that prohibited corporations and unions from engaging in independent expenditures for broadcast advertising, for or against identifiable candidates, 30 days before a primary or 60 days before a general election.[577]

But in *Citizens United v. Federal Election Commission*, the Court expressly overruled *Austin* and this aspect of *McConnell* and held that restrictions on independent expenditures from corporate treasuries (and, by implication, by unions)

---

[572] 494 U.S. 652 (1990).

[573] In *FEC v. National Right to Work Comm.*, 459 U.S. 197 (1982), the Court upheld a federal law that prohibited corporations and unions from making contributions for elections in connection with federal elections, but allowing them to create separate funds to solicit and spend money in connection with campaigns. However, in *FEC v. Massachusetts Citizens for Life, Inc.*, 479 U.S. 238 (1986), the Court held that this law could not be applied to a voluntary political association. The Court stressed that the antiabortion group was created to advance political ideas, not to amass wealth for its shareholders. But subsequently, the Court reaffirmed that the prohibition on corporate contributions constitutionally could be applied to prohibit advocacy corporations from contributing money to political candidates. In *Federal Election Commission v. Beaumont*, 539 U.S. 146 (2003), the Court held that the federal law prohibiting corporations from contributing directly to candidates for federal political office was constitutional as applied to advocacy corporations.

[574] 494 U.S. at 660 (citations omitted).

[575] *Id.*

[576] The law also created a distinction between media and nonmedia corporations. The law exempted from coverage expenditures by media corporations. The obvious purpose was to allow the press to editorialize in election campaigns. Yet the distinction among corporations is troubling because it discriminates in favor of some types of corporations in their ability to engage in freedom of speech over other corporations.

[577] 540 U.S. 93 (2003). Subsequently, in *Federal Election Commission v. Wisconsin Right to Life, Inc.*, 551 U.S. 449 (2007), the Court held that the restrictions on independent expenditures by corporations and unions was limited to the functional equivalent of express advocacy and to speech that would be understood by a reasonable person as an appeal to vote for or against a specific candidate.

violates the First Amendment.[578] Justice Kennedy wrote for the Court in a 5-4 decision and his opinion was joined by Chief Justice Roberts and Justices Scalia, Thomas, and Alito. The key difference from seven years earlier when the Court decided *McConnell* was Justice O'Connor, who had been in the five-Justice majority in that case, being replaced by Justice Alito, who joined the *McConnell* dissenters and Chief Justice Roberts (who took the same position as Chief Justice Rehnquist).

Justice Kennedy, writing for the Court, said that it had been established since *Bellotti* that corporations possess free speech rights and since *Buckley* that expenditures in election campaigns are core political speech. He said that *Austin* was anomalous in that it was the first time that the Court allowed restrictions based on the identity of the speaker. He wrote: "No case before *Austin* had held that Congress could prohibit independent expenditures for political speech based on the speaker's corporate identity."[579] The Court explained that "[p]olitical speech is indispensable to decisionmaking in a democracy, and this is no less true because the speech comes from a corporation rather than an individual."[580] The Court rejected *Austin*'s concern with preventing corporate wealth from distorting elections.

The Court concluded that the restrictions on independent expenditures by corporations and unions violated the First Amendment. The Court stated: "The censorship we now confront is vast in its reach. The Government has 'muffle[d] the voices that best represent the most significant segments of the economy.' And 'the electorate [has been] deprived of information, knowledge and opinion vital to its function.' By suppressing the speech of manifold corporations, both for-profit and nonprofit, the Government prevents their voices and viewpoints from reaching the public and advising voters on which persons or entities are hostile to their interests."[581] The Court, though, in an 8-1 ruling, upheld the disclosure requirements in the Bipartisan Campaign Finance Reform Act and Justice Kennedy's opinion stressed that these were a key way of preventing corruption or the appearance of corruption from large independent expenditures. He wrote: "The Court has explained that disclosure is a less restrictive alternative to more comprehensive regulations of speech."[582]

Justice Stevens wrote a lengthy and vehement dissent, which was joined by Justices Ginsburg, Breyer, and Sotomayor.[583] The dissent rejected the majority's premise that corporations are entitled to the same First Amendment rights as individuals. Justice Stevens stated: "In the context of election to public office, the distinction between corporate and human speakers is significant. Although they make

---

[578] 130 S. Ct. 876 (2010). For especially insightful commentaries on *Citizens United*, *see* Richard L. Hasen, *Citizens United* and the Illusion of Coherence, 109 Mich. L. Rev. 581 (2011); Kathleen M. Sullivan, The Supreme Court, 2009 Term: Two Concepts of Freedom of Speech, 124 Harv. L. Rev. 143, 145 (2010).

[579] *Id.* at 908.

[580] *Id.* (citation omitted).

[581] *Id.* at 907 (citations omitted).

[582] *Id.* at 915.

[583] *Id.* at 929 (Stevens, J., dissenting).

enormous contributions to our society, corporations are not actually members of it. They cannot vote or run for office. Because they may be managed and controlled by nonresidents, their interests may conflict in fundamental respects with the interests of eligible voters. The financial resources, legal structure, and instrumental orientation of corporations raise legitimate concerns about their role in the electoral process. Our lawmakers have a compelling constitutional basis, if not also a democratic duty, to take measures designed to guard against the potentially deleterious effects of corporate spending in local and national races."[584] Justice Stevens argued that the First Amendment was never intended to protect corporate speech.[585]

The dissent stressed that corporations (and unions) could engage in campaign spending through political action committees. Justice Stevens argued that the limits on spending directly from corporate and union treasuries was justified to prevent corruption and the appearance of corruption, the distorting effects of corporate wealth in elections, and the protection of corporate shareholders from having their funds spent against their beliefs. Justice Stevens concluded his dissent by declaring: "At bottom, the Court's opinion is thus a rejection of the common sense of the American people, who have recognized a need to prevent corporations from undermining self-government since the founding, and who have fought against the distinctive corrupting potential of corporate electioneering since the days of Theodore Roosevelt. It is a strange time to repudiate that common sense. While American democracy is imperfect, few outside the majority of this Court would have thought its flaws included a dearth of corporate money in politics."[586]

Citizens United raises many important questions. On a political level, what will it mean now that corporations (and by implication unions) can spend as much as they want from their treasuries to get candidates elected or defeated? On a doctrinal level, will other restrictions on corporate and union spending be allowed? Federal law prohibits corporations and unions from directly contributing money to candidates for federal elective office. But can this survive *Citizens United*'s holding that corporations and unions should have the same right to spend money in elections as individuals? More generally, Justices Scalia, Kennedy, and Thomas have taken the view that all contribution limits violate the First Amendment. Does *Citizens United* suggest that Chief Justice Roberts and Justice Alito will join them to create a majority and overrule this aspect of *Buckley*, which has been the basis for campaign finance law for the last 35 years?

---

[584] *Id.* at 930.

[585] *Id.* at 948-949. Justice Scalia wrote a separate concurring opinion that responded to this and defended the protection of corporate political spending from an originalist perspective. *Id.* at 925 (Scalia, J., concurring).

[586] *Id.* at 979.

§11.3.7   *Commercial Speech*

§11.3.7.1   Introduction

The Court's Initial Refusal to Protect
Commercial Speech

In *Valentine v. Chrestensen*, in 1942, the Supreme Court held that commercial speech was not protected by the First Amendment.[587] A city's ordinance prohibited the distribution of any "handbill . . . or other advertising matter . . . in or upon any street."[588] An individual was prosecuted for circulating an advertisement to visit a submarine that was being exhibited. Without analysis or explanation, the Supreme Court stated: "We are equally clear that the Constitution imposes such no restraint on government as respects purely commercial advertising."[589]

The Court followed *Valentine v. Chrestensen* in *Breard v. City of Alexandria*, where the Court upheld a law that prohibited sellers of goods from going door to door.[590]

The Constitutional Protection for Commercial Speech

Commercial speech remained unprotected by the First Amendment until 1975 when the Court decided *Bigelow v. Virginia*.[591] The Court in *Bigelow* declared unconstitutional a state law that made it a crime to encourage or prompt the procuring of abortions; specifically, the Court held that advertisements for abortion services in newspapers are protected by the First Amendment. The Court said that "speech is not stripped of First Amendment protection merely because it appears" as a commercial advertisement.[592] The Court said that "[t]he fact that the particular advertisement in appellant's newspaper had commercial aspects or reflected the advertiser's commercial interests did not negate all First Amendment guarantees."[593] The Court expressly said that the state court had erred in its conclusion "that advertising, as such, was entitled to no First Amendment protection."[594]

A year later, in *Virginia State Board of Pharmacy v. Virginia Citizens Consumer Council, Inc.*, the Court made it even clearer that commercial speech is protected by the First Amendment.[595] The Court declared unconstitutional a Virginia law

---

[587] 316 U.S. 52 (1942).

[588] *Id.* at 53.

[589] *Id.* at 54.

[590] 341 U.S. 622 (1951). The Court stressed the "commercial feature" of the transaction and distinguished the earlier case *Martin v. City of Struthers*, 319 U.S. 141 (1943), which had declared unconstitutional a city's ordinance that was used to punish a religious group that went door to door to solicit for their religion. The Court in *Martin* emphasized that it was religious speech and that it was in no way commercial.

[591] 421 U.S. 809 (1975).

[592] *Id.* at 818.

[593] *Id.*

[594] *Id.* at 825.

[595] 425 U.S. 748 (1976).

that prohibited pharmacists from advertising the prices of prescription drugs. The Court expressly held that speech that "does no more than propose a commercial transaction" is protected by the First Amendment.[596]

The Court observed that the economic interests of the speaker should not matter in deciding whether speech is protected by the First Amendment. Speech in labor disputes, for example, is protected even though there is a financial interest of the speakers. Nor should it matter that the speech is factual rather than opinions or ideas. Statements of fact obviously also are protected by the First Amendment, as in historical or scientific speech. Justice Blackmun's opinion stressed the importance of commercial speech: "As to the particular consumer's interest in the free flow of commercial information, that interest may be as keen, if not keener by far, than his interest in the day's most urgent political debate. . . . When drug prices vary as strikingly as they do, information as to who is charging what becomes more than a convenience. It could mean the alleviation of physical pain or the enjoyment of basic necessities."[597]

In fact, the Court said that commercial speech could have relevance to the political process. Justice Blackmun observed: "So long as we preserve a predominantly free enterprise economy, the allocation of our resources in large measure will be made through numerous private economic decisions. It is a matter of public interest that those decisions, in the aggregate, be intelligent and well informed. . . . [I]t is also indispensable to the formation of intelligent opinions as to how that system ought to be regulated or altered. Therefore, even if the First Amendment were thought to be primarily an instrument to enlighten public decisionmaking in a democracy, we could not say that the free flow of information does not serve that goal."[598]

The Court indicated that advertising of illegal activities or false and deceptive advertising would not be protected by the First Amendment.[599] But otherwise, the Court indicated grave reservations about any restriction of truthful information about entirely lawful activity.

Should Commercial Speech Be Protected by the First Amendment?

Since 1976, the Supreme Court has decided a large number of cases involving commercial speech. The Court, however, has never wavered from the basic holding of *Virginia State Board of Pharmacy*: Commercial speech is protected by the First Amendment. The issue thus arises as to whether such speech should be safeguarded.

Critics of the protection of commercial speech argue, in part, that the expression is not worthy of protection because it does not directly concern the political

---

[596] *Id.* at 762 (citation omitted).
[597] *Id.* at 763-764.
[598] *Id.* at 765.
[599] *Id.* at 771-772.

process and self-government.[600] Moreover, critics argue that the deference to government economic regulation since 1937 should include deference to government restrictions of commercial speech. Professors Thomas Jackson and John Jeffries argue that "in terms of relevance to political decision-making, advertising is neither more nor less significant than a host of other market activities that legislatures concededly may regulate. The decisive point is the absence of any principled distinction between commercial soliciting and other aspects of economic activity. . . . [E]conomic due process is resurrected, clothed in the ill-fitting garb of the first amendment."[601]

But defenders of the constitutional protection of commercial speech contend that the First Amendment is not limited to protecting speech about the political process.[602] Moreover, it is argued that, as Justice Blackmun concluded, commercial speech is important to individuals and thus worthy of First Amendment protection. Professor Martin Redish observed that "[i]f the individual is to achieve the maximum degree of material satisfaction permitted by his resources, he must be presented with as much information as possible concerning the relative merits of competing products."[603] Professor Robert Post has argued that commercial speech is deserving of constitutional protection because of its informational function, something also emphasized by Justice Blackmun in *Virginia State Board of Pharmacy*.[604]

Overview of the Section

Once the Court decided that commercial speech is protected by the First Amendment, the issue inevitably arises as to what is "commercial speech." This is discussed in §11.3.7.2. The question also occurs as to when the government may regulate commercial speech. Beginning with *Central Hudson Gas & Electric Corp. v. Public Service Commission of New York*, the Court has formulated and refined a test for when the government can regulate commercial speech.[605] This test, which is essentially a form of intermediate scrutiny, is reviewed in §11.3.7.3.

Under the *Central Hudson* test, four types of government regulations of commercial speech can be identified. First, there are laws that outlaw advertising of illegal activities. The Court consistently has held that such advertising is not protected by the First Amendment. Second, there is the prohibition of false and deceptive advertising. The Court also has always held that such ads are not protected by the First Amendment. Third, the Court has indicated that the government may

---

[600] *See* Vincent Blasi, The Pathological Perspective and the First Amendment, 85 Colum. L. Rev. 449, 486 (1985); C. Edwin Baker, Commercial Speech: A Problem in the Theory of Freedom, 62 Iowa L. Rev. 1 (1976).

[601] Thomas Jackson & John Jeffries, Jr., Commercial Speech: Economic Due Process and the First Amendment, 65 Va. L. Rev. 1, 18, 30 (1979).

[602] *See* Sylvia Law, Addiction, Autonomy, and Advertising, 77 Iowa L. Rev. 909, 932 (1992).

[603] Martin Redish, The First Amendment in the Marketplace: Commercial Speech and the Values of Free Expression, 39 Geo. Wash. L. Rev. 429, 433 (1971).

[604] Robert Post, The Constitutional Status of Commercial Speech, 48 UCLA L. Rev. 1 (2000).

[605] 447 U.S. 557 (1980).

prohibit true advertising that inherently risks becoming false or deceptive. For example, as discussed below, the government can prohibit professionals from advertising and practicing under trade names and can forbid attorneys from engaging in in-person solicitation of clients for profit. In both instances, the Court stressed the inherent danger of deception in such speech. Fourth, there are laws that limit commercial advertising to achieve other goals such as enhancing the image of lawyers, or decreasing consumption of alcohol or tobacco products, or preventing panic selling of houses in neighborhoods, or decreasing gambling. The largest number of cases have fit into this category, and they do not follow a consistent path. These four types of government regulation of commercial speech are discussed, respectively, in §11.3.7.4 to §11.3.7.7.

§11.3.7.2   What Is Commercial Speech?

No Clear Definition

In *Virginia State Board of Pharmacy*, the Court said that commercial speech was expression that "propose[s] a commercial transaction."[606] No one, of course, would disagree that advertising of prices for products is a form of commercial speech. The issue arises, though, as to what other speech, besides price advertising, should be regarded as commercial speech. Defining commercial speech as advertising is both overinclusive and underinclusive. Advertising can be pure political speech, such as in the advertisement that was the basis for *New York Times v. Sullivan*, which criticized the government's handling of civil rights demonstrations.[607] But defining commercial speech as advertising is also underinclusive because the commercial speech might take forms other than advertising, such as in direct solicitations by attorneys of prospective clients.

In *Central Hudson Gas & Electric Corp. v. Public Service Commission*, the Court said that commercial speech was "expression related solely to the economic interests of the speaker and its audience."[608] But this definition, too, is difficult to apply. A book publisher or a broadcast station might be motivated solely by economic interests in deciding what to publish or broadcast. Yet those decisions, even if related solely to economic considerations, are obviously protected by the First Amendment.

Bolger v. Youngs Drug Products Corp. is the only Supreme Court case to address directly the question of what is commercial speech.[609] A company that manufactured condoms prepared "informational pamphlets" with titles such as "Plain Talk About Venereal Disease" and "Condoms and Human Sexuality." Some of the pamphlets discussed condoms generally, while others described the specific products

---

[606] 425 U.S. at 762.
[607] 376 U.S. 254 (1964), discussed above in §11.3.5.2.
[608] 447 U.S. at 561.
[609] 463 U.S. 60 (1983).

made by Youngs Drug Products. The Supreme Court held that the brochures were a form of commercial speech.

The Court said: "The mere fact that these pamphlets are conceded to be advertisements clearly does not compel the conclusion that they are commercial speech. Similarly, the reference to a specific product does not by itself render the pamphlets commercial speech. Finally, the fact that Youngs has an economic motivation for mailing the pamphlets would clearly be insufficient by itself to turn the materials into commercial speech. The combination of *all these* characteristics, however, provides strong support for the . . . conclusion that the informational pamphlets are properly characterized as commercial speech."[610] In other words, under this approach, commercial speech has three characteristics: (1) It is an advertisement of some form, (2) it refers to a specific product, and (3) the speaker has an economic motivation for the speech.

Yet this definition, while seemingly specific, leaves many questions unanswered.[611] For example, are "image advertisements" meant to enhance the public's perception of a business or a particular product a form of commercial speech? If tobacco companies take out advertisements that discuss scientific studies about the harms of smoking, is that commercial speech? These are unanswered questions because, as Professor Steven Shriffin observed, "[t]he Court has yet to fully focus on the question of what speech outside advertising is to count as commercial speech."[612]

§11.3.7.3   The Test for Evaluating Government Regulation of Commercial Speech

The *Central Hudson* Test

In *Central Hudson Gas v. Public Service Commission*, the Supreme Court articulated a test for when the government may regulate commercial speech.[613] The issue in *Central Hudson* was the constitutionality of a state law prohibiting promotional advertising by an electrical utility. The state prohibited the utility from advertising because of the need for conservation of fuels and because the utility had a monopoly and therefore did not need to advertise to succeed relative to competitors.

The Court reaffirmed that commercial speech is protected by the First Amendment, but said that it nonetheless "recognized 'the commonsense distinction between speech proposing a commercial transaction, which occurs in an area traditionally subject to governmental regulation, and other varieties of speech.' "[614]

---

[610] *Id.* at 67 (citations omitted).

[611] *See* Laura Lin, Note, Corporate Image Advertising and the First Amendment, 61 S. Cal. L. Rev. 459 (1988).

[612] Steven Shiffrin, The First Amendment and Economic Regulation: Away from a General Theory of the First Amendment, 78 Nw. U. L. Rev. 1212, 1223 (1983).

[613] 447 U.S. 557 (1980).

[614] *Id.* at 562, quoting Ohralik v. Ohio State Bar Assn., 436 U.S. 447, 455-456 (1978).

The Court thus expressly declared that "[t]he Constitution therefore accords a lesser protection to commercial speech than to other constitutionally guaranteed expression."[615]

The Court then articulated a four-part analysis for analyzing government regulation of commercial speech. Justice Powell, writing for the majority, stated: "At the outset, we must determine whether the expression is protected by the First Amendment. For commercial speech to come within that provision, it at least must concern lawful activity and not be misleading. Next, we ask whether the asserted governmental interest is substantial. If both inquiries yield positive answers, we must determine whether the regulation directly advances the governmental interest asserted, and whether it is not more extensive than is necessary to serve that interest."[616]

The Court applied the test to the New York law and found that the utility's advertisements were truthful and not deceptive and that the government had a substantial interest in discouraging energy consumption. The Court also concluded that prohibiting advertising by the utility directly advanced the state's interest in energy conservation.[617] The Court accepted that "[t]here is an immediate connection between advertising and demand for electricity."[618]

However, the Court declared the ban on utility advertisements unconstitutional because the state could achieve its goal of encouraging energy conservation through means less restrictive of speech. The Court concluded that the state had failed to meet its burden of demonstrating that the "interest in conservation cannot be protected adequately by more limited regulation of . . . commercial expression."[619]

Thus, the *Central Hudson* test for commercial speech is: (1) Is the advertising false or deceptive or of illegal activities, areas that are unprotected by the First Amendment? (2) Is the government's restriction justified by a substantial government interest? (3) Does the law directly advance the government's interest? (4) Is the regulation of speech no more extensive than necessary to achieve the government's interest? The test is thus very similar, if not identical, to intermediate scrutiny in evaluating government regulation of truthful advertising for legal activities. In fact, the Court has expressly said that "we engage in 'intermediate scrutiny' of restrictions on commercial speech."[620]

The Court has ruled that the government has the burden of proof to demonstrate that the *Central Hudson* test is met in order to justify a restriction on commercial speech. The Court repeatedly has said that "[t]he party seeking to uphold a restriction on commercial speech carries the burden of justifying it."[621]

---

[615] 447 U.S. at 563.

[616] *Id.* at 566.

[617] *Id.* at 568-569.

[618] *Id.*

[619] *Id.* at 570.

[620] Florida Bar v. Went For It, Inc., 515 U.S. 618, 623 (1995).

[621] Bolger v. Youngs Drug Prods. Corp., 463 U.S. at 71 n.20; Edenfield v. Fane, 507 U.S. 761, 770 (1993).

In its subsequent commercial speech cases — *Greater New Orleans Broadcasting Association v. United States*,[622] *Lorillard Tobacco Co. v. Reilly*,[623] and *Thompson v. Western States Medical Center*[624] — the Supreme Court expressly relied on the *Central Hudson* test in invalidating government restrictions on commercial speech. These cases are discussed in detail below, but what is significant is that both used *Central Hudson* and both said that the test for commercial speech is whether the government regulation is narrowly tailored and substantially related to achieving an important government purpose.

Is Least Restrictive Alternative Analysis Applicable?

The Court has consistently invoked and applied the *Central Hudson* test in dealing with commercial speech issues. However, the Court has modified the fourth part of the test, the requirement that regulation be no more extensive than necessary to achieve the government's purpose. As of now, although the Court has not been clear or consistent, it appears that the government need not use the least restrictive alternative, but the regulation must be narrowly tailored to achieve the government's goal. In *Board of Trustees of the State University of New York v. Fox*, the Court held that government regulation of commercial speech need not use the least restrictive alternative.[625] *Fox* concerned a state regulation that prohibited commercial solicitations on campuses.[626]

The Court, in an opinion by Justice Scalia, expressly rejected the least restrictive alternative test for commercial speech. The Court said: "Our jurisprudence has emphasized that 'commercial speech [enjoys] a limited measure of protection, commensurate with its subordinate position in the scale of First Amendment values,' and is subject to 'modes of regulation that might be impermissible in the realm of noncommercial expression.' The ample scope of regulatory authority suggested by such statements would be illusory if it were subject to a least-restrictive-means requirement, which imposes a heavy burden on the State."[627] The Court said that while the government need not use the least restrictive alternative, it must use "a means narrowly tailored to achieve the desired objective."[628]

The Court in *Fox* also reaffirmed that overbreadth analysis is not used in analyzing government regulation of commercial speech.[629] The overbreadth doctrine

---

[622] 527 U.S. 173 (1999) (declaring unconstitutional prohibition of gambling advertisements).

[623] 533 U.S. 425 2404 (2001) (declaring unconstitutional restrictions on placement of advertisements for tobacco products).

[624] 535 U.S. 357 (2002) (declaring unconstitutional prohibition of advertisements for "compounded drugs").

[625] 492 U.S. 469 (1989).

[626] The regulation prohibited private commercial activities on campus facilities. The law was challenged on First Amendment grounds by a company that wanted to engage in commercial solicitations for students to buy its household goods and by students who claimed a desire to receive the solicitations.

[627] 492 U.S. at 477 (citations omitted).

[628] *Id.* at 480.

[629] *Id.* at 481-485. *See* Village of Hoffman Estates v. Flipside, Hoffman Estates, Inc., 455 U.S. 489, 496-497 (1982); Bates v. State Bar of Arizona, 433 U.S. 350, 380-381 (1977).

allows individuals whose speech may be constitutionally regulated to challenge a law that would be unconstitutional as applied to others; laws are deemed impermissibly overbroad if they regulate substantially more speech than the Constitution allows to be regulated.[630] The overbreadth doctrine is based on a concern that overbroad laws will chill constitutionally protected expression and that those for whom a law would be unconstitutional will refrain from speaking rather than challenge the regulation. The Court believes, however, that there is less reason to fear that commercial speech will be chilled because of the economic motivations that inspire such expression. Also, the Court has emphasized the lesser protection accorded to commercial speech under the First Amendment.

Although *Fox* expressly rejected least restrictive alternative analysis for commercial speech cases, in *Rubin v. Coors Brewing Co.*, the Court seemed to use it.[631] *Rubin* involved a challenge to a provision of the Federal Alcohol Administration Act that prevented beer labels from displaying their alcohol content. Interestingly, both sides in the case and the Court accepted that this constituted commercial speech. It, of course, is quite different from usual commercial speech, which is advertising for a particular product or service. Statements on labels about the alcohol content of beer are commercial speech in the sense that they may affect purchasers' decision whether to buy a particular product.

The Court said that government regulation of commercial speech must advance the government's interest "in a direct and material way," and "[t]hat burden 'is not satisfied by mere speculation and conjecture; rather, a governmental body seeking to sustain a restriction on commercial speech must demonstrate that the harms it recites are real and that its restriction will in fact alleviate them to a material degree.'"[632] The Court found that the government failed to meet this burden because of the "irrationality" of the regulatory scheme; the government did not prohibit listing of the alcohol content in advertisements for products, just on labels.[633] The Court also found that there were a number of alternative ways of preventing strength wars and that these options "could advance the Government's asserted interest in a manner less intrusive to respondent's First Amendment rights."[634] Indeed, the Court concluded its opinion by emphasizing "the availability of alternatives that would prove less intrusive to the First Amendment's protections for commercial speech."[635]

It is very difficult, if not impossible, to reconcile the language in *Rubin* with that in *Fox*. Where *Fox* says that government regulation of commercial speech need not use the least restrictive alternative, the *Rubin* Court says that a regulation of commercial speech is unconstitutional because less intrusive alternatives would

---

[630] The overbreadth doctrine is discussed in detail in §11.2.2.
[631] 514 U.S. 476 (1995).
[632] *Id.* at 487, quoting Edenfeld v. Fane, 507 U.S. 761, 767, 770-771 (1993).
[633] *Id.* at 488.
[634] *Id.* at 491.
[635] *Id.*

suffice. Even more troubling is that Justice Thomas's opinion for the Court does not even cite to *Fox*, let alone attempt to reconcile this inconsistency.[636]

Nor did the Court's decision in *44 Liquormart, Inc. v. Rhode Island* clarify this confusion.[637] In *44 Liquormart*, the Supreme Court declared unconstitutional a state law that prohibited advertisement of liquor prices. The plurality opinion—written by Justice Stevens and joined by Justices Kennedy, Souter, and Ginsburg—said: "The State also cannot satisfy the requirement that its restriction on speech be no more extensive than necessary. It is perfectly obvious that alternative forms of regulation that would not involve any restriction on speech would be more likely to achieve the State's goal of promoting temperance."[638] This is clearly the language of least restrictive alternative analysis. In the next paragraph, Justice Stevens invoked *Fox* and said that "even under the less than strict standard that generally applies in commercial speech cases, the State has failed to establish a 'reasonable fit' between its abridgement of speech and its temperance goal."[639]

The other opinions in *44 Liquormart* do not clarify this discrepancy either. Justice Thomas's opinion, concurring in the judgment, argued that the government should not be able to regulate truthful commercial speech based on the premise that people will be better off with less information.[640] Justice Scalia wrote a short opinion expressing doubts about the *Central Hudson* test and agreeing with Justice Thomas's analysis.[641] Justice O'Connor wrote an opinion concurring in the judgment—joined by Rehnquist, Souter, and Breyer—that expressly invoked *Fox* and said that "[w]hile the State need not employ the least restrictive means to accomplish its goal, the fit between means and ends must be 'narrowly tailored.' "[642] O'Connor concluded that the Rhode Island law failed this test.

Subsequent to *44 Liquormart*, in *Greater New Orleans Broadcasting Association v. United States*,[643] the Court expressly reaffirmed *Fox* and said the government regulation of commercial speech need not be the least restrictive alternative, though it must be narrowly tailored to achieving the government's goal. In *Greater New Orleans Broadcasting*, the Court declared unconstitutional a federal law that prohibited advertising by casinos. The Court expressly relied on the *Central Hudson* test, declaring that "*Central Hudson*, as applied in our more recent commercial speech cases, provides an adequate basis for decision."[644] The Court said that "[t]he fourth part of the test complements the direct-advancement inquiry of the third, asking whether the speech restriction is not more extensive than necessary to serve the interests that support it. The Government is not required to employ

---

[636] The result in *Rubin* was unanimous. Justice Stevens concurred in the judgment and challenged the premise that commercial speech is entitled to less protection than other types of expression. *Id.* at 491-492 (Stevens, J., concurring in the judgment).

[637] 517 U.S. 484 (1996).

[638] *Id.* at 507.

[639] *Id.*

[640] *Id.* at 518-520 (Thomas, J., concurring in part and concurring in the judgment).

[641] *Id.* at 517-518 (Scalia, J., concurring in part and concurring in the judgment).

[642] *Id.* at 529 (O'Connor, J., concurring in the judgment) (citation omitted).

[643] 527 U.S. 173 (1999).

[644] *Id.* at 184.

the least restrictive means conceivable, but it must demonstrate narrow tailoring of the challenged regulation to the asserted interest."[645] The Court said that this is "a fit that is not necessarily perfect, but reasonable; that represents not necessarily the single best disposition but one whose scope is in proportion to the interest served."[646] The Court cited to *Fox* as establishing this proposition. The Court then concluded that the federal law prohibiting advertising was not substantially related to achieving the objective of decreasing gambling because of the many exceptions in the law, such as in allowing advertising by casinos on Native American reservations and by state-run lotteries.

Thus, as of now, based on the Court's statements in *Greater New Orleans Broadcasting*, it appears that *Fox* is the law and least restrictive alternative analysis is not required in commercial speech cases, although the means must be "narrowly tailored." Yet there is some confusion because the Court's opinion in *Rubin* and Justice Stevens's plurality opinion in *44 Liquormart* use less restrictive alternative analysis. Moreover, the distinction between a narrow tailoring requirement and least restrictive alternative analysis is not always clear; a rigorous enough requirement for narrow tailoring would seem to approach the requirement for use of the least restrictive means.

§11.3.7.4   Advertising of Illegal Activities

Ads for Illegality Are Not Protected by the First Amendment

The Court consistently has held that advertising of illegality is not protected by the First Amendment.[647] The Court always has stated this as an axiom and offered little explanation. In some ways, it is a curious proposition. One would think that the government would welcome advertising of illegal activity; such ads, if they occurred, could help law enforcement. Moreover, speech that advocates illegal conduct is protected by the First Amendment unless it meets the test for incitement.[648] Yet advertising of illegality is unprotected by the First Amendment without any need to meet the test for incitement.

The only Supreme Court case to consider advertising of illegality, *Pittsburgh Press Co. v. The Pittsburgh Commission on Human Relations*, was actually decided before the Supreme Court held that commercial speech is protected by the First Amendment.[649] The Court upheld a decision by the Pittsburgh Human Relations Committee that a newspaper violated the city's Human Relations Ordinance by

---

[645] *Id.* at 188. The Court repeated exactly this language in *Lorillard Tobacco v. Reilly*, 533 U.S. 525 (2001), discussed below.

[646] 527 U.S. at 188.

[647] *See, e.g.,* Central Hudson Gas & Elec. Corp. v. Public Service Commn. of New York, 447 U.S. at 563-564.

[648] Incitement is discussed above in §11.3.2.

[649] 413 U.S. 376 (1973).

placing help-wanted advertisements in columns captioned "Jobs-Male Interest," "Jobs-Female Interest," and "Male-Female."

The Court emphasized that "[d]iscrimination in employment is not only commercial activity, it is *illegal* commercial activity under the Ordinance. We have no doubt that a newspaper constitutionally could be forbidden to publish a want ad proposing a sale of narcotics or soliciting prostitutes. . . . The illegality in this case may be less overt, but we see no difference in principle here."[650]

Pittsburgh Press is constantly approvingly cited as establishing that advertising of illegal activities is not protected by the First Amendment. Thus, such advertisements can be prohibited and punished, and be the basis for civil liability.[651]

§11.3.7.5   False and Deceptive Advertising

False and Deceptive Ads Are Not Protected by the First Amendment

It also is clearly established that false and deceptive advertisements are unprotected by the First Amendment. The Court frequently has declared that only truthful commercial speech is constitutionally protected.[652] The Supreme Court, however, has never decided a First Amendment case concerning false and deceptive ads.

False and deceptive advertisements do not contribute to the marketplace of ideas or the commercial marketplace in any useful way. In fact, false and deceptive advertisements distort those markets and thus are undeserving of First Amendment protection. Yet in contexts outside the commercial speech realm, it is clear that false speech is often protected. For example, in *New York Times v. Sullivan*, the Court said that erroneous "statement is inevitable in free debate, and . . . it must be protected if the freedoms of expression are to have the 'breathing space' that they 'need to survive.' "[653] The absence of protection for false commercial speech seems based on a judgment that such speech is more harmful, less likely to be chilled because of the profit motive, and more easily verified than most other types of expression.[654]

---

[650] *Id.* at 388.

[651] *See* Braun v. Soldier of Fortune Magazine, Inc., 968 F.2d 1110 (11th Cir. 1992). In *Braun*, the sons of a man murdered by an assassin hired in response to a personal service advertisement prevailed in their negligence suit against the magazine. The court held that the publisher was liable because "the advertisement on its face would alert a reasonably prudent publisher to the clearly identifiable unreasonable risk of harm to the public." *Id.* at 1115.

[652] *See, e.g.*, Central Hudson Gas & Elec. Corp. v. Public Serv. Commn. of New York, 447 U.S. at 566.

[653] 376 U.S. 254, 271-272 (1964) (citation omitted).

[654] *See* Friedman v. Rogers, 440 U.S. 1, 10 (1979) ("Because it relates to a particular product or service, commercial speech is more objective, hence more verifiable, than other varieties of speech. Commercial speech, because of its importance to business profits, and because it is carefully calculated, is also less likely than other forms of speech to be inhibited by proper regulation.").

§11.3.7.6   Advertising That Inherently Risks Deception

The Supreme Court has held that even true advertisements that inherently risk being deceptive are unprotected by the First Amendment. The Court has considered this in two areas: laws prohibiting professionals from advertising or practicing under trade names and laws restricting professionals from soliciting prospective clients.

Restrictions on Trade Names

In *Friedman v. Rogers*, the Supreme Court upheld a state law that prohibited optometrists from advertising and practicing under trade names.[655] The Court said that the use of trade names "is a form of commercial speech and nothing more."[656] Although there was no evidence that the optometrists bringing the challenge had engaged in any deception, the Court concluded that the state could prohibit trade names because of their inherent risk of deception. Bad optometrists could keep changing their trade names and thereby deceive the public as to their identity. A good optometrist could go out of business and a bad one could assume that name and fool the public. The Court concluded that "there is a significant possibility that trade names will be used to mislead the public."[657]

Friedman v. Rogers is important because it recognizes that even truthful advertising can be restricted if it is of a type that inherently risks becoming false and deceptive. Interestingly, the Court did not consider whether there would be ways of prohibiting the false and deceptive practices without prohibiting the truthful advertisements.

Attorney Solicitation of Prospective Clients

As discussed below, the Supreme Court has ruled that the government may not prohibit attorneys from engaging in truthful, nondeceptive advertising of their services.[658] However, the Supreme Court has held that the government may prohibit attorney in-person solicitation of prospective clients for profit. The underlying rationale is that such speech inherently risks becoming deceptive and thus even truthful solicitations can be forbidden when they are conducted in person and where the attorney would profit from the representation.

This rule emerged from a series of Supreme Court cases. In *Ohralik v. Ohio State Bar Assn.*, the Court found no violation of the First Amendment when a lawyer was punished for impermissible solicitation for approaching the victim of an automobile accident in her hospital room and offering to represent her on

---

[655]   440 U.S. 1 (1979).

[656]   *Id.* at 11.

[657]   *Id.* at 13.

[658]   *See* Bates v. State Bar of Arizona, 433 U.S. 350 (1977). Attorney advertising is discussed below in §11.3.7.7.

a contingency fee basis.[659] The Court noted that the government has a "compelling interest in preventing those aspects of solicitation that involve fraud, undue influence, intimidation, overreaching, and other forms of vexatious conduct."[660] The Court stressed that face-to-face solicitation inherently risks that prospective clients will be deceived and pressured because no one is there to monitor the communications.[661] Because of this danger, the Court said that it is not violative of the Constitution for a State to respond with what in effect is a "prophylactic rule."[662]

However, in another case decided the same day, *In re Primus,* the Supreme Court held that solicitations are protected by the First Amendment when the lawyer offers to represent a client without charge.[663] An attorney affiliated with the American Civil Liberties Union in South Carolina was disciplined for impermissible solicitation after the attorney offered to represent women for free. The women had been told by the welfare department that they had to be sterilized in order to continue to receive public medical assistance. The Supreme Court, however, held that the lawyer's speech was protected by the First Amendment.

The Court noted that "[t]he ACLU engages in litigation as a vehicle for effective political expression and association, as well as a means of communicating useful information to the public."[664] Thus, the Court said that South Carolina's action punishing the lawyer for offering free representation "must withstand the exacting scrutiny applicable to limitations on core First Amendment rights."[665] The Court expressly distinguished *Ohralik* on the ground that the attorney in *Primus* was not seeking to profit directly from the client. This distinction was important for the Court both in enhancing the importance of the speech as a form of political activity and in lessening the likelihood of deceptive practices by the attorney. The Court said that it was irrelevant that the ACLU attorney would seek attorneys' fees from the state if the plaintiff prevailed in the case.[666]

In *Shapero v. Kentucky Bar Association,* the Court declared unconstitutional a state law that prohibited targeted, direct mail solicitation by lawyers for pecuniary gain.[667] The Court explained that letter solicitation does not have the same risk of abuse as face-to-face solicitation. There is less danger of deception because there is a written record of the communication as compared to face-to-face solicitation where no one is present to monitor the conversations. There is less risk of pressure or undue influence because people are used to throwing away mail that is not of interest. The Court explained that "[l]ike print advertising, . . . letter[s] — and targeted, direct-mail solicitation generally — 'pose[] much less risk of overreaching or undue influence' than does in-person solicitation."[668]

---

[659] 436 U.S. 447 (1978).

[660] *Id.* at 462 (citation omitted).

[661] *Id.* at 465.

[662] *Id.* at 467.

[663] 436 U.S. 412 (1978).

[664] *Id.* at 431.

[665] *Id.* at 432 (citation omitted).

[666] *Id.* at 429.

[667] 486 U.S. 466 (1988).

[668] *Id.* at 475 (citation omitted).

Thus, *Ohralik, Primus,* and *Shapero* taken together establish the proposition that states may prohibit attorney in-person solicitation of clients for profit. Conversely, solicitation where the attorney would not profit directly from the client and solicitation by mail is generally protected by the First Amendment.

The Court, however, has carved one exception where mail solicitation by lawyers can be regulated. In *Florida Bar v. Went for It, Inc.,* the Supreme Court upheld a Florida law that prohibited attorneys from soliciting personal injury or wrongful death clients for 30 days after an accident.[669] The Court said that the "purpose of the 30-day targeted direct-mail ban is to forestall the outrage and irritation with the state-licensed legal profession that the practice of direct solicitation only days after accidents has engendered."[670] The Court, in its 5-to-4 decision, concluded that the regulation was justified to protect accident victims and their estates from "invasive conduct by lawyers and in preventing the erosion of confidence in the profession that such repeated invasions have engendered."[671]

Justice Kennedy wrote a dissenting opinion, joined by Justices Stevens, Souter, and Ginsburg. The dissent questioned whether letter solicitations are invasive and explained that they are important in informing people of their right to sue.[672] The state did not limit the ability of claims adjusters or insurance companies to settle claims during this 30-day period; thus, restricting communications from plaintiffs' attorneys could harm accident victims and their estates by denying them needed information. Moreover, the Court consistently had rejected the argument that attorney advertising could be restricted because of its negative impact on the image of the profession. Justice Kennedy said: "[F]or the first time since *Bates v. State Bar of Arizona,* the Court now orders a major retreat from the constitutional guarantees for commercial speech in order to shield its own profession from public criticism. . . . There is no authority for the proposition that the Constitution permits the State to promote the public image of the legal profession by suppressing information about the profession's business aspects."[673]

Solicitations by Accountants

The Supreme Court, however, has held that the government may not prohibit accountants from engaging in in-person solicitation of clients for profit. In *Edenfield v. Fane,* the Court declared unconstitutional a state law that prohibited certified public accountants from engaging in in-person solicitations.[674] The Court said that there was no evidence that accountants were engaged in abusive solicitations. The Court expressly distinguished *Ohralik,* which had upheld an identical rule for lawyers. Justice Kennedy, writing for the Court, said: "The solicitation here poses none of the same dangers. Unlike a lawyer, a CPA is not a 'professional

---

[669] 515 U.S. 618 (1995).
[670] *Id.* at 631.
[671] *Id.* at 635.
[672] *Id.* (Kennedy, J., dissenting).
[673] *Id.* at 644-645.
[674] 507 U.S. 761 (1993).

trained in the art of persuasion.' A CPA's training emphasizes independence and objectivity, not advocacy. The typical client of a CPA is far less susceptible to manipulation than the young accident victim in *Ohralik*."[675]

This distinction between attorneys and accountants seems highly questionable. Attorneys and accountants obviously are both capable of trying to pressure prospective clients. The Court in *Ohralik* upheld all prohibitions on in-person solicitations of clients, regardless of their sophistication; the Court in *Edenfield* invalidated all prohibitions of in-person solicitations by accountants, regardless of the client's lack of sophistication. As Justice O'Connor said in dissent, "[t]he attorney's rhetorical power derives not only from his specific training in the art of persuasion, but more generally from his professional expertise."[676] Nonetheless, the current law is that the government may prohibit attorney in-person solicitation for profit, but it may not prohibit accountants from engaging in such solicitations.

§11.3.7.7   Regulating Commercial Speech to Achieve Other Goals

The Issue

Perhaps the most difficult issue in the area of commercial speech concerns the ability of the government to regulate truthful, nondeceptive advertising of legal activities to achieve other goals. For example, may the government regulate commercial advertising to reduce sales of houses to preserve the racial balance in a neighborhood, or to decrease consumption of alcohol or tobacco products, or to lessen gambling, or to enhance the image of attorneys? In all of these areas, the restriction on commercial speech is based on a premise that seems at odds with the very core of the First Amendment: that people will be better off with less information.[677]

For the most part, the Supreme Court's commercial speech cases are consistent with this view, as the Court generally has rejected state laws that limit commercial speech based on the belief that people will be better off with less information. The primary exception has been in the area of gambling advertisements where the Court has allowed restrictions of commercial speech to achieve the goal of decreasing gambling.[678] But even here, in *Greater New Orleans Broadcasting v. United States*, the Court declared unconstitutional a federal law that prohibited advertising by gambling casinos.[679]

---

[675] *Id.* at 775.

[676] *Id.* at 779 (O'Connor, J., dissenting).

[677] *See* 44 Liquormart, Inc. v. Rhode Island, 517 U.S. at 526 (Thomas, J., concurring in the judgment) (arguing that the government never should be able to restrict commercial speech based on the assumption that people will be better off if they are kept in the dark about particular information).

[678] United States v. Edge Broad., 509 U.S. 418 (1993); Posadas de Puerto Rico Assocs. v. Tourism Co. of P.R., 478 U.S. 328 (1986).

[679] 527 U.S. 173 (1999).

§11.3 Types of Unprotected and Less Protected Speech

This section reviews these cases, focusing, in turn, on the Court's treatment of regulation of commercial speech concerning the sales of houses, traffic safety, alcohol products, gambling, tobacco products, contraceptives and abortions, and lawyers' and other professionals' services. In all of these cases, the issue is when the government may regulate truthful advertising of legal activities so as to achieve other objectives.

"For Sale" Signs on Houses

In *Linmark Associates, Inc. v. Township of Willingboro*, the Supreme Court declared unconstitutional an ordinance that outlawed the display of "For Sale" or "Sold" signs.[680] The city prohibited such signs "to prevent the flight of white homeowners from a racially integrated community."[681] The city's concern was that the pervasive presence of "For Sale" signs would encourage panic selling and white flight from the city.

The Court accepted that the ordinance serves a "vital goal . . . [in] promoting stable, racially integrated housing."[682] But the Court, in an opinion by Justice Thurgood Marshall, declared the ordinance unconstitutional because "the First Amendment disable[s] the State from achieving its goal by restricting the free flow of truthful information."[683] The Court questioned whether there was sufficient evidence of likely panic selling or that prohibiting "For Sale" signs would prevent this from occurring. But the Court said that the primary infirmity of the law was that the government suppressed truthful information based on the belief that people would be better off with less speech and knowledge. The Court unanimously held that this was unacceptable under the First Amendment.

Traffic Safety

The Court has allowed restrictions on commercial speech in areas where restrictions on noncommercial speech were not imposed because of the government's asserted interest in enhancing traffic safety. An early case in this vein, decided before the Court protected commercial speech under the First Amendment, was *Railway Express Agency v. New York*.[684] The Court upheld an ordinance that prohibited advertisements on trucks except where the advertisement was for the usual business of the owner of the truck. The law was challenged primarily on equal protection grounds, and the Court said that the ordinance was justified because "local authorities may well have concluded that those who advertise their own wares on their trucks do not present the same traffic problem in view of the nature or extent of the advertising which they use."[685]

---

[680] 431 U.S. 85 (1977).

[681] *Id.* at 86.

[682] *Id.* at 94.

[683] *Id.* at 95.

[684] 336 U.S. 106 (1949).

[685] *Id.* at 110. The equal protection aspects of the case are discussed in more detail in §9.2.3.

In *Metromedia, Inc. v. City of San Diego*, the Court considered a city's ordinance that prohibited all outdoor advertising display signs.[686] The Court upheld the law in its prohibition of commercial messages, but declared it unconstitutional in its prohibition of noncommercial messages. The Court applied the *Central Hudson* test in concluding that the prohibition of commercial advertising did not violate the First Amendment. The Court said that the city had substantial goals in attempting to enhance traffic safety and maintaining the appearance of the city. Justice White explained that "the city has a sufficient basis for believing that billboards are traffic hazards and are unattractive, [and] obviously the most direct and perhaps the only effective approach to solving the problems they create is to prohibit them. The city has gone no further than necessary in seeking to meet its ends."[687] However, the Court said that these goals did not warrant prohibiting billboards that contained messages that received greater First Amendment protection.

However, the continuing validity of *Metromedia* must be questioned in light of the Court's subsequent decision in *City of Cincinnati v. Discovery Network, Inc.*[688] In *Discovery Network*, the Court declared unconstitutional a city's ordinance that prohibited commercial newspapers from being distributed on newsracks while allowing other kinds of newspapers to be sold. The Court said that the content-based distinction drawn in the law was unconstitutional because it "bears no relationship whatsoever to the particular interests that the city has asserted."[689] In *Metromedia*, the distinction between commercial and noncommercial speech also bears no relationship to the particular interests asserted by the city; as in *Discovery Network*, there was no reason to believe that commercial billboards posed more of a risk of harm than noncommercial ones.

Moreover, in light of both *Metromedia* and *Discovery Network*, an earlier case, *Lehman v. City of Shaker Heights*, seems highly dubious.[690] In *Lehman*, the Court upheld a city's ordinance that prohibited public transportation from selling advertising space to candidates for public office. The restriction was exactly the opposite of the Court's holding in *Metromedia*; in *Lehman*, political ads were prohibited, but commercial ones were allowed. The Court stressed that advertising spaces on buses are not a public forum, that the city was engaged in a proprietary venture, and that the government had an interest in protecting a captive audience.

It is extremely difficult to reconcile *Lehman* with *Metromedia* and *Discovery Network* and the general prohibition against content-based discrimination. Once the government opens space to speech, it cannot engage in content-based distinctions, and the Court has rejected the idea that people can claim to be captive audiences outside their homes.[691] Furthermore, in light of *Metromedia*, it is hard to understand how *Lehman* could remain good law in allowing the government to favor commercial advertisements over political ones.

---

[686] 453 U.S. 490 (1981).
[687] *Id.* at 508.
[688] 507 U.S. 410 (1993).
[689] *Id.* at 424.
[690] 418 U.S. 298 (1974). *Lehman* is discussed in more detail below in §11.4.2.4.
[691] Cohen v. California, 403 U.S. 15, 19 (1971).

Alcohol Products

The Court has refused to allow the government to limit advertising of alcohol products based on its goal of decreasing consumption. For example, in *Rubin v. Coors Brewing Co.*, the Court declared unconstitutional a federal law that prohibited beer labels from stating the alcohol content of the product.[692] The Court accepted that the government had a substantial interest in preventing strength wars among malt beverage products. The Court said that government has "a significant interest in protecting the health, safety, and welfare of its citizens by preventing brewers from competing on the basis of alcohol strength, which could lead to greater alcoholism and its attendant social costs."[693]

However, the Court declared the federal law unconstitutional because the government could achieve this goal "in a manner less intrusive to respondent's First Amendment rights."[694] The Court identified "several alternatives, such as directly limiting the alcohol content of beers, prohibiting marketing efforts emphasizing high alcohol strength (which is apparently the policy in some other Western nations), or limiting the labeling ban only to malt liquors, which is the segment of the market that allegedly is threatened with a strength war."[695]

Subsequently, in *44 Liquormart, Inc. v. Rhode Island*, the Supreme Court declared unconstitutional a state law that prohibited price advertising of alcoholic beverages.[696] Justice Stevens, writing for a plurality, said that "when a State entirely prohibits the dissemination of truthful, nonmisleading commercial messages for reasons unrelated to the preservation of a fair bargaining process, there is far less reason to depart from the rigorous review that the First Amendment generally demands."[697] The plurality said that even if it accepted the importance of the state's goal of encouraging temperance, "without any findings of fact, or indeed any evidentiary support whatsoever, we cannot agree with the assertion that the price advertising ban will significantly advance the State's interest in promoting temperance."[698] The plurality said that it would be conjecture to speculate that prohibiting price advertising would decrease alcohol abuse.

Also, as described above, the plurality said that the state did not "satisfy the requirement that its restriction on speech be no more extensive than necessary."[699] The plurality said that many alternative forms of regulation that did not restrict speech would be more likely to achieve the state's goal of promoting temperance. The Court rejected the argument that the states' power to regulate sale of alcoholic beverages under the Twenty-first Amendment justified the law. The Court said that states must use their power under the Twenty-first Amendment in a manner consistent with other constitutional provisions, such as the First Amendment.

---

[692] 514 U.S. 476 (1995).
[693] *Id.* at 485.
[694] *Id.* at 491.
[695] *Id.* at 490-491.
[696] 517 U.S. 484 (1996).
[697] *Id.* at 501.
[698] *Id.* at 505.
[699] *Id.* at 507.

Justice Thomas wrote an opinion, concurring in part and concurring in the judgment, in which he argued that the government never should be able to regulate truthful speech based on the assumption that people are better off with less information.[700] Justice Scalia also wrote an opinion concurring in part and concurring in the judgment in which he agreed with Justice Thomas and urged reconsideration of the *Central Hudson* test.[701] Justice O'Connor wrote an opinion concurring in the judgment—joined by Rehnquist, Souter, and Breyer—and used the *Central Hudson* test to invalidate the law. Justice O'Connor argued that the Rhode Island law was not narrowly tailored because "[t]he State has other methods at its disposal—methods that would more directly accomplish this stated goal without intruding on sellers' ability to provide truthful, nonmisleading information to customers."[702]

Gambling

In sharp contrast to the Court's unwillingness to allow the government to regulate advertisements for alcohol products based on the desire to decrease consumption, the Court, in some cases, has permitted the government to prohibit gambling advertisements in order to attempt to reduce gambling. In *Posadas de Puerto Rico Associates v. Tourism Company of Puerto Rico,* the Supreme Court upheld a Puerto Rico law that prohibited advertising by casino gambling establishments.[703] The Court accepted Puerto Rico's argument that the government has an important interest in discouraging gambling and said that it had "no difficulty in concluding that the Puerto Rico Legislature's interest in the health, safety, and welfare of its citizens constitutes a 'substantial' governmental interest."[704]

The Court said that prohibiting advertising was sufficiently narrowly tailored to achieve this goal so as to meet the requirements of the First Amendment. The Court said that the law was not unconstitutional because it targeted advertising for casino gambling, but left advertising for other forms of gambling unregulated. The Court said that the "legislature felt that for Puerto Ricans the risks associated with casino gambling were significantly greater than those associated with the more traditional kinds of gambling in Puerto Rico."[705]

The Court also noted that the government could have banned all casino gambling. It concluded that it therefore could take the lesser step of just prohibiting advertisements. The Court said: "Here, on the other hand, the Puerto Rico Legislature could have prohibited casino gambling by the residents of Puerto Rico altogether. In our view, the greater power to completely ban casino gambling necessarily includes the lesser power to ban advertising of casino gambling."[706]

---

[700] *Id.* at 518 (Thomas, J., concurring in part and concurring in the judgment).

[701] *Id.* at 517 (Scalia, J., concurring in part and concurring in the judgment).

[702] *Id.* at 528 (O'Connor, J., concurring in the judgment).

[703] 478 U.S. 328 (1986).

[704] *Id.* at 341.

[705] *Id.* at 343.

[706] *Id.* at 545-546.

The Court followed the *Posadas* case in *United States v. Edge Broadcasting Co.*, where it upheld a federal law that prohibited lottery advertising by radio stations located in states that did not operate lotteries.[707] A radio station in southern Virginia wished to broadcast advertisements for the North Carolina lottery. Evidence demonstrated that over 92 percent of the broadcast station's audience resided in North Carolina, where lotteries were legal. However, the federal law prohibited the radio station from broadcasting such advertisements because it was located in Virginia, which did not have a lottery. Again, the Court upheld the law based on the government's substantial interest in discouraging gambling by limiting advertisements for it. The Court also stressed that the federal law served to effectuate the desires of each state by permitting advertising only in states that chose to have lotteries.

Posadas and *Edge Broadcasting* are troubling in many respects. They are based on the assumption that people will be better off with less speech. In neither case was there serious consideration of less intrusive alternatives for discouraging gambling. In contrast, in both *Rubin* and *44 Liquormart*, the Court emphasized the existence of other ways of decreasing alcohol consumption besides prohibiting advertising.

Finally, the *Posadas* Court's claim that "the greater includes the lesser" is problematic. Gambling is not protected by the Constitution but speech is. It therefore is not at all clear why the power to prohibit gambling has any relevance to the power to limit speech. Indeed, "the greater includes the lesser" argument seems to have been rejected in the *44 Liquormart* decision. States have the power to prohibit the sale of alcoholic beverages. Under the reasoning of *Posadas*, this would create a right to forbid advertising of them. But the *44 Liquormart* decision expressly held that states cannot prohibit price advertising by alcoholic beverage products.

In a subsequent case dealing with government regulation of gambling advertisements, *Greater New Orleans Broadcasting Association, Inc. v. United States*,[708] the Court came to a different conclusion and found a federal law that prohibited casinos from advertising to be unconstitutional. The Court expressly relied on the *Central Hudson* test, declaring that "*Central Hudson*, as applied in our more recent commercial speech cases, provides an adequate basis for decision."[709] The Court did not question the importance of the government's interest in discouraging gambling. Rather, the Court found the federal law unconstitutional because it was not substantially related to achieving the objective. The Court concluded that the federal law prohibiting advertising was not substantially related to achieving the objective of decreasing gambling because of the many exceptions in the law, such as in allowing advertising by casinos on Native American reservations and by state-run lotteries.[710] Justice Stevens concluded his majority opinion for a unanimous Court by declaring: "Had the federal government adopted a more coherent policy, or accommodated the rights of speakers in States that have legalized the

---

[707] 509 U.S. 418 (1993).
[708] 527 U.S. 173 (1999).
[709] *Id.* at 184.
[710] *Id.* at 190-191.

underlying conduct, . . . this might be a different case. But under current federal law, as applied to petitioners and the messages they wish to convey, the broadcast prohibition . . . violates the First Amendment."[711]

Greater New Orleans Broadcasting does not overrule the Court's earlier cases allowing regulation of gambling advertisements, *Posadas* and *Edge Broadcasting*. The cases might be reconciled by the Court finding the latter to have involved regulations that are sufficiently narrowly tailored and substantially related to achieving the government's goal of decreasing gambling. But there definitely seems to be a tension as *Greater New Orleans Broadcasting* used a more rigorous analysis of the relationship between the means and the ends than was present in the earlier cases.

Tobacco Advertising

In *Lorillard Tobacco Co. v. Reilly*, the Supreme Court considered the constitutionality of Massachusetts's regulations of tobacco advertising.[712] The most significant aspects of the regulations prevented advertising of tobacco products within 1,000 feet of a school or playground and required that places selling tobacco products place ads for these items at least 5 feet off the ground to avoid being at eye level for children. The state's goal for the regulations was decreasing tobacco consumption by children.

In evaluating the Massachusetts regulations, the Supreme Court distinguished between their application to cigarettes and to cigars and smokeless tobacco. The Supreme Court declared the regulations of cigarette advertising to be preempted by federal law. This aspect of the decision is discussed in Chapter 5. The federal law, however, concerns only cigarettes and not cigars or smokeless tobacco. Therefore, the Court considered whether the restrictions on advertising of these products violated the First Amendment.

Justice O'Connor, writing for the Court, repeated the *Central Hudson* test as the appropriate method for analyzing commercial speech issues. She acknowledged that the Court had been urged to overrule that case and use strict scrutiny, but she said that "we see no need to break new ground. *Central Hudson*, as applied in our more recent commercial speech cases, provides an adequate basis for decision."[713]

As for the prohibition of outdoor advertising, the Court said that the regulation failed the fourth part of the *Central Hudson* test because it was not narrowly tailored. Justice O'Connor explained that petitioners maintain "that this prohibition would prevent advertising in 87 percent to 91 percent of Boston, Worcester, and Springfield, Massachusetts."[714] Justice O'Connor said that "the substantial geographical reach of the Attorney General's outdoor advertising regulations is compounded by other factors. 'Outdoor' advertising includes not only advertising located outside an establishment, but also advertising inside a store if that

---

[711] *Id.* at 195-196.
[712] 533 U.S. at 525 (2001).
[713] *Id.* at 554-555.
[714] *Id.* at 563.

advertising is visible from outside the store. The regulations restrict advertisements of any size and the term advertisement also includes oral statements."[715]

Justice O'Connor also was particularly concerned about the extent to which the regulation, in its attempt to protect children, restricted constitutional speech desired by adults. She wrote: "In some geographical areas, these regulations would constitute nearly a complete ban on the communication of truthful information about smokeless tobacco and cigars to adult consumers. The breadth and scope of the regulations, and the process by which the Attorney General adopted the regulations, do not demonstrate a careful calculation of the speech interests involved."[716]

As for the regulation requiring that ads in stores be at least 5 feet above ground level, the Court concluded that this was not "substantially related" to the goal of protecting children. Justice O'Connor explained that children could still see the ads, and therefore it is not clear what the restriction would accomplish.[717] She said, "The 5-foot rule does not seem to advance that goal. Not all children are less than 5 feet tall, and those who are certainly have the ability to look up and take in their surroundings."[718]

Justice Thomas wrote a concurring opinion in which he said that he would use strict scrutiny in evaluating government regulation of commercial speech.[719] Justice Thomas questioned whether the government ever should be able to restrict advertising as a way of discouraging behavior that it regards as harmful. He said that if this were allowed, the government could stop advertisements for alcohol or any product that causes harm.[720]

The case seems particularly important in reaffirming that *Central Hudson*'s four-part test is used in evaluating government regulation of commercial speech. The decision also is significant in limiting the ability of the government to regulate advertising so as to discourage harmful behavior.

Contraceptives and Abortion

The Court consistently has held that the government may not prohibit advertising of abortions or contraceptives. As discussed earlier in this section, in *Bigelow v. Virginia*, the Court declared unconstitutional a state law that made it a crime to circulate any publication that encouraged or promoted abortions.[721] The Court said that a newspaper's ability to publish such ads is protected by the First Amendment.

In *Carey v. Population Services International*, the Court declared unconstitutional a state law that prohibited advertising of contraceptives.[722] The state argued that

---

[715] *Id.*

[716] *Id.* at 528.

[717] *Id.* at 566.

[718] *Id.*

[719] *Id.* at 575 (Thomas, J., concurring in part and concurring in the judgment).

[720] *Id.* at 535-590.

[721] 421 U.S. 809 (1975).

[722] 431 U.S. 678 (1977).

the ban on advertising was justified because "the advertisements of contraceptive products would be offensive and embarrassing to those exposed to them, and that permitting them would legitimize sexual activity of young people."[723] As to the former, preventing offense or embarrassment is never a sufficient justification for banning speech. As to the latter, while discouraging sexual activity among young people is a substantial state interest, there is no evidence that advertisements for contraceptives increase sexual activity or that there are not other ways of discouraging sexual activity that are less restrictive of speech.

The Court followed the same reasoning in *Bolger v. Youngs Drug Products Corp.*, which declared unconstitutional a federal statute that prohibited the mailing of unsolicited advertisements for contraceptives.[724] Again, the government's primary justification for banning the advertisements was preventing offense to recipients. But the Court said that the desire to prevent offense or embarrassment is not a substantial interest sufficient to warrant the restriction on speech. *Bolger*, together with *Bigelow* and *Carey*, establish that advertising of contraceptives is safeguarded by the First Amendment.

Advertising by Lawyers and Other Professionals

One of the most frequent topics of commercial speech before the Supreme Court has been state attempts to restrict advertising by lawyers and other professionals. The ability of states to regulate solicitations by attorneys and accountants is discussed above. Additionally, states have attempted to prohibit attorneys and other professionals from advertising and to restrict the content of the ads that are published. The Supreme Court repeatedly has made it clear that such advertisements are protected by the First Amendment so long as they are truthful and not deceptive.

The Court initially ruled that states cannot prohibit lawyers from advertising in *Bates v. State Bar of Arizona* in 1977.[725] A lawyer had been disciplined by the bar for an advertisement that stated prices for routine legal services such as uncontested divorces, name changes, and simple nonbusiness bankruptcies. The state presented a number of justifications for prohibiting and punishing the advertisement. It argued, for example, that such advertisements cause a negative public impression of attorneys, suggesting that they foment litigation and that they are inherently deceptive because inevitably legal services involve complications that cannot be foreseen. The Court rejected all of these justifications for prohibiting lawyer advertisements. The Court explained that it was far too tenuous and speculative to believe that lawyer advertising would have any of these ill effects.

As in *Virginia State Board of Pharmacy*, the Court stressed the value to consumers of receiving truthful information about prices and availability of services. Justice Blackmun, writing for the Court, said that the state's justifications were

---

[723] *Id.* at 701.
[724] 463 U.S. 60 (1983).
[725] 433 U.S. 350 (1977).

impermissibly "based on the benefits of public ignorance."[726] Justice Blackmun explained that the First Amendment precludes the state from acting on the premise that "the public is better kept in ignorance than trusted with correct but incomplete information."[727]

Repeatedly since *Bates* the Supreme Court has reiterated that truthful, non-deceptive advertisements by professionals are protected by the First Amendment. Many of these cases involved other efforts by states to restrict lawyer advertisements. For example, in *In re R.M.J.*, a lawyer was disciplined for not following state rules regulating lawyer advertising.[728] The attorney, for instance, listed his specialty as "real estate" and not "property" as prescribed in the rule. He also sent announcement cards to persons other than "lawyers, clients, former clients, personal friends, and relatives."[729] The Court held that the lawyer's speech and activities were protected by the First Amendment because the expression was true and not deceptive. The Court emphasized that the state could achieve all of its goals through means less restrictive of speech. In a unanimous decision, the Court said that "although the States may regulate commercial speech, the First and Fourteenth Amendments require that they do so with care and in a manner no more extensive than reasonably necessary to further substantial interests."[730]

In *Zauderer v. Office of Disciplinary Counsel of the Supreme Court of Ohio*, the Supreme Court again held that truthful advertisements are protected by the First Amendment, but that the government can punish deception including that which occurs through omission.[731] An attorney published advertisements offering to represent women who were injured by the Dalkon Shield. The lawyer was punished for three reasons. First, he was disciplined for violating a rule that prohibited advertisements that contained advice or information about a specific legal problem. Second, he was punished because his advertisement included an illustration, a drawing of a Dalkon Shield. Third, he was disciplined for deception; the advertisement stated that he would provide representation on a contingency fee basis and that the client would not have to pay any fee if the case was not won. The ad did not disclose that the clients were liable for litigation costs.

The Supreme Court rejected the first two grounds for discipline, but accepted the third. The Court said that a state could not prohibit advertisements that targeted a particular audience or a group of clients with a specific legal problem. The Court emphasized the difference from in-person solicitations in that "[p]rint advertise[ments] . . . lack the coercive force of the personal presence of a trained advocate."[732] Moreover, the Court said that illustrations were allowed in ads unless there was proof in a specific case that they were deceptive or misleading.

But the Court said that the omission of a statement about the client's liability for litigation costs could be the basis for discipline because its absence was

---

[726] *Id.* at 375.
[727] *Id.*
[728] 455 U.S. 191 (1982).
[729] *Id.* at 196.
[730] *Id.* at 207.
[731] 471 U.S. 626 (1985).
[732] *Id.* at 642.

deceptive. The Court rejected any claim that the lawyer had a First Amendment right to omit the information. The Court said: "Because the extension of First Amendment protection to commercial speech is justified principally by the value to consumers of the information such speech provides, [the] constitutionally protected interest in *not* providing any particular factual information in his advertising is minimal."[733]

In *Peel v. Attorney Registration and Disciplinary Commission of Illinois*, the Court invalidated a state law that limited the ability of attorneys to advertise specialties.[734] A lawyer had been disciplined for advertising himself as a trial specialist even though this was prohibited by a state bar rule. The plurality opinion by Justice Stevens emphasized that the statement on the attorney's letterhead about the receipt of a certificate of specialty was accurate and truthful. The plurality said that the state failed to meet its "heavy burden of justifying a categorical prohibition against the dissemination of accurate factual information to the public."[735]

The Court followed the same reasoning in *Ibanez v. Florida Department of Business and Professional Regulation Board of Accountancy*.[736] An attorney was disciplined for an advertisement listing that she also is a certified public accountant and a certified financial planner. The Court held that the information was accurate and thus could not be the basis for discipline.

The Court applied *In re R.M.J.* and *Zauderer* to uphold a federal law—the Bankruptcy Abuse Prevention and Consumer Protection Act of 2006—requiring that debt relief agencies, including attorneys, disclose in their advertisements that they are "debt relief agencies." In *Milavetz, Gallop & Milavetz, P.A. v. United States*,[737] the Court upheld this disclosure requirement and declared that it "share[s] the essential features of the rule at issue in *Zauderer*. As in that case, [the] required disclosures are intended to combat the problem of inherently misleading commercial advertisements—specifically, the promise of debt relief without any reference to the possibility of filing for bankruptcy, which has inherent costs. Additionally, the disclosures entail only an accurate statement identifying the advertiser's legal status and the character of the assistance provided, and they do not prevent debt relief agencies like Milavetz from conveying any additional information."[738]

The case law in this area is clear: Truthful, nondeceptive advertisements by lawyers are protected by the First Amendment. The Court refuses to allow the government to regulate attorney advertisements to improve the public's image of the bar, or out of concern that advertisements will foment litigation, or out of

---

[733] *Id.* at 651 (emphasis in original).

[734] 496 U.S. 91 (1990).

[735] *Id.* at 109.

[736] 512 U.S. 136 (1994).

[737] 130 S. Ct. 1324 (2010).

[738] *Id.* at 1340. The Court also upheld a provision of the law prohibiting debt relief agencies from advising clients to take on additional debt. This would seemingly prevent a lawyer from advising a client to get a mortgage, even where it would be lawful and nonfraudulent to do so. But the Court interpreted the provision to prevent such advice only where it was for the purpose of having the debt discharged in bankruptcy. *Id.* at 1335-1336.

unsupported fear that the public will not understand their content and thereby be deceived.

§11.3.8   Speech of Government Employees

§11.3.8.1   Adverse Actions Against Government Employees Because of Their Speech

Standard to Be Applied

In analyzing the speech of government employees, a crucial distinction exists depending on whether the speech is on the job in the scope of the employee's duties. The Court has held that there is no First Amendment protection for the speech of government employees while on the job in the scope of their duties.[739] For other speech by government employees, the Court has held that the government may not punish the speech of public employees if it involves matters of public concern unless the state can prove that the needs of the government outweigh the speech rights of the employee.

In other words, speech by public employees is clearly less protected than other speech. First Amendment protection does not exist if it is speech on the job in the scope of the employee's duties. For other speech by government employees, there is no First Amendment protection unless the expression is about public concern, and even then, the employee can be disciplined or fired if the government can show, on balance, that the efficient operation of the office justified the action.[740]

No Protection for Speech on the Job in the Scope of Duties

Garcetti v. Ceballos involved Richard Ceballos, a supervising district attorney in Los Angeles County, who concluded that a witness in one of his cases, a deputy sheriff, was not telling the truth.[741] He wrote a memo to this effect and felt that he was required by the Constitution to inform the defense of this. As a result of this speech, Ceballos alleged that his employers retaliated against him, including transferring him to a less desirable position and denying him a promotion.

The issue before the Supreme Court was whether Ceballos's speech was protected by the First Amendment. Although the Supreme Court long has held that there is constitutional protection for the speech of government employees,[742] it

---

[739] Garcetti v. Ceballos, 547 U.S. 410 (2006).

[740] The Court also has held that these protections apply to speech by government contractors. Board of County Commrs., Wabaunsee County, Kansas v. Umbehr, 518 U.S. 668 (1996) (applying the test for protecting speech of government employees to government contractors).

[741] 547 U.S. 410 (2006).

[742] *See, e.g.,* Pickering v. Board of Educ., 391 U.S. 563 (1968) (government employee's speech is protected by the First Amendment if it involves a matter of public concern and does not unduly interfere with the functioning of the workplace), discussed below.

ruled against Ceballos. The Court drew a distinction between speech "as a citizen" as opposed to "as a public employee"; only the former is protected by the First Amendment. Justice Kennedy stated: "[W]hen public employees make statements pursuant to their official duties, the employees are not speaking as citizens for First Amendment purposes, and the Constitution does not insulate their communications from employer discipline."[743] The Court expressed great concern about the disruptive effects of allowing employees to bring First Amendment claims based on their on the job speech. Justice Kennedy wrote that allowing such claims "would commit state and federal courts to a new, permanent, and intrusive role, mandating judicial oversight of communications between and among government employees and their superiors in the course of official business. This displacement of managerial discretion by judicial supervision finds no support in our precedents."[744] Kennedy observed that civil service protections provide safeguards for employees for retaliation for their speech.

Garcetti v. Ceballos was a 5-4 decision and the dissent strongly objected to the holding that there is *no* First Amendment protection for the speech of government employees on the job in the scope of their duties.[745] The dissent was expressly concerned about the whistleblower who exposes wrongdoing in the workplace, often benefiting the public, but who would have no protection from reprisals. The dissent noted that civil services protections are often nonexistent or limited.

Garcetti is thus an important limit on First Amendment protections for speech by government employees; it is a categorical exception from constitutional protection for speech that is on the job in the scope of the employee's duties. The Court acknowledged that it was leaving open many questions, for example, when should speech be regarded as "on the job" and in "the scope of duties." Justice Kennedy wrote: "We thus have no occasion to articulate a comprehensive framework for defining the scope of an employee's duties in cases where there is room for serious debate. We reject, however, the suggestion that employers can restrict employees' rights by creating excessively broad job descriptions. The proper inquiry is a practical one."[746] Also, the Court acknowledged that there may be distinct issues of academic freedom raised when the government employee works as an instructor. Justice Kennedy again said that this was left for future cases to address: "There is some argument that expression related to academic scholarship or classroom instruction implicates additional constitutional interests that are not fully accounted for by this Court's customary employee-speech jurisprudence. We need not, and for that reason do not, decide whether the analysis we conduct today would apply in the same manner to a case involving speech related to scholarship or teaching."[747]

Finally, the Court was explicit that it was not changing the First Amendment law with regard to other speech by government employees. The Court stated that its holding "relates only to the expressions an employee makes pursuant to his

---

[743] 547 U.S. at 421.
[744] *Id.* at 423.
[745] *Id.* at 428-429 (Souter, J., dissenting).
[746] *Id.* at 424.
[747] *Id.* at 425.

or her official responsibilities, not to statements or complaints (such as those at issue in cases like *Pickering* and *Connick*) that are made outside the duties of employment."[748] But this leads to the anomaly that Ceballos's speech would have been protected if he had written a memo to the *Los Angeles Times*, but not one to his supervisor.

The Court clarified the line between speech as a "citizen" and speech as a "government employee" in *Lane v. Franks*, where the Court unanimously held that a government employee's First Amendment rights were violated when he was fired for truthful testimony he gave in court pursuant to a subpoena.[749] Edward Lane was fired from his state job after he testified at a criminal trial, even though he appeared after being subpoenaed and testified truthfully. The Court said that under *Garcetti v. Ceballos* his speech was protected because it was speech as a "citizen" and not as a "government employee": "Truthful testimony under oath by a public employee outside the scope of his ordinary job duties is speech as a citizen for First Amendment purposes. That is so even when the testimony relates to his public employment or concerns information learned during that employment."[750]

On the one hand, it seems obvious that it violates the First Amendment to fire a government employee for truthful testimony given in court after a subpoena.[751] The employee obviously had no choice; he could not refuse to testify after being subpoenaed and could not commit perjury. On the other hand, the Court continues to use the problematic distinction between speech as a "citizen" as opposed to speech as a "government employee." For example, does this mean that there is no First Amendment protection for the truthful testimony of government employees, like police officers or social workers, who testify in court because of their jobs?

Other Speech by Government Employees

Pickering v. Board of Education is a key case in holding that other speech by government employees is protected by the First Amendment.[752] A teacher was fired for sending a letter to a local newspaper that was critical of the way school officials had raised money for the schools. The Supreme Court held that the firing violated the First Amendment. Justice Marshall, writing for the Court, said that its task was to balance the free speech rights of government employees with the government's need for efficient operation. Justice Marshall wrote: "[T]he State has interests as an employer in regulating the speech of its employees that differ significantly from those it possesses in connection with regulation of the speech of the citizenry in general. The problem in any case is to arrive at a balance between the interests

---

[748] *Id.* at 424.

[749] 134 S. Ct. 2369 (2014).

[750] *Id.* at 2378.

[751] However, the Court did not see it as obvious; it found that even though the defendant violated the First Amendment by firing Lane, the defendant was protected by qualified immunity because there was not clearly established law that this action violated the Constitution.

[752] 391 U.S. 563 (1968). *See also* Perry v. Sindermann, 408 U.S. 593, 597 (1973) (holding that the First Amendment limits the ability of the government to fire or discipline employees because of their speech activities).

of the teacher, as a citizen, in commenting upon matters of public concern and the interest of the State, as an employer, in promoting the efficiency of the public services it performs through its employees."[753]

The Court emphasized that there was no indication that Pickering's statements in any way interfered with the teacher's ability to perform or the operation of the school district. The Court also stressed that the speech concerned a matter of public concern: the operation of the school district. Indeed, the Court said that a teacher is likely to have unique and important insights as to the adequacy of educational funding. Although there were some factual inaccuracies in the statement, the Court held that "absent proof of false statements knowingly or recklessly made by him, a teacher's exercise of his right to speak on issues of public importance may not furnish the basis for his dismissal from public employment."[754]

In *Mt. Healthy City School District Board of Education v. Doyle*,[755] the Court articulated a test to be used in applying *Pickering*. An untenured teacher was not rehired after several speech-related incidents, including arguing with another teacher, making an obscene gesture to students, and informing a local radio station about the principal's memorandum on teacher dress and appearance. The Court reiterated that speech by public employees is protected by the First Amendment. The Court said, however, that a public employee who otherwise would have been fired does not deserve special protection because of the speech.

Thus, the Court said that a public employee challenging an adverse employment action must initially meet the burden of showing that "his conduct was constitutionally protected, and that this conduct was a 'substantial factor' or, to put it in other words, that it was a 'motivating factor' for the government's action."[756] If this is done, the burden shifts to the government to show "by a preponderance of the evidence that it would have reached the same decision . . . even in the absence of the protected conduct."[757]

The Requirement That the Speech Be on Matters of Public Concern

In *Connick v. Myers*,[758] the Court added an additional requirement to the *Pickering/Mt. Healthy* approach. An assistant district attorney, angry over a transfer to a different section in the office, circulated a memorandum soliciting the views of other attorneys in the office concerning the transfer policy, the level of morale, and the need for establishment of a grievance committee. The attorney was fired and sued alleging a violation of the First Amendment.

---

[753] *Id.* at 568.

[754] *Id.* at 574.

[755] 429 U.S. 274 (1977).

[756] *Id.* at 287.

[757] *Id.* This is the same approach the Court uses with regard to proof of discriminatory intent under the Fourteenth Amendment. *See* §9.3.3.2.

[758] 461 U.S. 138 (1983).

The Supreme Court ruled against the attorney, emphasizing that the speech was not protected by the First Amendment, because it did not involve comment upon matters of public concern. The Court, in an opinion by Justice White, said: "The repeated emphasis in *Pickering* on the right of a public employee 'as a citizen, in commenting upon matters of public concern,' was not accidental. . . . [When] employee expression cannot fairly be considered as relating to any matter of political, social, or other concern to the community, officials should enjoy wide latitude in managing their offices, without intrusive oversight by the judiciary in the name of the First Amendment."[759] The Court said that "[w]hether an employee's speech addresses a matter of public concern must be determined by the content, form, and context of a given statement."[760] Although Myers's statements related to the performance of supervisors and policy in a public office, the Court said that it did not involve matters of public concern, especially because she was not seeking to inform the public.

Accordingly, the Court also has expressly ruled that private statements that are not made publicly are protected by the First Amendment so long as they involve matters of public concern. In *Givhan v. Western Line Consolidated School District*, the Court unanimously held that it violated the First Amendment to fire a teacher because of her speech that privately communicated grievances about racially discriminatory policies.[761] The Court said that no First Amendment freedom "is lost to the public employee who arranges to communicate privately with his employer rather than to spread his views before the public."[762]

In *Rankin v. McPherson*, the Court applied *Connick* and found that a public employee's statement was protected by the First Amendment when she declared, after hearing of an assassination attempt directed at President Ronald Reagan, "If they go for him again, I hope they get him."[763] The Court held that firing the employee because of the statement violated the First Amendment because it concerned a matter of public concern. The Court, in an opinion by Justice Marshall, said that "[t]he statement was made in the course of a conversation addressing the policies of the president's administration. It came on the heels of a news bulletin regarding what is certainly a matter of heightened public attention: an attempt on the life of the president. . . . The inappropriate or controversial character of a statement is irrelevant to the question whether it deals with a matter of public concern."[764]

The Court said that if a statement is of public concern, then a court must balance the employee's First Amendment rights with the state's interest in the "effective functioning of the public employer's enterprise."[765] The Court found that the speech was protected by the First Amendment because there was no evidence that it interfered with the efficient functioning of the office.

---

[759] *Id.* at 143.
[760] *Id.* at 147-148.
[761] 439 U.S. 410 (1979).
[762] *Id.* at 415.
[763] 483 U.S. 378, 380 (1987).
[764] *Id.* at 386-387.
[765] *Id.* at 388.

The Test That Emerges

Thus, a four-step analysis can be derived from the cases: (1) The speech must not be expression on the job and within the scope of the employee's duties; if it is, there is no First Amendment protection for the speech; (2) the employee must prove that an adverse employment action was motivated by the employee's speech; if the employee does this, the burden shifts to the employer to prove by a preponderance of the evidence that the same action would have been taken anyway; (3) the speech must be deemed to be a matter of public concern; and (4) the court must balance the employee's speech rights against the employer's interest in the efficient functioning of the office. Phrased another way, the employee can prevail only if he or she convinces the court that speech was the basis for the adverse employment action, and if the court concludes that the speech related to matters of public concern, and if the court decides that, on balance, the speech interests outweigh the government's interests in regulating the expression for the sake of the efficiency of the office.

On the one hand, this lessened protection of the speech of government employees can be justified based on the Court's desire to minimize judicial interference with the government's role as employer. On the other hand, the test can be criticized for not providing adequate protection for the speech rights of government employees. The requirement that the speech be of public concern can be questioned because the First Amendment generally has no such limitation and because of the narrow definition of public concern in *Connick*; the employee's speech there concerned the functioning of an important public office. Moreover, the simple balancing test—weighing speech interests against the government's interest in administrative efficiency—can be questioned as failing to place sufficient weights on the First Amendment side of the scale.

How Is the Content of the Speech Determined?

The specific content of the employee's speech is obviously crucial in applying this test. Often, of course, there will be a dispute between employer and employee over exactly what was said. How is this dispute to be resolved? The Court addressed this issue in *Waters v. Churchill*.[766] A nurse was disciplined and ultimately fired from a public hospital for her speech, but there was a dispute between her and the employer over what she actually said.

Justice O'Connor, writing for a plurality of four, said that the trier of fact should accept the employer's account of what was said so long as it is reasonable to do so. Justice O'Connor said that there is no violation of the First Amendment when a government employer reasonably believes that speech does not involve matters of public concern. The plurality said that a court should side with the employer so long as the employer acted reasonably in obtaining information about what was said and so long as the employer's belief is reasonable.

---

[766] 511 U.S. 661 (1994).

Justice Scalia wrote an opinion concurring in the judgment, joined by two other Justices, and said that the employee was protected by the First Amendment only if she could prove that the firing was in retaliation for constitutionally protected speech.[767] Scalia objected to the plurality's requirement that employers use reasonable procedures to ascertain what was said.

Justice Stevens dissented, in an opinion joined by Justice Blackmun, and argued that the content of the speech was a question of fact that should be tried like any other factual issue.[768] Justice Stevens said that the issue is not whether the employer followed reasonable procedures or even whether the employer had a reasonable belief. The question is whether the speech is protected by the First Amendment, and that can be ascertained only by first deciding what was said.

§11.3.8.2　Freedom of Association for Government Employees: Subversive Organizations and Loyalty Oaths

The Emergence of First Amendment Protection

A key First Amendment issue during the 1950s and 1960s concerned the ability of the government to require its employees to take oaths swearing allegiance to the country and to deny employment to those who belonged to "subversive groups." Initially, the Court was very deferential to the government in this area, but as the hysteria of the McCarthy era subsided, the Court became much more protective of the speech and association rights of public employees.

In *Garner v. Board of Public Works of the City of Los Angeles*, in 1951, the Court upheld a law that required that every public employee swear that he or she did not advocate the overthrow of the government by unlawful means.[769] A year later, in *Adler v. Board of Education of the City of New York*, the Court upheld a New York law that prohibited civil service employment or public school teaching for any person who advocated the overthrow of the government by force or violence.[770] The Court said: "[The appellants] may work for the school system upon the reasonable terms laid down by the proper authorities of New York. If they do not choose to work on such terms, they are at liberty to retain their beliefs and associations and go elsewhere."[771]

Yet in the same year that *Adler* was decided, the Court also declared unconstitutional a state law that required public employees to take an oath that they were not members of the Communist Party or any group that advocated the overthrow of the government by force or violence. In *Wieman v. Updegraff*, the Court found this unconstitutional because the oath applied "solely on the basis of organizational membership, regardless of their knowledge" of the group's goals and regardless of

---

[767] *Id.* at 686 (Scalia, J., concurring in the judgment).
[768] *Id.* at 694 (Stevens, J., dissenting).
[769] 341 U.S. 716 (1951).
[770] 342 U.S. 485 (1952).
[771] *Id.* at 492.

the intent to further those objectives.[772] The Court distinguished *Garner* because in that case knowledge of the group's illegal goals was required, whereas in *Wieman* the mere fact of association was sufficient for denying employment.

In several subsequent cases, the Court invalidated similar loyalty oaths on vagueness and overbreadth grounds.[773] For instance, in *Baggett v. Bullitt*, the Court declared unconstitutional a state law that required that "employees swear that they were not a member of a subversive organization."[774] The Court found that the law's failure to define this term was void on vagueness grounds and the application even where individuals did not know of the illegal objectives was impermissibly overbroad.

By the mid-1960s, the Court expressly invalidated loyalty oath requirements as violating freedom of speech and association. In *Elfbrandt v. Russell*, the Court declared unconstitutional a state's loyalty oath and law that prohibited anyone from holding office if they were a member of a group such as the Communist Party.[775] The Court expressed grave concern that "[n]othing in the oath, the statutory gloss, or the construction of the oath and statutes given by the Arizona Supreme Court, purports to exclude association by one who does not subscribe to the organization's unlawful ends."[776] The Court said that it was impermissible for the government to punish individuals for being a member of a group without proof that the individual joined the organization knowing of its illegal objectives and with the specific intent to further them.

In *Keyishian v. Board of Regents of the State University of New York*,[777] the Court followed this approach and declared unconstitutional the same law that it had upheld in *Adler* 15 years earlier. The Court emphasized that the law punished mere membership in a "subversive" group, without any requirement for proof that the individual knew of the illegal objectives or intended to further them. Similarly, in *United States v. Robel*, the Court declared unconstitutional a federal law that denied federal employment to individuals who were members of designated Communist groups.[778] The Court stressed that the laws created guilt by association because mere membership was sufficient to deny employment. The Court held that the government could deny employment to an individual only if the person actively affiliated with a group, knowing of its illegal objectives, and with the specific intent to further those objectives.

However, not all loyalty oaths for public employees are unconstitutional. In *Cole v. Richardson*, the Court upheld a state law that required that state employees swear to "uphold and defend" the Constitution and to oppose the overthrow of the government by force or violence.[779] Unlike the oaths that were invalidated,

---

[772] 344 U.S. 183, 190 (1952).
[773] *See, e.g.,* Baggett v. Bullitt, 377 U.S. 360 (1964); Cramp v. Board of Pub. Instruction of Orange County, 368 U.S. 278 (1961); Shelton v. Tucker, 364 U.S. 479 (1960).
[774] 377 U.S. 360 (1964).
[775] 384 U.S. 11 (1966).
[776] *Id.* at 16.
[777] 385 U.S. 589 (1967).
[778] 389 U.S. 258 (1967).
[779] 405 U.S. 676 (1972).

Cole did not focus on the groups that an individual belonged to; the oath was seen as simply an affirmance of support for the country and its laws.

Thus, the law that emerged in this area is that the government may require that a public employee swear to uphold the Constitution of the country and its laws. The government, though, may not deny employment to individuals for their group memberships—or require an oath about them—unless the focus is solely on whether the person actively affiliated with the group, knowing of its illegal objectives, and with the specific intent of furthering those goals.

§11.3.8.3   Political Activities of Government Employees

Constitutionality of Restrictions on Government Employee Speech

The Supreme Court has held that the government may prohibit its employees from engaging in partisan political activities. The federal Hatch Act prohibited government employees from taking "an active part in political management or political campaigns."[780] In *United Public Workers v. Mitchell*, the Supreme Court initially upheld the Hatch Act and said that it was justified to prevent government officials from using employees in political activities and from pressuring them to participate in campaigns.[781] The Court said that "Congress may reasonably desire to limit party activity of federal employees so as to avoid a tendency toward a one-party system. It may have considered that parties would be more truly devoted to the public welfare if public servants were not over active politically."[782] The Court accepted Congress's concern that the Hatch Act was necessary to prevent the distortions in the political process that would result if government employers could use employees or pressure them to help in campaigns. The Court also accepted that this was desirable in order to improve the efficient operation of the government.[783]

The Court reaffirmed this in *United States Civil Service Commission v. National Association of Letter Carriers, AFL-CIO*.[784] The Court said that "[w]e unhesitatingly reaffirm . . . that Congress had, and has, the power to prevent [government employees] from holding a party office, working at the polls, and acting as party paymaster for other party workers. . . . Our judgment is that neither the First Amendment nor any other provision of the Constitution invalidates a law barring this kind of partisan political conduct by federal employees."[785]

The Court said that, in part, the prohibition on political activities by government employees was to ensure that "meritorious performance rather than political

---

[780] 5 U.S.C. §7324. This law has been substantially repealed; *see* 5 U.S.C. §7324 (1994).
[781] 330 U.S. 75 (1947).
[782] *Id.* at 100.
[783] *Id.* at 99.
[784] 413 U.S. 548 (1973).
[785] *Id.* at 556.

service" be the basis for hiring and promotions.[786] The Court reviewed the long history of such restrictions at both the federal and state levels and said that "they reflect the judgment that partisan political activities by federal employees must be limited if the Government is to operate effectively and fairly, elections are to play their proper part in representative government, and employees themselves are to be sufficiently free from improper influences."[787]

The issue posed in *Mitchell* and *Letter Carriers* is enormously difficult. The Hatch Act restricted political speech and association that is at the very core of the First Amendment. As the dissent in *Letter Carriers* argued, the government is certainly justified in prohibiting an employee from using time on the job for political activities, "[b]ut it is of no concern of Government what an employee does in his spare time, whether religion, recreation, social work, or politics is his hobby—unless what he does impairs efficiency or other facets of the merits of his job."[788] On the other hand, the Hatch Act was inspired by practical experience. Without it, and comparable state laws, there can be enormous pressure on government employees to participate in political activities. This risks distorting the political process, impairing efficient government operations, and undermining the freedoms of government workers.

Protection of Government Employees' Political Views

While *Mitchell* and *Letter Carriers* involved restrictions on the speech of government employees, the flip side of the coin is restrictions on the ability of the government to fire employees for their political views or permissible political party affiliations. *Elrod v. Burns* is the key case in this area.[789] A newly elected Democratic sheriff in Cook County, Illinois, replaced a Republican and fired all of the non–civil service Republican employees. The plaintiffs were a process server, a bailiff, and a security guard who were fired.

The Court recognized that the firings were a part of a system of patronage that has a long history in America. But the Court expressed concern that "[t]he cost of the practice of patronage is the restraint it places on freedoms of belief and association."[790] Firing individuals because of their political party affiliation or political views is inimical to the First Amendment's protection of freedom of speech.

The government argued in favor of patronage on the grounds that it improves effective government and the efficiency of public employees. The plurality opinion by Justice Brennan explained that the government's position was that "employees of political persuasions not the same as that of the party in control of public office will not have the same incentive to work effectively and may even be motivated to subvert the incumbent administration's efforts to govern effectively."[791]

---

[786] *Id.* at 557.

[787] *Id.* at 554.

[788] *Id.* at 597 (Douglas, J., dissenting).

[789] 427 U.S. 347 (1976).

[790] *Id.* at 355.

[791] *Id.* at 364.

The plurality rejected this argument and said that "it is doubtful that the mere difference of political persuasion motivates poor performance."[792] Besides, the plurality said, there were less drastic ways to ensure effective work; employees could be disciplined or fired for insubordination or poor job performance. Nor was the Court willing to accept that the patronage system was necessary to preserve the two-party system.

Justice Stewart wrote an opinion concurring in the judgment, joined by Justice Blackmun, that emphasized that the result only applied to "whether a nonpolicy-making, nonconfidential government employee can be discharged or threatened with discharge from a job that he is satisfactorily performing upon the sole ground of his political beliefs."[793] In *Branti v. Finkel*, the Court returned to exactly this issue: For what types of positions may political party affiliation be used as a criteria?[794] *Branti* involved two assistant public defenders who were fired because they were Republicans and thus did not have Democratic sponsorship when a Democratic public defender took office. The Court, based on *Elrod*, concluded that their discharge violated the First Amendment.

The Court noted that, as was observed in *Elrod*, "[political] party affiliation may be an acceptable requirement for some types of government employment."[795] Justice Stevens, writing for the Court, explained that there was no easy formula for deciding when political party affiliation is relevant. He said that the distinction between policymaking and nonpolicymaking positions was inadequate. There might be some who formulate "policy," like a football coach, where political party affiliation is irrelevant. There also might be some in nonpolicymaking positions, such as election judges in a system that requires one from each party for a county, where political party affiliation is crucial.

Thus, the Court concluded that "the ultimate inquiry is not whether the label 'policymaker' or 'confidential' fits a particular position; rather, the question is whether the hiring authority can demonstrate that party affiliation is an appropriate requirement for the effective performance of the public office involved."[796] The Court said that performance as an assistant public defender has nothing to do with political party, and thus the firings were unconstitutional.

The Court extended *Elrod* and *Branti* in *Rutan v. Republican Party of Illinois*, where it held that "the First Amendment not only limits firings because of political party affiliation, but also restricts decisions about promotions, transfers, and recalls after layoffs based on political affiliation or support."[797] Justice Scalia wrote a vehement dissent, joined by Rehnquist, Kennedy, and, in part, by O'Connor. Scalia advocated the repeal of this entire line of cases and stressed the long tradition of patronage in government.[798]

---

[792] *Id.* at 365.
[793] *Id.* at 375 (Stewart, J., concurring).
[794] 445 U.S. 507 (1980).
[795] *Id.* at 517.
[796] *Id.* at 518.
[797] 497 U.S. 62, 75 (1990).
[798] *Id.* at 95 (Scalia, J., dissenting).

However, in 1996, the Supreme Court strongly reaffirmed and extended *Elrod v. Burns*. In *O'Hare Truck Service Inc. v. Northlake, Ill.*, by a 7-to-2 decision, the Court held that the First Amendment precluded the government from terminating an independent contractor for refusing to support a political party or its candidate.[799] With only Justices Scalia and Thomas dissenting, the Court refused "to draw a line excluding independent contractors from the First Amendment safeguards of political association afforded to employees."[800]

§11.3.9   Attorneys' Speech

Protection of Speech About Judicial Proceedings

The Court repeatedly has held that speech about judicial proceedings is political speech protected by the First Amendment. Courts obviously are a part of government, and speech that reports on judicial proceedings or criticizes them serves an essential public purpose. For example, in *Bridges v. California*, the Court held that a publisher can be held in contempt for an out-of-court statement only if there is a clear and present danger of harm to the legal system.[801] A newspaper was held in contempt for a series of editorials concerning the pending sentencing of two members of a labor union who had been convicted of assaulting nonunion truck drivers. The editorial described the assailants as "thugs" and advocated prison sentences for them.

The Supreme Court overturned the contempt conviction and, in an opinion by Justice Black, forcefully declared that "[t]he assumption that respect for the judiciary can be won by shielding judges from published criticism wrongly appraises the character of American public opinion . . . and an enforced silence, however limited, solely in the name of preserving the dignity of the bench, would probably engender resentment, suspicion, and contempt much more than it would enhance respect."[802] The Court concluded that speech concerning the judicial process could be punished only if there was a clear and present danger of harm: "The substantive evil must be extremely serious and the degree of imminence extremely high before utterances can be punished."[803]

In other cases, as well, the Court has stressed the importance of speech about the judicial process and greatly restricted the government's ability to limit or punish such expression. In *Nebraska Press Association v. Stuart*, discussed above, the Court held that prior restraints on the press to prevent prejudicial pretrial publicity would be allowed only in the most extraordinary circumstances.[804] The Court

---

[799] 518 U.S. 712 (1996).

[800] *Id.* at 726. Also, on the same day, the Court held that the speech of government contractors is protected by the same standard as is applied to protect the speech of government employees. Board of County Commrs., Wabaunsee County, Kansas v. Umbehr, 518 U.S. 668 (1996).

[801] 314 U.S. 252 (1941).

[802] *Id.* at 270-271.

[803] *Id.* at 263. *See also* Wood v. Georgia, 370 U.S. 375 (1962) (overturning a contempt citation for an open letter written to the press and the grand jury).

[804] 427 U.S. 539 (1976), discussed above in §11.2.3.3.

said that such orders would be allowed only where there was reason to believe that the speech would jeopardize a fair trial, that no other alternative but a gag order could work, and that a prior restraint on media coverage would be successful in protecting a fair trial. In *Landmark Communications, Inc. v. Virginia*, also discussed above, the Court ruled that the press could not be punished for accurately report- ing about confidential judicial discipline proceedings.[805]

When Can Attorney Speech Be Punished?

Cases such as *Bridges*, *Nebraska Press*, and *Landmark* involve restrictions or punishments directed at the media. A distinct issue concerns when attorneys may be punished for their speech about pending judicial proceedings.[806] Are attor- neys "officers of the court" who can be punished for speech that otherwise would be deemed protected by the First Amendment? Or do attorneys retain their full free speech rights, especially because their information and views are essential in informing the public about the legal system?

In *Gentile v. State Bar of Nevada*, the Court held that attorney speech about pending cases is protected by the First Amendment, but that it can be punished if it poses a substantial likelihood of materially prejudicing an adjudicatory pro- ceeding.[807] A criminal defense attorney, Dominic Gentile, gave a press conference in which he said that his client was an innocent "scapegoat" who was the victim of "crooked cops."[808] After the client was acquitted, Nevada brought disciplinary proceedings against Gentile for violating the state's code of professional respon- sibility. Nevada had adopted a provision based on the American Bar Association's Model Rules of Professional Conduct that prohibits attorney speech that has a "substantial likelihood of materially prejudicing an adjudicatory proceeding."[809]

Gentile argued that an attorney should be subjected to discipline only if there is a "clear and present danger" to the fair administration of justice; he contended that the "substantial likelihood" test was not sufficiently speech protective. The Supreme Court, in a 5-to-4 decision, rejected this argument and upheld Nevada's ethical rule. The Court explained that attorneys are officers of the court and thus are more subject to regulation of their speech than others. The Court also noted that speech by attorneys could pose a greater risk to the fair administration of justice. Chief Justice Rehnquist, writing for the Court, said: "Because lawyers have special access to information through discovery and client communications, their extrajudicial statements pose a threat to the fairness of a pending proceeding since lawyers' statements are likely to be received as especially authoritative."[810] The Court thus concluded: "We agree with the majority of the States that the

---

[805] 435 U.S. 829 (1978), discussed above in §11.3.5.5.

[806] There also is the question of whether court orders directed at attorneys are constitutional. There is not a Supreme Court decision concerning this issue, and the lower court decisions are split. *See* §11.2.3.3.

[807] 501 U.S. 1030 (1991).

[808] *Id.* at 1034.

[809] ABA Model Rules of Professional Conduct, Rule 3.6(a).

[810] 501 U.S. at 1074.

'substantial likelihood of material prejudice' standard constitutes a constitutionally permissible balance between the First Amendment rights of attorneys in pending cases and the State's interest in fair trials."[811]

However, the Court also found that a particular provision in the Nevada rule was unconstitutional. The Court's decision upholding the substantial likelihood test was by a 5-to-4 margin. Justice O'Connor, who was part of the majority on that issue, joined with the dissenters to comprise a majority to declare that the "safe harbor" provisions of the law were impermissibly vague. For example, one exception said that lawyers could make statements about the nature of the defense. Justice Kennedy, writing for the Court on this issue, found that this safe harbor provision did not provide sufficient guidance as to what speech was allowed and what was protected.

Underlying *Gentile* is the assumption that speech and reporting about judicial proceedings can jeopardize the existence of a fair trial.[812] Based on these assumptions, restrictions on attorney speech makes sense in that this is the expression that is most likely to jeopardize the fairness of the proceedings. Also, attorneys, as licensed officers of the court, have a duty to the fair administration of justice that makes them more subject to regulation than the press.

On the other hand, there is no evidence that speech by attorneys—or extensive pretrial publicity generally—undermines the ability of defendants to receive fair trials. Also, the test approved by the Court is inherently vague; no lawyer can know what speech will later be found to have posed a substantial likelihood of materially prejudicing an adjudicatory proceeding. As a result, lawyers are likely to be chilled from expressing their views. In some instances, this could be to the detriment of their clients who might be better served by the points that would be made in the press. Indeed, there might be cases where the loss of attorney speech means that there is more inaccurate reporting as the media will need to rely on secondary and tertiary sources.

Punishing Attorneys for Speech Critical of Courts

An issue still unresolved by the Supreme Court is when a court may punish an attorney for speech critical of it and its judges. In *Standing Committee on Discipline v. Yagman*, the Ninth Circuit held that an attorney could be punished for such expression only if it was proved that there was actual malice.[813] An attorney was suspended from practice for two years for calling a judge a buffoon and accusing him of being anti-Semitic in applying sanctions. The discipline was for impugning the integrity of the courts and for attempting to interfere with the random

---

[811] *Id.*

[812] *See* Sheppard v. Maxwell, 384 U.S. 333 (1966) (overturning a conviction because of the "carnival atmosphere of the trial" and especially the failure of the judge to protect the jury from the publicity).

[813] 55 F.3d 1430 (9th Cir. 1995); *see also* United States Dist. Ct. for the Eastern Dist. of Washington v. Sandlin, 12 F.3d 861 (9th Cir. 1993) (upholding discipline of attorney for speech).

selection of judges; it was alleged that the attorney had spoken out to force the judge to recuse himself.

The Ninth Circuit, in an opinion by Judge Alex Kozinski, reversed. The Ninth Circuit emphasized the importance of speech about courts and judges and said that it could be punished only if there was actual malice. The court found that Yagman's statements either had been opinions or were factual allegations based on belief that they were true. The court rejected the claim that these statements would interfere with the random selection of judges because nothing would require that the criticized judge recuse himself.

In contrast, the United States Court of Appeals for the Seventh Circuit disagreed with the *Yagman* approach and accorded courts more ability to punish lawyers for their speech.[814] In an opinion by Judge Frank Easterbrook, the court upheld the disbarment of an attorney from practice in federal court for making false accusations against judges. The court expressly disagreed with the Ninth Circuit's ruling in the *Yagman* case and said that attorneys do not get the same freedom as others to participate in political debate. A key difference between rulings of the Ninth Circuit and the Seventh Circuit in these cases is that the former court emphasized that most of the statements by the lawyer were opinions protected by the First Amendment, while the latter court said that there were false factual statements implied in the statements of opinion.

§11.3.10 Labor Picketing and Protests

Lower Level of First Amendment Protection

The Court has recognized the need for the government to regulate labor disputes and thus has permitted more government latitude to restrict speech in this area than generally would be permitted under the First Amendment. Section 158 of the National Labor Relations Act defines "unfair labor practices."[815] Section 158(b)(4)(B) prohibits "forcing or requiring any person to cease using, selling, handling, transporting, or otherwise dealing in the products of any other producer, processor or manufacturer, or to cease doing business with any other person, or forcing or requiring any other employer to recognize or bargain with a labor organization as the representative of his employees."[816]

In *NLRB v. National Retail Store Employees, Local 1001 (Safeco)*, the Court found that picketing urging a general boycott of a secondary employer and urging it to end business with the union's primary antagonist was prohibited by §158(b)(4)(i) and (ii).[817] Specifically, the union was picketing title companies even though its real dispute was with the insurance company, Safeco. The union sought, via its picketing, to pressure the title companies to cancel their business with Safeco. Over 90 percent of the title company's income was from the sale of Safeco insurance.

---

[814] In the Matter of Michael Palmisano, 70 F.3d 483 (7th Cir. 1995).
[815] 29 U.S.C. §158(b)(4).
[816] §158(b)(4)(B).
[817] 447 U.S. 607 (1980).

The Supreme Court held that the picketing was not protected by the First Amendment and could be punished under the National Labor Relations Act. Justice Powell, writing for the plurality, said that the truthful picketing could be prohibited because it "spreads labor discord by coercing a neutral party to join the fray."[818] The plurality thus concluded that the prohibition of the picketing imposed "no impermissible restrictions upon constitutionally protected speech."[819]

What is troubling about *Safeco* is that it upheld a broad prohibition of truthful speech that would be protected in virtually any other context.[820] As Professor Theodore St. Antoine observed, "[*Safeco*] was the first time the Supreme Court had ever clearly sustained a ban on peaceful and orderly picketing addressed to, and calling for seemingly lawful responses by, individual consumers acting on their own."[821]

However, in *DeBartolo Corp. v. Florida Gulf Coast Building and Construction Trades Council,* the Court refused to extend *Safeco* to a union's peaceful handbilling of a business.[822] A union was in a dispute with the H.J. High Corporation over wages and benefits. The High Corporation had been hired by the H.J. Wilson Company to construct stores in a mall that was operated by the Edward J. DeBartolo Corporation. The union sought to place pressure on High and Wilson through leaflets asking customers not to shop at any of the stores in the mall "until the Mall's owner publicly promises that all construction at the Mall will be done using contractors who pay their employees fair wages and fringe benefits."[823] The handbills made it clear that the union was seeking a consumer boycott of the stores, not a secondary strike of those businesses by their employees.

The DeBartolo Corporation contended that the handbills were an unfair labor practice under §8(b)(4). The Court rejected that argument and found that the speech was protected by the First Amendment. The Court stressed that "[t]he handbills involved here truthfully revealed the existence of a labor dispute and urged potential customers of the mall to follow a wholly legal course of action, namely, not to patronize the retailers doing business in the mall. The handbilling was peaceful. No picketing or patrolling was involved."[824]

The Court found that the speech was not coercive and thus protected by the First Amendment. The Court explained that "[t]here is no suggestion that the leaflets had any coercive effect on customers of the mall. There was no violence, picketing, or patrolling and only an attempt to persuade customers not to shop in the mall."[825] The Court thus distinguished picketing from distribution of leaflets based on the likely degree of coercion.

---

[818] *Id.* at 616.

[819] *Id.*

[820] *See, e.g.,* NAACP v. Claiborne Hardware Co., 458 U.S. 886 (1982) (finding First Amendment protection for consumer boycott and picketing).

[821] For a thorough recent discussion of the law of labor picketing and the First Amendment, *see* Catherine L. Fisk & Jessica Rutter, Labor Protest Under the New First Amendment, 36 Berkeley J. Emp. & Lab. L. no. 2 (2015). *See also* James Pope, Labor and the Constitution: From Abolition to Deindustrialization, 65 Tex. L. Rev. 1071 (1987).

[822] 485 U.S. 568 (1988).

[823] *Id.* at 570.

[824] *Id.* at 575-576.

[825] *Id.* at 578.

§11.4 WHAT PLACES ARE AVAILABLE FOR SPEECH?

§11.4.1 Introduction

Importance of the Issue

Speech often requires a place for it to occur. Most people lack access to the mass media—television, radio, newspapers—to express their message. They need to have a place to distribute leaflets, or a corner to place a soapbox. Moreover, some types of expression require a larger area than a private person is likely to own. A protest rally or demonstration is an important way of attracting public attention and communicating that a large group shares a sentiment. Indeed, such activity is a form of "assembly" expressly protected by the First Amendment.

Thus, the issue arises as to what property is available for speech. Most of these cases involve claims of a right to use government property for speech purposes. The Court has dealt with this issue by identifying different types of government property—public forums, limited public forums, and nonpublic forums—and by articulating different rules as to when the government can regulate each. These cases are discussed in §11.4.2.

There have been claims of a right to use private property for speech, especially privately owned shopping centers. After initially deciding in the other direction, it is now clearly established that there generally is no right to use private property for speech purposes. Because it is privately owned, there is no state action and the Constitution does not apply. These cases are discussed in §11.4.3.

Finally, the identity of the places is sometimes relevant in another sense. The Supreme Court has treated speech in some government places differently based on the need for greater government control. These are authoritarian environments such as the military, prisons, and schools. Although the juxtaposition of these three places may seem odd, in each the Court has expressed a need for great deference to the government based on the authoritarian nature of the institution. These cases are discussed in §11.4.4.

§11.4.2 Government Properties and Speech

§11.4.2.1 Introduction

The Initial Rejection and Recognition of the Public Forum

Initially, the courts rejected any claim of a right to use government property for speech purposes. In *Davis v. Commonwealth of Massachusetts*, the Supreme Court upheld a Boston ordinance that prohibited "any public address" on publicly owned property "except in accordance with a permit from the mayor."[1] The

§11.4 [1] 167 U.S. 43 (1897).

Supreme Court affirmed a decision of the Massachusetts Supreme Judicial Court that found the ordinance constitutional. Oliver Wendell Holmes, then a Justice on the Massachusetts Court, concluded that the law was permissible because the government has the right to control the use of its property.[2] Holmes wrote that for "the Legislature absolutely or conditionally to forbid public speaking in a highway or public park is no more an infringement of the rights of a member of the public than for the owner of a private house to forbid it in his house."[3]

The United States Supreme Court affirmed and also spoke broadly of the government's ability to restrict the use of its property. The Court explained that the government's "right to absolutely exclude all right to use necessarily includes the authority to determine under what circumstances such use may be availed of, as the greater power contains the lesser."[4] The Court refused to recognize any First Amendment right to use government property for speech purposes.

Although occasionally the Supreme Court still speaks of the government's ability to control its property, including by prohibiting speech,[5] for the last 75 years the Court has recognized a right to use at least some government property under some circumstances for speech. *Hague v. CIO*[6] and *Schneider v. State of New Jersey*,[7] both decided in 1939, were crucial in recognizing this right. *Hague* involved an attempt by a mayor to prevent a union, the Council of Industrial Organizations, to organize in that city. An ordinance was enacted that prohibited all public meetings in the streets and other public places without a permit from the city. In a famous plurality opinion, Justice Owen Roberts found that there was a right to use government property for speech purposes. Roberts wrote: "Wherever the title of streets and parks may rest, they have immemorially been held in trust for the use of the public and, time out of mind, have been used for purposes of assembly, communicating thought between citizens, and discussing public questions. Such use of the streets and public places has, from ancient times, been a part of the privileges, immunities, rights, and liberties of citizens."[8]

In *Schneider*, the Court declared unconstitutional a city's ordinance that prohibited the distribution of leaflets on public property. The city maintained that it could do so in order to minimize litter and to maintain the appearance of its streets. The Court rejected this argument. The Court, again in an opinion by Justice Roberts, said: "We are of opinion that the purpose to keep the streets clean and of good appearance is insufficient to justify an ordinance which prohibits a person rightfully on a public street from handing literature to one willing to receive it. Any burden imposed upon the city authorities in cleaning and caring

---

[2] Commonwealth v. Davis, 162 Mass. 510, 39 N.E. 113 (1895).

[3] 39 N.E. 113, *aff'd*, 167 U.S. 43 (1897).

[4] 167 U.S. at 48.

[5] *See, e.g.*, Adderley v. Florida, 385 U.S. 39, 47 (1966) ("The State, no less than a private owner of property, has power to preserve the property under its control for the use to which it is lawfully dedicated.").

[6] 307 U.S. 496 (1939).

[7] 308 U.S. 147 (1939).

[8] 307 U.S. at 515 (Roberts, J., concurring).

for the streets as an indirect consequence of such distribution results from the constitutional protection of the freedom of speech and press."[9]

Schneider is important because it established that a city must allow speech on its property even if doing so will impose costs on the city.[10] Moreover, *Schneider* is significant because the Court expressly rejected the city's contention that it could restrict distribution of leaflets because other places were available for the speech. Justice Roberts wrote: "[T]he streets are natural and proper places for the dissemination of information and opinion; and one is not to have the exercise of his liberty of expression in appropriate places abridged on the plea that it may be exercised in some other place."[11]

What Government Property Under What Circumstances?

Once a right to use government property for speech is recognized, the issue inevitably arises: What publicly owned property must be made available for speech and under what circumstances?[12] For example, while *Hague* and *Schneider* recognize a presumptive right to use the sidewalks and the parks for speech purposes, there obviously would be problems with allowing speech in the middle of a courtroom during a trial or on the runways of a public-owned airport or in the middle of a highway during rush hour.

The Court has dealt with this issue by classifying different types of government property and articulating varying rules for when speech in each can be regulated. A clear statement of these categories and the rules applied for each is in *Perry Education Association v. Perry Local Educators' Association.*[13] The issue was whether it was permissible for a school to give the teachers' collective bargaining representative exclusive use of an interschool mail system in the district. A rival union wished to use the mail system and pointed to the fact that it was available to community groups, teachers, and the administration. The Court upheld the exclusion of the rival union from using the postal system and in doing so identified types of government property:

> The existence of a right of access to public property and the standard by which limitations upon such a right must be evaluated differ depending on the character of the property at issue. . . . In places which by long tradition or by government fiat have been devoted to assembly and debate, the rights of the state to limit expressive activity are sharply circumscribed . . . [such as] streets and parks. . . . In these

---

[9]   308 U.S. at 162.

[10]   *See* also Jamison v. Texas, 318 U.S. 413 (1943) (declaring unconstitutional a city's ordinance that prohibited the distribution of leaflets and expressly rejecting the city's argument of an absolute right to control speech on public property).

[11]   *Id.* at 163.

[12]   Excellent scholarship on this topic includes Lillian Bevier, Rehabilitating Public Forum Doctrine: In Defense of Categories, 1992 Sup. Ct. Rev. 79; Robert Post, Between Governance and Management: The History and Theory of the Public Forum, 34 UCLA L. Rev. 1713 (1987); Geoffrey Stone, Fora Americana: Speech in Public Places, 1974 Sup. Ct. Rev. 233; Harry Kalven, Jr., The Concept of the Public Forum: *Cox v. Louisiana*, 1965 Sup. Ct. Rev. 1.

[13]   460 U.S. 37 (1983).

quintessential public forums, the government may not prohibit all communicative activity. For the state to enforce a content-based exclusion it must show that its regulation is necessary to serve a compelling state interest and is narrowly drawn to achieve that end. . . . A second category consists of public property which the state has voluntarily opened for use by the public as a place for expressive activity. . . . Although a state is not required to indefinitely retain the open character of the facility, as long as it does so it is bound by the same standards as apply in a traditional public forum. . . . Public property which is not by tradition or designation a forum for public communication is governed by different standards. . . . [T]he state may reserve the forum for its intended purposes, communicative or otherwise, as long as the regulation on speech is reasonable and not an effort to suppress expression merely because public officials oppose the speakers' views.[14]

Thus, under *Perry* the constitutionality of a regulation of speech depends on the place and the nature of the government's action. In its most recent formulation, in *Christian Legal Society v. Martinez,* the Court articulated these categories somewhat differently.[15] In a footnote, Justice Ginsburg, writing for the Court, stated:

In conducting forum analysis, our decisions have sorted government property into three categories. First, in traditional public forums, such as public streets and parks, "any restriction based on the content of . . . speech must satisfy strict scrutiny, that is, the restriction must be narrowly tailored to serve a compelling government interest." Second, governmental entities create designated public forums when "government property that has not traditionally been regarded as a public forum is intentionally opened up for that purpose"; speech restrictions in such a forum "are subject to the same strict scrutiny as restrictions in a traditional public forum." Third, governmental entities establish limited public forums by opening property "limited to use by certain groups or dedicated solely to the discussion of certain subjects." As noted in text, "[i]n such a forum, a governmental entity may impose restrictions on speech that are reasonable and viewpoint-neutral."[16]

Interestingly, although prior cases speak of "non-public forums," government properties that the government can and does close to speech, this formulation does not mention them. All of the types of forums mentioned by Justice Ginsburg are opened for at least some speech activities. It is possible that the Court has collapsed nonpublic forums into the category of limited public forums since the test for both would be the same: Government regulation is allowed if it is reasonable and viewpoint neutral. Or it is possible that this was simply an omission because the Court in *Christian Legal Society v. Martinez* was dealing with what the Court deemed a "limited public forum" and did not have any occasion to consider non-public forums.[17]

---

[14] *Id.* at 44-46. The Court found that the school mail system was a nonpublic forum and that the regulation was constitutional because it was reasonable and viewpoint neutral.

[15] 130 S. Ct. 2971 (2010).

[16] *Id.* at 2984 n.11 (citations omitted).

[17] *Christian Legal Society v. Martinez* involved officially recognized student groups at a state university law school. It is discussed in detail below.

The law concerning each of these types of forums—public forums, designated public forums, limited public forums, and nonpublic forums—is reviewed in §§11.4.2.2 to 11.4.2.5.[18] An obvious and crucial question is what determines the category for a particular government property. Although the Court has ruled on many specific places, it never has articulated a clear set of criteria to be applied to determine how a particular property is to be categorized. Section 11.4.2.6 considers the criteria that have been used in this regard.

§11.4.2.2   Public Forums

Summary of the Law Concerning Public Forums

Public forums are government-owned properties that the government is constitutionally obligated to make available for speech. Sidewalks and parks are paradigm examples of the public forum. As the Court recently expressed: "It is no accident that public streets and sidewalks have developed as venues for the exchange of ideas. Even today, they remain one of the few places where a speaker can be confident that he is not simply preaching to the choir. With respect to other means of communication, an individual confronted with an uncomfortable message can always turn the page, change the channel, or leave the Web site. Not so on public streets and sidewalks."[19]

The government may regulate speech in public forums only if certain requirements are met. First, the regulation must be content-neutral unless the content restriction is justified by strict scrutiny. Second, it must be a reasonable time, place, or manner restriction that serves an important government interest and leaves open adequate alternative places for speech. Third, a licensing or permit system for the use of public forums must serve an important purpose, give clear criteria to the licensing authority that leaves almost no discretion, and provide procedural safeguards such as a requirement for prompt determination of license requests and judicial review of license denials. Finally, the Court has ruled that government regulation of speech in public forums need not use the least restrictive alternative, although it must be narrowly tailored to achieve the government's purpose. Each of these requirements is discussed in turn.

Content Neutrality

The general requirement that the government be content-neutral when regulating speech is discussed in §11.2.1. The Court has specifically ruled, such as in *Perry* and *Christian Legal Society* quoted above, that government regulation of speech in public forums must be content-neutral. At a minimum, this means that

---

[18] Although the Court in *Christian Legal Society* does not mention nonpublic forums, they are included here because of prior cases using this category and because it is not clear that the summary of the categories in the footnote was meant to eliminate this previously recognized category.

[19] McCullen v. Coakley, 134 S. Ct. 2518, 2529 (2014), discussed below.

the government cannot regulate speech based on its viewpoint or its subject matter unless strict scrutiny is met.[20]

Viewpoint restrictions of speech are virtually never allowed. The government obviously should not be able to advance a particular position by silencing those holding an opposite view. *Boos v. Berry* illustrates the impermissibility of viewpoint restrictions in government regulation of speech in public forums.[21] A District of Columbia ordinance prohibited the display of signs criticizing a foreign government within 500 feet of its embassy. The Court declared this unconstitutional because it was an obvious content-based restriction of speech. Whether the speech would be permitted depended on whether the content would embarrass a foreign government. The Court stressed that the regulation controlled political speech in a classic public forum, sidewalks.

The Court, however, upheld a separate part of the ordinance that allowed police to disperse demonstrators gathered within 500 feet of a foreign embassy if there was a threat to peace or security. The Court emphasized that this regulation was content-neutral and served important interests in public safety and order.

The requirement for subject matter neutrality reflects the ability of a government to control expression by prohibiting discussion of some topics. For example, if Southern states in the 1960s had prohibited discussion of civil rights in public parks or on public sidewalks, the ostensibly viewpoint neutral regulation would have had a dramatically disproportionate effect on those seeking to advance racial equality. Additionally, the Court has stressed the importance of equal access to public forums for speech purposes.[22] In fact, two leading cases, *Police Department of Chicago v. Mosley*[23] and *Carey v. Brown*,[24] expressly relied on the equal protection clause in declaring unconstitutional subject matter restrictions on speech on public sidewalks.

Mosley involved a Chicago ordinance that prohibited picketing or demonstrations within 150 feet of a school building while the school was in session, except for peaceful picketing in connection with a labor dispute. Earl Mosley frequently picketed the school, usually by himself, to protest what he perceived as race discrimination by the school. The protests were conceded by the city to be always peaceful, orderly, and quiet.[25]

The Supreme Court expressly used equal protection for analyzing the Chicago ordinance. Justice Marshall, writing for the Court, said: "Because Chicago treats some picketing differently from others, we analyze this ordinance in terms of the Equal Protection Clause of the Fourteenth Amendment."[26] The Court also

---

[20] *See, e.g.*, Niemotko v. Maryland, 340 U.S. 268 (1951) (declaring it unconstitutional for a city to deny Jehovah's Witnesses a permit to use a city park when other religious and political groups were able to do so).

[21] 485 U.S. 312 (1988).

[22] For an excellent discussion of the relationship of equality to freedom of speech, *see* Kenneth Karst, Equality as a Central Principle in the First Amendment, 43 U. Chi. L. Rev. 20 (1975).

[23] 408 U.S. 92 (1972).

[24] 447 U.S. 455 (1980).

[25] 408 U.S. at 92.

[26] *Id.* at 94-95.

recognized that the law restricted speech that was clearly protected by the First Amendment.

The Court concluded that the law was unconstitutional because it was an impermissible subject matter restriction on speech. Justice Marshall declared: "The central problem with Chicago's ordinance is that it describes permissible picketing in terms of its subject matter. Peaceful picketing on the subject of a school's labor-management dispute is permitted, but all other peaceful picketing is prohibited. The operative distinction is the message on a picket sign. But, above all else, the First Amendment means that government has no power to restrict expression because of its message, its ideas, its subject matter, or its content."[27]

Similarly, in *Carey v. Brown*, the Supreme Court declared unconstitutional an Illinois statute that prohibited picketing or demonstrations around a person's residence unless the dwelling is used as a place of business or is a place of employment involved in a labor dispute.[28] In other words, under the law, picketing in residential neighborhoods was allowed if it was a labor dispute connected to a place of employment, but otherwise generally speech was prohibited. The Court again applied equal protection and found the law unconstitutional. The Court applied *Mosley* and concluded: "[The] Act accords preferential treatment to the expression of views on one particular subject; information about labor disputes may be freely disseminated, but discussion of all other issues is restricted. . . . When government discriminates among speech-related activities in a public forum, the Equal Protection Clause mandates that the legislation be finely tailored to serve substantial interests, and the justifications offered for and distinctions it draws must be carefully scrutinized."[29]

In contrast, in *Hill v. Colorado*,[30] the Court upheld a regulation on protests outside abortion clinics based on its conclusion that the restrictions on speech were content-neutral. The Colorado law applied within 100 feet of the entrance to any health care facility and made it unlawful within that area for any person to "knowingly approach" within 8 feet of another person, without that person's consent, "for the purpose of passing a leaflet or handbill to, displaying a sign to, or engaging in oral protest, education, or counseling with such other person."[31]

The Supreme Court, in a 6-to-3 decision, upheld this as constitutional. Justice Stevens wrote for the majority and emphasized that the law applied no matter what the topic or viewpoint of the speech. Justice Stevens said that the law was content-neutral for three reasons: "First, it is not a 'regulation of speech.' Rather, it is a regulation of the places where some speech may occur. Second, it was not adopted 'because of disagreement with the message it conveys.' This conclusion is supported not just by the Colorado courts' interpretation of legislative history, but more importantly by the State Supreme Court's unequivocal holding that the statute's 'restrictions apply equally to all demonstrators, regardless of viewpoint, and

---

[27] *Id.* at 95.
[28] 447 U.S. 455 (1980).
[29] *Id.* at 461-462.
[30] 530 U.S. 703 (2000).
[31] Colo. Rev. Stat. §18-9-122(3).

the statutory language makes no reference to the content of the speech.' Third, the State's interests in protecting access and privacy, and providing the police with clear guidelines, are unrelated to the content of the demonstrators' speech. As we have repeatedly explained, government regulation of expressive activity is 'content neutral' if it is justified without reference to the content of regulated speech."[32]

Justice Scalia's dissent, joined by Justice Thomas, argued that the law was clearly content-based because it was adopted with the goal of stopping a particular message and had the effect of discriminating against it. He wrote: "What is before us is a speech regulation directed against the opponents of abortion, and it therefore enjoys the benefit of the 'ad hoc nullification machine' that the Court has set in motion to push aside whatever doctrines of constitutional law stand in the way of that highly favored practice. Having deprived abortion opponents of the political right to persuade the electorate that abortion should be restricted by law, the Court today continues and expands its assault upon their individual right to persuade women contemplating abortion that what they are doing is wrong. . . . I have no doubt that this regulation would be deemed content-based in an instant if the case before us involved antiwar protesters, or union members seeking to 'educate' the public about the reasons for their strike."[33]

Ultimately, the issue in *Hill* goes beyond how the government may regulate public forums; it is about the question of how to determine if a law is content-based or content-neutral. The majority says that it is irrelevant if the purpose and effect of a law are to restrict a particular message, so long as the law can be justified with other permissible, content-neutral purposes. The dissent says that when a law is adopted with the goal of restricting a specific message, the law should be deemed content-based, even if there are other justifications for the statute. The majority might have said, but did not say, that the compelling need to protect women and health care workers justified the restrictions even if they were content-based. Instead, both the majority and the dissent in *Hill* focused on whether the law is content-based.

The Court returned to the issue of buffer zones around health care facilities in *McCullen v. Coakley*.[34] A Massachusetts law created a 35-foot buffer zone around reproductive health care facilities. The only individuals allowed in this area were patients, employees, law enforcement personnel, and those needing to cross the space to get to an adjacent facility. Chief Justice Roberts, writing for the majority (joined by Justices Ginsburg, Breyer, Sotomayor, and Kagan) held that the law was unconstitutional because it restricted speech on public sidewalks and other traditional public forums, but was not sufficiently narrowly tailored.

The Court said that the Massachusetts law was content-neutral because it did not restrict speech based on its topic or viewpoint. But the Court explained that even a content-neutral regulation of speech in a public forum must be narrowly tailored and said that "[f]or a content-neutral time, place, or manner regulation to be narrowly tailored," it must not "burden substantially more speech than is

---

[32] 530 U.S. at 719-720.
[33] *Id.* at 741-742 (Scalia, J., dissenting).
[34] 134 S. Ct. 2518 (2014).

necessary to further the government's legitimate interests."[35] The Court focused especially on the "sidewalk counselors" who wanted to approach women entering the facilities and said that the restrictions on their speech was not narrowly tailored. The Court concluded: "The buffer zones burden substantially more speech than necessary to achieve the Commonwealth's asserted interest."[36]

Justice Scalia, joined by Justices Kennedy and Thomas, and Justice Alito wrote separate opinions concurring in the judgment and would have gone much further in limiting buffer zones around reproductive health care facilities. These Justices saw the Massachusetts law as content-based, restricting antiabortion speech. Justice Scalia expressly called for the overruling of *Hill v. Colorado*,[37] while Justice Alito implicitly did so.[38]

An area where the Court has upheld ordinances as content-neutral are laws that prohibited focused picketing at a person's home where the laws are completely subject matter neutral. In *Frisby v. Schultz*, the Court sustained an ordinance that prohibited picketing "before or about" any residence.[39] Although the law was adopted in response to targeted picketing by antiabortion protestors of a doctor's home, the Court concluded that the law was permissible because it was content-neutral and it was narrowly tailored to protect people's tranquility and repose in their homes. The Court stressed that the ordinance allowed picketing in the area and even on the street, but just not targeted at one person's home. Justice O'Connor, writing for the Court, said that "[t]he First Amendment permits the government to prohibit offensive speech as intrusive when the 'captive' audience cannot avoid the objectionable speech. The target of the focused picketing banned by the . . . ordinance is just such a 'captive.' The resident is figuratively, and perhaps literally, trapped within the home."[40]

Whether the analysis is under equal protection or solely under the First Amendment does not matter. The government cannot regulate speech in a public forum based on the viewpoint or subject matter of the speech unless it can meet strict scrutiny. Although history shows that strict scrutiny is rarely met, occasionally the Court finds that the test is satisfied. For example, in *Burson v. Freeman*, the Court found that there was a content-based regulation, used strict scrutiny, and upheld a law that prohibited distribution of campaign literature within 100 feet of the entrance of a polling place.[41] The Court said that the history of campaign workers intimidating voters around polling places created a compelling interest sufficient to justify the content-based restriction of speech.

---

[35] *Id.* at 2535.
[36] *Id.* at 2537.
[37] *Id.* at 2545 (Scalia, J., concurring in the judgment) ("I necessarily conclude that *Hill* should be overruled.).
[38] *Id.* at 2549 (Alito, J., concurring in the judgment).
[39] 487 U.S. 474 (1988).
[40] *Id.* at 487.
[41] 504 U.S. 191 (1992).

Time, Place, and Manner Restrictions

The concept of "time, place, and manner restrictions" is often uttered in connection with the First Amendment. It refers to the ability of the government to regulate speech in a public forum in a manner that minimizes disruption of a public place while still protecting freedom of speech. In *Heffron v. International Society for Krishna Consciousness, Inc.*, the Court said that it had often approved reasonable time, place, and manner restrictions "provided that they are justified without reference to the content of the regulated speech, that they serve a significant governmental interest, and that in doing so they leave open ample alternative channels for communication of the information."[42]

In *Heffron*, the Supreme Court upheld a regulation of speech at the Minnesota State Fair that prohibited the distribution of literature or the soliciting of funds except at booths. Booths were available on a first-come, first-serve basis. The Court said that the regulation was content-neutral because it applied to all literature and solicitations regardless of the speaker, viewpoint, or subject matter. The Court accepted the state's argument that the rule was justified by an important interest: regulating the flow of pedestrian traffic through the state fair grounds. The Court said the need for crowd control was "sufficient to satisfy the requirement that a place or manner restriction must serve a substantial state interest."[43] The Court also observed that the Krishna had other ways of reaching the audience, both off the fair grounds and at booths within the grounds.

In many other cases, the Court has upheld government restrictions of speech in public forums as permissible time, place, and manner restrictions. In *Kovacs v. Cooper*, the Court upheld a restriction on the use of sound amplification devices, such as loudspeakers on trucks.[44] The Court emphasized that the law did not prohibit all such devices, but rather was a reasonable time, place, and manner restriction.[45]

In *Grayned v. Rockford*, the Court upheld a city's ordinance that prohibited any "person, while on public or private grounds adjacent to any building in which a school or any class thereof is in session, [to make] any noise or diversion which disturbs or tends to disturb the peace or good order of such school."[46] The Court found that the restriction was a reasonable time, place, and manner restriction and affirmed a conviction for violating it. The Court said that the "crucial question is whether the manner of expression is basically incompatible with the normal activity of a particular place at a particular time."[47] The Court said that the ordinance was constitutional because it prohibited speech disruptive of schools

---

[42] 452 U.S. 640, 648 (1981).

[43] *Id.* at 654.

[44] 336 U.S. 77 (1949).

[45] In comparison, in *Saia v. New York*, 334 U.S. 558 (1948), the Court declared unconstitutional a restriction on sound trucks where the mayor had discretion as to whether to grant a permit. The Court's concern was that such discretion could open the door to content-based discrimination among speech.

[46] 408 U.S. 104, 107-108 (1972).

[47] *Id.* at 116.

and that was permissible based on the city's important interest in ensuring order sufficient for schooling.

In *Clark v. Community for Creative Non-Violence*, the Court approved a federal regulation and Park Service decision to keep a group protesting the plight of the homeless from sleeping in the park.[48] The National Park Service allowed the Community for Creative Non-Violence to erect a tent city in Lafayette Park and the Mall in Washington, D.C., as a symbolic protest, but refused to allow the demonstrators to sleep in the tents because of a regulation prohibiting camping in these parks. The Supreme Court accepted the contention that overnight sleeping as a part of this protest was a form of expressive conduct, but the Court upheld the regulation as a reasonable time, place, and manner restriction. The Court emphasized that the restriction was content-neutral, that it served the important purpose of preserving the attractiveness of the parks, and that it left adequate alternative ways of expressing the message. For example, the demonstrators could "feign" sleep in the tents, just not actually sleep there.

In several cases, the Court has upheld restrictions on protests outside abortion clinics as reasonable time, place, and manner restrictions. In *Madsen v. Women's Health Center*, the Court upheld a court order restricting speech in a 36-foot buffer zone around an abortion clinic.[49] A state court trial judge issued an order that, in part, created a buffer zone around the entrance to a clinic that provided abortions so as to protect the ability of people to enter and leave the facility. The Court upheld this, as well as noise restrictions, but struck down a ban on signs in the area, saying that this was unnecessary to achieve the government's goal of protecting the operation of the facility.

In *Schenck v. Pro-Choice Network of Western New York*, the Court again upheld a court order creating a buffer zone around an abortion clinic, though it invalidated a "floating buffer zone" around individuals using the facility.[50] After finding that repeated violence and harassment had occurred, a federal district court banned demonstrations within 15 feet of doorways, parking lot entrances, and driveways. The district court also prohibited approaching within 15 feet of any person or vehicle seeking to enter or leave the facility. Chief Justice Rehnquist wrote the opinion for the Court and held that the fixed buffer zone was constitutional; the Court emphasized the need for deference to the knowledge of trial courts that formulate such orders. But the Court invalidated floating buffer zones "because they burden more speech than is necessary to serve the relevant government interests."[51] The Court noted that the floating buffer zones prevent communicating a message from a normal conversational distance or from handing out leaflets.

Subsequently, in *Hill v. Colorado*,[52] the Court upheld a state law that restricted speech activities within 100 feet of the entrance to any health care facility. The law makes it unlawful within the regulated areas for any person to "knowingly

---

[48] 468 U.S. 288 (1984).
[49] 512 U.S. 753 (1994).
[50] 519 U.S. 357 (1997).
[51] *Id.* at 377.
[52] 530 U.S. 703 (2000).

approach" within 8 feet of another person, without that person's consent, "for the purpose of passing a leaflet or handbill to, displaying a sign to, or engaging in oral protest, education, or counseling with such other person."[53] The Court, in a 6-to-3 decision, upheld the law and stressed that this was a time, place, and manner restriction on speech that served the important interest of protecting patients and health care workers.[54]

While in *Heffron*, *Kovacs*, *Grayned*, *Clark*, *Madsen*, *Schenck*, and *Hill*, the Court upheld the regulations as permissible time, place, and manner restrictions, in other cases the Court has used this test and ruled against the government. For instance, in *Brown v. Louisiana*, the Court reversed the conviction of a group of African Americans who had conducted a silent sit-in as a protest at a racially segregated public library.[55] The plurality opinion stressed that it was a silent protest that did not interfere with the operation of the library. The plurality also was undoubtedly influenced by the importance of the protest. The plurality said that "the First Amendment protected the right in a peaceable and orderly manner to protest by silent and reproachful presence, in a place where the protestant has every right to be, the unconstitutional segregation of public facilities."[56]

In *United States v. Grace*, the Court declared unconstitutional a broad restriction of speech on the public sidewalks surrounding the Supreme Court's building.[57] In part, the regulation prohibited the display of "any flag, banner, or device designed or adapted to bring into public notice any party, organization, or movement."[58] The Court found that the rule was not a reasonable time, place, and manner restriction because a total ban on all speech was unnecessary to preserve order and prevent disruption of Supreme Court proceedings. Silent protests never would interfere with the Court, and the Court rejected the argument that protests could be prohibited to prevent the public from inferring that decisions were influenced by the demonstrations.

Looked at together, all of these cases indicate that the determination of whether a regulation is a reasonable time, place, and manner restriction is entirely contextual. In each instance, the Court has to assess whether the regulation serves an important interest and whether it leaves open adequate alternative places for expression.

Licensing and Permit Systems

As described in §11.2.3.4, a licensing or permit system is a classic form of prior restraint. The Court has made it clear that the government can require a license

[53] Colo. Rev. Stat. §18-9-122(3).
[54] But in *McCullen v. Coakley*, 134 S. Ct. 2518 (2014), discussed above, the Court declared unconstitutional a Massachusetts law that created a 35-foot buffer zone around reproductive health care facilities. The Court found that the law was not sufficiently narrowly tailored to meet First Amendment scrutiny for a content-neutral law restricting speech on a public forum.
[55] 383 U.S. 131 (1966).
[56] *Id.* at 142.
[57] 461 U.S. 171 (1983).
[58] *Id.*

for speech in public forums only if there is an important reason for licensing, there are clear criteria leaving almost no discretion to the licensing authority, and there are procedural safeguards such as a requirement for prompt determination of license requests and judicial review of license denials.

A permit system that meets all of these requirements will be allowed. For instance, in *Cox v. New Hampshire*, the Court upheld an ordinance that required that those wishing to hold a parade or demonstration obtain a permit and that allowed a permit to be denied only if the area already was in use by another group.[59] The Court found that the government had an important interest in requiring a permit for speech so as to make sure that there was only one demonstration in a place at a time. Professor Harry Kalven referred to this as "Robert's Rules of Order" for use of the public forum.[60] The Court emphasized that the "licensing board was not vested with arbitrary power or an unfettered discretion."[61]

In contrast, permit systems that leave significant discretion to the licensing authority are declared unconstitutional because they risk the government granting permits to favored speech and denying them to unpopular expression. In *Lovell v. City of Griffin*, the Court declared unconstitutional a city's ordinance that prohibited the distribution of leaflets, literature, or advertising without the written permission of the city manager.[62] The Court explained that the regulation was a prior restraint that "strikes at the very foundation of the freedom of the press by subjecting it to license and censorship. The struggle for freedom of the press was primarily directed against the power of the licensor."[63] The Court said that "[l]egislation of the type of the ordinance in question would restore the system of license and censorship in its baldest form."[64]

Similarly, in *Saia v. New York*, the Supreme Court declared unconstitutional an ordinance that required a permit in order to use a sound amplification system on a motor vehicle.[65] Although as described above the Court has upheld restrictions on such sound trucks,[66] an ordinance that gives unfettered discretion to government officials to decide who can use such vehicles violates the First Amendment. In *Kunz v. New York*, the Court invalidated an ordinance that prohibited the holding of a religious meeting on a public street without a permit.[67] The Court said that the government "cannot vest restraining control over the right to speak . . . in an administrative official where there are no appropriate standards to guide his action."[68]

[59] 312 U.S. 569 (1941).
[60] Harry Kalven, Jr., The Concept of the Public Forum: *Cox v. Louisiana*, 1965 Sup. Ct. Rev. 1, 26.
[61] 312 U.S. at 576.
[62] 303 U.S. 444 (1938).
[63] *Id.* at 451.
[64] *Id.* at 452.
[65] 334 U.S. 558 (1948).
[66] *See* Kovacs v. Cooper, 336 U.S. 77 (1949).
[67] 40 U.S. 290 (1951).
[68] *Id.* at 295.

In many other cases as well,[69] the Court has declared unconstitutional permit laws because of the extent of discretion vested in government officials. Likewise, the Court has held that the government cannot require a permit fee for demonstrations if government officials have discretion in setting the amount of the charge. In *Forsyth County, Georgia v. Nationalist Movement*, the Court declared unconstitutional an ordinance that required a permit in order for a demonstration to occur and that allowed government officials to charge a permit fee of up to $1,000.[70] The Court found that the licensing law was impermissible because "[t]here are no articulated standards either in the ordinance or in the county's established practice. The administrator is not required to rely on any objective factors. He need not provide any explanation for his decision, and that decision is unreviewable."[71] The Court concluded that "[n]othing in the law or its application prevents the official from encouraging some views and discouraging others through the arbitrary application of the fees. The First Amendment prohibits the vesting of such unbridled discretion in a government official."[72]

Nationalist Movement did not declare unconstitutional all permit fee requirements; it simply held that such charges are unconstitutional if government officials have discretion as to the amount. In *Cox v. New Hampshire*, described above, the Court upheld a licensing system that allowed the government to charge a permit fee of up to $300.[73] Although the discretion under this ordinance likely would make it unconstitutional under *Nationalist Movement*, the Court never has overruled its conclusion that the government can charge "a nominal fee . . . to defray the expenses of policing the activities in question."[74] But nor has the Court ever clarified what fees are permissible under what circumstances.

On the one hand, there is a strong argument that all charges for the use of public property for speech should be declared unconstitutional.[75] Any fee might keep some from speaking, and the loss is not just to the speaker's First Amendment rights, but to the rights of all who are denied hearing the message. If the government can charge demonstrators for use of public property or for police protection, that often will have the same effect as a complete ban on the speech. On the other hand, the government is almost never required to subsidize the exercise of constitutional rights. A prohibition of all permit fees would be forcing the government to subsidize the use of the public forum for speech purposes.

---

[69] *See, e.g.*, City of Lakewood v. Plain Dealer Publishing Co., 486 U.S. 750 (1988) (invalidating an ordinance requiring a permit for placement of a newsbox on city sidewalks where the mayor had discretion in issuing permits); Shuttlesworth v. City of Birmingham, 394 U.S. 147 (1969) (invalidating ordinance requiring a permit for parades); Staub v. City of Baxley, 355 U.S. 313 (1958) (invalidating permit requirement for solicitation of members of dues-paying organizations).

[70] 505 U.S. 123 (1992).

[71] *Id.* at 132.

[72] *Id.* at 133.

[73] 312 U.S. at 576-577.

[74] Murdock v. Pennsylvania, 319 U.S. 105, 113-114 (1943).

[75] For an excellent development of this argument, *see* David Goldberger, A Reconsideration of *Cox v. New Hampshire*: Can Demonstrators Be Required to Pay the Costs of Using America's Public Forums?, 62 Tex. L. Rev. 403 (1983).

No Requirement for Use of the Least
Restrictive Alternative

Finally, the Court has held that when the government regulates speech in the public forum, it need not use the least restrictive alternative, although any regulation must be narrowly tailored. In *Ward v. Rock Against Racism*, the Court upheld a requirement in New York City that any concert using the Bandshell in Central Park had to use city sound engineers and city sound equipment.[76] Concert producers and promoters argued that the city could achieve its goal of noise reduction through means less restrictive of speech; for example, they could impose decibel levels. The Court, however, said that "a regulation of the time, place, or manner of protected speech must be narrowly tailored to serve the government's legitimate, content-neutral interests but . . . it need not be the least restrictive or least intrusive means of doing so."[77]

The Court explained that the "requirement of narrow tailoring is satisfied so long as the regulation promotes a substantial governmental interest that would be achieved less effectively absent the regulation."[78] But the Court said that a time, place, or manner restriction may not "burden substantially more speech than is necessary to further the government's legitimate interests."[79] The Court concluded that "[s]o long as the means chosen are not substantially broader than necessary to achieve the government's interest, however, the regulation will not be invalid simply because a court concludes that the government's interest could be adequately served by some less-speech-restrictive alternative."[80]

In appraising *Ward*, there are two important questions, one normative and one descriptive. Normatively the issue is whether least restrictive alternative analysis should be used in evaluating government regulation of speech in public forums because of the importance of the right to use government property for speech. Descriptively the question is whether the distinction makes sense between a requirement for narrow tailoring and a demand for the least restrictive alternative. Although conceptually such a distinction can be drawn, in practice the distinction is difficult to apply.[81]

But even though a restriction need not be the least restrictive alternative, it still must be "narrowly tailored." The Court recently explained: "For a content-neutral time, place, or manner regulation to be narrowly tailored, it must not 'burden substantially more speech than is necessary to further the government's legitimate interests.' Such a regulation, unlike a content-based restriction of speech, 'need not be the least restrictive or least intrusive means of' serving the government's interests. But the government still 'may not regulate expression in

---

[76] 491 U.S. 781 (1989).
[77] *Id.* at 798.
[78] *Id.* at 782-783.
[79] *Id.* at 799.
[80] *Id.* at 800.
[81] For example, as discussed above, in the commercial speech context the Court also said that least restrictive alternative analysis was not required, but in subsequent cases has seemed to require just that in determining whether means were narrowly tailored. *See* §11.3.7.2.

such a manner that a substantial portion of the burden on speech does not serve to advance its goals.'"[82]

§11.4.2.3   Designated Public Forums

Government Regulation in Places Voluntarily Opened to Speech

A "designated" public forum is a place that the government could close to speech, but that the government voluntarily, affirmatively opens to speech. As described below, there are many places that the government can close to all speech activities. If, however, the government chooses to allow speech in such a place, it creates a limited or designated public forum. So long as the place is open to speech, all of the rules for public forums, described above, apply. The Court has stated: "[A] government entity may create 'a designated public forum' if government property that has not traditionally been regarded as a public forum is intentionally opened up for that purpose. Government restrictions on speech in a designated public forum are subject to the same strict scrutiny as restrictions in a traditional public forum."[83]

Analytical Difficulty with This Category

The difficulty, as described below, is that the third category—"limited public forums"—are places that the government opens only to some speakers or to some messages. This is far more common than the government opening a place that could be closed to all speech. However, there is a major difference in the rules: In a "designated public forum," the government must be both subject matter and viewpoint neutral and must have an important interest in regulating; in a "limited public forum," the government need be only viewpoint neutral and the regulation must be reasonable.

The analytical problem is that by restricting a place to particular speakers or messages, by definition, the government has created a limited public forum. Although subject matter restrictions in a designated public forum are supposed to meet strict scrutiny, the government's creating subject matter restrictions by definition makes the place a "limited public forum" where subject matter restrictions are permissible. In other words, any time a person challenged a subject matter restriction in a "designated public forum," the government's response could be that by having the subject matter restriction the government had created a limited public forum where subject matter restrictions are allowed.

This may explain why there are no Supreme Court cases that have ever deemed a place to be a "designated public forum" and applied the rules for designated

---

[82] McCullen v. Coakley, 134 S. Ct. 2518, 2535 (2014), discussed above.
[83] Pleasant Grove v. Summum, 555 U.S. 460, 468 (2009).

public forums. The closest case may be *Widmar v. Vincent*, where the Court held that a state university could not exclude religious student groups when it opened its classroom buildings to use by student groups.[84] The Court used strict scrutiny for content-based restrictions, as it would for a public forum or a designated public forum, and concluded that the exclusion of religious groups was impermissible.

The Court said that the university buildings were a public forum. The Court wrote: "In order to justify discriminatory exclusion from a public forum based on the religious content of a group's intended speech, the University must therefore satisfy the standard of review appropriate to content-based exclusions. It must show that its regulation is necessary to serve a compelling state interest and that it is narrowly drawn to achieve that end."[85] Yet this categorization seems problematic for many reasons. If these buildings were a public forum, then the government would be constitutionally required to make them available for speech. Never did the Court suggest that was the case. To the contrary, the Court emphasized that the government had made the choice to open the place to speech. The Court stated: "Through its policy of accommodating their meetings, the University has created a forum generally open for use by student groups."[86] This would indicate that under current categories it is a "designated" or "limited public forum," not a "public forum." Moreover, subsequent cases that deal with schools opening their facilities treat them as limited public forums and, as explained below, rely on *Widmar* to this effect.

§11.4.2.4 Limited Public Forums

In *Good News Club v. Milford Central School*, the Court said that "[w]hen the State establishes a limited public forum, the State is not required to and does not allow persons to engage in every type of speech. The State may be justified 'in reserving [its forum] for certain groups or for the discussion of certain topics.' The State's power to restrict speech, however, is not without limits. The restriction must not discriminate against speech on the basis of viewpoint, and the restriction must be 'reasonable in light of the purpose served by the forum.'"[87]

In *Good News Club*, the Court held unconstitutional an elementary school's exclusion of a group's using school property after school for religious activities including prayer and Bible study. The Court said that the parties had agreed that the place was a limited public forum and it assumed this for the purpose of its constitutional analysis.[88] The Court found that the exclusion of religious activities was "viewpoint" discrimination that was impermissible in a limited public forum.

---

[84] 454 U.S. 263 (1981).

[85] *Id.* at 269.

[86] *Id.* at 273.

[87] 533 U.S. 98, 106-107 (2001).

[88] The Court stated: "Because the parties have agreed that Milford created a limited public forum when it opened its facilities in 1992 . . . we simply will assume that Milford operates a limited public forum." *Id.* at 102.

The Court in *Good News* relied on its earlier decision in *Lamb's Chapel v. Center Moriches Union Free School District*, where the Court held that once a school district allowed community groups to use facilities during evenings and weekends, religious groups could not be excluded.[89] The Court said that "[w]ith respect to public property that is not a designated public forum open for indiscriminate public use for communicative purposes, we have said that '[c]ontrol over access to a nonpublic forum can be based on subject matter and speaker identity so long as the distinctions drawn are reasonable in light of the purpose served by the forum and are viewpoint neutral.'"[90] The Court ruled that the exclusion of religious groups violates this rule and that allowing them to use government property did not offend the establishment clause.

Lamb's Chapel, in turn, relied on *Widmar v. Vincent*, where the Court ruled that a university that allowed student groups to use school buildings could not exclude religious student groups from access.[91] As mentioned above, *Widmar* labeled the university buildings to be a "public forum," whereas *Good News Club* and *Lamb's Chapel* labeled the school facilities as a limited public forum.

The choice of labels has significance. If the school facilities are designated a public forum or a designated public forum, subject matter restrictions must meet strict scrutiny. In a limited public forum, though, subject matter restrictions are allowed. In *Good News Club*, *Lamb's Chapel*, and *Widmar*, the Court said that religious groups could not be excluded from using the facilities. This would seem to be a subject matter restriction that would be impermissible if the facilities are deemed a public forum or designated public forum, but allowed in a limited public forum. However, the Court declared the restrictions on religious speech impermissible in all three cases and in *Good News* explicitly said that the restriction was a "viewpoint" restriction in that it discriminated against religious viewpoints. The question, though, it why this should be regarded as a viewpoint restriction rather than a subject matter restriction, since the latter focuses on regulating speech based on its topic and that is exactly what the schools were doing.

An earlier case that can be more easily understood as involving a limited public forum is *Lehman v. City of Shaker Heights*.[92] A city sold advertising space on its buses, but refused to accept advertising on behalf of a candidate for public office. The Court upheld this limit as constitutional. The Court stressed that "the government was engaged in a commercial venture" and that the restriction was justified because "[t]here could be lurking doubts about favoritism, and sticky administrative problems might arise in parceling out limited space to eager politicians."[93] The Court said that "[i]n these circumstances, the managerial decision to limit car

---

[89] 508 U.S. 384 (1993). This case is discussed in more detail in §12.2.4.

[90] *Id.* at 392.

[91] 454 U.S. 263 (1981); *see also* Board of Educ. of the Westside Community Schools v. Mergens, 496 U.S. 226 (1990) (upholding the federal Equal Access Act, which requires that schools receiving federal funds allow all student groups equal access to facilities regardless of their religious, political, or philosophical views). These cases are discussed in more detail in §12.2.4.

[92] 418 U.S. 298 (1974).

[93] *Id.* at 304.

card space to innocuous and less controversial commercial and service oriented advertising does not rise to the dignity of a First Amendment violation."[94]

Justice Douglas, the fifth vote to uphold the regulation, wrote an opinion concurring in the judgment, emphasizing the need to protect the "captive audience" of bus riders.[95] He said that he voted to uphold the regulation because "there was not a constitutional right to spread his message before this captive audience."[96]

Although it was decided before the current vocabulary, *Lehman* can be understood as involving a limited public forum; the government created a place and reserved it to some messages. The regulation was allowed because it was reasonable and viewpoint neutral.

The most recent case involving nonpublic forums is *Christian Legal Society v. Martinez.*[97] The University of California, Hastings College of Law required that "Registered Student Organizations" accept "all-comers" and prohibited discrimination based on characteristics such as race, sex, religion, disability, or sexual orientation. For many years, the Christian Legal Society chapter at Hastings Law School complied with this policy. In 2004, the Christian Legal Society reconstituted itself and formed a relationship with the national Christian Legal Society. The Hastings Chapter then required that its members sign a "Statement of Faith," which affirmed a belief in Jesus Christ as the savior and also excluded "unrepentant homosexuals."[98] Hastings refused to recognize the Christian Legal Society as a "Registered Student Organization," which meant that it could not get student activity funds or officially reserve school facilities for its use.

The Supreme Court, in a 5-4 decision, ruled in favor of Hastings. The Court said that Hastings had created a "limited public forum." Justice Ginsburg, writing for the Court, stated: "[W]e are persuaded that our limited-public-forum precedents adequately respect both CLS's speech and expressive-association rights, and fairly balance those rights against Hastings' interests as property owner and educational institution."[99]

The Court said that since it was a limited public forum the regulation was to be allowed so long as it was reasonable and viewpoint neutral. The Court said that it was reasonable for Hastings to have an "all-comers" policy, requiring that every student group be open to all members in the school. The Court explained: "[T]he open-access policy ensures that the leadership, educational, and social opportunities afforded by [RSOs] are available to all students."[100] The Court also noted that "the Law School reasonably adheres to the view that an all-comers policy, to the extent it brings together individuals with diverse backgrounds and beliefs, 'encourages tolerance, cooperation, and learning among students.' . . .

---

[94] *Id.*

[95] *Id.* at 307 (Douglas, J., concurring).

[96] *Id.* at 308. The difficulty with this analysis is that the Court has held that people cannot object to being a captive audience when outside their home. Cohen v. California, 403 U.S. 15, 21 (1971), discussed at §11.3.4.6.

[97] 130 S. Ct. 2971 (2010).

[98] *Id.* at 2980.

[99] *Id.* at 2986.

[100] *Id.* at 2989.

[It] incorporates—in fact, subsumes—state-law proscriptions on discrimination, conveys the Law School's decision 'to decline to subsidize with public monies and benefits conduct of which the people of California disapprove.' "[101]

The Court found that the policy was, by definition, viewpoint neutral. A major dispute between the parties was whether Hastings actually administered its policy as an all-comers policy and the dissent focused on Hastings having previously recognized groups that did not follow this policy. But the Court emphasized that the parties had entered into a stipulation in the trial court that Hastings administered its policy without regard to belief and based on this stipulation found that the Hastings policy was viewpoint neutral.[102]

Justice Alito wrote a vehement dissent, joined by Chief Justice Roberts, Scalia, and Thomas. He focused on how Hastings actually had administered its policy and emphasized the infringement on freedom of association for the Christian Legal Society. He also expressed great concern that an "all-comers-policy would permit a small and unpopular group to be taken over by students who wish to silence its message."[103]

After *Christian Legal Society v. Martinez*, schools may follow an all-comers policy for officially recognized student groups. But where such policies exist, there can be challenges based on claims that the schools actually discriminate in recognizing student groups.

§11.4.2.5   Nonpublic Forums

Government Property That Constitutes Nonpublic Forums

Nonpublic forums are government properties that the government can close to all speech activities. The government may prohibit or restrict speech in nonpublic forums so long as the regulation is reasonable and viewpoint neutral. The Court has found many different types of government property to be nonpublic forums.[104]

For example, in *Adderley v. Florida*, the Court held that the government could prohibit speech in the areas outside prisons and jails.[105] Civil rights demonstrators

---

[101] *Id.* at 2990.

[102] The stipulation stated: "Hastings requires that registered student organizations allow *any* student to participate, become a member, or seek leadership positions in the organization, regardless of [her] status or beliefs. Thus, for example, the Hastings Democratic Caucus cannot bar students holding Republican political beliefs from becoming members or seeking leadership positions in the organization." *Id.* at 2982.

[103] *Id.* at 3019 (Alito, J., dissenting).

[104] As mentioned above, in its most recent formulation in *Christian Legal Society v. Martinez*, the Court does not mention this category of government properties. But there are many cases that fit within it and thus analytically it explains many of the cases. It is possible the Court is collapsing this category into "limited public forums," but the problem is that that confuses places open to some speech with those closed to all speech activities.

[105] 385 U.S. 39 (1966).

held a rally outside a jail after a group of their colleagues had been arrested for engaging in a civil rights protest. The Court, in an opinion by Justice Black, upheld the convictions of those protesting at the jail who did not disperse in response to an order from the sheriff. Although the Court emphasized the government's security interests, it also spoke very broadly about the government's ability to restrict speech in public places. Justice Black declared: "The State, no less than a private owner of property, has the power to preserve the property under its control for the use to which it is lawfully dedicated. . . . The United States Constitution does not forbid a State to control the use of its own property for its own lawful nondiscriminatory purpose."[106]

Justice Douglas wrote for the four dissenters and stressed the importance of the jail as a place for protest. He said: "The jailhouse, like an executive mansion, a legislative chamber, a courthouse, or the statehouse itself is one of the seats of government, whether it be the Tower of London, the Bastille, or a small county jail. And when it houses political prisoners or those who many think are unjustly held, it is an obvious center for protest."[107]

In *Greer v. Spock*, the Court held that military bases, even parts of bases usually open to the public, are a nonpublic forum.[108] Although civilians were allowed free access to nonrestricted areas of Fort Dix, a regulation prohibited "demonstrations, picketing, sit-ins, protest marches, [and] political speeches." The Supreme Court upheld this regulation and said that "it is the business of a military installation like Fort Dix to train soldiers, not to provide a public forum."[109] The Court said that the government could exclude such speech to insulate the military from political activities.[110]

In *Members of the City Council of the City of Los Angeles v. Taxpayers for Vincent*, the Court upheld an ordinance that prohibited the posting of signs on public property.[111] Specifically, the Court ruled that the government could prohibit the posting of political campaign signs on utility poles. The Court concluded that such poles are a nonpublic forum and that the government could prohibit the posting of signs to preserve "esthetic values."[112] The Court rejected the claim that the public property was a public forum because of the absence of a "traditional right of access respecting such items as utility poles for purposes of communication comparable to that recognized for public streets and parks. . . . [T]he mere fact that government property can be used as a vehicle for communication does not mean that the Constitution requires such uses to be permitted."[113]

---

[106] *Id.* at 47-48.

[107] *Id.* at 49 (Douglas, J., dissenting).

[108] 424 U.S. 828 (1976).

[109] *Id.* at 831.

[110] *See also* United States v. Albertini, 472 U.S. 675 (1985) (upholding the ability of the government to exclude from military bases individuals who had received a letter barring them from access). *But see* Flower v. United States, 407 U.S. 197 (1972) (where the bar letter was for earlier protected expression it could not be used as a basis for excluding a person from access to a military base).

[111] 466 U.S. 789 (1984).

[112] *Id.* at 805.

[113] *Id.* at 814.

In *Cornelius v. NAACP Legal Defense and Education Fund, Inc.*, the Court upheld a federal regulation limiting charitable solicitations of federal employees during working hours.[114] A federal regulation limited solicitations during working hours to those by the Combined Federal Campaign, which only raised money for tax-exempt charitable agencies that provided direct health and welfare services to individuals; legal defense and political organizations were excluded from receiving funds. The Court held that the Combined Federal Campaign is a nonpublic forum. Writing for the majority in a 4-to-3 decision, Justice O'Connor said that "access to a nonpublic forum can be based on subject matter and speaker identity so long as the distinctions drawn are reasonable in light of the purpose served by the forum and are viewpoint neutral."[115]

In *United States v. Kokinda*, the Court upheld a restriction on solicitations on post office properties.[116] Sidewalks, of course, are the paradigm public forum. But the plurality opinion of Justice O'Connor said that sidewalks on post office property were a nonpublic forum.[117] The plurality of four Justices concluded that a postal sidewalk does not "have the characteristics of public sidewalks traditionally open to expressive activity."[118] Justice O'Connor said that the "postal sidewalk was constructed solely to provide for the passage of individuals engaged in postal business."[119] Although others had been allowed to use the postal property for speaking, leafleting, and picketing, the plurality concluded that "this was not enough to transform it into a designated public forum because it did not add up to the dedication of postal property to speech activities."[120]

Justice Kennedy, the fifth vote for upholding the regulation, wrote an opinion concurring in the judgment and said that there were strong grounds for applying the standards for public forums because of the wide array of activities allowed on the sidewalks.[121] Justice Kennedy, however, said that the issue of how to characterize the forum did not need be resolved because the regulation was a reasonable time, place, and manner restriction.

In *International Society for Krishna Consciousness, Inc. v. Lee*, the Court ruled that airports are a nonpublic forum.[122] Chief Justice Rehnquist, writing for the Court, said that "precedents foreclose the conclusion that airport terminals are public fora. Reflecting the general growth of the air travel industry, airport terminals

---

[114] 473 U.S. 788 (1985).

[115] *Id.* at 806.

[116] 497 U.S. 720 (1990).

[117] In *United States Postal Service v. Council of Greenburgh Civic Associations*, 453 U.S. 114 (1981), the Court upheld a regulation prohibiting the placing of unstamped mailable matter in letter boxes. The Court said that home letter boxes were part of the nationwide system for delivery of the mails. The Court concluded that "[t]here is neither historical nor constitutional support for the characterization of a letterbox as a public forum." *Id.* at 128. The case is different from all of the other cases discussed in this section because it involved private property, mailboxes at private homes, and not government-owned property.

[118] 497 U.S. at 727.

[119] *Id.*

[120] *Id.* at 730.

[121] *Id.* at 737 (Kennedy, J., concurring in the judgment).

[122] 505 U.S. 672 (1992).

have only recently achieved their contemporary size and character. But given the lateness with which the modern air terminal has made its appearance, it hardly qualifies for the description of having 'immemorially . . . time out of mind' been held in the public trust and used for purposes of expressive activity."[123] The Court rejected the argument that the appropriate inquiry was the general openness of transportation facilities for speech; the issue, according to the Court, was solely about how airports should be characterized.

The Court also emphasized that airports are a commercial venture and that they obviously do not have as a "principal purpose promoting 'the free exchange of ideas.' "[124] Thus, the Court concluded that airports are a nonpublic forum, and regulations would be upheld so long as they are reasonable. The Court, by a 5-to-4 margin, decided that the prohibition of solicitation of funds in airports is reasonable. The Court said that the government has an important interest in preventing fraud, but because travelers are frequently on a tight schedule, "the airport faces considerable difficulty in achieving its legitimate interest in monitoring solicitation activity to assure that travelers are not interfered with unduly."[125]

But the Court also ruled by a 5-to-4 margin that the prohibition of the distribution of literature in airports was unconstitutional. Justice O'Connor, who voted with the majority in finding that airports are nonpublic forums and in upholding the ban on solicitation, joined with the four dissenters on those issues to create a majority to overturn the ban on distribution of literature. She concluded that the ban on leafleting was not reasonable and thus was impermissible even though the airport was a nonpublic forum.[126]

Finally, in *Arkansas Educational Television Commission v. Forbes*,[127] the Court held that a candidate debate sponsored by a government-owned television station is a nonpublic forum and that the exclusion of minor party candidates is not viewpoint discrimination. The State of Arkansas owns and operates a public television station that held a debate among candidates for a congressional seat. Only the Democratic and Republican candidates, and not the third-party candidates, were invited. A challenge was brought arguing that by holding the debate, the government created a limited public forum and, at the very least, excluding minor party candidates was a form of viewpoint discrimination that is impermissible even in nonpublic forums.

In an opinion by Justice Kennedy, the Court rejected both of these contentions and ruled in favor of the public television station. Justice Kennedy said that "[h]aving first arisen in the context of streets and parks, the public forum doctrine should not be extended in a mechanical way to the very different context of public television broadcasting. . . . In the case of television broadcasting, however, broad rights of access for outside speakers would be antithetical, as a general rule, to the discretion that stations and their editorial staff must exercise to fulfill their

---

[123] *Id.* at 680 (citation omitted).
[124] *Id.* at 682 (citation omitted).
[125] *Id.* at 684.
[126] *Id.* at 689-690 (O'Connor, J., concurring in the judgment).
[127] 523 U.S. 666 (1998).

journalistic purpose and statutory obligations."[128] Indeed, the Court said that a broadcaster's choice of content and selection of speakers is itself expressive activity protected by the First Amendment.

Nor was the Court persuaded that the government, by holding the debate, had created a limited public forum. Justice Kennedy explained: "[The] debate was not a designated public forum. To create a forum of this type, the government must intend to make the property 'generally available.' A designated public forum is not created when the government allows selective access for individual speakers rather than general access for a class of speakers. . . . [The] cases illustrate the distinction between 'general access,' which indicates the property is a designated public forum, and 'selective access,' which indicates the property is a nonpublic forum."[129] The Court was concerned that forcing the station to allow all candidates to participate could result in its choosing not to hold the debate at all.

The Court also rejected the claim that selecting major party candidates and rejecting those from third parties was viewpoint discrimination. Justice Kennedy said that the selection was based on the level of popular support and thus the likely viability of the candidacy and not the viewpoint expressed. He concluded: "There is no substance to Forbes' suggestion that he was excluded because his views were unpopular or out of the mainstream. His own objective lack of support, not his platform, was the criterion. . . . The broadcaster's decision to exclude Forbes was a reasonable, view point-neutral exercise of journalistic discretion consistent with the First Amendment."[130]

Justice Stevens, in a dissenting opinion joined by Justices Souter and Ginsburg, expressed concern over the lack of standards in the government's decision-making process.[131] The most troubling aspect of *Forbes* is whether the choice to include the Democratic and Republican candidates, while excluding third-party candidates, is viewpoint neutral. The Court said that the difference is in their degree of support, not their viewpoint. But the problem with this argument is that the less popular viewpoint is exactly the reason they are third-party candidates. Perhaps the case can be best understood as reflecting the majority's expressed judgment that candidate debates are extremely important and its concern that they will decrease if government-owned stations have to include every minor candidate.

§11.4.2.6   What Determines the Status of a Forum?

The Implicit Criteria

The Supreme Court never has articulated clear criteria for deciding whether a place is a public forum, a designated public forum, a limited public forum, or a nonpublic forum. Several criteria are implicit in the cases. Unfortunately,

---

[128] *Id.* at 672-673.
[129] *Id.* at 678-679.
[130] *Id.* at 683.
[131] *Id.* at 683-684 (Stevens, J., dissenting).

especially as applied in cases such as *Kokinda* and *Lee*, it will be very difficult to find that government property is a public forum.

One factor the Court considers is the tradition of availability of the place for speech. Sidewalks and parks, the classic public forums, are regarded as having been long available for speech purposes. But in recent cases, the Court's analysis has focused on whether the particular place has been open to speech. In *Kokinda*, for instance, the Court focused not on sidewalks generally, but on sidewalks on post office property; in *Lee*, the Court refused to consider places of transportation generally, but looked just at airports. Even as to airports, the Court said that because they are relatively new in American history, albeit decades old, they could not be regarded as places traditionally open to speech. This narrow focus makes it difficult to find that a place is a public forum based on a tradition of openness to speech.

Second, the Court considers the extent to which speech is incompatible with the usual functioning of the place. The greater the incompatibility, the more likely that the Court will find the place to be a nonpublic forum. For instance, in *Adderley*, the Court relied on security concerns to justify deeming areas outside prisons and jails to be a nonpublic forum. In *Vincent*, the Court found that the government's interest in aesthetics was incompatible with allowing postings on utility poles. However, these cases indicate that the Court requires little proof that speech actually will interfere with the functioning of the place. For instance, in *Adderley*, there was no evidence that the peaceful protest on a grassy area outside the jail was a security threat. In *Greer*, there was no proof that speech on the military base would interfere with its functioning or cause the appearance of political entanglement with the military.

Third, the Court considers whether the primary purpose of the place is for speech. In *Lee*, the Court observed that expression obviously is not the primary purpose of airports. In *Kokinda*, the plurality said that sidewalks on post office property were not even limited public forums because they had not been dedicated to speech activities. By this criteria, virtually no property ever would be a public forum or a limited public forum. Except for speaker's corner in Hyde Park in London, virtually no government property was created for the purpose of speech or has been dedicated to speech activities. Sidewalks are constructed primarily for pedestrian traffic, and parks are built for recreation.

Although these cases indicate a strong presumption for finding government property to be a nonpublic forum, the criteria can be applied in a more speech protective manner to safeguard expression in public property. Courts can find a tradition of availability to speech based on the use of that general type of property for expressive purposes. Even some incompatibility with the usual functioning of a place can be tolerated so as to accommodate First Amendment values. For example, in *Schneider*, the Court held that the government could not prohibit leafleting even though it had an important interest in preventing litter and in preserving aesthetics. Although a place's primary purpose may not be for speech, it should be found to be a limited public forum if the government has opened it to some speech. A place should be found to be a public forum, even though it obviously has other uses, if it is an important place for the communication of messages and there are not strong reasons for closing it to speech.

§11.4.3   Private Property and Speech

No First Amendment Right of Access to Private Property for Speech

The cases described above all involve claims of a right to use *government* property for speech purposes. There is not a right to use private property owned by others for speech. Because it is private property, the Constitution does not apply.[132]

Most of the cases involving a right to use private property for speech have concerned claims of a right to use privately owned shopping centers for expression. Initially, the Supreme Court recognized such a right and then later limited it and ultimately overruled it. In *Amalgamated Food Employees Union Local 590 v. Logan Valley Plaza,* in 1968, the Supreme Court held that a privately owned shopping center could not exclude striking laborers from picketing a store within it.[133] The Court relied on an earlier decision, *Marsh v. Alabama,* which held that a company-owned town could not exclude Jehovah's Witnesses who wished to distribute literature.[134] The Court in *Logan Valley* expressly analogized to *Marsh* and said that "[t]he similarities between the business block in *Marsh* and the shopping center . . . are striking. . . . The shopping center here is clearly the functional equivalent of the business district of Chickasaw involved in *Marsh.*"[135] The Court stressed that the shopping center was an important gathering place that served as the commercial center of town.

Four years later, in *Lloyd Corp. v. Tanner,* the Supreme Court held that a privately owned shopping center could exclude anti–Vietnam War protestors from distributing literature on its premises.[136] The Court explained that *Logan Valley* involved a labor protest related to the functioning of a store in the shopping center, whereas the speech in *Lloyd* was an antiwar protest unrelated to the conduct of the business. The problem with this distinction is that it is a content-based distinction among speech. Under *Lloyd,* speech in shopping centers could be the basis for a trespassing conviction unless its content concerned the functioning of the shopping centers. This was inconsistent with the basic principle, described at the beginning of this chapter, that speech cannot be regulated based on its content.

In *Hudgens v. National Labor Relations Board,*[137] the Court recognized these problems and expressly overruled *Logan Valley.* The Court said that "the reasoning of the Court's opinion in *Lloyd* cannot be squared with the reasoning of the Court's

---

[132] The requirement for state action is discussed in §6.4, and the lack of a constitutional right of access to private property for speech purposes is considered in §6.4.4.2.

[133] 391 U.S. 308 (1968).

[134] 326 U.S. 501 (1946). *Marsh* is discussed in detail in §6.4.4.2.

[135] 391 U.S. at 317.

[136] 407 U.S. 551 (1972).

[137] 424 U.S. 507 (1976).

opinion in *Logan Valley*."[138] The Court explained that if the First Amendment applies to privately owned shopping centers, then the law cannot permit a distinction based on the content of the speech.[139] The Court concluded that the First Amendment does not create a right to use privately owned shopping centers for speech.

Subsequent to *Hudgens*, in *PruneYard Shopping Center v. Robins*, the Supreme Court held that a state could create a state constitutional right of access to shopping centers for speech purposes.[140] The shopping center appealed to the Supreme Court and contended that forcing it to allow speakers violated its First Amendment rights and constituted a taking of its property without just compensation. The United States Supreme Court rejected both of these arguments and held that states could recognize a state constitutional right of access to shopping centers.[141]

§11.4.4 *Speech in Authoritarian Environments: Military, Prisons, and Schools*

Introduction

The place where speech occurs is relevant in another sense: The Court has held that some government-operated places are environments where great deference is required to regulations of speech. Specifically, the Court generally has sided with the government when regulating expression in the military, in prisons, and in schools.[142] Although there are obvious differences between these contexts, there are striking similarities, especially in the Court's treatment of them. All involve places where people often are involuntarily present. All are authoritarian environments that do not operate internally in a democratic fashion. In each, the Court has proclaimed a need for deference to authority and to the expertise of those managing the place.

The underlying issue as to each is whether the restrictions on speech upheld by the Court are appropriate or whether there is excessive deference. The Court has presumed that aggressive judicial review and significant protection of speech is inconsistent with the functioning of such authoritarian environments. But there is a strong argument that court protection of rights such as freedom of speech is essential in such places precisely because of the lack of political oversight and responsiveness to those in these places. The Court's decisions, described below, can be criticized as overly deferential in that they allowed restrictions of speech

---

[138] *Id.* at 518.

[139] *Id.* at 520.

[140] 447 U.S. 74 (1980).

[141] The issue of whether forcing privately owned shopping centers to allow access violates the First Amendment rights of shopping center owners is described above in §11.2.4.3.

[142] The juxtaposition of the military, schools, and prisons is borrowed from Geoffrey Stone et al., Constitutional Law 1362-1369 (3d ed. 1996).

without any proof that the expression actually would interfere with the functioning of the institution.

Military

The Supreme Court generally has been extremely deferential to the military in its ability to restrict constitutional rights; this also has been true for First Amendment freedoms. In *Parker v. Levy*, the Court upheld a court martial of an officer for making several statements to enlisted personnel that were critical of the Vietnam War and said that African-American soldiers should consider refusing to go to Vietnam because of how they were given the most hazardous duty there.[143] The Court said that "the military is, by necessity, a specialized society separate from civilian society."[144]

The Court explained that "[w]hile the members of the military are not excluded from the protection granted by the First Amendment, the different character of the military community and of the military mission requires a different application of those protections."[145] The Court said that the speech of the officer in this case, "that of a commissioned officer publicly urging enlisted personnel to refuse to obey orders which might send them into combat, was unprotected under the most expansive notions of the First Amendment."[146] Yet it should be noted that in any other context criticism of government policy, and even advocacy of illegal disobedience, would be allowed unless the constitutional test for incitement was met.[147]

In *Brown v. Glines*, the Court went even further in exempting the military from the application of the First Amendment.[148] *Brown* involved an Air Force regulation prohibiting members of the Air Force from posting or distributing printed materials at an Air Force installation without the permission of the commander. This, of course, is the most blatant form of prior restraint: a government licensing system for speech. Unlike *Parker v. Levy*, this was not punishment for specific speech that threatened the military's operation. Yet the Court upheld the prior restraint and concluded that "since a commander is charged with maintaining morale, discipline, and readiness, he must have authority over the distribution of materials that could affect adversely these essential attributes of an effective military."[149] Again, the underlying issue is whether this is necessary deference to military authority or excessive deference by allowing a system of prior restraint that would be permitted in virtually no other situation.

---

[143] 417 U.S. 733 (1974).
[144] *Id.* at 743.
[145] *Id.* at 751.
[146] *Id.* at 760.
[147] Incitement, and the test for when it can be punished, is discussed in §11.3.2.
[148] 444 U.S. 348 (1980).
[149] *Id.* at 356.

Prisons

The Court has held that the general test is that the government may restrict and punish the speech of prisoners if the action is reasonably related to a legitimate penological interest.[150] The Court has said that "[i]n a prison context, an inmate does not retain those First Amendment rights that are 'inconsistent with his status as a prisoner or with the legitimate penological objectives of the corrections system.'"[151] Most regulations of prisoner speech have been upheld under this test.

Procunier v. Martinez is the exceptional case; the Court declared unconstitutional a prison regulation that restricted the types of letters that prisoners can write.[152] The regulation said that prisoners could not write letters that would "magnify grievances" or that were "lewd, obscene, defamatory, or otherwise inappropriate."[153] The Court held that this restriction on the ability of prisoners to communicate with those outside the prison was unnecessary for the maintenance of order and discipline among prisoners. The prison had no legitimate interest in stopping prisoners from expressing their grievances to those outside the prison or in censoring the content of prisoner correspondence.

Yet *Procunier v. Martinez* is exceptional, even in the area of prisoner speech to those outside the prison. In other cases, the Court has allowed restrictions on prisoner correspondence and expression to those outside the institution. Indeed, it is highly questionable whether *Procunier* survives the later decisions. In *Turner v. Safley*, the Court upheld a prison regulation that prohibited correspondence between inmates at different prisons.[154] The Court accepted the government's claim that correspondence among prisoners could lead to comparisons that could provoke dissatisfaction and unrest. The Court also accepted the government's concern that unrest could spread among institutions through such correspondence.

In several cases, the Court upheld the ability of prisons to restrict the ability of the press to interview prisoners or have access to prisons. In *Pell v. Procunier*[155] and *Saxbe v. Washington Post Co.*,[156] the Court sustained prison regulations that prevented the media from interviewing particular prisoners.[157] The Court said that the regulations were justified because "press attention . . . concentrated on a relatively small number of inmates who, as a result, became virtual 'public figures' within the prison society and gained a disproportionate degree of notoriety and influence among their fellow inmates . . . and became the source of severe disciplinary problems."[158]

---

[150] Turner v. Safley, 482 U.S. 78 (1987).

[151] Jones v. North Carolina Prisoners' Labor Union, 433 U.S. 119, 129 (1977) (citation omitted).

[152] 416 U.S. 396 (1974).

[153] *Id.* at 399.

[154] 482 U.S. 78 (1987).

[155] 417 U.S. 817 (1974).

[156] 417 U.S. 843 (1974).

[157] The claim of the press to have a right of access to prisoners for the purpose of news gathering is discussed below in §11.6.3.

[158] *Pell*, 417 U.S. at 831-832.

In *Houchins v. KQED*, the Court held that the press did not have a right of access to prisons to observe conditions.[159] The media was allowed only monthly tours, without cameras or tape recorders, of the Greystone portion of the Santa Rita jail. There is obviously an important public interest in prison conditions and an inability to learn of them except through the press. The Court upheld the restriction, in part, based on the lack of any special First Amendment rights for the press to gather information and, in part, based on the need for government control over prisons.

The Court not only has restricted the ability of prisoners to communicate with those outside, but also has limited the ability of prisoners to receive information. In *Bell v. Wolfish*, the Court upheld a regulation that prevented jail inmates from receiving hardcover books except when mailed from publishers or bookstores.[160] The Court accepted the prison's concern that books could contain contraband and that the need for security required limiting the source for such books. The Court rejected the argument that the security concern could be satisfied by searching the books prior to delivery to the inmates.

Even more troubling, in *Thornburgh v. Abbott*, the Court upheld a federal prison regulation that limited the publications that could be received by prisoners.[161] The regulation was applied to prevent a prisoner from receiving a magazine that contained an article describing how a prisoner at a different institution died of an asthma attack because of the lack of adequate medical care within the facility. The Court emphasized the need for control within the prison and upheld the regulation as "reasonably related to legitimate penological interests."[162] Again, such a prior restraint is inconsistent with the most basic First Amendment principles, and the censorship was allowed based on conjecture about adverse effects of the speech.

Finally, in addition to restricting speech from and to prisoners, the Court also has limited speech among inmates in a prison and between prisoners at different institutions. In *Jones v. North Carolina Prisoners' Labor Union*, the Court upheld a prison regulation that prohibited prisoners from forming a union and that specifically forbid inmates from soliciting others to join the union and outlawed union meetings.[163] The Court expressed the need for great deference to prison authorities: "Because the realities of running a penal institution are complex and difficult, we have also recognized the wide-ranging deference to be accorded the decisions of prison administrators."[164] The Court allowed the prohibition of the prison union because of the prison's claim that it threatened discipline and order within the institution. The Court said that the "prison officials concluded that the presence, perhaps even the objectives, of a prisoners' labor union would be detrimental to order and security in the prisons. It is enough to say that they have

[159] 438 U.S. 1 (1978).
[160] 441 U.S. 520 (1979).
[161] 490 U.S. 401 (1989).
[162] *Id.* at 404.
[163] 433 U.S. 119 (1977).
[164] *Id.* at 126.

not been conclusively shown to be wrong in this view."[165] In any other context, the government would have to prove its justification for regulating speech; here, the Court upheld the restriction because the government's claim had not been proved wrong.

The cases concerning prisoner speech have emphatically reaffirmed the need for judicial deference to prison authorities' regulation of prisoners' speech. In *Shaw v. Murphy*,[166] a prisoner sent a letter containing legal advice to an inmate at another institution. Prison authorities intercepted it and did not deliver it. A suit was brought under the First Amendment.

The Supreme Court, in an opinion by Justice Thomas, unanimously held that there was no violation of the First Amendment rights of the prisoners. Justice Thomas reaffirmed that *Turner v. Safley* states the appropriate test: Prisoner speech may be regulated if it is rationally related to a legitimate penological interest. Justice Thomas stressed that this test is to be applied with great deference to prison authorities. He stated: "[U]nder *Turner* and its predecessors, prison officials are to remain the primary arbiters of the problems that arise in prison management. If courts were permitted to enhance constitutional protection based on their assessments of the content of the particular communications, courts would be in a position to assume a greater role in decisions affecting prison administration."[167]

The extent of the Court's deference to government officials is reflected in its willingness to uphold the prison's action in this case. Although the letter contained legal advice, the Court accepted the claim that such speech has sufficient risks to justify the prison's refusal to deliver it. Justice Thomas wrote: "Although supervised inmate legal assistance programs may serve valuable ends, it is 'indisputable' that inmate law clerks 'are sometimes a menace to prison discipline' and that prisoners have an 'acknowledged propensity . . . to abuse both the giving and the seeking of [legal] assistance.' Prisoners have used legal correspondence as a means for passing contraband and communicating instructions on how to manufacture drugs or weapons."[168]

In *Beard v. Banks*, the Court upheld a Pennsylvania prison regulation that prevented some prison inmates from having access to newspapers, magazines, or photographs.[169] The Court used the *Turner v. Safley* test allowing regulations that are reasonably related to a legitimate penological interest and found that it was met. Justice Breyer, writing for the Court in a 6-3 decision, said: "The Secretary in his motion set forth several justifications for the prison's policy, including the need to motivate better behavior on the part of particularly difficult prisoners, the need to minimize the amount of property they control in their cells, and the need to ensure prison safety, by, for example, diminishing the amount of material a prisoner might use to start a cell fire. We need go no further than the first justification, that of providing increased incentives for better prison behavior. Applying

---

[165] *Id.* at 132.
[166] 532 U.S. 223 (2001).
[167] *Id.* at 230.
[168] *Id.* at 231.
[169] 548 U.S. 521 (2006).

the well-established substantive and procedural standards . . . we find, on the basis of the record before us, that the Secretary's justification is adequate."[170]

Shaw v. Murphy and *Beard v. Banks*, like the earlier cases, raise the basic normative question about the appropriate role of the judiciary in evaluating prisoners' speech.[171] Is this, as the Court maintains, an area ill suited to judicial review and where the courts should defer to the choices of prison authorities? Or is this an area where more judicial protection is needed because prisoners should not lose more free speech rights than necessary to facilitate incarceration and because prison authorities and the political process are rarely sensitive to safeguarding their rights?

Schools

Schools, of course, are in many ways different from prisons and the military. An important function of schools is in teaching constitutional principles, such as the importance of freedom of speech. Restrictions of expression within schools are counter to that teaching. Also, while there is a need for discipline and order in schools, it is quite different in this regard from prisons or the military. However, courts tend to defer to the expertise of school officials and their need to make decisions about education and how to preserve discipline and order within the schools.

Some Supreme Court decisions have been very protective of student speech.[172] In *West Virginia State Board of Education v. Barnette*, discussed above in §11.2.4.3, the Court declared unconstitutional a state law that required that students salute the flag at the beginning of the school day.[173] Although the Court focused on the First Amendment's prohibition against compelled expression, the decision obviously accepted the protection of First Amendment rights in schools.

In *Tinker v. Des Moines Independent Community School District*, the Court said that the First Amendment protected the ability of students in a high school to wear black armbands to protest the Vietnam War.[174] In an opinion by Justice Fortas, the Court said that "First Amendment rights, applied in light of the special characteristics of the school environment, are available to teachers and students. It can hardly be argued that either students or teachers shed their constitutional rights to freedom of speech or expression at the schoolhouse gate."[175] The Court said that

[170] *Id.* at 531.

[171] In *Overton v. Bazzetta*, 539 U.S. 126 (2003), the Supreme Court upheld a law that regulated visits to prisoners. Michigan prison regulations prevented inmates from having noncontact family visits with any minor nieces and nephews and children as to whom parental rights had been terminated; prohibited inmates from visiting with former inmates; required children to be accompanied by family members or a legal guardian; and subjected inmates with two substance-abuse violations to a ban of visits for at least two years. The Court held that these regulations were constitutional because they were rationally related to legitimate penological objectives and thus did not violate substantive due process or freedom of association guaranteed by the First Amendment.

[172] *See also* the discussion of hate speech codes in colleges and universities, §11.3.3.4.

[173] 319 U.S. 624 (1943).

[174] 393 U.S. 503 (1969).

[175] *Id.* at 506.

§11.4 What Places Are Available for Speech?

"[i]n our system, state-operated schools may not be enclaves of totalitarianism. School officials do not possess absolute authority over their students. . . . [Students] are possessed of fundamental rights which the State must respect."[176]

The Court emphasized that the armbands were a silent protest that did not disrupt education within the schools.[177] The Court said that "[t]here is no indication that the work of the schools or any class was disrupted."[178] Justice Fortas wrote that the speech was protected absent a showing that it would materially and substantially interfere with the requirements of appropriate discipline in the operation of the school."[179]

The Court applied *Tinker* to the college context in *Papish v. Board of Curators of the University of Missouri*, where it held that a student could not be expelled for a political cartoon in a newspaper.[180] A student drew a cartoon in an off-campus underground newspaper that depicted a police officer raping the Statute of Liberty. Also, the student wrote an article that used the word "mother-fucker." The Court held that expelling the student for this speech violated the First Amendment: It was political speech; it was in an off-campus newspaper; it was at a university; and there was no showing of any disruption of the school's activities.[181]

In subsequent years, however, the Court has been much less protective of speech in school environments and much more deferential to school authorities. In *Bethel School District No. 403 v. Fraser*, the Court upheld the punishment of a student for a speech given at a school assembly, nominating another student for a position in student government, that was filled with sexual innuendo.[182] The student was suspended for a few days and kept from speaking at his graduation.

The Court upheld the punishment and emphasized the need for judicial deference to educational institutions. Chief Justice Burger, writing for the Court, said that "[t]he determination of what manner of speech in the classroom or school assembly is inappropriate properly rests with the school board."[183] The Court also distinguished *Tinker* on the ground that it had involved political speech, whereas the expression in *Bethel* was sexual in nature. Chief Justice Burger said that "it is a highly appropriate function of public school education to prohibit the use of vulgar and offensive terms in public discourse."[184] He concluded that "[a] high school assembly or classroom is no place for a sexually explicit monologue [and] it was perfectly appropriate for the school to disassociate itself to make the point to

---

[176] *Id.* at 511.

[177] The Court also stressed that other symbols worn by students were allowed in the school and that it was impermissible for the government to discriminate among them based on their message. *Id.* at 510.

[178] *Id.* at 508.

[179] *Id.* at 505 (citation omitted).

[180] 410 U.S. 667 (1973).

[181] *See also* Healy v. James, 408 U.S. 169 (1972) (holding that a college could not exclude a chapter of the Students for a Democratic Society because of its views, even if it expressed a philosophy of violence and destruction. The Court said that the speech was protected unless it met the test for incitement.).

[182] 478 U.S. 675 (1986).

[183] *Id.* at 683.

[184] *Id.*

the pupils that vulgar speech is wholly inconsistent with the 'fundamental values' of public school education."[185]

The Court went even further in its deference to school authorities in *Hazelwood School District v. Kuhlmeier.*[186] A school newspaper produced as part of a journalism class was going to publish, with the approval of its faculty advisor, stories about three students' experience with pregnancy and about the impact of divorce on students. No students' names were included in the article on pregnancy, and one was mentioned in the article on divorce (although the name had been deleted after the paper had been forwarded to the principal for review). The principal decided to publish the paper without these articles by deleting the two pages on which they appeared. The principal expressed the view that the articles on pregnancy discussed sexual activity and birth control in a manner that was inappropriate for some of the younger students at the school, that the three students in the article on pregnancy might be identified from other aspects of the article, and that the parents of the student identified in the article about divorce should have the opportunity to respond.

The Supreme Court upheld the principal's decision and rejected the First Amendment challenge. At the outset, Justice White, writing for the Court, quoted *Tinker*, that "[s]tudents in public schools do not 'shed their constitutional rights to freedom of speech or expression at the schoolhouse gate.' "[187] But he then added, quoting *Bethel*, that "the First Amendment rights of students in the public schools 'are not automatically coextensive with the rights of adults in other settings.' "[188] Justice White concluded that the school newspaper was a nonpublic forum and that as a result "school officials were entitled to regulate the content of [the school newspaper] in any reasonable manner."[189]

The Court emphasized the ability of schools to control curricular decisions, such as what appears in school newspapers published as part of journalism classes. Justice White wrote: "The question whether the First Amendment requires a school to tolerate particular student speech—the question that we addressed in *Tinker*—is different from the question whether the First Amendment requires a school affirmatively to promote particular student speech. The former question addresses educators' ability to silence a student's personal expression that happens to occur on the school premises. The latter question concerns educators' authority over school-sponsored publications, theatrical productions, and other expressive activities that students, parents, and members of the public might reasonably perceive to bear the imprimatur of the school."[190] The Court said in this context schools have broad authority to regulate student speech.

Hazelwood can be seen as a limited decision concerning the ability of schools to regulate expression that occurs as a part of official curricular activities. It reflects great judicial deference to choices by educators in this context. On the

---

[185] *Id.* at 685-686.
[186] 484 U.S. 260 (1988).
[187] *Id.* at 266.
[188] *Id.*
[189] *Id.* at 270.
[190] *Id.* at 270-271.

other hand, the decision can be criticized as excessively deferential. The articles concerned issues of vital interest to students: teenage pregnancy and dealing with divorce. The article on teen pregnancy did not glorify it; quite the contrary, the students strongly expressed regret over their situation. The Court can be criticized for dealing with the issue by characterizing the newspaper as a nonpublic forum and thereby using rational basis review. The case did not present a claim of a right of access to this government property. Instead, the issue was one of prior restraint of a school newspaper—a type of government control that generally would warrant strict scrutiny.

The most recent Supreme Court decision concerning student speech also evidenced great deference to school officials. In *Morse v. Frederick*,[191] the Court held that the First Amendment was not violated when a student was punished for displaying a banner with the inscription, "Bong Hits 4 Jesus." When the Olympic torch came through Juneau, Alaska, a high school released its students from class to watch and a student unfurled his banner. The principal, believing that the banner encouraged drug use, confiscated it and suspended the student who displayed it.

In an opinion by Chief Justice John Roberts, the Court, in a 5-4 decision, said that the principal could reasonably interpret the banner as encouraging illegal drug use and that schools have an important interest in stopping such speech. Chief Justice Roberts wrote: "The question thus becomes whether a principal may, consistent with the First Amendment, restrict student speech at a school event, when that speech is reasonably viewed as promoting illegal drug use. We hold that she may."[192]

Justice Alito wrote a concurring opinion, joined by Justice Kennedy, which stressed the narrowness of the Court's holding. Justice Alito explained that the Court was holding only that schools may punish speech that encourages illegal drug use. He wrote: "I join the opinion of the Court on the understanding that (a) it goes no further than to hold that a public school may restrict speech that a reasonable observer would interpret as advocating illegal drug use and (b) it provides no support for any restriction of speech that can plausibly be interpreted as commenting on any political or social issue, including speech on issues such as 'the wisdom of the war on drugs or of legalizing marijuana for medicinal use.' "[193]

Justice Stevens wrote a forceful dissent in which he questioned whether the majority's holding could be cabined so narrowly. He expressed concern that the Court did not require any showing that the speech would actually increase the likelihood of illegal drug use; he observed it is highly unlikely that any student, the smartest or the slowest, would be more likely to use drugs because of Frederick's banner.[194] He particularly lamented the abandonment of *Tinker's* prohibition on viewpoint discrimination in schools and its requirement of a showing of actual disruption to justify punishing student speech.

---

[191] 551 U.S. 393 (2007).

[192] *Id.* at 403. Justice Thomas wrote a concurring opinion in which he argued that the First Amendment does not apply at all in public schools. *Id.* at 410 (Thomas, J., concurring).

[193] *Id.* at 422 (Alito, J., concurring).

[194] *Id.* at 441-442 (Stevens, J., dissenting).

Although *Barnette, Tinker, Papish, Bethel, Hazelwood,* and *Morse* all focused on student speech, other First Amendment issues arise in schools as well. For example, in *Board of Education, Island Trees Union Free School District v. Pico,* the Court considered the ability of a school library to remove books because they were deemed objectionable.[195] The books included writings of authors such as Kurt Vonnegut, Desmond Morris, Langston Hughes, and Eldridge Cleaver. The Court said that the "First Amendment rights of students may be directly and sharply implicated by the removal of the books from the shelves of a school library."[196] The Court explained that the First Amendment protects a right to receive information and that the "special characteristics of the school *library* make that environment especially appropriate for the recognition of the First Amendment rights of students."[197]

The Court observed that it would clearly violate the First Amendment if a Democratic school board removed all books by Republican authors or if an all-white school board removed all books written by blacks or arguing for racial equality.[198] The Court said that "[o]ur Constitution does not permit the official suppression of ideas."[199] The Court concluded that whether the "removal of the books from their school libraries [violated the] First Amendment depends upon the motivation behind [the government's] action. If [the government] *intended* by their removal decision to deny respondents access to ideas with which petitioners disagreed, and if this intent was the decisive factor in petitioners' decision, then petitioners exercised their discretion in violation of the Constitution. . . . On the other hand, . . . an unconstitutional motivation would *not* be demonstrated if it were shown that petitioners had decided to remove the books at issue because those books were pervasively vulgar."[200] The Court remanded the case for a determination of this issue.

No school library can buy every book, and obtaining new volumes often means discarding old ones. Inherently, these choices are made based on the content of the books. Yet the Court also is obviously correct that a school board could not make these choices based on the political party affiliation or ideology of the authors. The problem is in courts striking the balance between deferring to the schools' inevitable choices and preventing school censorship of ideas or forms of expression that are unpopular, especially with some school board members. *Pico* attempts to do this by focusing on the motivation behind the decisions. Inevitably, this will turn on the content of the speech. It is difficult to imagine any permissible justification for a school library to remove from its shelves books by authors such as Kurt Vonnegut, Desmond Morris, Langston Hughes, or Eldridge Cleaver. On the other hand, no court would require that an elementary school library purchase *Hustler* magazine. As much as the prohibition of content-based discrimination is at the core of the First Amendment, this is an area where content-based choices are inescapable.

---

[195] 457 U.S. 853 (1982).
[196] *Id.* at 866.
[197] *Id.* at 868 (emphasis in original).
[198] *Id.* at 870-871.
[199] *Id.* at 871.
[200] *Id.*

§11.5   FREEDOM OF ASSOCIATION

§11.5.1   Introduction

Protection as a Fundamental Right

The Supreme Court has expressly held that freedom of association is a fundamental right protected by the First Amendment. Although "association" is not listed among those freedoms enumerated in the amendment, the Court has nonetheless declared that "freedom to engage in association for the advancement of beliefs and ideas is an inseparable aspect of the 'liberty' assured by the Due Process Clause of the Fourteenth Amendment, which embraces freedom of speech."[1]

Freedom of association is regarded as integral to the speech and assembly protected by the First Amendment. The Supreme Court explained that "[e]ffective advocacy of both public and private points of view, particularly controversial ones, is undeniably enhanced by group association."[2] Groups have resources—in human capital and money—that a single person lacks. The Court has observed that an "individual's freedom to speak, to worship, and to petition the Government for the redress of grievances could not be vigorously protected from interference by the state unless a correlative freedom to engage in group effort toward those ends were not also guaranteed."[3] Additionally, the very existence of group support for an idea conveys a message. Association is also important as people benefit from being with others in many ways.[4]

Issues Concerning Freedom of Association

Several issues concerning freedom of association have been discussed earlier in this chapter. For example, the issue of compelled association, such as through requiring employees to pay union dues or attorneys to pay bar dues, is discussed in §11.2.4.3. Also, many issues of freedom of association arise in the context of government regulation of campaign financing, which is considered in §11.3.6.3. Several questions concerning freedom of association involve the First Amendment rights of government employees, which are discussed in §11.3.8.

This section considers three issues that have not been discussed at length previously in this chapter. First, §11.5.2 considers when the government may prohibit

---

§11.5 [1] NAACP v. Alabama ex rel. Patterson, 357 U.S. 449, 460 (1958).

[2] *Id.*

[3] Roberts v. United States Jaycees, 468 U.S. 609, 622 (1984). For an excellent discussion of the rights of groups under the Constitution, *see* Ronald Caret, Community and Existence: The Rights of Groups, 56 S. Cal. L. Rev. 1001 (1983).

[4] The Court, however, generally has been unwilling to extend protection of freedom of association outside situations where it relates to First Amendment purposes. For instance, in *City of Dallas v. Stanglin*, 490 U.S. 19 (1989), the Court upheld a city ordinance that limited the ability of adults to gain access to teenage dance halls. The Court rejected a challenge based on freedom of association and emphasized that the restriction did not limit association for expressive purposes.

or punish membership in a group. Second, §11.5.3 focuses on when the government may require disclosure of membership, particularly where disclosure will chill association. Finally, §11.5.4 looks at when freedom of association protects a right of groups to discriminate.

§11.5.2   Laws Prohibiting or Punishing Membership

When May the Government Prohibit or Punish Group Membership?

Obviously, freedom of association is most directly infringed if the government outlaws and punishes membership in a group. The Court has held that the government may punish membership only if it proves that a person actively affiliated with a group, knowing of its illegal objectives, and with the specific intent to further those objectives.

For example, in *Scales v. United States*,[5] the Court affirmed the conviction of the chairman of the North Carolina and South Carolina Districts of the Communist Party under the "membership clause" of the Smith Act that made a felony "the acquisition or holding of knowing membership in any organization which advocates the overthrow of the Government by force or violence."[6] The Court said that "earlier precedents had established that the advocacy with which we are here concerned is not constitutionally protected speech, and it was further established that a combination to promote such advocacy, albeit under the aegis of what purports to be a political party, is not such association as is protected by the First Amendment."[7]

Justice Harlan, writing for the Court, said that the government's ability to prohibit such speech meant that it also had the authority to forbid associations to further these ideas and activities. Justice Harlan wrote: "We can discern no reason why membership, when it constitutes a purposeful form of complicity in a group engaging in this same forbidden advocacy, should receive any greater degree of protection from the guarantees of that Amendment."[8] The Court emphasized that "Scales was being punished for his active affiliation with the Communist Party, with knowledge of its illegal objectives, and with proof that he specifically intends to accomplish the aims of the organization by resort to violence."[9]

In contrast, in *Noto v. United States*, decided the same day, the Court reversed a conviction for membership in the Communist Party because of the absence of "illegal advocacy."[10] The Court stressed that the speech was advocacy of abstract

---

[5] 367 U.S. 203 (1961).

[6] 18 U.S.C. §2385. The language quoted is the Court's summary of the statute at 367 U.S. at 205. The Smith Act, and other cases construing its constitutionality, is discussed in more detail in §11.3.2.4.

[7] 367 U.S. at 228-229.

[8] *Id.* at 229.

[9] *Id.*

[10] 367 U.S. 290 (1961).

ideas and that there was not proof that the individual had the specific intent to further any illegal activities.

Public Employment

The Court has applied this test for punishing association in many contexts.[11] For example, the Court has held that the government may deny public employment to an individual based on group affiliation, or require that an individual take an oath concerning group affiliation, only if it is limited to situations where the individual actively affiliated with the group, knowing of its illegal activities, and with the specific intent to further those illegal goals.[12]

In *Elfbrandt v. Russell*, the Court declared unconstitutional a state's loyalty oath and law that prohibited anyone from holding office if they were a member of a group such as the Communist Party.[13] The Court applied the *Scales* test and said that it was impermissible for the government to punish individuals for being a member of a group without proof that the individual joined the organization knowing of its illegal objectives and with the specific intent to further them. The Court said that the law was unconstitutional because it "threatens the cherished freedom of association protected by the First Amendment."[14]

Similarly, in *Keyishian v. Board of Regents*, the Court declared unconstitutional a state law that denied employment as teachers to those who were part of organizations that advocated the overthrow of the government.[15] The Court emphasized that the law punished mere membership in a "subversive" group, without any requirement for proof that the individual knew of the illegal objectives or intended to further them. Similarly, in *United States v. Robel*, the Court invalidated a federal statute that denied employment to individuals who were members of designated Communist groups.[16] The Court explained that the statute created guilt by association because membership alone was enough to deny employment. The Court ruled that the government could deny employment to an individual only if the person actively affiliated with a group, knowing of its illegal objectives, and with the specific intent to further those objectives.

[11] *See, e.g.*, Communist Party of Indiana v. Whitcomb, 414 U.S. 441 (1974) (declaring unconstitutional a state law that said that political parties could not be listed on the ballot unless they filed an affidavit that they did not advocate the overthrow of the government by force or violence); Aptheker v. Secretary of State, 378 U.S. 500 (1964) (declaring unconstitutional a law that prohibited the use of a passport by a member of the Communist organization).

[12] The issue of government regulation of association of its employees is discussed in more detail in §11.3.8.2.

[13] 384 U.S. 11 (1966).

[14] *Id.* at 18.

[15] 385 U.S. 589 (1967).

[16] 389 U.S. 258 (1967).

Bar Membership

The same standards have been applied with regard to the ability of states to deny bar membership to individuals based on their group affiliations. In *Konigsberg v. State Bar*, the Court held that the government could deny bar membership to an individual who refused to answer questions concerning membership in the Communist Party.[17] But a decade later, the Court said that the government may require individuals to answer such questions only if they are narrowly focused on whether the individual actively affiliated with a group, knowing of its illegal objectives, and with the specific intent to further those goals.

In *Baird v. State Bar*[18] and *In re Stolar*,[19] the Court invalidated bar questions that asked whether a person was or ever had been a member of the Communist Party or any organization that advocated the overthrow of the government by force or violence. In contrast, in a companion case, *Law Students Civil Rights Research Council v. Wadmond*, the Court upheld a bar question that asked whether a person ever had joined a group knowing that its objective was the overthrow of the government by force or violence and, if so, whether the individual had the specific intent to advance those goals.[20] The difference among these cases is obviously the specificity of the questions. The inquiry is allowed only if it is narrowly focused on whether a person actively affiliated with a group that advocated the overthrow of the government, knowing of its goals, and with the specific intent to further them.

§11.5.3   Laws Requiring Disclosure of Membership

Disclosure of Group Membership

The Supreme Court has held that the government may require disclosure of membership, where disclosure will chill association, only if it meets strict scrutiny.[21] In *NAACP v. Alabama ex rel. Patterson*, in 1958, the Court declared unconstitutional an Alabama law that required that out-of-state corporations meet certain disclosure requirements.[22] In connection with this law, Alabama required that the NAACP disclose its membership lists. The Court, in an opinion by Justice Harlan, found the law unconstitutional and explained: "It is hardly a novel perception that compelled disclosure of affiliation with groups engaged in advocacy may constitute [an] effective . . . restraint on freedom of association. . . . This Court has recognized the vital relationship between freedom to associate and privacy in one's associations. Inviolability of privacy in group association may in many

---

[17]   366 U.S. 36 (1961). *See also* In re Anastaplo, 366 U.S. 82 (1961).
[18]   401 U.S. 1 (1971).
[19]   401 U.S. 23 (1971).
[20]   401 U.S. 154 (1971).
[21]   *But see* Communist Party of the United States v. Subversive Activities Control Bd., 367 U.S. 1 (1961); New York ex rel. Bryant v. Zimmerman, 278 U.S. 63 (1928) (upholding disclosure requirements).
[22]   357 U.S. 449 (1958).

circumstances be indispensable to preservation of freedom of association, particularly where a group espouses dissident beliefs."[23]

Similarly, in *Shelton v. Tucker*, the Court declared unconstitutional a state law that required that all teachers disclose their group memberships on an annual basis.[24] The Court again stressed the impact of such disclosures in chilling constitutionally protected association. The Court explained: "[To] compel a teacher to disclose his every associational tie is to impair that teacher's right of free association. [The] statute does not provide that the information it requires be kept confidential. . . . Even if there were no disclosure to the general public, the pressure upon a teacher to avoid any ties which might displease those who control his professional destiny would be constant and heavy."[25] Although the Court recognized the government's important interest in having competent teachers, it concluded that "the state cannot pursue the goal by means that broadly stifle fundamental personal liberties when the end can be more narrowly achieved."[26]

Campaign Finance Disclosure

A crucial aspect of many campaign finance laws is a requirement that candidates disclose their contributors. Such disclosures may chill contributions. Nonetheless, the Court generally has upheld such requirements because of the government's compelling interest in stopping corruption, except where there is reason to believe that the disclosure will chill contributions to a minor party or candidate.

In *Buckley v. Valeo*, the Court upheld a provision in the Federal Election Campaign Act of 1971 that required that every political candidate and political committee keep records of the names and addresses of all who contributed more than $10.[27] These records were required to be available to the Federal Election Commission and for public inspection and copying. There is no doubt that in some contexts people might be chilled from making a contribution because of the disclosure requirement. But the Court found that the requirement served significant government interests.

The Court said that "disclosure provides the electorate with information 'as to where political campaign money comes from' . . . in order to aid the voters in evaluating those who seek federal office."[28] The Court also observed that "the disclosure requirements discourage corruption and the appearance of corruption because of the light of publicity."[29] Finally, the Court explained that "such requirements are an essential means of gathering the data necessary to detect violations of the contribution limitations."[30]

---

[23] *Id.* at 462.
[24] 364 U.S. 479 (1960).
[25] *Id.* at 485.
[26] *Id.* at 488.
[27] 424 U.S. 1 (1976). *Buckley* is discussed in more detail in §11.3.6.3.
[28] *Id.* at 66.
[29] *Id.* at 67.
[30] *Id.* at 68.

The Court in *Buckley* recognized that disclosure might have a particularly harmful effect on a minor party and "[i]n some instances fears of reprisal may deter contributions to the point where the movement cannot survive."[31] The Court said that for a minor party there was much less need for disclosure to prevent corruption "for it is less likely that the candidate will be victorious."[32] Although no such parties were involved in *Buckley*, in *Brown v. Socialist Workers '74 Campaign Committee*, the Court held that it was unconstitutional to require the Socialist Workers Party to comply with a state campaign disclosure law.[33] The Court applied its dicta from *Buckley* and concluded that the Socialist Workers Party was a minor party that was historically unpopular so that disclosure requirements would serve little purpose and would likely chill contributions and associational activity.

In *Citizens United v. Federal Election Commission*, the Court invalidated restrictions on independent expenditures by corporations and unions, but once more upheld disclosure requirements.[34] The Court explained "that disclosure is a less restrictive alternative to more comprehensive regulations of speech. . . . The First Amendment protects political speech; and disclosure permits citizens and shareholders to react to the speech of corporate entities in a proper way. This transparency enables the electorate to make informed decisions and give proper weight to different speakers and messages."[35]

Disclosure of Signatures on Ballot Petitions

In *Doe v. Reed*, the Court rejected the argument that disclosing the identity of those who sign petitions for ballot initiatives and referenda inherently violate the First Amendment.[36] Washington State enacted a law expanding benefits for domestic partners. A group gathered signatures for a ballot referenda to overturn this law. Another group filed a request under the Washington Public Records Act for copies of these petitions. The group circulating the initiative filed a lawsuit in federal court objecting that disclosure would violate the First Amendment and would chill expression.

The Supreme Court, in an 8-1 decision, held that disclosure does not inherently violate the First Amendment, but ruled that there would be a constitutional claim if it could be shown in a particular instance that disclosure would lead to threats, intimidation, or reprisals. The Court said that disclosure raised a First Amendment issue and said that the First Amendment "standard requires a 'substantial relation' between the disclosure requirement and a 'sufficiently important' governmental interest."[37] The Court said that disclosure of ballot petitions serves important government interests "in preserving the integrity of the electoral process by combating fraud, detecting invalid signatures, and fostering government

---

[31] *Id.*
[32] *Id.* at 70.
[33] 459 U.S. 87 (1982).
[34] 130 S. Ct. 876 (2010). *Citizens United* is discussed in detail above in §11.3.6.3.
[35] *Id.* at 915.
[36] 130 S. Ct. 2811 (2010).
[37] *Id.* at 2818.

transparency and accountability."[38] For example, disclosure could reveal signatures by individuals who were not eligible or impermissible multiple signatures by the same person. However, the Court left open the possibility of challenging disclosure if there was a showing of likely resulting threats, reprisals, or intimidation.

Several Justices wrote separate opinions to address that possibility. Justice Alito wrote separately to indicate the likelihood of such a showing,[39] whereas Justice Sotomayor and Justice Stevens each wrote separate opinions to express the need for great deference to states in conducting their elections and in allowing such disclosures.[40] Justice Scalia concurred in the judgment and said that disclosure of ballot petitions raises no First Amendment issue.[41] Only Justice Thomas dissented and would have found a First Amendment violation from the disclosure of the ballot petitions under Washington's Public Records Act.[42]

§11.5.4   Laws Prohibiting Discrimination

Generally Does Not Protect Discrimination

Many state and local governments have adopted laws that prohibit discrimination by private groups and clubs. Frequently, challenges are brought to these laws by those wishing to discriminate; the claim is that freedom of association protects their right to discriminate and exclude whomever they want from their group. The Supreme Court has held that the compelling interest in stopping discrimination justifies interfering with such associational freedoms. The Court has indicated that freedom of association would protect a right to discriminate only if it is intimate association or where the discrimination is integral to express activity.

Roberts v. United States Jaycees is the initial and still leading case.[43] The Jaycees, a national organization of young men between ages 18 and 35, challenged the Minnesota Human Rights Act, which prohibited private discrimination based on characteristics such as race and sex.[44] The Jaycees claimed that freedom of association protected their right to exclude women and to be a place where men associated with each other. The Supreme Court reaffirmed that freedom of association is a fundamental right and agreed that "[t]here can be no clearer example of an intrusion into the internal structure or affairs of an association than a regulation that forces the group to accept members it does not desire."[45]

However, the Court said that freedom of association is not absolute and that "[i]nfringements on that right may be justified by regulations adopted to serve compelling state interests, unrelated to the suppression of ideas, that cannot be

---

[38]   *Id.* at 2819.
[39]   *Id.* at 2822 (Alito, J., concurring).
[40]   *Id.* at 2827 (Sotomayor, J., concurring); *id.* at 2829 (Stevens, J., concurring).
[41]   *Id.* at 2832 (Scalia, J., concurring in the judgment).
[42]   *Id.* at 2837 (Thomas, J., dissenting).
[43]   468 U.S. 609 (1984).
[44]   *Id.*
[45]   *Id.* at 623.

achieved through means significantly less restrictive of associational freedoms."[46] The Court concluded that the state's goal of prohibiting discrimination was unrelated to the suppression of any message and "plainly serves compelling state interests of the highest order."[47] The Court found no evidence that requiring the Jaycees to include women would undermine its expressive activities, and the Jaycees obviously was too large to be considered "intimate association."

Similarly, in *Board of Directors of Rotary International v. Rotary Club of Duarte*, the Court held that it did not violate the First Amendment rights of the members of Rotary Club to force them to admit women in compliance with a California law that prohibited private business establishments from discriminating based on characteristics such as gender.[48] In *New York State Club Association, Inc. v. City of New York*, the Court upheld the constitutionality of a city's ordinance that prohibited discrimination by clubs that have more than 400 members and that provide regular meal service.[49]

The Court in these cases acknowledged that the laws interfered with freedom of association. The Court, however, concluded that the government had a compelling interest in stopping discrimination that justified the infringement. Private clubs are places where business contacts are made, clients are recruited, and deals are done. If women and racial minorities are allowed to be excluded from these places, they will suffer in their careers.

The Court has recognized, however, that freedom of association would protect a right to discriminate in limited circumstances. For instance, if the activity is "intimate association"—a small private gathering—freedom of association would protect a right to discriminate.[50] Also, freedom of association would protect a right to discriminate where discrimination is integral to expressive activity. For example, the Klan likely could exclude African Americans or the Nazi party could exclude Jews because discrimination is a key aspect of their message.[51]

The Court applied these exceptions in a later, very important decision: *Boy Scouts of America v. Dale.*[52] In *Dale*, the Court, in a 5-to-4 decision, held that freedom of association protects the right of the Boy Scouts to exclude gays in violation of a state's antidiscrimination statute. Dale was a lifelong Scout who had reached the rank of Eagle Scout and had become an assistant scoutmaster. While in college he became involved in gay rights activities. Dale was quoted in a newspaper article after attending a seminar on the psychological needs of gay and lesbian teenagers and was identified in the article as the co-president of the Gay/Lesbian Alliance

---

[46] *Id.*

[47] *Id.* at 624.

[48] 481 U.S. 537 (1987).

[49] 487 U.S. 1 (1988).

[50] For an excellent discussion of the concept of intimate association, *see* Kenneth Karst, The Freedom of Intimate Association, 89 Yale L.J. 624 (1980).

[51] In Hurley v. Irish-American Gay, Lesbian, and Bisexual Group of Boston, 515 U.S. 557 (1995), the Court held that a private group that organized a St. Patrick's Day Parade could exclude a gay, lesbian, and bisexual group from participation. The unanimous decision said that organizing a parade is an inherently expressive activity and those doing so have a right to exclude messages inimical to their own. *Hurley* is discussed in detail in §11.2.4.3.

[52] 530 U.S. 640 (2000).

at Rutgers University. A scout official saw this article and then sent Dale a letter excluding him from further participation in the Scouts.

Dale sued under the New Jersey law that prohibits discrimination by places of public accommodation.[53] The New Jersey Supreme Court found that the Boy Scouts are a "public accommodation" within the meaning of the law and rejected the Boy Scouts claim that freedom of association protected their right to discriminate based on sexual orientation.[54]

The issue before the Supreme Court was whether the Boy Scouts' desire to exclude gays fit within either of the exceptions recognized in *Jaycees*. Since the Boy Scouts are a large national organization, they could not realistically claim to be "intimate association." Instead, their central argument was that they had an expressive message that was antigay and that forcing them to include homosexuals undermined this communicative goal.

The key question, then, was how to determine the expressive message of the Boy Scouts and whether forced inclusion harms this First Amendment right. In answering this question, the Court held that a group gets to determine its own expressive message, including during litigation, and that forced association undermines the expressive message of the group.

Determining a group's expressive message obviously is crucial in evaluating whether discrimination is integral to it. The Boy Scouts claimed to have an anti-gay expressive message, but as Justice Stevens pointed out in a lengthy dissent, there is virtually nothing in the organization's literature communicating this.[55] Justice Stevens carefully reviewed the Boy Scouts' mission statement, handbook, and other publications and found nothing expressing an antigay message.[56] There is one line stating that Boy Scouts should be "morally straight." But this obviously had nothing to do with sexual orientation when it was written. In fact, the Boy Scouts' literature instructs scout leaders and their assistants to refrain from discussing matters of sexuality.

Chief Justice Rehnquist's majority opinion acknowledged that "[o]bviously, the Scout Oath and Law do not expressly mention sexuality or sexual orientation."[57] But Chief Justice Rehnquist was willing to find such a goal based on the Boy Scouts' interpretation of its own words, such as its command that scouts be "morally straight," and from the position it had taken during litigation.[58]

In other words, the Court in *Boy Scouts of America v. Dale* essentially held that during litigation a group can define its own expressive message. Chief Justice Rehnquist said that its failure to clearly state such a communicative goal in advance is not determinative: "The fact that the organization does not trumpet its views from the housetops, or that it tolerates dissent within its ranks, does not mean that its views receive no First Amendment protection."[59]

---

[53] N.J. Stat Ann. §§10:5-4 and 10:5-5 (West Supp. 2000).
[54] 160 N.J. 562, 734 A.2d 1196 (1999).
[55] 530 U.S. at 665-671 (Stevens, J., dissenting).
[56] *Id.*
[57] *Id.* at 650.
[58] *Id.* at 650-655.
[59] *Id.* at 656.

Even if it is assumed that the Boy Scouts had an expressive message that was antigay, there still must be a determination of whether stopping it from discriminating undermined this communication. The Supreme Court in *Dale* recognized that this is crucial to any First Amendment claim. Chief Justice Rehnquist explained: "The forced inclusion of an unwanted person in a group infringes the group's freedom of expressive association if the presence of that person affects in a significant way the group's ability to advocate public or private viewpoints."[60]

But James Dale being a scout leader does not keep the Boy Scouts from expressing and advocating any message that it chooses. The Boy Scouts can advocate any viewpoint it wants with regard to sexual orientation in its publications, its legal briefs, its legislative testimony, and its statements to the media. Chief Justice Rehnquist said that "we give deference to an association's view of what would impair its expression."[61] He explained that "Dale's presence in the Boy Scouts would, at the very least, force the organization to send a message, both to youth organizations and the world, that the Boy Scouts accepts homosexual conduct as a legitimate form of behavior."[62]

On the one hand, *Boy Scouts of America v. Dale* can be defended as protecting freedom of association. The Court upheld the right of a group to determine its members and its message. But critics, such as the four dissenting Justices, argue that the Court has opened the door to discrimination. Any group that wants to discriminate and exempt itself from state antibias laws can do so by claiming, during litigation, that it has a discriminatory purpose. Moreover, critics argue that the Court erred in finding that requiring the Scouts to include Dale would undermine their ability to express their antigay views.

Freedom of association is unquestionably a fundamental right, and one of its core aspects is the right of a group to choose who is in and who is out. But antidiscrimination laws seek to keep people from being excluded based on invidious characteristics such as race, gender, religion, disability, and sexual orientation. Enforcing antidiscrimination laws against groups that want to exclude on such grounds intrudes on associational decisions. Refusing to apply antidiscrimination laws on this basis compromises the commitment to equality. *Boy Scouts of America v. Dale* is certainly not going to be the Court's last struggle with this difficult question. *Dale* is important because it is the first time that the Court has found that freedom of association protects a right to discriminate. Future cases will determine whether this is a limited exception or a basis for many groups to exempt themselves from antidiscrimination laws.[63]

---

[60] *Id.* at 648 (emphasis added).

[61] *Id.* at 653.

[62] *Id.*

[63] In *Christian Legal Society v. Martinez*, 130 S. Ct. 2971 (2010), the Court held that a public university law school could require that officially recognized student groups accept all-comers. Although there are obvious freedom of association implications, the Court did not decide the case on this basis. Instead, the Court found that the law school had created a "limited public forum" and that its regulation was allowed because it was reasonable and viewpoint neutral. *Christian Legal Society* is discussed in detail above in §11.4.2.4.

§11.6   FREEDOM OF THE PRESS

§11.6.1   Introduction

Are There Special Rights for the Press?

Although the First Amendment separately protects "freedom of the press," most of the issues concerning press freedom have been covered throughout this chapter. For example, the basic methodological issues concerning the First Amendment—such as the distinction between content-based and content-neutral laws, the requirement that laws not be vague or overbroad, and the prohibition of prior restraints—all apply to the press. Indeed, many of these cases, particularly those concerning prior restraints, arose in the context of actions against newspapers. Similarly, the categories of unprotected and less protected speech apply to all speakers, including the press.

This section focuses on issues that uniquely apply to the press. The underlying question is whether the press is entitled to any protections greater than others under the First Amendment. For example, does freedom of the press provide the media with an exemption from general government laws? Does it protect a right to news gathering and thus give the media special access to government places and papers?

On the one hand, freedom of the press is enumerated as a distinct right from freedom of speech. This arguably reflects the important and unique role of the press in informing the public and thereby checking government.[1] Sometimes the failure to protect the press as an institution will mean that the people will be denied significant information. For instance, arguably the refusal to allow reporters to keep their sources confidential will mean the loss of information that might have been available if secrecy could have been promised.

But others argue that the press is entitled to no special protections under the First Amendment.[2] In part, the argument against special status for the press is based on the framers' intent and the view that they used the words "speech" and "press" synonymously. In part, too, those who oppose special protections for the press argue that defining the press poses insurmountable obstacles. For example, if reporters can keep their sources confidential, is anyone who purports to be writing a story entitled to the privilege? Any distinctions could raise serious First Amendment and equal protection issues.[3] Opposition to special protections for the press also reflects a long-standing hostility to the media in American society. Some fear that special protection would unduly enlarge the power of the press.

---

[1] **§11.6** *See, e.g.,* David A. Anderson, The Origins of the Press Clause, 30 UCLA L. Rev. 455 (1983); Potter Stewart, Or of the Press, 26 Hastings L.J. 631 (1975).

[2] *See, e.g.,* Leonard W. Levy, Legacy of Suppression, 174 (1960); *see also* First Natl. Bank of Boston v. Bellotti, 435 U.S. 765, 797-801 (1978) (Burger, C.J., concurring).

[3] It should be noted, though, that many states have adopted reporter shield laws that have defined who is entitled to protection under them.

The Supreme Court generally has taken the latter view that the press is not entitled to any special rights or protections under the First Amendment. The issue remains, though, as to whether this is a desirable interpretation of the First Amendment and whether it adequately protects the need of the people to be informed.

Types of Issues Concerning Freedom of the Press

Two major types of issues arise concerning freedom of the press. First, does freedom of the press provide the media a shield that it can use to immunize itself from government regulation? Section 11.6.2 focuses on this issue and considers many specific issues. When do taxes on the press violate the First Amendment? Does freedom of the press exempt it from the application of general regulatory laws? Does the press have a constitutional right to keep its sources secret? Does the First Amendment protect the press from laws that create a right to use the media to reply to attacks?

A second major set of issues concerns whether freedom of the press can be used as a "sword" to gain access to government places and papers. There are two interrelated issues here: Does the First Amendment create a right of access for anyone to government places and papers; and does the press have a preferred right of access or any rights greater than the general population? As discussed in §11.6.3, the Court has found a First Amendment right for people to attend judicial proceedings, but otherwise has refused to find such a First Amendment right of access and has thus far failed to recognize greater rights for the press than others in society.

§11.6.2   Freedom of the Press as a Shield to Protect the Press from the Government

§11.6.2.1   Taxes on the Press

Unconstitutionality of Taxes Directed at the Press

The Supreme Court consistently has held that taxes that single out the press are unconstitutional; but the press can be required to pay general taxes applicable to all businesses. The obvious concern is that the government could use taxes to punish the press for aggressive reporting or pointed criticism. The fear of such taxes could chill the press. Justice O'Connor explained that there "is substantial evidence that differential taxation of the press would have troubled the Framers of the Constitution. . . . [When] a State singles out the press [for special taxation], the political constraints that prevent a legislature from passing crippling taxes of general applicability are weakened and the threat of burdensome taxes becomes acute. That threat can operate as effectively as a censor to check critical comment by the press."[4]

---

[4] Minneapolis Star & Tribune Co. v. Minnesota Commr. of Revenue, 460 U.S. 575, 583-585 (1983).

For example, in *Grosjean v. American Press Co.*, the Court declared unconstitutional a state statute imposing a license tax on advertisements in publications having a circulation of more than 20,000 copies a week.[5] The Court reviewed the history of the First Amendment and concluded that the framers clearly intended to prohibit taxes directed at the press because of fear that they could cripple or at least chill the press. The Court said that although the First Amendment did not exempt the press from ordinary taxation, it did provide immunity from taxes directed solely at them. Although the Court did not discuss the circumstances that caused Louisiana to adopt its tax on the press, it likely was influenced by the fact that it was initiated by Governor Huey Long as retaliation against newspapers that had opposed him.

The Court subsequently applied *Grosjean* in *Minneapolis Star & Tribune Co. v. Minnesota Commissioner of Revenue* and declared unconstitutional a print and ink tax.[6] Initially, the press was exempt from both sales and use taxes in Minnesota. The state then amended its law to tax ink and paper used in publications with the first $100,000 used being exempt. Justice O'Connor said that taxes, such as Minnesota's, directed solely at the press risk chilling reporting. She concluded: "[Differential] taxation of the press, then, places such a burden on the interests protected by the First Amendment and we cannot countenance such treatment unless the State asserts a counterbalancing interest of compelling importance that it cannot achieve without differential taxation."[7]

The Court found no such compelling interest to justify the Minnesota tax. The state argued that the paper and ink tax actually favored the press; it paid less taxes than it would have under the general sales tax.[8] But the Court said that was irrelevant because the very existence of a special tax, regardless of its level, posed a threat to press freedom. Once the press knows that it can be subject to a differential tax, it has reason to fear that a future greater tax might be adopted.

The taxes in *Grosjean* and *Minneapolis Star* both singled out the press and had a discriminatory effect among newspapers; larger papers would be taxed much more than smaller ones. In *Arkansas Writers' Project, Inc. v. Ragland*, the Court ruled that the government cannot discriminate among types of publications.[9] A state exempted from its sales tax special interest publications such as religious, professional, trade, and sports journals, but did not exempt general interest magazines. The Court emphasized that any differential taxation of the press—either of the press as opposed to others in society or at particular parts of the press—risked chilling reporting. The Arkansas law also was found unconstitutional on more basic grounds: It was content-based. The application of the tax turned entirely on the content of the publication and thus ran afoul of the fundamental prohibition against content-based discrimination except where necessary to serve a compelling purpose.

---

[5] 297 U.S. 233 (1936).

[6] 460 U.S. 575 (1983).

[7] *Id.* at 585.

[8] This also was the point emphasized by then-Justice Rehnquist in his dissenting opinion. *See id.* at 597-598 (Rehnquist, J., dissenting).

[9] 481 U.S. 221 (1987).

In light of these decisions, it is difficult to reconcile the Court's most subsequent decision concerning taxes on the press, *Leathers v. Medlock*.[10] *Leathers* involved a state law that exempted newspapers and magazines from a state gross receipts tax, but did not exempt cable television. Although the tax singled out a particular branch of the media, the Court found it constitutional. The Court said that unlike *Grosjean* and *Minneapolis Star*, the tax did not single out the press, and unlike the tax in *Ragland*, it was not content-based. The Court said that because the tax was not discriminatory on either of these grounds it was constitutional. Justice O'Connor, who also wrote the opinion for the Court in *Minneapolis Star*, stated for the majority that the "extension of [a state's] generally applicable sales tax to cable television, . . . while exempting the print media, does not violate the First Amendment."[11]

The cases can be reconciled by seeing the earlier decisions only as prohibiting the government from having a tax that is directed solely at the press or that distinguishes among the press.[12] *Leathers* does not involve either of these features, and thus the tax was upheld.[13] But if the earlier cases are seen as establishing a broader principle that the government should not be able to discriminate among parts of the press, then *Leathers* cannot be reconciled with the earlier precedents. The concern is that the government could retaliate against a particular branch of the press by a tax directed at it or denying it an exemption that other parts of the press are granted.

§11.6.2.2 Application of General Regulatory Laws

Refusal to Create Exemptions for the Press

The Supreme Court consistently has refused to find that the protection of freedom of the press entitles it to exemptions from general regulatory laws. For example, attempts by the press to receive constitutionally based exemptions to antitrust statutes, labor laws, and liability under state contract law have been expressly rejected.

---

[10] 499 U.S. 439 (1991).

[11] *Id.* at 453.

[12] In *Turner Broadcasting System, Inc. v. FCC*, 512 U.S. 622, 660-661 (1994), the Court expressed this distinction:

> It would be error to conclude, however, that the First Amendment mandates strict scrutiny for any speech regulation that applies to one medium (or a subset thereof) but not others. . . . The taxes invalidated in *Minneapolis Star and Arkansas Writers' Project*, for example, targeted a small number of speakers and . . . were structured in a manner that raised suspicions that their objective . . . was, in fact, the suppression of certain ideas. But such heightened scrutiny is unwarranted, when the differential treatment is . . . not structured in a manner that carries the inherent risk of undermining First Amendment interests.

[13] A distinct issue involves laws that treat the press better than others in society. *See* Austin v. Michigan State Chamber of Commerce, 494 U.S. 652 (1990) (upholding a law that prohibited corporations from using their corporate funds in political election campaigns, but permitting media corporations to do so in order to permit the media to editorialize and inform the public).

In *Associated Press v. United States*, the Court ruled against the claim that the First Amendment entitles the press to an exemption from federal antitrust laws.[14] An action was brought against an alleged monopoly in the dissemination of news through an association of member newspapers. Nonmembers were denied access to the association's news, and membership was restricted. Justice Black, writing for the Court, flatly rejected the claim that the First Amendment protected the press from antitrust liability. He said that "[f]reedom to publish is guaranteed by the Constitution, but freedom to combine to keep others from publishing is not. Freedom of the press from governmental interference under the First Amendment does not sanction repression of that freedom by private interests. The First Amendment affords not the slightest support for the contention that a combination to restrain trade in news and views has any constitutional immunity."[15] Indeed, the Court said that First Amendment values were served by the application of antitrust laws so as to ensure the widest possible dissemination of news.

The Court followed *Associated Press* in *Citizens Publishing Co. v. United States*,[16] which again rejected the claim of a First Amendment exemption to antitrust laws. *Citizens Publishing* involved an antitrust action against two newspapers in Tucson, Arizona, that formed a joint operating agreement that involved price fixing, profit pooling, and market controls. The Court upheld a finding of antitrust violations by the papers and noted that "[n]either news gathering nor news dissemination is being regulated by the present decree."[17] The Court invoked *Associated Press* for the proposition that antitrust laws enhance, not hinder, First Amendment values by encouraging diverse sources of information and news.

Likewise, the Court has rejected claims by the press that the First Amendment entitles it to exemptions from federal labor laws. In *Associated Press v. NLRB*, the Court disagreed with the argument that freedom of the press provided it an exemption from the National Labor Relations Act, which protects the right of employees to organize and bargain collectively.[18] The Court explained: "The business of the Associated Press is not immune from regulation because it is an agency of the press. The publisher of a newspaper has no special immunity from the application of general laws. He has no special privilege to invade the rights and liberties of others. He must answer for libel. He may be punished for contempt of court. He is subject to the antitrust laws. Like others he must pay equitable and nondiscriminatory taxes on his business. The regulation here in question has no relation whatever to the impartial distribution of news."[19]

In *Oklahoma Press Publishing Co. v. Walling*, the Court held that the First Amendment does not exempt the press from the Fair Labor Standards Act, which requires payment of the minimum wage and sets maximum hours limits for employees.[20] The Court said that *Associated Press* established that there was no

---

[14] 326 U.S. 1 (1945).
[15] *Id.* at 20.
[16] 394 U.S. 131 (1969).
[17] *Id.* at 139.
[18] 301 U.S. 103 (1937).
[19] *Id.* at 132-133.
[20] 327 U.S. 186 (1946).

merit to the claim that it violated the First Amendment to apply labor laws to the press. The Court said "[i]f Congress can remove obstructions to commerce by requiring publishers to bargain collectively with employees and refrain from interfering with their rights of self-organization, matters closely related to eliminating low wages and long hours, Congress likewise may strike directly at those evils when they adversely affect commerce."[21]

The strongest statement that the press is not exempt from general laws was in *Cohen v. Cowles Media Co.*[22] A newspaper published the identity of a source who had been promised that his name would not be disclosed. The Court rejected the argument that holding the newspaper liable for breach of contract would violate the First Amendment. The Court stressed that the case involved the application of a general law that in no way was motivated by a desire to interfere with the press. The Court said: "[G]enerally applicable laws do not offend the First Amendment simply because their enforcement against the press has incidental effects on its ability to gather and report the news. [E]nforcement of such general laws against the press is not subject to stricter scrutiny than would be applied to enforcement against other persons or organizations."[23]

All of these cases reflect the view that a law of general applicability applies to the press just like it applies to anyone else. Yet in none of these cases was there proof that application of the law would undermine First Amendment values. Indeed, in the antitrust cases and even in *Cohen* there were strong arguments that applying the general law would enhance the underlying constitutional values by fostering more news sources. If the press could prove in a particular case that the application of a general law significantly burdened its ability to function, the Court would need to consider whether an exemption from a general law is appropriate.

§11.6.2.3   Keeping Reporters' Sources and Secrets Confidential

Court's Refusal to Protect Secrecy of Sources

Confidential sources are often crucial to the media's gathering of information and being able to inform the public. Sometimes individuals may be willing to disclose important information to reporters only with a promise that their identity will be kept confidential. "Deep Throat"—the confidential source that provided the basis for many of the key stories by Washington Post reporters Carl Bernstein and Bob Woodward—was instrumental in helping to expose the criminal acts surrounding the Watergate cover-up and the actions of the Campaign to Re-elect President Nixon.

Thus, the press has claimed that the First Amendment gives it a right to resist subpoenas that require disclosure of the identity of confidential sources. The Supreme

---

[21] *Id.* at 193.
[22] 501 U.S. 663 (1991).
[23] *Id.* at 669-670.

Court, however, rejected this position in *Branzburg v. Hayes*.[24] *Branzburg* presented several cases to the Court where reporters had refused to appear before state and federal grand juries and disclose the identity of confidential sources. In a 5-to-4 decision, with the majority opinion written by Justice White, the Court rejected the claim that the First Amendment creates a shield for reporters that immunizes them from having to disclose their sources.

At the outset, the Court observed that news gathering is entitled to First Amendment protection and said that "without some protection for seeking out the news, freedom of the press could be eviscerated."[25] But the Court also said that "the First Amendment does not guarantee the press a constitutional right of special access to information not available to the public generally."[26] Justice White noted that the press is regularly kept from many places from which the public is excluded, ranging from grand jury proceedings to the Supreme Court's conferences to crime and disaster scenes.

The Court concluded that "the public interest in law enforcement and in ensuring effective grand jury proceedings" is sufficient to override the consequential, but uncertain, burden on news gathering that is said to result from insisting that "reporters, like other citizens, respond to relevant questions put to them in the course of a valid grand jury investigation or criminal trial."[27] In part, the Court's conclusion was based on its view that there was insufficient evidence that sources would dry up without First Amendment protection of confidentiality. In part, too, the Court said that creating a constitutional privilege would create serious problems in defining who was the press and thus entitled to refuse to answer questions from a grand jury.

It should be noted that Justice Powell, the fifth vote in the majority, wrote a concurring opinion in which he urged that a balancing test be used in particular cases to decide whether the First Amendment protected the ability of the press to keep its sources confidential. Powell said that "[t]he asserted claim to privilege should be judged on its facts by the striking of a proper balance between freedom of the press and the obligation of all citizens to give relevant testimony with respect to criminal conduct. The balance of these vital constitutional and societal interests on a case-by-case basis accords with the tried and traditional way of adjudicating such questions."[28] Some lower courts have relied on Justice Powell's opinion as the crucial fifth vote as creating a reporters' privilege, while other courts have rejected this position and found no such privilege under the First Amendment.[29]

---

[24]   408 U.S. 665 (1972).

[25]   *Id.* at 681.

[26]   *Id.* at 684.

[27]   *Id.* at 690.

[28]   *Id.* at 710 (Powell, J., concurring).

[29]   *Compare, e.g.*, United States v. Sterling, 724 F.3d 482 (4th Cir. 2013) (there was no First Amendment reporter's privilege that protected New York Times reporter James Risen from being compelled to testify about source); In re Grand Jury Subpoena, Judith Miller, 397 F.3d 964 (D.C. Cir.), *cert. denied*, 545 U.S. 1150 (2005) (rejecting a reporters' privilege), *with* Silkwood v. Kerr-McGee Corp., 563 F.2d 433 (10th Cir. 1977) (finding a reporters' privilege). *See* Rodney A. Smolla, Smolla and Nimmer on Freedom of Speech, 13-06 n.3; 13-07 n.39 (1994) (listing cases accepting and rejecting a reporter's privilege).

Branzburg reflects the principle described above that the press is not entitled to exemptions from general laws; anyone else would have to answer questions from a grand jury, so a reporter must also do so. But *Branzburg* can be criticized for failing to give adequate weight to the importance of confidential sources in informing the public and, at times, checking government. Although the Court was correct that there is not empirical proof of how many sources would vanish without assurances of confidentiality, this is something that would be impossible to measure. In fact, the Court has accepted the importance of other privileges, such as the attorney-client privilege, even though there also could not be proof of how many conversations would not occur without the promise of confidentiality. The importance of a reporter's privilege is reflected in the fact that a large number of states have adopted shield laws that protect reporters from having to disclose their sources.[30] The statutes vary greatly in their scope and exceptions. No such federal law exists, and thus there is still no basis for a reporter's privilege in federal courts.

Searches of Newsrooms

The Supreme Court has followed *Branzburg* in other cases in refusing to find First Amendment exemption for the press in court proceedings and law enforcement actions.[31] In *Zurcher v. Stanford Daily*, the Court upheld the ability of the police to search press newsrooms to gather information to aid criminal investigations.[32] A student newspaper published stories about a violent confrontation between students and the police at a demonstration. The police then obtained a warrant to search the newspaper's offices for negatives, films, and pictures that would help to identify the demonstrators. The search was conducted, though it did not yield any information that had not already been published.

The newspaper then sued the police for violating the First Amendment. The Court held that the First Amendment did not protect the press from valid searches pursuant to valid warrants. Justice White again wrote the opinion for the Court and once more rejected the claim of any special protection for the press under the First Amendment. He said: "Properly administered, the preconditions for a warrant—probable cause, specificity with respect to the place to be searched and the things to be seized, and overall reasonableness—should afford sufficient protection against the harms that are assertedly threatened by warrants for searching newspaper offices. . . . [Nor] are we convinced, any more than we were in [*Branzburg*], that confidential sources will disappear."[33]

---

[30] Forty-nine states and the District of Columbia have some form of reporters' shield laws, but there is not a federal statute creating such protection for reporters. *See generally* Kathryn A. Rosenbaum, Protecting More Than the Front Page: Protecting a Reporter's Privilege for Digital and Citizen Journalists, 89 Notre Dame L. Rev. 1427 (2014); RonNell Andersen Jones, Avalanche or Undue Alarm? An Empirical Study of Subpoenas Received by the News Media, 93 Minn. L. Rev. 585 (2008).

[31] *See, e.g.*, Herbert v. Lando, 441 U.S. 153 (1979) (the First Amendment did not protect the press from having to answer questions concerning its editorial process in a defamation action; the need for a public figure to prove "actual malice" warranted requiring the press to answer the questions).

[32] 436 U.S. 547 (1978).

[33] *Id.* at 565-566.

Zurcher is obviously consistent with *Branzburg* and the other cases described in this section that refused to recognize special protection for the press. Yet *Zurcher* is troubling because the search was not for evidence of any crimes committed by the newspaper or its reporters; the police were searching the newsroom to use in law enforcement the information that the paper gathered as the press. There is reason for concern that such searches would chill aggressive reporting and the willingness of confidential sources to speak to the press if their identity could be easily learned through the search of a newsroom. For this reason, almost immediately after *Zurcher*, Congress enacted the Privacy Protection Act of 1980 to protect the press from searches of newsrooms.[34] The law prohibits law enforcement from searches of those reasonably believed to be engaged in disseminating information to the public unless there is probable cause to believe that the person committed a crime or that giving notice by subpoena likely would result in the loss of evidence.

§11.6.2.4　Laws Requiring That the Media Make Access Available

Distinction Between Broadcast and Print Media

The issues described in the prior two sections focused on the application of general laws and law enforcement procedures to the press. A distinct issue arises concerning laws that attempt to regulate the press and require that it allow others to use it. Can the government require that the media make newspaper space or broadcast time available to respond to personal attacks? Arguably, such access laws enhance First Amendment values; they expand the voices that the public can hear. But the laws also infringe the First Amendment value of press autonomy; the ability of the media to control what it publishes or broadcasts is compromised when the government mandates access.[35]

Interestingly, the Court has found that the First Amendment is not violated by such requirements as applied to the broadcast media, but has invalidated these laws when applied to the print media. In *Red Lion Broadcasting Co. v. FCC*, the Court unanimously upheld the constitutionality of the fairness doctrine that required that broadcast stations present balanced discussion on public issues.[36] The law also provided that when the honesty or character of a person is attacked, he or she must be given notice, a transcript, and an opportunity to reply. Additionally, a station that endorsed a candidate in an election was required to provide notice to the opponent and provide a reasonable opportunity to respond.

The Court upheld these requirements and emphasized that "[i]t is the right of the viewers and listeners, not the right of broadcasters, which is paramount."[37]

---

[34] 42 U.S.C. §2000a.

[35] *See* FCC v. League of Women Voters, 468 U.S. 364 (1984) (declaring unconstitutional a federal law that prohibited noncommercial educational stations from editorializing as violating the First Amendment).

[36] 395 U.S. 367 (1969).

[37] *Id.* at 390.

The Court concluded that the fairness doctrine enhanced this right by expanding the views and voices that the public could hear. Justice White, writing for the Court, said that "[t]here is no sanctuary in the First Amendment for unlimited private censorship operating in a medium not open to all."[38] The Court stressed that broadcast frequencies are inherently scarce and that therefore the government was justified in regulating their use to increase the voices that the public could hear. Justice White declared: "In view of the scarcity of broadcast frequencies, the Government's role in allocating those frequencies, and the legitimate claims of those unable without governmental assistance to gain access to those frequencies for expression of their views, we hold the regulations . . . constitutional."[39]

However, just five years later, in *Miami Herald v. Tornillo*, the Court unanimously declared unconstitutional a right to reply law as applied to newspapers.[40] A Florida law required that a newspaper print a reply from any candidate for office whose character or official record had been attacked in its pages. The reply had to be printed free of charge in as conspicuous a place as the initial story. Without mentioning *Red Lion*, the Court struck down the Florida law as violating the First Amendment. The Court, in an opinion by Chief Justice Burger, said that "the Florida statute exacts a penalty on the basis of the content of a newspaper. The first phase of the penalty . . . is exacted in terms of the cost in printing and . . . in taking up space that could be devoted to other material the newspaper may have preferred to print. . . . Faced with [such a penalty], editors might well conclude that the safe course is to avoid controversy."[41] The Court stressed that forcing newspapers to publish a reply intrudes on editorial discretion that is protected by the First Amendment.

There is an obvious tension between *Red Lion* and *Tornillo*. Right to reply laws are allowed as to the broadcast media, but not the print media. In *Tornillo*, the Court emphasized the danger that such laws will chill coverage; yet in *Red Lion*, the Court rejected exactly this argument as unsupported conjecture. The distinction between *Red Lion* and *Tornillo* seems to be based on the inherent scarcity of the broadcast media.[42] Broadcast frequencies are inherently limited. But the economics of publishing are such that the number of newspapers is also likely to be scarce, and it is unclear why technological scarcity deserves more weight in First Amendment analysis than economically induced scarcity. In every city there are far more television and radio stations than newspapers. Indeed, the development of cable television and direct broadcast satellites undermines the claim that broadcast space is scarcer than print space, even if that was ever true. In fact, in 1987, the Federal Communications Commission repealed the fairness doctrine, although there have been repeated attempts to have it reinstituted by statute.

[38] *Id.* at 392.
[39] *Id.* at 400-401.
[40] 418 U.S. 241 (1974).
[41] *Id.* at 257.
[42] The Court had relied on the scarcity of the broadcast media as the justification for licensing stations and regulating them. *See* National Broad. Co. v. United States, 319 U.S. 190 (1943); *see also* FCC v. National Citizens Comm. for Broad., 436 U.S. 775 (1978) (upholding federal regulations that prevented common ownership of a broadcast station and a daily newspaper in the same area).

If the distinction between the print and broadcast media is rejected,[43] the issue then becomes whether it would be better to apply the *Red Lion* or the *Tornillo* approach to both media. Allowing right to reply laws has the benefit of enhancing the viewpoints that are heard.[44] But such laws also intrude on a crucial First Amendment value: press autonomy to decide what to publish.[45]

Cable Television and Emerging Technology

The Court faced this issue in another context involving the relatively newer technology of cable television. The federal Cable Act requires that cable companies carry local over-the-air broadcast stations. Cable companies challenged the law arguing that it violates their First Amendment right to decide what to include on their channels; forcing the inclusion of some stations will keep it from including other programming that it and its viewers would prefer. In *Turner Broadcasting System Inc. v. Federal Communications Commission*, the Supreme Court ruled that the First Amendment applied to this issue and remanded it to the lower court for the application of intermediate scrutiny.[46]

The Court expressly held that the principles of *Red Lion* should not be applied to cable television. Justice Kennedy, writing for the Court, said: "The rationale for applying a less rigorous standard of First Amendment scrutiny to broadcast regulation does not apply in the context of cable regulation. The justifications for our distinct approach to broadcast regulation rests upon the unique physical limitations of the broadcast medium. . . . The broadcast cases are inapposite in the present context because cable television does not suffer from the inherent limitations that characterize the broadcast medium."[47] The Court rejected the argument that the economics of the cable industry, where monopolies are granted for local areas, justified the application of the *Red Lion* standard.[48] Justice Kennedy said that "the mere assertion of a dysfunction or failure in a speech market, without more, is

---

[43] Professor Lee Bollinger has defended the distinction not on grounds of scarcity, but rather based on the desirability of having one media largely unregulated while the other is subjected to more government regulation. *See* Lee C. Bollinger, Jr., Freedom of the Press and Public Access: Toward a Theory of Partial Regulation of the Mass Media, 75 Mich. L. Rev. 1, 26-37 (1976).

[44] For an excellent development of this argument, *see* Jerome Barron, Access to the Press—A New First Amendment Right, 80 Harv. L. Rev. 1641 (1967).

[45] The Court has rejected the claim that there is a First Amendment right of access to use the broadcast media apart from statutes creating such a right. In *Columbia Broadcasting System v. Democratic Natl. Comm.*, 412 U.S. 94 (1973), the Court said that there was no obligation of the broadcast media to accept editorial advertisements apart from that created by the fairness doctrine. *See* §6.4.4.3 for a discussion of changes in broadcast regulations and their First Amendment implications; *see* Lili Levy, Reflections on the FCC's Recent Approach to Structural Regulation of the Electronic Mass Media, 52 Fed. Comm. L.J. 581 (2000).

[46] 512 U.S. 622 (1994).

[47] *Id.* at 638-39.

[48] *See also* City of Los Angeles v. Preferred Communications, Inc., 476 U.S. 488 (1986) (where the Court acknowledged that the grant of monopoly to cable companies raised First Amendment issues, but the Court did not decide them).

not sufficient to shield a speech regulation from the First Amendment standards applicable to nonbroadcast media."[49]

Justice Kennedy, at this point writing for a plurality, acknowledged that "must carry" rule intruded upon the autonomy of cable companies to decide what to broadcast. He said, however, that since it was a content-neutral regulation, intermediate scrutiny was the appropriate test. The plurality said that the law was content-neutral because it required that all local broadcasts be carried regardless of whether their content was news, sports, entertainment, religion, or education.[50] The case was remanded to the lower court for the application of intermediate scrutiny. After the remand, the Court upheld the "must carry" rule.[51] The Court held that the government has an important interest in protecting the free over-the-air broadcast media and that the "must carry" rule is substantially related to that goal.

Turner Broadcasting is likely just the beginning of the Court's considering the application of the First Amendment to new technologies. The Internet means that no longer does the press have a monopoly in conveying information; anyone with a modem can reach large numbers of people. Nor are there any longer technological limits on the number of available channels. Distinctions between print and broadcast media are illusory in a world where newspapers and television programming both can be received over computer screens. Undoubtedly, many of the most important constitutional issues in the years to come will involve the application of First Amendment principles to this rapidly developing new technology.

§11.6.3 Freedom of the Press as a Sword to Gain Access to Government Places and Papers

A First Amendment Right of Access to Government Places and Papers

The previous section considered the extent to which the First Amendment provides the press with a shield that protects it from government regulation. A distinct issue is whether the First Amendment provides the press a "sword" that it can use to gain access to government proceedings and papers. Actually, there are two interrelated subquestions here: First, does the First Amendment provide anyone such a right of access and, second, if so, does the press have a preferred right of access?

---

[49] *Id.* at 640.

[50] Justice Stevens would have upheld the Cable Act without a remand. Justices O'Connor, Scalia, Thomas, and Ginsburg would have declared the law unconstitutional. Justice O'Connor contended that the law was content-based because it was based on Congress's preference "for diversity of viewpoints, for localism, for educational programming, and for news and public affairs." *Id.* at 677 (O'Connor, J., concurring in part and dissenting in part). Justice O'Connor argued that strict scrutiny was therefore the appropriate test and would have invalidated the law.

[51] Turner Broadcasting System, Inc. v. FCC, 520 U.S. 180, 185 (1997).

Thus far, the Supreme Court has not answered either question in general terms but, rather, has dealt with the issues in two specific contexts. The Court has held that the public has a right of access to court proceedings, but has not recognized a preferred right of access for the press. In contrast, the Court has ruled that the public does not have a right of access to prison inmates and facilities, and the Court expressly has rejected any special right of access for the press. On the one hand, without a right of access to government papers and places the people will be denied information that is crucial in monitoring government and holding it accountable. The press obviously plays a crucial role in this regard. While it is not realistic to open a prison to all observers, the press can be the eyes and ears of the people. On the other hand, creating a right of access to government places and papers might be seen as better accomplished through statutes, such as freedom of information acts and open meeting laws, that can be drawn with specificity and balance competing interests. Additionally, any special rights for the press will raise the issue, described earlier, of defining who is entitled to the privileges.

Access to Judicial Proceedings

The Court has recognized a broad First Amendment right for people to attend judicial proceedings. Initially, the Court rejected such a right, at least for pretrial proceedings. In *Gannett Co. v. DePasquale*, the Court held that the press could be excluded from a pretrial proceeding that considered the suppression of a confession.[52] The prosecution and defense both consented to closing the courtroom for the hearing, and the trial judge had found a "reasonable probability of prejudice" to the defendant if the confession was deemed inadmissible but reported on in the press. The Court also emphasized that no one, including the press, had initially objected to the closure and that a transcript was made available once the proceedings were completed.

Yet it is questionable whether *Gannett* remains good law because the Court subsequently has consistently recognized a First Amendment right of access to court proceedings. *Richmond Newspapers v. Virginia* is the seminal case in the area.[53] In *Richmond Newspapers*, the Court held that there is a First Amendment right for the public and the press to attend criminal trials. The case involved a murder trial where the defendant previously had been tried three times for the crime; the first trial ended in a conviction that was reversed on appeal, and the latter two trials ended in mistrials. The trial court ordered that the fourth trial be closed to the public.

The Supreme Court declared that this closure was unconstitutional. Chief Justice Burger, writing for the plurality, said that "[t]he Bill of Rights was enacted against the backdrop of the long history of trials being presumptively open. . . . In guaranteeing freedoms such as those of speech and the press, the First Amendment can be read as protecting the right of everyone to attend trials so as to give meaning to those explicit guarantees."[54] The plurality thus concluded:

---

[52] 443 U.S. 368 (1979).
[53] 448 U.S. 555 (1980).
[54] *Id.* at 575.

"We hold that the right to attend criminal trials is implicit in the guarantees of the First Amendment; without the freedom to attend such trials, which people have exercised for centuries, important aspects of freedom of speech and of the press could be eviscerated."[55] The plurality did not describe the right as absolute, but said that "there would need to be an overriding interest articulated in findings" to justify closure.

Justice Brennan, in an opinion concurring in the judgment, joined by Justice Marshall, emphasized that as "a matter of law and virtually immemorial custom, public trials have been the essentially unwavering rule in ancestral England and in our own Nation."[56] Justice Brennan explained that open trials serve to inform people about the actions of a branch of the government and to enhance the fairness of judicial proceedings.[57]

In several subsequent cases, the Court applied *Richmond Newspapers* and declared unconstitutional the closure of judicial proceedings. In *Globe Newspaper Co. v. Superior Court*, the Court declared unconstitutional a Massachusetts law that allowed trial courts to exclude the press and the public from hearing the testimony of witnesses under age 18 who allegedly were the victims of sex crimes.[58] The Court said that *Richmond Newspapers* "firmly established . . . that the press and general public have a constitutional right of access to criminal trials."[59] The Court said, therefore, that "closing court proceedings would be allowed only if it was demonstrated to be necessitated by a compelling governmental interest, and is narrowly tailored to serve that interest."[60] The Court accepted that protecting minor victims was a compelling interest, but concluded that the state law that required closure in all cases was not sufficiently narrowly tailored; a case-by-case approach would adequately serve the state's interests.

In *Press-Enterprise Co. v. Superior Court*, the Court held that it violated the First Amendment for the court to close voir dire proceedings to the public and the press.[61] The Court explained that voir dire proceedings are a key phase of the trial. The Court said that "the presumption of openness may be overcome only by an overriding interest based on findings that closure is essential to preserve higher values and is narrowly tailored to serve that interest."[62] The Court acknowledged that "in some instances closure might be justified, where questioning of prospective jurors would pertain to deeply personal matters."[63] But even then closure should be regarded as a last resort because of the importance of the public monitoring what occurs during the crucial phase of jury selection. For example, during the O.J. Simpson murder case there were claims that the prosecution was

---

[55] *Id.* at 580.

[56] *Id.* at 593 (Brennan, J., concurring in the judgment).

[57] Justices Stewart and Blackmun also wrote opinions concurring in the judgment, and Justice Rehnquist dissented.

[58] 457 U.S. 596 (1982).

[59] *Id.* at 603.

[60] *Id.* at 606 (citation omitted).

[61] 464 U.S. 501 (1984).

[62] *Id.* at 510.

[63] *Id.* at 511.

treating prospective African-American jurors differently than white jurors during voir dire. This raised an important issue concerning the conduct of government officers and required that the press and public be present to observe and report on what occurred.

Although these cases emphatically recognize a First Amendment right of access to court proceedings, they leave many questions unanswered. Is *Gannett* still good law; can a court close pretrial proceedings involving the suppression of evidence? Arguably, press reporting on suppressed evidence could jeopardize the defendant's right to a fair trial. But suppression hearings are of great interest to the public: They concern the conduct of police and decisions by judges as to what evidence will be admitted.[64]

Another unanswered question concerns whether the press has a preferred right of access to judicial proceedings. If there are only a limited number of seats in a courtroom, must some of them be reserved for reporters? The values underlying the First Amendment would seem to require this because the public only can learn about what occurred in court if the press is present to observe and report. But the Court has not yet recognized a preferred right for the press and, as discussed throughout this section, has generally rejected any special protections for the press. In fact, in *Seattle Times Co. v. Rhinehart*, the Court held that the press did not have a right of access to information produced in discovery in a civil suit that was covered by a protective order.[65] Specifically, the press wanted to obtain a list of contributors to a controversial religious organization. The Court unanimously ruled against the newspaper and said that the press was not entitled to the information because the public would not have had a right to it. The Court concluded that where "a protective order is entered on a showing of good cause as required by Rule 26(c), is limited to the context of pretrial civil discovery, and does not restrict the dissemination of the information if gained from other sources, it does not offend the First Amendment."[66]

Prisons

The other context where the Supreme Court has considered a First Amendment right of access is with regard to prisons. Here the Court has expressly rejected such a right and has specifically ruled that the press is not entitled to any greater rights than the general public. In *Pell v. Procunier*[67] and *Saxbe v. Washington Post Co.*,[68] the Court upheld state and federal prison regulations that prohibited press interviews with particular inmates. The Court accepted the government's claim that such interviews created a "star" within the prison that undermined effective discipline and order. The Court also more generally declared: "The First

---

[64] *See also* Press Enterprise Co. v. Superior Court, 478 U.S. 1 (1986) (recognizing a First Amendment right to transcripts of a preliminary hearing).
[65] 467 U.S. 20 (1984).
[66] *Id.* at 37.
[67] 417 U.S. 817 (1974).
[68] 417 U.S. 843 (1974).

and Fourteenth Amendments bar government from interfering in any way with a free press. The Constitution does not, however, require government to accord to the press special access to information not shared by members of the public generally."[69] The Court expressly rejected the view that "the Constitution imposes upon government the affirmative duty to make available to journalists sources of information not available to members of the public generally."[70]

The Court followed this reasoning in *Houchins v. KQED*.[71] In *Houchins*, the press sought access to the Greystone facility in the Santa Rita jail. The jail had a no–press access policy except for monthly official tours of the facility. The press sought access to the jail to report on its conditions. A plurality opinion by Chief Justice Burger rejected this claim and again emphasized the lack of any special right of access for the press under the First Amendment. Burger wrote that "[t]his Court has never intimated a First Amendment guarantee of a right of access to all sources of information within governmental control. . . . There is an undoubted right to gather news 'from any source by means within the law,' but that affords no basis for the claim that the First Amendment compels others—private persons or government—to supply information."[72]

Justice Stewart, in an opinion concurring in the judgment, explicitly declared that the press is entitled to no privileges greater than those extended to the general public. He wrote: "The First and Fourteenth Amendments do not guarantee the public a right of access to information generated or controlled by government, nor do they guarantee the press any basic right of access superior to that of the public generally. The Constitution does no more than assure the public and the press equal access once government has opened its doors."[73]

Thus, *Houchins*, like the other prison cases, has strong language rejecting a First Amendment right of access to government places and any preferred rights for the press. Yet *Houchins* can be criticized for failing to recognize the importance of the press in informing the public about prison conditions. Without press access to the prisoners and prison facilities, the public might never learn of serious abusive conditions and be able to hold this aspect of government accountable.

---

[69] 417 U.S. at 834.

[70] *Id.*

[71] 438 U.S. 1 (1978). *Houchins* was a 4-to-3 decision, with two Justices not participating; the four consisted of a plurality of three and an opinion concurring in the judgment.

[72] *Id.* at 9, 11.

[73] *Id.* at 16 (Stewart, J., concurring).

CHAPTER 12

First Amendment: Religion

§12.1   INTRODUCTION

§12.1.1   *Constitutional Provisions Concerning Religion and the Tension Between Them*

First Amendment Provisions

The First Amendment begins with the words: "Congress shall make no law respecting an establishment of religion, or prohibiting the free exercise thereof."

These two clauses are commonly referred to, respectively, as the "establishment clause" and the "free exercise clause." The free exercise clause was first applied to the states through its incorporation into the due process clause of the Fourteenth Amendment in *Cantwell v. Connecticut* in 1940.[1] The establishment clause was first found to be incorporated and applied to the states in *Everson v. Board of Education* in 1947.[2]

The incorporation of the establishment clause is more controversial than the incorporation of the free exercise clause because the latter clearly safeguards individual liberty while the former seems directed at the government.[3] The Supreme Court, however, has explained that the establishment clause, too, protects liberty. Justice Brennan, concurring in *School District of Abington Township, Pa. v. Schempp*, explained that "the Establishment Clause [is] a co-guarantor, with the Free Exercise Clause, of religious liberty. The Framers did not entrust the liberty of religious beliefs to either clause alone."[4] As the Court declared in *Lee v. Weisman*, "[a] state-created orthodoxy puts at grave risk that freedom of belief and conscience which are the sole assurance that religious faith is real, not imposed."[5]

In recent years, Justice Clarence Thomas has argued that the Court was wrong in finding that the establishment clause applies to state and local governments.[6] His view is that the establishment clause was meant to prevent the federal government from establishing churches that would have competed with existing state churches. This view, of course, would mean a dramatic change in the law as state and local governments would be completely unconstrained by the establishment clause. To this point, no other Justice has taken this position.

The Compatibility and Tension Between the Provisions

To a large extent, the establishment and free exercise clauses are complementary.[7] Both protect freedom of religious belief and actions. Many government actions would simultaneously violate both of these provisions. For example, if the state were to create a religion and compel participation, it obviously would be establishing religion and, at the same time, denying free exercise to those who did not want to participate in religion or who wished to choose a different faith. Mandatory school prayers likewise involve the government both establishing

§12.1 [1] 310 U.S. 296 (1940). For an excellent history of the Supreme Court's development of the law concerning the religion clauses, *see* Jesse H. Choper, A Century of Religious Freedom, 88 Cal. L. Rev. 1709 (2000).

[2] 330 U.S. 1 (1947).

[3] *See* Edward Corwin, A Constitution of Powers in a Secular State 113-116 (1951).

[4] 374 U.S. 203, 256 (1963) (Brennan, J., concurring).

[5] 505 U.S. 577, 592 (1992).

[6] *See, e.g.,* Town of Greece v. Galloway, 134 S. Ct. 1811, 1835-1837 (2014) (Thomas, J., concurring in part and concurring in the judgment); Elk Grove Unified School Dist. v. Newdow, 542 U.S. 1, 46 (2004) (Thomas, J., concurring in the judgment); Zelman v. Simmons-Harris, 536 U.S. 639, 679 (2002) (Thomas, J., concurring).

[7] For a discussion of issues concerning the relationship between the religion clauses, *see* Ira C. Lupu, Threading Between the Religion Clauses, 63 Law & Contemp. Probs. 439 (2000).

religion and interfering with free exercise of religious beliefs for those who do not believe in the prayers.[8]

In a recent case, *Hosanna-Tabor Evangelical Lutheran Church and School v. EEOC*,[9] the Court found that both the establishment clause and the free exercise clause are violated if a religious institution is held liable under an employment discrimination law for its decision to fire a minister. The case involved a teacher at a parochial elementary school who took a leave of absence because of a serious illness. The Equal Employment Opportunity Commission sued on her behalf when the school filled her position when she was ill and then fired her when the school thought she might be contemplating an action under the Americans with Disabilities Act.

Chief Justice Roberts, writing for a unanimous Court, said that the teacher was deemed a "minister" by the school, having taken the requisite courses at a religious college and been approved by the board of the school for this designation. The Court said that it would be unconstitutional to hold the school liable under employment discrimination law for the choices it makes as to who will be its ministers. The Court stressed that this violated both religion clauses in the First Amendment and wrote: "By imposing an unwanted minister, the state infringes the Free Exercise Clause, which protects a religious group's right to shape its own faith and mission through its appointments. According the state the power to determine which individuals will minister to the faithful also violates the Establishment Clause, which prohibits government involvement in such ecclesiastical decisions."[10]

Yet there also is often a tension between the establishment and free exercise clauses. Government actions to facilitate free exercise might be challenged as impermissible establishments, and government efforts to refrain from establishing religion might be objected to as denying the free exercise of religion.[11] For instance, if the government pays for and provides ministers for those in the armed services, it arguably is establishing religion; but if the government refuses to do so on these grounds, it arguably is denying free exercise of religion.[12]

Indeed, the primary test used for the establishment clause—articulated in *Lemon v. Kurtzman*[13] and reviewed in detail below in §12.2.3—makes this tension inevitable. Under the *Lemon* test, the government violates the establishment clause if the government's primary purpose is to advance religion, or if the principal

---

[8] *See* Abington School Dist. v. Schempp, 374 U.S. at 222; Engel v. Vitale, 370 U.S. 421, 431 (1962) (concluding that school prayers violate the establishment clause), discussed more fully below at §12.2.5.1.

[9] 132 S. Ct. 694 (2012).

[10] *Id.* at 706.

[11] The Court acknowledged this tension in *Locke v. Davey*, 540 U.S. 712 (2004). The issue was whether the State of Washington's prohibition of the use of scholarships for "devotional studies" (instruction for the ministry) violates the establishment clause. Chief Justice Rehnquist's majority opinion said that the case involved "tension" and the "play in the joints" between the establishment and free exercise clauses. *Id.* at 718-719. As discussed below in §12.3.2.3, the Court upheld the Washington law and rejected the claim that it violated the free exercise clause.

[12] *See* Abington School Dist. v. Schempp, 374 U.S. at 309 (Stewart, J., dissenting) (noting this example as a tension between the clauses).

[13] 403 U.S. 602 (1971).

effect is to aid or inhibit religion, or if there is excessive government entanglement with religion. Yet any time the government acts to protect free exercise of religion, its primary purpose is to advance religion; any time the principal effect is to facilitate free exercise, the government is aiding religion. For example, if the government creates an exemption to a law solely for religion, it arguably violates the establishment clause; if the government fails to create such an exemption for religion, it arguably infringes on free exercise.[14]

The Court has recognized that this tension is inherent in the First Amendment and has noted the difficulty of finding "a neutral course between the two Religion Clauses, both of which are cast in absolute terms, and either of which, if expanded to a logical extreme, would tend to clash with the other."[15] Additionally, there is a tension between the First Amendment's protection of speech and its prohibition against establishment of religion. For example, allowing government financial aid to student religious groups[16] or permitting religious groups to use school facilities[17] arguably violates the establishment clause; but denying funds or facilities because of the religious content of the expression seems to infringe on the First Amendment's protection of freedom of speech. This tension between the establishment clause and freedom of speech has received a great deal of attention from the Supreme Court in recent years and is discussed below in §12.2.4.

History in Interpreting the Religion Clauses

As with all constitutional provisions, some look to history as a guide to the meaning of the religion clauses. This is particularly difficult for these provisions because there is no apparent agreement among the framers as to what they meant. Justice Brennan expressed this well when he stated: "A too literal quest for the advice of the Founding Fathers upon the issues of these cases seems to me futile and misdirected for several reasons. . . . [T]he historical record is at best ambiguous, and statements can readily be found to support either side of the proposition."[18] Yet Justices on all sides of the issue continue to invoke history and the framers' intent to support their position. Chief Justice Rehnquist has remarked that "[t]he true meaning of Establishment Clause can only be seen in its history."[19] In the Supreme Court's decision in *Rosenberger v. Rector and Visitors of the University of Virginia*, which concerned whether a public university could deny

---

[14] *See* Suzanna Sherry, *Lee v. Weisman*: Paradox Redux, 1992 Sup. Ct. Rev. 123 (arguing that the tension between the establishment and free exercise clauses is inherent and difficult to reconcile).

[15] Walz v. Tax Commn., 397 U.S. 664, 668-669 (1970). For efforts to reconcile these tensions, *see* Jesse Choper, The Religion Clauses of the First Amendment: Reconciling the Conflict, 41 U. Pitt. L. Rev. 673 (1980); William Marshall, Solving the Free Exercise Dilemma: Free Exercise as Expression, 87 Minn. L. Rev. 545 (1985).

[16] *See* Rosenberger v. Rector and Visitors of the Univ. of Virginia, 515 U.S. 819 (1995), discussed in §12.2.4.

[17] *See, e.g.*, Lamb's Chapel v. Center Moriches Union Free School Dist., 508 U.S. 384 (1993), discussed below at §12.2.4.

[18] Abington School Dist. v. Schempp, 374 U.S. at 237.

[19] Wallace v. Jaffree, 472 U.S. 38, 113 (1985) (Rehnquist, J., dissenting).

student activity funds to a religious group, both Justice Thomas in a concurring opinion and Justice Souter dissenting focused at length on James Madison's views of religious freedom.[20]

As Professor Laurence Tribe has cogently summarized, there were at least three main views of religion among key framers.[21]

> [A]t least three distinct schools of thought . . . influenced the drafters of the Bill of Rights: first, the evangelical view (associated primarily with Roger Williams) that "worldly corruptions . . . might consume the churches if sturdy fences against the wilderness were not maintained"; second, the Jeffersonian view that the church should be walled off from the state in order to safeguard secular interests (public and private) "against ecclesiastical depredations and incursions"; and, third, the Madisonian view that religious and secular interests alike would be advanced best by diffusing and decentralizing power so as to assure competition among sects rather than dominance by any one.[22]

These are quite distinct views of the proper relationship between religion and the government. Roger Williams was primarily concerned that government involvement with religion would corrupt and undermine religion, whereas Thomas Jefferson had the opposite fear that religion would corrupt and undermine the government. James Madison saw religion as one among many types of factions that existed and that needed to be preserved. He wrote that "[i]n a free government the security for civil rights must be the same as that for religious rights. It consists in the one case in the multiplicity of interests, and the other in the multiplicity of sects. The degree of security in both cases will depend on the number of interests and sects."[23]

The problem of using history in interpreting the religion clauses is compounded by the enormous changes in the country since the First Amendment was adopted. The country is much more religiously diverse today than it was in 1791. Justice Brennan observed that "our religious composition makes us a vastly more diverse people than were our forefathers. They knew differences chiefly among Protestant sects. Today the nation is far more heterogeneous religiously, including as it does substantial minorities not only of Catholics and Jews but as well of those who worship according to no version of the Bible and those who worship no God at all."[24]

Also, as discussed below, a significant number of cases involving the establishment clause have arisen in the context of religious activities in connection with schools. But public education, as it exists now, did not exist when the Bill of Rights was ratified, and it is inherently difficult to apply the framers' views to situations

---

[20] 515 U.S. 819, 854-858 (1995) (Thomas, J., concurring); *id.* at 868-873 (Souter, J., dissenting). James Madison issued his famous Remonstrance in arguing against a Virginia decision to renew a tax to support the church. This is reviewed in detail in *Everson v. Board of Education*, 330 U.S. 1, 12 (1947); *id.* at 31-34 (Rutledge, J., dissenting).

[21] Laurence H. Tribe, American Constitutional Law 1158-1160 (2d ed. 1988).

[22] *Id.* at 1158-1559 (citations omitted).

[23] James Madison, Federalist No. 51, The Federalist Papers 322 (C. Rossiter ed. 1961).

[24] Abington School Dist. v. Schempp, 374 U.S. at 240 (Brennan, J., concurring).

that they could not have imagined. Justice Brennan also remarked that "the structure of American education has greatly changed since the First Amendment was adopted. In the context of our modern emphasis upon public education available to all citizens, any views of the eighteenth century as to whether the exercises at bar are an 'establishment' offer little aid to decision."[25] Nonetheless, debates about history and the framers' intent are likely to remain a key aspect of decisions concerning the religion clauses. Members of the Supreme Court who follow an originalist philosophy of constitutional interpretation believe that the Constitution's meaning is to be ascertained solely from its text and from its framers' intent.[26] Also, the divergence of views among the framers, and the abstractness with which they were stated, makes it possible for those on all sides of the debate to invoke history in support of their positions.[27]

Article VI's Prohibition of Religious Tests for Government Office

In addition to the provisions of the First Amendment, the text of the Constitution contains one provision concerning religion. Article VI, clause 3, says: "The Senators and Representatives before mentioned, and the Members of the several State Legislatures, and all executive and judicial Officers, both of the United States and of the several States, shall be bound by Oath or Affirmation, to support this Constitution; but no religious Test shall ever be required as a Qualification to any Office or public Trust under the United States." Although the provision did not protect religious freedom for the general public, it did ensure that the government could not establish a religion as a condition for holding federal office or infringe on free exercise of religion for these individuals.

This provision was applied to the states in *Torcaso v. Watkins* in 1961.[28] *Torcaso* involved a challenge to Maryland's refusal to allow a man to be a notary public because he would not declare his belief in God. The Court stressed that the Constitution's framers sought "to put the people securely beyond the reach of religious test oaths."[29] The Court declared: "We repeat and again reaffirm that neither a State nor the Federal Government can constitutionally force a person to 'profess a belief or disbelief in any religion.' . . . This Maryland religious test for public office unconstitutionally invades the appellant's freedom of belief and religion and therefore cannot be enforced against him."[30]

---

[25] *Id.* at 238.

[26] Originalism and other philosophies of constitutional interpretation are discussed in detail in §1.4.

[27] *Compare* Phillip Hamburger, A Constitutional Right of Religious Exemption: An Historical Perspective, 60 Geo. Wash. L. Rev. 915 (1992); and Michael McConnell, Accommodation of Religion, 1985 Sup. Ct. Rev. 1 (both considering the historical intent behind the establishment clause).

[28] 367 U.S. 488 (1961).

[29] *Id.* at 491. *See also* Girouard v. United States, 328 U.S. 61, 69 (1946) ("The test oath is abhorrent to our tradition.").

[30] 367 U.S. at 495.

It also is inconsistent with the philosophy under this provision for the government to exclude clergy members from holding government offices. In fact, in *McDaniel v. Paty*, the Supreme Court declared unconstitutional a state law that prevented "Minister[s] of the Gospel, or priest[s] of any denomination whatever" from serving as delegates to the state constitutional convention.[31] Interestingly, the disqualification of ministers from legislative office existed in England before the Constitution and was followed by seven of the original states.[32] The Supreme Court, however, found that this history was not decisive and invalidated the state law. The plurality emphasized that the law infringed on free exercise of religion: Individuals had to choose between being a member of the clergy or holding government office.[33] An opinion concurring in the judgment stressed that the establishment clause "is a shield against any attempt by the government to inhibit religion as it has done here."[34]

§12.1.2 *What Is Religion?*

The Difficulty of Definition

Under both the establishment and the free exercise clauses the issue can arise as to what is "religion." Yet, not surprisingly, the Court has avoided trying to formulate a definition. It seems impossible to formulate a definition of religion that encompasses the vast array of spiritual beliefs and practices that are present in the United States.[35] As one commentator noted, "there is no single characteristic or set of characteristics that all religions have in common that makes them religions."[36] Moreover, any attempt to define religion raises concern that choosing a single definition is itself an establishment of religion.

Additionally, there is a desire for a broad definition of religion for purposes of the free exercise clause so as to maximize protection for religious conduct, but a narrow definition of religion for establishment clause analysis so as to limit the constraints on government. For instance, the issue has arisen in the lower courts as to whether a school's course in transcendental meditation violates the establishment clause.[37] Safeguarding the right of people to engage in transcendental meditation leads to the desire for a broad definition of religion that includes this

---

[31] 435 U.S. 618 (1978).

[32] *Id.* at 622.

[33] *Id.* at 626, 628.

[34] *Id.* at 641 (Brennan, J., concurring in the judgment).

[35] There is a rich literature focusing on the question of the definition of religion. *See, e.g.,* Stanley Ingber, Religion or Ideology: A Needed Clarification of the Religion Clauses, 41 Stan. L. Rev. 233 (1989); Jesse Choper, Defining "Religion" in the First Amendment, 1982 U. Ill. L. Rev. 579; Note, Toward a Constitutional Definition of Religion, 91 Harv. L. Rev. 1056 (1978).

[36] George C. Freeman, The Misguided Search for the Constitutional Definition of "Religion," 71 Geo. L.J. 1519, 1548 (1983).

[37] *See* Malnak v. Yogi, 592 F.2d 197 (3d Cir. 1979) (finding that a course in transcendental meditation violates the establishment clause).

practice, but wanting to allow schools to offer such a course causes a desire for a narrow definition of religion that excludes it.

Although some commentators have argued for separate definitions of religion for the establishment and the free exercise clauses,[38] the Supreme Court never has accepted this position. In fact, Justice Rutledge expressly rejected this approach in his opinion in *Everson v. Board of Education*: " 'Religion' appears only once in the Amendment. But the word governs two prohibitions and governs them alike. It does not have two meanings, one narrow to forbid 'an establishment' and another, much broader, for 'securing' the free exercise thereof."[39]

While the Supreme Court never has formulated a definition of religion, it has considered the issue in three contexts. First, in cases under the Selective Service Act, the Court struggled to define religion for purposes of the conscientious objector exemption. Second, the Court has said that a court can inquire as to whether a religious belief is sincerely held in deciding whether it is protected under the Constitution. Finally, the Court has made it clear that an individual's sincerely held religious belief is protected by the First Amendment even if it is not the dogma or dominant view within the religion. Each of these concepts is discussed in turn.

The Attempt to Define Religion Under the Selective Service Act

The primary effort by the Supreme Court to define religion has not been in First Amendment cases, but rather in decisions concerning the scope of a religious exemption to the Selective Service Act, which authorized the military draft. In other words, these cases involved statutory construction, rather than constitutional interpretation. Yet these cases are important as the only decisions to attempt to define religion. In *United States v. Seeger*, the Court construed a provision of the Universal Military Training and Selective Service Act that exempted for combat training and service in the armed forces those individuals "who by reason of their religious training and belief are conscientiously opposed to participation in war in any form."[40] The law defined "religious training and belief" as "an individual's belief in relation to a Supreme Being involving duties superior to those arising from any human relation, but [not including] essentially political, sociological, or philosophical views or a merely personal moral code."[41] *Seeger* involved an individual who sought a religious exemption from the draft, but denied any belief in a Supreme Being.

---

[38] For example, Professor Tribe took this position in the initial edition of his treatise and argued that all "that is 'arguably religious' should be considered religious in a free exercise analysis [and] anything 'arguably non-religious' should not be considered religious in applying the establishment clause." Laurence Tribe, American Constitutional Law 828 (1978). Professor Tribe, however, later shifted away from this approach and called it a "dubious solution" to the problem. *See* Laurence Tribe, American Constitutional Law 1186-1887 (2d ed. 1988).

[39] 330 U.S. at 32 (Rutledge, J., dissenting).

[40] 380 U.S. 163, 164-165 (1965).

[41] *Id.* at 165.

The Court broadly defined religion to include such nontheistic views. The Court said: "We believe that . . . the test of belief 'in a relation to a Supreme Being' is whether a given belief that is sincere and meaningful occupies a place in the life of its possessor parallel to that filled by the orthodox belief in God of one who clearly qualifies for the exemption."[42] The Court, however, offered no criteria for assessing whether a particular view is religious under this definition.

Nor did the Court do so in the subsequent case of *Welsh v. United States*.[43] *Welsh*, like *Seeger*, involved a person seeking an exemption from the draft on religious grounds. Welsh actually crossed out the words "religious training" on his form. The plurality opinion by Justice Black said that his situation was indistinguishable from Seeger's: "[B]oth Seeger and Welsh affirmed on those applications that they held deep conscientious scruples against taking part in wars where people were killed. Both strongly believed that killing in war was wrong, unethical, and immoral, and their consciences forbade them to take part in such an evil practice."[44] Again, the Court said that the crucial inquiry "in determining whether the registrant's beliefs are religious is whether these beliefs play the role of a religion and function as a religion in the registrant's life."[45]

The plurality explained that belief in God is characteristic of most religions, but not a prerequisite for religion. Justice Black wrote: "Most of the great religions of today and of the past have embodied the idea of a Supreme Being or a Supreme Reality—a God—who communicates to man in some way a consciousness of what is right and should be done, of what is wrong and therefore should be shunned. If an individual deeply and sincerely holds beliefs that are purely ethical or moral in source and content but that nevertheless impose upon him a duty of conscience to refrain from participating in any war at any time, those beliefs certainly occupy in the life of that individual 'a place parallel to that filled by . . . God' in traditionally religious persons."[46] The Court concluded that Welsh's moral opposition to war fit within this definition of religion.[47]

Although *Seeger* and *Welsh* involved the Court's interpreting a statutory provision and not the First Amendment, they likely would be the starting points for any cases that required the Court to define religion under the establishment and free exercise clauses. On the one hand, these cases can be praised for broadening the definition of religion to include nontheistic views. Many religions reject the idea of a Supreme Being, and *Seeger* and *Welsh* adopt an approach that allows these faiths to be protected by the First Amendment. Moreover, the broad definitions employed allow moral judgments to be protected whether they are based on religion or philosophy. This is desirable because it does not give special status to

---

[42] *Id.* at 165-166.

[43] 398 U.S. 333 (1970).

[44] *Id.* at 337.

[45] *Id.* at 339.

[46] *Id.* at 340.

[47] In *Gillette v. United States*, 401 U.S. 437 (1971), the Court held that the religious exemption was unavailable to individuals who objected to a particular war.

religious moral judgments over secular ones and thereby avoids an establishment clause problem.[48]

But on the other hand, these cases can be criticized because of the lack of guidance they provide in defining what is a religious belief. A judge in a future case has little guidance in deciding what is a belief that is "sincere and meaningful [and] occupies a place in the life of its possessor parallel to that filled by the orthodox belief in God of one who clearly qualifies for the exemption."[49]

Requirement for Sincerely Held Beliefs

The need to define "religion" might arise in the context of an individual who is seeking an exemption from a law because of views that he or she terms religious. For example, a case arose in Los Angeles of a woman who claimed to be a part of an ancient Egyptian religion where the sacrament was having sex with a high priestess and making a donation to her church. The woman attempted to defend a prostitution charge by claiming that she was engaged in a religious practice.[50] Several years ago, the United States Court of Appeals for the Tenth Circuit considered a case where a person charged with violating federal marijuana laws argued that his religion required the use of marijuana as a sacrament.[51]

How is a court to decide if these are religious beliefs? The Supreme Court has indicated that the judiciary can determine only if they are sincerely held views, not whether they are true or false. The Court drew this distinction in *United States v. Ballard*.[52] The leaders of the "I Am" religion were indicted for mail fraud because they asked people to send them donations in exchange for offering to cure them of diseases. The Court said that a jury could be asked to decide only if the defendants sincerely held their beliefs as religious views, not whether or not the defendants actually had curative powers. Justice William Douglas, writing for the Court, said: "Heresy trials are foreign to our Constitution. Men may believe what they cannot prove. They may not be put to the proof of their religious doctrines or beliefs. Religious experiences which are as real as life to some may be incomprehensible to others. Yet the fact that they may be beyond the ken of mortals does not mean that they can be made suspect before the law."[53] Justice Douglas said that "[i]f one

---

[48] However, the Court also has said that "[t]here is no doubt that 'only beliefs rooted in religion are protected by the Free Exercise Clause.' Purely secular views do not suffice." Frazee v. Illinois Dept. of Empl. Sec., 489 U.S. 829, 833 (1989) (citation omitted).

[49] United States v. Seeger, 380 U.S. at 166.

[50] High Priestess, Husband Sentenced for Prostitution, Los Angeles Times, Sept. 23, 1989, at Part 2, p. 3.

[51] United States v. Quaintance, 608 F.3d 717 (10th Cir. 2010) (rejecting the claim of a sincerely held religious belief); *see also* United States v. Kuch, 288 F. Supp. 429, 445 (D.D.C. 1968) (religion, the "Boo Hoos," claimed use of marijuana as a sacrament.)

[52] *Id.* 322 U.S. 78 (1944).

[53] *Id.* at 86-87. In *United States v. Quaintance*, 608 F.3d 717 (10th Cir. 2010), the Court rejected a claimed religious defense to a federal marijuana prosecution on the grounds that it was not a sincerely held religious belief.

could be sent to jail because a jury in a hostile environment found those teachings false, little indeed would be left of religious freedom."[54]

The problem, however, is whether it is possible to determine the sincerity of a person's beliefs without a view as to their truth or falsity. There is no measure for sincerity. Inevitably, if a view is regarded as false, such as the claim of curative powers, a jury is likely to be suspicious of its sincerity and think that it might be invented for economic profit. Justice Robert Jackson raised this concern in his dissenting opinion: "[A]s a matter of either practice or philosophy I do not see how we can separate an issue as to what is believed from considerations as to what is believable. The most convincing proof that one believes his statements is to show that they have been true in his experience. Likewise, that one knowingly falsified is best proved by showing that what he said happened never did happen. . . . If we try religious sincerity severed from religious verity, we isolate the dispute from the very considerations which in common experience provide its most reliable answer."[55] Moreover, Justice Jackson expressed doubt that sincerity of one's views ever could be ascertained by a jury or a court.[56]

The Relevance of Religious Dogma and Shared Beliefs

One way in which the sincerity of a religious belief might be assessed is with reference to the prevailing doctrines, if any, for that religion. In other words, what do others of that faith think with regard to the particular question? The problem, however, is that religion is inherently personal, as well as often group based, and an individual might have a sincere religious belief that departs from the dogma of his or her religion. In fact, for this reason, the Court has said that the dominant views in a faith are not determinative in assessing whether a particular belief is religious.

In *Thomas v. Review Board of the Indiana Employment Security Division*, the Court ruled that an individual could claim a religious belief even though it was inconsistent with the doctrines of his or her religion.[57] A person who was a member of Jehovah's Witnesses quit his job rather than be transferred to another department that produced turrets for military tanks. He claimed that producing armaments was contrary to his religious beliefs. The state denied him unemployment benefits because he had voluntarily left his job, but he sued under a line of cases holding that a state may not deny benefits to people who quit their jobs for religious reasons.[58]

The state argued that the Jehovah's Witnesses' faith did not prevent an individual from working in the armaments plant. The state pointed to others from that

---

[54] *Id.*

[55] *Id.* at 92-93 (Jackson, J., dissenting).

[56] *Id.* at 93 ("[A]ny inquiry into intellectual honesty in religion raises profound psychological problems.").

[57] 450 U.S. 707 (1981).

[58] *See, e.g.*, Sherbert v. Verner, 374 U.S. 398 (1963) (violation of the free exercise clause to deny unemployment benefits to a woman who quit her job rather than work on her Saturday Sabbath), discussed below in §12.3.2.2.

religion who worked on tank turrets and to testimony that such work was "scriptur-ally" acceptable.[59] The Court said, however, that this was irrelevant and declared: "[T]he guarantee of free exercise is not limited to beliefs which are shared by all of the members of a religious sect. Particularly in this sensitive area, it is not within the judicial function and judicial competence to inquire whether the petitioner or his fellow worker more correctly perceived the commands of their common faith. Courts are not arbiters of scriptural interpretation."[60]

Similarly, in *Frazee v. Illinois Department of Employment Security,* the Court allowed an individual to claim a religious basis for refusing to work on Sundays even though others of his and similar religions did not have such a proscription.[61] The Court said: "Undoubtedly, membership in an organized religious denomina-tion, especially one with a specific tenet forbidding members to work on Sunday, would simplify the problem of identifying sincerely held religious beliefs, but we reject the notion that to claim the protection of the Free Exercise Clause, one must be responding to the commands of a particular religious organization."[62]

Thus, the inquiry must be whether a particular individual holds a sincere religious belief. The problem, however, is that the Supreme Court has given little guidance in how to determine sincerity or what constitutes a "religious belief."

§12.2   THE ESTABLISHMENT CLAUSE

§12.2.1   *Competing Theories of the Establishment Clause*

There are three major competing approaches to the establishment clause.[1] Each has adherents on the Court, and each is supported by a body of scholarly literature. The theory chosen determines the approach used and often the result.

Strict Separation

The first theory often is termed "strict separation." This approach says that to the greatest extent possible government and religion should be separated. The government should be, as much as possible, secular; religion should be entirely

---

[59] 450 U.S. at 715.
[60] *Id.* at 715-716.
[61] 489 U.S. 829 (1989).
[62] *Id.* at 834.
[1] **§12.2** Although these theories have been presented and discussed most by the Justices and commentators in the context of the establishment clause, they also can be used in free exercise clause analysis. Also, these three theories are not exhaustive of all views, and there are variants of each.

in the private realm of society. This theory is perhaps best described by Thomas Jefferson's metaphor that there should be a wall separating church and state.[2] As the Supreme Court declared in *Everson v. Board of Education*, "[t]he First Amendment has erected a wall between church and state. That wall must be kept high and impregnable."[3]

Jefferson's famous words were uttered, as was Madison's Remonstrance, as part of a campaign against Virginia's renewing its tax to support the church. Justice Rutledge reviewed this history in describing the philosophy underlying the establishment clause: "The Amendment's purpose was not to strike merely at the official establishment of a single sect, creed or religion, outlawing only a formal relation such as had prevailed in England and some of the colonies. Necessarily it was to uproot all such relationships. But the object was broader than separating church and state in this narrow sense. It was to create a complete and permanent separation of the spheres of religious activity and civil authority by comprehensively forbidding every form of public aid or support for religion."[4]

A strict separation of church and state is seen as necessary to protect religious liberty.[5] When religion becomes a part of government, separationists argue, there is inevitable coercion to participate in that faith. Those of different faiths and those who profess no religious beliefs are made to feel excluded and unwelcome when government and religion become intertwined. Moreover, government involvement with religion is inherently divisive in a country with so many different religions and many people who claim no religion at all.[6]

There are problems, though, with the strict separation approach, as there are for all of the theories. A complete prohibition of all government assistance to religion would threaten the free exercise of religion. For example, a refusal by the government to provide police, fire, or sanitation services obviously would seemingly infringe on free exercise. Thus, a total wall separating church and state is impossible, and the issue becomes how to draw the appropriate line. Moreover, religion has traditionally been a part of many government activities, from the

---

[2] Thomas Jefferson, Letter to Messrs. Nehemiah Dodge and others, a Committee of the Danbury Baptist Association, Writings 510 (1984).

[3] 330 U.S. 1, 18 (1947).

[4] *Id.* at 31-32.

[5] *See* Alan Schwarz, No Imposition of Religion: The Establishment Clause Value, 77 Yale L.J. 692, 708 (1968).

[6] Justice Brennan has articulated these purposes behind the establishment clause:

The first, which is most closely related to the more general conceptions of liberty found in the remainder of the First Amendment, is to guarantee the individual right to conscience. . . . The second purpose of separation and neutrality is to keep the state from interfering in the essential autonomy of religious life, either by taking upon itself the decision of religious issues, or by unduly involving itself in the supervision of religious institutions or officials. The third purpose of separation and neutrality is to prevent the trivialization and degradation of religion by too close an attachment to the organs of government. . . . Finally, the principles of separation and neutrality help assure that essentially religious issues, precisely because of their importance and sensitivity, not become the occasion for battle in the political arena.

Marsh v. Chambers, 463 U.S. 783, 803-805 (1983) (Brennan, J., dissenting) (citations omitted).

phrase "In God We Trust" on coins to the invocation before Supreme Court sessions, "God save this honorable Court."[7]

Neutrality Theory

A second major approach to the establishment clause says that the government must be neutral toward religion; that is, the government cannot favor religion over secularism or one religion over others. Professor Philip Kurland, a key exponent of this approach to the religion clauses, wrote that "the clauses should be read as stating a single precept: that government cannot utilize religion as a standard for action or inaction because these clauses, read together as they should be, prohibit classification in terms of religion either to confer a benefit or to impose a burden."[8] Professor Douglas Laycock said that substantive neutrality means that "the religion clauses require government to minimize the extent to which it either encourages or discourages religious belief or disbelief, practice or nonpractice, observance or nonobservance."[9]

Several Supreme Court Justices have advanced a "symbolic endorsement" test in evaluating the neutrality of a government's action. Under this approach, the government violates the establishment clause if it symbolically endorses a particular religion or if it generally endorses either religion or secularism. For example, Justice O'Connor has written that "[e]very government practice must be judged in its unique circumstances to determine whether it constitutes an endorsement or disapproval of religion."[10]

Justice O'Connor explained the importance of such government neutrality: "As a theoretical matter, the endorsement test captures the essential command of the Establishment Clause, namely, that government must not make a person's religious beliefs relevant to his or her standing in the political community by conveying a message 'that religion or a particular religious belief is favored or preferred.' . . . If government is to be neutral in matters of religion, rather than showing either favoritism or disapproval towards citizens based on their personal religious choices, government cannot endorse the religious practices and beliefs of some citizens without sending a clear message to nonadherents that they are outsiders or less than full members of the political community."[11]

---

[7] Professor Lupu has argued that strict separation was the dominant theory for the establishment clause from 1947 to 1980, but that since then its role in Supreme Court decisions has greatly waned. Ira C. Lupu, The Lingering Death of Separationism, 62 Geo. Wash. L. Rev. 230 (1994).

[8] Philip Kurland, Of Church and State and the Supreme Court, 29 U. Chi. L. Rev. 1, 96 (1961).

[9] Douglas Laycock, Formal, Substantive and Disaggregated Neutrality Toward Religion, 39 DePaul L. Rev. 993, 1001 (1990).

[10] Lynch v. Donnelly, 465 U.S. 668, 694 (1984).

[11] County of Allegheny v. American Civil Liberties Union, Greater Pittsburgh Chapter, 492 U.S. 573, 627 (1989) (O'Connor, J., concurring in part and concurring in the judgment) (citations omitted).

§12.2   The Establishment Clause

The difficulty is in determining what government actions constitute a "symbolic endorsement" of religion.[12] Several Justices discussed this in *Capitol Square Review and Advisory Board v. Pinette*.[13] The issue in *Pinette* was whether it was unconstitutional for the government to preclude the Ku Klux Klan from erecting a large Latin cross in the park across from the Ohio Statehouse. Although there was no majority opinion for the Court, seven Justices voted that excluding the cross violated the Klan's free speech rights and that allowing it to be present would not violate the establishment clause. In the course of the establishment clause discussion, several of the Justices addressed what constitutes a symbolic endorsement.[14]

Justice O'Connor, in an opinion concurring in the judgment joined by Justices Souter and Breyer, concluded that the cross should be allowed because the reasonable observer would not perceive it as an endorsement of religion. O'Connor said that "[w]here the government's operation of a public forum has the effect of endorsing religion, even if the governmental actor neither intends nor actively encourages that result, the Establishment Clause is violated."[15] Justice O'Connor said that a reasonable observer would not likely perceive the cross as being endorsed by the government because there was "a sign disclaiming government sponsorship or endorsement" and this would "remove doubt about the State approval of [the] religious message."[16]

O'Connor said that the symbolic endorsement test is applied "from the perspective of a hypothetical observer who is presumed to possess a certain level of information that all citizens might not share."[17] She said that the reasonable observer "must be deemed aware of the history and context of the community and forum in which the religious display appears [and] the general history of the place in which the cross is displayed. [An] informed member of the community will know how the public space in question has been used in the past."[18]

Justices Stevens and Ginsburg dissented and argued that symbolic endorsement exists if a reasonable person passing by would perceive government support for religion. Justice Stevens wrote: "If a reasonable person could perceive a government endorsement of religion from a private display, then the State may not allow its property to be used as a forum for that display. No less stringent rule can adequately protect non-adherents from a well-grounded perception that their sovereign supports a faith to which they do not subscribe."[19] Justice Stevens

---

[12] For a prescient prediction of the development of the symbolic endorsement test and a description of its ambiguity, *see* William P. Marshall, "We Know It When We See It," the Supreme Court and Establishment, 59 S. Cal. L. Rev. 495 (1986).

[13] 515 U.S. 753 (1995).

[14] Justice Scalia—writing for a plurality of Rehnquist, Kennedy, and Thomas—rejected the symbolic endorsement test. He said that the symbolic endorsement approach "exiles private religious speech to a realm of less-protected expression. . . . [T]he Establishment Clause . . . was never meant to serve as an impediment to purely private religious speech connected to the State only through its occurrence in a public forum." *Id.* at 766-767.

[15] *Id.* at 777 (O'Connor, J., concurring in the judgment).

[16] *Id.* at 776.

[17] *Id.* at 780.

[18] *Id.* at 780-781.

[19] *Id.* at 799-800 (Stevens, J., dissenting).

argued that Justice O'Connor's "'reasonable person' comes off as a well-schooled jurist, a being finer than the tort-law model. . . . [T]his enhanced tort-law standard is singularly out of place in the Establishment Clause context. It strips of constitutional protection every person whose knowledge happens to fall below some 'ideal' standard."[20]

Thus, three different approaches to the symbolic endorsement test were expressed in *Pinette*. Justice Scalia, writing for the plurality, rejected using the test at all where the issue is private speech on government property. Justice O'Connor, writing for herself and Justices Souter and Breyer, said that the symbolic endorsement test should be applied from the perspective of the perceptions of a well-educated and well-informed observer. Justice Stevens, dissenting and joined by Justice Ginsburg, said that the symbolic endorsement test should look to the perceptions of the reasonable passerby.

The symbolic endorsement test is defended as a desirable approach to the establishment clause because it is a way of determining whether the government is neutral or whether it is favoring religion. A key purpose of the establishment clause is to prevent the government from making those who are not a part of the favored religion feel unwelcome. The symbolic endorsement test is seen as a way of assessing the likely perceptions of and reactions to government conduct.[21]

Those who criticize the symbolic endorsement test often focus on its ambiguity and indeterminacy.[22] People will perceive symbols in widely varying ways. The Court inevitably is left to make a subjective choice as to how people will perceive a particular symbol. Moreover, judges who are part of the dominant religion may be insensitive to how those of minority religions perceive particular symbols. At the same time, some argue that the endorsement test is too restrictive of government involvement with religion. Justice Kennedy, for example, said: "Either the endorsement test must invalidate scores of traditional practices recognizing the place religion holds in our culture, or it must be twisted and stretched to avoid inconsistency with practices we know to have been permitted in the past, while condemning similar practices with no greater endorsement effect simply by reason of their lack of historical antecedent. Neither result is acceptable."[23]

In a subsequent establishment clause case, a majority of the Justices used the symbolic endorsement test for determining the constitutionality of religious symbols on government property. In *Van Orden v. Perry*, the Court considered the constitutionality of a six-foot high, three-foot wide Ten Commandments monument between the Texas State Capitol and Texas Supreme Court.[24] Justices Stevens,

---

[20] *Id.* at 800 n.5.

[21] For a defense of the symbolic endorsement test, *see* Jesse Choper, Securing Religious Liberty: Principles for Judicial Interpretation of the Religion Clauses 28-29 (1995); Arnold H. Loewy, Rethinking Government Neutrality Towards Religion Under the Establishment Clause: The Untapped Potential of Justice O'Connor's Insight, 64 N.C. L. Rev. 1049 (1986).

[22] *See, e.g.*, Marshall, *supra* note 12, at 537; Steven D. Smith, Symbols, Perceptions, and Doctrinal Illusions: Establishment Neutrality and the "No Endorsement" Test, 86 Mich. L. Rev. 266, 283 (1987) (identifying this and other problems with the symbolic endorsement test).

[23] Allegheny County v. Greater Pittsburgh ACLU, 492 U.S. at 674.

[24] 545 U.S. 677 (2005).

O'Connor, Souter, and Ginsburg dissented and would have found the monument unconstitutional as an impermissible symbolic endorsement. Justice Breyer, though, concurred in the judgment and voted to uphold the monument's constitutionality. He expressly said that he agreed with the symbolic endorsement test, but concluded that there was not symbolic endorsement in this case because of the presence of many other secular monuments on the Texas State Capitol grounds and because the monument had been there for over 40 years without challenge.

Accommodation/Equality

A third major theory is termed an "accommodation" approach. Under this view, the Court should interpret the establishment clause to recognize the importance of religion in society and accommodate its presence in government. Specifically, under the accommodation approach the government violates the establishment clause only if it literally establishes a church, coerces religious participation, or favors one religion over others. Justice Kennedy, for example, has said that "the Establishment Clause . . . guarantees at a minimum that a government may not coerce anyone to support or participate in religion or its exercise, or otherwise act in a way which establishes a [state] religion or religious faith, or tends to do so."[25] In fact, Justice Kennedy said that "[b]arring all attempts to aid religion through government coercion goes far toward the attainment of [the] object [of the Establishment Clause]."[26] Justices taking this approach have described it in terms of the need for the government to treat religious beliefs and groups equally with nonreligious ones.[27] Whether termed accommodation or equality the approach is the same: Government should accommodate religion by treating it the same as nonreligious beliefs and groups; the government violates the establishment clause only if it establishes a church, coerces religious participation, or favors some religions over others.

A key question under this approach concerns what constitutes government "coercion." Several Justices discussed this in *Lee v. Weisman*, where the Court declared unconstitutional clergy-delivered prayers at public school graduations.[28] Justice Kennedy, writing for the Court, found that such prayers are inherently coercive because there is great pressure on students to attend their graduation ceremonies and to not leave during the prayers.[29]

Justice Blackmun, in an opinion joined by Justices Stevens and O'Connor, wrote to emphasize that the establishment clause can be violated even without coercion. He remarked that it "is not enough that the government refrain from

---

[25] Lee v. Weisman, 505 U.S. 577, 587 (1992).

[26] Allegheny County v. Greater Pittsburgh ACLU, 492 U.S. at 660 (Kennedy, J., concurring in the judgment in part and dissenting in part).

[27] *See, e.g.*, Mitchell v. Helms, 530 U.S. 793 (2000). Justice Thomas refers to this as the government being neutral in its treatment of religion. To avoid confusion with the "neutrality theory" described above, this is described here as requiring equal treatment for religious and nonreligious groups and activities.

[28] 505 U.S. 577 (1992).

[29] *Id.* at 593-595.

compelling religious practices; it must not engage in them either."[30] Likewise, Justice Souter, joined by Justices Stevens and O'Connor, wrote separately to stress that coercion is sufficient for a finding of the establishment clause, but it is not necessary; establishment clause violations exist without coercion if there is symbolic government endorsement for religion.[31]

The dissenting opinion by Justice Scalia, joined by Chief Justice Rehnquist and Justices White and Thomas, advocated the accommodation approach, but defined coercion much more narrowly than Justice Kennedy. Justice Scalia said that "[t]he coercion that was a hallmark of historical establishments of religion was coercion of religious orthodoxy and of financial support by force of law and threat of penalty."[32]

In other words, for the dissenters in *Lee*, coercion exists only if the law requires and punishes the failure to engage in religious practices. For Justice Kennedy, coercion can be found by more indirect pressures to engage in religious activity. The other Justices in *Lee* reject the accommodation approach that coercion is a prerequisite for finding an establishment clause violation.

Those who defend the accommodation approach argue that it best reflects the importance and prevalence of religion in American society. Professor Michael McConnell, an advocate of this view, said that it is desirable because it makes "religion . . . a welcome element in the mix of beliefs and associations present in the community. Under this view, the emphasis is placed on freedom of choice and diversity among religious opinion. The nation is understood not as secular but as pluralistic. Religion is under no special disability in public life; indeed, it is at least as protected and encouraged as any other form of belief and association — in some ways more so."[33] Anything less than accommodation, it is argued, is unacceptable hostility to religion.

Opponents of the accommodation approach argue that, especially as defined by Justice Scalia, little ever will violate the establishment clause.[34] Nothing except the government creating its own church or by force of law requiring religious practices will offend the provision. Those disagreeing with this theory argue that the establishment clause also should serve to prevent the government from making those of other religions feel unwelcome and to keep the government from using its power and influence to advance religion or a particular religion.[35] Justice O'Connor expressed this view when she wrote: "An Establishment Clause standard that prohibits only 'coercive' practices or overt efforts at government proselytization, but fails to take account of the numerous more subtle ways that government can show favoritism to particular beliefs or convey a message of disapproval to

[30] *Id.* at 604 (Blackmun, J., concurring).

[31] *Id.* at 618-619 (Souter, J., concurring).

[32] *Id.* at 640 (Scalia, J., dissenting).

[33] Michael W. McConnell, Accommodation of Religion, 1985 Sup. Ct. Rev. 1, 14.

[34] Professor Sherry argues that the coercion test "makes the Establishment Clause redundant. Any government action that coerces religious belief violates the Free Exercise Clause." Suzanna Sherry, *Lee v. Weisman*: Paradox Redux, 1992 Sup. Ct. Rev. 123, 134.

[35] For an excellent criticism of the accommodation approach, *see* Mark Tushnet, The Emerging Principle of Accommodation of Religion (Dubitante), 76 Geo. L.J. 1691 (1988).

others, would not, in my view, adequately protect the religious liberty or respect the religious diversity of the members of our pluralistic political community. Thus, this Court has never relied on coercion alone as the touchstone of Establishment Clause analysis."[36] Justices O'Connor and Souter have strongly objected that equality alone never has been regarded as the sole test of the establishment clause.[37]

The Theories Applied: An Example

The importance of these three theories in determining the inquiry and the results in establishment clause cases is reflected in *Allegheny County v. Greater Pittsburgh ACLU*.[38] The case concerned two different religious displays. One was a crèche—a representation of the nativity of Jesus—that was placed in a display case in a stairway in a county courthouse. The other display was in front of a government building and included a large Christmas tree, a large menorah (a candleholder used as part of the Chanukah celebration), and a sign saying that the city salutes liberty during the holiday season.

Three Justices—Stevens, Brennan, and Marshall—took a strict separation approach and argued that both symbols should be deemed unconstitutional as violating the establishment clause. Justice Stevens said that the "Establishment Clause should be construed to create a strong presumption against the display of religious symbols on public property."[39]

Four Justices—Kennedy, Rehnquist, Scalia, and White—took an accommodationist approach and would have allowed both symbols. Justice Kennedy wrote that "the principles of the Establishment Clause and our Nation's historic traditions of diversity and pluralism allow communities to make reasonable judgments respecting the accommodation or acknowledgement of holidays with both cultural and religious aspects."[40]

Justices Blackmun and O'Connor used a neutrality approach, specifically applying the symbolic endorsement test, and found that the menorah was constitutional, but the nativity scene was unconstitutional. From their perspective, the menorah was permissible because it was accompanied by a Christian symbol (a Christmas tree) and a secular expression concerning liberty. But the nativity scene was alone on government property and thus was likely to be perceived as symbolic endorsement for Christianity. Justice O'Connor concluded that "the city of Pittsburgh's

---

[36] Allegheny County v. Greater Pittsburgh ACLU, 492 U.S. at 627-628 (O'Connor, J., concurring in part and concurring in the judgment).

[37] Mitchell v. Helms, 530 U.S. at 836 (O'Connor, J., concurring); *id.* at 867 (Souter, J., dissenting). *Mitchell* is discussed below in detail at the end of §12.2.6.2 in text accompanying notes 304-309. For a discussion of the desirability of the Court's "equality" approach to the establishment clause, *see* Alan E. Brownstein, Interpreting the Religion Clauses in Terms of Liberty, Equality, and Free Speech Values—A Critical Analysis of "Neutrality" Theory and Charitable Choice, 13 Notre Dame J.L. Ethics & Pub. Poly. 243 (1999) (criticizing equality theory); Michael W. McConnell, State Action and the Supreme Court's Emerging Consensus on the Line Between Establishment and Private Religious Expression, 28 Pepp. L. Rev. 681 (2001) (defending equality approach).

[38] 492 U.S. 573 (1989).

[39] *Id.* at 650.

[40] *Id.* at 679 (Kennedy, J., concurring in the judgment in part and dissenting in part).

combined holiday display had neither the purpose nor the effect of endorsing religion, but that Allegheny County's crèche display had such an effect."[41]

Thus, the result was 5 to 4 that the nativity scene was unconstitutional but 6 to 3 that the menorah was permissible. The case clearly reflects the importance of the theories of the establishment clause. In *Allegheny County* in 1989 and in *Van Orden v. Perry* in 2005, no theory commanded support from a majority of the Justices. However, with changes in the composition of the Court, it is possible — indeed likely — that a majority of the Justices now take this accommodationist approach. Justices Scalia, Kennedy, and Thomas have repeatedly taken this position and it appears so far that Chief Justice Roberts and Justice Alito do as well. If so, there likely will be dramatic changes in the interpretation of the establishment clause in the years ahead.

§12.2.2   Government Discrimination Among Religions

Prohibition of Discrimination

It is firmly established that the government violates the establishment clause if it discriminates among religious groups. Such discrimination will be allowed only if strict scrutiny is met. All of the Justices on the current Court, regardless of their theory of the establishment clause, adhere to this principle. If there is not discrimination, the case is discussed under the *Lemon* test described in the next subsection. In *Hernandez v. Commissioner*, the Court explained: "[W]hen it is claimed that a denominational preference exists, the initial inquiry is whether the law facially differentiates among religions. If no such facial preference exists, we proceed to apply the customary three pronged Establishment Clause inquiry derived from *Lemon v. Kurtzman*."[42]

In *Larson v. Valente*, the Court declared unconstitutional a Minnesota law that imposed registration and reporting requirements on charitable organizations, but exempted religious institutions that received more than half of their financial support from members' contributions.[43]

The Court said that the "history and logic of the Establishment Clause [mean] that no State can 'pass laws which aid one religion' or that 'prefer one religion over another.'"[44] The Court concluded that the 50-percent requirement "clearly grants denominational preferences of the sort consistently and firmly deprecated

---

[41] *Id.* at 637 (O'Connor, J., concurring and concurring in the judgment).

[42] 490 U.S. 680, 695 (1989). In *Hernandez*, the Court upheld as constitutional a decision by the Commissioner of Internal Revenue to prevent payments to branch churches of the Church of Scientology for certain religious services from being deductible as charitable contributions. The Court said that disallowing the deduction did not discriminate among religious denominations and did not violate the *Lemon* test. *See also* Jimmy Swaggart Ministries v. Board of Equalization of Cal., 493 U.S. 378 (1990) (holding that religious groups had no constitutional right to refuse to pay general sales and use taxes for the sale of religious goods and literature).

[43] 456 U.S. 228 (1982).

[44] *Id.* at 246 (quoting Everson v. Board of Educ., 330 U.S. 1, 15 (1947)).

in our precedents" and thus could not be allowed unless strict scrutiny was met.[45] Religions that met the requirement, such as the Catholic Church, had the great benefit of being exempt from the burdens of the statute; religions that did not meet the requirement, such as the "Moonies," would have to comply with the law.[46] The Court found that there was no compelling interest to justify the discrimination and thus concluded that the "fifty percent rule sets up precisely the sort of official denominational preference that the Framers of the First Amendment forbade."[47]

The Court applied this neutrality principle in *Board of Education of Kiryas Joel Village School District v. Grumet* to declare unconstitutional a state law that created a separate school district for a small village that was inhabited by Hasidic Jews.[48] The Village Kiryas Joel was created by a sect known as Satmar Hasidim. They maintained two parochial schools, one for boys and one for girls. However, they did not have any services available for children with disabilities. Until the Supreme Court declared it unconstitutional in 1985, the government provided special education for such children within the parochial schools.[49] In response to these Supreme Court decisions, the State of New York adopted a law that created a public school district with boundaries identical to those of the Village of Kiryas Joel. The school board for the village was like all other school boards, except that all of its elected members were part of the Satmar Hasidic sect.

Justice Souter, writing for the Court, declared the New York law unconstitutional as impermissible preference for one religion over others. The government created a school district specifically to help one religion so that it could provide special education without its children having to attend school with those outside the faith. Justice Souter explained that "[t]he fundamental source of constitutional concern here is that the legislature itself may fail to exercise governmental authority in a religiously neutral way."[50]

In a part of the opinion that was joined only by a plurality, Justice Souter also said that the law violated the establishment clause because the government was impermissibly delegating government authority to a religious entity.[51] He said that creating a government entity contiguous with a religious community and thereby allowing the religion to control its political process was an impermissible "fusion of governmental and religious functions."[52]

---

[45] *Id.* at 246.

[46] *Id.* at 254-255.

[47] *Id.* at 255.

[48] 512 U.S. 687 (1994).

[49] Grand Rapids School Dist. v. Ball, 473 U.S. 373 (1985); Aguilar v. Felton, 473 U.S. 402 (1985), discussed below in §12.2.6.2. In 1997, in *Agostini v. Felton*, 521 U.S. 203 (1997), the Court overruled *Aguilar.* It, therefore, would not be necessary to try to create a special school district for public school teachers to provide remedial education in parochial schools.

[50] 512 U.S. at 703.

[51] *Id.* at 696. *See also* Larkin v. Grendel's Den, Inc., 459 U.S. 116 (1982) (declaring unconstitutional as an impermissible delegation to religious groups a law that allowed religious entities a power to veto applications for liquor licenses in areas near religious facilities).

[52] *Id.* at 702. Justice O'Connor wrote separately to express her view that creating the school district was an impermissible denominational preference. *Id.* at 712 (O'Connor, J., concurring in part and concurring in the judgment). Justice Kennedy concurred in the judgment and emphasized that

Thus, cases such as *Larson* and *Kiryas Joel* establish that a government action violates the establishment clause if it prefers one religion or sect over others.[53] In such instances, the Court invalidates the law without reaching the *Lemon* test. Yet the neutrality approach taken in cases such as *Larson* and *Kiryas Joel* is remarkably similar to the analysis under the first two prongs of the *Lemon* test: If the government is favoring one religion, it is acting with the purpose and there is the effect of fostering that religion.

§12.2.3   The *Lemon* *Test for the Establishment Clause*

The Test Summarized

If a law is not discriminatory, the Supreme Court says that a court should apply the three-part test articulated in *Lemon v. Kurtzman*.[54] The Court declared: "First, the statute must have a secular legislative purpose; second, its principal or primary effect must be one that neither advances nor inhibits religion; finally, the statute must not foster an excessive government entanglement with religion."[55] A law is unconstitutional if it fails any prong of the *Lemon* test.

Although there have been many instances where the Court decided establishment clause cases without applying this test,[56] it has been frequently used. While several Justices have criticized the test and called for it to be overruled, this has not occurred.[57] Indeed, Justice Scalia, the primary advocate for overruling the *Lemon* test, colorfully lamented its survival and analogized it to "a ghoul in a late-night horror movie that repeatedly sits up in its grave and shuffles abroad, after being repeatedly killed and buried. [It] is there to scare us [when] we wish it to do so, but we can command it to return to the tomb at will. When we wish to strike down

---

the denominational preference failed to meet strict scrutiny. *Id.* at 722 (Kennedy, J., concurring in the judgment). Justice Scalia dissenting, joined by Rehnquist and Thomas, argued that government entities should be allowed to engage in religious accommodation, such as by creating a school district to help the religion provide special education for its children without their having to attend school with those outside the faith.

[53] For a discussion of the *Kiryas Joel* case and its implications, *see* Abner S. Greene, *Kiryas Joel and Two Mistakes About Equality*, 96 Colum. L. Rev. 1 (1996); Ira C. Lupu, Uncovering the Village of Kiryas Joel, 96 Colum. L. Rev. 104 (1996).

[54] 403 U.S. 602 (1971).

[55] *Id.* at 612.

[56] *See, e.g.,* Town of Greece v. Galloway, 134 S. Ct. 1811 (2014) (upholding Christian prayers before town board meetings); Board of Educ. of Kiryas Joel Village School Dist. v. Grumet, 512 U.S. 687 (1994) (finding favoritism for one religion by creating a school district contiguous with a religious community violates the establishment clause); Lynch v. Donnelly, 465 U.S. 668 (1984) (allowing nativity scene on government property); Marsh v. Chambers, 463 U.S. 783 (1983) (allowing government payment of a legislative chaplain because of history of the practice).

[57] Justice Scalia has expressly called for the overruling of the *Lemon* test. *See, e.g.,* Lamb's Chapel v. Center Moriches Union Free School Dist., 508 U.S. 384, 399 (1993) (Scalia, J., concurring in the judgment); Lee v. Weisman, 505 U.S. 577, 644 (1992) (Scalia, J., dissenting).

a practice it forbids, we invoke it, when we wish to uphold a practice it forbids, we ignore it entirely."[58]

The *Lemon* test is favored and used by Justices taking the strict separationist approach to the establishment clause. It also is used by Justices taking the neutrality approach, although they emphasize whether the purpose or effect is to symbolically endorse religion.[59] Justices favoring the accommodationist approach urge the overruling of the *Lemon* test.

The current and future role of the *Lemon* test is uncertain. The test has not been expressly overruled or discarded, and it has been invoked in later cases.[60] On the other hand, with the change in the composition of the Court, there may be five Justices to overrule it, if Chief Justice Roberts and Justice Alito join with Justices Scalia, Kennedy, and Thomas in doing so.

The Requirement for a Secular Purpose

The first prong of the *Lemon* test is the requirement that there be a secular purpose for a law. For example, in *Stone v. Graham*, the Supreme Court declared unconstitutional a state law that required the Ten Commandments to be posted on the walls of every public school classroom.[61] The Court concluded that the law "has no secular legislative purpose" and therefore violated the establishment clause.[62] Similarly, in *Wallace v. Jaffree*, the Court invalidated a state law that authorized public school teachers to hold a one-minute period of silence for meditation or voluntary prayer.[63] The Court found that the purpose behind the law was to reintroduce prayer into public schools and deemed the law unconstitutional because it "was not motivated by any clearly secular purpose—indeed, the statute had *no* secular purpose."[64]

In *Edwards v. Aguillard*, the Court followed this reasoning and ruled unconstitutional a state law that required that public schools that teach evolution also teach "creation science."[65] Since "creation science" is a religious theory explaining the origin of human life, the Court concluded: "Because the primary purpose of

---

[58] Lamb's Chapel v. Center Moriches Union Free School Dist., 508 U.S. at 398-399 (Scalia, J., dissenting).

[59] *See, e.g.*, Lynch v. Donnelly, 465 U.S. at 690 (O'Connor, J., concurring) ("The purpose prong of the *Lemon* test asks whether government's actual purpose is to endorse or disapprove of religion. The effect prong asks whether, irrespective of government's actual purpose, the practice under review in fact conveys a message of endorsement or disapproval. An affirmative answer to either question should render the challenged practice invalid.").

[60] McCreary County, Ky. v. ACLU of Ky., 545 U.S. 844, 860 (2005). *See* Agostini v. Felton, 521 U.S. 203, 218, 232 (1997); Lamb's Chapel v. Center Moriches Union Free School Dist., 508 U.S. 384 (1993).

[61] 449 U.S. 39 (1980).

[62] *Id.* at 41.

[63] 472 U.S. 38 (1985).

[64] *Id.* at 56 (emphasis in original).

[65] 482 U.S. 578 (1987).

the Creationism Act is to endorse a particular religious doctrine, the Act furthers religion in violation of the establishment clause."[66]

Subsequently, in *McCreary County, Kentucky v. ACLU of Kentucky*, the Supreme Court declared unconstitutional a county's effort to post the Ten Commandments in county buildings.[67] Justice Souter's majority opinion stressed that the history of the county's actions left no doubt that it was acting with the purpose of advancing religion in violation of the first prong of the *Lemon* test. Justice Souter explained: "When the government acts with the ostensible and predominant purpose of advancing religion, it violates that central Establishment Clause value of official religious neutrality, there being no neutrality when the government's ostensible object is to take sides."[68] The Court concluded that the content of the Ten Commandments and the context of the county's actions left no doubt that it was acting with the purpose of advancing religion.

In contrast, in *McGowan v. Maryland*, the Supreme Court upheld the constitutionality of state laws requiring businesses to be closed on Sunday.[69] The Court acknowledged "the strongly religious origin of these laws."[70] Nonetheless, the Court found the laws permissible because "[t]he present purpose and effect of most of them is to provide a uniform day of rest for all citizens; the fact that this day is Sunday, a day of particular significance for the dominant Christian sects, does not bar the State from achieving its secular goals."[71]

Several of the Justices—especially Chief Justice Rehnquist and Justice Scalia—have criticized the first prong of the *Lemon* test. Rehnquist has argued that the requirement for a secular purpose "is a constitutional theory [that] has no basis in the history of the amendment it seeks to interpret, is difficult to apply and yields unprincipled results."[72] Scalia contended: "[D]iscerning the subjective motivation of those enacting the statute is, to be honest, almost always an impossible task. The number of possible motivations . . . is not binary, or indeed even finite. . . . To look for *the sole purpose* of even a single legislator is probably to look for something that does not exist."[73]

On the other hand, the Court considers legislative purpose, despite the difficulty in ascertaining it, in other areas of constitutional law, such as in the requirement for proof of a discriminatory purpose to prove a race or gender classification when there is a facially neutral law.[74] Justice Souter, writing for the Court, made exactly this point in defending retaining the first prong of the *Lemon* test: "Examination of purpose is a staple of statutory interpretation that makes up the daily fare of every appellate court in the country, and governmental purpose is a

---

[66] *Id*. at 594.

[67] 545 U.S. 844 (2005).

[68] *Id*. at 860.

[69] 366 U.S. 420 (1961).

[70] *Id*. at 433.

[71] *Id*. at 445. In Braunfeld v. Brown, 366 U.S. 599 (1961), discussed below in §12.3.2, the Court rejected a free exercise challenge to Sunday closing laws.

[72] Wallace v. Jaffree, 472 U.S. at 112 (Rehnquist, J., dissenting).

[73] Edwards v. Aguillard, 482 U.S. at 636-637 (Scalia, J., dissenting).

[74] *See, e.g.*, Washington v. Davis, 426 U.S. 229 (1976), discussed in §9.3.3.2.

key element of a good deal of constitutional doctrine."[75] The rationale for the first prong of the *Lemon* test is that the very essence of the establishment clause is to keep the government from acting to advance religion.

The Requirement for a Secular Effect

The second prong of the *Lemon* test requires that the principal or primary effect of a law must be one that neither advances nor inhibits religion. In recent years, this often has been expressed in terms of symbolic endorsement: The government's action must not symbolically endorse religion or a particular religion.[76] *Estate of Thornton v. Caldor* is an example where the Court used the second part of the *Lemon* test to invalidate a law.[77] A Connecticut statute provided that no person may be required by an employer to work on his or her Sabbath. The Supreme Court declared the law unconstitutional and emphasized that the law created an absolute and unqualified right for individuals to not work for religious reasons and thus favored religion over all other interests. The Court concluded that "the statute goes beyond having an incidental or remote effect of advancing religion. The statute has a primary effect that impermissibly advances a particular religious practice."[78]

However, in other cases, the Court has upheld exemptions from laws for religion. In *Corporation of Presiding Bishop of the Church of Jesus Christ of Latter-Day Saints v. Amos*,[79] the Court found constitutional an exemption for religious organizations from Title VII's prohibition against discrimination in employment based on religion.[80] The Court concluded that the exemption met the first prong of the *Lemon* test because it was a permissible purpose "to alleviate significant government interference with the ability of religious organizations to define and carry out their religious missions."[81]

More significantly, the Court found that the exemption was not inconsistent with the second part of the *Lemon* test. Justice White, writing for the majority, said that "[a] law is not unconstitutional simply because it *allows* churches to advance religion, which is their very purpose. For a law to have forbidden 'effects' under

---

[75] McCreary County, Ky. v. ACLU of Ky., 544 U.S. at 861.

[76] *See, e.g.*, Board of Educ. of Westside Community Schools v. Mergens, 496 U.S. 226, 249-253 (1990) (plurality opinion) (using the symbolic endorsement test to determine whether the effect of a government action was to advance religion impermissibly). *Mergens* is discussed below in §12.2.4.

[77] 472 U.S. 703 (1985).

[78] *Id.* at 710 (citation omitted).

[79] 483 U.S. 327 (1987). Also, in *Hosanna-Tabor Evangelical Lutheran Church and School v. EEOC*, 132 S. Ct. 694 (2012), the Court held that religious institutions have an exemption from employment discrimination laws that would limit their choices as to who will be their ministers. The case involved a teacher in a parochial elementary school who had been designated a minister and sued under the Americans with Disabilities Act to challenge her firing. The Court found that it would violate the establishment clause (and the free exercise clause) to hold a religious institution liable for the decisions it makes as to who will be its ministers. This case is discussed above in §12.1.

[80] 42 U.S.C. §2000e-l.

[81] 483 U.S. at 335.

Lemon, it must be fair to say that the *government itself* has advanced religion through its own activities and influence."[82]

The difference between *Thornton* and *Amos* is that the latter involved an exemption in a statute for religion, whereas the former concerned a law that provided a benefit solely for religion. The Court found that the latter was permissible, but that the former was the government advancing religion through its own activities and influence. Yet the distinction is difficult to defend because both laws granted a preference for religion alone.

The Prohibition of Excessive Entanglement

The final prong of the *Lemon* test forbids government actions that cause excessive entanglement with religion. The Court has said that a law violates the establishment clause when it requires a "comprehensive, discriminating, and continuing state surveillance."[83] The Court also has said that "apart from any specific entanglement of the State in particular religious programs, assistance . . . [violates the establishment clause if it] carries the [grave] potential for entanglement in the broader sense of continuing political strife over aid to religion."[84]

For example, the Supreme Court traditionally has held that the government cannot pay teacher salaries in parochial schools, even for teachers of secular subjects or for special education teachers.[85] If the government paid such salaries, it would need to monitor whether the teachers were teaching secular or religious material. Any such monitoring would be excessive government entanglement with religion.

As discussed below, in *Mitchell v. Helms,*[86] the Supreme Court held, without a majority opinion, that the government may give instructional equipment to parochial schools so long as it is not used for religious instruction. Actually, four Justices would have allowed the instructional equipment—computers, audiovisual equipment, and the like—to be used for religious education so long as all religions are treated equally. Three Justices would have prohibited the government from giving such aid to parochial schools because it could be used for religious education. Two Justices said that such aid is allowed so long as it is not actually used for religious instruction. It is unclear as to how *Mitchell* affects the no-entanglement prong of the *Lemon* test. The Court did not explicitly overrule or disavow the entanglement

---

[82] *Id.* at 337 (emphasis in original). Also, in *Cutter v. Wilkinson,* 544 U.S. 709 (2005), the Court rejected an establishment clause challenge to the Religious Land Use and Institutionalized Persons Act, which requires that the government meet strict scrutiny if it substantially burdens religion in its land use decisions or for institutionalized persons. The Court concluded that the accommodation of religion was not a violation of the establishment clause. *Cutter* is discussed in more detail below in §12.3.2.4.

[83] Lemon v. Kurtzman, 403 U.S. at 619.

[84] Committee for Public Educ. v. Nyquist, 413 U.S. 756, 794 (1973).

[85] *See, e.g.,* Grand Rapids Sch. Dist. v. Ball, 473 U.S. 373 (1985); Aguilar v. Felton, 473 U.S. 402 (1985), discussed in §12.2.6.2. In *Agostini v. Felton,* 521 U.S. 203 (1997), the Court expressly overruled *Aguilar.* Now public school teachers may provide remedial education in parochial schools, but beyond that the Court has not allowed the government to pay teachers' salaries in parochial schools.

[86] 530 U.S. 793 (2000).

inquiry. But it is difficult to see how this prong can survive the Court allowing much more government aid to religious schools. In *Mitchell*, Justices O'Connor and Breyer, concurring in the judgment and the decisive votes to uphold the program, seemed unconcerned about entanglement in allowing such aid.

As with all of the establishment clause, there is uncertainty over the future direction of the law because of the change in the composition of the Supreme Court. Three Justices—Scalia, Kennedy, and Thomas—clearly want to abandon the entanglement inquiry and the *Lemon* test. Two Justices want to keep the *Lemon* test—Ginsburg and Breyer—though Breyer may be willing to abandon or modify the last prong based on his vote in *Mitchell v. Helms*. If Chief Justice Roberts and Justice Alito agree with Scalia, Kennedy, and Thomas, the third prong and indeed the entire *Lemon* test will be overruled. Moreover, as of this writing, it is still unknown how the two newest Justices—Sotomayor and Kagan—will deal with this issue.

§12.2.4   *Religious Speech and the First Amendment*

Overview

A significant number of cases concerning the establishment clause have involved free speech claims. Specifically, these cases concern situations where the government chooses to restrict private religious speech on government property or with government funds because of a desire to avoid violating the establishment clause. The Supreme Court consistently has held that excluding such religious speech violates the First Amendment's protection of freedom of speech because it is an impermissible content-based restriction of expression.[87]

These cases mark a significant development in establishment clause jurisprudence that changes the way many cases will be litigated and decided. If a government action can be characterized as a restriction of private religious speech, it can be challenged as violating the First Amendment's protection of freedom of speech and the challenger has a strong likelihood of prevailing; no longer will such cases be seen as exclusively or even predominantly involving the establishment clause.

Religious Group Access to School Facilities

The initial Supreme Court cases in this area concerned efforts by the government to restrict religious groups from using school facilities so as to avoid violating the establishment clause. In *Widmar v. Vincent*, the Supreme Court declared unconstitutional a state university's policy of preventing student groups from using school facilities for religious worship or religious discussion.[88] The University of

---

[87] For a discussion of the First Amendment principle that content-based discrimination is permissible only if strict scrutiny is met, *see* §11.2.1.

[88] 454 U.S. 263 (1981).

Missouri at Kansas City allowed registered student groups to use its facilities, but forbid their use "for purposes of religious worship or religious teaching."[89]

The Court said that the university "discriminated against student groups and speakers based on their desire to use a generally open forum to engage in religious worship and discussion. These are forms of speech and association protected by the First Amendment."[90] The Court expressly rejected the dissent's argument that religious worship is not speech protected by the free speech guarantee of the First Amendment.[91] The Court said that the university had created a public forum by opening these places to speech and said that "[i]n order to justify discriminatory exclusion from a public forum based on the religious content of a group's intended speech, the University must therefore satisfy the standard of review appropriate to content-based exclusions. It must show that its regulation is necessary to serve a compelling state interest and that it is narrowly drawn to achieve that end."[92]

The Court then concluded that excluding religious speech was not necessary in order to be consistent with the establishment clause. The Court applied the *Lemon* test and said that opening school facilities to all groups served the secular purpose of providing a forum for student meetings. The Court said that any effect in advancing religion would be "incidental."[93] The Court concluded that allowing religious groups to use school facilities was not excessive entanglement with religion; no state monitoring would be necessary if the university allowed secular and religious groups to use the facilities.

The Court followed similar reasoning in *Board of Education of Westside Community Schools v. Mergens*.[94] *Mergens* involved a constitutional challenge to the federal Equal Access Act, which applies to any public school that receives federal financial assistance. The Equal Access Act says that any such school that opens its facilities to noncurricular student groups may not deny equal access to any students who wish to conduct meetings on similar terms because of the religious, political, philosophical, or other content of their speech.[95]

Justice O'Connor, writing for the plurality, said that "the logic of *Widmar* applies."[96] Justice O'Connor used the *Lemon* test and concluded that preventing discrimination against speech because of its religious, political, or philosophical content was a legitimate secular purpose. She said that the effect was not to advance religion because allowing religious groups to use school facilities was not likely to be perceived as a symbolic government endorsement of religion. Justice O'Connor wrote that "secondary school students are mature enough and are likely to understand that a school does not endorse or support student speech

---

[89] *Id.* at 265 n.3.
[90] *Id.* at 269.
[91] *Id.* at 269-270 n.6.
[92] *Id.* at 269-270.
[93] *Id.* at 274.
[94] 496 U.S. 226 (1990).
[95] 20 U.S.C. §4071 (1994).
[96] *Mergens*, 496 U.S. at 248.

that it merely permits on a nondiscriminatory basis."[97] Finally, Justice O'Connor concluded that there was not excessive entanglement with religion because faculty sponsors were not allowed to participate actively in religious groups' meetings.

Justices Brennan and Marshall concurred in the judgment and emphasized that schools had the constitutional duty to make it clear that the government was not endorsing the views or activities of the religious groups.[98] Justices Kennedy and Scalia also concurred in the judgment, though they used an accommodationist approach rather than the *Lemon* test.[99] They said that the only relevant inquiries were whether the government aid was so extensive as to have a clear tendency to establish a state religion or whether the government was coercing student religious participation. They concluded that the establishment clause was not violated because there was neither the establishment of a state religion nor coercion of religious activities.

In *Lamb's Chapel v. Center Moriches Union Free School District*, the Court followed this reasoning and declared unconstitutional a school district's policy of excluding religious groups from using school facilities during evenings and weekends.[100] Pursuant to state law, a school district opened its facilities to community and civic groups during evenings and weekends, but said that "school premises shall not be used by any group for religious purposes."[101]

The Court expressly followed the reasoning in *Widmar* and said that once the government chose to open its facilities to community groups, it could not discriminate against those engaging in religious speech unless strict scrutiny was met.[102] The Court again rejected the claim that avoiding violation of the establishment clause provided such a compelling interest. The Court said: "We have no more trouble than did the *Widmar* Court in disposing of the claimed defense on the ground that the posited fears of an Establishment Clause violation are unfounded. The showing of this film series would not have been during school hours, would not have been sponsored by the school, and would have been open to the public, not just to church members."[103] The Court concluded that "[a]s in *Widmar*, permitting District property to be used . . . would not have been an establishment of religion under the three-part test articulated in *Lemon v. Kurtzman*. The challenged governmental action has a secular purpose, does not have the principal or primary effect of advancing or inhibiting religion, and does not foster an excessive entanglement with religion."[104]

---

[97] *Id.* at 250.

[98] *Id.* at 264 (Marshall, J., concurring in the judgment).

[99] *Id.* at 258 (Kennedy, J., concurring in part and concurring in the judgment).

[100] 508 U.S. 384 (1993).

[101] *Id.* at 387.

[102] *Id.* at 394.

[103] *Id.* at 395.

[104] *Id.* at 395 (citations omitted). Justices Kennedy and Scalia, the latter joined by Justice Thomas, wrote separately to object to the use of the *Lemon* test. *Id.* at 397 (Kennedy, J., concurring in part and concurring in the judgment).

Subsequently, in *Good News Club v. Milford*,[105] the Supreme Court followed *Lamb's Chapel* and held that an elementary school could not exclude a religious group from using school facilities after school. The school opened its facilities to community groups to conduct activities for the students after school. A religious group, Good News Club, wanted access, but was denied because of the religious content of its activities. The Supreme Court, in a 6-to-3 decision, ruled that excluding the group violated its free speech rights and that allowing it did not infringe the establishment clause.

Justice Thomas wrote the opinion for the Court. At the outset, he said that the school, by opening its facilities to community groups, created a "limited public forum."[106] In a limited public forum, the government's regulation of speech must be viewpoint neutral. Justice Thomas relied expressly on *Lamb's Chapel* and *Rosenberger* to conclude that the exclusion of religious speech was not viewpoint neutral. Secular groups could use the school facilities to discuss their positions on various issues with the students; but religious groups were precluded from expressing their views on the same matters. Justice Thomas thus declared: "Applying *Lamb's Chapel*, we find it quite clear that Milford engaged in viewpoint discrimination when it excluded the Club from the after-school forum. [T]he exclusion of the Good News Club's activities, like the exclusion of Lamb's Chapel's films, constitutes unconstitutional viewpoint discrimination."[107]

The Court then considered whether allowing Good News Club to use the school facilities would violate the establishment clause. Neither the district court nor the United States Court of Appeals had reached this issue because each had found that the Good News Club did not have a right to use the school facilities. Indeed, the dissent strongly objected to the majority's considering this issue without it having been considered by the lower courts.[108] The majority found no violation of the establishment clause in allowing the religious group to use the school's facilities on the same basis as they were available to secular organizations.

Justice Thomas began by noting that the Court had not yet ruled as to whether complying with the establishment clause is a compelling interest sufficient to justify viewpoint discrimination: "We have said that a state interest in avoiding an Establishment Clause violation 'may be characterized as compelling,' and therefore may justify content-based discrimination. However, it is not clear whether a State's interest in avoiding an Establishment Clause violation would justify viewpoint discrimination. . . . We need not, however, confront the issue in this case, because we conclude that the school has no valid Establishment Clause interest."[109] This is a potentially important, unresolved issue that could arise in instances in which allowing religious speech would violate the establishment

---

[105] 533 U.S. 98.

[106] Limited public forums referred to government-owned properties that the government could close to speech, but that the government chooses to open to some topics or speakers, but without discriminating among them based on viewpoint. The rules for limited public forums are discussed in detail in §11.4.

[107] 553 U.S. at 110.

[108] *Id.* at 136 (Souter, J., dissenting).

[109] *Id.* at 112-113.

clause. For example, if teachers were involved and the school actively encouraged students to participate, there would be a strong argument that the religious activity violated the establishment clause. Justice Thomas's majority opinion says this nonetheless might be allowed to avoid viewpoint discrimination among speech. This would be a dramatic change in the law because it always has been assumed that government actions that violate the establishment clause are impermissible and no further analysis, such as free speech considerations, could save them.

Justice Thomas emphasized that here there would be no violation of the establishment clause because the government would be "neutral" with regard to religion; that is, it would be treating religious and secular groups the same.[110] Moreover, Justice Thomas noted the absence of coercive pressures by the government for students to participate in the religious activities.[111] The dissent objected that earlier cases were distinguishable in that Good News Club wanted to engage in religious activities immediately after classes in an elementary school.[112] The majority, however, rejected these distinctions and found no violation of the establishment clause in allowing the religious group to use the facilities under these circumstances.

Good News Club follows cases like *Lamb's Chapel* in that the Court held that excluding religious groups from using government property was impermissible discrimination based on the content of the speech. But *Good News Club* is important in extending the earlier decisions to elementary schools and the time immediately after school. There still remains the possibility of "as applied" challenges to religious groups' use of school facilities. For example, if the school participates in a manner that might be seen as "coercive" — such as teachers encouraging participation or religious activities during school — the result might well be different.

Student Religious Group Receipt of Government Funds

The Court applied these cases in *Rosenberger v. Rector and Visitors of the University of Virginia* to declare unconstitutional a state university's refusal to give student activity funds to a Christian group that published an expressly religious magazine.[113] Justice Kennedy wrote the opinion for the majority in the 5-to-4 decision and was joined by Chief Justice Rehnquist and Justices O'Connor, Scalia, and Thomas.

Kennedy reasoned in two steps. First, he said that denying funds to the religious student group was impermissible content-based discrimination against religious speech. Kennedy expressly relied on *Widmar, Mergens,* and *Lamb's Chapel* to conclude that the government unconstitutionally was discriminating against the Christian group because of the religious content of its speech. He said that although the government has wide discretion when it chooses to allocate scarce financial resources, "[i]t does not follow . . . that viewpoint-based restrictions are

[110] *Id.* at 114-115.
[111] *Id.*
[112] *Id.* at 142-143.
[113] 515 U.S. 819 (1995).

proper when the University does not itself speak or subsidize transmittal of a message it favors but instead expends funds to encourage a diversity of views from private speakers."[114] Kennedy said that "[v]ital First Amendment speech principles are at stake here. The first danger to liberty lies in granting the State the power to examine publications to determine whether or not they are based on some ultimate idea and if so for the State to classify them. The second, and corollary, danger is to speech from the chilling of individual thought and expression."[115]

Second, Justice Kennedy concluded that providing funds to the religious group would not violate the establishment clause. He emphasized that "[t]he governmental program here is neutral toward religion."[116] The government was acting with the purpose and effect of helping student groups and fostering a wide array of activities and viewpoints on campus. Justice Kennedy cited to *Widmar*, *Mergens*, and *Lamb's Chapel* and said that "[t]here is no difference in logic or principle, and no difference of constitutional significance, between a school using its funds to operate a facility to which students have access, and a school paying a third-party contractor to operate the facility on its behalf."[117] Justice Kennedy's majority opinion concluded: "There is no Establishment Clause violation in the University's honoring its duties under the Free Speech Clause."[118]

Justice Souter dissented and was joined by Justices Stevens, Ginsburg, and Breyer. He emphasized that this was the first time that the Court ever had allowed, let alone required, direct government financial subsidies to a religious group. Souter stated that "[u]sing public funds for the direct subsidization of preaching the word is categorically forbidden under the Establishment Clause, and if the Clause was meant to accomplish nothing else, it was meant to bar this use of public money."[119] He concluded that "[t]he principle against direct funding with public money is patently violated by the contested use of today's student activity fee."[120]

Private Placement of Religious Symbols on Government Property

The Court also used a free speech approach to resolve an establishment clause dispute issue in *Capitol Square Review and Advisory Board v. Pinette*.[121] In *Pinette*, a

---

[114] *Id.* at 834.

[115] *Id.* at 835.

[116] *Id.* at 840.

[117] *Id.* at 843.

[118] *Id.* at 846. The Court did not reach the issue of whether students could bring a free speech challenge by objecting to the use of their money to support religious speech that they do not wish to subsidize. *See, e.g.*, Keller v. State Bar of Cal., 496 U.S. 1 (1990); Abood v. Detroit Bd. of Educ., 431 U.S. 209 (1977) (finding unconstitutional compelled subsidies), discussed in §11.2.4.3.

[119] *Id.* at 868. Justice Souter relied on James Madison's Memorial and Remonstrance Against Religious Assessments, which objected to a state tax to aid the church. *Id.* at 868-871. Justice Thomas, in a concurring opinion, offered a different view of Madison's Remonstrance: as prohibiting preferential treatment of some religions over others with government funds. *Id.* at 854-858 (Thomas, J., concurring).

[120] *Id.* at 873.

[121] 515 U.S. 753 (1995). *Pinette* is discussed above in §12.2.1, text accompanying notes 13-20.

state agency refused to allow the Ku Klux Klan to build a large Latin cross in a park across from the state capitol. The Court ruled that the government violated the free speech guarantee of the First Amendment by excluding the religious speech.

There was no majority opinion for the Court. Justice Scalia wrote a plurality opinion, joined by Rehnquist, Kennedy, and Thomas. He began by expressly citing *Widmar, Mergens,* and *Lamb's Chapel* as establishing that "private religious speech, far from being a First Amendment orphan, is as fully protected under the Free Speech Clause as secular private expression."[122] Scalia said that the government's exclusion of the cross because of its religious significance was content-based discrimination against speech.

Scalia then observed that "[t]here is no doubt that compliance with the Establishment Clause is a state interest sufficiently compelling to justify content-based restrictions on speech."[123] Scalia's plurality opinion again invoked *Widmar* and *Lamb's Chapel* as ruling that the government does not violate the establishment clause if it permits religious speech on government property in the same manner as secular speech is allowed.

Justice O'Connor wrote an opinion concurring in the judgment that was joined by Justices Souter and Breyer.[124] Justice O'Connor recognized that excluding the cross was content-based discrimination, but said that the establishment clause also required analysis as to whether allowing the religious symbol would be perceived as government endorsement for religion. She concluded that there was not a violation of the establishment clause because "there is no realistic danger that the community would think that the [State] was endorsing religion or any particular creed."[125] Justice O'Connor said that "when the reasonable observer would view a government practice as endorsing religion, . . . it is our *duty* to hold the practice invalid."[126] She said, however, that the reasonable observer would not perceive the cross as government endorsement for religion because of a sign accompanying it and because the "reasonable observer in the endorsement inquiry must be deemed aware of the history and context of the community and forum in which the religious display appears."[127]

Justices Stevens and Ginsburg wrote dissenting opinions.[128] Stevens contended that the "Establishment Clause should be construed to create a strong presumption against the installation of unattended religious symbols on public property."[129] Stevens also argued that an observer coming upon a large cross in a public park could have perceived it as government endorsement of Christianity; "[e]ven on private property, signs and symbols are generally understood to express the

---

[122] *Id.* at 760.

[123] *Id.*

[124] *Id.* at 772 (O'Connor, J., concurring in part and concurring in the judgment). Justice Souter also wrote such an opinion, joined by Justices O'Connor and Breyer. *Id.* at 783 (Souter, J., concurring in part and concurring in the judgment).

[125] *Id.* at 765 (citation omitted).

[126] *Id.* at 777 (emphasis in original).

[127] *Id.* at 780.

[128] *Id.* at 797 (Stevens, J., dissenting); *id.* at 817 (Ginsburg, J., dissenting).

[129] *Id.* at 797 (Stevens, J., dissenting).

owner's views."[130] Stevens argued that it was inappropriate to define the reasonable observer from the perspective of an educated observer familiar with the history and politics surrounding a symbol. He said that therefore the "Constitution generally forbids the placement of a symbol of a religious character in, on, or before a seat of government."[131]

It must be emphasized that *Pinette* was about *private* placement of religious symbols on government property. Obviously, government placement of religious symbols on government property does not raise free speech issues, but rather is entirely about whether the establishment clause is violated.

Rejection of Prayer at Student Football Games

But not every attempt to use speech analysis to allow more religious presence in government activities has succeeded. In *Santa Fe Independent School District v. Doe*, the Court declared unconstitutional student-delivered prayers at high school football games and expressly rejected the argument that this was impermissible discrimination against religious speech.[132] The school district defended its policy, in part, based on the free speech rights of students; it argued that excluding prayer was an unconstitutional content-based restriction on speech. Justice Stevens, writing for the Court, disagreed. He emphasized that the school had not created a forum where students could say anything they wanted. Quite the contrary, the message was restricted by the school.

In other words, the Court did not see the student-delivered prayers as private speech. Rather, the Court viewed the school as encouraging and facilitating prayer, while preventing many other types of speech. In this context, the exclusion of prayer was not a violation of the speech protections of the First Amendment.

Implications

Many traditional establishment clause issues might be reconceptualized in light of these cases being considered as involving government content-based discrimination against speech. For example, whether student-delivered prayers are allowed at public school graduation might be analyzed in terms of whether allowing them is a violation of the establishment clause and also whether prohibiting them is an impermissible content-based discrimination against religious speech.[133] In fact, it even is conceivable that the Court might revisit the issue of government aid to parochial schools from the perspective of whether denying such money

---

[130] *Id.* at 800.

[131] *Id.* at 806-807. Justice Ginsburg, in a separate dissenting opinion, said that the disclaimer of government involvement was insufficient and said that the case did not present the more difficult question of whether there would be an establishment clause violation if there were "a sturdier disclaimer." *Id.* at 818 (Ginsburg, J., dissenting).

[132] 530 U.S. 290 (2000), discussed more fully below in §12.2.5.1 at text accompanying notes 161-165.

[133] *See, e.g.*, ACLU of N.J. v. Black Horse Pike Regional Bd. of Educ., 84 F.3d 1471 (3d Cir. 1996); Jones v. Clear Creek Indep. School Dist., 977 F.2d 963 (5th Cir. 1992).

is impermissibly discriminating against such institutions because of the religious content of the speech that occurs there.

The underlying issue is whether and when allowing private religious speech to use government property or to receive government funds violates the establishment clause. From one perspective, there is a strong presumption, if not an irrebuttable one, that all such activity violates the establishment clause; complying with the establishment clause is a compelling interest that requires the exclusion of religion from government property and from the receipt of government funds. From another perspective, the inquiry in each case is whether the government action would be perceived, from the perspective of the reasonable observer, as government symbolic endorsement for religion; only then would it violate the establishment clause and require government exclusion. But from yet another view, the government may never exclude such religious speech unless there was the extremely unlikely possibility that allowing it would be tantamount to the government creating a church or coercing religious participation.

§12.2.5   When Can Religion Become a Part of Government Activities?

Overview

Many cases under the establishment clause have involved issues of when, if at all, religion can become a part of government activities. For example, a large number of decisions have concerned the question of when does religion impermissibly become a part of public school education. The Court has considered this topic in evaluating laws that allow children to be released from school for religious education, in considering prayers in public schools, and in evaluating curricular decisions made for religious reasons. These cases are discussed in §12.2.5.1.

The Court also has considered religion as a part of government activities in a series of cases concerning when religious symbols, especially holiday displays such as nativity scenes and menorahs, can be on government property. These cases are considered in §12.2.5.2. Section 12.2.5.3 examines the constitutionality of prayers before legislative sessions. Finally, §12.2.5.4 considers an approach advocated by Justice O'Connor that some types of government religious activities be allowed because they are "ceremonial deism" and not the "establishment" of religion.

§12.2.5.1   Religion as a Part of Government Activities: Schools

Release Time

The first Supreme Court cases to consider religion as a part of public school activities concerned policies that allowed students to be released from classes to receive religious instruction. The Court said that this was impermissible if the religious teaching occurred on school premises, but allowed if the students were released to receive religious training elsewhere.

In *McCollum v. Board of Education*, the Court declared unconstitutional a school's policy of allowing students to be released, with parental permission, to religious instruction classes conducted during regular school hours in the school building by outside teachers.[134] The superintendent of schools approved the religious teachers, and attendance records were kept and reported to school authorities in the same way as for other classes. Students not attending the religion classes continued their regular secular studies.

The Court, in an opinion by Justice Black, found the law unconstitutional as violating the "wall of separation between church and state."[135] Justice Black explained: "Here not only are the state's tax-supported public school buildings used for the dissemination of religious doctrines. The State also affords sectarian groups an invaluable aid in that it helps to provide pupils for their religious classes through use of the State's compulsory public school machinery. This is not separation of Church and State."[136]

A few years later, in *Zorach v. Clauson*, the Supreme Court upheld a school board policy that allowed students to be released, during the school day, for religious instruction outside the school.[137] Although Justice Douglas, writing for the Court, said that "[t]here cannot be the slightest doubt that the First Amendment reflects the philosophy that Church and State should be separated,"[138] he also said, "We are a religious people whose institutions presuppose a Supreme Being."[139] The Court concluded that allowing students to receive religious instruction during school hours was simply accommodating religion and not a violation of the establishment clause since government funds and facilities were not used. Douglas wrote: "We would have to press the concept of separation of Church and State to these extremes to condemn the present law on constitutional grounds. . . . When the state encourages religious instruction or cooperates with religious authorities by adjusting the schedule of public events to sectarian needs, it follows the best of our traditions. For it then respects the religious nature of our people and accommodates the public service to their spiritual needs."[140]

The Court distinguished *McCollum* because there "the classrooms were used for religious instruction and the force of the public school was used to promote that instruction."[141] In contrast, in *Zorach*, all of the religious education occurred off school premises.

[134] 333 U.S. 203 (1948).
[135] *Id.* at 211.
[136] *Id.* at 212.
[137] 343 U.S. 306 (1952).
[138] *Id.* at 312.
[139] *Id.* at 313.
[140] *Id.* at 313-314.
[141] *Id.* at 315.

School Prayers and Bible Reading

Few Supreme Court decisions have been as controversial as those that declared unconstitutional prayers and Bible readings in public schools. The Supreme Court has invalidated prayer in public schools, including voluntary prayers led by instructors and a government-mandated moment of "silence" for "meditation or silent prayer." The Court also has followed this reasoning to invalidate clergy-delivered prayers at public school graduations. The Court, however, has not yet ruled as to whether a government-mandated moment of silent reflection would be allowed; nor has it decided the constitutionality of student-delivered prayers at public school graduations.

Engel v. Vitale was the initial Supreme Court case holding prayers in public schools to be unconstitutional.[142] *Engel* invalidated a school policy of having a "non-denominational prayer," composed by the state's Board of Regents, recited at the beginning of each school day. The prayer was: "Almighty God, we acknowledge our dependence upon Thee, and we beg Thy blessings upon us, our parents, our teachers and our Country."[143]

The Court, in an opinion by Justice Black, said that "[t]here can be no doubt that New York's state prayer program officially establishes the religious beliefs embodied in the Regents' prayer. . . . Neither the fact that the prayer may be denominationally neutral nor the fact that its observance on the part of the students is voluntary can serve to free it from the limitations of the Establishment Clause."[144] The Court said that the establishment clause rests on the "belief that a union of government and religion tends to destroy government and to degrade religion. . . . The Establishment Clause thus stands as an expression of principle on the part of the Founders of our Constitution that religion is too personal, too sacred, too holy, to permit its 'unhallowed perversion' by a civil magistrate."[145]

The Court emphasized the unconstitutionality of the government writing prayers and directing that they be read within the public schools. Justice Black expressly rejected the argument that forbidding prayers constituted hostility to religion: "It is neither sacrilegious nor antireligious to say that each separate government in this country should stay out of the business of writing or sanctioning official prayers and leave that purely religious function to the people themselves and to those the people choose to look to for religious guidance."[146]

A year later, in *Abington School District v. Schempp*, the Court declared unconstitutional a state's law and a city's rule that required the reading, without comment, at the beginning of each school day of verses from the Bible and the recitation of the Lord's Prayer by students in unison.[147] Although *Schempp*, unlike *Engel*, did not involve a state-composed prayer, the laws requiring Bible reading and reciting of the Lord's Prayer were deemed to violate the establishment clause. The Court

---

[142] 370 U.S. 421 (1962).
[143] *Id.* at 422.
[144] *Id.* at 430.
[145] *Id.* at 431-432.
[146] *Id.* at 435.
[147] 374 U.S. 203 (1963).

emphasized that these religious exercises were prescribed as part of the curricular activities of students, conducted in school buildings, and supervised by teachers.

The Court distinguished studying the Bible in a literature or comparative religion course, which would be permissible. The Court said that "the exercises here do not fall into those categories. They are religious exercises, required by the States in violation of the command of the First Amendment that the Government maintain strict neutrality, neither aiding nor opposing religion."[148]

In *Wallace v. Jaffree*, the Court followed *Engel* and *Schempp* and declared unconstitutional an Alabama law that authorized a moment of silence in public schools for "meditation or voluntary prayer."[149] The legislative history of the law was clear that its purpose was to reintroduce prayer into the public schools.[150] The Court said that the record was "unambiguous" that the law "was not motivated by any clearly secular purpose—indeed, the statute had *no* secular purpose."[151]

The Court did not resolve the question of whether a moment of "silent reflection" would be permissible absent legislative history that indicated that its purpose was to reintroduce prayer into public schools. For some people, there seems little objectionable about teachers asking students to be silent for a moment at the beginning of the school day to collect their thoughts and mentally prepare for learning. But for others, government-mandated moments of silent reflection and prayer seem unnecessary; students surely have been saying silent prayers as long as teachers have been giving tests.[152]

The Court reaffirmed and extended the ban on prayers in the public school in *Lee v. Weisman*.[153] In *Lee*, the Court declared unconstitutional clergy-delivered prayers at public school graduations. Justice Kennedy, writing for the Court, said that cases such as *Engel*, *Schempp*, and *Wallace* were controlling and indistinguishable. He said: "[T]he controlling precedents as they relate to prayer and religious exercise in primary and secondary public schools compel the holding here. . . . The State's involvement in the school prayers challenged today violates these central principles [of the establishment clause.]"[154] The school decided that there should be a religious invocation and benediction, chose a clergy member to perform the prayers, and gave instructions concerning them.

Justice Kennedy stressed the inherent coercion in allowing prayer at graduations. Although no student was required to attend graduation, it is an important event in a person's life and students likely feel psychological pressure not to absent

---

[148] *Id.* at 225.

[149] 472 U.S. 38 (1985).

[150] Justice Powell noted in his concurring opinion that "[t]he record before us . . . makes clear that Alabama's purpose was solely religious in character." *Id.* at 65 (Powell, J., concurring).

[151] *Id.* at 56.

[152] *See also* Norman Redlich, Separation of Church and State: The Burger Court's Tortuous Journey, 60 Notre Dame L. Rev. 1094, 1136 (1985) ("When the state encourages silent prayer, it endorses a practice that is unacceptable to those whose faith requires that they pray only in a place of worship, or before some religious symbol. Some faiths may forbid praying with members of another faith, or with the opposite sex; some require believers to stand, or face a certain direction, or sit down, or wear certain apparel, or be led by ordained spiritual leaders.").

[153] 505 U.S. 577 (1992).

[154] *Id.* at 586-587.

themselves during the prayer. He wrote that there "are heightened concerns with protecting freedom of conscience from subtle coercive pressure in the elementary and secondary public schools. [What] to most believers may seem nothing more than a reasonable request that the nonbeliever respect their religious practices, in a school context may appear to the nonbeliever or dissenter to be an attempt to employ the machinery of the State to enforce a religious orthodoxy."[155]

Justice Blackmun, in a concurring opinion joined by Justices Stevens and O'Connor, emphasized that prayers in public schools are unconstitutional even in the absence of coercion. He said that "it is not enough that the government restrain from compelling religious practices: it must not engage in them either. . . . Our decisions have gone beyond prohibiting coercion."[156] Likewise, Justice Souter, in a concurring opinion joined by Justices Stevens and O'Connor, argued that the establishment clause is violated by prayers at public school events regardless of whether there is a finding of coercion.[157]

But Justice Scalia, joined by Chief Justice Rehnquist and Justices White and Thomas, vehemently dissented and disagreed with the view that there was anything coercive about a clergy-delivered prayer at a public school graduation.[158] Scalia said that even if a student did feel subtly coerced to stand during the prayer, this was acceptable because maintaining "respect for the religious observance of others is a fundamental civic virtue that government can and should cultivate."[159] For Scalia, the prohibition of prayer constitutes impermissible hostility to religion. He wrote: "The reader has been told much in this case about the personal interest of [the plaintiffs], and very little about the personal interests on the other side. They are not inconsequential. Church and state would not be such a difficult subject if religion were, as the Court apparently thinks it to be, some purely personal avocation that can be indulged entirely in secret, like pornography, in the privacy of one's room. For most believers it is not that, and has never been. . . . But the longstanding American tradition of prayer at official ceremonies displays with unmistakable clarity that the Establishment Clause does not forbid the government to accommodate it."[160]

Subsequent Supreme Court decisions concerning prayers in the public schools continue to find that such activity is impermissible at official school activities, particularly where the school encourages and facilitates prayer. In *Santa Fe Independent School District v. Doe*, the Supreme Court, in a 6-to-3 decision, held that student-delivered prayers at high school football games violate the establishment clause.[161] A public high school in Texas had a tradition of having a student deliver a prayer before varsity football games. After this was challenged in litigation, the school adopted a policy where students would hold two elections; one was to

---

[155] *Id.* at 592.
[156] *Id.* at 604, 606 (Blackmun, J., concurring).
[157] *Id.* at 618-619 (Souter, J., concurring).
[158] *Id.* at 632 (Scalia, J., dissenting).
[159] *Id.* at 638.
[160] *Id.* at 645.
[161] 530 U.S. 290 (2000).

decide whether to have invocations before football games and, if so, the second was to select the student to give the invocation.

Justice Stevens, writing for the Court, emphasized that the school had encouraged and facilitated the prayer at an official school event. The school claimed that the student prayers were private speech, but the Court emphatically disagreed. Justice Stevens explained: "[W]e are not persuaded that the pregame invocations should be regarded as 'private speech.' These invocations are authorized by a government policy and take place on government property at government-sponsored school-related events."[162] The Court noted how the school encouraged the delivery of prayers, both in its official policies and in its traditional support for prayer at football games. The result is both actual and likely perceived government endorsement for religion. Justice Stevens stated: "The actual or perceived endorsement of the message, moreover, is established by factors beyond just the text of the policy. Once the student speaker is selected and the message composed, the invocation is then delivered to a large audience assembled as part of a regularly scheduled, school-sponsored function conducted on school property. The message is broadcast over the school's public address system, which remains subject to the control of school officials."[163]

Justice Stevens also noted the coercive aspects of the school's policy in that many students—football players, band members, cheerleaders—were required to be present in order to receive academic credit, as well as the benefits from participating in an extracurricular activity. The Court said that forcing students to choose between attending the game and avoiding religion itself violated the establishment clause: "The Constitution, moreover, demands that the school may not force this difficult choice upon these students for it is a tenet of the First Amendment that the State cannot require one of its citizens to forfeit his or her rights and benefits as the price of resisting conformance to state-sponsored religious practice."[164]

It is notable that Justice Stevens's majority opinion avoided choosing among the theories of the establishment clause; he explained why the prayers failed scrutiny under any of the leading tests. The dissent, written by Chief Justice Rehnquist, saw the exclusion of prayer as undue hostility to religion. He wrote: "But even more disturbing than its holding is the tone of the Court's opinion; it bristles with hostility to all things religious in public life. Neither the holding nor the tone of the opinion is faithful to the meaning of the Establishment Clause, when it is recalled that George Washington himself, at the request of the very Congress which passed the Bill of Rights, proclaimed a day of 'public thanksgiving and prayer,' to be observed by acknowledging with grateful hearts the many and signal favors of Almighty God."[165] Chief Justice Rehnquist's dissent thus is similar to Justice Scalia's lament in dissent in *Lee v. Weisman* that the Court was wrongly ignoring the interests of those who want prayer.

---

[162] *Id.* at 302.
[163] *Id.* at 307.
[164] *Id.* at 312 (citations omitted).
[165] *Id.* at 318 (Rehnquist, C.J., dissenting).

Engel, Schempp, Wallace, Lee, and *Doe* establish that prayer—even if voluntary, nondenominational, or silent—is impermissible in public schools.[166] The cases embody the view that government-directed prayer is inherently religious activity and therefore does not belong in public schools. Students are required by compulsory attendance laws to be present, and even voluntary prayers are coercive.[167] Students who do not believe in religion or are part of religions that do not believe in prayers are inherently made to feel unwelcome and to be outsiders when prayer occurs in the classroom. Yet critics of the Court's decision argue that prayer should be allowed in schools because of its importance in students' lives and because it is not coercive so long as it is voluntary. Former Solicitor General Erwin Griswold said: "No compulsion is put upon him. He need not participate. But he, too, has the opportunity to be tolerant. He allows the majority of the group to follow their own tradition, perhaps coming to understand and to respect what they feel is significant to them."[168]

Doe is clear that prayer at school functions is impermissible if the government encourages or facilitates the religious activity. The unresolved question concerns the permissibility of prayer at school events when there is not such participation by the government. For example, are student-delivered prayers at public school graduations constitutional? After *Doe,* such prayers would be clearly impermissible if the school encouraged them or significantly participated in facilitating their occurrence. The unresolved question is whether the establishment clause is violated if a student makes the voluntary choice to deliver or lead a prayer at graduation ceremonies. Is *Lee* controlling in prohibiting this, or is the exclusion of prayer a violation of the students' free speech rights? The Circuits are split on this question, and the Supreme Court has not yet considered it, though it has had the opportunity to do so.[169]

---

[166] The one situation where prayer would be permissible would be if it were conducted by students as part of a noncurricular use of school facilities. The Supreme Court has held that government may not exclude student religious groups from using school facilities on the same terms as nonreligious groups (Widmar v. Vincent, 454 U.S. 263 (1981)) and has upheld the federal Equal Access Act that prohibits schools receiving federal funds from discriminating against student groups in access to facilities based on their religious or philosophical activities or beliefs. Board of Educ. of Westside Community Schools v. Mergens, 496 U.S. 226 (1990). *Widmar* and *Mergens* are discussed in detail in §12.2.4.

[167] *See* Paul G. Kauper, Prayer, Public Schools and the Supreme Court, 61 Mich. L. Rev. 1031, 1046 (1963) ("immature and impressionable children are susceptible to a pressure to conform and to participate in the expression of religious beliefs that carry the sanction and compulsion of the state's authority").

[168] Erwin Griswold, Absolute Is in the Dark: A Discussion of the Approach of the Supreme Court to Constitutional Questions, 8 Utah L. Rev. 167, 177 (1963).

[169] *See, e.g.,* Adler v. Duval County School Bd., 250 F.3d 1330 (11th Cir. 2001) (unrestricted student message at graduation did not facially violate the establishment clause); *cf.* Cole v. Oroville Union High School Dist., 228 F.3d 1092 (9th Cir. 2000) (school district's refusal to allow student to deliver a sectarian invocation at graduation was necessary to avoid an establishment clause violation).

Curricular Decisions

The Supreme Court has declared unconstitutional government decisions concerning the curriculum that were motivated by religious purposes. These cases primarily have concerned state laws prohibiting the teaching of evolution or requiring the teaching of "creationism" when evolution is taught.[170]

In *Epperson v. Arkansas*, the Court declared unconstitutional an Arkansas law that made it unlawful for a teacher in a state-supported school or university "to teach the theory or doctrine that mankind ascended or descended from a lower order of animals" or "to adopt or use in any such institution a textbook that teaches" this theory.[171] The Court held that the law prohibiting teaching of evolution was motivated by a religious purpose and thus violated the establishment clause. The Court explained: "The overriding fact is that Arkansas' law selects from the body of knowledge a particular segment which it proscribes for the sole reason that it is deemed to conflict with a particular religious doctrine; that is, with a particular interpretation of the Book of Genesis by a particular religious group."[172] The Court observed that "[t]here is and can be no doubt that the First Amendment does not permit the State to require that teaching and learning must be tailored to the principles or prohibitions of any religious sect or dogma."[173] The Arkansas law did exactly that: preclude teaching of evolution because it was a theory opposed by some religions.[174]

In *Edwards v. Aguillard*, the Court followed this same reasoning and declared unconstitutional a Louisiana law that prohibited the teaching of the theory of evolution in public schools unless accompanied by instruction in "creation science."[175] The Court noted that, as in *Epperson*, the "same historic and contemporaneous antagonisms between the teachings of certain religious denominations and the teaching of evolution are present in this case."[176] The Court said that the law's "primary purpose was to change the science curriculum of public schools in order to provide persuasive advantage to a particular religious doctrine that rejects the factual basis of evolution in its entirety."[177] The Court thus concluded: "Because the primary purpose of the Creationism Act is to advance a particular religious belief, the Act endorses religion in violation of the First Amendment."[178]

---

[170] Another example is *Stone v. Graham*, 449 U.S. 39 (1980), where the Court declared unconstitutional, because of the absence of a secular purpose, a state law requiring the Ten Commandments to be posted in every public school classroom. *Stone* is discussed in §12.2.3.

[171] 393 U.S. 97, 98-99 (1968).

[172] *Id.* at 103.

[173] *Id.* at 106.

[174] A similar law in Tennessee was the subject of the famous Scopes trial. The case, however, never made it past the trial level, where the famous battle occurred between William Jennings Bryan and Clarence Darrow. Nor did a court declare the antievolution law unconstitutional. *See* Irving Stone, Clarence Darrow for the Defense 426-465 (1941); Edward J. Larson, Summer for the Gods (1997).

[175] 482 U.S. 578 (1987).

[176] *Id.* at 591.

[177] *Id.* at 592.

[178] *Id.* at 593.

§12.2.5.2 Religion as a Part of Government Activities: Religious Symbols on Government Property

Nativity Scenes and Menorahs

The Supreme Court has ruled that nativity scenes, menorahs, and other religious symbols are allowed on government property as long as they do not convey symbolic government endorsement for religion or for a particular religion. In *Lynch v. Donnelly*, the Supreme Court upheld the constitutionality of a nativity scene in a park.[179] The Christmas display included, among other things, a Santa Claus house, reindeer pulling Santa's sleigh, a Christmas tree, hundreds of colored lights, and a crèche. All of the display was owned by the city and placed in a park maintained by a nonprofit organization.

The Court, in an opinion by Chief Justice Burger, found that the nativity scene did not violate the establishment clause. Burger began by reviewing the many ways in which religion has traditionally been a part of government, from President George Washington's Thanksgiving Day proclamation to the slogan "In God We Trust" on currency.[180] Burger concluded that the nativity scene was permissible because it was motivated by a secular purpose: celebrating Christmas. He wrote: "The narrow question is whether there is a secular purpose for Pawtucket's display of the crèche. The display is sponsored by the city to celebrate the Holiday and to depict the origins of that Holiday. These are legitimate secular purposes."[181]

Yet from the perspective of both Christians and non-Christians this view of the nativity scene seems questionable. The crèche is a "re-creation of an event that lies at the heart of the Christian faith."[182] For Christians, it is a basic religious symbol and therefore is likely perceived that way by non-Christians as well.

In *Allegheny County v. Greater Pittsburgh ACLU*, the Court recognized the inherent religious nature of the nativity scene.[183] As described above, this case involved two December holiday displays: One was a crèche placed in a staircase display by the Roman Catholic Church; the other was a December holiday display that included a menorah, a Christmas tree, and a sign saluting liberty. The Court, without majority opinion, invalidated the nativity scene, but allowed the menorah. The key difference, at least for Justices Blackmun and O'Connor who cast the decisive votes, was that the nativity scene was by itself and thus conveyed symbolic endorsement for Christianity; the menorah, in contrast, was accompanied by symbols of other religions and secular symbols.[184]

Three Justices—Stevens, Brennan, and Marshall—would have found that both the nativity scene and the menorah on government property violated

---

[179] 465 U.S. 668 (1984).

[180] *Id.* at 675-676.

[181] *Id.* at 681.

[182] *Id.* at 711 (Brennan, J., dissenting).

[183] 492 U.S. 573 (1989). This case is discussed in §12.2.1.

[184] *Id.* at 632 (O'Connor, concurring in part and concurring in the judgment).

the establishment clause.[185] Four Justices—Kennedy, Rehnquist, Scalia, and White—argued that allowing neither symbol violated the establishment clause.[186] Justices O'Connor and Blackmun felt that the nativity scene, standing alone in the large display case in the county courthouse, constituted symbolic endorsement for Christianity. The menorah, on the other hand, was not such an endorsement because it was accompanied by a Christmas tree and a sign proclaiming liberty. Thus, the decision was 5 to 4 that the nativity scene was unconstitutional and 6 to 3 that the menorah was permissible.

Other Religious Symbols on Government Property

The importance of the endorsement test in evaluating the constitutionality of religious symbols on government property is reflected in *Capitol Square Review and Advisory Board v. Pinette.*[187] As described above,[188] *Pinette* involved the Ku Klux Klan placing a large Latin cross in a public park across from the Ohio state capitol. The Supreme Court, again without majority opinion, found that the government's attempt to exclude the cross was unconstitutional discrimination against religious speech.

Justice Scalia wrote the plurality opinion, joined by Rehnquist, Kennedy, and Thomas. He emphasized that the First Amendment's protection of speech includes religious expression and concluded that excluding the cross was impermissible content-based discrimination.[189] He concluded that "[r]eligious expression cannot violate the Establishment Clause where it (1) is purely private and (2) occurs in a traditional or designated forum, publicly announced and open to all on equal terms."[190]

Justice O'Connor concurred in part and concurred in the judgment and was joined by Justices Souter and Breyer. O'Connor said that the key question was whether allowing the cross would be perceived, by the reasonable observer, as government symbolic endorsement for religion.[191] O'Connor said that a reasonable observer would see the sign indicating the private origin of the cross and also would know the history surrounding its placement.

Justices Stevens and Ginsburg dissented. Justice Stevens argued for a strong presumption against allowing such religious symbols on government property. He also criticized Justice O'Connor's focus on the educated observer and said that the establishment clause was violated because "[t]he 'reasonable observer' of any symbol placed unattended in front of any capitol in the world will normally assume that the sovereign—which is not only the owner of that parcel of real estate but also the lawgiver for the surrounding territory—has sponsored and facilitated its

---

[185] *Id.* at 646 (Stevens, J., concurring in part and dissenting in part).
[186] *Id.* at 655 (Kennedy, J., concurring in the judgment in part and dissenting in part).
[187] 515 U.S. 753 (1995).
[188] *Pinette* is discussed in §§12.2.1 and 12.2.4.
[189] 515 U.S. at 760.
[190] *Id.* at 770.
[191] *Id.* at 773. (O'Connor, J., concurring in part and concurring in the judgment).

message."[192] Justice Ginsburg dissented and stressed the inadequacy of the disclaimer of government involvement accompanying the cross.[193]

In 2005, the Court considered two cases concerning Ten Commandments displays on government property. In *McCreary County, Kentucky v. ACLU of Kentucky*, the Court, by a 5-to-4 decision, ruled that Ten Commandments displays in Kentucky county courthouses were unconstitutional because the government had the impermissible purpose of advancing religion.[194] The counties were clear that they wanted the Ten Commandments posted because of the religious content and significance of the Decalogue. In *Van Orden v. Perry*, the Court, in a 5-to-4 decision without a majority opinion, upheld the constitutionality of a six-foot high, three-foot wide Ten Commandments monument that sits between the Texas State Capitol and the Texas Supreme Court.[195] Chief Justice Rehnquist wrote a plurality opinion joined by Justices Scalia, Kennedy, and Thomas, and declared that the government may place religious symbols on government property. Justice Breyer concurred in the judgment and stressed that the presence of the monument for over 40 years, the surrounding secular displays and monuments, and its donation by the Fraternal Order of Eagles all convinced him that the government was not impermissibly symbolically endorsing religion.

In trying to make sense of these decisions it is important to remember that only one Justice—Stephen Breyer—saw a distinction between them. Four Justices—Rehnquist, Scalia, Kennedy, and Thomas—would have upheld both displays. Four Justices—Stevens, O'Connor, Souter, and Ginsburg—would have invalidated both. Only Breyer was in the majority, both in striking down the Kentucky display and in upholding the Texas monument.

Five Justices, including Breyer, agreed that the government cannot place religious symbols on government property in a manner that symbolically endorses religion. For these five Justices, in determining whether a particular display is a symbolic endorsement of religion, courts must look at its history, its purpose, and its context. For Justice Breyer, these were the key factors that distinguished the Kentucky and the Texas displays. But this means that every religious symbol on government property will have to be analyzed based on its unique facts and circumstances.

However, it must be remembered that Justice O'Connor was one of the five Justices in the majority in *McCreary County* and one of the five who argued that the government may not symbolically endorse religion. With her departure and replacement by Justice Alito, the law could change dramatically. Also, it is unknown where Justices Sotomayor and Kagan will line up on this issue, though few expect them to be with the conservatives.

The only Roberts Court case so far concerning religious symbols on government property, *Salazar v. Buono*, did not change the law, but it also did not decide

---

[192] *Id.* at 801-802.
[193] *Id.* at 812 (Ginsburg, J., dissenting).
[194] 545 U.S. 844 (2005).
[195] 545 U.S. 677 (2005).

the establishment clause question presented.[196] The case concerned a large cross in a federal park in the Mojave Desert. A federal district court found that this violated the establishment clause and the Ninth Circuit affirmed. Both courts reasoned that a cross is a quintessential religious symbol and only of Christian faiths. Congress then passed a law transferring ownership of the small parcel of land where the cross is located to a private veterans group. The district court found that this was a sham transfer and the Ninth Circuit once more affirmed. The courts stressed that the reasonable observer seeing a cross in a large federal park would still see this as a government endorsement of religion. Also, the Federal Park Service still is responsible for maintaining the land around the cross. Besides, there was the concern that the government could put a religious symbol any place on government property and make it permissible by transferring the small piece of land where it is located.

The Supreme Court, in a 5-4 decision without a majority opinion, reversed the Ninth Circuit. Justice Kennedy announced the judgment of the Court in an opinion joined by Chief Justice Roberts and Justice Alito. He said that the lower courts had not adequately considered whether the federal statute transferring ownership was a basis for modifying the injunction to remove the cross. Justice Kennedy wrote: "The District Court failed to consider whether, in light of the change in law and circumstances effected by the land-transfer statute, the 'reasonable observer' standard continued to be the appropriate framework through which to consider the Establishment Clause concerns invoked to justify the requested relief. As a general matter, courts considering Establishment Clause challenges do not inquire into 'reasonable observer' perceptions with respect to objects on private land."[197]

Justices Scalia and Thomas concurred in the judgment. They would have dismissed the case on standing grounds, concluding that no one is injured by the presence of a religious symbol on government property.[198] Justice Scalia concluded his opinion by stating: "But adhering to Article III's limits upon our jurisdiction respects the authority of those whom the people have chosen to make and carry out the laws. In this case Congress has determined that transferring the memorial to private hands best serves the public interest and complies with the Constitution, and the Executive defends that decision and seeks to carry it out. Federal courts have no warrant to revisit that decision—and to risk replacing the people's judgment with their own — unless and until a proper case has been brought before them. This is not it."[199] This would clearly suggest that Justices Scalia and Thomas believe that no one is injured by a religious symbol on government property and would deny standing to all such challenges.

Justices Stevens, Ginsburg, Breyer, and Sotomayor dissented. They would have affirmed the district court and the Ninth Circuit, finding that a cross in the middle of a federal park violates the establishment clause and that the transfer of ownership to a private veterans group does not make this permissible.

---

[196]   130 S. Ct. 1803 (2010).
[197]   *Id.* at 1819.
[198]   *Id.* at 1824 (Scalia, J., dissenting).
[199]   *Id.* at 1828.

Thus, the case decided relatively little about the establishment clause. But with Justice Alito having replaced Justice O'Connor, the prospect for a major change in the law in this area remains.

§12.2.5.3   Religion as a Part of Government Activities: Prayers Before Legislative Sessions

Marsh v. Chambers

In *Marsh v. Chambers*, the Supreme Court upheld the constitutionality of a state legislature employing a Presbyterian minister for 18 years to begin each session with a prayer.[200] The Nebraska legislature had employed Robert E. Palmer, a Presbyterian minister, since 1965 to open each legislative day with a prayer. The Court upheld this as constitutional because of the long history and tradition of religious invocations before legislative sessions.

Chief Justice Burger, writing for the Court, said that "[t]he opening of sessions of legislative and other deliberative public bodies with prayer is deeply embedded in the history and tradition of this country. From colonial times through the founding of the Republic and ever since, the practice of legislative prayer has coexisted with the principles of disestablishment and religious freedom."[201] After reviewing this history in detail, Burger concluded that "[t]his unique history leads us to accept the interpretation of the First Amendment draftsmen who saw no real threat to the Establishment Clause arising from a practice of prayer similar to that now challenged."[202]

It is notable that the Court decided the issue solely on the basis of historical practice and did not apply the *Lemon* test in evaluating the constitutionality of legislative prayers and state employment of a minister for almost 20 years. The Court said: "In light of the unambiguous and unbroken history of more than 200 years, there can be no doubt that the practice of opening legislative sessions with prayer has become part of the fabric of our society. . . . Nor is the compensation of the chaplain from public funds a reason to invalidate the Nebraska Legislature's chaplaincy: Remuneration is grounded in historic practice initiated . . . by the same Congress that drafted the Establishment Clause of the First Amendment."[203] The dissent, though, stressed that the purpose of legislative prayers and paying a minister seems obviously to advance religion.[204] For the dissent, paying a minister, from one faith, for 18 years from public funds clearly seems to have the effect of advancing that religion and of entangling government with religion.[205]

---

[200] 463 U.S. 783 (1983).

[201] *Id.* at 786.

[202] *Id.* at 791.

[203] *Id.* at 792-793.

[204] *See id.* at 797 (Brennan, J., dissenting) ("That the 'purpose' of legislative prayer is preeminently religious rather than secular seems to me to be self-evident.").

[205] *Id.* at 798-799.

Town of Greece v. Galloway

The Court returned to the issue of prayers before legislative sessions in *Town of Greece v. Galloway*, which held that it does not violate the establishment clause for a town board to begin virtually every meeting over a ten-year period with a prayer by a Christian minister.[206] The Town of Greece is a suburb of Rochester, New York of about 100,000 people. Its town board opened meetings with a moment of silence until 1999 when the town supervisors initiated a policy change. The town began inviting ministers to begin meetings each month with a prayer. From 1999-2007, the town invited exclusively Christian ministers, most of whom gave explicitly Christian prayers.

In 2007, complaints were made to the Town Board about this and for four months clergy from other religions were invited. But then for the next 18 months, the Town Board reverted to inviting only Christian clergy and their prayers were almost always Christian in their content.

The Court, in a 5-4 decision, held that the Town of Greece did not violate the establishment clause. The Court stressed the long history of prayers before legislative sessions, including explicitly Christian prayers, and said that *Marsh* "teaches . . . that the Establishment Clause must be interpreted 'by reference to historical practices and understandings.' "[207] The Court said that for it to require nonsectarian prayers would put the government and the courts unduly in the position of monitoring the content of the prayers delivered by others: "To hold that invocations must be nonsectarian would force the legislatures that sponsor prayers and the courts that are asked to decide these cases to act as supervisors and censors of religious speech, a rule that would involve government in religious matters to a far greater degree than is the case under the town's current practice of neither editing or approving prayers in advance nor criticizing their content after the fact."[208]

The Court expressed great deference to the government in having prayers before legislative sessions and held: "Absent a pattern of prayers that over time denigrate, proselytize, or betray an impermissible government purpose, a challenge based solely on the content of a prayer will not likely establish a constitutional violation."[209]

Justice Thomas wrote an opinion concurring in part and concurring in the judgment, which was joined in part by Justice Scalia. Writing for just himself, Justice Thomas reiterated his view that the establishment clause does not apply to state and local governments; it was, in his view, meant only to keep Congress from creating a national church that could rival state churches.[210] In a part of the opinion joined by Justice Scalia, Justice Thomas argued that the establishment

---

[206] 134 S. Ct. 1811 (2014).
[207] *Id.* at 1819.
[208] *Id.* at 1822.
[209] *Id.* at 1825.
[210] *Id.* at 1835 (Thomas, J., concurring in part and concurring in the judgment). Justice Alito also wrote a concurring opinion.

clause is violated only if there is "actual legal coercion" to participate in religious activities.[211]

Justice Kagan wrote a dissent, which was joined by Justices Ginsburg, Breyer, and Sotomayor.[212] The dissent found that the Town Board violated the establishment clause by inviting virtually only Christian clergy over a long period of time and their usually delivering explicitly Christian prayers. Justice Kagan wrote: "[T]he Town of Greece's prayer practices violate that norm of religious equality—the breathtakingly generous constitutional idea that our public institutions belong no less to the Buddhist or Hindu than to the Methodist or Episcopalian."[213] Justice Kagan explicitly distinguished *Marsh v. Chambers*: "The practice at issue here differs from the one sustained in *Marsh* because Greece's town meetings involve participation by ordinary citizens, and the invocations given—directly to those citizens—were predominantly sectarian in content. Still more, Greece's Board did nothing to recognize religious diversity: In arranging for clergy members to open each meeting, the Town never sought (except briefly when this suit was filed) to involve, accommodate, or in any way reach out to adherents of non-Christian religions. So month in and month out for over a decade, prayers steeped in only one faith, addressed toward members of the public, commenced meetings to discuss local affairs and distribute government benefits. In my view, that practice does not square with the First Amendment's promise that every citizen, irrespective of her religion, owns an equal share in her government."[214]

The practical effect of *Town of Greece v. Galloway* is that there will be Christian prayers before legislative sessions in many parts of the country. But it certainly will not end litigation over legislative prayers. The Court said that there cannot be "a pattern of prayers that over time denigrate, proselytize, or betray an impermissible government purpose."[215] But what this means and how it will be applied are uncertain.

§12.2.5.4   Ceremonial Deism?

In *Elk Grove Unified School Dist. v. Newdow*, Justice O'Connor attempted to offer a principle to separate the permissible from the impermissible in the area of religious involvement in government.[216] The issue in *Newdow* was whether the words "under God" in the Pledge of Allegiance violate the establishment clause in public schools. The Supreme Court dismissed the case for lack of standing on the grounds that Michael Newdow, the plaintiff, lacked standing to sue on behalf

---

[211] *Id.* at 1838.

[212] Justice Breyer also wrote a dissenting opinion and stated: "[T]he town of Greece failed to make reasonable efforts to include prayer givers of minority faiths, with the result that, although it is a community of several faiths, its prayer givers were almost exclusively persons of a single faith. Under these circumstances, I would affirm the judgment of the Court of Appeals that Greece's prayer practice violated the Establishment Clause." *Id.* at 1841 (Breyer, J., dissenting).

[213] *Id.* at 1841 (Kagan, J., dissenting).

[214] *Id.* at 1841-1842 (Kagan, J., dissenting).

[215] *Id.* at 1825.

[216] 542 U.S. 1, 36-44 (2004) (O'Connor, J., concurring in the judgment).

of his daughter because he did not have legal custody over her. Justice O'Connor wrote an opinion concurring in the judgment in which she urged the Court to draw a distinction based on whether an activity was "ceremonial deism."

Justice O'Connor identified four factors that would make religious presence in government permissible ceremonial deism, rather than a violation of the establishment clause: "History and ubiquity," "Absence of worship or prayer," "Absence of reference to particular religion" and "Minimal religious content."[217] For example, Justice O'Connor found that "under God" in the Pledge of Allegiance was permissible because of a long history, the absence of worship or prayer, the absence of reference to a particular religion, and minimal religious content. Obviously, these factors may point in differing directions and require a balancing by a court as to which considerations deserve the most weight. But they do provide criteria that the Court may use in future years for deciding when the presence of religion in government violates the establishment clause.

§12.2.6   When Can Government Give Aid to Religion?

The Need for Line-Drawing

Many establishment clause cases have involved the issue of government assistance to religion. Decisions in this area are numerous, but often difficult to reconcile. The Court inevitably is involved in line-drawing. Total government subsidy of churches or parochial schools undoubtedly would violate the establishment clause. Indeed, the famous statement of Thomas Jefferson concerning the need for a wall separating church and state and James Madison's Memorial and Remonstrance Against Religious Assessments were made in the context of opposing a state tax to aid the church.[218] But it also would be clearly unconstitutional if the government provided no public services—no police or fire protection, no sanitation services—to religious institutions. Such discrimination surely would violate equal protection and infringe on free exercise of religion.[219]

Therefore, the Court must draw a line between aid that is permissible and that which is forbidden. No bright-line test exists or likely ever will exist. Any aid provided to a religious institution or a parochial school frees resources that can be used to further its religious mission.[220] The dominant approach for the past half

---

[217] *Id.* at 36-44.

[218] Madison's Remonstrance is reprinted in Everson v. Board of Educ., 330 U.S. 1, 63 (1947).

[219] *See, e.g.,* Lemon v. Kurtzman, 403 U.S. at 614 ("Fire inspections, building and zoning regulations, and state requirements under compulsory school attendance laws are examples of necessary and permissible contacts.").

[220] In the initial case concerning government aid to parochial schools, *Everson v. Board of Education,* 330 U.S. 1 (1947), the Court upheld the constitutionality of the government's reimbursing parents for the costs of bus transportation to and from parochial school. The Court recognized that "[t]here is even a possibility that some of the children might not be sent to the church schools if the parents were compelled . . . to pay their children's bus fares out of their own pockets . . . when transportation to a public school would have been paid for by the State." *Id.* at 17.

century has been to apply the test from *Lemon v. Kurtzman* and ask whether there is a secular purpose for the assistance, whether the aid has the effect of advancing religion, and whether the particular form of assistance causes excessive government entanglement with religion.[221] But not every case has used the *Lemon* test.[222]

In one of its most recent decisions concerning aid to parochial schools, *Mitchell v. Helms*,[223] there was no approach that received support from a majority of the Justices. As discussed in more detail below, the issue in *Mitchell* was whether the government could provide instructional equipment, such as computers and audiovisual equipment, to parochial schools. The Court overruled earlier decisions precluding such aid,[224] but without a majority opinion. Justice Thomas, in a plurality opinion joined by Chief Justice Rehnquist and Justices Scalia and Kennedy, said that any aid—even for religious education—should be allowed, so long as the government does not discriminate among religions.[225] Justice O'Connor, in an opinion concurring in the judgment joined by Justice Breyer, said that aid to parochial schools is permissible so long as it is not actually used for religious purposes.[226] Finally, Justices Stevens, Souter, and Ginsburg dissented and argued that the Court should have adhered to its prior approach precluding aid if it is of a type that likely could be used for religious instruction.[227]

Therefore, it is quite uncertain how the Court will deal with important future issues concerning aid to religious institutions, such as school vouchers and aid to faith-based organizations (often called charitable choice).[228] Especially with Justice Alito having replaced Justice O'Connor, there could be a significant shift in the Court and it may be that there will be a majority (Chief Justice Roberts and Justices Scalia, Kennedy, Thomas, and Alito) willing to allow much more aid to parochial schools.

---

[221] 403 U.S. 602 (1971), discussed above in §12.2.3.

[222] It also should be noted that such cases raise standing questions because they usually involve taxpayers challenging government expenditures. The Court has allowed federal taxpayers to challenge government expenditures of funds, Flast v. Cohen, 392 U.S. 83 (1968), but not government grants of property to religious institutions, Valley Forge Christian College v. Americans United for Separation of Church and State, 454 U.S. 464 (1982). However, the Court has allowed state and local taxpayers to challenge both funding and material support for religious schools. Grand Rapids School Dist. v. Ball, 473 U.S. 373, 380 n.5 (1985). The standing issue is discussed more fully in §2.5.5.

[223] 530 U.S. 793 (2000).

[224] Meek v. Pittenger, 421 U.S. 349 (1975); Wolman v. Walter, 433 U.S. 229 (1977) (precluding the government from giving aid to parochial schools because of the possibility that it could be used for religious instruction).

[225] *Mitchell*, 530 U.S. at 809-810.

[226] *Id.* at 836, 840 (O'Connor, J., concurring).

[227] *Id.* at 867, 868-869 (Souter, J., dissenting).

[228] For a discussion of constitutional issues concerning "charitable choice," *see* David J. Freedman, Wielding the Ax of Neutrality: The Constitutional Status of Charitable Choice in the Wake of *Mitchell v. Helms*, 35 U. Rich. L. Rev. 313 (2001); Alan E. Brownstein, Interpreting the Religion Clauses in Terms of Liberty, Equality, and Free Speech Values—A Critical Analysis of "Neutrality Theory" and Charitable Choice, 13 Notre Dame J.L. Ethics & Pub. Poly. 243 (1999). In *Hein v. Freedom from Religion Foundation, Inc.*, 551 U.S. 587 (2007), the Court dismissed on standing grounds a challenge to the Bush administration's use of executive revenue to facilitate government funds going to faith-based institutions. This case is discussed in §2.5.5.

There have been four major areas where the Court has considered government aid to religion: tax exemptions for religious institutions, assistance to parochial elementary and secondary schools, aid to religious colleges and universities, and assistance to religious institutions other than schools. These are discussed, in turn, in §§12.2.6.1 to 12.2.6.4.

§12.2.6.1   Tax Exemptions for Religious Organizations

Are the Tax Exemptions Available Only for Religions?

Tax exemptions that benefit only religion are unconstitutional, but those that benefit other groups along with religion, such as charitable and educational institutions, are permissible. In *Walz v. Tax Commission*, the Court upheld a state law that provided property tax exemptions for real or personal property used exclusively for religious, educational, or charitable purposes.[229] The plaintiffs argued that the establishment clause was violated by the tax exemption for religious property that was used solely for religious worship. The Supreme Court disagreed and emphasized that the government "granted exemption to all houses of religious worship within a broad class of property owned by nonprofit, quasi-public corporations which include hospitals, libraries, playgrounds, scientific, professional, historical, and patriotic groups."[230]

The Court said that "[t]he legislative purpose of a property tax exemption is neither the advancement nor the inhibition of religion; it is neither sponsorship nor hostility."[231] Rather, the goal is to help nonprofit institutions that the government regards as important to the community. The Court also concluded that granting the tax exemption did not entail excessive government involvement with religion. In fact, the Court said that "[e]limination of exemption would tend to expand the involvement of government by giving rise to tax valuation of church property, tax liens, tax foreclosures, and the direct confrontations and conflicts that follow in the train of those legal processes."[232]

In contrast, in *Texas Monthly, Inc. v. Bullock*, the Court declared unconstitutional a tax exemption that was available only for religious organizations.[233] A Texas law provided an exemption from the state sales and use tax for periodicals that were published or distributed by a religious faith and that consisted solely of writings promulgating the teaching of the faith, and for books that consisted wholly of writings sacred to a religious faith. The plurality opinion by Justice Brennan, and joined by Justices Marshall and Stevens, emphasized that *Walz* was distinguishable because there "the benefits derived by religious organizations flowed to a large

---

[229]   397 U.S. 664 (1970).
[230]   *Id.* at 673.
[231]   *Id.* at 672.
[232]   *Id.* at 674.
[233]   489 U.S. 1 (1989).

number of nonreligious groups as well."[234] Justice Brennan explained: "Insofar as that subsidy is conferred upon a wide array of nonsectarian groups as well as religious organizations . . . , the fact that religious groups benefit incidentally does not deprive the subsidy of the secular purpose and primary effect mandated by the Establishment Clause. However, when government directs a subsidy exclusively to religious organizations that is not required by the Free Exercise Clause . . . , it provide[s] unjustifiable awards of assistance to religious organizations and cannot but 'convey a message of endorsement' to slighted members of the community."[235]

Justice Scalia dissented and was joined by Chief Justice Rehnquist and Justice Kennedy. Scalia objected in strong language claiming that "[a]s a judicial demolition project today's decision is impressive,"[236] and that the "decision introduces a new strain of irrationality in our Religion Clause jurisprudence."[237] Scalia lamented that laws such as this, which existed in 15 states, were declared unconstitutional. For the dissent, the tax exemption for religious publications was a permissible accommodation of religion and did not have the purpose or effect of advancing religion or entail excessive government entanglement with religion.

Thus, *Walz* and *Texas Monthly* together indicate that states may give tax exemptions to religious groups only if nonreligious charitable organizations also are beneficiaries. A tax exemption solely for religious groups violates the establishment clause.[238]

§12.2.6.2 Aid to Parochial Elementary and Secondary Schools

Criteria for Evaluating Whether Aid Is Permissible

The most frequent source of litigation, by far, concerning the constitutionality of government aid to religious institutions has concerned assistance to parochial elementary and secondary schools. The Court has considered the constitutionality of a vast array of different types of assistance, ranging from tuition tax credits to textbooks to audiovisual equipment to medical diagnostic tests to many other kinds of aid.

The decisions often seem difficult to reconcile. For example, the Court has upheld the government providing buses to take children to and from parochial schools,[239] but not buses to take parochial school students on field trips.[240] The Court has permitted the government to pay for administering standard-

---

[234] *Id.* at 11 (plurality opinion).

[235] *Id.* at 14-15. The Court also rejected the argument that the denial of a tax exemption to religion would violate the free exercise clause. This aspect of the case is discussed below in §12.3.2.2.

[236] *Id.* at 29 (Scalia, J., dissenting).

[237] *Id.* at 45.

[238] However, the Court upheld an exemption solely for religious groups from Title VII's prohibition of employment discrimination based on religion. *See* Corporation of the Presiding Bishop of the Church of Jesus Christ of Latter-Day Saints v. Amos, 483 U.S. 327 (1987), discussed in §12.2.3.

[239] Everson v. Board of Educ., 330 U.S. 1 (1947).

[240] Wolman v. Walter, 433 U.S. 229 (1977).

ized tests in parochial schools,[241] but not for essay examinations assessing writing achievement.[242]

Although these distinctions often seem arbitrary, it is possible to identify several criteria that explain them. While not every case fits the pattern, in general, the Court is likely to uphold aid if three criteria are met. First, the aid must be available to all students enrolled in public and parochial schools; aid that is available only to parochial school students is sure to be invalidated. Second, the aid is more likely to be allowed if it is provided directly to the students than if it is provided to the schools. Third, the aid will be permitted if it is not actually used for religious instruction.

These criteria help explain the seemingly arbitrary distinctions described above. For example, buses to take children to and from school are provided to students at all schools and are not involved in education itself, but buses for field trips might be to see cathedrals or religious icons. The content of state-prescribed standardized tests is secular, but teacher-written essay examinations might be on religious subjects. Each of the three criteria is examined in turn.

In examining these criteria, it is important to recognize the extent to which the law in this area is changing and that some of the earlier decisions may be vulnerable. In the last few years, the Court has overruled a number of precedents limiting aid to parochial schools. In 1997, in *Agostini v. Felton*,[243] the Court expressly overruled *Aguilar v. Felton*,[244] which had ruled that public school teachers could not go on the premises of parochial schools to provide religious education. In 2000, in *Mitchell v. Helms*,[245] the Court overruled *Wolman v. Walter*[246] and *Meek v. Pittenger*,[247] which had prohibited the government from giving aid to parochial schools. In 2002, in *Zelman v. Simmons-Harris*,[248] the Court upheld voucher programs that allowed use of the aid in religious schools, taking a very different approach than it did in *Committee for Public Education v. Nyquist*.[249] Other precedents limiting aid to parochial schools also might be reconsidered in the future.

The uncertainty is compounded by the lack of a majority supporting a test for evaluating the constitutionality of government aid to parochial schools. In *Agostini*, at the end of the majority opinion, Justice O'Connor purported to summarize the current law regarding aid to parochial schools as prohibiting assistance (1) if it is used for government indoctrination in religion, (2) if the aid favors some religions over others by defining its recipients by reference to religion, or (3) if the aid creates an excessive government entanglement with religion.[250] This might be seen as a new test allowing more government aid to religion or, depending on how

---

[241] Committee for Pub. Educ. and Religious Liberty v. Regan, 444 U.S. 646 (1980).
[242] Levitt v. Committee for Pub. Educ., 413 U.S. 472 (1973).
[243] 521 U.S. 203 (1997).
[244] 473 U.S. 402 (1985).
[245] 530 U.S. 793 (2000).
[246] 433 U.S. 229 (1977).
[247] 421 U.S. 349 (1975).
[248] 536 U.S. 639 (2002).
[249] 413 U.S. 756 (1973).
[250] 521 U.S. at 234.

its requirements are interpreted, it might be seen as restating in different words existing law.

In *Mitchell v. Helms*, in 2000, Justice Thomas's plurality opinion invoked and applied this test, but five Justices rejected his approach. As described below, in *Mitchell*, four Justices would allow any aid to parochial schools, so long as the government treats all religions equally. Two Justices would allow aid so long as it is not actually used for religious education. And three Justices would allow assistance to parochial schools only if it is a type that likely cannot be used for religious instruction.

All of this, together with four new Justices since *Mitchell v. Helms*, make it very difficult to state the current law or predict what the Court will do with regard to aid to parochial schools. There now may be a majority willing to reconsider the law in this area and allow much more aid to parochial schools.

Is the Aid Available to All Students?

Aid that is available only to parochial school students is sure to be invalidated, but that same assistance is likely to be allowed if it is given to public school students as well and meets the other criteria. For example, in *Committee for Public Education v. Nyquist*[251] and *Sloan v. Lemon*,[252] the Court declared unconstitutional state laws that provided reimbursement and tax credits to students attending nonpublic schools. In *Nyquist*, a New York statute provided for reimbursement and tax credits for costs of nonpublic school elementary and secondary education for up to one-half of the costs of tuition for low- and middle-income students. Specifically, the law provided for reimbursement payments to families with incomes below $15,000 and tax credits for families with incomes below $25,000.[253] *Sloan* involved a Pennsylvania law that provided funds to reimburse parents for a portion of tuition expenses incurred in sending their children to nonpublic schools. Unlike the New York law in *Nyquist*, the Pennsylvania statute allowed families of all incomes to receive funds.

The Supreme Court declared both of these laws unconstitutional even though the aid went directly to the families rather than the schools. The Court emphasized that the aid was available only to nonpublic school students. The Court concluded that the aid "has a 'primary effect that advances religion' and offends the constitutional prohibition 'respecting an establishment of religion.' "[254]

In contrast, in *Mueller v. Allen*, the Court upheld a program of tax credits that were available to all students at both public and parochial schools.[255] A Minnesota law allowed taxpayers to deduct certain expenses incurred in providing education to their children from their state income taxes. The deduction was limited to actual expenses for tuition, textbooks, and transportation and could not exceed

---

[251]   413 U.S. 756 (1973).
[252]   413 U.S. 825 (1973).
[253]   413 U.S. at 765-767.
[254]   *Id.* at 798.
[255]   463 U.S. 388 (1983) (citation omitted).

$500 per dependent for grades kindergarten through 6, and $700 per student in grades 7 through 12.

By a 5-to-4 decision, the Court applied the *Lemon* test and upheld the income tax credits as constitutional. As to the first part of the *Lemon* test, the Court said that "[a] State's decision to defray the cost of educational expenses incurred by parents—regardless of the type of schools their children attend—evidences a purpose that is both secular and understandable. An educated populace is essential to the political and economic health of any community, and a State's efforts to assist parents in meeting the rising cost of educational expenses plainly serves this secular purpose of ensuring that the State's citizenry is well educated."[256]

In applying the second prong of the *Lemon* test, the Court emphasized that the tax credits were one of many deductions available and were limited in size. The Court said that the "[l]egislature's judgment that a deduction for educational expenses fairly equalizes the tax burden of its citizens and encourages desirable expenditures for educational purposes is entitled to substantial deference."[257] Most important, the Court stressed that the "deduction is available for educational expenses incurred by *all* parents, including those whose children attend public schools and those whose children attend nonsectarian private schools or sectarian private schools."[258] The Court saw this as the key distinction with *Nyquist* where the aid was available only to students attending nonpublic schools.

Finally, the Court concluded that allowing the tax credits did not entail government entanglement with religion. No government monitoring was involved in the program; the government was not required by the law to oversee any aspect of the parochial schools.

Justice Marshall dissented and was joined by Justices Brennan, Blackmun, and Stevens. Justice Marshall contended that the establishment clause prohibits the government from subsidizing parochial schools, even if it is providing the same assistance to public school students. Justice Marshall said: "The Establishment Clause of the First Amendment prohibits a State from subsidizing religious education, whether it does so directly or indirectly. In my view, this principle of neutrality forbids not only the tax benefits struck down in *Committee for Public Education v. Nyquist,* but any tax benefit, including the tax deduction at issue here, which subsidizes tuition payments to sectarian schools."[259]

Although there are some Justices who would allow financial aid in the form of tax credits available just for nonpublic school students and while there are some Justices who would not allow any such assistance to be received by parochial school students, the majority of the Court has drawn a distinction between programs that benefit all students and those just available for nonpublic school students. An assistance program benefiting only nonpublic school students violates the establishment clause. But a program available to all students is permissible unless it violates the other criteria discussed below.

---

[256] *Id.* at 395.

[257] *Id.* at 396.

[258] *Id.* at 397 (emphasis in original).

[259] *Id.* at 404 (Marshall, J., dissenting).

This distinction was made clear in the Court's important decision concerning vouchers, *Zelman v. Simmons-Harris*.[260] Ohio created a voucher program for students in the Cleveland schools. First, the program provides tuition aid in the form of a voucher for students in kindergarten through eighth grade. Students could use the vouchers to attend a participating school of their parent's choosing. By the terms of the program, students could use the vouchers in any private school, secular or religious. Second, the program provides tutorial aid for students who choose to remain enrolled in public school.

Tuition aid was distributed on a financial need basis, with the government paying a greater amount for poorer students. Vouchers were for $2,250 and for the poorest students, the government paid 90 percent of that amount.[261]

Almost all of the vouchers were used in religious schools. Ninety-six percent of all of the vouchers were used in parochial schools and 82 percent of the schools receiving vouchers were religiously affiliated.

Nonetheless, the Supreme Court upheld the program as constitutional. Chief Justice Rehnquist, writing for the Court in a 5-to-4 decision, said that prior decisions "make clear that where a government aid program is neutral with respect to religion, and provides assistance directly to a broad class of citizens who, in turn, direct government aid to religious schools wholly as a result of their own genuine and independent private choice, the program is not readily subject to challenge under the Establishment Clause."[262]

The United States Court of Appeals for the Sixth Circuit had invalidated the program as having been structured in a manner that encouraged parents to send their children to parochial schools and thus having the impermissible effect of advancing religion. The Supreme Court reversed and disagreed. Chief Justice Rehnquist stressed the program's neutrality: "Program benefits are available to participating families on neutral terms, with no reference to religion. The only preference stated anywhere in the program is a preference for low-income families, who receive greater assistance and are given priority for admission at participating schools. There are no 'financial incentive[s]' that 'ske[w]' the program toward religious schools. Such incentives [are] not present . . . where the aid is allocated on the basis of neutral, secular criteria that neither favor nor disfavor religion, and is made available to both religious and secular beneficiaries on a nondiscriminatory basis."[263]

The Court explained that the government was acting out of the important secular purpose of improving education for children in Cleveland and that if the aid ends up being spent in religious schools, it is because of parent choices not government decisions.

Justice O'Connor wrote a concurring opinion to emphasize that she did not see the decision as departing from precedent and to explain that parents had

---

[260] 536 U.S. 639 (2002).
[261] *Id.* at 663.
[262] *Id.* at 652.
[263] *Id.* at 653 (citations omitted).

a range of choices in Cleveland that made the voucher program acceptable.[264] Justice Thomas wrote a concurring opinion in which he discussed the need to improve education for inner-city children from minority races.[265] He also questioned whether the establishment clause should apply to the states at all.

There were four dissenters and three dissenting opinions. Justice Stevens wrote a brief dissent in which he argued that none of the characteristics of the program, such as the educational need of the students or the range of choices available, excused the government in providing such aid to parochial schools.[266] Justice Souter in a lengthy dissent criticized what he saw as an unprecedented transfer of government funds to religious coffers.[267] Justice Breyer's dissent emphasized the inherent divisiveness of the government giving such aid to religion.[268]

The 5-to-4 decision in *Zelman* reflects very different views between the majority and the dissent over the need for restrictions on government aid to religious schools. As a descriptive matter, *Zelman* largely resolves the constitutional issues concerning vouchers under the First Amendment. There still might be litigation, for example, over what types of choices must be available for voucher programs to be constitutional. In all likelihood, though, serious challenges to the constitutionality of voucher programs will be under state constitutions, many of which contain provisions preventing any direct or indirect aid to religion.[269]

Is the Aid Provided to the Students or to the Schools?

The Supreme Court has indicated that there is a strong presumption against government assistance that is provided to the schools, whereas the same types of aid might be permissible if they are provided directly to the students. The Court has observed that "the State may not grant aid to a religious school, whether cash or in kind, where the effect of the aid is that of a direct subsidy to the religious school from the State."[270]

For example, in *Committee for Public Education v. Nyquist*, the Court declared unconstitutional a portion of the state law that authorized "direct money grants from the State to 'qualifying' nonpublic schools to be used for the 'maintenance and repair of . . . school facilities and equipment to ensure the health, welfare and safety of enrolled pupils.' "[271] The Court found that the government violated the establishment clause when it provided funds directly to religious institutions.

Similarly, in *Levitt v. Committee for Public Education*, the Court declared unconstitutional a state law that provided nonpublic schools a sum of money for each pupil to reimburse it for costs incurred in complying with requirements for

---

[264] *Id.* at 663 (O'Connor, J., concurring).

[265] *Id.* at 676 (Thomas, J., concurring).

[266] *Id.* at 684 (Stevens, J., dissenting).

[267] *Id.* at 687 (Souter, J., dissenting).

[268] *Id.* at 719 (Breyer, J., dissenting).

[269] For example, in early 2006, the Florida Supreme Court invalidated a voucher program in that state as violating the Florida Constitution. Bush v. Holmes, 919 So. 2d 392 (Fla. 2006).

[270] Witters v. Washington Dept. of Servs. for the Blind, 474 U.S. 481, 487 (1986) (citation omitted).

[271] 413 U.S. at 762.

standardized testing and record keeping.[272] The Court concluded that the "lump sum payments . . . violate the Establishment Clause."[273]

In contrast, the Court is more likely to uphold aid when it is received by students and their families directly, rather than when it is provided to the schools. In *Mueller v. Allen*, described above, the Court allowed the tuition tax credits that were provided to parents of children in all public and private schools. Subsequently, in *Zelman v. Simmons-Harris*, the Court upheld a voucher program where aid could be used for parochial schools, in part, because the assistance was given to parents who could choose where to spend the vouchers.

Although this factor—whether the aid is provided to students or to the schools—is important, it is not necessarily decisive. Some aid provided directly to parochial schools has been upheld, such as in *Committee for Public Education and Religious Liberty v. Regan*, which allowed the state to reimburse private schools for expenses of compiling state-required data, such as student attendance records, and of administering and grading state-mandated standardized tests.[274] Also, some aid provided directly to students has been invalidated. For instance, in *Aguilar v. Felton*, the Court declared unconstitutional a program for sending government employees into parochial schools to treat students' learning disabilities.[275]

Nonetheless, the cases indicate that there is a presumption against aid received by schools rather than students. As explained below, the Court will allow assistance directly to parochial schools only if it is of a type that cannot be used for religious instruction. Also, a direct grant of money, as in *Nyquist* or *Levitt*, is objectionable because it so easily could be used for religious purposes and because it appears to be an endorsement of religion.

Is It Aid That Is Used for Religious Instruction?

A crucial factor in many of the cases is whether it is aid that is actually used for religious education. For example, as mentioned above, in *Everson v. Board of Education*, the Court allowed a state program that provided reimbursement for all parents of the cost of bus transportation to take children to and from school.[276] After carefully reviewing the history of the establishment clause, Justice Black, writing for the Court, declared: "The State contributes no money to the schools. It does not support them. Its legislation, as applied, does no more than provide a general program to help parents get their children, regardless of their religion, safely and expeditiously to and from accredited schools."[277]

In contrast, in *Wolman v. Walter*, the Court declared unconstitutional the government's paying for field trip transportation for parochial school students.[278]

---

[272] 413 U.S. 472 (1973).

[273] *Id.* at 482.

[274] 444 U.S. 646 (1980).

[275] 473 U.S. 402 (1985).

[276] 330 U.S. 1 (1947).

[277] *Id.* at 18.

[278] Wolman v. Walter, 433 U.S. 229 (1977). In *Mitchell v. Helms*, 530 U.S. 793 (2000), the Court overruled the part of *Wolman* concerning the ability of the government to give instructional equipment to parochial schools.

The government provided funds for commercial transportation or the use of state school buses for field trips. Because the trips could be to advance religious education, the Court found that the government could not pay for them.

Likewise, the Court has said that the government may reimburse schools for the costs of administering standardized tests,[279] but not for the expenses incurred in teacher-written and graded examinations.[280] The difference is that teacher-written tests could cover religious material and thus advance the religious mission of parochial schools.

Perhaps the clearest and most important example of the prohibition against the government providing aid that might be used for religious instruction is that the government may not pay teachers' salaries in parochial schools, even for teachers of secular subjects. These decisions are based on the concern that teachers could be giving instruction in religious matters and any government monitoring would mean excessive government entanglement with religion. In *Lemon v. Kurtzman*, the Supreme Court declared unconstitutional state laws that provided state aid to church-related elementary and secondary schools and for their teachers of secular subjects.[281] A Pennsylvania law provided state funds directly to private schools to purchase secular educational services such as teacher salaries, textbooks, and educational materials. A Rhode Island statute, also considered in *Lemon*, provided funds to supplement teachers' salaries in parochial schools.

The Supreme Court stressed that such payments to schools for teacher salaries inevitably foster religion. Chief Justice Burger, writing for the Court, explained: "We need not and do not assume that teachers in parochial schools will be guilty of bad faith or any conscious design to evade the limitations imposed by the statute and the First Amendment. We simply recognize that a dedicated religious person, teaching in a school affiliated with his or her faith and operated to inculcate its tenets, will inevitably experience great difficulty in remaining religiously neutral. Doctrines and faith are not inculcated or advanced by neutrals. . . . [T]he potential for impermissible fostering of religion is present."[282]

The Court said that the government would have to monitor to be sure that the teachers were engaged in only secular instruction, and this would mean constant government entanglement with religion. Chief Justice Burger wrote that "[a] comprehensive, discriminating, and continuing state surveillance will inevitably be required to ensure that these restrictions are obeyed and the First Amendment otherwise respected. . . . These prophylactic contacts will involve excessive and enduring entanglement between state and church."[283]

However, in *Agostini v. Felton*,[284] the Court allowed the government to send remedial education teachers on to parochial school premises to provide

---

[279] Committee for Pub. Educ. and Religious Liberty v. Regan, 444 U.S. 646 (1980); Wolman v. Walter, 433 U.S. 229 (1977).

[280] Levitt v. Community for Public Educ., 413 U.S. 472 (1973).

[281] 403 U.S. 602 (1971).

[282] *Id.* at 618-619.

[283] *Id.* at 619.

[284] 521 U.S. 203 (1997).

instruction. This overruled a decision from a decade earlier and eliminated the rigid rule preventing government subsidies of teachers in religious schools.[285] But it is unclear whether this is a very limited exception to the government's ability to pay teacher salaries in parochial schools or whether it marks the beginning of the end of this traditional limit on government aid to religious institutions.

It should be noted that even before *Agostini*, not every form of state-subsidized instructional personnel is unconstitutional. The Court has held that the government may provide its employees to parochial schools to supply diagnostic services for testing children for health and educational problems.[286] The Court also has ruled that the government may provide therapeutic services for health and educational disabilities for parochial school students at sites outside those schools.[287]

In *Zobrest v. Catalina Foothills School District*, the Court, by a 5-to-4 margin, upheld the constitutionality of the government providing sign interpreters for parochial school students.[288] Chief Justice Rehnquist, writing for the Court, emphasized that the aid was available for all students needing them in both parochial and public schools.[289] Rehnquist also stressed that the direct beneficiary of the aid was the student; the school was helped only indirectly.[290]

Perhaps most important, Rehnquist distinguished sign interpreters from teachers or guidance counselors. He wrote: "[T]he task of a sign-language interpreter seems to us quite different from that of a teacher or guidance counselor. . . . Nothing in this record suggests that a sign-language interpreter would do more than accurately interpret whatever material is presented to the class as a whole."[291]

The dissent disagreed with this characterization and objected that the "placement in a parochial school classroom of a public employee whose duty consists of relaying religious messages . . . violate[s] the establishment clause."[292] Justice Blackmun, joined by the other three dissenters, argued that at the parochial school, "where the secular and the sectarian are 'inextricably intertwined,' governmental assistance to the educational function of the school necessarily entails governmental participation in the school's inculcation of religion."[293] The law is simply unsettled now as to what subsidies for teachers are permissible.

Finally, the Court has held that the government may give instructional equipment to parochial schools.[294] Previously, the Court drew a distinction between textbooks and audiovisual equipment. In *Board of Education v. Allen*, the Court upheld the constitutionality of the government providing textbooks for secular subjects

---

[285] Aguilar v. Felton, 473 U.S. 402 (1985).

[286] Wolman v. Walter, 433 U.S. 229 (1977).

[287] *Id.*

[288] 509 U.S. 1 (1993).

[289] *Id.* at 10 ("The service at issue in this case is part of a general government program that distributes benefits neutrally to any child qualifying as 'disabled' . . . , without regard to the 'sectarian-nonsectarian, or public-nonpublic nature' of the school the child attends.").

[290] *Id.* at 12-13.

[291] *Id.* at 13.

[292] *Id.* at 14 (Blackmun, J., dissenting).

[293] *Id.* at 19.

[294] Mitchell v. Helms, 530 U.S. 793 (2000).

to all public and parochial school students.[295] But in *Meek v. Pittenger*, the Court declared unconstitutional a state law that provided instructional materials, including audiovisual equipment, to parochial schools.[296] The instructional materials that could be lent to parochial schools included "periodicals, photographs, maps, charts, sound recordings, films, or any other printed and published materials" and instructional equipment included "projection equipment, recording equipment, and laboratory equipment."[297] The Court emphasized that this material and equipment could be easily used for religious instruction. The Court explained that the "direct aid to Pennsylvania's predominantly church-related, nonpublic elementary and secondary schools, even though ostensibly limited to wholly neutral, secular instructional material and equipment, inescapably results in direct and substantial advancement of religious activity, and thus constitutes an impermissible establishment of religion."[298]

But in *Mitchell v. Helms*,[299] the Court expressly overruled *Meek*. *Mitchell* involved Louisiana providing instructional equipment to parochial schools. Justice Thomas, writing for a plurality of four, said that the aid should be allowed because it is provided equally to all schools, religious and nonreligious.[300] He said that the key question is whether the government was participating in religious indoctrination. He wrote: "In distinguishing between indoctrination that is attributable to the State and indoctrination that is not, we have consistently turned to the principle of neutrality, upholding aid that is offered to a broad range of groups or persons without regard to their religion. If the religious, irreligious, and areligious are all alike eligible for governmental aid, no one would conclude that any indoctrination that any particular recipient conducts has been done at the behest of the government."[301] He rejected the argument that aid is impermissible because it might be diverted to religious use because any assistance could free funds that end up being used for religious purposes.

Justice Thomas emphatically rejected the view that the government cannot give aid that is actually used for religious education. He also sharply criticized the traditional law preventing the government from giving aid to "pervasively sectarian" institutions. He said that this phrase was born of anti-Catholic bigotry and

---

[295] 392 U.S. 236 (1968). However, in *Norwood v. Harrison*, 413 U.S. 455 (1973), the Court declared unconstitutional a Mississippi program that allowed segregated private schools to receive school books. *Norwood* is discussed in more detail in §6.4.4.3.

[296] 421 U.S. 349 (1975). In *Mitchell v. Helms*, 530 U.S. 793 (2000), the Court overruled the part of *Meek* concerning the permissibility of the government giving instructional equipment to parochial schools.

[297] 421 U.S. at 355.

[298] *Id.* at 366 (citation omitted).

[299] 530 U.S. 793 (2000). For competing views of the equality theory the Court follows in *Mitchell, see* Alan E. Brownstein, Interpreting the Religion Clauses in Terms of Liberty, Equality, and Free Speech Values—A Critical Analysis of "Neutrality Theory" and Charitable Choice, 13 Notre Dame J.L. Ethics & Pub. Poly. 243 (1999) (criticizing equality theory); Michael W. McConnell, State Action and the Supreme Court's Emerging Consensus on the Line Between Establishment and Private Religious Expression, 28 Pepp. L. Rev. 681 (2001) (defending equality approach).

[300] 530 U.S. at 809.

[301] *Id.*

wrote that "hostility to aid to pervasively sectarian schools has a shameful pedigree that we do not hesitate to disavow."[302] He declared: "[T]he inquiry into the recipient's religious views required by a focus on whether a school is pervasively sectarian is not only unnecessary but also offensive. It is well established, in numerous other contexts, that courts should refrain from trolling through a person's or institution's religious beliefs."[303] Taken literally, this would seem to require the government to give aid to parochial schools any time it is assisting secular private schools.

Justice O'Connor wrote an opinion concurring in the judgment, joined by Justice Breyer, in which she sharply disagreed with Justice Thomas's approach. Justice O'Connor said that equality never had been the sole measure of whether a government action violated the establishment clause. She wrote: "[W]e have never held that a government-aid program passes constitutional muster solely because of the neutral criteria it employs as a basis for distributing aid. I also disagree with the plurality's conclusion that actual diversion of government aid to religious indoctrination is consistent with the Establishment Clause."[304] Justice O'Connor said that the test should be whether aid actually is used for religious instruction, in which case the establishment clause is violated.[305] Because she found no indication here that the aid was used for religious education in more than a negligible way, she found that the Louisiana program did not violate the First Amendment.

Justice Souter's dissenting opinion, joined by Justices Stevens and O'Connor, urged the Court to adhere to its precedents and find that aid is impermissible when it is of a type, like instructional materials, that can be used for religious education.[306] Justice Souter began by observing: "The establishment prohibition of government religious funding serves more than one end. It is meant to guarantee the right of individual conscience against compulsion, to protect the integrity of religion against the corrosion of secular support, and to preserve the unity of political society against the implied exclusion of the less favored and the antagonism of controversy over public support for religious causes."[307] He strongly disagreed with the plurality's view that equality is the sole test for the establishment clause and identified a number of factors that prior cases require to be considered in determining whether aid is impermissible.[308] Justice Souter powerfully concluded his dissent by stating: "[I]n rejecting the principle of no aid to a school's religious mission the plurality is attacking the most fundamental assumption underlying the Establishment Clause, that government can in fact operate with neutrality in its relation to religion. I believe that it can, and so respectfully dissent."[309]

---

[302] *Id.* at 828.
[303] *Id.*
[304] *Id.* at 839-840 (O'Connor, J., concurring in the judgment).
[305] *Id.* at 840-841.
[306] *Id.* at 867 (Souter, J., dissenting).
[307] *Id.* at 868.
[308] *Id.* at 868-869.
[309] *Id.* at 913.

Conclusion

The Court's decisions in this area can be criticized by those who believe that more government aid to parochial schools should be allowed and also by those who think that less should be permitted. The rulings can be attacked as drawing a series of distinctions that appear to be arbitrary. Yet this is an area where inevitably "lines must be drawn."[310] Overall, the cases concerning aid to parochial schools rest on three recurring principles. First, aid will not be allowed if it is received only by nonpublic schools and their students; to be permissible the assistance must be equally available to public school pupils. Second, there is a presumption against aid that is directly received by the schools; assistance is more likely to be upheld if it is provided directly to the students. Finally, aid will not be allowed if it is actually used in religious education. Beyond that, the law is uncertain, especially because, at least for now, no approach has support from a majority of the Court.

§12.2.6.3   Aid to Religious Colleges and Universities

Aid to the Institutions

The Court has been more lenient in allowing government assistance to religious colleges and universities. The Court has distinguished colleges and universities on the grounds that they are not likely to be as permeated with religious doctrine and dogma as are elementary and secondary schools. Also, the Court has emphasized the difference in the age of the students and their ability to understand that government assistance is not endorsement of religion. Additionally, the Court has stressed that aid to colleges and universities is much less likely to produce the political divisiveness that seems inherent to assistance to parochial elementary and secondary schools.

In *Tilton v. Richardson*, the Court upheld the constitutionality of religious colleges and universities receiving federal money for the construction of facilities that would not be used for religious instruction.[311] *Tilton* concerned Title I of the Higher Education Facilities Act of 1963, which provided construction grants for buildings and facilities used exclusively for secular purposes.[312] The Court applied the *Lemon* test and concluded that it was permissible for religious schools to receive the assistance. The Court concluded that the purpose of the aid was to expand facilities in colleges and universities to "accommodate rapidly growing numbers of youth who aspire to a higher education."[313] The Court said that this is a "legitimate secular objective entirely appropriate for governmental action."[314]

---

[310] Grand Rapids School Dist. v. Ball, 473 U.S. at 398.
[311] 403 U.S. 672 (1971).
[312] *Id.* at 674-675.
[313] *Id.* at 678.
[314] *Id.* at 679.

Moreover, the Court found that the aid did not have the effect of advancing religion because the law "was carefully drafted to ensure that the federally subsidized facilities would be devoted to the secular and not the religious function of the recipient institutions. It authorizes grants and loans only for academic facilities that will be used for defined secular purposes and expressly prohibits their use for religious instruction, training or worship."[315] The Court, however, invalidated a part of the Act that allowed the facilities to be used for religious purposes after 20 years. The Court said that allowing the building to be converted to religious use at that time would impermissibly have the "effect of advancing religion."[316]

Finally, the Court concluded that allowing the aid would not cause excessive government entanglement with religion. The Court said that "[t]here are generally significant differences between the religious aspects of church-related institutions of higher learning and parochial elementary and secondary schools. . . . [C]ollege students are less impressionable and less susceptible to religious indoctrination. . . . Since religious indoctrination is not a substantial purpose or activity of these church-related colleges and universities, there is less likelihood than in primary and secondary schools that religion will permeate the area of secular education."[317]

Justices Douglas, Black, Marshall, and Brennan dissented. They argued that direct government financial aid to religious institutions, including at the college and university level, violates the establishment clause. Justice Douglas said that "even a small amount coming out of the pocket of taxpayers and going into the coffers of a church was not in keeping with our constitutional ideal."[318]

In *Hunt v. McNair*, the Court followed the same reasoning as in *Tilton* and allowed the use of state revenue bonds for religious colleges and universities.[319] A state's Educational Facilities Authority issued bonds to finance the construction of facilities in colleges and universities in the state. Beneficiaries included religious schools, but they were not allowed to use the funds for the construction of facilities to be used for religious activities and the bonds had to be repaid by the schools. The Court relied on *Tilton* to uphold the aid, again emphasizing that the use of the funds was restricted, that the money was available to secular and religious schools, and that the institution was not permeated with religious instruction in the same way as an elementary or secondary school.

In *Roemer v. Board of Public Works*, the distinction between colleges and universities as compared to elementary and secondary schools was even clearer as the Court upheld a program of direct state financial aid to religious colleges and universities.[320] Maryland created a program whereby it provided for grants to private colleges and universities. The aid was calculated at 15 percent of the amount per student that the state spent in the public college system. Religious schools, except

---

[315] *Id.* at 679-680.
[316] *Id.* at 683.
[317] *Id.* at 685-687.
[318] *Id.* at 697 (Douglas, J., dissenting).
[319] 413 U.S. 734 (1973).
[320] 426 U.S. 736 (1976).

for seminaries, were allowed to receive the aid. The Court, by a 5-to-4 margin, but without a majority opinion, upheld the program.

Justice Blackmun's plurality opinion invoked *Tilton* and *Hunt* and found that the requirements of the *Lemon* test were met. Justice Blackmun said that the "purpose of Maryland's aid program is the secular one of supporting private higher education generally, as an economic alternative to a wholly public system."[321] Moreover, he said that the "institutions are not so permeated by religion that the secular side cannot be separated from the sectarian."[322] Therefore, the effect was not to advance religion because the state law required that "state funds not be used to support specifically religious activity."[323] Finally, the plurality opinion concluded that there was not excessive entanglement because there was minimal state oversight required and because "the danger of political divisiveness is substantially less when the aided institution is not an elementary or secondary school, but a college, whose student constituency is not local but diverse and widely dispersed."[324] Justices White and Rehnquist concurred in the judgment and criticized the *Lemon* test, but agreed that this aid was not motivated by a religious purpose and did not have a primary effect of advancing religion.

Thus, it is clear that much more financial assistance to religious colleges and universities will be allowed than to parochial elementary and secondary schools. Although there is a presumption against direct receipt of aid by the latter, no such presumption exists against receipt of aid by colleges and universities. Moreover, direct grants of money to parochial elementary and secondary schools have been declared unconstitutional in cases such as *Levitt* and *Lemon,* but *Roemer* approves just that.

The key question is whether the Court's distinctions are persuasive. Is there an inherent difference between elementary and secondary schools, on the one hand, and colleges and universities, on the other, in terms of their religious mission and the pervasiveness of religion in instruction? The Court assumes that there is such a clear distinction, but it is likely that there is an enormous range of schools at all levels. There are parochial elementary and secondary schools with relatively little overt religious influence and religious colleges and universities where religion is omnipresent.

Aid to Students in Religious Schools

In *Witters v. Washington Department of Services for the Blind,* the Court unanimously found constitutional a state program that provided vocational rehabilitation assistance to physically disabled students and that was used by a blind student at a Christian college.[325] The Court used the *Lemon* test and noted the "unmistakably secular purpose of the Washington program. That program was designed

---

[321] *Id.* at 754.
[322] *Id.* at 759 (citation omitted).
[323] *Id.*
[324] *Id.* at 765 (citation omitted).
[325] 474 U.S. 481 (1986).

to promote the well-being of the visually handicapped through the provision of vocational rehabilitation services, and no more than a minuscule amount of the aid awarded under the program is likely to flow to religious institutions."[326]

The Court also found that the effect was not to advance religion. The Court stressed that the aid was available to all qualifying students "without regard to the sectarian-nonsectarian, or public-nonpublic nature of the institution benefitted."[327] Nor was there any government monitoring involved that would entail excessive government entanglement with religion.

Although *Witters* involved aid for a college-level program, its reasoning is quite similar to that described above for aid in the elementary and secondary school context. The Court in *Witters* focused on the aid being available to all students at public and parochial schools, on the assistance being received by the student and not the school, and on the total amount of aid to religious colleges and universities being insignificant. Indeed, the subsequent decision in *Zobrest*, described above, relied heavily on *Witters* in upholding the constitutionality of the government providing a sign interpreter to a hearing-impaired student in a parochial school.[328]

§12.2.6.4   Aid to Religious Institutions Other Than Schools

Great Deference to the Government

Relatively few cases have involved attempts by the government to give assistance to religious institutions other than schools. The decisions thus far indicate that the Court is more likely to be deferential to the government, as in reviewing aid to colleges and universities, than it is to be more vigilant in its review, as it is concerning aid to elementary and secondary schools.

In *Bradfield v. Roberts*, in 1899, the Court upheld the constitutionality of the government building a new facility for a church-affiliated hospital.[329] The Court allowed the government aid to a hospital that was operated by members of the Roman Catholic Church under the auspices of the Church. The Court noted that the hospital did not discriminate based on religion and said that it was "wholly immaterial" that the hospital was run by a religious group.[330]

Subsequently, in *Bowen v. Kendrick*, the Court deemed constitutional the Adolescent Family Life Act, which provided for grants to organizations to provide counseling and care to pregnant adolescents and their parents, and also to provide counseling to prevent adolescent sexual activity.[331] The law specifically authorized receipt of grants by religious, as well as nonreligious, organizations. The law

---

[326] *Id.* at 485-486.
[327] *Id.* at 487 (citation omitted).
[328] 509 U.S. at 8-13.
[329] 175 U.S. 291 (1899).
[330] *Id.* at 298.
[331] 487 U.S. 589 (1988).

prohibited the use of any federal funds for family planning services, for abortion counseling, or for abortions.

Chief Justice Rehnquist wrote for the majority in the 5-to-4 decision and applied the *Lemon* test to uphold the law. Rehnquist said that the law "was motivated primarily, if not entirely, by a legitimate secular purpose—the elimination or reduction of social and economic problems caused by teenage sexuality, pregnancy, and parenthood."[332]

The Court also said that the law did not have an impermissible effect of advancing religion, even though it specifically encouraged organizations to allow religious groups to play a role. The Court concluded that the law did not favor or disfavor religious groups compared to secular ones and thus was permissible. Rehnquist stressed that the statute was successful in its "maintenance of a course of neutrality among religions and between religion and nonreligion."[333] The Court said that it was "important that the aid is made available regardless of whether it will ultimately flow to a secular or sectarian institution."[334] In fact, the Court invoked *Bradfield v. Roberts* as establishing the proposition that "religious institutions are [not] disabled by the First Amendment from participating in publicly sponsored social welfare programs."[335]

Finally, the Court said that there was not excessive entanglement with religion. Although the law did not require monitoring by the government, the Court said that most of the cases that had applied the entanglement test had involved elementary and secondary schools that "were pervasively sectarian and had as a substantial purpose the inculcation of religious values."[336] The Court said that "[h]ere, by contrast, there is no reason to assume that the religious organizations which may receive grants are pervasively sectarian in the same sense as the Court has held parochial schools to be."[337]

Justice Blackmun wrote a dissenting opinion joined by Justices Brennan, Marshall, and Stevens. Blackmun focused on the Act's subsidizing religious teaching. He said that the "statute encouraged the use of public funds for such instruction, by giving religious groups a central pedagogical and counseling role without imposing any restraints on the sectarian quality of the participation."[338] Blackmun particularly objected to the Court's claim that the groups were not pervasively sectarian; he questioned both the relevance of this factor and the characterization of the particular groups that would receive funds.[339] Blackmun argued that the law clearly had the effect of advancing religion: "Government funds are paying for religious organizations to teach and counsel impressionable adolescents on a highly sensitive subject of considerable religious significance, often on the

---

[332] *Id.* at 602.
[333] *Id.* at 607 (citations omitted).
[334] *Id.* at 609.
[335] *Id.*
[336] *Id.* at 616 (citations omitted).
[337] *Id.* at 616.
[338] *Id.* at 626 (Blackmun, J., dissenting).
[339] *Id.* at 631-633.

premises of a church or parochial school and without any effort to remove religious symbols from the sites."[340]

It seems difficult to reconcile *Bowen v. Kendrick* from the cases invalidating aid to parochial elementary and secondary schools. The Court in *Bowen* approved funding that would go directly to religious institutions. Perhaps *Bowen* reflects the Court's judgment that aid to elementary and secondary schools is different from aid to all other religious institutions. Yet from an establishment clause perspective, the issue must be whether this is a distinction that should make a difference. Government subsidies to religions to engage in religious teaching seem to run afoul of the First Amendment. *Bowen* is likely to be very important as courts consider the constitutionality of "charitable choice programs," which allow faith-based organizations to receive government funds to provide social service programs.

§12.3   THE FREE EXERCISE CLAUSE

§12.3.1   Introduction

Religious Beliefs and Actions

The Supreme Court repeatedly has stated that the government may not compel or punish religious beliefs; people may think and believe anything that they want. In *Reynolds v. United States*, the first case to construe the free exercise clause, Chief Justice Waite wrote that "Congress was deprived of all legislative power over mere opinion, but was left free to reach actions."[1] Likewise, in *Braunfeld v. Brown*, Chief Justice Warren declared that "[t]he freedom to hold religious beliefs and opinions is absolute."[2]

The free exercise clause, however, obviously does not provide absolute protection for religiously motivated conduct. The Court has thus said that the free exercise clause "embraces two concepts—freedom to believe and freedom to act. The first is absolute but, in the nature of things, the second cannot be."[3] Similarly, the Court has spoken of the "distinction between the absolute constitutional protection against governmental regulation of religious beliefs on the one hand, and the qualified protection against the regulation of religiously motivated conduct."[4]

Governments, though, do not adopt laws prohibiting or requiring thoughts; statutes invariably regulate conduct. Thus, the free exercise clause is invoked in several situations. One is when the government prohibits behavior that a person's religion requires. For example, in *Reynolds v. United States*, the Supreme Court

---

[340] *Id.* at 635.

§12.3 [1] 98 U.S. (8 Otto)145, 164 (1878).

[2] 366 U.S. 599, 603 (1961).

[3] Cantwell v. Connecticut, 310 U.S. 296, 303-304 (1940).

[4] Employment Div. v. Smith, 485 U.S. 660, 670 n.13 (1988).

upheld the constitutionality of a law forbidding polygamy even though Mormons claimed that it was required by their religion.[5]

The free exercise clause also is invoked when the government requires conduct that a person's religion prohibits. For instance, the Court rejected a challenge by Amish individuals who claimed that the requirement that they obtain Social Security numbers and pay Social Security taxes violated their religious beliefs.[6]

Additionally, the free exercise clause is invoked when individuals claim that laws burden or make more difficult religious observances. An illustration of this is the many cases where the Court held that the government impermissibly burdens religion if it denies benefits to individuals who quit their jobs for religious reasons.[7]

Overview of the Historical Development of the Law

Over time, the law of the free exercise clause has changed dramatically. Prior to the 1960s, the Court did not formulate a test for the free exercise clause, although it did invalidate laws that precluded solicitation for religious purposes or that taxed such activity as infringing freedom of speech and religion.[8]

In *Sherbert v. Verner*, in 1963, the Court expressly held that strict scrutiny should be used in evaluating laws burdening free exercise of religion and declared unconstitutional the denial of unemployment benefits to a woman who was discharged from her job rather than work on her Saturday Sabbath.[9] For the next 27 years, the Court usually purported to apply strict scrutiny to religion clause claims but, nonetheless, generally sided with the government when individuals claimed that laws infringed their free exercise of religion. Sometimes the Court did not use the language of strict scrutiny, but instead spoke of the need for an "overriding" government purpose to justify infringing religion.[10]

For instance, the Court rejected the free exercise claim of an Orthodox Jewish military doctor who wished to wear a yarmulke while on duty even though it was prohibited by military dress regulations.[11] Likewise, the Court rejected free exercise clause challenges to laws requiring payment of the minimum wage,[12] mandating payment of Social Security taxes,[13] and prohibiting racial discrimination.[14] There actually were only two areas during this time where the Court upheld free exercise

[5] 98 U.S. 145 (1878).

[6] United States v. Lee, 455 U.S. 252 (1982).

[7] *See, e.g.*, Thomas v. Review Board, 450 U.S. 707 (1981); Sherbert v. Verner, 374 U.S. 398 (1963).

[8] *See, e.g.*, Cantwell v. Connecticut, 310 U.S. 296 (1940); Murdock v. Pennsylvania, 319 U.S. 105 (1943).

[9] 374 U.S. 398 (1963).

[10] *See, e.g.*, United States v. Lee, 455 U.S. 252, 257-258 (1982).

[11] Goldman v. Weinberger, 475 U.S. 503 (1986).

[12] Tony and Susan Alamo Found. v. Secretary of Labor, 471 U.S. 290 (1985).

[13] United States v. Lee, 455 U.S. 252 (1982).

[14] Bob Jones Univ. v. United States, 461 U.S. 574 (1983).

clause challenges: to compulsory school attendance laws by Amish parents,[15] and to the denial of benefits to those who quit their jobs for religious reasons.[16]

In 1990, in *Employment Division v. Smith*, the law of the free exercise clause changed significantly.[17] The Court held that the free exercise clause cannot be used to challenge a neutral law of general applicability. In other words, no matter how much a law burdens religious practices, it is constitutional under *Smith* so long as it does not single out religious behavior for punishment and was not motivated by a desire to interfere with religion. For example, in *Smith*, the Court said that a law prohibiting consumption of peyote, a hallucinogenic substance, did not violate the free exercise clause even though such use was required by some Native American religions. The Court explained that the state law prohibiting consumption of peyote applied to everyone in the state and did not punish conduct solely because it was religiously motivated. In contrast, in *Church of the Lukumi Babalu Aye, Inc. v. Hialeah*, the Court declared unconstitutional a city ordinance that prohibited ritual sacrifice of animals because it was directed solely at a particular religious sect.[18]

After these cases, the law is that a neutral law of general applicability only has to meet rational basis review, but laws that are directed at religious practices have to meet strict scrutiny. Congress attempted to change this through the Religious Freedom Restoration Act of 1993, which declared its purpose as negating the effects of the *Smith* decision and restoring strict scrutiny for free exercise clause analysis.[19] The Religious Freedom Restoration Act required that courts use strict scrutiny in analyzing free exercise clause claims, even as to neutral laws of general applicability. In 1997, in *City of Boerne v. Flores*,[20] the Supreme Court declared the Act unconstitutional as applied to state and local governments as exceeding the scope of Congress's powers under §5 of the Fourteenth Amendment.[21] However, as discussed below, the Religious Freedom Restoration Act remains in force and is applied to the federal government, as reflected in the Court's recent decision in *Burwell v. Hobby Lobby*.[22] Additionally, in 2000, Congress passed and President Clinton signed the Religious Land Use and Institutionalized Persons Act,[23] which requires strict scrutiny of government decisions concerning land use or affecting institutionalized persons that significantly burden religion.[24]

---

[15] Wisconsin v. Yoder, 406 U.S. 205 (1972).

[16] Frazee v. Illinois Dept. of Employment Sec., 489 U.S. 829 (1989); Thomas v. Review Bd., 450 U.S. 707 (1981); Sherbert v. Verner, 374 U.S. 298 (1963).

[17] 494 U.S. 872 (1990).

[18] 508 U.S. 520 (1993).

[19] 42 U.S.C. §2000bb.

[20] 521 U.S. 507 (1997).

[21] *City of Boerne v. Flores*, and its holding that Congress exceeded the scope of its §5 powers, is discussed in detail in §3.7.2.

[22] 134 S. Ct. 2751 (2014). Also, in *Gonzales v. O Centro Espirita Beneficente União do Vegetal*, 546 U.S. 418 (2006), the Court used the Religious Freedom Restoration Act to rule in favor of a religion that wanted to use a controlled substance in its religious rituals.

[23] 42 U.S.C. §2000cc.

[24] In *Cutter v. Wilkinson*, 544 U.S. 709 (2005), the Supreme Court rejected a challenge to this law based on the claim that it violated the establishment clause by favoring religion. The Court left open other issues, such as whether the law fits within the scope of Congress's powers.

Overview of Organization

Section 12.3.2 reviews the development of this law in detail and is organized in chronological order. Section 12.3.2.1 looks at the free exercise clause cases before 1960, and then §12.3.2.2 considers the free exercise clause cases between 1960 and 1990. *Smith* and its application are discussed in §12.3.2.3. Finally, the Religious Freedom Restoration Act and the Religious Land Use and Institutionalized Persons Act are examined more fully in §12.3.2.4. The chronological order is chosen so as to show the development of the law. Also, although *Smith* is the controlling test for the free exercise clause, the earlier cases remain important in that laws to overturn that decision and restore the prior case law remain valid in limited areas: to the federal government, pursuant to the Religious Freedom Restoration Act, and to state and local government actions concerning land use and institutionalized persons, pursuant to the Religious Land Use and Institutionalized Persons Act.

The underlying issue is whether religion should be a basis for exemptions from general laws. Some believe that strict scrutiny is essential when the government significantly burdens religion.[25] This was the Supreme Court's stated view before *Smith*, and it is Congress's position in laws such as the Religious Freedom Restoration Act and the Religious Land Use and Institutionalized Persons Act. The basic idea is that free exercise of religion is a fundamental right and that government burdening of it should be justified as needed to achieve a compelling purpose. But others believe that there should not be religious exemptions from general laws.[26] This is the Supreme Court's current position as reflected in *Smith*. This view leaves protection from burdensome laws to the political process; it emphasizes the inappropriateness of favoring religious over secular justifications for exemptions and the lack of a historical basis for exempting religion.

The chapter concludes in §12.3.3 by considering a specific and distinct free exercise clause problem: When, if at all, may the government become involved in religious disputes?

§12.3.2   Challenges to Laws Regulating or Burdening Religious Conduct

§12.3.2.1   Decisions Prior to 1960 Initial Cases

The Supreme Court's earliest treatment of free exercise of religion was in *Reynolds v. United States*.[27] A federal law prohibited polygamy in the territories, and

---

[25] *See, e.g.,* Douglas Laycock, Religious Liberty as Liberty, 7 J. Contemp. Legal Issues 313 (1996); Michael W. McConnell, Accommodation of Religion: An Update and Response to the Critics, 60 Geo. Wash. L. Rev. 685 (1992).

[26] *See, e.g.,* Frederick Mark Gedicks, An Unfirm Foundation: The Regrettable Indefensibility of Religious Exemptions, 20 U. Ark. Little Rock L.J. 555 (1998); William P. Marshall, The Case Against the Constitutionally Compelled Free Exercise Exemption, 40 Case W. Res. L. Rev. 357 (1990).

[27] 98 U.S. (8 Otto) 145 (1878).

a defendant argued that his Mormon religion required that he have multiple wives. The Supreme Court rejected the free exercise clause argument and the claim that the constitutional provision required an exemption from otherwise valid criminal laws. Chief Justice Waite wrote: "[A]s a law of the organization of society under the exclusive dominion of the United States, it is provided that plural marriages shall not be allowed. Can a man excuse his practices to the contrary because of his religious belief? To permit this would be to make the professed doctrines of religious belief superior to the law of the land, and in effect to permit every citizen to become a law unto himself. Government could exist only in name under such circumstances."[28]

The Court thus drew a distinction between beliefs and action; the free exercise clause limited government regulation of the former, but not the latter. Chief Justice Waite said: "Congress was deprived of all legislative power over mere opinion, but was left free to reach actions which were in violation of social duties or subversive of good order."[29]

Protection of Religion Under Other Constitutional Provisions

The Supreme Court first applied the free exercise clause to the states in *Cantwell v. Connecticut* in 1940.[30] Prior to this time, the Court protected religious freedom under other constitutional provisions, especially the due process clause of the Fourteenth Amendment.[31]

For example, in *Pierce v. Society of Sisters*, the Court declared unconstitutional an Oregon law prohibiting private and parochial school education.[32] The Court concluded that the law infringed on the right of parents to control the upbringing of their children and thus impermissibly violated the liberty guaranteed under the due process clause of the Fourteenth Amendment.[33]

Restrictions on Religious Solicitations

The Supreme Court's initial explicit protection of free exercise of religion occurred in a series of cases that involved laws restricting religious groups from soliciting funds. For example, *Cantwell v. Connecticut* overturned the convictions of several Jehovah's Witnesses who were convicted of soliciting money without a

---

[28] *Id.* at 166-167.

[29] *Id.* at 164.

[30] 310 U.S. 296 (1940).

[31] The Court also rejected due process challenges in matters concerning religion. *See, e.g.*, Hamilton v. Regents of the Univ. of Cal., 293 U.S. 245 (1934) (rejecting a due process challenge to a law requiring male college students to take military training courses); Jacobson v. Massachusetts, 197 U.S. 11 (1905) (finding that a state's compulsory vaccination law was a permissible exercise of its police power).

[32] 268 U.S. 510 (1925).

[33] *Pierce* is discussed in §10.2.4 in connection with the right of parents to control the upbringing of their children.

license.[34] Although the Court recognized that freedom of religious conduct was not absolute, it said that "[i]n every case the power to regulate must be so exercised as not, in attaining a permissible end, unduly to infringe the protected freedom."[35] The Court said that a licensing system for religious solicitations violated both the free exercise and free speech clauses of the First Amendment.[36]

Similarly, in *Murdock v. Pennsylvania*[37] and *Follett v. Town of McCormick*,[38] the Supreme Court said that it was unconstitutional for a state to apply a license tax to a Jehovah's Witness who went door to door soliciting funds for the religion and distributing literature. In *Murdock*, the Court found unconstitutional a flat license tax for the privilege of soliciting within a municipality when it was applied to individuals who were disseminating religious material and soliciting for their religion.[39]

Similarly, in *Follett v. McCormick*, the Court declared unconstitutional a city's tax on agents selling books when the tax was applied to the distributor of religious literature.[40] The Court, again in an opinion by Justice Douglas, found that the tax infringed on free exercise of religion. Justice Douglas wrote: "Freedom of religion is not merely reserved for those with a long purse. Preachers of the more orthodox faiths are not engaged in commercial undertakings because they are dependent on their calling for a living. Whether needy or affluent they avail themselves of the constitutional privilege of a 'free exercise' of their religion when they enter the pulpit to proclaim their faith. The priest or preacher is as fully protected in his function as the parishioners are in their worship."[41]

Murdock and *Follett* involved license taxes directed at First Amendment activity: distributing literature and soliciting funds. They do not involve constitutional challenges to the application of general taxes, such as sales taxes, to sales of religious materials.[42] Also, the free exercise and free speech claims were intertwined; the defendants in both cases were engaged in religious activity, but their conduct also was protected speech under the First Amendment.[43]

Although the Court protected religious solicitation, the Court also made it clear during this time period that the government could impose limits on such activities. In *Prince v. Massachusetts*, the Court held that a state could prohibit

---

[34] 310 U.S. 296 (1940).

[35] *Id.* at 304.

[36] *Id.* at 307.

[37] 319 U.S. 105 (1943).

[38] 321 U.S. 573 (1944).

[39] 319 U.S. at 114.

[40] 321 U.S. at 573.

[41] *Id.* at 576-577.

[42] The Court later upheld such a tax in Jimmy Swaggart Ministries v. Board of Equalization of Cal., 493 U.S. 378 (1990).

[43] *See also* West Va. State Bd. of Educ. v. Barnette, 319 U.S. 624 (1943), which declared unconstitutional the state's flag salute law. Although the challenge was brought by Jehovah's Witnesses, the Court relied on a broad First Amendment principle against forced speech. *Barnette* is discussed in detail in §11.2.4.3.

children from being used in solicitations and rejected claims based on free exercise of religion and the right of parents to control the upbringing of their children.[44]

§12.3.2.2   Strict Scrutiny, at Least in Theory: The Cases from 1960 to 1990

Articulation of Strict Scrutiny

In *Sherbert v. Verner,*[45] the Supreme Court expressly held that strict scrutiny was the appropriate test in evaluating government laws burdening religious freedom.[46] A state denied unemployment benefits to a woman, a member of the Seventh-day Adventist Church, who quit her job rather than work on her Saturday Sabbath. The Court concluded that the denial of benefits imposed a substantial burden on religion; the woman had to choose between an income and her faith. The Court thus said that the issue was "whether some compelling state interest enforced in the eligibility provisions of the . . . statute justifies the substantial infringement of appellant's First Amendment right."[47] The Court found no such compelling interest and ruled that the denial of benefits constituted a violation of the free exercise clause.

Although *Sherbert* clearly stated that strict scrutiny was to be used in evaluating laws infringing on free exercise of religion, following *Sherbert*, the Court rarely struck down laws on this basis. In fact, there were only two areas where the Court invalidated laws for violating free exercise: laws, like the statute in *Sherbert*, that denied benefits to those who quit their jobs for religious reasons; and the application of a compulsory school law to the Amish. In all other free exercise clause cases between 1960 and 1990, the Court upheld the laws.

Government Benefit Cases

In several later cases, the Court reaffirmed its holding in *Sherbert v. Verner* that the government could not deny benefits to individuals who left their jobs because of religious reasons. For example, in *Thomas v. Review Board,* the Court held that the government could not deny unemployment benefits to an individual who quit his job rather than accept a transfer to work in an armaments section of the factory.[48] The individual said that he was quitting for religious reasons, and the Court said it accepted this explanation even though others of his faith saw no problem in working in that part of the factory. The Court said that it was not for the judiciary

---

[44] 321 U.S. 158 (1944).
[45] 374 U.S. 398 (1963).
[46] The right of parents to control the upbringing of their children is discussed in §10.2.4.
[47] *Sherbert,* 374 U.S. at 406.
[48] 450 U.S. 707 (1981).

to evaluate the proper content of religious doctrines and said that it was "clear that Thomas terminated his employment for religious reasons."[49]

In *Hobbie v. Unemployment Appeals Commission of Florida*, the Court applied *Sherbert* and *Thomas* and held that the state was required to provide unemployment benefits to a woman who was fired when she refused to work on her Saturday Sabbath.[50] Similarly, in *Frazee v. Illinois Department of Employment Security*, the Court found that a state law that required unemployed individuals to be available for work seven days a week infringed on free exercise when it was applied to deny benefits to an individual who refused to work on his Sunday Sabbath.[51] The Court said that it was immaterial that the individual was not a member of an organized church, sect, or denomination. His sincere religious belief was impermissibly burdened by the denial of benefits.

Wisconsin v. Yoder

The only other case where the Court found a violation of the free exercise clause during this time was in *Wisconsin v. Yoder*,[52] where the Court held that free exercise of religion required that Amish parents be granted an exemption from compulsory school laws for their 14- and 15-year-old children. The Court noted that the "Amish objection to formal education beyond the eighth grade is firmly grounded in these central religious concepts. They object to the high school, and higher education generally, because the values they teach are in marked variance with Amish values and the Amish way of life; they view secondary school education as an impermissible exposure of their children to a 'worldly' influence in conflict with their beliefs."[53]

The Court accepted this argument and found that requiring 14- and 15-year-old Amish children to attend school violated the free exercise clause and also infringed on the right of parents to control the upbringing of their children.[54] Chief Justice Burger, writing for the Court, said that "the record in this case abundantly supports the claim that the traditional way of life of the Amish is not merely a matter of personal preference, but one of deep religious conviction, shared by an organized group, and intimately related to daily living."[55] The Court concluded that "[t]he impact of the compulsory-attendance law on respondents' practice of the Amish religion is not only severe, but inescapable, for the Wisconsin law affirmatively compels them, under threat of criminal sanction, to perform acts undeniably at odds with . . . their religious beliefs. . . . [E]nforcement of the State's requirement of compulsory formal education after the eighth grade would gravely endanger if not destroy the free exercise of respondents' religious beliefs."[56]

[49] *Id.* at 716.
[50] 480 U.S. 136 (1987).
[51] 489 U.S. 829 (1989).
[52] 406 U.S. 205 (1972).
[53] *Id.* at 210-211.
[54] The right of parents to control the upbringing of their children is discussed in §10.2.4.
[55] 406 U.S. at 216.
[56] *Id.* at 218-219.

The Court concluded that the "self-sufficient" nature of Amish society made education for 14- and 15-year-old children unnecessary.[57] The Court said that the lack of "two additional years of compulsory education will not impair the physical or mental health of the child, or result in an inability to be self-supporting or to discharge the duties and responsibilities of citizenship, or in any other way materially detract from the welfare of society."[58]

Cases Rejecting Exemptions Based on the Free Exercise Clause

Other than the employment compensation cases and *Yoder*, the Court during this period never found another law to violate the free exercise clause. The Court was asked in many cases to allow an exemption to a law based on free exercise.[59] In each, the Court rejected the constitutional claim. As the Court noted in *Employment Division v. Smith*: "We have never invalidated any government action on the basis of the *Sherbert* test except the denial of unemployment compensation. Although we have sometimes purported to apply the *Sherbert* test in contexts other than that, we have always found the test satisfied. In recent years we have abstained from applying the *Sherbert* test (outside the unemployment compensation field) at all."[60]

The cases rejecting free exercise challenges occurred in a wide variety of contexts. For example, two years before *Sherbert*, in *Braunfeld v. Brown*, the Supreme Court rejected a free exercise clause challenge to Sunday closing laws.[61] Orthodox Jews argued that their religion required that their businesses be closed on Saturdays and that it was difficult for them to adhere to their religion if they also had to be closed on Sundays. Chief Justice Warren, writing for the plurality, rejected this argument and said: "[T]he statute before us does not make criminal the holding of any religious belief or opinion, nor does it force anyone to embrace any religious belief. . . . To strike down legislation which imposes only an indirect burden on the exercise of religion would radically restrict the operating latitude of the legislature."[62] The Court accepted the state's argument that Sunday closing laws served the important government interest of providing a uniform day of rest.

There is, however, an obvious tension between *Braunfeld* and *Sherbert*; in the latter, economic burdens on religion were deemed sufficient to trigger strict scrutiny, while in the former, the Court rejected such financial concerns as a basis for a

---

[57] *Id.* at 235.

[58] *Id.* at 234.

[59] There is a rich scholarly literature reviewing the framers' intent behind the free exercise clause and debating the extent to which it was meant to be a basis for exemptions from laws. *See, e.g.,* Michael W. McConnell, The Origins and Historical Understanding of Free Exercise of Religion, 103 Harv. L. Rev. 1409 (1990); Ira Lupu, Where Rights Begin: The Problem of Burdens on the Free Exercise of Religion, 102 Harv. L. Rev. 933 (1989).

[60] 494 U.S. at 883.

[61] 366 U.S. 599 (1961). The Court also rejected establishment clause challenges to these laws; *see* McGowan v. Maryland, 366 U.S. 420 (1961), discussed above in §12.2.3.

[62] *Id.* at 603, 606.

free exercise clause challenge. Moreover, the importance of a uniform day of rest, especially compared to the religious claim, can be questioned.

In many cases during this time period, the Court rejected challenges to tax laws based on free exercise of religion. For example, in *United States v. Lee*, the Court rejected a claim by an Amish individual that the requirement for paying Social Security taxes violated the free exercise clause.[63] The argument was that "the Amish believe it sinful not to provide for their own elderly and therefore are religiously opposed to the national social security system."[64] The Court found, however, that this restriction on religious freedom was "essential to accomplish an overriding governmental interest."[65] The Court concluded that mandatory participation in the Social Security system was "indispensable to [its] fiscal vitality."[66]

In *Jimmy Swaggart Ministries v. Board of Equalization of California*, the Court rejected a free exercise challenge to the payment of sales and use taxes for the sale of goods and literature by religious groups.[67] The Court distinguished the earlier cases, *Murdock* and *Follett*, discussed above, on the ground that they involved laws that taxed only the First Amendment activity of soliciting. In contrast, in *Jimmy Swaggart Ministries*, the Court said that free exercise did not create a basis for an exemption from a general tax law.[68]

Another case involving a claim for an exemption to a tax law on religious grounds was *Bob Jones University v. United States*, where the Court held that the denial of tax-exempt status to private schools that racially discriminated because of sincere religious beliefs did not violate the free exercise clause.[69] The Court, in an opinion by Chief Justice Burger, explained: "[T]he Government has a fundamental, overriding interest in eradicating racial discrimination in education [which] substantially outweighs whatever burden denial of tax benefits places on petitioners' exercise of their religious beliefs."[70] The Court found that eliminating discrimination was a compelling government interest and that "no less restrictive means are available to achieve the government interest."[71]

In *Bowen v. Roy*, the Court rejected the claim for a religious exemption to the requirement that individuals provide Social Security numbers in order to receive welfare benefits.[72] Individuals argued that their religion was violated by the requirement for Social Security numbers. The Court denied this claim and declared: "Never to our knowledge has the Court interpreted the First Amendment

---

[63]   455 U.S. 252 (1982).

[64]   *Id.* at 255.

[65]   *Id.* at 257-258.

[66]   *Id.* at 258. *See also* Hernandez v. Commissioner, 490 U.S. 680 (1989) (rejecting free exercise clause challenge to payment of income taxes alleged to make religious activities more difficult).

[67]   493 U.S. 378 (1990).

[68]   In *Tony and Susan Alamo Foundation v. Secretary of Labor*, 471 U.S. 290 (1985), the Court rejected the argument that complying with state minimum wage laws violated the free exercise of religion. The Court said that the law did not burden religion because individuals who did not wish to be paid could return their salaries to the religion. *Id.* at 304.

[69]   461 U.S. 574 (1983).

[70]   *Id.* at 604.

[71]   *Id.*

[72]   476 U.S. 693 (1986).

to require the Government *itself* to behave in ways that the individual believes will further his or her spiritual development. . . . [The] Free Exercise Clause affords an individual protection from certain forms of governmental compulsion; it does not afford an individual a right to dictate the conduct of the Government's internal procedures."[73]

In other contexts, besides those involving taxation and government benefits, the Court also rejected free exercise challenges. Some of these cases involved the military. For instance, in *Gillette v. United States*, the Court held that the free exercise clause did not require that individuals who objected to a particular war on religious grounds be given an exemption from the draft.[74] The Court said that "the impact of conscription on objectors to particular wars is far from unjustified. The conscription laws, applied to such persons as to others, are not designed to interfere with any religious ritual or practice, and do not work a penalty against any theological position."[75] The Court said that the draft laws that did not create a religious exemption for those opposed to particular wars "are strictly justified by substantial government interests."[76]

The Court also rejected a free exercise challenge to the military in *Goldman v. Weinberger*, where the Court, by a 5-to-4 margin, denied the claim of an Orthodox Jewish doctor in the Air Force who said that his religion required that he wear a yarmulke in violation of the dress code.[77] Simcha Goldman, a clinical psychologist in the Air Force, was an Orthodox Jew and an ordained rabbi. He was ordered not to wear his yarmulke on duty because it was inconsistent with the Air Force dress code.

The Court proclaimed the need for deference to the military and said that "[o]ur review of military regulations challenged on First Amendment grounds is far more deferential than constitutional review of similar laws or regulations designed for civilian society."[78] The Court said that "to accomplish its mission the military must foster instinctive obedience, unity, commitment and espirit de corps. The essence of military service is the subordination of the desires and interests of the individual to the needs of the service."[79] The Court said that it accepted the "considered professional judgment of the Air Force . . . that the traditional outfitting of personnel in standardized uniforms encourages the subordination of personal preferences and identities in favor of the overall group mission."[80] Justice Rehnquist, writing for the Court, concluded that the "First Amendment does not require the military to accommodate such practices in the face of its view that they would detract from the uniformity sought by the dress regulations."[81]

---

[73] *Id.* at 699.
[74] 401 U.S. 437 (1971).
[75] *Id.* at 462.
[76] *Id.*
[77] 475 U.S. 503 (1986).
[78] *Id.* at 507.
[79] *Id.*
[80] *Id.* at 508.
[81] *Id.* at 509-510.

All of these cases reflect the Court's refusal to uphold free exercise challenges to specific laws. In *Lyng v. Northwest Indian Cemetery Protective Association*, the Court made this even more explicit and rejected a free exercise clause challenge to the federal government's building a road and allowing timber harvesting in a national forest that contained sacred Indian burial grounds.[82] The Court recognized that the construction would "virtually . . . destroy the Indians' ability to practice their religion"[83] because it would irreparably damage "sacred areas which are an integral and necessary part of their belief systems."[84] Nonetheless, the Court said that "[t]he Free Exercise Clause simply cannot be understood to require the Government to conduct its own internal affairs in ways that comport with the religious beliefs of particular citizens. . . . [The] Free Exercise Clause affords an individual protection from certain forms of government compulsion; it does not afford an individual a right to dictate the conduct of the Government's internal procedures."[85]

These cases thus reflect a variety of techniques that the Court used to deny free exercise clause claims. Sometimes, as in *Bowen*, the Court applied strict scrutiny, but found it to be met. In other cases, such as *Lee* and *Goldman*, the Court did not use strict scrutiny.[86] In each of these cases, the Court rejected the claim of an exemption to a law based on free exercise of religion.

§12.3.2.3 *Employment Division v. Smith* and Its Application

Employment Division v. Smith

In *Employment Division v. Smith*, the Court expressly changed the law of the free exercise clause.[87] *Smith* involved a challenge by Native Americans to an Oregon law prohibiting use of peyote, a hallucinogenic substance. Specifically, individuals challenged the state's determination that their religious use of peyote, which resulted in their dismissal from employment, was misconduct disqualifying them from receipt of unemployment compensation benefits.

Justice Scalia, writing for the majority, rejected the claim that free exercise of religion required an exemption from an otherwise valid law. Scalia said that "[w]e have never held that an individual's religious beliefs excuse him from compliance with an otherwise valid law prohibiting conduct that the State is free to regulate. On the contrary, the record of more than a century of our free exercise

---

[82] 485 U.S. 439 (1988).

[83] *Id.* at 451.

[84] *Id.* at 442.

[85] *Id.* at 448 (citation omitted).

[86] The Court expressly rejected the use of strict scrutiny for free exercise challenges in the prison context in *O'Lone v. Estate of Shabazz*, 482 U.S. 342 (1987), which said that restrictions of free exercise in prison were allowed if they were reasonably related to legitimate penological interests. The Court in *O'Lone* rejected a prisoner's claim of an exemption from prison work requirements in order to attend worship services.

[87] 494 U.S. 872 (1990).

jurisprudence contradicts that proposition."[88] Scalia thus declared "that the right of free exercise does not relieve an individual of the obligation to comply with a 'valid and neutral law of general applicability on the ground that the law proscribes (or prescribes) conduct that his religion prescribes (or proscribes).' "[89]

Justice Scalia's opinion then reviewed the cases where free exercise clause challenges had been upheld—such as *Cantwell, Murdock, Follett, Pierce,* and *Yoder*—and said that none involved free exercise clause claims alone. All involved "the Free Exercise Clause in conjunction with other constitutional protections, such as freedom of speech and of the press, or the right of parents to direct the education of their children."[90] The Court said that *Smith* was distinguishable because it did not involve such a "hybrid situation," but was a free exercise claim "unconnected with any communicative activity or parental right."[91]

Moreover, the Court said that the *Sherbert* line of cases applied only in the context of the denial of unemployment benefits; it did not create a basis for an exemption from criminal laws. Scalia wrote that "[e]ven if we were inclined to breathe into *Sherbert* some life beyond the unemployment compensation field, we would not apply it to require exemptions from a generally applicable criminal law."[92]

The Court expressly rejected the use of strict scrutiny for challenges to neutral laws of general applicability that burden religion. Justice Scalia said that "[p]recisely because 'we are a cosmopolitan nation made up of people of almost every conceivable religious preference,' and precisely because we value and protect that religious divergence, we cannot afford the luxury of deeming presumptively invalid, as applied to the religious objector, every regulation of conduct that does not protect an interest of the highest order."[93] The Court said that those seeking religious exemptions from laws should look to the democratic process for protection, not the courts.

Justice O'Connor concurred in the judgment and argued that the Court should uphold the Oregon law under the existing test for the free exercise clause by finding that a compelling interest was served in preventing the use of peyote.[94] O'Connor disagreed with the majority's description of the prior cases and especially its leaving the protection of minority religions to the political process. She said that the "First Amendment was enacted precisely to protect the rights of those whose religious practices are not shared by the majority and may be viewed with hostility."[95] She said that strict scrutiny is appropriate for free exercise challenges

---

[88] *Id.* at 878-889.

[89] *Id.* at 879 (citation omitted).

[90] *Id.* at 881.

[91] *Id.* at 882.

[92] *Id.* at 884.

[93] *Id.* at 888 (citation omitted).

[94] *Id.* at 906 (O'Connor, J., concurring in the judgment) ("I believe that granting a selective exemption in this case would seriously impair Oregon's compelling interest in prohibiting possession of peyote by its citizens.").

[95] *Id.* at 902.

because "[t]he compelling interest test reflects the First Amendment's mandate of preserving religious liberty to the fullest extent possible in a pluralistic society."[96]

Justice Blackmun wrote a dissenting opinion that was joined by Justices Brennan and Marshall. The dissenting Justices agreed with Justice O'Connor that the majority had mischaracterized precedents, such as in describing *Yoder* as a "hybrid" case rather than as one under the free exercise clause.[97] The dissent also argued that strict scrutiny should be used in evaluating government laws burdening religion.

There is no doubt that *Smith* changed the test for the free exercise clause. Strict scrutiny was abandoned for evaluating laws burdening religion; neutral laws of general applicability only have to meet the rational basis test, no matter how much they burden religion. However, what is uncertain is how much this change in legal doctrine matters and whether it is desirable.[98]

On the one hand, *Smith* seems a radical change in the law. For instance, prior to *Smith*, if a county had a law prohibiting all consumption of alcoholic beverages, there is no doubt that a free exercise exemption could have been obtained by a priest who wanted to use wine in communion or a Jewish family that wanted to use wine at a Sabbath or seder dinner. Yet after *Smith*, it is clear that the priest or the Jewish family would lose in their free exercise claim. The prohibition of the consumption of alcohol is a neutral law of general applicability; it applies to all in the county and was not motivated by a desire to interfere with religion.

On the other hand, it can be argued that *Smith* simply changed the doctrine of the free exercise clause to reflect the actual pattern of decisions. As reviewed above, the Court had rejected all free exercise clause claims since 1960 except for the employment benefit cases and *Yoder*. *Smith* provided a legal doctrine to explain this outcome: The free exercise clause is not violated by a neutral law of general applicability.

In addition to disagreement over the impact of *Smith*, there also is debate as to whether it is desirable. *Smith* can be criticized as providing inadequate protection for religion. Critics argue, as Justice O'Connor and Justice Blackmun did in their opinions in *Smith*, that free exercise is a fundamental right and that laws burdening it should be subjected to strict scrutiny.[99] But *Smith*'s defenders argue that creating exemptions to general laws for free exercise of religion runs afoul of the establishment clause and that *Smith* appropriately avoids this conflict.[100]

---

[96] *Id.* at 903.

[97] *Id.* at 908-909.

[98] *See, e.g.,* Michael McConnell, Free Exercise Revisionism and the *Smith* Decision, 57 U. Chi. L. Rev. 1109 (1990); Douglas Laycock, The Remnants of Free Exercise, 1990 Sup. Ct. Rev. 1; Jesse H. Choper, The Rise and Decline of the Constitutional Protection of Religious Liberty, 70 Neb. L. Rev. 651 (1991) (criticizing *Smith*); Mark Tushnet, Of Church and State and the Supreme Court: *Kurland* Revisited, 1989 Sup. Ct. Rev. 373; William P. Marshall, In Defense of *Smith* and Free Exercise Revisionism, 58 U. Chi. L. Rev. 308 (1991).

[99] *See, e.g.,* McConnell, *id.* at 1111; Choper, *id.* at 687.

[100] Tushnet, *supra* note 98, at 390; Marshall, *supra* note 98, at 310.

Church of the Lukumi Babalu Aye, Inc. v. Hialeah

There only has been one Supreme Court decision interpreting and applying *Smith*: *Church of the Lukumi Babalu Aye, Inc. v. Hialeah*.[101] The Santería religion uses animal sacrifice as one of its principal forms of worship. Animals are killed and then cooked and eaten in accord with Santería rituals. After the Santerías announced plans to establish a house of worship, a school, a cultural center, and a museum in Hialeah, Florida, the city adopted an ordinance prohibiting ritual sacrifice of animals. The law defined "sacrifice" as killing animals "not for the primary purpose of food consumption."[102] The law applied only to an individual or group that "kills, slaughters, or sacrifices animals for any type of ritual, regardless of whether or not the flesh or blood of the animal is to be consumed."[103]

All of the Justices agreed the law was unconstitutional, with Justice Kennedy writing the opinion for the Court. At the outset, Justice Kennedy reaffirmed the *Smith* test and declared that "our cases establish the general proposition that a law that is neutral and of general applicability need not be justified by a compelling governmental interest even if the law has the incidental effect of burdening a particular religious practice."[104] Kennedy said, however, that "[a] law failing to satisfy these requirements must be justified by a compelling interest and must be narrowly tailored to advance that interest."[105]

The Court decided that the Hialeah law was not neutral because its clear object was to prohibit a religious practice. Justice Kennedy's majority opinion noted that the text of the law spoke of "sacrifice" and "ritual" and that its purpose was clearly to prohibit the practice of the Santería religion.[106] The Court also focused on the exceptions to the law that allowed killing of animals by other religions, such as in kosher slaughtering of animals, and that allowed killing of animals for nonreligious purposes.[107] The Court said that this further indicated the lack of neutrality of the law. The Court concluded that "the neutrality inquiry leads to one conclusion: The ordinances had as their object the suppression of religion."[108]

The Court also said that the law was not one of "general applicability." The Court again noted that "[d]espite the city's proffered interest in preventing cruelty to animals, the ordinances are drafted with care to forbid few killings but those occasioned by religious sacrifice. Many types of animal deaths or kills are either not prohibited or approved by express provision."[109]

Because it concluded that the ordinance was neither neutral nor of general applicability, the Court applied strict scrutiny. The Court found the law

---

[101]   508 U.S. 520 (1993).
[102]   *Id.* at 527.
[103]   *Id.*
[104]   *Id.* at 531 (citing *Smith*).
[105]   *Id.* at 531-532.
[106]   *Id.* at 534-535.
[107]   *Id.* at 536-537.
[108]   *Id.* at 543.
[109]   *Id.*

unconstitutional because the government could achieve the goals of safe and sanitary disposal of animal remains without targeting the Santería religion.

Justice Scalia, in an opinion concurring in part and concurring in the judgment and joined by Chief Justice Rehnquist, wrote separately to argue that the purpose behind a law should not be relevant in determining whether it is neutral and of general applicability.[110] Justice Souter also wrote an opinion concurring in part and concurring in the judgment. He argued that the Court should reconsider and overrule *Smith*.[111] Justice Blackmun concurred in the judgment, in an opinion joined by Justice O'Connor, and "emphasize[d] that the First Amendment's protection of religion extends beyond those rare occasions on which the government explicitly targets religion (or a particular religion) for disfavored treatment."[112]

After *Smith* and *Hialeah*, the law of the free exercise clause was that the provision is not violated by a neutral law of general applicability unless it fails rational basis review, but a law that is not neutral or of general applicability would be found unconstitutional unless it met strict scrutiny.[113]

Lower Court Applications

In the two decades since *Smith,* the lower courts have upheld many laws burdening religion on the ground that they are neutral laws of general applicability. But laws that are seen as targeting a particular religion are subjected to strict scrutiny and are struck down. For example, the United States Court of Appeals for the Ninth Circuit rejected a free exercise challenge to a law requiring individuals to disclose their Social Security number in order to receive a driver's license; the court said that the law was constitutional as a neutral law of general applicability.[114] Similarly, the Tenth Circuit ruled that the Bald and Golden Eagle Protection Act

---

[110] *Id.* at 558-559 (Scalia, J., concurring in part and concurring in the judgment).

[111] *Id.* at 559 (Souter, J., concurring in part and concurring in the judgment).

[112] *Id.* at 577-578.

[113] The Court also distinguished *Employment Division v. Smith* in *Hosanna Tabor Evangelical Lutheran Church and School v. EEOC*, 132 S. Ct. 694 (2012), discussed above in §12.1. The Court found that it violated the free exercise clause (as well as the establishment clause) to hold a religious school liable for the choices it makes as to who will be its ministers. The argument was that it did not violate the free exercise clause because of *Smith*: The federal law prohibiting disability discrimination, and retaliation against those who make claims under the Americans with Disabilities Act, is a neutral law of general applicability. But the Court rejected this argument and distinguished *Smith*: "It is true that the ADA's prohibition on retaliation, like Oregon's prohibition on peyote use, is a valid and neutral law of general applicability. But a church's selection of its ministers is unlike an individual's ingestion of peyote. *Smith* involved government regulation of only outward physical acts. The present case, in contrast, concerns government interference with an internal church decision that affects the faith and mission of the church itself. The contention that *Smith* forecloses recognition of a ministerial exception rooted in the Religion Clauses has no merit." *Id.* at 707. This suggests an exception to *Smith*: There can be challenges based on the free exercise clause to neutral laws of general applicability if the claim is that the law interferes with internal church decision making.

[114] Miller v. Reed, 176 F.3d 1202 (9th Cir. 1999).

did not violate the free exercise rights of Native Americans because the law was neutral and of general applicability.[115]

On the other hand, courts have invalidated laws that target religions and thus are not regarded as neutral and of general applicability. For example, the Seventh Circuit invalidated a prison regulation that forbids crosses unless they include a rosary; the court said that by favoring Catholic and not allowing Protestant symbols the law was unconstitutional.[116] The Third Circuit invalidated a police policy prohibiting beards as violating the free exercise rights of Muslims because it had secular exceptions, but none for religion.[117]

Lower courts have done relatively little to clarify when a claim should be regarded as a "hybrid" under *Smith*, combining a free exercise argument with another constitutional right, and thus triggering strict scrutiny. Many courts have ruled that merely alleging another constitutional violation along with free exercise of religion is not enough to trigger strict scrutiny.[118] But beyond this, it is not clear when a case presents a "hybrid claim" and warrants strict scrutiny. For example, there is a split among the lower courts as to whether a challenge to school uniforms based on free exercise of religion and the right of parents to control the upbringing of their children triggers strict scrutiny.[119]

Is the Denial of Funding a Violation of the Free Exercise Clause?

The Court has confronted one other important free exercise issue since *Smith*: Whether the refusal to allow aid to be used for religious education impermissibly violates free exercise of religion. *Locke v. Davey* held that a state government can restrict its college scholarships so as to prevent them from being used by those studying for the ministry.[120] The Court emphasized that while the government may constitutionally allow such use of its scholarships, it is not constitutionally required to do so.

Locke v. Davey arose from Washington's program of giving scholarships to students who qualify academically and financially and who attend college in the state. Students can attend any public or private college, including a religiously affiliated college, and may study whatever they choose. But there is one limit: Students must not be pursuing a degree that is "devotional"; that is, the student cannot use the scholarship to study for training to become a minister. Washington justified this restriction based on a provision in its state constitution that provides that

---

[115] United States v. Wilgus, 2001 U.S. App. LEXIS 17700, 2001 Colo. J. C.A.R. 3976 (10th Cir. 2001); *rehearing en banc granted by* United States v. Hardman, 260 F.3d 1199 (10th Cir. 2001).

[116] Sasnett v. Litscher, 197 F.3d 290 (7th Cir. 1999).

[117] FOP Network Lodge No. 12 v. City of Newark, 170 F.3d 359 (3d Cir. 1999).

[118] *See, e.g.*, Miller v. Reed, 176 F.3d 1202 (9th Cir. 1999); Swanson v. Guthrie Indep. School Dist., 135 F.3d 694 (10th Cir. 1998).

[119] Littlefield v. Forney Indep. School Dist., 108 F. Supp. 2d 681 (N.D. Tex. 2000) (only rational basis review); Hicks v. Halifax County Bd. of Educ., 93 F. Supp. 2d 649 (E.D.N.C. 1999) (strict scrutiny for a hybrid claim).

[120] 540 U.S. 712 (2004).

"[n]o public money or property shall be appropriated for or applied to any religious worship, exercise or instruction, or the support of any religious establishment."[121]

Joshua Davey, a recipient of a Promise Scholarship, chose to attend Northwest College, a private Christian college affiliated with the Assemblies of God denomination. Davey sought to become a minister and had a double major in pastoral ministries and business management/administration. When Davey was informed that he could not receive the Promise Scholarship if he pursued training to become a minister, he refused the aid and filed a lawsuit challenging the restriction. Davey argued that Washington violated the free exercise clause of the First Amendment by allowing students to receive scholarship assistance if they pursued secular, but not religious, studies.

In a 7-to-2 decision, with the majority opinion written by Chief Justice Rehnquist, the Court rejected that contention and ruled in favor of the State of Washington. At the outset, the Court emphasized that Washington could, if it wanted, allow its scholarships to be used by students studying to be clergy members. In *Witters v. Washington Dept. of Services for the Blind*,[122] the Supreme Court unanimously ruled that it did not violate the establishment clause of the First Amendment for the government to permit students receiving scholarship assistance to study for the ministry.

But the Court explained that denying Davey scholarship money to study to be a minister does not interfere with his free exercise of religion in any way. He still can receive training to be a pastor, just without it being subsidized by the government. The Court stressed that many states historically have sought to limit use of their taxpayers' money to subsidize religious institutions.

A contrary ruling would have dramatically changed the law and would have meant that any time the government provides assistance to private secular entities it would be required to give the same aid to religious institutions. Ultimately, *Locke v. Davey* means that government at all levels can choose how it wants to spend taxpayers' money and the extent, if any, it wants to financially support religion. The Court recognized that the case posed an issue where there is some tension between the establishment clause and the free exercise clause, but it concluded that it is a choice to be made by the political process and not the courts.

§12.3.2.4   The Religious Freedom Restoration Act, Its Invalidity, and the Religious Land Use and Institutionalized Persons Act

The Religious Freedom Restoration Act of 1993 was adopted to negate the *Smith* test and require strict scrutiny for free exercise clause claims.[123] Indeed, the findings section of the Act notes that *Smith* "virtually eliminated the requirement that the government justify burdens on religious exercise imposed by laws neutral

---

[121] Washington Constitution, Art. I, §11.
[122] 474 U.S. 481 (1986), discussed above in §12.2.6.3.
[123] 42 U.S.C. §2000bb.

toward religion."[124] The Act declares that its purpose is "to restore the compelling interest test as set forth in *Sherbert v. Verner* and *Wisconsin v. Yoder*, and to guarantee its application in all cases where free exercise of religion is substantially burdened; and to provide a claim or defense to persons whose religious exercise is substantially burdened by government."[125] The key provision of the Act states: "Government shall not substantially burden a person's exercise of religion even if the burden results from a rule of general applicability, except . . . [g]overnment may substantially burden a person's exercise of religion only if it demonstrates that application of the burden to the person (1) is in furtherance of a compelling governmental interest; (2) is the least restrictive means of furthering that compelling government interest."[126]

The Religious Freedom Restoration Act thus sought to overrule *Smith* and make strict scrutiny the test for all free exercise clause claims.

In *City of Boerne v. Flores*, the Supreme Court declared unconstitutional the Religious Freedom Restoration Act.[127] The Court, in a 6-to-3 decision, ruled that Congress exceeded the scope of its power under §5 of the Fourteenth Amendment in enacting the law. Justice Kennedy, writing for the majority, stated that §5 empowers Congress to enact laws "to enforce" the amendment, but Congress is not "enforcing" when it creates new constitutional rights or expands the scope of rights.[128] The Court held that Congress under §5 may act only to prevent or remedy the violation of rights recognized by the courts. Such laws must be narrowly tailored; they must be proportionate and congruent to prevent and remedy the constitutional violations.[129] The Religious Freedom Restoration Act was deemed to fail these requirements and was declared unconstitutional.

City of Boerne clearly invalidated the Religious Freedom Restoration Act as applied to state and local governments, but its reasoning does not speak to the constitutionality of the law as applied to the federal government. The congressional authority to regulate state and local governments was claimed to be §5 of the Fourteenth Amendment; but this provision, like the entire Fourteenth Amendment, does not apply to the federal government. Therefore, the constitutionality of the Religious Freedom Restoration Act as applied to the federal government is not resolved by *City of Boerne v. Flores* and has not been addressed by the Supreme Court since.

But in subsequent cases, the Court has applies the Religious Freedom Restoration Act to the federal government. In 2006, in *Gonzales v. O Centro Espirita Beneficente União do Vegetal*, the Court used the Religious Freedom Restoration Act

---

[124] Section (a)(4) of the Act.

[125] Section (b) (citations omitted).

[126] Section (1)(a) and (b).

[127] 521 U.S. 507 (1997).

[128] *Id.* at 519-520. I have criticized this aspect of *City of Boerne v. Flores* in Erwin Chemerinsky, The Religious Freedom Restoration Act Is a Constitutional Expansion of Rights, 39 Wm. & Mary L. Rev. 601 (1998).

[129] 521 U.S. at 508. The scope of Congress's §5 powers, including *City of Boerne v. Flores*, is discussed in detail in §3.7.2.

to unanimously rule in favor of a religion and against the federal government.[130] The case involved a small religion that used a controlled substance in making a tea used in its religious rituals. The Court, in an opinion by Chief Justice Roberts, used strict scrutiny under the Religious Freedom Restoration Act and ruled in favor of the religion, concluding that the government failed to show that keeping this small religion from using the controlled substance would serve a compelling government interest. The Court did not expressly consider the constitutionality of the Religious Freedom Restoration Act as applied to the federal government, but it assumed this in unanimously ruling in favor of the religious group.

Most recently and most dramatically, in *Burwell v. Hobby Lobby*, the Court held that it violates the Religious Freedom Restoration Act to require that a closely held corporation provide insurance coverage for contraceptives that violates its owners' religious beliefs.[131] A federal law required that the Department of Health and Human Services promulgate regulations requiring that health insurance provided by employers include preventative health care coverage for women. These regulations mandate that employer-provided insurance include contraceptive coverage for women. Although religious institutions and nonprofit corporations affiliated with religious institutions may exempt themselves from this requirement, for-profit companies must comply.

In a 5-4 decision, the Supreme Court held that it violated the federal Religious Freedom Restoration Act to require a closely held for-profit corporation to provide coverage for contraceptives that it says violate the religious beliefs of its owners. Justice Alito wrote the majority opinion. The Court said that Congress "included corporations within RFRA's definition of 'persons.'"[132] The Court held that corporations can claim to have religious beliefs and religious free exercise. It stated: "A corporation is simply a form of organization used by human beings to achieve desired ends. . . . When rights, whether constitutional or statutory, are extended to corporations, the purpose is to protect the rights of these people."[133]

The Court said that it had "little trouble concluding" that the contraceptive mandate substantially burdened the religious beliefs of owners of closely held corporations who opposed certain contraceptives.[134] The Court said that it would assume that the government has a compelling interest in ensuring the availability of contraceptives for women, but that there were less restrictive alternatives: Congress could directly pay for these contraceptives or Congress could allow for-profit companies the same ability to opt out that it had given to not-for-profit companies that are affiliated with religions that oppose contraception. The Court thus concluded that "[t]he contraceptive mandate, as applied to closely held corporations, violates RFRA."[135]

Justice Ginsburg wrote a vigorous dissent, joined by Justices Breyer, Sotomayor, and Kagan, and disagreed with every aspect of the majority's opinion. The dissent

---

[130] 546 U.S. 418 (2006).
[131] 134 S. Ct. 2751 (2014).
[132] *Id.* at 2768.
[133] *Id.*
[134] *Id.* at 2775.
[135] *Id.* at 2785.

disagreed that for-profit corporations can have religious beliefs or religious free exercise and stated that "until today, religious exemptions had never been extended to any entity operating in the commercial, profit-making world."[136] The dissent also disagreed that there is a substantial burdening of religious belief from requiring employers to provide insurance that includes coverage for contraceptives. Justice Ginsburg wrote: "The requirement carries no command that Hobby Lobby or Conestoga purchase or provide the contraceptives they find objectionable. Instead, it calls on the companies covered by the requirement to direct money into undifferentiated funds that finance a wide variety of benefits under comprehensive health plans. . . . Any decision to use contraceptives made by a woman covered under Hobby Lobby's or Conestoga's plan will not be propelled by the Government, it will be the woman's autonomous choice, informed by the physician she consults."[137]

The dissent also disagreed with the majority's conclusion that there are less restrictive alternatives. Justice Ginsburg's dissenting opinion stressed that this will open the door to other claims under RFRA for an exemption to providing health insurance coverage. She wrote: "Would the exemption the Court holds RFRA demands for employers with religiously grounded objections to the use of certain contraceptives extend to employers with religiously grounded objections to blood transfusions (Jehovah's Witnesses); antidepressants (Scientologists); medications derived from pigs, including anesthesia, intravenous fluids, and pills coated with gelatin (certain Muslims, Jews, and Hindus); and vaccinations (Christian Scientists, among others)?"[138]

The dissent was concerned, too, that this could lead to claims for religious exemptions to other federal laws, such as antidiscrimination statutes. The majority opinion responded to this by denying this possibility because "[t]he Government has a compelling interest in providing an equal opportunity to participate in the workforce without regard to race, and prohibitions on racial discrimination are precisely tailored to achieve that critical goal."[139]

Hobby Lobby was a 5-4 decision and very politically controversial. Its defenders see it as applying a federal statute to protect the sincere religious views of the owners of family-held businesses. Its critics see it as an unprecedented expansion of protection of rights for corporations and a precedent that opens the door to exemptions to other federal laws.

In addition to the Religious Freedom Restoration Act, in 2000, in response to *City of Boerne v. Flores*, the Religious Land Use and Institutionalized Persons Act was adopted.[140] This law requires that the government meet strict scrutiny when it significantly burdens religion in two areas: land use decisions and institutionalized persons. Congress justified acting to regulate land use decisions under its commerce power and to regulate institutionalized persons under its spending power

---

[136] *Id.* at 2795 (Ginsburg, J., dissenting).

[137] *Id.* at 2799.

[138] *Id.* at 2805.

[139] *Id.* at 2783. It is worth noting that the Court said that there was a compelling interest in stopping race discrimination, but did not mention gender or sexual orientation discrimination.

[140] 42 U.S.C. §2000cc.

as a condition on federal funds. In *Cutter v. Wilkinson,* the Court rejected a constitutional challenge that the law violated the establishment clause by impermissibly favoring religion. In a unanimous opinion written by Justice Ginsburg, the Court concluded that the government's accommodation of religion and protection of free exercise of religion did not impermissibly establish religion. The Court left open the issue of whether the law was a permissible exercise of Congress's powers.

§12.3.3   Government Involvement in Religious Disputes

Refusal of Courts to Become Involved in Internal Disputes

When disputes arise within a religion, especially as to the ownership of property, the matter may be brought to the courts for a resolution. The problem, of course, is that such cases often ask the judiciary to rule on internal religious matters.[141] The Supreme Court has made it clear that it is impermissible for the courts to decide questions of religious doctrine in handling such cases. Moreover, the Court has said that when a religion has a hierarchical structure for deciding church matters, the judiciary must defer to decisions emanating from that decision-making structure.

The Supreme Court first considered judicial involvement in church disputes in *Watson v. Jones.*[142] The Court was asked to decide which of two competing groups had control over church property. Although the Court decided on nonconstitutional grounds, its analysis has been invoked in subsequent First Amendment decisions.[143] The Court said: "In this country, the full and free right to entertain any religious belief, to practice any religious principle, and to teach any religious doctrine which does not . . . infringe personal rights, is conceded to all. The law knows no heresy, and is committed to the support of no dogma, the establishment of no sect. . . . [I]t would be a vain consent and would lead to the total subversion of religious bodies, if any one aggrieved by one of their decisions could appeal to the secular courts and have them reversed."[144]

In *Gonzalez v. Roman Catholic Archbishop of Manila,* the Court said that the judiciary could not decide the qualifications of a chaplain of the Roman Catholic Church.[145] An estate left money for the establishment of chaplaincy in the Church and specified that the funds should be given to the deceased's nearest male relative. The Church refused to allow an individual to have the position based on its

---

[141] Although this issue is discussed under the free exercise clause, it also could be phrased as an establishment clause question: When does government or court involvement in church disputes violate the establishment clause? Analytically, it does not seem to matter whether this issue is characterized as a free exercise clause issue or one involving the establishment clause.

[142] 80 U.S. (13 Wall.) 679 (1871).

[143] *See* Presbyterian Church in the United States v. Mary Elizabeth Blue Hull Meml. Presbyterian Church, 393 U.S. 440, 446 (1969).

[144] 80 U.S. at 728-729.

[145] 280 U.S. 1 (1929).

religious principles. The Supreme Court said that the judiciary could not resolve the dispute. The Court emphasized that the Church through its hierarchical structure could decide who was qualified to be chaplain.

Similarly, in *Presbyterian Church v. Mary Elizabeth Blue Hull Memorial Presbyterian Church*, the judiciary was asked to resolve a property dispute when two local churches attempted to withdraw from the national Presbyterian Church.[146] The Court said that "First Amendment values are plainly jeopardized when church property litigation is made to turn on the resolution by civil courts of controversies over religious doctrine and practice. . . . Hence, States, religious organizations, and individuals must structure relationships involving church property so as not to require civil courts to resolve ecclesiastical questions."[147] The Court said that the judiciary could not be in the position of interpreting church doctrine.

The Court has indicated that the courts can resolve internal church disputes over ownership of property only if the decision will turn entirely on secular legal principles and will not require the courts to decide any issues of religious doctrine. For example, in *Jones v. Wolf*, the Court remanded a case to the state courts to decide whether a disagreement over ownership of property could be resolved under traditional property law principles or whether inquiry into the religion was required.[148] The Court said that the former—a decision with no inquiry into religion—was permissible; but any judicial determination of religious beliefs was not allowed under the First Amendment.

In *Serbian Eastern Orthodox Diocese for the United States of America and Canada v. Milivojevich*, the judiciary was asked to review the decision of a religion to defrock and remove one of its bishops.[149] The Court noted that "[t]he basic dispute is over control of the Serbian Eastern Orthodox Diocese for the United States of America and Canada, its property, and its assets."[150] The Court reversed a state court decision resolving the dispute and said that the state court ruling "rests upon an impermissible rejection of the decisions of the highest ecclesiastical tribunals of this hierarchical church upon the issues in dispute, and impermissibly substitutes its own inquiry into church polity."[151]

The Court said that "where resolution of the disputes cannot be made without extensive inquiry by civil courts into religious law and polity, the First and Fourteenth Amendments mandate that civil courts shall not disturb the decisions of the highest ecclesiastical tribunal within a church of hierarchical polity, but must accept the decisions as binding on them, in their application to the religious issues of doctrine or polity before them."[152] The Court thus concluded that it was not for the judiciary to review the appropriateness of the defrocking and removal of the bishop.

---

[146] 393 U.S. 440 (1969).
[147] *Id.* at 449.
[148] 443 U.S. 595 (1979).
[149] 426 U.S. 696 (1976).
[150] *Id.* at 698.
[151] *Id.* at 708.
[152] *Id.* at 709.

Laws Resolving Church Disputes

These cases all involved attempts to use the judiciary to resolve internal church disputes. The Court also has said that the legislature, by statute, may not attempt to decide such controversies. In *Kedroff v. St. Nicholas Cathedral*, the Court declared unconstitutional a state law that granted ownership of church property to the American branch of the Russian Orthodox Church.[153] The Court concluded that the law violated free exercise of religion by interfering with an internal church dispute. The Court explained that in the context of an internal church dispute, the state law was deciding who was the "true" church. The Court said that the hierarchical church had to decide for itself, through its own processes, who owned the church's property.

---

[153]   344 U.S. 94 (1952).

APPENDIX

The Constitution of the United States of America

We the People of the United States, in Order to form a more perfect Union, establish Justice, insure domestic Tranquility, provide for the common defence, promote the general Welfare, and secure the Blessings of Liberty to ourselves and our Posterity, do ordain and establish this Constitution for the United States of America.

ARTICLE I

SECTION 1. All legislative Powers herein granted shall be vested in a Congress of the United States, which shall consist of a Senate and House of Representatives.

SECTION 2. The House of Representatives shall be composed of Members chosen every second Year by the People of the several States, and the Electors in each State shall have the Qualifications requisite for Electors of the most numerous Branch of the State Legislature.

No person shall be a Representative who shall not have attained to the Age of twenty five Years, and been seven Years a Citizen of the United States, and who shall not, when elected, be an Inhabitant of that State in which he shall be chosen.

Representatives and direct Taxes shall be apportioned among the several States which may be included within this Union, according to their respective Numbers, which shall be determined by adding to the whole Number of free Persons, including those bound to Service for a Term of Years, and excluding Indians not taxed, three fifths of all other Persons. The actual Enumeration shall be made within three Years after the first Meeting of the Congress of the United States, and within every subsequent Term of ten Years, in such Manner as they shall by Law direct. The Number of Representatives shall not exceed one for every thirty Thousand, but each State shall have at Least one Representative; and until such enumeration shall be made, the State of New Hampshire shall be entitled to chuse three, Massachusetts eight, Rhode-Island and Providence Plantations one,

Connecticut five, New-York six, New Jersey four, Pennsylvania eight, Delaware one, Maryland six, Virginia ten, North Carolina five, South Carolina five, and Georgia three.

When vacancies happen in the Representation from any State, the Executive Authority thereof shall issue Writs of Election to fill such Vacancies.

The House of Representatives shall chuse their Speaker and other Officers; and shall have the sole Power of Impeachment.

SECTION 3. The Senate of the United States shall be composed of two Senators from each State, chosen by the Legislature thereof, for six Years; and each Senator shall have one Vote.

Immediately after they shall be assembled in Consequence of the first Election, they shall be divided as equally as may be into three Classes. The Seats of the Senators of the first Class shall be vacated at the Expiration of the second Year, of the second Class at the Expiration of the fourth Year, and of the third Class at the Expiration of the sixth Year, so that one third may be chosen every second Year; and if Vacancies happen by Resignation, or otherwise, during the Recess of the Legislature of any State, the Executive thereof may make temporary Appointments until the next Meeting of the Legislature, which shall then fill such Vacancies. No Person shall be a Senator who shall not have attained to the Age of thirty Years, and been nine Years a Citizen of the United States, and who shall not, when elected, be an Inhabitant of that State for which he shall be chosen.

The Vice President of the United States shall be President of the Senate, but shall have no Vote, unless they be equally divided.

The Senate shall chuse their other Officers, and also a President pro tern-pore, in the Absence of the Vice President, or when he shall exercise the Office of President of the United States.

The Senate shall have the sole Power to try all Impeachments. When sitting for that Purpose, they shall be on Oath or Affirmation. When the President of the United States is tried, the Chief Justice shall preside: and no Person shall be convicted without the Concurrence of two thirds of the Members present.

Judgment in Cases of Impeachment shall not extend further than to removal from Office, and disqualification to hold and enjoy any Office of honor, Trust or Profit under the United States: but the Party convicted shall nevertheless be liable and subject to Indictment, Trial, Judgment and Punishment, according to Law.

SECTION 4. The Times, Places and Manner of holding Elections for Senators and Representatives, shall be prescribed in each State by the Legislature thereof; but the Congress may at any time by Law make or alter such Regulations, except as to the Places of chusing Senators.

The Congress shall assemble at least once in every Year, and such Meeting shall be on the first Monday in December, unless they shall by Law appoint a different Day.

SECTION 5. Each House shall be the Judge of the Elections, Returns and Qualifications of its own Members, and a Majority of each shall constitute a Quorum to do Business; but a smaller Number may adjourn from day to day, and may be authorized to compel the Attendance of absent Members, in such Manner, and under such Penalties as each House may provide.

Article I

Each House may determine the Rules of its Proceedings, punish its Members for disorderly Behaviour, and, with the Concurrence of two thirds, expel a Member.

Each House shall keep a Journal of its Proceedings, and from time to time publish the same, excepting such Parts as may in their Judgment require Secrecy; and the Yeas and Nays of the Members of either House on any question shall, at the Desire of one fifth of those Present, be entered on the Journal.

Neither House, during the Session of Congress, shall, without the consent of the other, adjourn for more than three days, nor to any other Place than that in which the two Houses shall be sitting.

SECTION 6. The Senators and Representatives shall receive a Compensation for their Services, to be ascertained by Law, and paid out of the Treasury of the United States. They shall in all Cases, except Treason, Felony and Breach of the Peace, be privileged from Arrest during their Attendance at the Session of their respective Houses, and in going to and returning from the same; and for any Speech or Debate in either House, they shall not be questioned in any other Place.

No Senator or Representative shall, during the Time for which he was elected, be appointed to any civil Office under the Authority of the United States, which shall have been created, or the Emoluments whereof shall have been encreased during such time; and no Person holding any Office under the United States, shall be a Member of either House during his Continuance in Office.

SECTION 7. All Bills for raising Revenue shall originate in the House of Representatives; but the Senate may propose or concur with Amendments as on other Bills.

Every Bill which shall have passed the House of Representatives and the Senate, shall, before it become a Law, be presented to the President of the United States; If he approve he shall sign it, but if not he shall return it, with his Objections to that House in which it shall have originated, who shall enter the Objections at large on their Journal, and proceed to reconsider it. If after such Reconsideration two thirds of that House shall agree to pass the Bill, it shall be sent, together with the Objections, to the other House, by which it shall likewise be reconsidered, and if approved by two thirds of that House, it shall become a Law. But in all such Cases the Votes of both Houses shall be determined by Yeas and Nays, and the Names of the Persons voting for and against the Bill shall be entered on the Journal of each House respectively. If any Bill shall not be returned by the President within ten days (Sunday excepted) after it shall have been presented to him, the Same shall be a Law, in like Manner as if he had signed it, unless the Congress by their Adjournment prevent its Return in which Case it shall not be a Law.

Every Order, Resolution, or Vote to which the Concurrence of the Senate and House of Representatives maybe necessary (except on a question of Adjournment) shall be presented to the President of the United States; and before the Same shall take Effect, shall be approved by him, or being disapproved by him, shall be repassed by two thirds of the Senate and House of Representatives, according to the Rules and Limitations prescribed in the Case of a Bill.

SECTION 8. The Congress shall have Power To lay and collect Taxes, Duties, Imposts and Excises, to pay the Debts and provide for the common Defence and general Welfare of the United States; but all Duties, Imposts and Excises shall be uniform throughout the United States;

To borrow Money on the credit of the United States;

To regulate Commerce with foreign Nations, and among the several States, and with the Indian Tribes;

To establish an uniform Rule of Naturalization, and uniform Laws on the subject of Bankruptcies throughout the United States;

To coin Money, regulate the Value thereof, and of foreign Coin, and fix the Standard of Weights and Measures;

To provide for the Punishment of counterfeiting the Securities and current Coin of the United States;

To establish Post Offices and post Roads;

To promote the Progress of Science and useful Arts, by securing for limited Times to Authors and Inventors the exclusive Right to their respective Writings and Discoveries;

To constitute Tribunals inferior to the supreme Court;

To define and punish Piracies and Felonies committed on the high Seas, and Offences against the Law of Nations;

To declare War, grant Letters of Marque and Reprisal, and make Rules concerning Captures on Land and Water;

To raise and support Armies, but no Appropriation of Money to that Use shall be for a longer Term than two Years;

To provide and maintain a Navy;

To make Rules for the Government and Regulation of the land and naval Forces;

To provide for calling forth the Militia to execute the Laws of the Union, suppress Insurrections and repel Invasions;

To provide for organizing, arming, and disciplining, the Militia, and for governing such Part of them as may be employed in the Service of the United States, reserving to the States respectively, the Appointment of the Officers, and the Authority of training the Militia according to the discipline prescribed by Congress;

To exercise exclusive Legislation in all Cases whatsoever, over such District (not exceeding ten Miles square) as may, by Cession of particular States, and the Acceptance of Congress, become the Seat of the Government of the United States, and to exercise like Authority over all Places purchased by the Consent of the Legislature of the State in which the Same shall be, for the Erection of Forts, Magazines, Arsenals, dock-Yards, and other needful Buildings;—And

To make all Laws which shall be necessary and proper for carrying into Execution the foregoing Powers, and all other Powers vested by this Constitution in the Government of the United States, or in any Department or Officer thereof.

SECTION 9. The Migration or Importation of such Persons as any of the States now existing shall think proper to admit, shall not be prohibited by the Congress prior to the Year one thousand eight hundred and eight, but a Tax or duty may be imposed on such Importation, not exceeding ten dollars for each Person.

The Privilege of the Writ of Habeas Corpus shall not be suspended, unless when in Cases of Rebellion or Invasion the public Safety may require it.

No Bill of Attainder or ex post facto Law shall be passed.

No Capitation, or other direct, Tax shall be laid, unless in Proportion to the Census or Enumeration herein before directed to be taken.

No Tax or Duty shall be laid on Articles exported from any State.

No Preference shall be given by any Regulation of Commerce or Revenue to the Ports of one State over those of another: nor shall Vessels bound to, or from, one State, be obliged to enter, clear, or pay Duties in another.

No Money shall be drawn from the Treasury, but in Consequence of Appropriations made by Law; and a regular Statement and Account of the Receipts and Expenditures of all public Money shall be published from time to time.

No Title of Nobility shall be granted by the United States: And no Person holding any Office of Profit or Trust under them, shall, without the Consent of the Congress, accept of any present, Emolument, Office, or Title, of any kind whatever, from any Bang, Prince, or foreign State.

SECTION 10. No State shall enter into any Treaty, Alliance, or Confederation; grant Letters of Marque and Reprisal, coin Money; emit Bills of Credit; make any Thing but gold and silver Coin a Tender in Payment of Debts; pass any Bill of Attainder, ex post facto Law, or Law impairing the Obligation of Contracts, or grant any Title of Nobility.

No State shall, without the Consent of the Congress, lay any Imposts or Duties on Imports or Exports, except what may be absolutely necessary for executing its inspection Laws: and the net Produce of all Duties and Imposts, laid by any State on Imports or Exports, shall be for the Use of the Treasury of the United States; and all such Laws shall be subject to the Revision and Controul of the Congress.

No State shall, without the Consent of Congress, lay any Duty of Tonnage, keep Troops, or Ships of War in time of Peace, enter into any Agreement or Compact with another State, or with a foreign Power, or engage in War, unless actually invaded, or in such imminent Danger as will not admit of delay.

ARTICLE II

SECTION 1. The executive Power shall be vested in a President of the United States of America. He shall hold his Office during the Term of four Years, and, together with the Vice President, chosen for the same Term, be elected as follows:

Each State shall appoint, in such Manner as the Legislature thereof may direct, a Number of Electors, equal to the whole Number of Senators and Representatives to which the State may be entitled in the Congress: but no Senator or Representative, or Person holding an Office of Trust or Profit under the United States, shall be appointed an Elector.

The Electors shall meet in their respective States, and vote by Ballot for two Persons, of whom one at least shall not be an Inhabitant of the same State with themselves. And they shall make a List of all the Persons voted for, and of the Number of Votes for each; which List they shall sign and certify, and transmit sealed to the Seat of the Government of the United States, directed to the

President of the Senate. The President of the Senate shall, in the Presence of the Senate and House of Representatives, open all the Certificates, and the Votes shall then be counted. The Person having the greatest Number of Votes shall be the President, if such Number be a Majority of the whole Number of Electors appointed; and if there be more than one who have such Majority, and have an equal Number of Votes, then the House of Representatives shall immediately chuse by Ballot one of them for President; and if no Person have a Majority, then from the five highest on the List the said House shall in like Manner chuse the President. But in chusing the President, the Votes shall be taken by States, the Representation from each State having one Vote; A quorum for this Purpose shall consist of a Member or Members from two thirds of the States, and a Majority of all the States shall be necessary to a Choice. In every Case, after the Choice of the President, the Person having the greatest Number of Votes of the Electors shall be the Vice President. But if there should remain two or more who have equal Votes, the Senate shall chuse from them by Ballot the Vice President.

The Congress may determine the Time of chusing the Electors, and the Day on which they shall give their Votes; which Day shall be the same throughout the United States.

No Person except a natural born Citizen, or a Citizen of the United States, at the time of the Adoption of this Constitution, shall be eligible to the Office of President; neither shall any Person be eligible to that Office who shall not have attained to the Age of thirty five Years, and been fourteen Years a Resident within the United States.

In Case of the Removal of the President from Office, or of his Death, Resignation, or Inability to discharge the Powers and Duties of the said Office, the Same shall devolve on the Vice president, and the Congress may by Law provide for the Case of Removal, Death, Resignation or Inability, both of the President and Vice President, declaring what Officer shall then act as President, and such Officer shall act accordingly, until the Disability be removed, or a President shall be elected.

The President shall, at stated Times, receive for his Services, a Compensation, which shall neither be encreased nor diminished during the Period for which he shall have been elected, and he shall not receive within that Period any other Emolument from the United States, or any of them.

Before he enter on the Execution of his Office, he shall take the following Oath or Affirmation:—"I do solemnly swear (or affirm) that I will faithfully execute the Office of President of the United States, and will to the best of my Ability, preserve, protect and defend the Constitution of the United States."

SECTION 2. The president shall be Commander in Chief of the Army and Navy of the United States, and of the Militia of the several States, when called into the actual service of the United States; he may require the Opinion, in writing, of the principal Officer in each of the executive Departments, upon any Subject relating to the Duties of their respective Offices, and he shall have Power to grant Reprieves and Pardons for Offences against the United States, except in Cases of Impeachment.

He shall have Power, by and with the Advice and Consent of the Senate, to make Treaties, provided two thirds of the Senators present concur; and he shall nominate, and by and with the Advice and Consent of the Senate, shall appoint Ambassadors, other public Ministers and Consuls, Judges of the supreme Court, and all other Officers of the United States, whose Appointments are not herein otherwise provided for, and which shall be established by Law: but the Congress may by Law vest the Appointment of such inferior Officers, as they think proper, in the President alone, in the Courts of Law, or in the Heads of Departments.

The President shall have Power to fill up all Vacancies that may happen during the Recess of the Senate, by granting Commissions which shall expire at the End of their next Session.

SECTION 3. He shall from time to time give to the Congress Information of the State of the Union, and recommend to their Consideration such Measures as he shall judge necessary and expedient; he may, on extraordinary Occasions, convene both Houses, or either of them, and in Case of Disagreement between them, with Respect to the Time of Adjournment, he may adjourn them to such Time as he shall think proper; he shall receive Ambassadors and other public Ministers; he shall take Care that the Laws be faithfully executed, and shall Commission all the Officers of the United States.

SECTION 4. The President, Vice President and all civil Officers of the United States, shall be removed from Office on Impeachment for, and Conviction of, Treason, Bribery, or other high Crimes and Misdemeanors.

ARTICLE III

SECTION 1. The judicial Power of the United States, shall be vested in one supreme Court, and in such inferior Courts as the Congress may from time to time ordain and establish. The Judges, both of the supreme and inferior Courts, shall hold their Offices during good Behaviour, and shall, at stated Times, receive for their Services, a Compensation, which shall not be diminished during their Continuance in Office.

SECTION 2. The judicial Power shall extend to all Cases, in Law and Equity, arising under this Constitution, the Laws of the United States, and Treaties made, or which shall be made, under their Authority;—to all Cases affecting Ambassadors, other public Ministers and Consuls;—to all Cases of admiralty and maritime Jurisdiction;—to Controversies to which the United States shall be a Party;—to Controversies between two or more States;—between a State and Citizens of another State;—between Citizens of different States;—between Citizens of the same State claiming Lands under Grants of different States, and between a State, or the Citizens thereof, and foreign States, Citizens or Subjects.

In all cases affecting Ambassadors, other public Ministers and Consuls, and those in which a State shall be Party, the supreme Court shall have original Jurisdiction. In all the other Cases before mentioned, the supreme Court shall have appellate Jurisdiction, both as to Law and Fact, with such Exceptions, and under such Regulations as the Congress shall make.

The Trial of all Crimes, except in Cases of Impeachment, shall be by Jury; and such Trial shall be held in the State where the said Crimes shall have been committed; but when not committed within any State, the Trial shall be at such Place or Places as the Congress may by Law have directed.

SECTION 3. Treason against the United States, shall consist only in levying War against them, or in adhering to their Enemies, giving them Aid and Comfort. No Person shall be convicted of Treason unless on the Testimony of two Witnesses to the same overt Act, or on Confession in open Court.

The Congress shall have Power to declare the Punishment of Treason, but no Attainder of Treason shall work Corruption of Blood, or Forfeiture except during the Life of the Person attainted.

ARTICLE IV

SECTION 1. Full Faith and Credit shall be given in each State to the public Acts, Records, and judicial Proceedings of every other State. And the Congress may by general Laws prescribe the Manner in which such Acts, Records and Proceedings shall be proved, and the Effect thereof.

SECTION 2. The Citizens of each State shall be entitled to all Privileges and Immunities of Citizens in the several States.

A Person charged in any State with Treason, Felony, or other Crime, who shall flee from Justice, and be found in another State, shall on Demand of the executive Authority of the State from which he fled, be delivered up, to be removed to the State having Jurisdiction of the Crime.

No Person held to Service or Labour in one State, under the Laws thereof, escaping into another, shall, in Consequence of any Law or Regulation therein, be discharged from such Service or Labour, but shall be delivered up on Claim of the Party to whom such Service or Labour may be due.

SECTION 3. New States may be admitted by the Congress into this Union; but no new State shall be formed or erected within the Jurisdiction of any other State; nor any State be formed by the Junction of two or more States, or Parts of States, without the Consent of the Legislatures of the States concerned as well as of the Congress.

The Congress shall have Power to dispose of and make all needful Rules and Regulations respecting the Territory or other Property belonging to the United States; and nothing in this Constitution shall be so construed as to Prejudice any Claims of the United States, or of any particular State.

SECTION 4. The United States shall guarantee to every State in this Union a Republican Form of Government, and shall protect each of them against Invasion; and on Application of the Legislature, or of the Executive (when the Legislature cannot be convened) against domestic Violence.

ARTICLE V

The Congress, whenever two thirds of both Houses shall deem it necessary, shall propose Amendments to this Constitution, or, on the Application of the Legislatures of two thirds of the several States, shall call a Convention for proposing Amendments, which, in either Case, shall be valid to all Intents and Purposes, as Part of this Constitution, when ratified by the Legislatures of three fourths of the several States, or by Conventions in three fourths thereof, as the one or the other Mode of Ratification may be proposed by the Congress; provided that no Amendment which may be made prior to the Year One thousand eight hundred and eight shall in any Manner affect the first and fourth Clauses in the Ninth Section of the first Article; and that no State, without its Consent, shall be deprived of its equal Suffrage in the Senate.

ARTICLE VI

All Debts contracted and Engagements entered into, before the adoption of this Constitution, shall be as valid against the United States under this Constitution, as under the Confederation.

This Constitution, and the Laws of the United States which shall be made in Pursuance thereof; and all Treaties made, or which shall be made, under the Authority of the United States, shall be the supreme Law of the Land; and the Judges in every State shall be bound thereby, any Thing in the Constitution or Laws of any State to the Contrary notwithstanding.

The Senators and Representatives before mentioned, and the Members of the several State Legislatures, and all executive and judicial Officers, both of the United States and of the several States, shall be bound by Oath or Affirmation, to support this Constitution; but no religious Test shall ever be required as a Qualification to any Office or public Trust under the United States.

ARTICLE VII

The Ratification of the Conventions of nine States, shall be sufficient for the Establishment of this Constitution between the States so ratifying the Same.

Articles in Addition to, and Amendment of, the Constitution of the United States of America, Proposed by Congress, and Ratified by the Several States, Pursuant to the Fifth Article of the Original Constitution

AMENDMENT I [1791]

Congress shall make no law respecting an establishment of religion, or prohibiting the free exercise thereof; or abridging the freedom of speech, or of the press; or the right of the people peaceably to assemble, and to petition the Government for a redress of grievances.

AMENDMENT II [1791]

A well regulated Militia, being necessary to the security of a free State, the right of the people to keep and bear Arms, shall not be infringed.

AMENDMENT III [1791]

No Soldier shall, in time of peace be quartered in any house, without the consent of the Owner, nor in time of war, but in a manner to be prescribed by law.

AMENDMENT IV [1791]

The right of the people to be secure in their persons, houses, papers, and effects, against unreasonable searches and seizures, shall not be violated, and no Warrants shall issue, but upon probable cause, supported by Oath or affirmation, and particularly describing the place to be searched, and the persons or things to be seized.

AMENDMENT V [1791]

No person shall be held to answer for a capital, or otherwise infamous crime, unless on a presentment or indictment of a Grand Jury, except in cases arising in the land or naval forces, or in the Militia, when in actual service in time of War or public danger; nor shall any person be subject for the same offence to be twice put in jeopardy of life or limb; nor shall be compelled in any criminal case to be a witness against himself, nor be deprived of life, liberty, or property, without due process of law; nor shall private property be taken for public use, without just compensation.

AMENDMENT VI [1791]

In all criminal prosecutions, the accused shall enjoy the right to a speedy and public trial, by an impartial jury of the State and district wherein the crime shall have been committed, which district shall have been previously ascertained by law, and to be informed of the nature and cause of the accusation; to be confronted with the witnesses against him; to have compulsory process for obtaining witnesses in his favor, and to have the Assistance of Counsel for his defence.

AMENDMENT VII [1791]

In Suits at common law, where the value in controversy shall exceed twenty dollars, the right of trial by jury shall be preserved, and no fact tried by a jury, shall be otherwise re-examined in any Court of the United States, than according to the rules of the common law.

AMENDMENT VIII [1791]

Excessive bail shall not be required, nor excessive fines imposed, nor cruel and unusual punishments inflicted.

AMENDMENT IX [1791]

The enumeration in the Constitution, of certain rights, shall not be construed to deny or disparage others retained by the people.

AMENDMENT X [1791]

The powers not delegated to the United States by the Constitution, nor prohibited by it to the States, are reserved to the States respectively, or to the people.

AMENDMENT XI [1798]

The judicial power of the United States shall not be construed to extend to any suit in law or equity, commenced or prosecuted against one of the United States by citizens of another state, or by citizens or subjects of any foreign state.

AMENDMENT XII [1804]

The electors shall meet in their respective states and vote by ballot for President and Vice-President, one of whom, at least, shall not be an inhabitant of the same state with themselves; they shall name in their ballots the person voted for as President, and in distinct ballots the person voted for as Vice-President, and they shall make distinct lists of all persons voted for as President, and of all persons voted for as Vice-President, and of the number of votes for each, which lists they shall sign and certify, and transmit sealed to the seat of the government of the United States, directed to the President of the Senate;—The President of the Senate shall, in the presence of the Senate and House of Representatives, open all the certificates and the votes shall then be counted;—the person having the greatest number of votes for President, shall be the President, if such number be a majority of the whole number of electors appointed; and if no person have such majority, then from the persons having the highest numbers not exceeding three on the list of those voted for as President, the House of Representatives shall choose immediately, by ballot, the President. But in choosing the President, the votes shall be taken by states, the representation from each state having one vote; a quorum for this purpose shall consist of a member or members from two-thirds of the states, and a majority of all the states shall be necessary to a choice. And if the House of Representatives shall not choose a President whenever the right of choice shall devolve upon them, before the fourth day of March next following, then the Vice-President shall act as President, as in the case of the death or other constitutional disability of the President. The person having the greatest number of votes as Vice-President, shall be the Vice-President, if such number be a majority of the whole number of electors appointed, and if no person have a majority, then from the two highest numbers on the list, the Senate shall choose the Vice-President; a quorum for the purpose shall consist of two-thirds of the whole number of Senators, and a majority of the whole number shall be necessary to a choice. But no person constitutionally ineligible to the office of President shall be eligible to that of Vice-President of the United States.

AMENDMENT XIII [1865]

SECTION 1. Neither slavery nor involuntary servitude, except as a punishment for crime whereof the party shall have been duly convicted, shall exist within the United States, or any place subject to their jurisdiction.

SECTION 2. Congress shall have power to enforce this article by appropriate legislation.

AMENDMENT XIV [1868]

SECTION 1. All persons born or naturalized in the United States, and subject to the jurisdiction thereof, are citizens of the United States and of the state wherein they reside. No state shall make or enforce any law which shall abridge the privileges or immunities of citizens of the United States; nor shall any state deprive any person of life, liberty, or property, without due process of law; nor deny to any person within its jurisdiction the equal protection of the laws.

SECTION 2. Representatives shall be apportioned among the several states according to their respective numbers, counting the whole number of persons in each state, excluding Indians not taxed. But when the right to vote at any election for the choice of electors for President and Vice President of the United States, Representatives in Congress, the executive and judicial officers of a state, or the members of the legislature thereof, is denied to any of the male inhabitants of such state, and citizens of the United States, or in any way abridged, except for participation in rebellion, or other crime, the basis of representation therein shall be reduced in the proportion which the number of such male citizens shall bear to the whole number of male citizens twenty-one years of age in such state.

SECTION 3. No person shall be a Senator or Representative in Congress, or elector of President and Vice President, or hold any office, civil or military, under the United States, or under any state, who, having previously taken an oath, as a member of Congress, or as an officer of the United States, or as a member of any state legislature, or as an executive or judicial officer of any state, to support the Constitution of the United States, shall have engaged in insurrection or rebellion against the same, or given aid or comfort to the enemies thereof. But Congress may by a vote of two-thirds of each House, remove such disability.

SECTION 4. The validity of the public debt of the United States, authorized by law, including debts incurred for payment of pensions and bounties for services in suppressing insurrection or rebellion, shall not be questioned. But neither the United States nor any state shall assume or pay any debt or obligation incurred in aid of insurrection or rebellion against the United States, or any claim for the loss or emancipation of any slave; but all such debts, obligations and claims shall be held illegal and void.

SECTION 5. The Congress shall have power to enforce, by appropriate legislation, the provisions of this article.

AMENDMENT XV [1870]

SECTION 1. The right of citizens of the United States to vote shall not be denied or abridged by the United States or by any state on account of race, color, or previous condition of servitude.

SECTION 2. The Congress shall have power to enforce this article by appropriate legislation.

AMENDMENT XVI [1913]

The Congress shall have power to lay and collect taxes on incomes, from whatever source derived, without apportionment among the several states, and without regard to any census or enumeration.

AMENDMENT XVII [1913]

The Senate of the United States shall be composed of two Senators from each state, elected by the people thereof, for six years; and each Senator shall have one vote. The electors in each state shall have the qualifications requisite for electors of the most numerous branch of the state legislatures.

When vacancies happen in the representation of any state in the Senate, the executive authority of such state shall issue writs of election to fill such vacancies: Provided, that the legislature of any state may empower the executive thereof to make temporary appointments until the people fill the vacancies by election as the legislature may direct.

This amendment shall not be so construed as to affect the election or term of any Senator chosen before it becomes valid as part of the Constitution.

AMENDMENT XVIII [1919]

SECTION 1. After one year from the ratification of this article the manufacture, sale, or transportation of intoxicating liquors within, the importation thereof into, or the exportation thereof from the United States and all territory subject to the jurisdiction thereof for beverage purposes is hereby prohibited.

SECTION 2. The Congress and the several states shall have concurrent power to enforce this article by appropriate legislation.

SECTION 3. This article shall be inoperative unless it shall have been ratified as an amendment to the Constitution by the legislatures of the several states, as provided in the Constitution, within seven years from the date of the submission hereof to the states by the Congress.

AMENDMENT XIX [1920]

The right of citizens of the United States to vote shall not be denied or abridged by the United States or by any state on account of sex.

Congress shall have power to enforce this article by appropriate legislation.

AMENDMENT XX [1933]

SECTION 1. The terms of the President and Vice President shall end at noon on the 20th day of January, and the terms of Senators and Representatives at noon on the 3d day of January, of the years in which such terms would have ended if this article had not been ratified; and the terms of their successors shall then begin.

SECTION 2. The Congress shall assemble at least once in every year, and such meeting shall begin at noon on the 3d day of January, unless they shall by law appoint a different day.

SECTION 3. If, at the time fixed for the beginning of the term of the President, the President elect shall have died, the Vice President elect shall become President. If a President shall not have been chosen before the time fixed for the beginning of his term, or if the President elect shall have failed to qualify, then the Vice President elect shall act as President until a President shall have qualified; and the Congress may by law provide for the case wherein neither a President elect nor a Vice President elect shall have qualified, declaring who shall then act as President, or the manner in which one who is to act shall be selected, and such person shall act accordingly until a President or Vice President shall have qualified.

SECTION 4. The Congress may by law provide for the case of the death of any of the persons from whom the House of Representatives may choose a President whenever the right of choice shall have devolved upon them, and for the case of the death of any of the persons from whom the Senate may choose a Vice President whenever the right of choice shall have devolved upon them.

SECTION 5. Sections 1 and 2 shall take effect on the 15th day of October following the ratification of this article.

ARTICLE 6. This article shall be inoperative unless it shall have been ratified as an amendment to the Constitution by the legislatures of three-fourths of the several states within seven years from the date of its submission.

AMENDMENT XXI [1933]

SECTION 1. The eighteenth article of amendment to the Constitution of the United States is hereby repealed.

SECTION 2. The transportation or importation into any state, territory, or possession of the United States for delivery or use therein of intoxicating liquors, in violation of the laws thereof, is hereby prohibited.

SECTION 3. This article shall be inoperative unless it shall have been ratified as an amendment to the Constitution by conventions in the several states, as provided in the Constitution, within seven years from the date of the submission hereof to the states by the Congress.

AMENDMENT XXII [1951]

SECTION 1. No person shall be elected to the office of the President more than twice, and no person who has held the office of President, or acted as President, for more than two years of a term to which some other person was elected President shall be elected to the office of the President more than once. But this article shall not apply to any person holding the office of President when this article was proposed by the Congress, and shall not prevent any person who may be holding the office of President, or acting as President, during the term within which this article becomes operative from holding the office of President or acting as President during the remainder of such term.

SECTION 2. This article shall be inoperative unless it shall have been ratified as an amendment to the Constitution by the legislatures of three-fourths of the several states within seven years from the date of its submission to the states by the Congress.

AMENDMENT XXIII [1961]

SECTION 1. The District constituting the seat of government of the United States shall appoint in such manner as the Congress may direct:

A number of electors of President and Vice President equal to the whole number of Senators and Representatives in Congress to which the District would be entitled if it were a state, but in no event more than the least populous state; they shall be in addition to those appointed by the states, but they shall be considered, for the purposes of the election of President and Vice President, to be electors appointed by a state; and they shall meet in the District and perform such duties as provided by the twelfth article of amendment.

SECTION 2. The Congress shall have power to enforce this article by appropriate legislation.

AMENDMENT XXIV [1964]

SECTION 1. The right of citizens of the United States to vote in any primary or other election for President or Vice President, for electors for President or Vice President, or for Senator or Representative in Congress, shall not be denied or abridged by the United States or any state by reason of failure to pay any poll tax or other tax.

SECTION 2. The Congress shall have power to enforce this article by appropriate legislation.

AMENDMENT XXV [1967]

SECTION 1. In case of the removal of the President from office or of his death or resignation, the Vice President shall become President.

SECTION 2. Whenever there is a vacancy in the office of the Vice President, the President shall nominate a Vice President who shall take office upon confirmation by a majority vote of both Houses of Congress.

SECTION 3. Whenever the President transmits to the President pro tempore of the Senate and the Speaker of the House of Representatives his written declaration that he is unable to discharge the powers and duties of his office, and until he transmits to them a written declaration to the contrary, such powers and duties shall be discharged by the Vice President as Acting President.

SECTION 4. Whenever the Vice President and a majority of either the principal officers of the executive departments or of such other body as Congress may by law provide, transmit to the President pro tempore of the Senate and the Speaker of the House of Representatives their written declaration that the President is unable to discharge the powers and duties of his office, the Vice President shall immediately assume the powers and duties of the office as Acting President.

Thereafter, when the President transmits to the President pro tempore of the Senate and the Speaker of the House of Representatives his written declaration that no inability exists, he shall resume the powers and duties of his office unless the Vice President and a majority of either the principal officers of the executive department or of such other body as Congress may by law provide, transmit within four days to the President pro tempore of the Senate and the Speaker of the House of Representatives their written declaration that the President is unable to discharge the powers and duties of his office. Thereupon Congress shall decide the issue, assembling within forty-eight hours for that purpose if not in session. If the Congress, within twenty-one days after receipt of the latter written declaration, or, if Congress is not in session, within twenty-one days after Congress is required to assemble, determines by two-thirds vote of both Houses that the President is unable to discharge the powers and duties of his office, the Vice President shall continue to discharge the same as Acting President; otherwise, the President shall resume the powers and duties of his office.

AMENDMENT XXVI [1971]

SECTION 1. The right of citizens of the United States, who are 18 years of age or older, to vote, shall not be denied or abridged by the United States or any state on account of age.

SECTION 2. The Congress shall have the power to enforce this article by appropriate legislation.

AMENDMENT XXVII [1992]

No law, varying the compensation for the services of the Senators and Representatives, shall take effect, until an election of Representatives shall have intervened.

Table of Cases

Table of Cases

Table of Cases

Table of Cases

Table of Cases

Table of Cases

Table of Cases

Table of Cases

Table of Cases

Table of Cases

Table of Cases

Table of Cases

Table of Cases

Table of Cases

Table of Cases

Table of Cases

Table of Cases

Table of Cases

Table of Cases

Index

Index

Index

Index

Index

Index

Index

Index

Unconstitutional conditions doctrine, 582-583, 830, 1028-1033
Underinclusiveness, 702
Undocumented aliens, 420-421, 425-427, 809-810. *See also* Immigration
Undue burden
  abortion, 568, 853, 860-875
  interstate commerce, 4, 411, 443, 445
Unenumerated rights, 18, 502
Uniform Code of Military Justice, 344, 402
Unions, 177, 644-645, 653
Universal Military Training and Selective Service Act, 1254-1256

Van Alstyne, William, 39
Veto power, 152
Vice presidential power
  impeachment and removal from office, 403
  independent candidates, 125-126, 941
  method of choosing, 2, 13
  terms of office, 2
  Twelfth Amendment, 13
  Twenty-fifth Amendment, 13
Vining, Joseph, 59
Violence Against Women Act, 251, 272, 275, 303-304
Virginia Freedom of Information Act, 495
Virginia plan, 10
Voting, 908-945. *See also* Elections; Fifteenth Amendment
  age, 13
  apportionment, 920-925
  at-large elections, 937-939
  balancing test, 920
  candidacy restrictions, 939-945
  constitutional protections, 908
  counting inequalities within states, 928-936
  dilution of right, 920-928
  districting based on race, 779-782
  durational residency requirements, 913
  equal protection, 908-909, 935, 936
  Fifteenth Amendment, 313, 908, 936
  filing fee requirements, 944-945
  as fundamental right, 908-909
  gender discrimination, 14
  gerrymandering. *See* Gerrymandering
  literacy tests, 913-915
  minor parties and candidates, 940-944
  multimember districts, 937-939
  one-person, one-vote rule, 920-925
  photo identification requirement, 919-920
  poll taxes, 910-911
  primaries and party affiliation, 917-919
  prisoners and convicted criminals, 915-916
  property ownership requirement, 911-913
  racial discrimination, 13-14, 298-299, 310-313, 936-939
  residency requirements, 899, 900
  restrictions on, 909-920
  strict scrutiny, 939-940
Voting Rights Act of 1965, 304-305, 310-313, 319, 742, 781, 914
War, determinations of beginning or ending, 148

War on Terrorism. *See* Terrorism, war on
War powers, 149, 295-296, 391-394
War Powers Resolution, 296, 393
Watergate, 324, 326, 372, 374, 405, 1236
Water Pollution Control Act, 278
Wealth classifications, 819-821
Wechsler, Herbert, 329-330
Wellington, Harry, 972
Westen, Peter, 702
White Primary Cases, 544, 548-550
Wright, Charles Alan, 210, 211

Yudof, Mark, 738

Zone of activities, 250-251, 255-256
Zone of interest test, 103-107. *See also* Standing
  application of, 105-107
  creation of, 104
  defined, 103-104
  desirability of, 105
Zoning, 678-680, 1077-1079